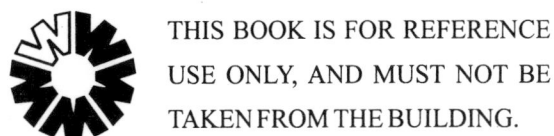

The Grants Register®

2007

Twenty-fifth Edition

palgrave
macmillan

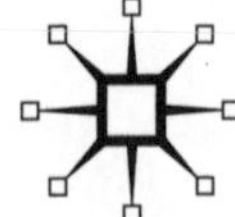

The editor of *The Grants Register* cannot undertake any correspondence in relation to grants listed in this volume.

This edition published 2006 by
PALGRAVE MACMILLAN
Houndmills, Basingstoke, Hampshire RG21 6XS and
175 Fifth Avenue, New York, N.Y. 10010
Companies and representatives throughout the world.

PALGRAVE MACMILLAN is the global academic imprint of the Palgrave Macmillan division of St. Martin's Press, LLC and of Palgrave Macmillan Ltd. Macmillan™ is a registered trademark in the United States, United Kingdom and other countries. Palgrave is a registered trademark in the European Union and other countries.

ISBN 13 978-1-4039-9254-3
ISSN 10 1-4039-9254-1
ISSN 0072-5471

This book is printed on paper suitable for recycling and made from fully managed and sustained forest sources.

A catalogue record for this book is available from the British Library.

A catalog record for this book is available from the Library of Congress.

10 9 8 7 6 5 4 3 2 1
15 14 13 12 11 10 09 08 07 06

Printed in China

LIST OF CONTENTS

PREFACE

The twenty-fifth edition of *The Grants Register* provides a detailed, accurate and comprehensive survey of awards intended for students at or above the postgraduate level, or those who require further professional or advanced vocational training.

Student numbers around the world continue to grow rapidly, and overseas study is now the first choice for many of these students. *The Grants Register* provides comprehensive, up-to-date information about the availability of, and eligibility for, non-refundable postgraduate and professional awards worldwide.

We remain grateful to the institutions which have supplied information for inclusion in this edition, and would also like to thank the International Association of Universities for continued permission to use their subject index within our Subject and Eligibility Guide to Awards.

The Grants Register database is updated continually in order to ensure that the information provided is the most current available. Therefore, if your details have changed or you would like to be included for the first time, please contact The Reference Administrator (The Grants Register), at address below. If you wish to obtain further information relating to specific application procedures, please contact the relevant grant-awarding institution, rather than the publisher.

The Grants Register
Palgrave Macmillan
Houndmills
Basingstoke
RG21 6XS
United Kingdom
Tel: +44 (0)1256 329242
Fax: +44 (0)1256 357268
Fax: +44 (0)1256 479476

Website: http://www.palgrave.com
Email: grants.register@palgrave.com

HOW TO USE THE GRANTS REGISTER

For ease of use, *The Grants Register 2007* is divided into five sections:

- *The Grants Register*
- Subject and Eligibility Guide to Awards
- Index of Awards
- Index of Discontinued Awards
- Index of Awarding Organisations

The Grants Register

Information in this section is supplied directly by the awarding organisations. Entries are arranged alphabetically by name of organisation, and awards are listed alphabetically within the awarding organisation. This section includes details on subject area, eligibility, purpose, type, numbers offered, frequency, value, length of study, study establishment, country of study, and application procedure. Full contact details appear with each awarding organisation and also appended to individual awards where additional addresses are given.

ACADIA UNIVERSITY

Wolfville, NS, B4P 2R6, Canada
Tel: (1) 902 585 1498
Fax: (1) 902 585 1096
Email: elaine.schofield@acadiau.ca
Website: www.acadiau.ca
Contact: Ms Elaine Schofield, Manager

Acadia University is an institution that is committed to providing a liberal education based on the highest standards. The University houses a scholarly community that aims to ensure a broadening life experience for students, faculty and staff.

Acadia Graduate Awards

Subjects: English, political science, sociology, biology, chemistry, computer science, geology, psychology, education and recreation management, mathematics and statistics.
Purpose: To financially support students.
Eligibility: Open to registered full-time graduate students at Acadia University.
Level of Study: Postgraduate.
Type: Award.
Value: Up to Canadian $9,000.
Length of Study: 1–2 years.

Subject and Eligibility Guide to Awards

Awards can be located through the Subject and Eligibility Guide to Awards. This section allows the user to find an award within a specific subject area. *The Grants Register* uses a list of subjects endorsed by the International Association of Universities (IAU), the information centre on higher education, located at UNESCO, Paris (please see pp. xxx-xxx for the complete subject list). It is further subdivided into eligibility by nationality. Thereafter, awards are listed alphabetically within their designated category, along with a page reference where full details of the award can be found.

ENGINEERING

GENERAL

Any Country

Alberta Research Council Karl A Clark Memorial Scholarship, 617
Andrew Stratton Scholarship, 632
Association for Women in Science Educational Foundation Predoctoral Awards, 104
Predoctoral Awards, 117
AUC Assistantships, 84
AUC Laboratory Instruction Graduation Fellowships in Engineering and Computer Science, 85
AUC University Fellowships, 86
Berthold Leibinger Innovationspreis, 125
BFWG: M H Joseph Prize, 143

Index of Awards

All awards are indexed alphabetically with a page reference.

Index of Discontinued Awards

This Index lists awards previously included within *The Grants Register* which are no longer being offered, have been replaced by another programme, or are no longer relevant for inclusion in the publication.

Index of Awarding Organisations

A complete list of all awarding organisations, with country name and page reference.

THE GRANTS REGISTER

A-T CHILDREN'S PROJECT

668 South Military Trail, Deerfield Beach, FL, 33442,
United States of America
Tel: (1) 954 481 6611
Fax: (1) 954 725 1153
Email: info@atcp.org
Website: www.atcp.org
Contact: Dr Cynthia Rothblum-Oviatt, Science Co-ordinator

The A-T Children's Project is a non-profit organization that raises funds to support and co-ordinate biomedical research projects, scientific conferences and a clinical centre aimed at finding a cure for ataxia-telangiectasia, a lethal genetic disease that attacks children, causing progressive loss of muscle control, as well as cancer and immune system problems.

Direct Research on Ataxia-Telangiectasia

Subjects: ATM biology.
Purpose: To accelerate first-rate, international scientific research in the area of ATM biology to help find a cure or life-improving treatments for children with ataxia-telangiectasia.
Eligibility: Open to applicants of all ages and nationalities.
Level of Study: Research
Type: Grant
Value: Up to US$75,000
Length of Study: 1–2 years
Frequency: Annual
Application Procedure: Applicants via website.
Closing Date: There are no deadlines for the submission of grant proposals
Funding: Private

AARON SISKIND FOUNDATION

School of Visual Arts, MFA Photography, 214 East 21st Street,
New York, NY 10010,
United States of America
Tel: (1) 609 348 5650
Fax: (1) 609 572 1243
Email: info@aaronsiskind.org
Website: www.aaronsiskind.org

The Foundation works to preserve and protect Aaron Siskind's artistic legacy, and foster knowledge of and appreciation of his art.

Individual Photographer's Fellowship

Subjects: Photography-based art. Eligible work must be based on the idea of the lens-based still image, but grant recipients work in forms as diverse as digital imagery, video, installations documentary projects and photo-generated print media.
Purpose: To stimulate excellence and the promise of future achievement in the photographic field.
Eligibility: Applicants must be citizens or permanent residents of the United States of America. Applications sent from outside the United States of America will not be accepted.
Level of Study: Postgraduate
Type: Fellowship
Value: Up to US$5,000
Country of Study: United States of America
Application Procedure: Applicants must send an application form, 10 x 35 mm slides of their work, a slide list, stamped addressed return envelope together with their curriculum vitae and statement of plans for intended work to main address.
Closing Date: October 15th
Funding: Private
Additional Information: The application procedure is explicit and applicants are advised to check the website.

AAUW EDUCATIONAL FOUNDATION

1111 16 Street North West, Washington, DC, 20036,
United States of America
Tel: (1) 202 728 7602
Fax: (1) 202 872 1425
Email: foundation@aauw.org
Website: www.aauw.org
Contact: Tara McLoughlin, Director of Programs

The AAUW Educational Foundation is composed of three corporations. These are the Association, a 150,000 member organization with more than 1,500 branches nationwide that lobbies and advocates for education and equity; the AAUW Educational Foundation, which funds pioneering research on girls and education, community action projects, and fellowships and grants for outstanding women around the globe; and the AAUW Legal Advocacy Fund, which provides funds and a support system for women seeking judicial redress for sexual discrimination in higher education.

AAUW Career Development Grants

Subjects: All subjects.
Purpose: To support course work beyond a bachelor's degree.
Eligibility: Grants are given to women who hold a bachelor's degree and are preparing to advance their careers, change careers, or re-enter the work force. Special consideration is given to AAUW members, women of color, and women pursuing their first advanced degree.
Level of Study: Professional development
Type: Grant
Value: US$2,000–7,000
Frequency: Annual
Study Establishment: Any accredited Institution
Country of Study: United States of America
Application Procedure: Apply online.
Closing Date: December 15th
Additional Information: Funds are not available for doctoral-level work.

AAUW Community Action Grants

Subjects: All subjects.
Purpose: To provide seed money to individual women, local community-based non-profit organizations, AAUW branches and AAUW state organizations for innovative programmes or non-degree research projects that engage girls in mathematics, science and technology.
Eligibility: Applicants must be women who are citizens or permanent residents of the United States of America. Special consideration will be given to AAUW members and AAUW branch and state applicants who seek partners for collaborative projects. Collaborators can include local schools or school districts, businesses and other community-based organizations. 2 year grants are restricted to projects focused on girls' achievement in mathematics, science or technology. Projects must involve community and school collaboration. The fund supports planning and coalition-building activities during the 1st year and implementation and evaluation the following year.
Type: Grant
Value: US$2,000–7,000 for 1-year projects and US$5,000–10,000 for 2-year projects
Length of Study: 1 or 2 years
Frequency: Annual
No. of awards offered: 5
Application Procedure: Applicants must write for an application form, which is also available from the website.
Closing Date: January 15th
Funding: Private
Additional Information: Two types of grant are available. 1-year grants are for short-term projects. Topic areas are unrestricted but should have a clearly defined educational activity. 2-year grants are for longer term programmes and are restricted to projects focused on K-12 girls achievement in mathematics, science and/or technology. Funds support planning activities and coalition-building during the 1st year and implementation and evaluation the following year.

AAUW Educational Foundation American Fellowships

Subjects: All subjects.
Purpose: To offset a scholar's living expenses while she completes her final year of dissertation writing, or to increase the number of women in tenure-track faculty positions and promote equality for women in higher education.
Eligibility: Open to women who are citizens or permanent residents of the United States of America.
Level of Study: Doctorate, postdoctorate, research
Type: Fellowship
Value: US$20,000 for the Dissertation Award, US$30,000 for the Postdoctoral Research Leave Award and US$6,000 for the Research Publication Grant
Length of Study: 1 year for dissertation and postdoctorate, summer for the Research Publication Grant
Frequency: Annual
Country of Study: United States of America or other countries if appropriate
No. of awards offered: 77
Application Procedure: Applicants must write for an application package or download materials from website. They must then return the application form, a narrative autobiography, a curriculum vitae, a statement of project, transcripts, three letters of recommendation and a filing fee. Applications may be downloaded from the website or requested from the Customer Service office via the website.
Closing Date: Postmarked November 15th
Funding: Private
No. of awards given last year: 77
No. of applicants last year: 677

AAUW Eleanor Roosevelt Teacher Fellowships

Subjects: Gender equality.
Purpose: To support professional development for teachers, educational opportunities for girls and the advancement of gender equity in the classroom, school or district.
Eligibility: Open to all public school, K–12 women teachers who are citizens of the United States of America or permanent residents. Applicants must be committed to teaching for 3 years including the fellowship year.
Level of Study: Professional development
Type: Fellowship
Value: US$5,000
No. of awards offered: Approx. 25
Application Procedure: Applicants must write for an application form, which is also available from the website.
Closing Date: January 10th
Funding: Private

AAUW International Fellowships Program

Subjects: All subjects.
Purpose: To support women studying at the graduate or postgraduate level at a United States Institute of Higher Education.
Eligibility: Open to women who are not citizens of the United States of America or permanent residents, who hold a United States of America Bachelor's degree or equivalent. Applicants must be planning to return to their home country upon completion of degree and/or research. English proficiency is required.
Level of Study: Doctorate, predoctorate, graduate, postgraduate, postdoctorate, research
Type: Fellowship
Value: US$30,000 for the Postdoctoral Fellowship, US$20,000 for the Doctoral Fellowship and US$18,000 for the Master's Fellowship
Length of Study: 1 year
Frequency: Annual
Study Establishment: Any accredited institution
Country of Study: United States of America
No. of awards offered: 57
Application Procedure: Applicants must complete an application for each year applying. Applications must be obtained from the customer service centre or the AAUW website between August 1st and December 15th. Three letters of recommendation, transcripts and a minimum score of 550 on the Test Of English as a Foreign Language (213 computer-based) are also required.
Closing Date: Postmarked December 15th
Funding: Private
No. of awards given last year: 57
No. of applicants last year: 1200+
Additional Information: These awards are non-renewable.

AAUW LAF Plaintiff Travel Grants

Subjects: All subjects.
Purpose: To help states and regions increase knowledge of LAF and equity issues in higher education.
Eligibility: See website for conditions.
Level of Study: Postgraduate, research
Type: Grant
Value: Air travel and accommodation
Frequency: Annual
Application Procedure: Apply online.
Closing Date: October 15th

AAUW Selected Professions Fellowships

Subjects: Architecture, computer/information sciences, engineering, mathematics/statistics, business administration, law, medicine.
Eligibility: Fellowships are restricted to women of color, who have been underrepresented in these fields. Special consideration is given to applicants who show professional promise in innovative or neglected areas of research or practice in areas of public interest.
Level of Study: Postdoctorate, postgraduate
Type: Fellowship
Value: US$5,000–20,000
Length of Study: 1 year
Frequency: Annual
Study Establishment: Any accredited institution
Country of Study: United States of America
Application Procedure: Apply online.
Closing Date: January 10th

AAUW University Scholar-in-Residence

Subjects: Educational equity for women and girls.
Purpose: To enable a female scholar to undertake and disseminate research on gender equality for women and girls.
Level of Study: Postdoctorate, research
Type: Grant
Value: Not to exceed US$100,000 for a 2-year project
Length of Study: 2 years
Frequency: Annual
Country of Study: United States of America
No. of awards offered: 1
Application Procedure: Institutional applicants must submit a proposal including both activities on gender and educational equity, and dissemination of findings. Successful proposals will be crafted to achieve impact across the institution or among departments or schools, rather than in a single department programme. Proposals must also include confirmation by an authorized institutional official confirming the institutions commitment to the project and cost share provided.
Closing Date: October 15th
Funding: Private
No. of awards given last year: 1
No. of applicants last year: 22
Additional Information: Applicants should contact the foundation for proposal guidelines or visit the website www.aauw.org/fga

THE ABBEY AWARDS

43 Carson Road, London, SE21 8HT, England
Tel: (44) 20 8761 7980
Email: administrator@abbey.org.uk
Website: www.abbey.org.uk
Contact: Ms Jane Reid, Administrator

The Abbey Awards offer all-expenses-paid residencies for painters in excellent studio apartments at the British School in Rome. The 9-month Abbey Scholarship is awarded to an emergent artist while the

3-month Abbey Fellowships are for mid-career painters with an established record of achievement.

Abbey Fellowships in Painting

Subjects: Painting.
Purpose: To enable mid-career painters with an established record of achievement to live and work at the British School in Rome.
Eligibility: Open to citizens of the United Kingdom and United States of America only, and to citizens of other countries provided that they have been and are currently living in the United Kingdom or the United States of America for at least 5 years. There are no age restrictions. Fellowships are for painters only.
Level of Study: Professional development, graduate
Type: Fellowship
Value: All expenses and spending money
Length of Study: 3 months
Frequency: Annual
Study Establishment: The British School in Rome
Country of Study: Italy
No. of awards offered: 2 or 3
Application Procedure: Applicants must send for an application form, enclosing a stamped addressed envelope. Alternatively, applicants can download application forms from the website.
Closing Date: Mid-January
Funding: Private
Contributor: The Incorporated Edwin Austin Abbey Memorial Scholarships
No. of awards given last year: 3
No. of applicants last year: 63

Abbey Harris Mural Fund

Subjects: Mural painting.
Purpose: To provide grants to artists who have been commissioned to create murals in public places or in charitable institutions in the United Kingdom.
Eligibility: Awards are for mural painters and the work must be carried out in the United Kingdom. There are other restrictions.
Level of Study: Unrestricted
Type: Grant
Value: Approx. UK £3,000
Frequency: Annual
Country of Study: United Kingdom
No. of awards offered: 2
Application Procedure: Applicants must send for an application form, enclosing a stamped addressed envelope. Application forms can also be requested by email.
Closing Date: Applications are accepted at any time. Decisions may be made at twice-yearly meetings of the Trustees in May and November
Funding: Private
Contributor: E A Abbey Memorial Trust Fund for Mural Painting in Great Britain and E Vincent Harris Fund for Mural Decoration
No. of awards given last year: 2
No. of applicants last year: 6

Abbey Scholarship in Painting

Subjects: Painting.
Purpose: To enable an exceptionally promising emergent painter to live and work at the British School in Rome.
Eligibility: Open to citizens of the United Kingdom and United States of America only, and to citizens of other countries provided that they have been and are currently living in the United Kingdom or the United States of America for at least 5 years. There are no age restrictions. Awards are for painters only.
Level of Study: Postgraduate, graduate
Type: Scholarship
Value: All expenses and spending money
Length of Study: 9 months
Frequency: Annual
Study Establishment: The British School in Rome
Country of Study: Italy
No. of awards offered: 1
Application Procedure: Applicants must send for an application form, enclosing a stamped addressed envelope. Alternatively, applicants can download application forms from the website.
Closing Date: Mid-January
Funding: Private
Contributor: The Incorporated Edwin Austin Abbey Memorial Scholarships
No. of awards given last year: 1
No. of applicants last year: 71

ABDUS SALAM INTERNATIONAL CENTRE FOR THEORETICAL PHYSICS (ICTP)

Strada Costiera 11, Trieste, I-34014, Italy
Tel: (39) 040 224 0111
Fax: (39) 040 224 163
Email: sci_info@ictp.it
Website: www.ictp.it
Contact: Public Information Officer

The Abdus Salam International Centre for Theoretical Physics (ICTP) is an institution for research and high-level training in physics and mathematics, mainly for scientists from developing countries. It also maintains a network of associate members and federated institutes.

Abdus Salam ICTP Fellowships

Subjects: Physics and mathematics.
Purpose: To enable qualified applicants to pursue research in the fields of condensed matter physics, mathematics and high-energy physics.
Eligibility: Open to qualified applicants of any nationality who have a PhD in physics or mathematics.
Level of Study: Postdoctorate
Type: Fellowship
Value: Monthly stipend, round-trip expenses where applicable and allowances according to the length of the visit
Length of Study: Up to 1 year
Frequency: Dependent on funds available
Study Establishment: ICTP
Country of Study: Italy
No. of awards offered: Varies
Application Procedure: Applicants must request appropriate application forms from the secretariat, or visit the ICTP website.
Closing Date: Applications are accepted at any time
Funding: Government
Contributor: The Italian government, IAEA and UNESCO

ACACIA INFORMATION AND COMMUNICATION TECHNOLOGIES (ICT)

250 Albert Street PO Box 8500, Ottawa, Canada
Tel: (1) 613 236 6163 ext. 2164
Fax: (1) 613 567 7749
Email: maldikpo@idrc.ca
Website: www.idrc.ca/acacia
Contact: Morenike Ladikpo

The Acacia Information and Communication Technologies (ICTs) initiative empowers sub-Saharan communities with the ability to apply ICT's own social and economic development.

The Acacia ICT R&D Grants Programme

Subjects: Policy impact, gender equity, social equality, sustainable communities, and technology diffusion to rural areas.
Purpose: To promote an active ICT research environment in Africa for issues relating to development applications, policy research and their impacts.
Eligibility: Solid participation by organization from Africa must be outlined in the submitted proposal.
Level of Study: Postgraduate

Type: Grant
Value: All approved costs
Length of Study: Varies
Frequency: Annual
Country of Study: Africa
No. of awards offered: Varies
Application Procedure: All information on the application process is available on the website.
Closing Date: September 12th
Additional Information: Copyright for project results will reside with the programme initiative.

ACADEMY OF MOTION PICTURE ARTS AND SCIENCES

Aademy Foundation, 1313 Vine Street, Hollywood, CA 90028, United States of America
Tel: (1) 310 247 3010
Fax: (1) 310 247 3794
Email: nicholl@oscars.org
Website: www.oscars.org/nicholl
Contact: Mr Greg Beal, Programme Co-ordinator

The Academy of Motion Picture Arts and Sciences annually presents Academy Awards for motion picture artistic achievement. The Academy Film Archive is a leader in preservation and restoration and the Academy's Margaret Herrick Library holds a vast array of film-related materials. The Student Academy Awards honours achievements by talented student filmmakers.

Don and Gee Nicholl Fellowships in Screenwriting

Subjects: Screenwriting.
Purpose: To foster the development of new writers.
Eligibility: Open to writers in English who have not earned more than US$5,000 writing for film or television. Adaptations are not eligible.
Level of Study: Unrestricted
Type: Fellowship
Value: US$30,000
Length of Study: 1 year
Frequency: Annual
Country of Study: Any country
No. of awards offered: Up to 5
Application Procedure: Applicants must complete an application form. This is available after January 1st and can be obtained by sending a written request via post or email or by visiting the website.
Closing Date: May 1st
Funding: Private
No. of awards given last year: 5
No. of applicants last year: 5879
Additional Information: In addition to the Academy Awards or Oscars and the Nicholl Fellowships, the Academy offers Student Film Awards for films completed by students at an accredited college or university.

ACADEMY OF NATURAL SCIENCES

1900 Benjamin Franklin Parkway, Philadelphia, PA 19103, United States of America
Tel: (1) 215 299 1000
Fax: (1) 215 299 1028
Email: kuter@acnatsci.org
Website: www.acnatsci.org/research/jessupinfo.html
Contact: Dr Lois Kuter, Volunteer Coordinator

Founded in 1812, the academy of natural sciences is the oldest continually operating museum of its kind in the Western Hemisphere. The Academy' s mission is to create the basis for a healthy and sustainable planet through exploration, research, and education.

The Bohlke Memorial Endowment Fund

Subjects: Ichthyology.
Purpose: To support graduate students and postdoctoral researchers to work with Ichthyology collection and library at the academy.
Eligibility: Open to all postgraduates and postdoctoral research workers.
Level of Study: Postdoctorate
Value: US$500, travel expenses and modest living accommodations
Study Establishment: Academy of Natural Sciences
Country of Study: United States of America
Application Procedure: A letter of application outlining proposed research and tentative budget should be sent.

For further information contact:

Academy of Natural Sciences
Contact: Dr John Lundberg

Academy of Natural Sciences
Contact: Dr Dominique Dagit

Jessup and McHenry Awards

Subjects: The Jessup award is for zoology and the McHenry award is for botany.
Purpose: To assist predoctoral and postdoctoral students working with biological collections at the Academy of Natural Sciences in Philadelphia.
Eligibility: Students commuting within the Philadelphia area are ineligible, otherwise eligibility is unrestricted.
Level of Study: Postgraduate, postdoctorate, doctorate, predoctorate
Type: Fellowship
Value: The stipend for subsistence is US$300 per week. Fellowships may include round trip travel costs of up to a total of US$500 for North American applicants, including Mexico and the Caribbean, and US$1,000 for applicants from other parts of the world. This is not guaranteed.
Length of Study: 2–12 weeks
Frequency: Annual
Study Establishment: The Academy of Natural Sciences
Country of Study: United States of America
Application Procedure: Applicants must send queries, requests for information and supporting information to the given address.
Closing Date: March 1st or October 1st
Funding: Private
No. of awards given last year: 3
Additional Information: The provision of scientific supplies and equipment is the responsibility of the student and the sponsoring curator.

John J. and Anna H. Gallagher Fellowship

Purpose: To offer an opportunity for postdoctoral research on the systematics of microscopic invertebrates.
Eligibility: Open to all postdoctorates.
Level of Study: Postdoctorate
Length of Study: 1 year
Study Establishment: The Academy of Natural Sciences
Country of Study: United States of America
Application Procedure: Application materials may be sent by email or post.

For further information contact:

Chair, Gallagher Fellowship Committee, c/o Ted Daeschler Academy of Natural Sciences

ACADIA UNIVERSITY

Wolfville, NS, B4P 2R6, Canada
Tel: (1) 902 585 1498
Fax: (1) 902 585 1096
Email: elaine.schofield@acadiau.ca
Website: www.acadiau.ca
Contact: Ms Elaine Schofield, Manager, Division of Research and Graduate Studies

Acadia University is an institution that is committed to providing a liberal education based on the highest standards. The University houses a scholarly community that aims to ensure a broadening life experience for students, faculty and staff.

Acadia Graduate Awards

Subjects: English, political science, sociology, biology, chemistry, computer science, geology, psychology, education and recreation management, mathematics and statistics.
Purpose: To financially support students.
Eligibility: Open to registered full-time graduate students at Acadia University.
Level of Study: Postgraduate
Type: Award
Value: Up to Canadian $9,000
Length of Study: 1–2 years
Frequency: Annual
Study Establishment: The Division of Research and Graduate Studies at Acadia University
Country of Study: Canada
No. of awards offered: Limited
Application Procedure: Applicants must write for details.
Closing Date: February 1st
Additional Information: Recipients of an Acadia Graduate Award should expect to undertake certain duties during the academic year (up to a minimum of 10 hours per week and a maximum of 100 hours per semester) as a condition of tenure of the award. The specific duties will be established by agreement at the beginning of each academic year.

Acadia University Research Fund

Subjects: All subjects.
Purpose: To support research.
Eligibility: Applicants must be either professors or librarians. Employed by Acadia University.
Level of Study: Research
Value: Canadian $2,500 per year
Length of Study: Up to 2 years
Frequency: Annual
Study Establishment: Acadia University
Country of Study: Canada
No. of awards offered: Varies
Application Procedure: Applicants must download the application form from the research and graduate studies website. The original and seven copies (typewritten, typeface no smaller than 12 font) must be submitted to the Dean of Research and Graduate Studies.
Closing Date: February 1st and October 1st
No. of awards given last year: Varies each year
No. of applicants last year: Varies

ACTION CANADA

515 West Hastings Street, c/o Morris J. Wosk Centre for Dialogue, Simon Fraser University, Vancouver, BC, V6B 5K3, Canada
Tel: (1) 604 268 7961
Fax: (1) 604 268 7956
Email: actioncanada@sfu.ca
Website: www.actioncanada.ca

Action Canada is a national organization committed to building leadership for the future of Canada through an innovative fellowship program.

Action Canada Fellowships

Subjects: All subjects.
Purpose: To support applicants in the early years of their careers.
Eligibility: Open to applicants who are citizens of Canada.
Level of Study: Postgraduate
Type: Fellowship
Value: Canadian $20,000 each
Frequency: Annual
Country of Study: Canada
No. of awards offered: 20
Application Procedure: A completed application form along with a curriculum vitae and proof of Canadian citizenship must be submitted. See the website for details.
Closing Date: February 15th
Contributor: Action Canada

ACTION CANCER

1 Marlborough Park, Belfast, BT9 6XS, Northern Ireland
Tel: (44) 28 9080 3344
Fax: (44) 28 9080 3356
Email: info@actioncancer.org
Website: www.actioncancer.org
Contact: Mr Robin McRoberts, Chief Executive

Action Cancer is a Northern Ireland cancer charity that relies entirely on voluntary donations. Founded in 1973, it offers awareness and health promotion, free early-detection clinics for men and women concerned about cancer and a support service for cancer patients and their families. Action Cancer also provides funding for research at local universities.

Action Cancer Pilot Grants

Subjects: Cancer-related projects.
Purpose: To help researchers in Northern Ireland carry out cancer-related projects by contributing to the cost of equipment or materials. Preference will be given to the support of individuals early in their career.
Eligibility: Researchers must be working in Northern Ireland.
Level of Study: Postdoctorate
Type: Grant
Value: UK £10,000
Length of Study: 1 year
Frequency: Annual
Country of Study: United Kingdom
No. of awards offered: 5
Application Procedure: Awards are advertised in the local press in March. Applicants must submit an application form, based on which a decision is made by the Scientific and Research Committee.
Closing Date: Early May
Funding: Private
Contributor: Voluntary donations
No. of awards given last year: 8
No. of applicants last year: 26

Action Cancer Project Grant

Subjects: Cancer-related projects.
Purpose: To help researchers in Northern Ireland carry out significant cancer-related projects by contributing to salaries, the purchase of materials and equipments and to other appropriate costs.
Eligibility: Researchers must be working in Northern Ireland.
Level of Study: Postdoctorate
Type: Project grant
Value: Up to UK £45,000 per year for up to 3 years
Length of Study: 3 years
Frequency: Every 2 years
Country of Study: United Kingdom
No. of awards offered: 1
Application Procedure: Awards are advertised in the local press in March. Applicants must submit a form, based on which a decision is taken by the Action Cancer Scientific and Research Committee, which also takes advice from external reviewers.
Closing Date: Early May
Funding: Private
Contributor: Voluntary donations
No. of awards given last year: None

Action Cancer Research Studentship

Subjects: Cancer-related projects.
Purpose: To provide an opportunity for an outstanding graduate in an appropriate chemical, biological or biomedical science, to work on a cancer-related research project and undergo research training with a view to being awarded a PhD from the Queen's University of Belfast or the University of Ulster.
Eligibility: Supervisors must be researchers in Northern Ireland.
Level of Study: Doctorate
Type: Studentship
Value: Approx. UK £17,800 per year
Length of Study: 3 years
Frequency: Annual

Country of Study: United Kingdom
No. of awards offered: 1
Application Procedure: Awards are advertised in the local press in December. Supervisors must submit an application form, and on receipt of the award must advertise for an appropriate student. Applications are reviewed externally and a decision is taken on the award by Action Cancer's Scientific and Research Committee.
Closing Date: Early January
Funding: Private
Contributor: Voluntary donations
No. of awards given last year: 1
No. of applicants last year: 10

ACTION MEDICAL RESEARCH

Vincent House, Horsham, West Sussex, RH12 2DP, England
Tel: (44) 14 0321 0406
Fax: (44) 14 0321 0541
Email: info@action.org.uk
Website: www.action.org.uk

Action Medical Research is a national research charity dedicated to preventing and treating disabling diseases. The charity supports a broad spectrum of research with the objective of preventing disease and disability, regardless of age group, and alleviating physical handicap. Emphasis is placed on clinical research, or research at the clinical and basic interface.

Action Medical Research Project Grants

Subjects: Preventing disease and disability regardless of cause or age group and alleviating physical handicap. The exceptions are cancer, cardiovascular, HIV and AIDS research.
Purpose: To support one precisely formulated line of research.
Eligibility: Open to researchers based in the United Kingdom. Grants are not awarded to MRC units, other charities or for higher education.
Level of Study: Unrestricted
Type: Grant
Value: Varies
Length of Study: Up to 3 years, assessed annually
Frequency: Dependent on funds available, see the website
Study Establishment: Hospitals, universities and recognized research establishments
Country of Study: United Kingdom
No. of awards offered: Varies
Application Procedure: Applicants must submit a one-page outline of the project before an application form can be issued. Full details and outline proposals are available on the website.
Closing Date: Please contact the Charity or visit the website
Funding: Private
Contributor: Voluntary income
No. of awards given last year: 15
No. of applicants last year: 99

Action Medical Research Training Fellowship

Subjects: Preventing disease and disability regardless of cause or age group and alleviating physical handicap. The exceptions are cancer, cardiovascular, HIV and AIDS research.
Purpose: To enable the training of young medical and non-medical graduates in research techniques and methodology in areas of interest to Research Action.
Eligibility: Open to medical and non-medical graduates, preferably between 23 and 32 years old, as this is a training position. Although it is not limited to United Kingdom citizens, those who do not hold United Kingdom citizenship must be able to show that they have all the required statutory documentation, eg. work permits, to cover the period of the fellowship. No grants are made purely for higher education.
Level of Study: Doctorate, postdoctorate, postgraduate
Type: Fellowship
Value: Varies
Length of Study: Up to 3 years
Study Establishment: A hospital or university department
Country of Study: United Kingdom
No. of awards offered: Varies
Application Procedure: Applicants must submit a one-page outline of the project before an application form can be issued. Full details and outline proposal forms are available on the website.
Closing Date: Please contact the Charity or visit the website
Funding: Private
Contributor: Voluntary income
No. of awards given last year: 5
No. of applicants last year: 51
Additional Information: Fellowships are advertised separately each year in late November.

THE ACTUARIAL FOUNDATION

475 North Martingale Road, Suite 600, Schaumburg, IL 60173-2226, United States of America
Tel: (1) 847 706 3565
Fax: (1) 847 706 3599
Email: sbaker@soa.org
Website: www.soa.org
Contact: Sheree Baker, Business Manager

The Committee on Knowledge Extension of the SOA and the AERF committee of The Actuarial Foundation carry out research and education projects in actuarial science and studies specific projects that could be advanced under this mechanism.

The AERF/CKER Individual Grants Competition

Subjects: Actuarial science.
Purpose: To produce publications that will advance actuarial science, especially with regard to practical applications.
Eligibility: Proposals are invited from members of the seven sponsoring actuarial organizations (AAA, ASPA, CIA, CAS, CONAC, CCA and SoA), from faculty members of universities or colleges who have teaching and research responsibilities in actuarial or related fields and by others who are qualified by knowledge and experience to contribute to their goals.
Level of Study: Unrestricted
Type: Grant
Value: Varies, approx. US$10,000–15,000
Length of Study: Projects should generally be of less than 1 year in duration
Frequency: Annual
Country of Study: Any country
No. of awards offered: Varies
Application Procedure: Applicants must submit a letter of intent and an application form.
Funding: Private
Contributor: The Actuarial Foundation and the Canadian Institute of Actuary and individuals.
Additional Information: The project may be either theoretical or empirical in nature. A key criteria is that the project should have the potential to contribute significantly to the advancement of knowledge in actuarial science. The Actuarial Foundation and the SOA give preference to projects relating to current policy issues or having direct applications and those that further the basic or continuing education of actuaries. Proposals for innovative developments in actuarial education are also considered by The Actuarial Foundation and the SOA. More information is available from the website.

THE ADA FOUNDATION

211 East Chicago Avenue, Chicago, IL, 60611-2678, United States of America
Tel: (1) 312 440 2567
Fax: (1) 312 440 3526
Email: adaf@ada.org
Website: www.ada.org
Contact: The Director

The purpose of the ADA Foundation Charitable Assistance Programs is to provide a measure of financial assistance to individuals who have financial hardship, whether due to educational needs, chemical dependency, disability or disaster.

ADA Foundation Allied Dental Health Scholarship

Subjects: Dental hygiene, dental assisting and dental laboratory technology.
Purpose: To defray study expenses including tuition fees, books, and living expenses.
Eligibility: Open to citizens of the United States of America only. Applicants must either be entering their 1st year (Dental Assisting) or final year (Dental Laboratory Technology and Dental Hygiene). Applicants must have a minimum grade point average of 3.0 based on a 4.0 scale and show financial need of at least US$1,000.
Level of Study: Professional development
Type: Scholarship
Value: US$1,000
Frequency: Annual
Country of Study: United States of America
No. of awards offered: 15 dental hygiene, 10 dental assisting and 5 dental laboratory technology
Application Procedure: Application forms are available from the dental hygiene, dental laboratory technology and dental assisting programme directors, and are distributed by school officials. Application forms must be original, typed, completed and signed with the assistance of school officials. Applicants must submit a completed application form, including the Academic Achievement Record Form and Financial Needs Assessment Form signed by school officials, two typed reference forms sealed and noted on the back of the envelopes by the referees and a typed biographical sketch.
Closing Date: August 15th for dental hygiene and dental laboratory technology or September 15th for dental assisting.
Funding: Private
Contributor: The ADA Foundation
No. of awards given last year: 15 for dental hygiene, 10 for dental assisting and 5 for dental laboratory technology
Additional Information: This scholarship is not renewable.

ADA Foundation Dental Student Scholarship

Subjects: Dentistry.
Purpose: To defray school expenses including tuition, fees, books, supplies and living expenses.
Eligibility: Open to citizens of the United States of America only. Applicants must be full-time entering 2nd year students enrolled in a dental school accredited by the Commission on Dental Accreditation of the American Dental Association. Applicants must have a minimum grade point average of 3.0 based on a 4.0 scale and show financial need of at least US$2,500.
Level of Study: Postgraduate
Type: Scholarship
Value: US$2,500
Frequency: Annual
Country of Study: United States of America
No. of awards offered: 15–25
Application Procedure: Application forms are available only at dental schools and are distributed by school officials. Forms must be original, typed, completed and signed with the assistance of school officials. Applicants must submit a completed application form, including the Academic Achievement Record Form and Financial Needs Assessment Form signed by school officials, two typed reference forms sealed and noted on the back of the envelopes by the referrers and a typed biographical sketch.
Closing Date: July 31st
Funding: Private
Contributor: The ADA Foundation
No. of awards given last year: 25
No. of applicants last year: 83
Additional Information: This scholarship is not renewable.

ADELPHI UNIVERSITY

School of Business, Hagedorn Hall of Enterprise, Room 121,
1 South Avenue, P.O. BOX 701, Garden City, NY, 11530-0701,
United States of America
Tel: (1) 516 877 4670
Fax: (1) 516 877 4607
Email: GradBusInquiries@adelphi.edu
Website: www.business.adelphi.edu

Adelphi University is the oldest Institution of Higher Education for liberal arts and sciences on Long Island.

Adelphi University Dean's Award

Subjects: All subjects.
Level of Study: Postgraduate
Type: Scholarship
Value: US$4,000–9,500
Frequency: Annual
Study Establishment: Adelphi University
Application Procedure: Students must file an admissions application.
Closing Date: February 15th
Funding: Private

Adelphi University Presidential Scholarship

Subjects: All subjects.
Purpose: To reward exceptional academic achievement.
Level of Study: Postgraduate
Type: Scholarship
Length of Study: US$12,500–14,500
Study Establishment: Adelphi University
Application Procedure: Students must file an admissions application.
Closing Date: February 15th
Funding: Private

Adelphi University Provost Scholarship

Subjects: All subjects.
Level of Study: Postgraduate
Type: Scholarship
Value: US$10,000–12,000
Frequency: Annual
Study Establishment: Adelphi University
Application Procedure: Students must file an admissions application.
Closing Date: February 15th
Funding: Private

Adelphi University Talent Awards

Subjects: Theatre, dance, art, music.
Level of Study: Postgraduate
Type: Scholarship
Value: US$4,000–9,500
Frequency: Annual
Study Establishment: Adelphi University
Application Procedure: Students must file an admissions application.
Closing Date: February 15th

Adelphi University Trustee Scholarship

Subjects: All subjects.
Level of Study: Postgraduate
Type: Scholarship
Value: Full tuition fees
Length of Study: 1 year
Application Procedure: Students must file an admissions application.
Closing Date: February 15th
Funding: Private
Contributor: Adelphi University

Adephi University Athletic Grants

Subjects: Athletics.
Level of Study: Postgraduate
Type: Scholarship
Value: Full tuition fees
Frequency: Annual
Study Establishment: Adephi University
Application Procedure: Students must file an admissions application.
Closing Date: February 15th

ADOLPH AND ESTHER GOTTLIEB FOUNDATION, INC.

380 West Broadway, New York, NY 10012, United States of America
Tel: (1) 212 226 0581
Fax: (1) 212 226 0584
Email: sross@gottliebfoundation.org
Website: www.gottliebfoundation.org
Contact: Sheila Ross, Grants Manager

The Adolph and Esther Gottlieb Foundation is a non-profit corporation registered with the state of New York. It was established to award financial aid to mature creative painters, sculptors and printmakers.

Gottlieb Foundation Emergency Assistance Grants

Subjects: Painting, sculpture and printmaking.
Purpose: To provide interim financial assistance to creative visual artists whose need is the result of unforeseen catastrophic incident.
Eligibility: Open to painters, sculptors and printmakers who can demonstrate a minimum of 10 years of involvement in a mature phase of their work and who do not have the resources to meet the costs incurred by a catastrophic event e.g. fire, flood or emergency medical expenses. The disciplines of film, photography or related forms are not eligible unless the work involves directly, or can be interpreted as, painting or sculpture.
Level of Study: Unrestricted
Type: Grant
Value: Up to US$10,000. US$4,000 is typical on a one time basis only
Frequency: Dependent on funds available
Country of Study: Any country
No. of awards offered: Varies
Application Procedure: Applicants must complete and submit an application form which is available from the Foundation throughout the year and may be requested by telephone. Second party requests are honoured only when the applicant is physically unable to communicate with the Foundation.
Closing Date: Please write for details
Funding: Private
Contributor: An endowment
Additional Information: Maturity is based on the level of technical, intellectual and creative development of the artist. The programme does not cover general indebtedness, dental work, unemployment, capital improvements, long-term disabilities or project funding. Review procedures for completed applications begin as soon as they are received. Full review generally takes about four weeks from the time an application is complete. Situations with imminent deadlines will receive priority. When a situation warrants it, reviews can be completed within 24 to 48 hours.

Gottlieb Foundation Individual Support Grants

Subjects: Painting, sculpture and printmaking.
Purpose: To recognize and support serious, fully committed painters, sculptors and printmakers who are in financial need.
Eligibility: Open to creative painters, sculptors and printmakers who have been in a mature phase of their work for at least 20 years and require financial assistance to continue this work. United States residency is not required. The Gottlieb Foundation does not provide funding for organizations, projects of any type, educational institutions, students, graphic artists or those working in crafts. The disciplines of photography, film, video or related forms are not eligible unless the work directly involves, or can be interpreted as, painting or sculpture.
Level of Study: Unrestricted
Type: Grant
Value: Varies
Length of Study: 1 year
Frequency: Annual
Country of Study: Any country
No. of awards offered: 12
Application Procedure: Applicants must include a current application form, available from the foundation, and a small group of slides of the artist's work that illustrates the progressive development of the art for at least a 20-year period. These slides must be properly labelled and dated. Applicants must also include a written statement in narrative form. This statement should include outside jobs which have helped support the artist's career, changes in artistic approach that have occurred, and other facts which can aid the review panel in forming an accurate picture. All aspects of artistic history, ie. education, exhibitions, etc., should be described, and dates must be provided for all information. Financial disclosure, which entails completing a disclosure page and submitting a copy of a federal tax return for the past year, is necessary in the determination of financial need. A stamped addressed envelope for the return of supplementary materials must also be included.
Closing Date: December 15th. Awards are distributed the following March
Funding: Private
Contributor: An endowment
Additional Information: Artists who have been awarded a grant must allow one year to elapse before reapplication. Only first person written requests for application forms will be honoured.

AFRICAN NETWORK OF SCIENTIFIC AND TECHNOLOGICAL INSTITUTIONS (ANSTI)

PO Box 30592, Nairobi, Kenya
Tel: (254) 2 622 619
Fax: (254) 2 622 750
Email: info@ansti.org
Website: www.ansti.org
Contact: Administrative Assistant

The African Network of Scientific and Technological Institutions (ANSTI) is an organ of co-operation that embraces institutions engaged in the fields of science and technology. To date it has 126 member institutions in 33 countries in Sub-Saharan Africa.

ANSTI Postgraduate Fellowships

Subjects: Basic and engineering sciences.
Purpose: To enable students to pursue Master's and PhD courses in the basic and engineering sciences.
Eligibility: Open only to African nationals who are staff members of ANSTI member institutions. Applicants must possess a good Bachelor's degree and must be below 36 years of age.
Level of Study: Doctorate, postgraduate
Type: Fellowship
Value: Varies, approx. US$12,000
Length of Study: Varies, approx. 1.5 years
Frequency: Annual
Study Establishment: ANSTI member institutions
Application Procedure: Applicants must complete an application form, available by contacting ANSTI by mail, fax or email, or by visiting our website.
Closing Date: March 31st
Funding: Government
Contributor: DAAD/UNESCO
No. of awards given last year: 5
No. of applicants last year: 52
Additional Information: The applicant is responsible for gaining admission into the university of his or her choice. Preference is given to graduates with a few years of experience.

AFRO-ASIAN INSTITUTE (AAI) IN VIENNA AND CATHOLIC WOMEN'S LEAGUE OF AUSTRIA

Student Division, Türkenstrasse 3, A-1090 Vienna, Austria
Tel: (43) 310 5145
Fax: (43) 310 5145 213
Email: s.angerler@aai-wien.at
Website: www.aai-wien.at
Contact: Mr Maga. Susanne Angerler, Study Advisor

The Afro-Asian Institute (AAI)'s major function is to aid students from the developing countries of Africa, Asia and Latin America. Presently, the AAI provides services for more than 5,000 students from developing countries, which counts as an acknowledged contribution to Austrian development aid.

One World Scholarship Program

Subjects: All subjects.
Purpose: To promote cultural exchange, international development and international co-operation aid.
Eligibility: Open to nationals of developing countries in Africa, Asia and Latin America aged 18–35 years who have had adequate previous study or vocational practice in the specific field for which the scholarship is applied. Preference is given to candidates who are able to speak German. Only those in financial need will be considered, and the applicability of the special branch of study or training in the applicant's home country is essential. It is expected that scholars will return to their home country after studying. Good, and sometimes excellent, study results are also required. Preference is given to applicants from the least developed countries. It is a requirement that applicants have already started their studies in Austria.
Level of Study: Doctorate, graduate, unrestricted
Type: Scholarship
Value: UK £475–510 per month
Frequency: Annual
Study Establishment: Universities
Country of Study: Austria
No. of awards offered: Varies
Application Procedure: Applicants must complete an application form, which is available from the Institute. Only personal applications will be considered. Postal applications from abroad will not be answered.
Closing Date: Please contact the organization
Funding: Private, government
Contributor: The Catholic Church
Additional Information: It is one of AAI's essential aims to establish a 'partnership' contact between assisted students and the scholarship donor that continues beyond the termination of studies. Only about 10 per cent of applicants can be accepted.

AGRICULTURAL HISTORY SOCIETY

Minard Hall, North Dakota State University, Fargo, North Dahota, Iowa, 58105, United States of America
Tel: (1) 701 231 5831
Fax: (1) 701 231 5832
Email: ndsu.agricultural.history@ndsu.nodak.edu
Website: www.agriculturalhistory.ndsu.nodak.edu
Contact: Editor

The Agricultural History Society recognizes the roles of agriculture and agri-business in shaping the political, economic, social and historical profiles of different countries worldwide. Since 1927, the Society's publication, *Agricultural History*, has been the international journal for the field and publishes innovative research on agricultural and rural history.

Everett E Edwards Awards in Agricultural History

Subjects: Agricultural and rural history.
Purpose: To encourage and reward scholarly work in the field. The award was established in 1953 in memory and recognition of the outstanding services of Everett Eugene Edwards, a long-time agricultural historian and editor of *Agricultural History* from 1931 to 1951.
Eligibility: Open to any graduate or doctoral student submitting an article to *Agricultural History* during the calendar year.
Level of Study: Graduate
Type: Award
Value: US$200 plus publication in the Journal
Frequency: Annual
Country of Study: Any country
No. of awards offered: 1
Application Procedure: Applicants must submit three copies of their manuscript, prepared in accordance with the latest edition of the *Chicago Manual of Style*, to the editor.
Closing Date: December 31st
Additional Information: The award is presented annually to the author of the winning article at the Agricultural History Society's Presidential Luncheon. In addition, the winning submission is published in the fall issue of *Agricultural History*. Further information is available on request.

Gilbert C Fite Dissertation Award

Subjects: Agricultural and rural history.
Purpose: To reward the best dissertation.
Eligibility: Open to any doctoral student who has completed a PhD dissertation.
Level of Study: Doctorate
Type: Award
Value: US$300
Frequency: Annual
Country of Study: Any country
No. of awards offered: 1
Application Procedure: Applicants must complete forms and send three copies to the editor.
Closing Date: Please contact the organization
Additional Information: Further information is available on request.

Theodore Saloutos Award

Subjects: Agricultural and rural history in the United States of America.
Purpose: To reward the best book published annually in the United States of America on the subject of agricultural history.
Eligibility: Open to nationals of any country. Books must be based on substantial primary research and should represent a major new scholarly interpretation or reinterpretation of agricultural history scholarship.
Level of Study: Unrestricted
Type: Prize
Value: US$500
Frequency: Annual
Country of Study: Any country
Application Procedure: Applicants must send four copies of the book to the editor. Books may be nominated by their authors, the publisher, a member of the award committee, or a member of the Society.
Closing Date: Please contact the organization
Additional Information: Further information is available on request.

Vernon Carstensen Award in Agricultural History

Subjects: Agricultural and rural history.
Purpose: To promote research and publication. The award was established in 1980 to recognize Vernon Carstensen's services to agricultural history by his former students.
Eligibility: Open to any author published in the quarterly journal *Agricultural History* during the calendar year.
Level of Study: Doctorate, postdoctorate
Type: Award
Value: US$200
Frequency: Annual
Country of Study: Any country
No. of awards offered: 1
Application Procedure: All published articles per issue and year are considered.
Closing Date: The Autumn issue of the Journal each year
Additional Information: Vernon Carstensen served as editor of Agricultural History from 1953 to 1957 and as president of the *Agricultural History* Society from 1957 to 1958. Further information is available on request.

AIDS ACTION

1906 Sunderland Place NW, Washington, DC, 20036, United States of America
Tel: (1) 202 530-8030
Fax: (1) 202 530-8031
Email: Zamora@aidsaction.org
Website: www.aidsaction.org
Contact: Coordinator, Pedro Zamora Fellowship Program

AIDS Action, founded in 1984, is the National AIDS Organization dedicated to the development, analysis, cultivation, and encouragement of sound policies and programs in response to the HIV epidemic.

The Pedro Zamora Public Policy Fellowship

Subjects: Research into a variety of public health and civil rights issues related to HIV prevention, treatment and care.
Purpose: To fund both undergraduate and postgraduate students seeking experience in public policy and government affairs focussed on HIV/AIDS issues.
Level of Study: Postgraduate, graduate
Type: Fellowship
Value: Stipend plus expenses
Length of Study: 26 weeks
Frequency: 3 times per year
Country of Study: United States of America
Application Procedure: Applicants must apply with covering letter, curriculum vitae, writing sample and essay. Check website for up-to-date details.
Closing Date: November 1st, March 15th, July 15th
Funding: Private

THE AIREY NEAVE TRUST

PO Box 36800, Fifth Floor, 40 Bernard Street, London, WC1N 1WJ, England
Tel: (44) 20 7833 4440
Email: hanthoc@aol.com
Website: www.aireyneavetrust.org.uk
Contact: The Trustees

Initiated in 1979, the Airey Neave Trust sponsors research into the protection of personal freedom under the law against the threat of terrorism, political violence and torture. It also provides financial support for any person who is a refugee, with particular emphasis on postgraduates and those retraining in their professions.

The Airey Neave Research Fellowships

Subjects: Research into the protection of personal freedom under the law against the threat of terrorism, political violence and torture.
Purpose: To support serious research connected with national and international law and human freedom.
Level of Study: Postdoctorate, research, fellowships
Type: Fellowship
Value: UK £20,000
Length of Study: Up to 3 years
Study Establishment: An institution attached to a particular university in the United Kingdom
Country of Study: United Kingdom
No. of awards offered: 1 to 3 per year
Application Procedure: Contact the organization for more details. No application form required but copy of an up to date curriculum vitae, certificate of mental fitness 2 referees research plan up to 500 words.
Closing Date: None
Funding: Trusts
No. of awards given last year: 2
No. of applicants last year: 2
Additional Information: The trust also supports work in the following areas: (i) research into transnational networks and their implications for international security. The study will investigate the use of networks by criminal and terrorist organizations for activities such as money-laundering and arms sales (Centre of International Studies, Cambridge University); and (ii) research assistance to the Metropolitan Police in preventing, deterring, disrupting and detecting terrorist activity, particularly in its preparatory stages.

The Airey Neave Trust Scholarship

Purpose: To provide help for postgraduate refugees.
Eligibility: Postgraduate refugees. Applicants who have applied for and got British citizenship excluded applicants who have applied for and got British citizenship excluded.
Level of Study: Professional development, postgraduate, postdoctorate, doctorate, medical doctors
Value: Grants average UK £1,000–1,500 per year
Frequency: Annual
Country of Study: United Kingdom
No. of awards offered: 20
Application Procedure: Applications are in March every year and must include completed application forms, two references and copies of home office documents confirming that the applicant is a refugee or has indefinite leave to stay in the United Kingdom.
Closing Date: May 31st
No. of awards given last year: 21
No. of applicants last year: 30

ALABAMA BANKERS ASSOCIATION (ABA)

543 Adams Avenue, Nontgomery, Alabama, 36104, United States of America
Tel: (1) 334 834 1890
Fax: (1) 334 834 4443
Email: info@alabamabankers.org
Website: www.alabamabankers.org

The ABA, founded in 1890, is the state's largest and oldest banking industry trade organization representing 155 banks with more than US$100 billion in total assets. The association provides a variety of member services, including publications, educational seminars and schools, as well as state and federal legislative updates.

Adams Foundation Banking School Scholarship

Subjects: Banking.
Purpose: To enhance the banking skills of the students.
Eligibility: Open to candidates who are good, sound bankers and business people.
Level of Study: Postgraduate
Type: Scholarship
Length of Study: 3 years
Frequency: Annual
Application Procedure: A completed application form must be submitted.
Funding: Foundation
Contributor: The Adams Foundation

Kenneth R. McCartha Scholarship

Subjects: Banking.
Purpose: To assist students who aspire to a career in banking.
Eligibility: Open to students with above-average academic achievement.
Level of Study: Postgraduate
Type: Scholarship
Value: US$1,500
Frequency: Annual
Country of Study: United States of America
Application Procedure: A completed application form must be submitted.

Mary Zoghby Award

Subjects: Financial education.
Purpose: To recognize education coordinators for their effort in promoting financial education in their community.
Eligibility: Open to all education coordinators who demonstrate outstanding economic education efforts in their community.
Level of Study: Postgraduate
Type: Scholarship
Value: US$500
Frequency: Annual
Application Procedure: A completed application form must be submitted.

ALBAN PROGRAMME

Association Grupo Stander, Universidade do Porto, Rua de Ceuta 118-5-5/35, PORTA, 4050-150, Portugal
Tel: (351) 22 2046 159
Email: info@programalban.org
Website: www.programalban.org

In 2002 the European commission adopted a high level scholarship programme specifically addressed to Latin America. The programme Alban aims at the reinforcement of the European union-Latin America co-operation in the area of higher education and cover studies for postgraduate as well as higher training for Latin American professionals.

Alban Scholarship

Subjects: All subjects.
Purpose: To support Latin American students who wish to pursue higher studies.
Eligibility: Open to Latin American students wishing to study at postgraduate level.
Level of Study: Postgraduate
Type: Scholarship
Value: 33% of tuition fees
Length of Study: 6 months–3 years
Frequency: Annual
No. of awards offered: 30
Application Procedure: Application form available on the website.
Closing Date: December 22nd
Contributor: Programme Alban

UFA Student Aid Programme

Subjects: Any subject.
Purpose: To help defray the cost of books, room and board, and the like.
Eligibility: Applicant must be of Ukranian ancestry.
Level of Study: Postgraduate
Type: Grant
Value: An annual stipend of US$300
Length of Study: 2 years
Frequency: Annual
Country of Study: United States of America
Application Procedure: Contact the association.
Closing Date: May 31st

THE ALBERT EINSTEIN INSTITUTION

427 Newbury Street, Boston, MA, 02115, United States of America
Tel: (1) 617 247 4882
Fax: (1) 617 247 4035
Email: einstein@igc.org
Website: www.aeinstein.org
Contact: Mr Ronald M McCarthy, Fellows Programme Director

The Albert Einstein Institution conducts programmes of publication, educational outreach, consulting and research in order to develop and disseminate knowledge of the potential for non-violent forms of struggles to contribute to the effective settlement of conflict. It focuses particularly on areas where violence may be employed to suppress the aspirations of peoples and groups.

The Albert Einstein Fellows Programme

Subjects: Political science, international relations, sociology, history.
Purpose: The primary goal of the programme is to promote and to encourage significant contributions to the study of non-violent action in relation to problems of political violence.
Eligibility: There are restrictions regarding citizenship, race, sex, or age. The programme supports candidates for doctoral degrees undertaking dissertation research or writing dissertations, advanced scholars undertaking specific research projects and practitioners in past or present non-violent struggles preparing documentation, description and analysis of conflicts.
Level of Study: Research, doctorate
Type: Fellowship
Value: The normal financial support for an Einstein Institution Fellow is a stipend that takes into consideration such factors as the applicant's level of preparation, need and prevailing academic salaries for comparable projects. Applicants may also submit requests for assistance in meeting expenses relating to the conduct of research and writing
Length of Study: 1 year (extension possible)
Study Establishment: The Albert Einstein Institute
Country of Study: United States of America
Application Procedure: Applications need not be submitted on a specific form.
Closing Date: Letter of intent may be submitted throughout the year. Proposal for academic year support must be received before January 1st

ALBERT ELLIS INSTITUTE

45 East 65th Street, New York, NY, 10021, United States of America
Tel: (1) 212 535 0822
Fax: (1) 212 249 3582
Email: info@albertellis.org
Website: www.rebt.org
Contact: Fellowships Office

The Albert Ellis Institute is a non-profit training and therapy institute chartered by the regents of the University of the State of New York, specializing in cognitive behaviour therapy and rational emotive behaviour therapy.

Albert Ellis Institute Clinical Fellowship

Subjects: Psychology and counselling.
Purpose: To provide in-depth, hands-on training in cognitive behavioural therapy and rational emotive behaviour therapy.
Eligibility: Applicants must be in a doctoral programme, hold a PhD, MSW, MD or RN and be licence-eligible in their place of practice. There are no other restrictions.
Level of Study: Postdoctorate, postgraduate, predoctorate
Type: Fellowship
Value: US$6,000
Length of Study: 2 years
Frequency: Annual
Country of Study: United States of America
No. of awards offered: Varies
Application Procedure: Applicants must obtain applications and further information by writing to the Institute.
Closing Date: February 15th
Funding: Private
No. of awards given last year: 6
Additional Information: The programme begins in mid-July.

ALBERTA HERITAGE FOUNDATION FOR MEDICAL RESEARCH (AHFMR)

1500 Bell Tower, 10104-103 Avenue, Edmonton, AB, T5J 4A7, Canada
Tel: (1) 780 423 5727
Fax: (1) 780 429 3509
Email: ahfmrinfo@ahfmr.ab.ca
Website: www.ahfmr.ab.ca
Contact: Dr Jacques Magnan, Director

The Alberta Heritage Foundation for Medical Research (AHFMR) supports a community of researchers who generate knowledge that improves the health and quality of life of Albertans and people throughout the world. The Foundation's long-term commitment is to fund basic patient and health research based on international standards of excellence and carried out by new and established investigators and researchers in training.

Alberta Heritage Clinical Fellowships

Subjects: Medical research.
Purpose: To provide an opportunity for research training to candidates who have completed clinical sub-speciality training requirements.

Eligibility: Open to candidates who hold an MD or DDS and who have received a significant portion of postgraduate training in Alberta.
Level of Study: Postgraduate
Type: Fellowship
Value: Canadian $3,000 research allowance plus stipend
Length of Study: 2 years, with a possibility of renewal for a further year
Study Establishment: An appropriate institution, usually in Alberta
Country of Study: Canada
No. of awards offered: Approx. 10
Application Procedure: Applicants must complete an application form.
Closing Date: March 1st and September 1st
Funding: Government
No. of awards given last year: 14
No. of applicants last year: 18

Alberta Heritage Full-Time Fellowships

Subjects: Medical research.
Purpose: To enable doctoral graduates to prepare for careers as independent investigators.
Eligibility: Open to graduates of science programmes relevant to AHFMR objectives or to health professional programmes who have received a PhD not more than five years prior to application. Professional health degrees should not have been received more than 10 years prior to application.
Level of Study: Postdoctorate
Type: Fellowship
Value: Canadian $3,000 research allowance plus stipend
Study Establishment: Usually at a university in Alberta
Country of Study: Canada
No. of awards offered: Varies
Application Procedure: Applicants must complete an application form.
Closing Date: March 1st and September 30th
Funding: Government
No. of awards given last year: 35
No. of applicants last year: 113

Alberta Heritage Full-Time Studentship

Subjects: Medical sciences.
Purpose: To enable academically superior students to undertake full-time research training in a discipline relevant to the objectives of the Foundation.
Eligibility: Open to candidates sponsored by a faculty supervisor. The supervisor must have a record of productive health orientated research and sufficient competitively acquired research funding to ensure the satisfactory conduct of the student's research during the term of the award. Students must be engaged in, or accepted into, a full-time university graduate programme in a health related discipline leading to a Master's or doctoral degree. Applicants must also hold a record of superior academic performance in studies relevant to the proposed training.
Type: Studentship
Value: Please write for details
Length of Study: 2 years with the possibility to renewal of a maximum of 5 years' support
Frequency: Annual
Study Establishment: A university in Alberta
Country of Study: Canada
No. of awards offered: Approx. 40–60
Application Procedure: Applicants must submit, in full, the original application to the Foundation's offices by either of the deadlines.
Closing Date: March 1st and September 30th
Funding: Government
No. of awards given last year: 92
No. of applicants last year: 260

Alberta Heritage Health Research Studentship

Subjects: Medical sciences.
Purpose: To enable academically superior students engaged in, or accepted in to, a full-time university programme to undertake full-time research training.
Value: Please write for details
Length of Study: 2 years with a possibility of renewal to a maximum of 5 years' support
Frequency: Annual
Study Establishment: A university in Alberta
Country of Study: Canada
No. of awards offered: Varies, approx. 10
Application Procedure: Applicants must submit the original application to the Foundation's offices by either of the deadlines. They must be completed in full to be entered into the competition.
Closing Date: March 1st and September 30th
Funding: Government
No. of awards given last year: 10
No. of applicants last year: 35

Alberta Heritage Part-Time Fellowships

Subjects: Medical research.
Purpose: To enable continuing active participation in research during professional education.
Eligibility: Open to graduates holding a PhD in a science relevant to AHFMR objectives or who are registered in a health professional programme in Alberta.
Level of Study: Postdoctorate
Type: Fellowship
Value: Pro-rated on full-time fellowship stipend and dependent on the amount of time spent in research
Length of Study: 1 year, renewable
Study Establishment: A university in Alberta
Country of Study: Canada
No. of awards offered: Approx. 5
Application Procedure: Applicants must complete an application form.
Closing Date: March 1st and September 30th
Funding: Government
No. of awards given last year: 5
No. of applicants last year: 6

Alberta Heritage Part-Time Studentship

Subjects: Medical research.
Purpose: To enable full-time degree students to continue research training on a part-time basis.
Eligibility: Open to students enrolled in a full-time professional degree programme who wish to continue research training on a part-time basis during the academic year.
Type: Studentship
Value: Pro-rated on full-time stipend rate of Canadian $16,500 and dependent on the amount of time spent in research
Length of Study: 2 years, to a maximum of 5 years' support
Study Establishment: A university in Alberta
Country of Study: Canada
No. of awards offered: Approx. 5
Application Procedure: Applicants must complete an application form.
Closing Date: March 1st and September 30th
Funding: Government
No. of awards given last year: 1
No. of applicants last year: 1

Dr Lionel E Mcleod Health Research Scholarship

Subjects: Health.
Purpose: To enable academically superior students engaged in, or accepted on to, a full-time university programme to undertake full-time research training.
Eligibility: Open to Canadian citizens or permanent residents who attend the Universities of Alberta, Calgary or British Columbia.
Level of Study: Postgraduate
Type: Scholarship
Value: Canadian $7,000–9,000
Frequency: Annual
Country of Study: Canada
No. of awards offered: 1
Application Procedure: Applicants must write for details.
Funding: Government, private

Heritage Health Research Career Renewal Awards

Subjects: Epidemiology, biostatistics, psychosocial sciences or clinical experimental method and design.
Purpose: To enable carefully selected Alberta faculty members with a demonstrated interest in clinical or health research to obtain training.
Eligibility: Open to candidates proposed and sponsored by an Alberta institution, which is prepared to ensure an adequate environment for the candidate on their return to the province. This environment should encompass fostering the development of a group of scientists to be capable of independent research and to be able to assist others in the design of patient based and population based research.
Level of Study: Postdoctorate
Value: Please write for details
Frequency: Annual, but dependent upon tenure of current scholarship
Country of Study: Canada
No. of awards offered: Varies
Application Procedure: Applicants must write for details.
Closing Date: March 1st and September 30th
Funding: Government
No. of awards given last year: 1
No. of applicants last year: 3

ALCOHOL BEVERAGE MEDICAL RESEARCH FOUNDATION

1122 Kenilworth Drive, Suite 407, Baltimore, MD, 21204, United States of America
Tel: (1) 410 821 7066
Fax: (1) 410 821 7065
Email: info@abmrf.org
Website: www.abmrf.org
Contact: Dr Robin A Kroft, Vice President

The Alcohol Beverage Medical Research Foundation is a non-profit independent research organization that provides support for scientific studies on the use of alcoholic beverages. It awards grants to study changes in drinking patterns, effects of moderate use of alcohol on health and well being and the mechanisms underlying the behavioural and biomedical effects of alcohol.

Alcohol Beverage Medical Research Foundation Research Project Grant

Subjects: Medical and behavioural sciences.
Purpose: To support new knowledge in order to prevent alcohol-related problems.
Level of Study: Doctorate
Type: Project grant
Value: Up to US$50,000 per year
Length of Study: Up to 2 years
Study Establishment: Non-profit universities and research institutions
Country of Study: United States of America or Canada
No. of awards offered: 30–40
Application Procedure: Applicants must complete an application form, available on request or from the website.
Closing Date: February 1st or September 1st
Funding: Private
No. of awards given last year: 40
No. of applicants last year: 150

ALCOHOL EDUCATION AND REHABILITATION FOUNDATION LTD.

PO Box 19 Deakin West, ACT 2600, Australia
Tel: (61) 02 6122 8600
Fax: (61) 02 6232 4400
Email: aerf@aerf.com.au
Website: www.aerf.com.au
Contact: Grants Officer

Our primary aim is to encourage responsible consumption of alcohol and emphasize the dangers of licit substance misuse. We do so by funding individuals that are directly in touch with these issues in their communities.

Alcohol Education and Rehabilitation Scholarship Grant

Subjects: Health services and support, medicine.
Level of Study: Postgraduate
Type: Scholarship
Length of Study: 3 years
Frequency: Annual
Closing Date: There is no application closing date
Funding: Foundation

ALCOHOL EDUCATION AND RESEARCH COUNCIL (AERC)

Room 408, Horseferry House, Dean Ryle Street, London, SW1P 2AW, England
Tel: (44) 20 7217 8028
Fax: (44) 20 7217 8847
Email: andrea.tilouche@aerc.org.uk
Website: www.aerc.org.uk
Contact: Andrea Tilouche, Committees and Grants Manager

AERC Research Grant

Subjects: Research on alcohol-related issues.
Purpose: To develop individuals as well as research in the alcohol field.
Level of Study: Research
Type: Grant
Value: UK £50,000
Length of Study: 1–3 years
Country of Study: United Kingdom
No. of awards offered: 4–5
Application Procedure: To apply, applicants must download the application form from the website and return the form as an email attachment after completion.
Contributor: The Alcohol Education and Research Council
Additional Information: Priority will be given to applications that focus upon the council's priorities.

AERC Small Grant

Subjects: Alcohol-related issues.
Purpose: To fund innovation and to increase the capacity of individuals and organizations in dealing with alcohol-related issues, and to develop the evidence base relating to these issues.
Level of Study: Unrestricted
Type: Grant
Value: UK £5,000
Country of Study: United Kingdom
No. of awards offered: Up to 10
Application Procedure: To apply, applicants download the application form from the website and return the filled application form as an email attachment.
Closing Date: No deadline
Contributor: The Alcohol Education and Research Council
Additional Information: Small grants are rapidly processed throughout the year.

AERC Studentship Grant

Subjects: Alcohol-related issues.
Purpose: To assist students who are working in the alcohol field and who wish to acquire professional qualifications by following a taught course.
Eligibility: Applicants must be resident in the United Kingdom and be registered at a United Kingdom educational institution. The applicant

should normally be working in the alcohol field for a voluntary agency in a paid capacity.
Type: Studentship
Value: UK £9,000 for full-time students (UK £11,000 within the city of London or Metropolitan Police Districts), UK £2,030 per year for part-time students
Length of Study: 1 year
Frequency: Annual
Country of Study: United Kingdom
Application Procedure: To apply, applicants must download the application form from the website: www.aerc.org.uk/grantsstud.html and return the filled application form as an email attachment.
Closing Date: May 6th
Contributor: The Alcohol Education and Research Council
Additional Information: The amounts and rates of the awards and the conditions that apply are similar to those of the Economic and Social Research Council.

ALEXANDER GRAHAM BELL ASSOCIATION FOR THE DEAF AND HARD OF HEARING

3417 Volta Place North West, Washington, DC, 20007, United States of America
Tel: (1) 202 337 5220
Fax: (1) 202 337 8314
Email: info@agbell.org
Website: www.agbell.org
Contact: Ms Lisa Ruffin Schauf, Financial Aid Coordinator

The Alexander Graham Bell Association for the Deaf and Hard of Hearing was established in 1890 to empower hearing-impaired persons to function independently by promoting universal rights and optimal opportunities to learn to use, maintain and improve all aspects of their verbal communications, including their abilities to speak, speech-read, use residual hearing and process both spoken and written language.

Alexander Graham Bell Scholarship Awards

Subjects: All subjects.
Purpose: To encourage severely or profoundly hearing-impaired students to attend regular hearing colleges. A G Bell offers financial aid and scholarships through four major programmes, which are parent-infant (0–6 years), school age, arts and sciences and college scholarships.
Eligibility: Open to auditory oral students born with profound hearing loss, 80 dB loss in the better ear, average, or a severe hearing loss, 60–80 dB loss, who experienced such a loss before acquiring language. Candidates must use speech and residual hearing and/or speech reading as their preferred customary form of communication and demonstrate a potential for leadership. In addition, applicants must have applied to, or already be enrolled in, a regular full-time college or university programme for hearing students.
Level of Study: Unrestricted
Type: Scholarship
Value: US$250–2,000
Frequency: Annual
Country of Study: United States of America
No. of awards offered: Varies
Application Procedure: Applicants must request an application form in writing between September 1st and January 1st. Fax copies or telephone applications will not be accepted. Applicants may visit the website or send an email to financialaid@agbell.org for current information.
Closing Date: March 1st
Funding: Private
Contributor: Members and donors
No. of awards given last year: 20
No. of applicants last year: Approx. 100

ALEXANDER S ONASSIS PUBLIC BENEFIT FOUNDATION

56 Amalias Avenue, Athens, GR-10558, Greece
Tel: (30) 210 371 3000
Fax: (30) 210 371 3013
Email: pubrel@onassis.gr
Website: www.onassis.gr
Contact: Deputy Director, Human Resource Manager

The Alexander S Onassis Public Benefit Foundation establishes and supports public benefit projects, offers services and makes contributions to other public benefit institutions for medical care, education, literature, religion, science, research, journalism, art, cultural matters, history, archaeology and sport. It also awards prizes, grants and scholarships to both Greeks and foreigners.

Onassis Foreigners' Fellowship Programme Educational Scholarships Category B

Subjects: Greek language, Greek literature, Greek history and civilization.
Purpose: To render possible the acquaintance, collaboration and exchange of information between the scholarship recipients and their Greek colleagues in Greek schools, education or other relevant departments of Greek universities.
Eligibility: Open to active elementary or high school foreign teachers who teach the Greek language, modern or ancient, Greek literature, Greek history and Greek civilization. Only persons of other than Greek nationality are eligible. However, persons of Greek descent, second generation and on, are also eligible providing they are permanently residing and working abroad or currently studying in foreign universities.
Type: Scholarship
Value: A monthly allowance plus hotel accommodation and a round trip air ticket
Length of Study: A maximum of 2 months
Frequency: Annual
Country of Study: Greece
No. of awards offered: 5
Application Procedure: Copies of the Announcement and the relevant nomination and application forms are available daily at the Foundation's Secretariat or from the website.
Closing Date: Please contact the organization
Additional Information: The programme presupposes that the scholarship recipients will continue offering their services to their country of origin after they have completed their training in Greece.

Onassis Foreigners' Fellowship Programme Educational Scholarships Category C

Subjects: All subjects.
Purpose: To render possible the acquaintance, collaboration and exchange of information between the scholarship recipients and their Greek colleagues in Greek schools, education or other relevant departments of Greek universities.
Eligibility: Open to foreign postgraduate students and PhD candidates up to 40 years of age who pursue studies in universities, scholarly or research centres or fine art schools either outside Greece or in Greece.
Level of Study: Doctorate, postgraduate
Type: Scholarship
Value: A monthly allowance plus hotel accommodation and a round trip air ticket
Length of Study: 5–10 months
Frequency: Annual
Country of Study: Greece
No. of awards offered: 17
Application Procedure: Copies of the Announcement and the relevant nomination and application forms are available daily at the Foundation's Secretariat or from the website.
Closing Date: Please contact the organization
Additional Information: The programme presupposes that the scholarship recipients will continue offering their services to their country of origin, after they have completed their training in Greece.

Onassis Foreigners' Fellowships Programme Research Grants Category AI

Subjects: Humanistic sciences, political sciences and the arts.
Purpose: To enable full members of national academies and full university professors whose scholarly or artistic work has been widely acclaimed and who wish to visit Greece in order to conduct scholarly research or to collaborate with educational institutions, research institutions or organizations.
Eligibility: Only persons of other than Greek nationality are eligible. However, persons of Greek descent, second generation and on, are also eligible providing they are permanently residing and working abroad or currently studying in foreign universities. Applicants must have had a professional academic career of at least 10 years.
Level of Study: Postdoctorate
Type: Research grant
Value: A monthly allowance plus a round trip air ticket and hotel accommodation
Length of Study: 1 month
Frequency: Annual
Country of Study: Greece
No. of awards offered: 10
Application Procedure: Copies of the Announcement and the relevant nomination and application forms are available daily at the Foundation's Secretariat or from the website.
Closing Date: Please contact the organization
Additional Information: Any person wishing to apply under this programme should specify the category in which they want to be considered in order to receive the relevant nomination and application form. Only one application form for one of the categories can be submitted.

Onassis Foreigners' Fellowships Programme Research Grants Category AII

Subjects: All subjects.
Purpose: To enable university or equivalent institutions' faculty, researchers, PhD holders, artists and musicians, and translators of Greek literature who wish to come to Greece either for scholarly research co-operation with a Greek university, research centre or institute or for their artistic creation or translation.
Eligibility: Only persons of other than Greek nationality are eligible. However, persons of Greek descent, second generation and on, are also eligible providing they are permanently residing and working abroad or currently studying in foreign universities. Applicants must have had a professional academic career of at least 10 years.
Level of Study: Postdoctorate
Type: Fellowship
Value: A monthly allowance plus hotel accommodation and a round trip air ticket
Length of Study: Up to 6 months
Frequency: Annual
Country of Study: Greece
No. of awards offered: 15
Application Procedure: Copies of the Announcement and the relevant nomination and application forms are available daily at the Foundation's Secretariat or from the website.
Closing Date: Please contact the organization
Additional Information: Any person wishing to apply under this programme should specify the category in which they want to be considered in order to receive the relevant nomination and application form. Only one application form for one of the categories can be submitted.

ALEXANDER VON HUMBOLDT FOUNDATION

Jean-Paul Strasse 12, Bonn, 53173, Germany
Tel: (49) 228 833 0
Fax: (49) 228 833 199
Email: info@avh.de
Website: www.humboldt-foundation.de
Contact: Dr Barbara Sheldon

The Alexander von Humboldt Foundation grants research fellowships to foreign scholars who hold doctorates and have not yet reached the age of 40. The Foundation also offers research awards to internationally recognized foreign scholars of any age, enabling them to spend lengthy periods of research in Germany.

Feodor Lynen Research Fellowships for German Scholars

Subjects: All subjects.
Purpose: To enable highly qualified German scholars up to the age of 38 to conduct a long-term period of research of their choice at the home institutions of non-German recipients of Humboldt fellowships and awards abroad.
Eligibility: Open to German nationals or those who have been living and working in Germany for more than 5 years.
Level of Study: Postdoctorate
Type: Fellowship
Value: €2,100–3,500, depending on the host country
Length of Study: 1–4 years
Frequency: Annual
Study Establishment: Research institutions or universities
No. of awards offered: Up to 150 per year
Application Procedure: Applicants must complete an application form, available from the internet.
Closing Date: Applications can be made at any time
Funding: Government
No. of awards given last year: 110
No. of applicants last year: 245

Friedrich Wilhelm Bessel Research Award

Subjects: All subjects.
Purpose: To enable internationally recognized top-flight foreign scientists and scholars up to the age of 45 to conduct research projects of their own choice in Germany.
Eligibility: Open to all scholars and scientists from abroad.
Level of Study: Research
Type: Prize
Value: €55,000
Length of Study: 6 months–1 year
Frequency: Annual, Selection twice a year
Study Establishment: Universities and research institutions
Country of Study: Germany
No. of awards offered: Approx. 20 per year
Application Procedure: Applicants are nominated by eminent German scientists and scholars directly to the Foundation in Bonn. Direct applications are not accepted.
Closing Date: Nominations are accepted throughout the year
Funding: Government
No. of awards given last year: 17
No. of applicants last year: 42
Additional Information: Selection committee meetings are held twice a year in March and October.

Georg Forster Research Fellowships

Subjects: Any subject with emphasis on development policy, particularly the transfer of knowledge and methods to Fellows' home countries.
Purpose: To provide opportunities for highly qualified scholars from developing countries up to the age of 45 to carry out long-term research projects of their own choice in Germany.
Eligibility: Open to highly qualified foreign academics from developing countries up to the age of 45, who have obtained a PhD degree or equivalent and can furnish proof of independent research through academic publications in internationally recognized journals. Candidates in the humanities should possess sound German language ability if it is needed to carry out the project successfully. Those in the natural, medical and engineering sciences should possess English language ability. Candidates should already have established relations with a German research institute where the project can be realized.
Level of Study: Postdoctorate
Type: Fellowship
Value: €2,100–3,000 per month

Length of Study: 6–12 months, with the possibility of extension to up to 24 months
Frequency: Annual, 3 selections per year
Study Establishment: Universities or research institution
Country of Study: Germany
No. of awards offered: approx. 50 per year
Closing Date: Applications are accepted at any time
Funding: Government
No. of awards given last year: 42
No. of applicants last year: 115
Additional Information: Applications should be forwarded directly to the Foundation, or through diplomatic or consular offices of the Federal Republic of Germany in the candidate's respective countries.

Humboldt Research Awards to Outstanding Scholars Resident Outside Germany

Subjects: All subjects.
Purpose: To enable internationally recognized foreign scientists and scholars to conduct research on a project of their own choice in Germany.
Eligibility: Open to all scholars and scientists from abroad.
Level of Study: Research
Type: Prize
Value: Up to €75,000
Length of Study: 6 months–1 year
Frequency: Annual
Study Establishment: Universities and research institutions
Country of Study: Germany
No. of awards offered: Up to 100 per year
Application Procedure: Applicants are nominated by eminent German scientists and scholars directly to the Foundation in Bonn. Direct applications are not accepted.
Closing Date: Nominations are accepted throughout the year
Funding: Government
No. of awards given last year: 66
No. of applicants last year: 182
Additional Information: Selection committee meetings are held twice a year in March and October.

Humboldt Research Fellowships

Subjects: All subjects.
Purpose: To provide opportunities for young, highly qualified scientists and scholars up to the age of 40 of all nationalities holding a doctorate, to carry out research projects of their own choice in Germany.
Eligibility: Open to young, highly qualified foreign academics who are up to 40 years of age, have obtained a PhD degree or equivalent and can furnish proof of independent research through academic publications in internationally recognized journals. Candidates in the humanities should possess sound German language ability if it is needed to carry out the project successfully. Those in the natural, medical and engineering sciences should possess English language ability. Candidates should already have established relations with a German research institute where the project can be realized.
Level of Study: Postdoctorate
Type: Fellowship
Value: €2,100–3,000 per month
Length of Study: 6 months–1 year, with the possibility of extension for up to 2 years
Frequency: Annual, 3 selections each year
Study Establishment: Universities or research institutions
Country of Study: Germany
No. of awards offered: Up to 600 per year
Application Procedure: Information regarding the application procedure is available from the Foundation's website.
Closing Date: Applications are accepted at any time
Funding: Government
No. of awards given last year: 544
No. of applicants last year: 1534
Additional Information: Applications should be forwarded directly to the Foundation or through diplomatic or consular offices of the Federal Republic of Germany in the candidates' respective countries.

JSPS Research Fellowships

Subjects: All subjects.
Purpose: To enable highly qualified scholars up to the age of 38 to carry out research projects of their own choice in Japan.
Eligibility: Open to German nationals only.
Level of Study: Postdoctorate
Type: Fellowship
Value: Yen 392,000 per month plus travel and housing allowance
Length of Study: 6–24 months
Frequency: Annual, 3 selection meetings per year
Study Establishment: A university or other research institution
Country of Study: Japan
No. of awards offered: Up to 42 per year
Application Procedure: Applicants must complete an application form.
Closing Date: Applications can be made at any time
Funding: Government

Konrad Adenauer Research Award

Subjects: Humanities and social sciences.
Purpose: To promote academic relations between Canada and Germany.
Eligibility: Open to highly qualified Canadian scholars, whose research work in the humanities or the social sciences has brought them international recognition and who belong to the group of leading scholars in their respective area of specialization. The award will be made regardless of age, race, religion or sex.
Level of Study: Research
Type: Prize grant
Value: Up to €75,000
Length of Study: Up to 1 year
Frequency: Annual
Study Establishment: Universities and research institutions
Country of Study: Germany
No. of awards offered: Up to 1 per year
Application Procedure: Applicants must be nominated by their universities and their dossiers sent to the Awards Co-ordinator. Nomination forms and information may also be requested from the Awards Co-ordinator. Direct applications are not accepted.
Closing Date: January 31st
Funding: Government
No. of awards given last year: 1
No. of applicants last year: 1
Additional Information: Nominations will be made jointly by the Royal Society of Canada and the University of Toronto and submitted to the Humboldt Foundation.

For further information contact:

Awards Co-ordinator, The Royal Society of Canada, 283 Sparks Street, Ottawa, ON, K1R 7X9, Canada

Max Planck Research Award - International Research Award of the Alexander von Humboldt Foundation and the Max Planck Society

Subjects: All subjects.
Purpose: To enable highly-qualified foreign and German scientists and scholars who have already achieved international recognition and who are expected to continue to produce outstanding academic achievements to conduct long-term research.
Eligibility: Open to scientists and scholars of all nationalities.
Level of Study: Research
Type: Prize
Value: Up to €750,000
Length of Study: 3–5 years
Frequency: Annual
Study Establishment: Universities and research institutions
Country of Study: Germany or abroad
No. of awards offered: 2 per year, 1 to a German national and 1 to a non-German scientist or scholar

Application Procedure: Nominations have to be initiated in Germany and may be submitted by the President/Vice Chancellors and Deans of any academic Institution of Higher Education, the heads of the Academies of Science, the Fraunhofer Society, the Hermann von Helmholtz Association of German Research Centres, the Max Planck Society, the Caesar Foundation and the Scientific Association Gottfried Wilhelm Leibniz, the former winners of the Leibniz Award, the Max Planck Research Award or the Wolfgang Paul Award working in Germany or the chairpersons of specialist German Research Foundation committees in closely related disciplines.
Closing Date: Applicants must inquire at www.max-plaucls-award.select@avh.de
Funding: Government
Additional Information: Selection occurs once per year.

Roman Herzog Research Fellowships

Subjects: All subjects, but preference is given to law, economics and social sciences.
Purpose: To enable young highly qualified scholars from central and southeast Europe (including the Baltic states) to carry out research projects of their choice in Germany.
Eligibility: The research fellowship programme is open to candidates up to 35 years of age who hold doctoral degrees, can furnish proof of equivalent research achievements or are approaching their doctoral degrees, can furnish proof of independent research work through recognized academic publications and, in addition, have proven outstanding leadership qualities in research and teaching or through non-academic activities. This programme is open to nationals of the following countries: Albania, Bosnia-Herzegovina, Bulgaria, Estonia, Croatia, Latvia, Lithuania, Macedonia, Poland, Romania, Serbia and Montenegro, Slovenia, The Slovak Republic, The Czech Republic and Hungary.
Level of Study: Predoctorate
Type: Fellowship
Value: €1,600–2,100 per month
Length of Study: 6 months–1 year with the possibility of extension to 1.5 years
Frequency: Annual, 2 selections per year
Study Establishment: Universities or research institutions
Country of Study: Germany
No. of awards offered: Up to 12 per year
Application Procedure: Applicants can obtain information regarding the application procedure at the Foundation's website.
Closing Date: Applications may be submitted at any time
Funding: Government
Contributor: Non-profit Hertie Foundation
No. of awards given last year: 9
No. of applicants last year: 28

Sofja Kovalevskaja Award for Foreign Scientists and Scholars

Subjects: All subjects.
Purpose: To enable successful outstanding young scientists and scholars from abroad up to the age of 35 to establish working groups and to conduct high-level research on a project of their choice in Germany.
Eligibility: Open to all scholars and scientists from abroad.
Level of Study: Research
Type: Prize
Value: Up to €1.2 million
Length of Study: 4 years
Frequency: Every 2 years
Study Establishment: Universities and research institutions
Country of Study: Germany
No. of awards offered: 10
Application Procedure: Applicants may apply directly to the Humboldt Foundation.
Closing Date: Applicants must inquire at kovalevskaja.select@avh.de
Funding: Government
Additional Information: Selection committee meetings are held once every 2 years in September. This programme is subject to confirmation in the course of ongoing parliamentary procedure.

ALEXANDER VON HUMBOLDT FOUNDATION USA

Alexander von Humboldt Foundation, U.S. Liaison Office, 1012 14th Street NW, Suite 1015, Washington, DC, 20005, United States of America
Tel: (1) 202 783 1907
Fax: (1) 202 783 1908
Email: avh@verizon.net
Website: www.humboldt-foundation.de
Contact: The Grants Management Officer

The Alexander von Humboldt Foundation is a non-profit foundation established by the Federal Republic of Germany for the promotion of international cooperation in research. It enables highly qualified scholars not resident in Germany to spend extended periods of research in Germany and promotes the ensuring academic contacts. The Humboldt Foundation supports an active world-wide network of scholars; since 1953 it has sponsored over 20,000 scholars from 131 countries.

German Chancellor Scholarship Program

Subjects: Topics as selected by young citizens of the United States of America and of the Russian Federation who show outstanding potential for leadership in their Fields. Successful candidates have come from such fields as government, social and policy sciences, law, journalism, communications, management, finance, economics, architecture, public service, arts and humanities and environmental affairs.
Purpose: To promote international co-operation in research. The German Chancellor Scholarship Program sponsors individuals who demonstrate the potential to strengthen ties between Germany and their own country through their profession or studies.
Eligibility: Applicants must hold a Bachelor's degree and be under 35 years of age. Prior knowledge of German is not a requirement. Candidates must be citizens of the United States or the Russian Federation possess a bachelor's degree, and be under 35 years of age at the start of the award.
Level of Study: Postgraduate, professional development, requires at least a bachelor's degree
Type: Scholarship
Value: €2,000–3,500 monthly
Length of Study: 12 months and orientation/language training
Frequency: Annual
Study Establishment: A study centre or other suitable institute
Country of Study: Germany
No. of awards offered: 10 - to US citizens, 10 - to Russian citizens
Application Procedure: Applicants must download application forms and guidelines from the website.
Closing Date: October 31st
Funding: Private
No. of awards given last year: 10 - U.S. and 10 - Russia
No. of applicants last year: Approx. 200
Additional Information: Allowances are available for accompanying family members, travel expenses and introductory German language instruction in the United States.

For further information contact:

Alexander van Humboldt Foundation, Jean-Paul-Str. 12, Bonn, D-53173, Germany

ALFRED BRADLEY BURSARY AWARD

BBC Radio Drama, Room 2129, New Broadcasting House, Oxford Road, Manchester, M60 1SJ, England
Tel: (44) 161 244 4245
Fax: (44) 16 1244 4248
Contact: The Coordinator

Established in 1992, this bursary is a biennial award in commemoration of the life and work of the distinguished radio producer Alfred Bradley.

Alfred Bradley Bursary Award

Subjects: Drama.
Purpose: To encourage and develop new radio writing talent in the BBC North region.
Eligibility: Entrants must live in the North of England.
Level of Study: Professional development
Value: Up to UK £6,000 and a BBC Radio Drama commission
Length of Study: 2 years
Frequency: Every 2 years
Country of Study: United Kingdom
Application Procedure: Applicants must contact the co-ordinator.
Closing Date: Usually November
Funding: Private
No. of applicants last year: 290
Additional Information: There is a change of focus for each award, eg. previous years have targeted comedy, drama, verse drama, etc. In 2004, the brief was for a play suitable for the afternoon play slot.

ALFRED P SLOAN FOUNDATION

630 Fifth Avenue, Suite 2550, New York, NY 10111,
United States of America
Tel: (1) 212 649 1649
Fax: (1) 212 757 5117
Email: stella@sloan.org
Website: www.sloan.org
Contact: Erica Stella, Fellowship Administrator

The Alfred P Sloan Foundation, a philanthropic non-profit institution, was established in 1934 by Alfred P Sloan Jr, then President and Chief Executive Officer of the General Motors Corporation.

Sloan Research Fellowships

Subjects: Chemistry, computational and evolutionary molecular biology, computer science, economics, mathematics, neuroscience, physics.
Purpose: To enhance the careers of the very best young faculty members in specified fields of science.
Level of Study: Postdoctorate
Type: Fellowship
Frequency: Annual
No. of awards offered: 116
Application Procedure: Applicants must check the website for detailed procedure.
Closing Date: September 15th

ALFRED TOEPFER FOUNDATION

Georgsplatz 10, Hamburg, 20099, Germany
Tel: (49) 4033 4020
Fax: (49) 4033 5860
Email: mail@toepfer-fvs.de
Website: www.toepfer-fvs.de

Alfred Toepfer Scholarships

Subjects: Humanities, social sciences.
Purpose: To provide (only in well-founded cases) scholarships for doctoral candidates from the humanities and the social sciences who are in the final stages of research on European issues.
Eligibility: Candidates should be no older than 30 years and should preferably be from Central and Eastern Europe: Albania, Armenia, Azerbaijan, Belarus, Bosnia-Herzegovina, Bulgaria, Croatia, Czech Republic, Estonia, Georgia, Hungary, Kazakhstan, Kyrgyzstan, Latvia, Lithuania, Macedonia, Moldavia, Poland, Romania, Russia, Slovakia, Slovenia, Tajikistan, Turkmenistan, Ukraine, Uzbekistan or Yugoslavia. Applicants should have a good knowledge of German.
Level of Study: Doctorate
Type: Scholarship
Value: €920 per month
Length of Study: 1 year
Country of Study: Germany
Application Procedure: Applications need not be submitted on a special form.
Closing Date: May 31st and November 30th
Contributor: Alfred Toepfer Foundation

ALICIA PATTERSON FOUNDATION

1730 Pennsylvania Avenue NW, Suite 850, Washington, DC, 20006,
United States of America
Tel: (1) 202 393 5995
Fax: (1) 301 951 8512
Email: info@aliciapatterson.org
Website: www.aliciapatterson.org
Contact: Ms Margaret Engel, Executive Director

The Alicia Patterson Foundation gives grants to professional print reporters and photojournalists to investigate a subject of their choice. Their reports are published in a quarterly magazine, the *Alicia Patterson Foundation Reporter*, and on the Foundation's website.

Alicia Patterson Journalism Fellowships

Subjects: Journalism.
Purpose: To give working print journalists, a chance to spend a year researching and writing on a topic of their choosing.
Eligibility: Open to print journalists eg. reporters, editors, photographers with at least 5 years of full-time professional experience, who are citizens of the United States of the America.
Level of Study: Professional development
Type: Fellowship
Value: US$35,000
Length of Study: 1 year
Frequency: Annual
Country of Study: Any country
No. of awards offered: 5–9
Application Procedure: Applicants must use the Alicia Patterson Foundation application form and are also required to submit a three-page proposal, a two-page autobiographical essay, three clips, four letters of reference and a budget.
Closing Date: Postmarked October 1st
Funding: Private
No. of awards given last year: 6
No. of applicants last year: 231

ALL SAINTS EDUCATIONAL TRUST

St Katharine Cree Church, 86 Leadenhall Street, London, EC3A 3DH,
England
Tel: (44) 20 7283 4485
Fax: (44) 20 7621 9758
Email: clerk@aset.org.uk
Website: www.aset.org.uk
Contact: Mr Stephen Harrow FKC, Clerk to the Trustees

The Trust makes grants to help with the costs of the formal training or better qualification of individual teachers, and also funds educational advance by other means, eg. research. There is particular emphasis on religious education, home economics or related subjects, and multi-cultural endeavour linked to those areas. (UK/EU only.)

All Saints Educational Trust Corporate Awards

Subjects: Religious education, home economics and kindred subjects, as well as multicultural and interfaith education.
Purpose: To offer assistance to individuals and institutions within certain specified terms of reference.
Level of Study: Unrestricted
Type: Award
Value: Varies. UK £100,000 over 3 years is the maximum awarded
Length of Study: Up to 5 years
Country of Study: United Kingdom
No. of awards offered: Subject to the availability of funds
Application Procedure: Applicants must complete an application form, available on request from the Clerk to the Trust.
Closing Date: Applications are accepted at any time. March 31st is the deadline for the ensuing academic year
Funding: Private

No. of awards given last year: 9
No. of applicants last year: 22
Additional Information: The award must be used or applied for in the United Kingdom. Further information is available on request or from the website.

All Saints Educational Trust Personal Awards

Subjects: Religious education, home economics and multicultural education.
Purpose: To give support to persons who work in certain capacities associated with education.
Eligibility: Open to individuals over 18 years of age who are, or who intend to become, teachers. Grants for research are open to individuals. The award must be used with United Kingdom awards to commonwealth citizens will be for postgraduate study only.
Level of Study: Foundation programme, professional development, graduate, postgraduate
Type: Grant
Value: Varies, usually UK £500–10,000 but occasionally more
Length of Study: 1–3 years
Study Establishment: Recognized educational institutions in the United Kingdom
Country of Study: United Kingdom
No. of awards offered: Dependent on availability of funds
Application Procedure: Applicants must complete an application form, available on request from the Clerk to the Trust or from the website.
Closing Date: March 31st
Funding: Private
No. of awards given last year: 30
No. of applicants last year: 80
Additional Information: Enquiries should not be delayed until the offer of a place on a course of study has been confirmed. Late applications cannot be considered.

For further information contact:

Further information is available on request or from the website

THE ALLEN FOUNDATION, INC.

PO Box 1606, Midland, MI, 48641-1606, United States of America
Tel: (1) 989 832 5678
Fax: (1) 989 696 3445
Email: d-baum@tamu.edu
Website: www.allenfoundation.org
Contact: Dale Baum, Secretary

Established in 1975 by agricultural chemist William Webster Allen, the Allen Foundation makes grants to projects that benefit human nutrition in the areas of education, training and research.

Allen Foundation Grants

Subjects: Human nutrition in the areas of health, education, training and research.
Purpose: To assist in the field of human nutrition, to fund relevant nutritional research and to encourage the dissemination of information regarding healthful nutritional practices and habits.
Eligibility: Open to non-profit organizations that are able to provide a copy of their federal Internal Revenue Service certification of tax-exempt status. If applying from outside the United States of America, applicants must send their country's counterpart or equivalent of the tax-exempt form. Individuals, non-profit organizations without a current exempt status, conferences, seminars, symposia, sponsorship events, fund-raising events and religious organizations without a secular community designation are not eligible for the award. If a grant proposal involves primarily academic research, the grant should be conducted under the leadership of a full-time, principal investigator who is a regular faculty member with tenure or on a tenure track.
Level of Study: Research
Type: Grant
Country of Study: United States of America
No. of awards offered: 1
Application Procedure: Applicants must submit an application form via email only. Application forms and further information can be obtained from the website.
Closing Date: December 31st
Additional Information: Any applications received after this deadline will be reviewed for the following year's applications. The Board of Trustees will announce their decision for successful applicants in June. Because of the number of proposals received and the limited resources of the Foundation, applicants should never view possible declinations to fund their proposals or delays in reviewing their proposals as judgements on the actual merits of their proposals. The Foundation does not directly administer the programmes it funds. For further information, visit the website or contact the Allen Foundation Inc.

ALPHA KAPPA ALPHA-EDUCATIONAL ADVANCEMENT ORGANIZATION (AKA-EAF)

5656 South Stony Island, Chicago, IL, 60637,
United States of America
Tel: (1) 777 947 0026
Email: akaeaf@aol.com
Website: www.akaeaf.org

AKA-EAF Financial Need Scholarship

Subjects: All subjects.
Purpose: To provide financial assistance to students who need to complete a preferred course of study and to help those who have endured great hardship to accomplish their educational goals.
Eligibility: The applicants must have completed a minimum of 1 year in a degree course or be a student in a non-institutional-based programme that may offer degrees.
Level of Study: Graduate, postgraduate
Type: Scholarship
Value: US$750–1,500
Frequency: Annual
Closing Date: January 15th

AKA-EAF Merit Scholarships

Subjects: All subjects.
Purpose: To support education and lifelong learning.
Eligibility: The applicant must have completed a minimum of 1 year in a degree course and should demonstrate exceptional academic achievement as evidenced by a grade point average of 3.0 or higher. The applicant should also show evidence of leadership by participation in community activities.
Type: Scholarship
Value: US$1,000
Frequency: Annual
Closing Date: January 15th

ALZHEIMER'S RESEARCH TRUST

Livanos House, Granham's Road, Cambridge, Cambridgeshire, CB2 5LQ, England
Tel: (44) 12 2384 3899
Fax: (44) 12 2384 3325
Email: enquiries@alzheimers-research.org.uk
Website: www.alzheimers-research.org.uk
Contact: Rebecca Wood, Chief Executive

Alzheimer's Research Trust is the leading United Kingdom research charity for dementia. The Trust funds work in any area of research that promises to further understanding of the basic disease process in Alzheimer's and related dementias, or that is directed to early detection, identifying risk factors, or progress towards effective treatments.

Alzheimer's Research Trust Clinical Research Training Fellowship

Subjects: The basic disease process in Alzheimer's disease and related dementias.

Purpose: To support clinical research by a medically qualified applicant in the field of dementia.
Type: Fellowship
Value: Full salary and research expenses of UK £2,000
Length of Study: Up to 3 years initially
Frequency: Annual
Country of Study: United Kingdom
No. of awards offered: 1
Application Procedure: Applicants must submit a brief description of the proposal plus other information as laid down in the Guidelines for Applicants, together with a Grant Application Header Page. Applicants must visit the organization's website for full details.
Closing Date: February annually
Contributor: Charitable sources
No. of awards given last year: 0
No. of applicants last year: 3

Alzheimer's Research Trust Graduate Student Programme

Subjects: The basic disease processes in Alzheimer's disease and related dementias.
Purpose: To contribute towards research in the field, and to help ensure that bright young graduates are inducted into this area.
Eligibility: Must be UK-based supervisors to apply for grant.
Level of Study: Postgraduate
Type: Scholarship
Value: Full fees and UK £60,000 or UK £63,000 in London
Length of Study: 3 years
Frequency: Annual
Country of Study: United Kingdom
No. of awards offered: Up to 5
Application Procedure: Applications must be submitted by individual or joint prospective supervisors, as laid down in the Guidelines for Applicants. Applicants must visit the organization's website for full details.
Closing Date: November prior to commencement in October of the following year
Contributor: Charitable sources
No. of awards given last year: 5
No. of applicants last year: 12

Alzheimer's Research Trust Network Co-operation Grant

Subjects: The basic disease process in Alzheimer's disease and related dementias.
Purpose: To promote collaborative research between members of the Trust's network.
Eligibility: Lead applicant must be a member of the Alzheimer's Research Trust network, but application can include non-network and non-United Kingdom researchers.
Level of Study: Research
Type: Grant
Value: Up to UK £50,000
Frequency: Twice a year if appropriate
Country of Study: United Kingdom or elsewhere
No. of awards offered: 1 or more
Application Procedure: Lead applicants must submit a research proposal as laid down in the Guidelines for Applicants, together with a Grant Application Header Page. Applicants must visit the organization's website for full details.
Closing Date: Can be submitted at any time
Contributor: Charitable sources
No. of awards given last year: 1
No. of applicants last year: 2

Alzheimer's Research Trust Pilot Project Grant

Subjects: The basic disease process in Alzheimer's disease and related dementias.
Purpose: To fund innovative research projects and pilot studies.
Eligibility: Lead applicant must be based in the UK.
Level of Study: Research
Type: Grant
Value: Up to UK £30,000
Length of Study: Up to 2 years
Frequency: Twice a year
Country of Study: United Kingdom
No. of awards offered: 1 or more
Application Procedure: Applicants must submit a research proposal of not more than four sides of A4, plus other information as laid down in the Guidelines for Applicants, together with a Grant Application Header Page. Applicants must visit the organization's website for full details.
Closing Date: November and March annually
Contributor: Charitable sources
No. of awards given last year: 13
No. of applicants last year: 38

Alzheimer's Research Trust Research Equipment Grant

Subjects: The basic disease processes in Alzheimer's disease and related dementias.
Purpose: To speed up and increase the accuracy and efficiency of research.
Eligibility: Must be UK-based.
Level of Study: Research
Type: Grant
Value: UK £10,000–100,000
Frequency: Twice a year
No. of awards offered: 1 or more
Application Procedure: Applicants must submit an application as laid down in the Guidelines for applicants, together with a Grant Application Header Page. Applicants must visit the organization's website for full details.
Closing Date: November and March annually
Contributor: Charitable sources
No. of awards given last year: 5
No. of applicants last year: 11

Alzheimer's Research Trust Research Fellowships

Subjects: The basic disease process in Alzheimer's disease and related dementias.
Purpose: To allow junior postdoctoral researchers of demonstrated ability and high potential to carry out further research.
Eligibility: Sponsor must be UK-based.
Level of Study: Postdoctorate
Type: Fellowship
Value: Full salary plus contribution towards research and travel costs
Length of Study: 3 years
Frequency: Annual, twice a year
Country of Study: United Kingdom
No. of awards offered: Up to 3 annually
Application Procedure: Applicants must submit a research proposal of not more than five pages plus other information as laid down in the Guidelines for Applicants, together with a Fellowship Application Header Page. Applicants must visit the organization's website for full details.
Closing Date: February annually
Contributor: Charitable sources
No. of awards given last year: 5
No. of applicants last year: 15

Alzheimer's Research Trust Research Major Grants

Subjects: The basic disease processes in Alzheimer's disease and related dementias.
Purpose: To support imaginative and high-quality research.
Eligibility: Collaborations with researchers outside the UK will be considered providing the lead applicant is UK-based.
Level of Study: Research
Type: Grant
Value: UK £150,000–1,000,000
Length of Study: 3–5 years
Frequency: Annual
Country of Study: United Kingdom
No. of awards offered: 1 or more
Application Procedure: Applicants must submit a preliminary proposal as laid down in the Guidelines for Applicants, together with a Grant Application Header Page. Applicants must visit the organization's website for full details.

Closing Date: Preliminary applications in November. Full submissions in March
Contributor: Charitable sources
No. of awards given last year: 3
No. of applicants last year: 23

Alzheimer's Research Trust Emergency Support Grant

Subjects: The basic disease processes in Alzheimer's disease and related dementias.
Purpose: To bridge funding shortfalls in research.
Eligibility: Members of the Alzheimer's Research Trust network only.
Level of Study: Research
Type: Grant
Value: Up to UK £30,000
Length of Study: A few weeks–2 years
Frequency: As necessary
No. of awards offered: As necessary
Application Procedure: Applicants must submit a proposal as laid down in the Guidelines for Applicants, together with a Grant Application Header Page. Applicants must visit the organization's for full details.
Closing Date: Can submit at any time
Contributor: Charitable sources
No. of awards given last year: 5
No. of applicants last year: 11

ALZHEIMER'S SOCIETY

Gordon House, 10 Greencoat Place, London, SW1P 1PH, England
Tel: (44) 20 7306 0606
Fax: (44) 20 7306 0808
Email: qrd@alzheimers.org.uk
Website: www.alzheimers.org.uk
Contact: Dr Richard Harvey, Director of Research

The Alzheimer's Society is the leading care and research charity for people with all forms of dementia, their families and carers.

Alzheimer's Society Research Grants

Subjects: All forms of dementia, particularly Alzheimer's disease and vascular dementia.
Purpose: To support research into the cause, cure and care of dementia.
Eligibility: Awards may only be held by United Kingdom institutions. Non-United Kingdom-based researchers may be subcontractors.
Level of Study: Research, postdoctorate
Value: UK £1,000,000 per year is committed to research. Fellowship Grants are approx. UK £250,000. Project Grants are approx. UK £650,000
Length of Study: Up to 5 years
Country of Study: United Kingdom
No. of awards offered: Varies
Application Procedure: Applicants must complete an application form, available from the website.
Closing Date: The deadline for Fellowship Grants is in October. Deadlines for Project Grants applications are in July and January
Funding: Trusts, commercial, private, government
No. of awards given last year: 7
No. of applicants last year: 71

AMERICA-ISRAEL CULTURAL FOUNDATION (AICF)

32 Allenby Road, Tel Aviv, 63325, Israel
Tel: (972) 3 517 4177
Fax: (972) 3 517 8991
Email: aicf@netvision.net.il
Website: www.aicf.webnet.org
Contact: Mr Gideon Paz, Executive Director

The America–Israel Cultural Foundation (AICF) has been promoting and supporting the arts in Israel for over 60 years. Through its Sharett Scholarship Program, the AICF grants hundreds of study scholarships each year to Israeli students of the arts, music, dance, visual arts, film, television and theatre, mainly for studies in Israel. The AICF also provides short-term fellowships to artists and art teachers and financially supports various projects in art schools, workshops, master classes, etc.

AICF Sharett Scholarship Program

Subjects: Performing arts, visual arts, design, film or television.
Eligibility: Open to Israeli citizens only.
Level of Study: Unrestricted
Type: Scholarship
Value: US$750–2,000
Length of Study: Varies
Frequency: Annual
Country of Study: Any country
No. of awards offered: Approx. 1,100 scholarships, fellowships and grants, mostly for students in Israel
Application Procedure: Applicants must complete and submit an application form with recommendations and prerequired repertoire. Application forms are available from February 1st of each year.
Closing Date: End of February
Funding: Private
Contributor: America–Israel Cultural Foundation
No. of awards given last year: 1,110
No. of applicants last year: 2,100
Additional Information: The programme is revised on an annual basis. For more detailed information, please contact the Foundation after February 1st.

AMERICAN ACADEMY OF CHILD AND ADOLESCENT PSYCHIATRY

3615 Wisconsin Avenue North West, Washington, DC, 20016, United States of America
Tel: (1) 202 966 7300
Fax: (1) 202 966 2891
Email: esilberstein@aacap.org
Website: www.aacap.org
Contact: Deputy Director of Research & Training

The American Academy of Child and Adolescent Psychiatry is a national, professional medical association established in 1953 as a non-profit organization to support and improve the quality of life for children, adolescents and families affected by mental illnesses.

Jeanne Spurlock Minority Medical Student Clinical Fellowship in Child and Adolescent Psychiatry

Subjects: Psychiatry and mental health.
Purpose: To support work during the summer with a child and adolescent psychiatrist mentor.
Eligibility: Applications are accepted from African American, Asian American, Native American, Alaskan Native, Mexican American, Hispanic and Pacific Islander students in accredited United States of America medical schools.
Level of Study: Graduate
Type: Fellowship
Value: Up to US$2,500
Length of Study: 12 weeks
Frequency: Annual
Country of Study: United States of America
No. of awards offered: Up to 14
Application Procedure: For updated application information, applicants must visit the AACAP website at www.aacap.org/awards/index.htm
Closing Date: March 1st
Funding: Government
Contributor: CMHS
No. of awards given last year: 12

Jeanne Spurlock Research Fellowship in Drug Abuse and Addiction for Minority Medical Students

Subjects: Psychiatry and mental health.
Purpose: To support work during the Summer with a child and adolescent psychiatrist research mentor.

Eligibility: Applications are accepted from African American, Asian American, Native American, Alaskan Native, Mexican American, Hispanic and Pacific Islander students in accredited United States of America medical schools. All applications must relate to substance abuse research.
Level of Study: Graduate
Type: Fellowship
Value: Up to US$2,500
Length of Study: 12 weeks
Frequency: Annual
Country of Study: United States of America
No. of awards offered: Up to 5
Application Procedure: For updated application information on the 2005 Spurlock Fellowships, applicants must visit the AACAP website at www.aacap.org/awards/index.htm
Closing Date: March 1st
Funding: Government
Contributor: NIDA
No. of awards given last year: 1

Pfizer Travel Grants

Subjects: Child and adolescent psychiatry.
Purpose: To help defray the cost of attending the AACAP's Annual Meeting in Toronto, Canada.
Eligibility: Applicants must be child and adolescent psychiatry residents at the time of the AACAP Annual Meeting and must be currently enrolled in a residency programme in the United States of America. All awardees must attend the Young Leaders Awards Luncheon and other stated events, and serve as a monitor for 1 day at the Annual Meeting.
Level of Study: Postdoctorate
Type: Travel grant
Value: US$1000
Frequency: Annual
Country of Study: United States of America
No. of awards offered: 50
Application Procedure: For updated application guidelines, applicants must visit the AACAP website at www.aacap.org/awards/pfizertravel.htm
Closing Date: August 1st
Contributor: Pfizer Pharmaceuticals
No. of awards given last year: 50

Presidential Scholar Award

Subjects: Child and adolescent psychiatry.
Purpose: To recognize specialized competence among child and adolescent psychiatry residents in research, public policy and innovative service systems.
Eligibility: Awardees must be AACAP resident members by the time of the Annual Meeting.
Level of Study: Research
Type: Award
Value: Up to US$2,500 for travel and lodging for 1 week's tutorial and exchange in the specified area of study. Travel and hotel expenses for participation in the Academy's Annual Meeting are also paid
Country of Study: United States of America
No. of awards offered: Up to 5
Application Procedure: Nominations must be made by programme or training directors and must include a statement in support of the nomination, the nominee's curriculum vitae and a statement from the nominee about his or her specific area of interest, be it research, public policy, administration or other, plans for the tutorial and exchange and plans for the presentation to the home programme. While applicants are responsible for contacting their potential mentors, the Program Director for this award can help locate potential mentors for those awardees who need assistance.
Closing Date: March 15th
Funding: Private
Contributor: Bristol-Myers Squibb
No. of awards given last year: 5

THE AMERICAN ACADEMY OF FACIAL PLASTIC AND RECONSTRUCTIVE SURGERY (AAFPRS) FOUNDATION

310 Henry Street, Alexandria, VA, 22314,
United States of America
Tel: (1) 703 299 9291
Fax: (1) 703 299 8898
Email: info@aafprs.org
Website: www.aafprs.org
Contact: Research Programme

The American Academy of Facial Plastic and Reconstructive Surgery (AAFPRS) Foundation represents 2,700 facial plastic and reconstructive surgeons throughout the world. Its main mission is to promote the highest quality facial plastic surgery through education, the dissemination of professional information and the establishment of professional standards. The AAFPRS was created to address the medical and scientific issues confronting facial plastic surgeons.

Leslie Bernstein Grant

Subjects: Facial plastic and reconstructive surgery.
Purpose: To encourage original research projects that will advance facial plastic and reconstructive surgery.
Eligibility: Open to all AAFPRS members.
Level of Study: Professional development
Value: US$25,000
Length of Study: 3 years
Study Establishment: The recipient's practice or institution
Country of Study: Any country
No. of awards offered: 1
Application Procedure: Applicants must submit an application form and other documentation including a curriculum vitae and research proposal. Application forms and guidelines are available on the web at www.entlink.net//research/grant/foundation.funding-opportunities.cfm
Closing Date: January 15th
Funding: Private
Contributor: Dr Leslie Bernstein
No. of awards given last year: 1
No. of applicants last year: 3
Additional Information: All applications must be submitted through the Centralized Otolaryngology Research Efforts (CORE) programme (see the website listed above for information and application).

Leslie Bernstein Investigator Development Grant

Subjects: Facial plastic surgery or clinical or laboratory research.
Purpose: To support the work of a young faculty member in facial plastic surgery conducting significant clinical or laboratory research, as well as the training of resident surgeons in research.
Eligibility: Open to AAFPRS members who are involved in the training of resident surgeons.
Level of Study: Postgraduate
Type: Research grant
Value: US$15,000
Length of Study: 2 years
Frequency: Annual
Study Establishment: The recipient's institution
Country of Study: United States of America
No. of awards offered: 1
Application Procedure: Applicants must submit an application form and other documentation including a curriculum vitae and research proposal. Application forms and guidelines are available on the web at www.entlink.net//research/grant/foundation-funding-opportunities.cfm
Closing Date: January 15th
Funding: Private
Contributor: Dr Leslie Bernstein
No. of awards given last year: 1
No. of applicants last year: 2
Additional Information: All applications must be submitted through the Centralized Otolaryngology Research Efforts (CORE) programme (see the website listed above for information and application).

Leslie Bernstein Resident Research Grants

Subjects: Facial plastic surgery.
Purpose: To stimulate resident research in projects that are well conceived and scientifically valid.
Eligibility: Open to AAFPRS members. Residents at any level may apply even if the research work will be done during their fellowship year. All applicants are required to have the sponsorship and oversight of the department chair or an AAFPRS member as mentor.
Level of Study: Postgraduate
Type: Research grant
Value: US$5,000
Length of Study: 2 years
Frequency: Annual
Study Establishment: The recipient's institution
Country of Study: United States of America
No. of awards offered: Up to 2
Application Procedure: Applicants must submit an application form and other documentation including a curriculum vitae and research proposal. Application forms and guidelines are available on the web www.entlink.net//research/grant/foundation-funding-opportunities.cfm
Closing Date: January 15th
Funding: Private
Contributor: Dr Leslie Bernstein
No. of awards given last year: 1
No. of applicants last year: 4
Additional Information: Residents are encouraged to enter early in their training so that their applications may be revised and resubmitted if not accepted the first time. All applications must be submitted through the Centralized Otolaryngology Research Efforts (CORE) programme (see the website listed above for information and application).

THE AMERICAN ALPINE CLUB (AAC)

710 Tenth Street, Suite 100, Golden, CO 80401, United States of America
Tel: (1) 303 384 0110
Fax: (1) 303 384 0111
Email: getinfo@americanalpineclub.org
Website: www.americanalpineclub.org
Contact: Corporate Support Co-ordinator

The American Alpine Club (AAC) is a national non-profit organization that has represented mountaineers and rock climbers for almost a century. Since its inception in 1902, the AAC has been the only national climbers' organization devoted to the exploration and scientific study of high mountain elevations and polar regions of the world, and the promotion and dissemination of knowledge about the mountains and mountaineering through its meetings, publications and libraries. It is also dedicated to the conservation and preservation of mountain regions and other climbing areas and the representation of the interests and concerns of the American climbing community.

AAC Mountaineering Fellowship Fund Grants

Subjects: Rock climbing.
Purpose: To encourage young American climbers to visit remote areas and seek out climbs more technically demanding than they would normally undertake.
Eligibility: Applicants must be 25 years of age or under, citizens of the United States of America and experienced climbers. Membership of the American Alpine Club is not a prerequisite. Members of a single expedition may apply individually, but organized groups or expeditions are ineligible. Grants are not available for the purpose of climbing instruction.
Level of Study: Unrestricted
Type: Grant
Value: US$300–800
Country of Study: United States of America
No. of awards offered: 5–16
Application Procedure: Applicants must write for application forms, which are also available from the website.
Closing Date: April 1st and November 1st
Funding: Private
Additional Information: Grants will be based on the excellence of the proposed project and evidence of mountaineering experience. A report must be written upon project completion.

AAC Research Grants

Subjects: Scientific research focusing on mountain and polar areas.
Purpose: To recognize a specific contribution to scientific endeavour germane to mountain regions and alpine research projects.
Eligibility: There are no restrictions on eligibility, but grants will not be awarded for academic tuition. Applications are considered in terms of their scientific or technical quality and the purposes for which the funds and the AAC are established.
Level of Study: Postgraduate
Type: Research grant
Value: US$200–500
Frequency: Annual
Country of Study: Any country
No. of awards offered: Varies
Application Procedure: Applicants must write for application forms, which are also available from the website.
Closing Date: March 1st
Funding: Private
Additional Information: A report must be submitted upon completion of the project.

AMERICAN ANTIQUARIAN SOCIETY (AAS)

185 Salisbury Street, Worcester, MA, 01609-1634, United States of America
Tel: (1) 508 755 5221
Fax: (1) 508 754 9069
Email: cfs@mwa.org
Website: www.americanantiquarian.org
Contact: Ms Caroline F Scoat, Director of Scholarly Programmes

The American Antiquarian Society (AAS) is a learned society that was founded in 1812 in Worcester, MA. The Society maintains a research library of American history and culture up to 1876 in order to collect, preserve and make available for study the printed records of the United States of America.

AAS 'Drawn to Art' Fellowship

Subjects: American art, visual culture or other projects that will make substantial use of graphic materials as primary sources.
Purpose: To support research.
Eligibility: Applicants are selected on the basis of their scholarly qualifications, the scholarly significance of the project and the appropriateness of the proposed study to the Society's collections.
Level of Study: Postdoctorate, doctorate
Type: Fellowship
Value: US$1,000
Length of Study: 1 month
Frequency: Annual
Study Establishment: The Society's Library in Worcester, Massachusetts
Country of Study: United States of America
No. of awards offered: 1
Application Procedure: All application material is available from our website: www.americanantiquarian.org
Closing Date: January 15th
Funding: Private
Contributor: Diana Korzenik
No. of awards given last year: 1

AAS American Society for 18th Century Studies Fellowships

Subjects: American 18th century studies.
Eligibility: Open to suitably qualified scholars. Degree candidates are not eligible. Membership in the American Society for 18th century studies is required upon taking up an award, but not for making an application.

Level of Study: Postdoctorate
Type: Fellowship
Value: US$1,000 per month
Length of Study: 1 year
Frequency: Annual
Study Establishment: The Society's Library in Worcester, Massachusetts
Country of Study: United States of America
No. of awards offered: 1
Application Procedure: All application material is available from our website: www.americanantiquarian.org
Closing Date: January 15th
Funding: Private
Contributor: The American Society for 18th Century Studies and the AAS
No. of awards given last year: 2

AAS Joyce Tracy Fellowship

Subjects: Early American history and culture.
Purpose: To support research on newspapers or magazines for projects using these resources as primary documentation.
Eligibility: Applicants are selected on the basis of their scholarly qualifications, the scholarly significance to the project and the appropriateness of the proposed study to the Society's collections.
Level of Study: Doctorate, postdoctorate
Type: Fellowship
Value: US$1,000 per month
Length of Study: 1 year
Frequency: Annual
Study Establishment: The Society's Library in Worcester, Massachusetts
Country of Study: United States of America
No. of awards offered: 1
Application Procedure: All application material is available from our website: www.americanantiquarian.org
Closing Date: January 15th
Contributor: An endowment established in memory of Joyce Tracy
No. of awards given last year: 1

AAS Kate B and Hall J Peterson Fellowships

Subjects: Early American history to 1876.
Purpose: To enable persons, who might not otherwise be able to do so, to travel to the Society in order to make use of its research facilities.
Eligibility: Open to individuals engaged in scholarly research and writing, including foreign nationals and persons at work on doctoral theses.
Level of Study: Doctorate, postdoctorate
Type: Fellowship
Value: US$1,000 per month
Length of Study: 1–3 months
Frequency: Annual
Study Establishment: The Society's Library in Worcester, Massachusetts
Country of Study: United States of America
No. of awards offered: 6–10
Application Procedure: All application material is available from our website: www.americanantiquarian.org
Closing Date: January 15th
Funding: Private
Contributor: The late Hall J Peterson and his wife Kate B Peterson
No. of awards given last year: 12

AAS Reese Fellowship

Subjects: American bibliography and the history of the book in America to 1876.
Purpose: To support research.
Eligibility: Applicants are selected on the basis of their scholarly qualifications, the scholarly significance of the project and the appropriateness of the proposed study to the Society's collections.
Level of Study: Doctorate, postdoctorate
Type: Fellowship
Value: US$1,000
Length of Study: 1 month
Frequency: Annual
Study Establishment: The Society's Library in Worcester, Massachusetts
Country of Study: United States of America
No. of awards offered: 1
Application Procedure: All application material is available from our website: www.americanantiquarian.org
Closing Date: January 15th
Contributor: The William Reese Company, New Haven, CT
No. of awards given last year: 1

AAS-National Endowment for the Humanities Visiting Fellowships

Subjects: Early American history and culture.
Purpose: To make the Society's research facilities more readily available to qualified scholars.
Eligibility: Fellowships may not be awarded to degree candidates or for study leading to advanced degrees, nor may they be granted to foreign nationals unless they have been resident in the United States of America for at least 3 years immediately prior to receiving the award.
Level of Study: Postdoctorate
Type: Fellowship
Value: The maximum stipend available is US$40,000
Length of Study: Either 4–5 months or 6 months–1 year
Frequency: Annual
Country of Study: United States of America
No. of awards offered: 3
Application Procedure: All application material is available from our website: www.americanantiquarian.org
Closing Date: January 15th
Funding: Government
Contributor: NEH
No. of awards given last year: 3
Additional Information: Fellows may not accept teaching assignments or undertake any other major activities during the tenure of the award. Other major fellowships may be held concurrently.

AAS-North East Modern Language Association Fellowship

Subjects: American literary studies.
Purpose: To support research.
Eligibility: Applicants are selected on the basis of their scholarly qualifications, the scholarly significance of the project and the appropriateness of the proposed study to the Society's collections.
Level of Study: Postdoctorate
Type: Fellowship
Value: US$1,000 per month
Length of Study: 1–3 months
Frequency: Annual
Study Establishment: The Society's Library in Worcester, Massachusetts
No. of awards offered: 1
Closing Date: January 15th
Funding: Private
Contributor: Jointly funded by NEMLA and AAS
No. of awards given last year: 1

ACLS Frederick Burkhardt Fellowship

Subjects: All subjects supported by the AAS library.
Purpose: To support research.
Eligibility: Applicants must be recently tenured humanists selected on the basis of their scholarly qualifications, the scholarly significance of the project and the appropriateness of the proposed study to the Society's collections.
Level of Study: Postdoctorate
Type: Fellowship
Value: A maximum stipend of US$65,000
Length of Study: 1 year
Frequency: Annual
Study Establishment: The Society's Library in Worcester, Massachusetts

Country of Study: United States of America
Application Procedure: All application material is available from our website: www.americanantiquarian.org
Closing Date: October 2nd
Funding: Private
Contributor: The Andrew W Mellon Foundation and ACLS
No. of awards given last year: 8, 1 at AAS

American Historical Print Collectors Society Fellowship

Subjects: American prints of the 18th and 19th centuries.
Purpose: To support research or projects using prints as primary documentation.
Eligibility: Applicants are selected on the basis of their scholarly qualifications, the scholarly significance of the project and the appropriateness of the proposed study to the Society's collections.
Level of Study: Doctorate, postdoctorate
Type: Fellowship
Value: US$1,000 monthly
Length of Study: 1 month
Frequency: Annual
Study Establishment: The Society's Library in Worcester, Massachusetts
Country of Study: United States of America
Application Procedure: All application material is available from our website: www.americanantiquarian.org
Closing Date: January 15th
Funding: Private
Contributor: The American Historical Print Collectors Society and the AAS
No. of awards given last year: 1

Stephen Botein Fellowship

Subjects: The history of the book in American culture to 1876.
Eligibility: Open to suitably qualified scholars.
Level of Study: Doctorate, postdoctorate
Type: Fellowship
Value: US$1,000 per month
Length of Study: Up to 2 months
Frequency: Annual
Study Establishment: The Society's Library in Worcester, Massachusetts
Country of Study: United States of America
No. of awards offered: 1–2
Application Procedure: All application material is available from our website: www.americanantiquarian.org
Closing Date: January 15th
Funding: Private
Contributor: An endowment established by the family and friends of the late Mr Botein
No. of awards given last year: 2

AMERICAN ASSOCIATION FOR CANCER RESEARCH (AACR)

615 Chestnut Street, 17th Floor, Philadelphia, PA, 19106-4404, United States of America
Tel: (1) 215 440 9300
Fax: (1) 215 440 9372
Email: awards@aacr.org
Website: www.aacr.org
Contact: Ms Sheri Ozard, Program Co-ordinator

The American Association for Cancer Research (AACR) is a scientific society of over 17,000 laboratory and clinical cancer researchers. It was founded in 1907 to facilitate communication and dissemination of knowledge among scientists and others dedicated to the cancer problem, and to foster research in cancer and related biomedical sciences. It is also dedicated to encouraging the presentation and discussion of new and important observations in the field, fostering public education, science education and training, and advancing the understanding of cancer aetiology, prevention, diagnosis and treatment throughout the world.

AACR Career Development Awards in Cancer Research

Subjects: Cancer research.
Purpose: To support cancer research by junior faculty.
Eligibility: Open to junior faculty. Candidates must have completed productive postdoctoral research and demonstrated independent, investigator-initiated research. Employees of national government or private industry are not eligible.
Level of Study: Postdoctorate, research
Type: Grant
Value: US$50,000 per year
Length of Study: 2 years
Frequency: Annual
Study Establishment: Universities or research institutions
Country of Study: Any country
No. of awards offered: Varies
Application Procedure: Applicants must be nominated by a member of AACR and must be an AACR member or apply for membership by the time the application is submitted. Associate members may not be nominators. The online application is available at the AACR website.
Closing Date: Fall of each year
Funding: Private
Contributor: The Cancer Research and Prevention Foundation, the Susan G Komen Breast Cancer Foundation, Genentech Inc., the Pancreatic Cancer Action Network and Fondation Nélia et Amadeo Barletta
No. of awards given last year: 6
No. of applicants last year: 75

AACR Gertrude B Elion Cancer Research Award

Subjects: Cancer research.
Purpose: To foster meritorious basic, clinical or translational cancer research.
Eligibility: Open to tenure-track scientists at the level of assistant professor at an institution worldwide, who have completed their postdoctoral studies or clinical research by July 1st of the award year, and ordinarily not more than 5 years earlier. Candidates must be members of the AACR or apply for membership by the time the applications are submitted.
Level of Study: Postdoctorate, research
Type: Research grant
Value: US$50,000
Length of Study: 1 year
Frequency: Annual
Study Establishment: Universities or research institutions
Country of Study: Any country
No. of awards offered: 1
Application Procedure: Applicants must be nominated by a member of the AACR. The online application is available at the AACR website.
Closing Date: Fall of each year
Funding: Private
Contributor: GlaxoSmithKline
No. of awards given last year: 1
No. of applicants last year: 10

AACR Research Fellowships

Subjects: Cancer research.
Purpose: To foster meritorious cancer research.
Eligibility: Candidates must have completed a PhD or other doctoral degree and currently be a postdoctoral or clinical research Fellow. Academic faculty holding the rank of Instructor or higher, graduates and medical students, medical residents, permanent government employees and employees of private industry are not eligible.
Level of Study: Postdoctorate
Type: Fellowship
Value: US$30,000–40,000 per year
Length of Study: 1–3 years
Frequency: Annual
Study Establishment: Universities or research institutions
Country of Study: Any country
No. of awards offered: Varies
Application Procedure: Applicants must be nominated by a member of the AACR or apply for membership by the time the application is submitted. The online application is available from the AACR website.

Closing Date: Fall of each year
Funding: Private
Contributor: Amgen, Inc., AstraZeneca, Bristol-Myers Squibb Oncology, the Cancer Research and Prevention Foundation and Genentech BioOncology, Inc, MedImmune
No. of awards given last year: 7
No. of applicants last year: 125

AACR Scholar-in-Training Awards

Subjects: Cancer research.
Purpose: To allow individuals to attend the AACR Annual Meeting and Special Conferences.
Eligibility: Open to first authors of an abstract submitted for presentation at the AACR Annual Meeting or Special Conference. Eligible candidates are graduate students, medical students and residents, clinical fellows or equivalent and postdoctoral Fellows.
Level of Study: Postgraduate, graduate, postdoctorate, predoctorate, doctorate
Type: Travel grant
Value: US$400–2,000
Frequency: Annual
No. of awards offered: Varies
Application Procedure: No application is needed. Qualified persons who want to be considered should follow the instructions included in the abstract submission materials for the AACR Annual Meetings or Special Conference. If a candidate is eligible based on the above criteria, a certification form confirming his or her status will be requested at a later date.
Closing Date: Varies, please contact AACR for details
Funding: Private
Contributor: AFLAC Inc., AstraZeneca, Aventis, Bristol-Myers Squibb Oncology, Genentech, GlaxoSmithKline, ILEX, ITO EN Limited, Novartis Pharmaceuticals, the Avon Foundation, Susan G. Komen Breast Cancer Foundation and Pezcoller Foundation
No. of awards given last year: 300
No. of applicants last year: Approx. 2,000

AMERICAN ASSOCIATION FOR RESPIRATORY CARE

Education Recognition Award, American Respiratory Care Foundation, 9425 N. MacArthur Blvd Suite 100, Irving, TX, 75063-4706, United States of America
Tel: (1) 972 243 2272
Fax: (1) 972 484 2720
Email: info@aarc.org
Website: www.aarc.org
Contact: Administrative Assistant

The American Respiratory Care Foundation is dedicated to the art, science, quality and technology of respiratory care. It is a non-profit organization formed for the purpose of supporting research, education and charitable activities and to promote prevention, quality treatment and management of respiratory-related diseases.

NBRC/AMP Gareth B Gish, MS RRT Memorial Postgraduate Recognition Award

Subjects: Respiratory care and prevention.
Purpose: To assist qualified individuals in the pursuit of training leading to an advanced degree.
Eligibility: Open to professional respiratory therapists who have at least a baccalaureate degree with a 3.0 cumulative grade point average or better on a 4.0 scale or equivalent. Candidates must be able to provide proof of acceptance into an advanced degree programme of a fully accredited school and proof that the applicant is a candidate for degree.
Level of Study: Postgraduate, professional development
Type: Award
Value: Up to US$1,500 plus airfare, a certificate of recognition, one night's lodging and registration for the AARC International Respiratory Congress
Frequency: Annual
Country of Study: United States of America
No. of awards offered: 1
Application Procedure: Applicants must return a completed, signed and notarized application form, provide three letters of reference attesting to the applicant's character, academic ability and professional commitment and supply an essay of at least 1,200 words. This must describe how the award will assist the applicant in reaching the objective of an advanced degree and the candidate's ultimate goals of leadership in healthcare. Application forms can be downloaded and printed out from the website.
Closing Date: May 31st

Parker B Francis Respiratory Research Grant

Subjects: Respiratory care and related topics.
Purpose: To provide financial assistance for research programmes.
Eligibility: Open to qualified investigators in the field of respiratory care. The principal investigator may be a physician or respiratory therapist. However, a respiratory therapist must be the co-principal investigator if a physician is the principal applicant for the award.
Level of Study: Professional development
Type: Research grant
Value: The award is at the discretion of the Board of Trustees and is dependent on the quality of the proposal
Frequency: Annual
Country of Study: United States of America
Application Procedure: Applicants must apply directly to the Foundation Executive Office. Complete details can be found in the Application for Research Grant packet available from the Foundation.
Funding: Private
Contributor: Parker B Francis Foundation
Additional Information: In 1993, the Parker B Francis Foundation provided an endowment to the American Respiratory Care Foundation to make funds available to provide financial assistance for research programmes.

William F Miller, MD Postgraduate Education Recognition Award

Subjects: Respiratory care and prevention.
Purpose: To assist a professional therapist pursuing postgraduate education which will lead to an advanced degree.
Eligibility: Open to professional respiratory therapists who have at least a baccalaureate degree with a 3.0 cumulative grade point average or better on a 4.0 scale or equivalent. Candidates must be able to provide proof of acceptance into an advanced degree programme of a fully accredited school and proof that the applicant is a candidate for degree.
Level of Study: Postgraduate, professional development
Value: Up to US$1,500 plus airfare, certificate of recognition, one night's lodging and registration for the AARC International Respiratory Congress
Frequency: Annual
Country of Study: United States of America
No. of awards offered: 1
Application Procedure: Applicants must return a completed, signed and notarized application form, provide three letters of reference attesting to the applicant's character, academic ability and professional commitment and supply an essay of at least 1,200 words. This must describe how the award will assist the applicant in reaching the objective of an advanced degree and the candidate's ultimate goals of leadership in healthcare.
Closing Date: May 31st
Funding: Private

AMERICAN ASSOCIATION FOR WOMEN RADIOLOGISTS (AAWR)

4550 Post Oak Place, Suite 342, Houston, Texas, TX 77027, United States of America
Tel: (1) 713 965 0566
Fax: (1) 713 960 0488
Email: admin@aawr.org
Website: www.aawr.org
Contact: AAWR Account Manager

Alice Ettinger Distinguished Achievement Award

Subjects: Radiology.
Purpose: To recognize outstanding residents on the basis of contributions to clinical care, teaching, research or public service.
Eligibility: Open to residents in the field of radiation oncology who are members of the AAWR as of January 1st of the year of the award.
Level of Study: Unrestricted
Type: Award
Frequency: Annual
Country of Study: Any country
No. of awards offered: 1
Application Procedure: Applicants must submit an application including a nominating letter from the residency director, a letter of concurrence from the department chair, a curriculum vitae and a personal statement.
Closing Date: July 1st
Funding: Private
Contributor: Membership dues
Additional Information: Expenses to accept the award will be provided to the winner.

Eleanor Montague Distinguished Resident Award in Radiation Oncology

Subjects: Radiation oncology.
Purpose: To honour a resident radiation oncologist on the basis of outstanding contributions to clinical care, teaching, research and/or public service.
Eligibility: Open to residents in the field who are members of the AAWR as of January 1st of the year of the award.
Level of Study: Unrestricted
Value: US$500 and reimbursement of expenses including travel and lodging per day
Frequency: Annual
Country of Study: Any country
No. of awards offered: 1
Application Procedure: Applicants must submit an application including a letter of nomination, a letter of concurrence and a curriculum vitae.
Closing Date: July 1st
Funding: Private

Lucy Frank Squire Distinguished Resident Award in Diagnostic Radiology

Subjects: Radiology.
Purpose: To honour a resident diagnostic radiologist on the basis of outstanding contributions to clinical care, teaching, research and/or public service.
Eligibility: Open to residents in the field of diagnostic radiology who are members of the AAWR as of January 1st of the year of the award.
Level of Study: Unrestricted
Value: US$500 and reimbursement of expenses including travel and lodging per day
Frequency: Annual
Country of Study: Any country
No. of awards offered: 1
Application Procedure: Applicants must submit an application including a curriculum vitae, a letter of nomination and a letter of concurrence.
Closing Date: July 1st
Funding: Private
Contributor: Membership dues

Marie Curie Award

Subjects: Radiology.
Purpose: To honour an individual who has made an outstanding contribution to the field.
Eligibility: There are no nationality restrictions and nominees need not be members of the AAWR.
Level of Study: Unrestricted
Type: Award
Frequency: Annual
Country of Study: Any country
No. of awards offered: 1
Application Procedure: Applicants must submit an application including a letter of nomination, at least one letter of support and a curriculum vitae.
Closing Date: July 1st
Funding: Private
Contributor: Membership dues
Additional Information: Expenses to accept the award will be provided to the winner.

AMERICAN ASSOCIATION OF CRITICAL-CARE NURSES (AACN)

101 Columbia, Aliso Viejo, CA, CA 92656-4109,
United States of America
Tel: (1) 800 899 2226
Fax: (1) 949 362 2020
Email: info@aacn.org
Website: www.aacn.org
Contact: Research Department

The American Association of Critical-Care Nurses (AACN) is the world's largest nursing speciality organization with approx. 68,000 members worldwide. The AACN is committed to providing the highest quality resources to maximize nurses' contributions to caring and improving the healthcare of critically ill patients and their families.

AACN Certification Corporation Research Grant

Subjects: Certified practice including, but not limited to, studies focusing on continued competency, the Synergy Model, the value of certification as it relates to patient care and/or nursing practice, and credentialing concepts.
Purpose: To fund research.
Eligibility: Applicants need not be members of the AACN. The proposed research may be used to meet the requirements of an academic degree.
Value: Up to US$10,000
No. of awards offered: Up to 4
Application Procedure: Applicants must submit completed application materials and proposals. Details are available directly from the organization or from the website.
Closing Date: February 1st
Additional Information: For more information regarding AACN Certification Corporation and the Synergy Model, visit the website www.certcorp.org

AACN Clinical Practice Grant

Subjects: The AACN clinical research properties.
Purpose: To support research.
Eligibility: Principal investigators must be nurses holding current AACN membership. Investigators who have received funding from the AACN are ineligible to receive additional funding during the lifetime of their original award. They may apply for a new award when their original award obligations have been met. Research conducted in fulfilment of an academic degree is acceptable.
Level of Study: Research
Type: Grant
Value: Up to US$6,000
Frequency: Annual
No. of awards offered: Varies
Application Procedure: Applicants must submit completed application materials and proposals. Details are available directly from the organization or from the website.
Closing Date: October 1st

AACN Critical Care Grant

Subjects: Critical care nursing practice.
Purpose: To fund research.
Eligibility: Principal investigators must be nurses holding current AACN membership. Investigators who have received funding from the AACN are ineligible to receive additional funding during the lifetime of their original award. They may apply for a new award when their original award obligations have been met. The proposed research may not be used to meet the requirements of an academic degree.

Level of Study: Research
Type: Research grant
Value: Up to US$15,000
Frequency: Annual
No. of awards offered: Varies
Application Procedure: Applicants must submit completed application materials and a proposal. Details and forms are available directly from the organization or from the website.
Closing Date: February 1st

AACN Sigma Theta Tau Critical Care Grant

Subjects: Critical care nursing.
Purpose: To fund research.
Eligibility: Applicants must either be a member of Sigma Theta Tau or AACN.
Level of Study: Research
Type: Grant
Value: US$10,000
Frequency: Annual
No. of awards offered: Varies
Application Procedure: Applicants must submit completed application materials and a proposal. Details are available directly from the organization or from the website.
Closing Date: October 1st
Contributor: Co-sponsored by the AACN and Sigma Theta Tau International

AACN Datex Ohmeda Grant

Subjects: Nutritional assessment in the critically ill patient.
Purpose: To provide research support for a study to be conducted by a critical care nurse.
Eligibility: Principal investigators must be nurses holding current AACN membership. Investigators who have received funding from the AACN are ineligible to receive additional funding during the lifetime of their original award. They may apply for a new award when their original award obligations have been met. Research conducted in fulfilment of an academic degree is acceptable.
Type: Grant
Value: Up to US$5,000
Application Procedure: Applicants must submit completed application materials and proposals. Details are available directly from the organization or from the website.
Closing Date: February 1st

American Nurses Foundation Research Grant

Subjects: Clinical research.
Purpose: To encourage the research career development of nurses.
Eligibility: Principal investigators must be nurses holding current AACN membership. Investigators who have received funding from the AACN are ineligible to receive additional funding during the lifetime of their original award. They may apply for a new award when their original award obligations have been met.
Level of Study: Research
Type: Research grant
Value: Up to US$5,000 is awarded by the American Nurses Foundation
No. of awards offered: Varies
Application Procedure: Applicants must obtain information and application forms from the American Nurses Foundation, and should see the website for further details.
Closing Date: May 1st
Contributor: The AACN

For further information contact:

The American Nurses Foundation, 600 Maryland Avenue SW, Suite 100W, Washington, DC, 20024-2571, United States of America
Tel: (1) 202 651 7298
Email: anf@ana.org
Website: www.nursingworld.org/anf

AMERICAN ASSOCIATION OF LAW LIBRARIES (AALL)

Scholarship Committee, Suite 940, 53 West Jackson Boulevard, Chicago, IL, 60604, United States of America
Tel: (1) 312 939 4764
Fax: (1) 312 431 1097
Email: aallhq@aall.org
Website: www.aallnet.org

The American Association of Law Libraries (AALL) was founded in 1906 to promote and enhance the value of law libraries to legal and public communities, to foster the profession of law librarianship and to provide leadership in the field of legal information. Today, the AALL represents law librarians and related professionals who are affiliated with a wide range of institutions including law firms, law schools, corporate legal departments and courts, and local, state and federal government agencies.

AALL and West–George A Strait Minority Scholarship Endowment

Subjects: Law librarianship.
Eligibility: Open to degree candidates in an accredited library or law school. Preference is given to individuals with previous service to, or interest in, law librarianship and who intend to pursue a career in law librarianship. Applicants must be members of a minority group as defined by the current United States of America government guidelines.
Level of Study: Graduate
Type: Scholarship
Value: Up to US$3,500 for tuition and school-related expenses
Frequency: Annual
Study Establishment: Accredited library schools or accredited law schools
Country of Study: Any country
No. of awards offered: Varies
Application Procedure: Applicants must write for details or download an application form from the website.
Closing Date: April 1st

AALL James F Connolly LexisNexis Academic and Library Solutions Scholarship

Subjects: Law librarianship.
Eligibility: Awarded to library school graduates with law library experience who are presently attending an accredited law school with the intention of pursuing a career as a law librarian. Preference will be given to individuals who have demonstrated an interest in government documents.
Level of Study: Graduate
Type: Scholarship
Value: Up to US$2,000 for tuition and school-related expenses
Frequency: Annual
Study Establishment: ABA-accredited Law Schools
Country of Study: Any country
No. of awards offered: Varies
Application Procedure: Applicants must write for details or download an application form from the website.
Closing Date: April 1st

AALL LexisNexis/John R Johnson Memorial Scholarship Endowment

Subjects: Law librarianship.
Eligibility: Candidates who apply for AALL educational scholarships, types I–IV, become automatically eligible to receive the LexisNexis/John R Johnson Memorial Scholarship.
Level of Study: Graduate
Type: Scholarship
Value: Up to US$2,000 for tuition and school-related expenses
Frequency: Annual
Study Establishment: ALA-accredited library schools or ABA-Accredited Law Schools
Country of Study: Any country
No. of awards offered: Varies

Application Procedure: Applicants must write for details or download an application form from the website.
Closing Date: April 1st

AALL Scholarship (Type I)

Subjects: Law librarianship.
Eligibility: Open to law graduates who have the intention of pursuing a career as a law librarian and who are candidates for a library degree in an accepted library school. Preference is given to all members and persons with meaningful law library experience. Evidence of financial need must be submitted.
Level of Study: Graduate
Type: Scholarship
Value: Up to US$2,000 for tuition and school-related expenses
Frequency: Annual
Study Establishment: ALA-accredited library schools
Country of Study: Any country
No. of awards offered: Varies
Application Procedure: Applicants must write for details or download an application form from the website.
Closing Date: April 1st

AALL Scholarship (Type II)

Subjects: Law.
Eligibility: Open to library school graduates working towards a degree in an accredited law school who have no more than 36 semester credit hours remaining before qualifying for the law degree, who have law library experience and who have the intention of pursuing a career as a law librarian. Preference is given to members of the AALL.
Level of Study: Graduate
Value: Up to US$2,000 for tuition and school-related expenses
Frequency: Annual
Study Establishment: ABA-accredited law schools
Country of Study: Any country
No. of awards offered: Varies
Application Procedure: Applicants must write for details or download an application form from the website.
Closing Date: April 1st

AALL Scholarship (Type III)

Subjects: Law librarianship.
Purpose: To assist persons with meaningful law library experience.
Eligibility: Open to degree graduates who hold an award from an accredited library school. The candidate should have the intention of pursuing a career path as a law librarian. Preference is given to applicants working for degrees with an emphasis on courses in law librarianship.
Level of Study: Graduate
Type: Scholarship
Value: Up to US$2,000 for tuition and school-related expenses
Frequency: Annual
Study Establishment: ALA-accredited library schools
Country of Study: Any country
No. of awards offered: Varies
Application Procedure: Applicants must write for details or download an application form from the website.
Closing Date: April 1st

AALL Scholarship (Type IV)

Subjects: Law librarianship.
Eligibility: Awarded to library school graduates who are degree candidates in an area, other than law, that will be beneficial to the development of a professional career in law librarianship and who intend to have a career as a law librarian. Scholarship restricted to members of AALL. Evidence of financial need must be submitted.
Level of Study: Graduate
Type: Scholarship
Value: Up to US$2,000 for tuition and school-related expenses
Frequency: Annual
Country of Study: Any country
No. of awards offered: Varies
Application Procedure: Applicants must write for details or download an application form from the website.
Closing Date: April 1st

AALL Scholarship (Type V)

Subjects: Law librarianship.
Purpose: To assist law librarians who are registrants in continuing education courses.
Eligibility: Open to members of the AALL. Preference is given to permanent residents of the United States of America and Canada. Applicants must have a degree from an accredited library or law school and be registrants in continuing education courses related to law librarianship.
Level of Study: Postgraduate, professional development
Type: Scholarship
Value: Up to US$500 for tuition
Country of Study: Any country
No. of awards offered: Varies
Application Procedure: Applicants must write for details or download an application form from the website.
Closing Date: April 1st, October 1st or February 1st
Funding: Private

AMERICAN ASSOCIATION OF NEUROLOGICAL SURGEONS (AANS)

5550 Meadowbrook Drive, Rolling Meadows, IL, 60008, United States of America
Tel: (1) 847 378 0500
Fax: (1) 847 378 0600
Email: info@aans.org
Website: www.aans.org
Contact: Laurie Singer

Founded in 1931 as the Harvey Cushing Society, the American Association of Neurological Surgeons (AANS) is a scientific and educational association with more than 6,500 members worldwide. The AANS is dedicated to advancing the speciality of neurological surgery in order to provide the highest quality of neurosurgical care to the public. All active members of the AANS are certified by the American Board of Neurological Surgery, The Royal College of Physicians and Surgeons (Neurosurgery) of Canada or the Mexican Council of Neurological Surgery, AC. Neurological surgery is the medical speciality concerned with the prevention, diagnosis, treatment and rehabilitation of disorders that affect the entire nervous system including the spinal column, spinal cord, brain and peripheral nerves.

NREF Research Fellowship

Subjects: Any field of neurosurgery.
Purpose: To provide training for neurosurgeons who are preparing for academic careers as clinician investigators.
Eligibility: Open to MDs who have been accepted into, or who are in, an approved residency training programme in neurological surgery in North America.
Level of Study: Postdoctorate
Type: Fellowship
Value: US$40,000 for a 1-year fellowship and US$70,000 for a 2-year fellowship
Length of Study: 1–2 years
Frequency: Annual
Country of Study: Other
Application Procedure: Applicants must send a completed application, sponsor statement, programme director comments and letters of recommendation. Responses to questions 1–9, a curriculum vitae and photographic images must also be submitted. Applications are available at the website www.aans.org
Closing Date: October 31st
Funding: Private
Contributor: Corporations and membership
No. of awards given last year: 5
No. of applicants last year: 25
Additional Information: Notification of awards will be made by February 28th. After notification of the award, the applicant must in-

dicate acceptance, in writing, no later than April 1st. If unwilling to accept the award by that date, funds will be awarded to the first runner-up. A report of findings and accounting of funds will be expected at the halfway point and upon completion of the fellowship. Normally, no more than one award per year will be made to any one institution. Individuals who accept a grant from another source, NIH or private, for the same research project will become ineligible for the award. A budget must be prepared by the applicant and the sponsor indicating how the grant funds will be expended. It is the policy of the NREF to fund only direct costs involved with the research awards. This means no fringe benefits, publication costs or travel expenses. The signature representing the applicant's institution's financial officer on page four should be that of their chief financial officer or grants and contracts manager. The award will be made payable to the institution and disbursed by it according to its institutional policy.

NREF Young Clinician Investigator Award

Subjects: Any field of neurosurgery.
Purpose: To fund pilot studies that provide preliminary data used to strengthen applications for more permanent funding from other sources.
Eligibility: Applicants must be neurosurgeons who are full-time faculty in teaching institutions in North America and in the early years of their careers.
Level of Study: Postdoctorate
Type: Fellowship
Value: US$40,000
Length of Study: 1 year
Frequency: Annual
Application Procedure: Applicants must send a completed application, sponsor statement, programme director comments and letters of recommendation. Responses to questions 1–9, a curriculum vitae and photographic images must also be submitted. Applications are available at the website www.aans.org
Closing Date: October 31st
Funding: Private
Contributor: Corporations and membership
No. of awards given last year: 3
No. of applicants last year: 20
Additional Information: Notification of awards will be made by February 28th. After notification of the award, the applicant must indicate acceptance, in writing, no later than April 1st. If unwilling to accept the award by that date, funds will be awarded to the first runner-up. A summary report and an accounting of funds will be expected upon completion of the award. Normally, no more than one award per year will be made to any one institution. Individuals who accept a grant from another source, NIH or private, for the same research project will become ineligible for the award. The award is for those budget items necessary to pursue proper research. It may be used entirely, or in part, for stipend. A budget must be prepared by the applicant and sponsor indicating how the award funds will be expended. It is the policy of the NREF to fund only direct costs involved with the research awards. This means no fringe benefits, publication costs or travel expenses.

William P Van Wagenen Fellowship

Subjects: Any field of neurosurgery.
Purpose: To fund quality research in which the plan for a period abroad has been designed.
Eligibility: All senior neurological residents in approved neurosurgery residency programs.
Level of Study: Postdoctorate
Type: Travelling fellowship
Value: US$60,000
Length of Study: 6 months–1 year
Frequency: Annual
Country of Study: Country of study must be different than the country of residence
No. of awards offered: 1
Application Procedure: Application should be submitted with letters of reference, including one from the applicant's Program Director. A letter from the proposed sponsor and documentation of intent to pursue an academic career, while not required, will strengthen the application.
Closing Date: October 1st
Funding: Private
Contributor: William P Van Wagenen
No. of awards given last year: 1
No. of applicants last year: 6
Additional Information: By December 31st, the Chairman of the Van Wagenen Selection Committee will notify the winning applicant, who will be expected to implement the fellowship within 6 months following notification. A formal announcement of the award will be made at the Annual Meeting of the AANS. Applications and additional information regarding the William P Van Wagenen Fellowship can be located at www.aans.org

For further information contact:

Email: tlb@aans.org

AMERICAN ASSOCIATION OF OCCUPATIONAL HEALTH NURSES FOUNDATION (AAOHN)

2920 Brandywine Rd. Suite 100, Atlanta, GA 30341, United States of America
Tel: (1) 455 7757
Fax: (1) 455 7271
Website: www.aaohn.org

Securing the future by improving the health and safety of the Nation's workers.

AAOHN Professional Development Scholarship

Subjects: Occupational and Environmental Health.
Eligibility: Candidates must be employed in the field of occupational and environmental health nursing.
Level of Study: Professional development, postgraduate
Value: US$1,000–1,500
Length of Study: 1
Frequency: Annual
No. of awards offered: 13
Application Procedure: Submit and application form, a narrative of 500 words or less describing career goals and how the scholarship will enable continued education activity, and also supply a letter of support.
Closing Date: December 1st

THE AMERICAN ASSOCIATION OF PETROLEUM GEOLOGISTS (AAPG) FOUNDATION

125 West 15th Street, Tulsa, OK, 74119, United States of America
Tel: (1) 918 560 2644
Fax: (1) 918 560 2642
Email: rgriffin@aapg.org
Website: www.foundation.aapg.org/gia/index.cfm
Contact: Ms Rebecca Griffin, Administrative Coordinator

Established by the American Association of Petroleum Geologists (AAPG) in 1967, the AAPG Foundation is a public foundation, qualified to receive gifts that are tax-deductible for United States of America taxpayers, in support of worthwhile educational and scientific programmes or projects related to the geosciences.

American Association of Petroleum Geologists Foundation Grants-in-Aid

Subjects: Earth and geological sciences.
Purpose: To support graduate (Master's or PhD) students whose research can be applied to the search for, and development of, petroleum and energy-minerals resources, and to related environmental geology issues.

Eligibility: Open to graduate and doctorate students of any nationality.
Level of Study: Doctorate, graduate
Type: Grant
Value: A maximum of US$2,000
Country of Study: Any country
No. of awards offered: Varies
Application Procedure: Applicants must complete an application form and submit certified college academic transcripts and signed statements from professors commenting on the applicant's academic credentials and endorsements. Applicants must apply online. Website to apply: http://aapg.gia.confex.com/aapg-gia/2006/index.html
Closing Date: January 31st
Funding: Foundation
No. of awards given last year: 88
No. of applicants last year: 303
Additional Information: Grants are to be applied to expenses directly related to the student's thesis work, such as Summer fieldwork, analytical analyses, etc. Funds are not to be used to purchase capital equipment, or to pay salaries, tuition or room and board during the school year.

AMERICAN CHEMICAL SOCIETY (ACS)

1155 sixteenth Street, NW, Washington, DC, 20036,
United States of America
Tel: (1) 202 872 4600
Fax: (1) 202 776 8258
Email: awards@acs.org
Website: www.chemistry.org

The Petroleum Research Fund (PRF) was established in 1944 by seven major oil companies. The American Chemical Society (ACS) must use the funds for advanced scientific education and fundamental research in the petroleum field, which may include any field of pure science that affords a basis for subsequent research directly connected with the petroleum field. Since the first ACS/PRF grants were approved in 1954, several grant programmes have evolved to serve segments of the scientific community. ACS/PRF does not support scholarships or scholarships. PRF funding commitments in 2002 totalled US$28 million.

ACS Ahmed Zewail Award in Ultrafast Science and Technology

Subjects: Physics, chemistry, biology, or related fields.
Purpose: To recognize outstanding and creative contributions to fundamental discoveries or inventions in ultrafast science and technology.
Level of Study: Postgraduate
Type: Grant
Value: US$5,000
Frequency: Annual
Application Procedure: See website for details.
Closing Date: February 1st
Funding: Trusts
Contributor: Ahmed Zewail Endowment Fund

ACS Award for Achievement in Research for the Teaching and Learning of Chemistry

Subjects: Chemical sciences.
Purpose: To recognize outstanding contributions to experimental research that have increased our understanding of chemical pedagogy.
Level of Study: Postgraduate
Type: Grant
Value: US$5,000
Length of Study: 1 year
Frequency: Annual
No. of awards offered: 1
Application Procedure: See website for details.
Closing Date: February 1st
Funding: Commercial
Contributor: Prentice-Hall Publishers
Additional Information: Experimental research should include one or more recognized techniques and designed such as: control-group designs with random assignments of subjects or the use of in-tact class sections; factorial designs, bi-variate or multivariate correlation studies, etc.

ACS Award for Creative Advances in Environmental Science and Technology

Subjects: Environmental science.
Purpose: To encourage creativity in research and technology.
Eligibility: Open to all applicants without regard to age or nationality.
Level of Study: Postgraduate
Type: Award
Value: US$5,000 and a certificate
Frequency: Annual
Application Procedure: See the website.
Closing Date: November 1st
Contributor: Air products and chemicals, Inc.

ACS Award for Creative Research and Applications of Iodine Chemistry

Subjects: Chemistry.
Purpose: To promote global research of iodine chemistry.
Eligibility: Open to applicants who have performed outstanding research related to iodine chemistry.
Level of Study: Postgraduate
Type: Award
Value: US$10,000, travel expenses of up to US$1,000 and a certificate
Frequency: Every 2 years
Application Procedure: A completed nomination form and curriculum vitae must be sent.
Closing Date: November 1st
Contributor: Sociedad Quimica y Minera de chile S.A. (SQM S.A.)

ACS Award for Creative Work in Synthetic Organic Chemistry

Subjects: Organic chemistry.
Purpose: To recognize and encourage creative work in synthetic organic chemistry.
Eligibility: Open to applicants who have accomplished outstanding creative work in synthetic organic chemistry, which has been published.
Level of Study: Postgraduate
Type: Award
Value: US$5,000 and a certificate. In addition up to US$1,000 is provided for travel expenses to the meeting.
Frequency: Annual
Application Procedure: See the website www.chemistry.org
Closing Date: November 1st
Contributor: Aldrich Chemical Company, Inc.

ACS Award for Encouraging Disadvantaged Students into careers in the Chemical Sciences

Subjects: Chemistry.
Purpose: To recognize individuals who are fostered the interest of economically disadvantaged students in chemistry.
Eligibility: Open to all applicants of any nationality.
Level of Study: Postgraduate
Type: Award
Value: US$5,000 and a certificate along with a travel allowance of US$1,500.
Frequency: Annual
Country of Study: United States of America
Application Procedure: Completed nomination and optional support forms must be submitted to the awards office.
Closing Date: November 1st
Contributor: The Camille and Henry Dreyfus Foundation, Inc.
Additional Information: A grant of US$10,000 will be made to an academic institution chosen by the recipient.

For further information contact:

The Awards Office
Email: awards@acs.org

ACS Award for Encouraging Women into Careers in Chemical Sciences

Subjects: Chemistry.
Purpose: To recognize individuals who have significantly stimulated the interests of women in chemistry.
Eligibility: Open to candidates of all nationalities.
Level of Study: Professional development
Type: Award
Value: US$5,000 and a certificate plus US$1,500 towards travel expenses
Frequency: Annual
No. of awards offered: 1
Application Procedure: See the website.
Closing Date: November 1st

ACS Award in Chromatography

Subjects: Chemistry.
Purpose: To recognize outstanding contributions to the fields of chromatography.
Eligibility: Open to all applicants.
Level of Study: Postgraduate
Type: Award
Value: US$5,000 and a certificate
Frequency: Annual
Application Procedure: See the website www.chemistry.org
Closing Date: November 1st
Contributor: SUPELCO, Inc.

For further information contact:

The Awards Office
Email: awards@acs.org

ACS Award in Colloid and Surface Chemistry

Subjects: Chemistry.
Purpose: To recognize outstanding scientific contributions to colloid and/or surface chemistry in North America.
Eligibility: Open to applicants who are residents of North America.
Level of Study: Postgraduate
Type: Award
Value: US$5,000 and a certificate
Frequency: Annual
Application Procedure: Completed nomination and optional support forms must be submitted.
Closing Date: November 1st
Contributor: Procter & Gamble Company

For further information contact:

The Awards Office
Email: awards@acs.org

ACS National Awards

Subjects: Chemical sciences.
Purpose: To recognize premier chemical professionals in extraordinary ways.
Level of Study: Postgraduate
Type: Grant
Length of Study: 2 years
Frequency: Annual
No. of awards offered: 57
Application Procedure: See website for details.
Closing Date: February 1st

ACS Petroleum Research Fund

Subjects: Petroleum-related chemistry science.
Type: Grant
Value: US$90,000
Length of Study: 1–3 years
Frequency: Annual
Application Procedure: See website for details.
Closing Date: December 9th
Funding: Trusts
Contributor: Petroleum Research Fund

ACS PRF Type AC Grants

Subjects: Chemistry, the earth sciences, chemical engineering and related fields such as polymers and materials science.
Eligibility: Open to non-profit institutions in the United States of America and other countries. Grants are made in response to proposals. Recently, PRF support has been restricted to faculty holding tenure or a tenure track appointment. This is the largest PRF grant programme and usually funds proposals from graduate departments.
Level of Study: Professional development
Type: Grant
Value: Up to US$120,000 over 3 years
Frequency: Annual
Country of Study: Any country
No. of awards offered: Varies
Closing Date: Applications are accepted at any time
Funding: Private
Contributor: A private trust
No. of awards given last year: 201
No. of applicants last year: 627
Additional Information: Most grants begin on September 1st, but an earlier start can be negotiated. The PRF Advisory Board normally meets to review proposals in February, May and October. Prospective applicants should check the PRF website for current information on dates of submission and consideration.

ACS Priestley Medal

Subjects: Chemistry.
Purpose: To recognize distinguished services to chemistry.
Eligibility: Open to applicants of any nationality who may or may not be members of the Society.
Level of Study: Doctorate
Type: Award
Value: A gold medallion, a presentation box and a certificate
Frequency: Annual
Application Procedure: Applicants must send their nominations to the ACS Board of Directors.
Closing Date: November 1st
Funding: Trusts
Contributor: The American Chemical Society

For further information contact:

The Awards Office
Email: awards@acs.org

ACS Roger Adams Award

Subjects: Organic chemistry.
Purpose: To recognize and encourage outstanding contributions to research in organic chemistry.
Eligibility: Open to applicants of any nationality.
Type: Award
Value: US$25,000, a medallion and a certificate
Frequency: Every 2 years
Application Procedure: A completed nomination form must be sent as an email attachment. See the website www.chemistry.org for further details.
Closing Date: November 1st
Contributor: Organic Reactions, Inc. and Organic Synthesis, Inc.

ACS Stanley C. Israel Regional Award

Subjects: Chemical sciences.
Purpose: To recognize individuals who have advanced diversity in the chemical sciences and significantly stimulated or fostered activities that promote inclusiveness within the region.
Level of Study: Postgraduate
Type: Grant
Value: US$1,000
Frequency: Annual

Application Procedure: See website for details.
Closing Date: July 13th

For further information contact:

Committee on Minority Affairs American Chemical Society 1155 16th Street NW, Washington, DC 20036, United States of America
Tel: (1) 800 227 5558 ext. 6122
Email: p.christopher@acs.org
Contact: Paula Christoper

ACS Summer Research Fellowships

Subjects: Chemistry science.
Purpose: To support faculty guest researchers from non-doctoral institutions.
Level of Study: Postgraduate
Type: Fellowship
Value: US$8,000
Frequency: Annual
Application Procedure: See website for details.
Closing Date: December 2nd
Additional Information: Up to US$1,000 of the US$8,000 may be used towards research expenses.

ACS Supplements for underepresented Minority Research

Subjects: Chemistry sciences.
Purpose: To support a student who is a member of a minority group underrepresented in science, ie., African American, Hispanic/Latino, or American Indian.
Level of Study: Postgraduate
Type: Grant
Value: US$5,000
Frequency: Annual
Application Procedure: See website for details.
Closing Date: December 2nd

ACS/PRF Scientific Education Grants

Subjects: Scientific education and fundamental research in the petroleum field.
Purpose: To provide partial funding for foreign speakers at major symposia.
Eligibility: Open to non-profit institutions throughout the United States of America and worldwide for speakers coming to conferences in the United States of America, Canada and Mexico and speaking within the PRF Trust.
Level of Study: Unrestricted
Type: Grant
Value: Up to US$1,200 per speaker or up to US$3,600 per symposium
Frequency: Annual
Country of Study: United States of America
No. of awards offered: Varies
Closing Date: Applications are accepted at any time
Funding: Private
Contributor: A private trust

ACS/PRF Type B Grants

Subjects: Chemistry, the earth sciences, chemical engineering and related fields such as polymers and materials science.
Eligibility: Open to non-profit institutions in the United States of America and other countries. Grants are made in response to proposals. Recently, PRF support has been restricted to faculty holding tenure or a tenure track appointment. Type B grants are restricted to departments that do not award PhDs. Grants are intended for research involving undergraduates. Graduate or postdoctoral students may not be supported by Type B funds.
Level of Study: Professional development
Type: Grant
Value: Up to US$50,000
Length of Study: 3 years
Frequency: Annual
Country of Study: Any country
No. of awards offered: Varies
Closing Date: Applications are accepted at any time
Funding: Private
Contributor: A private trust
No. of awards given last year: 50
No. of applicants last year: 119
Additional Information: Most grants begin on September 1st, but an earlier start can be negotiated. The PRF Advisory Board normally meets to review proposals in February, May and October. Prospective applicants should check the PRF website for information on dates of submission and consideration.

ACS/PRF Type G Starter Grants

Subjects: Chemistry, the earth sciences, chemical engineering and related fields such as polymers and materials science.
Eligibility: Open to non-profit institutions in the United States of America only. Grants are made in response to proposals. These grants are intended for new faculty within the first 3 years of teaching and without extensive postdoctoral research experience eg. more than 5 years.
Level of Study: Professional development
Type: Grant
Value: US$35,000 over 2 years
Length of Study: 2 years
Frequency: Annual
Country of Study: United States of America
No. of awards offered: Varies
Closing Date: Applications are accepted at any time
Funding: Private
Contributor: A private trust
No. of awards given last year: 125
No. of applicants last year: 352
Additional Information: Most grants begin on September 1st, but an earlier start can be negotiated. The PRF Advisory Board normally meets to review proposals in February, May and October. Prospective applicants should check the PRF website for information on dates of submission and consideration. A detailed budget is not required.

Alfred Burger Award in Medicinal Chemistry

Subjects: Medicinal chemistry.
Purpose: To acknowledge outstanding contributions to research in medicinal chemistry.
Eligibility: Open to all applicants without regard to age or nationality.
Level of Study: Postgraduate
Type: Award
Value: US$3,000 and a certificate
Frequency: Annual
Application Procedure: A completed nomination form available on the website www.chemistry.org must be sent as an email attachment.
Closing Date: November 1st
Contributor: Glaxo Smithkline

Anselme Payen Award

Subjects: Chemistry.
Purpose: To encourage outstanding professional contributions to the science and chemical technologies of cellulose and its allied products.
Eligibility: Open to all scientists conducting research in the field of cellulose.
Level of Study: Postgraduate
Type: Award
Value: US$3,000 and a bronze medal
Frequency: Annual
Application Procedure: A completed nomination form available on the website www.membership.acs.org must be sent.
Closing Date: December 1st
Contributor: Cellulose, paper and textile division, ACS

For further information contact:

Awards committee chair National Bioenergy Center 1617 Cole Boulevard, Golden, CO 80401
Tel: 384 6123
Fax: 384 6363
Contact: Dr Stephen S. Kelley

Arthur C. Cope Award

Subjects: Organic chemistry.
Purpose: To recognize outstanding achievement in the field of organic chemistry.
Eligibility: Open to all candidates irrespective of their nationality and age.
Level of Study: Postgraduate
Type: Award
Value: US$25,000, a medallion and a certificate
Frequency: Annual
Application Procedure: See the website.
Closing Date: November 1st
Additional Information: An unrestricted grant-in-aid of US$150,000 for research in organic chemistry will be made to the university selected by the recipient.

Cognis Corporation Graduate Research Fellowship in Colloid and Surface Chemistry

Subjects: Chemistry.
Purpose: To support outstanding graduate students during their final 2 years of doctoral thesis research.
Eligibility: Open to candidates who are enrolled in a full-time graduate programme leading to a PhD degree at an accredited university within the United States.
Level of Study: Research
Type: Award
Value: US$20,000
Length of Study: 2 years
Frequency: Annual
Study Establishment: Any accredited university
Country of Study: United States of America
Application Procedure: See the website www.membership.acs.org
Closing Date: Novermber 1st
Funding: Corporation
Contributor: The Cognis Corporation

For further information contact:

Department of chemical and Materials Engineering University of Kentucky, Lexington, KY 40506-0046
Contact: Professor Mark A. Keane

Earle B. Barnes Award for Leadership in Chemical Research Management

Subjects: Chemistry and chemical engineering.
Purpose: To recognize outstanding achievements in chemical research management.
Eligibility: Open to applicants who are citizens of the United States.
Level of Study: Postgraduate
Type: Award
Value: US$5,000 and a certificate
Frequency: Annual
Application Procedure: A completed nomination form must be submitted to awards @acs.org as an email attachment.
Closing Date: November 1st
Contributor: The DOW Chemical Company

Ernest Guenther Award in the Chemistry of Natural Products

Subjects: Organic chemistry.
Purpose: To recognize and encourage outstanding achievements in analysis, structure elucidation and chemical synthesis of natural products.
Eligibility: Open to all applicants for their accomplished outstanding work.
Type: Award
Value: US$5,000 plus up to US$2,500 for travel expenses
Frequency: Annual
Application Procedure: A completed nomination form and optional support forms must be mailed to awards@acs.org
Closing Date: November 1st

F. Albert Cotton Award in Synthetic Inorganic Chemistry

Subjects: Inorganic chemistry.
Purpose: To recognize distinguished work in synthetic inorganic chemistry.
Eligibility: Open to all candidates of all nationalities.
Level of Study: Postgraduate
Type: Award
Value: US$5,000
Frequency: Annual
Application Procedure: A completed application form to be submitted as an email attachment to awards@acs.org
Closing Date: November 1st
Funding: Private
Contributor: F. Albert Cotton Endowment Fund

Frederic Stanley Kipping Award in Silicon Chemistry

Subjects: Chemistry.
Purpose: To recognize distinguished contributions to the field of silicon chemistry.
Eligibility: Open to all candidates who have contributed to the field of silicon chemistry. There are no limits on age or on nationality.
Level of Study: Postgraduate
Type: Award
Value: US$5,000 and a certificate
Frequency: Every 2 years
Application Procedure: A completed nomination form to be mailed to awards@acs.org
Closing Date: November 1st
Funding: Corporation
Contributor: Dow Corning Corporation

Glenn T. Seaborg Award for Nuclear Chemistry

Subjects: Chemistry.
Purpose: To recognize and encourage research in nuclear and radiochemistry or their applications.
Eligibility: Open to all applicants without regard to nationality or age.
Level of Study: Postgraduate
Type: Award
Value: US$3,000 and a certificate
Frequency: Annual
Application Procedure: See the website.
Closing Date: November 1st
Contributor: ACS Division of Nuclear Chemistry and Technology

For further information contact:

The Awards Office
Email: awards@acs.org

Herbert C. Brown Award for Creative Research in Synthetic Methods

Subjects: Chemistry.
Purpose: To recognize and encourage outstanding and creative contributions to research in synthetic methods.
Eligibility: Open to all applicants without regard to age or nationality.
Level of Study: Postgraduate
Type: Award
Value: US$5,000 a medallion with a presentation box and a certificate
Frequency: Annual
Application Procedure: A completed application form available on the website must be sent as an email attachment to awards@acs.org
Closing Date: November 1st
Contributor: Aldrich Chemical Company, Inc.

Ipatieff Prize

Subjects: Chemistry.
Purpose: To recognize outstanding chemical experimental work in the field of catalysis.
Eligibility: Open to applicants of any nationality and not over 40 years of age.
Level of Study: Postgraduate
Type: Award
Value: Approx. US$5,000

Frequency: Every 3 years
Country of Study: Any country
Application Procedure: Contact the awards office.
Closing Date: November 1st
Contributor: Ipatieff Trust Fund
Additional Information: Preference will be given to American Chemists.

For further information contact:

The Awards Office
Email: awards@acs.org

Irving Langmuir Award in Chemical Physics

Subjects: Chemistry and physics.
Purpose: To encourage research in chemistry and physics.
Eligibility: Open to candidates who are residents of the United States.
Level of Study: Postgraduate
Type: Award
Value: US$10,000 and a certificate
Frequency: Every 2 years
Country of Study: United States of America
Application Procedure: Contact the Awards office.
Closing Date: November 1st
Funding: Foundation
Contributor: The General Electric Foundation

James Bryant Conant Award in High School Chemistry Teaching

Subjects: Teaching.
Purpose: To recognize outstanding teachers.
Eligibility: Open to candidates who are actively engaged in the teaching of chemistry in high school.
Level of Study: Postgraduate
Type: Award
Value: US$5,000 and a certificate
Frequency: Annual
Country of Study: United States of America
Application Procedure: A completed nomination form must be submitted as an email attachment.
Closing Date: November 1st
Contributor: The American Chemical Society

For further information contact:

Email: awards@acs.org
Contact: The Awards Office

Peter Debye Award in Physical Chemistry

Subjects: Physical chemistry.
Purpose: To encourage and reward outstanding research.
Eligibility: Open to all candidates without regard to age or nationality.
Level of Study: Postgraduate
Type: Award
Value: US$5,000 and a certificate
Frequency: Annual
Application Procedure: A completed nominations form to be sent as an email attachment to awards@acs.org
Closing Date: November 1st

Pfizer Graduate Travel Awards in Analytical Chemistry

Subjects: Analytical chemistry.
Purpose: To provide funds for students to travel to an ACS National meeting and present the results of their research.
Eligibility: Open to candidates who are U.S. citizens and permanent residents.
Level of Study: Postgraduate
Type: Award
Value: US$1,000
Frequency: Annual
Study Establishment: Open to candidates who are U.S. citizens and permanent residents
No. of awards offered: 5
Application Procedure: A completed application form, which may be downloaded from the website, must be sent.
Closing Date: October 21st
Contributor: The Division of Analytical Chemistry of the ACS

For further information contact:

Department of Chemistry The College of Wooster, Ohio, Wooster, 44691
Email: pedmiston@wooster.edu
Contact: Dr Paul Edmiston

Ronald Breslow Award for Achievement in Biomimetic Chemistry

Subjects: Chemistry.
Purpose: To recognize outstanding contributions to the field of biominetic chemistry.
Eligibility: Open to all candidates without regard to age or nationality.
Level of Study: Postgraduate
Type: Award
Value: US$5,000 and a certificate
Frequency: Annual
Application Procedure: A completed application form along with a curriculum vitae must be submitted as an email attachment to awards@acs.org
Closing Date: November 1st
Funding: Trusts
Contributor: The Breslow Endowment

Victor K. LaMer Award for Graduate Research in Colloid and Surface Chemistry

Subjects: Chemistry.
Purpose: To award outstanding PhD thesis.
Eligibility: Open to candidates whose PhD thesis is accepted by a US Canadian university.
Level of Study: Research, postgraduate
Type: Award
Value: Varies
Frequency: Annual
Application Procedure: Applicants must submit a nomination letter along with 5 copies of the thesis and a supporting letter.
Closing Date: November 30th
Contributor: The Division of Colloid and Surface Chemistry of ACS

AMERICAN COLLEGE OF OBSTETRICIANS AND GYNECOLOGISTS (ACOG)

409 12th Street South West, PO Box 96920, Washington, DC 20090-6920, United States of America
Tel: (1) 202 863 2577
Fax: (1) 202 863 4992
Email: lcummings@acog.org
Website: www.acog.org
Contact: Mrs Lee Cummings, Director of Corporate Relations

The American College of Obstetricians and Gynecologists (ACOG) is a membership organization of obstetricians and gynaecologists dedicated to the advancement of women's health through education, advocacy, practice and research.

ACOG/3M Pharmaceuticals Research Awards in Human Papillomavirus

Subjects: Obstetrics and gynaecology. One grant is awarded in the area of vulvar disease due to human papilomavirus (HPV). Topics may include pathogenesis, mechanisms of transmission, diagnosis, treatment, histology, immunology and preventive measures.
Purpose: To provide seed grant funds to junior investigators for clinical research.
Eligibility: Applicants must be ACOG Junior Fellows or Fellows in an approved obstetrics or gynaecology residency programme, or within 3

years of postresidency. Applicants must be citizens of the United States of America or Canada.
Level of Study: Postgraduate
Type: Research grant
Value: US$7,500 plus a US$1,000 travel stipend to attend the ACOG Annual Clinical Meeting
Length of Study: 1 year
Frequency: Annual
Country of Study: United States of America or Canada
No. of awards offered: 1
Application Procedure: Applicants must submit six copies of a proposal consisting of a hypothesis, objectives, specific aims, background and significance, experimental design and methods. These must not exceed six typewritten pages in total. A curriculum vitae, letter of support from the programme director, departmental chair or laboratory director, references and a one-page budget must also be submitted.
Closing Date: October 1st
Funding: Commercial
Contributor: 3M Pharmaceuticals
No. of awards given last year: 1
No. of applicants last year: 5

ACOG/Berlex Laboratories Research Award in PMS/PMDD

Subjects: Effective diagnosis and treatment of PMS and PMDD and/or overall impact of PMS/PMDD on quality of life.
Purpose: To provide seed grant funds to a junior investigator for clinical research in the area of PMS/PMDD.
Eligibility: Applicants must be ACOG Junior Fellows or Fellows in an approved obstetrics or gynaecology residency programme, or within 3 years of postresidency.
Level of Study: Postdoctorate
Type: Research grant
Value: US$25,000 plus US$1,000 travel stipend to attend the ACOG Annual Clinical Meeting
Length of Study: 1 year
Frequency: Annual
Country of Study: United States of America or Canada
No. of awards offered: 1
Application Procedure: Applicants must submit six copies of a proposal consisting of a hypothesis, objectives, specific aims, background and significance, experimental design and references. A one-page budget, applicant's curriculum vitae and a letter of support from the programme director, departmental chair, or laboratory director are required.
Closing Date: October 1st
Funding: Commercial
Contributor: Berlex Laboratories Inc.
No. of awards given last year: 1
No. of applicants last year: 4

ACOG/Berlex, Inc. Research Award in Contraception

Subjects: Obstetrics and gynaecology.
Purpose: To provide seed grant funds to junior investigators for clinical research in an area of contraception such as estrogen supplementation during the traditional hormone-free interval.
Eligibility: Applicants must be ACOG Junior Fellows or Fellows who are in an approved obstetrics or gynaecology residency programme or within 3 years of postresidency.
Level of Study: Postgraduate
Type: Research grant
Value: US$25,000 plus funds for travel expenses to attend the ACOG Annual Clinical Meeting
Length of Study: 1 year
Frequency: Annual
Country of Study: United States of America or Canada
No. of awards offered: 1
Application Procedure: Applicants must submit six copies of a proposal consisting of a hypothesis, objectives, specific aims, background and significance, experimental design and methods. These must not exceed six typewritten pages in total. A curriculum vitae, letter of support from the programme director, departmental chair or laboratory director, references and a one-page budget must also be submitted.
Closing Date: October 1st
Funding: Commercial
Contributor: Organon, Inc
No. of awards given last year: 1
No. of applicants last year: 6

ACOG/Berlex, Inc. Research Award in PMS/PMDD

Subjects: The basic research should include one or more of the following: effective diagnosis and treatment of PMS and PMDD and/or overall impact of PMS/PMDD on quality of life. Suggested research topics include, but are not limited to, the following: development and validation of a retrospective screen for diagnosis of PMS/PMDD; qualification of socioeconomic impact of PMS/PMDD or, impact of treatments (DRSP/EE OCs, SSRIs and/or calcium) in improving PMS/PMDD patient's quality of life.
Purpose: To provide seed grant funds to a junior investigator for clinical research in the area of PMS/PMDD.
Eligibility: Applicants must be an ACOG Junior Fellow or Fellow and in an approved obstetrics-gynecology residency program or within three years post-residency.
Level of Study: Postgraduate
Type: Research grant
Value: US$25,000 plus a US$1,000 travel stipend to attend the ACOG annual clinical meeting
Length of Study: 1 year
Frequency: Annual
Country of Study: United States of America or Canada
No. of awards offered: 1
Application Procedure: Applicants must submit six (6) copies of a research proposal, written in eight (8) pages or less, and should include the following: Hypothesis; Objectives; Specific Aims; Background and Significance; Experimental Design; and, References. A one-page budget, curriculum vitae, and letter of support from the program director, departmental chair, or laboratory director must also be submitted.
Closing Date: October 1st
Funding: Commercial
Contributor: Berley, Inc.
No. of awards given last year: 1
No. of applicants last year: 2

ACOG/Kenneth Gottesfeld-Charles Hohler Memorial Foundation Research Award in Ultrasound

Subjects: To provide grant funds to a junior investigator to support research or advanced training that is ultrasound specific and dedicated to a practical clinical use in a new or unique approach.
Purpose: To provide grant funds to support work in ultrasound and its application to obstetrics and gynaecology.
Eligibility: Applicants must be ACOG Junior Fellows or Fellows who are in an approved obstetrics/gynaecology residency programme, or within five years of completion of their residency or fellowship.
Level of Study: Postdoctorate
Value: One grant of US$10,000 or two grants of US$5,000 will be provided at the discretion of the review committee plus US$1,000 travel stipend to attend the ACOG Annual Clinical Meeting
Length of Study: 1 year
Frequency: Annual
Country of Study: United States of America or Canada
No. of awards offered: 1 or 2
Application Procedure: Applicants must submit six copies of a proposal or eight pages or less consisting of a hypothesis; objectives, specific aims, background and significance, and experimental design, and references. An advanced training proposal must be eight pages or less and include the site, the dates, the proposed curriculum and the individuals responsible for the training. A one-page budget is required and applicant's curriculum vitae.
Closing Date: October 1st
Funding: Foundation
Contributor: Kenneth Gottesfeld Charles Hohler Memorial Foundation
No. of awards given last year: 2

No. of applicants last year: 9
Additional Information: Further information can be found on the member side of the website www.acog.org

ACOG/Ortho Women's Health Academic Training Fellowships in Obstetrics and Gynaecology

Subjects: Obstetrics and gynaecology.
Purpose: To provide opportunities for especially qualified residents or Fellows to spend an extra year involved in responsibilities that will train them for academic positions in the speciality.
Eligibility: Open to ACOG Junior Fellows or Fellows who have completed at least 1 year of training, and are considered by the director of their residency programme to be especially fitted for a career in medical education or academic obstetrics and gynaecology.
Level of Study: Postgraduate
Type: Research grant
Value: US$30,000 stipend plus travel expenses to attend the ACOG Annual Clinical Meeting
Length of Study: 1 year
Frequency: Annual
Study Establishment: 1971
Country of Study: United States of America or Canada
No. of awards offered: 2
Application Procedure: Applicants must submit six copies of a proposal consisting of a hypothesis, objectives, specific aims, background and significance, experimental design and methods. These must not exceed six typewritten pages in total. A curriculum vitae, letter of support from the programme director, departmental chair or laboratory director, references and a one-page budget must also be submitted.
Closing Date: October 1st
Funding: Commercial
Contributor: Ortho-Women's Health
No. of awards given last year: 2
No. of applicants last year: 20

ACOG/Solvay Pharmaceuticals Research Award in Menopause

Subjects: Obstetrics and gynaecology focusing on issues related to the menopause. Relevant subjects include the physiological changes of the postreproductive woman, hormonal receptor site distribution, or other investigation deemed appropriate to furthering the basic understanding of the menopause.
Purpose: To advance knowledge in the field through encouraging basic research.
Eligibility: Open to ACOG Fellows or Junior Fellows in an approved obstetrics or gynaecology residency programme or within 3 years of postresidency.
Level of Study: Postgraduate
Type: Research grant
Value: US$15,000 plus a US$1,000 travel stipend to attend the ACOG Annual Clinical Meeting
Length of Study: 1 year
Frequency: Annual
Country of Study: United States of America or Canada
No. of awards offered: 1
Application Procedure: Applicants must submit six copies of a proposal consisting of a hypothesis, objectives, specific aims, background and significance, experimental design and methods. These must not exceed six typewritten pages in total. A curriculum vitae, letter of support from the programme director, departmental chair or laboratory director, references and a one-page budget must also be submitted.
Closing Date: October 1st
Funding: Commercial
Contributor: Solvay Pharmaceuticals Inc.
No. of awards given last year: 1
No. of applicants last year: 8

Warren H Pearse/Wyeth Pharmaceuticals Women's Health Policy Research Award

Subjects: Obstetrics and gynaecology focusing on an aspect of policy that either defines, assists or restricts the ability of the physician to deliver healthcare to women in general or in a specific area.
Purpose: To provide funds to support research.
Eligibility: The principal or co-principal investigator must be an ACOG Junior Fellow or Fellow. Proposals will be considered with regard to innovation, potential utility of the research, ability to generalize results and demonstrated capability of the investigator.
Level of Study: Postgraduate
Type: Research grant
Value: US$15,000 plus $1,000 travel stipend to attend the ACOG Annual Clinical Meeting
Length of Study: 1 year
Frequency: Annual
Country of Study: United States of America or Canada
No. of awards offered: 1
Application Procedure: Applicants must submit six copies of a proposal consisting of a hypothesis, objectives, specific aims, background and significance, experimental design and methods. These must not exceed six typewritten pages in total. A curriculum vitae, letter of support from the programme director, departmental chair or laboratory director, references and a one-page budget must also be submitted.
Closing Date: October 1st
Funding: Commercial
Contributor: Wyeth Pharmaceuticals
No. of awards given last year: 1
No. of applicants last year: 7

AMERICAN COLLEGE OF PROSTHODONTICS (ACP)

211 East Chicago Avenue Suite 1000, Chicago, IL 6011,
United States of America
Tel: (1) 312 573 1260
Fax: (1) 312 573 1257
Website: www.prosthodontics.org

The ACP is the official sponsoring organization for the specialty of prosthodontics, which is one of nine recognized specialties of the American Dental Association.

Claude R. Baker Predoctoral Faculty Award

Subjects: Prosthodontics.
Purpose: To acknowledge excellence in teaching.
Eligibility: Open to all dental school junior faculty member, recipients are chosen by a standing committee of the academy.
Level of Study: Postgraduate
Value: US$1000 and travel reimbursement to attend the academy meeting
Frequency: Annual

John J. Sharry Research Competition

Subjects: Prothodontics.
Purpose: To acknowledge original research is prothodontics by students.
Eligibility: Open to students enrolled in a post-doctoral programme.
Level of Study: Postgraduate
Type: Scholarship
Value: US$1,250
Frequency: Annual
Closing Date: June 27th
Funding: Foundation
Contributor: ACP Education Foundation

For further information contact:

University of Iowa College of Dentistry N447 Dental Science Building
Iowa City, IA 52242
Tel: (319) 335-7381
Fax: (319) 335-8895
Contact: Clark M. Stanford

Research Fellowship in Complete Dentures

Subjects: Prosthetic dentistry.
Purpose: To support research by dental scientists-in-training.
Eligibility: Open to all trainee dental scientists.
Level of Study: Research
Value: US$6,000
Frequency: Annual
Closing Date: October 15th
Funding: Foundation
Contributor: Procter and Gamble Denture care and ACP

For further information contact:

N447 Dental Science Building College of Dentistry Iowa City, Iowa, 52242
Contact: Clark M. Stanford

Research Fellowship in Geriatric Prosthodontics

Subjects: Prosthetic dentistry.
Purpose: To support promising research by dental scientists-in-training.
Eligibility: Open to all dental scientists-in-training.
Level of Study: Postdoctorate
Type: Fellowship
Value: US$6,000
Frequency: Annual
Closing Date: October 15th
Funding: Foundation
Contributor: American college of Prosthodontics and ESPE

For further information contact:

N447 Dental Science Building College of Dentistry Iowa City, Iowa, 52242
Tel: (319) 335-7381
Fax: (319) 335-8895
Contact: Dr Clark M. Stanford, ACP Research Committee Chair

Tylman Research Program

Subjects: Dentistry.
Purpose: To promote and support research in the field of fixed prosthodontics by graduate students.
Eligibility: Open to full-time students in the United States and Canada enrolled in any graduate or postgraduate programme who are conducting research pertinent to fixed prosthodontics. Proposals must be endorsed by the programme director of an accredited prosthodontic programme. Priority will be given to students in prosthodontic programmes. Predoctoral dental students are not eligible.
Level of Study: Postgraduate
Type: Grant
Value: Please contact the organization
Frequency: Annual
Country of Study: United States of America
Application Procedure: Applicants must submit the protocol of the research project to the Academy Research Committee. The six best protocols are funded. The student must submit progress reports and a final manuscript of the completed project.
Funding: Private

AMERICAN COLLEGE OF RHEUMATOLOGY

American College of Rheumatology, 1800 Century Place, Suite 250, Atlanta, GA 30345-4300, United States of America
Tel: (1) 404 633 3777
Fax: (1) 404 633 1870
Email: ref@rheumatology.com
Website: www.rheumatology.org

The American College of Rheumatology (ACR) is the professional organization of rheumatologists and associated health professionals who share a dedication to healing, preventing disability, and curing more than 100 types of arthritis and related disabling and sometimes fatal disorders of the joints, muscles and bones.

ACF/REF/Paula De Merieu Rheumatology Fellowship Award

Subjects: Rheumatic diseases.
Purpose: To help ensure that a diverse and highly trained workforce is available to provide competent clinical care to those affected by the rheumatic diseases.
Eligibility: Only training directors at ACGME-accredited institutions in good standing may apply. The trainee must be an underrepresented minority or a woman, ie., either Black American, Native American (American Indian, Alaska Native, Native Hawaiian), Mexican American, Puerto Rican or any other minority category. Award applicant must be a citizen or non-citizen national of the United States of America, or be in lawful possession of a permanent resident card. Individuals on temporary (J1, H1) or student visas are not eligible.
Level of Study: Professional development
Type: Fellowship
Value: US$25,000
Length of Study: 1 year
Frequency: Annual
Country of Study: United States of America
Application Procedure: Applications forms are available on website.
Closing Date: August 1st
Funding: Private
Contributor: The Dr Paula de Merieux estate

ACR/REF Clinician Scholars Educator Award

Subjects: Rheumatology.
Purpose: To recognize and support rheumatologists dedicated to providing high-quality clinical educational experience to trainees.
Eligibility: Candidates must be ACR members with experience in the training of medical students, residents and fellows in rheumatology. Candidates must be affiliated with an LCCME-accredited school or an ACGME-accredited training programme in internal medicine, paediatrics or rheumatology. A faculty appointment is not essential. If the candidate is not a citizen or non-citizen national of the United States of America, the candidate must provide evidence that he or she is eligible to remain in the United States of America throughout the period of the award.
Level of Study: Professional development
Type: Award
Value: US$50,000 per year
Length of Study: 3 years
Frequency: Annual
Country of Study: United States of America
Application Procedure: Application forms are available on website.
Closing Date: August 1st
Funding: Corporation
Contributor: Pfizer Inc.
No. of awards given last year: 3

ACR/REF Health Professional Graduate Student Research Preceptorship

Subjects: Rheumatic diseases.
Purpose: To introduce students to rheumatology-related healthcare by supporting full-time research by a graduate student in the broad area of rheumatic diseases.
Eligibility: Only students enrolled in graduate school are eligible. Preceptors are responsible for selecting student applicants and must be members of the ARHP.
Level of Study: Doctorate, postgraduate
Value: US$3,500 student stipend, US$1,000 for laboratory expenses, US$1,500 stipend for the mentor and up to US$1,000 for travel funds for the student to attend the ACR/ARHP annual scientific meeting.
Length of Study: 8 weeks
Frequency: Annual
Country of Study: United States of America
No. of awards offered: Up to 3
Application Procedure: Application forms are available on website.
Closing Date: February 7th
Contributor: Abbott Endowment for Rheumotology Development
No. of awards given last year: 4

ACR/REF Health Professional Investigator Award

Subjects: Rheumatic diseases.
Purpose: To provide support to health professionals in the research fields related to rheumatic diseases and to sustain individuals committed to a career in rheumatology-related research.
Eligibility: Applicants must have a doctoral degree and be members of the ARHP. Applicants should not apply for the health professional investigator award and the health professional new investigator award during the same cycle.
Level of Study: Research
Type: Award
Value: US$50,000 per year
Length of Study: 2 years
Frequency: Annual
Country of Study: United States of America
Application Procedure: Application forms are available on website.
Closing Date: August 1st
Funding: Private
Contributor: ACR
No. of awards given last year: 2

ACR/REF Health Professional New Investigator Award

Subjects: Rheumatology.
Purpose: To provide support to health professionals new to rheumatology and to individuals committed to a career in rheumatology-related research.
Eligibility: Applicants must be within 5 years of receiving their doctoral degree, have no existing or past NIH funding as principal investigators and be members of the ARHP.
Level of Study: Professional development
Type: Award
Value: US$50,000 per year
Length of Study: 2 years
Frequency: Annual
Country of Study: United States of America
Application Procedure: Application forms are available on website.
Closing Date: August 1st
Funding: Private
Contributor: ACR
No. of awards given last year: 2

ACR/REF Medical and Pediatric Resident Research Award

Subjects: Rheumatology.
Purpose: To motivate outstanding residents to pursue subspecialty training in rheumatology by providing an opportunity to attend the ACR annual scientific meeting.
Eligibility: A candidate must be a resident enrolled in an ACGME-accredited paediatric, medicine or combined medicine/paediatric residency programme who is interested in rheumatology. The candidate must be an author or co-author of an abstract submitted to the upcoming ACR annual meeting. Award applicant must be a citizen or non-citizen national of the United States of America, or be in lawful possession of a permanent resident card. Individuals on temporary (J1, H1) or student visas are not eligible.
Level of Study: Professional development
Type: Prize
Value: US$750 cash prize plus US$1,000 to cover travel expenses and hotel accommodations for the ACR annual scientific meeting. Registration fees will be waived
Frequency: Annual
Country of Study: United States of America
Closing Date: August 1st
Funding: Foundation
Contributor: Abbott Endowment for Rheumatology
No. of awards given last year: 5

ACR/REF Physician Scientist Development Award

Subjects: Arthritis and rheumatic diseases.
Purpose: To encourage qualified physicians without significant prior research experience to embark on careers in biomedical and/or clinical research in arthritis and rheumatic diseases.
Eligibility: Applicants must have received an MD, DO, or equivalent medical degree from an accredited institution; completed training in internal medicine or paediatrics; and will have completed at least 1 year of speciality training in rheumatology at the start of the award. MD/PhDs, and PhDs are not eligible for this award. Only physicians are eligible to apply. Award applicant must be a citizen or non-citizen national of the United States of America, or be in lawful possession of a permanent resident card. Individuals on temporary (J1, H1) or student visas are not eligible.
Level of Study: Postdoctorate
Type: Award
Value: US$50,000 per year
Length of Study: 3 years
Frequency: Annual
Country of Study: United States of America
Application Procedure: Application forms are available on website.
Closing Date: August 1st
Funding: Corporation
Contributor: Centocor Inc.
No. of awards given last year: 6

ACR/REF Rheumatology Fellowship Training Award

Subjects: Rheumatic diseases.
Purpose: To help ensure that a highly trained workforce is available to provide competent clinical care to those affected by rheumatic diseases.
Eligibility: Only training directors at ACGME-accredited institutions in good standing may apply. The rheumatology fellowship training programme director at the institution will be responsible for the selection and appointment of trainees. Award applicant must be a citizen or non-citizen national of the United States of America, or be in lawful possession of a permanent resident card. Individuals on temporary (J1, H1) or student visas are not eligible.
Level of Study: Professional development
Type: Fellowship
Value: US$25,000 and US$1,500 for travel costs
Length of Study: 1 year
Frequency: Annual
Country of Study: United States of America
Application Procedure: Application forms are available on website.
Closing Date: August 1st
Funding: Corporation
Contributor: Amgen Inc.
No. of awards given last year: 20

ACR/REF/Amgen Pediatric Rheumatology Research Award

Subjects: Rheumatology.
Purpose: To recognize and promote scholarship in the field of paediatric rheumatology.
Eligibility: Candidates must be trainees enrolled in a recognized ACGME-accredited paediatric rheumatology programme or a related research laboratory. Trainees must be preparing for a career in paediatric rheumatology. In addition, candidates must submit an abstract to the upcoming ACR Annual Scientific Meeting. There are no citizenship requirements for this award.
Level of Study: Research
Type: Award
Value: US$1,000
Length of Study: 1 year
Frequency: Annual
Country of Study: United States of America
Application Procedure: Application forms are available online at www.rheumatology.org
Closing Date: August 1st
Contributor: Amgen Inc.
No. of awards given last year: 4

ACR/REF/Arthritis Investigator Award

Subjects: Arthritis.
Purpose: To provide support to physicians and scientists in research fields related to arthritis for the period between the completion of

postdoctoral fellowship training and establishment as an independent investigators.
Level of Study: Research
Type: Award
Value: US$75,000 for the first 2 years and US$90,000 per year after renewal
Length of Study: 2–4 years
Frequency: Annual
Country of Study: United States of America
Application Procedure: Application forms are available on website.
Closing Date: September 1st
Funding: Foundation
Contributor: The Arthritis Foundation

ACR/REF/Association of Subspecialty Professors Junior Career Development Award in Geriatric Medicine

Subjects: Geriatrics, rheumatology.
Purpose: To provide support to academicians interested in careers focused on the geriatric and gerontology aspects of rheumatology.
Eligibility: To be eligible for the award, the candidate must: be a member of the ACR; have completed a rheumatology fellowship leading to certification by the ABIM and be within the first 3 years of his/her faculty appointment; and possess a faculty appointment at the time of the award. Award applicant must be a citizen or non-citizen national of the United States of America, or be in lawful possessions of a permanent resident card. Individuals on temporary (J1, H1) or student visas are not eligible.
Level of Study: Professional development
Type: Award
Value: US$75,000 per year plus US$3,000 in travel grants
Length of Study: 2 years
Frequency: Annual
Country of Study: United States of America
Application Procedure: Application forms are available on website.
Closing Date: August 1st
Funding: Private
Contributor: Association of Subspecialty Professors
No. of awards given last year: 1

ACR/REF/Clinical Investigator Fellowship Award

Subjects: Rheumatology.
Purpose: To provide a training programme to rheumatology fellows or rheumatologists in the early stages of their career on aspects of clinical investigations through a structured, formal training programme.
Eligibility: Applicant must be an ACR member and a physician licenced to practice in the United States of America. Applicants may apply only within 6 years after starting their rheumatology training programme. MD/PhD candidates are not eligible. Applicant must be a citizen or non-citizen national of the United States of America or a lawful permanent resident. Individuals on temporary (J1, H1) or student visas are not eligible.
Level of Study: Research, professional development
Type: Fellowship
Value: US$90,000 per year
Length of Study: Up to 2 years
Frequency: Annual
Country of Study: United States of America
Application Procedure: Application forms are available online at www.rheumatology.org
Closing Date: August 1st
Funding: Corporation
Contributor: Merck and Co., Inc.
No. of awards given last year: 3

ACR/REF/Lupus Research Institute Lupus Investigator Fellowship Award

Subjects: Systemic lupus erythematosus.
Purpose: To encourage qualified physicians without significant prior research experience to develop a research career that will emphasize the better understanding of systemic lupus erythematosus.
Eligibility: Applicants must have received an MD, DO, or equivalent degree from an accredited institution; completed training in internal medicine or paediatrics; and will have completed at least 1 year of speciality training in rheumatology at the start of the award. MD/PhDs, DO/PhDs, and PhDs are not eligible for this award. Only physicians, with not more than 1 year of research training at the time of application, are eligible. Award applicant must be a citizen or non-citizen national of the United States of America, or be in lawful possession of a permanent resident card. Individuals on temporary (J1, H1) or student visas are not eligible.
Level of Study: Research, professional development, doctorate
Type: Fellowship
Value: US$50,000 per year
Length of Study: 3 years
Frequency: Annual
Country of Study: United States of America
Application Procedure: Application forms are available on website.
Closing Date: August 1st
Funding: Foundation
Contributor: Lupus Research Institute
No. of awards given last year: 1

ACR/REF/Medical and Graduate Student Achievement Awards

Subjects: Rheumatology.
Purpose: To recognize outstanding medical and graduate students for significant work in the field of rheumatology and provide an opportunity to attend the ACR annual scientific meeting.
Eligibility: Medical student candidates must be enrolled in an LCCME-accredited medical school; graduate student candidates must be enrolled in an accredited institution. In addition, students must submit an abstract to the annual scientific meeting. The student must have made a significant contribution to the work submitted in order to be considered for the award. Award applicant must be a citizen or non-citizen national of the United States of America, or be in lawful possession of a permanent resident card. Individuals on temporary (J1, H1) or student visas are not eligible.
Level of Study: Graduate, postgraduate, doctorate
Type: Award
Value: US$750 cash award, waiver of registration fees and hotel and travel expenses to attend the ACR annual scientific meeting
Length of Study: 1 year
Frequency: Annual
Application Procedure: Application forms are available on website.
Closing Date: August 1st
Contributor: Abbott Endowment for Rheumatology Development
No. of awards given last year: 17

ACR/REF/Resident Research Preceptorship

Subjects: Rheumatology.
Purpose: To introduce residents to the speciality of rheumatology by supporting a full-time research experience.
Eligibility: Residents currently enrolled in ACGME-accredited training programmes in internal medicine, paediatrics, or med/paeds are eligible. Applicants may apply during any year of their residency; however preference is given to 1st and 2nd year residents. Preceptors are responsible for approving the research plan and must be members of the ACR. Applicant must be a citizen or non-citizen national of the United States of America or be in lawful possession of a permanent resident card. Individuals on temporary (J1, H1) or student visas are not eligible.
Level of Study: Research
Value: Up to US$15,000
Length of Study: 3 months
Frequency: Annual
Country of Study: United States of America
Application Procedure: Application forms are available on website.
Closing Date: February 7th
Funding: Private
Contributor: ACR

Lawren H Daltroy Fellowship in Patient-Clinician Communication

Subjects: Rheumatology.
Purpose: To improve patient-clinician interactions through the development of more qualified and trained clinicians and investigators in the field of patient–clinician communication.
Eligibility: Eligible applicants must be ARHP members. An applicant must have either a doctoral degree or a clinical degree and apply in partnership with a mentor possessing a doctoral degree. The award is not intended for physician members of the ACR or ARHP.
Level of Study: Professional development
Type: Fellowship
Value: Up to US$6,000 per year
Length of Study: 1 year
Frequency: Annual
Country of Study: United States of America
Application Procedure: Application forms are available on website.
Closing Date: August 1st
Contributor: Rheuminations, Inc.
No. of awards given last year: 1

AMERICAN CONGRESS ON SURVEYING AND MAPPING (ACSM)

6 Montgomery Village Avenue Suite # 403 Gaithersburg, Maryland, United States of America
Tel: (1) (240) 632-9716
Fax: (1) (240) 632-1321
Website: www.acsm.net

The ACSM is a nonprofit association dedicated to serving the public interest and advancing the profession of surveying and mapping.

AAGS Graduate Fellowship Award

Subjects: Geodetic surveying.
Purpose: To support students in the field of geodetic surveying.
Eligibility: Open to students enrolled in a programme in geodetic surveying.
Level of Study: Postgraduate
Type: Fellowship
Value: US$2,000
Length of Study: 2–4 years
Frequency: Annual
Application Procedure: See the website.
Closing Date: December 1st
Contributor: American Association for Geodetic Surveying (AAGS)

AAGS Joseph F. Dracup Scholarship Award

Subjects: Surveying.
Purpose: To offer better opportunities to students in geodetic science programmes.
Eligibility: Open to students enrolled in 4-year programme in surveying.
Value: US$2,000
Frequency: Annual
Application Procedure: A completed application form must be submitted.
Closing Date: December 1st

Berntsen International Scholarship

Subjects: Surveying technology.
Purpose: To encourage exceptional students in surveying and mapping.
Eligibility: Open to students who are registered in a 2-year programme in surveying technology.
Level of Study: Postgraduate
Type: Scholarship
Value: US$500
Length of Study: 2–4 years
Frequency: Annual
Application Procedure: A completed application form must be submitted.
Closing Date: December 1st
Contributor: Bernsten International Inc., of Madison, Wisconsin

The Cady McDonnell Memorial Scholarship

Eligibility: Open to female candidates who are residents of Alaska, Arizona, California, Colorado, Hawaii, Idaho, Montana, Nervada, New Mexico, Oregon, Utah, Washington.
Level of Study: Postgraduate
Type: Scholarship
Value: US$1,000
Length of Study: 2–4 years
Frequency: Annual
No. of awards offered: 1
Application Procedure: A completed application along with proof of ACSM membership website form must be submitted. See the website for further information.
Closing Date: December 17th
Contributor: National Society of Professional Surveyors

Netlie Dracup Memorial Scholarship

Subjects: Geodetic surveying.
Purpose: To provide financial assistance.
Eligibility: Open to candidates who are citizens of United States of America.
Level of Study: Postgraduate
Type: Scholarship
Value: US$2,000
Frequency: Annual
Application Procedure: See the website for further details.
Closing Date: December 1st
Contributor: American Congress on Surveying and Mapping

NSPS Forum for Equal Opportunity/Mary Feindt Scholarship

Subjects: Surveying and mapping.
Purpose: To support female students in the field of surveying and mapping.
Eligibility: Open to female members of ACSM who are enrolled in a 4-year degree programme in surveying.
Level of Study: Postgraduate
Type: Scholarship
Value: US$1,000
Frequency: Annual
Country of Study: United States of America
Application Procedure: A completed application form and proof of membership in ACSM must be submitted.
Closing Date: December 1st

The NSPS Scholarships

Purpose: To recognize outstanding students enrolled in surveying programs.
Eligibility: Open to students enrolled full-time in surveying programs.
Level of Study: Postgraduate
Type: Scholarship
Value: US$1,000
Frequency: Annual
No. of awards offered: 2
Application Procedure: See the website.
Closing Date: December 1st
Contributor: National Society of Professional Surveyors (NSPS)

The Schonstedt Scholarships in Surveying

Subjects: Surveying.
Purpose: To provide opportunities for students in surveying.
Eligibility: Open to students enrolled in a four-year degree programme in surveying.
Level of Study: Postgraduate
Type: Scholarship
Value: US$1,500
Frequency: Annual
No. of awards offered: 2
Application Procedure: See the website.

Closing Date: December 1st
Contributor: Schonstedt Instrument Company of Kearneysville

Tri State Surveying and Photogrammetry Kris M. Kunze Memorial Scholarship

Subjects: Surveying.
Purpose: To provide financial assistance.
Eligibility: Open to candidates who are citizens of United States of America.
Level of Study: Postgraduate
Type: Scholarship
Value: US$1,000
Frequency: Annual
Application Procedure: A completed application form along with proof of ACSM membership must be submitted. See the website for further information.
Closing Date: December 1st

AMERICAN COUNCIL OF LEARNED SOCIETIES (ACLS)

Office of Fellowships and Grants, 633 Third Avenue, New York, NY, 10017-6795, United States of America
Tel: (1) 212 697 1505
Fax: (1) 212 949 8058
Email: sfisher@acls.org
Website: www.acls.org

ACLS American Research in the Humanities in the People's Republic of China

Subjects: Humanities.
Purpose: To enable scholars to carry out research in the People's Republic of China.
Eligibility: Open to United States citizens and permanent residents. Applicants must hold a PhD or equivalent.
Level of Study: Postdoctorate
Type: Research grant
Value: Monthly stipend and travel allowance
Length of Study: 4–12 months
Frequency: Annual
Study Establishment: A university or research institute
Country of Study: China
No. of awards offered: Approx. 5
Application Procedure: Applicants must write for details.
Closing Date: November 15th
Contributor: The National Endowment for the Humanities

ACLS Charles A. Ryskamp Research Fellowship

Subjects: Humanities.
Purpose: To provide time and resources to enable research under optional conditions.
Level of Study: Postdoctorate
Type: Fellowship
Value: US$64,000 stipend, plus a US$2,500 travel allowance
Frequency: Annual
Country of Study: United States of America
Application Procedure: Apply online.
Closing Date: September 28th
Funding: Foundation
Contributor: Andrew W. Mellon Foundation
Additional Information: An additional US$14,222 is available if justified by a persuasive case.

ACLS Chinese Fellowships for Scholarly Development

Subjects: Humanities.
Eligibility: Open to Chinese Scholars.
Level of Study: Postdoctorate
Type: Fellowship
Value: Living allowance, health insurance and international airfare
Length of Study: 1–2 semesters
Frequency: Annual
Application Procedure: Apply online.
Funding: Foundation
Contributor: Li Foundation

ACLS Committee on Scholarly Communication with China

Subjects: Humanities.
Purpose: To find research in the People's Republic of China.
Level of Study: Postdoctorate
Type: Fellowship
Value: A monthly stipend and travel allowance
Length of Study: 4–12 months
Frequency: Annual
Country of Study: China
Application Procedure: Apply online.
Funding: Foundation
Contributor: National Endowment for the Humanities Foundation

ACLS Contemplative Practice Fellowships

Subjects: Art, humanities and humanities-related sciences and social sciences.
Purpose: To support individual or collaborative research leading to the development of courses and teaching materials that integrate contemplative practices into courses.
Eligibility: Individual scholars, partnerships or groups of scholars may apply. Regular full-time faculty members of accredited academic institutions in the United States of America are eligible.
Type: Fellowship
Value: US$10,000
Length of Study: 1 academic year
No. of awards offered: 6
Application Procedure: Applications materials for this programme are provided online. A copy of the application packet may also be requested from grants@acls.org
Closing Date: November 10th

For further information contact:

Office of Fellowships and Grants, American Council of Learned Societies, 633 Third Avenue, New York, NY, 10017-6795, United States of America

ACLS Contemplative Program Development Fellowships

Subjects: All subjects.
Purpose: To support groups of faculty and administrators who are developing curricular activities in contemplative studies of both a formal and informal character.
Eligibility: Regular full-time faculty members and administrators with faculty status at accredited academic instructions in the United States of America are eligible to apply.
Type: Fellowship
Value: US$20,000
Length of Study: 1 academic year
No. of awards offered: 3
Application Procedure: Application materials for this programme are provided online. A copy of the application packet may also be requested from grants@acls.org
Closing Date: November 10th

For further information contact:

Office of Fellowship and Grants, American Council of Learned Societies, 633 Third Avenue, New York, NY, 100176-6795, United States of America

ACLS Digital Innovation Fellowship

Subjects: Computing and networking.
Level of Study: Postdoctorate
Type: Fellowship
Length of Study: An annual US$55,000 stipend, plus an allowance of US$25,000
Frequency: Annual
Country of Study: United States of America
No. of awards offered: 5
Application Procedure: Apply online.

Closing Date: November 10th
Funding: Foundation
Contributor: Andrew W. Mellon Foundation

ACLS Fellowships for Postdoctoral Research

Subjects: Social sciences and humanities.
Purpose: To allow Scholars to undertake a period of full-time research.
Eligibility: Open to United States citizens and permanent residents only.
Level of Study: Postdoctorate
Type: Fellowship
Value: Up to US$50,000. The funds are intended primarily as salary replacements and may be used to supplement sabbatical salaries or awards from other sources, provided they would intensify or extend the contemplated research
Length of Study: At least 6 months
Frequency: Annual
Study Establishment: Approved universities or research institutions
Country of Study: United States of America
No. of awards offered: Approx. 5–7
Application Procedure: Apply online.
Closing Date: September 28th
Additional Information: The product of the proposed work must be disseminated in English.

ACLS Henry Luce Foundation/ACLS Dissertation Fellowships in American Art

Subjects: Art history, focusing on a topic in the history of the visual arts of the United States.
Purpose: To assist students at any stage of PhD dissertation research or writing.
Eligibility: Applicants must be United States citizens and have completed all requirements for a PhD except the dissertation before beginning tenure. They must also be in a department of art history. A student whose degree will be granted by another department may be eligible if the principal dissertation advisor is in a department of the history of art. In all cases the dissertation topic should be object orientated. Students preparing theses for the Master of Fine Arts Degree are not eligible.
Level of Study: Graduate, predoctorate
Type: Fellowship
Value: US$20,000
Length of Study: 1 year, non renewable
Country of Study: United States of America
No. of awards offered: 10
Application Procedure: Applicants must contact the organization.
Closing Date: November 15th
Contributor: The Henry Luce Foundation

ACLS Library of Congress Fellowships in International Studies

Subjects: Arts, humanities or social sciences.
Purpose: To support research using the foreign language collections of the Library of Congress.
Eligibility: Applicants must hold a PhD and preference will be given to those at an early stage in their careers ie. within seven years of their degree. Applicants must also be United States citizens or permanent residents as of the application deadline and may be affiliated with any academic institution. Independent Scholars are also welcome to apply.
Level of Study: Postdoctorate
Type: Fellowship
Value: US$3,500 per month
Length of Study: 4–9 months
Frequency: Annual
No. of awards offered: Up to 10
Application Procedure: Applicants must write to the organization or visit the website.
Closing Date: November 1st
Contributor: The Andrew W. Mellon Foundation, the Association of American Universities and the Library of Congress. The Henry Luce Foundation has enabled the Library of Congress to provide funding for research concerning East or South East Asia
Additional Information: Applicants must demonstrate the need for use of the Library of Congress foreign language holdings, and must document competence in the appropriate language at a level that would suffice to conduct research, and present a record of work that promises a high quality research work of a publishable nature. Applicants will be asked to submit a general overview of the material they expect to consult, a time table for the completion of their research and anticipated outcomes such as publications and presentations.

ACLS New York Public Library Fellowship

Subjects: Arts and Humanities.
Level of Study: Postdoctorate
Type: Fellowship
Value: US$30,000–50,000
Length of Study: 6–12 months
Frequency: Annual
Country of Study: United States of America
Application Procedure: Apply online.
Closing Date: September 28th

ACLS/Andrew W Mellon Fellowships for Junior Faculty

Subjects: Humanities or social sciences.
Eligibility: Open to citizens of America or permanent residents only. Applicants must have at least two years of teaching experience and a PhD. However, an established Scholar who can demonstrate the equivalent of a PhD in publications and professional experience may also qualify. Scholars currently enrolled for any degree are not eligible.
Level of Study: Postgraduate, postdoctorate
Type: Fellowship
Value: Varies
Length of Study: 6–12 months
No. of awards offered: 22
Application Procedure: Applicants must write for details.
Closing Date: October 1st

ACLS/SSRC/NEH International and Area Studies Fellowships

Subjects: The societies and cultures of Asia, Africa, the Near and Middle East, Latin America and the Caribbean, Eastern Europe and the former Soviet Union.
Purpose: To encourage humanistic research in area studies.
Eligibility: Applicants must be citizens or permanent residents of the United States as of the application deadline date, and hold a PhD degree. However, an established Scholar who can demonstrate the equivalent of a PhD in publications and professional experience may also qualify. Scholars pursuing research and writing on the societies and cultures of Asia, Africa, the Near and Middle East, Latin America and the Caribbean, East Europe and the Former Soviet Union are eligible. Scholars currently enrolled for any degree are not eligible.
Level of Study: Postdoctorate
Type: Fellowship
Value: Up to US$50,000 for full professor and equivalent, US$40,000 for associate professor and equivalent and US$30,000 for assistant professor and equivalent
Length of Study: 6–12 months
No. of awards offered: Approx. 10
Application Procedure: Applications must be made to the ACLS Fellowship Program and all requirements and provisions of that programme must be met. The Fellow must submit a final report to both NEH and ACLS. Note that applications must also be made to the competition for residential fellowships administered separately by the NYPL Center for Scholars and Writers.
Closing Date: Please consult the organization

For further information contact:

Center for Scholars & Writers, The New York Public Library Humanities & Social Sciences Library, Fifth Avenue & 42nd Street, New York, NY, 10018-2788, United States of America
Email: csw@nypl.org

Frederick Burkhardt Residential Fellowships

Subjects: Humanities.
Purpose: To encourage more adventurous, more wide-ranging and longer-term patterns of research.
Level of Study: Postdoctorate
Type: Fellowship
Value: US$75,000 stipend
Length of Study: 1 year
Frequency: Annual
Study Establishment: A participating national research centre
Country of Study: United States of America
No. of awards offered: 11
Application Procedure: Apply online.
Closing Date: September 28th
Funding: Foundation
Contributor: Rockefeller Foundation

AMERICAN COUNCIL ON RURAL SPECIAL EDUCATION (ACRSE)

Utah State University, 2865 Old Main Hill, Logan, UT 84322-2865, United States of America
Tel: (1) 735 747 0697
Fax: (1) 735 747 3572
Email: davidf@cc.usu.edu
Website: www.acres.sped.org
Contact: David Forbush, Headquarters Co-ordinator

ACRES Scholarship

Subjects: Special education in the areas of the handicapped, those with specific learning disabilities and the socially disadvantaged.
Purpose: To give a rural teacher an opportunity to pursue education and training not otherwise affordable within his or her district.
Eligibility: Applicants must be citizens of the United States of America, currently employed by a rural school district as a certified teacher in regular or special education, working with students with disabilities or with regular education students and retraining to a special education career.
Level of Study: Graduate
Type: Scholarship
Value: Up to US$1,000
Length of Study: 1 year
Frequency: Annual
Country of Study: United States of America
No. of awards offered: 1
Application Procedure: Applicants must complete and submit an application form with an essay and two letters of recommendation. Applicants should access application materials online.
Closing Date: February 1st
Funding: Private
Additional Information: The award will be announced at the March ACRES conference.

AMERICAN DIABETES ASSOCIATION (ADA)

1701 North Beauregard Street, Alexandria, VA, 22311, United States of America
Tel: (1) 703 549 1500
Fax: (1) 703 549 1715
Website: www.diabetes.org/research
Contact: Research Department

The American Diabetes Association (ADA) is the nation's leading non-profit health organization providing diabetes research information and advocacy. The mission of the organization is to prevent and cure diabetes, and to improve the lives of all people affected by diabetes. To fulfil this mission, the ADA funds research, publishes scientific findings and provides information and other services to people with diabetes, their families, healthcare professionals and the public.

ADA Career Development Awards

Subjects: Diabetes-related research.
Purpose: To allow exceptionally promising new investigators to conduct research.
Eligibility: Open to citizens of the United States of America and permanent residents or those who have applied for permanent resident status, who have MD or PhD degrees or, in the case of other health professions, an appropriate health- or science-related degree. Applicants must hold an assistant professorship or provide documentation that he or she will receive this position upon receipt of this award. Career Development Award applicants no more than seven years out of their post-doctoral fellowship may apply. All applicants must have independent lab space and must be publishing independently in order to be eligible for this Award. Career Development Award applicants may hold an R01 at the time of applying provided that the R01 does not overlap with the ADA award. Applicants currently holding awards with similar intent from NIH or other agencies (ie., career development award, new investigator award, etc) are *not* eligible for applying or holding an ADA Career Development Award. However, applicants can have previously been recipients of an NIH KO1 or KO8 awards. If awarded the ADA Career Development Award and another Career development award from another funding agency, the PI must relinquish one of the awards.
Level of Study: Postdoctorate, professional development
Type: Research grant
Value: Up to US$150,000 per year and an additional 15 per cent for indirect costs. The funds are to be divided by the recipient between the salary of the principal investigator and other grant support. Each year of funding, after the first, is contingent upon approval by the ADA of the recipient's research progress report, and the availability of funds
Length of Study: 5 years, non-renewable
Frequency: Twice a year
Country of Study: United States of America
No. of awards offered: Varies, depending on funds available
Application Procedure: Applicants must write for details. All applications must be submitted online via the website at www.diabetes.org
Closing Date: Deadlines: January 15th for July 1st funding and July 15th for January 1st funding

ADA Clinical Research Grants

Subjects: Diabetes-related research. For the purpose of this programme, clinical research is defined as research involving humans directly.
Purpose: To support patient-orientated research.
Eligibility: Open to citizens of the United States of America and permanent residents or those who have applied for permanent resident status, who have MD or PhD degrees or, in the case of other health professions, an appropriate health- or science-related degree, and who hold full-time faculty positions or the equivalent at university-affiliated institutions within the United States of America and its possessions. Support will be provided for studies that focus on intact human subjects in which the effects of a change in the individual's external or internal environment is evaluated.
Level of Study: Research
Value: Up to US$200,000 per year for 3 years. Up to US$20,000 per year may be used for principal investigator salary support, and up to 15 per cent for indirect costs. Each year of funding after the first is contingent upon approval by the ADA of the recipient's research progress report and the availability of funds
Length of Study: 3 years
Frequency: Twice per year
Country of Study: United States of America
No. of awards offered: Varies, depending on funds available
Application Procedure: Applicants must write for details. All applications must be submitted online via the website at www.diabetes.org/research
Closing Date: January 15th for July 1st funding and July 15th for January 1st funding

ADA Junior Faculty Awards

Subjects: Diabetes.
Purpose: To support investigators who are establishing their independence as diabetes researchers.

Eligibility: Open to citizens of the United States of America and permanent residents or those who have applied for permanent resident status, who have an MD or a PhD degree or an appropriate health- or science-related degree. Junior Faculty Award applicants may be senior post-doctoral or clinical fellows (more than 3 years of experience since doctoral degree) and will receive their first faculty position by the starting date of the award; or junior faculty less than 4 years from completion of post-doctoral/clinical fellowship at time of application submission are eligible. Exceptions to these rules will be considered on an individual basis for applicants who experienced a major career change or interruption. Applicants in this situation must verify their eligibility with the ADA's Research Programs Department prior to preparing their application. Applicants currently holding or having held awards with similar intent from NIH or other agencies (i.e., career development award, KO1 or KO8 award, new investigator award, etc) are *not* eligible for applying or holding an ADA Junior Faculty Award. If awarded the ADA Junior Faculty Award and another career development award from another funding agency, the PI must relinquish one of the awards. Applicants who currently hold or have held an RO1 or VA Merit Review award are not eligible for the junior faculty Award. If an RO1 or VA Merit Review award is obtained during the 3 years after ADA funding has begun, the applicant will not be required to relinquish his/her ADA award.
Level of Study: Postdoctorate, professional development
Type: Research grant
Value: Up to US$120,000 per year, and up to 15 per cent for indirect costs plus up to US$10,000 per year towards repayment of the principal on loans for a doctoral degree such as the MD or PhD
Length of Study: 3 years
Frequency: Twice per year
Country of Study: United States of America
No. of awards offered: Varies, depending on funds available
Application Procedure: Applicants must write for details. All applications must be submitted online via the website at www.diabetes.org/research
Closing Date: January 15th for July 1st funding and July 15th for January 1st funding

ADA Medical Scholars Program

Subjects: Diabetes.
Purpose: To produce leaders in the fields of research, teaching and patient care, by giving physicians in training the opportunity to contribute to the process of discovery in basic and clinical research laboratories. The Medical Scholars Program will supply a unique opportunity to effectively integrate medical students into the process of discovery.
Eligibility: Open to institutions within the United States of America and its possessions. The application must be initiated by the student, and the student must have a qualified sponsor. The student must have completed at least 1 year of medical school and the sponsor must hold a faculty position within an accredited medical school in the United States of America and be a citizen of the United States of America or a permanent resident.
Level of Study: Postgraduate
Type: Scholarship
Value: Support for 1 year in a clinical or basic science research environment. The award will be up to US$30,000 per student, US$20,000 for the student's support and US$10,000 for materials, supplies and travel to the Association's scientific sessions
Length of Study: 1 year
Frequency: Annual
Country of Study: United States of America
No. of awards offered: Varies
Application Procedure: Applicants must write for details. All applications must be submitted online via the website at www.diabetes.org/research
Closing Date: January 15th for July 1st funding

ADA Mentor-Based Postdoctoral Fellowship Program

Subjects: Diabetes.
Purpose: To support the training of scientists in an environment most conducive to beginning a career in research.
Eligibility: There are no citizenship requirements for the Fellow. However, the investigator must be a citizen of the United States of America or a permanent resident, and must also hold an appointment at a United States of America research institution and have sufficient research support to provide an appropriate training environment for the Fellow. The Fellow selected by the investigator must hold an MD or PhD degree and must not be serving an internship or residency during the fellowship period. The Fellow must not have more than 3 years of postdoctoral research experience in the field of diabetes or endocrinology at the commencement of this fellowship.
Level of Study: Postdoctorate
Type: Fellowship
Value: Up to US$45,000 per year
Length of Study: Up to 4 years
Frequency: Annual
Country of Study: United States of America
No. of awards offered: Varies, depending on funds available
Application Procedure: Applicants must complete an application form. All applications must be submitted online via the website at www.diabetes.org/research
Closing Date: July 15th for July 1st funding

ADA Research Awards

Subjects: Aetiology and pathophysiology of diabetes.
Purpose: To assist investigators, new or established, who have a particularly novel and exciting idea for which they need support.
Eligibility: Open to citizens of the United States of America and permanent residents or those who have applied for permanent resident status, who have MD or PhD degrees, or, in the case of other health professions, an appropriate health- or science-related degree. Applicants must hold full-time faculty positions or the equivalent at university-affiliated institutions within the United States of America and its possessions.
Level of Study: Research
Type: Research grant
Value: US$20,000–100,000 per year, for a maximum of 3 years, of which a maximum of US$20,000 can be used for principal investigator salary support, and up to 15 per cent for indirect costs. Each year of funding after the first is contingent upon approval by the ADA of the recipient's research progress report, and the availability of funds
Length of Study: Up to 3 years
Frequency: Twice per year
Country of Study: United States of America
No. of awards offered: Varies, depending on funds available
Application Procedure: All applications must be submitted online via the website at www.diabetes.org/research
Closing Date: January 15th for July 1st funding and July 15th for January 1st funding

AMERICAN FEDERATION FOR AGING RESEARCH (AFAR)

70 West 40th Street, 11th Floor, New York, NY 10018, United States of America
Tel: (1) 212 703 9977
Fax: (1) 212 997 0330
Email: afarapplication@afar.org
Website: www.afar.org
Contact: Odette van der Willik, Director, Grant Programs

The American Federation for Aging Research (AFAR) is a leading non-profit organization supporting biomedical aging research. Since its founding in 1981, AFAR has provided approx. US$87 million to more than 2,100 new investigators and students conducting cutting-edge biomedical research on the aging process and age-related diseases. The important work AFAR supports leads to a better understanding of the aging process and to improvements in the health of all Americans as they age.

AFAR Research Grants

Subjects: Biomedical and clinical topics. Basic mechanisms of aging.
Purpose: To help junior faculty to carry out research that will serve as the basis for longer term research efforts.

Eligibility: Open to junior faculty with an M.D. or Ph.D. degree.
Level of Study: Research, postdoctorate
Type: Research grant
Value: US$60,000 for junior faculty and US$50,000 to postdoctoral fellows
Length of Study: 1–2 years
Frequency: Annual
Country of Study: United States of America
No. of awards offered: Approx. 15
Application Procedure: Applicants must complete and return the application by the annual deadline. These are available from the website.
Closing Date: December 15th
Funding: Foundation, private
Contributor: AFAR and the Glenn Foundation for Medical Research

The Cart Fund, Inc.

Subjects: Alzheimers disease.
Purpose: To encourage exploratory and developmental Alzheimers disease research projects.
Eligibility: Open to applicants whose projects have the potential to advance biomedical research.
Level of Study: Research
Value: US$250,000
Frequency: Annual
No. of awards offered: 1
Application Procedure: A letter-of-intent that includes sufficient details of the study must be submitted.
Closing Date: December 15th

The Cart Fund, Inc. Coins for Alzheimer's Research Trust

Subjects: Our goal is to encourage exploratory and developmental AD research projects by providing support for the early and conceptual plans of those projects that may not yet be supported by extensive preliminary data but have the potential to substantially advance biomedical research. This proposal should be distinct from those projects designed to increase knowledge in a well established area unless it is intended to extend previous discoveries towards new directions or applications.
Eligibility: Research must be conducted at U.S. public and private institutions.
Level of Study: Research
Value: US$250,000
Length of Study: Up to 2 years
Frequency: Annual
Country of Study: United States of America
Application Procedure: Letter-of-intent due on December 15th.
Funding: Private
Additional Information: Additional information available on www.afar.org

For further information contact:

Email: gocar@hargray.com

Ellison Medical foundation/AFAR senior postdoctoral fellows research program.

Subjects: Fundamental mechanism of aging.
Purpose: To further the career of postdoctoral fellows in the fundamental mechanism of aging.
Eligibility: Open to applicants with a minimum of 3 and maximum of 5 years.
Level of Study: Postdoctorate
Type: Fellowship
Value: US$100,000
Length of Study: 2 years
Frequency: Annual
No. of awards offered: 3
Closing Date: December 15th

Ellison Medical Foundation/AFAR Senior Postdoctoral Research Program

Subjects: Fundamental mechanisms of aging.
Purpose: To encourage and further the careers of postdoctoral fellows.
Eligibility: Open to MDs and PhDs with at least 3 and no more than 5 years of prior postdoctoral training at the time of the award. Award must be completed at a non-for profit institution in the United States.
Level of Study: Postdoctorate
Type: Research grant
Value: US$100,000
Length of Study: 2 years
Frequency: Annual
Country of Study: United States of America
No. of awards offered: Up to 3
Application Procedure: Application available on the AFAR website, www.afar.org
Closing Date: December 15th
Funding: Private

The Glenn/AFAR Breakthroughs in Gerontology Awards

Subjects: Projects that focus on genetic controls of aging and longevity, on delay of aging by pharmacological agents or dietary means, or which elucidate the mechanisms by which alterations in hormones, antioxidant defenses, or repair processes promote longevity are all well within the intended scope of this competition. Projects that focus instead on specific diseases or on assessment of health care strategies will receive much lower priority, unless the research plan makes clear and direct connections to fundamental issues in the biology of aging. Studies of invertebrates, mice, human clinical materials or cell lines are all potentially eligible for funding. Although preliminary data are always helpful for evaluating the feasibility of the experiments proposed, the emphasis in review will be on creativity and the likelihood that the findings will open new vistas and approaches to aging research that might merit intensive follow-up studies.
Eligibility: To be eligible, applicants must at the time they submit their proposal be full-time faculty members at the rank of Assistant Professor or higher. A strong record of independent publication beyond the postdoctoral level is a requirement. Applications from individuals not previously engaged in aging research are particularly encouraged, as long as the research proposals show high promise for leading to important new discoveries in biological gerontology.Applicants who are employees in the NIH Intramural program are not eligible. The proposed research must be conducted at any type of not-for-profit setting in the United States.
Level of Study: Research
Frequency: Dependent on funds available
Closing Date: May 1st
Funding: Private
Contributor: The Glenn Foundation for Medical Research
No. of awards given last year: 2

For further information contact:

Email: afarapplication@afar.org

Glenn/AFAR Breakthroughs in Gerontology Awards

Subjects: Geriatrics.
Purpose: To support pilot research programmes.
Eligibility: Open to full-time faculty members at the rank of Assistant professor or higher.
Level of Study: Research
Type: Grant
Value: US$125,000
Frequency: Annual
No. of awards offered: 4
Application Procedure: All candidates must submit applicants enclosed by their institution.
Closing Date: May 2nd

The Julie Martin Mid-Career Award in Aging Research

Subjects: Aging research.
Purpose: To encourage outstanding mid-career scientists.

Eligibility: Open to scientists whose research could lead to novel approaches to aging, and also whose research is high risk.
Type: Award
Value: US$500,000, in addition up to US$50,000 may be requested for indirect costs.
Length of Study: 4 years
No. of awards offered: 4
Closing Date: December 15th
Funding: Foundation
Contributor: Ellison Medical Foundation

Medical Student Summer Research Training in Aging Program

Eligibility: Any allopathic or osteopathic medical student in good standing, who will have successfully completed one year of medical school at a U.S. institution by June 2006. Evidence of such likelihood must be provided at the time of application. Applicants must be citizens or non-citizen nationals of the United States, or must have been lawfully admitted for permanent residence (ie., in procession of a currently valid Alien Registration Receipt Card I-551, or some other legal verification of such status.) Individuals on temporary or student visas and individuals holding PhD, MD, DVM, or equivalent doctoral degrees in the health sciences are not eligible. The NIA and other sponsoring organizations have a strong interest in continuing to diversify the research workforce committed to advancing the fields of aging and geriatric research. Therefore, students who are members of ethnic or racial groups underrepresented in these fields, students with disabilities, or students whose background and experience are likely to diversify the research or medical questions being addressed, are encouraged to apply.
Level of Study: Graduate, medical student
Frequency: Annual
Application Procedure: Applications can be completed through www.afar.org
Closing Date: February 7th
Funding: Government, private

For further information contact:

Email: afarapplication@afar.org

Paul Beeson Career Development Award

Subjects: Medical sciences.
Purpose: To bolster the current severe shortage of academic physicians who have the combination of medical, academic and scientific training relative to caring for other people.
Eligibility: Applicants must be citizens of the United States of America or permanent residents, be full-time faculty members with clear potential for long-term faculty appointments, and, at the time of application, have received their MD degree in 1990 or later. To be eligible a candidate must: (1) Have clinical doctoral degree (eg., MD, DO, DDS) or its equivalent and have completed clinical training. (2) Commit at least 75% of his/her full-time professional effort to the goals of this award. (3) Be a U.S. citizen, non-citizen national of the United States or a permanent resident alien. (4) Be at a for-profit or non-profit organization, public or private institution (such as universities, colleges, hospitals, and laboratories), units of state and local governments or eligible agencies of the federal government provided the demonstrated environment has a commitment to the geriatric population and capacity to support the Scholar's career development.
Level of Study: Research, professional development
Type: Grant
Value: US$600,000–US$800,000
Length of Study: 3–5 years
Frequency: Annual
Country of Study: United States of America
No. of awards offered: Up to 11
Application Procedure: Applicants must complete and return the application by the annual deadline. These are available from the website (below). Application can be found at: http://grants1.nih.gov/grants/guide/rfa-files/rfa-ag-06-005.html or www.afar.org
Closing Date: November 23rd
Funding: Government, private
Contributor: The National Institute on Aging, John A Hartford Foundation, Commonwealth Fund, Atlantic Philanthropies and Starr Foundation

For further information contact:

Website: www.grants1.nih.gov/grants/guide/rfa-files/RFA-AG-05-001.html

AMERICAN FOUNDATION FOR AGING RESEARCH (AFAR)

Biochemistry Department, North Carolina State University,
Campus Box 7622, Polk Hall, Raleigh, NC, 27695,
United States of America
Tel: (1) 919 515 5679
Fax: (1) 919 515 2047
Email: afar@bchserver.bch.ncsu.edu
Website: www.ncsu.edu/project/afar/
Contact: Dr Paul F Agris, President

The American Foundation for Aging Research (AFAR) aims to promote and support research that will elucidate the basic processes involved in the biology of aging and age associated disease, by awarding scholarships and fellowships to young, motivated scientists.

Wilson-Fulton and Robertson Awards in Aging Research, Cecille Gould Memorial Fund Award in Cancer Research, Richard Shepherd Fellowship

Subjects: Aging and cancer research.
Purpose: To encourage young people to pursue research in age related health problems and the biology of aging.
Eligibility: Open to graduates enrolled in degree programmes eg. MS, PhD, MD or DDS at institutions within the United States of America. They must be working on specific projects in the fields of ageing or cancer. Sociological and psychological research is not accepted in these programmes.
Level of Study: Graduate, postgraduate, doctorate
Type: Fellowship
Value: US$1,000 per semester or summer
Length of Study: Between 4 months and 1 year
Frequency: Annual
Study Establishment: Educational institutions
Country of Study: United States of America
No. of awards offered: 5–10
Application Procedure: Applicants must undertake the two levels of review: a pre-application form to determine eligibility, and a full application. Applicants should submit a request for a pre-application. A cheque or money order to AFAR for US$3 to cover handling and postage should be included with the completed pre-application. There is no charge for the submission of the full application.
Closing Date: There is no deadline
Funding: Private
No. of awards given last year: 3
No. of applicants last year: 115
Additional Information: AFAR is a national, tax-exempt, non-profit, educational and scientific charity not affiliated with North Carolina State University.

AMERICAN FOUNDATION FOR AIDS RESEARCH (AMFAR)

Grants Administration Department, 120 Wall Street,
13th Floor, New York, NY, 10005-3908,
United States of America
Tel: (1) 212 806 1600
Fax: (1) 212 806 1601
Email: grants@amfar.org
Website: www.amfar.org

AMFAR is a leading non-profit organization dedicated to the support of AIDS research, AIDS prevention, treatment education and the advocacy of sound AIDS-related policy.

AMFAR Basic Research Grant

Subjects: The prevention of HIV infection and the disease and death associated with it and protection of the human rights of all people threatened by the epidemic of HIV/AIDS.
Purpose: To support a researcher in the various financial obligations incurred in the course of an HIV/AIDS - related investigation.
Eligibility: Applicants must be working with a suitable non-profit organization.
Level of Study: Postdoctorate
Type: Grant
Value: Costs of salaries for professional and technical personnel, laboratory supplies and equipment travel and the publication of findings plus overhead costs limited to a maximum of 20 per cent of direct costs
Frequency: Annual
Study Establishment: Suitable non-profit institution
Country of Study: United States of America
No. of awards offered: Approx. 100 per year
Application Procedure: Applicants must write to the organization for detailed guidelines. Applicant's projects are subject to peer-review.
Funding: Private
Additional Information: The committee will assess scientific merit, relevance of the research to the control of the epidemic or to the benefit of patients with AIDS or AIDS-related conditions, the qualifications, experience and productivity of the investigators and the facilities available.

AMFAR Clinical Research Fellowship

Subjects: The prevention of HIV infection and the disease and death associated with it and protection of the human rights of all people threatened by the epidemic of HIV/AIDS.
Purpose: To support a postdoctoral investigator with limited experience in the field of HIV/AIDS to redirect or embark on a career in biological, clinical or psychosocial HIV/AIDS research.
Eligibility: Applicants must be working with a suitable non-profit organization.
Level of Study: Postdoctorate
Type: Grant
Frequency: Apply as needed
Study Establishment: Suitable non-profit institution
Country of Study: United States of America
No. of awards offered: Approx. 100 per year
Application Procedure: Applicants must write to the organization for detailed guidelines. Applicant's projects are subject to peer-review.
Funding: Private
Additional Information: The committee will assess scientific merit, relevance of the research to the control of the epidemic or to the benefit of patients with AIDS or AIDS-related conditions, the qualifications, experience and productivity of the investigators, the facilities available.

AMERICAN FOUNDATION FOR PHARMACEUTICAL EDUCATION (AFPE)

One Church Street, Suite 202, Rockville, MD, 20850-4158, United States of America
Tel: (1) 301 738 2160
Fax: (1) 301 738 2161
Email: info@afpenet.org
Website: www.afpenet.org
Contact: Administrative Assistant

The mission of the AFPE is to advance and support pharmaceutical sciences education at U.S. schools and colleges of pharmacy.

AAPS/AFPE Gateway Scholarships

Subjects: Pharmaceutics.
Purpose: To encourage graduates from any discipline to pursue a PhD in a pharmacy graduate programme.
Eligibility: Open to students who are enrolled in the last three years of a Bachelor of Science or PharmD programme at a United States school or college of pharmacy, or Baccalaureate degree programme in a related field of scientific study at any college. Candidates must have a demonstrated interest in, and potential for, a career in any of the pharmaceutical sciences and be enrolled for at least one full academic year following the award of the scholarship. United States citizenship or permanent resident status is not required.
Level of Study: Professional development, postgraduate
Type: Scholarship
Value: No less than US$4,000 is provided as a student stipend for a full calendar year
Frequency: Annual
Country of Study: United States of America
No. of awards offered: 12
Application Procedure: Applicants must write for details.
Closing Date: January 27th

AFPE Clinical Pharmacy Post-PharmD Fellowships in the Biomedical Research Sciences Program

Subjects: Pharmacology including topics such as cost benefit and cost effectiveness of pharmaceuticals, the impact of current or future legislation on drug innovation and healthcare in the nation, the economics of healthcare and the quality of life in changing patterns of healthcare delivery systems, the contribution of the pharmaceutical industry, the economic impact of research and new drugs, and healthcare cost containment issues.
Eligibility: Open to all pharmacy faculty members who have a strong record of research.
Level of Study: Doctorate, postdoctorate
Type: Fellowship
Value: US$27,500 per year
Length of Study: 1–2 years
Frequency: Annual
Study Establishment: An Institute of Higher Education
Country of Study: United States of America
No. of awards offered: 2
Application Procedure: Applicants must complete an application form and should write for details.
Closing Date: February 15th

AFPE Gateway Research Scholarship Program

Subjects: Pharmacology.
Purpose: To encourage individuals in a pharmacy college to pursue a PhD within a pharmacy college.
Eligibility: Open to students who are enrolled in the last three years of a Bachelor of Science or PharmD programme at a United States school or college of pharmacy, or Baccalaureate degree programme in a related field of scientific study at any college. Candidates must have a demonstrated interest in, and potential for, a career in any of the pharmaceutical sciences and will be enrolled for at least one full academic year following the award of the scholarship. United States citizenship or permanent resident status is not required.
Level of Study: Professional development, postgraduate
Type: Scholarship
Value: No less than US$4,000 is provided as a student stipend for a research project
Frequency: Annual
Study Establishment: An approved college of pharmacy
Country of Study: United States of America
No. of awards offered: 12
Application Procedure: Applicants must write for details.
Closing Date: January 27th

AFPE Predoctoral Fellowships

Subjects: Any of the pharmaceutical sciences, including pharmaceutics, pharmacology, manufacturing pharmacy and medicinal chemistry.
Purpose: To offer fellowship support leading to a PhD degree.
Eligibility: Open to students who have completed at least three semesters of graduate study and who have no more than three years remaining to obtain a PhD degree in a graduate programme in the pharmaceutical sciences administered by, or affiliated with, a United States school or college of pharmacy. The award is also open to students enrolled in joint PharmD and PhDs, if a PhD degree will be awarded within three additional years. Applicants must be United States citizens or permanent residents.

Level of Study: Doctorate, postgraduate, postdoctorate
Type: Fellowship
Value: US$6,000 stipend
Length of Study: 1 year, renewable for 2 additional years
Frequency: Annual
Study Establishment: An appropriate university
Country of Study: United States of America
No. of awards offered: 70
Application Procedure: Applicants must write for details.
Closing Date: March 1st

AMERICAN FOUNDATION FOR SUICIDE PREVENTION (AFSP)

120 Wall Street, 22nd Floor, New York, NY 10005,
United States of America
Tel: (1) 2123633500
Fax: (1) 212 363 6237
Email: bkoestner@afsp.org
Website: www.afsp.org
Contact: Ms Bethany Koestner, Research Administrator

The American Foundation for Suicide Prevention (AFSP) is dedicated to preventing suicide through its support of research, treatment initiatives and professional and public education. The Foundation also offers programmes for those who have lost a family member or a friend to suicide.

AFSP Distinguished Investigator Awards

Subjects: The clinical, biological or psychosocial aspects of suicide.
Purpose: Awarded to investigators at the level of associate professor or higher with a proven history of research in the area of suicide.
Level of Study: Postdoctorate, research
Type: Grant
Value: Up to US$100,000
Length of Study: 1–2 years
Frequency: Annual
Country of Study: United States of America
No. of awards offered: Varies
Application Procedure: Applicants should consult the website or contact the organization for full details. Application form must be completed.
Closing Date: December 15th
Funding: Private
Additional Information: Decisions regarding awards are made in May and funding begins in July.

AFSP Pilot Grants

Subjects: The clinical, biological or psychosocial aspects of suicide.
Level of Study: Postdoctorate, research
Type: Grant
Value: Up to US$20,000
Length of Study: 1–2 years
Frequency: Annual
Country of Study: United States of America
No. of awards offered: Varies
Application Procedure: Applicants should consult the website or contact the organization for full details. Application form must be completed.
Closing Date: December 15th, April 15th, August 15th
Funding: Private
Additional Information: Decisions regarding awards are made 3 times a year.

AFSP Postdoctoral Research Fellowships

Subjects: The clinical, biological or psychosocial aspects of suicide.
Purpose: Awarded to investigators who have received a PhD, an MD, or other doctoral degrees within the preceding 3 years.
Eligibility: Applicants must have received a PhD 3 years prior to application for the fellowship.
Level of Study: Postdoctorate, research
Type: Fellowship
Value: US$42,000–46,000
Length of Study: Up to 2 years
Frequency: Annual
Country of Study: United States of America
No. of awards offered: Varies
Application Procedure: Applicants should consult the website or contact the organization. Application form must be completed.
Closing Date: December 15th
Funding: Private
Additional Information: Decisions regarding awards are made in May and funding begins in July.

AFSP Standard Research Grants

Subjects: The clinical, biological or psychosocial aspects of suicide.
Purpose: Awarded to individual investigators at any level.
Level of Study: Postdoctorate, research
Type: Grant
Value: Up to US$60,000
Length of Study: 1–2 years
Frequency: Annual
Country of Study: United States of America
No. of awards offered: Varies
Application Procedure: Applicants should consult the website or contact the organization. Application form must be completed.
Closing Date: December 15th
Funding: Private
Additional Information: Decisions regarding awards are made in May and funding begins in July.

AFSP Young Investigator Award

Subjects: The clinical, biological or psychosocial aspects of suicide.
Purpose: Awarded to those at the level of assistant professor or lower.
Level of Study: Research
Type: Award
Value: Up to US$70,000
Length of Study: Up to 2 years
Frequency: Annual
Country of Study: United States of America
No. of awards offered: Varies
Application Procedure: Applicants should consult the website or contact the organization. Application form must be completed.
Closing Date: December 15th
Funding: Private
Additional Information: Decisions regarding awards are made in May and funding begins in July. Investigators should be at the level of assistant professor or lower.

AMERICAN GEOPHYSICAL UNION (AGU)

2000 Florida Avenue North West Zip-1277, Washington, DC 20009,
United States of America
Tel: (1) 202 462 6900
Fax: (1) 202 328 0566
Email: service@agu.org
Website: www.agu.org
Contact: Director, Outreach and Research Support

The American Geophysical Union (AGU) is an international scientific society with more than 36,000 members, primarily research scientists, dedicated to advancing the understanding of Earth and solar system and making the results of the AGU's research available to the public.

F.L. Scarf Award

Subjects: Solar-planetary science.
Purpose: To award outstanding dissertation research that contributes directly to solar-planetary science.
Eligibility: Open to all candidates with a Ph.D. (or equivalent) degree.
Level of Study: Doctorate
Value: US$1,000
Frequency: Annual
Application Procedure: Nominations to be sent to outreach administrator at AGU.

Closing Date: October 1st
Contributor: The space Physics and Aeronomy section of AGU

Horton (Hydrology) Research Grant

Subjects: Hydrology including its physical, chemical or biological aspects, life sciences, physical sciences, social sciences, school of public affairs, school of law.
Purpose: To support research in hydrology and water resources.
Eligibility: There are no eligibility restrictions.
Level of Study: Postdoctorate
Type: Grant
Value: US$10,000
Frequency: Annual
No. of awards offered: 2
Application Procedure: Applicants must submit four copies of the application form, an executive summary, a statement of purpose, a detailed budget and two letters of recommendation. Applicants should contact the Union for further details.
Closing Date: March 1st
No. of awards given last year: 2
No. of applicants last year: 27

The Mineral and Rock Physics Outstanding Student Award

Subjects: Mineral and rock physics.
Purpose: To recognize outstanding contributions by young scientists.
Eligibility: Open to students who have completed their PhD.
Level of Study: Doctorate
Type: Award
Value: US$500, a certificate and public recognition at the annual mineral and rock physics reception at the AGU fall meeting
Frequency: Annual
No. of awards offered: Varies
Application Procedure: A letter of nomination along with a curriculum vitae and 3 repents of the nominee's work should be sent.
Closing Date: May 15t
Contributor: Mineral and Rock Physics community at AGU

For further information contact:

Crystallography Laboratory Department of Geosciences Virginia Polytechnic Institute and State University, Blacksburg, VA 24060, United States of America
Tel: (1) 540 231 7974
Fax: (1) 540 231 3386
Email: vangel@vt.edu
Contact: Dr Ross Angle

AMERICAN HEAD AND NECK SOCIETY (AHNS)

11300 W. Olympic Boulevard, Suite 600, Los Angeles, CA, 90064, United States of America
Tel: (1) 310 437 0559
Fax: (1) 310 437 0585
Email: admin@ahns.info
Website: www.headandneckcancer.org
Contact: Joyce Hasper, Research Grants Enquiries

The purpose of the American Head and Neck Society (AHNS) is to promote and advance the knowledge of prevention, diagnosis, treatment and rehabilitation of neoplasms and other diseases of the head and neck.

AHNS Career Development Award

Subjects: Diseases of the head and neck.
Purpose: To facilitate research in connection with career development.
Eligibility: Applicants must be a member or candidate member of AHNS.
Level of Study: Postgraduate
Type: Award
Value: US$40,000 per year
Length of Study: 2 years
Frequency: Annual
Study Establishment: A university in the United States of America
Country of Study: United States of America
Funding: Private

AHNS Pilot Research Grant

Subjects: Diseases of the head and neck.
Purpose: To support students who wish to try a pilot project in head and neck-related research.
Eligibility: Open to residents and fellows in the junior faculty.
Level of Study: Doctorate, postgraduate
Type: Award
Value: US$10,000
Length of Study: 1 year
Frequency: Annual
Study Establishment: A university in the United States of America
Country of Study: United States of America
No. of awards offered: 1
Funding: Private

AHNS Surgeon Scientist Career Development Award

Subjects: Cancer and other diseases of the head and neck.
Purpose: To support research in the pathogenesis, pathophysiology, diagnosis, prevention or treatment of head and neck neoplastic disease.
Eligibility: Open to surgeons beginning a clinician-scientist career.
Level of Study: Postdoctorate
Type: Award
Value: US$35,000 per year
Length of Study: 2 years
Frequency: Annual
Study Establishment: A university in the United States of America
Country of Study: United States of America
No. of awards offered: 1
Funding: Private

AHNS The Young Investigator Award

Subjects: Cancer and other diseases of the head and neck.
Purpose: To support research in neoplastic disease of the head and neck.
Eligibility: Candidate must be a member of AHNS.
Level of Study: Doctorate
Type: Award
Value: US$10,000 per year
Length of Study: Up to 2 years
Frequency: Annual
Study Establishment: A university in the United States of America
Country of Study: United States of America
No. of awards offered: 1
Funding: Private

AMERICAN HEALTH ASSISTANCE FOUNDATION (AHAF)

22512 Gateway Center Drive, Clarksburg, MD 20871, United States of America
Tel: (1) 301 948 3244
Fax: (1) 301 258 9454
Email: psenda@ahaf.org
Website: www.ahaf.org
Contact: Dr Pam Senda, Grants Manager

The American Health Assistance Foundation (AHAF) is a non-profit charitable organization that funds research and public education on age related and degenerative diseases including: Alzheimer's disease, macular degeneration, glaucoma and heart and stroke diseases. The organization also provides emergency financial assistance to Alzheimer's disease patients and their care givers.

AHAF Alzheimer's Disease Research Grant

Subjects: Neurology, biomedicine, biochemistry, biophysics, molecular biology and pharmacology.
Purpose: To enable basic research on the causes of and treatments for Alzheimer's disease.
Eligibility: The principal investigator must hold the rank of assistant professor or equivalent, or higher.
Level of Study: Postdoctorate, doctorate, postgraduate
Type: Grant
Value: Standard grants are for US$150,000 per year for up to two years. Pilot project grants can receive US$50,000 per year up to two years.
Length of Study: 1–2 years
Frequency: Annual
Study Establishment: Non-profit institutions and organizations
Country of Study: Any country
No. of awards offered: Varies
Application Procedure: Applicants must complete an application form. The current application form should be requested for each year or can be downloaded from the website.
Closing Date: October 11th
Funding: Private
No. of awards given last year: 14
No. of applicants last year: 89

AHAF Macular Degeneration Research

Subjects: Ophthalmology, biomedicine, biochemistry, biophysics, genetics, molecular biology and pharmacology.
Purpose: To enable basic research on the causes of, or the treatment for, macular degeneration.
Eligibility: The principal investigator must hold a tenure track or tenured position and the rank of assistant professor or higher.
Level of Study: Research
Type: Grant
Value: Up to US$50,000. Grants may be renewed on a competitive peer review basis
Length of Study: 1 year
Frequency: Annual
Study Establishment: Non-profit institutions and organizations
Country of Study: Any country
No. of awards offered: Varies
Application Procedure: Applicants must complete an application form. The current application form should be requested for each year or can be downloaded from the website.
Closing Date: Letters of intent due July of each year. Application due in October
Funding: Private
No. of awards given last year: 7
No. of applicants last year: 31

AHAF National Glaucoma Research

Subjects: Ophthalmology, biomedicine and pharmacology.
Purpose: To enable basic research on the causes of, or treatments for, glaucoma.
Eligibility: The principal investigator must hold the rank of assistant professor or equivalent, or higher.
Level of Study: Doctorate, research
Type: Grant
Value: Up to US$45,000 per year for up to two years
Length of Study: 1–2 years
Frequency: Annual
Study Establishment: Non-profit institutions and organizations
Country of Study: Any country
No. of awards offered: Varies
Application Procedure: Applicants must complete an application form. The current application form should be requested for each year and can also be downloaded from the website.
Closing Date: October 11th
Funding: Private
No. of awards given last year: 9
No. of applicants last year: 28

AHAF National Heart Foundation

Subjects: Cardiology, biomedicine, physiology and pharmacology.
Purpose: To provide start up grants for new investigators into the causes of, or treatments for, cardiovascular disease and stroke.
Eligibility: Open to young investigators who are beginning independent research careers at the assistant professor level and are head of an independent research laboratory group.
Level of Study: Professional development, predoctorate, research, postgraduate
Type: Grant
Value: Up to US$25,000 may be requested for one year
Length of Study: 1 year, renewable for a further year
Frequency: Annual
Study Establishment: Non-profit institutions and organizations
Country of Study: Any country
No. of awards offered: Varies
Application Procedure: Applicants must complete an application form. The current application form should be requested for each year or can be downloaded from the website.
Closing Date: November 2nd
Funding: Private
No. of awards given last year: 5
No. of applicants last year: 18

AMERICAN HERPES FOUNDATION

433 Hackensack Avenue, 9th Floor, Hackensack, NJ, 07601, United States of America
Tel: (1) 201 883 5852
Fax: (1) 201 342 7555
Website: www.herpes-foundation.org
Contact: Dr Jennifer Warf, Program Manager

American Herpes Foundation is a non-profit organization dedicated to improving the management of herpes virus infections. Our initiatives focus primarily on clinician education and awareness.

American Herpes Foundation Stephen L Sacks Investigator Award

Subjects: Research areas include HSV1 and 2, VZV, EBV, CMV, and HHV6 and 8.
Purpose: To recognize and encourage newer researchers who have completed significant research in the herpes virus area.
Eligibility: Residents, fellows or junior faculty up to the 5th year of faculty appointment are eligible.
Level of Study: Physicians-in-training or researchers-in-training
Type: Cash prize
Value: US$5,000 cash prize
Frequency: Annual
No. of awards offered: 2
Application Procedure: Candidates must submit a letter of nomination, completed application form, curriculum vitae, biographical sketch and documentation of research.
Closing Date: Call for details
Funding: Private
Contributor: GlaxoSmithKline, Novartis and Roche
No. of awards given last year: 1
No. of applicants last year: 12

AMERICAN HISTORICAL ASSOCIATION

400 A Street South East, Washington, DC, 20003, United States of America
Tel: (1) 202 544 2422
Fax: (1) 202 544 8307
Email: hpensack@historians.org
Website: www.historians.org
Contact: Executive Office

The American Historical Association (AHA) is a non-profit membership organization founded in 1884 and was incorporated by Congress in 1889 for the promotion of historical studies, the preservation of historial documents and artefacts and the dissemination of historical research.

Albert J Beveridge Grant

Subjects: The history of the United States of America, Latin America or Canada, from 1492 to the present.
Purpose: To promote and honour outstanding historical writing and to support research in the history of the western hemisphere.
Eligibility: Open to American Historical Association members only.
Level of Study: Postgraduate, postdoctorate, doctorate
Type: Grant
Value: A maximum of US$1,000
Frequency: Annual
Country of Study: Any country
No. of awards offered: Varies
Application Procedure: Applicants must apply online at www.historians.org/prizes/beveridgegrantinfo.htm
Closing Date: February 15th
Funding: Private

Bernadotte E Schmitt Grants

Subjects: The history of Europe, Asia and Africa.
Purpose: To support research in the history of Europe, Africa, and Asia, and to further research in progress.
Eligibility: Open to American Historical Association members only.
Level of Study: Postdoctorate, postgraduate, doctorate
Type: Grant
Value: Up to US$1,000
Frequency: Annual
Country of Study: Any country
No. of awards offered: Varies
Application Procedure: Applicants must apply online at www.historians.org/prizes/schmittgrantinfo.htm
Closing Date: February
Funding: Private

J Franklin Jameson Fellowship

Subjects: The collections of the Library of Congress.
Purpose: To support significant scholarly research for 1 semester in the collections of the Library of Congress by scholars at an early stage in their careers in history.
Eligibility: Applicants must hold a PhD degree or equivalent, must have received this degree within the past 7 years, and must not have published or had accepted for publication a book-length historical work. The fellowship will not be awarded to complete a doctoral dissertation.
Level of Study: Postdoctorate
Type: Fellowship
Value: US$5,000
Length of Study: 1 semester
Frequency: Annual
Country of Study: United States of America
No. of awards offered: 1
Application Procedure: Applicants must refer to the website www.historians.org/prizes/jameson_fellowship.htm for instructions.
Closing Date: January
Funding: Government, private

Littleton-Griswold Research Grant

Subjects: American legal history, law and society.
Purpose: To further research in progress.
Eligibility: Open to American Historical Association members only.
Level of Study: Postdoctorate, doctorate, postgraduate
Type: Research grant
Value: Up to US$1,000
Frequency: Annual
Country of Study: Any country
No. of awards offered: Varies
Application Procedure: Applicants must apply online at www.historians.org/prizes/littleton_griswoldgrantinfo.htm
Closing Date: February 15th
Funding: Private

AMERICAN INNS OF COURT

1229 King Street, 2nd Floor, Alexandria, VA 22314,
United States of America
Tel: (1) (703) 684 3590
Fax: (1) (703) 684 3607
Email: info@innsofcourt.org
Website: www.innsofcourt.org

American Inns of Court is designed to improve the skills professionalism and ethics of the bench and bar. An American Inn of Court is an amalgam of judges, lawyers, and in some cases law professors and law students. In short it is our mission to foster excellence in professionalism, ethics, civility, and legal skills.

Pegasus Scholarship Trust Program for Young Lawyers

Subjects: English legal system.
Purpose: To support talented young American lawyers travel to London, England.
Eligibility: Refer to website.
Level of Study: Graduate
Type: Scholarship
Value: All transportation costs to and from the United States, accommodation and a stipend sufficient for meals and public transport
Length of Study: 6 weeks
Frequency: Annual
Country of Study: United Kingdom
No. of awards offered: 2
Application Procedure: Complete available online application.
Closing Date: October 1st

AMERICAN INSTITUTE FOR ECONOMIC RESEARCH (AIER)

PO Box 1000, Great Barrington, MA, 01230,
United States of America
Tel: (1) 413 528 1216
Fax: (1) 413 528 0103
Email: info@aier.org
Website: www.aier.org
Contact: Ms Susan J Gillette, Assistant to the President

The American Institute for Economic Research (AIER), founded in 1933, is an independent scientific educational organization. The Institute conducts scientific enquiry into general economics with a focus on monetary issues. Attention is also given to business cycle analysis and forecasting as well as monetary economics.

AIER Summer Fellowship

Subjects: Scientific procedures of enquiry, monetary economics, business cycle analysis and forecasting.
Purpose: To further the development of economic scientists.
Eligibility: Open to graduating seniors who are entering doctoral programmes in economics, or those enrolled in doctoral programmes in economics for no longer than 2 years. The programme is not designed for those enrolling into business school.
Level of Study: Postgraduate
Type: Fellowship
Value: US$250 weekly stipend plus room and full board
Length of Study: Two 4-week sessions
Frequency: Annual
Study Establishment: The AIER
Country of Study: United States of America
No. of awards offered: 10–12
Application Procedure: Applicants must submit a completed application form, curriculum vitae, personal statement, writing sample, an outline of the proposed course of study and official transcripts. Scholastic references should be sent directly to the director from the referees.
Closing Date: March 31st
Funding: Private
No. of awards given last year: 17
No. of applicants last year: 47

THE AMERICAN INSTITUTE OF BAKING (AIB)

1213 Bakers Way, PO Box 3999, Manhattan, Kansas, KS, 66505-3999, United States of America
Tel: (1) 785 537 4750
Fax: (1) 785 537 1439
Email: info@aibonline.org
Website: www.aibonline.org
Contact: Mr Ken Embers, Registrar

The AIB is a non-project corporation, founded by the North American wholesale and retail baking industries in 1991. AIB's staff includes experts in the fields of baking production; research related to experimental baking, cereal science and nutrition; food safety and hygiene; occupational safety and maintenance engineering.

Baking Industry Scholarship

Subjects: Food processing.
Purpose: To support students who are planning to seek employment in the baking or food processing industry.
Eligibility: Open to applicants who are enrolled at the American Institute of Banking.
Level of Study: Postgraduate
Type: Scholarship
Length of Study: US$4,400
Frequency: Annual
Country of Study: United States of America
Application Procedure: See the website.

AMERICAN INSTITUTE OF INDIAN STUDIES (AIIS)

1130 East 59th Street, Chicago, Illinois, IL 60637, United States of America
Tel: (1) 773 702 8638
Email: aais@uchicago.edu
Website: www.indiastudies.org
Contact: Mr Ralph W Nicholas, President

The American Institute of Indian Studies (AIIS) is a consortium of American colleges and universities that supports the understanding of India, its people and cultures. AIIS offers a range of fellowships for research in India. It also supports individuals studying the performing arts, operates language programmes in India and offers research facilities to scholars in India.

AIIS Junior Research Fellowships

Subjects: India, its people and culture.
Purpose: To support the advancement of knowledge and understanding.
Eligibility: Open to doctoral candidates at United States of America colleges and universities.
Level of Study: Doctorate
Length of Study: Up to 11 months
Frequency: Annual
Study Establishment: An Indian university
Country of Study: India
Application Procedure: Applicants must write for further information.
Closing Date: July 1st

AIIS Senior Performing and Creative Arts Fellowships

Subjects: Performing and creative arts.
Eligibility: Open to accomplished practitioners of the performing arts of India and creative artists who demonstrate that study in India would enhance their skills, develop their capabilities to teach or perform in the United States of America, enhance American involvement with India's artistic traditions and strengthen their links with peers in India.
Level of Study: Unrestricted
Type: Fellowship
Frequency: Annual
Country of Study: India
Application Procedure: Applicants must write for further information.
Closing Date: July 1st

AIIS Senior Research Fellowships

Subjects: South Asian studies.
Purpose: To enable scholars to pursue further research in India.
Eligibility: Open to scholars who hold a PhD or its equivalent and are either citizens of the United States of America or resident aliens teaching full-time at United States of America colleges and universities.
Level of Study: Postdoctorate
Type: Fellowship
Length of Study: Up to 9 months
Frequency: Annual
Country of Study: India
Application Procedure: Applicants must write for further information.
Closing Date: July 1st

AIIS Senior Scholarly/Professional Development Fellowships

Subjects: India, its people and culture.
Purpose: To support the advancement of knowledge and understanding.
Eligibility: Open to established scholars who have not previously specialized in Indian studies and to established professionals who have not previously worked or studied in India.
Level of Study: Professional development
Type: Fellowship
Length of Study: 6–9 months
Frequency: Annual
Country of Study: India
No. of awards offered: Varies
Application Procedure: Applicants must write for further information.
Closing Date: July 1st

AMERICAN JEWISH ARCHIVES

3101 Clifton Avenue, Cincinnati, OH, 45220, United States of America
Tel: (1) 513 221 7444
Fax: (1) 513 221 7812
Email: aja@huc.edu
Website: www.americanjewisharchives.org
Contact: Mr Kevin Proffitt, Director, Fellowship Programmes

The Marcus Center of the American Jewish Archives was founded by Dr Jacob Rader Marcus in 1947 in the aftermath of World War II and the Holocaust. It is committed to preserving a documentary heritage of the religious, organizational, economic, cultural, personal, social and family life of American Jewry. It contains nearly 5,000 linear feet of archives, manuscripts, newsprint materials, photographs, audio and video tapes, microfilm and genealogical materials.

Bernard and Audre Rapoport Fellowships

Subjects: American Jewish studies.
Eligibility: Open to postdoctoral candidates of any nationality.
Level of Study: Postgraduate, doctorate, predoctorate, postdoctorate
Type: Fellowship
Value: Award is determined at the discretion of the selection committee
Length of Study: 1 month
Study Establishment: The Archives
Country of Study: Any country
Application Procedure: Applicants must provide an up-to-date curriculum vitae, a research proposal, evidence of published research and two recommendations from academic colleagues.
Closing Date: March 1st

Ethel Marcus Memorial Fellowship

Subjects: American Jewish studies.
Eligibility: Open to ABDs.
Level of Study: Postgraduate, doctorate, postdoctorate, predoctorate
Type: Fellowship

Value: Award is determined at the discretion of the selection committee
Length of Study: 1 month
Study Establishment: The Archives
Country of Study: Any country
Application Procedure: Applicants must provide an up-to-date curriculum vitae, a research proposal and three faculty recommendations including one from the dissertation supervisor.
Closing Date: March 1st

The Joseph and Eva R Dave Fellowship

Subjects: American Jewish studies.
Purpose: To facilitate research and writing using the vast collection at the American Jewish Archives, and to preserve a documentary heritage of the religious, organizational, economic, cultural, personal, social and family life of American Jewry and impart it to the next generation.
Eligibility: Open to ABDs.
Level of Study: Postgraduate, doctorate, postdoctorate, predoctorate, senior or independent scholars
Type: Fellowship
Value: Award is determined at the discretion of the selection committee
Length of Study: 1 month
Frequency: Annual
Study Establishment: The Archives
Country of Study: Any country
No. of awards offered: 1
Application Procedure: Applicants must provide an up-to-date curriculum vitae, which details the precise nature of the applicant's research interests and demonstrates clearly how the resources and holdings of the American Jewish archives are vital to the applicant's research. Proposals should be no more than five double-spaced, typewritten pages. Applicants must provide two recommendations. PhD students should include one from the dissertation supervisor.
Closing Date: March 18th in the year of proposed study
Funding: Private

Loewenstein-Wiener Fellowship Awards

Subjects: American Jewish studies.
Eligibility: Open to ABDs who have completed all but the dissertation requirement, and to postdoctoral candidates.
Level of Study: Predoctorate, postdoctorate, doctorate, postgraduate
Type: Fellowship
Value: Award is determined at the discretion of the selection committee
Length of Study: 1 month
Study Establishment: The Archives
Country of Study: Any country
Application Procedure: Applicants must provide an up-to-date curriculum vitae, a research proposal and evidence of published research where possible. ABDs must provide three faculty recommendations including one from the dissertation supervisor and postdoctoral candidates must provide two recommendations from academic colleagues. These will constitute the application.
Closing Date: March 1st

Marguerite R Jacobs Memorial Award

Subjects: American Jewish studies.
Eligibility: Open to postdoctoral candidates of any nationality.
Level of Study: Postdoctorate, doctorate, predoctorate, postgraduate, senior or independent scholars
Value: Award is determined at the discretion of the selection committee
Length of Study: 1 month
Frequency: Annual
Study Establishment: The Archives
Country of Study: Any country
No. of awards offered: 1
Application Procedure: Applicants must provide an up-to-date curriculum vitae, a research proposal, evidence of published research, where possible and two recommendations from academic colleagues.
Closing Date: March 1st
Funding: Private

The Natalie Feld Memorial Fellowship

Subjects: American Jewish studies.
Purpose: To facilitate research and writing using the vast collection at the American Jewish Archives, and to preserve a documentary heritage of the religious, organizational, economic, cultural, personal, social and family life of American Jewry for the next generation.
Eligibility: Open to ABDs.
Level of Study: Postgraduate, predoctorate, doctorate, postdoctorate, senior or independent scholars
Type: Fellowship
Value: Award is determined at the discretion of the selection committee
Frequency: Annual
Study Establishment: The Archives
Country of Study: Any country
No. of awards offered: 1
Application Procedure: Applicants must provide an up-to-date curriculum vitae, which details the precise nature of the applicant's research interests and demonstrates clearly how the resources and holdings of the American Jewish archives are vital to the applicant's research. Proposals should be no more than five double-spaced, typewritten pages. Applicants must provide two recommendations. PhD students should include one from the dissertation supervisor.
Closing Date: March 18th in the year of the proposed study
Funding: Private

Rabbi Frederic A Doppelt Memorial Fellowship

Subjects: American Jewish studies.
Purpose: To honour Rabbi Doppelt by providing fellowships for research and writing using the vast collection at the American Jewish Archives, and to preserve a documentary heritage of the religious, organizational, economic, cultural, personal, social, and family life of American Jewry and impart it to the next generation.
Eligibility: Open to ABDs. Preference will be given to candidates from Eastern Europe or those working on a topic related to East European Jewry in the American context.
Level of Study: Postgraduate, predoctorate, postdoctorate, doctorate, senior or independent scholars
Type: Fellowship
Value: Award is determined at the discretion of the selection committee
Length of Study: 1 month
Frequency: Annual
Study Establishment: The Archives
Country of Study: Any country
No. of awards offered: 1
Application Procedure: Applicants must provide an up-to-date curriculum vitae, which details the precise nature of the applicant's research interests and demonstrates clearly how the resources and holdings of the American Jewish Archives are vital to the applicant's research. Proposals should be no more than five double-spaced, typewritten pages. Applicants must provide two recommendations. PhD students should include one from the dissertation supervisor.
Closing Date: March 18th in the year of the proposed study
Funding: Private

The Rabbi Harold D Hahn Memorial Fellowship

Subjects: American Jewish studies, preserving a documentary heritage of the religious, organizational, economic, cultural, personal, social and family life of American Jewry and imparting it to the next generation.
Purpose: A perpetual scholarship created to enable scholars to conduct independent research in subject areas relating to the history of North American Jewry.
Eligibility: Open to ABDs.
Level of Study: Doctorate, predoctorate, postdoctorate, postgraduate, senior or independent scholars
Type: Fellowship

Value: Award is determined at the discretion of the Selection Committee
Length of Study: 1 month
Frequency: Annual
Study Establishment: The Archives
Country of Study: Any country
No. of awards offered: 1
Application Procedure: Applicants must provide an up-to-date curriculum vitae that details the precise nature of the applicant's research interests, and demonstrates clearly how the resources and holdings of the American Jewish archives are vital to the applicant's research. Proposals should be no more than five double-spaced, typewritten pages. Applicants must provide two recommendations. PhD students should include one from the dissertation supervisor.
Closing Date: March 18th in year of proposed study
Funding: Private

The Rabbi Joachin Prinz Memorial Fellowship

Subjects: American Jewish studies.
Purpose: To enable the recipient to conduct an extensive study of the Rabbi Joachin Prinz collection in preparation for a doctoral dissertation or other scholarly publication.
Eligibility: Open to ABDs.
Level of Study: Predoctorate, postdoctorate, doctorate, postgraduate, senior or independent scholars
Type: Fellowship
Value: Award is determined at the discretion of the selection committee
Length of Study: 1 month
Frequency: Annual
Study Establishment: The Archives
Country of Study: Any country
No. of awards offered: 1
Application Procedure: Applicants must provide an up-to-date curriculum vitae, which details the precise nature of the applicant's research interests and demonstrates clearly how the resources and holdings of the American Jewish Archives are vital to the applicant's research. Proposals should be no more than five double-spaced, typewritten pages. Applicants must provide two recommendations. PhD students should include one from the dissertation supervisor.
Closing Date: March 18th in the year of the proposed study
Funding: Private
Contributor: Deutsche Bank American Foundation

Rabbi Levi A Olan Memorial Fellowship

Subjects: American Jewish studies.
Eligibility: Open to ABDs.
Level of Study: Predoctorate, doctorate, postgraduate, postdoctorate
Type: Fellowship
Value: Award is determined at the discretion of the selection committee
Length of Study: 1 month
Study Establishment: The Archives
Country of Study: Any country
Application Procedure: Applicants must provide an up-to-date curriculum vitae, a research proposal and three faculty recommendations, including one from a dissertation supervisor.
Closing Date: March 1st

Rabbi Theodore S Levy Tribute Fellowship

Subjects: American Jewish studies.
Eligibility: Open to ABDs.
Level of Study: Doctorate, postgraduate, postdoctorate, predoctorate, senior or independent scholars
Type: Fellowship
Value: Award is determined at the discretion of the selection committee
Length of Study: 1 month
Frequency: Annual
Study Establishment: The Archives
Country of Study: Any country
No. of awards offered: 1
Application Procedure: Applicants must provide an up-to-date curriculum vitae, a research proposal and three faculty recommendations, including one from a dissertation supervisor.
Closing Date: March 1st
Funding: Private

Starkoff Fellowship

Subjects: American Jewish studies.
Eligibility: Open to ABDs.
Level of Study: Postgraduate, doctorate, postdoctorate, predoctorate
Type: Fellowship
Value: Award is determined at the discretion of the committee
Length of Study: 1 month
Study Establishment: The Archives
Country of Study: United States of America
Application Procedure: Applicants must provide an up-to-date curriculum vitae, a research proposal and three faculty recommendations, including one from a dissertation supervisor.
Closing Date: March 1st

AMERICAN LIBRARY ASSOCIATION (ALA)

50 East Huron Street, Chicago, IL, 60611,
United States of America
Tel: (1) 800 545 2433 ext. 3247
Fax: (1) 312 944 6131
Email: awards@ala.org
Website: www.ala.org/work/awards
Contact: Ms Cheryl Malden, ALA Awards Co-ordinator

Each year the American Library Association (ALA) and its member units sponsor awards to honour distinguished service and foster professional growth.

ALA 3M/NMRT Professional Development Grant

Subjects: Library studies.
Purpose: To allow librarians to attend the Annual Conference of the ALA.
Eligibility: Open to members of the ALA and the New Members Round Table (NMRT).
Level of Study: Professional development
Type: Grant
Value: Airfare, hotel, conference registration and US$250
Frequency: Annual
Country of Study: Any country
No. of awards offered: 3
Application Procedure: Applicants must submit nominations to the NMRT Professional Development Grant at ALA.
Closing Date: December 15th
Funding: Commercial
Contributor: 3M

ALA AASL Frances Henne Award

Subjects: Library media.
Purpose: To enable an individual to attend an AASL national conference or ALA Annual Conference for the first time.
Eligibility: Open to school library media specialists with less than 5 years in the profession.
Level of Study: Unrestricted
Type: Grant
Value: US$1,250
Frequency: Annual
Country of Study: Any country
No. of awards offered: 1
Application Procedure: Applicants must write for details.
Funding: Commercial
Contributor: R R Bowker

ALA AASL Highsmith Research Grant

Subjects: Library science.
Purpose: To enable an individual to conduct innovative research aimed at measuring and evaluating the impact of school library media programmes on learning and education.
Eligibility: Open to qualified researchers of any nationality.
Level of Study: Professional development
Type: Research grant
Value: Up to US$5,000
Frequency: Annual
Country of Study: Any country
No. of awards offered: 1
Application Procedure: Applicants must write for details.
Funding: Commercial
Contributor: The Highsmith Company

ALA AASL Information Technology Pathfinder Award

Subjects: Library media.
Purpose: To recognize and honour a school library media specialist for demonstrating vision and leadership through the use of information technology to build lifelong learners.
Eligibility: Open to school library media specialists, supervisors or educators.
Level of Study: Professional development
Type: Scholarship
Value: US$1,000 to the specialist and US$500 to the library, a citation and travel expenses to the ALA Annual Conference
Frequency: Annual
Country of Study: Any country
No. of awards offered: 1
Application Procedure: Applicants must write for details.
Funding: Commercial
Contributor: Information Plus

ALA Beta Phi Mu Award

Subjects: Education for librarianship.
Purpose: To recognize distinguished service.
Eligibility: Open to library school faculty members or others in the library profession.
Level of Study: Professional development
Value: US$500 and a citation
Frequency: Annual
No. of awards offered: 1
Application Procedure: Applicants must submit six copies of nominations to the ALA Awards Program Office.
Closing Date: December 1st
Funding: Private
Contributor: The Beta Phi Mu International Library Science Honorary Society
No. of awards given last year: 1

ALA Bogle-Pratt International Library Travel Fund

Subjects: Library science.
Purpose: To enable ALA members to attend their first international conference.
Eligibility: Open to ALA members.
Level of Study: Professional development
Type: Travel grant
Value: US$1,000
Frequency: Annual
Country of Study: Any country
No. of awards offered: 1
Application Procedure: Applicants must write for details.
Closing Date: January 1st
Funding: Private
Contributor: The Bogle Memorial Fund
No. of awards given last year: 1

ALA Bound to Stay Bound Book Scholarships

Subjects: Library science.
Purpose: To support study in the field of library service to children in an ALA-accredited programme.
Eligibility: Open to qualified applicants of any nationality who have not started the programme.
Level of Study: Postgraduate
Type: Scholarship
Value: US$6,000 each
Frequency: Annual
Country of Study: United States of America or Canada
No. of awards offered: 2
Application Procedure: Applicants must write or email for details.
Closing Date: March 1st
Funding: Commercial
Contributor: Bound to Stay Bound Books, Inc.

ALA Carroll Preston Baber Research Grant

Subjects: Library service.
Purpose: To encourage innovative research that could lead to an improvement in library services to any specified group or groups of people.
Level of Study: Unrestricted
Type: Research grant
Value: Up to US$3,000
Frequency: Annual
Country of Study: Any country
No. of awards offered: 1
Application Procedure: Applicants must submit an application including a research proposal.
Funding: Private
Contributor: Eric R Baber
No. of awards given last year: 1
No. of applicants last year: 5
Additional Information: The project should aim to answer a question that is of vital importance to the library community and the researchers should plan to provide documentation of the results of their work. The jury would welcome proposals that involve innovative uses of technology and proposals that involve co-operation between libraries and other agencies, or between librarians and persons in other disciplines.

ALA Christopher J Hoy/ERT Scholarship

Subjects: Library and information studies.
Purpose: To allow individuals to attend an ALA-accredited programme of library and information studies.
Eligibility: Open to applicants who will be attending an ALA-accredited programme of library and information studies leading to a Master's degree.
Level of Study: Postgraduate
Type: Scholarship
Value: US$3,000
Frequency: Annual
Country of Study: Any country
No. of awards offered: 1
Application Procedure: Applicants must write for details.
Funding: Private
Contributor: The family of Christopher J Hoy

ALA David H Clift Scholarship

Subjects: Library science.
Purpose: To enable a worthy candidate to begin a Master's degree.
Eligibility: Open to qualified citizens of Canada or the United States of America pursuing a Master's degree in library science in an ALA-accredited programme.
Level of Study: Postgraduate
Type: Scholarship
Value: US$3,000
Frequency: Annual
Country of Study: Any country
No. of awards offered: 1
Application Procedure: Applicants must write for details.

ALA David Rozkuska Scholarship

Subjects: Library science.
Purpose: To provide financial assistance to an individual who is currently working with government documents in a library.

Eligibility: Open to applicants currently completing a Master's programme in library science.
Level of Study: Postgraduate
Type: Scholarship
Value: US$3,000
Frequency: Annual
Country of Study: Any country
No. of awards offered: 1
Application Procedure: Applicants must write for details.

ALA EBSCO Conference Sponsorship

Subjects: Library science.
Purpose: To allow librarians to attend the ALA Annual Conference.
Eligibility: Open to librarians.
Level of Study: Professional development
Type: Travel grant
Value: Up to US$1,000 for expenses
Frequency: Annual
Country of Study: Any country
No. of awards offered: 10
Application Procedure: Applicants must write for details.
Closing Date: December 1st
Funding: Commercial
Contributor: EBSCO Subscription Services

ALA Eli M Oboler Memorial Award

Subjects: Intellectual freedom and freedom to read.
Purpose: To award the best published work in the field.
Eligibility: There are no eligibility restrictions.
Level of Study: Unrestricted
Type: Award
Value: US$1,500
Frequency: Every 2 years
Country of Study: Any country
No. of awards offered: 1
Application Procedure: Applicants must submit the nominated documents with nominating form.
Closing Date: December 1st
Funding: Private

ALA Elizabeth Futas Catalyst for Change Award

Subjects: Library science.
Purpose: To recognize and honour a librarian who invests time and talent to make positive changes in the profession of librarianship by taking risks to further the cause, helping new librarians grow and achieve, working for change within the ALA or other library organizations and inspiring colleagues to excel or make the impossible possible.
Type: Award
Value: US$1,000 and a citation
Frequency: Annual
No. of awards offered: 1
Application Procedure: Applicants must write for details.
Contributor: An endowment administered by the ALA
No. of awards given last year: 1

ALA Equality Award

Subjects: Pay equity, affirmative action, legislative work and non-sexist education.
Purpose: To recognize an outstanding contribution towards the promotion of equality in the library profession. The contribution may be either a sustained one or a single outstanding accomplishment.
Eligibility: Open to members of the library profession.
Level of Study: Professional development
Value: US$500 plus a citation
Frequency: Annual
No. of awards offered: 1
Application Procedure: Applicants must submit six copies of nominations to the ALA Awards Program Office.
Funding: Commercial
Contributor: The Scarecrow Press
No. of awards given last year: 1

ALA Facts on File Grant

Subjects: Library science.
Purpose: To award a library for imaginative programming that would make current affairs more meaningful to an adult audience. Programmes, bibliographies, pamphlets, and innovative approaches of all types and in all media are eligible.
Eligibility: Open to adult librarians.
Level of Study: Professional development
Type: Grant
Value: US$2,000
Frequency: Annual
Country of Study: Any country
No. of awards offered: 1
Application Procedure: Applicants must submit a proposal accompanied by a statement of objective, identification of the current issues, the target audience and the extent of community involvement planned, an outline of planned activities for conducting and promoting the project, a budget summary and details of how the project will be evaluated.
Funding: Commercial
No. of awards given last year: 1

ALA Frances Henne/YALSA/VOYA Research Grant

Subjects: Library science.
Purpose: To provide seed money to an individual, institution or group for a project to encourage research on library service to young adults.
Eligibility: Open to applicants of any nationality.
Level of Study: Unrestricted
Type: Research grant
Value: US$500 minimum
Frequency: Annual
Country of Study: Any country
No. of awards offered: 1
Application Procedure: Applicants must write for details.

ALA Frederick G Melcher Scholarships

Subjects: Library service to children.
Purpose: To provide financial assistance for the professional education of men and women who intend to pursue children's librarianship.
Eligibility: Open to qualified young persons who have been accepted for admission to an appropriate school.
Level of Study: Graduate
Type: Scholarship
Value: US$5,000
Frequency: Annual
Study Establishment: An ALA-accredited school
Country of Study: United States of America or Canada
No. of awards offered: 2
Application Procedure: Applicants must write or email for details.
Closing Date: April 1st
Funding: Private

ALA Grolier Foundation Award

Subjects: Library work with children and young people to high school age.
Purpose: To recognize a librarian whose unusual contribution to the stimulation and guidance of reading by children and young people exemplifies outstanding achievement in the profession. The award is given either for outstanding continuing service, or in recognition of one particular contribution of lasting value.
Eligibility: Open to community and school librarians.
Level of Study: Professional development
Value: US$1,000 plus a citation
Frequency: Annual
No. of awards offered: 1
Application Procedure: Applicants must submit six copies of the application to the ALA Awards Program Office.
Funding: Commercial
Contributor: Grolier Publishing Company
No. of awards given last year: 1

ALA H W Wilson Library Staff Development Grant

Subjects: Library science.
Purpose: To award a library organization whose application demonstrates greatest merit for a programme of staff development designed to further goals and objectives of the library organization.
Type: Grant
Value: US$3,500 and a citation
Frequency: Annual
No. of awards offered: 1
Application Procedure: Applicants must submit six copies of the application and documentation to the ALA Awards Program Office.
Contributor: The H W Wilson Company
No. of awards given last year: 1

ALA Jesse H Shera Award for Excellence in Doctoral Research

Subjects: Library science.
Level of Study: Doctorate
Type: Prize
Value: US$500, multiple authors will divide the award
Frequency: Annual
Country of Study: Any country
No. of awards offered: 1
Application Procedure: Applicants must send three copies of a research paper, together with a cover letter stating that they own copyright to it.
Closing Date: Postmarked no later than February 15th
Funding: Private
Additional Information: The text of any submitted research paper must not exceed 10,000 words. Research papers should be drawn from work completed in pursuit of doctoral studies.

ALA Jesse H Shera Award for Research

Subjects: Library science.
Purpose: To honour an outstanding and original paper reporting the results of research related to libraries.
Eligibility: Authors of nominated articles need not be Library Research Round Table (LRRT) members but the nominations must be made by LRRT members. All entries must be research articles published in English during the calendar year previous to the competition. All nominated articles must relate in at least a general way to library and information studies.
Level of Study: Unrestricted
Type: Prize
Value: US$500
Frequency: Annual
Country of Study: Any country
No. of awards offered: 1
Application Procedure: Applicants wishing to nominate research articles for this award should send three copies of each article together with a covering letter stating that they are a current member of LRRT or that they are acting in their role as journal editor.
Closing Date: February 15th
Funding: Private
No. of awards given last year: 1
No. of applicants last year: 12

ALA John Philip Immroth Award for Intellectual Freedom

Subjects: Intellectual freedom.
Purpose: To recognize a notable contribution to intellectual freedom fuelled by personal courage.
Eligibility: Open to intellectual freedom fighters.
Level of Study: Unrestricted
Type: Award
Value: US$500 plus a citation
Frequency: Annual
Country of Study: Any country
No. of awards offered: 1
Application Procedure: Applicants must submit a detailed statement explaining why the nominator believes that the nominee should receive the award. Nominations should be submitted to IFRT Staff Liaison at the ALA.
Closing Date: December 1st
Funding: Private

ALA Joseph W Lippincott Award

Subjects: Library work with professional library associations.
Purpose: To recognize distinguished service in the profession of librarianship, including outstanding participation in professional library activities, notable published professional writing or other significant activities.
Eligibility: Open to librarians.
Level of Study: Professional development
Type: Award
Value: US$1,000 plus a citation
Frequency: Annual
No. of awards offered: 1
Application Procedure: Applicants must submit six copies of nominations to the ALA Awards Program Office.
Funding: Private
Contributor: The late Joseph W Lippincott
No. of awards given last year: 1

ALA Ken Haycock Award for Promoting Librarianship

Subjects: Library science.
Purpose: Honours an individual for contributing significantly to the public recognition and appreciation of librarianship through professional performance, teaching or writing.
Type: Award
Value: US$1,000 and a citation
Frequency: Annual
No. of awards offered: 1
Funding: Private
Contributor: Kenneth Haycock, PhD

ALA Lexis/Nexis/GODORT/ALA Documents to the People Award

Subjects: Library science.
Purpose: To provide funding for research in the field of documents librarianship or in a related area that would benefit the individual's performance as a documents librarian or make a contribution to the field.
Eligibility: Open to individuals and libraries, organizations and other appropriate non-commercial groups.
Level of Study: Unrestricted
Type: Award
Value: US$3,000
Frequency: Annual
Country of Study: Any country
No. of awards offered: 1
Application Procedure: Applicants must submit nominations to the GODORT Staff Liaison at the ALA.
Funding: Commercial
Contributor: Lexis/Nexis

ALA Library Research Round Table Research Award

Subjects: Library science.
Purpose: To encourage excellence in research.
Eligibility: Open to library science researchers.
Level of Study: Unrestricted
Type: Research grant
Value: US$1,000
Frequency: Annual
Country of Study: Any country
No. of awards offered: 1
Application Procedure: Applicants must request guidelines from ALA.
Closing Date: February 2nd
No. of awards given last year: 1
No. of applicants last year: 4
Additional Information: Papers must not exceed 50 pages in length and will be judged on the definition of the research problem, application of research methods, clarity of reporting and the significance of conclusions. Research papers completed in pursuit of an academic

degree are not eligible. Candidates should submit their entries to the jury chair, whose name is available each year from the ALA.

ALA Loleta D Fyan Public Library Research Grant

Subjects: Library service.
Purpose: To facilitate the development and improvement of public libraries and the services they provide.
Eligibility: Applicants can include but are not limited to local, regional or state libraries, associations or organizations including units of the ALA, library schools or individuals.
Level of Study: Unrestricted
Type: Research grant
Value: Up to US$10,000
Frequency: Annual
Country of Study: Any country
No. of awards offered: 1 or more
Application Procedure: Applicants must submit an application form in addition to a proposal and budget.
Closing Date: Applications are accepted at any time
Funding: Private
No. of awards given last year: 1
No. of applicants last year: 10
Additional Information: The project must result in the development and improvement of public libraries and the services they provide, have the potential for broader impact and application beyond meeting a specific local need, should be designed to effect changes in public library services that are innovative and responsive to the future and should be capable of completion within 1 year.

ALA Marshall Cavendish Excellence in Library Programming

Subjects: Library science.
Purpose: To recognize a school or public library for programmes that have community impact and respond to community needs.
Type: Award
Value: US$2,000 and a citation
Frequency: Annual
No. of awards offered: 1
Funding: Corporation
Contributor: Marshall Cavendish Corporation

ALA Mary V Gaver Scholarship

Subjects: Library science.
Purpose: To assist library support staff specializing in youth services.
Eligibility: Open to library support staff who are citizens of the United States of America or Canada who are pursuing a Master's degree in library science.
Level of Study: Unrestricted
Type: Scholarship
Value: US$3,000
Frequency: Annual
Country of Study: Any country
No. of awards offered: 1
Application Procedure: Applicants must write for details.
Closing Date: March 1st
No. of awards given last year: 1

ALA Melvil Dewey Medal

Subjects: Library science.
Purpose: To award an individual or group for recent creative professional achievement in library management, training, cataloguing, classification and the tools and techniques of librarianship.
Type: Award
Value: Medal and citation
Frequency: Annual
No. of awards offered: 1
Application Procedure: Applicants must write for details.
Contributor: The OCLC Forest Press
No. of awards given last year: 1

ALA Miriam L Hornback Scholarship

Subjects: Library science.
Purpose: To assist an individual pursuing a Master's degree.
Eligibility: Open to ALA or library support staff who are pursuing a Master's degree in library science and who are citizens of the United States of America or Canada.
Level of Study: Postgraduate
Type: Scholarship
Value: US$3,000
Frequency: Annual
No. of awards offered: 1
Application Procedure: Applicants must write for details.
Closing Date: March 1st
No. of awards given last year: 2

ALA New Leaders Travel Grant

Subjects: Library science.
Purpose: To enhance professional development and improve the expertise of individuals new to the field by making possible their attendance at major professional development activities.
Eligibility: Open to qualified public librarians.
Level of Study: Professional development
Type: Travel grant
Value: Plaque and travel grant of up to US$1,500 per applicant
Frequency: Annual
Country of Study: Any country
No. of awards offered: 1
Application Procedure: Applicants must write for details.

ALA NMRT/EBSCO Scholarship

Subjects: Library science.
Purpose: To enable an individual to begin an MLS degree in an ALA-accredited programme.
Eligibility: Open to citizens of the United States of America and Canada.
Level of Study: Postgraduate
Type: Scholarship
Value: US$1,000
Frequency: Annual
Country of Study: Any country
No. of awards offered: 1
Application Procedure: Applicants must write for details.
Closing Date: April 1st

ALA Penguin Putnam Books for Young Readers Award

Subjects: Library science.
Purpose: To allow children's librarians to attend the Annual Conference of the ALA.
Eligibility: Open to members of the Association for Library Service to Children with between 1 and 10 years of experience who have never attended an ALA Annual Conference.
Level of Study: Professional development
Type: Award
Value: US$600
Frequency: Annual
Country of Study: Any country
No. of awards offered: 4
Application Procedure: Applicants must telephone or email for details.
Closing Date: December 1st
Funding: Commercial
Contributor: Penguin Group, USA
No. of awards given last year: 4

ALA Primark Student Travel Award

Subjects: Library science.
Purpose: To enable a student interested in a career as a business librarian to attend an ALA Annual Conference.
Eligibility: Open to qualified Master's students in an ALA-accredited programme.
Level of Study: Postgraduate
Type: Travel grant
Value: US$1,000
Frequency: Annual
Country of Study: Any country
No. of awards offered: 1

Application Procedure: Applicants must write for details.
Funding: Commercial
Contributor: Disclosure, Inc.

ALA Samuel Lazerow Fellowship for Research in Acquisitions or Technical Services

Subjects: Acquisitions or technical services.
Purpose: To foster advances in acquisitions or technical services by providing a fellowship for travel or writing in those fields.
Eligibility: Open to qualified librarians.
Level of Study: Professional development
Type: Fellowship
Value: US$1,000 plus a citation
Frequency: Annual
Country of Study: Any country
No. of awards offered: 1
Application Procedure: Applicants must write for details and are advised to refer to the awards section of the ACRL website www.ala.org/acrl
Closing Date: Early December
Contributor: Thomson ISI
No. of awards given last year: 1

ALA Schneider Family Book Award

Subjects: Library science.
Purpose: The Schneider Family Book Awards honour an author or illustrator for a book that embodies an artistic expression of the disability experience for child and adolescent audiences.The book must emphasize the artistic expression of the disability experience for children and or adolescent audiences. The book must portray some aspect of living with a disability or that of a friend or family member, whether the disability is physical, mental or emotional.
Type: Award
Value: US$5,000 and a citation for each winner
Frequency: Annual
No. of awards offered: 3
Funding: Private
Contributor: Katherine Schneider

ALA Shirley Olofson Memorial Awards

Subjects: Library science.
Purpose: To allow individuals to attend ALA conferences.
Eligibility: Open to members of the ALA who are also current or potential members of the New Members Round Table. Applicants should not have attended any more than five conferences.
Level of Study: Unrestricted
Type: Award
Value: US$1,000
Frequency: Annual
Country of Study: Any country
No. of awards offered: Varies
Application Procedure: Applicants must write for details.
Closing Date: December 15th

ALA SIRSI Leader in Library Technology Grant

Subjects: Library science.
Purpose: To encourage and enable continued advancements in quality library services for a project that makes creative or groundbreaking use of technology to deliver exceptional services to its community. Eligible libraries are public, academic, school and special (ie. medical, law, government, corporate or museum).
Type: Grant
Value: US$10,000 and a citation
Frequency: Annual
No. of awards offered: 1
Funding: Corporation
Contributor: SIRSI Corporation

ALA Spectrum Initiative Scholarship Program

Subjects: Library and information studies.
Purpose: To encourage admission to an ALA recognized Master's degree programme by the four largest underrepresented minority groups.
Eligibility: Open to citizens of the United States of America or Canada only, from one of the largest underrepresented groups. These are African American or African Canadian, Asian or Pacific Islander, Latino or Hispanic and native people of the United States of America or Canada.
Level of Study: Postgraduate
Type: Scholarship
Value: US$5,000
Frequency: Annual
Country of Study: United States of America or Canada
No. of awards offered: 25–50
Application Procedure: Applicants must request details via fax or visit the website.
Closing Date: April 1st

ALA Sullivan Award for Public Library Administrators Supporting Services to Children

Subjects: Library science.
Purpose: To an individual who has shown exceptional understanding and support of public library service to children while having general management/supervisory/administrative responsibility that has included public library service to children in its scope.
Type: Award
Value: Citation and commemorative gift
Frequency: Annual
No. of awards offered: 1
Funding: Private
Contributor: Peggy Sullivan, PhD

ALA Tom C Drewes Scholarship

Subjects: Library science.
Purpose: To assist a library support staff person.
Eligibility: Open to library support staff pursuing a Master's degree who are citizens of the United States of America or Canada.
Level of Study: Postgraduate
Type: Scholarship
Value: US$3,000
Frequency: Annual
Country of Study: Any country
No. of awards offered: 1
Application Procedure: Applicants must write for details.

ALA W Y Boyd Literary Award

Subjects: The writing and publishing of outstanding war-related fiction.
Purpose: To award an author who has written a military novel that honours the service of American veterans and military personnel during a time of war: 1861–1865, 1914–1918 or 1939–1945.
Type: Award
Value: US$5,000 and a citation
Frequency: Annual
No. of awards offered: 1
Application Procedure: Applicants must write for details.
Closing Date: December 1st
Funding: Private
Contributor: William Young Boyd II

ALA YALSA/Baker and Taylor Conference Grants

Subjects: Library science.
Purpose: To allow young adult librarians who work directly with young adults in either a public library or a school library, to attend the Annual Conference of the ALA.
Eligibility: Open to members of the Young Adult Library Services Association with between 1 and 10 years of library experience who have never attended an ALA Annual Conference.
Level of Study: Professional development
Type: Grant
Value: US$1,000
Frequency: Annual
Country of Study: Any country
No. of awards offered: 2

Application Procedure: Applicants must submit applications to the Young Adult Library Services Association, ALA.
Closing Date: December 1st

ALA/Information Today Library of the Future Award

Subjects: Library science.
Purpose: To honour an individual library, library consortium, group of librarians or support organization for innovative planning for applications of, or development of, patron training programmes about information technology in a library setting.
Type: Award
Value: US$1,500 and a citation
Frequency: Annual
No. of awards offered: 1
Application Procedure: Applicants must write for details.
Funding: Private
Contributor: Information Today, Inc.
Additional Information: The American Library Association offers a number of other awards in various fields related to library science, including the following medals and citations with no cash prizes: the Randolph Caldecott Medal, the James Bennett Childs Award, the Dartmouth Medal, the John Newberry Medal, the Laura Ingalls Wilder Medal, the ASCLA Exceptional Service Award, the Armed Forces Librarians Achievement Citation, the Francis Joseph Campbell Citation, the Margaret Mann Citation, the Isadore Gilbert Mudge Citation, the Esther J Piercy Award, the Distinguished Library Service Award for School Administrators and the Trustees Citations. A full list of awards is available from the ALA.

AMERICAN MUSIC CENTER, INC.

30 West 26th Street, Suite 1001, New York, NY, 10010-2011,
United States of America
Tel: (1) 212 366 5260
Fax: (1) 212 366 5265
Email: Anna@amc.net
Website: www.amc.net
Contact: Anna Smith, Manager of Grantmaking Programs

The American Music Center is a non-profit membership and service organization. The Center's mission is to build a national community for new American music.

American Music Center Composer Assistance Program

Subjects: Music.
Purpose: To support individual composers to realize their music in performance.
Eligibility: American composers in good standing with the American Music Center.
Level of Study: Professional development
Type: Fellowship
Value: Up to US$5,000
Length of Study: Variable
Frequency: Annual
Country of Study: United States of America
Application Procedure: Applicants must download guidelines from website.
Closing Date: February 1st, May 1st, October 1st
Funding: Private
Contributor: The Helen F Whitaker Fund

Margaret Fairbank Jory Copying Assistance Program

Subjects: Musical composition.
Purpose: To assist composers with copying expenses for a première performance.
Eligibility: Open to American composers who are members of the American Music Center and in good standing at the time of application. The performance must advance the professional career of the composer. Performers, presenters or ensembles are not eligible to apply. Funds are available for copying parts for the première performance of large-scale works for four or more instrumental and/or vocal parts. The composer must have a written commitment for at least one public performance of the work by a professional ensemble of recognized artistic merit.
Level of Study: Professional development
Type: Grant
Country of Study: Any country
No. of awards offered: Approx. 75
Application Procedure: Applicants must complete an application form and submit this with supporting materials. These include a brief statement of the significance of this performance to the composer's career, a brief professional curriculum vitae with a list of other recent performances, written confirmation of the exact premiere performance date, background on the performing organization, a list of estimated expenses that totals the amount requested, and the amount for which support is requested.
Closing Date: February 1st, June 1st or October 1st
Funding: Private
Contributor: The Mary Flager Cary Charitable Trust, the Helen F Whitaker Fund, JP Morgan Chase, the Arts Alive Foundation and individuals
No. of awards given last year: Approx. 75
No. of applicants last year: Approx. 200
Additional Information: Applicants should visit the website for further information.

THE AMERICAN MUSIC SCHOLARSHIP ASSOCIATION, INC. (AMSA)

441 Vine Street, Suite 1030, Cincinnati, OH, 45202,
United States of America
Tel: (1) 513 421 5342
Fax: (1) 513 421 2672
Email: info@amsa-wpc.org
Website: www.amsa-wpc.org
Contact: Chief Executive Officer

The American Music Scholarship Association (AMSA) produces the annual world piano competition in Cincinnati. AMSA also provides outreach programmes to Cincinnati children (eg. The Bach, Beethoven, and Brahms Club) and worldwide performances. The young artist division winners perform at Carnegie Hall and the gold medallist of the artist division performs at Lincoln Center's Alice Tully Hall.

AMSA World Piano Competition

Subjects: Musical performance on the piano.
Purpose: To encourage the careers of aspiring young pianists and expose them to the performances of great musicians.
Eligibility: Open to piano students of any nationality who are between the ages of 5 and 30.
Level of Study: Unrestricted
Type: Scholarship
Value: The Artist Division's first prize is US$10,000 plus a fully managed debut recital at the Lincoln Center in New York. The second prize is US$3,000, the third US$2,000, the fourth US$1,000, the fifth US$500 and the sixth US$300. The Young Artists Division grand prize at levels 9–12 is US$1,500
Country of Study: Any country
Application Procedure: Applicants must apply in compliance with the full competition rules and regulations, which are available on request and on the website.
Closing Date: June 25th
Funding: Private

AMERICAN MUSICOLOGICAL SOCIETY (AMS)

Department of Music, 201 South 34th Street, Philadelphia, PA,
19104-6313, United States of America
Tel: (1) 215 898 8698
Fax: (1) 215 573 3673
Email: ams@sas.upenn.edu
Website: www.ams-net.org
Contact: Executive Director

The American Musicological Society (AMS) was founded in 1934 as a non-profit organization, with the aim of advancing research in the various fields of music as a branch of learning and scholarship. In 1951, the Society became a constituent member of the American Council of Learned Societies.

Alfred Einstein Award

Subjects: Musicology.
Purpose: To honour a musicological article of exceptional merit by a scholar in the early stages of his or her career.
Eligibility: Open to citizens or permanent residents of Canada or the United States of America.
Level of Study: Professional development
Type: Prize
Value: Varies
Frequency: Annual
No. of awards offered: 1
Application Procedure: Applicants must be nominated. The committee will entertain articles from any individual, including eligible authors who are encouraged to nominate their own articles. Nominations should include the name of the author, the title of the article and the name and year of the periodical or other collection in which it was published. A curriculum vitae is also required.
Closing Date: June 1st
Funding: Private

Alvin H Johnson AMS 50 Dissertation One Year Fellowships

Subjects: Any field of musical research.
Purpose: To encourage research in the various fields of music as a branch of learning and scholarship.
Eligibility: Open to full-time students registered for a doctorate at a North American university, in good standing, who have completed all formal degree requirements except the dissertation at the time of full application. Open to all students without regard to nationality, race, religion or gender.
Level of Study: Postgraduate, doctorate
Type: Fellowship
Value: US$14,000
Length of Study: 1 year
Frequency: Annual
Country of Study: United States of America or Canada
No. of awards offered: 5–6
Application Procedure: Application forms will be sent via the Directors of Graduate Study at all doctorate-granting institutions in North America. They will also be available directly from the Society and the website. Applications must include a curriculum vitae, certification of enrolment and degree completed and two supporting letters from faculty members, one of whom must be the principal adviser of the dissertation. A detailed dissertation prospectus and a completed chapter or comparable written work on the dissertation should accompany the full application. All documents should be submitted in triplicate.
Closing Date: January 15th
Funding: Private
Additional Information: Any submission for a doctoral degree in which the emphasis is on musical scholarship is eligible. The award is not intended for support of early stages of research and it is expected that a recipient's dissertation will be completed within the fellowship year. An equivalent major award from another source may not normally be held concurrently unless the AMS award is accepted on an honorary basis.

AMS Subventions for Publications

Subjects: Musicology.
Purpose: To help individuals with expenses involved in the publication of works of musical scholarship, including books, articles and works in non-print media.
Eligibility: Open to younger scholars and scholars in the early stages of their careers. Proposals for projects that make use of newer technologies are welcomed.
Level of Study: Professional development
Type: Grant
Value: US$500–2,000 with a maximum of US$2,500 available
Application Procedure: Applicants must submit a short, written abstract of up to 1,000 words describing the project and its contribution to musical scholarship, a copy of the article or other equivalent sample, a copy of a contract or letter of agreement from the journal editor or publisher indicating final acceptance for publication, and a detailed budget and explanation of the expenses to which the subvention would be applied. Wherever possible expenses should be itemized. If the publication is a book a representative chapter should be submitted.
Closing Date: March 15th or September 15th
Additional Information: No individual can receive a subvention more than once in a 3-year period.

Howard Mayer Brown Fellowship

Subjects: Musicology.
Purpose: To increase the presence of minority scholars and teachers in musicology.
Eligibility: Open to candidates who have completed at least 1 year of academic work at an institution with a graduate programme in musicology and who intend to complete a PhD in the field. Applicants must be members of a group historically underrepresented in the discipline, including African Americans, Native Americans, Hispanic Americans and Asian Americans. Candidates will normally be citizens or permanent residents of the United States of America or Canada. There are no restrictions on age or gender.
Level of Study: Postgraduate
Type: Fellowship
Value: US$12,000
Length of Study: 1 year
Frequency: Annual
Study Establishment: An institution which offers a graduate programme in musicology
Country of Study: United States of America or Canada
Application Procedure: Applicants must be nominated. Nominations may come from a faculty member of the institution at which the student is enrolled, from a member of the AMS at another institution, or directly from the student. Supporting documents must include a letter summarizing the candidate's academic background, letters of support from three faculty members and samples of the applicant's work such as term papers or any published material.
Closing Date: April 1st of the year in which the fellowship is awarded
Funding: Private
Additional Information: The AMS encourages the institution at which the recipient is pursuing his or her degree to offer continuing financial support. Further information is available on request.

Noah Greenberg Award

Subjects: Musicology.
Purpose: To provide a grant-in-aid to stimulate active co-operation between scholars and performers by recognizing and fostering outstanding contributions to historical performing practices.
Eligibility: Both scholars and performers may apply. Applicants need not be members of the Society.
Level of Study: Professional development
Type: Award
Value: Varies
Frequency: Annual
No. of awards offered: 1–2
Application Procedure: Applicants must submit three copies of a description of the project, a detailed budget and supporting materials such as articles or tapes of performances which are relevant to the project. Applications must be sent to the chair of the Noah Greenberg Award Committee.
Funding: Private

Otto Kinkeldey Award

Subjects: Musicology.
Purpose: To award the work of musicological scholarship such as a major book, edition or other piece of scholarship that best exemplifies the highest quality of originality, interpretation, logic, clarity of thought and communication.

Eligibility: The work must have been published during the previous year in any language and in any country by a scholar who is a citizen or permanent resident of Canada or the United States of America.
Level of Study: Professional development
Type: Prize
Value: Varies
Frequency: Annual
Application Procedure: Applicants must write for details.
Funding: Private
Additional Information: Further information is available on request.

Paul A Pisk Prize

Subjects: Musicology.
Purpose: To encourage scholarship.
Eligibility: Open to graduate students whose abstracts have been submitted to the Program Committee of the Society and papers accepted for inclusion in the Annual Meeting. Open to all students without regard to nationality, race, religion or gender.
Level of Study: Graduate
Type: Prize
Value: US$1,000
Frequency: Annual
Country of Study: United States of America or Canada
No. of awards offered: 1
Application Procedure: Applicants must submit three copies of the complete text paper to the chair of the Pisk Prize Committee. The submission must be accompanied by a statement from the student's academic adviser affirming the graduate student status of the applicant.
Closing Date: September 1st
Funding: Private
Additional Information: Further information is available on request.

AMERICAN NUCLEAR SOCIETY (ANS)

555 North Kensington Avenue, La Grange Park, Illinois 60526, United States of America
Tel: (1) 708 352 6611
Fax: (1) 708 352 0499
Email: outreach@ans.org
Website: www.ans.org
Contact: Scholarship Programme

The American Nuclear Society (ANS) is a non-profit, international, scientific and educational organization. It was established by a group of individuals who recognized the need to unify the professional activities within the diverse fields of nuclear science and technology.

Alan F Henry/Paul A Greebler Scholarship

Subjects: Reactor physics.
Purpose: To aid students pursuing studies in the field of nuclear science.
Eligibility: Open to full-time graduate students at a North American university engaged in Master's or PhD research in the area of nuclear reactor physics or radiation transport. Applicants may be of any nationality.
Level of Study: Postdoctorate, graduate
Type: Scholarship
Value: US$3,500
Length of Study: Varies
Frequency: Annual
Study Establishment: An accredited institution
Country of Study: United States of America
No. of awards offered: 1
Application Procedure: Applicants must complete an application form available from the organization. An official grade transcript and three completed confidential reference forms are also required.
Closing Date: February 1st
No. of awards given last year: 1
Additional Information: Further information is available either on request or from the website.

ANS Best Paper Awards

Subjects: Writing.
Purpose: To recognize the best paper presented at the ASEE annual conference.
Level of Study: Postgraduate
Type: Award
Value: US$3,000 and a plaque
Frequency: Annual
Application Procedure: A nomination form to be sent.

ANS Edward Teller Award

Subjects: Nuclear engineering.
Purpose: To recognize pioneering research in the use of laser and ion-particle beams.
Eligibility: Open to candidates with significant achievements and accomplishments in the field.
Level of Study: Postgraduate
Type: Scholarship
Value: US$2,000 and a silver medal embedded in a solid oak plaque
Frequency: Every 2 years
Application Procedure: See the website.
Closing Date: April 1st

ANS Gerald C. Pomraning Memorial Award

Subjects: Mathematics and/or computation.
Purpose: To provide recognition to individuals who have made outstanding contributions toward the advancement of the fields of mathematics and/or computation.
Eligibility: Open to candidates with outstanding original research and technical leadership.
Level of Study: Postgraduate
Type: Award
Value: An engraved plaque and a monetary award
Frequency: Every 2 years
Application Procedure: Eight copies of the application form (or one electronic version) and supporting documents must be submitted.
Funding: Private
Contributor: Dr. Pomraning

For further information contact:

PO Box 7909, 1110 Burlington Engineering Laboratory, 2500 Stinson Drive, North Carolina, State University, Raleigh, NC 27695-7909
Contact: Dr Paul J. Turinsky

ANS Incoming Freshman Scholarship

Subjects: Science, mathematics and/or technical courses.
Purpose: To encourage high school seniors pursuing science, mathematics and/or technical courses.
Eligibility: Open to all graduate high school seniors.
Level of Study: Postgraduate
Type: Scholarship
Value: US$2,000
No. of awards offered: Up to 5
Application Procedure: A completed special application form and appropriate documents should be sent to the ANS headquarters.
Closing Date: April 1st

ANS Mishima Award

Subjects: Materials science and technology.
Purpose: To recognize outstanding contributions in research.
Eligibility: Open to candidates who may or may not be members of ANS.
Level of Study: Postgraduate
Type: Award
Value: An engraved plaque and a monetary award
Frequency: Annual
Application Procedure: Eight sets of the nomination form and supporting materials must be submitted.
Closing Date: March 1st

ANS Outstanding Achievement Award

Subjects: Nuclear science.
Purpose: To recognize professional excellence and leadership.
Eligibility: Open to members of ANS.
Level of Study: Postgraduate
Type: Award
Frequency: Annual
Application Procedure: Nominations must be sent before the deadline.
Closing Date: May 31st

For further information contact:

Center for Energy Research 460 EBU II, La Jolla, CA 92093-0438
Contact: Professor Farrokh Najmabadi

ANS Pioneer Award

Subjects: Nuclear science.
Purpose: To recognize the efforts of distinguished individuals who have been instrumental in the design, development, implementation and management of nuclear training and education.
Application Procedure: See the website.

ANS Radiation Science and Technological Award

Subjects: Radiation science and engineering.
Purpose: To recognize outstanding creative applications of radiation sciences and engineering principles.
Eligibility: Open to members of the Canadian Association of law libraries.
Level of Study: Postgraduate
Type: Award
Value: US$1,000 and an engraved plaque
Frequency: Annual
Application Procedure: Eight sets of the nomination form and supporting documents must be submitted.
Closing Date: April 15th
Contributor: Isotopes and Radiation Division

ANS Ray Goertz Award

Subjects: Remote technology.
Purpose: To recognize and honor Robotic and Remote Systems Division (RRSD) members who have made outstanding contributions to the field of remote technology.
Eligibility: Open to applicants who are current or retired members of the RRSD.
Level of Study: Postgraduate
Type: Award
Value: US$2,500 and a certificate of recognition
Frequency: Every 2 years
Application Procedure: A completed application form along with a 300–500 word summary explaining the qualifications and contributions to the field of remote technology must be sent.
Closing Date: October 15th

ANS Reactor Technology Award

Subjects: Reactor technology.
Purpose: To honor excellent contributions to the advancement of reactor technology.
Eligibility: Open to candidates who may or may not be numbers of ANS.
Level of Study: Postgraduate
Type: Scholarship
Value: US$2,000 and and engraved plaque
Frequency: Annual
Application Procedure: See the website.
Closing Date: July 1st

ANS Training Excellence Award

Subjects: Nuclear science.
Purpose: To recognize outstanding, innovative, unique and cost-effective contributions to the field of nuclear training and education.
Eligibility: Open to practitioners in International and US commercial, government/contractor and union nuclear training, and post-secondary education fields.
Level of Study: Postgraduate
Type: Award
Value: Varies
Frequency: Annual
Application Procedure: Filled-in nomination forms must be sent.

ANS Undergraduate/Graduate Scholarship

Subjects: Nuclear science and technology.
Value: US$2,000/Undergraduate, US$3,000/Graduate
Frequency: Annual
Study Establishment: An accredited institution
Country of Study: United States of America
Closing Date: February 1st

Arthur Holly Compton Award in Education

Subjects: Nuclear science and engineering.
Purpose: To encourage outstanding contributions to education in nuclear science and engineering.
Eligibility: Open to candidates who have made outstanding contributions to education in the field of nuclear science and engineering.
Level of Study: Postgraduate
Type: Award
Value: US$2,000 and an engraved plaque
Frequency: Annual
Application Procedure: Eight sets of the nomination form and supporting materials to be sent.
Closing Date: March 1st
Contributor: Wife of Edward MalincKrodt, and George E. MalincKrodt

Delayed Education Scholarship for Women

Subjects: Must be a mature woman whose undergraduate studies in nuclear science, nuclear engineering, or a nuclear-related field have been delayed.
Level of Study: Undergraduate
Value: US$4,000
Frequency: Annual
Study Establishment: An accredited institution
Country of Study: United States of America
Closing Date: February 1st

Everitt P Blizard Scholarship

Subjects: Radiation protection and shielding.
Purpose: To aid students pursuing studies in the field of radiation protection and shielding.
Eligibility: Open to full-time graduate students in a programme leading to an advanced degree in nuclear science, nuclear engineering or a nuclear-related field. Applicants must be citizens of the United States of America or permanent residents and be enrolled in an accredited institution in the United States of America.
Level of Study: Graduate
Type: Scholarship
Value: US$3,000
Length of Study: Varies
Frequency: Annual
Study Establishment: An accredited institution
Country of Study: United States of America
No. of awards offered: 1
Application Procedure: Applicants must complete an application form available from the organization. An official grade transcript and three completed confidential reference forms are also required.
Closing Date: February 1st
No. of awards given last year: 1
Additional Information: Further information is available either on request or from the website.

Fellow of ANS Award

Subjects: Nuclear science and engineering.
Purpose: To honor outstanding accomplishment.

Eligibility: Open to candidates who are at least 35 years of age and have served as an active, voting member of the society for a period of at least 5 countries years.
Level of Study: Postgraduate
Type: Award
Frequency: Annual
Application Procedure: Complete nominations must be submitted to ANS headquarters.
Closing Date: February 1st

George C. Laurence Pioneering Award
Subjects: Nuclear engineering.
Purpose: To recognize outstanding pioneering contributions to the field of nuclear reactor safety.
Eligibility: Open to outstanding candidates who may or may not be a member of ANS.
Level of Study: Postgraduate
Type: Award
Value: A certificate, plaque and a monetary award
Frequency: Dependent on funds available
Application Procedure: Nominations to be submitted to the NSID Honors and Awards Committee Chair.
Closing Date: Nominations to be submitted at any time
Contributor: Nuclear Installations Safety Division

Gerald C. Pomraning Memorial Award
Subjects: Mathematics and computation.
Purpose: To recognize achievements in the fields of mathematics and computation.
Level of Study: Postgraduate
Value: An engraved plaque and monetary award
Frequency: Every 2 years
No. of awards offered: 1
Application Procedure: Eight copies of the nomination form and supporting documents to be submitted.

For further information contact:

P.O. box 7909, 1110 Burlington Engineering Laboratory, 2500 Stinson Drive, Raleigh, NC 27695-7909
Contact: Dr Paul J. Turinsky

Glenn T. Seaborg Congressional Science and Engineering Fellowship
Subjects: Engineering.
Purpose: To bring a reasoned and knowledgeable view of nuclear matters to congress.
Eligibility: Open to US citizens who have been a national member of ANS.
Level of Study: Doctorate
Type: Fellowship
Value: A stipend of US$45,000 plus a small travel allowance
Length of Study: 1 year
Frequency: Annual
Application Procedure: See the website.

Henry Dewolf Smyth Nuclear Statesman Award
Subjects: Nuclear energy.
Purpose: To recognize outstanding and states manlike contributions to many aspects of nuclear energy activities.
Eligibility: Open to candidates of any nationality.
Level of Study: Postgraduate
Type: Award
Value: An engraved medal
Application Procedure: Nomination to be sent, see the website for further information.
Closing Date: February 15th
Contributor: ANS and Nuclear Energy Institute

James F Schumar Scholarship
Subjects: Materials science and technology for nuclear applications.
Eligibility: Open to citizens of the United States of America or holders of a permanent resident visa who are full-time graduate students enrolled in a programme leading to an advanced degree.
Level of Study: Graduate
Type: Scholarship
Value: US$3,000
Frequency: Annual
Study Establishment: An accredited institution
Country of Study: United States of America
No. of awards offered: 1
Application Procedure: Applicants must submit a request for an application form that includes the name of the university the candidate will be attending, the year the candidate will be in during the Autumn of the award, the major course of study and a stamped addressed envelope. Completed applications must include a grade transcript and three confidential reference forms. Candidates must be sponsored by an ANS section, division, student branch, committee, member or organization member. The applicant should indicate on the nomination form that he or she is applying for the MSTD Scholarship.
Closing Date: February 1st
No. of awards given last year: 1
Additional Information: Further information is available either on request or from the website.

John and Muriel Landis Scholarship Awards
Subjects: Nuclear physics and engineering.
Purpose: To help students who have greater than average financial need.
Eligibility: Candidates should be planning to pursue a career in nuclear engineering or a nuclear-related field. Candidates must have greater than average financial need, and consideration will be given to conditions or experiences that render the student disadvantaged. Applicants need not be citizens of the United States of America.
Level of Study: Graduate
Type: Scholarship
Value: US$4,000
Frequency: Annual
Study Establishment: An accredited institution
Country of Study: United States of America
No. of awards offered: Up to 8
Application Procedure: Applicants must request an application form and include the name and a letter of commitment from the university the candidate will be attending, the year the candidate will be in the Autumn of the award, the major course of study and a stamped addressed envelope. Completed applications must include a grade transcript and three confidential reference forms. Candidates must be sponsored by an ANS section, division, student branch, committee, member or organization member.
Closing Date: February 1st

John R. Lamash Scholarship
Subjects: Nuclear science and technology.
Value: US$2,000
Frequency: Annual
Study Establishment: An accredited institution
Country of Study: United States of America
Closing Date: February 1st
No. of awards given last year: 1

Landis Public Communication and Education Award
Subjects: Nuclear technology.
Purpose: To award outstanding efforts in furthering public education.
Eligibility: Open to both members and non-members of ANS.
Level of Study: Postgraduate
Type: Award
Length of Study: US$1,000 and an engraved plaque
Frequency: Annual
Application Procedure: Eight sets of the completed application form and supporting documents must be sent.
Closing Date: August 1st
Contributor: The Landis Public Communication and Education Award

Landis Young Member Engineering Achievement Award

Subjects: Engineering.
Purpose: To recognize outstanding achievement in the field of engineering.
Eligibility: Open to candidates who are members of ANS below the age of 40 years.
Level of Study: Postgraduate
Type: Award
Value: An engraved plaque and US$2,000
Frequency: Annual
Application Procedure: Eight sets of the completed application form and supporting documents to be submitted.
Closing Date: March 1st

Mark Mills Award

Subjects: Science and engineering.
Purpose: To award the best original technical paper contributing to the advancement of science and engineering.
Eligibility: Open to students who have been registered in a recognized institution of the higher learning for one year prior to the award.
Level of Study: Postgraduate
Type: Award
Value: Varies
Frequency: Annual
Application Procedure: Eight sets of the nomination form and paper must be submitted.
Closing Date: June 1st

Mary Jane Oestmann Professional Women's Achievement Award

Subjects: Nuclear science and engineering.
Purpose: To recognize outstanding personal dedication by a women.
Eligibility: Open to female candidates who need not be members of ANS but should be affiliated with the nuclear community in some manner.
Application Procedure: Eight sets of the nomination form and supporting documents be submitted.
Closing Date: July 1st

National Academics Christine Mirzayan Science and Technology Policy Graduate Fellowship Program

Subjects: Science, engineering, medicine, veterinary medicine, business and law.
Purpose: To engage students in science and technology policy.
Level of Study: Postgraduate
Type: Fellowship
Length of Study: 10 weeks
Frequency: Annual
Application Procedure: A completed application form must be submitted. Application forms are available on the website.
Closing Date: November 1st

Octave J. Du Temple Award

Subjects: Nuclear science.
Purpose: To recognize consistent effort and significant contribution of meritorious service to the society by an ANS staff member.
Eligibility: Open to full-time members of the ANS staff who have been employed for a minimum of 5 years.
Level of Study: Postgraduate
Type: Award
Frequency: Annual
Application Procedure: See the website.

Operations and Power Division Award

Subjects: Nuclear science and technology.
Level of Study: Undergraduate
Value: US$2,500
Frequency: Annual
Study Establishment: An accredited institution
Country of Study: United States of America
Closing Date: February 1st

Ray Goertz Award

Subjects: Remote technology.
Purpose: To recognize outstanding contributions to the field of remote technology.
Eligibility: Open to current or retired members of the RRSD.
Level of Study: Postgraduate
Type: Award
Value: US$2,500 and a certificate of recognition
Frequency: Every 2 years
Application Procedure: Nominations should be sent to the RRSD.
Closing Date: October 15th
Contributor: Robotics and Remote Systems Division (RRSD)

Robert A Dannels Memorial Scholarship

Subjects: Nuclear science or nuclear engineering.
Eligibility: Open to citizens of the United States of America or holders of a permanent resident visa who are full-time graduate students enrolled in a programme leading to an advanced degree or in graduate-level course of study leading towards a degree in mathematics and computation. Handicapped persons are encouraged to apply.
Level of Study: Graduate
Type: Scholarship
Value: US$3,500
Frequency: Annual
Study Establishment: An accredited institution
Country of Study: United States of America
No. of awards offered: 1
Application Procedure: Applicants must submit a request for an application form that includes the name of the university the candidate will be attending, the year the candidate will be in during the Autumn of the award, the major course of study and a stamped addressed envelope. Completed applications must include a grade transcript and three confidential reference forms. Candidates must be sponsored by an ANS section, division, student branch, committee, member or organization member.
Closing Date: February 1st

Rockwell Award

Subjects: Radiation protection and shielding.
Purpose: To honor lifetime achievement in research.
Eligibility: Open to long-time active members of ANS.
Level of Study: Postgraduate
Value: US$500 and a plaque
Frequency: Annual
Application Procedure: Nominations accompained by supporting documentation to be submitted.

For further information contact:

Radiation Protection and Shielding Division Oak Rigge National Laboratory, Oak Ridge, TN 2008
Tel: 37831-6363
Contact: Bernadette L. Kirt

Samuel Glasstone Award

Subjects: Nuclear science and engineering.
Purpose: To recognize achievement in public service.
Eligibility: Open to all ANS student branches.
Level of Study: Postgraduate
Type: Award
Value: US$500 and a plaque
Frequency: Annual
Application Procedure: A written report of the branch activities to be sent. See the website for more details.
Closing Date: May 1st

Samuel Untermyer Award

Subjects: Nuclear science.
Purpose: To recognize pioneering work in the development of safe, water-cooled nuclear power reactors.
Level of Study: Postgraduate
Type: Award
Value: US$2,500 and an engraved bronze medal.
Frequency: Annual

Application Procedure: Eight copies of the completed application form and supporting materials must be sent.
Closing Date: March 1st

Theos J. (Tommy) Thompson Award

Subjects: Nuclear Science.
Purpose: To recognize individuals who have made outstanding contributions to the field of nuclear reactor safety.
Eligibility: Open to individuals who have provided outstanding wisdom to key elements of the world nuclear safety activities.
Level of Study: Postgraduate
Type: Award
Value: A plaque and monetary award
Frequency: Annual
Application Procedure: The nominee's name and a written justification are to be submitted. See the website for further information.
Contributor: Nuclear Installation Safety Division (NISD)

U.S. Nuclear Regulatory Commission Master's and Doctoral Fellowship in Science and Engineering

Subjects: Nuclear science and engineering.
Purpose: To support individuals who wish to pursue studies and work in areas requiring highly specialized scientific and technical knowledge and skills.
Eligibility: Open to US citizens.
Level of Study: Doctorate
Type: Fellowship
Value: Monthly stipend, full tuition and fees, and an annual academic allowance
Frequency: Annual
Application Procedure: See the website www.orau.gov/nrced for information.
Closing Date: September 30th

Verne R Dapp Memorial Scholarship

Subjects: Nuclear science or nuclear engineering.
Eligibility: Open to citizens of the United States of America or holders of a permanent resident visa who are full-time graduate students enrolled in a programme leading to an advanced degree.
Level of Study: Graduate
Type: Scholarship
Value: US$3,000
Frequency: Every 2 years
Study Establishment: An accredited institution
Country of Study: United States of America
No. of awards offered: 1
Application Procedure: Applicants must submit a request for an application form that includes the name of the university the candidate will be attending, the year the candidate will be in during the Autumn of the award, the major course of study and a stamped addressed envelope. Completed applications must include a grade transcript and three confidential reference forms. Candidates must be sponsored by an ANS section, division, student branch, committee, member or organization member.
Closing Date: February 1st

Vogt Radiochemistry

Subjects: Student must be enrolled in or proposing to undertake research in radioanalytical chemistry, analytical chemistry, or analytical applications of nuclear science.
Level of Study: Graduate, or undergraduate
Value: US$2,000 if awarded to an undergraduate (Junior/Senior) US$3,000 if awarded to a graduate.
Country of Study: United States of America
No. of awards offered: 1 per year
Closing Date: February 1st
No. of awards given last year: 1

Walter Meyer Scholarship

Subjects: Nuclear physics and engineering.
Eligibility: Open to full-time graduate students in a programme leading to an advanced degree in nuclear science, nuclear engineering or a nuclear-related field. Applicants must be citizens of the United States of America or permanent residents and be enrolled in an accredited institution in the United States of America.
Type: Scholarship
Value: US$3,000
Length of Study: Varies
Frequency: Every 2 years
Study Establishment: An accredited institution
Country of Study: United States of America
No. of awards offered: 1
Application Procedure: Applicants must complete an application form available from, the organization. An official grade transcript and three completed confidential reference forms are also required.
Closing Date: February 1st
Additional Information: Further information is available either on request or from the website.

AMERICAN NUMISMATIC SOCIETY (ANS)

96 Fulton Street, New York, NY 10038,
United States of America
Tel: (1) 212 571 4470
Fax: (1) 212 571 4479
Email: info@amnumsoc.org
Website: www.amnumsoc.org
Contact: Dr Ute Wartenberg Kagan, Executive Director

The mission of the American Numismatic Society (ANS) is to be the pre-eminent national institution advancing the study and appreciation of coins, medals and related objects of all cultures as historical and artistic documents. It aims to do this by maintaining the foremost numismatic collection and library, supporting scholarly research and publications, and sponsoring educational and interpretative programmes for diverse audiences.

Donald Groves Fund

Subjects: Early American numismatics involving material dating no later than 1800.
Purpose: To promote publications in the field.
Level of Study: Research, postgraduate
Value: Varies. Funding is available for travel and other expenses in association with research as well as for publication costs
Frequency: Annual
Country of Study: United States of America
No. of awards offered: Varies
Application Procedure: Applicants must address applications to the Secretary of the Society and must include an outline of the proposed research, the method of accomplishing the research, the funding requested and the specific use to which the funding will be put. Applications will be reviewed periodically by the Donald Groves Fund Committee.
Closing Date: Applications are accepted at any time
Funding: Private

Frances M Schwartz Fellowship

Subjects: Numismatic methodology and museum practice.
Purpose: To assist the Fellow in the study of Greek and Roman fields relevant to the subject.
Eligibility: Open to students of numismatics who possess a Bachelor of Arts or equivalent degree.
Level of Study: Postgraduate, professional development
Type: Fellowship
Value: Up to US$5,000
Frequency: Annual
Country of Study: United States of America
No. of awards offered: Varies
Application Procedure: Applicants must write for details.
Closing Date: March 1st
Funding: Private
Additional Information: Further information is available by emailing metcalf@amnumsoc.org

Grants for ANS Summer Seminar in Numismatics
Subjects: Numismatics.
Purpose: To provide a selected number of graduate students with a deeper understanding of the contribution that this subject makes to other fields.
Eligibility: Open to applicants who have had at least one year's graduate study at a university in the United States of America or Canada and who are students of classical studies, history, near eastern studies or other humanistic fields.
Level of Study: Postgraduate
Type: Grant
Value: US$3,000
Length of Study: 9 weeks during the Summer
Frequency: Annual
Study Establishment: Museum of the American Numismatic Society
Country of Study: United States of America
No. of awards offered: Approx. 10
Application Procedure: Applicants must write well in advance for details of the application process.
Closing Date: March 1st
Funding: Private
No. of awards given last year: 12
No. of applicants last year: 21
Additional Information: One or two students from overseas are usually accepted to the seminar but will not receive a grant.

AMERICAN OCCUPATIONAL THERAPY FOUNDATION (AOTF)

4720 Montgomery Lane, PO Box 31220, Bethesda, MD 20824-1220, United States of America
Tel: (1) 301 652 6611
Fax: (1) 301 656 3620
Email: aotf@aotf.org
Website: www.aotf.org

The AOTF is a charitable, non-profit organization created in 1965 to advance the science of occupational therapy and increase public understanding of its value.

The A. Jean Ayres Award
Subjects: Occupational therapy.
Purpose: To recognize occupational therapy clinicians, educators and researchers who have made significant contributions to their profession.
Eligibility: Open to candidates who are members of the American Occupational Therapy Association.
Level of Study: Doctorate
Type: Award
Value: US$500, a plaque and acknowledgement at the Annual conference of the American Occupational Therapy Association
Frequency: Annual
No. of awards offered: 2
Application Procedure: Five copies of the nomination package must be sent to the chairman of the AOTF Awards of Recognition Committee.
Contributor: American Occupational Therapy Foundation

The Adelaide Ryerson Smith Memorial Award
Subjects: Occupational therapy.
Eligibility: Open to applicants who are members of the Arizona Occupational Therapy Association.
Level of Study: Postgraduate
Type: Scholarship
Value: US$1,000
Frequency: Annual
Study Establishment: Any accredited occupational therapy educational programme
Country of Study: United States of America
Application Procedure: A completed application form and all official transcripts must be submitted.
Closing Date: January 15th

AOTF Certificate of Appreciation
Subjects: Occupational therapy.
Purpose: To recognize outstanding service toward the Foundation.
Eligibility: Open to any individual, agency, business or other institutions.
Level of Study: Doctorate, postgraduate
Type: Award
Value: A certificate of appreciation and acknowledgement at the annual conference
Frequency: Annual
Application Procedure: Four copies of a letter of nomination and candidate's curriculum vitae must be sent.
Funding: Foundation
Contributor: American Occupational Therapy Foundation

The Chris Ebbers Scholarship
Subjects: Occupational therapy.
Eligibility: Open to candidates who are residents of South Carolina.
Level of Study: Postgraduate
Type: Scholarship
Value: US$750
Frequency: Annual
Study Establishment: Any accredited occupation therapy programme in South Carolina
Country of Study: United States of America
Application Procedure: See the website.

The Florence Wood Scholarship
Subjects: Occupational therapy.
Eligibility: Open to applicants who are Arkansas residents enrolled in an occupational therapy programme in Arkansas.
Level of Study: Postgraduate
Type: Scholarship
Value: US$500
Frequency: Annual
Study Establishment: Any accredited occupational therapy programme in Arkansas
Country of Study: United States of America
Application Procedure: Application forms and details are available online at www.aotf.org
Closing Date: January 15th
Contributor: Arkansas Occupational Therapy Association

For further information contact:

AROTA, PO Box 22082, Liute Rock, AR 72221
Contact: Kathryn White

The Karen Jacobs Scholarship
Subjects: Occupational therapy.
Eligibility: Open to applicants who are residents of Massachusetts who are enrolled in an occupational therapy educational programme in New England.
Level of Study: Postgraduate
Type: Scholarship
Value: US$500
Frequency: Annual
Study Establishment: Any accredited occupational therapy programme in Massachusetts
Country of Study: United States of America
No. of awards offered: 1
Application Procedure: See the website.

The Mary Eileem Dixey Scholarship
Subjects: Occupational therapy.
Eligibility: Open to candidates who are residents of New Hampshire.
Type: Scholarship
Value: US$2,000
Frequency: Annual
Study Establishment: Any authorized occupational therapy programme in New Hampshire
Country of Study: United States of America
No. of awards offered: 1
Application Procedure: See the website.

AMERICAN ORCHID SOCIETY

16700 AOS Lane, Delray Beach,
West Palm Beach, FL, 33446-4351,
United States of America
Tel: (1) 561 404 2000
Fax: (1) 561 404 2100
Email: theaos@aos.org
Website: www.aos.org
Contact: Ms Pamela Giust, Awards Registrar

Grants for Orchid Research

Subjects: Orchid research.
Purpose: To advance scientific study of orchids in every respect and to assist in the publication of scholarly and popular scientific literature on orchids.
Eligibility: There are no eligibility restrictions.
Level of Study: Postgraduate
Type: Grant
Value: US$500–12,000
Length of Study: Up to 3 years
Country of Study: Any country
No. of awards offered: Varies
Application Procedure: Applicants must write for guidelines.
Closing Date: January 1st and July 1st

AMERICAN ORIENTAL SOCIETY

Hatcher Graduate Library, University of Michigan,
Ann Arbor, MI, 48109-1205,
United States of America
Tel: (1) (734) 647-4760
Fax: (1) (734) 763-6743
Email: jrodgers@umich.edu
Website: www.umich.edu/~aos
Contact: Grants Management Officer

The American Oriental Society is primarily concerned with the encouragement of basic research in the languages and literatures of Asia.

Louise Wallace Hackney Fellowship

Subjects: Chinese art, with special relation to painting, and the translation into English of works on the subject.
Purpose: To remind scholars that Chinese art, like all art, is not a disembodied creation, but the outgrowth of the life and culture from which it has sprung. It is requested that scholars give special attention to this approach in their study.
Eligibility: Open to United States citizens who are doctoral or post-doctoral students and have successfully completed at least three years of Chinese language study at a recognized university, and have some knowledge or training in art. In no case shall a fellowship be awarded to Scholars of well-recognized standing, but shall be given to either men or women who show aptitude or promise in the said field of learning.
Level of Study: Postdoctorate
Type: Fellowship
Value: US$8,000
Length of Study: 1 year
Frequency: Annual
Study Establishment: Any institution where paintings and adequate language guidance is available
Country of Study: Any country
No. of awards offered: 1
Application Procedure: Applicants must submit the following materials in duplicate: a transcript of their undergraduate and graduate course work, a statement of personal finances, a four page summary of the proposed project to be undertaken including details of expense, and no less than three letters of recommendation.
Closing Date: March 1st
Funding: Private
Additional Information: It is possible to apply for a renewal of the fellowship, but this may not be done in consecutive years.

AMERICAN OTOLOGICAL SOCIETY (AOS)

2720 Tartan Way, Springfield, IL 62711,
United States of America
Tel: (1) 483 6966
Fax: (1) 483 6966
Email: segossard@aol.com
Website: www.itsa.ucsf.edu
Contact: Ms Shirley Gossard, Administrative Office

The AOS is a society focused upon aural medicine.
The society's mission is to advance and promote medical and surgical otology, encouraging research in the related disciplines.

American Otological Society Research Grants

Subjects: All aspects of otosclerosis, Meniere's disease and related disorders.
Eligibility: Open to physicians and doctorate level investigators.
Level of Study: Postdoctorate, postgraduate
Type: Research grant
Value: Up to US$55,000 per year. No funding is provided for the investigator's salary
Length of Study: 1 year, renewable
Frequency: Annual
Country of Study: United States of America or Canada
No. of awards offered: Varies
Closing Date: January 31st
Funding: Private
No. of awards given last year: 3
No. of applicants last year: 10

For further information contact:

University of California, San Diego 200 W. Arbor Drive, 8895, California, San Diego, 92103–8895, United States of America
Tel: (1) 543–7896
Fax: (1) 543–5521
Contact: Harris Jeffrey P., Research Fund of the American Otologic Society, Inc. Professor and Chairman

American Otological Society Research Training Fellowships

Subjects: All aspects of otosclerosis, Meniere's disease and related disorders.
Purpose: To support research.
Eligibility: Open to physicians, residents and medical students in the United States of America and Canada.
Level of Study: Postgraduate
Type: Fellowship
Value: Up to US$40,000 depending on position and institutional norms
Length of Study: 1–2 years
Frequency: Annual
Country of Study: United States of America or Canada
No. of awards offered: Varies
Closing Date: January 31st
No. of awards given last year: 1
No. of applicants last year: 1
Additional Information: The organization requires institutional documentation that facilities and faculty are appropriate for the requested research.

For further information contact:

University of California, San Diego 200 W. Arbor Drive, 8895, California, San Diego, 92103-8895, United States of America
Tel: (1) 543-7896
Fax: (1) 543-5521
Contact: Harris Jeffrey P., Research Fund of the American Otologic Society, Inc. Professor and Chairman

AMERICAN PHILOSOPHICAL SOCIETY

104 South Fifth Street, Philadelphia, PA, 19106-3387,
United States of America
Tel: (1) 440 3400
Fax: (1) 440 3423
Website: www.amphilsoc.org
Contact: Eleanor Roach, Research Administrator

The American Philosophical Society is an eminent scholarly organization of international reputation, and promotes useful knowledge in the sciences and humanities through excellence in scholarly research, professional meetings, publications, library resources and community outreach.

Daland Fellowships in Clinical Investigation

Subjects: Medicine, neurology, paediatrics, psychiatry and surgery.
Purpose: To award a limited number of fellowships for research in clinical medicine including the fields of internal medicine, neurology, paediatrics, psychiatry and surgery. For the purposes of this award, the committee emphasizes patient-orientated research.
Eligibility: Candidates are expected to have held the MD degree for less than 8 years. The fellowship is intended to be the first postclinical fellowship, but each case will be decided on its merits. Preference is given to candidates who have less than 2 years of postdoctoral training. Applicants must expect to perform their research at an institution in the United States of America, under the supervision of a scientific adviser.
Level of Study: Research
Type: Fellowship
Value: US$50,000 each for the first and second year
Length of Study: 1 year, with renewal for a further year if satisfactory progress is demonstrated.
Frequency: Annual
Application Procedure: Applicants must complete an application form. Information and forms are available from the website. If electronic access is denied, forms can be requested by mail and must indicate when the MD degree was awarded. Candidates must be nominated by their department chairman in a letter providing assurance that the nominee will work with the guidance of a scientific adviser of established reputation who has guaranteed adequate space, supplies, etc. for the Fellow. The adviser need not be a member of the department nominating the Fellow, nor need the activities of the Fellow be limited to the nominating department. As a general rule, no more than one fellowship will be awarded to a given institution in the same year of competition. Application forms must be sent to the Daland Fellowship Committee.
Closing Date: September 1st
Funding: Private
No. of awards given last year: 2
No. of applicants last year: 20

Franklin Research Grant Program

Subjects: Scholarly research: as the term is used here, covers most kinds of scholarly inquiry by individuals leading to publication. It does not include journalistic or other writing for general readership, the preparation of textbooks, case books, anthologies or other materials for use by students or the work of creative and performing artists.
Purpose: To contribute towards the cost of scholarly research in all areas of knowledge, except those in which support by government or corporate enterprise is more appropriate.
Eligibility: Applicants are normally expected to have a doctorate, but applications are considered from persons whose publications display equivalent scholarly achievement. Grants are rarely made to persons who have held the doctorate less than a year, and never for predoctoral study or research. It is the Society's long standing practice to encourage younger scholars. The Committee will seldom approve more than two grants to the same person within any 5-year period. Applicants may be residents of the United States of America, citizens of the United States of America on the staffs of foreign institutions or foreign nationals whose research can only be carried out in the United States of America. Institutions are not eligible to apply. Applicants expecting to conduct interviews in a foreign language must possess sufficient competence in that language, and must be able to read and translate all source materials.
Level of Study: Research
Type: Grant
Value: The maximum grant is US$6,000. The budget year corresponds to the calendar year, not the academic year. If an applicant receives an award for the same project from another granting institution, the Society will consider limiting its award to costs that are not covered by the other grant
Frequency: Annual
Country of Study: United States of America
Application Procedure: Applicants must complete an application form. Information and forms are available from the website. If electronic access is denied, forms can be requested by mail. These must indicate the eligibility of both applicant and project, state the nature of the research, eg. laboratory, archival or fieldwork and proposed use of the grant, eg. travel or purchase of microfilm. Foreign nationals must specify the objects of their research, only available in the United States of America, eg. indigenous plants, archival materials or architectural sites. A stamped addressed envelope should also be included. If forms are downloaded from the website, applicants must ensure that the page format is maintained and must print enough copies of the form for the letters of support.
Closing Date: October 1st and December 1st
Funding: Private
Additional Information: If an award is made and accepted, the recipient is required to provide the Society with a 250-word report on the research accomplished during the tenure of the grant, and a one-page financial statement.

Library Resident Research Fellowships

Subjects: Library collections research.
Purpose: To support research in the American Philosophical Society library's collections.
Eligibility: Scholars who reside beyond a 75-mile radius of Philadelphia. The fellowships are open to both citizens of the United States of America and foreign nationals who are holders of a PhD or equivalent, PhD candidates who have passed their preliminary exams and independent scholars. Applicants in any relevant field of scholarship may apply.
Level of Study: Research
Type: Fellowship
Value: US$2,000 per month
Length of Study: 1–3 months
Frequency: Annual
Application Procedure: Applicants must complete an application form. A complete application includes all information requested on the form, a project statement, the applicant's curriculum vitae and two letters of support; if the applicant is a graduate student, one of the letters must be from the dissertation supervisor. The project statement should briefly describe the project and how it relates to existing scholarship, state the specific relevance of the American Philosophical Society's collections to the project, and indicate expected results of the research, such as publications.
Closing Date: March 1st for a decision by May
Funding: Private
No. of awards given last year: 23
No. of applicants last year: 90
Additional Information: Published guides to the Society's collections are available in most research libraries. Applicants are strongly encouraged to consult the library staff by mail or phone regarding the collections. A list of these guides and further information can be found on the website or by contacting the American Philosophical Society Library.

Phillips Fund Grants for Native American Research

Subjects: Native American linguistics and ethnohistory, and the history of the study of Native Americans in the continental United States of America and Canada.
Purpose: To financially support research.
Eligibility: Open to graduate students who have passed their qualifying examinations for either the Master's or doctoral degrees. Postdoctoral applicants are eligible.

Level of Study: Research
Value: The average award is approx. US$2,000 and grants rarely exceed US$3,000. This is to cover travel, tapes and informants' fees and is not for general maintenance or the purchase of permanent equipment
Length of Study: 1 year
Frequency: Annual
Application Procedure: Applicants must complete an application form. A complete application includes all information requested on the form, the correct number of copies and three confidential letters supporting the application. It is the applicant's responsibility to ensure that all materials reach the Society on time. Information and forms are available from the website. If electronic access is denied, forms can be requested by mail. These must indicate eligibility of both applicant and project, and state whether the field of research is linguistics or ethnohistory. Applications should be addressed to Phillips Fund for Native American Research at the main address.
Closing Date: March 1st
Funding: Private
Additional Information: If an award is made and accepted, the recipient is required to provide the Society's Library with a brief formal report and copies of any tape recordings, transcriptions, microfilms, etc., that may be acquired in the process of the grant-funded research, and a release for scholarly use.

Sabbatical Fellowship for the Humanities and Social Sciences

Subjects: Humanities and social sciences.
Purpose: To support the second half of an awarded sabbatical year.
Eligibility: Open to mid-career faculty of universities and 4-year colleges in the United States of America who have been granted a sabbatical or research year, but for whom financial support from the parent institution is available for only the first half of the year. Candidates must not have had a financially supported leave during the 3 years prior to date of application. At the discretion of the review panels, the fellowship may be used to supplement another external award of similar purpose. The total external support cannot exceed the half-year salary. The Society encourages candidates to use the resources of the American Philosophical Society Library, but this is not a requirement of the fellowship. There is no restriction on where the Fellow resides during the fellowship year, but an indication of the appropriateness of the available library resources should be given.The PhD must have been awarded no fewer than 7 and no more than 2–3 years prior to the date of application.
Level of Study: Research
Type: Award
Value: US$30,000–40,000
Length of Study: Tenure of the fellowship is for the second half of the academic year
Frequency: Annual
Application Procedure: Applicants must submit an application form. Information and forms are available from the website. If electronic access is denied, applicants can request forms by mail, but must be sure to state the date that their PhD was awarded, the end date of the last financially supported leave and beginning date of sabbatical.
Closing Date: October 15th
Funding: Private
No. of awards given last year: 20
No. of applicants last year: More than 250

AMERICAN PHYSIOLOGICAL SOCIETY (APS)

9650 Rockville Pike, Bethesda, MD, 20814-3991, United States of America
Tel: (1) 301 634 7118
Fax: (1) 301 634 7241
Email: info@the-aps.org
Website: www.the-aps.org
Contact: Ms Linda Jean Dresser, Executive Assistant

The American Physiological Society (APS) is a non-profit scientific society devoted to fostering education, scientific research and the dissemination of information in the physiological sciences. By providing a spectrum of physiological information, the Society strives to play a role in the progress of science and the advancement of knowledge. The Society has integrated a prestigious award programme providing funding to outstanding APS members, young investigators and scientists in need of funding to continue their research in physiology. Through its functions and activities, the Society plays an important role in the progress of science and the advancement of knowledge. The Society maintains staff and offices on the campus of the Federation of American Societies for Experimental Biology (FASEB) in Bethesda, Maryland.

APS Conference Student Award

Subjects: Biology and physiology.
Purpose: To encourage the participation of young scientists in training at the APS conferences.
Eligibility: Open to graduate students wishing to present a contributed paper at an APS conference.
Level of Study: Graduate
Type: Award
Value: Cash award and complimentary conference registration
Length of Study: The duration of the conference
Frequency: Dependent upon meetings scheduled
Study Establishment: Any APS conference
Country of Study: United States of America
No. of awards offered: Varies
Application Procedure: Applicants must submit an abstract to the APS. Candidates must indicate on the abstract page a desire to be considered for the award and should contact the APS for further details.
Closing Date: Please write for details

APS Mass Media Science and Engineering Fellowship

Subjects: Physiology or any related subject.
Purpose: To enable promising young scientists to work in the newsroom of a newspaper, magazine, radio or television station, sharpening their ability to communicate complex scientific issues to non-scientists and helping to improve public understanding of science.
Eligibility: Open to graduate or postgraduate students of physiology, or a related subject, preferably with a background in scientific writing.
Level of Study: Graduate, postgraduate
Type: Studentship
Value: Subsistence and travel costs
Length of Study: 10 weeks
Frequency: Annual
Study Establishment: The newsroom of a newspaper, magazine or radio or television station
Country of Study: United States of America
No. of awards offered: 1
Application Procedure: Applicants must complete an application form, available from Alice Ra'anan, Public Affairs Office, American Physiological Society.
Closing Date: January 15th
No. of awards given last year: 1

APS Minority Travel Fellowship Awards

Subjects: Biology and physiology.
Purpose: To increase the participation of predoctoral and postdoctoral minority students in the physiological sciences.
Eligibility: Open to advanced predoctoral and postdoctoral students. Students in the APS Porter Physiology Development programme are also eligible. Minority faculty members at MBRS and MARC eligible institutions may also submit applications.
Level of Study: Postdoctorate, predoctorate
Type: Travel grant
Value: Funds for travel to attend either the Experimental Biology meeting or one of the APS conferences
Length of Study: The duration of the conference or meeting
Country of Study: United States of America
No. of awards offered: Varies

Application Procedure: Applicants must contact the Education Office of the APS for further details.
Closing Date: Please write for details
Contributor: NIDDK and NIGMS

Caroline tum Suden/Frances Hellebrandt Professional Opportunity Awards

Subjects: Biology and physiology.
Purpose: To provide funds for junior physiologists to attend and fully participate in the Experimental Biology meeting.
Eligibility: Open to graduate students or postdoctoral Fellows who are APS members or sponsored by an APS member.
Level of Study: Postdoctorate, graduate
Type: Award
Value: US$500 per award, complimentary registration for the meeting
Length of Study: The duration of the conference
Frequency: Annual
Study Establishment: An APS Experimental Biology meeting
Country of Study: United States of America
No. of awards offered: 36
Application Procedure: Applicants must submit an abstract to APS and should contact the Education Office for further details.
Closing Date: Please write for details
No. of awards given last year: 36
Additional Information: Recipients are obliged to attend the Experimental Biology meeting and present a paper.

Procter and Gamble Professional Opportunity Awards

Subjects: Biology and physiology.
Purpose: To provide funds to predoctoral students allowing them to fully participate in the Experimental Biology meeting.
Eligibility: Open to predoctoral students who are within 1–1.5 years of completing a PhD degree and wish to present a paper at the meeting. Applicants must be student members of the APS or have an adviser or a supporting sponsor who is an APS member.
Level of Study: Predoctorate
Type: Award
Value: US$500 per award and complementary registration for the Experimental Biology meeting
Length of Study: The duration of the conference
Frequency: Annual
Study Establishment: The APS Experimental Biology meeting
Country of Study: United States of America
No. of awards offered: Varies
Application Procedure: Applicants must submit an abstract to APS and should contact the Education Office for further details.
Closing Date: Please write for details
No. of awards given last year: 9

William T Porter Fellowship Award

Subjects: Biology and physiology.
Purpose: To support the training of talented students entering careers in physiology by providing predoctoral fellowships for underrepresented students (African Americans, Hispanics, Native Americans, Native Alaskans and Native Pacific Islanders).
Eligibility: Open to underrepresented ethnic minority applicants, ie. African Americans, Hispanics, Native Americans, Native Alaskans or Native Pacific Islanders who are citizens or permanent residents of the United States of America or its territories.
Level of Study: Graduate, postdoctorate, predoctorate
Type: Fellowship
Value: US$18,000 annual stipend
Length of Study: Varies
Frequency: Annual
Study Establishment: Universities or research establishments
Country of Study: United States of America
No. of awards offered: Varies
Application Procedure: Applicants must contact the Education Office of the APS for further details.
Closing Date: January 15th and June 15th
No. of applicants last year: Varies

AMERICAN POLITICAL SCIENCE ASSOCIATION (APSA)

1527 New Hampshire Avenue, North West Zip-1206,
Washington, DC 20036,
United States of America
Tel: (1) 202 483 2512
Fax: (1) 202 483 2657
Email: apsa@apsanet.org
Website: www.apsanet.org

Founded in 1903, the American Political Science Association (APSA) is the leading professional organization for the study of political science and serves more than 15,000 members in over 80 countries. With a range of programmers and services for individuals, departments and institutions, APSA brings together political scientists from all fields of inquiry, regions and occupational endeavours within and outside academia in order to expand awareness and understanding of politics.

APSA Congressional Fellowship Program (Journalists)

Subjects: Politics, government.
Purpose: To expand knowledge and awareness of the United States of America Congress through direct participation.
Eligibility: Applicant must be a citizen of the United States of America or a permanent resident and hold a Bachelor's degree. Print journalists must have 2–10 years of continuous, full-time professional experience with a newspaper or magazine at the time of application, and a background in reporting or editing. Broadcast journalists must have 2–10 years of continuous, full-time professional experience in radio or television and a background in reporting, producing, directing or writing.
Level of Study: Doctorate
Type: Fellowship
Value: US$38,000
Frequency: Annual
Country of Study: United States of America
Application Procedure: There are no application forms. Applicants must submit seven envelopes containing the following: a detailed resume; a 500-word personal statement explaining how the Congressional Fellowship relates to their professional goals; contact information for three professional references; three letters of recommendation and five clips of best writing (print journalists) or reporting (broadcast journalists).
Closing Date: November 1st
Funding: Foundation

APSA Congressional Fellowship Program (Political Scientists)

Subjects: Politics, government.
Purpose: To expand knowledge and awareness of the United States of America congress through direct participation.
Eligibility: Applicant must be a citizen of the United States of America or have a permanent citizen status classification, must have a PhD completed within 15 years or a dissertation near completion and a scholarly interest in Congress and the policy making process.
Level of Study: Doctorate
Type: Fellowship
Length of Study: US$38,000
Frequency: Annual
Country of Study: United States of America
Application Procedure: There are no application forms. The applicant must submit seven packets containing the following: a detailed resume; a personal statement explaining how the Congressional Fellowship relates to the applicant's professional goals; the names and contact information for three professional references and a complete sample of the applicant's best work.
Closing Date: November 1st
Funding: Foundation
Additional Information: For detailed information visit the website or write to the association.

APSA Congressional Fellowship Program for Political Scientists

Subjects: Legislative process.
Purpose: To allow participants to learn about the field through direct participation.
Eligibility: Open to mid career political scientists with a PhD completed within the past 15 years or near completion who can show scholarly interest in Congress and the policy making process. Minorities are encouraged to apply.
Level of Study: Postdoctorate
Type: Fellowship
Value: A stipend of US$38,000, plus a small travel allowance
Length of Study: 10 months
Frequency: Annual
Country of Study: United States of America
No. of awards offered: Varies
Application Procedure: Applicants must contact APSA for details. All information is available from the website.
Closing Date: November 1st
Funding: Private

APSA Congressional Fellowships for Journalists

Subjects: Legislative process.
Purpose: To allow participants to learn more about the field through direct participation.
Eligibility: Open to mid career professionals with a Bachelor's degree and an interest in Congress. Preference is given to candidates with a background in political reporting but without extensive experience in Washington. Candidates should have an absolute minimum of two years of full-time professional level experience in newspaper, magazine, radio or television reporting at the time of application. Candidates with more than 10 years of experience will not be considered.
Level of Study: Professional development
Type: Fellowship
Value: US$38,000
Length of Study: 10 months
Frequency: Annual
Country of Study: United States of America
No. of awards offered: Varies
Application Procedure: Applicants must visit the website for further information.
Closing Date: November 1st
Funding: Private
Additional Information: Applicants not currently living in the United States must be able to fund their own transportation for an interview should they be selected as finalists.

Edward S. Corwin Award

Subjects: Public Law.
Level of Study: Postgraduate
Type: Grant
Value: US$750
Frequency: Annual
No. of awards offered: Varies
Application Procedure: Contact award committee.
No. of awards given last year: 1

For further information contact:

University of Georgia, Political Science, Baldwin Hall, Room 306A, Athens, 9A 30602
Contact: Jeff Yates

Frank Goodnow Award

Subjects: Teaching politics.
Purpose: To honour service to the community of teachers.
Level of Study: Professional development
Type: Grant
Frequency: Annual
Application Procedure: Apply to the APSA direct.
Closing Date: January 15th
Funding: Foundation
Contributor: American Political Science Association

Gabriel A. Almond Award

Subjects: Theory in comparative politics.
Level of Study: Postgraduate
Type: Grant
Value: US$750
Frequency: Annual
Country of Study: United States of America
No. of awards offered: 1
Application Procedure: Contact award committee.

For further information contact:

Ohio State University, Political Science, 2140 Dorby Hall, Columbus, OH 43210
Contact: Timathy Frey

Harold D. Laswell Award

Subjects: Public policy.
Level of Study: Postgraduate
Type: Grant
Value: US$1,000
Frequency: Annual
No. of awards offered: 1
Application Procedure: Contact award committee.
Funding: Foundation
Contributor: Political Studies Organization
No. of awards given last year: 1

For further information contact:

University of California, Berkeley, Political Science, Barows Hall, 210, Berkeley, MC 1950, CA 94720-1950
Contact: J. Nicholas Ziegler

Ithiel de Sola Pool Award

Subjects: Political theory, political behaviour, political communication, science and technology policy, and international affairs.
Purpose: To explore the implications of research on issues of policies.
Level of Study: Professional development
Type: Grant
Frequency: Every 3 years
No. of awards offered: 1
Application Procedure: Contact APSA.
No. of awards given last year: 2

John Gaus Award

Subjects: Political science and public administration.
Purpose: To reward exemplary scholarship.
Level of Study: Professional development
Type: Grant
Value: US$1,500
Frequency: Annual
No. of awards offered: 1
Application Procedure: Contact award committee.
No. of awards given last year: 1

For further information contact:

George Washington University, School of Public Policy, 805 21st Street, Washington, NW, Suite 601, DC 20052-0001, United States of America
Contact: Kathryn Newcomer

Ralph J Bunche Award

Subjects: Political science.
Purpose: To help talented minority students.
Eligibility: Open to African American Latinola, and American students.
Level of Study: Postgraduate
Type: Grant
Value: All tuition fees
Length of Study: 5 weeks
Frequency: Annual
Study Establishment: Ralphe Bunche Summer Institute

Country of Study: United States of America
No. of awards offered: 20
Application Procedure: Apply online.
Closing Date: February 15th

William Anderson Award

Subjects: Local government, public administration and intergovernmental relations.
Level of Study: Postgraduate
Type: Grant
Value: US$750
Frequency: Annual
Country of Study: United States of America
No. of awards offered: 1

AMERICAN PSYCHOLOGICAL ASSOCIATION (APA)

Minority Fellowships Program (MFP), 750 First Street North East, Washington, DC, 20002-4242, United States of America
Tel: (1) 202 336 6127
Fax: (1) 202 336 6012
Email: mfp@apa.org
Website: www.apa.org/mfp
Contact: Administrative Assistant

The American Psychological Association Minority Fellowships Program's (APA/MFP) objective is to increase the knowledge of issues related to ethnic minority mental health and to improve the quality of mental health and substance abuse treatment delivered to ethnic minority populations as consistent with Healthy People 2010, the Surgeon General's report on mental health, and other federal initiatives to reduce health disparities. This is done by providing financial support and professional guidance to individuals pursuing doctoral degrees in psychology and neuroscience.

Diversity Program in Neuroscience Doctoral Fellowship

Subjects: Behavioural neuroscience, cellular neurobiology, cognitive neuroscience, computational neuroscience, developmental neurobiology, membrane biophysics, molecular neurobiology, neuroanatomy, neurobiology, neurobiology of ageing, neurobiology of disease, neurochemistry, neurogenetics, neuroimmunology, neuropathology, neuropharmacology, neurophysiology, neurotoxicology or systems neuroscience.
Purpose: To increase the representation of underrepresented ethnic minorities in neuroscience as well as to increase the pool of researchers and teachers whose work focuses on ethnic minority persons and issues.
Eligibility: Applicants must be citizens of the United States of America or permanent residents who are enrolled full-time in a doctoral programme. An important goal of the programme is to increase the representation of Black or African American, Alaskan Native, American Indian, Asian American, Hispanic or Latino and Pacific Islander students within neuroscience. However, the programme welcomes applications from all students, especially those interested in increasing the representation of underrepresented ethnic minorities in neuroscience as well as in increasing the pool of researchers and teachers in the field.
Level of Study: Doctorate
Type: Fellowship
Frequency: Annual
Country of Study: United States of America
Application Procedure: Applicants must submit a completed application, essay, references, transcripts, and Graduate Record Examination scores. Further information and application forms are available on request.
Closing Date: January 15th
Funding: Government
Contributor: National Institute of Mental Health

Diversity Program in Neuroscience Postdoctoral Fellowship

Subjects: Behavioural neuroscience, cellular neurobiology, cognitive neuroscience, computational neuroscience, developmental neurobiology, membrane biophysics, molecular neurobiology, neuroanatomy, neurobiology of ageing, neurobiology of disease, neurochemistry, neurogenetics, neuroimmunology, neuropathology, neuropharmacology, neurophysiology, neurotoxicology or systems neuroscience.
Purpose: To increase the number of ethnic minorities in neuroscience who conduct research in areas of importance to the National Institute of Mental Health.
Eligibility: Open to citizens or permanent residents of the United States of America with a PhD or MD degree and prior graduate training in neuroscience or in other basic sciences.
Level of Study: Postdoctorate, predoctorate
Type: Fellowship
Frequency: Annual
Application Procedure: Applicants must visit the website.
Closing Date: January 15th
Additional Information: Benefits include travel funds to visit universities being considered for postdoctoral training, travel funds to attend the Society for Neuroscience's annual meeting and opportunities for mentoring and networking with neuroscientists.

MFP Mental Health and Substance Abuse Services Doctoral Fellowship

Subjects: Clinical, counselling and school psychology.
Purpose: To improve the quality of mental health treatment and research on issues of concern to ethnic minority populations by providing financial support and professional guidance to individuals pursuing doctoral degrees in psychology and by increasing the knowledge of issues related to ethnic minority health.
Eligibility: Applicants must be citizens or permanent residents of the United States of America enrolled full-time in an APA-accredited doctoral programme at the time the fellowship is awarded. An additional factor among the many considered is the applicant's ethnic minority group including, but not limited to, Blacks or African Americans, Alaskan Natives, American Indians, Asian Americans, Hispanics or Latinos and Pacific Islanders, and/or those who can demonstrate commitment to a career in psychology related to ethnic minority health.
Level of Study: Doctorate
Type: Fellowship
Frequency: Annual
Country of Study: Any country
Application Procedure: Applicants must submit a completed application, essay, references, transcripts and Graduate Record Examination scores. Further information and application forms are available on request.
Closing Date: January 15th
Funding: Government
Contributor: The Substance Abuse and Mental Health Administration

AMERICAN PUBLIC POWER ASSOCIATION (APPA)

2301 M Street North West, Suite 300, Washington, DC 20037, United States of America
Tel: (1) 202 467 2900
Fax: (1) 202 467 2910
Email: mrufe@appanet.org
Website: www.appanet.org/DEED
Contact: Ms Michelle Ghosh, DEED Administrator

The APPA is the service organization for the nation' s more than 2,000 community-owned electric utilities that serve more than 43 million Americans. Its purpose is to advance the public policy interests of its members and their consumers, and provide member services to ensure adequate, reliable electricity at a reasonable price with the proper protection of the environment.

DEED (Demonstration of Energy-Efficient Developments) Student Research Grant/Internship

Subjects: Engineering, mathematics or computer science.
Purpose: To promote the involvement of students studying in energy related disciplines in the public power industry and to increase awareness of career opportunities in public power.
Eligibility: Open to students studying in energy-related disciplines.
Level of Study: Postdoctorate, graduate, doctorate, postgraduate
Type: Grant
Value: US$4,000
Frequency: Annual
Country of Study: United States of America
No. of awards offered: 10
Application Procedure: Applications must be completed, sponsored and submitted by a DEED member utility, with the required signatures. An official transcript must accompany the application or be sent separately to the attention of the DEED administrator by the deadline. A second copy of the application must be sent to the local DEED Board regional director. A listing of addresses for these are available on the website.
Closing Date: February 15th and August 15th
Funding: Private
No. of awards given last year: 10
Additional Information: Currently only the United States of America has DEED members. Applicants should visit the website for a listing of members.

AMERICAN RESEARCH CENTER IN EGYPT (ARCE)

Emory Briarcliff Campus, 1256 Briarcliff Road North East, Building A, Suite 423W, Atlanta, GA, 30306, United States of America
Tel: (1) 404 712 9854
Fax: (1) 404 712 9849
Email: arce@emory.edu
Website: www.arce.org
Contact: Dr Susanne Thomas, Co-ordinator

The American Research Center in Egypt (ARCE) is the professional society in the United States of America for specialists on all periods of Egypt's cultural history. It is also a consortium of universities and museums that supports archaeological and academic research in Egypt via fellowships, and whose membership is open to the public.

ARCE Fellowships

Subjects: Arts and humanities, Near East studies and humanistic social sciences.
Purpose: To support research in Egypt.
Eligibility: Open to citizens of the United States of America who are predoctoral candidates. Postdoctoral candidates should be nationals of the United States of America or foreign nationals who have been teaching at an American university for 3 years or more.
Level of Study: Doctorate, postdoctorate, museum curators
Type: Fellowship
Value: Varies
Length of Study: 3 months–1 year
Frequency: Annual
Study Establishment: ARCE
Country of Study: Egypt
No. of awards offered: 10–17
Application Procedure: Applicants must write for materials or download them from the website.
Closing Date: January 5th
Funding: Government
No. of awards given last year: 17
No. of applicants last year: 31

AMERICAN RESEARCH INSTITUTE IN TURKEY (ARIT)

University of Pennsylvania Museum, 3260 South Street, Philadelphia, Pennsylvania, PA 19104-6324, United States of America
Tel: (1) 215 898 3474
Fax: (1) 215 898 0657
Email: leinwand@sas.upenn.edu
Website: www.ccat.sas.upenn.edu/ARIT
Contact: Administrative Assistant

The American Research Institute in Turkey's (ARIT) main aim is to support scholarly research in all fields of the humanities and social sciences in Turkey through administering fellowship programmes at the doctoral and postdoctoral level and through maintaining research centres in Ankara and Istanbul.

ARIT Humanities and Social Sciences Fellowships

Subjects: All fields of the humanities and social sciences.
Purpose: To encourage research on Turkey in ancient, medieval and modern times.
Eligibility: Open to scholars and advanced graduate students engaged in research in the field. Student applicants must have fulfilled all requirements for the doctorate except the dissertation. Applicants must be citizens of the United States of America and/or be members in good standing of educational institutions in the United States of America or Canada. While grants for tenures of up to 1 year will be considered, some preference is given to projects of shorter duration.
Level of Study: Doctorate, postdoctorate
Type: Fellowship
Value: Varies, depending on the length of the study period
Length of Study: 1 year, though preference is given to shorter periods of study
Frequency: Annual
Study Establishment: Either of ARIT's two research establishments in Ankara or Istanbul
Country of Study: Turkey
Application Procedure: Applicants must submit six copies of an original application. Student applicants must provide a copy of their graduate transcript.
Closing Date: November 15th
Funding: Private, government
Contributor: The United States Information Agency (USIA)
Additional Information: Hostel, research and study facilities are available at ARIT's branch centres in Istanbul and Ankara.

ARIT-Bosphorus University Language Fellowships

Subjects: Turkish language.
Purpose: To provide students with an opportunity of studying advanced Turkish language.
Eligibility: Open to graduate students enrolled in a degree programme or postdoctoral students. Applicants must be citizens or permanent residents of the United States of America and have at least 2 years of college-level Turkish language study or its equivalent.
Level of Study: Postgraduate
Type: Fellowship
Value: Tuition, travel and a maintenance stipend of varying amounts
Frequency: Annual
Study Establishment: Bosphorus University, Istanbul
Country of Study: Turkey
Application Procedure: Applicants must submit an application form, statement and references.
Funding: Government, private

ARIT-National Endowment for the Humanities Advanced Fellowships for Research in Turkey

Subjects: All subjects of the humanities and interdisciplinary approaches to art, archaeology, language and history.
Purpose: To support research on ancient, medieval or modern times.

Eligibility: Open to scholars who hold a PhD or who have completed their professional training. Applicants are expected to have an affiliation with educational institutions in the United States of America or Canada and must be either citizens of the United States of America or have resided in the United States of America for 3 years.
Level of Study: Professional development, postdoctorate
Type: Fellowship
Value: Stipends generally range US$13,335–40,000
Length of Study: 4 months–1-year
Study Establishment: Either of ARIT's two research establishments in Ankara or Istanbul
Country of Study: Turkey
No. of awards offered: 2–4
Application Procedure: Applicants must submit an application form, project statement and references.
Closing Date: November 15th
Funding: Government
Contributor: The United States Information Agency (USIA)

Mellon Postdoctoral Fellowships In Turkey For East European Scholars

Subjects: Humanities and social sciences.
Purpose: To bring Eastern and Central European scholars to Turkey to carry out research.
Eligibility: Open to Bulgarian, Czech, Slovak, Polish, Hungarian and Romanian nationals as well as Estonia, Latvia, Lithuania. Preference will be given to scholars in the early stages of their careers who have not had an opportunity for extensive travel.
Level of Study: Postdoctorate
Type: Fellowship
Value: Up to US$11,500
Length of Study: 2–3 months
Frequency: Annual
Study Establishment: Either of ARIT's two research establishments in Ankara or Istanbul
Country of Study: Turkey
No. of awards offered: 3–4
Application Procedure: Applicants must submit an application form, project statement and references.
Closing Date: March 5th
Funding: Private
Contributor: The Mellon Foundation
Additional Information: Further information is available on request or from the website www.mellon.org

Samuel H Kress Foundation Graduate Fellowships in Archaeology and the History of Art

Subjects: The history of art and archaeology.
Purpose: To fund doctoral dissertation research in the field.
Eligibility: Applicants must be degree candidates who have completed all preliminary requirements for a PhD in art history and/or archaeology and who are enrolled at United States of America or Canadian institutions.
Level of Study: Doctorate
Type: Fellowship
Value: Up to US$15,000
Length of Study: 1 academic year. Awards for shorter periods of time are also available
Frequency: Annual
Study Establishment: Either of ARIT's two research establishments in Ankara or Istanbul
Country of Study: Turkey
No. of awards offered: 2–4
Application Procedure: Applicants must submit an application form accompanied by three letters of recommendation.
Closing Date: November 15th
Funding: Private
Contributor: The Samuel H Kress Foundation
No. of awards given last year: 2
No. of applicants last year: 14

AMERICAN SCHOOL OF CLASSICAL STUDIES AT ATHENS (ASCSA)

6-8 Charlton Street, Princeton, NJ, 08540-5232, United States of America
Tel: (1) 609 683 0800
Fax: (1) 609 924 0578
Email: ascsa@ascsa.org
Website: www.ascsa.edu.gr
Contact: Ms Mary E Darlington, Executive Assistant

Established in 1881, the American School of Classical Studies at Athens (ASCSA) offers both graduate students and scholars the opportunity to study Greek civilization, first hand, in Greece. The ASCSA supports and encourages the teaching of the archaeology, art, history, language and literature of Greece from early times to the present.

ASCSA Advanced Fellowships

Subjects: Classical art history, history of architecture, study of pottery.
Eligibility: Open to students from the United States of America or Canadian institutions who have completed 1 year as a regular or student associate member of the ASCSA.
Level of Study: Postgraduate, predoctorate
Type: Fellowship
Value: Room and board, school fees and stipend of US$10,000
Length of Study: 1 academic year
Frequency: Annual
Study Establishment: ASCSA
Country of Study: Greece
No. of awards offered: 4–6
Application Procedure: Applicants must submit the following to the Director of the school: an up-to-date curriculum vitae; a project statement no longer than three, single-spaced pages; a list of other fellowships, if any applied for, with dates of notification of these awards; and one letter of reference from the applicant's dissertation advisor on the feasibility of the applicant's work. Applicants who were not at the School in the preceding year should also get a letter of reference from a scholar who can evaluate what they have done since they left the School.
Closing Date: February 21st
Funding: Private
No. of applicants last year: 24
Additional Information: The fellowships include: the Edward Capps, the Doreen C Spitzer and the Eugene Vanderpool Fellowships (subject unrestricted); the Samuel H Kress Fellowships in art history; the Gorham P Stevens Fellowship in the history of architecture; and the Homer A and Dorothy B Thompson Fellowship in the study of pottery. Ione mylonas Shean in Mycenaean Archaeology or Athenian architecture.

For further information contact:

The American School of Classical Studies at Athens, 54 Soudias Street, Athens, GR-10676, Greece
Tel: (30) 210 723 6313
Fax: (30) 210 725 0584
Contact: School Director

ASCSA Fellowships

Subjects: Classical philology and archaeology, post-classical Greek studies or a related field.
Eligibility: Open to students who hold a Bachelor of Art degree but not a PhD, and who are preparing for an advanced degree in classical studies or a related field. Applicants must be affiliated with a college or university in the United States of America or Canada.
Level of Study: Graduate, postgraduate, predoctorate
Type: Fellowship
Value: US$10,000 stipend plus fees, room and partial board
Length of Study: 1 academic year
Frequency: Annual
Study Establishment: ASCSA
Country of Study: Greece

No. of awards offered: 13
Application Procedure: Applicants must complete an official application, either available on request or from the website. Applications are judged on the basis of credentials and competitive examinations in Greek language, history and archaeology.
Closing Date: January 15th
Funding: Private
No. of awards given last year: 13
No. of applicants last year: 15

ASCSA Research Fellowship in Environmental Studies
Subjects: Earth sciences, geological sciences and archaeological sciences.
Purpose: To support research on studies from archaeological contexts in Greece.
Eligibility: Doctoral candidates working on their dissertation and postdoctoral scholars with well-defined projects that can be completed during the academic year of the fellowship.
Level of Study: Doctorate, postdoctorate, postgraduate
Type: Fellowship
Value: US$15,500–25,000 stipend depending on seniority and experience
Length of Study: 1 academic year
Frequency: Annual
Study Establishment: The Malcolm H Wiener Research Laboratory for Archaeological Science, ASCSA
Country of Study: Greece
No. of awards offered: 1
Application Procedure: Applicants must contact the Chair of the Wiener Laboratory by fax or email. Alternatively, they should contact Dr Sherry C Fox by fax at (30) 210 725 0584, or by email at sfox@ascsa.edu.gr for application guidelines and further information.
Closing Date: January 15th
Funding: Private
No. of awards given last year: 1
No. of applicants last year: 11

ASCSA Research Fellowship in Faunal Studies
Subjects: Biological sciences, life sciences and archaeological sciences.
Purpose: To study faunal remains from archaeological contexts in Greece.
Eligibility: Doctoral candidates working on their dissertation and postdoctoral scholars with well-defined projects that can be completed during the academic year of the fellowship. There is no citizenship requirement.
Level of Study: Postdoctorate, postgraduate, doctorate
Type: Fellowship
Value: US$15,500–25,000 stipend depending on seniority and experience
Length of Study: 1 academic year
Frequency: Annual
Study Establishment: The Malcolm H Wiener Research Laboratory for Archaeological Science, ASCSA
Country of Study: Greece
No. of awards offered: 1
Application Procedure: Applicants must contact the Chair of the Wiener Laboratory by fax or email. Alternatively, they should contact Dr Sherry C Fox by fax at (30) 210 725 0584, or by email at sfox@ascsa.edu.gr for application guidelines and further information.
Closing Date: January 15th
Funding: Private
No. of awards given last year: 1
No. of applicants last year: 11

ASCSA Research Fellowship in Geoarchaeology
Subjects: Earth sciences, geological sciences and archaeological sciences.
Purpose: To support research on a geoarchaeological topic in Greece.
Eligibility: Doctoral candidates working on their dissertation and postdoctoral scholars with well-defined projects that can be completed during the academic year of the fellowship. There is no citizenship requirement.
Level of Study: Doctorate, postdoctorate, postgraduate
Type: Fellowship
Value: US$15,500–25,000 stipend depending on seniority and experience
Length of Study: 1 academic year
Frequency: Annual
Study Establishment: The Malcolm H Wiener Research Laboratory for Archaeological Science, ASCSA
Country of Study: Greece
No. of awards offered: 1
Application Procedure: Applicants must contact the Chair of the Wiener Laboratory by fax or email. Alternatively, they should contact Dr Sherry C Fox by fax at (30) 210 725 0584, or by email at sfox@ascsa.edu.gr for application guidelines and further information.
Closing Date: January 15th
Funding: Private
No. of awards given last year: 1
No. of applicants last year: 11

J Lawrence Angel Fellowship in Human Skeletal Studies
Subjects: Biological sciences, life sciences and archaeological sciences.
Purpose: To study human skeletal remains from archaeological contexts in Greece.
Eligibility: Doctoral candidates working on dissertations and scholars holding a PhD or equivalent degree.
Level of Study: Doctorate, postgraduate, postdoctorate
Type: Fellowship
Value: US$15,500–25,000 stipend, depending on seniority and experience
Length of Study: 1 academic year
Frequency: Annual
Study Establishment: The Malcolm H Wiener Research Laboratory for Archaeological Science, ASCSA
Country of Study: Greece
No. of awards offered: 1
Application Procedure: Applicants must contact Dr Sherry C Fox by fax at (30) 210 725 0584, or by email at sfox@ascsa.edu.gr for application guidelines and further information.
Closing Date: January 15th
Funding: Private
Contributor: The Malcolm H Wiener Research Laboratory for Archaeological Sciences at the American School at Athens
No. of awards given last year: 1
No. of applicants last year: 11

Jacob Hirsch Fellowship
Subjects: Pre-classical, classical or post-classical archaeology.
Purpose: To support individuals completing a project that requires a lengthy residence in Greece.
Eligibility: Open to graduate students of American or Israeli institutions who are writing a dissertation and to recent PhD graduates completing a project such as a dissertation for publication. Applications will be judged on the basis of appropriate credentials including referees.
Level of Study: Predoctorate, postgraduate, postdoctorate
Type: Fellowship
Value: US$10,000 stipend plus room, board and waiver of fees
Length of Study: 1 academic year, non-renewable
Frequency: Annual
Study Establishment: ASCSA
Country of Study: Greece
No. of awards offered: 1
Application Procedure: Applicants must submit three letters of recommendation, transcripts and a detailed description of projects to be pursued in Greece. Applicants must apply for membership at the School simultaneously with the application for the fellowship.
Closing Date: January 15th
Funding: Private
No. of awards given last year: 1
No. of applicants last year: 5

M Alison Frantz Fellowship in Post-Classical Studies at the Gennadius Library

Subjects: Post-classical studies in late antiquity, Byzantine studies, post-Byzantine studies and modern Greek studies.
Eligibility: Open to PhD candidates. Applicants from institutions in the United States of America or Canada must be recent PhD candidates and all candidates must show a need to use the Gennadius Library.
Level of Study: Predoctorate, doctorate, postdoctorate
Type: Fellowship
Value: US$10,000 stipend plus room, board and waiver of fees
Length of Study: 1 academic year
Frequency: Annual
Study Establishment: The Gennadius Library
Country of Study: Greece
No. of awards offered: 1
Application Procedure: Applicants must submit a curriculum vitae, project description and two letters of support to the Chair of Gennadius Library Committee.
Closing Date: January 15th
Funding: Private
No. of awards given last year: 1
No. of applicants last year: 8
Additional Information: This fellowship was formerly known as the Gennadeion Fellowship.

NEH Fellowships

Subjects: Ancient, classical and post-classical studies, including but not limited to the history, philosophy, language, art and archaeology of Greece and the Greek world, art history, literature, philology, architecture, archaeology, anthropology, metallurgy and environmental studies from prehistoric times to the present.
Eligibility: Open to doctoral and postdoctoral scholars who are citizens of the United States of America or foreign nationals with 3 years residency in the United States of America immediately preceding the application deadline.
Level of Study: Doctorate, postdoctorate
Type: Fellowship
Value: A maximum stipend of US$20,000 for a 5-month project and US$40,000 for a 10-month project
Length of Study: 1 academic year
Frequency: Annual
Study Establishment: ASCSA
Country of Study: Greece
No. of awards offered: 2–5
Application Procedure: Applicants must write for details or visit the website.
Closing Date: November 15th
Funding: Government
No. of awards given last year: 3: 1 academic year, 2 partial year
No. of applicants last year: 21

AMERICAN SOCIETY FOR EIGHTEENTH-CENTURY STUDIES (ASECS)

PO Box 7867, Wake Forest University, Winston-Salem, NC 27109, United States of America
Tel: (1) 727 4694
Fax: (1) 727 4697
Email: asecs@wfu.edu
Website: www.asecs.press.jhu.edu

The American Society for Eighteenth-Century studies is an interdisciplinary group dedicated to the advancement of scholarships in all aspects of the period from the later seventeenth through to the early nineteenth century.

Annibel Jenkins Biography Prize

Subjects: Writing.
Purpose: To award the author of the best book-length biography of a late seventeenth or eighteenth-century.
Eligibility: Open to candidates who are members of the society.
Type: Award
Value: US$1,000
Frequency: Every 2 years
Application Procedure: A completed application form must be sent.
Closing Date: November 15th

ASECS Innovative Course Design Competition Award

Subjects: Teaching.
Purpose: To encourage excellence in teaching of the eighteenth century.
Level of Study: Professional development
Type: Award
Length of Study: US$500
Frequency: Annual
Application Procedure: Five copies of 3–5 page proposal to be sent. See the website for complete details.
Closing Date: October 1st

ASECS Women's Caucus Editing and Translation Fellowship

Subjects: Editing and translation.
Purpose: To support an editing or a translation work in progress on a feminist or a women's studies subject.
Eligibility: Open to candidates working on projects related to women's studies.
Level of Study: Doctorate
Type: Fellowship
Value: US$1,000
Frequency: Annual
Application Procedure: Five copies of eligible proposals must be sent directly to the ASECS office. See website for further information.
Closing Date: January 15th

Catharine Macaulay Award

Subjects: Women's studies.
Purpose: To recognize the best paper on a feminist or women's studies subject.
Level of Study: Postgraduate
Type: Award
Value: US$200
Frequency: Annual
Application Procedure: Three copies of the papers must be sent.
Closing Date: September 1st

Emilie Du Chatelet Award for Independent Scholarship

Subjects: Women's studies.
Purpose: To support research on women's studies.
Eligibility: Open to candidates researching on subject related to women's studies.
Level of Study: Doctorate
Type: Scholarship
Value: US$500
Frequency: Annual
Application Procedure: Applicant must send a curriculum vitae and 3–5 page research proposal.
Closing Date: January 16th

The James L. Cifford Prize

Subjects: Writing.
Purpose: To honour author of an article on an outstanding study of some aspect of eighteenth-century culture.
Eligibility: Open to authors who are members of the society.
Level of Study: Postgraduate
Type: Award
Value: US$500
Frequency: Annual
Application Procedure: See the website.
Closing Date: January 1st

Percy Adams Article Prize

Subjects: History.
Purpose: To recognize excellence in scholary studies.
Eligibility: Open to members of SEASECS.
Level of Study: Postgraduate

Type: Award
Length of Study: US$500
Frequency: Annual
Application Procedure: See the website.
Closing Date: January 1st
Contributor: Southeastern American Society for Eighteenth-century studies (SEASECS)

AMERICAN SOCIETY FOR ENGINEERING EDUCATION (ASEE)

1818 North Street North West, Suite 600 Zip-2479, Washington, DC, 20036, United States of America
Tel: (1) 202 331 3500
Fax: (1) 202 265 8504
Email: sttp@asee.org
Website: www.asee.org
Contact: Mr Michael More, Projects Department

The American Society for Engineering Education (ASEE) is committed to furthering education in engineering and engineering technology. This mission is accomplished by promoting excellence in instruction, research, public service and practice, exercising worldwide leadership, fostering the technological education of society and providing quality products and services to members.

Air Force Summer Faculty Fellowship Program

Subjects: Engineering.
Eligibility: Applicants to the Air Force Summer Faculty Fellowship Program (SFFP) must be citizens or legal permanent residents of the United States. Applicants must hold a full-time appointment at a U.S. college or university. Participants are expected to conduct research at an Air Force Research Laboratory Directorate, U.S. Air Force Academy, or the Air Force Institute of Technology.
Level of Study: Doctorate, postdoctorate, postgraduate
Type: Fellowship
Value: Weekly stipend US$1,250–1,650
Length of Study: 8–12 weeks
Frequency: Annual
Country of Study: United States of America
Application Procedure: Apply online.
Closing Date: November
Funding: Government
Contributor: U.S. Air Force Academy and the Air Force Institute of Technology

ASEE Helen T Carr Fellowship Program

Subjects: Engineering.
Purpose: To increase the number of engineering professors for the historically Black engineering colleges by providing financial aid for doctoral study in engineering.
Eligibility: Open to African American faculty members, graduate students and other African Americans who have completed at least the equivalent of 1 academic year of full-time engineering graduate study. Candidates must be sponsored by the Dean of one of the historically Black engineering colleges at which they later intend to teach.
Level of Study: Doctorate
Value: Up to US$10,000
Length of Study: 1 year, renewable as funding allows
Frequency: Annual
Country of Study: United States of America
Application Procedure: Applicants must first submit a letter to the Dean of a historically Black engineering college asking to be sponsored. Transcripts of undergraduate and graduate course credits and at least three references testifying to intellectual capacity and educational attainments, which give promise of satisfactory performance in advanced study, must then be submitted to the ASEE. A covering letter from the sponsoring Dean is required, and a single copy of each of these documents is to be sent to the committee through its secretary at ASEE headquarters.
Closing Date: Applications for fellowships to begin in August or September should be submitted by January 15th and by May 15th for fellowships to begin the following January or February
Funding: Government, private, commercial
Contributor: The Allied-Signal Foundation, the AMOCO Foundation, AT&T-Bell Laboratories, El Dupont De Numours & Co., the Exxon Education Foundation, the General Electric Foundation, the IBM Corporation, the Mobil Oil Corporation, NASA, RCA and the Union Carbide

NASA Faculty Fellowships Program

Subjects: Aeronautical and aerospace engineering.
Purpose: To fund research and provide access to NASA's Jet Propulsion Laboratory.
Level of Study: Doctorate
Type: Fellowship
Length of Study: 1 Semester
Frequency: Annual
Country of Study: United States of America
No. of awards offered: 1

For further information contact:

Email: m.khalkho@asee.org
Contact: Magali Khalkho

NASA Summer Faculty Research Opportunities (NSFRO)

Subjects: Science technology, engineering and mathematics.
Level of Study: Postdoctorate
Type: Fellowship
Length of Study: 1 Semester
Frequency: Annual
Country of Study: United States of America
No. of awards offered: Varies
Funding: Government

For further information contact:

Email: m.khalkho@asee.org
Contact: Magali Khalkho

Naval Research Laboratory Post Doctoral Fellowship Program

Subjects: Computer science, artificial intelligence, plasma physics, acoustics, radar, fluid dynamics, chemistry, materials, science and many more specialist fields.
Purpose: To increase the involvement of creative and highly trained scientists to scientific and technical areas of interest and relevance to the U.S. Navy.
Level of Study: Doctorate, postdoctorate
Type: Fellowship
Frequency: Annual
Study Establishment: Naval Research Laboratory
Country of Study: United States of America
No. of awards offered: 40
Funding: Government
Contributor: U.S. Navy

For further information contact:

Tel: (202) 331 3525
Fax: (202) 265 8504
Email: r.kempinski@asee.org

SMART Defense Scholarship Program

Subjects: Science, mathematics and engineering.
Purpose: To support the education of future scientists and engineers.
Level of Study: Postdoctorate, doctorate
Type: Scholarship
Frequency: Annual
Country of Study: United States of America
No. of awards offered: Varies
Closing Date: March 4th
Funding: Government

Contributor: U.S. Department of Defense
No. of awards given last year: 36

AMERICAN SOCIETY FOR MICROBIOLOGY (ASM)

1752 N Street North West, Washington, DC, 20036-2904, United States of America
Tel: (1) 202 942 9225
Fax: (1) 202 942 9353
Email: awards@asmusa.org
Website: www.asm.org
Contact: Ms Peggy McNult, Manager, Awards Programme

The American Society for Microbiology (ASM) is the oldest and largest single life science membership organization in the world. With 43,000 members throughout the world. The ASM represents all disciplines of microbiological specialization including microbiology education. The ASM's mission is to promote research and research training in the microbiological sciences and to assist communication between scientists, policymakers and the public to improve health, the environment and economic well- being.

Abbott Laboratories Award in Clinical and Diagnostic Immunology

Subjects: Clinical or diagnostic immunology.
Purpose: To honour a distinguished scientist in the field.
Eligibility: There are no eligibility restrictions.
Level of Study: Unrestricted
Type: Award
Value: US$2,000 cash prize, a commemorative medal and domestic travel to the ASM General Meeting
Frequency: Annual
Country of Study: Any country
No. of awards offered: 1
Application Procedure: Self-nominations will not be accepted. Nominations must consist of a nomination cover page that includes a specific description of the nominee's contributions, a curriculum vitae including a list of the nominee's publications and two additional supporting letters.
Closing Date: October 1st
Funding: Commercial
Contributor: Abbott Laboratories, Diagnostic Division
No. of awards given last year: 1
No. of applicants last year: 5
Additional Information: ASM awards are granted at the discretion of award selection committees and may not be awarded every year.

Abbott-ASM Lifetime Achievement Award

Subjects: Microbiology.
Purpose: To honour a distinguished scientist for a lifetime of outstanding contributions in fundamental research in any of the microbiological sciences.
Eligibility: Open to mature scientists, both active and retired, from all relevant areas of microbiology.
Level of Study: Unrestricted
Type: Award
Value: US$20,000 cash prize, a commemorative medal and travel to the ASM General Meeting
Country of Study: Any country
No. of awards offered: 1
Application Procedure: Self-nominations will not be accepted. Nominations must consist of a nomination cover page that includes a description of the nominee's outstanding research accomplishments, a curriculum vitae including a list of nominee's publications and two additional letters of support.
Closing Date: October 1st
Funding: Commercial
Contributor: Abbott Laboratories
No. of awards given last year: 1
No. of applicants last year: 15
Additional Information: ASM awards are granted at the discretion of the award selection committees and may not be awarded every year.

ASM BD Award for Research in Clinical Microbiology

Subjects: Clinical microbiology.
Purpose: To honour a distinguished microbiologist for outstanding research accomplishments leading to or forming the foundation for important applications in the field.
Eligibility: Open to clinical microbiologists.
Level of Study: Unrestricted
Type: Award
Value: US$2,000 cash prize, a commemorative medal and travel expenses to the ASM General Meeting
Frequency: Annual
Country of Study: Any country
No. of awards offered: 1
Application Procedure: Self-nominations will not be accepted. Nominations must consist of a nomination cover page that describes the nominee's activities and accomplishments pertinent to the award, a curriculum vitae including a list of publications and two additional supporting letters.
Closing Date: October 1st
Funding: Commercial
Contributor: BD Diagnostic Systems
No. of awards given last year: 1
No. of applicants last year: 4
Additional Information: ASM awards are granted at the discretion of award selection committees and may not be awarded every year.

ASM Graduate Microbiology Teaching Award

Subjects: Microbiology.
Purpose: To recognize an individual for distinguished teaching and mentoring of students at the graduate and postgraduate level and for encouraging them to subsequent achievement.
Eligibility: Nominees must be currently teaching microbiology in a recognized college or university, have devoted a substantial portion of their time during the past 5 years to teaching graduate students in microbiology and have a minimum of 10 years of total teaching experience. Nominees may have engaged in research or other concerns, provided that teaching graduate students remained a substantial activity.
Level of Study: Unrestricted
Type: Award
Value: US$2,000 cash prize, a commemorative medal and travel to the ASM General Meeting
Frequency: Annual
Country of Study: Any country
No. of awards offered: 1
Application Procedure: Self-nominations will not be accepted. Nominations must consist of a nomination cover page that specifically addresses how the nominee fulfils the award eligibility, including a record of teaching responsibilities, manifests of distinguished teaching, innovations, publications, special awards or other pertinent information, a curriculum vitae including a list of the nominee's publications and two additional supporting letters.
Closing Date: October 1st
Funding: Private
Contributor: American Society for Microbiology
No. of awards given last year: 1
No. of applicants last year: 8
Additional Information: ASM awards are granted at the discretion of award selection committees and may not be awarded every year.

bioMérieux Sonnenwirth Award for Leadership in Clinical Microbiology

Subjects: Microbiology.
Purpose: To honour a distinguished microbiologist who has exhibited exemplary leadership, recognizes the promotion of innovation in clinical laboratory science and demonstrates high dedication and commitment to ASM and to the advancement of clinical microbiology as a profession.
Eligibility: Open to distinguished microbiologists.
Level of Study: Unrestricted
Value: US$2,000 cash prize, commemorative medal and travel to the ASM general meeting
Frequency: Annual

Country of Study: Any country
No. of awards offered: 1
Application Procedure: Self-nominations will not be accepted. Nominations must consist of a nomination cover page that describes the nominee's activities and accomplishments pertinent to the award, a curriculum vitae including a list of publications and two additional supporting letters.
Closing Date: October 1st
Funding: Commercial
Contributor: bioMérieux Inc.
No. of awards given last year: 1
No. of applicants last year: 7
Additional Information: ASM awards are granted at the discretion of award selection committees and may not be awarded every year.

Carski Foundation Distinguished Undergraduate Teaching Award

Subjects: Science education.
Purpose: To recognize a mature individual for distinguished teaching of microbiology to pre-baccalaureate students and who has encouraged them to subsequent achievements.
Eligibility: Nominees must be currently teaching microbiology in a recognized college or university. A substantial portion of his or her time during the past 5 years must have been devoted to teaching undergraduate students in microbiology and a minimum of 10 years total teaching experience is required. Nominees may have engaged in research or other concerns, provided that teaching undergraduates remained a substantial activity.
Level of Study: Unrestricted
Type: Award
Value: US$2,000 cash prize, commemorative medal and travel to the ASM General Meeting
Frequency: Annual
Country of Study: Any country
No. of awards offered: 1
Application Procedure: Self-nominations will not be accepted. Nominations must consist of a nomination cover page, a nominating letter detailing teaching responsibilities, manifests of distinguished teaching, innovations, publications and special awards, a curriculum vitae and two additional supporting letters.
Closing Date: October 1st
Funding: Foundation, private
Contributor: The Carski Foundation
No. of awards given last year: 1
No. of applicants last year: 11
Additional Information: ASM awards are granted at the discretion of award selection committees and may not be awarded every year.

Dade Behring MicroScan Young Investigator Award

Subjects: Microbiology.
Purpose: To recognize research excellence and potential and to further the educational or research objectives of an outstanding young clinical scientist.
Eligibility: There are no eligibility restrictions.
Level of Study: Postdoctorate
Type: Award
Value: US$2,000 cash prize, a commemorative medal and travel to the ASM General Meeting
Frequency: Annual
Country of Study: Any country
No. of awards offered: 1
Application Procedure: Self-nominations will not be accepted. Nominations must consist of a nomination cover page, a curriculum vitae including a list of publications, abstracts and manuscripts in preparation, a one- or two-page statement from the nominee that describes how educational or research objectives will be enhanced by the award, and two additional supporting letters documenting the nominee's research excellence and anticipated impact of the award on achievement of the nominee's career objectives.
Closing Date: October 1st
Funding: Commercial
Contributor: Dade Behring Inc., MicroScan Microbiology Systems
No. of awards given last year: 1
No. of applicants last year: 8
Additional Information: ASM awards are granted at the discretion of award selection committees and may not be awarded every year.

Eli Lilly and Company Research Award

Subjects: Microbiology and immunology.
Purpose: To reward fundamental research of unusual merit.
Eligibility: Nominees must be working in the United States of America or Canada at the time of application and must be actively involved in the line of research for which the award is to be made. They must not have reached their 45th birthday by April 30th of the year the award is given.
Level of Study: Unrestricted
Type: Award
Value: US$5,000 cash prize, a commemorative medal and travel expenses to the ASM General Meeting
Frequency: Annual
Country of Study: Any country
No. of awards offered: 1
Application Procedure: Self-nominations will not be accepted. Nominations must consist of a nomination cover page, a nominating letter that includes a specific description of the research on which the nomination is based, verification of the date of birth, ie. a photocopy of driver's licence, passport or birth certificate, a curriculum vitae including a list of publications and two additional supporting letters.
Closing Date: October 1st
Funding: Commercial
Contributor: Eli Lilly and Company
No. of awards given last year: 1
No. of applicants last year: 5
Additional Information: ASM awards are granted at the discretion of award selection committees and may not be awarded every year.

ICAAC Young Investigator Award

Subjects: Microbiology, including the discovery and application of chemotherapeutic agents and other sciences associated with infectious diseases.
Purpose: To recognize and reward young investigators for excellence and research.
Eligibility: Nominees must have completed postdoctoral research training in microbiology or infectious diseases no more than 3 years prior to presentation of the award, must reside in North America and have performed significant research in North America.
Level of Study: Doctorate, postdoctorate
Type: Award
Value: US$2,500 cash prize and commemorative medal
Country of Study: Any country
No. of awards offered: Up to 2
Application Procedure: Self-nominations will not be accepted. Nominations must consist of a nomination cover page including a specific description of research, a curriculum vitae including a list of publications and two additional supporting letters.
Closing Date: April 1st
Funding: Commercial
Contributor: The Human Health Division of Merck USA
No. of awards given last year: 2
No. of applicants last year: 12
Additional Information: ASM awards are granted at the discretion of award selection committees and may not be awarded every year.

Procter & Gamble Award in Applied and Environmental Microbiology

Subjects: Environmental microbiology, applied microbiology.
Purpose: To recognize distinguished achievement in research and development.
Eligibility: Nominees must show outstanding accomplishment in research or development in the appropriate field. They must be actively engaged in research or development at the time that the award is presented.
Level of Study: Unrestricted
Type: Award
Value: US$2,000 cash prize, a commemorative medal and travel to the ASM General Meeting

Frequency: Annual
Country of Study: Any country
No. of awards offered: 1
Application Procedure: Self-nominations will not be accepted. Nominations must consist of a nomination cover page that describes the work that has stimulated the nomination, a curriculum vitae including a list of publications and awards and two additional supporting letters.
Closing Date: October 1st
Funding: Commercial
Contributor: Procter & Gamble
No. of awards given last year: 1
No. of applicants last year: 10
Additional Information: ASM awards are granted at the discretion of award selection committees and may not be awarded every year.

Promega Biotechnology Research Award

Subjects: Biotechnology.
Purpose: To honour outstanding contributions to the application of biotechnology through fundamental research, developmental research or reduction to practice.
Eligibility: An outstanding contribution can be a single exceptionally significant achievement or the aggregate of a number of exemplary achievements.
Level of Study: Unrestricted
Type: Award
Value: US$5,000 cash prize, a commemorative medal and travel to the ASM General Meeting
Frequency: Annual
Country of Study: Any country
No. of awards offered: 1
Application Procedure: Self-nominations will not be accepted. Nominations must consist of a nomination cover page, a nominating letter that includes a description of the nominee's research, a curriculum vitae including a list of publications and two additional supporting letters.
Closing Date: October 1st
Funding: Commercial
Contributor: The Promega Corporation
No. of awards given last year: 1
No. of applicants last year: 15
Additional Information: ASM awards are granted at the discretion of the selection committee and may not be awarded every year.

Sanofi-Aventis Pharmaceuticals Award

Subjects: Microbiology.
Purpose: To stimulate research in antimicrobial chemotherapy and honour outstanding sustained achievement.
Eligibility: Nominees must be actively engaged in research involving development of new agents, investigation of antimicrobial action or resistance to antimicrobial agents and the pharmacology, toxicology or clinical use of those agents. They must not have served on an ICAAC Program Committee within the past 2 years.
Level of Study: Unrestricted
Type: Award
Value: US$20,000 cash prize, a commemorative medal and travel expenses
Frequency: Annual
Country of Study: Any country
No. of awards offered: 1
Application Procedure: Self-nominations will not be accepted. Nominations must consist of a nomination cover page that includes a specific description of the research on which the nomination is based, a curriculum vitae including a list of publications and two additional supporting letters.
Closing Date: April 1st
Funding: Commercial
Contributor: Sanofi-Aventis Pharmaceuticals
No. of awards given last year: 1
No. of applicants last year: 15
Additional Information: ASM awards are granted at the discretion of award selection committees and may not be awarded every year.

William A Hinton Research Training Award

Subjects: Microbiology.
Purpose: To honour an individual who has made outstanding significant contributions towards fostering the research training of underrepresented minorities in microbiology.
Eligibility: Nominees must have contributed to the research training of undergraduate students, graduate students, postdoctoral Fellows or health professional students. Their efforts must have led to the increased participation of underrepresented minorities in microbiology.
Level of Study: Unrestricted
Type: Award
Value: US$2,000 cash prize, a commemorative medal and travel to the ASM General Meeting
Frequency: Annual
Country of Study: Any country
No. of awards offered: 1
Application Procedure: Self-nominations will not be accepted. Nominations must consist of a cover page, a nominating letter highlighting the nominee's activities and accomplishments pertinent to the award, a curriculum vitae and two additional supporting letters.
Closing Date: October 1st
Funding: Private
Contributor: ASM
No. of awards given last year: 1
No. of applicants last year: 3
Additional Information: ASM awards are granted at the discretion of award selection committees and may not be awarded every year.

AMERICAN SOCIETY OF HEATING, REFRIGERATING AND AIR CONDITIONING ENGINEERS, INC. (ASHRAE)

1791 Tullie Circle North East, Atlanta, GA, 30329,
United States of America
Tel: (1) 404 636 8400
Fax: (1) 404 321 5478
Email: mvaughn@ashrae.org
Website: www.ashrae.org
Contact: Mr Michael R Vaughn, Manager of Research and Technical Services

The American Society of Heating, Refrigerating and Air Conditioning Engineers, Inc. (ASHRAE) is an international organization of 50,000 people with chapters all over the world. The Society is organized for the sole purpose of advancing the arts and sciences of heating, ventilation, air conditioning and refrigerating for public's benefit through research, standards writing, continuing education and publications.

ASHRAE Grants-in-Aid for Graduate Students

Subjects: Heating, refrigeration, air conditioning and ventilation.
Purpose: To stimulate interest through the encouragement of original research.
Eligibility: Open to graduate engineering students capable of undertaking appropriate and scholarly research.
Level of Study: Postgraduate, doctorate
Type: Grant
Value: Up to US$10,000 depending upon the needs and nature of request
Length of Study: Usually for 1 year or less, non-renewable
Frequency: Annual
Study Establishment: The grantee's institution
Country of Study: Any country
No. of awards offered: 12–18
Application Procedure: Applicants must complete an application form, available from the website. An application form must also be submitted by the faculty advisor.
Closing Date: December 15th
Funding: Private
No. of awards given last year: 18
No. of applicants last year: 48

AMERICAN SOCIETY OF HEMATOLOGY (ASH)

1900 M Street North West, Suite 200, Washington, DC, 20036, United States of America
Tel: (1) 202 776 0544
Fax: (1) 202 776 0545
Email: ash@hematology.org
Website: www.hematology.org
Contact: Administrative Assistant

American Society of Hematology Minority Medical Student Award Program

Subjects: Haematology.
Purpose: To provide support for a research programme of 6–8 weeks and for travel to the Society's annual meeting.
Eligibility: Applicants must be minority medical students enrolled in either MD, MD/PhD or equivalent DO programmes and must be citizens or permanent residents of the United States of America or Canada.
Level of Study: Professional development, research
Type: Grant
Value: US$6,000 plus US$1,000 travel allowance
Length of Study: 6–8 weeks
Frequency: Annual
Country of Study: United States of America or Canada
No. of awards offered: 10
Application Procedure: All applicants must complete the Minority Medical Student Award Program application available from the website.
Closing Date: February 15th
Funding: Commercial
Additional Information: For additional information, please contact LaFaundra Neville, Executive Assistant, at lneville@hematology.org or by phone at 202 776 0544, ext. 1106. Notification of awards will be by April 15th.

American Society of Hematology Scholar Award

Subjects: Haematology.
Purpose: To encourage haematologists to begin a career in research by providing partial salary or other support.
Eligibility: To be eligible for the Junior Faculty Scholar Award, applicants must be within the first 2 years of their initial faculty appointment as an assistant professor, and for the Fellow Scholar Award, applicants must have more than 2 years, but less than 6 years of postdoctoral research training. Applicants must work in a United States of America or Canadian institution.
Level of Study: Research
Type: Award
Value: US$100,000 for Fellow Scholars and US$150,000 for Junior Faculty Scholars
Length of Study: 2–3 years
Frequency: Annual
Application Procedure: A letter of intent must be submitted by May 4th and it should include a signed cover letter, abstract of the proposed project (350 words or less), applicant's curriculum vitae and should identify which award category the applicant is applying for.
Closing Date: September 1st
Funding: Commercial, foundation
Additional Information: For detailed information, applicants must visit the website or contact Karin Lombardi at the American Society of Hematology.

American Society of Hematology Trainee Award Program

Subjects: Haematology.
Purpose: To provide support for a research project of 3 months and for travel to the Society's annual meeting.
Eligibility: Applicants must be medical students or residents. The programme is open to ACGME-accredited institutions in the United States of America, Mexico and Canada that have a training programme director in haematology or a related area.
Level of Study: Professional development
Value: US$4,000 plus US$1,000 for travel
Length of Study: 3 months
Frequency: Annual
No. of awards offered: 1
Application Procedure: All applicants and institutions must complete the Trainee Award application form available from the website.
Closing Date: March 15th
Funding: Commercial
Additional Information: For any additional information regarding the programme, please contact Nancy Kuhn, Director of Education and Training, at 202 776 0544.

American Society of Hematology Travel Award

Subjects: Haematology.
Purpose: To help individuals to defray annual meeting expenses.
Eligibility: Applicants must be medical students graduate students, resident physicians or postdoctoral Fellows who are both first author and present of an abstract.
Level of Study: Professional development
Type: Travel grant
Value: US$500
Frequency: Annual
Funding: Foundation, commercial

American Society of Hematology Visiting Trainee Program

Subjects: Haematology.
Purpose: To provide scientists and haematologists in developing countries an opportunity to gain valuable clinical experience, technology training or laboratory experience.
Eligibility: Applicants must be scientists and haematologists from developing countries as defined by the American Society of Hematology.
Level of Study: Professional development
Type: Grant
Length of Study: Up to 12 weeks
Frequency: Annual
Application Procedure: Applicants must complete the visiting trainee programme application and submit it with a letter of recommendation from the proposed host institution. They will need to identify a site and host for their proposed short-term clinical or laboratory experience and give a clear statement of the topic or goal of the training programme. Application forms are available from the website.
Closing Date: April 1st
Funding: Commercial
Additional Information: For any additional information regarding the programme, please contact Lafaundra Neville, Executive Assistant, by email at lneville@hematology.org or phone at 202 776 544 Ext. 1106.

AMERICAN SOCIETY OF INTERIOR DESIGNERS (ASID) EDUCATIONAL FOUNDATION, INC.

608 Massachusetts Avenue North East, Washington, DC, 20002-6006, United States of America
Tel: (1) 202 546 3480
Fax: (1) 202 546 3240
Email: education@asid.org
Website: www.asid.org
Contact: Education Department

The American Society of Interior Designers (ASID) Educational Foundation represents the interests of more than 30,500 members including interior design practitioners, students and industry and retail partners. ASID's mission is to be the definitive resource for professional education and knowledge sharing, advocacy of interior designers' right to practice and expansion of interior design markets.

ASID/Joel Polsky-Fixtures Furniture Academic Achievement Award

Subjects: Interior design.
Purpose: To recognise an outstanding student's interior design research or thesis project.

Eligibility: Open to applicants of any nationality. Research papers or doctoral and Master's theses should address such interior design topics as educational research, behavioural science, business practice, design process, theory or other technical subjects.
Level of Study: Postgraduate
Type: Prize
Value: US$1,000
Frequency: Annual
Country of Study: Any country
No. of awards offered: 1
Application Procedure: Applicants must write for details.
Closing Date: April 30th
Additional Information: Entries will be judged on actual content, breadth of material, comprehensive coverage of topic, innovative subject matter and bibliography or references.

ASID/Joel Polsky-Fixtures Furniture Prize

Subjects: Interior design.
Purpose: To recognise outstanding academic contributions to the discipline of interior design through literature or visual communication.
Eligibility: Entries should address the needs of the public, designers and students on topics such as educational research, behavioural science, business practice, design process, theory or other technical subjects.
Level of Study: Unrestricted
Type: Prize
Value: US$1,000
Frequency: Annual
Country of Study: Any country
No. of awards offered: 1
Application Procedure: Applicants must write for details.
Closing Date: April 30th
Additional Information: Material will be judged on innovative subject matter, comprehensive coverage of topic, organization, graphic presentation and bibliography or references.

ASID/Mabelle Wilhelmina Boldt Memorial Scholarship

Subjects: Interior design.
Eligibility: Applicants must have been practising designers for a period of at least five years prior to returning to graduate level. Preference will be given to those with a focus on design research. The scholarship will be awarded on the basis of academic or creative accomplishment, as demonstrated by school transcripts and a letter of recommendation.
Level of Study: Graduate
Type: Scholarship
Value: US$2,000
Frequency: Annual
Study Establishment: A degree granting institution
Country of Study: Any country
No. of awards offered: 1
Application Procedure: Applicants must write for details.
Closing Date: April 30th

AMERICAN SOCIETY OF MECHANICAL ENGINEERS (ASME INTERNATIONAL)

Three Park Avenue, New York, NY 10016-5990,
United States of America
Tel: (1) 212 591 8131
Fax: (1) 212 591 7143
Email: oluwanifiset@asme.org
Website: www.asme.org/education/enged/aid
Contact: Theresa Oluwanifise, Coordinator Educational Operations

Founded in 1880 as the American Society of Mechanical Engineers (ASME International), today ASME International is a non-profit educational and technical organization serving a worldwide membership.

ASME Graduate Teaching Fellowship Program

Subjects: Mechanical engineering.
Purpose: To encourage outstanding students, especially women and minorities, to pursue a doctorate in mechanical engineering teaching and to encourage the engineering education as a profession.
Eligibility: Open to PhD students in mechanical engineering, with a demonstrated interest in a teaching career. A Master's degree or passage of qualifying exam is required as is a lecture responsibility/teaching assistantship commitment from the applicant's department. In addition, the applicant should be a citizen of the United States of America or permanent resident, with an undergraduate degree from an ABET-accredited programme, and a student member of ASME. The student must also study in the United States of America.
Level of Study: Postgraduate, doctorate
Type: Fellowship
Value: US$5,000 per year
Length of Study: 2 years
Frequency: Annual
Country of Study: United States of America
No. of awards offered: 4
Application Procedure: Applicants must submit an undergraduate grade point average, Graduate Record Examination scores, two letters of recommendation from faculty or their MS committee, a graduate transcript, transcripts of all academic work, a statement about faculty career and a current curriculum vitae.
Closing Date: October 20th
No. of awards given last year: 4
No. of applicants last year: 10
Additional Information: In the terms of the fellowship, the awardee must teach at least one lecture course. The applicant's department head must certify, prior to the award or continuation notice, the commitment of a teaching assistantship and the lecture assignment anticipated.

Elisabeth M and Winchell M Parsons Scholarship

Subjects: Mechanical engineering.
Purpose: To assist ASME student members working towards a doctoral degree.
Eligibility: Selection is based on academic performance, character, need and ASME participation. Applicants must be citizens of the United States of America and be enrolled in a United States of America school in an ABET-accredited mechanical engineering department. No student may receive more than one auxiliary scholarship or loan in the same academic year.
Level of Study: Doctorate
Type: Grant
Value: US$2,000
Frequency: Annual
Country of Study: United States of America
No. of awards offered: Approx. 2
Application Procedure: Application forms are available from the website.
Closing Date: March 15th

For further information contact:

102 Meadowridge Drive, Lynchburg, VA, 24503-3829, United States of America
Tel: (1) 434 384 1057
Email: mrsnyder@aol.com

Marjorie Roy Rothermel Scholarship

Subjects: Mechanical engineering.
Purpose: To assist students working towards a Master's degree.
Eligibility: Selection is based on academic performance, character, need and ASME participation. Applicants must be citizens of the United States of America and must be enrolled in a United States of America school in an ABET-accredited mechanical engineering department. No student may receive more than one auxiliary scholarship or loan in the same academic year.
Level of Study: Graduate
Type: Scholarship
Value: US$2,000
Frequency: Annual
Country of Study: United States of America
No. of awards offered: 6–8

Application Procedure: Application forms are available from the website.
Closing Date: March 15th

For further information contact:

332 Valencia Street, Gulf Breeze, FL, 32561, United States of America
Tel: (1) 850 932 3698
Email: eprocha340@aol.com

Rice-Cullimore Scholarship

Subjects: Mechanical engineering.
Purpose: To aid a foreign student pursuing graduate work for a Master's or doctoral degree in the United States of America.
Eligibility: Open to candidates from any country except the United States of America. Selection is based on academic performance, character, need and ASME participation. No student may receive more than one auxiliary scholarship or loan in the same academic year.
Level of Study: Doctorate
Type: Scholarship
Value: US$2,000
Length of Study: 1 year
Frequency: Annual
Country of Study: United States of America
Application Procedure: Applicants must apply in their home country through the local institute of International Education Embassy (IEE) or Education Offices at the United States of America Embassy. Only applications received from the IEE will be considered.
Closing Date: Please contact the organization

AMERICAN SOCIETY OF NEPHROLOGY (ASN)

1725 I Street NW, Suite 510, Washington, DC, 20006, United States of America
Tel: (1) 202 659 0599
Fax: (1) 202 659 0709
Email: email@asn-online.org
Website: www.asn-online.org
Contact: Grants Co-ordinator

The American Society of Nephrology (ASN) was founded in 1967 as a non-profit corporation to enhance and assist the study and practice of nephrology, to provide a forum for the promulgation of research and to meet the professional and continuing education needs of its members.

ASN M James Scherbenske Grant

Subjects: Nephrology.
Purpose: To provide bridge funding for investigators from R01 to R01 whose application was scored, but not funded.
Eligibility: Applicants must be an active member of the ASN and hold an MD or PhD or equivalent degree. The applicants appointment to full-time faculty must be confirmed in writing by the department chair, indicating the date of first full-time faculty appointment, and providing assurance that the department will provide needed resources for conducting independent research.
Type: Grant
Value: US$100,000
Length of Study: 1 year
Frequency: Annual
Country of Study: United States of America
Application Procedure: Applicants must submit four copies of the grant application form, available online, and the NIH grant proposal.
Closing Date: March 15th, June 15th, November 15th
Funding: Private
Contributor: ASN
Additional Information: Applicants will be considered ineligible should they submit more than one ASN grant application during any particular grants cycle. For detailed information contact Benjamin Schuster by email at bschuster@asn-online.org

ASN-ASP Junior Development Grant in Geriatric Nephrology

Subjects: Geriatric and gerontologic aspects of nephrology.
Purpose: To support developing academic subspecialists interested in careers in the field.
Eligibility: Open to individuals who are within the first 3 years of a faculty appointment. Candidates must have completed a subspecialty internal medicine fellowship leading to a certification in nephrology by the American Board of Internal Medicine. All candidates must have United States of America citizenship or permanent resident status classification in the United States of America, and must be active ASN members at the time of application.
Type: Grant
Value: US$75,000 per year. The award will also include a one-time travel grant of US$3,000, which must be used to attend the meetings of the American Geriatrics Society and the ASN during the second year of the award
Length of Study: 2 years
Frequency: Annual
No. of awards offered: 1
Application Procedure: Applicants must submit four copies of the grant application form, available online, which must include the department chairman's letter, division director's letter (if applicable) and three letters of reference.
Closing Date: March 11th
Contributor: ASP ASN
No. of awards given last year: 2
No. of applicants last year: 7

ASN-AST John Merrill Grant in Transplantation

Subjects: Biomedical research related to transplantation.
Purpose: To foster the independent careers of young investigators in biomedical research related to transplantation.
Eligibility: Applicant must be an active member of the ASN and hold an MD or PhD or equivalent degree. At the time of submission the applicant's membership must be current and their dues paid. Appointment to full-time faculty must be confirmed in writing by the department chair.
Level of Study: Postdoctorate, postgraduate
Value: US$100,000
Length of Study: 2 years
Frequency: Annual
Study Establishment: ASN and AST
Country of Study: United States of America
Application Procedure: Applicants must submit four copies of the grants application form, letters from the chairman and division director, a curriculum vitae and a research proposal (no longer then 10 pages).
Closing Date: March 11th
Additional Information: For more information contact Benjamin Schuster by email at bschuster@asn-online.org

Carl W Gottschalk Research Scholar Grant

Subjects: Nephrology.
Purpose: To provide funding for young faculty to foster evolution to an independent research career.
Eligibility: Applicants must an active member of the ASN and hold an MD or PhD or equivalent degree. At the time of submission the applicant's membership must be current and their dues paid. Appointment to full-time faculty must be conformed in writing by the department chair.
Level of Study: Postgraduate, postdoctorate
Type: Grant
Value: US$100,000 for 2 years. A maximum of 10 per cent of the whole amount can be used to cover indirect costs at the candidate's sponsoring institution
Length of Study: 2 years
Frequency: Annual
Country of Study: United States of America
Application Procedure: Applicants must submit four copies of the grant application form, the letters from the chairman and division director, a curriculum vitae and a research proposal (no longer than 10 pages).

Closing Date: March 11th
Contributor: Co-sponsored by the Kidney and Urology Foundation of America
Additional Information: For detailed information contact Benjamin Schuster by email at bschuster@asn-online.org

KUFA-ASN Research Grant

Subjects: Nephrology.
Purpose: To provide funding for young faculty to foster evolution to an independent research career.
Eligibility: Applicants must be an active member of the ASN and hold an MD or a PhD or equivalent degree. At the time of submission the applicant's membership must be current and their dues paid. Appointment to full-time faculty must be confirmed in writing by the department chair.
Level of Study: Postgraduate, postdoctorate
Type: Grant
Value: US$100,000 annually for 2 years. A maximum of 10 per cent of the whole amount can be used to cover indirect costs at the candidate's institution
Length of Study: 2 years
Frequency: Annual
Country of Study: United States of America
Application Procedure: Applicants must submit four copies of the grant application form, letters from the chairman and division director, a curriculum vitae and a research proposal (no longer than 10 pages).
Closing Date: March 11th
Contributor: Co-sponsored by Kidney and Urology Foundation of America
Additional Information: For detailed information contact Benjamin Schuster by email at bschuster@asn.online.org

AMERICAN SOCIETY OF TRAVEL AGENTS (ASTA) FOUNDATION, INC.

Myriam Lechuga 1101 King ST Suite 200, Alexandria, VA 22314-2944, United States of America
Tel: (1) 703 739 2782
Fax: (1) 703 684 8319
Email: askasta@astahq.com
Website: www.astanet.com

ASTA is the world's largest association of travel professionals. Its mission is to enhance the professionalism and profitability of member agents through effective representation in industry and government affairs, education and training, and by identifying and meeting the needs of the traveling public.

Alaska Airlines Scholarship

Subjects: Travel and tourism.
Purpose: To encourage students pursuing a career in the field of travel and tourism.
Eligibility: Open to applicants who are enrolled in a four-year travel and tourism program at a university.
Level of Study: Postgraduate
Type: Scholarship
Value: US$2,000
Frequency: Annual
No. of awards offered: 1
Application Procedure: Application form can be downloaded from the website.
Closing Date: August 30th
Funding: Foundation
Contributor: ASTA Foundation

Arizona Chapter Gold Scholarship

Subjects: Travel and tourism.
Purpose: To encourage serious academic study in the field of travel and tourism.
Eligibility: Open to students enrolled in an accredited university in the state of Arizona.
Level of Study: Postgraduate
Type: Scholarship
Value: US$3,000
Length of Study: 4 years
Frequency: Annual
Country of Study: United States of America
No. of awards offered: 1
Application Procedure: Application form available on the website.
Closing Date: August 30th
Funding: Foundation
Contributor: ASTA Foundation

Healy Scholarship

Subjects: Travel and tourism.
Eligibility: Open to candidates enrolled in a four year college/university course of study.
Level of Study: Postgraduate
Type: Scholarship
Value: US$2,000
Length of Study: 4 years
Application Procedure: See the website.
Closing Date: August 30th
Funding: Foundation
Contributor: ASTA Foundation

Southern California Chapter/Pleasant Hawaiian

Subjects: Travel and tourism.
Purpose: To encourage people to take up travel and tourism business as their profession.
Eligibility: Open to US citizens enrolled in a 4-year college/university course of study.
Level of Study: Postgraduate
Type: Scholarship
Value: US$2,500
Length of Study: 4 years
Frequency: Annual
Application Procedure: A completed form and general application requirements must be submitted.
Closing Date: August 30th
Contributor: ASTA Foundation

AMERICAN SOCIOLOGICAL ASSOCIATION (ASA)

1307 New York Avenue NW, Suite 700, Washington, DC, 20005-4701, United States of America
Tel: (1) 202 383 9005 ext. 321
Fax: (1) 202 638 0882
Email: minority.affairs@asanet.org
Website: www.asanet.org
Contact: Minority Affairs Program

The American Sociological Association (ASA), founded in 1905, is a non-profit membership association dedicated to advancing sociology as a scientific discipline and profession serving the public good. With over 13,200 members, the ASA encompasses sociologists who are faculty members at colleges and universities, researchers, practitioners and students. About 20 per cent of the members work in government, business or non-profit organizations.

ASA Minority Fellowship Program

Subjects: Sociological research on mental health and mental illness including attention to prevention and causes, consequences, adaptations and interventions.
Purpose: To support the development and training of minority sociologists, to attract talented minority students interested in mental health issues and to facilitate their placement, work and success in an appropriate graduate programme.
Eligibility: Open to citizens, non-citizen nationals or permanent residents of the United States of America. Applicants must have been accepted or be enrolled in a full-time sociology doctoral programme in the United States of America and must be members of one of the following minority racial and ethnic groups: Black/African American; Latino, eg. Chicano, Cuban, Puerto Rican; American Indian or Alaskan Native; Asian, eg. Chinese, Japanese, Korean, or South East

Asian; or Pacific Islander, eg. Hawaiian, Guamanian, Samoan or Filipino.
Level of Study: Graduate, predoctorate
Type: Fellowship
Value: US$20,772
Length of Study: 1 year, renewable for up to 3 years
Frequency: Annual
Study Establishment: Varies
Country of Study: United States of America
No. of awards offered: Varies
Application Procedure: Applicants must submit their complete application package to the Minority Fellowship Program in one package. The complete application package consists of a fellowship application, essays, three letters of recommendation, official transcripts and other optional supporting documents such as a curriculum vitae, published research papers and Graduate Record Examination scores.
Closing Date: January 31st
Funding: Government, private
Contributor: NIMH
No. of awards given last year: 8
No. of applicants last year: 60
Additional Information: Dissertation support is available through an NIMH Dissertation Research Grant to Fellows who have completed all coursework and who have advanced to degree candidacy.

AMERICAN TINNITUS ASSOCIATION (ATA)

PO Box 5, Portland, OR 97207-0005, United States of America
Tel: (1) 503 248 9985
Fax: (1) 503 248 0024
Email: barbara@ata.org
Website: www.ata.org
Contact: Ms Barbara Tabachnick Sanders

The American Tinnitus Association's (ATA) mission is to silence ringing in the ears.

American Tinnitus Association Scientific Research Grants

Subjects: Tinnitus.
Purpose: To identify the mechanisms of tinnitus, to improve treatments and to identify a cure.
Level of Study: Postdoctorate
Value: Varies, maximum US$50,000 up to US$100,000 per year for exceptional projects
Length of Study: 1–3 years
Country of Study: Any country
No. of awards offered: Varies
Application Procedure: Applicants must write for grant application policies and a procedures brochure. These documents can also be downloaded from the website.
Closing Date: June 30th and December 31st
Funding: Private
Contributor: Sufferers of tinnitus
No. of awards given last year: 3
No. of applicants last year: 8

THE AMERICAN UNIVERSITY IN CAIRO (AUC)

P.O. Box 2511, 113 Sharia Kasr El Aini, Cairo, 11511, Egypt
Tel: (20) 2 794 2964
Fax: (20) 2 795 7565
Email: aucgrad@aucegypt.edu
Website: www.aucegypt.edu/graduate
Contact: Mrs Sawsan Mardini, Office of Graduate Studies & Research

The American University in Cairo (AUC) provides quality higher and continuing education for students from Egypt and the surrounding region. The University is an independent, non-profit, apolitical, non-sectarian and equal opportunity institution. English is the primary language of instruction. The University is accredited in the United States of America by the Commission of Higher Education of the Middle States Association of Colleges and Schools.

AUC African Graduate Fellowship

Subjects: Arts, humanities, business administration, engineering or information science.
Purpose: To enable outstanding young men and women from Africa to study for a Master's degree.
Eligibility: Open to African nationals, not including Egyptians, with Bachelor's degrees, an academic record of not less than 'Very Good' and an overall grade point average of 3.0 on a 4.0 scale or the equivalent. Candidates must also show proficiency in the English language by either submitting a Test of English as a Foreign Language with TWE score of 550 or above, or taking the AUC's ELPET exam.
Level of Study: Graduate
Type: Fellowship
Value: A waiver of tuition, incidental and graduation fees, health insurance on the AUC plan, a monthly stipend and, if needed, a housing allowance or accommodation at the University's residence
Length of Study: 2 academic years and the intervening Summer session
Frequency: Annual
Study Establishment: AUC only
Country of Study: Egypt
No. of awards offered: 5
Application Procedure: Applicants must complete an application form available from the Office of Graduate Studies and Research.
Closing Date: February 1st
Funding: Private
No. of awards given last year: 3
No. of applicants last year: 45

AUC Arabic Language Fellowships

Subjects: All subjects.
Purpose: To support fully admitted international graduate students who need to satisfy their degree requirement.
Eligibility: Open to candidates from any country except Egypt. Candidates must be full-time graduate students who need to take Arabic language classes in order to satisfy their requirements at AUC and would like to enrol in the Arabic Language Institute's (ALI) full-time Summer Arabic programme or take up to 6 credits of ALING classes in the Arabic Language not towards a degree.
Level of Study: Graduate, postgraduate
Type: Fellowship
Value: 50 per cent waiver of tuition fees for the ALI full-time summer Arabic programme or 50 per cent of up to six credits of ALING classes (non-credit classes) during the academic year
Length of Study: 1 Summer session or 2 courses during the academic year
Frequency: Annual, every semester
Study Establishment: AUC
Country of Study: Egypt
No. of awards offered: 5
Application Procedure: Applicants must submit a completed application form, which can be found on the website www.aucegypt.edu/academic/gradstudies/Fellowship/arabic.html
Closing Date: February 1st for the Summer session, November 1st for Spring and June 1st for Fall
No. of awards given last year: 3
No. of applicants last year: 3
Additional Information: Fellows are assigned 5 hours per week of related academic or administrative work.

AUC Assistantships

Subjects: Arts, humanities, business administration, engineering and information science.
Purpose: To support graduate-level teaching or research assistants who do not receive tuition waivers.
Eligibility: Fully accepted graduate students enrolled in two or more courses or actively engaged in thesis work are given preference over

those not enrolled in the graduate programme. Applicants who have completed their MA or MS, are preparing for a PhD, and have or are receiving academic degree training may also receive assistantships as postmaster's assistants.
Level of Study: Graduate
Type: Award
Value: Holders of a Master's degree receive monthly stipends of Egyptian £35 per hour of load per week. Bachelor's degree holders receive monthly stipends of Egyptian £29 per hour of load per week
Length of Study: 1 semester, renewable
Study Establishment: AUC
Country of Study: Egypt
Application Procedure: Applications must be made to the relevant department.
Closing Date: September 7th, February 2nd or June 7th. First week of every semester and summer session

AUC Graduate Merit Fellowships

Subjects: Business, communication, computer science, social and behavioural sciences.
Purpose: To recognize and reward outstanding new or continuing graduate students who wish to pursue full-time study in one of the graduate programmes.
Eligibility: Open to students who are fully admissible to one of the graduate programmes at AUC and who have a BA or BSc degree with a minimum overall grade point average of 3.4 on a 4.0 scale and a minimum of 3.5 in their major. Students who are already enrolled in one of AUC's graduate programmes and have a minimum grade point average of 3.7 in their graduate courses are also eligible to apply.
Level of Study: Graduate
Type: Fellowship
Value: A waiver of tuition, student services and activities fees of approx. US$4,320 per year and a monthly stipend of Egyptian £532 for 11 months
Length of Study: 1 year, although the award may be renewed for a 2nd year with the approval of the school Dean
Frequency: Annual
Study Establishment: AUC
Country of Study: Egypt
No. of awards offered: 18
Application Procedure: Applicants must write to the Office of Graduate Studies and Research or the Dean's offices, or download forms from the web under Fellowships www.aucegypt.edu/academic/gradstudies/Fellowships/merit.html
Closing Date: Mid-May
Contributor: AUC
No. of awards given last year: 18
No. of applicants last year: 100
Additional Information: Please note that the Merit Fellowship provides a partial tution waiver to international students.

AUC International Graduate Fellowships in Arabic Studies, Middle East Studies and Sociology/Anthropology

Subjects: Arabic studies, Middle East studies, sociology or anthropology.
Purpose: To recognize and award outstanding new international graduate students who wish to pursue full-time study.
Eligibility: Open to candidates from any country except Egypt. Candidates must have completed an appropriate undergraduate degree with a minimum overall grade point average of 3.4 on a 4.0 scale or equivalent.
Level of Study: Graduate, postgraduate
Type: Fellowship
Value: A waiver of tuition fees, a monthly stipend and housing allowance or accommodation in the University's residence. The award also includes medical insurance
Length of Study: 2 years
Frequency: Annual
Study Establishment: AUC
Country of Study: Egypt
No. of awards offered: 2
Application Procedure: Applicants must complete an application form, available from the website.
Closing Date: February 1st
No. of awards given last year: 2
No. of applicants last year: 30
Additional Information: Fellows are assigned 18 hours per week of related academic or administrative work.

AUC Laboratory Instruction Graduate Fellowships in Engineering and Computer Science

Subjects: Computer science and engineering.
Purpose: To recognize and support outstanding graduate students who wish to pursue full-time study in either engineering or computer science.
Eligibility: Students must have a BSc degree with a minimum overall grade point average of 3.2 on a 4.0 scale or its equivalent. Students already enrolled in a graduate programme with a minimum grade point average of 3.2 are also eligible.
Level of Study: Graduate
Type: Fellowship
Value: A waiver of tuition, student services and activities fees of approx. US$3,200 per year and a monthly stipend of Egyptian £460 for 10 months
Length of Study: Reviewed every semester and may be renewed for a maximum period of 2 years. The fellowship may cover a Summer session
Frequency: Annual
Study Establishment: AUC
Country of Study: Egypt
No. of awards offered: 13
Application Procedure: Application forms are available from the Departments of Engineering and Computer Science as well as the Office of Graduate Studies and Research, and are also downloadable from the web site under Fellowships www.aucegypt.edu/academic/gradstudies/Fellowships/lab.html
Closing Date: Mid-May

AUC Nadia Niazi Mostafa Fellowship in Islamic Art and Architecture

Subjects: Islamic art and architecture.
Purpose: To recognize and award outstanding Egyptian graduate students who wish to pursue full-time study in the programme. The award is for 2nd-year Egyptian students already enrolled in the programme.
Eligibility: Open to Egyptians. Candidates must be 2nd-year students enrolled in the graduate programme in Islamic art and architecture and have completed 12 credit hours with a minimum grade point average of 3.2.
Level of Study: Postgraduate
Type: Fellowship
Value: A waiver of tuition fees of up to US$4,320 and a monthly stipend over a period of 10 months
Length of Study: 1 academic year
Frequency: Annual
Study Establishment: AUC
Country of Study: Egypt
No. of awards offered: 1
Application Procedure: Application forms are available from the Office of Graduate Studies and Research or the Department of Arabic Studies.
Closing Date: May 15th
Funding: Private
No. of awards given last year: 1
Additional Information: Fellows are assigned 12 hours per week of related academic or administrative work.

AUC Ryoichi Sasakawa Young Leaders Graduate Scholarship

Subjects: Arts, humanities and social sciences.
Purpose: To educate outstanding young men and women who have demonstrated a high potential for future leadership in international affairs, public life and private endeavour.

Eligibility: Applicants must have a Bachelor's degree with a grade point average of 3.2 or above and have actively participated in extra-curricular activities. Preference is given to those students who require four semesters to complete their degree. The award is contingent upon full admission to one of AUC's graduate programmes in the humanities and social sciences.
Level of Study: Graduate
Type: Scholarship
Value: A waiver of tuition, incidental and AUC medical service fees, a textbook allowance and a stipend towards living expenses of US$1,600 per year for Egyptians and US$3,600 for non-Egyptians
Length of Study: 2 years
Frequency: Annual
Study Establishment: AUC only
Country of Study: Egypt
No. of awards offered: 3
Application Procedure: Graduate application forms are available from the Office of Graduate Studies and Research or can be downloaded from the website.
Closing Date: February 1st
Funding: Private
Contributor: The Tokyo Foundation
No. of awards given last year: 3
No. of applicants last year: 25

AUC Sheikh Kamal Adham Fellowship

Subjects: Television journalism.
Purpose: To assist students undertaking postgraduate study.
Eligibility: Open to non-Egyptian graduate students who are MA candidates in the journalism and mass communication department, specializing in television journalism. Selection is made on the basis of financial need and academic performance. Professional experience is also considered where applicable.
Level of Study: Graduate
Type: Fellowship
Value: A partial waiver of tuition fees of US$5,000 per year
Length of Study: 1 year, with the possibility of renewal
Frequency: Annual
Country of Study: Egypt
No. of awards offered: 1
Application Procedure: Applicants must write to the director of the Kamal Adham Center for Television Journalism for details or telephone (20) 2 797 5424.
Closing Date: Mid-May
No. of awards given last year: 1
Additional Information: Applicants must serve as an assistant in the Adham Center for 40 hours per month during the academic year.

AUC Teaching Arabic as a Foreign Language Fellowships

Subjects: Arabic, education and teacher training.
Purpose: To acquire language teaching skills.
Eligibility: Open to individuals who have Teaching Arabic as a Foreign Language experience or excellent qualifications in the Arabic language.
Level of Study: Graduate
Type: Fellowship
Value: A tuition waiver of US$4,320 and a monthly stipend of Egyptian £607 and medical insurance
Length of Study: 2 academic years and the intervening Summer session
Frequency: Annual
Study Establishment: AUC
Country of Study: Egypt
No. of awards offered: 3
Application Procedure: Applicants must write to the Office of Graduate Admissions and the Arabic Language Institute.
Closing Date: February 1st
Contributor: AUC
No. of awards given last year: 3
No. of applicants last year: 10

AUC Teaching English as a Foreign Language Fellowships

Subjects: Education.
Purpose: To acquire language teaching experience.
Eligibility: Special consideration is given to applicants with previous Teaching English as a Foreign Language experience and/or excellent qualifications in the English language.
Level of Study: Graduate
Type: Fellowship
Value: A waiver of tuition fees and a monthly stipend of Egyptian £550 and medical insurance. Non-residents of Egypt are provided with accommodation in the University dormitory or with a monthly housing allowance of Egyptian £620 and one-way home travel
Length of Study: 2 academic years and the intervening Summer session
Frequency: Annual
Study Establishment: AUC
Country of Study: Egypt
Application Procedure: Applicants must write to the English Language Institute in Cairo or the New York office at aucegypt@aucnyo.edu The downloadable application for the TEFL fellowship is avaliable www.aucegypt.edu/academic/gradstudies/Fellowships/tefl.html apply.
Closing Date: February 1st
Contributor: AUC
No. of awards given last year: 10
No. of applicants last year: 50

AUC University Fellowships

Subjects: Art and humanities, business administration and management, engineering, mass communication and information, mathematics and computer science, social and behavioural sciences.
Purpose: To assist new and continuing graduate students who display superior performance in their academic endeavours and who wish to pursue full-time study.
Eligibility: Students must have a BSc or a BA degree with a minimum overall grade point average of 3.2 on a 4.0 scale or its equivalent. Students already enrolled in one of these graduate programmes with a minimum grade point average of 3.2 are also eligible. Preference is given to outstanding graduate students who are already enrolled.
Level of Study: Graduate
Type: Fellowship
Value: A waiver of tuition, student services and activities fees of approx. US$4,320 per year and a monthly stipend of Egyptian £197 for 10 months
Length of Study: Reviewed every semester and may be renewed for a maximum period of 2 years. The fellowship may cover a Summer session
Frequency: Annual
Study Establishment: AUC
Country of Study: Egypt
Application Procedure: Applicants must complete applications, available from the chosen department in May.
Closing Date: June
Contributor: AUC
No. of awards given last year: 18
No. of applicants last year: 123
Additional Information: Fellows are assigned 10–12 hours per week of work with faculty members in teaching and research activities.

AUC Writing Center Graduate Fellowships

Subjects: English, grammar, education and native language, literacy education, teaching and learning.
Purpose: To provide outstanding students with valuable teaching, academic experience and to involve them as tutors in AUC's Writing Center.
Eligibility: Open to students who are fully admissible to the graduate programme in English and Comparative Literature at AUC and who have a Bachelor of Arts degree with a minimum overall grade point average of 3.2 on a 4.0 scale or its equivalent. Students already enrolled in one of these graduate programmes with a minimum grade point average of 3.4 are also eligible.
Level of Study: Graduate

Type: Fellowship
Value: Up to US$4,320 waiver of tuition, student services and activities fee and a monthly stipend of Egyptian £242 for 10 months
Length of Study: Reviewed every semester and may be renewed for a maximum period of 2 years. The fellowship may cover a Summer session
Frequency: Annual
Study Establishment: AUC
Country of Study: Egypt
No. of awards offered: 1
Application Procedure: Applicants must write for details to the Chair of the Department of English and Comparative Literature, and the Office of Graduate Studies and Research.
Closing Date: The end of April
Contributor: AUC
No. of awards given last year: 1
No. of applicants last year: 5
Additional Information: As part of their fellowship and in support of their professional training, Fellows are assigned 10 hours of work per week in the Writing Center.

AMERICAN VENOUS FORUM FOUNDATION

PMB 311, 203 Washington Street, Salem, MA 01970, United States of America
Tel: (1) 978 744 5005
Fax: (1) 978 744 5029
Website: www.venous-info.com

The American Venous Forum Foundation grants research awards and prizes that stimulate and recognize excellence in published (science) writing on laboratory and clinical research in the study of venous disease.

The BSN-Jobst Inc. Research Award

Subjects: Venous disease.
Purpose: To award a grant to a research Fellow or a resident in an ACGME programme who has a specific interest in the diagnosis and treatment of venous disease.
Level of Study: Graduate, doctorate, postdoctorate
Type: Research grant
Value: US$25,000
Frequency: Annual
Country of Study: United States of America
No. of awards offered: 1
Application Procedure: Applicants must visit the website for details.
Closing Date: September 1st
Contributor: BSN-Jobst Inc. and the American Venous Forum Foundation
No. of awards given last year: 1
No. of applicants last year: 4

Sigvaris Travelling Fellowship

Subjects: Venous disease.
Purpose: To enable young physicians to travel throughout the United States of America and abroad to visit centres of excellence in the management of venous disease.
Level of Study: Doctorate, postdoctorate, graduate
Type: Travelling fellowship
Value: US$12,000
Frequency: Annual
Country of Study: United States of America and abroad
No. of awards offered: 1
Application Procedure: Applicants must visit the website for details.
Closing Date: December 15th
Contributor: Sigvaris Inc. and the American Venous Forum Foundation
No. of awards given last year: 1

AMERICAN WATER WORKS ASSOCIATION (AWWA)

6666 West Quincy Avenue, Denver, CO, 80235, United States of America
Tel: (1) 303 347 6206
Fax: (1) 303 347 0804
Email: acarabetta@awwa.org
Website: www.awwa.org
Contact: Administrative Assistant

The American Water Works Association (AWWA) is an international non-profit scientific and educational society dedicated to the improvement of drinking water quality and supply. The Association has more than 57,000 members who represent the full spectrum of the drinking water community, eg. treatment plant operators and managers, scientists, environmentalists, manufacturers, academics, regulators and others who have a genuine interest in water supply and public health.

AWWA Abel Wolman Fellowship

Subjects: Water supply and treatment.
Purpose: To encourage and support promising students from countries with AWWA sections to pursue advanced training and research.
Eligibility: Open to candidates who anticipate completing the requirements for their PhD degree within 2 years of the award. Applicants must be citizens of a country that has an AWWA section, ie. the United States of America, Canada or Mexico. Applicants will be considered without regard to colour, gender, race, creed or country of origin.
Level of Study: Doctorate
Type: Fellowship
Value: Up to US$20,000
Length of Study: Initially 1 year, renewable for 1 further year on submission of evidence of satisfactory progress and approval by a review committee
Frequency: Annual
Country of Study: United States of America, Canada or Mexico
No. of awards offered: 1
Application Procedure: Applicants must submit an official application form, official transcripts of all university education, official copies of Graduate Record Examination scores, three letters of recommendation, a proposed curriculum of study, and brief plans of dissertation research study.
Closing Date: January 15th
Funding: Private

For further information contact:

Email: swheeler@awwa.org.

AWWA Academic Achievement Award

Subjects: Water supply and treatment.
Purpose: To encourage academic excellence by recognizing contributions to the field.
Eligibility: Open to all Master's theses and doctoral dissertations that are relevant to the water supply industry. The manuscript must reflect the work of a single author and be submitted during the competition year in which it was submitted for the degree. The competition is open to students majoring in any subject provided the work is directly related to the drinking water supply industry.
Level of Study: Doctorate, postgraduate
Type: Award
Value: US$3,000 for 1st place and US$1,500 for 2nd place
Frequency: Annual
Country of Study: United States of America, Canada or Mexico
No. of awards offered: 4 (2 are for doctoral dissertations and 2 are for Master's theses)
Application Procedure: Applicants must submit an entry form with the names of the author, school and department, major professor, the degree sought, a one-page abstract of the manuscript plus a letter of endorsement from the major professor or department chair. Manuscripts submitted to the Academic Achievement Award Committee should be unbound.

Closing Date: October 1st
Funding: Commercial
Contributor: AWWA

AWWA Holly A Cornell Scholarship

Subjects: Water supply and treatment.
Purpose: To encourage and support outstanding students to pursue advanced training in the field.
Eligibility: Open to female and/or minority Master's students. Applicants must be citizens of the United States of America.
Level of Study: Postgraduate
Type: Scholarship
Value: US$5,000
Frequency: Annual
Country of Study: United States of America, Canada or Mexico
No. of awards offered: 1
Application Procedure: Applicants must submit an official application form, official transcripts of all university education, official copies of Graduate Record Examination scores, three letters of recommendation, a proposed curriculum of study and a brief statement describing the student's career objectives.
Closing Date: January 15th
Funding: Commercial

AWWA Larson Aquatic Research Support

Subjects: Corrosion control, treatment and distribution of domestic and industrial water supplies, aquatic chemistry, analytical chemistry and environmental chemistry.
Purpose: To provide support and encouragement to outstanding students preparing for a career in one of the fields of science or engineering to which Dr Thurston E Larson made significant contributions and who will provide leadership in efforts to improve water quality.
Eligibility: Open to candidates pursuing a Master's or PhD at an Institute of Higher Education located in Canada, Guam, Puerto Rico, Mexico or the United States of America. The requirements for the degree must be completed in the year of the award. Selection of scholarship recipients is based upon the excellence of their academic record and their potential to provide leadership in one of the fields served by Dr Larson.
Level of Study: Postdoctorate, doctorate
Type: Scholarship
Value: US$5,000 for Master's students and US$7,000 for a PhD students
Frequency: Annual
Country of Study: United States of America, Canada or Mexico
No. of awards offered: 2
Application Procedure: Applicants must submit an official application form, a curriculum vitae, official transcripts of all postsecondary education, official copies of Graduate Record Examination scores, three letters of recommendation, a proposed plan of study, and a statement of educational plans and career objectives demonstrating or declaring an interest in an appropriate field of endeavour, or, if applicable, a research plan.
Closing Date: January 15th for the MS for receipt in the following year and January 15th for the PhD for receipt in the same year
Funding: Private
Contributor: Private donations
Additional Information: Scholarship recipients will be publicly recognized at the annual conference of the American Water Works Association in June.

AWWA Thomas R Camp Scholarship

Subjects: Water supply and treatment.
Purpose: To support and encourage outstanding students undertaking applied research in the drinking water field.
Eligibility: Open to doctoral students in even years and to Master's students in odd years. Applicants will be considered without regard to colour, gender, race, creed or country of origin.
Level of Study: Doctorate, postgraduate
Type: Scholarship
Value: US$5,000
Frequency: Annual
Country of Study: United States of America, Canada or Mexico
No. of awards offered: 1
Application Procedure: Applicants must submit a completed application form, a curriculum vitae, official transcripts of all post secondary education, official copies of Graduate Record Examination scores, quantitative, verbal and analytical, three letters of recommendation, a one page statement of educational plans and career objectives demonstrating or declaring an interest in the drinking water field and a two-page proposed plan of research.
Closing Date: January 15th
Funding: Commercial
Contributor: Camp Dresser and McKee, Inc.

THE AMERICAN-SCANDINAVIAN FOUNDATION (ASF)

58 Park Avenue, New York, NY 10016, United States of America
Tel: (1) 212 879 9779
Fax: (1) 212 249 3444
Email: grants@amscan.org
Website: www.amscan.org
Contact: Director of Fellowships and Grants

The ASF is a publicity supported, non-profit organization that promotes international understanding through educational and cultural exchange between the U.S. and the Nordic countries

ASF Grants and Fellowships for Advanced Study or Research in Denmark, Finland, Iceland, Norway and Sweden

Subjects: All subjects.
Purpose: To encourage advanced study and research, and to increase understanding between the United States of America and Scandinavia.
Eligibility: Applicants must be citizens of the United States of America or permanent residents who have a well-defined research or study project that makes a stay in Scandinavia essential. Team projects are eligible, but each member must apply as an individual. Some ability in the language of the host country is desirable. Priority will be given to applicants who have not previously received an ASF award.
Level of Study: Postgraduate, professional development, research
Type: Fellowship
Value: Grants are usually US$4,000, fellowships are up to US$20,000
Length of Study: A maximum of 1 year
Frequency: Annual
Country of Study: Denmark, Finland, Iceland, Norway or Sweden
No. of awards offered: 25–30
Application Procedure: Applicants must complete an official application form and submit this with an application fee of US$20.
Closing Date: November 1st
Funding: Private
No. of awards given last year: 24
No. of applicants last year: 100
Additional Information: For further information please contact Ellen McKey via email or visit the website.

ANGLO-AUSTRIAN MUSIC SOCIETY

Richard Tauber Prize for Singers, 158 Rosendale Road, London, SE21 8LG, England
Tel: (44) 20 8761 0444
Fax: (44) 20 8766 6151
Email: info@aams.org.uk
Website: www.aams.org.uk
Contact: Jane Avery, Secretary

The Anglo-Austrian Music Society promotes lectures and concerts and is closely associated with its parent organization, the Anglo-Austrian Society, which was founded in 1944 to promote friendship and understanding between the people of the United Kingdom and Austria through personal contacts, educational programmes and cultural exchanges.

Richard Tauber Prize for Singers
Subjects: Vocal musical performance.
Eligibility: Open to British and Austrian resident singers. Male applicants must be aged 21–32 years and female applicants aged 21–30 years. All applicants must ordinarily be resident in the United Kingdom or Austria.
Level of Study: Postgraduate
Type: Prize
Value: First prize: UK £5,000 plus public recital in London; second prize: UK £2,500, Additional prizes of UK £1,000 and UK £500
Frequency: Every 2 years
Country of Study: Any country
No. of awards offered: 2
Application Procedure: Applicants must complete an application form.
Closing Date: February 7th
Funding: Private
Additional Information: Preliminary auditions are held in London and Vienna in March. Applicants must attend these auditions at their own expense. A final public audition is held in London in June.

ANGLO-BRAZILIAN SOCIETY

32 Green Street, London, W1K 7AU, England
Tel: (44) 20 7493 8493
Email: info@anglobraziliansociety.org
Website: www.anglobraziliansociety.org
Contact: Ms Eliane Dell'Aglio, Secretary

The Anglo-Brazilian Society was formed in 1943, to promote close and friendly relations between Brazil and the United Kingdom and to further in the United Kingdom a knowledge of Brazil, its people and its culture, with the participation of Brazilians resident in the United Kingdom.

Anglo-Brazilian Society Scholarship
Subjects: Any aspect of Brazil, including its culture, history, geography, literature, economy and medicine.
Purpose: To promote close and friendly relations between Brazil and the United Kingdom by providing a contribution to the cost of a working and/or research visit to Brazil.
Eligibility: Open to British nationals normally resident in the United Kingdom.
Level of Study: Postgraduate, graduate
Type: Scholarship
Value: UK £1,000
Frequency: Annual
Country of Study: Brazil
No. of awards offered: 1
Application Procedure: Applicants must contact the Society and are selected by means of an essay competition and presentation of an outline of their proposed study in Brazil. The outline must be approximately 3,000 words. Recipients travel to Brazil later in the same year and are expected to deliver a lecture to the Society on their return. Final selection is by interview in London in March.
Closing Date: February 1st
Funding: Private
Contributor: Events run by the Anglo-Brazilian Society
No. of awards given last year: 1
No. of applicants last year: 3

THE ANGLO-DANISH SOCIETY

Anglo-Danish Society, c/o 6 Keats Avenue, Littleover, Derbyshire, Derby, DE23 4ED, England
Tel: (44) 1332 517 160
Fax: (44) 1332 517 323
Email: info@anglo-danishsociety.org.uk
Website: www.anglo-danish.society.org.uk
Contact: Mrs Margit Staehr, Administrator

Anglo-Danish (London) Scholarships
Subjects: Anglo–Danish cultural and scientific interests.
Purpose: To promote Anglo-Danish relations.
Eligibility: Open to graduates of Danish and British nationality.
Level of Study: Doctorate, postgraduate, postdoctorate, professional development
Type: Scholarship
Value: UK £250 per month
Length of Study: A maximum of 6 months
Frequency: Dependent on funds available
Study Establishment: Universities
No. of awards offered: 4–6
Application Procedure: Applicants must complete an application form, available from October 1st – December 31st. Applicants should enclose a stamped addressed envelope or international reply coupons.
Closing Date: January 12th
Funding: Commercial, private
No. of awards given last year: 6
No. of applicants last year: 80

ANGLO-JEWISH ASSOCIATION

Suite 5, 107 Gloucester Place, London, W1U 6BY, England
Tel: (44) 20 7486 5055
Fax: (44) 20 7486 5155
Email: info@anglojewish.co.uk
Website: www.anglojewish.co.uk
Contact: Julia Samuel, Chairman, Education Committee

Anglo-Jewish Association Bursary
Subjects: All subjects.
Purpose: To assist Jewish students in full-time higher education who are in financial need.
Eligibility: Open to Jewish students of any nationality in financial need up to the age of 35.
Level of Study: Unrestricted
Type: Bursary
Value: Up to UK £3,000 per year
Frequency: Annual
Study Establishment: University
Country of Study: United Kingdom
No. of awards offered: 100–120
Application Procedure: Application form must be completed and returned with all enclosures. This form can be downloaded from the website.
Closing Date: April 29th
Funding: Trusts
No. of awards given last year: 130
No. of applicants last year: 950

THE APEX FOUNDATION FOR RESEARCH INTO INTELLECTUAL DISABILITY LIMITED

PO Box 311, Mount Evelyn, VIC, 3796, Australia
Tel: (61) 3 9736 1261
Email: morrish@c031.aone.net.au
Website: www.apexfoundation.org.au
Contact: Secretary

The Apex Foundation for Research into Intellectual Disability supports research into the prevention and treatment of intellectual disability utilizing the funds raised some years ago by the Association of Apex Clubs. The Foundation manages these funds and makes annual research grants in support of selected research projects.

Apex Foundation Annual Research Grants
Subjects: Disability.
Purpose: To support research projects that are concerned with the causes, diagnosis, prevention or treatment of intellectual disability.
Eligibility: Open to suitably qualified researchers of any nationality, but the research must be carried out within the Commonwealth of Australia.
Level of Study: Research

Value: Varies. The total annual funds available are approx. Australian $60,000
Length of Study: Varies
Frequency: Annual
Country of Study: Australia
No. of awards offered: Varies
Application Procedure: Applicants must complete an application form, available from the Secretary of the Foundation.
Closing Date: July 31st
Funding: Foundation
No. of awards given last year: 5
No. of applicants last year: 11

APPRAISAL INSTITUTE

550 West Van Buren Street, Suite 1000, Chicago, IL, 60607, United States of America
Tel: (1) 312 335 4129
Fax: (1) 312 335 4200
Email: sdavila@appraisalinstitute.org
Website: www.appraisalinstitute.org
Contact: Sylvia Davila, Education Trust

Educating real estate appraisers for over 60 years, the Appraisal Institute is the acknowledged leader in residential and commercial appraisal education, research, publishing and professional membership designation programmes. Appraisal Institute members are identified by their experience and knowledge of real estate valuation, and adhere to a strictly enforced code of professional ethics and standards of professional appraisal practice.

Appraisal Institute Education Trust Scholarship

Subjects: Real estate appraisal, land economics, real estate and allied fields.
Purpose: The Education Trust scholarship is awarded on the basis of academic excellence and is intended to help finance the education endeavors of individuals concentrating in the fields listed.
Eligibility: Full Time College, United States University or Community College. United States citizens, graduate and undergraduate students majoring in Real Estate Appraisal, land Economics, Real Estate or Allied Fields.
Level of Study: Postgraduate, graduate
Type: Scholarship
Value: Undergraduates US$2,000, graduates US$3,000
Length of Study: 1 year
Frequency: Annual
Country of Study: United States of America
No. of awards offered: Varies
Application Procedure: A written statement from the Dean of your college recommending your application; A signed statement regarding your general activities and intellectual interests in college. (This statement should not exceed 1,000 words.); Official copies of all collegiate grade records; A proposed student program, including a brief description of each course you plan to pursue in working toward the degree indicated, and a certificate of approval of this program signed by the Dean of the college in which the work is to be completed; A graduate student must have served, or is about to serve, an internship with an appraiser or the appraisal department of a corporation (letter from employer required); Request two individuals to write a letter regarding your qualifications and character and to forward these letters to the Appraisal Institute, at the address below; Student must submit four copies of all information (one original and three copies).
Closing Date: March 15th
Funding: Private
Additional Information: Applications are available in November. If you would like to receive further information or request an application to be sent via email or mail. Please write to the attention of Olivia Carreon, Project Coordinator at the Appraisal Institute at the address listed, or email ocarreon@appraisalinstitute.org or call 312-335-4100. If you have any further questions, please free to contact me at 312-335-4129 or email sdvila@appraisalinstitute.org

For further information contact:

Appraisal Institute
Tel: 312 335 4100
Email: ocarreon@appraisalinstitute.org
Contact: Olivia Carreon, Project Coordinator

Minorities and Women Educational Scholarship Program

Subjects: Real estate appraisal or related fields.
Purpose: The Minority and Women Educational Scholarship is geared towards college students working towards a degree in real estate appraisal or a related field. The scholarship is to help offset the cost of tuition.
Eligibility: Open to citizens of the United States of America. Applicant must be a member of a racial, ethnic or gender group underrepresented in the appraisal profession and full- or part-time student enrolled-in real estate related courses at a degree-granting college/ university or junior college/university. Individuals must have proof a cumulative grade point average of no less than 2.5 on 4.0 scale and have demonstrated financial need.
Level of Study: Graduate, postgraduate
Type: Scholarship
Value: Minimum of US$1,000 per person
Frequency: Annual
Country of Study: United States of America
No. of awards offered: Varies
Application Procedure: Applicants must provide an official student transcript, a 500-word written essay stating why they should be awarded the scholarship, an attestation that the scholarship will be applied towards tuition and book expenses and two letters of recommendation from previous employers and/or college professors. Students must also submit three copies of all information (one original and two copies).
Closing Date: April 15th
Funding: Private
Additional Information: For further information or request for an application, contact Wendy Woodburn at 312-335-4191 or via email wwoodburn@appraisalinstitute.org

For further information contact:

Appraisal Institute
Tel: 312 335 4100
Email: sbarnes@appraisalinstitute.org
Contact: Shella Barnes

ARAB-BRITISH CHAMBER CHARITABLE FOUNDATION (ABCCF)

Longmead, Benhall Green, Saxmundham, Suffolk, IP17 1HU, England
Tel: (44) 17 2860 3359
Fax: (44) 17 2860 3359
Email: abccf@abcc.org.uk
Website: www.abcc.org.uk
Contact: Mr Michael Payne, Secretary to the Trustees

The Arab-British Chamber Charitable Foundation (ABCCF) provides funding for Arab postgraduate students studying at British universities.

ABCCF Student Grant

Subjects: Agriculture, forestry and fishery, architecture and town planning, business administration and management, education and teacher training, engineering, mathematics and computer science, mass communication and information science, social sciences or transport.
Purpose: To assist Arab nationals in financial need, while they are at United Kingdom universities, to undertake studies in subjects of potential value to the Arab world.
Eligibility: Open to nationals of an Arab League State. The maximum age is 40 and applicants must have United Kingdom student visa status. Applicants must show a commitment to return to the Arab world on completion of the postgraduate programme.
Level of Study: Postgraduate, doctorate

Type: Grant
Value: Up to UK £2,000 per academic year
Length of Study: 3–4 years
Frequency: Annual
Study Establishment: A university in the United Kingdom
Country of Study: United Kingdom
No. of awards offered: Up to 30
Application Procedure: Applicants must complete an application form that is sent only to applicants who have confirmed that their circumstances meet with the ABCCF's criteria. Other supporting documentation is required, eg. transcripts of degrees, academic references, proof of citizenship and visa status, university acceptance or registration and a written undertaking to return to the Arab world after graduation.
Closing Date: None
Funding: Commercial
Contributor: The Arab–British Chamber of Commerce, London
No. of awards given last year: 30
No. of applicants last year: 200

THE ARC OF THE UNITED STATES

1010 Wayne Avenue, Suite 650, Silver Spring, MD, 20910, United States of America
Tel: (1) 301 565 3842
Fax: (1) 301 565 5342
Email: info@thearc.org
Website: www.thearc.org
Contact: Dr Sharon Davis, Professional & Family Services Director

The Arc of the United States works to include all children and adults with cognitive, intellectual and developmental disabilities in every community.

Distinguished Research Award

Subjects: The prevention or improvement of mental retardation.
Purpose: To reward an individual or individuals whose research has had a significant impact on the prevention or improvement of mental retardation.
Type: Award
Value: The recipient of the award will receive a plaque, US$1,000 and a trip to speak at the Research and Prevention Luncheon of The Arc's National Convention
Frequency: Every 2 years
No. of awards offered: 1
Application Procedure: Applicants must send the original and five copies of a nomination to The Arc.
Closing Date: April 15th
Funding: Private
No. of awards given last year: 1
No. of applicants last year: 3

ARCTIC INSTITUTE OF NORTH AMERICA (AINA)

The University of Calgary, 2500 University Drive North West, Calgary, AB, T2N 1N4, Canada
Tel: (1) 403 220 7515
Fax: (1) 403 282 4609
Email: wkjessen@ucalgary.ca
Website: www.ucalgary.ca/aina
Contact: Ms Karla Jesson Williamson, Executive Director

Created in 1945, the Arctic Institute of North America (AINA) is a non-profit membership organization and a multidisciplinary research institute for the University of Calgary.

Jennifer Robinson Memorial Scholarship

Subjects: Northern biology.
Purpose: To award a graduate who best exemplifies the qualities of scholarship that the late Jennifer Robinson brought to her studies at the Kluane Lake Research Station. The scholarship committee looks for evidence of Northern relevance and a commitment to field orientated research.
Eligibility: Applicants should contact the organization for eligibility details and guidelines.
Level of Study: Graduate
Type: Scholarship
Value: Canadian $5,000
Length of Study: 1 year, with the possibility of renewal
Frequency: Annual
Country of Study: Canada
No. of awards offered: 1
Application Procedure: There is no application form. Applicants must submit a brief description, of 2–3 pages, of the proposed research, including a clear hypothesis, relevance, title and statement of the purpose of the research, the area and type of study, and the methodology and plan for the evaluation of findings. Any collaborative relationship or work should be briefly identified. Three academic reference letters, a complete curriculum vitae with copies and a separate sheet of paper listing current sources and amounts of research funding including scholarships, grants and bursaries should also be submitted. Applicants are requested to include their email address upon submitting applications, if they have one.
Closing Date: January 10th
Funding: Private
No. of awards given last year: 1
Additional Information: The winning applicant will be notified by the selection committee in February.

Jim Bourque Scholarship

Subjects: Education, environmental studies or traditional knowledge of telecommunications.
Purpose: To financially support those in postsecondary training.
Eligibility: Open to Canadian Aboriginal mature or matriculating students who are enrolled in postsecondary training in the relevant subject areas.
Type: Scholarship
Value: Canadian $1,000
Length of Study: 1 year
Frequency: Annual
Country of Study: Canada
No. of awards offered: 1
Application Procedure: There is no application form. Applicants must submit, in 500 words or less, a description of their intended programme of study and the reasons for their choice. In addition, applicants must include a copy of their most recent college or university transcript, a signed letter of recommendation from a community leader eg. Town or Band Council, Chamber of Commerce, Metis Local, a statement of financial need indicating funding already received or expected and a proof of enrolment into, or application for, a post-secondary institution. Applications are evaluated based on need, relevance of study, achievements, return of investment and overall presentation of the application.
Closing Date: July 15th

Lorraine Allison Scholarship

Subjects: Canadian issues.
Purpose: To promote the study of Northern issues.
Eligibility: Open to any student enrolled at a Canadian university in a programme of graduate study related to Northern issues, whose application best addresses academic excellence, a demonstrated commitment to Northern research and a desire for research results to be beneficial to Northerners, especially Native Northerners. Candidates in biological science fields will be preferred, but a social science topic will also be considered. Scholars from Yukon, the North West Territories and Nunavut are encouraged to apply.
Level of Study: Graduate
Type: Scholarship
Value: Canadian $2,000
Length of Study: 1 year with the possibility of renewal following receipt of a satisfactory progress report and reapplication
Frequency: Annual
Country of Study: Canada
No. of awards offered: 1

Application Procedure: Applicants must submit a two-page description of the Northern studies programme and relevant projects being undertaken, three letters of reference from the applicant's current or past professors, a complete curriculum vitae with academic transcripts and a separate sheet of paper listing current sources and amounts of research funding, including scholarships, grants and bursaries. There is no application form.
Closing Date: January 10th
Funding: International Office, trusts
Additional Information: The selection committee will notify the winning applicant in February.

ARD INTERNATIONAL MUSIC COMPETITION

Bayerischer Rundfunk, Munich, 80300, Germany
Tel: (49) 89 5 900 2471
Fax: (49) 89 5 900 3573
Email: ard.musikwettbewerb@brnet.de
Website: www.ard-musikwettbewerb.de

The International Music Competition, held annually in September, covers various categories and is open to all nationalities. The 2007 competition is for Oboe, Trombone, Percussion and Piano Trio categories. The International Music Competition is part of all Germans Broadcast stations, situated in Munich, Germany.

ARD International Music Competition Munich

Subjects: Music, categories vary annually.
Purpose: To support and reward a selection of young musicians who are at concert standard.
Eligibility: Open to musicians of any nationality. Age restrictions apply.
Level of Study: Graduate
Type: Competition
Frequency: Annual
Study Establishment: Conservatories, university schools of music and music academies, but also includes advanced private studies
Country of Study: Any country
No. of awards offered: The competition includes either 4 or 5 categories. For each category 3 prizes are offered
Application Procedure: Applicants must complete and submit an application form, an application fee and an audio cassette. There is an entry fee of €90 per soloist, €120 for duos.
Closing Date: April 30th
Funding: Commercial
Contributor: Public radio stations in Germany
No. of awards given last year: 150
No. of applicants last year: 450

Prize Winner of the ARD International Music Competition Munich

Subjects: Music (categories are Singer, Solo instruments and chamber music ensembles categories vary annually).
Purpose: To support and reward a selection of young musicians who are at concert standard.
Eligibility: Open to musicians of any nationality. Age restrictions apply. Further information can be found in the brochure, which is available on request and on the website.
Level of Study: Graduate
Type: Prize
Value: €99,000 in cash awards per year. Please contact the organization for details
Frequency: Annual
Study Establishment: Conservatories, university schools of music and music academies, but also includes advanced private studies
Country of Study: Any country
No. of awards offered: The competition includes either 4 or 5 categories. For each category 3 prizes are offered
Application Procedure: Applicants must complete and submit an application form, an application fee and an audio cassette.
Closing Date: April 30th
Funding: Commercial
Contributor: Public radio stations in Germany
No. of awards given last year: 13
No. of applicants last year: 450
Additional Information: Categories in 2007: Oboe, Trombone, Percussion and Piano Trio.

ARISTOTLE UNIVERSITY OF THESSALONIKI

University Campus, Thessaloniki, GR 541 24, Greece
Tel: (30) 2310 994168, 996771
Fax: (30) 2310 995112
Email: dps@rect.auth.gr
Website: www.auth.gr/services/admin/studies_department.en.php3
Contact: Studies Department

Aristotle University of Thessaloniki Scholarships

Subjects: Modern Greek language.
Purpose: To encourage foreigners to learn the language and to diffuse Greek language and civilization.
Eligibility: Open to foreign citizens of any origin.
Level of Study: Unrestricted
Type: Scholarship
Value: Tuition fee waiver and €420 grant
Length of Study: Approx. 1 month, between August 16th and September 15th
Frequency: Annual
Study Establishment: The Aristotle University of Thessaloniki
Country of Study: Greece
No. of awards offered: 70
Application Procedure: Applicants must complete an application form, available on request from the Studies Department or from the website. Completed application form and supporting documents must be sent to the Department of Studies by surface mail.
Closing Date: February 28th
Funding: Government
Contributor: The Aristotle University of Thessaloniki
No. of awards given last year: 70
No. of applicants last year: 480
Additional Information: Information leaflet and application form also available via email.

For further information contact:

Aristotle University Department of Studies, University Campus, Hellas, Thessaloniki, 54 124, Greece

ARKANSAS SINGLE PARENT SCHOLARSHIP FUND (ASPSF)

614 East Emma Avenue, Suite 119, Springdale, AR 72764, United States of America
Tel: (1) 479 927 1402
Fax: (1) 479 751 1110
Website: www.aspsf.org

The ASPSF is a private, nonprofit corporation, which was established in 1990 in recognition of the severe impoverishment of single-parent families in Arkansas.

Arkansas Single Parent Scholarships

Subjects: All subjects.
Purpose: To provide financial assistance to single parents who are pursuing a course of instruction that will improve their income-earning potential.
Eligibility: Open to applicants who are single parents living in Arkansas who are considered economically disadvantaged.
Level of Study: Professional development
Type: Scholarship
Value: US$500
Frequency: Annual

Country of Study: United States of America
Application Procedure: See the website.

Business and Professional Women's (BPN) Foundation Career Advancement Scholarship

Subjects: All subjects.
Purpose: To promote equity for all women in the workplace through advocacy, education and information.
Eligibility: Open to female candidates who are US citizens or US nationals and are above the age of 25.
Level of Study: Professional development
Type: Scholarship
Frequency: Annual
Country of Study: United States of America
Application Procedure: Application forms and details are available on the website.
Closing Date: April 15th
Funding: Foundation
Contributor: The BPW Foundation

Jeannette Rankin Foundation Grant

Subjects: All subjects.
Purpose: To financially support low-income women in their education.
Eligibility: Open to female candidates who are US citizens and 35 years of age or older.
Level of Study: Professional development
Type: Grant
Value: Up to US$2,000
Frequency: Annual
Country of Study: United States of America
No. of awards offered: 60
Application Procedure: Application form can be downloaded from the website.
Funding: Private

ARMAUER HANSEN RESEARCH INSTITUTE (AHRI)

PO Box 1005, Addis Ababa, Ethiopia
Tel: (251) 1 21 13 34
Fax: (251) 1 21 15 63
Email: ahri@telecom.net.et; ahridir@telecom.net.et
Website: www.telecom.net.et/˜ahri
Contact: Dr Howard Engers, Scientific Director

The Armauer Hansen Research Institute (AHRI) is an Ethiopian biomedical research institute mainly devoted to work on infectious diseases including tuberculosis, leprosy, malaria, meningitis and HPV. AHRI has recently joined the Ethiopian Ministry of Health.

AHRI African Fellowship

Subjects: Medical sciences, parasitology or tropical medicine, immunology and microbiology.
Purpose: To promote biomedical science in Africa.
Eligibility: Open to African researchers who hold an MSc, MD or PhD. Women are especially encouraged to apply.
Level of Study: Doctorate
Type: Fellowship
Value: Accommodation and salary costs are covered
Length of Study: 1 year
Frequency: Annual
Study Establishment: AHRI
Country of Study: Ethiopia
No. of awards offered: 1
Application Procedure: Applicants must contact the AHRI for details.
Closing Date: October 1st
Funding: Government
Contributor: NORAD, SIDA/SAREC
No. of awards given last year: 1
No. of applicants last year: 1

ARTHRITIS NATIONAL RESEARCH FOUNDATION (ANRF)

200 Oceangate, Suite 830, Long Beach, CA, 90802, United States of America
Tel: (1) 800 588 2873
Fax: (1) 562 983 1410
Email: anrf@ix.netcom.com
Website: www.curearthritis.org
Contact: Ms Helene Belisle, Executive Director

The Arthritis National Research Foundation (ANRF) provides funding for highly qualified postdoctoral researchers associated with major research institutes, universities and hospitals seeking to discover new knowledge for the prevention, treatment and cure of arthritis and related rheumatic diseases. The ANRF fills a much-needed niche in the field of rheumatic disease research by providing support for young postdoctoral investigators, often providing the first major funding in their research careers.

ANRF Research Grants

Subjects: Arthritis, rheumatic diseases and related immune disorders.
Purpose: To support research focusing on high-incidence diseases, such as osteoarthritis, rheumatoid arthritis, lupus and related rheumatic and autoimmune diseases.
Eligibility: Applicants must hold an MD or PhD degree. Applicants need not be citizens of the United States of America, but must conduct their research at United States of America institutions. Applications will be accepted from postdoctorates and faculty members, with priority going to those scientists who do not already hold awards from the NIH or the Arthritis Foundation.
Level of Study: Postdoctorate, research
Type: Research grant
Value: Grants may range from US$20,000 to 50,000
Length of Study: 1 year, with potential for renewal
Frequency: Annual
Study Establishment: Qualifying non-profit institutions in the United States of America
Country of Study: United States of America
No. of awards offered: 10–15
Application Procedure: Applicants must visit the website for further information or request a copy of the grants guidelines via telephone or email.
Closing Date: January 16th
Funding: Individuals, private
No. of awards given last year: 11
No. of applicants last year: 36

ARTHRITIS RESEARCH CAMPAIGN (ARC)

Copeman House, St Mary's Court, St Mary's Gate, Chesterfield, S41 7TD, England
Tel: (44) 12 4655 8033
Fax: (44) 12 4655 8007
Email: info@arc.org.uk
Website: www.arc.org.uk
Contact: Mr Michael Patnick, Head of Research & Education Funding

The Arthritis Research Campaign (arc) is the fourth largest medical research charity in the United Kingdom, and the only charity in the country dedicated to finding the cause of and cure for arthritis, relying entirely upon voluntary donations to sustain its wide-ranging research and educational programmes.

ARC Allied Health Professional Training Fellowship

Subjects: Arthritis and related musculoskeletal diseases.
Purpose: To promote the training of allied health professionals by financing a higher degree course.
Eligibility: Open to HPC-Registered, allied health professionals committed to the care of patients with arthritis and related

musculoskeletal diseases. Candidates must have at least 3 years relevant postgraduate experience.
Level of Study: Postgraduate, professional development
Type: Fellowship
Value: Fees
Length of Study: Varies, full-time or part-time
Frequency: Annual
Study Establishment: A university, hospital or recognized research institute
Country of Study: United Kingdom
No. of awards offered: Varies
Application Procedure: Applicants must complete an application form, available from the website.
Closing Date: February 13th
Funding: Private
Contributor: Voluntary charitable donations
No. of awards given last year: 10

ARC Allied Health Professionals Educational Travel/ Training Bursaries

Subjects: Arthritis and related musculoskeletal diseases.
Purpose: To promote awareness and understanding of rheumatology among allied health professionals through research, practical experience, presentation of research or formal education by attending a national or international congress or a short training course.
Eligibility: Open to HPC-Registered allied health professionals committed to the care of patients with Arthritis and related musculoskeletal diseases. Applicants must have at least 3 years of postregistration work experience and 1 year of experience in rheumatology.
Level of Study: Professional development, postgraduate, unrestricted
Type: Bursary
Value: 90 per cent of fares, registration, accommodation and subsistence
Length of Study: Short courses only
Frequency: 3 times a year
Study Establishment: A recognized training establishment, a national or an international congress
Country of Study: United Kingdom
No. of awards offered: Varies
Application Procedure: Applicants must complete an application form, available from the website.
Closing Date: April, July and December
Funding: Private
Contributor: Voluntary charitable donations
No. of awards given last year: 21

ARC Barbara Ansell Fellowships in Paediatric Rheumatology

Subjects: Paediatric rheumatology.
Purpose: To provide an opportunity for paediatricians or rheumatologists to develop research interests in paediatric rheumatology.
Eligibility: Open to medical graduates of the United Kingdom who are at specialist registrar level. Successful applicants will be expected to develop projects in paediatric rheumatology for further fellowship support.
Level of Study: Research, professional development, postgraduate
Type: Fellowship
Value: Salary plus reasonable laboratory expenses
Length of Study: 1 year
Frequency: Annual
Study Establishment: A university department, hospital or recognized research institution
Country of Study: United Kingdom
No. of awards offered: Varies
Application Procedure: Applicants must complete an application form, available from the website.
Closing Date: There is no deadline date
Funding: Private
Contributor: Voluntary charitable donations
No. of awards given last year: None
No. of applicants last year: None
Additional Information: These entry-level training fellowships are offered by ARC in memory of Dr Barbara Ansell.

ARC Clinician Scientist Fellowship

Subjects: Arthritis and related musculoskeletal diseases.
Purpose: To combine a period of clinical training with a period of postdoctoral research.
Eligibility: Open to medical graduates who have completed their first period of research training and, in most cases, have obtained a PhD.
Level of Study: Postdoctorate, research, professional development
Type: Fellowship
Value: Salary plus supporting technician, running costs and essential equipment
Frequency: Annual
Study Establishment: A university, hospital or recognized research institute
Country of Study: United Kingdom
No. of awards offered: Varies
Application Procedure: Applicants must complete an application form, available from the website.
Closing Date: July 10th
Funding: Private
Contributor: Voluntary charitable donations
No. of awards given last year: 2

ARC Educational Project Grants

Subjects: Arthritis and related musculoskeletal diseases.
Purpose: To encourage education work in the field of arthritis and musculoskeletal disease.
Eligibility: Open to medical, scientific or educational professionals with an interest in relevant educational research.
Level of Study: Professional development, research
Type: Project grant
Value: Varies
Length of Study: Varies
Frequency: 3 times a year
Study Establishment: A university, hospital or recognized research institute
Country of Study: United Kingdom
No. of awards offered: Varies
Application Procedure: Applicants must complete an intent form in the first instance, available from the website.
Closing Date: The last Monday in February, June and October
Funding: Private
Contributor: Voluntary charitable contributions
No. of awards given last year: 3

ARC Educational Research Fellowships

Subjects: Arthritis and related musculoskeletal diseases.
Purpose: To provide an opportunity for an individual to gain training in educational research methodology and medical education.
Eligibility: Open to clinicians, allied health professionals and non-clinicians in institutions within the United Kingdom.
Level of Study: Postgraduate, research, professional development
Type: Fellowship
Value: Salary with lecturership scale, plus supporting technician, running costs and essential equipment
Length of Study: 2 or 3 years, full-time or part-time
Frequency: Twice a year
Study Establishment: A university, hospital or recognized research institute
Country of Study: United Kingdom
No. of awards offered: Varies
Application Procedure: Applicants must complete an application form, available from the website.
Closing Date: January 23rd and September
Funding: Private
Contributor: Voluntary charitable contributions
No. of awards given last year: 2

ARC Equipment Grants

Subjects: Arthritis and related musculeskeletal diseases.
Purpose: To fund major items of equipment costing in excess of UK £20,000 that will facilitate multiple projects and make

a lasting impact on rheumatological research over many years.
Eligibility: Open to established units with a track record of research in arthritis and musculoskeletal disease.
Level of Study: Research
Type: Grant
Value: Varies
Length of Study: Up to 3 years
Frequency: 3 times a year
Study Establishment: A university, hospital or recognized research institute
Country of Study: United Kingdom
No. of awards offered: Varies
Application Procedure: Applicants must complete an application form, available from the website.
Closing Date: The last Monday of February, June and October
Funding: Private
Contributor: Voluntary charitable contributions

ARC Non-Clinical Career Development Fellowships

Subjects: Arthritis and related musculoskeletal diseases.
Purpose: To attract and retain talented scientists in rheumatological research.
Eligibility: Open to candidates working in institutions in the United Kingdom who should normally have between 3 and 6 years of postdoctoral research experience.
Level of Study: Research, professional development, postdoctorate
Type: Fellowship
Value: Salary usually within 1A or II range plus reasonable running costs
Length of Study: Up to 5 years, with a possibility of renewal subject to satisfactory review
Frequency: Annual
Study Establishment: A university department or similar research institute preferably within a multidisciplinary research group
Country of Study: United Kingdom
No. of awards offered: Varies
Application Procedure: Applicants must complete an application form, available from the website.
Closing Date: March 6th
Funding: Private
Contributor: Voluntary charitable contributions
No. of awards given last year: 3

ARC Orthopaedic Clinical Research Fellowship

Subjects: Arthritis and related musculoskeletal diseases.
Purpose: To encourage trainee orthopaedic surgeons to undertake research relevant to arthritis and related musculoskeletal diseases.
Eligibility: Open to fellows or members of the Royal College of Surgeons of Edinburgh and the Royal College of Surgeons of England and in good standing.
Level of Study: Professional development, research, doctorate
Type: Fellowship
Value: Varies
Length of Study: Up to 3 years
Frequency: Annual
Study Establishment: A university, hospital or recognized research institute
Country of Study: United Kingdom
No. of awards offered: One
Application Procedure: Applicants must complete an application form, available from the website.
Closing Date: April 24th
Funding: Private
Contributor: Voluntary charitable contributions
No. of awards given last year: 6

ARC PhD Studentships

Subjects: Arthritis and related musculoskeletal diseases.
Purpose: To encourage the best young science graduates to embark on a research career in rheumatology.
Eligibility: Open to university departments allied to rheumatology.
Level of Study: Postgraduate, research, doctorate, professional development
Type: Studentship
Value: Incremental stipend, United Kingdom tuition fees and limited running costs
Length of Study: 3 years
Frequency: Annual
Study Establishment: A university, hospital or recognized research institute
Country of Study: United Kingdom
No. of awards offered: Varies
Application Procedure: Applicants must complete an application form, available from the website.
Closing Date: August 14th
Funding: Private
Contributor: Voluntary charitable donations
No. of awards given last year: 3

ARC Programme Grants

Subjects: Arthritis and related musculoskeletal diseases.
Purpose: To support work that cannot be carried out in the short-term, to attract and maintain high-quality staff in an effective research team and to enable established research workers of proven ability to concentrate their efforts in a specific area.
Eligibility: Established groups undertaking research relevant to the aims of arc, and which have a substantial research track record based on either arc support or peer-reviewed funding from other sources.
Level of Study: Research
Type: Grant
Value: Varies
Length of Study: Up to 5 years
Frequency: Annual
Study Establishment: A university, hospital or recognized research institute
Country of Study: United Kingdom
No. of awards offered: Varies
Application Procedure: Applicants must submit an outline proposal form in the first instance, available from the website.
Closing Date: June 5th
Funding: Private
Contributor: Voluntary charitable contributions
No. of awards given last year: 3
Additional Information: Applicants should note that up to 1 year should be allowed for the full process of the programme grant evaluation to take place.

ARC Project Grants

Subjects: Arthritis and related musculoskeletal diseases.
Purpose: To further research into arthritis and musculoskeletal disease.
Eligibility: Open to candidates working at institutions in the United Kingdom. Candidates must have previous investigation and research experience.
Level of Study: Research, professional development
Type: Project grant
Value: Varies
Length of Study: Up to 3 years
Frequency: 3 times a year
Study Establishment: A university, hospital or recognized research institute
Country of Study: United Kingdom
No. of awards offered: Varies
Application Procedure: Applicants must complete an application form, available from the website.
Closing Date: The last Monday of February, June and October
Funding: Private
Contributor: Voluntary charitable contributions
No. of awards given last year: 35
Additional Information: Grants are made in support of specific research projects.

ARC Senior Research Fellowships

Subjects: Arthritis and related musculoskeletal diseases.
Purpose: To further research into arthritis and musculoskeletal disease and to attract high-flying medical or scientific researchers into rheumatology.

Eligibility: Open to medical or scientific graduates with between 6 and 12 years of postdoctoral research experience. Candidates should have proven ability in establishing an independent research programme.
Level of Study: Research, professional development
Type: Fellowship
Value: Salary plus supporting technician, running costs and essential equipment
Length of Study: Up to 5 years, with a possibility of renewal subject to satisfactory review
Frequency: Annual
Study Establishment: A university, hospital or recognized research institute
Country of Study: United Kingdom
No. of awards offered: Varies
Application Procedure: Applicants must complete an application form, available from the website.
Closing Date: July 10th
Funding: Private
Contributor: Voluntary charitable contributions
No. of awards given last year: 3

ARC Travelling Fellowships

Subjects: Arthritis and related musculoskeletal diseases.
Purpose: To provide training and experience for doctors committed to a career in clinical rheumatology.
Eligibility: Open to doctors up to and including senior registrar status and postdoctoral scientists.
Level of Study: Professional development, research
Type: Fellowship
Value: Salary and travelling costs
Length of Study: 1 year
Frequency: Annual
Study Establishment: A research centre of the Fellow's choice, subject to arc's approval
Country of Study: Any country
No. of awards offered: Varies
Application Procedure: Applicants must complete an application form, available from the website.
Closing Date: January 16th
Funding: Private
Contributor: Voluntary charitable contributions
No. of awards given last year: None

THE ARTHRITIS SOCIETY

393 University Avenue, Suite 1700, Toronto, ON, M5G 1E6, Canada
Tel: (1) 416 979 3353
Fax: (1) 416 979 1149
Email: bthorn@arthritis.ca
Website: www.arthritis.ca
Contact: Ms Bonnie Thorn, Chief Science/Medical Officer

The Arthritis Society is Canada's only non-profit agency dedicated solely to funding and promoting arthritis research and care.

Arthritis Society Industry Program

Subjects: Arthritis.
Purpose: To foster new collaborative efforts through shared funding between The Arthritis Society and industry in relevant research.
Eligibility: Applicants should write to the Society for details or refer to the website www.arthritis.ca
Level of Study: Research, postdoctorate
Length of Study: 1–3 years
Frequency: Annual
Country of Study: Canada
No. of awards offered: Varies
Application Procedure: Applicants must write to the Society for details.
Closing Date: December 15th
Funding: Private
Contributor: Public donors

Arthritis Society Research Fellowships

Subjects: Arthritis.
Purpose: To provide financial support so that candidates can pursue full-time research.
Eligibility: Open to highly qualified candidates with preference given to candidates intending to embark on a research career in Canada. Candidates must hold a PhD, MD, DDS, DVM, PharmD or the equivalent.
Level of Study: Postdoctorate
Type: Fellowship
Value: Based on institution scales
Length of Study: 2 years, usually beginning on July 1st with a possibility of renewal
Frequency: Annual
Study Establishment: Ordinarily, universities. Out-of-country training may be arranged in order to obtain specific expertise
Country of Study: Canada
No. of awards offered: Varies
Application Procedure: Applicants must complete and submit an application form with further documentation as outlined in the regulations.
Closing Date: December 1st
Funding: Private
Contributor: Public donors
No. of awards given last year: 7
No. of applicants last year: 13
Additional Information: Fellowships are awarded by the Society on the advice of the Review Panel. The Society reserves the right to approve or decline any application without stating its reasons.

Geoff Carr Lupus Fellowship

Subjects: Lupus.
Purpose: To provide advanced training to a rheumatologist.
Eligibility: Open to nationals of any country specializing in lupus at an Ontario lupus clinic.
Level of Study: Postdoctorate
Type: Fellowship
Value: Canadian $55,000
Length of Study: 1 year
Frequency: Annual
Study Establishment: An approved Ontario lupus clinic
Country of Study: Canada
No. of awards offered: 1
Application Procedure: Applicants must submit an application with three letters of recommendation and a letter of acceptance from a proposed supervisor. The letter of acceptance must include an outline proposed training programme and a certified transcript of their undergraduate record.
Closing Date: December 1st
Funding: Private
Contributor: The Ontario Lupus Association

Metro A Ogryzlo International Fellowship

Subjects: Clinical rheumatology.
Purpose: To provide advanced training to individuals from a developing country.
Eligibility: The successful candidate will have completed his or her training in general medicine and have a substantial prospect of returning to an academic position in his or her own country. Canadian citizens or landed immigrants are not eligible.
Level of Study: Postdoctorate
Type: Fellowship
Value: Up to a maximum of Canadian $31,000 per year
Length of Study: 1 year, non-renewable
Frequency: Annual
Study Establishment: A rheumatic disease unit or arthritis centre
Country of Study: Canada
No. of awards offered: 1
Application Procedure: Applicants must submit an application including letters of recommendation from three sponsors, letter of acceptance from the proposed supervisor, an outline of the proposed training programme and a certified transcript of their undergraduate record.

Closing Date: December 1st
Funding: Private
Contributor: Public donors
Additional Information: Fellows may not receive remuneration for any other work or hold a second major scholarship, except that, with the approval of their supervisors, they may engage in and accept remuneration for such departmental activities as are conducive to their development as clinicians, teachers or investigators. Ordinarily, a Fellow who is not a graduate of a medical school in the United States of America, the United Kingdom, Republic of Ireland, Australia, New Zealand or South Africa must take the Medical Council of Canada evaluating examination to obtain the Medical Council of Canada certificate before an education licence can be issued.

ARTHUR RUBINSTEIN INTERNATIONAL MUSIC SOCIETY

12 Huberman Street, Tel Aviv, 64075, Israel
Tel: (972) 3 685 6684
Fax: (972) 3 685 4924
Email: competition@arims.org.il
Website: www.arims.org.il
Contact: Ms Idith Zui, Director

The Arthur Rubinstein International Music Society was founded by Jan Jacob Bistritzky in 1980 in tribute to the artistry of Arthur Rubinstein (1887–1982) and to maintain his spiritual and artistic heritage in the art of the piano. The Society organizes and finances the Arthur Rubinstein International Piano Master Competition and the Hommage à Rubinstein worldwide concert series and festivals, awards scholarships, runs music courses and master classes, organizes lectures and memorial festivals and issues publications and recordings.

Arthur Rubinstein International Piano Master Competition

Subjects: Piano.
Purpose: To reward talented pianists with the capacity for multifaceted creative interpretation of composers, ranging from the pre-classic to the contemporary era.
Eligibility: Candidates must be 18–32 years of age.
Level of Study: Professional development
Type: Prize
Value: The first prize is a competition gold medal plus US$25,000, the second prize is a competition silver medal plus US$15,000 and the third prize is a competition bronze medal plus US$10,000. The fourth, fifth and sixth prizes are US$3,000 each.
Frequency: Every 3 years
Country of Study: Any country
No. of awards offered: 10
Application Procedure: Applicants must complete an application form according to the rules stipulated in the prospectus of the Arthur Rubinstein International Piano Master Competition. Details are available from the organization.
Closing Date: October
Funding: Government, private
No. of applicants last year: 185
Additional Information: Next competition: March 28th–April 14th.

ARTIST TRUST

1835 12th Ave, Seattle, WA, 98122,
United States of America
Tel: (1) 206 467 8734
Fax: (1) 206 467 9633
Email: info@artisttrust.org
Website: www.artisttrust.org

Artist Trust is a non-profit organization whose sole mission is to support and encourage individual artists working in all disciplines in order to enhance community life throughout Washington State.

Artist Fellowship Program

Subjects: Art.
Purpose: To reward practicing professional artists of exceptional talent and demonstrated ability. The fellowship is a merit-based, not a project-based award.
Eligibility: Applicants must be 18 years or older, and should not be a matriculated student. Only Washington State residents may apply.
Level of Study: Unrestricted, students may not apply
Type: Fellowship
Value: US$6,000
Frequency: Annual, Awarded in two-year cycles: music, media, literature and crafts disciplines are awarded in odd-numbered years. Dance, Design, Theater and Visual Arts disciplines are awarded in even-numbered years.
No. of awards offered: 21
Application Procedure: Applicants must complete an application form (available online), submit work samples, proof of Washington State residency, a curriculum vitae and a work sample description.
Closing Date: June
Funding: Government, individuals, commercial, foundation, private, corporation
Contributor: Washington State Arts Commission
No. of awards given last year: 21
No. of applicants last year: 333 applicants in visual arts, dance, design, theatre

GAP (Grants for Artist Projects) Program

Subjects: Art.
Purpose: To provide support for artist-generated projects, which can include (but are not limited to) the development, completion or presentation of new work.
Eligibility: All applicants must be 18 years or older, and Washington State residents. All disciplines and interdisciplinary projects are eligible.
Level of Study: Unrestricted, students may not apply
Type: Grant
Value: A maximum of US$1,400 for projects
Frequency: Annual
No. of awards offered: Varies
Application Procedure: Applicants must submit an application form (available online), work sample, proof of Washington State residency, a curriculum vitae and a work sample description.
Closing Date: February
Funding: Private, government, commercial
No. of awards given last year: 40
No. of applicants last year: 675

Grants for Artist Projects (GAP)

Subjects: Art.
Purpose: To provide support for artist-generated projects.
Eligibility: Open to applicants who are residents of Washington state, 18 years of age or older and who are practicing artists.
Level of Study: Unrestricted
Type: Grant
Value: Up to US$1,400
Frequency: Annual
Country of Study: United States of America
No. of awards offered: 50–100
Application Procedure: A completed application form and other supporting materials must be submitted.
Closing Date: February
Funding: Commercial, individuals, foundation, government, corporation, private
No. of awards given last year: 58
No. of applicants last year: 698

Twining Humber Award for Lifetime Artistic Achievement

Subjects: Visual arts.
Purpose: To reward a female visual artist over the age of 60 from Washington State.
Eligibility: Artists must be nominated. Nominees must be female, over the age of 60, a Washington State resident and a visual artist who has been practicing for 25 years or more.

Level of Study: Unrestricted
Type: Award
Value: US$10,000
Frequency: Annual
No. of awards offered: 1
Application Procedure: Nomination forms are available by mail or online.
Closing Date: January
Funding: Commercial, foundation, government, individuals, private, corporation
Contributor: Mrs Twining Humber (deceased)
No. of awards given last year: 1
No. of applicants last year: 12

ARTS AND HUMANITIES RESEARCH COUNCIL (AHRC)

Postgraduate Awards Division, Whitefriars, Lewins Mead, Bristol, BS1 2AE, England
Tel: (44) 11 7987 6543
Fax: (44) 11 7987 6544
Email: pgenquiries@ahrc.ac.uk
Website: www.ahrc.ac.uk
Contact: Ms Alrson Henry, Head of Postgraduate Programmes

The Arts and Humanities Research Council (AHRC) funds postgraduate study and research within the United Kingdom's Institutions of Higher Education. The AHRC supports Master's courses and doctoral research within a huge subject domain ranging from history, modern languages and English literature, to music and the creative and performing arts. The AHRC makes awards on the basis of academic excellence.

AHRC Doctoral Awards Scheme

Subjects: Archaeology, classics and ancient history, cultural and media studies, English language and literature, history of art and architecture, law, linguistics, modern languages, music, drama, dance and performing arts, philosophy, religious studies, art and design, creative writing, musical performance, museum studies, librarianship and information studies and medieval and modern history.
Purpose: To support full-time and part-time study for students undertaking a doctoral degree in the arts and humanities.
Eligibility: Applicants must be resident in the United Kingdom or the European Union and be graduates of a recognized Institute of Higher Education or be expecting to graduate by July 31st preceding the start of the course. Applicants should refer to the AHRC guide for full details.
Level of Study: Doctorate
Type: Studentship
Value: UK £14,000 per year maintenance grant for London-based full-time students and UK £12,000 per year for full-time students based elsewhere. Tuition fees up to UK £3,085 per year, plus a study visit and conference costs
Length of Study: Up to 3 years full-time and 5 years part-time
Frequency: Annual
Study Establishment: Any approved Institute of Higher Education
Country of Study: United Kingdom
No. of awards offered: Varies
Application Procedure: Applicants must download and complete an application form available on the website.
Closing Date: May 2nd
Funding: Government
No. of awards given last year: 632
No. of applicants last year: 2,588

Professional Preparation Master's Scheme

Subjects: Art and design, interpreting and translation, librarianship, archives and information management, museum studies and heritage management, creative writing, archaeology, classics and literature, linguistics, modern languages, music, drama, dance and performing arts and medieval and modern history, conservation.
Purpose: To provide funding to allow students to undertake Master's or postgraduate diploma courses that focus on developing high-level skills and competencies for professional practice.
Eligibility: Applicants must be resident in the United Kingdom or the European Union and be graduates of a recognized Institute of Higher Education or be expecting to graduate by July 31st preceding the start of the course. Applicants should refer to the AHRC guide for full details.
Level of Study: Postgraduate
Type: Studentship
Value: UK £9,350 in London, UK £7,350 elsewhere, plus tuition fees of up to UK £3,085. These amounts are subject to change. Please consult the organization
Length of Study: 9 months–1 year
Frequency: Annual
Study Establishment: An Institute of Higher Education
Country of Study: United Kingdom
No. of awards offered: Varies
Application Procedure: Applicants must download and complete an application form available on the website.
Closing Date: May 2nd
Funding: Government
No. of awards given last year: 324
No. of applicants last year: 1,272

Research Preparation Master's Scheme

Subjects: Archaeology, classics and ancient history, cultural and media studies, English language and literature, history of art and architecture, law, linguistics, modern languages, music, drama, dance and performing arts, philosophy, religious studies, art and design, medieval and modern history, museum studies, librarianship, and information studies.
Purpose: To support students undertaking Master's courses that focus on advanced study and research training explicitly intended to provide a foundation for further research at doctoral level.
Eligibility: Applicants must be resident in the United Kingdom or the European Union, be graduates of a recognized Institute of Higher Education or be expecting to graduate by July 31st preceding the start of the course. Applicants should refer to the AHRC guide for full details.
Level of Study: Postgraduate
Type: Studentship
Value: UK £10,350 per year maintenance grant for London-based students and UK £8,350 per year for students based elsewhere plus tuition fees up to UK £3,085 per year
Length of Study: 1–2 years
Frequency: Annual
Study Establishment: An approved Institute of Higher Education
Country of Study: United Kingdom
No. of awards offered: Varies
Application Procedure: Applicants must download and complete an application form available on the website.
Closing Date: May 2nd
Funding: Government
No. of awards given last year: 534
No. of applicants last year: 1,858

THE ARTS COUNCIL OF WALES

Museum Place, CF10 3NX, Wales, Cardiff, United Kingdom
Tel: (44) 29 2037 6500
Fax: (44) 29 2022 1447
Email: info@artswales.org.uk
Website: www.artswales.org.uk
Contact: Angela Blackburn

The Arts Council of Wales is the national organization with specific responsibility for the funding and development of the arts in Wales. Most of its funds come from the National Assembly for Wales, but it also distributes National Lottery funds to the arts in Wales.

The Arts Council of Wales Fiction Factory Grant

Subjects: Arts.
Purpose: To fund short film production.

Level of Study: Professional development
Type: Grant
Value: UK £30,000
Frequency: Annual
Country of Study: United Kingdom
Application Procedure: See the website.
Funding: Government

For further information contact:

Tel: 029 2030 0320
Fax: 029 2030 0321
Contact: Ms Fizzi Oppe

BBC National Orchestra of Wales Grant

Subjects: Arts.
Purpose: To support projects.
Level of Study: Professional development
Type: Grant
Value: UK £759,119
Frequency: Annual
Country of Study: United Kingdom
Funding: Government
Contributor: Arts Council of Wales

For further information contact:

Tel: 029 2032 2442
Fax: 029 2032 2575
Email: david.murray.01@bbc.co.uk
Contact: Mr David Murray

Community Dance Wales Grants

Subjects: Arts.
Purpose: To promote professional interest in community dance in Wales.
Level of Study: Professional development
Type: Grant
Value: UK £25,342
Frequency: Annual
Country of Study: United Kingdom
Funding: Government

For further information contact:

Tel: 01495 224425
Fax: 01495 226457
Email: roonem@caerphilly.gov.uk
Contact: Ms Margaret Rooney

Cultural Enterprise Service Grant

Subjects: Arts.
Purpose: To provide financial assistance in the purchase of equipment, software and consultancy.
Level of Study: Professional development
Type: Grant
Value: UK £10,000
Frequency: Annual
Country of Study: United Kingdom
Application Procedure: See the website.
Funding: Government
Contributor: The Arts Council of Wales

For further information contact:

Tel: 029 2034 3205
Fax: 029 2034 5436
Email: stephan@cultural-enterprise.com
Contact: Mr Stephan Caddict

Diversions Dance Company Ltd Grant

Subjects: Arts.
Purpose: To provide secure funding for the programmes of Community Arts Organizations.
Eligibility: Open to community arts organizations across Wales.
Level of Study: Professional development
Type: Grant
Value: UK £436,280
Frequency: Annual
Country of Study: United Kingdom
Application Procedure: See the website.
Funding: Government
Contributor: Arts Council of Wales

For further information contact:

Tel: 029 2046 5345
Fax: 029 2046 5346
Email: diversions@diversionsdance.co.uk
Contact: Mr Phillip Morgan

Forget About it Film & TV Grant

Subjects: Arts.
Purpose: To support creativity.
Type: Grant
Value: UK £20,000
Frequency: Annual
Country of Study: United Kingdom
Application Procedure: Application details available on the website www.forgetaboutit.tv
Funding: Government
Contributor: The Arts Council of Wales

For further information contact:

Market House, Market Road, Canton, Cardiff, CF5 1QE
Tel: 029 2040 4048
Fax: 029 2040 4048
Contact: Ms Suzanne Phillips

Organic Films/Fertile Ground Ltd. Grant

Subjects: Arts.
Purpose: To finance short film production.
Level of Study: Professional development
Type: Grant
Length of Study: UK £27,000
Frequency: Annual
Country of Study: United Kingdom
Application Procedure: See the website.
Funding: Government
Contributor: The Arts Council of Wales

For further information contact:

Tel: 029 20651954
Contact: Mr Keir Alexander

Wales One World Film Festival Grant

Subjects: Arts.
Purpose: To present audiences with the best in wolrd cinema through the Festival.
Level of Study: Professional development
Type: Grant
Value: UK £24,936
Length of Study: 2 years
Frequency: Annual
Country of Study: United Kingdom
Application Procedure: See the website.
Funding: Government
Contributor: The Media Agency for Wales and the Arts Council of Wales

For further information contact:

Tel: 01239 615066
Fax: 01239 615066
Email: sa3657@eclipse.co.uk
Contact: Mr David Gillam

Welsh Independent Dance Grant
Subjects: Arts.
Purpose: To develop a successful dance sector in Wales.
Level of Study: Professional development
Type: Grant
Length of Study: UK £71,296
Frequency: Annual
Country of Study: United Kingdom
Application Procedure: See the website.
Funding: Government
Contributor: The Arts Council of Wales

For further information contact:

Tel: 029 2038 7314
Fax: 029 2038 7314
Email: welshindance@btconnect.com
Contact: Ms Kate Long

THE ASCAP FOUNDATION

10701 Ranch Road, Culver City, CA 90230,
United States of America
Tel: (1) 212 621 6219
Fax: (1) 212 595 3342
Email: concertmusic@ascap.com
Website: www.ascap.com
Contact: Dr Deon Nielsen Price, Concert Music Administrator

The American Society of Composers, Authors and Publishers (ASCAP) is a membership association of over 200,000 composers, songwriters, lyricists and music publishers. ASCAP's function is to protect the rights of its members by licensing and paying royalties for the public performances of their copyrighted works.

ASCAP Foundation Morton Gould Young Composer Awards
Subjects: Music composition.
Purpose: To encourage talented young composers by providing recognition, appreciation and monetary awards.
Eligibility: Open to United States citizens or permanent residents who have not reached their 30th birthday by March 1st in the year of competition. Original concert music of any style will be considered. However, works which have previously earned awards or prizes in any other national competition are ineligible. Arrangements are also ineligible.
Level of Study: Unrestricted
Type: Award
Value: US$30,000 in total (last year, Approx. US$40,000 in prizes)
Frequency: Annual
No. of awards offered: Varies from year to year
Application Procedure: Applicants must complete an application form and other materials.
Closing Date: Postmarked March 1st
Funding: Private

The ASCAP Foundation Rudolf Nissim Prize
Subjects: Music composition.
Purpose: To encourage talented composers of concert music by providing recognition, appreciation and a monetary award to the composer of the winning score.
Eligibility: Open to all living concert composer members of ASCAP. Prior winners of this Prize are ineligible. The bound score (copy, not original manuscript), of one published or unpublished original concert work (no arrangements) requiring a conductor scored for full orchestra, chamber orchestra, or large wind/brass ensemble (with or without soloists and/or chorus) will be considered. The work must not have been previously premiered by paid professionals.
Level of Study: Unrestricted
Type: Award
Value: US$5,000
Frequency: Annual
No. of awards offered: 1
Application Procedure: Applicants must complete an application form and other materials.
Closing Date: Postmarked November 15th
Additional Information: For guidelines and application: www.ascap.com/concert/nissimapp.pdf

The ASCAP Foundation Young Jazz Composer Awards
Subjects: Music composition.
Purpose: To encourage talented young jazz composers by providing recognition, appreciation and monetary awards.
Eligibility: Open to United States citizens or permanent residents who have not reached their 30th birthday by December 31st in the year of the competition. Only completely original music will be considered. Arrangements are not eligible. Compositions which have previously earned awards or prizes in any other national competition are ineligible.
Level of Study: Unrestricted
Type: Award
Value: US$25,000
Frequency: Annual
No. of awards offered: Varies from year to year
Application Procedure: Applicants must complete an application form and other materials.
Closing Date: Postmarked December 1st
Additional Information: For guidelines and application: www.ascapfoundation.org/youngjazz/youngjazz.pdf

ASCAP/CBDNA Frederick Fennell Prize for the Best Original Score for Concert Band
Subjects: Music composition.
Purpose: ASCAP and the College Band Directors National Association (CBDNA) seek to recognize talented young composers who write for Concert Band.
Eligibility: Open to United States citizens or permanent residents who are under 30 years of age. Only original music for concert band will be considered. Arrangements are not eligible. Compositions which have previously earned awards or prizes in any other national competition are ineligible.
Level of Study: Unrestricted
Type: Award
Value: US$5,000
Frequency: Every 2 years
Country of Study: Any country
No. of awards offered: 1
Application Procedure: Applicants must complete an application form and other materials.
Closing Date: Postmarked September 15th
Additional Information: The winning score will be performed at the ensuing CBDNA national conference. For guidelines and application: www.ascap.com/about/sbdna.pdf

ASCAP/Lotte Lehmann Foundation Song Cycle Competition
Subjects: Music composition.
Purpose: ASCAP and the Lotte Lehmann Foundation seek to recognize talented young composers who write for voice.
Eligibility: Open to United States citizens or permanent residents who are below the age of 30 for next competition. Only one original work with English text will be considered. Arrangements are not eligible.
Level of Study: Unrestricted
Type: Commission
Value: US$3,500 (first prize); US$1,000 (second prize); US$500 (third prize)
Frequency: Every 2 years
No. of awards offered: 3
Application Procedure: Applicants must complete an application form and other materials.
Closing Date: Postmarked September 15th
Additional Information: For guidelines and application: www.ascap.com/concert/lottelehmann/LLCompetition.pdf

ASCAP/LUS Awards Program

Subjects: Writing.
Purpose: To recognize active and established writers.
Eligibility: Open to writers who earn less than US$250,000 in annual domestic performance royalties.
Level of Study: Professional development, postgraduate
Type: Award
Frequency: Annual
Closing Date: June 1st

ASHRIDGE MANAGEMENT COLLEGE

Berkhamsted, Hertfordshire, HP4 1NS, England
Tel: (44) 14 4284 1143
Fax: (44) 14 4284 1144
Email: jane.tobin@ashridge.org.uk
Website: www.ashridge.org.uk
Contact: Ms Jane Tobin, MBA Admissions Manager

Ashridge Business School's expertise, built up through many years of experience as a provider of executive development, has deliberately shaped their mission to help practicing and experienced managers become even more effective as leaders, and in so doing, fulfil their individual potential and that of the organization.

Ashridge Management College-Full-Time MBA and Executive MBA Scholarships

Subjects: MBA studies.
Purpose: To fund students pursuing a full-time MBA.
Eligibility: Applicant must be accepted in a full-time MBA programme. Preferably, the applicant should be an individual applying from a non-profit organization, a female applicant or a need-based applicant. Applicants must have 3–5 years business or managerial experience.
Level of Study: MBA
Type: Scholarship
Value: UK £6,000
Length of Study: 1 year
Frequency: Annual
Study Establishment: Ashridge Business School
Country of Study: United Kingdom
No. of awards offered: 5
Application Procedure: Applicants must submit a form, with two references and either a Graduate Management Admission Test score or an Ashridge test score. English language skill is required. All candidates are asked to come for an interview.
Closing Date: December 1st
Funding: Commercial
Contributor: Natwest Bank, the Bank of Scotland and the Association of MBAs
No. of awards given last year: 5
No. of applicants last year: 7
Additional Information: Ashridge also awards two bursaries per year to suitable applicants who are employed in the charity sector, provided that the applicants carry out their project work for their employing charitable organization.

ASIAN CULTURAL COUNCIL (ACC)

437 Madison Avenue, 37th Floor, New York, NY, 10022, United States of America
Tel: (1) 212 812 4300
Fax: (1) 212 812 4299
Email: acc@accny.org
Website: www.asianculturalcouncil.org
Contact: Mr Ralph Samuelson, Director

The Asian Cultural Council (ACC) supports cultural exchange in the visual and performing arts between the United States of America and the countries of Asia. The emphasis of the ACC's programme is on providing individual fellowships to artists, scholars and specialists from Asia undertaking research, study and creative work in the United States of America. Grants are also made to United States of America citizens pursuing similar work in Asia.

ACC Fellowship Grants Program

Subjects: Visual and performing arts.
Purpose: To provide fellowship opportunities for research, training, travel and creative work.
Eligibility: Open to individuals from East and South East Asia, Burma, Japan and citizens or permanent residents of the United States of America. Artists seeking aid for personal exhibitions or performances cannot be considered.
Level of Study: Professional development, postgraduate, doctorate, postdoctorate
Value: Varies
Length of Study: 1 month–1 year
Frequency: Annual
No. of awards offered: Approx. 130
Application Procedure: Applicants must send a brief project description to the Council. If the proposal falls within the Council's guidelines, application forms will be forwarded to individual candidates or more detailed information will be requested from institutional applicants.
Closing Date: February 1st or August 1st
Funding: Private
No. of awards given last year: 133
No. of applicants last year: 606

ASIAN DEVELOPMENT BANK (ADB)

PO Box 789 0980, Manila, Philippines
Tel: (63) 632 4444
Fax: (63) 636 2444
Website: www.adb.org

The Asian development bank is a multilateral development financial institution. Its work is aimed at improving the welfare of the people in Asia and the Pacific.

ADB Fully funded Internships

Subjects: Finance.
Purpose: To help gain a deeper understanding of development finance and the impact of ADB.
Eligibility: Open to candidates enrolled in a Master's or PhD-level programme at a recognized academic institution.
Level of Study: Postgraduate
Type: Internship
Value: A daily stipend, round trip airfare and suitable accommodation and a certificate of completion to successful participants.
Frequency: Annual
No. of awards offered: 6
Application Procedure: See the website.
Closing Date: January 31st

ADB Research Fellowships

Subjects: All subjects.
Purpose: To support research.
Eligibility: Open to nationals of one of ADB's member countries.
Type: Fellowship
Value: All costs covered by the fellow's academic institution or grant agenc.
Frequency: Annual
No. of awards offered: Up to 5
Application Procedure: A completed application form along with curriculum vitae must be submitted.

ADB-Japan Scholarship Program

Subjects: Economics, management, science and technology.
Purpose: To provide an opportunity for further studies.
Eligibility: Open to applicants who are not more than 35 years of age.
Level of Study: Postgraduate
Type: Scholarship
Value: Full tuition fees, a monthly subsistence and housing allowance, travel expenses and an excellence for books
Length of Study: 1–2 years
Frequency: Annual
Application Procedure: See the website.

ASSOCIATED BOARD OF THE ROYAL SCHOOLS OF MUSIC

24 Portland Place, London, W1B 1LU, England
Tel: (44) 20 7636 5400
Fax: (44) 20 7637 0234
Email: abrsm@abrsm.ac.uk
Website: www.abrsm.org
Contact: Director of Finance & Administration

The Associated Board of the Royal Schools of Music is the world's leading provider of graded music examinations with over 500,000 candidates each year in over 80 countries. It is also a major music publisher and a provider of professional development courses and seminars for music teachers.

Associated Board of the Royal Schools of Music Scholarships

Subjects: Instrumental and vocal performance.
Purpose: To enable exceptionally talented young musicians to study at one of the four Royal Schools of Music.
Eligibility: Candidates should normally be at least 21 years of age by January 31st in the year of entry. Entries can be received from any of the countries where the Associated Board organizes examinations. Candidates must have a good standard of general education and must normally have qualified by passing, with distinction, Grade 8 in a practical examination of the Board's, the Advanced Certificate or the LRSM diploma, plus one other practical examination of the Board's above Grade 5.
Level of Study: Professional development, postgraduate
Type: Scholarship
Value: Full course fees, a contribution to air travel and UK £3,000 per year towards living expenses
Length of Study: 1–4 years, according to designated course
Frequency: Annual
Study Establishment: The Royal Academy of Music, the Royal College of Music, the Royal Northern College of Music or the Royal Scottish Academy of Music and Drama
Country of Study: United Kingdom
No. of awards offered: 2
Application Procedure: Applicants must submit an application form, health certificate, examination marks, forms, testimonials, and an authenticated cassette tape of recent performance. Candidates should apply to the Board's representative in their own country or directly to the Board in London.
Closing Date: December 31st of the year preceding year of entry
Funding: Private

ASSOCIATION FOR INTERNATIONAL PRACTICAL TRAINING (AIPT)

10400 Little Patuxent parkway Suite 250,
Columbia, MD 21044-3519,
United States of America
Tel: (1) 997 2200
Fax: (1) 992 3924
Email: aipt@aipt.org
Website: www.aipt.org

The AIPT is a non-profit organization that promotes international understanding through cross-cultural, on-the-job, practical training exchanges for students and professionals.

Jessica King Scholarship Fund

Subjects: Hotel management.
Purpose: To inspire young hospitality students and professionals.
Eligibility: Open to young Americans who wish to succeed in the international hospitality field.
Level of Study: Postgraduate
Type: Scholarship
Value: US$1,000
Frequency: Annual
Application Procedure: Contact AIPT.
Contributor: The King Family

For further information contact:

Email: aipt@aipt.org

ASSOCIATION FOR LIBRARY SERVICE TO CHILDREN

American Library Association, 50 East Huron, Chicago, IL 60611-2795, United States of America
Tel: (1) 800/545 2433 ext. 2163
Fax: (1) 312 280 5271
Email: alsc@ala.org
Website: www.ala.org

The Association for Library Service to Children develops and supports the profession of children's librarianship by enabling and encouraging its practitioners to provide the best library service to our nation's children.

The Bound to stay Bound Books Scholarship.

Subjects: Library science.
Purpose: To support library services to children.
Eligibility: See the website.
Level of Study: Postgraduate
Type: Scholarship
Length of Study: US$6,500
Frequency: Annual
Country of Study: United States of America
No. of awards offered: 4

The Frederic G. Melcher Scholarship

Subjects: Library science.
Purpose: To provide financial assistance to professionals who plan to work in children's librarianship.
Eligibility: Open to candidates with academic excellence, leadership qualities, and desire to work with children.
Level of Study: Postgraduate
Type: Scholarship
Value: US$6,000
Frequency: Annual
Country of Study: United States of America
No. of awards offered: 2
Application Procedure: See the website.

ASSOCIATION FOR SPINA BIFIDA AND HYDROCEPHALUS (ASBAH)

ASBAH House, 42 Park Road, Peterborough, Cambridgeshire, PE1 2UQ, England
Tel: (44) 17 3355 5988
Fax: (44) 17 3355 5985
Email: lynr@asbah.org
Website: www.asbah.org
Contact: Mrs L Rylance, Secretary to the Directorate

The Association for Spina Bifida and Hydrocephalus (ASBAH) is a voluntary organization that works for people with spina bifida and hydrocephalus. The charity lobbies for improvements in legislation and provides advisory and support services to clients and their families or carers, in addition to supplying information to professionals and sponsoring medical, social and educational research.

ASBAH Bursary Fund

Subjects: Any subject that will improve the chances of employment for people with spina bifida, hydrocephalus or both.
Purpose: To help with expenses of further or higher education courses approved by, but not organized by, ASBAH.
Eligibility: Open to individuals with spina bifida and hydrocephalus. Applicants must be resident in the United Kingdom.
Level of Study: Unrestricted

Type: Bursary
Value: Course fees and other expenses
Length of Study: Varies
Frequency: Dependent on funds available
Study Establishment: Varies
Country of Study: England, Wales and Northern Ireland only
No. of awards offered: Varies
Application Procedure: Applicants must complete an application form, available from Mrs M Malcolm, the Assistant Director of Services.
Closing Date: Applications are accepted at any time
Funding: Private
Contributor: Charitable donations
No. of awards given last year: None
No. of applicants last year: 3
Additional Information: Applicants are normally visited by an ASBAH Area Adviser prior to an award being considered.

ASBAH Research Grant

Subjects: Medical sciences, natural sciences, education and teacher training, recreation, welfare and protective services.
Purpose: To support research in an area directly related to spina bifida and/or hydrocephalus, and to explore ways of improving the quality of life for people with these conditions, those being medical, scientific, educational and social research.
Eligibility: Applicants must be resident in the United Kingdom.
Level of Study: Postgraduate
Value: Varies
Length of Study: Varies
Frequency: Dependent on funds available
Study Establishment: Varies
Country of Study: United Kingdom
No. of awards offered: Varies
Application Procedure: Applicants must make an initial enquiry to the Executive Director. If the proposed research is considered to be interesting, the applicant will be asked to complete an application form. Applications should be made in good time for submission to the committees which meet in February and September to October.
Closing Date: January 1st and August 1st
Funding: Private
Contributor: Charitable donations

ASSOCIATION FOR WOMEN IN SCIENCE EDUCATIONAL FOUNDATION

7008 Richard Drive, Bethesda, MD 20817-4838,
United States of America
Email: awisedfd@awis.org
Website: www.awis.org/ed_foundation.html
Contact: Dr Barbara Filner, President

The Association for Women in Science Educational Foundation provides fellowships to assist women students studying the sciences.

Association for Women in Science Educational Foundation Predoctoral Awards

Subjects: Life, physical, behavioural or social science and engineering.
Purpose: To promote the participation of women in engineering and the sciences.
Eligibility: Open to female students enrolled in any life, physical, behavioural or social science or engineering programme leading to a PhD degree. Applicant must have passed the departmental qualifying exam and except to complete the PhD within two-and-one-half years, at the time of application.
Level of Study: Doctorate, predoctorate
Value: Varies, usually US$300–1,000
Length of Study: 2 years
Frequency: Annual
Study Establishment: An Institute of Higher Education
Country of Study: Anywhere for United States of America citizens; in the United States of America for others
No. of awards offered: Varies
Application Procedure: Applicants must submit an application including a basic form, a five-page summary of the candidate's dissertation research, two recommendation report forms and official transcripts of all coursework conducted at postsecondary institutions. Forms are available on the website.
Closing Date: Mid-January
Funding: Foundation
No. of awards given last year: 10
No. of applicants last year: 100
Additional Information: Winners are notified by email in June and announced publicly in the Autumn issue of the AWIS Magazine.

ASSOCIATION OF AMERICAN GEOGRAPHERS (AAG)

1710 Sixteenth Street North West, Washington, DC, 20009-3198,
United States of America
Tel: (1) 202 234 1450
Fax: (1) 202 234 2744
Email: ekhater@aag.org
Website: www.aag.org
Contact: Ms Ehsan Khater, Office Coordinator

The Association of American Geographers (AAG) is a non-profit organization founded in 1904 to advance professional studies in geography and to encourage the application of geographic research in business, education and government. The AAG was amalgamated with the American Society of Professional Geographers (ASPG) in 1948.

AAG Dissertation Research Grants

Subjects: Geography.
Purpose: To support dissertation research.
Eligibility: Open to candidates without a doctorate at the time of the award, who have been AAG members for at least 1 year at the time of application and who have completed all PhD requirements except the dissertation by the end of the semester or term following the approval of the award. The candidates' dissertation supervisor must certify eligibility and proposals should demonstrate high standards of scholarship.
Level of Study: Postdoctorate
Type: Research grant
Value: A maximum of US$500
Frequency: Dependent on funds available
Country of Study: United States of America
No. of awards offered: 3
Application Procedure: Applicants must complete an application form, available on request from the executive assistant, Ehsan M Khater. Also, applicants must submit seven copies of a dissertation proposal of no more than 1,000 words and seven copies of the completed forms. The proposal should describe the problem that is to be solved, outline the methods and data to be used and summarize the results expected to be found. Budget items should also be included within the body of the proposal.
Closing Date: December 31st
Funding: Private
Contributor: Members
No. of awards given last year: 6
No. of applicants last year: 8
Additional Information: By accepting an AAG dissertation grant, awardees agree to submit a copy of the dissertation, and a report that documents expenses charged to the grant, to the AAG Executive Director. AAG support must also be acknowledged in presentations and publications. The awards include the Robert D Hodgson Memorial PhD Dissertation Fund the Paul Vouras Fund and the Otis Paul Starkey Fund. Please visit the website for any further information.

AAG General Research Fund

Subjects: Geography.
Purpose: To support research and field work expenses.
Eligibility: Open to candidates who have been AAG members for at least 2 years at the time of application. Proposals that, in the opinion of the committee, offer the prospect of obtaining substantial subsequent

support from private foundations or federal agencies and that address questions of major import to the discipline will be given preference.
Level of Study: Professional development, postdoctorate
Type: Research grant
Value: US$500–1,000
Country of Study: Any country
No. of awards offered: Varies
Application Procedure: Applicants must complete and send seven application forms, available on request from the executive assistant, Ehsan M Khater. Successful award applicants will be announced on or about March 31st.
Closing Date: December 31st
Funding: Private
Contributor: AAG members
No. of awards given last year: 5
No. of applicants last year: 8
Additional Information: No awards are made if proposals are not suitable or for Master's and doctoral dissertation research. Guidelines are printed in the AAG Newsletter.

Anne U White Fund
Subjects: Geochemistry.
Purpose: To enable people, regardless of any formal training in geography, to engage in useful field studies and to have the joy of working alongside their partners.
Eligibility: Open to candidates who have been AAG members for at least 2 years at the time of application. Proposals that, in the opinion of the committee, best meet the purposes for which Anne and Gilbert White set up the funds will be given preference.
Level of Study: Professional development
Type: Research grant
Value: US$1,000–5,500 each
Frequency: Annual
Application Procedure: Applicants must complete seven application forms, available from the website or by request from the executive assistant, Ehsan M Khater. Successful applicants will be announced on or about March 31st.
Closing Date: December 31st
Funding: Private
No. of awards given last year: 6
No. of applicants last year: 9
Additional Information: By accepting the Anne U White grant, awardees agree to submit a two-page report that summarizes results and documents expenses underwritten by the grant to the AAG Executive Director. In 1989, Gilbert and Anne White donated a sum of money to the Association of American Geographers to establish the Anne U White Fund. Gilbert White and other donors have subsequently added substantially to the original gift.

The George and Viola Hoffman Fund
Subjects: Historical, contemporary, systematic and regional geographic studies.
Purpose: To provide financial support towards a Master's thesis or doctoral dissertation on a geographical subject in Eastern Europe.
Level of Study: Doctorate, postgraduate
Type: Grant
Value: US$500
Length of Study: 1 year
Frequency: Annual
No. of awards offered: 1
Application Procedure: Applicants must obtain application forms and precise guidelines from the main organization, or write to the Chair of the Hoffman Award, Michelle Behr, Western New Mexico University, behrm@cs.wnmu.edu
Closing Date: October 31st

For further information contact:

Email: behrm@cs.wnmu.edu

IGU Travel Grant
Subjects: Geography.
Purpose: To provide Travel Grants to the IGU conference.
Eligibility: Open to United States of America scholars and citizens.
Level of Study: Professional development
Type: Grant
Value: US$1,000–1,750
Frequency: Annual
Country of Study: As applicable
No. of awards offered: 20
Application Procedure: Applicant must apply to the main organization address or download a form from the website.

Visiting Geographical Scientist Program
Subjects: Geography.
Purpose: To stimulate interest in geography.
Level of Study: Professional development
Type: Grant
Value: US$500
Frequency: Annual
Study Establishment: Institution with an active chapter of Gamma Theta Upsilon
Country of Study: United States of America
Application Procedure: Applicants must write to Oscar Laron, VGSP Coordinator, at the main organization address.

For further information contact:

Email: olarson@aag.org

Warren Nystrom Fund Awards
Subjects: Geography.
Purpose: To support a paper based upon recent dissertations in geography.
Eligibility: Open to AAG members who have received their doctorate within the last 2 years. The paper submitted should be based on the student's dissertation.
Level of Study: Postdoctorate, doctorate
Value: Varies
Frequency: Annual
Country of Study: Any country
No. of awards offered: Varies
Application Procedure: Applicants must apply to the Association for information.
Closing Date: Mid-September for the following year
Funding: Private
Contributor: AAG members
No. of awards given last year: 1
No. of applicants last year: 15
Additional Information: Awards are made for papers presented at the annual meeting of the Association.

ASSOCIATION OF BRITISH SCIENCE WRITERS

Wellcome Wolfson Building, 165 Queen's Gate, London, SW7 5HE, England
Tel: (44) (0) 870 770 3361
Fax: (44) (0) 7733 330344
Email: sr@spr.net
Website: www.absw.org.uk
Contact: Sallie Robins

The ABSW exists to help those who write and broadcast about science and technology, and to improve the standard of science journalism in the United Kingdom. The association's members include print and broadcast journalists, authors, scriptwriters and producers, journalism or science communication students and others active in the field of communicating science and technology.

ABSW Student Bursaries funded by the Wellcome Trust
Subjects: Science communication and journalism including broadcast journalism.
Purpose: ABSW student bursaries aim to identify and train the excellent science communicators of the future.
Eligibility: Applicants need to be United Kingdom-based with a background in science and a demonstrable aptitude for communication.

Level of Study: Professional development, postgraduate
Type: Bursary
Value: UK £5,000 part-time, UK £10,000 full-time
Length of Study: Usually 1 year full-time, 2 years part-time
Frequency: Annual
Study Establishment: An Individual may choose.
Country of Study: United Kingdom
No. of awards offered: Varies, but usually 2 part-time and 7 full-time
Application Procedure: Application forms can be obtained from the ABSW Office or downloaded from the website. Part of the application process involves writing two articles on scientific subjects for a specified audience. Applicants are shortlisted based on written applications, with the shortlisted candidates being interviewed for final selection of awardees.
Closing Date: Usually end of February
Funding: Trusts
Contributor: The Wellcome Trust
No. of awards given last year: 9
No. of applicants last year: 42

ASSOCIATION OF CALIFORNIA WATER AGENCIES (ACWA)

910 K street, suit 100, Sacramento, CA, United States of America
Tel: (1) 916 441 4545
Fax: (1) 916 325 4849
Email: acwabox@acwa.com
Website: www.acwa.com

The Association of California Water Agencies has been a leader in California water issues since 1910. Its primary mission is to assist its members in promoting the development, management and reasonable beneficial use of water in an environmentally balanced manner.

ACWA Scholarship

Subjects: Water resources.
Purpose: To support students in water resources-related fields.
Eligibility: Open to applicants who are residents of California.
Level of Study: Postgraduate
Type: Scholarship
Value: US$1,500
Frequency: Annual
No. of awards offered: 6
Application Procedure: See the website.
Closing Date: April 1st

Clair A. Hill Scholarship

Purpose: To provide financial assistance to students in the water-related fields.
Eligibility: Open to applicants who are residents of California attending a California University.
Level of Study: Postgraduate
Type: Scholarship
Value: US$3,000
Frequency: Annual
Country of Study: United States of America
Application Procedure: See the website.
Closing Date: February 7th
Contributor: Association of California Water Agencies

ASSOCIATION OF CLINICAL PATHOLOGISTS

189 Dyke Road, Hove, East Sussex, BN3 1TJ, England
Tel: (44) 12 7377 5700
Fax: (44) 12 7377 3303
Email: info@pathologists.org.uk
Website: www.pathologists.org.uk
Contact: Administrative Assistant

The Association of Clinical Pathologists promotes the practice of clinical pathology by running postgraduate education courses and national scientific meetings and has a membership of 2,000 worldwide.

Student Research Fund

Subjects: Research projects within laboratory medicine (undergraduate) or to support students undertaking BSc/BMED Sci.
Purpose: To support medical students undertaking BSc degrees in any pathology discipline and contribute to the living expenses during their year of study or to fund small educational projects up to a maximum of UK £1,000.
Type: Scholarship
Value: Up to UK £5,000
Frequency: Annual
No. of awards offered: Up to 5
Application Procedure: Written application including a brief statement (400 words) outlining their interest in laboratory medicine; together with a full curriculum vitae. applications should include details of work to be undertaken as a part of the project or during the BSc and must be supported in writing by the project supervisor or head of the department in which the students will be placed.
Closing Date: Applications for BSc support must be received by June 30th. For project funding applications are considered throughout the year
Contributor: Association of Clinical Pathologists
No. of awards given last year: 3
No. of applicants last year: 5

ASSOCIATION OF COMMONWEALTH UNIVERSITIES (ACU)

John Foster House, 36 Gordon Square, London, WC1H 0PF, England
Email: info@acu.ac.uk
Website: www.acu.ac.uk
Contact: Director

ACU Titular Fellowships

Subjects: All subjects, but preference is given to those fields that are needed in developing countries.
Purpose: To enable the universities of the commonwealth to develop the human resources of their institutions and countries through the interchanging of people, knowledge, skills and technologies. Not intended for degree courses, or for immediately postdoctoral programmes.
Eligibility: Applicants must be on the staff of member universities under the ACU, the Commonwealth interuniversity organization or working in industry, commerce or public service in a Commonwealth country. Applicant must be within 28–50 years of age.
Level of Study: Professional development
Type: Scholarship
Value: UK £5,000 for travel, board, insurance and fees where the approved programme includes a training programme
Length of Study: 6 months
Frequency: Annual
Study Establishment: ACU member university or in industry, commerce or public sector
Country of Study: Commonwealth countries
No. of awards offered: Up to 20
Application Procedure: Candidates must be nominated by executive heads of ACU member universities or by the chief executive officer of a Commonwealth interuniversity organization. Full application details on ACU website.
Closing Date: August 31st
Contributor: ACU

ACU/FCO Chevening Scholarships

Subjects: Human resource management.
Purpose: To support full-time study in the United Kingdom on Master's degree in human resource management offered by the University of Westminister. The principal aim of the programme is to improve human resource management in higher education in developing countries.

Eligibility: Open to persons currently working in human resource or personnel departments in ACU member universities in developing countries. Award holders must undertake to return to their employing university at the end of the scholarship.
Level of Study: Postgraduate
Type: Scholarship
Value: Full cost of study, including return airfare fees and maintenance allowance
Length of Study: 1 year
Frequency: Annual
Study Establishment: University of Westminister
Country of Study: United Kingdom
No. of awards offered: Up to 2 annually
Application Procedure: Application should be sent directly to ACU. Must be nominated for this award by the vice-chancellor or executive head of their employee ACU member university. Full application details on ACU website.
Closing Date: April
Contributor: Funded jointly by ACU, FCO, the University of Westminister and International Students House, London
Additional Information: Preference is given to candidates who have a combination of strong record of achievement in their careers to date and clear plans on how the benefits of the scholarships would be used in future. For details on the university and course check website www.wmin.ac.uk

ACU/FCO Chevening Scholarships: Public Relations, Media and Communications Programme

Subjects: Public communication and public relations.
Purpose: To support full-time study in the United Kingdom for a Master's degree in Public Communication and Public Relations offered by the University of Westminister. (The principal aim is to allow members to share best practice in this fast-growing field.) Intended for administrative or related staff currently employed by ACU render universities in developing commonwealth countries who wish to develop their success in media, public relations or marketing.
Eligibility: Open to administrative or related staff currently employed by ACU member universities in developing countries to develop their skills in public relations, media and external communications. Candidates should hold a good Honours degree or equivalent, although other professional qualifications or substantial work experience may also be acceptable. Award holders must undertake to return to their own university at the end of the scholarship.
Level of Study: Postgraduate
Type: Scholarship
Value: Full cost of study, including return airfare, fees and maintenance allowance
Frequency: Annual
Study Establishment: University of Westminister
Country of Study: United Kingdom
No. of awards offered: Up to 2
Application Procedure: Application should be sent directly to the ACU. Even candidates must be nominated for this award of the vice-chancellor or executive members of their employing ACU member university. Full application details on ACU website.
Closing Date: April 30th
Funding: Foundation
Contributor: ACU, FCO, the University of Westminister and International Students House, London
Additional Information: For details on the University and course check the website www.wmiw.ac.uk or contact the Director, Human Capacity Development, ACU.

British Academy/Association of Commonwealth Universities: Grants for International Collaboration

Subjects: Humanities and social sciences.
Purpose: To support international joint activities involving British scholars in collaboration with Commonwealth partners.
Eligibility: Open to staff of ACU member institutions.
Level of Study: Research, postdoctorate
Type: Grant
Value: Up to UK £5,000. Intended to cover travel, maintenance costs plus approved necessary expenditure (not intended to cover institutional overheads or permanent staff costs)
Length of Study: 1 year
Frequency: Annual
Study Establishment: An advanced research institution
Country of Study: Commonwealth countries
No. of awards offered: Up to 12
Application Procedure: Application should be submitted by the British partner. Full application details on ACU website.
Closing Date: September 30th
Contributor: British academy and ACU
Additional Information: Priority is given to new programmes with an expectation of continued collaboration or a defined overcome such as a joint publication.

Canada Memorial Foundation Scholarship

Subjects: All subjects.
Purpose: To fund postdoctorate study in Canada.
Eligibility: The candidate must be a United Kingdom citizen and must hold a First Class (Honours) Degree or equivalent (with at least Upper Second Class Honours), and should not be more than 30 years of age. To cover one year of taught postgraduate study. Not intended for doctoral level study.
Level of Study: Postgraduate
Type: Scholarship
Value: Maintenance allowance, return airfare, approved fees, book, thesis, travel and health insurance allowances
Length of Study: 1 year
Frequency: Annual
Study Establishment: Any institution or university in Canada approved by the Canada Memorial Foundation
Country of Study: Canada
No. of awards offered: Up to 2
Application Procedure: Application form and full application details on ACU website.
Closing Date: Third Friday in October
Funding: Foundation
Contributor: Canada Memorial Foundation

Commonwealth Academic Fellowships

Subjects: All subjects. But preventive given to applications which clearly fit with the development plans of the candidates home institutions.
Purpose: To support the cost of up to six months work in the United Kingdom, for staff of universities in certain developing commonwealth countries.
Eligibility: Open to Commonwealth citizens or British protected persons who have completed their doctorate in no less than 5 years by the time of taking up an award. Candidates should be a permanent resident of and a teaching staff of a university in a developing Commonwealth country. Candidates should not be more than 50 years of age with at least 2 years of teaching experience.
Level of Study: Postdoctorate, professional development
Type: Fellowship
Value: Maintenance and travel allowances
Length of Study: 6 months
Frequency: Annual
Study Establishment: A university-level institution
Country of Study: United Kingdom
No. of awards offered: 70
Application Procedure: Application by nomination only. Full application details, including special requirements for awards involving clinical training in nursing and dentistry, available of CSFP website.
Closing Date: December 31st
Additional Information: For detailed information check the website www.csfp-online.org

Commonwealth Academic Staff Scholarships

Subjects: All subjects.
Purpose: To enable promising staff members from universities and similar institutions in the developing commonwealth to obtain experience in a higher education institution in the UK.

Eligibility: Open to Commonwealth citizens or British protected persons who are permanently resident in Commonwealth countries other than the United Kingdom, not older than 42 years of age and holding or returning to a teaching appointment in a university in a developing Commonwealth country.
Level of Study: Postgraduate, research
Type: Scholarship
Value: University fees, scholar's return travel, allowance for books, apparatus, approved travel within the country of tenure, and personal maintenance (plus family allowances for awards over 1 year in duration)
Length of Study: 1–2 years initially, maximum 3 years
Frequency: Annual
Study Establishment: An approved Institution of Higher Education
Country of Study: United Kingdom
No. of awards offered: 45–50
Application Procedure: Applicant should be nominated by the executive head of the university to which the candidate belongs. Full application details available on CSFP website.
Closing Date: December 31st
Additional Information: For detailed information check the website www.cspf-online.org, To be incorporated into given scholarship scheme with effect from 2006.

Commonwealth Professional Fellowships

Subjects: Education, engineering, environment, governance, public health and technology.
Purpose: To enable mid-career professionals to visit the United Kingdom for professional updating purposes.
Eligibility: Open to citizens and residents of Commonwealth countries with at least 5 years of appropriate experience in a profession. Fellows can be drawn from any sector, but must not hold a full-time residential appointment.
Level of Study: Professional development
Type: Scholarship
Value: Maintenance and travel allowances, with fixed contributions to the costs of the host organization. Appropriate conference/short course fees are also available
Length of Study: 3–6 months
Frequency: Annual
Study Establishment: Appropriate host organizations in the United Kingdom
Country of Study: United Kingdom
No. of awards offered: 50
Application Procedure: Application by nomination from a range of professional, charitable, public and private sector organizations based in the United Kingdom. Nominating and host organizations are expected to be the same wherever possible, though not essential. Full application details available on CSFP website.
Closing Date: May 31st
Funding: Foundation
Additional Information: The scholarship is not intended for those undertaking full-time study, those seeking assistance for commencing or completing formal academic or professional qualifications or to develop academic research for its own sake. Fellowships are not open to full-time academic staff.

Commonwealth Scholarships

Subjects: All subjects.
Purpose: Awards to commonwealth citizens for postgraduate study in commonwealth countries other than their own.
Eligibility: Open to Commonwealth citizens or British protected persons who have completed a First Class (Honours) Degree or Master's degree, and who are permanently resident in Commonwealth countries other than the United Kingdom. Candidates should hold a good Honours degree or equivalent.
Level of Study: Postgraduate, research
Type: Scholarship
Value: University fees, scholar's return travel, allowance for books, apparatus, approved travel within the country of tenure, personal maintenance (plus family allowances for over 1 year in duration)
Length of Study: 1–2 years initially, maximum 3 years
Frequency: Annual
Study Establishment: An approved Institution of Higher Education
Country of Study: United Kingdom
No. of awards offered: Up to 200
Application Procedure: Application by nomination through the Commonwealth Scholarship Agency in the country in which the scholar resides. Application forms and detailed application information available from CSFP agencies in relevant country. Full application details available on CSFP website.
Closing Date: Varies according to the country in which the candidate applies, usually some 12–18 months before the intended period of study
Additional Information: For detailed information check the website www.csfp-online.org

Commonwealth Shared Scholarship

Subjects: Subjects related to economic, social on technological development of the candidates; home country.
Purpose: To provide financial assistance to students from developing Commonwealth countries wishing to pursue a talent Master's degree in the United Kingdom.
Eligibility: Open to students from developing Commonwealth countries who are not living or studying in a developing country. Priority is given to candidates from poorer developing countries and to those under 30 years of age. Age limit is 35 years. Fluency in English is required. Candidates should not have previously studied for one term or none in a developed country.
Level of Study: Postgraduate
Type: Scholarship
Value: Full cost of study, including return airfare, maintenance and thesis allowances
Length of Study: 1 year
Frequency: Annual
Study Establishment: Participants institution in the UK (information on these available on the CSFP website)
Country of Study: United Kingdom
No. of awards offered: Between 150 and 200 annually
Application Procedure: Application must be made to participating institutions, not directly to the ACU. Full application details available on CSFP website.
Closing Date: April/May
Contributor: Department for International Development (DFID)

Commonwealth Split-Site Doctoral Scholarships

Subjects: All subjects.
Purpose: To support attendance for one year at a UK university, for those students for a PhD in a developing commonwealth country.
Eligibility: Open to Commonwealth citizens and British protected persons who are permanently resident in Commonwealth countries other than the United Kingdom. Candidates should hold a good Honours degree or equivalent and should be studying for a doctoral degree at their home institution.
Level of Study: Doctorate
Type: Scholarship
Value: University fees, scholar's return travel, allowances for books, apparatus, approved travel, personal maintenance (and family allowances for awards over 1 year in duration). Awards does not support the period of study at the home country university
Length of Study: 1 year of full-time study or two 6-month periods of full-time study
Frequency: Annual
Study Establishment: An approved Institution of Higher Education in the UK
Country of Study: United Kingdom
No. of awards offered: 30–35
Application Procedure: Applications are accepted directly from certain developing country universities as well as from United Kingdom university departments that have an established link with a university in the developing Commonwealth. Otherwise, by nomination through the Commonwealth Scholarship Agency in the country in which candidate permanently resides. Full application details on the CSFP website.
Closing Date: December 31st
Additional Information: For detailed information check the website: www.csfp-online.org

Scholarships by Distance Learning

Subjects: All subjects.
Purpose: To support study by distance learning for courses at UK universities chosen on the grounds of their impact on international development and oriented in partnership with institutions in developing commonwealth countries.
Eligibility: Open only to Commonwealth citizens.
Level of Study: Postgraduate
Type: Scholarship
Value: Fees
Frequency: Annual
Study Establishment: UK universities in partnership with institutions in developing commonwealth countries
Country of Study: United Kingdom
No. of awards offered: Depends on the availability of funds
Application Procedure: Application can be sent directly to United Kingdom providers. Full application details on CSFP website.
Closing Date: Third Friday in October
Additional Information: For details check the website www.csfp-online.org

ASSOCIATION OF RHODES SCHOLARS IN AUSTRALIA

University of Melbourne, VIC, 3010, Australia
Tel: (61) 3 8344 6937
Fax: (61) 3 9347 6739
Email: g.swafford@unimelb.edu.au
Website: www.unimelb.edu.au/research
Contact: Dr Glenn Swafford, Director, Melbourne Research & Innovation Office

Association of Rhodes Scholars in Australia Scholarship

Subjects: All subjects.
Purpose: To enable an overseas Commonwealth student to undertake research in Australia.
Eligibility: Open to graduates of a Commonwealth university approved by the committee administering the bursary. Graduates must currently be enrolled as higher degree research students at their home university, be Commonwealth citizens and may not be graduates of an Australian or New Zealand university.
Level of Study: Research, postgraduate
Type: Scholarship
Value: Australian $20,000 including travel expenses and a monthly stipend
Length of Study: 6 months
Frequency: Dependent on funds available
Study Establishment: A university
Country of Study: Australia
No. of awards offered: 1
Application Procedure: Applicants must apply for information and application forms, available through the website.
Funding: Private
Contributor: Charitable donations from former Australian Rhodes Scholars
Additional Information: For further information visit the website at www.research.unimelb.edu.au/admin/rhodes/arsa.html

ASSOCIATION OF SURGEONS OF GREAT BRITAIN AND IRELAND

The Royal College of Surgeons of England, 35-43 Lincoln's Inn Fields, London, WC2A 3PN, England
Tel: (44) 20 7973 0300
Fax: (44) 20 7430 9235
Email: admin@asgbi.org.uk
Website: www.asgbi.org.uk
Contact: Mrs Nechema Lewis, Administrative Assistant

The founding objectives of the Association of Surgeons of Great Britain and Ireland, in 1920, were the advancement of the science and art of surgery and the promotion of friendship among surgeons. As other surgical specialities developed, the Association came to represent general surgery, encompassing breast, colorectal, endocrine, laparoscopic, transplant, upper gastrointestinal and vascular surgery.

Moynihan Travelling Fellowship

Subjects: General surgery.
Purpose: To enable specialist registrars or consultants to broaden their education, and to present and discuss their contribution to British or Irish surgery overseas.
Eligibility: Open to either specialist registrars approaching the end of their higher surgical training or consultants in general surgery within 5 years of appointment after the closing date for applications. Candidates must be nationals of and residents of the United Kingdom or the Republic of Ireland, but need not be Fellows or affiliate Fellows of the Association. They may be engaged in general surgery or a sub-speciality thereof.
Level of Study: Postdoctorate
Type: Fellowship
Value: Up to UK £5,000
Frequency: Annual
Country of Study: Any country
No. of awards offered: 1
Application Procedure: Applicants must submit 12 copies of an application, which must include a full curriculum vitae giving details of past and present appointments and publications, a detailed account of the proposed programme of travel, costs involved and the object to be achieved. Applications must be addressed to the Honorary Secretary at the Association of Surgeons.
Closing Date: October 2nd
Funding: Private
Contributor: Charitable association funds
No. of awards given last year: 1
No. of applicants last year: 6
Additional Information: Shortlisted candidates will be interviewed by the Scientific Committee of the Association, which will pay particular attention to the originality, scope and feasibility of the proposed itinerary. The successful candidate will be expected to act as an ambassador for British and Irish surgery and should therefore be fully acquainted with the aims and objectives of the Association of Surgeons and its role in surgery. After the completion of the fellowship, the successful candidate will be asked to address the Association at its annual general meeting and to provide a written report for inclusion in the Executive Newsletter. A critical appraisal of the centres visited should form the basis of the report.

THE ASSOCIATION OF TEACHERS AND LECTURERS (ATL)

7 Northumberland Street, London, WC2N 5RD, England
Tel: (44) 20 7930 6441
Fax: (44) 20 7930 1359
Email: info@atl.org.uk
Website: www.atl.org.uk
Contact: Ms Thelma Meredith, Personal Assistant to General Secretary

The Association of Teachers and Lecturers (ATL) is the leading professional organization and trade union for teachers and lecturers with over 150,000 members in England, Wales and Northern Ireland. The Association is committed to protecting and promoting the interests of its members and maintaining the highest quality professional support for them.

ATL Walter Hines Page Scholarships

Subjects: Observation and study of teaching and the educational system in the United States of America.
Purpose: To promote the exchange of educational ideas between the United Kingdom and the United States of America.
Eligibility: Open to British teachers who are members of the ATL and who wish to visit the United States of America.
Level of Study: Professional development
Type: Scholarship
Value: UK £1,100 plus full hospitality

Length of Study: 2 weeks
Frequency: Annual
Country of Study: United States of America
No. of awards offered: 2
Application Procedure: Applicants must write, telephone or email the ATL for details.
Closing Date: November 30th
No. of awards given last year: 2
No. of applicants last year: 15
Additional Information: These awards are given in conjunction with the English-Speaking Union of the Commonwealth.

ASSOCIATION OF UNIVERSITIES AND COLLEGES OF CANADA (AUCC)

Higher Education Scholarships Association of Universities and Colleges of Canada, Corporate Services and Scholarships Division, 350 Albert Street, Ottawa, Suite 600, ON K1R 1B1, Canada
Tel: (1) 613 563 1236
Fax: (1) 613 563 9745
Email: awards@aucc.ca
Website: www.aucc.ca
Contact: Mr Luc Poulin

The AUCC is a non-profit, non-governmental association that represents Canadian universities at home and abroad. The Association's mandate is to foster and promote the interests of higher education in the firm belief that strong universities are vital to the prosperity and wellbeing of Canada.

AUCC Cable Telecommunications Research Fellowship

Subjects: Electrical engineering communications systems.
Purpose: To encourage students at the Master's or PhD level to tackle topics in the engineering of communications systems for video, voice and data signals or for computer applications to cable TV requirements.
Eligibility: Open to Canadian citizens or permanent residents who are enrolled or planning to enrol in a graduate degree programme at a university in Canada. Applicants must intend to use the fellowship to assist them in completing a graduate degree which includes a thesis on a topic in the engineering of broadband communication systems or computer application to cable TV.
Level of Study: Postgraduate, doctorate
Type: Fellowship
Value: Canadian $5,000
Length of Study: 1 year, with the possibility of renewal for a further year
Frequency: Annual
Study Establishment: Any university which is a member, or affiliated to a member, of the AUCC
Country of Study: Canada
No. of awards offered: 1
Application Procedure: Applicants must complete an application form. Further information and application forms available on request or from the website.
Closing Date: March 28th
Additional Information: Further information is available on request or from the website.

Department of National Defence Security and Defence Forum Internship Program

Subjects: Studies relating to current and future Canadian national security and defence issues including their political, international, historical, social, military, industrial and economic dimensions. Research in the pure and applied sciences is ineligible.
Purpose: To help recent MA graduates with a background in security and defence studies to obtain work experience.
Eligibility: Open to Canadian citizens or permanent residents who hold a Master's degree before taking up the award.
Level of Study: Intership
Type: Internship
Value: Up to Canadian $35,000
Length of Study: Up to 12 months, non-renewable
Frequency: Annual
Study Establishment: Private sector or non-governmental organizations. Contact the AUCC to obtain a list of potential organizations.
Country of Study: Canada
No. of awards offered: Upto 4
Application Procedure: Applicants must contact the AUCC or visit the National Defense website (www.dnd.ca/admpol/eng/academic/sdf_e.htm) to obtain an application package.
Closing Date: Postmarked February 1st
Funding: Government
Additional Information: On completion of the award a reasonable detailed account of the internship and any research undertaken must be submitted to the AUCC who will forward it to the Department of National Defence. Further information is available on request or from the website.

Department of National Defence Security and Defence Forum MA Scholarship Program

Subjects: Current and future Canadian national security and defence issues including their political, international, historical, social, military, industrial and economic dimensions. Research in the pure or applied sciences is ineligible.
Eligibility: Open to Canadian citizens or permanent residents who, as a minimum requirement, hold a Bachelor's (Honours) Degree or its equivalent before taking up the award.
Level of Study: Graduate, mba
Type: Scholarship
Value: Up to Canadian $10,000
Length of Study: At least 1 year, with possible renewal for a further year if evidence of satisfactory academic achievement is found
Frequency: Annual
Country of Study: Canada
No. of awards offered: Approx. 8
Application Procedure: Applicants must contact the AUCC or visit the National Defense wesite (www.dnd.ca/admpol/eng/academic/sdf_e.htm) to obtain an application package.
Closing Date: Postmarked February 1st
Funding: Government
Additional Information: Successful applicants may not hold more than one award from the federal government.

Department of National Defense Security and Defence Forum PhD Scholarship Program Including the Dr Ronald Baker Doctoral Scholarship

Subjects: Studies relating to current and future Canadian national security and defence issues including their political, international, historical, social, military, industrial and economic dimensions. Research in the pure or applied science is ineligible.
Eligibility: Applicants must be Canadian citizens or permanent residents at the time of application and, as a minimum requirement, hold a Master's degree or its equivalent before taking up the award.
Level of Study: Doctorate, graduate
Value: Up to Canadian $20,000. The Dr Ronald Baker Doctoral Scholarship is up to Canadian $22,500
Length of Study: 1 year, non renewable
Frequency: Annual
Country of Study: Canada
No. of awards offered: PhD Scholarship: 4 Ronald Baker PhD Scholarship: 1
Application Procedure: Applicants must contact the AUCC or visit the National Defense website (www.dnd.ca/admpol/eng/academic/sdf_e.htm) to obtain an application package.
Closing Date: Postmarked February 1st
Funding: Government
Additional Information: On completion of the scholarship one copy of the dissertation or a reasonable detailed account of the research undertaken must be submitted to the AUCC who will forward it to the Department of National Defence.

Department of National Defense Security and Defense Forum Postdoctoral Fellowship including the R B Byers Postdoctoral Fellowship

Subjects: Studies relating to current and future Canadian national security and defence issues including their political, international,

historical, social, military, industrial and economic dimensions. Research in the pure and applied sciences is ineligible.
Eligibility: Open to Canadian citizens or permanent residents who hold a PhD or its equivalent before taking up the award. Individuals who hold a tenure or tenure track appointment at any level are not eligible.
Level of Study: Postdoctorate, postgraduate
Type: Fellowship
Value: Up to Canadian $27,000
Length of Study: 1 year, non renewable
Frequency: Annual
Country of Study: Canada
Application Procedure: Applicants must contact the AUCC or visit the National Defense website (www.dnd.ca/admpol/eng/academic/sdf_e.htm) to obtain an application package.
Closing Date: Postmarked February 1st
Funding: Government
Additional Information: On completion of the award period a reasonably detailed account of the research undertaken, as well as copies of publications and unpublished conference presentations resulting from the award, are to be submitted to the AUCC who will forward them to the Department of National Defence. Successful applicants may not hold more than one award from the federal government.

Frank Knox Memorial Fellowships

Subjects: Arts and sciences including engineering, business administration, design, divinity studies, education, law, public administration at the John F Kennedy School of Government, medicine, dental medicine and public health.
Purpose: To offer an opportunity to students from Canada who wish to graduate from the Harvard University.
Eligibility: Open to Canadian citizens or permanent residents who have recently graduated or who are about to graduate from an institution in Canada which is a member or affiliated to a member of the AUCC. Applications from students presently studying in the United States of America will not be considered, although applications will be considered from recent graduates who are working in the United States of America and will be applying to the MBA programme.
Level of Study: Postgraduate, mba
Type: Fellowship
Value: US$19,500 plus tuition fees and student health insurance
Length of Study: 1 academic year
Frequency: Annual
Study Establishment: Harvard University
Country of Study: United States of America
No. of awards offered: Up to 3
Application Procedure: Applicants must apply directly to the graduate school of their choice. Applicants are responsible for gaining admission to Harvard University by the deadline set by the various faculties. Further information and application forms are available on request or from the website.
Closing Date: November 30
Additional Information: Holders of this award may not accept any other grant for the period of this fellowship unless approved by the Committee on General Scholarships and the Sheldon Fund of Harvard University.

Frederick T Metcalf Award Program

Subjects: Disciplines related to new media companies and delivering cable communications services such as business finance and marketing, economics, television production, mass communications and engineering.
Purpose: To support students pursuing a Master's degree in a programme related to the cable communication services.
Eligibility: Open to qualified full-time students pursuing a Master's degree in a field directly related to the development and delivery of cable in Canada.
Level of Study: Postgraduate
Type: Scholarship
Value: Canadian $5,000
Length of Study: 1 year, non renewable
Frequency: Annual
Study Establishment: Any university which is a member of the AUCC, or affiliated to a member of the AUCC
Country of Study: Canada
No. of awards offered: 1
Application Procedure: Applicants must complete an application form, which are available on request or from the website.
Closing Date: March 31st
Contributor: The Canadian Cable Television Association

Public Safety and Emergency Preparedness Canada Research Fellowship in Honour of Stuart Nesbitt White

Subjects: 1. Cybersecurity relating to critical infrastructure protection, preferably in disciplines such as computer/software/electrical/mechanical engineering, computer science, and/or areas such as systems science, and risk modelling and management. Multidisciplinary studies are encouraged. 2. Disaster and emergency management, and physical critical infrastructure studies, preferably in disciplines such as urban and regional planning, geography, sociology, economics, engineering, and environmental sciences, and/or areas such as risk assessment and modelling. Multidisciplinary studies are encouraged.
Purpose: Public Safety and Emergency Preparedness Canada is seeking to encourage PhD. research in two areas of its mission, which is to enhance the safety and security of Canadians in their physical and cyber environments.
Eligibility: Open to Canadian citizens or permanent residents. Candidates must hold a Master's degree and be pursuing a degree at the doctorate level and have demonstrated interest in research with respect to emergencies. Applicants must pursue full time studies and be studying under the supervision of a faculty member or an academic committee. Awards are granted based on academic standing and demonstrated potential for advanced study and research.
Level of Study: Doctorate
Type: Fellowship
Value: Canadian $19,250
Length of Study: 1 year, not renewable but may re-apply
Frequency: Annual
Country of Study: Canada
No. of awards offered: 8
Application Procedure: Applicants must write for details or refer to the website.
Closing Date: May 15th
Funding: Government
Additional Information: Further information is available on request or from the website.

THE ASTHMA FOUNDATION OF NEW SOUTH WALES

Level 7, 35 Chandos St, St Leonards, NSW 2065, Australia
Tel: (61) 2 9906 3233
Fax: (61) 2 9906 4493
Email: ask@asthmansw.org.au
Website: www.asthmansw.org.au
Contact: Executive Director

The vision of the Asthma Foundation of New South Wales is to eliminate asthma as a major cause of illness and disruption within the New South Wales community. Fundraising efforts assist with the promotion and funding of research activities that are aimed at helping the Foundation to achieve this vision.

Ann J Woolcock Research Fellowship

Subjects: Asthma research.
Purpose: To provide an outstanding researcher in biomedical science with an opportunity for independent research.
Eligibility: Open to Australian citizens or permanent residents who hold a PhD or equivalent doctorate in a health-related field of research. Applicants must also have a demonstrated ability in research in the form of publications, and an intention to remain active in research. Candidates should have been actively engaged in research, in Australia or overseas, within the 2 years prior to application, and

should normally have no more than 8 years of postdoctoral experience from the date that the doctoral thesis was passed.
Level of Study: Postdoctorate
Type: Fellowship
Value: Up to Australian $100,000. This sum includes salary and up to Australian $15,000 for equipment, running expenses and travel. The value of a part-time fellowship will be adjusted on a pro rata basis
Length of Study: Applicants may elect to carry out research full or part-time with remaining time spent in clinical practice. The full-time fellowship is for a period of up to 3 years and the part-time fellowship is for up to 4 years
Frequency: Every 3 years
Study Establishment: A recognized and approved institution, teaching hospital or university in New South Wales or the Australian Central Territories
Country of Study: Australia
Application Procedure: All applications must be submitted on the correct application form, which, together with details of the conditions associated with the fellowship, can be found on the website.
Funding: Private
Contributor: Private donors

Asthma Foundation of New South Wales Biomedical and Medical Postgraduate Research Scholarships

Subjects: Medical, scientific and clinical research into asthma, its causes, triggers and impact.
Purpose: To expand the body of knowledge towards the causes of asthma and its possible cure.
Level of Study: Postdoctorate, postgraduate
Type: Scholarship
Value: Australian $20,000
Length of Study: 1 year
Frequency: Annual, (dependent on funds available)
Country of Study: Australia
No. of awards offered: Varies
Application Procedure: Applicants must complete application forms. Short-listed candidates will be interviewed.
Closing Date: Mid-October
Funding: Private
Contributor: Private donors
No. of awards given last year: 2
No. of applicants last year: 3

Asthma Foundation of New South Wales Medical Research Project Grant

Subjects: Medical, scientific and clinical research into asthma, its causes, triggers and impact.
Purpose: To expand the body of knowledge towards the causes of asthma and its possible cure.
Level of Study: Postdoctorate, postgraduate
Type: Project grant
Value: Australian $50,000
Length of Study: 1 year
Frequency: Annual, (dependent on funds available)
Country of Study: Australia
No. of awards offered: Varies
Application Procedure: Applicants must complete application forms. Short-listed candidates will be interviewed.
Closing Date: Mid-November
Funding: Private
Contributor: Private donors
No. of awards given last year: 4
No. of applicants last year: 11

ATAXIA UK

10 Winchester House, Kennington Park, London, SW9 6EJ, England
Tel: (44) 20 7820 3900
Fax: (44) 20 7582 9444
Email: office@ataxia.org.uk
Website: www.ataxia.org.uk
Contact: Ms Julia Greenfield, Research Liaison Officer

Ataxia UK is the leading charity in the United Kingdom working with and for people with ataxia. It will support research projects and related activities in order to enhance scientific understanding of ataxia, develop and evaluate therapeutic and supportive strategies and encourage wider involvement with ataxia research.

Ataxia UK Project Grant

Subjects: Any aspect of both inherited and sporadic progressive ataxias including Friedreich's and other cerebellar ataxias.
Purpose: To enhance scientific understanding of ataxia and to develop and evaluate therapeutic and supportive strategies.
Eligibility: Proposals are accepted from academic institutions, private sector research companies and suitably qualified individuals. There are no restrictions on age, nationality or residency.
Level of Study: Research
Type: Project grant
Value: Varies, maximum of UK £50,000 per year
Length of Study: Up to 3 years
Frequency: Dependent on funds available
Study Establishment: Any academic institution or private sector company
Country of Study: Any country
No. of awards offered: Varies
Application Procedure: Applicants must complete an application form available from Ataxia's Research Liaison Officer at research@ataxia.org.uk
Closing Date: No closing dates
Funding: Private, commercial
Additional Information: There are a number of priority areas of research and these can be obtained from the Research Liaison Officer.

Ataxia UK Research Studentships

Subjects: Any aspect of both inherited and sporadic progressive ataxias, including Friedreich's ataxia and other cerebellar ataxias.
Purpose: To enhance scientific understanding of ataxia, to develop and evaluate therapeutic and supportive strategies and to increase awareness of ataxia in the research community.
Eligibility: Proposals are accepted from academic institutions, private sector research companies and suitably qualified individuals. There are no restrictions on age, nationality or residency.
Level of Study: Doctorate
Type: Studentship
Value: UK £10,000–50,000
Length of Study: 3 years
Frequency: Dependent on funds available
Study Establishment: Any academic institution
Country of Study: Any country
No. of awards offered: Dependent on funds available
Application Procedure: Applicants must complete an application form available from Ataxia UK's Research Projects Manager at research@ataxia.org.uk
Closing Date: No closing dates
Funding: Commercial, private
Additional Information: There are a number of priority areas of research and these can be obtained from the Research Projects Manager.

Ataxia UK Satellite Meeting at Major Symposium on Related Disorders

Subjects: Any aspect of both inherited and sporadic progressive ataxias including Friedreich's and other cerebellar ataxias.
Purpose: To raise awareness of ataxia research and to enhance collaboration with researchers within the ataxia field and related disciplines.
Eligibility: Proposals are accepted from academic institutions, private sector research companies and suitably qualified individuals. There are no restrictions on age, nationality or residency.
Level of Study: Research
Type: Award
Value: Dependent on the meeting
Frequency: Dependent on funds available
Country of Study: Any country
No. of awards offered: Varies

Application Procedure: Applicants must complete an application form available from Ataxia's Research Liaison Officer at research@ataxia.org.uk
Closing Date: No closing dates
Funding: Commercial, private
Additional Information: There are a number of priority areas of research and these can be obtained from the Research Liaison Officer.

Ataxia UK Travel Award

Subjects: Any aspect of both inherited and sporadic progressive ataxias including Friedreich's ataxia and other cerebellar ataxias.
Purpose: To enable researchers to present their ataxia research at national and international conferences.
Eligibility: Proposals are accepted from academic institutions, private sector research companies and suitably qualified individuals. There are no restrictions on age, nationality or residency.
Level of Study: Unrestricted
Type: Travel grant
Value: Dependent on the conference
Frequency: Dependent on funds available
Country of Study: Any country
No. of awards offered: Varies
Application Procedure: Applicants must complete an application form available from Ataxia's Research Liaison Officer at research@ataxia.org.uk
Closing Date: No closing dates
Funding: Commercial, private
Additional Information: There are a number of priority areas of research and these can be obtained from the Research Liaison Officer.

ATHENAEUM INTERNATIONAL CULTURAL CENTRE

3 Adrianou Street, Athens, GR-105 55, Greece
Tel: (30) 210 321 1987
Fax: (30) 210 321 1196
Email: athenm@attglobal.net
Website: www.athenaeum.ids.gr
Contact: Mrs Irene Mega, Executive Secretary

The Athenaeum International Cultural Centre is a non-profit association dedicated to preserving the memory of Maria Callas. The organization was founded in 1974 by a group of inspired artists who wanted to contribute to the development and evolution of musical education and culture in Greece.

Maria Callas Grand Prix

Subjects: Singing and the piano.
Purpose: To recognize outstanding artists.
Eligibility: Open to nationals from any country.
Level of Study: Unrestricted
Type: Competition
Value: Please contact the organization
Frequency: Every 2 years
Country of Study: Any country
No. of awards offered: 1 for each category
Application Procedure: Applicants must complete an application form and submit this with the documentation as detailed in the prospectus of the Grand Prix. There is a registration fee of €120.
Closing Date: December 31st
Funding: Government, private
No. of awards given last year: 3 in opera and 3 in piano
No. of applicants last year: 45 for opera and 63 for piano
Additional Information: Concert appearances are arranged for the winners.

Maria Callas Grand Prix for Opera and Oratorio-Lied

Subjects: Opera and oratorio-lied.
Purpose: To recognize outstanding singers.
Eligibility: Open to singers of any nationality. Female singers should not be older than 30 years of age and male singers not older than 32 years of age.
Level of Study: Unrestricted
Type: Competition
Value: Please contact the organization
Frequency: Every 2 years
Country of Study: Any country
No. of awards offered: 1 for each category and then second and third prize
Application Procedure: Applicants must complete an application form and pay the registration fee of €120. Candidates must contact the Centre for further details.
Closing Date: December 15th
Funding: Government, private
No. of awards given last year: 3
No. of applicants last year: 45
Additional Information: Concert appearances are arranged for the winners.

Maria Callas Grand Prix for Pianists

Subjects: Musical performance on the piano.
Purpose: To recognize outstanding pianists.
Eligibility: Open to pianists of any nationality, up to 32 years of age.
Level of Study: Unrestricted
Type: Competition
Value: Please contact the organization
Frequency: Every 2 years
Country of Study: Any country
No. of awards offered: 3
Application Procedure: Applicants must contact the Centre for details. There is a registration fee of €120.
Closing Date: December 15th
Funding: Private, government
No. of awards given last year: 3
No. of applicants last year: 63
Additional Information: Concert appearances are arranged for the Grand Prix winner.

Maria Callas International Music Competition

Subjects: Musical performance, although disciplines vary with each competition. Singing such as opera, oratorio-lied and the piano.
Purpose: To recognize outstanding artists.
Eligibility: Open to musicians of all nationalities.
Level of Study: Unrestricted
Type: Competition
Value: Please contact the organization
Country of Study: Any country
No. of awards offered: Varies according to the category
Application Procedure: Applicants must request full details and application procedures or visit the website. There is a registration fee of €120.
Closing Date: December 15th
Funding: Government, private
No. of awards given last year: 3 in opera and 3 in piano
No. of applicants last year: 45 for singing and 63 for the piano competition
Additional Information: Concert appearances are arranged for the winners.

ATLANTIC SALMON FEDERATION (ASF)

PO Box 5200, St Andrews, NB, E5B 3S8, Canada
Tel: (1) 506 529 4581
Fax: (1) 506 529 4438
Email: asfres@nbnet.nb.ca
Website: www.asf.ca/awards/awards.html
Contact: Ms Ellen Merrill, Executive Assistant

The Atlantic Salmon Federation (ASF) is an international, non-profit organization that promotes the conservation and management of the Atlantic salmon and its environment. ASF has a network of seven regional councils, a membership of over 150 river associations and 40,000 volunteers. Regional offices cover the salmon's freshwater range in Canada and the United States of America.

Olin Fellowship

Subjects: Salmon biology, management and conservation.
Purpose: To support individuals seeking to improve their knowledge or skills in advanced fields, while looking for solutions to current problems in Atlantic salmon biology, management and conservation.
Eligibility: Open to citizens and legal residents of the United States of America or Canada. Applicants need not be enrolled in a degree programme to be eligible.
Level of Study: Unrestricted
Type: Fellowship
Value: Canadian $1,000–3,000
Frequency: Annual
Study Establishment: Any accredited university, research laboratory or active management programme
Country of Study: United States of America or Canada
No. of awards offered: Varies
Application Procedure: Applicants must complete an application form, available on request or from the website. www.asf.ca/awards/awards
Closing Date: March 15th
Funding: Private
Contributor: Memberships and foundation grants
No. of awards given last year: 6
No. of applicants last year: 8

AUDI DESIGN FOUNDATION

Yeomans Drive, Blakelands, Milton Keynes,
MK14 5AN, England
Tel: (44) 19 0860 1570
Fax: (44) 19 0860 1943
Email: audidesignfoundation@audidesignfoundation.org
Website: www.audidesignfoundation.org

Since 1997, Audi Design Foundation has awarded nearly £0.75m of funding through the pioneering grant programme. Hundreds of projects from a variety of design disciplines have received grants, and there have partly been car-related from water-bikes to medical equipment, grant winners work to their own briefs and retain all intellectual property rights. By giving support to such a wide range of projects, we enable creative individuals across the UK to develop their talents and become an innovative force in the world of design ideas.

Audi Design Foundation Award

Subjects: Design.
Purpose: To encourage young people to enjoy, innovate and take risks in design and technology, and help make their ideas a reality.
Eligibility: Applicants may be individuals or small groups, not younger than 16 or older than 35. The foundation can only support applicants who are resident in the United Kingdom; however, applicants can be citizens of any European country.
Level of Study: Unrestricted
Type: Grant
Value: Dependent on amount required to develop and produce a prototype. As set out in applicant's initial grant request document and approved by the Audi Design Foundation grant panel
Frequency: Ad hoc: Up to 10 times a year
Application Procedure: There is no standard application form. Each applicant must produce their own document and content will be assessed by the Grants Panel. A minimum of two sides of A4-size paper summary of the project with accompanying illustrative material will be required. Application must include name, age and contact details as well as an expected timescale for the project. For further information, please visit www.audidesignfoundation.org and follow the links under grants programme'.
Closing Date: None: ongoing process
Funding: Commercial
Contributor: Audi UK
No. of awards given last year: 15
No. of applicants last year: Approx. 60

THE AUSTRALIA COUNCIL (OZCO)

PO Box 788, Strawberry Hills, NSW 2012, Australia
Tel: (61) 2 9215 9000
Fax: (61) 2 9215 9111
Email: mail@ozco.gov.au
Website: www.ozco.gov.au

The Australia Council is the Australian Government's arts funding and advisory body. We support and promote the practice and enjoyment of the arts.

Aboriginal and Torres Strait Islander Arts Fellowship

Subjects: Craft art, literature, performing arts, new media.
Purpose: To support an Aboriginal and Torres Strait Islander artist undertaking a major creative project.
Eligibility: Open to practicing Aboriginal and Torres Strait Islander artists who are able to demonstrate at least 10 years experience as a practicing professional artist.
Level of Study: Postgraduate
Type: Fellowship
Value: Australian $40,000 annual stipend
Length of Study: 2 years
Frequency: Annual
Country of Study: Australia
Application Procedure: Apply online.
Closing Date: November 15th
Funding: Government

For further information contact:

Email: atsia@ozco.gov.au

Aboriginal and Torres Strait Islander New Work Grant

Subjects: Theatre, writing, music.
Purpose: To support Aboriginal and Torres Strait Islander artists organizing community oriented works.
Eligibility: Open to Aboriginal and Torres Strait Islander artists who demonstrate artistic merit and innovation.
Level of Study: Professional development
Type: Grant
Value: Varies
Length of Study: Up to 12 months
Frequency: Annual
Country of Study: Australia
Application Procedure: Apply online.
Closing Date: July 15th and November 15th
Funding: Government

For further information contact:

Email: atsia@ozco.gov.au

International Market Development Program

Subjects: Music.
Purpose: International Pathways aims to assist with strategic international artistic and market development activities for Australian music and musicians.
Eligibility: Applicants must have a commercially available CD, and touring experience.
Level of Study: Professional development
Type: Grant
Value: Australian $2,500–20,000
Length of Study: A maximum of 3 years
Frequency: Annual
Country of Study: Australia
Application Procedure: Contact the department.
Closing Date: No deadline
Funding: Government

For further information contact:

Tel: 02 9215 9115
Email: music@ozco.gov.au
Contact: Andy Ratzen

OZCO Community Cultural Development Fellowship

Subjects: Community-based arts.
Purpose: To enhance the capacity of artists and artsworkers to provide leadership in the field.
Level of Study: Postgraduate, professional development
Type: Fellowship
Value: Australian $40,000
Length of Study: 2 years
Frequency: Annual
Country of Study: Australia
No. of awards offered: Varies
Application Procedure: Contact the department.
Closing Date: April 15th
Funding: Government

For further information contact:

Tel: 61 2 9215 9029
Email: ccd@ozco.gov.au

OZCO Community Culture Development Grant Residency

Subjects: Arts.
Purpose: To afford an artist or arts worker the opportunity to take time out of project-based work and focus on professional development, reflection or individual arts practice.
Eligibility: Artists applying require a driver's licence.
Level of Study: Professional development
Type: Grant
Value: Australian $14,000 and an Australian $1,000 materials allowance
Frequency: Annual
Study Establishment: Hastings Council and Camden Haven Community College Inc.
Country of Study: Australia
Application Procedure: Contact the department.
Closing Date: August 1st
Funding: Government

For further information contact:

Tel: 02 9215 9034
Email: m.martin@ozco.gov.au

OZCO Dance Fellowship

Subjects: Dance.
Purpose: To strengthen an artist's current practice and ability to seek new challenges or test a new direction.
Level of Study: Postdoctorate, professional development
Type: Fellowship
Value: Australian $40,000
Length of Study: 2 years
Frequency: Annual
Country of Study: Australia
No. of awards offered: Varies
Application Procedure: Contact the department.
Closing Date: November 15th
Funding: Government

For further information contact:

Email: dance@ozco.gov.au

OZCO Dance Grant Initiative: Take Your Partner

Subjects: Dance and movement arts.
Purpose: To support young and emerging dance artists and art workers to forge a new relationship or build on an existing one through a specific project.
Level of Study: Professional development
Type: Grant
Value: Australian $15,000
Frequency: Annual
Country of Study: Australia
Application Procedure: Contact the department.
Closing Date: May–June
Funding: Government

For further information contact:

Tel: 2 9215 9179
Email: s.woo@ozco.gov.au
Contact: Sandi Woo

OZCO Literature Fellowships

Subjects: Fiction, literary non-fiction (defined by the Literature Board as autobiography, biography, essays, histories criticism or other analytical prose); children's and young adult literature; poetry; and creative writing for performance or new media.
Purpose: To support excellence in Australian literature.
Eligibility: Applications will only be accepted from individuals who have had a minimum of major works published or performed and have achieved substantial critical recognition.
Level of Study: Professional development, postgraduate
Type: Fellowship
Value: Australian $40,000
Length of Study: 2 years
Frequency: Annual
Country of Study: Australia
No. of awards offered: Varies
Application Procedure: Contact the department.
Closing Date: May 15th
Funding: Government

For further information contact:

Email: literature@ozco.gov.au

OZCO Literature Grants Initiative: Write in Your Face

Subjects: Writing in zines, e-zines, comics, multimedia, multi-art forms, websites, live performance and spoken word.
Purpose: To support young writers using language in innovative ways.
Eligibility: Applicant must be aged 30 years or under.
Level of Study: Professional development
Type: Grant
Value: A maximum of Australian $5,000
Frequency: Annual
Country of Study: Australia
No. of awards offered: Varies
Application Procedure: Contact the department.
Closing Date: December 9th

For further information contact:

Tel: 29215 9058
Email: j.jones@ozco.gov.au
Contact: J. Jones

OZCO Music Fellowship

Subjects: Music.
Purpose: To provide musicians with a record of outstanding achievement with financial support.
Level of Study: Professional development, postdoctorate
Type: Fellowship
Value: Australian $40,000
Length of Study: 2 years
Frequency: Annual
Country of Study: Australia
No. of awards offered: Varies
Application Procedure: Contact the department.
Closing Date: June 1st
Funding: Government
Additional Information: Fellowship recipients may apply for funding from other categories during the term of the Fellowship, with the exception of the project Fellowships initiative.

For further information contact:

Email: music@ozco.gov.au

OZCO Music Project Fellowship

Subjects: Music.
Purpose: To fund artists for significant projects that will benefit their artistic development.
Eligibility: Music artists working in music theatre and indigenous music artists are particularly encouraged to apply.
Level of Study: Postgraduate, professional development
Type: Fellowship
Value: Australian $20,000
Length of Study: 1 year
Frequency: Annual
Country of Study: Australia
No. of awards offered: Varies
Application Procedure: Contact the department.
Closing Date: June 1st
Funding: Government

For further information contact:

Email: music@ozco.gov.au

OZCO New Media Fellowship

Subjects: New media arts.
Purpose: To allow an outstanding artist to take two years out from other paid employment to enable them to create new work.
Eligibility: Open to artists with outstanding professional achievement and outstanding artistic potential.
Level of Study: Professional development, postdoctorate
Type: Fellowship
Value: Australian $40,000
Length of Study: 2 years
Frequency: Annual
Country of Study: Australia
Application Procedure: See website.
Closing Date: August
Funding: Government

For further information contact:

nma@ozco.gov.au

OZCO New Media Residency

Subjects: New Media Arts.
Purpose: To support hybrid and new media study abroad.
Level of Study: Postgraduate, postdoctorate
Type: Fellowship
Length of Study: 1 year
Frequency: Annual
Study Establishment: Banff Centre for the Arts
Country of Study: Canada
No. of awards offered: Varies
Application Procedure: Apply online.
Closing Date: November 1st
Funding: Government

For further information contact:

Email: nma@ozco.gov.au

OZCO Theatre Fellowship

Subjects: Theatre studies.
Purpose: To financially support an individuals professional development.
Eligibility: It is for artists with a record of outstanding achievement.
Level of Study: Postgraduate, professional development
Type: Fellowship
Value: Australian $40,000
Length of Study: 2 years
Frequency: Annual
Country of Study: Australia
Application Procedure: It is strongly recommended that you discuss your application with staff before applying.
Closing Date: November 15th
Funding: Government

For further information contact:

Email: theatre@ozco.gov.au

OZCO Visual Arts Fellowship

Subjects: Visual Arts.
Purpose: To provide financial support to visual artists, craftspeople and specialist visual arts and craft writers of outstanding achievement to enable them to create new work and further develop their practice.
Level of Study: Postgraduate
Type: Fellowship
Value: Australian $40,000
Length of Study: A maximum of 2 years
Frequency: Annual
Country of Study: Australia
Application Procedure: Apply online.
Closing Date: April 15th
Funding: Government
Additional Information: Fellowships are granted only once in an artist's lifetime.

For further information contact:

Email: vac@ozco.gov.au

AUSTRALIAN ACADEMY OF THE HUMANITIES (AAH)

GPO Box 93, Canberra, ACT, 2601, Australia
Tel: (61) 2 6125 9860
Fax: (61) 2 6248 6287
Email: aah@anu.edu.au
Website: www.humanities.org.au
Contact: Administration Officer

The Australian Academy of the Humanities (AAH) was established under Royal Charter in 1969 for the advancement of the scholarship, interest in and understanding of the humanities. Humanities disciplines include, but are not limited to, history, classics, English, European languages and cultures, Asian studies, philosophy, the arts, linguistics, prehistory and archaeology and cultural and communications studies.

AAH Humanities Travelling Fellowships

Subjects: Humanities disciplines as per the Academy's charter.
Purpose: To enable short-term study abroad.
Eligibility: Open to scholars resident in Australia and who are working in the field of humanities. Fellows of the Academy are ineligible for awards. Preference shall be given to scholars in the earlier stages of their careers, and who are not as well placed to receive funding from other sources. They should have a project going forward that requires a short visit overseas for its completion or advancement. The proposed work should not form part of the requirement for a higher degree. Funds are not given for conference attendance.
Level of Study: Postdoctorate, doctorate
Type: Fellowship
Value: Australian $4,000 each
Length of Study: At least 2 weeks
Frequency: Annual
Study Establishment: An appropriate research centre
Country of Study: Any country
No. of awards offered: 10
Application Procedure: Applicants can download application form and guidelines from the academy website www.humanities.org.au
Closing Date: July 31st
Funding: Government
No. of awards given last year: 9
No. of applicants last year: 36
Additional Information: Please visit the Academy's website, www.humanities.org.au for detailed information and application procedures.

AUSTRALIAN BIO SECURITY-CRC (AB-CRC)

Brisbane, OLD Building 76 Molecular Biosciences The University of Queens land, ST. Lucia, QLd 4072, Australia
Tel: (61) (0) 7 3346 8866
Fax: (61) (0) 7 3346 8862
Email: info@aberc.org.au

The mission of the ABCRC is to protect Australia's public health, livestock, wildlife and economic resources through research and education that strengthens the national capability to detect, diagnose, identify, monitor, assess, predict and to respond to emerging infectious disease threats.

AB-CRC Honours Scholarships

Subjects: Biosecurity and emerging infectious diseases.
Purpose: To encourage students of high academic ability to take the first step in their career path as a researcher.
Eligibility: Scholarships will be awarded preferentially to Australian residents and students from the Asia-Pacific region.
Level of Study: Postgraduate
Type: Scholarship
Value: Australian $5,000
Length of Study: 1 year
Frequency: Annual
Study Establishment: AB-CRC participating university
Country of Study: Australia
Application Procedure: Contact the scholarships Administrator officer.
Closing Date: November 16th

For further information contact:

Tel: 08 9266 1634
Email: debra.gendle@abcrc.org.au
Contact: Debra Gendle

AB-CRC PhD and Masters-by-Research Scholarships

Subjects: Bio security and emerging infectious diseases.
Purpose: To expand training opportunities.
Level of Study: Doctorate, postdoctorate, postgraduate
Type: Scholarship
Value: An annual stipend of up to Australian $25,000 and a development allowance of Australian $2,000
Length of Study: 1–3 years
Frequency: Annual
Study Establishment: AB-CRC participating university
Country of Study: Australia
Application Procedure: Request application form.
Closing Date: October 24th

AB-CRC Professional Development Scholarships

Subjects: Bio Security and emerging infectious diseases.
Purpose: To expand our capability to support the training of specialists.
Level of Study: Professional development
Type: Scholarship
Length of Study: Australian $2,000–Australian $6,000
Frequency: Annual
Study Establishment: AB-CRC participating university
Country of Study: Australia
No. of awards offered: 5
Application Procedure: Contact the Scholarships Administration officer.
Closing Date: November 16th
Additional Information: Candidates will be required to sign a confidentially agreement.

For further information contact:

Email: debra.gendle@abcrc.org.uk
Contact: Debra Gendle

THE AUSTRALIAN FEDERATION OF UNIVERSITY WOMEN, SOUTH AUSTRALIA, INC. TRUST FUND (AFUW-SA, INC.)

GPO Box 634, Adelaide, SA, 5001, Australia
Website: www.afuwsa-bursaries.com.au
Contact: Ms Heather Latz, Fellowships Trustee

The Australian Federation of University Women's (AFUW) main activity is assisting women in tertiary education in Australia via bursaries. Funds for the bursaries are raised through volunteer work, academic dress hire, donations and bequests.

AFUW-SA Barbara Crase, Doreen McCarthy, Cathy Candler and Brenda Nettle Bursaries

Subjects: All subjects.
Purpose: To assist in the completion of a Master's or PhD research degree.
Eligibility: Open to men and women of any nationality. Applicants must have completed 1 year of postgraduate research excluding the honours year, and must be enrolled at a university in South Australia.
Level of Study: Postgraduate, doctorate
Type: Bursary
Value: Australian $5,000
Length of Study: The bursary must be used within 1 year of the date of the award
Frequency: Annual
Study Establishment: A South Australian university
Country of Study: Australia
No. of awards offered: 4
Application Procedure: Candidates should complete an application form and submit this with evidence of enrolment at the institution at which the qualification will be obtained, as well as copies of official transcripts, a curriculum vitae and a list of publications. Application forms can be downloaded from the website and sent by post.
Closing Date: March 1st
Funding: Private
No. of awards given last year: 10
No. of applicants last year: 24

AFUW-SA Diamond Jubilee Bursary

Subjects: All subjects.
Purpose: To assist in the completion of a coursework postgraduate degree.
Eligibility: Open to men or women of any nationality, who are enrolled in a postgraduate degree by coursework at a South Australian University.
Level of Study: Postgraduate, doctorate
Type: Bursary
Value: Australian $4,000
Length of Study: The bursary must be used within 1 year of the date of the award
Frequency: Annual
Study Establishment: A South Australian university
Country of Study: Australia
No. of awards offered: 1
Application Procedure: Candidates should complete an application form and submit this with evidence of enrolment at the institution at which the qualification will be obtained, as well as copies of official transcripts and a curriculum vitae. Application forms can be downloaded from the website and sent by post.
Closing Date: March 1st
Funding: Private
No. of awards given last year: 3
No. of applicants last year: 9

AFUW-SA Padnendadlu Bursary

Subjects: All subjects.
Purpose: To assist in the completion of a postgraduate degree.
Eligibility: Applicants must be Australian indigenous women undertaking postgraduate degrees at South Australian universities.
Level of Study: Doctorate, postgraduate
Type: Bursary
Value: Australian $5,000, for those undertaking research degrees or Australian $4,000 for those undertaking course work degrees
Frequency: Annual
Study Establishment: A South Australian university
Country of Study: Australia
No. of awards offered: 1, however, runners up may be awarded less than the bursary amount

Application Procedure: Candidates should complete an application form and submit this with evidence of enrolment at the institution at which the qualification will be obtained, as well as copies of official transcripts and a curriculum vitae. Application forms can be downloaded from the website and sent by post.
Closing Date: March 1st
Funding: Private
No. of awards given last year: 2
No. of applicants last year: 2
Additional Information: Eligible applicants undertaking a postgraduate degree by coursework must apply for the Diamond Jubilee Bursary, and those undertaking a postgraduate degree by research must apply for the Doreen McCarthy, Barbara Crase, Cathy Candler and Brenda Nettle Bursaries. In each case, completion of a declaration of indigenous status will ensure that applicants are considered for the Padnendadlu Bursary.

AFUW-SA Thenie Baddams Bursary, Jean Gilmore Bursary and Daphne Elliott Bursary

Subjects: All subjects.
Purpose: To assist women to complete a Master's or PhD degree by research.
Eligibility: Open to female graduates who are enrolled at an Australian tertiary institution and have completed at least 1 year of postgraduate research, excluding their Honours year. Applicants must hold a good Honours degree or equivalent, and must not be in full-time paid employment or study leave during tenure.
Level of Study: Doctorate, postgraduate
Type: Bursary
Value: Up to Australian $6,000 each; however, runners-up can be awarded a lesser amount
Length of Study: The bursary must be used within 1 year of the date of the award
Frequency: Annual
Study Establishment: A recognized Australian Institute of Higher Education
Country of Study: Australia
No. of awards offered: 3
Application Procedure: Applicants must complete an application form and submit this with evidence of enrolment at the institution at which the qualification is to be obtained, as well as copies of official transcripts, a curriculum vitae and list of publications. There is an Australian $12 lodgement fee. Application forms can be downloaded from the website and sent by post.
Closing Date: March 1st
Funding: Private
No. of awards given last year: 13
No. of applicants last year: 138

AFUW-SA Winifred E Preedy Postgraduate Bursary

Subjects: Dentistry or a related field.
Purpose: To assist women in the completion of a higher degree.
Eligibility: Open to women who are past or present students of the Faculty of Dentistry at the University of Adelaide and who are enrolled as graduate students in dentistry or an allied field at the University of Adelaide or at such other institutions of tertiary education as the trustees may approve. The applicant must have completed 1 year of her postgraduate degree.
Level of Study: Doctorate, postgraduate
Type: Bursary
Value: Australian $4,000
Length of Study: The bursary must be used within 1 year of the date of the award
Frequency: Annual
Study Establishment: Anywhere, if the applicant is a past student at the University of Adelaide's Dental Faculty in Australia. Otherwise the applicant must be a student at the University of Adelaide Dental Faculty
Country of Study: Australia
No. of awards offered: 1
Application Procedure: Applicants must complete an application form and submit this with evidence of enrolment at the institution at which the qualification will be obtained, as well as copies of official transcripts, a curriculum vitae and list of publications. Application forms can be downloaded from the website and sent by post.
Closing Date: March 1st
Funding: Private
No. of awards given last year: None
No. of applicants last year: None

AFUW-SA, Inc. Trust Fund Bursary

Subjects: All subjects.
Purpose: To assist women to complete coursework postgraduate degrees.
Eligibility: Open to women enrolled for coursework postgraduate degrees at any Australian university. Applicants must not be in full-time paid employment or on fully paid study leave during the tenure of the bursary.
Level of Study: Postgraduate, doctorate
Type: Bursary
Value: Australian $4,000
Length of Study: The bursary must be used within 1 year of the date of the award
Frequency: Annual
Study Establishment: A recognized Australian tertiary institution
Country of Study: Australia
No. of awards offered: 1
Application Procedure: Applicants must complete an application form and submit this with evidence of enrolment at the institution at which the qualification is to be obtained, as well as copies of official transcripts, a curriculum vitae and list of publications. Application forms can be downloaded from the website and sent by post.
Closing Date: March 1st
Funding: Private
No. of awards given last year: 2
No. of applicants last year: 39

AUSTRALIAN KIDNEY FOUNDATION

GPO Box 9993, Adelaide, SA, 5001, Australia
Tel: (61) 8 8334 7555
Fax: (61) 8 8334 7540
Email: teresa.taylor@adelaide.kidney.org.au
Website: www.kidney.org.au
Contact: National Communications Manager

Founded in 1968, the Australian Kidney Foundation's mission is to be recognized as the leading non-profit national organization providing funding for, and taking the initiative in, the prevention of kidney and urinary tract diseases.

Australian Kidney Foundation Biomedical Scholarships

Subjects: Medical and Scientific kidney and urology-related research.
Purpose: To provide scholarships for individuals wishing to study full-time for the research degrees.
Eligibility: Open to applicants who are graduates, or proposing to graduate in the current academic year.
Level of Study: Postgraduate, doctorate
Value: Australian $25,000 for science and Australian $31,000 for medical
Length of Study: Up to 2 years for a Master's by research or up to 3 years for a PhD degree
Frequency: Annual
Closing Date: August 30th
Contributor: Kidney Health Australia

For further information contact:

Kidney Health Australia, GPO Box 9993, Adelaide, SA 5001
Tel: 08 8334 7555
Contact: The Medical Director

Australian Kidney Foundation Medical Research Grants and Scholarships

Subjects: The functions and disease of the kidney, urinary tract and related organs.
Purpose: To support medical research.

Eligibility: Open to Australian citizens who are graduates of Australian medical schools or overseas graduates who are eligible for Australian citizenship and for registration as medical practitioners in Australia.
Level of Study: Postgraduate, doctorate
Type: Scholarship
Value: Please contact the organization
Length of Study: Up to 3 years
Frequency: Annual
Study Establishment: Any approved medical centre, university or research institute
Country of Study: Australia
No. of awards offered: Up to 6
Application Procedure: Guidelines at www.kidney.org.au
Closing Date: Grants applications closes on June 30th and Scholarships application on September 30th

Australian Kidney Foundation Seeding and Equipment Grants

Subjects: The functions or diseases of the kidney, urinary tract and related organs, or relevant problems, dialysis, transplantation, organ donation and research.
Purpose: To provide financial support for research projects related to the kidney and urinary tract.
Eligibility: Open to Australian citizens connected with Australian universities or medical centres with requisite research facilities.
Level of Study: Unrestricted
Type: Grant
Value: Up to Australian $15,000 per year
Length of Study: Up to 2 years
Frequency: Annual
Study Establishment: Any medical centre, university or research institute
Country of Study: Australia
No. of awards offered: 30–35
Application Procedure: Applicants must contact the Foundation for details.
Closing Date: June 30th

Investigator Driven Research Grants and Scholars

Purpose: To award investigators who have applied to the NHMRC for funding but have just missed the cut-off mark.
Eligibility: Open to projects that are ranked as worthy of funding.
Type: Scholarship
Frequency: Annual
No. of awards offered: 1
Contributor: Kidney Health Australia

AUSTRALIAN NATIONAL UNIVERSITY (ANU)

Building 11, Canberra, ACT, 0200, Australia
Tel: (61) 2 6249 5949
Fax: (61) 2 6125 5931
Email: ressch.enq@anu.edu.au
Website: www.anu.edu.au
Contact: Research & Scholarships Office

The Australian National University (ANU) was founded by the Australian Government in 1946 as Australia's only completely research-orientated university. It comprises eight research schools, six teaching faculties, a graduate school and over a dozen other academic schools or centres.

ANU Alumni Association PhD Scholarships

Subjects: All subjects.
Purpose: To assist international students with study in Australia.
Eligibility: Open to nationals of Hong Kong, Japan, Malaysia, Thailand and Singapore.
Level of Study: Doctorate
Type: Scholarship
Value: Approx. Australian $19,231 per year (tax-free), payment of the programme fee for the duration of the stipend, an additional allowance for dependent children of married scholars, travel to Canberra and a grant for the reimbursement of some removal expenses. A thesis reimbursement allowance is also available
Length of Study: Normally tenable for 3 years, renewable for 6 months
Country of Study: Australia
No. of awards offered: 1 each for nationals of eligible countries
Application Procedure: Applicants must complete an application form, available on request or from the website.
Closing Date: Published through the Alumni Association of each country
Contributor: The Australian National University

ANU Graduate School Scholarships

Subjects: All subjects.
Purpose: To fund postgraduate study.
Eligibility: Open to individuals who are permanent residents of Australia. They need not necessarily have been resident in Australia for twelve months prior to the closing date. Applicants who have been in receipt of a PhD scholarship funded in the University for one year or more are ineligible.
Level of Study: Doctorate
Type: Scholarship
Value: A stipend of Australian $17,609 per year tax free, travel to Canberra from within Australia and a grant for the reimbursement of some removal expenses is available
Length of Study: 3 years in the first instance, with a possible extension of 6 months
Frequency: Annual
Country of Study: Australia
Application Procedure: Applicants must complete an application form, available on request or from the website.
Contributor: The Australian National University

ANU Indigenous Graduate Scholarship

Subjects: All subjects.
Purpose: To assist an Aboriginal or Torres Strait Islander to undertake a graduate diploma, Master's degree course or a course leading to a PhD.
Eligibility: Open to indigenous Australians who are Aborigines or Torres Strait Islanders.
Level of Study: Postgraduate
Type: Scholarship
Value: Benefits accord with those of the ANU PhD or Master's degree scholarships
Length of Study: Dependent upon the programme for which the scholarship is awarded
Frequency: Annual
Country of Study: Australia
No. of awards offered: 1
Application Procedure: Applicants must complete an application form, available on request or from the website.
Closing Date: October 31st
Contributor: The Australian National University
Additional Information: Open only to Australians citizens of indigenous.

ANU Master's Degree Scholarships

Subjects: All subjects.
Purpose: To assist study in most graduate school programmes for courses leading to a Master's degree by research, by coursework or by a combination of the two.
Eligibility: Open to candidates holding a Bachelor's degree with at least Upper Second Class (Honours), and, if wishing to undertake a degree by research only, applicants must have a proven capability for research.
Level of Study: Postgraduate, research
Type: Scholarship
Value: Basic stipend of Australian $19,231 per year tax free, an additional allowance for dependent children of married international scholars, travel to Canberra, excluding the international part of the

airfare for those recruited from overseas, and a grant for the reimbursement of some removal expenses
Length of Study: 1 year, but may be extended
Frequency: Annual
Country of Study: Australia
No. of awards offered: Varies
Application Procedure: Applicants must complete an application form, available on request or from the website.
Contributor: The Faculties

ANU PhD Scholarships

Subjects: All subjects.
Purpose: To assist research.
Eligibility: Applicants should write for details.
Level of Study: Doctorate
Type: Scholarship
Value: A stipend of Australian $19,231 per year tax free, and if applicable, an additional allowance for dependent children of international scholars plus economy travel to Canberra and a grant for the reimbursement of some removal expenses thesis reimbursement allowance
Length of Study: 3 years, renewable for 6 months
Frequency: Annual
Country of Study: Australia
No. of awards offered: Varies
Application Procedure: Applicants must complete an application form, available on request or from the website.
Closing Date: October 31st for citizens or permanent residents of Australia and New Zealand, and August 31st for international applicants
Additional Information: Initial correspondence concerning graduate courses and scholarships should be sent to the main address or sent by email.

ANU Re-entry Scholarships for Women

Subjects: All subjects.
Purpose: To assist graduates to resume their studies.
Eligibility: Open to women graduates who have taken a break from their studies of at least three years since formal enrolment in a university course, the break normally being due to fulfilment of family obligations. Applicants must be Australian citizens or permanent residents. The scholarship may be awarded to undertake a graduate diploma, a Master's degree course or a PhD and applicants must hold qualifications appropriate to the level of course for which they wish to apply.
Level of Study: Doctorate, research
Type: Scholarship
Value: Benefits accord with those of ANU PhD or Master's degree scholarships and tenure is dependent upon the programme for which the scholarship is awarded
Length of Study: Tenure is dependent upon the course to which the scholarship applies
Frequency: Annual
Country of Study: Australia
No. of awards offered: 1 or 2
Application Procedure: Applicants must submit a completed application form with a letter setting out the applicant's case for award of the scholarship and indicating their circumstances in terms of the eligibility criteria. Application forms are available on request or from the website.
Contributor: The Australian National University
Additional Information: Open only to Australian citizens or permanent residents of Australia.

Australian Development Scholarships (ADS)

Subjects: All subjects.
Level of Study: Graduate
Type: Scholarship
Value: Return airfare to Australia, tuition fees, an establishment allowance and a living allowance are available
Country of Study: Australia
Application Procedure: Applicants must write to the Australian Diplomatic Mission or the Australian Education Centre in their home country.
Closing Date: Varies

AUSTRALIAN RESEARCH COUNCIL (ARC)

GPO Box 2702, Canberra, ACT, 2601, Australia
Tel: (61) 2 6284 6600
Fax: (61) 2 6284 6601
Email: ncgp@arc.gov.au
Website: www.arc.gov.au
Contact: Grants Management Officer

The Australian Research Council (ARC) plays a key role in the Australian Government's investment in the future prosperity and well-being of the Australian community. Its mission is to advance Australia's capacity to undertake quality research. ARC has various funding programmes under the umbrella of the National Competitive Grants Programme.

ARC Discovery Projects Postdoctoral Fellow (APD)

Subjects: All areas of science except clinical medicine or dentistry.
Purpose: To strengthen Australia's national research and development capability by providing opportunities for researchers to undertake research of national and international significance, and to broaden their research experience.
Eligibility: Applicants must have submitted their PhD thesis before the commencement of the fellowship. No more than 3 years should have elapsed since the awarding of their PhD and an excellent academic record is required.
Level of Study: Postdoctorate
Type: Fellowship
Value: Australian $67,494, including 26 per cent of costs
Length of Study: 3 years
Frequency: Annual
Country of Study: Australia
No. of awards offered: Approx. 110
Application Procedure: Applicants must submit applications through an Australian host institution. It is the responsibility of the applicant to approach potential host institutions.
Closing Date: March 8th
Funding: Government
No. of awards given last year: 112
No. of applicants last year: 568
Additional Information: Candidates must obtain Australian citizenship or temporary residency status at the time of commencing the fellowship.

ARC Discovery Projects: Australian Research Fellow/ Queen Elizabeth II Fellow (ARF/QEII)

Subjects: All areas of science except clinical medicine or dentistry.
Purpose: To strengthen Australia's national research and development capability by providing opportunities for established researchers to undertake research of national and international significance.
Eligibility: Open to candidates with a PhD and an excellent academic record. Applicants should have more than 3 years, but not more than 8 years of professional experience since the awarding of their PhD.
Level of Study: Postdoctorate
Type: Fellowship
Value: Australian Research Fellows are awarded Australian $84,252 and Queen Elizabeth II Fellows are awarded Australian $100,126. This includes 26 per cent of costs
Length of Study: 5 years
Frequency: Annual
Country of Study: Australia
No. of awards offered: Approx. 15 of each
Application Procedure: Applicants must submit applications through an Australian host institution. It is the responsibility of the applicant to approach potential host institutions.
Closing Date: March 8th
Funding: Government

No. of awards given last year: 30
No. of applicants last year: 265
Additional Information: Candidates must obtain Australian citizenship or temporary residency status at the time of commencing the fellowship.

ARC Projects: Professional Fellow (APF)

Subjects: All areas of science except clinical medicine or dentistry.
Purpose: To provide opportunities for outstanding researchers with proven international reputations to undertake research that is both of major importance in its field and of significant benefit to Australia. Senior Research Fellowships are the premier fellowships offered by the Australian Research Council and, consequently, are highly sought after and extremely competitive.
Eligibility: Open to researchers who normally have more than 8 years of professional experience since the awarding of their PhD and extremely high-profile expatriate Australians and non-Australian researchers who wish to pursue their research in Australia.
Level of Study: Postdoctorate
Type: Fellowship
Value: Australian $115,656–135,822 including 26 per cent of costs
Length of Study: 5 years
Frequency: Annual
Country of Study: Australia
No. of awards offered: Approx. 15
Application Procedure: Applicants must submit applications through an Australian host institution. It is the responsibility of the applicant to approach potential host institutions.
Closing Date: March 8th
Funding: Government
No. of awards given last year: 23
No. of applicants last year: 176
Additional Information: Candidates must obtain Australian citizenship or temporary residency status at the time of commencing the fellowship.

Australian Postgraduate Award to Industry

Subjects: All areas of study other than clinical medicine, public health research and dental medicine.
Purpose: To provide industry-based research training to prepare high-calibre postgraduate research students and to produce a national pool of world-class researchers to meet the needs of Australian industry.
Level of Study: Doctorate
Type: Award
Value: Australian $24,148 per year
Length of Study: 3 years
Frequency: Twice per year
Study Establishment: Australian universities
Country of Study: Australia
No. of awards offered: Varies, typically several hundred per year
Application Procedure: Applications are submitted according to the Linkage Project funding rules, available on the ARC website.
Closing Date: Typically in May and November (see Funding Rules available on the ARC website)
Funding: Government
No. of awards given last year: 461
No. of applicants last year: 1012
Additional Information: This scholarship is awarded under the Linkage Project Scheme to Australian Universities by the Australian Research Council.

AUSTRALIAN-AMERICAN FULBRIGHT COMMISSION

PO Box 9541, Deakin, ACT 2600, Australia
Tel: (61) 2 6260 4460
Fax: (61) 2 6260 4461
Email: lwilson@fulbright.com.au
Website: www.fulbright.com.au
Contact: Ms Lyndell Wilson, Programme Manager

The Australian–American Fulbright Commision is a non-profit organization in Australia, established through a binational treaty between the Australian and United States governments in 1949 under the auspices of the United States Educational Foundation (USEFA) in Australia. The mission of the Commission is to further mutual understanding between the people of Australia and the United States through educational and cultural exchange.

Coral Sea Business Administration Scholarship

Subjects: Business and industry.
Purpose: To investigate a problem or opportunity relevant to Australian business or industry in the United States of America.
Eligibility: Open to resident Australian citizens who hold a degree or diploma. Candidates should have relevant business or industry experience. Applications are encouraged from those with a record of achievement poised for advancement in their professional field.
Level of Study: Professional development
Type: Scholarship
Value: Up to Australian $13,000
Length of Study: Up to 3 months
Frequency: Annual
Country of Study: United States of America
No. of awards offered: 1
Application Procedure: Applicants must complete and submit an application form along with three reference reports, already included in the application pack and documentation of citizenship and qualifications. Further information and application packs are available from the website.
Closing Date: August 31st
Funding: Commercial

Fulbright Awards

Subjects: All subjects.
Purpose: To undertake an approved course of study for an American higher degree or 8–12 months research relevant to an Australian degree.
Eligibility: Open to Australian postgraduate and postdoctoral students, senior scholars and professionals.
Level of Study: Professional development, research, doctorate, postgraduate, postdoctorate
Value: Postgraduate students receive up to Australian $40,000 and postdoctoral Fellows receive up to Australian $40,000. Senior scholars receive up to Australian $30,000 and professionals up to Australian $20,000
Length of Study: 8–12 months. Longer without funding
Frequency: Annual
Study Establishment: A university, college, research establishment
Country of Study: United States of America
No. of awards offered: Up to 13
Application Procedure: Applicants must complete and submit an application form along with three reference reports, already included in the application pack, documentation of citizenship and qualifications. Further information and application packs are available from the website.
Closing Date: August 31st
Funding: Commercial, government

Fulbright Postdoctoral Fellowships

Subjects: All subjects.
Purpose: To enable those who have recently completed their PhD to conduct postdoctoral research, to further their professional training or lecture at a university in the United States of America.
Eligibility: Open to Australian citizens by birth or naturalization. Those holding dual United States of America and Australian citizenship are not eligible. Applicants should have recently completed their PhD, normally less than 3 years prior to application, although those who have completed their PhD 4 or 5 years prior to application will be considered.
Level of Study: Postdoctorate
Type: Fellowship
Value: Up to Australian $30,000
Length of Study: 3–12 months
Frequency: Annual

Study Establishment: A university, college or research establishment or reputable private practice
Country of Study: United States of America
No. of awards offered: 1
Application Procedure: Applicants must complete and submit an application form along with three reference reports, already included in the application pack, documentation of citizenship and qualifications. Further information and application packs are available from the website.
Closing Date: August 31st
Funding: Government

Fulbright Postgraduate Awards

Subjects: All subjects.
Purpose: To enable students to undertake an approved course of study for an American higher degree or equivalent, or to engage in research relevant to an Australian higher degree.
Eligibility: Open to Australian citizens by birth or naturalization. Those holding dual United States of America and Australian citizenship are not eligible.
Level of Study: Doctorate, postgraduate
Type: Studentship
Value: Up to Australian $40,000
Length of Study: 8–12 months funded, renewable for up to 5 years unfunded
Frequency: Annual
Study Establishment: An accredited institution
Country of Study: United States of America
No. of awards offered: Up to 12
Application Procedure: Applicants must complete an application form and submit this with three reference reports, already included in the application pack, and documentation of citizenship and qualifications. Naturalized citizens must provide a certificate of Australian citizenship with their application, and native-born Australians must provide a copy of their birth certificate. Further information and application packs are available from the website.
Closing Date: August 31st
Funding: Government
Additional Information: As the award does not include any provision for maintenance payments, applicants must be able to demonstrate that they have sufficient financial resources to support themselves and any dependants during their stay in the United States of America.

Fulbright Postgraduate Student Award for Engineering

Subjects: Engineering.
Purpose: To enable candidates to undertake an approved course of study for an American higher degree, or engage in research relevant to an Australian higher degree.
Eligibility: Open to Australian citizens. Those with dual United States of America and Australian citizenship are not eligible.
Level of Study: Doctorate, postgraduate
Value: Up to Australian $40,000
Length of Study: 8–12 months funded or up to 4 years unfunded
Frequency: Annual
Study Establishment: An accredited institution
Country of Study: United States of America
No. of awards offered: 1
Application Procedure: Applicants must complete and submit an application form along with three reference reports, already included in the application pack, documentation of citizenship and qualifications. Further information and application packs are available from the website.
Closing Date: August 31st
Funding: Commercial, government
Contributor: Clough Engineering Limited

Fulbright Postgraduate Student Award for Science and Engineering

Subjects: Science and engineering.
Purpose: To enable candidates to undertake an approved course of study for an American higher degree, or to engage in research relevant to an Australian higher degree.
Eligibility: Open to Australian citizens. Those with dual United States of America and Australia citizenship are not eligible.
Level of Study: Doctorate, postgraduate
Value: Up to Australian $40,000
Length of Study: 8–12 months funded or up to 4 years unfunded
Frequency: Annual
Study Establishment: An accredited institution
Country of Study: United States of America
No. of awards offered: 1
Application Procedure: Applicants must complete and submit an application form along with three reference reports, already included in the application pack, documentation of citizenship and qualifications. Further information and application packs are available from the website.
Closing Date: August 31st
Funding: Commercial, government
Contributor: Billiton Pvt. Ltd.

Fulbright Postgraduate Student Award for the Visual and Performing Arts

Subjects: Fine and applied arts.
Purpose: To enable candidates to undertake a higher degree, or carry out research towards an Australian higher degree.
Eligibility: Open to Australian citizens. Those with dual United States of America and Australian citizenship are not eligible.
Level of Study: Professional development, doctorate, postgraduate
Value: Up to Australian $40,000
Length of Study: 8–12 months funded or up to 4 years unfunded
Frequency: Annual
Country of Study: United States of America
No. of awards offered: 1
Application Procedure: Applicants must complete and submit an application form along with three reference reports, already included in the application pack, documentation of citizenship and qualifications. Further information and application packs are available from the website.
Closing Date: August 31st
Funding: Commercial, government
Contributor: Anthony Joseph Pratt

Fulbright Professional Award

Subjects: All professional fields. Programmes should include an academic as well as a practical aspect.
Purpose: These awards are available to professionals from public and private sectors (junior to middle level staff poised for advancement to a senior level research or undertaking a programme of professional development in the United States of America.
Eligibility: Open to resident Australian citizens with a record of achievement poised for advancement to a senior management or policy role. Those holding dual United States of America and Australian citizenship are not eligible.
Level of Study: Professional development
Type: Award
Value: Up to Australian $25,000
Length of Study: 3–4 months. Programmes of longer duration may be proposed, but without additional funding
Frequency: Annual
Country of Study: United States of America
No. of awards offered: 4
Application Procedure: Applicants must complete and submit an application form along with three reference reports, already included in the application pack, documentation of citizenship and qualifications. Further information and application packs are available from the website.
Closing Date: August 31st
Funding: Government

Fulbright Professional Award for Vocational Education and Training

Subjects: All subjects.
Purpose: To enable candidates to visit institutions or organizations and people in the United States of America from their own field.

Eligibility: Open to Australian citizens employed in the vocational education and training sector. Those holding dual United States of America and Australian citizenship are not eligible.
Level of Study: Professional development
Value: Up to Australian $20,000
Length of Study: 3–4 months funded
Frequency: Annual
Country of Study: United States of America
No. of awards offered: 1
Application Procedure: Applicants must complete and submit an application form along with three reference reports, already included in the application pack, documentation of citizenship and qualifications. Further information and application packs are available from the website.
Closing Date: August 31st
Funding: Government
Contributor: The Australian National Training Authority
No. of awards given last year: 1

Fulbright Senior Scholar Awards

Subjects: All subjects.
Purpose: To allow candidates to teach, undertake research, be an invited speaker or visit institutions within their field.
Eligibility: Open to Australian citizens by birth or naturalization. Those holding dual United States of America and Australian citizenship are not eligible. Applicants should be either scholars of established reputation working in an academic institution, who intend to teach or research in the United States of America, leaders in the arts, eg. music, drama, visual arts or senior members of the academically based professions who are currently engaged in the private practice of their profession.
Level of Study: Professional development
Value: Up to Australian $30,000
Length of Study: 4–6 months
Frequency: Annual
Study Establishment: A university, college, research establishment or reputable private organization
Country of Study: United States of America
No. of awards offered: 2
Application Procedure: Applicants must complete an application form and submit this with three reference reports, already included in the application pack, documentation of citizenship and qualifications. Further information and application packs are available from the website. Naturalized citizens must provide a certificate of Australian citizenship with their application, and native-born Australians must provide a copy of their birth certificate.
Closing Date: August 31st
Funding: Government

AUSTRIAN ACADEMY OF SCIENCES

Institute of Limnology, Mondseestrasse 9, A-5310 Mondsee, Austria
Tel: (43) 623 240 79
Fax: (43) 623 235 78
Email: ipgl.mondsee@oeaw.ac.at
Website: www.ipgl.at
Contact: Mr Gerold Winkler, IPGL Course Administrator

The Institute of Limnology of the Austrian Academy of Sciences performs ecological research on inland waters. The overall research goal is to understand the structure, function and dynamics of freshwater ecosystems. Although the Institute primarily conducts basic research, aspects of applied research are also considered. The Institute at Mondsee, located close to Salzburg, was established in 1981 and has a staff of 26, including 13 scientists. Currently, the Institute's main fields of research are tropic interactions and food-web structures in lakes.

Austrian Academy of Sciences, MSc Course in Limnology and Wetland Ecosystems

Subjects: Aquatic systems.
Purpose: To provide an overall insight into aquatic systems through lectures, laboratory exercises, appropriate technology, group work, role play and field studies.
Eligibility: Open to candidates from developing countries who are maximum 35 years of age, have a good working knowledge of English and have an academic degree in science, agriculture or veterinary medicine from a university or any other recognized Institute of Higher Education. Applicants should have 3 years practical experience in at least one special subject in their field of professional training. All applications are considered on their individual merits.
Level of Study: Postgraduate
Type: Scholarship
Value: US$626 paid monthly to cover food, lodging and personal needs plus free tuition, health insurance, study material and equipment for laboratory work, field work and travelling expenses
Length of Study: 18 months
Frequency: Annual
Study Establishment: Institute for Limnology, Mondsee; Institute UNESCO-IHE, Delft, The Netherlands; Makerere University, Kampala, Uganda; Egerton University, Kenya; Czech Academy of Sciences, Trebon, Czech Republic; Austrian Universities and Federal Institutes in Austria
No. of awards offered: 4
Application Procedure: Applicants must obtain application forms from the website. Filled application forms can be sent to IPGL-Office, institute for limnology, mondseestrasse 9, A-5310 Mondsee, Austria, directly.
Closing Date: End of January
Funding: Government
Contributor: The Austrian Development Co-operation
No. of awards given last year: 4
No. of applicants last year: 70
Additional Information: No provisions are made for dependants. It is strongly advised that dependants do not accompany fellows due to frequent moves during the course. Fellows must also provide their own transportation to and from Austria.

Austrian Academy of Sciences, Short Course Tropical Limnology

Subjects: Tropical limnology.
Purpose: To assist students studying the special characteristics of tropical river and lake ecosystems, its interactions with activities, processes in the watershed and relevant ecosystem services.
Eligibility: Open to candidates from East African countries who have a good working knowledge of English and have an academic degree either in science, agriculture or veterinary medicine from a university or other recognised Institute of Higher Education. Applicants should have practical experience within at least one special subject in their field of professional training.
Level of Study: Postgraduate
Type: Scholarship
Value: US$21 paid per day including accommodation, full board and US$2,500 d.s.a. plus free tuition, health insurance, study material and equipment for laboratory work, field work and travelling expenses
Length of Study: 3 weeks
Frequency: Annual
Study Establishment: Egerton University, Kenya, Sagana Fish Farm, Kenya
No. of awards offered: 10
Application Procedure: Applicants must obtain application forms and further information from IPGL-Office, Mondsee, Mondseestraseg, A-5310 Mondsee, Austria or Prof. Dr. J. Mathooko, Dept. of Zoology, Egerton University, mathookoj@yahoo.com. Application forms are also available from the website.
Closing Date: July 15th
Funding: Government
Contributor: The Austrian Development Co-operation
No. of awards given last year: 10
No. of applicants last year: 58
Additional Information: No provisions are made for dependants. It is strongly advised that dependants do not accompany Fellows due to frequent moves during the course. Fellows must also arrange their own transportation to and from Kenya.

Institute for Limnology Postgraduate Training Fellowships

Subjects: Limnology.
Purpose: To provide an overall insight into the various problems of limnology so that researchers may be better equipped to implement necessary research in their home countries in order to find solutions to their practical problems.
Eligibility: Open to candidates from developing countries who are 25–35 years of age, have a good working knowledge of English and have an academic degree either in science, agriculture or veterinary medicine from a university or other recognized Institute of Higher Education. Applicants should have practical experience within at least one special subject in their field of professional training.
Level of Study: Postgraduate
Type: Fellowship
Value: Please contact the organization
Length of Study: 6 months
Frequency: Annual
Country of Study: Austria
No. of awards offered: 12
Application Procedure: Applicants must obtain application forms and further information from the Austrian Diplomatic Mission, Cultural Attaché or Cultural Institute in the applicant's home country, or from the address shown. Application forms are also available from the website.
Closing Date: November 30th
Additional Information: No provisions are made for dependants. It is strongly advised that dependants do not accompany Fellows due to frequent moves during the course. Fellows must also arrange their own transportation to and from Austria. Participants originating from certain developing countries will be further assisted by the Austrian Government so that travel expenses will be fully covered.

AUSTRIAN SCIENCE FUND (FWF)

Weyringergasse 35, Vienna, A-1040, Austria
Tel: (43) 150 567 40
Fax: (43) 150 567 39
Email: office@fwf.ac.at
Website: www.fwf.ac.at
Contact: Scientific Administrator

The Austrian Science Fund (FWF) is Austria's central body for the promotion of basic research. It is equally committed to all branches of science and in all its activities it is guided solely by the standards of the international scientific community. Its mission is the promotion of high-quality basic research, education and training through research and scientific culture and knowledge transfer.

Charlotte Bühler Habilitation Fellowships

Subjects: All subjects.
Purpose: To support and encourage young female scientists to become future university lecturers.
Eligibility: Open to female scientists up to the age of 40, who are residents of Austria.
Level of Study: Postdoctorate
Type: A variable number of fellowships
Value: Please contact the organization
Length of Study: 1–2 years
Frequency: 6 times per year
No. of awards offered: Varies
Application Procedure: Applicants must complete an application form, available from the Austrian Science Fund, from the website or by email.
Closing Date: Applications are accepted at any time
Funding: Government

Erwin Schrödinger Fellowships

Subjects: All subjects.
Purpose: To offer citizens the opportunity to work in leading foreign research institutions and research programmes.
Eligibility: Open to highly qualified Austrian citizens up to the age of 35.
Level of Study: Postdoctorate
Type: Fellowship
Value: Please contact the organization
Length of Study: 10 months–2 years
Frequency: 6 times per year
Study Establishment: Universities or research institutions
No. of awards offered: Varies
Application Procedure: Applicants must complete an application form, available from the Austrian Science Fund, from the website or by email. All necessary details can be found on the website www.fwf.ac.at/en/projects/erwin-schroedinger.html
Closing Date: Applications are accepted at any time
Funding: Government
No. of awards given last year: 55
No. of applicants last year: 117

Hertha Firnberg Research Positions for Women

Subjects: All subjects.
Purpose: To support and encourage young female scientists and expand scientific career opportunities for women.
Eligibility: Open to female scientists up to the age of 40 who are residents of Austria.
Level of Study: Postdoctorate
Type: Position (Employment)
Value: Please contact the organization
Length of Study: 3 years
Frequency: Annual
Study Establishment: Any university
Country of Study: Austria
No. of awards offered: 10
Application Procedure: Applicants must complete an application form, available from the Austrian Science Fund, from the website or by email. All necessary details can be found on the website www.fwf.ac.at/en/projects/firnberg.html
Closing Date: December
Funding: Government
No. of awards given last year: 11
No. of applicants last year: 43

Lise Meitner Program

Subjects: All subjects.
Purpose: To offer foreign scientists an opportunity to carry out research in Austria and to enhance the Austrian scientific community through international contacts.
Eligibility: Open to highly qualified foreign scientists up to the age of 40.
Level of Study: Postdoctorate
Type: Position (Employment)
Value: Please contact the organization
Length of Study: 1–2 years
Frequency: 6 times per year
Study Establishment: Universities or research institutions
Country of Study: Austria
No. of awards offered: Varies
Application Procedure: Applicants must complete an application form, available from the Austrian Science Fund, from the website or by email. All necessary details can be found on the website: www.fwf.ac.at/en/projects/meitner.html
Closing Date: Applications are accepted at any time
Funding: Government
No. of awards given last year: 35
No. of applicants last year: 86

AUSTRO-AMERICAN ASSOCIATION OF BOSTON

47 Windermere Road, Auburndale, MA, 02466-2521, United States of America
Tel: (1) 617 332 4055
Email: george_hauser@hms.harvard.edu
Website: www.austria-boston.org
Contact: Professor George Hauser, Chairman of Scholarship Committee

Membership of the Austro-American Association of Boston is open to any individual interested in any aspect of Austrian history, economy, culture, politics and tourism.

Austro-American Association of Boston Scholarship

Subjects: Austrian cultural studies, humanities, literature, music, fine and applied arts and film.
Purpose: To promote the appreciation and dissemination of Austrian culture.
Eligibility: Only students who are studying in a college in New England are eligible.
Level of Study: Unrestricted
Type: Scholarship
Value: US$1,000
Frequency: Dependent on funds available
Study Establishment: Any in New England
Country of Study: United States of America
No. of awards offered: 1
Application Procedure: Applicants must submit a detailed description of the project including budget, a curriculum vitae and two letters of recommendation from people familiar with the applicant's achievement and potential.
Closing Date: April 15th
Funding: Private
Contributor: Association members
No. of awards given last year: 1
No. of applicants last year: 5
Additional Information: The award is limited to individuals living or studying in New England. Projects funded in the past have included the preparation of musical or dramatic performances, the facilitation of appropriate publications and research trips to Austria. Culture is defined to include the humanities and the arts. The recipient is expected to present the results of the project at an event of the Austro-American Association.

THE AWARD AND RESEARCH GRANT PROGRAM

5005 LBJ Freeway, Suite 250, Dallas, TX, 75244, United States of America
Tel: (1) 972 855 1656
Fax: (1) 972 855 1640
Email: grants@komen.org
Website: www.komen.org
Contact: National Grants and Sponsored Programs Office

It is the mission of the Susan G Komen Breast Cancer Foundation to eradicate breast cancer as a life-threatening disease by advancing research, education, screening and treatment.

Susan G Komen Breast Cancer Foundation Basic Clinical and Translational Breast Cancer Research

Subjects: The cause, treatment, prevention and cure of breast cancer.
Purpose: To foster investigation.
Eligibility: MD, PhD, DO, DPH or equivalent doctoral degree.
Level of Study: Research
Type: Research grant
Value: Up to US$250,000 combined direct and indirect costs
Length of Study: 2–3 years
Frequency: Annual
Country of Study: Any country
No. of awards offered: Dependent on funds available
Application Procedure: Applicants must register before submitting an application. Registration is available on the website. Candidates should contact the main address for more information. All applications must be submitted electronically.
Closing Date: See the website
Funding: Private

Susan G Komen Breast Cancer Foundation Population Specific Research Project

Subjects: Unique needs, trends and barriers to breast healthcare among populations such as African American, Asian Pacific Islander, Hispanic/Latino, Native American, Lesbian, low literacy, breast cancer survivors and other defined communities.
Purpose: To fund innovative research projects addressing breast cancer and epidemiology within specific populations at risk for the disease.
Eligibility: Independent investigators at any stage of their research careers are eligible to apply.
Level of Study: Research
Type: Research grant
Value: Up to US$250,000 combined direct and indirect costs
Length of Study: 2–3 years
Frequency: Annual
Country of Study: Any country
No. of awards offered: Dependent on funds available
Application Procedure: Applicants must register before submitting an application. Registration is available on the website. Candidates should contact the main address for more information. All applications must be submitted electronically.
Closing Date: See the website
Funding: Private

Susan G Komen Breast Cancer Foundation Postdoctoral Fellowship in Breast Cancer Research, Public Health or Epidemiology

Subjects: Breast health and breast cancer.
Purpose: To encourage young scientists to begin a career in breast cancer research or to support continued research and independent investigations in breast health and breast cancer.
Eligibility: Candidates must be no more than 3 years postcompletion of a PhD. MD candidates must be no more than 3 years postcompletion of their clinical fellowship or 5 years postcompletion of residency.
Level of Study: Postdoctorate
Type: Fellowship
Value: US$45,000 per year
Length of Study: 2–3 years
Frequency: Annual
Country of Study: Any country
No. of awards offered: Dependent on funds available
Application Procedure: Applicants must register before submitting an application. Registration is available on the website. Candidates should contact the address for more information. All applications must be submitted electronically.
Closing Date: See the website
Funding: Private

AWSCPA

Administrative Offices, 136 South Keowee Street, Dayton, OH 45402, United States of America
Tel: (1) 937 222 1872
Fax: (1) 937 222 5794
Email: info@awscpa.org
Website: www.awscpa.org

The American Woman's Society of CPA provides annual scholarships to women working towards an accounting degree as well as to those working towards their Certified Public Accountant License.

AWSCPA National Scholarship

Subjects: Accounting.
Purpose: To fund women working towards an accounting degree.
Eligibility: Applicants must meet the minimum educational requirements to sit for the CPA exam within 1 year of the award of the scholarship.
Level of Study: Postgraduate
Type: Scholarship
Value: Approx. US$2,500
Frequency: Annual
No. of awards offered: 1 per year
Application Procedure: Apply through website.

Closing Date: March 15th
Funding: Foundation
Contributor: AWSCPA members and supporters
No. of awards given last year: 1
No. of applicants last year: 30

B P CONSERVATION PROGRAMME

Birdlife International/FFI, Wellbrook Court, Girton Road, Cambridge, Cambridgeshire, CB3 0NA, England
Tel: (44) 12 2327 7318
Fax: (44) 12 2327 7200
Email: bp-conservation-programme@birdlife.org.uk
Website: www.conservation.bp.com
Contact: The Programme Manager

Since 1985, the BP Conservation Programme has supported and encouraged international conservation projects that address global conservation priorities at a local level. This is achieved through a comprehensive system of advice, training and awards. The programme is managed through a partnership between BP, FFI, CI, WCS and Birdlife International.

BP Conservation Programme Awards

Subjects: Awards are presented annually to innovative international student conservation projects. All projects must: address a conservation priority of global importance, have local support and collaboration, and have a majority of team members in either university education, or who are early career conservationists.
Purpose: To research species, sites and habitats with the highest priority for biodiversity conservation worldwide and develop the skills and networks of future generations of young professionals.
Eligibility: The project must address a globally recognized conservation priority, involve people, have host government approval, be run by teams of at least three people, be student-led, have over 50 per cent students registered, last for less than 1 year and take place in Africa, Asia Pacific, Middle East, Eastern Europe, Latin America or the Carribean.
Level of Study: Doctorate, postgraduate, graduate, undergraduate
Type: Team
Value: Awards range from US$7,500 to 75,000
Length of Study: Projects should be less than 1 year in length
Frequency: Annual
Country of Study: This is a global programme
No. of awards offered: Up to 30
Application Procedure: Application forms are available from the website. Applications should be made electronically.
Closing Date: December 16th
Funding: Private
Contributor: BP, BirdLife International, Conservation International, WildLife Conservation Society and Fauna and Flora International
No. of awards given last year: 29
No. of applicants last year: 360

BACKCARE

16 Elmtree Road, Teddington, Middlesex, TW11 8ST, England
Tel: (44) 20 8977 5474
Fax: (44) 20 8943 5318
Email: info@backcare.org.uk
Website: www.backcare.org.uk
Contact: Mrs Nia Taylor, Chief Executive

BackCare is a national charity dedicated to educating people about how to avoid preventable back pain and to supporting those living with back pain. BackCare provides education and information through its publications, telephone helpline, local branches and website. It also funds research and campaigns to raise the profile of issues surrounding back pain.

BackCare Research Grants

Subjects: Studies related to back pain.
Purpose: To reduce the incidences of disability from back pain and to improve its treatment by gaining, through research, a better understanding of its manifestation and causes.
Eligibility: Open to appropriately qualified and experienced persons.
Level of Study: Postgraduate
Value: Varies, dependent on funds available
Length of Study: Up to 2 years
Frequency: Dependent on funds available
Study Establishment: Suitable establishments
Country of Study: United Kingdom
Application Procedure: Applicants must refer to the website for details of the application procedure.
Closing Date: February 1st, May 1st, August 1st, November 1st
Funding: Individuals, trusts, private
No. of awards given last year: 4
No. of applicants last year: 20

THE BANFF CENTRE

Arts Programming, Box 1020, Station 28, Banff, AB, T1L 1H5, Canada
Tel: (1) 403 762 6180/1 800 565 9989 (Canada and U.S.A.)
Fax: (1) 403 762 6345
Email: arts_info@banffcentre.ca
Website: www.banffcentre.ca
Contact: Registrar

The Banff Centre is a catalyst for creativity, with a transformative impact on those who attend the programmes, conferences and events. Our alumni create, produce and perform works of art all over the world, lead our institutions, organizations and businesses, and play significant roles in our cultural, social, intellectual and economic well-being, and in the preservation of our environment.

Banff Centre Financial Assistance

Subjects: Studio art, photography, ceramics, performance art, video art, theatre production and design, stage management, opera, singing, dance, drama, music, writing, creative non-fiction and cultural journalism, publishing, media arts, television and video, audio recording, computer applications, research, audio engineering work study, theatre production, design stage management work study, Aboriginal arts programmes in dance training, programme publicity and theatre production work study and screenwriting.
Purpose: To provide financial assistance to deserving artists for a residency at The Banff Centre.
Eligibility: Open to advanced students who have been accepted for a residency at the Banff Centre.
Level of Study: Professional development, postgraduate
Type: Grant
Value: A major contribution towards tuition
Length of Study: Varies
Frequency: Annual
Study Establishment: The Banff Centre, Arts Programming
Country of Study: Canada
No. of awards offered: Varies
Application Procedure: Applicants must submit a completed application form, accompanied by requested documentation. See website for details.
Closing Date: Varies according to programme
Funding: Private, government
Contributor: Individual donations and Banff Centre revenues
No. of awards given last year: 1,000

Paul D. Fleck Fellowships in the Arts

Purpose: To allow artists in all disciplines to participate in independent artists residencies at the Banff centre to create new work or collaborate with other arts programmes at the centre.
Eligibility: Nomination.
Level of Study: Professional development, research, postgraduate
Type: Fellowship /Scholarship
Value: Tuition, accommodation, meals and is approved circumstances, a travel award

Frequency: Annual
Study Establishment: Arts programming, The Banff Centre
Country of Study: Canada
No. of awards offered: Varies
Application Procedure: See website for details.
Closing Date: Spring
Funding: Private, trusts, individuals
No. of awards given last year: Varies
No. of applicants last year: Varies

Susan and Graeme Mc Donald Music Scholarships
Purpose: To bring gifted musicians together from across Canada and around the world for transformational learning experiences in Banff centre music programs.
Level of Study: Graduate, professional development
Type: Scholarship
Value: Varies
Length of Study: Varies
Frequency: Annual
Study Establishment: Music Programs, The Banff Centre
Country of Study: Canada
No. of awards offered: Varies
Application Procedure: See website for details.
Closing Date: Varies according to programme
Funding: Trusts, private
No. of awards given last year: Varies

BATTEN DISEASE SUPPORT AND RESEARCH ASSOCIATION

120 Humphries Drive, Suite 2, Reynoldsburg, OH, 43068, United States of America
Tel: (1) 740 927 4298
Email: bdsra1@bdsra.org
Website: www.bdsra.org
Contact: Mr Lance W Johnston, Executive Director

The Batten Disease Support and Research Association provides information, education, medical referrals and support to families that have children with NCL or Batten Disease. The Association also provides funding for research into Batten Disease.

Batten Disease Support and Research Association Research Grant Awards
Subjects: NCL or Batten Disease in the areas of genetics, biochemistry, molecular biology and related areas with the eventual goal of developing a viable treatment.
Purpose: To support work that identifies genes, proteins, enzymes or additional NCLs and the development of novel therapeutic treatments.
Eligibility: There are no eligibility restrictions.
Level of Study: Research, doctorate, postdoctorate
Value: Up to US$40,000
Length of Study: Research is for 1 year and doctorate and postdoctorate are up to 3 years
Frequency: Annual
Country of Study: Any country
Application Procedure: RFP (request for proposals) will be posted on website: www.bdsra.org, follow instructions contained in RFP.
Closing Date: June 15th
Funding: Private
No. of awards given last year: 10
No. of applicants last year: 24

BEINECKE SCHOLARSHIP PROGRAM

c/o Office of International Education and Fellowship Programs, Box 208351 Yale Station, New Haven, CT 06520-8351, United States of America
Tel: (1) 203 432 8685
Website: www.beineckescholarship.org

The Beinecke Scholarship Program, established in 1970, seeks to encourage and enable highly motivated students to take the fullest advantage of graduate opportunities available to them and be courageous in the selection of graduate study programmes.

Beinecke Scholarship
Subjects: Liberal arts mathematics and natural sciences.
Purpose: To encourage and enable highly motivated students to pursue opportunities available to them.
Eligibility: Open to U.S. citizens or U.S. national from American Samoa or the commonwealth of Northern Mariana Islands with superior standards of intellectual ability, scholastic achievement and personal.
Level of Study: Postgraduate
Type: Scholarship
Value: US$32,000
Length of Study: 1–5 years
Study Establishment: Any accredited university
No. of awards offered: 20
Application Procedure: Request and submit a completed application form a curriculum vitae, a personal statement of 1,000 words and three letters of recommendation from faculty members.
Funding: Corporation
Contributor: The Sperry Fund

For further information contact:

Scholarship Connection 301 Compbell Hall
Email: scholarships@learning.berkeley.edu
Website: www://scholarships.berkeley.edu

BEIT MEMORIAL FELLOWSHIPS

c/o Institute of Molecular Medicine, John Radcliffe Hospital, Headington, Oxford, Oxfordshire, OX3 9DS, England
Contact: Mrs Melanie J Goble, Administrative Secretary

Beit Memorial Fellowships for Medical Research
Subjects: Medical research.
Purpose: To promote research into medicine and allied sciences.
Eligibility: Open to postdoctoral level or medically qualified applicants who are graduates of any faculty at an approved university in the United Kingdom, or in any country that is or has been, since 1910, a British Dominion, Protectorate or Mandated Territory.
Level of Study: Postdoctorate, research
Type: Fellowship
Value: United Kingdom salary plus research expenses
Length of Study: 3 years
Frequency: Annual
Study Establishment: An approved university, research institute or medical school
No. of awards offered: Approx. 4
Application Procedure: Applicants must write for details.
Closing Date: March 1st

BEIT TRUST (ZIMBABWE, ZAMBIA AND MALAWI)

PO Box CH 76, Chisipite, Harare, Zimbabwe
Tel: (263) 4 496132
Fax: (263) 4 494046
Email: beitrust@africaonline.co.zw
Contact: T M Johnson, Representative

Beit Trust Postgraduate Fellowships
Subjects: All subjects.
Purpose: To support postgraduate study or research.
Eligibility: Open to persons under 30 years of age or 35 for medical doctors, who are university graduates domiciled in Zambia, Zimbabwe or Malawi. Applicants must be nationals of those countries.
Level of Study: Postgraduate
Type: Fellowship
Value: A variable personal allowance and fees plus book, clothing, thesis and departure allowances
Length of Study: 1–3 years depending on course sought

Frequency: Annual
Study Establishment: Approved universities and other institutions in South Africa, Britain and Ireland
No. of awards offered: 10
Application Procedure: Applicants must complete an application form.
Closing Date: August 31st
Funding: Private
No. of awards given last year: 8
No. of applicants last year: 400
Additional Information: Zambian applicants should contact BEIT Trust UK office.

For further information contact:

The BEIT Trust, BEIT House, Grove Road, Woking, Surrey, GU21 5JB, England
Tel: (44) 01483 772 575
Fax: (44) 01483 725 833
Email: enquiries@beittrust.org.uk

BELGIAN AMERICAN EDUCATIONAL FOUNDATION (BAEF)

Egmontstraat 11 Rue d'Egmont 1000 Brussels, Belgium
Tel: (32) 2 513 59 55
Fax: (32) 2 672 53 81
Email: mail@baef.be
Website: www.baef.be

The BAEF is a nonprofit organization, funded by the general public under United States Law, and engaged in fostering the higher education of deserving Belgians and Americans.

BAEF Alumni Award

Subjects: Arts and humanities.
Purpose: To encourage young researchers in Human Science.
Eligibility: Open to Belgian researchers who are below the age of 36 years.
Level of Study: Postgraduate
Type: Award
Length of Study: €5,000
Frequency: Annual
Application Procedure: A completed application form along with 10 copies of curriculum vitae and summary of complete scientific work must be sent.
Closing Date: March 1st

Fellowships for study or Research in the U.S.

Subjects: All subjects.
Purpose: To support advanced study or research.
Eligibility: Open to candidates who are below the age of 30 years with a reading and speaking knowledge of Dutch, French or German.
Type: Fellowship
Value: US$18,000 plus health insurance
Length of Study: 1 year
Frequency: Annual
Country of Study: Belgium
No. of awards offered: 8
Application Procedure: A completed application form along with three letters of recommendation must be sent.
Closing Date: October 31st

THE BERMUDA BIOLOGICAL STATION FOR RESEARCH, INC.

17 Biological Lane, Ferry Reach, St George's, GE 01, Bermuda
Tel: (1 441) 297 1880
Fax: (1 441) 297 8143
Email: education@bbsr.edu
Website: www.bbsr.edu
Contact: Ms Gillian Hollis, Assistant to Director

Bermuda Biological Station for Research Grant In Aid

Subjects: Oceanography, biological and life sciences.
Purpose: To provide financial assistance to help defray the costs of in house charges for visiting scientists.
Level of Study: Unrestricted
Type: Grant
Value: Varies, Bermuda $500–3,000
Length of Study: As required
Frequency: Annual
Study Establishment: The Bermuda Biological Station for Research, Inc.
Country of Study: Bermuda
No. of awards offered: Varies
Application Procedure: Applicants must submit grant proposals with their curriculum vitae and a budget. Proposals should be concise and contain an abstract, background, objectives, methods and the significance of proposed research.
Closing Date: January 15th
Funding: Private
No. of awards given last year: 10
No. of applicants last year: 10

BERTHOLD LEIBINGER FOUNDATION

Johann-Maus-Strasse 2, D-71254 Ditzingen, Germany
Tel: (49) 715 630 35205
Fax: (49) 715 630 3208
Email: innovationspreis@leibinger-stiftung.de
Website: www.leibinger-stiftung.de
Contact: Mr Sven Ederer, Project Manager

Berthold Leibinger Innovation Prize

Subjects: Applied laser technology.
Purpose: To promote the advancement of science.
Eligibility: Open to individuals and project groups who have completed an innovative scientific or technical development work on utilizing or generating laser light.
Level of Study: Unrestricted
Type: Prize
Value: €20,000, €10,000 and €5,000
Frequency: Every 2 years
No. of awards offered: 3
Application Procedure: Applicants must submit a completed application form, short documentation of up to ten pages in accordance with stipulated structure, biography and explanation describing the context of work upto eight nominees are invited to present their work in the jury session. Suggestions for the prize must include the reasons for the project's merit.
Closing Date: Varying, refer to the website
Funding: Private
Contributor: Berthold Leibinger
No. of awards given last year: 3
No. of applicants last year: Approx. 30
Additional Information: The foundation bears travelling expenses for nominees to jury session and for prize winners to the prize ceremony.

For further information contact:

Berthold Leibinger Foundation, Innovation Prize, D-71252 Ditzingen, Germany

BETA PHI MU

College of Information Studies, Florida State University, Tallahassee, FL, 32306-2100, United States of America
Tel: (1) 850 644 3907
Fax: (1) 850 644 9763
Email: beta_phi_mu@lis.fsu.edu
Website: www.beta-phi-mu.org
Contact: Mr Wayne Wiegand Executive, Secretary

Beta Phi Mu is a library and information studies society, founded in 1948, with over 25,000 graduates of the ALA-initiated accredited professional programmes. Beta Phi Mu was founded at the University of Illinois by a group of leading librarians and library educators. Aware of the notable achievements of honour societies in other professions, they believed that such a society would have much to offer librarianship and library education.

Blanche E Woolls Scholarship for School Library Media Service

Subjects: Library science.
Purpose: To assist a new student who plans to become a school media specialist.
Eligibility: Open to new students who have not completed more than 12 hours by Autumn. Applicants must be accepted into an ALA-accredited programme.
Level of Study: Graduate
Type: Scholarship
Value: US$1,500
Frequency: Annual
Study Establishment: An ALA-accredited school
Country of Study: United States of America
Application Procedure: Applicants must send three references and a completed application form, available by sending a stamped addressed envelope to Beta Phi Mu headquarters.
Closing Date: March 15th
No. of awards given last year: 1

Doctoral Dissertation Scholarship

Subjects: Library science and information studies.
Purpose: To support library and information science doctoral students who are working on their dissertations.
Eligibility: Applicants must be doctoral students who have completed their coursework and are ABD' at the time of application. Scholarships will be awarded based on the usefulness of the research topic to the profession.
Level of Study: Doctorate
Type: Scholarship
Value: US$2,000
Length of Study: 1 year
Frequency: Annual
Country of Study: Any country
No. of awards offered: 1
Application Procedure: Applicants must provide a 300-word abstract of dissertation, a curriculum vitae, a letter from their Dean or Director approving a topic and a work plan for the study.
Closing Date: March 15th
Funding: Private
No. of awards given last year: 1

Eugene Garfield Doctoral Dissertation Fellowship

Subjects: Library and information science.
Purpose: To fund library and information science doctoral students who are working on their dissertations.
Eligibility: All requirements for the degree except the writing and defense of dissertation must have been completed.
Level of Study: Doctorate
Type: Fellowship
Value: US$3,000
Frequency: Annual
Study Establishment: Florida State University
Country of Study: United States of America
No. of awards offered: 6
Application Procedure: Applicants should provide a personal statement not exceeding 500 words relating to post-dissertation plans, three letters of reference, a completed application form, abstract of dissertation (300-word limit) and a letter of approval of topic from the Dean or Director.
Closing Date: March 15th
Funding: Government

Frank B Sessa Award

Subjects: Library science or information studies.
Purpose: To enable the continuing professional education of a Beta Phi Mu member.
Eligibility: Open to Beta Phi Mu members only.
Level of Study: Professional development
Type: Scholarship
Value: US$1,250
Frequency: Annual
Country of Study: Any country
Application Procedure: Applicants must request an application form from Beta Phi Mu. Further details are also available from the website.
Closing Date: March 15th
Funding: Private
No. of awards given last year: 1

Harold Lancour Scholarship For Foreign Study

Subjects: Library science.
Purpose: To assist a librarian or library school student to undertake short-term research in a foreign country.
Eligibility: Open to nationals of any country.
Level of Study: Unrestricted
Type: Scholarship
Value: US$1,500
Frequency: Annual
Country of Study: Any country
No. of awards offered: 1
Application Procedure: Applicants must write to Beta Phi Mu for further details, enclosing a stamped addressed envelope. Further details are also available from the website.
Closing Date: March 15th
Funding: Private
No. of awards given last year: 1
No. of applicants last year: 10

Sarah Rebecca Reed Award

Subjects: Library and information science.
Purpose: To assist a new student in library and information science at an ALA-accredited school.
Eligibility: Open to beginning students who have not completed more than 12 hours by Autumn. Applicants must also be accepted into an ALA-accredited programme and provide five references. Nationals of any country can apply.
Level of Study: Graduate
Type: Scholarship
Value: US$2,000
Frequency: Annual
Study Establishment: An ALA-accredited school
Country of Study: United States of America
No. of awards offered: 1
Application Procedure: Applicants must request an application from the address shown, enclosing a stamped addressed envelope. Further details are also available from the website.
Closing Date: March 15th
Funding: Private
No. of awards given last year: 1
No. of applicants last year: 30

BFWG CHARITABLE FOUNDATION (FORMERLY CROSBY HALL)

28 Great James Street, London,
WC1N 3ES, England
Tel: (44) 20 7404 6447
Fax: (44) 20 7404 6505
Email: bfwg.charity@btinternet.com or jean.c@blueyonder.co.uk
Website: www.bcfgrants.org.uk
Contact: Ms Jean V Collett, Grants Administrator

The BFWG Charitable Foundation offers grants to help women graduates with their living expenses (not fees) while registered for study or research at an approved Institute of Higher Education in Great Britain.

BFWG Charitable Foundation Grants and Emergency Grants

Subjects: All subjects.
Purpose: To financially assist female graduates. Registered for study or research at an approved institution of Higher Education within the G7.
Eligibility: Open to female graduates who have completed their 1st year of graduate study, doctoral study or research. Foundation Grants are awarded to female students in their final year of a PhD. There is no restriction on nationality or age.
Level of Study: Doctorate, postgraduate, postdoctorate
Type: Grant
Value: Foundation Grants are up to UK £2,500 and Emergency Grants are typically UK £500. (these values are being reviewed)
Length of Study: Courses that exceed 1 year full-time in length
Frequency: Annual, Annually for main Foundation Grants and three times a year for Emergency Grants.
Study Establishment: Approved Institutes of Higher Education
Country of Study: United Kingdom
No. of awards offered: Approx. 30–40 Foundation Grants and approx. 50–60 Emergency Grants
Application Procedure: Applicants must complete an application form and submit this with two references, a copy of their graduate certificate, evidence of acceptance for the year, a cheque for UK £12 and a brief summary of thesis, if applicable, for Foundation Grants. Requests for application forms must be made by email.
Closing Date: The deadline for Foundation Grants is May 6th and the deadlines for Emergency Grants are January 2nd, May 31st and October 13th
Funding: Private
Contributor: Investment income
No. of awards given last year: 17 Foundation Grants and 19 Emergency Grants
No. of applicants last year: 231 Foundation Grants and Emergency Grants

BIAL FOUNDATION

Avenida da Siderurgia Nacional A, 4745-457, S. Mamede do Coronado, Portugal
Tel: (351) 22 986 6100
Fax: (351) 22 986 6190
Email: fundacao@bial.com
Website: www.bial.com
Contact: Chairman

The BIAL Foundation, a non-profit institution, was set up in 1994 with the aim of encouraging and supporting research focused on humans. It manages the BIAL award, one of the most distinguished awards for Health in Europe, and the BIAL Fellowship Programme, which focuses largely on psychophysiology and parapsychology.

BIAL Award

Subjects: Medical sciences and clinical medicine.
Purpose: To award intellectual written work in the subject area of health. To award work of a high quality in clinical practice.
Eligibility: At least one of the authors must be a physician.
Level of Study: Graduate
Type: Prize
Value: €230
Frequency: Every 2 years
No. of awards offered: 6
Application Procedure: Applicants must submit six copies of an original written specimen in either English or Portuguese to the Foundation. Further requirements are listed on its regulation, which will be forwarded to prospective applicants on request or can be downloaded at www.bial.com
Closing Date: October 31st
Funding: Private
Contributor: The BIAL Foundation
No. of awards given last year: 5
No. of applicants last year: 19

THE BIBLIOGRAPHICAL SOCIETY

Fellowship & Bursaries Subcommitte, The bibliographical Society, Centre for Urban History, University of Leicester, Leicester, LE1 7RH, England
Tel: (44) 0116 252 5925
Fax: (44) 0116 252 5769
Email: jh241@le.ac.uk
Website: www.bibsoc.org.uk
Contact: Dr John Hinks, Secretary

Founded in 1892, the Bibliographical Society is the senior learned society dealing with the study of the book and its history.

Antiquarian Booksellers Award

Subjects: Book trade and history of publishing.
Purpose: To support research into the history of the book trade and publishing industry.
Eligibility: Applicants may be of any age or nationality and need not be members of the Society.
Level of Study: Research
Type: Grant
Value: Up to US$1,500
Frequency: Annual
No. of awards offered: 1
Application Procedure: Application form (obtainable from the society's administrator), supported by letters from two referees familiar with the applicant's work.
Closing Date: December 1st in preceding year
Funding: Private
Contributor: Antiquarian Booksellers Association
No. of awards given last year: 1
Additional Information: Successful applicants will be asked to report briefly on the progress of their project by December of the same year.

Barry Bloomfield Bursary

Subjects: Research.
Purpose: To honour Barry Bloomfield by supporting research in bibliography, particularly pertaining to book history in areas of the former British Empire.
Eligibility: Applicants may be of any age or nationality and need not be members of the society.
Level of Study: Research
Type: Bursary
Value: Up to UK £2,000
Frequency: Annual
No. of awards offered: 1
Application Procedure: Application form (obtainable from the Society's administrator) supported by letters from two referees familiar with the applicant's work.
Closing Date: December 1st for preceding year
Funding: Private
Additional Information: Successful applicants will be asked to report briefly on the progress of their project by December of the same year.

Bibliographical Society Small Grants

Subjects: Bibliographic research.
Purpose: To support bibliographic research projects by providing small grants for specific purposes.
Eligibility: Applicants may be of any age or nationality and need not be members of the society.
Level of Study: Research
Type: Grant
Value: UK £50–200
Frequency: Any time
Application Procedure: Application by letter to the above address. If the applicant is registered for a research degree the application should be accompanied by a letter of support from their academic supervisor.
Closing Date: Applications are accepted any time
Funding: Private

Falconer Madan Award

Subjects: Any subject connected with Oxford or available to research specifically in an Oxford library.

Purpose: To support a scholar's research in an Oxford library.
Eligibility: Applicants may be of any age or nationality.
Level of Study: Research
Value: Up to UK £500 plus eligibility for accommodation at Wolfson College, Oxford
Frequency: At the discretion of the Society
Study Establishment: An Oxford library
Country of Study: United Kingdom
No. of awards offered: 1
Application Procedure: Application form (obtainable from the Society's administrator) supported by letters from two referees familiar with the applicant's work.
Closing Date: December 1st in preceding year
Funding: Private
Contributor: Oxford Bibliographical Society
Additional Information: Successful applicants will be asked to report briefly on the progress of their project by December of the same year.

The Fredson Bowers Award

Subjects: Bibliographic research.
Purpose: To support a bibliographic research project in the name of Fredson Bowers.
Eligibility: Applicants may be of any age or nationality and need not be members of the society.
Level of Study: Research
Type: Award
Value: US$1,500
Frequency: Annual
No. of awards offered: 1
Application Procedure: Application form (obtainable from the society's administrator) supported by letters from two referees familiar with the applicant's work.
Closing Date: December 1st in preceding year
Funding: Private
Contributor: The Bibliographical Society of America
Additional Information: Successful applicants will be asked to report briefly on the progress of their project by December of the same year.

Royal Oak Foundation Bursary

Subjects: Bibliographical research.
Purpose: To support bibliographical research projects involving work on National Trust Collections.
Eligibility: Applicants may be of any age or nationality and need not be members of the society.
Level of Study: Research
Type: Bursary
Value: UK £500
Frequency: Annual
No. of awards offered: 1
Application Procedure: Application form (obtainable from the society's administrator) supported by letters from two referees familiar with the applicant's work.
Closing Date: December 1st for preceding year
Funding: Private
Contributor: The National Trust
No. of awards given last year: None
No. of applicants last year: None
Additional Information: Successful applicants will be asked to report briefly on the progress of their project by December of the same year.

BIBLIOGRAPHICAL SOCIETY OF AMERICA (BSA)

PO Box 1537, Lenox Hill Station, New York, NY, 10021, United States of America
Tel: (1) 212 452 2710
Fax: (1) 212 452 2710
Email: bsa@bibsocamer.org
Website: www.bibsocamer.org
Contact: Ms Michele Randall, Executive Secretary

The Bibliographical Society of America (BSA) invites applications for its annual short-term fellowships, which supports bibliographical inquiry as well as research in the history of the book trades and in publishing history.

BSA Fellowship Program

Subjects: Books or manuscripts as historical evidence. Topics may include establishing a text or studying the history of book production, publication, distribution, collecting or reading.
Purpose: To support bibliographical inquiry and research in the history of the book trades and publishing.
Eligibility: This programme is open to applicants of any nationality.
Level of Study: Postgraduate, doctorate, postdoctorate
Type: Fellowship
Value: US$2,000
Length of Study: 1 month
Frequency: Annual
Country of Study: Any country
No. of awards offered: 10
Application Procedure: Applicants must complete an application form. The original plus six photocopies must be posted to the Executive Secretary of the Fellowship Committee at the Bibliographical Society of America.
Closing Date: December 1st
Funding: Private
No. of awards given last year: 10
Additional Information: For applications now only available on website visit the BSA's website.

BILKENT UNIVERSITY

Faculty of Business Administration, MBA Programme, Office of the Dean, Ankara, 06800, Turkey
Tel: (90) 312 290 1596
Fax: (90) 312 266 4958
Email: fba@bilkent.edu.tr
Website: www.bilkent.edu.tr
Contact: MBA Admissions Officer

Bilkent University is a non-profit research university. Courses are conducted in English. The University has more than 11,000 students and an international teaching staff of 1,000.

Bilkent Industrial Engineering Fellowship

Subjects: Industrial Engineering and Operations Research.
Eligibility: Open to application who have the necessary qualifications and show promise of scholarly achievement. The student is also expected to pass a qualifying examination.
Level of Study: Doctorate
Type: Fellowship
Value: A monthly stipend and a tuitions waiver
Frequency: Annual
Study Establishment: Bilkent University
Country of Study: Turkey
Application Procedure: Application forms can be obtained either from the Graduate admissions office or online.

For further information contact:

Department of Industrial Engineering
Tel: +90 (312) 290 1262
Fax: +90 (312) 266 4054
Email: barbaros@bilkent.edu.tr
Website: www.ie.bilkent.edu.tr
Contact: Dr Barbaros Tansel, Department of Chairman

Bilkent International Relations Fellowship

Subjects: International relations theory, strategic studies, comparative foreign politics, and/or area studies.
Purpose: To develop skills in international political analysis.
Eligibility: Candidates are selected on the basis of past academic achievement and references.
Level of Study: Doctorate
Type: Fellowship
Value: A monthly stipend and a tuition waiver
Frequency: Annual

Study Establishment: Bilkent University
Country of Study: Turkey
No. of awards offered: 1
Application Procedure: Contact the Department of International Relations.

For further information contact:

Tel: +90 (312) 266 4195
Fax: +90 (312) 266 4326
Email: ir@bilkent.edu.tr
Contact: Dr Ali Karaosmano

Bilkent Mathematics Fellowship

Subjects: Pure mathematics.
Eligibility: Preference is given to research proposals focused on non-linear differential equations and general relativity.
Level of Study: Postdoctorate, doctorate
Type: Fellowship
Value: A monthly stipend and a tuition fee waiver
Frequency: Annual
Study Establishment: Bilkent University
Country of Study: Turkey
No. of awards offered: 1
Application Procedure: Contact the department.

For further information contact:

Tel: +90 312 266 4377
Fax: +90 312 266 4579
Email: kocatepe@fen.bilkent.edu.tr
Contact: Dr Metharet Kocatepe

Bilkent MIAPP Fellowship

Subjects: Politics, economics and international law.
Purpose: To fund International and European affairs and executives who, understand and can deal with the increasing complex problems of a rapidly changing world.
Level of Study: Doctorate, postdoctorate
Type: Fellowship
Value: A monthly stipend and a tuition fee waiver
Length of Study: 2 year
Frequency: Annual
Study Establishment: Bilkent University
Country of Study: Turkey
Application Procedure: Contact the Department.

For further information contact:

Tel: +90 312 2901 249
Fax: +90 312 266 4960
Email: muge@bilkent.edu.tr
Contact: Dr Ali Karaosman

Bilkent Political Science Fellowship

Subjects: Political science.
Purpose: To provide a sophisticated conceptual framework and the analytical skills to specialize in a particular aspect of Turkish or comparative politics.
Eligibility: Applicants are required to have an M.A. degree in Political Science, Public Administrator or International Relations.
Level of Study: Doctorate
Type: Fellowship
Value: A monthly stipend and a tuition fee waiver
Frequency: Annual
Study Establishment: Bilkent University
Country of Study: Turkey
Application Procedure: Contact the department.

For further information contact:

Tel: +90 312 290 1931
Fax: +90 312 290 2792
Email: cindoglu@bilkent.edu.tr
Contact: Dr Dilek Cindo

Bilkent Turkish Literature Fellowship

Subjects: Turkish literature.
Purpose: To enhance the standards of Turkish literary studies and universalize the field.
Eligibility: Candidates will be required to take written and/or oral exams to prove their competence in Turkish, Ottoman and English.
Level of Study: Doctorate
Type: Fellowship
Value: A monthly stipend and a tuition fee waiver
Length of Study: 3 years
Frequency: Annual
Study Establishment: Bilkent University
Country of Study: Turkey
Application Procedure: Contact the department.

For further information contact:

Tel: +90 312 290 2711
Fax: +90 312 266 4059
Email: turkedeb@bilkent.edu.tr
Contact: Professor Talat S. Halman

Bilkent University MBA Scholarships

Subjects: MBA.
Eligibility: Open to students who have a cumulative grade point average of 300 or higher or students with a minimum Graduate Management Admission Test score of 650.
Level of Study: MBA
Type: Scholarship
Value: Various from tuition waiver to providing a stipend in addition to tuition waiver
Frequency: Annual
Study Establishment: Bilkent University
Country of Study: Turkey
No. of awards offered: Varies
Application Procedure: Applicants must apply for the MBA in the usual way and upon admission to the programme, scholarships of various degrees may be awarded.
Closing Date: Please contact the organization
Contributor: Bilkent University
No. of awards given last year: 15
No. of applicants last year: 45
Additional Information: For 2nd-year students, a tuition waiver is possible based on their academic achievement during the first year.

THE BIOCHEMICAL SOCIETY

The Biochemical Society, Third Floor, Eagle House, 16 Procter Street, London, W1CV 6NX, England
Tel: (44) 207 280 4131
Fax: (44) 207 280 4170
Email: alison.mcwhinnie@biochemistry.org
Website: www.biochemistry.org
Contact: Miss Alison McWhinnie, Head of Human Resources and Corporate Affairs

Serving biochemistry and biochemists since 1911, the aim of The Biochemical Society is to promote the advancement of the science of biochemistry. It does so in the context of cellular and molecular life sciences. Through its regular scientific meetings with special interest groups, its publishing company Portland Press Limited and its policy, professional and education contacts, the Society provides a forum for current research to be shared.

The Biochemical Society General Travel Fund

Subjects: Biochemistry.
Purpose: To assist scientists who wish to attend scientific meetings, or for short visits to other laboratories.
Eligibility: Postdoctorate, postgraduates in the 3rd year of a PhD programme, applicants who have been members of the British Biochemical Society for 1 year.

Level of Study: Postdoctorate, predoctorate
Type: Varies
Value: UK £500–750 (25–40 per cent of projected costs)
Country of Study: Any country
No. of awards offered: Varies
Application Procedure: Applicants must submit five copies of the completed form, registration form, abstract of the research to be presented at the meeting and a reference by the applicant's head of department. The form must demonstrate that the most cost effective form of transport and accommodation are to be utilized. All parts of the form must be completed.
Closing Date: January 1st, March 1st, May 1st, June 1st, September 1st and November 1st
Funding: Private
Additional Information: Faxed or emailed applications will not be accepted.

The Krebs Memorial Scholarship

Subjects: Biochemistry or allied biomedical science.
Purpose: To help candidates who wish to study for their PhD degree, but whose careers have been interrupted for non-academic reasons and/or who are unlikely to qualify for an award from public funds.
Eligibility: Postgraduate in biochemistry or allied biomedical science.
Level of Study: Postgraduate
Type: Scholarship
Value: A maintenance grant and all necessary fees
Length of Study: 1 year, maximum of 3 years
Frequency: Every 2 years, if award to current holder does not last for 3 years only one scholarship holder at any one
Study Establishment: Any British university
Country of Study: United Kingdom
No. of awards offered: 1
Application Procedure: Applications should be completed and forwarded through the head of department concerned, who will place the applicant in the top 5 per cent of PhD candidates. Two references are required.
Closing Date: April 1st
Funding: Private
Contributor: Sir Hans Krebs' pupils, colleagues and admirers
No. of awards given last year: 1
Additional Information: The scholarship is aimed at PhD students, but the award of a postdoctoral fellowship might be considered depending on the circumstances of the candidate.

BIRMINGHAM COLLEGE OF FOOD, TOURISM AND CREATIVE STUDIES

Summer Row, Birmingham, B3 1JB, England
Tel: (44) 12 1604 1000
Fax: (44) 12 1608 7100
Website: www.bcftcs.ac.uk
Contact: Student Scholarships

Gill Boydol Scholarship

Subjects: Hospitality subjects.
Purpose: Reduction in tuition fee for new international students.
Type: Scholarship
Value: Up to UK £1,500
Length of Study: 1 year
Frequency: Annual
Study Establishment: Birmingham College of Food, Tourism and Creative Studies
Country of Study: United Kingdom
No. of awards offered: 2
Closing Date: 1 month before the start of the programme

James Liu Scholarship

Subjects: Hospitality, tourism.
Purpose: Reduction in tuition fee for international students from the continent of Asia.
Level of Study: Unrestricted
Type: Scholarship
Value: Up to UK £1,500
Length of Study: 1 year
Frequency: Annual
Study Establishment: Birmingham College of Food, Tourism and Creative Studies
Country of Study: United Kingdom
No. of awards offered: 5
Closing Date: 1 month before the start of the programme

Tim Brighouse Scholarship

Subjects: Childcare, care subjects.
Purpose: Reduction in tuition fees for new international students.
Level of Study: Unrestricted
Type: Scholarship
Value: Up to UK £1,500
Length of Study: 1 year
Frequency: Annual
Study Establishment: Birmingham College of Food, Tourism and Creative Studies
Country of Study: United Kingdom
No. of awards offered: 2
Closing Date: 1 month before the start of the programme

BIRTH DEFECTS FOUNDATION

BDF Centre, Hemlock Way, Cannock, Staffordshire, WS11 7GF, England
Tel: (44) 15 4346 8888
Fax: (44) 15 4346 8999
Email: sbrown@bdfcharity.co.uk
Website: www.bdfcharity.co.uk
Contact: Mrs Sheila Brown, Chief Executive Officer

The Birth Defects Foundation, more recently known as BDF Newlife, is a United Kingdom registered charity whose mission is to improve child health, aid families and raise awareness. BDF Newlife is committed to funding basic, clinical and ethically approved research into the causes, prevention and treatment of birth defects.

BDF Newlife- Full and Small Grants Schemes

Subjects: Aetiology, prevention and treatment of birth defects.
Level of Study: Graduate, research, postgraduate
Type: Fellowship
Value: Varies. Small grants up to UK £10,000, full grants up to UK £80,000
Length of Study: Varies
Frequency: Annual, Small Grants available throughout the year.
No. of awards offered: Varies
Application Procedure: Applicants must fill in an application form for the full grant. Application for the small grant is by a brief proposal and then by application form if the proposal is of interest to the Foundation.
Closing Date: For full grants, applicants should consult advertisements and the website in June and July for the closing date. There is no closing date for small grants
Contributor: Charitable trading activity
No. of awards given last year: 14
No. of applicants last year: Over 30

BLACKLOCK NATURE SANCTUARY (BNS)

Catherine Jordan, Artists Fellowship Programs, 3853 County Line Road, P.O. 426, Moose Lake, MN 55767-0426, United States of America
Tel: (1) 823 6257
Email: jorda021@tc.umn.edu
Website: www.blacklock.org

The Blacklock Nature Sanctuary, founded in 1994, is dedicated to preserving undeveloped land in Minnesota and providing artists and naturalists with working space.

BNS Arts Administrator Renewal Fellowship

Subjects: Arts.
Purpose: To recognize the contributions made by artists.
Eligibility: Open to administrators who manage Minnesota arts organization or programmes.
Level of Study: Postgraduate
Type: Scholarship
Value: Up to US$300 per week
Frequency: Annual
Country of Study: United States of America
Application Procedure: See website.
Funding: Foundation
Contributor: Jerome Foundation

BNS Emerging Artists Fellowship

Subjects: Arts.
Purpose: To recognize the valuable cultural contributions of artists to society.
Eligibility: Open to candidates who are not less than 21 years of age and who are residents of Minnesota for at least one year.
Level of Study: Postgraduate
Type: Scholarship
Value: Up to US$2,000
Frequency: Annual
Country of Study: United States of America
Application Procedure: A completed application form must be submitted.
Contributor: Jerome Foundation

The Nadine Blacklock Nature Photography for women

Subjects: Photography.
Purpose: To give recognition to women working in the nature photography genre.
Eligibility: Open to all women nature photographers who are at least 21 years of age.
Level of Study: Postgraduate
Type: Scholarship
Value: Free use of Sanctuary land and studios plus accommodation
Length of Study: One month
Frequency: Annual
Country of Study: United States of America
Application Procedure: See the website www.blacklockgallery.com
Contributor: Blacklock Nature Photography

BLISS

68 South Lambeth Road, London, SW8 1RL, England
Tel: (44) 20 7820 9471
Fax: (44) 20 7820 9571
Email: information@bliss.org.uk
Website: www.bliss.org.uk
Contact: Mr Rob Williams, Chief Executive

BLISS is dedicated to make sure that more babies born prematurely or sick at birth survive and that each one has the best possible quality of life.

BLISS Research Awards

Subjects: Neonatal medicine and appropriate family support, development of aids and equipment.
Purpose: To support researchers whose project work will make a practical difference to the care of premature and sick newborn babies.
Eligibility: We do not accept applications for clinical research.
Level of Study: Research
Type: Grant
Value: Variable
Length of Study: Variable
Frequency: Apply as needed
Study Establishment: Any suitable institute in the United Kingdom
Country of Study: United Kingdom
Application Procedure: Applicants must contact Bonnie Green at BLISS.
Funding: Private

THE BLUE MAINTAINS HOTEL SCHOOL (BMHS)

45 Hume Street PO Box 905 Crows Nest, NSW 2065, Australia
Tel: (61) 9437 0300
Fax: (61) 9437 0299
Website: www.hotelschool.com

The Blue Mountain Hotel School is a university level institution, recognized and accredited in Australia by the vocational education and training accreditation board.

BMHS Hospitality and Tourism Management Scholarship

Subjects: Hospitality and tourism management.
Purpose: To encourage students in the field of hospitality and tourism.
Eligibility: Open to any Australian student.
Type: Scholarship
Value: Australian $15,000
Length of Study: 2–5
Frequency: Annual
No. of awards offered: 2
Application Procedure: A completed application form must be sent.
Closing Date: April 30th

BOEHRINGER INGELHEIM FONDS

Schlossmühle, Grabenstrasse 46, 55262 Heidesheim, Germany
Tel: (49) 6132 89 85 0
Fax: (49) 6132 89 85 11
Email: secretariat@bifonds.de
Website: www.bifonds.de

PhD scholarships (B.I.F.)

Subjects: Biomedicine.
Purpose: The exclusive and direct promotion of basic research in biomedicine.
Eligibility: Candidates must not be older than 27 years for doctoral research. All nationalities are eligible to apply. European citizens are supported while in Europe and overseas; non-European citizens receive support while conducting research in Europe.
Level of Study: Doctorate
Type: Scholarship
Value: €1,400 per month plus an additional flat rate sum of €100 per month to cover minor project-related costs and spouse allowance (no child allowance). A supplement for the respective country may be added
Length of Study: Up to 2 years for doctoral research (extension possible up to 1 additional year)
No. of awards offered: 45 per year
Application Procedure: Applications need not be submitted on a special form. Applications may be submitted in English. Consultation with scientific supervisors is recommended.
Closing Date: February 1st, June 1st, October 1st
Funding: Commercial
Contributor: C.H. Boehringer Sohn (Boehringer Ingelheim)
No. of awards given last year: 44
No. of applicants last year: 494
Additional Information: The foundation sponsors participation in research-oriented courses and summer or winter schools, where the selected participants learn special techniques in practical exercises as well as in lectures and discussions.

BOLOGNA CENTER OF THE JOHNS HOPKINS UNIVERSITY

Via Belmeloro 11, 40126 Bologna, Italy
Tel: (39) 051 291 7811
Fax: (39) 051 228 505
Email: admission@jhubc.it
Website: www.jhubc.it
Contact: Ms Bernadette O'Toole, Assistant Registrar

The Bologna Center is an integral part of the Paul H. Nitze School of Advanced International Studies (SAIS), one of the leading United States of America graduate schools devoted to the study of international relations. The programme seeks to merge the wisdom of universities, business and labour with the knowledge and expertise of those presently engaged in government, foreign affairs and international economic practice.

Paul H. Nitze School of Advanced International Studies (SAIS) Financial Aid and Fellowships

Subjects: International economics, European studies, international relations and international development In addition to fundamental courses, international economics covers European economic integration, environmental and resource economics, commercial policies, corporate finance, economic development and public sector economics. European studies examines history, economics, contemporary politics and culture, as well as demographic and enlargement issues. International relations explores international law, international non-governmental organizations, human rights, conflict management, ethnic conflict and security issues. The International Development Program takes a comprehensive approach to the economic, social, political, and environmental aspects of development as they interact within each nation's particular cultural and historical setting.
Purpose: To facilitate graduate study in International relations.
Eligibility: Open to students who have completed their first university degree. Students who are in the process of completing their first degree may apply providing they are awarded the degree prior to entry to the Bologna Center in the Autumn. All candidates must have an excellent command of written and spoken English and ideally have some background knowledge in economics, history, political or other social sciences. All fellowships and financial aid awards are based on need as well as academic merit.
Level of Study: Postgraduate
Type: Fellowships and financial aid
Value: Varies. Grants may cover partial or, occasionally, full tuition. Maintenance stipends are rarely provided
Frequency: Annual
Study Establishment: The Bologna Center of the Johns Hopkins University and the Paul H. Nitze School of Advanced International Studies
Country of Study: Italy
No. of awards offered: Varies, depending on funds available
Application Procedure: Applicants must submit an application form and financial aid application. Certain donor organizations require a separate application. Admission and financial aid for citizens of United States of America and permanent residents are administered by SAIS in Washington and all enquiries from United States of America students should be addressed to the Admissions Office in Washington. Financial aid and admission for non-United States of America students is administered in Bologna and all enquiries from non-United States of America students should be addressed to the Registrar's Office in Bologna.
Closing Date: The deadline for United States of America applicants is January 15th and February 1st for non-United States of America students
Funding: Commercial, private, government
No. of applicants last year: 600
Additional Information: A few courses are also offered in the United States of America foreign policy, as well as Latin American, African and Mediterranean issues. Language instruction is offered in the major Modern European languages. Special fellowships administered by the Bologna Center on behalf of other donor organizations have certain restrictions, which vary depending upon the donor. Many of the fellowships available to non-United States of America students are provided by government ministries and other European organizations and are reserved for citizens of the country providing the fellowship.

For further information contact:

United States of America Citizens: Admissions Office, 1740 Massachusetts Avenue North West, Washington, DC 20036, United States of America
Email: admission.sais@jhu.edu

Non-United States of America Citizens: Registrar's Office, Bologna Center, Via Belmeloro 11, 40126 Bologna, Italy
Email: admission@jhubc.it

THE BOSTON SOCIETY OF ARCHITECTS (BSA)

52 Broad Street, 4th Floor, Boston, MA 02109-4301,
United States of America
Tel: (1) 617 951 1433
Fax: (1) 617 951 0845
Email: kmiller@architects.org
Website: www.architects.org
Contact: Kate Miller, Awards Committee

The Boston Society of Architects (BSA) is the regional and professional association of over 3,000 architects and 1,000 affiliate members. The BSA's affiliate members include engineers, contractors, clients or owners, public officials, other allied professionals, students and lay people. The BSA administers many programmes that enhance the public understanding of design as well as the practice of architecture.

BSA Research Grants

Purpose: To encourage inquiry on specific research topics as well as on how the design and building process as well as results constitute research.
Level of Study: Unrestricted
Type: Research grant
Value: Varies
Length of Study: 1 year
Frequency: Annual
No. of awards offered: Varies
Application Procedure: Proposal response must be submitted according to requirements available on www.architects.org/grants
Closing Date: February 15th
No. of awards given last year: 5

For further information contact:

Website: www.architects.org/grants

Rotch Travelling Scholarship

Subjects: Architecture.
Purpose: To provide young architects with the opportunity to travel and study in foreign countries.
Eligibility: Open to United States of America architects who will be under 35 years of age on March 10th of the year of the competition and who have a degree from an accredited school of architecture plus 1 full year of professional experience in an architectural office.
Level of Study: Professional development
Type: Fellowship
Value: A stipend of US$35,000
Length of Study: 9 months
Frequency: Annual
Country of Study: Other
No. of awards offered: 1–2
Application Procedure: Applicants must complete an application form, available on written request.
Closing Date: January 1st for application requests
Funding: Private
Additional Information: The scholar is selected through a two-stage design competition. The 1 year of professional experience required should be completed prior to the beginning of the preliminary competition. Scholars are required to return to the United States of America after the duration of the scholarship and submit a report of their travels.

BRADFORD CHAMBER OF COMMERCE AND INDUSTRY

Devere House, Vicar Lane, Little Germany, Bradford, Yorkshire, BD1 5AH, England
Tel: (44) 12 7477 2777
Fax: (44) 12 7422 4549
Email: john.speak@bradfordchamber.co.uk
Website: www.bradfordchamber.co.uk
Contact: Julie Snook

The Bradford Chamber of Commerce and Industry represents member companies in the Bradford and district area. It works with local partners to develop the economic health of the district and has a major voice within the British Chamber of Commerce movement in order to promote the needs of local business on a national basis.

John Speak Trust Scholarships

Subjects: Modern languages.
Purpose: To promote British trade abroad by assisting people in perfecting their basic knowledge of a foreign language.
Eligibility: Open to British-born nationals intending to follow a career connected with the export trade in the United Kingdom. Applicants must be over 18 years of age with a sound, basic knowledge of at least one language.
Level of Study: Professional development
Type: Scholarship
Value: Sufficient to cover reasonable living expenses plus an amount towards the cost of travel
Length of Study: Between 3 months and 1 full academic year abroad depending on the circumstances and each candidate's level of knowledge of the language. It is non-renewable
Frequency: Annual
Study Establishment: A recognized college or university
No. of awards offered: 10
Application Procedure: Applicants must complete an application form and undertake an interview.
Closing Date: February 28th, May 31st or October 31st
Funding: Private
No. of awards given last year: 10
No. of applicants last year: 14

BRAIN TUMOR SOCIETY

124 Watertown Street, Suite 3H, PO BOX 5225, Carefree, AZ, 85377, United States of America
Tel: (1) 800 770 8287
Email: grants@tbts.org
Website: www.tbts.org
Contact: Carrie Treadwell, Director of Research Programs

The Brain Tumor Society exists to find a cure for brain tumours. It strives to improve the quality of life of brain tumour patients and their families. It disseminates educational information and provides access to psycho-social support. It raises funds to advance carefully selected scientific research projects, improve clinical care and find a cure.

BTS Research Grant

Subjects: Brain tumours.
Purpose: To fund scientific research aimed at finding a cure for brain tumours, and to support students working on a doctoral thesis in the subject.
Level of Study: Postgraduate, doctorate
Type: Scholarship
Value: US$100,000 per year
Length of Study: 2 years
Country of Study: United States of America
Application Procedure: Applicants must check the website.
Closing Date: April 16th
Funding: Private

BRANDON UNIVERSITY

The Scholarship Office, School of Music, 270 18th Street, Brandon, Manitoba, R7A 6A9, Canada
Tel: (1) 204 728 9520
Fax: (1) 204 726 4573
Email: wood@brandonu.ca
Website: www.brandonu.ca
Contact: Professor Janet Olmsteed Wood, Graduate Music Programmes

Brandon University is linked to the international community through the exchange of people and ideas. At an informal level, faculty may collaborate with researchers from around the world in pursuit of knowledge in their respective disciplines. In addition, the university has a number of joint programmes and exchange opportunities with institutions in other countries.

Brandon University Graduate Assistantships

Subjects: Music education, performance and literature.
Purpose: To afford graduate students the opportunity to gain professional experience while studying and to provide monetary assistance.
Eligibility: Open to candidates with a Bachelor's degree in music or music education and with a minimum grade point average of 3.0 during their final year.
Level of Study: Graduate
Type: Scholarship
Value: Varies
Length of Study: Normally 2 years
Frequency: Annual
Study Establishment: The School of Music, Brandon University
Country of Study: Canada
No. of awards offered: 1
Application Procedure: Applicants must complete an application form.
Closing Date: May 1st
Additional Information: Candidates for the performance and literature major are also required to show, by audition, high potential as performers. For the music education major, candidates should have adequate related professional experience, preferably teaching.

BREAST CANCER CAMPAIGN

Clifton Centre, 110 Clifton Street, London, EC2A 4HT, England
Tel: (44) 20 7749 3700
Fax: (44) 20 7749 3701
Email: info@bcc-uk.org
Website: www.breastcancercampaign.org
Contact: Grants Officer Chairman of the Trustees

Breast Cancer Campaign is the only charity that specializes in funding independent breast cancer research throughout the United Kingdom. The organization presently funds 51 projects, representing UK £6 million worth of research funds.

Breast Cancer Campaign PhD Studentships

Subjects: Breast cancer research including prevention, causes, diagnosis, treatment and management.
Purpose: To improve diagnosis and treatment of cancer, to achieve a better understanding of how it develops and ultimately to cure or prevent the disease.
Level of Study: Postdoctorate, postgraduate
Type: Studentship
Value: Please look at funding information on our website: www.breastcancercampaign.org
Length of Study: 3 years
Country of Study: United Kingdom
No. of awards offered: Variable

Breast Cancer Campaign Project Grants

Subjects: Breast cancer research including prevention, causes, diagnosis, treatment and management.

Purpose: To improve diagnosis and treatment of cancer, to achieve a better understanding of how it develops and ultimately to cure or prevent the disease.
Level of Study: Postdoctorate, postgraduate
Type: Studentship
Value: Not more than UK £50,000 per year
Length of Study: 3 years
Frequency: Twice yearly
Country of Study: United Kingdom
No. of awards offered: Variable
Application Procedure: Applicants must complete an application form. These can be downloaded from the website www.breastcancercampaign.org
Closing Date: The beginning of January and July. Please contact the campaign office for the precise dates.
No. of awards given last year: 20
No. of applicants last year: 110

Breast Cancer Campaign Scientific Fellowships

Subjects: Breast cancer research including prevention, causes, diagnosis, treatment and management.
Purpose: To improve diagnosis and treatment of cancer, to achieve a better understanding of how it develops and ultimately to cure or prevent the disease.
Level of Study: Postdoctorate, postgraduate
Type: Grant
Value: No more than UK £450,000 over 5 years
Length of Study: 5 years
Frequency: Annual
Country of Study: United Kingdom
No. of awards offered: Fellowship

Breast Cancer Campaign Small Pilot Grants

Subjects: Breast cancer research including prevention, causes, diagnosis, treatment and management.
Purpose: To improve diagnosis and treatment of cancer, to achieve a better understanding of how it develops and ultimately to cure or prevent the disease.
Level of Study: Postgraduate, postdoctorate
Type: Grant
Value: No more than UK £15,000
Length of Study: Up to 1 year
Frequency: Twice a year
No. of awards offered: Variable
Application Procedure: Applicants must complete an application form. These can be downloaded from the website.
Closing Date: The beginning of January and July. Please contact the campaign office for the precise dates.
No. of awards given last year: 20 in total awarded in 2004 for PhDs and project grants
Additional Information: Launch of new scientific fellowships and small pilot grants.

BRIAN MAY TRUST

ffrench Commercial Lawyers, PO box 2656 Southport, QLD 4215, Australia
Tel: (61) 07 5591 7555
Fax: (61) 07 55917 450
Email: gallison@ffcomlaw.com.au
Website: www.brianmayscholarship.org

The Trust is a charitable testamentary trust established under the will of the late Brian May, Australia's leading film composer to finance promising Australian film composers.

The Brian May Scholarship

Subjects: Creative arts.
Purpose: To provide financial assistance to promising Australian film composers to study film scoring.
Level of Study: Postgraduate
Type: Scholarship
Value: Australian $80,000
Frequency: Every 2 years
Study Establishment: Thornton School of Music
Country of Study: United States of America
No. of awards offered: 1
Application Procedure: Contact the trust or apply online.
Funding: Trusts
Contributor: The Brian May Trust
No. of awards given last year: 1

THE BRITISH ACADEMY

10 Carlton House Terrace, London, SW1Y 5AH, England
Tel: (44) 20 7969 5200
Fax: (44) 20 7969 5300
Email: secretary@britac.ac.uk
Website: www.britac.ac.uk
Contact: Ms Jane Lyddon, Assistant Secretary (International Relations)

The British Academy is the premier national learned society in the United Kingdom devoted to the promotion of advanced research and scholarship in the humanities and social sciences.

British Academy 44th International Congress of Americanists Fund

Subjects: Latin American studies.
Purpose: To enable British scholars to visit Latin America or Latin American scholars to visit Britain.
Eligibility: Open to support British or Latin American scholars. Applicants must be resident in the UK.
Level of Study: Postdoctorate
Type: Travel grant
Value: Awards do not generally exceed UK £1,000
Frequency: Annual
No. of awards offered: Varies
Closing Date: See the website
Funding: Private

British Academy Ancient Persia Fund

Subjects: Iranian, Central Asian studies in the pre-Islamic period.
Purpose: To encourage and support the study of Iranian or Central Asian studies in the pre-Islamic period. Grants are offered towards travel costs.
Eligibility: Preference will be given to scholars undertaking archaeological research or engaged in an archaeological project.
Level of Study: Postdoctorate
Type: Travel grant
Value: Awards do not generally exceed UK £500
Length of Study: Tenable for 1 year
Frequency: Annual
Country of Study: Any country
No. of awards offered: 1–2 annually
Closing Date: See the website
Funding: Private
Additional Information: For United Kingdom residents, an application to this fund for travel costs may be combined with an application for a small research grant for other costs, up to a total of UK £5,000.

British Academy Elie Kedourie Memorial Fund

Subjects: Middle Eastern, modern European history and political thought.
Purpose: To promote the study of Middle Eastern, modern European history or history of political thought.
Eligibility: Awards are offered to support any aspect of research, including travel and publication.
Level of Study: Postdoctorate
Frequency: Annual
Country of Study: Any country
No. of awards offered: 1–2 annually
Closing Date: See the website
Funding: Private

Additional Information: Funds are not available to support travel to or attendance at conferences, workshops or seminars, either in the United Kingdom or elsewhere.

British Academy Larger Research Grants

Subjects: Humanities and social sciences.
Purpose: To support research projects at the postdoctoral level in the humanities and social sciences.
Eligibility: Applicants must be resident in the United Kingdom.
Level of Study: Postdoctorate
Type: Grant
Value: Upper limit of UK £20,000 in any 1 year
Frequency: Annual
Country of Study: Any country
No. of awards offered: Approx. 50
Closing Date: See the website
Funding: Government

British Academy Overseas Conference Grants

Subjects: Humanities and social sciences.
Purpose: To help meet the costs of travel by British scholars to overseas conferences.
Eligibility: Open to scholars presenting an academic paper. Applicants must be resident in the United Kingdom and of postdoctoral or equivalent status. Postgraduate students are not eligible to apply.
Level of Study: Postdoctorate
Type: Grant
Value: Usually restricted to a maximum of UK £800
Country of Study: Any country
No. of awards offered: Approx. 800
Closing Date: See the website
Funding: Government

British Academy Postdoctoral Fellowships

Subjects: Academic career development in humanities and social science.
Purpose: To enable outstanding young scholars to obtain experience of research and teaching in the university environment, which will strengthen their curriculum vitae and improve their prospects of obtaining permanent posts by the end of the fellowship.
Eligibility: Applicants must have obtained their doctorate no earlier than July 1st 2004 and must not have held an established teaching post in an Institute of Higher Education. Applicants must be United Kingdom nationals, or nationals of any country who have a doctorate from United Kingdom university or European Union nationals resident in the United Kingdom.
Level of Study: Postdoctorate
Type: Fellowship
Value: Salary starting from UK £22,643
Length of Study: Tenable for 3 years and not renewable
Frequency: Annual
Country of Study: United Kingdom
No. of awards offered: Up to 40
Application Procedure: Applications must be made on the postdoctoral fellowship application form.
Closing Date: February 28th. See the British Academy website
Funding: Government
No. of awards given last year: See the website
No. of applicants last year: 518

British Academy Sino-British Fellowship Trust

Subjects: Humanities and social sciences.
Purpose: To support individual or co-operative research projects.
Eligibility: Research may be conducted either in the United Kingdom or China, or in both countries and must involve person to person contact.
Level of Study: Postdoctorate
Type: Grant
Frequency: As per availability of funds
No. of awards offered: 3–4
Closing Date: See the website
Funding: Private
Contributor: Sino-British Fellowship Trust (SBFT)
Additional Information: Successful applications will be forwarded to the SBFT for approval in the Autumn of each year. It should be noted that the Academy will be unable to offer support should the SBFT decline to confirm funding.

British Academy Small Research Grants

Subjects: Humanities and social sciences.
Purpose: For original research at postdoctoral level.
Eligibility: Applicants must be resident in the United Kingdom and be of postdoctoral or equivalent status. Postgraduate students are not eligible to apply.
Level of Study: Postdoctorate
Type: Grant
Value: Maximum UK £7,500
Frequency: As per availability of funds
Country of Study: Any country
No. of awards offered: Approx. 500
Closing Date: See the website
Funding: Government

British Academy Stein-Arnold Exploration Fund

Subjects: History, geography and the arts.
Purpose: To encourage research into the antiquities or historical geography or early history or arts of those parts of Asia that come within the sphere of the ancient civilizations of India, China and Iran, including Central Asia.
Eligibility: Research should be as far as possible by means of exploratory work. Applicants must be British or Hungarian subjects.
Level of Study: Postdoctorate
Type: Grant
Value: Awards do not generally exceed UK £2,500
Frequency: Annual
No. of awards offered: 3–4 annually
Closing Date: See the website
Funding: Private

British Academy Worldwide Congress Grant

Subjects: Humanities and social sciences.
Purpose: To help meet the costs of organizing major international congresses in the United Kingdom, but only where the congress is one of an established series and where it is clearly the United Kingdom's turn to host the conference.
Eligibility: Open to organizers of worldwide congresses in the United Kingdom.
Level of Study: Postdoctorate
Type: Grant
Value: Maximum UK £15,000
Frequency: Dependent on funds available
Country of Study: Any country
No. of awards offered: 2–3 per year
Application Procedure: Applicants must apply on the prescribed forms, and there is a two-stage consideration procedure.
Closing Date: See the website
Funding: Government

British Conference Grants

Subjects: Humanities and social sciences.
Purpose: To bring key speakers to conferences held in the United Kingdom.
Eligibility: Applicants must be resident in the United Kingdom and be of postdoctoral or equivalent status.
Level of Study: Postdoctorate
Type: Grant
Value: UK £500–2,000
Frequency: As per availability of funds.
Country of Study: United Kingdom
No. of awards offered: Approx. 200
Closing Date: See the website
Funding: Government

Elisabeth Barker Fund

Subjects: Recent European history, particularly of Eastern and Central Europe.

Purpose: To support research or small conferences.
Eligibility: Open to scholars of postdoctoral or equivalent status ordinarily resident in the United Kingdom. Applicants need not be British nationals. Applications must be made by a British resident and not a foreign scholar.
Level of Study: Postdoctorate
Value: Up to UK £1,000
Frequency: Annual
No. of awards offered: Up to 6
Closing Date: See the website
Funding: Private

Neil Ker Memorial Fund

Subjects: Western medieval manuscripts, particularly those of British interest.
Purpose: To promote the study of Western medieval manuscripts.
Eligibility: Open to both younger and established scholars of any nationality for research at postdoctoral level.
Level of Study: Postdoctorate
Type: Grant
Value: Approx. UK £2,000
Frequency: Annual
Country of Study: Any country
No. of awards offered: 3–4 annually
Closing Date: See the website
Funding: Private

Thank-Offering to Britain Fellowships

Subjects: Topics of an economic, industrial, social, political, literary or historical character relating to the British Isles. Preference will be given to projects in the modern period.
Purpose: To fund a research fellowship.
Eligibility: Open to persons ordinarily resident in the United Kingdom and of postdoctoral status. Candidates should be in mid-career and must be employed at a United Kingdom university in an established teaching post.
Level of Study: Postdoctorate
Type: Fellowship
Value: Within the first two points of the Grade A university lecturers' scale. The award also pays for a replacement to undertake the teaching and administrative duties of the award holders for 1 year
Length of Study: Normally for 1 year
Frequency: Annual
Country of Study: United Kingdom
No. of awards offered: 1
Closing Date: See the British Academy website
Funding: Private
Contributor: Association of Jewish Refugees
No. of awards given last year: 1
No. of applicants last year: 51

BRITISH ASSOCIATION FOR AMERICAN STUDIES (BAAS)

Department of Humanities, University of Central Lancashire, Preston, PR1 2HE, United Kingdom
Tel: (44) 17 7289 3040
Fax: (44) 17 7289 2970
Email: hrsmacpherson@uclan.ac.uk
Website: www.baas.ac.uk
Contact: Dr Heidi Macpherson, Secretary (STA)

The British Association for American Studies (BAAS), established in 1955, promotes research and teaching in all aspects of American studies. The Association organizes annual conferences and specialist regional meetings for students, teachers and researchers. The publications produced are The Journal of American Studies with Cambridge University Press, BAAS Paperbacks with Edinburgh University Press and British Records Relating to America in Microform with Microform Publishing.

BAAS Short Term Awards

Subjects: Culture and society of the United States of America.
Purpose: To fund travel to the United States of America for short-term research projects.
Eligibility: Open to residents in the United Kingdom. Preference is given to young postgraduates and to members of BAAS.
Level of Study: Doctorate, postgraduate, professional development, postdoctorate
Type: Award
Value: UK £500
Frequency: Annual
Country of Study: United States of America
No. of awards offered: 5–10
Application Procedure: Applicants must complete an application form.
Closing Date: December 15th
No. of awards given last year: 6
No. of applicants last year: 35
Additional Information: Successful candidates must write a report and acknowledge BAAS assistance in any related publication.

BRITISH ASSOCIATION FOR CANADIAN STUDIES (BACS)

21 George Square, Edinburgh, EH8 9LD, Scotland
Tel: (44) 13 1662 1117
Fax: (44) 13 1662 1118
Email: jodie.robson@ed.ac.uk
Website: www.canadian-studies.net
Contact: Ms Jodie Robson

In response to the growing academic interest in Canada, the British Association for Canadian Studies (BACS) was established in 1975. Its aim is to foster teaching and research on Canada and Canadian issues by locating study resources in Britain, facilitating travel and exchange schemes for professorial staff and ensuring that the expertise of Canadian scholars who visit the United Kingdom is put to effective use. Principal activities include the publication of The British Journal of Canadian Studies and the BACS Newsletter, and the organization of the Association's annual multidisciplinary conference, which attracts scholars from Canada and Europe as well as from the United Kingdom.

Molson Research Awards

Subjects: Canadian studies, humanities and social sciences.
Purpose: To encourage and fund visits to Canada directly related to the applicant's actual or proposed teaching or research. The awards are intended to increase contact between academics and other scholars in Canada and the United Kingdom, and to assist in the preparation of teaching about Canada.
Eligibility: Open to academics from universities, colleges of higher education and polytechnics of the United Kingdom. Applicants must be citizens or long-term residents of the United Kingdom. Priority will be given to BACS members.
Level of Study: Postdoctorate, doctorate
Type: Travel grant
Value: Up to UK £500
Frequency: Annual
Study Establishment: Universities or research institutions
Country of Study: Canada
No. of awards offered: 3–5
Application Procedure: Applicants must complete an application form and submit this with a covering letter, curriculum vitae and the names of two referees.
Closing Date: October 1st, February 1st or May 1st
No. of awards given last year: 6
No. of applicants last year: 20
Additional Information: The BACS administers these awards on behalf of the Foundation for Canadian Studies in the United Kingdom.

Prix du Québec Award

Subjects: Humanities and social sciences.
Purpose: To assist British academics carrying out research related to Québec.

Eligibility: Open to citizens or long-term residents of the United Kingdom.
Level of Study: Professional development, doctorate, postdoctorate
Type: Award
Value: UK £1,000
Frequency: Dependent on funds available
Study Establishment: Universities, research institutions and schools
Country of Study: Canada
No. of awards offered: 1 award to doctoral and postdoctoral students and 1 award to full-time teaching staff
Application Procedure: Applicants must contact Jodie Robson, Administrative Secretary of BACS, for application guidelines.
Closing Date: March 1st
Funding: Government
Contributor: The Office of the Government of Québec in the United Kingdom
No. of awards given last year: 2
Additional Information: The award also seeks to encourage projects that incorporate Québec in a comparative approach. The Québec component must be more than 50 per cent.

BRITISH ASSOCIATION OF PLASTIC SURGEONS (BAPS)

The Royal College of Surgeons, 35-43 Lincoln's Inn Fields, London, WC2A 3PE, England
Tel: (44) 20 7831 5161
Fax: (44) 20 7831 4041
Email: secretariat@baps.co.uk
Website: www.baps.co.uk
Contact: Ms Angela Rausch, Administrator

The British Association of Plastic Surgeons (BAPS) was founded in 1946 with the objective of relieving sickness and protecting and preserving public health by the promotion and development of plastic surgery. The aim of the association is to advance education in the field of plastic surgery.

BAPS Student Bursaries

Subjects: Plastic surgery.
Purpose: To help medical students to cover expenses of travel and research related to plastic surgery.
Eligibility: Medical students in the United Kingdom.
Level of Study: Predoctorate
Type: Bursary
Value: UK £500
Length of Study: Varies
Frequency: Annual
Study Establishment: Hospital plastic surgery units or research laboratories
Country of Study: Any country
No. of awards offered: 10
Application Procedure: Application forms are available on request from the BAPS or from the BAPS website: www.baps.co.uk
Closing Date: December 31st
Funding: Private
Contributor: BAPS
No. of awards given last year: 10
No. of applicants last year: 19

BAPS Travelling Bursary

Subjects: Plastic surgery.
Purpose: To enable a plastic surgeon in the United Kingdom to study new techniques abroad.
Eligibility: Open to members of the Association who are either specialist registrars in years 4–6, enrolled in a recognized training programme or who have not had more than 3 years as consultant plastic surgeons.
Level of Study: Professional development
Type: Bursary
Value: Up to UK £5,000
Length of Study: Varies
Frequency: Annual
Study Establishment: Any approved hospital plastic surgery units
Country of Study: Any country
No. of awards offered: 5
Application Procedure: Applicants must complete an application form and submit this with a proposed itinerary giving details of costs and reasons for wanting to attend a particular unit. A curriculum vitae of not more than two pages must also be submitted.
Closing Date: December 31st
Funding: Private
Contributor: BAPS
No. of awards given last year: 4
No. of applicants last year: 8

Paton/Masser Memorial Fund

Subjects: Plastic surgery.
Purpose: To provide funds towards research projects.
Eligibility: Open to consultants and specialist registrars in plastic surgery working in the British Isles.
Level of Study: Research
Value: UK £10,000
Length of Study: Varies
Frequency: Annual
Study Establishment: A hospital or research laboratory
Country of Study: United Kingdom
No. of awards offered: Varies
Application Procedure: Application forms available on the BAPS website, www.baps.co.uk or by e-mail request to secretariat@baps.co.uk
Closing Date: December 31st
Funding: Private
Contributor: BAPS
No. of awards given last year: 2 of UK £2,500 each
No. of applicants last year: 5

BRITISH COLUMBIA CENTRE FOR INTERNATIONAL EDUCATION

141-6200 Mckay Ave PO Box 543, Vancouver, BC, V5H 4M9, Canada
Tel: (1) 992 6022
Fax: (1) 992 6023
Email: bccie@bccie.bc.ca
Website: www.bccie.bc.ca

The British Columbia Centre for International Education (BCCIE), established in 1990, is a non-governmental agency and non-profit society funded through membership fees and fee for services activities. The BCCIE has been a leader in the successful development and promotion of international education in British Columbia.

British Columbia Asia Pacific Students' Awards

Subjects: All subjects.
Purpose: To provide an opportunity to students to gain a better understanding of the cultures, economics and languages of Asian countries.
Eligibility: Open to outstanding students who are citizens of Canada or landed immigrants.
Level of Study: Postgraduate
Type: Award
Value: Varies according to the country of study
Frequency: Annual
Study Establishment: Any accredited university or institution
Country of Study: Any country
Application Procedure: Contact BCCIE.

BRITISH DENTAL ASSOCIATION

64 Wimpole Street, London, W1G 8YS, United Kingdom
Tel: (44) 20 7563 4174
Fax: (44) 20 7563 4556
Email: students@bda.org
Website: www.bda.org
Contact: Miss Sarah Leithead, Marketing Executive

The British Dental Association (BDA) is the national professional association for dentists. With over 20,000 members, the Association strives to enhance the science, art and ethics of dentistry, improve the nation's oral health and promote the interests of its members.

BDA/Dentsply Student Support Fund

Subjects: Dentistry, maxillo-facial surgery.
Purpose: To give financial assistance to students who are in severe financial hardship. Only open to 4th- and 5th-year BDS students or postgraduates.
Eligibility: Open to BDA members only. All applicants must be registered students at a United Kingdom Dental School.
Level of Study: Postgraduate, graduate
Type: Scholarship/Hardship fund
Value: Varies
Frequency: Annual
Country of Study: United Kingdom
No. of awards offered: Varies, up to 10
Application Procedure: Applicants must complete and submit application forms, accompanied by an academic reference or supporting letter. Application forms can be found in the student section of the BDA website.
Closing Date: January 4th and July 1st
Funding: Commercial
Contributor: Dentsply UK Ltd
No. of awards given last year: 7
No. of applicants last year: 30
Additional Information: For BDS/Dental Students only.

BRITISH DIETETIC ASSOCIATION

The British Dietetic Association, 5th floor, Charles House, 148/9 Great Charles Street Queensway, Birmingham, B3 3HT, England
Tel: (44) 01 2120 0802
Fax: (44) 01 2120 8081
Website: www.bda.uk.com
Contact: Mr Nula Marnell, Assistant to the Chief Executive

The British Dietetic Association (BDA) is the professional body for dietitians in the United Kingdom and provides grants for research into human nutrition and dietetic practice that advances the profession.

Elizabeth Washington Award

Subjects: Educational work, nutrition education, health promotion, other educational topics.
Purpose: To reward a dietitian's published scientific work in 2004 broadly within the discipline of nutrition and dietetics.
Eligibility: Award open to all BDA members. Applications may be from a sole author or a multi-author publication or from two or more BDA members in equal joint partnership.
Level of Study: Research
Type: Grant
Value: UK £1,250
Frequency: Annual
Application Procedure: Four copies of the published work together with BDA membership number, name and address and place of published work to be submitted, anonymized and clearly marked 'Elizabeth Washington Award'.
Closing Date: January
Funding: Trusts
Additional Information: Dietitians can submit items previously submitted for other external awards.

Pace Award

Subjects: Nutrition, dietetics, education programme.
Purpose: For the development or implementation of a nutrition education programme for staff addressing the problem of undernutrition.
Eligibility: Applicants should be full members of the BDA and resident in the United Kingdom or Eire.
Level of Study: Research
Type: Grant
Value: UK £500 to fund the development of the project and UK £300 worth of pace learning units for staff to use
Frequency: Annual
Application Procedure: To apply, dietitians are to submit an outline of the proposed education programme that includes: which staff is targeted, subject area and level of the programme, which format will be taken, how the learner will be assessed, what effect it will have on nutritional care and how it will raise the profile of nutrition in your organization, potential benefits to employers and estimated cost of development and implementation. Four copies of the application are to be submitted.
Closing Date: January 28th
Additional Information: Applications should not exceed 1,000 words.

Rose Simmonds Award

Subjects: Scientific work in dietetics.
Purpose: To reward a dietitian's published scientific work in 2004.
Eligibility: Award open to all BDA members. Dietitian must be an acknowledged author and should have published his/her work. Applicant may be a sole author, the principal author of a multi-author publication or two or more BDA members in joint partnership.
Level of Study: Research
Type: Grant
Value: UK £1,250
Frequency: Annual
Application Procedure: The published work, with BDA membership number, name and address, and place of publication on a separate sheet of paper, should be submitted to the address. The submission must be supported by recommendations from entrants manager or senior colleagues in another discipline that significant contribution has been made to the project. Four copies of the entry, anonymized and marked Rose Simmonds Award' should be submitted. Application form must be completed.
Closing Date: January
Funding: Trusts
Additional Information: Members may submit more than one entry but the same piece of work cannot be submitted for the other awards.

BRITISH ECOLOGICAL SOCIETY (BES)

26 Blades Court, Putney, London, SW15 2NU, England
Tel: (44) 20 8871 9797
Fax: (44) 20 8871 9779
Email: dominic@britishecologicalsociety.org; grants@britishecologicalsociety.org
Website: www.britishecologicalsociety.org
Contact: Mr Dominic Burton, Grants Officer

As a learned society and registered charity, the British Ecological Society (BES) is an independent organization receiving no outside funds. The aims of the Society are to promote the science of ecology through research, publications and conferences and to use the findings of such research to educate the public and to influence policy decisions that involve ecological matters. The BES is an active and thriving organization with something to offer anyone with an interest in ecology. Academic journals, teaching resources, meetings for scientists and policy makers, career advice and grants for ecologists are first a few of the society's areas of activity.

BES Early Career Project Grants

Subjects: Ecology.
Purpose: To assist promising young ecologists by supporting innovative or important research of a pure or applied nature, and to provide an opportunity for ecologists recently appointed to academic posts to establish themselves.
Eligibility: Applicants must be in the early stages of their career and will normally be expected to have a PhD before applying. Must be a current BES member.
Type: Grant
Value: Up to UK £25,000
Frequency: Annual
Application Procedure: Applicants must complete an application form, available from the BES office. Application form available from BES and from website.

Closing Date: January 31st
No. of awards given last year: 6
No. of applicants last year: 39
Additional Information: Successful applicants will be expected to submit a brief report within 15 months of receipt of the award. Further information is available on request or from the website.

BES Overseas Bursary

Subjects: Ecology.
Purpose: To support ecologists from developing countries in undertaking innovative ecological research.
Eligibility: Be a scientist and a citizen or a country in Africa or its associated Islands. Have at least an MSc or equivalent degree. Be working at a university or research institution (including field centres NGO's museums etc) That provides basic research facilities. The research will be done in a developing country.
Level of Study: Professional development
Type: Grant
Value: Up to UK £7,000
Length of Study: 18 months
Frequency: Annual
Country of Study: Africa
Application Procedure: Applicants must complete an application form, available from the BES office. Further information is available on request and from the website. By application available from BES and BES website.
Closing Date: September 1st
Contributor: Education, Training and Careers Committee

BES Small Ecological Project and Ecological Project Support

Subjects: Ecological research and ecological survey.
Purpose: To promote all aspects of ecological research and ecological survey.
Eligibility: Open to ecological researchers. Support will not normally be given to projects forming part of an expedition proposal. All recipients will be required to submit a report on the work undertaken. (1) Must be a current BES member. (2) Must not be as part of a degree. (3) Applications require two referees. (4) UEPG's are given to an individual student who is responsible for completion of a report can be as part of an expedition but applicant has to take responsibility of completing own part of expedition.
Level of Study: Professional development
Type: Project grant
Value: Up to UK £1,000 for travel and up to UK £1,500 for other costs
Frequency: Annual
Country of Study: Any country
Application Procedure: Applicants must complete an application form, available from the BES office. The original form and seven copies must be submitted. Application form on website.
Closing Date: May 1st and December 1st
No. of awards given last year: 37
No. of applicants last year: 450
Additional Information: Published papers and reports to other organizations should include an acknowledgement of the support from the BES. Other conditions may apply. The Coalbourn Trust is an independent trust that looks to the BES to nominate suitable projects for funding. Recommendations for funding will be made from among the applicants for Small Ecological Project Grants. All applicants for Small Ecological Project Grants will automatically be eligible for funding from the Coalbourn Trust. Further information is available on request or from the website.

BES Specialist Course Grants

Subjects: Ecology.
Purpose: To help meet the costs of specialist field courses.
Eligibility: Open to postgraduates and recent graduates who are not in full-time employment. The Society will not fund applicants where a specialist course is a formal part of a credit-bearing programme eg. a degree, diploma, or certificate. There are a limited number of grants, which are allocated on a first-come first-served basis.
Level of Study: Graduate, postgraduate
Type: Grant
Value: The course fee, which may also include accommodation
Frequency: Annual
Country of Study: United Kingdom
Application Procedure: Applicants must complete an application form, available from the BES office. See the BES and the BES website.
Closing Date: As advertised in the Bulletin and on BES website
Additional Information: The Education, Training and Careers Committee decides upon the courses that will receive available grants. Successful applicants are bound by the booking conditions of the institution running the course, and non-attendance on a booked course will result in the applicants being personally liable for the cancellation fee. Grantees are required to produce a short report on the course. Further information is available from the website.

INTECOL-EURECO Attendance Funding

Subjects: Ecology.
Purpose: To aid attendance at the triennial European Ecological Congress and the INTECOL Congress.
Eligibility: Open to ecologists including students wishing to attend events co-sponsored by BES or for which the Society has elected to provide support. Preference is given to those individuals who are presenting a paper or poster at the conference. Must be a BES member.
Type: Travel grant
Application Procedure: Applicants must refer to the Bulletin, where the special application procedures are advertised. Application form available on BES website.
Closing Date: By closing dates for relevant conferences

Student Support for Attendance at BES and Specialist Group

Subjects: Ecology.
Purpose: To support students attending the Society's Winter and Annual General Meeting, Annual Symposium and Special Symposium.
Eligibility: Open to students. Applications must be endorsed by the student's Head of Department or research supervisor. Bulk applications on behalf of a group of students are not accepted. Undergraduates who at the time of the meeting will have graduated but not yet be enrolled on a postgraduate course and postgraduates. Unemployed post docs must be current BES member.
Level of Study: Graduate, postgraduate
Type: Grant
Value: 50 per cent of the cost of the registration fee plus meals and accommodation while at the meeting can only be claimed on a first-come first served basis on the online registration form
Frequency: Annual
No. of awards offered: Varies
Application Procedure: Applicants must complete an application form, available from the BES office. When all funds have been committed the price reduction for students will not be available on the online registration form.
Closing Date: By registration deadline of the Annual meeting. Other meetings are advertised in the Bulletin and on BES website
Additional Information: For a list of specialist group organized meeting please visit BES website. Registration procedure and form available online at the BES website.

Student Support Non-BES Meeting

Subjects: Ecology.
Purpose: To provide support to allow participants to attend meetings organized by the European congress on conservation science and the student conservation conference.
Eligibility: Eligibility is advertised in the Bulletin.
Level of Study: Postgraduate, research
Value: Travel and accommodation expenses for participants, who should be prepared to play a full part in the meetings, including the possibility of giving a seminar on their work
Frequency: Annual
Application Procedure: Application details can be found in each of the journals.
Closing Date: Advertised in the Bulletin

Additional Information: Courses will vary from year to year and will be advertised in the Bulletin and in the EEF Newsletter as and when details become available.

Travel Grants for Ecologists from Developing Countries to Attend BES Meetings

Subjects: Ecology.
Purpose: To make travel grants available to ecologists who wish to attend Society Annual meetings and Symposia within the UK.
Eligibility: Open to scientists and citizens of a country that is classified as low-income or low-middle-income economies.
Type: Grant
Value: UK £2,000
Country of Study: United Kingdom
Application Procedure: A completed application form along with supporting statements from the UK host institution and the applicant's institution should be submitted.
Closing Date: April 1st

BRITISH EYE RESEARCH FOUNDATION

Lincoln House, 75 Westminster Bridge Road, London, SE1 7HS, England
Tel: (44) 20 7928 7743
Fax: (44) 20 7928 7919
Email: info@berf.org.uk
Website: www.berf.org.uk
Contact: Cheif executive

Fight for sight the British Eye Research Foundation supports nationwide research into the prevention, treatment and cure of all forms of blindness and serious eye disorders, whether inherited, congenital or acquired. The Foundation also focuses on current needs by sponsoring screening programmes and helping ophthalmology departments purchase vital innovative equipment when funds are unavailable from other sources.

Fight for Sight, British Eye Research Foundation Grants for Research and Equipment (Ophthalmology)

Subjects: Ophthalmology.
Purpose: To prevent and cure blindness and serious eye disorders. To research into causes, diagnosis and prevention of blindness and treatment of eye disease.
Eligibility: Open to suitably qualified individuals. Applications must be submitted by qualified consultant ophthalmologists or equivalent for research under his or her supervision. Research projects can only take place in the United Kingdom.
Level of Study: Postgraduate, research, postdoctorate
Type: Grant
Value: As funds become available
Length of Study: Usually for a maximum of 3 years
Frequency: Annual
Country of Study: United Kingdom
No. of awards offered: Varies
Application Procedure: Applicants must submit six copies of the application form as well as supporting paperwork.
Funding: Commercial, private, trusts, individuals

BRITISH FEDERATION OF WOMEN GRADUATES (BFWG)

4 Mandeville Courtyard, 142 Battersea Park Road, London, SW11 4NB, England
Tel: (44) 20 7498 8037
Fax: (44) 20 7498 5213
Email: awards@bfwg.demon.co.uk
Website: www.bfwg.org.uk
Contact: Secretary

The British Federation of Women Graduates (BFWG) promotes women's opportunities in education and public life. BFWG works as part of an international organization to improve the lives of women and girls, fosters local, national and international friendship and offers scholarships for final-year postgraduate research.

AAUW Rose Sidgwick Memorial Fellowship

Subjects: All subjects.
Purpose: To assist with study or research that demonstrates a continued interest in the advancement of women.
Eligibility: Open to applicants who have earned the equivalent of a US bachelor's degree, are not US citizens, and are below 30 years of age. They must be studying in Great Britain and be members of BFWG.
Level of Study: Graduate, postgraduate, postdoctorate, research
Type: Fellowship
Value: From US$18,000–30,000. The fellowship does not cover travel costs
Length of Study: 1 year
Frequency: Annual
Study Establishment: An Institute of Higher Education
Country of Study: United States of America
No. of awards offered: 1
Application Procedure: Applicants studying in Great Britain must write to BFWG for details, enclosing a stamped addressed envelope. Information can also be downloaded from the website.
Closing Date: Early April
Funding: Private
Contributor: BFWG members
Additional Information: Recipients must submit a written report within 6 months of concluding the research.

AAUW/IFUW International Fellowships

Subjects: All subjects.
Purpose: To assist study or research that demonstrates a continued interest in the advancement of women.
Eligibility: Open to applicants who have earned the equivalent of a US bachelor's degree, are not US citizens and are members of IFUW/NFA.
Level of Study: Graduate, postdoctorate, research, postgraduate
Type: Fellowships
Value: From US$18,000–30,000. These fellowships do not cover travel costs
Length of Study: 1 year
Frequency: Annual
Study Establishment: An Institute of Higher Education
Country of Study: United Kingdom
No. of awards offered: 6
Application Procedure: Applicants must apply through their respective IFUW federation or association. Applicants studying in Great Britain should write to the BFWG for details, enclosing a stamped addressed envelope. A list of IFUW national federations can be sent on request or downloaded from the IFUW website, www.ifuw.org
Closing Date: December 15th in the year preceding the competition
Funding: Private
Contributor: AAUW members
Additional Information: A money order of US$20 must accompany all applications to be a member of an IFUW/NFA, applicants studying in Great Britain would need to be members of BFWG.

For further information contact:

AAUW Educational Foundation, Customer Service Centre, PO Box 4030, 2201 North Dodge Street, Iowa City, IA 52243-4030, United States of America
Website: aauw.org/fga/fellowships_grants/index.cfm
Contact: AAUW Fellowship Chair

AFFDU Jeanne Chaton Award

Subjects: Human rights and peace.
Purpose: To assist research on status of women, human rights and international contacts.
Eligibility: Open to female members of the BFWG or another international federation or association of the IFUW.
Level of Study: Predoctorate, postdoctorate, research
Type: Bursary
Value: €300–1,500

Length of Study: 3 months
Frequency: Annual
Study Establishment: An Institute of Higher Education
Country of Study: France
No. of awards offered: 1
Application Procedure: Application materials can be downloaded from AFFDU's website.
Closing Date: April 1st of the year preceding the competition
Funding: Private
Contributor: AFFDU members

For further information contact:

AFFDU, 4 Rue de Chevreuse, Paris, F-75006, France
Website: www.int-evry.fr/affdu

AFFDU Maryronne Stephan Award

Subjects: Agriculture.
Purpose: To assist research on agricultural management in the river area of Senegal.
Eligibility: Open to female members of an IFUW/NFA who speak French.
Level of Study: Postgraduate, research
Type: Bursary
Value: €300–1,500. The award does not cover travel costs
Length of Study: Up to 1 year
Frequency: Annual
Study Establishment: A university or institution of university status
Country of Study: Senegal
No. of awards offered: 1
Application Procedure: Application materials can be downloaded from AFFDU's website www.int.evry.fr/affdu
Closing Date: March 31st
Contributor: AFFDU members
Additional Information: To be a member of an IFUW/NFA applicants studying in Great Britain would need to be members of BFWG.

For further information contact:

AFFDU, 4 rue de Chevreuse, F-75006, Paris, France

AFUW Australian Capital Territory Bursary

Subjects: All subjects.
Purpose: To offer free board and lodging in Canberra.
Eligibility: Open to female graduate or final year honours students who are members of an IFUW/NFA.
Level of Study: Postgraduate, research
Type: Bursary
Value: Australian $1,000 onwards
Length of Study: 2 months
Frequency: Annual
Study Establishment: An Institute of Higher Education in Canberra
Country of Study: Australia
Application Procedure: Applicants must apply through their respective federation or association. Applicants studying in Great Britain should write for details from the BFGW enclosing a stamped addressed envelope. A list of IFUW national federations can be sent upon request or downloaded from the IFUW website www.afuw.org.au
Closing Date: July 31st of the year preceding the competition
Funding: Private
Contributor: AFUW members
Additional Information: Recipients must submit a written report within 6 months of concluding the bursary.

For further information contact:

AFUW-ACT Inc., GPO Box 1453, Canberra, ACT 2601, Australia
Fax: (61) 6125 5011
Email: reverett@netspace.net.au
Website: www.afuw.org.au
Contact: Fellowship Convenor

AFUW Georgina Sweet Fellowship

Subjects: All subjects.
Purpose: To support a female postgraduate student to undertake an advanced post-first degree.
Eligibility: Open to female candidates who are not Australian citizens and studying in Great Britain and are members of BFWG. Candidates must have started the 2nd year of research to which their application refers at the time of application and must be studying for 3 or more years. Taught Master's degrees do not count as research, although research undertaken for an MPhil may count on the assumption that it will be upgraded to a PhD.
Level of Study: Research, postgraduate
Type: Fellowship
Value: Australian $4,000 awards. The fellowship does not cover travel costs
Length of Study: 4–12 months
Frequency: Every 2 years
Study Establishment: A university or status
Country of Study: Australia
No. of awards offered: 1
Application Procedure: Applicants studying in Great Britain must write to BFWG for details, enclosing a stamped addressed envelope. Information can also be downloaded from the website www.bfwg.org.uk
Closing Date: Early April in the year preceding the competition
Funding: Private
Contributor: IFUW members
Additional Information: Recipients must submit a written report within 6 months of concluding their research.

AFUW Western Australian Bursaries

Subjects: Mathematics, science, humanities or social science.
Purpose: To assist in the completion of higher degree.
Eligibility: Open to female graduate members of BFWG or another national federation or association of the IFUW.
Level of Study: Research, postgraduate
Type: Bursary
Value: Australian $2,500–4,000. The bursaries do not cover travel costs
Length of Study: 4–12 months
Frequency: Annual
Study Establishment: An Institute of Higher Education in Western Australia
Country of Study: Australia
No. of awards offered: Varies
Application Procedure: Applicants must apply through their respective federation or association. Applicants studying in Great Britain should write for details from the BFWG, enclosing a stamped addressed envelope. A list of IFUW national federations can be sent upon request or downloaded from the IFUW website, www.ifuw.org
Funding: Private
Contributor: AFUW members
Additional Information: To be a member of IFUW/NFA, applicants studying in Great Britain would need to be members of BFWG.

For further information contact:

AFUW (WA), Inc., PO Box 48, Nedlands, WA 6909, Australia
Fax: (61) +61 8 9386 3570
Website: www.afuw.org.au
Contact: Bursary Liaison Officer

ASFDU/SVA International Fellowship

Subjects: All subjects.
Purpose: To support postgraduate study and research in Switzerland.
Eligibility: Open to female candidates who are members of an IFUW/NFA but do not live in Switzerland. Preference will be given to younger women starting their careers.
Level of Study: Research, postgraduate
Type: Scholarship
Value: Swiss francs 12,000
Length of Study: Up to 1 year
Frequency: Annual
Study Establishment: An Institute of Higher Education
Country of Study: Switzerland
No. of awards offered: 1

Application Procedure: Applicants must apply through their respective federation or association. Materials may be downloaded from ASFDU/SVA's website www.unifemmes.ch
Closing Date: Spring of the year preceding the competition
Funding: Private
Additional Information: Recipients must submit a written report within 6 months of concluding the research.

For further information contact:

AFFDU/SVA, Rue des Forgerons b, Fribourg, CH-1700, Swaziland
Tel: (268) 323 46 76
Website: www.unifemmes.ch
Contact: Fellowship Secretariat

BFWG Beryl Mavis Green Scholarship

Subjects: All subjects.
Purpose: To assist final-year postgraduate research.
Eligibility: Open to female candidates, regardless of nationality, whose studies take place in the United Kingdom. Research students should be in the final year of formal study towards a PhD degree. Taught Master's degrees do not count as research, although MPhil research students would need to be upgraded to a PhD during the dates of the competition.
Level of Study: Research, postgraduate
Type: Scholarship
Value: From UK £1,000
Frequency: Annual
Study Establishment: A university or institution of university status
Country of Study: United Kingdom
No. of awards offered: 1
Application Procedure: Applicants must write to BFWG for details enclosing a stamped addressed envelope or download information from the BFWG website.
Closing Date: Early April in the year of the competition
Funding: Private
Additional Information: Recipients must submit a written report within 6 months of concluding the research.

BFWG Eila Campbell Scholarship

Subjects: Geography.
Purpose: To assist final-year PhD research.
Eligibility: Open to female candidates, regardless of nationality, studying in Great Britain. Research students will be in the final year of formal study towards a PhD degree. Taught Master's degrees do not count as research, although MPhil research students would need to be upgraded to a PhD around the close of the competition.
Level of Study: Research, predoctorate
Type: Scholarship
Value: Up to UK £3,000
Length of Study: 1 year
Frequency: Annual
Study Establishment: A university or institution of university status
Country of Study: Great Britain
No. of awards offered: Normally 1
Application Procedure: Applicants studying in Great Britain must write to BFWG for details, enclosing a stamped addressed envelope, or download information from the BFWG website www.bfwg.org.uk
Closing Date: Early April for the academic year commencing in the Autumn
Funding: Private
Contributor: BFWG members
No. of awards given last year: 1
No. of applicants last year: 100
Additional Information: The competition opens on December 1st. Recipients must submit a written report within 6 months of being awarded their PhD.

BFWG Elen Vanstone Scholarship

Subjects: All subjects.
Purpose: To assist final-year postgraduate research.
Eligibility: Open to female candidates, regardless of nationality, whose studies take place in the United Kingdom. Research students will be in the final year of formal study towards a PhD degree. Taught Master's degrees do not count as research, although MPhil research students would need to be upgraded to a PhD during the dates of the competition.
Level of Study: Research, postgraduate
Type: Scholarship
Value: From UK £1,000
Frequency: Annual
Study Establishment: A university or institution of university status
Country of Study: United Kingdom
No. of awards offered: 1
Application Procedure: Applicants must write to BFWG for details, enclosing a stamped addressed envelope or download details from the BFWG website.
Closing Date: Early April in the year of the competition
Funding: Private
Additional Information: Recipients must submit a written report within 6 months of concluding the research.

BFWG J Barbara Northend Scholarship

Subjects: All subjects, although preference will be given to modern languages or computer studies.
Purpose: To assist final-year postgraduate research.
Eligibility: Open to female candidates, regardless of nationality, whose studies take place in Great Britain. Research students will be in the final year of formal study towards a PhD degree. Taught Master's degrees do not count as research though MPhil research students would need to be upgraded to PhD during the dates of the competition.
Type: Scholarship
Value: From UK £1,000
Frequency: Annual
Study Establishment: A university or institution of university status
Country of Study: Great Britain
No. of awards offered: 1
Application Procedure: Applicants studying in Great Britain must write to BFWG for details, enclosing a stamped addressed envelope, or download information from the BFWG website.
Closing Date: Early April in the year competition
Funding: Private
Additional Information: Recipients must submit a written report within 6 months of concluding the research.

BFWG Johnstone and Florence Stoney Studentship

Subjects: Biological, geological, meteorological or radiological science.
Purpose: To assist final-year PhD research.
Eligibility: Open to female candidates who are studying in Great Britain. Research students should be in the final year of formal study towards a PhD degree. Taught Master's degrees do not count as research, although MPhil research students would need to be upgraded to a PhD award the close of the competition.
Level of Study: Predoctorate, postgraduate, research
Type: Studentship
Value: Up to UK€3,000 the studentship does not cover travel costs
Frequency: Annual
Study Establishment: A university or institution of university status
No. of awards offered: Varies
Application Procedure: Applicants studying in Great Britain must write to BFWG for details, enclosing a stamped addressed envelope or download information from the BFWG website www.bfwg.org.uk
Closing Date: Early April for the academic year commencing in the Autumn
Funding: Private
Contributor: BFWG members
No. of awards given last year: 1
No. of applicants last year: 100
Additional Information: The competition opens on December 1st. The recipient must submit a written report within 6 months of being awarded their PhD.

BFWG Kathleen Hall Fellowship

Subjects: All subjects.
Purpose: To assist final-year PhD research students.

Eligibility: Open to female students from countries of low per capita income who are studying in Great Britain and who will be entering into their final year of formal study towards a PhD degree. Taught Master's degrees do not count as research, although MPhil research students would need to be upgraded to a PhD during the dates of the competition.
Level of Study: Predoctorate, research
Type: Fellowship
Value: Up to UK £3,000
Length of Study: 1 year
Frequency: Annual
Study Establishment: A university or institution of university status
Country of Study: United Kingdom
No. of awards offered: Normally 1
Application Procedure: Applicants must write to BFWG for details, enclosing a stamped addressed envelope or download information from the BFWG website www.bfwg.org.uk
Closing Date: Early April for the academic year commencing in the Autumn
Funding: Private
Contributor: BFWG members
No. of applicants last year: 100
Additional Information: The competition opens on December 1st. Recipients must submit a written report within 6 months of being awarded their PhD.

BFWG M H Joseph Prize

Subjects: Architecture or engineering.
Purpose: To assist final-year PhD research.
Eligibility: Open to female candidates who are studying in Great Britain. Research students should be in the final year of formal study towards a PhD degree. Taught Master's degrees do not count as research, although MPhil research students would need to be upgraded to a PhD around the close of the competition.
Level of Study: Predoctorate, research
Type: Prize
Value: Up to UK £3,000
Length of Study: 1 year
Frequency: Annual
Study Establishment: A university or institution of university status
Country of Study: United Kingdom
No. of awards offered: Normally 1
Application Procedure: Applicants must write to BFWG for details, enclosing a stamped addressed envelope or download information from the BFWG website www.bfwg.org.uk
Closing Date: Early April for the academic year commencing in the Autumn
Funding: Private
Contributor: BFWG members
No. of applicants last year: 100
Additional Information: The competition opens on December 1st. Recipients must submit a written report within 6 months of being awarded their PhD.

BFWG Margaret K B Day Scholarship

Subjects: All subjects.
Purpose: To assist final-year postgraduate research.
Eligibility: Open to female candidates regardless of nationality, whose studies take place in the United Kingdom. Research students should be in the final year of formal study towards a PhD degree. Taught Master's degrees do not count as research, although MPhil research students would need to be upgraded to a PhD during the dates of the competition.
Level of Study: Postgraduate, research
Type: Scholarship
Value: UK £1,000
Frequency: Annual
Study Establishment: A university or institution of university status
Country of Study: Great Britain
No. of awards offered: 1
Application Procedure: Applicants must write to BFWG for details, enclosing a stamped addressed envelope or download information from the BFWG website.
Closing Date: Early April in the year of the competition
Funding: Private
Additional Information: Recipients must submit a written report within 6 months of concluding the research.

BFWG Marjorie Shaw Scholarship

Subjects: All subjects.
Purpose: To assist final-year postgraduate research.
Eligibility: Open to female candidates, regardless of nationality, whose studies take place in the United Kingdom. Research students should be in the final year of formal study towards a PhD degree. Taught Master's degrees do not count as research, although MPhil research students would need to be upgraded to a PhD during the dates of the competition.
Level of Study: Postgraduate, research
Type: Scholarship
Value: UK £1,000
Frequency: Annual
Study Establishment: A university or institution of university status
Country of Study: United Kingdom
No. of awards offered: 1
Application Procedure: Applicants must write to BFWG for details enclosing a stamped addressed envelope or download details from the BFWG website.
Closing Date: Early April in the year of the competition
Funding: Private
Additional Information: Recipients must submit a written report within 6 months of concluding the research.

BFWG Mary Bradburn Scholarship

Subjects: Mathematics.
Purpose: To assist final-year postgraduate research.
Eligibility: Open to female candidates, regardless of nationality, whose studies take place in the United Kingdom. Research students should be in the final year of formal study towards a PhD degree in mathematics. Taught Master's degrees do not count as research, although MPhil research students would need to be upgraded to a PhD during the dates of the competition.
Level of Study: Postgraduate, research
Type: Scholarship
Value: UK £1,000
Frequency: Annual
Study Establishment: A university or institution of university status
Country of Study: United Kingdom
No. of awards offered: 1
Application Procedure: Applicants must write to BFWG for details enclosing a stamped addressed envelope or download details from the BFWG website.
Closing Date: Early April in the year of the competition
Funding: Private
Additional Information: Recipients must submit a written report within 6 months of concluding the research.

BFWG Ruth Bowden Scholarship

Subjects: Medical sciences.
Purpose: To assist final-year PhD research.
Eligibility: Open to female students who are studying in their final year of formal study towards a PhD degree at a university in Great Britain. Taught Master's degrees do not count as research, although MPhil research students would need to be upgraded to a PhD around the close of the competition.
Level of Study: Predoctorate, research
Type: Scholarship
Value: Up to UK £3,000
Length of Study: 1 year
Frequency: Annual
Study Establishment: A university or institution of university status
Country of Study: United Kingdom
No. of awards offered: Normally 1
Application Procedure: Applicants must write to BFWG for details enclosing a stamped addressed envelope or download details from the BFWG website www.bfwg.org.uk

Closing Date: Early April for the academic year commencing in the Autumn
Funding: Private
Contributor: BFWG members
No. of awards given last year: 1
No. of applicants last year: 100
Additional Information: The competition opens on December 1st. Recipients must submit a written report within 6 months of being awarded their PhD.

BFWG Scholarships

Subjects: Research in any discipline.
Purpose: To assist final-year PhD research.
Eligibility: Academic excellence as evidenced by a proven ability to carry out independent research is the chief criterion. Open to female candidates, regardless of nationality, whose studies take place in Great Britain. Research students should be in the final year of formal study towards a PhD degree. Taught Master's degrees do not count as research, although MPhil research students would need to be upgraded to a PhD during the dates of the competition.
Level of Study: Predoctorate, research
Type: Scholarship
Value: Up to UK £3,000
Frequency: Annual
Study Establishment: A university or institution of university status
Country of Study: United Kingdom
No. of awards offered: 1–8
Application Procedure: Applicants must write to BFWG for details, enclosing a stamped addressed envelope or download information from the BFWG website www.bfwg.org.uk
Closing Date: Early April in the year of the competition
Funding: Private
Contributor: BFWG members
No. of awards given last year: 7
No. of applicants last year: 100
Additional Information: Recipients must submit a written report within 6 months of being awarded their PhD. The BFWG scholarships include the Mary Bradburn, Margaret KB Day, Beryl Maris Green, J Barbara North end, Marjorie Shaw and Elen Wynne Vanstone Scholarships.

IAUW International Scholarship

Subjects: Arts and humanities, jewish area and cultural studies, international law.
Purpose: To foster friendly relations between university women in Israel and abroad.
Eligibility: Open to female candidates who are postgraduates and are members of an IFUW/NFA.
Level of Study: Postgraduate, research
Type: Scholarship
Value: US$3,000 onwards
Length of Study: Up to 1 year
Frequency: Dependent on funds available
Study Establishment: An Institute of Higher Education
Country of Study: Israel
No. of awards offered: 1
Application Procedure: Application materials can be downloaded from IAUW's website www.ifuw.org
Closing Date: July 31st of the year preceding the competition
Funding: Private
Contributor: IAVW members
Additional Information: Recipients must submit a written report within 6 months of concluding the research.

For further information contact:

IAUW, PO Box 7505, Jerusalem, 91074, Israel
Fax: (972) 35 353185
Website: www.ifuw.org/israel
Contact: Chairwoman Fellowship Committee

IFUW International Fellowships

Subjects: All subjects.
Purpose: To assist research, study or training.
Eligibility: Open to female members of BFWG or another national federation or association of the IFUW.
Level of Study: Doctorate, research, predoctorate
Type: Fellowship
Value: Varies. The awards do not cover travel costs
Length of Study: Up to 12 months
Frequency: Every 3 years
Study Establishment: An Institute of Higher Education
Country of Study: Any country
No. of awards offered: Up to 8
Application Procedure: Applicants studying in Great Britain should write for details to BFWG, enclosing a stamped addressed envelope. Information can also be downloaded from the website.
Closing Date: Early April in the year preceding the competition
Funding: Private
Contributor: IFUW/NFA members
Additional Information: Recipients must submit a written report within 6 months of concluding their research.

IFUWA Amy Rustomjee International Scholarship

Subjects: All subjects.
Purpose: To offer free accommodation undertaking advanced research in Mumbai.
Eligibility: Open to female candidates with postgraduate degrees and proof of ability to carry out research in Mumbai.
Type: Scholarship
Value: A stipend. The scholarship does not cover travel costs
Length of Study: Up to 1 year
Frequency: Annual
Study Establishment: A university or institution of university status
Country of Study: India
No. of awards offered: 1
Application Procedure: Application materials can be downloaded from IFUWA's website www.ifuw.org/india
Funding: Private
Contributor: IFUWA members
Additional Information: To be a member of an IFUW/NFA applicants studying in Great Britain would need to be members of BFWG.

For further information contact:

Scholarship Committee, Women Graduate Union, Union Road, Colaba, Mumbai, 400 005, India
Contact: Chairman

IFUWA Sarojini Naidu Memorial Scholarship

Subjects: Area and cultural studies, arts and cultural studies, arts and humanities.
Purpose: To foster better international understanding and to promote studies on Indian culture and other areas.
Eligibility: Open to female members of the BFWG or another international federation or association of the IFUW.
Level of Study: Postgraduate, research
Type: Scholarship
Value: Indian rupees 600 per month
Length of Study: 12 months
Frequency: Annual
Study Establishment: An Institute of Higher Education
Country of Study: India
No. of awards offered: 1
Application Procedure: Materials can be downloaded from IFUWA's website www.ifuw.org/India
Closing Date: July 31st of the year preceding the competition
Funding: Private
Contributor: IFUWA members
Additional Information: Recipients must submit a written report within 6 months of concluding the research.

For further information contact:

Scholarship Committee, University Women's Association of Delhi, 6 Bhagwandas Road, New Delhi, 110 001, India
Website: www.ifuw.org/india
Contact: Chairman

JAUW International Fellowship

Subjects: All subjects.
Purpose: To assist independent research or advanced study in Japan.
Eligibility: Open to female candidates who are members of BFWG or another national federation or association of the IFUW. Candidates must have started the 2nd year of research to which their application refers at the time of the application and must be studying for 3 or more years. Taught Master's degrees do not count as research, although research undertaken for an MPhil may count on the assumption that it will be upgraded to a PhD.
Level of Study: Research, postgraduate
Type: Fellowship
Value: Yen 600,000–1,000,000. The fellowships do not cover travel costs
Length of Study: 3 months minimum
Frequency: Annual
Study Establishment: An Institute of Higher Education
Country of Study: Japan
No. of awards offered: 2
Application Procedure: Information can be downloaded from the BFWG's website, www.bfwg.org.uk
Closing Date: Early April in the year preceding the competition
Funding: Private
Contributor: JAUW members
Additional Information: Recipients must submit a written report within 6 months of concluding the research.

For further information contact:

BFWG, 4 Mandeville Courtyard, 142 Battersea Park Road, London, SW11 4NB

NKA Ellen Gleditsch Scholarship

Subjects: All subjects.
Purpose: To assist independent research or advanced studies.
Eligibility: Open to female members of the BFWG or another national federation or association of the IFUW. Candidates must have started the 2nd year of research to which their application refers at the time of application and must be studying for 3 or more years. Taught Master's degrees do not count as research, although research undertaken for an MPhil may count on the assumption that it will be upgraded to a PhD.
Level of Study: Research, doctorate, postdoctorate
Type: Scholarship
Value: Norwegian krone 40,000
Length of Study: 3–4 months
Frequency: Every 3 years
Study Establishment: An Institute of Higher Education
Country of Study: Norway
No. of awards offered: 1
Application Procedure: Applicants studying in the Great Britain should write to BFWG for details, enclosing a stamped addressed envelope. Information can also be downloaded from the website.
Closing Date: Early April in the year preceding the competition
Funding: Private
Additional Information: Recipients must submit a written report within 6 months of concluding their research.

For further information contact:

BFWG, 4 Manderille Court Yard, 142 Battersea Park Road, London, SW11 4NB, United Kingdom

SAAWG International Fellowship

Subjects: All subjects.
Purpose: To enable a non-South African postgraduate female student to undertake research in South Africa.
Eligibility: Open to postgraduate women who are members of IFUW/NFA.
Level of Study: Postgraduate, research
Type: Fellowship
Value: Rand 2,500
Length of Study: 1 year
Frequency: Every 3 years
Study Establishment: An Institute of Higher Education
Country of Study: South Africa
No. of awards offered: 1
Application Procedure: Applicants must apply through their respective federation or association. Applicants studying in the United Kingdom should write to BFWG for details, enclosing a stamped addressed envelope. A list of IFUW national federations can be sent upon request or downloaded from the IFUW website.
Closing Date: August 31st of the year preceding the competition
Funding: Private
Contributor: SAAWG members
Additional Information: Recipients must submit a written report within 6 months of concluding the research.

For further information contact:

PO Box 1879, Bedfordview 2008, Gauteng, South Africa
Fax: (27) 11 453 0025
Website: www.ifuw.org
Contact: Fellowship Secretariat

BRITISH HEART FOUNDATION (BHF)

14 Fitzhardinge Street, London, W1H 6DH, England
Tel: (44) 20 7935 0185
Fax: (44) 20 7486 5820
Email: internet@bhf.org.uk
Website: www.bhf.org.uk
Contact: Ms Valerie Mason, Research Funds Manager

The British Heart Foundation (BHF) exists to encourage research into the causes, diagnosis, prevention and advances of cardiovascular disease, to inform doctors throughout the country of advances in the diagnosis, cure and treatment of heart diseases, and to improve facilities for the treatment of heart patients where the National Health Service is unable to help.

Basic Science Lectureships

Subjects: Cardiovascular.
Purpose: To enable non-clinical researchers who have shown outstanding ability in carrying out original and independent research to undertake a five year programme of research in the UK.
Eligibility: Open to applicants from the EEA who hold a PhD degree and have at least three years post doctoral research experience.
Level of Study: Professional development
Type: Fellowship
Value: Varies
Length of Study: Five years
Frequency: Annual
Study Establishment: University
Country of Study: United Kingdom
No. of awards offered: Varies
Application Procedure: Complete the appropriate form with a detailed research proposal, full curriculum vitae and letter of support from the head of department. Shortlisted applicants will normally be interviewed.
Closing Date: Varies
Funding: Trusts, government, private, corporation, individuals
No. of awards given last year: 2
No. of applicants last year: 11

BHF Clinical PhD Studentships

Purpose: For medically qualified candidates to obtain a PhD degree.
Eligibility: Candidates must be medically registered and members of the EEA.
Level of Study: Doctorate
Value: Varies
Length of Study: Three years
Frequency: Every three months
Study Establishment: Universities and medical schools
Country of Study: United Kingdom

Application Procedure: Complete the appropriate application form attaching a full research proposal, curriculum vitae and supporting letter from the head of department.
Closing Date: Varies
Funding: Individuals, government, corporation, trusts, private
No. of awards given last year: 10
No. of applicants last year: 22

BHF Clinical Science Fellowships

Subjects: The cardiovascular system.
Purpose: To enable training for clinicians who have demonstrated an interest in, and outstanding potential for academic clinical research.
Eligibility: Open to applicants from the European Economic Area. Who have completed their basic specialist training and obtained a PhD or MD.
Level of Study: Professional development
Type: Fellowship
Value: This award reimburses for salary commensurate with seniority within the health service and carries a consumables allowance of up to UK £10,000 per year. The salary of a technician may also be requested for up to three years
Length of Study: Four years
Frequency: Every three months
Study Establishment: University of medical school
Country of Study: United Kingdom
No. of awards offered: Varies
Application Procedure: Applicants must submit the appropriate form with the approval of the head of department. The application must include a full research protocol and/or training programme together with the curriculum vitae of the proposed Fellow. Short-listed applicants will normally be required to attend an interview. Application forms and further information are available on request.
Closing Date: Details are available on request
Funding: Corporation, government, individuals, private, trusts

BHF Intermediate Research Fellowships

Subjects: Basic or applied clinical cardiology.
Purpose: To enable highly qualified independent researchers to pursue their research objectives.
Eligibility: Open to applicants from the European Economic Area. Who have a PhD or MD and have been engaged in post-doctoral research for at least two years.
Level of Study: Professional development
Type: Fellowship
Value: A salary commensurate with seniority within the university or NHS scale. Up to UK £10,000 per year may be applied for to cover running expenses. Running expenses must be fully justified
Length of Study: Up to 3 years
Frequency: Every three months
Study Establishment: Universities and medical schools
Country of Study: United Kingdom
No. of awards offered: Varies
Application Procedure: Applicants must submit the appropriate form, with the approval of the head of department. The application must include a full research protocol together with the curriculum vitae of the Fellow.
Closing Date: Details are available on request
Funding: Individuals, corporation, trusts, government, private
No. of awards given last year: 9
No. of applicants last year: 30
Additional Information: These fellowships are unlikely to be awarded to those who are unable to obtain advancement within the health services.

BHF International Fellowships

Subjects: Cardiology.
Purpose: To support experienced clinical and non-clinical researchers who wish to undertake a research project in an approved center outside the UK.
Eligibility: Open to applicants with an MD or PhD degree and 2 years, post-doctoral experience.
Level of Study: Professional development
Type: Fellowship
Value: Salary and one advance booking economy return travel fare.
Length of Study: 1 year-renewable
Frequency: Annual
Study Establishment: Approved research centre
Country of Study: Any country
Application Procedure: A completed application form and a detailed research proposal to be submitted.
Closing Date: Varies
Funding: Individuals, trusts, government, private, corporation
No. of awards given last year: 1
No. of applicants last year: 4

BHF Junior Research Fellowships

Subjects: Basic or applied clinical cardiology.
Purpose: To enable individuals to be trained in academic research.
Eligibility: Open to applicants from the European Economic Area who wish to be trained in academic research under the direct supervision of senior and experienced research workers.
Level of Study: Postdoctorate, postgraduate
Type: Fellowship
Value: A salary, not higher than the top of the registrar scale or equivalent, and up to UK £7,000 per year to cover running expenses
Length of Study: 2 years, but subject to review at the end of the 1st year, dependent on the Foundation's approval and upon the head of department submitting a progress report on the candidate's work to date
Frequency: Every three months
Study Establishment: Universities and medical schools
Country of Study: United Kingdom
No. of awards offered: Varies
Application Procedure: Applicants must submit the appropriate form completed by the planned supervisor and with the approval of the head of department. The application must include a full research protocol together with the curriculum vitae of the proposed Fellow.
Closing Date: Details are available on request
Funding: Private, corporation, government, individuals, trusts
No. of awards given last year: 18
No. of applicants last year: 56

BHF MBPhd Studentships

Subjects: Cardiovascular Research.
Purpose: To obtain a PhD degree.
Eligibility: Open to UK institutions which participate in MBPhD programmes for named candidates only who hold a first class or upper second class honours degree. Candidates should have undertaken their pre-clinical training in the UK and have completed an intercalated BSc.
Level of Study: Postgraduate
Type: Fellowship
Value: BHF stipend rate, university fees and up to £7,000 a year for fully justified research consumables
Length of Study: Up to three years
Frequency: Every three months
Study Establishment: Universities and medical schools
Country of Study: United Kingdom
No. of awards offered: Varies
Application Procedure: Applicants must submit the appropriate form and attach a detailed research protocol, curriculum vitae of the candidate, references and a letter of support from the faculty tutor.
Closing Date: Varies
Funding: Private, individuals, trusts, government, corporation

BHF Overseas Visiting Fellowships

Subjects: Basic or applied clinical cardiology.
Purpose: To enable senior overseas research workers to undertake research in the United Kingdom.
Eligibility: Open to established research workers of proven outstanding talent who are able to contribute to the work of the host department.
Level of Study: Professional development
Type: Fellowship
Value: The Fellow's salary and up to UK £7,000 per year as a contribution towards research expenses. The applicant must confirm that

no additional financial support is necessary in order to carry out the project. Application may be made for funds to cover one economy return travel fare for the Fellow
Length of Study: Up to 2 years
Frequency: Every three months
Study Establishment: A recognized research centre in the United Kingdom
Country of Study: United Kingdom
No. of awards offered: Varies
Application Procedure: Applications must be made by the head of department in the United Kingdom institution on behalf of the Fellow and should include a full research protocol. The role of the Visiting Fellow in the research should be clearly stated. A curriculum vitae of the proposed Fellow and two letters of recommendation from the Fellow's country of origin should be included, and a brief curriculum vitae of the main collaboration in the host department with a letter of support from the head of the department in the UK.
Closing Date: Details are available on request
Funding: Private, trusts, government, individuals, corporation
No. of awards given last year: 1
No. of applicants last year: 1
Additional Information: These fellowships are not given for training.

BHF PhD Studentships

Subjects: Basic or applied clinical cardiology.
Purpose: To enable graduates to proceed to a PhD degree.
Eligibility: Open to candidates who have obtained the minimum of an Upper Second Class (Honours) Degree and who are from the European Economic Area.
Level of Study: Doctorate
Type: Studentship
Value: The level of the stipend is set by the BHF. Applicants may apply for funds to cover university fees. Up to UK £7,000 per year may also be applied for to cover research consumables
Length of Study: 3 years
Frequency: Every three months
Study Establishment: An appropriate university
Country of Study: United Kingdom
No. of awards offered: Varies
Application Procedure: Applications must be made by heads of department and may be made for named or unnamed candidates, although priority will be given to named candidates. Applications must be made on the appropriate form and must include a full research protocol, curriculum vitae of the candidate, two letters of reference and supporting letter from the head of department.
Closing Date: Details are available on request
Funding: Individuals, government, trusts, private, corporation
No. of awards given last year: 45
No. of applicants last year: 81

BHF Programme Grants

Subjects: Cardiovascular research.
Purpose: For long term support on a five year rolling basis.
Eligibility: Applicants from the European economic area who should be senior researchers.
Level of Study: Postdoctorate
Value: Varies
Length of Study: Five years
Frequency: Every three months
Study Establishment: Universities and medical schools
Country of Study: United Kingdom
No. of awards offered: Varies
Application Procedure: Relevant application form following approval of a preliminary outline proposal.
Closing Date: Varies
Funding: Corporation, individuals, trusts, private, government
No. of awards given last year: 9
No. of applicants last year: 33
Additional Information: See www.bhf.org.uk

BHF Project Grants

Subjects: Cardiology.
Purpose: To support short-term research projects.
Eligibility: Open to all post-doctoral researchers.
Level of Study: Postdoctorate, predoctorate
Type: Grant
Value: Grants may cover salaries, research consumables and equipment
Length of Study: Up to 3 years
Frequency: No closing dates
Study Establishment: Any approved research establishment
Country of Study: United Kingdom
Application Procedure: A completed application form and a detailed research proposal must be submitted.
Closing Date: No closing dates
Funding: Individuals, government, private, trusts, corporation
No. of awards given last year: 132
No. of applicants last year: 310
Additional Information: See www.bhf.org.uk

BHF Research Awards

Subjects: Cardiovascular research.
Purpose: To encourage and support research.
Eligibility: Open to applicants from the European Economic Area.
Level of Study: Postdoctorate
Value: Varies
Length of Study: Varies
Frequency: Varies
Study Establishment: Universities and medical schools
Country of Study: United Kingdom
No. of awards offered: Dependent on funding
Application Procedure: Applicants must write for details. Relevant application form must be completed.
Closing Date: Varies, according to the committee
Funding: Trusts, corporation, private, individuals, government
No. of awards given last year: 244
No. of applicants last year: 730
Additional Information: An annual report is available upon request. See www.bhf.org.uk

BHF Senior Research Fellowships

Subjects: Basic or applied clinical cardiology.
Purpose: To enable researchers with an international reputation of outstanding ability to pursue their research interests.
Eligibility: Open to applicants from the European Economic Area. The applicant should have been engaged in original research for at least 2 years and have published results, and should show outstanding ability both in original thought and practical application. This ability should already have been recognized outside the applicant's institution by invitations to talk to societies both at home and abroad. The applicant's career plans should be academic medicine and research. Senior Research Fellowships are awarded to those thought likely to gain a tennured chair or readership within five to eight years.
Level of Study: Professional development
Type: Fellowship
Value: Salary is commensurate with seniority within the university and health service plus rsearch consumables and items of equipment
Length of Study: Five years
Frequency: Annual
Study Establishment: University or medical school
Country of Study: United Kingdom
No. of awards offered: Varies
Application Procedure: Applicants must complete the appropriate form and submit this, with the approval of the head of department, together with a full research protocol and curriculum vitae of the proposed Fellow. Short-listed applicants will be required to attend an interview.
Closing Date: Details are available on request
Funding: Trusts, individuals, government, private
No. of awards given last year: 2
No. of applicants last year: 5
Additional Information: A Senior Research Fellow may apply to the Committee for a second 5-year period by the end of which it would be expected that the Fellow would have secured a permanent and more senior position. In this case an interview will be required.

BHF Travelling Fellowships (To and from UK)

Subjects: Basic or applied clinical cardiology.
Purpose: To enable established research workers to undertake research abroad, or acquire special knowledge that would assist them in their research after their return, or to enable heads of departments in the UK to invite a names researcher from overseas to train members of the department in a new research technique.
Eligibility: Applicants should be established research workers of proven outstanding talent.
Level of Study: Professional development
Type: Fellowship
Value: The proposed Fellow may apply for funds to cover the cost of economy travel and a reasonable subsistence allowance at the place of work. It is expected that the Fellow's salary would continue to be paid by the university or institution during his or her absence abroad
Length of Study: Up to 6 months
Frequency: Every three months
Study Establishment: University or medical school
Country of Study: Outside the United Kingdom
No. of awards offered: Varies
Application Procedure: Applicants must submit the appropriate form together with details of the purpose of the visit and what the Fellow expects to gain as a result of the visit. The applicant's curriculum vitae and a letter of acceptance by the host institution must be included in the application.
Closing Date: Details are available on request
Funding: Corporation, individuals, government, private, trusts
No. of awards given last year: 3
No. of applicants last year: 3

BRITISH INSTITUTE IN EASTERN AFRICA

PO Box 30710, Nairobi, GPO 00100, Kenya
Tel: (254) 020 43 43330/43190
Fax: (254) 020 43 43365
Email: bieanairobi@africaonline.co.uk
Contact: Dr Paul Lane, Director

The British Institute in Eastern Africa encourages research by individual scholars in African archaeology, history and cognate fields, and works closely with the universities, museums and antiquities services of the East African countries. It is based in Nairobi where it maintains a centre for field research and a comprehensive reference library.

British Institute in Eastern Africa Graduate Attachments

Subjects: Pre-colonial history and archaeology in East Africa through field research.
Purpose: To provide opportunities for recent graduates in history, archaeology, anthropology and related disciplines to gain practical field experience in East Africa.
Eligibility: Open to citizens of East African countries, the United Kingdom and the Commonwealth who are over 21 years of age. Candidates should have a Bachelor of Arts degree or equivalent and graduate training in African studies, archaeology, social anthropology or African history.
Level of Study: Postgraduate
Value: Varies
Length of Study: 3–6 months
Frequency: Annual
Study Establishment: The British Institute in Eastern Africa
No. of awards offered: Varies
Application Procedure: Applicants must submit a letter of application to the Director with the names of two academic referees and a curriculum vitae.
Closing Date: May 15th
Funding: Government
No. of awards given last year: 9
No. of applicants last year: 47
Additional Information: Small grants and assistance may be offered on a discretionary basis to scholars of other nationalities. Archaeology students may be required to assist in excavation carried out by the Institute's staff. Details of activities are published in the *Archaeology Abroad* bulletin and in the Institute's annual report, copies of which are available on request.

British Institute in Eastern Africa Research Grants

Subjects: Humanities and social sciences with some emphasis on archaeology, African history, anthropology and related subjects.
Purpose: To assist scholars undertaking original research in Eastern Africa in any field of the humanities and social sciences.
Eligibility: Open to scholars undertaking original research in East Africa and in any area of humanities or social sciences. Priority will be given to research on the urban history of East Africa and research on areas bordering Victoria Nyanza focusing on settlement history and the use of space, environmental history, management and technology and style and exchange.
Level of Study: Postgraduate
Value: Up to UK £1,000 for Minor Research Grants. Grants are normally awarded as contributions towards research costs and do not include institutional overheads or any stipendiary element
Frequency: Dependent on funds available
Study Establishment: The British Institute in Eastern Africa
No. of awards offered: Varies
Application Procedure: Applicants must submit both references and grant applications on the same form to the Director. Application forms can be obtained from the Director from June 1st onwards. It is the applicant's responsibility to ensure that references are received by the Director before the deadline dates for each grant and to send a copy of their completed application to the referees. All application forms and references must be received by the set deadlines. Late applications will not be considered after that date and late references will put the applicant at a serious disadvantage.
Closing Date: November 30th and May 30th for Minor Research Grants
Funding: Government
No. of awards given last year: 10
No. of applicants last year: 19
Additional Information: Applicants must contact the Director for further information on relevant topics likely to receive support. Those awarded grants will be required to keep the Institute regularly informed of the progress of their research, to provide a preliminary statement of accounts within 18 months of the award dates and to provide the Institute with copies of all relevant publications. They are encouraged to discuss with the Director the possibility of publishing their results in the Institute's journal, *Azania*. Results for the Minor Grants Award may be expected within 2 months of either May 30th or November 30th. Those awarded grants are required to become members of the BIEA.

For further information contact:

Email: pjlane@insightkenya.com

BRITISH JOURNAL OF SURGERY

John Wiley & Sons Limited, The Atrium, Southern Gate, Chichester, West Sussex, PO19 8SQ, England
Tel: (44) 1243 770384
Fax: (44) 1243 770460
Email: bjs@wiley.co.uk
Website: www.bjssoc.com
Contact: The Editor

British Journal of Surgery Research Bursaries

Subjects: Surgical research.
Purpose: To further surgical research.
Level of Study: Postgraduate
Type: Grant
Value: UK £10,000
Frequency: Annual
No. of awards offered: Up to 3
Application Procedure: Applicants must visit the website for application details.
Closing Date: July 31st
Funding: Private
Contributor: The British Journal of Surgery Society

BRITISH LEPROSY RELIEF ASSOCIATION (LEPRA)

28 Middle Borough, Colchester, England, Essex, CO1 1TG, United Kingdom
Tel: (44) 12 0656 2286
Fax: (44) 12 0676 2151
Email: lepra@lepra.org.uk
Website: www.lepra.org.uk
Contact: Ms Debbie Sharp, Programmes Department

The British Leprosy Relief Association (LEPRA) is a medical development charity that works to restore health, hope and dignity to those affected by leprosy.

LEPRA Grants

Subjects: Leprosy.
Purpose: To encourage and support research that is directly relevant to the understanding, prevention and care of leprosy.
Level of Study: Postgraduate
Type: Grant
Value: Dependent on funds available and the nature of the research or training
Length of Study: Up to 3 years
Frequency: Dependent on funds available
Study Establishment: As appropriate to the nature of the research or training
Country of Study: Any country
No. of awards offered: Varies
Application Procedure: Applicants must complete a research application pack, available on request. Applications must be submitted using the appropriate forms and should observe the time scales involved in the approval process.
Closing Date: Applications are accepted at any time

BRITISH LIBRARY-MAP LIBRARY

96 Euston Road, London, NW1 2DB, England
Tel: (44) 20 7412 7702
Fax: (44) 20 7412 7780
Email: maps@bl.uk
Website: www.maphistory.info/wallis.html
Contact: Mr Peter Barber, Map Librarian

Helen Wallis Fellowship

Subjects: The history of cartography, preferably with an international dimension.
Purpose: To promote the extended and complementary use of the British Library's book and cartographic collections in historical investigation.
Eligibility: Applicants should write for details.
Level of Study: Postdoctorate
Type: Fellowship
Value: Up to UK £300
Length of Study: 6 months–1 year
Frequency: Annual
Study Establishment: British Library, London
Country of Study: United Kingdom
No. of awards offered: 1
Application Procedure: Applicants must submit a letter indicating the proposed period and outlining the research project together with a full curriculum vitae and the names of three references.
Closing Date: May 1st
Funding: Private
No. of awards given last year: 1
Additional Information: The award honours the memory of Dr Helen Wallis, OBE (1924–1995), Map Librarian at the British Museum and then the British Library between the years 1967–1986. Further information can be found on the website.

BRITISH LUNG FOUNDATION

73-75 Goswell Road, London, EC1V 7ER, England
Tel: (44) 20 7688 5555
Fax: (44) 20 7688 5556
Email: blf@britishlungfoundation.com
Website: www.lunguk.org
Contact: Julia Heidsta, Research Manager

The British Lung Foundation provides information to the public on lung conditions and all aspects of lung health. The Foundation provides support to those who live with a lung condition every day of their lives through the Breathe Easy Club, a nationwide network of local voluntary support groups, and finds solutions to lung disease by funding world-class medical research.

British Lung Foundation Project Grants

Subjects: Respiratory diseases.
Purpose: To promote medical research into the prevention, diagnosis and treatment of all types of lung diseases.
Eligibility: Open to graduates working within the United Kingdom who have relevant research experience. The principal applicant must be based in a research centre in the United Kingdom.
Level of Study: Professional development, postgraduate, postdoctorate, doctorate, predoctorate, research
Type: Project grant
Value: Up to UK £120,000
Length of Study: Up to 3 years
Frequency: Annual
Study Establishment: An approved research centre
Country of Study: United Kingdom
No. of awards offered: Approx. 10
Application Procedure: Applicants must complete an application form, available from the British Lung Foundation.
Closing Date: Spring, for preliminary applications for awards in October
Funding: Private, commercial
Contributor: Voluntary donations
No. of awards given last year: Approx. 10
No. of applicants last year: 132

BRITISH MEDICAL ASSOCIATION (BMA)

Board of Science & Education, Tavistock Square, London, WC1H 9JP, England
Tel: (44) 20 7383 6755
Fax: (44) 20 7383 6383
Email: info.sciencegrants@bma.org.uk
Website: www.bma.org.uk
Contact: Emily Hoy, Research Grants Executive

The British Medical Association (BMA) is a professional association of doctors, representing their interests and providing services for its 128,000 plus members. It is an independent trade union, a scientific and educational body and a publishing house.

Albert McMaster Research Grant

Subjects: Research into the causes of blindness.
Purpose: To assist and support research.
Eligibility: Members of the BMA only.
Level of Study: Research
Type: Research grant
Value: Approx. UK £4,000
Length of Study: 3 years
Frequency: Every 2 years
Country of Study: United Kingdom
No. of awards offered: 1
Application Procedure: Applicants must complete an application form.
Closing Date: Mid-March
Funding: Private
No. of awards given last year: 1
Additional Information: Grants are advertised in January, on the BMA website and in the *British Medical Journal*.

Charlotte Eyck Research Grant
Subjects: Kidney research.
Purpose: To assist and support research.
Eligibility: Registered medical practitioners in the United Kingdom.
Level of Study: Research
Type: Research grant
Value: Approx. UK £8,500
Length of Study: 3 years
Frequency: Every 2 years
Country of Study: United Kingdom
No. of awards offered: 1
Application Procedure: Applicants must complete an application form.
Closing Date: Mid-March
Funding: Private
No. of awards given last year: None
Additional Information: Grants are advertised in January, on the BMA website and in the *British Medical Journal.*

Doris Hillier Research Grant
Subjects: Research into rheumatism and arthritis (and every 3rd year into Parkinson's disease).
Purpose: To assist and support research.
Eligibility: Open to registered medical practitioners in the United Kingdom.
Level of Study: Research
Type: Research grant
Value: Approx. UK £20,000
Length of Study: 3 years
Frequency: Annual
Country of Study: United Kingdom
No. of awards offered: 1
Application Procedure: Applicants must complete an application form.
Closing Date: Mid-March
Funding: Private
No. of awards given last year: 1
Additional Information: Grants are advertised in January, on the BMA website and in the *British Medical Journal.*

H C Roscoe Research Grant
Subjects: Research into the common cold and/or other viral diseases of the human respiratory system.
Purpose: To assist and support research.
Eligibility: Open to members of the BMA and non-medical scientists working in association with a BMA member.
Level of Study: Research
Type: Research grant
Value: Approx. UK £30,000
Length of Study: 3 years
Frequency: Annual
No. of awards offered: 1
Application Procedure: Applicants must complete an application form.
Closing Date: Mid-March
Funding: Private
No. of awards given last year: 2
Additional Information: Grants are advertised in January, on the BMA website and in the *British Medical Journal.*

Helen Lawson Research Grant
Subjects: Research in the field of heart diseases.
Purpose: To assist and support research.
Eligibility: Registered in the field of heart disease.
Level of Study: Research
Type: Research grant
Value: Approx. UK £7,500
Length of Study: 3 years
Frequency: Every 2 years
Country of Study: United Kingdom
No. of awards offered: 1
Application Procedure: Applicants must complete an application form.
Closing Date: Mid-March
Funding: Private
No. of awards given last year: None
Additional Information: Grants are advertised in January.

Helen Tomkinson Research Grant
Subjects: Research into public health relating to cancer.
Purpose: To assist and support research.
Eligibility: Medical practitioners or non-medical scientists in the United Kingdom.
Level of Study: Research
Type: Research grant
Value: Approx. UK £7,000
Length of Study: 3 years
Frequency: Every 2 years
Country of Study: United Kingdom
No. of awards offered: 1
Application Procedure: Applicants must complete an application form.
Closing Date: Mid-March
Funding: Private
No. of awards given last year: 1
Additional Information: Grants are advertised in January, on the BMA website and in the *British Medical Journal.*

Insole Research Grant
Subjects: Research on the cause, prevention and treatment of disease.
Purpose: To assist and support research.
Eligibility: Open to members of the BMA.
Level of Study: Research
Type: Research grant
Value: Approx. UK £750
Length of Study: 3 years
Frequency: Every 3 years, Not available in 2005
Country of Study: United Kingdom
No. of awards offered: 1
Application Procedure: Applicants must complete an application form.
Closing Date: Mid-March
Funding: Private
No. of awards given last year: None
Additional Information: Grants are advertised in January.

The James Trust Research Grant
Subjects: Research into asthma.
Purpose: To assist and support research.
Eligibility: Open to members of the BMA.
Level of Study: Research
Type: Research grant
Value: Approx. UK £30,000
Length of Study: 3 years
Frequency: Annual
Country of Study: United Kingdom
No. of awards offered: 1
Application Procedure: Applicants must complete an application form.
Closing Date: Mid-March
Funding: Private
No. of awards given last year: 1
Additional Information: Grants are advertised in January, on the BMA website and in the *British Medical Journal.*

Joan Dawkins Research Grant
Subjects: Research into the genetic basis of diseases.
Purpose: To assist and support research.
Eligibility: Open to registered medical practitioners. Non-medical scientists may also apply. Projects must relate to the United Kingdom.
Level of Study: Research
Type: Research grant
Value: Approx. UK £30,000
Length of Study: 3 years
Frequency: Annual

Country of Study: United Kingdom
No. of awards offered: 1
Application Procedure: Applicants must complete an application form.
Closing Date: Mid-March
Funding: Private
No. of awards given last year: 1
Additional Information: Grants are advertised in January, on the BMA website and in the *British Medical Journal.*

John William Clark Research Grant

Subjects: Research into the causes of blindness.
Purpose: To assist and support research.
Eligibility: Open to members of the BMA.
Level of Study: Research
Type: Research grant
Value: Approx. UK £6,000
Length of Study: 3 years
Frequency: Every 2 years
No. of awards offered: 1
Application Procedure: Applicants must complete an application form.
Closing Date: Mid-March
Funding: Private
No. of awards given last year: 1
Additional Information: Grants are advertised in January, on the BMA website and in the *British Medical Journal.*

Josephine Lansdell Research Grant

Subjects: Research in the field of heart disease.
Purpose: To assist and support research.
Eligibility: Registered medical practitioners in the United Kingdom.
Level of Study: Research
Type: Research grant
Value: Approx. UK £7,500
Length of Study: 3 years
Frequency: Every 2 years
Country of Study: United Kingdom
No. of awards offered: 1
Application Procedure: Applicants must complete an application form.
Closing Date: Mid-March
Funding: Private
No. of awards given last year: 1
Additional Information: Grants are advertised in January, on the BMA website and in the *British Medical Journal.*

Margaret Temple Research Grant

Subjects: Research into schizophrenia.
Purpose: To assist and support research.
Eligibility: Open to medical practitioners. Non-medical scientists may also apply. Projects must relate to the United Kingdom.
Level of Study: Research
Type: Research grant
Value: Approx. UK £20,000
Length of Study: 3 years
Frequency: Annual
Country of Study: United Kingdom
No. of awards offered: 1
Application Procedure: Applicants must complete an application form.
Closing Date: Mid-March
Funding: Private
No. of awards given last year: 1
Additional Information: Grants are advertised in January, on the BMA website and in the *British Medical Journal.*

Samuel Strutt Research Grant

Subjects: Kidney research.
Purpose: To assist and support research.
Eligibility: Registered Medical practitioners in the UK.
Level of Study: Research
Type: Research grant
Value: Approx. UK £1,500
Length of Study: 3 years
Country of Study: United Kingdom
No. of awards offered: 1
Application Procedure: Applicants must complete an application form.
Closing Date: Mid-March
Funding: Private
No. of awards given last year: 1
Additional Information: Grants are advertised in January, on BMA website and in the *British Medical Journal.*

T P Gunton Research Grant

Subjects: Research into public health relating to cancer.
Purpose: To assist and support research.
Eligibility: Open to both medical practitioners and non-medical scientists in the United Kingdom.
Level of Study: Research
Type: Research grant
Value: Approx. UK £18,000
Length of Study: 3 years
Frequency: Annual
Country of Study: United Kingdom
No. of awards offered: 1
Application Procedure: Applicants must complete an application form.
Closing Date: Mid-March
Funding: Private
No. of awards given last year: None
Additional Information: Grants are advertised in January, on the BMA website and in the *British Medical Journal.*

Vera Down Research Grant

Subjects: Research into neurological disorders.
Purpose: To assist and support research.
Eligibility: Open to registered medical practitioners in the United Kingdom.
Level of Study: Research
Type: Research grant
Value: Approx. UK £10,000
Length of Study: 3 years
Frequency: Every 2 years
Country of Study: United Kingdom
No. of awards offered: 1
Application Procedure: Applicants must complete an application form.
Closing Date: Mid-March
Funding: Private
No. of awards given last year: 1
Additional Information: Grants are advertised in January, on the BMA website and in the *British Medical Journal.*

BRITISH MOUNTAINEERING COUNCIL (BMC)

177-179 Button Road, Manchester, M20 2BB, United Kingdom
Tel: (44) (0) 870 010 4878
Fax: (44) (0) 161 445 4500
Email: office@thebmc.co.uk
Website: www.thebmc.co.uk

The BMC is the representative body that exists to protect the freedoms and promote the interests of climbers, hill walkers and mountaineers.

Alpine Ski Club Kenneth Smith Scholarship

Subjects: Ski research.
Purpose: To support exploratory expedition.
Level of Study: Professional development
Type: Grant
Value: UK £600
Length of Study: 1 year
Frequency: Annual

No. of awards offered: 2
Application Procedure: Contact organization.
Closing Date: December 15th
Funding: Trusts
Contributor: Kenneth Smith Trust

For further information contact:

The ASC Awards Sub-Committee, 22 Hatton Court, Hatton of Fintray, Aberdeenshire, AB21 OYA
Contact: Mrs Jay Turner

BMC Grant

Purpose: To fund innovative-style ascents in the greater mountain ranges by professional mountaineers.
Level of Study: Professional development
Type: Grant
Value: UK £1,000
Length of Study: 1 year
Frequency: Annual
No. of awards offered: Varies
Application Procedure: Contact the British Mountaineering Council.
Closing Date: No closing date

BRITISH RETINITIS PIGMENTOSA SOCIETY (BRPS)

PO Box 350, Buckingham, Buckinghamshire, MK18 1GZ, England
Tel: (44) 12 8082 1334
Fax: (44) 12 8081 5900
Email: info@brps.org.uk
Website: www.brps.org.uk
Contact: Mrs Lynda Cantor MBE, Trustee/Honorary Secretary

The British Retinitis Pigmentosa Society (BRPS) is a membership organization run by volunteers with 27 branches throughout the United Kingdom. The BRPS aims to raise funds for scientific research to provide treatments leading to a cure for retinitis pigmentosa. The Society provides a welfare support and guidance service to its members and their families.

BRPS Research Grants

Subjects: Retinitis pigmentosa.
Purpose: To financially support research into treatments leading to a cure for retinitis pigmentosa.
Eligibility: Please contact the Society.
Level of Study: Postgraduate
Type: Research grant
Value: Varies
Length of Study: Varies
Frequency: Twice a year
Country of Study: Any country
No. of awards offered: Varies
Application Procedure: Applicants must submit their application to the BRPS office.
Closing Date: Grant applications should reach the BRPS office at least 6 weeks prior to the Board of Trustees meeting. Dates of these meetings are supplied on request from the Honorary Secretary
Funding: Individuals, private, trusts

BRITISH SCHOOL AT ATHENS

52 Souedias Street, Athens, 106 76, Greece
Tel: (30) 210 721 0974
Fax: (30) 210 723 6560
Email: admin@bsa.ac.uk
Website: www.bsa.gla.ac.uk
Contact: Assistant Director

The British School at Athens promotes research into the archaeology, architecture, art, history, language, literature, religion and topography of Greece in ancient, medieval and modern times. It consists of the Library, Fitch Laboratory for Archaeological Science, Archive, Museum, hostel and a second base at Knossos for research and fieldwork.

Hector and Elizabeth Catling Bursary

Subjects: Greek studies including the archaeology, art, history, language, literature, religion, ethnography, anthropology or geography of any period and all branches of archaeological science.
Eligibility: Open to researchers of British, Irish or Commonwealth nationality.
Level of Study: Doctorate, postdoctorate, postgraduate
Type: Bursary
Value: A maximum of UK £500 per bursary to assist with travel and maintenance costs incurred in fieldwork, to pay for the use of scientific or other specialized equipment in or outside the laboratory in Greece or elsewhere and to buy necessary supplies
Study Establishment: The British School at Athens
No. of awards offered: 1–2
Application Procedure: Applicants must submit a curriculum vitae and state concisely the nature of the intended work, a breakdown of budget, the amount requested from the Fund and how this will be spent. Applications should include two sealed letters of reference. Bursary holders must submit a short report to the Committee upon completion of the project.
Closing Date: December 15th
Funding: Private
Additional Information: The bursary is not intended for publication costs, and cannot be awarded to an excavation or field survey team.

BRITISH SCHOOL AT ROME (BSR)

The British Academy, 10 Carlton House Terrace, London, SW1Y 5AH, England
Tel: (44) 20 7969 5202
Fax: (44) 20 7969 5401
Email: bsr@britac.ac.uk
Website: www.bsr.ac.uk
Contact: Dr Gill Clark, Registrar

The British School at Rome (BSR) is an interdisciplinary research centre for the humanities, visual arts and architecture. Each year, the School offers a range of awards in its principal fields of interest. These interests are further promoted by public lectures, conferences, publications, archaeological research and an excellent reference library.

Abbey Fellowships in Painting

Subjects: Painting.
Purpose: To give mid-career artists the opportunity of working in Rome.
Eligibility: Open to mid-career painters with an established record of achievement. Applicants must be citizens of the United Kingdom or United States of America or have been resident in either country for at least 5 years.
Level of Study: Postdoctorate, professional development, doctorate, postgraduate, research
Type: Fellowship
Value: UK £700 per month plus full board and lodging
Length of Study: 3 months
Frequency: Annual
Study Establishment: The British School at Rome
Country of Study: Italy
No. of awards offered: 23
Application Procedure: Applicants must complete an application form and pay an application fee.
Closing Date: Early to mid-January
Funding: Private
Contributor: The Abbey Council
No. of awards given last year: 3

For further information contact:

Abbey Awards, 43 Carson Road, London, SE21 8HT, England
Contact: The Administrator

Abbey Scholarship in Painting

Subjects: Painting.
Purpose: To give exceptionally promising emergent painters the opportunity to work in Rome.
Eligibility: Open to citizens of the United Kingdom and United States of America and to those of any other nationality provided that they have been resident in either country for at least 5 years.
Level of Study: Postgraduate, graduate, postdoctorate, doctorate
Type: Scholarship
Value: UK £500 per month plus board and lodging
Length of Study: 9 months
Frequency: Annual
Study Establishment: The British School at Rome
Country of Study: Italy
No. of awards offered: 1
Application Procedure: Applicants must complete an application form and pay an application fee.
Closing Date: Early to mid-January
Funding: Private
Contributor: The Abbey Council
No. of awards given last year: 1

For further information contact:

Abbey Awards, 43 Carson Road, London, SE21 8HT, England
Contact: The Administrator

Arts Council of England Helen Chadwick Fellowship

Subjects: Visual arts.
Purpose: To allow artists to pursue a project that could be made possible or enhanced by spending time in Rome and Oxford.
Eligibility: Open to visual artists who have established their practices in the years following graduation. Applicants must be United Kingdom nationals or have been continuously resident in the United Kingdom for the last three years.
Level of Study: Graduate, postgraduate, professional development, postdoctorate, research
Type: Fellowship
Value: UK £1,000 per month plus travel and materials allowances, and board and lodging at the British School at Rome and in Oxford
Length of Study: 6 months
Frequency: Annual
Study Establishment: The British School at Rome and the Ruskin School of Drawing and Fine Art at the University of Oxford
Country of Study: United Kingdom and Italy
No. of awards offered: 1
Application Procedure: Applicants must write for details of the application procedure.
Closing Date: Early January
Contributor: Arts Council England
No. of awards given last year: 1

Arts Council of Northern Ireland Fellowship

Subjects: Visual arts.
Eligibility: Visual artists resident in Northern Ireland.
Level of Study: Doctorate, postgraduate, professional development, graduate
Value: UK £650 per month plus board and lodging
Length of Study: 9 months
Frequency: Every 2 years
Study Establishment: The British School at Rome
Country of Study: Italy
No. of awards offered: 1
Application Procedure: Application form must be completed.
Funding: Government

For further information contact:

The Arts Council of Northern Ireland, MacNeice House, 77 Malone Road, Belfast, BT9 6AQ

Balsdon Fellowship

Subjects: Archaeology, art history, history, society and culture of Italy from prehistory to the modern period.
Purpose: To enable senior scholars engaged in research to spend time in Rome to further their studies.
Eligibility: Open to established scholars normally in post in a university of the United Kingdom. Applicants must either be nationals of the United Kingdom or Commonwealth or have been working professionally or studying at the graduate level for over 3 years within the United Kingdom or a Commonwealth country.
Level of Study: Research, postdoctorate, professional development
Type: Fellowship
Value: UK £650 plus board and lodging
Length of Study: 3 months
Frequency: Annual
Study Establishment: The British School at Rome
Country of Study: Italy
No. of awards offered: 1
Application Procedure: Applicants must complete an application form.
Closing Date: Early January
Funding: Private
Contributor: A bequest to the British School at Rome
No. of awards given last year: 1

Derek Hill Foundation Scholarship

Subjects: Painting, drawing.
Purpose: To enable an artist whose work demonstrates proficiency in drawing and who has a commitment to portrait and landscape painting to spend time in Rome.
Eligibility: Open to those who are of British or Irish nationality who will be aged 24 or over on September 1st of the academic year in which the award would be taken up. Applicants who have not previously received an art-based scholarship or bursary may be favoured.
Level of Study: Postgraduate, professional development
Type: Scholarship
Value: Approx. UK £950 per month plus full board and lodging at the British School at Rome
Length of Study: 3 months
Frequency: Annual
Study Establishment: The British School at Rome
Country of Study: Italy
No. of awards offered: 1
Application Procedure: Applicants must complete an application form and pay an entry fee.
Closing Date: Early December
Funding: Foundation
Contributor: Derek Hill Foundation
No. of awards given last year: None

Geoffrey Jellicoe Scholarship in Landscape Architecture

Subjects: Landscape architecture.
Purpose: To encourage a recent graduate or an individual in mid-career to propose a contemporary response to the Roman landscape and to pursue a topic with direct bearing on modern design in the landscape.
Eligibility: Open to United Kingdom or Commonwealth citizens and to those who have been working professionally or studying at postgraduate level for more than 3 years in the United Kingdom or Commonwealth.
Level of Study: Professional development, doctorate, graduate, postdoctorate, postgraduate, research
Type: Scholarship
Value: Approx. UK £500 per month plus full board and lodging at the British School at Rome
Length of Study: 3 months
Frequency: Every 2 years
Study Establishment: The British School at Rome
Country of Study: Italy
No. of awards offered: 1
Application Procedure: Applicants must complete an application form and pay an entry fee.
Closing Date: Early January
No. of awards given last year: New award

For further information contact:

The Landscape Foundation, 3rd Floor, 11 Northburgh Street, London, EC1R 0BD, England

Hugh Last Fellowship

Subjects: Classical antiquity.
Purpose: To enable established scholars to collect research material concerning classical antiquity.
Eligibility: Open to established scholars normally inpost at a United Kingdom university who are either United Kingdom or Commonwealth nationals, or who have been working professionally or studying at graduate level for more than 3 years within the United Kingdom or a Commonwealth country.
Level of Study: Research, postdoctorate, professional development
Type: Fellowship
Value: Board and lodging at the British School at Rome plus a research grant of UK £650
Length of Study: 3 months
Frequency: Annual
Study Establishment: The British School at Rome
Country of Study: Italy
No. of awards offered: 1
Application Procedure: Applicants must complete an application form.
Closing Date: Early January
Funding: Private
Contributor: A bequest to the British School at Rome
No. of awards given last year: 1

Paul Mellon Centre Rome Fellowship

Subjects: The Grand Tour and Anglo-Italian cultural and artistic relations.
Purpose: To assist research on grand tour subjects or on Anglo-Italian cultural and artistic relations.
Eligibility: Open to established scholars in the United Kingdom, United States of America or elsewhere. Applicants should be fluent in Italian.
Level of Study: Postdoctorate, doctorate, graduate, postgraduate, professional development, research
Type: Fellowship
Value: Full board at the British School at Rome. For independent scholars, the fellowship offers a stipend of UK £6,000 plus travel to and from Rome. For scholars in full-time university employment, the fellowship offers an honorarium of UK £2,000, travel to and from Rome and a sum of UK £6,000 towards replacement teaching costs for a term at the Fellow's home institution
Length of Study: 4 months
Frequency: Annual
Study Establishment: The British School at Rome
Country of Study: Italy
No. of awards offered: 1
Application Procedure: Applicants must contact the Paul Mellon Centre for Studies in British Art for details.
Closing Date: January
Funding: Private
Contributor: The Paul Mellon Centre for Studies in British Art
No. of awards given last year: 1

For further information contact:

The Paul Mellon Centre for Studies in British Art, 16 Bedford Square, London, WC1B 3JA, England
Email: info@paul-mellon-centre.ac.uk
Website: www.paul-mellon-centre.ac.uk/support/PDFs/4rome.pdf
Contact: The Grants Administrator

Rome Awards

Subjects: Archaeology, art history, history, society and culture of Italy from prehistory to the modern period.
Purpose: To enable persons engaged in research, either for a higher degree or at early postdoctoral level, to spend time in Rome to further their studies.
Eligibility: Open to United Kingdom or Commonwealth citizens and to those who have been working professionally or studying at postgraduate level for more than 3 years in the United Kingdom or a Commonwealth country. Applicants should normally have begun a programme of research in the general field for which the award is being sought, whether or not they are registered for a higher degree. Normally, applicants should be attached to or registered at a university in the United Kingdom.
Level of Study: Doctorate, graduate, postdoctorate, postgraduate, research
Type: Grant
Value: UK £150 per month plus UK £180 travel with board and lodging
Length of Study: Up to 4 months
Frequency: Annual
Study Establishment: The British School at Rome
Country of Study: Italy
No. of awards offered: Varies
Application Procedure: Applicants must complete an application form.
Closing Date: Early January
Funding: Private
No. of awards given last year: 4

Rome Fellowship

Subjects: Archaeology, art history, history, society and culture of Italy from prehistory to the modern period.
Purpose: To enable those who have been awarded their doctorate prior to taking up the award to launch a major piece of postdoctoral research.
Eligibility: Open to United Kingdom or Commonwealth citizens and to those who have been working professionally or studying at postgraduate level for more than 3 years in the United Kingdom or Commonwealth. Successful applicants will need to have been awarded their doctorate prior to taking up the award. Normally, applicants should be attached to, registered at or working at a university in the United Kingdom.
Level of Study: Doctorate, research, graduate, postdoctorate
Type: Fellowship
Value: UK £475 per month plus full board and lodging at the British School at Rome
Length of Study: 9 months
Frequency: Annual
Study Establishment: The British School at Rome
Country of Study: Italy
No. of awards offered: Varies
Application Procedure: Applicants must complete an application form.
Closing Date: Early January
Funding: Private
No. of awards given last year: 2

Rome Scholarship in Architecture

Subjects: Architecture and urbanism relevant to Rome and Italy.
Purpose: To encourage the pursuit of projects in architecture and urbanism relevant to Rome and Italy.
Eligibility: Open to architects, students of architecture and associated disciplines of at least postdiploma level who are United Kingdom or Commonwealth nationals, and to those who have been working professionally or studying at postgraduate level for more than 3 years in the United Kingdom or Commonwealth.
Level of Study: Doctorate, postdoctorate, graduate, postgraduate, professional development, research
Type: Scholarship
Value: UK £500 per month plus board and lodging
Length of Study: 3–9 months
Frequency: Annual
Study Establishment: The British School at Rome
Country of Study: Italy
No. of awards offered: 1–2
Application Procedure: Applicants must complete an application form and pay an application fee. Application forms are available from the British School at Rome Registrar.
Closing Date: Mid-January

Funding: Private
No. of awards given last year: 1

Rome Scholarships in Ancient, Medieval and Later Italian Studies

Subjects: Archaeology, art history, history, society and culture of Italy from prehistory to the modern period.
Purpose: To enable persons engaged in research, at a predoctoral level, to spend time in Rome to further their studies.
Eligibility: Open to United Kingdom or Commonwealth citizens and to those who have been working professionally or studying at postgraduate level for more than 3 years in the United Kingdom or Commonwealth. Applicants should normally have begun a programme of research in the general field for which the scholarship is being sought, whether or not they are registered for a higher degree. Normally, applicants should be attached to or registered at a university in the United Kingdom.
Level of Study: Doctorate, graduate, postgraduate, research
Type: Scholarship
Value: UK £444 plus board and lodging
Length of Study: 9 months
Frequency: Annual
Study Establishment: The British School at Rome
Country of Study: Italy
No. of awards offered: Varies
Application Procedure: Applicants must complete an application form.
Closing Date: Early January
Funding: Private
No. of awards given last year: 3

Rome Scholarships in the Fine Arts

Subjects: Painting, printmaking, sculpture and other suitable media including fine art video and photography.
Purpose: To give emerging, early and mid-career artists the opportunity to work in Rome.
Eligibility: Open to United Kingdom or Commonwealth citizens who have been working professionally or studying at postgraduate level for more than 3 years in the United Kingdom or Commonwealth.
Level of Study: Doctorate, professional development, graduate, research, postgraduate, postdoctorate
Type: Scholarship
Value: UK £500 per month plus board and lodging
Length of Study: 3–9 months
Frequency: Annual
Study Establishment: The British School at Rome
Country of Study: Italy
No. of awards offered: Varies
Application Procedure: Applicants must complete an application form and pay an application fee.
Closing Date: Early December
Funding: Private
No. of awards given last year: 2

SAIA Rome Scholarship in Architecture

Subjects: Architecture.
Level of Study: Graduate, postdoctorate, research, doctorate, postgraduate
Value: tbc
Length of Study: 9 months
Frequency: Dependent on funds available

For further information contact:

The South African Institute of Architects Private Bag X10063 Randburg 2125, South Africa

Sainsbury Scholarship in Painting and Sculpture

Subjects: Painting and sculpture.
Purpose: To give emerging artists the opportunity to work in Rome.
Eligibility: Open to United Kingdom citizens and to those who have been working professionally or studying at the postgraduate level for at least last 5 years in the United Kingdom. Applicants must be under 30 on October 1st in the year in which they would begin to hold the scholarship.
Level of Study: Doctorate, research, postdoctorate, postgraduate, graduate
Type: Scholarship
Value: UK £750 per month plus board, lodging and a travel grant of UK £1,000
Length of Study: 1 year, with an opportunity for a further 9 months in the following academic year, at the discretion of the selection committee
Frequency: Annual
Study Establishment: The British School at Rome
Country of Study: Italy
No. of awards offered: 1
Application Procedure: Applicants must complete an application form and pay an application fee.
Closing Date: Early December
Funding: Trusts
Contributor: The Linbury Trust
No. of awards given last year: 2

Sargant Fellowship

Subjects: Visual art and architecture.
Purpose: To enable a distinguished artist or architect to research and make new work within the historical context of Rome, away from the pressures associated with exhibiting and deadlines.
Eligibility: Open to United Kingdom or Commonwealth citizens and to those who have been working professionally or studying at postgraduate level for more than 3 years in the United Kingdom or Commonwealth.
Level of Study: Research, postdoctorate, graduate, professional development, postgraduate
Type: Fellowship
Value: UK £2,000 per month plus board and lodging at the British School at Rome
Length of Study: 3 or 6 months
Study Establishment: The British School at Rome
Country of Study: Italy
No. of awards offered: 1
Application Procedure: Applicants must complete an application form and pay an entry fee.
Closing Date: Mid-December
Funding: Private
Contributor: A bequest to the British School at Rome
No. of awards given last year: 1

Tim Potter Memorial Award

Subjects: Archaeology.
Purpose: To promote the study of Italian archaeological material by those of high academic potential who have had limited previous opportunity to visit Italy.
Eligibility: Open to United Kingdom or Commonwealth citizens and to those who have been working professionally or studying at postgraduate level for more than 3 years in the United Kingdom or Commonwealth. Applicants must have graduated prior to taking up the Award, but need not necessarily be registered for postgraduate study. Applications are also invited from those working in museums who could benefit from studying comparable Italian material.
Level of Study: Research, graduate, doctorate, professional development
Type: Grant
Value: UK £150 per month plus UK £500 travel allowance and full board and lodging at the British School at Rome
Length of Study: 2–4 months
Frequency: Annual
Study Establishment: The British School at Rome
Country of Study: Italy
No. of awards offered: Varies
Application Procedure: Applicants must complete an application form.
Closing Date: Early January
Funding: Private
No. of awards given last year: New award

Wingate Rome Scholarship in the Fine Arts

Subjects: Painting, printmaking, sculpture and other suitable media including fine art video and photography.
Purpose: To give emerging, early and mid-career artists an opportunity to work in Rome.
Eligibility: Open to citizens of the United Kingdom and other Commonwealth countries, Ireland, Israel or citizens of another European Union country provided that they are, during the period of application and have been for at least 3 years, resident in the United Kingdom. All applicants must be aged 24 or over at the beginning of the academic year (ie. on September 1st) in which the award falls.
Level of Study: Doctorate, graduate, postdoctorate, research, postgraduate, professional development
Type: Scholarship
Value: UK £500 per month plus board and lodging
Length of Study: 5
Frequency: Annual
Study Establishment: The British School at Rome
Country of Study: Italy
No. of awards offered: 1
Application Procedure: Applicants must complete an application form and pay an application fee.
Closing Date: Early December
Funding: Foundation
Contributor: The Harold Hyam Wingate Foundation
No. of awards given last year: 1

BRITISH SCHOOL OF ARCHAEOLOGY IN IRAQ

10 Carlton House Terrace, London, SW1Y 5AH, England
Tel: (44) 20 7969 5274
Fax: (44) 20 7969 5401
Email: bsai@britac.ac.uk
Website: www.britac.ac.uk/institutes/iraq/
Contact: The Secretary

The British School of Archaeology in Iraq's aim is to encourage and support the study of, and research relating to, the archaeology, history and languages of Iraq and its neighbouring countries, including East Syria and the Gulf, from the earliest times.

British School of Archaeology in Iraq Grants

Subjects: Archaeology, history and the languages of Iraq and neighbouring countries from the earliest times to the 17th century.
Purpose: To encourage and support research into the archaeology (and cognate subjects), history and languages of Iraq and its neighbouring countries.
Eligibility: Open to United Kingdom or Commonwealth citizens who are graduates or postgraduates with a knowledge of Western-Asiatic archaeology.
Level of Study: Graduate, postgraduate, postdoctorate, doctorate
Type: Grant
Value: Usually between UK £500–1,000, depending on the nature of the research
Length of Study: 1 academic year
Frequency: Twice a year
No. of awards offered: Varies
Application Procedure: The School considers applications for individual research grants twice a year in Spring and Autumn. Information and application forms are available from either the Secretary or the website. Two academic references are required.
Closing Date: April 15th and October 15th for grants of up to UK £1,000. October 15th is the preferred date for major research grants of over UK £1,000, grants may not be awarded for research funded by the British Academy
Funding: Government, trusts
Contributor: British Academy
No. of awards given last year: 12
Additional Information: Details of the British School of Archaeology in Iraq are available on the website under 'Institutes Overseas and Sponsored Societies.' Grantees will be required to provide a written report of their work and abstracts from these reports will be published in future issues of the School's newsletter. Individual research and travel grants are offered.

BRITISH SKIN FOUNDATION

19 Fitzroy Square, London, W1T 6EH, England
Tel: (44) 20 7383 0266
Fax: (44) 20 7388 5263
Email: bsf@bad.org.uk
Website: britishskinfoundation.org.uk
Contact: Mr James Stalley

The British Skin Foundation exists to support research and education into skin diseases. Working closely with patient support groups as well as many of the country's leading dermatology departments, the foundation aims to help the 7 million people in the United Kingdom who suffer with a serious skin condition.

British Skin Foundation Small Grants

Subjects: Available to anybody wishing to carry out United Kingdom-based research into skin disease or for the purchase of equipment.
Level of Study: Unrestricted
Value: Up to UK £10,000
Frequency: Annual
Funding: Commercial, private

BRITISH SOCIOLOGICAL ASSOCIATION (BSA)

Bailey Suite, Palatine House, Belmont Business Park, Belmont, Durham, DH1 1TW, England
Tel: (44) 19 1383 0839
Fax: (44) 19 1383 0782
Email: enquiries@britsoc.org.uk
Website: www.britsoc.co.uk/index.htm
Contact: Deborah Brown, Office Manager

The British Sociological Association (BSA) is the learned society and professional association for sociology in Britain. The Association was founded in 1951 and membership is drawn from a wide range of backgrounds, including research, teaching, students and practitioners in many fields. The BSA provides services to all concerned with the promotion and use of sociology and sociological research.

BSA Support Fund

Subjects: Sociology.
Purpose: To enable members of the association to pursue their research interests in the way of fieldwork/interview costs. Conference attendance in the UK and overseas (including non-BSA events). Photocopying and theses-production costs.
Eligibility: Only fully paid-up members of the association are eligible to apply, who are registered under the United Kingdom Concessionary or United Kingdom Lower Payment category. New members are eligible to apply, and there is no holding period.
Level of Study: Postgraduate, research, unrestricted
Type: Grant
Value: Up to UK £150 per year, to cover costs associated with research, but not tuition fees, equipment or textbook purchase
Frequency: As and when received, no submission deadline.
Country of Study: United Kingdom
No. of awards offered: Approx. 60
Application Procedure: The application from is available to download from the BSA website-see www.britsoc.co.uk Students Section. Applications are processed upon receipt and applications can expect a response within 14 days.
Closing Date: There is no closing date – applications are considered as and when received by the Support Fund Committee.
Funding: Private
No. of awards given last year: 48
No. of applicants last year: 48

THE BRITISH UNIVERSITIES NORTH AMERICA CLUB (BUNAC)

16 Bowling Green Lane, London, EC1R 0QH, England
Tel: (44) 20 7251 3472
Fax: (44) 20 7251 0215
Email: scholarships@bunac.org.uk
Website: www.bunac.org
Contact: Scholarships Department

The British Universities North America Club (BUNAC) is a leader in the field of international work and travel exchange programmes. A non-profit, non-political organization offering an ever-increasing range of programmes worldwide, BUNAC is dedicated to serving students and other young people everywhere by providing opportunities to live and work abroad legally.

BUNAC Educational Scholarship Trust (BEST)

Subjects: All subjects. Some awards are specifically for sports and geography-related courses.
Purpose: To help further transatlantic understanding.
Eligibility: Open to citizens of the United Kingdom who have graduated from a United Kingdom university within the last 5 years.
Level of Study: Postgraduate
Type: Scholarship
Value: Approx. US$5,000 per award
Length of Study: 3 months–3 years
Frequency: Annual
Country of Study: United States of America or Canada
No. of awards offered: Up to 10
Application Procedure: Applicants must complete an application form, available in January of each year.
Closing Date: Mid-March
Funding: Foundation
No. of awards given last year: 5
No. of applicants last year: 70

BRITISH VASCULAR FOUNDATION

Fides House, 10 Chertsey Road, Woking, Surrey, GU21 5AB, England
Tel: (44) 14 8372 6511
Fax: (44) 14 8372 6522
Email: bvf@care4free.net
Website: www.bvf.org.uk
Contact: K Lody, Office Manager

The British Vascular Foundation aims to provide research funding to find cures, better treatments and improve diagnosis of vascular disease. The Foundation also hopes to raise awareness of the disease's prevalence and impact and to provide information and support to sufferers, their families and friends.

Owen Shaw Award

Subjects: The rehabilitation of amputees.
Purpose: To devise better methods of helping patients to attain early mobilization.
Eligibility: Open to all those with an interest in amputee rehabilitation.
Level of Study: Unrestricted
Value: UK £3,000
Length of Study: 1 year
Frequency: Annual
Study Establishment: Any restricted research establishment
Country of Study: United Kingdom
No. of awards offered: 1
Application Procedure: Applicants must complete an outline proposal form, available from the Foundation.
Closing Date: January 31st
Funding: Trusts, private
Contributor: Owen Shaw
No. of awards given last year: 1
No. of applicants last year: 8

BRITISH VETERINARY ASSOCIATION

7 Mansfield Street, London, W1G 9NQ, England
Tel: (44) 20 7636 6541
Fax: (44) 20 7637 4769
Email: bvahq@bva.co.uk
Website: www.bva.co.uk
Contact: Mrs Helena Cotton

The British Veterinary Association's chief interests are the standards of animal health and veterinary surgeons' working practices. The organization's main functions are the development of policy in areas affecting the profession, protecting and promoting the profession in matters propounded by government and other external bodies and the provision of services to members.

Harry Steele-Bodger Memorial Travelling Scholarship

Subjects: Veterinary science and agriculture.
Purpose: To further the aims and aspirations of the late Harry Steele-Bodger.
Eligibility: Open to graduates of veterinary schools in the United Kingdom or the Republic of Ireland who have been qualified for not more than 3 years, and to penultimate or final-year students at those schools.
Level of Study: Unrestricted
Type: Scholarship
Value: Approx. UK £1,100
Frequency: Annual
Study Establishment: A veterinary or agricultural research institute or some other course of study approved by the governing committee
Country of Study: Any country
No. of awards offered: 1 or 2
Application Procedure: Applicants must complete an application form, available on request.
Closing Date: April 5th
Funding: Private
No. of awards given last year: 1
No. of applicants last year: 4
Additional Information: Recipients must be prepared to submit a record of their study abroad.

BROAD MEDICAL RESEARCH PROGRAM (BMRP)

The Eli and Edythe L Broad Foundation, 10900 Wilshire Boulevard, 12th Floor, Los Angeles, CA 90024-6532, United States of America
Tel: (1) 310 954 5091
Fax: (1) 310 954 5092
Email: info@broadmedical.org
Website: www.broadmedical.org
Contact: Dr Daniel Hollander, Director

The Eli and Edythe L Broad Foundation established the Broad Medical Research Program (BMRP) for Inflammatory Bowel Disease (IBD) Grants in 2001. The BMRP funds innovative and early exploratory clinical and basic research projects that will improve the lives of patients with IBD in the forseeable future.

BMRP for Inflammatory Bowel Disease Grants

Subjects: Understanding, treating and preventing IBD, particularly Crohn's disease and ulcerative colitis.
Purpose: The BMRP is interested in providing funding for clinical or basic research in IBD that will improve the lives of patients with IBD in the forseeable future, is scientifically sound, is innovative and will open new directions in IBD research and is in the early stages of exploration.
Eligibility: Open to non-profit organizations, such as universities, hospitals and research institutes. There are no other eligibility restrictions. In addition to experienced IBD researchers, the BMRP encourages applications from well-trained scientists who are not presently working in IBD to apply their knowledge, expertise and techniques to IBD research. Interdisciplinary collaboration is strongly encouraged.

Level of Study: Research
Type: Research grant
Value: Budgets should be commensurate with the scope of the work. Those who will need significantly more than US$100,000 per year should contact the BMRP before preparing their letters of interest
Length of Study: 1–2 years, with possible renewal
Country of Study: Any country
No. of awards offered: Varies
Application Procedure: Applicants must submit a brief letter of interest of up to three pages and also visit the website for further information. Investigators whose letters of interest appear to fit the BMRP's aims will be invited to submit full proposals.
Closing Date: There are no deadlines for receipt of letters of interest
Funding: Foundation
Contributor: Eli and Edythe L Broad
No. of awards given last year: 27
No. of applicants last year: 149

BROADCAST EDUCATION ASSOCIATION (BEA)

Scholarship Committee, 344 Moore Hall, Central Michigan University, Mount Pleasant, MI 48859, United States of America
Tel: (1) 989 774 3851
Fax: (1) 989 774 2426
Email: orlik1pb@cmich.edu
Website: www.beaweb.org
Contact: Dr Peter B Orlik, Scholarship Chair

The Broadcast Education Association (BEA) is the professional association for professors, industry professionals and graduate students interested in teaching and research related to television, radio and the electronic media industry.

BEA Abe Voron Scholarship

Subjects: Radio.
Purpose: To assist study towards a career in radio.
Eligibility: Open to individuals who can show substantial evidence of superior academic performance and potential to be an outstanding radio professionals.
Level of Study: Unrestricted
Type: Scholarship
Value: US$5,000
Frequency: Annual
Study Establishment: BEA member institutions
No. of awards offered: 1
Application Procedure: Applicants must obtain an official application form from the BEA or from campus faculty. Applicants should refer to the website for more details.
Closing Date: September 15th
Funding: Private
Contributor: The Abe Voron Committee
No. of awards given last year: 1
No. of applicants last year: 45

BEA Alexander M Tanger Scholarship

Subjects: Broadcasting.
Purpose: To assist study for a career in any area of broadcasting.
Eligibility: The applicant must be able to show substantial evidence of superior academic performance and potential to be an outstanding electronic media professional.
Level of Study: Unrestricted
Type: Scholarship
Value: US$5,000
Frequency: Annual
Study Establishment: BEA member institutions
No. of awards offered: 1
Application Procedure: Applicants must obtain an official application form from the BEA or from campus faculty. Applicants should refer to the website for more details.
Closing Date: September 15th
Funding: Private
Contributor: Alexander M Tanger
No. of awards given last year: 1
No. of applicants last year: 94

BEA Andrew M Economos Scholarship

Subjects: Radio.
Purpose: To support study towards a career in radio.
Eligibility: The applicant must be able to show substantial evidence of superior academic performance and potential to be an outstanding electronic media professional.
Level of Study: Unrestricted
Type: Scholarship
Value: US$3,500
Frequency: Annual
Study Establishment: BEA member institutions
No. of awards offered: 1
Application Procedure: Applicants must obtain an official application form from the BEA or campus faculty. Applicants should refer to the website for more details.
Closing Date: September 15th
Funding: Private
Contributor: The RCS Charitable Foundation
No. of awards given last year: 1
No. of applicants last year: 40

BEA Harold E Fellows Scholarship

Subjects: Broadcasting.
Purpose: To assist those who are studying towards a career in broadcasting.
Eligibility: The applicant must be able to show substantial evidence of superior academic performance and potential to be an outstanding electronic media professional.
Level of Study: Unrestricted
Value: US$1,250
Frequency: Annual
Study Establishment: BEA member institutions
No. of awards offered: 4
Application Procedure: Applicants must obtain an official application form from the BEA or campus faculty. Applicants should refer to the website for more details.
Closing Date: September 15th
Funding: Private
Contributor: National Association of Broadcasters (NAB)
No. of awards given last year: 4
No. of applicants last year: 55

BEA Helen J Sioussat/Fay Wells Scholarships

Subjects: Any area of broadcasting.
Purpose: To assist study in any area of broadcasting.
Eligibility: The applicant must be able to show substantial evidence of superior academic performance and potential to be an outstanding electronic media professional.
Level of Study: Unrestricted
Type: Scholarship
Value: US$1,250 each
Frequency: Annual
Study Establishment: BEA member institutions
No. of awards offered: 2
Application Procedure: Applicants must obtain an official application form from the BEA or campus faculty. Applicants should refer to the website for more details.
Closing Date: September 15th
Funding: Private
Contributor: Broadcasters' Foundation
No. of awards given last year: 2
No. of applicants last year: 96

BEA Philo T Farnsworth Scholarship

Subjects: Any area of broadcasting.
Purpose: To assist those who are studying towards a career in broadcasting.
Eligibility: The applicant must be able to show substantial evidence of superior academic performance and potential to be an outstanding electronic media professional.

Level of Study: Unrestricted
Value: US$1,500
Frequency: Annual
Study Establishment: BEA member institutions
No. of awards offered: 1
Application Procedure: Applicants must obtain an official application form from the BEA or campus faculty. Applicants should refer to the website for more details.
Closing Date: September 15th
Funding: Private
Contributor: BEA members and participating companies
No. of awards given last year: 1
No. of applicants last year: 94

BEA Vincent T Wasilewski Scholarship

Subjects: Broadcasting.
Purpose: To assist graduate study in any area of broadcasting.
Eligibility: The applicant must be able to show substantial evidence of superior academic performance and potential to be an outstanding electronic media professional.
Level of Study: Graduate
Type: Scholarship
Value: US$2,500
Frequency: Annual
Study Establishment: BEA member institutions
No. of awards offered: 1
Application Procedure: Applicants must obtain an official application form from the BEA or campus faculty. Applicants should refer to the website for more details.
Closing Date: September 15th
Funding: Private
Contributor: Patrick Communications Corporation
No. of awards given last year: 1
No. of applicants last year: 30

Broadcast Education Two year College Scholarship

Subjects: Electronic media.
Purpose: To assist study towards an electronic media career.
Eligibility: The applicant must be able to show substantial evidence of superior academic performance and potential to be an outstanding electronic media professional. There should be compelling evidence that the applicant possesses high integrity and a well articulated sense of personal and professional responsibility. Applicant must be studying at, or have studied at, a BEA two-year campus.
Type: Scholarship
Value: US$1,500
Frequency: Annual
Study Establishment: BEA member institutions
No. of awards offered: 2
Application Procedure: Applicants must obtain an official application form from the BEA or campus faculty. Applicants should refer to the website for more details.
Closing Date: September 15th
Funding: Private
Contributor: Sponsored by the Broadcast Education Association
No. of awards given last year: 2
No. of applicants last year: 22

NAB Harold E Fellows Scholarships

Subjects: Broadcasting.
Purpose: To assist study in any area of broadcasting.
Eligibility: The applicant must be able to show substantial evidence of superior academic performance and potential to be an outstanding electronic media professional. The applicant must have worked for pay or college credit at an NAB-member station.
Level of Study: Unrestricted
Type: Scholarship
Value: US$1,250 each
Frequency: Annual
Study Establishment: BEA member institutions
No. of awards offered: 4
Application Procedure: Applicants must obtain an official application form from the BEA or campus faculty. Applicants should refer to the website for more details.
Closing Date: September 15th
Funding: Private
Contributor: NAB
No. of awards given last year: 4
No. of applicants last year: 80

NAB Walter S Patterson Scholarships

Subjects: Radio.
Purpose: To assist study towards a career in radio.
Eligibility: The applicant must be able to show substantial evidence of superior academic performance and potential to be an outstanding electronic media professional.
Level of Study: Unrestricted
Type: Scholarship
Value: US$1,250 each
Frequency: Annual
Study Establishment: BEA member institutions
No. of awards offered: 2
Application Procedure: Applicants must obtain an official application form from the BEA or campus faculty. Applicants should refer to the website for more details.
Closing Date: September 15th
Funding: Private
Contributor: NAB
No. of awards given last year: 2
No. of applicants last year: 35

BROOKHAVEN NATIONAL LABORATORY

Brookhaven Women in Science, PO Box 5000, Upton, New York, NY 11973-5000, United States of America
Tel: (1) 631 344 8000
Email: bwisawards@bnl.gov
Website: www.bnl.gov
Contact: Ms Loralie Smart

Brookhaven National Laboratory is a multi-programme national laboratory operated by Brookhaven Science Associates for the United States Department of Energy. The Laboratory's broad mission is to produce excellent science in a safe, environmentally benign manner with the co-operation, support and appropriate involvement of many communities.

Renate W Chasman Scholarship

Subjects: Natural sciences, engineering and mathematics.
Purpose: To encourage women whose education was interrupted to pursue formal studies or a career in the natural sciences, engineering or mathematics.
Eligibility: Open to re-entry women residing in Nassau County, Suffolk County, Brooklyn or Queens, who must be citizens of the United States of America or permanent residents. They must be currently enrolled in or have applied for a degree-orientated programme at an accredited institution.
Level of Study: Postgraduate
Type: Scholarship
Value: US$2,000
Frequency: Annual
Country of Study: Any country
No. of awards offered: 1
Application Procedure: Applicants must submit a completed application, academic record, letters of reference and a short essay on career goals.
Closing Date: April 1st
Funding: Private
No. of awards given last year: 1
Additional Information: Please write to the given address for further information. Application forms are also available in PDF on the website.

BUCKINGHAMSHIRE CHILTERNS UNIVERSITY COLLEGE

Queen Alexandra Road, High Wycombe, Buckinghamshire, HP11 2JZ, England
Tel: (44) 1494 522141
Fax: (44) 14 9460 5047
Email: amurra01@bcuc.ac.uk
Website: www.bcuc.ac.uk
Contact: Anne Murray, Faculty Research Officer

Buckinghamshire Chilterns University College is committed to providing high academic standards in the areas of teaching, learning, scholarship and research. Primarily, our core vision is to create a vibrant academic community that is respected and valued throughout the university sector.

BCUC Research Student Bursary

Subjects: Leisure and tourism education, and leisure and tourism organization and society.
Eligibility: Applicant must hold a 1st degree from a United Kingdom university or its equivalent. Applicants whose mother tongue is not English should also have a certificate of English language competence.
Level of Study: Doctorate
Type: Bursary
Value: UK £7,500 per year
Length of Study: 3 years
Frequency: Dependent on funds available
Study Establishment: Leisure and Tourism Research Centre, Buckinghamshire Chilterns University College
Country of Study: United Kingdom
Application Procedure: Applicants must contact the Faculty Research Officer for further details and application form.

For further information contact:

Faculty of Leisure & Tourism, Wellesbourne Campus, Kingshill Road, High Wycombe, Buckinghamshire, HP13 5BB, England
Contact: Faculty Research Officer, BCUC

BCUC Research Student Bursary (Art and Design)

Subjects: Art and design.
Eligibility: Applicant must hold a 1st degree from a United Kingdom university or its equivalent. Applicants whose mother tongue is not English should also have a certificate of English language competence.
Level of Study: Doctorate
Type: Bursary
Value: UK £7,500 per year
Length of Study: 3 years
Frequency: Dependent on funds available
Study Establishment: Material Knowledge Research Centre, Buckinghamshire Chilterns University College
Country of Study: United Kingdom
Application Procedure: Applicants must contact the Faculty Research Officer for further details and application form.

For further information contact:

Faculty of Design, Queen Alexandra Road, High Wycombe, Buckinghamshire, HP11 2JZ, England
Contact: Faculty Research Officer, BCUC

BCUC Research Student Bursary (Business Systems)

Subjects: Business systems infrastructure, pattern recognition, image processing and GIS.
Eligibility: Applicant must hold a 1st degree from a United Kingdom university or its equivalent. Applicants whose mother tongue is not English should also have a certificate of English language competence.
Level of Study: Doctorate
Type: Bursary
Value: UK £7,500 per year
Length of Study: 3 years
Frequency: Dependent on funds available
Study Establishment: Centre for Applied Computing, Buckinghamshire Chilterns University College
Country of Study: United Kingdom
Application Procedure: Applicants must contact the Faculty Research Officer for further details and application form.

For further information contact:

Faculty of Technology, Queen Alexandra Road, High Wycombe, Buckinghamshire, HP11 2JZ, England
Contact: Faculty Research Officer, BCUC

BCUC Research Student Bursary (Furniture design)

Subjects: Furniture design and manufacture, furniture history, furniture conservation and restoration, 20th-century furniture, and forest products technology.
Eligibility: Applicant must hold a 1st degree from a United Kingdom university or its equivalent. Applicants whose mother tongue is not English should also have a certificate of English language competence.
Level of Study: Doctorate
Type: Bursary
Value: UK £7,500 per year
Length of Study: 3 years
Frequency: Dependent on funds available
Study Establishment: Research Centre for Furniture Studies, Buckinghamshire Chilterns University College
Country of Study: United Kingdom
Application Procedure: Applicant must contact the Faculty Research Officer for further details and application form.

For further information contact:

Faculty of Design, Queen Alexandra Road, High Wycombe, Buckinghamshire, HP11 2JZ, England
Contact: Faculty Research Officer, BCUC

BCUC Research Student Bursary (Management)

Subjects: International management and business forecasting.
Eligibility: Applicant must hold a 1st degree from a United Kingdom university or its equivalent. Applicants whose mother tongue is not English should also have a certificate of English language competence.
Level of Study: Doctorate
Type: Bursary
Value: UK £7,500 per year
Length of Study: 3 years
Frequency: Dependent on funds available
Study Establishment: Business and Management Research Centre, Buckinghamshire Chilterns University College
Country of Study: United Kingdom
Application Procedure: Applicants must contact the Faculty Research Officer for further details and application form.

For further information contact:

Buckinghamshire Business School, Chalfont Campus, Gorelands Lane, Chalfont St. Giles, Buckinghamshire, HP8 4AD, England
Contact: Faculty Research Officer, BCUC

BCUC Research Student Bursary (Medicine)

Subjects: Cardiovascular research, health psychology, telehealth, nutrition, oncology, and tissue viability.
Eligibility: Applicant must hold a 1st degree from a United Kingdom university or its equivalent. Applicants whose mother tongue is not English should also have a certificate of English language competence.
Level of Study: Doctorate
Type: Bursary
Value: UK £7,500 per year
Length of Study: 3 years
Frequency: Dependent on funds available
Study Establishment: Research Centre for Health Studies, Buckinghamshire Chilterns University College
Country of Study: England

Application Procedure: Applicants must contact the Faculty Research Officer for further details and application form.

For further information contact:

Faculty of Health Studies, Chalfont Campus, Gorelands Lane, Chalfont St. Giles, Buckinghamshire, HP8 4AD, England
Contact: Faculty Research Officer, BCUC

BUDAPEST INTERNATIONAL MUSIC COMPETITION

Philharmonia Budapest, Fòkai U.6, Budapest, H-1066, Hungary
Tel: (36) 1 266 1459, 302 4961
Fax: (36) 1 302 4962
Email: liszkay.maria@hu.inter.net
Contact: Ms Maria Liszkay, Secretary

The Budapest Music Competition has been held since 1933. Competitions in different categories alternate annually.

Budapest International Music Competition

Subjects: Musical performance.
Eligibility: Open to young artists of all nationalities who are under 32 years of age.
Level of Study: Professional development
Type: Competition
Value: Up to €24,000
Frequency: Annual
Country of Study: Any country
No. of awards offered: 3
Application Procedure: Applicants must complete an application form to be submitted with other required documentation and should contact the office for further information.
Closing Date: May 1st
Funding: Government
No. of awards given last year: 3

THE BUPA FOUNDATION

Bupa House, 15-19 Bloomsbury Way, London, WC1A 2BA, United Kingdom
Tel: (44) 20 7656 2591
Fax: (44) 20 7656 2708
Email: saunderl@bupa.com
Website: www.bupafoundation.co.uk
Contact: L Saunders, Research administrator

The BUPA Foundation is an independent medical research charity that funds medical research to prevent, relieve and cure sickness and ill health.

BUPA Medical Research Grant for Health at Work

Subjects: Health in the workplace.
Purpose: To support research into the feasibility and potential value of workplace conditions for health promotion and active management of employee health.
Eligibility: Open to health professionals and health researcher.
Level of Study: Doctorate, research, postdoctorate, postgraduate
Type: Grant
Length of Study: A maximum of 3 years
Frequency: Twice yearly
Application Procedure: For all queries contact Lee Saunders, the foundation's administrator. An application form is available online.
Closing Date: July for November intake and October for February intake
Funding: Foundation
Contributor: BUPA Foundation

BUPA Medical Research Grant for information and communication

Subjects: Health communication.
Purpose: To support research designed to enhance partnership between health professionals and public/patients.
Eligibility: Open to health professional and health researchers.
Level of Study: Postgraduate, postdoctorate, doctorate, research
Type: Grant
Length of Study: Maximum of 3 years
Frequency: Twice yearly
Application Procedure: For all queries contact Lee Saunders, the foundation's administrator. An application is available online.
Closing Date: July for November intake and October for February intake
Funding: Foundation
Contributor: BUPA Foundation

BUPA Medical Research Grant for preventive health

Subjects: Preventive health.
Purpose: To support research for projects in all health environments from epidemiology to health maintenance.
Eligibility: Open to health professionals and health researchers.
Level of Study: Postdoctorate, postgraduate, research, doctorate
Type: Grant
Length of Study: A maximum of 3 years
Application Procedure: For all queries contact Lee Saunders, the Foundation's administrator. An application form is available online.
Closing Date: July for November intake and October for February intake
Funding: Foundation
Contributor: BUPA Foundation

BUPA Medical Research Grant for Surgery

Subjects: Surgery.
Purpose: To support research into surgical practice, outcomes and new surgical techniques.
Eligibility: Open to health professionals and health researchers.
Level of Study: Postgraduate, doctorate, postdoctorate, research
Type: Grant
Length of Study: A maximum of 3 years
Frequency: Twice yearly
Application Procedure: For all queries contact Lee Saunders, the foundation's administrator. An application form is available online.
Closing Date: July for November intake and October for February intake
Funding: Foundation
Contributor: BUPA Foundation

BUPA Medical Research Grant for work on Older people

Subjects: Prevention, treatment and palliative care of mental ill health in older people.
Purpose: To support research into dementia depression, psychoses and other relevant conditions.
Eligibility: Open to health professionals and health researchers.
Level of Study: Research, doctorate, postdoctorate, postgraduate
Type: Grant
Length of Study: A maximum of 3 years
Frequency: Twice yearly
Application Procedure: For all queries contact Lee Saunders, the foundation's administrator. An application form is available online.
Closing Date: July for November intake and October for February intake
Funding: Foundation
Contributor: BUPA Foundation

THE CALEDONIAN RESEARCH FOUNDATION

The Carnegie Trust for the Universities of Scotland, Cameron House, Abbey Park Place, Dunfermline, Fife, KY12 7PZ, Scotland
Tel: (44) 1383 62 2148
Fax: (44) 1383 62 2149
Email: jgray@carnegie-trust.org
Website: www.carnegie-trust.org
Contact: Secretary & Treasurer

The Caledonian Research Foundation is a Scottish charity that has supported independent research in Scotland since 1990.

Caledonian Scholarship

Subjects: All subjects in the university curriculum. At least one scholarship each year is made in a non-scientific discipline.
Purpose: To support postgraduate research in any subject.
Eligibility: Open to persons possessing a First Class (Honours) Degree from a Scottish university.
Level of Study: Postgraduate
Type: Scholarship
Value: UK £10,800 plus tuition fees and allowances
Length of Study: Up to 3 years subject to annual renewal
Frequency: Annual
Study Establishment: Any university
Country of Study: Scotland
No. of awards offered: 2–3
Application Procedure: Applicants must write for details.
Closing Date: March 15th
Funding: Private
No. of awards given last year: 2
No. of applicants last year: 126
Additional Information: This award is considered along with Carnegie Scholarships.

THE CAMARGO FOUNDATION

BP 75, F-13714 Cassis Cedex, France
Tel: (33) 4 42 01 11 57
Fax: (33) 4 42 01 36 57
Website: www.camargofoundation.org
Contact: Mr Michael Pretina Jr, Executive Director

The Camargo Foundation maintains a study centre for the benefit of scholars who wish to pursue projects in the humanities and social sciences related to French and Francophone cultures.

Camargo Fellowships

Subjects: Humanities and social sciences, visual arts, music composition and creative writing.
Purpose: To assist scholars who wish to pursue projects in the humanities and social sciences related to French and Francophone cultures, and to support projects by visual artists, photographers, filmmakers, video artists, media artists, composers and writers.
Eligibility: Open to members of university and college faculties who wish to pursue special studies while on leave from their institutions, independent scholars working on specific projects and graduate students whose academic residence and general examination requirements have been met and for whom a stay in France would be beneficial in completing the dissertation required for their degree. The award is also open to writers, visual artists, photographers, filmmakers, video artists, multimedia artists and composers with specific projects to complete.
Level of Study: Postgraduate, doctorate, professional development
Type: Residency
Value: The use of furnished apartments, the reference library, darkroom, artist's studio and music composition studio, and a stipend of US$3,500
Length of Study: Varies
Frequency: Annual
Study Establishment: The Camargo Foundation, study centre in Cassis
Country of Study: France
No. of awards offered: Varies, approx. 20–26
Application Procedure: Applicants must submit a completed application form, a curriculum vitae, a detailed description of their project of up to 1,000 words in length and three letters of recommendation by individuals familiar with the applicant's professional work. At least two of the letters should come from persons outside the applicant's own institution; graduate students are exempt from this requirement. Artists should submit 10 slides showing samples of their work, composers should submit a score, cassette or compact disc and writers should send 10–20 pages of text or a copy of a published work. For further information and application forms applicants should log on to the Foundation's website at: www.camargofoundation.org
Closing Date: January 15th of the following academic year
Funding: Private
Contributor: The Jerome Hill endowment
No. of awards given last year: 26
No. of applicants last year: 200
Additional Information: A written report will be required at the end of the stay.

For further information contact:

The Camargo Foundation, 125 Park Square Court, 400 Sibley Street, St Paul, MN 55101-1928, United States of America
Tel: (1) 651 238 8805

CAMBRIDGE COMMONWEALTH TRUST, CAMBRIDGE OVERSEAS TRUST AND ASSOCIATED TRUSTS

Cambridge Trusts, Trinity College, Trinity Street, Cambridge, CB2 1TQ, United Kingdom
Tel: (44) 1223 351 449
Fax: (44) 1223 323 322
Email: info@overseastrusts.cam.ac.uk
Website: www.admin.cam.ac.uk

The Cambridge Commonwealth Trust and the Cambridge Overseas Trust (formerly the Chancellor's Fund) were established in 1982 by the University of Cambridge under the Chairmanship of his Royal Highness the Prime of Wales to provide financial assistance for students from overseas who, without help, would be unable to take up their places at Cambridge. Since 1982, the Cambridge Commonwealth Trust has brought 6,600 students from 51 countries to Cambridge, the Cambridge Overseas trust 4,252 students from 76 countries.

Aola Richards Studentships for PhD Study

Subjects: Biological sciences, with preference given to those who have done research in entomology.
Purpose: To financially support study towards a PhD.
Eligibility: Applicants must be citizens of Australia or New Zealand, must apply to the University of Cambridge and be offered a place at Cambridge in the normal way. All applicants must have a First Class or High Second Class (Honours) Degree or equivalent and normally be under 26. All applicants must be successfully nominated for an Overseas Research Student (ORS) award.
Level of Study: Predoctorate, doctorate
Type: Studentship
Value: The University Composition Fee at the home rate, approved college fees, a maintenance allowance sufficient for a single student and a contribution towards return economy airfare
Length of Study: Up to 3 years
Study Establishment: The University of Cambridge
Country of Study: United Kingdom
No. of awards offered: 1
Application Procedure: Preliminary application forms should be sent to the address relevant to that particular country. The final application forms should be sent to the Secretary, the Board of Graduate Studies.
Contributor: Offered in collaboration with the Aola Richards Fund

For further information contact:

The Board for Graduate Studies, 4 Mill Lane, Cambridge, Cambridgeshire, CB2 1RZ, England
Contact: The Secretary

Arab-British Chamber Charitable Foundation Scholarships

Subjects: All subjects.
Purpose: To financially support those undertaking postgraduate study.
Eligibility: Applicants must be citizens of Algeria, the Comoro Islands, Djibouti, Egypt, Jordan, Mauritania, Morocco, Palestine, Somalia, Sudan, Syria, Tunisia or the Yemen, must apply to the University of Cambridge and be offered a place at Cambridge in the normal way. All applicants must have a First Class or High Second Class (Honours) Degree or equivalent and normally be under 26.

Type: Scholarship
Value: The University Composition Fee at the overseas rate, approved college fees, a maintenance allowance sufficient for a single student and a contribution towards return economy airfare
Length of Study: 1 year
Frequency: Annual
Study Establishment: The University of Cambridge
Country of Study: United Kingdom
No. of awards offered: 5
Application Procedure: Applicants must complete a preliminary application form, which can be obtained from local universities, offices of the British Council or the Trust. Completed forms must be returned to the main address. Shortlisted candidates will be sent forms for admission to the University of Cambridge. The preliminary application form can also be downloaded from www.admin.cam.ac.uk/offices/gradstud/admissions/forms/
Closing Date: February 28th
Contributor: Offered in collaboration with the Arab-British Chamber Charitable Foundation and the Foreign and Commonwealth Office (FCO)

Argentina Cambridge Scholarships for PhD Study

Subjects: All subjects, particularly those relevant to the needs of Argentina.
Purpose: To financially support and encourage individuals to complete a PhD at the University of Cambridge.
Eligibility: Open to students from Argentina. Applicants must apply to the University of Cambridge and be offered a place at Cambridge in the normal way. All applicants must have a First Class or High Second Class (Honours) Degree or equivalent and normally be under 26. All applicants must be successfully nominated for an Overseas Research Student (ORS) award.
Level of Study: Doctorate, predoctorate
Type: Scholarship
Value: The award covers the University Composition Fee at the appropriate rate, approved college fees, a maintenance allowance sufficient for a single student and a contribution towards return economy airfare
Length of Study: Up to 3 years
Frequency: Annual
Study Establishment: The University of Cambridge
Country of Study: United Kingdom
No. of awards offered: Up to 2
Application Procedure: Applicants must complete a preliminary application form, which can be obtained from local universities, offices of the British Council or the Trust. Completed forms must be returned to the main address. Shortlisted candidates will be sent forms for admission to the University of Cambridge. The preliminary application form can also be downloaded from www.admin.cam.ac.uk/offices/gradstud/admissions/forms/
Funding: Government
Contributor: Offered in collaboration with the Ministry of Education in Argentina

Argentina Cambridge Scholarships for Postgraduate Study

Subjects: All subjects, particularly those relevant to the needs of Argentina.
Purpose: To financially support those undertaking postgraduate study.
Eligibility: Open to students from Argentina. Applicants must apply to the University of Cambridge and be offered a place at Cambridge in the normal way. All applicants must have a First Class or High Second Class (Honours) Degree or equivalent and normally be under 26. All applicants must be successfully nominated for an Overseas Research Student (ORS) award.
Level of Study: Postgraduate
Type: Scholarship
Value: The award covers the University Composition Fee at the overseas rate, approved college fees, a maintenance allowance sufficient for a single student and a contribution towards return economy airfare
Length of Study: 1 year
Frequency: Annual
Study Establishment: The University of Cambridge
Country of Study: United Kingdom
No. of awards offered: Up to 5
Application Procedure: Applicants must complete a preliminary application form, which can be obtained from local universities, offices of the British Council or the Trust. Completed forms must be returned to the main address. Shortlisted candidates will be sent forms for admission to the University of Cambridge. The preliminary application form can also be downloaded from www.admin.cam.ac.uk/offices/gradstud/admissions/forms/
Closing Date: February 28th
Funding: Government
Contributor: Offered in collaboration with the Ministry of Education, Argentina

BAT Cambridge Scholarships for PhD Study (China)

Subjects: All subjects.
Purpose: To financially support study towards a PhD.
Eligibility: Open to students from China. Applicants must apply to the University of Cambridge and be offered a place at Cambridge in the normal way. All applicants must have a First Class or High Second Class (Honours) Degree or equivalent and normally be under 26.
Level of Study: Postdoctorate, doctorate
Type: Scholarship
Value: The University Composition Fee at the appropriate rate, approved college fees, a maintenance allowance sufficient for a single student and a contribution towards return economy airfare
Length of Study: 3 years
Frequency: Annual
Study Establishment: The University of Cambridge
Country of Study: United Kingdom
No. of awards offered: Varies
Application Procedure: Applicants must complete a preliminary application form, which can be obtained from local universities, offices of the British Council or the Trust. Completed forms must be returned to the main address. Shortlisted candidates will be sent forms for admission to the University of Cambridge. The preliminary application form can also be downloaded from www.admin.cam.ac.uk/offices/gradstud/admissions/forms/
Contributor: Offered in collaboration with the British-American Tobacco (BAT) Company

BAT Cambridge Scholarships for PhD Study (Russia)

Subjects: All subjects.
Purpose: To financially support study towards a PhD.
Eligibility: Open to citizens of Russia. Applicants must apply to the University of Cambridge and be offered a place at Cambridge in the normal way. All applicants must have a First Class or High Second Class (Honours) Degree or equivalent and normally be under 26. All applicants must be successfully nominated for an Overseas Research Student (ORS) award.
Level of Study: Doctorate, predoctorate
Type: Scholarship
Value: The University Composition Fee at the appropriate rate, approved college fees, a maintenance allowance sufficient for a single student and a contribution towards return economy airfare
Length of Study: Up to 3 years
Frequency: Annual
Study Establishment: The University of Cambridge
Country of Study: United Kingdom
No. of awards offered: Varies
Application Procedure: Applicants must complete a preliminary application form, which can be obtained from local universities, offices of the British Council or the Trust. Completed forms must be returned to the main address. Shortlisted candidates will be sent forms for admission to the University of Cambridge. The preliminary application form can also be downloaded from www.admin.cam.ac.uk/offices/gradstud/admissions/forms/
Contributor: Offered in collaboration with the British-American Tobacco (BAT) Company

BAT Cambridge Scholarships for Postgraduate Study (China)

Subjects: All subjects.
Purpose: To financially support those undertaking postgraduate study.
Eligibility: Open to students from China. Applicants must apply to the University of Cambridge and be offered a place at Cambridge in the normal way. All applicants must have a First Class or High Second Class (Honours) Degree or equivalent and normally be under 26.
Level of Study: Postgraduate
Type: Scholarship
Value: The University Composition Fee at the appropriate rate, approved college fees, a maintenance allowance sufficient for a single student and a contribution towards return economy airfare
Length of Study: 1 year
Frequency: Annual
Study Establishment: The University of Cambridge
Country of Study: United Kingdom
No. of awards offered: Varies
Application Procedure: Applicants must complete a preliminary application form, which can be obtained from local universities, offices of the British Council or the Trust. Completed forms must be returned to the main address. Shortlisted candidates will be sent forms for admission to the University of Cambridge. The preliminary application form can also be downloaded from www.admin.cam.ac.uk/offices/gradstud/admissions/forms/
Closing Date: February 28th
Contributor: Offered in collaboration with the British-American Tobacco (BAT) Company

BAT Cambridge Scholarships for Postgraduate Study (Russia)

Subjects: All subjects.
Purpose: To financially support those undertaking postgraduate study.
Eligibility: Open to citizens of Russia. Applicants must apply to the University of Cambridge and be offered a place at Cambridge in the normal way. All applicants must have a First Class or High Second Class (Honours) Degree or equivalent and normally be under 26.
Level of Study: Postgraduate
Type: Scholarship
Value: The University Composition Fee at the appropriate rate, approved college fees, a maintenance allowance sufficient for a single student and a contribution towards return economy airfare
Length of Study: 1 year
Frequency: Annual
Study Establishment: The University of Cambridge
Country of Study: United Kingdom
No. of awards offered: Varies
Application Procedure: Applicants must complete a preliminary application form, which can be obtained from local universities, offices of the British Council or the Trust. Completed forms must be returned to the main address. Shortlisted candidates will be sent forms for admission to the University of Cambridge. The preliminary application form can also be downloaded from www.admin.cam.ac.uk/offices/gradstud/admissions/forms/
Closing Date: February 28th
Contributor: Offered in collaboration with the British–American Tobacco (BAT) Company

BP Cambridge Chevening Scholarships for Postgraduate Study (Russia)

Subjects: All subjects.
Purpose: To financially support those undertaking postgraduate study.
Eligibility: Open to citizens of Russia. Applicants must apply to the University of Cambridge and be offered a place at Cambridge in the normal way. All applicants must have a First Class or High Second Class (Honours) Degree or equivalent and normally be under 26.
Level of Study: Postgraduate
Type: Scholarship
Value: The University Composition Fee at the overseas rate, approved college fees, a maintenance allowance sufficient for a single student and a contribution towards return economy airfare
Length of Study: 1 year
Frequency: Annual
Study Establishment: The University of Cambridge
Country of Study: United Kingdom
No. of awards offered: Varies
Application Procedure: Applicants must complete a preliminary application form, which can be obtained from local universities, offices of the British Council or the Trust. Completed forms must be returned to the main address. Shortlisted candidates will be sent forms for admission to the University of Cambridge. The preliminary application form can also be downloaded from www.admin.cam.ac.uk/offices/gradstud/admissions/forms/
Closing Date: February 28th
Contributor: Offered in collaboration with BP and the Foreign and Commonwealth Office

BP Cambridge Scholarships for PhD Study (Egypt)

Subjects: All subjects.
Purpose: To financially support study towards a PhD.
Eligibility: Candidates must be citizens of Egypt. All applicants must apply for an Overseas Research Student (ORS) award and also apply to the University of Cambridge and be offered a place at Cambridge in the normal way. All applicants must have a First Class or High Second Class (Honours) Degree or equivalent and normally be under 26.
Level of Study: Doctorate, predoctorate
Type: Scholarship
Value: The University Composition Fee at the overseas rate, approved college fees, a maintenance allowance sufficient for a single student and a contribution towards return economy airfare
Length of Study: Up to 3 years
Frequency: Annual
Study Establishment: The University of Cambridge
Country of Study: United Kingdom
No. of awards offered: 2
Application Procedure: Applicants must complete a preliminary application form, which can be obtained from local universities, offices of the British Council or the Trust. Completed forms must be returned to the main address. Shortlisted candidates will be sent forms for admission to the University of Cambridge. The preliminary application form can also be downloaded from www.admin.cam.ac.uk/offices/gradstud/admissions/forms/
Contributor: Offered in collaboration with BP

BP Cambridge Scholarships for Postgraduate Study (Egypt)

Subjects: All subjects.
Purpose: To financially support those undertaking postgraduate study.
Eligibility: Open to citizens of Egypt. Applicants must apply to the University of Cambridge and be offered a place at Cambridge in the normal way. All applicants must have a First Class or High Second Class (Honours) Degree or equivalent and normally be under 26.
Level of Study: Postgraduate
Type: Scholarship
Value: The University Composition Fee at the appropriate rate, approved college fees, a maintenance allowance sufficient for a single student and a contribution towards return economy airfare
Length of Study: 1 year
Frequency: Annual
Study Establishment: The University of Cambridge
Country of Study: United Kingdom
No. of awards offered: 2
Application Procedure: Applicants must complete a preliminary application form, which can be obtained from local universities, offices of the British Council or the Trust. Completed forms must be returned to the main address. Shortlisted candidates will be sent forms for admission to the University of Cambridge. The preliminary application form can also be downloaded from www.admin.cam.ac.uk/offices/gradstud/admissions/forms/

Closing Date: February 28th
Contributor: Offered in collaboration with BP

Britain-Australia Bicentennial Scholarships for Postgraduate Study

Subjects: All subjects.
Purpose: To financially support those undertaking postgraduate study.
Eligibility: Candidates must be citizens of Australia, must apply to the University of Cambridge and be offered a place at Cambridge in the normal way. All applicants must have a First Class or High Second Class (Honours) Degree or equivalent and normally be under 26.
Level of Study: Postgraduate
Type: Scholarship
Value: The University Composition Fee at the overseas rate, approved college fees, a maintenance allowance sufficient for a single student and a contribution towards return economy airfare
Length of Study: 1 year
Frequency: Annual
Study Establishment: Jesus College, the University of Cambridge
Country of Study: United Kingdom
No. of awards offered: 2
Application Procedure: Applicants must contact the Board of Graduate Studies.
Closing Date: February 28th
Contributor: Offered in collaboration with the Foreign and Commonwealth Office (FCO) and Jesus College, Cambridge

For further information contact:

The Board of Graduate Studies, 4 Mill Lane, Cambridge, Cambridgeshire, CB2 1RZ, England
Contact: The Secretary

British Chevening Brockmann Cambridge Scholarships

Subjects: Engineering.
Purpose: To financially support those undertaking postgraduate study.
Eligibility: Applicants must be from Mexico, must apply to the University of Cambridge and be offered a place at Cambridge in the normal way. All applicants must have a First Class or High Second Class (Honours) Degree or equivalent and normally be under 26.
Level of Study: Postgraduate
Type: Scholarship
Value: The University Composition Fee at the overseas rate, approved college fees and a maintenance allowance sufficient for a single student
Length of Study: 1 year
Frequency: Annual
Study Establishment: The University of Cambridge
Country of Study: United Kingdom
No. of awards offered: Up to 2
Application Procedure: Applicants must complete a preliminary application form, which can be obtained from local universities, offices of the British Council or the Trust. Completed forms must be returned to the main address. Shortlisted candidates will be sent forms for admission to the University of Cambridge. The preliminary application form can also be downloaded from www.admin.cam.ac.uk/offices/gradstud/admissions/forms/
Closing Date: February 28th
Contributor: Offered in collaboration with the Brockmann Foundation and the Foreign and Commonwealth Office (FCO)

British Chevening Cambridge Australia Trust Scholarships for Postgraduate Study

Subjects: All subjects.
Purpose: To financially support those undertaking postgraduate study.
Eligibility: Open to citizens of Australia. Applicants must apply to the University of Cambridge and be offered a place at Cambridge in the normal way. All applicants must have a First Class or High Second Class (Honours) Degree or equivalent and normally be under 26.
Level of Study: Doctorate
Type: Scholarship
Value: The University Composition Fee at the overseas rate, approved college fees, a maintenance allowance sufficient for a single student and a contribution towards return economy airfare
Frequency: Annual
Study Establishment: The University of Cambridge
Country of Study: United Kingdom
No. of awards offered: 2
Application Procedure: Applicants must contact the Board of Graduate Studies.
Closing Date: February 28th
Contributor: Offered in collaboration with the Foreign and Commonwealth Office (FCO) and the Cambridge Australia Trust
Additional Information: Further information is available on request. For details of scholarships offered in collaboration with the Cambridge Australia Trust please see the website www.anu.edu.au/graduate/scholarships

For further information contact:

The Board of Graduate Studies, 4 Mill Lane, Cambridge, Cambridgeshire, CB2 1RZ, England
Contact: The Secretary

British Chevening Cambridge Scholarship for PhD Study (Mexico)

Subjects: All subjects.
Purpose: To financially support study towards a PhD.
Eligibility: Open to citizens of Mexico. Applicants must apply to the University of Cambridge and be offered a place at Cambridge in the normal way. All applicants must have a First Class or High Second Class (Honours) Degree or equivalent and normally be under 26. All applicants must be successfully nominated for an Overseas Research Student (ORS) award.
Level of Study: Doctorate
Type: Scholarship
Value: The University Composition Fee at the appropriate rate, approved college fees and a maintenance allowance sufficient for a single student
Length of Study: Up to 3 years
Frequency: Annual
Study Establishment: The University of Cambridge
Country of Study: United Kingdom
No. of awards offered: 1
Application Procedure: Applicants for this scholarship must complete a preliminary application form, which can only be obtained from the British Council in Mexico City.
Contributor: Offered in collaboration with the Foreign and Commonwealth Office (FCO)

For further information contact:

The British Council, Maestro Antonio Caso 127, Col. San Rafael, Delegacion Cuauhtemoc, Apartado postal 30-588, Mexico City, DF 06470, Mexico

British Chevening Cambridge Scholarship for PhD Study (Uganda)

Subjects: All subjects.
Purpose: To financially support study towards a PhD.
Eligibility: Open to students from Uganda. Applicants must apply to the University of Cambridge and be offered a place at Cambridge in the normal way. All applicants must have a First Class or High Second Class (Honours) Degree or equivalent and normally be under 26. All applicants must be successfully nominated for an Overseas Research Student (ORS) award.
Level of Study: Doctorate
Type: Scholarship
Value: The University Composition Fee at the appropriate rate, approved college fees, a maintenance allowance sufficient for a single student and a contribution towards return economy airfare
Length of Study: Up to 3 years
Frequency: Annual
Study Establishment: The University of Cambridge

Country of Study: United Kingdom
No. of awards offered: 1
Application Procedure: Applicants must complete a preliminary application form, which can be obtained from local universities, offices of the British Council or the Trust. Completed forms must be returned to the main address. Shortlisted candidates will be sent forms for admission to the University of Cambridge. The preliminary application form can also be downloaded from www.admin.cam.ac.uk/offices/gradstud/admissions/forms/
Contributor: Offered in collaboration with the Foreign and Commonwealth Office (FCO)

British Chevening Cambridge Scholarship for Postgraduate Study (East and West Africa)

Subjects: All subjects.
Purpose: To financially support those undertaking postgraduate study.
Eligibility: Applicants must be from Ghana, Sierra Leone, Tanzania or Uganda, must apply to the University of Cambridge and be offered a place at Cambridge in the normal way. All applicants must have a First Class or High Second Class (Honours) Degree or equivalent and normally be under 26.
Level of Study: Postgraduate
Type: Scholarship
Value: The University Composition Fee at the overseas rate, approved college fees, a maintenance allowance sufficient for a single student and a contribution towards return economy airfare
Frequency: Annual
Study Establishment: The University of Cambridge
Country of Study: United Kingdom
No. of awards offered: Up to 7. Up to 3 are for students from Ghana, 1 for students from Sierra Leone, 1 for students from Uganda and 1 is for students from Tanzania
Application Procedure: Applicants must complete a preliminary application form, which can be obtained from local universities, offices of the British Council or the Trust. Completed forms must be returned to the main address. Shortlisted candidates will be sent forms for admission to the University of Cambridge. The preliminary application form can also be downloaded from www.admin.cam.ac.uk/offices/gradstud/admissions/forms/
Closing Date: February 28th
Contributor: Offered in collaboration with the Foreign and Commonwealth Office (FCO)

British Chevening Cambridge Scholarship for Postgraduate Study (Namibia)

Subjects: All subjects.
Purpose: To financially support those undertaking postgraduate study.
Eligibility: Applicants must be from Namibia, must apply to the University of Cambridge and be offered a place at Cambridge in the normal way. All applicants must have a First Class or High Second Class (Honours) Degree or equivalent and normally be under 26. All applicants must be successfully nominated for an Overseas Research Student (ORS) award.
Level of Study: Postgraduate
Type: Scholarship
Value: The University Composition Fee at the overseas rate, approved college fees and a maintenance allowance sufficient for a single student
Length of Study: 1 year
Frequency: Annual
Study Establishment: The University of Cambridge
Country of Study: United Kingdom
No. of awards offered: 1
Application Procedure: Applicants must complete a preliminary application form, which can be obtained from local universities, offices of the British Council or the Trust. Completed forms must be returned to the main address. Shortlisted candidates will be sent forms for admission to the University of Cambridge. The preliminary application form can also be downloaded from www.admin.cam.ac.uk/offices/gradstud/admissions/forms/
Closing Date: February 28th
Contributor: Offered in collaboration with the Malaysian Commonwealth Studies Centre and the Foreign and Commonwealth Office (FCO)

British Chevening Cambridge Scholarships (Hong Kong)

Subjects: All subjects.
Purpose: To financially support those undertaking postgraduate study.
Eligibility: Applicants must be from Hong Kong, must apply to the University of Cambridge and be offered a place at Cambridge in the normal way. All applicants must have a First Class or High Second Class (Honours) Degree or equivalent and normally be under 26.
Level of Study: Postgraduate
Type: Scholarship
Value: The University Composition Fee at the overseas rate, approved college fees, a maintenance allowance sufficient for a single student and a contribution towards return economy airfare
Length of Study: 1 year
Frequency: Annual
Study Establishment: The University of Cambridge
Country of Study: United Kingdom
No. of awards offered: Up to 8
Application Procedure: Applicants must complete a preliminary application form, which can be obtained from local universities, offices of the British Council or the main address. Completed forms must be returned to the main address. Shortlisted candidates will be sent forms for admission to the University of Cambridge and a scholarship application form. These forms must be returned to the Board of Graduate Studies at the address below.
Closing Date: February 28th
Contributor: Offered in collaboration with the Foreign and Commonwealth Office (FCO)

For further information contact:

The Board of Graduate Studies, 4 Mill Lane, Cambridge, Cambridgeshire, CB2 1RZ, England
Contact: The Secretary

British Chevening Cambridge Scholarships (The Philippines)

Subjects: All subjects.
Purpose: To financially support those undertaking postgraduate study.
Eligibility: Applicants must be from the Philippines, must apply to the University of Cambridge and be offered a place at Cambridge in the normal way. All applicants must have a First Class or High Second Class (Honours) Degree or equivalent and normally be under 26.
Level of Study: Postgraduate
Type: Scholarship
Value: The University Composition Fee at the overseas rate, approved college fees, a maintenance allowance sufficient for a single student and a contribution towards return economy airfare
Length of Study: 1 year
Frequency: Annual
Study Establishment: The University of Cambridge
Country of Study: United Kingdom
No. of awards offered: 3
Application Procedure: Applicants must complete a preliminary application form, which can be obtained from local universities, offices of the British Council or the Trust. Completed forms must be returned to the main address. Shortlisted candidates will be sent forms for admission to the University of Cambridge. The preliminary application form can also be downloaded from www.admin.cam.ac.uk/offices/gradstud/admissions/forms/
Closing Date: February 28th
Contributor: Offered in collaboration with the Foreign and Commonwealth Scholarships

British Chevening Cambridge Scholarships (Vietnam)

Subjects: All subjects.
Purpose: To financially support those undertaking postgraduate study.

Eligibility: Applicants must be from Vietnam, must apply to the University of Cambridge and be offered a place at Cambridge in the normal way. All applicants must have a First Class or High Second Class (Honours) Degree or equivalent and normally be under 26. They must be successfully nominated for an Overseas Research Student (ORS) award.
Level of Study: Postgraduate
Type: Scholarship
Value: The University Composition Fee at the overseas rate, approved college fees, a maintenance allowance sufficient for a single student and a contribution towards return economy airfare
Length of Study: 1 year
Frequency: Annual
Study Establishment: The University of Cambridge
Country of Study: United Kingdom
No. of awards offered: 2
Application Procedure: Applicants for these scholarships should apply directly to the British Embassy in Vietnam.
Closing Date: February 28th
Contributor: Offered in collaboration with the Foreign and Commonwealth Office (FCO)

For further information contact:

The British Embassy, 16 Ly Thuong Kiet, Hanoi, Vietnam

British Chevening Cambridge Scholarships for Postgraduate Study (Australia)

Subjects: All subjects.
Purpose: To financially support those undertaking postgraduate study.
Eligibility: Open to citizens of Australia. Applicants must apply to the University of Cambridge and be offered a place at Cambridge in the normal way. All applicants must have a First Class or High Second Class (Honours) Degree or equivalent and normally be under 26.
Level of Study: Postgraduate
Type: Scholarship
Value: The University Composition Fee at the overseas rate, approved college fees, a maintenance allowance sufficient for a single student and a contribution towards return economy airfare
Length of Study: 1 year
Frequency: Annual
Study Establishment: The University of Cambridge
Country of Study: United Kingdom
No. of awards offered: 4
Application Procedure: Applicants must write for information.
Closing Date: February 28th
Contributor: Offered in collaboration with the Foreign and Commonwealth Office (FCO)

For further information contact:

The Board of Graduate Studies, 4 Mill Lane, Cambridge, Cambridgeshire, CN2 1RZ, England
Contact: The Secretary

British Chevening Cambridge Scholarships for Postgraduate Study (Chile)

Subjects: All subjects.
Purpose: To financially support study towards a PhD.
Eligibility: Applicants must be from Chile, must apply to the University of Cambridge and be offered a place at Cambridge in the normal way. All applicants must have a First Class or High Second Class (Honours) Degree or equivalent and normally be under 26. They must be successfully nominated for an Overseas Research Student (ORS) award.
Level of Study: Postgraduate
Type: Scholarship
Value: The University Composition Fee at the overseas rate, approved college fees and a maintenance allowance sufficient for a single student
Length of Study: 1 year
Frequency: Annual
Study Establishment: The University of Cambridge
Country of Study: United Kingdom
No. of awards offered: 1
Application Procedure: Applicants for this scholarship must apply directly to the British Council in Chile.
Contributor: Offered in collaboration with the Foreign and Commonwealth Office (FCO)

For further information contact:

The British Council, Eliodoro Yanez 832, Santiago de Chile, Chile

British Chevening Cambridge Scholarships for Postgraduate Study (Cuba)

Subjects: All subjects.
Purpose: To financially support those undertaking postgraduate study.
Eligibility: Open to citizens of Cuba. Applicants must apply to the University of Cambridge and be offered a place at Cambridge in the normal way. All applicants must have a First Class or High Second Class (Honours) Degree or equivalent and normally be under 26.
Level of Study: Postgraduate
Type: Scholarship
Value: The University Composition Fee at the overseas rate, approved college fees, a maintenance allowance sufficient for a single student and a contribution towards return economy airfare
Length of Study: 1 year
Frequency: Annual
Study Establishment: The University of Cambridge
Country of Study: United Kingdom
No. of awards offered: 2
Application Procedure: Applicants must complete a preliminary application form, which can be obtained from local universities, offices of the British Council or the Trust. Completed forms must be returned to the main address. Shortlisted candidates will be sent forms for admission to the University of Cambridge. The preliminary application form can also be downloaded from www.admin.cam.ac.uk/offices/gradstud/admissions/forms/
Closing Date: February 28th
Contributor: Offered in collaboration with the Foreign and Commonwealth Office (FCO)

British Chevening Cambridge Scholarships for Postgraduate Study (Eastern Europe)

Subjects: All subjects.
Purpose: To financially support those undertaking postgraduate study.
Eligibility: Open to students from Poland, Romania or Yugoslavia. Applicants must apply to the University of Cambridge and be offered a place at Cambridge in the normal way. All applicants must have a First Class or High Second Class (Honours) Degree or equivalent and normally be under 26.
Level of Study: Postgraduate
Type: Scholarship
Value: The University Composition Fee at the overseas rate, approved College fees, a maintenance allowance sufficient for a single student and a contribution towards return economy airfare
Length of Study: 1 year
Frequency: Annual
Study Establishment: The University of Cambridge
Country of Study: United Kingdom
No. of awards offered: Up to 6
Application Procedure: Applicants must complete a preliminary application form, which can be obtained from local universities, offices of the British Council or the Trust. Completed forms must be returned to the main address. Shortlisted candidates will be sent forms for admission to the University of Cambridge. The preliminary application form can also be downloaded from www.admin.cam.ac.uk/offices/gradstud/admissions/forms/
Closing Date: February 28th
Contributor: Offered in collaboration with the Foreign and Commonwealth Office (FCO)

British Chevening Cambridge Scholarships for Postgraduate Study (European Union)

Subjects: All subjects.
Purpose: To financially support those undertaking postgraduate study.
Eligibility: Open to citizens of Belgium, Denmark, Finland, Germany, Greece, Ireland, Italy, Luxembourg, the Netherlands, Portugal and Sweden.
Level of Study: Postgraduate
Type: Scholarship
Value: Applicants must contact local offices of the British Council
Length of Study: 1 year
Frequency: Annual
Study Establishment: The University of Cambridge
Country of Study: United Kingdom
No. of awards offered: Varies
Application Procedure: Applicants must contact the local offices of the British Council for details of the application procedure. Candidates are advised to apply well in advance of their proposed date of entry to the University of Cambridge.
Closing Date: February 28th
Contributor: Offered in collaboration with the Foreign and Commonwealth Office (FCO)
Additional Information: In Sweden these awards are known as the Prince Bertil Memorial Cambridge Scholarships.

British Chevening Cambridge Scholarships for Postgraduate Study (Hong Kong)

Subjects: All subjects.
Purpose: To financially support those undertaking postgraduate study.
Eligibility: Open to citizens of Hong Kong.
Level of Study: Postgraduate
Type: Scholarship
Value: The University Composition Fee at the overseas rate, approved college fees, a maintenance allowance sufficient for a single student and a contribution towards return economy airfare
Length of Study: 1 year
Frequency: Annual
Study Establishment: The University of Cambridge
Country of Study: United Kingdom
No. of awards offered: 8
Application Procedure: Applicants must contact the organization.
Closing Date: February 28th

British Chevening Cambridge Scholarships for Postgraduate Study (Mexico)

Subjects: All subjects.
Purpose: To financially support those undertaking postgraduate study.
Eligibility: Applicants must be from Mexico, must apply to the University of Cambridge and be offered a place at Cambridge in the normal way. All applicants must have a First Class or High Second Class (Honours) Degree or equivalent and normally be under 26.
Level of Study: Postgraduate
Type: Scholarship
Value: The University Composition Fee at the overseas rate, approved college fees and a maintenance allowance sufficient for a single student
Length of Study: 1 year
Frequency: Annual
Study Establishment: The University of Cambridge
Country of Study: United Kingdom
No. of awards offered: 1
Application Procedure: Applicants for this scholarship must complete a preliminary application form, which can only be obtained from the British Council, Mexico City.
Closing Date: February 28th
Contributor: Offered in collaboration with the Foreign and Commonwealth Office (FCO)

For further information contact:

The British Council, Maestro Antonio Caso 127, Col San Rafael, Delegacion Cuauhtemoc, Apartado Postal 30-588, Mexico City, DF, 06470, Mexico

British Chevening Cambridge Scholarships for Postgraduate Study (Mozambique)

Subjects: All subjects.
Purpose: To financially support those undertaking postgraduate study.
Eligibility: Applicants must be from Mozambique, must apply to the University of Cambridge and be offered a place at Cambridge in the normal way. All applicants must have a First Class or High Second Class (Honours) Degree or equivalent and normally be under 26. They must be successfully nominated for an Overseas Research Student (ORS) award.
Level of Study: Postgraduate
Type: Scholarship
Value: The University Composition Fee at the overseas rate, approved college fees, a maintenance allowance sufficient for a single student and a contribution towards return economy airfare
Length of Study: 1 year
Frequency: Annual
Study Establishment: The University of Cambridge
Country of Study: United Kingdom
No. of awards offered: Up to 4
Application Procedure: Applicants must complete a preliminary application form, which can be obtained from local universities, offices of the British Council or the Trust. Completed forms must be returned to the main address. Shortlisted candidates will be sent forms for admission to the University of Cambridge. The preliminary application form can also be downloaded from www.admin.cam.ac.uk/offices/gradstud/admissions/forms/
Closing Date: February 28th
Contributor: Offered in collaboration with the Malaysian Commonwealth Studies Centre and the Foreign and Commonwealth Office (FCO)

British Chevening Cambridge Scholarships for Postgraduate Study (Peru)

Subjects: All subjects.
Purpose: To financially support those undertaking postgraduate study.
Eligibility: Open to students from Peru. Applicants must apply to the University of Cambridge and be offered a place at Cambridge in the normal way. All applicants must have a First Class or High Second Class (Honours) Degree or equivalent and normally be under 26. They must be successfully nominated for an Overseas Research Student (ORS) award.
Level of Study: Postgraduate
Type: Scholarship
Value: The University Composition Fee at the appropriate rate, approved college fees, a maintenance allowance sufficient for a single student and a contribution towards return economy airfare
Length of Study: 1 year
Frequency: Annual
Study Establishment: The University of Cambridge
Country of Study: United Kingdom
No. of awards offered: 1
Application Procedure: Applicants must contact the British Council in Peru.
Closing Date: February 28th
Contributor: Offered in collaboration with the Foreign and Commonwealth Office (FCO)

For further information contact:

The British Council, Calle Alberto Lynch 110, San Isidro, Lima, 27, Peru

British Chevening Cambridge Scholarships for Postgraduate Study (Thailand)

Subjects: All subjects.
Purpose: To financially support those undertaking postgraduate study.
Eligibility: Applicants must be from Thailand, must apply to the University of Cambridge and be offered a place at Cambridge in the normal way. All applicants must have a First Class or High Second

Class (Honours) Degree or equivalent and normally be under 26. They must be successfully nominated for an Overseas Research Student (ORS) award.
Level of Study: Postgraduate
Type: Scholarship
Value: The University Composition Fee at the overseas rate, approved college fees, a maintenance allowance sufficient for a single student and a contribution to a return economy airfare
Length of Study: 1 year
Frequency: Annual
Study Establishment: The University of Cambridge
Country of Study: United Kingdom
No. of awards offered: 2
Application Procedure: Applicants must complete a preliminary application form, which can be obtained from local universities, offices of the British Council or the Trust. Completed forms must be returned to the main address. Shortlisted candidates will be sent forms for admission to the University of Cambridge. The preliminary application form can also be downloaded from www.admin.cam.ac.uk/offices/gradstud/admissions/forms/
Closing Date: February 28th
Contributor: Offered in collaboration with the Cambridge Thai Foundation and the Foreign and Commonwealth Office (FCO)

British Chevening Malaysia Cambridge Scholarship for PhD Study

Subjects: All subjects.
Purpose: To financially support study towards a PhD.
Eligibility: Open to students from Malaysia. Applicants must apply to the University of Cambridge and be offered a place at Cambridge in the normal way. All applicants must have a First Class or High Second Class (Honours) Degree or equivalent and normally be under 26. They must be successfully nominated for an Overseas Research Student (ORS) award.
Level of Study: Doctorate
Type: Scholarship
Value: The University Composition Fee at the appropriate rate, approved college fees, a maintenance allowance sufficient for a single student and a contribution towards return economy airfare
Length of Study: Up to 3 years
Frequency: Annual
Study Establishment: The University of Cambridge
Country of Study: United Kingdom
No. of awards offered: 1
Application Procedure: Applicants must complete a preliminary application form, which can be obtained from local universities, offices of the British Council or the Trust. Completed forms must be returned to the main address. Shortlisted candidates will be sent forms for admission to the University of Cambridge. The preliminary application form can also be downloaded from www.admin.cam.ac.uk/offices/gradstud/admissions/forms/
Contributor: Offered in collaboration with the Foreign and Commonwealth Office (FCO)

British Chevening Malaysia Cambridge Scholarships for Postgraduate Study

Subjects: All subjects.
Purpose: To financially support those undertaking postgraduate study.
Eligibility: Applicants must be from Malaysia, must apply to the University of Cambridge and be offered a place at Cambridge in the normal way. All applicants must have a First Class or High Second Class (Honours) Degree or equivalent and normally be under 26.
Level of Study: Postgraduate
Type: Scholarship
Value: The University Composition Fee at the overseas rate, approved college fees, a maintenance allowance sufficient for a single student and a contribution towards return economy airfare
Length of Study: 1 year
Frequency: Annual
Study Establishment: The University of Cambridge
Country of Study: United Kingdom
No. of awards offered: 4
Application Procedure: Applicants must complete a preliminary application form, which can be obtained from local universities, offices of the British Council or the Trust. Completed forms must be returned to the main address. Shortlisted candidates will be sent forms for admission to the University of Cambridge. The preliminary application form can also be downloaded from www.admin.cam.ac.uk/offices/gradstud/admissions/forms/
Closing Date: February 28th
Contributor: Offered in collaboration with the Foreign and Commonwealth Office (FCO)

For further information contact:

Cambridge (Malaysia) Foundation, PO Box 10139, Kuala Lumpur, 50704, Malaysia
Contact: The Secretary

British Chevening Scholarships for Postgraduate Study (Pakistan)

Subjects: All subjects.
Purpose: To financially reward students of outstanding academic merit.
Eligibility: Open to citizens of Pakistan who are of outstanding academic merit. Applicants must apply to the University of Cambridge and be offered a place at Cambridge in the normal way. All applicants must have a First Class or High Second Class (Honours) Degree or equivalent and normally be under 26.
Level of Study: Postgraduate
Type: Scholarship
Value: The University Composition Fee at the overseas rate, approved college fees, a maintenance allowance sufficient for a single student and a contribution towards return economy airfare
Length of Study: 1 year
Frequency: Annual
Study Establishment: The University of Cambridge
Country of Study: United Kingdom
No. of awards offered: 20
Application Procedure: Applicants must complete a preliminary application form, which can be obtained from local universities, offices of the British Council or the Trust. Completed forms must be returned to the main address. Shortlisted candidates will be sent forms for admission to the University of Cambridge. The preliminary application form can also be downloaded from www.admin.cam.ac.uk/offices/gradstud/admissions/forms/
Closing Date: October 7th
Contributor: Offered in collaboration with the Foreign and Commonwealth Office (FCO)

For further information contact:

The Board of Graduate Studies, 4 Mill Lane, Cambridge, Cambridgeshire, CB2 1RZ, England
Contact: The Secretary

British Prize Cambridge Scholarships

Subjects: All subjects.
Purpose: To financially support those undertaking postgraduate study.
Eligibility: Applicants must be from either Barbados or the Eastern Caribbean, have a First Class or High Second Class (Honours) Degree or equivalent and normally be under 26.
Level of Study: Postgraduate
Type: Scholarship
Value: The University Composition Fee at the overseas rate, approved college fees, maintenance allowance for a single student and a contribution towards return economy airfare
Length of Study: 1 year
Frequency: Dependent on funds available
Study Establishment: The University of Cambridge
Country of Study: United Kingdom
No. of awards offered: Up to 2
Application Procedure: Applicants must apply to the University of Cambridge and be offered a place at Cambridge in the normal way. Applicants should complete only one scholarship application form,

which will enable them to be considered for all awards for which they are eligible. Application forms can be downloaded from the website.
Closing Date: February 28th
Funding: Trusts

C T Taylor Studentship for PhD Study

Subjects: Biotechnology, computer science, chemical engineering, engineering, earth sciences and geography, genetics, land economy, mathematics, physics and chemistry, plant sciences and zoology.
Purpose: To financially support study towards a PhD.
Eligibility: Open to citizens of Australia, New Zealand and Canada. Applicants must apply to the University of Cambridge and be offered a place at Cambridge in the normal way. All applicants must have a First Class or High Second Class (Honours) Degree or equivalent and normally be under 26. They must be successfully nominated for an Overseas Research Student (ORS) award.
Level of Study: Doctorate
Type: Studentship
Value: Up to UK £5,000 towards the costs of study at Cambridge, to be determined in the light of the student's own resources
Length of Study: Up to 3 years
Frequency: Annual
Study Establishment: The University of Cambridge
Country of Study: United Kingdom
No. of awards offered: 1
Application Procedure: Applicants must complete a preliminary application form and send it to the address relevant to that particular country. The final application forms must be sent to the Secretary of the Board of Graduate Studies.
Closing Date: July 31st
Contributor: The C T Taylor Fund

For further information contact:

The Registry, The Old Schools, Cambridge, Cambridgeshire, CB2 1TN, England

Calbee Cambridge Scholarship

Subjects: All subjects.
Purpose: To financially support postgraduate study.
Eligibility: Applicants must be from Japan, must have a First Class or High Second Class (Honours) Degree or equivalent and normally be under 26.
Level of Study: Postgraduate
Value: Contribution towards fees
Length of Study: 1 year
Frequency: Annual
Study Establishment: The University of Cambridge
Country of Study: United Kingdom
No. of awards offered: 1
Application Procedure: Applicants must apply to the university of Cambridge and be offered a place at Cambridge in the normal way. Applicants should complete only one scholarship form, which will enable them to be considered for all awards for which they are eligible. Application forms can be downloaded from the website.
Closing Date: February 28th
Funding: Trusts
Contributor: Cambridge Trusts

Cambridge DFID Scholarships for Postgraduate Study

Subjects: All subjects.
Purpose: To partly support those undertaking postgraduate study.
Eligibility: Open to citizens from developing countries of the Commonwealth–The Falkland Islands, St Helena, Tristan de Cunha, Cameroon, Gambia, Ghana, Kenya, Sierra Leone, Tanzania, Uganda, India, Mauritius, the Seychelles, Fiji, Kiribati, Nauru, Papua New Guinea, Pitcairn, the Solomon Islands, Tonga, Tuvalu, Vanuatu, Western Samoa, South Africa, Botswana, Lesotho, Malawi, Mozambique, Namibia, Swaziland, Zambia, Zimbabwe and the Commonwealth countries of the Caribbean. Applicants must apply to the University of Cambridge and be offered a place at Cambridge in the normal way. All applicants must have a First Class or High Second Class (Honours) Degree or equivalent and be under the age of 35 on October 1st of the year they are applying for, with priority given to those candidates under the age of 30.
Level of Study: Postgraduate
Type: Scholarship
Value: The University Composition Fee at the overseas rate, approved college fees, a maintenance allowance sufficient for a single student and a contribution towards return economy airfare
Length of Study: 1 year
Frequency: Annual
Study Establishment: The University of Cambridge
Country of Study: United Kingdom
No. of awards offered: 40
Application Procedure: Applicants must complete a preliminary application form, which can be obtained from local universities, offices of the British Council or the Trust. Completed forms must be returned to the main address. Shortlisted candidates will be sent forms for admission to the University of Cambridge. The preliminary application form can also be downloaded from www.admin.cam.ac.uk/offices/gradstud/admissions/forms/
Closing Date: February 28th
Contributor: Offered in collaboration with the Department for International Development (DFID)

Cambridge European Trust Bursaries

Subjects: All subjects.
Purpose: To financially support those undertaking postgraduate study.
Eligibility: Open to citizens of the European Union, excluding the United Kingdom.
Level of Study: Postgraduate
Type: Bursary
Value: Part cost bursaries
Length of Study: 1 year
Frequency: Annual
Study Establishment: The University of Cambridge
Country of Study: United Kingdom
No. of awards offered: Varies
Application Procedure: Applicants should contact the organization.
Closing Date: February 28th

Cambridge Foundation Scholarships for Postgraduate Study (Chile)

Subjects: All subjects, particularly those relevant to the needs of Chile.
Purpose: To financially support those undertaking postgraduate study.
Eligibility: Open to citizens of Chile. Applicants must apply to the University of Cambridge and be offered a place at Cambridge in the normal way. All applicants must have a First Class or High Second Class (Honours) Degree or equivalent and normally be under 26. They must be successfully nominated for an Overseas Research Student (ORS) award.
Level of Study: Postgraduate
Type: Scholarship
Value: The University Composition Fee at the appropriate rate, approved college fees, a maintenance allowance sufficient for a single student and a contribution towards return economy airfare
Length of Study: 1 year
Frequency: Annual
Study Establishment: The University of Cambridge
Country of Study: United Kingdom
No. of awards offered: Varies
Application Procedure: Applicants must complete a preliminary application form, which can be obtained from local universities, offices of the British Council or the Trust. Completed forms must be returned to the main address. Shortlisted candidates will be sent forms for admission to the University of Cambridge. The preliminary application form can also be downloaded from www.admin.cam.ac.uk/offices/gradstud/admissions/forms/
Closing Date: February 28th
Contributor: Offered in collaboration with the Cambridge Foundation in Chile

Cambridge Nehru Scholarships for PhD Study

Subjects: All subjects.
Purpose: To financially support study towards a PhD.
Eligibility: Applicants must be from India, must be successful in winning an Overseas Research Student (ORS) award. Those who have a First Class Master's Degree or equivalent, in addition to a First Class (Honours) Degree, may be given preference.
Level of Study: Doctorate, predoctorate
Type: Scholarship
Value: The University Composition Fee at the home rate, approved college fees, a maintenance allowance sufficient for a single student and a contribution towards return economy airfare
Length of Study: Up to 3 years
Frequency: Annual
Study Establishment: The University of Cambridge
Country of Study: United Kingdom
No. of awards offered: Up to 8
Application Procedure: Applicants may obtain further details and a preliminary application form by writing before August 16th of the year before entry to the Joint Secretary of the Nehru Trust for Cambridge University at the address given below with details of academic qualifications.
Contributor: Offered in collaboration with the Nehru Trust for Cambridge University

For further information contact:

The Nehru Trust for Cambridge University, Teen Murti House, Teen Murti Marg, New Delhi, 110011, India

Cambridge Raffles Scholarships

Subjects: All subjects.
Purpose: To financially support those undertaking postgraduate study.
Eligibility: Applicants must be from Singapore, must apply to the University of Cambridge and be offered a place at Cambridge in the normal way. All applicants must have a First Class or High Second Class (Honours) Degree or equivalent and normally be under 26.
Level of Study: Postgraduate
Type: Scholarship
Value: The University Composition Fee at the overseas rate, approved college fees, a maintenance sufficient for a single student and a contribution towards return economy airfare
Length of Study: 1 year
Frequency: Annual
Study Establishment: The University of Cambridge
Country of Study: United Kingdom
No. of awards offered: 2
Application Procedure: Applicants must complete a preliminary application form, which can be obtained from local universities, offices of the British Council or the Trust. Completed forms must be returned to the main address. Shortlisted candidates will be sent forms for admission to the University of Cambridge. The preliminary application form can also be downloaded from www.admin.cam.ac.uk/offices/gradstud/admissions/forms/
Closing Date: February 28th
Contributor: Offered in collaboration with the Foreign and Commonwealth Office (FCO)

Cambridge Thai Foundation Scholarship for PhD study

Subjects: All subjects.
Purpose: To financially support study towards a PhD.
Eligibility: Applicants must be from Thailand, must apply to the University of Cambridge and be offered a place at Cambridge in the normal way. All applicants must have a First Class or High Second Class (Honours) Degree or equivalent and normally be under 26. For PhD study they be successfully nominated for an Overseas Research Student (ORS) award.
Level of Study: Doctorate
Type: Scholarship
Value: The University Composition Fee at the appropriate rate, approved college fees, a maintenance allowance sufficient for a single student and a contribution towards return economy airfare
Length of Study: Up to 3 years
Frequency: Annual
Study Establishment: The University of Cambridge
Country of Study: United Kingdom
No. of awards offered: 1
Application Procedure: Applicants must complete a preliminary application form, which can be obtained from local universities, offices of the British Council or the main address. Completed forms must be returned to the main address. Shortlisted candidates will be sent forms for admission to the University of Cambridge. These forms must be returned to the Board of Graduate Studies.
Contributor: Offered in collaboration with the Cambridge Thai Foundation

Cambridge Thai Foundation Scholarship for Postgraduate Study

Subjects: All subjects.
Purpose: To financially support those undertaking postgraduate study.
Eligibility: Applicants must be from Thailand, must apply to the University of Cambridge and be offered a place at Cambridge in the normal way. All applicants must have a First Class or High Second Class (Honours) Degree or equivalent and normally be under 26 years of age. They must be successfully nominated for an Overseas Research Student (ORS) award.
Level of Study: Postgraduate
Type: Scholarship
Value: The University Composition Fee at the overseas rate, approved college fees, a maintenance allowance sufficient for a single student and a contribution towards return economy airfare
Length of Study: 1 year
Frequency: Annual
Study Establishment: The University of Cambridge
Country of Study: United Kingdom
No. of awards offered: 2
Application Procedure: Applicants must complete a preliminary application form, which can be obtained from local universities, offices of the British Council or the Trust. Completed forms must be returned to the main address. Shortlisted candidates will be sent forms for admission to the University of Cambridge. The preliminary application form can also be downloaded from www.admin.cam.ac.uk/offices/gradstud/admissions/forms/
Closing Date: February 28th
Contributor: The Cambridge Thai Foundation

Canada Cambridge Scholarships for PhD Study

Subjects: All subjects.
Purpose: To financially support study towards a PhD.
Eligibility: Open to students from Canada. Applicants must apply to the University of Cambridge and be offered a place at Cambridge in the normal way. All applicants must have a First Class or High Second Class (Honours) Degree or equivalent and normally be under 26. They must be successfully nominated for an Overseas Research Student (ORS) award.
Level of Study: Predoctorate, doctorate
Type: Scholarship
Value: The University Composition Fee at the home rate and approved college fees
Length of Study: Up to 3 years
Frequency: Annual
Study Establishment: The University of Cambridge
Country of Study: United Kingdom
No. of awards offered: Up to 5
Application Procedure: Application forms for the scholarship will be sent out to eligible candidates once the completed form for admission to the University of Cambridge has reached the Board of Graduate Studies.

For further information contact:

The Board of Graduate Studies, 4 Mill Lane, Cambridge, Cambridgeshire, CB2 1RZ, England
Contact: The Secretary

CEU FCO Cambridge Non-Degree Research Scholarships

Subjects: All subjects.
Purpose: To financially support the pursuit of non-degree research.
Eligibility: Applicants must be current PhD students at the Central European University. They must be applying to pursue research at Cambridge in the same subject area that they are following at the Central European University.
Level of Study: Predoctorate, doctorate
Type: Scholarship
Value: The University Composition Fee at the appropriate rate, approved college fees, a maintenance allowance sufficient for a single student and return economy airfare
Length of Study: Up to 1 year
Frequency: Annual
Study Establishment: The University of Cambridge
Country of Study: United Kingdom
No. of awards offered: Up to 6
Application Procedure: Applicants must apply through the scholarships office at the Central European University.
Closing Date: December 16th
Contributor: Offered in collaboration with the Central European University (CEU) and the Foreign and commonwealth office (FCO)

CIALS Cambridge Scholarships

Subjects: Law.
Purpose: To support study towards the Master of Law (LLM) degree.
Eligibility: Open to graduates of Canadian law schools who have completed a Bachelor of Law degree on or before June 1st. Applicants must be Canadian citizens. Applicants must apply to the University of Cambridge and be offered a place at Cambridge in the normal way. All applicants must have a First Class or High Second Class (Honours) Degree or equivalent and normally be under 26.
Level of Study: Postgraduate
Type: Scholarship
Frequency: Annual
Study Establishment: The University of Cambridge
Country of Study: United Kingdom
No. of awards offered: 2
Application Procedure: Applicants must apply in writing to the Executive Director of the Canadian Institute for Advanced Legal Studies (CIALS).
Closing Date: December 31st
Contributor: Offered in collaboration with the CIALS

For further information contact:

The Canadian Institute of Advanced Legal Studies, 4 Beechwood Avenue, Ottawa, ON, K1L 8L9, Canada
Contact: Mr Frank E McArdle, Executive Director

Citibank Cambridge Scholarship for the MPhil degree in Management Studies

Subjects: Management studies.
Eligibility: Applicants must apply to the University of Cambridge and be offered a place at Cambridge in the normal way. All applicants must have a First Class or High Second Class (Honours) Degree or equivalent and normally be under 26. For students liable to pay fees at the overseas rate.
Level of Study: Postgraduate
Type: Scholarship
Value: University Composition Fee at the home rate, approved college fees, maintenance allowance sufficient for a single student, contribution towards return economy airfare
Length of Study: 1 year
Study Establishment: The University of Cambridge
Country of Study: United Kingdom
No. of awards offered: 1
Application Procedure: Applicants must complete a preliminary application form, which can be obtained from local universities, offices of the British Council or the main address. Completed application forms must be returned to the main address. Candidates short-listed will be sent forms for admission to the University of Cambridge and must be returned to The Board of Graduate Studies.
Closing Date: February 28th
Contributor: In collaboration with the Judge Institute of Management Studies

For further information contact:

The Board of Graduate Studies, 4 Mill Lane, Cambridge, Cambridgeshire, CB2 1RZ, England
Contact: The Secretary

Citigroup Cambridge Scholarships

Subjects: Finance, economics or management studies.
Purpose: To financially support those undertaking postgraduate study.
Eligibility: Open to citizens of Australia, New Zealand, Sri Lanka, Hong Kong, India, Malaysia, Philippines, Singapore and Thailand. Applicants must apply to the University of Cambridge and be offered a place at Cambridge in the normal way. All applicants must have a First Class or High Second Class (Honours) Degree or equivalent and normally be under 26.
Level of Study: Postgraduate
Type: Scholarship
Value: The University Composition fee at the overseas rate, approved college fees, a maintenance allowance sufficient for a single student and a contribution towards return economy airfare
Length of Study: 1 year
Study Establishment: The University of Cambridge
Country of Study: United Kingdom
No. of awards offered: 1
Application Procedure: Applicants must complete a preliminary application form, which can be obtained from local universities, offices of the British Council or the Trust. Completed forms must be returned to the main address. Shortlisted candidates will be sent forms for admission to the University of Cambridge. The preliminary application form can also be downloaded from www.admin.cam.ac.uk/offices/gradstud/admissions/forms/
Closing Date: February 28th
Contributor: Offered in collaboration with Citibank

Citigroup Cambridge Scholarships for Postgraduate Study (Czech Republic, Hungary, Poland and Slovakia)

Subjects: Economics and finance.
Purpose: To allow candidates to pursue a 1-year diploma at Cambridge, and, subject to a satisfactory performance in the diploma, to proceed to a 1-year MPhil degree.
Eligibility: Applicants must apply to the University of Cambridge and be offered a place at Cambridge in the normal way. All applicants must have a First Class or High Second Class (Honours) Degree or equivalent and normally be under 26.
Level of Study: Postgraduate
Type: Scholarship
Value: The University Composition Fee at the overseas rate, approved college fees, a maintenance allowance sufficient for a single student and a contribution towards return economy airfare
Length of Study: 1 year
Frequency: Annual
Study Establishment: The University of Cambridge
Country of Study: United Kingdom
No. of awards offered: 2
Application Procedure: Applicants must complete a preliminary application form, which can be obtained from local universities, offices of the British Council or the Trust. Completed forms must be returned to the main address. Shortlisted candidates will be sent forms for admission to the University of Cambridge. The preliminary application form can also be downloaded from www.admin.cam.ac.uk/offices/gradstud/admissions/forms/
Closing Date: February 28th
Contributor: Offered in collaboration with Citigroup

Computer Laboratory ORS Equivalent Awards

Subjects: Computer science.
Purpose: To financially support study towards a PhD.
Eligibility: Open to candidates studying for a PhD in the Computer Laboratory. Applicants must apply to the University of Cambridge and be offered a place at Cambridge in the normal way. All applicants must

have a First Class or High Second Class (Honours) Degree or equivalent and normally be under 26.
Level of Study: Postgraduate
Type: Award
Value: Up to the difference between the home and overseas rate of the University Composition Fee
Length of Study: Up to 3 years
Study Establishment: The University of Cambridge
Country of Study: United Kingdom
No. of awards offered: 1
Application Procedure: Applicants must contact the organization.

Corpus Christi ACE Scholarship for Postgraduate Study

Subjects: Conservation, development or the environment.
Purpose: To financially support those undertaking postgraduate study.
Eligibility: Open to students from the developing world with a preference for applicants from Eastern Europe. Applicants must apply to the University of Cambridge and be offered a place at Cambridge in the normal way. All applicants must have a First Class or High Second Class (Honours) Degree or equivalent and normally be under 26.
Level of Study: Postgraduate
Type: Scholarship
Value: The University Composition Fee at the overseas rate, approved college fees, a maintenance allowance sufficient for a single student and a contribution towards return economy airfare
Length of Study: 1 year
Frequency: Annual
Study Establishment: Corpus Christi College, the University of Cambridge
Country of Study: United Kingdom
No. of awards offered: 1
Application Procedure: Applicants must complete a preliminary application form, which can be obtained from local universities, offices of the British Council or the Trust. Completed forms must be returned to the main address. Shortlisted candidates will be sent forms for admission to the University of Cambridge. The preliminary application form can also be downloaded from www.admin.cam.ac.uk/offices/gradstud/admissions/forms/
Closing Date: February 28th
Contributor: Offered in collaboration with the Association for Cultural Exchange (ACE) and Corpus Christi College, the University of Cambridge

Cyprus Cambridge Scholarships For PhD Study

Subjects: All subjects.
Purpose: To financially support study towards a PhD.
Eligibility: Open to citizens of Cyprus. Candidates must sign an undertaking with the Cyprus State Scholarship Authority to return to work in Cyprus for a minimum of three years. This requirement may be deferred if, eg. the Scholar obtains a subsequent award for further studies. The Trust cannot admit students to the University or any of its colleges. Applicants for awards from the Trusts must, therefore, also apply to the University of Cambridge and be offered a place at Cambridge in the normal way. All applicants must have a First Class or High Second Class (Honours) Degree or equivalent and normally be under 26. Candidates must apply for an Overseas Research Student (ORS) award, which covers the difference between the home and overseas rate of the University Composition Fee.
Level of Study: Doctorate
Type: Scholarship
Value: The scholarships will take into account the financial resources of the applicant and will cover up to the University Composition Fee at the overseas rate, approved college fees, a maintenance allowance sufficient for a single student and a contribution towards return economy airfare
Length of Study: Up to 3 years
Study Establishment: The University of Cambridge
Country of Study: United Kingdom
No. of awards offered: 1
Application Procedure: Applicants must complete a preliminary application form, which can be obtained from local universities, offices of the British Council or the Trust. The preliminary application form can also be downloaded from www.admin.cam.ac.uk/offices/gradstud/admissions/forms/ completed forms must be returned to the main address. Shortlisted candidates will be sent forms for admission to the University of Cambridge.
Closing Date: February 28th
Contributor: Offered in collaboration with the Cyprus State Scholarship Authority

Developing World Education Fund Cambridge Scholarships for Postgraduate Study (China)

Subjects: All subjects.
Purpose: To financially support those undertaking postgraduate study.
Eligibility: For students from a number of countries including China. Applicants must apply to the University of Cambridge and be offered a place at Cambridge in the normal way. All applicants must have a First Class or High Second Class (Honours) Degree or equivalent and normally be under 26.
Level of Study: Postgraduate
Type: Scholarship
Value: The University Composition Fee at the overseas rate, approved college fees, a maintenance allowance sufficient for a single student and a contribution towards return economy airfare
Length of Study: 1 year
Frequency: Annual
Study Establishment: The University of Cambridge
Country of Study: United Kingdom
No. of awards offered: Up to 2
Application Procedure: Applicants must complete a preliminary application form, which can be obtained from local universities, offices of the British Council or the Trust. Completed forms must be returned to the main address. Shortlisted candidates will be sent forms for admission to the University of Cambridge. The preliminary application form can also be downloaded from www.admin.cam.ac.uk/offices/gradstud/admissions/forms/
Closing Date: February 28th
Contributor: Offered in collaboration with the Developing World Education Fund

Dharam Hinduja Cambridge DFID Shared Scholarships

Subjects: All subjects.
Purpose: To offer financial support.
Eligibility: Applicants must be from India, and must be under the age of 35 on October 1st, with priority given to those candidates under the age of 30. Applicants must not be employed by a national or local government department or by a parastatal organization, or at present be living or studying in a developed country. Priority will be given to candidates wishing to pursue a course of study related to the economic and social development of their country.
Level of Study: Postgraduate
Type: Scholarship
Value: The University Composition Fee at the appropriate rate, approved college fees, a maintenance allowance sufficient for a single student and a contribution towards return economy airfare
Length of Study: 1 year
Frequency: Annual
Study Establishment: The University of Cambridge
Country of Study: United Kingdom
No. of awards offered: 2
Application Procedure: Applicants may obtain further details and a preliminary application form by writing before August 16th of the year before entry to the address given below with details of academic qualifications.
Closing Date: February 28th
Contributor: Offered in collaboration with the Hinduja Cambridge Trust and the Department for International Development

For further information contact:

The Nehru Trust for Cambridge University, Teen Murti House, Teen Murti Marg, New Delhi, 110011, India
Contact: The Joint Secretary

Dharam Hinduja Cambridge Scholarships

Subjects: All subjects.
Purpose: To financially support study towards a PhD.
Eligibility: Applicants must be from India, and must be successful in winning an Overseas Research Student (ORS) award. Those who have, in addition, to a First Class (Honours) Degree, a First Class Master's Degree or its equivalent may be given preference.
Level of Study: Doctorate
Type: Scholarship
Value: The University Composition Fee at the home rate, approved college fees, a maintenance allowance sufficient for a single student and a contribution towards return economy airfare
Length of Study: Up to 3 years
Frequency: Annual
Study Establishment: The University of Cambridge
Country of Study: United Kingdom
No. of awards offered: 2
Application Procedure: Applicants must obtain further details and a preliminary application form by writing before August 16th of the year before entry to the address given below with details of academic qualifications.
Contributor: Offered in collaboration with the Hinduja Cambridge Trust

For further information contact:

The Nehru Trust for Cambridge University, Teen Murti House, Teen Murti Marg, New Delhi, 110011, India
Contact: The Joint Secretary

Entente Cordiale Scholarships for Postgraduate Study

Subjects: All subjects.
Purpose: To financially support those undertaking postgraduate study.
Eligibility: Applicants must be citizens of France.
Level of Study: Postgraduate
Type: Scholarship
Value: Applicants must contact the British Council for details
Length of Study: 1 year
Frequency: Annual
Study Establishment: The University of Cambridge
Country of Study: United Kingdom
No. of awards offered: Up to 6
Application Procedure: Applicants must obtain details of the application procedure from the British Council.
Closing Date: February 28th
Contributor: Offered in collaboration with the United Kingdom's Foreign and Commonwealth Office (FCO)

For further information contact:

British Council, 9-11 rue de Constantine, 75007 Paris, France
Tel: (33) 1 49 55 73 43180
Fax: (33) 1 47 05 77 02

FCO-China Chevening Fellowships for Postgraduate Study (China)

Subjects: All subjects.
Purpose: To financially support those undertaking postgraduate study.
Eligibility: Open to citizens of China. Applicants must apply to the University of Cambridge and be offered a place at Cambridge in the normal way. All applicants must have a First Class or High Second Class (Honours) Degree or equivalent and normally be under 26.
Level of Study: Postgraduate
Type: Scholarship
Value: The University Composition Fee at the overseas rate, approved college fees, a maintenance allowance sufficient for a single student and a contribution towards return economy airfare
Length of Study: 1 year
Frequency: Annual
Study Establishment: The University of Cambridge
Country of Study: United Kingdom
No. of awards offered: 3
Application Procedure: Applicants must complete a preliminary application form, which can be obtained from local universities, offices of the British Council or the Trust. Completed forms must be returned to the main address. Shortlisted candidates will be sent forms for admission to the University of Cambridge. The preliminary application form can also be downloaded from www.admin.cam.ac.uk/offices/gradstud/admissions/forms/
Closing Date: February 28th
Contributor: Offered in collaboration with the Foreign and Commonwealth Office (FCO)

First Canadian Donner Foundation Research Cambridge Scholarships for PhD Study

Subjects: All subjects.
Purpose: To financially support study towards a PhD.
Eligibility: Open to citizens of Canada who excel in sport. Candidates must gain admission to Magdalene College, Cambridge in the normal way. All applicants must be successfully nominated for an Overseas Research Student (ORS) award.
Level of Study: Predoctorate, doctorate
Type: Scholarship
Length of Study: 3 years
Frequency: Annual
Study Establishment: Magdalene College, the University of Cambridge
Country of Study: United Kingdom
No. of awards offered: 1
Application Procedure: Applicants must contact the Board of Graduate Studies.

For further information contact:

The Board of Graduate Studies, 4 Mill Lane, Cambridge, Cambridgeshire, CB2 1RZ, England
Contact: The Secretary

French Embassy Bursaries

Subjects: Engineering.
Purpose: To financially support those undertaking postgraduate study.
Eligibility: Open to citizens of France.
Level of Study: Postgraduate
Type: Bursary
Length of Study: 1 year
Frequency: Annual
Study Establishment: The Department of Engineering, the University of Cambridge
Country of Study: United Kingdom
No. of awards offered: Up to 4
Application Procedure: Applicants should contact the organization.
Closing Date: February 28th
Contributor: Offered in collaboration with the French Embassy in London

Guan Ruijin Memorial Bursary

Subjects: All subjects.
Purpose: To support postgraduate study.
Eligibility: Preference will be given to students from Peking University. Applicants must have a First Class or High Second Class (Honours) Degree or equivalent and normally be under 26.
Level of Study: Postgraduate
Type: Bursary
Value: Part-cost contribution towards the fees of the bursar
Length of Study: 1 year
Frequency: Dependent on funds available
Study Establishment: Wolfson College, Cambridge
Country of Study: United Kingdom
No. of awards offered: 1
Application Procedure: Applicants must apply to the university of Cambridge and be offered a place at Cambridge in the normal way. Applicants should complete only one scholarship form, which will enable them to be considered for all awards for which they are eligible. Application forms can be downloaded from the website.
Closing Date: February 28th
Contributor: Wolfson College and Cambridge Trusts

Guy Clutton-Brock Scholarship for PhD Study

Subjects: All subjects.
Purpose: To financially support those undertaking postgraduate study.
Eligibility: For a student from Zimbabwe who has been offered a place at Magdalene College, Cambridge in the normal way. All applicants must have a First Class or High Second Class (Honours) Degree or equivalent and normally be under 26. They must be successfully nominated for an Overseas Research Student (ORS) award.
Level of Study: Predoctorate, doctorate
Type: Scholarship
Value: The University Composition Fee at the home rate, approved college fees, a maintenance allowance sufficient for a single student and a contribution towards return economy airfare
Length of Study: Up to 3 years
Study Establishment: Magdalene College, the University of Cambridge
Country of Study: United Kingdom
No. of awards offered: 1
Application Procedure: Applicants must complete a preliminary application form, which can be obtained from local universities, offices of the British Council or the Trust. Completed forms must be returned to the main address. Shortlisted candidates will be sent forms for admission to the University of Cambridge. The preliminary application form can also be downloaded from www.admin.cam.ac.uk/offices/gradstud/admissions/forms/
Contributor: Offered by the Government of Zimbabwe in collaboration with Magdalene College, Cambridge in honour of Guy Clutton-Brock, hero of Zimbabwe

Guy Clutton-Brock Scholarship for Postgraduate Study

Subjects: All subjects.
Purpose: To financially support those undertaking postgraduate study.
Eligibility: Open to students from Zimbabwe who have been offered a place at Magdalene College, Cambridge in the normal way. All applicants must have a First Class or High Second Class (Honours) Degree or equivalent and normally be under 26. They must be successfully nominated for an Overseas Research Student (ORS) award.
Level of Study: Postgraduate
Type: Scholarship
Value: The University Composition Fee at the overseas rate, approved college fees, a maintenance allowance sufficient for a single student and a contribution towards return economy airfare
Length of Study: 1 year
Study Establishment: Magdalene College, the University of Cambridge
Country of Study: United Kingdom
No. of awards offered: 1
Application Procedure: Applicants must complete a preliminary application form, which can be obtained from local universities, offices of the British Council or the Trust. Completed forms must be returned to the main address. Shortlisted candidates will be sent forms for admission to the University of Cambridge. The preliminary application form can also be downloaded from www.admin.cam.ac.uk/offices/gradstud/admissions/forms/
Closing Date: February 28th
Contributor: Offered by the Government of Zimbabwe in collaboration with Magdalene College, Cambridge, in honour of Guy Clutton-Brock, hero of Zimbabwe

Hamilton Cambridge Scholarship for PhD Study

Subjects: All subjects.
Purpose: To financially support study towards a PhD.
Eligibility: Applicants must apply to the University of Cambridge and be offered a place at Cambridge in the normal way. All applicants must have a First Class or High Second Class (Honours) Degree or equivalent and normally be under 26. They must be successfully nominated for an Overseas Research Student (ORS) award.
Level of Study: Doctorate
Type: Scholarship
Value: The University Composition Fee at the home rate, approved college fees, a maintenance allowance sufficient for a single student and a contribution towards return economy airfare
Length of Study: Up to 3 years
Study Establishment: Selwyn College, the University of Cambridge
Country of Study: United Kingdom
No. of awards offered: 1
Application Procedure: Applicants must complete a preliminary application form, which can be obtained from local universities, offices of the British Council or the Trust. Completed forms must be returned to the main address. Shortlisted candidates will be sent forms for admission to the University of Cambridge. The preliminary application form can also be downloaded from www.admin.cam.ac.uk/offices/gradstud/admissions/forms/
Contributor: Offered in collaboration with Selwyn College, Cambridge

For further information contact:

The Board of Graduate Studies, 4 Mill Lane, Cambridge, Cambridgeshire, CB2 1RZ, England
Contact: The Secretary

Hinduja Cambridge ODA Scholarships

Subjects: All subjects.
Purpose: To financially support postgraduate study.
Eligibility: Applicants must be from India, have a First Class (Honours) Degree or equivalent from a recognized university and return to their home country upon completion of the course. Applicants employed by a government department, by a parastatal organization or at present living or studying in a developed country are not eligible.
Level of Study: Postgraduate
Value: Tuition fees, a maintenance allowances and airfares
Length of Study: 1 year
Study Establishment: The University of Cambridge
Country of Study: United Kingdom
Application Procedure: Applicants must apply to the university of Cambridge and be offered a place at Cambridge in the normal way. Applicants should complete only one scholarship form, which will enable them to be considered for all awards for which they are eligible. Application forms can be downloaded from the website.
Closing Date: September 1st
Funding: Trusts, private
Contributor: Hinduja Cambridge Trust

For further information contact:

The Nehru Trust for Cambridge University, Teen Murti House, Teen Murti Marg, New Delhi, 110011, India
Contact: The Joint Secretary

Hong Kong Cambridge Scholarships for PhD Study

Subjects: All subjects.
Purpose: To financially support study towards a PhD.
Eligibility: Preference is given to graduates of the Chinese University of Hong Kong and the University of Hong Kong, must apply to the University of Cambridge and be offered a place at Cambridge in the normal way. All applicants must have a First Class or High Second Class (Honours) Degree or equivalent and normally be under 26.
Level of Study: Predoctorate, doctorate
Type: Scholarship
Value: The University Composition Fee at the appropriate rate, approved college fees, a maintenance allowance sufficient for a single student and a contribution towards return economy airfare
Length of Study: Up to 3 years
Frequency: Annual
Study Establishment: The University of Cambridge
Country of Study: United Kingdom
No. of awards offered: Up to 5
Application Procedure: Applicants must complete a preliminary application form, which can be obtained from local universities, offices of the British Council or the Trust. Completed forms must be returned to the main address. Shortlisted candidates will be sent forms for admission to the University of Cambridge. The preliminary application

form can also be downloaded from www.admin.cam.ac.uk/offices/gradstud/admissions/forms/
Contributor: Offered in collaboration with the Malaysian Commonwealth Studies Centre

Huntsman Tioxide Cambridge Scholarship for Postgraduate Study

Subjects: Chemical engineering.
Purpose: To financially support those undertaking postgraduate study.
Eligibility: Applicants must be from Malaysia, South Africa or Singapore, must apply to the University of Cambridge and be offered a place at Cambridge in the normal way. All applicants must have a First Class or High Second Class (Honours) Degree or equivalent and normally be under 26.
Level of Study: Postgraduate
Type: Scholarship
Value: The University Composition Fee at the overseas rate, approved college fees, a maintenance allowance sufficient for a single student and a contribution towards return economy airfare
Length of Study: 1 year
Frequency: Dependent on funds available
Study Establishment: The University of Cambridge
Country of Study: United Kingdom
No. of awards offered: 1
Application Procedure: Applicants must complete a preliminary application form, which can be obtained from local universities, offices of the British Council or the Trust. Completed forms must be returned to the main address. Shortlisted candidates will be sent forms for admission to the University of Cambridge. The preliminary application form can also be downloaded from www.admin.cam.ac.uk/offices/gradstud/admissions/forms/
Closing Date: February 28th
Contributor: Offered in collaboration with Huntsman Tioxide

Hutchison Whampoa Chevening Cambridge Scholarships

Subjects: All subjects.
Purpose: To financially support those undertaking postgraduate study.
Eligibility: Open to students from China and Hong Kong. Applicants must apply to the University of Cambridge and be offered a place at Cambridge in the normal way. All applicants must have a First Class or High Second Class (Honours) Degree or equivalent.
Type: Scholarship
Value: The University Composition Fee at the overseas rate, approved college fees, a maintenance allowance sufficient for a single student and a contribution towards return economy airfare
Length of Study: 1 year
Study Establishment: The University of Cambridge
Country of Study: United Kingdom
No. of awards offered: Up to 21
Application Procedure: Applicants must complete a preliminary application form, which can be obtained from local universities, offices of the British Council or the Trust. Completed forms must be returned to the main address. Shortlisted candidates will be sent forms for admission to the University of Cambridge. The preliminary application form can also be downloaded from www.admin.cam.ac.uk/offices/gradstud/admissions/forms/
Closing Date: February 28th
Contributor: In collaboration with Hutchison Whampoa and the Foreign and Commonwealth Office (FCO)

Isaac Newton Trust European Research Studentships

Subjects: All subjects.
Purpose: To support research leading to a PhD.
Eligibility: Open to candidates from the European Union.
Level of Study: Doctorate
Type: Studentship
Value: UK £2,000 per year
Length of Study: 3 years
Frequency: Annual
Study Establishment: The University of Cambridge
Country of Study: United Kingdom
No. of awards offered: 33
Application Procedure: Applicants must contact the Trust.
Contributor: Offered in collaboration with the Isaac Newton Trust and the Cambridge European Trust

Jawaharlal Nehru Memorial Fund Cambridge Scholarship for PhD Study

Subjects: The broad fields of science policy, technology, global restructuring, philosophy and history of science, comparative studies in religion and culture, international relations and constitutional studies, Indian history, civilization and culture, interface of social change and economic development, environmental ecology and sustainable development.
Purpose: To financially support study towards a PhD.
Eligibility: Applicants must be from India, and must be successful in winning an Overseas Research Student (ORS) award. Those who have, in addition, to a First Class (Honours) Degree, a First Class Master's Degree or equivalent, may be given preference.
Level of Study: Predoctorate, doctorate
Type: Scholarship
Value: The University Composition Fee at the home rate, approved college fees, a maintenance allowance sufficient for a single student and a contribution towards return economy airfare
Length of Study: Up to 3 years
Frequency: Annual
Study Establishment: The University of Cambridge
Country of Study: United Kingdom
No. of awards offered: 1
Application Procedure: Applicants may obtain further details and a preliminary application form by writing before August 16th of the year before entry to the Joint Secretary of the Nehru Trust for Cambridge University, giving details of academic qualifications.
Contributor: Offered in collaboration with the Jawaharlal Nehru Memorial Fund

For further information contact:

The Nehru Trust for Cambridge University, Teen Murti House, Teen Murti Marg, New Delhi, 110011, India
Contact: The Joint Secretary

Jawaharlal Nehru Memorial Trust Cambridge DFID Scholarships

Subjects: All subjects.
Purpose: To offer financial support.
Eligibility: Open to citizens from India. All applicants must be under the age of 35 on October 1st with priority given to those candidates under the age of 30. They must not be employed by a national or local government department or by a parastatal organization, nor at present be living or studying in a developed country and not have undertaken studies lasting a year or more in a developed country. Priority will be given to candidates wishing to pursue a study related to the economic and social development of their country.
Level of Study: Postgraduate
Type: Scholarship
Value: The University Composition Fee at the overseas rate, approved college fees, a maintenance allowance sufficient for a single student and a contribution towards return economy airfare
Length of Study: 1 year
Frequency: Annual
Study Establishment: The University of Cambridge
Country of Study: United Kingdom
No. of awards offered: 2
Application Procedure: Applicants may obtain further details and a preliminary application form by writing before August 16th of the year before entry to the Joint Secretary of the Nehru Trust for Cambridge University, giving details of their academic qualifications.
Closing Date: February 28th
Contributor: Offered in collaboration with the Jawaharlal Nehru Memorial Trust and the Department of International Development (DFID)

For further information contact:

The Nehru Trust for Cambridge University, Teen Murti House, Teen Murti Marg, New Delhi, 110011, India
Contact: The Joint Secretary

Jawaharlal Nehru Memorial Trust Cambridge Scholarships

Subjects: All subjects.
Purpose: To financially support study towards a PhD.
Eligibility: Open to candidates from India. All applicants must be successful in winning an Overseas Research Student (ORS) award. Those who have, in addition to a First Class (Honours) Degree, a First Class Master's Degree or equivalent, may be given preference.
Level of Study: Doctorate
Type: Scholarship
Value: The University Composition Fee at the overseas rate, approved college fees, a contribution towards a maintenance allowance and a contribution to return economy airfare
Length of Study: 2 years
Frequency: Annual
Study Establishment: Trinity College, the University of Cambridge
Country of Study: United Kingdom
No. of awards offered: 1
Application Procedure: Applicants may obtain further details and a preliminary application form by writing before August 16th of the year before entry to the Joint Secretary of the Nehru Trust for Cambridge University, giving details of academic qualifications.
Contributor: Offered in collaboration with the Jawaharlal Nehru Memorial Trust and Trinity College, Cambridge

For further information contact:

The Nehru Trust for Cambridge University, Teen Murti House, Teen Murti Marg, New Delhi, 110011, India
Contact: The Joint Secretary

Kalimuzo Cambridge DFID Scholarships

Subjects: All subjects.
Purpose: To offer a scholarship in memory of Professor Frank Kalimuzo, former Vice-Chancellor of Makerere University.
Eligibility: Open to students from Uganda. All applicants must be under the age of 35 on October 1st with priority given to those candidates under the age of 30. They must not be employed by a national or local government department or by a parastatal organization, nor at present be living or studying in a developed country. Priority will be given to candidates wishing to pursue a course of study related to the economic and social development of their country.
Level of Study: Postgraduate
Type: Scholarship
Value: The University Composition Fee at the overseas rate, approved college fees, a maintenance allowance sufficient for a single student and a contribution towards return economy airfare
Length of Study: 1 year
Frequency: Annual
Study Establishment: The University of Cambridge
Country of Study: United Kingdom
No. of awards offered: 3
Application Procedure: Applicants must complete a preliminary application form, which can be obtained from local universities, offices of the British Council or the Trust. Completed forms must be returned to the main address. Shortlisted candidates will be sent forms for admission to the University of Cambridge. The preliminary application form can also be downloaded from www.admin.cam.ac.uk/offices/gradstud/admissions/forms/
Closing Date: February 28th
Contributor: Offered in collaboration with the Department of International Development (DFID)

Kalimuzo Cambridge Scholarship for PhD Study

Subjects: All subjects.
Purpose: To financially support study towards a PhD.
Eligibility: Open to students from Uganda. Applicants must apply to the University of Cambridge and be offered a place at Cambridge in the normal way. All applicants must have a First Class or High Second Class (Honours) Degree or equivalent and normally be under 26. They must be successfully nominated for an Overseas Research Student (ORS) award.
Level of Study: Doctorate
Type: Scholarship
Value: The University Composition Fee at the appropriate rate, approved college fees, a maintenance allowance sufficient for a single student and a contribution towards return economy airfare
Length of Study: 3 years
Frequency: Annual
Study Establishment: The University of Cambridge
Country of Study: United Kingdom
No. of awards offered: 1
Application Procedure: Applicants must complete a preliminary application form, which can be obtained from local universities, offices of the British Council or the Trust. Completed forms must be returned to the main address. Shortlisted candidates will be sent forms for admission to the University of Cambridge. The preliminary application form can also be downloaded from www.admin.cam.ac.uk/offices/gradstud/admissions/forms/
Additional Information: The scholarship is awarded in the memory of Professor Frank Kalimuzo, former Vice Chancellor of Makerere University.

Kapitza Cambridge Scholarships

Subjects: All subjects.
Eligibility: Open to students from countries of the former Soviet Union. Applicants must apply to the University of Cambridge and be offered a place at Cambridge in the normal way. All applicants must have a First Class or High Second Class (Honours) Degree or equivalent and normally be under 26.
Level of Study: Postdoctorate
Type: Scholarship
Value: The University Composition Fees at the overseas rate, approved college fees, a maintenance allowance sufficient for a single student and a contribution towards return economy airfare
Length of Study: 1 year
Frequency: Annual
Study Establishment: The University of Cambridge
No. of awards offered: Varies
Application Procedure: Applicants must complete a preliminary application form, which can be obtained from local universities, offices of the British Council or the Trust. Completed forms must be returned to the main address. Shortlisted candidates will be sent forms for admission to the University of Cambridge. The preliminary application form can also be downloaded from www.admin.cam.ac.uk/offices/gradstud/admissions/forms/
Closing Date: February 28th

Karim Rida Said Cambridge Scholarship for PhD Study

Subjects: All subjects.
Purpose: To financially support study towards a PhD.
Eligibility: Applicants must be from Jordan, Lebanon, Palestine or Syria, must apply to the University of Cambridge and be offered a place at Cambridge in the normal way. All applicants must have a First Class or High Second Class (Honours) Degree, or equivalent and may be up to the age of 40. They must be successfully nominated for an Overseas Research Student (ORS) award.
Level of Study: Doctorate, predoctorate
Type: Scholarship
Value: The University Composition Fee at the appropriate rate, approved college fees, a maintenance allowance sufficient for a single student and a contribution towards return economy airfare
Length of Study: Up to 3 years
Frequency: Annual
Study Establishment: The University of Cambridge
Country of Study: United Kingdom
No. of awards offered: 2
Application Procedure: Applicants must complete a preliminary application form, which can be obtained from local universities, offices of the British Council or the Trust. Completed forms must be returned to the main address. Shortlisted candidates will be sent forms for

admission to the University of Cambridge. The preliminary application form can also be downloaded from www.admin.cam.ac.uk/offices/gradstud/admissions/forms/
Contributor: Offered in collaboration with the Karim Rida Said Foundation
Additional Information: This scholarship is offered in memory of Karim Rida Said.

Karim Rida Said Cambridge Scholarship for Postgraduate Study

Subjects: All subjects.
Purpose: To financially support those undertaking postgraduate study.
Eligibility: Applicants must be from Jordan, Lebanon, Palestine or Syria. Applicants must apply to the University of Cambridge and be offered a place at Cambridge in the normal way. All applicants must have a First Class or High Second Class (Honours) Degree or equivalent and may be up to the age of 40. They must be successfully nominated for an Overseas Research Student (ORS) award.
Level of Study: Postgraduate
Type: Scholarship
Value: The University Composition Fee at the overseas rate, approved college fees, a maintenance allowance sufficient for a single student and a contribution towards a return economy airfare
Length of Study: 1 year
Frequency: Annual
Study Establishment: The University of Cambridge
Country of Study: United Kingdom
No. of awards offered: 4
Application Procedure: Applicants must complete a preliminary application form, which can be obtained from local universities, offices of the British Council or the Trust. Completed forms must be returned to the main address. Shortlisted candidates will be sent forms for admission to the University of Cambridge. The preliminary application form can also be downloaded from www.admin.cam.ac.uk/offices/gradstud/admissions/forms/
Closing Date: February 28th
Contributor: Offered in collaboration with the Karim Rida Said Foundation
Additional Information: This scholarship is offered in memory of Karim Rida Said.

Kenneth Sutherland Memorial Cambridge Scholarship

Subjects: Engineering.
Purpose: To support study towards a PhD.
Eligibility: Applicants must be from Canada and must be successfully nominated for an ORS award. All applicants must have a First Class or High Second Class (Honours) Degree or equivalent and normally be under 30.
Level of Study: Doctorate
Length of Study: 3 years
Frequency: Dependent on funds available
Study Establishment: Jesus College
Country of Study: United Kingdom
No. of awards offered: 1
Application Procedure: Applicants must apply to the university of Cambridge and be offered a place at Cambridge in the normal way. Applicants should complete only one scholarship form, which will enable them to be considered for all awards for which they are eligible. Application forms can be downloaded from the website. Candidates must also apply for an ORS award.
Closing Date: February 28th
Funding: Trusts
Contributor: Cambridge Trust and Jesus college

Kenya Cambridge DFID Scholarship

Subjects: All subjects.
Purpose: To offer financial support to students from Kenya.
Eligibility: Open to students from Kenya. All applicants must be under the age of 35 on October 1st with priority given to those candidates under the age of 30. Applicants must not be employed by a government department or by a parastatal organization, nor at present be living or studying in a developed country. Priority will be given to candidates wishing to pursue a course of study related to the economic and social development of their country.
Level of Study: Postgraduate
Type: Scholarship
Value: The University Composition Fee at the overseas rate, approved college fees, a maintenance allowance sufficient for a single student and a contribution towards return economy airfare
Length of Study: 1 year
Frequency: Annual
Study Establishment: The University of Cambridge
Country of Study: United Kingdom
No. of awards offered: 1
Application Procedure: Applicants must complete a preliminary application form, which can be obtained from local universities, offices of the British Council or the Trust. Completed forms must be returned to the main address. Shortlisted candidates will be sent forms for admission to the University of Cambridge. The preliminary application form can also be downloaded from www.admin.cam.ac.uk/offices/gradstud/admissions/forms/
Closing Date: February 28th
Contributor: Offered in collaboration with the Kenya Cambridge Commonwealth Trusts and the Department of International Development (DFID)

Kenya Cambridge Scholarship for PhD Study

Subjects: All subjects.
Purpose: To financially support study towards a PhD.
Eligibility: Applicants must be citizens of Kenya, must apply to the University of Cambridge and be offered a place at Cambridge in the normal way. All applicants must have a First Class or High Second Class (Honours) Degree or equivalent and normally be under 26. They must be successfully nominated for an Overseas Research Student (ORS) award.
Level of Study: Doctorate
Type: Scholarship
Value: The University Composition Fee at the home rate, approved college fees, a maintenance allowance sufficient for a single student and a contribution towards return economy airfare
Length of Study: Up to 3 years
Frequency: Annual
Study Establishment: The University of Cambridge
Country of Study: United Kingdom
No. of awards offered: 1
Application Procedure: Applicants must complete a preliminary application form, which can be obtained from local universities, offices of the British Council or the Trust. Completed forms must be returned to the main address. Shortlisted candidates will be sent forms for admission to the University of Cambridge. The preliminary application form can also be downloaded from www.admin.cam.ac.uk/offices/gradstud/admissions/forms/
Contributor: Offered in collaboration with the Kenya Cambridge Commonwealth Trust

The Laboratory of Molecular Biology (LMB) Cambridge Scholarships for PhD Study

Subjects: Molecular biology.
Purpose: To financially support study towards a PhD.
Eligibility: Applicants must apply to the University of Cambridge and be offered a place at Cambridge in the normal way. All applicants must have a First Class or High Second Class (Honours) Degree or equivalent and normally be under 26.
Level of Study: Doctorate, predoctorate
Type: Scholarship
Value: Full maintenance allowance at the single student rate, after taking account of other awards from public sources towards maintenance for which the students are eligible and have received funding
Length of Study: Up to 3 years
Frequency: Annual
Study Establishment: The Laboratory of Molecular Biology (LMB), the University of Cambridge
Country of Study: United Kingdom
No. of awards offered: Up to 3

Application Procedure: Candidates for LMB Cambridge Scholarships should apply directly to the LMB by: nominating up to four possible PhD supervisors and projects from the list of available projects as published by the LMB; providing a personal statement of not more than one page (for each proposed supervisor) explaining why they wish to work in that chosen area of research and their reasons for nominating that supervisor; providing a copy of an up-to-date curriculum vitae; and providing a copy of their transcripts.
Closing Date: December 13th

For further information contact:

The MRC Laboratory of Molecular Biology, Hills Road, Cambridge, Cambridgeshire, CB2 2QH, England
Website: www.mrc-lmb.cam.ac.uk
Contact: Director of Studies

The Laboratory of Molecular Biology (LMB) Newton Cambridge Scholarships

Subjects: Molecular biology.
Purpose: To support and encourage candidates to pursue a course of research leading to a PhD.
Eligibility: Open to candidates from the European Union.
Level of Study: Doctorate
Type: Scholarship
Value: Full maintenance allowance at the single student rate, after taking account of other awards from public sources towards maintenance for which the students are eligible and have received
Length of Study: 3 years
Frequency: Annual
Study Establishment: The Laboratory of Molecular Biology (LMB), the University of Cambridge
Country of Study: United Kingdom
No. of awards offered: 3
Application Procedure: Applicants must apply directly to the LMB by: nominating up to four possible PhD supervisors and projects from the list of available projects as published by the LMB; providing a personal statement of not more than one page (for each proposed supervisor) explaining why they wish to work in that chosen area of research and their reasons for nominating that supervisor; providing a copy of an up-to-date curriculum vitae and providing a copy of their transcripts.
Contributor: Offered in collaboration with the LMB, the Isaac Newton Trust and the Cambridge European Trust

For further information contact:

The MRC Laboratory of Molecular Biology (LMB), Hills Road, Cambridge, Cambridgeshire, CB2 2QH, England
Website: www.mrc-lmb.cam.ac.uk
Contact: Director of Studies

Lady Noon Bursary

Subjects: All subjects.
Purpose: To financially support study towards a second Bachelor's degree as an affiliated student.
Eligibility: Applicants must be from Pakistan.
Level of Study: Graduate
Type: Bursary
Value: A substantial contribution towards the costs of study, to be determined in the light of the student's own resources
Frequency: Annual
Study Establishment: The University of Cambridge
Country of Study: United Kingdom
No. of awards offered: 1
Application Procedure: Applicants must complete a preliminary application form, which can be obtained from local universities, offices of the British Council or the Trust. The preliminary application form can also be downloaded from www.admin.cam.ac.uk/offices/gradstud/admissions/forms/ completed application forms must be returned to the main address. Candidates shortlisted will be sent forms for admission to the University of Cambridge and a scholarship application form. These forms must be returned to the Board of Graduate Studies at the address below.
Closing Date: February 28th
Contributor: In association with the Lady Noon Trust

For further information contact:

The Board of Graduate Studies, 4 Mill Hill, Cambridge, Cambridgeshire, CB2 1RZ, England

Lady Noon Cambridge DFID Scholarships

Subjects: All subjects.
Purpose: To financially support those undertaking postgraduate study.
Eligibility: Open to students from Pakistan. All applicants must be under the age of 35 on October 1st with priority given to those candidates under the age of 30. They must not be employed by a national or local government department or by a parastatal organization, nor at present be living or studying in a developed country. Priority will be given to candidates wishing to pursue a course of study related to the economic and social development of their own country.
Level of Study: Postgraduate
Type: Scholarship
Value: The University Composition Fee at overseas rate, approved college fees, a maintenance allowance sufficient for a single student and a contribution towards return economy airfare
Length of Study: 1 year
Frequency: Annual
Study Establishment: The University of Cambridge
Country of Study: United Kingdom
No. of awards offered: Varies
Application Procedure: Applicants must complete a preliminary application form, which can be obtained from local universities, offices of the British Council or the Trust. Completed forms must be returned to the main address. Shortlisted candidates will be sent forms for admission to the University of Cambridge. The preliminary application form can also be downloaded from www.admin.cam.ac.uk/offices/gradstud/admissions/forms/
Closing Date: February 28th
Contributor: Offered in collaboration with the Lady Noon Trust and the Department for International Development (DFID)

Link Foundation/FCO Chevening Cambridge Scholarships for Postgraduate Study

Subjects: All subjects.
Purpose: To financially support those undertaking postgraduate study.
Eligibility: Open to citizens of New Zealand. Applicants must apply to the University of Cambridge and be offered a place at Cambridge in the normal way. All applicants must have a First Class or High Second Class (Honours) Degree or equivalent and normally be under 26.
Level of Study: Postgraduate
Type: Scholarship
Value: Up to UK £10,000 towards the costs of study and UK £1,000 towards the return airfare to the United Kingdom
Length of Study: 1 year
Frequency: Annual
Study Establishment: The University of Cambridge
Country of Study: United Kingdom
No. of awards offered: 3
Application Procedure: Applicants must contact the Board of Graduate Studies.
Closing Date: February 28th
Contributor: Offered in collaboration with the Link Foundation for UK-New Zealand Relations (formerly known as the Waitangi Foundation) and the Foreign and Commonwealth Office (FCO)

For further information contact:

The Board of Graduate Studies, 4 Mill Hill, Cambridge, Cambridgeshire, CB2 1RZ, England
Contact: The Secretary

Mandela Cambridge Scholarships for PhD Study

Subjects: All subjects.
Purpose: To financially support study towards a PhD.

Eligibility: Applicants must be from South Africa. Applicants must apply to the University of Cambridge and be offered a place at Cambridge in the normal way. All applicants must have a First Class or High Second Class (Honours) Degree or equivalent and normally be under 26. They must be successfully nominated for an Overseas Research Student (ORS) award.
Level of Study: Doctorate, predoctorate
Type: Scholarship
Value: The University Composition Fee at the appropriate rate, approved college fees, a maintenance allowance sufficient for a single student and a contribution to return economy airfare
Length of Study: Up to 3 years
Frequency: Annual
Study Establishment: The University of Cambridge
Country of Study: United Kingdom
No. of awards offered: Up to 5
Application Procedure: Applicants must complete a preliminary application form, which can be obtained from local universities, offices of the British Council or the Trust. The preliminary application form can also be downloaded from www.admin.cam.ac.uk/offices/gradstud/admissions/forms/ completed forms must be returned to the main address. Shortlisted candidates will be sent forms for admission to the University of Cambridge.
Contributor: Offered by the Malaysian Commonwealth Studies Centre, the Cambridge Local Examinations Syndicate, Trinity College, Cambridge, and the Cambridge University Press
Additional Information: These scholarships are offered in honour of former South African President Nelson Mandela.

Mandela Cambridge Scholarships for Postgraduate Study

Subjects: All subjects.
Purpose: To financially support those undertaking postgraduate study.
Eligibility: Applicants must be from South Africa, must apply to the University of Cambridge and be offered a place at Cambridge in the normal way. All applicants must have a First Class or High Second Class (Honours) Degree or equivalent and normally be under 26. They must be successfully nominated for an Overseas Research Student (ORS) award.
Level of Study: Postgraduate
Type: Scholarship
Value: The University Composition Fee at the overseas rate, approved college fees, a maintenance allowance sufficient for a single student and a contribution towards return economy airfare
Length of Study: 1 year
Frequency: Annual
Study Establishment: The University of Cambridge
Country of Study: United Kingdom
No. of awards offered: Up to 20
Application Procedure: Applicants must complete a preliminary application form, which can be obtained from local universities, offices of the British Council or the Trust. The preliminary application form can also be downloaded from www.admin.cam.ac.uk/offices/gradstud/admissions/forms/ completed forms must be returned to the main address. Shortlisted candidates will be sent forms for admission to the University of Cambridge.
Closing Date: February 28th
Contributor: Offered by the Malaysian Commonwealth Studies Centre, the Cambridge Local Examinations Syndicate, Trinity College, Cambridge, and the Cambridge University Press
Additional Information: These scholarships are offered in honour of former South African President Nelson Mandela.

Mandela Magdalene College Scholarships for Postgraduate Scholarships

Subjects: All subjects.
Purpose: To financially support those undertaking postgraduate study and research.
Eligibility: Students must have been offered a place at Magdalene College, Cambridge and be citizens of South Africa. All applicants must have a First Class or High Second Class (Honours) Degree or equivalent and normally be under 26.
Level of Study: Postgraduate
Type: Scholarship
Value: The University Composition Fee at the overseas rate, approved college fees, a maintenance allowance sufficient for a single student and a contribution to return economy airfare
Length of Study: 1 year
Frequency: Annual
Study Establishment: Magdalene College, the University of Cambridge
Country of Study: United Kingdom
No. of awards offered: Up to 3
Application Procedure: Applicants must complete a preliminary application form, which can be obtained from local universities, offices of the British Council or the Trust. Completed forms must be returned to the main address. Shortlisted candidates will be sent forms for admission to the University of Cambridge. The preliminary application form can also be downloaded from www.admin.cam.ac.uk/offices/gradstud/admissions/forms/
Closing Date: February 28th
Contributor: Offered in collaboration with Magdalene College, Cambridge and Mr Chris von Christierson

Mehmed Fuad Köprülü Scholarships for Turkey

Subjects: All subjects.
Purpose: To financially support study towards a PhD.
Eligibility: Applicants must be from Turkey and must apply for an Overseas Research Student (ORS) award. Applicants must apply to the University of Cambridge and be offered a place at Cambridge in the normal way. They must have a First Class or High Second Class (Honours) Degree or equivalent and normally be under 26.
Level of Study: Postdoctorate
Type: Scholarship
Value: The University Composition Fee at the appropriate rate, approved college fees, a maintenance allowance sufficient for a single student and a contribution towards return economy airfare
Length of Study: Up to 3 years
Frequency: Annual
Study Establishment: The University of Cambridge
Country of Study: United Kingdom
No. of awards offered: 10
Application Procedure: All applicants must complete an application for admission to the University of Cambridge as a graduate student and return it to the Turkish Council for Higher Education (YÖK).
Contributor: Offered in collaboration with the YÖK

For further information contact:

The Turkish Council for Higher Education (YÖK), Binasi Bilkent, Ankara, 06539, Turkey

Michael Miliffe Cambridge Scholarships

Subjects: All subjects.
Purpose: To financially support study towards a second Bachelor's degree as an affiliated student.
Eligibility: Open to citizens of developing countries. The Trusts cannot admit students to the University or any of its colleges. Applicants for awards from the Trusts must, therefore, also apply to the University of Cambridge and be offered a place at Cambridge in the normal way. All applicants must have a First Class or High Second Class (Honours) Degree or equivalent and normally be under 26.
Level of Study: Graduate
Type: Scholarship
Value: A substantial contribution of up to UK £5,000 per year towards the student's costs, to be determined in the light of the student's own resources
Length of Study: 2 years
Frequency: Annual
Study Establishment: Gonville and Caius College, the University of Cambridge
Country of Study: United Kingdom
No. of awards offered: 2
Application Procedure: Applicants must contact the organization.
Closing Date: February 28th
Contributor: Offered in collaboration with the Michael Miliffe Fund and Gonville and Caius College, the University of Cambridge

Ministry of Education (Malaysia) Scholarships for Postgraduate Study

Subjects: All subjects.
Purpose: To financially support those undertaking postgraduate study.
Eligibility: Applicants must be from Malaysia, and must be nominated by the Ministry of Education. Applicants must apply to the University of Cambridge and be offered a place at Cambridge in the normal way. They must have a First Class or High Second Class (Honours) Degree or equivalent and normally be under 26.
Level of Study: Postgraduate
Type: Scholarship
Value: The University Composition Fee at the overseas rate, approved college fees, a maintenance allowance sufficient for a single student and a contribution to return economy airfare
Length of Study: 1 year
Frequency: Annual
Study Establishment: The University of Cambridge
Country of Study: United Kingdom
No. of awards offered: 4
Application Procedure: Applicants must complete a preliminary application form, which can be obtained from local universities, offices of the British Council or the Trust. Completed forms must be returned to the main address. Shortlisted candidates will be sent forms for admission to the University of Cambridge. The preliminary application form can also be downloaded from www.admin.cam.ac.uk/offices/gradstud/admissions/forms/
Closing Date: February 28th
Contributor: Offered in collaboration with the Malaysian Commonwealth Studies Centre and the Ministry of Education, Government of Malaysia

For further information contact:

The Cambridge (Malaysia) Foundation, PO Box 10139, Kuala Lumpur, 50704, Malaysia

Ministry of Science, Technology and the Environment Scholarships for Postgraduate Study (Malaysia)

Subjects: All subjects.
Purpose: To financially support those undertaking postgraduate study.
Eligibility: Applicants must be from Malaysia, and must be nominated by the Ministry of Science, Technology and the Environment. Applicants must apply to the University of Cambridge and be offered a place at Cambridge in the normal way. They must have a First Class or High Second Class (Honours) Degree or equivalent and normally be under 26.
Level of Study: Postgraduate
Type: Scholarship
Value: The University Composition Fee at the overseas rate, approved college fees, a maintenance allowance sufficient for a single student and a contribution to return economy airfare
Length of Study: 1 year
Frequency: Annual
Study Establishment: The University of Cambridge
Country of Study: United Kingdom
No. of awards offered: Up to 10
Application Procedure: Applicants must complete a preliminary application form, which can be obtained from local universities, offices of the British Council or the Trust. Completed forms must be returned to the main address. Shortlisted candidates will be sent forms for admission to the University of Cambridge. The preliminary application form can also be downloaded from www.admin.cam.ac.uk/offices/gradstud/admissions/forms/
Closing Date: February 28th
Contributor: Offered in collaboration with the Malaysian Commonwealth Studies Centre and the Ministry of Science, Technology and the Environment, Government of Malaysia

For further information contact:

The Cambridge (Malaysia) Foundation, PO Box 10139, Kuala Lumpur, 50704, Malaysia

Nehru Centenary Chevening Cambridge Scholarships

Subjects: All subjects.
Purpose: To financially support study towards a second Bachelor's degree as an affiliated student.
Eligibility: Applicants must be from India. The Trusts cannot admit students to the University or any of its colleges. Applicants for awards from the Trusts must, therefore, also apply to the University of Cambridge and be offered a place at Cambridge in the normal way. All applicants must have a First Class or High Second Class (Honours) Degree or equivalent and normally be under 26.
Level of Study: Graduate
Type: Scholarship
Value: The University Composition Fee at the overseas rate, approved college fees, a contribution towards a maintenance allowance and a contribution towards return economy airfare
Length of Study: 2 years
Frequency: Annual
Study Establishment: The University of Cambridge
Country of Study: United Kingdom
No. of awards offered: Up to 5
Application Procedure: Applicants may obtain further details and a preliminary application form by writing before August 16th of the year before entry to the Joint Secretary giving details of academic qualifications.
Closing Date: February 28th
Contributor: Offered in collaboration with the Foreign and Commonwealth Office (FCO)

For further information contact:

The Nehru Trust for Cambridge University, Teen Murti House, Teen Murti Marg, New Delhi, 110011, India
Contact: The Joint Secretary

Nehru Trust for the Indian Collections V&A Cambridge DFID Scholarship

Subjects: Archaeology, focusing on archaeological heritage and museums or social anthropology, with special reference to the work of a museum.
Purpose: To financially support those undertaking postgraduate study.
Eligibility: Applicants must be from India, and must be under the age of 35 on October 1st with priority given to those candidates under the age of 30. Applicants must not be employed by a national or local government department or by a parastatal organization, nor at present be living or studying in a developed country. Priority will be given to candidates wishing to pursue a course of study related to the economic and social development of their country.
Level of Study: Postgraduate
Type: Scholarship
Value: The University Composition Fee at the overseas rate, approved college fees, a maintenance allowance sufficient for a single student and a contribution to return economy airfare. In addition a supplementary allowance to cover a short period of practical training at the Victoria and Albert Museum, or other approved institution, will be given
Length of Study: 1 year
Frequency: Annual
Study Establishment: The University of Cambridge
Country of Study: United Kingdom
No. of awards offered: 1
Application Procedure: Applicants may obtain further details and a preliminary application form by writing before August 16th of the year before entry to the Joint Secretary at the address given below with details of academic qualifications.
Closing Date: February 28th
Contributor: Offered in collaboration with the Nehru Trust for the Indian Collections at the Victoria and Albert (V&A) Museum and the Department for International Development (DFID)

For further information contact:

The Nehru Trust for Cambridge University, Teen Murti House, Teen Murti Marg, New Delhi, 110011, India
Contact: The Joint Secretary

Nepal Cambridge Scholarships

Subjects: All subjects.
Purpose: To financially support those undertaking postgraduate study.
Eligibility: Applicants must be from Nepal, must apply to the University of Cambridge and be offered a place at Cambridge in the normal way. All applicants must have a First Class or High Second Class (Honours) Degree or equivalent and normally be under 26.
Level of Study: Postgraduate
Type: Scholarship
Value: The University Composition Fee at the overseas rate, approved college fees, a maintenance allowance sufficient for a single student and a contribution towards return economy airfare
Length of Study: 1 year
Frequency: Annual
Study Establishment: The University of Cambridge
Country of Study: United Kingdom
No. of awards offered: 1
Application Procedure: Applicants must complete a preliminary application form, which can be obtained from local universities, offices of the British Council or the Trust. Completed forms must be returned to the main address. Shortlisted candidates will be sent forms for admission to the University of Cambridge. The preliminary application form can also be downloaded from www.admin.cam.ac.uk/offices/gradstud/admissions/forms/
Closing Date: February 28th
Contributor: Offered in collaboration with the British Embassy in Kathmandu

OSI Chevening Cambridge Scholarships for Postgraduate Study

Subjects: Social sciences and humanities.
Purpose: To financially support those undertaking postgraduate study.
Eligibility: Open to students from Albania, Bosnia, Croatia, Estonia, Kosovo, Latvia, Lithuania, Macedonia, Slovenia, Ukraine or the Federal Republic of Yugoslavia. Applicants must apply to the University of Cambridge and be offered a place at Cambridge in the normal way. All applicants must have a First Class or High Second Class (Honours) Degree or equivalent and normally be under 26.
Level of Study: Postgraduate
Type: Scholarship
Value: The University Composition Fee at the overseas rate, approved college fees, a maintenance allowance sufficient for a single student and a contribution towards return economy airfare
Frequency: Annual
Study Establishment: The University of Cambridge
Country of Study: United Kingdom
No. of awards offered: Up to 34
Application Procedure: Applicants must complete a preliminary application form, which can be obtained from local universities, offices of the British Council or the Trust. Completed forms must be returned to the main address. Shortlisted candidates will be sent forms for admission to the University of Cambridge. The preliminary application form can also be downloaded from www.admin.cam.ac.uk/offices/gradstud/admissions/forms/
Closing Date: February 28th
Contributor: Offered in collaboration with the Open Society Institute (OSI) and the Foreign and Commonwealth Office (FCO)

OSI Noon Chevening Cambridge Scholarships

Subjects: All subjects relevant to the needs of Pakistan.
Purpose: To financially support postgraduate study.
Eligibility: Candidates should be nationals of and normally resident in, Pakistan during the academic year in which they apply for an award. They must preferably have not already spent a full academic year or more studying in an Institution of Higher Education in the West, and must return to their home country at the end of their scholarship period to continue their studies/work there.
Level of Study: Postgraduate
Type: Scholarship
Length of Study: 1 year
Study Establishment: University of Cambridge
Country of Study: United Kingdom
No. of awards offered: 5
Application Procedure: Applicants must complete a preliminary application form, which can be obtained from local universities, offices of the British Council or the Trust. Completed forms must be returned to the main address. Shortlisted candidates will be sent forms for admission to the University of Cambridge. The preliminary application form can also be downloaded from www.admin.cam.ac.uk/offices/gradstud/admissions/forms/
Closing Date: February 28th
Funding: Foundation, trusts
Contributor: Cambridge Trusts, Noon Educational Foundation, Foreign and Commonwealth Office and the Open Society Institute (OSI)

Oxford and Cambridge Society of Bombay Cambridge DFID Scholarship

Subjects: All subjects.
Purpose: To financially support those undertaking postgraduate study.
Eligibility: Open to a resident of Bombay City or the State of Maharashtra whose application is supported by the Oxford and Cambridge Society of Bombay. All applicants must be under the age of 35 on October 1st with priority given to those candidates under the age of 30. They must not be employed by a national or local government department or by a parastatal organization, nor at present be living or studying in a developed country. Priority will be given to candidates wishing to pursue a study related to the economic and social development of their country.
Level of Study: Postgraduate
Type: Scholarship
Value: The University Composition Fee at the overseas rate, approved college fees, a maintenance allowance sufficient for a single student and a contribution to return economy airfare
Length of Study: 1 year
Frequency: Annual
Study Establishment: The University of Cambridge
Country of Study: United Kingdom
No. of awards offered: 1
Application Procedure: Applicants may obtain further details and a preliminary application form by writing before August 16th of the year before entry to the Joint Secretary at address given below with details of academic qualifications.
Closing Date: February 28th
Contributor: Offered in collaboration with the Department for International Development (DFID)

For further information contact:

The Nehru Trust for Cambridge University, Teen Murti House, Teen Murti Marg, New Delhi, 110011, India
Contact: The Joint Secretary

Pegasus Cambridge Scholarships for Postgraduate Study

Subjects: Law.
Purpose: To financially assist students who have gained an offer of a place to read for the Master of Law degree (LLM).
Eligibility: Applicants must be from one of the following countries: Australia, New Zealand, Canada, Bermuda and the Commonwealth countries of the Caribbean, Kenya, Nigeria, Zambia, Zimbabwe, Hong Kong, Singapore or India. Applicants must apply to the University of Cambridge and be offered a place at Cambridge in the normal way. All applicants must have a First Class or High Second Class (Honours) Degree or equivalent and normally be under 26. They must be successful in winning an Overseas Research Student (ORS) award.
Level of Study: Postgraduate
Type: Scholarship
Frequency: Annual
Study Establishment: The University of Cambridge
Country of Study: United Kingdom
No. of awards offered: Up to 6
Application Procedure: Applicants must complete a preliminary application form, which can be obtained from local universities, offices

of the British Council or the Trust. Completed forms must be returned to the main address. Shortlisted candidates will be sent forms for admission to the University of Cambridge. The preliminary application form can also be downloaded from www.admin.cam.ac.uk/offices/gradstud/admissions/forms/
Closing Date: February 28th
Contributor: Offered in collaboration with the Pegasus Scholarships Trust and the Foreign and Commonwealth Office (FCO)

President Árpad Göncz Scholarship for Postgraduate Study

Subjects: All subjects.
Purpose: To commemorate the visit of the President of Hungary to the University of Cambridge.
Eligibility: Applicants must be Hungarian nationals, must apply to the University of Cambridge and be offered a place at Cambridge in the normal way. All applicants must have a First Class or High Second Class (Honours) Degree or equivalent and normally be under 26.
Level of Study: Postgraduate
Type: Scholarship
Value: The University Composition Fees at the overseas rate, approved college fees, a maintenance allowance sufficient for a single student and a contribution to return economy airfare
Length of Study: 1 year
Frequency: Annual
Study Establishment: The University of Cambridge
Country of Study: United Kingdom
No. of awards offered: 1
Application Procedure: Applicants must complete a preliminary application form, which can be obtained from local universities, offices of the British Council or the Trust. Completed forms must be returned to the main address. Shortlisted candidates will be sent forms for admission to the University of Cambridge. The preliminary application form can also be downloaded from www.admin.cam.ac.uk/offices/gradstud/admissions/forms/
Closing Date: February 28th

President's Cambridge Scholarships for PhD Study

Subjects: All subjects.
Purpose: To financially support study towards a PhD.
Eligibility: Open to students from Ghana. Applicants must apply to the University of Cambridge and be offered a place at Cambridge in the normal way. All applicants must have a First Class or High Second Class (Honours) Degree or equivalent and normally be under 26. They must be successfully nominated for an Overseas Research Student (ORS) award.
Level of Study: Doctorate
Type: Scholarship
Value: The University Composition Fee at the appropriate rate, approved college fees, maintenance allowance sufficient for a single student and a contribution to a return economy airfare
Length of Study: Up to 3 years
Frequency: Annual
Study Establishment: The University of Cambridge
Country of Study: United Kingdom
No. of awards offered: Up to 5
Application Procedure: Applicants must complete a preliminary application form, which can be obtained from local universities, offices of the British Council or the Trust. Completed forms must be returned to the main address. Shortlisted candidates will be sent forms for admission to the University of Cambridge. The preliminary application form can also be downloaded from www.admin.cam.ac.uk/offices/gradstud/admissions/forms/
Contributor: Offered in collaboration with the Malaysian Commonwealth Studies Centre

President's Cambridge Scholarships for Postgraduate Study

Subjects: All subjects.
Purpose: To financially support those undertaking postgraduate study.
Eligibility: Applicants must be from Ghana, must apply to the University of Cambridge and be offered a place at Cambridge in the normal way. All applicants must have a First Class or High Second Class (Honours) Degree or equivalent and normally be under 26.
Level of Study: Postgraduate
Type: Scholarship
Value: The University Composition Fee at the appropriate rate, approved college fees, a maintenance allowance sufficient for a single student and a contribution towards return economy airfare
Length of Study: 1 year
Frequency: Annual
Study Establishment: The University of Cambridge
Country of Study: United Kingdom
No. of awards offered: Up to 5
Application Procedure: Applicants must complete a preliminary application form, which can be obtained from local universities, offices of the British Council or the Trust. Completed forms must be returned to the main address. Shortlisted candidates will be sent forms for admission to the University of Cambridge. The preliminary application form can also be downloaded from www.admin.cam.ac.uk/offices/gradstud/admissions/forms/
Closing Date: February 28th
Contributor: Offered in collaboration with the Malaysian Commonwealth Studies Centre

Prince of Wales (Cable and Wireless) Cambridge Scholarships

Subjects: All subjects.
Eligibility: Open to citizens of Japan. Applicants must apply to the University of Cambridge and be offered a place at Cambridge in the normal way. All applicants must have a First Class or High Second Class (Honours) Degree or equivalent and normally be under 26.
Level of Study: Postgraduate
Type: Scholarship
Value: The University Composition Fee at the appropriate rate, approved college fees, a maintenance allowance sufficient for a single student and a contribution towards a return economy airfare
Length of Study: 1 year
Frequency: Annual
Study Establishment: The University of Cambridge
Country of Study: United Kingdom
No. of awards offered: 10
Application Procedure: Applicants must complete a preliminary application form, which can be obtained from local universities, offices of the British Council or the Trust. Completed forms must be returned to the main address. Shortlisted candidates will be sent forms for admission to the University of Cambridge. The preliminary application form can also be downloaded from www.admin.cam.ac.uk/offices/gradstud/admissions/forms/
Closing Date: February 28th

Prince of Wales (Cable and Wireless) Cambridge Scholarships for PhD Study

Subjects: All subjects.
Purpose: To financially support study in subjects related to the needs of the scholar's country.
Eligibility: Open to citizens of a number of countries including Anguilla, Antigua and Barbuda, Barbados, Bermuda, the British Virgin Islands, the Cayman Islands, Dominica, Grenada, Jamaica, Montserrat, St Kitts-Nevis, St Lucia, St Vincent, Trinidad and Tobago, and the Turks and Caicos Islands. Applicants must apply to the University of Cambridge and be offered a place at Cambridge in the normal way. All applicants must have a First Class or High Second Class (Honours) Degree or equivalent and normally be under 26. They must be successfully nominated for an Overseas Research Student (ORS) award.
Level of Study: Doctorate, predoctorate
Type: Scholarship
Value: The University Composition Fee at the appropriate rate, approved college fees, a maintenance allowance sufficient for a single student and a contribution towards return economy airfare
Length of Study: 3 years
Frequency: Annual
Study Establishment: The University of Cambridge
Country of Study: United Kingdom

No. of awards offered: 10
Application Procedure: Applicants must complete a preliminary application form, which can be obtained from local universities, offices of the British Council or the Trust. Completed forms must be returned to the main address. Shortlisted candidates will be sent forms for admission to the University of Cambridge. The preliminary application form can also be downloaded from www.admin.cam.ac.uk/offices/gradstud/admissions/forms/
Closing Date: February 28th
Contributor: Offered in collaboration with Cable and Wireless

Prince of Wales (Cable and Wireless) Chevening Cambridge Scholarships for Postgraduate Study

Subjects: Development studies, economics, economics and development, engineering, environment and development, finance, international relations, law or management studies.
Purpose: To financially support study in subjects related to the needs of the scholar's country.
Eligibility: Open to citizens of Anguilla, Antigua and Barbuda, Barbados, Bermuda, the British Virgin Islands, the Cayman Islands, Dominica, Grenada, Jamaica, Montserrat, St Kitts-Nevis, St Lucia, St Vincent, Trinidad and Tobago, and the Turks and Caicos Islands. Applicants must apply to the University of Cambridge and be offered a place at Cambridge in the normal way. They must have a First Class or High Second Class (Honours) Degree or equivalent and normally be under 26.
Level of Study: Postgraduate
Type: Scholarship
Value: The University Composition Fee at the appropriate rate, approved college fees, a maintenance allowance sufficient for a single student and a contribution towards return economy airfare
Length of Study: 1 year
Frequency: Annual
Study Establishment: The University of Cambridge
Country of Study: United Kingdom
No. of awards offered: 10
Application Procedure: Applicants must complete a preliminary application form, which can be obtained from local universities, offices of the British Council or the Trust. Completed forms must be returned to the main address. Shortlisted candidates will be sent forms for admission to the University of Cambridge. The preliminary application form can also be downloaded from www.admin.cam.ac.uk/offices/gradstud/admissions/forms/
Closing Date: February 28th
Contributor: Offered in collaboration with Cable and Wireless and the Foreign and Commonwealth Office (FCO)

Prince of Wales Scholarships for PhD Study

Subjects: All subjects.
Purpose: To financially support study towards a PhD.
Eligibility: Candidates must be citizens of New Zealand, must apply to the University of Cambridge and be offered a place at Cambridge in the normal way. All applicants must have a First Class or High Second Class (Honours) Degree or equivalent and normally be under 26. They must be successfully nominated for an Overseas Research Student (ORS) award.
Level of Study: Predoctorate, doctorate
Type: Scholarship
Value: The University Composition Fee at the home rate, approved college fees, a maintenance allowance sufficient for a single student and a contribution to return economy airfare
Length of Study: Up to 3 years
Frequency: Annual
Study Establishment: The University of Cambridge
Country of Study: United Kingdom
No. of awards offered: Up to 5
Application Procedure: Applicants must apply directly to the Scholarships Officer at their own university. Otherwise, they should apply directly to the New Zealand Vice Chancellor's Committee.
Closing Date: February 28th
Contributor: Offered in collaboration with the New Zealand Vice Chancellor's Committee

For further information contact:

The New Zealand Vice Chancellor's Committee, Level 11, 94 Dixon Street, Wellington 6034, P.O. Box 11-915, New Zealand
Contact: Scholarships Officer

Prince Philip Graduate Exhibitions For PhD Study

Subjects: All subjects.
Purpose: To financially support study towards a PhD.
Eligibility: Students who have graduated from the Chinese University of Hong Kong and the University of Hong Kong. Applicants must apply to the University of Cambridge and be offered a place at Cambridge in the normal way. All applicants must have a First Class or High Second Class (Honours) Degree or equivalent and normally be under 26. They must be successfully nominated for an Overseas Research Student (ORS) award.
Level of Study: Doctorate
Type: Scholarship
Value: The University Composition Fee at the appropriate rate, approved college fees, a maintenance allowance sufficient for a single student and a contribution to return economy air fare
Length of Study: Up to 3 years
Frequency: Annual
Study Establishment: The University of Cambridge
Country of Study: United Kingdom
No. of awards offered: 2
Application Procedure: Applicants must complete a preliminary application form, which can be obtained from local universities, offices of the British Council or the Trust. Completed forms must be returned to the main address. Shortlisted candidates will be sent forms for admission to the University of Cambridge. The preliminary application form can also be downloaded from www.admin.cam.ac.uk/offices/gradstud/admissions/forms/
Contributor: Offered in collaboration with the Friends of Cambridge University in Hong Kong

PTDF Cambridge Scholarships

Subjects: Science-related subjects.
Purpose: To financially support postgraduate study.
Eligibility: Candidates must be from Nigeria, must apply to the University of Cambridge and be offered a place at Cambridge in the normal way. All applicants must have a First Class or High Second Class (Honours) Degree or equivalent and normally be under 26. They must be successfully nominated for an Overseas Research Student (ORS) award.
Level of Study: Postgraduate
Type: Scholarship
Length of Study: 1 year
Study Establishment: University of Cambridge
Country of Study: United Kingdom
Application Procedure: Applicants must complete a preliminary application form, which can be obtained from local universities, offices of the British Council or the Trust. Completed forms must be returned to the main address. Shortlisted candidates will be sent forms for admission to the University of Cambridge. The preliminary application form can also be downloaded from www.admin.cam.ac.uk/offices/gradstud/admissions/forms/
Closing Date: February 28th
Funding: Trusts
Contributor: Cambridge Trusts and Robert Gordon University, Aberdeen

For further information contact:

Training, PTDF, Head Office, Plot 672, Port-Harcourt Crescent, Off Gimbiya Street, Area-11-Garlci, Abuja, Nigeria
Tel: (234) 234 9 3148843
Email: ambabi@yahoo.com
Contact: Ibifubara Wasiro

Rajiv Gandhi Cambridge Bursaries

Subjects: All subjects.
Purpose: To financially support study towards a PhD.

Eligibility: Applicants must be from India, must apply to the University of Cambridge and be offered a place at Cambridge in the normal way. All applicants must have a First Class (Honours) Degree. Those with a First Class Master's Degree may be given preference.
Level of Study: Postgraduate
Type: Bursary
Value: A substantial contribution towards the student's costs, to be determined in the light of the student's own resources
Length of Study: 2 years
Frequency: Annual
Study Establishment: The University of Cambridge
Country of Study: United Kingdom
No. of awards offered: 1
Application Procedure: Applicants must contact the organization.
Closing Date: February 28th
Contributor: Offered in collaboration with the Rajiv Gandhi Foundation

For further information contact:

The Nehru Trust for Cambridge University, Teen Murti House, Teen Murti Marg, New Delhi, 110011, India
Contact: The Joint Secretary

Raymond and Helen Kwok Research Scholarship

Subjects: Any subject relevant to China's needs.
Purpose: To financially support study leading to a PhD.
Eligibility: Applicants must be from China, and must have been awarded a First Class (Honours) Degree or equivalent.
Level of Study: Doctorate
Length of Study: 3 years
Frequency: Annual
Study Establishment: Jesus College
Country of Study: United Kingdom
No. of awards offered: 2
Application Procedure: Applicants must complete a preliminary application form, which can be obtained from local universities, offices of the British Council or the Trust. Completed forms must be returned to the main address. Shortlisted candidates will be sent forms for admission to the University of Cambridge. Applicants must also apply for an ORS award. The preliminary application form can also be downloaded from www.admin.cam.ac.uk/offices/gradstud/admissions/forms/
Closing Date: March 31st
Funding: Individuals, trusts
Contributor: Mr Raymond Kowk and Jesus College

Schlumberger Cambridge Scholarships

Subjects: All subjects.
Purpose: To offer financial assistance to a student undertaking PhD study from a developing country.
Eligibility: Open to students from a developing country. Applicants must apply to the University of Cambridge and be offered a place at Cambridge in the normal way. All applicants must have a First Class or High Second Class (Honours) Degree or equivalent and normally be under 26. They must be successfully nominated for an Overseas Research Student (ORS) award.
Level of Study: Doctorate, predoctorate
Type: Scholarship
Value: The University Composition Fee at the overseas rate, approved college fees, a maintenance allowance sufficient for a single student and a contribution to return economy airfare
Length of Study: Up to 3 years
Frequency: Annual
Study Establishment: The University of Cambridge
Country of Study: United Kingdom
No. of awards offered: 1
Application Procedure: Applicants must complete a preliminary application form, which can be obtained from local universities, offices of the British Council or the Trust. Completed forms must be returned to the main address. Shortlisted candidates will be sent forms for admission to the University of Cambridge. The preliminary application form can also be downloaded from www.admin.cam.ac.uk/offices/gradstud/admissions/forms/
Closing Date: February 28th
Contributor: Offered in collaboration with Schlumberger Cambridge Research Limited

Shell Centenary Cambridge Scholarships (Countries Outside of the Commonwealth)

Subjects: Applied sciences and technology, environmental science, business management or economics.
Purpose: To financially support those undertaking postgraduate study.
Eligibility: Open to citizens from a number of non-Commonwealth countries, including China, Kazakhistan, Russia, Egypt, Iran, Oman, Saudi Arabia, Syria, Argentina, Brazil, Chile, Peru and Thailand. Applicants must apply to the University of Cambridge and be offered a place at Cambridge in the normal way. All applicants must have a First Class or High Second Class (Honours) Degree or equivalent.
Level of Study: Postgraduate
Type: Scholarship
Value: The University Composition Fee at the overseas rate, approved college fees, a maintenance allowance sufficient for a single student and a contribution towards return economy airfare
Length of Study: 1 year
Frequency: Annual
Study Establishment: The University of Cambridge
Country of Study: United Kingdom
No. of awards offered: Up to 12
Application Procedure: Applicants must complete a preliminary application form, which can be obtained from local universities, offices of the British Council or the Trust. Completed forms must be returned to the main address. Shortlisted candidates will be sent forms for admission to the University of Cambridge. The preliminary application form can also be downloaded from www.admin.cam.ac.uk/offices/gradstud/admissions/forms/
Closing Date: February 28th
Contributor: Offered in collaboration with Shell International Limited

Shell Centenary Chevening Scholarships for Postgraduate Study

Subjects: Applied sciences and technology, including environmental sciences, business management and economics.
Purpose: To financially support those undertaking postgraduate study.
Eligibility: Open to citizens of Pakistan, China, Russia, Nigeria, India, Malaysia, Singapore, Brazil and Thailand. Applicants must apply to the University of Cambridge and be offered a place at Cambridge in the normal way. All applicants must have a First Class or High Second Class (Honours) Degree or equivalent and normally be under 26.
Level of Study: Postgraduate
Type: Scholarship
Value: The University Composition Fee at the overseas rate, approved college fees, a maintenance allowance sufficient for a single student and a contribution to return economy airfare
Length of Study: 1 year
Frequency: Annual
Study Establishment: The University of Cambridge
Country of Study: United Kingdom
No. of awards offered: 10
Application Procedure: Applicants must complete a preliminary application form, which can be obtained from local universities, offices of the British Council or the Trust. Completed forms must be returned to the main address. Shortlisted candidates will be sent forms for admission to the University of Cambridge. The preliminary application form can also be downloaded from www.admin.cam.ac.uk/offices/gradstud/admissions/forms/
Closing Date: February 28th
Contributor: Offered in collaboration with Shell International Limited and the Foreign and Commonwealth Office (FCO)

Shell Centenary Scholarships (Developing Countries of the Commonwealth)

Subjects: Applied sciences and technology, environmental science, business management or economics.

Purpose: To financially support those undertaking postgraduate study.
Eligibility: Open to citizens of developing countries of the Commonwealth, including Pakistan, Nigeria and India. Applicants must apply to the University of Cambridge and be offered a place at Cambridge in the normal way. All applicants must have a First Class or High Second Class (Honours) Degree or equivalent, must be under 35 on October 1st with priority given to those under the age of 30. They must not be employed by a government department (local or national) or by a parastatal organization nor at present be living or studying in a developed country. Candidates wishing to pursue a study related to the economic and social development of their country will be given priority.
Level of Study: Postgraduate
Type: Scholarship
Value: The University Composition Fee at the overseas rate, approved college fees, a maintenance allowance sufficient for a single student and a contribution to return economy airfare
Length of Study: Varies
Frequency: Annual
Study Establishment: The University of Cambridge
Country of Study: United Kingdom
No. of awards offered: Up to 10
Application Procedure: Applicants must complete a preliminary application form, which can be obtained from local universities, offices of the British Council or the Trust. Completed forms must be returned to the main address. Shortlisted candidates will be sent forms for admission to the University of Cambridge. The preliminary application form can also be downloaded from www.admin.cam.ac.uk/offices/gradstud/admissions/forms/
Closing Date: February 28th
Contributor: Offered in collaboration with the Department for International Development (DFID) and Shell International Limited

Shell Centenary Scholarships at Cambridge (Commonwealth Countries)

Subjects: Applied sciences and technology, including environmental sciences, business management or economics.
Purpose: To financially support those undertaking postgraduate study.
Eligibility: Open to students from a number of Commonwealth countries, including Malaysia, the Philippines, Singapore and South Africa. Applicants must apply to the University of Cambridge and be offered a place at Cambridge in the normal way. All applicants must have a First Class or High Second Class (Honours) Degree or equivalent and normally be under 26.
Level of Study: Postgraduate
Type: Scholarship
Value: The University Composition Fee at the overseas rate, approved college fees, a maintenance sufficient for a single student and a contribution to return economy airfare
Length of Study: 1 year
Frequency: Annual
Study Establishment: The University of Cambridge
Country of Study: United Kingdom
No. of awards offered: Up to 10
Application Procedure: Applicants must complete a preliminary application form, which can be obtained from local universities, offices of the British Council or the main address. Completed forms must be returned to the main address. Shortlisted candidates will be sent forms for admission to the University of Cambridge and a scholarship application form. These forms must be returned to the Board of Graduate Studies.
Closing Date: February 28th
Contributor: Offered in collaboration with Shell International Limited

Shell Centenary Scholarships at Cambridge (Non-OECD Countries)

Subjects: Applied sciences and technology, including environmental sciences, business management or economics.
Purpose: To financially support those undertaking postgraduate study.
Eligibility: Open to students from non-organization for Economic Co-operation and Development (OECD) countries. Applicants must apply to the University of Cambridge and be offered a place at Cambridge in the normal way. All applicants must have a First Class or High Second Class (Honours) Degree or equivalent and normally be under 26.
Level of Study: Postgraduate
Type: Scholarship
Value: The University Composition Fee at the overseas rate, approved college fees, a maintenance allowance sufficient for a single student and a contribution towards return economy airfare
Frequency: Annual
Study Establishment: The University of Cambridge
Country of Study: United Kingdom
No. of awards offered: Up to 22
Application Procedure: Applicants must complete a preliminary application form, which can be obtained from local universities, offices of the British Council or the main address. Completed forms must be returned to the main address. Shortlisted candidates will be sent forms for admission to the University of Cambridge and a scholarship application form. These forms must be returned to the Board of Graduate Studies.
Closing Date: February 28th
Contributor: Offered in collaboration with Shell International Limited

For further information contact:

The Board of Graduate Studies, 4 Mill Lane, Cambridge, Cambridgeshire, CB2 1RZ, England

Sir Patrick Sheehy Scholarships

Subjects: International relations.
Eligibility: Applicants must apply to the University of Cambridge and be offered a place at Cambridge in the normal way. All applicants must have a First Class or High Second Class (Honours) Degree or equivalent and normally be under 26. They must be successfully nominated for an Overseas Research Student (ORS) award.
Level of Study: Doctorate, predoctorate
Type: Scholarship
Value: The University Composition Fee at the appropriate rate, approved college fees, a maintenance allowance sufficient for a single student and a contribution to return economy airfare
Length of Study: Up to 3 years
Frequency: Annual
Study Establishment: The University of Cambridge
Country of Study: United Kingdom
No. of awards offered: Varies
Application Procedure: Applicants must complete a preliminary application form, which can be obtained from local universities, offices of the British Council or the Trust. Completed forms must be returned to the main address. Shortlisted candidates will be sent forms for admission to the University of Cambridge. The preliminary application form can also be downloaded from www.admin.cam.ac.uk/offices/gradstud/admissions/forms/
Closing Date: February 28th
Additional Information: This award is offered to mark the retirement of Sir Patrick Sheehy, the Chairman of the British-American Tobacco (BAT) Company Limited.

Smuts MCSC Bursaries for Commonwealth Studies

Subjects: Commonwealth studies.
Purpose: To financially support study towards a PhD.
Eligibility: The Trusts cannot admit students to the University or any of its colleges. Applicants for awards from the Trusts must, therefore, also apply to the University of Cambridge and be offered a place at Cambridge in the normal way. All applicants must have a First Class or High Second Class (Honours) Degree or equivalent and normally be under 26.
Level of Study: Doctorate, predoctorate
Type: Bursary
Value: The value of the bursaries will be determined in the light of the financial circumstances of the applicant
Frequency: Annual
Study Establishment: The University of Cambridge
Country of Study: United Kingdom
No. of awards offered: Up to 4

Application Procedure: Applicants must complete a preliminary application form, which can be obtained from local universities, offices of the British Council or the Trust. Completed forms must be returned to the main address. Shortlisted candidates will be sent forms for admission to the University of Cambridge. The preliminary application form can also be downloaded from www.admin.cam.ac.uk/offices/gradstud/admissions/forms/
Contributor: Offered in collaboration with the Malaysian Commonwealth Studies Centre

Smuts ORS Equivalent Awards

Subjects: Commonwealth studies.
Purpose: To financially support study towards a PhD.
Eligibility: Applicants must apply to the University of Cambridge and be offered a place at Cambridge in the normal way. All applicants must have a First Class or High Second Class (Honours) Degree or equivalent and normally be under 26.
Level of Study: Postdoctorate
Type: Award
Value: Please contact the organization
Frequency: Annual
Study Establishment: The University of Cambridge
Country of Study: United Kingdom
No. of awards offered: 2
Application Procedure: Applicants must complete a preliminary application form, which can be obtained from local universities, offices of the British Council or the Trust. Completed forms must be returned to the main address. Shortlisted candidates will be sent forms for admission to the University of Cambridge. The preliminary application form can also be downloaded from www.admin.cam.ac.uk/offices/gradstud/admissions/forms/

South African College Bursaries

Subjects: All subjects.
Purpose: To enable citizens of South and Southern Africa to study at the University of Cambridge.
Eligibility: Applicants must be from South or Southern Africa, must apply to the University of Cambridge and be offered a place at Cambridge in the normal way. All applicants must have a First Class or High Second Class (Honours) Degree or equivalent and normally be under 26. They must be successfully nominated for an Overseas Research Student (ORS) award.
Level of Study: Postgraduate
Type: Bursary
Value: The University Composition Fee at the overseas rate, approved college fees, a maintenance allowance sufficient for a single student and a contribution to return economy airfare
Length of Study: 1 year
Study Establishment: The University of Cambridge
Country of Study: United Kingdom
No. of awards offered: Varies
Application Procedure: Applicants must complete a preliminary application form, which can be obtained from local universities, offices of the British Council or the Trust. Completed forms must be returned to the main address. Shortlisted candidates will be sent forms for admission to the University of Cambridge. The preliminary application form can also be downloaded from www.admin.cam.ac.uk/offices/gradstud/admissions/forms/
Closing Date: February 28th
Contributor: Offered in collaboration with Churchill College, Newnham College, Selwyn College, St Catherine's College and Sidney Sussex College, Cambridge
Additional Information: The bursaries are normally held in conjunction with other awards from the Cambridge Commonwealth Trust and other sources.

St Edmund's Commonwealth and Overseas Studentships

Subjects: All subjects.
Purpose: To financially support those undertaking postgraduate study.
Eligibility: Applicants must be from South or Southern Africa, must apply to the University of Cambridge and be offered a place at Cambridge in the normal way. All applicants must have a First Class or High Second Class (Honours) Degree or equivalent and normally be under 26. They must be successfully nominated for an Overseas Research Student (ORS) award.
Level of Study: Postgraduate
Type: Studentship
Value: The University Composition Fee at the overseas rate, approved college fees, a maintenance allowance sufficient for a single student and a contribution towards return economy airfare
Length of Study: 1 year
Frequency: Annual
Study Establishment: The University of Cambridge
Country of Study: United Kingdom
Application Procedure: Applicants must complete a preliminary application form, which can be obtained from local universities, offices of the British Council or the Trust. Completed forms must be returned to the main address. Shortlisted candidates will be sent forms for admission to the University of Cambridge. The preliminary application form can also be downloaded from www.admin.cam.ac.uk/offices/gradstud/admissions/forms/
Closing Date: February 28th

Sun Hung Kai Cambridge Scholarships

Subjects: All subjects.
Purpose: To financially support study towards a PhD.
Eligibility: Open to students from China. All applicants must have a First Class or High Second Class (Honours) Degree or equivalent and normally be under 26. They must be successfully nominated for an Overseas Research Student (ORS) award.
Level of Study: Doctorate
Type: Scholarships
Value: University Composition Fee, approved college fees, maintenance allowance for a single student, contribution to return economy airfare
Length of Study: Up to 3 years
Frequency: Annual
No. of awards offered: 2
Application Procedure: Applicants must complete a preliminary application form, which can be obtained from local universities, offices of the British Council or the Trust. Completed forms must be returned to the main address. Shortlisted candidates will be sent forms for admission to the University of Cambridge. The preliminary application form can also be downloaded from www.admin.cam.ac.uk/offices/gradstud/admissions/forms/
Contributor: Cambridge Trusts and Sun Hung Kai properties limited

Tanzania Cambridge DFID Scholarships

Subjects: All subjects.
Purpose: To offer financial support to students from Tanzania.
Eligibility: Open to candidates from Tanzania. All applicants must be under the age of 35 on October 1st with priority given to those candidates under the age of 30. Applicants must not be employed by a government department or by a parastatal organization, nor at present be living or studying in a developed country. Priority will be given to candidates wishing to pursue a study related to the economic and social development of their country.
Level of Study: Postgraduate
Type: Scholarship
Value: The University Composition Fee at the overseas rate, approved college fees, a maintenance allowance sufficient for a single student and a contribution to return economy airfare
Length of Study: 1 year
Frequency: Annual
Study Establishment: The University of Cambridge
Country of Study: United Kingdom
No. of awards offered: Up to 4
Application Procedure: Applicants must complete a preliminary application form, which can be obtained from local universities, offices of the British Council or the Trust. Completed forms must be returned to the main address. Shortlisted candidates will be sent forms for admission to the University of Cambridge. The preliminary application form can also be downloaded from www.admin.cam.ac.uk/offices/gradstud/admissions/forms/
Closing Date: February 28th

Contributor: Offered in collaboration with the Department of International Development (DFID)

Tanzania Cambridge Scholarship for PhD Study

Subjects: All subjects.
Purpose: To financially support study towards a PhD.
Eligibility: Open to students from Tanzania. All applicants must have a First Class or High Second Class (Honours) Degree or equivalent and normally be under 26. They must be successfully nominated for an Overseas Research Student (ORS) award.
Level of Study: Doctorate, predoctorate
Type: Scholarship
Value: The University Composition Fee at the appropriate rate, approved college fees, a maintenance allowance sufficient for a single student, and a contribution to return economy airfare
Length of Study: Up to 3 years
Frequency: Annual
Study Establishment: The University of Cambridge
Country of Study: United Kingdom
No. of awards offered: 1
Application Procedure: Applicants must complete a preliminary application form, which can be obtained from local universities, offices of the British Council or the Trust. Completed forms must be returned to the main address. Shortlisted candidates will be sent forms for admission to the University of Cambridge.The preliminary application form can also be downloaded from www.admin.cam.ac.uk/offices/gradstud/admissions/forms/

Tidmarsh Cambridge Scholarship for PhD Study

Subjects: All subjects.
Purpose: To financially support study towards a PhD.
Eligibility: Open to citizens of Canada. Applicants must apply to the University of Cambridge and be offered a place at Cambridge in the normal way. All applicants must have a First Class or High Second Class (Honours) Degree or equivalent and normally be under 26. They must have been successfully nominated for an Overseas Research Student (ORS) award.
Level of Study: Doctorate
Type: Scholarship
Value: The University Composition Fee at the home rate, approved college fees and a maintenance allowance sufficient for a single student
Study Establishment: Trinity Hall, the University of Cambridge
Country of Study: United Kingdom
No. of awards offered: 1
Application Procedure: Application forms for the scholarship will be sent out to eligible candidates once the completed form for admission to the University of Cambridge has reached the Board of Graduate Studies.
Closing Date: February 28th
Contributor: A benefaction from Dr Evan Schulman

For further information contact:

The Board of Graduate Studies, 4 Mill Lane, Cambridge, Cambridgeshire, CB2 1RZ, England
Contact: The Secretary

TNK/BP Kapitza Cambridge Scholarships for Russia

Subjects: All subjects.
Purpose: To financially support study towards a PhD.
Eligibility: Open to citizens of Canada. Applicants must apply to the University of Cambridge and be offered a place at Cambridge in the normal way. All applicants must have a First Class or High Second Class (Honours) Degree or equivalent and normally be under 26. They must have been successfully nominated for an Overseas Research Student (ORS) award.
Level of Study: Doctorate
Type: Scholarship
Frequency: Annual
Study Establishment: Trinity College
Country of Study: United Kingdom
No. of awards offered: 8
Application Procedure: Application forms for the scholarship will be sent out to eligible candidates once the completed form for admission to the University of Cambridge has reached the Board of Graduate Studies.

UK Commonwealth (Cambridge) Scholarships for PhD Study

Subjects: All subjects.
Purpose: To offer the opportunity for individuals with proven academic merit to study towards a PhD at Cambridge.
Eligibility: Open to candidates from Australia, New Zealand and Canada. It is not a pre-requisite for successful United Kingdom Commonwealth Scholars to be nominated for an Overseas Research Student (ORS) award; however, candidates for a PhD will be expected to apply for an ORS award.
Level of Study: Predoctorate, doctorate
Type: Scholarship
Value: The University Composition Fee at the home rate, approved college fees, a maintenance allowance sufficient for a single student and a contribution towards return economy airfare
Length of Study: Up to 3 years
Frequency: Annual
Study Establishment: The University of Cambridge
Country of Study: United Kingdom
No. of awards offered: Up to 15
Application Procedure: Candidates must apply to the local Commonwealth scholarship agency in their home country.
Contributor: Offered in collaboration with the Commonwealth Scholarship Commission in the United Kingdom

UK Commonwealth (Cambridge) Scholarships for PhD Study (Developing Countries)

Subjects: All subjects.
Eligibility: Open to candidates from developing countries of the Commonwealth. It is not a pre-requisite for successful United Kingdom Commonwealth Scholars to be nominated for an Overseas Research Student (ORS) award; however, candidates for a PhD will be expected to apply for an ORS award.
Value: The University Composition Fee at the home rate, approved college fees, a maintenance allowance sufficient for a single student and a contribution towards return economy airfare
Study Establishment: The University of Cambridge
No. of awards offered: Varies
Application Procedure: Candidates must apply to the local Commonwealth scholarship agency in their home country.

UK Commonwealth (Cambridge) Scholarships for Postgraduate Study

Subjects: All subjects.
Purpose: To financially support those undertaking postgraduate study.
Eligibility: Open to candidates from Australia, New Zealand and Canada. It is not a pre-requisite for successful United Kingdom Commonwealth Scholars to be nominated for an Overseas Research Student (ORS) award; however, candidates for a PhD will be expected to apply for an ORS award.
Level of Study: Postgraduate
Type: Scholarship
Value: The University Composition Fee at the overseas rate, approved college fees, a maintenance allowance sufficient for a single student and a contribution towards return economy airfare
Length of Study: 1 year
Study Establishment: The University of Cambridge
Country of Study: United Kingdom
No. of awards offered: Up to 15
Application Procedure: Candidates must apply to the local Commonwealth scholarship agency in their home country.
Closing Date: February 28th
Contributor: Offered in collaboration with the Commonwealth Scholarship Association in the United Kingdom

UK Commonwealth (Cambridge) Scholarships for Postgraduate Study (Developing Countries)

Subjects: All subjects.
Eligibility: Open to candidates from developing countries of the Commonwealth. It is not a pre-requisite for successful United Kingdom Commonwealth Scholars to be nominated for an Overseas Research Student (ORS) award; however, candidates for a PhD will be expected to apply for an ORS award.
Value: The University Composition Fee at the home rate, approved college fees, a maintenance allowance sufficient for a single student and a contribution towards return economy airfare
Study Establishment: The University of Cambridge
No. of awards offered: Varies
Application Procedure: Candidates must apply to the local Commonwealth scholarship agency in their home country.
Closing Date: February 28th

UK-Germany Millenium Studentships

Subjects: All subjects.
Purpose: To financially support PhD study.
Eligibility: Applicants must be German nationals. All applicants must have a First Class or High Second Class (Honours) Degree or equivalent and normally be under 26.
Level of Study: Doctorate
Type: Studentship
Value: UK £2,000 per year
Frequency: Annual
Study Establishment: St Edmund's College, Cambridge
No. of awards offered: 2
Application Procedure: Applicants must apply to the University of Cambridge and be offered a place at Cambridge in the normal way. Applicants should complete only one scholarship form, which will enable them to be considered for all awards for which they are eligible. Application form can be downloaded from the website.
Contributor: Cambridge Trusts and St Edmund's College

W A Frank Downing Studentship in Law

Subjects: Law.
Purpose: To financially support those undertaking the Master of Law degree (LLM).
Eligibility: Open to citizens of Australia. Applicants must apply to the University of Cambridge and be offered a place at Cambridge in the normal way. All applicants must have a First Class or High Second Class (Honours) Degree or equivalent and normally be under 26.
Level of Study: Doctorate
Type: Studentship
Value: The University Composition Fee at the overseas rate, approved college fees, a maintenance allowance sufficient for a single student and a contribution towards return economy airfare
Length of Study: 1 year
Study Establishment: The University of Cambridge
Country of Study: United Kingdom
No. of awards offered: 1
Application Procedure: Applicants must contact the Board of Graduate Studies.
Closing Date: February 28th
Contributor: Offered in collaboration with the Cambridge Australia Trust
Additional Information: For details of scholarships offered in collaboration with the Cambridge Australia Trust please see the website www.anu.edu/cabs/scholarships/cambridge/cambridge-austrust.html

For further information contact:

The Board of Graduate Studies, 4 Mill Lane, Cambridge, Cambridgeshire, CB2 1RZ, England
Contact: The Secretary

William and Margaret Brown Cambridge Scholarship for PhD Study

Subjects: Engineering, natural sciences, physical sciences or political sciences.
Purpose: To financially support study towards a PhD.
Eligibility: Open to students from Canada. Applicants must apply to the University of Cambridge and be offered a place at Cambridge in the normal way. All applicants must have a First Class or High Second Class (Honours) Degree or equivalent and normally be under 26. They must be successfully nominated for an Overseas Research Student (ORS) award.
Level of Study: Predoctorate, doctorate
Type: Scholarship
Value: The University Composition Fee at the home rate and approved college fees
Length of Study: Up to 3 years
Study Establishment: The University of Cambridge
Country of Study: United Kingdom
No. of awards offered: 1
Application Procedure: Application forms for the scholarship will be sent out to eligible candidates once the completed form for admission to the University of Cambridge has reached the Board of Graduate Studies.
Contributor: A benefaction from Dr Donald Pinchin

For further information contact:

The Board of Graduate Studies, 4 Mill Hill, Cambridge, Cambridgeshire, CB2 1RZ, England
Contact: The Secretary

Wing Yip Cambridge Scholarships

Subjects: All subjects.
Eligibility: Applicants must be from China and be members of either Peking University or Tsinghun University. They must have a First Class or High Second Class (Honours) Degree or equivalent and normally be under 26.
Level of Study: Postgraduate
Value: University Composition Fee, approved college fees, maintenance allowance, return economy airfare
Length of Study: 1 year
Frequency: Annual
Study Establishment: Churchill College
No. of awards offered: 2
Application Procedure: Applicants must apply to the University of Cambridge and be offered a place at Cambridge in the normal way. Applicants should complete only one scholarship form, which will enable them to be considered for all awards for which they are eligible. Application forms can be downloaded from the website.
Closing Date: February 28th
Contributor: Cambridge Trusts, Mr Wing Yip and the Education Section of the Chinese Embassy, London

Wolfson Bursaries

Subjects: All subjects.
Eligibility: All applicants must have a First Class or High Second Class (Honours) Degree or equivalent and normally be under 26.
Level of Study: Unrestricted
Type: Bursary
Frequency: Annual
Study Establishment: Wolfson College, the University of Cambridge
Country of Study: United Kingdom
No. of awards offered: Varies
Application Procedure: Applications should be made directly to the college.
Closing Date: February 28th

World Bank Cambridge Scholarships

Subjects: Subjects related to development.
Eligibility: Candidates must have a First Class or High Second Class Degree from a recognized university in a development-related field, 2–5 years of recent full-time professional experience in public services, and must return to their home country upon completion of their studies.
Level of Study: Postgraduate
Value: University Composition Fee, approved college fee, maitanance allowance, contribution to return economy airfare
Length of Study: 1 year
Frequency: Annual

Application Procedure: Applicants must apply to the university of Cambridge and be offered a place at Cambridge in the normal way. Applicants should complete only one scholarship form, which will enable them to be considered for all awards for which they are eligible. Application forms can be downloaded from the website.
Closing Date: February 28th

World Bank Cambridge Scholarships for Postgraduate Study

Subjects: Subjects related to development.
Purpose: To financially support those undertaking postgraduate study.
Eligibility: Candidates must be nationals of a World Bank member country, be under the age of 45, with priority given to those candidates under 35, have or be about to obtain a First Class or High Second Class Degree from a recognized university in a development-related field. Other prerequisites include 2, but preferably 4–5 years of recent full-time professional experience in their home country or other developing country, usually in public service. Candidates must not hold resident status in the United States of America or another industrialized country. They should not hold a Master's degree or diploma or at present be studying towards a Master's degree or diploma from an industrialized country.
Level of Study: Postgraduate
Type: Scholarship
Value: The University Composition Fee at the overseas rate, approved college fees, a maintenance allowance sufficient for a single student and a contribution towards return economy airfare
Length of Study: 1 year
Frequency: Annual
Study Establishment: The University of Cambridge
Country of Study: United Kingdom
No. of awards offered: Up to 20
Application Procedure: Applicants must contact the organization.
Closing Date: February 28th
Contributor: Offered in collaboration with the World Bank

Zambia Cambridge Scholarships for PhD Study

Subjects: All subjects.
Purpose: To financially support study towards a PhD.
Eligibility: Candidates must be from Zambia, must apply to the University of Cambridge and be offered a place at Cambridge in the normal way. All applicants must have a First Class or High Second Class (Honours) Degree or equivalent and normally be under 26. They must be successfully nominated for an Overseas Research Student (ORS) award.
Level of Study: Predoctorate, doctorate
Type: Scholarship
Value: The University Composition Fee at the home rate, approved college fees, a maintenance allowance sufficient for a single student and a contribution towards return economy airfare
Length of Study: Up to 3 years
Study Establishment: The University of Cambridge
Country of Study: United Kingdom
No. of awards offered: 1
Application Procedure: Applicants must complete a preliminary application form, which can be obtained from local universities, offices of the British Council or the Trust. Completed forms must be returned to the main address. Shortlisted candidates will be sent forms for admission to the University of Cambridge. The preliminary application form can also be downloaded from www.admin.cam.ac.uk/offices/gradstud/admissions/forms/
Contributor: Offered in collaboration with the Zambia Cambridge Trust

Zambia Cambridge Scholarships for Postgraduate Study

Subjects: All subjects.
Purpose: To financially support those undertaking postgraduate study.
Eligibility: Candidates must be from Zambia, must apply to the University of Cambridge and be offered a place at Cambridge in the normal way. All applicants must have a First Class or High Second Class (Honours) Degree or equivalent and normally be under 26. They must be successfully nominated for an Overseas Research Student (ORS) award.
Level of Study: Postgraduate
Type: Scholarship
Value: The University Composition Fee at the appropriate rate, approved college fees, a maintenance allowance sufficient for a single student and a contribution towards return economy airfare
Length of Study: 1 year
Study Establishment: The University of Cambridge
Country of Study: United Kingdom
No. of awards offered: 1
Application Procedure: Applicants must complete a preliminary application form, which can be obtained from local universities, offices of the British Council or the Trust. Completed forms must be returned to the main address. Shortlisted candidates will be sent forms for admission to the University of Cambridge. The preliminary application form can also be downloaded from www.admin.cam.ac.uk/offices/gradstud/admissions/forms/
Closing Date: February 28th
Contributor: Offered in collaboration with the Zambia Cambridge Trust

Zimbabwe Cambridge Scholarships for PhD Study

Subjects: All subjects.
Purpose: To financially support study towards a PhD.
Eligibility: Applicants must be from Zimbabwe, must apply to the University of Cambridge and be offered a place at Cambridge in the normal way. All applicants must have a First Class or High Second Class (Honours) Degree or equivalent and normally be under 26. They must be successfully nominated for an Overseas Research Student (ORS) award.
Level of Study: Predoctorate, doctorate
Type: Scholarship
Value: The University Composition Fee at the appropriate rate, approved college fees, a maintenance allowance sufficient for a single student and a contribution towards return economy airfare
Length of Study: Up to 3 years
Study Establishment: The University of Cambridge
Country of Study: United Kingdom
No. of awards offered: 1
Application Procedure: Applicants must complete a preliminary application form, which can be obtained from local universities, offices of the British Council or the Trust. Completed forms must be returned to the main address. Shortlisted candidates will be sent forms for admission to the University of Cambridge. The preliminary application form can also be downloaded from www.admin.cam.ac.uk/offices/gradstud/admissions/forms/
Contributor: Offered in collaboration with the Cambridge Local Examinations Syndicate and the Zimbabwe Cambridge Trust

Zimbabwe Cambridge Scholarships for Postgraduate Study

Subjects: All subjects.
Purpose: To financially support those undertaking postgraduate study.
Eligibility: Applicants must be from Zimbabwe, must apply to the University of Cambridge and be offered a place at Cambridge in the normal way. All applicants must have a First Class or High Second Class (Honours) Degree or equivalent and normally be under 26. They must be successfully nominated for an Overseas Research Student (ORS) award.
Level of Study: Postgraduate
Type: Scholarship
Value: The University Composition Fee at the overseas rate, approved college fees, a maintenance allowance sufficient for a single student and a contribution towards return economy airfare
Length of Study: 1 year
Study Establishment: The University of Cambridge
Country of Study: United Kingdom
No. of awards offered: 1
Application Procedure: Applicants must complete a preliminary application form, which can be obtained from local universities, offices of the British Council or the Trust. Completed forms must be returned to the main address. Shortlisted candidates will be sent forms for admission to the University of Cambridge. The preliminary application

form can also be downloaded from www.admin.cam.ac.uk/offices/gradstud/admissions/forms/
Closing Date: February 28th
Contributor: Offered in collaboration with the Cambridge Local Examinations Syndicate and the Zimbabwe Cambridge Trust

THE CANADA COUNCIL FOR THE ARTS

350 Albert Street, PO Box 1047, Ottawa, ON, K1P 5V8, Canada
Tel: (1) 613 566 4414 ext 5060
Fax: (1) 613 566 4390
Email: lise.rochon@canadacouncil.ca
Website: www.canadacouncil.ca
Contact: Ms Lise Rochon

The Canada Council for the Arts is a national agency that provides grants and services to professional Canadian artists and art organizations in dance, media arts, music, theatre, writing and publishing, interdisciplinary work, performance art and the visual arts.

Canada Council Grants for Professional Artists

Subjects: Art, dance, music, theatre, media arts, visual arts, creative writing and publishing and inter-arts.
Purpose: To help professional Canadian artists pursue professional development in independent artistic creation or production.
Eligibility: Open to Canadian citizens or permanent residents of Canada who have finished their basic training in the arts or are recognized as professionals within their own disciplines.
Level of Study: Postgraduate
Value: Canadian $3,000–20,000 (or up to Canadian $34,000 for established visual artists only)
Frequency: Annual
Country of Study: Any country
No. of awards offered: Varies
Closing Date: Varies
Additional Information: Interested Canadian individuals should see the website for detailed information on the financial assistance offered by the Canada Council for the Arts.

Canada Council Travel Grants

Subjects: Art.
Purpose: To enable Canadian artists to travel on occasions important to their professional careers.
Eligibility: Open to Canadian citizens or permanent residents of Canada who have finished their basic training in the arts or are recognized as professionals within their own disciplines.
Level of Study: Postgraduate, undergraduate
Type: Travel grant
Value: A maximum of Canadian $2,800 to cover travel costs, may include an allowance of Canadian $100 per day for up to 5 days to help defray living expenses
Frequency: Annual
Country of Study: Any country
No. of awards offered: Varies
Additional Information: Interested Canadian individuals should see the website for detailed information on the financial assistance offered by the Canada Council for the Arts.

J B C Watkins Award

Subjects: Architecture, music, theatre.
Purpose: To allow Canadian artists to pursue graduate study outside Canada in media arts, theatre, architecture and music.
Eligibility: Open to Canadian artists who are graduates of a Canadian university or postsecondary art institution or training school in the above subjects.
Level of Study: Postgraduate
Value: Up to Canadian $5,000
Frequency: Annual
No. of awards offered: 5
Application Procedure: Applicants must see the Canada Council's website for details. www.canadacouncil.ca/prizes/jbc_watkins
Closing Date: Varies
Additional Information: Interested individuals should request the Grants to Artists Programme for their arts discipline for detailed information on the financial assistance offered by the Canada Council for the Arts.

Killam Prizes

Subjects: Health sciences, natural sciences, engineering, social sciences or humanities.
Purpose: Intended to honour eminent Canadian scholars actively engaged in research in Canada in universities, hospitals, research and scientific institutes or other equivalent or similar institutions.
Eligibility: Prize winners must have had a distinguished career and exceptional achievements.
Level of Study: Postgraduate
Type: Prize
Value: Canadian $100,000
Length of Study: Varies
Frequency: Annual
Study Establishment: Universities, hospitals, research institutes or scientific institutes
Country of Study: Canada
No. of awards offered: 5
Application Procedure: Scholars may not apply on their own behalf; three experts in their field must nominate them. All three may sign a single letter. Information is available on the Canada Council website www.canadacouncil.ca/prizes/killam
Closing Date: November 1st
Funding: Private
Contributor: Dorothy J Killam
No. of awards given last year: 5
Additional Information: Detailed guidelines for the application process are available from main organization.

Killam Research Fellowships

Subjects: Humanities, social sciences, natural sciences, health sciences, engineering and studies linking any of the disciplines within these broad fields.
Purpose: To support Canadian scholars of exceptional ability engaged in advanced research projects.
Eligibility: Open to Canadian citizens or permanent residents of Canada. Killam Research Fellowships are aimed at established scholars who have demonstrated outstanding ability through substantial publications in their fields over a period of several years.
Level of Study: Postgraduate
Type: Fellowship
Value: Canadian $70,000, paid to the university or research institution which employs the fellow.
Length of Study: Up to 2 years
Frequency: Annual
No. of awards offered: Varies
Application Procedure: Requests must be submitted using the Canada Cancil's on-line internet application system (http://killam.canadiancouncil.ca)
Closing Date: May 15th
Funding: Private
No. of awards given last year: 7

Robert Fleming Prize

Subjects: Composition in classical music.
Purpose: To encourage young Canadian composers.
Eligibility: It is intended to encourage the career development of young composers and is awarded to the most talented Canadian music composer in the competition for Canada Council Grants to Professional musicians in classical music.
Level of Study: Postgraduate
Value: Canadian $2,000
Length of Study: Up to 1 year
Frequency: Annual
Country of Study: Any country
No. of awards offered: 1
Closing Date: March 1st
Funding: International Office
Additional Information: Artists may not apply for this prize. All successful candidates in the Canada Council Grants to professional musicians in classical music are considered automatically.

Saidye Bronfman Award

Subjects: Any discipline within the fine crafts.
Purpose: To recognize excellence in the fine crafts. The award is made to a Canadian craftsperson judged to be an outstanding practitioner in his/her field, shown by his/her output over a working life and his/her current level of achievement.
Eligibility: Open to Canadian citizens or individuals who have permanent resident status. The nominee must have made a significant contribution to the development of fine crafts in Canada over a significant period of time, usually more than 10 years.
Level of Study: Unrestricted
Value: Canadian $25,000
Frequency: Annual
No. of awards offered: 1
Application Procedure: Please write for details. Information is available on the Canada Council website www.canadacouncil.ca/prizes/saidye_bronfman.
Closing Date: January 30th
Funding: Private
Contributor: Samuel and Saidye Bronfman Family Foundation

CANADIAN ACADEMIC INSTITUTE IN ATHENS/CANADIAN ARCHAEOLOGICAL INSTITUTE IN ATHENS (CAIA)

59 Queens Park Crescent, Toronto, ON, M5S 2C4, Canada
Tel: (1) 416 926 7290
Fax: (1) 416 926 7292
Email: caia-icaa@caia-icaa.gr
Website: www.caia-icaa.gr
Contact: Grants Management Officer

Homer and Dorothy Thompson Fellowship

Subjects: Modern Greek, classical languages and literatures, history, archaeology, history of art and music.
Purpose: To support the studies of a person who needs to work in Greece.
Eligibility: Open to Canadian citizens or landed immigrants.
Level of Study: Postdoctorate, predoctorate, postgraduate, doctorate, graduate
Type: Fellowship
Value: Approx. Canadian $6,000 plus reduced rent in the CAIA hostel for the period of the fellowship
Length of Study: 1 year
Frequency: Every 2 years
Study Establishment: CAIA
Country of Study: Greece
No. of awards offered: 1
Application Procedure: Applicants must write enclosing a curriculum vitae and an outline of the proposed research. Applicants must also arrange for three referees to send letters to the Canadian address.
Closing Date: March 15th
Funding: Private
No. of awards given last year: 1
Additional Information: In addition to studies related to the fellowship, the Fellow will assist the director of CAIA with office work for 10 hours per week. Some previous experience in Greece and knowledge of modern Greek is recommended.

CANADIAN ASSOCIATION FOR THE PRACTICAL STUDY OF LAW IN EDUCATION (CAPSLE)

c/o Secretariat (Lori Pollock) 37 Moultrey Crescent, Ontario, Georgtown, LTG 4NY, Canada
Tel: (1) 905 702 1710
Fax: (1) 905 873 0662
Email: info@capsle.ca
Website: www.capsle.ca

CAPSLE is a national organization whose aim is to provide an open forum for the practical study of legal issues related to and affecting the education system and its stakeholders.

CAPSLE Fellowship

Subjects: Law.
Purpose: To provide an open forum for the practical study of legal issues affecting education.
Eligibility: Open to Canadian citizens or landed immigrants enrolled in a faculty of law or a Graduate School of Education at Canadian university.
Level of Study: Postgraduate
Type: Fellowship
Value: Canadian $3,000
Frequency: Annual
Study Establishment: Any accredited university or institution
Country of Study: Canada
Application Procedure: See the website.
Closing Date: December 31st

CANADIAN ASSOCIATION OF BROADCASTERS (CAB)

PO Box 627, Station B, Ottawa, ON, K1P 5S2, Canada
Tel: (1) 613 233 4035
Fax: (1) 613 233 6961
Email: cab@cab-acr.ca
Website: www.cab-acr.ca
Contact: Vanessa Dawson, Special Events and Projects Co-ordinator

The Canadian Association of Broadcasters (CAB) is the collective voice of Canada's private radio and television stations and speciality services. The CAB develops industry-wide strategic plans, works to improve the financial health of the industry, and promotes private broadcasting's role as Canada's leading programmer and local service provider.

BBM Scholarship

Subjects: Statistical and quantitative research methodology.
Purpose: To ensure that there is an investment in the development of individuals, skilled and knowledgeable in research, who may be of future benefit to the Canadian broadcasting industry.
Eligibility: Open to students enrolled in a graduate studies programme, or in the final year of an Honours degree with the intention of entering a graduate programme, anywhere in Canada. Candidates must have demonstrated achievement in, and knowledge of, statistical and/or quantitative research methodology in a course of study at a Canadian university or postsecondary institution.
Level of Study: Graduate
Type: Scholarship
Value: Canadian $2,500
Frequency: Annual
Country of Study: Canada
No. of awards offered: 1
Application Procedure: Applicants must complete an application form and submit a 250-word essay outlining their interest in audience research. Application forms are available from the website. Three references should be attached to the completed application form, including one from the course director.
Closing Date: June 30th
Funding: Private
Contributor: The BBM Bureau of Measurement and the Canadian Association of Broadcasters

CANADIAN BAR ASSOCIATION (CBA)

Suite 500, 865 Carling Avenue, Ottawa, ON, K1S 5S8, Canada
Tel: (1) 613 237 2925
Fax: (1) 613 237 0185
Email: info@cba.org
Website: www.cba.org
Contact: Senior Director of Communications

The Canadian Bar Association (CBA) is the essential ally and advocate of all members of the legal profession. It is the voice of and for all members of the profession and its primary purpose is to serve its members. It is also the premier provider of personal and professional development and support to all members of the legal profession, promoting fair justice systems, facilitating effective law reform and promoting equality in the legal profession. The CBA is devoted to the elimination of discrimination.

Viscount Bennett Fellowship

Subjects: Law.
Purpose: To encourage a high standard of legal education, training and ethics.
Eligibility: Open to Canadian citizens only.
Level of Study: Postgraduate
Type: Fellowship
Value: Canadian $25,000
Length of Study: 1 year
Frequency: Annual
Study Establishment: An approved institution
Country of Study: Any country
No. of awards offered: 1
Application Procedure: Please refer to www.cba.org/cba/awards/viscount_bennett for full details and an application form.
Closing Date: November 15th
Funding: Trusts
No. of awards given last year: 1
No. of applicants last year: Average: 48

CANADIAN BLOOD SERVICES (CBS)

1800 Alta Vista Drive, Ottawa, ON, K1G 4J5, Canada
Tel: (1) 613 739 2300
Fax: (1) 613 731 1411
Email: elaine.konecny@bloodservices.ca
Website: www.bloodservices.ca
Contact: Ms Elaine Konecny, Administrative Assistant, Research & Development

Canadian Blood Services (CBS) is a non-profit, charitable organization whose sole mission is to manage the blood system for Canadians. CBS collects approx. 850,000 units of blood annually and processes it into components and products that are administered to thousands of patients each year.

CBS Graduate Fellowship Program

Subjects: Blood transfusion science focusing on aspects of the collection and preparation of blood from volunteer donors as well as on the biological materials derived from blood or their substitutes obtained through biotechnology. Research may encompass a broad variety of disciplines including, but not restricted to, epidemiology, surveillance, social sciences, blood banking, immunohaematology, haematology, infectious diseases, immunology, genetics, protein chemistry, molecular and cell biology, clinical medicine, laboratory sciences, virology, bioengineering, process engineering or biotechnology.
Purpose: To attract and support young investigators to initiate or continue training in the field of blood or blood products research.
Eligibility: Open to graduate students who are undertaking full-time research training leading to a PhD degree. Students registering solely for a Master's degree will not be considered and only those demonstrating acceptance into a PhD programme will receive continued support. Candidates must have completed sufficient academic work to be admitted in good standing to a graduate school by the time the award is to take effect, or be already engaged in a PhD programme. Applicants possessing a medical degree but not licensed to practice medicine in Canada are eligible to apply for this award providing they meet the above criteria.
Level of Study: Graduate
Value: Canadian $20,000 per year plus a yearly research and travel allowance of Canadian $1,000 per year
Length of Study: Up to 4 years. The initial term is for 2-years, with the option for a 2 year renewal. Renewals must be requested in the form of a complete new application
Country of Study: Canada
Application Procedure: Candidates are required to submit a completed application form (GFP-01) that is available either from the website, from or the main address.
Closing Date: July 30th and November 15th
Funding: Government
No. of awards given last year: 6
No. of applicants last year: 16

CBS Postdoctoral Fellowship (PDF)

Subjects: Transfusion science. The CBS has active research programmes within transfusion science emphasizing platelets, stem cells, plasma proteins, infectious disease, epidemiology and chemical transfusion practice.
Purpose: To support Fellows working with CBS-affiliated research and development groups across Canada and to foster careers related to transfusion science in Canada.
Eligibility: Candidates must hold a recent PhD or equivalent research degree or an MD, DDS, DVM, plus a recent research degree in an appropriate health field (minimum of a MSc) or equivalent research experience, neither must be registered for a higher degree at the time of acceptance of the award and nor undertake formal studies for such a degree during the period of appointment.
Level of Study: Postdoctorate, professional development
Type: Fellowship
Value: The value of each fellowship is related to the major degree(s) and experience that the applicant holds. The fellowship offers a stipend based on current Medical Research Council rates for each of the 3 years as well as a 1st year research allowance of Canadian $10,000
Length of Study: 1–3 years
Frequency: Annual
Country of Study: Canada
No. of awards offered: 6
Application Procedure: Applicants must complete CBS Form RD40. Applications must be made through and with the support of a CBS-affiliated scientist. Application forms and guidelines are available from any of the CBS centres or from the main address.
Closing Date: July 1st
Funding: Government
No. of awards given last year: 4
No. of applicants last year: 9

CBS Research and Development Program Individual Grants

Subjects: Blood.
Purpose: To carry out research into all areas of the collection, testing, processing and therapeutic use of blood and blood products in order to maximize effectiveness, to minimize risk to the health of donor and recipient, to minimize cost of products and service and to ensure that all applicable and validated scientific advances in blood transfusion therapy and related fields are incorporated in a timely fashion for the benefit of the public.
Eligibility: Available to principal investigators who are staff members at one of the CBS centers or head office.
Type: Grant
Value: Materials, supplies, equipment, travel and laboratory personnel
Length of Study: 1–2 years
Frequency: Annual
Country of Study: Canada
Application Procedure: Applicants must complete CBS form RD10. Application forms and guidelines are available from any of the Canadian Blood Service Centers or from the main address.
Closing Date: The deadline for the letter of intent is December 15th, and the deadline for the full application is April 3rd
Funding: Government
No. of awards given last year: 7
No. of applicants last year: 26

CBS Research and Development Program Major Equipment Grants

Subjects: Blood.
Purpose: To carry out research into all areas of the collection, testing, processing and therapeutic use of blood and blood products in order to

maximize effectiveness, to minimize risk to the health of donor and recipient, to minimize cost of products and service and to ensure that all applicable and validated scientific advances in blood transfusion therapy and related fields are incorporated in a timely fashion for the benefit of the public.
Eligibility: Open to principal investigators who are staff members at one of the CBS centres or head office.
Type: Grant
Value: To cover the purchase of specific items of permanent and otherwise unavailable equipment costing more than Canadian $10,000 necessary for research relevant to the CBS research and development programme. Less expensive items of equipment are provided for under the Individual and Group Grants and the Request for Proposal
Frequency: Annual
Country of Study: Canada
Application Procedure: Applicants must complete CBS form RD30. Application forms and guidelines are available from any of the Canadian Blood Service Centres or from the main address.
Closing Date: The deadline for the letter of intent is December 15th, and the deadline for the full application is April 13rd
Funding: Government
No. of awards given last year: 0
No. of applicants last year: 1

CBS Research Fellowship In Haemostasis (RFH)

Subjects: Haemostasis management.
Purpose: To fund an original research proposal.
Eligibility: Generally open to individuals who are within 4 years of completion of graduate or clinical fellowship training in an appropriate speciality. The proposed research will contribute to further understanding of the processes of haemostasis and may be of a basic, preclinical or clinical nature.
Level of Study: Professional development, postdoctorate
Type: Fellowship
Value: Canadian $50,000
Length of Study: 1 year
Frequency: Annual
No. of awards offered: 1
Application Procedure: Candidates for this fellowship are required to complete a NNCI/CBS RFH application form (RFH-2001). Application forms and guidelines are available from the main address, as well as in electronic format on the CBS website.
Closing Date: November 1st
Funding: Commercial
Contributor: Novo Nordisk Canada, Inc.
No. of awards given last year: 1
No. of applicants last year: 2
Additional Information: Although it is not a requirement of the award, the fellowship may include some active participation in a clinical programme within a Canadian healthcare facility.

CBS Small Projects Fund

Subjects: Any area of relevance to the CBS.
Purpose: To provide funding for CBS staff, including medical staff, to participate in the CBS research and development effort. Projects may address any area of obvious relevance to the mandate of CBS.
Eligibility: Projects must be based in CBS Blood Centres. Project leaders must be CBS staff members but co-applicants may be from other institutions. Designation as project leader implies that the individual is actively engaged in conducting the study or project and assumes the major responsibility and leadership for the project. CBS scientists (associate scientist, scientist, senior scientists or adjunct scientist) are not eligible to apply to this programme as project leaders and are directed to the Intramural Grants Programme.
Value: Up to Canadian $15,000
Length of Study: 1 year
Study Establishment: CBS Blood Centres
Country of Study: Canada
Application Procedure: Requests for funding must be submitted as a completed application form (SPF-01) that is available from the main address or by email.
Closing Date: July 31st or November 15th, March 15th
Funding: Government
No. of awards given last year: 3
No. of applicants last year: 4

CANADIAN CENTENNIAL SCHOLARSHIP FUND

Canadian Women's Club, MacDonald House, 1 Grosvenor Square, London, W1K 4AB, England
Tel: (44) 20 7258 6344
Fax: (44) 20 7258 6637
Email: info@canadianwomenlondon.org
Website: www.canadianscholarshipfund.co.uk
Contact: The Bursar

The Canadian Centennial' Scholarship fund gives annual awards to Canadian men and women who are already studying in the United Kingdom. Scholarships are awarded on the basis of high academic standards, financial need and relevance of the proposed course of study to Canada.

Canadian Centennial Scholarship Fund

Subjects: All subjects.
Purpose: To assist Canadians studying in the United Kingdom.
Eligibility: Canadian citizens currently enrolled in a United Kingdom programme of studies are eligible to appply.
Level of Study: Postgraduate, doctorate, mba, professional development, graduate
Type: Scholarship
Value: UK £500–2,000
Length of Study: 1 year. Recipients may re-apply
No. of awards offered: 12–15
Application Procedure: Candidates submit a written application and those short listed are interviewed. Applications can be downloaded from our website.
Closing Date: March 16th
Funding: Trusts
Contributor: Maple Leaf Trust
No. of awards given last year: 14
No. of applicants last year: 80+

CANADIAN CYSTIC FIBROSIS FOUNDATION (CCFF)

2221 Yonge Street, Suite 601, Toronto, ON, M4S 2B4, Canada
Tel: (1) 416 485 9149
Fax: (1) 416 485 0960
Email: kethier@cysticfibrosis.ca
Website: www.cysticfibrosis.ca
Contact: Manager, Research Programs

Since 1960, the Canadian Cystic Fibrosis Foundation (CCFF) has worked to provide a brighter future for every child born with cystic fibrosis. Through its research and clinical programmes, the Foundation helps to provide outstanding care for affected individuals, while pursuing the quest for a cure or control.

CCFF Clinic Incentive Grants

Subjects: Cystic fibrosis.
Purpose: To enhance the standard of clinical care available to Canadians with cystic fibrosis, by providing funds to initiate a comprehensive programme for patient care, research and teaching or to strengthen an existing programme.
Eligibility: Canadian hospitals and medical schools are eligible to apply. Applicants must demonstrate the regional need for specialized clinical care for cystic fibrosis, the need of the institution for assistance and its plans to attract complementary funding from other sources to develop a complete cystic fibrosis programme, the potential for the development of a comprehensive programme for care, clinical research and teaching and the desire to collaborate with the CCFF and other Canadian cystic fibrosis clinics.
Level of Study: Research

Type: Grant
Value: Honorarium and travel allowance
Length of Study: 1 year, renewable on an annual basis
Frequency: Annual
Country of Study: Canada
Application Procedure: Applicants must complete an application form. Late applications will be subject to a penalty equal to 10 per cent of the value of the award. This penalty will be deducted from the clinic director's honorarium.
Closing Date: October 1st

CCFF Fellowships

Subjects: Cystic fibrosis.
Purpose: To support basic or clinical research training in areas of the biomedical or behavioural sciences pertinent to cystic fibrosis.
Eligibility: Applicants must hold a PhD or MD. Medical graduates should have already completed basic residency training and must be eligible for Canadian licensure. Equitable consideration will be given to Fellowship applicants from outside of Canada, who intend to return to their own country on completion of a fellowship.
Level of Study: Postgraduate
Type: Fellowship
Value: Dependent upon academic qualifications and research experience, Canadian $40,000–50,000 stipend and Canadian $1,200 travel allowance
Length of Study: 2 years, renewable for up to 1 more year
Frequency: Annual, Twice per year
Study Establishment: An approved university department, hospital or research institute in Canada
Country of Study: Canada
Application Procedure: Applicants must arrange to send three letters of recommendation, one of which should be from the applicant's current or most recent supervisor.
Closing Date: October 1st, April 1st

CCFF Research Grants

Subjects: Cystic fibrosis.
Purpose: To facilitate scientific investigation.
Eligibility: A principal investigator should hold a recognized, full-time faculty appointment in a relevant discipline at a Canadian university or hospital. Under exceptional circumstances and at the discretion of the Research Subcommittee, applications from other individuals may be evaluated on a case-by-case basis.
Level of Study: Doctorate
Type: Research grant
Value: Determined by the Medical or Scientific Advisory Committee following a detailed review of the applicant's proposed budget
Length of Study: Usually 1 or 2 years or, in a limited number of instances, 3 years
Frequency: Annual
Study Establishment: A Canadian institution
Country of Study: Canada
Application Procedure: Applicants must write for details. Incomplete or late applications will be returned to the applicant.
Closing Date: October 1st
Additional Information: Investigators are eligible to hold more than one Research Grant. No more than one initial application may be submitted to a single competition, and it is a requirement that the focus of a second grant be clearly delineated from the first one. The specific aims of a second grant should represent new approaches to the cystic fibrosis problem and not an extension of an existing research programme.

CCFF Scholarships

Subjects: Cystic fibrosis.
Purpose: To provide salary support for a limited number of exceptional investigators, offering them an opportunity to develop outstanding cystic fibrosis research programmes, unhampered by heavy teaching or clinical loads. Intended to attract gifted investigators to cystic fibrosis research.
Eligibility: Open to holders of an MD or PhD degree who are sponsored by the Chairman of the appropriate department and by the Dean of Faculty. They may have recently completed training or be established investigators wishing to devote major research effort to cystic fibrosis. The beginning investigator should have demonstrated promise of ability to initiate and carry out independent research and the established investigator should have a published record of excellent scientific research.
Level of Study: Doctorate, postgraduate
Type: Scholarship
Value: Salary support, which is dependent on the qualifications and experience of the successful candidate, will be determined by prevailing Canadian scholarship rates and the nominating university. The salary of the scholar may be supplemented by the institution or by clinical income and up to 50 per cent of the salary will be paid by the Foundation
Length of Study: 3 years, renewable for an additional 2 years on receipt of a satisfactory progress report. In no case will an award be for more than 5 years
Frequency: Annual
Study Establishment: Any approved university, hospital or research institute
Country of Study: Canada
No. of awards offered: Varies, subject to availability of funds
Application Procedure: Applicants must write for details.
Closing Date: October 1st
Additional Information: Applications will be accepted only in odd-numbered years.

CCFF Senior Scientist Research Training Award

Subjects: Cystic fibrosis.
Purpose: To provide support to a limited number of cystic fibrosis investigators by offering them an opportunity to obtain additional training that will enhance their capacity to conduct research directly relevant to cystic fibrosis.
Eligibility: Applicants must have held a recognized, full-time faculty appointment in a relevant discipline at a Canadian university or hospital for at least 6 years.
Level of Study: Postgraduate
Type: Training award
Value: Canadian $30,000
Length of Study: 3 months–1 year
Frequency: Annual
Study Establishment: An approved university department or hospital in Canada
Country of Study: Canada
Application Procedure: Applications must be received by the Foundation no later than October 1st. Incomplete or late applications will be returned to the applicant.
Closing Date: October 1st
Additional Information: This award can be used for sabbatical support for qualified individuals.

CCFF Small Conference Grants

Subjects: Cystic fibrosis.
Purpose: To support small conferences that are focused on subjects of direct relevance to cystic fibrosis and to facilitate the exchange of special expertise between larger, university-based cystic fibrosis clinics and smaller, more remote clinics.
Eligibility: Open to clinic directors and CCFF-funded investigators.
Level of Study: Professional development
Type: Grant
Value: Grants to conferences will be up to a maximum of Canadian $2,500 and grants for the exchange of expertise will not normally exceed Canadian $1,000
No. of awards offered: Dependent on availability of funds
Application Procedure: Applicants must make applications in the form of a letter. For medical and/or scientific conferences, the application should indicate who is organizing and attending the conference, and the specific topics and purpose of the conference. For inter-clinic exchanges, the application should specify the proposed arrangements for, and the specific purpose of the exchange.
Closing Date: Applications may be submitted at any time, but the Foundation should be consulted in advance with respect to the availability of funds

Additional Information: Grants are available on a first-come, first-served basis. Frequency of application from any particular individual or group should be reasonable.

CCFF Special Travel Allowances

Subjects: Cystic fibrosis.
Purpose: To enable fellows and students to attend and participate in scientific meetings related to cystic fibrosis.
Eligibility: Fellows and other CCFF-supported scientists.
Level of Study: Doctorate, postgraduate
Type: Award
Value: Travel and meal allowance
Length of Study: As determined by seminar length
Frequency: Annual
Study Establishment: Appropriate seminar
Country of Study: Any country
Application Procedure: Applications should be made in the form of a letter and must be submitted prior to travel.
Closing Date: Any time, but the Foundation must be consulted

CCFF Studentships

Subjects: Cystic fibrosis.
Purpose: To support highly qualified graduate students who are registered for a higher degree, and who are undertaking full-time research training in areas of the biomedical or behavioural sciences relevant to cystic fibrosis.
Eligibility: Applicants must be highly qualified graduate students who are registered for a higher degree and who are undertaking full-time research training in areas relevant to cystic fibrosis, or highly qualified students who are registered in a joint MD/MSc or MD/PhD programme. Equitable consideration will be given to studentship applicants from outside of Canada who intend to return to their own country on completion of a studentship.
Level of Study: Doctorate, postgraduate
Type: Studentship
Value: Salary and cost-of-living award at the discretion of the Medical/Scientific Advisory Committee
Length of Study: Master's level: 2–3 years, doctorate level: 2–5 years
Frequency: 3 times per year
Study Establishment: Studentships are tenable only at Canadian universities
Country of Study: Canada
Application Procedure: The Foundation sponsors a studentship competition in October and April. Candidates for initial awards are eligible to apply to either competition. Similar to all CCFF grants, studentships are subject to the availability of funds, and the availability of funds is generally more certain with respect to the October competition.
Closing Date: April 1st, July 1st, October 1st
Additional Information: Studentships are awarded for studies at the Master's or doctoral level. If a student receiving support for studies leading to a Master's degree elects to continue to a doctorate degree, he or she must reapply for an initial CCFF studentship at the doctoral level.

CCFF Transplant Centre Incentive Grants

Subjects: Cystic fibrosis.
Purpose: To enhance the quality of care available to cystic fibrosis transplant candidates by providing eligible centres with supplementary funding.
Eligibility: Open to any Canadian lung transplant centre that currently has one or more individuals with cystic fibrosis listed for transplant. Please note that under no circumstances will funding be provided to more than one transplant centre in the same city. Applicants must demonstrate how funds awarded would serve to enhance the quality of care available to patients in their centre.
Level of Study: Research
Type: Grant
Value: Determined in accordance with a formula that takes account of the number of patients assessed, accepted and followed pre-operatively, transplanted and followed postoperatively in a given centre during the calendar year ending December 31st of the year preceding the application
Length of Study: 1 year
Frequency: Annual
Country of Study: Canada
Application Procedure: Applicants must contact the Foundation. Applicants must provide a rationale for the funding request and a detailed report on patient care and research within the lung transplant programme. All applications will be adjudicated by the Clinic Subcommittee of the Canadian Cystic Fibrosis Foundation.
Closing Date: October 1st
Additional Information: Late applications will be subject to a penalty equal to 10 per cent of the value of the award.

CCFF Visiting Scientist Awards

Subjects: Cystic fibrosis.
Purpose: To enable senior investigators to travel to Canada from abroad who are invited to engage in cystic fibrosis research at a Canadian institution or to assist junior or senior investigators who wish to work in another laboratory in Canada or abroad. This experience should, in some way, benefit the Canadian cystic fibrosis research effort.
Eligibility: A senior investigator can be considered such if he or she has attained at least the position of an associate professor, or has 6 years of equivalent experience.
Level of Study: Professional development, doctorate
Type: Award
Value: Varies
Length of Study: Varies
Frequency: Dependent on funds available
Country of Study: Any country
Application Procedure: Applicants must send an application letter, accompanied by supporting letters from the head of the appropriate department of the host university. Supporting letters should also be provided by the Head of the Department and the Dean of the Faculty of the applicant's own university.

CCFF/Canadian Institutes of Health Research (CIHR) Fellowships

Subjects: Cystic fibrosis.
Eligibility: The general CIHR fellowship eligibility and award guidelines apply. Please consult the Foundation for details.
Type: Fellowship
Value: The value of the award will be in accordance with regular CIHR stipends. A yearly research and travel allowance is provided
Length of Study: 1–3 years, based on peer review recommendations
Frequency: Annual
No. of awards offered: Up to 5
Application Procedure: Applications are to be submitted to the Canadian Institutes of Health Research using the CIHR Fellowship application package.
Closing Date: November 1st

CANADIAN EMBASSY (USA)

501 Pennsylvania Avenue North West Zip-2114, Washington, DC 20001, United States of America
Tel: (1) 202 682 1740
Fax: (1) 202 682 7619
Email: daniel.abele@international.qc.ca
Website: www.canadianembassy.org
Contact: Daniel Abele, Academic Relations Officer

Canadian Embassy (USA) Faculty Enrichment Program

Subjects: Priority topics include bilateral trade and economics, Canada United States border issues, cultural policy and values, environment, natural resources, energy issues and security co-operation, projects that examine Canadian politics, economics, culture and society as well as Canada's role in international affairs.
Purpose: To provide faculty members with the opportunity to develop or redevelop courses with substantial Canadian content that will be

offered as part of their regular teaching load, or as a special offering to select audiences in continuing or distance education.
Eligibility: Open to full-time, tenured or tenure track faculty members at accredited four year United States colleges and universities. Candidates should be able to demonstrate that they are already teaching, or will be authorized to teach, courses with substantial Canadian content (33 per cent or more). Team teaching applications are welcome. Applicants are ineligible to receive the same grant in two consecutive years or to receive two individual category Canadian Studies grants in the same grant period.
Value: Up to US$6,000
Frequency: Annual
Country of Study: United States of America
No. of awards offered: Varies
Application Procedure: Applicants must contact the organization for an application form.
Closing Date: October 31st
Additional Information: The Embassy especially encourages the use of new Internet technology to enhance existing courses, including the creation of instructional websites, interactive technologies and distance learning links to Canadian Universities.

Canadian Embassy (USA) Graduate Student Fellowship Program

Subjects: Business and economic issues, Canadian values and culture, communications, environment, national and international security or natural resources eg. energy, fisheries, forestry and trade.
Purpose: To offer graduate students the opportunity to conduct part of their doctoral research in Canada.
Eligibility: Open to full-time doctoral students at accredited four year colleges and universities in the United States or Canada whose dissertations are related in substantial part to the study of Canada, Canada and the United States or Canada and North America. Candidates must be citizens or permanent residents of the United States and should have completed all doctoral requirements except the dissertation when they apply for a grant.
Level of Study: Graduate
Type: Fellowship
Value: A maximum amount of US$850 per month may be awarded for a designated period of up to nine months
Frequency: Annual
Study Establishment: An accredited four year college or university
Country of Study: Other
Application Procedure: Applicants must provide six copies of the following in the order listed: the completed application form, a concise letter of three to four pages which will explain clearly the present status of the candidate's doctoral studies, describe the candidate's study plans in Canada, list Canadian contacts such as Scholars, research institutes, academic institutions or libraries, state clearly the exact number of months for which financial support is needed, provide a complete and detailed budget, indicate what other funding sources are available, give the names and addresses of two referees, one of which must be the dissertation advisor, contain the dissertation prospectus which must identify the key issues or the main theoretical problem, justify the methodology and indicate clearly the nature of the dissertation's contribution to the advancement of Canadian Studies. An unofficial transcript of grades, a curriculum vitae and proof of United States citizenship or permanent residency must also be included. Application forms are available on request.
Closing Date: October 31st
Funding: Government
Additional Information: The Graduate Student Fellowship Program promotes research in the social sciences and humanities with a view to contributing to a better knowledge and understanding of Canada and its relationship with the United States or other countries of the world.

Canadian Embassy (USA) Research Grant Program

Subjects: Business and economic issues, Canadian values and culture, communications, environment, national and international security or natural resources eg. energy, fisheries, forestry and trade.
Purpose: To assist individual scholars or a group of scholars in writing an article length manuscript of publishable quality and reporting their findings in scholarly publications.
Eligibility: Open to full-time faculty members at accredited four year United States colleges and universities, as well as scholars at American research and policy planning institutes who undertake significant research projects concerning Canada, Canada and the United States, or Canada and North America. Recent PhD recipients who are citizens or permanent residents of the United States are also eligible to apply.
Level of Study: Postgraduate
Value: Individual applicants may request funding for up to US$10,000. The principal investigator, on behalf of a group, may request funding for up to US$15,000
Frequency: Annual
Study Establishment: An accredited four year college or university
Country of Study: United States of America
Application Procedure: Applicants must provide six copies of the following in this order: the completed application form, a concise proposal of four-eight pages which will identify all members of the research team, if a team project, and specify each member's affiliation and role in the study, identify the key issues or the main theoretical problem, describe and justify the appropriate methodology, present a general schedule of research activities, indicate clearly both the nature and scope of the projects contribution to the advancement of Canadian Studies, include a detailed budget including all other funding sources and a description of anticipated expenditures. A curriculum vitae, and the names and addresses of two scholars from whom the applicants will solicit recommendations should also be included. Application forms are available on request.
Closing Date: September 30th
Funding: Government
Additional Information: The Research Grant Program promotes research in the social sciences and humanities with a view to contributing to a better knowledge and understanding of Canada and its relationship with the United States or other countries of the world.

Canadian Embassy Conference Grant Program

Subjects: Social science and humanities.
Purpose: To assist an institution in holding a conference and publishing the resulting papers and proceedings in a scholarly fashion.
Eligibility: Open to U.S. institutions and universities who wish to undertake a conference on Canada–U.S. issues.
Level of Study: Postgraduate
Type: Grant
Value: US$15,000
Frequency: Annual
Country of Study: United States of America
Application Procedure: Applicants must complete the online application form.
Closing Date: June 15th
Funding: Government
Contributor: Foreign Affairs Canada

Canadian Embassy Program Enhancement Grant

Subjects: International relations.
Purpose: To encourage innovative projects that promote awareness among students and the public about Canada–U.S. relations.
Eligibility: Open to U.S. colleges, research institutions and universities who wish to undertake professional academic activities.
Level of Study: Postgraduate
Type: Grant
Value: Up to US$18,000 per year
Length of Study: 1 year
Frequency: Annual
Country of Study: United States of America
Application Procedure: A completed online application form must be submitted.
Closing Date: June 15

CCFF Outreach Grant

Subjects: Teacher training.
Purpose: To encourage training and resource development.

Eligibility: Open to all K–12 teacher who teach about Canada or Canada – U.S. relations.
Level of Study: Professional development
Type: Grant
Frequency: Annual
Country of Study: United States of America
Application Procedure: Contact the academic relations officer.
Funding: Government
Contributor: Foreign Affairs Canada

Embassy International Research Linkages Grant

Subjects: Canadian studies.
Purpose: To facilitate international collaboration between U.S. and Canadian institutions.
Eligibility: Open to all U.S. and Canadian institutions.
Level of Study: Postgraduate
Type: Grant
Value: Up to US$10,000
Frequency: Annual
Country of Study: United States of America
Application Procedure: Contact academic relations officer.
Funding: Government
Contributor: Foreign Affairs Canada

CANADIAN FEDERATION OF UNIVERSITY WOMEN (CFUW)

251 Bank Street, Suite 600, Ottawa, ON, K2P 1X3, Canada
Tel: (1) 613 234 2732; (1) 613 214 8252
Fax: (1) 613 234 8221
Email: cfuwfls@rogers.com
Website: www.cfuw.org
Contact: Betty A Dunlop, Fellowships Programme Manager

Found in 1919, the Canadian Federation of University Women (CFUW) is a voluntary, non-partisan, non-profit, self-funded bilingual organization of 10,000 women university graduates. CFUW members are active in public affairs, working to raise the social, economic, and legal status of women as well as to improve education, the environment, peace, justice and human rights.

Margaret McWilliams Predoctoral Fellowship

Subjects: All subjects.
Purpose: To provide funding for full-time doctoral study.
Eligibility: Open to female Canadian citizens or women who have held landed immigrant status for at least 1 year prior to the submission of an application. Candidates should hold a Bachelor's degree or its equivalent from a recognized university, not necessarily in Canada, and be a full-time student at an advanced stage, ie. at least 1 year into her doctoral programme.
Level of Study: Doctorate
Type: Fellowship
Value: Canadian $12,000 paid in two 6 monthly instalments
Frequency: Annual
Study Establishment: A recognized university
Country of Study: Any country
No. of awards offered: 1
Application Procedure: Applicants must complete an application, available from the Federation website.
Closing Date: November 1st
Funding: Private
No. of awards given last year: 1
No. of applicants last year: 119
Additional Information: The fellowship is not renewable.

CANADIAN FORESTRY FOUNDATION

185 Somerset Street West, Suite 203, Ottawa, ON, K2P 0J2, Canada
Tel: (1) 613 232 1815
Fax: (1) 613 232 4210
Email: cfa@canadianforestry.com
Website: www.canadianforestry.com
Contact: Administrative Assistant

The Canadian Forestry Foundation is a registered charity whose purpose is to support the educational programmes of the Canadian Forestry Association in promoting understanding and co-operation in the wise use and environmentally sound sustainable development of Canada's forests.

Canadian Forestry Foundation Forest Capital of Canada Award

Subjects: Forestry awareness.
Purpose: To recognize, annually, one community in Canada that is distinct because of its commitment to, and dependence on, the forest and the civic-minded recognition of the importance of the forest to the community.
Eligibility: Open to forest communities in Canada that fulfil the terms of the purpose of the award.
Level of Study: Unrestricted
Type: Award
Length of Study: 1 year
Frequency: Annual
Country of Study: Canada
No. of awards offered: 3
Application Procedure: Applicants must write for details.
Closing Date: December 31st
Additional Information: Information on annual recipients is available on the website.

Canadian Forestry Foundation Forest Education Scholarship

Subjects: Forest education and communication.
Purpose: To encourage students to consider a career in the education and communications side of forestry.
Eligibility: Open to Canadian citizens currently enrolled in a graduate forestry programme at a recognized Canadian university. Applicants with backgrounds in communications or education who are registered in a forestry technical school may also be considered. Students with a formal forestry background who are currently studying education at the university level may also apply.
Level of Study: Postgraduate
Type: Scholarship
Value: Canadian $500
Length of Study: 1 academic year
Frequency: Annual
Study Establishment: A recognized Canadian university or forestry technical school
Country of Study: Canada
No. of awards offered: 1
Application Procedure: Applicants must submit applications in writing.
Closing Date: May 30th

CANADIAN HIGH COMMISSION

Academic Relations Unit, Canada House, Trafalgar Square, London, SW1Y 5BJ, England
Tel: (44) 20 7258 6692
Fax: (44) 20 7258 6476
Email: vivien.hughes@international.gc.ca
Website: www.dfait-maeci.gc.ca/london
Contact: Ms Vivien Hughes, Canadian Studies Project Officer

Canadian Department of Foreign Affairs Faculty Enrichment Program

Subjects: Social sciences and humanities, including architecture and town planning, business administration and management, education and teacher training, fine art, law, mass communication and information, transport and communication, recreation, welfare and protection, politics, international relations, history, geography, Canadian literature in English, Canadian literature in French, sociology.
Purpose: To assist in the undertaking of studies relating to Canada or comparative Canada–United Kingdom topics in order to devise a new course on Canada or to modify or extend significantly the Canadian component of an existing course.

Eligibility: Open to full-time, permanent teaching members of staff from a recognized Institution of Higher Education within the United Kingdom.
Level of Study: Faculty
Value: Up to a maximum of Canadian $4,400, paid in two instalments
Length of Study: 3–4 weeks
Frequency: Annual
Country of Study: Canada
No. of awards offered: Varies
Application Procedure: Applicants must complete an application form, available from the Academic Relations Unit at the Canadian High Commission.
Closing Date: October 31st
Funding: Government

Canadian Department of Foreign Affairs Faculty Research Program

Subjects: Social sciences and humanities in relation to Canada, comparative Canada–United Kingdom topics or aspects of Canada's bilateral relations with the United Kingdom. Purely scientific subjects are ineligible.
Purpose: To promote research about Canada, comparative Canada–United Kingdom topics or aspects of Canada's bilateral relations with the United Kingdom, leading to the publication of articles in the scholarly press.
Eligibility: Open to full-time academic staff members and professors emeritus of universities, colleges of higher education or equivalent degree-granting institutes of the United Kingdom. Scholars at research and policy-planning institutions who undertake significant Canadian, or comparative Canadian–United Kingdom projects or Canada's bilateral relations research projects may also apply.
Level of Study: Faculty
Value: Up to a maximum of Canadian $4,400, paid in two instalments
Length of Study: 3–4 weeks
Frequency: Annual
Country of Study: Canada
No. of awards offered: Varies
Application Procedure: Applicants must complete an application form, available from the Academic Relations Unit at the Canadian High Commission.
Closing Date: October 31st
Funding: Government

CANADIAN HOME ECONOMICS ASSOCIATION (CHEA)

307-151 Slater Street, Ottawa, ON, K1P 5H3, Canada
Tel: (1) 613 238 8817
Fax: (1) 613 238 8972
Email: general@chea-acef.ca
Website: www.chea-acef.ca
Contact: Ms Lisa Pearson, Administration Assistant

The Canadian Home Economics Association (CHEA) is the national organization for home economics professionals and has worked to improve life in Canadian homes and communities since 1939. More than 60 years later, CHEA continues to be an advocate for positive change in the home both across Canada and abroad.

Mary A Clarke Memorial Scholarship, Silver Jubilee Scholarship and Fiftieth Anniversary Scholarship

Subjects: Home economics, human ecology, textiles or consumer science.
Purpose: To promote study towards an advanced degree in home economics or an allied field such as human ecology, textiles, family and consumer science.
Eligibility: Open to Canadian citizens or permanent residents who are graduates in home economics and proceeding to a higher degree in the field.
Level of Study: Postgraduate, doctorate
Type: Scholarship
Value: Canadian $4,000
Length of Study: 1 year
Study Establishment: An appropriate institution
Country of Study: Any country
No. of awards offered: 1
Application Procedure: Applicants must complete an application form, available through faculty offices or from CHEA.
Closing Date: January 15th
Funding: Private
Contributor: The Canadian Home Economics Association
No. of awards given last year: 3
No. of applicants last year: 20
Additional Information: The award was established as a tribute to Mary Clarke, a valued member of CHEA and 1952–1954 President.

Robin Hood Multifoods Scholarship

Subjects: Home economics.
Purpose: To financially support individuals planning a career in business, consumer service, food or food service management.
Eligibility: Open to Canadian citizens or landed immigrants who are Master's or doctoral students planning a career in business related consumer food services or food service management. Applicants must have been members of the Canadian Home Economics Association for at least two years and proof of acceptance to a graduate programme must be available. The award is based on academic achievement, personal qualities and past or potential contribution to the home economics profession. The applicant must be registered in a relevant academic programme in September.
Level of Study: Doctorate, postgraduate
Type: Scholarship
Value: Canadian $1,000
Frequency: Annual
Study Establishment: An appropriate institution
Country of Study: Any country
No. of awards offered: 1
Application Procedure: Applicants must complete an application form, available through faculty offices or from CHEA.
Closing Date: January 15th
Funding: Commercial
Contributor: Robin Hood Multifoods Inc
No. of awards given last year: 1
No. of applicants last year: 20

Ruth Binnie Scholarship

Subjects: Home economics and home economics education.
Purpose: To support students studying for a Master's degree in home economics education.
Eligibility: Open to applicants who are Canadian citizens or permanent residents from the field of home economics education.
Level of Study: Doctorate, postgraduate
Type: Scholarship
Value: Canadian $3,000
Frequency: Annual
Study Establishment: An appropriate institution
Country of Study: Any country
No. of awards offered: 2
Application Procedure: Applicants must complete an application form, available through faculty offices or from CHEA.
Closing Date: January 15th
Funding: Private
Contributor: The Ruth Binnie Bequest to the Canadian Home Economics Association
No. of awards given last year: 3
No. of applicants last year: 20

CANADIAN HOSPITALITY FOUNDATION

300 Adelaide Street East, Suite 213, Toronto, ON M5A 1N1, Canada
Tel: (1) 363 3401
Fax: (1) 363 3403
Email: chf@theohi.ca
Website: www.chfscholarships.com

The Canadian Hospitality Foundation is Canada's largest industry driven source of scholarships for students pursuing careers in the foodservice/hospitality industry.

Canadian Hospitality Foundation Scholarship

Subjects: Hotel, food, tourism.
Level of Study: Postgraduate
Type: Scholarship
Value: Canadian $1,000–2,000
Frequency: Annual
Study Establishment: University of Calgary, University of Guelph, Ryerson Polytechnical Institute or Mount Saint Vincent University
Country of Study: Canada
No. of awards offered: 8
Application Procedure: More information and application forms available online.
Closing Date: March 20th

CANADIAN INSTITUTE FOR ADVANCED LEGAL STUDIES

Suite 203, 4 Beechwood Avenue, Ottawa, ON, K1L 8L9, Canada
Tel: (1) 613 744 6166
Fax: (1) 613 744 5766
Contact: Mr Frank McArdle, Executive Director

The Canadian Institute for Advanced Legal Studies conducts legal seminars for judges and lawyers in Cambridge, England and Strasbourg, France.

Right Honorable Paul Martin Scholarship

Subjects: Law.
Purpose: To study for an LLM at the University of Cambridge.
Eligibility: Open to graduates of Canadian faculties of law at the time of application, law students in their articling year at the time of application, or to students registered in their Bar Admission course at the time of application.
Level of Study: Postgraduate
Type: Scholarship
Value: Canadian $14,000
Length of Study: 1 year
Frequency: Annual
Study Establishment: The University of Cambridge
Country of Study: England
No. of awards offered: 2
Application Procedure: Applicants must submit a letter of application, undergraduate and faculty of law transcripts and no more than three letters of recommendation. There is no application form.
Closing Date: December 31st
Funding: Private
No. of awards given last year: 2
No. of applicants last year: 36
Additional Information: The scholarship may be held with another small award as approved by the Institute.

CANADIAN INSTITUTE OF UKRAINIAN STUDIES (CIUS)

University of Alberta, 450 Athabasca Hall, Edmonton, AB, T6G 2E8, Canada
Tel: (1) 780 492 2972
Fax: (1) 780 492 4967
Email: cius@ualberta.ca
Website: www.cius.ca
Contact: Ms Khrystyna Jendyk, Administrator

The Canadian Institute of Ukrainian Studies (CIUS) is part of the University of Alberta under the jurisdiction of the University's Vice President of Research. It was founded in 1976 in order to provide an institutional home to develop Ukrainian scholarship and Ukrainian language education in Canada. It also supports such studies internationally, through organizing research and scholarship in Ukrainian and Ukrainian and Canadian studies, by publishing books and a scholarly journal, developing materials for Ukrainian language education largely for the bilingual school programme, and organizing conferences, lectures and a seminar series. Policy is developed by the director in consultation with CIUS units, programme directors and an advisory council.

CIUS Research Grants

Subjects: Ukrainian or Ukrainian and Canadian studies in history, literature, language, education, social sciences and library sciences.
Purpose: To fund research by scholars on Ukrainian or Ukrainian-Canadian topic in the humanities and social sciences.
Eligibility: Please write for details.
Level of Study: Research, postdoctorate
Value: Up to Canadian $8,000
Length of Study: 1 year
Frequency: Annual
Country of Study: Any country
No. of awards offered: 1
Application Procedure: Applicants may request an application form and guide either from the main address or by email, or download from them the website.
Closing Date: March 1st
Funding: Private

Helen Darcovich Memorial Doctoral Fellowship

Subjects: Ukrainian or Ukrainian and Canadian topics in education, history, law, humanities, social sciences, women's studies and library sciences.
Purpose: To aid students to complete a thesis on a Ukrainian or Ukrainian and Canadian topic in education, history, law, humanities, social sciences, women's studies or library sciences.
Eligibility: Open to qualified applicants of any nationality. For non-Canadian applicants, preference will be given to students enrolled at the University of Alberta.
Level of Study: Doctorate
Type: Fellowship
Value: Up to Canadian $12,000
Length of Study: 1 academic year
Frequency: Annual
Study Establishment: Any approved Institute of Higher Education
Country of Study: Any country
No. of awards offered: 1
Application Procedure: Applicants may write to the main address for application form and guide. Application forms can also be downloaded from the website or received by email.
Closing Date: March 1st
Funding: Private
Contributor: The Helen Darcovich Memorial Endowment Fund
No. of awards given last year: 3
Additional Information: Only in exceptional circumstances may an award be held concurrently with other awards.

John Kolasky Memorial Fellowship

Subjects: Research in social sciences or humanities specializing in Ukrainian studies.
Purpose: To allow scholars from Ukraine to undertake research in Candada.
Eligibility: Limited to scholar from Ukraine.
Level of Study: Postdoctorate
Type: Fellowship
Value: Canadian $7,500–30,000
Length of Study: 3–12 months
Frequency: Annual
No. of awards offered: 1 or more
Funding: Private

Marusia and Michael Dorosh Master's Fellowship

Subjects: Ukrainian or Ukrainian and Canadian topic in education, history, law, humanities, social sciences, women's studies and library sciences.

Purpose: To aid a student to complete a thesis on a Ukrainian or Ukrainian and Canadian topic in education, history, law, humanities, social sciences, women's studies or library sciences.
Eligibility: Open to qualified applicants of any nationality. For non-Canadian applicants, preference will be given to students enrolled at the University of Alberta.
Level of Study: Graduate
Type: Fellowship
Value: Up to Canadian $8,000
Length of Study: 1 academic year
Frequency: Annual
Study Establishment: Any approved Institute of Higher Education
Country of Study: Any country
No. of awards offered: 1
Application Procedure: Applicants may write to the main address for application form. Information and application forms can also be obtained by email or downloaded from the website.
Closing Date: March 1st
Funding: Private
Contributor: The Marusia and Michael Dorosh Endowment Fund
No. of awards given last year: 1
Additional Information: Only in exceptional circumstances may an award be held concurrently with other major awards.

Neporany Doctoral Fellowship

Subjects: Awarded to one or more doctoral students specializing on Ukraine in political science, economics and related fields (social sciences and political, economic, and social history).
Purpose: To fund research of doctoral students writing dissertation in Ukrainian studies.
Eligibility: Applicants must be a PhD student writing a PhD thesis on Ukrainian studies.
Level of Study: Doctorate, postdoctorate
Type: Fellowship
Value: Up to Canadian $15,000
Length of Study: 1 academic year
Frequency: Annual
Country of Study: Any country
No. of awards offered: 1 or more
Application Procedure: Applicants must write for further details to the main address. Information can be obtained by email or downloaded from the website.
Closing Date: March 1st
Funding: Private
Contributor: The Osyp and Josaphat Neporany Educational Fund
No. of awards given last year: 1

CANADIAN INSTITUTES OF HEALTH RESEARCH (CIHR)

160, Elgin Street, 9th Floor, Address Locator 4809A,
Ottawa, ON, K1A 0W9, Canada
Tel: (1) 613 954 1968
Fax: (1) 613 954 1800
Email: info@cihr.ca
Website: www.cihr.ca
Contact: Awards Officer

CIHR Canadian Graduate Scholarships Doctoral Awards

Purpose: To provide special recognition and support to students who are pursuing a doctoral degree in a health-related field in Canada.
Eligibility: These candidates are expected to have an exceptionally high potential for future research achievement and productivity.
Level of Study: Doctorate
Value: Canadian $30,000 annual stipend and Canadian $5,000 annual research allowance
Length of Study: Maximum of 3 years
Frequency: Annual
Study Establishment: A Canadian Institution
Country of Study: Canada
Application Procedure: Applicants must complete an application form in accordance with programme guidelines, available on the website.
Closing Date: October 15th
Funding: Government
No. of awards given last year: 86

CIHR Doctoral Research Awards

Subjects: General medical sciences and health sciences.
Purpose: To provide recognition and funding to students early in their academic research career, providing them with an opportunity to gain research experience. To provide a reliable supply of highly skilled and qualified researchers.
Eligibility: Open to students engaged in full-time research training in a graduate school, who, at the time of application, have completed at least 12 months of graduate study at Master's or PhD level but have been registered for no more than 26 months as a full-time student in a doctoral programme. Candidates must be Canadian citizens or permanent residents of Canada and have an exceptionally high potential for future research achievement and productivity. Individuals with a health professional degree who seek support for Doctoral research training are eligible to apply, but should also consult the guidelines for the CIHR Fellowship program.
Level of Study: Graduate
Type: Award
Value: An annual stipend of Canadian $21,000 for awards held inside Canada and Canadian $26,000 for awards held outside Canada, Awards are valued in Canadian dollars and are taxable
Length of Study: A maximum of 3 years
Frequency: Annual
Study Establishment: Universities or research institutions
Country of Study: Canada and abroad
No. of awards offered: Varies
Application Procedure: Applicants must complete an application form in accordance with programme guidelines, available on the CIHR website.
Closing Date: October 15th
Funding: Government
Contributor: CIHR
No. of awards given last year: 86
No. of applicants last year: 804
Additional Information: Please consult the CIHR website for the complete programme description.

CIHR Fellowships Program

Subjects: Applicants must hold, or be completing, a PhD, health professional degree or equivalent. The health professional degree must be in a regulated health profession such as medicine, dentistry, pharmacy, optometry, veterinary medicine, chiropractic, nursing or rehabilitative science which requires at least a bachelor's degree to be eligible for licensure in Canada.
Purpose: To provide support for highly qualified candidates at the post PhD or post health professional degree stages to add to their experience by engaging in health research either in Canada or abroad.
Eligibility: Candidates must hold or be completing a PhD or health professional degree. Candidates with more than three years of post-PhD training by the competition deadline are not eligible to apply. Candidates may not hold more than three years of federal to undertake post PhD studies. Please consult CIHR's website for full eligibility requirements. www.cihr-irsc.ge.cale/22340.html
Level of Study: Postdoctorate, doctorate, graduate, postgraduate, research
Type: Fellowship
Value: Depending on the experience, a stipend of Canadian $20,000–$47,500 per annum including a further and travel allowance of Canadian $3,500 per annum. Recipients holding the award outside Canada will receive an annual stipend supplement of Canadian $5,000
Length of Study: 5 years maximum for health professionals intending to proceed to a PhD degree, 4 years maximum for health professionals who do not intend to proceed to a PhD degree, 3 years maximum for those with a PhD degree or a PhD and health professional degree

Study Establishment: Universities or research institutions
Country of Study: Any country
No. of awards offered: Varies
Application Procedure: Applicants must submit a training module, a curriculum vitae module for both the candidate and the supervisor(s), official transcripts of the candidate's graduate and/or professional training including proof of any degrees completed, proof of Canadian licensure, three assessments from persons under whom the candidate has studied and a letter of support from the proposed supervisor of foreign candidates and proof of residency/ citizenship for Canadians wishing to hold their award outside of Canada.
Closing Date: February 1st and October 1st
Funding: Government
No. of awards given last year: 160
No. of applicants last year: 914
Additional Information: Consult the CIHR website, www.cihr-irsc.gc.ca for the full programme description.

CIHR MD/PhD Studentships

Subjects: General medical sciences.
Purpose: To promote promising students embarking on a combined MD or PhD programme at approved Canadian Universities.
Eligibility: Candidates for this Studentship Award must be enrolled in a combined MD/PhD programme at one of the approved Canadian institutions. Research supervisors should normally be holders of operating grants or salary funding obtained through a CIHR peer review process.
Level of Study: Doctorate, graduate, research
Type: Studentship
Value: A stipend of Canadian $20,000 per year plus a yearly research allowance of Canadian $500 is provided
Length of Study: 6 years maximum
Study Establishment: The universities of British Columbia, Calgary, Dalhousie, Manitoba, McGill, Memorial, Montreal, Toronto, Western Ontario, Alberta, Sherbrooke
Country of Study: Canada
Application Procedure: Applicants must be nominated by the director of the MD/PhD programme at each institution.
Closing Date: Please write for details
Funding: Government
Contributor: CIHR
Additional Information: For further information please contact the CIHR or refer to the website.

CANADIAN INTERNATIONAL DEVELOPMENT AGENCY (CIDA)

200 Promenade du Portage, Quebee, Gatineau,
K1A 0G4, Canada
Tel: (1) 997 5006
Fax: (1) 953 6088
Email: info@acdi-cida.gc.ca
Website: www.acdi-cida.gc.ca

The CIDA is a Canadian government agency, which administers foreign aid programmes in developing countries.

CIDA Awards for Excellence in Writing on International cooperation

Subjects: Writing.
Purpose: To assist writers.
Eligibility: Open to applicants who are Canadian citizens.
Level of Study: Postgraduate
Type: Scholarship
Value: Funding for a guided tour of international projects in a developing country
Frequency: Annual
Country of Study: Canada
No. of awards offered: 2
Application Procedure: See the website.
Contributor: The Canadian Community Newspapers Association

CIDA Research Grant

Subjects: Areas related to international development.
Purpose: To support research.
Eligibility: Open to candidates who are Canadian residents.
Level of Study: Postgraduate
Type: Grant
Value: Canadian $15,000
Frequency: Annual
Country of Study: Canada
Application Procedure: See the website.
Closing Date: January 31st

CANADIAN LIBRARY ASSOCIATION

Scholarships and Awards Committee, CLA, Membership Services,
328 Frank Street, Ottawa, ON, K2P 0X8, Canada
Tel: (1) 613 232 9625
Fax: (1) 613 563 9895
Email: info@cla.ca
Website: www.cla.ca
Contact: B Shields, Member Services

The Canadian Library Association works to maintain a tradition of commitment to excellence in library education and to advance continuing research in the field of library and information science.

CLA Dafoe Scholarship

Subjects: Library science.
Eligibility: Open to Canadian citizens and landed immigrants.
Level of Study: Postgraduate
Type: Scholarship
Value: Canadian $5,000
Length of Study: 1 year
Frequency: Annual
Study Establishment: An accredited library school
Country of Study: United States of America or Canada
No. of awards offered: 1
Application Procedure: Applicants must complete an application form, available on request. Applicants must submit transcripts, references and proof of admission to a library school.
Closing Date: May 1st
Funding: Commercial
No. of awards given last year: 1

CLA Research and Development Grants

Subjects: Library and information science.
Purpose: To support theoretical and applied research in library and information science.
Eligibility: Open to Canadian citizens and landed immigrants who are members of the CLA.
Level of Study: Unrestricted
Value: Canadian $1,000
Length of Study: 1 year
Frequency: Annual
Country of Study: Canada
No. of awards offered: Varies
Application Procedure: Applicants must write for application guidelines.

H W Wilson Scholarship

Subjects: Library science.
Eligibility: Open to Canadian citizens or landed immigrants. Scholarship candidates must be commencing studies for their first professional library or information studies degree.
Level of Study: Postgraduate
Type: Scholarship
Value: Canadian $2,000
Length of Study: 1 year
Frequency: Annual
Study Establishment: An accredited library school
Country of Study: United States of America or Canada
No. of awards offered: 1

Application Procedure: Applicants must write, telephone or visit the website for further information.
Closing Date: May 1st
Funding: Private
Contributor: The H W Wilson Company
No. of awards given last year: 1

World Book Graduate Scholarship in Library Science

Subjects: Library science.
Eligibility: Open to Canadian citizens or landed immigrants with a BLS or MLS degree. In exceptional circumstances, the scholarship may be given to an outstanding candidate with a degree in another discipline who wishes to obtain a BLS or MLS degree.
Level of Study: Postgraduate
Type: Scholarship
Value: Canadian $2,500
Length of Study: 1 year
Frequency: Annual
Study Establishment: An accredited library school
Country of Study: United States of America or Canada
No. of awards offered: 1
Closing Date: May 1st
Funding: Private
Contributor: World Book Incorporated
No. of awards given last year: 1
Additional Information: The scholarship is given for study leading to a further library degree or related to library work in which the candidate is currently engaged, or to library work that will be undertaken upon completion of the studies.

CANADIAN LIVER FOUNDATION

2235 Sheppard Avenue East, Suite 1500, Toronto, ON, M2J 5B5, Canada
Tel: (1) 416 491 3353
Fax: (1) 416 491 4952
Email: clf@liver.ca
Website: www.liver.ca
Contact: National Director of Health Promotion and Patient Services

The Canadian Liver Foundation provides support for research and education into the causes, diagnosis, prevention and treatment of diseases of the liver.

Canadian Liver Foundation Graduate Studentships

Subjects: Hepatology, chemistry and biochemistry.
Purpose: To enable academically superior students to undertake full-time studies in a Canadian university in a discipline relevant to the objectives of the Foundation.
Eligibility: Candidates must be accepted into a full-time university graduate science programme in a medically related discipline related to a Master's or doctoral degree, and hold a record of superior academic performance in studies relevant to the proposed training.
Level of Study: Postgraduate, doctorate
Type: Studentship
Value: Canadian $16,500 per year
Length of Study: 2 years, renewable once. Transfer from an MSc to a PhD programme will permit the student to renew the award for a total of 4 years support
Country of Study: Canada
No. of awards offered: Dependent on availability of funds
Application Procedure: Applicants must submit application forms along with supporting documents. Application forms can be obtained from the applicant's institution or from the Canadian Liver Foundation website.
Closing Date: March 30th
Funding: Private
No. of awards given last year: 3
No. of applicants last year: 19
Additional Information: A student supported by the Foundation must not hold a current stipend award from another granting agency.

Canadian Liver Foundation Operating Grant

Subjects: Hepatology.
Purpose: To support research projects directed towards a defined objective.
Eligibility: Open to hepatobiliary research investigators who hold an academic appointment in a Canadian university or affiliated institution.
Level of Study: Research
Type: Grant
Value: Up to Canadian $60,000 per year
Length of Study: 2 years, after which time renewal may be sought
Country of Study: Canada
No. of awards offered: Dependent on availability of funds
Application Procedure: Applicants must submit application forms along with supporting documentation. Application forms can be obtained from the applicant's institution or from the Canadian Liver Foundation website.
Closing Date: March 15th
Funding: Private
No. of awards given last year: 5
No. of applicants last year: 30

CANADIAN MORTGAGE AND HOUSING CORPORATION (CMHC)

700 Montreal Road, Ottawa, ON K1A 0P7, Canada
Tel: (1) 748 2300 ext. 3061
Fax: (1) 748 2402
Email: erp@cmhc-schl.gc.ca
Website: www.cmhc-schl.gc.ca

The CMHC is Canada's national housing agency, which is committed to helping Canadians access a wide choice of quality, affordable homes, while making vibrant, healthy communities and cities a reality across the country.

CMHC External Research Program Fund

Subjects: Housing related professions and businesses.
Purpose: To assist Canadian researchers carry out investigations on topics related to housing.
Eligibility: Open to applicants who are Canadian citizens or permanent residents in Canada.
Level of Study: Postgraduate
Type: Scholarship
Value: Canadian $25,000
Frequency: Annual
Country of Study: Canada
Application Procedure: A completed application form must be submitted.
Closing Date: October 31st

CMHC Housing Awards Program

Subjects: Housing.
Purpose: To recognize individuals and organizations that have implemented innovations to improve the quality of housing for Canadians.
Eligibility: Open to applicants who are Canadian citizens or have permanent residents studies in Canada.
Level of Study: Postgraduate
Type: Award
Frequency: Annual
Country of Study: Canada
No. of awards offered: 16
Application Procedure: Refer to Housing Awards Guidelines and Application form on the website, for complete details.
Closing Date: April 5th

Community–University Research Alliance Grant

Subjects: Housing.
Purpose: To help organizations within communities and universities combine forces and tackle issues of common concern.
Eligibility: Open to applicants who are affiliated with a Canadian postsecondary institution.
Level of Study: Postgraduate

Type: Grant
Value: Varies
Frequency: Annual
Country of Study: Canada
Application Procedure: See the website.
Contributor: The social sciences and Humanities Research Council

THE CANADIAN NATIONAL INSTITUTE FOR THE BLIND (CNIB)

1929 Bayview Avenue, Toronto, ON, M4G 3E8, Canada
Tel: (1) 416 486 2500
Fax: (1) 416 480 7677
Email: barbara.marjeram@cnib.ca
Website: www.cnib.ca
Contact: Ms Barbara J. Marjeram, Corporate Secretary

The Canadian National Institute for the Blind (CNIB) is a voluntary, non-profit rehabilitation agency that provides services for people who are blind, visually impaired or deafblind. The CNIB provides consultation in safe and efficient travel training, Braille, tape and electronic information, employment, environmental accessibility, government and community entitlements, technology, sight enhancement, eye banks and community integration. Through the E A Baker Foundation it provides fellowships and Research Grants into blindness prevention.

Barbara Tuck/Mac Phee Family Vision Research Award in Macular Degeneration

Subjects: Ophthalmology and optometry.
Purpose: Provide a one-year grant of in support of research in macular degeneration.
Level of Study: Research
Type: Grant
Value: Up to Canadian $50,000
Length of Study: One year
Frequency: Annual
Country of Study: Canada
No. of awards offered: Varies
Application Procedure: See application website www.cnib.ca
Closing Date: December 1st
Funding: Private
No. of awards given last year: 2
No. of applicants last year: 2

CNIB Winston Gordon Award

Subjects: The award consists of a two-troy-ounce 24 carat gold medal and $15,000 Canadian.
Purpose: The award is given for significant advances in, or applications of, Archnology that are demonstrated to provide benefits to people who are blind or visually impaired.
Eligibility: The significant advances in, or application of, technology must have occurred within 10 years of nomination. The device or application must have a documented benefit to people who are blind or visually impaired. The award may be presented to an individual, group, or organization, including corporations and academic institutions.
Level of Study: Product Development assistive technology for the blind.
Value: Canadian $15,000
Country of Study: Any country
No. of awards offered: One annually
Application Procedure: Application form-www.cnib.ca
Closing Date: April 1st
Funding: Private
No. of awards given last year: 1
No. of applicants last year: 7

E A Baker Fellowship/Grant

Subjects: Ophthalmology and optometry.
Purpose: To further the prevention of blindness in Canada.
Eligibility: Open to Canadians for research or study in Canada, or abroad if returning to practice in Canada, with priority given to university teaching.
Level of Study: Professional development, postgraduate, research
Type: Fellowship or Grant
Value: Canadian $40,000
Length of Study: 2 years
Frequency: Annual
Country of Study: Any country
No. of awards offered: Varies
Application Procedure: Applicants must visit the website for information and an application form. Application form see: www.cnib.ca
Closing Date: December 1st
Funding: Private
No. of awards given last year: 6 including 2 awarded 2 year
No. of applicants last year: 8
Additional Information: Award is co-funded with the Canadian Institute of Health Research.

The E.(Ben) & Mary Hochhausn Fund for Research in Adaptive Technology for Blind & Visually Impaired Persons

Subjects: Research awards may be applied to: research projects, study at centers of excellence in Archnology, fellowships, development of prototypes and development costs of bringing important new products to market.
Purpose: To support research in the field of adaptive Archnology for blind visually impaired persons by means of financial award.
Eligibility: The award will be available to individuals, including CNIB staff, volunteers and clients, with a post-secondary degree.
Level of Study: Research
Type: Research award
Value: Canadian $10,000
Country of Study: International
No. of awards offered: One annually
Application Procedure: See website for details www.cnib.ca
Closing Date: July 30th
Funding: Private
No. of awards given last year: 0
No. of applicants last year: 0

E.A. Baker Applied Research Division Research Fund

Subjects: Research focused on the social educational cultural needs of Canadians who are blind or visually impaired.
Purpose: To promote non medical applied research that will enhance the Luis of the blind or visually impaired.
Level of Study: Research
Type: Grant
Value: Varies
Length of Study: One year
Frequency: Annual
Country of Study: Canada
No. of awards offered: Varies
Application Procedure: Application form-www.cnib.ca
Closing Date: December 1st
Funding: Private
No. of awards given last year: 2
No. of applicants last year: 4

E.A. Baker Research Fund

Purpose: To further the prevention of blindness in Canada.
Level of Study: Postdoctorate, research, professional development
Type: Grant
Value: Up to Canadian $40,000
Length of Study: 1 year
Frequency: Annual
Country of Study: Canada
No. of awards offered: Varies
Application Procedure: Application form-www.cnib.ca
Closing Date: December 1st
Funding: Private
No. of awards given last year: 6
No. of applicants last year: 14

F.J.L. Woodcock/Sir Arthur Pearson Association of war Blinded Scholarship Foundation

Purpose: To provide scholarships to students who have not more than 20/70 vision after corrections, and who are continuing either their vocational or academic education at the post-secondary level.
Eligibility: See website for further information www.cnib.ca
Level of Study: Post-secondary
Type: Scholarship
Value: Canadian $1,000
Length of Study: One year
Frequency: Dependent on funds available
Country of Study: Canada
No. of awards offered: Varies
Application Procedure: Application form www.cnib.ca
Closing Date: April 28th
Funding: Private

F.J.L. Woodcock/Sir Arthur Pearson Association of war Blinded Scholarship Foundation to Mohawk College

Purpose: To provide scholarships to students who have not more than 20/70 vision after corrections, and who are continuing either their vocational or academic education at the post-secondary level.
Level of Study: Post-secondary
Type: Scholarship
Value: Varies
Length of Study: One year
Frequency: Dependent on funds available
Country of Study: Canada
No. of awards offered: Varies
Application Procedure: Application form-www.cnib.ca
Closing Date: April 28th
Funding: Private

Ross C. Purse Doctoral Fellowship

Subjects: The fellowship will be awarded for research in social sciences, engineering and other fields of study that relate to blindness and visual impairment.
Purpose: To encourage and support theoretical and practical research and studies at the post graduate or doctoral level in the fields of blindness and visual impairment in Canada.
Eligibility: Applications will be considered from persons studying at a Canadian University or college, or at a foreign University, where a commitment to work in the field of blindness in Canada for at least two years can be demonstrated.
Level of Study: Doctorate, postgraduate
Type: Fellowship
Value: Up to Canadian $12,500
Length of Study: Two years
Frequency: Annual
Country of Study: Any country
No. of awards offered: One annually
Application Procedure: Application form-www.cnib.ca
Closing Date: April 1st
Funding: Private
No. of awards given last year: 1
No. of applicants last year: 4

Walter and Wayne Gretzy Scholarship Foundation for the Blind Youth of Canada

Subjects: The Gretzy family continue a tradition of assisting the blind youth of Canada to pursue their academic and lifelong dreams.
Purpose: To provide scholarships to eligible blind and visually impaired students planning to study at the post-secondary level.
Eligibility: All applicants must be blind or visually impaired, a graduate from secondary school entering their first year of post-secondary education, and a Canadian citizen.
Level of Study: Post secondary for blind or visually impaired students.
Type: Scholarship
Length of Study: Canadian $3,000
Frequency: Annual
Country of Study: Canada
No. of awards offered: 20
Application Procedure: Application form-www.cnib.ca
Closing Date: July 31st
Funding: Private
No. of awards given last year: 22

CANADIAN NURSES FOUNDATION (CNF)

50 Driveway, Ottawa, ON, K2P 1E2, Canada
Tel: (1) 613 237 2159
Fax: (1) 613 237 3520
Email: info@cnursesfdn.ca
Website: www.canadiannursesfoundation.com
Contact: CNF Scholarship Co-ordinator

The Canadian Nurses Foundation (CNF) is a registered charity founded in 1962. It is committed to promoting the health of Canadians through the advancement of the nurses' profession by financially supporting Canadian nurses in pursuing further education, research, or certification in their speciality. CNF is funded through donations from corporations, nursing associations and individuals.

CNF Scholarships and Fellowships

Subjects: All nursing specialities. Several awards are identified for neurosurgery, oncology, community health nursing, epidemiology, gerontology, child or family healthcare, nursing administration, occupational health, dialysis nursing, home care nursing and aplastic anaemia.
Purpose: To assist Canadian nurses pursuing further education and research.
Eligibility: Open to Canadian nurses who are members of the Foundation.
Level of Study: Doctorate, predoctorate, professional development, graduate, research, postgraduate, baccalaureate
Type: Scholarships, fellowships, bursaries
Value: US$3,000–3,500
Length of Study: 1 year
Frequency: Annual
Country of Study: Canada
No. of awards offered: Varies
Application Procedure: Applicants must visit the website for the application forms, criteria and requirements at www.canadiannursesfoundation.com
Closing Date: April 15th
Funding: Private
Contributor: Corporations, other foundations, individuals
No. of awards given last year: 35
Additional Information: Recipients must submit a summary of any thesis, study or major paper undertaken as part of the course to the CNF.

CANADIAN SOCIETY FOR CHEMICAL ENGINEERING

Suite 550, 130 Slater Street, Ottawa, ON K1P 6E2, Canada
Tel: (1) 613 232 6252 ext 235
Fax: (1) 613 232 5862
Email: awards@cheminst.ca
Website: www.chemeng.ca
Contact: Ms Rita Afeltra, Conferences & Awards Co-ordinator

The Canadian Society for Chemical Engineering (CSCHE), one of the three constituent societies of the Chemical Institute of Canada, is the national technical association representing the field of chemical engineering and the interests of chemical engineers.

CIC Award for Chemical Education

Subjects: Chemistry and chemical engineering.
Purpose: To recognize a person who has made outstanding contributions in Canada to education at the past secondary level in the field of chemistry or chemical engineering.
Level of Study: Professional development
Type: Award

Value: A framed scroll, a cash prize of Canadian $1,000 and up to Canadian $400 travel expenses
Frequency: Annual
Country of Study: Canada
No. of awards offered: 1
Application Procedure: Applicants must be nominated. CIC nomination and curriculum vitae with letters of support.
Closing Date: July 2nd
Funding: Private
Contributor: CIC Chemical Education Fund

CIC Catalysis Award

Subjects: Chemistry/chemical engineering.
Purpose: To recognize an individual who has made a distinguished contribution to the field of catalysis while resident in Canada.
Level of Study: Professional development
Type: Award
Value: A rhodium-plated silver medal and travel expenses to present the Award Lecture
Frequency: Every 2 years
Country of Study: Canada
No. of awards offered: 1
Application Procedure: Applicants must be nominated. (1) Nomination form, (2) curriculum vitae, (3) bio and citation, (4) letters of support.
Closing Date: October 1st (odd number years only)
Funding: Private
Contributor: Catalysis Foundation

CIC Environmental Improvement Award

Subjects: Environmental pollution, treatment and remediation.
Purpose: To award a company, individual, team or organization in Canada for a significant achievement in pollution prevention, treatment or remediation in Canada.
Eligibility: Demonstrated practical application. Nature of achievement based primarily on chemical or chemical engineering principles. Process must result in a demonstratable net improvement. Magnitude of environmental improvement, novelty of approach capacity to conserve resources. Economic benefits, improved industry or public awareness.
Level of Study: Professional development
Type: Award
Value: A plaque and certificate for each nominated individual and travel assistance of up to Canadian $500
Country of Study: Canada
No. of awards offered: 1
Application Procedure: Applicants must be nominated. Nomination form, curriculum vitae, Bio and Citation letters of support.
Closing Date: July 2nd
Funding: Private
Contributor: The CIC Environment Division

CIC Macromolecular Science and Engineering Lecture Award

Subjects: Macromolecular science and engineering.
Purpose: To recognize an individual who has made a distinguished contribution to macromolecular science or engineering.
Level of Study: Professional development
Type: Award
Value: A framed scroll, a cash prize of Canadian $1,500 and travel expenses
Frequency: Annual
Country of Study: Canada
No. of awards offered: 1
Application Procedure: Applicants must be nominated. Nomination form, curriculum vitae, bio and citation and letters of support.
Closing Date: July 2nd
Funding: Private
Contributor: NOVA Chemicals Limited
No. of awards given last year: 1

CIC Medal

Subjects: Chemistry and chemical engineering.
Purpose: To recognize a person who has made an outstanding contribution to the science of chemistry or chemical engineering in Canada.
Level of Study: Professional development
Type: Award
Value: A medal and travel expenses
Frequency: Annual
Country of Study: Canada
No. of awards offered: 1
Application Procedure: Applicants must be nominated. (1) Nomination form, (2) curriculum vitae, (3) bio and citation, (4) letters of support.
Closing Date: July 2nd
Funding: Private
No. of awards given last year: 1

CIC Montreal Medal

Subjects: Chemistry and chemical engineering.
Purpose: To honour a person who has shown significant leadership in or outstanding contribution to the profession of chemistry or chemical engineering in Canada.
Eligibility: Open to administrative contributions within the Chemical Institute of Canada and other professional organizations that contribute to the advancement of the professions of chemistry and chemical engineering. Contributions to the sciences of chemistry and chemical engineering are not considered. Administrative contributions to the CIC, contributions by chemical educators and by staff members of chemical industries and single individual exploits which contribute to the advancement of the chemical profession.
Level of Study: Professional development
Type: Award
Value: A medal and travel expenses if required
Frequency: Annual
Country of Study: Canada
No. of awards offered: 1
Application Procedure: Applicants must be nominated. Application form, curriculum vitae, bio and citation and letters of support.
Closing Date: July 2nd
Funding: Private
Contributor: Montréal CIC Local Section

CIC Pestcon Graduate Scholarship

Subjects: Any area of pesticide and contaminant research including alternative pest control strategies.
Purpose: To support postgraduate work.
Eligibility: Open to Canadian citizens, including landed immigrants, for graduate study in any area of pesticide and contaminant research. Preference will be given to students already in their 2nd year of a PhD programme.
Level of Study: Postgraduate
Type: Scholarship
Value: Canadian $3,000 in two instalments
Length of Study: 1 year
Frequency: Annual
Country of Study: Canada
No. of awards offered: 1
Application Procedure: Applicants must submit a written application including a curriculum vitae and a brief description of no more than 500 words of the research programme undertaken and the progress to date. Applications must be accompanied by an official transcript of the candidate's academic records, the names of their supervisors and a second academic referee. Pestcon application form. 500 word description of research. Official transcriptsLetter of support from supervisor. Pestcon application form, (2) 9 Page maximum curriculum vitae, (3) 500 word description of research, (4) official transcripts, (5) Letters of support from supervisor.
Closing Date: March 1st
Funding: Private
Contributor: The 5th International Congress of Pesticide Chemistry

CIC/Lanxyss, Inc. Award for High School Chemistry Teachers

Subjects: Chemistry.
Purpose: To recognize excellence in the teaching of chemistry at the secondary level. This award pays tribute to outstanding contributions in high school chemistry teaching, stimulates interest in the CIC among teachers and facilitates the Institute's efforts to improve chemistry teaching at the high school level.
Level of Study: Professional development
Type: Award
Value: A cash prize of Canadian $500 and 1 year of membership of the CIC
Frequency: Annual
Study Establishment: Any secondary school
Country of Study: Canada
No. of awards offered: Up to 2
Application Procedure: Applicants must be nominated.
Closing Date: December 1st
Funding: Private
Contributor: Bayer, Inc.

CANADIAN SOCIETY FOR CHEMICAL TECHNOLOGY

130 Slater Street, Suite 550, Ottawa, ON, K1P 6E2, Canada
Tel: (1) 613 232 6252 ext 235
Fax: (1) 613 232 5862
Email: awards@cheminst.ca
Website: www.chem-tech.ca
Contact: Bita Aeltra, Awards Co-ordinator

The Canadian Society for Chemical Technology is the national technical association of chemical and biochemical technicians and technologists with members across Canada who work in industry, government or academia. The purpose of the Society is the advancement of chemical technology, the maintenance and improvement of practitioners and educators and the continual evaluation of chemical technology in Canada. The Society hopes to maintain a dialogue with educators, government and industry, to assist in the technology content of the education process of technologists, to attract qualified people into the professions and the Society, to develop and maintain high standards and enhance the usefulness of chemical technology to both the industry and the public.

Boehringer Ingelheim Award for Organic or Bioorganic Chemistry

Subjects: Organic chemistry.
Purpose: For a Canadian citizen or landed immigrant whose PhD. thesis in the field of organic or bioorganic chemistry who was formally accepted by a Canadian university in the 12 month period preceding the nomination deadline and whose doctoral research is judged to be of outstanding quality.
Level of Study: Postdoctorate
Value: A framed scroll, Canadian $2,000 cash, reasonable travel expenses
Frequency: Annual
No. of awards offered: 1
Application Procedure: Curriculum vitae, nomination form, brief synopsis of PhD thesis and 2 letters of support.
Closing Date: July 2nd
Funding: Corporation
Contributor: Boehringer ingelheim (Canada) Ltd.

CIC Fellowships

Subjects: Chemistry, chemical engineering, chemical technology.
Purpose: A senior class of membership that recognizes the merits of CIC members who have made outstanding contributions.
Frequency: Annual
No. of awards offered: Multiple
Application Procedure: Nomination form, Letters of support must be member of CIC for a minimum of 10 years.
Closing Date: October 1st

CIC Honorary Fellowship

Subjects: Chemistry, chemical engineering.
Purpose: To an individual for exceptional contributions in the chemical profession (no more than 25 living honorary fellows).
Frequency: Annual
Application Procedure: Nomination form.

CNC/IUPAC Travel Awards

Subjects: Chemistry, chemical engineering.
Purpose: Helps young Canadian scientists and engineers who are within 10 years of gaining their PhD. present a paper at an IUPAC-sponsored conference.
Eligibility: Evidence of an independent research programme. High quality publication record. Ability to attract research funding.
Level of Study: Postdoctorate
Value: Up to US$2,000
No. of awards offered: Multiple
Application Procedure: Curriculum vitae, 2 letters of reference, name and location of conference amount ($) needed.
Closing Date: October 14th
Funding: Private
Contributor: Gendron Fund and CNC/IUPAC company associates

CSCT Norman and Marion Bright Memorial Award

Subjects: Chemical technology.
Purpose: To reward an individual who has made an outstanding contribution in Canada to the furtherance of chemical technology.
Eligibility: Open to chemical sciences technologists or persons from outside the field who have made significant or noteworthy contributions to its advancement. May be either a chemical sciences technologist or a person from outside the field who has made a significant and noteworthy contribution to its advancement.
Type: Award
Value: An engraved medallion and a cash prize
Frequency: Annual
Country of Study: Canada
No. of awards offered: 1
Application Procedure: Applicants must complete a nomination form. (1) nomination form (2) curriculum vitae, (3) bio and citation, (4) letters of support.
Closing Date: December 1st
Funding: Trusts
Contributor: Norman and Marion Bright Trust Fund
Additional Information: Award winners are welcome to submit papers at either the CSC or CSChE conferences.

CANADIAN SOCIETY FOR CHEMISTRY (CSC)

130 Slater Street, Suite 550, Ottawa, ON K1P 6E2, Canada
Tel: (1) 613 232 6252 ext 235
Fax: (1) 613 232 5862
Email: awards@cheminst.ca
Website: www.chemistry.ca
Contact: Ms Rita Afettra, Conferences and Awards Co-ordinator

The Canadian Society for Chemistry (CSC), one of three constituent societies of The Chemical Institute of Canada, is the national scientific and educational society of chemists. The purpose of the CSC is to promote the practice and application of chemistry in Canada.

Ichikizaki Fund for Young Chemists

Subjects: Synthetic organic chemistry.
Purpose: To provide financial assistance to young chemists who are showing unique achievements in basic research by facilitating their participation in international conferences or symposia.
Eligibility: Open to members of the Canadian Society for Chemistry who have not passed their 34th birthday as of December 31st of the year in which the application is submitted, who have a research

speciality in synthetic organic chemistry and are scheduled to attend an international conference or symposium directly related to synthetic organic chemistry within 1 year. be a member of the CSC or the Chemical Society of Japan, not have passed 34th birthday as of December 30 of the year of application, have a research specialty in synthetic organic chemistry and be scheduled to attend an international conference in the year of after submission.
Level of Study: Professional development, doctorate, postgraduate, postdoctorate
Value: The maximum value of any one award is Canadian $10,000. Successful applicants may re-apply in subsequent years, provided the cumulative total of all awards does not exceed Canadian $15,000
Frequency: Annual
Study Establishment: Ichikizaki Fund
Country of Study: Any country
Application Procedure: Applicants must submit an application, including a curriculum vitae, copies of recent research papers, the title and brief description of the conference that the applicant wishes to attend, the title and abstract, if available, of the research paper that the applicant intends to present and a proposed budget. Applications from graduate students must be accompanied by a letter of reference from the research supervisor. Resume, research papers, description of conference attending, title and abstract and budget and letter of reference.
Closing Date: December 31st for conferences scheduled between March 1st and February 28th of the following year
Funding: Private
Additional Information: The number of applicants to be recommended by the Society is limited to 10 per year. Although the awards are intended primarily for established researchers, applications from postgraduate students and postdoctoral Fellows will be considered. However, only one application per year from a graduate student can be recommended to the Fund.

THE CANADIAN SOCIETY FOR CLINICAL INVESTIGATION (CSCI)

774 Echo Drive, Ottawa, ON, K1S 5N8, Canada
Tel: (1) 613 730 6240
Fax: (1) 613 730 8194
Email: csci@rcpsc.edu
Website: www.csci-scrc.medical.org
Contact: Mrs C Frewer, Executive Director

Canadian Research Awards for Specialty Residents (Medicine, Surgery)

Subjects: Medicine and surgery.
Purpose: To provide national recognition for original work by postgraduate trainees.
Level of Study: Postgraduate
Value: Canadian $2,000 each and a certificate
Frequency: Annual
Country of Study: Any country
No. of awards offered: Varies
Application Procedure: Applicants write for details.
Funding: Private
Additional Information: These awards are adjudicated by the CSCI. The winners will present their work at one of the scientific sessions of the Annual Meeting of the Royal College or CSCI or a relevant speciality meeting.

CSCI Trainee Awards

Subjects: Medical research.
Purpose: To reward selected trainees who have been involved in programmes of research that have led to the development of an abstract for submission to the Annual Meeting of the Society.
Level of Study: Postgraduate
Value: Canadian $500, a certificate and 1-year complimentary CSCI associate membership. The trainee's supervisor is responsible for the cost of the awardee to attend the meeting
Frequency: Annual
Country of Study: Any country
No. of awards offered: 1
Application Procedure: Applicants must write for details.
Funding: Private

CSCI/CIHR Resident Research Awards

Subjects: Medical research.
Purpose: Prizes will be awarded annually for the best resident research project conducted during an RCPSC/CFPC training programme at each Canadian Medical School.
Level of Study: Postdoctorate
Value: US$1,000
Frequency: Annual
Study Establishment: Canadian Medical Schools
Country of Study: Canada
Application Procedure: Candidates will be selected by each faculty following the criteria outlined by the CSCI and submitted by them to the CSCI.
Funding: Private

Joe Doupe Young Investigators Award

Subjects: Medical research.
Purpose: To reward a significant and/or innovative piece of work.
Eligibility: Open to a new young investigator within 5 years of having completed formal research training or still engaged in that training.
Level of Study: Postdoctorate
Value: Canadian $1,000 and plaque
Frequency: Annual
Country of Study: Any country
No. of awards offered: 1
Application Procedure: Applicants must write for details.
Funding: Private
Contributor: Nickerson Trust Fund/University of Manitoba

CANADIAN SOCIETY FOR MEDICAL LABORATORY SCIENCE (CSMLS)

PO 2830, LCD1, Hamilton, ON L8N 3N8, Canada
Tel: (1) 905 528 8642
Fax: (1) 905 528 4968
Email: sandraw@csmls.org
Website: www.csmls.org
Contact: Sandra Wagner, Director, Educational Development

The CSMLS is the certifying body and professional association for laboratory technologists in Canada. Its purpose is to promote and maintain a nationally accepted standard of medical laboratory technology by which other health professionals and the public are assured of effective and economical laboratory services and to promote, maintain and protect the professional identity and interest of medical laboratory technologists and of the profession.

CSMLS Founders' Fund Award

Subjects: Medical laboratory technology.
Purpose: To assist members with costs of professional continuing education.
Eligibility: Open to certified members in good standing at the time of application.
Level of Study: Professional development
Type: Grant
Value: Varies, at the discretion of the Founders' Fund Committee
Frequency: Dependent on funds available
Country of Study: Canada
No. of awards offered: Varies
Application Procedure: Applicants may submit applications at any time during the year and will be dealt with at the next scheduled meeting of the Founders' Fund Committee. These are held in conjunction with the meetings of the Board of Directors, usually in February, June, September, November and December. The decision to grant an award and the actual amount of the award shall be at the discretion of the Founders' Fund Committee. Applicants may only apply for one award for any activity.
Funding: Private
Contributor: A member supported trust fund

Quebec CE Fund Grants

Subjects: Medical technology.
Purpose: To promote continuing education among medical laboratory technologists who are Francophones.
Eligibility: Open to any person or group who is able to establish or co-ordinate the continuing education programmes for Francophone members of the CSMLS. This would include individual CSMLS members, an affiliated society or branch, the Ordre Professionnelle des Technologistes Médicaux du Québec (OPTMQ) and institutions which teach medical technology.
Level of Study: Postgraduate
Type: Grant
Value: Varies
Country of Study: Canada
No. of awards offered: Varies
Application Procedure: Applicants must request an application form. All applications must include the amount of the grant requested from the fund, an outline of the proposed programme, a comprehensive budget including a breakdown of expenses, a statement of other support to be received or being applied for, development times and the dates that progress reports will be submitted during development, evidence of the need for the programme, and a signed statement declaring that CSMLS members will be permitted to participate in the finished programme at no increased differential fee.
Funding: Private
Additional Information: It is the policy of CSMLS that continuing education programmes should normally be financially self-supporting through the fees charged for the programme. However, there are some situations in which a programme is needed in a particular location, but the programme cannot be self-supporting without charging unacceptably high fees. There may also be a need to fund development costs for certain types of programmes. All requests for the use of the Quebec CE funds shall be reviewed and approved or rejected by the Quebec CE Fund Committee and then considered for ratification at the next CSMLS Board of Directors meeting.

CANADIAN THORACIC SOCIETY (CTS)

The Lung Association, National Office, 3 Raymond Street, Suite 300, Ottawa, ON, K1R 1A3, Canada
Tel: (1) 613 569 6411
Fax: (1) 613 569 8860
Email: info@lung.ca
Website: www.lung.ca/cts
Contact: Grants Management Officer

The Canadian Thoracic Society (CTS) is the medical section of the Canadian Lung Association. It advises the Association on scientific matters and programmes including policies regarding support for research and professional education. The CTS provides a forum whereby medical practitioners and investigators may join in the study of thoracic diseases and other medical fields that may come within the scope of the Lung Association. The CTS's objectives are to maintain the highest professional and scientific standards in all aspects of respiratory diseases, to collect, interpret and distribute scientific information, to encourage epidemiological, clinical and other scientific studies in the prevention, diagnosis and treatment of respiratory diseases and to stimulate and support undergraduate, postgraduate and continuing medical education in respiratory diseases.

CTS Fellowships

Subjects: Pulmonary disease.
Purpose: To support research training in pulmonary disease.
Eligibility: Applicants must be Canadian citizens or permanent residents of Canada. Candidates for the award must have obtained an MD or PhD degree or the equivalent and must not hold a university-level academic position. Those expected to receive a PhD degree within the following year are eligible to apply but may not begin the fellowship until the PhD requirements have been completed. CLA Fellows may not work on projects that have not been approved by the appropriate institutional ethics committees.
Level of Study: Postdoctorate, postgraduate
Type: Fellowship
Length of Study: 2 years, with a possibility of renewal for a further year
Frequency: Annual
Country of Study: Canada
Application Procedure: Applicants must submit applications on CIHR forms.
Closing Date: November 1st
Funding: Government, commercial
Contributor: The Canadian Lung Association, the Canadian Institutes of Health Research, Industry Partners, eg. Glaxo Smithkline Inc., Merck Frosst Can, Bayer Inc, Boehringer Ingelheim and Astrazeneca
Additional Information: Recipients are selected based on priority ratings provided by the CIHR and are subject to the approval of the Canadian Thoracic Society and the Canadian Lung Association (CLA) Board of Directors. Applicants are screened to ensure proposed research areas are appropriate to the goals of the CLA. Fellowships are awarded in each case for research training in a specific institution, and may not be transferred without the explicit approval of both institutions involved.

For further information contact:

Canadian Institutes of Health Research, 410 Laurier Avenue West, 9th Floor, Address Locator 4209A, Ottawa, ON, KIA 0W9, Canada
Website: www.cihr.ca

CANADIAN TOBACCO CONTROL RESEARCH INITIATIVE (CTCRI)

CCS/NCIC National Office, 10 Acom Ave., Toronto, Suite 200, ON M4V 3B1, Canada
Tel: (1) 416 934 5666
Fax: (1) 416 961 4189
Email: aodonohue@ctcri.ca
Website: www.ctcri.ca
Contact: Dr Agnes O'Donohue, Research Grants Manager

The Canadian Tobacco Control Research Initiative (CTCRI) is a national partnership of research organizations working to increase capacity and innovation in research relevant to tobacco control policies and programmes. The goal of the CTCRI is to provide strategic leadership to catalyse, co-ordinate and sustain research that has a direct impact on programmes and policies aimed at reducing toacco abuse and nicotine addiction.

CTCRI Best Knowledge Synthesis Grants RFA

Subjects: Tobacco-related cancer research.
Purpose: To aid interdisciplinary research teams of researchers, practitioners and decision makers to conduct collaborative reviews of evidence for particular tobacco control interventions.
Eligibility: Open to applicant teams that include both researchers and those responsible for tobacco policy or programmes. International co-applicants are welcome.
Value: Up to Canadian $80,000
Length of Study: 1 year
Country of Study: Canada
No. of awards offered: Up to 4
Application Procedure: Applicants must visit the website for application details.
Closing Date: September 1st and April 1st
Contributor: Canadian Career Society/National Cancer Institute of Canada and Canadian Institutes of Health Research
No. of awards given last year: 3
No. of applicants last year: 7

CTCRI Community Based Research Grants

Subjects: Child and youth health, sex and gender study.
Purpose: To support community-based, multisectoral research related to nicotine addiction.
Level of Study: Postgraduate
Type: Grant
Value: Canadian $250,000
Length of Study: 1–5 years

Frequency: Annual
Country of Study: Canada
No. of awards offered: 2
Application Procedure: Applicants must visit the website for details.
Closing Date: October 1st
Funding: Government

CTCRI Idea Grants

Subjects: Tobacco-related research.
Purpose: To support innovative research and young researchers in the health and social sciences in the area of tobacco control and encourage unique to original research that has the potential to advance knowledge in this area.
Eligibility: Open to Canadian citizens or those residing legally in Canada. Applicants will have to sign a waiver affirming lack of support from tobacco companies International applicants welcome in all grant programmes.
Level of Study: Graduate, research
Value: Up to Canadian $50,000
Country of Study: Canada
Application Procedure: Applicants must visit the website for details.
Closing Date: April 1st and October 1st
Funding: Government
Contributor: NCIC

CTCRI Policy Research Grants

Subjects: Tobacco-related research.
Purpose: To stimulate research that will influence and guide policy decisions in tobacco control.
Level of Study: Postgraduate
Type: Grant
Value: Canadian $80,000
Length of Study: 2 years
Frequency: Annual
Country of Study: Canada
No. of awards offered: 6
Application Procedure: Applicants must visit the website for details.
Closing Date: October 1st
Funding: Government

CTCRI Research Planning Grants

Subjects: Tobacco-related research.
Purpose: To bring together new multisectoral and interdisciplinary research teams to construct research proposals.
Level of Study: Postgraduate
Type: Grant
Value: Canadian $15,000
Length of Study: 1 year
Frequency: 4 competitions per year
Country of Study: Canada
No. of awards offered: 2
Application Procedure: Applicants must visit the website for details.
Closing Date: February 28th, May 30th, August 30th, November 30th
Funding: Government

CTCRI Research Planning Grants

Subjects: Tobacco-related research, literature review or other background information gathering.
Purpose: To aid the development of new interdisciplinary research teams for the purpose of developing a well-formed and competitive research proposal for submission to traditional funding sources in tobacco control.
Eligibility: Open to Canadian citizens or permanent residents living legally in Canada. Applicants will be required to sign a waiver affirming lack of support from tobacco companies.
Level of Study: Research, professional development
Value: Up to Canadian $15,000
Country of Study: Canada
No. of awards offered: 8
Application Procedure: Applicants must visit the website for details.
Closing Date: February 28th, May 30th, August 30th and November 30th
Funding: Government
Contributor: National Cancer Institute of Canada/Canadian Cancer Society
No. of awards given last year: 4
No. of applicants last year: 10

CTCRI Researcher Travel Grant

Subjects: Tobacco-related cancer, social, behavioural research.
Purpose: To support travel for a student or member of a non-profit community group to attend a conference or similar event and present results of their research or high-quality evaluation.
Eligibility: Open to students or members of community groups who are not affiliated with a university, government or business.
Level of Study: Research, professional development, graduate, postgraduate
Value: Up to Canadian $3,000
Country of Study: Canada
No. of awards offered: 10
Application Procedure: Applicants must visit the website for details.
Closing Date: September 30th, January 10th, April 1st and June 30th
Funding: Private, government
Contributor: National Cancer Institute of Canada/Canadian Cancer Society
No. of awards given last year: 18
No. of applicants last year: 20

CTCRI Secondary Analysis Grants

Subjects: Tobacco-related research.
Purpose: To provide an opportunity for expert analysis of existing data sets and by doing so, improve the availability of evidence for decision making.
Level of Study: Postgraduate
Type: Grant
Value: Canadian $40,000
Length of Study: 1 year
Frequency: Annual
Country of Study: Canada
No. of awards offered: 1
Application Procedure: Applicants must visit the website for details.
Closing Date: May 1st
Funding: Government

CTCRI Student Research Grant

Subjects: Tobacco-control research.
Purpose: To support graduate research training in the health and social sciences, specifically in the area of tobacco-control research.
Eligibility: Open to students enrolled at an accredited university in Canada. Candidates must be Canadian citizens living legally in Canada and will be expected to sign a waiver affirming lack of support from a tobacco company.
Value: Up to Canadian $10,000
Country of Study: Canada
No. of awards offered: 16
Application Procedure: Applicants must visit the website for details.
Closing Date: March 30th, June 30th, September 30th and December 20th
Funding: Government, private
Contributor: CCS/WCIC

CTCRI Workshop and Learning Opportunity Grants

Subjects: Tobacco-related research.
Purpose: To support events that aim to build research capacity.
Level of Study: Postgraduate
Type: Grant
Value: Canadian $15,000
Length of Study: 1 year
Frequency: Annual
Country of Study: Canada
No. of awards offered: 6
Application Procedure: Applicants must visit the website for details.
Closing Date: Rolling deadline
Funding: Government

THE CANCER COUNCIL N.S.W.

Research Strategy Unit, New South Wales Cancer Council, PO Box 572, Kings Cross, NSW 1340, Australia
Tel: (61) 2 9334 1766
Fax: (61) 2 9326 9328
Email: rong@nswcc.org.au
Website: www.cancercouncil.com.au
Contact: Mr Ron Gale, Administrative Assistant

The Cancer Council NSW is one of the leading cancer charity organizations in New South Wales. Its mission is to defeat cancer and is working to build a cancer-smart community. In building a cancer-smart community, the Council undertakes high-quality research and is an advocate on cancer issues, providing information and services to the public and raising funds for cancer programmes.

The Cancer Council NSW Research Project Grants

Subjects: All aspects of cancer that elucidate its origin, cause and control at a fundamental and applied level. Grants are open to all research disciplines relevant to cancer including behavioural, biomedical, clinical, epidemiological, psychosocial and health services.
Purpose: To provide flexible support for cancer researchers.
Eligibility: Open to Australian residents from New South Wales. Recipients of tobacco sponsorship are ineligible. Applicants must complete an application form available through the NHMARC website. Applications are submitted through the researches institution to the NHMRC.
Level of Study: Unrestricted
Type: Project grant
Value: Generally a maximum of Australian $100,000 per year for 3 years
Length of Study: 1–3 years
Frequency: Annual
Study Establishment: An approved institution in New South Wales
Country of Study: Australia
No. of awards offered: Varies
Application Procedure: Applicants must complete an application form, available on request or from the website. Applications are submitted through the researcher's institution to NHMRC.
Closing Date: Expressions of Internet - 3 March Full applications - 8 May
Funding: Private
Contributor: Community fund-raising
No. of awards given last year: 10 grants awarded in 2005
No. of applicants last year: 70

For further information contact:

NHMRC, GPO Box 9848, Canberra, ACT, 2601, Australia

THE CANCER COUNCIL SOUTH AUSTRALIA

202 Grenhill Road, Eastwood, SA 5063, Australia
Tel: (61) 8 8291 4111
Fax: (61) 8 8291 4122
Email: msmith@cancersa.org.au
Website: www.cancersa.org.au
Contact: Ms Nicole Polglase, Executive Assistant Research & Development

The Cancer Council South Australia is a community-based charity independent of government control that has developed since 1928 with the support of South Australians. The Foundation's mission is to pursue the eradication of cancer through research and education on the prevention and early detection of cancer, thus enhancing the quality of life for people living with cancer.

Cancer Council South Australia Research Grants

Subjects: Any scientific or medical field directly concerned with the cause, diagnosis, prevention and treatment of cancer.
Purpose: To assist postgraduate research workers undertaking research into cancer.
Eligibility: Open to postgraduate research workers who show promise of establishing themselves or to those who have already established themselves in the field of cancer research.
Level of Study: Postdoctorate
Type: Research grant
Value: Varies according to the needs of the proposed research project and available funds
Length of Study: 1–2 years
Frequency: Annual
Study Establishment: An appropriate research organization
Country of Study: Australia
No. of awards offered: Approx. 20
Application Procedure: Visit our website for details. Visit our website www.cancersa.org.au
Closing Date: February
Funding: Private
Contributor: South Australian community
No. of awards given last year: 21
No. of applicants last year: 56

THE CANCER RESEARCH SOCIETY, INC.

625 Avenue du President-Kennedy, Suite 402, Montréal, QC H3A 3S5, Canada
Tel: (1) (26) 514 861 9227
Fax: (1) 514 861 9220
Email: grants@cancerresearchsociety.ca
Website: www.cancerresearchsociety.ca
Contact: Ms Louise Langlois, Executive Director

The Cancer Research Society, founded in 1945, is a national organization that devotes its funds exclusively to research on cancer. The Society is committed to funding basic cancer research or seed money for original ideas. The funds are allocated in the form of grants and fellowships to universities and hospitals across Canada.

Cancer Research Society, Inc. (Canada) Postdoctoral Fellowships

Subjects: Basic medical sciences.
Purpose: To provide financial support to recent PhD and MD's.
Eligibility: Open to holders of a PhD or MD degree of any nationality.
Level of Study: Postdoctorate
Type: Fellowship
Value: Canadian $35,000
Length of Study: 1 year, renewable
Frequency: Annual
Study Establishment: Universities and their affiliated institutions
Country of Study: Canada
No. of awards offered: Varies
Application Procedure: Applicants must visit the website for details.
Closing Date: February 15th
Funding: Private, commercial
No. of awards given last year: 3
No. of applicants last year: 50

Cancer Research Society, Inc. (Canada) Research Grants

Subjects: Fundamental research on cancer.
Purpose: To provide support for new or continuing research activities by independent scientists or groups of investigators in the field of cancer.
Eligibility: Candidates must hold an academic position on the staff of a Canadian university.
Level of Study: Research, professional development, doctorate
Type: Grant
Value: Canadian $30,000–60,000 to cover the cost of research. No equipment or travel is permitted
Frequency: Annual
Study Establishment: Universities and their affiliated institutions
Country of Study: Canada
No. of awards offered: Varies
Application Procedure: Applicants must visit the website for details of application procedures.
Closing Date: February 15th

Funding: Commercial, private
No. of awards given last year: 60
No. of applicants last year: 110

Grant Research Program on Pancreatic Cancer

Type: Research grant
Frequency: Special offering 2 years
No. of awards offered: 1
Funding: Private

Strategic Research Program on Genomics and Proteomics of Metastasic Cancer

Subjects: Medicine.
Purpose: To support basic research in cancer.
Level of Study: Doctorate, research
Type: Grant
Value: Canadian $150,000
Length of Study: 3 years
Frequency: Dependent on funds available
Application Procedure: Application forms are available on the website.
Closing Date: February 26th
Funding: Private
Contributor: Cancer Research Society, Inc.

CANCER RESEARCH UK

London Research Institute, PO Box 123, Lincoln's Inn Fields, London, WC2A 3PX, England
Tel: (44) 20 7269 3609
Fax: (44) 20 7269 3585
Website: www.cancerresearch.org
Contact: Mrs Yvonne Harman, Graduate Programme Administrator

Cancer Research UK London Research Institute is part of CR-UK, which is a registered United Kingdom charity dedicated to saving lives through research into the causes, prevention, treatment and cure of cancer.

Cancer Research UK LRI Clinical Research Fellowships

Subjects: All areas of cancer research.
Purpose: To enable research training.
Eligibility: Open to medical graduates of registrar or senior registrar status. Applicants must have obtained an MRCP, FRCS or other higher medical qualifications.
Level of Study: Doctorate, postdoctorate
Type: Fellowship
Value: Remuneration based on current National Health Service salary scales
Length of Study: Up to 4 years
Frequency: Annual
Study Establishment: Cancer Research UK LRI laboratories
Country of Study: United Kingdom
No. of awards offered: Approx. 5
Application Procedure: Applicants must refer to the advertisements that list procedure information, or alternatively, make direct applications to laboratory heads.
Additional Information: Fellowships are advertised in scientific and medical journals.

Cancer Research UK LRI Graduate Studentships

Subjects: All areas of cancer research.
Purpose: To enable research training.
Eligibility: Open to candidates who have normally been resident in the United Kingdom for more than 3 years and have obtained, or are about to obtain, a First or Upper Second Class (Honours) Degree in science. Applicants must also be aged 25 years or younger. Non-residents are not excluded from consideration.
Level of Study: Doctorate
Type: Studentship
Value: Approx. UK £13,701–14,821 per year, depending on location
Length of Study: 3 years
Frequency: Annual
Study Establishment: Cancer Research UK LRI laboratories
Country of Study: United Kingdom
No. of awards offered: Approx. 20
Application Procedure: Applicants must refer to the advertisements that list procedure information.

Cancer Research UK LRI Research Fellowships

Subjects: All areas of cancer research.
Purpose: To assist postdoctoral research.
Eligibility: Applicants must have been awarded a PhD or equivalent or must be able to show written proof of having submitted their thesis.
Level of Study: Postdoctorate
Type: Fellowship
Value: The starting salary is approx. UK £19,945–26,839 plus location allowances per year depending on experience
Length of Study: Up to 3 years
Frequency: Every 2 months
Study Establishment: Cancer Research UK, London Research Institute laboratories
Country of Study: United Kingdom
No. of awards offered: Approx. 30
Application Procedure: Applicants must refer to the advertisements that list procedure information or alternatively make direct applications to laboratory heads.

THE CANON FOUNDATION IN EUROPE

Borenkerkerweg 59-61, 1185 XB Amstelveen, Netherlands
Tel: (31) 20 5458934
Fax: (31) 20 7128934
Email: foundation@canon-europe.com
Website: www.canonfoundation.org
Contact: Secretary

The Canon Foundation is a non-profit, grant-making philanthropic organization founded to promote, develop and spread science, knowledge and understanding, in particular, between Europe and Japan.

Canon Foundation Award

Subjects: Academic education and cultural understanding, in particular, between Europe and Japan.
Purpose: To contribute to scientific knowledge and international understanding through a teaching assignment that can be combined with collaborative research.
Eligibility: Open to Japanese and European nationals only.
Level of Study: Research, doctorate, professional development, postdoctorate
Type: Award
Value: A maximum award of €3,780 per month
Length of Study: 1–3 months
Frequency: Annual
No. of awards offered: 1–3
Application Procedure: The host institution must complete a nomination form, which is to be submitted with a curriculum vitae, a list of papers and two photographs.
Closing Date: September 15th
Funding: Private
Contributor: Canon Europa NV
No. of awards given last year: 1
No. of applicants last year: 3

For further information contact:

Postbus 2262, 1180 EG Amstelveen, Netherlands

Canon Foundation Research Fellowships

Subjects: All subjects.
Purpose: To contribute to scientific knowledge and international understanding, in particular, between Europe and Japan.
Eligibility: Open to Japanese and European nationals only.
Level of Study: Doctorate, mba, postgraduate, research, postdoctorate
Type: Fellowship

Value: A maximum of award of €27,500
Length of Study: 1 year maximum
Frequency: Annual
No. of awards offered: 10–15
Application Procedure: Applicants must complete an application form, which is to be submitted with two reference letters, a curriculum vitae, a list of papers, two photographs and copies of certificates of higher education.
Closing Date: September 15th
Funding: Private
Contributor: Canon Europa NV
No. of awards given last year: 12
No. of applicants last year: 106

For further information contact:

Postbus 2262, 1180 EG Amstelveen, Netherlands

CANTERBURY HISTORICAL ASSOCIATION

c/o History Department, University of Canterbury, Private Bag, Christchurch, New Zealand
Fax: (64) 3 364 2003
Email: geoff.rice@canterbury.ac.nz
Website: www.hist.canterbury.ac.nz
Contact: Dr G W Rice, Secretary

The Canterbury Historical Association (founded 1922, but in recess between 1940 and 1953) aims to foster public interest in all fields of history by holding meetings for the discussion of historical issues, and to promote historical research and writing through its administration of the J M Sherrard Award in New Zealand local and regional history.

J M Sherrard Award

Subjects: New Zealand regional and local history writing.
Purpose: To foster high standards of scholarship in New Zealand regional and local history.
Eligibility: Open to qualified applicants from New Zealand only. Major awards are normally restricted to substantial monograph length publications that meet scholarly standards. Small-scale works, biographies and family histories are not eligible.
Level of Study: Unrestricted
Type: Prize
Value: New Zealand $1,000
Country of Study: New Zealand
No. of awards offered: Varies
Application Procedure: No application is required, as judges assess all potential titles appearing in the New Zealand National Bibliography.
Funding: Private
No. of awards given last year: 3 major awards
No. of applicants last year: 45 works considered, 10 were shortlisted
Additional Information: The prize money is often divided among two or three finalists. A commendation list is also published.

CARDIFF UNIVERSITY

Cardiff University, CF10 3XQ, Wales, United Kingdom
Tel: (44) 29 2087 4000
Email: graduate@cardiff.ac.uk
Website: www.cardiff.ac.uk

Cardiff University is recognized in independent government assessments as one of the United Kingdom's leading teaching and research universities. Founded by Royal Charter in 1883, the University today combines impressive modern facilities and a dynamic approach to teaching and research with its proud heritage of service and achievement. Having gained national and international standing, Cardiff University's vision is to be recognized as a world-class university and to achieve the associated benefits for its students, staff and all other stakeholders.

Cardiff University MSc/Diploma in Housing Studentship

Subjects: Housing.
Purpose: To fund a postgraduate course in housing.
Eligibility: Studentships are available to United Kingdom applicants with a First or Upper Second Class (Honours) Degree only.
Level of Study: Postgraduate
Type: Studentship
Value: University fees and maintenance grant
Length of Study: 2 years
Frequency: Annual
Study Establishment: Cardiff University
Country of Study: United Kingdom
No. of awards offered: 12
Application Procedure: Applicants must contact the School of City and Regional Planning.
Closing Date: Around June

For further information contact:

Cardiff School of City and Regional Planning, Glamorgan Building, King Edward VII Avenue, Cardiff, CF10 3WA, Wales, United Kingdom
Tel: (44) 29 2087 6092
Email: cardpd@cardiff.ac.uk
Contact: Pauline Card

Cardiff University PhD Business Management Studentship

Subjects: Business management.
Purpose: To fund research in business management.
Eligibility: Open to students with a First or Upper Second Class (Honours) Degree.
Level of Study: Doctorate
Type: Studentship
Value: Tuition fees and living expenses
Length of Study: 3 years
Frequency: Annual
Study Establishment: Cardiff University
Country of Study: United Kingdom
Application Procedure: Applicants must contact the Cardiff Business School.
Closing Date: Feburary 25th

For further information contact:

Cardiff Business School, Aberconway Building, Colum Drive, Cardiff, CF10 3EU, Wales, United Kingdom
Tel: (44) 29 2087 4198
Fax: (44) 29 2087 4419
Contact: Elsie Phillips

Cardiff University PhD Innovative Manufacturing Research Studentship

Subjects: Innovative manufacturing research.
Purpose: To fund PhD study in innovative manufacturing research.
Eligibility: A good Honours degree with knowledge and experience of dynamic modelling and simulation. Overseas applicants should have a minimum International English Language Testing System score of 6.5.
Level of Study: Doctorate
Type: Studentship
Value: Tuition fees and maintenance grant
Length of Study: 3 years
Frequency: Annual
Study Establishment: Cardiff University
Country of Study: United Kingdom
No. of awards offered: 1
Application Procedure: Applicants must complete the standard postgraduate application form and mark on the front of the form CU-IMRC studentship application.
Closing Date: February 25th

For further information contact:

Cardiff Business School, Aberconway Building, Colum Drive, Cardiff, CF10 3EU, Wales, United Kingdom
Tel: (44) 29 2087 4198

Fax: (44) 29 2087 4419
Contact: Elsie Phillips

Cardiff University PhD Music Studentship

Subjects: Music.
Purpose: To fund doctoral study in music.
Eligibility: Applicants should have a good Honours degree in Music, be a United Kingdom or European Union citizen or have been a resident for at least 3 years for reasons other than education.
Level of Study: Doctorate
Type: Studentship
Value: Tuition fees and maintenance
Length of Study: 3 years
Frequency: Annual
Study Establishment: Cardiff University
Country of Study: United Kingdom
No. of awards offered: 2
Application Procedure: Applicants must contact the School of Music. They will need to have received an offer of a place to study before they can apply for financial support.
Closing Date: Around June

For further information contact:

School of Music, 31 Corbett Road, Cardiff, CF10 3EB, Wales, United Kingdom
Tel: (44) 29 2087 4816
Fax: (44) 29 2087 4379
Email: music-pg@cardiff.ac.uk

Cardiff University PhD Pharmacy Studentship

Subjects: Pharmacy.
Purpose: To fund PhD study in pharmacy.
Eligibility: Applicants must have a First or Upper Second Class (Honours) Degree.
Level of Study: Doctorate
Type: Studentship
Value: Tuition fees and a stipend of UK £10,500
Length of Study: 3 years
Frequency: Annual
Study Establishment: Cardiff University
Country of Study: United Kingdom
No. of awards offered: Up to 25
Application Procedure: Applicants must contact the Welsh School of Pharmacy. They will need to have received an offer of a place to study before they can apply for financial support.
Closing Date: Around June

For further information contact:

Postgraduate Admissions, Welsh School of Pharmacy, Redwood Building, King Edward VII Avenue, Cardiff, CF10 3XF, Wales, United Kingdom
Tel: (44) 29 2087 4151
Contact: Mrs Lynne Terrett

Cardiff University PhD Social Sciences Studentship

Subjects: Social theory, environment and public policy, sociology of science and expertise, economic and social change, health, welfare and risk, lifelong learning, work and labour markets, young people, education and disadvantage, educational policy and schooling, human development and learning, crime risk and governance.
Purpose: To fund PhD study in social sciences.
Eligibility: Only United Kingdom and European Union students with a First or Upper Second Class (Honours) Degree can apply for a PhD studentship.
Level of Study: Doctorate
Length of Study: 3 years
Frequency: Annual
Study Establishment: Cardiff University
Country of Study: United Kingdom
Application Procedure: Applicants must contact the School of Social Sciences. They will need to have received an offer of a place before they can apply for financial support.
Closing Date: Around June

For further information contact:

School of Social Sciences, Glamorgan Building, King Edward VII Avenue, Cardiff, CF10 3WT, Wales, United Kingdom
Fax: (44) 29 2087 4436
Email: renton@cardiff.ac.uk
Tel: 29 2087 4972
Contact: Elizabeth Renton

Cardiff University Postgraduate Studentships

Subjects: All subjects.
Purpose: To fund postgraduate training. Awards are available for selected Master's and PhD programmes.
Eligibility: Usually, applicants require a First or Upper Second Class (Honours) Degree, although there are a few exceptions. Most studentships are available to United Kingdom and European Union students only, although in some subjects non-European Union students are also considered for school awards.
Level of Study: Postgraduate
Type: Studentship
Length of Study: Generally 1 year for Master's schemes and 3 years for PhD studentships
Frequency: Annual
Study Establishment: Cardiff University
Country of Study: United Kingdom
No. of awards offered: Approx. 70 per year
Application Procedure: Applicants should contact the School in which they are interested in studying to find out about any funding available. They will need to have received an offer of a place to study before they can apply for financial support. The School will then nominate the applicants they consider most deserving.
Closing Date: Variable, but usually around May or June each year
Additional Information: Cardiff University also has a strong track record of obtaining funding from the Research Council for postgraduate study. Subject-specific enquiries should be directed to the relevant schools. For more general enquiries, please contact the Postgraduate Recruitment Office by email.

EPSRC Geoenvironmental Engineering Studentship

Subjects: Geoenvironmental engineering.
Purpose: To fund postgraduate (MSc) study in geoenvironmental engineering.
Eligibility: Only United Kingdom and European Union students with a First or upper Second Class (Honours) Degree are are eligible for the studentship.
Level of Study: Postgraduate
Type: Studentship
Value: UK £6,800 and tuition fees
Length of Study: 1 year
Frequency: Annual
Study Establishment: Cardiff University
Country of Study: United Kingdom
No. of awards offered: 6
Application Procedure: Applicants must contact the School of Engineering. They will need to have received an offer of a place before they can apply for financial support.
Closing Date: Around June

EPSRC Molecular Modelling Studentship

Subjects: Molecular modelling.
Purpose: To fund postgraduate study in molecular modelling.
Eligibility: Only United Kingdom and European Union students with a good degree in chemistry or a related discipline are eligible for awards.
Level of Study: Postgraduate
Type: Studentship
Value: UK £8,000 and tuition fees
Length of Study: 1 year
Frequency: Annual
Study Establishment: Cardiff University
Country of Study: United Kingdom

No. of awards offered: 10
Application Procedure: Applicants must contact the school of Chemistry. They will need to have received an offer of a place before they can apply for financial support.
Closing Date: Around June

For further information contact:

School of Chemistry, The Main Building, Park Place, Cathays, Cardiff, CF10 3YE, Wales, United Kingdom
Contact: Dr Jamie Platts

ESRC (1+3) Sociology Studentship

Subjects: Sociology and social policy.
Purpose: To fund postgraduate training.
Eligibility: Applicants must have a First or Upper Second Class (Honours) Degree.
Level of Study: Postgraduate
Type: Studentship
Length of Study: 1 year for MSc and 3 years for PhD
Frequency: Annual
Study Establishment: Cardiff University
Country of Study: United Kingdom
No. of awards offered: 8
Application Procedure: Applicants must contact the School of Social Sciences.
Closing Date: Around June

For further information contact:

School of Social Sciences, Glamorgan Building, King Edward VII Avenue, Cardiff, CF10 3WT, Wales, United Kingdom
Tel: (44) 29 2087 4972
Fax: (44) 29 2087 4436
Email: renton@cardiff.ac.uk
Contact: Elizabeth Renton

International Engineering MSc Studentship

Subjects: Civil engineering, water engineering, structural engineering, geoenvironmental engineering.
Purpose: To fund postgraduate study in areas of engineering.
Eligibility: First or Upper Second Class (Honours) Degree.
Level of Study: Postgraduate
Type: Studentship
Value: UK £1,500
Length of Study: 1 year
Frequency: Annual
Study Establishment: Cardiff University
Country of Study: United Kingdom
Application Procedure: Applicants must contact the School of Engineering.
Closing Date: Around June
Additional Information: There is no need to apply seperately for scholarships as eligible applicants will be considered on the basis of their application forms.

For further information contact:

Admission Office, Cardiff School of Engineering, Cardiff University, Cardiff, CF24 0YZ, Wales, United Kingdom
Tel: (44) 29 2087 4656
Email: engineering-pg@cardiff.ac.uk

International Engineering Research Bursary

Subjects: Engineering.
Purpose: To assist well-qualified international students who wish to join the Cardiff School of Engineering.
Eligibility: Applicants must have been offered a place in a full-time PhD programme at Cardiff school of Engineering. Applicants require a First or Upper Second Class (Honours) Degree.
Level of Study: Doctorate
Type: Bursary
Value: UK £1,500
Length of Study: 1 year
Frequency: Annual
Study Establishment: Cardiff University
Country of Study: United Kingdom
No. of awards offered: 10
Application Procedure: Applicants must contact the School of Engineering.
Closing Date: Around June

For further information contact:

Admission Office, Cardiff School of Engineering, Cardiff University, Cardiff, Wales, CF24 0YZ, United Kingdom
Tel: (44) (0) 29 2087 4070
Fax: (44) (0) 29 2087 4716

CARNEGIE TRUST FOR THE UNIVERSITIES OF SCOTLAND

Cameron House, Abbey Park Place, Dunfermline, Fife, KY12 7PZ, Scotland
Tel: (44) 13 8362 2148
Fax: (44) 13 8362 2149
Email: jgray@carnegie-trust.org
Website: www.carnegie-trust.org
Contact: Ms Jackie Gray, Assistant Secretary

The Carnegie Trust for the Universities of Scotland, founded in 1901, is one of the many philanthropic agencies established by Andrew Carnegie. The trust aims to offer assistance to students, to aid the expansion of the Scottish universities and to stimulate research.

Carnegie Grants

Subjects: All subjects in the universities' curriculum.
Purpose: To support personal research projects or aid in the publication of books likely to benefit the universities of Scotland.
Eligibility: Open to graduates of Scottish universities and to full-time members of staff of Scottish universities.
Level of Study: Professional development, postgraduate
Type: Grant
Value: Varies according to requests but the maximum is usually UK £2,000
Length of Study: Up to 3 months
Country of Study: Any country
No. of awards offered: Varies
Application Procedure: Applicants must complete an application form, available from the Trust office.
Closing Date: January 15th, May 15th or October 15th prior to Executive Committee meetings in February, June and November
Funding: Private
No. of awards given last year: 262
No. of applicants last year: 281

Carnegie Scholarships

Subjects: All subjects in the universities' curriculum.
Purpose: To support postgraduate research.
Eligibility: Open to candidates possessing a First Class (Honours) Degree from a Scottish university.
Level of Study: Postgraduate
Type: Scholarship
Value: UK £13,000 per year plus tuition fees and allowances
Length of Study: Up to 3 years, subject to annual review
Frequency: Annual
Study Establishment: Any university
Country of Study: United Kingdom
No. of awards offered: 12–15
Application Procedure: Applicants must be nominated by a senior member of staff at a Scottish university and an application form completed, available from the Trust office.
Closing Date: March 15th
Funding: Private
No. of awards given last year: 12
No. of applicants last year: 133

CATHOLIC ACADEMIC EXCHANGE SERVICE (KAAD)

Hausdorffstrasse 151, 53129, Bonn, Germany
Tel: (49) 228 91758 0
Fax: (49) 228 91758 58
Email: zentrale@kaad.de
Website: www.kaad.de

Research Scholarships: Eastern Europe Programme

Subjects: All subjects.
Purpose: To support study and research visits of East European nationals in Germany who are preparing their theses (doctoral/postdoctoral).
Eligibility: Applicants must be young academics from Asia, Africa, Latin America, Near and Middle East or Eastern Europe, with a commitment to return to their home country upon completion of their research stay.
Level of Study: Doctorate, postdoctorate
Type: Scholarship
Value: In accordance with KAAD scholarship guidelines
Length of Study: 2 years for doctoral research, 6 months for short-term research stays
Study Establishment: A German university
Country of Study: Germany
Application Procedure: Application forms are available on request. Applications can be submitted to the KAAD partner organizations in the home country, which in turn will propose the applicants to the KAAD.
Closing Date: January 15th and June 15th
Contributor: Catholic Academic Exchange Service (KAAD)

Research Scholarships: Programme I

Subjects: All subjects.
Purpose: To support candidates from developing nations, who are still in their home countries, for doctoral and postdoctoral research.
Eligibility: Applicants must be young academics from Asia, Africa, Latin America, Near and Middle East or Eastern Europe, with a commitment to return to their home country upon completion of their research stay.
Level of Study: Doctorate, postdoctorate
Type: Scholarship
Value: In accordance with KAAD scholarship guidelines
Length of Study: 1 year (extendable up to 3 years)
Study Establishment: A German university
Country of Study: Germany
Application Procedure: Application forms are available on request. Applications can be submitted to the KAAD partner organizations in the home country, which in turn will propose the applicants to the KAAD.
Closing Date: January 15th and June 15th
Contributor: Catholic Academic Exchange Service (KAAD)

Research Scholarships: Programme II

Subjects: All subjects.
Purpose: To support candidates from developing nations, who are already in Germany and are in an advanced stage of their research and whose research is not yet promoted by KAAD.
Eligibility: Applicants must be young academics from Asia, Africa, Latin America, Near and Middle East or Eastern Europe, with a commitment to return to their home country upon completion of their research stay.
Level of Study: Doctorate, postdoctorate
Type: Scholarship
Value: In accordance with KAAD scholarship guidelines
Length of Study: 1 year (extendable up to 3 years)
Study Establishment: A German university
Country of Study: Germany
Application Procedure: Application forms are available on request. Applications can be submitted to the KAAD partner organizations in the home country, which in turn will propose the applicants to the KAAD.
Closing Date: January 15th and June 15th
Contributor: Catholic Academic Exchange Service (KAAD)

CATHOLIC LIBRARY ASSOCIATION (CLA)

100 North Street, Suite 224, Pittsfield, MA 01201-5109, United States of America
Tel: (1) 413 443 2252
Fax: (1) 413 442 2252
Email: cla@clatha.org
Website: www.cathla.org
Contact: Jean R Bostley, SSJ, Executive Director

The Catholic Library Association (CLA) represents all segments of the library community. Members strive to initiate, foster and encourage any activity or library programme that will promote literature and libraries, not only of a Catholic nature, but also of an ecumenical spirit.

Rev Andrew L Bouwhuis Memorial Scholarship

Subjects: Library science.
Purpose: To encourage promising and talented individuals to enter librarianship and to foster advanced study in the library profession.
Eligibility: Open to individuals who have been accepted into a graduate school programme, show promise of success based on collegiate record and who demonstrate the need for financial aid.
Level of Study: Graduate, postgraduate
Type: Scholarship
Value: US$1,500
Frequency: Annual
Country of Study: United States of America
No. of awards offered: 1
Application Procedure: Applicants must complete an application form, available on request. Please send a stamped addressed envelope.
Closing Date: February 1st
Funding: Private
No. of awards given last year: 1

World Book, Inc. Grant

Subjects: Continuing education in school or children's librarianship.
Purpose: Establish scholarships for continuing education in school or children's librarianship.
Eligibility: Open to national members of the CLA.
Level of Study: Postgraduate, professional development
Type: Grant
Value: US$1,500 to be divided among no more than three recipients
Frequency: Annual
Study Establishment: Special workshops, institutes, or seminars and summer sessions at Institutes of Higher Education
Country of Study: Any country
No. of awards offered: 1–3
Application Procedure: Applicants must send a stamped addressed envelope for details.
Closing Date: March 15th
Funding: Commercial
No. of awards given last year: 3
Additional Information: This award may not be used for study leading to a degree in library science.

CAUZ GROUP

PO Box 777, Randwick, NSW 2031, Australia
Tel: (61) 2 9332 1559
Fax: (61) 2 9332 1298
Email: trustawards@cauzgroup.com.au
Website: www.trust.com.au
Contact: Mr Petrea Salter, Director

Cauz Group is the administrator and PR agency for a number of high profile awards and scholarships. These include the Miles Franklin Literary Award, Kathleen Mitchell Award (literary), Portia Geach Memorial Award (for female artists), the Sir Robert Askin Operatic

Travelling Scholarship (for male singers), the Lady Mollie Askin Ballet Travelling Scholarship, and the Marten Bequest Travelling Scholarship.

Lady Mollie Askin Ballet Travelling Scholarship

Subjects: Dancing or classical ballet.
Purpose: To support the advancement of culture and education in Australia and elsewhere. To reward Australian citizens of outstanding ability and promise in ballet.
Eligibility: Open to Australian citizens who are aged 17–30 at the closing date for entries for the award.
Level of Study: Unrestricted
Type: Scholarship
Value: Australian $15,000
Length of Study: More than 2 years
Frequency: Every 2 years
Country of Study: Any country
No. of awards offered: 1
Application Procedure: Applicants must complete an application form to be submitted with specified documents and enclosures.
Closing Date: November
Funding: Private
Contributor: The Estate of Lady Mollie Askin
No. of awards given last year: 1
No. of applicants last year: 30

Marten Bequest Travelling Scholarships

Subjects: Instrumental music, painting, singing, sculpture, architecture, ballet, prose, poetry and acting.
Purpose: To augment a scholar's own resources towards affording them a cultural education by means of a travelling scholarship.
Eligibility: Applicants must have been born in Australia, and be aged 21–35 or 17–35 for ballet.
Level of Study: Unrestricted
Type: Scholarship
Value: Australian $18,000 over 2 years
Length of Study: 2 years
Frequency: Annual
Country of Study: Any country
No. of awards offered: 12 per year
Application Procedure: Applicants must complete an application form and submit this with a study outline and supporting material as required.
Closing Date: The last Friday in October of the year preceding the award
Funding: Private
Contributor: The Estate of the late John Chisholm Marten
No. of awards given last year: 12
No. of applicants last year: 200

Miles Franklin Literary Award

Subjects: Writing.
Purpose: To reward the novel of the year that is of the highest literary merit and that presents Australian life in any of its phases.
Eligibility: Genres not eligible for the award are farce, musical comedy, biographies, collections of short stories, poetry and children's books.
Level of Study: Unrestricted
Type: Award
Value: Australian $42,000
Frequency: Annual
Country of Study: Any country
No. of awards offered: 1
Application Procedure: Applicants must complete an application form and enter their novel.
Closing Date: 2nd Friday in December
Funding: Private
Contributor: The Estate of the late Miss S M S Miles Franklin
No. of awards given last year: 1
No. of applicants last year: 55
Additional Information: If there is no novel worthy of the prize the award may be given to the author of a play.

Portia Geach Memorial Award

Subjects: Fine and applied arts.
Purpose: To award the best portraits painted from life of a man or woman distinguished in art, letters or the sciences by a female artist.
Eligibility: Entrants must be female Australian residents who are either Australian or British-born or naturalized. Works must be executed entirely in the previous year.
Type: Award
Value: Australian $18,000
Frequency: Annual
No. of awards offered: 1
Application Procedure: Applicants must complete an application form and submit this with an entry fee and the work.
Closing Date: The last Friday in August
Funding: Private
Contributor: The Estate of the late Miss Florence Kate Geach
No. of awards given last year: 1
No. of applicants last year: 315
Additional Information: The winning portrait and selected works are exhibited for 1 month at the S H Ervin Gallery in Sydney, Australia.

Sir Robert Askin Operatic Travelling Scholarship

Subjects: Operatic singing.
Purpose: To support the advancement of culture and education in Australia and elsewhere. To reward male Australian citizens of outstanding ability and promise as an operatic singer.
Eligibility: Applicants must be male Australian citizens and be aged 18–30 at the time of application.
Level of Study: Unrestricted
Type: Scholarship
Value: Australian $15,000
Length of Study: 2 years
Frequency: Every 2 years
Country of Study: Any country
No. of awards offered: 1
Application Procedure: Applicants must complete an application form to be submitted along with specified documents and enclosures.
Closing Date: November
Funding: Private
Contributor: The Estate of Sir Robert Askin
No. of awards given last year: 1
No. of applicants last year: 30

CDS INTERNATIONAL, INC.

871 United Nations Plaza, New York, NY 10017-1814,
United States of America
Tel: (1) 212 497 3513
Fax: (1) 212 497 3535
Email: rdelfino@cdsintl.org
Website: www.cdsintl.org
Contact: Ms Anna F Oberle, Programme Officer

CDS International, Inc. is a non-profit organization that administers work exchange programmes. CDS International's goal is to further the international exchange of knowledge and technological skills, and to contribute to the development of a pool of highly trained and interculturally experienced business, academic and government leaders.

Congress Bundestag Youth Exchange for Young Professionals

Subjects: Business, technical, computer science, social and service fields.
Purpose: To foster the exchange of knowledge and culture between German and American youth, while providing career-enhancing theoretical and practical work experience.
Eligibility: Open to citizens of the United States of America and permanent residents aged 18–24 years who have well-defined career goals and related part or full-time work experience. Applicants must be able to communicate and work well with others, have maturity enabling them to adapt to new situations, an intellectual curiosity and a sense of diplomacy.
Level of Study: Professional development

Type: Scholarship
Value: International airfare and partial domestic transportation, language training and study at a German professional school, seminars, including transportation and insurance, host family stay
Length of Study: One year: 2-month language; 4-month study; 5-month internship
Frequency: Annual
Study Establishment: A field-specific postsecondary professional school
Country of Study: Germany
No. of awards offered: 75
Application Procedure: Applicants must complete an application form, available on request by mail, email or from the website.
Closing Date: December 1st
Funding: Government
Contributor: U.S. Congress and German Bundestag
No. of awards given last year: 75
No. of applicants last year: 250
Additional Information: Participants must have US$300–350 pocket money per month. During the year of the award, American exchange students will have the opportunity to improve their skills through formal study and work experience. The programme also includes intensive language instruction and housing with a host family or in a dormitory.

CEC ARTSLINK

435 Hudson Street, 8th Floor, New York, NY 10014, United States of America
Tel: (1) 212 643 1985
Fax: (1) 212 643 1996
Email: al@cecartslink.org
Website: www.cecartslink.org
Contact: Tamalyn Miller, Program Coordinator, ArtsLink Awards

CEC Artslink is an international arts service organization. Our programmes encourage and support exchange of artists and cultural managers between the United States and Central Europe, Russia and Eurasia. We believe that the arts are a society's most deliberate and complex means of communication.

ArtsLink Bang on a Can Music Institute

Subjects: Music performance.
Purpose: To establish mutually beneficial exchange of ideas and expertise with U.S. and other international musicians and composers.
Eligibility: Applicants must be citizens of, and reside in one of the eligible countries; Kazakhstan, Kyrgystan, Tajikstan, Uzbekistan.
Level of Study: Postgraduate
Type: Fellowship
Value: Airfare, Visa and health insurance
Length of Study: 1 month
Frequency: Annual
Study Establishment: Vermont Studio Center New York
Country of Study: United States of America
Application Procedure: Contact the Foundation.
Closing Date: December 15th
Funding: Trusts, private

ArtsLink Independent Projects

Subjects: Performing, design, media, literary and visual arts.
Type: Fellowship
Value: US$5,000
Length of Study: 1 year
Frequency: Annual
Country of Study: United States of America
Application Procedure: Complete online application form.
Closing Date: November 7th
Funding: Trusts, private
No. of awards given last year: 41

ArtsLink Jubliee Fellowship Program

Purpose: To contribute to the development of new audiences for Russian culture in Russia and the U.S.
Eligibility: Open to rising young arts managers from all parts of Russia.
Type: Fellowship
Value: Airfare, accommodation, visa and health insurance.
Length of Study: 25 days
Frequency: Annual
Country of Study: United States of America
Application Procedure: Complete online application form.
Funding: Trusts, private
No. of awards given last year: 4

ArtsLink Projects

Subjects: Performing Arts, visual and media arts.
Level of Study: Postgraduate
Type: Fellowship
Value: US$2,500–10,000
Length of Study: 1 year
Frequency: Annual
Application Procedure: Complete online application form.
Closing Date: January 17th
Funding: Private, trusts
No. of awards given last year: 274

ArtsLink Residencies

Subjects: Literature and performing arts.
Type: Fellowship
Length of Study: 5 weeks
Frequency: Annual
Country of Study: United States of America
No. of awards offered: 14
Application Procedure: Complete online application form.
Closing Date: November 7th
Funding: Trusts, private
No. of awards given last year: 14

ArtsLink VisArt Central Asia

Subjects: Arts.
Eligibility: Applicants must be citizens of and reside in one of the eligible countries; Kazakhstan, Kyrgystan, Tajikstan, Uzbekistan.
Level of Study: Postgraduate
Type: Fellowships
Value: Airfare, health insurance, and living and work expenses
Length of Study: 1 month
Frequency: Annual
Study Establishment: Vermont Studio Center New York
Country of Study: United States of America
No. of awards offered: 2
Application Procedure: Contact the Foundation.
Closing Date: February 1st
Funding: Private, trusts

THE CENTER FOR CROSS-CULTURAL STUDY (CC-CS)

446 Main Street, Massachusetts, Amherst, 01002-2314, United States of America
Tel: (1) 256 0011
Fax: (1) 256 1968
Website: www.cccs.com

The CC-CS provides unique learning experiences for students in a true cross-cultural exchange by inviting them to expand their world-view through intense immersion in Seville, Havana and Cordoba. The CC-CS has developed it's reputation from an emphasis on the personal growth of students.

CC-CS Scholarship Program

Subjects: Cultural studies, Spanish studies.
Purpose: To fund continuing excellence in Spanish studies.
Eligibility: Open to all students enrolled on the cross-cultural scholarship programme in Spain, Argentina and Cuba.
Level of Study: Postdoctorate, postgraduate, doctorate

Value: Up to US$2,000
Length of Study: 1 year
Frequency: Annual
Study Establishment: The center for cross-cultural study
Country of Study: Argentina
No. of awards offered: Varies
Application Procedure: Submit application accompanied by an original essay in Spanish, Portuguese and English, and a faculty recommendation.
Closing Date: 60 days prior to taking up a past
No. of awards given last year: 11

CENTER FOR DEFENSE INFORMATION (CDI)

1779 Massachusetts Avenue North West, Washington, DC 20036-2109, United States of America
Tel: (1) 202 332 0600
Fax: (1) 202 462 4559
Email: info@cdi.org
Website: www.cdi.org
Contact: Development Director

The Center for Defense Information (CDI) provides responsible, non-partisan research and analysis on the social, economic, environmental, political and military components of national and global security, and aims to educate the public and inform policy makers about these issues. The organization is staffed by retired senior government officials and knowledgeable researchers and is directed by Dr Bruce G Blair.

CDI Internship

Subjects: Weapons proliferation, military spending, military policy, diplomacy and foreign affairs.
Purpose: To support the work of CDI's senior staff while gaining exposure to research, issues and communications related to national security and foreign policy.
Eligibility: There are no eligibility restrictions. Paid internships are available for nationals of the United States of America and legal immigrants.
Level of Study: Unrestricted
Type: Internship
Value: US$1,000 per month
Length of Study: 3–5 months
Study Establishment: CDI
Country of Study: Any country
No. of awards offered: 5 per trimester, 15 per year
Application Procedure: Applicants must submit a curriculum vitae, covering letter, brief writing sample, transcript and two letters of recommendation.
Closing Date: July 1st for the Autumn deadline, October 1st for the Spring deadline and March 1st for the Summer deadline
Funding: Private
No. of awards given last year: 12
No. of applicants last year: 200

World Security Institute Internship

Subjects: Policy issues, including; weapons proliferation, military spending and reform, diplomacy and foreign affairs, small aims trade, terrorism, missile defense and space weaponization.
Purpose: To support work of one of the World Security Institute's four divisions: the Center of Defense Information, Azimuth Media, International Media, or International Programs.
Level of Study: Postgraduate
Type: Internship
Value: All fees and agreed allowance
Length of Study: 1 year
Frequency: Annual
Study Establishment: World Security Institute
No. of awards offered: 18
No. of awards given last year: 16

CENTER FOR HELLENIC STUDIES

3100 Whitehaven Street North West, Washington, DC 20008, United States of America
Tel: (1) 202 745 4400
Fax: (1) 202 332 8688
Email: chs@fas.harvard.edu
Website: www.chs.harvard.edu
Contact: Programs Officer

The Center for Hellenic Studies (Trustees for Harvard University) offers residential research fellowships for professional scholars in ancient Greek studies.

Center for Hellenic Studies Junior Fellowships

Subjects: Ancient Greek studies, primarily literature, language, philosophy, history, religion, archaeology and art history, with restrictions.
Purpose: To provide selected classics scholars fairly early in their careers with an academic year free of other responsibilities to work on a publishable project.
Eligibility: Open to scholars and teachers of Ancient Greek studies with a PhD degree or equivalent qualification and some published work.
Level of Study: Postdoctorate
Type: Fellowship
Value: Up to US$24,000, plus private living quarters and a study at the Center building. Limited funds for research expenses and research related travel are available
Length of Study: 9 months from September–June, non-renewable
Frequency: Annual
Study Establishment: The Center for Hellenic Studies, Washington, DC
Country of Study: United States of America
No. of awards offered: 12
Application Procedure: Applicants must submit an application form, a curriculum vitae, description of research project, samples of publications and three letters of recommendation. Enquiries about eligibility and early applications are encouraged. Applicants who are unable to stay for the full academic year may apply for a one-semester fellowship and should include a note explaining the circumstances that make this necessary with their application.
Closing Date: October 15th
Funding: Private
Additional Information: Residence at the Center is required.

CENTER FOR INTERNATIONAL STUDIES, UNIVERSITY OF MISSOURI-ST LOUIS

366 Social Sciences and Business Building, University of Missouri-St. Louis, One University Boulevard, St Louis, MO, 63121-4400, United States of America
Tel: (1) 314 516 5753
Fax: (1) 314 516 6757
Email: jglassman@umsl.edu
Website: www.umsl.edu
Contact: Mr Robert Baumann, Assistant Director

The Center for International Studies supports a wide range of academic programmes designed to promote research and interest in international studies and to improve the teaching of international affairs.

Theodore Lentz Postdoctoral or Sabbatical Fellowship in Peace and Conflict Resolution Research

Subjects: International relations.
Purpose: To provide an opportunity for the recipient to conduct research projects in peace and conflict resolution, and to teach an introductory peace studies course in the Autumn semester and one course in the Spring semester at the University of Missouri-St. Louis.
Eligibility: A completed PhD is required and preference is given to graduates of university programmes in peace studies and conflict resolution. Graduates of political science, international relations and

other social science programmes who specialize in peace and conflict resolution are also invited to apply.
Level of Study: Postdoctorate
Type: Fellowship
Value: Approx. US$23,400 and university benefits and US$1,000 travel and expense allowance
Length of Study: 9 months
Frequency: Annual
Study Establishment: The University of Missouri-St Louis
Country of Study: United States of America
No. of awards offered: 1
Application Procedure: Applicants must submit a curriculum vitae, a letter of application, evidence of completion of PhD, three letters of recommendation and a research proposal of approx. 750 words.
Closing Date: April 15th
Funding: Private
Contributor: The Lentz Peace Research Association
No. of awards given last year: 1
No. of applicants last year: 10
Additional Information: Supported in part by the Lentz Peace Research Association.

CENTRAL INTELLIGENCE AGENCY (CIA)

Office of Public Affairs, Washington, DC 20505,
United States of America
Tel: (1) 402 0623
Fax: (1) 482 1739
Website: www.cia.gov

The Central Intelligence Agency (CIA) is an agency exclusively devoted to the business of intelligence. The CIA engages in research, development and deployment of technology for intelligence purposes.

CIA Graduate Studies Program Scholarship

Subjects: International affairs, languages, economics, geography, cartography, physical sciences and engineering.
Purpose: To offer programmes that relate to the respective college major.
Eligibility: Open to candidates who are US citizens.
Level of Study: Postgraduate
Type: Scholarship
Value: Varies.
Frequency: Annual
Country of Study: United States of America
Application Procedure: See the website.
Closing Date: November 1st
Funding: Government

CENTRE FOR THE HISTORY OF SCIENCE, TECHNOLOGY AND MEDICINE (CHSTM)

Simon Building, Oxford Road. The University of Manchester,
Manchester, M13 9PL, England
Tel: (44) 16 306 6000
Email: chstm@manchester.ac.uk
Website: www.manchester.ac.uk/chstm

The Centre for the History of Science, Technology and Medicine (CHSTM) maintains teaching and research programmes of the highest standards. It acts as a focus for the history of science, technology and medicine in the northwest of England. CHSTM houses a Welcome Unit for the History of Medicine and the National Archive for the History of Computing.

AHRB Studentships

Subjects: The history of science, technology and medicine.
Purpose: To support students working for their MSc in the history of science, technology and medicine.
Level of Study: Postgraduate
Type: Studentship
Frequency: Annual
Study Establishment: CHSTM
Country of Study: United Kingdom
Application Procedure: The AHRB deadline is May 1st. In order to ensure completion of paperwork and prompt submission of applications, the CHSTM deadline for AHRB forms is April 12th. We expect to work closely with applicants as they complete the forms, so early contact with CHSTM staff is advisable.
Closing Date: April 1st in any given year
Funding: Government
Contributor: Arts and Humanities Research Board

The Economic and Social Research Council (ESRC) Studentships

Subjects: The history of science, technology and medicine.
Purpose: To fund students working for the MSc in research methods in history of science, technology and medicine.
Eligibility: Open to applicants for our MSc in research methods in history of science, technology and medicine.
Level of Study: Postgraduate
Type: Studentship
Frequency: Annual
Study Establishment: CHSTM
Country of Study: United Kingdom
Application Procedure: The deadline for receipt of application is May 1st. In order to ensure completion of paperwork and prompt submission of applications, the CHSTM deadline for receipt of ESRC forms is April 12th. We expect to work closely with applicants as they complete the forms so early contact with CHSTM staff is advisable. Contact postgraduate co-ordinator at the University.
Closing Date: May 1st
Funding: Government
Contributor: ESRC

Wellcome Trust Studentships

Subjects: The history of medicine.
Purpose: To support applicants whose main interests are in the history of medicine.
Level of Study: Doctorate, research, postgraduate, graduate
Type: Studentship
Frequency: Annual
Study Establishment: CHSTM
Country of Study: United Kingdom
No. of awards offered: Varies
Application Procedure: Applicants must complete the university application form (with two references), the Wellcome Trust Studentship application form and submit a curriculum vitae and samples of written work.
Closing Date: May 1st each year
Funding: Foundation
Contributor: Wellcome Trust
Additional Information: Applicants are encouraged to discuss their application informally with Professor Michael Worboys and to submit their applications as soon as possible.

CENTRO DE INVESTIGACIÓN Y ESTUDIOS AVANZADOS DEL IPN (CINVESTAV-IPN)

Departmento De Matematicas Del CINVESTAV,
Apartado Postal 14-740, Mexico City, 07000, Mexico
Tel: (52) +52 (55) 50 61 3871
Fax: (52) +52 (55) 50 61 3876
Email: matemat@math.cinvestav.mx
Website: www.math.cinvestav.mx
Contact: Dr Enrique Ramirez de Arellano, Head

The Mathematics Department of the Centro de Investigación y Estudios Avanzados Del IPN (CINVESTAV-IPN) offers the Solomon Lefschetz Instructorships to young mathematicians with doctorates who show definite promise in research.

Solomon Lefschetz Instructorships
Subjects: Mathematics and statistics.
Purpose: To support young mathematicians.
Eligibility: Open to applicants with a doctoral degree. Some knowledge of Spanish is also desirable.
Level of Study: Postdoctorate
Type: Fellowship
Value: The salary is equivalent to that of an assistant professor in the mathematics department. An allowance for moving expenses is also provided
Length of Study: 1 year, with a possibility of renewal for an extra year
Country of Study: Mexico
No. of awards offered: 2
Application Procedure: Applicants must submit a curriculum vitae, a short 1–3 page research statement and arrange for at least three letters of recommendation to be sent to the centre.
Closing Date: December 31st
Funding: Government
Contributor: The Mexican Office of Education
Additional Information: Teaching duties generally include one course per semester.

For further information contact:

Soloman Lefschetz Instructorships, Mathematics Department, Cinvestav del IPN, Apartado Postal 14-740, 07000, D.F., Mexico
Tel: (52) (52-5) 747-7103
Fax: (52) (52-5) 747-7104

CEREBRA FOUNDATION

Principality Buildings, 13 Guildhall Square, Carmarthen, Carmarthenshire, SA31 1PR, Wales
Tel: (44) 12 6724 4200
Fax: (44) 12 6724 4201
Email: davidw@cerebra.org.uk
Website: www.cerebra.org.uk
Contact: David Williams, Head of Research

Cerebra works to ensure that up-to-date evidence-based knowledge is available and applied for the prevention of brain damage and for proven treatments.

Cerebra Foundation Research Grant
Subjects: Paediatric neurology.
Purpose: To support research relating to the prevention, detection, early diagnosis, subsequent treatment, therapy and management of paediatric neurological disorders.
Eligibility: Applicants must read all guidelines from the website.
Level of Study: Postgraduate
Value: Varies
Length of Study: Varies
Study Establishment: A suitable reputable institution
Application Procedure: Applicants must write a letter of proposal. Full details are available from the website.
Closing Date: No specific closing date
Funding: Private

CERIES (CENTRE DE RECHERCHES ET D'INVESTIGATIONS EPIDERMIQUES ET SENSORIELLES)

20 rue Victor Noir, 92200, Neuilly-sur-Seine, France
Tel: (33) 146 434 900
Fax: (33) 146 434 600
Email: contact@ceries.com
Website: www.ceries.com

CERIES (Centre de Recherches et d'Investigations Epidermiques et Sensorielles or Centre for Epidermal and Sensory Research and Investigation) is the healthy skin research centre of Chanel.

CERIES Research Award
Subjects: The biology and physiology of healthy skin and/or its reactions to environmental factors.
Purpose: To honour a scientific researcher for a fundamental or clinical research project in the field of healthy skin.
Eligibility: There are no eligibility restrictions.
Level of Study: Research
Value: €40,000
Length of Study: 2 years
Frequency: Annual
Country of Study: Any country
Application Procedure: Applicants must consult the website.
Closing Date: June 2nd
Funding: Private
Contributor: Chanel
No. of awards given last year: 1
No. of applicants last year: 26

CERN EUROPEAN LABORATORY FOR PARTICLE PHYSICS

Human Resources Division, CH-1211 Geneva 23, Switzerland
Tel: (41) 22 767 2735
Fax: (41) 22 767 2750
Email: recruitment.service@cern.ch
Website: www.cern.ch
Contact: Administrative Assistant

CERN European Laboratory for Particle Physics is the world's leading laboratory in its field, that being the study of the smallest constituents of matter and of the forces that hold them together. The laboratory's tools are its particle accelerators and detectors, which are among the largest and most complex scientific instruments ever built.

CERN Summer Student Programme
Subjects: Physics, computing and engineering.
Purpose: To awaken the interest of undergraduates in CERN's activities by offering them hands-on experience during their long summer vacation.
Eligibility: Open to all interested students who have completed at least 3 years of full-time studies at university level.
Value: Travel allowance and a daily stipend
Length of Study: 8–13 weeks
Study Establishment: CERN
Country of Study: Switzerland
Application Procedure: A completed application and curriculum vitae along with 2 references must be submitted to CERN.
Closing Date: January 31

For further information contact:

CERN Recruitment Services via the e-recruitment system
Email: jkrich@umich.edu

CERN Technical Student Programme
Subjects: Accelerator physics, computing, mathematics, engineering, geotechnics, instrumentation for accelerators and particle physics experiments, low temperature physics and superconductivity, materials science, radiation protection, environmental and safety engineering, solid state, surface physics and ultra-high vacuum.
Purpose: To provide placements for students who are specializing in different technical fields.
Eligibility: Open to applicants attending an educational establishment in a CERN member state and following a full-time course in one of the subjects listed, at university or advanced technical level. Students must be less than 30 years of age at the time of the Selection Committee meeting. Candidates must be nationals of the member states of CERN. Students specializing in theoretical or experimental particle physics are not eligible for the programme.
Value: A subsistence allowance of Swiss franc 3,164 per month to cover the expenses of a single person in the Geneva area and medical costs arising from illnesses and accidents of a professional

and non-professional nature. Travel expenses equivalent to a second class return rail fare to Geneva for one person may be paid
Length of Study: Appointments can last for 6 consecutive months, but mostly 1 year. Appointments can start throughout the year
Study Establishment: The European Laboratory for Particle Physics
Country of Study: Switzerland
No. of awards offered: Approx. 80–90
Application Procedure: Applications must be made electronically via the website.
Closing Date: February 16th, July 15th or October 14th
Funding: Government
No. of awards given last year: Approx. 80–90
No. of applicants last year: Approx. 240
Additional Information: The official languages of CERN are English and French. A good knowledge of at least one of these languages is essential. CERN member states include Austria, Belgium, Bulgaria, the Czech Republic, Denmark, Finland, France, Germany, Greece, Hungary, Italy, the Netherlands, Norway, Poland, Portugal, Slovakia Republic, Spain, Sweden, Switzerland and the United Kingdom.

CERN-Asia Associate Programme

Subjects: Scientific research.
Purpose: To offer short-term associateship positions to scientists who are on a leave of absence from their institutes.
Eligibility: Open to scientists who are under 40 years of age and are nationals of Asian countries.
Level of Study: Postdoctorate
Type: Fellowship
Application Procedure: Contact Recruitment office at CERN.
Closing Date: September 30
Contributor: CERN

For further information contact:

Recruitment Services, Human Resources Department, CERN, Geneva 23, CH-1211, Switzerland

CERN-Japan Fellowship Programme

Purpose: To support young researchers who are interested in LHC data analysis and physics studies.
Eligibility: Open to young researchers with Japanese nationality.
Level of Study: Doctorate
Value: A stipend that is calculated individually, travel expense and insurance coverage
Length of Study: Up to 3 years
Frequency: Annual
Application Procedure: A completed electronic application form along with a curriculum vitae should be submitted.
Closing Date: September 30
Contributor: CERN

For further information contact:

Recruitment Service, Human Resource Department, CERN, Geneva 23, CH-1211, Switzerland
Email: recruitment.science@cern.ch

Marie Curie Fellowships for Early Stage Training at CERN

Subjects: Scientific training.
Purpose: To offer structured scientific and/or technological training and to encourage participants to take up long-term research careers.
Eligibility: Open to researchers in the first 4 years of their research activity. Persons who have obtained a doctorate are ineligible.
Study Establishment: CERN
Application Procedure: Candidates should register and apply for the Marie Curie Fellowship programme using the CERN e-recruitment system.
Contributor: European Comission

For further information contact:

Please contact the Recruitment Service
Email: recruitment.service@cern.ch

THE CHARLES A AND ANNE MORROW LINDBERGH FOUNDATION

2150 Third Avenue North, Suite 310, Anoka, MN 55303-2200, United States of America
Tel: (1) 763 576 1596
Fax: (1) 763 576 1664
Email: info@lindberghfoundation.org
Website: www.lindberghfoundation.org
Contact: Ms Shelley Nehl, Grants Administrator

The Charles A and Anne Morrow Lindbergh Foundation is dedicated to improving the quality of life through balance between nature and technology.

Lindbergh Grants

Subjects: Adaptive technology, waste minimization and management, agriculture, aviation, aerospace, conservation of natural resources, humanities, education, arts, intercultural communication, exploration, biomedical research, health and population sciences.
Purpose: To provide grants to individuals whose initiative in a wide spectrum of disciplines seeks to actively further a better balance between technology and the natural environment.
Eligibility: Open to nationals of any country.
Level of Study: Unrestricted, research
Type: Research grant
Value: A maximum of US$10,580
Length of Study: 1 year
Frequency: Annual
Country of Study: Any country
No. of awards offered: Approx. 10
Application Procedure: Applicants must complete an application form.
Closing Date: The second Thursday in June
Funding: Private
Contributor: Individuals, corporations and foundations
No. of awards given last year: 8
No. of applicants last year: 163

CHARLES BABBAGE INSTITUTE (CBI)

University of Minnesota, 211 Andersen Library, 222 21st Avenue South, Minneapolis, MN 55455, United States of America
Tel: (1) 612 624 5050
Fax: (1) 612 625 8054
Email: yostx003@tc.umn.edu
Website: www.cbi.umn.edu
Contact: Jeffrey Yost, CBI Assoc. Director

The Charles Babbage Institute (CBI) is a research centre dedicated to promoting the study of the history of computing, its impact on society and preserving relevant documentation. CBI fosters research and writing in the history of computing by providing fellowship support, archival resources and information to scholars, computer scientists and the general public.

Adelle and Erwin Tomash Fellowship in the History of Information Processing

Subjects: The history of computing and information processing.
Purpose: To advance the professional development of historians in the field.
Eligibility: Open to graduate students whose dissertations deal with a historical aspect of information processing. Priority will be given to students who have completed all requirements for the doctoral degree except the research and writing of the dissertation.
Level of Study: Doctorate
Type: Fellowship
Value: US$10,000 stipend plus up to US$2,000 to be used for tuition, fees, travel and other research expenses
Length of Study: 1 year
Frequency: Annual
Country of Study: Any country
No. of awards offered: 1

Application Procedure: Applicants must send their curriculum vitae, a five page statement and justification of the research problem, and a discussion of methods, research materials and evidence of faculty support for the project. Applicants should also arrange for three letters of reference and certified transcripts of graduate school credits to be sent directly to the Institute.
Closing Date: January 15th
Funding: Private

For further information contact:

Charles Babbage Institute University of Minnesota 103 Walter Library 117 Pleasant Street, SE, Minneapolis, MN 55455
Tel: 624-5050
Fax: 625-8054
Email: cbi@tx.umn.edu
Contact: Associative Director

CHARLES DARWIN UNIVERSITY (CDU)

Research Branch, Darwin, NT, 0909, Australia
Tel: (61) 8 8946 6405
Fax: (61) 8 8946 7075
Email: charles.webb@ntu.edu.au
Website: www.ntu.edu.au
Contact: Professor Charles Webb

The Charles Darwin University (CDU) offers programmes from certificate level to PhD, incorporating the full range of vocational education courses. CDU has a distinctive research profile, reflecting the priorities appropriate to its location. It is a participating member of several CRCs and hosts the ARC Key Centre for Tropical Wildlife Management.

CDU Senior Research Fellowship

Subjects: Indigenous and tropical health, health services delivery, environmental, cultural and natural resource management, education and learning, education services delivery and society, communication and identity.
Purpose: To provide opportunities for outstanding researchers with proven international reputations to undertake research that is both of major importance in its field and of benefit to Australia.
Eligibility: All applicants must have an outstanding track record in a relevant field of research.
Level of Study: Postdoctorate
Type: Fellowship
Value: Australian $66,178–76,308 per year plus allowances, and Australian $20,000 establishment grant
Length of Study: 3 years
Frequency: Dependent on funds available
Study Establishment: CDU
Country of Study: Australia
Application Procedure: Applicants must contact the Research Branch at the University for application forms, which are also available from the website.
Closing Date: See the website
Funding: Private
Contributor: The University

CDU Three Year Postdoctoral Fellowship

Subjects: Indigenous and tropical health, health services delivery, environmental, cultural and natural resource management, education and learning, education services delivery and society, communication and identity.
Purpose: To foster research in designated areas of research strength and developing priority.
Eligibility: All applicants must have completed their PhD within 5 years of the date of application.
Level of Study: Postdoctorate
Type: Fellowship
Value: Australian $47,809–$51,321 per year plus allowances, and Australian $3,500 per year research support
Length of Study: 3 years
Frequency: Dependent on funds available
Study Establishment: CDU
Country of Study: Australia
Application Procedure: Applicants must contact the Research Branch at the University for application forms, which are also available from the website.
Closing Date: Check the website
Funding: Private
Contributor: The University

CHARLES H HOOD FOUNDATION

95 Berkeley Street, Suite 201, Boston, MA 02116, United States of America
Tel: (1) 617 695 9439
Fax: (1) 617 423 4619
Email: research@tmfnet.org
Website: www.tmfnet.org/grantmake.html
Contact: Grants Administrator

The Charles H. Hood Foundation, a New England based entity, was incorporated in 1942 for the support of child health research. Its emphasis is on the initiation and furtherance of medical research that will help to diminish health problems affecting large numbers of children.

Charles H Hood Foundation Child Health Research Grant

Subjects: The initiation and furtherance of medical research that will help diminish health problems affecting large numbers of children.
Purpose: To assist junior faculty who are initiating independent research in paediatrics health and have limited federal grant experience.
Eligibility: Awards can be given to applicants from the residents of New England states of Maine, Vermont, New Hampshire, Massachusetts, Rhode Island and Connecticut only.
Level of Study: Research
Type: Research grant
Value: US$75,000 per year or US$150,000 over 2 years
Length of Study: 2 years
Frequency: Twice a Year
Country of Study: United States of America
No. of awards offered: 10 per year
Application Procedure: Application forms must be completed and submitted along with letters of recommendation, a curriculum vitae, a non-technical summary, a scientific summary and an itemized budget. Applicants should visit the website for further information.
Closing Date: April and October; exact dates vary each year
Funding: Private
Contributor: The Charles H Hood Foundation
No. of awards given last year: 10
No. of applicants last year: 52

CHEMICAL HERITAGE FOUNDATION (CHF)

315 Chestnut Street, Philadelphia, PA 19106-2702, United States of America
Tel: (1) 215 925 2222
Fax: (1) 215 925 1954
Email: fellowships@chemheritage.org
Website: www.chemheritage.org
Contact: Mr Josh McIlvain, Staff Researcher & Fellowship Coordinator

The Beckman Center for the History of Chemistry is the historical unit of the Chemical Heritage Foundation (CHF), which is located in Philadelphia. The Center is devoted to preserving, making known and applying the history of the chemical and molecular science technologies and associated industries.

Charles C Price Fellowship

Subjects: Chemistry.
Purpose: To fund scholars who are pursuing research.
Eligibility: Open to scholars pursuing research on the history of the chemical sciences; preference given to projects in the history of polymers.

Type: Fellowship
Length of Study: 1 academic year
Frequency: Annual
No. of awards offered: 1
Application Procedure: Applicants must visit the website for details on application procedure.
Closing Date: January 15th

Glenn E and Barbara Hodsdon Ullyot Scholarship

Subjects: The history of science.
Purpose: To advance understanding of the importance of the chemical sciences to the public's welfare.
Eligibility: To fund students to pursue postgraduate research.
Level of Study: Postgraduate
Type: Scholarship
Length of Study: A minimum of 2 months
Frequency: Annual
No. of awards offered: 1
Application Procedure: Applicants must submit a completed application form, a one-page description of the proposed research and an outline of a specific product as an outcome of the scholarship. Application forms are available on request.
Closing Date: January 15th

Gordon Cain Fellowship

Subjects: The history of the development of the chemical industry. The outcome of the research should further the understanding of the relationship between technology, policy, management and entrepreneurship and should shed light on the complex development of modern society and commerce.
Purpose: To support historical research.
Eligibility: Open to a scholar with a PhD who will carry out historical research on the development of chemical industries.
Level of Study: Postgraduate
Type: Fellowship
Value: Varies
Length of Study: 1 academic year
Frequency: Annual
Application Procedure: Applications must include a proposal of no more than 1,000 words outlining the applicant's research project, with specific reference to how the work advances scholarship and how the outcome might be published. All applications must be sent to Josh McIlvain at the main address.
Closing Date: January 15th

Société de Chimie Industrielle (American Section) Fellowship

Subjects: The history of science.
Purpose: To stimulate public understanding of the chemical industries, using both terms in their widest sense.
Eligibility: Applications are encouraged from writers, journalists, educators and historians of science, technology and business.
Level of Study: Postgraduate
Type: Fellowship
Length of Study: A minimum of 3 months
Frequency: Annual
Study Establishment: Chemical Heritage Foundation
Country of Study: United States of America
No. of awards offered: 1
Application Procedure: Applicants must submit a one-page research proposal outlining the specific project to be completed while in residence at CHF, and showing how the project will further public understanding of the chemical industries.
Closing Date: February 15th
Funding: Private

THE CHICAGO TRIBUNE

Tribune Books, 435 North Michigan Avenue, Chicago, IL, 60611, United States of America
Tel: (1) 312 222 4429
Fax: (1) 312 222 3751
Website: www.chicagotribune.com

The Chicago Tribune is the Midwest's leading newspaper. The Chicago Tribune Literary Awards are part of a continued dedication to readers, writers and ideas.

Nelson Algren Awards

Subjects: Short fiction.
Purpose: To award writers of short fiction.
Eligibility: Submissions must be unpublished, written by an American writer, and within 2,500–10,000 words in length.
Level of Study: Unrestricted
Type: Award
Frequency: Annual
Country of Study: Any country
No. of awards offered: 4
Application Procedure: Applicants must send a stamped addressed envelope with a request for written guidelines. The competition will begin accepting entries from November 1st.
Funding: Corporation

CHILDREN'S LITERATURE ASSOCIATION

PO Box 138, Battle Creek, MI 49016-0138, United States of America
Tel: (1) 269 965 8180
Fax: (1) 269 965 3568
Email: kkiessling@childlitassn.org
Website: www.ebbs.english.vt.edu/chal/.index.html
Contact: Ms Kathy Kiesling, Administrator

The Children's Literature Association is an international organization of persons interested in the promotion of scholarship about children's literature. The goals of the association are to enhance the professional stature of the graduate and undergraduate teaching of childrens literature and to encourage serious scholarships and research.

ChLA Beiter Scholarships for Graduate Students

Subjects: Children's literature.
Purpose: To fund proposals of original scholarship with the expectation that the undertaking will lead to a publication or a conference presentation and contribute to the field.
Eligibility: Winners must be, or become, members of the Children's Literature Association. Students of the ChLA Executive Board members or Scholarship Committee members are not eligible to apply. Previous recipients are not eligible to reapply until the third year from the date of the first award.
Level of Study: Postdoctorate, graduate, doctorate
Type: Scholarship
Value: From US$500–1,000, which may be used to purchase supplies and materials eg. books and videos, and as research support eg. photocopying, or to underwrite travel to special collections or libraries
Frequency: Annual
Country of Study: Any country
No. of awards offered: 1–4
Application Procedure: Applicants must send five copies of their contact details including email address, academic institution and status, the expected date of their degree, a detailed description of the research proposal, a curriculum vitae and three letters of reference, one of which must be from the applicant's dissertation or thesis advisor.
Closing Date: February 1st
Funding: Private
No. of awards given last year: 1
No. of applicants last year: 5
Additional Information: Applicants should visit the website for further details. If applicants wish to receive guidelines by mail, a stamped addressed envelope must be provided.

ChLA Research Fellowships and Scholarships

Subjects: Children's literature.
Purpose: To award proposals dealing with criticism or original scholarship with the expectation that the undertaking will lead to publication and make a significant contribution to the field of children's literature in the area of scholarship or criticism.
Eligibility: Applicants must be, or become, members of the Children's Literature Association.

Level of Study: Unrestricted
Type: Other
Value: Up to US$1,000. Individual awards may range from US$250–1,000 and may be used only for research-related expenses such as travel to special collections or materials and supplies. Funds are not intended for work leading to the completion of a professional degree
Frequency: Annual
Country of Study: Any country
No. of awards offered: 1–4
Application Procedure: Applicants must send five copies of the application in English including three letters of reference and a curriculum vitae. Applications must include the applicant's name, address, telephone number and email address, details of the academic institution the applicant is affiliated with and a detailed description of the research proposal, not exceeding three single spaced pages, and indicating the nature and significance of the project, where it will be carried out and the expected date of completion.
Closing Date: February 1st
Funding: Private
No. of awards given last year: 1
No. of applicants last year: 2
Additional Information: In honour of the achievement and dedication of Dr Margaret P Esmonde, proposals that deal with critical or original work in the areas of science fantasy or science fiction for children or adolescents will be awarded the Margaret P Esmonde Memorial Scholarship. Applicants should visit the website for further details. If applicants wish to receive guidelines by mail, a stamped addressed envelope must be provided.

For further information contact:

Department of English Miami University Oxford, Ohio, 45056, United States of America
Contact: Dr Anita Wilson

ChLA Research Grants

Subjects: Children's literature.
Purpose: To reward proposals dealing with criticism or original scholarship in the field of children's literature.
Eligibility: Applicants must either be members of the Children's Literature Association (ChLA) or join the association before they receive any funds. The awards may not be used for obtaining advanced degrees, for researching or writing a thesis or dissertation, for textbook writing or for pedagogical projects.
Level of Study: Unrestricted
Type: Grant
Value: US$500–1,000
Length of Study: 1 year
Frequency: Annual
Country of Study: United States of America
No. of awards offered: Varies
Application Procedure: Applicants must send five copies of the proposal. The application and supporting materials should be written in or translated into English. Proposals should include a cover sheet with the contact information of the applicant, applicant's academic affiliation, a detailed description of the research proposal that does not exceed three single-spaced pages and a curriculum vitae.
Closing Date: February 1st
Funding: Private
Additional Information: The awards honour the achievement and dedication of Dr Margaret P Esmonde. Proposals that deal with critical or original work in the areas of fantasy or science fiction for children or adolescents will be awarded the Margaret P Esmonde Memorial Grant.

CHILDREN'S MEDICAL RESEARCH INSTITUTE

Locked Bag 23, Wentworthville, NSW, 2145, Australia
Tel: (61) 2 9687 2800
Fax: (61) 2 9687 2120
Email: prowe@cmri.usyd.edu.au
Website: www.cmri.com.au
Contact: Professor P B Rowe, Director

The Children's Medical Research Institute is an independent research institute affiliated with the University of Sydney and the New Children's Hospital. Supported by grants and a state government infrastructure grant, it conducts basic research in the fields of vertebrate development, cellular immortalization and oncogenesis, cellular signalling and gene therapy.

Children's Medical Research Institute Graduate Scholarships and Postgraduate Fellowships

Subjects: Muscle genetics, neurosciences, oncogenesis, embryology, gene imprinting, gene therapy, genevector design for the treatment of inherited and acquired disease, cell signalling and membrane biology in neurotransmission.
Purpose: To allow individuals to undertake research.
Eligibility: Open to permanent residents of Australia with suitable qualifications, usually an Honours Degree for postgraduate studies.
Level of Study: Postdoctorate, postgraduate
Type: Scholarships, fellowships
Value: The award value is based on the National Health and Medical Research Council of Australia scale
Length of Study: 3–5 years
Frequency: Annual
Study Establishment: A biomedical research institute affiliated to the University of Sydney
Country of Study: Australia
No. of awards offered: Up to 4 postgraduate scholarships and 2 postdoctoral fellowships
Application Procedure: Applicants must submit a letter outlining their background, interests and referees. No application form is required.
Funding: Government, private
Contributor: An investment trust
No. of awards given last year: 6
No. of applicants last year: 32
Additional Information: There are no course requirements.

Children's Medical Research Institute Postdoctoral Fellowship

Subjects: Biophysics and molecular biology, embryology and reproduction biology, genetics and neurosciences.
Purpose: To allow individuals to obtain further professional training in their fields of interest.
Eligibility: Open to qualified applicants of any nationality who must meet temporary visa requirements. Knowledge of English is essential.
Level of Study: Postdoctorate
Type: Fellowship
Value: Varies depending on experience, but is generally Australian $47,000 for a 1st-year PhD
Length of Study: Up to 3 years
Frequency: Dependent on funds available
Study Establishment: A research centre
Country of Study: Australia
No. of awards offered: 2
Application Procedure: Applicants must submit a letter of intent with a curriculum vitae, transcript, references and any other appropriate documentation.
Closing Date: Applications are accepted at any time
Funding: Government, private
Contributor: Investment Trust
No. of awards given last year: 2
No. of applicants last year: 20

Children's Medical Research Institute Postgraduate Scholarship

Subjects: Biophysics and molecular biology, embryology and reproduction biology, genetics and neurosciences.
Purpose: To support research-based study for the award of the degrees of PhD or MSc (Med) at the University of Sydney.
Eligibility: Open to Australian residents only.
Level of Study: Postgraduate, doctorate
Type: Scholarship
Value: More than Australian $18,500 per year
Length of Study: 3–4 years

Frequency: Dependent on funds available
Study Establishment: A research centre
Country of Study: Australia
No. of awards offered: Up to 4
Application Procedure: Applicants must submit a letter of intent with a curriculum vitae, transcript, references and any other appropriate support documents. There is no application form.
Funding: Government, private
Contributor: Investment Trust
No. of awards given last year: 4
No. of applicants last year: 12

THE CHINA SCHOLARSHIP COUNCIL

160 Fuxingmennei Street, Beijing, 100031, China
Tel: (86) 86 10 664 3249
Fax: (86) 86 10 664 3198
Website: www.csc.edu.cn

The China Scholarship council (CSC) is a non-profit institution, which is affiliated with the ministry of education. The main objective of the CSC is to develop the educational, scientific and technological, and cultural exchanges and economic and trade cooperation between China and other countries.

The Barbara and Fred Kort Chinese Fellowship Program

Subjects: All subjects.
Eligibility: Open to Chinese scholars who wish to do post-doctoral research at Bar-Ilan university.
Level of Study: Postdoctorate
Type: Fellowship
Value: US$15,000 per year
Length of Study: 1 year
Frequency: Annual
Study Establishment: Bar-Ilan University
Country of Study: Israel
Application Procedure: The candidates should obtain formal approval from the academic supervisors of Bar-Ilan universtiy.
Funding: Government
Contributor: China Scholarship Council and Bar-Ilan University, Israel

Hang Seng Bank Overseas Scholarships Program

Subjects: All Subjects.
Type: Scholarship
Value: Tuition fees, textbooks, livings expenses
Length of Study: 2 Years
Frequency: Annual
Study Establishment: Harvard University and Princeton University
Country of Study: United States of America
No. of awards offered: 2
Application Procedure: See the website.
Funding: Government

K C Wong Postgraduate Scholarship Programme

Subjects: All subjects.
Purpose: To support students who intend to study further at King's College London.
Eligibility: Open to applicants who are citizens and permanent residents of People's Republic of china.
Type: Scholarship
Value: UK £8,400
Length of Study: 3 years
Frequency: Annual
Study Establishment: King's College London
Country of Study: United Kingdom
No. of awards offered: Up to 5
Application Procedure: A completed application form, which is available online, must be sent.
Closing Date: March 1st
Funding: Government
Contributor: K C Wong Education Foundation

For further information contact:

Quality Assurance Section King's College London 7.38 James Derk Maxwell Building 57 Waterloo Road, London, SE1 8WA, United Kingdom

Sino-French Training Programme in the Law in Europe

Subjects: French language, law.
Purpose: To provide training in French language and one-year training in law in Europe.
Eligibility: Open to young teachers and postgraduate students in law.
Type: Scholarship
Value: Living expenses and international airfares.
Frequency: Every 2 years
Country of Study: Europe, Germany
No. of awards offered: 10
Application Procedure: A completed application form must be submitted.
Funding: Government
Contributor: French Government and European union

CHINESE AMERICAN MEDICAL SOCIETY (CAMS)

281 Edgewood Avenue, Teaneck, NJ 07666, United States of America
Tel: (1) 201 833 1506
Fax: (1) 201 833 8252
Email: hw5@columbia.edu
Website: www.camsociety.org
Contact: Dr H H Wang, Executive Director

The Chinese American Medical Society (CAMS) is a non-profit, charitable, educational and scientific society that aims to promote the scientific association of medical professionals of Chinese descent. It also aims to advance medical knowledge and scientific research with emphasis on aspects unique to the Chinese and to promote the health status of Chinese Americans. The Society makes scholarships available to medical dental students and provides summer fellowships for students conducting research in health problems related to the Chinese.

CAMS Scholarship

Subjects: Medical or dental studies.
Purpose: To help defray the cost of study.
Eligibility: Open to Chinese Americans, or Chinese students who are residing in the United States of America. Applicants must be full-time medical or dental students at approved schools within the United States of America and must be able to show academic proficiency and financial hardship.
Level of Study: Doctorate
Type: Scholarship
Value: US$1,000–2,000
Frequency: Annual
Country of Study: United States of America
No. of awards offered: 3–6
Application Procedure: Applicants must complete an application form and send it together with a letter for the Dean of Students verifying good standing, two to three letters of recommendation, a personal statement, a curriculum vitae and a financial statement.
Closing Date: March 31st
Funding: Private
Contributor: Membership and fund-raising
No. of awards given last year: 6
No. of applicants last year: 30

CHINOOK REGIONAL CAREER TRANSITIONS FOR YOUTH

3305-18 Avenue North, Lethbridge, AB T1H ss1, Canada
Tel: (1) 403 328 3996
Fax: (1) 403 320 2365
Website: www.careertransitionsnews.ca

The Chinook regional career transitions for youth aims to improve the school-to-work transitions for students, promoting lifelong learning and coordinating and implementing career development activities and programming for youth.

Alberta Blue Cross 50th Anniversary Scholarships

Subjects: All subjects.
Purpose: To provide financial support.
Eligibility: Open to applicants who are registered Indian, Inuit, or Melis and are residents of Alberta.
Level of Study: Postgraduate
Type: Scholarship
Value: Canadian $375–1,250
Frequency: Annual
Country of Study: Canada
No. of awards offered: 3
Application Procedure: A completed application form must be sent. For further information, see the website www.ab.bluecross.ca
Closing Date: June 1st

For further information contact:

Alberta Scholarship Programs, 9th Floor, 9940-106 Street, Box 28000 Station Main, Edmonton, AB 75J 4R4

Canadian Millenium Excellence Awards

Subjects: Social welfare.
Purpose: To recognize talented Canadians who make positive and significant contributions to the betterment of communities across the country.
Eligibility: Open to applicants who are Canadian citizens.
Level of Study: Professional development
Type: Award
Value: Canadian $4,000–20,000
Frequency: Annual
Country of Study: Canada
No. of awards offered: 931
Application Procedure: More information and application forms are available online.
Closing Date: January 21st

For further information contact:

Canadian Milleniuni Scholarship Foundation, P.O. Box 1386, Station M, Calgary, AB T2P 2L6

The CanWest Global System Broadcasters of the Future Awards

Subjects: Broadcasting.
Purpose: To encourage careers in Canadian broadcast industry.
Eligibility: Open to citizens of Canadian with strong English language communications skills.
Level of Study: Professional development
Type: Scholarship
Value: Up to Canadian $10,000
Length of Study: 4 months
Frequency: Annual
No. of awards offered: 1
Application Procedure: A completed application form and copy of transcript of marks must be sent.
Closing Date: August 30th

For further information contact:

CanWest Global System Broadcasters of the Future Awards, 81 Barber Greene Road, Don Mills, Ontario, M3C 2A2

Robin Roussean Memorial Mountain Achievement Scholarship

Subjects: Mountain leadership and safety.
Purpose: To bring about awareness of ways to improve safety in the mountains.
Eligibility: Open to all applicants who demonstrate volunteer commitment.
Level of Study: Professional development
Type: Scholarship
Length of Study: Course fee
Frequency: Annual
No. of awards offered: 1
Application Procedure: A completed application form must be sent.
Closing Date: January 30th

For further information contact:

Alberta Scholarship Programs, Box 28000 Stn. Mam, Edmonton, AB T5J 4R4

Terry Fox Humanitarian Award

Subjects: Social services.
Purpose: To encourage voluntary humanitarian work.
Eligibility: Open to Canadian citizens who are not more than 25 years of age.
Level of Study: Professional development
Type: Scholarship
Value: Canadian $3,500–7,000
Frequency: Annual
No. of awards offered: 20
Application Procedure: A completed application form must be submitted.
Closing Date: February 1st

For further information contact:

AQ5003, Simon Fraser University, Burnaby, BC V5A 153

Toyota Earth Day Scholarship Program

Subjects: Environmental community service.
Purpose: To encourage community service.
Eligibility: Open to students who have achieved academic excellence and distinguished themselves in environmental community service and extracurricular and volunteer activities.
Level of Study: Professional development
Type: Scholarship
Value: Canadian $5,000
Frequency: Annual
No. of awards offered: 3
Application Procedure: Application form available online.
Closing Date: January 31st

For further information contact:

Toyota Earth Day Scholarship Program, III Peter Street, Suite 503, Toronto, ON M5V 2H1

CHOIRS ONTARIO

330 Walmer Road, Toronto, ON, M5R 2Y4, Canada
Tel: (1) 416 923 1144
Fax: (1) 416 929 0415
Email: info@choirsontario.org
Website: www.choirsontario.org
Contact: Melva Graham

Choirs Ontario is an arts service organization dedicated to the promotion of choral activities and standards of excellence. Established in 1971 as the Ontario Choral Federation, Choirs Ontario provides services to choirs, conductors, choristers, composers, administrators and educators as well as anyone who enjoys listening to the sound of choral music. Choirs Ontario operates with the financial assistance of the Ministry of Culture, the Ontario Arts Council, the Trillium Foundation, the Toronto Arts Council and numerous foundations, corporations and individual donors.

Choirs President's Leadership Award

Subjects: Music.
Purpose: To recognize individuals who have made an exceptional contribution to the promotion of choral music in the community.
Eligibility: Open to individuals who reside in Ontario with at least 5 years experience in choral music.
Level of Study: Professional development

Type: Award
Frequency: Annual
Application Procedure: A completed application form with three letters of recommendation must be submitted.

Leslie Bell Competition For Conducting

Subjects: Conducting.
Purpose: To award a prize for the winning entry in the category of choral conducting.
Level of Study: Unrestricted
Type: Prize
Value: Canadian $7,000
Frequency: Every 2 years
Country of Study: Canada
Application Procedure: Applicants must contact the organization.
Funding: Private
Contributor: Leslie Bell Scholarship Fund and Ontario Arts Council

For further information contact:

OAC Communications, Canada
Tel: (1) 416 969 7403
Email: kgunter@arts.on.ca
Contact: Kirsten Gunter

Ruth Watson Henderson Choral Competition

Subjects: Singing: treble voice choirs.
Purpose: To reward new choral works.
Eligibility: This year's competition is for an SSA work for treble voice choir. Suggested time limit is 4–8 minutes. Compositions may be a capella or accompanied by up to three instruments. Texts may be sacred or secular and need not be limited to English. Submissions must not have been previously commissioned or published and must have been composed within the last 2 years. Composers must be Canadian citizens or landed immigrants. There is no age limit.
Level of Study: Unrestricted
Type: Award
Value: Canadian $1,000
Frequency: Every 2 years
Country of Study: Canada
Application Procedure: Applicants must submit four legible photocopies of the score (not original manuscripts). More than one entry may be submitted, but each entry must be accompanied by a separate entry form and a fee of Canadian $20. The composer's name must not appear on any score. Scores will be returned if a stamped addressed envelope is included. Application forms can be downloaded from the website www.choirsontario.org/ruthwatsonhenderson.html
Closing Date: September 1st
Funding: Private
Contributor: Choirs Ontario
Additional Information: Ruth Watson Henderson, one of Canada's foremost musicians, is internationally known both as a composer and pianist. Her compositions have been commissioned, performed and recorded worldwide.

Ruth Watson Henderson Choral Composition Competition

Subjects: Choral music, particularly composition.
Purpose: To award new choral composition.
Eligibility: Candidates must be Canadian citizens or landed immigrants who are permanent residents of Ontario.
Level of Study: Postgraduate
Type: Prize
Value: Canadian $1,000
Country of Study: Any country
No. of awards offered: 1
Application Procedure: Further information available on the website.
Closing Date: There are various deadlines
Funding: Private

CHRISTOPHER REEVE PARALYSIS FOUNDATION (CRPF)

636 Morris Tumpike, Suite 3A, Short Hills, NJ, NJ 07078, United States of America
Tel: (1) 973 379 2690
Fax: (1) 973 912 9433
Email: dlandsman@crpf.org
Website: www.ChristopherReeve.org
Contact: Dr Douglas S Landsman, Director of Individual Grants

The Christopher Reeve Paralysis Foundation (CRPF) is committed to funding research that develops treatments and cures for paralysis caused by spinal cord injury and other central nervous system disorders. The Foundation also vigorously works to improve the quality of life for people living with disabilities through its grants programme, paralysis resource centre and advocacy efforts.

CRPF Research Grant

Subjects: Spinal cord injury-related research.
Purpose: To fund research that will lead to effective treatments and ultimately a cure for spinal cord injury.
Eligibility: Open to American and international investigators located at institutions that have clearly established lines of accountability and fiscal responsibility. Institutional assurances regarding animal research and human subjects are required.
Level of Study: Postdoctorate, research
Value: US$75,000 per year for a maximum total of US$150,000
Length of Study: A maximum of 2 years
Frequency: Annual
Country of Study: Any country
No. of awards offered: Usually 40 per year. Varies depending on the level of science and the amount of funds available
Application Procedure: Applicants must complete an application form and forward seven copies of it to the Foundation. Forms are available from the website.
Closing Date: December 15th and June 15th
Funding: Private, foundation
Contributor: Private sector donations
No. of awards given last year: 40
No. of applicants last year: 200
Additional Information: The intent of these awards is to promote innovative and ground-breaking work, not to provide ongoing long-term support. CRPF funds activities that hold promise of identifying therapies for paralysis. For further information visit the website.

CHRONIC DISEASE RESEARCH FOUNDATION (CDRF)

St Thomas' Hospital, 1st Floor, South Wing, Lambeth Palace Road, London, SE1 7EH, England
Tel: (44) 20 7633 9990
Fax: (44) 20 7188 6761
Email: ChristelMB77@aol.com
Website: www.cdrf.org.uk
Contact: Ms Christel Barnetson, Chief Administrator

The Chronic Disease Research Foundation (CDRF) was established to look at new ways of exploring the genetics of diseases associated with ageing. Its mission is to target those common diseases such as osteoporosis, arthritis, back pain, migraine, asthma and diabetes, which we inherit from our parents, and prevent and alleviate them now and for future generations. Its principal focus is on comparative studies of identical and non-identical twins, undertaken at the Twin Research Unit of St Thomas' Hospital.

CDRF Project Grants

Subjects: The genetic basis of diseases associated with ageing.
Purpose: To carry out comparative studies of identical and non-identical twins to pinpoint the genetic cause of common diseases associated with ageing.
Level of Study: Research, postgraduate
Type: Project grant

Value: UK £30,000–150,000
Length of Study: 2–3 years
Frequency: Dependent on funds available
Country of Study: United Kingdom
No. of awards offered: Dependent on availability of funds
Application Procedure: Applicants must submit a preliminary proposal of no more than one side of A4-size paper including an outline of the proposal, a list of principal aims and objectives and scale of funding. Provided the CDRF's panel of experts considers the project to be of relevance, applicants must then submit a full grant proposal.
Funding: Private
No. of awards given last year: None

CDRF Research Fellowship

Subjects: The genetic basis of disease associated with ageing.
Purpose: To promote postgraduate education and enable the charity to carry out further research projects.
Level of Study: Postgraduate, research
Type: Fellowship
Value: UK £30,000–175,000
Length of Study: 2–5 years
Frequency: Dependent on funds available
Country of Study: United Kingdom
No. of awards offered: Dependent on availability of funds
Application Procedure: Applicants must submit a preliminary proposal of no more than one side of A4-size paper including an outline of proposal, a list of principal aims and objectives and the scale of funding. If the CDRF's panel of experts consider the project to be of relevance, applicants must then submit a full-grant proposal.
Funding: Private
No. of awards given last year: 2

CHRONIC GRANULOMATOUS DISORDER (CGD) RESEARCH TRUST

Manor Farm, Wimborne St Giles, Dorset, BH21 5NL, England
Tel: (44) 17 2551 7977
Fax: (44) 17 2551 7977
Email: cgd@cgdrt.co.uk
Website: www.cgd.org.uk
Contact: Ms Rosemary Rymer, General Secretary

The CGD Research Trust is a member of the Association of medical research charities and the International Patient Organization of Primary Immueficiencies (IPOPI). The Trust, founded in 1991, exists to promote research into the case, inheritance, management, symptoms and cure of CGD.

CGD Research Trust Grants

Subjects: Topics pertaining to the cause, inheritance, management and symptoms of chronic granulomatous disorder.
Purpose: To support thorough research that aims to increase understanding of the cause, inheritance, management and symptoms of chronic granulomatous disorder, and to disseminate the useful results of such research.
Level of Study: Predoctorate, postgraduate, doctorate, research
Type: Grant
Value: UK £40,000–250,000
Length of Study: Usually 1–3 years depending on the programme
Frequency: Annual
No. of awards offered: 2–3 each year
Application Procedure: Grants are advertised annually every April in Nature. Applicants must initially submit a one-page outline. A number of these are then invited to complete full applications. These are then subject to a peer review. The medical panel then makes recommendations and trustees announce grant offers the following January.
Closing Date: Usually the end of August
Funding: Private
Contributor: Voluntary donations
No. of awards given last year: 3
No. of applicants last year: 12

CIIT-CENTERS FOR HEALTH RESEARCH

Human Resources, PO Box 12137, Research Triangle Park, NC 27709, United States of America
Tel: (1) 919 558 1331
Fax: (1) 919 558 1430
Email: bramlage@ciit.org
Website: www.ciit.org
Contact: Rusty Bramlage, Human Resources

Founded in 1974, the CIIT - Centers for Health Research is a non-profit toxicology research institute dedicated to providing an improved scientific basis for understanding and assessing the potential adverse effects of chemicals, pharmaceuticals and consumer products on human health. Many CIIT researchers are on the faculties of the University of North Carolina at Chapel Hill, North Carolina State University in Raleigh and Duke University in Durham, the three institutions that form North Carolina's Research Triangle. CIIT is supported by 36 major companies and the American Chemistry Council.

CIIT-Centers for Health Research Postdoctoral Fellowships

Subjects: Toxicology including genetic toxicology, biochemical toxicology, pathology, teratology, carcinogenesis, inhalation toxicology, risk assessment and molecular biology.
Purpose: To support persons undergoing further training in toxicology.
Eligibility: Open to those who hold a recently awarded PhD degree in a discipline related to toxicology. Applicants holding a recently awarded DVM or MD degree are expected to have substantial research experience. Candidates on the J-1 Exchange Visitor Programme are approved.
Level of Study: Postdoctorate
Type: Fellowship
Value: approx. US$40,000, depending upon the number of years of experience
Length of Study: 2–3 years
Frequency: Annual
Study Establishment: CIIT
Country of Study: United States of America
No. of awards offered: Varies
Application Procedure: Applicants must apply for information, available on request or from the website.
Closing Date: Applications are accepted at any time
Funding: Private
Contributor: CIIT
No. of awards given last year: 20
No. of applicants last year: 35
Additional Information: Fellowships are granted only for conduct of research at the Institute's facility in Research Triangle Park, NC.

CIIT-Centers for Health Research Predoctoral Traineeships

Subjects: Fields related to toxicology including biochemistry, pharmacology, chemistry, zoology and biology.
Purpose: To support persons enrolled in a programme of study leading to a doctoral degree. Trainees will pursue a PhD while conducting dissertation research at CIIT.
Eligibility: Open to persons who have been accepted into a course of graduate study in a subject related to toxicology by a degree granting institution.
Level of Study: Predoctorate
Type: Fellowship
Value: US$8,000–12,000 per year, plus tuition and fees
Length of Study: 3–4 years
Frequency: Annual
Study Establishment: The University of North Carolina at Chapel Hill, North Carolina State University or Duke University in the Research Triangle area, for the duration of the programme
Country of Study: United States of America
No. of awards offered: 4–6
Application Procedure: Applicants must apply for information, available on request or from the website.
Closing Date: Applications are accepted at any time

Funding: Private
Contributor: CIIT
No. of awards given last year: 1
No. of applicants last year: 10
Additional Information: Preference is given to individuals who wish to conduct their dissertation research at CIIT in conjunction with local university programmes of study.

CLARA HASKIL COMPETITION

Case postale 234, 31 rue du Conseil, 1800 Vevey 1, Switzerland
Tel: (41) 21 922 6704
Fax: (41) 21 922 6734
Email: clara.haskil@bluewin.ch
Website: www.regart.ch/clara-haskil
Contact: Mr Patrick Peikert, Director

The Clara Haskil Competition exists to recognize and help a young pianist whose approach to piano interpretation is of the same spirit that constantly inspired Clara Haskil, and that she illustrated so perfectly.

Clara Haskil Competition

Subjects: Piano performance.
Purpose: To recognize and financially help a young pianist.
Eligibility: Open to pianists of any nationality and either sex who are no more than 27 years of age.
Level of Study: Postgraduate
Type: Prize
Value: Swiss Francs 20,000
Frequency: Every 2 years
Country of Study: Any country
No. of awards offered: 1
Application Procedure: Applicants must pay an entry fee of Swiss Franc 260.
Closing Date: April 30th
Additional Information: The competition is usually held during the last weeks of August or the beginning of September.

THE CLAUDE LEON FOUNDATION

PO Box 13187, Mowbray 7705, Cape Town, South Africa
Tel: (27) 21 531 6910
Email: tanya@conferencewise.co.za
Website: www.leonfoundation.co.za
Contact: Mrs Tanya Stone, Postdoctoral Fellowships Administrator

The Claude Leon Foundation is a charitable trust, resulting from a bequest by Claude Leon (1887–1972). A founder and managing director of the Elephant Trading Company, a wholesale business based in Johannesburg, Claude Leon also helped develop several well-known South African companies, including Edgars, OK Bazaars and the mining house Anglo Transvaal (later Anglovaal). He served for many years on the Council of the University of the Witwatersrand, which in 1971 awarded him an honorary Doctorate of Law. The university postdoctoral fellowship award programme is now in its eighth year, and has as its goal the building of research capacity at South African universities and technikons.

Postdoctoral Fellowships (Claude Leon)

Subjects: Science, engineering, medical sciences.
Purpose: To fund postdoctoral research.
Eligibility: South African and foreign nationals may apply. Preference will be given to candidates who have received their doctoral degrees in the last 5 years and are currently underrepresented in South African science, engineering and medical science.
Level of Study: Postdoctorate
Type: Fellowship
Value: Rand 90,000 per year
Length of Study: 2 years
Frequency: Annual
Study Establishment: South African universities and technikons
Country of Study: South Africa
Application Procedure: Application forms are available from the website or the Postdoctoral Fellowships Administrator.
Closing Date: May 31st
Funding: Foundation
Contributor: The Claude Leon Foundation

CLEMSON UNIVERSITY

MBA Office, Admissions Office, 124 Sirrine Hall, Clemson, SC, 29634-1315, United States of America
Tel: (1) 864 656 3975
Fax: (1) 864 656 0947
Email: mba@clemson.edu
Website: www.clemson.edu
Contact: Associate Director

Uemson University is a selective, public, land-grant university, which is committed to world-class teaching, research and public service in the context of general education, student development and continuing education.

Abney Scholarship

Subjects: All subjects.
Purpose: To financially support students who wish to study further.
Level of Study: Postgraduate
Type: Scholarship
Frequency: Annual
Closing Date: March 1st

Clemson Graduate Assistantships

Subjects: MBA.
Eligibility: Decisions regarding the awarding of these assistantships and the duties and work period assigned are separately determined by each university department or office that employs graduate assistants.
Level of Study: MBA
Type: Graduate assistantship
Value: The assistantships pay stipends starting at US$6.18 per hour. The pay depends upon job duties and candidate qualifications. In addition, graduate assistants are granted partial remission of academic fees and enjoy some benefits provided to the University faculty and staff. Graduate assistantship presently pay US$1,044 per semester in tuition and fees
Length of Study: 2 years
Frequency: Dependent on funds available, on an annual or 9-month basis
Study Establishment: Clemson University
Country of Study: United States of America
No. of awards offered: Varies
Application Procedure: Applicants must contact the various university departments or offices for information or submit a general application with a curriculum vitae to the MBA office.

CLEVELAND INSTITUTE OF MUSIC

11201 East Boulevard, Cleveland, OH 44106, United States of America
Tel: (1) 216 791 5000 Ext. 262
Fax: (1) 216 795 3141
Email: kxg26@cwru.edu
Website: www.cim.edu
Contact: Kristie Gripp, Director of Financial Aid

The Cleveland Institute of Music's mission is to provide talented students with a professional, world-class education in the art of music. The Institute ranks among the top tier music schools across the nation, granting degrees up to the doctoral level. More than 80 per cent of the Institute's alumni perform in major national and international orchestras and opera companies, while others hold prominent teaching positions.

Cleveland Institute of Music Scholarships and Accompanying Fellowships

Subjects: Music.
Eligibility: Candidates for the accompanying fellowships should have a Bachelor of Music Degree or equivalent and must be proficient in English.

Level of Study: Postgraduate, graduate
Type: Scholarships and fellowships
Value: US$1,000–25,000 for scholarships and US$1,000–3,000 for accompanying fellowships. No travel grants are provided
Length of Study: 1 academic year for scholarships or from August to the following May for accompanying fellowships. Scholarships are renewable
Frequency: Annual
Study Establishment: The Cleveland Institute of Music
Country of Study: United States of America
No. of awards offered: Approx. 400 scholarships and 15 accompanying fellowships
Application Procedure: Applicants must apply online.
Closing Date: December 1st
Funding: Private

COLORADO DEPARTMENT OF EDUCATION (CDE)

201 East Colfax Avenue, Denver, Co 80203-1799, United States of America
Tel: (1) 303 866 6600
Fax: (1) 303 866 0793
Website: www.cde.state.co.us

The Colorado Department of Education is the administrative arm of the Colorado State Board of Education. With an organization commitment to high standards, challenging assessments and rigorous accountability measures, CDE serves the prek-12 public education, adult education and family literacy and library communities of Colorado.

Robert C. Byrd Honors Scholarship

Subjects: All subjects.
Purpose: To promote exceptional achievements in students with academic excellence.
Eligibility: Open to U.S. citizens or legal residents of the State in which the students apply.
Level of Study: Postgraduate
Type: Scholarship
Value: Up to US$1,500 per year
Length of Study: 4 years
Frequency: Annual
Application Procedure: Contact the respective State Education Agency (SEA) for application information.
Closing Date: Application deadlines are set forth by the respective SEA

COLT FOUNDATION

New Lane, Havant, Hampshire, PO9 2LY, England
Tel: (44) 23 9249 1400
Fax: (44) 23 9249 1363
Email: jackie.douglas@uk.coltgroup.com
Website: www.coltfoundation.org.uk
Contact: Ms Jackie Douglas, Director

The primary interest of the Colt Foundation is the promotion of research into medical and environmental problems created by commerce and industry and is aimed particularly at discovering the cause of illnesses arising from conditions at the place of work. The Foundation also makes grants to students taking higher degrees in related subjects.

Colt Foundation PhD Fellowship

Subjects: Medical and natural sciences including public health and hygiene, sports medicine, biological and life sciences, physiology or toxicology.
Purpose: To encourage the young scientists of the future.
Eligibility: Open to any student proposing to take a PhD in the correct subject area in a United Kingdom university or college.
Level of Study: Doctorate
Type: Fellowship
Value: UK £46,500
Length of Study: 3 years
Frequency: Annual
Application Procedure: Applicants must visit the website where details are posted in August each year.
Closing Date: Normally October 31st
No. of awards given last year: 3

THE COMMONWEALTH FUND OF NEW YORK

Harkness House, 1 East 75th Street, New York, NY, 1002, United States of America
Tel: (1) 212 606 3809
Fax: (1) 212 606 3875
Email: ro@cmwf.org
Website: www.cmwf.org
Contact: Ms Robin Osborn, International Programs in Health Policy Director

The Commonwealth Fund of New York is a philanthropic foundation established in 1918. The Fund supports independent research on health and social issues and makes grants to improve healthcare practice and policy.

The Commonwealth Fund/Harvard University Fellowship in Minority Health Policy

Subjects: Health policy, public health and management, with special programme activities on minority health issues.
Purpose: To create physician-leaders who will pursue careers in minority health policy.
Eligibility: Open to physicians who are citizens of the United States of America and who have completed their residency. Additional experience beyond residency is preferred. Applicants must demonstrate an awareness of, or interest and experience in dealing, with the health needs of minority populations, strong evidence of past leadership experience, as related to community efforts and health policy and the intention to pursue a career in public health practice, policy, or academia.
Level of Study: Postgraduate, research
Type: Fellowship
Value: US$50,000 stipend, full tuition, health insurance, books, travel and related expenses
Length of Study: 1 year
Frequency: Annual
Study Establishment: Harvard Medical School
Country of Study: United States of America
Application Procedure: Applications available online at the website: www.cmwf.org/fellowships.
Closing Date: First week of January each year
Funding: Foundation

For further information contact:

Minority Faculty Development Program, 164 Longwood Avenue, 2nd Floor, Boston, MA 02115, United States of America
Contact: Programme Co-ordinator

Harkness Fellowships in Healthcare Policy

Subjects: Healthcare policy and health services research.
Purpose: To encourage the professional development of promising healthcare policy researchers and practitioners who will contribute to innovation in healthcare policy and practice in the United States of America and their home countries.
Eligibility: Open to individuals who have completed a Master's degree or PhD in health services or health policy research. Applicants must also have shown significant promise as a policy-orientated researcher or practitioner, eg. physicians or health service managers, journalists and government officials, with a strong interest in policy issues. Candidates should also be at the research Fellow to senior lecturer level, if academically based; be in their late 20s to early 40s, and have been nominated by their department chair or the director of their institution.

Level of Study: Research, professional development, postgraduate
Type: Fellowship
Value: Basic expenses of travel, residence and research, up to a maximum of US$95,000
Length of Study: Up to 1 year. A minimum of 6 months must be spent in the United States of America
Frequency: Annual
Study Establishment: An academic or other research policy institution
Country of Study: United States of America
No. of awards offered: 2 for Australia, 2 for New Zealand and 6 for the United Kingdom
Application Procedure: Applicants must complete a formal application available online at the website www.cmwf.org/fellowships. Applicants must be submitted via email.
Closing Date: September 15th
Funding: Private
Contributor: The Commonwealth Fund
Additional Information: Successful candidates will have a policy orientated research project, on a topic relevant to the Fund's programme areas. Projects will be supervised by senior researchers and each Fellow will be expected to produce a publishable report contributing to a better understanding of health policy issues.

For further information contact:

Associate Professor & Director (Australia), Center for Health Economics Research & Evaluation, University of Sydney, Mallett Street Campus, 88 Mallett Street, Level 6, Building F, Camperdown, NSW, 2050, Australia
Tel: (61) 2 9351 0900
Fax: (61) 2 9351 0930
Email: sylviab@pub.health.usyd.edu.au
Contact: Dr Jane Hall

Policy Representative, Executive Director (New Zealand), New Zealand-United States Educational Foundation, PO Box 3465, Wellington, New Zealand
Tel: (64) 4 722 065
Fax: (64) 4 995 364
Email: jennifer@fulbright.org.nz
Contact: Ms Jennifer M Gill

Ian Axford (New Zealand) Fellowships in Public Policy

Subjects: Public policy.
Purpose: To provide American professionals with the opportunity to study, travel and gain practical experience in public policy in New Zealand, including first hand knowledge of economic, social and political reforms and management of the government sector.
Eligibility: Open to mid-career professionals active in any part of the public, business or non-profit sectors. Applicants must be citizens of the United States of America with at least 5 years of experience in their professions. There are no formal age limits, but the focus of the fellowships is on mid-career development and successful candidates are likely to be in their late 20s to early 40s.
Level of Study: Professional development
Type: Fellowship
Value: Fellows on paid leave will receive an allowance of New Zealand $1,700 per month on top of their salaries and will be entitled to family and other allowances. Fellows unable to obtain paid leave will receive a living allowance of New Zealand $4,000 per month, intended to cover basic expenses of residence in New Zealand, and will be entitled to family and other allowances.
Length of Study: 6 months
Frequency: Annual
Country of Study: New Zealand
Application Procedure: Applicants must complete a formal application, including a project proposal. Candidates should show that their proposed project will inform public policy in New Zealand and the United States of America and contribute something of value to the policy of their field. Applications are available online at the website and must be submitted via email.
Closing Date: March 1st
Funding: Government
Additional Information: Applications are welcome equally from men and women, from members of any ethnic group and regardless of physical disabilities.

Packer Fellowships

Subjects: Health policy issues in Australia and the United States of America, and shared lessons of both policies.
Purpose: To allow outstanding, mid-career health policy researchers from the United States of America to spend up to 10 months in Australia conducting original research and working with leading Australian health policy experts on issues relevant to both countries.
Eligibility: Accomplished, mid-career health policy researchers and practitioners including academics, physicians, decision makers in managed care and other private organizations, federal and state health officials and journalists.
Level of Study: Research
Type: Fellowship
Value: Australian $50,000 plus family allowance
Length of Study: Up to 10 months
Frequency: Annual
Study Establishment: Suitable establishment in Australia
Country of Study: Australia
Application Procedure: Applicants must submit a formal application, including a project proposal that falls within an area of mutual policy interest, such as: healthcare quality and safety, the private/public mix of insurance and providers, the fiscal sustainability of health systems, the healthcare workforce and investment in preventive care strategies. Applications are available online (www.cmwf.org/fellowships) and must be submitted via email.
Closing Date: August 15th
Funding: Government

COMMONWEALTH SCHOLARSHIP COMMISSION IN THE UNITED KINGDOM

c/o Association of Commonwealth Universities, John Foster House, 36 Gordon Square, London, WC1H 0PF, England
Tel: (44) 20 7380 6700
Fax: (44) 20 7387 2655
Email: info@acu.ac.uk
Website: www.acu.ac.uk
Contact: Awards Administrator

The Commonwealth Scholarship Commission in the United Kingdom was set up as the body responsible for the United Kingdom's participation in the Commonwealth Scholarship and Fellowship Plan in 1959. It is responsible for the selection and placement of recipients coming to the United Kingdom and for the selection of candidates from the United Kingdom to be put forward for awards in other Commonwealth countries.

Commonwealth Academic Fellowships

Subjects: All subjects, but preference given to applications which fit with the development plans of the candidate's none institution.
Purpose: To support the cost of up to six months in the united for staff of universities in certain developing commonwealth countries.
Eligibility: Open to commonwealth citizens or British protected persons who have completed their doctorate in no less than 5 years by the time of taxing up an award. Candidates should be a permanent resident of and a teaching staff of a university in a developing commonwealth country candidates should not be more than 50 years of age with at least 2 years of teaching experience.
Level of Study: Postdoctorate
Type: Fellowship
Value: Maintenance and travel allowances
Length of Study: 6 months
Frequency: Annual
Study Establishment: A university level institution
Country of Study: United Kingdom
No. of awards offered: Approx. 80

Application Procedure: Application by nomination only. Full application details, including special for awards involving clinical training in available on CSFP website.
Closing Date: December 31st for receipt of nominations in London
Funding: Government
Contributor: Commonwealth Scholarship Commission
Additional Information: Fellows are required to sign an undertaking to return to and resume their academic post in their country on completion of the fellowships. Candidates must be nominated by the vice chancellor of the university on whose permanent staff the applicant serves. Heads of Indian universities should send their nominations to the University Grants Commission in New Delhi, heads of Pakistani universities to the Ministry of Education in Islamabad, heads of Sri-Lankan universities to the Ministry of tertiary education and training in Colombo and heads of Bangladeshi universities to the University Grants Commission in Dhaka. The fellowship may not be held concurrently with other awards or with paid employment.

Commonwealth Academic Staff Scholarships

Subjects: All subjects.
Purpose: To help universities in the developing countries of the Commonwealth to increase the numbers and enhance the experience of their locally born staff. The scholarships are intended to enable promising staff members from universities and similar institutions in the developing Commonwealth to obtain experience in a university or other appropriate institution in the United Kingdom.
Eligibility: Open to Commonwealth citizens or British protected persons who are permanently resident in Commonwealth countries other than the UK, not older than 42 years of age and holding a teaching appointment in a university in a developing commonwealth country.
Level of Study: Postgraduate
Type: Scholarship
Value: Return airfare to the United Kingdom, approved tuition, laboratory and examination fees, a personal maintenance allowance, a grant for books and equipment, a grant towards the expense of preparing a thesis or dissertation, where applicable, a grant for approved travel within the United Kingdom, an initial clothing allowance in special cases and in certain circumstances, a marriage and child allowance. The emoluments are not subject to United Kingdom income tax
Length of Study: 1–3 years
Frequency: Annual
Study Establishment: An approved institution of higher education
Country of Study: United Kingdom
No. of awards offered: 45–50
Application Procedure: Applicants must be nominated by the executive head of the university to which the candidate belongs. Full applications details available on CSFP website.
Closing Date: December 31st for receipt of nominations in London
Additional Information: Scholars are required to sign an undertaking to return to and resume their academic post in their own country on completion of the scholarship.

Commonwealth Scholarships

Subjects: All subjects.
Purpose: To enable students of high intellectual promise to pursue studies in Commonwealth countries other than their own so that on their return home they can make a distinctive contribution to life in their own countries and to advance mutual understanding in the Commonwealth.
Eligibility: Open to Commonwealth citizens under 35 years of age who are normally resident in some part of the Commonwealth other than the particular awarding country. Applicants must be graduates of high intellectual promise with a Master's degree within the last 10 years at the time of nomination.
Level of Study: Postgraduate
Type: Scholarship
Value: Fares to and from the United Kingdom, payment of tuition fees, allowances for books, special clothing, local travel and a personal maintenance allowance
Length of Study: 1–3 academic years
Frequency: Annual
Study Establishment: Universities, colleges and other educational institutions
Country of Study: Designated Commonwealth countries other than candidates own
No. of awards offered: Approx. 200 per year
Application Procedure: Applicants must apply to the appropriate national scholarship agency in their country of normal residence. These agencies distribute prospectuses and application forms for the various awards and will usually be the best local centres to obtain information. For detailed application procedures and appropriate contact addresses visit the website: www.csfp-online.org
Closing Date: Varies according to the country in which the candidate applies, usually some 12–18 months before the intended period of study
Funding: Government
Additional Information: Award holders must undertake to return to their own countries on completion of their studies overseas.

CONCORDIA UNIVERSITY

École des Études Supérieures, 1455 boulevard de Maisonneuve, Montréal, QC, H3G 1M8, Canada
Tel: (1) 514 848 3809
Fax: (1) 514 848 2812
Email: verret@vax2.concordia.ca
Website: www.concordia.ca
Contact: Ms Patricia Verret, Graduate Awards Manager

Concordia University is the result of the 1974 merger between Sir George Williams University and Loyola College. The University incorporates superior teaching methods with an interdisciplinary approach to learning and is dedicated to offering the best possible scholarship to the student body and to promoting research beneficial to society.

Bank of Montréal Pauline Varnier Fellowship

Subjects: Business and administration management.
Eligibility: Open to women with 2 years of cumulative business experience who are Canadian citizens or landed immigrants intending to pursue a full-time course of study for the MBA. This is an entrance fellowship.
Level of Study: MBA
Type: Fellowship
Value: Canadian $10,000 per year
Length of Study: 2 years
Frequency: Annual
Study Establishment: Concordia University
Country of Study: Canada
No. of awards offered: 1
Application Procedure: Applicants must submit a completed application form, three letters of recommendation and official transcripts of all university studies by the closing date.
Closing Date: April 30th
Funding: Private
No. of awards given last year: 1
Additional Information: Academic merit is the prime consideration in the granting of the awards.

Concordia University Graduate Fellowships

Subjects: All subjects.
Eligibility: Open to graduates of any nationality. Candidates must be planning to pursue full-time Master's or doctoral study at the University.
Level of Study: Postgraduate
Type: Fellowship
Value: Canadian $2,900 per term for Master's level and Canadian $3,600 per term for doctoral level
Length of Study: A maximum of 4 terms at the Master's level and 9 terms at the doctoral level, calculated from the date of entry into the programme
Frequency: Annual
Study Establishment: Concordia University
Country of Study: Canada
No. of awards offered: Varies

Application Procedure: Applicants must submit a completed application form, three letters of recommendation and official transcripts of all university studies by the closing date.
Closing Date: December 15th
Funding: Government, private
No. of awards given last year: 25
No. of applicants last year: 1050
Additional Information: Academic merit is the prime consideration in the granting of the award.

David J Azrieli Graduate Fellowship

Subjects: All subjects.
Eligibility: Open to Master's or doctoral students of any nationality. Candidates must be planning to pursue full-time Master's or doctoral study at the University.
Level of Study: Postgraduate
Type: Fellowship
Value: Canadian $17,500 per year
Length of Study: 1 year, non-renewable
Frequency: Annual
Study Establishment: Concordia University
Country of Study: Canada
No. of awards offered: 1
Application Procedure: Applicants must submit a completed application form, three letters of recommendation and official transcripts of all university studies by the closing date.
Closing Date: December 15th
Funding: Private
No. of awards given last year: 1
No. of applicants last year: 1050
Additional Information: Academic merit is the prime consideration in the granting of the award.

J W McConnell Memorial Fellowships

Subjects: All subjects.
Eligibility: Open to Canadian citizens and permanent residents of Canada who are planning to pursue full-time Master's or doctoral study at the University. Fellowships are awarded on academic merit.
Level of Study: Postgraduate
Type: Fellowship
Value: Canadian $2,900 per term at the Master's level and Canadian $3,600 per term at the doctoral level
Length of Study: A maximum of 4 terms at the Master's level and 9 terms at the doctoral level, calculated from the date of entry into the programme
Frequency: Annual
Study Establishment: Concordia University
Country of Study: Canada
No. of awards offered: Varies
Application Procedure: Applicants must submit a completed application form, three letters of recommendation and official transcripts of all university studies by the closing date.
Closing Date: December 15th
Funding: Private
No. of awards given last year: 15
No. of applicants last year: 800
Additional Information: Academic merit is the prime consideration in the granting of the awards.

John W O'Brien Graduate Fellowship

Subjects: All subjects.
Eligibility: Open to full-time graduate students of any nationality. Candidates must be planning to pursue full-time Master's or doctoral study at the University.
Type: Fellowship
Value: Canadian $3,300 per term at the Master's level and Canadian $4,000 per term at the doctoral level
Length of Study: A maximum of 3 terms
Frequency: Annual
Study Establishment: Concordia University
Country of Study: Canada
No. of awards offered: 1
Application Procedure: Applicants must submit a completed application form, three letters of recommendation and official transcripts of all university studies by the closing date.
Closing Date: December 15th
Funding: Private
No. of awards given last year: 1
No. of applicants last year: 1050
Additional Information: Academic merit is the prime consideration in the granting of awards.

Stanley G French Graduate Fellowship

Subjects: All subjects.
Eligibility: Open to graduates of any nationality. Candidates must be planning to pursue full-time Master's or doctoral study at the University.
Level of Study: Postgraduate
Type: Fellowship
Value: Canadian $3,300 per term for Master's level and Canadian $4,000 per term for doctoral level
Length of Study: A maximum of 3 terms
Frequency: Annual
Study Establishment: Concordia University
Country of Study: Canada
No. of awards offered: 1
Application Procedure: Applicants must submit a completed application form, three letters of recommendation and official transcripts of all university studies by the closing date.
Closing Date: December 15th
Funding: Private
No. of awards given last year: 1
No. of applicants last year: 1050
Additional Information: Academic merit is the prime consideration in the granting of awards.

CONSERVATION TRUST

National Geographic Society 1/45 17th Street NW, Washington, DC 20090-8244, United States of America
Email: conservationtrust@ngs.org
Website: www.nationalgeographic.com/conservation

The objective of the Conservation Trust is to support conservation activities around the world as they fit within the mission of the National Geographic Society. The trust will fund projects that contribute significantly to the presentation and sustainable use of the Earth's biological, cultural, and historical resources.

National Geographic Conservation Trust Grant

Subjects: Conservation.
Purpose: To support cutting programmes that contribute to the preservation and sustainable use of the Earth's resources.
Eligibility: Applicants must provide a record of prior research or conservation action. Researchers planning work in foreign countries should include at least one local collaboration as part of their research teams. Grants recipients are excepted to provide the National Geographic Society with rights of first refusal for popular publication of their findings.
Level of Study: Research
Type: Research grant
Value: US$15,000–20,000
Frequency: Annual
No. of awards offered: Varies
Application Procedure: Apply online.
Closing Date: 8 months prior to anticipated field dates
Funding: Trusts
Contributor: National Geographic Society

COOLEY'S ANEMIA FOUNDATION

Suite 203, 129-09 26th Avenue, Flushing, NY 11354, United States of America
Tel: (1) 718 321 2873
Fax: (1) 718 321 3340
Email: info@cooleysanemia.org
Website: www.cooleysanemia.org
Contact: Ms Sophie Buicynski, Accounting Department

The Cooley's Anemia Foundation is dedicated to serving people afflicted with various forms of thalassemia, most notably the major form of this genetic blood disease, Cooley's anemia/thalassemia major.

Cooley's Anemia Foundation Research Fellowship

Subjects: Clinical or basic research related to thalassemia. Applications on topics such as cardiac and endocrine complications of iron overload, hepatitis C, osteoporosis, bone marrow transplantation, iron chelation and gene therapy are encouraged.
Purpose: The research fellowship programme of the Cooley's Anemia Foundation exists to promote an increased understanding of Cooley's anemia, develop improved treatment and achieve a final cure for this life-threatening genetic blood disorder.
Eligibility: Fellows must have adequate preceptorship and guidance by an experienced investigator. The application is expected to be the original work of the candidate, but should reflect the close advice of the interested and involved sponsor. Applicants who are Fellows must have an MD, PhD or equivalent degree, and must not hold a faculty position. Applicants who are junior faculty must have an MD, PhD or equivalent degree, and must have completed less than 5 years at the assistant professor level at the time the applications are due.
Level of Study: Postgraduate
Type: Fellowship
Value: US$40,000
Length of Study: 1 year
Frequency: Annual
Study Establishment: Any suitable establishment
Country of Study: Any country
No. of awards offered: 10–15
Application Procedure: Qualified applicants should download an application form from the website.
Closing Date: March 7th
Funding: Private
Contributor: Study is supported by a grant from the Cooley's Anemia Foundation
No. of awards given last year: 11
Additional Information: The foundation seeks to make an extraordinary commitment towards recruiting doctors to pursue a career investigating thalassemia, especially due to the relatively small patient base in the United States of America.

CORE

3 St Andrew's Place, London, NW1 4LB, England
Tel: (44) 20 7486 0341
Fax: (44) 20 7224 2012
Email: info@corecharity.org.uk
Website: www.corecharity.org.uk
Contact: Research Grants Administrator

CORE (the new name for the Digestive Disorders Foundation) supports research into the cause, prevention and treatment of digestive disorders, including digestive cancers, ulcers, irritable bowel syndrome, inflammatory bowel disease, diverticulitis, liver disease and pancreatitis. CORE also provides information for the public that explains the symptoms and treatment of these and other common digestive conditions.

CORE Fellowships and Grants

Subjects: Gastroenterology, such as basic or applied clinical research into normal and abnormal aspects of the gastrointestinal tract, liver and pancreas, and the prevention of and treatment for digestive disorders.
Purpose: To provide funding for gastroenterological research.
Eligibility: Open to applicants resident within the United Kingdom. Fellowship projects must contain an element of basic science training.
Level of Study: Doctorate, postgraduate, postdoctorate, research
Type: Fellowship or Grant
Value: Up to UK £50,000 for Research Grants and up to UK £2,000 for Travel Grants. For fellowships, payment of a full-time, if medically qualified, is available
Length of Study: 1, 2 or 3 years
Frequency: Dependent on funds available
Study Establishment: Recognized and established research centres
Country of Study: United Kingdom
No. of awards offered: Approx. 10 annually
Application Procedure: Applicants must complete an application form for consideration in a research competition. Details are available from the website.
Funding: Trusts, private, individuals, commercial
Contributor: Charitable donations
No. of applicants last year: Varies
Additional Information: Conditions are advertised in the medical press. Research grants are awarded for specific projects in the same field of interest. Travel grants are awarded to assist researchers by enabling them to visit overseas institutions with the aim of learning new techniques or otherwise advancing their own research.

CORNELL UNIVERSITY

Center for the Humanities, Andrew D White House,
27 East Avenue, Ithaca, NY 14853-1101,
United States of America
Tel: (1) 607 255 9274
Email: humctr-mailbox@cornell.edu
Website: www.arts.cornell.edu/sochum
Contact: Program Administrator

Cornell University is a learning community that seeks to serve society by educating the leaders of the future and extending the frontiers of knowledge. The university aims to pursue understanding beyond the limitations of existing knowledge, ideology and disciplinary structure, and to affirm the value of the cultivation and enrichment of the human mind to individuals and society.

Mellon Postdoctoral Fellowships

Subjects: Arts and humanities.
Eligibility: Open to citizens of the United States of America and Canada and permanent residents who have completed requirements for a PhD before the application deadline and within the last 4–5 years.
Level of Study: Postdoctorate
Type: Fellowship
Value: US$40,000
Length of Study: 9 months
Frequency: Annual
Study Establishment: Cornell University
Country of Study: United States of America
No. of awards offered: 3–4
Application Procedure: Applicants must write for details.
Closing Date: Postmarked on or before October 1st
No. of awards given last year: 5
No. of applicants last year: 200
Additional Information: While in residence at Cornell, postdoctoral Fellows have department affiliation, limited teaching duties and the opportunity for scholarly work. Areas of specialization change each year.

Society for the Humanities Postdoctoral Fellowships

Subjects: Humanities.
Eligibility: Open to holders of a PhD degree who have at least 1 or 2 years of teaching experience at the college level. Applicants should be scholars with interests that are not confined to a narrow humanistic speciality and whose research coincides with the focal theme for the year. Fellows of the Society devote most of their time to research writing, but they are encouraged to offer a weekly seminar related to their special projects.
Level of Study: Postdoctorate
Type: Fellowship
Value: US$40,000
Length of Study: 1 academic year
Frequency: Annual
Study Establishment: Cornell University
Country of Study: United States of America
No. of awards offered: 6–7

Application Procedure: Applicants must contact the office to receive information on the theme and application materials.
Closing Date: Postmarked on or before October 1st
No. of awards given last year: 6
No. of applicants last year: 180
Additional Information: Information about this year's theme is available upon request.

THE CORPORATION OF YADDO

Box 395, Saratoga Springs, NY, 12866,
United States of America
Tel: (1) 518 584 0746
Fax: (1) 518 584 1312
Email: yaddo@yaddo.org
Website: www.yaddo.org
Contact: Ms Lesley M Leduc, Public Affairs Co-ordinator

The Corporation of Yaddo is an artists' community located on a 400-acre estate in Saratoga Springs, New York. Its mission is to nurture the creative process by providing an opportunity for artists to work without interruption in a supportive environment. Yaddo awards approximately 200 residences per year of between 2 weeks and 2 months in length and is among the United States of America's first and most acclaimed artists' communities.

Yaddo Residency

Subjects: Choreography, film, literature, musical composition, painting, performance art, photography, printmaking, sculpture and video.
Purpose: To provide uninterrupted time and space for creative artists to think, experiment and create.
Eligibility: Open to all artists who are working at the professional level in their fields. Applications are welcomed from artists from the United States of America and abroad. Open to visual artists, writers, composers and artists working in film and/or video, choreography and performance art. An abiding principle at Yaddo is that applications for residency are judged on the quality of the artist's work and professional promise.
Level of Study: Professional development
Type: Residency
Value: Room, board and studio space. There is no stipend. Limited help towards travel expenses available
Length of Study: 2 weeks–2 months
Frequency: Annual
Study Establishment: Yaddo
Country of Study: United States of America
No. of awards offered: Approx. 200
Application Procedure: Applicants must send a large stamped addressed envelope to the Admissions Committee. The requirements include a completed application form, letters from two sponsors, copies of a professional curriculum vitae, work samples and the US$20 non-refundable application fee.
Closing Date: January 1st or August 1st
Funding: Individuals, private, corporation
Contributor: Endowment
No. of awards given last year: 207
No. of applicants last year: 1,229

THE COSTUME SOCIETY

32 Nore Road, Portishead, Bristol, BS20 7HN,
United Kingdom
Tel: (44) 12 7584 3264
Email: ler@lakegrounds.fsnet.co.uk
Contact: Mr Lindsay Evans Robertson

The Patterns of Fashion Award

Subjects: Art and design, drama, history of art and design.
Purpose: To help students To help students studying theatre design and, in particular studying the production of costume per performance.
Eligibility: The award is open to United Kingdom Full-time students studying theatre design and wardrobe.
Level of Study: Graduate, postgraduate
Type: Grant
Value: UK £500
Length of Study: As applicable to the course
Frequency: Annual
Study Establishment: Not specified
Country of Study: United Kingdom
No. of awards offered: 1
Application Procedure: Applicants must submit photographs of a finished garment reconstructed from a pattern selected from one of the patterns of Fashion Books by Janel Arnold. The application must be supported by the Head of Department and Academic Supervisor of the course on which the applicant is enrolled.
Closing Date: April 30th
Funding: Trusts
Contributor: The Costume Society
Additional Information: Full details of the Award are published on the Society's web site www.costumesociety.org.uk and with Costumes, the annual Journal of the Society.

For further information contact:

The awards Co-ordinater, The Patterns of Fashion Award, The Costume Society, c/o Moore Stephens, St. Paul's House, 8 Warwick Lane, London, EC4P 4BN, England

The Student Bursary

Subjects: History of dress stage and Fashion design and associated studies such as textiles and jewelry design.
Purpose: To offer full attendance at an annual symposium dedicated to the study of the history of dress.
Eligibility: Open to UK students at graduate and postgraduate level engaged in research directed towards a dissertation or thesis on the history and theory of dress. The research should reflect the theme of the Costume Society's current symposium or be an object-based project on the history of dress.
Level of Study: Postgraduate, graduate
Type: Bursary
Value: Full-time attendance at the three-day symposium inclusive of accommodation, meals, and lecturer visits
Length of Study: The award offers an intensive three-day study course
Frequency: Annual
Study Establishment: Not specified
Country of Study: United Kingdom
No. of awards offered: 1
Application Procedure: The applicant should submit a curriculum vitae and a proposal of no more than 200 words identifying the subject area of the proposed research. The applicant should specify the institution and course attended and the names of the Head of Department and the academic supervisor who will be required as referees on awarding the bursary.
Closing Date: April 30th
Funding: Trusts
Contributor: The Costume Society
No. of awards given last year: 1
Additional Information: Full details of the Award are published on the Society's website www.costumesociety.org.uk and with Costume, the annual journal of the Society.

For further information contact:

The Student Bursary, The Costume Society, c/o Moore Stephens, St. Paul's House, 8 Warwick Lane, London, EC4P 4BN
Contact: The Awards Co-ordinator

THE COSTUME SOCIETY OF AMERICA (CSA)

PO Box 73, Earleville, MD 21919, United States of America
Tel: (1) 410 275 1619
Fax: (1) 410 275 8936
Email: national.office@costumesocietyamerica.com
Website: www.costumesocietyamerica.com
Contact: Administrative Assistant

The Costume Society of America (CSA) advances the global understanding of all aspects of dress and appearance. The Society seeks as members those who are involved in the study, education, collection, preservation, presentation and interpretation of dress and appearance in past, present and future societies.

CSA Adele Filene Travel Award

Subjects: Cultural heritage, museum studies and related areas.
Purpose: To assist student members in their travel to the CSA National Symposium to present an accepted paper or poster.
Eligibility: Open to current students with CSA membership who have been accepted to present a juried paper or poster at the CSA National Symposium.
Level of Study: Unrestricted
Type: Travel grant
Value: Up to US$500
Frequency: Annual
Country of Study: United States of America
No. of awards offered: 1–3
Application Procedure: Applicants must send three letters of support with a copy of the juried abstract and a one-page letter of application.
Closing Date: Approx. 2 months before the event
No. of awards given last year: 4
No. of applicants last year: 3

CSA Stella Blum Research Grant

Subjects: North American costume.
Purpose: Support for research projects on North American costume by CSA student members.
Eligibility: Open to student members of the Society, who are enrolled on a degree programme at an accredited institution.
Level of Study: Doctorate, postgraduate, graduate, predoctorate, postdoctorate
Type: Grant
Value: Up to US$3,500. Allowable costs include transportation to and from the research site, living expenses at the research site, supplies such as film, photographic reproductions, books, paper, computer disks, postage and telephone and services such as typing, computer searches and graphics. In addition, up to US$500 is available for travel and related expenses to present a paper based on research at the annual meeting and symposium
Frequency: Annual
Study Establishment: An accredited institution
Country of Study: United States of America
No. of awards offered: 1
Application Procedure: Applicants must complete an application form, available upon request.
Closing Date: May 1st
No. of awards given last year: 1
No. of applicants last year: 4
Additional Information: The award will be given based on merit rather than need. Judging criteria will include creativity and innovation, specific awareness of and attention to costume matters, impact on the broad field of costume, awareness of the interdisciplinary nature of the field, ability to successfully implement the proposed project in a timely manner and faculty adviser recommendation.

CSA Travel Research Grant

Subjects: Textile and fashion design, museum studies and related areas.
Purpose: To allow an individual to travel to collections for research purposes.
Eligibility: Applicants must be current, non-student CSA members and must have held membership for 2 years or more. Applicants must give proof of work in progress and indicate why the particular collection is important to the project.
Level of Study: Professional development
Value: Up to US$1,500
Frequency: Annual
Country of Study: Any country
No. of awards offered: 1
Application Procedure: Applicants must send a letter of application of no more than two pages and include the name of the collection and projected date of visit, a description of the project underway, evidence of work accomplished to date, reasons for visiting the designated collection, projected completion date of project, what audience the project will be directed to, as well as a current curriculum vitae.
Closing Date: September 1st
No. of awards given last year: 1
No. of applicants last year: 3

THE COUNCIL FOR BRITISH RESEARCH IN THE LEVANT (CBRL)

The British Academy, 10 Carlton House Terrace, London, SW1Y 5AH, England
Tel: (44) 20 7969 5296
Fax: (44) 20 7969 5401
Email: cbrl@britac.ac.uk
Website: www.britac.ac.uk/institutes/cbrl

In 1998, the British Institute at Amman for Archaeology and History and the British School of Archaeology in Jerusalem amalgamated to create the Council for British Research in the Levant (CBRL). The CBRL promotes the study of the humanities and social sciences as relevant to the countries of the Levant (Cyprus, Israel, Jordan, Lebanon, Palestinian Territories and Syria).

CBRL Research Award

Subjects: Humanities and social sciences subjects, eg. archaeology, economics, geography, historical studies, legal studies, languages and literature, linguistics, music, philosophy, politics, social anthropology, sociology and theology or religious studies.
Purpose: To support research projects from initial exploratory work through to publication.
Eligibility: Applicants must be of British nationality or ordinarily resident in the United Kingdom, Isle of Man or the Channel Islands.
Level of Study: Postdoctorate, research
Type: Research award
Value: The value of individual awards does not normally exceed UK £10,000 and in most cases will be below that level
Frequency: Annual
Study Establishment: Council for British Research in the Levant
No. of awards offered: Varies
Application Procedure: Applicants must complete an application form, available from the United Kingdom Secretary at the main address or from the website.
Closing Date: December 1st
Funding: Government
Contributor: The British Academy
No. of awards given last year: 10
No. of applicants last year: 17

CBRL Travel Grant

Subjects: Humanities and social sciences subjects, eg. archaeology, economics, geography, historical studies, legal studies, languages and literature, linguistics, music, philosophy, politics, social anthropology, sociology and theology or religious studies.
Purpose: To cover the travel and subsistence costs of students, academics and researchers undertaking reconnaissance tours or smaller research projects in the countries of the Levant.
Eligibility: Applicants must be of British nationality, a citizen of the European Union or ordinarily resident in the United Kingdom, Isle of Man or the Channel Islands, or registered for a full-time undergraduate or postgraduate degree in a United Kingdom university.
Level of Study: Unrestricted
Type: Travel grant
Value: A maximum of UK £800
Frequency: Annual
Study Establishment: Council for British Research in the Levant
No. of awards offered: Varies
Application Procedure: Applicants must complete an application form, available from the United Kingdom Secretary at the main address or from the CBRL website.
Closing Date: January 31st
Funding: Government

Contributor: The British Academy
No. of awards given last year: 15
No. of applicants last year: 38

COUNCIL FOR INTERNATIONAL EXCHANGE OF SCHOLARS (CIES)

3007 Tilden Street North West, Suite 5L, Washington, DC 20008-3009, United States of America
Tel: (1) 202 686 4000
Fax: (1) 202 362 3442
Email: apprequest@cies.iie.org
Website: www.cies.org
Contact: Ms Nancy Gainer, Director of External Relations

The Council for International Exchange of Scholars (CIES) is a private, non-profit organization that facilitates international exchanges in higher education. Under a co-operative agreement with the United States of America Department of State Bureau of Educational and Cultural Affairs, it assists in the administration of the Fulbright Scholar Program for faculty and professionals. CIES is affiliated with the Institute of International Education.

Fulbright Distinguished Chairs Program

Subjects: American studies (history, politics and literature), humanities, law, social sciences, computer science and e-commerce, business and management, fine arts, mass communications and journalism.
Purpose: To increase mutual understanding between the people of the United States of America and other countries and to promote international educational co-operation.
Eligibility: Open to citizens of the United States of America who hold a PhD or equivalent qualification. Candidates should have a prominent record of scholarly achievement.
Level of Study: Postdoctorate
Value: Varies by country
Length of Study: From 3 months to 1 academic year
Frequency: Annual
No. of awards offered: Approx. 30
Application Procedure: Applicants must submit a letter of intent and an eight-page curriculum vitae, and should telephone CIES or visit the website for more information.
Closing Date: May 1st
Funding: Private, government
No. of awards given last year: 30
No. of applicants last year: 300
Additional Information: Applicants must contact Dario Teutonico at dteutonico@cies.iie.org for more information.

Fulbright Postdoctoral Research and Lecturing Awards for Non-US Citizens

Subjects: All subjects.
Eligibility: Open to nationals of countries and territories holding United States of America diplomatic or consular posts who have a doctoral degree or equivalent qualification. Preference is given to those persons who have not had extensive previous experience within the United States of America.
Level of Study: Postdoctorate
Type: Grant
Value: A maintenance allowance and international travel expenses
Length of Study: 3 months–1 academic year
Frequency: Annual
Country of Study: United States of America
No. of awards offered: Varies, approx. 800
Application Procedure: Applicants must make applications to the Binational Educational Commission, or the United States of America Embassy or consulate in their home country.
Closing Date: Varies depending on the country
Funding: Private, government
Contributor: The United States of America Government and the Fulbright Commission
No. of awards given last year: More than 800

Fulbright Scholar Awards for Research and Lecturing Abroad for US Citizens

Subjects: All subjects.
Purpose: To increase mutual understanding between the people of the United States of America and the people of other nations, to strengthen the ties that unite the United States of America with other nations and to promote international co-operation for educational and cultural advancement.
Eligibility: Open to citizens of the United States of America with a PhD or comparable professional qualification. University or college teaching experience is normally expected for lecturing awards. For selected assignments, proficiency in a foreign language may be required.
Level of Study: Postdoctorate, professional development
Type: Award
Value: Varies by country
Length of Study: 2 months–1 academic year
Frequency: Annual
No. of awards offered: 800
Application Procedure: Applicants must complete an application, available on request from CIES or from the website.
Closing Date: August 1st
Funding: Private, government
No. of awards given last year: 800
No. of applicants last year: 2,000
Additional Information: Individual countries' programmes are described in the Council's publication and online. Applicants must email apprequest@cies.iie.org for more information.

Fulbright Scholar Program for US Citizens

Subjects: The humanities, social sciences, applied, natural and physical sciences and professional fields such as architecture, business, law, museum work and creative arts, etc. Clinical medicine is excluded.
Purpose: To increase mutual understanding between the United States of America and other countries of the world.
Eligibility: Open to citizens of the United States of America.
Level of Study: Postdoctorate
Type: Grant
Value: A maintenance allowance and international travel expenses
Length of Study: 3 months–1 academic year
Frequency: Annual
No. of awards offered: Approx. 800
Closing Date: August 1st
No. of awards given last year: 800
No. of applicants last year: 2,000
Additional Information: Applicants should visit the website for further information.

Fulbright Senior Specialists Program

Subjects: Anthropology, archaeology, business administration, communications and journalism, economics, education, environmental science, information technology, law, library science, political science, public administration, sociology, social work, United States of America studies and urban planning.
Purpose: To offer short-term grants and encourage new types of activities in the Fulbright context. The programme also aims to advance mutual understanding, establish long-term co-operation and create opportunities for institutional linkages.
Eligibility: Open to citizens of the United States of America with a PhD or comparable professional qualification.
Level of Study: Postdoctorate, professional development
Type: Grant
Value: An honorarium and international travel expenses
Length of Study: 2–6 weeks
Frequency: Annual
Country of Study: Other
No. of awards offered: Varies
Application Procedure: Applicants must complete the application form, available on the CIES website.
Closing Date: Applications and grants are processed on a rolling basis
Funding: Government

Additional Information: Successful candidates are expected to lecture, lead seminars, work with foreign counterparts on curriculum and program and institutional development. Applicants must contact fulspec@cies.iie.org for more information.

COUNCIL FOR THE ADVANCEMENT OF SCIENCE WRITING, INC. (CASW)

PO Box 910, Hedgesville, WV 25427, United States of America
Tel: (1) 304 754 5077
Fax: (1) 304 754 5076
Email: diane@casw.org
Website: www.casw.org
Contact: Ms Diane McGurgan, Administration Secretary

The CASW is a group of distinguished journalists and scientists committed to improving the quality of science news reaching the general public.

Taylor/Blakeslee Fellowships for Graduate Study in Science Writing

Subjects: Journalism.
Purpose: To support graduate study in science writing.
Eligibility: Applicants must have a degree in science or journalism and must convince the CASW selection committee of their ability to pursue a career in science writing for the general public.
Level of Study: Postgraduate
Type: Fellowship
Value: A maximum of US$2,000
Length of Study: 1 year
Frequency: Annual
Country of Study: United States of America
No. of awards offered: 2–4
Application Procedure: Applicants must submit four collated sets of a completed application form, a curriculum vitae, a transcript of undergraduate studies if a student, three faculty recommendations or employer recommendations, three samples of writing on 8.5 by 11 inch sheets only and a short statement of career goals.
Closing Date: July 1st
Funding: Private
No. of awards given last year: 4
No. of applicants last year: 16
Additional Information: Science writing is defined as writing about science, medicine, health, technology and the environment for the general public via the mass media.

COUNCIL FOR THE DEVELOPMENT OF SOCIAL SCIENCE RESEARCH IN AFRICA (CODESRIA)

Avenue Cheikh Anta Diopx Canal IV BP 3304, Dakar, 18524, Senegal
Tel: (221) 825 98 22/23
Fax: (221) 824 12 89
Email: codesria@codesria.sn
Website: www.codesria.org

Initiated in 1988 CODESRIA has awarded grants to over one thousand laureates from various universities in Africa. By focusing on a younger generation of scholars CODESRIA aims to reinforce the capacity building of the African scholar in higher education.

CODESRIA Small Grants Programme

Purpose: To provide graduate researchers with the basic requirements they need to carry out their fieldwork.
Level of Study: Postgraduate
Type: Grant
Length of Study: 1 year
Frequency: Annual
Study Establishment: Any African University
Country of Study: Africa
Application Procedure: Contact the organization.
No. of awards given last year: 1

COUNCIL OF SUPPLY CHAIN MANAGEMENT PROFESSIONALS (CSCMP)

2805 Butterfield Road, Suite 200, Oak Brook, IL 60523-1170, United States of America
Tel: (1) 630 574 0985
Fax: (1) 630 574 0989
Email: khedland@cscmp.org
Website: www.cscmp.org
Contact: Kathleen Hedland, Director Education and Roundtable Services

The Council of Supply Chain Management Professionals (CSCMP) is a non-profit organization of business personnel who are interested in improving their logistics management skills. CSCMP works in co-operation with private industry and various organizations to further the understanding and development of the logistics concept. This is accomplished through a continuing programme of organized activities, research and meetings designed to develop the theory and understanding of the logistics process, promote the art and science of managing logistics systems, and foster professional dialogue and development within the profession.

CSCMP Distinguished Service Award

Subjects: Logistics.
Purpose: To recognize all those involved in logistics.
Eligibility: Open to all individuals who have provided exemplary service to the profession.
Type: Award
Frequency: Annual

CSCMP Doctoral Dissertation Award

Subjects: Logistics.
Purpose: To encourage research leading to advancement of the theory and practice to logistics management.
Eligibility: Open to all candidates whose doctoral dissertation demonstrates signified originality and contributes to the logistics knowledge base.
Level of Study: Postdoctorate
Frequency: Annual

CSCMP George A Gecowets Graduate Scholarship Program

Subjects: Logistics management.
Purpose: To acknowledge the importance of logistics in a tangible way, while emphasising the Council's commitment to promote the art and science of managing logistics systems.
Eligibility: Applicants must be planning to pursue a career in logistics management, be a senior at an accredited four year college or university, and already be enrolled in the first year of a logistics or logistics related Master's degree programme.
Level of Study: Graduate
Type: Scholarship
Frequency: Annual
Application Procedure: Applicants must submit a completed application, official college transcripts, Graduate Record Examination scores or Graduate Management Admission Test scores, and notification of any changes in address, school enrolment, or other pertinent information. The Citizens' Scholarship Foundation of America (CSFA) will then send a complete application package upon request.
Closing Date: Postmarked April 1st
Funding: Private
Contributor: The Council of Logistics Management
Additional Information: The Council wishes to make high potential students aware of the tremendous opportunities and challenges that await them in a career in logistics management, as the last 10 years have seen an exponential increase in the importance of the logistics manager.

For further information contact:

Council of Supply Chain Management Professionals, George A Gecowets Graduate Scholarship Program, Scholarship Management Services CSFA, 1505 Riverview Road, PO Box 297, St Peter, MN 56082, United States of America

COUNCIL ON FOREIGN RELATIONS (CFR)

The Harold Pratt House, 58 East 68th Street,
New York, NY 10021,
United States of America
Tel: (1) 212 434 9489
Fax: (1) 212 434 9801
Email: fellowships@cfr.org
Website: www.cfr.org
Contact: Ms Elise Lewis, Vice President, Membership and Fellowship Affairs

The Council on Foreign Relations (CFR) is dedicated to increasing America's understanding of the world and contributing ideas to United States of America foreign policy. The Council accomplishes this mainly by promoting constructive debates and discussions, clarifying world issues and publishing *Foreign Affairs*, the leading journal on global issues.

CFR International Affairs Fellowship Program in Japan

Subjects: International relations.
Purpose: To cultivate the United States of America's understanding of Japan and to strengthen communication between emerging leaders of the two nations.
Eligibility: Open to citizens of the United States of America aged 27–45 who have not had prior substantial experience in Japan. Fellows will be drawn from academia, government institutions, the business community and the media. The programme does not fund pre- or postdoctoral scholarly research, work towards a degree or the completion of projects on which substantial progress has been made prior to the fellowship period. Knowledge of the Japanese language is not a requirement.
Level of Study: Professional development
Type: Fellowship
Value: Living expenses in Japan plus international transportation, health and travel insurance and necessary research expenses
Length of Study: 3 months to 1 year
Frequency: Annual
Country of Study: Japan
No. of awards offered: 2–5
Application Procedure: Application is primarily by invitation, on the recommendation of individuals in academic, government and other institutions who have occasion to know candidates particularly well suited for the experience offered by this fellowship. Others who inquire directly and who meet preliminary requirements may also be invited to apply without formal nomination. Those invited to apply will be forwarded application materials.
Closing Date: September 15th is the deadline for nominations and October 31st is the application deadline. Nominations and applications will also be accepted out of cycle
Funding: Private
Contributor: Hitachi Limited
No. of awards given last year: 3–5
No. of applicants last year: 10
Additional Information: While the Fellow is not required to produce a book, article or report, it is hoped that some written output will result.

CFR International Affairs Fellowships

Subjects: Important problems in international affairs and their implications for the interests and policies of the United States of America, foreign states or international organizations.
Purpose: To bridge the gap between analysis and action in foreign policy by supporting a variety of policy studies and active experiences in policy making.
Eligibility: Open to United States citizens aged 27–35. While a PhD is not a requirement, successful candidates should generally hold advanced degrees and possess a solid record of work experience. The programme does not fund pre- or postdoctoral research, work towards a degree, or the completion of projects for which substantial progress has been made prior to the fellowship period.
Level of Study: Research, professional development
Type: Fellowship
Value: Determined according to individual budget statements in consultation with the programme administration. The programme will attempt to meet the major portion of a Fellow's current income, up to a maximum of US$60,000. The programme does not provide support for research assistance. Fellows may receive a travel grant of up to US$3,000
Length of Study: 1 year
Frequency: Annual
Country of Study: Any country
No. of awards offered: 8–12
Application Procedure: Application is primarily by invitation, on the recommendation of individuals in academic, government and other institutions who have occasion to know candidates particularly well suited for the experience offered by this fellowship. Others who enquire directly and who meet preliminary requirements may also be invited to apply without formal nomination. Those invited to apply will be forwarded application materials.
Closing Date: September 15th is the deadline for nominations and October 31st is the application deadline
Funding: Private
No. of awards given last year: 12
No. of applicants last year: 50
Additional Information: While the Fellow is not required to produce a book, article or report, it is hoped that some written output will result.

Edward R Murrow Fellowship for Foreign Correspondents

Subjects: Issues in international affairs and their implications for the interests and policies of the United States of America, foreign states or international organizations.
Purpose: To help the Fellow increase his or her competency in reporting and interpreting events abroad and to give him or her a period of nearly a year of sustained analysis and writing, free from the daily pressures that characterize journalistic life.
Eligibility: Open to any correspondent, editor or producer for radio, television, a newspaper or a magazine widely available in the United States of America who has covered international news.
Level of Study: Professional development
Type: Fellowship
Value: A stipend equivalent to the salary relinquished, not to exceed US$65,000 for 9 months
Length of Study: Normally a period of 9 months
Frequency: Annual
Study Establishment: The Council headquarters in New York City
No. of awards offered: 1
Application Procedure: Application is primarily by nomination. A nomination letter must be submitted to the main address. The nomination letter may be submitted by a Council member, a former or current Murrow Fellow, the candidate's employer, or the candidates themselves. The nomination letter should confirm the candidate's eligibility as well as provide a brief description of their background and why the nominator believes the candidate to be an appropriate prospect for the Fellowship. For those candidates who choose to nominate themselves, their letter should address the same aforementioned issues in addition to providing a copy of their most recent curriculum vitae. Nominees who meet the criteria of the programme will then be forwarded an application form.
Closing Date: February
Funding: Private
No. of awards given last year: 1
No. of applicants last year: 12

COUNCIL ON SOCIAL WORK EDUCATION (CSWE)

1725 Duke Street, Suite 500, Alexandria, VA 22314-3457, United States of America
Tel: (1) 703 683 8080
Fax: (1) 703 683 8099
Email: eafrancis@cswe.org
Website: www.cswe.org
Contact: Dr E Aracelis Francis, Director, Minority Fellowship Programmes

The Council on Social Work Education (CSWE) provides national leadership and a forum for collective action designed to ensure the preparation of competent and committed social work professionals. Founded in 1952, CSWE is a non-profit, tax exempt, national organization representing 2,700 individual members as well as 650 graduate and undergraduate programmes of professional social work education. CSWE's goals include improving the quality of social work education, preparing competent human service professionals and developing new programmes to meet the demands of the changing services delivery systems.

CSWE Doctoral Fellowships in Social Work for Ethnic Minority Students Preparing for Leadership Roles in Mental Health and/or Substance Abuse

Subjects: Mental health or substance abuse.
Purpose: To equip ethnic minority individuals for the provision of leadership, teaching, consultation, training, policy development and administration in mental health or substance abuse programmes and to enhance the development and dissemination of knowledge that is required for the provision of relevant clinical and social services to ethnic minority individuals and communities.
Eligibility: Applicants must be citizens or permanent residents of the United States of America, including, but not limited to, persons who are American Indian or Alaskan Native, Asian or Pacific Islander, Chinese, East Indian and other South Asians, Filipino, Hawaiian, Japanese, Korean or Samoan, black or Hispanic, eg. Mexican or Chicano, Puerto Rican, Cuban, Central or South American. This programme is open to students who have a Master's degree in social work and who will begin full-time study leading to a doctoral degree in social work or who are currently enrolled as full-time students in a doctoral social work programme.
Level of Study: Graduate
Type: Fellowship
Value: Monthly stipends to help defray living expenses. Some tuition support may be provided depending upon the availability of funds
Length of Study: 1 year
Frequency: Annual
Study Establishment: Schools of Social Work
Application Procedure: Applicants must write to the CSWE for an application pack and further information or visit the website.
Closing Date: February 28th
Funding: Government
Contributor: The Substance Abuse and Mental Health Services Administration
Additional Information: Applicants should demonstrate potential for assuming leadership roles, as well as potential for success in doctoral studies and commitment to a career in providing mental health and/or substance abuse services to ethnic minority clients and communities.

CSWE Doctoral Fellowships in Social Work for Ethnic Minority Students Specializing in Mental Health

Subjects: Mental health research.
Purpose: To educate leaders of the nation's next generation of mental health researchers.
Eligibility: Applicants must be citizens of the United States of America or permanent residents, including, but not limited to, persons who are American Indian or Alaskan Native, Asian or Pacific Islander, Chinese, East Indian and other South Asians, Filipino, Hawaiian, Japanese, Korean or Samoan, black or Hispanic, eg. Mexican or Chicano, Puerto Rican, Cuban, Central or South American. This programme is open to students who have a Master's degree in social work and who will begin full-time study leading to a doctoral degree in social work or are currently enrolled as full-time students in a doctoral social work programme.
Level of Study: Graduate
Type: Fellowship
Value: Monthly stipends to help defray living expenses. Tuition support provided according to the National Insitiute of Health tuition formula.
Length of Study: 1 year, although the award is renewable upon reapplication if the Fellow maintains satisfactory progress towards degree objectives and funding is available
Frequency: Annual
Study Establishment: Schools of Social Work
Country of Study: United States of America
No. of awards offered: 20
Application Procedure: Applicants must write to the CSWE for an application pack and further information or visit the website.
Closing Date: February 28th
Funding: Government
Contributor: The Division of Epidemiology and Services Research, NIMH
No. of awards given last year: 22
No. of applicants last year: 50
Additional Information: Applicants should demonstrate potential for, and interest in, mental health research, as well as potential for success in doctoral studies and commitment to a career in mental health research.

CSWE Mental Health Minority Fellowship Program

Subjects: Social work.
Purpose: To equip ethnic minority individuals for the provision of leadership, teaching, consultation, training, policy, development and administration in mental health or substance abuse programmes and to enhance the development and dissemination of knowledge necessary for the provision of relevant clinical and social services to ethnic minority individuals and communities.
Eligibility: Applicants must have a Master's degree in social work and must be citizens of the United States of America.
Level of Study: Graduate
Type: Fellowship
Value: US$10,008 per year, with a possible US$1,800 available towards tuition costs
Length of Study: 1 year, renewable for up to 3 years
Frequency: Dependent on funds available
Study Establishment: Approved Schools of Social Work
Country of Study: United States of America
No. of awards offered: 12
Application Procedure: Applicants must request application materials.
Closing Date: February 28th
Funding: Government
No. of awards given last year: 25
No. of applicants last year: 45

THE COUNTESS OF MUNSTER MUSICAL TRUST

Wormley Hill, Godalming, Surrey, GU8 5SG, England
Tel: (44) 14 2868 5427
Fax: (44) 14 2868 5064
Email: admin@munstertrust.org.uk
Website: www.munstertrust.org.uk
Contact: Mrs Gillian Ure, Secretary

The Countess of Munster Musical Trust provides financial assistance towards the cost of studies and maintenance of outstanding postgraduate students who merit further training at home or abroad. Each year, the Trust is able to offer a small number of interest-free loans for instrument purchase to former beneficiaries.

Countess of Munster Musical Trust Awards

Subjects: Musical studies.
Purpose: To enable students, selected after interview and audition, to pursue a course of specialist or advanced performance studies.
Eligibility: Open to United Kingdom or British Commonwealth citizens who are aged 18–24 years (for instrumentalists, conductors and composers) or under 28 (for singers) who show outstanding musical ability and potential.
Level of Study: Professional development, postgraduate, doctorate
Type: Grant
Value: By individual assessment to meet tuition fees and maintenance according to need, usually between UK £500–5,000
Length of Study: 1 year, with the possibility of renewal
Frequency: Annual
Country of Study: Any country
No. of awards offered: Up to 100 per year
Application Procedure: Applicants must complete an application form and will have to attend an audition and interview.
Closing Date: Application forms must be received between January and the second week of February for awards to go through in September
Funding: Private
No. of awards given last year: 62
No. of applicants last year: 256

CRANFIELD UNIVERSITY

School of Industrial or Manufacturing & Science Cranfield University, Bedfordshire, Cranfield, MK43 OAL, England
Tel: (44) 1234 754902
Fax: (44) 1234 754109
Email: sims.enquiries@cranfied.ac.uk
Website: www.cranfield.ac.uk/sims
Contact: Felicity Hull

The school of industrial or manufacturing science is recognized globally for its multidisciplinary approach to teaching and research in the key areas of manufacturing, materials, nanotechnology and sustainable systems our focus is on fundamental research and its application, together with teaching, to meet the needs of industry and society.

Cranfield University Overseas Bursary

Subjects: Any MSc programme offered by Cranfield University in the area of natural resources, Earth observation, soil and water management, environmental diagnostics, environmental management for business, medical diagnostics, molecular translational medicine, bioinformatics and land reclamation.
Purpose: To assist postgraduate study.
Eligibility: Open to students classified as overseas' for fee purposes. Must have a good UK honours degree or equivalent and have been offered a place on a 1-year MSc programme at Cranfield university Silsoe.
Level of Study: Predoctorate
Type: Bursary
Value: Up to UK £3,000
Length of Study: 1 year
Frequency: Annual
Study Establishment: Cranfield university
Country of Study: United Kingdom
No. of awards offered: Approx. 10
Application Procedure: Applicants must apply directly to the university.
Closing Date: July
Contributor: Cranfield university
No. of awards given last year: 10
No. of applicants last year: 250

NERC Awards

Subjects: Available for students wishing to study MSc water management (environmental water management option).
Purpose: To assist postgraduate study.
Eligibility: Open to UK candidates only who have a good UK honours. Degree or equivalent and have been offered a place on the MSc in water management.
Level of Study: Predoctorate
Value: Half tuition fees and stipend (approx UK £3,940)
Length of Study: 1 year
Frequency: Annual
Study Establishment: Cranfield university
Country of Study: United Kingdom
No. of awards offered: Up to 10
Application Procedure: Applicants must apply directly to the university.
Closing Date: July
Funding: Government
Contributor: NERC
No. of awards given last year: 0
No. of applicants last year: 75+

School of Industrial and Manufacturing Science Overseas Scholarships

Subjects: A wide range of disciplines, including advanced materials, motorsport engineering, nanotechnology, offshore engineering, welding, manufacturing, enterprise integration, water sciences, waste management and sustainability.
Purpose: To complement an individual overseas student's fees (50 per cent of total).
Level of Study: Postgraduate
Type: Scholarship
Value: Approx. UK £8,000
Length of Study: 1 year
Frequency: Annual
Study Establishment: Cranfield University School of Industrial and Manufacturing Science
Country of Study: United Kingdom
No. of awards offered: 5
Application Procedure: Complete and submit an application form along with two references.
Closing Date: April of each year although early application is advised; decision made in May
Funding: Trusts
Contributor: School of Industrial and Manufacturing Science
No. of awards given last year: 5
No. of applicants last year: 48
Additional Information: Candidates must demonstrate their ability to fund the remaining 50 per cent of the overseas fees and to be able to support themselves while at Cranfield University.

Silsoe Awards

Subjects: Any MSc programme option offered by Cranfield University in the area of natural resources, Earth observation, soil and water management, environmental diagnostics, environmental management for business medical diagnostics, molecular medicine, translational medicine bioinformatics and land reclamation.
Purpose: To assist postgraduate study.
Eligibility: Open to European Union citizens who have a good United Kingdom (Honours) Degree or equivalent and have been offered a place in a 1-year MSc programme at Cranfield University at Silsoe.
Level of Study: Predoctorate
Type: Bursary
Value: Tuition fees or half of tuition fees
Length of Study: 1 year
Frequency: Annual
Study Establishment: Cranfield University
Country of Study: United Kingdom
No. of awards offered: Approx. 50
Application Procedure: Applicants must apply directly to the University.
Closing Date: July
Contributor: Cranfield University
No. of awards given last year: 45
No. of applicants last year: 250

Williams F1-Cranfield Motorsport

Subjects: High-performance engineering: motorsport.
Purpose: To support high-calibre United Kingdom graduates wishing to undertake Cranfield university's MSc motorsport engineering and management programme.

Level of Study: Postgraduate
Type: Scholarship
Value: UK £4,800
Length of Study: 1 year
Frequency: Annual
Study Establishment: Cranfield University School of Industrial and Manufacturing Science
Country of Study: United Kingdom
No. of awards offered: 2
Application Procedure: When completing the application for a place on the MSc motorsport engineering and management programme, the candidate should indicate that they wish to be considered for the Williams F1 Scholarship. Complete and submit an application form along with two references.
Closing Date: September of each year although early application is advised
Funding: Commercial
Contributor: Williams F1
No. of awards given last year: 2
No. of applicants last year: 12
Additional Information: Candidates have to be accepted into the MSc motorsport engineering and management programme and then meet Williams F1's requirements. Awards are intended for those whose interest is in mechanical/design engineering in the context of motorsport.

CRIMINOLOGY RESEARCH COUNCIL (CRC)

GPO Box 2944, Canberra, ACT 2601, Australia
Tel: (61) 2 6260 9295
Fax: (61) 2 6260 9201
Email: crc@aic.gov.au
Website: www.aic.gov.au/crc
Contact: Administrator

The Criminology Research Council (CRC) funds methodologically sound research in the areas of sociology, psychology, law, statistics, police, judiciary, corrections, mental health, social welfare, education and related fields. The research to be conducted is policy-orientated, and research outcomes should have the potential for application nationally or in other jurisdictions.

CRC Grants

Subjects: Criminological research in the areas of sociology, psychology, law, statistics, police, judiciary and corrections, etc. From time to time the Council will call for research in specific areas.
Eligibility: Open to Australian residents or visitors (actual or intending) who are pursuing or intend to pursue studies of consequence to the furtherance of criminological research in Australia. Grants are not likely to be given for assistance with research leading to the award of postgraduate degrees.
Level of Study: Postdoctorate, doctorate
Type: Grant
Value: Usually Australian $25,000 paid in three instalments
Length of Study: Usually 1 year, with a possibility of renewal for up to 3 years
Frequency: Annual
Country of Study: Australia
No. of awards offered: Approx. 6
Application Procedure: Applicants must complete an application form, available from the CRC.
Closing Date: 12 weeks prior to meetings
Funding: Government
No. of awards given last year: 9
No. of applicants last year: 35
Additional Information: The Council does not ordinarily consider applications involving travelling expenses outside Australia. Meetings are held in March, July and November. The November meeting is for general grants funding in any area the council deems relevant.

THE CROHN'S AND COLITIS FOUNDATION OF AMERICA

386 Park Avenue South, 17th Floor, New York, NY, 10016-8804, United States of America
Tel: (1) 212 685 3440
Fax: (1) 212 779 4098
Email: info@ccfa.org
Website: www.ccfa.org
Contact: Ms Carol M Cox, Research Co-ordinator

The Crohn's and Colitis Foundation of America is a non-profit, voluntary health organization dedicated to improving the quality of life for persons with Crohn's disease or ulcerative colitis. It supports basic and clinical scientific research to find the causes and cure for these diseases, provides educational programmes for patients, medical and healthcare professionals and the general public, alongside offering supportive services to patients, their families and friends.

Crohn's and Colitis Foundation Career Development Award

Subjects: Crohn's disease and ulcerative colitis.
Purpose: To stimulate and encourage innovative research that is likely to increase our understanding of the aetiology, pathogenesis, therapy and prevention of Crohn's disease and ulcerative colitis (IBD).
Eligibility: Candidates should hold an MD and must have 5 years of experience (with 2 years of research relevant to IBD).
Level of Study: Research, postdoctorate
Value: Not to exceed US$90,000 per year
Length of Study: 1–3 years
Study Establishment: An approved research institute
Country of Study: United States of America
Application Procedure: All applicants must submit completed applications that consist of one CD ROM or disk in PDF or Word format, one master copy and four copies. The complete application must be compiled and saved as a single document.
Funding: Foundation, corporation

Crohn's and Colitis Foundation First Award

Subjects: Crohn's disease and ulcerative colitis.
Purpose: To underwrite the first independent investigative efforts of an individual, to provide a reasonable opportunity to demonstrate creativity, productivity and further promise and to help in the transition to traditional types of research project grants.
Eligibility: The applicant must be independent of a mentor yet at the same time must be at the beginning stages of his or her research career, with no more than 5 years of research experience since completing postdoctoral research training. The applicant must hold an MD, PhD or equivalent and be employed by an institution within the United States of America engaged in healthcare at the time of application.
Level of Study: Postdoctorate
Value: A maximum of US$60,000 in direct costs per year and indirect costs at 15 per cent of direct cost
Length of Study: A maximum of 3 years
Frequency: Annual
Study Establishment: Approved research institutions
Country of Study: United States of America
No. of awards offered: Varies
Application Procedure: Applicants must complete an application form in accordance with the guidelines. Please write for details.
Closing Date: January 14th or July 1st
Funding: Private
No. of awards given last year: 4

Crohn's and Colitis Foundation Research Fellowship Awards

Subjects: Crohn's disease and ulcerative colitis (IBD).
Purpose: To stimulate and encourage innovative research that is likely to increase our understanding of the aetiology, pathogenesis, therapy and prevention of Crohn's disease and ulcerative colitis (IBD).
Eligibility: Applicants must hold an MD, PhD or equivalent with at least 2 years of research experience.

Level of Study: Postdoctorate, research
Value: Not to exceed US$58,000 per year
Length of Study: 1–3 years
Study Establishment: An approved research institute
Country of Study: United States of America
Application Procedure: All completed applications must include one CD ROM or disk in PDF or Word format, one master copy and four copies. The complete application must be compiled and saved as a single document.
Funding: Individuals, foundation, corporation

Crohn's and Colitis Foundation Research Grant Program

Subjects: Inflammatory bowel disease including its cause, pathogenesis or treatment.
Purpose: To provide financial support for innovative basic and clinical research.
Eligibility: Open to qualified investigators in the United States of America and abroad.
Level of Study: Postdoctorate
Type: Research grant
Value: A maximum of US$100,000 for direct costs. Requests for purchases of major equipment totalling more than US$5,000 are not generally considered and the maximum amount allowed for overhead is 15 per cent of total direct costs
Length of Study: 2 years with a possibility of renewal for a further year
Frequency: Every 2 years
Country of Study: Any country
No. of awards offered: Varies
Application Procedure: Applicants must complete an application form in accordance with the guidelines.
Closing Date: January 14th or July 1st
Funding: Private
No. of awards given last year: 13

Crohn's and Colitis Foundation Senior Research Award

Subjects: Crohn's disease and ulcerative colitis (IBD).
Purpose: To stimulate and encourage innovative research that is likely to increase our understanding of the aetiology, pathogenesis, therapy and prevention of Crohn's disease and ulcerative colitis (IBD).
Eligibility: Applicants should be researchers who hold an MD, PhD or equivalent.
Level of Study: Postdoctorate, research
Type: Research award
Value: Up to US$100,000 direct cost per year plus indirect cost of 15 per cent of direct cost (or US$15,000, whichever is less)
Length of Study: Up to 2 years
Frequency: Annual
Study Establishment: An approved research institute
Country of Study: United States of America
Application Procedure: All completed applications must include one CD ROM or disk in PDF or Word format, one master copy and four copies. The complete application must be compiled and saved as a single document.
Closing Date: January 14th and July 1st
Funding: Corporation, foundation, individuals

Crohn's and Colitis Foundation Student Research Fellowship Awards

Subjects: Crohn's disease and ulcerative colitis (IBD).
Purpose: To stimulate and encourage innovative research that is likely to increase our understanding of the aetiology, pathogenesis, therapy and prevention of Crohn's disease and ulcerative colitis (IBD).
Eligibility: Applicants should be a medical student or graduate student studying at an accredited North American institution.
Level of Study: Postgraduate
Length of Study: US$2,500 per year
Frequency: Annual
Study Establishment: An approved research institute
Country of Study: United States of America
No. of awards offered: 16
Application Procedure: All completed applications must include one CD ROM or disk in PDF or Word format, one master copy and four copies collated in order per checklist. The complete application must be compiled and saved as a single document.
Closing Date: March 15th or June 15th
Funding: Individuals, foundation, corporation

THE CROSS TRUST

PO Box 17, 25 South Methven Street, Perth, Perthshire, PH1 5ES, Scotland
Tel: (44) 17 3862 0451
Fax: (44) 17 3863 1155
Contact: Mrs Dorothy Shaw, Assistant Secretary

The aim of the Cross Trust is to provide opportunities to young people of Scottish birth or parentage to extend the boundaries of their knowledge of human life. Proposals are to be of demonstrable merit from applicants with a record of academic distinction.

Cross Trust Grants

Subjects: Any approved subject.
Purpose: To enable young people to extend the boundaries of their knowledge and experience or to encourage performance and participation in drama or opera.
Eligibility: Open to graduates of Scottish universities, Scottish secondary school pupils or graduates of central institutions in Scotland. Applicants must be of Scottish birth or parentage.
Level of Study: Unrestricted
Type: Grant
Value: Varies
Length of Study: Varies
Frequency: Annual
Study Establishment: Any approved institute
Country of Study: Any country
No. of awards offered: Varies
Application Procedure: Applicants must complete an application form.
Closing Date: There is no deadline
Funding: Private
No. of awards given last year: 118
No. of applicants last year: 450
Additional Information: Awards will only be considered from postgraduate students who have part funding in place from another organization. The Trust may support the pursuit of studies or research.

THE CROUCHER FOUNDATION

Suite 501, Nine Queen's Road Central, Hong Kong
Tel: (852) 2 736 6337
Fax: (852) 2 730 0742
Email: cfadmin@croucher.org.hk
Website: www.croucher.org.hk
Contact: Ms Elaine Sit, Administrative Officer

Founded to promote education, learning and research in the areas of natural science, technology and medicine, the Croucher Foundation operates a scholarship and fellowship scheme for individual applicants who are permanent residents of Hong Kong wishing to pursue doctoral or postdoctoral research overseas. The Foundation otherwise makes grants to institutions only.

Croucher Foundation Fellowships and Scholarships

Subjects: Natural science, medicine and technology.
Purpose: To enable selected students of outstanding promise to devote themselves to full-time postgraduate study or research in approved academic institutions outside Hong Kong.
Eligibility: Open to permanent residents of Hong Kong. Fellowships are intended for recent PhD graduates and not for the funding of career vacancies in universities. Scholarships are intended for those undertaking a research degree, such as a PhD programme.
Level of Study: Postdoctorate, doctorate

Type: Scholarships, fellowships
Value: UK £17,280 per year for fellowships, and UK £9,960 per year and tution fees for scholarships, plus airfare assistance and other allowances
Length of Study: 1–2 years for fellowships, 1–3 years for scholarships
Frequency: Annual
Country of Study: Outside Hong Kong
No. of awards offered: Approx. 20–25
Application Procedure: Applicants must write requesting an application form stating whether they are applying for a scholarship or fellowship, and enclose a stamped addressed envelope, or download an application form from the website.
Closing Date: November 17th. Applicants should visit the website for the exact date every year
Funding: Private
No. of awards given last year: 28
No. of applicants last year: 138

CYSTIC FIBROSIS FOUNDATION (CFF)

Office of Grants Management, 6931 Arlington Road,
Bethesda, MD, 20814,
United States of America
Tel: (1) 301 951 4422
Fax: (1) 301 951 6378
Email: grants@cff.org
Website: www.cff.org
Contact: Grants Division

The mission of the Cystic Fibrosis Foundation (CFF) is to assure the development of the means to cure and control cystic fibrosis and to improve the quality of life for those with the disease.

CFF Research Programmes in Cystic Fibrosis

Subjects: Cystic fibrosis.
Purpose: To offer competitive awards for research.
Eligibility: Applicants must be citizens of the United States of America or have permanent resident status.
Level of Study: Doctorate, professional development
Type: Research grant
Value: Please contact the organization
Frequency: Annual
Country of Study: Any country
No. of awards offered: 8
Additional Information: The names of the awards are as follows: Therapeutics Development Grants, Pilot Feasibility Awards, Research Grants, Leroy Matthews Physician/Scientist Award, Harry Shwachman Clinical Investigator Award, Clinical Research Grants, CFF/NIH Funding Award and Special Research Awards. Applicants are advised to email the Foundation for further information as grants are currently under review.

CFF Training Programmes in Cystic Fibrosis

Subjects: Cystic fibrosis.
Purpose: To support individuals interested in careers related to cystic fibrosis research and care.
Eligibility: Open to citizens of the United States of America and permanent residents only.
Level of Study: Professional development, doctorate
Type: Varies
Value: From US$1,500–45,000
Frequency: Annual
Country of Study: Any country
No. of awards offered: 4 programmes
Application Procedure: Applicants must write for an application form.
Additional Information: The names of the specific awards are: Postdoctoral Research Fellowships, Clinical Fellowships, Student Traineeships and Summer Scholarships in Epidemiology. Applicants are advised to email the Foundation for further information as grants are currently under review.

CYSTIC FIBROSIS TRUST (CFT)

11 London Road, Bromley, Kent, BR1 1BY, England
Tel: (44) 20 8464 7211
Fax: (44) 20 8313 0472
Email: researchgrants@cfttrust.org.uk
Website: www.cftrust.org.uk
Contact: Research administrator

The Cystic Fibrosis Research Trust (CFRT) funds medical and scientific research aimed at understanding, treating and curing cystic fibrosis, and ensuring that sufferers receive the best possible care and support in all aspects of their lives.

CFT Fibrosis Trust

Subjects: Cystic fibrosis.
Purpose: To support research into cystic fibrosis.
Level of Study: Postgraduate, research, doctorate
Type: Studentship
Length of Study: Up to 3 years
Country of Study: United Kingdom
No. of awards offered: Varies
Application Procedure: Application form on request.
Closing Date: August 14th
Funding: Private

CFT Innovative Awards

Subjects: Cystic fibrosis.
Purpose: To provide support for a short-term, small-scale pilot research project.
Eligibility: Open to all established researchers within or outside of the CF field.
Type: Award
Value: Up to £45,000
Length of Study: 1 year
Study Establishment: University, hospital, medical school or other research institution

CFT PhD Studentships

Purpose: To encourage the best young science graduates to embark on a research career in CF.
Eligibility: Open to all science graduates who wish to pursue a research career in CF.
Level of Study: Postdoctorate, doctorate
Type: Grant
Value: Tax-free stipend, tuition fees and the running costs of the project

CFT Project Grants

Subjects: Cystic fibrosis.
Purpose: To provide support for a time-limited research projects.
Eligibility: University, hospital, medical school or other research institution.
Type: Grant
Value: Covers salary, running costs of the project and purchase of essential equipments
Length of Study: Up to 3 years

CYSTIC FIBROSIS WORLDWIDE

Administration office, P.O. Box 677, Eindhoven, 5600 AR,
Netherlands
Tel: (31) 40 2592 760
Fax: (31) 40 2592 701
Email: info@cfww.org
Website: www.cfww.org
Contact: Mrs Gina Steenkamer, Administration Office

Cystic Fibrosis Worldwide works to promote access to appropriate care and education to those people living with the disease in developing countries and to improve the knowledge of cystic fibrosis (CF) among medical professionals and governments worldwide.

CF Worldwide Scholarships

Subjects: Cystic fibrosis.
Purpose: To support individuals working in the field of clinical CF care wishing to improve their knowledge by undertaking research.
Eligibility: The applicant must come from a country or region where CF research is in need of improvement.
Level of Study: Postgraduate
Type: Scholarship
Value: Variable
Frequency: Annual
Application Procedure: Applicants must download details from the website.
Funding: Private

DAIMLER-BENZ FOUNDATION

Dr Carl-Benz-Platz 2, D-68526, Ladenburg, Germany
Tel: (49) 6203 1092 16
Fax: (49) 6203 1092 5
Email: info@daimler-benz-stiftung.de
Website: www.daimler-benz-stiftung.de

Research Scholarships (Diamler-Benz Foundation)

Subjects: All subjects.
Purpose: To support young foreigners to undertake doctoral research projects in Germany. The Foundation also supports selected research projects aimed at elucidating the interrelationships and interaction between humankind, the environment and technology.
Eligibility: Candidates of all nationalities may apply, but must not be older than 30 years.
Level of Study: Doctorate
Type: Scholarship
Value: €970 per month. Family allowance, conference allowance, travel grants
Length of Study: Up to 2 years
Country of Study: Germany
Application Procedure: Applications need not be submitted on a special form. Guidelines for applicants are available on request.
Closing Date: March 1st and October 1st
Contributor: Daimler-Benz Foundation

DALLAS COUNTY COMMUNITY COLLEGE DISTRICT (DCCCD) FOUNDATION, INC.

10 Elm Street, Suite 700, Dalls, TX 35202,
United States of America
Tel: (1) 214 860 2053
Fax: (1) 214 860 2040
Email: foundation@dcccd.edu
Website: www.dcccd.edu

The DCCCD Foundation created in 1973, is a vital resource for Dallas County, helping to foster ongoing partnerships between the DCCD and virtually all sectors of community life.

David McCopy Photography Scholarship

Subjects: Photography.
Purpose: To provide financial assistance to photography students attending Eastfield college.
Eligibility: Open to photography students attending Eastfield college who are in need of financial assistance.
Level of Study: Professional development
Type: Scholarship
Value: Up to US$250 per semester
Frequency: Annual
Study Establishment: Eastfield college
Country of Study: United States of America
No. of awards offered: Varies per available funds
Application Procedure: Contact Financial Aid office for further information.
Closing Date: Varies

DAMON RUNYON CANCER RESEARCH FOUNDATION

675 Third Avenue, New York, NY 10017, United States of America
Tel: (1) 212 455 0520
Email: awards@drcrf.org
Website: www.drcrf.org

The Damon Runyon Cancer Research Foundation identifies and supports extraordinary young scientists across the nation who are committed to discovering the causes and cures for cancer.

Damon Runyon Cancer Research Foundation Fellowship Award

Subjects: Understanding the causes and mechanisms of cancer and developing more effective cancer therapies and preventions.
Purpose: To encourage all theoretical and experimental research relevant to the study of cancer and the search for cancer causes, mechanisms, therapies and prevention.
Eligibility: Legal residents or citizens of the United States of America working abroad. Candidates must be at the beginning of their 1st full-time postdoctoral fellowship. Candidate cannot be in the sponsor's laboratory for more than 1 year.
Level of Study: Postdoctorate
Type: Fellowship
Value: US$39,000–57,000 per year
Length of Study: 3 years
Study Establishment: Suitable accredited establishment within the United States of America
Country of Study: United States of America
No. of awards offered: 50–60 per year
Application Procedure: Applicants should download an application from the website. Fellowship awards are to be approved by the Board of Directors of the Damon Runyon Cancer Research Foundation acting upon the recommendation of the Scientific Advisory Committee.
Funding: Private
No. of awards given last year: 53
No. of applicants last year: 477

Damon Runyon Scholar Award

Subjects: Understanding the causes and mechanisms of cancer and developing more effective cancer therapies and preventions.
Purpose: To support the development of outstanding scientists as independent investigators in the cancer field by helping foster their research productivity during the first few years of their first faculty position.
Eligibility: Researchers must show exceptional promise within the first 3 years of their appointment as assistant professor.
Level of Study: Professional development, postdoctorate
Type: Grant
Value: US$100,000 per year
Length of Study: 3 years
Frequency: Annual
Country of Study: United States of America
No. of awards offered: 5
Application Procedure: The application must be made within 3 years of the initial faculty appointment. The institution and department must guarantee, in written form, a commitment to the individual and the development of their laboratory and career.
Closing Date: July 1st
Funding: Private
No. of awards given last year: 5
No. of applicants last year: 87
Additional Information: The award will be allocated to the awardee's institution, with the understanding that it is to be used for the awardee's salary, technical support and/or equipment. The award may not be used for institutional overhead or indirect costs.

The Damon Runyon-Lilly Clinical Investigator Award

Subjects: Understanding the causes and mechanisms of cancer and developing more effective cancer therapies and preventions.
Purpose: To support young scientists conducting patient-orientated cancer research.
Eligibility: This award is specifically intended to provide outstanding young physicians with the resources and training

structure essential to becoming independent clinical investigators.
Level of Study: Professional development, research
Type: Grant
Value: US$100,000, stipend US$75,000, research allowance US$30,000, mentor stipend up to US$100,000 payment of medical student debt
Length of Study: Up to 5 years
Frequency: Annual
Study Establishment: Suitable facilities within the United States of America
Country of Study: United States of America
No. of awards offered: 5
Application Procedure: Application form can be downloaded from the website.
Closing Date: March 1st
Funding: Private
Contributor: Eli-Lilly
No. of awards given last year: 5
No. of applicants last year: 41

DANISH CANCER SOCIETY

Strandboulevarden 49, DK-2100, Copenhagen, Denmark
Tel: (45) 3525 7500
Fax: (45) 3525 7701
Email: info@cancer.dk
Website: www.cancer.dk
Contact: Ms Birgit Christensen, Head Secretary

The Danish Cancer Society's mission is to fight cancer and its consequences through research, preventative measures and support for patients and their families. Patient's interests in relation to authorities are also represented.

Danish Cancer Society Psychosocial Research Award

Subjects: Psychology.
Purpose: To support research on cancer-related projects in psychology.
Eligibility: Only cancer-related projects will be granted.
Level of Study: Research
Length of Study: Up to 5 years
Frequency: Annual
Country of Study: Denmark
Application Procedure: Applicants should visit the website for details.
Funding: Private
Contributor: Legacies, testamentary gifts and investment income lotteries
No. of awards given last year: 30
No. of applicants last year: 49

Danish Cancer Society Scientific Award

Subjects: Medical and natural sciences.
Purpose: To support research on cancer-related projects.
Eligibility: Only cancer-related projects will be granted.
Level of Study: Research
Length of Study: Up to 5 years
Frequency: Annual
Country of Study: Denmark
Application Procedure: Applicants should visit the website for details.
Funding: Private
Contributor: Legacies, testamentary gifts and investment income lotteries
No. of awards given last year: 179
No. of applicants last year: 370

DEAKIN UNIVERSITY

221 Burwood Highway, Burwood, Victoria, 3125, Australia
Tel: (61) 3 9244 5095
Fax: (61) 3 9244 5094
Website: www.deakin.edu

Established in the 1970s, Deakin University is one of Australia's largest universities providing all the resources of a major university to more than 32,000 award students. The University's reputation for excellent teaching and innovative course delivery has been recognized through many awards over the past few years.

Coltman Scholarship

Subjects: Biomedical science.
Purpose: To recognize outstanding achievement and ability within the student's particular area of research.
Eligibility: Open to students undertaking research in biomedical sciences.
Level of Study: Postgraduate
Type: Scholarship
Value: Australian $3,000 and a framed certificate
Frequency: Annual
Application Procedure: Contact the website.

Edward Wilson Scholarship for Graduate Diploma of Journalism

Subjects: Journalism.
Purpose: To assist students pursuing journalism.
Eligibility: Open to Australian citizens undertaking postgraduate studies in journalism.
Level of Study: Postgraduate
Type: Scholarship
Value: Tuition fees
Length of Study: 2 years
Frequency: Annual
No. of awards offered: 1
Application Procedure: A completed application form must be submitted.
Closing Date: October 7th

Helen Macpherson Smith Trust Scholarship

Subjects: Arts and entertainment management.
Purpose: To financially support outstanding students.
Eligibility: Open to students who may benefit from financial assistance.
Level of Study: Postgraduate
Type: Scholarship
Value: Australian $500
Length of Study: 1 year
Frequency: Annual
No. of awards offered: 2
Application Procedure: See the website.
Closing Date: October 31st

The Isi Leibler Prize

Subjects: Area and cultural studies.
Purpose: To advance knowledge of multiculturism and community relations in Australia.
Eligibility: Open to students who have submitted a postgraduate or doctoral thesis at the university.
Level of Study: Doctorate, postgraduate
Type: Award
Value: Australian $250
Frequency: Annual
Study Establishment: Deakin University
Country of Study: Australia
Application Procedure: Completed application form plus additional information must be submitted.
Closing Date: January 20

For further information contact:

Vice-Chancellor's Prizes Committee, Academic Administrative Services Division, Geelong Waterfront Campus, Deakin University, Geelong, Vic 3217

Rex Williamson Prize

Subjects: Chemistry.
Purpose: To award students showing the best research potential and academic merit.

Eligibility: Open to students enrolled within the school of biological and chemical sciences.
Level of Study: Postgraduate
Type: Award
Value: Australian $1,200 and a framed certificate
Frequency: Annual
Application Procedure: See the website.

Tennis Australia Prize

Subjects: Sport management.
Purpose: To recognize outstanding achievement.
Eligibility: Open to outstanding students of Master's/graduate certificate of business.
Level of Study: Postgraduate
Type: Award
Value: Australian $750
Frequency: Annual
Application Procedure: A completed application form must be submitted.
Closing Date: October 31st

DEBRA UK

DEBRA House, 13 Wellington Business Park, Dukes Ride, Crowthorne, Berkshire, RG45 6LS, England
Tel: (44) 13 4477 1961
Fax: (44) 13 4476 2661
Email: debra@debra.org.uk
Website: www.debra.org.uk

DEBRA UK is the national charity working on behalf of people with the genetic skin blistering condition, epidermolysis bullosa (EB).

DEBRA UK Research Grant Scheme

Subjects: Epidermolysis bullosa.
Purpose: To fund research into epidermolysis bullosa (EB).
Eligibility: Applicants must be productive postdoctorates, usually with a track record as a principal investigator.
Level of Study: Postdoctorate
Type: Project grant
Value: Average UK £40,000–50,000 per year
Length of Study: Grants for projects are usually for 1–3 years
Frequency: Twice yearly
No. of awards offered: Varies
Application Procedure: Application form can be downloaded from the website www.debra-international.org or from the DEBRA UK Office.
Closing Date: April 1st and October 1st each year
Funding: Private
Contributor: Charitable funding
No. of awards given last year: 11
No. of applicants last year: 15

DELTA SOCIETY

875 124th Ave NE Ste 101, Bellevue, WA, 98005-2531, United States of America
Tel: (1) 425 226 7357
Fax: (1) 425 235 1076
Email: info@deltasociety.org
Website: www.deltasociety.org
Contact: Administrative Assistant

The Delta Society's mission is to improve human health through service and therapy animals. The Society does this by expanding awareness of the positive effects animals can have on family health and human development, reducing barriers to the involvement of animals in everyday life, delivering animal assisted therapy to more people and by increasing the availability of well-trained service dogs.

James M Harris/Sarah W Sweatt Student Travel Grant

Subjects: Veterinary medicine, general medical sciences and general education.
Purpose: To provide an annual grant for transportation costs for a student to attend the Delta Society Training Conference.
Eligibility: Open to students who are enrolled full-time in a veterinary or human health professional training programme pursuing a Master's or doctoral degree.
Level of Study: Postgraduate
Type: Travel grant
Value: Transportation costs
Frequency: Annual
Country of Study: United States of America
No. of awards offered: 1
Application Procedure: Applicants must contact the Society for details.
Closing Date: Varies

DEMOCRATIC NURSING ORGANIZATION OF SOUTH AFRICA (DENOSA)

PO Box 1280, Pretoria, 0001, South Africa
Tel: (27) 12 343 2315
Fax: (27) 12 344 0750
Email: info@denosa.org.za
Website: www.denosa.org.za
Contact: Executive Director

The Democratic Nursing Organization of South Africa (DENOSA) is a professional organization and labour union for nurses in South Africa.

DENOSA Bursaries, Scholarships and Grants

Subjects: Nursing.
Purpose: To encourage postbasic studies at a South African teaching institution.
Eligibility: Open to members of the organization in good standing who hold the required registered nursing qualifications.
Level of Study: Doctorate, graduate, professional development, postgraduate
Type: Bursary
Value: Varies
Study Establishment: A South African teaching institution
No. of awards offered: Varies
Application Procedure: Applicants must complete an application form.
Closing Date: January 31st
Funding: Private
Contributor: Donor funding
No. of awards given last year: 125
No. of applicants last year: 158

THE DENMARK-AMERICA FOUNDATION

Fiolstraede 24, 3rd Floor, DK-1171, Copenhagen, Denmark
Tel: (45) 3312 8323
Fax: (45) 3332 5323
Email: daf-fulb@daf-fulb.dk
Website: www.daf-fulb.dk
Contact: Ms Marie Monsted, Executive Director

The Denmark-America Foundation was founded in 1914 as a private foundation, and today its work remains based on donations from Danish firms, foundations and individuals. The Foundation offers scholarships for studies in the United States of America at the graduate and postgraduate university level and also has a trainee programme.

Denmark-America Foundation Grants

Subjects: All subjects.
Purpose: To further understanding between Denmark and the United States of America.
Eligibility: Open to Danes and Danish-American citizens.
Level of Study: Professional development, mba, postdoctorate, graduate, postgraduate, research

Type: Bursary
Value: Varies
Length of Study: 3 months–1 year
Frequency: Annual
Country of Study: United States of America
No. of awards offered: Varies
Application Procedure: Applicants must complete a special application form, available by contacting the secretariat.
Funding: Private
No. of awards given last year: 34–35
No. of applicants last year: 250

DENTISTRY CANADA FUND (DCF)

Scilan House, 427 Gilmour Street, Ottawa, ON, K2P 0R5, Canada
Tel: (1) 613 236 4763
Fax: (1) 613 236 3935
Email: information@dcf-fdc.ca
Website: www.dcf-fdc.ca
Contact: Co-ordinator Administration

The Dentistry Canada Fund (DCF) is the national charitable foundation dedicated to assisting in the encouragement of optimal oral health in Canada through education, research and promotion.

DCF Biennial Research Award

Subjects: Dentistry.
Purpose: To encourage research.
Eligibility: Open to graduate or postgraduate students who have conducted their research in association with a Canadian dental faculty. Applicants must either be in their graduating year or the ensuing year.
Level of Study: Postgraduate, graduate
Type: Research grant
Value: Canadian $2,000 plus a commemorative plaque
Frequency: Every 2 years
Country of Study: Canada
No. of awards offered: 1
Application Procedure: Applicants must submit one typewritten double-spaced copy, not exceeding 25 pages, and four copies of an original research project in the form of a paper. The manuscript should not be a previously published paper of the candidate's graduate work currently in press or already published in a scientific journal. Each applicant must also send a current curriculum vitae.
Closing Date: October 1st
Additional Information: Each entry will be reviewed by three referees appointed by the CDA Committee on Dental Materials and Devices. The decision of the Committee is final.

DCF Fellowships for Teacher/Researcher Training

Subjects: Dentistry.
Purpose: To provide financial assistance to students who wish to pursue a career in dentistry research or teaching at the graduate level.
Eligibility: Applicants must be Canadian citizens or permanent residents who have completed a course in dentistry, a dental hygiene programme or a programme in science and also be eligible for admission to a graduate or other advanced education programme.
Level of Study: Postgraduate
Type: Fellowship
Value: The value of the award is dependent on the funds available and the number of applications received.
Country of Study: Canada
Application Procedure: Applicants must submit an application including official transcripts of previous postsecondary education and a letter of recommendation from a faculty member of the applicant's postsecondary institution and from the administrative head of the institution and department where he or she expects to be employed. All applications must include a curriculum vitae.
Closing Date: February 1st
Funding: Corporation
Contributor: Pfizer Canada
No. of awards given last year: 2
No. of applicants last year: 5

DEPARTMENT FOR EMPLOYMENT AND LEARNING

Adelaide House, 39-49 Adelaide Street, Belfast, BT2 8FD, Northern Ireland
Tel: (44) 28 9025 7710
Fax: (44) 28 9025 7747
Email: del@nics.gov.uk
Website: www.delni.gov.uk
Contact: Mrs Siobhan Woods

The Department for Employment and Learning makes available research and advanced course studentships, to provide for both the payment of approved fees and the maintenance of students who are being trained in methods of research and undertaking approved postgraduate courses of instruction.

DEL Postgraduate Studentships and Bursaries for Study in Northern Ireland

Subjects: Science, technology, social sciences and humanities.
Purpose: To provide students ordinarily resident in the United Kingdom with bursaries.
Eligibility: Open to United Kingdom and European Union residents only. Applicants for studentships must have at least an Upper Second Class (Honours) Degree. Bursaries are open to United Kingdom residents who must be ordinarily resident in Northern Ireland on the date of the application for an award and hold a university degree or qualification regarded by the department as equivalent to a degree.
Level of Study: Postgraduate
Type: Bursary and scholarship
Value: In line with the other United Kingdom awarding bodies
Length of Study: Varies
Frequency: Annual
Study Establishment: Appropriate institutions
Country of Study: Northern Ireland
No. of awards offered: Varies, determined by universities
Application Procedure: Applicants must complete an application form, available from universities in Northern Ireland.
Closing Date: Deadlines are determined by the institution concerned
Funding: Government

DEPARTMENT OF EDUCATION AND SCIENCE (IRELAND)

International Section, Training College Building, Marlborough Street, Dublin, 1, Ireland
Tel: (353) 1 889 6400
Fax: (353) 1 889 2376
Email: dolores_ronane@education.gov.ie
Website: www.education.ie
Contact: Ms Ivanna D'Arcy, International Section

The Department of Education and Science's (Ireland) International Section deals with International Scholarships from foreign governments with whom Ireland has a cultural agreement.

Department of Education and Science (Ireland) Exchange Scholarships and Postgraduate Scholarships Exchange Scheme

Subjects: All subjects.
Purpose: To allow students to pursue study or research in Ireland.
Eligibility: Open to Australian, Austrian, Belgian, Chinese, Finnish, German, Greek, Italian, Japanese, Dutch, Norwegian, Russian Federation, Spanish and Swiss nationals who are university graduates and have completed at least three years of academic study. A good knowledge of English or Irish is necessary, depending on the course taken.
Level of Study: Postgraduate, graduate
Type: Scholarship
Value: Please contact the association for details
Length of Study: 8 months
Frequency: Annual

Study Establishment: An Irish University or Institute of Higher Education
Country of Study: Ireland
No. of awards offered: 28
Application Procedure: Applicants must apply to the appropriate institution in their home country.
Closing Date: April 30th
Funding: Government
No. of awards given last year: 25

Department of Education and Science (Ireland) Summer School Exchange Scholarships

Subjects: All subjects.
Purpose: To allow European students to attend a summer school in Ireland.
Eligibility: Open to Belgian, French, Finnish, German, Hungarian, Italian, Dutch, Czech Republic, Russian Federation and Spanish nationals who are university graduates. A good knowledge of English or Irish is necessary, depending on the course taken.
Level of Study: Unrestricted
Type: Scholarship
Value: Please contact the association for details
Length of Study: 2 weeks–1 month
Frequency: Annual
Study Establishment: Summer schools at University College Dublin, University College Galway or University College Cork
Country of Study: Ireland
No. of awards offered: 34
Application Procedure: Applicants must apply to the appropriate institution in their home country.
Closing Date: April 30th
Funding: Government
No. of awards given last year: 20
No. of applicants last year: 20

DESCENDANTS OF THE SIGNERS OF THE DECLARATION OF INDEPENDENCE (DSDI)

DSDI Scholarship Committee, PO Box 224, Suncook, NH 03275, United States of America
Website: www.dsdi1776.com
Contact: Mr Phillip Kennedy, DSDI Scholarship Chairman

Descendants of the Signers of the Declaration of Independence Scholarships

Subjects: All subjects.
Purpose: To financially assist descendants of the signers of the Declaration of Independence (those who prove eligibility and become members of this Society) to pursue their goals in higher education.
Eligibility: Open to proven direct lineal descendants of a signer of the Declaration of Independence. Proof of lineage must be established before an application is sent. Applicants must give the name of their ancestor signer in their first communication or they will not receive a reply. Applicants must be attending an accredited 4-year college or university course full-time, in graduate or undergraduate study.
Level of Study: Unrestricted
Type: Scholarship
Value: US$3,000, paid directly to the institution. Funds may be applied towards any costs chargeable to the students college account, ie. room, board, books, fees, tuition
Frequency: Annual
Country of Study: United States of America
No. of awards offered: 3
Closing Date: March 15th
Funding: Private
No. of awards given last year: 3
No. of applicants last year: 25
Additional Information: Only those with proven descent (a Society member number) will receive an application. Competition among eligible applicants is based on merit, need and length of time to graduation.

DEUTSCHE FORSCHUNGSGEMEINSCHAFT (DFG)

Kennedyallee 40, Bonn, 53175, Germany
Tel: (49) 0228 885 1
Fax: (49) 0228 885 2777
Email: postmaster@dfg.de
Website: www.dfg.de

The DFG is a central, self-governing research organization, which promotes research at universities and other publicity financial research institutions in Germany. The DFG serves all branches of science and the humanities by funding research projects and facilitating cooperation among researchers.

Albert Maucher Prize

Subjects: Geosciences.
Purpose: To promote outstanding young scientists and scholars in the field of geosciences.
Eligibility: Open to promising young scientists and scholars up to the age of 35 years who are German nationals or permanent residents of Germany.
Level of Study: Postdoctorate
Type: Award
Value: Please contact the organization
Length of Study: Varies
Frequency: Every 2 years
Study Establishment: Approved universities or research institutions
Country of Study: Germany
Application Procedure: Applicants must write for details or visit the website. Application is by nomination.
Contributor: Professor Albert Maucher

Copernicus Award

Subjects: All subjects.
Purpose: To promote young researchers to further advance research and contribute to the German–Polish research cooperation.
Eligibility: Open to outstanding researchers in Germany and Poland who work at universities or research institutions.
Type: Award
Value: €50,000
Length of Study: 5 years
Frequency: Every 2 years
No. of awards offered: 2
Application Procedure: A completed application form along with the required documents should be submitted.
Contributor: The Foundation for Polish Science and the DFG

For further information contact:

Tel: (0) 228 885 2372
Email: torsten.fischer@dfg.de
Contact: Dr Torsten Fischer

DFG Collaborative Research Grants

Subjects: All subjects.
Purpose: To promote long-term co-operative research in universities and academic research.
Eligibility: Open to promising groups of German nationals and permanent residents of Germany.
Level of Study: Postdoctorate, research
Type: Research grant
Value: Dependent on the requirements of the project
Length of Study: Up to 12 years
Study Establishment: Universities and academic institutions
Country of Study: Germany
No. of awards offered: Varies
Application Procedure: Applicants must write or visit the website for further information. Applications must be formally filed by the universities.
Closing Date: No submission deadline
Additional Information: A list of collaborative research centres is available in Germany only from the DFG.

DFG Individual Research Grants

Subjects: All subjects.
Purpose: To foster the proposed research projects of promising academic scientists or scholars.
Eligibility: Open to promising researchers and scholars who are German nationals or permanent residents of Germany.
Level of Study: Doctorate
Type: Grant
Value: Dependent on the requirements of the project
Length of Study: Based on individual project needs
Study Establishment: Universities
Country of Study: Any country
No. of awards offered: Varies
Application Procedure: Applicants must submit a proposal for a research project. Applicants must write for more details or visit the website.
Closing Date: Applications are accepted at any time

DFG Mercator Programme Guest Professorships

Subjects: All subjects.
Purpose: To support stays of foreign scientists at German universities.
Eligibility: Open to foreign scientists whose individual research is of special interest to research and teaching in Germany.
Level of Study: Postdoctorate
Type: Fellowship
Value: Dependent on the duration of the stay
Length of Study: 3 months–1 year
Frequency: Annual
Study Establishment: German universities
Country of Study: Germany
No. of awards offered: Varies
Application Procedure: A proposal must be submitted by the university intending to host the guest professor.

DFG Priority Programme Funds

Subjects: All subjects.
Purpose: To promote proposals made by interested groups of scientists in selected fields.
Eligibility: Open to interested groups of scientists from Germany or any country participating in the scheme.
Level of Study: Research, postdoctorate
Type: Grant
Value: The Senate decides on the financial ceiling for each programme
Length of Study: Up to 6 years
Frequency: Annual
Study Establishment: Universities or academic establishments
Country of Study: Germany
No. of awards offered: 30
Application Procedure: Applicants must write or visit the website for further information. Priority programmes are operated through calls for proposals, with all applications subject to open panel review, usually after discussion with the applicants.
Closing Date: November 15th

DFG Research Training Grant

Subjects: All subjects.
Purpose: To promote high-quality graduate studies at the doctoral level through the participation of graduate students recruited through countrywide calls in research programmes.
Eligibility: Open to highly qualified graduate and doctoral students of any nationality.
Level of Study: Postgraduate, predoctorate
Type: Grant
Length of Study: Up to 9 years
Frequency: Annual
Study Establishment: Any approved university
Country of Study: Germany
No. of awards offered: Varies
Application Procedure: Applications should be submitted in response to calls. For further information applicants must visit the website.
Closing Date: April 1st and October 1st, preliminary version to be submitted 3 months prior to these dates
Additional Information: A list of graduate colleges presently funded is available (in Germany only) from the DFG.

DFG Research Unit Grants

Subjects: All subjects.
Purpose: To promote intensive co-operation between highly qualified researchers in one or several institutions in fields of high scientific promise.
Eligibility: Open to interested groups of German nationals and permanent residents of Germany.
Level of Study: Postdoctorate, research
Type: Research grant
Value: Dependent on the requirements of the project
Length of Study: Up to 6 years
Frequency: Annual
Study Establishment: An approved university
Country of Study: Germany
No. of awards offered: Varies
Application Procedure: Applicants must submit proposals to the Senate of the DFG. Applicants must write or visit the website for further information.
Closing Date: No submission deadline
Additional Information: A list of currently operating research groups is available in Germany only from the DFG.

Emmy Noether Programme

Subjects: All subjects.
Purpose: To give outstanding young scholars the opportunity to obtain the scientific qualifications needed to be appointed as a lecturer.
Eligibility: Open to promising young postdoctoral scientists up to 30 years of age, who are German nationals or permanent residents of Germany within 5 years of receiving their PhD.
Level of Study: Postdoctorate
Type: Project grant
Value: For the 2 years of research spent abroad the candidate will receive a project grant in keeping with the requirements of the project including an allowance for subsistence and travel. For the 3 years of research spent at a German university or research institution the candidate will receive a project grant
Length of Study: 5 years
Frequency: Annual
Study Establishment: Universities or research institutions
Country of Study: Any country
No. of awards offered: 100
Application Procedure: Applicants must complete an application form. For further information applicants must write or visit the website.
Closing Date: Applications may be submitted at any time.

For further information contact:

Tel: (0) 228 885 2124
Email: vera.herkommer@dfg.de
Contact: Dr Vera Herkommer

Eugen and Ilse Seibold Award

Subjects: Humanities, social science, law, economics, natural sciences, engineering and medicine.
Purpose: To promote outstanding young scientists and scholars who have made significant contributions to the scientific interchange between Japan and Germany.
Eligibility: Open to outstanding young German or Japanese scholars.
Level of Study: Postdoctorate
Type: Award
Value: €10,000
Length of Study: Varies
Frequency: Every 2 years
Study Establishment: Universities or research institutions
No. of awards offered: 2
Application Procedure: Applicants must write for details or visit the website. Application is by nomination.
Closing Date: August 31st

For further information contact:

Tel: (0) 228 885 2724
Email: ina.sauer@dfg.de
Contact: Dr Ina Sauer

Gottfried Wilhelm Leibniz Prize

Subjects: All subjects.
Purpose: To promote outstanding scientists and scholars in German universities and research institutions.
Eligibility: Open to outstanding scholars in German universities.
Level of Study: Predoctorate, research
Type: Research grant
Value: Please contact the organization
Length of Study: 5 years
Frequency: Annual
Study Establishment: Any approved university or research institution
Country of Study: Germany
No. of awards offered: Varies
Application Procedure: Applicants must write for details or visit the website. Application is by nomination. Nominations are restricted to selected institutions such as DFG member organizations or individuals eg. former prize winners or chairpersons of DFG review committees.
Additional Information: A list of prize winners is available in Germany only from the DFG.

Heinz Maier-Leibnitz Prize

Subjects: All subjects.
Purpose: To promote outstanding young scientists at the doctorate level.
Eligibility: Open to promising young scholars up to 33 years of age, who are German nationals or permanent residents of Germany.
Level of Study: Postdoctorate, doctorate
Type: Award
Value: €16,000
Length of Study: Varies
Frequency: Annual
Study Establishment: Any approved university or research institution
Country of Study: Germany
No. of awards offered: 6
Application Procedure: Applicants must write for details or visit the website. Application is by nomination.
Closing Date: August 31st
Funding: Government
Contributor: The Federal Ministry of Education and Research

For further information contact:

Tel: (0) 228 885 2724
Email: ina.sauer@dfg.de
Contact: Dr Ina Sauer

Heisenberg Programme

Subjects: All subjects.
Purpose: To promote outstanding young scientists.
Eligibility: Open to high-calibre young scientists up to the age of 35 years who are German nationals or permanent residents of Germany.
Level of Study: Postdoctorate
Type: Scholarship
Value: Varies
Length of Study: 5 years
Frequency: Annual
Study Establishment: Any approved university or research institution
Country of Study: Germany
No. of awards offered: Varies
Application Procedure: Applicants must submit a research proposal, a detailed curriculum vitae, copies of degree certificates, a copy of the thesis, a letter explaining the choice of host institution, a list of all previously published material and a letter outlining financial requirements in duplicate. For further information applicants must contact the DFG.
Closing Date: Applications are accepted at any time

For further information contact:

Tel: (0) 228 885 2398
Email: paul.heuermann@dfg.de
Contact: Paul Heuermann

Ursula M. Handel Animal Welfare Prize

Subjects: Animal welfare.
Purpose: To award scientists who have a significant contribution to the welfare of animals in research.
Eligibility: Open to scientists who aim at improving the welfare of animals in research.
Level of Study: Postdoctorate
Type: Award
Value: €25,000
Frequency: Annual
No. of awards offered: Varies
Application Procedure: A completed application form and required documents must be submitted.
Funding: Trusts
Contributor: Mrs. Ursula M. Handel

For further information contact:

Tel: +49 (0) 228-885-2297
Email: hans joachim.bode@dfg.de
Contact: Dr Hans Joachim Bode

DIABETES RESEARCH & WELLNESS FOUNDATION

Office 101-102, Northney Marina, Hayling Island, Hampshire, PO11 0NH, England
Tel: (44) 23 9263 7808
Fax: (44) 23 9263 6137
Email: drwf@drwf.org.uk
Website: www.drwf.org.uk
Contact: Mrs S. Dixon, Grants Administrator

The Diabetes Research & Wellness Foundation was established in 1998 to fund research into finding a cure for diabetes. Each year this goal becomes more important as the number of people diagnosed continues to rise. The organization hopes to make diabetes a thing of the past, and, until then, alleviate its awful complications.

DRWF Open Funding

Subjects: Endocrinology or diabetes.
Purpose: To encourage research.
Level of Study: Doctorate, postgraduate, research
Type: Grant
Value: Up to UK £30,000
Length of Study: 1 year
Frequency: Annual
Study Establishment: A recognized institution or research group in the United Kingdom
Country of Study: United Kingdom
No. of awards offered: Up to 6, depending on grant amount
Application Procedure: Applications should be no more than 4 sides of A4 paper, typed using single-line spacing and an 11 or 12 point clearly readable font. They should include (as appropriate): applicant's name, qualifications, present post and contact details; name and address of the institution(s) where the work will be carried out; head of department/institution and major participants in the project; signed verification of funding application by HOD, outline of the proposed research comprising title, research question, relevance to diabetes, expected outcome; lay summary of the research question; any additional information to support the application; amount of funding requested, with a general breakdown of costs; and a (brief) curriculum vitae of the main applicant on separate single sheet of A4.
Closing Date: September 8th
Funding: Private, commercial
No. of awards given last year: 5

No. of applicants last year: 33
Additional Information: Notification of awards in November.

DRWF Research Fellowship

Subjects: Endocrinology or diabetes.
Purpose: To encourage research.
Eligibility: Open to suitable candidates who are working at an institution within the United Kingdom in an established position.
Level of Study: Doctorate, research, postdoctorate
Type: Fellowship
Value: Up to UK £195,000 for the non-clinical fellowship and up to UK £130,000 for the clinical fellowship
Length of Study: Up to 3 years for the non-clinical fellowship and up to 2 years for the clinical fellowship
Frequency: Annual
Study Establishment: A recognized institution or research group in the United Kingdom
Country of Study: United Kingdom
No. of awards offered: 1
Application Procedure: Applicants must undergo a three-stage selection procedure starting with a pre-application. This is a single side of A4 paper, with single-line spacing and a clearly readable font in 11 or 12 points. The pre-application must include the applicant's name, qualifications, contact details and present post. The pre-application must also include the name of the head of the group, see open funding addition where the grant will be held, the post held or expected post to be held within the group and the relevant contact details of the group. There should also be a 300-word abstract of the proposed research work including the title, a research question of approximately 300 words, relevance to diabetes, expected outcome and any additional information to support the application, but no references. Lastly, a brief curriculum vitae of the applicant on a separate single sheet of A4 paper must be provided. Successful applicants at the pre-selection stage are required to submit a full application by August.
Closing Date: April 28th
Funding: Private, commercial
No. of awards given last year: 1
No. of applicants last year: 10
Additional Information: Fellowships are alternated between clinical and non-clinical, year by year. Final interviews of selected candidates are held in October. The recipient of the fellowship is expected to take it up early in the following year.

DIABETES UK

10 Parkway, London, NW1 7AA, England
Tel: (44) 20 7424 1833
Fax: (44) 20 7424 1082
Email: eleanor.kennedy@diabetes.org.uk
Website: www.diabetes.org.uk
Contact: Dr Eleanor Kennedy, Research Manager

Diabetes UK's overall aim is to help and care for both people with diabetes and those closest to them, to represent and campaign for their interests and to fund research into diabetes. Diabetes UK continues to encourage research into all areas of diabetes.

Diabetes UK Equipment Grant

Subjects: Endocrinology, diabetes and subjects relevant to diabetes.
Purpose: To enable the purchase of equipment that is required only for a single project or programme and is solely concerned with diabetes research.
Eligibility: Open to suitably qualified members of the medical or scientific professions who are resident in the United Kingdom.
Level of Study: Postdoctorate
Type: Grant
Value: More than UK £5,000
Frequency: 3 times a year
Country of Study: United Kingdom
No. of awards offered: Varies
Application Procedure: Applicants must complete an application form, which will be assessed by a peer review. Please write or telephone for details. Details can be found on the website.
Closing Date: April 1st, August 1st and December 1st
Funding: Private
Contributor: Voluntary contributions
No. of awards given last year: 3

Diabetes UK Project Grants

Subjects: Endocrinology, diabetes and subjects relevant to diabetes.
Purpose: To provide funding for a well-defined research proposal of timeliness and promise that, in terms of the application, may be expected to lead to a significant advance in our knowledge of diabetes.
Eligibility: Open to suitably qualified members of the medical or scientific professions who are resident in the United Kingdom.
Level of Study: Postdoctorate
Type: Project grant
Value: A maximum of UK £50,000 per year
Length of Study: 1–3 years
Frequency: Every 3 years
Country of Study: United Kingdom
No. of awards offered: Varies
Application Procedure: Applicants must complete an application form, which will be assessed by a peer review and should write or telephone for details. Details can be found on the website.
Closing Date: April 1st, August 1st and December 1st
Funding: Private
Contributor: Voluntary contributions
No. of awards given last year: 9
No. of applicants last year: 10

Diabetes UK Research Fellowships

Subjects: Diabetes mellitus, diabetes or subjects relevant to diabetes.
Eligibility: Open to suitably qualified members of the medical or scientific professions who are resident in the United Kingdom.
Level of Study: Postdoctorate
Type: Fellowship
Value: Varies
Length of Study: 2–3 years
Frequency: Annual
Country of Study: United Kingdom
No. of awards offered: Varies
Application Procedure: Applicants must complete an application form and should write or telephone for details. Details can be found on the website.
Closing Date: June 1st
Funding: Private
Contributor: Members' donations and subscriptions
No. of awards given last year: 4
Additional Information: Availability is advertised annually in the scientific and medical press.

Diabetes UK Research Studentships

Subjects: Endocrinology, diabetes and subjects relevant to diabetes.
Purpose: To train basic scientists in diabetes research.
Eligibility: Open to potential supervisors in single departments or in collaborative projects between departments, preclinical or clinical. Applicants must be resident in the United Kingdom.
Level of Study: Postgraduate
Type: Studentship
Value: In London UK £11,500 maintenance and UK £5,000 laboratory expenses. Outside London UK £10,500 maintenance and UK £5,000 laboratory expenses
Length of Study: 3 years
Frequency: Annual
Country of Study: United Kingdom
No. of awards offered: Varies
Application Procedure: Applicants must complete an application form. Please write or telephone for details. Details can be found on the website.
Closing Date: September
Funding: Private
Contributor: Voluntary contributions
No. of awards given last year: 4
Additional Information: Availability is advertised annually in the scientific and medical press.

Diabetes UK Small Grant Scheme

Subjects: Endocrinology, diabetes and subjects relevant to diabetes.
Purpose: To enable research workers to develop new ideas in the field of diabetes research.
Eligibility: Open to suitably qualified members of the medical or scientific professions who are resident in the United Kingdom.
Level of Study: Postdoctorate
Type: Grant
Value: A maximum of UK £10,000
Length of Study: Varies
Country of Study: United Kingdom
No. of awards offered: Varies
Application Procedure: Applicants must complete an application form which will be assessed by a peer review within 6–8 weeks. Please write or telephone for details. Details can also be found on the website.
Closing Date: Applications are accepted at any time
Funding: Private
Contributor: Voluntary contributions
No. of awards given last year: 14
No. of applicants last year: 30

DIRKSEN CONGRESSIONAL CENTER

2815 Broadway, Pekin, IL, 61554,
United States of America
Tel: (1) 309 347 7113
Fax: (1) 309 347 6432
Email: fmackaman@dirksencenter.org
Website: www.dirksencenter.org
Contact: Executive Director

The Dirksen Congressional Center sponsors educational and research programmes to help people understand better the United States of America Congress, its members and leaders and the public policies it produces.

Dirksen Congressional Research Grants Program

Subjects: Political science and government.
Purpose: To fund the study of the United States of America Congress.
Eligibility: Open to citizens or residents of the United States of America. Awards are to individuals only. No institutional overhead charges are permitted.
Level of Study: Doctorate, research, postdoctorate
Type: Research grant
Value: Up to US$3,500
Length of Study: Varies
Frequency: Annual
Study Establishment: Unrestricted
Country of Study: United States of America
No. of awards offered: 10–15 per year
Application Procedure: Applicants should visit the Center's website for application information.
Closing Date: February 1st
Funding: Private

DONATELLA FLICK ASSOCIAZIONE

Donatella Flick Conducting Competition, P.O. Box 34227,
London, NW5 1XP, United Kingdom
Tel: (44) 20 7482 1353
Fax: (44) 20 7267 0068
Email: administrator@conducting.org
Website: www.conducting.org
Contact: The Administrator

The Donatella Flick Associazione organizes the Donatella Flick Conducting Competition, which, in association with the London Symphony Orchestra, aims to help advance career opportunities for young conductors. The award subsidizes study and concert engagements for the winner who will work as Assistant Conductor with the London Symphony Orchestra for 1 year.

Donatella Flick Conducting Competition

Subjects: Conducting.
Purpose: To assist a young conductor in establishing an international conducting career.
Eligibility: Open to conductors who are citizens of member states of the European Union and under 35 years of age.
Level of Study: Professional development
Type: Prize
Frequency: Every 2 years
Study Establishment: London Symphony Orchestra
Country of Study: Any country
Application Procedure: Applicants must complete an application form and submit this with references specific to the competition, as well as videos and other supporting documentation such as other prizes, reviews, a curriculum vitae etc.
Funding: Private
Contributor: Mrs Donatella Flick
Additional Information: Entry is by recommendation, documentation and supporting video. Finalists are then selected for audition, and three finalists conduct a public concert. The course of study of entrants must be approved by the organizing committee.

DR HADWEN TRUST FOR HUMANE RESEARCH

84A Tilehouse Street, Hitchin, Hertfordshire, SG5 2DY, England
Tel: (44) 14 6243 6819
Fax: (44) 14 6243 6844
Email: info@drhadwentrust.org.uk
Website: www.drhadwentrust.org.uk
Contact: Dr Carol Newman, Scientific Officer

The Dr Hadwen Trust for Humane Research is a registered charity, established in 1970, to promote research into techniques and procedures to replace the use of living animals in biomedical research, teaching and testing.

Dr Hadwen Trust for Humane Research Grants

Subjects: Scientific research to develop humane alternative methods to the use of living animals in biomedical research and testing.
Purpose: To advance medical progress and replace animal experiments.
Eligibility: Open to nationals from any country, but research must be based in the United Kingdom.
Level of Study: Postdoctorate, postgraduate, doctorate
Type: Grant
Value: Varies according to need and to funds available. Payments are usually made quarterly, and may be used as salary for the researcher, technical assistance, expenses incurred during the research, purchase of equipment or attendance at meetings
Length of Study: A maximum of 3 years, interim progress reports are required. Renewal past 3 years is awarded only in exceptional circumstances
Frequency: Dependent on funds available
Country of Study: United Kingdom
No. of awards offered: Varies
Application Procedure: Official application form must be completed.
Funding: Private
Contributor: Public donations
No. of awards given last year: 7
Additional Information: Recipients are required to sign an agreement not to use Trust funds for any procedure using living animals or animal tissues. Applications must be signed by the candidate's head of department and administrative authority.

Dr Hadwen Trust for Humane Research PhD Studentship

Subjects: Developing alternatives to animal experiments in biomedical fields.
Purpose: To encourage young graduates with a good honours degree to train in non-animal methods.
Eligibility: Open to applicants resident in the United Kingdom.
Level of Study: Postgraduate
Type: Studentship

Value: Outside London UK £8,600 per year, in London UK £11,210 plus an allowance for consumables
Length of Study: 3 years
Frequency: Dependent on funds available
Country of Study: United Kingdom
No. of awards offered: Varies
Application Procedure: Applicants must make initial enquiries by writing to the scientific adviser, Dr G Langley. Applications must be submitted by the project supervisor.
Funding: Private
Contributor: Donations from the general public

Dr Hadwen Trust Research Assistant or Technician

Subjects: The development, validation or implementation of a technique or procedure that would replace one currently using living animals.
Purpose: To provide additional scientific or technical support for a research project.
Eligibility: Open to applicants resident in the United Kingdom.
Value: Salary for research assistant or technician plus an allowance for consumables
Length of Study: 3 years
Frequency: Dependent on funds available
Study Establishment: Varies
Country of Study: United Kingdom
No. of awards offered: Varies
Application Procedure: Applicants must make initial enquiries by writing to the scientific adviser, Dr G Langley. Applications must be made by the senior researcher who will oversee the work.
Funding: Private

Dr Hadwen Trust Research Fellowship

Subjects: The development, validation or implementation of a technique or procedure that would replace one currently using living animals.
Purpose: To attract and retain talented young scientists in non-animal research fields. The funds provide personal support and a contribution to direct research costs.
Eligibility: Open to applicants resident in the United Kingdom.
Level of Study: Postdoctorate
Type: Fellowship
Value: Salary on research analogous salary scale grade 1A, up to spinal point 9 plus a London allowance where appropriate, and an allowance for consumables
Length of Study: 3 years
Frequency: Dependent on funds available
Study Establishment: Varies
Country of Study: United Kingdom
No. of awards offered: Varies
Application Procedure: Applicants must make initial enquiries by writing to the scientific adviser, Dr G Langley. Application forms must be submitted by a senior researcher who will oversee the work.
Funding: Private
Contributor: Public donations

DR M AYLWIN COTTON FOUNDATION

Albany Trustee Company Ltd, PO Box 232, Newport House,
St Peter Port, GY1 4LA, Guernsey
Tel: (44) 14 8172 4136
Fax: (44) 14 8171 0478
Email: info@cotton-foundation.org
Website: www.cotton-foundation.org
Contact: Administrator

Cotton Research Fellowships

Subjects: Archaeology, architecture, history, language and the arts of the Mediterranean.
Eligibility: Open to senior scholars.
Level of Study: Professional development
Type: Fellowship
Value: Up to UK £10,000, to cover the costs of accommodation, travel, photography, photocopying and all other expenses relating to the work for which the fellowship is awarded
Frequency: Annual
Country of Study: Any country
No. of awards offered: Varies
Application Procedure: Applicants must submit a curriculum vitae and an outline of the research they intend to undertake.
Closing Date: February 28th
Funding: Private
Contributor: Dr M Aylwin Cotton
No. of awards given last year: 7
No. of applicants last year: 36
Additional Information: The Foundation also provides grants annually to finance the publication costs of a completed work or a work due for publication in the immediate future.

DR WILLIAMS'S TRUST

14 Gordon Square, London, WC1H 0AR, England
Tel: (44) 20 7387 3727
Website: www.dwlib.co.uk/dwtrust/grants.html
Contact: The Director

The Dr Williams's Trust gives further education grants to dissenting Protestant ministers in the United Kingdom. It also owns the Dr Williams's Library in London.

Glasgow Bursary

Subjects: Religious studies, theology, Christian history, etc.
Purpose: To support an educated non-conformist ministry.
Eligibility: Open to graduate dissenting Protestant ministers for research leading to the degree of PhD.
Level of Study: Doctorate
Type: Bursary
Value: Approx. UK £14,500 per year plus fees paid each term
Length of Study: 3 years
Frequency: Dependent on funds available
Study Establishment: The University of Glasgow Faculty of Divinity
Country of Study: United Kingdom
No. of awards offered: 1
Application Procedure: Applicants must contact the Director of the Trust for details.
Closing Date: March 31st
Funding: Private
No. of awards given last year: Not advertised last year

DUBLIN INSTITUTE FOR ADVANCED STUDIES

10 Burlington Road, Dublin, 4, Ireland
Tel: (353) 1 614 0100
Fax: (353) 1 668 0561
Email: registrarsoffice@admin.dias.ie
Website: www.dias.ie
Contact: Ms Ruth Graham, Administrative Assistant

The Dublin Institute for Advanced Studies is a statutory corporation established in 1940, under the Institute for Advanced Studies Act of that year. It is a publicly funded independent centre for research in basic disciplines. Research is currently carried out in the fields of Celtic studies, theoretical physics and cosmic physics including astronomy, astrophysics and geophysics.

Dublin Institute for Advanced Studies Scholarship in Astronomy, Astrophysics and Geophysics

Subjects: Astronomy, astrophysics and geophysics.
Purpose: To enable training in advanced research methods in the fields of astronomy, astrophysics and geophysics.
Eligibility: Open to candidates from any country.
Level of Study: Doctorate, graduate, postgraduate, predoctorate, postdoctorate
Type: Scholarship

Value: Please contact the Institute for details
Length of Study: 1 year
Frequency: Annual
Study Establishment: The Dublin Institute for Advanced Studies
Country of Study: Ireland
No. of awards offered: 3
Application Procedure: Applicants must complete an application form, available upon request.
Closing Date: Please write for details
Funding: Government
Contributor: State
No. of awards given last year: 2
No. of applicants last year: 12

Dublin Institute for Advanced Studies Scholarship in Celtic Studies

Subjects: Celtic studies.
Purpose: To enable training in advanced research methods in the field of Celtic studies.
Eligibility: Open to nationals of any country.
Level of Study: Postgraduate, postdoctorate, predoctorate, doctorate
Type: Scholarship
Value: Please contact the Institute for details
Length of Study: 1 year
Frequency: Annual
Study Establishment: The Dublin Institute for Advanced Studies
Country of Study: Ireland
No. of awards offered: 3
Application Procedure: Applicants must complete an application form, available upon request.
Closing Date: Applications are accepted at any time
Funding: Government
No. of awards given last year: 3
No. of applicants last year: 10

Dublin Institute for Advanced Studies Scholarship in Theoretical Physics

Subjects: Physics.
Purpose: To enable training in advanced research methods in the field of theoretical physics.
Eligibility: Open to candidates of any country.
Level of Study: Postdoctorate
Type: Scholarship
Value: Please contact the Institute for details
Length of Study: 1 year
Frequency: Annual
Study Establishment: The Dublin Institute for Advanced Studies
Country of Study: Ireland
No. of awards offered: 5
Application Procedure: Applicants must complete an application form, available upon request.
Closing Date: Please write for details
Funding: Government
Contributor: State
No. of awards given last year: 3
No. of applicants last year: 30

DUMBARTON OAKS: TRUSTEES FOR HARVARD UNIVERSITY

1703, 32nd Street North West, Washington, DC, 20007, United States of America
Tel: (1) 202 339 6410
Email: DumbartonOaks@doaks.org
Website: www.doaks.org
Contact: Ms Carol A Sellery, Fellowship Programme Manager

Dumbarton Oaks houses important research and study collections in the areas of Byzantine and Medieval studies, landscape architecture studies and pre-Columbian studies. While the gallery holds exhibitions and the gardens are open to the public, the research facilities exist primarily to serve scholars who hold appointments at Dumbarton Oaks.

Dumbarton Oaks Fellowships and Junior Fellowships

Subjects: Byzantine civilization in all its aspects, including the late Roman and Early Christian period and the Middle Ages generally, studies of Byzantine cultural exchanges with the Latin West, Slavic and Near Eastern countries, pre-Columbian studies and garden and landscape studies.
Purpose: To promote study and research or to support writing of doctoral dissertations.
Eligibility: Junior fellowships are open to persons of any nationality who have passed all preliminary examinations for a higher degree and are writing a dissertation. Candidates must have a working knowledge of any languages required for the research. Fellowships are open to scholars of any nationality holding a PhD or relevant advanced degree and wishing to pursue research on a project of their own at Dumbarton Oaks.
Level of Study: Doctorate, postdoctorate
Type: Fellowship
Value: US$14,635 per year for junior fellowships, US$26,670 per year for fellowships. Both junior and regular Fellows receive furnished accommodation or a housing allowance and US$2,000, if needed, to assist with the cost of bringing and maintaining dependants in Washington plus an expense account of US$975 for approved research expenditure during the academic year. Fellows are also provided with travel assistance
Length of Study: Up to 1 academic year of full-time study, non-renewable
Frequency: Annual
Study Establishment: Dumbarton Oaks
Country of Study: United States of America
No. of awards offered: 10–11 fellowships in Byzantine studies and 3–4 in each of the other fields
Application Procedure: Applicants must contact Dumbarton Oaks for the current application brochure.
Closing Date: November 1st of the academic year preceding that for which the fellowship is required
No. of awards given last year: 35
No. of applicants last year: 200
Additional Information: Dumbarton Oaks also awards a limited number of Summer fellowships.

DUQUESNE UNIVERSITY, DEPARTMENT OF PHILOSOPHY

600 Forbes Avenue, Pittsburgh, Pennsylvania, PA 15282, United States of America
Tel: (1) 412 396 6500
Fax: (1) 412 396 5353
Email: thompson@duq.edu
Website: www.duq.edu
Contact: Ms Joan Thompson, Administrative Assistant

The PhD programme in the Department of Philosophy at Duquesne University emphasizes continental philosophy, ie. phenomenology, 20th-century French and German philosophy as well as the history of philosophy.

Duquesne University Graduate Assistantship

Subjects: Philosophy.
Purpose: To provide a stipend to enable students to obtain a PhD in philosophy.
Eligibility: Open to holders of a Bachelor's degree in philosophy or equivalent, who have a grade point average of at least 3.7 and an excellent Graduate Record Examination score. Candidates should have knowledge of a second language.
Level of Study: Doctorate
Type: Assistantship
Value: A stipend of approximately US$10,000 plus all tuition for coursework
Length of Study: 5–6 years
Frequency: Annual

Study Establishment: McAnulty College and Graduate School of Liberal Arts
Country of Study: United States of America
No. of awards offered: 13 including 2 for 1st year students, 13 this includes 2 for new incoming students
Application Procedure: Applicants must complete an application form letter a statement of intent, three letters of recommendation, Graduate Record Examination scores, application fee and Test of English as a Foreign Language scores.
Closing Date: February 15th before the Autumn term
Funding: Private
Contributor: Duquesne University
No. of awards given last year: 2
No. of applicants last year: 75

DYSTONIA SOCIETY

46-47 Britton Street, London, EC1M 5UJ, England
Tel: (44) 20 7490 5671
Fax: (44) 20 7490 5672
Email: info@dystonia.org.uk
Website: www.dystonia.org.uk
Contact: Administrative Assistant

The Dystonia Society exists to support people with any form of the neurological movement disorder or dystonia, and their families, through the promotion of awareness, research and welfare.

Jackie Deakin Dystonia Prize Essay Competition

Subjects: Neurology, movement disorders and dystonia.
Purpose: To promote awareness and understanding of dystonia among tomorrow's medical profession.
Eligibility: Open to 3rd, 4th and 5th year students at United Kingdom medical schools.
Type: Prize
Value: The 1st prize is UK £1,000, the 2nd is UK £500 and there are six further prizes of UK £250 each
Frequency: Every 2 years
Study Establishment: Medical schools
Country of Study: United Kingdom
No. of awards offered: 8
Application Procedure: Applicants must refer to the website or contact the Society directly.
Closing Date: Registration must be completed by November 30th and completion and submission of the essay must take place by January 15th
Funding: Private
Contributor: Voluntary donations
No. of awards given last year: 8
No. of applicants last year: 24

E-MAIL XPRESS

Rhett Spencer, 390 West 910 South, Heber City, Utah, 84032-2478, United States of America
Tel: (1) 657 2090
Fax: (1) 654 3555
Email: rhett@141.com
Website: www.141.com

E-mail Xpress, started in 1996, is a family-owned business, which has been functioning in the communication and paging field for 20 years and also has extensive experience in industrial and automation computer control systems.

E-Mail Xpress Scholarship

Subjects: Open source systems.
Purpose: To award students who can best exhibit the importance of e-mail and the Internet in their chosen field.
Level of Study: Postgraduate
Type: Scholarship
Value: US$500 plus US$100 of e-mail service
Length of Study: 1 year
Frequency: Annual
Country of Study: United States of America
No. of awards offered: 1
Application Procedure: A short essay about e-mail and the application form must be submitted.
Closing Date: January 31st
Funding: Corporation
Contributor: E-mail Xpress

EARLY AMERICAN INDUSTRIES ASSOCIATION

1324 Shallcross Avenue, Wilmington, DE, 19806, United States of America
Tel: (1) 302 652 7297
Email: eaiainfo@worldnet.att.net
Website: www.eaiainfo.org
Contact: Ms Justine J Mataleno, Co-ordinator

The Early American Industries Association seeks to encourage the study and better understanding of early American industries in the home, in the shop, on the farm and on the sea. It also wishes to discover, identify, classify and exhibit obsolete tools, implements and mechanical devices that were used in early America.

Early American Industries Association Research Grants Program

Subjects: Early American industrial development, including craft practices, industrial technology and identification and use of obsolete tools, implements and mechanical devices used prior to 1900.
Purpose: To encourage research leading to a publication, exhibition or audio-visual material for educational purposes.
Eligibility: Open to citizens or permanent residents of the United States of America. Individuals may be either sponsored by an institution or engaged in self-directed projects.
Level of Study: Postgraduate, predoctorate, postdoctorate, research, graduate, doctorate
Type: Grant
Value: Up to US$2,000
Length of Study: 1 year, non-renewable
Frequency: Annual
Country of Study: United States of America
No. of awards offered: 3–5
Application Procedure: Applicants must submit a completed application form plus three letters of recommendation.
Closing Date: March 15th
Funding: Private
Contributor: Membership dues and donations
No. of awards given last year: 3
No. of applicants last year: 14
Additional Information: Awards may be used to supplement existing financial awards. Successful applicants are required to file a project report on forms supplied by the Association. These are not scholarship funds.

EARTHWATCH INSTITUTE

Research Program, 3 Clock Tower Place, Suite 100, Maynard, MA, 01754, United States of America
Tel: (1) 978 461 0081
Fax: (1) 978 461 2332
Email: research@earthwatch.org
Website: www.earthwatch.org/research

Earthwatch Institute supports diverse research projects of high scientific merit worldwide that address critical environmental and social issues at local, national and international levels. Researchers are given both funding and field assistance from layperson volunteers. Volunteers are recruited by Earthwatch, who pay for the opportunity to assist them in the field.

Earthwatch Education Awards

Subjects: Science education, historical and cultural education.
Purpose: To give teachers and students the opportunity to experience field research first hand and share this experience with their students and local communities.
Level of Study: Professional development
Type: Fellowship
Length of Study: 2–3 weeks
Frequency: Annual
Country of Study: Any country
No. of awards offered: 265
Application Procedure: Applicants must complete an application form and submit it with the other requested documents. Incomplete applications will not be considered. Letters of recommendation are required and referees should explain how long and in what respect they know the applicant. There is an application fee of US$35, which includes a 1 year membership.
Closing Date: Applications are accepted on an ongoing basis
Funding: Private
Contributor: Over 40 donors including foundations and corporations
No. of awards given last year: 250
No. of applicants last year: 700
Additional Information: Recipients are limited to two education awards and cannot receive an award in two consecutive years.

Earthwatch Field Research Grants

Subjects: Disciplines include, but are not limited to, anthropology, archaeology, biology, botany, cartography, conservation, ethnology, folklore, geography, geology, hydrology, marine sciences, meteorology, musicology, nutrition, ornithology, restoration, sociology and sustainable development.
Purpose: To provide grants for field research projects that can constructively utilize teams of non-specialist field assistants in accomplishing their research goals.
Eligibility: There are no residency requirements or nomination processes. Preference is given to applicants who hold a PhD and have both field and teaching experience, however, support is also offered for outstanding projects by younger postdoctoral scholars and, in special cases, graduate students. Women and minority applicants are encouraged. Research teams must include qualified volunteers from the Earthwatch Institute.
Level of Study: Doctorate, postdoctorate, postgraduate, research
Type: Grant
Value: Varies. The normal range of support is US$7,000–130,000. Grants are awarded on a per capita basis, depending upon the number of volunteer participants who are recruited by Earthwatch
Length of Study: Teams last for 2–3 weeks and projects can go on all year
Frequency: Annual
Study Establishment: Research sites
Country of Study: Any country
No. of awards offered: Approx. 140
Application Procedure: Applicants must complete an application form, which can be obtained from the Earthwatch headquarters or by visiting the website. Preliminary proposals must be submitted 13 months prior to field dates.
Closing Date: There is no deadline
Funding: Private
Contributor: Volunteers' contributions
No. of awards given last year: 130
No. of applicants last year: 400

EAST LOTHIAN EDUCATIONAL TRUST

Finance Department, John Muir House, Haddington, East Lothian, EH41 3HA, Scotland
Tel: (44) 16 2082 7436
Fax: (44) 16 2082 7446
Website: www.eastlothian.gov.uk
Contact: Kim Brand, Clerk

The East Lothian Educational Trust provides grants to individuals who are undertaking studies, courses or projects of an educational nature, including scholarships abroad and educational travel. Applicants must be residents of East Lothian.

East Lothian Educational Trust General Grant

Subjects: All subjects, but must be of an educational nature.
Purpose: To provide supplementary support to individuals who undertake studies.
Eligibility: Open to residents of East Lothian, excluding Musselburgh, Wallyford and Whitecraig.
Level of Study: Unrestricted
Type: Grant
Value: Variable
Length of Study: Unrestricted
Frequency: Annual
No. of awards offered: Varies
Application Procedure: Applicants must complete an application form.
Closing Date: August 10th and November 10th
Funding: Private

ECONOMIC AND SOCIAL RESEARCH COUNCIL (ESRC)

Polaris House, North Star Avenue, Swindon, Wiltshire, SN2 1UJ, England
Tel: (44) 17 9341 3000
Fax: (44) 17 9341 3056
Email: ptd@esrc.ac.uk
Website: www.esrc.ac.uk
Contact: Ms Zoë Grimwood, Research Training & development

The Economic and Social Research Council (ESRC) is an independent, government-funded body set up by royal charter. The mission of the ESRC is to promote and support, by any means, high-quality basic, strategic and applied research and related postgraduate training in the social sciences. It also aims to advance knowledge and provide trained social scientists who meet the needs of users and beneficiaries, thereby contributing to the economic competitiveness of the United Kingdom, the effectiveness of public services and policy and quality of life. ESRC also provides advice, disseminates knowledge and promotes public understanding of the social sciences.

ESRC 1+3 Awards and +3 Awards

Subjects: Social sciences.
Purpose: To promote social science research and postgraduate training. The ESRC aims to provide continuous support for high-quality postgraduate training and research on issues of importance to business, the public sector and government.
Eligibility: Open to United Kingdom or European Community nationals with a First or Upper Second Class (Honours) Degree in any subject, or a United Kingdom professional qualification acceptable to the ESRC as of degree standard plus 3 years of subsequent full-time, relevant professional work experience. Candidates must have ordinarily been resident in Great Britain throughout the 3-year period preceding the date of application.
Level of Study: Postgraduate
Type: Studentship
Value: ESRC 1+3 awards cover fees and/or maintenance, depending on the student's situation, circumstances and the type of award
Length of Study: Up to 3 years
Frequency: Annual
Study Establishment: ESRC recognized institutional outlets and courses
Country of Study: United Kingdom
No. of awards offered: Varies
Application Procedure: Applicants must complete an application form. Information sheets and application forms are available from February each year and must be collected from the social science department of any university or Institute of Higher Education or career guidance outlet. Forms are available from the website. Studentships allocates under the quota system.
Closing Date: May 1st
Funding: Government

No. of awards given last year: 630
No. of applicants last year: 1093
Additional Information: The 1 refers to the 1-year Master's and the 3 refers to the 3-year PhD.

ECONOMICS EDUCATION AND RESEARCH CONSORTIUM (EERC)

NaUKMA vul.Voloska, 10, Suite 406, Kyiv, 04070, Ukraine
Tel: (380) 380 (044) 492 8012
Fax: (380) 388 (044) 492 8011
Email: eerc@eerc.kiev.ua
Website: www.eerc.kiev.ua

The EERC is a group of distinguished international donor organizations that joined forces in 1996 to modernize economics education and research in Ukraine and Russia.

EERC Professors Scholarship

Subjects: Economics.
Eligibility: Open to any citizen of Ukraine, Belarus, Moldova or the South Camcasus who meets the eligibility requirements (see website).
Level of Study: Postgraduate
Type: Scholarship
Value: US$2,841
Frequency: Annual
Study Establishment: EERC
No. of awards offered: 1
Application Procedure: See website.
Closing Date: June 23rd
Funding: Private

EERC Scholarships

Subjects: Economics.
Eligibility: Open to citizen of Ukraine, Belarus, Moldova or the South Caucasus who meets the eligibility requirements (see website).
Level of Study: Postgraduate
Type: Scholarship
Value: All tuition costs
Frequency: Annual
Study Establishment: EERC
No. of awards offered: 25
Application Procedure: See website.
Closing Date: June 23rd
Funding: Corporation
Contributor: Tetra Pak Ukraine

EDMUND NILES HUYCK PRESERVE, INC.

PO Box 189, Rensselaerville, NY, 12147, United States of America
Tel: (1) 518 797 3440
Fax: (1) 518 797 3440
Email: rlwyman@capital.net
Website: www.huyckpreserve.org/ggl.htm
Contact: Mr Richard Wyman, Executive Director

The Edmund Niles Huyck Preserve is a 2,000-acre nature preserve and biological research station with a newly expanded laboratory and housing for 20. The habitat is the north-eastern hardwood Hemlock forest with lakes, streams, bogs and plantations.

Edmund Niles Huyck Preserve, Inc. Graduate and Postgraduate Grants

Subjects: Ecology, behaviour evolution and natural resources of the area and conservation biology.
Purpose: To promote scientific research on the flora and fauna of the Huyck Preserve and its vicinity.
Eligibility: Open to all nationalities. Awards are made without regard to sex, colour, religion, ethnic origin or academic affiliation of the applicant, and support is based solely on the quality of the proposed research and its appropriateness to the natural resources and facilities of the Preserve.
Level of Study: Postdoctorate, graduate, doctorate, postgraduate
Type: Grant
Value: A maximum of US$2,500 plus laboratory space and lodging (renewable)
Length of Study: Varies
Frequency: Annual
Study Establishment: The Preserve
Country of Study: United States of America
No. of awards offered: 10
Application Procedure: Applicants must complete an application form, available on written request. Proposals must contain an abstract of not more than 200 words describing the background and significance of the proposal. A literature cited section should be included and an up-to-date curriculum vitae provided. The researcher should submit three references that deal specifically with their proposed work.
Closing Date: February 1st
Funding: Private
No. of awards given last year: 6
No. of applicants last year: 12

EDUCATION FOUNDATION (SME-EF)

PO Box 930, Dearborn, MI, 48121-0930, United States of America
Tel: (1) (313) 425 3301
Fax: (1) (313) 425 3411
Email: squinlan@sme.org
Website: www.sme.org/foundation
Contact: Mr Steve Quinlan, Senior Grants Program Officer Society of Manufacturing Engineers

The SME-EF provides the manufacturing professional with an outlet to support the development of the manufacturing workforce of the future. As one of the nation's leading organizations dedicated to advancing manufacturing education, the Foundation awards grants and scholarships and administers student outreach programmes designed in partnership with corporations, foundations, educational institutions and individual donors. Since 1998, the Foundation has awarded more than US$12 million in cash grants, scholarships and special awards.

SME Education Foundation Grants Program

Subjects: Manufacturing engineering.
Purpose: To establish a process that will stimulate the academic community to help improve the competency of the manufacturing workforce. It focuses on identifying and then closing competency gaps between industry's manufacturing workforce needs and what is currently provided by educational programmes.
Eligibility: Open to full-time university faculty representing manufacturing engineering or manufacturing engineering technology programmes which offer manufacturing courses. Applicants must be Canadian, American or Mexican.
Level of Study: Postgraduate
Type: Grant
Value: Funds are reimbursed upon receipt of an invoice and narrative report
Length of Study: 2 years
Frequency: Annual
Country of Study: United States of America, Canada or Mexico
No. of awards offered: Varies
Application Procedure: Applicants must submit a signed original application with seven copies to coincide with the request. Further information is available from the website.
Closing Date: The first Friday in December
Funding: Private
Contributor: SME members, chapters, regions and corporations
Additional Information: Grants must be matched dollar for dollar by the educational institution, industry or government unit.

EDUCATIONAL TESTING SERVICE (ETS)

Rosedale Road, Princeton, NJ, 08541-0001, United States of America
Tel: (1) 609 734 1806
Fax: (1) 609 734 1755
Email: ldelauro@ets.org
Website: www.ets.org
Contact: Ms Linda J DeLauro

The Educational Testing Service (ETS) is a non-profit organization whose goal is to help advance quality and equity in education by providing valid assessments, research, projects and services.

ETS Postdoctoral Fellowships

Subjects: Psychology, education, sociology of education, psychometrics, statistics, computer science, policy research or special education, minority issues in education, literacy.
Purpose: To provide research opportunities to individuals who hold a doctorate in education and related fields, and to increase the number of women and minority professionals conducting research in educational measurement.
Eligibility: The applicant should hold a doctorate in educational measurement or a related field. A background in second language education and assessment is highly desirable. The applicant should show evidence of a commitment to research and to achieving excellence in this field. Three Recommendations from established scholars in measurement and educational research are required.
Level of Study: Postdoctorate
Type: Fellowship
Value: US$50,000. In addition, limited relocation expenses, consistent with ETS guidelines, will be reimbursed upon presentation of receipts
Length of Study: 1 year, 2nd year renewable upon successful completion of first year, and mutual consent
Frequency: Annual, renewable
Country of Study: United States of America
No. of awards offered: Up to 3
Application Procedure: Applicants must submit a curriculum vitae, a five-page typed research proposal, a description of relevant work, interests and experience, publications and other relevant documents and materials, official transcripts of undergraduate and graduate studies and letters of recommendation from three people who are familiar with the applicant's work. There is no formal application form.
Closing Date: Materials must be postmarked by February 1st
Funding: Private
Contributor: ETS
No. of awards given last year: 5
No. of applicants last year: 35

ETS Summer Program in Research for Graduate Students

Subjects: Psychology, education, teaching, learning, psychometrics, statistics, computer science, linguistics, literacy, psycholinguistics, educational technology, minority issues, testing issues, including alternate forms of assessment for special populations and issues associated with new forms of assessment or policy research.
Purpose: To increase the number of women and minority professionals in educational measurement and related fields and to provide students with the opportunity to conduct independent research under the mentorship of an ETS researcher.
Eligibility: Open to graduate students who are pursuing a doctorate in a relevant discipline and have completed 2 years of coursework towards a PhD or EdD by June 1st of the internship year. The main criteria for selection will be scholarship and the match of applicant interests with participating ETS staff. Affirmative action goals will also be considered.
Level of Study: Predoctorate
Value: US$5,000 for the 2-month period. Participants will be reimbursed for limited travel to and from Princeton, consistent with the ETS travel policy
Length of Study: June–July
Frequency: Annual
Country of Study: United States of America
No. of awards offered: Up to 16
Application Procedure: Applicants must submit an application including a statement of interest, a curriculum vitae, electronic standard letter of recommendation available at the ETS website from two individuals who are familiar with the applicant's academic work and official transcripts of undergraduate and graduate studies.
Closing Date: February 1st
Funding: Private
Contributor: ETS
No. of awards given last year: 25
No. of applicants last year: 165
Additional Information: To request applications, email: internfellowships@ets.org or apply online at the website: www.ets.org/research/fellowships/html

ETS Sylvia Taylor Johnson Minority Fellowship Educational Measurement

Subjects: Educational research, educational measurement, policy research, minority issues in education, assessment: universal access to PRE-K assessment, teacher education and achievement.
Purpose: To promote excellence as well as to encourage original and significant research for early career scholars. Studies focused on issues concerning the education of minority students are especially encouraged.
Eligibility: Open to applicants who have received their doctoral degree within the past 10 years and who are citizens or permanent residents of the United States of America. Selections will be based on the applicant's record of accomplishment and proposed topic of research. Applicants should have a commitment to education and an independent body of scholarship that signals the promise of continuing outstanding contributions to educational measurement.
Level of Study: Postdoctorate
Type: Fellowship
Value: The stipend will be set in relation to the successful applicant's compensation at the home institution. In addition, limited relocation expenses, consistent with ETS guidelines, will be reimbursed
Length of Study: 1 year, renewal upon successful completion of first year by mutual consent
Frequency: Annual
Country of Study: United States of America
No. of awards offered: 1
Application Procedure: Applicants must submit a letter of intent, a current curriculum vitae, a detailed proposal of the research the applicant will conduct while at the ETS, a standardized letter of recommendation from three individuals, completed at the website electronically and samples of published research. Applicants will be notified of results by March 1st.
Closing Date: February 1st
Funding: Private
Contributor: ETS
No. of awards given last year: 1
No. of applicants last year: 11
Additional Information: Through her research, extensive writings and service to the educational community as an educator, editor, counsellor, committee member and collaborator during her lifetime, Sylvia Taylor Johnson had a significant influence in educational measurement and assessment nationally. In honour of Dr Johnson's important contributions to the field of education, the ETS has established the Sylvia Taylor Johnson Minority Fellowship in educational measurement.

THE EDWARD F ALBEE FOUNDATION, INC.

14 Harrison Street, New York, NY, 10013, United States of America
Tel: (1) 212 226 2020
Email: info@albeefoundation.org
Website: www.albeefoundation.org
Contact: Mr Jakob Holder, Foundation Secretary

The Edward F Albee Foundation provides residence and working space to writers and visual artists at its facilities in Montauk, New York. The residency is offered at no charge to the participants and imposes no obligations, except diligent application to their work and respect for the privacy of others.

William Flanagan Memorial Creative Persons Center

Subjects: Writing, painting, sculpting and musical composition.
Purpose: To provide accommodation.
Eligibility: Open to artists and writers in need who have displayed evidence of their talent.
Level of Study: Unrestricted
Value: Accommodation only

Length of Study: 4 months (June 1st–October 1st)
Frequency: Annual
Study Establishment: The William Flanagan Memorial Creative Persons Center in Montauk, Long Island
Country of Study: United States of America
No. of awards offered: 20
Application Procedure: Applicants must complete an application form. Forms are available upon request and should be accompanied by a stamped addressed envelope. Other materials are also required, and applicants should write for further details.
Closing Date: January 1st–April 1st
Funding: Private
No. of awards given last year: 20
No. of applicants last year: 300
Additional Information: The environment is communal and residents are expected to do their share in maintaining the conditions of the Center.

THE ELECTROCHEMICAL SOCIETY, INC.

65 South Main Street, Pennington, NJ, 08534, United States of America
Tel: (1) 609 737 1902
Fax: (1) 609 737 2743
Email: ecs@electrochem.org
Website: www.electrochem.org
Contact: Erin Goudwin, Electrochemical Society, Inc.

The Electrochemical Society is an international non-profit educational organization concerned with a broad range of phenomena relating to electrochemical and solid state science and technology. The Society has more than 8,000 individual members worldwide as well as roughly 100 corporations and laboratories that hold contributing membership.

Electrochemical Society Summer Fellowships

Subjects: Electrochemical and solid state science.
Purpose: To fund a student's research through the Summer months.
Eligibility: Awards are made without regard to sex, citizenship or financial need. They will be made to a graduate student pursuing work between the degrees of BS and PhD at a college or university, and who will continue their studies after the Summer period.
Level of Study: Unrestricted, doctorate, graduate, postgraduate, predoctorate
Type: Fellowship
Value: US$4,000
Length of Study: 3 months
Frequency: Annual
No. of awards offered: 4
Application Procedure: Applicants must submit an application and supporting materials.
Closing Date: January 1st
Funding: Private
No. of awards given last year: 4
No. of applicants last year: 4

ELIZABETH GLASER PEDIATRIC AIDS FOUNDATION

1140 Connecticut Avenue NW, Suite 200, Washington, DC 20036, United States of America
Tel: (1) 310 314 1459
Fax: (1) 310 314 1469
Email: research@pedaids.org
Website: www.pedaids.org
Contact: Research Grants Enquiries

Elizabeth Glaser Pediatric Scientist Award

Subjects: Research in paediatric HIV/AIDS.
Purpose: To build a network of scientists focusing on issues of paediatric HIV/AIDS and create a generation of children born free of this infection.
Eligibility: Applicants must have an MD, PhD, DDS or DVM degree.
Level of Study: Research
Type: Grant
Value: Up to US$650,000
Length of Study: 5 years
Frequency: Annual
No. of awards offered: 1
Application Procedure: Applicants must visit the website to download instructions for the letter of intent and application form.
Closing Date: September 10th
Funding: Foundation
Contributor: The Elizabeth Glaser Pediatric AIDS Foundation

International Leadership Award

Subjects: Research in paediatric HIV/AIDS.
Purpose: To invest in medically trained individuals in developing countries who have the potential to develop local programmes that will have a direct impact on the paediatric HIV epidemic, but who lack resources.
Eligibility: Applicants should be developing country leaders in HIV/AIDS programme implementation and research.
Level of Study: Professional development
Type: Grant
Value: Up to US$450,000
Length of Study: 3 years
No. of awards offered: 1
Application Procedure: Application forms and instructions for letter of intent can be downloaded from the website.
Closing Date: September 10th
Funding: Foundation
Contributor: The Elizabeth Glaser Pediatric AIDS Foundation

Targeted Research Program

Subjects: Research in paediatric HIV/AIDS.
Purpose: To fund research projects relevant to paediatric HIV vaccine issue.
Eligibility: Applicants must have an MD, PhD, DDS or DVM degree and be at the assistant professor level or above.
Level of Study: Postgraduate, postdoctorate, research
Type: Grant
Value: Up to US$450,000
No. of awards offered: 1–2
Application Procedure: Applicants must download instructions and the application form from the website.
Closing Date: August 6th
Funding: Foundation
Contributor: The Elizabeth Glaser Pediadric AIDS Foundation

Two-year International Scholar Awards

Subjects: Research in paediatric HIV/AIDS.
Purpose: To assist clinicians and scientists in paediatric HIV/AIDS.
Eligibility: Applicants must be clinicians and scientists from developing countries and must work in developing countries.
Level of Study: Postdoctorate, research
Type: Postdoctoral fellowship
Value: US$10,000–30,000 plus US$10,000
Length of Study: 2 years
Frequency: Annual
Application Procedure: Applicants must select an experienced sponsor who is a faculty member with an advanced degree and who will oversee the research, provide guidance to the applicant and can provide evidence of the institution's commitment to the career development of the applicant. Application form is available from the website.
Closing Date: September 10th
Funding: Foundation
Contributor: The Elizabeth Glaser Pediatric AIDS Foundation

Two-year Scholar Awards

Subjects: Research in paediatric HIV/AIDS.
Purpose: To assist clinicians and scientists in paediatric HIV/AIDS.
Eligibility: Applicants should be clinicians and scientists in developed countries.

Level of Study: Postdoctorate, research
Type: Postdoctoral fellowship
Value: US$30,000–46,000 plus US$10,000
Length of Study: 2 years
Frequency: Annual
Application Procedure: Applicants must select an experienced sponsor who is a faculty member with an advanced degree and who will oversee the research, provide guidance to the applicant and can provide evidence of the institution's commitment to the career development of the applicant. Application form is available from the website.
Closing Date: September 10th
Funding: Foundation
Contributor: The Elizabeth Glaser Pediatric AIDS Foundation

EMBASSY OF FRANCE IN AUSTRALIA

6 Perth Avenue, Yarralumla, Canberra, ACT, 2600, Australia
Tel: (61) 262 160 100
Fax: (61) 262 160 156
Email: language@ambafrance-au.org
Website: www.ambafrance-au.org
Contact: Mr Stéphane Grivelet, Higher Education Attaché

French Government Postgraduate Scholarships

Subjects: Engineering (general) 6.1 political sciences and government 17.2.
Eligibility: Open to Australian citizens who hold a Bachelor's degree and who have completed 3 years at a university.
Level of Study: Postgraduate
Type: Scholarship
Value: €730 monthly maintenance allowance plus medical cover
Length of Study: 2 years
Frequency: Annual
Study Establishment: An approved university
Country of Study: France
No. of awards offered: 2
Application Procedure: Applicants must submit an application after their admission to the postgraduate programme of a French university. Application forms are available from the website of the French Embassy: www.ambafrance-au.org
Closing Date: December 31st
Funding: Government
No. of awards given last year: 2 awards

Language Assistantships in Australia

Subjects: French language studies.
Purpose: To enable French assistants to take up positions supporting the teaching of French in Australian schools.
Eligibility: Open to French citizens only.
Level of Study: Postgraduate
Type: Other
Value: Please contact the organization
Length of Study: 1 year, non-renewable
Frequency: Annual
Country of Study: Australia
No. of awards offered: 26
Application Procedure: Applicants must apply to the French Ministry of Education in Paris or through the Centre International d'Etudes Pédagogiques (CIEP), 1 Avenue León-Journault, 92318 Sèvres Cedex, France; www.ciep.fr
Funding: Government
No. of awards given last year: 25 awards
Additional Information: These awards are organized by the Bureau de Co-opération pour le Francais of the Embassy of France in Australia (BCLE).

Language Assistantships in France and New Caledonia

Subjects: French language studies.
Purpose: To enable graduates who intend to teach French in the future or beginning teachers of French to improve their language skills.
Eligibility: Open to young Australian graduates and school teachers aged 20–30.
Level of Study: Graduate
Value: €902 living allowance plus medical cover in France, between €1250–1350 in overseas 'Départements' and between €1400 and €1600 in New Caledonia
Length of Study: 7 months
Frequency: Annual
Study Establishment: Any approved high school
No. of awards offered: 80 in France and 4 in New Caledonia
Application Procedure: Application forms are available on the website of the French Embassy: www.ambafrance-au.org
Closing Date: October 20th for New Caledonia, December 19th for Metropolitan France and overseas 'Départements'
Funding: Government
No. of awards given last year: 36
Additional Information: These awards are organized by the higher education office of the Embassy of France in Australia. Successful applicants will conduct English conversation classes with small groups of students for 12 hours per week.

Ministry of Foreign Affairs (France) International Teaching Fellowships

Subjects: French language education.
Purpose: To enable experienced teachers of French to spend time at a French primary school, a French college, or a French lycée.
Eligibility: Open to Australian teachers of French employed by state education authorities.
Level of Study: Professional development
Type: Fellowship
Length of Study: 1 year
Frequency: Annual
Study Establishment: A lycée, collège, primary school or Institut Universitaire de Formation de Maÿtres (IUFM)
Country of Study: France
No. of awards offered: 2
Application Procedure: Applicants must complete an application form, available from state departments of education and on the French Embassy website: www.ambafrance-au.org
Closing Date: April 30th
Funding: Government
No. of awards given last year: 2 awards
Additional Information: These awards are organized by the higher education office of the Embassy of France in Australia (BCF).

Ministry of Foreign Affairs (France) Tertiary Studies in French Universities (Baudin Travel Grants)

Subjects: All subjects.
Purpose: To encourage graduate and postgraduate students to study for a year at a French university.
Eligibility: Open to graduate or postgraduate students with a good knowledge of French.
Level of Study: Graduate, postgraduate
Type: Grant
Value: Australian $2,000 and medical cover (worth Australian $2,000)
Length of Study: 1 year
Frequency: Annual
Study Establishment: A university
Country of Study: France
No. of awards offered: 18
Application Procedure: Applicants must complete an application form, available on request from every Australian university's department or section of French studies and on the website of the French Embassy: www.ambafrance-au.org Students must apply for a course of study approved for credit by their home institution.
Closing Date: May 26th
Funding: Government
No. of awards given last year: 11 awards

Ministry of Foreign Affairs (France) University Study Tours (Nouméa)

Subjects: French language.
Purpose: To assist French language students to attend a 2-week course in Nouméa (New-Caledonia).

Eligibility: Open to French language students in Australian Universities.
Level of Study: Graduate
Value: Australian $500
Length of Study: 2 weeks
Frequency: Annual
No. of awards offered: 30
Application Procedure: Applicants must contact the French department at this university.
Closing Date: April 30th
Funding: Government
No. of awards given last year: 30 awards
Additional Information: The tours are currently organized at different times of the year by the French departments of the James Cook University of North Queensland, the Australian National University, Flinders University, Macquarie University and Melbourne and Monash Universities. Students from other universities are entitled to join one of these groups. Please contact the relevant French department for further information.

EMBASSY OF JAPAN IN PAKISTAN

P.O Box 1119, 53–70, Ramna 5/4 Diplomatic Enclave 1, Islamabad, 44000, Pakistan
Tel: (92) (51) 2279320, 2279330
Fax: (92) (51) 2279340
Email: japanemb@comsats.net.pk
Website: www.pk.emb-japan.go.jp

The Japan Exchange and Teaching (JET) Programme
Subjects: International relations.
Purpose: To enhance the mutual understanding and relations that currently exist between Japan and Pakistan.
Eligibility: Open to applicants who are interested in Japan and who are below the age of 40 years.
Type: Scholarship
Length of Study: Yen 3,600,000 per annum
Frequency: Annual
Country of Study: Japan
Application Procedure: A completed application form must be submitted.

Japanese Government (Bunka-Cho) Fellowship Programme
Subjects: Art.
Purpose: To encourage artists who wish to improve their artistic ability in Japan.
Eligibility: Open to candidates with professional experience in the field of arts who are between 18 and 35 years of age.
Level of Study: Postgraduate
Type: Fellowship
Value: A daily allowance of Yen 17,000
Length of Study: Up to 10 months
Frequency: Annual
Country of Study: Japan
Application Procedure: A completed application form which is field by a Japanese arts organizational artist must be sent.
Closing Date: February 28th

EMBASSY OF THE UNITED STATES IN KABUL

Humphrey Fellowship Program Public Affairs Section U.S. Embassy, Kabul, Afghanistan
Tel: (93) 20 230 0436
Fax: (93) 20 230 1364
Email: amirism@state.gov

By providing future leaders and policy makers with experience in the U.S. society, culture and professional fields, the Embassy of the United States in Kabul provides a basis for lasting, productive, ties between Americans and their professional counterparts overseas.

Hubert H. Humphrey Fellowship program
Subjects: Culture and professional fields.
Eligibility: Open to candidates who have completed a university degree programme, are proficient in written and spoken English, and also have five years of relevant professional experience.
Level of Study: Postdoctorate
Type: Fellowship
Length of Study: 1 year
Frequency: Annual
Country of Study: United States of America
No. of awards offered: Varies
Application Procedure: Applicants should submit a curriculum vitae along with copies of university transcripts and degrees.
Closing Date: June 30th
Funding: Government
Contributor: The U.S. Department of State Bureau of Educational and Cultural Affairs

EMBLEM CLUB SCHOLARSHIP FOUNDATION

PO Box 712, San Luis Rey, CA, 92068, United States of America
Tel: (1) 619 757 0619
Fax: (1) 619 757 0619
Email: perky2@home.com
Website: www.emblemclub.org
Contact: Administrative Secretary

Emblem Club Scholarship Foundation Grant
Subjects: Education and teacher training.
Purpose: To assist teachers who are working towards their Master's degree and accreditation in order to teach the deaf and hearing impaired. This does not include audiology or speech therapy.
Eligibility: Applicants must be citizens of the United States of America of no more than 50 years of age, and must agree to teach within the United States of America. There are no other restrictions as to minority, religion or language.
Level of Study: Postgraduate
Type: Grant
Value: Varies
Country of Study: United States of America
Application Procedure: Applicants must apply to the schools concerned.
Closing Date: March 1st, June 1st, September 1st or January 1st
Funding: Private

EMMANUEL COLLEGE OF VICTORIA UNIVERSITY

75 Queen's Park Crescent, Toronto, ON, M55 1K7, Canada
Tel: (1) 416 585 4539
Fax: (1) 416 585 4516
Email: ec.office@utoronto.ca
Website: www.vicu.utoronto.ca

Emmanuel College, set within Victoria University and the University of Toronto, is the United Church of Canada's largest theological college. The College offers four basic or first professional degrees and five advanced or graduate degrees. About 210 students are currently enrolled. Emmanuel College is one of seven member schools of the Toronto School of Theology.

Bertram Maura Memorial Entrance Scholarship
Subjects: Old and New Testament.
Purpose: To provide funding to doctoral students.
Eligibility: Open to outstanding doctoral students.
Level of Study: Doctorate
Type: Scholarship
Value: Dependent on funds available, but usually Canadian $10,000
Length of Study: 2 years
Frequency: Annual
Study Establishment: Emmanuel College

Country of Study: Canada
No. of awards offered: Usually 4
Closing Date: March 31st
Funding: Private

Bloor Lands Entrance Scholarship

Subjects: Theology.
Purpose: To assist newly admitted ThD or PhD students with potential for excellence in scholarship demonstrated by high achievement in previous theological studies.
Level of Study: Doctorate
Type: Scholarship
Value: Dependent on funds available, but usually Canadian $10,000
Length of Study: 2 years
Frequency: Annual
Study Establishment: Emmanuel College
Country of Study: Canada
No. of awards offered: Usually 3 or 4
Application Procedure: Admission to the Toronto School of Theology/Emmanuel College must be granted first. A scholarship application is then sent to the Director of Advanced Degree Studies.
Closing Date: January 31st
Funding: Private

Emmanuel College Finishing Scholarships

Subjects: Theology.
Purpose: To enable a doctoral student to finish his or her dissertation in the year in which the award is made.
Eligibility: Open to doctoral students at the end of the programme.
Level of Study: Doctorate
Type: Scholarship
Value: Varies
Length of Study: 1 year
Frequency: Annual
Study Establishment: Emmanuel College
Country of Study: Canada
No. of awards offered: Varies
Closing Date: March 31st
Funding: Private

Frank P Fidler Memorial Award

Subjects: Theology.
Purpose: To assist alumni returning for further study.
Eligibility: Applications from those interested in studying the Church's ministry with various types of families in today's changing world are particularly encouraged. Preference is given to graduates returning to Emmanuel to complete a ThM or second basic degree.
Level of Study: Doctorate
Type: Scholarship
Value: Varies
Length of Study: 1 year
Frequency: Annual
Study Establishment: Emmanuel College
Country of Study: Canada
No. of awards offered: 1
Closing Date: January 31st
Funding: Private

In-Course Scholarships

Subjects: Theology.
Purpose: To support doctoral study.
Eligibility: Open to doctoral students.
Level of Study: Doctorate
Type: Scholarship
Value: Varies
Length of Study: 2–3 years
Frequency: Annual
Study Establishment: Emmanuel College
Country of Study: Canada
No. of awards offered: Varies from year to year
Closing Date: March 31st
Funding: Private

Additional Information: These scholarships are awarded to students who have demonstrated academic excellence to assist them beyond the residency phase of their studies.

Vernon Hope Emory Entrance Scholarship

Subjects: Theology.
Purpose: To support an outstanding newly admitted ThD or PhD student.
Level of Study: Doctorate
Type: Scholarship
Value: Varies according to funds available
Length of Study: 2 years
Frequency: Annual
Study Establishment: Emmanuel College
Country of Study: Canada
No. of awards offered: 1
Application Procedure: Admission to the Toronto School of Theology/Emmanuel College must be granted first. Application must be sent to the Director of Advanced Degree Studies.
Closing Date: January 31st
Funding: Private

Victoria University Graduate Student Assistantships

Subjects: Theology, including Christian education, ethics, field education, history of Christianity, homiletics, the Old and New Testament, pastoral theology and systematic theology and worship.
Purpose: To provide funding for doctoral students.
Eligibility: Open to doctoral students.
Level of Study: Doctorate
Type: Scholarship
Value: Canadian $9,800 per year
Length of Study: 2 years
Frequency: Annual
Study Establishment: Emmanuel College
Country of Study: Canada
No. of awards offered: Usually 12 or 13
Application Procedure: Admission to the Toronto School of Theology/Emmanuel College must be granted first. A scholarship application is then sent to the Director of Advance Degree Studies.
Closing Date: February 28th
Funding: Private

ENGINEERING AND PHYSICAL SCIENCES RESEARCH COUNCIL (EPSRC)

Polaris House, North Star Avenue, Swindon, Wiltshire, SN2 1ET, England
Tel: (44) 17 9344 4239
Fax: (44) 17 9344 4007
Email: jan.tucker@epsrc.ac.uk
Website: www.epsrc.ac.uk
Contact: Ms Jan Tucker, Peer Review Operations

The Engineering and Physical Sciences Research Council (EPSRC) promotes and supports high quality, basic, strategic and applied research and related postgraduate training in engineering and physical sciences. It aims to advance knowledge and technology by providing trained scientists and engineers, in order to meet the needs of users and beneficiaries, and thereby contribute to economic competitiveness and quality of life.

EPSRC Advanced Research Fellowships

Subjects: Engineering, mathematics, physics, chemistry, materials and information technology with life sciences interface.
Purpose: To support outstanding young academic research workers in order that they may devote themselves to full-time research projects.
Eligibility: Open to candidates holding a PhD or equivalent standing in their profession along with at least 3 years of experience at the postdoctoral level upon the expected start date of the fellowship.
Level of Study: Postdoctorate
Type: Fellowship

Value: Funding for basic salary costs, which includes National Insurance and superannuation contributions. Successful candidates also receive a Fellowship Support Fund (FSF) of UK £4,000 per year. The salary is paid on an 'age for wage' basis
Length of Study: A maximum of 5 years
Frequency: Annual
Study Establishment: Any academic institution acceptable to the Council
Country of Study: United Kingdom
No. of awards offered: Up to 40
Application Procedure: Applicants must complete an application form, available on the website. After an initial sitting by EPSRC the subject area panel shortlists those candidates to be invited for interview. The interviewees are usually the top ranked 25–33 per cent of candidates. The remaining candidates not selected for interview are informed of this decision as soon as possible.
Closing Date: November
Funding: Government
No. of awards given last year: 41
No. of applicants last year: Approx. 300

EPSRC Doctoral Training Grants (DTGs)

Subjects: Engineering, mathematics, information technology, materials, chemistry and physics.
Purpose: To provide funds directly to universities to support doctoral training in subjects that lie broadly within the remit of the EPSRC.
Eligibility: Open to candidates at a university whose standards of training, supervision and career advice meet those set by the EPSRC. Students must meet eligibility requirements of the education (fees and awards) regulations 1997.
Level of Study: Postgraduate, doctorate, predoctorate
Type: Grant
Value: Payments will be profiled over the first 3 years, save an element held back to the final quarter pending reconciliation of actual expenditure against payments made. A separate grant will be awarded for each subsequent annual output from the research algorithm
Length of Study: 3 years
Frequency: Annual
Study Establishment: United Kingdom universities
Country of Study: United Kingdom
Application Procedure: Applicants are selected in accordance with the university's postgraduate admission requirements and should approach the university at which they wish to study.
Funding: Government
Additional Information: Students are selected and paid by the university.

EPSRC Postdoctoral Fellowships in Mathematics

Subjects: Mathematics.
Purpose: To provide support for outstanding individuals at various stages of their careers to give them the freedom to pursue their research interests full-time, free from the burden of academic duties.
Eligibility: Candidates should be within 3 years of completing their PhD, and should neither hold permanent academic posts nor have more than 4 years of postdoctoral experience. This fellowship is open to European Union citizens.
Level of Study: Postdoctorate
Type: Fellowship
Value: The successful candidates receive funding for basic salary costs on an 'age for wage' basis, plus appropriate employer's National Insurance and superannuation. There is a Fellowship Support fund (FSF), which is valued at UK £6,000 per year, to be used at the discretion of the Fellow
Length of Study: 3 years
Frequency: Annual
Study Establishment: Normally universities or research institutions in the United Kingdom
Country of Study: United Kingdom
No. of awards offered: 10
Application Procedure: Applicants must complete an application form, available on the website. The subject area panel shortlists those candidates to be invited for interview. The interviewees are usually the top ranked 25–33 per cent of candidates and interviews are usually held in December or January. The remaining candidates not selected for interview are informed of this decision as soon as possible. Applications are limited to one per year and applications for more than one type of fellowship will not be accepted.
Closing Date: January 8th
Funding: Government
No. of applicants last year: 50

EPSRC Postdoctoral Theory Fellowship in Physics

Subjects: Physics.
Purpose: To provide support for outstanding individuals at the start of their careers to give them the freedom to pursue their research interests full-time, normally shortly or immediately after completing a PhD.
Eligibility: Candidates should be within 3 years of completing their PhD at the time of the submission deadline and should not hold permanent academic posts. This fellowship is open to European Union citizens.
Level of Study: Postdoctorate
Type: Fellowship
Value: The successful candidates receive funding for basic salary costs on an 'age for wage' basis, plus appropriate employer's National Insurance and superannuation. There is a Fellowship Support fund (FSF), which is valued at UK £6,000 per year, to be used at the discretion of the Fellow
Length of Study: 3 years
Frequency: Annual
Study Establishment: Universities or research institutions in the United Kingdom
Country of Study: United Kingdom
No. of awards offered: Approx. 4
Application Procedure: Applicants must complete an application form, available on the website, and are required to ensure that their personal referees submit their comments on the correct forms. Letters of support are not accepted. The interviewees are usually the top ranked 25–33 per cent of candidates and interviews are usually held in February. The remaining candidates not selected for interview are informed of this decision as soon as possible. Applications are limited to one per year and applications for more than one type of fellowship will not be accepted.
Closing Date: January 8th
Funding: Government
No. of applicants last year: 20

EPSRC Senior Research Fellowships

Subjects: Engineering, mathematics, physics, chemistry, materials and information technology with life sciences interface.
Purpose: To enable outstanding established scientists and engineers at the peak of their capabilities to devote themselves to full-time research free of the restrictions imposed by their normal academic duties.
Eligibility: Open to scientists and engineers who are already established in their careers, having proved their exceptional research and interpretative ability. Applicants must be members of permanent staff of United Kingdom universities, technical colleges or similar United Kingdom academic institutions and must be at a level of Senior Lecturer/Reader/Professor or equivalent.
Level of Study: Professional development
Type: Fellowship
Value: Replacement of the Fellow's basic academic salary, excluding the superannuation and National Insurance contributions, as these must be covered by the academic host institution. The fellowship will include a Fellowship Support Fund (FSF), which is a fixed sum of UK £4,000 per year, over the period of the award
Length of Study: A maximum of 5 years
Frequency: Annual
Study Establishment: Any academic institution acceptable to the Council
Country of Study: United Kingdom
No. of awards offered: Up to 3
Application Procedure: Applicants must complete an application form, available on the EPSRC website. The application forms can be

downloaded via the links. An applicant is limited to one application for a fellowship each year.
Closing Date: November and May
Funding: Government
No. of awards given last year: 3
No. of applicants last year: Approx. 30–60
Additional Information: For further information applicants should visit the website.

MOD Joint Grants Scheme

Subjects: All subjects.
Purpose: To support high-quality research that has relevance to defence.
Eligibility: Open to anyone eligible for research council funding and particularly suited to the development of new research links. Funding is available to jointly support high-quality basic and strategic research of relevance to defence needs.
Type: Research grant
Value: Varies
Length of Study: Varies
Frequency: Dependent on funds available
Study Establishment: Universities and similar institutions
Country of Study: United Kingdom
No. of awards offered: Varies
Application Procedure: Applicants must visit the Defence Science and Technology Laboratory (DSTL) website: www.dstl.gov.uk where further details can be found about the scheme and contacts.
Closing Date: There is no closing date
Funding: Government

ENGLISH-SPEAKING UNION (ESU)

Dartmouth House, 37 Charles Street, London, W1J SED, England
Tel: (44) 20 7529 1550
Fax: (44) 20 7495 6108
Email: esu@esu.org
Website: www.esu.org
Contact: Cultural Affairs Officer

The English-Speaking Union (ESU) is an independent, non-political educational charity with members throughout the world, promoting international and human achievement through the worldwide use of the English language.

ESU Chautauqua Institution Scholarships

Subjects: Art (painting, ceramics and sculpture), music education, literature and international relations and drama.
Purpose: To enable teachers from the United Kingdom to study at the Chautauqua Institution's Summer School.
Eligibility: Open to teachers from the United Kingdom with a particular interest in the arts, aged 25–35.
Level of Study: Professional development
Type: Scholarship
Value: UK £850 plus board, room, tuition and lecture sessions at the Summer School
Length of Study: 6 weeks
Frequency: Annual
Study Establishment: Chautauqua Institution's Summer School
Country of Study: United States of America
No. of awards offered: 2
Application Procedure: Applicants must write for details.
Closing Date: November
Funding: Private

ESU Music Scholarships

Subjects: Music.
Purpose: To enable musicians of outstanding ability to study at summer schools in the United States of America, Canada, France, United Kingdom, Czech Republic or Hungary.
Eligibility: Candidates must be aged 30 or under, and be students or graduates from a recognized United Kingdom conservatory or university music department.
Level of Study: Professional development
Type: Scholarship
Value: Tuition, board and lodging and relevant flight costs
Length of Study: 2–9 weeks, depending on the particular scholarship
Frequency: Annual
Study Establishment: Summer school
No. of awards offered: 10
Application Procedure: Applications must be supported by a teacher's reference.
Funding: Commercial, private
Contributor: Private trust funds

ESU Travelling Librarian Award

Subjects: Library science.
Purpose: To encourage United States of America and United Kingdom contacts in the library world and establish links between pairs of libraries.
Eligibility: Open to professionally qualified United Kingdom and United States of America librarians.
Level of Study: Professional development
Type: Travel grant
Value: Board and lodging and relevant flight costs
Length of Study: A minimum of 3 weeks
Frequency: Annual
No. of awards offered: 1
Application Procedure: Applicants must submit a curriculum vitae and a covering letter explaining why they are the ideal candidates for the award.
Closing Date: Please write for details
Funding: Commercial, private
Additional Information: Applicants should contact the Librarian by telephone or email: library@esu.org

Lindemann Trust Fellowships

Subjects: Astronomy, chemistry, engineering, geology, geophysics, mathematics, physics and biophysics.
Purpose: To allow postdoctoral research to be carried out at a university in the United States of America.
Eligibility: Open to United Kingdom and Commonwealth citizens who are graduates of a United Kingdom university and to United Kingdom and Commonwealth citizens who are pursuing postgraduate research at a United Kingdom university, although are not graduates of that institution. Preference is given to those who have demonstrated their capacity for original research and who will be under 30 years of age on September 1st of the fellowship year, but candidates up to 35 years of age are not debarred.
Level of Study: Postdoctorate, postgraduate
Type: Fellowship
Value: US$30,000 stipend per year
Length of Study: 1 year
Frequency: Annual
Study Establishment: A university
Country of Study: United States of America
No. of awards offered: 2
Application Procedure: Applicants must write for details.
Closing Date: October
Funding: Private
Additional Information: Fellows are not required to work for an American degree, but are expected to be attached to a university, college or seat of advanced learning and technical repute in the United States of America. The place of study and research programme must be approved by the Committee. A limited amount of teaching as an adjunct to research activities is not excluded.

ENTENTE CORDIALE SCHOLARSHIPS

French Cultural Department, 23 Cromwell Road, London, SW7 2EL, England
Tel: (44) 20 7073 1300
Fax: (44) 20 7073 1326
Email: entente.cordiale@ambafrance.org.uk
Website: www.francealacarte.org.uk/entente
Contact: Administrative Officer

Launched by an agreement between the United Kingdom and French governments in 1995, the Entente Cordiale Scholarships enable outstanding British postgraduates to study or carry out research on the other side of the Channel, with a view to dispel preconceived ideas and promote good relations between the two countries.

Bourses Scholarships

Subjects: All subjects.
Purpose: To allow individuals to study or carry out research in France.
Eligibility: Open to British citizens.
Level of Study: Postgraduate
Type: Scholarship
Value: UK £8,000 for students living in Paris and UK £7,500 for those studying outside Paris
Length of Study: 1 academic year
Frequency: Annual
Study Establishment: Approved universities or grande écoles
Country of Study: France
No. of awards offered: 10
Application Procedure: Applicants must complete an application form, available from the website.
Closing Date: March 17th
Funding: Private
Contributor: Blue Circle (Lafarge), BP, Kingfisher PLC, EDF Energy, UBS, Xerox, Paul Minet, Sir Patrick Sheehy Schlumberger, French Embassy
No. of awards given last year: 9
No. of applicants last year: 60
Additional Information: Scholarships are also awarded to French postgraduates to study in the United Kingdom. Interested parties should contact the British Council in Paris.

EPILEPSY ACTION

New Anstey House, Gate Way Drive, Yeadon, Leeds, LS19 7XY, England
Tel: (44) 11 3210 8800
Fax: (44) 11 3391 0300
Email: research@epilepsy.org.uk
Website: www.epilepsy.org.uk
Contact: Margaret Rawnsley, Research Administration Officer

Epilepsy Action is the largest member-led epilepsy organization in the United Kingdom. As well as campaigning to improve epilepsy services and raise awareness of the condition, we offer assistance to people in a number of ways including a national network of branches, volunteers, free telephone and an email helpline.

Postgraduate Research Bursaries (Epilepsy Action)

Subjects: Social, healthcare and psychological aspects of epilepsy.
Purpose: To support postgraduate research in the social and medical aspect of epilepsy and all non-laboratory research into epilepsy.
Eligibility: Students should be registered for a postgraduate degree or study at a United Kingdom University.
Level of Study: Doctorate, postgraduate, postdoctorate, predoctorate
Type: Bursary
Value: UK £1,500
Length of Study: Varies
Frequency: Annual
Country of Study: United Kingdom
No. of awards offered: 3
Application Procedure: Applicants must contact the Research Administration Office.
Closing Date: October
Funding: Foundation
Contributor: Organization's own funds
No. of awards given last year: 3
No. of applicants last year: 7
Additional Information: Epilepsy Action is happy to consider any United Kingdom-based epilepsy research projects that address issues affecting the daily lives of people living with epilepsy.

EPILEPSY FOUNDATION (EF)

4351 Garden City Drive, Landover, MD, 20785, United States of America
Tel: (1) 301 459 3700
Fax: (1) 301 577 4941
Website: www.epilepsyfoundation.org
Contact: Ms Cassandra Richard, Research Co-ordinator

The Epilepsy Foundation (EF) is a national, charitable organization, founded in 1968 as the Epilepsy Foundation of America. It is the only organization wholly dedicated to the welfare of people with epilepsy and to working on their behalf through research, education, advocacy and service.

Behavioral Sciences Postdoctoral Fellowships

Subjects: Epilepsy research relevant to the behavioural sciences. Appropriate fields of study include sociology, social work, psychology, anthropology, nursing, political science and others fields relevant to epilepsy research and practice.
Purpose: To offer qualified individuals the opportunity to develop expertise in epilepsy research through a training experience or involvement in an epilepsy research project.
Eligibility: Open to individuals who have received their doctoral degree in a field of the behavioural sciences by the time the fellowship commences and desire additional postdoctoral research experience in epilepsy. Applications from women and minorities are encouraged.
Level of Study: Postdoctorate
Type: Fellowship
Value: Up to US$40,000 stipend, depending on the experience and qualifications of the applicant and the scope and duration of the proposed project
Length of Study: 1 year
Frequency: Annual
Study Establishment: An approved facility
Country of Study: United States of America
No. of awards offered: 1
Application Procedure: Applicants must complete an application form, available from the Foundation. Applicants may also visit the website research page for details.
Closing Date: March 1st
Funding: Private
No. of awards given last year: 1
Additional Information: The closing date for applications may vary from year to year. Applicants should email: cmorris@efa.org for details.

Postdoctoral Research Fellowships

Subjects: Basic or clinical epilepsy.
Purpose: To offer qualified individuals the opportunity to develop expertise in epilepsy research through involvement in an epilepsy research project.
Eligibility: Open to physicians and neuroscientist PhDs who desire postdoctoral research experience. Preference is given to applicants whose proposals have a paediatric or developmental emphasis. Research must address a question of fundamental importance. A clinical training component is not required. Applications from women and minorities are encouraged.
Level of Study: Postdoctorate
Type: Fellowship
Value: US$40,000 stipend
Length of Study: 1 year
Frequency: Annual
Study Establishment: A facility where there is an ongoing epilepsy research programme
Country of Study: United States of America or Canada
No. of awards offered: Varies
Application Procedure: Applicants must complete an application form, available from the Foundation. Applicants may also look at the website research page for details.
Closing Date: September 1st
Funding: Private

Research and Training Fellowships for Clinicians

Subjects: Basic or clinical epilepsy, with an equal emphasis on clinical training and clinical epileptology.
Purpose: To offer qualified individuals the opportunity to develop expertise in epilepsy research through training and involvement in an epilepsy research project.
Eligibility: Open to individuals who hold an MD degree and have completed their residency training. Applications from women and minorities are encouraged.
Level of Study: Postdoctorate, postgraduate
Type: Fellowship
Value: US$50,000 stipend
Length of Study: 1 year
Frequency: Annual
Study Establishment: A facility where there is an ongoing epilepsy research programme
Country of Study: United States of America
No. of awards offered: Varies
Application Procedure: Applicants must complete an application form, available from the Foundation. Applicants may also visit the website research page for details.
Closing Date: September 1st
Funding: Private
Additional Information: These fellowships include the Merrit-Putnam Fellowship.

Research Grants (EF)

Subjects: Basic biomedical, behavioural and social science.
Purpose: To support basic and clinical research that will advance the understanding, treatment and prevention of epilepsy.
Eligibility: Open to United States of America researchers. Priority is given to investigators just entering the field of epilepsy, to new or innovative projects or to investigators whose research is relevant to developmental or paediatric aspects of epilepsy. Applications from women and minorities are encouraged, while applications from established investigators with other sources of support are discouraged. Research grants are not intended to provide support for postdoctoral Fellows.
Level of Study: Postdoctorate, postgraduate
Value: Up to US$450,000 support, but this may vary
Length of Study: 1 year
Frequency: Annual
Country of Study: United States of America
No. of awards offered: Varies
Application Procedure: Applicants must complete an application form, available from the Foundation. Applicants may also visit the website research page for details.
Closing Date: September 1st
Funding: Private
Additional Information: The closing date for applications may vary from year to year. Applicants should email: cmorris@efa.org for details.

EPILEPSY RESEARCH FOUNDATION

PO Box 3004, London, W4 4XT, England
Tel: (44) 20 8995 4781
Fax: (44) 20 8995 4781
Email: info@erf.org.uk
Website: www.erf.org.uk
Contact: Ms Isabella Von Holstein

The Epilepsy Research Foundation promotes and supports basic and clinical scientific research into epilepsy. It seeks to identify medical research needs in epilepsy and raise money for independent research to be carried out by the best available research teams.

Epilepsy Research Foundation Equipment Grant

Purpose: To promote and support basic, clinical and qualitative research into the causes, treatment and prevention of epilepsy.
Eligibility: Open to researchers resident in United Kingdom. And affiliated to an academic institution in the United Kingdom. Applicants must be graduates in medicine or in one of the sciences allied to medicine.
Level of Study: Unrestricted
Type: Equipment grant
Value: A maximum of UK £10,000
Frequency: Annual
Country of Study: United Kingdom
No. of awards offered: 3
Application Procedure: Application is a two-stage process: A preliminary application form must be completed and submitted. If short listed, a full application form must be completed. further details can be got from the website.
Closing Date: The end of October
Funding: Private, trusts, individuals
No. of awards given last year: 5
No. of applicants last year: 35

Epilepsy Research Foundation Fellowship

Subjects: Epilepsy.
Purpose: To promote and support basic, clinical and qualitative research into the causes, treatment and prevention of epilepsy.
Eligibility: Open to researchers resident in the United Kingdom. And affiliated to an academic institution in the United Kingdom. Applicants must be graduates in medicine or in one of the sciences allied to medicine.
Level of Study: Unrestricted, research
Type: Fellowship
Value: Unrestricted
Length of Study: 1–3 years
Frequency: Annual
Country of Study: United Kingdom
No. of awards offered: 3
Application Procedure: Application is a two-stage process: A preliminary application form must be completed and submitted. If shortlisted, a full application form must be completed. Further details from our website. An interview may be required.
Funding: Private, individuals, trusts
No. of awards given last year: 5
No. of applicants last year: 35

Epilepsy Research Foundation Research Grant

Subjects: Epilepsy.
Purpose: To promote and support basic, clinical and qualitative research into the causes, treatment and prevention of epilepsy.
Eligibility: Open to researchers resident in the United Kingdom. And affiliated to an academic institution in the United Kingdom. Applicants must be graduates in medicine or in one of the sciences allied to medicine.
Level of Study: Research, unrestricted
Type: Research grant
Value: A maximum of UK £60,000
Length of Study: 1–3 years
Frequency: Annual
Country of Study: United Kingdom
No. of awards offered: 3
Application Procedure: Application is a two-stage process: A preliminary application form must be completed and submitted. If shortlisted, a full application form must be completed. Further details from our website.
Closing Date: The end of October
Funding: Individuals, private, trusts
No. of awards given last year: 5
No. of applicants last year: 35

EPISCOPAL CHURCH FOUNDATION

815 Second Avenue, New York, NY, 10017, United States of America
Tel: (1) 212 697 2858
Fax: (1) 212 297 0142
Email: all@episcopalfoundation.org
Website: www.episcopalfoundation.org
Contact: Fellows Program Manager

The Episcopal Church Foundation is an independent, lay-led organization that offers innovative programmes in leadership development, education and philanthropy for the clergy and laity of the Episcopal Church. It does not accept unsolicited grant proposals or extend aid to individuals.

Episcopal Church Foundation Graduate Fellowship Program

Subjects: Theological studies.
Purpose: To support doctoral study for Episcopalians planning teaching careers in theological education in the Episcopal Church in the United States of America.
Eligibility: Open to recent graduates of an accredited seminary who have been nominated by one of the 11 Episcopal seminaries, by the Harvard Divinity School or the Union Theological Seminary of New York. Scholars who are not graduates of these institutions may seek nomination through the Fellows Forum. Neither ordination nor a Master of Divinity degree is required. Priority consideration is given to applicants who are in the early stages of their doctoral studies.
Level of Study: Doctorate
Type: Fellowship
Value: US$10,000 regardless of financial need
Length of Study: 1 year, renewable for a further 2 years
Frequency: Annual
Study Establishment: Accredited institutions in the United States of America and abroad
Country of Study: Any country
No. of awards offered: 4
Application Procedure: Applicants must contact the Dean's office at any of the 11 accredited Episcopal seminaries, the Harvard Divinity School or the Union Theological Seminary for application materials.
Funding: Private
Additional Information: Applicants must be communicants of the Episcopal Church in the United States of America and show demonstrated evidence of commitment to this church.

THE ERIC THOMPSON TRUST

The Royal Philharmonic Society, 10 Stratford Place, London, W1C 1BA, England
Tel: (44) 20 7491 8110
Fax: (44) 20 7493 7463
Email: ett@royalphilharmonicsociety.org.uk
Website: www.etorgantrust.co.uk
Contact: Mr David Lowe, Clerk to The Trustees

The Eric Thompson Trust aims to provide modest grants to help aspiring professional organists. Preference will be given to students seeking assistance towards specific projects, rather than continuing academic tuition, eg. summer schools or special lessons in addition to normal studies and opportunities to play on historical instruments in the context of further study.

Eric Thompson Charitable Trust for Organists

Subjects: The organ.
Purpose: To provide aspiring professional organists with financial assistance for special studies such as summer schools, travel and subsistence for auditions or performance or other incidental costs incurred in their work.
Eligibility: Some professional training as an organist is required.
Level of Study: Professional development
Value: Determined by the Trustees, but normally limited to a contribution towards costs
Frequency: 6-monthly
Country of Study: Any country
No. of awards offered: Varies
Application Procedure: Applicants must send full details of their needs together with information on their training and career, two written references from organists of good standing in the profession and other relevant material to the Clerk to the Trustees.
Closing Date: December 31st or June 30th for consideration in January and July, respectively
Funding: Private
Contributor: Personal and corporate donors

ESADE

MBA Office, Avenue d'espluges 92-96, E-08034 Barcelona, Spain
Tel: (34) 93 495 2088
Fax: (34) 93 495 3828
Email: mba@esade.edu
Website: www.esade.edu
Contact: Ms Nuria Guilera, MBA Admissions Director

Established in 1958, ESADE is a private, non-profit Institute of Higher Education with a distinctly international outlook. It consists of three schools: the Business School, the Law School and the Language School. Located in one of Barcelona's most attractive residential areas, ESADE's three buildings provide a total of 26,850 square metres of space for teaching and study.

ESADE MBA Scholarships

Subjects: MBA (18-month MBA and One Year).
Purpose: To assist full-time MBA students with tuition fees.
Eligibility: All candidates admitted to the programme. Scholarships are awarded on the basis of applicants' academic records, professional experience, personal merits and how well they fit the required profile of the programme.
Level of Study: MBA
Type: Scholarship
Value: (1) ESADE Business School awards two grants for 20% of the tuition fees to female candidates of any nationality. These two grants are awarded based on the candidate's professional career, their personal qualifications and their suitability for an MBA programme. (2) ESADE Business School awards two grants for 20% of the tuition fees to candidates (men or women) from developing countries, especially from Eastern Europe and Asia. Selection will be based mainly on the candidate's international experience and professional career. (3) ESADE Business School awards a grant for 20% of the tuition fees to candidates (men or women) in recognition of their exceptional academic and professional career. (4) ESADE Business School, together with Foundatión Carolina, awards two grants covering 25% of the tuition fees, a return awardees will have access to favourable bank loan conditions to finance the rest of the programme. These grants are available as per suitability of each candidate to the programme.
Length of Study: 1 year–18 months
Frequency: Annual
Study Establishment: ESADE
Country of Study: Spain
No. of awards offered: 7
Application Procedure: Applicants must apply for a scholarship along with their course application. Scholarship applications are reviewed once candidates have been admitted to the MBA programme by the admissions committee.
Closing Date: May

For further information contact:

Website: www.mbafinaid@esade.edu

EUROPEAN CALCIFIED TISSUE SOCIETY

PO Box 337, Bristol, BS32 4ZR, England
Tel: (44) 14 5461 0255
Fax: (44) 14 5461 0255
Email: admin@actsoc.org
Website: www.ectsoc.org

The European Calcified Tissue Society is the major organization in Europe for researchers and clinicians working in the field of calcified tissues and related fields.

ECTS Career Establishment Award

Subjects: Calcified tissue and related fields.
Purpose: To assist newly appointed faculty members in launching a successful research career.
Eligibility: Applicants must be a member of the ECTS.
Level of Study: Set-up grant not dependent on study

Value: UK £50,000 (over 2–3 years)
Frequency: Dependent on funds available
No. of awards offered: Dependent on funds available
Application Procedure: Applicants must complete an application form, available from the website.
Closing Date: January 10th
Funding: Foundation
Contributor: ECTS
No. of awards given last year: 1

ECTS Exchange Scholarship Grants

Subjects: Calcified tissue and related fields.
Purpose: To enable researchers to spend time in another laboratory to learn new techniques.
Eligibility: Applicants must be member's of the ECTS.
Level of Study: Professional development
Type: Scholarship
Value: Depends on anticipated expenses
No. of awards offered: Dependent on funds
Application Procedure: Applicants must complete an application form, available from the website.
Closing Date: September 1st and March 1st
Funding: Foundation
Contributor: ECTS
No. of awards given last year: 2
No. of applicants last year: 3

EUROPEAN COMMISSION

Rue de la Loi 200, B-1049 Brussels, Belgium
Tel: (32) 33 2299 1111
Email: rtd-mariecurie-actions@cec.eu.int
Website: www.europa.eu.int
Contact: Marie Curie Prize

Marie Curie Development Host Fellowships

Subjects: All fields of scientific research.
Purpose: To provide an opportunity to institutions that are active in research Community's less-favourable regions to attain high-level research capacity in specific area of their choice.
Eligibility: All applicants must be nationals of a European Union member state or associated states or must have resided in the European Union for at least 5 years prior to their selection by the Commission. Applicants must be below 35 years, holding a doctoral degree, or having spent at least 4 years on full-time research at the postgraduate level.
Level of Study: Postdoctorate, research
Type: Fellowship
Value: Salary costs and social security contributions of the employer, a mobility allowance, research, management and travel costs
Length of Study: 1–2 years
Frequency: Dependent on funds available
Study Establishment: A research institution
Country of Study: European Union
Application Procedure: The institution/research group identifies areas where it needs to develop new competence and applies to the Commission to host a number of postdoctoral researchers. Young postdoctoral researchers with proven research experience in those specific areas apply directly to the hosts selected by the Commission.
Closing Date: Application deadlines vary. For details visit the website: www.cordis.lu/improving/code/calls.htm
Contributor: European Union

EUROPEAN LEAGUE AGAINST RHEUMATISM

Witikonerstrasse 15, CH-8032 Zurich, Switzerland
Tel: (41) 411 383 9690
Fax: (41) 411 383 9810
Email: secretariat@eular.org
Website: www.eular.org
Contact: Elly Wyss, EULAR Training Bursaries

EULAR Research Grants

Subjects: Research into diagnostic and therapeutic aspects of rheumatic diseases.
Purpose: To support work programmes that improve the quality of care in the field of rheumatology.
Level of Study: Research
Type: Project grant
Value: €100,000 per year
Length of Study: Up to 3 years
Frequency: Annual
Application Procedure: Applications for grants should include: an abstract, a rationale of the need and relevance of the project, an account of strategic objectives, resources, budget and organization, a description of the implementation and relevance of the project for EULAR, and a list of references of participating university/hospital centres relating to the topic of the proposal.
Closing Date: March 31st
Contributor: European League Against Rheumatism
Additional Information: For further information contact the EULAR Secretariat.

EUROPEAN MOLECULAR BIOLOGY ORGANIZATION (EMBO)

Postbox 1022.40, D-69012 Heidelberg, Germany
Tel: (49) 622 188 910
Fax: (49) 622 188 91200
Email: embo@embo.org
Website: www.embo.org
Contact: Mr Lindsay Johnson, Communications Officer

The European Molecular Biology Organization (EMBO) was established in 1964 to promote biosciences in Europe. Today EMBO supports transnational mobility, training and exchange through initiatives such as fellowships, courses, workshops and its young investigator activities.

EMBO Award for Communication in the Life Sciences

Subjects: Public communication of science.
Purpose: To promote and reward public communication of the life sciences and their applications by practising scientists in Europe.
Eligibility: Open to scientists working in active research in an area of life sciences at the time of nomination. Candidates must be working in Europe or Israel, and the criterion for consideration is excellence in public communication of science via any medium or activity.
Type: Monetary award and medal
Value: €5,000
Frequency: Annual
No. of awards offered: 1
Application Procedure: Applicants must apply using the forms available on the website.
Closing Date: May 31st
Funding: Private
Contributor: EMBO
No. of awards given last year: 1
No. of applicants last year: 27
Additional Information: For further information, email: Dr Andrew Moore at scisoc@embo.org

For further information contact:

EMBO, Meyerhofstrasse 1, D-69117 Heidelberg, Germany
Tel: (49) 622 188 91119
Fax: (49) 622 188 91200
Email: embo@embo.org
Website: www.embo.org

EMBO Long-Term Fellowships in Molecular Biology

Subjects: Molecular biology and disciplines relying on molecular biology.
Purpose: To promote the development of research in Europe and Israel.
Eligibility: Open to holders of a doctoral degree. EMBO fellowships are not awarded for exchanges between laboratories within any one

country. Applicants must be nationals from a European Molecular Biology Conference (EMBC) member state or be wishing to travel to a EMBC member state.
Level of Study: Postdoctorate
Type: Fellowship
Value: A return travel allowance for the Fellow and any dependants plus a stipend and dependants' allowance
Length of Study: 1 year, renewable for a further year
Frequency: Every 2 years
Study Establishment: A suitable laboratory
Country of Study: Any country
No. of awards offered: Approximately 150–200 per year
Application Procedure: Please see the EMBO website (www.embo.org/fellowships)
Closing Date: February 15th and August 15th
Funding: Government
Contributor: The 24 EMBC member states
No. of awards given last year: 190
No. of applicants last year: 1080
Additional Information: The following countries form the EMBC: Austria, Belgium, Croatia, the Czech Republic, Denmark, Finland, France, Germany, Greece, Hungary, Iceland, Ireland, Israel, Italy, the Netherlands, Norway, Poland, Portugal, Slovenia, Spain, Sweden, Switzerland, Turkey and the United Kingdom. Special provision is also made for applications involving Cyprus. For further information, email: fellows@embo.org

EMBO Science Writing Prize

Subjects: Public communication of science in written form.
Purpose: To promote and reward science communication by young scientists in Europe.
Eligibility: Open to any life scientist in Europe under 40 years of age. The preferred language is English and entries should not exceed 2000 words.
Level of Study: Unrestricted
Type: Monetary award and certificate
Value: €1,500
Frequency: Annual
No. of awards offered: 1
Application Procedure: Applicants must visit the website www.embo.org/projects/scisoc/writing_prize.html for full details.
Closing Date: September 15th
Funding: International Office
Contributor: EMBO
No. of awards given last year: 1
No. of applicants last year: 26

EMBO Short-Term Fellowships in Molecular Biology

Subjects: Molecular biology and disciplines relying on molecular biology.
Purpose: To advance molecular biology research by helping scientists to visit another laboratory with a view to applying a technique not available in the home laboratory and to foster collaboration.
Eligibility: Please see the EMBO website (www.embo.org/fellowships)
Level of Study: Predoctorate, doctorate, postdoctorate, postgraduate, research
Type: Fellowship
Value: Return travel for the Fellow and a daily subsistance for the duration of the fellowship
Length of Study: 2 weeks–3 months
Study Establishment: A suitable laboratory
No. of awards offered: Varies
Application Procedure: Application form and guidelines are available on the EMBO website.
Closing Date: There is no deadline, but applications should be made at least 3 months before proposed start date
Funding: Government
Contributor: The 24 EMBC member states
No. of awards given last year: 167
No. of applicants last year: 301

EMBO Young Investigator

Subjects: Molecular biology and disciplines relying on molecular biology.
Purpose: To promote the development of research in Europe and Israel.
Eligibility: Applicants should: be leading their first independent laboratory for at least one and not more then four years in an EMBC member state, have at least 2 years of post PhD scientific experience, have an excellent track record, be working in the very broadly defined area of Molecular Biology, be supported by sufficient funds to run their laboratories. have published at least one last author paper after establishing an independent laboratory.
Level of Study: Postdoctorate, professional development
Value: €15,000
Length of Study: 3 years
Frequency: Annual
Study Establishment: The applicant's own independent laboratory
No. of awards offered: Varies
Application Procedure: Applicants must visit the website for details on Application forms, letters of reference and on-line application.
Closing Date: April 1st
Funding: Government
Contributor: The 24 EMBC member states
No. of awards given last year: 20
No. of applicants last year: 166

EUROPEAN SOCIETY OF SURGICAL ONCOLOGY (ESSO)

Dept of Surgery, Umea University Hospital, Umea, S 90185, Sweden
Tel: (46) 2 537 3106
Fax: (46) 2 539 0374
Email: peter.naredi@surgery.umu.se
Website: www.esso-surgeonline.be
Contact: Ms Peter Naredi, ESSO Administrator

ESSO was founded to advance the art, science and practice of surgery for the treatment of cancer. ESSO endeavours to ensure that the highest possible standard of surgical treatment is available to cancer patients throughout Europe by organizing congresses, granting fellowships and publishing the *EJSO.*

ESSO Fellowships

Subjects: Surgical oncology.
Purpose: To allow young surgeons the chance to spend time in another specialist centre to either expand their experience or learn new techniques.
Eligibility: Applicants must refer to the ESSO website.
Level of Study: Postdoctorate
Type: Fellowship
Value: €2,500 for European fellowships and €10,000 for the major international training fellowship
Length of Study: 2–3 weeks for fellowships and 3 months for the major training fellowship
Frequency: Annual
Country of Study: Any country
No. of awards offered: 4 fellowships and 1 major training fellowship
Application Procedure: Applicants must submit a full curriculum vitae with their application, together with a note of their career intentions. Applicants should also outline what they hope to gain from the training fellowship, including what specific experience is sought and how this will fit in with the applicant's career development. Applicants should provide details as to which institution they wish to visit, together with details of the clinical or research training opportunities that the department can offer. A letter of support from the applicant's head of department must be included and this can be in the form of a reference. A letter of support from the head of the department they wish to visit must also be supplied, indicating that the department to be visited will be in a position to provide the experience required by the applicant.
Closing Date: August 31st
Additional Information: Applicants must be or become ESSO members.

For further information contact:

Department of Surgery, University Hospital, UMEA, S 90185, Sweden
Contact: Dr Peter Naredi

EUROPEAN SOUTHERN OBSERVATORY (ESO)

Karl-Schwarzschild-Strasse 2, D-85748 Garching bei Muenchen, Germany
Tel: (49) 893 200 60
Fax: (49) 893 202 362
Email: vacancy@eso.org
Website: www.eso.org
Contact: Mr Roland Block, Head of Personnel Department

The European Southern Observatory (ESO) is an intergovernmental organization for research in astronomy. At present ESO is operating the Very Large Telescope (VLT) at Cerro Paranal in Chile, the world's most powerful facility for optical astronomy, and La Silla Observatory.

ESO Fellowship
Subjects: Astronomy and astrophysics.
Purpose: To provide a unique opportunity to learn and participate in the process of observational astronomy while pursuing a research programme.
Level of Study: Postdoctorate
Type: Fellowship
Value: A basic monthly salary of not less than €2,918, to which is added an expatriation allowance as well as some family allowances, if applicable. The Fellow will also have an annual travel budget for scientific meetings, collaborations and observing trips
Length of Study: 1 year, with a possible extension to 3 years in Garching. Fellowships in Chile are for 1 year with a possible extension to 4 years
Frequency: Annual
Study Establishment: The European Southern Observatory
No. of awards offered: 6–9
Application Procedure: Applicants must visit the ESO website for an application form and further information.
Closing Date: October 15th
Funding: Government
Additional Information: Fellowships begin between April and October of the year in which they are awarded. Selected Fellows can join ESO only after having completed their doctorate.

EUROPEAN SYNCHROTRON RADIATION FACILITY (ESRF)

BP 220, F-38043 Grenoble, France
Tel: (33) 4 76 88 20 00
Fax: (33) 4 76 88 20 20
Email: stuck@esrf.fr
Website: www.esrf.fr
Contact: Ms Elizabeth Moulin

The European Synchrotron Radiation Facility (ESRF) supports scientists in the implementation of fundamental and applied research on the structure of condensed matter in fields such as physics, chemistry, crystallography, Earth science, biology, medicine, surface science and materials science.

ESRF Postdoctoral Fellowships
Subjects: Physics, biology, chemistry, mineralogy and crystallography, computer engineering and accelerators science.
Purpose: To enable postdoctoral Fellows to develop their own research programme and to motivate them to collaborate with external users.
Eligibility: Preference is given to member-country nationals, but other nationals may be accepted for the postdoctoral positions.
Level of Study: Postdoctorate
Value: €2,975 each month, plus a possible relocation allowance of up to €371 each month. These amounts correspond to a gross remuneration and are subject to social charges and income tax in France
Length of Study: 2–3 years
Frequency: Dependent on funds available
No. of awards offered: Up to 20
Application Procedure: Applicants must complete an application form, available on request from the personnel department of the ESRF.
Closing Date: Individual deadlines exist for each position. Please contact the organization
Funding: Private
Contributor: Public funds from 16 countries, mostly European
No. of awards given last year: 25
No. of applicants last year: 304
Additional Information: Member countries are Belgium, Denmark, Finland, France, Germany, Italy, the Netherlands, Norway, Spain, Sweden, Switzerland and the United Kingdom. New associated members are the Czech Republic, Israel, Portugal and the Republic of Hungary.

ESRF Thesis Studentships
Subjects: Physics, biology, chemistry, mineralogy and crystallography, computer engineering and accelerators science. The ESRF proposes subjects related to the use of synchrotron radiation or synchrotron or storage ring technology.
Purpose: To enable grant holders to pursue a PhD at the ESRF and to enable young scientists to acquire knowledge of the use of synchrotron radiation or its generation.
Eligibility: Preference is given to member country nationals, but other nationals may be accepted for the postdoctoral positions.
Level of Study: Doctorate
Value: €1,959 per month. These amounts correspond to a gross remuneration and are subject to social charges and income tax in France
Length of Study: 2–3 years
Frequency: Dependent on funds available
Study Establishment: Universities
No. of awards offered: Up to 10
Application Procedure: Applicants must complete an application form, available on request from the personnel department of the ESRF.
Closing Date: There is an individual deadline for each position
Funding: Private
Contributor: Public funds from 16 countries, mainly European
No. of awards given last year: 12
No. of applicants last year: 202
Additional Information: Member countries are Belgium, Denmark, Finland, France, Germany, Italy, the Netherlands, Norway, Spain, Sweden, Switzerland and the United Kingdom. Newly associated members are the Czech Republic, Israel, Portugal and the Republic of Hungary.

EUROPEAN UNIVERSITY INSTITUTE (EUI)

Via dei Roccettini 9, I-50016 San Domenico di Fiesole, Italy
Tel: (39) 55 468 51
Fax: (39) 55 468 5444
Email: applyres@iue.it
Website: www.iue.it
Contact: Mr Kenneth Hulley, Assistant Administrator (Academic Service)

The European University Institute's (EUI) main aim is to make a contribution to the intellectual life of Europe. Created by the European Union member states, it is a postgraduate research institution, pursuing interdisciplinary research programmes on the main issues confronting European society and the construction of Europe.

EUI Postgraduate Scholarships
Subjects: History and civilization, economics, law or political and social sciences.

Purpose: To provide the opportunity for study leading to the doctorate or Master's degree from the Institute.
Eligibility: Open to nationals of European Union member states. Candidates must possess a good Honours degree or its equivalent, and have full written and spoken command of at least two of the Institute's official languages. Nationals of countries other than the European Union may be admitted to the Institute subject to scholarship agreements being in place.
Level of Study: Postgraduate, doctorate
Type: Scholarship
Value: Varies, but approx. €1,060 per month
Length of Study: 1 year, renewable for up to an additional 3 years
Frequency: Annual
Study Establishment: EUI
Country of Study: Italy
No. of awards offered: Approx. 125–135
Application Procedure: Applications must be submitted online at www.iue.it
Closing Date: January 31st
Funding: Government
Contributor: Member states of the European Union
No. of awards given last year: 130
No. of applicants last year: 1,100
Additional Information: The annual scholarships are currently granted by the governments of 17 EU Members States to nationals of their own countries. Awards this year were distributed as follows: Germany-12, France-10, Italy-16, United Kingdom-12, Spain-10, The Netherlands-7, Denmark-4, Belgium-3, Sweden-5, Poland-11, Estonia-1. Switzerland and Norway have grant arrangements with the EUI and contribute approx. 2–3 scholarships each per year.

Fernand Braudel Senior Fellowships

Subjects: Humanities and social sciences, with special attention to problems related to the European Community and to the development of Europe's cultural and academic heritage.
Purpose: To encourage postdoctoral research.
Eligibility: Open mainly to candidates with a doctoral degree at an early stage of their academic career.
Level of Study: Postdoctorate
Type: Fellowship
Value: €1,200–3,000 per month depending on the type of the fellowship and whether the applicant is on a paid sabbatical or not
Length of Study: Depending on the type of the fellowship from 3 months to 2 years.
Frequency: Annual
Study Establishment: The EUI
Country of Study: Italy
No. of awards offered: 80
Application Procedure: Applicants must complete an online application form available via the internet at www.ine.it
Closing Date: October 25th for Max Weber and JeanMornet Fellowships; March 30th/September for Fernand Braudel Senior Fellowships
Contributor: The EU Commission/Members states of the European Union
No. of applicants last year: 750

Jean Monnet Fellowships

Subjects: Humanities and social sciences, with special attention to problems related to the European Community and to the development of Europe's cultural and academic heritage.
Purpose: To encourage postdoctoral research.
Eligibility: Open mainly to candidates with a doctoral degree at an early stage of their academic career.
Level of Study: Postdoctorate
Type: Fellowship
Value: €1,200–3,000 per month depending on the type of the fellowship and whether the applicant is on a paid sabbatical or not
Length of Study: Depending on the type of the fellowship from 3 months to 2 years
Frequency: Annual
Study Establishment: The EUI
Country of Study: Italy
No. of awards offered: 80
Application Procedure: Applicants must complete an online application form available via the Internet at www.ine.it
Closing Date: October 25th for Max Weber and Jean Honnet Fellowships; March 30th/September for Fernand Braudel Senior Fellowship
Funding: Government
Contributor: The EU commission Member states of the European Union
No. of applicants last year: 750

Max Weber Fellowships

Subjects: Humanities and social sciences, with special attention to problems related to the European Community and to the development of Europe's cultural and academic heritage.
Purpose: To encourage postdoctoral research.
Eligibility: Open mainly to candidates with a doctoral degree at an early stage of their academic career.
Type: Fellowship
Value: €1,200–3,000 per month depending on the type of the fellowship and whether the applicant is on a paid sabbatical or not
Length of Study: Depending on the type of the fellowship from 3 months to 2 years
Frequency: Annual
Study Establishment: The EUI
Country of Study: Italy
No. of awards offered: 80
Application Procedure: Applicants must complete an online application form available via the internet at www.ine.it
Closing Date: October 25th for Max Weber and Jean Mornet Fellowships; March 30th/September for Fernand Braudel Senior Fellowships
Contributor: The EU Commission/Members State of European Union
No. of applicants last year: 750

EVANGELICAL LUTHERAN CHURCH IN AMERICA (ELCA)

Division for Ministry, 8765 West Higgins Road, Chicago, IL, 60631-4195, United States of America
Tel: (1) 773 380 2873
Fax: (1) 773 380 2829
Email: pwilder@elca.org
Website: www.elca.org
Contact: Mr Pat Wilder, Executive Secretary

ELCA Educational Grant Program

Subjects: Theological studies.
Eligibility: Open to members of the Evangelical Lutheran Church in America who are enrolled in an accredited graduate institution for study in a PhD, EdD or ThD programme in a theological area appropriate to seminary teaching. Priority is given to women and minority students.
Level of Study: Doctorate
Type: Grant
Value: US$250–5,000. Funds are distributed according to need and the contribution the applicant will make towards the future of the Church
Length of Study: Grants are awarded for a maximum of 4 years with a 5th-year award for the dissertation
Frequency: Annual
Country of Study: United States of America
No. of awards offered: 40–65
Application Procedure: Applications are available online at www.elca.org/dm/te/grants.html in January. Two recommendations are required for each applicant.
Closing Date: March 15th
Funding: Private
No. of awards given last year: 65
No. of applicants last year: 72

EVRIKA FOUNDATION

PO Box 615, 1, Patriarch Evtimii Blvd, Sofia, BG-1000, Bulgaria
Tel: (359) 2 981 5181, (359) 2 981 37 99
Fax: (359) 2 981 5483
Email: bkadmonova@evrika.org /evrika@einet.bg
Website: www.evrika.org
Contact: Mr Boryana Kadmonova, Executive Director

The Evrika Foundation was established in 1990 by state and public organizations to promote the development of youth technical and scientific creativity, and to encourage youth economic enterprise and to assist youth education, specialization and training. The Evrika Foundation is a non-governmental, non-religious and apolitical organization.

Achievements of Science

Subjects: The award is given for an excellent defence of a dissertation before the High Atestation Commission of the Ministerial counsie of Bulgaria.
Purpose: Discovering and popularizing the experience of young people in the field of technics, engineering and natural sciences.
Eligibility: Less than 35 years old by the end of the year (37th XII) in which the award is given, Bulgarians living in Bulgaria.
Type: Scholarship
Value: Dependent on the type of award
Frequency: Annual
Country of Study: Bulgaria
No. of awards offered: 1 plus additional encouraging awards for excellent presentation
Application Procedure: A Competition by an application form, other documents and a conversation with a specialized jury.
Closing Date: December 10th
Funding: Foundation
Contributor: Foundation
No. of awards given last year: 1
No. of applicants last year: 13
Additional Information: Eligible to nationals of Bulgaria only. Besides the financial support, a certification and a statute statement are awarded.

The Evrika Award for Young Farmer

Subjects: The award is given to young people with both highly productive and highly profitable production.
Purpose: Discovering and popularizing the experience of young people in the field of agriculture and live stock breeding.
Eligibility: To be less than 35 years old by December 31st, the year that the award is given; the award is only for Bulgarians giving in Bulgaria.
Level of Study: MBA, graduate, postgraduate, predoctorate, secondary, vocational, specialized education
Type: Scholarship
Value: Dependent on the type of award
Frequency: Annual
Country of Study: Bulgaria
No. of awards offered: 1 plus additional encouraging awards for excellent presentation
Application Procedure: A competition by an application form, other documents, and a conversation with a specialized jury.
Closing Date: December 10th
Funding: Foundation, private
Contributor: Foundation
No. of awards given last year: 1
No. of applicants last year: 15
Additional Information: Eligible to nationals of Bulgaria only; besides the financial award, a certificate and a statuette are given.

The Evrika Award for Young Manager

Subjects: The award is given to a young person under 35, who has achieved the best results in the field of management and has proven his or her entrepreneurial spirit, assertiveness, communication ability and language or computer skills.
Purpose: Discovering and popularizing the experience of young people in the field of technology, engineering and management.
Eligibility: Less than 35 years old by the end of year in which the award is given. Bulgarians living in Bulgaria.
Level of Study: Predoctorate, research, mba, postgraduate, secondary, vocational, specialized education
Type: Scholarship
Value: Dependent on the type of award
Frequency: Annual
Country of Study: Bulgaria
No. of awards offered: 1 plus additional encouraging awards for excellent presentation
Application Procedure: A completion by an application form, other documents and a conversation with a specialized jury.
Closing Date: December 10th
Funding: Foundation, private
Contributor: Foundation
No. of awards given last year: 1
No. of applicants last year: 14
Additional Information: Eligible to nationals of Bulgaria only. Besides the financial support, a certification and a statuette are awarded.

The Evrika Awards for Young Inventor

Subjects: The award is given to a young inventor whose work has had a significant impact on scientific and technological progress on a world-wide scale and on the development of society.
Purpose: Discovering and popularizing the experience of young people in the field of technology, engineering and innovations.
Eligibility: Under the age of 35 by the date of application for the national pattern department and under the age of 39 by December 31st, the year the award is given. Bulgarians living is Bulgaria.
Level of Study: MBA, postdoctorate, doctorate, postgraduate, research
Type: Scholarship
Value: Dependent on the type of award
Frequency: Annual
Country of Study: Bulgaria
No. of awards offered: 1 plus additional encouraging awards for excellent presentation
Application Procedure: A competition by an application form, other documents and a conversation with a specialized jury.
Closing Date: December 10th
Funding: Foundation, private
Contributor: Foundation
No. of awards given last year: 1
No. of applicants last year: 12
Additional Information: Eligible to nationals of Bulgaria only. Besides the financial support, a certification and a statuette are awarded.

The Evrika Foundation Awards

Subjects: Science, technics, technology and management.
Purpose: To discover and popularize the experiences of young people.
Eligibility: Open to Bulgarian nationals only who are not more than 35 years of age.
Level of Study: MBA, postgraduate
Type: Award
Value: Varies
Frequency: Annual
Study Establishment: Any accredited university
Country of Study: Bulgaria
No. of awards offered: 10
Application Procedure: A completed application form along with other relevant documents must be submitted.
Closing Date: December 15th
Funding: Commercial, foundation, corporation, private
Contributor: Varies
No. of awards given last year: 50
No. of applicants last year: 194
Additional Information: Besides the financial support, a certification and a statuette are awarded scholarships, are also given to students who are winners in National and International Olympiads.

Evrika Foundation Awards

Subjects: Agriculture and farm management, management systems and techniques, engineering and natural sciences.

Purpose: To support young people with proven abilities and skills.
Eligibility: Open to Bulgarian nationals only, up to the age of 35. Scholarships are available to postgraduate students and grants and awards are reserved for Scholars who hold a Master's degree or PhD.
Level of Study: Graduate, doctorate
Type: Other
Value: Dependent on the type of award
Frequency: Annual
Country of Study: Other
No. of awards offered: 3–4
Application Procedure: Applicants must complete and submit an application form with references.
Closing Date: December 15th
Funding: Private
No. of awards given last year: 3
No. of applicants last year: 285

EXETER COLLEGE

Oxford, Oxfordshire, OX1 3DP, England
Tel: (44) 18 6527 9660
Fax: (44) 18 6527 9630
Email: joan.himpson@exeter.ox.ac.uk
Website: www.exeter.ox.ac.uk
Contact: Mrs Joan Himpson, Academic Administrator

Exeter College is one of the University of Oxford's oldest colleges. Founded in 1,314, the college currently has 478 students, of which 321 are undergraduates and 157 are postgraduate students.

Exeter College Senior Scholarship in Theology

Subjects: Theology or philosophy and theology.
Purpose: To support a graduate who wishes to read for the Final Honour School of Theology or philosophy and theology.
Eligibility: Applicants must hold at least a Second Class (Honours) Degree by the time of admission in a subject other than theology.
Level of Study: Postgraduate
Type: Scholarship
Value: A minimum value of UK £200, which may be supplemented up to a maximum of all college fees, university fees to the amount charged to home and European Union students and maintenance to the current maximum Local Education Authority maintenance grant
Length of Study: 2 years
Frequency: Every 3 years
Study Establishment: Exeter College, the University of Oxford
Country of Study: United Kingdom
No. of awards offered: 1
Application Procedure: Applicants must apply in writing to the Academic Administrator, with a curriculum vitae and the names of two academic references.
Funding: Private
Contributor: Endowment
No. of awards given last year: None
No. of applicants last year: None

Monsanto Senior Research Fellowship

Subjects: Molecular biology, cellular biology and biochemistry.
Purpose: To support research.
Eligibility: Open to qualified applicants of any nationality.
Level of Study: Postdoctorate
Type: Fellowship
Value: UK £17,626–26,491 stipend per year. Fellows are entitled to free lunch and dinner, free rooms in the college if unmarried and a housing allowance if not resident in the college
Length of Study: 3–5 years
Frequency: Every 3–5 years
Study Establishment: Exeter College, the University of Oxford
Country of Study: United Kingdom
No. of awards offered: 1
Application Procedure: Applicants must address enquiries to the Academic Administrator.
Funding: Private
No. of awards given last year: 1
No. of applicants last year: 76
Additional Information: The next award is not expected to be given until 2008.

Queen Sofia Research Fellowship

Subjects: Peninsular Spanish literature.
Purpose: To support research.
Eligibility: Applicants should be close to completing doctoral or postdoctoral work and must be under 31 years of age at the time of taking up the fellowship. They must also be fluent in Spanish.
Level of Study: Doctorate, postdoctorate
Type: Fellowship
Value: Up to UK £12,000 stipend per year. Fellows are entitled to free lunch and dinner, free rooms in the college if unmarried and a housing allowance if not resident in the college
Length of Study: 2–3 years
Frequency: Every 3 years
Study Establishment: Exeter College, the University of Oxford
Country of Study: United Kingdom
No. of awards offered: 1
Application Procedure: Applicants must address enquiries to the Academic Administrator.
Funding: Private
Contributor: Endowment
No. of awards given last year: 1
No. of applicants last year: 30

Staines Medical Research Fellowship

Subjects: Medical science.
Purpose: To support research in medical science.
Eligibility: Applicants should be close to completing doctoral or postdoctoral work and must be under 31 years of age at the time of taking up the fellowship.
Level of Study: Doctorate, postdoctorate
Type: Fellowship
Value: UK £300–10,240 stipend per year. Fellows are entitled to free lunch and dinner, free rooms in the college if unmarried and a housing allowance if not resident in the college
Length of Study: 2–3 years
Frequency: Every 5 years
Study Establishment: Exeter College, the University of Oxford
Country of Study: United Kingdom
No. of awards offered: 1
Application Procedure: Applicants must address enquiries to the Academic Administrator.
Funding: Private
Contributor: Endowment
No. of awards given last year: 1
No. of applicants last year: 65

THE EXPLORERS CLUB

Exploration Fund 46 East 70th Street, New York, NY 10021, United States of America
Tel: (1) 212 628 8383
Fax: (1) 212 288 4449
Email: asstmgr@explorers.org
Website: www.explorers.org

The Explores Club funds projects with scientific purpose to broaden our knowledge of the universe through remote travel and exploration.

Diversia Corporation Award

Subjects: Microbial science.
Level of Study: Postgraduate, professional development
Type: Grant
Length of Study: 1–2
Frequency: Annual
No. of awards offered: 1

Application Procedure: Request application form.
Closing Date: January 13th
Funding: Corporation
Contributor: Diversia Corporation

Explorers Club Exploration Fund

Purpose: To support scientific expeditions.
Level of Study: Professional development, postgraduate
Type: Grant
Value: US$1,200
Frequency: Annual
No. of awards offered: Varies
Application Procedure: Request application form.
Closing Date: January 13th

Scott Pearlman Field Award for Science and Exploration

Purpose: To support scientific expeditions.
Eligibility: Open to any professional artist, writer, photographer, filmmaker, or journalist who has excelled in their field.
Level of Study: Postgraduate, professional development
Type: Grant
Value: US$1,500
No. of awards offered: Varies
Application Procedure: Samples of the candidates work must be submitted alongside an application form and two references.
Closing Date: January 13th
Funding: Trusts
Contributor: Scott Pearlman Fund

For further information contact:

Scott Pearlman Field Awards The Explorers Club 46 East 70th Street, New York, NY 10021, United States of America
Contact: Executive Assistant

F BUSONI FOUNDATION

Conservatorio Statale di Musica 'C Monteverdi'-Piazza Domenicani, 25-PO Box 368, I-39100 Bolzano, Italy
Tel: (39) 047 197 6568
Fax: (39) 047 197 3579
Email: info@concorsobusoni.it
Website: www.concorsobusoni.it
Contact: Ms Maria Pia Venturi, Secretary

The Busoni International Piano Competition was first held in 1949 to commemorate the 25th anniversary of the death of composer Ferruccio Busoni. The aim of the competition is to create a forum for Busoni's music as well as for promising young pianists.

Foundation Busoni International Piano Competition

Subjects: Piano performance.
Purpose: To award excellence in piano performance.
Eligibility: Open to pianists of any nationality between 16 and 28 years of age.
Level of Study: Unrestricted
Type: Prize
Value: The 1st prize is €22,000 plus 60 important concert contracts, the 2nd prize is €10,000, the 3rd prize is €5,000, the 4th prize is €4,000, the 5th prize is €3,000 and the 6th prize is €2,500. There are also other special prizes
Frequency: Every 2 years
Country of Study: Italy
No. of awards offered: 10
Application Procedure: Applicants must complete and submit an application form with a birth certificate, reports or certificates of study, a brief curriculum vitae and documentation of any artistic activity. Three recent photographs, the entrance fee and written evidence of any prizes and international competitions should also be included.
Closing Date: May 31st
Funding: Commercial, government, private
Contributor: The Municipality of Bolzano
No. of awards given last year: 10
No. of applicants last year: 150
Additional Information: The competition lasts for 2 years, with the preselection phase taking place in the 1st year.

FANCONI ANEMIA RESEARCH FUND, INC.

1801 Willamette Street, Suite 200, Eugene, OR, 97401, United States of America
Tel: (1) 541 687 4658
Fax: (1) 541 687 0548
Email: info@fanconi.org
Website: www.fanconi.org
Contact: Ms Mary Ellen Eiler, Executive Director

To support research into effective treatments and a cure for Fanconi anaemia.

Fanconi Anemia Research Award

Subjects: Fanconi anaemia.
Purpose: To support research into effective treatments and a cure for Fanconi anaemia.
Eligibility: There are no restrictions on eligibility in terms of nationality, residency, age, gender, sexual orientation, race, religion or politics.
Level of Study: Doctorate, postdoctorate
Value: US$5,000–100,000
Length of Study: 1–2 years
Country of Study: Any country
No. of awards offered: Unlimited
Application Procedure: Applicants must email to obtain information about the application process and to complete an application form.
Closing Date: There is no closing date
Funding: Foundation
No. of awards given last year: 10
No. of applicants last year: 15
Additional Information: The Internal Revenue Service has confirmed that the Fund is not a private foundation for the purposes of tax-exempt donations but a public charitable organization under 501(c) 3 of the Internal Revenue Code.

FANNIE AND JOHN HERTZ FOUNDATION

2456 Research Drive Zip-3850, Livermore, CA, 94550, United States of America
Tel: (1) 925 373 1642
Fax: (1) 925 373 6329
Email: askhertz@aol.com
Website: www.hertzfndn.org
Contact: Ms Linda Kubiak, Fellowship Administrator

The Fannie and John Hertz Foundation runs a national competition for graduate fellowships in the applied physical sciences.

Fannie and John Hertz Foundation Fellowships

Subjects: Applied physical and biophysical sciences.
Purpose: To support students of outstanding potential in the applied physical sciences.
Eligibility: Open to citizens or permanent residents of the United States of America who have received a Bachelor's degree by the start of tenure and who propose to complete a programme of graduate study leading to a PhD. Students who have commenced graduate study are also eligible. The Foundation does not support candidates pursuing joint PhD and professional degree programmes.
Level of Study: Doctorate
Type: Fellowship
Value: US$28,000 per nine month academic year, plus cost-of education allowance
Length of Study: 1 academic year and may be renewed annually for up to 5 years
Frequency: Annual
Study Establishment: Specific universities listed on the website

Country of Study: United States of America
No. of awards offered: 20
Application Procedure: Applicants must complete a Hertz application form, four reference reports on the supplied specific forms and official transcripts of all college work must be submitted. The application form is available from the Foundation's website.
Closing Date: October 28th
Funding: Private
No. of awards given last year: 15
No. of applicants last year: Approx. 550

FEDERAL OFFICE FOR EDUCATION AND SCIENCE

Hallwylstrasse 4, CH-3003 Bern, Switzerland
Tel: (41) 31 323 2676
Fax: (41) 31 323 3020
Website: www.bbw.admin.ch
Contact: Federal Commission for Scholarships for Foreign Students

University Grant for Foreign Students

Subjects: All subjects.
Eligibility: Open to students up to the age of 35.
Level of Study: Postgraduate
Type: Grant
Value: Varies
Length of Study: 9 months
Frequency: Annual
Country of Study: Switzerland
No. of awards offered: Varies
Application Procedure: See website.
Closing Date: May
Funding: Government
Contributor: Any Swiss Institution of Higher Education

FEDERATION OF EUROPEAN MICROBIOLOGICAL SOCIETIES (FEMS)

Keverling Buismanweg 4, 2628 CL Delft, Netherlands
Tel: (31) 15 269 3920
Fax: (31) 15 269 3921
Email: fems@fems-microbiology.org
Website: www.fems-microbiology.org
Contact: Dr D Van Rossum, Executive Officer

The Federation of European Microbiological Societies (FEMS) is devoted to the promotion of microbiology in Europe. FEMS advances research and education in the science of microbiology within Europe, by encouraging joint activities and facilitating communication among microbiologists, supporting meetings and laboratory courses and publishing books and journals.

FEMS Fellowship

Subjects: Microbiology.
Purpose: To foster transnational research in microbiology and to enable young scientists to pursue a short-term research project in another European country.
Eligibility: The award is restricted to members of FEMS member societies.
Level of Study: Doctorate, postgraduate, research, graduate, predoctorate, professional development, postdoctorate
Type: Fellowship
Value: A maximum of €3,500
Length of Study: A maximum of 3 months
No. of awards offered: Approx. 50
Application Procedure: Applicants must complete and submit an application form to a society that is a member of FEMS. The delegate of the member society will handle the application and submit it to the Federation for funding. FEMS will then make a decision on the application. Addresses of the Federation's delegates are published on the website.
Closing Date: December 1st and June 15th
Funding: Foundation
No. of awards given last year: 35
No. of applicants last year: 37

FERRARI

Direzione e stablimento via Abetone int.4, Maranello (MO), I-41053, Italy
Tel: (39) 0536 949111
Email: carrerservice@mip.polimi.it
Website: www.ferrariworld.com

Born in 1947, Ferrari has always produced vehicles at its current site and has maintained its direction. Its has progressively widened it range using visionary planning to both on a design level and on the quality of work produced.

Ferrari Innovation Team Project Scholarship

Subjects: Mechanic/Electronic engineering focused on human machine interface, Complex Systems development Nanotechnologies, control systems, as well as material engineering focused on innovative materials applied to and planes.
Purpose: To create members of a new and innovative team for the new and innovative cars of the future.
Eligibility: Knowledge of ergonomics will be considered a plus.
Level of Study: Postgraduate, professional development
Type: Scholarship
Value: €25,000 and all accommodation and training
Length of Study: 1 year
Frequency: Annual
Study Establishment: Ferrari Spa
Country of Study: Italy
Closing Date: May 25th
Funding: Commercial
Contributor: Ferrari

For further information contact:

Email: cdozio@ferrari.it
Contact: Mr Claudio Dozio, HR Manager

THE FIELD PSYCH TRUST

301 Dixie Street, Carrollton, GA, 30117, United States of America
Tel: (1) 770 834 8143
Email: arichard@westga.edu
Website: www.fieldpsychtrust.org
Contact: Dr Anne C Richards, Trustee

The Field Psych Trust is a charitable trust honouring the professional life and contributions of psychologist/educator Dr Arthur W Combs. It provides grant funding to encourage graduate student research grounded in perceptual (field) psychology perspectives. It also supports the publication of manuscripts related to Dr Combs' professional life and work.

Field Psych Trust Grant

Subjects: As psychological theory, perceptual is (field) psychology applicable to any subject area in which links between human experience, meaning and/or perception and human behavior can be explored.
Purpose: To encourage graduate student research exploring the history, contributions and further development of perceptual (field) psychology as related to the research and writings of Arthur W Combs, PhD.
Eligibility: Open to graduate students in good standing through a competitive review process.
Level of Study: Doctorate, postdoctorate, graduate, predoctorate
Type: Research grant
Value: Varies according to the itemized budget request of successful applicants and their projects. Awards range from US$500–1,500
Length of Study: Varies, although 1 year is preferable
Frequency: Twice a year
Study Establishment: An accredited Institution of Higher Education

Country of Study: Any country
No. of awards offered: 2
Application Procedure: Applicants must complete an application form and submit references. Application forms can be found on the website. Applications are judged with respect to the relevance of the proposed project to the mission of the Field Psych Trust, substance, conceptual quality and clarity of the proposal, significance of the project in addressing matters of consequence to the human condition and the degree of confidence that the prospective grant recipient has the ability to produce the proposed project.
Closing Date: January 31st and October 5th of each year
Funding: Private
Contributor: The estate of Arthur W Combs
No. of awards given last year: 1
No. of applicants last year: 1
Additional Information: Awards are subject to conditions, which are described, and include an obligation to submit a final report upon conclusion of the project, which can take the form of a completed Master's thesis, research project report, doctoral dissertation or published manuscript. More information is available from the website, or by contacting Anne Richards at the main address.

FINE ARTS WORK CENTER IN PROVINCETOWN, INC.

24 Pearl Street, Provincetown, MA 02657, United States of America
Tel: (1) 508 487 9960
Fax: (1) 508 487 8873
Email: general@fawc.org
Website: www.fawc.org
Contact: Mr Hunter O'Hanian, Executive Director

Established in 1968, the Fine Arts Work Center offers 7-month fellowships to emerging visual artists and creative writers. Housing, studios and monthly stipends are provided to create a community of peers as a catalyst for artistic growth.

Fine Arts Work Center in Provincetown Fellowships

Subjects: Visual arts and creative writing in fiction and poetry.
Purpose: To give artists and writers the opportunity to work in a congenial and stimulating environment and to devote most of their time to art and writing.
Eligibility: Open to all, but preference is given to emerging artists of outstanding promise. Applicants are accepted on the basis of work submitted.
Level of Study: Unrestricted
Type: Fellowship
Value: US$650 per month, plus housing and studio space
Length of Study: 7 months
Frequency: Annual
Study Establishment: Provincetown, MA
Country of Study: United States of America
No. of awards offered: 10 for visual arts and 10 for writing
Application Procedure: Applicants must send a stamped addressed envelope for applications, the fee for which is US$35. Alternatively, application forms can be downloaded from the website.
Closing Date: February 1st for visual artists and December 1st for writers
Funding: Individuals, private, corporation, government
No. of awards given last year: 20
No. of applicants last year: 1,000
Additional Information: The Center is a working community, not a school.

FIRST (FLORICULTURE INDUSTRY RESEARCH AND SCHOLARSHIP TRUST)

PO Box 280, East Lansing, MI, 48826-0280, United States of America
Tel: (1) 517 333 4617
Fax: (1) 517 333 4494
Email: willbrandt@firstinfloriculture.org
Website: www.firstinfloriculture.org
Contact: Mr William Willbrandt, Executive Director

FIRST (Floriculture Industry Research and Scholarship Trust) is a leading organization for funding research and education in floriculture to improve the production and marketability of plants.

FIRST BioWorks Grant

Subjects: Integrated pest management.
Purpose: To fund students interested in programming EPA-registered biological pesticides as alternatives for chemical pesticides.
Level of Study: Research
Type: Grant
Length of Study: 1 year
Frequency: Annual
Study Establishment: An accredited college or university
Country of Study: United States of America
No. of awards offered: 1
Application Procedure: Apply online.
Funding: Commercial
Contributor: BioWorks

FIRST Fred Blackmore, Sr. Research Grant

Subjects: Horticulture and the horticultural Industry.
Purpose: To encourage research projects pertaining to greenhouse production.
Level of Study: Research
Type: Grant
Length of Study: 1 year
Study Establishment: An accredited college or university
Country of Study: United States of America
No. of awards offered: 1
Application Procedure: Apply online.
Funding: Commercial
Contributor: The Blackmore Company

FIRST Gus Poesch Research Grant

Subjects: Floriculture.
Purpose: To support top quality floriculture graduate students.
Level of Study: Postgraduate
Type: Grant
Length of Study: 1 year
Frequency: Annual
Study Establishment: An accredited college or university
Country of Study: United States of America
No. of awards offered: 1
Application Procedure: Apply online.
Funding: Private
Contributor: Gus Poesch Floriculture Endowment

FIRST Meister Research Fund

Subjects: Horticulture and the horticulture Industry.
Purpose: To fund a research assistantship for a student in a graduate degree programme.
Level of Study: Research
Type: Grant
Length of Study: 1 year
Frequency: Annual
Study Establishment: An accredited college or university
Country of Study: United States of America
No. of awards offered: 1
Application Procedure: Apply online.
Funding: Private
Contributor: Richard Meister

FIRST Research Grants

Subjects: Horticulture and the horticultural Industry.
Purpose: To improve the production and marketability of plants.
Level of Study: Research
Type: Grant
Value: Up to US$140,000
Length of Study: 1 year
Frequency: Annual
Study Establishment: An accredited college or university
Country of Study: United States of America
Application Procedure: Apply online.
No. of awards given last year: 14

FIRST Scholarship Program

Subjects: Horticulture and the horticultural industry.
Eligibility: Open to students who are studying horticulture or have a career interest in any aspect of the horticultural industry.
Type: Scholarship
Value: Varies
Frequency: Annual
Study Establishment: An accredited college or university
Country of Study: United States of America
No. of awards offered: Varies
Application Procedure: Applicants must contact FIRST directly to obtain the latest scholarship application form which lists all of the current scholarships and requirements. Application forms are available from January 1st to May 1st from the website or by sending a stamped addressed envelope or printed self-addressed mailing label to the main address.
Closing Date: May 1st
Additional Information: Applicants are requested to contact the Foundation directly for information on individual scholarships. Information regarding the Foundation's research grant programme is also available from the website.

FIRST Van Wingerden Research Fund

Subjects: Horticulture and the horticulture Industry.
Purpose: To support research on the promotion of the greenhouse industry.
Level of Study: Research
Type: Grant
Length of Study: 1 year
Frequency: Annual
Study Establishment: An accredited college or university
Country of Study: United States of America
No. of awards offered: 1
Application Procedure: Apply online.
Funding: Private
Contributor: A art and Cora Van Wingerden

FLORIDA FEDERATION OF GARDEN CLUBS (FFGC)

1400 South Denning Drive, Winter Park, FL 32789-5662, United States of America
Tel: (1) 647 7016
Fax: (1) 647 5479
Website: www.ffgc.org

The FFGC is the first state garden club on the Internet, which features FFGC activities, scholarships, youth programmes, floral design courses, arrangements, educational opportunities, tours, shows and special events of the various affiliated garden clubs in the state of Florida.

FFGC Scholarship in Ecology

Subjects: Ecology.
Purpose: To provide financial assistance to students in field of ecology.
Eligibility: Open to applicants who are residents of Florida and who demonstrate financial needs.
Level of Study: Postgraduate
Type: Scholarship
Value: US$1,500
Frequency: Annual
Country of Study: United States of America
No. of awards offered: 9
Application Procedure: See the website.
Closing Date: May 1st
Contributor: Florida Federation of Garden Clubs
No. of awards given last year: 9

FFGC Scholarship in Environmental Issues

Subjects: Environmental studies.
Purpose: To support students in the field of environmental studies.
Eligibility: Open to students who are residents of Florida.
Level of Study: Postgraduate
Type: Scholarship
Value: Up to US$3,500
Frequency: Annual
Country of Study: United States of America
Application Procedure: A completed application form must be submitted.
Closing Date: May 1st
Contributor: Florida Federation of Garden Clubs

FONDATION DES ETATS-UNIS

15 boulevard Jourdan, F-75690 Paris Cedex 14, France
Tel: (33) 1 53 80 68 80
Fax: (33) 1 53 80 68 99
Email: administration@feusa.org
Website: www.feusa.org
Contact: Mr Terence Murphy, Director

Harriet Hale Woolley Scholarships

Subjects: Art and music.
Purpose: To support the study of visual fine arts and music in Paris.
Eligibility: Open to citizens of the United States of America, who are 21–29 years of age and have graduated with high academic standing from a United States of America college, university or professional school of recognized standing. Preference is given to mature students who have already completed graduate study. Applicants should provide evidence of artistic or musical accomplishment. Applicants should have a good working knowledge of French, sufficient to enable the student to benefit from study in France. Grants are for those doing painting, printmaking or sculpture and for instrumentalists, not for research in art history, musicology or composition, nor for students of dance or of theatre.
Level of Study: Graduate, doctorate, postgraduate, predoctorate
Type: Scholarship
Value: A stipend of €8,500
Length of Study: 1 academic year
Frequency: Annual
Country of Study: France
No. of awards offered: 4–5
Application Procedure: Applicants must write for details.
Closing Date: January 31st
Funding: Private
No. of awards given last year: 4
No. of applicants last year: 25

FONDATION FYSSEN

194 Rue de Rivoli, F-75001 Paris, France
Tel: (33) 1 42 97 53 16
Fax: (33) 1 42 60 17 95
Email: secretariat@fondation-fyssen.org
Website: www.fondation-fyssen.org
Contact: Mrs Nadia Ferchal, Director

The aim of the Fyssen Foundation is to encourage all forms of scientific enquiry into cognitive mechanisms, including thought and reasoning, that underlie animal and human behaviour, their biological and cultural bases and phylogenetic and ontogenetic development.

Fondation Fyssen Postdoctoral Study Grants

Subjects: Disciplines relevant to the aims of the Foundation such as ethology, palaeontology, archaeology, anthropology, psychology, ethnology, neurobiology.
Purpose: To fund scientific research.
Eligibility: Open to French research scientists who wish to work in laboratories abroad and foreign research scientists who wish to work in French laboratories. Applicants should be under 35 years of age.
Level of Study: Postdoctorate
Type: Study grant
Value: €22,000

Length of Study: 2 years for researchers of neurobiology who are coming from the United States of America to France and 1 year for all others
Frequency: Annual
Application Procedure: Applicants must complete an application form, available from the secretariat of the Foundation or from the website.
Closing Date: The end of March
Funding: Private
No. of awards given last year: 53
No. of applicants last year: 188

FOOD AND DRUG LAW INSTITUTE (FDLI)

1000 Vermont Avenue NW, Suite 200, Washington, DC, 20005-4903, United States of America
Tel: (1) 202 371 1420
Fax: (1) 202 371 0649
Email: comments@fdli.org
Website: www.fdli.org
Contact: Mr Rita M. Fullem, Vice President-Programs Publications

The Food and Drug Law Institute (FDLI) is a non-profit educational association dedicated to advancing public health by providing a neutral forum for a critical examination of the laws, regulations and policies related to drugs, medical devices, other healthcare technologies and food.

H Thomas Austern Memorial Writing Competition–Food and Drug Law

Subjects: Current issues relevant to the food and drug field including relevant case law, legislative history and other authorities, particularly where the United States Food and Drug Administration is involved. Additional topic possibilities are available from the website.
Purpose: To encourage law students interested in the areas of law affecting foods, drugs, devices, cosmetics and biologics.
Eligibility: Entrants must currently be enrolled in a JD programme at any of the United States of America law schools. Anyone currently enrolled in a Juris Doctorate program in any U.S. college or university.
Level of Study: Postgraduate
Value: Two first prizes of US$1,500; two second prizes of US$1,000
Frequency: Annual
Country of Study: United States of America
No. of awards offered: 4
Application Procedure: Applicants must submit a typewritten, double-spaced paper on 8.5 by 11 inch paper or submit a Word document electronically. The cover sheet must list the applicant's full name, address and telephone number, law school and year, and the date of submission of the paper. Papers must not exceed 40 pages in length, including footnotes (for shorter paper competition). There is no page limit for papers longer than 41 pages.
Closing Date: June 15th
Funding: Private
Contributor: Association funds and Association member dues
No. of awards given last year: 4
No. of applicants last year: Approx. 50
Additional Information: Winning papers will be considered for publication in the *Food and Drug Law Journal.*

FORD FOUNDATION

320 East 43 Street, New York, NY 10017, United States of America
Tel: (1) 573-5000
Fax: (1) 351-3677
Email: office-secretary@fordfound.org
Website: www.fordfound.org
Contact: The Secretary

The aim of the Ford Foundation is to strengthen democratic values, reduce poverty and injustice, promote international cooperation and advance human achievement.

Ford Foundation Grant Program

Subjects: Asset building and community development, peace and social justice, and knowledge, creativity and freedom.
Purpose: To support the development of resources to advance social change, human achievement and understanding.
Eligibility: Support is not normally given for routine operating costs or for religious activities.
Level of Study: Postgraduate, postdoctorate
Type: Grant
Value: From a few thousand dollars to millions of dollars
Length of Study: 2 years
Frequency: Annual
No. of awards offered: 2,500
Application Procedure: Before a request is made a brief letter of inquiry should be submitted to determine whether the foundation's present interests and funds permit consideration of the request.
Closing Date: There are no deadlines for inquires and proposals
Funding: Foundation
Contributor: The Ford Foundation
No. of awards given last year: 2,091
No. of applicants last year: 41,000

FOULKES FOUNDATION

37 Ringwood Avenue, London, N2 9NT, England
Tel: (44) 20 8444 2526
Fax: (44) 20 8444 2526
Website: www.foulkes-foundation.org
Contact: M Foulkes, The Registrar

The aim of the Foulkes Foundation Fellowship is to promote medical research by providing financial support for postdoctoral science graduates who need a medical degree before they can undertake medical research, and similarly for medical graduates who need a science PhD degree.

Foulkes Foundation Fellowship

Subjects: All aspects of medical research, especially the areas of molecular biology and biological sciences.
Purpose: To promote research by providing financial support for postdoctoral study.
Eligibility: Open to recently qualified scientists and medical graduates who intend to contribute to medical research and who have a PhD or equivalent or proven research ability.
Level of Study: Postdoctorate
Type: Fellowship
Value: Varies depending on individual need, but the scale for the basic SRC Studentship is used as a guideline. Fellowships do not cover fees
Length of Study: Up to 3 years
Frequency: Annual
Country of Study: United Kingdom
No. of awards offered: Varies
Application Procedure: Applicants must send a stamped addressed envelope to the Registrar for additional information and an application form.
Closing Date: March 15th
Funding: Private
No. of awards given last year: 5
No. of applicants last year: 75

FOUNDATION FOR ANESTHESIA EDUCATION AND RESEARCH (FAER)

Wells Fargo 674, Mayo Clinic, 200 First Street South West, Rochester, MN, 55905, United States of America
Tel: (1) 507 266 6866
Fax: (1) 507 284 0120
Email: schrandt.mary@mayo.edu
Website: www.faer.org
Contact: Ms Mary Schrandt, Associate Director

The Foundation for Anesthesia Education and Research (FAER) strives to foster progress in anaesthesiology, critical care, pain and all areas of perioperative medicine. The organization aims to generate new knowledge that advances health and patient care by facilitating the career development of anaesthesiologists dedicated to research and education.

FAER Research Education Grant

Subjects: Anaesthesiology.
Purpose: To improve the quality and productivity of education and research.
Eligibility: Open to anaesthesiology residents or faculty.
Level of Study: Postgraduate
Type: Grant
Value: US$50,000 in the first year and US$50,000 in the second
Length of Study: 2 years
Frequency: Annual
Application Procedure: Applicants must visit the website.
Closing Date: February 15th and August 15th

FAER Research Fellowship Grant

Subjects: Anaesthesiology.
Purpose: To provide significant training in research techniques and scientific methods.
Eligibility: Open to anaesthesiology residents after CA-1 training and 6 months on a clinical scientist track.
Level of Study: Postdoctorate
Type: Fellowship
Value: US$50,000
Length of Study: 1 year
Frequency: Annual
Application Procedure: Applicants must visit the website.
Closing Date: February 15th or August 15th

FAER Research Starter Grants

Subjects: Anaesthesiology.
Purpose: To support and initiate a project for which an investigator will seek further support.
Eligibility: Applicants must be instructors or assistant professors who are within 5 years of their initial appointment.
Level of Study: Postdoctorate
Type: Grant
Value: US$35,000 in the first year and US$50,000 in the second
Length of Study: 2 years
Frequency: Annual
Application Procedure: Applicants must visit the website.
Closing Date: February 15th or August 15th

FAER Research Training Grant (RTG)

Subjects: Anaesthesiology.
Purpose: To allow the applicant to become an independent investigator.
Eligibility: Applicants must be instructors or assistant professors who are within 5 years of their initial appointment.
Level of Study: Postdoctorate
Type: Grant
Value: US$75,000 in the first year and US$100,000 in the second. Mentor stipend $40,000 per year
Length of Study: 2 years
Frequency: Annual
Application Procedure: Applicants must visit the website.
Closing Date: February 15th or August 15th

FOUNDATION FOR DIGESTIVE HEALTH AND NUTRITION

4930 Del Ray Avenue, Bethesda, MD, 20814,
United States of America
Tel: (1) 301 222 4005
Fax: (1) 301 222 4010
Email: rsmith@gastro.org
Website: www.fdhn.org
Contact: Ms Rochel Smith, Research Awards Manager

The Foundation for Digestive Health and Nutrition is the foundation of the American Gastroenterological Association (AGA), the leading professional society representing gastroenterological and heptatologists worldwide. It is separately incorporated and governed by a distinguished board of AGA physicians and members of the lay public. The Foundation raises funds for research and public education in the prevention, diagnosis, treatment and cure of digestive diseases. Along with the AGA, it conducts public education initiatives related to digestive diseases. The Foundation also administers the disbursement of grants on the behalf of the AGA and other funders.

AGA Astra Zeneca Fellowship/Faculty Transition Awards

Subjects: Medical science, specifically gastroenterology and hepatology.
Purpose: To prepare and support physicians for independent research careers in digestive diseases.
Eligibility: Applicants must be MDs currently in a gastroenterology-related fellowship at an accredited United States of America or Canadian institution and be committed to academic careers. They should have completed 2 years of research training at the start of this award. The additional training could be considered the equivalent of practical training ordinarily involved in a PhD programme. Therefore, individuals who hold a PhD are ineligible. Please note that non-United States of America or Canadian citizens based at United States of America or Canadian institutions are eligible to apply. Women and minority investigators are strongly encouraged to apply. Applicants must be AGA members or sponsored by an AGA member.
Level of Study: Postgraduate
Type: Award
Value: US$40,000 per year
Length of Study: 2 years
Frequency: Annual
Country of Study: The United States of America, Canada or Mexico
No. of awards offered: 4
Application Procedure: Electronic applications only.
Closing Date: September 5th
Funding: Private
Contributor: The AGA
Additional Information: At the end of the award, the recipient will be required to indicate how the funds were used, the accomplishments made during the training project and how this training has contributed to his or her research career development. A complete financial statement and scientific progress report are required annually and upon completion of the programme. All publications arising from work funded by this programme must acknowledge support of the award.

AGA Elsevier Research Initiative Award

Subjects: Medical science, specifically gastroenterology and hepatology.
Purpose: To provide non-salary funds for new investigators to help them establish their research careers and to support pilot projects that represent new research directions for established investigators. The intent is to stimulate research in gastroenterology or hepatology-related areas by permitting investigators to obtain new data that can ultimately provide the basis for subsequent grant applications of more substantial funding and duration.
Eligibility: Investigators must possess an MD, PhD or equivalent and must hold a faculty position at accredited United States of America or Canadian institutions. They may not hold awards on a similar topic from other agencies. Applicants must be members of the AGA. Women and minorities are strongly encouraged to apply. Applicants for this award may not simultaneously apply for the AGA/Miles and Shirley Fiterman Foundation Basic Research Award.
Level of Study: Postgraduate, predoctorate, postdoctorate
Type: Award
Value: US$25,000
Length of Study: 1 year
Frequency: Annual
Country of Study: The United States of America, Canada or Mexico
No. of awards offered: 1
Application Procedure: Electronic applications only.
Closing Date: January 16th

Funding: Private
Contributor: The AGA

AGA June and Donald O Castell, MD, Esophageal Clinical Research Award

Subjects: Oesophageal diseases.
Purpose: To support investigators who have demonstrated a high potential to develop an independent, productive research career.
Eligibility: Applicants must have an MD or PhD equivalent to hold a full-time faculty position at a United States of America or Canadian university or professional institute and be members of the AGA. The recipient must be at or below the level of assistant professor, and his/her initial appointment to the faculty position must have been within 7 years of the time of application. This award is not intended for Fellows, but for juniors who have demonstrated unusual promise, have some record of accomplishment in research and have established independent research programmes at the time of the award. Candidates must devote at least 50 per cent of their efforts to research related to oesophageal function or diseases. Applicants may not simultaneously apply for an AGA Research Scholar Award, AGA Fiterman Foundation Basic Research Award or AGA/Elsevier Research Initiative Award.
Level of Study: Graduate
Value: US$35,000
Length of Study: 1 year
Frequency: Annual
Country of Study: United States of America
No. of awards offered: 1
Application Procedure: Electronic applications only.
Closing Date: January 16th
Funding: Private

AGA Miles and Shirley Fiterman Foundation Basic Research Awards

Subjects: Medical science, specifically gastroenterology and hepatology.
Purpose: To provide research or salary support for junior faculty members involved in basic research in any area of gastrointestinal, liver function or related diseases.
Eligibility: Applicants must hold faculty positions at an accredited United States of America or Canadian university or professional institute and must hold an MD, PhD or equivalent. Applicants must be individual members of the AGA. The recipient must be at or below the level of assistant professor and his/her appointment to the faculty position must have been within 7 years of the time of application. This award is not intended for Fellows, but for junior faculty who have demonstrated unusual promise, have some record of accomplishment in research and have established an independent research programme at the time of the award. Candidates must devote at least 70 per cent of their efforts to research related to the gastrointestinal tract or the liver. Applicants for this award may not simultaneously apply for the AGA Research Scholar Award or the AGA/Elsevier Research Initiative Award.
Level of Study: Postgraduate
Type: Award
Value: US$35,000
Length of Study: 1 year
Frequency: Annual
Country of Study: The United States of America, Canada or Mexico
No. of awards offered: 2
Application Procedure: Electronic applications only.
Closing Date: January 16th
Funding: Private
Contributor: The Miles & Shirley Fiterman Foundation

AGA Miles and Shirley Fiterman Foundation Clinical Research in Gastroenterology or Hepatology/Nutrition Awards

Subjects: Medical science, specifically gastroenterology and hepatology.
Purpose: To recognize excellence in clinical research and to help support the clinical research of the recipients.
Eligibility: The award is not meant to be one that solely recognizes past achievements by a senior member of the academic gastroenterology community. The recipients of these awards should be active investigators whose research is ongoing. Nominees must be members of the AGA.
Type: Award
Value: US$35,000
Frequency: Annual
Country of Study: The United States of America, Canada or Mexico
No. of awards offered: 2
Application Procedure: Electronic applications only.
Closing Date: February 15th
Funding: Private
Contributor: The Miles and Shirley Fiterman Foundation
Additional Information: Two awards are offered: the Joseph B Kirsner Award in Gastroenterology and the Hugh R Butt Award in Hepatology or Nutrition. The award defines clinical research as studies related to patients or disease processes.

AGA R Robert and Sally D Funderburg Research Scholar Award in Gastric Biology Related to Cancer

Subjects: Gastric mucosal cell biology, regeneration and regulation of cell growth.
Purpose: To support an active established investigator working on novel approaches in the field of gastric cancer and who consequently enhances the fundamental understanding of gastric cancer pathobiology in order to ultimately develop a cure for the disease.
Eligibility: Applicants must hold faculty positions at accredited United States of America or Canadian institutions and must have established themselves as independent investigators in the field of gastric biology. Women and minority investigators are strongly encouraged to apply. Applicants must be individual members of the AGA.
Level of Study: Postgraduate
Type: Award
Value: US$25,000
Length of Study: 2 years
Frequency: Annual
Country of Study: The United States of America, Canada or Mexico
No. of awards offered: 1
Application Procedure: Electronic applications only.
Closing Date: September 5th
Contributor: The AGA, the late R Robert and the late Sally D Funderburg

AGA Research Scholar Awards

Subjects: Gastroenterology and hepatology.
Purpose: To ensure that a major proportion of young investigators' time is protected for research. The overall objective is to enable young investigators to develop independent and productive research careers in related fields and to support physicians or investigators who have the potential to develop independent, productive research careers.
Eligibility: Applicants must hold full-time faculty positions at United States of America or Canadian universities or professional institutes at the time of application and be members of the AGA. The award is not intended for Fellows, but for young faculty who have demonstrated unusual promise and have some record of accomplishment in research. Candidates should be in the beginning years of their careers. Those who have been at the assistant professor level or equivalent for more than 5 years at the time the award would begin are not eligible. Candidates must hold an MD, PhD or equivalent degree. Candidates must devote at least 70 per cent of their efforts to research related to the gastrointestinal tract or liver. Women and minority investigators are strongly encouraged to apply.
Level of Study: Graduate
Type: Research grant
Value: US$65,000 per year
Length of Study: 3 years
Frequency: Annual
Country of Study: United States of America
No. of awards offered: 6
Application Procedure: Electronic applications only.
Closing Date: September 5th
Funding: Private

Additional Information: A complete financial statement and scientific progress report are required upon completion of the programme. All publications arising from work funded by this programme must acknowledge the support of the award. Awardees must submit their work for presentation at Digestive Disease Week during the last year of the award.

AGA Student Research Fellowship Awards

Subjects: Medical science, specifically gastroenterology and hepatology.
Purpose: To stimulate interest in research careers in digestive diseases by providing salary support for research projects.
Eligibility: Candidates may be medical or graduate students, who are not yet engaged in their thesis research, at accredited United States of America or Canadian institutions. Candidates holding advanced degrees must be enrolled as medical or graduate students and they may not hold any similar support from other agencies, eg. American Liver Foundation, Crohn's and Colitis Foundation of America. Women and minority students are strongly encouraged to apply.
Level of Study: Graduate, postgraduate, professional development
Type: Award
Value: From US$2,000–3,000
Length of Study: A minimum of 10 weeks
Frequency: Annual
Country of Study: The United States of America, Canada or Mexico
No. of awards offered: Up to 20
Application Procedure: Applicants must visit the website.
Closing Date: March 3rd
Funding: Private
Contributor: The AGA

FOUNDATION FOR HIGH BLOOD PRESSURE RESEARCH

PO Box 13F, Monash University, VIC, 3800, Australia
Tel: (61) 3 9905 2555
Fax: (61) 3 9905 2566
Website: www.hbprca.com.au
Contact: Ms Jan Morrison, Administrative Officer

The Foundation for High Blood Pressure Research was established to support research into any aspect of blood pressure, hypertension and associated cardiovascular diseases.

Foundation for High Blood Pressure Research Postdoctoral Fellowship

Subjects: The understanding of the causes, prevention, treatment or effects of hypertension.
Purpose: To fund a scientist to perform research.
Eligibility: Open to applicants who are Australian citizens or have permanent residency in Australia, who have a degree in medicine or science, or an appropriate PhD.
Level of Study: Postdoctorate
Type: Fellowship
Value: Salary and associated costs, plus project maintenance
Length of Study: 2 years
Frequency: Annual
Study Establishment: An approved institute, university or hospital
Country of Study: Australia
No. of awards offered: 1
Application Procedure: Applicants must complete and submit an application with a curriculum vitae and relevant publications.
Closing Date: Please consult the Foundation
Funding: Private
Contributor: The Foundation
No. of awards given last year: 1
No. of applicants last year: 10
Additional Information: The award is advertised in Australia and overseas. Interested applicants should contact the Honorary Secretary for further information.

ISH Postdoctoral Award

Subjects: The understanding of the causes, prevention, treatment or effects of hypertension.
Purpose: To fund an international scientist to perform research at an Australian research institution.
Eligibility: Open to applicants who have a degree in medicine or science, or appropriate PhD.
Level of Study: Postdoctorate
Type: Fellowship
Value: Some assistance is provided to the employing institution comprising part salary only
Length of Study: 2 years
Frequency: Every 2 years
Study Establishment: An approved institute, university or hospital
Country of Study: Australia
No. of awards offered: 1
Application Procedure: Applicants must complete and submit an application with a curriculum vitae and relevant publications.
Closing Date: Please consult the Foundation
Funding: Private
Contributor: The Foundation
No. of awards given last year: 1
No. of applicants last year: 4
Additional Information: Details are advertised in Australia and overseas. Interested applicants should contact the Honorary Secretary for further information.

FOUNDATION FOR PHYSICAL THERAPY

1111 North Fairax Street, Alexandria, VA, 22314, United States of America
Tel: (1) 800 999 2782 ext 8505
Fax: (1) 703 706 8519
Email: foundation@apta.org
Website: www.apta.org/foundation
Contact: Ms Lucy Dickson, Scientific Review Administrator

The Foundation for Physical Therapy is a national, independent, non-profit corporation founded to support the physical therapy profession's research needs in the areas of scientific research, clinical research and health services research.

McMillan Doctoral Scholarships

Subjects: Physical therapy, rehabilitation medicine, neuroscience, sports medicine, paediatrics, medical sciences and social or preventative medicine.
Purpose: To assist physical therapists with outstanding potential for doctoral studies in the 1st year of study towards a doctorate.
Eligibility: Open to candidates who possess a licence to practice physical therapy in the United States of America and fulfil specific requirements with regard to research experience.
Level of Study: Doctorate
Type: Scholarship
Value: US$5,000
Length of Study: 1 year
Frequency: Annual
Country of Study: United States of America
Application Procedure: Applicants must check the website for full details.
Closing Date: August 11th
Funding: Private
No. of awards given last year: 6
No. of applicants last year: 10

New Investigator Fellowships Training Initiative (NIFTI)

Subjects: Physical therapy, rehabilitation medicine, neuroscience, sports medicine, paediatrics, medical sciences and social or preventative medicine.
Purpose: To fund doctorally prepared physical therapists as developing researchers and improve their competitiveness in securing external funding for future research.
Eligibility: Open to candidates who possess a licence to practice physical therapy in the United States of America, have received the

required postprofessional doctoral degree no earlier than 5 years prior to the year of application or, for those already holding a postprofessional doctorates, a professional education degree in physical therapy no earlier than 5 years prior to the year of application. Candidates must also have completed a research experience as part of their postprofessional doctoral education.
Level of Study: Postdoctorate
Type: Fellowship
Value: US$30,000
Length of Study: 1 year
Frequency: Annual
Country of Study: United States of America
No. of awards offered: Varies
Application Procedure: Applicants must complete an application form.
Closing Date: January 14th
Funding: Private
No. of awards given last year: None
No. of applicants last year: 2

Promotion of Doctoral Studies (PODS)

Subjects: Physical therapy, rehabilitation medicine, neuroscience, sports medicine, paediatrics, medical sciences and social or preventative medicine.
Purpose: To fund doctoral students who, having completed 1 full year of coursework, wish to continue their coursework or enter the dissertation phase.
Eligibility: Open to candidates who possess a licence to practice physical therapy in the United States of America and who are enrolled as students in a regionally accredited postprofessional, doctoral programme. The content of this programme should have a demonstrated relationship to physical therapy. Applicants must also be able to demonstrate continuous progress towards the completion of their postprofessional doctoral programme in a timely fashion and with a commitment to further the physical therapy profession through research and teaching within the United States of America and its territories.
Level of Study: Doctorate
Type: Scholarship
Value: Two levels, at US$7,500 or US$15,000
Length of Study: 1 year
Frequency: Annual
Country of Study: United States of America
No. of awards offered: Varies
Application Procedure: Applicants must complete an application form.
Closing Date: January 14th
Funding: Private
No. of awards given last year: 14
No. of applicants last year: 40

Research Grants (FPT)

Subjects: Physical therapy, rehabilitation medicine, neuroscience, sports medicine, paediatrics, medical sciences and social or preventative medicine.
Purpose: The purpose of the Foundation's Research Grant programme is to fund research studies in specific areas initiated by emerging investigators.
Eligibility: Open to citizens or permanent residents of the United States of America or its territories who possess a licence to practice physical therapy. Projects to be completed in fulfilment of requirements for an academic degree are not eligible to be funded by a Foundation Research Grant. A doctoral student in the latter stage of the dissertation phase of his/her programme may submit an application, but must provide evidence of completion of the degree by October 15th. In addition, the proposed study must differ substantially from any thesis research being conducted by graduate assistant(s) to be supported by this Research Grant.
Level of Study: Research
Type: Grant
Value: US$40,000
Frequency: Annual
Country of Study: United States of America
No. of awards offered: Varies
Application Procedure: Applicants must complete an application form.
Closing Date: August 12th
Funding: Private
No. of awards given last year: 1
No. of applicants last year: 10
Additional Information: Guidelines and application forms are available online in the spring at www.apta.org/foundation/ applications online. A paper version of the RFP is available from the Foundation.

FOUNDATION FOR SCIENCE AND DISABILITY, INC.

503 North West, 89th Street, Gainesville, FL, 32607, United States of America
Tel: (1) 352 374 5774
Fax: (1) 352 374 5781
Email: rmankin@gainesville.usda.ufl.edu
Website: www.as.wvu.edu/scidis/organizations
Contact: Dr Richard Mankin, Grants Committee Chair

The Foundation for Science and Disability aims to promote the integration of scientists with disabilities into all activities of the scientific community and of society as a whole, and to promote the removal of barriers in order to enable students with disabilities to choose careers in science.

Foundation for Science and Disability Student Grant Fund

Subjects: Engineering, mathematics, medicine, natural sciences and computer science.
Purpose: To increase opportunities in science for physically disabled students at the graduate or professional level.
Eligibility: Open to candidates from the United States of America.
Level of Study: Postdoctorate, postgraduate, doctorate
Type: Grant
Value: US$1,000
Length of Study: 1 year
Frequency: Annual
Country of Study: United States of America
No. of awards offered: 1–3
Application Procedure: Applicants must submit a completed application form, copies of official college transcripts, a letter from the research or academic supervisor in support of the request and a second letter from another faculty member.
Closing Date: December 1st
Funding: Private
No. of awards given last year: 2
No. of applicants last year: 8
Additional Information: The award may be used for an assistive device or instrument, or as financial support to work with a professor on an individual research project or for some other special need.

FOUNDATION PRAEMIUM ERASMIANUM

Jan van Goyenkade 5, Amsterdam, NL-1075 HN, Netherlands
Tel: (31) 20 676 0222
Fax: (31) 20 675 2231
Email: spe@erasmusprijs.org
Website: www.erasmusprijs.org
Contact: Y C Goester, Secretary

The Foundation Praemium Erasmianum operates internationally in the fields of social studies and the arts and humanities, through the awarding of the Erasmus Prize and other activities.

ERASMUS Prize

Subjects: Arts, humanities and social studies.
Purpose: To honour persons who have made an exceptional contribution to European culture.
Eligibility: There are no eligibility restrictions.
Level of Study: Unrestricted
Type: Money prize
Value: €150,000
Frequency: Annual
Country of Study: Any country
No. of awards offered: 1
Application Procedure: Applications by third parties only are considered.
Funding: Private

Foundation Praemium Erasmianum Study Prize

Subjects: Humanities and social sciences.
Purpose: To honour young academics who have written an excellent thesis in the field of humanities or social sciences.
Eligibility: Open to students of Dutch universities.
Level of Study: Postdoctorate
Type: Money prize
Value: €3,000
Frequency: Annual
Country of Study: Any country
No. of awards offered: 5
Application Procedure: Relevant faculties or universities nominate candidates, from which the Foundation selects five winners.
Closing Date: July 15th
Funding: Private
No. of awards given last year: 5
No. of applicants last year: 21

FRANCIS CHAGRIN FUND

Society for the Promotion of New Music (SPNM), 4th Floor, 18–20 Southwark Street, London, SE1 1TJ, England
Tel: (44) 20 7407 1640
Fax: (44) 20 7403 7652
Email: spnm@spnm.org.uk
Website: www.spnm.org.uk
Contact: Ms Gwendolyn Tietbe, Administrator

From contemporary jazz, classical and popular music to that written for film, dance and other creative media, SPNM is one of the main advocates of new music in the United Kingdom today.

Francis Chagrin Fund

Subjects: Composition.
Purpose: To help cover the costs of photocopying and binding incurred by composers in reproducing performance materials for unpublished works awaiting their first performance.
Eligibility: Applicants must be British composers or composers resident in the United Kingdom. Their works must be unpublished.
Level of Study: Professional development, unrestricted
Type: Grant
Value: UK £250 maximum
Length of Study: None
Frequency: Dependent on funds available
Study Establishment: None
No. of awards offered: Unlimited
Application Procedure: Applicants must submit an application form, curriculum vitae, two references and relevant invoices. Application forms are available from the SPNM.
Closing Date: There is no deadline
Funding: Private
Contributor: None
No. of awards given last year: None
No. of applicants last year: None
Additional Information: The committee meets approximately every other month.

FRANK KNOX MEMORIAL FELLOWSHIPS

3 Birdcage Walk, Westminster, London, SW1H 9JJ, England
Tel: (44) 20 7222 1151
Fax: (44) 20 7222 7189
Website: www.frankknox.harvard.edu
Contact: Ms Anna Mason, Secretary

The Frank Knox Memorial Fellowships were established at Harvard University in 1945 by a gift from Mrs Annie Reid Knox, widow of the late Colonel Frank Knox, to allow students from the United Kingdom to participate in an educational exchange programme.

Frank Knox Fellowships at Harvard University

Subjects: Arts, sciences including engineering and medical sciences, business administration and management, design, divinity, education, law, public administration and public health.
Eligibility: Open to citizens of the United Kingdom who, at the time of application, have spent at least 2 of the last 4 years at a university or university college in the United Kingdom and who will have graduated by the start of tenure. Fellowships are not awarded for postdoctoral study and no application will be considered from persons already in the United States of America. A period of full-time work since graduation is necessary prior to embarking on the MBA programme.
Type: Fellowship
Value: US$19,500 plus tuition fees. Unmarried Fellows may be accommodated in one of the university dormitories or halls
Length of Study: 1 academic year. Depending on the availability of sufficient funds fellowships may be renewed for those Fellows registered for a degree programme of more than 1 year
Frequency: Annual
Study Establishment: Harvard University
Country of Study: United States of America
No. of awards offered: 5 or 6
Application Procedure: Applicants must file an admissions application directly with the graduate school of their choice at an early date. Harvard University will try to arrange a suitable course for each individual.
Closing Date: October 27th
Funding: Private
Contributor: The estate of the late Frank Knox
No. of awards given last year: 5
No. of applicants last year: 117
Additional Information: Travel Grants are not awarded, although in cases of extreme hardship applications can be made to Harvard University for travel cost assistance.

FRANKLIN AND ELEANOR ROOSEVELT INSTITUTE

Franklin D Roosevelt Library, 4079 Albany Post Road, Hyde Park, NY 12538, United States of America
Tel: (1) 845 486 1150
Fax: (1) 845 486 1150
Email: info@feri.org
Website: www.feri.org
Contact: The Chairman, Grants Committee

The Franklin and Eleanor Roosevelt Institute is a private non-profit corporation dedicated to preserving the legacy and promoting the ideals of Franklin and Eleanor Roosevelt.

Roosevelt Institute Research Grant

Subjects: Research on the Roosevelt years and clearly related subjects.
Purpose: To encourage younger scholars to expand their knowledge and understanding of the Roosevelt period and to give continued support to more experienced researchers who have already made a mark in the field.
Eligibility: Open to qualified researchers of any nationality with a viable plan of work. Proposals are recommended for funding by an independent panel of Scholars which reports to the Institute Board.

Level of Study: Doctorate, graduate, postdoctorate
Type: Research grant
Value: Up to US$2,500
Study Establishment: The Franklin D Roosevelt Library, Hyde Park in New York
Country of Study: United States of America
No. of awards offered: 15–20
Application Procedure: Applicants must submit two copies of each of the following: an application front sheet, research proposal, relevance of holdings, travel plans, time estimate, curriculum vitae, three letters of reference and budget. Application forms and guidelines are available from the website or by emailing, faxing, or writing to the Roosevelt Institute.
Closing Date: February 15th and September 15th
Funding: Private

For further information contact:

The Franklin and Eleanor Roosevelt Institute, 511 Albany Post Road Hyde Park, NY 12538
Contact: Chairman, Grants Committee

FRAXA RESEARCH FOUNDATION

45 Pleasant Street, Newburyport, MA, 01950, United States of America
Tel: (1) 978 462 1866
Fax: (1) 978 463 9985
Email: info@fraxa.org
Website: www.fraxa.org
Contact: Ms Katherine Clapp, President

The FRAXA Research Foundation funds postdoctoral fellowships and investigator-initiated grants to support medical research aimed at the treatment of Fragile X Syndrome. FRAXA is particularly interested in preclinical studies of potential pharmacological and genetic treatments and studies aimed at understanding the function of the FMRI gene.

FRAXA Grants and Fellowships

Subjects: The treatment of Fragile X Syndrome, and potential pharmacological and genetic treatments and studies aimed at understanding the function of the FMRI gene.
Purpose: To promote research aimed at finding a specific treatment for Fragile X Syndrome.
Eligibility: There are no eligibility restrictions.
Level of Study: Postdoctorate, research
Value: Up to US$35,000 for postdoctoral fellowships. No limit for investigator-initiated grants
Length of Study: 1 year, renewable
Country of Study: Any country
No. of awards offered: 25–35 each year
Application Procedure: Applicants must complete an application form, available from the FRAXA Research Foundation or from the website. Potential applicants are welcome to submit a one-page initial inquiry letter describing the proposed research before submitting a full application.
Closing Date: May 1st or December 1st
Funding: Private
No. of awards given last year: 36
No. of applicants last year: 60

THE FREDERIC CHOPIN SOCIETY

Ostrogski Castle, Ul Okolnik 1, Warsaw, PL, 00-368, Poland
Tel: (48) 22 826 81 90
Fax: (48) 22 827 95 99
Email: konkurs@chopin.pl
Website: www.konkurs.chopin.pl
Contact: Administrative Assistant

The Frederic Chopin Society organizes the International Chopin Piano Competition, the Scholarly Piano Competition for Polish Pianists, the Grand Prix du Disque Frederic Chopin, courses in Chopin's music interpretation and Chopin music recitals as well as running a museum and collection.

International Frederic Chopin Piano Competition

Subjects: Piano performance of Chopin's music.
Purpose: To recognize the best artistic interpretation of Chopin's music and to encourage professional development.
Eligibility: Open to pianists of any nationality, born between 1977 and 1988.
Level of Study: Unrestricted
Type: Prize
Value: US$25,000 for the first prize, US$20,000 for the second prize, US$15,000 for the third prize, US$11,000 for the fourth prize, US$8,000 for the fifth prize, US$6,000 for the sixth prize and mentions of US$2,000 each for six remaining finalists
Frequency: Every 5 years
Country of Study: Any country
No. of awards offered: 6
Application Procedure: Applicants must complete and submit an application form attached with the rules.
Closing Date: March 1st
Funding: Private, government
No. of awards given last year: 14

FREDERICK DOUGLASS INSTITUTE FOR AFRICAN AND AFRICAN-AMERICAN STUDIES

University of Rochester, 302 Morey Hall, Rochester, NY, 14627-0440, United States of America
Tel: (1) 585 275 7235
Fax: (1) 585 256 2594
Email: fdi@troi.cc.rochester.edu
Website: www.cc.rochester.edu/college/aas
Contact: G R Radegonde-Eison, Administrative Assistant

The Frederick Douglass Institute for African and African-American Studies was established in 1986 to promote the development of African and African-American studies and graduate education through advanced research at the University of Rochester. It has served as an interdisciplinary centre, its focus being on the social sciences, though not excluding the humanities and the natural sciences.

Frederick Douglass Institute Postdoctoral Fellowship

Subjects: Historical and contemporary topics on the economy, society, politics and culture of Africa and its diaspora. Broadly conceived projects on human and technological aspects of energy development and agriculture in Africa are welcomed.
Purpose: To support the completion of a project.
Eligibility: Open to scholars who hold a PhD degree in a field related to the African and African American experience.
Level of Study: Postdoctorate
Type: Fellowship
Value: A stipend of US$35,000 as well as full access to the university's facilities and office space in the Institute. It also supports the completion of a research project for 1 academic year
Frequency: Annual
Country of Study: Any country
No. of awards offered: 1
Application Procedure: Applicants must submit a completed application, a curriculum vitae, a three- to five-page description of the project plus a short bibliography and a sample of published or unpublished writing on a topic related to the proposal. Three letters of recommendation that comment upon the value and feasibility of the work proposed are to be sent by referees.
Closing Date: January 31st
Additional Information: All Fellows receive office space in the Institute and opportunities to interact and collaborate with scholars of their respective disciplines within the University. Fellows must be in full-time residence during the tenure of their awards and are expected to be engaged in scholarly activity on a full-time basis. They must be available for consultation with students and professional colleagues,

make at least two formal presentations based upon their research and contribute generally to the intellectual discourse on African and African-American Studies.

Frederick Douglass Institute Predoctoral Dissertation Fellowship

Subjects: Historical and contemporary topics on the economy, society, politics and culture of Africa and its diaspora. Broadly conceived projects on human and technological aspects of energy development and agriculture in Africa are welcomed.
Purpose: To support the completion of a dissertation.
Eligibility: Open to graduate students of any university who study aspects of the African and African American experience. Applicants must have completed and passed all required courses, any qualifying oral and/or written exams and have written at least one chapter of the dissertation, which then becomes part of the application package, to qualify for this award.
Level of Study: Predoctorate
Type: Fellowship
Value: A stipend of US$18,000 as well as full access to the university's facilities and office space in the institute
Frequency: Annual
Country of Study: Any country
Application Procedure: Applicants must complete and send the FDI fellowship application form, a curriculum vitae, an official transcript showing completion of all preliminary coursework and qualifying examinations, the dissertation prospectus, a sample chapter from the dissertation and three letters of recommendation to be sent out by the referees, including one from the dissertation supervisor assessing the candidate's prospects for completing the project within a year.
Closing Date: January 31st
Additional Information: All Fellows receive office space in the Institute and opportunities to interact and collaborate with scholars of their respective disciplines within the University. Fellows must be in full-time residence during the tenure of their awards and are expected to be engaged in scholarly activity on a full-time basis. They must be available for consultation with students and professional colleagues, make at least two formal presentations based upon their research and contribute generally to the intellectual discourse on African and African-American Studies.

FRIEDRICH EBERT FOUNDATION

Godesberger Allee 149, Bonn, 53170, Germany
Tel: (49) 228 883 617
Fax: (49) 228 883 697
Email: adm@fes.de
Website: www.fes.de

Research Scholarships (FEF)

Subjects: All subjects.
Purpose: To support researchers of all disciplines who are registered at a state or state-recognized university in Germany focusing either on research leading to a doctorate at the German host university or short-term research visits.
Eligibility: Young scholars with a good academic record and a commitment towards social policy issues may apply.
Level of Study: Doctorate, research
Type: Scholarship
Value: €975 per month for research visits; €795 per month for doctoral research. Additional payments in the form of family allowance, health insurance contributions and travel grants are possible
Length of Study: Up to 1 year for research visits (extension not possible); up to 2 years for doctoral research (extension possible)
Study Establishment: Any state or state-recognized university in Germany
Country of Study: Germany
Application Procedure: Application forms are available on request.
Closing Date: There are no firm application deadlines
Contributor: Friedrich Ebert Foundation

FRIENDS OF FRENCH ART

100 Vanderlip Drive, Villa Narcissa, Rancho Palos Verdes, CA, 90275, United States of America
Tel: (1) 310 377 4444
Fax: (1) 310 377 4584
Email: villacisssa@aol.com
Website: www.arcat.com
Contact: Ms Elin Vanderlip, President

Friends of French Art restore art in peril, both in France and the United States of America.

Summer Art Restoration Program

Subjects: Art restoration and conservation.
Purpose: To give graduate students in the field of art conservation the opportunity to spend the summer in France.
Eligibility: Open to graduate students in the field of art restoration.
Level of Study: Postgraduate
Value: Approx. US$5,000, airfare to France and accommodation while working on a specific project
Length of Study: Summer programme
Frequency: Dependent on funds available
Country of Study: France
No. of awards offered: Varies
Application Procedure: Applicants should contact the organization for details.
Funding: Private
Contributor: Private donations through the Friends of French Art

For further information contact:

University of Delaware, Winterthur Art Conservation Department, Winterthur, DE, 19735, United States of America

FRIENDS OF ISRAEL EDUCATIONAL FOUNDATION

Academic Study Group, POB 42763, London, N2 0YJ, England
Tel: (44) 020 8883 0321
Fax: (44) 020 8444 0681
Email: info@foi-asg.org
Website: www.foi-asg.org
Contact: Mr John D A Levy

The Friends of Israel Educational Foundation and its sister operation, the Academic Study Group, aim to encourage a critical understanding of the achievements, hopes and problems of modern Israel, and to forge new collaborative working links between the United Kingdom and Israel.

Friends of Israel Educational Foundation Academic Study Bursary

Subjects: All subjects.
Purpose: To provide funding for British academics planning to pay a first research or study visit to Israel.
Eligibility: Open to research or teaching postgraduates. The Academic Study Group will only consider proposals from British academics who have already linked up with professional counterparts in Israel and agreed terms of reference for an initial visit.
Level of Study: Postdoctorate
Type: Bursary
Value: UK £300 per person
Frequency: Annual
Country of Study: Israel
No. of awards offered: 30
Application Procedure: Applicants must contact the organization. There is no application form.
Closing Date: November 15th or March 15th
Funding: Private
Contributor: Trusts and individual donations
No. of awards given last year: 10
No. of applicants last year: Approx. 50

Friends of Israel Educational Foundation Young Artist Award

Subjects: Fine arts.
Purpose: To enable a promising British artist to pay a working visit to Israel and prepare work for an exhibition on Israeli themes in the United Kingdom.
Eligibility: Open to promising young British painters, print makers and illustrators.
Level of Study: Postgraduate, professional development
Type: Award
Value: Airfares, accommodation and basic living costs
Length of Study: A minimum of 2 months
Frequency: Annual
Study Establishment: A kibbutz
Country of Study: Israel
No. of awards offered: 1–2
Application Procedure: Applicants must submit a personal curriculum vitae, an academic letter of reference, a statement of reasons for wishing to visit Israel and a representative selection of work.
Closing Date: May
Funding: Private
Contributor: Individual donations
Additional Information: Shortlisted candidates will be interviewed and artwork examined by a distinguished panel of judges.

Jerusalem Botanical Gardens Scholarship

Subjects: Botany and horticulture.
Purpose: To provide opportunities for botanists and horticulturists to work at the Jerusalem Botanical Gardens.
Eligibility: Preference is given to permanent residents of the United Kingdom who hold a degree in a relevant subject. Landscape architects with practical plant skills are also eligible.
Level of Study: Professional development, postgraduate
Type: Scholarship
Value: Return airfare to Israel, subsidized accommodation in the vicinity of the Hebrew University campus and a subsistence allowance that covers the full placement. Participants receive no formal salary
Length of Study: 6 months–1 year
Frequency: Annual
Study Establishment: The Jerusalem Botanical Gardens
Country of Study: Israel
No. of awards offered: Varies
Application Procedure: Applicants must submit a curriculum vitae, an academic letter of reference, a statement of reasons for wishing to work in Jerusalem, two passport-sized photographs and a handwritten covering letter.
Closing Date: March 31st
Funding: Private
Contributor: Trusts and individual donations
No. of awards given last year: 4

FRIENDS OF JOSÉ CARRERAS INTERNATIONAL LEUKEMIA FOUNDATION

1100 Fairview Avenue North, D5-100, Seattle, WA, 98109-1024, United States of America
Tel: (1) 206 667 7108
Fax: (1) 206 667 6124
Email: friendsjc@fhcrc.org
Website: www.carrerasfoundation.org
Contact: Administrator

The Friends of José Carreras International Leukemia Foundation funds Medical Research Fellowships.

Friends of José Carreras International Leukemia Foundation E D Thomas Postdoctoral Fellowship

Subjects: Medical sciences or leukaemia.
Purpose: To support research in the field of leukaemia or related haematological disorders.
Eligibility: Candidates must hold an MD or PhD degree and have completed at least 3 years of postdoctoral training but must be less than 10 years past their first doctoral degree when the award begins.
Type: Fellowship
Value: US$50,000 per year
Length of Study: 1 year, renewable for an additional 2 years
Frequency: Annual
Study Establishment: A suitable institution with the academic environment to provide adequate support for the proposal project
Country of Study: Any country
No. of awards offered: 1
Application Procedure: Applicants must complete an application form, available from the website. All applications must be typed, single spaced, in English and must follow the format specified in the application packet. Award announcements will be made by letter in January. Please do not contact the Foundation for results. Reapplication by unsuccessful candidates will be necessary for the following year.
Closing Date: Early November
Funding: Foundation
Contributor: Individual donors
No. of awards given last year: 1
No. of applicants last year: 15

THE FRINK SCHOOL OF FIGURATIVE ART & SCULPTURE

Cross St Mill, Leek, Staffs, ST13 6BL, United Kingdom
Tel: (44) 7989 149168
Email: info@frinkschool.org
Website: www.frinkschool.org
Contact: The Administrator

The Frink School of Figurative Sculpture is a Sculpture School, teaching the traditional art of sculpture not taught in mainstream education today.

Frink School Bursary

Subjects: The traditional art of sculpture, working with clay, steel, stone, cement and polystyrene. Life drawing is also taught.
Eligibility: Dependent upon applicant's financial circumstances.
Type: Bursary
Value: Up to UK £1,500 dependent on funds available
Length of Study: 1 year
Frequency: Dependent on funds available
Country of Study: United Kingdom
No. of awards offered: Dependent on funds available
Application Procedure: Applicants must submit written applications or apply via email.
Closing Date: September
Funding: Private
Contributor: Fubber Trust
No. of awards given last year: 4
No. of applicants last year: 10

FROMM MUSIC FOUNDATION

c/o Department of Music, Harvard University, Cambridge, MA, 02138, United States of America
Tel: (1) 617 495 2791
Fax: (1) 617 496 8081
Email: moncrieff@fas.harvard.edu
Website: www.fas.harvard.edu
Contact: Ms Jean Moncrieff

The Fromm Music Foundation at Harvard University, founded by the late Paul Fromm in the fifties, has been located at Harvard since 1972. Over, the course of its existence, the foundation has commissioned over 300 new compositions and their performances, and has sponsored hundreds of new music concerts and concert series.

Fromm Foundation Commission

Subjects: Music composition.
Purpose: To support compositions by young and lesser known composers who are citizens or residents of the United States of

America.The award includes a stipend for premiere performance of commissioned work.
Eligibility: There are no eligibility restrictions. Applicants must be citizens or residents of the United States of America.
Level of Study: Unrestricted
Frequency: Annual
Country of Study: Any country
No. of awards offered: Up to 12
Application Procedure: Applicants must obtain guidelines from the Fromm Music Foundation.
Closing Date: June 1st
Funding: Private
No. of awards given last year: 12
No. of applicants last year: 200

FULBRIGHT COMMISSION (ARGENTINA)

Viamonte 1653, 2 Piso, Buenos Aires, Capital Federal, 1055, Argentina
Tel: (54) 11 4814 3561
Fax: (54) 11 4814 1377
Email: info@fulbright.com.ar
Website: www.fulbright.edu.ar
Contact: M. Graciela Abarca, Educational Advisor

The Fulbright Programme is an educational exchange programme that sponsors awards for individuals approved by the J William Fulbright Board. The programme's major aim is to promote international co-operation and contribute to the development of friendly, sympathetic and peaceful relations between the United States and other countries in the world.

Fulbright Commission (Argentina) Awards for US Lecturers and Researchers

Subjects: All subjects except medical science.
Purpose: To enable United States lecturers to teach at an Argentine university for one semester, and to enable United States researchers to conduct research at an Argentine institution for three months.
Eligibility: Open to United States researchers and lecturers. Applicants must be proficient in spoken Spanish.
Level of Study: Professional development
Value: Varies according to professional experience
Length of Study: 3 months
Frequency: Annual
Country of Study: Argentina
Closing Date: July 31st
Funding: Government
Contributor: The United States of America and the Argentine governments

For further information contact:

The Council for International Exchange of Scholars, 3001 Tilden Street, Washington, N.W, D.C. 20008-3009
Tel: (202) 686-4000
Email: info@ciesnet.cies.org

Fulbright Commission (Argentina) Master's Program

Subjects: All subjects except medical science.
Purpose: To support Argentines pursuing a Master's degree in the United States of America.
Eligibility: Open to Argentines only.
Level of Study: Postgraduate
Frequency: Annual
Country of Study: United States of America
Application Procedure: Applicants must contact the Fulbright Commission in Argentina between February 1st and April 30th.
Funding: Government, private
Contributor: The Binational Commission and private sources

Fulbright Commission (Argentina) US Students Research Grant

Subjects: All subjects except medical science.
Purpose: To enable American students to study in Argentina.
Eligibility: Open to United States of America citizens who hold a Bachelor's degree, are writing a Master's thesis or PhD dissertation and are proficient in Spanish.
Level of Study: Postgraduate, graduate, doctorate
Type: Research grant
Length of Study: 8 months
Frequency: Annual
Country of Study: Argentina
No. of awards offered: 10–12
Application Procedure: Applicants must complete an application form.
Funding: Government
Contributor: The United States of America and Argentine government

Fulbright Institutional Linkages Program

Subjects: Social sciences, public administration, business, economics, law, journalism and communications and educational administration.
Purpose: To support educational partnerships between U.S. universities and foreign post-secondary institutions.
Level of Study: Postgraduate
Frequency: Annual
Contributor: The U.S. department of state's institutional linkage programmes

For further information contact:

Humphrey Fellowships and Institutional linkage Branch, Office of Global Educational Programs, Bureau of Educational and Cultural Affairs, SA-44, 301 4th street, Washington, S.W., D.C. 20547

Fulbright Scholar-in Residence

Subjects: Education administration.
Purpose: To enable visiting scholars to teach in the US about their home country or world region.
Eligibility: Open to candidates with strong international interest and some experience in study abroad and exchange programmes.
Level of Study: Professional development
Type: Grant
Value: Fulbright funding plus salary supplement and in-kind support from the host institution
Length of Study: 1 year
Frequency: Annual
Application Procedure: Candidates must submit a Fulbright visiting scholar application form and a brief project statement.

For further information contact:

Tel: (011) 4814-3561/62
Email: info@fulbright.edu.ar

Fulbright Student Awards

Purpose: To enable students working for their PhD dissertation or towards a Master's degree to carry out independent research.
Eligibility: Applications are restricted to U.S. citizens who are proficient in spoken and written Spanish.
Level of Study: Doctorate, postgraduate
Value: Round-trip international travel, monthly stipend and health insurance
Length of Study: 8 months
Frequency: Annual
Closing Date: October 31st

For further information contact:

U.S. Student Programs Institute of International Education, 809 United Nations Plaza New York, New York, 10017-3580
Tel: (212) 984-5330
Fax: (212) 984-5325

Fulbright Teacher and Administrator Exchange Awards–Elementary & High School Administrator

Subjects: Educational Administration.
Purpose: To support U.S. Administrators who wish to shadow an Argentine counterpart and then host a reciprocal visit of the Argentine counterpart in the U.S.

Eligibility: Open to both Argentine and U.S. candidates with considerable expenses as school principals, vice principal or other high level administrative position within the education sector.
Level of Study: Professional development
Type: Grant
Length of Study: 3 weeks
Frequency: Annual
Closing Date: May 14th

For further information contact:

Fulbright Teacher Exchange Program, 600 Maryland Avenue, SW, Room 235, Washington, D.C. 20024-2520, United States of America

Fulbright Teacher and Administrator Exchange Awards–Teacher Exchange Awards

Subjects: Educational administration.
Purpose: To enable U.S. teachers to exchange jobs for one semester with Argentine colleagues.
Eligibility: Applicants must have at least 3 years of teaching experience after graduation.
Level of Study: Professional development
Type: Grant
Value: Round-trip international travel, salary supplement and health services
Length of Study: One semester
Frequency: Annual
Closing Date: October 15th

For further information contact:

Fullbright Teacher Exchange Program, 600 Maryland Avenue, SW, Room 235, Washington, D.C. 20024-2520

Fulbright Teaching Assistant Awards

Purpose: To provide young English teachers of Argentina with an opportunity to work as Language Assistants at US college or universities.
Eligibility: Open to candidates with Argentine citizenship who show interest in interacting closely with the host community.
Level of Study: Professional development
Value: Roundtrip ticket, monthly stipend and health insurance
Length of Study: 9-10 months
Frequency: Annual
No. of awards offered: 15
Application Procedure: Download application form from the website.
Closing Date: November 12th

Hubert H. Humphrey Alumni Impact Awards

Purpose: To provide opportunities for Humphrey fellows to pursue objectives that expand the knowledge and skills that they gained during their Humphrey fellowship experiences.
Eligibility: Open to all Humphrey fellows.
Level of Study: Postdoctorate
Type: Grant
Value: US$5,000–10,000
Frequency: Annual
Application Procedure: Download application form from the website.
Closing Date: September 1st
Contributor: IIE and U.S. Department of State

Hubert H. Humphrey Alumni Mini Grants

Purpose: To help Humphrey alumni to maintain the networks of professional contacts formed during their fellowship year and to continue to further professional development in their fields.
Eligibility: Open to all alumni who have been home for at least 3 years.
Level of Study: Postdoctorate, professional development
Type: Grant
Value: Up to US$2,500
Frequency: Annual
Application Procedure: Download the application form from the website.

For further information contact:

Institute of International Education, 1400 K street, N.W., Washington, Suite 650, DC 20005
Tel: (202) 326-7701
Fax: (202) 326-7702

FULBRIGHT TEACHER EXCHANGE

600 Maryland Avenue SW, Room 320, Washington, DC, 20024, United States of America
Tel: (1) 202 314 3527
Fax: (1) 202 479 6806
Email: fulbright@grad.usda.gov
Website: www.fulbrightexchanges.org
Contact: Administrative Officer

Sponsored by the United States Department of State, the Fulbright Teacher Exchange arranges direct one-to-one classroom exchanges to over 30 countries for teachers at the elementary, secondary, 2-year and 4-year college levels. Administrators may participate in six-week seminars in eleven countries.

Fulbright Teacher and Administrator Exchange

Subjects: Education and cultural exchange.
Purpose: To promote cultural understanding between peoples of other countries and the people of the United States of America through educational exchange.
Eligibility: Open to administrators and teachers of all subjects and levels from elementary through to community college. Applicants must be citizens of the United States of America, be fluent in English, have a current full-time academic position, be in at least their 3rd year of teaching and hold a Bachelor's degree.
Level of Study: Professional development
Type: Grant
Value: Varies by country
Length of Study: 6 weeks–1 year
Frequency: Annual
Study Establishment: K-12 schools and, 2-year and 4-year colleges
Country of Study: Any country
No. of awards offered: Varies
Application Procedure: Applicants must submit a basic application that includes a two-page essay, three letters of recommendation, administrative approval and a peer interview.
Closing Date: October 15th
Funding: Government
No. of awards given last year: 250
No. of applicants last year: 800

FUND FOR THEOLOGICAL EDUCATION, INC.

825 Houston Mill Road Suite 250, Atlanta, GA, 30329, United States of America
Tel: (1) 404 727 1450
Fax: (1) 404 727 1490
Email: fte@thefund.org
Website: www.thefund.org
Contact: Ms Sharon Watson Fluker, Director

The Fund for Theological Education advocates excellence and diversity in pastoral ministry and theological scholarship. Through our initiatives, we enable gifted young people throughout the Christian community to explore and respond to God's calling in their lives. We seek to be a creative, informed catalyst for educational and faith communities in developing their own capacities to nurture men and women for vocations in ministry and teaching. We also aim to awaken the larger community to the contributions of pastoral leaders and educators who act with faith, imagination and courage to serve the common good.

Expanding Horizons-Dissertation Fellowship for African Americans

Subjects: Religion and theology.
Purpose: To support African American students in PhD and ThD programmes in the final writing stages of their dissertation.
Eligibility: Open to African American students in the final writing stages of their dissertation. The dissertation proposal must have been approved prior to application.
Level of Study: Doctorate
Type: Fellowship
Value: Up to US$15,000
Length of Study: 1 year, non-renewable
Frequency: Annual
Study Establishment: Graduate or theological schools
Country of Study: United States of America
No. of awards offered: Up to 10 per year
Application Procedure: Applicants must complete an application form, available from the programme office or the website.
Closing Date: February 1st
Funding: Private
Contributor: Lilly Endowment, Inc.
No. of awards given last year: 9
No. of applicants last year: Varies

Expanding Horizons-Doctoral Fellowship for African Americans

Subjects: Religion and theology.
Eligibility: Open to African American students entering the 1st year of a PhD or ThD programme and studying at an ATS (Association of Theological Schools) accredited school or in another accredited graduate programme in religion/theology.
Level of Study: Doctorate
Type: Fellowship
Value: Up to US$15,000
Length of Study: 1 year, with a possibility of renewal for a 2nd year
Frequency: Annual
Study Establishment: Graduate or theological schools
Country of Study: United States of America
No. of awards offered: Up to 10
Application Procedure: Applicants must complete an application form, available from the programme office or website.
Closing Date: March 1st
Funding: Private
Contributor: Lilly Endowment, Inc.
No. of awards given last year: 7
No. of applicants last year: Varies

Ministry Fellowship

Subjects: Religion, theology and divinity.
Purpose: To enrich theological education in a Master of Divinity degree programme.
Eligibility: Open to applicants aged 35 or younger and entering a Master of Divinity degree programme in the Autumn semester. The award is to be used for the design and implementation of creative projects during the Summer.
Level of Study: Postgraduate
Type: Fellowship
Value: US$5,000 plus conference attendance
Frequency: Annual
Study Establishment: A school accredited by the ATS of North America
Country of Study: United States of America or Canada
No. of awards offered: 40
Application Procedure: Applicants must complete and submit an application form together with supporting documentation. Forms are available from the website or by request.
Closing Date: April 1st
Funding: Private
No. of awards given last year: 40
No. of applicants last year: 165

North American Doctoral Fellowship

Subjects: Religion and theology.
Purpose: To support students from African American, Asian American, Hispanic American and Native American populations already in doctoral programmes leading towards completion of a PhD or ThD.
Eligibility: Open to students from targeted racial or ethnic groups at any point in their graduate programme, although preference is given to students further along in their programmes. Students must be currently enrolled in PhD or ThD programmes of religion or theology.
Level of Study: Doctorate
Type: Fellowship
Value: US$5,000
Length of Study: 1 year
Frequency: Annual
Country of Study: United States of America or Canada
No. of awards offered: 10–12 per year
Application Procedure: Applicants must complete an application form, available from the programme office or website.
Closing Date: March 1st
Funding: Private
Contributor: National Council of Churches and others
No. of awards given last year: 10
No. of applicants last year: Varies

FUNGAL RESEARCH TRUST

PO Box 482, Macclesfield, Cheshire,
SK10 9AR, England
Tel: (44) 16 2550 0228
Email: secretary@fungalresearchtrust.org
Website: www.fungalresearchtrust.org
Contact: Secretary

The Fungal Research Trust is a small charity that funds small research and travel grants and the aspergillus website (www.aspergillus.man.ac.uk). The website is the most comprehensive source of data on the aspergillus fungus and the diseases it causes.

Fungal Research Trust Travel Grants

Subjects: Fungal diseases and fungi.
Purpose: To enable researchers to attend national and international fungal meetings.
Eligibility: No restrictions.
Level of Study: Research, doctorate, postdoctorate, postgraduate, professional development
Type: Travel grant
Value: UK £1,000
Length of Study: Up to 1 week
Frequency: Dependent on funds available
No. of awards offered: Up to 3
Application Procedure: Applicants must submit a letter of application.
Closing Date: Applications are considered at any time, but 3 months notice before travel is required
Funding: Commercial, private
Contributor: Numerous
No. of awards given last year: 2
No. of applicants last year: 2
Additional Information: Advertisements for other awards are placed in the *Lancet*.

GENERAL BOARD OF HIGHER EDUCATION AND MINISTRY

PO Box 340007, Nashville, TN, 37203-0007,
United States of America
Tel: (1) 615 340 7388
Fax: (1) 615 340 7377
Email: bkohler@gbhem.org
Website: www@gbhem.org
Contact: Dr Robert F Kohler

The General Board of Higher Education and Ministry of the United Methodist Church prepares and assists those whose ministry in Christ is exercised through ordination, the diaconate, licencing or certification. It also provides general oversight and care for United Methodist Institutions of Higher Education and campus ministries as well as financial resources for students to attend Institutions of Higher Education through church offerings and investments.

Dempster Fellowship

Subjects: Theology.
Purpose: To increase the effectiveness of teaching in United Methodist schools of theology by assisting worthy PhD candidates who are committed to serving the church through theological education.
Eligibility: The fellowships are open only to members of the United Methodist Church who plan to teach in seminaries, or to teach one of the technological disciplines (Bible, church history, theology, ethics, and the arts of ministry) in universities or colleges. The applicant must have received the M.Div. degree or its equivalent from one of the United Methodist seminaries, or be in a PhD programme or its equivalent at a university affiliated with a United Methodist seminary at the time the award is granted.
Level of Study: Doctorate
Type: Fellowship
Value: Up to US$30,000 over a five year period
Length of Study: 1 year, with a possibility of renewal at the discretion of the Committee on Awards
Frequency: Annual
Country of Study: Any country
No. of awards offered: 5
Application Procedure: Applicants must submit a completed application form, transcripts of all previous academic work, letters of reference, a term or other paper of essay length, Graduate Record Examination scores, summary statement of academic plans and a curriculum vitae. Further information is available on request.
Closing Date: October 15th
Funding: Private
Contributor: The United Methodist Church
No. of awards given last year: 5
No. of applicants last year: 20

GENERAL SOCIAL CARE COUNCIL

Goldings House, 2 Hay's Lane, London, SE1 2HB, England
Tel: (44) 20 7397 5100
Fax: (44) 20 7397 5101
Email: info@bursaries.gscc.org.uk
Website: www.gscc.org.uk
Contact: Administrative Officer

The General Social Care Council is the first ever regulatory body for the social care profession in England. It was set up to establish codes of conduct and practice for social care workers, a register of practicing professionals and to regulate and support social work, education and training. It takes forwards some of the work of the Central Council for Education and Training in Social Work, which closed on September 28, 2001. Similar councils exist for Northern Ireland, Scotland and Wales.

General Social Care Council Additional Graduate Bursary

Subjects: Social work.
Purpose: To support those seeking the qualifications required for social work.
Eligibility: Open to graduates, who have ordinarily been resident in the United Kingdom for 3 years and comply with the LEA regulations for mandatory awards.
Level of Study: Postgraduate
Type: Bursary
Length of Study: 2 years
Frequency: Annual
Country of Study: United Kingdom
No. of awards offered: Approx. 1,000
Application Procedure: Applicants can obtain an application form by contacting Bursary information line (44) 20 7397 5835 or by email: bursaries@gscc.org.uk
Closing Date: June 7th. Late applications must be received by December 31st
Funding: Government
Contributor: The Department of Health
No. of awards given last year: 1,000

GEOLOGICAL SOCIETY OF AMERICA (GSA)

3300 Penrose Place, PO Box 9140, Boulder, CO 80301-9140, United States of America
Tel: (1) 303 447 2020
Fax: (1) 303 357 1070
Email: awards@geosociety.org
Website: www.geosociety.org
Contact: Ms Diane C Lorenz, Program Officer, Grants, Awards, and Recognition

Established in 1888, the GSA is a non-profit organization dedicated to the advancement of the science of geology. GSA membership is for the generalist and the specialist in the field of geology and offers something for everyone.

A L Medlin Scholarship Award and Field Research Award

Subjects: Geology.
Purpose: To financially support students who are involved in research in coal geology.
Eligibility: Open to full-time students involved in coal-geology research.
Level of Study: Research
Type: Scholarship and award
Length of Study: 1 year
Frequency: Annual
Application Procedure: For more information visit the GSA division web page.
Closing Date: February 15th
Funding: Corporation
Contributor: The Coal Geology Division of the GSA

For further information contact:

Box 25046, Denver Federal Center, Denver, CO 80225, United States of America
Fax: (1) 303 236 0459
Contact: Romeo Flores, U.S. Geological survey

Alexander & Geraldine Wanek Fund

Subjects: Earth and geological sciences.
Purpose: To support research projects.
Eligibility: Open to GSA members.
Level of Study: Research
Type: Award
Frequency: Annual
Closing Date: February 1st

Alexander Sisson Award

Subjects: Geology.
Purpose: To support research.
Eligibility: Open to candidates who wish to pursue studies in Alaska and the Caribbean.
Type: Award
Frequency: Annual
Application Procedure: Applications are available online.
Closing Date: February 1st
Contributor: Geological Society of America

Bruce L. Award

Subjects: Geology.
Purpose: To support students pursuing geologic research.
Eligibility: Open to candidates who are enrolled in a U.S., Canadian, Mexican, or Central American university or college.
Type: Award
Frequency: Annual

Application Procedure: For further details contact the Program Officer-Grants, Awards and Recognition.
Closing Date: February 1st
Funding: Private

Charles A. & June R.P. Ross Research Fund

Subjects: Biostratigraphy.
Purpose: To support research projects.
Eligibility: Open to GSA members.
Level of Study: Postgraduate
Type: Award
Frequency: Annual
Application Procedure: Applications available online.
Closing Date: February 1st

Claude C. Albritton, Jr. Scholarships

Subjects: Earth science and archaeology.
Purpose: To encourage students who want to pursue higher studies in the field of Earth science and archaeology.
Level of Study: Postgraduate
Type: Award
Length of Study: US$500
Frequency: Annual
Funding: Foundation
Contributor: GSA foundation

For further information contact:

Institute for Applied Sciences, P.O. Box 13078, University of North Texas, Denton, TX 76203
Contact: Reid Feming

Gladys W Cole Memorial Research Award

Subjects: Investigation of the geomorphology of semi-arid and arid terrain in the United States of America and Mexico.
Purpose: To provide financial support for research.
Eligibility: Open to GSA members or Fellows aged 30–65 who have published one or more significant papers on geomorphology. Funds cannot be used to pay for work already accomplished, but previous recipients may reapply if additional support is needed to complete their work. All qualified applicants are urged to apply.
Level of Study: Postdoctorate
Type: Research grant
Value: US$8,200
Frequency: Annual
Country of Study: Other
No. of awards offered: 1
Application Procedure: Applicants must complete an application form available from the website.
Closing Date: February 1st
Funding: Private
Contributor: Dr W Storrs Cole
No. of awards given last year: 1

Gretchen L. Blechschmidt Award

Subjects: Geological sciences.
Purpose: To support research by women interested in achieving a PhD.
Eligibility: Open to all women candidates who are GSA members and wish to achieve a PhD.
Level of Study: Postgraduate, postdoctorate, research
Type: Award
Frequency: Annual
Application Procedure: For additional contact: Program Officer Grants, Awards and Recognition.
Closing Date: February 1st

GSA Research Grants

Subjects: Earth science.
Purpose: To provide partial support for Master's and doctoral thesis research.
Eligibility: Open to students attending colleges and universities within the United States of America, Canada, Mexico and Central America. Applicants must be members of the GSA in order to apply.
Level of Study: Postgraduate, research
Type: Research grant
Value: There are no set limits
Length of Study: 1 year, renewable
Frequency: Annual
Country of Study: Other
No. of awards offered: Varies
Application Procedure: Applicants must complete current application forms.
Closing Date: February 1st
Funding: Government, private
Contributor: GSA's Penrose and Pardee endowments, the National Science Foundation, industry, individual GSA members through the GEOSTAR and Research Grants funds, and numerous dedicated research funds that have been endowed at the GSA Foundation by members
No. of awards given last year: 251
No. of applicants last year: 571
Additional Information: Grants are awarded on the basis of the scientific merits of the problem, the capability of the investigator and the feasibility of the budget, and as an aid to a research project, not to sustain the entire cost. Students may receive the award once at the Master's level and once at the PhD level.

Harold T. Stearns Fellowship Award

Subjects: Geology of Pacific Island and the circum-pacific region.
Purpose: To support research projects.
Eligibility: Open to GSA members.
Level of Study: Research
Type: Award
Frequency: Annual
Application Procedure: For more information contact the Program Officer-Grants, Awards and Recognition.
Closing Date: February 1st

History of Geology Student Award

Subjects: Geology.
Purpose: To award best proposals for a history of Geology paper.
Eligibility: Open to applicants who are enrolled in a U.S., Canadian, Mexican or Central American university or college.
Level of Study: Research
Type: Grant
Frequency: Annual
Application Procedure: Applications available online.
Closing Date: February 1st

J. Hoover Mackin and Arthur D. Howard Research Grants

Subjects: Quaternary geology/geomorphology.
Purpose: To support outstanding student research.
Eligibility: Applicants must be GSA members.
Level of Study: Research
Type: Grant
Frequency: Annual
No. of awards offered: 1–2
Application Procedure: Application forms are available online.
Closing Date: February 1st

John Montagne Fund

Subjects: Geomorphology.
Purpose: To support research.
Eligibility: Open to GSA members.
Type: Award
Frequency: Annual
Application Procedure: Applications are available online.
Closing Date: February 1st
Funding: Private

John T. Dillon Alaska Research Award

Subjects: Earth science.
Purpose: To support research on earth science problems.
Eligibility: Open to applicants who are GSA members.

Level of Study: Research
Type: Award
Frequency: Annual
Closing Date: February 1st

Lipman Research Award

Subjects: Volcanology and Petrology.
Purpose: To promote and support graduate research.
Eligibility: Open to applicants who are GSA members.
Level of Study: Research
Type: Award
Frequency: Annual
Application Procedure: Contact the Program officer for further information.
Closing Date: February 1st
Funding: Private

Parke D. Snavely, Jr., Cascadia Research Award Fund

Subjects: Geology.
Purpose: To support field-oriented graduate student research.
Eligibility: Open to applicants enrolled in a U.S., Canadian, Mexican or Central American university or college.
Level of Study: Research
Type: Award
Frequency: Annual
Application Procedure: For more information contact: Program Officer-Grants, Awards and Recognition.
Closing Date: February 1st

Robert K. Fahnestock Memorial Award

Subjects: Earth and geological science.
Purpose: To award applicants with the best application in the field of sediment transport.
Eligibility: Applicants must be enrolled in a U.S., Canadian, Mexican or Central American university or college and must be GSA members.
Level of Study: Research
Type: Award
Frequency: Annual
Application Procedure: For more details contact the Program Officer-Grants, Awards and Recognition.
Closing Date: February 1st

Roy J. Shlemon Scholarship Awards

Subjects: Engineering geology.
Purpose: To award best research proposals.
Eligibility: Open to student members of the Engineering Geology Division.
Level of Study: Doctorate, research
Type: Scholarship
Value: US$1,000 stipend and US$500 allowance
Frequency: Annual
No. of awards offered: 4
Application Procedure: Application forms are available online.
Closing Date: March 15th
Additional Information: The scholarship award committee strongly encouraged women, minorities and persons with disabilities to participate in this program.

For further information contact:

13376 Azores Avenue, Sylmar, CA 91342
Contact: Robert A. Larson

S.E. Dwornik Student Paper Awards

Subjects: Planetary geology.
Purpose: To encourage students to become involved with NASA and planetary science.
Eligibility: Open to all American students interested in planetary science.
Level of Study: Postgraduate
Type: Award
Value: US$500
Frequency: Annual
Application Procedure: Students must submit abstract of the paper along with the application form.

W Storrs Cole Memorial Research Award

Subjects: Invertebrate micropalaeontology.
Purpose: To support research into invertebrate micropalaeontology.
Eligibility: Open to GSA members or Fellows aged 30–65 who have published one or more significant papers on micropalaeontology. Funds cannot be used for work already accomplished but recipients of previous awards may reapply if additional support is needed to complete their work. All qualified applicants are urged to apply.
Level of Study: Postdoctorate
Type: Research grant
Value: US$7,500
Frequency: Annual
Application Procedure: Applicants must write for further details and an application form or visit the website.
Closing Date: Applications must be postmarked before February 1st
Funding: Private
Contributor: Dr W Storrs Cole
No. of awards given last year: 1

GEORGE WALFORD INTERNATIONAL ESSAY PRIZE (GWIEP)

12 Bloomfield Road, London, N6 4ET, England
Email: richenda@gwiep.net
Website: www.gwiep.net
Contact: Ms Richenda Walford, Trustee

The George Walford International Essay Prize (GWIEP) is a registered charity that awards a cash prize each year to the winner of an essay on the subject of systematic ideology.

George Walford International Essay Prize (GWIEP)

Subjects: Any subject.
Purpose: To award a prize to the best essay on systematic ideology.
Eligibility: Everyone is eligible, with the exception of the trustees and judges themselves. There are no bars regarding age, race, nationality or gender.
Level of Study: Unrestricted
Type: Prize
Value: UK £3,500
Length of Study: Varies
Frequency: Annual
Country of Study: Any country
No. of awards offered: 1
Application Procedure: Applicants must contact GWIEP for details. Information can be requested by mail though communication via email and the website is greatly preferred.
Closing Date: May 31st
Funding: Private
Contributor: The family of the late George Walford
No. of awards given last year: 1
Additional Information: For more information about the prize and systematic ideology, please visit the website.

GEORGIA LIBRARY ASSOCIATION (GLA)

GLA, P O Box 793, Rex, Georgia, GA 30273,
United States of America
Tel: (1) 770 961 3520
Fax: (1) 404 892 7879
Email: ebagley@gsu.edu
Website: www.library.gsu.edu/gla
Contact: Scholarship Committee Chair

The Georgia Library Association's (GLA) mission is to provide an understanding of the place that libraries should take in advancing the educational, cultural and economic life of the state, to promote the expansion and improvement of library service and to stimulate activities toward these ends.

Hubbard Scholarship

Subjects: Library science.
Purpose: To recruit excellent librarians for Georgia and provide financial assistance toward completing a degree in library science.
Eligibility: Open to United States citizens accepted for admission to a Master's programme at an American Library Association (ALA) accredited library school, who intend to complete the course of study within two years.
Level of Study: Postgraduate
Type: Scholarship
Value: US$3,000, paid in equal instalments at the beginning of each term, semester or quarter
Length of Study: 2 years
Frequency: Annual
Study Establishment: An ALA accredited school
Country of Study: United States of America
No. of awards offered: 1
Application Procedure: Applicants must submit an official form of application, proof of acceptance in an accredited library school and official transcripts of all academic work sent directly from each institution of higher education. Three letters of reference must also be sent directly from the referee.
Closing Date: May 1st
Additional Information: The Scholar is required to work in a library or library related capacity in Georgia for one year following completion of the programme, or agree to pay back a pro-rated amount of the scholarship plus interest within a two year period.

THE GERALDINE R. DODGE FOUNDATION

163 Madison Avenue, Post Office Box 1239, Morris town, NJ 07962-12 39, United States of America
Tel: (1) 973 540 8442
Fax: (1) 973 540 1211
Email: info@grdodge.org
Website: www.grdodge.org

The Geraldine R. Dodge Foundation was established in 1974 with funds from the will of Geraldine Rockefeller Dodge. The mission of the foundation is to support and encourage those educational, cultural, social and environmental values that contribute to making our society more humane and our world more livable.

Dodge Foundation Frontiers for Veterinary Medicine Fellowships

Subjects: Veterinary medicine.
Purpose: To provide opportunities to veterinary students to explore and bring new problem-solving perspectives to animal-related issues.
Eligibility: Open to candidates who are enrolled as full-time veterinary students at a U.S. or Canadian college of Veterinary medicine.
Level of Study: Postgraduate
Type: Fellowship
Length of Study: US$7,000
Frequency: Annual
Study Establishment: Any American Veterinary Medical Association accredited college of veterinary medicine
Country of Study: United States of America or Canada
Application Procedure: See the website.
Closing Date: December 16th

For further information contact:

Contact: Michelle Knapik, Director for Environmental and Welfare of Animals

Dodge Foundation Teacher Fellowships

Subjects: Teacher training.
Purpose: To enable teachers to grow as educational leaders to better impact their scholars and communities.
Eligibility: Open to K-12 full-time teachers who are employed in New Jersey public and public charter schools in Camden Country, New Jersey.
Level of Study: Postgraduate
Type: Fellowship
Value: US$2,000–7,500 for individuals, and between US$5,000 and 10,000 for teams
Frequency: Annual
Country of Study: United States of America
Application Procedure: Application form and details available on the website.
Closing Date: January 12th
Funding: Foundation

Dodge Foundation Visual Arts Initiative

Subjects: Visual art.
Purpose: To provide a unique professional infrastructure and sprinted network for the artist/educator.
Eligibility: Open to candidates who have taught the visual arts for at least 3 years and will be continuing as visual arts teachers.
Level of Study: Professional development
Type: Grant
Value: US$5,000 plus US$2,000 for visual arts project
Frequency: Annual
Country of Study: United States of America
No. of awards offered: 20
Application Procedure: See the website.
Closing Date: January 31st
Funding: Foundation

For further information contact:

Tel: 973 540 8443, ext. 118
Email: erastocky@grdodge.org
Contact: Elaine Rastocky

GERMAN HISTORICAL INSTITUTE

1607 New Hampshire Avenue North West, Washington, DC, 20009, United States of America
Tel: (1) 202 387 3355
Fax: (1) 202 483 3430
Email: info@ghi-dc.org
Website: www.ghi-dc.org
Contact: Dirk Schumann, Deputy Director

The German Historical Institute is an independent research institute dedicated to the promotion of historical research in the Federal Republic of Germany and the United States of America. The Institute supports and advises German and American historians and political scientists and encourages co-operation between them.

Bucerius Seminar

Subjects: American history.
Purpose: To familiarize participants with American research facilities (archives and libraries), provide a forum for discussing research methods and practical tips and help prepare them for their prospective dissertation research in the United States of America.
Eligibility: Open to PhD students in American history.
Level of Study: Doctorate
Type: Scholarship
Value: US$2,700
Length of Study: 12 days
Frequency: Annual
Country of Study: United States of America
Application Procedure: Applicants must refer to the website www.ghi-dc.org/scholarship-bucerius.html
Closing Date: April 30th
Funding: Foundation
Contributor: Ebelin and Gerd Bucerius ZEIT Foundation
No. of awards given last year: 10

Fritz Stern Dissertation Prize

Subjects: German history, history of Germans in North America, German–American relations.

Purpose: To award the two best doctoral dissertations submitted in German history, German–American relations or the history of Germans in North America. The winners are invited to the GHI to present their research at the annual symposium of the Friends each November. Candidates are nominated by their dissertation advisers at a North American university during the previous academic year.
Eligibility: Open to United States of America PhDs.
Level of Study: Doctorate
Type: Prize
Value: US$2,000 and reimbursement for the travel to Washington, DC
Frequency: Annual
Country of Study: United States of America
No. of awards offered: 2
Application Procedure: Applicants must refer to the website for further information.
Closing Date: May 1st
Funding: Private
Contributor: Friends of the German Historical Institute
No. of awards given last year: 2

German Historical Institute Collaborative Research Program for Postdoctoral Scholars

Subjects: German and United States of America post-World War II history, transatlantic studies and comparative studies in social, cultural and political history.
Purpose: To support a research programme for postdoctoral scholars on the topic of continuity, change and globalization in postwar Germany and the United States of America.
Eligibility: Open to German and United States of America postdoctoral students. Applications from women and minorities are especially encouraged.
Level of Study: Postdoctorate
Type: Fellowship
Value: US$20,000–40,000, dependent on length of study
Length of Study: 6 months–1 year
Frequency: Dependent on funds available
Country of Study: United States of America
Application Procedure: Applicants must refer to the website for details.
Closing Date: Refer to the website
Funding: Government
Contributor: The National Endowment for Humanities
No. of awards given last year: 1

German Historical Institute Doctoral and Postdoctoral Fellowships

Subjects: Humanities and social sciences, comparative studies in social, cultural and political history, studies of German–American relations and transatlantic studies.
Purpose: To give support to German and United States of America doctoral and postdoctoral students working on topics related to the Institute's general scope of interest.
Eligibility: Open to German and United States of America doctoral students. Applications from women and minorities are especially encouraged.
Level of Study: Postdoctorate, doctorate
Type: Fellowship
Value: US$1,350 for doctoral students, US$2,650 for postdoctoral students
Length of Study: Up to 6 months
Frequency: Annual
Country of Study: United States of America
No. of awards offered: Open
Application Procedure: Applicants must refer to the website for details.
Closing Date: May 20th and October 15th
Funding: Government
No. of awards given last year: 14
No. of applicants last year: 50
Additional Information: All candidates are expected to evaluate source material in the United States of America that is important for their research. At the end of the scholarship they are required to report on their findings or give a presentation at the GHI.

German Historical Institute Summer Seminar in Germany

Subjects: German handwriting, German archives, German history and transatlantic studies.
Purpose: To introduce students to German handwriting of previous centuries by exposing them to a variety of German archives, familiarizing them with major research topics in German culture and history and encouraging the exchange of ideas among the next generation of United States of America scholars.
Eligibility: Open to United States of America doctoral students. Applications from women and minorities are especially encouraged.
Level of Study: Doctorate
Type: Scholarship
Value: US$2,500
Length of Study: 2 weeks
Frequency: Annual
Country of Study: Germany
Application Procedure: Applicants must refer to the website for details.
Closing Date: December 31st
Funding: Government
No. of awards given last year: 13

German Historical Institute Transatlantic Doctoral Seminar in German History

Subjects: German history and transatlantic studies.
Purpose: To bring together young scholars from Germany and the United States of America who are nearing completion of their doctoral degrees. It provides an opportunity to debate doctoral projects in a transatlantic setting.
Eligibility: Open to German and United States of America doctoral students. Applications from women and minorities are especially encouraged.
Level of Study: Doctorate
Type: Scholarship
Value: US$2,000
Length of Study: 4 days
Frequency: Annual
Country of Study: Other
Application Procedure: Applicants must refer to the website for details.
Closing Date: December 1st
Funding: Government
No. of awards given last year: 16

Kade-Heideking Fellowship

Subjects: American history, German history in the 20th century, comparative international history, German–American relations.
Purpose: To support a German doctoral student working in one of the three areas to which the late Professor Jürgen Heideking made significant contributions: American history and German–American relations from the early modern period to the present; international history of the 19th and 20th centuries, including the history of international relations and the comparative history of colonial systems and societies; and 20th-century German history, with an emphasis on the United States of America's influence on German society between 1918 and 1949.
Eligibility: Open to German doctoral students only.
Level of Study: Doctorate
Type: Fellowship
Value: US$30,000
Length of Study: 1 year
Frequency: Annual
Country of Study: United States of America
No. of awards offered: 1
Application Procedure: Applicants must refer to the website for details.
Closing Date: November 15th
Funding: Private
Contributor: Annette Kade Charitable Trust Fund
No. of awards given last year: 1

Medieval History Seminar

Subjects: Medieval history.
Purpose: The Medieval History Seminar is devoted to the latest research in the field of European medieval studies. Similar to the Transatlantic Doctoral Seminar, this programme invites 16 doctoral students from Europe and North America to discuss their dissertation projects with peers and senior scholars from both sides of the Atlantic.
Eligibility: Open to citizens of the United States of America and Europe.
Level of Study: Doctorate
Type: Grant
Value: US$2,000
Length of Study: 4 days
Frequency: Every 2 years
Country of Study: United States of America and Europe
No. of awards offered: 16
Application Procedure: Applicants must refer to the website for details.
Closing Date: May 1st
Funding: Government
No. of awards given last year: 16

Thyssen–Heideking Fellowship

Subjects: American history, German history in the 20th century, comparative international history, German–American relations.
Purpose: To support American scholars working in one of the three areas to which the late Professor Jürgen Heideking made important contributions: American history and German–American relations from the early modern period to the present; international history of the 19th and 20th centuries, including the history of international relations and the comparative history of colonial systems and societies; and 20th-century German history, with emphasis on America's influence on German society between 1918 and 1949.
Eligibility: Open to American scholars only.
Level of Study: Postdoctorate
Type: Fellowship
Value: €21,250
Length of Study: 6 months–1 year
Frequency: Annual
Country of Study: Germany
No. of awards offered: 1
Application Procedure: Applicants must refer to the website for details.
Closing Date: November 15th
Funding: Private
Contributor: Fritz Thyssen Foundation
No. of awards given last year: 1

Young Scholars Forum

Subjects: Humanities and social sciences, comparative studies in social cultural and political history, studies of German–American relations, German history, European history.
Purpose: To gather together PhD candidates and recent PhD recipients from the United States of America and Europe who work in the fields of German, German–American or European history and to give them the opportunity to present their work to peers and distinguished academics from both sides of the Atlantic.
Eligibility: Open to applicants from the United States of America and Europe, and Germans in particular.
Level of Study: Doctorate, postdoctorate
Type: Grant
Value: US$2,000
Length of Study: 3 days
Frequency: Annual
Country of Study: United States of America
Application Procedure: Applicants must refer to the website for details.
Closing Date: January 10th
Funding: Government
No. of awards given last year: 15

GERMAN ISRAELI FOUNDATION FOR SCIENTIFIC RESEARCH AND DEVELOPMENT

GSF Forschungszentrum, Neuherberg,
Post box 1129, D-85758, Oberschleissheim,
Germany
Tel: (49) 89 3187 3106
Fax: (49) 89 3187 3365
Email: gif.stepper@gsf.de
Website: www.gifres.org.il
Contact: G I F Verbindungsbuero

German Israeli Foundation Young Scientist's Programme

Subjects: Natural sciences, social sciences and humanities.
Purpose: This new initiative aims to encourage young German and Israeli scientists to establish initial contacts with potential counterparts in Israel or Germany. An integral part of the programme will be a visit of at least 2–3 weeks to Germany or Israel, to give a presentation of their research activities and results and to meet possible partners for future co-operation.
Eligibility: Scientists below 40 years, within the first 7 years after receiving their PhD, MD or equivalent degree, and recognized staff members of a GIF-eligible institution with legal status are eligible to apply.
Level of Study: Research
Type: Grant
Value: Up to €40,000 for the 1-year programme, for project-related equipment, disposable materials, computer services, auxiliary personnel, foreign travel, reports and publications
Length of Study: 1 year
Study Establishment: Any GIF-eligible institution
Country of Study: Germany and Israel
Application Procedure: Application forms are available on request.
Closing Date: Application deadlines vary. For details see www.gifres.org.il

Research Grant (GIF)

Subjects: Natural sciences, social sciences and humanities.
Purpose: To promote doctoral studies as well as basic and applied research projects within the framework of co-operative research programmes.
Eligibility: GIF projects must involve active collaboration between Israeli and German scientists. Special consideration will be given to young scientists, partners applying for the first time, scientists from the former East Germany and new immigrants to Israel from the former Soviet Union. Scientists applying for grants must be recognized staff members of a GIF-eligible institution with legal status. The principal investigators must hold a doctoral degree or equivalent at the time of application.
Level of Study: Research, doctorate
Type: Grant
Value: €225,000–600,000 per project
Length of Study: 3 years
Study Establishment: Any GIF-eligible institution
Country of Study: Germany and Israel
Application Procedure: Doctoral candidates can apply to the GIF project co-ordinators, either in Germany or Israel, to pursue their doctoral research within the framework of the co-operative research project.
Closing Date: Application deadlines vary. For details see website.
Contributor: German Israeli Foundation for Scientific Research and Development
Additional Information: The joint research programme must be presented as a single, co-ordinated proposal in which the roles and tasks of both groups are clearly defined. If institutional academic regulations permit the granting of fellowships, the GIF may support a fellowship for tasks within the research plan.

GERMAN MARSHALL FUND OF THE UNITED STATES (GMF)

1744 R Street NW, Washington, DC 20009,
United States of America
Tel: (1) 202 745 6686
Fax: (1) 202 265 1662
Email: lrosenbohm@gmfus.org
Website: www.gmfus.org
Contact: Lea Rosenbohm, Administrative Assistant

The German Marshall Fund of the United States (GMF) is an American institution that stimulates the exchange of ideas and promotes co-operation between the United States and Europe in the spirit of the post war Marshall Plan. GMF was created in 1972 by a gift from Germany as a permanent memorial to Marshall Plan Aid.

GMF Journalism Fellowships

Subjects: Journalism.
Purpose: To contribute to better reporting on transatlantic issues by both American and European journalist.
Eligibility: Open to American and European journalists who have an outstanding record in reporting on foreign affairs.
Level of Study: Postdoctorate, professional development
Type: Fellowship
Value: US$2,000–25,000 and funds for travel
Frequency: Annual
Application Procedure: Applicants including a description of the proposed project, current resume and samples of previous work must be sent.
Funding: Foundation
Contributor: The German Marshall Fund

For further information contact:

Email: usoyez@gmfus.org
Contact: Ursula Soyez

GMF Research Fellowships Program

Subjects: Understanding of economic, political and social developments relating to Europe.
Purpose: To support research projects that seek to improve the understanding of significant contemporary economic, political and social developments involving the United States of America and Europe.
Eligibility: Open to citizens of the United States and permanent residents only. Special consideration will be given to applicants seeking support for dissertation fieldwork in one or more European countries and to projects involving parallel or collaborative research by both established and younger Scholars, including projects designed on a transatlantic basis.
Level of Study: Doctorate, postdoctorate, postgraduate
Type: Fellowship
Value: For dissertation fieldwork in Europe the grants are worth US$20,000. The support for advanced research grants will not exceed US$40,000
Length of Study: For dissertation fieldwork in Europe up to 1 year, and for advanced research support not less than 1 semester and not greater than 1 year
Frequency: Annual
Study Establishment: There is no restriction on the place of tenure
Country of Study: Other
No. of awards offered: Approx. 20
Application Procedure: Applicants must visit the website for information and downloadable application forms.
Closing Date: November 15th for dissertation or advanced research
No. of awards given last year: 22
No. of applicants last year: 120
Additional Information: All award recipients are responsible for arranging their own housing, insurance, benefits and travel, including a visa if applicable. Submissions will be reviewed by a committee of established Scholars from various disciplines. An independent selection committee of Scholars will make recommendations to the Fund.

Manfred Wörner Seminar

Purpose: To provide an opportunity to broaden professional networks.
Level of Study: Professional development
Value: Travel, accommoadation and meals
Length of Study: 10 days
Frequency: Annual
Country of Study: Germany
No. of awards offered: 30
Funding: Government
Contributor: The German Government

For further information contact:

Email: nhagen@gmfus.org
Website: www.gmfus.org/fellowships/manfred.cfm
Contact: Nicola Hagen, Program assistant

Marshall Memorial Fellowship

Subjects: Politics, government business, media and non-profit sector committed to strengthening the transatlantic relationship.
Purpose: To provide opportunities for emerging leaders from the United States and Europe to explore societies, institutions and people from the other side of the Atlantic.
Eligibility: Open to candidates who are citizens or permanent residents of one of the 15MMF countries.
Level of Study: Postdoctorate
Length of Study: 3–4 weeks
Frequency: Annual
Application Procedure: Candidates are required to submit a written application and undergo an interview in person.
Closing Date: Varies
Contributor: German Marshall Fund

For further information contact:

Website: www.gmfus.org/fellowships/mmf.cfm

Peter R.Weitz Journalism Prize

Subjects: Journalism.
Purpose: To acknowledge outstanding coverage of transatlantic and European issues by American media.
Eligibility: The senior prize is open to all journalists covering European issues and the young journalist prize is open to American journalists under 35 years of age.
Type: Award
Value: Senior prize worth US$10,000 and junior prize US$5,000
Frequency: Annual
Application Procedure: A completed application form must be submitted.
Closing Date: February 28th
Funding: Foundation
Contributor: The German Marshall Fund

Transatlantic Community Foundation Fellowship

Subjects: International relations.
Purpose: To create strengthen networks of people and share international expenses.
Eligibility: Open to staff of American and European community foundation.
Level of Study: Postdoctorate, professional development
Value: Roundtrip airfare, a daily stipend and reimbursement for car rental expenses as needed
Frequency: Annual
No. of awards offered: 10
Funding: Foundation
Contributor: Charles Stewart Mott Foundation

For further information contact:

Website: www.gmfus.org/fellowships/tcff.cfm

Transatlantic Fellows Program

Subjects: Foreign policy, international security, trade and economic development, immigration and other topics important to transatlantic cooperation.

Purpose: To build important networks of policymakers analysts in the Euro-Atlantic community.
Eligibility: Open to senior policy-practitioners, journalists businesspeople and academics.
Level of Study: Postdoctorate
Frequency: Annual

For further information contact:

Website: www.gmfus.org/fellowships/taf.cfm

GERMAN STUDIES ASSOCIATION

340 E 15th Street, Tempe, AZ, 85281, United States of America
Tel: (1) 480 966 2245
Fax: (1) 480 966 2239
Email: thegsa@yahoo.com
Website: www.g-s-a.org
Contact: Gerald R. Kleinfeld, Exectuive Director

The German Studies Association (GSA) is a non-profit educational organization that promotes the research and study of Germany, Austria and Switzerland. The GSA Endowment Fund provides financial support to Association projects, the annual conference, and general operations.

Berlin Program Fellowship

Subjects: Modern and contemporary German and European affairs.
Purpose: To support doctoral dissertation research as well as postdoctoral research leading to the completion of a monograph.
Eligibility: Applicants for a dissertation fellowship must be full-time graduate students who have completed all coursework required for the PhD and must have achieved ABD status by the time the proposed research stay in Berlin begins. Also eligible are United States of America and Canadian PhDs who have received their doctorates within the past 2 calendar years.
Level of Study: Postdoctorate, doctorate
Type: Fellowship
Value: €1,100 per month for dissertation fellows, €1,400 per month for postdoctoral fellows
Length of Study: 10 months–1 year
Frequency: Annual
Study Establishment: Freie Universität Berlin
Country of Study: Germany
No. of awards offered: 12
Application Procedure: Applicants must submit a single application packet consisting of completed application forms, a proposal, three letters of reference, language evaluation(s) and graduate school transcripts. Proposals should be no longer than 2,500 words or 10 pages, followed by a one- or two-page bibliography or bibliographic essay.
Closing Date: December 1st
Contributor: Halle Foundation and the National Endowment for the Humanities

For further information contact:

Berlin Program for Advanced German and European Studies, Freie Universität Berlin, Garystrasse 45, D-14195, Berlin, Germany
Tel: (49) 30 838 56671
Fax: (49) 30 838 56672
Email: bprogram@zedat.fu-berlin.de
Website: www.userpage.fu-berlin.de/˜bprogram

THE GETTY GRANT PROGRAM, J PAUL GETTY TRUST

1200 Getty Center Drive, Suite 800, Los Angeles, CA, 90049-1685, United States of America
Tel: (1) 310 440 7320
Fax: (1) 310 440 7703
Email: researchgrants@getty.edu
Website: www.getty.edu/grants
Contact: Senior Programme Officer

The J Paul Getty Trust is a privately operating foundation dedicated to the visual arts and the humanities. The Getty supports a wide range of projects that promote research in fields related to the history of art, the advancement of the understanding of art and the conservation of cultural heritage.

The Getty Trust Collaborative Research Grants

Subjects: History of art and related fields.
Purpose: To provide opportunities for teams of scholars to collaborate on interpretative research projects that offer new explanations of art and its history.
Eligibility: Collaborative Research Grant teams must consist of two or more art historians, or of an art historian and one or more scholars from other disciplines. Funding is also available for the research and planning of scholarly exhibitions. Teams for these projects must include scholars from both museums and universities.
Level of Study: Postdoctorate, postgraduate, professional development
Type: Research grant
Value: Varies according to the needs of the project
Length of Study: 1–2 years
Frequency: Annual
Country of Study: Any country
No. of awards offered: Varies
Application Procedure: Applicants must complete an application form. Additional information, detailed guidelines and application forms are available from the website or by contacting the Getty Grant Program Office.
Closing Date: November 1st
Funding: Private
Additional Information: Further information is available on request.

The Getty Trust Curatorial Research Fellowships

Subjects: History of art and related fields.
Purpose: To support the professional scholarly development of curators by providing them with time off from regular museum duties to undertake short-term research or study projects.
Eligibility: Open to full-time curators who have a minimum of 3 years of professional experience and are employed at museums with art collections.
Level of Study: Professional development
Type: Fellowship
Value: Please contact the organization
Length of Study: 1–3 months
Frequency: Annual
Country of Study: Any country
No. of awards offered: Varies
Application Procedure: Applicants must complete an application form. Additional information, detailed guidelines and application forms are available from the website or by contacting the Getty Grant Program Office.
Closing Date: November 1st
Funding: Private
Additional Information: Further information is available on request.

Postdoctoral Fellowships (Getty)

Subjects: History of art or related fields.
Purpose: To provide support for outstanding scholars in the early stages of their careers to pursue interpretative research projects that make a substantial and original contribution to the understanding of art and its history.
Eligibility: Open to scholars of all nationalities who have earned a doctoral degree within the past 6 years.
Level of Study: Postdoctorate
Type: Fellowship
Value: Please contact the organization
Length of Study: 1 year
Frequency: Annual
Country of Study: Any country
Application Procedure: Applicants must complete an application form. Additional information, detailed guidelines and application forms are available from the website or by contacting the Getty Grant Program Office.

Closing Date: November 1st
Funding: Private
Additional Information: Further information is available on request.

Residential Grants at the Getty Center

Subjects: Arts and humanities.
Purpose: To provide support for established scholars to undertake research related to a specific theme while in residence at the Getty Center in Los Angeles.
Eligibility: Open to established scholars who are working on projects that address the given scholarly theme.
Level of Study: Research, postgraduate, professional development, postdoctorate
Type: Grant
Value: Please contact the organization
Frequency: Annual
Country of Study: Any country
No. of awards offered: Varies
Application Procedure: Applicants must complete an application form. Additional information, detailed guidelines and application forms are available from the website or by contacting the Getty Grant Program office.
Closing Date: November 1st
Funding: Private

GÉZA ANDA FOUNDATION

Bleicherweg 18, CH-8002, Zurich, Switzerland
Tel: (41) 44 205 1423
Fax: (41) 44 205 1429
Email: info@gezaanda.org
Website: www.gezaanda.org
Contact: Ms Ruth Bossart

The Géza Anda Foundation was established in 1977 in memory of the pianist, Géza Anda. It holds the Géza Anda Concours, an international piano competition, every 3 years, awarding prize winners and special prizes, and providing an opportunity for the laureates to appear as soloists in concerts and recitals.

International Géza Anda Piano Competition

Subjects: Piano playing.
Purpose: To sponsor young pianists in the musical spirit of Géza Anda.
Eligibility: Open to pianists born after June 8th, 1974.
Level of Study: Unrestricted
Type: Prize
Value: Cash prizes of Swiss francs 60,000 and other benefits such as free concert management services for 3 years
Frequency: Every 3 years
Country of Study: Switzerland
No. of awards offered: 3
Application Procedure: Applicants must complete four rounds in the competition: an audition, a recital, Mozart and a final concert with orchestra.
Closing Date: March 1st
Funding: Private
No. of awards given last year: 3 official awards and 4 special awards

GILBERT MURRAY TRUST

5 Warnborough Road, Oxford, OX2 6HZ, England
Tel: (44) 18 6555 6633
Contact: Mrs Mary Bull, Secretary, International Studies Committee

Gilbert Murray Trust Junior Awards

Subjects: International affairs or international law.
Purpose: To study the purposes and work of the United Nations.
Eligibility: Open to persons of any nationality who are, or who have been, students at a university or similar institution in the United Kingdom. Candidates should currently be taking or should have taken part in a course of international affairs or international law and must not be over 25 years of age, although consideration will be given to those over that age in special cases.
Level of Study: Postgraduate, undergraduate
Type: Award
Value: UK £300
Frequency: Annual
Country of Study: Any country
No. of awards offered: 10
Application Procedure: Applicants must submit five copies, typed and on one side only, of a letter of application, a curriculum vitae, an outline of their intention with regard to a future career, full particulars of the purpose for which the award would be used and a supporting testimonial from a person capable of judging the candidate's ability to use the award profitably.
Closing Date: April 1st
Funding: Private
Contributor: Small individual contributions
No. of awards given last year: 10
No. of applicants last year: 22
Additional Information: Awards are only given to support a specific project, such as a research visit to the headquarters of an international organization, or to a particular country, or a short research course at an institution abroad that will assist the applicant in his or her study of international affairs in relation to the purpose and work of the United Nations. The Junior Awards are not intended as general financial support for the study of international affairs.

GILCHRIST EDUCATIONAL TRUST (GET)

28 Great James Street, London, WC1N 3EY, England
Tel: (44) 020 7404 1672
Contact: Mrs Everidge, Secretary

GET Grants

Subjects: All subjects.
Purpose: To promote the advancement of education and learning.
Eligibility: Open to: students in the United Kingdom who have made proper provision to fund a degree or higher education course but find themselves facing unexpected financial difficulties which may prevent completion of it; students who are required to spend a short period abroad as part of their course; and British expeditions proposing to carry out scientific research in another country.
Level of Study: Doctorate, postgraduate
Type: Grant
Frequency: Dependent on funds available
Study Establishment: Any university
Country of Study: United Kingdom
No. of awards offered: Varies
Application Procedure: Expedition teams are required to complete an application form. Eligible individuals are sent a list of information required.
Closing Date: February 28th for expeditions. No deadline for applications from individuals
Funding: Private

Gilchrist Fieldwork Award

Subjects: All scientific subjects.
Purpose: To fund a period of fieldwork by established scientists or academics.
Eligibility: Open to teams wishing to undertake a field season of over 6 weeks in relation to one or more scientific objectives. Teams should consist of not more than 10 members, most of whom should be British and holding established positions in research departments at universities or similar establishments. The proposed research must be original and challenging, achievable within the timetable and preferably of benefit to the host country or region.
Type: Grant
Value: UK £15,000
Frequency: Every 2 years
Country of Study: Any country
No. of awards offered: 1
Application Procedure: Applicants must write for details.
Closing Date: March 15th in even-numbered years

Funding: Private
Additional Information: The award is competitive.

GILROY AND LILLIAN P ROBERTS CHARITABLE FOUNDATION

10 Presidential Boulerard, Suite 250, bala Cynwyd, PA 19004, United States of America
Tel: (1) 610 862 1998
Fax: (1) 610 862 3200
Contact: Mr Stanley Merves, Grants Enquiries

Private foundation funded under the will of Gilroy Roberts, designer of the obverse side of the Kennedy half-dollar when he was Chief Engraver of the US Mint.

Gilroy Roberts Art of Engraving Fellowship

Subjects: Fine and applied arts.
Purpose: To gain knowledge in bas relief and engraving.
Eligibility: Recipients should have art background. Sculpture and/or engraving.
Level of Study: Professional development, unrestricted
Type: Tuition, room and board and a small stipend
Value: US$2,000
Length of Study: 1 week
Frequency: Annual
Study Establishment: Colorado College
Country of Study: United States of America
No. of awards offered: 5
Application Procedure: Applicants can obtain an application form available from the American Numismatic Association, 919 North Cascade, Colorado Springs, CO, 80903-3279, United States of America.
Closing Date: As stated on application (changes annually)
Funding: Private
Contributor: Gilroy and Lillian P Roberts Charitable Foundation
No. of awards given last year: 5
No. of applicants last year: 15
Additional Information: The Art of Engraving course is offered annually.

GLADYS KRIEBLE DELMAS FOUNDATION

521 Fifth Avenue, Suite 1612, New York, NY, 10175-1699, United States of America
Tel: (1) 212 687 0011
Fax: (1) 212 687 8877
Email: info@delmas.org
Website: www.delmas.org
Contact: Ms Shirley Lockwood

The Gladys Krieble Delmas Foundation promotes the advancement and perpetuation of humanistic enquiry and artistic creativity by encouraging excellence in scholarship and in the performing arts, and by supporting research libraries and other institutions that preserve the resources that transmit this cultural heritage.

Gladys Krieble Delmas Foundation Grants

Subjects: The history of Venice, the former Venetian empire and contemporary Venetian society and culture. Disciplines of the humanities and social sciences are eligible areas of study, including but not limited to art, architecture, archaeology, theatre, music, literature, political science, economics and law.
Purpose: To promote research into Venice and the Veneto.
Eligibility: Open to citizens and permanent residents of the United States of America who have some experience in advanced research. Graduate students must have fulfilled all doctoral requirements except for completion of the dissertation. The dissertation proposal must, however, have been approved by the time of application for the grant. There is also a programme for scholars from Commonwealth countries.
Level of Study: Predoctorate, postdoctorate
Type: Grant
Value: US$500–19,900 depending on the length of study. At the discretion of the trustees and advisory board of the Foundation, funds may be made available for aid on the publication of results
Length of Study: Up to 1 academic year
Frequency: Annual
Country of Study: Italy
No. of awards offered: Usually 15–25
Application Procedure: Applicants must complete an application form. Instruction sheets and forms are available from the website.
Closing Date: December 15th
Funding: Private
No. of awards given last year: 17
No. of applicants last year: 43

For further information contact:

2 Lansdowne Circus, Leamington Spa, Warwickshire, CV32 4SW, England
Contact: Professor M E Mallett

GLASGOW EDUCATIONAL AND MARSHALL TRUST

21 Beaton Road, Glasgow, G41 4NW, Scotland
Tel: (44) 14 1423 2169
Fax: (44) 14 1424 1731
Website: www.gemt.org.uk
Contact: R R McLean, Administrator

The Glasgow Educational and Marshall Trust is a charitable trust that meets quarterly and awards bursaries to, among others, mature students and postgraduate students to aid travel and school trips.

Glasgow Educational and Marshall Trust Bursary

Subjects: All subjects.
Purpose: To offer financial support to those who have lived, or are currently living within the Glasgow Municipal Boundary.
Eligibility: Applicants must have a minimum of 5 years of residence within the Glasgow Municipal Boundary, as it was prior to 1975. Years spent within the Boundary purely for the purpose of study do not count.
Level of Study: Unrestricted
Type: Bursary
Value: UK £100–1,000
Frequency: Annual
Country of Study: United Kingdom
Application Procedure: Applicants must complete and submit an application form together with two written references prior to the start of the course. No retrospective awards are available.
Closing Date: July 31st
Funding: Private
No. of awards given last year: 74
No. of applicants last year: 240

GLAUCOMA RESEARCH FOUNDATION

251 Post Street, Suite 600, San Francisco, CA 94108, United States of America
Tel: (1) 415 986 3162
Fax: (1) 415 986 3763
Email: research@glaucoma.org
Website: www.glaucoma.org
Contact: Ms Jennifer Rulon, Research Manager

The Glaucoma Research Foundation is a national non-profit organization working to protect the sight and independence of people with glaucoma, through research and education.

Pilot Project Grants Program

Subjects: Glaucoma.
Purpose: To provide funds for research.
Eligibility: Applicants must hold a graduate degree.
Level of Study: Postgraduate
Value: US$15,000–40,000

Length of Study: 1 year
Frequency: Annual
Country of Study: United States of America
No. of awards offered: Varies
Application Procedure: Applicants must write, telephone or visit the website for details.
Closing Date: August 1st
No. of awards given last year: 5
No. of applicants last year: 20

GLAXOSMITHKLINE

Medicines Research Centre, Gunnels Wood Road, Stevenage, SG1 2NY, England
Tel: (44) 14 3876 3280
Fax: (44) 14 3876 3276
Email: ms3845@gsk.com
Website: www.glaxosmithkline.co.uk
Contact: Director, European Academic Liaison

GlaxoSmithKline is a pharmaceutical and healthcare company, committed to improving the quality of human life by enabling people to do more, feel better and live longer. The focus of the company is health care, treatment, prevention and diagnosis including the concept of proactive health living. GlaxoSmithKline comprises three integrated businesses: pharmaceuticals, consumer healthcare and clinical diagnostics.

GlaxoSmithKline Collaborative Research Projects

Subjects: Pharmaceuticals, consumer healthcare and clinical diagnostic services.
Purpose: To target people whose research activities fit into the company's own research programme.
Eligibility: Open to groups who are carrying out relevant research activities. Speculative approaches are also welcome from the academic sector.
Level of Study: Graduate, doctorate
Type: Studentship
Value: Please contact the organization
Length of Study: 1–3 years
Frequency: Annual
Study Establishment: Any university
Country of Study: Any country
Application Procedure: Applicants must write for details.
Closing Date: Applications are accepted at any time
Funding: Commercial, government
Contributor: The majority of studentships are jointly funded with the Research Councils and a small number are totally funded by them

GlaxoSmithkline Services to Academia

Subjects: Pharmacology, chemistry, biotechnology and toxicology.
Eligibility: Open to students excelling in the listed subject areas during their studies.
Level of Study: Professional development
Value: Varies
Frequency: Annual
Country of Study: Any country
No. of awards offered: Varies
Application Procedure: Organizations must approach the company in writing.
Closing Date: Applications are accepted at any time
Funding: Commercial

THE GOLDA MEIR MOUNT CARMEL INTERNATIONAL TRAINING CENTRE (MCTC)

PO Box 6111, Haifa, 31060, Israel
Tel: (972) 4 837 5904
Fax: (972) 4 837 5913
Email: mctc@mctc.co.il
Contact: Mrs Mazal Renford, Director

The Golda Meir Mount Carmel International Training Centre (MCTC) devotes its resources to training women and men from developing countries and societies in transition. Its underlying philosophy stresses the importance of grassroots development and recognition of women's contributions. It conducts courses and workshops at the MCTC and abroad in three key areas: community development, early childhood education and management of microenterprises.

MCTC Assistance for Courses

Subjects: Courses in community organization and management of human services, preschool education, organization and management of income-generating projects and small-scale industries, and the management of non-governmental organizations (NGOs).
Purpose: To assist developing countries and transitional societies in training personnel engaged in socio-economic development.
Eligibility: Open mainly to women aged 25–45 years of age from developing countries. Male students are also accepted. Participants must have completed at least 12 years of schooling, have undergone relevant professional training and have work experience. A good knowledge of the language in which the course will be given is essential.
Level of Study: Postgraduate, professional development
Value: Tuition, lodging and board
Length of Study: 3 or 6 weeks
Frequency: Annual
Study Establishment: MCTC
Country of Study: Israel
No. of awards offered: 28
Application Procedure: Applicants must apply to the Israeli diplomatic representative in their country for admission to the course.
Closing Date: 3 months prior to the commencement of the course
Funding: Government
Contributor: MASHAV-Centre for International Cooperation, Ministry of Foreign Affairs, Israel
No. of awards given last year: 400
No. of applicants last year: 1,400
Additional Information: Courses are given in English, French or Spanish and include lectures, discussion groups, study tours and fieldwork.

MCTC Tuition and Maintenance Scholarships

Subjects: Community organization and management of human services, preschool education, organization and management of income generating projects and small-scale industries or management of non-governmental organizations (NGOs).
Eligibility: Open to nationals of developing countries and transitional societies.
Level of Study: Professional development, postgraduate
Type: Scholarship
Value: US$3,000 per month
Length of Study: 3 or 6 weeks
Frequency: Annual
Study Establishment: MCTC
Country of Study: Israel
No. of awards offered: 28
Application Procedure: Applicants must complete an application form including a health form and copies of their diplomas. Forms can be obtained from the nearest Israeli diplomatic representative.
Closing Date: 3 months prior to the course start date
Funding: Government
Contributor: MASHAV-Centre for International Co-operation, Ministry of Foreign Affairs, Israel
No. of awards given last year: 400
No. of applicants last year: 1,400
Additional Information: Courses are given in English, French or Spanish and includes lectures, discussion groups, study tours and fieldwork.

THE GOLDSMITHS' COMPANY

Goldsmiths' Hall, Foster Lane, London, EC2V 6BN, England
Tel: (44) 20 7606 7010
Fax: (44) 20 7606 1511
Email: education@thegoldsmiths.co.uk
Website: www.thegoldsmiths.co.uk
Contact: The Assistant Clerk

The Goldsmiths' Company is one of the Twelve Great Companies of the City of London. It has been responsible for hallmarking since 1300 and today, operates the London Assay Office and supports the craft and industry of silversmithing and precious metal jewellery.

Goldsmiths' Company Science for Society Courses

Subjects: Genetics, particle physics, complementary medicine, astrophysics, sustainable development and materials science.
Purpose: To provide teachers of A levels with first-hand, practical experience of the theory that they teach.
Eligibility: Open to United Kingdom science teachers of secondary age children, but teachers from other disciplines are also accepted.
Level of Study: Professional development
Value: Free tuition, accommodation and travel after joining
Length of Study: 1 week in July
Frequency: Annual
Study Establishment: Various locations around the United Kingdom
Country of Study: United Kingdom
No. of awards offered: Approx. 120 vacancies each year
Application Procedure: Please write for details.
Closing Date: Vacancies are on a first come, first served basis
Funding: Private

GRADUATE INSTITUTE OF INTERNATIONAL STUDIES, GENEVA

132, rue de Lausanne, Case postale 36, Genève 21, CH-1211, Switzerland
Tel: (41) 22 908 5700
Fax: (41) 22 908 5710
Email: info@hei.unige.ch
Website: www.hei.unige.ch

The Graduate Institute of International Studies is a teaching and research establishment devoted to the scientific study of contemporary international relations. The international character of the Institute is emphasized by the use of both English and French as working languages. Its plural approach, which draws upon the method of history and political science, law and economics, reflects its aim to promote a broad approach and in-depth understanding of international relations.

Graduate Institute of International Studies (HEI-Geneva) Scholarships

Subjects: History and international politics, international economics, international law and political science.
Eligibility: Open to any applicant who can prove sound knowledge of the French language and sufficient prior study in political science, economics, law or modern history through the presentation of a college or university degree.
Level of Study: Postgraduate, doctorate
Type: Scholarship
Value: Swiss francs 1,500 per month on 10 months
Length of Study: 1 year, possibly renewable
Frequency: Annual
Study Establishment: Graduate Institute of International Studies, Geneva
Country of Study: Switzerland
No. of awards offered: 50
Application Procedure: Applicants must contact the Institute for details.
Closing Date: March 1st
Funding: Government
Contributor: The Canton of Geneva and the Swiss Confederation
No. of awards given last year: 24
No. of applicants last year: 49
Additional Information: Scholars are exempt from Institute fees, but not from the obligatory fees of the University of Geneva, which confers the degree.

GRAINS RESEARCH AND DEVELOPMENT CORPORATION (GRDC)

PO Box 5367, Kingston, ACT 2604, Australia
Tel: (61) 2 6272 5525
Fax: (61) 2 6271 6430
Email: grdc@grdc.com.au
Website: www.grdc.com.au
Contact: Ms Sonia Yanni, Program Support Coordinator

The Grains Research and Development Corporation's (GRDC) mission is to invest in innovation for the greatest benefit stakeholders. This will be achieved by being a global leader in linking science, technology and its adoption with industry and community needs. The Corporation's vision is for a profitable, internationally competitive and ecologically sustainable grains industry.

GRDC Grains Industry Research Scholarships

Subjects: Fields of high priority to the grains industry.
Purpose: To give support to students of excellence proceeding to postgraduate study in a field relevant to the future of the Australian grains industry.
Eligibility: Open to permanent residents of Australia who hold academic qualifications equivalent to a First Class (Honours) Degree or have otherwise demonstrated a high level of postgraduate achievement in research, teaching or extension activities.
Level of Study: Doctorate, postgraduate
Type: Scholarship
Value: A tax-free stipend of Australian $25,000 with no allowances for dependants. An additional grant of up to Australian $5,000 per year may be provided to the host organization to support the work
Length of Study: 3 years
Frequency: Annual
Study Establishment: Any university with a record of achievement for full-time research in the subject area leading to a DPhil
Country of Study: Australia
No. of awards offered: Several
Application Procedure: Applicants must complete an application form, available on request. Applications (six copies) should include the curriculum vitae of the applicant and the report of at least two referees. Evidence that the university and collaborating organizations will provide facilities and supervision of the project must also be supplied.
Closing Date: October for the following year
Funding: Government
Contributor: The government and Australian grain growers
No. of awards given last year: 13
No. of applicants last year: Approx. 30
Additional Information: The Corporation's 5-year research and development plan outlines the objectives and programmes to be covered. Copies of this may be obtained from the Secretariat.

GRDC In-Service Training

Subjects: Grains research and development.
Purpose: To support training on an industry-wide basis by funding younger scientists, technical staff or other persons engaged in work relevant to the Corporation's objectives who may not be eligible for other forms of support. Funds may be provided for travel, secondment or interchange between institutions.
Eligibility: Open to permanent residents of Australia only.
Level of Study: Unrestricted
Type: Grant
Value: Personal travel costs, including economy-class airfares and a contribution to living expenses for a maximum of 6 months
Length of Study: Up to 6 months
Frequency: Annual
Country of Study: Any country
Application Procedure: Applicants must submit six copies of a curriculum vitae, details of the proposed in-service training, the names, positions and locations of the proposed collaborators and training venue and approximate dates for the programme, which must fall within the appropriate funding year. Details of any travel directly related to the proposed programme, a proposed budget, including the

cost of travel and expected accommodation and living expenses, an indication of other forms of support available to the applicant, evidence that the proposed collaborators are agreeable to the training programme, supporting comments from two referees and a covering letter should also be included.
Closing Date: October for the following year
Contributor: The government and Australian grain growers
Additional Information: On completion of their award, trainees must provide the Board with a report.

GRDC Industry Development Awards

Subjects: Grains research and development.
Purpose: To fund study tours or for other purposes approved by the Corporation.
Eligibility: Open to permanent residents of Australia who are experienced growers, processors or other contributors to the work of the Corporation who are not engaged in research and development activity.
Level of Study: Unrestricted
Type: Award
Value: Up to a total of Australian $15,000 towards personal travel costs, including economy class airfares and contribution to living expenses
Frequency: Annual
Country of Study: Any country
No. of awards offered: Several
Application Procedure: Applicants must submit five copies of the nominee's curriculum vitae, details of the proposed programme, the names, positions and locations of the proposed collaborators, approximate dates for the programme and details of any internal travel directly related to the proposed programme. A proposed budget, including the cost of international and internal travel, and expected accommodation and living expenses, an indication of other forms of support available to the nominee, evidence that the proposed collaborators are agreeable to the programme, supporting comments from two referees and a covering letter should also be included.
Closing Date: End of March and September each year
Contributor: The government and Australian grain growers
Additional Information: On completion of the award, a report must be given to the Board. Preference may be given to applicants who have access to matching funds.

GRDC Senior Fellowships

Subjects: Grains research and development.
Purpose: To allow experienced research and development personnel to enhance their experience and their potential to contribute to the work of the Corporation by working at an institution in Australia or overseas.
Eligibility: Open to permanent residents of Australia only.
Level of Study: Unrestricted
Type: Fellowship
Value: Up to a total of Australian $50,000 towards personal travel costs, including economy class airfares and a contribution to living expenses
Length of Study: Up to 1 year
Frequency: Annual
Country of Study: Any country
No. of awards offered: Up to 2 per year
Application Procedure: Applicants must submit six copies of the following documentation: the nominee's curriculum vitae, including a list of publications, details of the nominee's research project and its relationship to the host institution's programme of research (this should include evidence that the host institution already has an interest and competence in the area of research proposed by the applicant and that it is relevant to the Corporation's objectives) and the names, positions and major publications of the proposed collaborators, together with a letter of invitation from the Head of the host institution. They should also include approximate dates for the programme, which must fall within the appropriate funding year, details of any internal travel directly related to the proposed programme, a proposed budget, including the cost of international and internal travel, and expected accommodation and living expenses, an indication of other forms of support available to the applicant, evidence that the host institution has available the necessary facilities and is willing to accept the Fellow, supporting comments from two referees, and a covering letter. On completion of their award Fellows must furnish the Board with a report. Preference may be given to applicants who have access to matching funds.
Closing Date: October for the following year
Funding: Government
Contributor: The government and Australian grain growers

GRDC Visiting Fellowships

Subjects: Grains research and development.
Purpose: To give support and stimulus to research programmes supported by the Corporation by funding visits by overseas personnel who could enhance those programmes.
Eligibility: Open to candidates of any nationality.
Level of Study: Postgraduate
Type: Fellowship
Value: The Corporation will consider paying the nominee's personal travel costs, contributing to living expenses and providing some support to the host institution or company. The maximum total level of support will normally be Australian $17,500
Length of Study: Up to 1 year
Frequency: Annual
Country of Study: Australia
No. of awards offered: Several
Application Procedure: Applicants must submit six copies of the following documentation: the nominee's curriculum vitae, details of the nominee's research project or itinerary for study and its relationship to the host institution's or company's programme of research, development or other industry contribution, the name, position and industry contributions of the person proposing the nominee, together with a letter of support from the Head of the host institution or company, where appropriate, the names, positions and institutions of collaborators of the proposed project or study tour. They should also include approximate dates for the programme, which must fall within the appropriate funding year, details of any travel directly related to the proposed programme, a proposed budget, including the cost of international and internal travel, and expected accommodation and living expenses, an indication of other forms of support available to the nominee, including those from the home institution or company, evidence that the host institution or company has accepted the nomination, supporting comments from two referees and a covering letter.
Closing Date: October for the following year
Contributor: The government and Australian grain growers
No. of awards given last year: 4
No. of applicants last year: 6
Additional Information: On completion of the award, a report must be given to the Board. Preference may be given to nominees who have access to matching funds.

GREEK MINISTRY OF NATIONAL EDUCATION AND RELIGIOUS AFFAIRS

General Secretary's Office Mitropoles 15, Athens, 10185, Greece
Website: www.ypeplh.gr

Greek Language Summer Course Scholarships in Indian University

Subjects: Greek language.
Purpose: To encourage candidates who wish to learn Greek.
Eligibility: Open to candidates from Azerbaijan Egypt, Argentina, Armenia, Bosma and Herzegovina, Bulgaria, China, Crotia, Georgia, Indonesia, Iran, Israel, Jordan, Khazakstan, Korea, Kyrgyzstan, Lebanon, Mexico, Moldavia, Uzbekistan, Ukraine, Rumania, Russia, Serbia and Montenegro, Srilanka, Sudan, Syria, Thailand, Turkey and Chile.
Level of Study: Postgraduate
Type: Scholarship
Value: Tuition fees, accommodation and food expenses
Length of Study: 1 month
Frequency: Annual
No. of awards offered: Varies

Application Procedure: See the website.
Closing Date: June 15th

Greek Scholarship

Subjects: All subjects.
Purpose: To enable an Irish postgraduate student to study in Greece.
Eligibility: Open to Irish postgraduate students.
Level of Study: Postgraduate
Type: Scholarship
Value: Varies
Frequency: Annual
Country of Study: Greece
No. of awards offered: 1
Application Procedure: See the website.
Closing Date: February 24th
Contributor: The Ministry of Education in Greece

Scholarships Granted by the GR Government to Foreign Citizens

Subjects: All subjects.
Purpose: To support candidates who wish to study or conduct research project in Greek Universities.
Eligibility: Open to candidates who are accepted in a postgraduates programme in a recognized Greek university.
Level of Study: Postgraduate
Type: Scholarship
Value: €550
Frequency: Annual
Study Establishment: Any recognized Greek university
Application Procedure: See website.
Closing Date: March 31st
Funding: Government

GRIFFITH UNIVERSITY

Highridge Plaza, 25 Redmond Drive, Unit Suite 4, Hamilton, Ontario, Canada
Tel: (1) 905 318 8200
Email: m.mitchell@griffith.edu.au
Website: www.gu.edu.au
Contact: Griffith University Scholarships

In the pursuit of excellence in teaching, research and community service, Griffith University is committed to innovation, bringing disciplines together, internationalization, equity and social justice and lifelong learning, for the enrichment of Queensland, Australia and the international community.

Griffith University Postgraduate Research Scholarships

Subjects: All subjects.
Purpose: To provide financial support for candidates undertaking full-time research leading to the award of the degree of MPhil or PhD.
Eligibility: Open to any person, irrespective of nationality, holding or expecting to hold a First Class (Honours) Degree or equivalent from a recognized institution. Applicants must demonstrate proficiency in the English language by scoring an overall score of 6.5 in the International English Language Testing System test, or have a score of at least 580 on the Teaching of English as a Foreign Language test or hold a test score of 237 (new Teaching of English as a Foreign Language) with an essay rating of 5.0.
Level of Study: Postgraduate
Type: Scholarship
Value: Australian $18,484 per year, tax exempt
Length of Study: Up to 2 years for a research Master's and up to 3 years for PhD candidates, with a possible extension of up to 6 months for the PhD, subject to satisfactory progress
Frequency: Annual
Study Establishment: Griffith University
Country of Study: Australia
No. of awards offered: Varies
Application Procedure: Applicants must complete an application form.
Closing Date: October 31st
Additional Information: The scholarship does not cover the cost of tuition fees, which ranges from Australian $15,000 to 19,000 per year.

Jackson Memorial Fellowship

Subjects: The application of the social, political, economic, environmental or technological sciences to the analysis and resolution of substantial policy issues at the national or regional levels.
Purpose: To consolidate links with a variety of institutions in South East Asia and to provide funding to facilitate visits to Griffith University by faculty staff of the Association of South East Asian Institutions of Higher Learning (ASAIHL) member institutions.
Eligibility: Open to senior members of faculty staff of the ASAIHL member institutions.
Level of Study: Professional development
Type: Fellowship
Frequency: Annual
Study Establishment: Griffith University
Country of Study: Australia
Application Procedure: Applicants must apply through the heads of their employing institutions.
Closing Date: September 15th
Funding: Private
No. of awards given last year: 1
No. of applicants last year: Varies

Sir Allan Sewell Visiting Fellowship

Subjects: All subjects offered by Griffith University.
Purpose: To commemorate the distinguished service of Sir Allan Sewell to Griffith University by offering awards to enable visits by distinguished scholars engaged in academic work who can contribute to research and teaching in one or more areas of interest at a faculty or college of the university.
Eligibility: Open to researchers of any nationality.
Level of Study: Professional development
Type: Fellowship
Frequency: Annual
Study Establishment: Griffith University
Country of Study: Australia
Application Procedure: Applicants must be invited to apply by faculties or colleges of the University.
Closing Date: September 15th
Funding: Private
No. of awards given last year: Varies
No. of applicants last year: Varies

GROUPE DE RECHERCHE SUR LE SYSTÈME NERVEUX CENTRAL

Faculty of Medicine, University of Montréal, PO Box 6128, Station Centre-Ville, Montréal, QC, H3C 3J7, Canada
Tel: (1) 514 343 6366
Fax: (1) 514 343 6113
Email: grsnc@umontreal.ca
Website: www.grsnc.umontreal.ca
Contact: Dr Trevor Drew, Director

Founded in 1991, the Groupe de Recherche sur le Système Nerveux Central (GRSNC) is a multidisciplinary research group that includes researchers from several departments within the Faculties of Medicine and Dentistry at the University of Montréal. It receives funding from both the University and from the provincial government to support its research infrastructure. It organizes an annual international symposium and has weekly research seminars by invited speakers.

Herbert H Jasper Fellowship

Subjects: Neurology and neurosciences.
Purpose: To enable the use of the exceptional research facilities of the Groupe de Recherche sur le Système Nerveux Central of the University of Montréal.
Eligibility: Open to Canadian citizens or permanent residents.
Level of Study: Postdoctorate
Type: Fellowship
Value: Canadian $40,000 per year

Length of Study: 2 years
Frequency: Annual
Study Establishment: Group de Recherche sur le Système Nerveux Central, University of Montréal
Country of Study: Canada
No. of awards offered: 1
Application Procedure: Applicants must complete an application form, which can be obtained from the website or by writing to the Fellowship Committee.
Closing Date: January 31st
Funding: Government
No. of awards given last year: 1
No. of applicants last year: 20
Additional Information: The fellowship provides the opportunity for the recipient to work closely with the investigator of his or her choice within a large active group of neuroscientists who are members of the group.

THE GRUNDY EDUCATIONAL TRUST

Jeffard Cottage, 3 Parkside Lane, Hants S024 0BB, Ropley, England
Tel: (44) 1962 773118
Fax: (44) 1590 677846
Email: chrisgrundy@adelphia.net
Website: www.grundyeducationaltrust.org.uk
Contact: Mrs A Hardy, Secretary to the Trustees

The Grundy Educational Trust was established in 1991 to advance education by providing or assisting in the provision of graduate and post-graduate awards to students for research and higher learning at institutions in the United Kingdom.

Grundy Educational Trust

Subjects: Technologically or scientifically based disciplines in industry and commerce.
Purpose: To assist in covering maintenance costs while obtaining postgraduate or second degrees.
Eligibility: Open to United Kingdom citizens under 30 years of age.
Level of Study: Postgraduate
Type: Award
Value: Up to UK £3,000
Length of Study: 1–5 years
Frequency: Annual
Study Establishment: Birmingham, Loughborough, Imperial College, Southampton, Surrey, UMIST or Nottingham
Country of Study: United Kingdom
No. of awards offered: Up to 16
Application Procedure: Applicants must apply through the seven selected universities only.
Closing Date: May 31st
Funding: Private
No. of awards given last year: 11
No. of applicants last year: 25

For further information contact:

Grundy Educational Trust, Shirley Holms, Lymington, Hampshire, S041 8NG, England
Contact: PG Grundy, The Secretary

GUIDE DOGS FOR THE BLIND ASSOCIATION

Hillfields Burghfield Common, Reading, Berkshire, RG7 3YG, England
Tel: (44) 11 8983 5555
Fax: (44) 11 8983 5433
Email: guidedogs@guidedogs.org.uk
Website: www.guidedogs.org.uk
Contact: Ms Diana Patten, Ophthalmic Research Officer

Founded in 1931, the Guide Dogs for the Blind Association's mission is to provide guide dogs, mobility and other rehabilitation services that meet the needs of blind and partially sighted people. The Association also supports other activities that enhance the quality of life of visually impaired people, including funding research into eye conditions.

Guide Dogs Ophthalmic Research Grant

Subjects: The causes, treatment, prevention and cure of sight-threatening diseases and conditions, especially those that involve large numbers of people, require improved therapeutic regimens or that are likely to lead to a clinical application.
Purpose: To promote high-quality research into the causes, treatment, prevention and cure of sight-threatening diseases and conditions.
Eligibility: Applicants and any research workers must be resident in the United Kingdom. The principal applicant must be in a tenured post for the duration of the requested grant.
Level of Study: Research
Value: Up to UK £60,000 per year
Length of Study: Maximum of 3 years
Frequency: Annual
Study Establishment: Specialist ophthalmic departments or organizations
Country of Study: United Kingdom
No. of awards offered: 6–10, depending on funds
Application Procedure: Applicants must submit an application in accordance with Guide Dogs Ophthalmic Research Grant application guidelines.
Closing Date: The last Friday in September
Funding: Private
Contributor: Donations to the Guide Dogs for the Blind Association
No. of awards given last year: 7
Additional Information: The Guide Dogs for the Blind Association is committed to avoiding the use of experimental animals or tissues from laboratory animals in funded research and will not accept any application that involves these procedures.

GUILLAIN-BARRÉ SYNDROME SUPPORT GROUP

Lincolnshire County Council Offices, Eastgate, Sleaford, Lincolnshire, NG34 8NR, England
Tel: (44) 15 2930 0328
Fax: (44) 15 2930 0328
Email: admin@gbs.org
Website: www.gbs.org.uk
Contact: Ms Anne Bennegt, Secretary

The Guillain-Barré Syndrome Support Group provides emotional support, personal visits and comprehensive literature to patients and their relatives and friends. The Group also educates the public and the medical community about the Support Group and maintains their awareness of the illness. The Group fosters research into the causes, treatment and other aspects of the illness and encourages fund raising and support for its activities.

Guillain-Barré Syndrome Support Group Research Fellowship

Subjects: Any aspect of Guillain-Barré syndrome (GBS) or related diseases including chronic inflammatory demyelinating polyradiculoneuropathy (CIDP).
Purpose: To advance research into the prevention and cure of GBS and CIDP.
Level of Study: Doctorate, research, professional development, postgraduate
Type: Fellowship
Value: Up to UK £65,000
Length of Study: Up to 3 years
Frequency: Dependent on funds available
Study Establishment: Any suitable hospital, university laboratory or department
No. of awards offered: 1
Application Procedure: Applicants must write for an application form.
Closing Date: Please contact the organization
Contributor: Members' donations, fund raising and trust funds

No. of awards given last year: 1
Additional Information: Further information is available on request.

THE GYPSY LORE SOCIETY

5607 Greenleaf Road, Cheverly, MD, 20785, United States of America
Tel: (1) 301 341 1261
Fax: (1) 301 341 1261
Email: headquarters@gypsyloresociety.org
Website: www.gypsyloresociety.org
Contact: Ms Sheila Salo, Treasurer

The Gypsy Lore Society, an international association of persons interested in Gypsy Studies, was formed in the United Kingdom in 1888. The Gypsy Lore Society, North American Chapter, was founded in 1977 in the United States of America and since 1989, has continued as the Gypsy Lore Society. The Society's goals include the promotion of the study of the Gypsy peoples and analogous itinerant or nomadic groups, dissemination of information aimed at increasing understanding of Gypsy culture in its diverse forms and establishment of closer contacts among Gypsy scholars.

Gypsy Lore Society Young Scholar's Prize in Romani Studies

Subjects: Any topic in Romani (Gypsy) studies.
Purpose: To recognize outstanding work by young scholars in Romani (Gypsy) studies.
Eligibility: An unpublished paper not under consideration for publication is eligible for this award as well as self-contained scholarly articles of publishable quality that treat a relevant topic in an interesting and insightful way.
Level of Study: Postdoctorate, graduate, doctorate, graduate students beyond the 1st year of study and phd holders no more than 3 years beyond the degree
Type: Cash prize
Value: US$500
Frequency: Annual, if worthy work is submitted. Committee reserves the right not to award prize in a given year
Study Establishment: Any
Country of Study: Any country
No. of awards offered: 1
Application Procedure: Applicants must submit four copies of their paper along with an abstract of fewer than 250 words, and a cover sheet with the title of the paper, the author's name, affiliation, mailing address, email address, telephone and fax numbers, date of entrance into an appropriate graduate programme or awarding of the PhD and United States of America Social Security number, if the author has one.
Closing Date: October 30th
Funding: Corporation
Contributor: Gypsy Lore Society
No. of applicants last year: 3

For further information contact:

Gypsy Lore Society Prize Competition, Institute of Musicology, Hungarian Academy of Sciences, H-1250 Budapest, Pf 28, Hungary
Email: kovalcsik@zti.hu
Contact: Katalin Kovalcsik

HAGLEY MUSEUM AND LIBRARY

PO Box 3630, Wilmington, Delaware, DE 19807-0630, United States of America
Tel: (1) 302 658 2400 ext. 243
Fax: (1) 302 655 3188
Email: clockman@hagley.org
Website: www.hagley.org
Contact: Ms Carol Ressler Lockman, Center Co-ordinator

Located along the Brandywine River on the site of the first du Pont black powder works, the Hagley Museum and Library provide a unique glimpse into American life at home and at work in the 19th century. Set among more than 230 acres of trees and flowering shrubs, Hagley offers a diversity of restorations, exhibits and live demonstrations for visitors of all ages.

Hagley Museum and Library Grants-in-Aid of Research

Subjects: American economic and technological history and 18th century French history.
Purpose: To support travel to the Hagley Library for scholarly research in the collections.
Eligibility: Open to degree candidates and advanced scholars of any nationality. Research must be relevant to Hagley's collections.
Level of Study: Postdoctorate, graduate, predoctorate, doctorate
Value: Up to US$1,400 per month
Length of Study: 2–8 weeks
Study Establishment: The Library
Country of Study: United States of America
No. of awards offered: 25
Application Procedure: Applicants must submit a completed application form with a five-page proposal.
Closing Date: March 30th, June 29th or October 30th
Funding: Private
Contributor: Foundation funds
No. of awards given last year: 19
No. of applicants last year: 40
Additional Information: Candidates may apply for research in the imprint, manuscript, pictorial and artefact collections of the Hagley Museum and Library. In addition the resources of the 125 libraries in the greater Philadelphia area will be at the disposal of the visiting scholar. The Research Fellowship is to be used only in the Hagley Library.

Hagley/Winterthur Arts and Industries Fellowship

Subjects: Business and economics, design, architecture, crafts, fine arts, technology and industrial history focusing on historical and cultural relationships between economic life and the arts.
Purpose: To support scholarly research at the Hagley and Winterthur Libraries.
Eligibility: Open to advanced scholars, graduate students and independent researchers.
Level of Study: Postdoctorate, doctorate, professional development
Type: Fellowship
Value: US$1,400 per month
Length of Study: Up to 3 months
Frequency: Annual
Country of Study: United States of America
No. of awards offered: 6
Application Procedure: Applicants must submit a completed application form with a five-page proposal and two recommendations.
Closing Date: December 1st
Funding: Private
Contributor: Foundation funds
No. of awards given last year: 2
No. of applicants last year: 14
Additional Information: The scholar must travel to Delaware to use the collections at both the Hagley and Winterthur libraries.

Henry Belin du Pont Dissertation Fellowship in Business, Technology and Society

Subjects: Business and technology.
Purpose: To aid students whose research on important historical questions would benefit from the use of Hagley's research collections.
Eligibility: Open to graduate students or PhD candidates.
Level of Study: Graduate, predoctorate
Type: Fellowship
Value: US$6,000, free housing, use of computer, email and internet access and an office
Length of Study: 4 months
Frequency: Annual
Study Establishment: The Center for the History of Business, Technology and Society at Hagley
Country of Study: United States of America
Application Procedure: Applicants must submit an application dossier including a dissertation prospectus, a statement concerning the relevance of Hagley's research collections to the project and at least

two letters of recommendation. Writing samples are also welcome. Potential applicants are strongly encouraged to consult with Hagley staff prior to submitting their dossier.
Closing Date: November 15th
Funding: Private
Additional Information: Recipients are expected to have no other obligations during the term of the fellowship, to maintain continuous residence at Hagley for its duration and to participate in events organized by Hagley's Center for the History of Business, Technology and Society. Towards the end of the residency the recipient will make a presentation at Hagley based on research conducted during the Fellowship. Hagley should also receive a copy of the dissertation, as well as any publications aided by the Fellowship.

Henry Belin du Pont Fellowship
Subjects: Areas of study relevant to the Library's archival and artefact collections.
Purpose: To support access to and use of Hagley's research collections and to enable individual out-of-state scholars to pursue their own research and to participate in the interchange of ideas among the Center's scholars.
Eligibility: Open to applicants who have already completed their formal professional training. Consequently, degree candidates and persons seeking support for degree work are not eligible to apply. Applicants must not be residents of Delaware and preference will be given to those whose travel costs to Hagley will be higher. Research must be relevant to Hagley's collections.
Level of Study: Doctorate, postdoctorate
Type: Fellowship
Value: US$1,500 stipend per month
Length of Study: 2–6 months
Frequency: Annual
Study Establishment: The Library
Country of Study: United States of America
No. of awards offered: Varies
Application Procedure: Applicants must submit a completed application form with a five-page proposal.
Closing Date: March 31st, June 30th or October 30th
Funding: Private
Contributor: Foundation funds
No. of awards given last year: 3
No. of applicants last year: 10
Additional Information: Fellows must devote all their time to study and may not accept teaching assignments or undertake any other major activities during the tenure of their fellowships. At the end of their tenure, Fellows must submit a final report on their activities and accomplishments. As a centre for advanced study in the humanities, Hagley is a focal point of a community of scholars. Fellows are expected to participate in seminars, which meet periodically, as well as attend colloquia, lectures, concerts, exhibits and other public programmes offered during their tenure. Research fellowships are to be used in the Hagley Library only, not as scholarships for college.

THE HAGUE ACADEMY OF INTERNATIONAL LAW

Peace Palace, Carnegieplein 2, The Hague, NL-2517 KJ, Netherlands
Tel: (31) 70 302 4154
Fax: (31) 70 302 4153
Email: hagueacademy@registration
Website: www.hagueacademy.nl
Contact: The Secretariat

The Hague Academy of International Law's purpose is to gather together young international lawyers of a high standard from all parts of the world who will undertake original research work within the framework of the subject matter of the concerned year. The results of this research work may, if appropriate, be published collectively.

Hague Academy of International Law/Doctoral Scholarships
Subjects: International law.
Purpose: To aid individuals with the completion of their theses through the assistance of the Academy.
Eligibility: Open to doctoral candidates up to the age of 40 years from developing countries who reside in their home country and do not have access to scientific sources.
Level of Study: Doctorate
Type: Scholarship
Value: Please contact the Academy for details
Length of Study: 2 months
Frequency: Annual
Country of Study: The Netherlands
No. of awards offered: 4
Application Procedure: Applicants must submit their applications with a letter of recommendation from the professor under whose direction the thesis is being written. The thesis may be concerned with either private or public international law and the title should be mentioned.
Closing Date: March 1st
Funding: Private
Contributor: The Hague Academy of International Law
No. of awards given last year: 4
No. of applicants last year: 30

Hague Academy of International Law/Scholarships for Sessions of Courses
Subjects: International private or public law.
Purpose: To assist students with living expenses, including the registration fee, during summer courses.
Eligibility: Open to candidates up to the age of 40 years, who have not yet received an Academy scholarship. Applicants must have sufficient knowledge of English or French.
Level of Study: Doctorate
Type: Scholarship
Value: Applicants should contact the Academy for details. Scholars are exempt from registration fees and examination fees. Travelling expenses will not be refunded
Length of Study: 3 weeks
Frequency: Annual
Study Establishment: The Hague Academy of International Law
Country of Study: The Netherlands
No. of awards offered: Varies
Application Procedure: Applicants must apply personally by submitting a curriculum vitae, one photograph and a statement of evidence that the candidate considers to be of value in support of their application. Every application must be typed and accompanied by a recommendation from a professor of international law. As documents forwarded by applicants are not returned, university certificates or other documents must be submitted in the form of copies, duly verified by a competent authority. The teaching period for which the candidate wants to be registered should be stated clearly.
Closing Date: March 1st
Funding: Private
Contributor: Foundations, institutions and personalities
No. of awards given last year: 119
No. of applicants last year: 600

THE HAMBIDGE

PO Box 339, Rabun Gap, GA, 30568, United States of America
Tel: (1) 706 746 5718
Fax: (1) 706 746 9933
Email: center@hambidge.org
Website: www.hambidge.org
Contact: The Residency Director

The Hambidge Center's primary function is an artist residency programme with the following aims: to provide artists with time and space to pursue their work, to enhance their communities' art environment, provide public accessibility and to protect and sustain the natural environment, land and endangered species. The Center is set in 600 acres of mountain and valley terrain with waterfalls and nature trails.

Hambidge Residency Program Scholarships
Subjects: Any field or discipline of creative work.
Purpose: To provide applicants with an environment for creative work in the arts and sciences.

Eligibility: Open to qualified applicants in all disciplines who can demonstrate seriousness, dedication and professionalism. International residents are welcome. The Fulton County Arts Council Fellowship is open to residents of Fulton County, Georgia only.
Level of Study: Unrestricted
Type: Fellowship
Length of Study: 2 weeks–2 months
Frequency: Dependent on space available
Study Establishment: Hambidge
Country of Study: United States of America
Application Procedure: Applicants must submit an application form and a stamped addressed envelope to the centre marked for the attention of the Residency Program. The application form can be downloaded from the website. Applicants for the Fulton County Arts Council Fellowship should contact Fulton County Arts Council.
Closing Date: January 15th, April 15th, September 15th
Funding: Private, government
Additional Information: The scholarships that are offered by the Center are the Nellie Mae Rowe Fellowship, the Fulton County Arts Council Fellowship and teaching fellowships at public or independent schools.

For further information contact:

The Fulton County Arts Council, 121 Pryor Street South West, Atlanta, GA, 30303, United States of America
Tel: (1) 404 730 5780

Nellie Mae Rowe Fellowship

Subjects: Any field or discipline of creative work.
Purpose: The scholarship was established to serve the memory of Nellie Mae Rowe, to recognize the creativity of those artists who come to Hambidge in her name and to encourage the artistic growth of African American visual artists.
Level of Study: Unrestricted
Type: Fellowship
Length of Study: 2 weeks
Study Establishment: Hambidge
Country of Study: United States of America
No. of awards offered: 1
Contributor: Judith Alexander
No. of awards given last year: 1

Rabun Gap-Nacoochee School Teaching Fellowship

Subjects: Any field or discipline of creative work.
Purpose: To develop the caliber of creative thinkers.
Level of Study: Unrestricted
Type: Fellowship
Value: All fees
Study Establishment: Hambridge
Country of Study: United States of America
No. of awards offered: 1
No. of awards given last year: 1

HAMDARD UNIVERSITY

Mohammed Bin Qasin Avenue, Karachi, 74600, Pakistan
Tel: (92) 9221 6440035/42
Fax: (92) 9221 6440045
Email: admissions.karachi@hamdard.edu.pk
Contact: Madinat al Hikmah

Responding to its tradition as an institution with a strong social welfare commitment, the university offers a broad based and liberal financial assistance programme for the meritorious as well as deserving students.

Hamdard Fellowship in Business Administration

Subjects: Marketing, finance and management.
Purpose: To bridge the gap between the requirements of business organizations and the academic curricula in educational institutions.
Eligibility: Open to academically qualified students with a minimum of two years of full time work experience.
Level of Study: Professional development, postgraduate
Type: Fellowship
Value: 100% concession of tuition fee
Length of Study: 1–3 years
Frequency: Annual
Study Establishment: Hamdard University
Country of Study: Pakistan
Application Procedure: Obtain an Application package and submit along with copies of all certificates and degrees, transcripts of academic work and two letters of recommendation.

Hamdard Fellowship in Eastern Medicine

Subjects: Medicine.
Purpose: To give more impetus to scientific, clinical, and technological research and development.
Eligibility: Open to students possessing a five year Bachelor's degree in Eastern Medicine (BEMS) or equivalent.
Level of Study: Postdoctorate, doctorate
Type: Fellowship
Value: 100% concession of tuition fee
Length of Study: 1–3 years
Frequency: Annual
Study Establishment: Hamdard University
Country of Study: Pakistan
No. of awards offered: 1
Application Procedure: Contact admissions office.

Hamdard Fellowship in Engineering and Information Technology

Subjects: Engineering.
Purpose: To develop scholars who can contribute to existing knowledge in modern society.
Eligibility: Open to candidates with specialization in the following areas; civil engineering, electronic engineering, environmental science, material engineering and telecommunication engineering; subject to an entrance examination.
Level of Study: Postdoctorate, doctorate
Type: Fellowship
Value: 100% concession of tuition fee
Length of Study: 1–3 years
Frequency: Annual
Study Establishment: Hamdard University
Country of Study: Pakistan
No. of awards offered: 1
Application Procedure: Contact admissions department.
Funding: Corporation
Contributor: FEST

HAND WEAVERS, SPINNERS & DYERS OF ALBERTA (HWSDA)

228 Park Ridge Close, Camrose, AB T4V 4 P1, United States of America
Tel: (1) 672 2551
Email: studioword@studioword.com
Website: www.hwsda.org

The HWSDA is an exciting network of fibre artisans whose objectives are to foster and promote the development of fine craft in the province of Alberta for both amateur and professional crafts people.

HWSDA Scholarship Program

Subjects: Textile design.
Purpose: To gain more knowledge in the field of weaving, spinning, dying, felting, basketry.
Eligibility: Open to applicants who are involved in the art of textile design and who need financial help.
Level of Study: Professional development
Type: Scholarship
Value: Up to US$600 in total
Frequency: Annual
Application Procedure: A complete application form should be submitted.

Funding: Foundation
Contributor: The memorial scholarship fund

HARNESS TRACKS OF AMERICA

4640 East Sunrise Drive, Suite 200, Tucson, AZ 85718, United States of America
Tel: (1) 529 2525
Fax: (1) 529 3235
Email: info@harnesstracks.com
Website: www.harnesstracks.com

Harness Tracks of America, Inc. is an association of the finest harness racing establishments in the world, dedicated to the advancement and progress of the sport.

Harness Track of America Scholarship

Subjects: Sports.
Purpose: To provide financial assistance to young people actively engaged in the harness racing industry.
Eligibility: Open to applicants with active harness racing involvement.
Level of Study: Professional development
Type: Scholarship
Value: US$5,000
Length of Study: 1 year
Frequency: Annual
No. of awards offered: 4% of the applications
Application Procedure: A completed application form and official academic transcripts must be submitted.
Closing Date: June 15th

HARRY FRANK GUGGENHEIM FOUNDATION (HFG)

527 Madison Avenue, New York, NY, 10022-4301, United States of America
Tel: (1) 212 644 4907
Fax: (1) 212 644 5110
Email: info@hfg.org
Website: www.hfg.org
Contact: Administrative Assistant

The Harry Frank Guggenheim Foundation (HFG) sponsors scholarly research on problems of violence, aggression and dominance. The Foundation provides both research grants to established scholars and dissertation fellowships to graduate students during the dissertation writing year. The *HFG Review of Research* is published twice a year.

HFG Dissertation Fellowship

Subjects: Any discipline that includes the study of dominance, aggression and violence.
Purpose: To support a PhD candidate at the writing stage of a dissertation. Work must be relevant to HFG programme interests in the study of violence and aggression.
Eligibility: Open to PhD candidates of any nationality.
Level of Study: Doctorate
Type: Fellowship
Value: US$15,000
Length of Study: 1 year
Frequency: Annual
Study Establishment: Any university
Country of Study: Any country
No. of awards offered: 10
Application Procedure: Applicants must submit an application form, research proposal and letter from their adviser. Candidates should contact the Foundation for application materials.
Closing Date: February 1st
Funding: Foundation
No. of awards given last year: 10
No. of applicants last year: 150
Additional Information: It is mandatory that a final report be given to the Foundation. Recipients of dissertation fellowships must submit a copy of the dissertation, approved and accepted by the home university or college, within 6 months of the end of the award year. The award is only available in circumstances where all necessary research has been done and the dissertation will be complete within 1 year.

HFG Research Program

Subjects: The social, behavioural and biological sciences. Research that is related to the Foundation's programme will be considered regardless of the disciplines involved.
Purpose: To promote understanding of the human social condition through the study of the causes and consequences of dominance, aggression and violence.
Eligibility: Open to individuals or institutions in any country.
Level of Study: Postdoctorate, postgraduate
Value: Up to US$35,000 per year. Applicants should contact the organization for more details
Length of Study: 1 year, but 2 or 3 year projects may also be considered
Frequency: Annual
Country of Study: Any country
No. of awards offered: 15–35 per year
Application Procedure: Applicants must submit an application form and research proposal along with a curriculum vitae and budget request. Application materials are available by contacting the Foundation.
Closing Date: August 1st
Funding: Foundation
No. of awards given last year: 15
No. of applicants last year: 200
Additional Information: The Foundation operates a programme of specific and innovative study and research. Proposals should be for a specific project and should describe well-defined aims and methods, not general institutional support.

THE HARRY S TRUMAN LIBRARY INSTITUTE

500 West US Highway 24, Independence, MO 64050-1798, United States of America
Tel: (1) 816 268 8200
Fax: (1) 816 268 8295
Email: lisa.sullivan@nara.gov
Website: www.trumanlibrary.org
Contact: Lisa Sullivan, Grants Administrator

The Harry S Truman Library Institute is a non-profit partner of the Harry S Truman Library. The institute's purpose is to foster the Truman Library as a center for research and as a provider of educational and public programmes.

Harry S Truman Library Institute Dissertation Year Fellowships

Subjects: The public career of Harry S Truman and the history of the Truman administration.
Purpose: To encourage historical scholarship in the Truman era.
Eligibility: Open to graduates who have completed their dissertation research and are ready to begin writing. Dissertations must be on some aspect of the life and career of Harry S Truman or of the public and policy issues that were prominent during the Truman years.
Level of Study: Graduate, postgraduate
Type: Fellowship
Value: US$16,000, payable in two instalments
Length of Study: 1 year
Frequency: Annual
Country of Study: United States of America
No. of awards offered: 1–2
Application Procedure: Application forms are available from the website.
Closing Date: February 1st for notification in April
Funding: Private
Additional Information: Recipients will not be required to come to the Truman Library but will be expected to furnish the Library with a copy of their dissertation.

THE HASTINGS CENTER

21 Malcolm Gordon Road, Garrison, NY, 10524,
United States of America
Tel: (1) 845 424 4040
Fax: (1) 845 424 4545
Email: visitors@thehastingscenter.org
Website: www.thehastingscenter.org
Contact: Ms Lori P Knowles, Executive Vice President

The Hastings Center is an independent, non-profit research and educational institute that studies ethical, social and legal issues in medicine, the life sciences, health policy and environment policy.

Hastings Center International Visiting Scholars Program

Subjects: Ethical, legal and policy issues in medicine, the life sciences and the professions.
Purpose: To enable international visiting scholars to spend time at the Center for advanced study and research.
Eligibility: Open to international scholars.
Level of Study: Doctorate, graduate, predoctorate, professional development, unrestricted, postdoctorate, research, postgraduate
Type: Grant
Value: Assistance with accommodation costs is available based on need
Length of Study: Usually 4–6 weeks
Frequency: Annual
Study Establishment: The Hastings Center
Country of Study: United States of America
No. of awards offered: Varies
Application Procedure: Applicants must visit the website for applications. A detailed description of a research topic and work plan is also required as well as a copy of a recent writing sample, a curriculum vitae and the names and addresses of two referees.
Closing Date: Applications are accepted at any time, but should be submitted at least 3 months prior to the proposed stay
Funding: Private
No. of awards given last year: 13
No. of applicants last year: 15
Additional Information: Participation in the ongoing activities of the Center such as conferences, seminars and workshops is encouraged.

HATTORI FOUNDATION

72E Leopold Road, London, SW19 7JQ, England
Tel: (44) 20 8944 5319
Fax: (44) 20 8946 6970
Email: admin@hattorifoundation.org.uk
Website: www.hattorifoundation.org.uk
Contact: Ms Sarah C Hallan, Administrator

The chief aim of the Hattori Foundation is to encourage and assist exceptionally talented young instrumental soloists or chamber ensembles who are British nationals or resident in the United Kingdom, and whose talent and achievement give promise of an international career.

Hattori Foundation Awards

Subjects: Instrumental, solo performance and ensembles.
Purpose: To assist young instrumentalists of exceptional talent in establishing a solo or chamber music career at international level.
Eligibility: Open to British or foreign nationals aged 21–27 years studying full-time in the United Kingdom. Foreign applicants must have won a major prize in an international competition or won a national competition. Candidates should be of postgraduate performance level.
Level of Study: Postgraduate, professional development
Type: Award
Value: No pre-determined amounts. The grant is based on the requirements of the approved project
Length of Study: Varies
Frequency: Annual
Country of Study: British Nationals can study in any country. Foreign nationals must be resident in the United Kingdom only
No. of awards offered: Up to 20
Application Procedure: Applicants must submit a completed application form with reference forms and a 30 minute performance (recital) on cassette tape or compact disc.
Closing Date: April 30th
Funding: Private
Contributor: Hattori family
No. of awards given last year: 12
No. of applicants last year: 59
Additional Information: Grants may be made for study, concert experience and international competitions, but course fees and the purchase of instruments are not funded. Projects must be submitted for approval and discussion with the Director of Music and the trustees. Auditions take place in June and are in two stages.

HAYSTACK MOUNTAIN SCHOOL OF CRAFTS

PO Box 518, Deer Isle, ME, 04627,
United States of America
Tel: (1) 207 348 2306
Fax: (1) 207 348 2307
Email: haystack@haystack-mtn.org
Website: www.haystack-mtn.org
Contact: Ms Lesley Lichko, Development Director

The Haystack Mountain School of Crafts studio programme in the arts offers 1, 2 and 3 week workshops in a variety of craft and visual media including blacksmithing, clay, wood, glass, metals, fibres and graphics.

Haystack Scholarship

Subjects: Fine crafts.
Purpose: To allow craftspeople of all skill levels to study at Haystack sessions for 1, 2 or 3 week periods. Technical assistant and work study positions as well as minority scholarships and fellowships are awarded.
Eligibility: Open to nationals of any country, who are 18 years or older. Technical Assistant Scholarship: One year of graduate specialization or the equivalent in the craft area for which is requested. Work study Scholarship: Intended for those who show high promise in their craft field. Criteria include stated financial need, commitment to and growing knowledge of the craft area for which application is made, and the ability to work in a supportive, close-knit community. Minority Scholarship: Haystack awards up to six full scholarships to students of colour. Same criteria as work study scholarships.
Level of Study: Research, unrestricted
Type: Scholarships and fellowships
Value: US$600–1,800
Length of Study: 1, 2- and 3-week sessions
Frequency: Annual
Country of Study: Any country
No. of awards offered: 100
Application Procedure: Applications available *on the website or by contacting the school. Applicants must include references and supporting materials in their application.*
Closing Date: March 25th
Funding: Foundation, private, individuals
No. of awards given last year: 100
No. of applicants last year: 300
Additional Information: Technical assistance are responsible for assisting the instructor and for shop maintenance and organization. Expected to be familiar with general technical requirements of the particular studio/medium. Responsibilities take precedence, but there is ample time for personal work and study. Work study and minority scholarship students will be assigned periodic tasks in the kitchen, or around the school campus. Assigned tasks will not exceed three hours daily, and students have ample time for personal work and study in the studio.

HEALTH RESEARCH BOARD (HRB)

Research & Development for Health, 73 Lower Baggot Street, Dublin, 2, Ireland
Tel: (353) 1 676 1176
Fax: (353) 1 661 1856
Email: hrb@hrb.ie
Website: www.hrb.ie
Contact: The Research Grants Manager

The Health Research Board (HRB) comprises 16 members appointed by the Minister of Health, with eight of the members being nominated on the co-joint nomination of the universities and colleges. The main functions of the HRB are to promote or commission health research, to promote and conduct epidemiological research as may be appropriate at national level, to promote or commission health services research, to liase and co-operate with other research bodies in Ireland and overseas in the promotion of relevant research and to undertake such other cognate functions as the Minister may from time to time determine.

Clinical Research Training Fellowship in Nursing and Midwifery

Subjects: Nursing and midwifery.
Purpose: The purpose of Fellowships is to provide experienced nurses and midwives with an opportunity to carry out research in clinical nursing or midwifery, leading to a postgraduate degree at the Master's or doctoral level. These fellowships will provide nurses with the research experience necessary to develop their expertise as specialists in their chosen field of nursing or midwifery.
Eligibility: To be eligible for a fellowship a candidate must: be registered as a nurse or midwife; have practised professional nursing or midwifery for at least 5 years; hold a post in nursing or midwifery practice or a post related to nursing or midwifery; have been employed in the Irish health services or an Irish academic Department of Nursing and/or Midwifery, within 2 years prior to the closing date for application to the Fellowship; confirm support approval from Head of Department in which the research study is being carried out; and provide evidence of academic supervision from a suitably qualified nurse or a midwife.
Level of Study: Postgraduate, graduate
Type: Fellowship
Value: Personnel costs and consumables together approx. €67,000 p.a.
Length of Study: Up to 3 years
Frequency: Annual
Study Establishment: Fellowships are tenable by nurses or midwives employed in a recognized health service or an Irish academic Department of Nursing and/or Midwifery and registered with an academic Department of Nursing and/or Midwifery or other relevant academic department
Country of Study: Ireland
Application Procedure: Applicants can obtain an application form from our website.
Closing Date: January 13th
Funding: Government
No. of awards given last year: 4
No. of applicants last year: 20

Clinician Scientist Award for Clinical Health Professionals

Subjects: Word class research clinical and translational research with a strong relevance to human health.
Purpose: To release outstanding medically or professionally qualified researchers in the health professions from some or all of their service commitment to conduct.
Eligibility: Medical consultants in the Irish health system or senior clinicians in health related disciplines who are qualified to hold a post in the Irish health service.
Level of Study: Research
Value: €1.5 million
Length of Study: 5 years
Frequency: Annual
Study Establishment: Any Irish teaching hospital or academic institution
Country of Study: Ireland
No. of awards offered: 2–3
Application Procedure: Online application form available from website. Full applications from invited applicants only.
Closing Date: September 30th
Funding: Government
No. of awards given last year: 2
No. of applicants last year: 13

Health Research Board PhD Training Sites

Subjects: Medical, epidemiological, health and health services research.
Purpose: To enhance the training of postgraduates in the health-related sciences.
Eligibility: Teams of at least four scientists.
Level of Study: Predoctorate
Value: Up to €2 million
Length of Study: 5 years
Frequency: PhD training programme for up to 8 students per year for 2 consecutive years
Study Establishment: Any academic institution
Country of Study: Ireland
No. of awards offered: 2
Application Procedure: Applicants must complete an online application form.
Closing Date: Consult the HRB website
Funding: Government
No. of awards given last year: 2
No. of applicants last year: 13

Health Services Research Fellowships

Subjects: Clinical, epidemiological, public health, statistics, health economics, social science, operational and management disciplines.
Purpose: To enable graduates with some appropriate relevant experience to pursue a career in health devices and research in Ireland.
Eligibility: Candidates must normally hold a primary degree in a discipline relevant to health services research, have acquired appropriate postgraduate experience in the field of health services and research, have support from an approved academic department or centre, have obtained the prior approval of a head of department for the research study being proposed and be Irish citizens or graduates from overseas with a permanent Irish resident status.
Level of Study: Graduate
Type: Fellowship
Value: Please consult the organization salary on a postdoctorate scale up to €7,500 p.a for consumables
Length of Study: The maximum period of the award will be 3 years,
Frequency: Annual
Study Establishment: Institutions approved by the Board, such as teaching hospitals, universities, research institutes and health boards in Ireland
Country of Study: Ireland
No. of awards offered: Varies
Application Procedure: Applicants must complete an online application form, available from the website.
Closing Date: October 14th
Funding: Government
No. of awards given last year: 4
No. of applicants last year: 17

HRB Clinical Research Training Fellowships

Subjects: Biomedicine.
Purpose: To enable medical and dental graduates at any stage in their career to gain specialized research training in the biomedical field in Ireland.
Eligibility: Candidates should be graduates in medicine or dentistry from postregistration up to and including senior registrar or equivalent academic level.
Level of Study: Postgraduate, postdoctorate
Value: Please consult the organization salary on registrar's scale consumables of €15,000 p.a.
Length of Study: Normally 2 years
Frequency: Annual

Study Establishment: At an appropriate academic department in the Republic of Ireland
Country of Study: Ireland
No. of awards offered: Varies
Application Procedure: Applicants must apply with the support of the head of an appropriate sponsoring laboratory in the Republic of Ireland. Candidates may apply to remain in their current laboratory, to return to one where they have worked before or to move to a new laboratory. Applicants have to fill in on online form available the on website.
Funding: Government
No. of applicants last year: 42
Additional Information: Proposals may be submitted for specialized research training or for training in a basic subject relevant to a particular clinical interest.

HRB Equipment Grants

Subjects: Health related research.
Purpose: To facilitate the purchase of items of equipment aimed at improving the quality or broadening the scope of a scientific research investigation being undertaken at an Irish academic institution in the biomedical sciences.
Eligibility: Applicants should hold a full-time academic post in an Irish university or college and be actively engaged in biomedical research in Ireland.
Level of Study: Research, postdoctorate
Value: Awards will be in the range €50,000–500,000 per piece of equipment. A contribution towards essential running and maintenance costs may be allowed in the first 3 months
Frequency: Dependent on funds available
Country of Study: Ireland
No. of awards offered: Varies, depending on the quality of the applications received and the amount of funding made available from the Department of Health
Application Procedure: Applications for equipment that is essential for the conduct of biomedical research may be made and applications will be assessed on the basis of the research case presented. Please write for further details.
Funding: Government
No. of awards given last year: 37
No. of applicants last year: 52
Additional Information: Applications reflecting interdepartmental collaboration are particularly welcome.

HRB Postdoctoral Research Fellowships

Subjects: Researchers who hold a PhD and who want to develop their career, as an advanced level in a health-related discipline.
Purpose: Career development in health related disciplines.
Eligibility: Applicants must be postdoctorates with less than 5 years of postdoctoral experience.
Level of Study: Postdoctorate
Type: Fellowship
Value: Salary on senior postdoctorate scale plus consumables of €15,000 p.a.
Length of Study: Up to 3 years
Frequency: Annual
Study Establishment: A university, research hospital or institute
Country of Study: Ireland
No. of awards offered: Varies
Application Procedure: Applicants must complete an online application form, available from the website.
Funding: Government
No. of awards given last year: 8
No. of applicants last year: 42

HRB Project Grants-General

Subjects: Biomedical sciences, public health and epidemiology, health services research or health research.
Purpose: To facilitate research in biomedical sciences, public health, epidemiology and health service research.
Eligibility: Post-doctoral researches can apply for their own salary support his or her speciality should be within the range of disciplines stated in the subject index. Applicants must reside in the Republic of Ireland and grants are tenable in this country.
Type: Project funding
Value: Please consult the organization €70,000 p.a. if employing salarised researcher €55,000 p.a if training PhD student
Length of Study: Up to 3 years
Frequency: Annual
Study Establishment: An Irish academic institution of research
Country of Study: Ireland
No. of awards offered: Varies
Application Procedure: Applicants must complete an online application form, available from the website.
Closing Date: November 25th
Funding: Government
No. of awards given last year: 75
No. of applicants last year: 307

HRB Summer Student Grants

Subjects: Medical, dental science, health service and science.
Purpose: To develop interest in research and give the student the opportunity to become familiar with research techniques.
Eligibility: Open to students from medical, dental science or health service-related disciplines.
Level of Study: Graduate
Type: Grant
Value: €200 per week for up to 8 weeks
Length of Study: 8 weeks
Frequency: Annual
Study Establishment: A university, research hospital or institution
Country of Study: Ireland
No. of awards offered: Varies
Application Procedure: Applicants must fill in or online an application form, available from the website.
Funding: Government
No. of awards given last year: 50
No. of applicants last year: 100

HRB Translational research programmes

Purpose: To enable researchers to establish and support teams working full-time or extensive or long-term research programmes that have a clear link to patient care.
Value: €1.5 million
Length of Study: 5 years
Study Establishment: Any Irish academic or research institution
Country of Study: Ireland
Application Procedure: Online application form available from the HR3 website.
Closing Date: September 23rd

HEART RESEARCH UK

Suite 12D, Joseph's Well, Leeds, LS3 1AB, England
Tel: (44) 11 3234 7474
Fax: (44) 11 3297 6208
Email: mail@heartresearch.org.uk
Website: www.heartresearch.org.uk

Since 1967, Heart Research UK has provided a lifeline of support for research into the prevention, treatment and cure of heart disease. The fund is a visionary charity leading the way in funding ground-breaking, innovative medical research projects at the cutting edge of science into the prevention, treatment and cure of heart disease. There is a strong emphasis on clinical and surgical projects and young researchers. Heart Research UK encourages and supports original health lifestyle initiatives exploring novel ways of preventing heart disease in all sectors of the community.

Heart Research UK Basic Science Medical Research Grant

Subjects: Basic science research projects on ways to fight heart disease for patients of all ages.
Purpose: To support ground-breaking, innovative medical research into the prevention, treatment and cure of heart disease.

Eligibility: Graduates or those studying for a recognized professional qualification. Research must be carried out in the United Kingdom at a host institution with the proper supervision.
Level of Study: Unrestricted, research
Type: Studentship, postdoctorate fellowship or project grant
Value: Average UK £54,000, maximum UK £85,000
Length of Study: Maximum 3 years
Frequency: Annual, 1 main round, but more if funds are available
Study Establishment: Centres of health and educational establishments
Country of Study: United Kingdom
No. of awards offered: No fixed number
Application Procedure: Applicants must send 15 copies of application outlining aims and objectives to the Heart Research Medical Review Panel on the appropriate form.
Closing Date: Basic Science Round March 31st (noon)
Funding: Private, trusts
Contributor: Voluntary funding from supporters, grant-making trusts
No. of awards given last year: 7
No. of applicants last year: 31

Heart Research UK Clinical Medical Research Grant

Subjects: Clinical research projects on ways to fight and treat heart disease for patients of all ages.
Purpose: To support ground-breaking, innovative medical research into the prevention, treatment and cure of heart disease.
Eligibility: Graduates or those studying for a recognized professional qualification research must be carried out in the United Kingdom and at a host institution with the proper supervision.
Level of Study: Unrestricted, research
Type: Studentship, postdoctorate fellowship or project grant
Value: Average UK £54,000, maximum UK £85,000
Length of Study: Maximum 3 years
Frequency: Annual, 1 main round, but more if funds available
Study Establishment: Centres of health and educational establishments
Country of Study: United Kingdom
No. of awards offered: No fixed number
Application Procedure: Applicants must send 15 copies of application, outlining aims and objectives, to the Heart Research Medical Review Panel on the appropriate form.
Closing Date: Clinical Round, September 30th (noon)
Funding: Private, trusts
Contributor: Voluntary funding from supporters, grant-making trusts
No. of awards given last year: 9
No. of applicants last year: 30

Heart Research UK Emerging Technologies Grant

Subjects: Research projects into ways to fight and treat heart disease for patients of all ages.
Purpose: To support ground-breaking, innovative medical research into the prevention, treatment and cure of heart disease.
Eligibility: Graduates or those studying for a recognized professional qualification. Research must be carried out in the United Kingdom at a host institution with the proper supervision.
Level of Study: Research, unrestricted
Type: Studentship, postdoctorate fellowship or project grant
Value: Maximum UK £200,000
Length of Study: Maximum 3 years
Frequency: Annual, 1 main round, but more if funds available
Study Establishment: Centres of health and educational establishments
Country of Study: United Kingdom
No. of awards offered: No fixed number
Application Procedure: Applicants must send 10 copies of application, outlining aims and objectives, to the Heart Research Medical Review Panel on the appropriate form.
Closing Date: Please call for details
Funding: Trusts
Contributor: Voluntary funds from supporters, grant-making trusts

HEART UK

Wheldon Events and Conferences, 49A Anchor Road, Aldridge, West Midlands, WS9 8PT, England
Tel: (44) 19 2245 7984
Fax: (44) 19 2245 5238
Email: natashadougall@wheldonevents.freeserve.co.uk
Website: www.heartuk.org.uk
Contact: Ms Natasha Dougall, Meetings Organizer

Heart UK is a charity that combines the skills of research scientists and epidemiologists, with the expertise of doctors, nurses and dietitians in partnership with the patients. The charity specializes in the treatment of a genetic condition called Familial Hypercholesterolaemia (FH) that affects around 1 in 500 of the population.

Sue McCarthy Travelling Scholarship

Subjects: Medical sciences.
Purpose: The award is designed to support career development for healthcare professionals or for doctors or scientists in training.
Eligibility: Open to medical and scientific professionals.
Level of Study: Unrestricted
Type: Scholarship
Value: UK £1,500
Frequency: Annual
Study Establishment: A university, hospital or research institution
Country of Study: United Kingdom
No. of awards offered: 1
Application Procedure: Applicants must request an application form from Heart UK.
Closing Date: March 24th
Funding: Private
No. of awards given last year: 1
No. of applicants last year: 11

HEBREW IMMIGRANT AID SOCIETY (HIAS)

333 Seventh Avenue, 16th Floor, New York, NY, 10001, United States of America
Tel: (1) 212 967 4100
Fax: (1) 212 967 4483
Email: info@hias.org.il
Website: www.hias.org
Contact: Scholarship Co-ordinator

The Hebrew Immigrant Aid Society (HIAS) is the United States of America's oldest international and refugee resettlement agency dedicated to assisting persecuted and opressed people worldwide and delivering them to safe havens. HIAS has helped more than 4.5 million people in its 124 years of existence.

HIAS Scholarship Awards Competition

Subjects: All subjects.
Purpose: To help HIAS-assisted refugees and asylees in pursuing higher education.
Eligibility: Open to HIAS-assisted refugees and asylees in the United States of America. United States of America applicants must have completed 1 year, ie. two semesters, at a United States of America high school, college, or graduate school, college or graduate school. The student must have immigrated after January 1, 1980.
Level of Study: Research, graduate, doctorate, predoctorate, mba, postdoctorate, postgraduate, professional development, and trade programmes
Type: Scholarship
Value: Average US$1,500
Length of Study: 1 year must be completed in a U.S. School prior to beginning the award and applicant must be poised to start another academic year
Frequency: Annual
Country of Study: United States of America
No. of awards offered: Varies, approx. 150

Application Procedure: Applicants must complete an official application form, which must be completed online. Application forms are available from mid-December each year.
Closing Date: March 15th
Funding: Private
No. of awards given last year: 150
No. of applicants last year: 370
Additional Information: Applications are judged on financial need, academic scholarship and community service. The HIAS Scholarship Awards Competition in Israel has a different deadline, award amount, specifications, etc. For further information visit the website: www.hias.org/scholarships/apply.html

HENRY A MURRAY RESEARCH CENTER

Radcliffe Institute for Advanced Study, Harvard University,
10 Garden Street, Cambridge, MA, 02138,
United States of America
Fax: (1) 617 496 2982
Email: mrc@radcliffe.edu
Website: www.murray.hmdc.harvard.edu/
Contact: Programme Co-ordinator

The Henry A Murray Research Center is a centre for research on the changing lives of American women. The Center's purpose is to promote the use of existing social science data to explore human development and social change. The archive holds over 230 studies available for new research.

Henry A Murray Adolescent and Youth Research Award

Subjects: Social and behavioural sciences.
Purpose: To support predoctoral and postdoctoral researchers who focus on adolescent development projects drawing on the Center's data.
Eligibility: Predoctoral applicants must be enrolled in a doctoral programme in a relevant field, and must have their dissertation proposal approved by an advisor or committee before the grant application is made.
Level of Study: Doctorate, postdoctorate, predoctorate
Type: Research grant
Value: Up to US$5,000 for predoctoral candidates and up to US$10,000 for postdoctoral candidates
Frequency: Annual
Country of Study: Any country
Application Procedure: Applicants must submit five copies of a curriculum vitae including social security number, permanent home address and the name and address of a referee who has been asked to send a letter of recommendation directly to the programme. Also, an application for the Use of Data form and a Computer Data Request form should be submitted if applicable, as well as six copies of a proposal that describes the intended research, and a covering page.
Closing Date: The deadline for predoctoral applications is April 1st, and for postdoctoral applications is October 15th or March 15th
Contributor: The W T Grant Foundation
No. of awards given last year: 7
No. of applicants last year: Varies

Henry A Murray Dissertation Award Program

Subjects: Social and behavioural studies.
Purpose: To enable doctoral students to undertake projects that focus on some aspect of the study of lives, concentrating on issues in human development or personality. Priority will be given to projects drawing on Center data.
Eligibility: Applicants must be enrolled in a doctoral programme in a relevant field and must have had their dissertation proposal approved by an adviser or committee before the grant application is made.
Level of Study: Doctorate, predoctorate
Type: Research grant
Value: Up to US$5,000
Length of Study: 1 year
Frequency: Annual
Country of Study: Any country
Application Procedure: Applicants must submit six copies of a curriculum vitae including their social security number, permanent home address and the name and address of a referee who has been asked to send a letter of recommendation directly to the programme. Also, an application for the Use of Data form and a Computer Data Request form should be submitted if applicable, as well as six copies of a proposal that describes the intended research and a covering form.
Closing Date: April 1st
Funding: Private
Contributor: The Radcliffe Institute
No. of awards given last year: 3
No. of applicants last year: Varies

Jeanne Humphrey Block Dissertation Award

Subjects: Social and behavioural studies.
Purpose: To enable a female doctoral student to undertake research on gender differences or some developmental issue of particular concern to girls or women. Projects drawing on Center data will be given priority, although this is not a requirement.
Eligibility: Female applicants must be enrolled in a doctoral programme in a relevant field and must have had their dissertation proposal approved by an adviser or committee before the grant application is made.
Level of Study: Doctorate, predoctorate
Type: Award
Value: Up to US$5,000
Length of Study: 1 year
Frequency: Annual
Country of Study: Any country
No. of awards offered: 1
Application Procedure: Applicants must submit six copies of a curriculum vitae including their social security number, permanent home address and the name and address of a referee who has been asked to send a letter of recommendation directly to the programme. Also, an application for the Use of Data form and a Computer Data Request form should be submitted if applicable, as well as six copies of a proposal that describes the intended research and a covering page.
Closing Date: April 1st
Contributor: Murray Center Endowment
No. of awards given last year: 1
No. of applicants last year: Varies

Studying Diverse Lives Research Grant

Subjects: Social sciences.
Purpose: To allow social science researchers to use the Henry A Murray Research Center's Diversity Archive.
Eligibility: Open to postdoctoral researchers looking for data with racially and ethnically diverse samples to use in their work who have received their doctorate within the last 10 years.
Level of Study: Postdoctorate
Type: Research grant
Value: Up to US$10,000
Frequency: Annual
Country of Study: Any country
Application Procedure: Applicants must submit six copies of a curriculum vitae including their social security number, permanent home address and the name and address of a referee, who has been asked to send a letter of recommendation directly to the programme, should be attached to the proposal. Also, an application for the Use of Data form and a Computer Data Request form should be submitted if applicable, as well as six copies of a proposal that describes the intended research and a covering page.
Closing Date: February 1st and October 15th
Funding: Government
Contributor: The National Institute of Mental Health
No. of awards given last year: 2
No. of applicants last year: 9
Additional Information: Grant recipients will be required to attend one of two research meetings at Harvard to discuss their work.

HENRY COGSWELL COLLEGE

3002 Colby Avenue, Washington, Everett, 98201, United States of America
Tel: (1) 258 3351
Fax: (1) 257 0405
Email: admissions@henrycogswell.edu
Website: www.henrycogswell.edu

Henry Cogswell College is a private, non-profit, independent, four-year college offering professional degrees and continuing education opportunities for students of all ages.

Boeing Company Diversity Program Scholarship

Subjects: Engineering, science and business.
Purpose: To encourage diversity in engineering, science and business.
Eligibility: Open to candidates who are US citizens and belong to the low income/minority group.
Type: Scholarship
Value: US$3,000
Frequency: Annual
Study Establishment: Henry Cogswell College
Country of Study: United States of America
No. of awards offered: 2
Application Procedure: A completed application form, which is available on the website must be submitted.
Closing Date: February 1st
Contributor: The Boeing Company

Henry Cogswell Active Duty Military Scholarship

Subjects: All subjects.
Eligibility: Open to candidates who are actively serving in one of the U.S. armed forces.
Level of Study: Postgraduate
Type: Scholarship
Value: 75% of tution fees
Frequency: Annual
Study Establishment: Henry Cogswell College
Country of Study: United States of America
Application Procedure: A completed application form must be submitted.
Closing Date: One month prior to start of trimester
Funding: Private

Henry Cogswell Director Scholarship Program

Subjects: Engineering.
Purpose: To provide financial assistance to students transferring from a Puget sound area community college to complete their studies at Henry Cogswell College.
Eligibility: Open to students who have enrolled at the college as a full-time student.
Level of Study: Postgraduate
Type: Scholarship
Value: 100% of tuition fees
Length of Study: 1 year
Frequency: Annual
Study Establishment: Henry Cogswell College
Country of Study: United States of America
No. of awards offered: 12
Application Procedure: A completed application form must be submitted along with official transcripts of all prior college work.
Funding: Private

J. W. Sutton Scholarship

Subjects: All subjects.
Purpose: To encourage students who have a strong academic record.
Eligibility: Open to applicants who are enrolled in Henry Cogswell college.
Level of Study: Postgraduate
Type: Scholarship
Value: US$2,500
Length of Study: Renewable
Frequency: Three times a year
Study Establishment: Henry Cogswell College
Country of Study: United States of America
No. of awards offered: 4
Application Procedure: See the website.
Closing Date: One month prior to start of trimester

For further information contact:

Henry Cogswell College
Contact: Financial Aid Director

THE HENRY MOORE INSTITUTE

74 The Headrow, Leeds, LS1 3AH, United Kingdom
Tel: (44) 11 3246 7467
Fax: (44) 11 3246 1481
Email: hmi@henry-moore.ac.uk
Website: www.henry-moore-fdn.co.uk/hmi
Contact: Ellen Tait

The Henry Moore Institute aims to enlarge the understanding of how sculpture makes meaning at different times and in different places through a programme of exhibitions, talks, conferences, publications and through its collection activities and research fellowship programme.

Henry Moore Institute Research Fellowship

Subjects: Sculpture, both historical and contemporary.
Purpose: To enable scholars to use the Institute's facilities, which include the sculpture collection, library, archive and slide library, to assist them in researching their particular field.
Eligibility: There are no restrictions.
Level of Study: Research, postgraduate, postdoctorate, doctorate
Type: Fellowship
Value: Accommodation, travel and daily living expenses
Length of Study: 1 month
Frequency: Annual
Study Establishment: The Henry Moore Institute
Country of Study: United Kingdom
No. of awards offered: 4
Application Procedure: Applicants must send a letter of application (marked RF), a proposal (maximum 1,000 words) and a curriculum vitae.
Closing Date: January 9th
Funding: Private
Contributor: The Henry Moore Foundation
No. of awards given last year: 4
No. of applicants last year: 70

For further information contact:

Henry Moore Institute 74 Tue Headrow, Leeds, LS1 3AH

Henry Moore Senior Fellowships

Subjects: Sculpture, both historical and contemporary.
Purpose: To provide senior scholars with time and space to develop a research project away from usual work commitment.
Level of Study: Senior Academic
Value: Accommodation, Travel and daily living expenses
Length of Study: 1 month
Frequency: Annual
Study Establishment: Tue Henry Moore Institute
Country of Study: United Kingdom
No. of awards offered: 2
Application Procedure: Letter of Application, a proposal and a curriculum vitae.
Closing Date: January 5th
Funding: Private
Contributor: Tue Henry Moore Foundation
No. of awards given last year: 1
No. of applicants last year: 40

For further information contact:

Henry Moore Institute 74 Tue Headrow, Leed, LS1 3AH

THE HERB SOCIETY OF AMERICA, INC.

9019 Kirtland Chardon Road, Kirtland, OH, 44094,
United States of America
Tel: (1) 440 256 0514
Fax: (1) 440 256 0541
Email: herbs@herbsociety.com
Website: www.herbsociety.org
Contact: Ms Michelle Milks, Office Administrator

The aim of the Herb Society of America Inc. is to promote the knowledge, use and delight of herbs through educational programmes, research and sharing the experience of its members with the community.

Herb Society of America Research Grant

Subjects: Herbal projects.
Purpose: To further the knowledge and use of herbs and to contribute the results of study and research to the records of horticulture, science, literature, history, art or economics.
Eligibility: Open to persons with a proposed programme of scientific, academic or artistic investigation of herbal plants.
Level of Study: Unrestricted
Value: Up to US$5,000
Length of Study: Up to 1 year
Frequency: Annual
Country of Study: Any country
Application Procedure: Applicants must submit an application clearly defining all their research in 500 words or less and a proposed budget with specific budget items listed. Requests for funds will not be considered unless accompanied by five copies of the application form and proposal.
Closing Date: January 31st
Contributor: Members
No. of awards given last year: 0
No. of applicants last year: 45
Additional Information: Finalists will be interviewed.

HSA Grant for Educators

Subjects: Herbal projects.
Purpose: To deliver herbal education in schools, communities, or any public forum.
Level of Study: Unrestricted
Value: Up to US$5,000
Length of Study: Up to 1 year
Frequency: Annual
Country of Study: Any country
Application Procedure: Please submit application cover sheet, statement of qualifications, a comprehensive descriptions of the programme, and detailed budget (8 copies).
Closing Date: April 15th
Contributor: Members
No. of awards given last year: 1
Additional Information: Finalists will be interviewed.

HERBERT HOOVER PRESIDENTIAL LIBRARY ASSOCIATION

302 Parkside Drive, PO Box 696, West Branch, IA, 52358,
United States of America
Tel: (1) 319 643 5327
Fax: (1) 319 643 2391
Email: info@hooverassociation.org
Website: www.hooverassociation.org
Contact: Ms Patricia A Hand, Manager of Promotions & Academic Programs

The Herbert Hoover Presidential Library Association is a private, non-profit support group for the Herbert Hoover Presidential Library Museum and National Historic Site in West Branch, Iowa.

Herbert Hoover Presidential Library Association Travel Grants

Subjects: American history, journalism, political science and economic history.
Purpose: To encourage the scholarly use of the holdings, and to promote the study of subjects of interest and concern to Herbert Hoover, Lou Henry Hoover and other public figures.
Eligibility: Open to current graduate students, postdoctoral students and qualified independent scholars. Priority is given to well-developed proposals that utilize the resources of the Library, have the greatest likelihood of publication and subsequently, greatest likelihood of use by educators, students and policy makers.
Level of Study: Postdoctorate, professional development, graduate, doctorate, research, postgraduate, predoctorate
Type: Travel grant
Value: US$500–1,500 to cover the cost of a trip to the Library. There is no money available for any purpose other than to defray the expense of travel to West Branch, IA
Length of Study: Varies by individual
Frequency: Annual
Study Establishment: The Herbert Hoover Presidential Library-Museum in West Branch, IA
Country of Study: United States of America
No. of awards offered: Varies
Application Procedure: Applicants must submit a completed application form, a project proposal of up to 1,200 words and three letters of reference, mailed separately. The application form can be obtained from the website.
Closing Date: March 1st
Funding: Private
No. of awards given last year: 10
No. of applicants last year: 14
Additional Information: For archival holdings information please contact the Hoover Library on (1) 319 643 5301, email: hoover.library@nara.gov or visit the website: www.hoover.archives.gov

HERBERT SCOVILLE JR PEACE FELLOWSHIP

322 4th Street, NE, Washington, DC, 20002,
United States of America
Tel: (1) 202 543 4100
Fax: (1) 202 543 6297
Email: scoville@clw.org
Website: www.scoville.org
Contact: Paul Revsine, Program Director

The Herbert Scoville Jr Peace Fellowship was established in 1987 to provide college graduates with the opportunity to gain a Washington perspective on key issues of peace and security.

Herbert Scoville Jr Peace Fellowship

Subjects: Arms control and disarmament.
Purpose: To provide a unique educational experience to outstanding graduates, that will allow them to develop leadership skills that can serve them throughout a career in arms control or a related area of public service, to contribute to the work of the participating arms control and disarmament organizations and to continue the work of Herbert Scoville Jr.
Eligibility: Open to United States of America college graduates with experience or interest in arms control, disarmament, international security and/or peace issues. A fellowship is awarded periodically to a foreign national from a country of arms proliferation concern to the United States of America.
Level of Study: Postgraduate
Type: Fellowship
Value: Please contact the organization
Length of Study: 4–6 months
Country of Study: United States of America
Application Procedure: Applicants must telephone, write or consult the website for information on application requirements.

HERZOG AUGUST LIBRARY

Post box 1364, D-38299, Wolfenbuettel, Germany
Tel: (49) 5331 808 208
Fax: (49) 5331 808 266
Email: bepler@hab.de
Website: www.hab.de
Contact: Dr Gillian Bepler

The Herzog August Library is an independent research library devoted to the study of the cultural history of Europe from the middle ages to the early modern period. Its rich book manuscript holdings were founded in the 17th century and have survived intact until today.

Findel Scholarships and Schneider Scholarships

Subjects: History and related disciplines.
Purpose: The Herzog August Library administers the doctoral fellowships funded by the Dr Guenther Findel Foundation and Rolf and Ursula Schneider Foundation towards the advancement of history and other related disciplines.
Eligibility: Outstanding doctoral candidates from all over the world, whose research requires an intensive use of the rich collections at Herzog August Library, may apply.
Level of Study: Doctorate, predoctorate
Type: Scholarship
Value: €700 per month. Additionally, the Herzog August Library provides accommodation for Fellows in its guest house
Length of Study: 3–6 months
Frequency: Twice a year
Study Establishment: Herzog August Library
Country of Study: Germany
Application Procedure: An application form is available on request.
Closing Date: April 1st and November 1st
Funding: Foundation
Contributor: Findel and Schneider Foundations
No. of awards given last year: 15
Additional Information: If researchers are already supported by another grant/fellowship, the foundation will only provide free accommodation, but no subsistence allowance.

Herzog August Library Fellowship

Subjects: History and all related disciplines.
Purpose: Awards to post-doctoral researchers whose projects are based on the historical book and manuscript holdings of the Wolfenbuettel Library.
Eligibility: Qualified researchers whose projects are partly or fully based on the library's holdings.
Type: Fellowship
Value: €1,600 per month
Length of Study: 2–12 months
Study Establishment: Herzog August Library
Country of Study: Germany
Application Procedure: Application forms available on request.
Closing Date: January 31st
Contributor: State of Lower Saxony
No. of awards given last year: 20
No. of applicants last year: 80
Additional Information: Fellowship holders have a residence requirement in Wolfenbuttel during their tenure. The library has its own guest accomodation.

Mellon Research Fellowships

Subjects: Humanities.
Eligibility: Postdoctoral researchers from Bulgaria, Hungary, Poland, Rumania, Czech Republic, Slovakia and Baltic countries, whose research requires an intensive use of the rich collections at Herzog August Library, are eligible to apply.
Level of Study: Postdoctorate
Type: Fellowship
Value: US$11,500
Length of Study: 3 months
Study Establishment: Herzog August Library
Country of Study: Germany
Application Procedure: Application forms are available on request.
Closing Date: January 31st and March 31st
Contributor: Andrew W. Mellon Foundation
No. of awards given last year: 3

HIGHER EDUCATION COMMISSION

Islamabad, H-9, Pakistan
Tel: (92) 92 51 9257651 60
Fax: (92) 92 51 9290128
Email: info@hec.gov.pk
Website: www.hec.gov.pk

The Higher Education Commission has been set up to facilitate the development of the universities of Pakistan to be world-class centers of education, research and development.

HEC Commonwealth Scholarship

Subjects: All subjects.
Eligibility: Open to candidates who are Pakistan nationals.
Level of Study: Postgraduate
Value: Varies
Length of Study: 6 months
Frequency: Annual
Country of Study: United Kingdom
No. of awards offered: Up to 80
Application Procedure: A completed application form must be sent. Application form is available on the website.
Closing Date: December 20th
Funding: Government

HEC Overseas Scholarship for Masters/PhD at AIT, Bangkok

Subjects: Science, engineering and technology.
Purpose: To support candidates pursuing Master's/PhD study.
Eligibility: Open to Pakistani/AJK nationals who are below the age of 45 years.
Level of Study: Doctorate, postgraduate
Type: Scholarship
Value: Living allowance, tuition fee, thesis allowance, visa extension fee and one time return air fare
Frequency: Annual
Study Establishment: Asia Institute of, Technology (AIT)
No. of awards offered: 7 (4 for Master's and 3 for PhD)
Application Procedure: A completed application form must be sent.
Closing Date: February 6th
Funding: Government

HEC Overseas Scholarships for Master's in Engineering

Subjects: Engineering.
Purpose: To provide opportunity for Master's degree programme in European countries.
Eligibility: Open to Pakistani/AJK Nationals who are below the age of 40 years.
Type: Scholarship
Value: Living allowance, tuition fee, study, research allowance and one time return air fare
Frequency: Annual
Country of Study: Germany
No. of awards offered: 36
Application Procedure: A completed application form must be sent.
Closing Date: February 6th

International Research Support Initiative Program

Subjects: All subjects.
Purpose: To provide a training programme.
Eligibility: Open to candidates who have completed their PhD. studies and who are under the age of 45 years.
Level of Study: Doctorate
Type: Scholarship
Value: Travel costs (up to Rs 80,000), monthly stipend (up to Rs 70,000) and bench fee (up to Rs 200,000)
Length of Study: 6 months
Frequency: Annual

Application Procedure: A completed application form, which is available on the website, must be sent.
Closing Date: November 21st
Funding: Government
Additional Information: The candidates will have to enter into a bond with HEC to serve the country at least for 3 years.

Overseas Scholarship for MS (Engineering) in South Korean Universities

Subjects: Engineering.
Purpose: To create a critical mass of highly qualified engineering manpower in high-tech field.
Eligibility: Open to Pakistan and AJK nationals who are the below the age of 35 years.
Level of Study: Doctorate
Type: Scholarship
Value: US$9,600 and round-trip expenses from South Korea
Length of Study: 24 months
Frequency: Annual
Country of Study: South Africa
No. of awards offered: 250
Application Procedure: A completed application form along with all other requirements must be sent.
Funding: Government

For further information contact:

HRD Divison Higher Education Commission
Contact: Reznana Siddiqui, Project Director (SK/FFSP)

Partial Support for PhD Studies Abroad

Subjects: All subjects.
Purpose: To financially support Pakistan students who are in the final stage of completion of their PhD studies aborad.
Eligibility: Open to candidate who are Pakistan nationals who are studying abroad.
Level of Study: Doctorate
Type: Scholarship
Value: Up to US$15,000
Frequency: Annual
Application Procedure: A completed application form along with photocopies of all academics documents must be sent.
Funding: Government
Additional Information: An awardee is required to execute a bond with HEC to serve Pakistan for 2 years.

HILDA MARTINDALE EDUCATIONAL TRUST

Royal Holloway University of London, Egham, Surrey, TW20 0EX, England
Tel: (44) 17 8443 4455
Fax: (44) 17 8443 7520
Contact: Miss J L Hurn, Secretary to the Trustees

The Hilda Martindale Educational Trust was set up by Miss Hilda Martindale in order to help women of the British Isles with the costs of vocational training for any profession or career likely to be of use or value to the community. Applications are considered annually by six women trustees.

Hilda Martindale Exhibitions

Subjects: Any vocational training for a profession or career likely to be of value to the community.
Purpose: To assist with the costs of vocational training.
Eligibility: Open to women of the British Isles over 21 years of age. Assistance is not given for short courses, courses abroad, elective studies, intercalated BSc years, access courses or academic research. Awards are not given to those who are eligible for grants from research councils, the British Academy or other public sources.
Level of Study: Professional development, graduate, postgraduate
Type: Grant
Value: Varies, normally UK £200–1,000
Length of Study: 1 year
Frequency: Annual
Study Establishment: Any establishment approved by the trustees
Country of Study: United Kingdom
No. of awards offered: 15–20
Application Procedure: Applicants must complete two copies of an application form, which must be obtained from and returned to the Secretary to the Trustees.
Closing Date: March 1st for the following academic year. Late or retrospective applications will not be considered
Funding: Private
Contributor: Private trust
No. of awards given last year: 20 awards
No. of applicants last year: 100

HILGENFELD FOUNDATION FOR MORTUARY EDUCATION

PO Box 4311, Fullerton, CA, 92834, United States of America
Contact: Mr Chester Gromaki, President

Hilgenfeld Foundation Grant

Subjects: Mortuary science education.
Purpose: To support scholarships and research.
Eligibility: Open to nationals of the United States of America only. Applicant must be enrolled in an approved institution teaching funeral service education or teaching in an approved programme for funeral service education.
Level of Study: Graduate, professional development, postgraduate
Type: Grant
Value: Varies
Length of Study: Varies
Frequency: Annual
Country of Study: United States of America
No. of awards offered: Approx. 20
Application Procedure: Applicants must submit an application on forms provided by the Hilgenfeld Foundation.
Closing Date: Applications are accepted at any time
Funding: Private
Contributor: The Hilgenfeld Family
No. of awards given last year: 10
No. of applicants last year: 100
Additional Information: Scholarship grants are awarded through a co-operative effort between the Hilgenfeld Foundation and the American Board of Funeral Service.

For further information contact:

Margre Hilgenfeld Field, Hilgenfeld Foundation for Mortuary Education, 120 E. Broadway, Anaheim, CA 92805, United States of America

THE HINRICHSEN FOUNDATION

10-12 Baches Street, London, N1 6DN, England
Contact: L E Adamson, Administrator

Hinrichsen Foundation Awards

Subjects: Contemporary music composition, performance and research.
Purpose: To promote the written areas of music.
Eligibility: Preference will be given to United Kingdom applicants and projects taking place in the United Kingdom. Grants are not given for recordings, for the funding of commissions, for degree or other study courses or for the purchase of instruments or equipment.
Level of Study: Unrestricted
Value: Varies
Frequency: Dependent on funds available
No. of awards offered: Varies
Application Procedure: Applicants must submit a completed application form along with two references.
Closing Date: Applications are accepted at any time
No. of awards given last year: 37 grants, 1 composition bursary
No. of applicants last year: 105

For further information contact:

The Hinrichsen Foundation PO Box 309 KT22 2AT

HISTORY OF SCIENCE SOCIETY (HSS)

Executive Office, PO Box 117360, University of Florida, Gainesville, FL 32611-7360, United States of America
Tel: (1) 352 392 1677
Fax: (1) 352 392 2795
Email: info@hssonline.org
Website: www.hssonline.org
Contact: Mr Robert J Malone, Executive Director

The History of Science Society (HSS) is the world's largest society dedicated to understanding science, technology, medicine, and their interactions with society within their historical context.

Derek Price/Rod Website Prize

Subjects: History of science.
Purpose: To recognize an outstanding published article.
Level of Study: Postgraduate
Type: Award
Value: US$1,000
Frequency: Annual
No. of awards offered: 1
Contributor: Marjorie Webster

The George Sarton Medal Award

Subjects: History of science.
Purpose: To honor an outstanding historian of science for lifetime scholarly achievement.
Eligibility: Open to candidates who have devoted their entire career to the field of history of science.
Level of Study: Postgraduate
Type: Award
Value: The George Sarton Medal
Frequency: Annual
Application Procedure: A completed application form that is available online must be sent.
Closing Date: April 1st
Contributor: Dibner Fund

HSS Travel Grant

Subjects: The history of science from ancient to modern times.
Purpose: To allow an individual to travel to the annual HSS meeting.
Eligibility: Eligibility is restricted to those who participate in the annual meeting. Preference is given to HSS members and those who have not been awarded a travel grant in the past two years.
Level of Study: Postdoctorate, postgraduate, doctorate
Type: Travel grant
Value: US$10–1,000
Frequency: Annual
Country of Study: United States of America
No. of awards offered: Approx. 50
Application Procedure: Applicants must apply to the HSS Executive Office.
Closing Date: June 1st
Funding: Government
Contributor: The National Science Foundation
No. of awards given last year: 43
No. of applicants last year: 48
Additional Information: Other awards include the Marguret W. Rossiter History of Women in Science Prize, Watson Davis and Helen Miles Davis Prize, Derek Price Rod Webster Award, Nathan Reingold Prize, Pfizer Prize, Joseph H Hazen Education Prize and the Suzanne J. Lovingon Prize.

Joseph H. Hazen Education Prize

Subjects: Science education.
Purpose: To promote exemplary teaching and educational service.
Eligibility: Open to applicants who have made outstanding contributions to the teaching of history sciences.
Level of Study: Postgraduate
Type: Award
Value: US$1,000
Frequency: Annual
Application Procedure: A completed application form along with the nomenee's curriculum vitae must be sent.
Closing Date: April 1st

Margaret W. Rossiter History of Women in Science Prize

Subjects: Medicine, technology, social and national sciences.
Purpose: To recognize an outstanding book on the history of women in science.
Eligibility: Open to authors of books/articles that have been published no more than 4 years before the year of award.
Level of Study: Postgraduate
Type: Award
Value: US$1,000
Frequency: Annual
No. of awards offered: 1
Application Procedure: A completed application form, available on the website, must be sent.
Closing Date: April 1st

The Nathan Reingold Prize

Subjects: History of science.
Purpose: To recognize an outstanding student essay in the history of science and its cultural influences.
Eligibility: Open to all original student essays that have not been published.
Level of Study: Postgraduate
Type: Prize
Value: US$500 and up to US$500 towards travel reimbursement
Frequency: Annual
No. of awards offered: 1
Application Procedure: A complete application form along with 3 copies of the essay and proof of student status must be submitted.
Closing Date: April 1st
Contributor: Friends and family of Nathan Reingold

Pfizer Award

Subjects: History of science.
Purpose: To honour outstanding books related to the history of science.
Eligibility: Open to authors books of that are published in the last 3 years.
Level of Study: Postgraduate
Type: Award
Value: US$2,500
Frequency: Annual
Application Procedure: A completed application form that is available on the website must be sent.
Closing Date: April 1st

Watson Davis and Helen Miles Davis Prize

Subjects: Writing.
Purpose: To promote a book that helps in public understanding of the history of science.
Eligibility: Open to authors of books published in the last 3 years.
Level of Study: Postgraduate
Type: Prize
Value: US$1,000
Frequency: Annual
Application Procedure: A completed application form that is available on the website must be submitted.
Closing Date: April 1st

HONDA FOUNDATION

6-20 Yaesu 2-chome, Chuo-ku, Tokyo, 104, Japan
Tel: (81) 3 3274 5125
Fax: (81) 3 3274 5103
Email: xv6m-nkmr@asahi-net.or.jp
Website: www.soc.nii.ac.jp/hf
Contact: Yutaka Ishihara, Secretary General

The Honda Foundation was established in December 1977 to contribute to the creation of true human civilization on the basis of the philosophy of the late Mr Soichiro Honda, the founder of Honda Motor Company Limited.

Honda Prize

Subjects: Eco-technology.
Purpose: To recognize a distinguished achievement in the field of ecótechnology.
Eligibility: Open to individuals or an organization, irrespective of nationality.
Type: Prize
Value: The prize includes a donation of Yen 10,000,000 and a medal
Frequency: Annual
Closing Date: March 31st
Funding: Private
Contributor: The late Mr Soichiro Honda, the founder of Honda Motor Company Limited
No. of awards given last year: 1
No. of applicants last year: 1
Additional Information: Eco-technology is the new concept that harmonizes the progress of technology and civilization, rather than pursuing technology designed solely for efficiency and profit.

THE HOROWITZ FOUNDATION FOR SOCIAL POLICY

Post Office Box 7, Rocky Hill, NJ, 08553-0007,
United States of America
Tel: (1) 609 921 1479
Fax: (1) 732 445 3138
Email: ihorowitz@transactionpub.com
Website: www.horowitz-foundation.org
Contact: Mr Irving Louis Horowitz, The Chairman

An independent foundation for the support and advancement of social science research in related to issues of social and economic policies in press related to issue of social and economic policies.

Eli Ginzberg Award

Subjects: Social sciences, including anthropology, area studies, economics, political science, psychology, sociology and urban studies as well as newer areas such as evaluation research.
Purpose: To support a project involving solutions to major urban health problems in urban settings.
Eligibility: Open to nationals of any country. Candidates may propose new projects, and they may also solicit support for research in progress, travel or preparing a work for publication.
Level of Study: Unrestricted
Type: Grant
Value: US$2,000–5,000 with an additional stipend
Length of Study: 1 year
Frequency: Annual
Country of Study: Any country
No. of awards offered: 1
Application Procedure: Application forms may be requested from the Horowitz Foundation or downloaded from the website. The application should be accompanied by a cover sheet listing the name of the applicant, the title of the project, a 50-word abstract stating what is to be done and why including methodology to be used and a 50-word summary of the policy implications of the research. The application must be signed.
Closing Date: December 31st in the preceding year
Funding: Private

Horowitz Foundation for Social Policy Grant

Subjects: Social sciences, including psychology, anthropology, sociology, economics, urban affairs, area studies, political sciences, communication studies, demography, criminology, health and welfare and other disciplines.
Purpose: To directly assist individual scholars who require small grants to further their research with emphasis on policy-orientated studies, and to support the advancement of research and understanding in major fields of social sciences.
Eligibility: Preference will be given to advanced graduate students and untenured assistant professors and instructors.
Level of Study: Graduate, professional development
Type: Grant
Value: US$3,000–5,000 per grant
Frequency: Annual
No. of awards offered: 10
Application Procedure: Completed applications (in English) should be sent to the Foundation's mailing address. Cover sheet must be filled carefully. Applications should include a curriculum vitae, project budget and letters of support. Email letters of support are not accepted. Applicants should not send originals. Applications can be sent via email, but a signed hard copy of the application must also be sent before the deadline.
Closing Date: January 31st
Funding: Foundation
Additional Information: The cover sheet in the application is the most important, as it is the basis for the initial screening of prospects.

John L Stanley Award

Subjects: Social sciences, including anthropology, area studies, economics, political science, psychology, sociology and urban studies as well as newer areas such as evaluation research.
Purpose: To support a work that seeks to expand our understanding of the political and ethical foundations of policy research.
Eligibility: Open to nationals of any country. Candidates may propose new projects and they may also solicit support for research in progress, including final work on a dissertation, supplementing research in progress, travel funds, preparing a work for publication.
Level of Study: Unrestricted, graduate
Type: Grant
Value: US$2,000–5,000 with additional stipend
Length of Study: 1 year
Frequency: Annual
Country of Study: Any country
No. of awards offered: 1
Application Procedure: Application forms may be requested from the Horowitz Foundation or downloaded from the website. The application should be accompanied by a cover sheet listing the name of the applicant, the title of the project, a 50-word abstract stating what is to be done and why including methodology to be used and a 50-word summary of the policy implications of the research. The application must be signed.
Closing Date: December 31st in the preceding year
Funding: Private
Additional Information: The cover sheet in the application is the most important, as it is the basis for the initial screening of prospects.

Joshua Feigenbaum Award

Subjects: Social sciences, including anthropology, area studies, economics, political science, psychology, sociology and urban studies as well as newer areas such as evaluation research.
Purpose: To support empirical research on policy aspects of the arts and popular culture, with special reference to mass communication.
Eligibility: Open to nationals of any country. Candidates may propose new projects, and they may also solicit support for research in progress, including final work on a dissertation, supplementing research in progress, travel funds, preparing a work for publication.
Level of Study: Unrestricted
Type: Grant
Value: US$2,000–5,000 with additional stipend
Length of Study: 1 year
Frequency: Annual
Country of Study: Any country
No. of awards offered: 1
Application Procedure: Applications forms may be requested from The Horowitz Foundation or downloaded from the website. The application should be accompanied by a cover sheet using the name of the applicant, the title of the project, a 50-word abstract stating what is to be done and why including methodology to be used and a 50-word

summary policy implication of the research. The application must be signed.
Closing Date: December 31st in the preceding year
Funding: Private
Additional Information: The cover sheet in the application is the most important, as it is the basis for the initial screening of prospects.

Robert K Merton Award

Subjects: Social sciences including anthropology, area studies, economics, political science, psychology, sociology and urban studies as well as newer areas such as evaluation research.
Purpose: To support studies in the relation between social theory and public policy.
Eligibility: Open to nationals of any country. Candidates may propose new projects, and they may also solicit support for research in progress, travel funds or preparing a work for publication.
Level of Study: Unrestricted
Type: Grant
Value: US$2,000–5,000 with additional stipend
Length of Study: 1 year
Frequency: Annual
Country of Study: Any country
No. of awards offered: 1
Application Procedure: Application forms may be requested from the Horowitz Foundation or downloaded from the website. The application should be accompanied by a cover sheet listing the name of the applicant, the title of the project, a 50-word abstract stating what is to be done and why including methodology to be used and a 50-word summary of the policy implications of the research. The application must be signed.
Closing Date: December 31st in the preceding year
Funding: Private
Additional Information: The cover sheet in the application is the most important, as it is the basis for the initial screening of prospects.

HORSERACE BETTING LEVY BOARD (HBLB)

52 Grosvenor Gardens, London, SW1W 0AU, England
Tel: (44) 20 7333 0043
Fax: (44) 20 7333 0041
Email: vet.grants@hblb.org.uk
Website: www.hblb.org.uk
Contact: Equine Grants Team

The Horserace Betting Levy Board (HBLB) operates in accordance with the Betting, Gaming and Lotteries Act 1963. It assesses and collects contributions from bookmakers and the Horserace Totalizator Board and uses these for the advancement of equine veterinary science and education and other improvements within the horseracing industry.

Horserace Betting Levy Board Senior Equine Clinical Scholarships

Subjects: Equine veterinary studies with emphasis on the thoroughbred.
Purpose: To support postgraduate veterinary clinical training.
Eligibility: Open to holders of degrees, registerable with the RCVS, in veterinary science or medicine who have had at least 2 years of practical experience following graduation and who wish to undertake specialized higher clinical training in the equine veterinary field.
Level of Study: Postgraduate
Type: Scholarship
Value: UK £17,660 stipend in year 1 with increments for years 2 and 3. The institution receives UK £8,510 to cover expenses directly relevant to the scholarship
Length of Study: Up to 3 years, subject to satisfactory progress
Frequency: Annual
Study Establishment: At any of the six veterinary schools, or at any appropriate university department or research institute or veterinary practice in the United Kingdom
Country of Study: United Kingdom
No. of awards offered: Up to 6
Application Procedure: The study establishment must submit applications on appropriate forms.
Closing Date: March 1st
Funding: Government
No. of awards given last year: 2
No. of applicants last year: Up to 10
Additional Information: Awards normally commence on October 1st. The study establishment is responsible for the appointment of clinical scholars.

Horserace Betting Levy Board Veterinary Research Training Scholarship

Subjects: Equine veterinary medicine or science, with emphasis on the thoroughbred.
Purpose: To support postgraduate equine veterinary research training.
Eligibility: Open to holders of a degree, registerable with the RCVS, in veterinary medicine or science, who wish to undertake full-time training in research in the equine veterinary field leading to a PhD.
Level of Study: Postgraduate
Type: Scholarship
Value: UK £16,190–17,660 stipend in year 1, depending on experience, with increments for years 2 and 3. UK £3,600 (accountable) per year for fees and expenses, and UK £4,810 (unaccountable) per year to the department in which the holder works. Scales are reviewed annually
Length of Study: Up to 3 years, subject to satisfactory progress
Frequency: Annual
Study Establishment: Any of the six veterinary schools or at any appropriate university department, research institute or veterinary practice in the United Kingdom
Country of Study: United Kingdom
No. of awards offered: Up to 6
Application Procedure: Applicants must submit applications on appropriate forms.
Closing Date: March 1st
Funding: Government
No. of awards given last year: 3
No. of applicants last year: Up to 10
Additional Information: Candidates must be nominated by a professor, lecturer, director or head of department of an eligible institution. Candidates will be interviewed by the Board's Veterinary Advisory Committee. Awards normally commence on October 1st.

HORTICULTURAL RESEARCH INSTITUTE

1000 Vermont Street North West, Suite 300, Washington, DC, 20005, United States of America
Tel: (1) 202 789 2900 ext. 3014
Fax: (1) 202 789 1893
Email: hriresearch@anla.org
Website: www.anla.org/research
Contact: Ms Teresa A Jodon, Endowment Program Administrator

The aim of the Horticultural Research Institute is to direct, fund, promote and communicate research that increases the quality and value of plants, improves the productivity and profitability of the nursery and landscape industry and protects and enhances the environment.

Horticultural Research Institute Grants

Subjects: Nursery and landscape industry, especially woody and perennial landscape plants, their production, marketing, landscape, water management or the environment.
Purpose: To support necessary research for the advancement of the nursery, greenhouse and landscape industry.
Eligibility: Open to nationals and permanent residents of the United States of America and Canada. Candidates must submit an appropriate project that the Institute feels is deserving of support.
Level of Study: Unrestricted
Type: Grant
Value: US$5,000–30,000
Length of Study: 1 year, occasionally renewable by reapplication

Frequency: Annual
Study Establishment: State or federal research laboratories, land grant universities, forest research stations, botanical gardens and arboreta
Country of Study: United States of America
No. of awards offered: 15–30
Application Procedure: Applicants must submit the application electronically.
Closing Date: May 15th
Funding: Private
Contributor: Nursery and landscape firms, as well as state and regional nursery and landscape associations
No. of awards given last year: 18
No. of applicants last year: 105
Additional Information: Applicants should visit the website to download an application form.

HOSPITAL FOR SICK CHILDREN RESEARCH TRAINING CENTRE (RESTRACOMP)

Hospital for Sick Children, 555 University Avenue, Toronto, ON, M5G 1X8, Canada
Tel: (1) 416 813 7781
Fax: (1) 416 813 8142
Email: nadia.ramsundar@sickkids.ca
Website: www.sickkids.on.ca
Contact: N. Ramsundar

RESTRACOMP Research Fellowship

Subjects: Paediatric research, biomedical research.
Purpose: To provide funds to postgraduate students or Fellows seeking research training.
Eligibility: Open to those nominated by the active senior staff of the Research Institute of the Hospital for Sick children. Postdoctoral trainees at the hospital for Sick Children, working under sick kids scientific staff.
Level of Study: Graduate, postdoctorate, postgraduate
Type: Fellowship
Value: Up to Canadian $31,750 per year
Length of Study: 2 years
Frequency: Biannual
Study Establishment: The Hospital for Sick Children, Toronto
Country of Study: Canada
No. of awards offered: 20–30 per annum
Application Procedure: Applicants must submit a completed application form.
Closing Date: Applications are accepted in mid-April and mid-October
Funding: Foundation
No. of applicants last year: 30% success rate

HOUBLON-NORMAN FUND

Bank of England, Threadneedle Street, London, EC2R 8AH, England
Tel: (44) 20 7601 5213
Fax: (44) 20 7601 4423
Email: laura.edmunds@bankofengland.co.uk
Website: www.bankofengland.co.uk/education/fellowships/index.htm
Contact: Miss Laura Edmunds, Business Support Unit

Houblon-Norman Fellowships/George Fellowships

Subjects: Economics and finance.
Purpose: To promote research into and disseminate knowledge and understanding of the working, interaction and function of financial and business institutions in the United Kingdom and elsewhere and the economic conditions affecting them.
Eligibility: Open to distinguished research workers as well as younger postdoctoral or equivalent applicants of any nationality. Preference will be given to the United Kingdom and European Union nationals.
Level of Study: Postdoctorate
Type: Fellowship
Value: The value of a fellowship is dependent on the candidate's circumstances and will be of such amount as seems necessary for undertaking the work. It might take the form of payment to the individual's employer
Length of Study: 1 month–1 year
Frequency: Annual
Study Establishment: The Bank of England
Country of Study: United Kingdom
No. of awards offered: Varies
Application Procedure: Applicants must complete an application form. Advertised through one economist, one Royal economic society and our website where an application form can be found www.bankofengland.co.uk/education/fellowships/index.htm
Closing Date: As advertised in the press
No. of awards given last year: 3
No. of applicants last year: 13

HUDSON RIVER FOUNDATION (HRF)

17 Battery Place, Suite 915, New York, NY 10004, United States of America
Tel: (1) 212 924 8290
Fax: (1) 212 924 8325
Email: info@hudsonriver.org
Website: www.hudsonriver.org
Contact: Grants Management Officer

The Hudson River Foundation (HRF) supports scientific research, education and projects to enhance public access to the Hudson River. The purpose of the Foundation is to make science integral to the decision-making process with regard to the Hudson River and its watershed and to support competent stewardship of this extraordinary resource.

HRF Graduate Fellowships

Subjects: The Hudson River system.
Purpose: To assist advanced graduate students in conducting research on the Hudson River system.
Eligibility: Applicants must be enrolled in an accredited programme, have a thesis advisor and advisory committee (if appropriate to the institution), and have a thesis research plan approved by the student's institution or department.
Level of Study: Doctorate, graduate
Type: Fellowship
Value: Please contact the organization
Frequency: Annual
No. of awards offered: Up to 6
Application Procedure: Applicants must obtain an HRF Call for proposals booklet, available on request or from the website. Applications must include an HRF proposal cover page, letter of interest, description of the project of up to ten pages, timetable, statement of the significance and relevance of the project to the HRF's objectives, an estimate of the cost of supplies and travel using the HRF's Proposal Budget Summary Page, and a letter from the university stating that the student will receive a tuition waiver or reimbursement for the period of the fellowship. Two letters of recommendation, sent under a separate cover, are also required, one of which must be from the student's advisor and should certify the student's current status, evaluate the student's capabilities, and rate the student's project on technical merit. The original and ten copies of the proposal must be submitted to the Science Director.
Additional Information: The award is conditional upon a full tuition waiver or reimbursement by the University.

Hudson River Expedition Grants

Subjects: Emergency situations such as unexpected natural or human-induced events, or research efforts for which additional funds are needed to enhance an existing research effort prior to the Foundation's next formal funding cycle.
Purpose: To facilitate the study of emergency situations affecting the Hudson River.
Level of Study: Postgraduate

Type: Grant
Value: Variable
Length of Study: Variable
Frequency: Dependent on need
Application Procedure: Proposals to include proposal cover page, abstract, description, list of personnel and reasons for expedited review. Please submit an original and ten copies to the Science Director, Dennis Suszkowski, at the main organization address.
Closing Date: None because of the nature of the award

Hudson River Graduate Fellowships

Subjects: Research on the resources, key species, toxic substances, abundances of key organisms, dynamics of Hudson River trophic webs, hydrodynamics, sediment transport, public policy and social science of the Hudson Bay River.
Purpose: To fund research fellowships to advanced graduate students conducting research on the Hudson River system.
Eligibility: Applicants must be in an accredited doctoral programme, and must have a thesis advisor and a research plan approved by the applicant's institution.
Level of Study: Doctorate, postgraduate
Type: Full-time research fellowship
Value: US$11,000 stipend plus US$1,000 expenses for Master's and US$15,000 stipend plus US$1,000 expenses for doctorate
Length of Study: 1 year
Frequency: Annual
Study Establishment: Any
Country of Study: Any country
No. of awards offered: Up to 6
Application Procedure: Applicants must supply a description, timetable, statement of significance and relevance, estimate of the cost, curriculum vitae and two letters of recommendation. The original and ten copies of the proposal must be forwarded to the Science Director at the main organization address.
Closing Date: April 14th

Hudson River Research Grants

Subjects: Research designed to compare and contrast the Hudson River with other estuarine ecosystems through literature review as well as laboratory or field experiments.
Purpose: To elucidate the dynamic interactions among the physical, chemical and biological processes that are important to the Hudson River ecosystem.
Eligibility: There are no eligibility restrictions.
Level of Study: Graduate
Type: Grant
Length of Study: Up to 2 years
Frequency: Annual
Study Establishment: The Foundation prefers, but does not require, that unaffiliated researchers seek some institutional affiliation for the purpose of conducting the proposed research
Country of Study: Any country
Application Procedure: Applicants must submit a preproposal consisting of a cover page, a project description of no more than three single-spaced pages and an estimated budget. 25 copies of the proposal to be submitted.
Closing Date: September 23rd
Additional Information: Hudson River Research Grants are made after a rigorous review process, including peer review.

Hudson River Travel Grants

Subjects: Research designed to compare and contrast the Hudson River with other estuarine ecosystems through literature review as well as laboratory or field experiments.
Purpose: Travel Grants are available for travel related to the research goals of the Hudson River Fund.
Level of Study: Postgraduate
Type: Grant
Value: As appropriate, with budget and references
Length of Study: Variable
Frequency: As needed
Application Procedure: Applicants must send an original plus ten copies to the Science Director, Dennis Suszkowski, (1) 212-924-8290, at the main organization address.
Closing Date: Any time of year, but as far in advance of anticipated need as possible

Tibor T Polgar Fellowship

Subjects: All aspects of the environment of the Hudson River, from Troy, New York, to the New York Harbor and Bight. Previous projects have studied hydrodynamics, larval fish, zooplankton, terrapins, landscape ecology, nutrients and public policy.
Purpose: To fund Summer research on the Hudson River.
Eligibility: There are no eligibility restrictions.
Level of Study: Graduate
Type: Fellowship
Value: US$3,800 and limited research funds
Length of Study: From May–June to August–September
Frequency: Annual
Country of Study: United States of America
No. of awards offered: 8 every Summer
Application Procedure: Applicants must submit the original and five copies of their application, which must include letters of interest from the student and of support from the sponsor, a short description of the research project including its significance of between four and six pages, a detailed timetable for the completion of the project, a detailed budget with estimated cost of supplies, travel and other expenses, and the student's curriculum vitae. Because of the training and educational aspects of this programme, each potential fellow must be sponsored by a primary advisor. The advisor must be willing to commit sufficient time for supervision of the research and to attend at least one meeting to review the progress of the research. Advisors will receive a stipend of US$500.
Closing Date: February 28th in each year
Funding: Private
Additional Information: The objectives of the programme are to gather important information on all aspects of the river and to train students in conducting estuarine studies and public policy research. Polgar Fellowships may be awarded for studies anywhere within the tidal Hudson estuary from the Federal Dam at Troy, to the New York Harbor.

HUMANE RESEARCH TRUST

The Humane Research Trust, Brook House, 29 Bramhall Lane South, Bramhall, Stockport, Cheshire, SK7 2DN, England
Tel: (44) 161 439 8041
Fax: (44) 161 439 3713
Email: info@humaneresearch.org.uk
Website: www.humaneresearch.org.uk
Contact: Jane McAllister, Trust Administrator

The Humane Research Trust is a national charity, which funds a range of unique medical research programmes into human illness at hospitals and universities around the country. In keeping with the philosophy of the Trust, none of the research involves animals and much of it seeks to establish and develop pioneering techniques that will replace animal intensive experiments.

Humane Research Trust Grant

Subjects: Humane research.
Purpose: To encourage scientific programmes where the use of animals is replaced by other methods.
Eligibility: Open to established scientific workers engaged in productive research. Nationals of any country are considered but for the sake of overseeing, projects should be undertaken in a United Kingdom establishment.
Level of Study: Unrestricted
Type: Grant
Value: Varies
Length of Study: Varies
Frequency: Dependent on funds available
Study Establishment: Various
Country of Study: United Kingdom

No. of awards offered: Varies
Application Procedure: Applicants must complete an application form, available on request.
Closing Date: Varies
Funding: Private
Contributor: Supporters and legacies
No. of awards given last year: 8
No. of applicants last year: 27
Additional Information: The Trust is a registered charity and donations are encouraged.

HUMANITARIAN TRUST

27 St James Place, London, SW1A 1NR, England
Contact: Mrs M Myers, Secretary of Trustees

The Humanitarian Trust was set up to support general charitable purposes.

Humanitarian Trust Awards

Subjects: All academic subjects, but not journalism, theatre, music or any arts subjects, nursing, medical auxiliaries, midwifery, radiology, treatment techniques or medical technology.
Eligibility: Open to applicants already holding an original grant who can show evidence of an approx. UK £200 shortfall. Candidates are only considered when studying academic subjects and the awards cannot be used for travel, overseas courses and fieldwork.
Level of Study: Postgraduate, graduate
Type: Award
Value: UK £200 (Top-up on fees)
Length of Study: 1 year, non-renewable
Frequency: Annual
Study Establishment: Any approved institution
Country of Study: United Kingdom
No. of awards offered: Approx. 15
Application Procedure: Applicants must write in and submit two references preferably from tutors or heads of department, a breakdown of anticipated income and expenditure and a curriculum vitae.
Funding: Private
No. of awards given last year: 6
No. of applicants last year: 100

HUMANITIES RESEARCH CENTRE (HRC)

Australian National University (ANU), Canberra, ACT, 0200, Australia
Tel: (61) 2 6125 2700
Fax: (61) 2 6248 0054
Email: administration.hrc@anu.edu.au
Website: www.anu.edu.au/hrc
Contact: Ms Judy Buchanan, Administrator

The Humanities Research Centre (HRC) was established in 1972, specifically to stimulate humanities research and debate at the Australian National University (ANU), within Australia and beyond.

HRC Visiting Fellowships

Subjects: Humanities. The HRC interprets this generously, recognizing that new methods of theoretical enquiry have done much to break down the traditional distinction between the humanities and the social sciences, recognizing too, the importance of establishing dialogue between the humanities and the natural and technological sciences and the creative arts.
Purpose: To provide scholars with time to pursue their own work in congenial and stimulating surroundings.
Eligibility: Open to candidates of any nationality who are at the postdoctoral level.
Level of Study: Postdoctorate
Type: Fellowship
Value: Return economy airfare up to Australian $2,700, plus accommodation
Length of Study: 12 weeks
Frequency: Annual
Study Establishment: The Humanities Research Centre at the Australian National University
Country of Study: Australia
No. of awards offered: Up to 20
Application Procedure: Applicants must complete a formal application, available from the website.
Closing Date: End of November
Funding: Government
No. of awards given last year: 20
Additional Information: Fellows are required to spend all of their time in residence at the Centre, but are encouraged to visit other institutions. Please refer to the website for further information.

THE HUNTINGTON

1151 Oxford Road, San Marino, CA, 91108, United States of America
Tel: (1) 626 405 2194
Fax: (1) 626 449 5703
Email: cpowell@huntington.org
Website: www.huntington.org
Contact: Ms Carolyn Powell, Committee on Awards

The Huntington is an independent research center with holdings in British and American history, literature, art history and the history of science and medicine.

Barbara Thom Postdoctoral Fellowship

Subjects: British and American history, literature, art history, and history of science.
Purpose: To support a non-tenured faculty member while they are revising a manuscript for publication.
Eligibility: Preference will be given to scholars who are 4 or 5 years beyond the award of PhD.
Level of Study: Postdoctorate
Type: Fellowship
Value: US$40,000
Length of Study: 1 year
Frequency: Annual
Study Establishment: The Huntington
Country of Study: United States of America
No. of awards offered: 2
Application Procedure: Applicants must contact the Chair of the Committee on Awards.
Closing Date: Applications are accepted between October 1st and December 15th
Funding: Private
No. of awards given last year: 2
No. of applicants last year: 19

Huntington Short-Term Fellowships

Subjects: British and American history, literature, art history, and history of science.
Purpose: To enable outstanding scholars to carry out significant research in the collections of the Library and Art Gallery, by assisting in balancing the budgets of such persons, on leave at reduced pay and living away from home.
Eligibility: Open to nationals of any country who have demonstrated, to a degree commensurate with their age and experience, unusual abilities as scholars through publications of a high order of merit. Attention is paid to the value of the candidate's project and the degree to which the special strengths of the Library and Art Gallery will be used.
Level of Study: Postdoctorate, postgraduate
Type: Fellowship
Value: US$2,000 per month
Length of Study: 1–5 months
Frequency: Annual
Study Establishment: The Huntington
Country of Study: United States of America
No. of awards offered: Approx. 100, depending on funds available
Application Procedure: Applicants must contact the Chair of the Committee on Awards.
Closing Date: Applications are accepted between October 1st and December 15th

Funding: Private
No. of awards given last year: 122
No. of applicants last year: 358
Additional Information: Fellowships are available for work towards doctoral dissertations.

Mellon Postdoctoral Research Fellowships

Subjects: British and American history, literature, art history, and history of science.
Purpose: To support scholarship study in a field appropriate to the Huntington's collections.
Eligibility: Preference will be given to scholars who have not held a major award in the 3 years preceding the year of this award.
Level of Study: Postdoctorate
Type: Fellowship
Value: US$40,000
Length of Study: 1 year
Frequency: Annual
Study Establishment: The Huntington
Country of Study: United States of America
No. of awards offered: 2
Application Procedure: Applicants must contact the Committee on Fellowships.
Closing Date: Applications are accepted between October 1st and December 15th
Funding: Private
No. of awards given last year: 2
No. of applicants last year: 50

National Endowment for the Humanities Fellowships

Subjects: British and American history, literature, art history, and history of science.
Purpose: To support scholarship in a field appropriate to the Huntington's collections.
Eligibility: Preference will be given to scholars who have not held a major award in the 3 years preceding the year of this award.
Level of Study: Postdoctorate
Type: Fellowship
Value: Up to US$40,000
Length of Study: 4 months–1 year
Frequency: Annual
Study Establishment: The Huntington
Country of Study: United States of America
No. of awards offered: 3
Application Procedure: Applicants must contact the Chair of the Committee on Awards.
Closing Date: Applications are accepted between October 1st and December 15th
Funding: Government
No. of awards given last year: 3
No. of applicants last year: 39

W M Keck Foundation Fellowship for Young Scholars

Subjects: British and American history, literature, art history, and history of science.
Purpose: To encourage outstanding young scholars to pursue their own lines of enquiry, complete dissertation research or begin a new project in the fields of British and American history, literature, art history or the history of science.
Eligibility: There are no restrictions on age, nationality or citizenship.
Level of Study: Postdoctorate, postgraduate
Type: Fellowship
Value: US$2,300 per month
Length of Study: 1–3 months
Frequency: Annual
Study Establishment: The Huntington
Country of Study: United States of America
No. of awards offered: Varies
Application Procedure: Applicants must contact the Chair of the Committee on Awards.
Closing Date: Applications are accepted between October 1st and December 15th
Funding: Private
No. of awards given last year: 15

HUNTINGTON'S DISEASE ASSOCIATION

108 Battersea High Street, London, SW11 3HP, England
Tel: (44) 20 7223 7000
Fax: (44) 20 7223 9489
Email: info@hda.org.uk
Website: www.hda.org.uk
Contact: Ms Eileen Cook, The Administrator

HDA Research Project Grants

Subjects: Furthering the understanding of Huntington's Disease, improving its treatment or otherwise improving the quality of life for patients and their carers.
Purpose: To support research projects on Huntington's Disease in a direct way. Preference given to small 'pump priming grants' likely to lead to support from a major funding body.
Eligibility: Open to suitably qualified researchers of any nationality.
Level of Study: Research, postgraduate
Value: Up to UK £25,000
Length of Study: 1–3 years
Frequency: Annual
Study Establishment: A suitable United Kingdom institution
Country of Study: United Kingdom
Application Procedure: Applicants should apply to the main organization.
Closing Date: March 1st
Funding: Private

HDA Studentship

Subjects: Furthering understanding into Huntington's Disease, improving its treatment or otherwise improving the quality of life for patients and their carers.
Purpose: To support a postgraduate student undertaking research into Huntington's Disease.
Level of Study: Postgraduate
Type: Studentship
Value: Payment of registration fees, UK £8,000 maintenance grant, contribution of UK £4,000 towards the running costs up to a maximum of UK £4,000 per year
Length of Study: Up to 3 years
Frequency: Annual
Study Establishment: A suitable United Kingdom academic institution
Country of Study: United Kingdom
Application Procedure: Applicants should apply to the main organization.
Closing Date: March 1st

THE HURSTON-WRIGHT FOUNDATION

6525 Belcrest Road, Suite 531, Hyattsville, MD, 20782, United States of America
Tel: (1) 301 683-2134
Email: info@hurston-wright.org
Website: www.hurston-wright.org

The Foundation was established in September 1990 by novelist Marita Golden. Our mission is to develop, nurture and sustain the world community of writers of African descent.

The Hurston-Wright Award for College Writers

Subjects: Fiction or nonfiction writing in any genre.
Purpose: To support students of African descent enrolled full time as undergraduate or graduate students in any college or university in the United States of America.
Eligibility: Students of African descent from any area of the diaspora.
Level of Study: Graduate, postgraduate
Type: Scholarship
Value: US$1,000 or US$500
Length of Study: Varies

Frequency: Annual
Study Establishment: Any suitable college or university
Country of Study: United States of America
No. of awards offered: 3
Application Procedure: Applicants must submit an application form to the main organization. Please check the website for details.
Closing Date: December 31st
Funding: Private
No. of awards given last year: 3

Hurston-Wright Legacy Award

Subjects: Works by published writers of African descent from any area of the diaspora.
Purpose: To support published writers of African descent in furthering their art.
Eligibility: Writers of African descent from any area of the diaspora.
Level of Study: Unrestricted, professional development
Type: Scholarship
Value: US$10,000 or US$5,000
Length of Study: Varies
Frequency: Annual
No. of awards offered: 9
Application Procedure: Book must be submitted by the publisher with permission of the writer.
Closing Date: December 8th
Funding: Private
No. of awards given last year: 9

The Hurston-Wright Writer's Week Scholarships

Subjects: Fiction or nonfiction writing in any genre.
Purpose: To support promising writers attending Writer's Week.
Eligibility: Students of African descent from any area of the diaspora.
Level of Study: Professional development
Type: Scholarship
Value: Up to US$1,100
Length of Study: Duration of workshop
Frequency: Annual
Study Establishment: Howard University, Washington, DC
Country of Study: United States of America
No. of awards offered: Variable
Application Procedure: Applicants must write a brief letter of no more than two paragraphs stating their financial situation and the amount of assistance they are requesting.
Closing Date: June 11th
Funding: Private

THE HYPERTENSION TRUST

113-119 High Street, Hampton Hill, Middlesex, TW12 INJ, England
Tel: (44) 20 8979 8300
Fax: (44) 20 8979 6700
Email: gmccarthy@hamptonmedical.com
Website: www.hypertensiontrust.org
Contact: Mrs G McCarthy, Administrator

The Hypertension Trust is a registered charity established to support research in hypertension and related cardiovascular conditions. Funds are available to support annual awards for Research Fellowships and Research Studentships.

Hypertension Trust Fellowship

Subjects: Hypertension and related cardiovascular conditions.
Purpose: To support research into hypertension and related cardiovascular conditions.
Eligibility: Applicants must hold a medical degree or higher degree in science, eg. doctorate, and provide evidence of research aptitude or clinical experience in hypertension. The fellowship is open to United Kingdom citizens or European Union nationals working in the United Kingdom.
Level of Study: Postgraduate, graduate
Type: Fellowship
Value: A salary of approx. UK £20,000–30,000 per year. Up to UK £5,000 per year in expenses is available
Length of Study: 2 years
Frequency: Annual
Country of Study: United Kingdom
No. of awards offered: 1
Application Procedure: Applicants must complete an application form.
Closing Date: March 3rd
Contributor: Surplus funds following the 16th Scientific Meeting of the International Society of Hypertension in June 1996
No. of awards given last year: 2
No. of applicants last year: 13
Additional Information: Applicants should visit the website for additional information.

Hypertension Trust Studentship

Subjects: Hypertension and related cardiovascular conditions.
Purpose: To support research into hypertension and related cardiovascular conditions.
Eligibility: Open to graduates of a European Union university or those currently working in a United Kingdom or Republic of Ireland hospital or institution.
Level of Study: Graduate, postgraduate
Type: Studentship
Value: A salary based on MRC rates and PhD fees and up to UK £5,000 in expenses
Length of Study: 3 years
Frequency: Annual
No. of awards offered: 1
Application Procedure: Applicants must complete an application form.
Closing Date: March 3rd
Contributor: Surplus funds following the 16th Scientific Meeting of the International Society of Hypertension in June 1996
No. of awards given last year: 1
No. of applicants last year: 3
Additional Information: Applicants should visit the website for additional information.

IAN KARTEN CHARITABLE TRUST

The Mill House, Newark Lane, Ripley, Surrey, GU23 6DP, England
Fax: (44) 14 8322 2420
Email: iankarten@aol.com
Contact: Mr Tim Simon, Trustee & Administrator

The Ian Karten Charitable Trust aims to improve the quality of life and independence of people with severe physical, sensory, cognitive or learning disabilities by providing for them centres for computer-aided training, education and communications (CTEC centres). It also aims to support higher education by funding lectureships and studentships for postgraduate studies and research at universities in the United Kingdom.

Ian Karten Scholarship

Subjects: Most subjects, with varying levels of priority.
Purpose: To assist eligible students with the costs of postgraduate programmes of research at selected universities in the United Kingdom.
Eligibility: The scholarships will be available on a competitive basis for postgraduate students taking selected courses leading to Master's degrees or PhDs.
Level of Study: Doctorate, postgraduate
Type: Scholarship
Value: Varies
Frequency: Annual
Study Establishment: Selected Universities
Country of Study: United Kingdom
No. of awards offered: 100
Application Procedure: Applicants must address enquiries about the availability of Ian Karten Scholarships and about the procedure for applying to the institution concerned.
Closing Date: May 31st
Funding: Private

Contributor: Ian H Karten
No. of awards given last year: 160
No. of applicants last year: 500

ICELANDIC MINISTRY OF EDUCATION

University of Iceland, Sundurgata 1, 101 Reykjavik, Iceland
Tel: (354) 354 525 4000
Fax: (354) 354 552 1331
Email: hi@hi.is
Website: www.hi.is

The University of Iceland is a state university, founded in 1911. During its first year of operation 45 students were enrolled. Today, the university serves a nation of approximately 283,000 people and provides instruction for some 8,000 students studying in eleven faculties.

Icelandic Studies Scholarships

Subjects: Icelandic language, literature and history.
Eligibility: See website.
Type: Scholarship
Value: A monthly stipend of IKR 69,000 and all registration fees
Length of Study: 8 months
Frequency: Annual
Study Establishment: The University of Iceland
Country of Study: Iceland
No. of awards offered: 28
Closing Date: April 1st
Funding: Government
Contributor: Icelandic Ministry of Education, Science and Culture
Additional Information: No one will be granted a scholarship more than 3 times.

IEDC BLED SCHOOL OF MANAGEMENT

Pre cesta 33, 4260 Bled, Slovenia
Tel: (386) 386 457 92500
Fax: (386) 386 457 92501
Email: info@iedc.si
Website: www.iedc.si

The school is a center of excellence in management development and a business meeting point, where leaders and potential leaders come to learn and reflect. We offer a unique environment for developing leadership and management potential of international business executives at every stage of their careers.

IEDC MBA Scholarship

Subjects: Business management.
Purpose: To finance an MBA programme for outstanding candidates from Moldova and Ukraine.
Eligibility: Only outstanding candidates from Moldova and Ukraine will be considered.
Level of Study: Professional development
Value: All tuition fees
Length of Study: 1 year
Frequency: Annual
Study Establishment: IEDC
No. of awards offered: Varies
Application Procedure: See website.
Closing Date: October 30th

For further information contact:

Tel: 386 457 92506
Email: emba@iedc.si

TRIMO MBA Scholarship

Subjects: International business.
Purpose: To finance an outstanding candidate from Serbia.
Eligibility: The candidate must be from Serbia.
Level of Study: Professional development
Type: Scholarship
Value: All tuition fees and agreed costs
Length of Study: 1 year
Frequency: Annual
Study Establishment: IEDC
No. of awards offered: 1
Application Procedure: See website.
Closing Date: December 1st
Funding: Corporation
Contributor: Trimo d.d. Slovenia
Additional Information: The successful candidate will be offered a position at Trimo In ženjering d.o.o Serbia.

For further information contact:

Tel: 386 457 92506
Email: emba@iedc.si

IEEE (INSTITUTE OF ELECTRICAL AND ELECTRONICS ENGINEERS, INC.) HISTORY CENTER

39 Union Street, New Brunswick, NJ, 08901, United States of America
Tel: (1) 732 932 1066
Fax: (1) 732 932 1193
Email: history@ieee.org
Website: www.ieee.org/history_center
Contact: Mr Robert Colburn, Research Co-ordinator

The mission of the IEEE History Center is to preserve, research and promote the history of information and electrical technologies.

IEEE Fellowship in Electrical History

Subjects: The history of electrical engineering and computer technology.
Purpose: To support graduate work in the history of electrical engineering.
Eligibility: Open to suitably qualified graduate students.
Level of Study: Postdoctorate, postgraduate, doctorate
Type: Fellowship
Value: US$17,000 plus US$3,000 research budget
Length of Study: 1 year
Frequency: Annual
Study Establishment: A college or university of recognized standing
Country of Study: Any country
No. of awards offered: 1
Application Procedure: Applicants must submit a completed application, transcripts, three letters of recommendation and a research proposal. Application material may be downloaded from www.ieee.org/history_center/fellowship.html
Closing Date: February 1st
Funding: Corporation
Additional Information: The fellowship is made possible by a grant from the IEEE Life Member Fund and is awarded by the IEEE History Committee. Application materials become available in October.

IESE BUSINESS SCHOOL

21 08034 Barcelona, Spain
Tel: (34) 34 93 253 4229
Fax: (34) 34 93 253 4343
Website: www.iese.edu
Contact: Avenida Peason

Created in 1964 the school prepares students to lead in today's global business environment. Becoming part of a close-knit community, students gain the necessary skills to make informed and ethical business decisions to later affect positive change in the corporate world and society as a whole.

The Cámara de Comercio Scholarship
Subjects: Business management.
Eligibility: Preference is given to students from developing countries.
Level of Study: MBA
Type: Scholarship
Value: All tuition fees
Length of Study: 1 year
Frequency: Annual
Study Establishment: IESE
Country of Study: Spain
No. of awards offered: 2
Application Procedure: See website.
Closing Date: April 26th
Funding: Corporation
Contributor: Cámara de Comercio, Industria, Navegació de Barcelona

Ficosa International Scholarship
Subjects: Business management.
Eligibility: Preference is given to students from Central or Eastern Europe.
Level of Study: MBA
Type: Scholarship
Value: All agreed costs
Length of Study: 1 year
Frequency: Annual
Study Establishment: IESE
Country of Study: Spain
No. of awards offered: 1
Application Procedure: See website.
Closing Date: April 26th
Funding: Corporation
Contributor: Ficosa International

Fundación Ramón Areces Scholarship
Subjects: Business management.
Eligibility: Open to applicants of Spanish nationality only.
Level of Study: MBA
Type: Scholarship
Value: All tuition fees
Length of Study: 1 year
Frequency: Annual
Study Establishment: IESE
Country of Study: Spain
Application Procedure: See website.
Closing Date: April 26th
Funding: Foundation
Contributor: Fudación Ramón Arces

IESE AECI/Becas MAE
Subjects: Business management.
Eligibility: Preference is given to candidates from nations designated as priority countries by the plan Director de la Cooperación Espaola.
Level of Study: Professional development
Type: Scholarship
Value: All living expenses
Length of Study: 1 year
Frequency: Annual
Study Establishment: IESE
Country of Study: Spain
No. of awards offered: Varies
Application Procedure: See website.
Funding: Government
Contributor: The Spanish Ministry of Foreign Affairs

For further information contact:

Website: www.becasmal.es

IESE Alumini Association Scholarships
Subjects: Business management.
Purpose: To reward candidates who have demonstrated excellent work experience and personal merit.
Eligibility: See website for conditions.
Level of Study: MBA
Type: Scholarship
Value: 50% of tuition fees
Length of Study: 1 year
Frequency: Annual
Study Establishment: IESE
Country of Study: Spain
No. of awards offered: 4
Application Procedure: Contact Admission's office.
Closing Date: June 28th

For further information contact:

MBA Admissions Department, Avda. Pearson 21, Barcelona, 08034, Spain

IESE Donovan Data Systems Anniversary
Subjects: Business management.
Purpose: To commemorate 30 years of DDS partnership with the advertising industry.
Eligibility: Preference is given to students interested in pursuing a career in advertising, marketing or communications.
Level of Study: Professional development
Type: Scholarship
Value: All agreed costs
Length of Study: 1 year
Frequency: Annual
No. of awards offered: 1
Application Procedure: See website.
Funding: Corporation
Contributor: Donovan Data Systems
Additional Information: The scholarship alternates each year between a European studying in North American and a North American Studying in Europe.

For further information contact:

Website: www.donovanadata.com

IESE Private Foundation Scholarships
Subjects: Business management.
Eligibility: Priority is given to students from developing countries.
Level of Study: MBA
Type: Scholarship
Value: All agreed costs
Length of Study: 1 year
Frequency: Annual
Study Establishment: IESE
Country of Study: Spain
No. of awards offered: 4
Application Procedure: See website.
Closing Date: April 26th
Funding: Private

IESE Trust Scholarships
Subjects: Business management.
Eligibility: See website for conditions.
Level of Study: Professional development
Type: Scholarship
Value: All tuition fees
Length of Study: 1 year
Frequency: Annual
Study Establishment: IESE
Country of Study: Spain
No. of awards offered: Varies
Application Procedure: Contact Admissions Office.
Closing Date: June 28th
Funding: Trusts

For further information contact:

MBA Admissions Department, Avda. Pearson, 21, Barcelona, 08034, Spain

ILLINOIS TEACHERS ESOL & BILINGUAL EDUCATION ITBE

PMB 232 8926 N. Greenwood, Niles, IL 60714-5163, United States of America
Tel: (1) 409 4770
Email: awards@itbe.org
Website: www.itbe.org

The ITBE is a non-profit organization of individuals involved in professional development legislation, government issues and specialist interest groups for the teaching of English to speakers of other languages and bilingual education.

ITBE Graduate Scholarship

Subjects: Bilingual education.
Level of Study: Postgraduate
Type: Scholarship
Value: US$1,000
Length of Study: 1 year
Frequency: Annual
Application Procedure: Submit application form and follow further instructions on the website.
Closing Date: December 1st

For further information contact:

Illinois TESOL-BE Awards Chair c/o Adult Learning Resource Center 1855 Mt. Prospect Road, DES PLAINES, IL 60018

INDIAN EDUCATION DEPARTMENT

Government of India, Ministry of Human Resource Department, Shastri Bhavan, New Delhi, 110001, India
Tel: (91) 91 11 23382947
Fax: (91) 91 11 23381355
Email: webmaster.edu@nic.in
Website: www.education.nic.in

The origin of the Indian Education Department, Government of India, dates back to pre-independence days when for the first time a separate Department was created in 1910 to look after education. However, soon after India achieved its independence, a full fledged ministry of Education was established.

Government of India SC/ST Scholarship

Subjects: Any subject.
Purpose: To provide financial assistance to students.
Eligibility: Open to candidates belonging to the SC/ST communities.
Level of Study: Postdoctorate
Type: Scholarship
Length of Study: 2 years
Frequency: Annual
Country of Study: India
Application Procedure: A written application to be submitted for approval of the university Authorities.
Funding: Government
Contributor: The Governments of Tamil Nadu, Kerala, Andhra, Karnataka, Maharastra and the Union Territory Pondichery

Indian Institute of Geomagnetism Research Scholarship

Subjects: Geomagnetism.
Purpose: To offer scholarships for a doctoral programme in Geomagnetism.
Eligibility: Open to any student holding postgraduate degree in physics, applied physics, geophysics or applied mathematics.
Level of Study: Research, doctorate
Type: Scholarship
Value: Rs 8,000/- per month (first and second years), Rs 9,000/- per month (subsequent years). A book grant of Rs 6,000/- per annum is available for PhD students
Frequency: Annual
Study Establishment: Indian Institute of Geomagnetism
Country of Study: India
Application Procedure: Applicants must submit a written application.
Funding: Government
Contributor: Department of Science and Technology

For further information contact:

The Department of Science and Technology, Govt. of India, Plot No. 5, Sector-18, Kalamboli Highway, New Panvel, Navi Mumbai, 410218, India

National Board for Higher Mathematics Scholarship

Subjects: Mathematics.
Purpose: To find students pursuing further study in mathematics.
Eligibility: Open to students with a good academic record, below the age of 22 years as on January 1, may apply.
Level of Study: Postgraduate
Type: Scholarship
Value: Rs 1,200/- per month
Length of Study: 2 years
Frequency: Annual
Study Establishment: National Board for Higher Mathematics
Country of Study: India
Application Procedure: Applicants must submit a written application for approval.
Closing Date: August 16th
Funding: Government
Contributor: Department of Atomic Energy

For further information contact:

The Department of Atomic Energy, Govt. of India, Anushakti Bhavan, C.S.M. Marg, Mumbai, 400 001, India

INSEAD

Boulevard de Constance, F-77305 Fontainebleau Cedex, France
Tel: (33) 1 60 72 43 92
Fax: (33) 1 60 74 55 35
Email: mba.info@insead.fr
Website: www.insead.edu/mba
Contact: Ms Helen Henderson, Director, Financial Aid

INSEAD is widely recognized as one of the most influential business schools in the world. With its second campus in Asia to complement its established presence in Europe, INSEAD is setting the pace in globalizing the MBA. The 1-year intensive MBA programme is focused on international general management.

INSEAD Alumni Fund (IAF) Scholarship for the Asian Campus

Subjects: MBA.
Eligibility: Open to candidates admitted to and starting their course at INSEAD's Asian campus.
Level of Study: MBA
Type: Scholarship
Value: Varies
Frequency: Annual
Study Establishment: INSEAD
Country of Study: Singapore
No. of awards offered: 3
Application Procedure: Applicants must complete a specific assignment, details of which are available from the organization or from the website.
Closing Date: May 5th for the September intake of the same year and September 30th for the January intake of the following year
Contributor: Alumni and a gift from a private individual

INSEAD Alumni Fund (IAF) Scholarships

Subjects: MBA.
Purpose: To assist candidates admitted to the MBA programme.
Eligibility: Open to applicants from emerging or developing countries.
Level of Study: MBA
Type: Scholarship
Value: From €3,000–10,000
Frequency: Annual
Study Establishment: INSEAD
No. of awards offered: Varies
Application Procedure: Applicants must complete a specific assignment, details of which are available from the website.
Closing Date: May 5th for the September intake of the same year and September 30th for the January intake of the following year
Contributor: Alumni

INSEAD Antoine Rachid Irani/Bissada Scholarship

Subjects: MBA.
Purpose: To financially support MBA candidates.
Eligibility: Open to candidates of Lebanese or Egyptian nationality who are fluent in Arabic, preferably have a minimum of 3 years in a Lebanese university, who have obtained excellent academic and professional results and have been admitted to the INSEAD MBA programme.
Level of Study: MBA
Type: Scholarship
Value: Full tuition fees, but in order to lengthen the period of the scholarship, winners must pledge to repay 10 per cent of the value of the scholarship 2 years after graduating from INSEAD and an additional 10 per cent 3 years after graduating
Frequency: Annual
Study Establishment: INSEAD
No. of awards offered: 1
Application Procedure: Applicants must complete a specific assignment, details of which are available from the organization or from the website.
Closing Date: May 5th for the September class of the same year and September 30th for the January class of the following year
Contributor: Bissada Management

INSEAD Belgian Alumni and Council Scholarship Fund

Subjects: MBA.
Purpose: To assist MBA participants.
Eligibility: Open to candidates of merit of Belgian nationality and those who have lived in Belgium for at least 5 years. Priority will be given to admitted applicants who intend to return to Belgium after their MBA.
Level of Study: MBA
Type: Scholarship
Value: €6,400
Frequency: Annual
Study Establishment: INSEAD
No. of awards offered: 2
Application Procedure: Applicants must complete a specific assignment, details of which are available from the organization or from the website.
Closing Date: May 5th for the September class of the same year and September 30th for the January class of the following year
Contributor: Alumni and the Belgian Council

INSEAD Børsen/Danish Council Scholarship

Subjects: MBA.
Purpose: To assist MBA participants.
Eligibility: Open to candidates of Danish nationality, admitted to the INSEAD MBA programme.
Level of Study: MBA
Type: Scholarship
Value: Please contact the organization
Frequency: Annual
Study Establishment: INSEAD
Country of Study: Other
No. of awards offered: 2
Application Procedure: Applicants must complete an application form, available from the website.
Closing Date: May 15th for the September class of the same year and September 15th for the January class of the following year
Contributor: The Danish Council/Børsen

INSEAD Canadian Foundation Scholarship

Subjects: MBA.
Purpose: To provide financial assistance and scholarships to deserving Canadians admitted to the INSEAD MBA programme.
Eligibility: Open to candidates of Canadian nationality, preferably resident in Canada, who have been admitted to the INSEAD MBA programme and who intend to return to Canada.
Level of Study: MBA
Type: Scholarship
Value: Up to Canadian $10,000
Frequency: Annual
Study Establishment: INSEAD
No. of awards offered: Varies
Application Procedure: Applicants must submit the following in support of their application: a covering letter requesting a scholarship specifying which campus the applicant is applying to, a budget detailing the need for financial assistance including current and expected sources of funding, a copy of a completed INSEAD admission form with essay and supporting documents, a copy of reference letters submitted in support of application to INSEAD, a copy of Graduate Management Admissions Test results, a copy of university transcripts and a copy of confirmation of admission to INSEAD.
Closing Date: June 30th for candidates admitted to the September intake of the same year and October 31st for candidates admitted to the January class of the following year
Contributor: Alumni
Additional Information: The Canadian INSEAD Foundation is a non-profit corporation whose purpose is to encourage Canadian students to develop an international business understanding and perspective.

For further information contact:

The Board of Trustees, Canadian INSEAD Foundation, c/o Richard Tarte, Société générale de financement du Québec, 600 de La Gauchetière Street, West Suite 1700, Montréal, QC, H3B 4L8, Canada
Tel: (1) 514 876 9290 ext 2171

INSEAD Eli Lilly and Company Innovation Scholarship

Subjects: MBA.
Eligibility: Open to students of merit who demonstrate the capacity for innovative thinking and actions. Nationals from Africa, Asia, Central and Eastern Europe, Middle East, Central and South America, Turkey and Canada may apply.
Level of Study: MBA
Type: Scholarship
Value: Partial tuition
Frequency: Annual
Study Establishment: INSEAD
No. of awards offered: 2 per class
Application Procedure: Applicants must complete a specific assignment, details of which are available from the organization or from the website.
Closing Date: May 5th for the September intake of the same year and September 30th for the January intake of the following year
Contributor: Eli Lilly Foundation
Additional Information: Eli Lilly creates and delivers innovative pharmaceutical-based healthcare solutions that enable people worldwide to live longer, healthier and more active lives.

INSEAD Elmar Schulte Diversity Scholarship

Subjects: MBA.
Purpose: To encourage diversity in the INSEAD MBA programme.
Eligibility: Open to candidates from non-traditional MBA backgrounds who have been admitted to the programme.
Level of Study: MBA
Type: Scholarship
Value: Varies

Frequency: Annual
Study Establishment: INSEAD
No. of awards offered: Varies
Application Procedure: Applicants must complete an application form, available from the website.
Closing Date: May 5th for the September intake of the same year and September 30th for the January intake of the following year
Contributor: Alumni

INSEAD Elof Hansson Scholarship Fund

Subjects: MBA.
Purpose: To assist MBA participants.
Eligibility: Open to candidates of Swedish nationality who have been admitted to the INSEAD MBA programme.
Level of Study: MBA
Type: Scholarship
Value: €6,000
Frequency: Annual
Study Establishment: INSEAD
No. of awards offered: 2
Application Procedure: Applicants must complete an application form, available from the website.
Closing Date: May 15th for the September class of the same year and September 15th for the January class of the following year
Contributor: The Elof Hansson Foundation

INSEAD Freshfields Scholarship

Subjects: MBA.
Eligibility: Open to candidates of Asian nationality admitted to the INSEAD MBA programme, who will spend some time studying at INSEAD's Asian campus.
Level of Study: MBA
Type: Scholarship
Value: Up to €17,500
Frequency: Annual
Study Establishment: INSEAD
Country of Study: Singapore
No. of awards offered: 2
Application Procedure: Applicants must complete an application form, available from the website.
Closing Date: May 5th for the September class of the same year and September 30th for the January class of the following year
Contributor: Freshfields
Additional Information: Freshfields is a major international law firm and market leader in international transactions that has an appreciation of the importance of the Asia Pacific region.

INSEAD Giovanni Agnelli Scholarship

Subjects: MBA.
Purpose: To support MBA participants.
Eligibility: Open to Italian candidates of high merit, admitted to the INSEAD MBA programme.
Level of Study: MBA
Type: Scholarship
Value: €1,500
Frequency: Annual
Study Establishment: INSEAD
No. of awards offered: 1–2
Application Procedure: Applicants must complete an application form, available from the website.
Closing Date: May 5th for the September class of the same year and September 30th for the January class of the following year
Contributor: Fiat
Additional Information: This endowed scholarship is offered by the Fiat Group.

INSEAD Henry Grunfeld Foundation Scholarship

Subjects: MBA.
Purpose: To aid MBA students who can demonstrate a commitment to a career in investment banking.
Eligibility: Open to participants from a United Kingdom background with an interest in pursuing a career in investment banking.
Level of Study: MBA
Type: Scholarship
Value: Up to €16,000
Frequency: Annual
Study Establishment: INSEAD
Country of Study: Other
No. of awards offered: 1
Application Procedure: Applicants must complete a specific assignment, details of which are available from the organization or from the website.
Closing Date: May 5th for the September class of the same year and September 30th for the January class of the following year
Contributor: The Henry Grunfeld Foundation
Additional Information: Henry Grunfeld was a co-founder of S G Warburg, the United Kingdom investment bank that became one of the largest securities firms in the world, combining merchant banking, securities broking and market-making.

INSEAD Jean François Clin MBA Scholarship

Subjects: MBA.
Purpose: To assist MBA participants from Francophone Africa.
Eligibility: Open to applicants from Burkino Faso, Guinea, Côte D'Ivoire, Mali, Niger, Senegal, Togos, Cambodia, Laos, Myanmar, Thailand and Vietnam who have already gained admission to the INSEAD MBA programme and have close ties with his or her country of origin. Candidates must have had at least secondary education in his or her country of origin although university-level education may have been undertaken abroad. Scholarships will be awarded to candidates for either the September or January classes, on the basis of both merit and need.
Level of Study: MBA
Type: Scholarship
Value: Partial tuition
Frequency: Annual
Study Establishment: INSEAD
No. of awards offered: 3
Application Procedure: Applicants must complete a specific assignment, details of which are available from the organization or from the website.
Closing Date: May 5th for the September intake of the same year and September 30th for the January intake of the following year
Contributor: Jean François Clin
Additional Information: Jean François Clin, an alumnus of INSEAD who has a general interest in the economic development of Francophone West Africa and South East Asia, believes that managers in the region will need to be better equipped to face increasing competition, globalization of businesses and demands on productivity.

INSEAD Judith Connelly Delouvrier Scholarship

Subjects: MBA.
Purpose: To support women undertaking the MBA.
Eligibility: Open to deserving American women admitted to the September MBA programme.
Level of Study: MBA
Type: Scholarship
Value: US$15,000
Frequency: Annual
Study Establishment: INSEAD
No. of awards offered: 1
Application Procedure: Applicants must complete a specific assignment, details of which are available from the website.
Closing Date: May 5th for the September class of the same year
Contributor: Alumni
Additional Information: This scholarship is offered in memory of Judith Connelly Delouvrier, wife of Phillippe Delouvrier, an INSEAD MBA of 1977, who was a victim of the TWA Flight 800 tragedy in 1996.

INSEAD L'Oréal Scholarship

Subjects: MBA.
Purpose: To foster creativity, diversity and entrepreneurial spirit within the MBA population.
Eligibility: Open to candidates of any nationality who demonstrate a capacity for creativity, innovation and entrepreneurial activity and who can demonstrate financial need.

Level of Study: MBA
Type: Scholarship
Value: Partial tuition fees
Length of Study: 1 year
Frequency: Annual
Study Establishment: INSEAD
No. of awards offered: 2 per year, 1 per intake
Closing Date: May 5th for the September class of the same year and September 30th for the January class of the following year
Contributor: L'Oréal

INSEAD Lord Kitchener National Memorial Scholarship

Subjects: MBA.
Purpose: To assist MBA participants from the United Kingdom.
Eligibility: Open to candidates who are British subjects and have served, or are the son or daughter of a parent who has at any time served or is serving on a full-time engagement in HM Armed Forces. This includes members and former members of the Territorial Army and other Reserve Forces of the Crown, and their sons and daughters, providing that the former have served an element of full-time or permanent service for a minimum consecutive period of 3 months.
Level of Study: MBA
Type: Scholarship
Value: UK £2,000 each
Frequency: Annual
Study Establishment: INSEAD
No. of awards offered: 2 per year, 1 per intake
Application Procedure: Applicants must complete an application form, available from the website and send it to INSEAD with documentary evidence of either the candidate's or the candidate's parent's service in the British Armed Forces.
Closing Date: May 5th for the September class of the same year and September 30th for the January class of the following year
Additional Information: The Lord Kitchener National Memorial Fund was created in memory of the first Earl Kitchener of Khartoum who died in action in June 1916 when he went down with his ship.

INSEAD Louis Franck Scholarship

Subjects: MBA.
Eligibility: Open to candidates of United Kingdom nationality admitted to INSEAD. Financial need is neither a necessary nor a sufficient condition for being granted an award. Nevertheless, the candidate's financial position will be taken into account, and awards will not necessarily be granted to the best candidates if there is a sound candidate who is in financial need. Selected scholars are required to write a thesis or report, the subject of which is to be agreed upon with the trustees, and is to be presented to the trustees within 3 months of graduation.
Type: Scholarship
Value: Varies, approx. UK £5,000 each
Frequency: Annual
Study Establishment: INSEAD
No. of awards offered: Up to 8
Application Procedure: Applicants must complete a specific assignment, details of which are available from the website.
Closing Date: May 5th for the September class of the same year and September 30th for the January class of the following year
Funding: Private
Contributor: The Louis Franck Trust
Additional Information: This scholarship was established in 1983 by Louis Franck, who served for many years on the Board of INSEAD.

INSEAD Sasakawa (SYLLF) Scholarships

Subjects: MBA.
Purpose: To encourage candidates to broaden their knowledge and enhance their career leadership through the INSEAD MBA programme.
Eligibility: Open to candidates of any nationality. The awards will be made on a competitive basis.
Level of Study: MBA
Type: Scholarship
Value: €3,000–11,000 depending on the number and quality of applications
Frequency: Annual
Study Establishment: INSEAD
No. of awards offered: 1 or more per intake
Application Procedure: Applicants must complete a specific assignment, details of which are available from the website.
Closing Date: May 5th for the September class of the same year and September 30th for the January class of the following year
Funding: Private
Contributor: The Sasakawa Young Leaders Fellowship Fund (SYLFF)

INSEAD Sisley-Marc d'Ornano Scholarship

Subjects: MBA.
Purpose: To support young graduates seeking further education in order to contribute to the economic development of Poland.
Eligibility: Open to Polish nationals admitted to the INSEAD MBA programme who demonstrate a commitment to work in Poland for 3 years after the INSEAD MBA programme. The winner of the scholarship will agree to take up a professional activity in Poland for at least 3 years, and if not, the candidate is obliged to reimburse the scholarship.
Level of Study: MBA
Type: Scholarship
Value: Tuition fees and a living allowance. Partial scholarships, ie. tuition fees only, may be awarded for residence outside Poland
Frequency: Annual
Study Establishment: INSEAD
No. of awards offered: 1
Application Procedure: Applicants must submit an essay addressing the following question: Give the main reason for your applying for the scholarship and describe your aspirations for your future career development. Scholarship applications may be submitted with the admissions application form. Application forms are available from the website.
Closing Date: May 5th for the September intake of the same year and September 30th for the January intake of the following year
Contributor: Sisley
Additional Information: This scholarship is offered in memory of the late Marc d'Ornano, who lost his life in a car accident while at the start of an excellent career.

INSTITUT FRANÇAIS DE WASHINGTON

238 Dey Hall, CB 3170, UNC-CH, Chapel Hill, NC, 27599-3170, United States of America
Tel: (1) 919 962 2032
Fax: (1) 919 962 5457
Email: cmaley@email.unc.edu
Website: www.unc.edu/depts/institut
Contact: Dr Catherine A Maley, President

The purpose of the Institut Français de Washington is to promote the study of French civilization, history, literature and art in the United States of America.

Edouard Morot-Sir Fellowship in Literature

Subjects: French studies in the areas of art, economics, history, history of science, linguistics, literature or social sciences.
Eligibility: Open to those in the final stage of a PhD dissertation or who have held a PhD for no longer than 6 years before the application deadline.
Level of Study: Postdoctorate, doctorate
Type: Fellowship
Value: US$1,500
Length of Study: At least 2 months
Frequency: Annual
Country of Study: France
Application Procedure: Applicants must write a maximum of two pages describing the research project and planned trip and enclose a curriculum vitae. A letter of recommendation from the dissertation director is also required.
Closing Date: January 15th
Funding: Private, foundation

No. of awards given last year: 1
No. of applicants last year: 45
Additional Information: Awards are for maintenance during research in France and should not be used for travel.

Gilbert Chinard Fellowships

Subjects: French studies in the areas of art, economics, history, history of science, linguistics, literature or social sciences.
Eligibility: Open to those in the final stage of a PhD dissertation or who have held a PhD for no longer than 6 years before the application deadline.
Level of Study: Doctorate, postdoctorate
Type: Fellowship
Value: US$1,500
Length of Study: At least 2 months
Frequency: Annual
Country of Study: France
No. of awards offered: 3
Application Procedure: Applicants must write a maximum of two pages describing the research project and planned trip and enclose a curriculum vitae. A letter of recommendation from the dissertation director is also required for PhD candidates.
Closing Date: January 15th
Funding: Private
No. of awards given last year: 2
No. of applicants last year: 45
Additional Information: Awards are for maintenance during research in France and should not be used for travel.

Harmon Chadbourn Rorison Fellowship

Subjects: French studies in the areas of art, economics, history, history of science, linguistics, literature or social sciences.
Eligibility: Open to those in the final stage of a PhD dissertation or who have held a PhD for no longer than 6 years before the application deadline.
Level of Study: Postdoctorate, doctorate
Type: Fellowship
Value: US$1,500
Length of Study: At least 2 months
Frequency: Every 2 years
Country of Study: France
No. of awards offered: 1
Application Procedure: Applicants must write a maximum of two pages describing the research project and planned trip and enclose a curriculum vitae. A letter of recommendation from the dissertation director is also required for PhD candidates.
Closing Date: January 15th
Funding: Foundation, private
No. of awards given last year: 1
No. of applicants last year: 45
Additional Information: Awards are for maintenance during research in France and should not be used for travel.

THE INSTITUT MITTAG-LEFFLER

Auravägen 17, SE-18260 Djursholm, Sweden
Tel: (46) 8 6220560
Fax: (46) 8 6220589
Email: koskull@mittag-leffler.se
Website: www.mittag-leffler.se
Contact: Marie-Louise Koskull, Administrator of the Visiting Programme

The Institut Mittag-Leffler is a Nordic research institute for mathematics, under the auspices of the Royal Swedish Academy of Sciences, created by Gösta and Signe Mittag-Leffler, who donated their house, library and fortune to the Academy.

Institut Mittag-Leffler Grants

Subjects: Mathematics. The specific topics vary every 6 to 12 months.
Eligibility: Open to recent PhDs and advanced graduate students. Preference will be given to applications for long stays.
Level of Study: Doctorate
Type: Grant
Value: Krona 15,000 per month or Krona 135,000 for those who stay for the full duration of the programme, plus a family allowance
Length of Study: 1 academic year, from September through to June 15th. Sometimes there are two different topics during one academic year
Frequency: Annual, semi-annual, depending on the length of the topic
Country of Study: Sweden
No. of awards offered: Varies
Application Procedure: Applicants must complete an application form.
Closing Date: January 31st

INSTITUTE FOR ADVANCED STUDIES IN THE HUMANITIES

University of Edinburgh, Hope Park Square, Edinburgh, EH8 9NW, Scotland
Tel: (44) 13 1650 4671
Fax: (44) 13 1668 2252
Email: iash@ed.ac.uk
Website: www.ed.ac.uk/iash
Contact: Ms Anthea Taylor, Assistant to Director

The Institute for Advanced Studies in the Humanities aims to promote scholarship in the humanities, and, wherever possible, to foster interdisciplinary enquiries. This is achieved by means of fellowships awarded for the pursuit of relevant research and by the public dissemination of findings in seminars, lectures, conferences, exhibitions, cultural events and publications.

Andrew W Mellon Foundation Fellowships in the Humanities

Subjects: Humanities.
Purpose: To promote advanced research within the field of humanities and to sponsor interdisciplinary research.
Eligibility: Open to Bulgarian, Czech, Estonian, Hungarian, Latvian, Lithuanian, Polish, Romanian and Slovak scholars only. Fellows must be able to speak English and be under 45 years of age.
Level of Study: Postdoctorate
Type: Grant
Length of Study: 3 months
Frequency: Annual
Study Establishment: The Institute for Advanced Studies in the Humanities at the University of Edinburgh
Country of Study: Scotland
No. of awards offered: 4
Application Procedure: Applicants must complete an application form, available from the Institute.
Closing Date: March 31st
Funding: Private
No. of awards given last year: 4
No. of applicants last year: 33

Institute for Advanced Studies in the Humanities Visiting Research Fellowships

Subjects: Archaeology, history of art, classics, English literature, history, European and oriental languages and literature, linguistics, philosophy, Scottish studies, history of science, law, divinity, music and social sciences.
Purpose: To promote advanced research within the field and also to sponsor interdisciplinary research.
Eligibility: Open to scholars of any nationality holding a doctorate or offering equivalent evidence of aptitude for advanced studies. Degree candidates are not eligible.
Level of Study: Postdoctorate
Type: Fellowship
Value: Most fellowships are honorary, but limited support towards expenses is available to a small number of candidates
Length of Study: 2–6 months

Frequency: Annual
Study Establishment: The Institute for Advanced Studies in the Humanities at the University of Edinburgh
Country of Study: United Kingdom
No. of awards offered: 15
Application Procedure: Applicants must complete an application form, available from the Institute. Candidates should advise their referees to write on their behalf directly to the Institute.
Closing Date: December 1st. Candidates should ensure that their references are received in Edinburgh before January 10th
Funding: Private
No. of awards given last year: 14
No. of applicants last year: 23
Additional Information: Fellows have the use of study rooms at the Institute, near the library and within easy reach of the National Library of Scotland, the Central City Library, the National Galleries and Museums, the Library of the Society of Antiquaries in Scotland and the National Archives of Scotland.

INSTITUTE FOR ADVANCED STUDY

Einstein Drive, Princeton, NJ, 08540, United States of America
Tel: (1) 609 734 8000
Fax: (1) 609 924 8399
Email: cferrara@ias.edu
Website: www.ias.edu
Contact: Ms Christine Ferrara, Public Affairs Officer

The Institute for Advanced Study is an independent, private institution whose mission is to support advanced scholarship and fundamental research in historical studies, mathematics, natural sciences and social science. It is a community of scholars where theoretical research and intellectual enquiry are carried out under the most favourable conditions.

Institute for Advanced Study Postdoctoral Residential Fellowships

Subjects: Social science, history, astronomy, theoretical physics, mathematics or theoretical biology.
Purpose: To support advanced study and scholarly exploration.
Eligibility: There are no restrictions on eligibility.
Level of Study: Postdoctorate
Type: Fellowship
Value: US$40,000–50,000
Length of Study: Generally 1 year
Frequency: Annual
Country of Study: United States of America
No. of awards offered: Approx. 190
Application Procedure: Applicants must complete an application. Materials are available from the school administrative officers.
Closing Date: Varies, but is between November 15th and December 15th
No. of awards given last year: Approx. 190
No. of applicants last year: Approx. 2,400

INSTITUTE FOR ECUMENICAL AND CULTURAL RESEARCH

PO Box 6188, Collegeville, MN, 53621-6188, United States of America
Tel: (1) 320 363 3366
Fax: (1) 320 363 3313
Email: iecr@iecr.org
Website: www.iecr.org
Contact: Patrick Henry, Executive Director

The Institute for Ecumenical and Cultural Research seeks to discern the meaning of Christian identity and unity in a religiously and culturally diverse nation and world and to communicate that meaning for the mission of the church and the renewal of human community. The Institute is committed to research, study, prayer, reflection and dialogue, in a place shaped by the Benedictine tradition of worship and work.

Bishop Thomas Hoyt Jr Fellowship

Subjects: Ecumenical and cultural research.
Purpose: To provide the Institute's residency fee to a North American person of colour writing a doctoral dissertation, in order to help the churches to increase the number of persons of colour working in ecumenical and cultural research.
Eligibility: Open to a North American, Canadian or Mexican person of colour writing a doctoral dissertation within the general area of the Institute's concern.
Level of Study: Postgraduate
Type: Fellowship
Value: US$3,600, this figure is slated to rise gradually in future years; check the website for projections
Length of Study: 1 academic year
Frequency: Annual
Study Establishment: The Institute
Country of Study: United States of America
No. of awards offered: 1 each year (or 2 if for semesters)
Application Procedure: Applicants must apply in the usual way to the Resident Scholars Programme (see separate listing). If invited by the admissions committee to be a Resident Scholar, the person will then be eligible for consideration for the Hoyt Fellowship.
Closing Date: November 1st
Funding: Private
No. of awards given last year: None
No. of applicants last year: None

INSTITUTE FOR HUMANE STUDIES (IHS)

3301 North Faifax Drive, Suite 440, Arlington, VA, 22201-4432, United States of America
Tel: (1) 703 993 4880
Fax: (1) 703 993 4890
Email: abrand@gmu.edu
Website: www.theihs.org
Contact: Ms Amanda Bland, Director of Academic Programs

The Institute for Humane Studies (IHS) is a unique organization that assists graduate students worldwide with a special interest in individual liberty. IHS awards over US$400,000 a year in scholarships to students from universities around the world. They also sponsor the attendance of hundreds of students at free summer seminars and provide various forms of career assistance. Through these and other programmes, IHS and a network of faculty associates promote the study of liberty across a broad range of disciplines, encouraging understanding, open enquiry, rigorous scholarship and creative problem-solving.

Hayek Fund for Scholars

Subjects: Social sciences, law, the humanities, journalism.
Purpose: To help offset expenses for participating in professional conferences and job interviews.
Eligibility: Open to graduate students and untenured faculty members.
Level of Study: Postgraduate
Value: US$1,000
Frequency: Annual
Country of Study: Any country
Application Procedure: For application requirements visit the website.

For further information contact:

George Mason University, 4400 University Drive, Fairfax, VA, 22030, United States of America
Tel: (1) 703 323 1055
Fax: (1) 703 425 1536
Contact: Keri Anderson, Programme Director

IHS Felix Morley Memorial Journalism Competition

Subjects: Current issues from a classical liberal perspective.
Purpose: To encourage writing that reflects an interest in the classical liberal tradition.
Eligibility: Open to full-time students or under 25 years old.

Level of Study: Unrestricted
Type: Other
Value: First prize US$2,500, second prize US$1,500, third prize US$1,000, five runners-up prizes US$500
Frequency: Annual
Country of Study: Any country
Application Procedure: Download an application at www.theihs.org/morley
Closing Date: December 1st

For further information contact:

George Mason University 4400 University Drive, Fairfax, VA, 22030, United States of America
Tel: (1) 703 323 1055
Fax: (1) 703 425 1536
Contact: Keri Landerson, Programme Director

IHS Film & Fiction Scholarships

Subjects: Filmmaking, fiction writing and playwriting.
Eligibility: Open to graduate students pursuing a Master of Fine Arts degree. Applicants should have a demonstrated interest in classical liberal ideas and their application in contemporary society. They should also demonstrate the desire, motivation and creative ability to succeed in their chosen profession.
Level of Study: Graduate
Type: Scholarship
Value: Up to US$10,000
Frequency: Annual
Application Procedure: Applicants must apply online at www.theihs.org/film&fiction
Closing Date: January 15th
Funding: Private

IHS Humane Studies Fellowships

Subjects: Arts and humanities, fine and applied art, law, mass communication and information, religion and theology and social and behavioural science.
Purpose: To support outstanding students with a demonstrated interest in the classical liberal tradition intent on pursuing an intellectual and scholarly career.
Eligibility: Open to graduate students who have enrolled for the next academic year at accredited colleges and universities.
Level of Study: Graduate, postgraduate
Type: Fellowship
Value: Up to US$12,000
Frequency: Annual
Country of Study: Any country
Application Procedure: Applicants must complete and submit an application form with three completed evaluations, three essays, official test scores, official transcripts and a term paper or writing sample. Applications can be downloaded at www.theihs.org/hsf
Closing Date: December 30th
Funding: Private
No. of awards given last year: 100
No. of applicants last year: 650

IHS Liberty & Society Summer Seminars

Subjects: Foundations of liberty, liberty and culture, liberty and current issues, the crisis of liberty, social change workshop and liberal society.
Purpose: To allow individuals to learn and exchange ideas.
Level of Study: Graduate
Value: All free summer seminars include room and board, lectures and seminars, materials and books. Each seminar spot is worth approx. US$1,000
Frequency: Annual
Study Establishment: The IHS
Country of Study: United States of America
Application Procedure: Applicants must apply online at www.theihs.org
Closing Date: The final deadline is March 30th

IHS Summer Graduate Research Fellowship

Subjects: The humane sciences, eg. history, political and moral philosophy, political economy, economic history, legal and social theory.
Purpose: To give students who share an interest in scholarly research in the classical liberal tradition the opportunity to work on a thesis chapter or a paper of publishable quality and to participate in interdisciplinary seminars under the guidance of a faculty supervisor.
Eligibility: Open to graduate students in the humanities, social sciences and law who intend to pursue academic careers and who are currently pursuing research in the classical liberal tradition.
Level of Study: Graduate, doctorate, postgraduate
Type: Fellowship
Value: US$5,000
Frequency: Annual
Country of Study: United States of America
No. of awards offered: 8–10
Application Procedure: Applicants must submit a proposal, curriculum vitae, a copy of Graduate Record Examination scores or Law School Admission Test scores and transcripts, a writing sample and reference details. Visit the website for further information.
Closing Date: February 15th
Funding: Private

IHS Young Communicators Fellowship

Subjects: Journalism, film, writing (fiction or nonfiction), publishing or free-market-orientated public policy.
Purpose: To help place Fellows in strategic positions that can enhance their abilities and credentials to pursue targeted careers.
Eligibility: Open to advanced students and recent graduates who have a clearly demonstrated interest in the classical liberal tradition of individual rights and market economies.
Level of Study: Professional development
Type: Fellowship
Value: US$5,000, to include stipend, housing and travel
Frequency: Annual
Country of Study: Any country
No. of awards offered: Varies
Application Procedure: Applicants must submit a proposal of 500–1,000 words explaining what specific Summer position, similar short-term position, or training programme they could pursue if they were supported by a Fellowship, how the proposed opportunity would enhance the applicant's career prospects and how the proposed opportunity could contribute to the applicant's understanding of classical liberal principles and their application to today's issues. A current curriculum vitae listing educational background, including major field and any academic honours received, current educational status, work experience, including Summer positions and internships, and citations of any publications should also be included. Candidates should also submit a writing sample or other sample of work appropriate to the intended career and provide the name, address, and phone number of an academic and/or professional reference.
Closing Date: March 15th for Summer positions and 10 weeks prior to the start of other positions

THE INSTITUTE FOR SUPPLY MANAGEMENT (ISM)

2055 East Centennial Circle, PO Box 22160, Tempe, AZ, 85285-2160, United States of America
Tel: (1) 480 752 6276
Fax: (1) 480 752 7890
Email: jcavinato@ism.ws
Website: www.ism.ws
Contact: Dr Joseph L Cavinato, Senior Vice President

The Institute for Supply Management (ISM) is a non-profit association that provides national and international leadership in purchasing and supply management research and education. ISM provides more than 46,000 members with opportunities to expand their professional skills and knowledge.

ISM Doctoral Grants

Subjects: Purchasing materials and supply management.
Purpose: To financially assist individuals in preparation for a career in the field, for university teaching and to encourage research.
Eligibility: Open to doctoral candidates who are pursuing a PhD or DBA in purchasing, business, logistics, management, economics, industrial engineering or a related field and who are at the dissertation stage. Applicants must be enrolled in an accredited United States of America university to be eligible for the award.
Level of Study: Doctorate
Type: Grant
Value: Up to US$10,000
Frequency: Annual
Country of Study: United States of America
No. of awards offered: 4
Application Procedure: Applicants must submit an application form and documents including letters of recommendation, transcripts and a research proposal.
Closing Date: January 31st
Funding: Private
Contributor: ISM
No. of awards given last year: 4
No. of applicants last year: 20
Additional Information: Upon successful completion of the research, the ISM will be interested in the publication of material from the study. Nominations are invited from departments of economics, management, marketing and business administration at United States of America universities offering a doctoral degree in appropriate fields.

ISM Senior Research Fellowship Program

Subjects: Topics include but are not limited to the integration of purchasing with other functions, the impact of globalization on purchasing, the role of purchasing in supply chain management, measuring purchasing effectiveness, historical analysis of trends in purchasing, objective measures of supplier performance, the application of electronic commerce in purchasing and supply, the use of purchasing as a strategic tool, the identification of educational or training tools and skills for purchasing and supply management, forecasting methods, ERP and purchasing, alliances and supplier development.
Purpose: To help support emerging, high-potential scholars who teach and conduct research in purchasing and supply management.
Eligibility: Open to assistant professors, associate professors or equivalent who have demonstrated exceptional academic productivity in research and teaching. Candidates are chosen from those who can help produce useful research that can be applied to the advancement of purchasing and supply management. Candidates must be full-time faculty members within or outside the United States of America and be present or past members of ISM committees, groups, forums or affiliated organizations. An assistant professor should have 3 or more years of post-degree experience. Previous awardees are ineligible.
Level of Study: Predoctorate
Type: Fellowship
Value: US$5,000
Frequency: Annual
Country of Study: United States of America
No. of awards offered: 2
Application Procedure: Applicants must submit four copies of each of the following items in one complete package: a letter of application explaining qualifications for the fellowship, a research proposal of not more than five pages including a problem statement or hypothesis, research methodology with data sources, collection and analysis, value to the field of purchasing and supply and a curriculum vitae including works in progress.
Closing Date: April 1st
Funding: Private
Contributor: ISM
No. of applicants last year: 5–10
Additional Information: It is expected that the ISM Fellows will present the results of their research at an ISM forum, eg. research symposium, ISM Annual International Purchasing Conference and/or an NAPM publication such as *The Journal of Supply Chain Management*.

THE INSTITUTE FOR THE STUDY OF AGING

767 Fifth Avenue, Suite 4600, New York, NY, 10153,
United States of America
Tel: (1) 212 572 4086
Fax: (1) 212 572 4094
Email: tlee@aging-institute.org
Website: www.aging-institute.org
Contact: Ms Tonya Lee, Grants Manager

The Institute for the Study of Aging is a non-profit foundation based in New York City. The Institute supports research on Alzheimer's disease and cognitive decline.

Institute for the Study of Aging Grants Program

Subjects: Early identification, prevention and treatment of Alzheimer's disease and cognitive decline. The Institute focuses its efforts on facilitating drug discovery and development in this field.
Purpose: To promote the research and development of technology and therapies to identify, treat and prevent cognitive decline, Alzheimer's disease and related dementias.
Eligibility: There are no eligibility restrictions.
Level of Study: Unrestricted
Type: Grant
Value: Negotiable
Length of Study: 1–3 years
Frequency: There is no funding cycle
Study Establishment: A non-profit family foundation
Country of Study: Any country
Application Procedure: Applicants must submit a brief lay summary, a research proposal of up to five pages including background, aims, supporting data, experimental design and methods, a biosketch, a summary of resources and a budget with justification.
Closing Date: Applications are accepted at any time
Funding: Private
No. of awards given last year: 29
Additional Information: In addition to funding research activities, the Institute sponsors and/or co-sponsors conferences, scientific and medical workshops to advance knowledge on issues related to Alzheimer's disease and cognitive vitality.

For further information contact:

Email: lrefolo@aging-institute.org
Contact: Lorenzo Refolo, Scientific Director

Email: hfillit@aging-institute.org
Contact: Howard Fillit, Executive Director

INSTITUTE OF ADVANCED LEGAL STUDIES (IALS)

School of Advanced Study, Charles Clore House, 17 Russell Square, London, WC1B 5DR, England
Tel: (44) 20 7862 5883
Fax: (44) 20 7862 5850
Email: dphillip@sas.ac.uk
Website: www.ials.sas.ac.uk
Contact: Mr D E Phillips, Administrative Secretary

The Institute of Advanced Legal Studies (IALS) plays a national and international role in the promotion and facilitation of legal research. It possesses one of the leading research libraries in Europe and organizes a regular programme of conferences, seminars and lectures. It also offers postgraduate taught and research programmes and specialized training courses.

Howard Drake Memorial Fund

Subjects: Law and library science.
Purpose: To encourage collaboration and exchanges between legal scholars and law librarians, especially between those of different countries, and to promote the study of law librarianship and the training of law librarians.

Eligibility: There are no restrictions on eligibility.
Level of Study: Professional development
Type: Grant
Value: Up to approx. UK £800 per grant
Frequency: Dependent on funds available
Study Establishment: The IALS
Country of Study: United Kingdom
No. of awards offered: 1–2
Application Procedure: Applicants must make applications to the Administrative Secretary. There is no official application form.
No. of awards given last year: None
No. of applicants last year: None

IALS Visiting Fellowship in Law Librarianship

Subjects: Law and library science.
Purpose: To enable experienced law librarians, who are undertaking research in, appropriate fields, to relate their work to activities in which the Institutes own library is involved.
Eligibility: Open to experienced law librarians from any country.
Level of Study: Unrestricted
Type: Fellowship
Value: Non-stipendary
Length of Study: A minimum of 3 months and a maximum of 1 year
Frequency: Annual
Study Establishment: The IALS
Country of Study: United Kingdom
No. of awards offered: 1
Application Procedure: Applicants must submit a full curriculum vitae, the names, addresses and telephone numbers of two referees and a brief statement of the research programme to be undertaken to the Administrative Secretary.
Closing Date: January 31st in respect of the following academic year
No. of awards given last year: 1
No. of applicants last year: 1

IALS Visiting Fellowship in Legislative Studies

Subjects: Law.
Purpose: To enable individuals in the field to undertake research.
Eligibility: Open to established academics and practitioners from any country. This award is not available for postgraduate research.
Level of Study: Unrestricted
Type: Fellowship
Value: Non-stipendary
Length of Study: A minimum of 3 months and a maximum of 1 year
Frequency: Annual
Study Establishment: The IALS
Country of Study: United Kingdom
No. of awards offered: 1
Application Procedure: Applicants must submit a full curriculum vitae, the names, addresses and telephone numbers of two referees and a brief statement of the research programme to be undertaken.
Closing Date: January 31st for the following academic year
No. of awards given last year: None
No. of applicants last year: 1

IALS Visiting Fellowships

Subjects: Law.
Eligibility: Open to nationals of any country who are established legal scholars and are undertaking research in appropriate fields.
Level of Study: Unrestricted
Type: Fellowship
Value: Non-stipendary
Length of Study: A minimum of 3 months and a maximum of 1 year
Frequency: Annual
Study Establishment: The IALS
Country of Study: United Kingdom
No. of awards offered: Up to 6
Application Procedure: Applicants must submit a full curriculum vitae, the names, addresses and telephone numbers of two referees and a brief statement of the research programme to be undertaken.
Closing Date: January 31st for the following academic year
No. of awards given last year: 7
No. of applicants last year: 16

Additional Information: This award is not available for postgraduate research.

THE INSTITUTE OF CANCER RESEARCH (ICR)

Genetic Epidemiology Building, Sutton, Surrey, SM2 5NG, England
Tel: (44) 20 8643 8901 ext 4253
Fax: (44) 20 8643 6940
Email: joanna.richards@icr.ac.uk
Website: www.icr.ac.uk
Contact: Simon Hobson, Registrar

Over the past 90 years, the Institute of Cancer Research (ICR) has become one of the largest, most successful and innovative cancer research centres in the world. The Institute and the Royal Marsden NHS Trust exist side by side in Chelsea and on a joint site at Sutton, and this close association allows for maximum interaction between fundamental laboratory work and clinical environment.

ICR Studentships

Subjects: Cancer research.
Purpose: Research degree studentships.
Eligibility: First class Master's or upper second class Master's undergraduate degree required in a relevent subject.
Level of Study: Doctorate
Type: Studentship
Value: A generous stipend, consumables and fees
Length of Study: Up to 4 years
Frequency: Annual
Study Establishment: The Institute of Cancer Research, University of London
Country of Study: United Kingdom
No. of awards offered: 15–20
Application Procedure: See website.
Closing Date: January
Funding: Government
Contributor: Cancer Research UK
No. of awards given last year: 14
No. of applicants last year: 212
Additional Information: A limited number of Institute postdoctoral fellowships are offered from time to time as vacancies occur.

INSTITUTE OF CURRENT WORLD AFFAIRS

4 West Wheelock Street, Hanover, NH, 03755,
United States of America
Tel: (1) 603 643 5548
Fax: (1) 603 643 9599
Email: icwa@valley.net
Website: www.icwa.org
Contact: Brent Jacobson

Institute of Current World Affairs Fellowships

Subjects: International affairs.
Purpose: To enable young adults of outstanding promise and character to study and write about areas or issues of the world outside the United States of America.
Eligibility: Open to individuals under 36 who have finished their formal education. Applicants must have a good command of spoken and written English.
Level of Study: Professional development, postgraduate
Type: Fellowship
Value: Full support for Fellows and their immediate families
Length of Study: A minimum of 2 years
Frequency: Annual
Country of Study: Any country
No. of awards offered: 4
Application Procedure: Applicants must write to the Executive Director and briefly explain their personal background and the professional experience that would qualify them in the Institute's current

areas of concern, details of which are available upon request. They should also describe the activities they would like to carry out during the 2 years overseas. This initial letter is followed by a more detailed written application process and must be completed prior to the deadline.
Closing Date: Deadlines for completed applications are April 1st for a June decision and September 1st for a December decision
Funding: Private
Additional Information: Fellowships are not awarded to support work toward academic degrees nor to underwrite specific studies or research projects. The Institute is also known as the Crane-Rogers Foundation.

INSTITUTE OF EDUCATION

20 Bedford Way, London, WC1H 0AL, England
Tel: (44) 20 7612 6000
Fax: (44) 20 7612 6126
Email: info@ioe.ac.uk
Website: www.ioe.ac.uk
Contact: Josie Charlton, Head of Marketing and Development

Founded in 1902, the Institute of Education is a world-class centre of excellence for research, teacher training, higher degrees and consultancy in education and education-related areas of social science. Our pre-eminent scholars and talented students from all walks of life make up an intellectually rich and diverse learning community.

Nicholas Hans Comparative Education Scholarship

Subjects: Comparative education.
Purpose: To assist a well-qualified student to study for a PhD in comparative education at the Institute.
Eligibility: Candidates must be registered Institute students not normally resident in the United Kingdom.
Level of Study: Doctorate
Type: Scholarship
Value: Value of 1 year's full time tuition fees
Length of Study: 3–7 years
Frequency: Annual
Study Establishment: Institute of Education
Country of Study: United Kingdom
No. of awards offered: 1
Application Procedure: Candidates are required to submit an extended essay of 25,000–30,000 words, based upon their research or proposed research, that exemplifies, extends or develops by critique the concerns of Nicholas Hans in comparative education.
Closing Date: June 1st
Funding: Trusts
Contributor: Trust fund based upon money left in the will of Nicholas Hans' widow
No. of awards given last year: 3-7 years
No. of applicants last year: None

INSTITUTE OF EUROPEAN HISTORY

Alte Universitätsstrasse 19, D-55116 Mainz, Germany
Tel: (49) 613 1393 9360
Fax: (49) 613 1393 0154
Email: ieg2@ieg-mainz.de
Website: www.ieg-mainz.de
Contact: Dr Joachim Berger, Staff unit/management

The Institute of European History in Mainz, founded in 1950, is dedicated to the promotion of interdisciplinary historical research that focuses on European communication and transfer processes since 1450. Its Abteilung für Religionsgeschichte Universalgeschichte specialize on the interplay of religious, political and social phenomena relating to these processes.

Institute of European History Fellowships

Subjects: Transnational and comparative history of Europe, especially religious and politics.
Purpose: To support young scientists in the completion of their doctoral work or in the execution of shorter postdoctoral projects. Participation in the Institute's research projects is particularly welcome.
Eligibility: Open to holders of a Master's degree and to Fellows in the advanced stages of graduate work, at least 2 years after admission to doctoral candidacy. Applicants must have successfully completed their comprehensive oral examinations.
Level of Study: Postdoctorate, doctorate
Type: Fellowship
Value: A monthly stipend, a family allowance, health insurance and a travel allowance, all of which are in line with the guidelines of the German Academic Exchange Service (DAAD)
Length of Study: 6 months–1 year
Frequency: Annual
Study Establishment: The Institute of European History
Country of Study: Germany
Application Procedure: Applicants must contact the directors of the institute. For details and deadlines see the website.
Closing Date: February and September
Funding: Government
No. of awards given last year: 20
No. of applicants last year: 100

INSTITUTE OF FOOD TECHNOLOGISTS (IFT)

525 W. Van Buren, Suite 1000, Chicago, IL 60607, United States of America
Tel: (1) 312 782 8424
Fax: (1) 312 782 8348
Email: info@ift.org
Website: www.ift.org
Contact: Scholarship Department

The Institute of Food Technologists (IFT), founded in 1939, is a nonprofit scientific society with 29,000 members working in food science, technology and related professions in industry, academia and government. IFT's mission is to advance the science and technology of food through the exchange of knowledge. As a society for food science and technology, IFT brings a scientific perspective to the public discussion of food issues.

Congressional Support for Science Award

Subjects: Food science.
Purpose: To recognize outstanding contributions to science-based food policies.
Eligibility: Open to the members of the United States Congress.
Level of Study: Postgraduate
Type: Award
Value: Varies
Frequency: Annual
No. of awards offered: 2
Application Procedure: Application forms and details available on the website.
Closing Date: December 1st
Contributor: Institute of Food Technologists

For further information contact:

IFT Congressional Support for Science Awards Jury, Institute of Food Technologists, 1025 Connecticut Avenue, NW, Suite 503, Washington, DC 20036

IFT Graduate Fellowships

Subjects: Food technology and food science.
Purpose: To encourage and support outstanding research.
Eligibility: Open to current graduates pursuing a course of study leading to an MS or PhD degree. Candidates must possess an above-average interest in research together with demonstrated scientific aptitude.
Level of Study: Postgraduate, graduate, doctorate
Type: Fellowship
Value: Varies

Frequency: Annual
Study Establishment: Any educational institution that is conducting fundamental investigations in the advancement of food science and technology
Country of Study: United States of America or Canada
Application Procedure: Applicants must contact IFT for details.
Funding: Private, commercial
Contributor: Contributors include General Mills, Inc., the Coca-Cola Foundation and Proctor & Gamble Company

Marcel Loncin Research Prize

Subjects: Food processing.
Purpose: To provide funds for research in food processing.
Eligibility: Open to all individuals who are capable of conducting research.
Level of Study: Research
Type: Prize
Value: US$50,000 and a plaque
Frequency: Every 2 years
Application Procedure: A completed application form accompanied by a grant proposal and a biographical sketch must be submitted.
Closing Date: December 1st
Contributor: Institute of Food Technologists

INSTITUTE OF HISTORICAL RESEARCH (IHR)

Senate House, Malet Street, London, WC1E 7HU, England
Tel: (44) 20 7862 8740
Fax: (44) 20 7862 8811
Email: ihrsec@sas.ac.uk
Website: www.ihr.sas.ac.uk
Contact: Director

The Institute of Historical Research (IHR) is a centre for advanced study in history. It is the meeting place for scholars from around the world, housing the largest open access collection of primary sources for historians in the United Kingdom, administering research and providing courses, seminars and conferences.

IHR Past and Present Postdoctoral Fellowships in History

Subjects: History.
Purpose: To fund 1 year of postdoctoral research.
Eligibility: Applicants may be of any nationality and their PhD may have been awarded in any country. Those who have previously held another postdoctoral fellowship will normally not be eligible. The fellowship may not be held in conjunction with any other award. Fellowships will begin on October 1st each year and it is a strict condition of these awards that a PhD thesis should have been submitted by that date.
Level of Study: Postdoctorate
Type: Fellowship
Value: Approx. UK £15,000
Length of Study: 1 year
Frequency: Dependent on funds available
Study Establishment: IHR
Country of Study: United Kingdom
No. of awards offered: 2 (may vary according to funds)
Application Procedure: Applicants must complete an application form, available from the Fellowship Officer in early January.
Closing Date: Early April
Funding: Private
Contributor: The Past and Present Society and IHR
No. of awards given last year: 2

Isobel Thornley Research Fellowship

Subjects: Medieval history, modern history or contemporary history.
Purpose: To help candidates at an advanced stage of a PhD to complete their doctorates.
Eligibility: Open to nationals of any country, but only to those who are registered for a PhD at the University of London.
Level of Study: Doctorate
Type: Fellowship
Value: UK £10,000
Length of Study: 1 year
Frequency: Dependent on funds available
Study Establishment: IHR
Country of Study: United Kingdom
No. of awards offered: 1
Application Procedure: Applicants must complete an application form, available from the Fellowship Assistant in early January.
Closing Date: Early March
Funding: Private
Contributor: Isobel Thornley Bequest
No. of awards given last year: 1

Royal History Society Fellowship

Subjects: Medieval history, modern history and contemporary history.
Purpose: To help candidates at an advanced stage of a PhD to complete their doctorates.
Eligibility: Open to nationals of any country.
Level of Study: Doctorate
Type: Fellowship
Value: Approx. UK £10,000
Length of Study: 1 year
Frequency: Dependent on funds available
Study Establishment: IHR
Country of Study: United Kingdom
No. of awards offered: 1
Application Procedure: Applicants must complete an application form, available from the Fellowship Officer in early January.
Closing Date: Early March
Funding: Private
Contributor: The Royal Historical Society
No. of awards given last year: 1

Scouloudi Fellowships

Subjects: Medieval history, modern history and contemporary history.
Purpose: To help candidates at an advanced stage of a PhD to complete their doctorates.
Eligibility: Only open to United Kingdom citizens or to candidates with a first degree from a United Kingdom university.
Level of Study: Doctorate
Type: Fellowship
Value: Approx. UK £10,000
Length of Study: 1 year
Frequency: Dependent on funds available
Study Establishment: IHR
Country of Study: United Kingdom
No. of awards offered: 5
Application Procedure: Applicants must complete an application form, available from the Fellowship Officer in early January.
Closing Date: Early March
Funding: Private
Contributor: The Scouloudi Foundation
No. of awards given last year: 4

INSTITUTE OF HORTICULTURE (IOH)

14/15 Belgrave Square, London, SW1X 8PS, England
Tel: (44) 20 7245 6943
Fax: (44) 20 7245 6943
Email: ioh@horticulture.org.uk
Website: www.horticulture.org.uk
Contact: A Clarke, General Secretary

The Institute of Horticulture (IOH) is the professional institute for horticulturists of all disciplines in the industry.

Martin McLaren Horticultural Scholarship

Subjects: Horticulture, botany and landscape architecture.
Purpose: To fund 1 year of an MSc course at an American university.
Eligibility: Applicants must have gained a botany, horticulture or landscape architecture degree, and be in the early stages of their career. The age limit is 27 years of age.
Level of Study: Postgraduate

Type: Scholarship
Value: US$29,000
Length of Study: 1 year
Frequency: Annual
Study Establishment: A university
Country of Study: United States of America
No. of awards offered: 1
Application Procedure: Applicants must complete an application form, available from the IOH.
Closing Date: November 10th
Funding: Private
Contributor: The Martin McLaren Trust
No. of awards given last year: 1

INSTITUTE OF IRISH STUDIES

Queen's University of Belfast, Belfast, BT7 INN, Northern Ireland
Tel: (44) 28 9097 3386
Fax: (44) 28 9097 3388
Email: irish.studies@qub.ac.uk
Website: www.qub.ac.uk/iis
Contact: Director

The Institute of Irish Studies at Queen's University was established in 1965 and was one of the first of its kind. It is one of the leading centres for research-based teaching in Irish studies and is an internationally renowned centre of interdisciplinary Irish scholarship attracting academics from all over the world.

Institute of Irish Studies Research Fellowships

Subjects: Any field of Irish studies.
Purpose: To promote research.
Eligibility: Candidates must hold at least a Second Class (Honours) Degree, have research experience and a viable research proposal.
Level of Study: Postdoctorate
Type: Fellowship
Value: UK £19,000
Length of Study: 1 year
Frequency: Annual
Study Establishment: The Institute of Irish Studies, Queen's University Belfast
Country of Study: Northern Ireland
No. of awards offered: Up to 3
Application Procedure: Applicants must see the website for details. Awards are usually advertised in February to March.
Closing Date: Varies
Funding: Government
No. of awards given last year: 3
No. of applicants last year: 50

Institute of Irish Studies Senior Visiting Research Fellowship

Subjects: Irish studies.
Purpose: To promote research.
Eligibility: Open to established scholars of senior standing with a strong publication record.
Level of Study: Postdoctorate
Type: Fellowship
Value: UK £19,000
Length of Study: 1 year
Frequency: Annual
Study Establishment: The Institute of Irish Studies, Queen's University Belfast
Country of Study: Northern Ireland
No. of awards offered: Up to 2
Application Procedure: Awards are usually advertised in February to March.
Closing Date: Varies
No. of awards given last year: 0
No. of applicants last year: Varies

Mary McNeill Scholarship in Irish Studies

Subjects: Irish studies.
Eligibility: Open to well-qualified students enrolled in the 1-year MA course in Irish studies at Queen's University. Applicants must be citizens of the United States of America or Canada and be enrolled as overseas students in this course.
Level of Study: Postgraduate
Type: Scholarship
Value: UK £3,000
Length of Study: 1 year
Frequency: Dependent on funds available
Study Establishment: Queen's University Belfast
Country of Study: Northern Ireland
No. of awards offered: 1
Application Procedure: Applicants must write to the Secretary of the Institute for an application form.
Closing Date: May 31st
No. of awards given last year: 1

THE INSTITUTE OF MATERIALS, MINERALS AND MINING

Danum House, South Parade, Doncaster, South Yorkshire, DN1 2DY, England
Tel: (44) 44 (0) 1780 759211
Fax: (44) 13 0238 0900
Email: diane.talbot@iom3.org
Website: www.iom3.org
Contact: Dr Rachel Brooks, Awards Administrator

The Institute of Materials, Minerals and Mining is a qualifying body and learned society for individuals seeking to be recognized or already practising as professionals in the international minerals and materials industry.

Bosworth Smith Trust Fund

Subjects: Metal mining and non-ferrous extraction metallurgy or mineral dressing.
Purpose: To assist research.
Eligibility: Open to applicants who possess a degree in a relevant subject.
Level of Study: Postgraduate
Value: Approx. UK £5,500 to cover working expenses, visits to mines and plants in connection with research and the purchase of apparatus
Length of Study: 1 year
Frequency: Annual
Study Establishment: An approved university
Country of Study: United Kingdom
No. of awards offered: Varies
Application Procedure: Applicants must complete an application form, available on request.
Closing Date: March 15th

Edgar Pam Fellowship

Subjects: All subjects within IMechE's field of interest ranging from explorative geology to extractive metallurgy.
Eligibility: Open to young graduates resident in Australia, Canada, New Zealand, South Africa or the United Kingdom who wish to undertake advanced study or research in the United Kingdom.
Level of Study: Postgraduate
Type: Fellowship
Value: UK £2,000
Length of Study: 1 year
Frequency: Annual
Study Establishment: Approved universities
Country of Study: United Kingdom
No. of awards offered: 1
Application Procedure: Applicants must complete an application form, available on request.
Closing Date: March 15th

G Vernon Hobson Bequest

Subjects: Mining geology.
Purpose: To advance the teaching and practice of geology as applied to mining.
Eligibility: Open to university staff throughout the United Kingdom.
Level of Study: Professional development
Value: Approx. UK £1,300 to cover travel, research or other objects in accordance with the terms of the bequest
Frequency: Annual
Country of Study: United Kingdom
No. of awards offered: More than 1
Application Procedure: Applicants must complete an application form, available on request.
Closing Date: March 15th

Malcolm Ray Travelling Scholarship

Subjects: Materials engineering.
Purpose: To help candidates advance both personal skills and professional knowledge.
Eligibility: Open to applicants studying materials engineering and who are under the age of 28, and can put forward an imaginative and testing project outside the UK.
Level of Study: Professional development
Type: Scholarship
Value: UK £6,000
No. of awards offered: 1
Closing Date: April 20th
Contributor: Malcolm Ray Travelling Scholarship

For further information contact:

Tel: +44 (0)1273 858700

Mining Club Award

Subjects: Mineral industry operations.
Purpose: To enable candidates to study in the United Kingdom or overseas, to present a paper at an international minerals industry conference or to assist the candidate in attending a full-time course of study related to the minerals industry outside the United Kingdom.
Eligibility: Open to British citizens aged 21–35 years who are actively engaged in full or part-time postgraduate study or employment in the minerals industry.
Level of Study: Postgraduate, professional development
Type: Award
Value: Approx. UK £1,500
Frequency: Annual
Country of Study: Any country
No. of awards offered: Varies
Application Procedure: Applicants must complete an application form, available on request.
Closing Date: March 15th

Stanley Elmore Fellowship Fund

Subjects: Extractive metallurgy and mineral processing.
Purpose: To provide funds for research to related to metallurgy and mineral processing.
Level of Study: Postdoctorate, doctorate
Type: Fellowship
Value: UK £14,000
Length of Study: 1 year
Frequency: Annual
No. of awards offered: 2

The Tom Seaman Travelling Scholarship

Subjects: Mining and/or related technologies.
Purpose: To assist the study for an aspect of engineering in the minerals industry.
Eligibility: Open to candidates who are training or have been trained for a career in mining.
Level of Study: Postgraduate, professional development
Type: Scholarship
Value: Up to UK £5,500
Frequency: Annual
Application Procedure: A complete application must be submitted.
Closing Date: April 8th

For further information contact:

The Institute of Materials, Minerals and Mining
Tel: (0) 1302 320486
Fax: (0) 1302 380900
Contact: Dr GJM Woodrow, Deputy Chief Executive

THE INSTITUTE OF SPORTS MEDICINE

Royal Free and University College Medical School, Charles Bell House, 67-73 Riding House Street, London, W1W 7EJ, England
Tel: (44) 01628-851199
Email: john@hotmail.com
Contact: Miss D Meynell, Secretary

The Institute of Sports Medicine is a postgraduate medical institute that was established to develop research, teaching and treatment in sports medicine. It offers national awards to medical practitioners and runs courses on different aspects of this specialist subject. Now that it is based at University College London, the Institute hopes to work closely with the College in the fulfilment of its objectives.

Duke of Edinburgh Prize for Sports Medicine

Subjects: Sports medicine in the community.
Purpose: To promote postgraduate work and to signify standards of excellence.
Eligibility: Open to medical practitioners in the United Kingdom.
Level of Study: Postgraduate
Type: Prize
Value: Varies, but usually a substantial cash prize
Frequency: Annual
Country of Study: United Kingdom
No. of awards offered: 1
Application Procedure: Applicants must write for an entry or nomination form in the first instance.
Closing Date: Varies annually. The exact date is specified in the conditions of entry
Funding: Private
No. of applicants last year: 3

Sir Robert Atkins Award

Subjects: Sports medicine.
Purpose: To increase medical support and active involvement in the field and to recognize a doctor who has provided the most consistently valuable medical, clinical or preventive service to a national sporting organization or sport in general.
Eligibility: Open to medical practitioners in the United Kingdom.
Level of Study: Postgraduate
Type: Award
Value: Varies, but usually a substantial cash prize
Frequency: Annual
Country of Study: United Kingdom
No. of awards offered: 1
Application Procedure: Applicants must write for an entry or nomination form in the first instance.
Closing Date: Varies
Funding: Private
No. of applicants last year: 1

THE INSTITUTE OF TURKISH STUDIES

Interculture Centre, Box 571033, Georgetown University, Washington, DC, 20057-1033, United States of America
Tel: (1) 202 687 0295
Fax: (1) 202 687 3780
Email: institute_turkishstudies@yahoo.com
Website: www.turkishstudies.org
Contact: Postdoctoral Research Travel Grants

Dissertation Writing Grants for Graduate Students

Subjects: Social sciences and humanities.
Purpose: To fund advanced students who have finished the research stage of their dissertation.
Eligibility: Applicants must be graduate students currently enrolled in a PhD degree programme in the United States of America, expected to complete all PhD requirements except their dissertation by March. Open to citizens of the United States of America or permanent residents.
Level of Study: Doctorate
Type: Grant
Value: US$5,000–10,000
Length of Study: 1 academic year
Frequency: Annual
Application Procedure: A complete application must include the two-page grant application cover sheet completed in full, a project proposal (maximum six double-spaced pages), a budget statement, three letters of recommendation sent directly to ITS, an updated curriculum vitae and academic transcripts of all graduate work.
Closing Date: March 11th
Funding: Private
Additional Information: Decisions on applications will be announced in May. For further details check the website.

Postdoctoral Summer Travel-Research Grants

Subjects: Social sciences and humanities.
Purpose: To provide partial support for travel and research to Turkey.
Eligibility: Applicants must hold a PhD in a social sciences or humanities discipline. To be eligible, applicants must be citizens of the United States of America or permanent residents and currently live or work in the United States of America.
Level of Study: Postgraduate
Type: Grant
Value: Round-trip air fare to Turkey
Length of Study: Varies, minimum of 4 weeks
Frequency: Annual
Application Procedure: A complete application must include the two-page grant application cover sheet completed in full, a project proposal (maximum five double-spaced pages), a budget statement, three letters of recommendation sent directly to ITS and an updated curriculum vitae.
Closing Date: March 11th
Funding: Private
Additional Information: Decisions on applications will be announced in May. For further details check the website.

Research Grants in Comparative Studies of Modern Turkey

Subjects: Political science.
Purpose: To fund scholars in the United States of America who study aspects of the Republic of Turkey (post-1922) in a comparative context.
Eligibility: Applicants must be citizens of the United States of America or permanent residents and affiliated with a United States of America university. Applicants must be graduate students at the dissertation research stage or postdoctoral scholars.
Level of Study: Doctorate, postgraduate, postdoctorate
Type: Grant
Value: US$10,000
Length of Study: 1 academic year
Frequency: Annual
Application Procedure: A complete application must include the two-page grant application cover sheet completed in full, a project proposal (maximum five double-spaced pages), a budget statement, three letters of recommendation sent directly to ITS, an updated curriculum vitae and academic transcripts of all graduate work.
Closing Date: March 11th
Funding: Private
Additional Information: Decisions on applications will be announced in May. For further details check the website.

Summer Language Study Grants in Turkey for Graduate Studies

Subjects: Turkish language.
Purpose: To fund summer travel to Turkey for language study in preparation for graduate research.
Eligibility: Applicants must be graduate students in any field of the social sciences or humanities, currently enrolled in a university in the United States of America. Open to citizens of the United States of America or permanent residents.
Level of Study: Graduate
Type: Grant
Value: US$1,000–2,000
Length of Study: Varies, minimum of 2 months
Frequency: Annual
Study Establishment: An established Ottoman or Turkish language training facility
Application Procedure: A complete application must include the two-page grant application cover sheet completed in full, a project proposal (maximum three double-spaced pages), a budget statement, three letters of recommendation sent directly to ITS, an updated curriculum vitae and academic transcripts of all graduate work.
Closing Date: March 11th
Funding: Private
Additional Information: Decisions on applications will be announced in May. For further details check the website.

Summer Research Grants in Turkey for Graduate Students

Subjects: Social sciences and humanities.
Purpose: To fund summer travel to carry out projects.
Eligibility: Applicants must be graduate students in any field of the social sciences or humanities in the United States of America, currently not engaged in dissertation writing. Applicants must be citizens of the United States of America or permanent residents.
Level of Study: Postgraduate, graduate
Type: Grant
Value: US$1,000–2,000
Length of Study: Varies, minimum of 2 months
Frequency: Annual
Application Procedure: A complete application must include the grant application cover sheet completed in full, a project proposal (maximum five double-spaced pages), a detailed budget stating the amount requested from ITS, three letters of recommendation sent directly to ITS, an updated curriculum vitae and academic transcripts of all graduates work.
Closing Date: March 11th
Funding: Private
Additional Information: Decisions on applications will be announced in May. For further details check the website.

THE INSTITUTION OF CIVIL ENGINEERS

1-7 Great George Street, Westminster, London, SW1P 3AA, England
Tel: (44) 20 7665 2110
Fax: (44) 20 7233 0515
Email: helen.moger@ice.org.uk
Website: www.ice.org.uk
Contact: Ms Ellen Ryan, Education Officer

QUEST C H Roberts Bequest

Subjects: Civil engineering.
Purpose: To promote the exchange of engineering graduates between the United Kingdom and Spain for the purpose of furthering their academic studies and engineering training.
Eligibility: Open to British or Spanish nationals who are members or associate members of the Institution.
Level of Study: Postgraduate
Type: Bursary
Value: Approx. UK £2,000
Length of Study: 6–9 months
Frequency: Annual
Country of Study: Spain for United Kingdom candidates and the United Kingdom for Spanish candidate

No. of awards offered: 2
Application Procedure: Applicants must complete an application form, available from Ms Coverdale.
Closing Date: March 31st
Funding: Private
Contributor: The British Council
Additional Information: Successful applicants are encouraged under the terms of the bequest to learn the language of the other country (some prior knowledge is essential) and to acquire a knowledge of its people by residence, study and engineering experience. They will be required to further their knowledge of the language by spending 1–2 hours weekly on additional language study with an approved institute or teacher, whose fees will be covered by the award. Practical experience gained in Spain under the award will be accepted towards the experience required for permission to take the professional examination.

QUEST Institution of Civil Engineers Continuing Education Award

Subjects: Civil engineering.
Purpose: To enable approved persons to undertake MSc courses after some years of industrial experience.
Eligibility: Open to graduates of any nationality who hold an accredited First Class Degree in civil engineering and have been members of the Institution at any grade for not less than 2 years.
Level of Study: Postgraduate
Type: Award
Value: Up to UK £2,000
Frequency: Annual
Country of Study: United Kingdom
No. of awards offered: 10–15
Application Procedure: Applicants must complete an application form, available from Ms Coverdale.
Closing Date: March 31st
No. of awards given last year: 13
No. of applicants last year: 20

QUEST Institution of Civil Engineers Overseas Travel Awards

Subjects: Civil engineering, environmental engineering, transportation and agricultural engineering.
Purpose: To support overseas travel by institution members to overseas universities, specific overseas projects and mid-career support and development.
Eligibility: Open to institution members, preference being given to postgraduate applicants proposing individual overseas projects or requiring mid-career support.
Level of Study: Postgraduate
Value: Up to UK £2,000
Length of Study: 3 months–1 year
Frequency: Annual
Country of Study: Any country
No. of awards offered: Approx. 15
Application Procedure: Applicants must complete an application form, available from Mrs Coverdale.
Closing Date: March 31st
Additional Information: Applications are not necessarily restricted to technical developments, but may be concerned with organizational, managerial or financial aspects of civil engineering. Awards will be judged on merit.

THE INSTITUTION OF ELECTRICAL ENGINEERS (IEE)

Michael Faraday House, Six Hills Way, Stevenage, Hertfordshire, SG1 2AY, England
Tel: (44) 20 7240 1871
Fax: (44) 20 7497 3633
Email: scholarships@iee.org
Website: www.iee.org.uk
Contact: The Scholarships Officer

The Institution of Electrical Engineers (IEE) seeks to promote the advancement of electrical, manufacturing and information engineering and facilitate the exchange of knowledge and ideas. The IEE wishes to provide a broad range of services to members, to assist them in developing their careers by improving their capabilities as engineers, and to enable them to play their full part in contributing to society.

D H Thomas Travel Bursary

Subjects: Electrical, electronic, information engineering, manufacturing engineering and related disciplines.
Purpose: To support IEE members undertaking research in Europe.
Eligibility: Open to IEE members undertaking personal and professional research. Preference is given to research taking place in Germany.
Level of Study: Professional development, doctorate, research, postgraduate, postdoctorate
Type: Travel grant
Value: UK £500
Length of Study: Up to 3 years
Frequency: Every 2 years
Country of Study: Europe, Germany
No. of awards offered: 1
Application Procedure: Applicants must complete an application form. Given that there are a limited number of awards, applicants are advised to apply as early as possible.
Closing Date: April 30th, July 31st and November 30th
Funding: Trusts

Hudswell Bequest Travelling Fellowships

Subjects: Electrical, electronic, manufacturing, engineering and related disciplines.
Purpose: To allow IEE members to pursue study overseas.
Eligibility: Open to IEE members undertaking postgraduate research in the United Kingdom.
Level of Study: Postgraduate
Type: Fellowship
Value: Up to UK £1,000
Frequency: Annual
Country of Study: United Kingdom
No. of awards offered: 4
Application Procedure: Applicants must complete an application form. Given that there are a limited number of awards, applicants are advised to apply as early as possible.
Closing Date: April 30th, July 31st and November 30th
Funding: Trusts
No. of awards given last year: 2

Hudswell International Research Scholarships

Subjects: Electrical, electronic, information technology, manufacturing engineering and related disciplines.
Purpose: To assist members of the IEE with advanced research work, leading to the award of a doctorate, to be undertaken outside the applicant's home country.
Eligibility: Open to those who have been members of the IEE for a minimum of 2 years before an application is submitted. It is expected that applicants should have attained Chartered Membership of the IEE, but applications may be accepted from applicants whose research studies may lead to Chartered Membership on completion of the approved doctorate.
Level of Study: Postgraduate, doctorate
Type: Scholarship
Value: UK £5,000
Length of Study: 1 year
Frequency: Annual
Study Establishment: Internationally recognized universities or research establishments with a high reputation for research
Country of Study: Any country
No. of awards offered: 3
Application Procedure: Applicants must complete an application form. Given that there are a limited number of awards available, applicants are advised to apply as early as possible.
Closing Date: October 15th
Funding: Trusts
No. of awards given last year: 3

IEE Master's Degree Research Scholarship

Subjects: Electrical, electronic, manufacturing and information engineering.
Purpose: To assist IEE members undertaking advanced postgraduate research studies for MRes or MPhil degrees.
Eligibility: Applicants must be IEE members who have satisfied the IEE educational requirements for Chartered Membership or whose course of studies will lead to Chartered Membership of the IEE. Applicant must have been an IEE member for not less than 2 years.
Level of Study: Postgraduate
Type: Scholarship
Value: UK £1,500
Frequency: Annual
Country of Study: United Kingdom
No. of awards offered: 6
Application Procedure: Applicants must complete an application form.
Closing Date: October 15th
Funding: Trusts
Additional Information: Given that there are a limited number of awards available, applicants are advised to apply as early as possible.

IEE Postgraduate Scholarships

Subjects: Electrical, electronic, communications, manufacturing and power engineering.
Purpose: To assist IEE members with research studies.
Eligibility: Open to research students holding qualifications which have been accepted by the IEE and to members wishing to complete a research programme that will lead to Chartered Membership. The qualifications must satisfy the IEE's educational requirements for Chartered Membership.
Level of Study: Postgraduate, doctorate, research
Type: Scholarship
Value: UK £1,250
Length of Study: 1 year
Frequency: Annual
Study Establishment: University in the UK
Country of Study: United Kingdom
No. of awards offered: 3
Application Procedure: Applicants must complete an application form and are advised to apply as early as possible.
Closing Date: October 15th
Funding: Trusts
No. of awards given last year: 3

IEE Younger Members Conference Bursary

Subjects: Electrical engineering and related disciplines.
Purpose: To assist IEE members with presenting papers at IEE conferences.
Eligibility: Open to members of the IEE who are full-time students and/or aged under 30, who have had papers accepted for presentation at an IEE conference. Applicants must also have no other sources of funding towards the registration fee or accommodation while attending the event.
Level of Study: Professional development, postgraduate
Type: Travel grant
Value: Up to UK £350
Frequency: Annual
No. of awards offered: 2 per conference
Application Procedure: Applicants must complete an application form.
Closing Date: 2 months prior to the date of the conference
No. of awards given last year: 3
Additional Information: This award is subject to complete revision and substantial changes in terms and conditions.

J R Beard Travelling Fund

Subjects: Electrical, electronic, manufacturing and related engineering.
Purpose: To enable members of the IEE to travel overseas and thus broaden their professional experience.
Eligibility: Open to IEE members intending to expand their experience in the field of manufacturing techniques conducted overseas. Applicants must currently be studying in the United Kingdom. Grants are available to assist, in particular, younger IEE members to broaden their professional experience through overseas travel.
Level of Study: Unrestricted
Type: Travel grant
Value: Up to UK £500
Frequency: Annual
Country of Study: Any country
No. of awards offered: 6
Application Procedure: Applicants must complete an application form. Given that there are a limited number of awards applicants are advised to apply as early as possible.
Closing Date: April 30th, July 31st and November 30th
Funding: Private

Leonard Research Grant

Subjects: Electrical, electronic, manufacturing and related engineering.
Purpose: To assist engineering graduates who might not otherwise be able to undertake or complete work leading to a higher degree.
Eligibility: Applicants should currently be resident in the United Kingdom and must have satisfied the educational requirement for Chartered Membership. Applicants must be IEE Members.
Level of Study: Postgraduate, doctorate
Type: Research grant
Value: UK £1,000 per annum
Frequency: Every 3 years
Study Establishment: A suitable university
Country of Study: United Kingdom
No. of awards offered: 1
Application Procedure: Applicants must complete an application form.
Closing Date: October 15th
Funding: Trusts

Leslie H Paddle Fellowship

Subjects: Electronic and radio engineering.
Purpose: To assist IEE members with research studies.
Eligibility: Open to first year research students currently resident in the United Kingdom. Applicants must possess qualifications accepted by the IEE as fulfilling the educational requirements for Chartered Membership.
Level of Study: Postgraduate, doctorate
Type: Fellowship
Value: UK £10,000
Length of Study: 2 years
Frequency: Annual
Study Establishment: A suitable university in the UK
Country of Study: United Kingdom
No. of awards offered: 1
Application Procedure: Applicants must complete an application form. Given that there are a limited number of awards, applicants are advised to apply as early year as possible.
Closing Date: October 15th
No. of awards given last year: 1
Additional Information: It is hoped that the fellowship will encourage co-operation between industry and the higher education sector and that an industrial organization will be associated with the fellowship. Leslie H Paddle Fellowship holders who satisfactorily complete their research studies may use the appendage IEE Scholar.

Lord Lloyd of Kilgerran Memorial Prize

Subjects: Mobile radio and RF engineering.
Purpose: To aid a candidate who intends to undertake an MSc, MPhil or PhD in mobile radio and RF engineering.
Eligibility: Applicants should currently be resident in the United Kingdom and should have been professional, practising engineers for a minimum of 3 years.
Level of Study: Postgraduate
Type: Prize
Value: UK £1,000
Length of Study: 1 year for full-time study, 2 years for part-time study
Frequency: Annual

Study Establishment: A suitable university
Country of Study: United Kingdom
No. of awards offered: 1
Application Procedure: Applicants must complete an application form.
Closing Date: December 31st
No. of awards given last year: 2

Princess Royal Scholarship

Subjects: Engineering work commensurate with the activities of the IEE.
Purpose: To enable an IEE member to use his or her professional knowledge and experience in a way that is beneficial to an underprivileged community in a developing country.
Eligibility: Open to applicants undertaking a specific programme of work with a charitable organization. The nature of the work must be commensurate with the activities of the IEE. The programme must be undertaken for a period of not less than 3 months and conducted in co-operation with an organization in the receiving country.
Level of Study: Postgraduate
Type: Scholarship
Value: UK £1,000
Frequency: Annual
Country of Study: Any developing country
No. of awards offered: 1
Application Procedure: Applicants must complete an application form. Given that there are a limited number of awards, applicants are advised to apply as early as possible.
Closing Date: October 15th
No. of awards given last year: 1

Robinson Research Scholarship

Subjects: Electrical, electronic, communications, information or manufacturing engineering and related disciplines.
Purpose: To assist IEE members with research leading to the award of a PhD or postdoctoral qualification.
Eligibility: Open to first-year research students currently resident in the United Kingdom. Applicants must possess qualifications which have been accepted by the IEE as fulfilling the educational requirements for Chartered Membership.
Level of Study: Doctorate, postdoctorate, postgraduate
Type: Scholarship
Value: UK £1,250 per year
Length of Study: 2 years
Frequency: Annual
Study Establishment: A suitable university or research establishment
Country of Study: United Kingdom
No. of awards offered: 2
Application Procedure: Applicants must complete an application form.
Closing Date: October 15th
Funding: Trusts
No. of awards given last year: 2
Additional Information: Given that there are a limited number of awards available, applicants are advised to apply as early as possible.

Vodafone Scholarships

Subjects: Mobile telecommunications and related subjects.
Eligibility: Open to members of the IEE studying postgraduate courses in telecommunications.
Level of Study: Postgraduate
Type: Scholarship
Value: UK £1,250 per year for two years
Frequency: Annual
Study Establishment: Any university in the UK
Country of Study: United Kingdom
No. of awards offered: 2
Closing Date: October 15th
Additional Information: The scholarships are sponsored by the Vodafone United Kingdom Foundation.

INSTITUTION OF MECHANICAL ENGINEERS (IMECHE)

Northgate Avenue, Bury St Edmunds, Suffolk, IP32 6BN, England
Tel: (44) 12 8471 8617
Fax: (44) 12 8476 5172
Email: prizesandawards@imeche.org.uk
Website: www.imeche.org.uk
Contact: The Prizes and Awards Officer

The Institution of Mechanical Engineers (IMechE) was founded in 1847 by engineers. They formed an institution to promote the exchange of ideas and encourage individuals or groups in creating inventions that would be crucial to the development of the world as a whole. Now, over 150 years later, IMechE is one of the largest engineering institutions in the world, with over 88,000 members in 120 countries.

Donald Julius Groen Prizes

Subjects: Engineering.
Purpose: To award the author of outstanding papers or for outstanding achievements in the group's sphere of activity.
Eligibility: Open to authors of papers or those who have achievements of a sufficiently high standard to warrant the award of an IMechE prize. As a general rule, but with certain exceptions, grants are normally awarded only to members of the Institution.
Type: Prize
Value: UK £250
Frequency: Annual
No. of awards offered: 14
Application Procedure: Applicants must contact the Institution of Mechanical Engineers for details.
Funding: Private

Flatman Grants

Subjects: Mechanical engineering.
Purpose: To help individuals to further their education or to obtain special experience overseas.
Eligibility: Open to IMechE members under 30 years of age.
Level of Study: Postgraduate, professional development
Type: Grant
Value: Up to UK £750
Frequency: Annual
Country of Study: Any country
No. of awards offered: Approx. 10
Application Procedure: Applicants must submit a completed application form with three references.
Closing Date: 3 months before a decision is required
Funding: Private
Additional Information: A report is required within 3 months of completion of the project.

James Clayton Awards

Subjects: Mechanical engineering.
Purpose: To enable the recipient to pursue advanced postgraduate studies or programmes of research.
Eligibility: Open to IMechE members who hold an accredited engineering degree or who have satisfied the academic requirements for IMechE membership by other means. Applicants must not have had less than 2 years of acceptable professional training in mechanical engineering.
Level of Study: Postgraduate
Type: Grant
Value: Up to UK £1,000 per year
Length of Study: Up to 3 years
Frequency: Annual
Study Establishment: An approved centre
Country of Study: United Kingdom
No. of awards offered: Approx. 10
Application Procedure: Applicants must complete and submit an application form with three references.
Closing Date: 3 months before a decision is required
Funding: Private

Additional Information: A report is required within 3 months of the completion of the project.

James Clayton Lectures

Subjects: Mechanical engineering.
Purpose: To provide for the expenses of the person presenting the lecture that is to take place at an ordinary meeting of the Institution on a subject relating to mechanical engineering science, research, invention or experimental work.
Level of Study: Postgraduate
Type: Grant
Value: UK £500
Frequency: Annual
Country of Study: United Kingdom
No. of awards offered: 1
Application Procedure: Applicants must write for details.
Funding: Private

James Clayton Overseas Conference Travel for Senior Engineers

Subjects: Mechanical engineering.
Purpose: To assist members of the Institution who have been invited to contribute in some way to a conference or who could be expected to make a significant contribution to the aims of a conference by their attendance.
Eligibility: Open to IMechE members over the age of 40 years.
Level of Study: Professional development
Type: Travel grant
Value: Up to UK £1,000
Country of Study: Any country
No. of awards offered: Varies
Application Procedure: Applicants must submit a completed application form with 3 references.
Funding: Private
Additional Information: A report is required three months after the conference.

James Clayton Postgraduate Hardship Award

Subjects: Mechanical engineering.
Purpose: To assist outstanding postgraduates who experience hardship while undertaking courses of advanced study, training or research work on a course approved by the Institution.
Eligibility: Open to candidates who have completed a degree course in mechanical engineering accredited by IMechE and who have gained graduate membership of IMechE.
Level of Study: Postgraduate
Type: Grant
Value: Up to UK £1,000
Length of Study: 1 year
Frequency: Annual
Country of Study: United Kingdom
No. of awards offered: Up to 3
Application Procedure: Applicants must complete and submit an application form with three references.
Closing Date: 3 months before a decision is required
Funding: Private
Additional Information: A report is required 3 months after the activity has been completed.

James Watt International Medal

Subjects: Mechanical engineering.
Purpose: To award an eminent engineer who has attained worldwide recognition in mechanical engineering.
Eligibility: Open to United Kingdom engineers and those nominated from overseas.
Type: Prize
Frequency: Every 2 years (odd-numbered years)
No. of awards offered: 1
Application Procedure: Applicants must write for details.
Funding: Private
Additional Information: This award is the premier international award of the Institution.

Neil Watson Grants

Subjects: Mechanical engineering, power generation and internal combustion engines.
Purpose: To enable young engineers to attend conferences and seminars, to study engineering practices overseas or to attend suitable training courses in the field of power generation and in particular, internal combustion engines.
Eligibility: Usually only open to non-corporate members of IMechE, under the age of 31.
Level of Study: Postgraduate
Type: Grant
Value: UK £500
Frequency: Annual
Country of Study: Any country
No. of awards offered: Varies
Application Procedure: Applicants must complete and submit an application form with three references.
Funding: Private
Additional Information: A report is required 3 months after the activity has been completed.

INSTITUTO NACIONAL DE METEOROLOGIA (INM)

Camino de las Morenas S/N Ciudad Universitaria, Madrid, E-28040, Spain
Tel: (34) 91 581 9860
Fax: (34) 91 581 9892
Email: carlos.legaz@inm.es
Website: www.inm.es
Tel: 2247 LEMMC
Contact: Dr Carlos Garcia-Legaz Martinez

INM Fellowship for (Curso Internacional de Técnico en Meteorologia General Applicada)

Subjects: Atmospheric sciences and meteorology.
Eligibility: Candidates should have a background of training and professional experience in sciences, engineering or meteorology. A good knowledge of the Spanish language is required.
Level of Study: Professional development
Type: Fellowship
Value: Please contact the organization for details
Length of Study: 21 months
Frequency: Every 2 years
Study Establishment: INM training centre
Country of Study: Spain
No. of awards offered: 15–20
Application Procedure: Applicants must complete an application form, distributed by the INM. Candidates should be supported by a meteorological or academic authority. Applications can be submitted through the WMO in Geneva.
Funding: Government
No. of awards given last year: 15
No. of applicants last year: 60

INM Short-term Fellowship

Subjects: Atmospheric sciences and meteorology.
Purpose: To support on-the-job training in different departments of the INM.
Eligibility: Candidates must be staff of the meteorological service in their country. A good knowledge of English or the Spanish language is required.
Level of Study: Professional development
Type: Fellowship
Value: Please contact the organization for details
Length of Study: 2 months
Frequency: Annual
Study Establishment: INM technical departments
Country of Study: Spain
No. of awards offered: 10–15
Application Procedure: Applicants must complete an application, but no form is required, through the permanent

representatives of their countries with WMO expressing their support of the candidate.
Closing Date: The beginning of June for fellowships to be initiated in the second semester
Funding: Government
No. of awards given last year: 15
No. of applicants last year: 100

INTEGRATIVE GRADUATE EDUCATION AND RESEARCH TRAINEESHIP (IGERT)

PO Box 607, Damariscotta, ME 04543,
United States of America
Tel: (1) 593 9103
Email: questions@igert.org

The IGERT programme is a National Science Foundation. Initiated in 1997 and comprising of approximately 150 projects nationwide, the helps foundation helps universities develop new graduate programs to foster collaborative, innovative and interdisciplinary research.

IGERT Program

Subjects: Science, technology, engineering and mathematics.
Purpose: To give students the edge needed to become leaders in their chosen fields and agents for change in their careers.
Eligibility: The major criteria for selection are academic excellence and outstanding research potential.
Level of Study: Postdoctorate
Type: Scholarship
Value: A monthly stipend and tuition fee support
Frequency: Annual
Country of Study: United States of America
No. of awards offered: Determined by the National Science Foundation
Application Procedure: Apply online.
Contributor: The National Science Foundation

For further information contact:

The National Recruitment Program, PO Box 607, Damariscotta, ME 04543
Tel: (806) 593-9103

INTEL CORPORATION

Intel Public Affairs International Contribution 2200 Mission College Blud-Santa Clara, CA 95052,
United States of America
Tel: (1) 800 628 8686
Website: www.intel.com/community

Intel Corporation is committed to maintaining and enhancing the quality of life in the communities where the company has a major presence.

Intel Public Affairs China Grant

Subjects: Science, mathematics, environmental studies and technology education.
Purpose: To support further study programmes with educational and technological components in India.
Eligibility: Each request will be evaluated on the basis of the services offered and the program's impact on the community and the potential for Intel employee involvement.
Level of Study: Professional development
Type: Grant
Value: Varies
Length of Study: 1 year
Frequency: Annual
Country of Study: China
No. of awards offered: Varies
Application Procedure: Apply online or contact the office.
Funding: Corporation
Contributor: Intel Corporation

For further information contact:

Intel Technology (China) Ltd, Shanghai city
Tel: +86 21 504818818 ext. 32707
Contact: Joanna Chen, Community Affairs Manger

Intel Public Affairs Costa Rica Grant

Subjects: Science, mathematics, environmental studies and technology education.
Purpose: To support further study programmes with educational and technological components Costa Rica.
Eligibility: Each request will be evaluated on the basis of the services offered and the programme's impact on the community and the potential for Intel employee involvement.
Level of Study: Professional development
Type: Grant
Value: Varies
Length of Study: 1 year
Frequency: Annual
Country of Study: Costa Rica
No. of awards offered: Varies
Application Procedure: Apply online or contact the office.
Funding: Corporation
Contributor: Intel Corporation

For further information contact:

Intel Education Program Components Intel de Costa Rica Calle 129 La Ribera de Belen, Heredia, Costa Rica
Tel: (506) 256-6032
Contact: Public Affairs

Intel Public Affairs India Grant

Subjects: Science, mathematics, environmental studies and technology education.
Purpose: To support further study programmes with educational and technological components India.
Eligibility: Each request will be evaluated on the basis of the services offered and the programme's impact on the community and the potential for Intel employee involvement.
Level of Study: Professional development
Type: Grant
Value: Varies
Length of Study: 1 year
Frequency: Annual
Country of Study: India
No. of awards offered: Varies
Application Procedure: Apply online or contact the office.
Funding: Corporation
Contributor: Intel Corporation

For further information contact:

Intel Technology India Ltd Upper Ground Floor International Trade Tower Nehru place, New Delhi, 110019, India
Tel: (91) 11 51226055
Fax: (91) 11 51226000

Intel Public Affairs Malaysia Grant

Subjects: Science, mathematics, environmental studies and technology education.
Purpose: To support further study programmes with educational and technological components in Malaysia.
Eligibility: Each request will be evaluated on the basis of the services offered and the programme's impact on the community and the potential for Intel employee involvement.
Level of Study: Professional development
Type: Grant
Value: Varies
Length of Study: 1 year
Frequency: Annual
Country of Study: Malaysia
No. of awards offered: Varies
Application Procedure: Apply online or contact the office.
Funding: Corporation
Contributor: Intel Corporation

For further information contact:

Intel Technology Sdn Bhd Selina Saiu, Public Affairs Dept. Bayan Lepas Free International Zone Phase 3, Halaman Kampung Jawa, Penang, 11900, Malaysia
Tel: (60) 604-6422222
Fax: (60) 604-8596403

Intel Public Affairs Russia Grant

Subjects: Science, mathematics, environmental students and technology education.
Purpose: To support further study programmes with educational and technological components in Russia.
Eligibility: Each request will be evaluated on the basis of the services offered and the programme's impact on the community and the potential for Intel employee involvement.
Type: Grant
Frequency: Annual
Country of Study: Russia
No. of awards offered: Varies
Application Procedure: Apply online or contact the office.
Funding: Corporation
Contributor: Intel Corporation

For further information contact:

Intel Russia 30 Turgenev Street, Novgorod, Nizhny, 603950, Russia
Tel: (7) (8312) 16 2496
Email: paris@intel.com
Contact: Mr Evgeny Zakablukovsky, Public Affairs Manager

INTENSIVE CARE SOCIETY (ICS)

29B Montague Street, London, WC1B 5BH, England
Tel: (44) 20 7291 0690
Fax: (44) 20 7580 0689
Email: shaba@ics.ac.uk
Website: www.ics.ac.uk
Contact: Shaba Haque, Research Grant and Visiting Scholarship Enquiries & Educational Events Team Leader

The Intensive Care Society (ICS) is a charitable organization promoting advances in the care of the critically ill. This is largely accomplished through educational means and promoting research activity.

ICS Research Grants

Subjects: Any aspect of intensive care medicine and care of the critically ill.
Purpose: To promote research.
Eligibility: Applicants must be ICS members.
Level of Study: Unrestricted
Type: Research grant
Value: Please contact the organization
Frequency: Dependent on funds available
Country of Study: Any country
No. of awards offered: Varies
Application Procedure: Applicants must complete an application form, available from the website.
Closing Date: Please contact the organization
Funding: Private
Additional Information: Further information is available on the Society's website.

ICS Visiting Fellowship

Subjects: Medicine.
Purpose: To provide the cost of travel to ICS members who wish to travel to an institution other than their own, either within the UK, or overseas.
Eligibility: Open to all members of ICS.
Level of Study: Postdoctorate, doctorate
Type: Fellowship
Value: Up to UK £5,000
Application Procedure: A written proposal of not more than 1000 words should be submitted, outlining the proposed use of the grant, appropriate costs and the benefits accruing from the visit.
Closing Date: June 24th

INTER AMERICAN PRESS ASSOCIATION (IAPA)

Inter American Press Association, Jules Dubois Building, 1801 SW, 3rd Avenue, 8th Floor, Miami, FL 33129, United States of America
Tel: (1) 305 634-2465
Fax: (1) 305 635-2272
Email: gbryan@sipiapa.org
Website: www.sipiapa.org
Contact: Gloria Bryan, Assistant to the Executive Director

The Inter American Press Association (IAPA) was established in 1942 to defend and promote the right of the peoples of the America to be fully and freely informed through an independent press.

IAPA Grand Prize for Press Freedom

Subjects: Journalism.
Purpose: To recognize outstanding work by one or more persons in the Americas in defence of freedom of the press.
Eligibility: Applicants must be from North or South America and authors of published news items. Books, essays, theses and any other work that has not been published as a news article in a newspaper, periodical or magazine are excluded. Members, directors or staff members of the IAPA are not eligible.
Level of Study: Unrestricted
Type: Prize
Value: US$2,000 and plaque
Frequency: Annual
Application Procedure: Applicants must submit two originals or photocopies of the complete work, folded and pasted to one or more sheets of letter or A4 size paper, along with a copy of the edition of the newspaper, periodical or magazine in which the entry was published.
Closing Date: February 1st
Funding: Private

IAPA Scholarship Fund, Inc.

Subjects: Journalism in the print media.
Purpose: To help develop more rounded journalists through cultural exposure and study in a foreign country.
Eligibility: Open to all journalists or journalism school seniors between 21 and 35 years of age.
Level of Study: Postgraduate, professional development
Type: Scholarship
Value: US$13,000 and a one-time round-trip airfare for the year
Length of Study: 1 year
Frequency: Annual
Study Establishment: An American or Canadian university school of journalism approved by the Fund for Latin American and West Indian candidates, or an approved university or field work in a Latin American country for United States and Canadian candidates
Country of Study: Other
No. of awards offered: 4–6
Application Procedure: Applicants must complete an application form, available from the Scholarships Director.
Closing Date: December 31st
Additional Information: Candidates should have good command of the language of the country they intend to visit. United States and Canadian Scholars must take a minimum of three university courses, participate in the Fund's Reporting Program, and undertake a major research project. The Association also gives IAPA awards of US$500–1,000 and a scroll or plaque to Latin American and American journalists.

INTERNATIONAL AGENCY FOR RESEARCH ON CANCER (IARC)

150 cours Albert Thomas, F-69372 Lyon Cedex 08, France
Tel: (33) 4 72 73 84 48
Fax: (33) 4 72 73 80 80
Email: fel@iarc.fr
Website: www.iarc.fr
Contact: Ms Eve Elakroud, Administrative Assistant IARC Fellowship Programme

The International Agency for Research on Cancer (IARC) is part of the World Health Organization. IARC's mission is to co-ordinate and conduct research into the causes of human cancer and the disease's mechanisms and to develop scientific strategies for cancer control. The Agency is involved in both epidemiological and laboratory research and disseminates scientific information through publications, meetings, courses and fellowships.

IARC Postdoctoral Fellowships for Training in Cancer Research

Subjects: Epidemiology and biostatistics of cancer, environmental chemical carcinogenesis, cancer etiology and prevention, infection and cancer molecular cell biology, molecular genetics, molecular pathology and mechanisms of carcinogenesis.
Purpose: To provide training in cancer research to junior scientists from low- or medium-resource countries.
Eligibility: Applicants from any country other than those classified as high-income economies by the World Bank are eligible. Candidates should have spent less than 5 years abroad (including doctoral studies), have finished their doctoral degree within 5 years of the closing date for application and be under the age of 40 at the time of application. The working languages at IARC are English and French. Candidates must be proficient in English at a level sufficient for scientific communication. Candidates should contact the host group of their choice at IARC before application in order to establish a proposed programme of mutual interest. Candidates already working as a postdoctoral fellow at the Agency at the time of application or who have had any contractual relationship with IARC during the 6 months preceding the deadline for applications cannot be considered.
Level of Study: Postdoctorate
Type: Fellowship
Value: Travel for the Fellow and for dependents if accompanying the Fellow for at least 8 months; an annual stipend of approx. €25,000, net of tax; an annual family allowance of €400 for spouses and €450 for each child; and health insurance cover
Length of Study: 2 years, the 2nd year being subject to satisfactory appraisal
Frequency: Annual
Study Establishment: IARC in Lyon, France
Country of Study: France
No. of awards offered: Approx. 4
Application Procedure: Applicants must complete and submit an application form and include with it a letter of acceptance from the host Group at IARC. Applications must be supported by the Director of the applicant's own institution.
Closing Date: November 30th
No. of awards given last year: 10
No. of applicants last year: 44
Additional Information: Applicants should provide evidence of their ability to return to their home country at the end of the fellowship and to continue their work in cancer research.

INTERNATIONAL AIRLINE TRAINING FUND (IATF)

33, Route de l'Aeroport PO Box 416, Gineva - 15 Airport, CH-1215, Switzerland
Tel: (41) 22 799 2605
Fax: (41) 22 799 2682
Email: iatf@iata.org
Website: www.iata.org
Contact: IATF Co-ordinator

The International Airline Training Fund's (IATF) mission is to provide vocational training opportunities for staff of IATA member airlines based in countries with developing economies. It does so by providing scholarships and other training opportunities to enable worthy candidates to follow vocational training courses conducted by the IATA Aviation Training & Development Institute, the Aviation MBA at Concordia University, as well as several other courses.

IATF Aviation MBA Scholarship

Subjects: Aviation law, business administration and management.
Purpose: To allow candidates to study for their global aviation MBA course.
Eligibility: Open to staff from IATA member airlines from countries with developing economies. Applications for IATF Scholarships will be considered only after the applicant has gained acceptance onto the course by Concordia University.
Level of Study: MBA, postgraduate
Type: Scholarship
Value: Please contact the organization
Frequency: Annual
Study Establishment: Concordia University
Country of Study: Canada
Application Procedure: Applicants must first complete a course application form, available from Concordia University, followed by a scholarship application form, available from the human resources director of the applicant's airline or from the IATF secretariat.
Closing Date: May 31st
Funding: Commercial
Contributor: IATA member airlines and aviation industry suppliers
Additional Information: All applicants have to take the Graduate Management Admissions Test and should accordingly make timely arrangements to do so at the nearest testing point to their place of residence.

For further information contact:

Concordia University, Annex FB 801, 1455 de Maisonneuve Boulevard West, Montréal, H3G 1M8, Canada

IATF Global Aviation MBA Scholarship (GAMBA)

Subjects: Business administration and management.
Purpose: To allow candidates to study for their global aviation MBA course.
Eligibility: Open to staff from IATA member airlines from countries with developing economies.
Level of Study: MBA, postgraduate
Type: Scholarship
Value: Please contact the organization
Frequency: Annual
Application Procedure: Applicants must first complete a course application form, available from Concordia University. They must then complete a scholarship application form, available from the human resources director of the applicant's airline or from the IAFT secretariat.
Funding: Commercial
Additional Information: All applicants have to take the Graduate Management Admissions Test and should accordingly make timely arrangements to do so at the nearest testing point to their place of residence. This programme is the same as the Aviation MBA but has a distance learning format and runs over two academic years.

IATF IATA Aviation Training and Development Institute (ATDI) Scholarships

Subjects: Business administration and management in the field of aviation training and development.
Purpose: To enable staff of IATA member airlines based in countries with developing economies to follow short courses of specialist vocational training provided under the auspices of the IATA Aviation Training & Development Institute (ATDI).
Eligibility: Open to staff from IATA member airlines from countries with developing economies.
Level of Study: Postgraduate
Type: Scholarship
Value: Please contact the organization

Country of Study: Switzerland, the United States of America or Singapore
No. of awards offered: Varies
Application Procedure: Applicants must channel applications through the human resources director of the IATA member airline which employs the applicant for an IATF-IATDI scholarship.
Funding: Private, commercial
Contributor: IATA member airlines and aviation industry suppliers
Additional Information: The scholarship committee meets quarterly to assess accumulated applications as of that date and to make awards. The ATDI seeks to offer skills training for managers, supervisors and other airline industry specialist staff who wish to add to their professional knowledge and ability. The range of courses taught is wide, with courses in heavy demand being repeated during the course of the year.

INTERNATIONAL ANESTHESIA RESEARCH SOCIETY

2 Summit Park Drive, Suite 140, Cleveland, Ohio 44131, United States of America
Tel: (1) 216 642 1124
Fax: (1) 216 642 1127
Email: iarshq@iars.org
Website: www.iars.org

An International society committed to improving clinical care, education and research in anaesthesia, pain management and peri-operative medicine.

Clinical Scholar Research Award

Subjects: Anaesthesiology.
Purpose: To further the understanding of clinical practice in anaesthesiology through clinical investigations.
Type: Research grant
Value: US$80,000 maximum per award
Length of Study: 2 years
Study Establishment: International Anesthesia Research Society
No. of awards offered: 5
Application Procedure: Applicants must submit a formal application to the IARS by the deadline. Applicants must be a member of the IARS.
Closing Date: June 6th
No. of awards given last year: 4
No. of applicants last year: 25–30

Frontiers in Anesthesia Research Award

Subjects: Anaesthesiology.
Purpose: To foster innovation and creativity by an individual researcher in the field of anaesthesiology.
Level of Study: Unrestricted
Type: Research grant
Value: US$500,000
Length of Study: 3–5 years
Frequency: Every 2 years
No. of awards offered: 1
Application Procedure: Applicants must submit a formal application to the IARS by the published deadline. Applicants must be a member of the IARS.
Closing Date: September
Funding: Corporation
Contributor: International Anesthesia Research Society
No. of applicants last year: 13–15

Teaching Recognition Award

Subjects: Anaesthesiology.
Purpose: To recognize an individual with outstanding teaching skills.
Level of Study: Unrestricted
Type: Grant
Value: US$5,000; disbursement: US$1,000 to the recipient, US$4,000 to the recipient's institution.
Frequency: Annual
Study Establishment: International Anesthesia Research Society
No. of awards offered: 1
Application Procedure: Application must be submitted to the IARS by the published deadline. Applicant must be a member of the IARS.
Closing Date: May 2nd
No. of awards given last year: 1
No. of applicants last year: 2

INTERNATIONAL ASSOCIATION FOR THE PROMOTION OF CO-OPERATION WITH SCIENTISTS FROM THE NEW INDEPENDENT STATES OF THE FORMER SOVIET UNION (INTAS)

58/8 Avenue des Arts, B-1000 Brussels, Belgium
Tel: (32) 2 549 01 11
Fax: (32) 2 549 01 56
Email: intas@intas.be
Website: www.intas.be
Contact: INTAS Secretariat

Young Scientist PhD Fellowships (NIS)

Subjects: All subjects.
Purpose: To enable the researchers to carry out research in the NIS, including two visits to a scientific organization in an INTAS member state for the purpose of project-related research.
Eligibility: Young scientists, not older than 35 years of age, from New Independent States of the former Soviet Union (NIS)-Armenia, Azerbaijan, Belarus, Georgia, Kazakhstan, Kyrgyzstan, Moldova, Russia, Tajikistan, Turkmenistan, Ukraine and Uzbekistan may apply. The young NIS scientists who are in the 1st year of a PhD programme in an NIS institution may apply for a fellowship for the 2nd and 3rd years of their PhD. The work programme must include a minimum of 2 visits each of 2–3 months to an INTAS member state research institute for the purpose of collaborative research.
Level of Study: Doctorate, research
Type: Fellowship
Value: Up to €16,400 for 2 years. This may include a monthly grant of €300 while in the NIS, travel costs, 10 per cent overheads for the NIS institute and a monthly allowance of up to €1,200 while working in an INTAS member state
Length of Study: 2 years
Study Establishment: Any NIS Institute
Closing Date: April 30th

Young Scientist Postdoctoral Fellowships

Subjects: Open to all academic discipline.
Purpose: To enable the researchers to carry out research in the NIS, including two visits to a scientific organization from an INTAS member state for the purpose of project-related research.
Eligibility: Young postdoctoral fellows, not older than 35 years of age, holding a full-time research position at an Institute in one of the New Independent States of the former Soviet Union (NIS)-Armenia, Azerbaijan, Belarus, Georgia, Kazakhstan, Kyrgyzstan, Moldova, Russia, Tajikistan, Turkmenistan, Ukraine, and Uzbekistan may apply. The work programme must include a minimum of 2 visits each of 2 to 3 months to an INTAS member state research institute for the purpose of collaborative research.
Level of Study: Postdoctorate
Type: Fellowship
Value: Up to €20,400 for 2 years. This may include a monthly grant of €400 while in the NIS, travel costs, 10 per cent overheads for the NIS institute and a monthly allowance of up to €1,500 while working in an INTAS member state
Length of Study: 2 years
Study Establishment: Any NIS Institute
Application Procedure: Application forms are available on request or on the INTAS website.
Closing Date: April 30th

INTERNATIONAL ASSOCIATION FOR THE STUDY OF INSURANCE ECONOMICS

53 Route de Malagnou, CH-1208 Geneva, Switzerland
Tel: (41) 22 707 6600
Fax: (41) 22 736 7536
Email: secretariat@genevaassociation.org
Website: www.genevaassociation.org
Contact: Professor Patrick Liedtke, Secretary General

The International Association for the Study of Insurance Economics was established in 1973 for the purpose of promoting economic research in the sector of risk and insurance.

Ernst Meyer Prize

Subjects: Risk and insurance economics.
Purpose: To recognize research work that makes a significant and original contribution.
Eligibility: Open to professors, researchers or students of economics.
Level of Study: Unrestricted
Type: Prize
Value: Swiss Francs 5,000
Frequency: Annual
Country of Study: Any country
No. of awards offered: 1
Application Procedure: Applicants must write for details.
Closing Date: September 30th
Funding: Private
No. of applicants last year: 7

Geneva Association

Subjects: Topics of interest in risk management or insurance.
Purpose: To defray printing costs of university theses.
Eligibility: Open to authors of university theses already submitted.
Level of Study: Postdoctorate, doctorate
Type: Grant
Value: Swiss Francs 3,000 to help defray printing costs
Frequency: Annual
Application Procedure: Applicants must write for further information.
Closing Date: September 30th
Funding: Private

International Association for the Study of Insurance Economics Research Grants

Subjects: Risk management and insurance economics.
Purpose: To promote economic research.
Eligibility: Open to graduates involved in research for a thesis leading to a doctoral degree in economics.
Level of Study: Postgraduate
Type: Research grant
Value: Swiss Francs 10,000
Length of Study: 10 months
Frequency: Annual
Country of Study: Any country
No. of awards offered: 2
Application Procedure: Applicants must submit an application accompanied by a personal history, a description of the research undertaken and a letter of recommendation from two professors of economics.
Closing Date: September 30th
Funding: Private
Additional Information: The Association reserves the right to support research on other subjects for which applications are submitted. The Association also grants authors of university theses already submitted, dealing in depth with a subject in the field of risk and insurance economics, a subsidy of up to Swiss francs 3,000 towards printing costs.

INTERNATIONAL ASSOCIATION FOR THE STUDY OF OBESITY

231 North Gower Street, London, NW1 2NS, England
Tel: (44) 20 7691 1900
Fax: (44) 20 7387 6033
Email: kate.Baillie@iaso.org
Website: www.iaso.org
Contact: Kate Baillie, Director

The International Association for the Study of Obesity (IASO) aims to improve global health by promoting the understanding of obesity and weight-related diseases through scientific research and dialogue whilst encouraging the development of effective policies for their prevention and management. IASO is the leading global professional organization concerned with obesity, operating in over 50 countries around the world.

The IASO New Investigator Award

Subjects: Obesity research.
Purpose: To promote interest in obesity research among investigators who are still in training. IASO aims to increase the number of individuals choosing a career in the field and encourage attendance of students, fellows and mentors at the International Congress of Obesity.
Eligibility: Applicant must be a member of an IASO National Association.
Level of Study: Research, doctorate, postgraduate
Type: Award
Value: Cash prize of US$500 and a commemorative plaque
Length of Study: Variable
Frequency: Every 4 years
Study Establishment: Any
Country of Study: Any country
No. of awards offered: 1
Application Procedure: Applicants must check the website for details.

Per Björntorp Travelling Fellowship

Subjects: Obesity research.
Purpose: In memory of Professor Per Björntorp, to provide travel grants to enable young researchers to attend the International Congress of Obesity.
Eligibility: Applicant must be a member of an IASO National Association.
Level of Study: Research, postgraduate, predoctorate, doctorate, postdoctorate
Type: Travelling bursary
Value: Return economy flights, Congress Registration and hotel accommodation at the International Congress of Obesity
Frequency: 4 years
Study Establishment: Any
Country of Study: Any country
Application Procedure: Applicant must check the website for details.

INTERNATIONAL ASSOCIATION OF FIRE CHIEFS (IAFC) FOUNDATION

4025, Fair Ridge Drive, Fairfax, VA, 22033, United States of America
Tel: (1) 703 273 0911
Fax: (1) 703 273 9363
Email: iafcfoun@msn.com
Contact: Ms Patricia Hessenauer

Each year, the International Association of Fire Chiefs (IAFC) Foundation co-ordinates a scholarship programme made possible through the generosity of corporations throughout the United States of America as well as donations from individuals and persons sponsoring a scholarship as a memorial to a friend or colleague.

IAFC Foundation Scholarship

Subjects: All subjects.
Purpose: To assist fire service personnel towards college degrees.

Eligibility: Open to any person who is an active member of a state, county, provincial, municipal, community, industrial or federal fire department who has demonstrated proficiency as a member. Dependants of members are not eligible.
Level of Study: Graduate, doctorate, professional development, postdoctorate, mba, postgraduate, predoctorate
Type: Scholarship
Value: US$250–4,000
Frequency: Annual
Country of Study: Any country
No. of awards offered: 20
Application Procedure: Applicants must complete an application form. This includes a 250-word statement outlining reasons for applying for assistance and an explanation as to why the candidate thinks that the course will be useful in their chosen field of course description.
Closing Date: August 1st
Funding: Commercial, individuals, private
No. of awards given last year: 13
No. of applicants last year: 65
Additional Information: In evaluating the applications, preference will be given to those demonstrating need, desire and initiative.

INTERNATIONAL ASTRONOMICAL UNION (IAU)

98bis, boulevard Arago, F-75014 Paris, France
Tel: (33) 1 43 25 83 58
Fax: (33) 1 43 25 26 16
Email: iau@iap.fr
Website: www.iau.org
Contact: Administrative Assistant

The mission of the International Astronomical Union (IAU), founded in 1919, is to promote and safeguard the science of astronomy in all its aspects through international co-operation. The IAU, through its 12 scientific divisions and 40 commissions covering the full spectrum of astronomy, continues to play a key role in promoting and co-ordinating worldwide co-operation in astronomy.

IAU Travel Grant

Subjects: Astronomy and astrophysics.
Purpose: To provide funds to qualified individuals to enable them to visit institutions abroad. It is intended that the visitors have ample time and opportunity to interact with the intellectual life of the host institution. It is a specific objective of the programme that astronomy in the home country is enriched after the applicant returns.
Eligibility: Open to faculty members, staff members, postdoctoral Fellows or graduate students at any recognized educational or research institution.
Level of Study: Postgraduate, postdoctorate, graduate, research
Value: One return economy fare between home and host institutions
Length of Study: At least 3 months at a single host institution
Country of Study: Any country
No. of awards offered: 12–15 per year
Application Procedure: Applicants must submit an application including a curriculum vitae, a plan of scientific activity, letters of support from the home and host institutions, information on responsibility for subsistence at the host institution, and information on the lowest available fare. Applications should be submitted in time for the Officers of the Commission to consult by post.
Closing Date: There is no deadline
Contributor: Academy of Sciences
No. of awards given last year: 15
No. of applicants last year: 30

For further information contact:

University of Virginia - University of Station, Box 3818, Charlottesville, VA, 22 903 0818, United States of America
Tel: (1) 4349247494
Fax: (1) 434 924 3104
Email: crt@viginia.edu
Contact: Dr Charles R Tolbert, President

University of Toronto, Erindale College, Mississauga, ON, L5l 1C6, Canada
Tel: (1) 905 828 5351
Fax: (1) 905 828 5328
Email: jpercy@credit.erin.utoronto.ca
Contact: John R Percy, Vice-President

INTERNATIONAL ATOMIC ENERGY AGENCY (IAEA)

Vienna International Centre, Wagramerstrasse 5,
PO Box 100, A-1400 Vienna, Austria
Tel: (43) 1 26 00 0
Fax: (43) 1 26 00 7
Email: crp.research@iaea.org
Website: www.crp.iaea.org
Contact: Research Contract Administrator

Research Contracts (IAEA)

Subjects: Any scientific or technical field related to the peaceful uses of atomic energy and the use of radio-isotopes in agriculture, industries, medicine, research, etc.
Purpose: To encourage and assist research on the development and practical application of atomic energy for peaceful use throughout the world.
Eligibility: Institutions with research projects developed in line with the overall goals of the agency. Priority is normally given to proposals received from institutions in developing countries.
Level of Study: Research
Type: Research
Value: Approx. US$5,000 per year per contract
Length of Study: 1 year (extension possible up to 3 years)
Application Procedure: Application forms are available on request or can be downloaded from www.iaea.org/programs/ri/uc.html Research proposals could be submitted either based on a proposal made by the agency or a proposal developed by the research institute itself.
Closing Date: May 31st

INTERNATIONAL BEETHOVEN PIANO COMPETITION

Universität für Musik und darstellende Kunst Wien,
Anton-Von-Webernplatz 1,
A-1030 Vienna, Austria
Tel: (43) 171 155 6050
Fax: (43) 171 155 6059
Email: beethoven-comp@mdw.ac.at
Website: www.mdw.ac.at/beethoven-competition
Contact: Ms Elga Ponzer, Secretary General

International Beethoven Piano Competition

Subjects: Piano.
Purpose: To encourage the artistic development of young pianists.
Eligibility: Open to pianists of all nationalities born between January 1st 1973 and December 31st 1988.
Level of Study: Unrestricted
Type: Competition
Value: The first prize is €7,122, a Bosendorfer Model 200 piano and engagements, the second prize is €5,087, the third prize is €4,069, and there are three further prizes of €1,500
Frequency: Every 4 years
Country of Study: Austria
No. of awards offered: 6
Application Procedure: Applicants must write for details.
Closing Date: September 30th
Funding: Government, private
No. of awards given last year: 6
No. of applicants last year: 248

INTERNATIONAL CENTER FOR JOURNALISTS (ICFJ)

1616 H Street, NW Third floor, Washington, DC 20006, United States of America
Tel: (1) 1 202 737 3700
Fax: (1) 1 202 737 0530
Email: editor@icfj.org
Website: www.icfj.com

Since 1984 the ICFJ has sought to share professional knowledge and information with journalists and their news organizations around the world, promoting excellence in news coverage of critical community and global issues.

Knight International Press Fellowship

Subjects: Journalism, media.
Level of Study: Postdoctorate
Type: Fellowship
Value: Transportation costs, living expenses and a daily US$100 honorarium
Length of Study: 2–9 months
Frequency: Annual
Study Establishment: International Center for Journalists
No. of awards offered: 25
Application Procedure: Apply online.
Closing Date: February 15th and August 15th
Funding: Foundation
Contributor: Knight Foundation

The McGee Journalism Fellowship in Southern Africa

Subjects: Journalism and technical, management and business aspects of the media.
Purpose: To help journalists improve the skills and standards they need to carry out their work.
Eligibility: Open candidates of outstanding personal and professional achievement in journalism, with experience of teaching overseas, a readiness to work under difficult conditions and an interest in Southern Africa.
Level of Study: Postdoctorate
Type: Fellowship
Value: The fellowship covers all travel, housing, health insurance, living expenses and an honorarium of US$100 per day
Frequency: Annual
Study Establishment: An approved South African University
Country of Study: South Africa
No. of awards offered: 1
Application Procedure: Submit a completed application form, an essay of 500 words or less and three letters of personal or professional recommendation.
Closing Date: April 15th
Funding: Foundation
Contributor: McGee Foundation

INTERNATIONAL CENTRE FOR GENETIC ENGINEERING AND BIOTECHNOLOGY (ICGEB)

Padriciano 99, I-34012 Trieste, Italy
Tel: (39) 040 375 71
Fax: (39) 040 226 555
Email: fellowships@icgeb.org
Website: www.icgeb.org
Contact: Human Resources Unit

The International Centre for Genetic Engineering and Biotechnology (ICGEB) is an organization devoted to advanced research and training in molecular biology, with special regard to the needs of the developing world. The component host countries are Italy and India. The full member states of ICGEB are the following: Afghanistan, Algeria, Argentina, Bangladesh, Bhutan, Bosnia and Herzegovina, Brazil, Bulgaria, Chile, China, Colombia, Costa Rica, Côte d'Ivoire, Croatia, Cuba, Ecuador, Egypt, FYR Macedonia, Hungary, Iran, Iraq, Jordan, Kuwait, Kyrgyzstan, Mauritius, Mexico, Morocco, Nigeria, Pakistan, Panama, Peru, Poland, Romania, Russia, Senegal, Serbia and Montenegro, Slovakia, Slovenia, South Africa, Sri Lanka, Sudan, Syria, Tanzania, Trinidad and Tobago, Tunisia, Turkey, United Arab Emirates, Uruguay, Venezuela and Vietnam.

ICGEB Flexible Fellowship Programme

Subjects: Molecular biology, proteomics, molecular medicine, tumour virology, microbiology, bacteriology, protein structure and bioinformatics, molecular pathology, molecular immunology, biosafety, biotechnology development, human molecular genetics, leukocyte biology, molecular virology, mouse molecular genetics, muscle molecular biology, mammalian biology, malaria, biotechnology, plant biology, plant molecular biology, plant transformation, insect resistance and plant resistance, molecular/haematology, plant virology/bacteriology.
Purpose: To provide short-term training in genetic engineering and biotechnology for scientists from the member states of ICGEB, and to promote academic and industrial research in an international context.
Eligibility: Open to promising pre-and postdoctoral students, who are nationals of one of the member states of ICGEB and have already made contact with an ICGEB.
Level of Study: Predoctorate, postdoctorate
Type: Fellowship
Value: €125,000–195,000 per fellow per month
Length of Study: 3–12 months
Frequency: Annual
Study Establishment: ICGEB laboratories in Trieste, Italy; New Delhi, India; and at ICGEB outstations at Monterotondo (Rome) and Ca' Tron (Treviso), Italy
Country of Study: India or Italy
No. of awards offered: Varies
Application Procedure: Applicants must submit a completed application form through the ICGEB Liaison Officer of the applicant's country of origin. Application forms can be found on the website.
Closing Date: Applications are accepted at any time
Additional Information: For further information please refer to the website.

ICGEB Long-Term Postdoctoral Fellowship Programme

Subjects: The New Delhi laboratory is concerned with mammalian biology, virology, immunology, malaria, recombinant gene products, plant biology, plant molecular biology, insect resistance and plant resistance. Research in Trieste comprises molecular biology, proteomics, molecular medicine, tumour virology, microbiology, bacteriology, protein structure and bioinformatics, molecular pathology, tumour molecular immunology biosafety, biotechnology development, human molecular genetics, leukocyte biology, molecular virology, mouse molecular genetics, muscle molecular biology. Outstations at Monterotondo (Rome) and Ca' Tron (Treviso) are concerned with molecular/haematology and plant bacteriology/plant virology, respectively.
Purpose: To provide long-term training in genetic engineering and biotechnology for scientists from the member states and to promote state-of-the art academic and industrial research training in an international context. The fellowship aims to effectively contribute to the scientific development of the Fellow's home country. Training is proposed within the scope of biotechnological and genetic engineering research and offers an opportunity for individuals to broaden their scientific background or to extend their research in health, nutrition, industrial development, environmental protection and energy production.
Eligibility: Open to promising postdoctoral or established research students under the age of 35, who are nationals of one of the ICGEB member states.
Level of Study: Postdoctorate
Type: Fellowship
Value: €16,000–29,000 per Fellow per year, depending on the place of study, as well as travel costs and medical insurance
Length of Study: 1–2 years
Frequency: Annual
Study Establishment: ICGEB laboratories in Trieste, Italy; New Delhi, India; and Outstations at Monterotondo (Rome) and Ca' Tron (Treviso), Italy

Country of Study: India or Italy
No. of awards offered: Varies
Application Procedure: Applicants must submit a completed application form through the respective National Liaison Officer in their country of origin.
Closing Date: Refer to website
Additional Information: For further information please refer to the website.

Predoctoral Fellowship Programme ICGEB International PhD Programme

Subjects: Molecular biology, molecular medicine, tumour virology, microbiology, bacteriology, protein structure and bioinformatics, molecular pathology, molecular immunology, proteomics, human molecular genetics, molecular virology, mouse molecular genetics.
Purpose: To enable promising young students to attend and complete the PhD programme at ICGEB Trieste in Italy. The programme is in collaboration with the Scuola Normale Superiore (SNS) Pisa, Italy and is validated by the Open University, UK.
Eligibility: Open to promising predoctoral students under the age of 32 from any member state of the ICGEB.
Level of Study: Predoctorate, postgraduate
Type: Fellowship
Value: €15,600
Length of Study: 3–4 years
Frequency: Annual
Study Establishment: ICGEB component laboratories in Trieste
Country of Study: Italy
No. of awards offered: Various
Application Procedure: Applicants must refer to the website.
Closing Date: Refer to website
Additional Information: For more information on this programme please refer to the website.

Predoctoral Fellowship Programme ICGEB JNU PhD Programme in Life Sciences

Subjects: Mammalian biology, virology, immunology, malaria and biotechnology, plant biology, plant molecular biology, plant transformation, insect and plant resistance.
Purpose: To offer postgraduate training with the aim of obtaining a PhD degree in the field of life sciences at the Jawaharlal Nehru University in New Delhi, in collaboration with the ICGEB.
Eligibility: Open to promising young students in possession of an MSc from a recognized university, who are nationals of one of the ICGEB member states.
Level of Study: Postgraduate, predoctorate
Type: Fellowship
Value: €10,200
Length of Study: 3–4 years
Frequency: Annual
Study Establishment: Jawaharlal Nehru University in New Delhi
Country of Study: India
No. of awards offered: Various
Application Procedure: Applicants must refer to the website.
Closing Date: Refer to website
Additional Information: For more information on this programme please refer to the website.

INTERNATIONAL CENTRE FOR PHYSICAL LAND RESOURCES

Geological Institute, University of Ghent, Krijgslaan 281/S8, B-9000 Ghent, Belgium
Tel: (32) 9 264 4626
Fax: (32) 9 264 4991
Email: plrprog.adm@rug.ac.be
Website: www.allserv.rug.ac.be/˜amtanghe/main.html
Contact: Professor E Van Ranst

The International Centre for Physical Land Resources has a long-standing tradition in academic formation and training in physical land resources, including soil science, soil survey, land evaluation, agricultural applications and eremology, eg. dryland and desertification. Since 1997, the scope of the courses has been widened with courses on the non-agricultural use and application of physical land resources. Students can major in either soil science or in engineering geology. Teaching is provided by lecturers of the University of Ghent and of the Free University of Brussels.

Postgraduate Studies in Physical Land Resources Scholarship

Subjects: Fundamental soil science, soil genesis, prospection and classification, non-agricultural use and applications of land and soils, geotechnical engineering, soil mechanics and hydrogeology, management of physical and land resources, agricultural applications, soil fertility, soil erosion and conservation or land evaluation.
Purpose: To provide postgraduate/MSc training opportunities to nationals from developing countries.
Eligibility: Open to nationals of the developing world or non-European Union members.
Level of Study: Postgraduate
Type: Scholarship
Value: €850 per month
Length of Study: 1 year, with a possible maximum extension to 2 years
Frequency: Annual
Study Establishment: Ghent University
Country of Study: Belgium
No. of awards offered: Approx. 2
Application Procedure: Applicants must complete an application form and submit this with certified diplomas and transcripts to the Programme Secretariat to obtain academic admission.
Closing Date: March 31st
Funding: Government
No. of awards given last year: 1
No. of applicants last year: 45

INTERNATIONAL CHAMBER MUSIC COMPETITION

UFAM, 8 rue du Dôme, F-75116 Paris, France
Tel: (33) 1 47 04 76 38
Fax: (33) 1 47 27 35 03
Email: ufam@wanadoo.fr
Website: www.infoservice.fr/ufam
Contact: Mrs Dominique Bertrand, President

International Chamber Music Competition

Subjects: Groups of wind and string instruments, with or without the piano.
Purpose: To enable musicians to play engagements across the world.
Eligibility: Open to groups of musicians of any nationality who are not more than 36 years of age. The average age of the group should not exceed 34 years.
Level of Study: Postgraduate
Type: Prize
Value: €25,000 plus special prizes. Please contact the organization for details
Frequency: Every 2 years
Country of Study: Any country
No. of awards offered: Varies
Application Procedure: Applicants must request a brochure.
Closing Date: September 12th in the year of the competition
Funding: Private

Paris International Singing Competition

Subjects: Singing, opera and melody.
Purpose: To help young singers in starting their career.
Eligibility: Open to female singers aged 32 years and younger and male singers aged 34 years and younger. There are no nationality restrictions.
Level of Study: Unrestricted
Type: Prize

Value: Please contact the organization. There is free accommodation for competitors and winners are offered important singing engagements
Frequency: Every 2 years
Country of Study: Any country
No. of awards offered: 8
Application Procedure: Applicants must request a brochure.
Closing Date: May

INTERNATIONAL COUNCIL FOR CANADIAN STUDIES (ICCS)

250 City Centre Avenue, Suite 303, Ontario, Ottawa, K1ON K1P 5E7, Canada
Tel: (1) 613 789 7828
Fax: (1) 613 789 7830
Email: reception@iccs-ciec.ca
Website: www.iccs-ciec.ca
Contact: Luc Asselin, Program Assistant

The International Council for Canadian Studies (ICCS) administers programmes for Canadian students (CSFP, FGA, OAS and PRA) on behalf of the Department of Foreign Affairs and International Trade (DFAIT). The ICCS is also responsible for the administration aspects of scholarships and study programmes offered to students of foreign countries, funded by DFAIT.

Canada-Asia-Pacific Awards

Subjects: International research.
Purpose: To assist scholars in higher education institutions in Asia Pacific Region to undertake short-term research.
Eligibility: Open to students from the Asia-Pacific region.
Level of Study: Postgraduate
Type: Award
Value: Canadian $5,000–$10,000
Frequency: Annual
Country of Study: Canada
No. of awards offered: Up to 2
Application Procedure: A completed application form must be submitted.
Closing Date: September 30th

For further information contact:

Website: www.iccs-ciec.ca/pages/5_govprogs/e_capacaw.html

Canadian Commonwealth Scholarship and Fellowship Plan

Subjects: Science, Law, environment studies, economics, sociology, geography, electronics and education.
Purpose: To offer scholarships to citizens of other common wealth countries to study in Canada.
Eligibility: Open to candidates who are not more than 40 years of age with completion of tertiary education from a English medium.
Level of Study: Postgraduate
Type: Scholarship
Value: Expenses of travel, living and study
Length of Study: 2–4 years
Frequency: Annual
Country of Study: Canada
Application Procedure: Further information available on the website.
Closing Date: September 30th

Canadian Prime Minister's Awards for Publishing (CPMA)

Subjects: Area and cultural studies.
Purpose: To increase the amount of published material related to Canada available in Japanese.
Eligibility: Open to Japanese publishers who are likely to increase the knowledge and understanding of contemporary Canada.
Level of Study: Postgraduate
Type: Scholarship
Frequency: Annual
Application Procedure: Further information available on the website.
Closing Date: November 15th

For further information contact:

Academic Relations (CPMA), Public Affairs, embassy of Canada, 7-3-38 Akasaku, Minato-Ku, Tokyo, 107-8503
Tel: (03) 5412 6305
Fax: (03) 5412 6287
Email: tokyo.lib-bib@international.gc.ca
Website: www.iccs-ciec.ca/pages/5_govprogs/l_pmaward.html

Canadian Studies Postdoctoral Fellowship

Subjects: Area and cultural studies.
Purpose: To enable young academics who have completed a doctoral thesis to visit a Canadian university.
Eligibility: Open to students with a doctoral degree.
Level of Study: Postdoctorate
Type: Fellowship
Value: Canadian $2,500 per month plus the cost of a return airline ticket
Length of Study: 1–3 months
Frequency: Annual
Study Establishment: Any accredited Canadian university
Country of Study: Canada
Application Procedure: Application form and a recommendation from the national Canadian studies Association must be submitted.
Closing Date: December 31st

For further information contact:

Canadian Studies Postdoctoral Fellowships, International Council for Canadian Studies, 250 City Centre, S-303, Ottawa, ON K1R 6K7
Tel: (613) 789 7834
Email: reception@iccs-ciec.ca
Website: www.iccs-ciec.ca/pages/4_ICCSprogs/b_intern.html

ICCS Doctoral Student Research

Subjects: Social sciences and humanities.
Purpose: To assist students to undertake doctoral research in Canada.
Eligibility: Open to applicants whose dissertations are related in substantial part to Canada.
Level of Study: Postgraduate
Value: Assistance towards international airfare and a monthly allowance.
Length of Study: 8 months
Frequency: Annual
Study Establishment: Any accredited Canadian university
Country of Study: Canada
Application Procedure: A completed application form must be submitted.
Closing Date: November 25th
Funding: Government
Contributor: Department of Foreign Affairs and International Trade

For further information contact:

Public Affairs Section, The Canadian Embassy
Website: www.iccs-ciec.ca/pages/5_govprogs/d_doctresrch.html

ICCS Graduate Student Scholarships

Subjects: Social sciences and humanities.
Purpose: To provide access to crucial scholarly information and resources in Canada in support of a thesis/dissertation.
Eligibility: Open to students at the thesis or dissertation stage in the field of social sciences or humanities.
Type: Scholarship
Value: Canadian $3,500
Frequency: Annual
Study Establishment: Any accredited Canadian University
Country of Study: Canada
No. of awards offered: 10
Application Procedure: A completed application form and all supporting materials should be submitted.
Closing Date: December 31st

For further information contact:

Tel: (613) 789 7834 ext. 242
Email: csppec@iccs-ciec.ca
Website: www.iccs-ciec.ca/pages/4_ICCSprogs/a_gradstu.html#
Contact: Canadian Studies Programs Assistant

Organization of American States (OAS) Fellowships Programs

Subjects: Human development.
Purpose: To fund education of Canadian residents and nationals in other American nations.
Eligibility: Open to Canadian residents and nationals.
Type: Fellowship
Length of Study: 3 months–3 years
Frequency: Annual
Application Procedure: A completed application form must be submitted.

For further information contact:

Website: www.scholarships-bourses-ca.org/pages/OASout/aOAS_Intro-en.html

THE INTERNATIONAL DAIRY-DELI-BAKERY ASSOCIATION

IDDBA, PO Box 5528, Madison, W1 53705 0528,
United States of America
Tel: (1) 608 238 7908
Fax: (1) 608 238 6330
Website: www.iddba.org

Our mission is to expand our leadership role in promoting the growth and development of daily, deli and bakery sales in the food industry. Our vision is to be the essential resource for relevant information and services that add value across all food channels for the dairy, deli and bakery categories.

IDDBA Graduate Scholarships

Subjects: Culinary arts, baking/party arts, food service, business and marketing.
Purpose: To support employees of IDDBA-member companies.
Eligibility: Applicants must be a current full- or part-time employee of an IDDBA member company with an academic background in a food-related field.
Level of Study: Postgraduate
Type: Scholarship
Value: US$250–1,000
Length of Study: 1 year
Frequency: Annual
Country of Study: United States of America
No. of awards offered: Varies
Application Procedure: Contact the Education Information Specialist.
Closing Date: January 1st, April 1st, July 1st, October 1st
Funding: Foundation
Contributor: IDDBA

For further information contact:

Email: kpeckham@iddba.org

INTERNATIONAL DEVELOPMENT RESEARCH CENTRE (IDRC)

Centre Training & Awards Program, 250 Albert Street, PO Box 8500,
Ottawa, ON K1G 3H9, Canada
Tel: (1) 613 236 6163
Fax: (1) 613 563 0815
Email: cta@idrc.ca
Website: www.idrc.ca/awards
Contact: Mrs Jennifer Chauhan, Program Assistant

The International Development Research Centre (IDRC) is a public corporation created by the Canadian government to help communities in the developing world find solutions to social, economic and environmental problems through research.

Canadian Window on International Development

Subjects: One award is for research that explores the relationship between Canadian aid, trade, immigration and diplomatic policy and international development and the alleviation of global poverty, and a second award will be granted for research into a problem that is common to First Nations or Inuit communities in Canada and a developing region of the world.
Eligibility: Successful candidates will propose comparative research requiring data from both Canada and a developing region of the world to better understand the common, interrelated problem or issue identified for in-depth study. Selection will favour those proposals that demonstrate the relevance of the research topic for Canada and for the less-developed country or countries being studied, and the close linkage between the international and national character of the topic. Competition is open to Canadian citizens, permanent residents of Canada and developing country nationals.
Level of Study: Graduate, postgraduate, doctorate
Value: Up to Canadian $20,000
Length of Study: 3 months–1 year
Frequency: Annual
Study Establishment: Universities
Country of Study: Canada
No. of awards offered: 2 or 3 per year
Application Procedure: Applicants must complete an application form. Please refer to the website: www.idrc.ca/awards
Closing Date: April 1st
Funding: Government
No. of awards given last year: Varies
No. of applicants last year: Varies

Community Forestry: Trees and People - John G Bene Fellowship

Subjects: Forestry management.
Purpose: To assist Canadian graduate students in undertaking research on the relationship of forest resources to the social, economic and environmental welfare of people in developing countries.
Eligibility: Open to Canadian citizens and permanent residents who are registered at a Canadian university at the Master's or doctoral level. Applicants must have an academic background that combines forestry or agroforestry with social sciences.
Level of Study: Graduate, postgraduate, doctorate
Type: Fellowship
Value: Canadian $15,000
Length of Study: 3 months–1 year
Frequency: Annual
Study Establishment: Universities
Country of Study: Canada
No. of awards offered: 1
Application Procedure: Applicants must submit a summary of their research proposal, budget of proposed research, application form, curriculum vitae, two references, a letter from the institution confirming affiliation, transcripts, confirmation from their academic advisor that coursework is complete and proof of Canadian citizenship or permanent residency.
Closing Date: March 1st
Funding: Private
Contributor: Endowment
No. of awards given last year: Varies
No. of applicants last year: Varies

Ecosystem Approaches to Human Health Awards

Subjects: The interactions between multiple determinates of health within defined ecosystems, using transdisciplinary, participatory and gender-integrative approaches, moving from an exclusive health service response to an ecosystem management response to human health problems.

Purpose: To provide financial assistance to graduate students undertaking research projects that look at the relationships between the environment and human health.
Eligibility: Research questions and methods need to address the implications of gender and social differences as these relate to ecosystem approaches to human life. Awards will be granted for training and research proposals that use ecosystem approaches to improve human health. Priority will be given to proposals for research on ecosystems that are stressed through agriculture, urbanization or mining activities.
Level of Study: Graduate, postgraduate, doctorate
Type: Award
Value: Up to Canadian $15,000
Length of Study: Up to 1 year
Frequency: Annual
Study Establishment: Universities
No. of awards offered: Up to 6
Application Procedure: Applicants must write for details.
Funding: Government
Contributor: Canadian Government
No. of awards given last year: Varies
No. of applicants last year: Varies

IDRC Doctoral Research Awards

Subjects: IDRC's research activities focus on four programme areas: social and economic equity, environment and natural resource management and information, communication techniques (ICTs) for development, innovation, policy and science.
Purpose: To promote the growth of Canadian capacity in research on sustainable and equitable development from an international perspective.
Eligibility: Open to Canadian citizens and permanent residents and developing country nationals. Applicants must be registered at a Canadian university, have a research proposal for a doctoral thesis and provide evidence of affiliation and complete coursework prior to taking on research.
Level of Study: Doctorate
Type: Award
Value: Up to Canadian $20,000
Length of Study: 3 months–1 year
Frequency: Annual
Study Establishment: Universities. Normally, such research is conducted in Latin America, Africa, the Middle East or Asia
Country of Study: Canada
No. of awards offered: Varies
Application Procedure: Applicants must complete and submit an application form with a research proposal, budget, curriculum vitae, two references, a letter from the institution of affiliation, approval of thesis by committee, transcripts, confirmation from their adviser that coursework will be complete before the start of research, and proof of Canadian citizenship or permanent residency, or citizenship of a developing country.
Closing Date: April and November
Funding: Government
Contributor: The Canadian government
No. of awards given last year: Varies
No. of applicants last year: Varies

Use of Fertility-Enhancing Food, Forage and Cover Crops in Sustainably Managed Agroecosystems: The Bentley Fellowship

Subjects: Use of fertility-enhancing plants such as leguminous forages, cover crops and grain legumes in subsistence tropical agriculture.
Purpose: To provide assistance to those who wish to undertake applied on-farm research in a developing country with co-operating farmers.
Eligibility: Open to Canadian or developing country students or researchers with a university degree in agriculture, forestry or biology.
Level of Study: Postdoctorate, postgraduate, unrestricted, graduate, doctorate
Type: Fellowship
Value: Up to Canadian $30,000
Length of Study: 1.5–2 years
Frequency: Every 2 years
Study Establishment: Universities
No. of awards offered: 1–2
Application Procedure: Applicants must complete an application form, available on request.
Closing Date: October
Funding: Private
No. of awards given last year: Varies
No. of applicants last year: Varies

INTERNATIONAL FEDERATION OF LIBRARY ASSOCIATIONS AND INSTITUTIONS (IFLA)

PO Box 95312, The Hague, NL-2509 CH, Netherlands
Tel: (31) 70 314 0884
Fax: (31) 70 383 4827
Email: ifla@ifla.org
Website: www.ifla.org
Contact: Ms Josche Neven, Communications Manager

Established in 1927, the primary function of the International Federation of Library Associations and Institutions (IFLA) is to encourage, sponsor and promote research and development in all aspects of library activity and to share its findings with the library community as a whole for the greater good of librarianship.

The Guust van Wesemael Literacy Prize

Subjects: Library science.
Purpose: To recognize an achievement in the field of literacy promotion in a developing country.
Eligibility: Open to candidates from developing countries.
Level of Study: Unrestricted
Value: €2,725
Frequency: Every 2 years
Country of Study: Any country
No. of awards offered: 1
Application Procedure: Applicants must complete an application form, available from IFLA headquarters.
Closing Date: March 1st every odd-numbered year
Funding: Private
No. of awards given last year: 2
Additional Information: The prize should be used for follow-up activities such as purchasing targeted collections of appropriate books.

Hans-Peter Geh Grant for Conference Participation

Subjects: Library and information science.
Purpose: To sponsor a librarian from the geographic region previously called the Soviet Union, including the Baltic States, to attend an IFLA seminar or conference in Germany or elsewhere in order to become acquainted with new international developments in the field of information.
Eligibility: Applicants must be IFLA affiliates or employees of IFLA members. Open only to librarians from the former Soviet region or the Baltic States.
Level of Study: Professional development
Value: €1,135
Frequency: Annual
Country of Study: Any country
Application Procedure: Applicants must complete an application form, available from IFLA headquarters.
Closing Date: February 1st
Funding: Private
No. of awards given last year: 1

INTERNATIONAL FEDERATION OF UNIVERSITY WOMEN (IFUW)

8 rue de l'Ancien-Port, CH-1201 Geneva, Switzerland
Tel: (41) 22 731 2380
Fax: (41) 22 738 0440
Email: ifuw@ifuw.org
Website: www.ifuw.org
Contact: Grants Management Officer

The International Federation of University Women (IFUW) is a non-profit, non-governmental organization comprising graduate women working locally, nationally and internationally to advocate the improvement of the status of women and girls at the international level, to promote lifelong education and to enable graduate women to use their expertise to effect change.

British Federation Crosby Hall Fellowship

Subjects: All subjects.
Purpose: To encourage advanced scholarship and original research.
Eligibility: Open to female applicants who are either members of one of IFUW's national federations or associations or, in the case of female graduates living in countries where there is not yet a national affiliate, independent members of IFUW. Applicants should be well started on a research programme and should have completed at least 1 year of graduate work.
Level of Study: Research, postdoctorate, doctorate
Type: Fellowship
Value: UK £2,500
Study Establishment: An approved Institute of Higher Education
Country of Study: United Kingdom
No. of awards offered: 1
Application Procedure: Applicants must apply through their respective federation or association. A list of IFUW national federations can be sent upon request or obtained from the website. IFUW independent members and international individual members must apply directly to the IFUW headquarters in Geneva.
Closing Date: Early September in the year preceding the competition
Funding: Private
No. of awards given last year: 1
Additional Information: Applicants in the United States and the United Kingdom should write to the addresses shown for those countries, all others should write to the main address.

For further information contact:

AAUW/IFUW Liason, 1111 Sixteenth Street NW, Washington, DC, 28036, United States of America
Fax: (1) 202 872 1425

BFWG, 4 Mandeville Courtyard, 142 Battersea Park Road, London, SW11 4NB, England
Tel: (44) 20 7498 8037

Ida Smedley Maclean, CFUW/A Vibert Douglas, IFUW and Action Fellowship

Subjects: All subjects.
Purpose: To encourage advanced scholarship and original research.
Eligibility: Open to female applicants who are either members of one of IFUW's national federations or associations or, in the case of female graduates living in countries where there is not yet a national affiliate, independent members of IFUW. Applicants should be well started on a research programme and should have completed at least 1 year of graduate work.
Level of Study: Postdoctorate, postgraduate, doctorate
Type: Fellowship
Value: The Maclean Fellowship is Swiss Francs 8,000–10,000, the Douglas Fellowship is Canadian $12,000 and the SAAP Fellowship is Swiss francs 8,000–10,000
Length of Study: More than 8 months
Study Establishment: An approved Institute of Higher Education other than that in which the applicant received her education
Country of Study: Any country
No. of awards offered: 1 of each fellowship
Application Procedure: Applicants must write for details enclosing a stamped addressed envelope. Applicants should apply through their respective federation or association. A list of IFUW national federations can be sent upon request or obtained from the website.
Closing Date: Early September in the year preceding the competition
Funding: Private
No. of awards given last year: 1 of each
Additional Information: Applicants from the United States of America and the United Kingdom should write to the addresses shown for those countries, all others should write to the main address.

For further information contact:

AAUW/IFUW Liaision, 1111 Sixteenth Street NW, Washington, DC, 28036, United States of America
Fax: (1) 202 872 1425

BFWG, 4 Mandeville Courtyard, 142 Battersea Park Road, London, SW11 4NB, England
Tel: (44) 20 7498 8037

Winifred Cullis and Dorothy Leet Grants, NZFUW Grants

Subjects: All subjects.
Purpose: To enable recipients to carry out research, obtain specialized training essential to research or training in new techniques.
Eligibility: Open to female applicants who are either a member of one of IFUW's national federations or associations or, in the case of female graduates living in countries where there is not yet a national affiliate, an independent member of IFUW. Applicants should be well started on a research programme and should have completed at least one year of graduate work.
Level of Study: Doctorate, postgraduate, graduate, postdoctorate
Type: Grant
Value: Swiss Franc 3,000–6,000
Length of Study: A minimum of 2 months
Country of Study: Any country
No. of awards offered: Varies
Application Procedure: Applicants must write for details enclosing a stamped addressed envelope. Applicants should apply through their respective federation or association. A list of IFUW national federations can be sent upon request or obtained from the Internet. Applicants in the United States of America and the United Kingdom should write to the addresses shown for those countries and all others should write to the main address.
Closing Date: Early September in the year preceding the competition
Funding: Private
No. of awards given last year: 15–20
Additional Information: Further information is available from the website.

For further information contact:

AAUW/IFUW Liason, 1111 Sixteenth Street NW, Washington, DC, 28036, United States of America
Fax: (1) 202 872 1425

BFWG, 4 Mandeville Courtyard, 142 Battersea Park Road, London, DC, SW11 4NB, England
Tel: (44) 20 7498 8037

INTERNATIONAL FOUNDATION FOR ETHICAL RESEARCH (IFER)

53 West Jackson Boulevard, Suite 1552, Chicago, IL, 60604, United States of America
Tel: (1) 312 427 6025
Fax: (1) 312 427 6524
Email: ifer@navs.org
Website: www.ifer.org
Contact: Mr Peter O'Donovan, Deputy Director

The International Foundation for Ethical Research (IFER) supports the development and implementation of viable, scientifically valid alternatives to the use of animals in research, product testing and classroom education. IFER is dedicated to the belief that through new technologies and diligent research, solutions can be found that will create a better world for all, without using animals.

IFER Fellowship for Alternatives in Scientific Research

Subjects: Tissue cultures, cell cultures, organ cultures, gas chromatography, mathematical and computer models and clinical and epidemiological surveys.
Purpose: To develop, validate and disseminate alternatives to the use of live animals in research, education and product testing. Alternatives are defined as methods that replace, refine or reduce the number of animals traditionally used.
Eligibility: Open to students enrolled in Master's and PhD programmes.
Level of Study: Postgraduate, graduate
Type: Fellowship
Value: Up to US$500 and US$2,500 for supplies
Length of Study: 1 year, renewable for up to 3 years based on eligibility and funding
Frequency: Annual
Country of Study: Any country
No. of awards offered: Varies
Application Procedure: Applicants must write for details or refer to the website.
Funding: Private

INTERNATIONAL FOUNDATION FOR SCIENCE (IFS)

Karlavägen 108, 5th Floor, SE-115 26 Stockholm
Sweden
Tel: (46) 85 458 1800
Fax: (46) 85 458 1801
Email: info@ifs.se
Website: www.ifs.se
Contact: Head of Finance & Administration

Founded in 1972, the International Foundation for Science (IFS), a non-government organisation, has its largest presence in developing countries where it contributes to the strengthening of capacity to conduct relevant and high-quality research on the management, use and conservation of biological resources and the environment in which these resources occur and upon which they depend.

HFSPO IFS Research Grant

Subjects: The renewable utilization of biological resources such as projects in agriculture, forestry, natural products and aquatic resources as well as research on the sustainable utilization and conservation of natural ecosystems.
Purpose: To build scientific capacity in developing countries.
Eligibility: Open to scientists who are citizens of developing countries, in possession of an academic degree of not less than an MSc or the equivalent, currently working at a university or research institution in a developing country, normally under 40 at the time of their first application for a grant and at the beginning of their research careers.
Level of Study: Research
Value: Awards are limited to US$12,000 per research period and may be renewed twice. IFS also gives other support to help grantees further their research. IFS funding is not intended for travel or study, but should be used for purchasing the basic tools of research such as equipment, expendable supplies and literature
Frequency: Bi-Annually
Country of Study: Any developing country
No. of awards offered: 200–250 per year
Application Procedure: Applicants must complete an application form. This is available from the IFS website or on request in English or French.
Closing Date: Applications are accepted at any time
Funding: Private, government
Contributor: Regular financing comes from France, Germany, the Netherlands, Norway, Sweden and Switzerland. A number of national and international development agencies contribute to the IFS granting and supporting programmes
Additional Information: Research proposed by applicants shall be conducted in a developing country and be relevant to the needs of a developing country.

IFS Carolina MacGillavry Fellowship

Eligibility: Applicants must be from, and do research in, a developing country. Countries in Eastern Europe, Turkey, Cyprus and the former Soviet Union are not eligible for support.
Level of Study: Postgraduate
Type: Fellowship
Value: Up to US$12,000 and the purchase and delivery of equipment, supplies and literature
Frequency: Annual
Funding: Foundation
Contributor: International Foundation for Science

IFS Research Grants

Subjects: Aquatic resources, animal production, crop science, forestry/agroforestry, food science and natural products.
Purpose: To provide opportunities for young researchers to contribute to the generation of scientific knowledge.
Eligibility: Applicants must be from, and do research in, a developing country. Countries in Eastern Europe, Turkey, Cyprus and the former Soviet Union are not eligible for support.
Level of Study: Postdoctorate, research
Type: Grant
Value: Up to US$12,000
Length of Study: 1–3 year
Frequency: Annual
Application Procedure: Applications can be downloaded.
Closing Date: December 31st
Funding: Foundation
Contributor: International Foundation for Science

For further information contact:

International Foundation for Science, Grev Turegatan 19, Stockholm, SE-11438, Sweden
Tel: (46) 545 818 00
Fax: (46) 545 818 01
Email: info@ifs.se
Website: www.ifs.se

INTERNATIONAL HARP CONTEST IN ISRAEL

4 Aharonowitz Street, IL-63566 Tel Aviv,
Israel
Tel: (972) 3 528 233
Fax: (972) 3 629 9524
Email: harzimco@netvision.net.il
Website: www.harpcontest-israel.org.il
Contact: Ms Ilana Barnea, Director

The International Harp Contest takes place in Israel every 3 years and is judged by a jury of internationally known musicians. It was founded in 1959, and since then, harpists from all over the world gather in Jerusalem to participate in the contest, the only one of its kind.

International Harp Contest in Israel

Subjects: Harp playing.
Purpose: To encourage excellence in harp playing.

Eligibility: Open to harpists of any nationality who are aged 35 years or younger.
Level of Study: Professional development
Type: Prize
Value: The first prize is a grand concert harp from the House of Lyon and Healy, Chicago, the second prize is US$6,000 and the third prize is US$4,000. The Propes Prize is US$1,500 for the best performance of the required Israeli composition in stage one and the Herlitz Prize is US$1,000 for the best performance of a contemporary piece in stage three. The Chamber Music Prize is US$1,000 for the best performance of Ravel's Introduction and Allegro in stage three. Board and lodging is provided by the Contest Committee. The Gulbenkian Prize is awarded for a contemporary work
Frequency: Every 3 years
Country of Study: Any country
No. of awards offered: 7
Application Procedure: Applicants must complete an application form and submit this with recommendations, a record of concert experience, curriculum vitae and birth certificate. There is a registration fee of US$150.
Closing Date: April 1st
Funding: Trusts, private, government
Contributor: Culture Authority, the Government of Israel, the Ministry of Culture, foundations and donors
No. of awards given last year: 6
No. of applicants last year: 36

THE INTERNATIONAL HUMAN FRONTIER SCIENCE PROGRAM ORGANIZATION (HFSPO)

12 quai Saint-Jean, BP 10034, F-67080 Strasbourg Cedex, France
Fax: (33) 388215289
Email: jhusser@hfsp.org
Website: www.hfsp.org

The Human Frontier Science Program (HFSP) promotes basic research in the life sciences that is original, interdisciplinary and requires international collaboration. The support and training of young investigators is given special emphasis.

HFSPO Career Development Award (CDA)

Subjects: Life sciences, biology. The Human Frontier Science Program supports basic research focused on the elucidation of the complex mechanisms of living organisms. The fields support range from biological functions at the molecular level to higher brain functions.
Purpose: To promote a global network of young, independent investigators. The CDA provides former HFSP Long-Term and Cross-Disciplinary fellows with support to establish their own programmes in their home country.
Eligibility: The award is open to Long-Term and Cross-Disciplinary Fellows who return to their home country at the end of their HFSP Fellowship. For details, see HFSP website.
Level of Study: Research
Type: Fellowship
Value: US$180,000 over 2–3 years
Length of Study: 2–3 years
Frequency: Annual
Country of Study: Home Country
No. of awards offered: Varies
Application Procedure: Applications must be submitted online.
Closing Date: October/November
Funding: Government
Contributor: Management Supporting Parties now include Canada, France, Germany, Italy, Japan, Republic of Korea Switzerland, United Kingdom, United States of America, European Union
No. of awards given last year: 18
No. of applicants last year: 47
Additional Information: CDA awardees are eligible to apply for HFSP research grants and HFSP Short-Term Fellowships during the tenure of their CDA.

HFSPO Cross-Disciplinary Fellowships

Subjects: Life sciences, biology. The aim is to support basic research focused on elucidating the complex mechanisms of living organisms. The fields supported range from biological functions at the molecular level to higher brain functions.
Purpose: Cross-Disciplinary Fellowships are intended for postdoctoral Fellows with a PhD in the physical sciences, chemistry, mathematics, engineering or computer science who wish to receive training in biology. The fellowships provide young scientists with up to 3 years of postdoctoral research training in an outstanding laboratory in another country. The conditions are the same as for Long-Term Fellowships.
Eligibility: For details, see HFSP website.
Level of Study: Postdoctorate
Type: Fellowship
Value: Approx. US$46,000 per year, including allowances for travel and research expenses
Frequency: Annual
Country of Study: Nationals of one of the supporting countries can apply to receive training in any country. Nationals of any other country must apply to train in a supporting country.
No. of awards offered: Varies
Application Procedure: Applications must be submitted online.
Closing Date: September
Funding: Government
Contributor: Management Supporting Parties now include: Australia, Canada, France, Germany, Italy, Japan, Republic of Korea Switzerland, United Kingdom, United States of America, European Union
No. of awards given last year: 12
No. of applicants last year: 65
Additional Information: Former awardees are eligible to apply for a Career Development Award upon repatriation to their home country to help fellowships for up to 3 years. The third year can be used to support 1 year of postdoctoral training in the home country and can be deferred for up to 2 years as independent investigators.

HFSPO Long-Term Fellowships

Subjects: Life sciences, biology. The aim is to support basic research focused on elucidating the complex mechanisms of living organisms. The fields supported range from biological functions at the molecular level to higher brain functions.
Purpose: Long-Term Fellowships provide young scientists with up to 3 years of postdoctoral research training in an outstanding laboratory in another country.
Eligibility: Applicants must see the website for details.
Level of Study: Postdoctorate
Type: Fellowship
Value: Approx. US$45,000 per year, including allowances for travel and research expenses
Frequency: Annual
Country of Study: Worldwide
No. of awards offered: Varies
Application Procedure: Applications must be submitted online.
Closing Date: September
Funding: Government
Contributor: Management Supporting Parties now include: Australia, Canada, France, Germany, Italy, Japan, Republic of Korea, Switzerland, United Kingdom, United States of America, European Union
No. of awards given last year: 89
No. of applicants last year: 609
Additional Information: Former awardees are eligible to apply for a Career Development Award upon repatriation to their home country to help establish themselves as independent investigators. fellowships for up to 3 years. The third year can be used to support 1 year of postdoctoral training in the home country and can be deferred for up to 2 years.

HFSPO Program Grant

Subjects: Life sciences, biology. The aim is to support basic research focused on elucidating the complex mechanisms of living organisms. The fields supported range from biological functions at the molecular level to higher brain functions.

Purpose: To enable to teams of independent researchers at any stage of their career to develop new lines of research.
Eligibility: Independent investigators early in their careers are encouraged to apply.
Level of Study: Research
Type: Collaborative research grant
Value: Up to US$450,000 per grant per year
Length of Study: Max 3 years
Frequency: Annual
Country of Study: The Principal applicant must have his/her laboratory in a member country. Atleast one other team member must be located in another country.
No. of awards offered: Varies
Application Procedure: Application online, by letter of intent, submission of full application, by invitation.
Closing Date: Spring. See website for details
Funding: Government
Contributor: Management Supporting Parties now include: Australia, Canada, France, Germany, Italy, Japan, Republic of Korea Switzerland, United Kingdom, United States of America, European Union
No. of awards given last year: 27
No. of applicants last year: 590 letters of intent 66 full applications received

HFSPO Short-Term Fellowships

Subjects: Life sciences, biology. The aim is to support basic research focused on elucidating the complex mechanisms of living organisms. The fields supported range from biological functions at the molecular level to higher brain functions.
Purpose: Short-Term Fellowships enable researchers who are early in their careers to spend 2 weeks–3 months working in a laboratory in another country to learn new techniques or establish new collaborations.
Eligibility: Applicants must see the website for details.
Level of Study: Postdoctorate
Type: Fellowship
Value: Travel and per diem support
Length of Study: 2 weeks–3 months
Frequency: Applications are received throughout the year
Country of Study: Nationals of one of the supporting countries can apply to receive training in any country. Nationals of any other country must apply to train in a supporting country.
No. of awards offered: Varies
Application Procedure: Applications must be submitted online.
Closing Date: Applications are accepted throughout the year
Funding: Government
Contributor: Management Supporting Parties now include: Australia, Canada, France, Germany, Italy, Japan, Republic of Korea, Switzerland, United Kingdom, United States of America, European Union
No. of awards given last year: 27
No. of applicants last year: 73
Additional Information: Former holders of HFSP Long-term or Cross-disciplinary Fellowships who have returned to their home country are also eligible to use HFSP Short-Term Fellowships to return to their former host laboratory to complete or extend the research.

HFSPO Young Investigator Grant

Subjects: Life sciences, biology. The aim is to support basic research focused on elucidating the complex mechanisms of living organisms. The fields supporter range firm biological at the molecular level to higher brain.
Purpose: Young investigator grants are awarded to teams of researchers, all of whom are within the first 5 years of obtaining an independent position (eg. Assistant Professor, Lecturer or equivalent). They must also be within 10 years of receiving their PhD before the deadline for submission of the letter of intent.
Level of Study: Research
Type: Collaborative research grant
Value: Up to US$450,000 per grant, per year
Length of Study: Maximum 3 years
Frequency: Annual
Country of Study: The Principal applicant must have his/her laboratory in a member country. Atleast one other team member must be located in another country.
No. of awards offered: Varies
Application Procedure: Application online by letter of intent submission of full application by invitation.
Closing Date: Spring. See website for details
Funding: Government
Contributor: Management Supporting Parties now include: Australia, Canada, France, Germany, Italy, Japan, Republic of Korea, Switzerland, United Kingdom, United States of America, European Union
No. of awards given last year: 7
No. of applicants last year: 129 letters of intent and 20 full applications

INTERNATIONAL INSTITUTE FOR MANAGEMENT DEVELOPMENT (IMD)

Chemin de Bellerive 23, PO Box 915, CH-1001 Lausanne, Switzerland
Tel: (41) 21 618 0298
Fax: (41) 21 618 0615
Email: mbainfo@imd.ch
Website: www.imd.ch/mba
Contact: Ms Janet Shaner, Director, MBA Marketing

The International Institute for Management Development (IMD), created by industry to serve industry, develops cutting-edge research and programmes that meet real world needs. Their clients include dozens of leading international companies and their experienced faculty incorporate new management practices into the small and exclusive MBA programme. With no nationality dominating, IMD is truly global, practical and relevant.

IMD Future Leaders Scholarships

Subjects: MBA.
Purpose: To financially support candidates with exceptionally strong leadership potential undertaking an MBA at IMD.
Eligibility: Candidates must have gained acceptance into the MBA programme and demonstrate strong leadership potential.
Level of Study: MBA
Type: Scholarship
Value: Swiss Franc 30,000 towards tuition fees and book expenses
Length of Study: 1 year
Frequency: Annual
Study Establishment: IMD
Country of Study: Switzerland
No. of awards offered: 3
Application Procedure: Applicants must complete and submit the IMD MBA application form. In addition, candidates must submit an essay of maximum of 750 and should contact the organization for details.
Closing Date: September 30th
No. of awards given last year: 3
No. of applicants last year: 43

The IMD MBA Service Industry Scholarship

Subjects: MBA.
Purpose: To financially support candidates with a strong interest in the service industry undertaking an MBA at IMD.
Eligibility: Candidates must have gained acceptance into the MBA programme and demonstrate a keen interest or past experience in the service industry.
Level of Study: Graduate, mba
Type: Scholarship
Value: Swiss Franc 25,000 towards tuition fees and book expenses
Length of Study: 1 year
Frequency: Annual
Study Establishment: IMD
Country of Study: Switzerland
No. of awards offered: 1
Application Procedure: Applicants must complete and submit the IMD MBA application form. In addition, candidates must submit an essay of maximum of 750 words on the topic: 'What are the essential

leadership skills for the service industry and how do they impact the success of a business?'
Closing Date: September 30th
Funding: Private
No. of awards given last year: 1
No. of applicants last year: 8

MBA4 Association Scholarship

Subjects: MBA.
Purpose: To financially support candidates from developing countries undertaking an MBA at IMD.
Eligibility: Candidates must have gained acceptance into the MBA programme, demonstrate financial need and a desire to make a difference in their home country.
Level of Study: MBA, graduate
Type: Scholarship
Value: Swiss Franc 30,000 towards tuition fees and book expenses
Length of Study: 1 year
Frequency: Annual
Study Establishment: IMD
Country of Study: Switzerland
No. of awards offered: 1
Application Procedure: Applicants must complete and submit the IMD MBA application form. In addition, candidates must submit an essay of maximum of 750 words and should contact the organization for details.
Closing Date: September 30th
Funding: Private
Contributor: Alumni
No. of awards given last year: 2
No. of applicants last year: 17

Nestlé Scholarship for Women

Subjects: MBA.
Purpose: To financially support women undertaking an MBA at IMD.
Eligibility: Candidates must be female, have gained acceptance into the MBA course and show financial need.
Level of Study: MBA, graduate
Type: Scholarship
Value: Swiss Francs 25,000 towards tuition and living expenses
Length of Study: 1 year
Frequency: Annual
Study Establishment: IMD
Country of Study: Switzerland
No. of awards offered: 1
Application Procedure: Applicants must submit an additional essay of a maximum 750 words, on the topic: Does Diversity in Management impact the bottom line? If so, how?' along with their completed IMD MBA application form for financial assistance.
Closing Date: September 30th
Funding: Commercial
No. of awards given last year: 1
No. of applicants last year: 9

Shell and IMD MBA Alumni Scholarships

Subjects: MBA.
Purpose: To financially support applicants from Africa, Asia, Latin America and Eastern Europe undertaking an MBA at IMD.
Eligibility: Candidates must have gained acceptance into the IMD MBA programme, provide evidence of financial need, and show high potential for successful careers in private, public or governmental sectors of business.
Level of Study: Graduate, mba
Type: Scholarship
Value: Swiss Francs 30,000 towards tuition fees and book expenses
Frequency: Annual
Study Establishment: The International Institute for Management Development (IMD)
Country of Study: Switzerland
No. of awards offered: 4
Application Procedure: Applicants must complete and submit the IMD MBA application form for financial assistance and the MBA application form. In addition, applicants must write an essay and should contact the organization for details.
Closing Date: September 30th
Funding: Private
Contributor: IMD Alumni Loan Fund
No. of awards given last year: 4
No. of applicants last year: 22

Staton Scholarship

Subjects: MBA.
Purpose: To financially support applicants from South America (Excluding Brazil) undertaking an MBA at IMD.
Eligibility: Candidates must be from South America, must have already gained acceptance into the IMD MBA programme, and must return to South America (Except Brazil) for at least 3 years after graduation.
Level of Study: MBA, graduate
Type: Scholarship
Value: US$50,000 towards tuition fees and book expenses
Length of Study: 1 year
Frequency: Annual
Study Establishment: IMD
Country of Study: Switzerland
No. of awards offered: 1
Application Procedure: Applicants must complete and submit the IMD MBA application form for financial assistance and the MBA application form. In addition, applicants must submit a 750-word essay on the topic: The Role of Entrepreneurship in Moving My Country Forward and my contribution to that goal.
Closing Date: September 30th
Funding: Private
Contributor: Woods Staton
No. of awards given last year: 1
No. of applicants last year: 3
Additional Information: It is a condition of the scholarship that candidates return to South America for at least 3 years after graduation.

Von Muralt-Lo Scholarship

Subjects: MBA.
Purpose: To financially support two candidates from China, Hong Kong, Estonia, Czech Republic, Bulgaria, Rumania, Hungary, Slovenia or Switzerland undertaking an MBA at IMD.
Eligibility: Candidates must be based in China, Hong Kong, Estonia Czech Republic, Bulgaria, Rumania, Hungary, Slovenia or Switzerland and they must have already gained acceptance into the IMD MBA programme.
Level of Study: Graduate, mba
Type: Scholarship
Value: Swiss Francs 25,000
Length of Study: 1 year
Frequency: Annual
Study Establishment: IMD
Country of Study: Switzerland
No. of awards offered: 2
Application Procedure: Applicants must complete and submit the IMD MBA application form for financial assistance and the MBA application form. In addition, candidates must submit a 500-word essay and contact the organization for details.
Closing Date: September 30th
Funding: Private
Contributor: Mr and Mrs Peter von Muralt-Lo
No. of awards given last year: 2
No. of applicants last year: 3
Additional Information: Candidates need to clearly demonstrate their desire to further contribute to their country.

INTERNATIONAL MATHEMATICAL UNION (IMU)

Institute for Advanced Study, Einstein Drive, Princeton, NJ, 08540, United States of America
Tel: (1) 609 734 8200
Fax: (1) 609 683 7605
Email: imu@ias.edu
Website: www.mathunion.org
Contact: Ms Linda Geraci

The International Mathematical Union (IMU) is an international, non-governmental and non-profit scientific organization, with the purpose of promoting international co-operation in mathematics. It belongs to the International Council of Scientific Unions (ICSU).

Carl Friedrich Gauss Prize for Applications of Mathematics

Subjects: Mathematical contributions with significant practical applications outside mathematics.
Purpose: To honour scientists whose research has had an impact outside mathematics in technology, business or people's everyday lives.
Eligibility: An individual or group of individuals who have made outstanding mathematical contributions that have found significant practical applications outside of mathematics are eligible to apply.
Level of Study: Unrestricted
Type: Prize
Value: €10,000
Frequency: Every 4 years
Study Establishment: Any establishment
Country of Study: Any country
No. of awards offered: 1
Application Procedure: Applicants must be nominated by other mathematicians.
Closing Date: January 1st
Funding: International Office, foundation
Contributor: German Mathematical Union and International Mathematical Union

IMU Fields Medals

Subjects: Mathematics.
Purpose: To reward outstanding achievements.
Eligibility: Open to young mathematicians up to 40 years old and of any nationality.
Type: Prize
Frequency: Every 4 years
Country of Study: Any country
No. of awards offered: 2–4
Application Procedure: Applicants must be nominated by other mathematicians.
Closing Date: Jan 31st
Funding: Private
Contributor: The Fields Foundation
No. of awards given last year: 2 awards

Rolf Nevanlinna Prize

Subjects: Mathematical aspects of information science.
Eligibility: Open to young mathematicians up to 40 years old and of any nationality.
Level of Study: Unrestricted
Type: Prize
Frequency: Every 4 years
Country of Study: Any country
No. of awards offered: 1
Application Procedure: Applicants must be nominated by other mathematicians.
Closing Date: Jan 31st
Contributor: The University of Helsinki/IMU
No. of awards given last year: 1

INTERNATIONAL MUSIC FESTIVAL SION-VALAIS

International Music Festival of Sion Valais Case postale
1429 CH-1951 Sion, Valais, Switzerland
Tel: (41) 27 323 43 17
Fax: (41) 27 323 46 62
Email: info@sion-festival.ch
Website: www.sion-festival.ch
Contact: Mr Boris Dupont, General Manager

International Classical Music Festival held in August and September every year with a dozen concerts under the highs auspices of Maestro Shlomo Mintz, artistic Director.

International Violin Competition of Sion Valais

Subjects: International Violin Competition.
Purpose: Help discover and promote new talents, enrich the musical experience and practice of the participants and encourage and support prize winners in their future careers under the high auspices of Maestro Shlomo Mintz, President of the International Jury.
Eligibility: Open to violinists of any nationality aged between 15 and 32.
Level of Study: Unrestricted
Type: Prize
Value: The first prize is US$15,000. The total prize money is US$35,000
Length of Study: 14 days
Frequency: Annual
Country of Study: Switzerland
No. of awards offered: 6 prizes and 3 special prizes
Application Procedure: Applicants must complete an application form (available online at www.sion-festival.ch) and submit it with two pictures, a curriculum vitae, a DVD and a receipt showing payment of the entrance fee of Swiss Franc 100.
Closing Date: March 30th
Funding: Private, government
No. of awards given last year: 6 prizes and 3 special prizes
No. of applicants last year: 25
Additional Information: Up to 30 candidates are invited to the international Violin Competition of Sion Valais. All rounds are public and free of entrance. The first 3 prize winners will be invited to perform in 2 or 3 gala concerts in Switzerland and Europe with a symphonic orchestra immediately after the final.

INTERNATIONAL NAVIGATION ASSOCIATION (PIANC)

Graaf de Ferraris Building, 11th Floor, Boulevard du Roi Albert II, 20-Box 3, B-1000 Brussels, Belgium
Tel: (32) 2 553 7160
Fax: (32) 2 553 7145
Email: info@pianc-aipcn.org
Website: www.pianc-aipcn.org
Contact: Secretary General

The International Navigation Association (PIANC) is a worldwide non-political and non-profit technical and scientific organization of private individuals, corporations and national governments. PIANC's objective is to promote the maintenance and operation of both inland and maritime navigation by fostering progress in the planning, design, construction, improvement, maintenance and operations of inland and maritime waterways, ports and coastal areas for general use in industrialized and industrializing countries. Facilities for fisheries, sport and recreational navigation are included in PIANC's activities.

De Paepe - Willems Award

Subjects: The design, construction, improvement, maintenance or operation of inland and maritime waterways such as rivers, estuaries, canals, port, inland and maritime ports and coastal areas and related fields.
Purpose: To encourage young professionals to submit for presentation outstanding technical articles in the fields of interest to PIANC.
Eligibility: Open to members of PIANC or candidates sponsored by a member, who are under the age of 35.
Level of Study: Unrestricted
Type: Award
Value: A monetary award of €5,000 and free membership of PIANC for a 5-year period. Free hotel accommodation will be provided, together with a coverage of travel expenses to the venue of the General Assembly
Frequency: Annual
Country of Study: Any country
No. of awards offered: 1
Application Procedure: Applicants must complete an application form, available on request from the PIANC General Secretariat or on

the PIANC website, and submit this together with the article. Articles must be written by a single author, not have been previously published elsewhere, not exceed 12,000 words, be in type script, and in English or French with a summary in the same language. Articles may be accompanied by illustrations or diagrams.
Closing Date: October 31st
Funding: Private, government
Additional Information: The prize will be awarded to the individual candidate who submits the most outstanding article in the calendar year preceding the Annual General Assembly at which the prize is awarded, provided the article is judged to be of sufficiently high standard. The prize winner will be invited to present a commentary on his or her article during the General Assembly of the PIANC or during the Congress. In judging the articles the jury shall take into account their technical level, originality and practical value and the quality of presentation. Candidates are advised that the Bulletin is designed for readers with a wide range of engineering interests and highly specialized articles should be written with this in mind.

INTERNATIONAL PEACE SCHOLARSHIP FUND

PEO, 3700 Grand Avenue, Des Moines, IA, 50312,
United States of America
Tel: (1) 515 255 3153
Fax: (1) 515 255 3820
Website: www.peointernational.org
Contact: Ms Carolyn J Larson, Project Supervisor

PEO International Peace Scholarship

Subjects: All subjects.
Purpose: To support international women studying for graduate degrees.
Eligibility: Applicants of any nationality may apply, with the exception of candidates from the United States of America or Canada. Eligibility is based on financial need, nationality, degree, full-time status and residence.
Level of Study: Doctorate, graduate, postgraduate
Type: Scholarship (grant-in-aid)
Value: US$8,000 maximum per year
Length of Study: A maximum of 2 years
Frequency: Annual
Country of Study: United States of America or Canada
No. of awards offered: Approx. 200
Application Procedure: Eligibility must be established before application material is sent. Candidates should write to the main address and request an eligibility form or download from our website: www.peointernational.org If the applicant is deemed eligible, an application form is sent.
Closing Date: December 15th for receipt of the eligibility form and January 31st for receipt of the application form
Funding: Private
Contributor: PEO members
No. of awards given last year: 200
No. of applicants last year: 340
Additional Information: Scholarships cannot be used for travel, research dissertations, internships or practical training. An applicant must have a contact person who is a citizen of the United States of America or Canada and who will act as a non-academic adviser. Applicants must also have round-trip return travel expense guaranteed at the time of the application and promise return to their own country within 60 days on completion of their studies.

INTERNATIONAL READING ASSOCIATION

800 Barksdale Road, PO Box 8139, Newark, DE, 19714-8139,
United States of America
Tel: (1) 302 731 1600 ext 423
Fax: (1) 302 731 1057
Email: research@reading.org
Website: www.reading.org
Contact: Marcella Moore, Research & Policy Division

The International Reading Association seeks to promote high levels of literacy for all by improving the quality of reading instruction through studying the reading processes and teaching techniques, serving as a clearing house for the dissemination of reading research through conferences, journals and other publications and actively encouraging the lifetime reading habit.

Albert J Harris Award

Subjects: Reading and literacy.
Purpose: To recognize outstanding published works on the topics of reading disabilities and the prevention, assessment or instruction of learners experiencing difficulty learning to read.
Eligibility: Articles must be single- or joint-authored research-based articles. Nominees for this award do not need to be members of the International Reading Association. Publications that have appeared in a refereed professional journal or monograph within the last 18 months are eligible and may be submitted by the author or anyone else.
Level of Study: Postgraduate
Type: Prize
Value: US$1,000
Frequency: Annual
Country of Study: Any country
No. of awards offered: 1
Application Procedure: Applicants must obtain guidelines with specific information from the main address or by visiting the website.
Closing Date: September 1st
Funding: Private

Dina Feitelson Research Award

Subjects: Literacy.
Purpose: To recognize an outstanding empirical study that was published in English in a refereed journal that specifically reports on an investigation of aspects of literary acquisition such as phonemic awareness, the alphabetic principle, bilingualism, home influences on literacy development or cross-cultural studies of beginning reading.
Eligibility: Articles must have been published in a refereed journal within the past 18 months and may be submitted by the author or anyone else. Empirical studies involve the collection of original data from direct experimentation or observation, and articles that develop theory without data, secondary reviews of the literature or descriptions of the theory are not eligible for this competition. Nominees for this award do not need to be members of the International Reading Association.
Level of Study: Unrestricted
Type: Prize
Value: US$500
Frequency: Dependent on funds available
Country of Study: Any country
No. of awards offered: 1
Application Procedure: Applicants must obtain guidelines with specific information from the main address or by visiting the website.
Closing Date: September 1st
Funding: Private
Additional Information: The Dina Feitelson Research Award was established to honour the memory of Dina Feitelson. This award began in 1997.

Elva Knight Research Grant

Subjects: Literacy education.
Purpose: To assist a researcher in a reading and literacy project that addresses significant questions about literacy instruction and practice.
Eligibility: Applicants must be members of the International Reading Association and projects should be completed within 2 years.
Level of Study: Postgraduate, research
Value: Upto a maximum of US$10,000
Length of Study: 2 years
Frequency: Annual
Country of Study: Any country
No. of awards offered: Up to 4 awards. It is expected that at least 1 award will go to a researcher outside the United States of America and/or Canada and at least 1 to a teacher-initiated research project
Application Procedure: Applicants must obtain guidelines with specific information from the main address or by visiting the website.

Closing Date: January 15th
Funding: Private
Additional Information: This award began in 1982.

Helen M Robinson Award

Subjects: Literacy education.
Eligibility: Open to all doctoral students at the early stages of their dissertation research worldwide who are members of the International Reading Association.
Level of Study: Doctorate
Value: US$1,000
Frequency: Annual
Country of Study: Any country
No. of awards offered: 1
Application Procedure: Applicants must obtain guidelines with specific information from the main address or by visiting the website.
Closing Date: January 15th
Funding: Private
Additional Information: This award began in 1991.

International Reading Association Outstanding Dissertation of the Year Award

Subjects: Reading and literacy.
Purpose: To recognize dissertations in the field of reading and literacy.
Eligibility: Open to all doctoral students worldwide who are members of the International Reading Association.
Level of Study: Doctorate
Type: Prize
Value: US$1,000
Frequency: Annual
Country of Study: Any country
No. of awards offered: 1
Application Procedure: Applicants must obtain guidelines with specific information from the main address or by visiting the website.
Closing Date: October 1st
Funding: Private
Additional Information: This award began in 1964. Should there be more than one winner, the US$1,000 prize will be split.

International Reading Association Teacher as Researcher Grant

Subjects: Literacy.
Purpose: To support teachers in their enquiries about literacy learning and instruction.
Eligibility: All applicants must be members of the International Reading Association and practicing pre-K-12 teachers with full-time teaching responsibilities, including librarians, classroom teachers and resource teachers. Applicants are limited to one proposal per year. There must be a span of 3 years before past grant recipients can apply for another Teacher as Researcher Grant.
Level of Study: Research
Value: Up to US$5,000 maximum, but priority is given to smaller grants of between US$1,000 and 2,000
Frequency: Annual
Country of Study: Any country
No. of awards offered: Several
Application Procedure: Applicants must obtain guidelines with specific information from the main address or by visiting the website.
Closing Date: January 15th
Funding: Private
Additional Information: This award began in 1997.

Jeanne S Chall Research Fellowship

Subjects: Reading and literacy.
Purpose: To encourage and support doctoral research investigating issues in beginning research, readability, reading difficulty and stages of reading development.
Eligibility: Open to doctoral students who are members of the International Reading Association and are planning or beginning dissertations.
Level of Study: Research, doctorate
Type: Fellowship
Value: US$6,000 maximum
Frequency: Annual
Country of Study: Any country
No. of awards offered: 1
Application Procedure: Applicants must obtain guidelines with specific information from the main address or by visiting the website.
Closing Date: January 15th
Funding: Private
Additional Information: This award began in 1997.

Nila Banton Smith Research Dissemination Support Grant

Subjects: Reading and literacy.
Purpose: To facilitate the dissemination of literacy research to the educational community.
Eligibility: Open to all members of the International Reading Association worldwide.
Level of Study: Professional development, research
Type: Grant
Value: US$5,000
Length of Study: 2–10 months
Frequency: Annual
No. of awards offered: 1
Application Procedure: Applicants must obtain guidelines with specific information from the main address or by visiting the website.
Closing Date: January 15th
Additional Information: This award began in 1991.

Reading/Literacy Research Fellowship

Subjects: Literacy education.
Purpose: To provide support to a researcher who has shown exceptional promise in reading or literacy research.
Eligibility: Open to any International Reading Association member outside the United States of America or Canada.
Level of Study: Postdoctorate
Type: Fellowship
Value: US$1,000
Frequency: Annual
No. of awards offered: 1
Application Procedure: Applicants must obtain guidelines with specific information from the main address or by visiting the website.
Closing Date: January 15th
Funding: Private
Additional Information: This award began in 1974.

INTERNATIONAL RESEARCH AND EXCHANGE BOARD (IREX)

2121 K Street North West, Suite 700, Washington, DC, 20037, United States of America
Tel: (1) 202 628 8188
Fax: (1) 202 628 8189
Email: irex@irex.org
Website: www.irex.org
Contact: Ms Michelle Duplissis, Senior Program Officer

The International Research and Exchange Board (IREX) is an international non-profit organization specializing in education, independent media, internet development and civil society programmes. Through training, partnerships, education, research and grant programmes, IREX develops the capacity of individuals to contribute to their societies. Since its founding in 1968, IREX has supported over 15,000 students, scholars, policymakers, business leaders, journalists and other professionals.

ECA/IREX/FSA Contemporary Issues Fellowship Program

Subjects: Business administration, civic education, educational policy, economics, energy policy, environmental policy, human rights, international relations, the internet, journalism and media, law enforcement, military/security issues, non-governmental organization

development and management, political science, public administration (government), public health policy, rule of law and social welfare.
Purpose: To provide opportunities for experienced professionals and specialists to conduct policy-orientated research in the United States of America.
Eligibility: Open to citizens and residents of Armenia, Azerbaijan, Belarus, Georgia, Kazakhstan, Kyrgyzstan, Moldova, the Russian Federation, Tajikistan, Turkmenistan, Ukraine or Uzbekistan. Candidates must be aged 25–55, have an academic degree at least equivalent to a United States of America Master's degree, have at least 3 years experience in the listed topic of research and possess a high level of proficiency in written and spoken English. Applicants must not have participated in a United States of America government-sponsored grant of more than 6 weeks in the past 2 years.
Level of Study: Professional development
Type: Fellowship
Value: Travel, housing, a stipend, medical insurance, a research allowance and return trip transportation from the home city to the placement city
Length of Study: 4 months
Frequency: Annual
Study Establishment: A university, research centre, government institution or non-governmental organization
Country of Study: United States of America
No. of awards offered: Approx. 60
Application Procedure: Applicants must submit a completed application form, research proposal, two letters of recommendation, curriculum vitae and a short personal biography. All applications must contain developed and focused research projects that are policy-driven with practical application in Eurasia. Please contact the organization for further details.
Closing Date: November
Funding: Government
Contributor: The Bureau of Cultural and Educational Affairs, at the United States of America Department of State
No. of awards given last year: 100
No. of applicants last year: 1000
Additional Information: Prospective applicants are encouraged to contact IREX's Eurasia field offices and educational advising centres before submitting an application. Further information and field office contacts are available on the website.

IREX Individual Advanced Research Opportunities

Subjects: Policy-relevant research in the social sciences and humanities.
Purpose: To provide opportunities for scholars from the United States of America wishing to pursue research in the humanities and social sciences in Europe and Eurasia.
Eligibility: Open to citizens and 3-year permanent residents of the United States of America. Applicants must hold a PhD or other terminal graduate degree or be pursuing a PhD or a Master's degree. Doctoral candidates must have completed all requirements for the PhD except for the dissertation. Master's candidates are eligible for grants of 1–3 months to conduct policy relevant research for a thesis or comparable project. Normally, command of the host country's language sufficient for advanced research is required of all applicants. Further details can be found on the website.
Level of Study: Doctorate, graduate, professional development, predoctorate, postdoctorate, postgraduate, mba, research
Type: Grant
Value: Up to a maximum of US$40,000. Covers travel and visa fees, dollar stipend and a housing allowance
Length of Study: 2–9 months
Frequency: Annual
Study Establishment: Appropriate institutions
No. of awards offered: Varies
Application Procedure: Applicants must visit the website for application forms and further information.
Closing Date: November 1st
Funding: Government, private
Contributor: The United States of America Department of State (Title VIII) and the IREX Scholar Support Fund
No. of awards given last year: 25
Additional Information: Applicants must study in one of the following countries: Albania, Armenia, Azerbaijan, Belarus, Bosnia and Herzegovina, Bulgaria, Croatia, Czech Republic, Estonia, Georgia, Hungary, Iran, Kazakhstan, Kyrgyzstan, Latvia, Lithuania, Macedonia, Moldova, Mongolia, Romania, Russia, Serbia and Montenegro, Slovakia, Slovenia, Tajikistan, Turkey, Turkmenistan, Ukraine and Uzbekistan. Further information is available on request; however, please contact IREX for programme information well in advance of the deadline.

IREX Policy-Connect Collaborative Research Grants Program

Subjects: Social sciences concerned with Europe, Eurasia, the Near East and Asia. Applicants should refer to the website as there will be a theme each year limiting the geographical focus and the eligible fields of research.
Purpose: To provide grants for collaborative cutting-edge research.
Eligibility: Open to citizens and 3-year permanent residents of the United States of America. Applicants must hold a PhD or other terminal graduate degree at the time of application. Collaborative research programmes involving international colleagues are strongly encouraged.
Level of Study: Postdoctorate, postgraduate
Type: Grant
Value: Up to US$30,000
Length of Study: Up to 1 year
Frequency: Annual
No. of awards offered: 4
Application Procedure: Applicants must contact IREX or visit the website for application forms.
Closing Date: April 1st
Funding: Government, private
Contributor: United States of America Department of State (Title VIII), John J and Nancy Lee Roberts
No. of awards given last year: 1
Additional Information: Further information is available on request. The programme is limited to specific geographic areas and topics each year.

IREX Short-Term Travel Grants

Subjects: Policy-relevant research.
Purpose: To provide opportunities for scholars from the United States of America to pursue research in the social sciences in Europe and Eurasia.
Eligibility: Open to citizens and permanent residents of the United States of America who have a PhD or other terminal graduate degree and need project support.
Level of Study: Postgraduate, postdoctorate
Type: Travel grant
Value: Up to US$3,500 travel expenses. Airfare on a United States of America flag carrier is provided through IREX as well as per diem for food, lodging and local transport. The grant may also cover incidental expenses such as visa fees, photocopying and medical evacuation insurance
Length of Study: Up to 60 days
Frequency: Annual
Country of Study: Eastern Europe and Eurasia
No. of awards offered: Varies
Application Procedure: Applicants must contact Amy Schulz, Program Officer, at stg@irex.org for details or application guidelines. Application forms can be downloaded from the website.
Closing Date: February 1st
Funding: Government
Contributor: The United States of America Department of State's Title VIII Program
No. of awards given last year: Approx. 40
No. of applicants last year: Varies
Additional Information: Applicants will be notified of award decisions approx. 8 weeks after the application deadline. Applicants must study in one of the following countries: Albania, Armenia, Azerbaijan, Belarus, Bosnia and Herzegovina, Bulgaria, Croatia, Czech Republic, Estonia, Georgia, Hungary, Kazakhstan, Kyrgyzstan, Latvia,

Lithuania, Macedonia, Moldova, Poland, Romania, Russia, Serbia and Montenegro, Slovakia, Tajikistan, Turkmenistan, Ukraine or Uzbekistan.

THE INTERNATIONAL SCHOOL FOR ADVANCED STUDIES (SISSA)

Via Beirut 2-4, Trieste, I-34014, Italy
Tel: (39) (39) 040 37811
Fax: (39) (39) 040 3787 528
Website: www.sissa.it
Contact: Scientific Secretariat

The International School for Advanced Studies (SISSA) is a centre for research and postgraduate studies leading to the PhD degree (equivalent to the Italian Dottore di Ricerca) in the fields of astrophysics, mathematics, neuroscience, elementary particles and condensed matter physics and functional and structural genomics.

SISSA Fellowships

Subjects: Applied mathematics, astrophysics, functional and structural genomics, mathematical analysis, mathematical physics, statistical and biological physics, neurosciences, theory of elementary particles or the theory of computational physics of condensed matter.
Purpose: To financially support PhD studies.
Eligibility: Open to candidates over the age of 30 at the beginning of the academic year.
Level of Study: Doctorate
Type: Fellowship
Value: Please contact the School for details
Frequency: Annual
Study Establishment: The International School for Advanced Studies (SISSA)
Country of Study: Italy
No. of awards offered: 58
Application Procedure: Applicants must complete the application form which can be found on the website.
Funding: Government
Contributor: The Italian Government

INTERNATIONAL SCHOOL OF CRYSTALLOGRAPHY, E MAJORANA CENTRE

Dip to Scienze Della Terra Geo Ambientoli, Piazza di Porta San Donato 1, I-40126 Bologna, Italy
Tel: (39) 051 209 4912
Fax: (39) 051 209 4904
Email: riva@geomin.unibo.it
Website: www.geomin.unibo.it
Contact: Professor L Riva Di Sanseverino

The International School of Crystallography is an international organizing committee that offers, once a year, short advanced courses of 9–11 days on frontier topics in crystallography, solid state chemistry, materials science, structure activity relationship, molecular biology and biophysics.

International School of Crystallography Grants

Subjects: Frontier topics in crystallography, eg. high pressure crystallography, polymorphism and drug design via crystallography.
Purpose: To enable postgraduates to attend short high-level courses held at Erice once a year.
Eligibility: Open to all who have scientific interests related to the topic chosen each year at a PhD or postdoctoral level. English language proficiency is mandatory.
Level of Study: Postdoctorate, postgraduate, doctorate
Type: Grant
Value: Fees, board and lodging during the course
Length of Study: 8–12 days
Frequency: Annual
Study Establishment: E Majorana Centre, Erice, Sicily, Italy
Country of Study: Italy
No. of awards offered: Approx. 30–40
Application Procedure: Young applicants must submit a letter of recommendation stating their financial needs, personal data and details of scientific interests. Further details can be found at www.crystalerice.org
Closing Date: The end of November
Funding: Government
Contributor: NATO, the European Commission and the Italian National Research Council
No. of awards given last year: 70
No. of applicants last year: 250

For further information contact:

Department of Organic Chemistry, Via Marzolo 1, I-35131 Padova, Italy
Tel: (39) 49 827 5275
Fax: (39) 49 827 5239
Email: paola.spadon@unipd.it
Contact: Dr Paola Spadon

INTERNATIONAL SOCIETY OF NEPHROLOGY

Global Headquarters, Avenue Gaulois 7,
B-1040 Brussels, Belgium
Tel: (32) 2 743 1546
Fax: (32) 2 743 1550
Email: info@isn-online.org
Website: www.isn-online.org

The International Society of Nephrology (ISN) pursues the goal of worldwide advancement of education, science and patient care in nephrology. ISN achieves this through its journal *Kidney International*, organizing international congresses, symposia, specific programmes and fellowships. As a result, ISN helps to improve renal science and renal patient care worldwide, especially in emerging countries.

ISN Fellowship Awards

Subjects: Nephrology.
Purpose: To offer training opportunities to young nephrologists in emerging countries with the ultimate goal of improving the standards of nephrology practice in their home institutions upon their return.
Eligibility: Open to young nephrologists from emerging countries, as defined by World Bank criteria. Applicants must have received sufficient training in internal medicine or other fields to pass all host country examinations that are necessary for the care of patients. Fellowships are primarily offered for clinical training in nephrology, but in some circumstances research training may be allowed, priority can be considered for training in epidemiology.
Level of Study: Postdoctorate, predoctorate
Type: Fellowship
Value: The stipends are subject to indexation based on-the-cost-of-living in their host country; the top and bottom level grants are respectively US$26,000 and US$20,000 for 12 months of training. If the host country is contributing funds then this is subtracted from the standard fund
Length of Study: Short-term fellowships are for 3–6 months and long-term fellowships are for 12 months. Extensions are possible.
Frequency: Annual
Study Establishment: Any suitable university, scientific institution or hospital
No. of awards offered: Up to 40 each year
Application Procedure: Applicants must complete an application form, which is subjected to the review of an international committee. Applicants must provide evidence of a guaranteed position in a medical institution upon return to their home country. The applicant must agree to return to their home country upon completion of the training; if not, the recipient will have to refund the ISN fellowship in full.
Closing Date: Deadlines are the end of January and the end of July each year. The selection is made in May and November each year
Funding: Foundation, private

Contributor: Offered in collaboration with sister societies and industry, the American Society of Nephrology, the National Kidney Research Fund in the United Kingdom, Fresenius Medical care in Germany and the European renal Association
No. of awards given last year: 44
Additional Information: The selection procedure has three parts: data verification, where information provided by applicants is verified and evaluated through correspondence; evaluation, where 7 members of the Committee, one from each Continent, score each application according to standard format; and finally, selection, which is largely based on the aforementioned scores but also considers the geographical balance, urgent needs in certain regions and the preference of certain sponsors.

For further information contact:

ISN Global Headquarters Av. Tervueren 300 1150 Brussels, Belgium
Email: an@associationhg.com
Website: www.isn-online.org

ISN Travel Grants

Subjects: Nephrology.
Purpose: To encourage young physicians and scientists to attend conferences, especially those from emerging countries. Travel grants are offered to facilitate attendance at the ISN International Congress and the ISN Forefronts Commission Conference.
Eligibility: Applicants must have training and experience in an area of research relevant to the conference and an infrastructure at their home institutions to allow the pursuit of techniques and approaches discussed at the conference. Young physicians and scientists are preferred as are ISN Fellows. A portion of the grants are reserved for applicants from emerging countries.
Level of Study: Research, postdoctorate, doctorate, postgraduate
Type: Travel grant
Value: The size of the grant is decided according to each conference and congress
Length of Study: Varies
No. of awards offered: 120 travel grants for each International Congress of Nephrology and 6 travel grants for young scientists from emerging countries to attend each ISN Forefront Conference
Application Procedure: Applicants must complete an application form, which can be downloaded from the ISN website or requested from the ISN Secretary General a year prior to the Congress. Applications can also be obtained from the Directors of the ISN Forefront Programmes.
Closing Date: Please contact the organization
Funding: Foundation, private
Contributor: Offered in collaboration with sponsors of ISN
No. of awards given last year: 120
No. of applicants last year: 395

For further information contact:

ISN Secretary General, Cairo Kidney Centre, 3 Hussein El-Memar Street, Antikhana, PO Box 91, Bab El-Louk, Cairo, 11513, Egypt
Tel: (20) 2 579 0267
Email: Isn@rusys.eg.net
Contact: Dr Rashad Barsoum

ISN Visiting Scholars Program

Subjects: Nephrology.
Purpose: To improve the long-term quality of patient care, education and research in fields relevant to the kidney at the host institution, and enable senior physicians or scientists who are experts in nephrology and related disciplines to spend between 6 weeks and 3 months at an institution in the developing world.
Eligibility: Applicants must focus primarily on hands-on activities that are the focus of this award, eg. the establishment of a new clinical programme, research programme or laboratory technique. ISN visiting scholars should spend the duration of their study time at an institution in the developing world. Applicants must be experts in nephrology and related disciplines.
Level of Study: Postdoctorate, research
Type: Scholarship
Value: US$20,000, inclusive of travel and expenses, for 3 months or a pro rata amount for a shorter period of time
Length of Study: 6 weeks–3 months
Frequency: At the discretion of the ISN
No. of awards offered: At the discretion of the ISN but usually up to 2 scholarships per year
Application Procedure: Applicants must send a description of the programme, its objectives, personal references and a letter of acceptance from the host institution to the ISN Secretary General. Applicants must be members of the ISN.
Closing Date: Please contact the organization
Funding: Foundation, private
No. of awards given last year: 2
No. of applicants last year: 2

For further information contact:

Cairo Kidney Centre, 3 Hussein El-Memar Street, Antikhana, PO Box 91, Bab El-Louk, Cairo, 11513, Egypt
Tel: (20) 2 579 0267
Email: isn@rusys.eg.net

THE INTERNATIONAL SPINAL RESEARCH TRUST (ISRT)

Unit 8a, Bramley Business Centre, Station Road, Bramley, Guildford, Surrey, GU5 0AZ, England
Tel: (44) 14 8389 8786
Fax: (44) 14 8389 8763
Email: research@spinal-research.org
Website: www.spinal-research.org
Contact: Head of Research

The International Spinal Research Trust (ISRT) organizes fund raising to support research projects that have the aim of repairing or restoring the loss of function that occurs as a result of injury to the spinal cord. A structured research strategy has been developed to target funds towards relevant research topics.

ISRT Project Grant

Subjects: Furthering the understanding of mammalian spinal cord injury and approaches towards the repair and restoration of function.
Purpose: To provide support for laboratory or clinically based projects.
Eligibility: Open to suitably qualified and experienced principal investigators.
Level of Study: Postdoctorate, research
Type: Grant
Value: Please contact the organization
Length of Study: Up to 3 years
Frequency: Dependent on funds available
Study Establishment: An appropriate university or research institution
Country of Study: Any country
No. of awards offered: According to funds available
Application Procedure: Calls for proposals on a specific theme will be advertised periodically. Short-listed applicants will be required to complete a full application form.
Closing Date: Varies, as advertised
Funding: Private
Additional Information: Each call for proposals is on a specific theme. Proposals must be within the charity's remit.

INTERNATIONAL TROPICAL TIMBER ORGANIZATION (ITTO)

International Organizations Center, 5th floor Pacifico-Yokohama 1-1-1, Minato-Mirai, Nishi-ku, Yokohama, 220-0012, Japan
Tel: (81) 45 223 1110
Fax: (81) 45 223 1111
Email: itto@itto.or.jp
Website: www.itto.or.jp

ITTO is an intergovernmental organization promoting the conservation and sustainable management, use and the trade of tropical forest resources.

International Tropical Timber Organization (ITTO) Fellowship Programme

Subjects: Forestry management.
Purpose: To promote human resource development and to strengthen professional expertise in tropical forestry.
Eligibility: Only nationals of ITTO member countries are eligible to apply and fellowships are awarded mainly to nationals of developing member countries.
Level of Study: Postgraduate, professional development, research
Type: Fellowship
Value: US$10,000
Frequency: Annual
No. of awards offered: Varies
Closing Date: April 21st
Funding: Government
Contributor: International Tropical Timber Organization

INTERNATIONAL UNION AGAINST CANCER (UICC)

Fellowships Department, 3 rue de Conseil-Général, CH-1205 Geneva, Switzerland
Tel: (41) 22 809 1840
Fax: (41) 22 809 1810
Email: bbaker@uicc.org
Website: www.uicc.org
Contact: Mrs Brita M. Baker, Head, UICC Fellowships

The International Union Against Cancer (UICC) Fellowships Programme provides long-, medium- and short-term fellowships to qualified investigators, clinicians and nurses, who are actively involved in cancer research, clinical oncology or oncology nursing.

ACLS/SSRC/NEH International and Area Studies Fellowships

Subjects: Research and writing on the societies and cultures of Asia, Africa, the Middle East, Latin America and the Caribbean, East Europe, and the former Soviet Union.
Purpose: To encourage humanistic research in area studies.
Eligibility: Applicant must have a PhD conferred prior to September 30, 2002, or in the case of an established Scholar, the equivalent of a PhD. Most recent supported research leave must have concluded prior to July 1, 2002–2003, and the applicant must be citizen of the United States of America or permanent resident who has lived in the United States of America continuously for at least 3 years by the application deadline.
Level of Study: Research, postdoctorate
Type: Fellowship
Value: US$30,000–50,000
Frequency: Annual
Country of Study: United States of America
No. of awards offered: Up to 10
Application Procedure: Applicants must submit a completed application form, a proposal (no more than 5 pages, double spaced), a bibliography (no more than 2 pages), a publication list (no more than 2 pages) and 2 reference letters.
Closing Date: September 30th
Funding: Foundation, private, individuals
Contributor: Andrew W. Mellon Foundation, Ford Foundation, Rockefeller Foundation, National Endowment for the Humanities and the Willam and Flora Hewlett Foundation

American Cancer Society UICC International Fellowships for Beginning Investigators (ACSBI)

Subjects: Oncology.
Purpose: To facilitate cancer investigators and clinicians, who are in the early stages of their careers, to conduct cancer research projects into the pre-clinical, clinical, epidemiological, psychological, behavourial, health services, health policy, outcomes and cancer-control aspects of the disease.
Eligibility: Candidates must be investigators and clinicians who are in the early stages of their careers and hold assistant professorships or similar positions in their home institutes.
Level of Study: Research
Type: Fellowship
Value: US$40,000
Length of Study: 1 year
Frequency: Annual
No. of awards offered: 6–8 per year
Application Procedure: Application forms can be obtained from the fellowships department or downloaded from the UICC website.
Closing Date: December 1st
Funding: Commercial
Contributor: American Cancer Society
Additional Information: Awards are conditional on the return of the fellow to the home institute at the end of fellowship and on the availability of appropriate facilitites and resources to apply the newly acquired skills.

Reverse UICC International Cancer Technology Transfer Fellowships

Subjects: Basic, clinical, behavourial and epidemiological aspects of cancer research, cancer control and prevention, clinical management, and diagnostic and therapeutic skills.
Purpose: To facilitate teaching and training courses on cancer research.
Eligibility: Applicants should be internationally recognized leaders in their respective fields.
Level of Study: Teaching
Type: Fellowship
Value: US$2,000
Length of Study: 1 week
Frequency: Annual
No. of awards offered: 10–20 per year
Application Procedure: Application forms can be obtained from the UICC fellowships department or downloaded from the website.
Closing Date: Accepted at any time
Funding: Private
Contributor: The fellowships are funded by a group of cancer institutes, societies, leagues, associations and governmental agencies in North America, Europe and Australia.
Additional Information: Awards are subject to the UICC general conditions for fellowships.

Trish Greene UICC International Oncology Nursing Fellowships

Subjects: Nursing.
Purpose: To provide an opportunity for qualified nurses to augment their professional knowledge and experience in the field of cancer treatment.
Eligibility: Registered nurses or nurse educators who are actively engaged in the management of cancer patients or the training of nurses in middle- and low-income countries, and who can communicate effectively in the language of the host centre, are eligible to apply.
Level of Study: Professional development
Type: Fellowship
Value: US$2,800
Length of Study: 1 month
Frequency: Annual
Country of Study: Australia, North America, United Kingdom, India, Singapore, France or Spain
No. of awards offered: 10–15 per year
Application Procedure: Application forms can be obtained from the UICC fellowships department or downloaded from the website.
Closing Date: November 1st
Funding: Private
Contributor: The Oncology Nursing Society (USA) and related corporations: the ONS Foundation, Oncology Education Services and the Oncology Nursing Certification Corporation
Additional Information: Awards are subject to the UICC general conditions for fellowships.

UICC Asia-Pacific Cancer Society Training Grants

Subjects: Oncology.
Purpose: To increase the capacity of volunteers and staff of voluntary cancer societies located in the Asia Pacific region by participating in, and learning from activities conducted by established collaborating cancer societies in the region.
Level of Study: Unrestricted, professional development
Type: Grant
Value: US$1,800
Length of Study: 1 week
Frequency: Annual
Country of Study: India, Australia, Singapore
No. of awards offered: 3–5 per year
Application Procedure: Candidates must choose one of the projects offered and submit their curriculum vitae together with a letter of justification to the host society with a request for a formal invitation to participate in the specific project. The letter of justification must describe why a specific project was chosen, how candidates and their organizations would benefit from this experience and how they would disseminate the new skills upon return. All application material can be obtained from the UICC Fellowships Department or downloaded from the website.
Closing Date: September 1st
Funding: Trusts
Contributor: William Rudder Memorial Fund (Australia)
Additional Information: Selection results will be notified in mid-December. Awards are subject to the UICC general conditions for fellowships.

UICC International Cancer Research Technology Transfer Fellowships (ICRETT)

Subjects: Cancer control and prevention, epidemiology and cancer registration, public education and behavioural sciences.
Purpose: To facilitate the rapid international transfer of cancer research and clinical technology; to exchange knowledge and enhance skills in basic, clinical, behavourial and epidemiological areas of cancer research, and in cancer control and prevention; and to acquire up-to-date clinical management, diagnostic and therapeutic expertise.
Eligibility: Investigators and clinicians should be working in places where such teaching is not yet available and where the necessary facilities exist to apply and disseminate the new skills upon return. Qualified cancer investigators should be at the early stages in their careers, while clinicians should be well established in their oncology practice.
Level of Study: Professional development
Type: Fellowship
Value: US$3,000
Length of Study: 1–3 months
Study Establishment: A suitable host institute abroad
Country of Study: Any country
No. of awards offered: 120 per year
Application Procedure: Application forms can be obtained from the fellowships department or downloaded from the UICC website.
Closing Date: Any time
Funding: Private, government, commercial
Contributor: The fellowships are funded by a group of cancer institutes societies, leagues, associations and governmental agencies in North America, Europe and Australia
Additional Information: Candidates who are already physically present at the proposed host institute while their applications are under consideration are not eligible for a UICC fellowship.

UICC International Cancer Technology Transfer Fellowships (ICRETT) for Bilateral Exchanges Between Indonesia and the Netherlands

Subjects: Cancer control and prevention, epidemiology and cancer registration, public education or behavioural sciences.
Purpose: To foster the acquisition of up to date clinical management, diagnostic and therapeutic expertise, exchange knowledge and enhance skills in cancer control and prevention and facilitate rapid transfer of cancer research and technology.
Eligibility: Eligible to nationals of Indonesia and experts from any country who have been invited to teach these specialised skills at institutes abroad. Qualified cancer investigators should be in the early stages of their careers while clinicians should be fully established in their oncology practise.
Level of Study: Research, professional development, postdoctorate, postgraduate
Type: Fellowship
Value: One month stipend and travel of US$3,000. Home and/or host institutions are expected to cover living costs for any additional periods. UICC also contributes to the least expensive international return air fares or other appropriate form of transport. Travel estimates should not include costs for internal travel within the home and/or host countries. These and extra costs for visa, passports, airport taxes and insurance are the responsibility of the Fellow. No allowances are made for accompanying dependants
Length of Study: A maximum of 3 months
Frequency: Annual
Study Establishment: A suitable host institution
Country of Study: The Netherlands
No. of awards offered: 10
Application Procedure: Applicants must complete an application form, available from the Fellowships Department or from the website.
Closing Date: Applications are accepted at any time
Funding: Private
No. of awards given last year: 3
No. of applicants last year: 6

UICC Translational Cancer Research Fellowships (TCRF)

Subjects: Oncology.
Purpose: To enhance the translation of basic, experimental and applied research insights into clinical or population applications in the form of new ideas, diagnostics, drugs and treatments, vaccines and other effective cancer prevention or intervention strategies.
Eligibility: Candidates and hosts should be experienced scientists or clinicians (such as those eligible for a mid-career or sabbatical break) and willing to enter into an enduring collaboration.
Level of Study: Research
Type: Fellowship
Value: US$55,500
Length of Study: 1 year
Frequency: Annual
Country of Study: Any country
No. of awards offered: 2 per year
Application Procedure: Application forms can be obtained from the fellowships department or downloaded from the UICC website.
Closing Date: December 1st
Funding: Commercial
Contributor: National Cancer Institute, United States of America and Novartis, Switzerland
Additional Information: A telephone interview will be conducted by an expert reviewer with both the candidate and the host. Any clinical applications resulting from such a collaboration should benefit both the country of the candidate and the country of the host.

UICC Trish Greene International Oncology Nursing Fellowships

Subjects: Training for nursing cancer patients.
Purpose: To support nurses who are actively engaged in the care of cancer patients and who come from developing and Eastern European countries.
Eligibility: Open to English or French speaking nurses who are actively engaged in the care of cancer patients in their home institutes and who come from developing or East European countries where specialist cancer nurse training is not yet widely available.
Level of Study: Professional development
Type: Fellowship
Value: The average stipend is US$2,800
Length of Study: 1–3 months with stipend support for 1 month
Frequency: Annual
Study Establishment: The Comprehensive Cancer Centre
Country of Study: Any country
No. of awards offered: 15
Application Procedure: Applicants must submit applications complete with supporting documentation to the UICC Geneva Office by the

application closing date. Application forms can be obtained from the Fellowships department or the website.
Closing Date: November 1st for notification in mid February
Funding: Private
Contributor: The Oncology Nursing Society (USA) and the Norwegian Cancer Society
No. of awards given last year: 15
No. of applicants last year: 24

UICC Yamagiwa-Yoshida Memorial International Cancer Study Grants

Subjects: Cancer research.
Purpose: To enable cancer investigators from any country to carry out bilateral research projects that exploit complementary materials or skills, including advanced training in experimental methods or special techniques.
Eligibility: Open to appropriately qualified investigators from any country who are actively engaged in cancer research. Candidates who are already physically present at the proposed host institute are not eligible.
Level of Study: Professional development
Type: Grant
Value: The average stipend is US$9,000. If a Fellow's return home is delayed beyond the extra approved period, 50 per cent of the travel award, the return portion has to be reimbursed to the UICC. Calculation of travel and stipend awards are based on the candidate's estimates which are adjusted, if need be, to published fares and UICC scales. Travel awards contribute to the least expensive international return air fares or other appropriate form of transport. Travel estimates should not include costs for internal travel within the home or host countries. These and extra costs for visa, passports, airport taxes and insurance are the responsibility of the Fellow. No financial support is provided for dependants
Length of Study: 3 months. May be extended by their original duration, subject to written approval of the home and host supervisors. Funding for these additional periods may be secured from other funding agencies
Frequency: Annual
Country of Study: Any country
No. of awards offered: 15
Application Procedure: Applicants must complete an application form, available from the Fellowships Department or from the website.
Closing Date: January 1st for notification by mid April, July 1st for notification by mid October
Funding: Private, commercial
Contributor: Kyowa Hakko Kyoga Company Limited, Toray Industries, Inc. and the Japan National Committee for UICC
No. of awards given last year: 14
No. of applicants last year: 16

Yamagiwa-Yoshida Memorial (YY) UICC International Cancer Study Grants

Subjects: Cancer research.
Purpose: To enable cancer investigators to carry out bilateral research projects abroad that exploit complementary materials or skills, including advanced training in experimental methods or special techniques.
Level of Study: Research, professional development
Type: Grant
Value: US$10,000
Length of Study: 3 months
Frequency: Annual
Country of Study: Any country
No. of awards offered: 15
Application Procedure: Application forms can be obtained from the fellowships department or downloaded from the UICC website at www.uicc.org
Closing Date: January 1st, July 1st
Funding: Private
Contributor: Kyowa Hakko Kogyo Company Ltd., Toray Industries Incorporated, Tokyo and the Japan National Committee for UICC
Additional Information: Grants are subject to the UICC general conditions for fellowships.

INTERNATIONAL UNION FOR VACUUM SCIENCE AND TECHNOLOGY (IUVSTA)

84 Oldfield Drive, Vicars Cross, Chester, CH3 5LW, United Kingdom
Tel: (44) 12 44 34 2675
Fax: (44) 77 1340 3525
Email: iuvsta.secretary.general@ronreid.me.uk
Website: www.iuvsta.org
Contact: Dr R J Reid, Secretary General

The International Union for Vacuum Science and Technology (IUVSTA) is a non-government organization whose member societies represent all vacuum scientists, engineers and technologists in their country.

Welch Foundation Scholarship

Subjects: Vacuum science.
Purpose: To encourage promising scholars who wish to study vacuum science, techniques or their application in any field.
Eligibility: Open to applicants of any nationality who hold the minimum of a Bachelor's degree, although preference is given to those holding a doctoral degree.
Level of Study: Postgraduate, doctorate, postdoctorate
Type: Scholarship
Value: US$15,500
Length of Study: 1 year
Frequency: Annual
Study Establishment: An appropriate laboratory
Country of Study: Any country
No. of awards offered: 1
Application Procedure: Applicants must complete and submit an application form with a research proposal, a curriculum vitae and two letters of reference. More information and application forms can be obtained from the website.
Closing Date: April 15th
Funding: Private
Contributor: IUVSTA
No. of awards given last year: 1
No. of applicants last year: 4

For further information contact:

Canadian Photorics Fabrication Centre, Institute for Microstructural Sciences, National Research Council, Building M-50, Montréal Road, Ottawa, ON, K1A 0R6, Canada
Email: Frank.Shepherd@nrc-cnrc.gc.ca
Contact: Dr FR Shepherd, Administrator Technical Manager

INTERNATIONAL UNIVERSITY OF JAPAN

Kokusai-cho, Minami Uonuma-shi, Nilgata, 949-7277, Japan
Tel: (81) 25 779 1111
Fax: (81) 25 779 4441
Website: www.iuj.ac.jp

From our vantage point in the heart of Asia, we offer a unique perspective of the world in a lively global setting. Our culturally diverse campus, coupled with our location and our insight, will enrich your educational experience.

Japanese Grant Aid for Human Resource Development Scholarship

Purpose: To provide students in Cambodia with opportunities for academic research at a Japanese University and thereby enhance bilateral relations between Cambodia and Japan.
Eligibility: Open to all University Graduates with advanced English language skills, and who are between the ages of 22 and 34 and nations of: Bangladesh, Cambodia, china, Indonesia, Laos, Mongolia, Myanmar, Phillipines, Uzbekistan, or Vietnam.
Level of Study: Postgraduate
Value: The scholarship includes tuition, a living allowance and travel expenses.
Frequency: Annual

Country of Study: Japan
No. of awards offered: 20
Application Procedure: Submit application form available online.
Closing Date: September 9th
Contributor: The Ministry of Education, youth and sport

For further information contact:

JICE JDS Project Office PO Box 1592, Phnom Penh, Cambodia,

INTERNATIONAL VIOLIN COMPETITION "PREMIO PAGANINI"

Secretariat of the International Violin Competition Premio Paganini, Comune di Genova, Via Sottoripa, 5, I-16124 Genova, Italy
Tel: (39) 010 557 4215
Fax: (39) 010 557 4326
Email: violinopaganini@comune.genova.it
Website: www.paganini.comune.genova.it
Contact: Ms Anna Rita Certo, Secretary General

The international violin competition is a competition for young violinists. It offers prizes for a total amount of €40,000 plus special prizes and an opportunity for the winner to play Paganini's violin on October 12th, on the occasion of the closing ceremony of the Christopher Columbus Celebrations.

International Violin Competition

Subjects: Violin.
Purpose: To discover new, talented, young violinists and to encourage them to spread the values which Paganini himself, and his music, stands for.
Eligibility: Open to violinists of any nationality born between May 2nd, 1973 and May 2nd, 1990.
Level of Study: Unrestricted
Type: Prize
Value: The first prize is €12,000, the second €7,000, the third €4,500, the fourth €2,700, the fifth €2,200 and the sixth €1,600
Frequency: Every 2 years
Country of Study: Italy
No. of awards offered: 6 awards and 4 special prizes
Application Procedure: Applicants must write for an application and registration form. Registration fee of €100 to be paid only after having passed the preselection. Forms can be downloaded from the website, but must be mailed to the competition address.
Closing Date: May 2nd
Funding: Government
Contributor: Comune di Genova
No. of awards given last year: 6 awards and 4 special prizes
No. of applicants last year: 116
Additional Information: The competition is held from September 21st to October 1st.

International Violin Competition Permio Paganini

Subjects: Violin.
Purpose: To discover new talented young violinists and encourage them to spread the values which Paganini himself and his music stands for.
Level of Study: Unrestricted
Type: Award
Value: €5,000–25,000
Frequency: Every 2 years
Country of Study: Italy
No. of awards offered: 3
Application Procedure: Applicants must send the application form by mail together with the documents required to the address indicated below. A printed application form may be obtained by writing to the Competition Secretariat or downloaded at: www.paganini.commune.genova.it
Closing Date: End of April
Funding: Government
Contributor: Comune di Genova
No. of awards given last year: 5
No. of applicants last year: 116
Additional Information: Registration fee of €100 to be paid only after having passed the pre-selection.

For further information contact:

Segreteria del Cancorso Internazionale di Violino Premio Paganini, Comune di Genova-Archivio Generale, Via XX Settember, 15-2 Piano, I-16121 Genova, Italy

INTERNATIONALER ROBERT-SCHUMANN-WETTBEWERB ZWICKAU

Stadtvevwaltung Zwickau, Kuetuvamt, 08009 Zwickau, PF 200933, Germany
Tel: (49) 375 834130
Fax: (49) 375 834 130
Email: kulturbuero@zwickau.de
Website: www.zwickau.de

International Robert Schumann Competition

Subjects: Piano performance and individual singing.
Purpose: To support the interpretation of the work of Robert Schumann.
Eligibility: Open to pianists up to the age of 30 and to individual singers up to the age of 32.
Level of Study: Professional development
Type: Competition
Value: Please contact the organization
Frequency: Every four years
Country of Study: Germany
No. of awards offered: 10
Application Procedure: Applicants must write for further details.
Funding: Government, commercial

IOTA SIGMA PI

National Honor Society for Women in Chemistry Hydrogen Chapter University of California, Berkeley, United States of America
Website: www.iotasigmapi.info

Iota Sigma Pi, founded in 1902, is a National Honor Society that serves to promote the advancement of women in chemistry by granting recognition to women who have demonstrated superior scholastic achievement and high professional competence by election into Iota Sigma Pi.

Agnes Fay Morgan Research Award

Subjects: Chemistry and biochemistry.
Purpose: To acknowledge research achievements in chemistry or biochemistry.
Eligibility: Open to female applicants who are not more than 40 years of age.
Level of Study: Postgraduate
Type: Award
Value: US$500
Frequency: Annual
Study Establishment: Any accredited institution
Country of Study: Any country
Application Procedure: See the website.
Closing Date: January 15th
Contributor: Iota Sigma Pi

For further information contact:

PO Box 6949 Radford university, Radford, VA 24142
Email: chermann@radford.edu
Contact: Dr Christine Hermann, Chemistry of Physics Department

Anna Louise Hoffman Award

Subjects: Chemistry.
Purpose: To recognize outstanding achievement in research.
Eligibility: Open to applicants who are full-time degree students and who may or may not be member of Iota Sigma Pi.

Level of Study: Postgraduate
Type: Scholarship
Value: US$500 and a certificate
Frequency: Annual
Study Establishment: Any accredited institution
Country of Study: Any country
Application Procedure: A completed application form along with two recommendations must be sent.
Closing Date: February 15th
Contributor: Iota Sigma Pi

Gladys Anderson Emerson Scholarship

Subjects: Chemistry and biochemistry.
Purpose: To award excellence in chemistry or biochemistry.
Eligibility: Open to applicants who are members of Iota Sigma Pi.
Level of Study: Postgraduate
Type: Scholarship
Value: US$2,000 and a certificate
Frequency: Annual
Study Establishment: Any accredited institution
Country of Study: Any country
Application Procedure: A completed application form, available on the website, must be sent.
Contributor: Iota Sigma Pi

For further information contact:

University of North Dakota Chemistry Department, Box 9024, Grand Forks, ND 58202-9024
Email: kthomasson@mail.chem.und.nodak.edu
Contact: Kathryn A. Thomasson

Iota Sigma Pi Centennial Award

Subjects: Chemistry, biochemistry.
Purpose: To award excellence in teaching chemistry, biochemistry or chemistry-related subjects.
Eligibility: Open to female applicants who are chemists or biochemists.
Level of Study: Postgraduate
Type: Award
Value: US$500, a certificate and membership in Iota Sigma Pi with a waiver of dues for one year
Frequency: Annual
Application Procedure: See the website.
Closing Date: January 15th
Contributor: Iota Sigma Pi

For further information contact:

Email: paisners@research.ge.com
Contact: Dr Sara Paisner

Iota Sigma Pi National Honorary Member Award

Subjects: Chemistry.
Purpose: To honor outstanding women chemists.
Eligibility: Open to female candidate with exceptional achievements in chemistry. Applicants may or may not be members of Iota Sigma Pi.
Type: Award
Value: US$1,000 a certificate and membership in Iota Sigma Pi with a lifetime waiver of dues
Frequency: Every 3 years
Application Procedure: See the website.
Closing Date: January 15th

For further information contact:

GE Global Research One Research Circle K1-4D17, Niskayuna, NY 12309
Email: paisners@research.ge.com
Contact: Dr Sara Paisner, Director for Professional Awards

Members-at-Large (MAL) Reentry Award

Subjects: Chemistry.
Purpose: To recognize potential excellence in chemistry and related fields.
Eligibility: Open to female candidates who have returned to academic studies after an absence of 3 or more years.
Level of Study: Postgraduate
Type: Award
Value: US$1,000, a certificate and a year's complimentary membership in Iota Sigma Pi
Study Establishment: Any accredited institution
Country of Study: Any country
Application Procedure: A completed application form must be sent.
Closing Date: March 20th
Contributor: Iota Sigma Pi

For further information contact:

Joanne Bedlek-Anslow, PhD Camden High School 1022 Ehrenclou Drive, Camden, SC 29020
Contact: MAL National Coordinator

Violet Diller Professional Excellence Award

Subjects: Chemistry.
Purpose: To recognize significant accomplishments in academic, governmental or industrial chemistry.
Eligibility: Open to female applicants who have contributed to the scientific community or society on a national level.
Level of Study: Postgraduate
Type: Award
Value: US$1,000 a certificate and membership in Iota sigma Pi with a lifetime of dues
Frequency: Every 3 years
Application Procedure: See the website.
Closing Date: January 15th
Contributor: Iota Sigma Pi

For further information contact:

One Research Circle K1-4D17, Niskayuna, NY 12309
Email: paisners@research.ge.com
Contact: Dr Sara Paisner

IOWA STATE UNIVERSITY

Iowa State University, Ames, IA, 50011, United States of America
Tel: (1) 515 2944111
Website: www.iastate.edu
Contact: Dr James R Bloedell, Dean

Iowa State University of Science and Technology is a public land-grant institution serving the people of Iowa, the nation and the world.

AICPA Accountemps Student Scholarship

Subjects: Accounting, finance and information systems.
Purpose: To support a full-time declared student of accounting towards postgraduate study and a career in accounting.
Eligibility: Not eligible to students who have already gained their CPA.
Level of Study: Postgraduate
Type: Scholarship
Value: $2,500
Frequency: Annual
Study Establishment: Iowa State University
Country of Study: United States of America
No. of awards offered: 2
Closing Date: April 1st
Funding: Private
Contributor: AICPA

For further information contact:

AICPA/Accountemps Student Scholarship Program, AICPA-Team 331, 1211 Avenue of the Americas, NY, 10036-8775, United States of America

Air and Waste Management Association Midwest Section Scholarship Award

Subjects: Environment-related studies.
Purpose: To support a postgraduate student pursuing a course of study and research leading to a career in environment-related studies.

Level of Study: Postgraduate
Type: Scholarship
Length of Study: 1 year
Frequency: Annual
Study Establishment: Iowa State University
Country of Study: United States of America or Canada
Closing Date: June 1st
Funding: Commercial
Contributor: Air and Waste Management Association

For further information contact:

A&WMA-Midwest Section, RMK Consultants, Kansas city, MO 64113, United States of America
Tel: (1) 515 294 4111
Contact: Ralph Keller, Scholarship Program

AMBUCS Scholarship

Subjects: Physical therapy, occupational therapy, speech language pathology and hearing audiology.
Purpose: To provide financial assistance to needy postgraduate students studying therapy.
Eligibility: Candidates must document financial need and express intent to enter clinical produce in the relevant discipline.
Level of Study: Postgraduate
Type: Scholarship
Frequency: Annual
Study Establishment: Iowa State University
Country of Study: United States of America
Closing Date: April 15th
Funding: Private
Contributor: AMBUCS

For further information contact:

AMBUCS Resource Center, PB 5127, High Point, NC, 27262, United States of America
Contact: National Scholarships Committee

American Electroplaters and Surface Finishers Society Scholarship

Subjects: Metallurgy, metallurgical engineering, materials science or engineering, chemistry, chemical engineering and environmental engineering.
Purpose: To support postgraduate students to continue their studies in metallurgical engineering and related disciplines.
Eligibility: Candidates must intend to study full-time for the year of the scholarship.
Level of Study: Postgraduate
Type: Scholarship
Length of Study: 1 year
Frequency: Annual
Study Establishment: Iowa State University
Country of Study: United States of America
Closing Date: April 15th
Funding: Private
Contributor: AESFS

For further information contact:

Central Florida Research Park, 12644 Research Parkway, Orlando, FL, 32826-3298, United States of America
Contact: Scholarship Committee AFSFS

American Society of Naval Engineers Scholarship

Subjects: Naval engineering.
Purpose: To support a postgraduate student for 1 year of full-time study leading to a designated engineering or physical science degree.
Eligibility: The candidate must be a citizen of the United States of America and have demonstrated or expressed a genuine interest in a career in naval engineering.
Level of Study: Postgraduate
Type: Scholarship
Value: US$3,500
Length of Study: 1 year
Frequency: Annual
Study Establishment: Iowa State University
Application Procedure: Selection criteria will be based on the candidate's academic record, work history, professional promise and interest in naval engineering.
Closing Date: February 15th
Funding: Private
Contributor: American Society of Naval Engineers

For further information contact:

1452 Duke Street, Alexandria, VA, 22314-3458, United States of America
Contact: The American Society of Naval Engineers

Charles and Kathleen Manatt Democracy Studies

Subjects: International relations, political science, public administration.
Purpose: To support students who have completed their undergraduate studies and who are working towards a graduate degree.
Level of Study: Postgraduate
Type: Fellowship
Value: US$1,800
Length of Study: 6 weeks
Frequency: Annual
Study Establishment: Iowa State University
Country of Study: United States of America
No. of awards offered: 2
Closing Date: May 22nd
Funding: Private

For further information contact:

1101 15th Street NW, Third Floor, Washington, DC, 20005, United States of America
Contact: Mr Dorin Tudoran, Director of Research & Communications

Charles E Fahmey Education Foundation Scholarship

Subjects: Any subject as approved by Iowa State University.
Purpose: To support a graduate student who is a resident of Wapello County.
Eligibility: Selection is made without regard to sex, race, age, religion or marital status.
Level of Study: Postgraduate
Type: Scholarship
Value: US$2,500
Frequency: Annual
Study Establishment: Iowa State University
Country of Study: United States of America
Closing Date: February 15th
Funding: Private
Contributor: Charles E Fahmey Foundation

For further information contact:

Firstar Bank, NA 123 East Third Street, Ottumwa, IA, 52501-8003, United States of America
Contact: Trust Department

John L Carey Scholarship

Subjects: Accountancy.
Purpose: To support a graduate student with a liberal arts degree who is interested in pursuing a CPA certificate.
Level of Study: Postgraduate
Type: Scholarship
Value: US$5,000 per year
Length of Study: 2 years
Frequency: Annual
Study Establishment: Iowa State University
Country of Study: United States of America
No. of awards offered: 5
Application Procedure: Candidates must supply two letters of recommendation as well as transcripts from both undergraduate and graduate entrance tests.

Closing Date: April 1st
Funding: Private
Contributor: American Institute of Certified Public Accountants
Additional Information: Students must maintain scholastic progress in order to quality for the 2nd year.

For further information contact:

AICPA, 1211 Avenue of the Americas, New York, NY, 10036–8775, United States of America
Contact: AICPA Carey Scholarships Program

IRELAND ALLIANCE

2800 darendon Boulevard # 502, Arlington, VA 22201, United States of America
Tel: (1) 703/841-5843
Email: vargo@us-irelandalliance.org
Website: www.us-irelandalliance.org
Contact: Trina Vargo, President

The US-Ireland Alliance is a proactive, non-partisan, non-profit organization dedicated to consolidating existing relations between the United States and Ireland and building that relationship for the future.

George J. Mitchell Scholarships
Subjects: All subjects.
Purpose: To familiarize and connect the next generation of American leadership with the island of Ireland.
Eligibility: Open to American citizens between the ages of 18 and 30.
Type: Scholarship
Value: Tuition, housing a stipend of US$12,000 and international travel expenses.
Length of Study: 1 year
Frequency: Annual
Study Establishment: Any accredited institution of higher learning
Country of Study: United Kingdom
No. of awards offered: 12
Application Procedure: Applications forms are available online.
Closing Date: October 10th
Funding: Foundation
Contributor: US–Ireland Alliance
No. of applicants last year: 20

IRISH-AMERICAN CULTURAL INSTITUTE (IACI)

1 Lackawanna Place, Morristown, NJ, 07960, United States of America
Tel: (1) 973 605 1991
Fax: (1) 973 605 8875
Email: info@iaci-usa.org
Website: www.iaci-usa.org

The Irish–American Cultural Institute (IACI), a non-profit educational institute, is dedicated to preserving and promoting the highest standards of artistic development, education, research and entertainment in fostering the cultural understanding of Irish heritage in America. With international headquarters in Morristown, NJ, the Institute has a long history of supporting the arts and humanities through grants and awards as well as through programming. The Institute is strictly non-political and non-sectarian. Founded in 1962, the IACI is the sole United States of America organization with the distinction of having the President of Ireland as patron.

IACI Visiting Fellowship in Irish Studies at the National University of Ireland, Galway
Subjects: Irish studies.
Purpose: To allow scholars whose work relates to any aspect of Irish studies to spend a semester at the University of Ireland, Galway.
Eligibility: Open to Scholars who normally reside in the United States of America, and whose work relates to any aspect of Irish studies.
Level of Study: Postgraduate
Type: Fellowship
Value: A stipend of US$13,000 plus transatlantic transportation
Length of Study: A period of not less than 4 months
Frequency: Annual
Country of Study: Ireland
No. of awards offered: 1
Application Procedure: Applicants must complete an application form and submit this with a current curriculum vitae and list of publications. Application forms are available on request.
Closing Date: December 31st for the forthcoming academic year
Contributor: Jointly funded with University College Galway (UCG)
Additional Information: The holder of the fellowship will be provided with services appropriate to a visiting faculty member during his or her time at UCG. There are certain relatively minor departmental responsibilities expected of the holder during his or her time at UCG, and certain other expectations regarding publication, upon completion of the fellowship.

Irish Research Funds
Subjects: All subjects; historical research has predominated, but other areas of research will be given equal consideration.
Purpose: To promote scholarly enquiry and publication regarding the Irish–American experience.
Eligibility: Open to individuals of any nationality. Media production costs and journal subventions will not be considered for funding.
Level of Study: Postgraduate
Type: Grant
Value: US$1,000–5,000
Frequency: Annual
Country of Study: Any country
No. of awards offered: Varies
Application Procedure: Applicants must complete an application form.
Funding: Private

THE ISLAMIC DEVELOPMENT BANK (IDB)

PO Box 5925 Jeddah 21432 Kingdom of Saudi Arabia, Saudi Arabia
Tel: (966) 636 6871
Fax: (966) 636 6871
Email: idbarchives@isdb.org
Website: www.isdb.org

The Islamic Development Bank is an international financial institution, which aims to foster the economic development and social progress of member countries and Muslim countries.

IDB Merit Scholarship for High Technology
Subjects: Science and high technology.
Purpose: To encourage advanced studies/research in science and high technology areas.
Eligibility: Open to scholars between the age of 25 and 40 years.
Level of Study: Postgraduate
Type: Scholarship
Value: Tuition allowance, insurance and ticket allowance.
Frequency: Annual
Application Procedure: See the website.

IDB Scholarship Programme in Science and Technology
Subjects: Science, technology, engineering and medicine.
Purpose: To assist IDB least developed member countries in the development of science and technology.
Eligibility: Open to candidates from least developed member countries, who are below the age of 30 years.
Level of Study: Postgraduate
Type: Scholarship
Value: Living allowance, book allowance, medical coverage, a return airticket and prepaid tuition fee
Length of Study: 2 years
Frequency: Annual
Application Procedure: A completed application form must be sent.

ISMA CENTRE

The University of Reading, Whiteknights Park, PO Box 242, Reading, Berkshire, RG6 6BA, England
Tel: (44) 11 8378 8239
Fax: (44) 11 8931 4741
Email: admin@ismacentre.rdg.ac.uk
Website: www.ismacentre.rdg.ac.uk
Contact: Ms Julie Stewart, Marketing & Recruitment Manager

The ISMA Centre at the University of Reading is a leader in the research and education of applied securities and investment banking education. Its graduate study opportunities include Master's degrees and doctoral research programmes. The Centre is part of the School of Business at the University, but is housed in its own facilities with two financial dealing rooms.

ISMA Centre Doctoral Scholarship

Subjects: A topic relating to fixed income, market microstructure, corporate finance, risk management, financial regulation and theoretical and applied financial econometrics.
Purpose: To support research in the field.
Eligibility: Open to candidates with an excellent academic background who have completed, or who are in the process of completing, a Master's degree with grade averages at distinction level, in a course containing a significant proportion of finance.
Level of Study: Doctorate
Type: Scholarship
Value: UK £10,000 paid quarterly plus PhD fee waiver
Length of Study: 3 years
Frequency: Annual
Study Establishment: ISMA Centre, University of Reading
Country of Study: United Kingdom
No. of awards offered: 3
Application Procedure: Applicants must complete an application form, available from the Centre.
Funding: Commercial
Contributor: ISMA Centre and the University of Reading
No. of awards given last year: 3
No. of applicants last year: 120

ITALIAN INSTITUTE FOR HISTORICAL STUDIES

Via Benedetto Croce 12, I-80134 Naples, Italy
Tel: (39) 081 551 7159
Fax: (39) 081 551 4813
Email: istituto@iiss.it
Website: www.iiss.it
Contact: Ms Marta Herling, Secretary

The Italian Institute for Historical Studies is a postgraduate institute for the study of history and philosophy. The study of history is seen in connection with the disciplines of philosophy, the arts, economics and literature. The Institute offers two annual scholarships for non-Italian postgraduates specializing in humanities and social sciences.

Adolfo Omodeo Scholarship

Subjects: History and philosophy. The study of history is seen in connection with the disciplines of philosophy, the arts, economics and literature.
Purpose: To allow students to participate in life at the Institute while completing a personal research project with the assistance of its staff.
Eligibility: Open to nationals of all countries. Applicants must possess a Bachelor's degree.
Level of Study: Postgraduate
Type: Scholarship
Value: Please contact the Institute for details
Length of Study: 12 months
Frequency: Annual
Study Establishment: The Italian Institute for Historical Studies
Country of Study: Italy
No. of awards offered: 1
Application Procedure: Applicants must submit an application including a copy of their birth certificate, proof of citizenship, university diploma, scholarly work, curriculum vitae, programme of research, letters of reference and copies of publications.
Closing Date: September 30th
Funding: Private, government
No. of awards given last year: 2
No. of applicants last year: 2

Frederico Chabod Scholarship

Subjects: History and philosophy. The study of history is seen in connection with the disciplines of philosophy, the arts, economics and literature.
Purpose: To allow students to participate in life at the Institute, while completing a personal research project with the assistance of its staff.
Eligibility: Open to nationals of all countries. Applicants must possess a Bachelor's degree.
Level of Study: Postgraduate
Type: Scholarship
Value: Please contact the Institute for details
Length of Study: 8 months
Frequency: Annual
Study Establishment: The Italian Institute for Historical Studies
Country of Study: Italy
No. of awards offered: 1
Application Procedure: Applicants must submit an application including a copy of their birth certificate, proof of citizenship, university diploma, scholarly work, curriculum vitae, programme of research, letters of reference and copies of publications.
Closing Date: September 30th
Funding: Government, private
No. of awards given last year: 12
No. of applicants last year: 2

IWHM BERNARD BUTLER TRUST FUND

37 Oasthouse Drive, Fleet, Hampshire, GU51 2UL, United Kingdom
Tel: (44) 12 5262 7748
Fax: (44) 12 5262 7748
Email: info@bernardbutlertrust.org
Website: www.bernardbutlertrust.org
Contact: The Secretary

The Trust was established in 1998 from the assets of the Institution of Works and Highways Management after the merger of its professional activities with the Institution of Civil Engineers in 1994.

The Bernard Butler Trust Fund

Subjects: Engineering.
Purpose: To encourage men and women engaged in the engineering field to improve their education, training and professional standing together with aiding and promoting individuals/organizations to advance engineering training, safety and methods of working.
Eligibility: Those who can show practical and personal qualities needed to promote engineering.
Level of Study: Postgraduate, graduate, professional development, research
Type: Training, education and research grants
Value: UK £750 upwards depending on submission
Study Establishment: Variable
Country of Study: Worldwide
Application Procedure: Applicants must download an application form from the website or on request from the Trust secretary.
Closing Date: None
Funding: Private
Contributor: Institution of Works and Highways Management
No. of awards given last year: 13
No. of applicants last year: 14

J N TATA ENDOWMENT

Bombay House, 2nd floor 24 Homi Mody Street Fort, Mumbai, 400001, India
Tel: (91) 022 5665 7643
Fax: (91) 022 2204 5432
Email: gjkerawalla@tata.com
Website: www.tata.com
Contact: J. N. Tata Endowment, Director

The J N Tata Endowment awards loan scholarships to scholars of conspicuous distinction for postgraduate, PhD or postdoctoral studies abroad in all fields. Mid-career professionals with an outstanding academic background and experience in the field, who are going abroad for further specialization, are also considered for the scholarship.

J N Tata Endowment Loan Scholarship

Subjects: All subjects.
Purpose: To provide an opportunity to the gifted to pursue higher studies abroad in all disciplines.
Eligibility: Open only to Indian nationals. Applicants must be graduates of a recognized Indian university with a sound academic and extracurricular record. Deserving mid-career professionals are also eligible.
Level of Study: Doctorate, mba, postgraduate, postdoctorate, professional development, research
Type: Loan scholarship
Value: Please contact the organization
Length of Study: Minimum 1 year; minimum 6 months for mid-career professionals
Frequency: Annual
Country of Study: Any country except India
No. of awards offered: 100+
Application Procedure: Applicants must complete an application form. Forms are issued against an application fee of Indian rupees 100 only.
Closing Date: February 15th for the Autumn and Spring semesters
Funding: Trusts, private
Contributor: Tata Trusts
No. of awards given last year: 120
No. of applicants last year: 606
Additional Information: The award is primarily for the Autumn semester. The selection of scholars is made on the basis of a personal interview that assesses the student's competence in the field of graduation, general knowledge and maturity and suitability for the proposed field of study. Interviews are conducted between March and June for the Autumn and Spring semesters.

For further information contact:

Administrative Office Mulla House, 4th Floor, 51, M. G. Road Fort, Mumbai, 400001, India
Contact: J. N. Tata, Endowment

Regd. Off: Bombay House, 2nd floor 24, Homi Mody Street Fort, Mumbai, 400 001, India
Contact: J. N. Tata Endowment

JACK KENT COOKE FOUNDATION

44115 Woodridge Parkway, Suite 200, Virginia, Lansdowne, 20176-5199, United States of America
Tel: (1) 703 723 8000
Fax: (1) 703 723 8030
Email: jck@jackkentcookefoundation.org
Website: ww.jackkentcookefoundation.org

The Jack Kent Cooke Foundation is a private, independent foundation, established in 2000 to help young people of exceptional reach their full potential through education.

Jack Kent Cooke Scholarship

Subjects: Any subjects.
Purpose: To goal of this scholarship is to enable the next generation of leaders to follow their dreams through graduate study..
Eligibility: Open to outstanding students from an accredited US college or university with financial need.
Level of Study: Postgraduate
Type: Scholarship
Value: US$50,000
Length of Study: Varies
Frequency: Annual
Study Establishment: A US University
Country of Study: United States of America
No. of awards offered: 45–50
Application Procedure: Application to be submitted which will undergo a rigorous review process by expert selection committee members. Visit Foundation website for information.
Closing Date: May 1st
Funding: Foundation
Contributor: Jack Kent Cooke Foundation

For further information contact:

Jack Kent Cooke Foundation, 44115 Woodridge Parkway, Suite 200, Virgina, Lansdowne, 20176-5199

JACOB'S PILLOW DANCE

358 George Canter Road, Becket, MA 01223, United States of America
Tel: (1) 413 243 9919
Fax: (1) 413 243 4744
Email: info@jacobspillow.org
Website: www.jacobspillow.org

Jacob's Pillow is America's premier dance festival. Founded in 1930s, the Pillow today is renowned not only for producing a premier festival, but also for its professional school, intern programme, archives of rare holdings, artist residencies and year-round community programmes.

Jacob's Pillow Intern Program

Subjects: The following fields related to Dance studies: Archives/ presentation, business, development, education, general management, marketing, photojournalism, technical theatre production, ticket services and video documentation.
Purpose: To offer on-the-job training and experience working alongside professional staff.
Eligibility: Open to all candidates without regard to age, gender or national or ethnic origin.
Level of Study: Professional development
Type: Internship
Value: US$500 stipend, free room and board and access to festival activities
Length of Study: 3 months
Frequency: Annual
Country of Study: United States of America
No. of awards offered: 30
Application Procedure: See the website.
Closing Date: March 3rd

For further information contact:

Jacobs Pillow Dance Festival, PO Box 287, Lee, MA 01238
Contact: Internship Coordinator

JAMES AND GRACE ANDERSON TRUST

32 Wardie Road, Edinburgh, EH5 3LG, Scotland
Tel: (44) 13 1552 4062
Fax: (44) 13 1467 1333
Email: tim.straton@virgin.net
Contact: Mr Tim Straton, Trustee

The James and Grace Anderson Trust funds research into the cure or alleviation of cerebral palsy.

James and Grace Anderson Trust Research Grant

Subjects: Research into cure or alleviation of cerebral palsy.
Purpose: To advance by investigation, research or any other way, knowledge with regard to the causes of cerebral

palsy and related conditions and, if possible, curing or alleviating the same.
Level of Study: Research
Type: Grant
Value: Maximum UK £25,000
Length of Study: 1–3 years
Frequency: Twice each year
Country of Study: Scotland
Application Procedure: Application must be made in writing, giving full details of the research being carried out and the anticipated value. A copy of the ethical approval, if granted, should also be included.
Closing Date: April 15th and October 15th
Funding: Private
No. of awards given last year: 5
No. of applicants last year: 22

THE JAMES BEARD FOUNDATION

The Beard House 167 West 12th Street, New York, NY 10011, United States of America
Tel: (1) 212 627 2308

It is our mission to celebrate, preserve, nurture American's culinary heritage and diversity in order to elevate the appreciation of our culinary excellence.

James Beard Scholarship

Subjects: Fine cuisine.
Purpose: To fund aspiring culinary professionals.
Level of Study: Professional development
Type: Scholarship
Value: US$20,000 (awarded in US$5,000 increments)
Length of Study: 1–4 years
Frequency: Annual
No. of awards offered: 50
Application Procedure: Supply two letters of reference, mailed with a completed application.
Closing Date: May
Funding: Foundation
Contributor: James Beard Foundation
No. of awards given last year: 50

James Beard Scholarship II

Subjects: Fine cuisine.
Purpose: To offer unstinting help and encouragement to people embracing on a culinary career.
Level of Study: Professional development
Type: Scholarship
Value: US$500–5,000
Length of Study: 1 year
Frequency: Annual
No. of awards offered: 50
Application Procedure: Supply two letters of reference, mailed with a completed application.
Closing Date: May
Funding: Foundation
Contributor: The James Beard Foundation
No. of awards given last year: 50

JAMES COOK UNIVERSITY

Graduate Research School, Townsville, QLD, 4811, Australia
Tel: (61) 7 4781 4575
Fax: (61) 7 4781 6204
Email: researchhigherdegrees@jcu.edu.au
Website: www.jcu.edu.au
Contact: Ms Susan Meehan, Manager

James Cook University prides itself on its international reputation for research and discovery and teaching that is enhanced and enlivened by that research activity.

James Cook University Postgraduate Research Scholarship

Subjects: All disciplines.
Purpose: To encourage full-time postgraduate research leading to a Master's or PhD degree.
Eligibility: Open to any student who has attained at least an Upper Second Class (Honours) Bachelor's Degree.
Level of Study: Postgraduate
Type: Scholarship
Value: Australian $18,484 per year. The award does not cover annual tuition fees for overseas students
Length of Study: 3 years with a possible additional 6 months in exceptional circumstances for the PhD, or 2 years for the Master's programme
Frequency: Annual
Study Establishment: James Cook University
Country of Study: Australia
No. of awards offered: Up to 12
Closing Date: October 31st

Noel and Kate Monkman Postgraduate Award

Subjects: Marine biology.
Purpose: To encourage full-time study towards an MSc or PhD degree in marine biology.
Eligibility: Open to Australian citizens or those with permanent resident status in Australia who hold, or are expecting to hold, an Upper Second Class (Honours) Degree, or its equivalent, in marine biology or a related science.
Level of Study: Postgraduate
Type: Scholarship
Value: To be determined
Length of Study: 3 years for the PhD or 2 years for the Master's programme
Frequency: Dependent on funds available
Study Establishment: James Cook University
Country of Study: Australia
No. of awards offered: 1

JAMES MADISON MEMORIAL FELLOWSHIP FOUNDATION

2000 K Street North West, Suite 303, Washington, DC, 20006, United States of America
Tel: (1) 202 653 8700
Fax: (1) 202 653 6111
Email: madison@act.org
Website: www.jamesmadison.com
Contact: Mr Lewis F Larsen, Director of Programs

The mission of the James Madison Memorial Fellowship Foundation is to strengthen the teaching of the principles, framing and development of the United States of America Constitution in secondary schools.

James Madison Fellowship Program

Subjects: History, political science and education.
Eligibility: Applicants must be citizens of the United States of America.
Level of Study: Graduate
Type: Fellowship
Value: Up to US$24,000
Length of Study: Up to 5 years
Frequency: Annual
Country of Study: United States of America
No. of awards offered: Up to 60
Application Procedure: Applicants must obtain an application form by calling (1) 800 525 6928. Applications may also be downloaded from the Foundation's website.
Closing Date: March 1st
Funding: Private, government
No. of awards given last year: 70

JAMES PANTYFEDWEN FOUNDATION

9 Market Street, Aberystwyth, Ceredigion, SY23 1DL, Wales
Tel: (44) 19 7061 2806
Fax: (44) 19 7061 2806
Email: pantyfedwen@btinternet.com
Contact: Mr Richard H Morgan, Executive Secretary

James Pantyfedwen Foundation Grants

Subjects: All subjects.
Purpose: To promote mainly postgraduate research.
Eligibility: Open to Welsh nationals, especially those who wish to train as ministers of religion of any denomination. The qualifying criteria for this are defined by the benefactor.
Level of Study: Postgraduate
Type: Grant
Value: Varies, usually linked to the cost of postgraduate tution fees (up to a maximum of UK £5,000)
Length of Study: Up to 3 years
Frequency: Annual
Country of Study: United Kingdom
No. of awards offered: Varies
Application Procedure: Applicants must submit applications on the appropriate forms, accepted on an ongoing basis. Closing date for students in each year is June 30th.
Closing Date: Please contact the organization by June 30th in each year
Funding: Private
Contributor: Exclusive to private investment portfolio
No. of awards given last year: 40
No. of applicants last year: 140

JANSON JOHAN HELMICH OG MARCIA JANSONS LEGAT

Blommeseter, Norderhov, N-3512, Hönefoss, Norway
Tel: (47) 3 213 5465
Fax: (47) 3 213 5626
Email: janlegat@online.no
Website: www.jansonslegat.no
Contact: Mr Reidun Haugen, Manager

Janson Johan Helmich Scholarships and Travel Grants

Subjects: All subjects.
Purpose: To support practical or academic training.
Eligibility: Open to qualified Norwegian postgraduate students with practical experience for advanced study abroad.
Level of Study: Professional development, doctorate, mba, postgraduate, research
Type: Scholarship
Value: A maximum of Norwegian Krone 75,000
Frequency: Annual
Country of Study: Any country
No. of awards offered: 30
Application Procedure: Applicants must complete an application form.
Closing Date: March 15th
No. of awards given last year: 32
No. of applicants last year: 238

JAPAN SOCIETY FOR THE PROMOTION OF SCIENCE (JSPS)

Japan Society for the Promotion of Science, Overseas Fellowship Division, 6 Ichiban-cho, Chiyoda-ku, Tokyo, 102-8471, Japan
Tel: (81) 3263 9094
Fax: (81) 3263 1854
Email: gaitoku@jsps.go.jp
Website: www.jsps.go.jp

The Japan Society for the Promotion of Science (JSPS) is an independent administrative institution, established for the purpose of contributing to the advancement of science in all fields of the natural and social sciences and the humanities. The JSPS plays a pivotal role in the administration of a wide specrum of Japan's scientific and academic programs.

JSPS Research Fellowships for Young Scientists

Subjects: Humanities, social sciences, natural sciences.
Purpose: To foster young researchers who will play an important role in future scientific research activities.
Eligibility: Postdoctoral researchers who conduct research activities at universities or research institutions on a non-employment basis and graduate students who conduct research in university doctoral programmes are eligible to apply.
Level of Study: Postdoctorate, doctorate
Type: Grant
Value: For doctorate: Yen 205,000 per month; for postdoctorate: Yen 373,000 per month; Research Grants: up to Yen 1,500,000 per year
Length of Study: 2–3 years for doctorate, 3 years for postdoctorate
Study Establishment: Any eligible host institution (see the website for details)
Country of Study: Japan

JSPS Award for Eminent Scientists

Subjects: Humanities, social sciences and natural sciences.
Purpose: To enable Nobel Laureates and other leading scientists to come to Japan for the purpose of associating directly with younger Japanese researchers so as to mentor, stimulate and inspire them to greater achievements.
Eligibility: Foreign researchers such as Nobel laureates, who possess a record of excellent research achievements and who are mentors and leaders in their respective fields are eligible to apply.
Level of Study: Professional development
Type: Award
Value: First class round-trip air tickets, Yen 42,000 as per day stipend and a family allowance of Yen 10,000
Length of Study: 1–3 years
Frequency: Annual
Study Establishment: Any eligible host institution (see the website for details)
Country of Study: Japan
No. of awards offered: Approx. 5
Application Procedure: JSPS invities universities and institutions in Japan that wish to invite a Nobel laureate or other leading scientists to their campus to submit an invitation plan. JSPS reviews the plan and decides whether or not to fund the award. JSPS does not accept applications directly. It is the host institution that submits the application and supports the invitee's stay in Japan.

JSPS Invitation Fellowship Programme for Research in Japan

Subjects: Humanities, social sciences, natural sciences.
Purpose: To enable Japanese scientists to invite their foreign colleagues to Japan to participate in co-operative work and other academic activities. This programme also aims to promote international co-operation in mutual understanding through scientific research.
Eligibility: The candidate must be a researcher with an excellent record of research achievements who is employed full time at an overseas research institution and is a citizen of a country that has diplomatic relations with Japan. Senior scientists, university professors and other persons with substantial professional experience are welcome to apply. Japanese applicants must have lived abroad and been engaged in research for over 10 years.
Level of Study: Research
Type: Fellowship
Value: Short-term fellowships: round-trip air ticket, Yen 18,000 per day and Yen 150,000 domestic travel allowance; long-term fellowships: round-trip air ticket, Yen 369,000 monthly stipend, Yen 100,000 domestic travel allowance Yen 40,000 and for research expenses
Length of Study: 14–60 days for short-term and 2–10 months for long-term fellowships
Study Establishment: Any eligible host institution (see the website for details)
Country of Study: Japan

No. of awards offered: 295 short-term and 78 long-term fellowships
Application Procedure: Applications for these programmes must be submitted to JSPS by a host scientist in Japan through the head of his/her university or institution. Foreign scientists wishing to participate in this programme are advised to establish contact with a Japanese or foreign-resident researcher in their field and to ask him/her to submit an application. An application form and all supporting documents must be submitted by the deadline.
Closing Date: September 10th or May 13th for short-term fellowships and September 10th for long-term fellowships

JSPS Postdoctoral Fellowships for Foreign Researchers
Subjects: Humanities, social sciences, natural sciences, engineering and medicine.
Purpose: To assist promising and highly qualified young foreign researchers wishing to conduct research in Japan.
Eligibility: Open to citizens of countries that have diplomatic relations with Japan. Applicants must have a doctoral degree.
Level of Study: Postdoctorate
Type: Fellowship
Value: Please contact the organization
Length of Study: 2 years but a minimum of 1 year
Frequency: Annual
Study Establishment: Universities and research institutions
Country of Study: Japan
No. of awards offered: Varies
Application Procedure: Applicants must write for details.
Application must be submitted to JSPS by the host researcher in Japan.
Closing Date: May and September
Funding: Government

JSPS Postdoctoral Fellowships for Research Abroad
Subjects: Humanities, social sciences, natural sciences.
Purpose: To enable young Japanese postdoctoral researchers to conduct research at foreign universities or research institutions.
Level of Study: Postdoctorate
Type: Fellowship
Value: Travel expenses, a stipend and a research grant
Length of Study: 2 years
Frequency: Annual
Study Establishment: Any foreign university or research institution
Country of Study: Any country
No. of awards offered: Approx. 100

JSPS Summer Programme Fellowship
Subjects: Humanities, social sciences and natural sciences.
Purpose: To provide opportunities for young pre- and postdoctoral researchers from North America and Europe to receive an orientation on Japanese culture and research systems and to pursue research under the guidance of host researchers at Japanese universities and research institutes.
Eligibility: Candidates must hold a doctorate, which must have been received within 6 years prior to April 1st of the year of the summer programme or must be enrolled in a university graduate programme. The candidate should also possess the nationality, citizenship, permanent residence or equivalent status in one of the countries represented by the five designated nominating agencies (ie. the United States of America, United Kingdom, France, Germany or Canada).
Type: Fellowship
Value: Maintenance allowance: Yen 534,000, domestic research trip allowance: Yen 58,500 and round-trip airfare
Length of Study: 2 months
Study Establishment: Eligible host institutes (see the website for details)
Country of Study: Japan
Application Procedure: Applicants must contact the nominating authority in their respective countries for detailed application procedures, and consult the website for further details.
Funding: Government

JAPANESE AMERICAN CITIZENS LEAGUE (JACL)

1765 Sutter Street, San Francisco, CA, 94115, United States of America
Tel: (1) 41 5921 5225
Fax: (1) 41 5931 4671
Email: jacl@jacl.org
Website: www.jacl.org
Contact: Scholarships Officer

The Japanese American Citizens League (JACL) was founded in 1929 to fight discrimination against people of Japanese ancestry. It is the largest and one of the oldest Asian American organizations in the United States of America. The JACL has over 24,500 members in 112 chapters located in 25 states, Washington, DC, and Japan. The organization operates within a structure of eight district councils, with headquarters in San Francisco, CA.

Abe & Esther Hagiwara Student Aid Award
Subjects: All subjects.
Purpose: To provide financial assistance to students who are JACL members.
Eligibility: Open to members of JACL who demonstrate financial needs.
Level of Study: Postgraduate
Type: Scholarship
Value: US$5,000
Frequency: Annual
Application Procedure: See the website.
Closing Date: April 1st
Contributor: Japanese American Citizens League

JAPANESE GOVERNMENT

Embassy of Japan, 112 Empire Circuit, Yarralumla, ACT, 2600, Australia
Tel: (61) 2 6273 3244
Fax: (61) 2 6273 1848
Email: cultural@japan.org.au
Website: www.japan.org.au
Contact: Ms Eriko Prior, Monbukagakusho Scholarship Co-ordinator

Japanese Government (Monbukagakusho) Scholarships In-Service Training for Teachers Category
Subjects: Teacher training.
Eligibility: Open to Australians under 35 years of age who are university or teacher training graduates currently in active service in primary or secondary schools, or who are on the staff at teacher training institutions or educational administrative institutions. Applicants must have at least 5 years of experience in their terms of service. University academic staff members should not be selected as grantees.
Level of Study: Postgraduate
Type: Scholarship
Value: Return airfare plus Yen 184,000 per month
Length of Study: 18 months
Frequency: Annual
Study Establishment: A Japanese university
Country of Study: Japan
No. of awards offered: 1–2
Application Procedure: Applicants must complete an application form available from the Embassy of Japan in their own country. Applications are not available from the main organization.
Closing Date: Late March
Funding: Government
No. of awards given last year: 2
No. of applicants last year: 6
Additional Information: Applicants must be willing to study the Japanese language.

Japanese Government (Monbukagakusho) Scholarships Research Category
Subjects: Humanities, social sciences, literature, history, aesthetics, law, politics, economics, commerce, pedagogy, psychology, sociology, music and fine arts, natural sciences, pure science, engineering,

agriculture, fisheries, pharmacology, medicine, dentistry and home economics.
Eligibility: Open to Australian graduates under 35 years of age.
Level of Study: Doctorate, postgraduate
Type: Scholarship
Value: Return airfare plus Yen 184,000 per month
Length of Study: 18–24 months
Frequency: Annual
Study Establishment: A Japanese university
Country of Study: Japan
No. of awards offered: Approx. 17
Application Procedure: Applicants must complete an application form available from the Embassy of Japan in their own country. Applications are not available from the main organization.
Closing Date: June
Funding: Government
No. of awards given last year: 17
No. of applicants last year: 50
Additional Information: Applicants must be willing to study the Japanese language.

JEAN SIBELIUS INTERNATIONAL VIOLIN COMPETITION

PB 31, Helsinki, Finland
Tel: (358) 50 408 4335
Fax: (358) 10 850 4760
Email: violin.competition@kolumbus.fi
Website: www.siba.fi/sibeliuscompetition
Contact: Mr Harri Pohjolainen, Competition Secretary

The International Jean Sibelius Violin Competition is organized by the Sibelius Society. The first competition was held in 1965 to mark the 100th anniversary of the maestro's birth.

Jean Sibelius International Violin Competition

Subjects: Musical performance on the violin.
Purpose: To recognize and reward exceptional young violinists.
Eligibility: Open to violinists of any nationality born in 1975 or later.
Level of Study: Unrestricted
Type: Prize
Value: The first prize is €20,000, the second prize is €15,000 and the third prize is €10,000. There are also five prizes of €2,000 and three special prizes of €1,500–2,000
Frequency: Every 5 years
Country of Study: Any country
No. of awards offered: 11
Application Procedure: Applicants must refer to the competition brochure for the rules, application forms and programme, which is published in May of the preceding year. The brochure will be sent to schools around the world, but can also be sent directly on request. Applicants should contact the Competition Secretary.
Closing Date: August 19th
Funding: Government
Contributor: The Ministry of Education
No. of awards given last year: 12
No. of applicants last year: 121
Additional Information: For further information please contact the Competition Secretary.

JEWISH COMMUNITY CENTERS ASSOCIATION (JCCA)

15 East 26th Street, New York, NY, 10010-1579, United States of America
Tel: (1) 212 532 4949 ext 246
Fax: (1) 212 481 4174
Email: info@jcca.org
Website: www.jccworks.com
Contact: Ms Naomi Marks, Scholarships Co-ordinator

The Jewish Community Centers Association (JCCA) of North America is the leadership network of, and central agency for, over 275 Jewish Community Centers, YM-YWHAs and camps in the United States of America and Canada, which annually serve more than one million members. The Association offers a wide range of services and resources to enable its affiliates to provide educational, cultural and recreational programmes to enhance the lives of North American Jewry. The JCCA is also the United States of America government-accredited agency for serving the religious and social needs of Jewish military personnel, their families and patients in Virginia hospitals through the JWB Chaplains Council.

JCCA Graduate Education Scholarship

Subjects: Social work, Jewish education, health, physical education, recreation, education and non-profit business administration.
Purpose: To provide scholarships for graduate study at the Master's level in areas leading to full-time professional employment at a Jewish Community Center.
Eligibility: Open to applicants who have obtained a BA (Honours) Degree with a grade point average of at least 3.0 and a strong commitment to the Jewish Community Center Movement. It is preferred that applicants have knowledge of Jewish community practices, customs, rituals and organization.
Level of Study: MBA, graduate
Type: Scholarship
Value: Up to US$10,000 for tuition costs
Length of Study: 1 year, renewable for 1 extra year based on satisfactory academic performance
Frequency: Annual
Country of Study: United States of America or Canada
No. of awards offered: 6–8
Application Procedure: Applicants must submit an application, reference letters, personal statement and transcripts. Application forms and information are available on the website. Applications are available online on: www.jccworks.com
Closing Date: February 1st
Funding: Private
No. of awards given last year: 7
No. of applicants last year: 50
Additional Information: Candidates must make the commitment of working at a Jewish Community Center for a minimum of 2 years following the completion of graduate work.

JEWISH FOUNDATION FOR EDUCATION OF WOMEN

135 East 64th Street, New York, NY, 10021, United States of America
Tel: (1) 212 288 3931
Fax: (1) 212 288 5798
Email: fdnscholar@aol.com
Website: www.jfew.org
Contact: Ms Marge Goldwater, Executive Director

The Jewish Foundation for Education of Women is a private, nonsectarian organization. It provides scholarship assistance for higher education to women with financial need within a 50-mile radius of New York City through several specific programmes.

Fellowship Programme for Émigrés Pursuing Careers in Jewish Education

Subjects: Religious education and Jewish studies.
Purpose: To provide fellowships for graduate work to women who are interested in pursuing careers in Jewish education.
Eligibility: Applicants must be women and must be residents of New York city or live within a 50-mile radius thereof. Students entering or enrolled in full-time rabbinical and cantorial programmes, or Master's and doctoral programmes in Jewish education or Jewish studies, are eligible.
Level of Study: Graduate, doctorate, professional development
Type: Fellowship
Value: US$10,000–20,000 per year
Length of Study: 2 years for the Master's degree and 4 years for the rabbinical, cantorial programmes and PhD

Frequency: Annual
Country of Study: United States of America
No. of awards offered: 5–10
Application Procedure: Applicants must request an application in writing or by email. In the application request, the candidate must indicate their current educational status and the programme for which financial aid is required.
Closing Date: March 15th
Funding: Private
Additional Information: The Foundation also provides recipients with the opportunity to meet the programme supervisor for enriched learning on a monthly basis and to productively share experiences as a means of learning how to teach more effectively.

Scholarships for Émigrés in the Health Professions

Subjects: Medicine, dentistry, dental hygiene nursing, pharmacy, occupational and physical therapy and physician assistant programmes.
Eligibility: Applicants must be female émigrés from the former Soviet Union who live within a 50-mile radius of New York City and demonstrate financial need.
Level of Study: Graduate
Type: Scholarship
Value: US$5,000 per year
Frequency: Annual
Study Establishment: Schools within a 50-mile radius of New York City
Country of Study: United States of America
No. of awards offered: Approx. 80
Application Procedure: Applicants must request an application in writing from the financial aid office. Application forms are available in late October.
Closing Date: May 15th
Funding: Private

JILA (FORMERLY JOINT INSTITUTE FOR LABORATORY ASTROPHYSICS)

440, University of Colorado, Boulder, CO, 80309-0440, United States of America
Tel: (1) 303 492 7789
Fax: (1) 303 492 5235
Email: jilavf@jila.colorado.edu
Website: www.colorado.edu
Contact: Programme Assistant

JILA's interests are at present research and applications in the fields of laser technology, opto-electronics, precision measurement, surface science and semiconductors, information and image processing, and materials and process science, as well as basic research in atomic, molecular and optical physics, precision measurement, gravitational physics, chemical physics, astrophysics and geophysical measurements. To provide an opportunity for persons actively contributing to these fields, JILA operates the Visiting Fellowship Programme as well as the Postdoctoral Research Associate Programme.

JILA Postdoctoral Research Associateship and Visiting Fellowships

Subjects: Natural sciences.
Purpose: To support additional training beyond the PhD and sabbatical research.
Eligibility: There are no restrictions other than those that might be required by the grant that supports the research.
Level of Study: Postdoctorate, professional development
Type: Fellowship
Value: Varies
Length of Study: Visiting fellowships are for 4–12 months and Postdoctoral Research Associateships are for 1 year or more
Frequency: Annual
Country of Study: United States of America
No. of awards offered: Varies
Funding: Government
Contributor: Varies

JOHN CARTER BROWN LIBRARY AT BROWN UNIVERSITY

Box 1894, Providence, RI, 02912, United States of America
Tel: (1) 401 863 2725
Fax: (1) 401 863 3477
Email: jcbl_fellowships@brown.edu
Website: www.jcbl.org
Contact: Ms Nan Sumner-Mack, Programme Administration

The John Carter Brown Library, an independently funded and administered institution for advanced research in history and the humanities, is located on the campus of Brown University. The Library supports research focused on the colonial history of the Americas, including all aspects of the European, African and Native American involvement.

Alexander O Vietor Memorial Fellowship

Subjects: European and American maritime history 1450–1800.
Purpose: To assist students conducting research into early maritime history.
Eligibility: Open to scholars engaged in predoctoral, postdoctoral or independent research. Graduate students must have passed their preliminary or general examinations at the time of application.
Level of Study: Predoctorate, doctorate, postdoctorate
Type: Fellowship
Value: US$1,600 per month
Length of Study: 2–4 months
Frequency: Annual
Country of Study: United States of America
No. of awards offered: 1
Application Procedure: Applicants must complete an application form. Candidates should write to, or email the Director.
Closing Date: January 15th
Funding: Private
No. of awards given last year: 1

Andrew W Mellon Postdoctoral Research Fellowship at Brown University

Purpose: To assist scholars in any area of research related to the Library's holdings.
Level of Study: Postdoctorate, research
Value: US$4,000 per month
Length of Study: 5–10 months
Frequency: Annual
Study Establishment: The John Carter Brown Library
Country of Study: United States of America
No. of awards offered: Approx. 4
Application Procedure: Applicants must complete an application form. Candidates should write to or email the Director.
Closing Date: January 15th
Funding: Government, private
Contributor: The Andrew W Mellon Foundation and the National Endowment for the Humanities

Barbara S Mosbacher Fellowship

Subjects: All aspects of the discovery, exploration, settlement and development of the New World and the related history of Europe and Africa prior to 1825.
Purpose: To assist scholars in any area of research related to the Library's holdings.
Eligibility: Open to scholars engaged in predoctoral, postdoctoral or independent research. Graduate students must have passed their preliminary or general examinations at the time of application.
Level of Study: Postdoctorate, predoctorate, research
Type: Fellowship
Value: US$1,600 per month
Length of Study: 2–4 months
Frequency: Annual
Country of Study: United States of America
No. of awards offered: Varies
Application Procedure: Applicants must complete an application form. Candidates should write to or email the Director.

Closing Date: January 15th
Funding: Private
No. of awards given last year: 1

Center for New World Comparative Studies Fellowship
Subjects: The early history of the Americas from the late 15th century to 1830 and all aspects of the discovery, exploration, settlements and development of the New World.
Purpose: To enable research with a definite comparative dimension relating to the history of the Americas prior to 1825.
Eligibility: Open to scholars engaged in predoctoral, postdoctoral or independent research. Graduate students must have passed their preliminary or general examinations at the time of application.
Level of Study: Predoctorate, postdoctorate, doctorate
Type: Fellowship
Value: US$1,600 per month
Length of Study: 2–4 months
Frequency: Annual
Country of Study: United States of America
No. of awards offered: 2
Application Procedure: Applicants must complete an application form. Candidates should write to or email the Director.
Closing Date: January 15th
Funding: Private
No. of awards given last year: 1

Charles H Watts Memorial Fellowship
Subjects: All aspects of the discovery, exploration, settlement and development of the New World and the related history of Europe and Africa prior to 1825.
Purpose: To assist scholars in any area of research related to the Library's holdings.
Eligibility: Open to scholars engaged in predoctoral, postdoctoral or independent research. Graduate students must have passed their preliminary or general examinations at the time of application.
Level of Study: Predoctorate, postdoctorate, research
Type: Fellowship
Value: US$1,600 per month
Length of Study: 2–4 months
Frequency: Annual
Country of Study: United States of America
No. of awards offered: Varies
Application Procedure: Applicants must complete an application form. Candidates should write to or email the Director.
Closing Date: January 15th
Funding: Private
No. of awards given last year: 1

Helen Watson Buckner Memorial Fellowship
Subjects: All aspects of the discovery, exploration, settlement and development of the New World and the related history of Europe and Africa prior to 1825.
Purpose: To assist scholars in any area of research related to the Library's holdings.
Eligibility: Open to scholars engaged in predoctoral, postdoctoral or independent research. Graduate students must have passed their preliminary or general examinations at the time of application.
Level of Study: Postdoctorate, predoctorate, research
Type: Fellowship
Value: US$1,600 per month
Length of Study: 2–4 months
Country of Study: United States of America
No. of awards offered: Varies
Application Procedure: Applicants must complete an application form. Candidates should write to or email the Director.
Closing Date: January 15th
Funding: Private
No. of awards given last year: 1

JCB William Reese Company Fellowship
Subjects: The discovery, exploration, settlement and development of the New World and the related history of Europe and Africa prior to 1825.
Purpose: To enable the study of American bibliography and the history of the book in the Americas.
Eligibility: Open to scholars engaged in predoctoral, postdoctoral or independent research. Graduate students must have passed their preliminary or general examinations at the time of application.
Level of Study: Research, postdoctorate, predoctorate
Type: Fellowship
Value: US$1,600 per month
Length of Study: 2–4 months
Frequency: Annual
No. of awards offered: 1
Application Procedure: Applicants must contact the organization for details.
Closing Date: January 15th
Funding: Commercial
No. of awards given last year: 25
No. of applicants last year: 46

Jeannette D Black Memorial Fellowship
Subjects: The early history of the Americas from the late 15th century to 1830 and all aspects of the discovery, exploration, settlements and development of the New World.
Purpose: To enable research into the history of cartography or a closely related area.
Eligibility: Open to scholars engaged in predoctoral, postdoctoral or independent research. Graduate students must have passed their preliminary or general examinations at the time of application.
Level of Study: Doctorate, postdoctorate, predoctorate
Type: Fellowship
Value: US$1,600 per month
Length of Study: 2–4 months
Frequency: Annual
Country of Study: United States of America
No. of awards offered: 1
Application Procedure: Applicants must write to, or email the Director.
Closing Date: January 15th
Funding: Private
No. of awards given last year: 1

Library Associates Fellowship
Subjects: All aspects of the discovery, exploration, settlement and development of the New World and the related history of Europe and Africa prior to 1825.
Purpose: To assist scholars in any area of research related to the Library's holdings.
Eligibility: Open to scholars engaged in predoctoral, postdoctoral or independent research. Graduate students must have passed their preliminary or general examinations at the time of application.
Level of Study: Postdoctorate, research, predoctorate
Type: Fellowship
Value: US$1,600 per month
Length of Study: 2–4 months
Frequency: Annual
Country of Study: United States of America
No. of awards offered: 1
Application Procedure: Applicants must complete an application form. Candidates should write to, or email the Director.
Closing Date: January 15th
Funding: Private
Contributor: Associates of the John Carter Brown Library

Maria Elena Cassiet Fellowships
Subjects: The history of the colonial period of the Americas.
Purpose: To sponsor historical research relating to Spanish America.
Eligibility: Open to scholars who are permanent residents of countries in Spanish America only and who are engaged in predoctoral, postdoctoral or independent research. Graduate students must have passed their preliminary or general examinations at the time of application.
Level of Study: Predoctorate, research, postdoctorate
Type: Fellowship
Value: US$1,600 per month

Length of Study: 2–4 months
Frequency: Annual
Study Establishment: The John Carter Brown Library
Country of Study: United States of America
No. of awards offered: 1–2
Application Procedure: Applicants must complete an application form. Candidates should write to, or email the Director.
Closing Date: January 15th
Funding: Private
No. of awards given last year: 1

NEH Research Fellowship

Subjects: All aspects of the discovery, exploration, settlement and development of the New World, including the related history of Europe and Africa prior to 1825.
Purpose: To assist scholars in any area of research related to the Library's holdings.
Eligibility: Open to citizens of the United States of America or those who have been resident in the United States of America for 3 years immediately preceding the term of the fellowship. Those living within commuting distance, classed as within approx. 50 miles of the Library, are ordinarily not eligible for JCB fellowships.
Level of Study: Postdoctorate, research
Type: Fellowship
Value: US$4,000 per month
Length of Study: 5–10 months
Frequency: Annual
Study Establishment: The John Carter Brown Library
Country of Study: United States of America
No. of awards offered: Approx. 4
Application Procedure: Applicants must complete an application form. Candidates should write to, or email the Director.
Closing Date: January 15th
Funding: Private, government
Contributor: The Andrew W Mellon Foundation and the National Endowment for the Humanities
No. of awards given last year: 4
No. of applicants last year: 14
Additional Information: Recipients are expected to relocate to Providence and be in continuous residence at the John Carter Brown Library for the entire term of the award.

Paul W McQuillen Memorial Fellowship

Subjects: All aspects of the discovery, exploration, settlement and development of the New World and the related history of Europe and Africa prior to 1825.
Purpose: To assist scholars in any area of research related to the Library's holdings.
Eligibility: Open to scholars engaged in predoctoral, postdoctoral or independent research. Graduate students must have passed their preliminary or general examinations at the time of application.
Level of Study: Postdoctorate, research, predoctorate
Type: Fellowship
Value: US$1,600 per month
Length of Study: 2–4 months
Frequency: Annual
Country of Study: United States of America
No. of awards offered: Varies
Application Procedure: Applicants must complete an application form. Candidates should write to, or email the Director.
Closing Date: January 15th
Funding: Private
No. of awards given last year: 1

Ruth and Lincoln Ekstrom Fellowship

Subjects: The history of women and the family in the Americas prior to 1825, including the question of cultural influences on gender formation.
Purpose: To sponsor historical research.
Eligibility: Open to scholars engaged in predoctoral, postdoctoral or independent research. Graduate students must have passed their preliminary or general examinations at the time of application.
Level of Study: Postdoctorate, research, predoctorate
Type: Fellowship
Value: US$1,600 per month
Length of Study: 2–4 months
Frequency: Annual
Country of Study: United States of America
No. of awards offered: 1–2
Application Procedure: Applicants must complete an application form. Candidates should write to, or email the Director.
Closing Date: January 15th
Funding: Private
No. of awards given last year: 1

Touro National Heritage Trust Fellowship

Subjects: Some aspect of the Jewish experience in the Western hemisphere prior to 1830.
Purpose: To sponsor historical research.
Eligibility: Open to graduates of any nationality engaged in predoctoral, postdoctoral or independent research. Applicants must have passed their preliminary or general examinations at the time of application.
Level of Study: Doctorate, predoctorate, postdoctorate
Type: Fellowship
Value: US$1,600 per month
Length of Study: 2–4 months
Frequency: Annual
Country of Study: United States of America
No. of awards offered: 1
Application Procedure: Applicants must complete and submit an application form. Candidates should write to or email the Director.
Closing Date: January 15th
Funding: Private
No. of awards given last year: 1
Additional Information: The Touro Fellow will be selected by an academic committee consisting of representatives from Brown University, the American Jewish Historical Society, Brandeis University, the Newport Historical Society and the John Carter Brown Library, as well as a representative of the Executive Committee of the Touro National Heritage Trust. The Touro Fellow must be prepared to participate in symposia or other academic activities organized by these institutions and may be called upon to deliver one or two public lectures.

JOHN DOUGLAS FRENCH ALZHEIMER'S FOUNDATION (JDFAF)

11620 Wilshire Boulevard, Suite 270, Los Angeles, CA, 90025, United States of America
Tel: (1) 310 445 4654
Fax: (1) 310 479 0516
Website: www.jdfaf.org
Contact: Gwen Waggoner, Director, Research Administration

The mission of The John Douglas French Alzheimer's Foundation is to provide seed money for promising research and scientists who might not otherwise be funded. It is our objective to support cutting-edge research, individual or collaborative, that can expedite the day when we might delay the onset and advancement of, and find a cure for Alzheimer's.

French Foundation Fellowships

Subjects: Alzheimer's disease.
Purpose: To aid the development of young scientists with demonstrated promise for a research career in Alzheimer's disease.
Eligibility: Candidates who are more than 6 research years beyond a PhD or residency are not ordinarily eligible. Not more than 6 research years out from PhD.
Level of Study: Postdoctorate
Type: Fellowship
Value: US$35,000 per year
Length of Study: A maximum of 2 years
Frequency: Annual
Country of Study: Any country
No. of awards offered: 1

Application Procedure: Applicants must complete an application form, available from the website and submit it in PDF format, as an E-mail attachment.
Closing Date: November 1st
Funding: Individuals, foundation, corporation

JOHN E FOGARTY INTERNATIONAL CENTER (FIC) FOR ADVANCED STUDY IN THE HEALTH SCIENCES

Division of International Training & Research Building 31, Room B2C39, Fogarty International Center, 31 Center Drive, MSC 2220, Bethesda, MD, 20892, United States of America
Tel: (1) 301 496 2075
Fax: (1) 301 594 1211
Email: ficinfo@nih.gov
Website: www.nih.gov/fic/programs.html
Contact: Program Officer

The John E Fogarty International Center (FIC) for Advanced Study in the Health Sciences, a component of the National Institutes of Health (NIH), promotes international co-operation in the biomedical and behavioural sciences. This is accomplished primarily through long- and short-term fellowships, small grants and training grants. This compendium of international opportunities is prepared by the FIC with the hope that it will stimulate scientists to seek research enhancing experiences abroad.

AIDS International Training and Research Programme (AITRP)

Subjects: Biomedical and behavioural research related to AIDS.
Purpose: To enable scientists from developing countries to increase their proficiency to undertake biomedical and behavioural research related to AIDS and HIV, related TB infections and to develop these acquired skills in clinical trials, prevention and related research.
Eligibility: Decisions about whom to accept for training are made by the programme directors. All current programme directors have developed collaborative activities with specific countries. The relevant United States programme director should be contacted for country specific information, necessary qualifications, eligibility and application procedures. Scientists from the participating countries are eligible to apply for these training programmes.
Level of Study: Research
Type: Research grant
Frequency: Annual
No. of awards offered: Varies
Application Procedure: Applications are accepted from United States institutions in response to a specific request for applications. Individuals who wish to become trainees must apply to the project director of an awarded grant. Application forms are available from the website.
Funding: Government

Fogarty International Research Collaboration Award (FIRCA)

Subjects: Biomedical and behavioural sciences.
Purpose: To foster international research partnerships between NIH supported United States scientists and their collaborators in regions of the developing world.
Eligibility: Open to principal investigators of a United States based NIH sponsored research project grant that will be active for at least one year beyond the submission date of the FIRCA application. It is also open to scientists affiliated with public and private research institutions in Africa, Asia, (except Japan, Singapore, South Korea and Taiwan), Central and Eastern Europe, Russia and the Newly Independent States of the Former Soviet Union, Latin America and the non United States Caribbean, the Middle East and the Pacific Islands except Australia and New Zealand. The United States scientist will apply as principal investigator with a colleague from a single laboratory or research site in an eligible country.
Level of Study: Unrestricted
Value: Up to US$32,000 in direct costs per year are available for up to three years. Additional funds are available for the purchase of supplies and equipment necessary to the collaborative research project, for the foreign collaborator's laboratory only, funds for travel for the United States principal investigator, the foreign collaborator and/or their research associates. In addition up to US$2,000 is allowed for conference travel for the foreign collaborator. No salaries are offered under these awards, but a stipend of up to US$5,000 may be allocated for the foreign collaborator, if justified
Length of Study: 1–3 years
Frequency: Annual
Study Establishment: The foreign collaborator's research site
Country of Study: Other
No. of awards offered: Approx. 35 depending on funds available
Application Procedure: Applicants must submit applications on the grant application form PHS 398. Special instructions and conditions apply. Please refer to the website for further information.
Closing Date: March 25th, July 25th or November 25th
Funding: Government

Global Health Research Initiative Program for New Foreign Investigators (GRIP)

Subjects: Medicine.
Purpose: To assist well-trained young investigators to contribute to health care advances in their home countries.
Eligibility: Open to all well-trained young investigators.
Level of Study: Postgraduate
Type: Grant
Value: US$50,000 per year
Length of Study: 5 years
Frequency: Annual
Application Procedure: Application form on request.
Funding: Foundation
Contributor: Fugarty International Center

For further information contact:

Email: butrumb@mail.nih.gov
Contact: Bruce Butrum, Grants Management Officer

Health, Environment, and Economic Development (HEED) Awards

Subjects: Environmental studies.
Purpose: To study the relationship between health, environment and economic development.
Level of Study: Postgraduate
Type: Grant
Value: US$100,000 for five-year research.
Length of Study: 5 years
Frequency: Annual
Closing Date: November 31th
Funding: Foundation
Contributor: Fogarty International Center

For further information contact:

Email: nugentra@mail.nih.gov
Contact: Rachel Nugent, Program Director

HIV-AIDS and Related Illnesses Collaboration Award (AIDS-FIRCA)

Subjects: HIV and AIDS research.
Purpose: To support co-operative research between NIH grant recipients and foreign institutions throughout the world.
Eligibility: Open to principal investigators of a United States based NIH sponsored research project grant that will be active during the proposed grant award period. The award is also open to scientists affiliated with public and private research institutions in other countries, who serve as co-investigators.
Type: Grant
Value: Up to US$32,000 in direct costs per year, for a maximum of three years to support direct costs. Funds are also available for supplies and equipment necessary to support the collaborative studies at the foreign and United States sites and for travel for the principal

investigator, the foreign collaborator and/or their research associates. In addition, up to US$2,000 is allowed for conference travel for a foreign collaborator from a developing country. No salaries are offered under these awards, but a stipend of up to US$50,000 may be allocated for a foreign collaborator from a developing country, if required
Length of Study: Up to 3 years
Application Procedure: Applicants must refer to the website for further information and application details.
Closing Date: September 1st, January 2nd or May 1st

John E Fogarty International Research Scientist Development Award

Subjects: Medical research.
Purpose: To forge working relationships between future heads of health research programmes in the United States of America and established researchers in developing countries that will lead to ongoing collaborations in the study of health problems of mutual interest.
Eligibility: Applicants must be American citizens or permanent residents, have a doctoral or medical degree, or the equivalent, in a health science field earned within the last seven years. Applicants must have a demonstrated commitment and competence in health research, and have an invitation from a sponsor affiliated with an internationally recognized research facility in Africa, Asia (except Japan, Singapore, South Korea and Taiwan), Central and Eastern Europe, Russia and the Newly Independent States of the Former Soviet Union, Latin America and the non United States Caribbean, the Middle East and the Pacific Islands except Australia and New Zealand. Applications to work in institutions in Sub-Saharan Africa are especially encouraged. Applicants must have a United States sponsor or mentor at a research institution with ongoing collaborative research funding in one of the eligible countries listed above.
Value: Up to US$50,000 based on the level of experience, an allowance of up to US$20,000 for materials and an administrative supplement of up to US$20,000 during the third year if the candidate is promoted to junior faculty status upon return. An economy class round trip airfare is also provided
Application Procedure: Applicants must refer to the website for further information and application forms.
Closing Date: February 13th

JOHN F AND ANNA LEE STACEY SCHOLARSHIP FUND

National Cowboy Hall of Fame, 1700 North East 63rd Street, Oklahoma City, OK, 73111, United States of America
Tel: (1) 405 478 2250
Email: emuno@nationalcowboymuseum.org
Contact: Mr Ed Muno

In accordance with the will of the late Anna Lee Stacey, a trust fund has been created for the education of young men and women who aim to make art their profession.

John F and Anna Lee Stacey Scholarships

Subjects: Painting and drawing in the classical tradition of western culture.
Purpose: To foster a high standard in the study of form, colour, drawing, painting, design and technique, as these are expressed in modes showing patent affinity with the classical tradition of western culture.
Eligibility: Open to citizens of the United States of America of 18–35 years of age who are skilled in printing and drawing and devoted to the classical or conservative tradition of western culture.
Level of Study: Graduate, postgraduate, high-school graduate
Type: Scholarship
Value: A total of approx. US$5,000
Length of Study: 1 year
Frequency: Annual
Country of Study: Any country
No. of awards offered: 1–5
Application Procedure: Applicants must complete and submit an application form with up to 10–35 mm slides of their work. Slides and completed application forms should be sent by United States of America mail, not rail or air express. Applicants should also enclose a recent photograph, a letter outlining plans and objectives and at least four letters of reference.
Closing Date: February 1st
Funding: Private
Contributor: A bequest from the John F and Anna Lee Stacey Foundation
No. of awards given last year: 5
No. of applicants last year: 100
Additional Information: The Committee does not maintain storage facilities, so applicants must not send slides or any materials before October 1st. Each successful competitor will be required to submit a brief quarterly report together with 35 mm slides of their work and a more complete report at the termination of the scholarship.

JOHN SIMON GUGGENHEIM MEMORIAL FOUNDATION

90 Park Avenue, New York, NY, 10016, United States of America
Tel: (1) 212 687 4470
Fax: (1) 212 697 3248
Email: fellowships@gf.org
Website: www.gf.org

The John Simon Guggenheim Memorial Foundation is concerned with encouraging and supporting scholars and artists to engage in research in any field of knowledge and creation within the arts. The Foundation was established by United States Senator Simon Guggenheim and his wife as a memorial to their son who died on April 26th, 1922.

Guggenheim Fellowships to Assist Research and Artistic Creation (Latin America and the Caribbean)

Subjects: Sciences, humanities, social sciences and creative arts.
Purpose: To further the development of scholars and artists by assisting them to engage in research in any field of knowledge and creation in any of the arts, under the freest possible conditions irrespective of race, colour or creed.
Eligibility: Open to citizens and permanent residents of countries of Latin America and the Caribbean who have demonstrated an exceptional capacity for productive scholarship or exceptional creative ability in the arts.
Level of Study: Professional development, postdoctorate
Type: Fellowship
Value: Grants will be adjusted to the needs of Fellows, taking into consideration their other resources and the purpose and scope of their plans. The average grant is US$33,000
Length of Study: Ordinarily for 1 year, but in no instance for a period shorter than 6 consecutive months
Frequency: Annual
Country of Study: Any country
No. of awards offered: 36
Application Procedure: Applicants must complete an application form. Further information is available on the Foundation's website.
Closing Date: December 1st
Funding: Private
Contributor: The Foundation
No. of awards given last year: 36
Additional Information: Members of the teaching profession receiving sabbatical leave on full or part salary are eligible for appointment, as are holders of other fellowships and of appointments at research centres. Fellowships are awarded by the Trustees upon nominations made by a committee of selection.

Guggenheim Fellowships to Assist Research and Artistic Creation (USA and Canada)

Subjects: Sciences, humanities, social sciences and creative arts.
Purpose: To further the development of scholars and artists by assisting them to engage in research in any field of knowledge and creation in any of the arts, under the freest possible conditions irrespective of race, colour or creed.

Eligibility: Open to citizens and permanent residents of the United States of America and Canada who have demonstrated an exceptional capacity for productive scholarship or exceptional creative ability in the arts.
Level of Study: Postdoctorate, professional development
Type: Fellowship
Value: Grants will be adjusted to the needs of Fellows, taking into consideration their other resources and the purpose and scope of their plans. The average grant is US$37,360
Length of Study: Ordinarily for 1 year, but in no instance for a period shorter than 6 consecutive months
Frequency: Annual
Country of Study: Any country
Application Procedure: Applicants must complete an application form. Further information is available on the Foundation's website.
Closing Date: October 1st
Funding: Private
Contributor: The Foundation
No. of awards given last year: 185
Additional Information: Members of the teaching profession receiving sabbatical leave on full or part salary are eligible for appointment, as are holders of other fellowships and of appointments at research centres. Fellowships are awarded by the Trustees upon nominations made by a committee of selection.

JOHNS HOPKINS UNIVERSITY

Bloomberg School of Public Health, Center for Alternatives to Animal Testing, 111 Market Place, Suite 840, Baltimore, MD, 21202, United States of America
Tel: (1) 410 223 1692
Fax: (1) 410 223 1603
Email: caat@jhsph.edu
Website: www.caat.jhsph.edu
Contact: Grants Co-ordinator

The vision of the Johns Hopkins Center for Alternatives to Animal Testing is to be a leading force in the development and use of reduction, refinement and replacement alternatives in research, testing and education to protect and enhance the health of the public.

CAAT Research Grants

Subjects: Alternatives to current testing methods to replace, reduce and refine the use of animals.
Purpose: To serve as starter grants.
Eligibility: No eligibility restrictions.
Level of Study: Unrestricted
Value: A maximum of US$20,000
Length of Study: 1 year
Frequency: Annual
Country of Study: United States of America
No. of awards offered: Approx. 12
Application Procedure: Applicants must complete a preproposal. After review, selected applicants are invited to submit a full application.
Closing Date: The preproposal deadline is March 15th
Funding: Private
No. of awards given last year: 12
No. of applicants last year: 30

THE JOSEPH ROWNTREE FOUNDATION

The Homestead, 40 Water End, York, YO30 6WP, England
Tel: (44) 19 0462 9241
Fax: (44) 19 0462 0072
Email: info@irf.org.uk
Website: www.jrf.org.uk
Contact: Dr Anne Harrop, Director of Research

The Joseph Rowntree Foundation is one of the largest social policy research and development charities in the United Kingdom. Working in partnership with academic and other bodies, the Foundation places great emphasis on disseminating its findings and engaging with policy makers and practitioners.

JRF Project Funding: Housing Benefit Payment Method

Subjects: Housing, sociology.
Purpose: To fund project proposals that search for better ways of tackling poor living conditions and social disadvantage through projects that investigate the understanding of and attitudes towards housing benefit and payment methods among tenants, and how attitudes and payment methods affect behaviour.
Level of Study: Research
Type: Project funding
Value: Up to UK £70,000
Frequency: Annual
No. of awards offered: 1–2
Application Procedure: Applicants must submit three unbound hard copies of all required documents, and email a Word version of the complete proposal and summary to Louise Ross. Forms can be downloaded from website.
Closing Date: January 10th
Funding: Foundation, corporation, individuals
Additional Information: Proposals are encouraged that fully involve people who have had direct experience of claiming housing benefit, where this is likely to improve the quality and potential impact of the research.

JRF Project Funding: Poverty and Disadvantage

Subjects: Sociology, poverty.
Purpose: To fund project proposals addressing areas within the broad remit of the poverty and disadvantage committee that do not readily fit within the existing programmes or themes of the oraganization, and that are relevant to policy and practice concerns in the field of poverty.
Level of Study: Research
Type: Project funding
Value: Varies
Frequency: Annual
Application Procedure: Applicants must submit three unbound hard copies of all required documents, and email a Word version of the complete proposal and summary to Louise Ross. Forms can be downloaded from website.
Closing Date: January 10th
Funding: Individuals, foundation, corporation
Additional Information: The Foundation wishes to avoid areas already covered by projects in existing programmes, work closely related to research being done by the Foundation's other committees and extensive overlaps with projects funded through other organizations.

JUNE BAKER TRUST

5 Forest Road, Kintore, Aberdeenshire, AB51 0US, Scotland
Tel: (44) 14 6763 2337
Email: ramseyph@lineone.net
Contact: Mrs Priscilla Ramsey, Chairman

June Baker collected, refurbished and arranged a collection of artefacts in her domestic environment. Her friends established the Trust in 1990, in memory of her life and death, to help individuals in the conservation of historic and artistic artefacts in Scotland or those training with the intention to do so.

June Baker Trust Awards

Subjects: Conservation of historic and artistic artefacts.
Purpose: To assist with travel, training and equipment. To encourage persons working in conservation in Scotland by giving small grants for specific short courses, equipment or travel.
Eligibility: Open to individuals from Scotland working or training in conservation in Scotland.
Type: Grant
Value: Up to UK £300 towards travel, training and purchase of equipment
Length of Study: Not available for full-time study fees
Frequency: Annual

Country of Study: Scotland
No. of awards offered: 1–4
Application Procedure: Applicants must complete an application form, available from the Chairman.
Closing Date: May 31st
Funding: Private
Contributor: Trust investments
No. of awards given last year: 3
No. of applicants last year: 8
Additional Information: Applicants must work, or intend to work in Scotland.

JUVENILE DIABETES FOUNDATION INTERNATIONAL/THE DIABETES RESEARCH FOUNDATION

120 Wall Street, 19th Floor, New York, NY, 10005-4001, United States of America
Tel: (1) 212 875 2562
Fax: (1) 212 785 9595
Email: info@jdrf.org
Website: www.jdrf.org
Contact: Grant Adminstrator

JDRF Career Development Award

Subjects: Diabetes: the prevention of diabetes and its recurrence, restoration of normal metabolism and the avoidance of and reversal of complications.
Purpose: To provide salary and research support for exceptional scientists in research related to diabetes who are beginning their careers as junior staff members.
Eligibility: Open to highly qualified researchers of all nationalities, holding a PhD, MD, DMD, DVM or equivalent at a college, university, medical school or other research facility who have directed their expertise to target JDRF research priority areas. Both new and established researchers are supported. Proposals must be for a scientific research project involving the cause, treatment, prevention and/or cure of diabetes and its complications.
Level of Study: Professional development
Type: Award
Value: US$125,000 per year including indirect costs
Length of Study: 5 years
Closing Date: Varies. For details see the JDRF website

JDRF Conference Grant

Subjects: Diabetes: the prevention of diabetes and its recurrence, restoration of normal metabolism and the avoidance of and reversal of complications.
Purpose: To support scientific meetings, conferences and workshops relevant to the JDRF's mission.
Eligibility: Open to highly qualified researchers of all nationalities, holding a PhD, MD, DMD, DVM or equivalent at a college, university, medical school or other research facility, who have directed their expertise to target JDRF research priority areas. Both new and established researchers are supported. Proposals must be for a scientific research project involving the cause, treatment, prevention and/or cure of diabetes and its complications.
Level of Study: Professional development
Type: Grant
Value: Up to US$10,000 or above
Closing Date: Varies. For details see the JDRF website

JDRF Innovative Grant

Subjects: Diabetes: the prevention of diabetes and its recurrence, restoration of normal metabolism and the avoidance of and reversal of complications.
Purpose: To support highly innovative basic and clinical research that is at the developmental stage.
Eligibility: Open to highly qualified researchers of all nationalities, holding a PhD, MD, DMD, DVM or equivalent at a college, university, medical school or other research facility, who have directed their expertise to target JDRF research priority areas. Both new and established researchers are supported. Proposals must be for a scientific research project involving the cause, treatment, prevention and/or cure of diabetes and its complications.
Level of Study: Research
Type: Grant
Value: US$55,000 for 1 year including indirect costs
Length of Study: 1 year
Closing Date: Varies. For details see the JDRF website

JDRF Postdoctoral Fellowships

Subjects: Diabetes: the prevention of diabetes and its recurrence, restoration of normal metabolism and the avoidance of and reversal of complications.
Purpose: To attract qualified, promising scientists entering their professional careers in diabetes.
Eligibility: Open to highly qualified researchers of all nationalities, holding a PhD, MD, DMD, DVM or equivalent at a college, university, medical school or other research facility, who have directed their expertise to target JDRF research priority areas. Both new and established researchers are supported. Proposals must be for a scientific research project involving the cause, treatment, prevention and/or cure of diabetes and its complications.
Level of Study: Postdoctorate
Type: Fellowship
Value: US$41,000–52,000
Length of Study: 2 years
Closing Date: Varies. For details see the JDRF website

JDRF Regular Research Grant

Subjects: Diabetes: the prevention of diabetes and its recurrence, restoration of normal metabolism and the avoidance of and reversal of complications.
Purpose: To support and fund research to find a cure for diabetes.
Eligibility: Open to highly qualified researchers of all nationalities, holding a PhD, MD, DMD, DVM or equivalent at a college, university, medical school or other research facility, who have directed their expertise to target JDRF research priority areas. Both new and established researchers are supported. Proposals must be for a scientific research project involving the cause, treatment, prevention and/or cure of diabetes and its complications.
Level of Study: Research
Type: Grant
Value: US$165,000 per year for 3 years including indirect costs
Length of Study: 3 years
Closing Date: Varies. For details see the JDRF website

KAY KENDALL LEUKAEMIA FUND

Allington House, 1st Floor, 150 Victoria Street, London, SW1E 5AE, England
Tel: (44) 20 7410 7045
Fax: (44) 20 7410 0332
Email: liz.storer@sfct.org.uk
Contact: Ms Elizabeth Storer, Trust Secretary

Kay Kendall Leukaemia Fund Research Fellowship

Subjects: Aspects of leukaemia or relevant studies on related haematological malignancies.
Purpose: To encourage researchers new to the field of leukaemia research to submit applications on their own account.
Eligibility: Open to applicants of any nationality intending to work mainly in the United Kingdom. Applicants must hold a recognized higher degree, but need not be medically qualified.
Level of Study: Postdoctorate
Type: Fellowship
Value: Salary and laboratory expenses
Length of Study: 3 years
Frequency: Annual
Country of Study: United Kingdom
No. of awards offered: 2–3

Application Procedure: Applicants must submit a research proposal form and details of support from the intended United Kingdom institution.
Closing Date: January
Funding: Private
No. of awards given last year: 2

KAZAN STATE TECHNICAL UNIVERSITY (KSTU)

10 K Marx Street, Kazan, Tatarstan, 420111, Russia
Tel: (7) 843 238 5044
Fax: (7) 843 236 6032
Email: agishev@kai.ru
Website: www.kai.ru
Contact: Professor Ravil R Agishev, Head of International Co-operation

The Kazan State Technical University (KSTU) aims to support joint international research projects relating to scientific and technical issues and to develop a young generation of local scientists and technicians.

KSTU Rector's Grant

Subjects: Scientific research.
Purpose: To support joint research on scientific and technical issues and to invite eligible applicants to deliver lectures on new scientific branches of mutual interest.
Eligibility: Applicants must be proficient in Russian or English, a PhD or DSc degree and not be more than 45 years of age.
Level of Study: Professional development, postdoctorate
Value: US$1,500 plus the monthly loan of the KSTU Professor
Length of Study: 3–6 months
Frequency: Annual
Study Establishment: KSTU
Country of Study: Russia
No. of awards offered: 2
Application Procedure: Applicants must complete an application form. An abstract must also be submitted including four pages of curriculum vitae with research aims and recommendations from three professors.
Closing Date: August 31st
Funding: Government
No. of awards given last year: 2
No. of applicants last year: 11

KENNAN INSTITUTE FOR ADVANCED RUSSIAN STUDIES

Woodrow Wilson International Center for Scholars, One Woodrow Wilson Plaza, 1300 Pennsylvania Avenue North West, Washington, DC, 20004-3027, United States of America
Tel: (1) 202 691 4100
Fax: (1) 202 691 4247
Email: kiars@wwic.si.edu
Website: www.wilsoncenter.org
Contact: Ms Edita Krunkaitytee, Program Assistant

The Kennan Institute for Advanced Russian Studies sponsors advanced research on the successor states to the USSR and encourages Eurasian studies with its public lecture and publication programmes, maintaining contact with scholars and research centres abroad. The Institute seeks to function as a forum where the scholarly community can interact with public policymakers.

Kennan Institute Research Scholarship

Subjects: Social sciences and humanities. Research proposals examining topics in Eurasian studies are eligible, with those topics relating to regional Russia, the NIS and contemporary issues especially welcome.
Purpose: To offer support to junior scholars studying in the former Soviet Union, allowing them time and resources in the Washington, DC area to work on their first published work or to continue their research.
Eligibility: Open to academic participants in the early stages of their career before tenure, or scholars whose careers have been interrupted or delayed. For non-academics, an equivalent degree or professional achievement is expected. U.S. Citizens or permanent residents.
Level of Study: Postdoctorate
Type: Scholarship
Value: US$3,000 per month plus research facilities, word processing support and some research assistance
Length of Study: 3–9 months
Frequency: Dependent on funds available
Study Establishment: The Kennan Institute
Country of Study: United States of America
No. of awards offered: 4
Application Procedure: Applicants must complete an application form. The application must include a project proposal, publications list, bibliography, biographical data and three letters of recommendation specifically in support of the research to be conducted at the Institute. Applications received by fax or email will not be accepted.
Closing Date: December 1st
Funding: Government
No. of awards given last year: 4
No. of applicants last year: 22

Kennan Institute Short-Term Grants

Subjects: Eurasian studies in the social sciences and humanities. Social sciences and humanities focusing on the (excluding the Baltic States).
Purpose: To support scholars in need of the academic and archival resources of the Washington, DC area in order to complete their research.
Eligibility: Open to academic participants with a doctoral degree or those who have nearly completed their dissertations. For non-academic participants, an equivalent level of professional development is required. Applicants can be citizens of any country, but must note their citizenship while applying.
Level of Study: Doctorate, postdoctorate
Type: Scholarship
Value: US$100 per day
Length of Study: Up to 31 days
Frequency: Dependent on funds available
Study Establishment: The Kennan Institute
Country of Study: United States of America
No. of awards offered: 4 are available to non-United States of America citizens and 4 to citizens of the United States of America
Application Procedure: Applicants must submit a concise description of their research project of 700–800 words, a curriculum vitae, a statement on preferred dates of residence in Washington, DC and two letters of recommendation specifically in support of the research to be conducted at the institute. No application form is required for short-term grants.
Closing Date: March 1st, June 1st, September 1st and December 1st
Funding: Government, private
No. of awards given last year: 27
No. of applicants last year: 63

KENNEDY MEMORIAL TRUST

3 Birdcage Walk, Westminster, London, SW1H 9JJ, England
Tel: (44) 20 7222 1151
Fax: (44) 20 7222 7189
Website: www.kennedytrust.org.uk
Contact: Ms Anna Mason, Secretary

As part of the British national memorial to President Kennedy, the Kennedy Memorial Trust awards scholarships to British postgraduate students for study at Harvard University or the Massachusetts Institute of Technology. The awards are offered annually following a national competition and cover tuition costs and a stipend to meet living expenses.

Kennedy Scholarships

Subjects: All fields of arts, science, social science and political studies.
Purpose: To enable students to undertake a course of study in the United States of America.
Eligibility: Open to resident citizens of the United Kingdom who have been wholly or mainly educated in the United Kingdom. At the time of application, candidates must have spent at least 2 of the last 5 years at a university in the United Kingdom and must either have graduated by the start of tenure in the following year or have graduated not more than 3 years prior to the commencement of studies. Applications will not be considered from persons already in the United States of America.
Level of Study: Postgraduate
Type: Scholarship
Value: US$19,500 to cover support costs, special equipment and some travel in the United States of America, plus tuition fees and travelling expenses to and from the United States of America
Length of Study: 1 year. In certain circumstances, students who are applying for PhD or 2-year Master's programmes may be considered for extra funding to help support a second year of study
Frequency: Annual
Study Establishment: Harvard University and the Massachusetts Institute of Technology (MIT), Cambridge, MA
Country of Study: United States of America
No. of awards offered: 10–12
Application Procedure: Applicants must submit a form, statement of purpose, references and a letter of endorsement from the applicant's university. Completed applications should be sent via the applicant's university.
Closing Date: November 3rd
Funding: Private
Contributor: Public donation
No. of awards given last year: 10
No. of applicants last year: 160
Additional Information: Scholars are not required to study for a degree in the United States of America, but are encouraged to do so if they are eligible and able to complete the requirements for it.

THE KENTUCKY RESTAURANT ASSOCIATION

133 Evergreen Road, Suite 201, Louisville, KY 40243,
United States of America
Tel: (1) 896 0464
Fax: (1) 896 0465
Email: info@kyra.org
Website: www.kyra.org

The Kentucky Restaurant Association is an organization dedicated to promoting the restaurant and foodservice industry in the state of Kentucky.

Kentucky Restaurant Association Governor's Scholarship

Subjects: Foodservice industry.
Purpose: To encourage and promote education in the foodservice industry.
Eligibility: Open to applicants who are Kentucky residents attending a Kentucky institution.
Level of Study: Postgraduate
Type: Scholarship
Value: US$5,000
Frequency: Annual
Country of Study: United States of America
No. of awards offered: 1
Application Procedure: A completed application form must be submitted.
Closing Date: November 15th
Contributor: Kentucky Restaurant Association

For further information contact:

512 Executive Park, Louisville, KY 40207
Contact: Betsy Byrd, Director of Member Relations

KONRAD ADENAUER FOUNDATION

Rathausallee 12, D-53757, Sankt Augustin,
Germany
Tel: (49) 2241 246 0
Fax: (49) 2241 246 591
Email: zentrale@kas.de
Website: www.kas.de

Research Fellowships (Konrad Adenauer)

Subjects: All subjects, except specializations in medicine, dentistry and veterinary sciences.
Purpose: To award scholarships to young academics for doctoral research.
Eligibility: Open to academics no older than 30 years, with outstanding academic qualifications, an involvement in social policy issues, a good knowledge of German and a willingness to return to their home country upon completion of the research project. Candidates are preferred from countries where the Foundation is represented either through projects or a branch office.
Level of Study: Doctorate
Type: Research
Value: Up to €920 per month (additional payments like family allowance, travel grants and grants for books are possible)
Length of Study: 2–3 years
Study Establishment: Any German research institution
Country of Study: Germany
Application Procedure: Applications need not be submitted on a special form. However, candidates should submit application papers to the Foundation's branch offices in the home country, which in turn will recommend the applicants to the Foundation.
Closing Date: Contact the Foundation

THE KOREA FOUNDATION

Fellowship Programme, 10th Floor, Diplomatic Center Building,
1376-1 Seocho-2-dong, Seocho-gu,
Seoul 137-863, Korea
Tel: (82) 2 3463 5614
Fax: (82) 2 3463 6075/6076
Email: fellow@kf.or.kr
Website: www.kf.or.kr
Contact: Ms Bo Myung KIM, Programme Officer

The Korea Foundation seeks to improve awareness and understanding of Korea worldwide as well as to foster co-operative relationships between Korea and foreign countries through a variety of exchange programmes.

Korea Foundation Advanced Research Grant

Subjects: Korea-related research in the humanities and social sciences, culture and arts, and comparative research related to Korea.
Purpose: To support scholarly research and writing activities of Korean studies students during their sabbatical leave to advance scholarship in Korean studies.
Eligibility: Open to overseas Korean studies scholars with a PhD degree in a subject related to Korea, who are currently engaged in Korea-related teaching and research activities. In the case of Korean nationals, only those with foreign residency status and regular faculty positions at foreign universities are eligible to apply. Candidates who are receiving support from other programmes administered by the Korea Foundation are not eligible to receive this grant at the same time.
Level of Study: Professional development, postdoctorate, research
Type: Research grant
Value: The grant amount is designed to supplement the sabbatical compensation of Korean studies scholars at different stages in their careers
Length of Study: 6 months–1 year
Frequency: Annual
Application Procedure: Applicants must complete an application form. Application forms are available from the Foundation or the website.
Closing Date: January 31st

Korea Foundation Fellowship for Field Research

Subjects: Korea-related research in the humanities and social sciences, culture and arts, and comparative research related to Korea.
Purpose: To promote Korean studies and support professional researchers in Korean studies by facilitating their research activities in Korea.
Eligibility: Open to university professors and instructors, doctoral candidates, researchers and other professionals. Candidates must be proficient in Korean or English. In the case of Korean nationals, only those with foreign residency status and regular faculty positions at foreign universities are eligible to apply. Fellows in this programme must concentrate on their research and may not enrol in any language courses or other university courses during the fellowship period. Candidates who are receiving support from other organizations or programmes administered by the Korea Foundation are not eligible to receive this fellowship at the same time.
Level of Study: Postdoctorate, doctorate, professional development, research
Type: Fellowship
Value: The grant amount will be determined by the Foundation according to the Fellow's research experience and current position. Awards range between US$1,000–1,600 monthly. The Foundation will also provide an international economy class airline ticket for round-trip transportation between the airport nearest to the Fellow's residence and Korea. Travellers' insurance is also provided
Length of Study: 3 months–1 year
Frequency: Annual
Country of Study: Korea
No. of awards offered: Varies
Application Procedure: Applicants must complete an application form. Application forms are available from the Foundation and the website.
Closing Date: July 31st
No. of awards given last year: 45
No. of applicants last year: 75

Korea Foundation Fellowship for Graduate Studies

Subjects: Korea-related research in the humanities and social sciences, culture and arts, and comparative research related to Korea.
Purpose: To promote Korean studies and foster young scholars in this field by providing graduate students majoring in Korean studies with scholarships for their coursework and/or research while enrolled at their home institutions.
Eligibility: Open to MA or PhD level students majoring in Korean studies at any university in the United States of America, Canada, Europe, Australia, New Zealand, China and Japan. Korean nationals are eligible to apply only if they have permanent residency status overseas. Candidates who are receiving support from other programmes administered by the Korea Foundation are not eligible to receive this fellowship at the same time.
Level of Study: Doctorate, postgraduate, predoctorate, graduate
Type: Scholarship
Value: A intended to cover living expenses and/or tuition costs, of an amount to be determined based on the country, region, institution and academic level of applicants
Length of Study: 1 academic year
Frequency: Annual
Country of Study: United States of America, Canada, Europe, Australia, New Zealand, China, Japan
No. of awards offered: Up to 110
Application Procedure: Applicants must complete an application form available from the Foundation or from the website.
Closing Date: Varies according to the region. Please contact the Foundation for details
No. of awards given last year: 170
No. of applicants last year: 350

Korea Foundation Fellowship for Korean Language Training

Subjects: Korean studies related to the humanities, culture and arts, social sciences or comparative research.
Purpose: To provide foreign scholars and graduate students who need systematic Korean language education with the opportunity to enrol in a Korean language programme at a language institute affiliated to a Korean university.
Eligibility: Candidates must have a basic knowledge of, and an ability to communicate in, the Korean language. In the case of Korean nationals, only those with foreign residency status are eligible to apply. Candidates who are receiving support from other organizations or programmes administered by the Korea Foundation are not eligible to receive this fellowship at the same time.
Level of Study: Postgraduate, graduate
Type: Fellowship
Value: The grant amount will be determined by the Foundation according to the Fellow's academic experience and current position. Awards range between US$700–850. The tuition for language training will be paid by the Foundation directly to the Korean language institute that the Foundation designates. Travel insurance is also provided. Please note that the cost of an international round-trip airline ticket is not covered under this fellowship
Length of Study: 6 months, 9 months or 1 year
Frequency: Annual
Study Establishment: A language institute affiliated to a Korean university
Country of Study: Korea
No. of awards offered: Varies
Application Procedure: Applicants must complete an application form are available from the Korean Foundation. Applicants must request an application form by supplying their curriculum vitae along with details of their including Korean language ability and previous study of Korean.
Closing Date: May 31st
No. of awards given last year: 92
No. of applicants last year: 127

Korea Foundation Postdoctoral Fellowship

Subjects: Korea-related research in the humanities and social sciences, culture and arts, and comparative research related to Korea.
Purpose: To provide promising and highly qualified PhD recipients with the opportunity to conduct research at leading universities in the field of Korean studies so that they can further develop their scholarship as well as have their dissertations published as manuscripts.
Eligibility: Open to non-Korean scholars who have received a PhD degree in a subject related to Korea within 5 years of their application, but do not currently hold a regular faculty position. Korean nationals with permanent resident status in foreign countries may apply. Candidates who are receiving support from other programmes administered by the Korea Foundation are not eligible to receive this fellowship at the same time.
Level of Study: Postdoctorate
Type: Fellowship
Value: Stipend support for a 1-year period, of an amount to be determined based on the country, region and institution where the Fellow will conduct his or her research
Length of Study: 1 year
Frequency: Annual
Country of Study: Any country
No. of awards offered: 4
Application Procedure: Applicants must complete an application form, available from the website.
Closing Date: January 15th

KOSCIUSZKO FOUNDATION

15 East 65th Street, New York, NY, 10021-6595,
United States of America
Tel: (1) 212 734 2130
Fax: (1) 212 628 4552
Email: thekf@aol.com
Website: www.kosciuszkofoundation.org
Contact: Mr Thomas J Pniewski, Director, Cultural Affairs

The Kosciuszko Foundation, founded in 1925, is dedicated to promoting educational and cultural relations between the United States of America and Poland and increasing American awareness of Polish culture and history. In addition to its grants and scholarships, which total more than US$1 million annually, the Foundation presents cultural programmes including lectures, concerts and exhibitions, promotes Polish culture in the United States of America and nurtures the spirit of multicultural co-operation.

Chopin Piano Competition

Subjects: Piano performance of Chopin or other composers.
Purpose: To encourage highly talented students of piano to study and play works of Chopin and other Polish composers.
Eligibility: Open to students between the age of 16 and 22 who are citizens of the United States of America or full-time international students in the United States of America with a valid visa who wish to pursue a career in piano performance.
Level of Study: Unrestricted
Type: Prize
Value: First prize of US$2,500, a second prize of US$1,500 and a third prize of US$1,000. Scholarships may be awarded in the form of shared prizes
Frequency: Annual
Country of Study: United States of America
No. of awards offered: 3
Application Procedure: Applicants must complete an application form, available in December via the Kosciuszko Foundation's Cultural Department. Applications should be marked Chopin Piano Competition.
Closing Date: The first week of March
Additional Information: The required repertoire is as follows: Chopin: one Mazurka of the contestant's choice and two major works; Szymanowski: one Mazurka of the contestant's choice; a major work by Bach, excluding The Well-Tempered Clavier; a complete sonata by Beethoven, Hadyn, Mozart or Schubert; a major 19th-century work (including Debussy, Ravel, Prokofiev and Rachmaninoff but excluding those already mentioned); and a substantial work by an American, Polish or Polish-American composer written after 1950. The competition is held on 3 consecutive days in mid-April.

Dr Marie E Zakrzewski Medical Scholarship

Subjects: Medical studies.
Purpose: To fund a young woman of Polish ancestry for the 1st, 2nd, or 3rd year of medical studies at an accredited school of medicine in the United States of America.
Eligibility: The applicant must be a woman of Polish descent who is a citizen of the United States of America or a Polish citizen with permanent residency status in the United States of America, entering the 1st, 2nd or 3rd year of studies towards an MD degree with a minimum grade point average of 3.0.
Level of Study: Postgraduate
Type: Scholarship
Value: US$3,500
Frequency: Annual
Study Establishment: An accredited school of medicine in the United States of America
Country of Study: United States of America
No. of awards offered: 1
Application Procedure: Applicants must submit a tuition scholarship application form, a US$25 non-refundable application fee and supporting materials to the Kosciuszko Foundation. Emailed and faxed materials will not be considered.
Closing Date: December 30th
Funding: Private
Additional Information: First preference is given to residents of the state of Massachusetts or former presentees of the federation ball. Qualified residents of New England are considered if no first-preference candidates apply.

Jozef Tischner Fellowships

Subjects: All academic disciplines related to IWM's main research fields.
Purpose: To fund a Polish junior researcher in any academic discipline to work in Vienna on research projects of their choice related to one of the Institute for Human Sciences' (IWM) main research fields.
Eligibility: Open to Polish citizens, permanent residents of Poland and Polish-American scholars with a recent PhD degree, not older than 35 years.
Level of Study: Research, doctorate
Type: Fellowship
Value: Fellowship and €7,850 stipend to cover accommodation, living expenses, travel, health insurance and incidentals during the stay
Length of Study: 6 months
Frequency: Annual
Study Establishment: The Institute for Human Sciences (IWM)
Country of Study: Austria
No. of awards offered: 1
Application Procedure: Applicants must send the application by mail to address below.
Closing Date: December 1st

For further information contact:

Institute Fur Die Wissenschaften Vom Menschen, Fellowship Coordinator, Spittelauer Lande 3, A-1090, Vienna, Austria
Fax: (43) 313 58 30
Email: fellowships@iwm.at

Kosciuszko Foundation Graduate and Postgraduate Studies and Research in Poland Program

Subjects: All subjects.
Purpose: To enable American students to pursue a course of graduate or postgraduate study and research in Poland for an academic year or semester.
Eligibility: Open to United States of America graduates and postgraduate students who wish to pursue a course of study and research at Institutes of Higher Education in Poland. University faculty members who wish to spend a sabbatical pursuing research in Poland are also eligible. All entrants must have the requisite Polish language ability commensurate with the proposed research project and must be under the supervision of a Polish university academic advisor.
Level of Study: Postgraduate, graduate
Type: Grant
Value: Housing, plus a monthly stipend from the Polish Ministry in Polish currency for living expenses, and additional funding of US$250 per month from the Foundation for expenses. Transportation to and from Poland is not included
Length of Study: 1 academic year or semester
Frequency: Annual
Country of Study: Poland
No. of awards offered: Varies
Application Procedure: Applicants must complete an application form, available in the Autumn by mail or from the website.
Closing Date: January 14th
Contributor: The Foundation and the Polish Ministry of National Education

Kosciuszko Foundation Tuition Scholarships

Subjects: Polish-American related issues and activities.
Purpose: To provide financial aid to students in the United States of America and Poland.
Eligibility: Open to citizens of the United States of America of Polish descent who are pursuing or Polish citizens who are legal and permanent residents who are pursuing graduate studies in any field at a United States of America Institute of Higher Education, or citizens of the United States of America who are pursuing a major in Polish studies at the graduate level. All entrants must have a grade point average of 3.0.
Level of Study: Graduate
Type: Scholarship
Value: US$1,000–5,000
Length of Study: 1 academic year, renewable for a further academic year
Frequency: Annual
Country of Study: United States of America
No. of awards offered: Varies
Application Procedure: Applicants must write for details.
Closing Date: January 14th

Additional Information: Information and guidelines are available all year round. A student can receive funding through the Tuition Scholarship programme no more than twice. Only one member per immediate family may receive a Tuition Scholarship during a given academic year.

The Kosciuszko Foundation Year Abroad Program at the Jagiellonian University in Krakow

Subjects: Polish language, history, literature and culture.
Eligibility: Open to citizens of the United States of America who are students in an MA or PhD programme, but not at the dissertation level.
Level of Study: Graduate, doctorate, postgraduate
Type: Grant
Value: Tuition and housing, a monthly stipend in Polish currency for living expenses from the Polish Ministry of National Education plus a monthly stipend of US$150 from the Foundation
Length of Study: 1 year
Frequency: Annual
Study Establishment: Polonia Institute at Jagiellonian University, Krakow
Country of Study: Poland
No. of awards offered: Varies
Application Procedure: Applicants must complete an application form, available in the Autumn by mail or from the website.
Closing Date: January 14th
No. of awards given last year: 12
Additional Information: Applicants should mention the Year Abroad Program in their request letter and complete a physician's certificate as part of the application procedure.

Marcella Sembrich Voice Competition

Subjects: Polish music.
Purpose: To encourage young singers to study the repertoire of Polish composers and to honour the great Polish soprano, Marcella Sembrich.
Eligibility: Open to all singers preparing for professional careers who are citizens of the United States of America or international full-time students with valid student visas, at least 18 years of age and born after May 13, 1969.
Level of Study: Unrestricted
Type: Scholarship
Value: 1st prize: US$1,000; 2nd prize: US$750; 3rd prize: US$500, (1st prize also includes round-trip airfare from New York City to the International Moniuszko competition in Warsaw, recital at the Moniuszko festival and an invitation to perform at the Sembrich Memorial Association (Lake George, NY)
Frequency: Every 3 years
Country of Study: Any country
No. of awards offered: 3
Application Procedure: Applicants must submit a competition application form and a non-refundable fee of US$35 with supporting documents, suggested programme and two copies of an audio cassette recording of approx. 10 min.
Closing Date: December 15th
Funding: Private

The Metchie J E Budka Award of the Kosciuszko Foundation

Subjects: Polish literature from the 14th century to 1939, and Polish history, the state, the nation and the people from 962 to 1939.
Purpose: To reward outstanding scholarly work in Polish literature, Polish history and Polish-American relations.
Eligibility: Applicants must be graduate students in colleges and universities of United States of America and doctoral degree recipients from these institutions who apply during, or at the close of, the first 3 years of their postdoctoral scholarly careers.
Level of Study: Graduate, doctorate
Type: Award
Study Establishment: Colleges and universities of United States of America
Country of Study: United States of America
Application Procedure: Applicants must send four copies of each complete submission together with a cover letter.
Closing Date: July 19th
Funding: Private
Additional Information: Materials to be submitted: two original articles, or comparable material written in English in a form appropriate for publication or published in a refereed scholarly journal, or annotated translations into English from the original Polish of one or more significant works, which fall within the designated guidelines.

The Moniuszko International Vocal Competition

Subjects: Music.
Purpose: To promote knowledge of the composer's works among young artists.
Type: Cash prize
Value: US$6,000–14,000
Frequency: Every 3 years
Study Establishment: Teatr Norodowy (National Theater)
Country of Study: Poland

For further information contact:

Teatr Norodowy, Plac Teatralny 1, 00-950, Warsaw, Poland
Fax: (48) 22 6920 742

The Polish-American Club of North Jersey Scholarships

Subjects: All subjects.
Purpose: To financially aid full-time graduate students in the United States of America.
Eligibility: Applicants must be citizens of the United States of America or permanent residents of Polish descent, active members of the Polish-American Club of North Jersey, have a minimum grade point average of 3.0 and be children or grandchildren of Polish-American Club of North Jersey members.
Level of Study: Postgraduate, predoctorate
Type: Scholarship
Value: US$1,000
Length of Study: 1 year
Frequency: Annual
Country of Study: United States of America
Application Procedure: Applicants must complete an application form, available on the website from October to the end of December.
Closing Date: December 30th
Additional Information: Only one member per immediate family may receive a Polish-American Club of North Jersey Scholarship during any given academic year.

THE KURT WEILL FOUNDATION FOR MUSIC

7 East, 20 Street, 3rd Floor, New York, NY, 10003,
United States of America
Tel: (1) 212 505 5240
Fax: (1) 212 353 9663
Email: kwfinfo@kwf.org
Website: www.kwf.org
Contact: Mr Brady Sansone, Office Manager

The Kurt Weill Foundation for Music is a non-profit, private foundation chartered to preserve and perpetuate the legacies of the composer Kurt Weill (1900–1950) and his wife, singer and actress Lotte Lenya (1898–1981). The Foundation awards grants and prizes, sponsors print and online publications, maintains the Weill-Lenya Research Center and administers Weill's copyrights.

Kurt Weill Foundation for Music Grants Program

Subjects: Any subject related to the perpetuation of Kurt Weill's artistic legacy. This includes performances or recordings of his compositions in their original form, scholarly projects focusing on Kurt Weill and other related activities as outlined in the printed guidelines.

Purpose: To fund projects that aim to perpetuate Kurt Weill's artistic legacy.
Eligibility: There are no eligibility restrictions.
Level of Study: Postdoctorate, postgraduate, doctorate, professional development
Value: For college and university production performances, a maximum of US$5,000; otherwise no restrictions on requested amounts
Frequency: Annual
Country of Study: Any country
No. of awards offered: Varies
Application Procedure: Applicants must complete an application form for all but performances over US$5,000. Guidelines and forms are available from the website or from the Foundation directly.
Closing Date: November 1st. There is no deadline for professional proposals over US$5,000
Funding: Private

Kurt Weill Prize

Subjects: Music theatre of the 20th century.
Purpose: To encourage scholarship focusing on musical theatre in the 20th century.
Eligibility: Open to nationals of any country.
Level of Study: Unrestricted
Type: Prize
Value: US$2,500 for books, US$500 for articles
Frequency: Every 2 years
Country of Study: Any country
No. of awards offered: 2
Application Procedure: Applicants must submit five copies of their published work. Works must have been published within the 2 years preceding the award year.
Closing Date: April 30th
Funding: Private

KUWAIT FOUNDATION FOR THE ADVANCEMENT OF SCIENCE (KFAS)

PO Box 25263, Safat, Kuwait City, 13113, Kuwait
Tel: (965) 242 5912
Fax: (965) 240 3912
Email: prize@kfas.org.kw
Website: www.kfas.org
Contact: Dr Ali A Al-Shamlan, Director General

The Kuwait Foundation for the Advancement of Science (KFAS) aims to support efforts for modernization and scientific development within Kuwait by sponsoring basic and applied research, awarding grants to support and encourage research and awarding grants, prizes and recognition to enhance intellectual development. The KFAS also grants scholarships and fellowships for academic or training purposes, holds symposia and scientific conferences and encourages, supports and develops research projects and scientific programmes.

Islamic Organization for Medical Sciences Prize

Subjects: Medical practice addressing professional and well-documented clinical and laboratory experiments as well as the appropriate documentation of Islamic medical heritage, including Islamic jurisprudence.
Purpose: To support and promote scientific research in the field of Islamic medical sciences.
Level of Study: Unrestricted
Type: Prize
Frequency: Every 2 years
No. of awards offered: 2
Application Procedure: Nominations must be proposed by universities, scientific institutes, international organizations, individuals, past recipients of the prize and academic bodies.
Closing Date: December 31st
Funding: Private
Contributor: KFAS
No. of awards given last year: 1
No. of applicants last year: 32

KFAS Kuwait Prize

Subjects: Basic sciences, applied sciences economics and social sciences, arts and letters and Arabic and Islamic scientific heritage.
Purpose: To recognize the scientific achievements of outstanding Arab and Kuwaiti researchers and scientists worldwide.
Level of Study: Unrestricted
Type: Prize
Value: Kuwaiti Dinar 30,000, which is approx. US$100,000, for each prize. The combined value of the prizes is more than US$1 million
Frequency: Annual
No. of awards offered: 10
Application Procedure: Applicants must apply themselves or through non-political organizations and may also be recommended by search committees.
Closing Date: October 31st
Funding: Private
Contributor: KFAS
No. of awards given last year: 3
No. of applicants last year: 75

LA TROBE UNIVERSITY

Bundoora Campus, Melbourne, VIC, 3083, Australia
Tel: (61) 3 9479 2971
Fax: (61) 3 9479 1464
Email: c.cocks@latrobe.edu.au
Website: www.latrobe.edu.au/rgso
Contact: Scholarships & Candidature Co-ordinator

La Trobe University is one of the leading research universities in Australia. The University has internationally regarded strengths across a diverse range of disciplines. It offers a detailed and broad research training programme and provides unique access to technology transfer and collaboration with end users of its research and training via its Research and Development Park.

Australian Postgraduate Awards

Subjects: Health sciences, humanities, social sciences, science, technology, engineering, law, management and education.
Purpose: To support research leading to Master's or doctoral degrees.
Eligibility: Open to applicants who have completed at least 4 years of tertiary education studies with a high level of achievement, eg. a First Class (Honours) Degree or its equivalent at an Australian university. Applicants must be Australian citizens or have permanent resident status and have lived in Australia continuously for the year prior to the closing date for application. Applicants who have previously held an Australian Government Award (APA, APRA or CPRA) for more than 3 months are not eligible for an APA and applicants who have previously held an Australian Postgraduate Course Award (APCA) may apply only for an APA to support PhD research. The awards may be held concurrently with other non-Australian government awards.
Level of Study: Postgraduate, doctorate, research
Type: Award
Value: Australian $19,231 per year full-time, which is tax exempt plus allowances and Australian $10,118 per year part-time, which is taxable plus allowances
Length of Study: 2 years for the Master's and 3 years for the PhD. Periods of study already undertaken towards the degree will be deducted from the tenure of the award
Frequency: Annual
Study Establishment: Bundoora Campus, La Trobe University
Country of Study: Australia
No. of awards offered: 36
Application Procedure: Applicants must write for application kits, available from the school in which the candidate wishes to study. Applications must be submitted in duplicate to the Research and Graduate Studies Office.
Closing Date: October 31st
Funding: Government
No. of awards given last year: 38
Additional Information: APA holders are required to pay the annual General Service Fee of Australian $357 for the Bundoora Campus or

Australian $310 for the Bendigo Campus. Paid work may be permitted for up to a maximum of 8 hours per week for the full-time award or up to 4 hours per week for the part-time award.

Endeavour International Postgraduate Research Scholarships (EIPRS)

Subjects: Health sciences, humanities, social sciences, science, technology, engineering, law, management and education.
Purpose: To attract top quality overseas postgraduate students to areas of research in Institutes of Higher Education and to support Australia's research efforts.
Eligibility: Open to suitably qualified overseas graduates (excluding New Zealand) eligible to commence a doctoral or Master's degree by research. The EIPRS may be held concurrently with a university research scholarship and applicants for an EIPRS are advised to apply for a La Trobe University Postgraduate Research Scholarship (LTUPRS). Applicants who have already commenced a Master's or PhD candidature or applicants for Master's candidature by coursework and a minor thesis are not eligible to apply for an EIPRS. EIPRSs are awarded on the basis of academic merit and research capacity alone.
Level of Study: Doctorate, research, postgraduate
Type: Scholarship
Value: Tuition fees.
Length of Study: 2 years for the Master's and 3 years for the PhD
Frequency: Annual
Study Establishment: Bundoora Campus, La Trobe University
Country of Study: Australia
No. of awards offered: 7
Application Procedure: Applicants must submit the application form for international candidates available from the International Programmes Office. Email: international@latrobe.edu.au for further information.
Funding: Government
Contributor: The Australian government
Additional Information: Applicants in most instances will become members of a research team working under the direction of senior researchers.

La Trobe University Postdoctoral Research Fellowship

Subjects: All subjects.
Purpose: To advance research activities on the various campuses of the University by bringing or retaining promising scholars in Australia.
Eligibility: Open to students who have been awarded their doctorates within the last 5 years. Applicants must hold a doctoral degree or equivalent on the date of appointment. The University may also take into account the relationship of proposed area of research to the University's research promotion and management strategy policies.
Level of Study: Postdoctorate
Type: Fellowship
Value: Australian $50,336–52,184 per year, plus airfares and a resettlement allowance
Length of Study: 2 years
Frequency: Annual
Country of Study: Australia
No. of awards offered: 1 or more, subject to funding
Application Procedure: Applicants must complete an application form available from the website, requested in writing or via email.
Closing Date: August
Funding: Government
No. of awards given last year: 3
No. of applicants last year: 55
Additional Information: A project must be proposed by the applicant in collaboration with a La Trobe University research worker or team. The approved project will be designated in the letter of offer and the major objectives of a Fellow's project shall not be altered without the written approval of the University.

For further information contact:

Grants and Fellowships
Tel: 3 9479 2049
Fax: 3 9479 1464
Email: b.murray@latrobe.edu.au
Contact: Dr Barbara Murray, Co-ordinator

La Trobe University Postgraduate Scholarship

Subjects: Education, engineering, health sciences, humanities and social sciences, law, management, science and technology.
Purpose: To provide financial assistance.
Eligibility: Open to applicants of any nationality having qualifications deemed to be equivalent to an Australian First Class (Honours) Degree.
Level of Study: Postgraduate, research, doctorate
Type: Scholarship
Value: Approx. Australian $19,200 per year. There is no spouse allowance, but Australian $919 per year is available per dependent child, along with a thesis allowance, partial removal and travel allowance. All amounts are dependent on funds available
Length of Study: Up to 2 years for the Master's and up to 3 years for the PhD
Frequency: Annual
Country of Study: Australia
No. of awards offered: Approx. 59
Application Procedure: Applicants must complete an application form, available directly from the department offering the relevant course of study.
Closing Date: September 30th for overseas applicants and October 31st for Australian citizens and permanent residents

LADY TATA MEMORIAL TRUST

Academic Department of Haematology, Royal Cytogenetics, Royal Marsden Hospital, Fulham Road, London, SW3 6JJ, United Kingdom
Tel: (44) +44 (0) 20-7235-8281
Fax: (44) +44 (0) 20-7351-6420
Website: www.icr.ac.uk/haemcyto/tata/index.html

Established in 1932, the Trust has an international advisory committee, based in London, which supports research on Leukaemia worldwide, and spends four-fifths of its income on this initiative.

Lady Tata Memorial Trust Scholarships

Subjects: Leukaemia.
Purpose: To encourage study and research in diseases of the blood, with special reference to leukaemias and furthering knowledge in connection with such diseases.
Eligibility: Open to qualified applicants of any nationality. No restrictions of age or country.
Level of Study: Postdoctorate, doctorate
Type: Scholarship
Value: Ranging between UK £2,000–15,000 per year
Length of Study: 1 year
Frequency: Annual
Country of Study: Any country
No. of awards offered: Normally 10
Application Procedure: Applicants must submit eight copies of the application, including form, summary of proposed research, and two letters of reference.
Closing Date: March 1st
Funding: Private
Contributor: Tata Memorial Trust (India)
No. of awards given last year: 1–2 years

For further information contact:

Tata Limited c/o Tata Awards or c/o Mrs Dafhne Harris, 18 Grosvenor Place, SWIX 7H5

LAHORE UNIVERSITY OF MANAGEMENT SCIENCES (LUMS)

Opposite Sector U, DHA, Lahore, 54792, Pakistan
Tel: (92) 92 42 5722670 9
Fax: (92) 92 42 5722591
Website: www.lums.edu.pk

The Lahore university of Management Sciences is a national university, which aims to provide rigorous academic and intellectual training and a viable alternative to education comparable to leading universities around the world.

HEC-USAID Scholarship

Subjects: Management.
Purpose: To support talented students who have a high financial need.
Eligibility: Open to candidates studying at Lahore university of Management Science.
Value: Tuition fees, books and matenals, lodging and transportation.
Study Establishment: LUMS
Country of Study: Pakistan
No. of awards offered: 21
Application Procedure: A completed application form must be sent.
Closing Date: January 25th
Contributor: Higher Education Commission

Unilever-LUMS MBA Fund for Women

Subjects: Management.
Purpose: To provide financial support for female candidates who aspire for a career in management.
Eligibility: Open to all female candidates from Pakistan.
Level of Study: Postgraduate
Type: Fellowship
Value: 7-year interest-free loan
Length of Study: 2 years
Frequency: Annual
Country of Study: Pakistan
No. of awards offered: 5
Application Procedure: A completed application form must be sent.
Contributor: Unilever Pakistan

LALOR FOUNDATION

c/o Grants Management Associates, 77 Summer Street, 8th Floor, Boston, MA 02110, United States of America
Tel: (1) 617 420 7080
Fax: (1) 617 426 7087
Email: pmaksy@grantsmanagement.com
Website: www.lalorfound.org
Contact: Administrative Assistant

The Lalor Foundation was incorporated in Delaware in 1935, under bequests from members of the Lalor family. A major objective of the Foundation has been to give assistance and encouragement to capable, young investigators who have embarked on teaching and research careers in universities and colleges. Since 1960, the foundation has concentrated its assistance on basic research in mammalian reproductive biology as related to the regulation of fertility by providing 647 postdoctoral grants for research in the United States of America and abroad.

Lalor Foundation Postdoctoral Fellowships

Subjects: Reproductive biology as related to the regulation of fertility.
Purpose: To promote intensive research and to assist and encourage able recent postdoctoral investigators in academic positions to follow research careers in reproductive physiology.
Eligibility: Open to tax-exempt institutions within or outside the United States of America. The individual nominated by the institution for the postdoctoral fellowship may be a citizen of any country and should have training and experience at least equal to the PhD or MD level. People who have held a doctoral degree for less than 5 years are preferred. The institution applying can nominate a Fellow either from its own staff or from elsewhere but, qualifications being equal, candidates external to the institution may carry modest preference. The institution nominating the candidate must provide the name and performance record of the nominated candidate on the application form.
Level of Study: Postdoctorate
Type: Fellowship
Value: Up to US$35,000 per year to cover a fellowship stipend, institutional overheads and miscellaneous expenses
Frequency: Annual
Study Establishment: An institution that is tax exempt
Country of Study: Any country
No. of awards offered: Approx. 20
Application Procedure: Applicants must submit an application form by mail, available from the website or on request.
Closing Date: January 15th
Funding: Private
No. of awards given last year: Approx. 20
No. of applicants last year: Approx. 75

LANCASTER UNIVERSITY

Postgraduate Admissions Office University House, Bailrigg, Lancaster LA1 4YW, England
Tel: (44) 1524 592030
Fax: (44) 1524 592065
Email: studentfinance@lancaster.ac.uk
Website: www.lancs.ac.uk/pgfunding
Contact: Diane E. Montgomery

Lancaster University is a campus university dedicated to excellence in teaching and research, offering a wide range of nationally and internationally recognized postgraduate courses. For updated information on all the University's Funding opportunities, please see our website: www.lancs.ac.uk/pgfunding

Cartmel College Scholarship Fund

Purpose: To assist prospective students who are unable to obtain adequate grants from other bodies.
Eligibility: Priority given to applicants who are past or present members of Cartmel College, however, all applications will be considered.
Level of Study: Postgraduate
Type: Bursary
Value: UK £500–1,000
Length of Study: 1 Year
Frequency: Annual
Application Procedure: Application form available from the Student Support Office.
Closing Date: June 1st
Funding: Government

For further information contact:

Student Support Office University House Lancaster University, Lancaster, LA1 4YW

Lancaster University International Bursaries

Subjects: All subjects.
Purpose: To offer financial support.
Eligibility: Open to nationals of India and China who have not previously studied at Lancaster University.
Level of Study: Postgraduate
Type: Bursary
Value: UK £2,000, offset against fees
Length of Study: 1 year or more
Frequency: Annual
Study Establishment: Lancaster University
Country of Study: United Kingdom
No. of awards offered: 3
Application Procedure: Applicants must complete an application, available on request from the International Office.
Closing Date: June 2nd
Funding: International Office

Lancaster University International Business

Subjects: All subjects.
Purpose: To assist students from certain counties with their costs of study.
Eligibility: Open to candidates of any nationality who have a place at Lancaster University. Candidates must be former members of County College.
Level of Study: Postgraduate

Value: UK £3,000
Length of Study: one year
Frequency: Annual
Study Establishment: Lancaster University
Country of Study: United Kingdom
No. of awards offered: 3
Application Procedure: Applicants must write to the Student Support Office for application details.
Closing Date: June 31st
Funding: Government
No. of awards given last year: 3

For further information contact:

Student Support Office University House Lancaster University, Lancaster, LA1 4YW

Peel Awards

Subjects: All subjects.
Purpose: To enable students who are unable to secure finance from other sources to study at Lancaster University.
Eligibility: Open to candidates of any nationality who have a place at Lancaster University and who will be over 21 years of age at the commencement of the course.
Level of Study: Postgraduate
Value: UK £1,500
Frequency: Annual
Study Establishment: Lancaster University
Country of Study: United Kingdom
No. of awards offered: 20–30
Application Procedure: Applicants must complete an application form, available on request from the Student Support Office.
Closing Date: June 1st
Funding: Private, trusts
Contributor: Peel (Dowager Countess Eleanor) Trust
No. of awards given last year: 21

Peel Awards

Subjects: All subjects.
Purpose: To enable students to study at Lancaster University.
Eligibility: Open to candidates of any nationality who have a place at Lancaster University and who will be over 21 years old at the commencement of their course.
Level of Study: Postgraduate
Value: UK £500–1,500
Frequency: Annual
Study Establishment: Lancaster University
Country of Study: United Kingdom
No. of awards offered: 20–30
Application Procedure: Application form, available on request from the student support office.
Closing Date: June 1st
Funding: Trusts
Contributor: Dowager Countess Eleanor Peel Trust
No. of awards given last year: 25

For further information contact:

Student Support Office University House Lancaster University, Lancaster, LA1 4YW,

LANCASTER UNIVERSITY MANAGEMENT SCHOOL

MBA Office, Lancaster University Management School, Lancaster, LA1 4YX, England
Tel: (44) 15 2459 4068
Fax: (44) 15 2459 2417
Email: mba@lancaster.ac.uk
Website: www.lums.lancs.ac.uk
Contact: Angela Graves

Lancaster University Management School (LUMS) is one of the only two United Kingdom to business schools have the coveted 6-star (6*) rating for research quality, and has been rated 'excellent' for teaching quality by the Higher Education Funding Council for England and Wales. LUMS is EQUIS-accredited and its MBA programmes are AMBA-accredited and winners of the Association of MBAs Student of the Year Award twice. In the Financial Times MBA rankings 2005, LUMS was placed joint 39th in the world, placing the Lancaster MBA 3rd in the United Kingdom and 10th in Europe.

Lancaster MBA Bursaries

Subjects: Full-time MBA.
Purpose: To assist candidates to pursue the full-time MBA.
Eligibility: These bursaries are open to applicants from any part of the world and will be awarded on the basis of exceptional ability and need.
Level of Study: Postgraduate, full-time MBA.
Value: UK £1000–5000
Length of Study: 1 year
Frequency: Annual
Study Establishment: Lancaster University Management School
Country of Study: United Kingdom
No. of awards offered: Dependent on demand
Application Procedure: Applicants should contact the MBA Office for full details. Candidates should send a 1,000-word statement demonstrating how, through their ideas and achievements, they will be an asset to the programme. Cases of exceptional need will also be considered. The School can only consider applications from candidates who already hold an offer of a place in the programme.
Closing Date: May 31st
Funding: Private
No. of awards given last year: None
No. of applicants last year: None

Lancaster MBA Scholarships

Subjects: Full-time MBA.
Purpose: To assist exceptional candidates to pursue the full-time MBA.
Eligibility: Students who meet specific academic and professional criteria, which are above our standard admissions requirements. Candidates must contact the MBA Office for details.
Level of Study: Postgraduate, full-time mba
Type: Scholarship
Value: UK £7,500
Length of Study: 1 year
Frequency: Annual
Study Establishment: Lancaster University Management School
Country of Study: United Kingdom
No. of awards offered: 5
Application Procedure: Applicants must contact the MBA Office for full details. Candidates should send a 1,000-word statement demonstrating significant achievement in their career to date and outlining how their career plan can benefit from the Lancaster MBA. The School can only consider applications from candidates who already hold an offer of a place in the programme.
Closing Date: May 31st
Funding: Private
No. of awards given last year: None
No. of applicants last year: None

LE CORDON BLEU AUSTRALIA

Tel: 8346 3700
Fax: 8346 3755
Email: australia@cordonbleu.edu
Website: www.lecordonbleu.com

Le Cordon bleu, a global leader hospitality education, provides professional development for existing executives.

Food Media Club Australia Scholarship

Subjects: Gastronomy.
Purpose: To support further studies.

Eligibility: Open to members of the club who are permanent Australian residents.
Level of Study: Postgraduate
Type: Scholarship
Value: Australian $12,750
Length of Study: 15–28 months
Frequency: Annual
Country of Study: Australia
Application Procedure: A completed application must be submitted see the website for full details.
Closing Date: October 27th

International Association of Culinary Professionals (IACP) and culinary Trust Scholarship
Subjects: Gastronomy.
Purpose: To provide financial assistance.
Eligibility: Open to candidates who may or may not members of IACP.
Level of Study: Postgraduate
Type: Scholarship
Value: Australian $5,000
Frequency: Annual
Country of Study: Australia
Application Procedure: See the website.

The James Beard Foundation Award
Subjects: Hotel & restaurant management.
Purpose: To provide financial assistance.
Level of Study: Postgraduate
Type: Scholarship
Value: Australian $5,000
Frequency: Annual
Country of Study: Australia
Application Procedure: A copy of educational history statement of culinary goals, financial statement and two letters of reference must be submitted.

For further information contact:

The Beard House 167 West 12th Street, New York, NY 10011

Le Cordon Bleu Master of Arts in Gastronomy Scholarship
Subjects: Gastronomy.
Purpose: To encourage candidates seeking a gastronomy-related career.
Eligibility: Open to those with a passion for anything culinary.
Level of Study: Postgraduate
Type: Scholarship
Value: Varies
Frequency: Annual
Country of Study: Australia
Application Procedure: A completed application form must be submitted.

Le Cordon Bleu Master of Business Administration Scholarship.
Subjects: Hotel and restaurant management.
Purpose: To help in advancement to senior or corporate management positions.
Eligibility: Open to Hoteliers restaurateurs, industry consultants and aspiring management executives.
Level of Study: Postgraduate
Type: Scholarship
Length of Study: Varies
Frequency: Annual
Country of Study: Australia
Application Procedure: See the website.

New Zealand Guild of Food Writers Scholarship
Purpose: Gastronomy.
Eligibility: Open to applicants who are permanent residents of New Zealand.
Level of Study: Postgraduate
Type: Scholarship
Value: Australian $12,750
Length of Study: 15–18 months
Frequency: Annual
Country of Study: New Zealand
Application Procedure: See the website.
Closing Date: October 27th

LEEDS INTERNATIONAL PIANOFORTE COMPETITION

Piano Competition Office, The University of Leeds, Leeds, LS 2 9JT, United Kingdom
Tel: (44) (0) 113 244 6586
Fax: (44) (0) 113 244 6586
Email: admin@leedspiano.bdx.co.uk
Website: www.leedspiano.com
Contact: Office Manager

The leeds International Pianoforte competition is a member of the World Federation of International Music competitions. It was founded in 1961 and since then has developed to become the world's greatest piano competition producing prizewinners who have gone onto successful international careers.

Henry Rudolf Meisels Bursary Awards
Subjects: Music.
Purpose: To award competitors accepted in the first stage of the competition.
Eligibility: Open to candidates who are accepted to perform in the first stage of the competition.
Level of Study: Professional development
Type: Scholarship
Value: UK £100
Frequency: Every 3 years
Study Establishment: The University of Leeds
Country of Study: United Kingdom
Contributor: Henry Rudolf Meisels Bequest
Additional Information: A non-refundable entrance fee of UK £50 must be paid no later than 1st February.

Leeds International Pianoforte Competition Award
Subjects: Music.
Purpose: To promote the careers of of the winners.
Eligibility: Open to young, talented, professional pianists, who were born on or after 1st September 1976.
Level of Study: Professional development
Type: Scholarship
Value: UK £65,750
Frequency: Every 3 years, Once every 3 years
Study Establishment: University of Leeds
Country of Study: United Kingdom
No. of awards offered: 33
Application Procedure: Application forms, completed in English, and repertoire to be submitted before the closing date.
Closing Date: February 1st
Funding: Foundation, trusts, private, individuals
Contributor: Leeds International Pianoforte Competition
No. of awards given last year: 36
Additional Information: A non-refundable entrance fee of UK £50 must be paid no later than 1st February.

LENTZ PEACE RESEARCH ASSOCIATION (LPRA)

c/o University of Missouri-St Louis, One University Boulevard, St Louis, MO, 63121-4400, United States of America
Tel: (1) 314 516 5798
Fax: (1) 314 516 6757
Email: bob.baumann@umsl.edu
Contact: Mr Robert Baumann, Board Member

The Lentz Peace Research Association, which Theodore F. Lentz founded originally in 1930 as the Character Research Institute, is the oldest continuously operating peace research center in the world.

Theodore Lentz Fellowship in Peace and Conflict Resolution Research

Subjects: International relations.
Purpose: To support research projects in peace and conflict resolution and to enable the recipient to teach an introductory peace studies course in the Fall semester and one course in the Spring semester at the University of Missouri-St Louis.
Eligibility: A completed PhD is required and preference is given to graduates of university programmes in peace studies and conflict resolution. Graduates of political science, international relations and other social science programmes that specialize in peace and conflict resolution are also invited to apply.
Level of Study: Postdoctorate
Type: Fellowship
Value: Approx. US$23,400 plus university benefits and US$1,000 travel and expense allowance
Length of Study: 9 months
Frequency: Annual
Study Establishment: The University of Missouri-St Louis
Country of Study: United States of America
No. of awards offered: 1
Application Procedure: Applicants must send a curriculum vitae, a letter of application, evidence of completion of the PhD, three letters of recommendation and a research proposal of approximately 750 words to the Center for International Studies.
Closing Date: April 15th
Funding: Private
Contributor: The Lentz Peace Research Association
No. of awards given last year: 1
No. of applicants last year: 18
Additional Information: The fellowship is supported in part by the University of Missouri-St Louis. The Fellow must serve in residence at University of Missouri-St Louis.

LEO BAECK INSTITUTE (LBI)

15 West 16th Street, New York, NY, 10011-6301,
United States of America
Tel: (1) 212 744 6400
Fax: (1) 212 988 1305
Email: lbaeck@lbi.cjh.org
Website: www.lbi.org
Contact: Secretary

The Leo Baeck Institute (LBI) is a research, study and lecture centre, a library and repository for archival and art materials. It is devoted to the preservation of original materials pertaining to the history and culture of German-speaking Jewry.

David Baumgardt Memorial Fellowship

Subjects: Modern intellectual history of German-speaking Jewry.
Purpose: To provide financial support to scholars whose research projects are connected with the writings of Professor David Baumgardt or his scholarly interests.
Level of Study: Postdoctorate, postgraduate, doctorate
Type: Fellowship
Value: US$3,000
Length of Study: 1 year
Frequency: Annual
Study Establishment: The Leo Baeck Institute
Country of Study: United States of America
No. of awards offered: 1
Application Procedure: Applicants must submit an application form, a curriculum vitae and a full description of the research project. Doctoral students must submit official transcripts of graduate and undergraduate work, written evidence that they are enrolled in a PhD programme and two letters of recommendation, one by their doctoral adviser and one by another scholar familiar with the work. Postdoctoral candidates must submit evidence of their degree, of which transcripts are not required, and two letters of recommendation from two colleagues familiar with their research.
Closing Date: November 1st
Funding: Private
Contributor: The Leo Baeck Institute
No. of awards given last year: 1
No. of applicants last year: 2

Fritz Halbers Fellowship

Subjects: Culture and history of German-speaking Jewry.
Purpose: To provide financial assistance to scholars whose projects are connected with the culture and history of German-speaking Jewry.
Level of Study: Graduate, postgraduate, predoctorate, doctorate, postdoctorate
Type: Fellowship
Value: US$3,000
Length of Study: 1 year
Frequency: Annual
Country of Study: United States of America
No. of awards offered: More than 1
Application Procedure: Applicants must submit an application form, curriculum vitae and a full description of the research project. Doctoral students must submit official transcripts of graduate and undergraduate work, written evidence that they are enrolled in a PhD programme and two letters of recommendation, one by their doctoral adviser and one by another scholar familiar with the work. Postdoctoral candidates must submit evidence of their degree, of which transcripts are not required, and two letters of recommendation from two colleagues familiar with their research.
Closing Date: November 1st
Funding: Private
Contributor: The Leo Baeck Institute
No. of awards given last year: 1
No. of applicants last year: 7

LBI/DAAD Fellowship for Research at the Leo Baeck Institute, New York

Subjects: Social, communal and intellectual history of German-speaking Jewry.
Purpose: To provide assistance to students for dissertation research and to academics for writing a scholarly essay or book.
Level of Study: Doctorate, graduate, postdoctorate
Type: Fellowship
Value: US$2,000
Length of Study: 1 year
Frequency: Annual
Study Establishment: The Leo Baeck Institute
Country of Study: United States of America
No. of awards offered: 2
Application Procedure: Applicants must submit an application form, a curriculum vitae and a full description of the research project. Doctoral students must submit official transcripts of graduate and undergraduate work, written evidence that they are enrolled in a PhD programme and two letters of recommendation, one by their doctoral adviser and one by another scholar familiar with the work. Postdoctoral candidates must submit evidence of their degree, of which transcripts are not required, and two letters of recommendation from two colleagues familiar with their research.
Closing Date: November 1st
Funding: Private
Contributor: The Leo Baeck Institute
No. of awards given last year: 2
Additional Information: The fellowship holders must agree to submit a brief report on their research activities after the period for which the fellowship was granted.

LBI/DAAD Fellowships for Research in the Federal Republic of Germany

Subjects: Social, communal and intellectual history of German-speaking Jewry.
Purpose: To provide financial assistance to doctoral students conducting research for their dissertation and to academics in the preparation of a scholarly essay or book.

Eligibility: Applicants must be citizens of the United States of America and PhD candidates or recent PhDs who have received their degrees within the preceding 2 years.
Level of Study: Doctorate, postdoctorate
Type: Fellowship
Value: Please contact the organization
Length of Study: 1 year
Frequency: Annual
Country of Study: Germany
No. of awards offered: 1–2
Application Procedure: Applicants must submit an application form, a curriculum vitae and a full description of the research project. Doctoral students must submit official transcripts of graduate and undergraduate work, written evidence that they are enrolled in a PhD programme and two letters of recommendation, one by their doctoral adviser and one by another scholar familiar with the work. Postdoctoral candidates must submit evidence of their degree, of which transcripts are not required, and two letters of recommendation from two colleagues familiar with their research.
Closing Date: November 1st
Funding: Private
Contributor: The Leo Baeck Institute
Additional Information: The fellowship holders must agree to submit a brief report on their research activities upon conclusion of their fellowship. These awards are in conjunction with awards offered by the German Academic Exchange Service (DAAD) in New York, United States of America.

THE LEONARD FOUNDATION

20 Eglinton Avenue West-7th Floor, Toronto, ON MAR 2EZ, Canada
Tel: (1) 361 8711
Email: info@leonardfnd.org
Website: www.leonardfnd.org

The Leonard Foundation, created in 1916, has a charitable Trust and also a Financial Assistance Program for students who, without help from the Foundation, would not be able to continue their education.

Leonard Foundation Financial Assistance Program

Subjects: All subjects.
Purpose: To provide financial assistance.
Eligibility: Preference given to offspring of clergy men, teachers, officers and people in the military.
Level of Study: Postgraduate
Type: Scholarship
Value: US$1,000–1,500
Frequency: Annual
No. of awards offered: 140
Application Procedure: Application forms are available on the website.
Closing Date: March 15th

LEUKAEMIA RESEARCH FUND

43 Great Ormond Street, London, WC1N 3JJ, England
Tel: (44) 20 7405 0101
Fax: (44) 20 7242 1488
Email: info@lrf.org.uk
Website: www.lrf.org.uk

The Leukaemia Research Fund is devoted exclusively to leukaemia, Hodgkin's disease and other lymphomas, myeloma, myelodysplastic syndromes, aplastic anaemia and the myeloproliferative disorders. The Fund is committed to finding causes, improving and developing new treatments and diagnostic methods as well as supplying free information booklets and answering written and telephone enquiries.

Gordon Piller Studentships

Subjects: All life science disciplines. The research topic must be applicable to leukaemia.
Purpose: To train graduates in life sciences in research and allow them to obtain a PhD degree.
Eligibility: Open to graduates of any nationality who work and reside in the United Kingdom.
Level of Study: Postgraduate
Type: Studentship
Value: Varies
Length of Study: 3 years
Frequency: Annual
Study Establishment: Universities, medical schools and research institutes
Country of Study: United Kingdom
No. of awards offered: 4
Application Procedure: Applicants must be invited to apply and must complete the appropriate form.
Closing Date: Advertised in *Nature* every January
No. of awards given last year: 4

Leukaemia Research Fund Clinical Research Training Fellowships

Subjects: All life science disciplines. The research topic must be applicable to leukaemia.
Purpose: To train registrar grade clinicians in research and allow them to obtain a higher degree.
Eligibility: Open to researchers of any nationality who work and reside in the United Kingdom.
Level of Study: Research
Type: Fellowship
Value: Varies
Length of Study: 3 years
Frequency: 3 times per year
Study Establishment: Universities, medical schools, research institutes and teaching hospitals
Country of Study: United Kingdom
No. of awards offered: Varies
Application Procedure: Applicants must complete an application form.
Closing Date: Varies, available on request

Leukaemia Research Fund Grant Programme

Subjects: All life science disciplines.
Purpose: To give long-term support to research groups studying the causes and treatment of haematological malignancies.
Eligibility: Open to researchers who work and reside in the United Kingdom.
Level of Study: Unrestricted
Type: Research grant
Value: Varies
Length of Study: Varies
Study Establishment: Universities, medical schools, research institutes and teaching hospitals
Country of Study: United Kingdom
No. of awards offered: Varies
Application Procedure: Applicants must complete an application form only after discussion with the Scientific Director.
Closing Date: Available on request

THE LEUKEMIA & LYMPHOMA SOCIETY OF CANADA (LLSC)

936 The East Mall, Toronto, ON,
M9B 6J9, Canada
Tel: (1) 416 661 9541
Fax: (1) 416 661 7799
Email: alil@lls.org
Website: www.lls.org/canada
Contact: CEO

The Leukaemia & Lymphoma Society of Canada's mission is to cure leukaemia, lymphoma, Hodgkin's disease and myeloma and to improve the quality of life of patients and their families. Since its founding, the Society has invested millions of dollars in research specifically targeting leukaemia, lymphoma and myeloma.

LLSC Awards

Subjects: Leukaemia, lymphoma (Hodgkin's and non-Hodgkin's) and myeloma.
Purpose: To support peer-reviewed research and fellowships in leukaemia, lymphoma (Hodgkin's and non-Hodgkin's) and myeloma.
Eligibility: Open to applicants with a faculty appointment at a Canadian university.
Level of Study: Research, postdoctorate
Type: Fellowship or Grant
Value: Varies
Length of Study: 1 year. (fellowships are renewable for a further year)
Frequency: Annual
Country of Study: Canada
No. of awards offered: Varies
Application Procedure: Applicants must complete an official application. Applications are available from Deans of Medicine, the LLSC Office, the website, by contacting (1) 877 668 8326 or via email alil@lls.org
Closing Date: February 1st
Funding: Private
Additional Information: A special grant is available for the study of CLL.

LEUKEMIA AND LYMPHOMA SOCIETY

1311 Mamoroneck Avenue, White Plains, NY, 10605, United States of America
Tel: (1) 914 821 8843
Fax: (1) 914 949 6691
Email: researchprograms@lls.org
Website: www.lls.org
Contact: Director of Research Administration

The Leukemia and Lymphoma Society is a national voluntary health agency dedicated to the conquest of leukaemia, lymphoma and myeloma through research. Through its research programme, the Society hopes to encourage and promote research activity of the highest quality. In addition, the Society also supports patient aid, public and professional education and community service programmes.

Career Development Program

Subjects: Leukaemia, lymphoma, Hodgkin's disease and myeloma research.
Purpose: To provide support for individuals pursuing careers in basic, clinical or translational research.
Eligibility: Applications may be submitted by individuals working in domestic or non-profit organizations such as universities, hospitals or units of state and local governments. International applicants are welcome to apply.
Level of Study: Postdoctorate
Type: Fellowship
Value: US$45,000–100,000 per year
Length of Study: 3–5 years, based on experience and training
Frequency: Annual
Study Establishment: International and domestic non-profit organizations, including hospitals, universities and research institutes
Country of Study: Any country
No. of awards offered: Varies
Application Procedure: Applicants can visit the website for details of the Career Development Award application packet at www.lls.org/cdp
Closing Date: October 1st
Funding: Private

Translational Research Program

Subjects: Leukaemia, lymphoma, Hodgkin's disease and myeloma research.
Purpose: To encourage and provide early stage support for clinical research.
Eligibility: Open to individuals working in domestic or foreign non-profit organizations such as universities, hospitals or units of state and local governments. International applicants are welcome to apply.
Level of Study: Research, postdoctorate
Value: Up to US$130,000 per year
Length of Study: 3 years, with the possibility of 2 additional years
Frequency: Annual
Study Establishment: International and domestic non-profit organizations, including hospitals, universities and research institutes
No. of awards offered: Varies
Application Procedure: Applicants must contact the Society or visit the website for details.
Funding: Private

THE LEVERHULME TRUST

Research Awards Advisory Committee, 1 Pemberton Row, London, EC4A 3BG, England
Tel: (44) 20 7822 6964
Fax: (44) 20 7822 5084
Email: jcater@leverhulme.org.uk
Website: www.leverhulme.org.uk
Contact: Mrs Bridget Kerr, Grants Administrative Officer

The Leverhulme Trust awards grants mainly for research but also, to a limited extent, for the support of students and areas of educational activity.

Leverhulme Trust Emeritus Fellowships

Subjects: All subjects.
Purpose: To assist experienced researchers in the completion of research already begun.
Eligibility: Open to individuals who have retired in the last 3 years or who are about to retire. Applicants must hold, or have recently held, teaching and/or research posts in universities or institutions of similar status in the United Kingdom. Applicants must also have an established record of research and be aged 59 or over at the age of retirement.
Level of Study: Postdoctorate
Type: Fellowship
Value: Up to UK £20,000 by individual assessment. The awards are to meet incidental costs and do not provide a personal allowance or pension supplementation
Length of Study: 3 months–2 years
Frequency: Annual
No. of awards offered: Approx. 30
Application Procedure: Applicants must complete an application form. Requests for application forms must be accompanied by an A4-sized stamped addressed envelope.
Closing Date: February 7th
Funding: Private
No. of awards given last year: 43
No. of applicants last year: 115

Leverhulme Trust Research Fellowships

Subjects: All subjects.
Purpose: To assist experienced researchers pursuing investigations who are prevented, by routine duties or other causes, from undertaking or completing a research programme.
Eligibility: Open to persons educated in the United Kingdom or the Commonwealth or who are permanent members of the United Kingdom scholarly community and who are normally resident in the United Kingdom. Awards are not normally made to those aged under 30 and are not made to those registered for first or higher degrees, professional or vocational qualifications.
Type: Fellowship
Value: Up to UK £25,000 by individual assessment
Length of Study: 3 months–2 years
Frequency: Annual
Country of Study: Any country
No. of awards offered: Approx. 90
Application Procedure: Applicants must complete an application form. Requests for application forms must be accompanied by an A4-sized stamped addressed envelope.
Closing Date: Mid-November
Funding: Private
No. of awards given last year: 92
No. of applicants last year: 532

Leverhulme Trust Study Abroad Studentships
Subjects: All subjects.
Purpose: To fund advanced study or research at a centre of learning.
Eligibility: Open to candidates who have obtained a first degree from a United Kingdom university at the time of application or who are able to show evidence of equivalent education in the United Kingdom. Applicants must also have been educated at a school or schools in the United Kingdom or other parts of the Commonwealth. They must be normally resident in the United Kingdom and under 30 years of age on June 1st. If older than this, candidates must make a strong and appropriate case for special consideration. Students wishing only to improve knowledge of modern languages are not eligible.
Level of Study: Doctorate, professional development, postgraduate, postdoctorate
Type: Studentship
Value: UK £15,000 per year plus return airfare and other allowances at the discretion of the Committee
Length of Study: 1 or 2 years
Frequency: Annual
Study Establishment: Any centre of learning
No. of awards offered: Approx. 20
Application Procedure: Applicants must complete an application form. Requests for application forms must be accompanied by an A4-sized stamped addressed envelope.
Closing Date: January 10th
Funding: Private
No. of awards given last year: 18
No. of applicants last year: 137

LEWIS & CLARK COLLEGE

Graduate School of Education, Lewis & Clark College,
0615 SW Palatine Hill Road, Portland, OR, 97219-7899,
United States of America
Tel: (1) 503 768 7090
Email: sfs@lclark.edu
Website: www.lclark.edu
Contact: The Bursar

The College was founded by Presbyterian pioneers as Albany Collegiate Institute in 1867. The school moved to the former Lloyd Frank estate in Portland's southwest hills in 1942 and took the name Lewis & Clark College.

Mary Stuart Rogers Scholarship
Subjects: Teacher education.
Purpose: To support postgraduate students by funding study at Master's degree or PhD level.
Level of Study: Postgraduate
Value: US$3,000
Frequency: Annual
Study Establishment: Lewis & Clark College
Country of Study: United States of America
No. of awards offered: Variable
Application Procedure: Applicants must contact the Department of Teacher Education.

LEWIS WALPOLE LIBRARY

154 Main Street, Farmington, CT, 06032-2958,
United States of America
Tel: (1) 860 677 2140
Fax: (1) 860 677 6369
Email: walpole@yale.edu
Website: www.library.yale.edu/Walpole
Contact: Dr Margaret K Powell, The Librarian

The Lewis Walpole Library is a research centre for the study of all aspects of English 18th-century studies and is a prime centre for the study of Horace Walpole and Strawberry Hill.

Lewis Walpole Library Fellowship
Subjects: 18th-century British studies including history, literature, theatre, drama, art, architecture, politics, philosophy or social history.
Purpose: To fund study into any aspect of the Library's collection of 18th-century British prints, paintings, books and manuscripts.
Eligibility: Applicants should normally be pursuing an advanced degree or must be engaged in postdoctoral or equivalent research.
Level of Study: Postgraduate, postdoctorate, doctorate, research
Type: Fellowship
Value: US$1,800 plus travel expenses and on-site accommodation
Length of Study: 1 month
Frequency: Annual
Study Establishment: Lewis Walpole Library, Yale University
Country of Study: United States of America
No. of awards offered: More than 2
Application Procedure: Applicants must submit a curriculum vitae, a brief research proposal of up to three pages and two confidential letters of recommendation.
Closing Date: January 15th
Funding: Private
No. of awards given last year: 13
No. of applicants last year: 35

LIBRARY AND INFORMATION TECHNOLOGY ASSOCIATION (LITA)

50 East Huron Street, Chicago, IL, 60611,
United States of America
Tel: (1) 312 280 4270
Fax: (1) 312 280 3257
Email: lita@ala.org
Website: www.lita.org
Contact: Grants Management Officer

The Library and Information Technology Association (LITA) provides a forum for discussion, an environment for learning and a programme for action on the design, development and implementation of automated and technological systems in the library and information science field.

LITA/Christian Larew Memorial Scholarship in Library and Information Technology
Subjects: Library and information science, with an emphasis on information technology.
Purpose: To encourage the entry of qualified people into the library and information technology field.
Eligibility: Open to students at the Master's degree level in an ALA-accredited programme.
Level of Study: Postgraduate
Type: Scholarship
Value: US$3,000
Frequency: Annual
Study Establishment: An ALA-accredited programme
Country of Study: United States of America
No. of awards offered: 1
Application Procedure: Candidates must send a statement indicating their previous experience in the field and what he or she can bring to the profession. Application forms and instructions are available from the website.
Contributor: The Electronic Business and Information Services (EBIS), a unit of Baker & Taylor, Inc.
Additional Information: Factors considered in awarding the scholarship are academic excellence, leadership, evidence of commitment to a career in library automation and information technology and prior activity and experience in those fields.

LITA/LSSI Minority Scholarship in Library and Information Technology
Subjects: Library science and information technology.
Purpose: To encourage the entry of qualified persons into the library automation field.

Eligibility: Open to citizens of the United States of America or Canada who are qualified members of a principal minority group: American Indian or Alaskan Native, Asian or Pacific Islander, African American or Hispanic.
Level of Study: Postgraduate
Type: Scholarship
Value: US$2,500
Frequency: Annual
Study Establishment: An ALA-accredited programme
Country of Study: United States of America
No. of awards offered: 1
Application Procedure: Applicants must write, phone or visit the website for application forms.
Funding: Commercial
Contributor: Library Systems and Service, Inc.

LITA/OCLC Minority Scholarship in Library and Information Technology

Subjects: Library information science, with an emphasis on library automation.
Purpose: To encourage the entry of qualified minority persons into the library automation field who plan to follow a career in that field and who evidence potential leadership in, and a strong commitment to, the use of automated systems in libraries.
Eligibility: Open to citizens of the United States of America or Canada who are qualified members of a principal minority group: American Indian or Alaskan Native, Asian or Pacific Islander, African American or Hispanic.
Level of Study: Postgraduate
Type: Scholarship
Value: US$3,000
Frequency: Annual
Study Establishment: An ALA-accredited programme
Country of Study: United States of America
No. of awards offered: 1
Application Procedure: Applicants must write, phone or visit the website for application forms.
Funding: Commercial
Contributor: Online Computer Library Center
Additional Information: Factors considered in awarding the scholarship are academic excellence, leadership, evidence of commitment to a career in library automation and information technology and prior activity and experience in those fields.

LITA/SIRSI Scholarship in Library and Information Technology

Subjects: Library information science, with an emphasis on library automation.
Purpose: To encourage the entry of qualified persons into the library automation field who plan to follow a career in that field.
Eligibility: Open to new students at the Master's degree level in an ALA-accredited programme.
Level of Study: Postgraduate
Type: Scholarship
Value: US$2,500
Frequency: Annual
Study Establishment: An ALA-accredited programme
Country of Study: United States of America
No. of awards offered: 1
Application Procedure: Applicants must write, telephone or visit the website for application forms. Applicants must illustrate their qualifications for this scholarship with a statement indicating the nature of their previous experience, letters of reference and a personal statement.
Funding: Commercial
Contributor: SIRSI
Additional Information: Factors considered in awarding the scholarship are academic excellence, leadership, evidence of commitment to a career in library automation and information technology and prior activity and experience in those fields.

LIBRARY COMPANY OF PHILADELPHIA

1314 Locust Street, Philadelphia, PA, 19107,
United States of America
Tel: (1) 215 546 3181
Fax: (1) 215 546 5167
Email: jgreen@librarycompany.org
Website: www.librarycompany.org
Contact: Fellowship Office

Founded in 1731, the Library Company of Philadelphia was the largest public library in America until the 1850s and contains printed materials on aspects of American culture and society in that period. It is a research library with a collection of 500,000 books, pamphlets, newspapers and periodicals, 75,000 prints, maps and photographs and 150,000 manuscripts.

Library Company of Philadelphia and Historical Society of Pennsylvania Research Fellowships in American History and Culture

Subjects: 18th- and 19th-century American social and cultural history, African American history, literary history or the history of the book in America.
Purpose: To offer short-term fellowships for research in residence in their collections.
Eligibility: The fellowship supports both postdoctoral and dissertation research. The project proposal should demonstrate that the Library Company and/or the Historical Society of Pennsylvania has a primary source central to the research topic. Candidates are encouraged to enquire about the appropriateness of a proposed topic before applying.
Level of Study: Doctorate, postdoctorate
Type: Fellowship
Value: US$1,800
Length of Study: 1 month
Frequency: Annual
Study Establishment: An independent research library
Country of Study: United States of America
No. of awards offered: Usually 25–30
Application Procedure: Applicants must send five copies each of a curriculum vitae, a description of the proposed project of 2–4 pages in length and a letter of reference.
Closing Date: March 1st. Fellows may take up residence at any time from the following June to May of the next year
Funding: Private
Contributor: The Andrew W Mellon Foundation, the Barra Foundation and McLean Contributionship
No. of awards given last year: 34
No. of applicants last year: 120
Additional Information: Fellows will be assisted in finding reasonably priced accommodation. International applications are especially encouraged since two fellowships, jointly sponsored with the Historical Society of Pennsylvania, are reserved for scholars whose residence is outside the United States of America. A partial catalogue of the Library's holdings is available through the website. This programme includes fellowships offered by the Library Company's programme in Early American Economy and Society and by the Balch Institute for Ethnic studies.

Library Company of Philadelphia Dissertation Fellowships

Subjects: 18th- and 19th-century American social, cultural and literary history, pre-1860 American economic and business history.
Purpose: To promote scholarship by offering long-term dissertation fellowships.
Eligibility: The fellowship supports dissertation research in the collections of the Library Company and other Philadelphia repositories.
Level of Study: Doctorate
Type: Fellowship
Value: US$9,000
Length of Study: 4.5 months (one semester)
Frequency: Annual
Study Establishment: An independent research library

Country of Study: United States of America
No. of awards offered: 4
Application Procedure: Applicants must send five copies each of a curriculum vitae, a description of the proposed project of 2–4 pages in length, two letters of recommendation and a relevant writing sample of up to 24 pages in length. Candidates are encouraged to enquire about the appropriateness of a proposed topic before applying.
Closing Date: March 1st. Fellows may take up residence for either the following Fall or the Spring semester
Funding: Private
No. of awards given last year: 4
No. of applicants last year: 21
Additional Information: Further information can be found on the website, which also includes fellowships offered by the Library Company's programme in early American economy and society.

Library Company of Philadelphia Postdoctoral Research Fellowship

Subjects: 18th- and 19th-century American social, cultural and literary history.
Purpose: To promote scholarship by offering long-term postdoctoral and advanced research fellowships.
Eligibility: The fellowship supports both postdoctoral and advanced research in the collections of the Library Company and often Philadelphia repositories. Applicants must hold a doctoral degree.
Level of Study: Research, postdoctorate
Type: Fellowship
Value: US$20,000
Length of Study: 4.5 months (1 semester)
Frequency: Annual
Study Establishment: An independent research library
Country of Study: United States of America
No. of awards offered: 4
Application Procedure: Applicants must send five copies of a curriculum vitae, a description of the proposed project of 2–4 pages in length, two letters of recommendation and a relevant writing sample of up to 24 pages in length. Candidates are encouraged to enquire about the appropriateness of a proposed topic before applying.
Closing Date: November 1st. Fellows may take up residence for either the following Fall or the Spring semester
Funding: Government, international office
No. of awards given last year: 4
No. of applicants last year: 20
Additional Information: Two of the fellowships are offered by the Library Company's programme in early American economy and society. Two are supported by the National Endowment for the Humanities.

THE LIFE COURSE CENTER

Department of Sociology, University of Minnesota, 909 Social Sciences Building, 267 19th Avenue South, Minneapolis, MN, 55455, United States of America
Tel: (1) 612 624 4064
Fax: (1) 612 624 7020
Email: morti002@atlas.socsci.umn.edu
Website: www.soc.umn.edu
Contact: Dr Jeylan T Mortimer

The Life Course Center at the University of Minnesota supports scholarly enquiry related to the life course. Through research, seminars and courses offered by the Center's faculty and visiting scholars, the Center provides an intellectual forum that enriches the research and educational activities of a broad range of faculty and students, as research assistants, in the department of sociology as well as in other units of the University.

National Research Service Award for Mental Health and Adjustment in the Life Course

Subjects: Topics include early work experience, mental health and the transition to adulthood, the joint development of autonomy and intimacy, the sources of competence and resilience in the face of adversity, physical and relational aggression, the life course consequences of victimization, cognitive and emotional factors in decision-making in criminal, delinquent and work behaviour, perceptions of criminal sanctions and their efficacy in inhibiting offending and female inmates' adaptations to prison life as a function of prior life experience or trajectories of deviance and reintegration.
Purpose: To provide opportunities for students to carry out longitudinal research into the psychosocial determinants of mental health and adjustment, with an emphasis on childhood, adolescence and the transition to adulthood.
Eligibility: Open to citizens of the United States of America or residents. Postdoctoral candidates must have received a PhD in a social science discipline or an equivalent degree such as an MD, public health or nursing degree.
Level of Study: Predoctorate, postdoctorate
Type: Fellowship
Value: A stipend in accordance with NRSA guidelines, providing tuition, fees and medical insurance
Length of Study: 3 years predoctoral students and 2 years for postdoctoral students. This award is subject to review at the end of the 1st year
Frequency: Every 2 years
Study Establishment: The University of Minnesota
Country of Study: United States of America
No. of awards offered: 4, 1 of which is postdoctoral
Application Procedure: Applicants must provide a letter describing current research interests, a complete curriculum vitae, a university transcript, three letters of recommendation and samples of written work.
Closing Date: November 15th. Applications will be accepted until the position is filled
Funding: Government
Contributor: The National Institute of Mental Health (NIMH)
Additional Information: The University of Minnesota is committed to the policy that all persons shall have equal access to its programmes, facilities and employment without regard to race, colour, creed, religion, national origin, sex, age, marital status, disability, public assistance status or sexual orientation.

LIFE SCIENCES RESEARCH FOUNDATION (LSRF)

Lewis Thomas Laboratories, Princeton University, Washington Road, Princeton, NJ, 08544, United States of America
Tel: (1) 609 258 3551
Email: sdirenzo@molbio.princeton.edu
Website: www.lsrf.org
Contact: Assistant Director

The Life Sciences Research Foundation (LSRF) solicits monies from industry, foundations and individuals to support postdoctoral fellowships in the life sciences. The LSRF recognizes that discoveries and the application of innovations in biology for the public's good will depend upon the training and support of the highest quality young scientists in the very best research environments. The LSRF awards fellowships across the spectrum of life sciences: biochemistry, cell, developmental, molecular, plant, structural, organismic population and evolutionary biology, endocrinology, immunology, microbiology, neurobiology, physiology and virology.

LSRF 3-Year Postdoctoral Fellowships

Subjects: Biological and life sciences.
Purpose: To offer research support for aspiring scientists.
Eligibility: Open to researchers of any nationality, who are graduates of medical or graduate schools in the biological sciences and who hold an MD or PhD degree. Awards will be based solely on the quality of the individual applicant's previous accomplishments and on the merit of the proposal for postdoctoral research.
Level of Study: Postdoctorate
Type: Fellowship
Value: US$50,000 per year. The salary scale begins at US$30,000 for a 1st-year postdoctoral Fellow and a 5 per cent raise thereafter. The Fellow will control expenditure of the remainder. It can be used for fringe benefits, travel to the host institution, travel to visit the sponsor

and to the LSRF annual meeting. However, its main purpose is to support the Fellow's research expenses
Length of Study: 3 years
Frequency: Annual
Study Establishment: Appropriate research institutions
No. of awards offered: 16–18
Application Procedure: Electronic submission only. See website.
Closing Date: October 1st
Funding: Private
No. of awards given last year: 16
No. of applicants last year: 820
Additional Information: LSRF Fellows must carry out their research at non-profit institutions. The fellowship cannot be used to support research that has any patent commitment or other kind of agreement with a commercial profit-making company.

LIGHT WORK

316 Waverly Avenue, Syracuse, NY 13244,
United States of America
Tel: (1) 315 443 1300
Fax: (1) 315 443 9516
Email: jjhoone@syr.edu
Website: www.lightwork.org
Contact: Jessica Heckman

Light Work is an artist-run space that focuses on providing direct support for artists working in photography through its Artist-in-Residence Program, exhibitions, publications, and online permanent collection.

Light Work Artist-in-Residence Program

Subjects: Photography and digital imaging.
Purpose: To support and encourage the production of new work by emerging and mid-career artists.
Eligibility: Open to artists of any nationality working in photography with experience and demonstrable, serious intent in the field. Students are not eligible.
Level of Study: Professional development
Type: Residency
Value: US$2,000 stipend plus a darkroom and apartment
Length of Study: 1 month, non-renewable
Frequency: Annual
Country of Study: United States of America
No. of awards offered: 12–15
Application Procedure: Applicants must send a letter of intent describing in general terms the project or type work they would like to accomplish while in residence. In addition, 20 slides of work or proof prints, a curriculum vitae, and a short statement about the work must be included with a stamped addressed envelope for the return of materials. There are no application forms.
Closing Date: Applications are accepted at any time
Funding: Government, private
No. of awards given last year: 11
No. of applicants last year: 300
Additional Information: Participants in the residency program are expected to use their month to pursue their own projects: photographing in the area, printing for a specific project or book, etc. Artists are not obligated to teach at our facility, though we hope that the artists are friendly and accessible to local artists. Work produced by the Artists-in-Residence will also be published in Light Work's publication *Contact Sheet*.

THE LIONEL MURPHY FOUNDATION

GPO Box 4545, Sydney, NS4 1044, Australia
Tel: (61) 9223 5151
Fax: (61) 9223 5267
Website: www.lionelmurphy.anu.edu

The Lionel Murphy Foundation was established in 1986 to provide a permanent institution and provide postgraduates scholarship opportunities for the study of law and/or science.

The Lionel Murphy Australian Postgraduate Scholarships

Subjects: All subjects.
Purpose: To support candidates who wish to study further.
Eligibility: Open to Australian Citizens.
Level of Study: Postgraduate
Type: Scholarship
Value: Australian $15,000
Length of Study: 1 year
Frequency: Annual
Study Establishment: Australian tertiary institution
Country of Study: Australia
No. of awards offered: Varies
Application Procedure: See the website.
Closing Date: September 1st

The Lionel Murphy Overseas Postgraduate Scholarships

Subjects: All subjects.
Eligibility: Open to Australian citizens.
Level of Study: Postgraduate
Type: Scholarship
Value: Australian $30,000
Frequency: Annual
Application Procedure: A completed application form must be submitted.
Closing Date: September 1st

THE LISTER INSTITUTE OF PREVENTIVE MEDICINE

The White House, 70 High Road, Bushey Heath,
Hertfordshire, WD23 1GG, England
Tel: (44) 20 8421 8808
Fax: (44) 20 8421 8818
Email: secretary@lister-institute.org.uk
Website: www.lister-institute.org.uk
Contact: Mr Keith Cowey, Secretary

The Lister Institute of Preventive Medicine, originally founded in 1891, operates as a medical research charity whose sole function is to award research prizes to young clinical and non-clinical scientists working in the biological and biomedical sciences. The prizes are awarded on the basis of the quality of the proposed research and its potential implications.

Lister Institute Research Prizes

Subjects: Biomedical and biological science.
Purpose: To promote biomedical excellence in the United Kingdom through the support of postdoctoral scientific research into the causes and prevention of disease in man, thereby enhancing the state of public health.
Eligibility: Open to residents of the United Kingdom who have obtained a PhD, DPhil, MD or MBBCh, with membership of the Royal College of Physicians. Candidates must have a minimum of 3 and a maximum of 10 years postgraduate research experience. Applicants must have guaranteed support for the period of the award. The bulk of the work should be United Kingdom-based.
Level of Study: Postdoctorate, research
Type: Research prize
Value: UK £150,000 to be spent in support of the recipient's research for a period of 3 years. The only restriction is 'no personal salaries'
Length of Study: 3 years
Frequency: Annual
Study Establishment: An employing United Kingdom university, research institute unit, hospital or charity laboratory
Country of Study: United Kingdom
No. of awards offered: 2–3
Application Procedure: Applicants must complete and submit an application form, curriculum vitae and two letters of reference.
Closing Date: The end of the second week in January
Funding: Private
Contributor: Investment income
No. of awards given last year: New scheme

Additional Information: Research topics are of the applicant's own choosing, but are primarily laboratory-based and targeted at generating understanding and underpinning knowledge through fundamental research. Epidemiological, bioinformatics and small clinical projects may also be considered but not social research. Projects are assessed on scientific merit and potential. The awards are personal and are transferable within the United Kingdom.

THE LONDON CHAMBER OF COMMERCE AND INDUSTRY EXAMINATIONS BOARD (LCCIEB)

Athena House, 112 Station Road, Sidcup, Kent, DA15 7BJ, England
Tel: (44) 20 8302 0261
Fax: (44) 20 8309 1473
Email: custserv@iccieb.org.uk
Website: www.lccieb.com
Contact: Ms Valerie Brasier

The London Chamber of Commerce and Industry Examinations Board (LCCIEB) is a leading international awarding body for business, information technology, secretarial, financial and marketing qualifications. Established over a century ago, the Board is active today in more than 125 countries worldwide.

LCCIEB Examinations Board Scholarships

Subjects: Business studies, marketing or finance.
Purpose: To award scholarships to qualified candidates wishing to take higher level qualifications or desiring to pursue LCCIEB qualifications.
Eligibility: Open to suitable candidates of any nationality. Candidates must have passed at least one LCCIEB qualification.
Level of Study: Unrestricted
Type: Scholarship
Value: Varies according to student requirements, but do not usually exceed UK £500 per application
Length of Study: Unrestricted
Frequency: Annual
Study Establishment: Unrestricted, but preference is normally given to candidates undertaking LCCIEB qualifications at LCCIEB registered training centres
Country of Study: Any country
Application Procedure: Applicants must complete an application form subject to recommendation from a registered LCCIEB centre. The LCCIEB centre must process the application on the applicant's behalf. Application forms can be downloaded from the website or by writing to Debbie Davis at the address given below.
Closing Date: Unrestricted
Funding: Private
Contributor: London Chamber of Commerce and Industry Commercial Education Trust
No. of awards given last year: 20
No. of applicants last year: 50

For further information contact:

LCCI CET, The Old School, Holly Walk Leamington SPA, Warwickshire, CV32 4GL
Tel: 19 2645 8600
Contact: Debbie Davis

LONDON METROPOLITAN UNIVERSITY

International Office, 166-220 Holloway Road, London, N7 8DB, United Kingdom
Tel: (44) (0) 20 7133 3317
Fax: (44) (0) 20 7133 2240
Email: international@londonmet.ac.uk
Website: www.londonmet.ac.uk

London Metropolitan University is one of Britain's largest universities, which offers a wide variety of courses in a huge range of subject areas. The University aims to provide education and training that will help students to achieve their potential and London to succeed us a world city.

BBC World Service/London Metropolitan University Scholarship

Subjects: Mass communication.
Purpose: To provide support to students from commonwealth of Independent States in the field of communication and to enable them to gain practical experience while studying.
Eligibility: Open to students from the commonwealth of Independent States (former Soviet States) who have been given an offer to study at London Metropolitan University in Mass communication.
Level of Study: Postgraduate
Type: Scholarship
Frequency: Annual
Study Establishment: London Metropolitan University
Country of Study: United Kingdom
No. of awards offered: 1
Application Procedure: A completed scholarship application together with all accompanying documentation and references should be submitted.
Closing Date: May 31st
Contributor: BBC and London Metropolitan University

For further information contact:

Scholarship office, 133 whitechapel High St., London, E1 7QA, United Kingdom

Cannon Collins Scholarship

Subjects: Public administration.
Purpose: To provide financial support and accommodation to international students in the centre of London.
Eligibility: Open to nationals of Botswana, Lesotho, Malawi, Mozambique, Namibia, South Africa, Zambia and Zimbabwe.
Level of Study: Postgraduate
Type: Scholarship
Value: Full-fee or half-fee waiver and support in the form of stipend, fares and books
Frequency: Annual
Study Establishment: London Metropolitan University
Country of Study: United Kingdom
Application Procedure: Application should be sent to the Canon Collins Trust and the Trust will forward it to the university.
Closing Date: March 15th
Funding: Trusts
Contributor: Cannon Collins Educational Trust and Department of Applied Social Sciences

For further information contact:

Canon Collins Educational Trust for Southern Africa, PO Box 34692, Groote Schuur, 7937 Cape Town, South Africa

The Chevening Scheme

Subjects: All subjects.
Purpose: To provide financial assistance to students from over 150 countries to study in the UK.
Eligibility: Open to all students with academic excellence.
Level of Study: Postgraduate
Type: Scholarship
Value: Tuition fees
Frequency: Annual
Country of Study: United Kingdom
Application Procedure: Application form and further details available on the website www.britishcouncil.org
Closing Date: End of November
Funding: Government
Contributor: UK Governments Foreign and Commonwealth Office (FCO) and Department for International Development (DFID)

ISH/London Metropolitan Scholarship Scheme

Subjects: All subjects.
Purpose: To support international students in the centre of London.

Eligibility: Open to students from Afghanistan, Algeria, Armenia, Botswana, Cameroon, Cuba, Democratic people's Republic of Korea, East Timor, Gambia, Iran, Libya, Nepal, Tanzania, Tibet, Uganda, Uzbekistan, Vietnam and Zimbabwe.
Level of Study: Postgraduate
Type: Scholarship
Value: Free tuition and accommodation
Length of Study: 1–2 years
Frequency: Annual
Study Establishment: London Metropolitan University
Country of Study: United Kingdom
Application Procedure: See the website.
Closing Date: May 31st
Contributor: International Students House (ISH) and London Metropolitan University

For further information contact:

Scholarship Section, c/o Student Recruitment Services, London Metropolitan, City Campus, 133 whitechapel High Street, London, E1 7QA, United Kingdom

The Katrina Mihaere Scholarship

Subjects: Sports Management.
Purpose: To honour the memory of Katrina Mihaere, a former London Metropolitan Women's Tennis team member.
Eligibility: Open to all women tennis players with an excellent track record in Women's sports.
Level of Study: Postgraduate
Type: Scholarship
Value: Full tuition and accommodation
Frequency: Annual
Study Establishment: London Metropolitan University
Country of Study: United Kingdom
Application Procedure: See the website.

For further information contact:

Email: i.jennings@londonmet.ac.uk
Contact: Ian Jennings, Sports Manager

The ODASS Scheme

Subjects: All subjects.
Purpose: To financially assist students of high academic merit from developing Commonwealth countries.
Eligibility: Open to students from developing Commonwealth.
Level of Study: Postgraduate
Type: Scholarship
Value: Full tuition fees and living allowance
Frequency: Annual
Study Establishment: London Metropolitan Society
Country of Study: United Kingdom
Application Procedure: See the website.
Funding: Government
Contributor: British Government's Aid Programme

For further information contact:

The Association of Commonwealth universities, 36 Gordon Square, London, WC1H OPF
Email: info@acu.ac.uk

Savoy Educational Trust Scholarships

Subjects: Hospitality and Tourism.
Purpose: To financially assist students wishing to pursue students in the field of Hospitality and Tourism.
Eligibility: Open to applicants from any country in the world.
Level of Study: Postgraduate
Type: Bursary
Value: UK £3,000
Frequency: Annual
Study Establishment: London Metropolitan University
Country of Study: United Kingdom
No. of awards offered: 1
Application Procedure: Contact the scholarship department at the university.
Closing Date: July 31st
Funding: Trusts
Contributor: Savoy Educational Trust

For further information contact:

Scholarship Department, c/o Student Recruitment Services, Room 210, London Metropolitan University, London, E1 7NT, United Kingdom

LONDON STRING QUARTET FOUNDATION

8 Woodlands Road, Romford, London, RM1 4HD, England
Tel: (44) 1708 761423
Fax: (44) 1708 761423
Email: info@playquartet.com
Website: www.playquartetet.com
Contact: General Manager

The London String Quartet Foundation is a registered charity whose purpose is to promote the discovery and development of talent and audiences for the string quartet. The main activity of the Foundation is organizing the triennial London International String Quartet Competition.

London International String Quartet Competition

Subjects: Musical performance.
Purpose: To encourage young string quartets to develop further on the world stage and take part in this prestigious competition.
Eligibility: There are no restrictions except that each musician in the quartet must be under 35 years of age on April 9th.
Level of Study: Unrestricted
Type: Award
Value: Prizes total UK £27,500, and are split into five different awards of differing amounts and a menu of development prizes for three prize winners. Concerts are also organized for the first three prize winners
Frequency: Every 3 years
Country of Study: Any country
No. of awards offered: 7
Application Procedure: Applicants must complete an application form, available on the website.
Closing Date: September 1st in the year preceding the award
Funding: Foundation, private, individuals, trusts, commercial

LORD DOWDING FUND FOR HUMANE RESEARCH

261 Goldhawk Road, London, W12 9PE, England
Tel: (44) 20 8846 9777
Fax: (44) 20 8846 9712
Email: info@ldf.org.uk
Website: www.ldf.org.uk
Contact: Head of Research

The Lord Dowding Fund for Humane Research is a department of the National Anti-Vivisection Society. It aims to support, sponsor and fund better methods of research for testing products and curing disease that work towards replacing the use of laboratory animals.

Lord Dowding Fund for Humane Research

Subjects: Medical research, veterinary science, toxicology and teaching. A wide range of techniques are supported, including cell, tissue or organ culture, computer simulation mathematical modelling, quantum pharmacology chemical analysis, epidemiology, genetic or tissue engineering, virology and pain research.
Purpose: To support research aimed at replacing the use of laboratory animals.
Eligibility: Applications on behalf of junior scientists must be made by a senior scientist, eg. a PhD supervisor or Head of Research. Projects

must not involve the use of animals and applicants must not hold a Home Office licence.
Level of Study: Research
Type: Award
Value: Up to UK £75,000
Length of Study: Up to 3 years
Frequency: Dependent on funds available
Study Establishment: Academic departments or hospitals
Country of Study: United Kingdom
No. of awards offered: Varies
Application Procedure: Applicants must complete an application form and submit a project proposal. An information pack can be requested from the organization, or is available by visiting the website. Applications are peer-reviewed.
Closing Date: February 1st, May 1st, August 1st and November 1st each year
Funding: Private
Contributor: Private subscribers, legacies and fund raising events
No. of awards given last year: 3
No. of applicants last year: 19

LOREN L ZACHARY SOCIETY FOR THE PERFORMING ARTS

2250 Gloaming Way, Beverly Hills, CA, 90210,
United States of America
Tel: (1) 310 276 2731
Fax: (1) 310 275 8245
Contact: Mrs Nedra Zachary, Director, National Vocal Competition

The Loren L Zachary Society for the Performing Arts was founded in 1972 by the late Dr Loren L Zachary and Nedra Zachary. The purpose of the organization is to help further the careers of young opera singers by providing financial assistance. The National Vocal Competition, now in its 33rd year, has helped over 80 singers to embark on international careers.

Loren L Zachary Society National Vocal Competition for Young Opera Singers

Subjects: Operatic singing.
Purpose: To assist in the development of the careers of young opera singers through competitive auditions and monetary awards.
Eligibility: Open to female singers between 21–33 years of age and male singers between 21–35 years of age who have completed operatic training and are fully prepared to pursue professional operatic stage careers. Applicants must reside in the United States of America, Mexico or Canada.
Level of Study: Professional development
Type: Competition
Value: US$10,000 for the top winner. A round-trip flight to Europe for opera-auditioning purposes may be awarded to a finalist. Approx. US$50,000 is distributed among the finalists and the minimum award is US$1,000
Frequency: Annual
Country of Study: Any country
No. of awards offered: 10
Application Procedure: Applicants must complete an application form accompanied by a proof of age and an application fee of US$35. For application forms and exact dates, singers should send a stamped addressed business-sized envelope to the Society in November. Faxed requests will not be accepted. Applications are not available by e-mail or website.
Closing Date: The deadline for the New York preliminary auditions is in January and the Los Angeles deadline is in March
Funding: Individuals, private
No. of awards given last year: 10
No. of applicants last year: 200
Additional Information: Applicants must be present at all phases of the auditions. Recordings are not acceptable. Preliminary and semifinal auditions take place in New York in February, and in Los Angeles in April. The grand finals and awards distribution occurs on May 21st 2006 in Los Angeles.

LOUGHBOROUGH UNIVERSITY

Leicestershire, LE11 3TU, United Kingdom
Tel: (44) 1509 263171
Email: international.office@loughboro.ac.uk
Website: www.lboro.ac.uk
Contact: The International Office

With 3,000 staff and 12,000 students Loughbrough, with its impressive 410 acre campus, is one of the largest university's in the UK. Our mission is to increase knowledge through research, provide the highest quality of educational experience and the widest opportunities for students, advance industry and the profession, and benefit society.

Business School Scholarships

Subjects: Finance, International and Marketing Management.
Level of Study: Postgraduate
Type: Scholarship
Value: UK £1,000
Length of Study: 1 year
Frequency: Annual
Study Establishment: Loughborough University
Country of Study: United Kingdom
No. of awards offered: 20
Application Procedure: See website.

For further information contact:

Email: msc.management@lboro.ac.uk

Design and Technology Scholarships

Subjects: Design and Technology.
Level of Study: Postgraduate
Type: Scholarship
Value: All tuition fees and agreed maintenance costs
Frequency: Annual
Study Establishment: Loughborough University
Country of Study: United Kingdom
Application Procedure: See website.

For further information contact:

Email: r.i.campbell@lboro.ac.uk

Eli Lilly Scholarship

Subjects: Chemistry.
Level of Study: Postgraduate
Type: Scholarship
Value: UK £1,000
Length of Study: 1 year
Frequency: Annual
Study Establishment: Loughborough University
Country of Study: United Kingdom
No. of awards offered: 1
Application Procedure: See website.

For further information contact:

Email: l.e.child@lboro.ac.uk

ESPRC Studentships

Subjects: Chemistry.
Level of Study: Postgraduate
Type: Studentship
Value: All tuition fees and maintenance grant up to UK £6,000 p.a.
Length of Study: 1 year
Frequency: Annual
Study Establishment: Loughborough University
Country of Study: United Kingdom
No. of awards offered: 8
Application Procedure: See website.
Funding: Government
Contributor: EPSRC

For further information contact:

Email: l.e.child@lboro.ac.uk

Industrial Design Studentship

Subjects: Industrial Design.
Eligibility: Open to British nationals, resident in UK, intending to make a career in British Industry normally aged 21–24, but older candidates may apply.
Level of Study: Doctorate
Type: Studentship
Value: All tuition fees, stipend of UK £9,000 p.a., allowance of UK £850 p.a. for materials and agreed travel costs
Length of Study: 1–3 years
Frequency: Annual
Study Establishment: Loughborough University
Country of Study: United Kingdom
Application Procedure: See website.
Funding: Foundation
Contributor: Royal Commission for the Exhibition of 1851

For further information contact:

Email: royalcom1851@imperial.ac.uk

IPTME (Materials) Scholarships

Subjects: Polymer Technology.
Level of Study: Postgraduate
Type: Scholarship
Value: All tuition fees
Length of Study: 1 year
Frequency: Annual
Study Establishment: Loughborough University
Country of Study: United Kingdom
No. of awards offered: 6
Application Procedure: See website.
Funding: Foundation
Contributor: Institute of Polymer Technology and Materials Engineering

For further information contact:

Email: iptme@lboro.ac.uk

Jean Scott Scholarships

Level of Study: Postgraduate
Type: Scholarship
Value: A maximum of US$5,000
Frequency: Annual
Study Establishment: Loughborough University
Country of Study: United Kingdom
No. of awards offered: 2
Application Procedure: See website.

For further information contact:

Email: msc.economics@lboro.ac.uk

Loughborough Sports Scholarships

Subjects: Athletics, Cricket, Football, Golf, Hockey, Rugby, Swimming, Tennis and Triathlon.
Purpose: To support elite athletes.
Type: Scholarship
Value: An annual UK £1,000 stipend, first class coaching, sports massage, expert nutritional advice and all
Frequency: Annual
Study Establishment: Loughborough University
Country of Study: United Kingdom
Application Procedure: See website.

For further information contact:

Email: sports-scholars@lboro.ac.uk

Mathematical Sciences Scholarship

Subjects: Industrial Mathematical Modelling.
Level of Study: Postgraduate
Type: Scholarship
Value: All tuition fees
Length of Study: 1–3 years
Frequency: Annual
Study Establishment: Loughborough University
Country of Study: United Kingdom
No. of awards offered: 3
Application Procedure: See website.

For further information contact:

Email: maths-admissions@lboro.ac.uk

MBA Scholarships

Subjects: Business Management.
Level of Study: MBA
Type: Scholarship
Value: UK £500 annual stipend
Length of Study: 1–2 years
Frequency: Annual
Study Establishment: Loughborough University
Country of Study: United Kingdom
No. of awards offered: 10
Application Procedure: See website.

For further information contact:

Email: exec.mba@lboro.ac.uk

Politics Scholarships

Subjects: Politics, International relations and European Studies.
Level of Study: Postgraduate
Type: Scholarship
Value: UK £1,000
Frequency: Annual
Study Establishment: Loughborough University
Country of Study: United Kingdom
Application Procedure: See website.

School of Art and Design Scholarships

Subjects: Art and Design.
Level of Study: Postgraduate
Type: Scholarship
Value: All UK/EU tuition fees
Length of Study: 1–3 years
Frequency: Annual
Study Establishment: Loughborough University
Country of Study: United Kingdom
No. of awards offered: 6
Application Procedure: See website.

For further information contact:

Email: p.sawdon@lboro.ac.uk

LOWE SYNDROME ASSOCIATION (LSA)

222 Lincoln Street, West Lafayette, IA, 47906-2732,
United States of America
Tel: (1) 765 743 3634
Email: info@lowesyndrome.org
Website: www.lowesyndrome.org
Contact: Ms Kaye McSpadden, Director of Public & Scientific Affairs

The Lowe Syndrome Association (LSA) is an international non-profit organization made up of families, friends and professionals dedicated to helping children with Lowe Syndrome and their families. Its main purposes are to foster communication among families, provide information and support research.

LSA Medical Research Grant

Subjects: Understanding and treatment of Lowe Syndrome.
Purpose: To support research projects that will lead to a better understanding of the metabolic basis of Lowe Syndrome, better treatments of the major complications of the disease and the prevention of and/or a cure for it.
Eligibility: Open to researchers who are affiliated with a non-profit institution.

Level of Study: Unrestricted
Type: Grant
Value: Varies, approx. US$30,000
Length of Study: 1 year
Frequency: Dependent on funds available
No. of awards offered: Varies
Application Procedure: Applicants must submit their application in writing. Specific instructions are available in the grant proposal guidelines document.
Closing Date: Varies
Funding: Private
Contributor: Members of the LSA and fund-raising events
No. of awards given last year: 1
No. of applicants last year: 1

THE MACDOWELL COLONY

100 High Street, Peterborough, NH, 03458, United States of America
Tel: (1) 603 924 3886
Fax: (1) 603 924 9142
Email: info@macdowellcolony.org, admissions@macdowellcolony.org
Website: www.macdowellcolony.org
Contact: Ms Courtney Bethel, Director

The MacDowell Colony was founded in 1907 to provide creative artists with uninterrupted time and seclusion to work and enjoy the experience of living in a community with gifted artists. Residencies are up to eight weeks for writers, and playwrights, composers, film and video makers, visual artists, architects and interdisciplinary artists. Artists in residence receive room, board and the exclusive use of a studio. There are no residency fees. A travel grant and limited writer's aid grant are available to artists in residence.

MacDowell Colony Residencies

Subjects: Creative writing, visual arts, musical composition, film and video making, architecture and interdisciplinary arts, playwriting.
Purpose: To provide a place where creative artists can take advantage of uninterrupted work time and seclusion in which to work and enjoy the experience of living in a community of gifted artists.
Eligibility: Open to established and emerging artists in the fields specified.
Level of Study: Unrestricted
Type: Residency
Value: Up to US$1,000 for writers in need of financial assistance, plus limited travel grants for any artist based on need
Length of Study: Usually 4 weeks
Frequency: Annual, 3 deadlines annually
Study Establishment: The Colony
Country of Study: United States of America
No. of awards offered: A total of 32 studios are available during each application period for individual residencies
Application Procedure: Applicants must write, telephone or refer to the website for information and an application form.
Closing Date: Summer (June 1st–September 30th), Autumn (October–January 31st), Winter-Spring (February 1st–May 31st)
Funding: Private
No. of awards given last year: 240 residencies
No. of applicants last year: 1400+
Additional Information: The studios are offered for the independent pursuit of the applicant's art. No workshops or courses are given and there are no stipends. Requests for information should be accompanied by a stamped addressed envelope.

MACKENZIE KING SCHOLARSHIP SELECTION COMMITTEE

Faculty of Law, University of British Columbia, 1822 East Mall, Vancouver, BC, V6T 1Z1, Canada
Tel: (1) 604 822 4564
Fax: (1) 604 822 8108
Email: blom@law.ubc.ca
Website: www.mkingscholarships.ca
Contact: Professor Joost Blom

The Mackenzie King Scholarship Trust consists of two funds established under the will of the Right Honourable William Lyon Mackenzie King (1874–1950). Both scholarships are to support postgraduate study for graduates of Canadian universities.

Mackenzie King Open Scholarship

Subjects: All subjects.
Eligibility: Open to graduates of any Canadian university. Applicants should be persons of unusual worth or promise as awards are determined on the basis of academic achievement, personal qualities and demonstrated aptitudes. Consideration is also given to the applicant's proposed programme of postgraduate study.
Level of Study: Postgraduate
Type: Scholarship
Value: Canadian $9,000
Length of Study: 1 year, non-renewable
Frequency: Annual
Country of Study: Any country
No. of awards offered: 1
Application Procedure: Applicants must complete an application form available from the Faculty of Graduate Studies at each Canadian university and from the website. Applications must be submitted to the Dean of Graduate Studies at the Canadian university from which the candidate most recently graduated.
Closing Date: February 1st
Funding: Private
No. of awards given last year: 1

Mackenzie King Travelling Scholarship

Subjects: International or industrial relations, including international aspects of law, history, politics and economics.
Purpose: To give Canadian students the opportunity to broaden their outlook and sympathies and to contribute in some measure to the understanding of the problems and policies of other countries.
Eligibility: Open to graduates of any Canadian university who propose to engage in postgraduate studies in the given fields in the United States of America or the United Kingdom.
Level of Study: Postgraduate
Type: Scholarship
Value: Canadian $9,000
Length of Study: 1 year, non-renewable
Frequency: Annual
Study Establishment: Suitable institutions
Country of Study: United Kingdom or United States of America
No. of awards offered: 4
Application Procedure: Applicants must complete an application form available from the Faculty of Graduate Studies at each Canadian university or from the website. Applications must be submitted to the Dean of Graduate Studies at the Canadian university from which the candidate most recently graduated.
Closing Date: February 1st
Funding: Private
No. of awards given last year: 4

MAKING MUSIC, THE NATIONAL FEDERATION OF MUSIC SOCIETIES (NFMS)

7-15 Rosebery Avenue, London, EC1R 4SP, England
Tel: (44) 87 0903 3780
Fax: (44) 87 0903 3785
Email: info@makingmusic.org.uk
Website: www.makingmusic.org.uk
Contact: Ms Kate Fearnley, Award Administrator

Making Music, The National Federation of Music Societies (NFMS), is the leading umbrella group for the voluntary and semi-professional music sector. Making Music represents and supports over 2,000 music groups throughout the United Kingdom. Making Music groups also promote over 8,000 performances, spend just over UK £8.9 million on professional artists per year and perform to audiences of around 1.5 million.

Philip and Dorothy Green Award for Young Concert Artists in Association with Making Music

Subjects: Music.
Purpose: To support young musicians at the start of their professional careers.
Eligibility: Open to singers under 30 years of age and instrumentalists under 28 years of age. All applicants must be European Community citizens normally resident within the United Kingdom.
Level of Study: Professional development
Type: Award
Value: Up to 50 engagements with affiliated societies throughout the United Kingdom and Northern Ireland, shared between the winners
Frequency: Annual
No. of awards offered: 4–5
Application Procedure: Applicants must submit a completed application form with their curriculum vitae.
Closing Date: As advertised in the national press and on the website
Funding: Private
No. of awards given last year: 5
No. of applicants last year: 60+

MANHATTAN SCHOOL OF MUSIC (MSM)

120 Claremont Avenue, New York, NY, 10027, United States of America
Tel: (1) 212 749 2802 ext 4463
Fax: (1) 212 749 3025
Website: www.msmnyc.edu
Contact: Ms Amy A Anderson, Director of Financial Aid

The Manhattan School of Music (MSM) is a major national and international force in the education of professional musicians. It is the largest private conservatory in the nation offering both classical and jazz training.

MSM Scholarships

Subjects: Music.
Purpose: To recognize outstanding talent, achievements and performance.
Eligibility: Open to all students who demonstrate, through performance, that they have attained excellence in music and have the capacity for further development. Students must demonstrate financial need and provide the necessary income documents in order to qualify. All necessary instructions can be found on our website: www.msmnyc.edu
Level of Study: Doctorate, postgraduate, graduate
Type: Scholarship
Value: Tuition expenses only, ranging from US$1,000 to the full tuition costs, payable in equal instalments by semester
Length of Study: 1 academic year, renewable for a total of 2 years
Frequency: Annual
Study Establishment: MSM
Country of Study: United States of America
No. of awards offered: Approx. 375
Application Procedure: Applicants who are citizens of the United States of America and permanent residents must submit a completed PROFILE and FAFSA form. International students must submit an in-house international application form.
Closing Date: December 1st for March auditions and March 1st for May auditions
Funding: Private
No. of awards given last year: 404
No. of applicants last year: 2300

MANITOBA LIBRARY ASSOCIATION (MLA)

606-100 Arthur Street, Winnipeg MB, R3B 1H3, Canada
Tel: (1) 204 943 4567
Fax: (1) 204 942 1555
Email: mla@uwinnipeg.ca
Website: www.mla.mb.ca

The Manitoba Association (MLA) is a provincial, voluntary, non-incorporated association that provides leadership in the promotion, development and support of library and information services in Manitoba.

Jean Thorunn Law Scholarship

Subjects: Library science.
Purpose: To encourage careers in library and information science.
Eligibility: Open to applicants who have completed 12 months of library employment in Manitoba.
Level of Study: Postgraduate
Type: Scholarship
Value: Up to Canadian $3,000
Frequency: Annual
Country of Study: Canada
Application Procedure: A completed application form, which is available online, must be sent.
Closing Date: June 15th

John Edwin Bissett Scholarship

Subjects: Library science.
Purpose: To encourage careers in library and information science.
Eligibility: Open to candidates attending an accredited library school.
Type: Scholarship
Value: Up to Canadian $6,500
Frequency: Annual
Country of Study: Canada
Application Procedure: See the website.
Closing Date: June 15th

The Manitoba Library Service Award

Subjects: Library science.
Purpose: To honour people who have made an important contribution to the development of libraries and library services.
Level of Study: Postgraduate
Type: Award
Frequency: Annual
Country of Study: Canada
Application Procedure: See the website.
Closing Date: April
Contributor: Manitoba Library Endowment Fund

MARINE CORPS HISTORICAL CENTER

Marine Corps Historical Division, 3079 Moreell Avenue, Quantico, Virginia, 22134, United States of America
Tel: (1) 202 433 4244
Fax: (1) 202 433 7265
Website: www.usmc.mil
Contact: Attn: Coordinator Grants and Fellowships

The Marine Corps Historical Center houses the History and Museums Divisions. The History Division provides reference services to the public and government agencies, maintains the Marine Corps' archives and oral history collection and produces official histories of Marine activities, units and bases. The Museums Division maintains the artefact and personal papers collection, and operates the Marine Corps Museum and the Air-Ground Museum.

General Lemed C. Shepherd, Jr. Memorial Dissertation Fellowship

Subjects: U.S. military and naval history, as well as history and history-based studies in the social and behavioural sciences, with a direct relationship to the history of the United States Marine Corps.
Purpose: To fund a doctoral dissertation pertinent to Marine Corps history.
Eligibility: Awards are based on merit, without regard to race, creed, color, or gender subject to a screening by the Director of Marine Corps History.
Level of Study: Postdoctorate
Type: Fellowship
Value: US$10,000
Country of Study: United States of America

No. of awards offered: 1
Closing Date: May 1st
Funding: Foundation
Contributor: The Marine Corps Heritage Foundation

Marine Corps Historical Center College Internships

Subjects: History.
Purpose: To offer opportunities for college students to participate on a professional level in the Marine Corps Historical Center's many activities. The programme aims to give promising and talented student interns a chance to earn college credits while gaining meaningful experience in fields in which they might choose to seek employment after school or pursue a vocational interest.
Eligibility: Applicants must be registered students at a college or university that will grant academic credit for work experience as interns in subject areas related to the student's course of study. While there are no restrictions on individuals applying for intern positions, it has been found that mature and academically superior students are most successful. The agreement of the academic institution to the internship for credit is essential.
Level of Study: Postgraduate
Type: Internship
Value: A small grant of daily expense money is provided. Any other costs of the internship must be made by the student
Frequency: Annual
Study Establishment: Internships are served either at the Marine Corps Historical Center or the Marine Corps Air Ground Museum, Marine Corps Development and Education Command in Quantico, Virginia
Country of Study: United States of America
No. of awards offered: Varies
Application Procedure: Applicants must contact the Chief Historian at the Center for further details.
Closing Date: Please contact the organization
Funding: Foundation, private
Contributor: The Marine Corps Heritage Foundation

Marine Corps Historical Center Dissertation Fellowships

Subjects: Topics in United States of America military and naval history, as well as history and history-based studies in the social and behavioural sciences with a direct relationship to the United States Marine Corps.
Purpose: To award a qualified graduate student working on a doctoral dissertation relevant to Marine Corps history.
Eligibility: Applicants must be citizens of the United States of America, enrolled in a recognized graduate school, must have completed, by September, all requirements for the doctoral degree except the dissertation and have an approved dissertation topic. A fellowship will not be awarded to an applicant who has held or accepted an equivalent fellowship from any other Department of Defence agency; however, recipients of the Marine Corps' Master's Thesis Fellowships may apply.
Level of Study: Doctorate
Type: Fellowship
Value: US$10,000
Frequency: Annual
Country of Study: United States of America
No. of awards offered: 1
Application Procedure: Applicants must complete an application form, available from the Chairman of the History Department of the applicant's university, or by writing to the Director of the Marine Corps History and Museums at the Center. The applicant is responsible for insuring that all required documentation is mailed before the closing date.
Closing Date: May 1st
Funding: Foundation, private
Contributor: The Marine Corps Heritage Foundation
No. of awards given last year: 1
No. of applicants last year: 1
Additional Information: Evaluation of applicants is on the basis of academic achievements, faculty recommendations and demonstrated research and writing ability. The nature of the topic must be of benefit to the study and understanding of Marine Corps history. All awards will be based on merit, without regard to race, creed, colour or sex. The Director of Marine Corps History and Museums will notify all applicants individually of the application committee's decision not later than mid-July.

Marine Corps Historical Center Master's Thesis Fellowships

Subjects: Topics in United States of America military and naval history, as well as history and history-based studies in the social and behavioural sciences, with a direct relationship to the United States Marine Corps. This programme gives preference to projects covering the pre-1975 period where records are declassified or can be most readily declassified and made available to scholars.
Purpose: To award a number of fellowships to qualified graduate students working on topics pertinent to Marine Corps history.
Eligibility: Applicants must be actively enrolled in an accredited Master's degree programme that requires a Master's thesis. The competition is limited to citizens or nationals of the United States of America. A fellowship will not be awarded to anyone who has held or accepted an equivalent fellowship from any other Department of Defence agency.
Level of Study: Postgraduate
Type: Fellowship
Value: US$3,500
Length of Study: 1–3 years
Frequency: Annual
Country of Study: United States of America
No. of awards offered: 2
Application Procedure: Applicants must complete an application form, available from the Chairman of the History Department of the applicant's university, or by writing to the Director of the Marine Corps History and Museums, at the Center. The applicant is responsible for insuring that all required documentation is mailed before the closing date.
Closing Date: May 1st
Funding: Foundation, private
Contributor: The Marine Corps Heritage Foundation
No. of awards given last year: 1
No. of applicants last year: 2
Additional Information: The Director of Marine Corps History and Museums will notify all applicants individually of the application committee's decision not later than mid-July.

Marine Corps Historical Center Research Grants

Subjects: Topics in United States of America military and naval history, as well as history and history-based studies in the social and behavioural sciences, with a direct relationship to the United States Marine Corps. This programme gives preference to projects covering the pre-1975 period where records are declassified or can be most readily declassified and made available to scholars.
Purpose: To encourage research.
Eligibility: While the programme concentrates on graduate students, grants are available to other qualified persons. Applicants for grants should have the ability to conduct advanced study in those aspects of American military history and museum activities related to the United States Marine Corps.
Level of Study: Research
Type: Grant
Value: US$400–3,000
Frequency: Annual
Country of Study: United States of America
Application Procedure: Applicants must submit a preliminary application to the Director of Marine Corps History and Museums outlining their qualifications, and either proposing a specific topic or requesting a suggested topic based on their interests and qualifications. If the evaluation of the preliminary application is favourable, the applicant will be asked to make a formal application on a form provided by the Center.
Closing Date: Please contact the organization
Funding: Foundation, private
Contributor: The Marine Corps Heritage Foundation

Michael Beller–Marine Raider Fellowship

Subjects: United States of America military and naval history, as well as history and history-based studies in the social and

behavioural sciences with a direct relationship to the United States Marine Corps.
Purpose: To encourage graduate level and advanced study of the combat contributions of enlisted marines.
Eligibility: The competition is limited to citizens or nationals of the United States of America.
Level of Study: Postgraduate
Type: Fellowship
Value: US$2,500
Length of Study: 1 year
Frequency: Annual
Country of Study: United States of America
No. of awards offered: 1
Application Procedure: Applicants must submit a preliminary application to the Director of Marine Corps History and Museums outlining their qualifications, and either proposing a specific topic or requesting a suggested topic based on their interests and qualifications. If the evaluation of the preliminary application is favourable, the applicant will be asked to make a formal application on a form provided by the Center. The applicant is responsible for insuring that all required documentation is mailed before the closing date.
Closing Date: May 1st
Funding: Foundation, private
Contributor: The Marine Corps Heritage Foundation
Additional Information: The Director of Marine Corps History and Museums will notify all applicants individually of the application committee's decision not later than mid-July.

MARINES' MEMORIAL ASSOCIATION

609 Sutter Street, San Francisco, California, 94102-1027, United States of America
Tel: (1) 673 6672
Fax: (1) 441 3649
Website: www.marineclub.com

The Marines' Memorial Association is a non-profit veterans organization chartered to honor the memory of and commemorate the valor of Marines who have sacrificed in the nation's wars.

The Marine Corps Law Enforcement Foundation Scholarship

Subjects: All subjects.
Purpose: To encourage the spiritual, moral, intellectual and physical development of children through education.
Eligibility: Open to children of active and former MMA members in pursuit of higher education.
Level of Study: Postgraduate
Type: Scholarship
Value: Varies
Length of Study: Renewable
Frequency: Annual
Country of Study: Any country
No. of awards offered: 2
Application Procedure: See the website
Funding: Foundation
Contributor: The Marine Corps Foundation

The Marine Corps Scholarship

Subjects: All subjects.
Purpose: To provide financial assistance to children of active and former members of the US Marines Corps.
Eligibility: Open to children of the MMA members scholastic aptitude, community involvement and civic spirit.
Level of Study: Postgraduate
Type: Scholarship
Value: Varies
Length of Study: Renewable
Frequency: Annual
Country of Study: Any country
No. of awards offered: 4
Application Procedure: See the website
Closing Date: April 15th
Funding: Foundation
Contributor: The Marine Corps Foundation

MARQUETTE UNIVERSITY

PO Box 1881, Milwaukee, WI, 53201-1881, United States of America
Tel: (1) 414 288 7137
Fax: (1) 414 288 1902
Email: mugs@marquette.edu
Website: www.grad.marquette.edu
Contact: Thomas Marek, Student Services Co-ordinator

Marquette University is a private, Jesuit university situated about 100 miles north of Chicago. It is a graduate research institution with 18 doctoral and over 40 Master's and certificate programmes.

Alpha Sigma Nu Graduate Scholarship

Subjects: All subjects.
Purpose: To offer tuition scholarships for members of Alpha Sigma Nu.
Eligibility: Open to 1st-year graduate students who are members of Alpha Sigma Nu.
Level of Study: Graduate
Type: Scholarship
Value: US$10,800
Length of Study: 2 years
Frequency: Annual
Country of Study: United States of America
No. of awards offered: 2
Application Procedure: Applicants must send a letter of application to the Graduate School.
Closing Date: February 15th
Funding: Private
No. of awards given last year: 2

Johnson's Wax Research Fellowship

Subjects: Engineering, chemistry and biology.
Purpose: To provide financial assistance for doctoral students.
Eligibility: Applicants must be admitted to a doctoral programme in engineering, biology or chemistry.
Level of Study: Doctorate
Type: Fellowship
Value: Approx. US$5,500 stipend and a tuition scholarship
Length of Study: 1 year
Frequency: Annual
No. of awards offered: 1
Application Procedure: Qualified applicants will be contacted by their department.
Closing Date: February 15th
Funding: Private
No. of awards given last year: 1
Additional Information: The award is offered to a different programme each year.

Marquette University Graduate Assistantship

Subjects: All subjects.
Purpose: To financially support teaching and research.
Eligibility: Open to full-time Master's and doctoral students.
Level of Study: Graduate
Type: Assistantship
Value: US$11,490 plus an 18-credit tuition scholarship, the value of which is approx. US$22,000
Length of Study: 1 year
Frequency: Annual
No. of awards offered: 289
Application Procedure: Applicants must submit an application to the Graduate School by the deadline. The graduate bulletin or the website should be consulted for further details.
Closing Date: February 15th for Autumn and November 15th for Spring
Funding: Private
Contributor: Marquette University
No. of awards given last year: 289

Marquette University Women's Club Fellowship

Subjects: All subjects.
Purpose: To support students who received their baccalaureate degrees from Marquette University.
Eligibility: Applicants must be admitted to a degree programme and have received a Bachelor's degree from Marquette University.
Level of Study: Graduate
Type: Fellowship
Value: US$2,000 stipend
Length of Study: 1 year
Frequency: Annual
No. of awards offered: 1
Application Procedure: Qualified students will be contacted by their department.
Closing Date: February 15th
Funding: Private
No. of awards given last year: 1
Additional Information: The award is offered to a different graduate programme each year.

Milwaukee Foundation's Frank Rogers Bacon Research Assistantship

Subjects: Electrical and computer engineering.
Purpose: To provide research support for students.
Eligibility: Open to full-time Master's and doctoral students.
Level of Study: Graduate
Type: Fellowship
Value: Up to US$11,490 stipend and possible scholarship
Length of Study: Varies
Frequency: Annual
Country of Study: United States of America
No. of awards offered: Varies depending on funds
Application Procedure: Applicants must contact the Department of Electrical and Computer Engineering at the University.
Closing Date: February 15th
Funding: Private
No. of awards given last year: 7

R A Bournique Memorial Fellowship

Subjects: Chemistry.
Eligibility: Open to graduate students in chemistry.
Level of Study: Graduate
Type: Fellowship
Value: Varies
Length of Study: The Summer
Frequency: Annual
No. of awards offered: 2
Application Procedure: Applicants must contact the Department of Chemistry.
Funding: Private
No. of awards given last year: 2

MARSHALL AID COMMEMORATION COMMISSION

ACU, John Foster House, 36 Gordon Square, London, WC1H 0PF, England
Tel: (44) 20 7380 6700
Fax: (44) 20 7387 2655
Email: info@marshallscholarship.org
Website: www.marshallscholarship.org
Contact: Administrative Assistant

The Marshall Aid Commemoration Commission is responsible for the selection and placement of recipients of Marshall scholarships from the United States of America to the United Kingdom. The first awards were presented in 1954.

Marshall Scholarships

Subjects: All subjects.
Purpose: To provide intellectually distinguished young Americans with the opportunity to study in the United Kingdom, and thus to understand and appreciate the British way of life.
Eligibility: Open to citizens of the United States of America who have graduated with a minimum grade point average of 3.7 or A- from an accredited United States of America college not more than 2 years previously. Recipients are required to take a degree at their United Kingdom university. Preference is given to candidates who combine high academic ability with the capacity to play an active part in the United Kingdom university.
Level of Study: Postgraduate
Type: Scholarship
Value: Approx. UK £19,000 per year, which comprises tuition fees, residence, travel and related costs
Length of Study: 2 academic years, with a possible extension for a third year
Frequency: Annual
Study Establishment: Any suitable institution
Country of Study: United Kingdom
No. of awards offered: 40
Application Procedure: Applicants must submit an application form, university or college endorsement and four references. Information and application forms can be obtained from the British consulate in selected cities. Full details on application procedures can be obtained from the website.
Closing Date: October
Funding: Government
No. of awards given last year: 40
No. of applicants last year: 800

For further information contact:

Cultural Department, British Embassy, 3100 Massachusetts Avenue NW, Washington, DC, 20008, United States of America

British Consulate-General, 33 North Dearborn Street, Chicago, IL, 60602, United States of America

British Consulate-General, 1 Sansome Street, San Francisco, CA, 94104, United States of America

British Consulate-General, 11766 Wiltshire Boulevard, Suite 400, Los Angeles, CA, 90025, United States of America

British Consulate-General, Wells Fayo Plaza, 1000 Louisiana, No 1900, Houston, TX, 77002, United States of America

British Consulate-General, Georgia Pacific Center, Suite 3400, 134 Peachtree Street NE, Atlanta, GA, 30303, United States of America

MARY ROBERTS RINEHART FUND

MSN 3E4, English Department, George Mason University, 4400 University Drive, Fairfax, VA, 22030-4444, United States of America
Tel: (1) 703 993 1180
Email: writing@gmu.edu
Website: www.gmu.edu/departments/writing/rinehart.htm
Contact: Mr William Miller, Director of Graduate Writing Program

The Mary Roberts Rinehart Fund is housed within a public university and was established to support and encourage unpublished writers.

Mary Roberts Rinehart Awards

Subjects: Writing, eg. works of fiction, poetry, biography, autobiography or history with a strong narrative quality.
Purpose: To encourage developing writers who need financial assistance, not otherwise available, to complete works in progress.
Eligibility: Open to new and relatively unknown writers, without regard to citizenship, sex, colour or creed. Published writers are ineligible. Applicants from any country are eligible, although only works in English will be read and awards will only be made in United States of America dollars.
Level of Study: Unrestricted
Type: Award
Value: Up to US$2,000
Country of Study: Any country

No. of awards offered: 3. (1 each in fiction, nonfiction and poetry)
Application Procedure: There are no formal application forms. The only way to have a work considered is to have it nominated by a sponsoring writer, agent, writing teacher or editor who is familiar with the author. Candidates are requested to provide their address and telephone number with their submission and should also include brief biographical information.
Closing Date: November 30th for announcement in the following March
Funding: Private
Contributor: The Mary Roberts Rinehart Foundation
No. of awards given last year: 3
No. of applicants last year: 500+

MARYLAND INSTITUTE COLLEGE OF ART (MICA)

1300 West Mount Royal Avenue, Baltimore, MD, 21217, United States of America
Tel: (1) 410 225 2256
Fax: (1) 410 225 2408
Email: graduate@mica.edu
Website: www.mica.edu
Contact: Mr Scott G Kelly, Director of Graduate Studies

The Maryland Institute College of Art (MICA) offers a Master of Fine Arts (MFA) degree in painting, sculpture, mixed media, photography, graphic design and digital imaging. It also offers excellent art education degrees such as an MAT and an MA in Art Education as well as Community Arts. The college has private studios, a strong visiting artists programme, housing and excellent exhibition opportunities.

MICA Fellowship

Subjects: Art.
Purpose: To serve as a tuition scholarship.
Eligibility: Each applicant is considered.
Level of Study: Graduate
Type: Fellowship
Value: US$6,000–12,000 per year
Length of Study: 1–2 years
Frequency: Annual
Study Establishment: MICA
Country of Study: United States of America
No. of awards offered: 11
Application Procedure: All accepted applicants are automatically considered.
Closing Date: February 15th
Funding: Private
Contributor: MICA
No. of awards given last year: 10
No. of applicants last year: 782

MICA International Fellowship Award

Subjects: Fine and applied arts.
Purpose: To serve as a tuition scholarship.
Eligibility: Open to all international students accepted to the Institute.
Level of Study: Graduate
Type: Fellowship
Value: US$12,000 per year
Length of Study: 1–2 years
Frequency: Annual
Study Establishment: MICA
Country of Study: United States of America
No. of awards offered: 1
Application Procedure: All accepted applicants are automatically considered.
Closing Date: February 15th
Funding: Private
Contributor: MICA
No. of awards given last year: 1
No. of applicants last year: 72

THE MATSUMAE INTERNATIONAL FOUNDATION

4-14-46 Kamiogi, Suginami-ku, Tokyo, 167-0043, Japan
Tel: (81) 3 3301 7600
Fax: (81) 3 3301 7601
Email: contact@matsumae-if.org
Website: www.matsumae-if.org
Contact: Mr S Nakajima

Matsumae International Foundation Research Fellowship

Subjects: Engineering, mathematics, medicine, natural sciences and agriculture.
Purpose: To provide an opportunity for foreign scientists to conduct research at Japanese institutions.
Eligibility: Open to applicants under 40 years of age, of non-Japanese nationality who hold a doctorate or have 2 years of research experience after the receipt of a Master's degree, and who have not been to Japan previously.
Level of Study: Professional development, postdoctorate
Type: Fellowship
Value: An air ticket, personal accident or sickness insurance and a research stipend plus Yen 300,000 on arrival in addition to Yen 200,000 monthly
Length of Study: 3–6 months
Frequency: Annual
Study Establishment: Unrestricted
Country of Study: Japan
No. of awards offered: 20
Application Procedure: Applicants must obtain the current issue of the fellowship announcement from the Foundation.
Closing Date: July 31st
Funding: Private
Contributor: Charitable donations from individuals
No. of awards given last year: 22
No. of applicants last year: 132
Additional Information: Priority will be given to the fields of science, engineering and medicine.

MCDONNELL CENTER FOR THE SPACE SCIENCES

Washington University, Campus Box 1169, One Brookings Drive, St Louis, MO, 63130-4899, United States of America
Tel: (1) 314 935 5332
Fax: (1) 314 935 7361
Email: phillips@wustite.wustl.edu
Website: www.mcss.wustl.edu
Contact: Professor Roger J Phillips, Director

The McDonnell Center for the Space Sciences exists to encourage scholarship and to promote collaborative research by Washington University scientists on space science-related problems.

McDonnell Center Astronaut Fellowships in the Space Sciences

Subjects: Space sciences, physics, Earth sciences, astronomy, chemistry and planetary studies.
Purpose: To encourage scholarship and research in accepted Washington University graduate students with an interest in space science.
Eligibility: Open to citizens of the United States of America who have applied for and been accepted into a graduate programme in the departments of physics, Earth and planetary sciences or chemistry at Washington University, St Louis. Candidates must have an excellent academic background and a particular interest in the space sciences.
Level of Study: Doctorate
Type: Fellowship
Value: Full tuition plus a stipend
Length of Study: 9 months, 1 academic year or 3 years
Frequency: Annual

Study Establishment: Washington University
Country of Study: United States of America
No. of awards offered: 3
Application Procedure: Applicants must apply to one of the standard science or engineering departments at the University.
Closing Date: January 15th
Funding: Private
No. of awards given last year: 1

McDonnell Graduate Fellowship in the Space Sciences

Subjects: Space sciences, physics, Earth sciences, astronomy, chemistry and planetary studies.
Purpose: To encourage graduate scholarship and research.
Eligibility: Open to candidates who have applied for and been accepted into a graduate programme in the department of physics or Earth and planetary sciences at Washington University, St Louis. Candidates must have an excellent academic background and a particular interest in the space sciences.
Level of Study: Doctorate
Type: Fellowship
Value: Full tuition plus a stipend
Length of Study: 3 years
Frequency: Annual
Study Establishment: Washington University
Country of Study: United States of America
No. of awards offered: 4–6
Application Procedure: Applicants who have been accepted into a Washington University graduate programme in physics, Earth and planetary sciences, chemistry, biology or electrical engineering and who have exhibited an interest in the space sciences are automatically considered for a McDonnell Center Fellowship.
Closing Date: January 15th
Funding: Private
No. of awards given last year: 4

MCGILL UNIVERSITY

3644 Peel Street, Montréal, 43A 1W9, Canada
Tel: (1) 514 398 6666
Fax: (1) 514 398 4659
Website: www.law.mcgill.ca
Contact: Ms Linda Coughlin, Faculty of Law

Maxwell Boulton QC Fellowship

Subjects: Law, especially with significance to the Canadian legal system and legal community.
Purpose: To provide young scholars with an opportunity to pursue a major research project or to complete the research requirements for a higher degree.
Eligibility: Open to candidates who have completed the residency requirements for a doctoral degree in law.
Level of Study: Postdoctorate, doctorate
Type: Fellowship
Value: Canadian $30,000–35,000 per year
Length of Study: 1 year
Frequency: Annual
Country of Study: Canada
No. of awards offered: 2
Application Procedure: Applicants must write for details.
Closing Date: February 1st
No. of awards given last year: 2
No. of applicants last year: 20

MEDICAL LIBRARY ASSOCIATION (MLA)

65 East Wacker Place, Suite 1900, Chicago, IL, 60601, United States of America
Tel: (1) 312 419 9094
Fax: (1) 312 419 8950
Email: mlapd2@mlahq.org
Website: www.mlanet.org
Contact: Professional Development Department

The Medical Library Association (MLA) is organized exclusively for scientific and educational purposes, and is dedicated to the support of health sciences research, education and patient care. MLA fosters excellence in the professional achievement and leadership of health sciences libraries and information professionals to enhance the quality of healthcare, education and research.

Cunningham Memorial International Fellowship

Subjects: Medical librarianship.
Purpose: To provide foreign medical librarians the opportunity to participate in and attend the Annual Meeting Library Association.
Eligibility: Open to those with a baccalaureate degree and a library degree who are working in a medical library. The applicant must submit a signed statement from a home country official stating that he or she is guaranteed a position in a medical library upon returning home. A satisfactory score must be achieved on the Test of English as a Foreign Language competency examination. Nationals of the United States of America or Canada are not eligible.
Level of Study: Professional development
Type: Fellowship
Value: Approximately US$2,000–3,000 to cover travel and expenses to MLA's Annual Meeting
Length of Study: 2–3 weeks
Frequency: Annual
Study Establishment: Medical libraries
Country of Study: United States of America or Canada
No. of awards offered: 3–4
Application Procedure: Applicants must submit a completed application form with three letters of reference in English, a project overview, a certificate of health, Test of English as a Foreign Language examination result and an audio or video tape.
Closing Date: December 1st
Funding: Private
No. of awards given last year: 1

MLA Continuing Education Grants

Subjects: The theoretical, administrative and technical aspects of library and information science.
Purpose: To provide professional health science librarians with the opportunity to continue their education.
Eligibility: Open to citizens of the United States of America or Canada or permanent residents who are medical librarians with a graduate degree in library science and at least 2 years of work experience at the professional level.
Level of Study: Professional development
Type: Fellowship
Value: US$100–500
Length of Study: 1 year
Frequency: Annual
Country of Study: United States of America
No. of awards offered: Usually 1
Application Procedure: Applicants must complete and submit an application form along with three references. Candidates should also identify a continuing education programme.
Closing Date: December 1st
Funding: Private
No. of awards given last year: 1
Additional Information: The award does not support work towards a degree or certificate.

MLA Doctoral Fellowship

Subjects: Medical librarianship and information science.
Purpose: To encourage superior students to conduct doctoral work in the field of health sciences librarianship or information sciences.
Eligibility: Open to citizens or permanent residents of the United States of America or Canada who are graduates of an ALA-accredited library school and are enrolled in a PhD programme with an emphasis on biomedical and health-related information science.
Level of Study: Doctorate
Type: Fellowship
Value: US$2,000
Length of Study: 1 year, non-renewable
Frequency: Every 2 years

Country of Study: United States of America or Canada
No. of awards offered: 1
Application Procedure: Applicants must submit a completed application form with two letters of reference, transcripts of graduate work completed, a summary of the project and a detailed budget plus a signed statement of terms and conditions.
Closing Date: December 1st
Funding: Commercial
Contributor: Thomson ISI
No. of awards given last year: 1
Additional Information: The award supports research or travel applicable to the candidate's study and may not be used for tuition.

MLA Research, Development and Demonstration Project Award

Subjects: Health science librarianship and the information sciences.
Purpose: To provide support for research, development and demonstration projects that will help to promote excellence in the field of health sciences librarianship.
Eligibility: Open to members of the Association who have a graduate degree in library science, are practicing medical librarians with at least 2 years of experience at the professional level and are citizens or permanent residents of the United States of America or Canada. Grants will not be given to support an activity that is only operational in nature or that has only local usefulness.
Level of Study: Postgraduate
Type: Award
Value: US$100–1,000
Length of Study: 1 year
Frequency: Annual
Country of Study: United States of America or Canada
No. of awards offered: Usually 1
Application Procedure: Applicants must submit a completed application form with three references, a detailed description of the project design and budget.
Closing Date: December 1st
Funding: Private
No. of awards given last year: 1

MLA Scholarship

Subjects: Library science.
Purpose: To provide an opportunity to study at an ALA-accredited library school.
Eligibility: Open to citizens and permanent residents of the United States of America or Canada who are entering an ALA-accredited library school or who have at least one half of the academic requirements of the programme to finish in the year following the granting of the scholarship.
Level of Study: Graduate
Type: Scholarship
Value: US$5,000
Length of Study: 1 academic year
Frequency: Annual
Country of Study: United States of America or Canada
No. of awards offered: 1
Application Procedure: Applicants must submit a completed application form with two letters of reference, official transcripts and a statement of career objectives.
Closing Date: December 1st
Funding: Private
No. of awards given last year: 1

MLA Scholarship for Minority Students

Subjects: Medical librarianship.
Purpose: To provide a minority student with the opportunity to begin or continue graduate study in the field of library and information science.
Eligibility: Open to Black, Hispanic, Asian, Pacific Island or Native American students who are entering an ALA-accredited library school and have at least one half of the academic requirements of the programme to finish in the year following the granting of the scholarship.
Level of Study: Graduate
Type: Scholarship
Value: US$5,000
Length of Study: 1 academic year
Frequency: Annual
Study Establishment: An ALA-accredited school
Country of Study: United States of America or Canada
No. of awards offered: 1
Application Procedure: Applicants must submit a completed application form with two letters of reference, official transcripts and a statement of career objectives.
Closing Date: December 1st
No. of awards given last year: 1

MEDICAL RESEARCH COUNCIL (MRC)

20 Park Crescent, London, W1B 1AL, England
Tel: (44) 20 7636 5422
Fax: (44) 20 7670 5002
Email: robert.hay@headoffice.mrc.ac.uk
Website: www.mrc.ac.uk
Contact: Mr Robert Hay, Fellowships Administrator

The Medical Research Council (MRC) offers support for talented individuals who want to pursue a career in the biomedical sciences, public health and health services research. It provides its support through a variety of personal award schemes that are aimed at each stage in a clinical or non-clinical research career.

Collaborative Career Development Fellowship in Stem Cell Research

Subjects: Biomedical sciences.
Purpose: To provide specialized training in stem cell research to support fundamental stem cell biology or work towards new stem cell-derived treatments for major diseases and disabilities.
Eligibility: Applicants are normally expected to have a PhD/DPhil in a relevant discipline or hold a relevant research-orientated Master's degree, and to have undertaken not less than 3 years of appropriate research training.
Level of Study: Postdoctorate
Type: Fellowship
Value: An appropriate clinical or academic salary along with a fixed sum for research expenses and a travel allowance for attendance at scientific conferences
Length of Study: Up to 3 years
Frequency: Annual
Study Establishment: A suitable university or similar institution
Country of Study: United Kingdom
No. of awards offered: Varies
Application Procedure: Applicants must submit a personal application. Forms and further details are available from the MRC.
Closing Date: Usually around February, but applicants are advised to check the website for details
Funding: Government
No. of awards given last year: 6
No. of applicants last year: 19
Additional Information: Awards may be jointly funded with the MRC, or funded by bodies other than the MRC. Please contact the Fellowships Section at the MRC for further details.

MRC Career Development Award

Subjects: Biomedical sciences.
Purpose: To award outstanding researchers who wish to consolidate and develop their research skills and make the transition from postdoctoral research and training to becoming independent investigators, but who do not hold established positions.
Eligibility: It is expected that all applicants will hold a PhD or MPhil in a basic science and will have at least 3 years of postdoctoral research experience.
Level of Study: Postdoctorate, research
Type: Fellowship
Value: Competitive personal salary support plus research support staff at the technical level, research expenses, capital equipment and a travel allowance for attendance at scientific conferences
Length of Study: Up to 4 years

Frequency: Annual
Study Establishment: A suitable university department or similar institution
Country of Study: United Kingdom
No. of awards offered: Up to 8
Application Procedure: Applicants must submit a personal application. Forms and further details are available from the MRC.
Closing Date: Usually around November, but applicants are advised to check the website for details
Funding: Government
No. of awards given last year: 10
No. of applicants last year: 80
Additional Information: Awards may occasionally be jointly funded with other bodies. Please contact the Fellowships Section at the MRC for further details.

MRC Clinical Research Training Fellowships

Subjects: Biomedical sciences.
Purpose: To provide an opportunity for specialized or further research training leading to the submission of a PhD, DPhil or MD.
Eligibility: Open to hospital doctors, dentists, general practitioners, nurses, midwives and allied health professionals. Residence requirements apply.
Level of Study: Postgraduate, research
Type: Fellowship
Value: An appropriate clinical academic salary will be provided along with a fixed sum for research expenses and a travel allowance for attendance at scientific conferences
Length of Study: Up to 3 years
Study Establishment: A suitable university department or similar institution
Country of Study: United Kingdom
No. of awards offered: Up to 32
Application Procedure: Applicants must submit a personal application. Forms and further details are available from the MRC.
Closing Date: Round one is in August/September, and round two is in January/February, but applicants are advised to check the website for details
Funding: Government
No. of awards given last year: 29
No. of applicants last year: 218
Additional Information: In addition to this scheme, the MRC also offers Joint Training Fellowships with the Royal Colleges of Surgeons of England and Edinburgh and the Royal College of Obstetricians and Gynaecologists. These awards are aimed at individuals whose long-term career aspirations involve undertaking academic clinical research. Fellowships may also be jointly funded with the MS Society or the Prior Group. Please contact the Fellowships Section at the MRC for further details.

MRC Clinician Scientist Fellowship

Subjects: Biomedical sciences.
Purpose: To provide an opportunity for outstanding clinical researchers who wish to consolidate their research skills and make the transition from postdoctoral research and training to becoming independent investigators.
Eligibility: The scheme is open to hospital doctors, dentists, general practitioners, nurses, midwives and allied health professionals. All applicants must have obtained their PhD or MD in a basic science or clinical project, or expect to have received their doctorate by the time they intend to take up an award, and must not hold tenured positions.
Level of Study: Research, postdoctorate
Type: Fellowship
Value: Competitive personal salary support plus research support staff at the technical level, research expenses, capital equipment and a travel allowance for attendance at scientific conferences
Length of Study: Up to 4 years
Frequency: Annual
Study Establishment: A suitable university department or similar institution
Country of Study: United Kingdom
No. of awards offered: Up to 7
Application Procedure: Applicants must submit a personal application. Forms and further details are available from the MRC.
Closing Date: August to December, but applicants are advised to check the website for details
Funding: Government
No. of awards given last year: 7
No. of applicants last year: 39

MRC Industrial Collaborative Studentships

Subjects: Any biomedical science.
Purpose: To enhance links between academia and industry in the provision of high-quality research training.
Eligibility: Candidates should have graduated with a good Honours Degree from a United Kingdom academic institution in a subject relevant to the MRC's scientific remit. This should be an Upper Second Class (Honours) Degree or higher. The MRC will, however, consider qualifications or a combination of qualifications and experience that demonstrates equivalent ability and attainment, eg. a Lower Second Class (Honours) Degree can be enhanced by a Master's degree. A copy of the regulations governing residence eligibility may be obtained from the Council.
Level of Study: Postgraduate
Value: A tax-free maintenance stipend depending on United Kingdom location, university tuition fees up to the current DFEE recommended limit plus college fees, where applicable. Awards also include a fixed sum for conference travel expenses and a support grant to the university department to help cover incidental costs of students' training. As a measure of interest and involvement the industrial company is expected to make a financial contribution to the cost of the studentship
Length of Study: Up to 4 years
Frequency: Annual
Study Establishment: Universities, medical schools, industry and other academic institutions
Country of Study: United Kingdom
No. of awards offered: Approx. 10
Application Procedure: The MRC does not make awards directly to students. Awards are made to industrial partners who apply for studentships by application. The individual or academic partner will then advertise for students to apply for their awards. Students who wish to apply for a studentship are advised to contact the department where they wish to study to see if it has an allocation of awards.
Closing Date: This competition is advertised in the Autumn
Funding: Commercial
No. of awards given last year: 9
Additional Information: The industrial company is expected to make a contribution.

MRC Master's Studentships

Subjects: Any biomedical science.
Purpose: To enable students to undertake early research training relevant to strategic research or strategic employment in a research-related capacity in academia or industry.
Eligibility: Candidates should have graduated with a good Honours Degree. A copy of the regulations governing residence eligibility may be obtained from the Council.
Level of Study: Postgraduate
Type: Studentship
Value: Tax-free maintenance stipend, depending on United Kingdom location, and university tuition fees up to the current DFEE recommended limit. Awards also include a fixed sum for conference travel expenses
Length of Study: 1 year
Frequency: Annual
Study Establishment: Universities, medical schools and other academic organizations
Country of Study: United Kingdom
Application Procedure: The MRC does not make awards directly to students. Awards are made to Institutes of Higher Education (IHE) based on the level of MCR grant and fellowship awards to that IHE. The IHE is responsible for recruiting students. Students who wish to apply for a studentship are advised to contact the department where they wish to study to see if it has an allocation of awards.

Closing Date: IHE's are notified of funding available for awards in March each year
Funding: Government
Additional Information: The MRC also has awards in strategic capacity building areas from time to time. Studentship awards have been replaced by Doctoral Training Accounts (DTA) from October 2004. Further details can be obtained from the MRC website.

MRC Research Studentships

Subjects: Any biomedical science.
Purpose: To enable individuals to undertake a training programme under the guidance of named supervisors that includes a research project plus training in research methods and personal key skills.
Eligibility: Candidates should have graduated with a good Honours Degree from a United Kingdom academic institution in a subject relevant to the MRC's scientific remit. This should be an Upper Second Class (Honours) Degree or higher. The MRC will, however, consider qualifications or a combination of qualifications and experience that demonstrates equivalent ability and attainment eg. a Lower Second Class (Honours) Degree can be enhanced by a Master's degree. A copy of the regulations governing residence eligibility may be obtained from the Council.
Level of Study: Predoctorate
Type: Studentship
Value: A tax-free maintenance stipend depending on United Kingdom location, university tuition fees up to the current DFEE recommended limit plus college fees, where applicable. Awards also include a fixed sum for conference travel expenses and a support grant to the university department to help cover incidental costs of students' training
Length of Study: Most studentships are 3 years, but they can be linked to a Master's course, making it a 4–year programme
Frequency: Annual
Study Establishment: Universities, medical schools, MRC research establishments and other academic organizations
Country of Study: United Kingdom
No. of awards offered: Approx. 400
Application Procedure: The MRC does not make awards directly to students. Awards are made to Institutes of Higher Education (IHE) based at the level of MRC grant and fellowship awards to that IHE. The IHE is responsible for recruiting students. Students who wish to apply for a studentship are advised to contact the department where they wish to study to see if it has an allocation of awards.
Closing Date: IHEs are notified of awards in March each year. The capacity building studentship competition is advertised in the Autumn
Funding: Government

MRC Royal College of Obstetricians and Gynaecologists (RCOG) Training Fellowship

Subjects: Biomedical sciences.
Purpose: To provide members of the RCOG with an opportunity for specialized or further research training in a basic science relevant to obstetrics and gynaecology leading to the submission of a PhD, DPhil or MD.
Eligibility: Open to members of the RCOG wishing to pursue research at PhD or MD level. Applicants must have a minimum of 1 year of experience in clinical obstetrics and gynaecology and hold part one membership of the college. Residence requirements apply.
Level of Study: Research, postgraduate
Type: Fellowship
Value: An appropriate clinical academic salary will be provided along with a fixed sum for research expenses and a travel allowance for attendance at scientific conferences
Length of Study: Up to 3 years
Frequency: Annual
Study Establishment: A suitable university or similar institution
Country of Study: United Kingdom
No. of awards offered: 1
Application Procedure: Applicants must contact the Fellowships Section, Research Career Awards of the MRC for details.
Closing Date: Applicants are advised to check the MRC website for details
Funding: Government
No. of awards given last year: 1
No. of applicants last year: 8

MRC Royal College of Surgeons of Edinburgh Training Fellowship

Subjects: Biomedical sciences.
Purpose: To provide an opportunity for specialized or further research training within the United Kingdom leading to the submission of a PhD, DPhil or MD.
Eligibility: Open to members of the Royal College of Surgeons of Edinburgh wishing to pursue research at the PhD or MD level. Residence requirements apply.
Level of Study: Postgraduate, research
Type: Fellowship
Value: An appropriate clinical academic salary will be provided along with a fixed sum for research expenses and a travel allowance for attendance at scientific conferences
Length of Study: Up to 3 years
Frequency: Annual
Study Establishment: A suitable university department or similar institution
Country of Study: United Kingdom
No. of awards offered: 1–2
Application Procedure: Applicants must submit a personal application. Forms and further details are available from the MRC.
Closing Date: Applicants are advised to check the MRC website for details
Funding: Government
No. of awards given last year: 2
No. of applicants last year: 24

MRC Royal College of Surgeons of England Training Fellowship

Subjects: Biomedical sciences.
Purpose: To provide an opportunity for specialized or further research training within the United Kingdom leading to the submission of a PhD, DPhil or MD.
Eligibility: Open to members of the Royal College of Surgeons of England wishing to pursue research at the PhD or MD level. Residence requirements apply.
Level of Study: Research, postgraduate
Type: Fellowship
Value: An appropriate clinical academic salary will be provided along with a fixed sum for research expenses and a travel allowance for attendance at scientific conferences
Length of Study: Up to 3 years
Frequency: Annual
Study Establishment: A suitable university department or similar institution
Country of Study: United Kingdom
No. of awards offered: Up to 2
Application Procedure: Applicants must submit a personal application. Forms and further details are available from the MRC.
Closing Date: Round one is in August/September, and round two is in January/February, but applicants are advised to check the website for details
Funding: Government
No. of awards given last year: 2
No. of applicants last year: 26

MRC Senior Clinical Fellowship

Subjects: Biomedical sciences.
Purpose: To provide an opportunity for clinical researchers of exceptional ability to concentrate on a period of research.
Eligibility: Open to nationals of any country. Applicants are expected to have proven themselves to be independent researchers, be well qualified for an academic research career and demonstrate the promise of becoming future research leaders. The scheme is open to hospital doctors, dentists, general practitioners, nurses, midwives and allied health professionals. Applicants must hold a PhD or MD in a

basic science or clinical project and have at least 3 years of postdoctoral research experience.
Level of Study: Postdoctorate, research
Type: Fellowship
Value: Competitive personal salary support is provided plus research support staff at the technical and postdoctoral level, research expenses, capital equipment and a travel allowance for attendance at scientific conferences
Length of Study: Up to 5 years, with a possibility of renewal through open competition for a further 5 years
Frequency: Annual
Study Establishment: A suitable university department or similar institution
Country of Study: United Kingdom
No. of awards offered: Up to 4
Application Procedure: Applicants must submit a personal application. Forms and further details are available from the MRC.
Closing Date: Usually around August, but applicants are advised to check the website for details
Funding: Government
No. of awards given last year: 3
No. of applicants last year: 14

MRC Senior Non-Clinical Fellowship

Subjects: Biomedical sciences.
Purpose: To provide support for non-clinical scientists of exceptional ability to concentrate on a period of research.
Eligibility: Open to nationals of any country. Applicants are expected to have proven themselves to be independent researchers, be well qualified for an academic research career and demonstrate the promise of becoming future research leaders. It is expected that all applicants will hold a PhD or DPhil in a basic science project, have at least 6 years of relevant postdoctoral research experience and not hold a tenured position.
Level of Study: Postdoctorate, research
Type: Fellowship
Value: Competitive personal salary support is provided plus research support staff at the technical and postdoctoral level, research expenses, capital equipment and a travel allowance for attendance at scientific conferences
Length of Study: Up to 5 years, with a possibility of renewal through open competition for a further 5 years
Frequency: Annual
Study Establishment: A suitable university department or similar institution
Country of Study: United Kingdom
No. of awards offered: Up to 6
Application Procedure: Applicants must submit a personal application. Forms and further details are available from the MRC.
Closing Date: Usually around September, but applicants are advised to check the website for details
Funding: Government
No. of awards given last year: 5
No. of applicants last year: 38

MRC Special Training Fellowships in Bioinformatics, Neuroinformatics and Computational Biology

Subjects: Biomedical sciences.
Purpose: To provide specialist, multidisciplinary research training at the doctoral or postdoctoral level.
Eligibility: The scheme is aimed at individuals from a variety of backgrounds such as non-biological as well as biological, non-clinical as well as clinical, and individuals with PhDs or MDs or with informatics research experience at the predoctoral level.
Level of Study: Postgraduate, research
Type: Fellowship
Value: An appropriate academic salary will be provided along with a fixed sum for research expenses and a travel allowance for attendance at scientific conferences
Length of Study: Up to 4 years
Frequency: Annual
Study Establishment: A suitable university department or similar institution
Country of Study: United Kingdom
No. of awards offered: Up to 4
Application Procedure: Applicants must submit a personal application. Forms and further details are available from the MRC.
Closing Date: Applicants are advised to check the website for details
Funding: Government
No. of awards given last year: 5
No. of applicants last year: 23
Additional Information: Award holders are encouraged to apply for a PhD or MD if they do not already have one.

MRC Special Training Fellowships in Health Services and Health of the Public Research

Subjects: Biomedical sciences in health services research and health of the public, as defined by the MRC.
Purpose: To provide support for researchers wishing to gain further training in multidisciplinary research to address problems of direct relevance to the health services within the United Kingdom.
Eligibility: Open to non-medical graduates, hospital doctors, dentists, general practitioners, nurses, midwives and allied health professionals who are seeking a research career in health services and research.
Level of Study: Research, postdoctorate
Type: Fellowship
Value: An appropriate academic salary will be provided along with a fixed sum for research expenses and a travel allowance for attendance at scientific conferences
Length of Study: Up to 4 years
Frequency: Annual
Study Establishment: A suitable university department or similar institution
Country of Study: United Kingdom
No. of awards offered: Up to 15
Application Procedure: Applicants must submit a personal application. Forms and further details are available from the MRC.
Closing Date: Usually around September/October, but applicants are advised to check the website for details
Funding: Government
No. of awards given last year: 10
No. of applicants last year: 42
Additional Information: Some awards are jointly funded with the Department of Health.

MRC/Academy of Medical Sciences Tenure Track Clinician Scientist Fellowship

Subjects: Biomedical sciences.
Purpose: To allow outstanding clinical researchers to consolidate their research skills and make the transition from postdoctoral research and training to becoming independent investigators, and to support career development and promote recruitment into clinical academic medicine.
Eligibility: Open to hospital doctors, dentists and general practitioners.
Level of Study: Research, postdoctorate
Type: Fellowship
Value: Competitive personal salary support plus research support staff at the technical level, research expenses, capital equipment and a travel allowance for attendance at scientific conferences
Length of Study: Up to 5 years
Frequency: Annual
Study Establishment: A suitable university department or similar institution
Country of Study: United Kingdom
No. of awards offered: Varies
Application Procedure: Applicants must submit a personal application. Forms and further details are available from the MRC.
Closing Date: August/December, but applicants are advised to check the website for details
Funding: Government
No. of awards given last year: 1
No. of applicants last year: 3

MEET THE COMPOSER, INC.

75 Ninth Avenue, 3R Suite C, New York, NY, 10011,
United States of America
Tel: (1) 212 645 6949
Fax: (1) 212 645 9669
Email: mtrevino@meetthecomposer.org
Website: www.meetthecomposer.org
Contact: Mr Edward Ficklin, Director of Programmes

Meet The Composer's mission is to increase artistic and financial opportunities for American composers by fostering the creation, performance, dissemination and appreciation of their music.

Commissioning Music/USA

Subjects: Music commissioning.
Purpose: To support the commissioning of new works.
Eligibility: Open to citizens of the United States of America only. Organizations that have been producing or presenting for at least 3 years are eligible and may be dance, chorus, orchestra, opera, theatre and music-theatre companies, festivals, arts presenters, public radio and television stations, internet providers, soloists and small performing ensembles of all kinds, eg. jazz, chamber, new music, etc.
Level of Study: Professional development
Type: Grant
Value: A single organization may apply for up to US$15,000 and a consortium for up to US$30,000
Frequency: Annual
Country of Study: United States of America
Application Procedure: Individuals cannot apply on their own. Host organizations must submit completed application forms and accompanying materials.
Closing Date: January 15th
Contributor: Offered in partnership with the National Endowment for the Arts
No. of awards given last year: 20–30
No. of applicants last year: 150–200

J P Morgan Chase Regrant Program for Small Ensembles

Subjects: Musical performance.
Purpose: To support small New York City-based ensembles and music organizations committed to performing the work of living composers and contemporary music.
Eligibility: Applicants must write for details.
Level of Study: Professional development
Type: Grant
Value: US$1,000–5,000
Frequency: Annual
Country of Study: United States of America
Application Procedure: Applicants must contact the organization.
Closing Date: March 4th
Funding: Commercial
Contributor: In partnership with J P Morgan Chase
No. of awards given last year: 15–20
No. of applicants last year: 75–100

Meet The Composer Fund

Subjects: Musical performance.
Purpose: To enable composers to participate actively in performances of their work and consequently build audiences for new music. Participation may include performing, conducting, speaking with the audience, presenting workshops, giving interviews and coaching performances.
Eligibility: Open to citizens of the United States of America only. Organizations may be choruses, dance, opera, theatre and music-theatre companies, symphonies, arts presenters, musical organizations, festivals, television production companies, radio stations and performing ensembles of all kinds, eg. jazz, chamber, new music etc. Awards are based solely on the overall quality of the application, which includes the merit of the composer, participation, level of audience or community involvement and general strength of the compositions.
Level of Study: Professional development
Type: Award
Value: Up to US$250–1,000 per composer
Country of Study: United States of America
Application Procedure: Varies from region to region, but individuals cannot apply themselves, as performing organizations apply on behalf of the composer. Interested parties should contact the organization for further details.
Closing Date: Application deadlines are quarterly: January 2nd, April 1st, June 1st and October 1st
No. of awards given last year: 85 per cent
No. of applicants last year: 800–1,000

Music Alive

Subjects: Music.
Purpose: To support composer residencies for professional composers to work with teachers, students and their families, nurturing creativity in the classroom while writing works for students to play and sing.
Eligibility: Open to all American Symphony Orchestra League and youth member orchestras.
Level of Study: Professional development
Type: Residency
Value: A composer's fee of US$2,500 per residency week, composer's expenses of up to one round trip for every 2-week residency and up to US$175 per day for food and lodging and orchestra expenses of up to US$1,000 per residency week
Length of Study: 2–8 week residencies
Frequency: Annual
Country of Study: United States of America
Application Procedure: Individuals cannot apply themselves, as performing organizations apply on behalf of the composer.
Closing Date: August 20th
Contributor: Offered in partnership with the American Symphony Orchestra League

Music Alive: Composers and Orchestras Together

Subjects: Musical performance.
Purpose: To financially support orchestras.
Eligibility: Open to all American Symphony Orchestra league professional and youth member orchestras. The residencies must be scheduled in conjunction with performances of the composer's work. The works may be a world premiere or an existing work by a living American composer. Performance of a world premiere or commissioned work is not a requirement of the programme. Residency weeks may be scheduled contiguously or divided into multiple visits, but must be of a 1-week minimum duration.
Level of Study: Professional development
Type: Grant
Value: A composer's fee of up to US$2,500 per residency per week, composer's expenses of up to one round trip for every 2 week residency, up to US$175 per day for food and lodging and orchestra expenses of up to US$1,000 per residency week
Length of Study: 2–8 weeks
Frequency: Annual
Country of Study: United States of America
Application Procedure: Individuals cannot apply themselves. Performing organizations must apply on behalf of the composer.
Closing Date: August 16th

MELVILLE TRUST FOR CARE AND CURE OF CANCER

Tods Murray LLP, Edinburgh Quay, 133 Fountain Bridge, Edinburgh, EH3 9AG, Scotland
Tel: (44) 131 656 2000
Fax: (44) 131 656 2020
Email: maildesk@todsmurray.com

Melville Trust for Care and Cure of Cancer Research Fellowships

Subjects: The care and cure of cancer.
Purpose: To fund innovative research work.
Eligibility: Applicants need not necessarily hold a medical qualification or have experience of research.

Level of Study: Research
Type: Fellowship
Length of Study: Up to 2 years
Frequency: Annual
Study Establishment: One of the clinical or scientific departments in Lothian, Borders, Fife or Dundee
Application Procedure: Applicants must complete an application form and then be interviewed.
Closing Date: March 31st
Funding: Private
No. of awards given last year: 2
No. of applicants last year: 4

For further information contact:

Tods Murray LLP Edinburgh Quay 133 Fountain Bridge, Edinburgh, EH3 9AG, Scotland

Melville Trust for Care and Cure of Cancer Research Grants

Subjects: The care and cure of cancer.
Purpose: To fund innovative research work.
Eligibility: Applicants need not necessarily hold a medical qualification or have experience of research.
Level of Study: Research
Type: Grant
Value: Up to UK £25,000
Length of Study: Up to 2 years
Frequency: Annual
Study Establishment: One of the clinical or scientific departments in Lothian, Borders, Fife or Dundee
Application Procedure: Applicants must complete an application form.
Closing Date: March 31st
Funding: Private
No. of awards given last year: 5
No. of applicants last year: 7

For further information contact:

Tods Murray LLP Edinburgh Quay 133 Fountain Bridge, Edingburgh, EH3 9AG, Scotland

MEMORIAL FOUNDATION FOR JEWISH CULTURE

50 Broadway, 34th Floor, New York, NY, 10004,
United States of America
Tel: (1) 212 425 6606
Fax: (1) 212 425 6602
Email: office@mfjc.org
Website: www.mfjc.org
Contact: Dr Jerry Hochbaum, Executive Vice President

The Memorial Foundation for Jewish Culture was established in 1965 to help assure a creative future for Jewish life throughout the world. The Foundation encourages Jewish scholarship, Jewish cultural creativity, and makes possible the training of professionals to serve in communities deprived of a large Jewish presence.

Memorial Foundation for Jewish Culture International Doctoral Scholarships

Subjects: Jewish studies.
Purpose: To assist in the training of future Jewish scholars for careers in Jewish scholarship and research, and to enable religious, educational and other Jewish communal workers to obtain advanced training for leadership positions.
Eligibility: Open to graduate students of any nationality who are specializing in a field of Jewish studies. Applicants must be officially enrolled or registered in a doctoral programme at a recognized university.
Level of Study: Doctorate
Type: Scholarship
Value: US$2,000–7,500 per year, but varies depending on the country where study is undertaken
Length of Study: 1 academic year, renewable for a maximum of 4 years
Frequency: Annual
Study Establishment: A recognized university
Country of Study: Any country
No. of awards offered: Varies
Application Procedure: Applicants must write requesting an application form.
Closing Date: October 31st

Memorial Foundation for Jewish Culture International Fellowships in Jewish Studies

Subjects: A specialized field of Jewish studies that will make a significant contribution to the understanding, preservation, enhancement or transmission of Jewish culture.
Purpose: To allow well-qualified individuals to carry out independent scholarly, literary or artistic projects.
Eligibility: Open to recognized or qualified scholars, researchers or artists of any nationality who possess the knowledge and experience to formulate and implement a project in a specialized field of Jewish studies.
Level of Study: Unrestricted
Type: Fellowship
Value: US$2,000–7,500, but varies depending on the country in which the project is undertaken
Length of Study: 1 academic year, in exceptional cases renewable for a further year
Frequency: Annual
Country of Study: Any country
No. of awards offered: Varies
Application Procedure: Applicants must write requesting an application form.
Closing Date: October 31st

Memorial Foundation for Jewish Culture International Scholarship Programme for Community Service

Subjects: The rabbinate, Jewish education, communal service or religious functionaries, eg. shohatim, mohalim.
Purpose: To assist well-qualified individuals for career training.
Eligibility: Open to any individual who is planning or who is currently undertaking training in his or her chosen field in a recognized Yeshiva, teacher training seminary, school of social work, university or other educational institution.
Level of Study: Unrestricted
Type: Scholarship
Value: US$1,000–4,000, but varies depending on the country in which the recipient is trained and other considerations
Length of Study: 1 year, renewable
Frequency: Annual
Study Establishment: Diaspora Jewish communities in need of such personnel
No. of awards offered: Varies
Application Procedure: Applicants must write for details.
Closing Date: November 30th
Additional Information: Recipients must commit themselves to serve a community of need. They should also be knowledgeable in the language and culture of that country or be prepared to learn it.

Memorial Foundation for Jewish Culture Scholarships for Post-Rabbinical Students

Subjects: Jewish studies.
Purpose: To assist in the training of future Jewish religious scholars and leaders and to assist newly ordained rabbis to obtain advanced training for careers as head of Yeshivot, as Dayanim and other leadership positions.
Eligibility: Open to recently ordained rabbis engaged in full-time studies at a Yeshiva, Kollel or rabbinical seminary.
Level of Study: Unrestricted
Type: Scholarship
Value: US$1,000–4,000
Length of Study: 1 year

Frequency: Annual
Country of Study: Any country
No. of awards offered: Varies
Application Procedure: Applicants must write for details.
Closing Date: November 30th
Additional Information: The Foundation also provides grants to bolster Jewish educational programmes in areas of need. Grants are awarded on the understanding that the recipient institution will assume responsibility for the programme following the initial limited period of Foundation support. Grants are made only for team or collaborative projects.

MENINGITIS RESEARCH FOUNDATION

Midland Way, Thornbury, Bristol, BS35 2BS, England
Tel: (44) 14 5428 1811
Fax: (44) 14 5428 1094
Email: lindaglennie@meningitis.org
Website: www.meningitis.org
Contact: Mrs Joy Pepper, Research Administrator

The Meningitis Research Foundation is a registered charity that supports an international programme of independently peer-reviewed research into the prevention, detection and treatment of meningitis and septicaemia. The Foundation also provides information for public and health professionals, runs medical and scientific meetings and provides support to people affected by the disease.

Meningitis Research Foundation Project Grant

Subjects: Meningitis and associated infections.
Purpose: To fight death and disability from meningitis and septicaemia by supporting research with the potential to produce results in immediate problem areas. Priority is given to work that is likely to bring clinical or public health benefits.
Eligibility: Meningitis Research Foundation research grants may be held in any country; nationality is not a restriction. Employees of commercial companies are not eligible to apply.
Level of Study: Research
Type: Project grant
Value: Up to UK £150,000 per year
Length of Study: Up to 5 years
Frequency: Twice a year, subject to availabily of funds
Study Establishment: Universities, research medical institutions and hospitals
Country of Study: Any country
No. of awards offered: 1
Application Procedure: Applicants must submit a two- or three-page outline proposal by email summarizing the work planned, the approximate cost and the duration of the project. This must include approximately ten lines explaining; (a) how the work described falls within the Foundation's research strategy; (b) the potential for clinical/public health benefit arising from this study and (c) why the applicant has chosen to apply to the Foundation for funding for this particular project. Applicants who are invited to apply in full, submit a details research plan with other supporting documents. These are accessed by external referees and the Foundations scientific advisory panel.
Closing Date: February 28th or August 31st
Funding: Private
Contributor: Voluntary donations from the public
No. of awards given last year: 1
Additional Information: Extension funding was given to one existing grant.

MENINGITIS TRUST

Fern House, Bath Road, Stroud, Gloucestershire, GL5 3TJ, England
Tel: (44) 14 5376 8000
Fax: (44) 14 5376 8001
Email: support@meningitis-trust.org.uk
Contact: Ms Sarah Booker, Education & Research Co-ordinator

The Meningitis Trust is an internationally respected charity with a strong community focus. It has three main aims: to provide care and support for people affected by meningitis, to educate both public and professionals and to fund life-saving medical research. The strategic aim of the Trust is to work towards the eradication of meningitis as a serious medical condition. Research priorities have been reviewed in relation to progress with the development of serogroup B meningococcal vaccine.

Meningitis Trust Research Award

Subjects: The after-effects of meningitis, the aftercare of patients and families who have been affected by meningitis and the recognition, diagnosis and management of meningitis.
Purpose: To contribute to the funding of research into all types of meningitis whether bacterial or viral.
Eligibility: Applicants must contact the Trust for eligibility requirements. Generally, funding is given for postgraduate study, but applications from those studying for a doctorate will be considered.
Level of Study: Unrestricted
Value: Up to UK £400,000 per year
Frequency: Dependent on funds available
Application Procedure: Applicants must submit a précis, and if accepted, they will be required to submit a completed full application.
Closing Date: Please contact the organization

THE MENZIES FOUNDATION

210 Clarendon Street, East Melbourne, Victoria, 3002, Australia
Tel: (61) 9419 5699
Fax: (61) 9417 7049
Email: menzies@vicnet.net.au
Website: www.menziesfoundation.org.au

The Sir Robert Menzies Memorial Foundation Limited is a non-profit, non-political organization created in 1979 to promote excellence in health research, education and post graduate scholarship by Australians.

NH MRC/RG Menzies Fellowship

Subjects: Medicine.
Eligibility: Open students who are Australian students.
Level of Study: Postgraduate
Type: Fellowship
Value: $5,000 per annum
Length of Study: Up to 4 years
Frequency: Annual
Study Establishment: Any approved institution
Country of Study: Any country
Application Procedure: See the website.
Funding: Foundation
Contributor: Menzies Foundation

The Robert Gordon Menzies Scholarship to Harvard

Subjects: All subjects.
Purpose: To encourage students who have gained admission to a Harvard graduate school.
Eligibility: Open to candidates who are Australian citizens who have graduated from an Australian University.
Level of Study: Postdoctorate
Type: Scholarship
Length of Study: US$50,000
Frequency: Annual
No. of awards offered: 1
Application Procedure: A completed application form with original academic transcripts must be submitted.
Funding: Foundation
Contributor: The Harvard club of Australia, the Menzies Foundation and the Australian National University

Sir Robert Menzies Memorial Research Scholarship in the Allied Health Sciences

Subjects: Health sciences.
Purpose: To support students who wish to pursue their education in the field of health sciences.

Eligibility: Open to students studying health sciences and enrolled for a PhD in an Australian University.
Level of Study: Doctorate
Type: Scholarship
Value: Australian $25,000
Length of Study: 2 years
Frequency: Annual
Study Establishment: Any accredited university
Country of Study: Australia
No. of awards offered: 2
Application Procedure: A completed application form must be submitted.
Funding: Foundation
Contributor: Menzies Foundation

Sir Robert Menzies Memorial Scholarships in Law

Subjects: Law.
Purpose: To sponsor students wishing to pursue their law studies in the UK.
Eligibility: Open to Australian citizens with a postgraduate degree in Law.
Level of Study: Postgraduate
Type: Scholarship
Value: Contribution towards university fees and living travel expenses
Length of Study: 1–2 years
Frequency: Annual
Country of Study: United Kingdom
No. of awards offered: 3
Application Procedure: See the website.
Closing Date: August 31st
Funding: Trusts
Contributor: The Sir Robert Menzies Memorial Trust in London

MESA STATE COLLEGE

PO Box 2647, 1100 North Avenue, Grand Junction, CO 81501, United States of America
Tel: (1) 970 248 1020
Fax: (1) 970 248 1973
Email: webmaster@mesastate.edu
Website: www.mesastate.edu
Contact: MBA Admissions Officer

Mesa State College, founded in 1925, is a comprehensive, liberal arts college that offers programmes at the Master's, baccalaureate, associate degree and certificate levels.

Brach, Louis and Betty Scholarship

Subjects: Natural science and mathematics.
Purpose: To provide financial assistance.
Eligibility: Open to full-time students who are in need of financial help.
Level of Study: Postgraduate
Type: Scholarship
Value: US$500–1,000
Length of Study: 1 year
Frequency: Annual
Study Establishment: Mesa State College
Country of Study: United States of America
Application Procedure: See the website.
Closing Date: March 1st

Bray and Company Leadership Scholarship

Subjects: Business administration.
Eligibility: Open to full-time students pursuing a Bachelor of Business Administration degree.
Level of Study: Postgraduate
Type: Scholarship
Value: US$250–550
Frequency: Annual
Study Establishment: Mesa State College
Country of Study: United States of America
Application Procedure: A completed application form must be submitted.
Closing Date: March 1st

Burkey Family Memorial Scholarship

Subjects: All subjects.
Eligibility: Open to candidates who are full-time seniors at the College.
Level of Study: Postgraduate
Type: Scholarship
Value: US$500
Length of Study: 1 year
Frequency: Annual
Study Establishment: Mesa State College
Country of Study: United States of America
Application Procedure: See the website.
Closing Date: March 1st

Hawkins, Edwin and Harriet History of Mathematics Scholarship

Subjects: Mathematics.
Eligibility: Open to full-time students enrolled in the spring mathematics course.
Level of Study: Postgraduate
Type: Scholarship
Value: US$500–1,000
Frequency: Annual
Study Establishment: Mesa State College
Country of Study: United States of America
Application Procedure: See the website.
Closing Date: March 1st

Mesa State College Academic (Colorado) Scholarship

Subjects: Natural sciences and mathematics.
Eligibility: Open to students of Meta State College who are citizens of United States of America.
Level of Study: Postgraduate
Type: Scholarship
Value: Up to US$1,000
Length of Study: 1 year
Frequency: Annual
Study Establishment: Mesa State College
Country of Study: United States of America
Application Procedure: A completed application form, available on the website, must be submitted.
Closing Date: March 1st

Reynolds Polymer Technology Scholarship

Subjects: Natural sciences and mathematics.
Purpose: To provide financial assistance.
Eligibility: Open to full-time students who are residents of Colorado.
Level of Study: Postgraduate
Type: Scholarship
Value: US$1,000
Frequency: Annual
Study Establishment: Mesa State College
Country of Study: United States of America
Application Procedure: A completed application form and relevant details must be submitted.
Closing Date: March 1st

THE METROPOLITAN MUSEUM OF ART

1000 Fifth Avenue, New York, NY, 10028-0198, United States of America
Tel: (1) 212 650 2763
Fax: (1) 212 570 3782
Email: communications@metmuseum.org
Website: www.metmuseum.org
Contact: Internship Programmes & Education

The Metropolitan Museum of Art is one of the world's largest and finest art museums. Its collections include more than two million works of art spanning 5,000 years of world culture, from prehistory to the present, and from every part of the world. As one of the greatest research institutions in the world, the Metropolitan Museum welcomes the responsibility to train future scholars and museum professionals. The Museum offers opportunities for students at several stages in their academic careers, from high school to the postgraduate level. Internships and apprenticeships can be either paid or unpaid, full- or part-time and can last from 9 weeks to an academic year.

Interdisciplinary Internship: Early German and Netherlandish Paintings, Department of European Paintings

Subjects: Art historical research.
Purpose: To encourage candidates interested in working with the technical investigation of the Museum's early German and The Netherlandish paintings.
Eligibility: Open to candidates who have completed their PhD and interested in the field of art historical research.
Level of Study: Doctorate
Type: Scholarship
Value: US$22,000; stipend of US$3,000 for research and educational travel
Frequency: Annual
Study Establishment: The Metropolitan Museum of Art
Country of Study: United States of America
Application Procedure: See the website.
Closing Date: January 20th

Metropolitan Museum of Art 6-Month Internship

Subjects: Art history and related fields.
Purpose: To promote greater diversity in the national pool of future museum professionals.
Eligibility: Open to candidates of any nationality.
Level of Study: Postgraduate, graduate
Type: Internship
Value: Please contact the organization for details
Length of Study: 6 months, full-time from June to December and participation in the Summer orientation programme
Frequency: Annual
Study Establishment: The Metropolitan Museum of Art
Country of Study: United States of America
No. of awards offered: Varies
Application Procedure: Applicants must submit a typed application including their name and address, a full curriculum vitae, two academic recommendations, official transcripts, a list of art history or other relevant courses taken and an essay or letter of not more than 500 words describing their career goals, interest in museum work and their reasons for applying. There are no application forms.
Closing Date: Please contact the Museum
Funding: Private
Additional Information: Interns are placed in one of the museum's departments, where they work on projects that suit their academic background, professional skills and career goals.

The Metropolitan Museum of Art Annette Kade Art History Fellowship

Subjects: Fine art.
Purpose: To allow foreign students to study in the United States of America.
Eligibility: Open to French and German predoctoral art history students.
Level of Study: Predoctorate
Type: Fellowship
Length of Study: 1 year
Frequency: Annual
Study Establishment: The Metropolitan Museum of Art, New York
Country of Study: United States of America
No. of awards offered: 1
Application Procedure: Applicants must submit a typed application in triplicate that includes the contact details of the applicant, a curriculum vitae, details of professional experience, a statement not exceeding 1,000 words describing what the applicant expects to accomplish in the fellowship period and how the Museum's facilities can be utilized to achieve these objectives, a tentative schedule of work to be accomplished, proposed start and end dates and three letters of recommendation, at least one of which should be professional and one academic. Master's degree and predoctoral applicants should only send the original plus two copies of their official undergraduate and graduate transcripts.
Closing Date: November
Funding: Private
Contributor: Annette Kade
Additional Information: Predoctoral Fellows will generally be expected to assist the hosting curatorial departments with projects that complement and are incidental to their approved scholarly subject. They will be asked to give a gallery talk during their fellowship term and be expected to participate in a Fellows' colloquium in the second half of their term, in which they will give a 20-minute presentation on their work in progress. Senior Fellows will also be invited to participate in these activities.

Metropolitan Museum of Art Internship in Educational Media

Subjects: Design, education and art history.
Purpose: To support students who wish to participate in the production of print, online and video publications created for families, teachers, students and the general museum public.
Eligibility: Open to candidates interested in careers in art museums.
Level of Study: Postgraduate
Type: Internship
Value: US$22,000
Length of Study: 1 year
Frequency: Annual
Study Establishment: The Metropolitan Museum of Art
Country of Study: United States of America
Application Procedure: For detailed information see the website.
Closing Date: January 20th

Metropolitan Museum of Art Lifchez/Stronach Curatorial Internship

Subjects: Art history.
Purpose: To support students interested in a curatorial career.
Eligibility: Open to students who are in need of financial assistance to pursue a career in art history.
Level of Study: Postgraduate
Type: Internship
Value: US$15,000
Frequency: Annual
Study Establishment: The Metropolitan Museum of Art
Country of Study: United States of America
Application Procedure: A typed application along with supporting materials must be sent.
Closing Date: January 20th
Contributor: Judith Lee Stronach and Raymond Lifchez

Metropolitan Museum of Art Roswell L Gilpatric Internship

Subjects: Museum studies.
Purpose: To support students showing an interest in museum careers.
Eligibility: Open to graduate students showing special interest in museum careers.
Level of Study: Graduate
Type: Internship
Value: Please contact organization for details
Length of Study: 9 weeks, from mid-June to mid-August
Frequency: Annual
Study Establishment: The Metropolitan Museum of Art
Country of Study: United States of America
No. of awards offered: Varies
Application Procedure: Applicants must submit a typed application including their name and address, a full curriculum vitae, two academic recommendations, official transcripts, a list of art history or other relevant courses taken and an essay or letter of not more than 500 words describing their career goals, interest in museum work and their reasons for applying. There are no application forms.

Closing Date: Please contact the Museum
Funding: Private
Contributor: The Thorne Foundation

Metropolitan Museum of Art Summer Internships for College Students

Subjects: Art history and related fields.
Purpose: To support students showing an interest in museum careers.
Eligibility: Open to recent graduates who have not yet entered graduate school. Candidates should have a strong background in art history and intend to pursue careers in art museums. It is not always possible to obtain a visa for foreign nationals.
Level of Study: Graduate
Type: Internship
Value: Varies
Length of Study: 10 weeks, full-time from June to August including 2 weeks of orientation
Frequency: Annual
Study Establishment: The Metropolitan Museum of Art
Country of Study: United States of America
No. of awards offered: Varies
Application Procedure: Applicants must submit a typed application including their name and address, a full curriculum vitae, two academic recommendations, official transcripts, a list of art history or other relevant courses taken and an essay or letter of not more than 500 words describing their career goals, interest in museum work and their reasons for applying. There are no application forms.
Closing Date: Please contact the Museum
Funding: Private
Contributor: The Lebensfeld Foundation, The Billy Rose Foundation, The Solow Art and Architecture Foundation and the Ittleson Foundation, Inc.

Metropolitan Museum of Art Summer Internships for Graduate Students

Subjects: Art history and related fields.
Purpose: To support students showing an interest in museum careers.
Eligibility: Open to individuals who have completed at least 1 year of graduate work in art history or an allied field and who intend to pursue careers in art museums. It is not always possible to obtain a visa for foreign nationals.
Level of Study: Graduate
Type: Internship
Value: US$3,250
Length of Study: 10 weeks, full-time
Frequency: Annual
Study Establishment: The Metropolitan Museum of Art
Country of Study: United States of America
No. of awards offered: Varies
Application Procedure: Applicants must submit a typed application including their name and address, a full curriculum vitae, two academic recommendations, official transcripts, a list of art history or other relevant courses taken and an essay or letter of not more than 500 words describing their career goals, interest in museum work and their reasons for applying. There are no application forms.
Closing Date: Please contact the Museum
Funding: Private
Contributor: The Lebensfeld Foundation, The Billy Rose Foundation, Francine LeFrak Friedburg, the Solow Art and Architecture Foundation and the Ittleson Foundation, Inc.
Additional Information: Graduate interns work on projects related to the Museum's collection or to a special exhibition as well as administrative areas.

The Tiffany & Co. Foundation Curatorial Internship in American Decorative Arts

Subjects: Museum management.
Eligibility: Open to postgraduates who are interested in careers in art museums.
Level of Study: Research, postgraduate
Type: Internship
Value: US$22,000; stipend of US$3,000 available for research and educational travel
Length of Study: 1 year
Frequency: Annual
Application Procedure: See the website.
Closing Date: January 20th

MICHIGAN SOCIETY OF FELLOWS

University of Michigan, 3572 Rackham Building, 915 E Washington Street, Ann Arbor, MI, 48109-1070, United States of America
Tel: (1) 734 763 1259
Email: society.of.fellows@umich.edu
Website: www.rackham.umich.edu/Faculty/society.html
Contact: Administrative Assistant

The Michigan Society of Fellows, founded in 1970, promotes academic and creative excellence in the humanities and the arts, the social, physical and life sciences and the professions. The objective of the Society is to provide financial and intellectual support for individuals selected for outstanding achievement, professional promise and interdisciplinary interests.

Michigan Society of Fellows Postdoctoral Fellowships

Subjects: All subjects.
Purpose: To provide financial and intellectual support for individuals selected for outstanding achievement, professional promise and interdisciplinary interests.
Eligibility: Applicants must be near the beginning of their professional careers and have completed a PhD or comparable professional or artistic degree 3 years prior to application.
Level of Study: Postdoctorate
Type: Fellowship
Value: A stipend of US$47,271 per year
Length of Study: 3 years
Frequency: Annual
Study Establishment: The University of Michigan
Country of Study: United States of America
No. of awards offered: 4
Application Procedure: Applicants must complete an application form available from the website.
Closing Date: September 29th
Funding: Private
Contributor: The University of Michigan
No. of awards given last year: 4
No. of applicants last year: 398

MINERVA FOUNDATION

Society for Research Ltd., Hofgartenstrasse 8, D-80539, Munich, Germany
Tel: (49) 89 2108 1242
Fax: (49) 89 2108 1451
Email: reichardt@mpg-gv.mpg.de
Website: www.minerva.mpg.de

Minerva Fellowships

Subjects: All subjects.
Purpose: To fund scientific visits of Israeli scholars and scientists and to promote Israeli-German scientific co-operation.
Eligibility: Open to young scientists and researchers working in Israeli research institutes and universities. Candidates may be young doctoral and postdoctoral scientists, senior scientists or university teaching staff.
Level of Study: Research, doctorate, postdoctorate
Type: Fellowship
Value: €1,128 per month for scientists working on their PhD thesis, €2,100 per month for scientists (PhD) with 2 years working experience and €2,300 per month for scientists (PhD) with 5 years working experience
Length of Study: 6 months–3 years for doctoral candidates, 6 months–2 years for postdoctoral candidates
Study Establishment: A German university or research institute

Country of Study: Germany
Closing Date: January 15th and July 15th

Minerva Seed Grants
Subjects: All subjects.
Purpose: To fund scientific visits of Israeli scholars and scientists and to promote Israeli–German scientific co-operation.
Eligibility: Candidates must be nominated by their supervisor.
Level of Study: Doctorate
Type: Grant
Length of Study: 2–3 months
Study Establishment: A German university or research institute
Country of Study: Germany
Closing Date: January 15th and July 15th

Minerva Short-Term Research Grants
Subjects: All subjects.
Purpose: To fund scientific visits of Israeli scholars and scientists and to promote Israeli–German scientific co-operation.
Eligibility: Open to young scientists and researchers working in Israeli research institutes and universities. Candidates may be young doctoral and postdoctoral scientists, senior scientists or university teaching staff.
Level of Study: Research
Type: Grant
Value: €300 per week for doctoral candidates and €425 per week for postdoctoral candidates. (Additional payments like travel grants and family allowances are possible, depending on the type of the fellowship/grant)
Length of Study: 1–8 weeks
Study Establishment: A German university or research institute
Country of Study: Germany

MINISTRY OF EDUCATION, SCIENCE AND CULTURE (ICELAND)

Sölvhólsgata 4, IS-150, Reykjavik, Iceland
Tel: (354) 545 9500
Fax: (354) 562 3068
Email: postur@mrn.stjr.is
Website: www.ministryofeducation.is
Contact: Mrs Thórunn Bragadóttir, Division for Higher Education, Science & Research

Ministry of Education, Science and Culture (Iceland) Scholarships in Icelandic Studies
Subjects: Icelandic for Foreign Students Icelandic Studies for Foreign Students provides students with a good practical and theoretical basis for the Icelandic language and Icelandic culture. It facilitates further study in linguistics, literature, history and translation.
Eligibility: Citizens of the following countries may apply: Austria, Belgium, Bulgaria, Canada (if Icelandic origin), China, Croatia, the Czech Republic, Denmark, Estonia, Faroe Islands, Finland, France, Germany, Greenland, Holland, Hungary, Ireland, Italy, Japan, Latvia, Lithuania, Norway, Poland, Russia, Slovakia, Slovenia, Spain, Sweden, Switzerland, Taiwan, the United Kingdom and United States of America. The scholarships are intended for students of language and literature. Preference will, as a rule, be given to a candidate under 35 years of age.
Level of Study: Unrestricted
Type: Scholarship
Value: Krona 550,000 plus tuition
Length of Study: 8 months
Frequency: Annual
Study Establishment: The University of Iceland, Reykjavik
Country of Study: Iceland
No. of awards offered: 27–28
Application Procedure: The scholarship authorities of each cooperating country are invited to present applications for up to 2–3 candidates. Applicants must therefore apply to the relevant government department in their own country. United States of America candidates should apply to the Institute of International Education. United Kingdom candidates should apply to the Icelandic Embassy. Candidates of Icelandic origin from Canada or the United States of America should apply to the Icelandic National League of North America, 103-94 1st Avenue, Gimli, MB ROC 1B1, Canada.
Closing Date: April 1st
Funding: Government
No. of awards given last year: 27
No. of applicants last year: 76
Additional Information: All applications must have been evaluated and forwarded to the Icelandic Ministry of Education, Science and Culture through the home country scholarship authorities. A special committee in Iceland will decide on the outcome of the applications and its evaluation will be announced to the candidates in June/July.

For further information contact:

Icelandic Embassy, 2A Hans Street, London, SW1X 0JE, England
Email: icemb.london@utn.stjr.is
Website: www.iceland.org/uk

MINISTRY OF EDUCATION, YOUTH AND SPORTS OF THE CZECH REPUBLIC

Karmelitska 7–8 118 12 Praha 1, Czech Republic
Tel: (42) 257193111
Email: info@msmt.cz
Website: www.msmt.cz

The ministry of Education, Youth and sports is the central authority of state administration for overall strategy, educational policy and the preparation of appropriate legislative standards and executive and operational activities.

Czech Republic Scholarships
Subjects: All subjects.
Purpose: To offer opportunity to foreign nationals to pursue independent research studies.
Eligibility: Open to foreign nationals who a PhD candidates and wish to accomplish a study or research stay at one of the Czech public institutions.
Level of Study: Postgraduate
Type: Scholarship
Value: CZK 7,500 per month
Length of Study: 2–10 months
Frequency: Annual
Country of Study: Czech Republic
Application Procedure: See the website for details.
Closing Date: March 31st
Funding: Government

MINTEK

Human Resources Division, Private Bag X3015, Randburg, 2125, South Africa
Tel: (27) 11 709 4648
Fax: (27) 11 709 4465
Email: bobt@mintek.co.za
Website: www.mintek.co.za
Contact: Head of Academic Support

Mintek is the partially state-funded South African metallurgical research organization. Its mission is to serve the national interest through high-calibre research and development and technology transfer that promotes mineral technology, and to foster the establishment of small, medium and large industries in the field of minerals and products derived from them.

Mintek Bursaries
Subjects: Chemical, metallurgical and electrical engineering, light current and electronics, chemistry, with an emphasis on inorganic, physical or analytical chemistry, metallurgy, extraction and mineralogy, geology and physics.

Purpose: To promote the training of research workers for the minerals industry in general and to meet its own needs for technically trained people.
Eligibility: Open to graduates of any nationality who possess an appropriate 4-year degree or higher qualification. A knowledge of English is essential. Preference is given to South African citizens. Merit and excellence are the criteria for selection. The project should be a promising development that will contribute to Mintek's activities and is in line with its strategic purpose. The student must have a strong academic background and show the potential to develop expertise that would benefit Mintek, and the institution where the project is carried out should be a centre of excellence in the subject.
Level of Study: Postgraduate
Type: Bursary
Value: Rand 32,400 per year for a MSc degree and Rand 40,200 per year for a PhD degree
Length of Study: Up to 2 years. Extension of this period can be granted by the President of Mintek
Frequency: Annual
Study Establishment: Any university or technikons in fields that complement its own activities
Country of Study: South Africa
No. of awards offered: 10–15
Application Procedure: Applicants must write for details.
Closing Date: There is no deadline
Funding: Government
Additional Information: Candidates are requested to sign a contract before starting their project. Usually, Mintek insists on a service commitment from the bursar on the completion of his or her studies on a year-to-year basis. Bursars are paid a monthly bursary-salary and Mintek pays the institution an amount to cover the project's running costs.

MISSOURI STATE UNIVERSITY

College of Business Administration, 400 David D Glass Hall, Springfield, MO 65897, United States of America
Tel: (1) 417 836 5646
Fax: (1) 417 836 4407
Email: mbaprogram@missouristate.edu
Website: www.coba.missouristate.edu
Contact: MBA Admissions Officer

Missouri State University is a college of business administration offering courses in various departments. The programme will provide the background knowledge necessary for professional practice in the field of business. In the eyes of MBA students at Missouri State University, educational value is defined by a high-quality programme, low tuition rates and low living costs in an attractive locale.

Missouri State University Carr Foundation Scholarship

Subjects: MBA.
Purpose: To assist students with expenses and to enhance learning.
Eligibility: Students must be enrolled in the MBA programme and display financial need.
Level of Study: Graduate
Type: Scholarship
Value: US$600
Length of Study: Varies
Study Establishment: Missouri State University
Country of Study: United States of America
No. of awards offered: 1
Application Procedure: Applicants must contact the organization for application details.
Closing Date: Please contact the organization
Additional Information: The scholarship is automatically renewed as long as the student maintains satisfactory academic progress; however, the recipient must reapply to renew.

Missouri State University Graduate Assistantships

Subjects: All subjects.
Purpose: To assist students with expenses and to enhance learning while studying for advanced degrees at SMSU.
Eligibility: Applicants must be admitted to a graduate programme at SMSU to be eligible. A minimum grade point average of 3.00 on the last 60 hours of undergraduate coursework or a minimum grade point average of 3.00 on 9 hours or more of graduate coursework is required. Graduate students who did not receive both their primary and secondary education where English was the primary language must meet the following requirements to qualify for graduate assistantships: successful completion of one semester of graduate studies at SMSU, during which they complete cultural orientation to prepare them for a teaching appointment and pass an SMSU-juried examination, in which the candidate must demonstrate his or her ability to interpret written English passages and to communicate orally in English in a classroom setting.
Level of Study: MBA, graduate
Value: A minimum stipend of US$6,450 for the academic year (9 months). In a few situations, a stipend of US$8,200 may be awarded
Length of Study: A maximum of 2 years (including Fall, Spring, and Summer)
Frequency: Annual
Study Establishment: Missouri State University
Country of Study: United States of America
No. of awards offered: Varies
Application Procedure: Applicants must submit an application directly to the department in which the assistantship is sought. It is wise to check with the department before applying. Information from an applicant must include employment history, academic history and the addresses of referees. Applications are available from the Graduate Research College and on the website.
Additional Information: For further information visit the website or contact the Graduate Research College.

Missouri State University Graduate of Business Professional Honor Society Scholarship

Subjects: MBA.
Purpose: To assist students with expenses and to enhance learning.
Eligibility: Applicants must be enrolled in either the MBA programme or the MACC programme, have a grade point average of not less than 3.33, have active membership in the Graduate of Business Professional Honor Society and have been a member of the Society for at least two semesters.
Level of Study: MBA
Type: Scholarship
Value: US$250
Frequency: Annual
Study Establishment: Missouri State University
Country of Study: United States of America
No. of awards offered: 1
Application Procedure: Applicants must contact the organization for application details.
Closing Date: Please contact the organization for details

Missouri State University Robert and Charlotte Bitter Graduate Scholarship

Subjects: MBA.
Purpose: To assist students with expenses and to enhance learning.
Eligibility: Applicants must have been admitted to the MBA or MACC programme, be enrolled in 12 hours or more each semester or enrolled in 6 hours or more each semester if the student is a graduate assistant, have a combined formula score (200 x grade point average Graduate Management Admission Test score) of 1,100 or higher and minimum 3.33 graduate grade point average, have completed a minimum of 24 hours or 15 hours if the student is a graduate assistant, and have completed all prerequisite courses or be currently enrolled in final prerequisite courses.
Level of Study: Graduate, mba
Type: Scholarship
Value: US$1,200
Length of Study: Varies
Study Establishment: Missouri State University
Country of Study: United States of America
No. of awards offered: 1
Application Procedure: Applicants must contact the organization for application details.
Closing Date: Please contact the organization

MIZUTANI FOUNDATION FOR GLYCOSCIENCE

Marunouchi Center Bldg. 10f, 1-6-1 Marunouchi, Chiyoda-ku, Tokyo, 100-0005, Japan
Tel: (81) 3 5220 8977
Fax: (81) 3 5220 8978
Email: info@mizutanifdn.or.jp
Website: www.mizutanifdn.or.jp
Contact: Keiichi Yoshida, Executive Secretary

The Mizutani Foundation for Glycoscience undertakes major programmes such as the worldwide distribution of research grants to qualified glycoscientists for their outstanding basic research, assistance of international exchanges between Japanese and foreign glycosciences, contributions to glycoscience-related meetings in Japan and practice of other activities that are necessary to achieve the aims of the Foundation.

Mizutani Foundation for Glycoscience Research Grants

Subjects: Glycoscience.
Purpose: To contribute to human welfare through the enhancement of glycoscience by awarding grants for creative research in glycoscience conducted by domestic and overseas researchers, by awarding grants for international exchanges and for convening conferences in the field of glycoscience.
Eligibility: Open to those with a doctorate corresponding to a PhD or MD in the United States of America in a field relevant to the proposed project, who have documented capability of performing independent studies and are members of a scientific institution where they can carry out the proposed study. An applicant who has been awarded the grant previously may reapply after 5 years.
Level of Study: Doctorate, postdoctorate
Value: Yen 3,000,000–7,000,000
Length of Study: 1 year
Frequency: Annual
Country of Study: Any country
No. of awards offered: 10–15
Application Procedure: Applicants must download an application form from the website.
Closing Date: July 1st and September 1st
Funding: Foundation
Contributor: The Seikagaku Corporation
No. of awards given last year: 15
No. of applicants last year: 118

MODERN LANGUAGE ASSOCIATION OF AMERICA (MLA)

26 Broadway 3rd Floor, New York, NY, 10004-1789, United States of America
Tel: (1) 646 576 5141
Fax: (1) 646 458 0030
Email: awards@mla.org
Website: www.mla.org
Contact: Ms Annie Reiser, Co-ordinator, MLA Book Prizes

The Modern Language Association of America (MLA) is a non-profit membership organization that promotes the study and teaching of language and literature in English and foreign languages.

Aldo and Jean Scaglione Prize for a Translation of a Literary Work

Subjects: Translation.
Purpose: To award an outstanding translation of a book-length literary work into English.
Eligibility: Open to translations published in the year preceding the year in which the award is given.
Type: Prize
Value: US$2,000
Frequency: Every 2 years
No. of awards offered: 1
Application Procedure: Applicants must send six copies of the work. For detailed information about specific prizes, applicants should contact the MLA.
Closing Date: April 1st
Funding: Private

Aldo and Jeanne Scaglione Prize for Comparative Literary Studies

Subjects: Comparative literary and cultural studies involving at least two literatures.
Purpose: To recognize outstanding scholarly work in comparative literary studies.
Eligibility: Open to books published in the year preceding the year in which the award is given. Authors must be members of the MLA.
Level of Study: Postdoctorate
Type: Prize
Value: US$2,000
Frequency: Annual
No. of awards offered: 1
Application Procedure: Applicants must send four copies of the work. For detailed information about specific prizes, applicants should contact the MLA.
Closing Date: May 1st
Funding: Private

Aldo and Jeanne Scaglione Prize for French and Francophone Literary Studies

Subjects: French and Francophone linguistic or literary studies.
Purpose: To recognize outstanding scholarly work.
Eligibility: Open to books published in the year preceding the year in which the prize is given. Authors must be members of the MLA.
Level of Study: Postdoctorate
Type: Prize
Value: US$2,000
Frequency: Annual
No. of awards offered: 1
Application Procedure: Applicants must send four copies of the work. For detailed information about specific prizes, applicants should contact the MLA.
Closing Date: May 1st
Funding: Private

Aldo and Jeanne Scaglione Prize for Italian Studies

Subjects: Italian literature, culture or comparative literature involving Italian.
Purpose: To award an outstanding scholarly work.
Eligibility: Open to books published in the year preceding the year in which the award is given. Authors must be members of the MLA.
Level of Study: Postdoctorate
Type: Prize
Value: US$2,000
Frequency: Every 2 years
No. of awards offered: 1
Application Procedure: Applicants must send four copies of the work. For detailed information about specific prizes, applicants should contact the MLA.
Closing Date: May 1st
Funding: Private

Aldo and Jeanne Scaglione Prize for Studies in Germanic Languages and Literatures

Subjects: The linguistics or literatures of any of the Germanic languages including Danish, Dutch, German, Norwegian, Swedish or Yiddish.
Purpose: To recognize an outstanding scholarly work.
Eligibility: Authors must be members of the MLA. Books must have been published in the 2 years preceding the year of the award.
Level of Study: Postdoctorate
Type: Prize
Value: US$2,000
Frequency: Every 2 years
No. of awards offered: 1

Application Procedure: Applicants must send four copies of the work. For detailed information about specific prizes, applicants should contact the MLA.
Closing Date: May 1st
Funding: Private

Aldo and Jeanne Scaglione Prize for Studies in Slavic Languages and Literatures

Subjects: Linguistic or literary study of a work in a Slavic language.
Purpose: To recognize an outstanding scholarly work.
Eligibility: Open to books published no more than two years preceding the year in which the prize is given. Authors need not be members of the MLA.
Level of Study: Postdoctorate
Type: Prize
Value: US$2,000
Frequency: Every 2 years
No. of awards offered: 1
Application Procedure: Applicants must send four copies of the work. For detailed information about specific prizes, applicants should contact the MLA.
Closing Date: May 1st
Funding: Private

Aldo and Jeanne Scaglione Prize for Translation of a Scholarly Study of Literature

Subjects: Translation.
Purpose: To recognize an outstanding translation of a book-length work of literary history, literary criticism, philology and literary theory into English.
Eligibility: Open to books published no more than two years preceding the year in which the prize is given. Authors need not be members of the MLA.
Level of Study: Postdoctorate
Type: Prize
Value: US$2,000
Frequency: Every 2 years
No. of awards offered: 1
Application Procedure: Applicants must send four copies of the work. For detailed information about specific prizes, applicants should contact the MLA.
Closing Date: May 1st
Funding: Private

Fenia and Yaakov Leviant Memorial Prize

Subjects: English translation of a Yiddish literary work and/or Yiddish literature and culture.
Purpose: To recognize an outstanding translation into English or an outstanding scholarly work in the field of Yiddish.
Eligibility: The prize is awarded alternately to a translational or scholarly work in the field of Yiddish.
Level of Study: Postdoctorate
Type: Prize
Value: US$500
Frequency: Every 2 years
No. of awards offered: 1
Application Procedure: Applicants must send four copies of the work. For detailed information about specific prizes, applicants should contact the MLA.
Closing Date: May 1st
Funding: Private

Howard R Marraro Prize

Subjects: Italian literature or comparative literature involving Italian.
Purpose: To award an outstanding scholarly work.
Eligibility: Authors must be members of the MLA.
Level of Study: Postdoctorate
Type: Prize
Value: US$1,000
Frequency: Every 2 years
No. of awards offered: 1
Application Procedure: Applicants must send four copies of the work. For detailed information about specific prizes, applicants should contact the MLA.
Closing Date: May 1st
Funding: Private

James Russell Lowell Prize

Subjects: Literary theory, media, cultural history and interdisciplinary topics.
Purpose: To recognize an outstanding literary or linguistic study, a critical edition of an important work or a critical biography.
Eligibility: Open to books published the year preceding the year in which the award is due to be given. Authors must be current members of the MLA.
Level of Study: Postdoctorate
Type: Prize
Value: US$1,000
Frequency: Annual
No. of awards offered: 1
Application Procedure: Applicants must send six copies of the work. For detailed information about specific prizes, applicants should contact the MLA.
Closing Date: March 1st
Funding: Private

Katherine Singer Kovacs Prize

Subjects: Latin American or Spanish literatures and cultures.
Purpose: To recognize an outstanding book published in English in the field.
Eligibility: Open to books published the year preceding the year in which the prize is given. Competing books should be broadly interpretative works that enhance the understanding of the interrelations among literature, the arts and society.
Level of Study: Postdoctorate
Type: Prize
Value: US$1,000
Frequency: Annual
No. of awards offered: 1
Application Procedure: Applicants must send six copies of the work. For detailed information about specific prizes, applicants should contact the MLA.
Closing Date: May 1st
Funding: Private

Kenneth W Mildenberger Prize

Subjects: The teaching of languages and literatures, other than English.
Purpose: To support work in the field of the teaching of languages and literatures, other than English.
Eligibility: Authors need not be members of the MLA. Open to books published in the year preceding the year in which the prize is given.
Level of Study: Postdoctorate
Type: Prize
Value: US$1,000
Frequency: Annual
No. of awards offered: 1
Application Procedure: Applicants must send seven copies of the work. For detailed information about specific prizes, applicants should contact the MLA.
Closing Date: May 1st
Funding: Private
Additional Information: The prize is given for a research article in odd-numbered years and a book in even-numbered years.

Lois Roth Award for a Translation of Literary Work

Subjects: Translation.
Purpose: To recognize an outstanding translation of a book-length literary work into English.
Eligibility: Open to translations published in the year preceding the year in which the prize is given. Translators need not be members of the MLA.
Level of Study: Postdoctorate

Type: Prize
Value: US$1,000
Frequency: Every 2 years
No. of awards offered: 1
Application Procedure: Applicants must send six copies of the work. For detailed information about specific prizes, applicants should contact the MLA.
Closing Date: April 1st
Funding: Private

Mina P Shaughnessy Prize

Subjects: Teaching English language, literature, rhetoric and composition.
Purpose: To recognize a research publication in the field of teaching English language, literature, rhetoric and composition.
Eligibility: Open to books published in the year preceding the year in which the prize is given. Authors need not be members of the MLA.
Level of Study: Postdoctorate
Type: Prize
Value: US$1,000
Frequency: Annual
No. of awards offered: 1
Application Procedure: Applicants must send seven copies of the work. For detailed information about specific prizes, applicants should contact the MLA.
Closing Date: May 1st

MLA Prize for a Distinguished Bibliography

Subjects: Bibliography.
Purpose: To award an outstanding enumerative or descriptive bibliography.
Eligibility: Editors need not be members of the MLA. Open to books published during the 2 years preceding the year in which the prize is given.
Level of Study: Postdoctorate
Type: Prize
Value: US$1,000
Frequency: Every 2 years
No. of awards offered: 1
Application Procedure: Applicants must send four copies of the work. For detailed information applicants should contact the MLA.
Closing Date: May 1st
Funding: Private

MLA Prize for a Distinguished Scholarly Edition

Subjects: Works in any of the modern languages.
Purpose: To recognize an outstanding scholarly edition.
Eligibility: At least one volume must have been published during the two years preceding the year in which the award is given. Editors need not be members of the MLA. Editions may be single or multiple volumes.
Level of Study: Postdoctorate
Type: Prize
Value: US$1,000
Frequency: Every 2 years
No. of awards offered: 1
Application Procedure: Applicants must send four copies of the work. For detailed information about specific prizes, applicants should contact the MLA.
Closing Date: May 1st
Funding: Private

MLA Prize for a First Book

Subjects: Literary theory, media, cultural history or interdisciplinary topics.
Purpose: To recognize an outstanding literary or linguistic study, or a critical biography.
Eligibility: Open to books published in the year preceding the year in which the prize is given as the first book-length publication of a current MLA member.
Level of Study: Postdoctorate
Type: Prize
Value: US$1,000
Frequency: Annual
No. of awards offered: 1
Application Procedure: Applicants must send six copies of the work. For detailed information about specific prizes, applicants should contact the MLA.
Closing Date: April 1st
Funding: Private

MLA Prize for Independent Scholars

Subjects: English or other modern languages and literatures.
Purpose: To award a scholarly book in the field of modern languages.
Eligibility: Open to books published in the year preceding the year in which the prize is given. At the time of publication of the book, the author must not be enrolled in a programme leading to an academic degree or hold a tenured, tenure-accruing or tenure-track position in postsecondary education. Authors need not be members of the MLA.
Level of Study: Postdoctorate
Type: Prize
Value: US$1,000
Frequency: Annual
No. of awards offered: 1
Application Procedure: Applicants must send six copies of the work. For detailed information about specific prizes, applicants should contact the MLA.
Closing Date: May 1st
Funding: Private

MLA Prize in Latina and Latino or Chicana and Chicano Literary and Cultural Studies

Subjects: Chicana and Chicano, Latina and Latino literary or cultural studies.
Purpose: To award an outstanding scholarly study.
Eligibility: Open to authors who are members of the MLA.
Level of Study: Postdoctorate
Type: Prize
Value: US$1,000
Frequency: Annual
No. of awards offered: 1
Application Procedure: Applicants must send four copies of their work. For detailed information about specific prizes, applicants should contact the MLA.
Closing Date: May 1st
Funding: Private

Morton N Cohen Award for A Distinguished Edition of Letters

Subjects: Edition of letters in any of the modern languages.
Eligibility: At least one volume must have been published during the two years preceding the year in which the award is given. Editors need not be members of the MLA. Editions may be single or multiple volumes.
Level of Study: Postdoctorate
Type: Award
Value: US$1,000
Frequency: Every 2 years
No. of awards offered: 1
Application Procedure: Applicants must send four copies of the work. For detailed information about specific prizes, applicants should contact the MLA.
Closing Date: May 1st
Funding: Private

William Sanders Scarborough Prize

Subjects: Black American literature and culture.
Purpose: To recognize an outstanding scholarly book in the field of Black American literature or culture.
Eligibility: Books that are primarily translations will not be considered.
Level of Study: Postdoctorate
Type: Prize
Value: US$1,000
Frequency: Annual
No. of awards offered: 1

Application Procedure: Applicants must send four copies of the work. For detailed information about specific prizes, applicants should contact the MLA.
Closing Date: May 1st

MONASH UNIVERSITY

Wellington Road, Clayton, VIC, 3168, Australia
Tel: (61) 3 9905 3009
Fax: (61) 3 9905 5042
Email: mrgs@adm.monash.edu.au
Website: www.monash.edu.au/phdschol
Contact: Monash Research Graduate School

Monash University is one of Australia's largest universities, with ten faculties covering every major area of intellectual activity, six campuses in Australia and an increasing global presence. Research at Monash covers the full spectrum from fundamental to applied research and ranges across the arts and humanities, social, natural, health and medical sciences and the technological sciences. The University is determined to preserve its strength in fundamental research, which underpins its successes in applied research, and to continue to make a distinguished contribution to intellectual and cultural life.

Monash International Postgraduate Research Scholarship (MIPRS)

Subjects: All subjects.
Purpose: To provide support for supervised full-time research at the Master's and doctoral level.
Eligibility: Open to graduates of any Australian or overseas university who hold a First Class (Honours) Bachelor's Degree or equivalent.
Level of Study: Doctorate, master's by research
Type: Scholarship
Value: The award meets the full cost of international tuition fees, amenities and OSHC (overseas student health cover)
Length of Study: Up to 2 years for the Master's degree and up to 3 years with the possibility of an additional 6-month extension for the doctoral degree
Frequency: Annual
Study Establishment: Monash University
Country of Study: Australia
No. of awards offered: 40
Application Procedure: Applicants must complete an application kit, which is available 4 months before the closing date.
Closing Date: October 31st
Additional Information: International students must meet English language proficiency requirements.

Monash University Silver Jubilee Postgraduate Scholarship

Subjects: Medicine, nursing and health sciences, science and pharmacy.
Purpose: To provide supervised full-time research at the Master's and doctoral level.
Eligibility: Open to graduates of any Australian or overseas university who hold a First Class (Honours) Bachelor's Degree or equivalent.
Level of Study: Doctorate, master's by research candidates
Type: Scholarship
Value: Australian $24,388 p.a. plus relocation, research and thesis allowance
Length of Study: Up to 2 years for the Master's degree and up to 3 years with the possibility of an additional 6-month extension for the doctoral degree
Frequency: Annual
Study Establishment: Monash University
Country of Study: Australia
No. of awards offered: 1
Application Procedure: Applicants must complete an application kit, which is available 4 months before the closing date.
Closing Date: October 31st
Additional Information: International students must meet English language proficiency requirements.

Sir James McNeill Foundation Postgraduate Scholarship

Subjects: Engineering, medicine, music and science.
Purpose: To enable a PhD scholar to pursue a full-time programme of research that is both environmentally responsible and socially beneficial to the community.
Eligibility: Open to graduates of any Australian or overseas university who hold a First Class (Honours) Bachelor's Degree or equivalent.
Level of Study: Doctorate
Type: Scholarship
Value: Australian $24,886 p.a. plus relocation, research and thesis allowance
Length of Study: Up to 3 years, with the possibility of an additional 6-month extension
Frequency: Annual
Study Establishment: Monash University
Country of Study: Australia
No. of awards offered: 1
Application Procedure: Applicants must complete an application kit, which is available 4 months before the closing date.
Closing Date: October 31st
No. of awards given last year: 1
No. of applicants last year: N/A
Additional Information: International students must meet English language proficiency requirements.

Vera Moore International Postgraduate Research Scholarships

Subjects: All subjects.
Purpose: To provide support for supervised full-time research at the Master's and doctoral level.
Eligibility: Open to graduates of any Australian or overseas university who hold a First Class (Honours) Bachelor's Degree or equivalent.
Level of Study: Doctorate
Type: Scholarship
Value: The full cost of tuition fees plus a research allowance of up to Australian $550 per year, amenities and overseas student health cover
Length of Study: Up to 2 years for the Master's degree and up to 3 years with the possibility of an additional 6–month extension for the doctoral degree
Frequency: Annual
Study Establishment: Monash University
Country of Study: Australia
No. of awards offered: 1
Application Procedure: Applicants must complete an application kit, which is available 4 months before the closing date.
Closing Date: October 31st
Additional Information: International students must meet English language proficiency requirements.

MONTANA STATE UNIVERSITY-BILLINGS

1500 University Drive, Billings, MT 59101-0298, United States of America
Tel: (1) 657 2244
Fax: (1) 657 1600
Website: www.msubllings.edu

The Montana State University-Billings is dedicated to the development of workforce capacity by providing top quality learning opportunities and services to meet a variety of career choices and customer needs by being responsive, flexible and market driven.

Abrahamson Family Endowed Scholarship

Subjects: All subjects.
Purpose: To provide financial assistance.
Eligibility: Open to full-time enrolled students who are residents of Montana or Wyoming.
Level of Study: Postgraduate
Type: Scholarship
Value: US$1,000
Frequency: Annual

Study Establishment: Montana State University-Billings
Country of Study: United States of America
Application Procedure: A completed application form along with scholarship application, which is available on the must be submitted at the earliest.
Closing Date: February 1st

The Berg Family Endowed Scholarship

Subjects: Humanities area including English, philosophy and history.
Purpose: To provide financial assistance.
Eligibility: Open to residents of Montana Community who are between the age of 18 and 22.
Level of Study: Postgraduate
Type: Scholarship
Length of Study: US$1,200
Frequency: Annual
Study Establishment: Montana State University-Billings
Country of Study: United States of America
No. of awards offered: 2
Application Procedure: Complete details available on the website.
Closing Date: February 1st
Contributor: The Billings Foundation

Billings Broadcasters MSU-Billings Media Scholarship

Subjects: Communication, public relations, marketing, business management, graphic design, information technology, promotions and other areas related to the broadcast industry.
Purpose: To support students by offering financial assistance.
Eligibility: Open to full-time students at MSU-Billings.
Level of Study: Postgraduate
Type: Scholarship
Value: US$2,000
Frequency: Annual
Study Establishment: Montana State University-Billings
Country of Study: United States of America
No. of awards offered: Varies
Application Procedure: A completed application form along with scholarship application must be submitted.
Closing Date: February 1st

For further information contact:

MSU-Billings University, Relations, McMuller Hall, Room 201

Briggs Distributing Co., Inc/John & Claudia Decker Endowed Scholarship

Subjects: All subjects.
Purpose: To provide financial assistance.
Eligibility: Open to full-time students with financial needs.
Level of Study: Postgraduate
Type: Scholarship
Value: US$2,500
Frequency: Annual
Study Establishment: Montana State University-Billings
Country of Study: United States of America
Application Procedure: See the website.
Closing Date: February 1st
Additional Information: Preference will be given to Children of employers of Briggs Distributing Co., Inc.

The Bruce H. Carpenter Non-Traditional Endowed Scholarship

Subjects: All subjects.
Purpose: To provide financial assistance.
Eligibility: Open to non-traditional students who reside in Montana.
Level of Study: Postgraduate
Type: Scholarship
Value: US$3,400
Frequency: Annual
Study Establishment: Montana State University-Billings
Country of Study: United States of America
Application Procedure: A completed application form along with 3 letters of recommendation and a copy of college transcript must be submitted.
Closing Date: February 1st

Ellen Shields Endowed Scholarship

Subjects: All subjects.
Purpose: To assist a student with economic need.
Eligibility: Open to candidates who are not entitled to scholarships provided by the larger companies based on achievement.
Level of Study: Postgraduate
Type: Scholarship
Value: US$7,500
Frequency: Annual
Study Establishment: Montana State University-Billings
Country of Study: United States of America
No. of awards offered: 1
Application Procedure: See the website for details.
Closing Date: February 1st

Eric Robert Anderson Memorial Scholarship

Subjects: Arts.
Purpose: To support art students.
Eligibility: Open to paid members of Art students league who are enrolled as full-time students.
Type: Scholarship
Value: US$1,000
Frequency: Annual
No. of awards offered: 2
Application Procedure: A completed application form along with curriculum vitae and artist's statement must be submitted. See the website for complete details.
Closing Date: February 1st

For further information contact:

MSU-Billings Art Office Secretary, First floor, liberal Arts Building

Frances S. Barker Endowed Scholarship

Subjects: All subjects.
Purpose: To support students with financial needs.
Eligibility: Open to full-time students who demonstrate a definite financial need.
Level of Study: Postgraduate
Type: Scholarship
Value: US$1,000
Frequency: Annual
Study Establishment: Montana State University-Billings
Country of Study: United States of America
No. of awards offered: 3
Application Procedure: See the website.
Closing Date: February 1st
Contributor: The MSU-Billings Foundation Athletics Scholarship Committee
Additional Information: Preference will be given to student athletes.

The Haynes Foundation Scholarships

Subjects: All subjects.
Purpose: To provide financial assistance.
Eligibility: Open to candidates who are residents of Montana.
Level of Study: Postgraduate
Type: Scholarship
Value: US$2,000
Frequency: Annual
Study Establishment: Montana State University-Billings
Country of Study: United States of America
Application Procedure: See the website.
Closing Date: February 1st

Jarussi Sisters Scholarships Endowment

Subjects: All subjects.
Eligibility: Open to applicants who have enrolled as full-time students.

Level of Study: Postgraduate
Type: Scholarship
Value: Up to US$5,300 each
Frequency: Annual
Study Establishment: Montana State University-Billing
Country of Study: United States of America
No. of awards offered: 2
Application Procedure: See the website.
Closing Date: February 1st

John F. and Winifred M. Griffith Endowed Scholarship

Subjects: All subjects.
Purpose: To encourage students who demonstrate academic and leadership potential.
Eligibility: Open to candidates who are full-time students at Montana State University-Billings.
Level of Study: Postgraduate
Type: Scholarship
Value: Up to US$6,000 each
Frequency: Annual
Study Establishment: Montana State University-Billing
Country of Study: United States of America
No. of awards offered: 3
Application Procedure: Contact the Financial Aid Office.
Closing Date: February 1st

Kenneth W. Heikes Family Endowed Scholarship

Subjects: Accounting and information system.
Purpose: To assist students who wish to study further.
Eligibility: Open to full-time students who demonstrate academic or disciplinary potential.
Level of Study: Postgraduate
Type: Scholarship
Value: US$2,000
Frequency: Annual
Study Establishment: Montana State University-Billings
Country of Study: United States of America
Application Procedure: See the website.
Closing Date: February 1st

MSU-Billing Energy Laboratories Chemistry Endowed Scholarship

Subjects: Chemistry.
Purpose: To encourage students who wish to major in chemistry.
Eligibility: Open to full-time students residing in Montana.
Level of Study: Postgraduate
Type: Scholarship
Value: US$2,200
Frequency: Annual
Study Establishment: Montana State University-Billings
Country of Study: United States of America
Application Procedure: See the website.
Closing Date: February 1st

MSU-Billings Chan Cellor's Excellence Awards

Subjects: All subjects.
Purpose: To recognize academic achievement and leadership qualities.
Eligibility: Open to applicants with evidence of leadership and a record of community service.
Level of Study: Postgraduate
Type: Scholarship
Value: US$2,500 per year
Length of Study: 4 years
Frequency: Annual
Study Establishment: Montana State University-Billings
Country of Study: United States of America
Application Procedure: A completed Chancellor's Excellence Awards application must be submitted.
Closing Date: January 15th
Additional Information: Chancellor Scholars who meet or exceed all awards criteria may have their awards renewed for 4 years for a maximum award of US$10,000.

For further information contact:

Chancellor's Excellence Awards Committee, Montana State University-Billings Foundation

MONTREAL NEUROLOGICAL INSTITUTE

McGill University, 3801 University Street, Montréal, QC, H3A 2B4, Canada
Tel: (1) 514 398 8998
Fax: (1) 514 398 8248
Email: fil.lumia@mcgill.ca
Website: www.mcgill.ca/mni
Contact: Ms Filomena Lumia, Personnel Liaison Officer

The Montreal Neurological Institute is dedicated to the study of the nervous system and neurological disorders. Its 70 principal researchers hold teaching positions at McGill University. The Institute is characterized by close interaction between basic science researchers and the clinicians at its affiliated hospital.

Jeanne Timmins Costello Fellowships

Subjects: Neurology, neurosurgery and neuroscience research and study.
Purpose: To support research.
Eligibility: Open to candidates of any nationality who have an MD or PhD degree. Those with MD degrees will ordinarily have completed clinical studies in neurology or neurosurgery.
Level of Study: Postgraduate, doctorate
Type: Fellowship
Value: Canadian $25,000 per year
Length of Study: 1 year, with the possibility of renewal for a further year
Frequency: Annual
Study Establishment: The Montreal Neurological Institute
Country of Study: Canada
No. of awards offered: 4
Application Procedure: Applicants must write for details.
Closing Date: October 15th
Funding: Private
Contributor: Jean Timmins Costello
No. of awards given last year: 4

Preston Robb Fellowship

Subjects: Neurology, neurosurgery and neuroscience.
Purpose: To support research.
Eligibility: Open to researchers of any nationality.
Level of Study: Postdoctorate, postgraduate, doctorate
Type: Fellowship
Value: Canadian $25,000
Length of Study: 1 year
Frequency: Annual
Country of Study: Canada
No. of awards offered: 1
Application Procedure: Applicants must write for details.
Closing Date: October 15th
Funding: Private
Contributor: Preston Robb
No. of awards given last year: 1

MOSCOW UNIVERSITY TOURO

20/12 Podsosenski Pereulok, Moscow, Russia
Tel: (7) (095) 917 4169
Email: admin@touro.ru
Website: www.touro.ru
Contact: Admissions Office

Moscow University Touro is an independent, non-profit institution of higher education, established in 1991, which promotes international-style business education in Russia.

Moscow University Touro Corporate Scholarships

Subjects: Any subject.
Purpose: To fund exceptionally talented students or employees with the intellectual potential to become future business leaders in Russia.
Eligibility: Candidates of award are determined by the company or association sponsor in consultation with Moscow University Touro.
Level of Study: Postgraduate
Type: Scholarship
Length of Study: 1 year
Frequency: Annual
Study Establishment: Moscow University Touro
Country of Study: Russia
Application Procedure: Apply online or contact the admissions office.
Closing Date: August 1st
Funding: Corporation
Contributor: Russian and International Corporations

Moscow University Touro Universal Scholarships

Subjects: Any subject.
Purpose: To provide financial assistance to ready student with strong scholarship potential.
Eligibility: Only available to student studying full time at the Moscow campus.
Level of Study: Postgraduate
Type: Scholarship
Value: Payment of an approved tuition sum
Length of Study: 1 year
Frequency: Annual
Study Establishment: Moscow University Touro
Country of Study: Russia
Application Procedure: Apply online or contact the admissions office.
Closing Date: August 1st

For further information contact:

Tel: +7 (0) 95 917 4052
Contact: Eugenij Pouchinkin

MOTOR NEURONE DISEASE ASSOCIATION

PO Box 246, Northampton, Northamptonshire, NN1 2PR, England
Tel: (44) 16 0425 0505
Fax: (44) 16 0463 8289
Email: research@mndassociation.org
Website: www.mndassociation.org
Contact: Mrs M D Reicale, Research Administrator

The Motor Neurone Disease Association supports research on fundamental aspects of motor neurone disease (MND) and on its management and alleviation. It provides information and advice to patients and carers, and runs a nationwide care service. MND paralyzes selectively or generally and is fatal, irreversible and at present, incurable.

MND PhD Studentship Award

Subjects: Research on all aspects of MND in all relevant disciplines.
Purpose: To stimulate interest in MND research by encouraging young scientists into the field.
Eligibility: Restricted to researchers from United Kingdom laboratories.
Level of Study: Postdoctorate
Type: Studentship
Value: Approx. UK £65,000
Length of Study: 3 years
Frequency: Annual
Country of Study: United Kingdom
No. of awards offered: 1–2
Application Procedure: Applicants must submit a summary of their proposal, which is first considered by three members of the research advisory panel (RAP). Full applications are invited thereafter and application forms are provided. Full applications are submitted to two or more independent referees and then to the RAP for consideration.
Closing Date: Summary applications must be received by May 13th (may be subject to change)
No. of awards given last year: 2
No. of applicants last year: 7
Additional Information: The studentships are awarded on the basis of scientific merit and the value of research training offered.

MND Research Project Grants

Subjects: Research into all aspects of MND in all disciplines.
Purpose: To understand and research the cause and effective treatments of MND.
Eligibility: Overseas applicants must have a project that is unique in concept or design and that involves some aspect of collaboration with a United Kingdom institute.
Type: Grant
Value: UK £50,000 per year, maximum
Length of Study: 1–3 years
Frequency: Annual
Study Establishment: A research institution
No. of awards offered: Varies
Application Procedure: Applicants must submit a summary of their proposal, which is first considered by three members of the research advisory panel (RAP). Full applications are invited thereafter and application forms are provided. Full applications are submitted to two or more independent referees and then to the RAP for consideration.
Closing Date: Summary applications must be received by November 3rd (may be subject to change)
No. of awards given last year: 1
No. of applicants last year: 6

MOUNT DESERT ISLAND BIOLOGICAL LABORATORY

PO Box 35, Department NIA, Old Bar Harbor Road,
Salisbury Cove, ME, 04672,
United States of America
Tel: (1) 207 288 3605
Fax: (1) 207 288 2130
Email: phand@mdibl.org
Website: www.mdibl.org
Contact: Ms Patricia Hand, Administrative Director

The Mount Desert Island Biological Laboratory is a marine and biomedical research laboratory that uses unique models such as shark, skate and flounder to solve questions related to human and environmental health.

Mount Desert Island New Investigator Award

Subjects: Biological and life sciences.
Purpose: To support independent investigators spending 2–3 months in the Summer doing physiological research on marine animals at the Mount Desert Island Biological Laboratory.
Eligibility: Open to scientists at all stages of their career who wish to use marine systems for research studies at the Laboratory.
Level of Study: Postdoctorate, professional development
Type: Fellowship
Value: US$4,000–12,000. Special awards from the Salisbury Cove Research Fund (Thomas H Maren Foundation) are available for up to US$20,000 depending on need and potential long-term commitment to the laboratory
Length of Study: 2–3 months
Study Establishment: Mount Desert Island Biological Laboratory
Country of Study: United States of America
No. of awards offered: 15–20
Application Procedure: *Applicants must obtain an application form from the organization.* Please visit the website for application information.
Closing Date: February 1st

Funding: Government, private, foundation
No. of awards given last year: 19
No. of applicants last year: 20
Additional Information: The Mount Desert Island Biological Laboratory, located in Salisbury Cove, Maine is a 105-year-old research institution and an international centre for comparative physiology, toxicology, tissue culture biology and marine functional genomics studies. Awards can be used to defray the cost of laboratory space, housing, equipment fees and other costs depending on individual needs. Additional information can be found on the website.

MULTIPLE SCLEROSIS SOCIETY OF CANADA (MSSC)

175 Bloor Street East, Suite 700, North Tower, Toronto, Ontario, M4W 3R8, Canada
Tel: (1) 416 922 6065
Fax: (1) 416 922 7538
Email: jackie.munroe@mssociety.ca
Website: www.mssociety.ca
Contact: Ms Jackie Munroe, Research Grants Programme Manager

The mission of the MSSC is to be a leader in finding a cure for multiple sclerosis and enabling people affected by the disease to enhance their quality of life.

MSSC Career Development Award

Subjects: Multiple sclerosis.
Purpose: To encourage full-time research.
Eligibility: Open to individuals holding a doctoral degree who have recently completed their training in research and are capable of carrying out independent research relevant to multiple sclerosis on a full-time basis.
Level of Study: Postdoctorate
Value: The salary scale, conditions of remuneration and allowable involvement in non research activities will be similar to Medical Research Council (MRC) scholarships
Length of Study: 1–3 years
Frequency: Annual
Study Establishment: A Canadian school of medicine
Country of Study: Canada
No. of awards offered: Limited
Application Procedure: Further information from Dean of graduate studies office.
Closing Date: October 1st
Funding: Private
No. of awards given last year: 0
No. of applicants last year: 1

MSSC Postdoctoral Fellowship

Subjects: Multiple sclerosis and allied diseases.
Purpose: To encourage research.
Eligibility: Open to qualified persons holding an MD or PhD degree and intending to pursue research work relevant to multiple sclerosis and allied diseases. The applicant must be associated to an appropriate authority in the field he or she wishes to study.
Level of Study: Postdoctorate
Type: Fellowship
Value: Salary scales will be similar to those suggested by the Canadian Institutes for Health Research
Length of Study: 1–3 years
Frequency: Annual
Study Establishment: A recognized institution which deals that problems relevant to multiple sclerosis
Country of Study: Other
No. of awards offered: Varies
Application Procedure: Contact Dean of Graduate studies office for further information.
Closing Date: October 1st
Funding: Private
No. of awards given last year: 19
No. of applicants last year: 21

MSSC Research Grant

Subjects: Multiple sclerosis.
Purpose: To fund research projects.
Eligibility: Open to researchers working in Canada or intending to return to Canada.
Level of Study: Postgraduate
Type: Research grant
Value: Varies
Length of Study: 1–3 years
Frequency: Annual
Study Establishment: An approved institution
Country of Study: Any country
No. of awards offered: Limited
Application Procedure: Contact Dean of Graduate studies office for further information.
Closing Date: October 1st
Funding: Private
No. of awards given last year: 15
No. of applicants last year: 30

MUSCULAR DYSTROPHY ASSOCIATION (MDA)

Research Department, 3300 East Sunrise Drive, Tucson, AZ, 85718, United States of America
Tel: (1) 520 529 2000
Fax: (1) 520 529 5300
Email: grants@mdausa.org
Website: www.mdausa.org
Contact: Grants Manager

The Muscular Dystrophy Association (MDA) supports research into over 40 diseases of the neuromuscular system to identify the causes of, and effective treatments for, the muscular dystrophies and related diseases including spinal muscular atrophies and motor neuron diseases, peripheral neuropathies, inflammatory myopathies, metabolic myopathies and diseases of the neuromuscular junction.

MDA Grant Programs

Subjects: The muscular dystrophies and related diseases.
Purpose: To support research into over 40 diseases of the neuromuscular system, and to identify the causes of, and effective treatments for, the muscular dystrophies and related diseases.
Eligibility: Open to persons who are professional or faculty members at appropriate educational, medical or research institutions, qualified to conduct and supervise a programme of original research, who have access to institutional resources necessary to conduct the proposed research project and who hold an MD or PhD.
Level of Study: Postdoctorate
Type: Grant
Value: Please contact the Association
Length of Study: Maximum of 3 years
Frequency: Annual
Country of Study: Any country
No. of awards offered: Varies
Application Procedure: Applicants must complete the Request for Research Grant Application.
Closing Date: Pre-applications are due no later than December 15th or June 15th
Funding: Private
Contributor: Voluntary contributions
No. of awards given last year: 140
Additional Information: Proposals from applicants outside the United States of America will only be considered for projects of highest priority to the MDA. Other conditions apply. Research is sponsored under the following grant programmes: Neuromuscular Disease Research and Neuromuscular Disease Research Development. Further information is available from the website.

MUSCULAR DYSTROPHY CAMPAIGN OF GREAT BRITAIN AND NORTHERN IRELAND

Research Department, 7-11 Prescot Place, London, SW4 6BS, England
Tel: (44) 20 7720 8055
Fax: (44) 20 7498 0670
Email: research@muscular-dystrophy.org
Website: www.muscular-dystrophy.org
Contact: Mrs Jenny Versnel, Head of Research

The Muscular Dystrophy Campaign is a United Kingdom-based charity funding medical research and support services for people with muscular dystrophy and related conditions.

Muscular Dystrophy Research Grants

Subjects: Muscular dystrophy and allied neuromuscular conditions.
Purpose: To provide continuity of funding for high-quality research of central importance to the Muscular Dystrophy Campaign's research objectives.
Eligibility: The MDC will only fund United Kingdom-based research. Principal Investigators must hold a contract that extends beyond the duration of the grant at an institution approved by the MDC.
Level of Study: Research, postdoctorate
Value: Salary of research staff, equipment and consumables. Salary of grant holder is not funded
Length of Study: 1–3 years
Frequency: Annual
Study Establishment: Universities, hospitals or research institutions
Country of Study: United Kingdom
No. of awards offered: Varies
Application Procedure: Applicants must contact the Head of Research with a summary of proposed research on A4-size paper. More details are available on the website.
Closing Date: October
Funding: Private
No. of awards given last year: 10
No. of applicants last year: 30

MUSEUM OF COMPARATIVE ZOOLOGY

26 Oxford Street, Cambridge, MA, 02138, United States of America
Tel: (1) 617 495 2460
Fax: (1) 617 496 8308
Email: ernstmayrgrant@oeb.harvard.edu
Website: www.mcz.harvard.edu
Contact: Ms Andrea Prill, Assistant to the Director

The Museum of Comparative Zoology was founded in 1859 through the efforts of Louis Agassiz (1807–1873). Agassiz, a zoologist from Neuchatel, Switzerland, served as the Director of the Museum from 1859 until his death in 1873. A brilliant lecturer and scholar, he established the Museum and its collections as a centre for research and education.

Ernst Mayr Travel Grant

Subjects: Animal systematics.
Purpose: To stimulate taxonomic work on neglected taxa.
Eligibility: There are no restrictions on eligibility. Preference is given to studies that use the Museum of Comparative Zoology's collections, although applications to work at other museums will be considered.
Level of Study: Research, unrestricted
Type: Travel grant
Value: Awards average about US$1,000
Length of Study: 1 year
Frequency: Twice a year
Study Establishment: An accredited museum
Country of Study: Any country
No. of awards offered: Varies
Application Procedure: Applicants must submit a short project description, itinerary, budget, a curriculum vitae and three letters of support. No proposal forms are required or provided. Proposals may be submitted through standard mail or electronically. Submissions through standard mail must include four copies of all materials and be received by the closing date. Proposals submitted electronically must be created in Microsoft Word or plain ASCII text format. For additional information visit the website.
Closing Date: October 15th and April 15th
Funding: Trusts
Contributor: Ernst Mayr
No. of awards given last year: 13
No. of applicants last year: 25
Additional Information: Announcements of awards will be made within 2 months of the closing date.

MUSICIANS BENEVOLENT FUND (MBF)

16 Ogle Street, London, W1W 6JA, England
Tel: (44) 20 7299 8356
Fax: (44) 20 7637 4307
Email: education@mbf.org.uk
Website: www.mbf.org.uk
Contact: Ms Susan Dolton, Education Administrator

The Musicians Benevolent Fund is the music business's own charity, the largest of its kind in the United Kingdom. Last year, it helped about 1,500 people of any age and in any area of the music business who were in need as a result of illness, accident or other misfortune, and spent over UK £2 million on its benevolent work. The MBF also plays a significant role in education, fulfilling its remit to encourage the next generation of young musicians.

Guilhermina Suggia Gift

Subjects: Musical performance of the cello.
Purpose: To assist with the studies of an outstanding cellist.
Eligibility: Open to cellists of any nationality, under 21 years of age.
Level of Study: Professional development
Value: Up to UK £3,000
Frequency: Annual
Country of Study: Any country
No. of awards offered: 1
Application Procedure: Applicants must complete an application form and provide two references.
Closing Date: Autumn
Funding: Private
No. of awards given last year: 1
No. of applicants last year: 13

Ian Fleming Charitable Trust Music Education Awards

Subjects: Musical performance.
Purpose: To help exceptionally talented young musicians.
Eligibility: Open to singers and instrumentalists possessing the potential to become first-class performers, who have been resident in the United Kingdom for 3 years. Instrumentalists must be under 25 years of age, and singers must be under 28 years of age.
Level of Study: Postgraduate, professional development
Value: Varies, to cover tuition, maintenance and the purchase of instruments. Awards range from UK £2,000–5,000
Frequency: Annual
Country of Study: Any country
No. of awards offered: Approx. 10
Application Procedure: Applicants must complete application forms and provide two references.
Closing Date: February 17th
Funding: Private
No. of awards given last year: 8
No. of applicants last year: 296
Additional Information: Selected applicants will be asked to audition in March or April.

Manoug Parikian Award

Subjects: Musical performance on the violin.
Purpose: To assist the studies of an outstanding young violinist.
Eligibility: Open to violinists under of any nationality, under 21 years of age.
Level of Study: Professional development

Value: UK £3,000
Frequency: Annual
Country of Study: Any country
No. of awards offered: 1
Application Procedure: Applicants must complete an application form and provide two references.
Closing Date: Autumn
Funding: Private
No. of awards given last year: 1
No. of applicants last year: 31
Additional Information: The Manoug Parikian Award is run in conjunction with the RPS Emily Anderson Prize. The Award must be used for study costs or instrument purchase.

MBF Awards for Accompanists and Repetiteurs

Subjects: Musical performance.
Purpose: To assist accompanists and repetiteurs.
Eligibility: Open to postgraduates and accompanists under 27 years of age and repetiteurs under 30 years of age. Applicants should have been resident in the United Kingdom for 3 years.
Level of Study: Postgraduate, professional development
Value: Up to UK £3,500 each
Frequency: Annual
Country of Study: Any country
No. of awards offered: 5–10
Application Procedure: Applicants must complete an application form and provide two references.
Closing Date: May
Funding: Private
No. of awards given last year: 6
No. of applicants last year: 25
Additional Information: Selected students will be asked to audition. The Sir Henry Richardson Scholarship of UK £3,500 will be awarded to the most outstanding musician heard in each discipline.

MBF Music Education Awards

Subjects: Musical performance.
Purpose: To help exceptionally talented young musicians.
Eligibility: Open to singers and instrumentalists possessing the potential to become first-class performers, who have been resident in the United Kingdom for 3 years. Instrumentalists must be under 25 years of age, and singers under 28 years of age.
Level of Study: Professional development, postgraduate
Value: Varies, to cover tuition maintenance and the purchase of instruments. Awards range from UK £1,000 to 5,000
Frequency: Annual
Application Procedure: Applicants must complete an application form and provide two references.
Closing Date: February 17th
Funding: Private
No. of awards given last year: 60
No. of applicants last year: 296
Additional Information: The following major awards are also available through these auditions: Ian Fleming Charitable Trust Music Education Awards, Professor Charles Leggett Awards, Emily English Scholarship and Maidment Scholarships.

Miriam Licette Scholarship

Subjects: Musical performance and song.
Purpose: To assist a female student of French song.
Eligibility: Open to soprano, mezzo-soprano or contralto singers for advanced study. Applicants should be in full-time study or in their first year in the profession and be under 30 years of age.
Level of Study: Postgraduate, professional development
Type: Scholarship
Value: UK £3,000
Frequency: Annual
Country of Study: Any country
No. of awards offered: 1. There may be further discretionary awards
Application Procedure: Selected students will be asked to audition. An application form must be completed and two references must be provided.
Closing Date: December 1st
Funding: Private
No. of awards given last year: 3
No. of applicants last year: 54
Additional Information: The award is run in conjunction with the Maggie Teyte Prize.

Myra Hess Trust

Subjects: Musical performance on strings and piano.
Purpose: To give assistance for the purchase of instruments, and for tuition, maintenance.
Eligibility: Open to outstanding young instrumentalists between 20 and 27 years of age. Preference is given to those entering a professional career as a soloist. Open to piano, violin, viola, cello and double bass students. Applicants may be of any nationality, but British and Irish applicants may not apply for funding for study/recitals outside the United Kingdom.
Level of Study: Postgraduate, professional development
Value: Up to UK £3,000 each
Frequency: Annual
Country of Study: Any country
No. of awards offered: 5–20
Application Procedure: Applicants must complete an application form and provide two references. Selected applicants are asked to audition in May/June.
Closing Date: April 24th
Funding: Private
No. of awards given last year: 18
No. of applicants last year: 76

Peter Whittingham Award

Subjects: Jazz.
Purpose: To promote both composition and performance through an innovative jazz project.
Eligibility: Open to individuals ordinarily resident in the United Kingdom to work independently or with a project group. The project should be in creation or performance in the field of cutting-edge jazz. Money is not given for course fees. All applicants should be under 26 years old.
Level of Study: Graduate, professional development, postgraduate
Value: UK £4,000
Frequency: Annual
No. of awards offered: 1
Application Procedure: A written description of the project must be provided together with a budget, a reference and a recording demonstrating composition and/or performance.
Closing Date: October
Funding: Private
No. of awards given last year: 1
No. of applicants last year: 7
Additional Information: Selected applicants will be asked to attend an interview.

Sybil Tutton Awards

Subjects: Musical performance in opera.
Purpose: To assist exceptionally talented students on a recognized course of operatic study.
Eligibility: Open to opera students under 30 years of age who have been resident in the United Kingdom for 3 years.
Level of Study: Postgraduate, professional development
Value: Up to UK £3,000 each
Frequency: Annual
Country of Study: Any country
No. of awards offered: 5–10
Application Procedure: Applicants must complete an application form and provide two references.
Closing Date: May 5th
Funding: Private
No. of awards given last year: 9
No. of applicants last year: 33
Additional Information: Selected students will be asked to audition in June.

THE MYASTHENIA GRAVIS FOUNDATION OF AMERICA

1821 University Ave W, Suite 8256, St Paul, MN 55104, United States of America
Tel: (1) 800 541 5454
Fax: (1) 651 917 1835
Email: mgfa@myasthenia.org
Website: www.myasthenia.org
Contact: Ms L J Taugher, Chief Executive

The Myasthenia Gravis Foundation of America's mission is to facilitate the timely diagnosis and optimal care of individuals affected by myasthenia gravis and to improve their lives through programmes of patient services, public information, medical research, professional education, advocacy and patient care.

Henry R Viets Medical/Graduate Student Research Fellowship

Subjects: The scientific basis of myasthenia gravis or related neuromuscular conditions.
Purpose: To promote research into the cause and cure of myasthenia gravis.
Eligibility: There are no eligibility restrictions.
Level of Study: Research, doctorate, graduate
Type: Fellowship
Value: US$3,000
Length of Study: Short-term
Frequency: Annual
Country of Study: Any country
No. of awards offered: 4–8
Application Procedure: Applicants must briefly describe, in abstract form, the question proposed for study, its association to myasthenia gravis or related neuromuscular conditions and research methodology. Further information may then be requested by the Foundation.
Closing Date: March 15th
Funding: Private
No. of awards given last year: 3
No. of applicants last year: 4

Myasthenia Gravis Nursing Research Fellowship

Subjects: Myasthenia gravis.
Purpose: To fund research specific to myasthenia gravis.
Eligibility: There are no eligibility restrictions.
Level of Study: Research, graduate, postgraduate
Type: Fellowship
Value: US$3,000
Length of Study: Short-term
Frequency: Dependent on funds available
Country of Study: Any country
No. of awards offered: 2–3
Application Procedure: Applicants must contact the Foundation for further details.
Closing Date: Applications are accepted at any time
Funding: Private
No. of awards given last year: None
No. of applicants last year: None

Osserman/Sosin/McClure Research Fellowship

Subjects: Research pertinent to myasthenia gravis that is concerned with neuromuscular transmission, immunology, molecular cell biology of the neuromuscular synapse and the aetiology and pathogenesis, diagnosis or treatment of the disease.
Purpose: To investigate the fundamental nature of myasthenia gravis.
Eligibility: There are no eligibility restrictions. The research preceptor must be an established investigator at an institution in the United States of America, Canada or abroad deemed appropriate by the MGFA Medical/Scientific Advisory Board. The applicant must either be (a) a permanent resident of the United States of America or Canada who has been accepted to work in the laboratory of an established investigator at an institution in the United States of America, Canada or abroad or (b) a foreign national who has been accepted to work in the laboratory of an established investigator at an institution in the United States of America or Canada deemed appropriate by the Medical/Scientific Advisory Board of MGFA.
Level of Study: Postdoctorate
Type: Fellowship
Value: US$50,000
Length of Study: 1 year
Frequency: Annual
Country of Study: Any country
No. of awards offered: 2–4
Application Procedure: Applicants must submit a ten-page proposal, a lay summary, budget, applicant's and preceptor's curriculum vitae and letters of recommendation.
Closing Date: October 1st
Funding: Private
No. of awards given last year: 1
No. of applicants last year: 8

NANTUCKET HISTORICAL ASSOCIATION (NHA)

15 Broad Street PO Box 1016, Nantucket, MA 02554, United States of America
Tel: (1) 508 228 1894
Fax: (1) 508 228 5618
Email: library@nha.org
Website: www.nha.org
Contact: Georgen Gilliam Charnes, Curator of Library and Archives

The Nantucket Historical Association (NHA) is the principal repository of Nantucket history, with extensive archives, collections of historic properties and art and artefacts that broadly illustrate Nantucket's past. The Research Library at the NHA contains a rich collection of primary and secondary sources that document all facets of Nantucket's cultural, social, economic and spiritual history for more than three centuries. More than 400 manuscript collections relate to Nantucket individuals and families, ships, businesses and trades, churches, schools and organizations. Searchable inventories of the library's manuscript, map and book holdings can be accessed via the NHA website. The NHA art and artefacts collections include paintings, drawings, prints, baskets, silver, whaling tools, scrimshaw, furniture and textiles. The particular strengths of the collection lie in artefacts that document Nantucket's whaling industry.

E Geoffrey and Elizabeth Thayer Verney Research Fellowship

Subjects: History.
Purpose: To enhance the public's knowledge and understanding of the heritage of Nantucket, Massachusetts.
Eligibility: Open to graduate students and independent Scholars in any field to conduct research in the collections of the NHA.
Level of Study: Graduate
Type: Residency
Value: A stipend of US$300 per week and travel expenses will be reimbursed for expenses up to US$600
Length of Study: 3 weeks
Frequency: Annual
Study Establishment: The NHA
Country of Study: United States of America
No. of awards offered: 1
Application Procedure: Applicants must send a full description of the proposed project, a preliminary bibliography and a complete curriculum vitae. An account of travel expenses must also be included with the anticipated time and duration of stay. Applications must be addressed to the Library Director.
Closing Date: December 1st
No. of awards given last year: 1
Additional Information: Applicants will be notified by December 21st.

NANYANG TECHNOLOGICAL UNIVERSITY (NTU)

MBA Office, Nanyang Business School, Nanyang Avenue, Singapore, 639798, Singapore
Tel: (65) (65) 6790 4899
Fax: (65) 6791 3561
Email: postgraduate@ntu.edu.sg
Website: www.ntu.edu.sg
Contact: Administrative Officer

The Nanyang Business School is one of Asia's top business schools. Its flagship programme is the Nanyang MBA, which has consistently been ranked one of the top in Asia and is ranked in the world top 100 by Economist intelligence unit, 2005.

NTU Alumni Scholarship

Subjects: MBA.
Purpose: To provide financial support to alumni of Nanyang Technological University admitted to the MBA programme on a full-time basis.
Eligibility: Open to alumni of Nanyang Technological University admitted to the MBA programme on a full-time basis. Recipients of other scholarships or bursaries are not eligible to apply.
Level of Study: MBA
Type: Scholarship
Value: US$3,000 per year
Length of Study: Each scholarship shall be tenable only for the academic year in which it is awarded
Frequency: Annual
Study Establishment: NTU
Country of Study: Singapore
No. of awards offered: 2 for MBA
Application Procedure: Applicants must submit a completed application form (available at www.ntu.edu.sg/alumni2/forms/postgrad-form.pdf).
Closing Date: End of July
Funding: Private
Contributor: NTU Alumni Fund
No. of awards given last year: None

For further information contact:

Nanyang Technological University, Level 5, Administrative Annexe 42 Nanyang Avenue, Singapore, 639798
Contact: The Director, Alumni and Endowment Office

NTU APEC Scholarship

Subjects: MBA.
Purpose: To allow outstanding candidates from the APEC member economies to pursue the MBA programme at NTU on a full-time basis.
Eligibility: Open to nationals from the following APEC member economies: Australia, Brunei Darussalem, Canada, Chile, Chinese Taipei, Hong Kong, China, Indonesia, Japan, Malaysia, Mexico, New Zealand, Papua New Guinea, People's Republic of China, Peru, Philippines, Republic of Korea, Russia, Thailand, United States of America and Vietnam. Singaporeans, Singapore permanent residents and recipients of other scholarships or bursaries are not eligible to apply.
Level of Study: MBA
Type: Scholarship
Value: Monthly stipend of US$1,400, book allowance of US$500, tuition fees, health insurance, examination fees and other approved fees, allowances and expenses, cost of one overseas Business Study Mission, cost of travel from home country to Singapore on award of the scholarship, and cost of travel from Singapore to home country on successful completion of the Master's programme. Each scholarship is tenable for a period of 4 trimesters only
Length of Study: Full-time for 16 months
Frequency: Annual
Study Establishment: NTU
Country of Study: Singapore
No. of awards offered: 2
Application Procedure: Application details are available at the University website.
Closing Date: December
Funding: Government
Contributor: NTU
No. of awards given last year: 2
No. of applicants last year: 50
Additional Information: Applications open in September/October and close in December each year. Invitations for applications will be placed in the newspapers in the capital cities of the APEC countries and on the University's website. International students have to apply for a student's pass from Singapore immigration in order to pursue a full-time course of study in Singapore. The University will assist successful international applicants in their applications for the student's pass.

NTU ASEAN Postgraduate Scholarship

Subjects: MBA.
Purpose: To allow outstanding candidates from the ASEAN (Association of South East Asian Nations) member economies, except Singapore, to pursue the MBA programme at NTU on a full-time basis.
Eligibility: Open to nationals of the member countries of ASEAN (Brunei Darussalem, Cambodia, Indonesia, Laos, Malaysia, Myanmar, Philippines, Thailand and Vietnam). Singaporeans, Singapore permanent residents and recipients of other scholarships or bursaries are not eligible to apply.
Level of Study: MBA
Type: Scholarship
Value: Monthly stipend of US$1,350; book allowance of US$500; tuition fees, health insurance, examination fees and other approved fees, allowances and expenses; cost of one overseas Business Study Mission; cost of travel from home country to Singapore on award of the scholarship; and cost of travel from Singapore to home country on successful completion of the Master's programme. Each scholarship is tenable for a period of 4 trimesters only
Length of Study: Full-time for 16 months
Frequency: Annual
Study Establishment: NTU
Country of Study: Singapore
No. of awards offered: 1–2
Application Procedure: Application details available at the University website.
Closing Date: December
Funding: Government
No. of awards given last year: 1
No. of applicants last year: 50
Additional Information: Applications open in September/October and close in December each year. Invitations for applications will be placed in the newspapers in the capital cities of the ASEAN countries and on the University's website. International students have to apply for a student's pass from Singapore immigration in order to pursue a full-time course of study in Singapore. The University will assist successful international applicants in their applications for the student's pass.

NTU MBA Scholarship

Subjects: MBA.
Purpose: To enable outstanding overseas candidates to pursue the MBA programme on a full-time basis.
Eligibility: Open to international applicants. Singaporeans, Singapore permanent residents and recipients of other scholarships or bursaries are not eligible to apply.
Level of Study: MBA
Type: Scholarship
Value: US$24,000 to cover the tuition fees of a full-time programme
Length of Study: Full-time for 16 months
Frequency: Annual
Study Establishment: NTU
Country of Study: Singapore
No. of awards offered: 4
Application Procedure: Applicants must submit only one application form for application to the NTU MBA and scholarship. Online application is available at www.nanyangmba.ntu.edu.sg/online.asp

Closing Date: End of February
Funding: Private
No. of awards given last year: 4
No. of applicants last year: 81
Additional Information: Applications open in October each year and close at the end of February each year. International students have to apply for a student's pass from Singapore immigration in order to pursue a full-time course of study in Singapore. The University will assist successful international applicants in their applications for the student's pass.

NTU SCCCF Business Scholarship

Subjects: MBA.
Purpose: To provide financial support to Singaporeans and permanent residents of Singapore.
Eligibility: Open to Singaporeans and Singapore permanent residents admitted to the MBA programme on either a full-time or part-time basis. Recipients of other scholarships or bursaries are not eligible to apply.
Level of Study: MBA
Type: Scholarship
Value: US$5,000
Length of Study: Full-time is 16 months and part-time is 24–32 months
Frequency: Annual
Study Establishment: NTU
Country of Study: Singapore
No. of awards offered: 3
Application Procedure: Applicants must apply in September and October each year. Invitations for applications will be placed on the notice boards of the MBA Office and the Graduate Studies Office.
Closing Date: To be decided by the donor, usually end of October
Funding: Commercial
Contributor: The Singapore Chinese Chamber of Commerce Foundation Business Scholarship
No. of awards given last year: None
No. of applicants last year: None

NARSAD, THE MENTAL HEALTH RESEARCH ASSOCIATION

60 Cutter Mill Road, Suite 404, Great Neck, NY, 11021, United States of America
Tel: (1) 516 829 5576
Fax: (1) 516 487 6930
Email: amoran@narsad.org
Website: www.narsad.org
Contact: Ms Audra Moran, Director, Research Grants Programme

NARSAD, The Mental Health Research Association raises and distributes funds for scientific research into the causes, cures, treatments and prevention of neurobiological disorders. NARSAD is the largest donor-supported organization devoted exclusively to supporting scientific research on psychiatric brain disorders in the world.

NARSAD Distinguished Investigator Awards

Subjects: Schizophrenia, major affective disorders, other serious mental illnesses such as bipolar disease, borderline disorders with depression or suicide and research on children's psychiatric disorders.
Purpose: To encourage experienced scientists to pursue innovative projects in diverse areas of neurobiological research.
Eligibility: Open to senior researchers at the rank of professor or equivalent who maintain their own laboratory.
Level of Study: Research, postdoctorate
Type: Grant
Value: Up to US$100,000
Length of Study: 1 year
Frequency: Annual
Country of Study: Any country
No. of awards offered: Varies
Application Procedure: Applicants must refer to the website for guidelines and a face sheet.
Closing Date: May 15th
Funding: Private
Contributor: Donors
No. of awards given last year: 20
No. of applicants last year: 176
Additional Information: Further information is available from the website.

NARSAD Independent Investigator Awards

Subjects: Schizophrenia, major affective disorders, other serious mental illnesses such as bipolar disease, borderline disorders with depression or suicide and research on children's psychiatric disorders.
Purpose: To facilitate innovative research opportunities in diverse areas of neurobiological research.
Eligibility: Open to scientists at the academic level of associate professor or equivalent. Candidates must have won national competitive support as a principal investigator.
Level of Study: Postdoctorate, research
Type: Grant
Value: Up to US$50,000 maximum per year
Length of Study: 2 years
Frequency: Annual
Country of Study: Any country
No. of awards offered: Varies
Application Procedure: Applicants must refer to the website for guidelines and a face sheet.
Closing Date: March 5th
Funding: Private
Contributor: Donors
No. of awards given last year: 45
No. of applicants last year: 211
Additional Information: Further information is available from the website.

NARSAD Young Investigator Awards

Subjects: Schizophrenia, major affective disorders, other serious mental illnesses such as bipolar disease, borderline disorders with depression or suicide and psychiatric research on children's psychiatric disorders.
Purpose: To enable promising investigators to either extend their research fellowship training or to begin careers as independent research faculty.
Eligibility: Open to investigators who have attained a doctorate or equivalent degree, are affiliated with a specific research institution and who have a mentor or senior collaborator who is performing significant research in an area relevant to schizophrenia, depression or other serious mental illnesses. Candidates should be at the postdoctoral to assistant professor level.
Level of Study: Research, postdoctorate
Type: Grant
Value: Up to US$30,000 maximum per year
Length of Study: 1 or 2 years
Frequency: Annual
Country of Study: Any country
No. of awards offered: Varies
Application Procedure: Applicants must refer to the website for guidelines and a face sheet.
Closing Date: July 25th
Funding: Private
Contributor: Donors
No. of awards given last year: 197
No. of applicants last year: 755
Additional Information: This award is intended to support only advanced Fellows through assistant professors or their equivalent. Further information is available from the website.

NATIONAL ALLIANCE FOR MEDIA ARTS AND CULTURE (NAMAC)

145 Ninth Street, Suite 205, San Francisco, CA 94103, United States of America
Tel: (1) 415 431 1391
Fax: (1) 415 431 1392
Website: www.namac.org

NAMAC, founded in 1980, is a non-profit association whose membership comprises a diverse mix of organizations and individuals dedicated to a common goal: the support and advocacy of independent film, video, audio and online/multimedia arts.

McKnight Artist Fellowship for Filmmakers

Subjects: Cinema and television.
Purpose: To honor the professional and artistic accomplishments of Minnesota artists working in the medium of film/video.
Eligibility: Open to candidates who are residents of Minnesota.
Level of Study: Postgraduate
Type: Fellowship
Value: Varies
Frequency: Annual
Country of Study: United States of America
Application Procedure: See the website.

McKnight Artists Fellowship for Screenwriters

Subjects: Screenwriting.
Purpose: To recognize screenwriters who have excelled in the artistic discipline of writing for cinema.
Eligibility: Open to resident screenwriters of Minnesota.
Level of Study: Postgraduate
Type: Fellowship
Value: Varies
Frequency: Annual
Country of Study: United States of America
Application Procedure: See the website.

NATIONAL ASSOCIATION BLACK JOURNALISTS (NABJ)

University of Maryland 8701-A Adelphi Road,
Adelphi, MD 20783-1716,
United States of America
Tel: (1) 445 7100
Fax: (1) 445 7101
Email: nabj@nabj.org
Website: www.nabj.org

NABJ is an organization of journalists, students and media-related professionals that provides quality programmes and services to black journalists worldwide.

Ethel Payne Fellowships

Subjects: Journalism.
Purpose: To fund journalists wanting international reporting experience through self-conceived assignments in Africa.
Eligibility: Applicants should be an NABJ member with five years journalism experience, full-time freelance.
Level of Study: Postdoctorate
Type: Fellowship
Value: US$5,000
Study Establishment: University of Maryland
Country of Study: United States of America
Application Procedure: A completed application should be submitted accompanied by an 800-word project proposal, a 300 word essay on the applicant's journalism experience, three samples of work published or aired and two letters of recommendation.
Closing Date: December 15th
Contributor: The National Association of black Journalists (NABJ)
No. of awards given last year: 2

For further information contact:

NABJ, Ethel Payne Fellowship 8701-A Adelphi RD, Maryland, Adelphi, 20783-1716
Contact: Kristie Jones

NATIONAL ASSOCIATION OF COMPOSERS

PO Box 49256, Barrington Station,
Los Angeles, CA, 90049,
United States of America
Tel: (1) 310 838 4465
Fax: (1) 310 838 4465
Email: info@music-usa.org/nacusa
Website: www.music-usa.org/nacusa
Contact: President

The National Association of Composers presents concerts of music by American composers throughout the United States of America, and sponsor a Young composers competition.

National Association of Composers Young Composers Competition

Subjects: Music composition.
Purpose: To foster the creation of new American concert hall music.
Eligibility: Open to nationals of any country between the ages of 18 and 30.
Level of Study: Postdoctorate, postgraduate, unrestricted
Type: Competition
Value: Please contact the organization
Frequency: Annual
Country of Study: Any country
No. of awards offered: 2
Application Procedure: Applicants must send in their music as there are no application forms.
Closing Date: October 30th
Funding: Private

NATIONAL ASSOCIATION OF DENTAL ASSISTANTS

900 St. Washington Street, Suite G-13,
Falls Church, VA, 22046,
United States of America
Tel: (1) 703 237 8616
Fax: (1) 703 533 1153
Contact: Scholarship Department

National Association of Dental Assistants Annual Scholarship Award

Subjects: Dental assistant certification, recertification, dental training, continuing dental education seminars or any course that is related to, or required in, the dental degree programme.
Purpose: To enable dental assistants to further their education.
Eligibility: Open to dental assistants who have a minimum of 2 years of membership in good standing. Applicants may also be a member's dependent, spouse or grandchild. All courses must be approved by the board.
Level of Study: Unrestricted
Type: Scholarship
Value: US$250, varies
Frequency: Annual
Study Establishment: Appropriate institutions
Country of Study: Any country
No. of awards offered: 1–2
Application Procedure: Applicants must submit one recommendation from their current or previous employer, one recommendation from someone other than a member, if a member's dependent, such as a school counsellor or another dental assistant, a completed application form and an updated student transcript.
Closing Date: May 31st
Funding: Commercial
No. of awards given last year: 2
No. of applicants last year: Approx. 10

NATIONAL ASSOCIATION OF SCHOLARS (NAS)

221 Witherspoon Street, 2nd Floor, Princeton, NJ, 08542-3215, United States of America
Tel: (1) 609 683 1437
Fax: (1) 609 683 0316
Email: brasor@nas.org
Website: www.nas.org
Contact: G C Brasor, Associate Director

The National Association of Scholars (NAS) is an organization of professors, graduate students, college administrators and independent scholars committed to rational discourse as the foundation of academic life in a free democratic society. The NAS works to enrich the substance and strengthen the integrity of scholarship and teaching, convinced that only through an informed understanding of the western intellectual heritage and the realities of the contemporary world can citizen and scholar be equipped to sustain civilization's achievements.

Barry R Gross Memorial Award

Subjects: Academic reform.
Purpose: To reward an NAS member for outstanding service, through the medium of the organization or responsible citizenship, to the cause of academic reform.
Eligibility: Candidates must be NAS-nominated.
Type: Award
Value: US$1,000, a plaque and travel expenses to attend the national conference and present a speech
Frequency: Every 2 years
Application Procedure: No direct applications are accepted.
Funding: Private
Additional Information: Established to honour the memory of Barry R Gross.

Peter Shaw Memorial Award

Subjects: Writing on issues pertaining to higher education and American intellectual culture.
Purpose: To recognize exemplary writing on issues pertaining to higher education and American intellectual culture.
Eligibility: Candidates must be NAS-nominated.
Type: Award
Value: US$1,000, a plaque and travel expenses to attend the national conference and present a speech
Frequency: Every 2 years, Every 18 months
Application Procedure: No direct applications are accepted.
Funding: Private
Additional Information: Established to honour the memory of Peter Shaw.

Sidney Hook Memorial Award

Subjects: The defence of academic freedom and integrity of academic life.
Purpose: To award an individual for distinguished contributions to the defence of academic freedom and the integrity of academic life.
Eligibility: Candidates must be NAS-nominated.
Type: Award
Value: US$2,500, a plaque and travel expenses to attend the national conference and present a speech
Frequency: Every 2 years
Application Procedure: No direct applications are accepted.
Funding: Private
Additional Information: The award was established to honour the memory of Sidney Hook.

NATIONAL BRAIN TUMOR FOUNDATION

22 Battery Street, Suite 612, San Francisco, CA 94111-5520, United States of America
Tel: (1) 510 839 9777
Fax: (1) 510 839 9779
Email: nbtf@braintumor.org
Website: www.braintumor.org
Contact: Director of Patient Services

The Andrew Christian Bryce Pediatric Grant

Subjects: Oncology.
Purpose: To support research in pediatric patients diagnosed with a PNET.
Level of Study: Research
Type: Grant
Value: US$25,000
Frequency: Annual
Application Procedure: See the website.
Closing Date: February 10th
Contributor: The Andrew Christian Bryce Foundation, Inc.

Charles B Wilson Brain Tumor Research Excellence Grant

Subjects: Neuro-oncology and neuroscience.
Purpose: To provide funding for general research.
Eligibility: Preference is given to translational research, but all types of applications are accepted.
Level of Study: Research
Type: Research grant
Value: A total value of US$100,000
Country of Study: United States of America or Canada

The GBM Research Fund

Subjects: Oncology.
Purpose: To fund research specifically focusing on glioblastoma multiforme.
Type: Grant
Value: US$50,000
Frequency: Annual
Application Procedure: See the website.
Closing Date: February 10th

NABTC/NABTT Research Grant

Subjects: Brain tumours.
Purpose: To financially fund research.
Eligibility: Applicants must be researchers at a member institution of the North American Brain Tumor Consortium (NABTC) or New Approaches to Brain Tumor Therapy (NABTT).
Level of Study: Research
Type: Grant
Value: US$100,000
Study Establishment: A member institution of the North American Brain Tumor Consortium (NABTC) or New Approaches to Brain Tumor Therapy (NABTT)
Country of Study: United States of America or Canada
No. of awards offered: 1
Application Procedure: Applicants must visit the website for further information.

NBTF Quality of Life Research Grant

Subjects: Brain tumours.
Purpose: To provide support for research into quality of life issues affecting both brain tumour patients and their caregivers.
Eligibility: Open to United States of America or Canadian researchers. Applicants should hold a Master's degree.
Level of Study: Doctorate, postgraduate, research
Type: Research grant
Value: US$15,000
Length of Study: 1 year (extendable for 1year)
Country of Study: United States of America or Canada
No. of awards offered: 1
Application Procedure: Applicants must visit the website for further information.

Oligo Brain Tumor Fund

Subjects: Neurology.
Purpose: To financially support research into oligodendroglioma tumours.
Level of Study: Research
Type: Research grant
Value: US$50,000

Frequency: Annual
Country of Study: United States of America or Canada
No. of awards offered: Varies
Application Procedure: Applicants must visit the website for further information.
Closing Date: March 4th
Funding: Private
Contributor: The Jeffrey Bein Family, supported by the Haberman Family and ongoing private donations

The Steven J. Bryant Research Grant

Subjects: Medicine.
Purpose: To award the best result-oriented research project.
Level of Study: Research
Type: Grant
Value: US$25,000
Frequency: Annual
Application Procedure: See the website.
Closing Date: February 10th
Contributor: The Steven J. Bryant Research Foundation

NATIONAL CANCER INSTITUTE OF CANADA (NCIC)

Research Programs, Suite 200, 10 Alcorn Avenue, Toronto, Ontario, M4V 3B1, Canada
Tel: (1) 416 934 5966
Fax: (1) 416 961 7327
Email: pmanzer@cancer.ca
Website: www.ncic.cancer.ca
Contact: Dr Patricia Manzer, Research Analyst

The National Cancer Institute of Canada (NCIC) is the largest non-government funder of cancer research in Canada. In concert with its partner, the Canadian Cancer Society, and with the Terry Fox Foundation, the NCIC provides support for research and related programmes undertaken at Canadian universities, hospitals and other research institutions.

CCS Feasibility Grants

Subjects: Cancer research.
Purpose: To provide a modest level of funding as the NCIC recognizes that it is difficult to submit a full application for a research grant without having first conducted preliminary studies.
Eligibility: This programme is open to all applicants but priority will be given where it is apparent that no other resources are available. These grants will not be awarded to support travel to conduct planning meetings. These funds will also not be awarded for conference travel or for the purchase of permanent equipment.
Level of Study: Postgraduate
Type: Grant
Value: Up to Canadian $35,000
Length of Study: 1 year, but funds may be spent over a 2 year period
Frequency: Annual
Country of Study: Canada
No. of awards offered: Varies
Application Procedure: Applicants must write for details or refer to the website.
Closing Date: Please contact the organization
Funding: Private
Contributor: The Canadian Cancer Society
Additional Information: Further information is available from the website.

NCIC Academic Oncology Fellowship

Subjects: Clinical cancer research.
Purpose: To assist outstanding individuals who hold a doctoral degree in medicine and who seek specialized training.
Eligibility: Open to Canadian citizens or residents who possess a doctoral degree in medicine from a recognized institution and be licensed to practice in Canada. Preference will be given to those who can demonstrate research commitment by having completed, or being enrolled in, a relevant graduate course.
Level of Study: Professional development, postdoctorate
Type: Fellowship
Value: Minimum Canadian $35,000 rising for each year of postdoctoral experience to a maximum of Canadian $47,500 per year
Length of Study: Up to 3 years
Frequency: Annual
Study Establishment: An approved institution
Country of Study: Canada, or abroad as approved
No. of awards offered: Varies
Application Procedure: Applicants must write for details or refer to the website.
Closing Date: September 15th
Funding: Private
Contributor: The Terry Fox Foundation and the Canadian Cancer Society
No. of applicants last year: 4
Additional Information: Further information is available from the website. Stipends are subject to annual review. Recipients of these fellowships are eligible to apply for a contribution of Canadian $1,200 towards the cost of conference travel per award year.

NCIC Equipment Grants for New Investigators

Subjects: Cancer research.
Purpose: To make it possible for new investigators to set up cancer research facilities in Canada. The award is designed to assist young investigators beginning their career.
Eligibility: Applicants should be new investigators who have no more than two years of experience as an independent investigator and have not received an operational research grant from the National Cancer Institute or another comparable agency.
Level of Study: Postgraduate
Type: Grant
Value: Up to Canadian $75,000
Frequency: Dependent on funds available
Country of Study: Canada
No. of awards offered: Varies
Application Procedure: Applicants must write for details or refer to the website.
Closing Date: October 17th
Funding: Private
Contributor: The Terry Fox Foundation
Additional Information: The award is not intended to facilitate the relocation of individuals from one laboratory to another. Further information is available from the website.

NCIC Post-PhD Research Fellowships

Subjects: Cancer research.
Purpose: To provide training in cancer research for outstanding candidates who plan a career in Canada in this field of investigation.
Eligibility: Candidates must be graduates of a university recognized by the NCIC and must be accepted for postdoctoral training in the field of cancer research in an academic environment also recognized. If the fellowship is to be taken outside Canada the applicant must be either a Canadian citizen or Canadian landed immigrant. Post MD candidates must be licensed to practice in Canada. For applicants with both PhD and MD degrees, the degree obtained most recently will determine the fellowship category for which they should apply.
Level of Study: Postdoctorate
Type: Fellowship
Value: Minimum Canadian $35,000 rising for each year of postdoctoral experience to a maximum of Canadian $47,500 per year
Length of Study: Up to a maximum of 3 years
Frequency: Annual
Study Establishment: A Canadian institute or abroad if the applicant is Canadian or a Canadian landed immigrant
Country of Study: Canada and abroad
No. of awards offered: Varies
Application Procedure: Applicants must refer to the website.
Closing Date: February 1st
Funding: Private
Contributor: The Terry Fox Foundation and the Canadian Cancer Society
No. of awards given last year: 19

No. of applicants last year: 43
Additional Information: Further information is available from the website.

NCIC Research Grants for New Investigators

Subjects: Cancer research.
Purpose: To facilitate the greatest possibility for new investigators to obtain grant support for cancer research. The award is designed to assist new investigators who are beginning a career in cancer research.
Eligibility: Applicants should be new investigators who have no more than two years of experience as an independent investigator and have not previously received a research grant from the National Cancer Institute of Canada or another comparable agency.
Level of Study: Postgraduate
Type: Research grant
Value: Varies
Frequency: Annual
Study Establishment: An approved institution
Country of Study: Canada
No. of awards offered: Varies
Application Procedure: Applicants must write for details or refer to the website.
Closing Date: October 17th
Funding: Private
Contributor: The Terry Fox Foundation
No. of awards given last year: 5
No. of applicants last year: 26

NCIC Research Grants to Individuals

Subjects: Cancer research.
Purpose: To stimulate Canadian investigators in a very broad spectrum of research.
Eligibility: Open to a researcher who is designated as the principal investigator and must be based in, or formally affiliated with, but not necessarily receive salary support from, an eligible Canadian host institution such as a university, research institute or healthcare agency. Graduate students, postdoctoral Fellows, research associates, technical support staff, or investigators based outside of Canada are not eligible to be a principal investigator.
Level of Study: Postgraduate
Type: Research grant
Value: Awards will be granted for the purchase and maintenance of animals, for expendable supplies, minor items of equipment, for payment of graduate students, postdoctoral Fellows and technical and professional assistants, and for research travel and permanent equipment. An allocation for conference travel may be added automatically by the NCIC. These grants do not provide for personal salary support of the principal investigator and/or co-applicants nor for institutional overhead costs
Length of Study: 3 years in the first instance, with possible renewals for periods of 1–5 years
Frequency: Annual
Study Establishment: Universities or other institutions
Country of Study: Canada
No. of awards offered: Varies
Application Procedure: Applicants must complete an application form. Further details are available on request or from the website.
Closing Date: October 15th
Funding: Private
Contributor: The Terry Fox Foundation and the Canadian Cancer Society
No. of awards given last year: 73
No. of applicants last year: 286
Additional Information: Further information is available from the website. Grants will be awarded to projects deemed worthy of support, provided that the basic equipment and research facilities are available in the institution concerned and that it will provide the necessary administrative services. Grants are made only with the consent and knowledge of the administrative head of the institution at which they are to be held and applications must be countersigned accordingly.

NCIC Research Scientist Awards

Subjects: Cancer research.
Purpose: To provide a career development opportunity for individuals committed to a high standard of cancer research.
Eligibility: Applicants must hold a PhD, MD or comparable degree and be conducting research in a field relevant to cancer or cancer control. An intention to remain in Canada is required. Candidates must have a minimum of three years of postdoctoral training in research and may not have more than five years of research experience calculated from the beginning of their independent research career. Applicants must also hold a nationally peer reviewed research grant relevant to cancer at the time of application.
Level of Study: Postdoctorate
Type: Research grant
Value: The initial salary will depend on the experience and competence of the individual. The University must be willing to provide space and two years of salary at the end of the award
Length of Study: A maximum of 6 years
Frequency: Annual
Study Establishment: An approved university or research establishment
Country of Study: Canada
No. of awards offered: Varies
Application Procedure: Applicants must refer to the website for details. Applications are made by the university in which the candidate will hold an academic appointment, and not directly from the applicants themselves.
Closing Date: February 1st
Funding: Private
Contributor: The Canadian Cancer Society
No. of awards given last year: 7
No. of applicants last year: 10
Additional Information: Further information is available from the website.

NCIC Research Studentships

Subjects: Cancer research.
Purpose: To award outstanding PhD students who plan a career in cancer research in Canada.
Eligibility: Applicants must be Canadian residents enrolled in a PhD programme at a Canadian institute. Applicants must have completed atleast two years of research training at graduate level or have equivalent research experience.
Level of Study: Postgraduate
Value: Canadian $21,500 per year
Length of Study: A maximum of 4 years
Frequency: Annual
Study Establishment: An approved institution
Country of Study: Canada
No. of awards offered: Varies
Application Procedure: Applicants must refer to the website for details and application forms.
Closing Date: Please contact the organization
Funding: Private
Contributor: The Terry Fox Foundation and the Canadian Cancer Society
No. of awards given last year: 20
No. of applicants last year: 37
Additional Information: Further information is available from the website. The NCIC invite all members of the research community to identify and approach qualified individuals, and encourage them to apply.

NCIC Travel Awards for Senior Level PhD Students

Subjects: Cancer research.
Purpose: To provide financial assistance by helping to defray the travel costs associated with making a scientific presentation at a conference, symposium or other appropriate professional gathering.
Eligibility: Applicants must be students enrolled in a PhD or MD programme at a Canadian institution and be in the final phase of their studies. Candidates must be attending a conference for the purpose of presenting data from a cancer related project on a first author basis.
Level of Study: Postgraduate

Type: Travel grant
Value: Up to Canadian $1,500
Country of Study: Canada
No. of awards offered: Up to 20 per calendar year
Application Procedure: Applicants must refer to the website.
Closing Date: April 1st, September 1st or December 1st
Funding: Private
Contributor: The Canadian Cancer Society
No. of awards given last year: 15
No. of applicants last year: 16
Additional Information: Further information is available from the website.

NATIONAL CENTER FOR ATMOSPHERIC RESEARCH (NCAR)

PO Box 3000, Advanced Study Programme, Boulder, CO, 80307-3000, United States of America
Tel: (1) 303 497 1601
Fax: (1) 303 497 1646
Email: barbm@ucar.edu
Website: www.asp.ucar.edu
Contact: Ms Barbara Hansford, Co-ordinator

The National Center for Atmospheric Research (NCAR) is a national research center focused on atmospheric science.

NCAR Faculty Fellowship Programme

Subjects: Atmospheric sciences.
Purpose: To facilitate residency study at NCAR.
Eligibility: Open to all faculty employed full-time at a college or university. Diversity concerns will also be addressed in the selection process.
Level of Study: Doctorate, postdoctorate
Type: Fellowships
Value: You may be eligible for the following: travel, salary, benefits, temporary living per Diem, shipping allowance.
Frequency: Annual
Study Establishment: The NCAR Centre
Country of Study: United States of America
No. of awards offered: 1
Application Procedure: Apply online.
Closing Date: March 15th
Additional Information: If you have any questions please work with Paula Fisher; and email: paulad@ucar.edu

NCAR Graduate Visitor Programme

Subjects: Atmospheric sciences.
Level of Study: Postgraduate
Type: Scholarship
Value: A US$1,000 stipend and travel expenses.
Length of Study: 3–12 months
Frequency: Annual
Study Establishment: The NCAR Center
Country of Study: United States of America
No. of awards offered: Varies
Application Procedure: Apply oline.
Closing Date: March 1st
Additional Information: If you have any questions about this new programme, please contact Paula Fisher; email: paulad@ucar.edu

NCAR IAI/NCAR Postdoctoral Fellowship

Subjects: Atmospheric sciences.
Purpose: To provide an opportunity for recent PhD scientists to continue to pursue their research interests in atmospheric and related science.
Eligibility: Limited to natives of IAI member courtries who are within 5 years of receiving a doctoral degree from an institution in an IAI member country. Candidates should be fluent in verbal and written English.
Level of Study: Doctorate, postdoctorate
Type: Fellowship
Value: The first year stipend is US$3,916 per month and the second year is US$4,083 per month
Length of Study: 2 years
Frequency: Annual
Study Establishment: The NCAR Centre
Country of Study: United States of America
No. of awards offered: Varies
Application Procedure: Apply online.
Closing Date: January 5th

NCAR Postdoctoral Appointments in the Advanced Study Program

Subjects: Atmospheric sciences.
Purpose: To assist and support research.
Eligibility: Open to those who have recently received their PhD and scientists with no more than 4 years of applicable experience since receiving their PhD. Foreign nationals may also apply.
Level of Study: Postdoctorate
Type: Fellowship
Value: US$45,000 per year for recent PhDs and US$47,000 for appointees in the second year at NCAR-ASP. All appointees are eligible for life and health insurance, and travel expenses to the center are reimbursed for the appointee and family. Fellows living abroad will have round-trip travel expenses for themselves and their families paid up to a maximum of US$2,500. A small allowance for moving and storing personal belongings is provided. Scientific travel and registration fees that cost up to US$1,500 per year are normally available
Length of Study: Up to 1 year, with a possibility of renewal for a further year
Frequency: Annual
Study Establishment: The Center
Country of Study: United States of America
No. of awards offered: 7–10
Application Procedure: Applicants must send transcripts of graduate university courses, a curriculum vitae including any scientific work experience, an abstract of doctoral thesis, four references, a short statement describing the applicant's interest in the atmospheric sciences and the work he or she would like to do during their visit to the National Center for Atmospheric Research. Applications should be addressed to Barbara Hansford at the main address or sent by express mail to the address below.
Closing Date: January 5th
Funding: Government
No. of awards given last year: 8
No. of applicants last year: 120
Additional Information: NCAR is an equal opportunity employer with an affirmative-action programme.

For further information contact:

1850 Table Mesa Drive, Boulder, CO, 80305, United States of America

NCAR Postdoctoral Fellowships

Subjects: Atmospheric dynamics, climate science, cloud physics, atmospheric chemistry and radiation, turbulences, upper-atmosphere physics, solar physics, oceanography.
Purpose: To provide considerable freedom to pursue research interests.
Eligibility: Open to applicants with a PhD or ScD degree granted in an area related to NCAR science during the four years preceding the application date. We encourage applications from women and minorities. There are no special restrictions for applicants.
Level of Study: Postdoctorate, doctorate
Type: Fellowship
Value: US$47,000 in the first year, and US$49,000 in the second year
Length of Study: 2 years
Frequency: Annual
Study Establishment: The NCAR Centre
Country of Study: United States of America
No. of awards offered: 7
Application Procedure: Apply online.
Closing Date: January 5th

THE NATIONAL COLLEGIATE ATHLETIC ASSOCIATION

NCAA Postgraduate Scholarship Program, National Collegiate Athletic Association, PO Box 6222, Indianapolis, IN, 46206-6222, United States of America
Tel: (1) 317 917 6222
Website: www.ncaa.org

The National Collegiate Athletic Association is the organization through which the nation's colleges and universities speak and act on athletics matters at the national level. It is a voluntary association of more than 1,265 institutions, conferences, organizations and individuals devoted to the sound administration of intercollegiate athletics.

NCAA Postgraduate Scholarship

Subjects: All subjects.
Purpose: To honour outstanding student-athletes who are also outstanding scholars.
Eligibility: Open to student-athletes enrolled at an NCAA member institution, in the last year of intercollegiate competition and with a minimum grade point average of 3.2 on a 4.0 scale or its equivalent.
Level of Study: Postgraduate
Type: Scholarship
Value: One-time grant of US$7,500. This is not earmarked for a specific area of postgraduate study but the awardee must use it as a part-time or full-time graduate student in a graduate or professional school of an academically accredited institution within 3 years of winning the award
Frequency: Each Academic year
Country of Study: Any country
No. of awards offered: 174
Application Procedure: Applicants must be nominated by their faculty athletics representative or designee. Student may be any nationality but must be attending an NCAA member institution and be in final year of eligibility in the sport they are nominated.
Closing Date: There are three deadlines (may vary slightly each year): December 9th for Fall sports; February 24th for Winter sports; and May 5th for Spring sports
Funding: Foundation
No. of awards given last year: 174
No. of applicants last year: 374

NATIONAL DAIRY SHRINE

1224 Atton Darby Creek Road, Columbus, OH 43228-9792, United States of America
Tel: (1) 614 870 5333
Fax: (1) 614 870 2622
Email: shrine@cobaselect.com
Website: www.dairyshrine.org
Contact: Maurice E. Core, Executive Director

Founded in 1949 by a small group of visionary dairy leaders, National Dairy Shrine brings together dairy producers, scientists, students, educators, marketers and others who share a desire to preserve the dairy heritage and keep the dairy industry strong.

Iager Dairy Scholarship

Subjects: Food science and production.
Purpose: To encourage students with an explicit interest in a career in the dairy industry.
Eligibility: Open to applicants studying in the agricultural schools.
Level of Study: Postgraduate
Type: Scholarship
Frequency: Annual
No. of awards offered: Varies
Application Procedure: A completed, typed, application form must be submitted to the National Dairy Shrine.
Closing Date: March 15th
Funding: Private
Contributor: Charles and Judy Iager

McCullough Scholarships

Subjects: Dairy science and agricultural journalism.
Purpose: To assist incoming college freshman who plan to major in dairy science or agricultural journalism.
Eligibility: Open to U.S. citizens.
Level of Study: Postgraduate
Type: Scholarship
Value: US$2,500 and 1,000
Frequency: Annual
No. of awards offered: 2
Application Procedure: A completed application form and letter of recommendation must be sent.
Closing Date: March 15th
Funding: Private
Contributor: Marshall McCullough

THE NATIONAL EDUCATION ASSOCIATION (NEA) FOUNDATION FOR THE IMPROVEMENT OF EDUCATION

1201 16th Street North West, Suite 234, Washington, DC, 20036-7840, United States of America
Tel: (1) 202 833 4000
Fax: (1) 202 822 7779
Email: cchirichella@nea.org
Website: www.nfie.org
Contact: Ms Christine Chirichella, Communications Officer

Established by NEA in 1969, the national foundation for the improvement of Education (NFIE) is a foundation created by educators. NFIE' s programs provide front-line practitioners the support they need to explore new frontiers in teaching and learning.

NEA Foundation Fine Arts Grant Program

Subjects: Art, music, theatre, dance, design, media and folk arts.
Purpose: To enable teachers to create and implement fine arts programmes that promote learning by students at risk of school failure.
Eligibility: Open to NEA member teachers of art, music, theatre, dance, design, media or folk arts.
Level of Study: Professional development
Type: Grant
Value: US$2,000
Length of Study: 1 year
Frequency: Annual
No. of awards offered: 10
Application Procedure: Applications must be submitted by local affiliates of the NEA. The local affiliate accepts the grant and administers the project.
Closing Date: February 1st

NEA Foundation Innovation Grants

Subjects: Education.
Purpose: To promote collaborative, innovative ideas that lead to student achievement of high standards.
Eligibility: Open to teams of two or more practising United States public school teachers in grades K–12, public school education support personnel, public higher education faculty and staff. Preference will be given to National Education Association members, and to educators who serve economically disadvantaged and/or underserved students.
Level of Study: Postgraduate
Type: Grant
Value: US$5,000
Length of Study: 12 months
Frequency: Annual
Country of Study: United States of America
Application Procedure: Applicants must consult the organization for details.
Closing Date: Applications may be submitted at any time

NEA Foundation Learning and Leadership Grants

Subjects: All subjects.
Purpose: To support high quality professional development that addresses specific student learning needs. Recipients must also

exercise professional leadership by sharing their new learning with their colleagues.
Eligibility: Open to practising public school classroom teachers, public school education support personnel and faculty and staff of public higher education institutions. Two or more collaborating educators may also apply for a group grant. Preference will be given to members of the NEA.
Level of Study: Professional development
Type: Grant
Value: US$2000 for individuals and US$5,000 for groups
Length of Study: 1 year
Frequency: Annual
Country of Study: United States of America
No. of awards offered: Up to 75
Application Procedure: Applicants should consult the organization for details.
Closing Date: Applications are accepted at any time

NATIONAL FEDERATION OF THE BLIND (NFB)

1800 Johnson Street, Baltimore, MD 21230, United States of America
Tel: (1) 410 659 9314
Fax: (1) 410 685 5653
Email: pmaurer@nfb.org
Website: www.nfb.org

Founded in 1940, the National Federation of the Blind (NFB) is the nation's largest and most influential membership organization of blind people. With 50,000 members, the NFB has affiliates in all 50 states as well as Washington, DC and Puerto Rico, and over 700 local chapters. As a consumer and advocacy organization, the NFB is considered the leading force in the blindness field today.

Charles and Melva T Owen Memorial Scholarship

Subjects: Any subject excluding religion and general or cultural education.
Purpose: To assist blind people and to recognize achievements by blind scholars.
Eligibility: All applicants for the scholarship must be legally blind and pursuing or planning to pursue a full-time postsecondary course.
Level of Study: Unrestricted
Type: Scholarship
Value: US$10,000
Frequency: Annual
Study Establishment: A United States of America institution
Country of Study: United States of America
No. of awards offered: 1
Application Procedure: All applications must include a personal letter from the applicant, two letters of recommendation, all transcripts related to institutions attended, a letter from a federation state president or designee and score reports (for high school seniors).
Closing Date: March 31st
Funding: Private
Additional Information: First established by Charles Owen in loving memory of his blind wife and now endowed by his last will and testament to honour the memory of both.

EU Parker Scholarship

Subjects: All subjects.
Purpose: To assist blind people and to recognize achievements by blind scholars.
Eligibility: All applicants for the scholarship must be legally blind and pursuing or planning to pursue a full-time postsecondary course.
Level of Study: Unrestricted
Type: Scholarship
Value: US$3,000
Frequency: Annual
Study Establishment: A United States of America Institution
Country of Study: United States of America
No. of awards offered: 1
Application Procedure: All applications must include a personal letter from the applicant, two letters of recommendation, all transcripts related to institutions attended, a letter from a federation state president or designee and score reports (for high school seniors).
Closing Date: March 31st
Funding: Private
Additional Information: Given in honour of a long-time leader of the NFB, E U Parker.

Hank Lebonne Scholarship

Subjects: All subjects.
Purpose: To assist blind people and to recognize achievements by blind scholars.
Eligibility: All applicants for the scholarship must be legally blind and pursuing or planning to pursue a full-time postsecondary course.
Level of Study: Unrestricted
Type: Scholarship
Length of Study: US$5,000
Frequency: Annual
Study Establishment: A United States of America Institution
Country of Study: United States of America
No. of awards offered: 1
Application Procedure: All applications must include a personal letter from the applicant, two letters of recommendation, all transcripts related to institutions attended, a letter from a federation state president or designee and score reports (for high school seniors).
Closing Date: March 31st
Funding: Private
Additional Information: The scholarship is given in the memory of Hank Lebonne.

Hermione Grant Calhoun Scholarship

Subjects: All subjects.
Purpose: To assist blind people and to recognize achievements by blind scholars.
Eligibility: All applicants for the scholarship must be legally blind and pursuing or planning to pursue a full-time postsecondary course. The applicant must be a woman.
Level of Study: Unrestricted
Type: Scholarship
Value: US$3,000
Frequency: Annual
Study Establishment: A United States of America Institution
Country of Study: United States of America
No. of awards offered: 1
Application Procedure: All applications must include a personal letter from the applicant, two letters of recommendation, all transcripts related to institutions attended, a letter from a federation state president or designee and score reports (for high school seniors).
Closing Date: March 31st
Funding: Private

Howard Brown Rickard Scholarship

Subjects: Law, medicine, engineering, achitecture and natural sciences.
Purpose: To assist blind people and to recognize achievements by blind people.
Eligibility: All applicants for the scholarship must be legally blind and pursuing or planning to pursue a full-time postsecondary course.
Level of Study: Unrestricted
Type: Scholarship
Value: US$3,000
Frequency: Annual
Study Establishment: A United States of America Institution
Country of Study: United States of America
No. of awards offered: 1
Application Procedure: All applications must include a personal letter from the applicant, two letters of recommendation, all transcripts related to institutions attended, a letter from a federation state president or designee and score reports (for high school seniors).
Closing Date: March 31st

Jennica Ferguson Memorial Scholarship

Subjects: All subjects.
Purpose: To assist blind people and to recognize achievements by blind scholars.

Eligibility: All applicants for the scholarship must be legally blind and pursuing or planning to pursue a full-time postsecondary course.
Level of Study: Unrestricted
Type: Scholarship
Value: US$5,000
Frequency: Annual
Study Establishment: A United States of America Institution
Country of Study: United States of America
No. of awards offered: 1
Application Procedure: All applications must include a personal letter from the applicant, two letters of recommendation, all transcripts related to institutions attended, a letter from a federation state president or designee and score reports (for high school seniors).
Closing Date: March 31st
Additional Information: The scholarship is given in the memory of Jennica Ferguson.

Kenneth Jernigan Scholarship

Subjects: All subjects.
Purpose: To assist blind people and to recognize achievements by blind scholars.
Eligibility: All applicants for the scholarship must be legally blind and pursuing or planning to pursue a full-time postsecondary course.
Level of Study: Unrestricted
Type: Scholarship
Value: US$12,000
Frequency: Annual
Study Establishment: A United States of America Institution
Country of Study: United States of America
No. of awards offered: 1
Application Procedure: All applications must include a personal letter from the applicant, two letters of recommendation, all transcripts related to institutions attended, a letter from a federation state president or designee and score reports (for high school seniors).
Closing Date: March 31st
Funding: Private
Contributor: The American Action Fund for Blind Children and Adults
Additional Information: The scholarship is given in memory of Kenneth Jernigan.

Kuchler-Killian Memorial Scholarship

Subjects: All subjects.
Purpose: To assist blind people and to recognize achievements by blind scholars.
Eligibility: All applicants for the scholarship must be legally blind and pursuing or planning to pursue a full-time postsecondary course.
Level of Study: Unrestricted
Type: Scholarship
Value: US$3,000
Frequency: Annual
Study Establishment: A United States of America Institution
Country of Study: United States of America
No. of awards offered: 1
Application Procedure: All applications must include a personal letter from the applicant, two letters of recommendation, all transcripts related to institutions attended, a letter from a federation state president or designee and score reports (for high school seniors).
Closing Date: March 31st
Funding: Private

Michael and Marie Marucci Scholarship

Subjects: Foreign languages, comparative literature, history, geography, political science with a concentration in international studies or any other discipline requiring study abroad.
Purpose: To assist blind people and to recognize achievements by blind scholars.
Eligibility: All applicants for the scholarship must be legally blind and pursuing or planning to pursue a full-time postsecondary course. The applicants must show evidence of competence in a foreign language.
Level of Study: Unrestricted
Type: Scholarship
Value: US$5,000
Frequency: Annual
Study Establishment: A United States of America Institution
Country of Study: United States of America
No. of awards offered: 1
Application Procedure: All applications must include a personal letter from the applicant, two letters of recommendation, all transcripts related to institutions attended, a letter from a federation state president or designee and score reports (for high school seniors).
Closing Date: March 31st
Funding: Private
Additional Information: Given by two dedicated and valued members of the NFB, Maryland.

National Federation of the Blind Computer Science Scholarship

Subjects: Computer science.
Purpose: To assist blind people and to recognize achievements by blind scholars.
Eligibility: All applicants must be legally blind and studying in the computer science field.
Level of Study: Unrestricted
Type: Scholarship
Value: US$3,000
Frequency: Annual
Study Establishment: A United States of America Institution
Country of Study: United States of America
No. of awards offered: 1
Application Procedure: All applications must include a personal letter from the applicant, two letters of recommendation, all transcripts related to institutions attended, a letter from a federation state president or designee and score reports (for high school seniors).
Closing Date: March 31st
Funding: Private

National Federation of the Blind Educator of Tomorrow Award

Subjects: Education.
Purpose: To assist blind people and to recognize achievements by blind scholars.
Eligibility: All applicants for the award must be legally blind and planning a career in elementary, secondary or postsecondary teaching.
Level of Study: Unrestricted
Type: Award
Value: US$3,000
Frequency: Annual
Study Establishment: At a United States of America Institution
Country of Study: United States of America
No. of awards offered: 1
Application Procedure: All applications must include a personal letter from the applicant, two letters of recommendation, all transcripts related to institutions attended, a letter from a federation state president or designee and score reports (for high school seniors).
Closing Date: March 31st

National Federation of the Blind Scholarships

Subjects: All subjects.
Purpose: To assist blind people and to recognize achievements by blind scholars.
Eligibility: All applicants for the scholarships must be legally blind.
Level of Study: Unrestricted
Type: Scholarship
Value: US$3,000 each
Frequency: Annual
Study Establishment: A United States of America Institution
Country of Study: United States of America
No. of awards offered: 16
Application Procedure: All applications must include a personal letter from the applicant, two letters of recommendation, all transcripts related to institutions attended, a letter from a federation state president or designee and score reports (for high school seniors).
Closing Date: March 31st
Funding: Private

Additional Information: Given for academic excellence, community service and financial need.

NFB Computer Science Scholarship

Subjects: Computer science.
Eligibility: Open to legally blind persons pursuing, or planning to pursue, a full-time post secondary course of training. The scholarship is awarded on the basis of academic excellence, service to the community and financial need. Candidates need not be members of the Federation.
Level of Study: Unrestricted
Type: Scholarship
Value: US$3,000
Frequency: Annual
Country of Study: United States of America
No. of awards offered: 1
Application Procedure: Applicants must complete an application form, available on request.
Closing Date: March 31st
Funding: Private

Sally S Jacobsen Scholarship

Subjects: Education.
Purpose: To assist blind people and to recognize achievements by blind scholars.
Eligibility: All applicants for the scholarship must be legally blind and pursuing or planning to pursue a full-time postsecondary course.
Level of Study: Unrestricted
Type: Scholarship
Value: US$5,000
Frequency: Annual
Study Establishment: A United States of America Institution
Country of Study: United States of America
No. of awards offered: 1
Application Procedure: All applications must include a personal letter from the applicant, two letters of recommendation, all transcripts related to institutions attended, a letter from a federation state president or designee and score reports (for high school seniors).
Closing Date: March 31st
Funding: Private
Additional Information: The scholarship is given in memory of a long-time New York state leader Sally S Jacobsen.

NATIONAL FISH AND WILDLIFE FOUNDATION

1120 Connecticut Avenue NW, Suite 900, Washington, DC, 20036, United States of America
Tel: (1) 202 857 0166
Fax: (1) 202 857 0162
Email: megan.oliver@nfwf.org
Website: www.nfwf.org
Contact: Ms Megan Oliver, Budweiser Scholarship Programme

The National Fish and Wildlife Foundation is a private, non-profit organization dedicated to the conservation of fish, wildlife and plants, and the habitats on which they depend. Our goals are to promote healthy populations of fish, wildlife and plants by generating new commerce for conservation.

Budweiser Conservation Scholarship

Subjects: The Budweiser Conservation Scholarship programme is designed to respond to many of the most significant challenges in fish, wildlife and plant conservation in the United States of America.
Purpose: To support and promote innovative research or study that seeks to respond to today's most pressing conservation issues.
Eligibility: To be eligible for consideration, a student must be a citizen of the United States of America, at least 21 years of age and enrolled in an accredited Institute of Higher Education in the United States of America. The applicant must be pursuing a graduate or undergraduate degree (sophomores and juniors in the current academic year only) in environmental science, natural resource management, biology, public policy, geography, political science or related disciplines.
Level of Study: Doctorate, graduate
Type: Scholarship
Value: US$10,000
Length of Study: 1 year
Frequency: Annual
Country of Study: United States of America
No. of awards offered: 10–15
Application Procedure: Our website at www.nfwf.org/budscholarship/ has application guidelines and an application form. Applicants must submit an application form, essay of 1,500 words, title for proposed research and short abstract, transcripts and three letters of recommendation.
Closing Date: January 27th (check website for future dates)
Funding: Corporation, government
Contributor: Anheuser-Busch Companies, Inc., United States of America; Fish and Wildlife Service
No. of awards given last year: 11
No. of applicants last year: 300+

NATIONAL FOUNDATION FOR INFECTIOUS DISEASES (NFID)

4733 Bethesda Avenue, Suite 750, Bethesda, MD, 20814, United States of America
Tel: (1) 301 656 0003
Fax: (1) 301 907 0878
Email: info@nfid.org
Website: www.nfid.org
Contact: Mr Charlotte Lazrus, Grants Manager

The National Foundation for Infectious Diseases (NFID) is a non-profit, non-governmental organization whose mission is public and professional education and promotion of research on the causes, treatment and prevention of infectious diseases.

NFID Advanced Vaccinology Course Travel Grant

Subjects: Immunology, vaccinology.
Purpose: To defray expenses related to attending the course, registration, airfare, ground transportation, lodging, meals and incidentals.
Eligibility: Applicants must be recent postdoctoral graduates (doctoral degree within past 3 years)/physicians who have completed speciality or subspeciality training within the past 2 years, with a demonstrated interest in a career in vaccinology. The applicant must be conducting research or working in a recognized and accredited United States of America Institution of Higher Learning or in a government agency.
Level of Study: Professional development
Type: Travel grant
Value: US$4,000
Length of Study: 10 days
Frequency: Annual
Study Establishment: Les Pensières, Veyrier-du-Lac
Country of Study: France
No. of awards offered: 2
Application Procedure: Applicant must submit an application and two copies, containing a letter from the applicant, letter of support from the department chairman, curriculum vitae and a copy of the application to the advanced vaccinology course, to be sent to the institution's main address.
Closing Date: November 15th
Funding: Foundation
Contributor: NFID Aventis Pasteur

NFID Colin L Powell Minority Postdoctoral Fellowship in Tropical Disease Research

Subjects: Tropical diseases.
Purpose: To encourage and assist a qualified minority researcher to become a specialist and investigator in the field of tropical disease research.
Eligibility: Open to applicants who hold a doctorate from a recognized university and who are permanent residents or citizens of the United States of America. Each applicant is required to have arranged

for an American or foreign laboratory in which to conduct his or her research. The laboratory should be supervised by a recognized leader in tropical disease research qualified to oversee the work of the selected Fellow. The fellowship may not be awarded if the applicant has received or will be receiving a major fellowship, research grant or traineeship from the federal government or another foundation in excess of the total amount of this award.
Level of Study: Postdoctorate
Type: Fellowship
Value: A stipend of US$30,000, of which US$3,000 may be used for travel and supplies, at the investigator's discretion. Although it is anticipated that the award will be tax exempt, no guarantee of internal revenue service rulings can be made. No overhead to the sponsoring institution will be paid but the stipend may be supplemented by other monies up to US$30,000 to achieve salary levels consistent with other Fellows within the supporting institution
Length of Study: 1 year
Frequency: Annual
No. of awards offered: 1
Application Procedure: Applicants must submit the original application and four copies no later than the deadline. The application should be addressed to the Grants Manager.
Closing Date: January 7th
Funding: Private
Contributor: NFID, GlaxoSmithKline
Additional Information: Minority in the context of this fellowship refers to underrepresented minorities in the biomedical sciences, eg. Black, Hispanic, American Indian, Alaskan Native and Asian or Pacific Islander from the United States Bureau of the Census.

NFID John P Utz Postdoctoral Fellowship in Medical Mycology

Subjects: Medical mycology.
Purpose: To encourage and assist a qualified physician to become a specialist and an investigator in medical mycology.
Eligibility: Open to physicians who are citizens of the United States of America. Applicants must demonstrate aptitude and training in research and must confirm arrangements for conduct of the proposed research in a recognized host laboratory. The applicant must be sponsored by a university-affiliated medical centre. The fellowship may not be awarded if the applicant has received or will receive a major fellowship, research grant or traineeship from the federal government or another foundation in excess of the amount of this award.
Level of Study: Postdoctorate
Type: Fellowship
Value: A stipend of US$40,000 plus US$1,000 for travel and supplies. Although it is anticipated that the award will be tax exempt, no guarantee of internal revenue service rulings can be made. No overhead will be paid to the sponsoring institution
Length of Study: 1 year
Frequency: Annual
Study Establishment: Approved research institutions
Country of Study: United States of America
No. of awards offered: 1
Application Procedure: Applicants must submit four copies of an original application including a letter from the laboratory director, curriculum vitae, description of applicant's proposed research project and a signed statement indicating that the applicant will acknowledge support received from the grant.
Closing Date: January 6th
Funding: Private
Contributor: IDSA, NFID and Pfizer, Inc
No. of awards given last year: 1

NFID Travelling Professorship in Rural Areas

Subjects: Infectious diseases education, antimicrobial resistance and antimicrobial stewardship, new and future antimicrobials, tuberculosis, adult and adolescent immunizations, etc.
Purpose: To provide support for the applicant to provide face-to-face infectious diseases education to practicing physicians in rural areas in the applicant's state of residence or primary practice.
Eligibility: Applicant must be board certified in infectious diseases and must be a citizen of the United States of America.
Level of Study: Professional development
Type: Professorship
Value: US$10,000
Length of Study: 5 working days
Frequency: Annual
Country of Study: United States of America
No. of awards offered: 1
Application Procedure: Applicant must submit an original application and four copies including cover letter, curriculum vitae and proposal (three pages), to be sent to the institution's main address.
Closing Date: January 7th
Funding: Foundation
Contributor: NFID Steven R. Mostow Endowment for Outreach Programs

THE NATIONAL GALLERY

Information Department, The National Gallery, Trafalgar Square, London, WC2N SDN, United Kingdom
Tel: (44) (0) 20 7747 2885
Fax: (44) (0) 20 7747 2423
Email: information@ng-london-org.uk
Website: www.nationalgallery.org.uk

The National Gallery, London houses one of the largest collections of European painting in the world.

The Pilgrim Trust Grants

Subjects: Art history.
Purpose: To fund research into regional collections, which will make a contribution to the National Inventory Research Project.
Level of Study: Research
Type: Grant
Value: A maximum of UK £5,000
Frequency: Twice yearly
Country of Study: United Kingdom
No. of awards offered: Varies
Application Procedure: There is no application form. Please submit a project plan including a list of paintings to be researched and a detailed budget, together with a letter of support from a senior curator or other responsible person and a curriculum vitae for the person who carry out the research.
Closing Date: April 30th and October 30th
Funding: Trusts
Contributor: The Pilgrim Trust
Additional Information: Researchers are most welcome to spend all or some part of the research period in the National Gallery Library, but this is not obligatory.

For further information contact:

Pilgrim Trust Grants, National Gallery Curatorial Department, The National Gallery, Trafalgar Square, London, WC2N 5DN

NATIONAL HEADACHE FOUNDATION

820 N Orleans, Suite 217, Chicago, IL, 60610, United States of America
Tel: (1) 1 888 NHF 5552
Fax: (1) 312 640 9049
Email: info@headaches.org
Website: www.headaches.org
Contact: Executive Director

The National Headache Foundation disseminates information, funds research, sponsors public and professional education programmes and has a nationwide network of support groups, with 20,000 subscribers. The Foundation is the recognized authority in headache and head pain, and offers the award winning newsletter NHF Head Lines, patient education brochures, and audio and video tapes.

National Headache Foundation Research Grant

Subjects: Treatment and causes of headache.
Purpose: To encourage better understanding and treatment of headache and head pain.

Eligibility: Open to researchers in neurology and pharmacology departments in medical schools throughout the United States of America. Submissions from other departments and individual investigators are also welcome.
Level of Study: Doctorate, postgraduate, postdoctorate
Type: Research grant
Value: Dependent on funds available. Grants only cover direct costs of carrying out research and do not cover overheads or salaries
Length of Study: 1 year
Frequency: Annual
Country of Study: United States of America
No. of awards offered: Varies, depending on funds available and the number of worthy projects submitted
Application Procedure: Applicants must complete an application form.
Closing Date: December 1st for notification by the following March
Funding: Private
Contributor: Dues and donations
No. of awards given last year: 8
No. of applicants last year: 15

NATIONAL HEALTH AND MEDICAL RESEARCH COUNCIL (NHMRC)

Centre for Research Management (MDP 33), GPO Box 9848, Canberra, ACT, 2601, Australia
Tel: (61) 2 6213 4153
Fax: (61) 2 6289 9132
Email: research@nhmrc.gov.au
Website: www.nhmrc.gov.au
Contact: Administrative Assistant

The National Health and Medical Research Council (NHMRC) (Australia) consolidates within a single national organization the often independent functions of research funding and development of advice. One of its strengths is that it brings together and draws upon the resources of all components of the health system, including governments, medical practitioners, nurses and allied health professionals, researchers, teaching and research institutions, public and private programme managers, service administrators, community health organizations, social health researchers and consumers.

Australian Clinical Research Postdoctoral Fellowship

Subjects: Scientific research, including the social and behavioural sciences, that can be applied to any area of clinical or community medicine.
Purpose: To provide training in scientific research methods.
Eligibility: Open to Australian citizens or graduates from overseas with permanent Australian resident status, who are not under bond to any foreign government. Candidates should hold a doctorate in a health-related field of research or have submitted a thesis for such by December of the year of application, be actively engaged in such research in Australia or overseas and have no more than 2 years postdoctoral experience at the time of application.
Level of Study: Postdoctorate
Type: Fellowship
Value: Australian $59,000 and Australian $5,000 per year
Length of Study: 4 years
Frequency: Annual
Study Establishment: Institutions approved by the NHMRC, such as teaching hospitals, universities and research institutes
Country of Study: Australia
No. of awards offered: Varies
Application Procedure: Application forms are available from the website.
Closing Date: First Friday in July each year
Funding: Government
No. of awards given last year: 7
No. of applicants last year: 26

Biomedical (Dora Lush) and Public Health Postgraduate Scholarships

Subjects: Biomedical sciences and public health.
Purpose: To encourage science honours or equivalent graduates of outstanding ability to gain full-time health and medical research experience.
Eligibility: Open to Australian citizens who have already completed a Science Honours Degree (or equivalent) at the time of submission of the application, science honours graduates and unregistered medical or dental graduates from overseas, who have permanent resident status and are currently residing in Australia. The scholarship shall be held within Australia.
Level of Study: Postgraduate
Type: Scholarship
Value: Varies
Length of Study: 1 year, renewable for up to 2 further years
Frequency: Annual
Study Establishment: Institutions approved by the NHMRC, such as teaching hospitals, universities and research institutes
Country of Study: Australia
No. of awards offered: Varies
Application Procedure: Applicants should visit the website at www.nhmrc.gov.au/funding/schlorships.htm for details.
Closing Date: First Friday of August each year
Funding: Government
No. of awards given last year: 95
No. of applicants last year: 220

Burnet Fellowships

Subjects: Any field of health and medical sciences.
Purpose: To attract back to Australia health and medical researchers of high calibre who have spent considerable time overseas and who have not returned because of the lack of suitable opportunities.
Eligibility: Open to Australian citizens or permanent residents who are not under bond to any foreign government. Candidates should have a current academic or hospital appointment overseas (for at least 7 years) equivalent to an Australian professor or associate professor, be actively engaged in research and apply in conjunction with a host institution, which must undertake to provide infrastructural support and administer the award.
Level of Study: Professional development
Type: Fellowship
Value: Allocation of Australian $400,000 per year
Length of Study: 5 years
Frequency: Dependent on funds available
Study Establishment: Australian research institutions
Country of Study: Australia
No. of awards offered: Varies
Application Procedure: Applicants must submit applications in writing with a curriculum vitae attached. There is no application form.
Closing Date: Applications are accepted at any time
Funding: Government
Additional Information: Enquiries should be directed to the Fellowships Office at the main address or by telephone on (61) 2 6289 9119 or by fax on (61) 2 6289 9131.

C J Martin Fellowships (Overseas Biomedical)

Subjects: Biomedical sciences.
Purpose: To enable Fellows to develop their research skills and work overseas on specific research projects within the biomedical sciences under nominated advisers.
Eligibility: Open to Australian citizens or graduates from overseas with permanent Australian resident status who are not under bond to any foreign government. Candidates should hold a doctorate in a medical, dental or related field of research, be actively engaged in such research in Australia and have no more than 2 years postdoctoral experience at the time of application.
Level of Study: Postdoctorate
Type: Fellowship
Value: Australian $60,000 and allowances per year
Length of Study: 4 years, the first 2 of which are to be spent overseas and the final 2 in Australia
Frequency: Annual
Study Establishment: Institutions approved by the NHMRC, such as teaching hospitals, universities and research institutes
Country of Study: Any country
No. of awards offered: Varies
Application Procedure: Application forms available from the website.

Closing Date: First Friday in July each year
Funding: Government
No. of awards given last year: 30
No. of applicants last year: 89

Career Development Awards
Subjects: Any human health-related research area.
Purpose: To help researchers to conduct research that is internationally competitive and to develop a capacity for independent research.
Eligibility: Open to Australian citizens or permanent residents, normally between 3 and 9 years postdoctoral experience.
Type: Fellowship
Value: Australian $87,000 per year
Length of Study: 5 years
Frequency: Annual
Study Establishment: Institutions approved by NHMRC, such as teaching hospitals, universities and research institutes
Country of Study: Australia
No. of awards offered: Varies
Application Procedure: Application forms available from the website at www.nhmrc.gov.au
Closing Date: Second Friday in April each year
Funding: Government
No. of awards given last year: 42
No. of applicants last year: 170

Howard Florey Centenary Fellowship
Subjects: Any human health-related research area.
Purpose: To provide a vehicle for Australian researchers working overseas to return to Australia to pursue medical research.
Eligibility: Open to Australian citizens currently researching overseas, normally with between 2 and 5 years postdoctoral experience.
Type: Fellowship
Value: Australian $70,000 and Australian $10,000 per year
Length of Study: 2 years
Frequency: Annual
Study Establishment: Institutions approved by the NHMRC, such as teaching hospitals, universities and research institutes
Country of Study: Australia
No. of awards offered: Varies
Application Procedure: Application forms available from the website.
Closing Date: First Friday in July each year
Funding: Government
No. of awards given last year: 8
No. of applicants last year: 25

Industry Fellowships
Subjects: Human health-related field.
Purpose: To enable Australian researchers to gain experience in industrial research and increase knowledge of commercial aspects of R & D within research institutions.
Eligibility: Open to Australian citizens or permanent residents, normally with between 3 and 9 years postdoctoral experience in medical research.
Type: Fellowship
Value: Australian $87,000 per year
Length of Study: 4 years
Frequency: Annual
Study Establishment: Institutions approved by the NHMRC, such as teaching hospitals, universities and research institutes
Country of Study: Any country
No. of awards offered: Varies
Application Procedure: Application forms available from the website.
Closing Date: Last Friday in June each year
Funding: Government
No. of awards given last year: 4
No. of applicants last year: 10

Neil Hamilton Fairley Fellowships (Overseas Clinical)
Subjects: Scientific research, including the social and behavioural sciences, that can be applied to any area of clinical or community medicine.
Purpose: To provide training in scientific research methods.
Eligibility: Open to Australian citizens or graduates from overseas with permanent Australian resident status who are not under bond to any foreign government. Candidates should hold a doctorate in a health-related field of research or have submitted a thesis for such by December of the year of application, be actively engaged in such research in Australia and have no more than 2 years postdoctoral experience at the time of application.
Level of Study: Postdoctorate
Type: Fellowship
Value: Australian $65,000 and allowances per year
Length of Study: 4 years, the first two of which are to be spent overseas and the final two in Australia
Frequency: Annual
Study Establishment: Institutions approved by the NHMRC, such as teaching hospitals, universities and research institutes
Country of Study: Any country
No. of awards offered: Varies
Application Procedure: Application form available from the website.
Closing Date: First Friday in July each year
Funding: Government
No. of awards given last year: 3
No. of applicants last year: 11

NHMRC Medical and Dental and Public Health Postgraduate Research Scholarships
Subjects: Medical or dental research.
Purpose: To encourage medical and dental graduates to gain full-time research experience.
Eligibility: Open to Australian citizens who are medical or dental graduates registered to practice in Australia, with the proviso that medical graduates can also apply during their intern year and that dental postgraduate research scholarships may be awarded prior to graduation provided that the evidence of high quality work is shown. Also open to medical and dental graduates from overseas who hold a qualification that is registered for practice in Australia, who have permanent resident status and are currently residing in Australia.
Level of Study: Postgraduate
Type: Scholarship
Value: Varies
Length of Study: 1 year, renewable for up to 2 further years
Frequency: Annual
Study Establishment: Institutions approved by the NHMRC such as teaching hospitals, universities and research institutes
Country of Study: Australia
No. of awards offered: Varies
Application Procedure: Available from the website at www.nhmrc.gov.au/funding/scholarships.htm
Closing Date: First Friday of August each year
Funding: Government
No. of awards given last year: 71
No. of applicants last year: 122

NHMRC/INSERM Exchange Fellowships
Subjects: Biomedical sciences.
Purpose: To enable Australian Fellows to work overseas on specific research projects in INSERM laboratories in France and vice versa.
Eligibility: Open to Australian citizens and permanent residents, who are not under bond to any foreign government, who hold a doctorate in a medical, dental or related field of research or have submitted a thesis for such by December in the year of application, are actively engaged in such research in Australia and have no more than 2 years postdoctoral experience at the time of application.
Level of Study: Postdoctorate
Type: Fellowship
Value: Australian $59,000 and allowances per year
Length of Study: 4 years, the first two of which are to be spent in France and the final two in Australia
Frequency: Annual
Study Establishment: Institutions approved by the NHMRC, such as teaching hospitals, universities and research institutes, and INSERM laboratories in France
Country of Study: France or Australia

No. of awards offered: 1
Application Procedure: Applications forms available from the website.
Closing Date: First Friday of July each year
Funding: Government
No. of awards given last year: 1
No. of applicants last year: 5
Additional Information: This fellowship is awarded in association with l'Institut National de la Santé et de la Recherche Médicale (INSERM), France.

Peter Doherty Fellowships (Australian Biomedical)

Subjects: Biomedical sciences.
Purpose: To provide a vehicle for training in clinical and basic research in Australia, and to encourage persons of outstanding ability to make medical research a full-time career.
Eligibility: Open to Australian citizens or graduates from overseas with permanent Australian resident status who are not under bond to any foreign government. Candidates should hold a doctorate in a medical, dental or related field of research or have submitted a thesis for such by December in the year of application, be actively engaged in such research in Australia or overseas and have no more than 2 years postdoctoral experience at the time of application.
Level of Study: Postdoctorate
Type: Fellowship
Value: Australian $59,000 and allowances per year
Length of Study: 4 years
Frequency: Annual
Study Establishment: Institutions approved by the NHMRC, such as teaching hospitals, universities and research institutes
Country of Study: Australia
No. of awards offered: Varies
Application Procedure: Application forms available from the website.
Closing Date: First Friday in July each year
Funding: Government
No. of awards given last year: 30
No. of applicants last year: 100

Public Health Fellowship (Australian)

Subjects: Public health.
Purpose: To provide full-time training in public health research in Australia.
Eligibility: Applicants should hold a doctorate in a health-related field of research or have submitted a PhD by December in the year of application and have no more than 2 years postdoctoral experience. Open to Australian citizens or permanent residents.
Type: Fellowship
Value: Australian $59,000 and Australian $5,000
Length of Study: 4 years
Frequency: Annual
Study Establishment: Institutions approved by the NHMRC, such as teaching hospitals, universities and research institutes
Country of Study: Australia
No. of awards offered: Varies
Application Procedure: Application forms available from the website.
Closing Date: First Friday in July each year
Funding: Government
No. of awards given last year: 11
No. of applicants last year: 38

Sidney Sax Fellowship (Overseas Public Health)

Subjects: Public health.
Purpose: To provide full-time training in public health research overseas in Australia.
Eligibility: Applicants should hold a doctorate in a health-related field of research or have submitted a PhD by December in the year of application and have no more than 2 years postdoctoral experience. Open to Australian citizens or permanent residents.
Type: Fellowship
Value: Australian $59,000 and allowances per year
Length of Study: 4 years
Frequency: Annual
Study Establishment: Institutions approved by the NHMRC, such as teaching hospitals, universities and research institutes
Country of Study: Any country
No. of awards offered: Varies
Application Procedure: Application forms available from the website.
Closing Date: First Friday in July each year
Funding: Government
No. of awards given last year: 3
No. of applicants last year: 9

Training Scholarship for Indigenous Health Research

Purpose: To encourage research with relevance to the health and well being of Aboriginal and Torres Strait Islander people.
Eligibility: Open to Australian citizens or Australian permanent residents enrolling in a diploma, certificate, an undergraduate degree or a postgraduate degree at a fully accredited institution, which will enable the applicant to pursue research relevant to Aboriginal and Torres Strait Islander health, healthcare, healthcare delivery or health research in the area of Aboriginal and Torres Strait Islander health.
Level of Study: Postdoctorate
Type: Scholarship
Length of Study: 1 year, renewable up to further 2 years
Frequency: Annual
Country of Study: Australia
Application Procedure: Available from the website at www.nhmrc.gov/funding/scholarships.htm
Closing Date: First Friday of August
Funding: Government
No. of awards given last year: 5
No. of applicants last year: 8

NATIONAL HEART FOUNDATION OF AUSTRALIA

411 King Street, West Melbourne, VIC, 3003, Australia
Tel: (61) 3 9329 8511
Fax: (61) 3 9326 3190
Email: research@heartfoundation.com.au
Website: www.heartfoundation.com.au
Contact: Research Manager

The National Heart Foundation of Australia is a non-government, non-profit health organization funded mostly by public donation. The Foundation's mission is to prevent early death and disability from heart disease and stroke. The Foundation funds biomedical research, provides clinical leadership and develops health promotion strategies and initiatives.

National Heart Foundation of Australia Career Development Fellowship

Subjects: Cardiovascular disease and related disorders.
Purpose: To enable a senior Australian researcher of exceptional merit and proven record in the cardiovascular field to undertake independent research.
Eligibility: Open to Australian citizens and permanent residents only.
Level of Study: Research
Type: Fellowship
Value: Please contact the organization
Length of Study: 5 years, non-renewable
Frequency: Annual
Study Establishment: Universities, hospitals or research institutions
Country of Study: Australia
Application Procedure: Applicants must be nominated by the head of the host department or institution.
Funding: Private

National Heart Foundation of Australia Overseas Research Fellowships

Subjects: Clinical, public health or basic medical sciences related to cardiovascular disease and related disorders.

Purpose: To allow Fellows to obtain skills in cardiovascular research.
Eligibility: Open to Australian citizens or permanent residents who are actively engaged in research in Australia on December 31st of the year prior to application.
Level of Study: Postdoctorate
Type: Fellowship
Value: Please contact the organization
Length of Study: 3 years
Frequency: Annual
Study Establishment: Approved institutions
Country of Study: Other
Application Procedure: Applicants must be nominated by the head of the host department or institution.
Funding: Private
Additional Information: Fellowships are awarded on the understanding that the Fellow will return to Australia to continue his or her career upon completion of the fellowship.

National Heart Foundation of Australia Postdoctoral Research Fellowship

Subjects: Cardiovascular disease and related disorders.
Purpose: To award graduates who have demonstrated expertise and significant achievement in cardiovascular research.
Eligibility: Open to Australian citizens and permanent residents only.
Level of Study: Postdoctorate
Type: Fellowship
Value: Please contact the organization
Frequency: Annual
Study Establishment: Universities, hospitals or research institutions
Country of Study: Australia
Application Procedure: Applicants must submit an application outlining a research proposal accompanied by the supervisor's reference and backing.
Funding: Private

National Heart Foundation of Australia Postgraduate Biomedical Research Scholarship

Subjects: Cardiovascular disease and related disorders.
Purpose: To allow graduates to undertake a period of training in research under the full-time supervision and tuition of a responsible investigator.
Eligibility: Open to Australian citizens and permanent residents only.
Level of Study: Postgraduate
Type: Scholarship
Value: Please contact the organization
Length of Study: Up to 3 years
Frequency: Annual
Study Establishment: Universities, hospitals or research institutions
Country of Study: Australia
Application Procedure: Applicants must submit an application outlining a research proposal accompanied by the supervisor's reference and backing.
Funding: Private

National Heart Foundation of Australia Postgraduate Clinical Research Scholarship

Subjects: Cardiovascular disease.
Purpose: To enable medical graduates to undertake a period of training in research under the full-time supervision and tuition of a responsible investigator.
Eligibility: Open to Australian citizens and permanent residents only.
Level of Study: Postgraduate
Type: Scholarship
Value: Please contact the organization
Length of Study: 3 years
Frequency: Annual
Study Establishment: Universities, hospitals and research institutions
Country of Study: Australia
No. of awards offered: Varies
Application Procedure: Applicants must submit an application outlining a research proposal accompanied by the supervisor's reference and backing.
Funding: Private

National Heart Foundation of Australia Postgraduate Public Health Research Scholarship

Subjects: Cardiovascular research and related disorders.
Purpose: To allow graduates to undertake a period of training in research under the full-time supervision and tuition of a responsible investigator.
Eligibility: Open to Australian citizens and permanent residents only.
Level of Study: Postgraduate
Type: Scholarship
Value: Please contact the organization
Length of Study: Up to 3 years
Frequency: Annual
Study Establishment: Universities, hospitals or research institutions
Country of Study: Australia
Application Procedure: Applicants must submit an application outlining a research proposal accompanied by the supervisor's reference and backing.
Funding: Private

National Heart Foundation of Australia Research Grants-in-Aid

Subjects: Basic, clinical and public health research.
Purpose: To support research in the cardiovascular field.
Eligibility: Open to Australian citizens and permanent residents only.
Level of Study: Research
Type: Grant
Value: Please contact the organization
Length of Study: Up to 2 years
Frequency: Annual
Study Establishment: An approved institution
Country of Study: Australia
Application Procedure: Applicants must submit an application outlining research proposal. References are also required.
Closing Date: Refer website each year (www.heartfoundation.com.au)
Funding: Private
No. of awards given last year: 39
No. of applicants last year: 191

NATIONAL HEART FOUNDATION OF NEW ZEALAND

PO Box 17-160, Greenlane, Newmarket, Auckland, New Zealand
Tel: (64) 9 571 9191
Fax: (64) 9 571 9190
Email: info@nhf.org.nz
Website: www.heartfoundation.org.nz
Contact: Ms Helen Stewart, Research Grants Manager

The National Heart Foundation of New Zealand aims to promote good health and to reduce suffering and premature death from diseases of the heart and circulation.

National Heart Foundation of New Zealand Fellowships

Subjects: Any aspect of cardiovascular disease including rehabilitation and education.
Purpose: To promote the aims of the National Heart Foundation of New Zealand.
Eligibility: Normally open to New Zealand graduates only.
Level of Study: Postgraduate
Type: Other
Value: Varies, according to the determination of the Scientific Committee and within an annual budget
Frequency: Annual
No. of awards offered: Varies
Application Procedure: Applicants must apply to the Foundation for the publication A Guide to Applicants for Research and Other Grants.
Closing Date: June 1st
Funding: Private
No. of awards given last year: 8
No. of applicants last year: 17

National Heart Foundation of New Zealand Limited Budget Grants

Subjects: Any aspect of cardiovascular disease including rehabilitation and education. Priority areas include modification of lifestyle with regard to cardiovascular disease, the socio-economic determinants of heart disease, Maori and Pacific Island health, diagnosis and management of patients with cardiovascular disease.
Purpose: To further the aims of the National Heart Foundation of New Zealand.
Eligibility: Normally open to New Zealand graduates only.
Level of Study: Postgraduate
Type: Grant
Value: Varies, according to the determination of the Scientific Committee and within an annual budget
Country of Study: New Zealand
No. of awards offered: Varies
Application Procedure: Applicants must write for details.
Closing Date: February 1st, June 1st or October 1st
Funding: Private
No. of awards given last year: 18
Additional Information: These grants cover small projects, eg. less than New Zealand $15,000 and grants-in-aid.

National Heart Foundation of New Zealand Maori Cardiovascular Research Fellowship

Subjects: Cardiovascular health.
Purpose: To financially support graduates who propose to engage in research to improve Maori cardiovascular health.
Eligibility: Open to medical graduates or to non-medical graduates enrolled for a higher degree. Preference will be given to those with a working knowledge of Te Reo Maori and who are committed to Maori health.
Level of Study: Predoctorate, doctorate, postgraduate
Type: Fellowship
Value: New Zealand $30,000
Length of Study: 2 years
Frequency: Annual
Country of Study: New Zealand
No. of awards offered: 1
Application Procedure: Applications will be considered at the annual meeting of the Scientific Committee.
Closing Date: February 1st
Funding: Private
No. of awards given last year: 1

National Heart Foundation of New Zealand Project Grants

Subjects: Any aspect of cardiovascular disease including rehabilitation and education. Priority areas include modification of lifestyle with regard to cardiovascular disease, the socio-economic determinants of heart disease, Maori and Pacific Islander health, diagnosis and management of patients with cardiovascular disease.
Purpose: To provide short-term support for a single individual or small group working on a clearly defined research project, which will promote the aims of the National Heart Foundation of New Zealand.
Eligibility: Normally open to New Zealand graduates only.
Level of Study: Postgraduate
Type: Grant
Value: Varies, according to the determination of the scientific committee and within an annual budget
Frequency: Annual
Country of Study: New Zealand
No. of awards offered: Varies
Application Procedure: Applicants must write for details.
Closing Date: March 1st
Funding: Private
No. of awards given last year: 10
No. of applicants last year: 21

National Heart Foundation of New Zealand Senior Fellowship

Subjects: Cardiovascular disease.
Purpose: To support graduates from New Zealand who have trained as cardiologists or other scientists working in the field of cardiovascular research.
Eligibility: Applicants must possess an appropriate postgraduate degree or diploma. The maximum age for appointment will normally be 40 years.
Level of Study: Postgraduate
Type: Fellowship
Value: Up to New Zealand $1,500 to enable research work to commence. In subsequent years, senior fellows may apply for working expenses not exceeding New Zealand $1,000 annually with no single item to exceed New Zealand $500
Length of Study: Up to 3 years
Country of Study: New Zealand
No. of awards offered: 1
Application Procedure: Applicants should follow the format outlined in the revised A Guide to Applicants for Research and Other Grants,' which is available from the website. Applications should be sent to Professor Norman Sharpe, Medical Director.
Closing Date: June 1st
Funding: Private
No. of awards given last year: 1
No. of applicants last year: 3
Additional Information: The fellowship must be taken up within 1 year of the award. Further research funding will require an application for project grant funds from the Foundation. Funding for conference expenses must be applied for separately.

National Heart Foundation of New Zealand Travel Grants

Subjects: Any aspect of cardiovascular disease including education. Priority areas include modification of lifestyle with regard to cardiovascular disease, the socio-economic determinants of heart disease, Maori and Pacific Island health, diagnosis and management of patients with cardiovascular disease.
Purpose: To enable medical or non-medical workers to travel in New Zealand or overseas for short-term study or to attend conferences.
Eligibility: Normally open to New Zealand graduates only.
Level of Study: Postgraduate
Type: Grant
Value: Varies, according to the determination of the scientific committee and within an annual budget
Country of Study: Any country
No. of awards offered: Varies
Application Procedure: Applicants must write for details.
Closing Date: February 1st, June 1st or October 1st
Funding: Private
No. of awards given last year: 15

NATIONAL HISTORICAL PUBLICATIONS AND RECORDS COMMISSION (NHPRC)

National Archives and Records Administration 700 Pennsylvania Avenue, NW, Room 111, Washington, DC 20408-0001, United States of America
Tel: (1) 202 501 5610
Fax: (1) 202 501 5601
Email: nancy.copp@nara.gov
Website: www.archives.gov
Contact: Nancy T. Copp, Management and Program Analyst

The National Historical Publications and Records Commission (NHPRC) is the grantmaking affiliate of the National Archives and Records Administration (NARA). The Commission has defined its purpose to carry out its statutory mission to ensure understanding of the nation's past by promoting, nationwide, the identification, preservation and dissemination of essential historical documentation.

NHPRC Fellowship in Archival Administration

Subjects: Library and archive studies.
Purpose: To provide experience in management and administration for archivists.
Eligibility: Open to individuals who must have spent two–five years working as an archivist, and be United States of America citizens. While not required, it is desirable that applicants have the equivalent of two semesters of full-time graduate training in a programme containing an archival education component.

Level of Study: Professional development
Type: Fellowship
Value: A stipend of US$35,000 plus an additional US$7,000 for fringe benefits
Length of Study: 9–12 months
Frequency: Annual
Country of Study: United States of America
No. of awards offered: 1
Application Procedure: Applicants must contact the Commission for guidelines and host institution information. This information is available before December of the preceding year.
Closing Date: Postmarked March 1st
Funding: Government

NHPRC Fellowship in Documentary Editing

Subjects: Documentary editing.
Purpose: To provide individuals with training in the field of historical documentary editing.
Eligibility: Open to applicants who hold PhD or have completed all requirements for the doctorate except the dissertation. Applicants may be working on their dissertation and must be United States of America citizens.
Level of Study: Doctorate, postdoctorate
Type: Fellowship
Value: US$41,250 including funds for fringe benefits
Length of Study: 11 months
Frequency: Annual
Country of Study: United States of America
No. of awards offered: 1
Application Procedure: Applicants must contact the Commission for guidelines and host institution information. This information is available before December of the preceding year.
Closing Date: Postmarked March 1st
Funding: Government
Additional Information: Further information is available from the website.

NATIONAL INSTITUTE OF GENERAL MEDICAL SCIENCES (NIGMS)

45 Center Drive, MSC 6200, Bethesda, MD, 20892-6200, United States of America
Tel: (1) 301 496 7301
Fax: (1) 301 402 0224
Email: pub_info@nigms.nih.gov
Website: www.nigms.nih.gov
Contact: Ms Jilliene Mitchell, Public Affairs

The National Institute of General Medical Sciences (NIGMS) is one of the National Institutes of Health (NIH), the principal biomedical research agency of the Federal Government. NIGMS primarily supports basic biomedical research that lays the foundation for advances in disease diagnosis, treatment, and prevention.

MARC Faculty Predoctoral Fellowships

Subjects: Biomedical or behavioural sciences.
Purpose: Awards provide an opportunity for eligible faculty who lack the PhD degree (or equivalent) to obtain the research doctorate.
Eligibility: Open to full-time, permanent faculty members in a biomedically related science or mathematics programme who have been at a minority or minority-serving institution for at least 3 years at the time of application. Candidates must be enrolled in, or have been accepted into, a PhD or combined MD-PhD training programme in the biomedical or behavioural sciences. Candidates must intend to return to the minority institution at the end of the training period.
Level of Study: Postgraduate, predoctorate
Type: Fellowship
Value: An applicant may request a stipend equal to his or her annual salary, but not to exceed the stipend of a level 1 postdoctoral Fellow, currently valued at US$38,976. The applicant may also request tuition and fees as determined by the training institution as well as an allowance of US$2,750 per year for training-related costs
Frequency: Annual
Study Establishment: An institution in the United States of America
Country of Study: United States of America
No. of awards offered: Varies
Application Procedure: Applicants must write to the main address for details or telephone Dr Adolphus Toliver, at (1) 301 594 3900. Further details are also available from the website, www.nigms.nih.gov
Funding: Government

NIGMS Fellowship Awards for Minority Students

Subjects: Biomedical or behavioural sciences.
Purpose: These awards provide up to 5 years of support for research training leading to a PhD or equivalent research degree, a combined MD-PhD degree or another combined professional doctorate-research PhD.
Eligibility: Open to highly qualified students who are members of minority groups that are underrepresented in the biomedical or behavioural sciences in the United States of America. These groups include African Americans, Hispanic Americans, Native Americans, including Alaska Natives and natives of the United States of America Pacific Islands.
Level of Study: Postgraduate, predoctorate
Type: Fellowship
Value: An annual stipend of US$20,772, a tuition and fee allowance, and an annual institution fee of US$2,750, which may be used for travel to scientific meetings and for laboratory and other training expenses
Length of Study: Up to 5 years
Frequency: Annual
Study Establishment: An institution in the United States of America
Country of Study: United States of America
No. of awards offered: Varies
Application Procedure: Applicants must write to the main address for details or telephone Dr Adolphus Toliver, at (1) 301 594 3900. Further details are also available from the website, www.nigms.nih.gov
Funding: Government

NIGMS Fellowship Awards for Students With Disabilities

Subjects: Biomedical and behavioural sciences.
Purpose: These awards provide up to 5 years of support for research training leading to a PhD or equivalent research degree, combined MD-PhD degree or another combined professional doctorate/research PhD degree in the biomedical or behavioural science.
Eligibility: Open to principal investigators at domestic institutions holding an active NIGMS research grant, programme project grant, centre grant or co-operative agreement research programme with a reasonable period of research support remaining.
Level of Study: Postdoctorate, predoctorate, doctorate, postgraduate, graduate
Type: Fellowship
Value: Varies
Length of Study: 2 years or more
Frequency: Annual
Study Establishment: An institution in the United States of America
Country of Study: United States of America
No. of awards offered: Varies
Application Procedure: Applicants must write to the main address for details or telephone Dr Anthony René, at (1) 301 594 3833. Further details are also available from the website, www.nigms.nih.gov
Funding: Government

NIGMS Postdoctoral Awards

Subjects: Biomedical and behavioural sciences.
Purpose: NIGMS welcomes NRSA applications from eligible individuals who seek postdoctoral biomedical research training in areas related to the scientific programmes of the Institute.
Eligibility: Open to applicants who have received the doctoral degree (domestic or foreign) by the beginning date of the proposed award.
Level of Study: Postdoctorate
Value: Up to US$51,036 per year, based on the salary of the applicant at the time of the award
Frequency: Annual

Study Establishment: The institutional setting may be domestic or foreign, public or private
Country of Study: Any country
No. of awards offered: Varies
Application Procedure: Applicants must write to the main address for details or telephone Dr Alison Cole, at (1) 301 594 3349. Further details are also available from the website, www.nigms.nih.gov
Funding: Government

NIGMS Program Project Grants

Subjects: Biomedical and behavioral sciences.
Purpose: Programme project grants are available to a group of several investigators with differing areas of expertise who wish to collaborate in research by pooling their talents and resources.
Level of Study: Postgraduate
Frequency: Annual
Funding: Government

NIGMS Research Center Grants

Purpose: The grants are multidisciplinary in scope and may focus more on an area or discipline of science then on a specific theme or goal.
Frequency: Annual

NIGMS Research Project Grants

Subjects: Biomedical and behavioural sciences.
Purpose: To support a discrete project related to the investigator's area of interest and competence.
Eligibility: Research Grants may be awarded to non-profit organizations and institutions, governments and their agencies, and occasionally to individuals who have access to adequate facilities and resources for conducting the research, as well as profit-making organizations. Foreign institutions and international organizations are also eligible to apply for these grants.
Level of Study: Postgraduate
Value: These grants may provide funds for reasonable costs of the research activity, as well as for salaries, equipment, supplies, travel and other related expenses
Frequency: Annual
Country of Study: United States of America
No. of awards offered: Varies
Application Procedure: Applicants must contact the Office of Extramural Outreach and Information Resources for details.
Funding: Government

For further information contact:

Office of Extramural Outreach and Information Resources, NIH, 6701 Rockledge Drive, MSC 7910, Room 6207, Bethesda, MD, 20892-7910, United States of America
Tel: (1) 301 435 0714
Email: grantsinfo@nih.gov

NIGMS Research Supplements for Underrepresented Minorities

Subjects: Biomedical and behavioural sciences.
Purpose: To help minority scientists and students develop their capabilities for independent research careers. Supplements are available to high school students, undergraduate students, post-baccalaureate, post-Master's degree and predoctoral students as well as minority individuals in postdoctoral training and minority staff and faculty.
Eligibility: Open to principal investigators at domestic institutions holding an active NIGMS research grant, programme project grant, centre grant or co-operative agreement research programme with a reasonable period of research support remaining.
Level of Study: Unrestricted
Type: Grant
Value: Varies
Length of Study: 2 years or more
Frequency: Annual
Study Establishment: An institution in the United States of America
Country of Study: United States of America
No. of awards offered: Varies
Application Procedure: Applicants must write to the main address for details or telephone Dr Anthony René, at (1) 301 594 3833. Further details are also available from the website, www.nigms.nih.gov
Funding: Government

NATIONAL INSTITUTE ON AGING

GW 218, Bethesda, MD, 20892, United States of America
Tel: (1) 301 496 9322
Fax: (1) 301 402 2945
Email: mk46u@nih.gov
Website: www.nih.gov
Contact: Dr Miriam Kelty, Associate Director

The National Institute on Aging conducts and supports research and research training in all areas of biological ageing, the neuroscience and neuropsychology of ageing, geriatrics and the social and behavioural sciences of ageing.

NIH Research Grants

Subjects: The biology of ageing, the neuroscience and neuropsychology of ageing, geriatrics and clinical gerontology and the social and behavioural sciences of ageing.
Purpose: To support research and training in the biological, clinical, behavioural and social aspects of ageing mechanisms and processes.
Eligibility: Varies, depending on the mechanism, but generally open to United States of America citizens only.
Level of Study: Postdoctorate
Type: Grants, fellowships, career development awards and institutional training awards
Value: Varies
Length of Study: 1–5 years
Frequency: Annual, 3 cycles a year
Country of Study: The United States of America or others depending on mechanisms
No. of awards offered: Varies
Application Procedure: Applicants must download the application form, available on the website. NIH is transitioning to electronic transmission through grants.gov (www.nih.gov)
Closing Date: Deadlines are staggered. Please see website
Funding: Government
Contributor: The United States of America government
Additional Information: Some award mechanisms are limited to citizens and permanent residents of the United States of America. Others are open to applicants from any country. Further information is available on the website.

NATIONAL KIDNEY RESEARCH FUND (NKRF)

King's Chambers, Priestgate, Peterborough, Cambridgeshire, PE1 1FG, England
Tel: (44) 1733 704658
Fax: (44) 1733 704685
Email: grants@nkrf.org.uk
Website: www.nkrf.org.uk
Contact: Mrs Elaine Davies, Grants Administration Manager

The National Kidney Research Fund (NKRF) aims to advance and promote research into kidney and renal disease. These may include epidemiological, clinical or biological approaches to relevant problems. All research must be carried out in the United Kingdom.

NKRF Research Project Grants

Subjects: Renal medicine.
Purpose: To support both basic scientific and clinical research projects, improving the understanding of renal disease, its causes, treatment and management.
Eligibility: Open to suitably qualified researchers of any nationality. Work must be carried out in the United Kingdom.
Level of Study: Unrestricted
Type: Project grant

Value: Up to UK £100,000 over 1–3 years for a full research project, and up to UK £30,000 over 1–2 years for a start-up research project
Length of Study: 1–3 years
Study Establishment: Any institution
Country of Study: United Kingdom
No. of awards offered: Varies
Application Procedure: Applicants must complete an application form available from the Grants Department or website.
Closing Date: Provisional dates: March 5th for round one, August 27th for round two
Funding: Private
Contributor: Public donations
No. of awards given last year: 10
No. of applicants last year: 61

NKRF Senior Fellowships

Subjects: Renal medicine and related scientific studies.
Eligibility: Open to postdoctoral researchers in the biomedical field with evidence of independent research or academic clinicians or those building towards this senior role. Applicants may be of any nationality but project work must be carried out in the United Kingdom.
Level of Study: Professional development, research, postdoctorate
Type: Fellowship
Value: Up to UK £285,000 over a maximum of 5 years. Salary will be at the Consultant/Senior Registrar or established academic level at the appropriate university scale. Includes a UK £12,000 per year bench allowance for consumables, minor equipment and technical support
Length of Study: 3–5 years, subject to review in the 3rd year
Frequency: Annual
Study Establishment: Any institution
Country of Study: United Kingdom
No. of awards offered: Varies
Application Procedure: Applicants must complete an application form available from the Grants Department or website.
Closing Date: November 28th, provisional November 26th
Funding: Private
Contributor: Public donations
No. of awards given last year: 1
No. of applicants last year: 6

NKRF Special Project Grants

Subjects: Renal disease.
Purpose: To provide support for substantial projects in scientific disciplines related to renal disease and its management.
Eligibility: Open to suitably qualified researchers of United Kingdom or European Union residency or nationality.
Level of Study: Research, professional development
Type: Grant
Value: Up to UK £150,000
Length of Study: 3 years
Frequency: Dependent on funds available
Country of Study: United Kingdom
No. of awards offered: Varies
Application Procedure: Applicants must complete application forms, available from the Grants Department and also via the website or email.
Closing Date: Please see the website
Funding: Government, commercial
No. of awards given last year: 2
No. of applicants last year: 12

NKRF Studentships

Subjects: Renal medicine.
Purpose: To enable postgraduates to start a career in renal medicine by completing a course of training including submitting a PhD thesis.
Eligibility: Open to applicants of any nationality. Work must take place in the United Kingdom.
Level of Study: Postgraduate
Type: Studentship
Value: Up to UK £50,000. University fees are met by the NKRF and a bench fee is available to the host institution
Length of Study: 3 years, subject to a satisfactory annual report
Frequency: Annual
Study Establishment: Any institution
Country of Study: United Kingdom
No. of awards offered: Varies
Application Procedure: Applicants must complete an application form available from the Grants Department or website.
Closing Date: November 28th, provisional date November 26th
Funding: Private
Contributor: Public donations
No. of awards given last year: 2
No. of applicants last year: 9

NKRF Training Fellowships

Subjects: Renal medicine and related scientific studies.
Purpose: To enable medical or scientific graduates to undertake specialized training in renal research.
Eligibility: Open to medical candidates of immediate postregistration to registrar level and to science candidates with a PhD or DPhil and at least 2 years of postdoctoral experience. Project work must be carried out in the United Kingdom.
Level of Study: Research, professional development, postdoctorate
Type: Fellowship
Value: Up to UK £150,000. The level of financial support will be based on an appropriate point on current NHS or university pay scales and includes a UK £5,000 per year United Kingdom bench allowance with fees where applicable
Length of Study: 1–3 years, subject to annual review
Frequency: Annual
Study Establishment: Any institution
Country of Study: United Kingdom
No. of awards offered: Varies
Application Procedure: Applicants must complete an application form available from the Grants Department, the website or via email.
Closing Date: November 28th, provisional November 26th
Funding: Private
Contributor: Public donations
No. of awards given last year: 3
No. of applicants last year: 24

NATIONAL LEAGUE OF AMERICAN PEN WOMEN, INC. (NLAPW)

1300 17th Street NW, Washington, DC, 20036-1973, United States of America
Tel: (1) 202 785 1997
Fax: (1) 202 452 6868
Email: nlapw1@juno.com
Website: www.americanpenwomen.org
Contact: Ms Elaine Waidelich, National Scholarship Chairperson

The National League of American Pen Women (NLAPW) exists to promote women in the creative arts including art, writing and music.

Virginia Liebeler Biennial Grants For Mature Women (Art)

Subjects: Art.
Purpose: To advance creative purpose in art.
Eligibility: Open to women over 35 years of age who wish to pursue special work in their field of art, letters or music. Applicants must be citizens of the United States of America. Current and past recipients are not eligible for this award.
Level of Study: Unrestricted
Type: Grant
Value: US$1,000. The award may be used for college, framing, research or any creative purpose that furthers a career in the creative arts
Frequency: Every 2 years
Country of Study: United States of America
No. of awards offered: 1
Application Procedure: Applicants must; (a) send proof of age and United States of America citizenship (copy of birth certificate, passport ID page, voter's registration card and a driver's license or a state ID, if possible). Driver's license alone is not proof of citizenship; (b) enclose a one-page cover letter describing how they intend to use the grant

money, if awarded the grant, and any relevant information about themselves; (c) enclose a US$8 check made payable to NLAPW with submission; (d) enclose a stamped addressed envelope/mailer with sufficient postage for the return of the submission; (e) provide their name, address, telephone number and e-mail address on the cover page of submission; submit three 4 X 6 or larger colour prints (no slides): oil, watercolor, acrylic, mixed media, original works on paper etc. submit three 4 X 6 or larger photos of sculpture; and for photography, submit three 4 X 6 or larger prints in colour or black and white.
Closing Date: October 15th
Funding: Private
Contributor: NLAPW
No. of applicants last year: 1000+
Additional Information: Interested parties must send a stamped addressed envelope to receive current information.

For further information contact:

1837 Grandview Avenue, El Paso, Sudbury, TX, 79902-5195, United States of America
Contact: Sister Marquita Margula

Virginia Liebeler Biennial Grants For Mature Women (Music)

Subjects: Music.
Purpose: To advance creative purpose in music.
Eligibility: Open to women over 35 years of age who wish to pursue special work in their field of art, letters or music. Applicants must be citizens of the United States of America. Current and past recipients are not eligible for this award.
Level of Study: Unrestricted
Type: Grant
Frequency: Every 2 years
Country of Study: United States of America
No. of awards offered: 1
Application Procedure: Applicants must; (a) send proof of age and United States of America citizenship (copy of birth certificate, passport ID page, voter's registration card and a driver's license or a state ID, if possible). Driver's license alone is not proof of citizenship; (b) enclose a one-page cover letter describing how they intend to use the grant money, if awarded the grant, and any relevant information about themselves; (c) enclose a US$8 check made payable to NLAPW with the submission; (d) enclose a stamped addressed envelope/mailer with sufficient postage for the return of submission; and (e) provide their name, address, telephone number and e-mail address on the cover page of their submission. Applicants must also submit two compositions: 3-minute minimum performance time, 5-minute maximum performance time.
Funding: Private
Contributor: NLAPW
Additional Information: Interested parties must send a stamped addressed envelope to receive current information.

For further information contact:

666 Wall Road, Napa, CA, 94558-9583, United States of America
Contact: Louise P Canepa

Virginia Liebeler Biennial Grants For Mature Women (Writing)

Subjects: Writing.
Purpose: To advance creative purpose in writing.
Eligibility: Open to women over 35 years of age who wish to pursue special work in their field of art, letters or music. Applicants must be citizens of the United States of America. Current and past recipients are not eligible for this award.
Level of Study: Unrestricted
Type: Grant
Value: US$1,000
Frequency: Every 2 years
Country of Study: United States of America
No. of awards offered: 1
Application Procedure: Applicants must (a) send proof of age and United States of America citizenship (copy of birth certificate, passport ID page, voter's registration card and a driver's license or a state ID, if possible). Driver's license alone is not proof of citizenship; (b) enclose a one-page cover letter describing how they intend to use the grant money, if awarded the grant, and any relevant information about themselves; (c) enclose a US$8 check made payable to NLAPW with their submission; (d) enclose a stamped addressed envelope/mailer with sufficient postage for the return of their submission; and (e) provide their name, address, telephone number and e-mail address on the cover page of the submission. Applicants must submit either a published or unpublished manuscript in any or all of the following categories: article, drama, essay, first chapter of a novel, narrative outline of a complete novel, three poems, short-story or TV script. The entry is not to exceed 4,000 words.
Closing Date: October 15th
Funding: Private
Contributor: NLAPW
No. of applicants last year: 1000+
Additional Information: Interested parties must send a stamped addressed envelope to receive current information.

For further information contact:

921 South Hill Avenue, DeLand, FL, 32724-7015, United States of America
Contact: Lorna Jean Hagstrom

NATIONAL LIBRARY OF AUSTRALIA

Canberra, ACT, 2600, Australia
Tel: (61) 2 6262 1258
Fax: (61) 2 6262 1516
Email: gpowell@nla.gov.au
Contact: Mr Graeme Powell, Manuscript Librarian

The National Library of Australia is responsible for developing and maintaining a comprehensive collection of Australian library materials and a strong collection of non-Australian publications, and for administering and co-ordinating a range of national bibliographical activities.

Harold White Fellowships

Subjects: There are few subject limitations but most fellowships fall within the categories of arts and humanities, fine and applied arts or social sciences.
Purpose: To promote the Library as a centre of scholarly activity and research, to encourage the scholarly and literary use of the collection and the production of publications based on them and to publicize the Library's collections.
Eligibility: Open to established scholars, writers and librarians from any country. Fellowships are not normally offered to candidates working for a higher degree.
Level of Study: Unrestricted
Type: Fellowship
Value: Australian $800 per week
Length of Study: 3–6 months
Frequency: Annual
Study Establishment: The National Library of Australia
Country of Study: Australia
No. of awards offered: 3–6
Application Procedure: Applicants must complete an application form available from the National Library.
Closing Date: April 30th
Funding: Government
No. of awards given last year: 5
No. of applicants last year: 50
Additional Information: Normally, Fellows will be expected to give a public lecture and at least one seminar on the subject of their research during their tenure. At least three quarters of the fellowship time should be spent in Canberra.

THE NATIONAL MULTIPLE SCLEROSIS SOCIETY

733 Third Avenue, New York, NY, 10017, United States of America
Tel: (1) 212 986 3240
Fax: (1) 212 986 7981
Email: nat@nmss.org
Website: www.nationalmssociety.org
Contact: Grants Management Officer

The National Multiple Sclerosis Society is dedicated to ending the devastating effects of multiple sclerosis.

National Multiple Sclerosis Society Junior Faculty Awards

Subjects: Neurosciences related to multiple sclerosis.
Purpose: To enable highly qualified persons who have concluded their research training and have begun academic careers as independent investigators to undertake independent research.
Eligibility: Open to citizens of the United States of America holding a doctoral degree, and who have had sufficient research training at the pre- or postdoctoral levels to be capable of independent research. Individuals who have already carried out independent research for more than 5 years are not eligible.
Level of Study: Professional development
Value: Approx. US$75,000 per year
Length of Study: 5 years
Frequency: Annual
Study Establishment: An approved university, professional or research institute
Country of Study: United States of America
No. of awards offered: Varies
Application Procedure: Applicants must complete an application form.
Closing Date: February 13th for awards beginning on August 1st
Funding: Private
No. of awards given last year: 1
No. of applicants last year: 2
Additional Information: The candidate will not be an employee of the Society but rather of the institution. It is expected that the institution will develop plans for continuing the candidate's appointment and for continued salary support beyond the 5-year period of the award. Fellows may not supplement their salary through private practice or consultation, nor accept another concurrent award. The grantee institution holds title to all equipment purchased with award funds.

National Multiple Sclerosis Society Pilot Research Grants

Subjects: Multiple sclerosis.
Purpose: To provide limited short-term support of novel high-risk research.
Eligibility: Open to suitably qualified investigators.
Level of Study: Research
Type: Research grant
Value: Up to US$40,000 in direct costs may be requested
Length of Study: 1 year
Frequency: Dependent on funds available
Country of Study: Any country
No. of awards offered: Varies
Application Procedure: Applicants must complete an application form.
Closing Date: Applications are accepted at any time
Funding: Private
No. of awards given last year: 38
No. of applicants last year: 97
Additional Information: Grants are awarded to an institution to support the research of the principal investigator. Progress reports are required.

National Multiple Sclerosis Society Postdoctoral Fellowships

Subjects: Multiple sclerosis.
Purpose: To provide postdoctoral training that will enhance the likelihood of performing meaningful and independent research relevant to multiple sclerosis.
Eligibility: Open to unusually promising recipients of MD or PhD degrees. Foreign nationals are welcome to apply for fellowships in the United States of America only. The Society will consider applications from established investigators who seek support to obtain specialized training in some field in which they are not expert, when such training will materially enhance their capacity to conduct more meaningful research. United States of America citizenship is not required for training in United States of America institutions but applicants who plan to train in other countries must be citizens of the United States of America.
Level of Study: Postdoctorate
Type: Fellowship
Value: Varies according to professional status, previous training, accomplishments in research and the pay scale of the institution in which the training is provided. Fellowships may be supplemented by other forms of support, with prior approval
Length of Study: 1–3 years
Frequency: Annual
Study Establishment: An institution of the candidate's choice
Country of Study: Any country
No. of awards offered: Varies
Application Procedure: Applicants must complete an application form.
Closing Date: February 13th for grants beginning on August 1st or thereafter
Funding: Private
No. of awards given last year: 18
No. of applicants last year: 62
Additional Information: Fellows are not considered employees of the Society but rather of the institution where the training is provided. The fellowship is to be administered in accordance with the prevailing policies of the sponsoring institution. It is the responsibility of the applicant to make all the necessary arrangements for their training with the mentor and institution of their choice.

National Multiple Sclerosis Society Research Grants

Subjects: Multiple sclerosis, the cause, prevention, alleviation and cure.
Purpose: To stimulate, co-ordinate and support fundamental or applied clinical or non-clinical research.
Eligibility: Open to suitably qualified investigators.
Level of Study: Professional development
Type: Research grant
Value: Funds may be used to pay the salaries of associated professional personnel, technical assistants and other non-professional personnel in proportion to the time spent directly on the project, in whole or in part. Salaries are made in accordance with the prevailing policies of the grantee institution. If requested, other expenses such as travel costs and fringe benefits may also be paid
Length of Study: 3 years
Country of Study: Any country
No. of awards offered: Varies
Application Procedure: Applicants must complete an application form.
Closing Date: February 1st for grants beginning on October 1st, August 1st for grants beginning on April 1st
Funding: Private
No. of awards given last year: 45
No. of applicants last year: 207
Additional Information: Grants are awarded to an institution to support the research of the principal investigator. Scientific equipment and supplies bought with grant funds become the property of the grantee institution. Progress reports are required and appropriate publication is expected.

NATIONAL ORCHESTRAL INSTITUTE

2110 Clarice Smith Performing Arts Center, University of Maryland, College Park, MD 20742-1620, United States of America
Tel: (1) 301 405 2317
Fax: (1) 301 314 9504
Email: noi@umd.edu
Website: www.noimusic.com

The National Orchestral Institute at the University of Maryland School of Music offers an intensive 3-week experience in orchestral musicianship and professional development for musicians on the threshold of their careers. Distinguished musicians and conductors work closely with participants to polish ensemble skills and orchestral excerpts.

National Orchestral Institute Scholarships

Subjects: Orchestral performance and chamber music.
Purpose: To provide an intensive 3-week orchestral training programme to enable musicians to rehearse and perform under internationally acclaimed conductors and study with principal musicians of the United States of America's foremost orchestras in preparation for careers as orchestral musicians.
Eligibility: Open to advanced musicians between 18 and 28 years of age, primarily students and postgraduates of United States of America universities, conservatories and colleges. Others, however, are welcome to apply, but must appear for an audition at the centre. String players, including harpists, who live more than 100 miles away from an audition centre, may audition by tape.
Level of Study: Unrestricted
Type: Scholarship
Value: Full tuition, room and board
Length of Study: 3 weeks
Frequency: Annual
Study Establishment: The University of Maryland
Country of Study: United States of America
No. of awards offered: Approx. 100
Application Procedure: Applicants must submit an application, a fee of US$50, curriculum vitae and (optional) letter of recommendation.
Closing Date: Before the regional auditions
Funding: Government
Contributor: The University of Maryland
No. of awards given last year: 100
No. of applicants last year: 720
Additional Information: Personal auditions are required at one of the audition centres throughout the country.

THE NATIONAL ORGANIZATION FOR RARE DISORDERS (NORD)

PO Box 1968, 55 Kenosia Avenue, Danbury, CT, 06813-1968, United States of America
Tel: (1) 203 744 0100
Fax: (1) 203 798 2291
Email: lcataldo@rarediseases.org
Website: www.rarediseases.org
Contact: Ms Linda M Cataldo, Field Services Co-ordinator

The National Organization for Rare Disorders (NORD) is a federation of voluntary health organizations dedicated to helping people with rare (orphan) diseases and assisting the organizations that serve them. NORD is committed to the identification, treatment and cure of rare disorders through programmes of advocacy, education, research and service.

NORD Clinical Research Grants

Subjects: New treatments or diagnostic tests for rare diseases.
Purpose: To support small clinical trials.
Eligibility: Open to academic scientists in the United States of America, Canada and Europe, or any country that adheres to the most recent guidelines for human subject protection as set forth by the NIH.
Level of Study: Research, doctorate, postdoctorate
Value: US$30,000 per year
Length of Study: 1 year
Frequency: Annual
Country of Study: Any country
No. of awards offered: 6–20
Application Procedure: Applicants must submit an application form, letter of intent and proposals. Forms are available from the website.
Closing Date: July–August
Funding: Private
Contributor: Public donations
No. of awards given last year: 22
No. of applicants last year: 100
Additional Information: Funding opportunities are announced during January–March.

NORD/Rosoe Brady Lysosomal Storage Diseases Fellowships

Subjects: Genetics, new treatments and diagnostics, and/or epidemiology of lysosomal storage diseases in general, or a specific lysosomal storage disease.
Purpose: To assist physicians who desire to establish careers in lysosomal storage diseases and clinical medicine.
Eligibility: Open to all countries that adhere to the most recent guidelines for human subject protection as set forth by the NIH. Applicants should have earned an MD degree within the past 10 years.
Level of Study: Doctorate, postdoctorate, research
Type: Fellowship
Value: US$50,000–70,000 per year
Length of Study: 1 year, but renewable for a 2nd year
Frequency: Annual
Country of Study: Any country
No. of awards offered: 1
Application Procedure: Application forms and required attachments may be obtained directly from the website.
Closing Date: March 25th
Funding: Private
Contributor: Public donations
No. of awards given last year: 3
No. of applicants last year: 14

NATIONAL OSTEOPOROSIS FOUNDATION (NOF)

1232 22nd Street North West, Washington, DC, 20037-1292, United States of America
Tel: (1) 202 223 2226
Fax: (1) 202 223 2237
Email: harriet@nof.org
Website: www.nof.org
Contact: Co-ordinator

The National Osteoporosis Foundation (NOF) is the United States of America's foremost voluntary, non-profit health organization dedicated to overcoming the widespread prevalence of osteoporosis. The Foundation provides up-to-date, medically sound information and programme materials on the prevention, diagnosis and treatment of osteoporosis through a network of individuals, healthcare professionals, organizations and the public.

NOF Scholar's, Foundation and Mazess Research Grants

Subjects: Epidemiology, pathogenesis and osteoporosis.
Purpose: To support clinical or basic research related to the epidemiology, pathogenesis, diagnosis and treatment of osteoporosis.
Eligibility: Applicants must have an MD, PhD or equivalent degree, United States of America citizenship or permanent resident status and be affiliated with non-profit institutions within the United States of America, its territories or the Commonwealth of Puerto Rico. Federal agencies and their employees are not eligible.
Level of Study: Postdoctorate, research
Type: Research grant
Value: US$50,000
Length of Study: 1 year
Frequency: Annual
Country of Study: United States of America
No. of awards offered: 3
Application Procedure: Applicants must visit the website for further information.
Closing Date: December 1st.
Funding: Private
No. of awards given last year: 5
No. of applicants last year: 63

NATIONAL RADIO ASTRONOMY OBSERVATORY

520 Edgemont Road, Charlottesville, VA, 22903-2475, United States of America
Tel: (1) 434 296 0221
Fax: (1) 434 296 0278
Email: brodrigu@nrao.edu
Website: www.nrao.edu/administration/directors_office/jansky-postdocs.shtml
Contact: Jansky Fellowship

The National Radio Astronomy Observatory designs, builds and operates the world's most sophisticated and advanced radio telescopes (the VLA, VLBA, GBT and ALMA), providing scientists from around the world the means to study all aspects of astronomy from planets in our Solar System to the most distant galaxies.

Jansky Fellowship

Subjects: Astronomy radio astronomy instrumentation, computation, and theory.
Purpose: The purpose of the programme is to provide an opportunity for young scientists to establish themselves as independent researchers so that they may more effectively compete for permanent positions. The placement of fellows at institutions other than the NRAO will help foster closer scientific ties between the NRAO and the U.S. astronomical community. Annual Jansky Fellows symposia are planned to ensure close contact among all Fellows and the NRAO.
Eligibility: Open to astronomers, physicists, electrical engineers and computer specialists. Preference will be given to recent PhD recipients.
Level of Study: Postdoctorate
Type: Fellowship
Value: US$49,000 per year with a research budget of US$7,000 per year for travel and computing requirements. In addition, page charge support, as well as vacation accrual, health insurance, and a moving allowance are provided, as well as up to US$3,000 per year to defray local institutional costs
Length of Study: 2 years, with a possibility of renewal for 1 further year
Frequency: Annual
Study Establishment: The Observatory's centres in Charlottesville, VA; Green Bank, WV; and Socorro, NM
Country of Study: Any country
No. of awards offered: Up to three appointments will be made annually for positions at any of the NRAO sites (Socorro, NM; Green Bank, WV; and Charlottesville, VA). Jansky Fellows are encouraged to spend time at universities working with collaborators during the course of their fellowship. In addition, up to three Jansky Fellowship appointments will be made annually for positions that may be located at a U.S. university or research institute. Frequent and/or long term visits to NRAO sites are encouraged
Application Procedure: Applications normally commence in September or October. There is no application form. The initial letter should include a statement of the individual's research interests together with his or her own appraisal of his or her qualifications for carrying out research. Applications should be single-sided with no staples. The applicant should have three letters of recommendation sent directly to the NRAO.
Closing Date: Please contact the organization
Funding: Government
Contributor: The National Science Foundation
No. of awards given last year: 6
No. of applicants last year: 63
Additional Information: Research associates may formulate and carry out investigations either independently or in collaboration with others.

NATIONAL RESEARCH COUNCIL OF CANADA (NRC)

1200 Montreal Road, Bldg. M-58, Ontario, Ottawa, K1A 0R6, Canada
Tel: (1) 613 993 9101'
Fax: (1) 613 952 9907
Email: info@nrc-cnrc.gc.ca
Website: www.nrc-cnrc.gc.ca
Contact: Research Associates Co-ordinator

The National Research Council of Canada (NRC) is a dynamic, nationwide research and development organization committed to helping Canada realize its potential as an innovative and competitive nation.

NRC Research Associateships

Subjects: Biological sciences, biotechnology, chemistry, molecular sciences, chemical engineering and process technologies, electrical engineering, astrophysics, industrial materials research, construction, mechanical engineering, aeronautics, physics, photonics, microstructural sciences, plant biotechnology, biochemistry, microbiology or advanced structural ceramics, bioinformatics, fuel cells, genomics, nanotechnology, nutraceuticals, proteomics, ocean engineering, aerospace, measurement standards, communication and technologies.
Purpose: To give promising scientists and engineers an opportunity to work in a challenging research environment during the early stages of their research careers.
Eligibility: Open to nationals of any country, although preference will be given to Canadians and permanent residents of Canada. Applicants should have acquired a PhD in natural science or a Master's degree in an engineering field within the last 5 years or should expect to obtain their degree before taking up the associateship. Selections will be made on a competitive basis with a demonstrated ability to perform original research of high quality in the chosen field as the main criterion.
Level of Study: Postgraduate
Value: Canadian $48,282 for a new PhD
Frequency: Annual
Study Establishment: Laboratories in the National Research Council of Canada
Country of Study: Any country
No. of awards offered: Approx. 50
Application Procedure: Applicants must fill out the online application form, available on the website www.careers-carrieres.nrc-cnrc.gc.ca
Closing Date: Applications are accepted at any time
Funding: Government
No. of awards given last year: 50
No. of applicants last year: 400
Additional Information: Salaries are revised annually. Further information is available from the website.

NATIONAL SCIENCE FOUNDATION (NSF)

Division of Earth Sciences, 4201 Wilson Boulevard, Arlington, VA, 22230, United States of America
Tel: (1) 703 292 8550
Fax: (1) 703 292 9025
Website: www.geo.nsf.gov/ear
Contact: Division Director

The National Science Foundation (NSF) supports research in the areas of geology, geophysics, geochemistry, paleobiology and hydrology, including interdisciplinary or multidisciplinary proposals that may involve one or more of these disciplines. Proposals for research in newly emerging areas of science that may not fit easily into one of these categories are especially welcome.

NSF Division of Earth Sciences

Subjects: The Earth's structure, properties, processes and evolution, including basic research in areas of practical importance. Support is provided in most fields of the Earth sciences including geology, geophysics, geochemistry surficial processes and hydrology.
Purpose: To advance the state of knowledge in the Earth sciences and enhance the ability of United States of America colleges and universities to conduct research and education in these fields.
Eligibility: Open to qualified research scientists at United States of America universities, colleges and other research institutions.
Level of Study: Unrestricted
Value: Award sizes vary greatly depending on the project proposed
Frequency: Annual
Study Establishment: Appropriate sites and institutions
Country of Study: Any country
No. of awards offered: Varies

Application Procedure: Applicants must consult the NSF Guide to Programs and Earth Sciences Research at NSF. Latest editions of these publications may be requested by mail from the forms and publications unit.
Funding: Government
No. of awards given last year: 400
No. of applicants last year: 2000
Additional Information: For detailed information on general application procedure, preparation of proposals and budgeting, please refer to the website www.nsf.gov. The Division is a participant in the National Earthquake Hazard Prevention Program and the United States of America Global Change Research Program.

NATIONAL STRENGTH AND CONDITIONING ASSOCIATION (NSCA)

1885 Bob Johnson Drive, Colorado Springs, CO 80906,
United States of America
Tel: (1) 719 632 6722
Fax: (1) 719 632 6367
Email: foundation@nsca-lift.org
Website: www.nsca-lift.org
Contact: Ms Karri Todd Baker, Membership Director

As the worldwide authority on strength and conditioning, we support and disseminate research-based knowledge and its practical application to improve athletic performance and fitness.

GNC Nutritional Research Grant

Subjects: Strength and conditioning.
Eligibility: Applicants must be NSCA members for at least 1 year prior to the application deadline date, and must be pursuing careers in strength and conditioning.
Level of Study: Graduate, postgraduate
Type: Grant
Value: US$2,500
Frequency: Annual
Study Establishment: Unrestricted
Country of Study: Any country
No. of awards offered: 1
Application Procedure: Applicants must submit a cover letter, completed application form, all original transcripts, an abstract and project proposal (ten single-spaced pages), references, itemized budget, proposed time schedule, Human Subject Consent Form, proof of institutional review board approval and abbreviated curriculum vitae of the faculty co-investigator. Beginning in 2006 we will require two copies of each students proposal. One regular copy for HQ filing purposes and one blinded copy for Research Committee.
Closing Date: March 15th must be received at the National Headquarters
Funding: Private
Contributor: GNC
No. of awards given last year: 1
No. of applicants last year: 3

NSCA Challenge Scholarship

Subjects: Strength and conditioning.
Purpose: To financially assist members in their pursuit of a career in the field of strength and conditioning.
Eligibility: Applicants must have been NSCA members for at least 1 year from the application deadline and must be seeking a graduate degree in a strength and conditioning-related field.
Level of Study: Graduate, postgraduate
Type: Scholarship
Value: US$1,000
Frequency: Annual
Study Establishment: Unrestricted
Country of Study: Any country
No. of awards offered: 12
Application Procedure: Applicants must submit a current curriculum vitae, a covering letter of application and three current letters of recommendation, an original copy of an authorized transcript from all postsecondary schools attended and an essay of no more than 500 words describing course of study, career goals and need. All materials must be mailed together and received at the National Headquarters by March 15th.
Closing Date: March 15th must be received at the National Head Quarters
Funding: Private
Contributor: Funding is made possible by the Bob Hoffman Foundation, NSCA Certification Commission and the NSCA National Office
No. of awards given last year: 12
No. of applicants last year: 27

NSCA Graduate Research Grant

Subjects: Strength and conditioning.
Purpose: To fund graduate student research that is directed by a graduate faculty member.
Eligibility: Open to NSCA members who have been members for at least 1 year from the application deadline. Graduate student members who are studying in the field of strength and conditioning are invited to apply. A graduate faculty member is required to serve as co-investigator in the study.
Level of Study: Postgraduate, graduate, research
Type: Grant
Value: Up to US$2,500
Length of Study: 1 year
Frequency: Annual
Study Establishment: Unrestricted
Country of Study: Any country
No. of awards offered: Varies, dependent on the number of applications
Application Procedure: Applicants must submit an application pack consisting of a covering letter of application, a completed application form, an original school transcript from each school attended or attending, an abstract, a proposal (including rationale, study purpose and methods), references, an itemized budget, proposed time schedule, a Human Subject Consent Form, proof of institutional review board approval and an abbreviated curriculum vitae of faculty co-investigator. Beginning in 2006 we will require two copies of each students proposal. One regular copy for HQ filing purposes and one blinded copy for Research Committee.
Closing Date: March 15th must be received at the National Headquarters
Funding: Private
Contributor: The NSCA Certification Commission and NSCA National Office
No. of awards given last year: 8
No. of applicants last year: 13
Additional Information: Application forms can be accessed via the website or by telephoning the organization.

NSCA Minority Scholarship

Subjects: Strength and conditioning.
Purpose: To financially assist minorities in the pursuit of a career in the field of strength and conditioning.
Level of Study: Graduate, postgraduate
Type: Scholarship
Value: US$1,000
Frequency: Annual
Study Establishment: Unrestricted
Country of Study: Any country
No. of awards offered: 2
Application Procedure: 1. Cover letter of application, 2. Completed application form, 3. Current resume, 4. Original school transcript from each school attended or attending, 5. Three (3) letters of recommendation 6. Essay of 500 words or less describing course of study, career goals, and financial need.
Closing Date: March 15th must be received at National Headquarters
Funding: Private
Contributor: The NSCA Certification Commission and NSCA National Office
No. of awards given last year: 2
No. of applicants last year: 4

NSCA Power Systems Professional Scholarship

Subjects: Strength and conditioning.
Purpose: To financially assist members in their pursuit of a career as a strength and conditioning coach.
Eligibility: Open to any NSCA member who has been a member for at least 1 year from the application deadline.
Level of Study: Graduate, postgraduate
Type: Scholarship
Value: US$1,000
Frequency: Annual
Study Establishment: Unrestricted
Country of Study: Any country
No. of awards offered: 1
Application Procedure: The head strength coach from the applicant's school must submit a letter of application. The applicant must submit an original, official transcript from all secondary schools attended, a current curriculum vitae and an essay of no more than 500 words describing career goals and objectives. The transcript must be mailed directly to the NSCA office by the school. To obtain an application form, applicants should telephone or visit the website. Only one candidate per school is permitted to apply.
Closing Date: March 15th must be received at the Nation Headquarters
Funding: Private
Contributor: Power Systems, Inc
No. of awards given last year: 1
No. of applicants last year: 4

NSCA Women's Scholarship

Subjects: Strength and conditioning.
Purpose: To financially assist women in the pursuit of a career in the field of strength and conditioning.
Level of Study: Postgraduate, graduate
Type: Scholarship
Value: US$1,000
Frequency: Annual
Study Establishment: Unrestricted
Country of Study: Any country
No. of awards offered: 2
Application Procedure: 1. Cover letter of application, 2. Completed application form, 3. Current resume, 4. Original school transcript from each school attended or attending, 5. Three (3) letters of recommendation 6. Essay of 500 words or less describing course of study, career goals, and financial need.
Closing Date: March 15th must be received at the National Headquarters
Funding: Private
Contributor: The NSCA Certification Commission and NSCA National Office
No. of awards given last year: 2
No. of applicants last year: 10
Additional Information: Applications forms can be accessed via the website or by telephoning the organization.

NATIONAL TRAPPERS ASSOCAITION (NTA)

NTA Headquarters, 524 5th Street, Bedford, IN 47421-2247, United States of America
Tel: (1) 812 277 9670
Fax: (1) 812 277 9672
Email: ntaheadquarters@nationaltrappers.com
Website: www.nationaltrappers.com

The NTA, established in 1959, is an organization of dedicated individuals who have joined together to promote and protect the appropriate conservative use of our fur bearing species.

Charles Dobbins Memorial Scholarship

Subjects: Wildlife management.
Purpose: To encourage students majoring in a field of study pertaining to wildlife management or related topics.
Eligibility: Open to applicants who are members of a state or national trappers association.
Level of Study: Postgraduate
Type: Scholarship
Length of Study: US$250
Frequency: Annual
No. of awards offered: 12
Application Procedure: A completed application form must be submitted.
Closing Date: July 1st

For further information contact:

National Trappers Association, 4170 St. Clair, Fallon, NV 89406
Contact: Jim Curran

NATIONAL UNION OF TEACHERS (NUT)

Central Co-ordinating Unit, Hamilton House, Mabledon Place, London, WC1H 9BD, England
Tel: (44) 20 7380 4704
Fax: (44) 20 7387 8458
Website: www.teachers.org.uk
Contact: Ms Angela Bush

NUT Page Scholarship

Subjects: A specific aspect of American education relevant to the recipient's own professional responsibilities.
Purpose: To promote the exchange of educational ideas between Britain and America.
Eligibility: Open to teaching members of the NUT aged 25–60 years, although 25–55 is preferred.
Level of Study: Professional development
Type: Scholarship
Value: Up to UK £1,700 pro rata daily rate with complete hospitality in the United States of America provided by the English-Speaking Union of the United States of America
Length of Study: 2 weeks. The scholarship must be taken during the American academic year, which is September–May
Frequency: Annual
Country of Study: United States of America
No. of awards offered: 1
Application Procedure: Applicants must complete an application form. An outline and synopsis of the project must accompany the form along with a curriculum vitae and scholastic and personal testimonials.
Closing Date: December 22nd
Funding: Private
Contributor: NUT
No. of awards given last year: 1
No. of applicants last year: 120
Additional Information: The scholarship is limited to the individual teacher and neither the spouse nor partner can be included in the travel, accommodation or study arrangements. Recipients are required to report on their visit to teacher groups and educational meetings in the United States of America and on their return home.

NATIONAL UNIVERSITY OF IRELAND

Postgraduate Admissions Office University Road, Galway, Ireland
Tel: (353) +353 (0) 91 524411
Email: postgrad@nuigalway.ie

The national university of Ireland, founded in 1845 as Queen's College Galway, is now an institution with over 15,000 students in several facilities.

Lady Gregory Fellowship Scheme

Purpose: Humanities, languages and literatures, and social and behavioral sciences.
Eligibility: Open to students who are in their first year of PhD programme.
Level of Study: Doctorate
Type: Fellowship
Value: €20,000 per year

Length of Study: 3 years
Frequency: Annual
No. of awards offered: 3
Application Procedure: A completed application form and other required information must be sent. See website for further details.
Closing Date: March 3rd

For further information contact:

Office of Faculty of Arts Room 217A, First floor Arts Millenium Building NU1 Galway, university road, Galway, Ireland
Contact: Mr Mairead Ni Dhomhnaill

NATIONAL UNIVERSITY OF SINGAPORE (NUS)

21 Lower Kent Ridge Road, Singapore, 119077, Singapore
Tel: (65) (0) 6775 6666
Fax: (65) (0) 6775 9330
Email: gradenquiry@nus.edu.sg
Website: www.nus.edu.sg
Contact: Grants Management Officer

NUS aspires to be a dynamic connected knowledge community imbued with a no walls culture that promotes the free flow of talent and ideas. Individual members of our community enjoy access to diverse opportunities for intellectual and professional growth and in twin add value to NUS becoming a global knowledge enterprise.

Asian Development Bank (ADB)-Japan Scholarship Program (JSP)

Subjects: Economics, management, science and technology, and other development-related fields.
Purpose: To provide an opportunity for well-qualified citizens of ADB's developing member countries to pursue postgraduate study.
Eligibility: Open to residents of Asian Development Bank member countries currently enrolled at NUS. Upon completion of their study programs, scholars are expected to contribute to the economic and social development of their home countries.
Level of Study: Postgraduate
Type: Scholarship
Value: A monthly stipend of S$1,350, all approved NUS fees, a book allowance of S$250 per semester and a return air ticket
Length of Study: 1 year
Frequency: Annual
Study Establishment: National University of Singapore
Country of Study: Singapore
Application Procedure: Apply online.
Closing Date: December 31st
Funding: Corporation
Contributor: Asian Development Bank (ADB)

For further information contact:

Email: LKYSPPmpp@nus.edu.sg

Law/Faculty Graduate Scholarship (FGS)

Subjects: Law.
Purpose: To reward an outstanding student of the faculty of Law.
Eligibility: Open to outstanding international applicants of any nationality (except Singapore citizens).
Level of Study: Postgraduate
Type: Scholarship
Value: A monthly stipend of S$300, a one-off air travel allowance of S$700, health insurance and all approved NUS fees
Frequency: Annual
Study Establishment: National University of Singapore
Country of Study: Singapore

Lee Kong Chian Graduate Scholarships

Subjects: Any subject.
Purpose: To reward proven academic excellence, leadership and exceptional promise.
Eligibility: Open to any student enrolled as a candidate for a PhD programme at the university.
Level of Study: Postdoctorate
Type: Scholarship
Value: A monthly stipend of S$3,000, all approved fees at NUS, an annual book allowance of S$500, one-off air travel allowance of two return tickets of up to S$4,000 (only for overseas students) and a one-off laptop allowance of S$1,500
Frequency: Annual
Study Establishment: National University of Singapore
Country of Study: Singapore
No. of awards offered: 5
Funding: Foundation
Contributor: Lee Foundation

Lee Kuan Yew School of Public Policy Scholarships (LKYSPPS)

Subjects: Public policy.
Purpose: To find further study in public policy implementation.
Eligibility: Open to all nationalities (except Singapore).
Level of Study: Postgraduate
Type: Scholarship
Value: A monthly stipend of S$1350, a one-off book allowance of S$500, a one-off settling-in allowance of S$500, all approved NUS fees.
Length of Study: 1 year
Frequency: Annual
Study Establishment: National University of Singapore
Country of Study: Singapore
Application Procedure: Apply online.
Closing Date: December 31st
Funding: Foundation
Contributor: Lee Kuan Yew Foundation

For further information contact:

Email: LKYSPPmpp@nus.edu.sg

National University of Singapore Fellowships

Subjects: Any subject.
Level of Study: Postdoctorate
Type: Fellowship
Value: A monthly stipend of S$3,100
Length of Study: 3–4 years
Frequency: Annual
Study Establishment: National University of Singapore
Country of Study: Singapore
Additional Information: Research scholars may be eligible for an additional stipend of up to S$500 per month.

National University of Singapore Master's Research Scholarships

Subjects: Any subject.
Purpose: To reward outstanding graduates for research leading to a higher degree at the university.
Level of Study: Postgraduate
Type: Scholarship
Value: Monthly stipend of S$1,500 and a full research fee subsidy. No travel or other allowances are provided
Length of Study: 2–2.5 years
Frequency: Annual
Study Establishment: National University of Singapore
Country of Study: Singapore
Additional Information: Research scholars may be asked to assist in departmental work for which they can earn up to S$ 16,000 (gross) per annum at the current rate of remuneration. However, please note that the university does not guarantee employment to research scholars upon completion of their candidature.

NUS Asean Scholarship

Subjects: Public health and occupational medicine.
Purpose: To enable a successful scholar to pursue full-time study.
Eligibility: Open to all Asean nationals, except Singaporeans.

Level of Study: Postgraduate
Type: Scholarship
Value: Payment of all NUS approved fees
Length of Study: 2–3 years
Frequency: Annual
Study Establishment: National University of Singapore
Country of Study: Singapore
Application Procedure: Download application form: www.med.nus.edu.sg/dgms

For further information contact:

Manager, Division of Graduate Medical Studies (DGMS), Young Loo Lin School of Medicine, National University of Singapore, Block MD5, Level 3, 12 Medical Drive, Singapore, 117598
Tel: 6516 3306
Fax: 6773 1462
Email: dgms@nus.edu.sg

NUS Design Technology Institute Scholarship

Subjects: Embedded system, rapid product development, mechatronics and industrial design.
Eligibility: Open to all nationalities with good Bachelor's degree with Honours in Engineering or Science.
Level of Study: Postgraduate
Type: Scholarship
Value: A monthly stipend S$1,500 with a possible monthly top-up of S$500 and all approved NUS fees
Length of Study: 2 years
Frequency: Annual
Study Establishment: National University of Singapore
Country of Study: Singapore
Closing Date: November
Additional Information: DTI Scholars who are international students will be required to serve a 2 years bond in Singapore upon graduation.

For further information contact:

Tel: 6874 1227
Fax: 6873 2175
Email: dtibox@nus.edu.sg
Contact: Mr Frederich Chang

Sanwa Bank Foundation Research Fellowship

Subjects: Business, commerce and economics.
Purpose: To promote international cultural exchange, mutual understanding and friendship between other countries and Japan.
Eligibility: Any (non-Japanese) student enrolled in a higher degree at the university.
Level of Study: Postgraduate, postdoctorate
Type: Fellowship
Value: S$5,000
Length of Study: 1 year
Frequency: Annual
Study Establishment: National University of Singapore
Country of Study: Singapore
Application Procedure: Complete and submit an application form online.
Funding: Foundation
Contributor: Sanwa Bank Foundation
Additional Information: Short-listed candidates will also be required to attend a selection interview in Singapore.

Singapore-MIT Alliance Scholarship

Subjects: Any subject.
Level of Study: Postdoctorate, postgraduate, doctorate
Type: Scholarship
Value: A monthly stipend of S$1,500–2,100 in addition, tuition fees, and all housing and living fees are paid for confirmed PhD candidates receive an additional top-up grant
Frequency: Annual
Study Establishment: National University of Singapore
Country of Study: Singapore
Funding: Foundation
Contributor: Singapore-MIT Alliance

For further information contact:

Tel: 6874 4787
Email: smart@nus.edu.sg

Temask/APEC Scholarship

Subjects: Public policy.
Purpose: To fund the knowledge and training to enable students to adopt a multi-disciplinary approach to the development and implementation of policy alternatives.
Eligibility: Open to nationals of permanent residents of member countries of ASEAN (except Singapore) and APEC (except Singapore).
Level of Study: Postgraduate
Type: Scholarship
Value: A monthly stipend of S$1,350, a one-off book allowance of S$500, a one-off settling-in allowance of S$500 all approved NUS fees
Length of Study: 1 year
Frequency: Annual
Study Establishment: National University of Singapore
Closing Date: December 31st
Funding: Foundation

NATO SCIENCE COMMITTEE

NATO, Scientific and Environmental Affairs Division, B-1110 Brussels, Belgium
Tel: (32) 2 707 4111
Fax: (32) 2 707 4232
Website: www.nato.int/science

NATO Science Fellowships

Subjects: Natural sciences, engineering, basic medical sciences.
Purpose: To prepare for the long-term future by training young researchers. Science fellowships provide opportunities for scientists of NATO's partner countries to pursue their research work or continue their training in a NATO country, and vice versa.
Eligibility: Candidates must be citizens of a NATO partner country. As a rule only scientists who are working at their home institutes are eligible to apply. Return to the home country at the end of the stay is compulsory. Candidates must hold a doctorate. There is no age limit, but the doctorate should have been acquired more than 5 years before the commencement of the fellowship.
Level of Study: Research
Type: Fellowship
Length of Study: 1–3 months
Country of Study: United Kingdom, West European countries and United States of America
Application Procedure: It is now possible to apply directly. For details see the website.
Closing Date: There are no firm application deadlines. However, it is recommended to submit applications latest by February each year
Additional Information: NATO partner countries include Albania, Armenia, former Yugoslav Republic of Macedonia, Georgia, Kazakhstan, Turkmenistan, Ukraine, and Uzbekistan.

NATURAL ENVIRONMENT RESEARCH COUNCIL (NERC)

Polaris House, North Star Avenue, Swindon, Wiltshire, SN2 1EU, England
Tel: (44) 17 9341 1500
Fax: (44) 17 9341 1501
Website: www.nerc.ac.uk/funding
Contact: Dr A E Allman, Process Manager

The Natural Environment Research Council (NERC) is one of the seven United Kingdom Research Councils that fund and manage research in the United Kingdom. NERC is the leading body in the United

Kingdom for research, survey, monitoring and training in the environmental sciences. NERC supports research and training in universities and in its own centres, surveys and units.

NERC Advanced Course Studentships

Subjects: Environmental sciences.
Purpose: To allow postgraduate students to undertake courses, recognized by NERC, that usually lead to an MSc or MRes. These courses are essentially vocational and are designed to prepare students for employment in industry or the public sector, or to advance their study.
Eligibility: Open to persons who, at the closing date of application for an award, have been ordinarily resident in the United Kingdom or Northern Ireland throughout the 3-year period preceding that date. Ordinarily, 'resident' means that no period of the candidate's residence during those 3 years has been wholly, or mainly, for the purpose of receiving full-time education. European Union candidates can receive fees only. Candidates must hold a First or Second Class (Honours) Degree in an appropriate branch of science or technology or the equivalent qualifications and/or experience. There is no age limit for studentships but the Council reserves the right to decline an application from a candidate if it considers that an award would not represent a good investment of public funds.
Level of Study: Predoctorate, postgraduate
Type: Studentship
Value: UK £7,500 maintenance grant per year for students outside London and UK £9,500 per year for students in London, payment of approved fees and assistance with travel and subsistence expenses under specified conditions, eg. fieldwork
Length of Study: 1 year
Frequency: Annual
Study Establishment: Any approved Institute of Higher Education
Country of Study: United Kingdom
No. of awards offered: Varies, approx. 290
Application Procedure: Applications must be submitted by the head of the department in which the student proposes to work. Applications will not be accepted directly from individual candidates. Awards are tenable only for those courses that are currently recognized by NERC for the purposes of its studentship scheme.
Closing Date: July 31st for student nominations
Funding: Government
No. of awards given last year: 349

NERC Advanced Research Fellowships

Subjects: The sciences of the natural environment.
Purpose: To enable outstanding mid-career researchers to develop into team leaders of international standing and devote themselves to personal research.
Eligibility: Open to candidates who hold a PhD and who have had at least 2 years of research experience at the postdoctoral level at the time of application, although not necessarily in the United Kingdom. They must also have proven their ability as individual research workers.
Level of Study: Postdoctorate
Type: Fellowship
Value: Awards are based on the United Kingdom universities non-clinical academic and related research staff scale and are related to age when taking up an appointment. Up to UK £10,000 per year is also available for small items of equipment, consumables and United Kingdom fieldwork. Funding for specified overseas fieldwork can also be requested
Length of Study: Depends on the individual scheme, but generally up to 5 years with a possible extension of a further 5 years
Frequency: Annual
Study Establishment: Universities and other approved research institutes
Country of Study: United Kingdom
No. of awards offered: Varies: 10–20 per year
Application Procedure: Applicants must refer to the fellowship handbook and application forms available via the NERC website.
Closing Date: November 15th
Funding: Government
No. of awards given last year: 9
Additional Information: All applications must carry the full support of the host institution, which will be expected to act as the Fellow's employer. As part of NERC's commitment to promoting equal opportunities, all fellowships may be held by suitably qualified candidates on a full- or part-time basis, subject to the agreement of the host institution. The NERC is particularly keen to attract applications from scientists in the areas of applied mathematics, physics or strongly quantitative disciplines wishing to develop a career in environmental science.

NERC Postdoctoral Research Fellowships

Subjects: The sciences of the natural environment.
Purpose: Early career development award to provide further postdoctoral experience and to support outstanding environmental scientists as they become independent investigators.
Eligibility: Candidates must hold a PhD or be able to demonstrate equivalent and relevant research experience. Applications will be accepted from PhD students but, if successful, awards may not start until NERC has received written confirmation of the outcome of the applicant's PhD viva. However, applicants are advised that some post-PhD experience can be an advantage when seeking a postdoctoral fellowship.
Level of Study: Postdoctorate, postgraduate
Type: Fellowship
Value: Awards are based on the United Kingdom universities non-clinical academic and related research staff scale. Starting salary is related to age when taking up appointment and UK £8,500 per year is also available for the purchase of small items of equipment, consumables and United Kingdom fieldwork. Funding for specified overseas fieldwork can also be requested
Length of Study: 3 years, with the possibility of extension for up to 2 further years
Frequency: Annual
Study Establishment: Universities and other approved research institutes
Country of Study: United Kingdom
No. of awards offered: Varies. 15–25 per year
Application Procedure: Applicants must refer to the fellowship handbook and application forms available via the NERC website.
Closing Date: November 15th
Funding: Government
No. of awards given last year: 25
Additional Information: All applications must carry the full support of the host institution, which will be expected to act as the Fellow's employer. As part of the NERC's commitment to promoting equal opportunities, all fellowships may be held by suitably qualified candidates on a full- or part-time basis, subject to the agreement of the host institution. The NERC is particularly keen to attract applications from scientists in the areas of mathematics, physics or other strongly quantitative disciplines wishing to develop a career in environmental science.

NERC Research Studentships

Subjects: Environmental sciences.
Purpose: To enable students to receive training in methods of research and to undertake research in particular scientific areas under the guidance of named supervisors.
Eligibility: Open to persons who, at the closing date of application for an award, have been ordinarily resident in the United Kingdom or Northern Ireland throughout the 3-year period preceding that date. Ordinarily, 'resident' means that no period of the candidate's residence during those 3 years has been wholly, or mainly, for the purpose of receiving full-time education. European Union candidates can receive fees only. Candidates must hold a First or Upper Second Class (Honours) Degree in an appropriate branch of science or technology or a combination of qualifications and experience, that demonstrates equivalent ability and attainment. There is no age limit for studentships but the Council reserves the right to decline an application from a candidate if it considers that an award would not represent a good investment of public funds.
Level of Study: Postgraduate

Type: Studentship
Value: A maintenance grant of UK £12,000 per year for students outside London and UK £14,000 per year for students in London, the payment of approved fees and assistance with travel and subsistence expenses under specified conditions, eg. fieldwork
Length of Study: Up to 3 years, part of which may be spent at an institution in Europe
Frequency: Annual
Study Establishment: Any approved Institute of Higher Education
Country of Study: Other
No. of awards offered: Varies, approx. 310
Application Procedure: Applications must be submitted by the head of the department in which the student proposes to work. Applications will not be accepted directly from individual candidates. To encourage research students to gain additional experience outside the academic sphere some of these awards are made as Co-operative Awards in Sciences of the Environment (CASE Studentships). CASE awards involve the joint supervision of the student by a member of staff of an academic institution and a scientist from industry, a public authority or government research institute.
Closing Date: July 31st for student nominations
Funding: Government
No. of awards given last year: 350
Additional Information: It is expected that the award will lead to the submission of a PhD thesis.

NATURAL HISTORY MUSEUM

Cromwell Road, London, SW7 5BD, England
Tel: (44) 20 7942 5530
Fax: (44) 20 7942 5841
Email: l.houseago@nhm.ac.uk
Website: www.nhm.ac.uk/science
Contact: L Houseago, Liaison Officer

The Natural History Museum's mission is to maintain and develop its collections and use them to promote the discovery, understanding, responsible use and enjoyment of the natural world.

Synthesys Visiting Fellowship

Subjects: Biomedical sciences.
Purpose: To provide access for researchers so that they can undertake short visits to utilize the facilities of 20 major museums and botanic gardens within Europe, including the Natural History Museum and its associates, the Royal Botanical Gardens, Kew and the Royal Botanic Garden Edinburgh.
Eligibility: Open to applicants from the European Union member states, and associated and accession states.
Level of Study: Postdoctorate, research, unrestricted, doctorate
Value: International travel, accommodation, local travel and subsistence along with all access and facility costs
Length of Study: Up to 60 working days
Frequency: Twice a year
Study Establishment: The Natural History Museum, London
Country of Study: United Kingdom
No. of awards offered: 30 per call
Application Procedure: Applications must be completed. Website: www.synthesys.info
Closing Date: Please refer to the website
Funding: Government
Contributor: The European Union IHP Programme
No. of awards given last year: 51
No. of applicants last year: 125
Additional Information: During the visit the user is assigned a host, according to their speciality. The role of the host is to familiarize the user with the department, collections and facilities and to give training where necessary. The visits are often collaborative, in which case the host will work directly with the user. Please note that projects that include one of the associated institutions must be collaborative with the Natural History Museum.

For further information contact:

Website: www.synthesys.info

NATURAL SCIENCES AND ENGINEERING RESEARCH COUNCIL OF CANADA (NSERC)

350 Albert Street, Ottawa, ON, K1A 1H5, Canada
Tel: (1) 61 3995 5521
Fax: (1) 61 3996 2589
Email: schol@nserc.ca
Website: www.nserc.ca
Contact: Corporate Account Executive

NSERC is Canada's instrument for promoting and supporting university research in the natural sciences and engineering, other than the health sciences. NSERC supports both basic university research through discovery grants and project research through partnerships among universities, governments and the private sector as well as the advanced training of highly qualified people.

NSERC Postdoctoral Fellowships

Subjects: Engineering and natural sciences.
Purpose: To provide support to a core of the most promising researchers at a pivotal time in their careers. The fellowships are also intended to secure a supply of highly qualified Canadians with leading edge scientific and research skills for Canadian industry, government and universities.
Eligibility: Open to Canadian citizens or permanent residents residing in Canada, who have recently received, or will shortly receive a PhD in one of the fields of research that NSERC supports.
Level of Study: Postdoctorate
Type: Fellowship
Value: Canadian $40,000 per year
Length of Study: 1 year, renewable for 1 additional year
Frequency: Annual
Study Establishment: A university or research institution of the Fellow's choice
Country of Study: Any country
Application Procedure: Applicants must complete Form 200. Information is available on request.
Closing Date: October 15th
Funding: Government
Additional Information: The information provided here is subject to change. Please visit the NSERC's website for up-to-date information.

NESTA

NESTA, Fishmonger's Chambers,
110 Upper Thames Street, London, EL4R 3TW,
United Kingdom
Tel: (44) (0) 20 7645 9500
Email: nesta@nesta.org.uk
Website: www.nesta.org.uk

Nesta's Fellowship Programme gives creative and innovative individuals who have demonstrated exceptional talent and originality, the time, space, resources and support to develop their ideas, pursue their goals, experiment, and push at the boundaries of knowledge and practice.

NESTA Creative Pioneer Programme

Purpose: To encourage the growth of new generation of creative entrepreneurs.
Level of Study: Professional development
Type: Grant
Value: UK £35,000 start up finance and long-term mentoring
Length of Study: Continuous
Frequency: Annual
Study Establishment: NESTA Academy
Country of Study: United Kingdom
Application Procedure: Contact NESTA.
Closing Date: September 6th
Funding: Foundation
Contributor: NESTA Creative Investor

NESTA Crucible Fellowship

Purpose: To finance creative scientists and engineers-from astrophysicists to zoologists.
Level of Study: Professional development
Type: Fellowship
Value: Lab space, all travel fees and any other reasonable costs, such as child care
Length of Study: 1 year
Frequency: Annual
Study Establishment: NESTA Academy
Country of Study: United Kingdom
No. of awards offered: 30
Application Procedure: Contact NESTA.
Closing Date: November 30th
Contributor: NESTA Creative Investor

NESTA Dream Time Fellowship

Subjects: Technology, engineering, science, arts.
Purpose: To finance exceptional achievers wishing to take structured time away from their work to pursue ideas which will benefit both themselves and their sector.
Eligibility: Applicants must have at least 10 years of work experience in their field.
Level of Study: Professional development
Type: Fellowship
Value: UK £40,000
Length of Study: 1 year
Frequency: Annual
Study Establishment: NESTA Academy
Country of Study: United Kingdom
Application Procedure: Contact NESTA.
Closing Date: September
Funding: Foundation
Contributor: NESTA Creative Investor

NETHERLANDS ORGANIZATION FOR INTERNATIONAL CO-OPERATION IN HIGHER EDUCATION (NUFFIC)

Kortenaerkade 11, 2118 AX Den Haag, Po Box 29777, 2502-LT, The Hague, Netherlands
Tel: (31) 70 4260260
Fax: (31) 70 4260399
Email: nuffic@nuffic.nl
Website: www.nuffic.nl
Contact: Ms Rosalien van Santen, Information Officer

Since its founding in 1952, the Netherlands Organization for International Co-operation in Higher Education (NUFFIC) has been an independent, non-profit organization. Its mission is to foster international co-operation in higher education. Special attention is given to development co-operation.

European Development Fund Awards for Citizens of ACP Countries

Subjects: All subjects.
Eligibility: Open to citizens of African, Caribbean and Pacific countries associated with the European Union.
Level of Study: Unrestricted
Value: Course fees, books and field trips, international travel expenses, insurance, a monthly allowance and a stipend to cover the initial expense of becoming established
Length of Study: The duration of the course
No. of awards offered: Varies
Application Procedure: Applicants must obtain information and application forms from the Netherlands Embassy in the candidate's country and the European Union Delegations and offices of the Commission. The application should be submitted through the candidate's employer and government.
Closing Date: Please contact the Commission for details

NFP Netherlands Fellowships Programme for Development Co-operation

Subjects: All subjects offered by the Institutes for International Education in the Netherlands.
Purpose: To develop human potential through education and training mainly in the Netherlands with a view to diminishing qualitative and quantitative deficiencies in the availability of trained manpower in developing countries.
Eligibility: Open to candidates who have the education and work experience required for the course as well as an adequate command of the language in which it is conducted. This is usually English but sometimes French. The age limit is 40 for men and 45 for women. It is intended that candidates, upon completion of training, return to their home countries and resume their jobs. When several candidates with comparable qualifications apply, priority will be given to women. Candidates for a fellowship must be nominated by their employer and formal employment should be continued during the fellowship period.
Level of Study: Postgraduate
Type: Fellowship
Value: Normal living expenses, fees and health insurance. International travel expenses are provided only when the course lasts 3 months or longer
Length of Study: The duration of the course
Country of Study: The Netherlands
No. of awards offered: Varies
Application Procedure: Applicants must contact the Netherlands Embassy in their own country for information on nationality eligibility and on the application procedure. Information on the courses for which the fellowships are available can be obtained from the website.
Funding: Government
Additional Information: As a rule the candidate's government is required to state its formal support, except in the case of certain development-orientated non-government organizations. Further information is available from the website www.studyin.nl

NUFFIC-NFP Fellowships for Master's Degree Programmes

Subjects: Any subject on the list of eligible Master's degree programmes.
Purpose: To allow candidates to receive a postgraduate education and to earn either an MA, MSc or Professional Master's degree.
Eligibility: Applicant must be a national of one of 57 developing countries and have been admitted by a Dutch institution to one of the Master's degree programmes on the course list. Applicants who have received their education in any language other than English must provide International English Language Testing System scores (at least 5.5) or Test of English as a Foreign Language scores (at least 550).
Level of Study: Postgraduate
Type: Fellowship
Value: Tuition fees, cost of international travel, subsistence, books and health insurance
Length of Study: 9 months–2 years
Frequency: Annual
Study Establishment: A Dutch institution
Country of Study: The Netherlands
Application Procedure: Applicants may apply for an NFP fellowship through the Netherlands embassy or consulate in their own country. To do this, applicants must complete an NFP Master's degree programme application form and submit it together with all the required documents and information to the embassy or consulate well before the deadline. Forms can be obtained from the embassy or consulate or downloaded from the website, www.nuffic.nl/nfp
Closing Date: September 1st, sometime in March
Additional Information: Applicants may not be employed by a large industrial, commercial and/or multinational firms.

For further information contact:

Contact the Netherlands embassy or consulate in home country

NUFFIC-NFP Fellowships for PhD Studies

Purpose: To allow candidates to pursue a PhD at one of 18 Dutch universities and institutes for international education.

Eligibility: Candidate must be a national of one of 57 developing countries and have been admitted to a Dutch institution as a PhD fellow. Priority will be given to female candidates and candidates from sub-Saharan Africa.
Level of Study: Doctorate
Type: Fellowship
Value: Up to €74,000
Length of Study: 4 years
Frequency: Annual
Study Establishment: Any one of 18 Dutch universities and institutes for international education. See list on website
Country of Study: The Netherlands
Application Procedure: After being accepted for admission to a Dutch institution, the candidate may submit a request for a PhD fellowship. Applicant must present a completed NFP PhD study application form to the Netherlands embassy or consulate in his/her own country. The application must be accompanied by the necessary documentation and by a research proposal that is supported by the supervisor(s). Form can be downloaded from website www.nuffic.nl/nfp.
Closing Date: July 1st and November 1st
Additional Information: A large portion of the PhD research must take place in the candidate's home country.

For further information contact:

Contact the Netherlands embassy or consulate in home country

THE NETHERLANDS ORGANIZATION FOR SCIENTIFIC RESEARCH (NWO)

Lann van Nieuw Oost Indie 131, PO Box 93138, The Hague, NL-2509 AC, Netherlands
Tel: (31) 70 344 0853
Fax: (31) 70 385 0971
Email: nwo@nwo.nl
Website: www.nwo.nl
Contact: Dr H. Weijma, Head Of Central Programmes

The Netherlands Organization for Scientific Research (NWO) is the central Dutch organization in the field of fundamental and strategic scientific research. NWO encompasses all fields of scholarship and consequently plays a key role in the development of science, technology and culture in the Netherlands. NWO is an independent organization that acts as the national research council in the Netherlands. NWO is the largest national sponsor of fundamental scientific research undertaken in the 13 Dutch universities and provides many types of funding for research driven by intellectual curiosity.

Dutch Russian Scientific Cooperation Programme

Subjects: Scientific research.
Purpose: To give a strong impulse to the scientific collaboration between the two countries.
Eligibility: Open to all talented Dutch researchers together with a Russian counterpart.
Level of Study: Postgraduate
Type: Fellowship
Value: €500,000
Length of Study: 5 years
No. of awards offered: 2
Contributor: The Netherlands Organization for Scientific Research

Rubicon Programme

Subjects: Scientific research.
Purpose: To encourage talented researchers at Dutch Universities to dedicate themselves to a career in postdoctoral research.
Eligibility: Open to postgraduates who are currently engaged in doctoral research.
Level of Study: Postdoctorate
Type: Grant
Value: €4.5 million a year
Length of Study: Up to 2 years
Application Procedure: A completed application form to be submitted via NOW's electronic submission system Iris.
Closing Date: 15 April, 15 September and 15 December
Contributor: The Netherlands Ministry of Education, Culture and Science

For further information contact:

Tel: (0)70-3440 565
Email: rubicon@nwo.nl
Website: www.nwo.nl/rubicon
Contact: Coordinator Rubicon

WOTRO DC Fellowships

Subjects: Natural and medical sciences, social sciences and humanities.
Purpose: To support high-quality PhD and postdoctorate research projects.
Eligibility: Open to project researchers with the appropriate degrees.
Level of Study: Doctorate
Value: A contribution to personal living costs and research costs
Length of Study: 4 years for PhD research and 2 years for postdoctorate research
Frequency: Annual
No. of awards offered: 20
Application Procedure: Applications must be formally submitted by a senior researcher employed at a Dutch research institution, together with a senior researcher from the home country as a co-applicant and as part of the supervising them.
Contributor: WOTRO

For further information contact:

National and Medical Sciences, The Hague, AC, Netherlands
Tel: (31) +31(0)70 344 0945
Email: dijk@nwo.nl
Contact: Ms Han van Dijk, Staff Member

THE NEUROBLASTOMA SOCIETY

Beverley House, Frilford, Abingdon, Oxfordshire, OX13 5NU, England
Tel: (44) 18 6539 1207
Email: antonya@hsoc.co.uk
Website: www.nsoc.co.uk
Contact: Antonya Cooper, Chairman

The Neuroblastoma Society was started in 1982 by a group of parents with children affected by neuroblastoma. The aim is to raise money to fund medical research towards better treatment and an eventual cure for this aggressive childhood tumour. The Society also aims to offer support to families affected by the disease.

Neuroblastoma Society Research Grants

Subjects: Paediatric oncology, specifically in neuroblastoma.
Purpose: To fund clinical research towards improvements in treatment and a cure for neuroblastoma.
Eligibility: There are no age or nationality restrictions but candidates must be based in the United Kingdom.
Value: Up to UK £150,000
Length of Study: 2–3 years
Frequency: Every 2 years
Study Establishment: A reputable research institution, usually a university or hospital
Country of Study: United Kingdom
No. of awards offered: Usually 3–4
Application Procedure: Applicants must apply to the Society for the terms of grant application. Application forms available on website.
Closing Date: December 31st
Funding: Private
Contributor: Members of the Society
No. of awards given last year: 3
No. of applicants last year: 9

For further information contact:

Website: www.nsoc.co.uk

THE NEW SCHOOL

66 West 12th Street, New York, NY 10011, United States of America
Tel: (1) (212) 229 5600
Email: nsadmission@newschool.edu
Website: www.newschool.edu

The New School is a legendary, progressive university comprising eight schools bound by a common, unusual intent: to prepare and inspire its 9,300 undergraduate and graduate students to bring actual, positive change to the world.

The New School Culinary Arts Scholarship

Subjects: Culinary arts.
Purpose: To financially assist students enrolled in culinary arts programme.
Eligibility: Open to individuals who wish to pursue professional-level instruction courses.
Level of Study: Professional development
Type: Scholarship
Value: Full tuition fees
Frequency: Annual
Study Establishment: The New School
Country of Study: United States of America
No. of awards offered: Varies
Application Procedure: A completed application form must be submitted.

For further information contact:

Scholarship Committee, Culinary Arts, 127 West 24th Street, 4th Floor, New York, NY 10011

NEW YORK STATE HISTORICAL ASSOCIATION

PO Box 800, Lake Road, Cooperstown, NY 13326-0800, United States of America
Tel: (1) 607 547 1491
Fax: (1) 607 547 1405
Email: mason@nysha.org
Website: www.nysha.org
Contact: Ms Catherine Mason, Assistant Editor

The mission of the New York State Historical Association is to instil and cultivate, in a broad public audience, an informed appreciation of the diversity of the American past, especially as represented and exemplified by the history of New York State, in order to better understand the present.

Dixon Ryan Fox Manuscript Prize of the New York State Historical Association

Subjects: The history of New York state.
Purpose: To honour the best unpublished book-length monograph.
Eligibility: Open to nationals of any country. Biographies and edited volumes may be included. Fiction and poetry are not eligible entries.
Level of Study: Postdoctorate, postgraduate, doctorate, professional development
Type: Prize
Value: US$3,000 plus assistance in publishing
Length of Study: Dependent on the book length
Frequency: Annual
No. of awards offered: 1
Application Procedure: Applicants must submit two copies of the manuscript, typed and double-spaced with at least 1 inch margins.
Closing Date: January 20th
Funding: Private
No. of awards given last year: 1
No. of applicants last year: 8

NEW ZEALAND VICE-CHANCELLORS COMMITTEE (NZVCC)

PO Box 11-915, Wellington, New Zealand
Tel: (64) 4 381 8510
Fax: (64) 4 381 8501
Website: www.nzvcc.ac.nz
Contact: Scholarships Officer

Claude McCarthy Fellowships

Subjects: All subjects.
Purpose: To enable graduates of a New Zealand university to undertake original work or research.
Eligibility: Open to any graduate of a New Zealand university.
Level of Study: Postgraduate, doctorate
Type: Fellowship
Value: Varies, according to country of residence during tenure, and the project itself. Assistance for expenses incurred in travel, employment of technical staff, special equipment, etc. may be provided
Length of Study: Usually no more than 1 year
Frequency: Annual
Country of Study: Any country
No. of awards offered: Varies, depending upon funds available, but usually 12–15
Application Procedure: Applicants must write for details.
Closing Date: August 1st
Funding: Private
Contributor: The Claude McCarthy Trust
Additional Information: Further information is available on request.

Gordon Watson Scholarship

Subjects: International relationships and social and economic conditions.
Purpose: To facilitate study abroad.
Eligibility: Candidates must be New Zealand citizens or permanent residents. Open to holders of an Honours degree, or a degree in theology from a university in New Zealand. Candidates must undertake to return to New Zealand after the scholarship period for not less than 2 years.
Level of Study: Postgraduate
Type: Scholarship
Value: New Zealand $12,000 per year
Length of Study: 3 years
Frequency: Annual
Study Establishment: Any approved university
No. of awards offered: 1
Application Procedure: Applicants must write for details.
Closing Date: October 1st
Funding: Private
Contributor: The Gordon Watson Trust
Additional Information: Further information is available on request.

L B Wood Travelling Scholarship

Subjects: All subjects.
Purpose: To allow graduates to undertake doctoral studies in the United Kingdom.
Eligibility: Open to all holders of postgraduate scholarships from any faculty of any university in New Zealand, provided that application is made within 3 years of the date of graduation.
Level of Study: Doctorate
Type: Scholarship
Value: New Zealand $3,000 per year, as a supplement to another postgraduate scholarship
Length of Study: Up to 3 years
Frequency: Annual
Study Establishment: A university or institution of university rank
Country of Study: United Kingdom
No. of awards offered: 1
Application Procedure: Applicants must write for details.
Closing Date: October 1st
Funding: Private
Contributor: The L B Wood Trust
Additional Information: Further information is available on request.

Shirtcliffe Fellowship

Subjects: Arts, science, law, commerce and agriculture.
Purpose: To provide further aid for New Zealand doctoral students.
Eligibility: Open to graduates of New Zealand universities.
Level of Study: Doctorate
Type: Fellowship
Value: New Zealand $2,000 as a supplement to the postgraduate scholarship emolument
Length of Study: Up to 3 years
Frequency: Annual
Study Establishment: A suitable Institute of Higher Education
No. of awards offered: 3
Application Procedure: Applicants must write for details.
Closing Date: October 1st
Funding: Private
Additional Information: Further information is available on request.

William Georgetti Scholarships

Subjects: All subjects.
Purpose: To encourage postgraduate study and research in a field that is important to the social, cultural or economic development of New Zealand.
Eligibility: Candidates must be New Zealand citizens or permanent residents. Open to graduates who have been resident in New Zealand for 5 years immediately before application and who are preferably aged between 21 and 28 years.
Level of Study: Postgraduate
Type: Scholarship
Value: Up to New Zealand $7,500 for study in New Zealand and up to New Zealand $15,000 for study overseas
Frequency: Annual
Study Establishment: Suitable universities
Country of Study: Any country
No. of awards offered: Varies
Application Procedure: Applicants must write for details.
Closing Date: October 1st
Funding: Private
Contributor: The Georgetti Trust
Additional Information: Further information is available on request.

NEWBERRY LIBRARY

60 West Walton Street, Chicago, IL, 60610, United States of America
Tel: (1) 312 255 3666
Fax: (1) 312 255 3680
Email: research@newberry.org
Website: www.newberry.org
Contact: Ms Erin Lucipo, Programme Assistant

The Newberry Library, open to the public without charge, is an independent research library and educational institution dedicated to the expansion and dissemination of knowledge in the humanities. With a broad range of books and manuscripts relating to the civilizations of Western Europe and the Americas, the Library's mission is to acquire and preserve research collections of such material, and to provide for and promote their effective use by a diverse community of users.

American Society for Eighteenth-Century Studies (ASECS) Fellowship

Subjects: Arts and humanities from 1660 to 1815.
Purpose: To support scholars wanting to use the Newberry's collections.
Eligibility: Open to members of the Society. The award is limited to scholars from outside the Chicago area.
Level of Study: Postdoctorate, doctorate
Type: Fellowship
Value: US$1,200 per month, pro rata
Length of Study: 1 month
Frequency: Annual
Study Establishment: The Newberry Library
Country of Study: United States of America
No. of awards offered: 1
Application Procedure: Applicants must submit a completed application form, a description of the project and three letters of reference.
Closing Date: March 1st
Funding: Private
Contributor: ASECS
No. of awards given last year: 1
No. of applicants last year: 28

Arthur Weinberg Fellowship for Independent Scholars

Subjects: Humanities.
Purpose: To assist scholars working outside the academy who have demonstrated excellence through publishing and are working in a field appropriate to the Newberry's collections.
Eligibility: Open to all scholars but preference is given to those working on historical issues related to social justice or reform.
Level of Study: Unrestricted
Type: Fellowship
Value: US$1,200
Length of Study: 1 month
Frequency: Annual
Study Establishment: The Newberry Library
Country of Study: United States of America
No. of awards offered: Varies
Application Procedure: Applicants must write for details. Application forms can be downloaded from the website.
Closing Date: March 1st
Funding: Private
No. of applicants last year: 2

Audrey Lumsden-Kouvel Fellowship

Subjects: Late medieval and renaissance studies.
Purpose: To enable scholars to use the Newberry's extensive holdings. The fellowship is intended to encourage scholars to pursue research at the Newberry during sabbaticals.
Eligibility: Open to postdoctoral scholars wishing to carry out extended research. Applicants must plan to be in continuous residence for at least 3 months. Preference will be given to projects focusing on romance cultures.
Level of Study: Postdoctorate
Type: Fellowship
Value: US$4,000
Length of Study: At least 3 months
Frequency: Annual
Study Establishment: The Newberry Library
Country of Study: United States of America
No. of awards offered: 1
Application Procedure: Applicants must write for details. Application forms can be downloaded from the website.
Closing Date: March 1st
Funding: Private
No. of awards given last year: 1
No. of applicants last year: 15

Center for Great Lakes Culture/Michigan State University Fellowship

Subjects: The cultural history and expressions of the diverse peoples of the Great Lakes or the Ohio Valley region, eg. Michigan, Illinois, Wisconsin, Minnesota, Ohio, Indiana, West Virginia, Kentucky and Ontario.
Purpose: To support projects using the Newberry Library collections.
Eligibility: Open to scholars with a PhD or the equivalent or an established record of scholarly research. Candidates for degrees are not eligible. The award is limited to scholars from outside the Chicago area.
Level of Study: Postdoctorate
Type: Fellowship
Value: US$1,250
Length of Study: 1 month
Frequency: Annual
Study Establishment: The Newberry Library
Country of Study: United States of America
No. of awards offered: 2

Application Procedure: Applicants must write for details. Application forms can be downloaded from the website.
Closing Date: March 1st
Funding: Government, private
Contributor: The Center for Great Lakes Culture and Michigan State University
No. of awards given last year: 2
No. of applicants last year: 7

Committee on Institutional Co-operation Faculty Fellowship

Subjects: American Indian studies.
Purpose: To support research at the Newberry by CIC faculty.
Eligibility: Open to faculty members of a CIC institution.
Level of Study: Postdoctorate
Type: Fellowship
Value: US$40,000
Length of Study: A minimum of 9 months
Frequency: Annual
Study Establishment: The Newberry Library
Country of Study: United States of America
No. of awards offered: 1
Application Procedure: Applicants must contact the CIC programme at the D'Arcy McNickle Centre for American Indian history at mcnickle@newberry.org
Closing Date: January 6th
Funding: Government, private
Contributor: The Committee on Institutional Co-operation
No. of awards given last year: 1
Additional Information: In addition to carrying out this independent research, the CIC Faculty Fellow will lead a Spring seminar at the Library for graduate students at CIC institutions on a topic appropriate to the Newberry's collections and the expertise of the Fellow.

Committee on Institutional Co-operation Graduate Student Fellowship

Subjects: American Indian studies.
Purpose: To support dissertation research.
Eligibility: Open to graduate students at CIC institutions.
Level of Study: Doctorate
Type: Fellowship
Value: US$1,500 per month
Length of Study: Up to 3 months
Frequency: Annual
Study Establishment: The Newberry Library
Country of Study: United States of America
No. of awards offered: Varies
Application Procedure: Applicants must contact the CIC programme at the D'Arcy McNickle Centre for American Indian history at mcnickle@newberry.org
Closing Date: January 6th
Funding: Private, government
Contributor: Committee on Institutional Co-operation
No. of awards given last year: 7

Frances C Allen Fellowships

Subjects: Humanities and social sciences.
Purpose: To encourage women of American Indian heritage in their studies through financial support.
Eligibility: Open to women of American Indian heritage who are pursuing an academic programme in any graduate or preprofessional field.
Level of Study: Postgraduate, graduate
Type: Fellowship
Value: Varies according to need and may include travel expenses. Up to US$8,000 in approved expenses is available
Length of Study: 1 month–1 year
Frequency: Annual
Study Establishment: The Newberry Library
Country of Study: United States of America
No. of awards offered: Varies
Application Procedure: Applicants must write for details. Application forms can be downloaded from the website.
Closing Date: March 1st
Funding: Private
Contributor: The Frances C Allen Fund
No. of awards given last year: 3
No. of applicants last year: 6
Additional Information: Allen Fellows are expected to spend a significant part of their tenure in residence at the Newberry's D'Arcy McNickle Centre for American Indian History.

Herzog August Bibliothek Wolfenbüttel Fellowship

Subjects: Humanities.
Purpose: To enable a period of residence in Wolfenbüttel, Germany for study of the collections housed in the Herzog August Bibliothek.
Level of Study: Postdoctorate
Type: Fellowship
Value: Please contact the organization
Length of Study: 3 months
Frequency: Annual
Study Establishment: The Herzog August Bibliothek in Wolfenbüttel
Country of Study: Germany
No. of awards offered: 1
Application Procedure: Applicants must write for details. Application forms may also be downloaded from the website.
Closing Date: January 10th for linked long-term fellowship, March 1st for linked short-term fellowship
Funding: Private

For further information contact:

60 W. Walton, Chicago, IL 60610, United States of America
Contact: Committee on Awards, The Newberry Library

Lester J Cappon Fellowship in Documentary Editing

Subjects: Editing and archiving.
Purpose: To support historical editing projects based on Newberry materials.
Eligibility: Open to scholars who live outside the Chicago area.
Level of Study: Postdoctorate
Type: Fellowship
Value: Up to US$5,000
Length of Study: Varies
Frequency: Annual
Study Establishment: The Newberry Library
Country of Study: United States of America
No. of awards offered: 1
Application Procedure: Applicants must write for details. Application forms can be downloaded from the website.
Closing Date: March 1st
Funding: Private
Contributor: Lester J Cappon
No. of awards given last year: 1
No. of applicants last year: 8

Lloyd Lewis Fellowship in American History

Subjects: Any field of American history appropriate to the collections of the Newberry Library.
Eligibility: Open to established scholars, holding a PhD, who have demonstrated excellence in the field through publications. Foreign nationals may apply if they have resided in the United States of America for 3 or more years.
Level of Study: Postdoctorate
Type: Fellowship
Value: Up to US$40,000
Length of Study: 6–11 months
Frequency: Annual
Study Establishment: The Newberry Library
Country of Study: United States of America
No. of awards offered: Varies
Application Procedure: Applicants must write for details. Application forms can be downloaded from the website.
Closing Date: January 10th
Funding: Private
Contributor: The Lloyd Lewis Memorial Fund
No. of awards given last year: 1

No. of applicants last year: 27
Additional Information: Lewis Fellows participate in the Library's scholarly community through regular participation in seminars, colloquia and other events. Lewis Fellowships may be combined with sabbaticals or other stipendiary support. Applicants may ask to be considered for NEH and Mellon Fellowships at the time of their application.

Mellon Postdoctoral Research Fellowship

Subjects: Humanities.
Purpose: To support residential research and writing.
Eligibility: Open to postdoctoral scholars in any field of relevance to the Library's collection.
Level of Study: Postdoctorate
Type: Fellowship
Value: Up to US$40,000
Length of Study: 6–11 months
Frequency: Annual
Study Establishment: The Newberry Library
Country of Study: United States of America
No. of awards offered: Varies
Application Procedure: Applicants must write for details. Application forms can be downloaded from the website. Completed applications must include three letters of recommendation.
Closing Date: January 10th
Funding: Private
Contributor: The Mellon Foundation
No. of awards given last year: 3
No. of applicants last year: 67
Additional Information: Fellows will become part of Newberry's community of scholars, participating in biweekly fellows seminars, colloquial and other events.

Monticello College Foundation Fellowship for Women

Subjects: Any field appropriate to the Library's collections.
Purpose: To offer young women the opportunity to undertake work in residence at the Library and to significantly enhance their careers through research and writing.
Eligibility: Open to women who hold a PhD and are in the early stages of their academic careers. This academic award is designed for a woman whose work gives clear promise of scholarly productivity and who would benefit significantly from 6 months of research, writing and participation in the intellectual life of the library. Other things being equal, preference is given to the applicant whose proposed study is concerned with the study of women.
Level of Study: Postdoctorate
Type: Fellowship
Value: US$15,000
Length of Study: 6 months
Frequency: Annual
Study Establishment: The Newberry Library
Country of Study: United States of America
No. of awards offered: 1
Application Procedure: Applicants must write for details. Application forms can be downloaded from the website.
Closing Date: January 10th
Funding: Private
Contributor: The Monticello College Foundation
No. of awards given last year: 1
No. of applicants last year: 10

National Endowment for the Humanities (NEH) Fellowships

Subjects: Any field appropriate to the Library's collections.
Purpose: To encourage scholarly research, and to deepen and enrich the opportunities for serious intellectual exchange through the active participation of Fellows in the library community.
Eligibility: Open to citizens of the United States of America or foreign nationals who have been resident in the United States of America for 3 years, who are established scholars at the postdoctoral level or its equivalent. Preference is given to applicants who have not held major fellowships for 3 years preceding the proposed period of residency.
Level of Study: Postdoctorate
Type: Fellowship
Value: Up to US$40,000
Length of Study: 6–11 months
Frequency: Annual
Study Establishment: The Newberry Library
Country of Study: United States of America
No. of awards offered: Varies
Application Procedure: Applicants must write for an application form. Completed application forms must include all letters of reference. Application forms can be downloaded from the website.
Closing Date: January 10th
Funding: Government
Contributor: The NEH
No. of awards given last year: 3
No. of applicants last year: 41
Additional Information: Applicants may combine this award with sabbatical or other stipendiary support. Scholars conducting research in American history may also ask to be considered for the Lloyd Lewis Fellowship at the time of their application.

Newberry Library British Academy Fellowship for Study in Great Britain

Subjects: Humanities.
Purpose: To allow an individual to study in the United Kingdom in any field in which the Newberry's collections are strong.
Eligibility: Open to established scholars at the postdoctoral level or equivalent. Preference is given to readers and staff of the Newberry Library and to established Scholars who have previously used the Newberry Library.
Level of Study: Postdoctorate
Type: Fellowship
Value: A stipend of UK £1,350 per month while in the United Kingdom
Length of Study: Up to 3 months
Frequency: Annual
Country of Study: United Kingdom
No. of awards offered: Varies
Application Procedure: Applicants must write for details. Application forms can be downloaded from the website.
Closing Date: January 10th
Funding: Private
Contributor: The British Academy
No. of awards given last year: 2
No. of applicants last year: 5
Additional Information: The home institution is expected to continue to pay the Fellow's salary.

Newberry Library Ecole des Chartes Exchange Fellowship

Subjects: Renaissance studies.
Purpose: To enable a graduate student to study at the Ecole des Chartes in Paris.
Eligibility: Preference is given to graduate students at institutions in the Renaissance Centre Consortium.
Level of Study: Doctorate
Type: Fellowship
Value: Varies, but provides a monthly stipend and free tuition
Length of Study: 3 months
Frequency: Annual
Study Establishment: The Ecole des Chartes
Country of Study: France
No. of awards offered: Varies
Application Procedure: Applicants must write for details. Application forms can be downloaded from the website.
Closing Date: January 10th
Funding: Private
Contributor: The Ecole des Chartes
No. of awards given last year: 1
No. of applicants last year: 5
Additional Information: The Ecole des Chartes is the oldest institution in Europe specializing in the archival sciences, including palaeography, bibliography, textual editing and the history of the book.

Newberry Library Short-Term Fellowship in the History of Cartography

Subjects: The history of cartography.
Purpose: To financially support work in residence at the Newberry on projects related to the history of cartography.
Eligibility: Open to established scholars of any nationality, but limited to scholars who live outside the Chicago area.
Level of Study: Postdoctorate, doctorate
Type: Fellowship
Value: US$1,200 per month
Length of Study: 1 week–2 months
Frequency: Annual
Study Establishment: The Newberry Library
Country of Study: United States of America
No. of awards offered: 1–2
Application Procedure: Applicants must submit an application, project description, curriculum vitae and letters of reference. Applicants must visit the website for further details and application forms.
Closing Date: March 1st
Funding: Private
Contributor: Arthur Holzheimer
No. of awards given last year: 3
No. of applicants last year: 9

Newberry Library Short-Term Resident Fellowships for Individual Research

Subjects: Any field appropriate to the Library's collections.
Purpose: To provide access to Newberry's collections for those who live beyond commuting distance from Chicago.
Eligibility: Open to nationals of any country who hold a PhD degree or have completed all requirements for the degree except the dissertation. Awards are limited to scholars from outside the Chicago area.
Level of Study: Doctorate, postdoctorate
Type: Fellowship
Value: US$1,200 per month
Length of Study: 1 week–2 months
Frequency: Annual
Study Establishment: The Newberry Library
Country of Study: United States of America
No. of awards offered: Varies
Application Procedure: Applicants must write for details. Application forms can be downloaded from the website.
Closing Date: March 1st
Funding: Private
No. of awards given last year: 24
No. of applicants last year: 112

South Central Modern Language Association Fellowship

Subjects: Humanities.
Purpose: To support residential research at the Library by members of the South Central Modern Language Association.
Eligibility: Open to scholars who live outside the Chicago area.
Level of Study: Doctorate
Type: Fellowship
Value: US$2,000
Length of Study: 1 month
Frequency: Annual
Study Establishment: The Newberry Library
Country of Study: United States of America
No. of awards offered: 1
Application Procedure: Applicants must write for details. Application forms can be downloaded from the website.
Closing Date: March 1st
Funding: Private
Contributor: The South Central Modern Language Association
No. of awards given last year: 1
No. of applicants last year: 1

Susan Kelly Power and Helen Hornbeck Tanner Fellowship

Subjects: American Indian heritage.
Purpose: To support residential research.
Eligibility: Open to applicants with American Indian heritage.
Level of Study: Doctorate, postdoctorate
Type: Fellowship
Value: US$1,200 per month
Length of Study: Up to 2 months
Frequency: Annual
Study Establishment: The Newberry Library
Country of Study: United States of America
No. of awards offered: 1
Application Procedure: Applicants must visit the website for application details and forms.
Closing Date: March 1st
Funding: Private
No. of awards given last year: 1
No. of applicants last year: 4

Weiss/Brown Publication Subvention Award

Subjects: Humanities, particularly European civilization before 1700 in the areas of music, theatre, French or Italian literature or cultural studies.
Purpose: To subsidize the publication of a scholarly book and books.
Eligibility: Open to authors of books already accepted for publication.
Level of Study: Unrestricted
Type: Award
Value: Variable, up to US$15,000
Frequency: Annual
No. of awards offered: Varies
Application Procedure: Applicants must write for details. Application guidelines can be downloaded from the website. Applicants will be asked to provide detailed information regarding the publication and the subvention request.
Closing Date: January 10th
Funding: Private
Contributor: Roger Weiss and Howard Brown
No. of awards given last year: 3
No. of applicants last year: 8

NEWBY TRUST LIMITED

Hill Farm, Froxfield, Petersfield, Hampshire, GU32 1BQ, England
Tel: (44) 17 3082 7557
Fax: (44) 17 3082 7938
Website: www.newby-trust.org.uk
Contact: Miss W Gillam, Company Secretary

The Newby Trust Limited is a grant-giving charity working nationally, whose principal aims are to promote medical welfare, education and training and the relief of poverty.

Newby Trust Awards

Subjects: All subjects.
Eligibility: Open to students of any nationality. Overseas students must have already started their course in the United Kingdom before applying.
Level of Study: Predoctorate, doctorate, professional development, postgraduate
Type: Grant
Value: Up to UK £1,000 for fees or maintenance
Frequency: Annual
Study Establishment: A suitable university
Country of Study: United Kingdom
No. of awards offered: Varies
Application Procedure: Applicants must submit in duplicate a personal letter with a curriculum vitae, two letters of academic reference, a statement of income and expenditure including fees and a stamped addressed envelope. Application forms are not supplied. Applications intended for the start of an academic year should be submitted at least 4 months in advance.
Closing Date: At least 2 weeks prior to the Director's meetings, which are usually held in April and July
Funding: Private
Contributor: Funds from the Trust
No. of awards given last year: 137

No. of applicants last year: 800
Additional Information: Funding is not available for Primary and Secondary Education First Degrees CPE Law exam, BSc Intercalated with a Medical Degree PhD's prior to commencement courses which are outside of the UK adventure or volunteer courses in general including EAP' year projects additionally, applications will only be considered for the final two years of study for postgraduate Medical/ Veterinary Degrees.

NEWCOMEN SOCIETY OF THE UNITED STATES

211 Welsh Pool Road, Suite 240, Exton, Pennsylvania, 19341, United States of America
Tel: (1) 610 363 6600
Fax: (1) 610 363 0612
Email: mstoner@newcomen.org
Website: www.newcomen.org
Contact: Ms Marcy J. Stoner, Executive Assistant

The Newcomen Society of the United States is a non-profit business educational foundation that studies and supports outstanding achievement in American business.

Newcomen Society Dissertation Fellowship in Business and American Culture

Subjects: American business history.
Purpose: To encourage students to pursue careers in studying and teaching in the field.
Eligibility: Open to United States doctoral students only.
Level of Study: Doctorate
Type: Fellowship
Value: US$10,000
Length of Study: 9 months full-time
Frequency: Annual
Country of Study: United States of America
No. of awards offered: 1
Application Procedure: Applicants must submit five copies of their curriculum vitae and a research programme, which must not exceed 10 double spaced pages, including references. Faxed proposals cannot be accepted. University transcripts and two letters of recommendation must be sent in support of applications.
Closing Date: February 15th

NORTH ATLANTIC TREATY ORGANIZATION (NATO)

Public Diplomacy Division Office Nb 106 Boulevard Leopold III, 1110, Brussels, Belgium
Tel: (32) 2 707 4111
Fax: (32) 32 2707 5457
Email: natodoc@hq.nato.int
Website: www.nato.int
Contact: Academic Affairs Officer

The North Atlantic Treaty was signed in Washington on April 4, 1949, creating an alliance of 12 independent nations committed to each other's defence. Four more European nations later acceded to the Treaty between 1952 and 1982. On March 12, 1999, the Czech Republic, Hungary and Poland were welcomed into the Alliance, which now numbers 19 members.

Manfred Wörner Fellowship

Subjects: International relations.
Purpose: To honour the memory of the late Secretary General by focusing attention on his leadership in the transformation of the alliance, including efforts at extending NATO's relations with CEE countries and promoting the principles and image of the Transatlantic partnership.
Eligibility: Open to applicants who are citizens of the EAPC countries with proven experience to carry out an important scholarly endeavour within the time limit of the Fellowship.
Level of Study: Professional development
Type: Fellowship
Value: US$20,000
Frequency: Annual
Country of Study: Any country
Application Procedure: Application forms can be downloaded from the NATO website.
Closing Date: December 31st
Funding: Government

For further information contact:

Public Diplomacy Division, NATO Academic Affairs Officer, Office Nb 106, Boulevard Leopold III, 1110 Brussels, Belgium
Fax: (32) +32 2707 5457
Email: academics@hq.nato.int
Website: www.nato.int/acad/fellow/mwooe.htm

NORTH DAKOTA UNIVERSITY SYSTEM

600 East Boulevard, Bismarck, ND, 58505, United States of America
Tel: (1) 701 328 2960
Email: ndus.office@ndus.nodak.edu
Website: www.ndus.nodak.edu
Contact: Ms Rhonda Shaver, Co-ordinator

The North Dakota University System, governed by the State Board of Higher Education, comprises 11 public campuses.

North Dakota Indian Scholarship

Subjects: All subjects.
Purpose: To assist Native American students in obtaining a basic college education.
Eligibility: Open to residents of North Dakota with a quarter degree of Indian blood who have been accepted for admission at an Institute of Higher Education or state vocational programme. Recipients must be enrolled full-time and have a grade point average above 2.0.
Level of Study: Doctorate, postgraduate
Type: Scholarship
Value: US$700
Frequency: Annual
Country of Study: United States of America
No. of awards offered: 140
Application Procedure: Applicants must complete an application form.
Closing Date: July 15th
Funding: Government
Contributor: The State
No. of awards given last year: 140

NORTH WEST CANCER RESEARCH FUND

22 Oxford Street, Liverpool, L7 7BL, England
Tel: (44) 15 1709 2919
Fax: (44) 15 1708 7997
Email: nwcrf@btclick.com
Website: www.cancerresearchnorthwest.co.uk
Contact: Mr A W Renison, General Secretary

North West Cancer Research Fund Research Project Grants

Subjects: All types of cancer, the mechanisms by which they arise and the way they exert their effects.
Purpose: To provide financial support for fundamental cancer research in northwest England and North and Mid-Wales.
Eligibility: Open to candidates undertaking cancer research studies at one of the universities named below in the Northwest. Grants are only available for travel costs associated with currently funded 3-year cancer research projects. No grants are awarded for buildings or for the development of drugs.
Level of Study: Research
Type: Grant

Value: Approx. UK £45,000 per year
Length of Study: Usually 3 years
Frequency: Dependent on funds available
Study Establishment: The University of Liverpool, Lancaster University and the University of Wales, Bangor
Country of Study: North West England, North and Mid-Wales
Application Procedure: The NWCRF Scientific Committee meets twice a year. All applications are subject to peer review.
Closing Date: April 1st and October 1st
Funding: Individuals, private
Contributor: Voluntary donations
No. of awards given last year: 10
No. of applicants last year: 50

For further information contact:

NWCRF Scientific Committee Department of Medicine, Duncan Building, Daulby Street, Liverpool, L69 3BX, England
Email: ricketts@liverpool.ac.uk
Contact: The Secretary

NORWEGIAN INFORMATION SERVICE IN THE UNITED STATES

825 Third Avenue, 38th Floor, New York, NY 10022-7584, United States of America
Tel: (1) 212 421 7333
Fax: (1) 212 754 0583
Email: norcons@interport.net
Website: www.norway.org
Contact: Grants and Scholarships Department

America-Norway Heritage Fund Grant

Subjects: All subjects.
Purpose: To award special grants to Americans of Norwegian descent who have made significant contributions to American culture, enabling them to visit Norway to share the results of their work through lectures, exhibitions or performances. In this way, it is hoped that Norwegians will become better acquainted with the cultural, economic, political and religious contributions made by Norwegian-Americans in the building of America.
Eligibility: Open to Americans of Norwegian descent.
Level of Study: Unrestricted
Type: Travel grant
Value: Travel expenses as well as an honorarium
Length of Study: 1–2 weeks. Activities should be scheduled between October and April
Frequency: Annual
Country of Study: Norway
Application Procedure: Applications are not accepted. Candidates will be selected by the Board of Directors of the Fund in co-operation with its connections in the United States of America. However, proposals for possible candidates will be appreciated.
Contributor: The Lutheran Brotherhood Insurance Company

For further information contact:

Norge-Amerika Foreningen, Rådhusgaten 23 B, Oslo, N-0158, Norway

American-Scandinavian Foundation (ASF)

Subjects: All subjects.
Purpose: To encourage Scandinavians to undertake advanced study and research programmes.
Eligibility: Applicants must be Scandinavians over the age of 21 (applicants from Denmark must be between 21 and 30). Applicants can be young professionals who have completed their formal education with related work experience in Scandinavia or Europe, or students who are currently enrolled in colleges and universities who need to undertake an internship. They should be fluent in English.
Level of Study: Postgraduate
Value: Grants are normally US$3,000, and fellowships can be up to US$18,000
Length of Study: 1 year
Frequency: Annual
Country of Study: United States of America
No. of awards offered: Varies
Application Procedure: Applicants must complete an application on ASF application forms, available on request from the Foundation.
Closing Date: November 1st

For further information contact:

American-Scandinavian Foundation (ASF), 56 Park Avenue, New York, NY, 10016, United States of America
Tel: (1) 212 879 9779
Fax: (1) 212 249 3444
Contact: Grants Management Officer

John Dana Archbold Fellowship Program

Subjects: All subjects.
Purpose: To support educational exchange between the United States of America and Norway.
Eligibility: Open to citizens of the United States of America citizens aged 20–35, in good health and of good character. Qualified applicants must show evidence of a high level of competence in their chosen field, indicate a seriousness of purpose, and have a record of social adaptability. There is ordinarily no language requirement.
Level of Study: Postgraduate, postdoctorate, professional development, research
Type: Fellowship
Value: Up to US$5,000. Individual grants vary, depending on the projected costs. Note that there will be no tuition at the University of Oslo. The maintenance stipend is sufficient to meet expenses for a single person. The travel allowance covers round trip airfare to Oslo
Length of Study: 1 year
Frequency: Annual
Study Establishment: The University of Oslo
No. of awards offered: 2
Application Procedure: Applicants must write to the Nansen Fund, Inc. for an application form.
Closing Date: January 15th
Funding: Private
Additional Information: The University of Oslo International Summer School offers orientation and Norwegian languages courses 6 weeks before the start of the regular academic year. For Americans, tuition is paid. Attendance is required. Americans visit Norway in even-numbered years and Norwegians visit the United States of America in odd-numbered years. For further information please contact the Nansen Fund, Inc.

For further information contact:

The Nansen Fund, Inc., 77 Saddlebrook Lane, Houston, TX, 77024, United States of America
Tel: (1) 713 680 8255

Memorial Fund of May 8th 1970

Subjects: All subjects.
Purpose: To promote cultural exchange between foreign countries and Norwegian residential experiential colleges by providing scholarships for residence, and to help prepare young people for everyday life in the community.
Eligibility: Open to candidates aged 18–22 years who do not have a permanent residence in Norway, and do not hold a Norwegian passport. Candidates must be planning to return to their home country after a year in Norway. Candidates must be aware of the kind of education the Memorial Fund bursaries cover, that being a year in a Norwegian residential colleges, not admission to education on a higher level, such as a university, or specialized training.
Level of Study: Unrestricted
Type: Scholarship
Value: The scholarship will cover board and lodging. In addition it is possible to apply for extra funds. Applicants from some countries may apply for required books and excursions arranged by the school. Also, extra support may be provided for short study trips and short courses before or after the school year. A fixed amount towards spending money may also be given. Normally the students must pay their own travelling expenses. The colleges do not charge tuition fees

Length of Study: 1 year
Frequency: Annual
Study Establishment: Norwegian residential experiential colleges
Country of Study: Norway
No. of awards offered: Approx. 25
Application Procedure: Applicants must request more information and application forms from the Memorial Fund of May 8th 1970 or to the nearest Norwegian Embassy. Applicants who require a scholarship to attend a Norwegian college should not apply to a them directly. In this case, the Board will place successful applicants at a college school based on their hobbies and interest. Residence permits must be applied for by each individual student when a scholarship has been granted.
Closing Date: March 15th
Funding: Government
No. of awards given last year: 25
No. of applicants last year: 700
Additional Information: A residential experiential college is a 1-year independent residential school, primarily for young adults, offering many non-traditional subjects of study. Each college has its own profile, but as a group, the Norwegian colleges teach classes covering almost all areas, including history, arts, crafts, music, sports, philosophy, theatre, photography etc.

For further information contact:

IKF, Grensen 9a N-0159 Oslo, Norway, Oslo, N-0159, Norway
Email: ikf@ikf.no

Norwegian Emigration Fund of 1975

Subjects: Emigration history and relations between the United States of America and Norway.
Purpose: To support for advanced or specialized study in Norway.
Eligibility: Open to citizens and residents of the United States of America. The fund may also give grants to institutions in the United States of America whose activities are primarily centred on the subjects mentioned.
Level of Study: Postgraduate, graduate
Type: Grant
Value: Norwegian Krone 5,000–20,000
Frequency: Annual
Country of Study: Norway
No. of awards offered: Varies
Application Procedure: Applicants must complete an application form and return it clearly marked Emigration Fund to Nordmanns-Forbundet. Applications as well as enclosures will not be returned.
Closing Date: February 1st
Funding: Government

Norwegian Information Service Fulbright Stipend

Subjects: All subjects.
Purpose: To award study and research.
Level of Study: Postgraduate, postdoctorate
Type: Award
Length of Study: 3 months to 1 year
Application Procedure: Applicants must contact the organization. Candidates with a PhD or more should contact the Council of International Exchange of Scholars.
Closing Date: Early Fall
Funding: Government

For further information contact:

US Student Program Institute of International Education 809 United States Plaza, New York, NY 10017, United States of America

Norwegian Marshall Fund

Subjects: Science and humanities.
Purpose: To provide financial support for Americans to come to Norway to conduct postgraduate study or research in areas of mutual importance to Norway and the United States of America, thereby increasing knowledge, understanding and strengthening the ties of friendship between the two countries.
Eligibility: Open to citizens of the United States of America, who have arranged with a Norwegian sponsor or research institution to pursue a research project or programme in Norway. Under special circumstances, the awards can be extended to Norwegians for study or research in the United States of America.
Level of Study: Postgraduate, research
Type: Research grant
Value: The size of the individual grants depends on the research subject, purpose and the intended length of stay in Norway. In previous years, the grants have varied from Norwegian Krone 10,000–30,000
Length of Study: Varies
Frequency: Annual
Study Establishment: Norwegian universities
Country of Study: Norway
No. of awards offered: 5–15
Application Procedure: Applicants must contact the Norway-America Association to receive an application. Application forms must be typewritten either in English or Norwegian and submitted in duplicate, including all supplementary materials. Each application must also be accompanied by a letter of support from the project sponsor or affiliated research institution in Norway. There is an application fee of Norwegian Krone 350.
Closing Date: March 23rd
Funding: Government

For further information contact:

The Norway-America Association, Rådhusgaten 23 B, Oslo, N-0158, Norway
Fax: (47) 2 335 7160
Email: namerika@online.no
Website: www.noram.no/index_am.html

Norwegian Ministry of Foreign Affairs Travel Grants

Subjects: Norwegian culture and society.
Purpose: To give financial assistance to teachers and graduate students visiting Norway for study and research purposes.
Eligibility: Open to citizens and residents of the United States of America who are members of NORTANA. They must be university or college teachers of Norwegian or other courses in Norwegian culture or society, or graduate students who have passed their preliminary examinations in these fields.
Level of Study: Professional development, graduate
Type: Travel grant
Value: US$750–1,500
Frequency: Annual
Country of Study: Norway
No. of awards offered: Varies
Application Procedure: Applicants must download an application form from the website.
Closing Date: February 16th
Funding: Government
Contributor: The Norwegian Ministry of Foreign Affairs

Norwegian Thanksgiving Fund Scholarship

Subjects: Fisheries, geology, glaciology, astronomy, social medicine and Norwegian culture.
Eligibility: Open to American graduate students.
Level of Study: Graduate
Type: Scholarship
Value: Up to US$3,000
Frequency: Annual
Country of Study: Norway
No. of awards offered: 1
Application Procedure: Applicants must contact the American Scandinavian Foundation.
Closing Date: November 1st
Funding: Individuals
Contributor: Former Norwegian students and friends

For further information contact:

The American Scandinavian Foundation, 58 Park Avenue, New York, NY, 10016, United States of America

Tel: (1) 212 879 9779
Fax: (1) 212 249 3444

NORWICH JUBILEE ESPERANTO FOUNDATION

37 Granville Court, Cheney Lane,
Oxford, Oxfordshire, OX3 0HS, England
Tel: (44) 18 6524 5509
Website: www.esperanto.org/uk/nojef
Contact: Dr Kathleen M Hall, Secretary to the Foundation

A registered charitable trust established in 1967, the Norwich Jubilee Esperanto Foundation was founded for the advancement of education in the study and practice of Esperanto. It can pay travelling expenses to enable young persons who have shown efficiency in the study of Esperanto to visit approved United Kingdom venues or foreign countries. It also awards prizes and encourages research.

Norwich Jubilee Esperanto Foundation Grants-in-Aid

Subjects: Esperanto.
Purpose: To encourage thorough study of Esperanto by enabling young students to travel abroad or to approved United Kingdom venues and promote research into the teaching of Esperanto.
Eligibility: Open to citizens under 26 years of age of any country, who require financial assistance and who have a high standard of competence in Esperanto. An efficiency test may be required but there are no set academic or age requirements for research grants.
Level of Study: Unrestricted
Type: Travel grant
Value: Approx. UK £50–200, up to UK £1,000
Length of Study: From 1 week to several months
Frequency: Dependent on funds available
Study Establishment: Any venue approved by the Foundation
Country of Study: United Kingdom or Other
No. of awards offered: Varies
Application Procedure: Applicants must submit a letter of application in Esperanto. An application may be completed later.
Closing Date: Applications are accepted at any time provided an adequate margin is left for processing
Funding: Private
Contributor: Legacies from past supporters
No. of awards given last year: 21
No. of applicants last year: 30
Additional Information: Visitors to the United Kingdom will be expected to speak in Esperanto to schools or clubs.

NSW ARCHITECTS REGISTRATION BOARD

NSW Architects Registration Board, Level 2, 156 Gloucester Street, Sydney, NSW, 2000, Australia
Tel: (61) 2 9241 4033
Fax: (61) 2 9241 6144
Email: mail@architects.nsw.gov.au
Website: www.architects.nsw.gov.au
Contact: Ms Mae Cruz, Deputy Registrar

Byera Hadley Travelling Scholarships

Subjects: Architecture.
Purpose: To allow candidates to undertake a course of study, research or other activity approved by the Board as contributing to the advancement of architecture.
Eligibility: Open to graduates or students of four accredited schools of architecture in New South Wales. Applicants must be Australian citizens.
Level of Study: Research, postgraduate, graduate
Type: Scholarship
Value: The total value of the combined awards is Australian $65,000, comprising two Registered Architect awards of Australian $30,000 and $11,000, one graduate award of Australian $8,000 and four student awards of Australian $4,000 each
Frequency: Annual
Country of Study: Any country
No. of awards offered: 7
Application Procedure: Applicants must write for details.
Closing Date: The deadline for all awards is July 30th
Funding: Private
Contributor: A bequest from the estate of the late Byera Hadley, an Australian architect
No. of awards given last year: 7
No. of applicants last year: 24
Additional Information: A report suitable for publication must be submitted within 3 years of the date of the award.

NSW Architects Registration Board Research Grant

Subjects: Any architectural topic approved by the board.
Purpose: To provide assistance to those wishing to undertake research on a topic approved by the Board to contribute to the advancement of architecture.
Eligibility: Open to candidates who are registered as architects in New South Wales.
Level of Study: Professional development
Value: Australian $12,000
Length of Study: 1 year
Frequency: Every 2 years
Country of Study: Australia
No. of awards offered: 1
Application Procedure: Applicants must write for details.
Closing Date: Variable
Funding: Government
No. of awards given last year: None
Additional Information: A report is to be submitted upon completion of tenure.

NURSES' EDUCATIONAL FUNDS, INC.

304 Park Avenue South, 11th Floor, New York, NY, 10010, United States of America
Tel: (1) 212 590 2443
Fax: (1) 212 590 2446
Email: info@n-e-f.org
Website: www.n-e-f.org

Nurses' Educational Funds, Inc. is an independent, non-profit organization that grants scholarships to registered nurses for graduate study. It is governed by a board of trustees of nursing and business leaders, and is supported by contributions from corporations, foundations, nurses and individuals interested in the advancement of nursing.

Nurses' Educational Funds Fellowships and Scholarships

Subjects: Administration, supervision, education, clinical specialization and research. Any nursing-related field.
Purpose: To provide the opportunity to registered nurses who seek to qualify through advanced study in a degree programme.
Eligibility: Baccalaureate-prepared registered nurses residing in any one of the 50 states and the District of Columbia who are pursuing either a Master's or doctoral degree in nursing are eligible to apply for NEF scholarship monies.
Level of Study: Graduate, doctorate
Type: Fellowship
Value: Please contact the organization
Frequency: Annual
Country of Study: United States of America
No. of awards offered: Varies
Application Procedure: Application available on the website.
Closing Date: March 1st
Funding: Private, trusts, corporation, individuals
No. of awards given last year: 10
No. of applicants last year: 70

THE O'REILLY FOUNDATION

Scholarship Programme, 2 Fitzwilliam Square, Dublin 2, Ireland
Tel: (353) (0) 1 294 6550
Fax: (353) (0) 1 294 6550
Email: info@oreillyfoundation.ie

The O'Reilly Foundation, established in 1998, is a charitable foundation, which aims to support charitable endeavours for the betterment of Ireland and to promote excellence, global vision, community responsibility and leadership.

The O'Reilly Scholarship Programme

Subjects: All subjects.
Purpose: To provide world-class educational opportunities for young Irish scholars.
Eligibility: Open to candidates who are residents of Ireland.
Level of Study: Postgraduate
Type: Scholarship
Value: €25,000
Length of Study: 2 years
Frequency: Annual
Study Establishment: Any accredited institution or university
No. of awards offered: 2
Application Procedure: See the website for further details.
Closing Date: November 11th

OKLAHOMA SCHOOL OF ART

University of Oklahoma 520 Parrington Oval, Room 202 Norman, Oklahoma, 73019-0550, United States of America
Tel: (1) 405 325 2691
Fax: (1) 405 325 1668
Email: infoart.ou.edu
Website: www.art.ou.edu

The School of Art is the largest, most comprehensive art school in Oklahoma, which provides excellent professional education and a focus for the study of visual arts. Additionally, the school is dedicated to promoting, pursuing and supporting creative activity and scholarly research in the visual arts.

Ben Barnett Scholarship

Subjects: Arts.
Eligibility: Open to applicants who are full-time art students in the School of Art.
Level of Study: Postgraduate
Type: Scholarship
Value: US$1,000
Frequency: Annual
Study Establishment: School of Art, University of Oklahoma
Country of Study: United States of America
No. of awards offered: 16
Application Procedure: See the website.
Closing Date: March 1st

Frances Weitzenhoffer Memorial Fellowship in Art History

Subjects: History of art.
Eligibility: Open to students enrolled for Art History at the School of Arts.
Level of Study: Postgraduate
Type: Fellowship
Value: US$8,000
Frequency: Annual
Study Establishment: School of Arts, University of Oklahoma
Country of Study: United States of America
No. of awards offered: 1
Application Procedure: See the website.
Closing Date: March 1st

Glenis Horn Scholarship

Subjects: Sculpture.
Purpose: To support art students who are majoring in Sculpture.
Eligibility: Open to applicants majoring in Sculpture in the School of Art.
Level of Study: Professional development
Type: Scholarship
Value: US$500–2,500
Frequency: Annual
Study Establishment: School of Art, University of Oklahoma
Country of Study: United States of America
No. of awards offered: 1
Application Procedure: The School of Art Scholarship application may be downloaded from the website.
Closing Date: March 1st

Kim and Paul Moore Scholarship

Subjects: Arts.
Eligibility: Open to full-time Art majors admitted to the studio programme at the School of Arts.
Level of Study: Postgraduate
Type: Scholarship
Value: Varies
Frequency: Annual
Study Establishment: School of Art, University of Oklahoma
Country of Study: United States of America
No. of awards offered: Varies
Application Procedure: Contact the scholarship office.
Closing Date: March 1st

Robert H. Monroe Memorial Scholarship

Subjects: Arts.
Eligibility: Open to applicants who are enrolled in either MA or MFA at the School of Arts.
Level of Study: Postgraduate
Type: Scholarship
Value: US$150 per credit hour
Frequency: Annual
Study Establishment: School of Art, University of Oklahoma
Country of Study: United States of America
Application Procedure: Contact the scholarship committee.
Closing Date: March 15th

Selma Naifeh Scholarship Fund

Subjects: Painting.
Eligibility: Open to applicants who are residents of Oklahoma.
Level of Study: Postgraduate
Type: Scholarship
Value: US$500–2,500
Frequency: Annual
Study Establishment: School of Art, University of Oklahoma
Country of Study: United States of America
No. of awards offered: 1
Application Procedure: A completed application form must be sent to the scholarship office.
Closing Date: March 1st

OMOHUNDRO INSTITUTE OF EARLY AMERICAN HISTORY AND CULTURE

PO Box 8781, Williamsburg, VA, 23187-8781, United States of America
Tel: (1) 757 221 1110
Fax: (1) 757 221 1047
Email: ieahc1@wm.edu
Website: www.wm.edu/oieahc
Contact: Ms Sally D Mason, Assistant to the Director

The Omohundro Institute of Early American History and Culture publishes books in its field of interest, the *William and Mary Quarterly* and a biannual newsletter, *Uncommon Sense*. It also sponsors conferences and colloquia and annually awards a 2-year NEH postdoctoral fellowship and a 1-year Andrew W Mellon postdoctoral research fellowship.

Andrew W Mellon Postdoctoral Research Fellowship at the Omohundro Institute

Subjects: The history and culture of North America's indigenous and immigrant peoples during the colonial, revolutionary and early national periods of the United States of America, and the related histories of Canada, the Caribbean, Latin America, the British Isles, Europe and Africa from 1500 to 1815.
Purpose: To revise the applicant's book manuscript into a first book that will make a distinguished contribution to scholarship, with publication by the Institute intended.
Eligibility: Applicants must not have previously published a book or have a book under contract, and must also have received their PhD at least 1 year prior to the application deadline.
Level of Study: Postdoctorate
Type: Fellowship
Value: US$45,000
Length of Study: 1 year, residential recommended but not mandatory
Frequency: Annual
Study Establishment: The Omohundro Institute of Early American History and Culture
Country of Study: United States of America
No. of awards offered: 1
Application Procedure: Applicants must complete an application form and submit this with a completed manuscript. Application forms are available on request and from the website.
Closing Date: November 1st
Funding: Private
Contributor: The Andrew W Mellon Foundation and the College of William and Mary
No. of awards given last year: 1
No. of applicants last year: 12

The National Endowment for Humanities (NEH) Institute Postdoctoral Fellowship

Subjects: The history and culture of North America's indigenous and immigrant peoples during the colonial, revolutionary and early national periods of the United States of America, and the related histories of Canada, the Caribbean, Latin America, the British Isles, Europe and Africa from 1500 to 1815.
Purpose: To revise a dissertation into a first book that will make a major contribution to the field of early American history and culture, for publication by the Institute.
Eligibility: Applicants must have been citizens of the United States of America for 3 years prior to applying.
Level of Study: Postdoctorate
Type: Fellowship
Value: US$40,000 annually
Length of Study: 2 years
Frequency: Annual
Study Establishment: The Omohundro Institute of Early American History and Culture
Country of Study: United States of America
No. of awards offered: 1
Application Procedure: Applicants must complete an application form, available on written request or from the website.
Closing Date: November 1st
Funding: Government
Contributor: The NEH and the College of William and Mary
No. of awards given last year: 1
No. of applicants last year: 17

ONCOLOGY NURSING FOUNDATION (ONS)

125 Enterprise Drive, RIDC Park West,
Pittsburgh, PA, 15275-1214,
United States of America
Tel: (1) 859-6100
Fax: (1) 859-6160
Email: found@ons.org
Website: www.ons.org
Contact: Director of Research

The mission of the Oncology Nursing Society (ONS) is to promote excellence in oncology nursing and quality cancer care. The Foundation works to fulfil this mission by providing nurses and healthcare professionals with access to the highest quality educational programmes, cancer care resources, research opportunities, and networks for peer support.

ONS Foundation Research Awards

Subjects: Oncology nursing research, including research proposals related to AIDS, neuro-oncology, community health, cancer related genetics, nursing outcomes, oncology nursing education, symptom assessment and management, pain, palliative care, nausea and vomiting, neutropenia or biotherapy.
Purpose: To promote excellence in oncology nursing and quality cancer care.
Eligibility: Open to health professionals working in the field of oncology.
Level of Study: Unrestricted
Type: Research grant
Value: Generally US$3,000–10,000
Length of Study: 2 years
Frequency: Dependent on funds available
Country of Study: Any country
No. of awards offered: 28
Application Procedure: Applicants must complete an application form, available on request. They must also include a research proposal.
Closing Date: November 1st

For further information contact:

501 Holiday Drive, Pittsburgh, PA, 15220–2749, United States of America
Tel: (1) 412 921 7373
Fax: (1) 412 921 6565
Contact: Dr Gail A Mallory, Director of Research

OPEN RUSSIA FOUNDATION

31a, Dubininskaya str, Moscow, 115054, Russia
Email: secretariat@openrussiafoundation.org
Website: www.openrussiafoundation.org

The Open Russia Foundation, founded in 2001, is an international, independent and charitable organization that supports a broad range of educational projects providing funds for their implementation.

Open Russia Foundation Grant

Subjects: Education.
Purpose: To support educational and cultural projects.
Eligibility: Open to those projects focusing on the themes and topics identified by the Board are eligible.
Level of Study: Postgraduate
Type: Grant
Value: US$3,000–50,000
Frequency: Annual
Application Procedure: Before submitting a full grant proposal please first send us a brief (one-page) preliminary project outline.
Contributor: YUKOS Oil Company

For further information contact:

Apply online.

OPPENHEIM-JOHN DOWNES MEMORIAL TRUST

50 Broadway, London, Westminster, SW1H OBL, England
Contact: Grants Management Officer

The Oppenheim-John Downes Memorial Trust makes annual awards in December to deserving artists of any kind unable to pursue their vocation by reason of poverty. Awards are restricted to persons over 30 years of age, who are natural born British subjects and of parents who are both natural born British subjects (534 Race Relations Act applies).

Oppenheim-John Downes Trust Grants

Subjects: Arts.
Purpose: To assist artists, musicians, writers, inventors, singers, actors and dancers of all descriptions who are unable to pursue their vocation by reason of their poverty.
Eligibility: Open to artists over 30 years of age, born in the British Isles of British parents and grandparents born after 1900. These qualifications are mandatory and applicants who do not qualify in all respects should not apply.
Level of Study: Unrestricted
Type: Grant
Value: UK £50–1,500 depending on requirement
Frequency: Annual
Country of Study: Any country
No. of awards offered: Approx. 30–40
Application Procedure: Applicants must write for details.
Closing Date: October 15th
Funding: Private
No. of awards given last year: 40
No. of applicants last year: 152

ORENTREICH FOUNDATION FOR THE ADVANCEMENT OF SCIENCE, INC. (OFAS)

855 Route 301, Cold Spring, NY, 10516-9802,
United States of America
Tel: (1) 845 265 4200
Fax: (1) 845 265 4210
Email: ofase@orentreich.org
Contact: Dr Rozlyn A Krajcik, Assistant Director Scientific Affairs

The Orentreich Foundation for the Advancement of Science, Inc. (OFAS) is an operating private foundation that performs its own research and collaborates on projects of mutual interest.

OFAS Grants

Subjects: Areas of interest to the Foundation, including ageing, dermatology, endocrinology and serum markers for human diseases.
Purpose: To allow an individual to conduct collaborative biomedical research or research at the Foundation.
Eligibility: Open to applicants at or above the postgraduate level in science or medicine at an accredited research institution in the United States of America. There are, however, no citizenship restrictions.
Level of Study: Unrestricted
Type: Grant
Value: Varies, depending on the needs, nature and level of OFAS interest in the project
Frequency: Annual
Country of Study: United States of America
Application Procedure: Applicants must submit an outline of proposed joint or collaborative research, including, as a minimum, a brief overview of the current research in the field of interest, a statement of scientific objectives, a protocol summary, a curriculum vitae of the principal investigator, funding needed and total estimated project funding. Applications are reviewed quarterly. OFAS is usually the initiator of joint projects.
Closing Date: Applications may be submitted at any time
Funding: Foundation, private
Additional Information: Individuals who have a research question relating to a human disease or disease prevention factor for which there is adequate scientific basis for a serum marker to justify the use of the Serum Treasury, should submit a brief overview of a proposal. Researchers will be asked for additional information after the initial screening process. Proposals will be evaluated on an ongoing basis. In certain cases where the research applies directly to the primary interests of OFAS, limited grants to fund collaborative studies are available.

ORGANIZATION OF AMERICAN HISTORIANS (OAH)

112 North Bryan Avenue, PO Box 5457, Bloomington, IN, 47408-5457, United States of America
Tel: (1) 812 855 9852
Fax: (1) 812 855 0696
Email: oah@oah.org
Website: www.oah.org
Contact: Administrative Assistant

The Organization of American Historians (OAH) was founded in 1907 as the Mississippi Valley Historical Association and originally focused on the history of the Mississippi Valley. Now, national in scope and with approx. 11,000 members, it is a large professional organization created and sustained for the investigation, study and teaching of American history.

ABC-Clio America: History and Life Award

Subjects: American history.
Purpose: For scholarship in American history in the journal literature advancing new perspectives on accepted interpretations or previously unconsidered topics.
Eligibility: Open to entrants who have published an article in an American historical journal. Nominations and applications are welcome from both individuals and editors. Each entry must have been published within a specified time period, prior to the application deadline.
Type: Award
Value: US$750
Frequency: Every 2 years
No. of awards offered: 1
Application Procedure: Applicants should visit the website for complete application requirements. There is no standard application form. Publishers are encouraged to enter one or more articles in the competition.
Closing Date: December 1st
Contributor: ABC-Clio America: History & Life
No. of awards given last year: 1
No. of applicants last year: 39

Avery O Craven Award

Subjects: The coming of the Civil War, the Civil War years or the Era of Reconstruction, with the exception of works of purely military history.
Purpose: For the most original book on the coming of the Civil war, civil war years, or the era of reconstruction, with the exception of works of purely military history.
Type: Award
Value: US$500
Frequency: Annual
No. of awards offered: 1
Application Procedure: Applicants should visit the website for complete application requirements. There is no standard application form. Publishers are encouraged to enter one or more articles in the competition.
Closing Date: October 1st
Contributor: OAH
No. of awards given last year: 1
No. of applicants last year: 33
Additional Information: The exception of works of purely military history recognizes and reflects the Quaker convictions of Avery Craven, President of the Organization of American Historians (1963–1964).

Binkley-Slephenson Award

Purpose: For the best scholarly article published in the *Journal of American History* during the preceding calendar year.
Value: US$500
Frequency: Annual
Closing Date: N/A
No. of awards given last year: 1

Additional Information: All articles published in the *Journal of American History* during the preceding calendar year are considered.

David Thelen Award

Subjects: Past issues of continuity and change, as well as events or processes that began, developed or ended in what is now the United States of America.
Purpose: Abiennial prize for the best article published in a foreign language.
Eligibility: Comparative and international studies that fall within these guidelines are welcomed. This prize is not open to articles whose manuscripts were originally submitted for publication in English or by other people for whom English is their first language.
Type: Prize
Value: The winning article will be printed in the *Journal of American History* and its author awarded a US$500 subvention for refining the article's English translation
Frequency: Every 2 years
No. of awards offered: 1
Application Procedure: Applicants must write a 1- to 2-page essay in English explaining why their article is a significant and original contribution to an understanding of American history. This and five copies of the article should be sent. The application must include the following information: name, mailing address, institutional affiliation, fax number and email address if available and the language of the submitted article. Authors of eligible articles are invited to nominate their work. Scholars who know of eligible publications written by others are urged to inform them of the prize. Applicants should visit the website for complete application requirements. There is no standard application form. Publishers are encouraged to enter one or more articles in the competition.
Closing Date: May 1st of odd-numbered years
Contributor: OAH
No. of awards given last year: 1
No. of applicants last year: 14

For further information contact:

The Chair, *Journal of American History*, 1215 East Atwater, Bloomington, IN, 47401, United States of America
Contact: David Nord

Department of Education, Teaching American History Grants (TAH Grants)

Subjects: Content standard for teachers, content stands for students, graduation and exit exam requirements related to the discipline of history teaching.
Level of Study: Professional development
Type: Grant
Frequency: Annual
Funding: Foundation
Contributor: The Gilder Lehrman Institute

Ellis W Hawley Prize

Subjects: Political economy, politics or institutions of the United States of America in its domestic or international affairs, from the Civil War to the present.
Purpose: For the best book-length historical study of the political economy politics, or institutions of the United States in its domestic or international affairs, from the civil war to the resent.
Eligibility: Eligible works shall include book-length historical studies, written in English and published during a given calendar year.
Type: Prize
Value: US$500
Frequency: Annual
No. of awards offered: 1
Application Procedure: Applicants should visit the website for complete application requirements. There is no standard application form. Publishers are encouraged to enter one or more articles in the competition.
Closing Date: October 1st
No. of awards given last year: 1
No. of applicants last year: 75

Erik Barnouw Award

Subjects: American history.
Purpose: To recognize outstanding reporting or programming on network television, cable television or in a documentary film, concerned with American history, the study of American history, and/or the promotion of history.
Level of Study: Professional development
Type: Award
Value: US$500
Frequency: Annual
No. of awards offered: 1–2
Application Procedure: Applicants should visit the website for complete application requirements. There is no standard application form. Companies are encouraged to enter one or more firms in the competition.
Closing Date: December 1st
No. of awards given last year: 1
No. of applicants last year: 15

Frederick Jackson Turner Award

Subjects: American history.
Purpose: For an author's first book dealing with significant phase of American history.
Eligibility: The work must be the first book-length study of history published by the author. If the author has a PhD, he or she must have received it no more than 7 years prior to the submission of the manuscript for publication. The work must be published in the calendar year before the award is given.
Type: Award
Value: US$1,000
Frequency: Annual
No. of awards offered: 1
Application Procedure: Applicants should visit the website for complete application requirements. There is no standard application form. Publishers are encouraged to enter one or more books in the competition.
Closing Date: October 1st
No. of awards given last year: 1
No. of applicants last year: 92

Friend of History award

Subjects: American history.
Purpose: To recognize an individual, who is not a professional historian, or an institution or organization for outstanding support for the pursuit of historical research, for the public presentation of history, or for the work of the OAH.
Level of Study: Unrestricted
Type: Award
Value: No money given
Frequency: Annual
No. of awards offered: 1
Application Procedure: See website.
Closing Date: No deadline
Funding: Foundation
Contributor: OAH
Additional Information: This is not an award for which individuals and organizations apply. The recipient(s) are chosen by the OAH Executive Board.

Huggins-Quarles Dissertation Award

Subjects: History, ethnic studies, whiteness studies, Afro-Caribbean studies, cultural studies (postcolonialism), feminist studies, popular culture and media studies, immigration history, environmental studies or diplomatic history.
Purpose: For graduate students of color at the dissertation research stage of their PhD programme.
Eligibility: Open to minority graduate students at the dissertation research stage of their PhD.
Level of Study: Postgraduate
Type: Award
Value: US$1,000
Frequency: Annual
No. of awards offered: 1–2

Application Procedure: Applicants should visit the website for complete application requirements. There is no standard application form.
Closing Date: December 1st
No. of awards given last year: 2
No. of applicants last year: 9

James A Rawley Prize
Subjects: The history of race relations in the United States of America.
Purpose: To reward a book dealing with the history of race relations in the United States of America.
Type: Prize
Value: US$1,000
Frequency: Annual
No. of awards offered: 1
Application Procedure: Applicants should visit the website for complete application requirements. There is no standard application form. Publishers are encouraged to enter one or more books in the competition.
Closing Date: October 1st
No. of awards given last year: 1
No. of applicants last year: 91

Japanese Residencies Program
Subjects: American history and culture, native Americans, the West, social, economic and political history of the 20th century.
Purpose: To contribute to the expansion of personal scholarly networks between Japan and the United States of America.
Eligibility: Applicants must be current members of the OAH, have a PhD and be scholars of American history or culture. The committee invites applicants from previous competitions as well as new applicants to apply.
Level of Study: Professional development
Type: Residency
Value: Modest daily expenses, round-trip expenses to Japan and accommodation
Length of Study: 2 weeks
Frequency: Annual
Country of Study: Japan
No. of awards offered: 3
Application Procedure: Applicants must send a two-page curriculum vitae emphasizing teaching experience and publications, three references, details of the institution to which the applicant wishes to apply and a personal statement no longer than two pages describing their interest in the programme, and the issues that their own history teaching has addressed. Postal applications must be addressed to the OAH Selection Committee. There is no standard application form.
Closing Date: December 1st
No. of awards given last year: 3
No. of applicants last year: 17
Additional Information: During the residency, the selected scholars will give lectures and seminars in their speciality and provide individual consultation to Japanese scholars, graduate students and sometimes undergraduates studying American history and culture. Visitors will also participate in the collegial life of their host institutions.

John Higham Travel Grant Fund
Purpose: For students to be used towards costs of attending the OAH/IEHS annual meeting.
Type: Travel grant
Value: US$500
Frequency: Annual
No. of awards offered: 3
Closing Date: December 1st
No. of applicants last year: 8

Lerner-Scott Dissertation Prize
Subjects: United States of America women's history.
Purpose: For the best doctoral dissertation in U.S. women's history.
Level of Study: Postdoctorate
Type: Prize
Value: US$1,000
Frequency: Annual
No. of awards offered: 1
Application Procedure: Each application must contain a letter of support from a faculty member at the degree-granting institution, along with an abstract, table of contents and a sample chapter from the dissertation. Email addresses for the applicants and the adviser should also be included if available. For further application details, candidates should visit the website. There is no standard application form.
Closing Date: October 1st
No. of awards given last year: 1
No. of applicants last year: 18

Liberty Legacy Foundation Award
Subjects: American history and the civil rights movement.
Purpose: For the best book on any aspect of the struggle for civil rights in the United States, from the nation's founding to the present.
Eligibility: Open to writers and publishers writing a book on any historical aspect of the struggle for human civil rights in the United States of America. Each entry must be published within a specified time period prior to the application deadline.
Level of Study: Professional development
Type: Competition
Value: US$2,000
Frequency: Annual
Country of Study: United States of America
No. of awards offered: 1
Application Procedure: Applicants should visit the website for complete application requirements. There is no standard application form. Publishers are encouraged to enter one or more books in the competition.
Closing Date: October 1st
No. of awards given last year: 2
No. of applicants last year: 49
Additional Information: This award was inspired by the OAH President Darlene Clark Hine's call in her 2002 OAH presidential address for more research on the origins of the civil rights movement in the period before 1954.

Louis Pelzer Memorial Award
Subjects: Any period or topic in the history of the United States of America.
Purpose: For the best essay in American history by a graduate student.
Type: Award
Value: The winning essay will be published in the *Journal of American History*. The organization offers a prize of US$500
Frequency: Annual
Application Procedure: Applicants must submit five copies of essays that should not exceed 7,000 words in length (including endnotes). The footnotes at the end of the text should be triple spaced. Manuscripts are judged anonymously; therefore, the author's name and graduate programme should appear only on a separate cover page. For further application details, candidates should visit the website. There is no standard application form.
Closing Date: December 1st
No. of awards given last year: 1
No. of applicants last year: 19

For further information contact:

The Committee Chair, Louis Pelzer Award Committee, Journal of American History, 1215 East Atwater Avenue, Bloomington, IN, 47401, United States of America
Contact: David Nord

Mary K Bonsteel Tachau Precollegiate Teaching Award
Subjects: History.
Purpose: To recognize the contributions made by precollegiate and classroom teachers to improve history education.
Eligibility: Applicants must be precollegiate teachers engaged at least half time in history teaching, with exceptional ability in initiating projects that involve students in historical research. They should also demonstrate ability in working with museums, historical preservation

societies or other public history associations, and in publishing or presenting scholarship that advances education or knowledge.
Level of Study: Professional development
Type: Award
Value: US$750, 1-year OAH membership and a 1-year subscription to the *OAH Magazine of History*. If the winner is an OAH member, the award will include a 1-year renewal of membership in the awardee's usual membership category. Finally, the winner's school will receive a plaque suitable for permanent public display
Frequency: Annual
No. of awards offered: 1
Application Procedure: Applicants should visit the website for complete application requirements. There is no standard application form.
Closing Date: December 1st
No. of awards given last year: 1
No. of applicants last year: 4

Merle Curti Award

Subjects: American social, intellectual or cultural history.
Purpose: To recognize books in the fields of American social, intellectual and cultural history.
Type: Award
Value: US$1,000
Frequency: Annual
No. of awards offered: 1
Application Procedure: Applicants must visit the website for complete application requirements. There is no standard application form. Publishers are encouraged to enter one or more books in the competition.
Closing Date: October 1st
Contributor: OAH
No. of awards given last year: 2
No. of applicants last year: 175

OAH Awards and Prizes

Subjects: American history.
Purpose: To recognize scholarly and professional achievement in the field of American history.
Eligibility: Open to applicants of any nationality.
Level of Study: Unrestricted
Type: Grant
Value: Varies, depending on award
Frequency: Other
No. of awards offered: Varies
Application Procedure: Applicants must obtain flyers for each award from the OAH office. The names and addresses of committee members are listed and submissions are sent directly to these members. There are no application forms to fill out and no application fees.
Closing Date: Deadlines vary
Funding: Foundation
Contributor: OAH

Ray Allen Billington Prize

Subjects: American frontier history.
Purpose: To award the best book in American frontier history, defined broadly so as to include the pioneer periods of all geographical areas and comparisons between American frontiers and others.
Type: Award
Value: US$1,000
Frequency: Every 2 years
No. of awards offered: 1
Application Procedure: Applicants must visit the website for complete application requirements. There is no standard application form. Publishers are encouraged to enter one or more books in the competition.
Closing Date: October 1st
Funding: Foundation
Contributor: OAH
No. of awards given last year: 1
No. of applicants last year: 76

Richard W Leopold Prize

Subjects: Foreign policy, military affairs broadly construed, the historical activities of the federal government or a biography in one of the aforementioned areas.
Purpose: To improve contacts and interrelationships within the historical profession, where an increasing number of historically trained scholars hold distinguished positions in governmental agencies. It is awarded to the best book written by a historian connected with federal, state or municipal government. Awarded every two years for the best book written by a historian connected with federal, state, or municipal government.
Eligibility: The winner must have been employed in a government position for the last 5 years. If the author has accepted an academic position the book must have been published within 2 years from the time of the change.
Type: Prize
Value: US$1,500
Frequency: Every 2 years
No. of awards offered: 1
Application Procedure: Applicants should visit the website for complete application requirements. There is no standard application form. Publishers are encouraged to enter one or more books in the competition.
Closing Date: October 1st
No. of awards given last year: 1
No. of applicants last year: 21

White House Historical Association Fellowships

Subjects: Cultural education.
Purpose: To award teachers and scholars whose work enhances the understanding of how the White House functions in all its various capacities as home, workplace, museum, structure and symbol.
Eligibility: Open to teachers and scholars. Studies dealing primarily with political or governmental policy issues will not be considered except for ones concerning the operation of the White House as a political institution.
Level of Study: Research
Type: Fellowship
Value: US$2,000 per month plus a travel stipend
Length of Study: 1–6 months
Frequency: Annual
Country of Study: United States of America
Application Procedure: Applicants must send a curriculum vitae, a 2-page summary of their project, including the proposed final product of the research and timetable with three professional references. Applicants should visit the website for complete application requirements. There is no standard application form.
Closing Date: December 1st
No. of awards given last year: 2

Willi Paul Adams Award

Subjects: American history, namely, the past and issues of continuity and change as well as events or processes that began, developed or ended in what is now the United States of America.
Purpose: For the best book on American history published in a foreign language.
Eligibility: This prize is not open to books whose manuscripts were originally submitted for publication in English or by people for whom English is their first language.
Type: Prize
Value: US$1,000
Frequency: Every 2 years
No. of awards offered: 1
Application Procedure: Applicants must write a two-page essay in English explaining why the book is a significant and original contribution to American history. This and four copies of the book should be sent to the Willi Paul Adams Award Committee at the main address of the organization. Authors of eligible books are invited to nominate their work. Scholars who know of eligible publications written by others are urged to inform them of the prize. Publishers are encouraged to enter one or more books in the competition. There is no standard application form.

Closing Date: May 1st in even years
Contributor: OAH
No. of awards given last year: 1
No. of applicants last year: 11

ORTHOPAEDIC RESEARCH AND EDUCATION FOUNDATION (OREF)

6300 N River Road, Suite 700, Rosemont, IL, 60018-4261, United States of America
Tel: (1) 847 698 9980
Fax: (1) 847 698 7806
Email: mcguire@oref.org
Website: www.oref.org
Contact: Mrs Jean McGuire, Vice President Grants

In 1955, leaders of the major professional organizations in the speciality, the American Orthopaedic Association, the American Academy of Orthopaedic Surgeons and the Orthopaedic Research Society, established the Orthopaedic Research and Education Foundation (OREF) as a means of supporting research and building the scientific base of clinical practice. Today, the Foundation raises over US$5 million per year and holds a unique place in medicine in the United States of America.

OREF Career Development Award
Subjects: Orthopaedic surgery.
Purpose: To encourage a commitment to scientific research in orthopaedic surgery.
Eligibility: Applicants must be orthopaedic surgeons, and are not eligible if they are holders of the NIH ROI award.
Level of Study: Professional development
Type: Award
Value: Up to US$75,000 per year
Length of Study: 3 years
Frequency: Annual
Country of Study: United States of America or Canada
No. of awards offered: 1–3
Application Procedure: Applicants must make a formal application together with letters of recommendation.
Closing Date: October 1st
Funding: Private
Contributor: Orthopaedic surgeons
No. of awards given last year: 2
No. of applicants last year: 16

OREF Clinical Research Award
Subjects: Orthopaedics.
Purpose: To recognize outstanding clinical research related to musculoskeletal disease or injury.
Eligibility: Restricted to members of the American Academy of Orthopaedic Surgeons, the Orthopaedic Research Society (ORS), the Canadian Orthopaedic Association or the Canadian Orthopaedic Research Society. Alternatively, candidates may be sponsored by a member.
Level of Study: Professional development
Type: Award
Value: US$20,000
Length of Study: 1 year
Frequency: Annual
Country of Study: United States of America or Canada
No. of awards offered: 1
Application Procedure: Applicants must submit an original manuscript.
Closing Date: July 1st
Funding: Private
Contributor: Orthopaedic surgeons
No. of awards given last year: 1
No. of applicants last year: 9

OREF Fellowship in Health Services Research
Subjects: Orthopaedics.
Purpose: To enable orthopaedic surgeons with research skills to manage health services and outcomes research.
Eligibility: Applicants must be orthopaedic surgeons in either Canada or the United States of America.
Level of Study: Postdoctorate
Type: Fellowship
Value: US$70,000 per year
Length of Study: 2 years
Frequency: Annual
Study Establishment: Participating institutions
Country of Study: United States of America
No. of awards offered: 1
Application Procedure: Applicants must make a formal application.
Closing Date: October 1st
Funding: Private
Contributor: Orthopaedic surgeons
No. of awards given last year: 1
No. of applicants last year: 5

OREF Prospective Clinical Research
Subjects: Orthopaedics.
Purpose: To provide funding for promising prospective clinical proposals.
Eligibility: Applicants must be orthopaedic surgeons.
Level of Study: Professional development
Type: Award
Value: Up to US$50,000 per year
Length of Study: 3 years
Frequency: Annual
Study Establishment: A medical centre
Country of Study: United States of America
No. of awards offered: 1–3
Application Procedure: Applicants must make a formal application.
Closing Date: October 1st
Funding: Private
Contributor: Orthopaedic surgeons
No. of awards given last year: 2
No. of applicants last year: 13

OREF Research Grants
Subjects: Sports medicine, surgery, rheumatology and treatment techniques.
Purpose: To encourage new investigators by providing seed money and start-up funding.
Eligibility: Open to orthopaedic surgeons who are principal investigators (PI) or co-PIs. PIs cannot have NIH ROI awards.
Level of Study: Postdoctorate
Type: Research grant
Value: Up to US$50,000 per year
Length of Study: 2 years
Frequency: Annual
Study Establishment: A medical centre
Country of Study: United States of America
No. of awards offered: 8–12
Application Procedure: Applicants must make a formal application.
Closing Date: October 1st
Funding: Private
Contributor: Orthopaedic surgeons and corporations
No. of awards given last year: 9
No. of applicants last year: 57

OREF Resident Research Award
Subjects: Orthopaedics.
Purpose: To encourage the development of research interests for residents and Fellows.
Eligibility: Applicants must be orthopaedic surgeon residents or Fellows in an approved residency programme in the United States of America.
Level of Study: Professional development
Type: Award
Value: US$15,000
Length of Study: 1 year

Frequency: Annual
Study Establishment: A medical centre
Country of Study: United States of America
No. of awards offered: Up to 10
Application Procedure: Applicants must make a formal application.
Closing Date: October 1st
Funding: Private
Contributor: Orthopaedic surgeons
No. of awards given last year: 11
No. of applicants last year: 52

OTTO BENECKE FOUNDATION

Kennedyalle 105-107, D-53175, Bonn, Germany
Tel: (49) 228 8163 217
Fax: (49) 228 8163 200
Email: hghrach@obs-ev.de
Website: www.obs-ev.de

Otto Benecke Foundation Scientific Internships

Subjects: Humanities, natural sciences and engineering.
Purpose: To support those who have completed their academic training and whose training needs to be complemented to qualify them for career integration.
Eligibility: Late repatriates and contingent refugees recognized by the Federal Expellee Law. Applicants must be between 30 and 50 years of age.
Level of Study: Unrestricted
Type: Internship
Value: Approx. €346 per month. Additionally, health insurance contributions and housing allowance will be paid
Length of Study: 1 year (extension not possible)
Country of Study: Germany
Application Procedure: Applications need not be submitted on a special form.
Closing Date: Application papers should not be submitted later than 3 years after the applicant's arrival, entry or stay in Germany

OUR WORLD-UNDERWATER SCHOLARSHIP SOCIETY

PO Box 4428, Chicago, IL 60680, United States of America
Tel: (1) 969 6690
Fax: (1) 969 6690
Email: vicepresident-EU@owuscholarship.org
Website: www.owuscholarship.org

The Our World Underwater Scholarship Society in an organization dedicated to promoting education in the underwater world.

Our World-Underwater Scholarship Society Scholarships

Subjects: Underwater-related disciplines.
Purpose: To provide hands-on intro to underwater and other aquatic-related endeavors.
Eligibility: Open to applicants who are certified scuba divers and above the age of 21 years.
Level of Study: Professional development
Type: Scholarship
Length of Study: 1 year
Frequency: Annual
No. of awards offered: 2
Application Procedure: Application form along with the required documents must be submitted before the deadline.
Closing Date: December 31st

For further information contact:

Our World-underwater Scholarship Society, PO Box 4428, Chicago, IL 60680
Contact: Scholarship Coordinator

PAINTING AND DECORATING CONTRACTORS OF AMERICA (PDCA)

11960 Westline Industrial Drive, Suite 201, St. Louis, MD 63146-3209, United States of America
Tel: (1) 800 332 7322
Fax: (1) 314 514 9417
Website: www.pdca.org

The PDCA was established in 1884 by a group of contractors to devise a means for assuring the public of the skill, honorable reputation, and probity of master painters.

A.E. Robert Friedman PDCA Scholarship

Subjects: All subjects.
Purpose: To provide scholastic and vocational aid.
Eligibility: Open to applicants who are under the age of 25 and are nominated by a PDCA member.
Level of Study: Postgraduate
Type: Scholarship
Value: Open to applicants who are under the age of 25 and are nominated by a PDCA member.
Length of Study: US$1,000
Frequency: Annual
Application Procedure: See the website.
Closing Date: November 30th

PALOMA O'SHEA SANTANDER INTERNATIONAL PIANO COMPETITION

Calle Hernán Cortés 3, E-39003 Santander, Spain
Tel: (34) 94 231 1451
Fax: (34) 94 231 4816
Email: concurso@albeniz.com
Website: www.albeniz.com
Contact: A Kaufmann, Secretariat General

The Paloma O'Shea Santander International Piano Competition is one of the best rated competitions in the world. It provides an opportunity for exceptionally talented pianists to enhance their careers. The jury is composed of renowned musicians in order to ensure that grants are made in a fair and unbiased manner.

Paloma O'Shea Santander International Piano Competition

Subjects: Piano performance.
Purpose: To give support to young pianists of exceptional talent.
Eligibility: Open to pianists of any nationality under 29 years of age.
Level of Study: Unrestricted
Type: Competition
Value: Please contact the organization for details
Length of Study: July 25th–August 7th
Frequency: Every 3 years
No. of awards offered: 7
Application Procedure: Applicants in the United States of America should contact Mrs Brookes McIntyre at the address below. Applicants from all other countries must contact the Secretariat General for details at the main address.
Closing Date: October 30th
Funding: Government, commercial, private
No. of awards given last year: 7
No. of applicants last year: 220
Additional Information: 20 pianists will participate in Santander in the First Phase with a performance of 50 minutes duration. Each one will be chosen from the pre-selection phase, which will be held in different cities of the world. 12 Participants will continue in the Second Phase and perform a recital of 40 minutes duration and a quintet for piano and strings. 6 pianists will go in the Semifinals and perform a concerto with chamber orchestra and a recital of 40 minutes duration. The final will consist of a concerto with symphony orchestra (3 finalists).

For further information contact:

PO Box 82743, Albuquerque, NM, 87198, United States of America
Tel: (1) 505 250 2341
Fax: (1) 505 265 8932
Contact: Mrs Brookes McIntyre

PAN AMERICAN HEALTH ORGANIZATION (PAHO) REGIONAL OFFICE OF THE WORLD HEALTH ORGANIZATION (WHO)

Regional Office for the Americas/Pan American Sanitary Bureau, 525 23rd Street North West, Washington, DC, 20037-2895, United States of America
Tel: (1) 202 974 3000
Fax: (1) 202 974 3663
Email: rgp@paho.org
Website: www.paho.org
Contact: Grants Administrator

The Pan American Health Organization (PAHO) is an international public health agency working to improve the health and living standards of the countries of the Americas. It serves as the specialized organization for health of the Inter-American System and as the regional office for the Americas of the World Health Organization.

PAHO Grants

Subjects: Public health studies.
Purpose: To contribute to the public health of the countries of the Americas (individual programme objectives vary). Programmes include graduate thesis grants, research training grants, regional research competitions (announced yearly) and special initiatives announced via the PAHO website.
Eligibility: Open to citizens and residents of Latin America and the Caribbean.
Level of Study: Research, postgraduate, doctorate, graduate
Type: Research grant
Value: Please contact the organization
Study Establishment: Varies
Country of Study: Latin America or Caribbean countries only
No. of awards offered: Varies according to the programme
Application Procedure: Applicants must complete an application form. Guidelines and application forms are available from the website.
Closing Date: Varies according to the programme
Funding: Government
Contributor: Member states and their agencies

PARALYZED VETERANS OF AMERICA

Paralyzed Veterans of America (PVA) Education & Training Foundation 801 18th Street North West, Washington, DC 20006, United States of America
Tel: (1) 202 416 7651
Fax: (1) 202 416 7652
Email: foundations@pva.org
Website: www.pva.org
Contact: Florence Montgomery

The Spinal Cord Injury Research Foundation aims to fund innovative educational projects that enhance the quality of life of individuals with spinal cord injury or disease (SCI/D) and/or increases the knowledge and effectiveness of health professionals in the SCI/D community.

PVA Educational Scholarship Program

Subjects: Spinal cord injury or dysfunction.
Purpose: To provide financial support for PVA members so that they can achieve their goals in the academic arena.
Eligibility: Open to all PVA members and their families.
Level of Study: Postgraduate
Type: Scholarship
Value: US$1,000
Frequency: Annual
No. of awards offered: 3 part-time and 14 full-time scholarships
Application Procedure: Details are available on the website.

PARAPSYCHOLOGY FOUNDATION, INC.

PO Box 1562, New York, NY 10021-0043, United States of America
Tel: (1) 212 628 1550
Fax: (1) 212 628 1559
Email: info@parapsychology.org
Website: www.parapsychology.org
Contact: Vice President

Established in 1951, the Parapsychology Foundation acts as a clearinghouse for information about parapsychology. Essentially an administrative organization, it maintains one of the largest libraries to do with parapsychology, the Eileen J Garret Library, as well as supporting various programmes that include the library, a grant and scholarship programme, a conference and lecture programme, and a speaker's bureau and publishing programme.

D Scott Rogo Award for Parapsychological Literature

Subjects: Parapsychology.
Purpose: To provide support to authors working on a manuscript pertaining to the science of parapsychology.
Eligibility: Open to nationals of any country.
Level of Study: Unrestricted
Type: Award
Value: US$3,000
Length of Study: 1 year
Frequency: Annual
Country of Study: Any country
No. of awards offered: 1
Application Procedure: Applicants must submit a brief synopsis of the proposed contents of manuscript, a list of previous writings and a sample writing of assistance.
Closing Date: April 15th for notification on May 1st

Eileen J Garrett Scholarship

Subjects: Parapsychology.
Purpose: To assist students attending an accredited college or university in pursuing the academic study of the science of parapsychology.
Eligibility: Open to nationals of any country.
Level of Study: Unrestricted
Type: Scholarship
Value: US$3,000
Length of Study: 1 year
Frequency: Annual
Study Establishment: An accredited college or university
Country of Study: Any country
No. of awards offered: 1
Application Procedure: Applicants must submit samples of writings on the subject with an application form from the Foundation. Letters of reference are required from three individuals, familiar with the applicant's work and/or studies in parapsychology.
Closing Date: July 15th for notification on August 1st

Parapsychology Foundation Grant

Subjects: Parapsychology.
Purpose: To support original study, research and experiments in parapsychology.
Eligibility: Open to nationals of any country.
Level of Study: Unrestricted
Type: Grant
Value: Up to US$3,000
Length of Study: 1 year
Frequency: Annual
Country of Study: Any country
No. of awards offered: 10
Application Procedure: Applicants must contact the organization for details.

Closing Date: Applications are accepted at any time
Additional Information: Funding for the Foundation Grant is limited but applicants are still welcome to submit a proposal on the off chance that the programme will be reviewed.

PARKER B FRANCIS FELLOWSHIP PROGRAM

Physiology Program, Harvard School of Public Health, Room 1411
Building 1665, Huntington Avenue, Boston, MA, 02115,
United States of America
Tel: (1) 617 432 4099
Fax: (1) 617 277 2382
Email: hoffmann@hsph.harvard.edu
Website: www.francisfellowships.org
Contact: Ms Rebecca Hoffmann, Executive Director

A private foundation dedicated to creating current and future generations of well-rounded individuals who are creative, life-long learners, striving to achieve their fullest potential within their communities.

Parker B Francis Fellowship Program

Subjects: Pulmonary research.
Purpose: To support rising stars in the field of pulmonary research as they make the transition from postdoctoral trainees to independent researchers.
Eligibility: Ideally, open to applicants with 2–7 years of postdoctoral research experience, published articles in leading journals and a clear trajectory in pulmonary research.
Level of Study: Postdoctorate
Type: Fellowship
Value: The total budget is limited to US$44,000 for the 1st year, US$46,000 for the 2nd and US$48,000 for the 3rd. These totals include a stipend plus fringe benefits and may include travel costs to a maximum of US$1,500. Direct research project costs and indirect costs are not covered. These expenses ought to be supported by research Project Grants, which are an essential part of the application in documenting the availability of sufficient research project support to make possible fulfilment of the Fellow's research aims
Length of Study: 3 years
Frequency: Annual
Country of Study: United States of America, Canada or Mexico
No. of awards offered: 15
Application Procedure: Applicants must submit a completed application form, biographical sketch and a brief statement of their career goals. They must also provide a letter from their mentor evaluating the applicant's qualifications and indicating their career goals in the field of pulmonary research, three letters of recommendation, a summary of the past training record of the primary mentor (including names of former trainees and their current positions, sources and level of support with grants pending and the extent of equipment and space for research training available to the primary mentor and trainee) and signatures of the primary mentor, department or division head and the fiscal officer responsible for administering the grant on the face page.
Closing Date: Mid-October
Funding: Private
Contributor: The Francis Family Foundation
No. of awards given last year: 15
No. of applicants last year: 55

Parkinson's
Disease
Foundation
Hope through Research • Education • Advocacy

THE PARKINSON'S DISEASE SOCIETY OF THE UNITED KINGDOM (PDS)

215 Vauxhall Bridge Road, London, SW1V 1EJ, England
Tel: (44) 20 7931 8080
Fax: (44) 20 7233 9908
Email: research@parkinsons.org.uk
Website: www.parkinsons.org.uk
Contact: Ms Catherine Fleming, Research Officer

The Parkinson's Disease Society of the United Kingdom (PDS) works with people who have Parkinson's disease, their families and health and social care professionals. The mission of the PDS is, through research, the conquest of Parkinson's disease and the alleviation of the suffering and distress it causes. The work of the PDS includes research into the cause, cure and prevention of the disease, improvements in treatments, and a helpline staffed by nurses offering advice on all aspects of Parkinson's disease including drug treatments, surgery, therapies, social and healthcare rights, benefits, driving, insurance and employment. The PDS also provides a wide range of publications, audio tapes and videos, a comprehensive education and training programme and a national network of field staff, branches and welfare visitors offering local information, support, advice and social activities.

PDS Research Project Grant

Subjects: Medical sciences, neurology, neurosciences, biochemistry, toxicology, pathology, genetics, geriatrics and pharmacy.
Purpose: To support research into the causes, cure and prevention of Parkinson's disease, its care and effective treatments.
Eligibility: The Parkinson's Disease Society supports Biomedical, Health and Social Care and Social Policy research and wishes to encourage research related to improving the quality of life for people with Parkinson's. Applications are invited for project grants for up to 3 years. Grants are tenable only at a United Kingdom University or NHS Trust or statutory Social Care organization.
Level of Study: Postdoctorate, professional development, research
Type: Project grant
Value: To include at least one salary plus consumables and equipment
Length of Study: Up to 3 years
Frequency: Annual
Study Establishment: A recognized research institution, university or hospital in the United Kingdom
Country of Study: United Kingdom
No. of awards offered: Varies
Application Procedure: Applicants must complete an application form, which is available from the Society's website.
Closing Date: Please refer to the website (mid-April & mid-September)
Funding: Private
Contributor: Donations
No. of awards given last year: 13
Additional Information: For further details visit the Society's website.

PDS Training Fellowships

Subjects: Medical sciences, neurology, neurosciences, biochemistry, toxicology, pathology, genetics, geriatrics and pharmacy.
Purpose: To support research into the causes, cure and prevention of Parkinson's disease, its care and effective treatments.
Eligibility: Fellowships are available to appropriately qualified professionals working in the UK.
Level of Study: Doctorate
Type: Fellowship
Value: UK £55,000 for non-clinical, UK £105,000 for clinical
Length of Study: Up to 3 years
Frequency: Annual
Study Establishment: A recognized teaching, research or clinical institution in the United Kingdom
Country of Study: United Kingdom
No. of awards offered: Varies
Application Procedure: Applicants must complete an application form, which is available from the Society's website.
Closing Date: Please refer to PDS website
Funding: Private
Contributor: Donations

Additional Information: The Society is currently implementing a new research strategy. For further details visit the Society's website.

PARTICLE PHYSICS AND ASTRONOMY RESEARCH COUNCIL (PPARC)

Polaris House, North Star Avenue, Swindon, Wiltshire, SN2 1SZ, England
Tel: (44) 1793 442000
Fax: (44) 1793 442125
Email: steve.cann@pparc.ac.uk
Website: www.pparc.ac.uk
Contact: Mr Steve Cann, E & T Section

The PPARC is the UK's strategic science investment agency. By directing, coordinating and research, education and training in particle physics and astronomy, PPARC delivers world leading science, technologies and people for the UK.

PPARC Advanced Fellowships

Subjects: Particle physics, astronomy and solar system science.
Level of Study: Postdoctorate
Type: Fellowship
Value: All agreed salary, travel and subsistence, equipment, additional costs, and a UK £1,500 stipend
Frequency: Annual
Country of Study: United Kingdom
No. of awards offered: 13
Application Procedure: Applications for a PPARC Fellowship must be submitted using the Je-S system.
Closing Date: October 13th
Additional Information: You may undertake up to a maximum of six hours teaching, including preparation each working week.

PPARC CASE Studentship

Subjects: Science, engineering.
Purpose: To give promising students experience outside a purely academic environment.
Eligibility: Advice on eligibility should be sought from the Registrar's Office.
Level of Study: Postgraduate
Type: Studentship
Value: Tuition fees only.
Length of Study: 3 months–3 years
Frequency: Annual
Country of Study: United Kingdom
Application Procedure: Contact the PPARC.
Closing Date: October 1st
Funding: Commercial

For further information contact:

Tel: 1793 442026
Email: steve.cann@pparc.ac.uk
Contact: Steve Cann

PPARC CASE-plus Studentship

Subjects: Science, engineering.
Purpose: To help students become more effective in promoting technology transfer.
Eligibility: Advice on eligibility should be sought from the Registrar's Office.
Level of Study: Postgraduate
Type: Studentship
Value: Tuition fees only
Length of Study: 3 years
Frequency: Annual
Country of Study: United Kingdom
Application Procedure: Contact the PPARC.
Closing Date: October 1st
Funding: Commercial

For further information contact:

Tel: 1793 442026
Email: steve.cann@pparc.ac.uk
Contact: Steve Cann

PPARC Communications/Media Programme

Subjects: Science communication.
Purpose: To support students undertake communications training.
Level of Study: Postgraduate
Type: Bursary
Value: All tuition fees
Length of Study: 1 academic year
Frequency: Annual
Study Establishment: Any approved university
Country of Study: United Kingdom
Application Procedure: Contact the PPARC Science and Society team.
Closing Date: October 13th

For further information contact:

Tel: 01793 442030
Email: pr.pus@pparc.ac.uk

PPARC Daphne Jackson Fellowships

Subjects: Particle physics, particle astrophysics, solar system science and astronomy.
Purpose: To enable high-level engineers and scientists to return to their professions after a career break for family or other reasons.
Eligibility: Open to promising engineers and scientists who have taken a career break.
Level of Study: Research, postdoctorate
Type: Fellowship
Value: Dependent on age and experience
Length of Study: 2 years
Frequency: Annual
Study Establishment: Any academic institution acceptable to the PPARC
Country of Study: United Kingdom
No. of awards offered: Varies
Application Procedure: Applicants must contact Jennifer Woolley, Trust Director, or Sue Smith, Fellowship Administrator, for application forms and further information.
Closing Date: Please write for details
Funding: Government
Additional Information: The Daphne Jackson Fellowship is also administered by the BBSRC and the EPSRC.

For further information contact:

The Daphne Jackson Trust, Department of Physics, University of Surrey, Guildford, Surrey, GU2 7XH, England
Tel: (44) 14 8368 9166

PPARC Exploring Entrepreneurship Programme

Subjects: Science communication.
Purpose: To support PhD Students develop skills, knowledge and insight into innovation and entrepreneurship.
Level of Study: Doctorate
Type: Bursary
Value: Tuition fees
Frequency: Biennial
Country of Study: United Kingdom
Application Procedure: See website.
Closing Date: October 13th

PPARC Gemini Studentship

Subjects: Astronomy.
Purpose: To enable promising South-American students to pursue a PhD in Great Britain.
Eligibility: Open to students from Argentina, Brazil or Chile only.
Level of Study: Doctorate

Type: Fellowship
Value: Agreed tuition costs and a maintenance allowance
Length of Study: 3 years
Frequency: Annual
Country of Study: United Kingdom
No. of awards offered: 3
Application Procedure: See website.
Closing Date: March 31st

PPARC Postdoctoral Fellowships

Subjects: Particle physics, astronomy and solar system science.
Level of Study: Postgraduate
Type: Fellowship
Value: All agreed salary, travel and subsistence, equipment, additional costs, and UK £1,500 stipend
Frequency: Annual
Country of Study: United Kingdom
No. of awards offered: 14
Application Procedure: Applications for a PPARC Fellowship must be submitted using the Je-S system.
Closing Date: October 13th
Additional Information: You may undertake up to a maximum of six hours teaching, including preparation each working week.

PPARC Postgraduate Studentships

Subjects: Particle physics, particle astrophysics, solar system science and astronomy.
Eligibility: Open to postgraduates from the United Kingdom and European Union countries.
Level of Study: Postgraduate
Type: Studentship
Length of Study: Up to 3 years
Frequency: Annual
Study Establishment: Any academic institution that is acceptable to the PPARC
Country of Study: United Kingdom
No. of awards offered: Approx. 185
Application Procedure: Applicants must refer to the PPARC website for application information.
Closing Date: July 31st
Funding: Government
Additional Information: Further information is available on request by emailing studentships@pparc.ac.uk

PPARC Research Grants in Astronomy and Particle Physics

Subjects: Particle physics, particle astrophysics, solar system science and astronomy.
Eligibility: For requirements please refer to the website.
Level of Study: Postdoctorate, research
Value: Varies
Study Establishment: Any academic institution that is acceptable to the PPARC
Country of Study: United Kingdom
No. of awards offered: Varies
Application Procedure: Applicants must refer to the PPARC website for application information.
Funding: Government

PPARC Senior Research Fellowships

Subjects: Particle physics, astronomy and solar system science.
Eligibility: Candidates should normally have completed five years in a permanent post at lecturer or above level.
Level of Study: Postdoctorate
Type: Fellowship
Value: All agreed salary, travel and subsistence, equipment additional costs, and a UK £2,000 stipend
Length of Study: 3 years
Frequency: Annual
Country of Study: United Kingdom
No. of awards offered: 7
Application Procedure: Applications for a PPARC Fellowship must be submitted using the Je-S system.
Closing Date: October 13th
Additional Information: You may undertake up to a maximum of six hours teaching, including preparation each working week.

PPARC Short Stays in European Centres Programme

Subjects: Particle physics, astronomy and solar system science.
Eligibility: Open to postgraduate students under 35 years of age.
Level of Study: Doctorate
Type: Studentship
Value: All agreed fees
Length of Study: 3 months–1 academic year
Frequency: Annual
Study Establishment: An approved Marie Curie Training Site
Application Procedure: See website.
Closing Date: October 13th
Funding: Government
Contributor: European Commission

PPARC Spanish (IAC) Studentship

Subjects: Astronomy.
Purpose: To support students of the Instituto de Astrofiscia de Canarias (IAC), Tenerite, Spain pursuing a PhD in Great Britain.
Eligibility: Open to Spanish students of the Instituto de Astrofiscia de Canarias (IAC) only.
Level of Study: Doctorate
Type: Studentship
Value: Agreed tuition costs and a maintenance allowance
Length of Study: 3 years
Frequency: Annual
Country of Study: United Kingdom
No. of awards offered: 2
Application Procedure: See website.
Closing Date: March 31st

PPARC Standard Research Studentship

Subjects: Science, engineering.
Purpose: To enable promising scientists and engineers to continue training.
Eligibility: Advice on eligibility should be sought from the Registrar's Office.
Level of Study: Postgraduate
Type: Studentship
Value: Tuition fees only
Length of Study: 1–3 years
Frequency: Annual
Country of Study: United Kingdom
Application Procedure: Contact the PPARC.
Closing Date: March 31st

For further information contact:

Tel: 1793 442026
Email: steve.cann@pparc.ac.uk
Contact: Steve Cann

PPARC Summer School

Subjects: Astronomy, solar terrestrial physics, theoretical elementary particle physics and elementary particle physics.
Level of Study: Graduate
Type: Studentship
Value: Tuition fees
Frequency: Annual
Country of Study: United Kingdom
Application Procedure: See website.
Closing Date: October 13th

PPARC UK Grad Programme

Subjects: Research skills relating to science.
Purpose: To enable research students to take control of their future.
Level of Study: Graduate
Type: Studentship
Value: All tuition fees

Length of Study: 1 academic year
Frequency: Annual
Study Establishment: Joint Research council Graduate School
Country of Study: United Kingdom
Application Procedure: See website.
Closing Date: October 13th

Robert Skills Training Funds

Subjects: Research.
Purpose: To support the promotion of generic and transferable skills training for research students.
Level of Study: Research, doctorate, postgraduate
Type: Grant
Value: Tuition fees
Frequency: Annual
Country of Study: United Kingdom
Application Procedure: See website.
Closing Date: October 13th

PATERSON INSTITUTE FOR CANCER RESEARCH

Christie Hospital NHS Trust, Manchester, M20 4BX, England
Tel: (44) 16 1446 3136
Fax: (44) 16 1446 3109
Email: gcowling@picr.man.ac.uk
Website: www.paterson.man.ac.uk
Contact: Dr Graham Cowling

The Paterson Institute for Cancer Research is a Cancer Research UK-funded centre for cancer research and forms the research arm of a specialist cancer hospital, the Christie Hospital NHS Trust. It carries out cancer research in a large number of areas and has 16 research groups and around 200 scientists.

Paterson 4-Year Studentship

Subjects: Molecular and cellular basis of cancer and translational cancer research.
Purpose: To support study towards a PhD.
Eligibility: Open to candidates who have obtained a First or Second Class (Honours) Bachelor of Science Degree. International First or 2.1 degree equivalent in biological science, medicine, or related subject.
Level of Study: Doctorate, postgraduate
Type: Studentship
Value: UK £12,500 as stipend per year, university fees and bench fees
Length of Study: 4 years
Frequency: Annual, 3 times per year
Study Establishment: The University of Manchester
Country of Study: United Kingdom
No. of awards offered: Up to 10 per year
Application Procedure: www.paterson.man.ac.uk for details and download application form.
Closing Date: 1st week of January, (1st week of May)
Funding: Private
Contributor: Cancer Research UK
No. of awards given last year: 8
No. of applicants last year: 350
Additional Information: All positions are advertised on the website. Self-funded students are accepted subject to qualifications and 3-year funding. Please use application form (website).

For further information contact:

Postgraduate Tutor, Paterson Institute
Email: gcowling@picr.man.ac.uk

THE PAUL & DAISY SOROS FELLOWSHIP PROGRAM

400 west 59th street, New York, 10019, United States of America
Tel: (1) 212 547 6926
Fax: (1) 212 548 4623
Email: pdsoros-fellows@sorasny.org
Website: www.pdsoros.org

The Paul & Daisy Soros Fellowship for New Americans

Subjects: Any subject.
Purpose: To provide opportunities for continuing generations of able and accomplished New Americans to achieve leadership in their chosen fields.
Eligibility: Open to New Americans: resident aliens (Green Card Holders) naturalized U.S. citizens and/or children of two naturalized parents.
Level of Study: Postdoctorate
Type: Fellowship
Value: US$20,000–30,000
Length of Study: 2 years
Study Establishment: Any accredited graduate University in the United States
Country of Study: United States of America
No. of awards offered: 30
Application Procedure: Apply online.
Closing Date: November 1st
Funding: Private
Contributor: Paul and Daisy Soros
No. of awards given last year: 30
No. of applicants last year: 84

THE PAUL FOUNDATION

Apeejay House, 15 Park Street, Kolkata 700 016, West Bengal, India
Tel: (91) 033 22295455
Website: www.thepaulfoundation.org

The Paul Foundation has been conceived to promote the individuals quest for intellectual excellence. To pursue higher studies in India and abroad, the Foundation supports those Indians who have shown ability in their specific areas of interest, to give them an opportunity to develop their potential and be recognized as leaders.

The Paul Foundation Postgraduate Scholarship

Subjects: Humanities, social sciences, basic sciences, applied sciences, law, management, medicine, engineering, fine arts and the performing arts.
Purpose: To encourage outstanding scholars who have the ability to produce thoughtful and thought-provoking work and make a difference to society.
Eligibility: Open to applicants who are Indian citizens and have completed their graduation from a UGC-recognized Indian university.
Level of Study: Postgraduate, doctorate
Type: Scholarship
Frequency: Annual
Country of Study: Any country
Application Procedure: A completed application form must be submitted.
Closing Date: February 28th
Funding: Foundation

THE PAULO CELLO COMPETITION

PL 1105, Helsinki, FIN-00101, Finland
Tel: (358) 4 0528 4876
Fax: (358) 9 2243 2879
Email: cello@paulo.fi
Website: www.cellocompetitionpaulo.org
Contact: Administrative Assistant

The Paulo Cello Competition organizes an international competition for cellists of all nations.

International Paulo Cello Competition

Subjects: Cello performance.
Eligibility: Open to cellists between 16 and 33 years of age.
Level of Study: Unrestricted
Type: Competition
Value: The 1st prize is €15,000, the 2nd prize is €12,000, the 3rd prize is €9,000 and the 4th, 5th and 6th prizes are €2,000
Frequency: Every 5 years

Country of Study: Finland
No. of awards offered: 6
Application Procedure: Applicants must write for a brochure, which contains details of the application and audition pieces.
Funding: Private
Contributor: The Paulo Foundation
No. of awards given last year: 6
No. of applicants last year: 66

PEN AMERICAN CENTER

588 Broadway, Suite 303, New York, NY 10012, United States of America
Tel: (1) 212 334 1660
Fax: (1) 212 334 2181
Email: pen@pen.org;awards@pen.org
Website: www.pen.org

PEN American Center is a fellowship of writers dedicated to to advance literature, depend free expression and foster international fellowship. The American Center is the largest of 141 international PEN centers worldwide.

The PEN Translation Fund Award

Subjects: Translations of works of fiction, creative nonfiction, poetry and drama.
Purpose: The fund seeks to encourage translators to undertake projects they might not otherwise have had the means to attempt.
Eligibility: Works that have not previously appeared in English or have appeared only in an egregiously flawed translation are eligible.
Level of Study: Unrestricted
Type: Grant
Value: US$2,000–10,000
Frequency: Annual
Application Procedure: All applications must include the cover sheet with all the items filled in, a sample of the translation and a curriculum vitae of the translator. Seven hard copies of the translation with the completed applications must be submitted. Visit website: www.pen.org
Closing Date: January 15th
Funding: Private
Additional Information: Anthologies with multiple translators, works of literary criticism and scholarly or technical texts do not qualify.

For further information contact:

Director of Literary Awards Translation Fund, PEN American Center
Email: peter@pen.org
Contact: Peter G Meyer

PEN Writer's Fund

Subjects: Writing and translation.
Purpose: To assist professional published writers facing emergency situations.
Eligibility: Open to published professional writers and produced playwrights who have a traceable record of writing and publication.
Level of Study: Unrestricted
Type: Grant
Value: Up to US$2,000
Frequency: Every 3 months
Country of Study: Any country
Application Procedure: Applicants must submit an application consisting of a two-page form, published writing samples, documentation of financial emergency, including bills, etc. and a professional curriculum vitae.
Closing Date: Applications are accepted at any time
Funding: Private
Additional Information: A separate fund exists for writers and editors with AIDS who are in need of emergency assistance. The funds are not for research purposes, to enable writers to complete unfinished projects, or to fund writing publications or organizations. Grants and loans are for unexpected emergencies only, for the support of working writers. PEN American Center also offers numerous annual awards to published writers to recognize distinguished writing, editing and translation.

PENN HUMANITIES FORUM

University of Pennsylvania 3619 Locust Walk, Philadelphia, PA, 19104-6213, United States of America
Tel: (1) 215 898 8220
Fax: (1) 215 746 5946
Email: humanities@sas.upenn.edu
Website: www.humanities.sas.upenn.edu
Contact: Jennifer Conway, Associate Director

The Penn Humanities Forum promotes interdisciplinary collaboration across University of Pennsylvania departments and schools and between the University and the Philadelphia region. Each year, a broad topic sets the theme for a research seminar for resident and visiting scholars, courses and public events involving Philadelphia's cultural institutions.

Mellon Postdoctoral Fellowships in the Humanities

Subjects: Humanities.
Purpose: To support research by untenured junior scholars.
Eligibility: Open to junior scholars who, at the time of application, have received a PhD (degree must be in hand no later than December of the year preceding the fellowship) but have not held it for more than 8 years nor been granted tenure. Applicants may not be tenured during the year of the fellowship. Research proposals must relate to the Forum's annual topic of study and are invited in all areas of humanistic studies, except educational curriculum-building and the performing arts. Other requirements include residency at the University of Pennsylvania and the teaching of one freshman seminar in each of the two semesters.
Level of Study: Postdoctorate
Type: Fellowship
Value: US$42,000 plus health insurance
Length of Study: 1 academic year, non-renewable
Frequency: Annual
Study Establishment: The University of Pennsylvania
Country of Study: United States of America
No. of awards offered: 5
Application Procedure: Applicants must complete an application form, which can be downloaded from the Forum's website.
Closing Date: October 1st
Funding: Private
No. of awards given last year: 5
No. of applicants last year: 200
Additional Information: Fellows may not normally hold other awards concurrently.

THE PERRY FOUNDATION

31 Rossendale, Chelmsford, Essex, CM1 2UA, England
Tel: (44) 12 4526 0805
Fax: (44) 12 4526 0805
Email: david.naylor@blueyonder.co.uk
Website: www.perryfoundation.co.uk
Contact: Mr D J Naylor, Secretary and Chief Executive

The Perry Foundation offers research awards and postgraduate scholarships in agriculture and related disciplines. Research awards are offered to universities and institutes in the United Kingdom and are normally for a 3-year period. Postgraduate scholarships are offered to holders of First or Second Class Degrees and are for a 3-year period leading to a PhD. Both research awards and postgraduate scholarships must be undertaken at a university, college or research establishment in the United Kingdom.

Perry Postgraduate Scholarships

Subjects: The production and utilization of crops for food and non-food uses, ecologically acceptable and sustainable farming systems, including, in particular, water and nutrient balances, integrated disease and pest control systems for both crops and livestock, socio-economic studies in the occupation and use of land, the rural economy and infrastructure and developments in marketing. Projects must be of definable benefit to United Kingdom agriculture.
Purpose: To enable postgraduates to undertake research and investigate work into agriculture and related fields and to build up a pool of highly competent researchers in the United Kingdom.
Eligibility: Applicants must hold a First or Upper Second Class (Honours) Degrees in appropriate subjects, and must who have been offered a place at a university, college or other establishment that will lead to the award of a PhD.
Level of Study: Doctorate
Type: Postgraduate scholarships
Value: UK £12,000 p.a. maintenance stipend, UK £3,085 p.a. tuition fees, plus bench fees to a maximum of UK £2,500 per academic year
Length of Study: 3 years
Frequency: Dependent on funds available
Study Establishment: Universities, colleges, research establishments and institutes in the U.K.
Country of Study: United Kingdom
No. of awards offered: 3–4 per year
Application Procedure: Applicants must write to or email the Foundation Secretary requesting an application form. Full details will be provided to suitable applicants.
Closing Date: November 30th
Funding: Private
No. of awards given last year: 2
No. of applicants last year: 100+
Additional Information: Projects must be of definable benefit to United Kingdom agriculture.

Perry Research Awards

Subjects: The production and utilization of crops for food and non-food uses, ecologically acceptable and sustainable farming systems, including, in particular, water and nutrient balances, integrated disease and pest control systems for both crops and livestock, socio-economic studies in the occupation and use of land, the rural economy and infrastructure and developments in marketing. Must be of definable benefit to United Kingdom agriculture.
Purpose: To support research projects at research establishments, universities and colleges in the United Kingdom and investigative work into agriculture and related fields.
Eligibility: Open to holders of First or Upper Second Class (Honours) Degrees in appropriate subjects, gained at a university in the United Kingdom.
Level of Study: Research
Type: Scholarship and Research award
Value: Research awards are normally UK £15,000 per year maximum
Length of Study: Normally 3 years
Frequency: Dependent on funds available
Study Establishment: Universities, colleges, institutes and research establishments
Country of Study: United Kingdom
No. of awards offered: 3–4, depending on the availability of funds
Application Procedure: Applicants must write to the Foundation Secretary for a brochure, which contains details of the application procedure and application forms. Applications submitted by individuals must be supported by their university, college, institute or other establishment.
Closing Date: November 30th for the postgraduate scholarships and October 31st for the research awards
Funding: Private
No. of awards given last year: 1
No. of applicants last year: More than 100 each year
Additional Information: The research awards must be of definable benefit to United Kingdom agriculture.

PETSAVERS

Woodrow House, 1 Telford Way, Waterwells Business Park, Quedgeley, Gloucestershire, GL2 2AB, England
Tel: (44) 14 5272 6700
Fax: (44) 14 5272 6701
Email: adminoff@bsava.com
Website: www.bsava.com
Contact: M J Berriman, Administrator

Petsavers was established in 1975 to promote clinical investigations into the many unsolved diseases of dogs, cats, rabbits and other small animals. In the past 20 years, Petsavers has given over UK £1 million towards numerous clinical studies, clinical research studentships and residencies. The British Small Animal Veterinary Association supports Petsavers with its administration costs, enabling all donations to benefit pets.

Petsavers Award

Subjects: Small animal veterinary medicine and surgery.
Purpose: To advance the science of small animal medicine and surgery.
Eligibility: Open to veterinary surgeons currently working in United Kingdom universities, centres of learning or veterinary practices.
Level of Study: Postgraduate, professional development
Type: Award
Value: Varies
Length of Study: 1–3 years
Frequency: Annual
Study Establishment: Universities, veterinary schools and veterinary practices
Country of Study: United Kingdom
No. of awards offered: Varies
Application Procedure: Applicants must write for details. An application can be downloaded from the petsaver website or from the association headquarters.
Closing Date: September 15th
Funding: Trusts, private
Contributor: Donations by practice clients
No. of awards given last year: 1
No. of applicants last year: 13
Additional Information: Projects must involve clinical cases only and no experimental animals.

PFIZER INC.

Pfizer MAP Program, Psymark Communications, 33 Main Street, Old Saybrook, CT, 06475, United States of America
Tel: (1) 800 201 1214
Website: www.promisingminds.com

As a reflection of our commitment to the advancement of healthcare, Pfizer Inc. is pleased to support medical innovation in a wide range of discipline through our Medical and Academic Partnership (MAP) grants and awards. Our Fellowships and Scholar Grants, which offer at career-building opportunities for academic researchers in basic, outcomes, and patient-oriented research, are key among these efforts. In addition, Pfizer Visiting Professorships continue to be a resource for in-depth, clinically focused exchange between medical scholars, host organizations and outside scholar-scientists. At Pfizer, we are proud to support the innovators and ideas that help make better treatments and cures possible.

AASM/Pfizer Professorships in Sleep Medicine

Subjects: Medicine.
Purpose: To provide opportunities for a academic institutions to host a recognized expert for three days for educational exchange.
Eligibility: Open to U.S. medical schools and/or teaching hospitals with clear educational objectives.
Level of Study: Professional development
Type: Grant
Value: US$7,500
Length of Study: 3 days
Frequency: Annual

Country of Study: United States of America
No. of awards offered: 8
Application Procedure: See the website.
Closing Date: January 27th
Funding: Corporation
Contributor: Pfizer Inc. and American Academy of Sleep Medicine (AASM)

ACCF/Pfizer Visiting Professorships in Cardiovascular Medicine

Subjects: Medicine.
Purpose: To provide opportunities for academic institutions to host a recognized expert for three days of educational exchange.
Eligibility: Open to U.S. medical schools and/or teaching hospitals.
Level of Study: Professional development
Type: Grant
Value: US$7,500
Length of Study: 3 days
Frequency: Annual
Country of Study: United States of America
No. of awards offered: 8
Application Procedure: See the website.
Closing Date: January 27th
Funding: Corporation
Contributor: The American College of Cardiology Foundation (ACCF) and Pfizer Inc.

AUAER/Pfizer Visiting Professorships in Urology

Subjects: Medicine.
Purpose: To provide opportunities for academic institutions to host a recognized expert for 3 days of educational exchange.
Eligibility: Open to U.S. medical schools and/or teaching hospitals.
Level of Study: Professional development, postgraduate
Type: Grant
Value: US$7,500
Frequency: Annual
Country of Study: United States of America
No. of awards offered: Up to 10
Application Procedure: See the website.
Closing Date: January 27th
Funding: Corporation
Contributor: The American Urological Association Education and Research Inc.

Pfizer Atorvastatin Research Awards Program

Subjects: Medicine.
Purpose: To support outstanding investigators at the early stages of their careers in academic research.
Eligibility: Open to U.S citizens who hold an M.D. or PhD.
Level of Study: Research
Type: Grant
Value: US$50,000
Length of Study: 2 years
Frequency: Annual
No. of awards offered: 20
Application Procedure: A proposal must be submitted. See the website for further information.
Closing Date: March 15th
Funding: Corporation

Pfizer Detrol LA Research Awards Program

Subjects: Urology.
Purpose: To support basic science investigations pertaining to any aspect of antimuscarinic therapy.
Eligibility: Open to all postdoctoral and clinical fellows.
Level of Study: Research
Type: Grant
Value: US$50,000
Frequency: Annual
No. of awards offered: 10
Application Procedure: A completed form must be submitted either online or by mail.

For further information contact:

Med point communications, Inc. 1603 Orrington Are Suite 1900, Evanston, IL 60201
Contact: Melissa Shapiro

Pfizer Fellowship in Biological Psychiatry

Subjects: Biological psychiatry.
Purpose: To provide training opportunities for promoting young physicians who wish to pursue research in an academic environment.
Eligibility: Open to applicants who are the citizens of the United States.
Level of Study: Postdoctorate
Type: Grant
Value: US$65,000
Length of Study: 3 years
Frequency: Annual
Application Procedure: A complete form must be submitted.
Closing Date: March 1st

For further information contact:

UF college of medicine, 392-5398, United States of America
Contact: Dr Kristen Madsen, Director, Grants Program Development

Pfizer Fellowships in Health Literary Clear Health Communication

Subjects: Medicine, health administration.
Purpose: To fund scientific research in health literary/clear health communication.
Eligibility: Open to US citizens who have undergone atleast one year of postdoctoral clinical training.
Level of Study: Professional development, doctorate
Type: Fellowship
Value: US$130,000
Length of Study: 2 years
Frequency: Annual
No. of awards offered: 1
Application Procedure: See the website.
Closing Date: January 6th
Funding: Corporation

The Pfizer Fellowships in Infectious Diseases

Subjects: Medicine.
Purpose: To support the career development of talented junior physician-scientists.
Eligibility: Open to U.S. Citizens who have at least one year of postdoctoral clinical training.
Level of Study: Postdoctorate, postgraduate
Type: Fellowship
Value: US$130,000
Length of Study: 2 years
Frequency: Annual
No. of awards offered: 2
Application Procedure: See the website.
Closing Date: January 6th
Funding: Commercial
Additional Information: Applications must demonstrate a strong career interest in academic infectious diseases.

The Pfizer Fellowships in Rheumatology/Immunology

Subjects: Rheumatology and immunology.
Purpose: To provide training opportunities for promising young physicians who wish to pursue research in an academic environment.
Eligibility: Open to applicants who demonstrate a strong career interest in academic research in rheumatology and immunology.
Level of Study: Postgraduate, postdoctorate
Type: Fellowship
Value: US$65,000
Length of Study: 3 years
Frequency: Annual
Application Procedure: See the website.
Closing Date: January 15th
Funding: Commercial

For further information contact:

VF College of Medicine, 392-5398
Contact: Dr Kristen Madsen, Director, Grants Program Development

Pfizer International HDL Research Awards Program
Subjects: Biology.
Purpose: To support outstanding investigators in the field of HDL biology.
Type: Grant
Value: US$110,000 per year
Length of Study: 2 years
Frequency: Annual
Application Procedure: See the website.
Closing Date: See the website
No. of awards given last year: 14

For further information contact:

International HDL Research Awards, 335 W. 16th Street., 4th Floor, New York, United States of America
Contact: Grants Co-ordinator

Pfizer Scholar's Grant in Clinical Epidemiology
Subjects: Epidemiology.
Purpose: To support the cancer development in epidemiology.
Eligibility: Open to individuals who are pursuing research in epidemiology relevant to human health.
Level of Study: Postgraduate
Type: Grant
Value: US$130,000
Length of Study: 2 years
Frequency: Annual
No. of awards offered: Up to 2
Application Procedure: A completed application form must be submitted.
Closing Date: January 6th
Funding: Commercial

Pfizer Scholars Grants in Public Health
Subjects: Health administration.
Purpose: To support the career development of faculty.
Eligibility: Open to US citizens who demonstrate that at least 75% their professional time will be devoted to research.
Level of Study: Postgraduate, professional development
Type: Grant
Value: US$130,000
Length of Study: 2 years
Frequency: Annual
No. of awards offered: Up to 2
Application Procedure: See the website.
Closing Date: January 6th

Pfizer Visiting Professorship in Neurology
Subjects: Neurology.
Purpose: To bring new educational value to the institution.
Eligibility: Open to accredited U.S. medical schools and/or affiliated teaching hospitals.
Level of Study: Postgraduate, professional development
Type: Grant
Value: US$7,500 each
Length of Study: 3 days
Frequency: Annual
No. of awards offered: Up to 8
Application Procedure: See the website.
Closing Date: January 27th
Contributor: Pfizer Inc.

Pfizer Visiting Professorships in Clear Health Literacy/ Clear Health Communication
Subjects: Health administration.
Purpose: To facilitate in-depth, educationally focused visits by prominent experts to U.S. healthcare organizations.
Eligibility: Open to U.S. medical schools and/or teaching hospitals.
Level of Study: Professional development
Type: Grant
Value: US$7,500 each
Length of Study: 3 days
Frequency: Annual
No. of awards offered: Up to 10
Application Procedure: See the website.
Funding: Corporation

Pfizer Visiting Professorships in Diabetes
Subjects: Endocrinology.
Purpose: To bring new educational value to the institution.
Eligibility: Open to all accredited U.S. medical schools (allopathic or osteopathic).
Level of Study: Professional development, postgraduate
Type: Grant
Value: US$7,500 each
Length of Study: 3 days
Frequency: Annual
No. of awards offered: Up to 8
Application Procedure: See the website.
Closing Date: January 27th

Pfizer Visiting Professorships in Oncology
Subjects: Oncology.
Purpose: To advance oncology.
Eligibility: Open to accredited US. Medical schools, teaching hospitals and/or academic or community cancer centers.
Level of Study: Professional development, postgraduate
Type: Grant
Value: US$7,500
Length of Study: 3 days
Frequency: Annual
No. of awards offered: Up to 10
Application Procedure: See the website.
Closing Date: January 27th
Funding: Corporation

Pfizer Visiting Professorships in Pulmonology
Subjects: Pulmonology.
Purpose: To bring new educational value to the institution.
Eligibility: Open to accredited US. Medical schools and/or affiliated teaching hospitals.
Level of Study: Postgraduate, professional development
Type: Grant
Value: US$7,500 each
Length of Study: 3 days
Frequency: Annual
No. of awards offered: Up to 8
Application Procedure: See the website.
Closing Date: January 27th

Pfizer Visiting Professorships Program
Subjects: Medicine.
Purpose: To create opportunities for selected institutions to invite a distinguished expert for three days of teaching.
Eligibility: Open to accredited medical schools and/or affiliated teaching hospitals.
Level of Study: Postgraduate
Type: Grant
Value: US$7,500 each
Frequency: Annual
No. of awards offered: Up to 10
Application Procedure: Applications available online.
Closing Date: January 27th

The Pfizer/AGS Foundation Junior Faculty Scholars Program
Subjects: Geriatrics.
Purpose: To offer/AGS development programmes.
Eligibility: Open to U.S. citizens who have completed at least one year of geriatric medicine.

Level of Study: Postgraduate
Type: Scholarship
Value: US$65,000 per year
Length of Study: 2 years
Frequency: Annual
No. of awards offered: 2
Application Procedure: A completed application form must be submitted.
Closing Date: December 2nd
Funding: Commercial
Contributor: AGS Foundation for Health in Aging

PHARMACEUTICAL RESEARCH AND MANUFACTURERS OF AMERICA FOUNDATION (PHRMAF)

1615 L Street NW, Suite 1260, Washington, DC, 20036, United States of America
Tel: (1) 202 572 7756
Fax: (1) 202 572 7799
Email: foundation@phrma.org
Website: www.phrmafoundation.org
Contact: Ms Eileen M McCarron, Executive Director

The Pharmaceutical Research and Manufacturers of America Foundation (PhRMAF) is a non-profit organization, established in 1965 to promote public health through scientific and medical research. It provides funding for research and for the education and training of scientists and physicians who have selected pharmacology, pharmaceutics, toxicology, informatics or health outcomes as a career choice.

PhRMAF Medical Student Fellowships

Subjects: Pharmacology, toxicology and clinical pharmacology.
Purpose: To support medical, dental or veterinary students who have substantial interests in research and teaching careers in pharmacology or clinical pharmacology and who are willing to work full-time in a specific research effort.
Eligibility: Open to applicants with a firm commitment from a university in the United States of America prior to applying for a PhRMAF award. All applicants must be citizens or permanent residents of the United States of America.
Level of Study: Predoctorate, graduate, postgraduate
Type: Fellowship
Value: Up to US$18,000
Length of Study: 3 months–2 years
Frequency: Annual
Study Establishment: An accredited school of medicine, or dentistry medicine
Country of Study: United States of America
Application Procedure: Applications are to be submitted by the appropriate representative of the applicant's school or university to the Director of Development at PhRMAF. Detailed application requirements are stated on the Foundation's website where the applicant can download an application form and read the specific requirements for each award.
Closing Date: September 1st
Funding: Private
Additional Information: Research projects involving animal subjects require a statement that the project will follow the guidelines set forth by the NIH Guide for the Care and Use of Laboratory Animals and that the project will be performed, reviewed and approved by a faculty committee of the university. The recipient school is expected to submit an annual report on the disposition of the funds awarded by PhRMAF. A final report is due within 60 days after the conclusion of the grant. These reports must be signed by the recipient's sponsor. Any publications, speeches, presentations and other materials that stem directly from the research supported by this grant must acknowledge the support of PhRMAF. Three reprints of each publication should be forwarded to PhRMAF for further information visit the Foundation's website.

PhRMAF Paul Calabresi Medical Student Research Fellowship

Subjects: Pharmacology, toxicology and clinical pharmacology.
Purpose: To support medical/dental students who have substantial interests in research and teaching careers in pharmacology/clinical pharmacology and who are willing to work full time in a specific research effort.
Eligibility: A candidate must be enrolled in a United States medical/dental school and have finished at least one year of the school curriculum. Priority consideration will be given to those candidates who project strong commitments to careers in the field of clinical pharmacology. Applicants must be citizens or permanent residents of the US.
Level of Study: Graduate, postgraduate, predoctorate
Study Establishment: An accredited school of medicine or dentistry.
Country of Study: United States of America
Application Procedure: Requests for the Paul Calabresi Medical Student Research Fellowship are to be submitted online by the appropriate representative of the school or university.
Closing Date: October 1st
Funding: Private
No. of awards given last year: 3

PhRMAF Postdoctoral Fellowships in Health Outcomes Research

Subjects: Health outcomes research, patient-reported outcomes or pharmacoeconomics.
Purpose: To support well-trained graduates from PharmD, MD and PhD programmes who seek to further develop and refine their research skills through formal postdoctoral training.
Eligibility: Open to full-time students who are citizens or permanent residents of the United States of America. Applicants must have a firm commitment from a university in the United States of America before applying for a PhRMAF award. The department's chair will be expected to verify the applicant's doctoral candidacy.
Level of Study: Graduate, postdoctorate, postgraduate
Type: Fellowship
Value: US$40,000 stipend per year
Length of Study: 1–2 years
Frequency: Annual
Study Establishment: An accredited school of medicine, pharmacy, dentistry, public health or nursing
Country of Study: United States of America
No. of awards offered: Varies
Application Procedure: Applications must include a research plan written by the applicant, the mentor's research record and a description of how the mentored experience will enhance the applicant's career development in health outcomes research. Applications are to be submitted online by the appropriate representative of the school or university to the Executive Director at PhRMAF. Detailed application requirements are stated on the Foundation's website where applicants can download an application form and read the specific requirements for each award.
Closing Date: October 1st
Funding: Private

PhRMAF Postdoctoral Fellowships in Informatics

Subjects: Informatics.
Purpose: To support well-trained graduates from PhD programmes who seek to further develop and refine their informatics research skills through formal postdoctoral training.
Eligibility: Open to full-time students who are citizens or permanent residents of the United States of America. Applicants must have a firm commitment from a university in the United States of America before applying for a PhRMAF award. The department's chair will be expected to verify the applicant's doctoral candidacy.
Level of Study: Postdoctorate
Type: Fellowship
Value: US$40,000 per year
Length of Study: 1–2 years
Frequency: Annual
Country of Study: United States of America
No. of awards offered: Varies

Application Procedure: Applicants must submit an application including a research plan written by the applicant, the mentor's research record and a description of how the mentored experience will enhance the applicant's career development in informatics. Applications are to be submitted online by the appropriate representative of the school or university to the Executive Director of at PhRMAF. Detailed application requirements are stated on the Foundation's website where the applicant can download an application form and read the specific requirements for each award.
Closing Date: September 1st
Funding: Private
Additional Information: Research projects involving animal subjects require a statement that the project will follow the guidelines set forth by the NIH Guide for the Care and Use of Laboratory Animals and that the project will be performed, reviewed and approved by a faculty committee of the university.

PhRMAF Postdoctoral Fellowships in Pharmaceutics

Subjects: Pharmaceutics.
Purpose: To encourage graduates to continue to develop and refine their pharmaceutics research skills through formal postdoctoral training.
Eligibility: Open to graduates from PhD programmes in pharmaceutics. Before an individual is eligible to apply for a PhRMAF award, the applicants must first have a firm commitment from a university in the United States of America. Applicants must be full-time students, and the department's chair is expected to verify the applicant's doctoral candidacy. All applicants must be citizens of the United States of America or permanent residents.
Level of Study: Postdoctorate, postgraduate
Type: Fellowship
Value: US$40,000 stipend per year
Length of Study: 1–2 years
Frequency: Annual
Study Establishment: Schools of pharmacy in the United States of America
Country of Study: United States of America
No. of awards offered: Varies
Application Procedure: Applicants must visit the Foundation's website where detailed application requirements are stated and application forms can be downloaded. Applications must include a research plan written by the applicant, the mentor's research record and a description of how the mentored experience will enhance the applicant's career development in pharmaceutics. Applications are to be submitted online by the appropriate representative of the school or university to the Executive Director at PhRMAF.
Closing Date: October 1st
Funding: Private
Additional Information: Research projects involving animal subjects require a statement that the project will follow the guidelines set forth by the NIH Guide for the Care and Use of Laboratory Animals and that the project will be performed, reviewed and approved by a faculty committee of the university.

PhRMAF Postdoctoral Fellowships in Pharmacology/ Toxicology

Subjects: Pharmacology and toxicology.
Purpose: To facilitate career entry into pharmacology or toxicology at the level of postdoctoral training and to provide funding for recent graduates from PhD programmes who seek to develop research skills through formal postdoctoral training.
Eligibility: Open to applicants with a firm commitment from a university in the United States of America, prior to applying for a PhRMAF award. Applications must be submitted online by an accredited United States of America school and all applicants must be citizens of the United States of America or permanent residents.
Level of Study: Postdoctorate
Type: Fellowship
Value: US$40,000 stipend per year
Length of Study: 1–2 years
Frequency: Annual
Study Establishment: An accredited school of medicine, pharmacy, dentistry or veterinary medicine
Country of Study: United States of America
No. of awards offered: Varies
Application Procedure: Applicants must visit the Foundation's website where detailed application requirements are stated and application forms can be downloaded. Applications must be submitted online by the appropriate representative of the school or university to the Executive Director at PhRMAF. An application must include a research plan written by the applicant, a mentor's research record and a description of how the mentored experience will enhance the applicant's career development on pharmacology or toxicology.
Closing Date: September 1st
Funding: Private
Additional Information: Research projects involving animal subjects require a statement that the project will follow the guidelines set forth by the NIH Guide for the Care and Use of Laboratory Animals and that the project will be performed, reviewed and approved by a faculty committee of the university.

PhRMAF Predoctoral Fellowships in Health Outcomes Research

Subjects: Health outcomes research, patient-reported outcomes and pharmacoeconomics.
Purpose: To support a student's PhD doctoral programme after coursework has been completed and the remaining training activity is the student's research project.
Eligibility: Open to applicants who have a firm commitment from a university in the United States of America. Applicants must be full-time students and the department's chair is expected to verify the applicant's doctoral candidacy. All applicants must be citizens of the United States of America or permanent residents.
Level of Study: Postgraduate
Type: Fellowship
Value: A stipend of US$20,000 per year, up to US$500 per year may be used for expenses associated with thesis preparation
Length of Study: 1–2 years
Frequency: Annual
Study Establishment: An accredited school of medicine, pharmacy, dentistry, public health or nursing
Country of Study: United States of America
No. of awards offered: Varies
Application Procedure: Applications are to be submitted online by the appropriate representative of the school or university to the Executive Director at PhRMAF. Detailed application requirements are stated on the Foundation's website where the applicant can download an application form and read the specific requirements for each award.
Closing Date: October 1st
Funding: Private
Additional Information: Research projects involving animal subjects require a statement that the project will follow the guidelines set forth by the NIH Guide for the Care and Use of Laboratory Animals and that the project will be performed, reviewed and approved by a faculty committee of the university.

PhRMAF Predoctoral Fellowships in Pharmaceutics

Subjects: Pharmaceutics.
Purpose: To support promising students during their thesis research.
Eligibility: Open to full-time students and citizens or permanent residents of the United States of America. Applicants must have a firm commitment from a university in the United States of America prior to applying for a PhRMAF award and the department's chair will be expected to verify the applicant's doctoral candidacy.
Level of Study: Postgraduate
Type: Fellowship
Value: A stipend of US$20,000 per year, which includes up to US$500 for expenses associated with thesis research
Length of Study: 1–2 years
Frequency: Annual
Study Establishment: A school of pharmacy
Country of Study: United States of America
No. of awards offered: Varies
Application Procedure: Applicants must visit the Foundation's website where detailed application requirements are stated and application forms can be downloaded. Applications must be submitted

online by the appropriate representative of the school or university to the Executive Director of at PhRMAF.
Closing Date: October 1st
Funding: Private
Additional Information: Research projects involving animal subjects require a statement that the project will follow the guidelines set forth by the NIH Guide for the Care and Use of Laboratory Animals and that the project will be performed, reviewed and approved by a faculty committee of the university.

PhRMAF Predoctoral Fellowships in Pharmacology/ Toxicology

Subjects: Pharmacology and toxicology.
Purpose: To support promising students during their thesis research.
Eligibility: Open to advanced students who have completed the bulk of their pre-thesis requirements and are starting their thesis research by the time the award is activated. Students just starting graduate school should not apply. Before an individual is eligible to apply for a PhRMAF award, the applicant must have a firm commitment from a university in the United States of America. The applicant must be a citizen or permanent resident of the United States of America.
Level of Study: Predoctorate
Type: Fellowship
Value: A stipend of US$20,000 per year, which includes up to US$500 for expenses associated with thesis research
Length of Study: 1–2 years
Frequency: Annual
Study Establishment: An accredited school of medicine, pharmacy, dentistry or veterinary medicine
Country of Study: United States of America
No. of awards offered: Varies
Application Procedure: Applicants must visit the Foundation's website where detailed application requirements are stated and application forms can be downloaded. Applications must be submitted online by the appropriate representative of the school or university to the Executive Director at PhRMAF.
Closing Date: September 1st
Funding: Private
Additional Information: Research projects involving animal subjects require a statement that the project will follow the guidelines set forth by the NIH Guide for the Care and Use of Laboratory Animals and that the project will be performed, reviewed and approved by a faculty committee of the university.

PhRMAF Research Starter Grants in Health Outcomes Research

Subjects: Health outcomes research, patient-reported outcomes and pharmacoeconomics.
Purpose: To support individuals beginning independent research careers in academia.
Eligibility: Open to applicants sponsored by the school or university at which the research is to be conducted. Applicants must be appointed to an entry level tenure track or equivalent permanent position in a department or unit responsible for pharmaceutical activities as part of its core mission. All applicants must be citizens or permanent residents of the United States of America.
Level of Study: Graduate, postgraduate
Type: Grant
Value: US$30,000 per year
Length of Study: 1–2 years
Frequency: Annual
Study Establishment: An accredited school of medicine, pharmacy, dentistry, public health or nursing
Country of Study: United States of America
No. of awards offered: Varies
Application Procedure: Applicants must visit the Foundations' website where detailed application requirements are stated and application forms can be downloaded. Applications must be submitted online by the appropriate representative of the school or university to the Executive Director of Development at PhRMAF. The description of an applicant's career goals and the departmental chair's description of institutional support for the applicant's salary are all important while evaluating an application.
Closing Date: October 1st
Funding: Private
Additional Information: Research projects involving animal subjects require a statement that the project will follow the guidelines set forth by the NIH Guide for the Care and Use of Laboratory Animals and that the project will be performed, reviewed and approved by a faculty committee of the university.

PhRMAF Research Starter Grants in Informatics

Subjects: Informatics.
Purpose: To offer support to new investigators beginning their independent research careers in academia at the faculty level.
Eligibility: Open to applicants sponsored by the school or university at which the research is to be conducted. Applicants must be appointed online to an entry level tenure track or equivalent permanent position in a department or unit responsible for informatics activities as part of its core mission. All applicants must be citizens or permanent residents of the United States of America.
Level of Study: Postdoctorate, postgraduate, graduate
Type: Grant
Value: US$30,000 per year
Length of Study: 1–2 years
Frequency: Annual
Country of Study: United States of America
No. of awards offered: Varies
Application Procedure: Applicants must visit the Foundation's website where detailed application requirements are stated and application forms can be downloaded. Applications must be submitted online by the appropriate representative of the school or university to the Executive Director at PhRMAF. The description of an applicant's career goals and the departmental chair's description of institutional support for the applicant's salary are all important while evaluating an application.
Closing Date: September 1st
Funding: Private
Additional Information: Research projects involving animal subjects require a statement that the project will follow the guidelines set forth by the NIH Guide for the Care and Use of Laboratory Animals and that the project will be performed, reviewed and approved by a faculty committee of the university.

PhRMAF Research Starter Grants in Pharmaceutics

Subjects: Pharmaceutics.
Purpose: To offer support to new investigators beginning their independent research careers in academia.
Eligibility: Open to applicants sponsored by the school or university at which the research is to be conducted. Applicants must be appointed to an entry level tenure track or equivalent permanent position in a department or unit responsible for pharmaceutical activities as part of its core mission. All applicants must be citizens or permanent residents of the United States of America.
Level of Study: Postgraduate, graduate, postdoctorate
Type: Grant
Value: US$30,000 per year
Length of Study: 1–2 years
Frequency: Annual
Study Establishment: Schools of pharmacy
Country of Study: United States of America
No. of awards offered: Varies
Application Procedure: Applicants must visit the website where detailed application requirements are stated and application forms can be downloaded. Applications must be submitted online by the appropriate representative of the school or university to the Executive Director at PhRMAF. The description of an applicant's career goals and the departmental chair's description of institutional support for the applicant's salary are all important while evaluating an application.
Closing Date: October 1st
Funding: Private
Additional Information: Research projects involving animal subjects require a statement that the project will follow the guidelines set forth by the NIH Guide for the Care and Use of Laboratory Animals and that the project will be performed, reviewed and approved by a faculty committee of the university.

PhRMAF Research Starter Grants in Pharmacology/ Toxicology

Subjects: Pharmacology and toxicology.
Purpose: To support individuals beginning independent research careers in academia.
Eligibility: Open to applicants sponsored by the school or university at which the research is to be conducted. Applicants must be appointed to an entry level tenure track or equivalent permanent position in a department or unit responsible for pharmacology or toxicology activities as part of its core mission. All applicants must be citizens or permanent residents of the United States of America.
Level of Study: Postdoctorate, graduate, postgraduate
Type: Grant
Value: US$30,000 per year
Length of Study: 1–2 years
Frequency: Annual
Study Establishment: An accredited school of medicine, pharmacy, dentistry or veterinary medicine
Country of Study: United States of America
Application Procedure: Applicants must visit the website where detailed application requirements are stated and application forms can be downloaded. Applications must be submitted online by the appropriate representative of the school or university to the Executive Director of at PhRMAF. The description of an applicant's career goals and the departmental chair's description of institutional support for the applicant's salary are all important while evaluating an application.
Closing Date: September 1st
Funding: Private
Additional Information: Research projects involving animal subjects require a statement that the project will follow the guidelines set forth by the NIH Guide for the Care and Use of Laboratory Animals and that the project will be performed, reviewed and approved by a faculty committee of the university.

PhRMAF Sabbatical Fellowships in Health Outcomes Research

Subjects: Health outcomes research, patient-reported outcomes and pharmacoeconomics.
Purpose: To support faculty members at all levels with active research programmes and the opportunity to work at other institutions to learn new skills or develop new collaborations that will enhance their research and research training activities in health outcomes.
Eligibility: Open to citizens or permanent residents of the United States of America. Applicants are expected to have approval for a sabbatical leave from their home institution and to provide an endorsement from the mentor who will sponsor their visiting scientific activity. Matching funds must be provided through the university.
Level of Study: Professional development, postdoctorate, postgraduate
Type: Fellowship
Value: A stipend of up to US$40,000
Length of Study: 6 months–1 year
Frequency: Annual
Study Establishment: An accredited school of medicine, pharmacy, dentistry, public health or nursing
Country of Study: United States of America
No. of awards offered: Varies
Application Procedure: Applications are to be submitted online by the appropriate representative of the school or university to the Executive Director at PhRMAF. Detailed application requirements are stated on the Foundation's website where applicants can download an application form and read the specific requirements for each award.
Closing Date: October 1st
Funding: Private
Additional Information: Research projects involving animal subjects require a statement that the project will follow the guidelines set forth by the NIH Guide for the Care and Use of Laboratory Animals and that the project will be performed, reviewed and approved by a faculty committee of the university.

PhRMAF Sabbatical Fellowships in Informatics

Subjects: Informatics.
Purpose: To give faculty members at all levels with active research programmes an opportunity to work at other institutions and to develop new collaborations that will enhance their research and research training activities in informatics.
Eligibility: Applicants are expected to have approval for a sabbatical leave from their home institution and provide an endorsement from the mentor who will sponsor their visiting scientific activity. Matching funds must be provided through the university. All applicants must be citizens of the United States of America or permanent residents.
Level of Study: Postgraduate, professional development, postdoctorate
Type: Fellowship
Value: Up to US$40,000 stipend
Length of Study: 6 months–1 year
Frequency: Annual
Country of Study: United States of America
No. of awards offered: Varies
Application Procedure: Applications are to be submitted online by the appropriate representative of the school or university to the Executive Director of at PhRMAF. Detailed application requirements are stated on the Foundation's website where the applicant can download an application form and read the specific requirements for each award.
Closing Date: September 1st
Funding: Private
Additional Information: Research projects involving animal subjects require a statement that the project will follow the guidelines set forth by the NIH Guide for the Care and Use of Laboratory Animals and that the project will be performed, reviewed and approved by a faculty committee of the university.

PhRMAF Sabbatical Fellowships in Pharmaceutics

Subjects: Pharmaceutics.
Purpose: To enable pharmaceutics faculty members at all levels with active research programmes an opportunity to work at other institutions and to develop new collaborations that will enhance their research and research training activities in pharmaceutics.
Eligibility: Open to citizens of the United States of America or permanent residents. Applicants are expected to have approval for a sabbatical leave from their home institution and provide an endorsement from the mentor who will sponsor their sabbatical activity. Matching funds must be provided through the university.
Level of Study: Professional development, postdoctorate, postgraduate
Type: Fellowship
Value: A stipend of up to US$40,000
Length of Study: 6 months–1 year
Frequency: Annual
Study Establishment: An approved institute
Country of Study: United States of America
Application Procedure: Applicants must visit the Foundation's website where detailed application requirements are stated and application forms can be downloaded. Applications must be submitted online by the appropriate representative of the school or university to the Executive Director of at PhRMAF.
Closing Date: October 1st
Funding: Private
Additional Information: Research projects involving animal subjects require a statement that the project will follow the guidelines set forth by the NIH Guide for the Care and Use of Laboratory Animals and that the project will be performed, reviewed and approved by a faculty committee of the university.

PhRMAF Sabbatical Fellowships in Pharmacology/ Toxicology

Subjects: Pharmacology and toxicology.
Purpose: To give faculty members at all levels with active research programmes an opportunity to work at other institutions to learn new skills or develop new collaborations that will enhance their research and research training activities in pharmacology or toxicology.
Eligibility: Open to applicants with approval for sabbatical leave from their home institution and who can provide an endorsement from the mentor who will sponsor their visiting scientific activity. Matching funds must be provided through the university. All applicants must be citizens or permanent residents of the United States of America.

Level of Study: Professional development, postgraduate, postdoctorate
Type: Fellowship
Value: Up to US$40,000 stipend
Length of Study: 6 months–1 year
Frequency: Annual
Study Establishment: An accredited school of medicine, pharmacy, dentistry or veterinary medicine
Country of Study: United States of America
No. of awards offered: Varies
Application Procedure: Applicants must visit the Foundation's website where detailed application requirements are stated and application forms can be downloaded. Applications must be submitted online by the appropriate representative of the school or university to the Executive Director of at PhRMAF.
Closing Date: September 1st
Funding: Private
Additional Information: Research projects involving animal subjects require a statement that the project will follow the guidelines set forth by the NIH Guide for the Care and Use of Laboratory Animals and that the project will be performed, reviewed and approved by a faculty committee of the university.

THE PHI BETA KAPPA SOCIETY

1606 New Hampshire Avenue NW, Washington, DC, 20009, United States of America
Tel: (1) 202 265 3808
Fax: (1) 202 986 1601
Email: esozzi@pbk.org
Website: www.pbk.org
Contact: Eugenia Sozzi, Awards Co-ordinator

The Phi Beta Kappa Society has pursued its mission of fostering and recognizing excellence in the liberal arts and sciences since 1776.

Mary Isabel Sibley Fellowship

Subjects: French language or literature in even-numbered years and Greek language, literature, history or archaeology in odd-numbered years.
Purpose: To recognize female scholars who have demonstrated their ability to carry out original research.
Eligibility: Open to unmarried women aged 25–35 who have demonstrated their ability to carry out original research. Candidates must hold the doctorate or have fulfilled all the requirements for the doctorate except the dissertation. There are no restrictions as to nationality and the award is not restricted to members of the Phi Beta Kappa Society.
Level of Study: Postgraduate, doctorate, postdoctorate
Type: Fellowship
Value: US$20,000
Length of Study: 1 year, non-renewable
Frequency: Annual
Country of Study: Any country
No. of awards offered: 1
Application Procedure: Applicants must complete an application form, available from the Society, and submit this with transcripts and references.
Closing Date: January 15th
Funding: Private
No. of awards given last year: 1
No. of applicants last year: 50

The Walter J Jensen Fellowship for French Language, Literature and Culture

Subjects: French language, literature and culture.
Purpose: To help educators and researchers improve education in Standard French language, literature and culture and in the study of Standard French in the United States of America.
Eligibility: Candidates must be under 40 years of age and must be able to certify their career that will involve active use of the French language.
Level of Study: Postgraduate
Type: Fellowship
Value: US$10,000, with additional support available for airfare and, if applicable, support of dependant(s)
Length of Study: This 1-year-long fellowship includes 6 months of residence and study
Frequency: Annual
Country of Study: France
No. of awards offered: 1 per year
Application Procedure: Applicants must complete self-managed application form and submit it along with academic records, references, plans for study and proof of superior competence in French according to the standards established by the American Association for Teachers of French.
Closing Date: October 1st of each year
Funding: Private
Contributor: Dr Walter J Jensen
No. of awards given last year: None
No. of applicants last year: None
Additional Information: Preference may be given to, though the eligibility is not restricted to, members of Phi Beta Kappa and teachers at the high school level or above. Standard French is defined to exclude a focus on Creole, Quebecois and other dialects.

PHILHARMONIA ORCHESTRA/MARTIN MUSICAL SCHOLARSHIP FUND

Beeches, Well Hill, Chelsfield, Kent, BR6 7PR, England
Tel: (44) 19 5953 2299
Fax: (44) 19 5953 2299
Email: info@philharmonia.co.uk
Website: www.philharmonia.co.uk
Contact: Mr Martyn Jones, Administrator

Emanual Hurwitz Award for Violinists of British Nationality

Subjects: Musical performance on violin only.
Purpose: To reward exceptional musical talent.
Eligibility: Open to British nationals only.
Level of Study: Postgraduate
Type: Award
Value: Varies
Frequency: Annual
Country of Study: Any country
No. of awards offered: Varies
Application Procedure: Applicants must write for details.
Closing Date: Please contact the organization

John E Mortimer Foundation Awards

Subjects: Musical performance on all instruments.
Purpose: To reward exceptional musical talent.
Eligibility: Applicants must write for details.
Level of Study: Postgraduate
Type: Award
Value: Prizes of varying value
Frequency: Annual
Country of Study: Any country
No. of awards offered: Varies
Application Procedure: Applicants must complete an application form and submit this with a stamped addressed envelope and a non-returnable registration fee of UK £10.
Closing Date: December 1st

June Allison Award

Subjects: Musical performance on woodwind only.
Purpose: To assist exceptional musical talent with specialist and advanced study, and to help bridge the gap between study and fully professional status.
Eligibility: Applicants must write for details.
Level of Study: Postgraduate
Type: Award
Value: UK £500 plus recital
Frequency: Annual

Country of Study: Any country
Application Procedure: Applicants must complete an application form and submit this with a stamped addressed envelope and a non-returnable registration fee of UK £10.
Closing Date: December 1st

Martin Musical Scholarships
Subjects: Musical performance.
Purpose: To assist exceptional musical talent with specialist and advanced study and to help in bridging the gap between study and fully professional status.
Eligibility: Open to practising musicians as well as students who are instrumental performers, including pianists, preparing for a career on the concert platform either as a soloist or orchestral player, and are of no more than 25 years of age. Preference is given to United Kingdom citizens.
Level of Study: Postgraduate
Type: Scholarship
Value: Varies
Length of Study: 2 years, with a possibility of renewal
Frequency: Annual
No. of awards offered: Varies
Application Procedure: Applicants must complete an application form.
Closing Date: October 1st
Funding: Private
No. of awards given last year: 50
No. of applicants last year: 71
Additional Information: It is not the present policy of the Fund to support organists, singers, conductors, composers, academic students or piano accompanists.

Reginald Conway Memorial Award for String Performers
Subjects: Musical performance on strings only.
Purpose: To reward exceptional musical talent.
Eligibility: Applicants must write for details.
Level of Study: Postgraduate
Type: Award
Value: Varies
Frequency: Annual
Country of Study: Any country
Application Procedure: Applicants must write for details.
Closing Date: Please contact the organization

Sidney Perry Scholarship
Subjects: Musical performance.
Purpose: To support postgraduate study.
Eligibility: Open to nationals of any country.
Level of Study: Postgraduate
Type: Scholarship
Value: Varies
Length of Study: Up to 2 years
Frequency: Annual
Country of Study: Any country
No. of awards offered: Varies
Application Procedure: Applicants must complete an application form.
Closing Date: October 1st
No. of awards given last year: 3

Trevor Snoad Memorial Trust
Subjects: Music performance on the viola.
Purpose: To reward exceptional musical talent.
Eligibility: Open to outstanding viola players. There is no limit to the number of times an unsuccessful candidate may apply. Each candidate is eligible to apply for two awards.
Level of Study: Postgraduate
Type: Award
Value: UK £500
Frequency: Annual
Country of Study: Any country
No. of awards offered: 1
Application Procedure: Applicants must complete an application form.
Closing Date: October 1st
No. of awards given last year: 1
No. of applicants last year: 3
Additional Information: An award is valid for 2 years and must be taken up within that time. Candidates are selected by audition. Preliminary auditions are held in the Autumn with final auditions in the Spring.

PHILLIPS EXETER ACADEMY

20 Main Street, Exeter, NH, 03833-2460,
United States of America
Tel: (1) 603 777 3405
Fax: (1) 603 777 4393
Email: beggers@exeter.edu
Website: www.exeter.edu
Contact: Ms Barbara Eggers, Dean of Faculty

Phillips Exeter Academy is a private secondary school with over 1,000 students.

George Bennett Fellowship
Subjects: Creative writing.
Purpose: To allow a person commencing a career as a writer the time and freedom from material considerations to complete a manuscript in progress.
Eligibility: Preference is given to writers who have not published a book with a major commercial publisher. Works must be in English.
Level of Study: Unrestricted
Type: Fellowship
Value: US$10,000 per year
Frequency: Annual
Study Establishment: Phillips Exeter Academy, Exeter, NH
Country of Study: United States of America
No. of awards offered: 1
Application Procedure: Applicants must send a manuscript, together with an application form, personal statement and US$5.
Closing Date: December 1st for the following academic year
Funding: Private
No. of awards given last year: 1
No. of applicants last year: 150
Additional Information: Duties include being in residence for 1 academic year while working on the manuscript and informal availability to student writers. For further information, please visit the Academy's website, www.Exeter.edu

THE PKD FOUNDATION

9221 Ward Parkway, Suite 400, Kansas City, MO, 64114-3367,
United States of America
Tel: (1) 816 931 2600 or (1) 800 PKD CURE
Fax: (1) 816 931 8655
Email: pkdcure@pkdcure.org
Website: www.pkdcure.org
Contact: Administrative Assistant

The PKD Foundation is the only organization worldwide solely devoted to promoting research into finding a cure for polycystic kidney disease (PKD) and to improving the care and treatment of those affected by it.

PKD Foundation Grant-In-Aid
Subjects: The cause of PKD and possible treatments and a cure.
Purpose: To encourage researchers to conduct a research on PKD.
Eligibility: Research Grants are open to basic and clinical principal investigators with quality projects relevant to finding a treatment and/or cure for PKD. Research Fellowships are open to promising post-doctoral researchers who have the potential to become productive, independent investigators in PKD research.
Level of Study: Postdoctorate, predoctorate, doctorate, research, graduate

Type: Research grant or fellowship
Value: Research Grants: US$65,000 per year; fellowships: US$50,000 per year
Length of Study: 2-years, renewable for a 3rd year, pending scientific review and availability of funding
Frequency: Annual
Country of Study: Any country
No. of awards offered: Approximately 40, dependent on funding
Application Procedure: Application must not exceed a total of 18 pages; otherwise, it will be returned without review. Application guidelines will be available on the PKD foundation website after April 1st. Late applications will not be accepted. Please visit the website for complete application information.
Closing Date: August 1st
Funding: Individuals, foundation, corporation, trusts, private
Contributor: Individuals
No. of awards given last year: 46
No. of applicants last year: 71

PLASTIC SURGERY EDUCATIONAL FOUNDATION (PSEF)

444 East Algonquin Road, Arlington Heights, IL, 60005, United States of America
Tel: (1) 847 228 9900
Fax: (1) 847 228 9131
Email: ml@plasticsurgery.org
Website: www.plasticsurgery.org
Contact: Ms Mary Lewis

The mission of the Plastic Surgery Educational Foundation (PSEF) is to develop and support domestic and international education as well as research and public service activities of plastic surgeons.

Plastic Surgery Basic Research Grant

Subjects: Plastic surgery.
Purpose: To encourage young investigators to conduct clinical research.
Eligibility: Open to plastic surgeons and holders of an MD or PhD working in plastic surgery. Residents, Fellows and non-members of the ASPRS or the PSEF require the sponsorship of a member or candidate from the ASPRS or the PSEF or the American Society for Aesthetic Plastic Surgery membership.
Level of Study: Postgraduate, professional development
Value: Research seed money up to US$5,000
Length of Study: 1 year
Frequency: Annual
Country of Study: Any country
No. of awards offered: Approx. 20
Application Procedure: Applicants must complete an application available on the website.
Closing Date: Mid-January
Funding: Private
Contributor: The Plastic Surgery Educational Foundation

Plastic Surgery Research Fellowship Award

Subjects: Cranofacial reconstructive, cleft lip and palate, paediatric reconstruction.
Purpose: To encourage research and academic career development in plastic and reconstructive surgery.
Eligibility: Open to surgical residents or Fellows, plastic surgery residents planning to interrupt their training for a research experience or recent residency graduates wishing to supplement their clinical training with a research experience. Residents, Fellows and non-members of the ASPS or the PSEF require the sponsorship of a member or candidate for membership of the ASPS or the PSEF.
Level of Study: Professional development, postgraduate
Type: Fellowship
Value: US$30,000
Length of Study: 1 year
Frequency: Annual
Country of Study: Any country
No. of awards offered: 2
Application Procedure: Applicants must complete an application available on the website.
Closing Date: November 15th
Funding: Corporation, trusts
Contributor: Lyndon Peer and Fresh Start Surgical Gifts
No. of awards given last year: 3

PSEF Scientific Essay Contest

Subjects: Plastic surgery.
Eligibility: Open to persons involved in research in the field of plastic surgery.
Level of Study: Postgraduate, professional development
Type: Prize
Value: US$500–3,000
Length of Study: 1 year
Frequency: Annual
Country of Study: Any country
No. of awards offered: 8
Application Procedure: Applicants must submit manuscripts that contain the results of original clinical or basic science research in an area of importance to plastic and reconstructive surgery. Information on essay content and format are available on the website.
Closing Date: February 15th
Funding: Corporation, trusts
Contributor: Bernard G Sarnat MD, D Ralph Millard from the Plastic Surgery Society and the Plastic Surgery Educational Foundation, Integra Foundation
No. of awards given last year: 8
No. of applicants last year: 24
Additional Information: Check on Medicine Professionals, then check on Research.

For further information contact:

Website: www.plasticsurgery.org

PLAYMARKET

P.O. Box 9767 Te Aro, Wellington, New Zealand
Tel: (64) 4 382 8462
Fax: (64) 4 382 8461
Email: info@playmarket.org.nz
Website: www.playmarket.org.nz
Contact: Ms Dilys Grant, Director

Playmarket was founded in 1973 to assist New Zealand playwrights with a professional production of their scripts. For 25 years Playmarket has offered script assessment, development and agency services. Playmarket is at the heart of New Zealand theatre and its focus is on playwrights.

The Bruce Mason Playwriting Award

Subjects: Playwriting.
Purpose: To recognize achievement at the beginning of a career.
Eligibility: Open to all potential applicants.
Level of Study: Unrestricted
Type: Award
Value: New Zealand $7,000
Length of Study: 1 year
Frequency: Annual
Country of Study: New Zealand
No. of awards offered: 1
Application Procedure: Applicants can obtain full details of the competition directly from playmarket.
Closing Date: October
Funding: Commercial
Contributor: Independent Newspapers Limited
No. of awards given last year: 1
No. of applicants last year: 13
Additional Information: It is expected that the award will be used to write or complete a work for the theatre.

For further information contact:

Playmarket, Level 2, 16 Cambridge Terrace, Wellington, PO BOX 9767

POLLOCK-KRASNER FOUNDATION, INC.

863 Park Avenue, New York, NY, 10021,
United States of America
Tel: (1) 212 517 5400
Fax: (1) 212 288 2836
Email: grants@pkf.org
Website: www.pkf.org
Contact: Programme Officer

The Pollock-Krasner Foundation's mission is to aid, internationally, those individuals who have worked as professional artists over a significant period of time.

Pollock-Krasner Foundation Grant

Subjects: Painting, sculpting, print-making, mixed media and installation art.
Purpose: To aid, internationally, individual artists of artistic merit with financial need.
Eligibility: Applicants may be painters, sculptors, print-makers, mixed media or installation artists. The Foundation has no age or geographic limits. Commercial artists, photographers, film-makers, craft-makers and students are not eligible.
Level of Study: Professional development
Type: Grant
Frequency: Annual
Application Procedure: Applicants must write, fax or email to the Foundation for an application and guidelines.
Closing Date: There is no deadline as grants are awarded throughout the year
Funding: Private
Additional Information: The Foundation does not fund academic study.

PONDICHERRY UNIVERSITY

R.V. Nagar Kalapet Pondicherry 605014 Tamil Nadu, India
Website: www.pondiuni.org

The Pondicherry University, which was established in 1985 by the Government of India, is a teaching-cum-affiliating central University. The University is known for its advanced teaching leading to in-depth research, consultancy and extension activities.

Government of Pondicherry Fellowship

Subjects: Any subject.
Purpose: To provide financial assistance to students.
Eligibility: Open to students who are residents/natives of Pondicherry.
Level of Study: Doctorate
Type: Fellowship
Value: Rs 800/- per month and an annual contingency of Rs 3,000/- for 2 candidates pursuing research in Tamil/French leading to PhD.
Frequency: Annual
Study Establishment: The Pondicherry University
Country of Study: India
No. of awards offered: 2
Application Procedure: A written application should be submitted for approval by the university authority.
Contributor: Government of Pondicherry

Pondicherry Junior Research Fellowship

Subjects: Any subject.
Purpose: To provide financial assistance to students.
Eligibility: The candidates must not be more than 28 years of age with a minimum of 55% marks in a postgraduate degree or equivalent examination.
Level of Study: Doctorate, postgraduate
Type: Fellowship
Value: Rs 8,000/- per month for 2 years, enhanced to Rs 9,000 on completion of 2 years; also eligible for a contingent grant of Rs 20,000/- per year
Length of Study: 2 years
Study Establishment: The Pondicherry University
Country of Study: India
Application Procedure: Application must submit written application.

Pondicherry Merit Scholarship

Subjects: Any subject.
Eligibility: Candidates must secure the highest percentage of marks in the postgraduate entrance examination.
Type: Scholarship
Value: Rs 500/- per month for semester 1 only
Length of Study: 2 years
Study Establishment: The Pondicherry University
Country of Study: India
Application Procedure: Applicants must submit a written application subject to the approval of the university.

Pondicherry Merit-Cum-Means Scholarship

Subjects: Any subject.
Purpose: To provide financial assistance to students.
Eligibility: Annual parental income of the student should not exceed Rs 30,000/-.
Level of Study: Postgraduate
Type: Scholarship
Value: Rs 500/- per month for semester 1
Length of Study: 2 years
Frequency: Annual
Study Establishment: The Pondicherry University
Country of Study: India
No. of awards offered: 10% of the students in each degree programme are eligible for this award.
Application Procedure: Written application to be submitted for approval by the university.

PONTIFICAL INSTITUTE OF MEDIEVAL STUDIES

59 Queen's Park Crescent East, Toronto, ON, M5S 2C4, Canada
Tel: (1) 416 926 7290
Fax: (1) 416 926 7276
Email: sheila.campbell@utoronto.ca
Website: www.pims.ca

Council of the Institute Awards

Subjects: Medieval studies.
Eligibility: Open to scholars engaged in medieval studies.
Level of Study: Postdoctorate
Type: Bursary and scholarship
Value: Varies, depending on funds available
Length of Study: 1 year
Frequency: Annual
Study Establishment: The Institute
Country of Study: Canada
No. of awards offered: Varies
Application Procedure: Applicants must complete an application form, available on request.
Closing Date: January 15th
Additional Information: The Institute also offers a small number of research associateships annually, without stipend, to postdoctoral students and senior scholars who wish to use the Institute's library for their research.

THE POPULATION COUNCIL

Policy Research Division, One Dag Hammarskjold Plaza,
New York, NY, 10017, United States of America
Tel: (1) 212 339 0500
Fax: (1) 212 755 6052
Email: ssfellowship@popcouncil.org
Website: www.popcouncil.org
Contact: Fellowship Co-ordinator

The Population Council is an international non-profit, non-governmental institution that seeks to improve the well being and reproductive health of current and future generations around the world and to help achieve a humane, equitable and sustainable balance between people and resources. The Council conducts biomedical, social science and public health research and helps build research capacities in developing countries.

Health and Population Innovation Fellowship Program

Subjects: Varies.
Purpose: To support mid-career individuals who have innovative ideas and the capacity to help shape public debate in the field of population, rights and reproductive health.
Level of Study: Professional development, postdoctorate
Type: Fellowship
Length of Study: 1 year
Frequency: Annual
Study Establishment: The Population Council, New Delhi
Country of Study: India
No. of awards offered: 12
Application Procedure: Request application form.
Closing Date: September 15th
Funding: Foundation
Contributor: John D. and Catherine T. MacArthur Foundation
No. of awards given last year: 12

For further information contact:

Population Council, India Habitat Centre, Zone 5A, Ground Floor, Lodi Road, New Delhi, 110003
Tel: +91 11 24642901
Fax: 91 11 24642903
Email: fellowships@pcindia.org
Contact: Komal Saxena

Population Council Fellowships in Population and Social Sciences

Subjects: Population studies including demography and public health in combination with a social science discipline, such as economics, sociology, anthropology, and geography, dealing with the developing world.
Purpose: To make a significant contribution to the advanced training of professionals in the broad field of population studies through the awarding of fellowships on a competitive basis, with particular emphasis on the training of nationals from developing countries.
Eligibility: Predoctoral fellowships are open to applicants who have completed all coursework requirements toward a PhD or an equivalent degree in one of the social sciences in combination with population studies. Applications requesting support for either the dissertation fieldwork or the dissertation writing period will be considered. Postdoctoral fellowships are open to persons having a PhD or equivalent degree who wish to undertake postdoctoral training and research at an institution other than the one at which they received their PhD degree. Awards are open to all qualified persons, but strong preference will be given to applicants from developing countries who have a firm commitment to return home upon completion of their training programmes. Applications by women are particularly encouraged.
Level of Study: Professional development, doctorate, postdoctorate
Type: Fellowship
Value: For predoctoral the value is US$24,000, for postdoctoral US$32,000, and for midcareer the value varies. A monthly stipend based on the type of fellowship and place of study, tuition payments and related fees, transportation expenses for the Fellow only and health insurance are also included. Some research related costs may also be part of the award. Tuition at the postdoctoral and midcareer academic levels is not included in the award
Length of Study: Up to 1 year
Frequency: Annual
Study Establishment: A training or research institution with a strong programme in population studies, regardless of geographic location
Country of Study: Any country
No. of awards offered: 15–20
Application Procedure: Applicants must submit an application and supporting documents in English. Application forms can be obtained from the website. Requests for application forms should include a brief description of candidates' academic and professional qualifications and a short statement about their research or study plans for the proposed fellowship period.
Closing Date: December 15th of each year for notification in March. If the 15th falls on a weekend or holiday then the due date is the next business day
No. of awards given last year: 14
No. of applicants last year: 111
Additional Information: Selection will be based on the recommendation of the Fellowship Committee, which consists of three distinguished Scholars in the field of population. Selection criteria will stress academic excellence and prospective contribution to the population field. Application for independent research funds, or for fieldwork not related to a dissertation, will not be considered. The Bernard Berelson Fellowships are for training at The Population Council's New York office. Prior to submitting a formal application to the Fellowship Office for consideration, the Berelson applicants are required to seek sponsorship from at least one council staff member from the New York office. There are two types of Bernard Berelson Fellowships, which are postdoctoral and midcareer.

Reproductive Biomedicine Postdoctoral Fellowships

Subjects: Physiology and Biochemistry.
Eligibility: Foreign applicants must return to his/her own country up on completion of the fellowship.
Level of Study: Professional development, postdoctorate, doctorate
Type: Fellowship
Length of Study: 1–2 years
Frequency: Annual
Study Establishment: The Population Council's Centre for Biomedical Research
Country of Study: United States of America
No. of awards offered: Varies
Application Procedure: Contact the center for Biomedical Research.
Closing Date: No deadlines for submission
No. of awards given last year: 17

For further information contact:

Center for Biomedical Research, 1230 York Avenue, Box 773, New York, NY 10021

PRADER-WILLI SYNDROME ASSOCIATION UK

125a London Road, Derby, DE1 2QQ, England
Tel: (44) 13 3236 5676
Fax: (44) 13 3236 0401
Email: website@pwsa-uk.demon.co.uk
Website: www.pwsa-uk.demon.co.uk
Contact: Administrative Assistant

PWSA UK Research Grants

Subjects: Prader-Willi syndrome.
Purpose: To improve understanding and/or treatment of Prader-Willi Syndrome.
Level of Study: Unrestricted
Frequency: Dependent on funds available
Country of Study: United Kingdom
Application Procedure: Applicants must write or call the PWSA (UK) for information.
Funding: Private

PREHISTORIC SOCIETY

University College London, Institute of Archaeology, 31-34 Gordon Square, London, WC1H 0PY, England
Fax: (44) 20 7383 2572
Email: prehistoric@ucl.ac.uk
Contact: Ms Tessa Machling, Administrative Assistant

The Prehistoric Society is open to professionals and amateurs alike and has over 2,000 members worldwide. Its main activities are lectures, study tours and conferences and it publishes an annual journal (*PPS*) and a newsletter (*PAST*), which is published three times a year.

Prehistoric Society Conference Fund

Subjects: Archaeology, especially prehistoric.
Purpose: To finance attendance at international conferences.
Eligibility: Preference is given first to scholars from developing countries, whether they are members of the Society or not, then to members of the Society not qualified to apply for conference funds available to university staff. Other members of the Society are also eligible.
Level of Study: Postgraduate
Type: Travel grant
Value: A maximum of UK £250
Length of Study: 1 year, renewals are considered
Frequency: Annual
Country of Study: Any country
No. of awards offered: 2
Application Procedure: Applicants must contact the Honorary Secretary for an application form.
Closing Date: December 31st
Funding: Private
Additional Information: Recipients are required to submit a short report on the conference to *PAST*, the Society's newsletter and their papers for the Society's proceedings if these are not to be included in a conference volume.

Prehistoric Society Research Fund Grant

Subjects: Prehistoric archaeology.
Purpose: To further research in prehistory by excavation or other means.
Eligibility: Open to all members of the Society. The Society may make specific conditions relating to individual applications.
Level of Study: Unrestricted
Type: Grant
Value: At the discretion of the Society
Length of Study: 1 year, renewals are considered
Frequency: Annual
Country of Study: Any country
No. of awards offered: Varies
Application Procedure: Applicants must complete an application form and include the names of two referees in their application.
Closing Date: December 31st
Funding: Private
Additional Information: Awards are made on the understanding that a detailed report will be made to the Society as to how the grant was spent.

Prehistoric Society Research Grant Conference Award

Subjects: Prehistoric archaeology.
Purpose: To fund initial projects and visits to conferences.
Eligibility: There are no eligibility restrictions.
Level of Study: Unrestricted
Value: Varies, but usually under UK £500
Frequency: Annual
Application Procedure: Applicants must complete an application form.
Closing Date: January 1st
Funding: Private

PRESS GANEY ASSOCIATES INC.

404 Columbia Place, South Bend, IN, 46601,
United States of America
Tel: (1) 800 232 8032
Fax: (1) 574 232 3485
Email: kleddy@pressganey.com
Website: www.pressganey.com
Contact: Ms Kelly Leddy, Research Specialist

The Press Ganey Associates, Inc. is the healthcare industry's top satisfaction measurement and improvement firm, serving more than 5,900 healthcare facilities and processing nearly 7,000,000 surveys annually. As one of the industry's market leaders, the company offers one of the world's largest comparative databases and unparalleled benchmarking opportunities.

Press Ganey Best Practices Research Program

Subjects: The subject of the grant is patient satisfaction in all aspects of the healthcare industry.
Purpose: To increase the systematic and rigorous study of patient satisfaction, through the funding of applied research that will identify best practices and that can be used throughout the healthcare industry.
Eligibility: There are no eligibility restrictions.
Level of Study: Research, unrestricted
Value: US$10,000
Frequency: Annual
No. of awards offered: 5
Application Procedure: Applicants must visit the website or email Kelly Leddy at kleddy@pressganey.com for application procedures.
Closing Date: March 14th
Contributor: Press Ganey Associates
No. of awards given last year: 2
No. of applicants last year: 28

PRIMATE CONSERVATION INC.

1411 Shannock Road, Charlestown, RI, 02813-3726,
United States of America
Tel: (1) 401 364 7140
Fax: (1) 401 364 6785
Email: nrowe@primate.org
Website: www.primate.org
Contact: The Grants Administrator

Primate Conservation Inc. gives small grants and matching funds for the conservation projects and studies of the least known and most endangered primates in their natural habitat.

Primate Conservation Inc. Grants

Subjects: Conservation and research projects on the least known and/or most endangered primates in habitat countries with wild populations.
Purpose: To protect and study the least known and/or most endangered primates in their natural habitats.
Eligibility: Applicants must be graduate students, qualified conservationists or primatologists.
Level of Study: Postgraduate, graduate, doctorate, research
Type: Grant
Value: Average US$2,500 maximum US$5,000
Length of Study: 2 months–2 years
Frequency: Twice a year
No. of awards offered: Varies with each funding season
Application Procedure: Applicants must submit a grant proposal on forms that can be downloaded from the website, and submit four copies of the application to the institution's main address. Proposal must be typed, double spaced and in English. One copy of the proposal should be emailed to nrowe@primate.org
Closing Date: September 20th and Febuary 1st
Funding: Private
Contributor: Private donation
No. of awards given last year: 20
No. of applicants last year: 55

PRINCIPALITY OF LIECHTENSTEIN STATE EDUCATIONAL SUPPORT

Government office, Educational Support 9490 Vaduz Principality of Liechtenstein, Switzerland
Tel: (41) 236 7681
Email: office@liechtenstein.li
Website: www.liechtenstein.li

The State provides educational assistance in the form of scholarships, loan, or contributions to expenses. Eligibility is determined on the basis of citizenship and the type of education.

Liechtenstein Scholarships and Loans

Subjects: All subjects.
Purpose: To awaken greater understanding of the Liechtenstein State by the domestic and foreign public.
Eligibility: Open to residents of Liechtenstein, expatriates or those whose mother, father, or spouse is a Liechtenstein citizen are eligible.
Level of Study: Postgraduate
Type: Scholarship
Frequency: Annual
Study Establishment: Liechtenstein Institute, Liechtenstein
Application Procedure: Applicants should first contact their chosen place of study.
Closing Date: No deadline
Funding: Government
Additional Information: All additional loans must be repaid within 6 years of completion of the course of study.

PROGRESSIVE SUPRANUCLEAR PALSY (PSP-EUROPE) ASSOCIATION

The Old Rectory, Wappenham, Towcester,
Northamptonshire, NN12 8SQ, England
Tel: (44) 13 2786 0299
Fax: (44) 13 2786 1007
Email: psp@pspeur.org
Website: www.pspeur.org
Contact: Administrative Assistant

Progressive Supranuclear Palsy (PSP) is a neuro-degenerative disease involving the death of neurons above the nuclei that control balance, movement, vision, speech and ability to swallow. The Progressive Supranuclear Palsy (PSP-Europe) Association is committed to promoting research worldwide into the cause, effective treatment and cure of PSP. Its objectives also include engendering awareness and providing information and support for afflicted families across Europe.

PSP Research Grants

Subjects: The cause effective treatment and cure of PSP.
Purpose: To sponsor research into PSP.
Eligibility: There are no eligibility restrictions.
Level of Study: Postgraduate, doctorate
Type: Research fellowship
Value: Normally less than UK £150,000 per grant
Length of Study: One to three year
Frequency: Annual
Country of Study: Any country
No. of awards offered: One to four each year
Application Procedure: Applications are submitted initially in one A4-page summary of proposed research, length and outline cost, together with a curriculum vitae. Those considered by the Medical Advisory Panel (MAP) to be relevant are then asked to submit a full application, copies of which are forwarded to each member of the MAP, who scores the application. The applications are also put out for peer review. The Chairman of the MAP then briefs the Trustees at the following Executive Committee Meeting, where funds available are assessed and awards made. These Executive Committee Meetings are held in May and November each year.
Closing Date: August 1st and February 1st
Contributor: Donor trusts
No. of awards given last year: 2
No. of applicants last year: 10

PROSTATE RESEARCH CAMPAIGN UK

10 Northfields Prospect, Putney Bridge Road, London,
SW18 1PE, England
Tel: (44) 20 8877 5840
Fax: (44) 20 8877 2609
Email: info@prostate-research.org.uk
Website: www.prostate-research.org.uk
Contact: Chief Executive

Prostate Research Campaign UK is a United Kingdom-registered charity (No. 1037063) that deals with all forms of prostate disease, benign and malignant (cancer). It seeks to limit the damage prostate diseases cause, by funding medical research, raising awareness and providing information. It provides free leaflets, videos, DVDs, a quarterly newsletter and a website.

Prostate Research Campaign UK Research Grants

Subjects: Research into prostate cancer, benign prostatic hyperplasia and prostatitis.
Purpose: To support research into both malignant and benign prostate diseases.
Eligibility: Available to English-speaking nationals of any country, of any mature age, resident in the United Kingdom and wishing to carry out research at a recognized United Kingdom hospital or institution into malignant or benign prostate disease. Bench space in a United Kingdom hospital/institution must be a prior condition for work to be carried out in the United Kingdom.
Level of Study: Professional development, research
Value: 3 categories: UK £10,000, UK £25,000 and UK £50,000
Country of Study: United Kingdom
No. of awards offered: Dependent on funds available
Application Procedure: Advertisements appear once a year in *The British Medical Journal* and *The British Journal Of Urology International* inviting applicants to describe research projects they wish to undertake and to indicate the level of funding sought. Abstracts of the proposed research not longer than two A4 pages, plus the agreement of the finance officer (of the United Kingdom institution where the award is tenable) to administer grant(s), should form part of the submission.
Closing Date: Specified in relevant advertisements
Contributor: Charitable funds raised by Prostate Research Campaign UK
No. of awards given last year: Approx. 20
No. of applicants last year: Approx. 40

PYMATUNING LABORATORY OF ECOLOGY (PLE)

University of Pittsburgh, 13142 Hartstown Road, Linesville, PA,
16424, United States of America
Tel: (1) 814 683 5813
Fax: (1) 814 683 2302
Email: ple@toolcity.net
Website: www.pitt.edu/~biology/pymatuning
Contact: Dr Gail F Johnston, Associate Director

The Pymatuning Laboratory of Ecology (PLE) is a University of Pittsburgh field station dedicated to environmental education and ecological research. Situated on the shores of the Pymatuning Reservoir in North Western Pennsylvania, PLE's land includes woods, wet lands, successional fields and experimental agricultural lands. Researchers from nine institutions conduct projects ranging from community and ecosystem ecology to evolutionary genetics and behaviour.

Darbaker Botany Prize

Subjects: Botany.
Purpose: To award funds for the pursuit of excellent graduate and recent postdoctoral research in botany.
Eligibility: Applicants must be graduate students, recent PhDs or senior researchers initiating new research at PLE.
Level of Study: Doctorate, postdoctorate, postgraduate

Type: Research grant
Value: US$500–1,500
Length of Study: 1 year
Frequency: Annual
Study Establishment: PLE
Country of Study: United States of America
No. of awards offered: 1–3
Application Procedure: Applicants must request guidelines from the PLE or refer to the website.
Closing Date: February 1st
Funding: Private
No. of awards given last year: 1
No. of applicants last year: 2

G M McKinley Research Fund

Subjects: Ecology.
Purpose: To fund research at the graduate and recent postdoctoral level in ecological science.
Level of Study: Postdoctorate, doctorate, postgraduate
Type: Research grant
Value: US$500–3,000
Length of Study: 1 year
Frequency: Annual
Study Establishment: PLE
Country of Study: United States of America
No. of awards offered: 1–5
Closing Date: February 1st
Funding: Private
Contributor: Dr G M McKinley
No. of awards given last year: 8
No. of applicants last year: 10

QUEEN ELISABETH INTERNATIONAL MUSIC COMPETITION OF BELGIUM

20 rue aux Laines, B-1000 Brussels, Belgium
Tel: (32) 2 213 4050
Fax: (32) 2 514 3297
Email: info@qeimc.be
Website: www.qeimc.be
Contact: Secretariat

The Queen Elisabeth International Music Competition of Belgium is a non-profit association, located in Brussels, whose principal aim is to organize major international competitions for music virtuosos. In this way, the competition participates in the Belgian and international music world, and gives its support to young musicians.

Queen Elisabeth International Music Competition of Belgium

Subjects: Music: piano, voice, violin and composition.
Purpose: To provide career support for young pianists, singers, violinists and composers.
Eligibility: Open to musicians of any nationality who are at least 17 years of age and not older than 27 for violin and piano, 30 years of age for singing and 40 for composers. The competition is made up of a first round, a semi-final and a final round.
Level of Study: Unrestricted
Value: A total amounting to more than €80,000
Country of Study: Any country
No. of awards offered: 12
Application Procedure: Applicants must obtain an application form from the Secretariat of the Competition or via the website.
Closing Date: January 15th for instrumental sessions November 10th for composers
Funding: Private
No. of awards given last year: 12
No. of applicants last year: Unrestricted
Additional Information: There are also master classes with jury members.

QUEEN MARGARET UNIVERSITY COLLEGE

Corstorphine Campus, Edinburgh, EH12 8TS, Scotland
Tel: (44) 13 1317 3000
Fax: (44) 13 1317 3256
Website: www.qmuc.ac.uk
Contact: Professor Anthony Cohen, Principal + Vice Patron

Queen Margaret University College provides vocationally relevant education in business and enterprise; drama and creative industries; health, including international health; and social sciences, media and communication. Its internationally recognized research activity informs our teaching. With around 4,500 students, our small size allows us to offer students a highly supportive environment.

Postgraduate Student Allowance Scheme (PSAS) (Queen Margaret)

Subjects: Cultural management programmes, art therapy, audiology and international health scheme.
Purpose: International Health Scheme.
Eligibility: United Kingdom and European Union nationals living in Scotland on the relevant date (conditions apply).
Level of Study: Postgraduate
Value: UK £3,010 towards tuition fees and an income-assessed maintenance grant
Length of Study: 2 years, full-time
Frequency: Annual
Study Establishment: Queen Margaret University College
Country of Study: United Kingdom
No. of awards offered: 4
Application Procedure: Applicants must complete an application and send it to the SAAS, once nominated by the institution.
Funding: Government
Contributor: Students Awards Agency for Scotland (SAAS)
No. of awards given last year: 2
Additional Information: Students cannot apply directly to the SAAS. They must have accepted an offer of a place and be nominated by the institution.

QMUC International Student Postgraduate Scholarship

Subjects: All subjects.
Purpose: To assist and attract greater numbers of international students to postgraduate courses at QMUC.
Eligibility: Any self-funding, postgraduate international (non-European Union) student.
Level of Study: MBA, postgraduate, graduate
Value: UK £1,000
Frequency: Annual
Country of Study: United Kingdom
No. of awards offered: 10 per year
Application Procedure: Applicants must complete the application form and submit it to the International Office before the stated closing date, after accepting an offer of a place by the institution.
Closing Date: Mid-to late September each year
No. of awards given last year: 10
No. of applicants last year: 55

For further information contact:

International Office, QMUC, Corstorphine Campus, Clerwoon Terrace, Edinburgh, EH12 8TS, Scotland

QUEEN MARY UNIVERSITY OF LONDON

Admissions and Research Student Office, London, E1 4NS, England
Tel: (44) 20 7882 5511
Fax: (44) 20 7882 5588
Email: admissions@qmul.ac.uk
Website: www.qmul.ac.uk
Contact: Mr Peter Smith, Admissions Assistant

Queen Mary is the fourth largest college in the University of London. Located on an attractive campus, it has more than 8,000 students studying in four faculties plus St Bartholomew's and the Royal London School of Medicine and Dentistry. Of these, more than 1,600 are pursuing postgraduate courses or undertaking research.

Queen Mary Research Studentships

Subjects: Arts, sciences, engineering, social sciences, law, medicine and dentistry.
Purpose: To provide the opportunity for full-time research leading towards an MPhil or PhD.
Eligibility: Open to suitably qualified candidates who hold at least an Upper Second Class (Honours) Degree or equivalent at first degree level, but preferably a relevant Master's degree.
Level of Study: Research
Type: Studentship
Value: Maintenance at the current research council rate plus tuition fees
Length of Study: 3 years full-time subject to a satisfactory academic report
Frequency: Annual
Study Establishment: Queen Mary University of London
Country of Study: United Kingdom
No. of awards offered: 20+
Application Procedure: Applicants must contact the Admission and Recruitment Office for further application details.
Closing Date: Mid-Summer
Funding: Government
No. of awards given last year: 30
No. of applicants last year: 200+
Additional Information: These studentships are not available to existing Queen Mary research students.

THE QUEEN'S NURSING INSTITUTE

3 Albemarle Way, Clerkenwell, London,
EC1V 4RQ, England
Tel: (44) 20 7490 4227
Fax: (44) 20 7490 1269
Email: mail@qni.org.uk
Website: www.qni.org.uk
Contact: Miss Sarah Perry, Assistant Director

The Queen's Nursing Institute exists to promote and support the best community nursing practice in order to foster the highest possible standards of public health. Through its unique Innovation and Creative Practice Award Scheme and its new Grants Scheme, it provides both professional and financial support for a range of community nurse-led initiatives throughout England, Wales and Northern Ireland.

Innovation and Creative Practice Award

Subjects: Implementation of good practice, or a project or an idea, within the community.
Purpose: To support nurses in a community setting to improve patient care through the development of innovative and creative practice.
Level of Study: Research, graduate, postgraduate, professional development
Type: Grant
Value: UK £6,000 for major projects, UK £2,000 for grants
Length of Study: Varies, usually 1 year
Frequency: Annual
Study Establishment: The Queen's Nursing Institute
Country of Study: United Kingdom
No. of awards offered: Varies, usually 6–10
Application Procedure: Applicants must submit a form, an application proposal and a curriculum vitae.
Closing Date: The last Friday in July for major projects and the first Monday in April and November for grants
Funding: Private
Contributor: National Gardens Scheme
No. of awards given last year: 8
No. of applicants last year: 120
Additional Information: Applicants are encouraged to discuss their application with a staff member before applying.

THE RADCLIFFE INSTITUTE FOR ADVANCED STUDY

34 Concord Avenue, Cambridge, MA, 02138, United States of America
Tel: (1) 617 495 8212
Fax: (1) 617 495 8136
Email: bunting_fellowships@radcliffe.harvard.edu
Website: www.radcliffe.edu
Contact: Administrator of Fellowships

The Radcliffe Institute for Advanced Study is a scholarly community where individuals pursue advanced work across a wide range of academic disciplines, professions and creative arts. Within this broad purpose, the Radcliffe Institute sustains a continuing commitment to the study of women, gender and society.

Radcliffe Institute for Advanced Study Fellowship Programme

Subjects: All subjects.
Purpose: To support women and men of exceptional promise and demonstrated accomplishment, who wish to pursue independent work.
Eligibility: Open to female and male scholars in any field who gained a doctorate or appropriate terminal degree at least 2 years prior to appointment, or female creative writers and visual or performing artists with a record of significant accomplishment and equivalent professional experience. Special eligibility requirements apply to creative artists.
Level of Study: Research, postdoctorate
Type: Fellowship
Value: Please consult the organization
Frequency: Annual
Study Establishment: Harvard University
Country of Study: United States of America
Application Procedure: Applicants must visit the website.
Closing Date: Please consult the organization

RADIO AND TELEVISION NEWS DIRECTORS FOUNDATION (RTNDF)

1000 Connecticut Avenue North West, Suite 615, Washington, DC, 20036, United States of America
Tel: (1) 202 659 6510
Fax: (1) 202 223 4007
Email: walts@rtndf.org
Website: www.rtndf.org
Contact: Ms Walt Swanston, Senior Project Director

The mission of the Radio and Television News Directors Foundation (RTNDF) is to promote excellence in electronic journalism through research, education and professional training in four principal programme areas: journalistic ethics and practices, the impact of technological change on electronic journalism, the role of electronic news in politics and public policy and cultural diversity in the electronic journalism profession.

Capitol Hill News Internships

Subjects: Electronic journalism.
Purpose: To provide an opportunity for students to make future contacts and learn the ropes of political coverage.
Eligibility: Open to recent college graduates whose career objective is electronic journalism. Preference is given to minority students.
Level of Study: Postgraduate
Type: Internship
Value: US$1,000 per month. Travel, housing and other living expenses are the responsibility of the intern
Length of Study: 3 months
Frequency: Annual
Country of Study: United States of America
No. of awards offered: 4
Application Procedure: Applicants must write or email for an application form, which they must submit along with a curriculum vitae and

a one-page essay on why they are interested in this programme. Late, incomplete or faxed applications will not be accepted.
Closing Date: The deadline for the Spring internships is January 19th, and April 1st for the Summer internships
Funding: Private
Contributor: The Radio-Television Correspondent's Association
Additional Information: Interns will be responsible for following newsworthy congressional activities and helping to co-ordinate these activities. Excellent writing skills are essential. Interns will get hands-on experience in the House and Senate Radio or TV galleries, working with the Washington press and congressional staff to cover the political process.

RTNDF Fellowships

Subjects: Electronic journalism.
Eligibility: To support young journalists in radio or television with up to 10 years of experience.
Level of Study: Postgraduate, professional development
Type: Fellowship
Value: Up to US$2,500
Frequency: Annual
Country of Study: United States of America
No. of awards offered: 8
Application Procedure: Applicants must write for application form.
Closing Date: May 4th
Funding: Private
Additional Information: The awards include: the Sandra Freeman Geller and Alfred Geller Fellowship, the Shirlee Barish Fellowship, the Michele Clark Fellowship for Minority News Professionals, the Jacque I Minotte Health Reporting Fellowship, the Vada and Barney Oldfield National Security Fellowship, RTNDF Environment and Science Reporting Fellowship, the Michael Burke News Management Fellowship and the NS Bienstock Fellowship for Minority Journalists.

RADIOLOGICAL SOCIETY OF NORTH AMERICA, INC. (RSNA)

820 Jorie Boulevard, Oak Brook, IL, 60523-2251, United States of America
Tel: (1) 630 571 7816
Fax: (1) 630 571 7837
Email: walter@rsna.org
Website: www.rsna.org
Contact: Mr Scott A Walter, Grant Review Process Manager

The Research and Education Foundation of the Radiological Society of North America (RSNA) provides grant support to medical students, residents, Fellows and full-time faculty members of departments of radiology, radiation oncology and nuclear medicine.

RSNA Derek Harwood-Nash International Fellowship

Subjects: Academic radiology.
Purpose: To supply travel and living expenses to international scholars whose educational goals can be met most appropriately by a course of study in a North American institution.
Eligibility: Promising international scholars who are embarking on a career in academic radiology and who demonstrate that their specific educational goals can be met most appropriately by a course of study in a North American institution.
Level of Study: Professional development
Type: Fellowship
Value: Up to US$10,000
Length of Study: 1 year
Frequency: Annual
Study Establishment: Committee on International Relations and Education (CIRE)-approved academic centre in North America
Country of Study: United States of America
Application Procedure: Applicants must complete an application form or be nominated. Forms are available from the website.
Closing Date: June 15th
No. of awards given last year: 1

RSNA Educational Scholar Program

Subjects: Radiology or related disciplines.
Purpose: To fund board-certified individuals who are seeking an opportunity to develop their expertise in the discipline of education in the radiological sciences.
Eligibility: Open to board-certified individuals in radiology or related disciplines who hold an MD, have a demonstrated interest in teaching and show that the pursuit of advanced training in education will impact the future education of radiologists. Applicants must be citizens of a North American country or have permanent resident status.
Level of Study: Predoctorate, postgraduate
Type: Grant
Value: Up to US$75,000 per year
Length of Study: 2 years
Frequency: Annual
No. of awards offered: 1
Application Procedure: Applicants must complete an application form, available from the website.
Closing Date: June 1st

RSNA Holman Pathway Research Seed Grant

Subjects: Any area of radiology-related research, including basic, clinical, developmental and healthcare planning, delivery and evaluation.
Purpose: To support residents selected by the American Board of Radiology (ABR) into the B Leonard Holman Research Pathway.
Eligibility: Applicants must be working on a new pilot project and must not have served as a principal investigator, co-principal investigator or co-investigator on grants totalling US$50,000 or more in a single calendar year.
Type: Research award
Value: 1-year grant of US$30,000 or less to support a specific research project. No salary support will be provided. An application for a 2nd year of support of up to US$30,000 may be made if the awardee shows significant progress towards the stated goals of the project
Frequency: Annual
Country of Study: United States of America
Application Procedure: Applicants must already have been accepted into the B Leonard Holman Research Pathway for their residency-training programme in radiology, radiation oncology or nuclear medicine. Applicants should download an application form from the RSNA website or from the main organization address.
Closing Date: January 15th each year, to begin July 1st

RSNA Institutional Clinical Fellowship in Cardiovascular Imaging

Subjects: Cardiovascular imaging.
Purpose: To provide opportunities for radiologists early in their careers to gain experience and expertise in cardiovascular imaging.
Eligibility: Open to citizens or permanent residents of a North American country who have completed their residency training in the radiological sciences. Fellows must also hold an MD or the equivalent as recognized by the American Medical Association and must be ACGME-certified in radiology or be eligible to sit for such certification.
Type: Fellowship
Value: US$50,000 per year paid to a department. The Foundation does not pay overhead or indirect costs
Length of Study: 3 years
Frequency: Annual
No. of awards offered: 1
Application Procedure: Applications must be submitted by a department in preparation for the recruitment of a Fellow into an existing cardiovascular imaging training programme. Application forms are available from the website.
Closing Date: June 1st

RSNA Institutional Fellowship in Radiological Informatics

Subjects: Radiology and related disciplines.
Purpose: To enable institutions with departments strong in information technology to provide training opportunities to young physicians in the radiologic sciences who are not yet professionally established in the area of radiologic informatics.
Eligibility: Fellows must be physicians or scientists in North America who have completed their residency or postdoctoral training.

Level of Study: Postdoctorate
Type: Fellowship
Value: US$50,000
Length of Study: 1 year
Frequency: Annual
Study Establishment: An approved department of radiology within North America
Country of Study: United States of America
Application Procedure: Applicants are selected by application or nomination.
Closing Date: June 1st
Funding: Private

RSNA International Radiology Program Educational Grant to 'Teach the Teachers' from Emerging Nations

Subjects: Radiology or related disciplines.
Purpose: To provide an opportunity for scientists and physicians in developed countries to use or develop educational materials specifically to educate the teachers in emerging countries who will return to their respective countries to improve clinical practice and education.
Eligibility: Open to individuals in the radiological sciences in developed countries throughout the world with the facilities and institutional support to establish the programme required to successfully compete for this grant.
Level of Study: Postgraduate
Type: Grant
Value: Up to US$100,000 per year. Each year's funding is based on successful progress towards the stated goals of the proposal. The Foundation does not pay institutional overhead costs or indirect costs
Length of Study: 3 years
Frequency: Annual
No. of awards offered: 1
Application Procedure: Applicants must complete an application form, available from the website.
Closing Date: June 1st

RSNA Introduction to Research for International Young Academics

Subjects: Academic radiology.
Purpose: To encourage young radiologists from countries outside North America to pursue careers in academic radiology.
Eligibility: Eligible candidates must be not more than 3 years out of training and must be fluent in English.
Level of Study: Postdoctorate
Type: Fellowship
Value: Complimentary registration and a stipend of US$1,000 to the individual's department to defray participant's travel expenses
Length of Study: 1 year
Frequency: Annual
Study Establishment: Any department approved by RSNA
Country of Study: Seminar attendance in United States of America
No. of awards offered: 15
Application Procedure: Applicants must be nominated by the candidate's department chairperson or training director.
Closing Date: April 15th

RSNA Medical Student Departmental Grant Program

Subjects: Diagnostic radiology, radiation oncology and nuclear medicine.
Purpose: To provide matching grants to enable departments of diagnostic radiology, radiation oncology or nuclear medicine allied with North American medical schools to offer research opportunities to medical students.
Eligibility: Open to departments of diagnostic radiology, radiation oncology or nuclear medicine that have been allied with fully accredited North American medical schools for 5 consecutive years.
Type: Grant
Value: US$1,000 per month for 3 or more months to be matched by the department
Frequency: Annual
Application Procedure: Applicants must complete an application form, available from the website. Departments must describe their commitment to research, provide details of the medical student's proposed activity and participation, and identify the method by which the student will be selected. They must also designate a scientific adviser to oversee the medical student's participation in the research programme.
Closing Date: January 8th

RSNA Medical Student/Scholar Assistant Program

Subjects: Radiology and related disciplines.
Purpose: To make radiology research opportunities available for medical students early in their training and encourage them to consider academic radiology as a career option.
Eligibility: Open to full-time medical students at an accredited North American medical school. Nominees must be citizens of a North American country or hold permanent resident status.
Type: Grant
Value: US$5,000
Length of Study: 1 year
Application Procedure: Applicants must be nominated by a current RSNA scholar grant recipient and work with the scholar on his or her designated research project.
Closing Date: There is no specific deadline. The scholar is notified of the option to nominate a medical student. The application must be prepared with the assistance of the nominating scholar

RSNA Research Fellow Program

Subjects: Medical sciences.
Purpose: To provide young investigators not yet professionally established in the radiological sciences an opportunity to gain further insight into scientific investigation and to develop competence in research techniques and methods.
Eligibility: Open to citizens or permanent residents of a North American country who have an MD, DO, DVM, DDS, DMD degree or equivalent as recognized by the American Medical Association. Individuals with a PhD or ScD, in addition to the appropriate medical degree, are not eligible for this award, although MD or PhDs who have their PhDs in areas other than medical research are eligible. Applicants should be near the end of their prescribed training and/or have completed the prerequisite training to sit for qualifying exams. Preference will be given to candidates who have a commitment from a North American educational institution for a faculty appointment after the fellowship is completed.
Level of Study: Predoctorate, doctorate, postdoctorate, postgraduate
Type: Fellowship
Value: US$45,000 for 1 year with US$5,000 to the institution, on request, to be applied to direct expenses. Applications for renewal for a 2nd year at US$50,000, plus US$5,000 to the institution, on request, will be considered. The Foundation does not pay overhead or indirect costs
Length of Study: 1 or 2 years
Frequency: Annual
No. of awards offered: 1
Application Procedure: Applicants must complete an application form, available from the website.
Closing Date: January 15th

RSNA Research Fellowship in Basic Radiologic Sciences

Subjects: Radiological sciences.
Purpose: To provide training and research opportunities for scientists who possess a PhD or equivalent degree to gain insight into scientific investigation and to develop competence in state-of-the-art research in basic radiological sciences.
Eligibility: Fellows must be within 5 years of completing their doctoral training in the radiological sciences and be eligible to join a department of diagnostic radiology, radiation oncology or nuclear medicine.
Level of Study: Postdoctorate
Type: Fellowship
Value: US$45,000 salary support for 1 year. Application for renewal for a 2nd year of salary support at US$50,000 will be considered based on progress towards the stated goals during the initial year. US$5,000 will be given to the institution each year to help cover direct expenses
Length of Study: Initially 1 year, further year by application
Frequency: Annual

Study Establishment: Any, which provides the necessary space, facilities and equipment
Country of Study: United States of America
No. of awards offered: Varies
Application Procedure: Applicants must download an application form from the website or contact the main organization address.
Closing Date: January 15th in same year. Award starts July 1st
Funding: Private
Additional Information: This programme is designed to promote and enhance the understanding and utilization of basic radiological sciences within departments of diagnostic radiology, radiation oncology and nuclear medicine. Research Fellows must be prepared to devote 100 per cent of their time to research under the guidance of a scientific advisor of their choice for the full-term of the fellowship.

RSNA Research Resident Program

Subjects: Radiology, radiation oncology and nuclear medicine.
Purpose: To provide opportunities for individuals to gain further insight into scientific investigation, and to develop competence in research and educational techniques and methods.
Eligibility: Open to citizens or permanent residents of a North American country. Applicants should be in residency training so that the award can occur during any year after the 1st year of training and should have an academic degree acceptable for a radiology residency.
Level of Study: Postgraduate
Type: Grant
Value: US$30,000 designed to replace a portion of the resident's salary
Length of Study: 1 year, non-renewable
Frequency: Annual
No. of awards offered: 1
Application Procedure: Applicants must complete an application form, available from the website.
Closing Date: January 15th

RSNA Scholars Program

Subjects: Medical sciences.
Purpose: To support junior clinical faculty members and allow them to gain experience in research early in their academic careers.
Eligibility: Open to citizens or permanent residents of a North American country who have completed advanced training and are within 5 years of an initial faculty appointment at a North American educational institution. Applicants must also be board certified or eligible to sit for certifying exams and have not served or not currently be serving as principal investigator or co-principal investigator on grants or contracts totalling US$50,000 or more in a single calendar year.
Level of Study: Postdoctorate, doctorate
Type: Award
Value: US$75,000 per year, payable to the institution, to be used exclusively as a stipend for the scholar
Length of Study: 2 years. In unusual circumstances, a 3rd year may be granted to provide bridge funding between the scholar award and additional funding obtained from other sources. A separate application is required to be considered for a 3rd year of funding
Frequency: Annual
No. of awards offered: 1
Application Procedure: Scholar applicants must be nominated by their host institution. If awarded, scholars will be required to take the Advanced Grant Writing Course offered through the RSNA Office of Research Development (ORD). Personal interviews will be conducted for selected finalists. Three letters of recommendation and a budget with details of the project and all sources of support are required.
Closing Date: January 15th

RSNA Seed Grant Research Program

Subjects: Diagnostic radiology, radiation oncology and nuclear medicine.
Purpose: To assist investigators in defining objectives and testing hypotheses before they apply for major grants from corporations, foundations or government agencies.
Eligibility: Applications are accepted from any country. Applicants must hold a full-time faculty position in an educational institution at the time the award commences and be in a department of diagnostic radiology, radiation oncology or nuclear medicine, having completed all advanced training. Applicants must not have served as a principal investigator co-principal investigator or co-investigator on grants totalling US$50,000 or more in a single calendar year. Any area of radiology-related research is eligible including basic, clinical, developmental and healthcare planning, delivery and evaluation.
Type: Research grant
Value: US$30,000 or less, payable to the recipient's department in two equal instalments
Length of Study: 1 year
Application Procedure: Applicants must complete an application form, available from the website.
Closing Date: January 15th

RSNA World Wide Web-Based Educational Program

Subjects: Radiology and related disciplines.
Purpose: To provide an opportunity for scientists and physicians to develop educational materials specifically for widespread distribution through the Internet.
Eligibility: Open to anyone in the radiological sciences from any country. Individuals who are not in the radiological sciences, such as computer or web specialists, may be involved as co-investigators.
Level of Study: Postgraduate, professional development
Type: Grant
Value: Up to US$75,000
Length of Study: 1 year
Application Procedure: Applicants must complete an application form, available from the website.
Closing Date: June 1st

The Rebecca Skelton Fund 

THE REBECCA SKELTON FUND

C/o School of Visual and Performing Arts, University College Chichester, Chichester west Sussex, P019 6PE, England
Tel: (44) 01243 816470
Fax: (44) 01243 816080
Website: www.ucc.ac.uk

The fund provides financial assistance towards the cost of dance study. Rebecca Skelton who died in 2005 was an accomplished dance performer, choreographer and researcher whose work was an inspiration to many. This fund has been set up in her memory.

The Rebecca Skelton Scholarship

Subjects: Dance improvization; skinner releasing technique, alignment therapy, feldenkrais technique, Alexander technique and other body-mind practices that focus on an inner awareness and use of the proprioceptive communication system or inner sensory mode.
Purpose: To assist students to pursue a course of specific or advanced performance studies or an appropriate or dance research project.
Eligibility: Open to anyone pursuing dance studies at postgraduate level.
Level of Study: Postgraduate
Type: Scholarship
Value: UK £100
Frequency: Annual
Country of Study: United Kingdom
No. of awards offered: 1–4
Application Procedure: Application form on request.
Closing Date: January 6th
Funding: Foundation
Contributor: The Rebecca Skelton Fund

For further information contact:

Contact: Fiona bunn, Research Administrator

REES JEFFREYS ROAD FUND

Rees Jeffreys Road Fund, Merriewood, Horsell Park, Woking, Surrey, GU21 4LW, England
Tel: (44) 1483 750758
Fax: (44) 1483 750758
Contact: Mr Brian Smith, Secretary

The Rees Jeffreys Road Fund makes grants for courses or research connected with roads and transportation. Within those subjects, it endows university teaching posts, pays bursaries for postgraduate students, sponsors research and contributes to research projects. It has a small budget for the provision of roadside rests and improving roadside environment.

Rees Jeffreys Road Fund Bursaries

Subjects: Transport-scholarship and research that will lead to the better understanding of transport issues and offer the prospect of new thinking and ideas for grappling with contemporary transport issues.
Purpose: To facilitate postgraduate study or research into transport.
Eligibility: Open to candidates of any nationality who hold at least an Upper Second Class (Honours) Degree at a United Kingdom university.
Level of Study: Postgraduate, doctorate
Type: Full bursaries for MSc students; transportation annual contributions to PhD research students
Value: Fees plus maintenance plus UK £1,000 for 1-year MSc courses; UK £3,000–6,000 per year for 1, 2 or 3-year PhD courses
Length of Study: 1–2 years
Frequency: Annual
Study Establishment: Universities and research institutions
Country of Study: United Kingdom
No. of awards offered: Approx. 5 to 7
Application Procedure: Applicants must be recommended by the intended institution of study.
Closing Date: July 1st for MSc courses
Funding: Private
No. of awards given last year: 7
No. of applicants last year: 21

Rees Jeffreys Road Fund Research Grants

Subjects: Transport.
Purpose: To facilitate research projects into roads and transportation.
Level of Study: Research
Value: UK £1,000–20,000, depending on the project
Frequency: Annual
Study Establishment: Universities and research institutions
Country of Study: United Kingdom
No. of awards offered: Approx. 10 per year
Application Procedure: Applicants must write a letter to the secretary.
Closing Date: There is no fixed deadline. Applications will be considered by the Trustees at one of the five meetings each year
Funding: Private
No. of awards given last year: 12
No. of applicants last year: 30

REGENTS BUSINESS SCHOOL

RBS London Inner Circle Regent's Park, London, NW1 4NS, United Kingdom
Tel: (44) 20 7477 2990
Fax: (44) 20 7477 2991
Email: info@RBSlondon.ac.uk
Website: www.rbslondon.ac.uk

RBS London is one of the faster growing business schools in London. Located in the heart of London, Europe's principle center, we are ideally placed to launch our graduates into global business world.

RBS London Academic Excellence Scholarships

Subjects: International business management.
Eligibility: These merit awards are awarded to students with strong academic achievements and potential.
Level of Study: Graduate
Value: Up to 50% of tuition fees is paid
Length of Study: 1 year
Frequency: Annual
Study Establishment: Regents Business School London
Country of Study: United Kingdom
Application Procedure: Contact the school, or apply online and submit a 500-word statement for the attention of the scholarship committee.
Closing Date: There is no application deadline

RBS London Work-Study Scholarships

Subjects: International business management.
Eligibility: These merit awards are awarded to students with strong academic achievements and potential, who can combine study and work without interfering with their academic progress.
Level of Study: Postgraduate, professional development
Type: Scholarship
Value: Partial remission of tuition fees
Length of Study: 1 year
Frequency: Annual
Study Establishment: Regents Business School London
Country of Study: United Kingdom
Application Procedure: Apply online submit a 500-word statement for the attention of the scholarship committee.
Closing Date: There is no application deadline
Additional Information: Scholarship holders are required to work a specified number of hours per week (normally 10 hours, up to a maximum of 20 hours) during term time.

THE REID TRUST FOR THE HIGHER EDUCATION OF WOMEN

53 Thornton Hill, Exeter, Devon, EX4 4NR, England
Contact: Mrs H M Harvey, Honorary Treasurer

The Reid Trust for the Higher Education of Women was founded in 1868 in connection with Bedford College for Women for the promotion and improvement of women's education. It is administered by a small committee of voluntary trustees.

Reid Trust For the Higher Education of Women

Subjects: All subjects.
Purpose: To promote the education of women.
Eligibility: Open to women educated in the United Kingdom who have appropriate academic qualifications and who wish to undertake further training or research in the United Kingdom.
Level of Study: Unrestricted
Type: Grant
Value: UK £50–750 each
Length of Study: Unrestricted
Frequency: Annual
Country of Study: United Kingdom
No. of awards offered: Usually 10–12
Application Procedure: Applicants must complete an application form, obtained by sending a stamped addressed envelope with a request.
Closing Date: May 31st
Funding: Private
No. of awards given last year: 16
No. of applicants last year: 200

REMEDI

The Old Rectory, Stanton Prior, Bath, BA2 9HT, England
Tel: (44) 17 6147 2662
Fax: (44) 17 6147 0662
Email: rosie.wait@remedi.org.uk
Website: www.remedi.org.uk
Contact: P D Mesquita OBE, Director

REMEDI, founded in 1973, supports pioneering research into all aspects of disability and disease to improve the quality of life.

REMEDI Research Grants

Subjects: Diabetes, amputees, childhood eczema, osteoporosis, rehabilitation of the elderly, speech therapy, stroke, autism and head injury.
Purpose: To support pioneering research into all aspects of disability and disease. The Trustees are particularly interested in funding or part funding initial grants where applicants find it difficult to obtain funding through larger organizations.
Eligibility: Open to English-speaking applicants living and working in the United Kingdom.
Level of Study: Unrestricted
Type: Research grant
Value: Varies
Length of Study: 1–3 years
Study Establishment: A hospital or university
Country of Study: United Kingdom
No. of awards offered: Varies
Application Procedure: Applicants must email the Director with a summary, including costs and start date on one side of A4-size paper. If the Chairman considers the research project to be of interest the Director will email an application form to be completed. Completed applications are sent to independent referees for peer review. The Trustees normally make awards twice a year in June and November.
Closing Date: Applications are accepted at any time
Funding: Private
Contributor: Trusts, companies and individuals
No. of awards given last year: 8
No. of applicants last year: 180
Additional Information: Grants will not be awarded for course fees, administration and university overheads. Cancer and cancer-related diseases are not normally supported. Trustees have decided to reduce the number of awards, but substantially increase the size of the grants.

REPORTERS COMMITTEE FOR FREEDOM OF THE PRESS

1101 Wilson Boulevard Suite 1100, Arlington, VA 22209-2275, United States of America
Tel: (1) 703 807 2100
Fax: (1) 703 807 2109
Email: rcfp@rcfp.org
Website: www.rcfp.org
Contact: Ms Maria Gowen, Office Manager

The Reporters Committee for Freedom of the Press is a voluntary, unincorporated association of reporters and editors, dedicated to protecting the First Amendment interests of the news media. From its office in Arlington, Virginia, the Reporters Committee staff provide cost free legal defence and research services to journalists and their attorneys throughout the United States and also operate the FOI service centre to assist the news media with federal and state open records and open meetings issues.

Jack Nelson Legal Fellowship

Subjects: Media law.
Purpose: To financially support a recent law school graduate to pursue a postgraduate study.
Eligibility: To be eligible for the programme, candidates must have been granted a law degree no later than August. Significant experience in print or electronic news reporting and strong legal research and writing skills are required.
Level of Study: Professional development, postgraduate
Type: Fellowship
Value: US$30,000 plus fully paid health benefits
Length of Study: 1 year
Frequency: Annual
Country of Study: United States of America
No. of awards offered: 1
Application Procedure: There is no application form. Applicants must submit a covering letter, curriculum vitae, contact details of three referees, news clips and a short legal writing sample to the attention of Gregg P Leslie, Acting Executive Director.
Closing Date: February 1st
Funding: Private
No. of awards given last year: 1
No. of applicants last year: 40
Additional Information: The Fellow will monitor significant developments in first amendment media law, assist with legal defence requirements from reporters, prepare legal memoranda, amicus briefs and other special projects. He or she will also write for The Reporter's Committee's publications, the quarterly magazines *The News Media* and *The Law* and the bi-weekly newsletter *News Media Update*.

Reporters Committee Legal Fellowship

Subjects: Media law.
Purpose: To financially support a recent law school graduate to pursue a postgraduate study.
Eligibility: Candidates must have received a law degree no later than August. Strong legal research and writing skills are required and a background in news reporting is very strongly preferred.
Level of Study: Postgraduate, professional development
Type: Fellowship
Value: US$30,000 plus fully paid health benefits
Length of Study: 1 year, September–August
Frequency: Annual
Country of Study: United States of America
No. of awards offered: 1
Application Procedure: There is no application form, but the applicants should submit a covering letter, contact details of three referees, a short legal writing sample and new clips or one non-legal writing sample may be submitted in lieu of news clips. Email applications will not be accepted.
Closing Date: February 1st
Funding: Private
No. of awards given last year: 1
No. of applicants last year: 40
Additional Information: Legal fellows monitor significant developments in first amendment media law, assist with legal defence requests from reporters, prepare legal memoranda, amicus briefs and other special projects. They write for the Committee's publications, the quarterly magazine The News Media and The Law and the bi-weekly newsletter, News Media Update.

Robert R McCormick Tribune Foundation Journalism Fellowship

Subjects: Media law.
Purpose: To financially support an experienced journalist with an interest in free press issues.
Eligibility: Candidates must possess a law degree and be admitted to the Bar of any state. They must have a minimum of 2 or 3 years of postgraduate legal experience in a law firm, public interest group, government agency or judicial clerkship. Substantial experience in appellate brief writing is mandatory and strong legal research and writing skills is required. A background in news reporting is strongly preferred.
Level of Study: Professional development, postgraduate
Type: Fellowship
Value: US$40,000
Length of Study: 1 year
Frequency: Annual
Country of Study: United States of America
No. of awards offered: 1
Application Procedure: There is no application form. Applicants must submit a covering letter, curriculum vitae and contact details of three referees, a sample appellate brief and news clips or another short non-legal writing sample to Gregg P Leslie, Acting Executive Director.
Closing Date: February 1st
Funding: Private
No. of awards given last year: 1
No. of applicants last year: 10

Robert R McCormick Tribune Foundation Legal Fellowship

Subjects: Media law.
Purpose: To financially support a law school graduate to pursue a postgraduate study.

Eligibility: Candidates must possess a law degree and be admitted to the Bar of any state. They must have a minimum of 2 or 3 years of postgraduate legal experience in a law firm, public interest group, government agency or judicial clerkship. Substantial experience in appellate brief writing is mandatory and strong legal research and writing skills is required. A background in news reporting is strongly preferred.
Level of Study: Postgraduate
Type: Fellowship
Value: US$42,000
Length of Study: 1 year
Frequency: Annual
Country of Study: United States of America
No. of awards offered: 1
Application Procedure: There is no application form. Applicants must submit a covering letter, curriculum vitae and contact details of three referees, a sample appellate brief and news clips or another short non-legal writing sample to Gregg P Leslie, Acting Executive Director.
Closing Date: February 1st
Funding: Foundation, private
Contributor: Robert R McCormick Tribune Foundation
No. of awards given last year: 1
No. of applicants last year: 10
Additional Information: The Fellow will be expected to draft approx. six appellate amicus briefs in significant cases involving First Amendment media law issues during the fellowship. The legal Fellow will also monitor significant developments in media law, assist with responding to legal defence requests from reporters, prepare legal memoranda and other special projects. In addition, the legal Fellow will write for the Committee's publications, the quarterly magazine The News Media and The Law and the bi-weekly newsletter News Media Update.

REPRESENTATION OF THE FLEMISH GOVERNMENT

Embassy of Belgium, 3330 Garfield Street NW, Washington, DC 20008, United States of America
Tel: (1) 202 625 5850
Fax: (1) 202 342 8346
Email: franm@wizard.net
Website: www.flanders.be
Contact: Cultural and Administrative Officer

The Government of Flanders offers bursaries to permit students to continue their studies in Flanders.

Fellowship for American College Students

Subjects: Study or research at universities, conservatories of music or art academics recognized by the Flemish community in the fields of art, music humanities, social and political sciences, law, economics, sciences and medicine.
Purpose: To enable students to continue their education in Flanders, Belgium.
Eligibility: Citizens of the United States of America who are already studying for a first or doctoral degree.
Level of Study: Doctorate, postgraduate, postdoctorate, graduate, predoctorate
Type: Fellowship
Value: A monthly stipend of approx. €674.27 at a Flemish institution, reimbursement of tuition fees, health insurance and public liability insurance in accordance with Belgian law. There is no reimbursement of travel expenses
Length of Study: Varies
Frequency: Annual
Study Establishment: Recognized institutes in Flanders
Country of Study: Belgium
No. of awards offered: 5
Application Procedure: Applicants must download an application form from the website or Cultural Officer, at the Belgian Embassy, Washington, DC.
Closing Date: January 14th to commence in September of the same year
Funding: Government
Additional Information: The decision to grant a fellowship is made by the Ministry of the Flemish community after consultation with the prospective host institution.

RESEARCH CORPORATION (USA)

4703 E Camp Lowell Drive Suite 201, Tucson, AZ, 85712, United States of America
Tel: (1) 520 571 1111
Fax: (1) 520 571 1119
Email: awards@rescorp.org
Website: www.rescorp.org
Contact: Ms Dena McDuffie, Editor, Science Advancement Programme

The Research Corporation (USA) was one of the first United States of America foundations, and is the only one wholly devoted to the advancement of academic science. An endowed organization, it makes grants totalling US$5–7 million annually for independently proposed research in chemistry, physics and astronomy at United States of America and Canadian colleges and universities.

Cottrell College Science Awards

Subjects: Physics, chemistry and astronomy.
Purpose: To support significant research that contributes to the advancement of science.
Eligibility: Open to faculty members at public and private Institutes of Higher Education in the United States of America or Canada. The principal investigator must have an appointment in a department of astronomy, chemistry or physics and the department must offer at least baccalaureate, but not doctoral degrees. The institution must demonstrate its commitment by providing facilities and opportunities for faculty and student research.
Level of Study: Doctorate
Type: Research award
Value: Equipment and supplies, student Summer stipends of up to US$3,500 and a faculty Summer stipend of up to US$7,500
Length of Study: Up to 5 years, possibly renewable
Study Establishment: Public and private universities with non-PhD-granting departments of astronomy, chemistry or physics
Country of Study: United States of America or Canada
No. of awards offered: 100+
Application Procedure: Applicants must complete an application form and should visit the website for guidelines and application request forms.
Closing Date: November 15th or May 15th
Funding: Private
Contributor: Foundation endowment
No. of awards given last year: 93
No. of applicants last year: 262

Cottrell Scholars Awards

Subjects: Physics, chemistry and astronomy.
Purpose: To encourage excellence in both research and teaching.
Eligibility: Open to faculty in the 3rd year of a first tenure-track position.
Level of Study: Doctorate
Type: Award
Value: US$75,000, which may be flexibly applied in keeping with the applicants' approved programme
Frequency: Annual
Study Establishment: Universities with PhD-granting departments of physics, chemistry and astronomy
Country of Study: United States of America or Canada
No. of awards offered: Varies
Application Procedure: Applicants must complete an application form and should visit the website for guidelines and application request forms.
Closing Date: September 1st
Funding: Private

Contributor: Foundation endowment
No. of awards given last year: 12
No. of applicants last year: 122
Additional Information: Candidates must provide both a research and teaching plan for peer review.

Research Corporation (USA) Research Opportunity Awards

Subjects: Physics, chemistry and astronomy.
Purpose: To assist mid-career faculty scientists in launching new research programmes.
Eligibility: Open to established faculty members in PhD departments in the United States of America or Canada.
Level of Study: Doctorate
Type: Research award
Value: Up to US$50,000
Study Establishment: Universities with PhD-granting departments of physics, chemistry and astronomy
Country of Study: United States of America or Canada
No. of awards offered: Varies
Application Procedure: Applicants must be nominated by the department chair and selected nominees are invited to submit applications on the forms provided. Interested parties should visit the website.
Closing Date: May 1st and October 1st are the deadlines for nominations
Funding: Private
Contributor: Foundation endowment
No. of awards given last year: 3
No. of applicants last year: 6
Additional Information: The chair of each PhD-granting physics, astronomy and chemistry department in the United States of America or Canada may make two nominations twice a year from tenured faculty without major research funding. Applications are invited from a selected group of these nominees.

THE RESEARCH COUNCIL FOR THE HUMANITIES AND SOCIAL SCIENCE (IRCHSS)

First floor, Brooklawn House, Crampton Avenue (off shelbourne road), Ballsbridge, Dublin, Ireland
Tel: (353) 353 (0) 1 660 3652
Fax: (353) 35 (0) 1 660 3728
Email: info@irchss.le
Website: www.irchss.le

The IRCHSS was established in 2000 by the Minister for the Education and science in response to the need to develop Ireland's research capacity and skills in a rapidly changing global environment.

IRCHSS Postdoctoral Fellowship

Subjects: Humanities and social sciences.
Purpose: To facilitate the integration of Irish researchers in the humanities and social sciences within the European research area.
Eligibility: Open to applicants of any nationality.
Level of Study: Postdoctorate
Type: Scholarship
Value: €31,745
Frequency: Annual
Country of Study: Ireland
Application Procedure: See the website. Application form is available online.
Closing Date: December 12th

IRCHSS Postgraduate Scholarships

Subjects: Arts and humanities, social sciences.
Purpose: To help build an expertise-driven research system in Ireland.
Eligibility: Open to applicants who are citizens of Ireland or citizens of a member state European union.
Level of Study: Postgraduate
Type: Scholarship
Value: €12,700
Length of Study: 1 year
Frequency: Annual
Country of Study: Ireland
Application Procedure: See the website for complete details.
Closing Date: January 16th

IRCHSS Senior Research Fellowship

Subjects: Humanities and social sciences, law and business studies.
Purpose: To support research.
Eligibility: Open to applicants who are members of the academic staff in a recognized third-level institution in Ireland.
Level of Study: Doctorate
Type: Scholarship
Value: €15,000
Length of Study: 1 year
Frequency: Annual
Country of Study: Ireland
Application Procedure: See the website.
Closing Date: December 12th

RESOURCES FOR THE FUTURE (RFF)

1616 P Street North West, Washington, DC, 20036, United States of America
Tel: (1) 202 328 5043
Fax: (1) 202 939 3460
Email: macauley@rff.org
Website: www.rff.org
Contact: Co-ordinator for Academic Programmes

Resources for the Future (RFF) is a non-profit and non-partisan think tank located in Washington, DC that conducts independent research rooted primarily in economics and other social sciences on environmental and natural resource issues.

Gilbert F White Postdoctoral Fellowship

Subjects: Social and policy sciences, environmental studies, energy and natural resources.
Purpose: To enable postdoctoral researchers to spend a year in residence conducting research in the social or policy sciences in areas related to the environment, energy or natural resources.
Eligibility: A strong economics background, or closely related discipline in the social or policy sciences, is required. Applicants must be postdoctorates.
Level of Study: Postdoctorate
Type: Fellowship
Value: Please visit the website for details
Length of Study: 11 months
Frequency: Annual
Country of Study: United States of America
No. of awards offered: 2
Application Procedure: Applicants must submit a covering letter and curriculum vitae with a proposal relating to budget and three letters of recommendation. No application form is required. Application forms sent by fax or email will not be accepted.
Closing Date: February 28th

Joseph L Fisher Dissertation Award

Subjects: Economics, policy sciences, environment and natural resources.
Purpose: To support PhD students in their last year of dissertation research in economics or other policy sciences on issues related to the environment, energy or natural resources.
Eligibility: Open to all nationalities. Students must be in the final year of dissertation research or writing.
Level of Study: Doctorate
Type: Award
Value: US$12,000
Length of Study: 1 year
Frequency: Annual
Country of Study: Any country
No. of awards offered: Varies

Application Procedure: Applicants must submit a letter of application, a curriculum vitae, graduate transcripts, a one-page abstract of the dissertation, a technical summary of the dissertation, a letter from the department chair and two letters of recommendation. Applications sent by fax or email will not be accepted.
Closing Date: February 28th

RFF Fellowships in Environmental Regulatory Implementation

Subjects: Environmental studies and natural resources.
Purpose: To support research that documents the implementation and outcomes of environmental regulations.
Eligibility: Open to scholars from universities and research establishments who have a doctorate or equivalent degree or professional research experience.
Level of Study: Postdoctorate
Type: Fellowship
Value: Negotiable stipend
Length of Study: 1–2 years
Frequency: Annual
Country of Study: United States of America
No. of awards offered: 2
Application Procedure: Applicants must submit a preproposal no longer than two pages, single spaced, with 11-point or larger font and 1-inch margins, containing full details of the proposed project. Applicants whose preproposals are selected for further review will then be invited to submit final proposals. These are limited to ten pages and are to follow a similar format. They must include all of the information contained in the preproposal but should offer further detailed description of the proposed research, anticipated contribution of the project and the importance of the results. Applicants must also include a curriculum vitae with the applicant's educational background, professional experience, a list of most relevant publications and honours and awards received. In addition, final proposals must include three letters of recommendation from fellow faculty members or colleagues. Applications sent by fax or email will not be accepted.
Closing Date: January 6th for preproposals and February 28th for final proposals
Funding: Private

RESUSCITATION COUNCIL (UK)

5th Floor, Tavistock House, North Tavistock Square,
London, WC1H 9HR, England
Tel: (44) 20 7388 4678
Fax: (44) 20 7383 0773
Email: enquiries@resus.org.uk
Website: www.resus.org.uk
Contact: Dr David Gabbott, Chair, Research Subcommittee

The Resuscitation Council (UK) is the expert advisory body on the training and practice of resuscitation in the United Kingdom. It also actively pursues and promotes research in the field of resuscitation medicine.

Resuscitation Council Research Fellowships

Subjects: All aspects of the science, practice and teaching of resuscitation.
Purpose: To fund the wages of researchers based in the United Kingdom to conduct research into the science and practice of resuscitation medicine.
Eligibility: Open to research Fellows carrying out work in a suitable venue in the United Kingdom. Applicants must be full or associate members of the Resuscitation Council (UK).
Level of Study: Research, postdoctorate, postgraduate, doctorate
Type: Fellowship
Value: Basic salary level including National Insurance and Superannuation contributions. The salary would be at the appropriate point on the applicant's salary scale
Length of Study: Up to 2 years
Frequency: Dependent on funds available
Country of Study: United Kingdom
Application Procedure: Applicants should visit the website for application procedures.
Funding: Private
Contributor: The Resuscitation Council (UK)
No. of awards given last year: 1
No. of applicants last year: 2

Resuscitation Council Research Grants

Subjects: All aspects of the science, practice and teaching of resuscitation techniques.
Purpose: To provide grants up to a maximum of UK £20,000 for capital cost, data analysis and administrative support for research into the science and practice of resuscitation medicine.
Level of Study: Unrestricted
Type: Grant
Value: Up to UK £20,000
Frequency: Dependent on funds available
Country of Study: United Kingdom
Application Procedure: Applicants should visit the website: www.resus.org.uk for application details.
Closing Date: No closing dates. Applications are considered on a rolling basis
Funding: Private
Contributor: The Resuscitation Council, United Kingdom
No. of awards given last year: 4
No. of applicants last year: 7

RHODES COLLEGE

2000 North Parkway Memphis, Tennessee, 38112-1690, United States of America
Tel: (1) 901 843 3000

Rhodes, founded in 1848, seeks to graduate students with a lifelong passion for learning, a compassion for others, and the ability to translate academic study and personal concern into effective leadership and action in their communities and world.

Jacob K. Jarits Fellowships

Subjects: Humanities, arts and social sciences.
Purpose: Support for higher students in the areas of humanities, arts and social sciences.
Eligibility: Open to candidates who are U.S. citizens, permanent residents of the U.S. or citizens of any one of the freely associated states.
Type: Fellowship
Value: US$30,000 per year
Length of Study: Up to 4 years
Frequency: Annual
Study Establishment: Rhodes College
Country of Study: United States of America
No. of awards offered: 48
Application Procedure: Submit applications to the Rhodes Faculty post graduate scholarship committee one month prior to deadline.
Closing Date: October 1st, FAFSA by January 31st
Funding: Government
Contributor: The U.S. Department of Education

For further information contact:

U.S. Department of Education, DPE Teacher and student Development Programs Service Jacob K. Jarits Fellowships Program 1990 k street, N.W., 6th floor, Washington, DC 20006-8524
Tel: (202) 502-7542
Fax: (202) 502-7859
Website: www.ed.gov/programs/jacobjarits

Luce Scholars Program

Subjects: Any subject.
Purpose: To develop better cultural exchange between Asia and the U.S.
Eligibility: Open to U.S. citizens with BA or equivalent degree, under 29 years of age with no significant exposure to Asia culture or study.
Level of Study: Postgraduate

Type: Scholarship
Length of Study: 1 year
Frequency: Annual
Country of Study: Asia
No. of awards offered: 15
Application Procedure: Requests for responsive or project grants should be submitted.
Closing Date: December 1st
Funding: Foundation
Contributor: Henry Luce Foundation

For further information contact:

The Henry Luce Foundation 111 West 50th street, New York, 10020
Tel: 212 489 7700
Website: www.hluce.org

Truman Scholarships

Subjects: Any subject.
Purpose: To support college juniors preparing for leadership in public service.
Eligibility: Candidates should be U.S. citizens and full-time students pursuing a Bachelor's degree.
Value: US$26,000
Frequency: Annual
Study Establishment: Rhodes College
Country of Study: United States of America
No. of awards offered: 75–80 from 600 applications
Application Procedure: Download application from the website.
Closing Date: Early February
Funding: Foundation
Contributor: Truman Scholarship Foundation

For further information contact:

712 Jackson Place NW, Washington, DC 20006
Tel: (202) 395-4831
Fax: (202) 395-6995

Watson Fellowship

Purpose: To offer college graduates a year of independent study and travel outside the United States.
Eligibility: Candidates must be graduating seniors.
Type: Fellowship
Value: US$25,000
Frequency: Annual
No. of awards offered: Up to 50
Application Procedure: A fellowship form along with a project application proposal and details in not more than 5 pages should be submitted electronically.
Closing Date: Early November
Contributor: Thomas J. Watson Foundation

For further information contact:

Watson Fellowship Program, 293 South Main Street, Providence, RI 02903
Tel: 401 274 1952
Fax: 401 274 1954
Email: tjw@watsonfellowship.org
Contact: Thomas J

RHODES UNIVERSITY

PO Box 94, Grahamstown, 6140, South Africa
Tel: (27) 46 603 8055
Fax: (27) 46 622 8444
Email: research-admin@ru.ac.za
Website: www.ru.ac.za/research
Contact: Miss Moira Pogrund, Dean of Research

Rhodes University is a small university campus in Grahamstown. The University offers excellent undergraduate and postgraduate education, provides opportunities for research and fosters personal development and leadership as well as team, social and communication skills among its diverse student body.

Allan Gray Senior Scholarship

Subjects: Commerce (accounting, economics, management and information systems).
Purpose: To encourage and enable previously disadvantaged South Africans to pursue their studies at Honours and Master's levels.
Eligibility: Open to previously disadvantaged South African students with the appropriate qualifications.
Level of Study: Postgraduate
Type: Scholarship
Value: Rand 25,000 for Honours and Rand 35,000 for Master's
Length of Study: 1 year, renewable upon reapplication for Master's
Frequency: Annual
Study Establishment: Rhodes University, Grahamstown
Country of Study: South Africa
No. of awards offered: 4
Application Procedure: Applicants must submit a curriculum vitae and a full academic record. Short-listed applicants will be required to complete an application form providing additional information and referee reports.
Closing Date: July 1st in the year preceding registration
Funding: Private
Contributor: Donor and investments
No. of awards given last year: 4
No. of applicants last year: Approx.100 per year
Additional Information: Postgraduate scholars must assist with teaching and/or research duties up to a maximum of 6 hours a week in their department of study, without additional remuneration. Awards are for full-time study in attendance at Rhodes University only.

Andrew Mellon Foundation Scholarship

Subjects: Humanities, commerce, education, law, pharmacy and science.
Purpose: To encourage and enable previously disadvantaged people to pursue their studies at the Honours, Master's or doctoral level at Rhodes University, as well as to enhance the recipients' ability to contribute to higher education in South Africa.
Eligibility: Open to previously disadvantaged individuals with the appropriate qualifications.
Level of Study: Postgraduate
Type: Scholarship
Value: Rand 35,000 for Master's and Rand 50,000 for doctoral
Length of Study: 1 year, renewable upon reapplication
Frequency: Annual
Study Establishment: Rhodes University, Grahamstown
Country of Study: South Africa
No. of awards offered: 25 at Honours level, 10 at Master's and doctoral level
Application Procedure: Applicants must submit a curriculum vitae and a full academic record. Short-listed applicants will be required to complete an application form providing additional information and referee reports.
Closing Date: July 1st in the year preceding registration
Funding: Private
Contributor: Donor and investments
No. of awards given last year: 25 at Honours level, 10 at Master's or doctoral level
No. of applicants last year: Approx. 250 per year
Additional Information: Scholars must assist with teaching and/or research duties up to a maximum of 6 hours a week in their department of study, without additional remuneration. Awards are for full-time study in attendance at Rhodes University only.

Henderson Postgraduate Scholarships

Subjects: Mathematical, physical, Earth, life and pharmaceutical sciences, accountancy and information systems.
Purpose: To encourage and enable students to pursue their studies at the Master's and doctoral levels, and to enhance recipients' research abilities and produce internationally competitive graduates with an innovative, analytical, articulate and well-rounded desire to learn.

Eligibility: Open to South African citizens with appropriate qualifications.
Level of Study: Postgraduate
Type: Scholarship
Value: Rand 35,000 for Master's and Rand 50,000 for doctoral
Length of Study: 1 year, renewable upon reapplication
Frequency: Annual
Study Establishment: Rhodes University, Grahamstown
Country of Study: South Africa
No. of awards offered: 1
Application Procedure: Applicants must submit a curriculum vitae and a full academic record. Short-listed applicants will be required to complete an application form, providing additional information and referee reports.
Closing Date: July 1st in the year preceding
Funding: Private
Contributor: Donor and investments
No. of awards given last year: 1
No. of applicants last year: Approx. 30
Additional Information: Scholars must assist with teaching and/or research duties up to a maximum of 6 hours a week in their department of study, without additional remuneration. Awards are for full-time study in attendance at Rhodes University only.

Hugh Kelly Fellowship

Subjects: Biochemistry and microbiology, botany, chemistry, computer science, statistics, mathematics, both pure and applied sciences, pharmaceutical sciences, physics and electronics, zoology and entomology, ichthyology, fisheries science, geography or geology, human kinetics and ergonomics.
Purpose: To enable senior scientists to devote themselves to advanced work.
Eligibility: Open to suitable senior postdoctoral scientists with a very well-established research output record. Preference is given to candidates willing to accept appointments for at least 4 months. Applicants must be English speakers.
Level of Study: Postdoctorate
Type: Fellowship
Value: Currently under review, but a package of approx. Rand 70,000. If the Fellow accepts an appointment for at least 4 months and is accompanied by a spouse, the spouse's air or rail fares will also be paid. University accommodation will be provided free of charge, but the provision of a telephone if available at the place of residence will be for the Fellow's personal account
Length of Study: Up to 1 year
Frequency: Every 2 years
Study Establishment: Rhodes University, Grahamstown
Country of Study: South Africa
No. of awards offered: 1
Application Procedure: Applicants must complete an application form, available from the Dean of Research or from the website.
Closing Date: July 31st of the year preceding the award
Funding: Private
Contributor: Donor and investments
No. of awards given last year: 1
No. of applicants last year: 6
Additional Information: The Fellow will be required to present a concise report on the work completed at the conclusion of the term of the fellowship.

Patrick and Margaret Flanagan Scholarship

Subjects: All subjects.
Purpose: To enable South African women graduates to attend a university in the United Kingdom in order to obtain a higher postgraduate qualification.
Eligibility: Open to women graduates, preferably those who are English-speaking applicants of South African descent. Selection is based initially on academic merit, as well as broader qualities of intellect and character.
Level of Study: Postgraduate
Type: Scholarship
Value: Rand 180,000 per year
Length of Study: 2 years
Frequency: Annual
Study Establishment: Rhodes University, Grahamstown
Country of Study: United Kingdom
No. of awards offered: 1
Application Procedure: Applicants must submit a curriculum vitae and full academic record. Candidates shortlisted will be sent an application form or additional information and referee reports.
Closing Date: August 1st of the year prior to registration abroad
Funding: Private
Contributor: Donor and investments
No. of awards given last year: 1
No. of applicants last year: Approx. 85

Rhodes University Postdoctoral Fellowship and The Andrew Mellon Postdoctoral Fellowship

Subjects: All subjects (Rhodes University Postdoctoral Fellowship), humanities (Andrew Mellon Postdoctoral Fellowship).
Purpose: To enable scholars to devote themselves to advanced work, that will closely complement existing programmes in the host department.
Eligibility: Open to any postdoctoral scholars of standing, with research publications to their credit and of exceptional merit. Applicants must be English speakers.
Level of Study: Postdoctorate
Type: Fellowship
Value: Rand 90,000 per year with an additional allocation of a maximum of Rand 5,000 (or Rand 10,000 for the Andrew Mellon postdoctoral Fellowship) to be used at the discretion of the head of department for running costs for the postdoctoral project or the transport of the candidate to Grahamstown
Length of Study: 1 year, but may be extended by mutual agreement, subject to the availability of funds
Frequency: Annual
Study Establishment: Rhodes University, Grahamstown
Country of Study: South Africa
No. of awards offered: 2–3
Application Procedure: Applicants must be nominated. Nominations should be made through heads of departments and directors of research institutes at Rhodes University. Nominations must include a full curriculum vitae, research proposal and the name of three referees who may be consulted. Further information may be obtained from the Dean of Research or from the website.
Closing Date: July 31st of the year preceding the award
Funding: Private
Contributor: Donor and investments
No. of awards given last year: 4 for Rhodes University Postdoctoral Fellowship, 2 for Andrew Mellon Postdoctoral Fellowship
No. of applicants last year: 34
Additional Information: Fellows are not expected to undertake teaching duties.

Rhodes University Postgraduate Scholarship

Subjects: Humanities, commerce, education, law, pharmacy and science.
Purpose: To encourage and enable students to pursue their studies at the Master's and doctoral levels, enhancing recipients' research abilities and producing internationally competitive graduates with an innovative, analytical, articulate, adaptable and well-rounded desire to learn.
Eligibility: Open to students with the appropriate qualifications. Academic merit will override eligibility criteria.
Level of Study: Postgraduate
Type: Scholarship
Value: Rand 35,000 for Master's and Rand 50,000 for doctoral
Length of Study: 1 year, renewable upon reapplication
Frequency: Annual
Study Establishment: Rhodes University, Grahamstown
Country of Study: South Africa
No. of awards offered: 4
Application Procedure: Applicants must submit a curriculum vitae and a full academic record. Short-listed applicants will be required to complete an application form providing additional information and referee reports.

Closing Date: July 1st in the year preceding registration
Funding: Private
Contributor: Donor and investments
No. of awards given last year: 4
No. of applicants last year: Approx. 40 per year
Additional Information: Scholars must assist with teaching and/or research duties up to a maximum of 6 hours per week in their department of study, without additional remuneration. Awards are for full-time study in attendance at Rhodes University only.

RICHARD III SOCIETY, AMERICAN BRANCH

2041 Christian Street, Philadelphia, PA, 19146,
United States of America
Email: feedback@r3.org
Website: www.r3.org
Contact: Ms Laura Blanchard, Schallek Fellowships

The Richard III Society was founded in 1924 in England as The Fellowship of the White Boar and was renamed the Richard III Society in 1959. The American Branch was founded in 1961. Today, the Society has more than 4,000 members worldwide, and American Branch membership is more than 800.

William B Schallek Memorial Graduate Fellowship Award

Subjects: Medieval history.
Purpose: To support graduate study of 15th-century English history and culture.
Eligibility: Applicants must be citizens of the United States of America, have made an application for first citizenship papers or be permanent resident aliens enrolled at a recognized educational institution.
Level of Study: Doctorate
Type: Fellowship
Value: US$500–2,000 depending on the need and/or quality of applicant
Length of Study: 1 year, renewals will be considered
Frequency: Annual
Study Establishment: Recognized and accredited degree-granting institutions
Country of Study: Any country
No. of awards offered: Varies
Application Procedure: Applicants must visit the website for guidelines, lists of past awards, their topics and application forms.
Closing Date: February 28th for the following academic year
No. of awards given last year: 3
No. of applicants last year: 7

RICS EDUCATION TRUST

12 Great George Street, London, SW1P 3AD, England
Tel: (44) 20 7334 3713
Fax: (44) 20 7334 3795
Email: jmacdonnell@rics.org
Website: www.rics-educationtrust.org
Contact: Ms Jenny MacDonnell

The Royal Institution of Chartered Surveyors (RICS) is the professional institution for the surveying profession.

RICS Education Trust Award

Subjects: The theory and practice of surveying in any of its disciplines including general practice, quantity surveying, building surveying, rural practice, planning and development, land surveying or minerals surveying.
Eligibility: Open to chartered surveyors and others carrying out research studies in relevant subjects.
Level of Study: Unrestricted
Type: Research grant
Value: Up to UK £5,000
Frequency: Twice per year
Country of Study: Any country
Application Procedure: Applicants must complete an application form.
Closing Date: September 30th or February 28th
Funding: Commercial
Contributor: RICS
No. of awards given last year: 20
No. of applicants last year: 40

RM EDUCATIONAL SOFTWARE, INC

Windmill Square Plaza, Unit 3C 3821 Falmouth Road,
Marstons Mills, MA 02648,
United States of America
Tel: (1) 508 420 8305
Fax: (1) 508 420 8310
Website: www.rmeducation.com

RM Educational Software, Inc, founded in 1973, is one of Europe's largest, most innovative and most respected suppliers of technology-based curriculum products for education.

The Easiteach Scholarship Award

Subjects: Teaching.
Purpose: To recognize excellence in teaching.
Eligibility: Open to North American K-12 educators.
Type: Scholarship
Value: Varies
Frequency: Annual
Application Procedure: See the website.
Closing Date: May 31st

ROB AND BESSIE WELDER WILDLIFE FOUNDATION

PO Drawer 1400, Sinton, TX, 78387,
United States of America
Tel: (1) 361 364 2643
Fax: (1) 361 364 2650
Email: welderwf@aol.com
Website: www.hometown.aol.com/welderwf/welderweb.html
Contact: Dr Lynn Drawe, Director

The Rob and Bessie Welder Wildlife Foundation is a private non-profit foundation whose mission is to conduct research and education in wildlife management and closely related fields. The Welder Foundation operates a wildlife refuge on a commercial ranch in the midst of an active oil field.

Welder Wildlife Foundation Fellowship

Subjects: Wildlife ecology and management.
Purpose: To provide support to individual graduate student research.
Eligibility: Open to citizens of the United States of America or legal aliens registered at a United States of America university for a graduate degree. Priority is given to students who wish to work at the Welder Foundation Refuge or in the Coastal Bend Region of Texas.
Level of Study: Doctorate, graduate
Type: Fellowship
Value: Up to US$17,000 per year, according to individual needs
Length of Study: The duration of a graduate degree programme
Frequency: Annual
Study Establishment: Any legitimate wildlife management or wildlife ecological department at any accredited university
Country of Study: United States of America
No. of awards offered: 10 at any given time, approx. 3 each year
Application Procedure: Applicants must write for details.
Closing Date: October 1st for fellowships to begin in January
Funding: Private
Contributor: Private endowment
No. of awards given last year: 2
No. of applicants last year: 15

ROBERT BOSCH FOUNDATION

CDS International, Inc., 871 United Nations Plaza, 15th Floor, First Avenue 49th Street, New York, NY, 10017-1814, United States of America
Tel: (1) 212 497 3518
Fax: (1) 212 497 3535
Email: info@cdsintl.org
Website: www.cdsintl.org
Contact: Weingart Carolin, Programme assistant

The Robert Bosch Foundation is one of the largest German industry foundations. Many of the foundation's international exchange programmes are aimed at providing young people with opportunities to improve their knowledge of other countries and cultures and to build up networks among future leaders in Europe and the United States of America.

Robert Bosch Foundation Fellowships

Subjects: Business administration, economics, public affairs, public policy, political science, law, journalism and mass communication.
Purpose: To promote the advancement of American and German–European relations, and to broaden the participants' professional competence and cultural horizons.
Eligibility: Open to citizens of the United States of America between the ages of 23 and 34 years with a graduate or professional degree or equivalent work experience in the above subject areas. Candidates must provide evidence of outstanding professional or academic achievement and a strong knowledge of the German language. For those candidates who are outstanding in other areas but lack sufficient knowledge of German, the Foundation will provide language training prior to programme participation.
Level of Study: Postgraduate, professional development
Type: Fellowship
Value: €1,800 per month stipend. Extra funding is available for family, language training and business travel
Length of Study: 9 months (from September–May)
Frequency: Annual
Country of Study: Germany
No. of awards offered: 20
Application Procedure: Applicants must complete an application form and attend a personal interview. Please visit the website for more details.
Closing Date: October 15th
Funding: Private
Additional Information: Programme participants receive internships in German institutions such as the Federal Parliament, private corporation headquarters, mass media and other elements within the framework of government or commerce. Internships will be at a high level, closely related to senior officials. The programme will follow the following schedule: an intensive course on German language, political, economic and cultural affairs, work experience, a visit to Berlin and the former East Germany, a visit to the European Economic Community (EEC) and NATO headquarters in Brussels, a group visit to France for an overview of the political, economic and cultural perspective of another European country and a final programme evaluation in Stuttgart. All activities are conducted in German.

THE ROBERT WOOD JOHNSON FOUNDATION

Route 1 & College Road East, PO Box 2316, Princeton, NJ 08543-2316, United States of America
Tel: (1) 800 734 7635
Email: hss@rwjf.org
Website: www.rwjf.org

Established in 1972 in memory of Robert Wood Johnson, who founded Johnson & Johnson.

The Robert Wood Johnson Health & Society Scholars Program

Subjects: A broad range of factors affecting the nation's health.
Purpose: To build the nation's capacity for research, leadership and action.
Eligibility: For eligibility information, please visit our website at www.healthandsocietyscholars.org
Level of Study: Postdoctorate
Type: Scholarship
Length of Study: 2 years
Frequency: Annual
Study Establishment: One of six universities
Country of Study: United States of America
No. of awards offered: 18
Application Procedure: The application for the Robert Wood Johnson Health and Society Scholars program is done through an online application system available on our website at www.healthandsocietyscholars.org
Closing Date: October 15th
Funding: Private
No. of awards given last year: 18

ROBERTO LONGHI FOUNDATION

Fondazione Roberto Longhi Via Benedetto Fortini 30, I-50125 Florence, Italy
Tel: (39) 55 658 0794
Fax: (39) 55 658 0794
Email: longhi@fondaborselonghi.it
Website: www.fondaborselonghi.it

The aim of the Roberto Longhi Foundation is to advance art historical studies. Applications are accepted annually from prospective Fellows who hold an advanced degree in art history. Fellows pursue individual and group research projects using the library and photo archive, participate in seminars and lectures by distinguished scholars at the Foundation and visit galleries, restorations and exhibitions.

Fondazione Roberto Longhi

Subjects: History of art.
Purpose: To aid those who want to seriously dedicate themselves to research in the history of art.
Eligibility: Open to citizens of Italy who possess a degree from an Italian university with a thesis in the history of art and to non-Italian citizens who have fulfilled the preliminary requirements for a doctoral degree in the history of art at an accredited university or an institution of equal standing. Students who have reached their 32nd birthday before the application deadline are not eligible.
Level of Study: Postgraduate, doctorate
Type: Fellowship
Value: €600 per month
Length of Study: 9 months
Frequency: Annual
Study Establishment: The Foundation
Country of Study: Italy
No. of awards offered: Up to 10
Application Procedure: Applicants must submit an application containing their biographical data including place and date of birth, domicile, citizenship, transcript of undergraduate and graduate records, a copy of the degree thesis if available and of other original works, a curriculum vitae including knowledge of foreign languages both spoken and written, letters of reference from at least two persons of academic standing who are acquainted with the applicant's work, the subject of the research proposed and two passport photographs.
Closing Date: May
Funding: Private
Contributor: Private funds and capital endowment
No. of awards given last year: 10
No. of applicants last year: 29
Additional Information: Successful candidates must give the assurance that they can dedicate their full time to the research for which the fellowship is assigned. They may not enter into any connection with other institutions, they must live in Florence for the duration of the fellowship, excepting travel required for their research. They may not exceed the periods of vacations fixed by the Institute and are required to attend seminars, lectures and other activities arranged by the Institute. The Fellows must, in addition, submit a written report at the end of their stay in Florence relating the findings of their individual

research undertaken at the Longhi Foundation. Once approved by the scientific committee the Fellows research must be published only in the Foundations annual journal *Proporzioni*. Non-compliance with the above conditions will be considered sufficient grounds for the cancellation of a fellowship. Further information is available on request.

ROCHE RESEARCH FOUNDATION

Building 92/8.08, F Hoffmann-La Roche Limited, CH-4070 Basel, Switzerland
Tel: (41) (44) 61 688 5227
Fax: (41) (44) 61 688 1460
Email: research.foundation@roche.com
Website: www.research-foundation.org
Contact: Ms Margrit Freiburghaus

The Roche Research Foundation is a charity sponsored by F Hoffmann-La Roche Limited subsidizing experimental scientific research in the life sciences.

Roche Research Foundation

Subjects: Biology, medicine and chemistry.
Purpose: To promote scientific research at Swiss universities and hospitals in the biomedical field, and to sponsor the experimental research of Swiss Fellows in biology, chemistry and medicine at universities and laboratories abroad.
Eligibility: Open to all qualified researchers for fellowships at Swiss universities or hospitals, and to qualified Swiss students for fellowships abroad.
Level of Study: Postgraduate, postdoctorate, doctorate
Type: Fellowship
Value: Living costs
Length of Study: 2 years
Frequency: Quarterly
Country of Study: Any country
Application Procedure: Applicants must complete an application form in English.
Closing Date: January 15th, April 15th, July 15th or October 15th
Funding: Private

ROHERDAM SCHOOL OF MANAGEMENT (RSM)

PO Box 1738, 3000 DR Roherdam, Netherlands
Tel: (31) 31 10 408 2222
Fax: (31) 31 10 452 9509
Email: info@rsm.nl
Website: www.rsm.nl

As one of the world's top business schools, RSM is a centre of excellence and innovation for management education and research. Our goal is to empower individuals to succeed amid the complexities of modern international commerce and become the business leaders of tomorrow.

RSM-Antoinette Scholarship

Subjects: Business management.
Eligibility: The scholarship competition is open to candidates from Turkey. Please refer to the website for further admissions requirements.
Level of Study: MBA
Type: Scholarship
Length of Study: 3 years
Frequency: Annual
Study Establishment: Erasmus University
Country of Study: The Netherlands
Application Procedure: See website.
Closing Date: May 31st
Funding: Foundation
Contributor: The Antoinette Foundation
Additional Information: Finalists must be able to attend (at their own cost) a panel interview in Istanbul in July.

RSM-ING Bank Loan Programme

Subjects: Business management.
Purpose: To finance outstanding Dutch students seeking to pursue a career in business.
Eligibility: Only candidates of Dutch nationality are eligible.
Level of Study: MBA
Type: Grant
Value: 50% of all tuition fees
Length of Study: 1 year
Frequency: Annual
Study Establishment: Erasmus University
Country of Study: The Netherlands
Application Procedure: Apply online.
Closing Date: May 31st
Funding: Corporation
Contributor: ING Bank

RSM-Intermediair EMBA Scholarship

Subjects: Business management.
Level of Study: MBA
Value: €15,000
Length of Study: 1 year
Frequency: Annual
Study Establishment: Erasmus University
Country of Study: The Netherlands
No. of awards offered: 2
Application Procedure: See website.
Closing Date: May 31st
Funding: Foundation
Contributor: Intermediair

RSM-NESO in Beijing Scholarship

Subjects: Business management.
Eligibility: Open to candidates from China only.
Level of Study: MBA
Type: Scholarship
Value: €17,000
Length of Study: 1 year
Frequency: Annual
Study Establishment: Erasmus University
Country of Study: The Netherlands
No. of awards offered: 2
Application Procedure: See website.
Closing Date: May 31st

RSM-NTIO in Taiwan Scholarship

Subjects: Business management.
Eligibility: Open to candidates from Taiwan only.
Type: Scholarship
Value: €34,000
Length of Study: 1 year
Frequency: Annual
Study Establishment: Erasmus University
Country of Study: The Netherlands
No. of awards offered: 1
Application Procedure: See website.
Closing Date: May 31st
Funding: Government
Contributor: Netherlands Education Support Office

ROSL (ROYAL OVER-SEAS LEAGUE) ARTS

Over-Seas House, Park Place, St James's Street, London, SW1A 1LR, England
Tel: (44) 20 7408 0214 ext 219
Fax: (44) 20 7499 6738
Email: culture@rosl.org.uk
Website: www.rosl.org.uk
Contact: Ms Elaine Mitchener, Promotions Officer

The principal aim of the ROSL (Royal Over-Seas League) ARTS is to provide performance and exhibition opportunities for prize-winning artists and musicians early in their careers, bringing their work to the attention of the professional arts community, the media and the general public.

ROSL Annual Music Competition

Subjects: Musical performance, in four solo classes such as strings (including the harp and guitar), woodwind, brass and percussion, keyboard, singers and an ensemble class.
Purpose: To support and promote young Commonwealth musicians.
Eligibility: Open to citizens of the Commonwealth, including the United Kingdom and former Commonwealth countries, who are not more than 28 years of age for instrumentalists or 30 years of age for singers.
Level of Study: Professional development
Type: Competition
Value: Over UK £30,000 in prizes, including a UK £5,000 first prize
Frequency: Annual
Country of Study: Any country
No. of awards offered: Varies
Application Procedure: Applicants must see the website: www.roslarts.co.uk
Closing Date: January 14th
Funding: Commercial, individuals, private, trusts
No. of awards given last year: 19
No. of applicants last year: 500

Royal Over-Seas League Travel Scholarship

Subjects: ROSL will consider work in any medium.
Purpose: To support and promote young United Kingdom and Commonwealth artists.
Eligibility: Open to citizens of Commonwealth, including the United Kingdom, and former Commonwealth countries, who are up to 35 years of age, on year of application.
Level of Study: Graduate, postgraduate, professional development, unrestricted
Value: UK £3,000
Frequency: Annual
Country of Study: United Kingdom or Commonwealth
No. of awards offered: 5 travel scholarships (regions change annually)
Application Procedure: Applicants must see the website: www.roslarts.co.uk
Closing Date: March 31st
Funding: Private, commercial, trusts
No. of awards given last year: 5
No. of applicants last year: 450
Additional Information: Each artist may be represented by one recent work only, any medium. Works must not exceed 152 cm in their largest dimension, inclusive of frame.

ROTARY FOUNDATION

One Rotary Center, 1560 Sherman Avenue, Evanston, IL, 60201-3698, United States of America
Tel: (1) 847 866 3000
Fax: (1) 847 328 8554
Email: scholarshipinquiries@rotaryintl.org
Website: www.rotary.org
Contact: Administrative Assistant

Through the Rotary Foundation, Rotarians worldwide strive to promote international understanding and relations between peoples of different nations.

Rotary Foundation Academic Year Ambassadorial Scholarships

Subjects: All subjects.
Purpose: To further international understanding and friendly relations among people of different countries.
Eligibility: Open to citizens of a country where there are Rotary clubs. The applicants should have completed more than 2 years of college-level coursework or equivalent professional experience before commencing their scholarship studies. Applicants must be proficient in the language of the proposed host country.
Level of Study: Unrestricted
Type: Scholarship
Value: Round-trip transportation, tuition, room and board expenses, some educational supplies and 1 month of language training if necessary, totalling up to US$25,000 or its equivalent
Length of Study: 1 academic year
Frequency: Annual
Study Establishment: A study institution assigned by the Trustees of the Rotary Foundation
No. of awards offered: Varies
Application Procedure: Applicants should contact a local Rotary club for details.
Closing Date: Varies according to the local Rotary club, but between March 15th and July 15th. Applicants must apply over a year in advance
Funding: Private
Additional Information: Scholars will not be assigned to study in areas of a country where they have previously lived or studied for more than 6 months. During the study year, scholars are expected to be outstanding ambassadors of goodwill through appearances before Rotary clubs, schools, civic organizations and other forums. Upon completion of the scholarship, scholars are expected to share the experiences of understanding acquired during the study year with the people of their home countries. Candidates should contact local Rotary clubs for information on the availability of particular scholarships. Not all Rotary districts are able to offer scholarships. Further details are available from the website.

Rotary Foundation Cultural Ambassadorial Scholarships

Subjects: Cultural immersion and intensive language study.
Purpose: To further international understanding and friendly relations among people of different countries, and to make possible intensive language study and cultural immersion in another country.
Eligibility: Open to citizens of a country where there are Rotary clubs. The applicants should have completed more than 2 years of college-level coursework or equivalent professional experience before commencing their scholarship studies. Applicants must have completed more than 1 year of college level coursework or equivalent in the proposed language of study.
Level of Study: Unrestricted
Type: Scholarship
Value: Round-trip transportation, language training expenses, and homestay living arrangements, totalling up to US$12,000 and US$19,000, respectively
Length of Study: 3 or 6 months
Frequency: Annual
Study Establishment: A language school assigned by the Trustees of the Rotary Foundation
Country of Study: Any country in which there is a Rotary Club
No. of awards offered: Varies
Application Procedure: Applicants should contact their local Rotary club for details. Applications are considered for candidates interested in studying Arabic, English, French, German, Hebrew, Italian, Japanese, Korean, Mandarin Chinese, Polish, Portuguese, Russian, Spanish, Swahili and Swedish.
Closing Date: Varies according to the local Rotary club, but between March 15th and July 15th. Applicants must apply over a year in advance
Funding: Private
Additional Information: During the study year, scholars are expected to be outstanding ambassadors of goodwill through appearances before Rotary clubs, schools, civic organizations and other forums. Candidates should contact local Rotary clubs for information on the availability of particular scholarships. Not all Rotary districts are able to offer scholarships. Further details are available from the website.

Rotary Foundation Multi-Year Ambassadorial Scholarships

Subjects: All subjects.
Purpose: To further international understanding and friendly relations among people of different countries and help defray the cost of pursuing a degree.

Eligibility: Open to citizens of a country where there are Rotary clubs. the applicants have completed more than 2 years of college-level coursework or equivalent professional experience before commencing their scholarship studies. Applicants must be proficient in the language of the proposed host country.
Level of Study: Postgraduate, unrestricted, graduate
Type: Scholarship
Value: The award provides a flat grant of US$12,500 or its equivalent per year to be applied towards the cost of a degree programme
Length of Study: 2 years
Frequency: Annual
Study Establishment: A foreign study institution approved by the trustees of the Rotary Foundation
Country of Study: Any country in which there is a Rotary Club
No. of awards offered: Varies
Application Procedure: Applicants should contact a local Rotary club for details.
Closing Date: Varies according to the local Rotary club, but between March 15th and July 15th. Applicants must apply over a year in advance
Funding: Private
Additional Information: Scholars will not be assigned to study in areas of a country where they have previously lived or studied for more than 6 months. During the study year, scholars are expected to be outstanding ambassadors of goodwill through appearances before Rotary clubs, schools, civic organizations and other forums. Upon completion of the scholarship, scholars are expected to share the experiences of understanding acquired during the study year with the people of their home countries. Candidates should contact local Rotary clubs for information on the availability of particular scholarships. Not all Rotary districts are able to offer scholarships. Further details are available from the website.

Rotary Grants for University Teachers

Subjects: All subjects of practical use to the host country.
Purpose: To build international understanding while strengthening higher education in low-income countries.
Eligibility: Open to candidates who have held a college or university appointment for 3 or more years and are proficient in the language of their prospective host country. Rotarians and relatives of rotarians are eligible.
Level of Study: Professional development
Type: Grant
Value: Up to US$12,500 for 3–5 months or up to US$22,500 for 6–10 months
Length of Study: 3–5 months or 6–10 months
Frequency: Annual, dependent on funds available
Study Establishment: A college/university located in a low-income country
Country of Study: Low-income countries only
No. of awards offered: Varies
Application Procedure: Applicants should contact a local Rotary club for details.
Closing Date: Varies according to the local Rotary club, but between March 15th and July 15th. Applicants must apply over a year in advance
Funding: Private
Additional Information: Grant recipients are expected to be outstanding ambassadors of goodwill to the people of their host and home countries through appearances to Rotary clubs. Not all Rotary districts are able to offer grants for university teachers. Further details are available from the website.

ROTARY YONEYAMA MEMORIAL FOUNDATION, INC.

8F ABC Building, 2-6-3 Shiba Koen, Minato-ku, Tokyo, 105-0011, Japan
Tel: (81) 3 3434 8681
Fax: (81) 3 3578 8281
Website: www.rotary-yoneyama.org.jp/english
Contact: Administrative Assistant

The Rotary Yoneyama Memorial Foundation, Inc. has been growing in service and organization annually through the endorsement and cooperation of Japanese Rotaries. It awards scholarships to students not only from Asian countries but also from the rest of the world who are residents of Japan and studying or conducting research at Japanese Institutes of Higher Education.

Rotary Yoneyama Scholarship

Subjects: All subjects.
Purpose: The purpose of this programme is, by supporting motivated and excellent students from the world, to promote international and mutual understanding, develop international friendships and exchanges and make a contribution to create and maintain peace in the world.
Eligibility: Open to non-Japanese candidates under 45 years of age with a 'college student' visa for the purpose of studies and research.
Level of Study: Postgraduate, graduate, doctorate
Type: Scholarship
Value: Yen 140,000 per month (graduate, postgraduate), Yen 100,000 per month (undergraduate)
Length of Study: A maximum of 2 years
Frequency: Annual
Study Establishment: Colleges and universities
Country of Study: Japan
No. of awards offered: Varies
Application Procedure: Applicants should contact the Foundation for details or visit the website.
Closing Date: Please contact the organization
Funding: Private
Contributor: Rotarians in Japan
No. of awards given last year: 1,002 (sum total of all the scholarship programmes)
No. of applicants last year: 1,600
Additional Information: It is recommended that applicants contact the Foundation directly, since requirements for certain applicants can be conditional. Selection is extremely competitive, as the number of awards is limited.

THE ROYAL ACADEMY OF ENGINEERING

29 Great Peter Street, London, SW1P 3LW, England
Tel: (44) 20 7222 2688
Fax: (44) 20 7233 0054
Website: www.raeng.org.uk
Contact: Dr Elizabeth Horwitz, MacRobert Award Scheme

The Royal Academy of Engineering's objectives may be summarized as the pursuit, encouragement and maintenance of excellence in the whole field of engineering in order to promote the advancement of the science, art and the practice of engineering for the benefit of the public.

Exxon Mobil Teaching Fellowships

Subjects: Chemical, petroleum and mechanical engineering, geology.
Purpose: To encourage able young engineering and Earth science lecturers to remain in the education sector in their early years.
Eligibility: Open to well-qualified graduates, preferably with industrial experience and full-time lecturing posts at Institutes of Higher Education in the United Kingdom. Applicants should have been in their current posts for at least 1 year. The post must include the teaching of chemical, petroleum or mechanical engineering to undergraduates through courses that are accredited for registration with professional bodies for qualifications such as chartered engineer. For applicants whose career path has been graduation at the age of 22, followed by academic or industrial posts, the age limit is generally 32 years (at the closing date). Older candidates who have taken time out, eg. for industrial experience, parenthood or voluntary service, will also be considered. Applicants should preferably be chartered engineers, or of equivalent professional status, or should be making progress towards this qualification.
Level of Study: Postdoctorate
Type: Fellowship

Value: UK £9,000
Length of Study: 4 years
Frequency: Annual
Study Establishment: The applicant's current university in the United Kingdom
Country of Study: United Kingdom
No. of awards offered: Up to 6
Application Procedure: Applicants must complete an application form.
Closing Date: October 1st
Funding: Commercial
Contributor: Exxon Mobile
Additional Information: A brochure is available on request. Enquiries about Exxon mobile university contacts should be sent to bowbricki@raeng.co.uk

Panasonic Trust Awards

Subjects: Engineering, particularly new engineering developments and new technologies.
Purpose: To encourage the technical updating and continuous professional development of qualified engineers through courses provided by United Kingdom Institutes of Higher Education at the Master's level.
Eligibility: Open to United Kingdom citizens who are qualified at the degree level in engineering or a related discipline. HND, HNC, OND, ONC or City and Guilds Full Technological Certificate qualifications are acceptable as a minimum. Applicants must be members, at any grade, of an engineering institution, working at the professional level in engineering in the United Kingdom and have several years of experience working at this level. Preference is given to those undertaking part-time modular Master's courses. The intended course of study must be relevant to the applicant's current or future career plans.
Level of Study: Professional development
Type: Award
Value: Usually 50 per cent of course fees up to a maximum of UK £1,000
Length of Study: The duration of the course
Frequency: Dependent on funds available
Country of Study: United Kingdom
No. of awards offered: Varies
Application Procedure: Applicants must write to the main address for application instructions, the application form and guidelines for employers and course co-ordinators.
Closing Date: Offered all year round
Funding: Private
Additional Information: Employers are expected to support an application in writing. The Trustees hope that the employer, once approached, might pay the full fees for the course. However, if this is not possible, a contribution from the employer is desirable. Applications must be supported by the course director or co-ordinator and confirm that the applicant is suitable for the course. Applications for grants of less than UK £1,000 should be submitted at least 4 weeks before the start of the course. Applications for larger grants should be submitted at least 6 weeks before the start of the course.

Royal Academy Engineering Professional Development

Subjects: Engineering.
Purpose: To ensure that the stills and knowledge of employees reflect the very latest in technological advances.
Eligibility: Open to UK citizens with a degree or HND/HNC in engineering or a closely allied subject. OND/ONC or City and Guilds Full Technological Certificate or NVQ level III qualifications are acceptable provided the individual has substantial industrial experience.
Level of Study: Professional development
Type: Grant
Value: Up to UK £10,000. In additions, prizes of UK £1,000 are being offered for each of the five most innovative applications.
Length of Study: 1 year
Frequency: Annual
Country of Study: United Kingdom
Application Procedure: For further information please contact the scheme manager Ian Bowbrick at the Academy.
Closing Date: October 21st

For further information contact:

Email: Ian.bowbrick@raeng.org.uk

Royal Academy Executive Engineering Programme

Subjects: Engineering.
Purpose: To ensure that top engineering graduates continue to develop as professional engineers in order to provide UK industry with the high caliber technical and commercial managers required by world class enterprises.
Eligibility: Open to permanent members of United Kingdom Institutes of Higher Education with an approved engineering qualification.
Level of Study: Postgraduate
Type: Scholarship
Value: All training programme fees
Length of Study: 1 year
Frequency: Annual
Study Establishment: An industrial or commercial company
Country of Study: United Kingdom
Application Procedure: Visit the programme website.
Closing Date: Offered all year round
Funding: Foundation
Contributor: Gatsby Charitable Foundation

For further information contact:

Email: peter.revell@raeng.org.uk

Royal Academy of Engineering Industrial Secondment Scheme

Subjects: All fields of engineering.
Purpose: To provide financial support for the secondment of academic engineering staff to industrial companies within the United Kingdom.
Eligibility: Open to permanent members of United Kingdom Institutes of Higher Education with an approved engineering qualification, teaching some aspects of engineering. Preference may be given to junior staff without previous industrial experience or to more senior members whose industrial experience may have taken place some years earlier.
Level of Study: Unrestricted
Type: Grant
Value: Varies
Length of Study: Usually 3–6 months
Frequency: Dependent on funds available
Study Establishment: An industrial or commercial company
Country of Study: United Kingdom
No. of awards offered: Varies
Application Procedure: Applicants must submit a completed application form with a curriculum vitae, personal statement outlining the nature and objectives of the proposed secondment, letter of support from the applicant's head of department, statement from the applicant's employer detailing the financial aspects of the application, statement from the host company confirming the agreed work programme and defining the benefits of the secondment to the company and detailing any contribution costs that the company may wish to make. Application forms are available from the main address.
Funding: Government
No. of awards given last year: 18
No. of applicants last year: 26
Additional Information: The main objective is to obtain up-to-date industrial experience, to improve teaching capabilities and generally to foster academic industrial links. Contact Mr A Eades for further information.

Royal Academy of Engineering International Travel Grants

Subjects: Engineering, materials technology and computing.
Purpose: To facilitate study visits overseas, generally for attendance at conferences, research institutions and/or industrial sites.
Eligibility: Open to postgraduate students, postdoctoral researchers, lecturers involved in research and chartered engineers in United Kingdom Institutes of Higher Education and in United Kingdom industry. Grants are not given to Fellows of The Royal Academy of

Engineering, civil servants, employees of the British Museum or other government bodies. To be eligible for funding applicants must be United Kingdom or European Union nationals or United Kingdom permanent residents. There are no age restrictions.
Level of Study: Postgraduate, postdoctorate, professional development, doctorate
Type: Travel grant
Value: 30–50 per cent of approved costs
Frequency: Dependent on funds available
No. of awards offered: Varies
Application Procedure: Applicants must submit a completed application form, nominating two referees of their choice, an abstract if an essay is being presented at a conference, publication list, photocopy of the personal details page from their passport, and a short paragraph of no more than 200 words, on a separate sheet of A4, justifying the relevance of the activity to their current work.
Closing Date: Applications are accepted at any time
Funding: Government
No. of awards given last year: Over 700
No. of applicants last year: Over 1,000
Additional Information: Applicants are urged to submit their forms at least 2 months prior to the departure date to enable APEX fares to be used.

Royal Academy of Engineering MacRobert Award

Subjects: The successful development of innovation in engineering or the other physical sciences.
Purpose: To recognize and reward outstanding contributions relating to innovation in engineering.
Eligibility: Open to individuals, independent teams and teams working for a firm, organization or laboratory. There should be no more than five members in a team.
Level of Study: Unrestricted
Type: Award
Value: UK £50,000 and a gold medal
Frequency: Annual
Country of Study: United Kingdom
No. of awards offered: 1
Application Procedure: Applicants must submit a 200–500 word summary of the engineering achievement, supported by 15 copies of relevant technical documentation. Further details and rules and conditions are available from the Royal Academy of Engineering.
Closing Date: January 30th
Funding: Private
No. of awards given last year: 1

Royal Academy Sir Angus Paton Bursary

Subjects: Engineering for development and water and environmental management.
Eligibility: Open to all suitably qualified engineer enrolled on a full-time Masters course related to the environment.
Level of Study: Postgraduate
Type: Bursary
Value: UK £7,000
Length of Study: 1 year
Frequency: Annual
Country of Study: United Kingdom
No. of awards offered: 1
Application Procedure: For further information please contact the scheme manager Ian Bowbrick at the Academy.
Closing Date: Offered all year round.
Funding: Private
Contributor: Sir Angus Paton

For further information contact:

Email: ian.bowbrick@raeng.org.uk

Royal Academy Sir Henry Royce Bursary

Subjects: Aerospace design, manufacture and management, automotive engineering design.
Eligibility: Open to qualified engineers enrolled on part-time modular Master's courses.
Level of Study: Postgraduate
Type: Bursary
Value: UK £1,000
Length of Study: 1 year
Frequency: Annual
Country of Study: United Kingdom
Application Procedure: For further information please contact the scheme manager Ian Bowbrick at the Academy.
Closing Date: Offered all year round
Funding: Foundation
Contributor: Sir Henry Royce Memorial Foundation
Additional Information: Each awardee will receive a commemorative certificate and, on successful completion of their studies and award of the degree, a medal from the Sir Henry Royce Memorial Foundation.

For further information contact:

Email: ian.bowbrick@raeng.org.uk

Royal Academy Visiting Professors Scheme

Subjects: Principles of engineering design, engineering design for sustainable development, integrated system design.
Purpose: To help universities to teach engineering design to undergraduates in a way that relates to real professional practice.
Level of Study: Research, postdoctorate, doctorate
Type: Fellowship
Length of Study: 1 year
Frequency: Annual
Country of Study: United Kingdom
No. of awards offered: 3
Application Procedure: Further information is available from the scheme manager David Foxley at the Academy.

Sainsbury Management Fellowships

Subjects: Engineering.
Purpose: To enable young chartered engineers of the highest career potential to undertake MBA courses at European business schools.
Eligibility: Open to United Kingdom citizens, who hold a First or Upper Second Class (Honours) Degree in engineering or a closely allied subject, have chartered engineer status or are making substantial progress towards it, have the potential and ambition to achieve senior management responsibility at an early age and be aged 26–34 years at the commencement of the proposed MBA course.
Level of Study: MBA, professional development, postgraduate
Type: Fellowship
Value: Course fees
Length of Study: 1 year
Frequency: Annual
Study Establishment: Awards are normally tenable at the following business schools: North America–Harvard, MIT, Stanford, Wharton, Columbia, Kellogg, University of Chicago; Europe–INSEAD (France), IMD (Switzerland), Erasmus (The Netherlands), IESE (Spain), SDA Bocconi (Italy)
Country of Study: Any country
No. of awards offered: 10
Application Procedure: Applicants must complete an application form, please contact the office for details.
Closing Date: Applications are accepted at any time
Funding: Private
Contributor: The Gatsby Charitable Foundation
No. of awards given last year: 10
No. of applicants last year: 46

Sainsbury Management Fellowships in the Life Sciences.

Subjects: Life science.
Purpose: To support young scientists of high career potential to undertake activities related to their Personal Development Plans.
Eligibility: Open to UK citizens with a PhD in a bio-related subject, following a career compatible with the scheme's objectives in the UK. The applicants should be aged between 25 and 38 years.
Level of Study: Postgraduate
Type: Fellowship
Value: The award covers the cost of activities related to an individuals personal development plan, subject to approval.

Frequency: Annual
Country of Study: Any country
Application Procedure: For further information please contact the scheme manager Ian Bowbrick at the Academy.
Closing Date: Offered all year round
Funding: Private
Contributor: Gatsby Charitable Foundation

For further information contact:

Email: ian.bowbrick@raeng.org.uk

ROYAL ACADEMY OF MUSIC

Marylebone Road, London, NW1 5HT, England
Tel: (44) 20 7873 7393
Fax: (44) 20 7873 7394
Email: go@ram.ac.uk
Website: www.ram.ac.uk
Contact: Examinations Officer

The Royal Academy of Music is a music college offering courses in music at postgraduate level. The Academy is part of the University of London.

Royal Academy of Music General Bursary Awards

Subjects: All relevant branches of music education and training.
Purpose: To help defray tuition fees and general living expenses for study at the Royal Academy of Music.
Eligibility: Open to any student offered a place at the Academy.
Level of Study: Postgraduate
Type: Scholarship/Bursary
Value: According to need and availability of funds
Length of Study: Normally for a complete academic year. Individual requirements may be imposed
Frequency: Annual
Study Establishment: The Royal Academy of Music
Country of Study: United Kingdom
No. of awards offered: Varies
Application Procedure: Applicants must complete an application form, which is sent automatically to all postgraduate students who are offered places.
Closing Date: January 31st for the following academic year
Funding: Trusts, individuals, private, commercial

ROYAL AERONAUTICAL SOCIETY

4 Hamilton Place, London, W1J 7BQ, England
Tel: (44) 20 7670 4300
Fax: (44) 20 7670 4309
Email: careers@raes.org.uk
Website: www.aerosociety.com
Contact: Careers Centre Manager

The Royal Aeronautical Society was founded in 1866 and is the only professional institution that covers all aspects of the aerospace industry including research, manufacture, operations and maintenance. Society membership unlocks a host of benefits for both the individual and organizations. Membership is open to anyone with an association or interest in aerospace.

Handley Page Award

Subjects: Aeronautics.
Purpose: To encourage the advancement of safety and reliability in air transport.
Eligibility: Open to citizens of the United Kingdom and the British Commonwealth who are suitably qualified undertake the proposed work.
Level of Study: Professional development
Type: Award
Value: Approx. UK £5,000 to be awarded in whole or in part to an individual or group
Frequency: Annual
No. of awards offered: 1
Application Procedure: Applicants must complete an application form, available on request.
Closing Date: May 30th
Funding: Private
Contributor: The Society Trust Fund

Royal Aeronautical Society Centennial Scholarship Award

Subjects: Aeronautics and aerospace-related subjects.
Purpose: To encourage the next generation of aerospace pioneers through the study of aeronautics and aerospace-related subjects and relevant projects to encourage young people.
Eligibility: Open to students studying aerospace-related (eg. aviation, aeronautical engineering, aeronautic-related) studies, and key organizations and research groups whose projects meet the aims and objectives of the fund.
Level of Study: Postdoctorate, postgraduate, doctorate, graduate, research, relevant projects of national reach that meet the aims and objectives of the end
Type: Scholarship
Value: As a guide, from UK £500 to 5,000
Length of Study: Most have already completed 1–2 years of relevant study
Study Establishment: Not specified
No. of awards offered: Varies
Application Procedure: Applicants must complete an application form, available on request and provide all documentation specified in the form.
Closing Date: March 31st - series 1, September 5th - series 2
Funding: Individuals, commercial
Contributor: A number of corporate, private and individual donors
No. of awards given last year: 8
No. of applicants last year: Approx. 25

ROYAL ANTHROPOLOGICAL INSTITUTE

50 Fitzroy Street, London, WTP 5BT, England
Tel: (44) 20 7387 0455
Fax: (44) 20 7383 4235
Email: admin@therai.org.uk
Website: www.therai.org.uk
Contact: Director of Grants

The Royal Anthropological Institute is a non-profit registered charity. It is entirely independent, with a Director and a small staff accountable to the Council, elected annually from the Fellowship. Council and Committee members and the editorial team of the Institute's principal journal, the *Journal of the Royal Anthropological Institute* (incorporating MAN), give their services without remuneration.

Emslie Horniman Anthropological Scholarship Fund

Subjects: Anthropology.
Purpose: To provide predoctoral grants for fieldwork in anthropology with a preference for research outside the United Kingdom.
Eligibility: Open to citizens of the United Kingdom, Commonwealth or Irish Republic who are university graduates or who can satisfy the trustees of their suitability for the study proposed. Preference is given to applicants whose proposals include fieldwork outside the United Kingdom. Graduates who already hold a doctorate in anthropology are not eligible. Open to individuals only, as no grants are given to expeditions or teams.
Level of Study: Postgraduate, predoctorate
Type: Scholarship
Value: UK £1,000–9,500
Frequency: Annual
Country of Study: Any country
No. of awards offered: Approx. 10
Application Procedure: Applicants must request an application form.
Closing Date: March 31st
Funding: Private
No. of awards given last year: 4

Additional Information: No grants are available for library research, university fees or subsistence in the United Kingdom.

ROYAL COLLEGE OF MIDWIVES

15 Mansfield Street, London, W1G 9NH, England
Tel: (44) 20 7312 3535
Fax: (44) 20 7312 3536
Email: info@rcm.org.uk
Website: www.rcm.org.uk
Contact: S E MacDonald, Education and Research Manager

The Royal College of Midwives is the major professional organization for midwives in the United Kingdom, and aims to contribute to the art and science of midwifery knowledge and practice. The RCM awards and scholarships provide opportunities for the development of good practice ultimately improving the care provided to women, their babies and families.

Hospital Savings Association (HSA) Charitable Trust Scholarships

Subjects: Midwifery and women's care.
Purpose: To provide financial support for midwives undertaking further academic studies relevant to the improvement of practice and care.
Eligibility: Open to midwives who are RCM members, employed in clinical practice in the NHS, returning to NHS, in non-profit charity employment. Applicants must be able to demonstrate that they can make a valuable contribution to healthcare delivery during the next 5 years, that they are undertaking studies of direct relevance to patient care, are studying in the United Kingdom and have not already received HSA funding.
Level of Study: Doctorate, professional development, graduate, postgraduate
Type: Scholarships
Value: UK £5,000 for midwives studying for a doctorate or Master's degree, UK £3,000 for midwives studying for a BSc, diploma or certificate and UK £1,000 for any study (except doctorate/Master's)
Frequency: Annual
Country of Study: United Kingdom
No. of awards offered: Several
Application Procedure: Applicants must email marlyn.gennace@rcm.org.uk for further information.
Closing Date: November
Funding: Commercial
Contributor: HSA Charitable Trust
No. of awards given last year: 16
No. of applicants last year: 34

Mary Seacole Nursing Leadership Award

Subjects: Midwifery, nursing, health visiting, health service needs of ethnic minority communities.
Purpose: To provide an opportunity for the development of professional practice, service development and leadership potential of black and minority ethic midwives, nurses and health visitors.
Eligibility: Applicants must be a nurse and, midwife or health visitor. Application should reflect the example set by Mary Seacole.
Level of Study: Graduate, research, professional development, doctorate
Type: Leadership awards
Value: UK £6,250
Length of Study: 1 year
Frequency: Annual
Country of Study: United Kingdom
No. of awards offered: 4
Application Procedure: Applicants must send a stamped addressed envelope to the Royal College of Nursing (RCN) to obtain details and an application form.
Closing Date: End of May
Funding: Government
Contributor: Department of Health
No. of awards given last year: 1
No. of applicants last year: 3

For further information contact:

Royal College of Nursing, 20 Cavendish Square, London, W1G 0RN, England
Contact: Mary Seacole Award Award, Officer

RCM Midwifery Awards

Subjects: Midwifery.
Purpose: To recognize and celebrate innovation in midwifery practice, education and research.
Eligibility: Applicants may be individuals or small groups and should meet the criteria of one of the 9 categories.
Level of Study: Research, professional development
Value: Varies (up to UK £20,000 in total)
Frequency: Annual
Country of Study: Projects Based in United Kingdom – though some requiring travel may involve external activity
No. of awards offered: 9
Application Procedure: Applicants must apply in writing or email to the address given below. The application must be accompanied by a 500-word description of the project. Short-listed candidates will be asked to attend an interview.
Closing Date: July 16th
Funding: Commercial
Contributor: Several
No. of awards given last year: 10 awards in 5 categories
No. of applicants last year: 110

For further information contact:

Gothic House, 3 The Green, Richmond, Surrey, TW9 1PL, England
Email: mail@chamberdunn.co.uk
Contact: Chamberlain Dunn Associates

Ruth Davies Research Bursary

Subjects: Midwifery.
Purpose: To promote and develop midwifery research and practice.
Eligibility: Open to practicing midwives who are RCM members, who have basic knowledge, skills and understanding of the research process, have access to research support in their trust or Institutes of Higher Education and who have been in practice for 2 years or more.
Level of Study: Graduate, professional development, postgraduate, postdoctorate, doctorate, research
Type: Bursary
Value: UK £5,000
Length of Study: 1 year
Frequency: Annual
Country of Study: United Kingdom
No. of awards offered: 2
Application Procedure: Applicants must submit a succinct curriculum vitae covering the previous 5 years, a research proposal of no more than 2,500 words and letters of support from both employers and academics who are familiar with the applicant's work.
Closing Date: July 16th
Funding: Commercial
Contributor: RNPFN/Liverpool Victoria Group
No. of awards given last year: 2
No. of applicants last year: 10

For further information contact:

Mrs Marlyn Gennace, Ruth Davies Research Bursary Administrator

ROYAL COLLEGE OF MUSIC

Prince Consort Road, London, SW7 2BS, England
Tel: (44) 20 7591 4377
Fax: (44) 20 7591 4856
Email: cpartridge@rcm.ac.uk
Website: www.rcm.ac.uk
Contact: Ms Celia Partridge, International & Awards Officer

The Royal College of Music, London, provides specialized musical education and professional training at the highest international level for performers and composers. This enables talented students to develop the musical skills, knowledge, understanding and resourcefulness that will equip them to contribute significantly to musical life in the United Kingdom and internationally.

Royal College of Music Junior Fellowship in Performance History

Subjects: Music performance history.
Purpose: To offer a young musician the opportunity to develop practical and scholarly skills.
Level of Study: Unrestricted
Type: Fellowship
Value: UK £8,000
Length of Study: 12 months
Frequency: Annual
Study Establishment: Royal College of Music
Country of Study: United Kingdom
No. of awards offered: 1
Application Procedure: See the website.
Closing Date: October 28th

For further information contact:

Website: www.cph.rcm.ac.uk

Royal College of Music Junior Scholarship

Subjects: Music performance, composition and conducting.
Purpose: To recognize merit in music performance, composition or conducting.
Eligibility: Applicants need to be able to demonstrate substantial successful in their specialism, the motivation and determination to continue intensive studies, and the desire to develop their skills by working regularly with other musicians within and outside the college.
Level of Study: Unrestricted
Type: Scholarship
Value: UK £6,000–10,000
Length of Study: 1–4 years
Frequency: Dependent on funds available
Study Establishment: Royal College of Music
Country of Study: United Kingdom
No. of awards offered: 20
Application Procedure: Contact the college.
Closing Date: March 10th
Additional Information: Junior fellows may take part in competitions as accompanists or ensemble members, but may not receive any prize money awarded.

Royal College of Music Scholarships

Subjects: Music performance, composition and conducting.
Purpose: To recognize merit in music performance, composition or conducting.
Eligibility: Applicants must be talented, young musicians enrolled in a course of study at the college.
Level of Study: Unrestricted
Type: Scholarship
Value: Up to UK £13,950 (full fees)
Length of Study: 1–4 years
Frequency: Annual
Study Establishment: Royal College of Music
Country of Study: United Kingdom
No. of awards offered: Approx. 140
Application Procedure: Applicants must apply only by application for a place of study.
Closing Date: October 1st
Funding: Private
No. of awards given last year: 85
No. of applicants last year: 1,500

ROYAL COLLEGE OF NURSING (RCN)

20 Cavendish Square, London, W1G 0RN, England
Tel: (44) 20 7409 3333
Fax: (44) 20 7647 3433
Email: moira.lambert@rcn.org.uk
Website: www.rcn.org.uk
Contact: Ms Moira Lambert, Awards Officer

The Royal College of Nursing of the United Kingdom (RCN) represents nurses and nursing, promotes excellence in practice and shapes health policies.

The Allen Iswlyn Giles Memorial Nursing Scholarship

Subjects: Nursing.
Purpose: To promote the advancement of the art and science of nursing.
Eligibility: Open to RCN members holding a statutory qualification in nursing and practicing in Wales.
Level of Study: Unrestricted
Type: Scholarship
Value: Up to UK £1,000
Frequency: Annual
Country of Study: United Kingdom
No. of awards offered: Varies
Application Procedure: Applicants must apply directly to the trustees of the fund.
Closing Date: May 31st
Funding: Private
Contributor: Allen Iswlyn Giles (Covenant)
No. of awards given last year: None
No. of applicants last year: 12

Barbers Company Clinical Nursing Scholarship

Subjects: All subjects related to nursing.
Purpose: To enable nurses making a career in clinical nursing to undertake further education, research or a clinical project.
Eligibility: The scholarship is offered for the fees or subsistence of a nurse, normally undertaking a taught masters programme relevant to nursing or research in an academic department in the U.K., or at an approved academic department of nursing overseas.
Level of Study: Predoctorate, postgraduate, doctorate
Type: Scholarship
Value: UK £5,000
Frequency: Annual
Study Establishment: Universities
Country of Study: United Kingdom
No. of awards offered: Varies
Application Procedure: Applicants must send in their curriculum vitae plus 500 words on the course/research or project and its intended application to: Miss Kate Monks, The Barbers Company Clinical Nursing Scholarship, RCN Institute, Radcliffe Infirmary, Woodstock Road, Oxford 02 6HE.
Closing Date: February 28th
Funding: Commercial
Contributor: Barber Surgeons (The Worshipful Company of Barbers)
No. of awards given last year: UK£5,000 shared among 4 successful awardees
No. of applicants last year: 40

For further information contact:

The Barbers Company Clinical Nursing Scholarship, RCN Institute, Radcliffe Infirmary, Woodstock Road, Oxford, 02 6HE, England

Ethicon Nurses Education Trust Fund

Subjects: Nursing, midwifery and health visiting.
Purpose: To further members' education and to enhance the standard of expertise in their chosen field of nursing.
Eligibility: Open to members of the RCN, NATN or ICNA only.
Level of Study: Postgraduate, professional development
Type: Grant
Value: Up to UK £1,000 each
Length of Study: Unrestricted
Frequency: Annual
Study Establishment: Unrestricted
Country of Study: Any country
No. of awards offered: Varies
Application Procedure: Applicants must contact Fitwise Drumcross Hall for an application form. Telephone no: 01506 811077.
Closing Date: March
Funding: Commercial
Contributor: Johnson & Johnson/Ethicon

No. of awards given last year: 9
No. of applicants last year: 48

For further information contact:

Fitwise Drumcross Hall, Bathgate, EH48 4JT, Scotland
Tel: (44) 01506 811077

HSA Charitable Trust Scholarships for Nurses and Midwives

Subjects: Nursing, midwifery and health visiting.
Purpose: To fund nurses and midwives in clinical practice towards course fees on postregistration study and enrolled nurses taking conversion courses.
Eligibility: Open to nurses, midwives and health visitors in the United Kingdom working in the NHS or caring for NHS patients and enrolled nurses in the NHS or non-profit organizations.
Level of Study: Professional development, doctorate, postgraduate, graduate, predoctorate
Type: Other
Value: UK £1,000–5,000 each
Length of Study: Unrestricted
Frequency: Annual
Study Establishment: A university
Country of Study: United Kingdom
No. of awards offered: Up to 60
Application Procedure: Applicants must request an application form by sending a stamped addressed envelope. Applications and enquiries will be dealt with between August and October each year.
Closing Date: November 1st
Funding: Commercial
Contributor: HSA charitable trust
No. of awards given last year: 43
No. of applicants last year: 124

For further information contact:

HSA Charitable Trust Scholarships, c/o Awards Officer, Royal College of Nursing, 20 Cavendish Square, London, W1G 0RN, England

Nuffield Trust/RCN/IHM Joint Travel Awards

Subjects: Nursing, midwifery and health visiting including public health, health policy and health education.
Purpose: To undertake a study overseas to pursue an area of innovation in health services. For nurses and healthcare managers to undertake joint study tours to improve patient experience.
Eligibility: Open to members of the RCN only.
Level of Study: Professional development, postgraduate
Type: Fellowship
Value: Up to UK £5,000 each
Length of Study: Unrestricted
Frequency: Annual
Study Establishment: Unrestricted
Country of Study: Any country
No. of awards offered: Varies
Application Procedure: Applicants must send a stamped addressed envelope for application requirements. Enquiries are dealt with between February and April.
Closing Date: April
Funding: Private
Contributor: Nuffield Trust
No. of awards given last year: 2
No. of applicants last year: 5

For further information contact:

RCN/Nuffield Trust Travelling Fellowship, c/o Award Officer, Royal College of Nursing, 20 Cavendish Square, London, W1G 0RN, England

RCN Grants

Subjects: Nursing, midwifery and health visiting.
Purpose: To assist RCN members to enhance their professional skills, knowledge and competence. Preregistration nursing students in RCN membership are also eligible.
Eligibility: Open to RCN members with 2 years of RCN membership for postregistration nurses or 1 year's membership for preregistration nursing students.
Level of Study: Professional development
Type: Grant
Value: Up to UK £250 each
Length of Study: Unrestricted
Frequency: Annual
Study Establishment: Unrestricted
Country of Study: Any country
No. of awards offered: Varies
Application Procedure: Applicants must request information by sending a stamped addressed envelope. Enquiries are dealt with between May and July.
Closing Date: August 1st
Funding: Private
Contributor: RCN Charitable Trust Funds
No. of awards given last year: 31
No. of applicants last year: 57

For further information contact:

RCN Grants (001-532), 20 Cavendish Square, London, W1G 0RN, England
Contact: Awards Officer

RCN Margaret Parkinson Scholarships

Subjects: Nursing and midwifery.
Purpose: To encourage graduates with a non-nursing degree to qualify as a nurse and for postregistration nurses to undertake study.
Eligibility: Open to graduates who have not yet started nurse training or postregistration nurses and midwives in membership of Royal College of Nursing.
Level of Study: Professional development, graduate
Type: Scholarship
Value: Up to UK £1,000 each per annum
Length of Study: Unrestricted
Frequency: Annual
Study Establishment: Usually universities
Country of Study: United Kingdom
No. of awards offered: Varies
Application Procedure: Applicants must send a stamped addressed envelope to the Awards Officer stating that they are a graduate or postregistration nurse. Enquiries will be dealt with between November and January.
Closing Date: February
Funding: Private
Contributor: Margaret Parkinson Scholarship Fund
No. of awards given last year: 8
No. of applicants last year: 34

RCN Scholarships Fund

Subjects: Nursing, midwifery and health visiting including public health, health policy and health education.
Purpose: To provide funding for a project, study visit or course to facilitate professional development with an emphasis on education, leadership, management or dementia care.
Eligibility: Open to applicants with 3 years RCN membership for a major scholarship and 1 year membership for other scholarships.
Level of Study: Postgraduate, predoctorate, doctorate, graduate, research, professional development
Type: Scholarship
Value: Varies, up to UK £4,000 each
Length of Study: Unrestricted
Frequency: Annual
Study Establishment: Unrestricted
Country of Study: Any country
No. of awards offered: Varies
Application Procedure: Applicants must request information by sending a stamped addressed envelope. Enquiries are dealt with between February and April.
Closing Date: May 1st
Funding: Private
Contributor: RCN Charitable Trust Funds

No. of awards given last year: 15
No. of applicants last year: 24

For further information contact:

RCN Scholarships, c/o Awards Officer, Royal College of Nursing, 20 Cavendish Square, London, W1G 0RN, England

RNPFN Student Nurse Travel Awards

Subjects: Nursing and midwifery.
Purpose: To fund nursing students taking overseas electives.
Eligibility: Open to nursing students in RCN membership.
Level of Study: Professional development, pre-registration nurses
Type: Scholarship
Value: UK £500 each
Length of Study: Unrestricted
Frequency: Annual
Study Establishment: Unrestricted
Country of Study: Any country
No. of awards offered: 4
Application Procedure: Applicants must send a stamped addressed envelope to the Awards Officer to receive an application form. Enquiries will be dealt with February to April.
Closing Date: April
Funding: Commercial
Contributor: Liverpool Victoria
No. of awards given last year: 4
No. of applicants last year: 34

For further information contact:

HSA Charitable Trust Awards For Healthcare Assistants, c/o Awards Officer, Royal College of Nursing, 20 Cavendish Square, London, W1G 0RN, England

ROYAL COLLEGE OF OBSTETRICIANS AND GYNAECOLOGISTS (RCOG)

27 Sussex Place, Regent's Park, London, NW1 4RG, United Kingdom
Tel: (44) 20 7772 6263
Fax: (44) 20 7772 6359
Website: www.rcog.org.uk
Contact: R. Deshmukh, Awards Administrator

The Royal College of Obstetricians and Gynaecologists (RCOG) is dedicated to the encouragement of the study, and the advancement of science and practice of obstetrics and gynaecology.

American Gynecological Club / Gynaecological Visiting Society Fellowship

Subjects: Obstetrics and gynaecology.
Purpose: To enable the recipient to visit, make contact with and gain knowledge from a specific centre offering new techniques or methods of clinical management within the speciality.
Eligibility: Open to specialist registrars in the United Kingdom, and to junior Fellows or those in residency programmes in the United States of America.
Level of Study: Professional development
Type: Fellowship
Frequency: Annual
Country of Study: United Kingdom or United States of America
No. of awards offered: 1
Application Procedure: Applicants must contact the Awards Secretary for details.
Closing Date: March 31st

Endometriosis Millennium Fund Award

Subjects: Endometriosis.
Purpose: To stimulate and encourage research, clinical or laboratory based, or to encourage clinicians to acquire extra clinical skills to manage patients.
Eligibility: Open to members of the College or members of the RCOG trainees register who are residents and working within the United Kingdom.
Level of Study: Postgraduate
Value: Up to UK £5,000
Frequency: Annual
Country of Study: United Kingdom
No. of awards offered: More than 1
Application Procedure: Applicants must submit an application on the requisite form, which can be downloaded from the website or can be obtained from the Awards Secretary at the RCOG. Applications must be accompanied by two references from supervisors or senior colleagues and written confirmation of availability of laboratory space or access for surgical training in the host institution must be provided with the application. An undertaking that a structured typewritten report will be provided at the end of the grant period and that the source of grant will be acknowledged in any related publications must also be submitted.
Closing Date: March 31st
Contributor: The Endometriosis Millennium Fund
Additional Information: The award may only be used for the purpose approved by the Assessment Committee.

RCOG Bernhard Baron Travelling Scholarships

Subjects: Obstetrics and gynaecology.
Purpose: To expand the recipient's knowledge in areas in which he or she already has some experience.
Eligibility: Open to Fellows and members of the College.
Level of Study: Postgraduate
Type: Scholarship
Value: Up to UK £6,000
Frequency: Annual
Country of Study: Any country
No. of awards offered: 1
Application Procedure: Applicants must contact the Awards Secretary for details.
Closing Date: March 31st
No. of awards given last year: 1
No. of applicants last year: 16

RCOG Eden Travelling Fellowship

Subjects: Obstetrics and gynaecology.
Purpose: To enable the recipient to gain additional knowledge and experience in the pursuit of a specific research project in which he or she is currently engaged.
Eligibility: Open to medical graduates of not less than 2 years standing from any approved university in the United Kingdom or Commonwealth.
Level of Study: Postgraduate
Type: Fellowship
Value: Up to UK £5,000, according to the project undertaken
Frequency: Annual
Study Establishment: Another department of obstetrics and gynaecology or of closely related disciplines
Country of Study: Any country
No. of awards offered: 1
Application Procedure: Applicants must include information on qualifications, areas of interest and/or publications in a specified area, centres to be visited with confirmation of arrangements from the head of that centre, estimated costs and the names of two referees.
Closing Date: March 31st

RCOG Edgar Gentilli Prize

Subjects: Obstetrics and gynaecology.
Purpose: To recognize original work done on the cause, nature, recognition and treatment of any form of cancer of the female genital tract.
Eligibility: Unrestricted.
Type: Prize
Value: UK £750 plus book tokens up to a value of UK £250
Frequency: Annual
No. of awards offered: 1
Application Procedure: Applicants must submit results of their research in the form of an original manuscript, adequately referenced

and written in a format comparable with that used for submission to a learned journal, or by means of reprint of a published article.
Closing Date: March 31st

RCOG Ethicon Travel Awards

Subjects: Obstetrics and gynaecology.
Purpose: To promote international goodwill in the speciality.
Eligibility: Open to RCOG members who have passed both Part I and II of the membership exams. Members from the United Kingdom must be trainees and overseas members must not be in independent practice.
Level of Study: Postgraduate
Type: Travel grant
Value: Up to UK £1,000
No. of awards offered: Up to 15
Application Procedure: Applicants must complete an application form, available from the Awards Secretary or from the website.
Closing Date: January 31st
Additional Information: Travel must take place within 1 year of the award being made.

RCOG Green-Armytage and Spackman Travelling Scholarship

Subjects: Obstetrics and gynaecology.
Purpose: To allow applicants to visit centres where work similar to their own is being carried out.
Eligibility: Open to Fellows and members of the College. Applicants should have shown a special interest in some particular aspect of obstetrical or gynaecological practice.
Level of Study: Postgraduate
Type: Scholarship
Value: Please contact the organization
Frequency: Every 2 years
Country of Study: Any country
No. of awards offered: 1
Application Procedure: Applicants must include information on qualifications, areas of interest and/or publications in a specified area, centres to be visited with confirmation from the head of that centre, estimated costs and the names of two referees.
Closing Date: March 31st

RCOG Harold Malkin Prize

Subjects: Obstetrics and gynaecology.
Purpose: To reward those undertaking the best original work while holding a specialist registrar post in a hospital.
Eligibility: Open to RCOG members or membership candidates.
Level of Study: Professional development
Type: Prize
Value: 1st prize UK £250, 2nd prize UK £150
Frequency: Annual
No. of awards offered: 2
Application Procedure: Applicants must contact the Awards Secretary for details.
Closing Date: March 31st

RCOG Overseas Fund

Subjects: Obstetrics and gynaecology.
Purpose: To allow individuals to travel to the United Kingdom for further training.
Eligibility: Open to RCOG members or the equivalent, working overseas.
Level of Study: Professional development
Type: Travel grant
Value: Up to UK £2,000
Frequency: Annual
No. of awards offered: Up to 8
Application Procedure: Applicants must see the website.
Closing Date: March 31st

RCOG Research Prize

Subjects: Obstetrics and gynaecology.
Purpose: To recognize the best research projects in any aspect of obstetrics and gynaecology.
Level of Study: Graduate
Value: UK £500–200
Frequency: Annual
Country of Study: United Kingdom, Northern Ireland and Republic of Ireland
Application Procedure: Applicants should submit research outline no more than 1,500 words, with reference to publications (if any). The research must have been carried out during the applicant's undergraduate course and in a relevant department.
Closing Date: February 15th
Funding: Private
Additional Information: Submissions may by sent by email or post (four copies of the typewritten submission on A4-size paper). Applicants must state clearly which award they are applying for and include their supervisor's name and address.

RCOG William Blair-Bell Memorial Lectureships in Obstetrics and Gynaecology

Subjects: Obstetrics and gynaecology.
Purpose: To allow an individual to give a lecture.
Eligibility: Open to Fellows or members of not more than 2 years standing.
Value: Honorarium of UK £500
Frequency: Annual
Application Procedure: Applicants must contact the Awards Secretary.
Closing Date: March 31st

RCOG/Wyeth Historical Lecture

Subjects: Obstetrics and gynaecology with a strong historical content.
Purpose: To allow an individual to give a lecture on a current development in the field.
Eligibility: Open to RCOG Fellows and members.
Type: Other
Value: An honorarium of UK £400. This amount may be subject to change and applicants should contact the organization
Frequency: Annual
No. of awards offered: 1
Application Procedure: Applicants must contact the Awards Secretary for details.
Closing Date: March 31st
Funding: Private
Contributor: Wyeth Laboratories

Richard Johanson Obstetric Prize

Subjects: Obstetrics and gynaecology.
Purpose: To reward the best project, report or published research paper on a topic pertinent to pregnancy, childbirth or the postpartum period.
Level of Study: Graduate
Type: Prize
Value: UK £250
Frequency: Annual
Country of Study: United Kingdom, Northern Ireland and Republic of Ireland
Application Procedure: Applicants should submit a research outline of no more than 1,500 words, with reference to publications, if any. The research must have been carried out during the applicant's undergraduate course and in a relevant department.
Closing Date: February 15th
Funding: Private

Tim Chard Case History Prize

Subjects: Obstetrics and gynaecology.
Purpose: To reward students showing the greatest understanding of a clinical problem in obstetrics and gynaecology.
Level of Study: Graduate
Value: First prize UK £500, second prize UK £200
Frequency: Annual
Study Establishment: An accredited medical school
Country of Study: United Kingdom, Northern Ireland and Republic of Ireland

Application Procedure: Applicants should submit one case history with discussion no longer than 1,500 words with 10 biographical references that includes the name and address of the applicant's supervisor. Submissions may be sent by email or post (four copies of the typewritten submission on A4-size paper). Applicants must state clearly which award they are applying for, and make separate applications for each. Applications that do not comply with the stipulations will not be accepted.
Closing Date: February 15th
Funding: Private
Contributor: Bart's and the London School of Medicine

THE ROYAL COLLEGE OF OPHTHALMOLOGISTS

17 Cornwall Terrace, London, NW1 4QW, England
Tel: (44) 20 7935 0702
Fax: (44) 20 7935 9838
Email: education@rcophth.ac.uk
Website: www.rcophth.ac.uk
Contact: Beth Barnes, Deputy

The college is responsible for promoting high standards of professional practice, setting curricula and conducting examinations, inspecting hospital eye units for their training suitability and providing professional support and advice for ophthalmologists. The college runs an annual scientific congress and seminars for opthalmologists and publishes a range of clinical guidelines.

The Royal College of Ophthalmologists Clinical Research Fellowships – The Keeler Scholarship

Subjects: Ophthalmology.
Purpose: To enable the scholar to study, research or acquire special skills, knowledge or experience at a suitable location in the United Kingdom or elsewhere for a minimum period of 6 months.
Eligibility: Fellows, members and affiliate members of the college are eligible to apply for the scholarship. The trustees will give special consideration to candidates intending to make a career in ophthalmology in the United Kingdom.
Level of Study: Postgraduate
Type: Scholarship
Value: Up to UK £20,000
Frequency: Every 2 years
Country of Study: United Kingdom or elsewhere
No. of awards offered: 1
Application Procedure: An application must be completed and copied five times and submitted with five copies of the candidate's curriculum vitae.
Closing Date: February 17th
Funding: Commercial
Contributor: Keeler LTD
No. of awards given last year: 1

The Royal College of Ophthalmologists Clinical Research Fellowships – The Pfizer Ophthalmic Fellowship

Subjects: Ophthalmology.
Purpose: To enable the scholar to study, research or acquire special skills, knowledge or experience at a suitable location in the United Kingdom or elsewhere for a minimum period of 6 months.
Eligibility: Applicants must be citizens of the United Kingdom and Fellows, members and affiliates of the Royal College of Ophthalmologists, in good standing.
Level of Study: Postgraduate
Type: Fellowship
Value: Up to UK £35,000
Frequency: Annual
Country of Study: United Kingdom or elsewhere
No. of awards offered: 1
Application Procedure: An application form must be completed and copied five times and submitted with five copies of the candidate's curriculum vitae.
Closing Date: To be arranged by October 28th
Funding: Commercial
Contributor: Pfizer Ltd.
No. of awards given last year: 1

The Royal College of Ophthalmologists Travel Awards – Ethicon Foundation Fund

Subjects: Ophthalmology.
Purpose: To prove financial assistance to members and Fellows of the Royal College of Ophthalmologists who are travelling abroad for research or training purposes.
Eligibility: Applicants must be members and Fellows of the Royal College of Ophthalmologists.
Level of Study: Postgraduate
Type: Travel award
Value: Generally UK £400–600 per award
Frequency: Annual
Country of Study: Any country
No. of awards offered: Varies
Application Procedure: An application form must be completed and copied five times and submitted with five copies of the candidates curriculum vitae.
Closing Date: To be announced
Funding: Commercial
Contributor: Ethicon Ltd.
No. of awards given last year: 4

The Royal College of Ophthalmologists Travel Awards – Sir William Lister Award

Subjects: Ophthalmology.
Purpose: To provide personal travel expenses to citizens of the United Kingdom who are travelling abroad for research or training.
Eligibility: Applicants must be citizens of the United Kingdom.
Level of Study: Postgraduate
Type: Travel award
Value: Generally UK £400–600 per award
Frequency: Annual
Country of Study: Any country
No. of awards offered: Varies
Application Procedure: An application form must be completed and copied five times and submitted with five copies of the candidate's curriculum vitae.
Closing Date: To be announced
Funding: Private

Royal College of Ophthalmologists Travel Awards – The Dorey Bequest

Subjects: Ophthalmology.
Purpose: To provide personal travel expenses to members and Fellows of the Royal College of Ophthalmologists who are travelling abroad for research or training.
Eligibility: Members and Fellows of the Royal College of Ophthalmologists.
Level of Study: Postgraduate
Type: Travel award
Value: Generally UK £300–600 per award
Frequency: Annual
Country of Study: Any country
No. of awards offered: Varies
Application Procedure: An application form must be completed and copied five times and submitted with five copies of the candidate's curriculum vitae.
Closing Date: To be announced
Funding: Private

ROYAL COLLEGE OF ORGANISTS (RCO)

Millennium point, Curzon street, Birmingham, B4 7XG, United Kingdom
Tel: (44) (0) 121 331 7222
Fax: (44) (0) 121 331 7220
Email: kim.gilbert@rco.org.uk
Website: www.rco.org.uk
Contact: Kim Gilbert, General Manager

The Royal College of Organists (RCO) is membership based. It promotes the art of organ playing as choral directing, and provides an organization with a library, events and examinations to further that object.

RCO Various Open Award Bequests

Purpose: To assist students who are training to become organists.
Eligibility: School and students in undergraduate and postgraduate education who are members of the college.
Level of Study: Postgraduate, professional development, school and undergradute
Type: Award
Value: Between €100 and €400 each
Frequency: Annual
Study Establishment: Various
No. of awards offered: Various
Application Procedure: Write for application form.
Closing Date: February 17th
Funding: Private

For further information contact:

Email: admin@rco.org.uk
Contact: The Registrar

William Robertshaw Exhibition

Subjects: Organ playing.
Purpose: To offer financial support for organ student to use towards tuition fees and/or cost of sheet music.
Eligibility: Student organ who is member of RCO; membership is open to everyone on payment of subscription.
Level of Study: Professional development, postgraduate, school and undergraduate
Value: €250 per annum
Frequency: Annual
No. of awards offered: Various
Application Procedure: Write for application form.
Closing Date: February 17
Funding: Private

ROYAL COLLEGE OF PAEDIATRICS AND CHILD HEALTH (RCPCH)

50 Hallam Street, London, W1W 6DE, England
Tel: (44) 20 7307 5600
Fax: (44) 20 7307 5693
Email: aaron.barham@rcpch.ac.uk
Website: www.rcpch.ac.uk
Contact: Mr Aaron Barham, Conference Organizer

The Royal College of Paediatrics and Child Health works to advance the art and science of paediatrics, to raise the standard of medical care provided to children, to educate and examine those concerned with health of children, and to advance the education of the public and, in particular, medical practitioners in child health.

Ashok Nathwani Visiting Fellowship

Subjects: Paediatrics.
Purpose: To enable young paediatricians from abroad to visit the United Kingdom.
Eligibility: Open to all Paediatricians.
Level of Study: Postdoctorate
Type: Fellowship
Value: A travel, accommodation and subsistence costs
Frequency: Annual
Country of Study: United Kingdom

Douglas Hubble Travel Bursary

Subjects: Paediatrics and Child Health.
Purpose: To provide financial support for young pediatricians, or paediatric research workers, who contribute to the British paediatric practice.
Eligibility: Open to all young paediatricians or paediatric research workers below consultant status.
Level of Study: Postgraduate
Type: Award
Frequency: Every 2 years
Funding: Foundation
Contributor: University of Birmingham and the Royal College of paediatrics and Child Health

For further information contact:

Royal College of Paediatrics and Child Health, 50 Hallam Street, London, W1W 6DE
Contact: Mrs Aaron Barham

Dr Michael Blacow Memorial Prize

Subjects: Paediatrics.
Purpose: To award the best plenary paper presented at the spring meeting.
Eligibility: Open to all trainee paediatricians.
Level of Study: Postgraduate
Type: Award
Value: UK £200
Frequency: Annual
Funding: Trusts, foundation
Contributor: The British Paediatric Association

Heinz Visiting and Travelling Fellowships

Subjects: Paediatrics.
Purpose: To enable paediatricians from any part of the Commonwealth to visit the United Kingdom and to attend the Spring meeting of the College, or to enable British paediatricians to spend time in a developing country.
Eligibility: Open to young paediatricians from any commonwealth country.
Level of Study: Professional development
Type: Fellowship
Value: Air fares and living expenses
Length of Study: Up to 12 weeks for Visiting Fellowships and up to 3 months for Travelling Fellowships
Frequency: Annual
Country of Study: United Kingdom for the visiting fellowship and up to three months for travelling fellowship
No. of awards offered: Varies
Application Procedure: Application form can be downloaded from the website.
Closing Date: Please write for details
Funding: Corporation, private
Contributor: H J Heinz Company
No. of awards given last year: 3

Honorary Joint RCPCH / Health Protection Agency (HPA) Training Fellowship

Subjects: Paediatrics.
Purpose: To provide information and practical experience in control of paediatric infectious diseases.
Eligibility: This award is restricted to paediatricians in training.
Level of Study: Postdoctorate, postgraduate
Type: Fellowship
Value: Bench fees to the HPA and registration fee of attending the annual infection meeting of CDSC will be waived
Length of Study: 6 months-1 year
Frequency: Annual
No. of awards offered: 3
Application Procedure: Please see the website for further details.
Closing Date: July
Contributor: Health Protection Agency and RCPCH

RCPCH / VSO Fellowship

Subjects: Paediatrics.
Purpose: To accredit one-year placements in developing countries as part of higher specialist training in paediatrics.
Eligibility: Open to specialist registrars undertaking type 1 training.

Level of Study: Postgraduate
Type: Fellowship
Length of Study: 1 year
Frequency: Annual
Application Procedure: Contact VSO enquiries team for further information.

RCPCH/Babes in Arms Fellowships

Subjects: Paediatrics.
Purpose: To support paediatricians researching into sudden infant death syndrome or associated problems.
Eligibility: Open to paediatricians in higher specialist praising.
Level of Study: Postdoctorate
Type: Fellowship
Value: UK £3,000
Frequency: Annual

VISITING FELLOWSHIPS (Including the Donal Court visiting Fellowship)

For further information contact:

Royal College of Paediatrics and Child Health, 50 Hallam Street, London, W1W 6DE
Contact: Mr Aaron Barham

Young Investigator of the Year Medal

Subjects: Paediatrics.
Purpose: To award young medically qualified research worker for excellence in research.
Eligibility: Open to all young, medically qualified research workers.
Level of Study: Postgraduate
Type: Award
Value: UK £5,000 and medal plus UK £500 to the department in which they work for other expenses with their research
Frequency: Annual
No. of awards offered: 1
Application Procedure: All nominations are from the Head of Department. Direct applications are not accepted.
Funding: Foundation
Contributor: Sport Aiding Medical Research for Kids (SPARKS)

ROYAL COMMISSION FOR THE EXHIBITION OF 1851

Sherfield Building, Imperial College, London, SW7 2AZ, England
Tel: (44) 20 7594 8790
Fax: (44) 20 7594 8794
Email: royalcom1851@imperial.ac.uk
Website: www.royalcommission1851.org.uk
Contact: Mr Malcolm Shirley, Secretary

The Royal Commission for the Exhibition of 1851 is an educational trust supporting innovation and creativity in science, technology and occasionally the arts, almost always at postgraduate level. Apart from the competitive schemes listed, assistance is sometimes given to suitable charities or individuals.

Royal Commission Industrial Design Studentship

Subjects: Industrial design.
Purpose: To fund engineering and science graduates for a postgraduate industrial design course.
Eligibility: Open to United Kingdom nationals only with a first degree in engineering.
Level of Study: Postgraduate
Type: Studentship
Value: UK £9,000 per year plus materials and fees
Length of Study: 1–2 years
Frequency: Annual
Study Establishment: Universities
Country of Study: Any country
No. of awards offered: Approx. 6
Application Procedure: Applicants must complete an application form and submit this with the required enclosures. Forms available from the commission or its website.
Closing Date: April 27th
Funding: Private
Contributor: The profits from the Great Exhibition
No. of awards given last year: 7
No. of applicants last year: 24

Royal Commission Industrial Fellowships

Subjects: Industrial and management engineering.
Purpose: To allow able graduates working in industry to carry out research and development leading to a higher degree or other career milestone.
Eligibility: Open to United Kingdom nationals only with a degree in science or engineering who are working in for a British company.
Level of Study: Doctorate, postgraduate
Type: Fellowship
Value: 50 per cent of salary, up to a maximum of UK £20,000 per annum plus university fees London weighting and travel upto UK £3,500 per annum
Length of Study: 3 years
Frequency: Annual
Study Establishment: Any approved university/British company
Country of Study: United Kingdom
No. of awards offered: Approx. 7
Application Procedure: Applicants must complete an application form.
Closing Date: January 26th
Funding: Private
Contributor: The profits from the Great Exhibition
No. of awards given last year: 7
No. of applicants last year: 30

Royal Commission Research Fellowship

Subjects: Pure and applied sciences including mathematics and any branch of engineering.
Purpose: To give employed young scientists or engineers of exceptional promise the opportunity to conduct research.
Eligibility: Open to citizens of the United Kingdom, the British Commonwealth, or the Republics of Ireland or Pakistan.
Level of Study: Postdoctorate
Type: Fellowship
Value: UK £22,800 in year 1, UK £24,000 in year 2, plus a London Weighting of UK £2,134 per year
Length of Study: 2 years
Frequency: Annual
Study Establishment: Any approved university
Country of Study: Any country
No. of awards offered: Approx. 7
Application Procedure: Applicants must complete an application form, available from all United Kingdom universities or from the website. Applications must be made by professors of United Kingdom universities on behalf of the applicants.
Closing Date: February 23rd
Funding: Private
Contributor: The profits from the Great Exhibition
No. of awards given last year: 7
No. of applicants last year: 170

ROYAL GEOGRAPHICAL SOCIETY (WITH THE INSTITUTE OF BRITISH GEOGRAPHERS)

1 Kensington Gore, London, SW7 2AR, England
Tel: (44) 20 7591 3073
Fax: (44) 20 7591 3031
Email: grants@rgs.org
Website: www.rgs.org/grants
Contact: Grants Officer

The Royal Geographical Society (with the Institute of British Geographers) is the United Kingdom's learned society for geography and geographers and a professional body. It supports and promotes many aspects of geography including geographical research, education and teaching, field training and small expeditions, the public understanding and popularization of geography and the provision of geographical information.

British Airways Travel Bursary

Subjects: Tourism research.
Purpose: To support tourism-related field research.
Eligibility: Individuals under 35.
Level of Study: Postdoctorate, postgraduate, doctorate
Type: Bursary
Value: Free return flight
Length of Study: Above 1 month
Frequency: Twice yearly
Country of Study: Outside the United Kingdom
No. of awards offered: 4
Application Procedure: Applicants must submit a typed proposal.
Closing Date: January 13th and September 30th
Funding: Corporation
Contributor: British Airways
No. of awards given last year: 4
No. of applicants last year: Approx 20
Additional Information: Flights must be on existing BA routes. Some conditions apply.

EPSRC Geographical Research Grants

Subjects: (1) 21st century infrastructure, (2) waste, pollution and urban land use, urban transport and urban design, an inclusive environment, impacts of climate change, and flooding.
Purpose: To support postdoctoral research in the Engineering and Physical Sciences Research Council's field of interest.
Eligibility: Applicants should hold a PhD; individuals only.
Level of Study: Postdoctorate, doctorate
Type: Grant
Value: Up to UK £3,000
Length of Study: Unspecified
Frequency: Annual
No. of awards offered: 510
Application Procedure: Applicants must submit a completed application form.
Closing Date: December 31st
No. of awards given last year: Approx. 5
No. of applicants last year: Approx. 10

Gilchrist Fieldwork Award

Subjects: Natural sciences and geography.
Purpose: To finance an overseas research proposal that will enable original and challenging research to take place, preferably of potential applied benefit to the host country.
Eligibility: Open to teams of up to 10 members, the majority of which must be British and hold established posts in university departments.
Level of Study: Postdoctorate, doctorate
Type: Grant
Value: UK £12,000
Length of Study: More than 6 weeks
Frequency: Every 2 years
Country of Study: Outside the United Kingdom
No. of awards offered: 1
Application Procedure: Applicants must submit a proposal, following the guidelines, to the Grants Co-ordinator by the closing date. There is no application form.
Closing Date: March 15th
Funding: Commercial

For further information contact:

Gilchrist Educational Trust, Mary Trevewyan Hall, 10 York Terrace East, London, NW1 4PT, England
Contact: The Secretary

Henrietta Hotton Research Grants

Subjects: Geographical field research.
Purpose: To support female geographers.
Eligibility: Female undergraduate/postgraduate geography students (under 25) are eligible to apply.
Level of Study: Postgraduate, graduate
Type: Grant
Value: UK £500
Length of Study: Above 4 weeks
Frequency: Annual
No. of awards offered: 2
Application Procedure: Applicants must submit a written proposal.
Closing Date: January 25th
No. of awards given last year: 2
No. of applicants last year: 10
Additional Information: Applicants who are members of RGS-IBG supported teams may additionally apply to this award.

Hong Kong Research Grant

Subjects: Field research in China, Taiwan, Macau, Sar and Hong Kong Sar.
Purpose: To support postgraduate research in greater China.
Level of Study: Postgraduate
Type: Grant
Value: UK £2,500
Length of Study: Above 4 weeks
Frequency: Annual
Country of Study: Greater China
No. of awards offered: 1
Application Procedure: Applicants must submit a typed proposal.
Closing Date: December 2nd
Contributor: Royal Geographical Society Hong Kong
No. of awards given last year: 2
No. of applicants last year: 6

Innovative Geography Teaching Grants

Subjects: Geography.
Purpose: To support new ideas in geography teaching.
Eligibility: Practicing geography teachers are eligible to apply.
Level of Study: Teachers
Type: Grant
Value: Up to UK £800
Length of Study: Unspecified
Frequency: Annual
Country of Study: Worldwide
No. of awards offered: 5
Application Procedure: Applicants must submit a typed proposal.
Closing Date: September 1st
No. of awards given last year: 3
No. of applicants last year: 8
Additional Information: One award is usually reserved for NQTs. All applicants must be teaching secondary school pupils.

John Radford Award for Geographical Photography

Purpose: To support a geographically orientated photo assignment.
Eligibility: Aged between 18 and 30.
Type: Award/Grant
Value: UK £700
Frequency: Annual
Country of Study: Unrestricted
No. of awards offered: 1
Closing Date: March 31st
No. of awards given last year: 1
No. of applicants last year: 7

Journey of a Lifetime Award

Purpose: To support an inspiring journey and encourage new broadcast talent.
Eligibility: Unrestricted.
Level of Study: Unrestricted
Type: Travelling bursary
Value: UK £4,000
Length of Study: Unspecified

Frequency: Annual
Country of Study: Outside the United Kingdom
No. of awards offered: 1
Application Procedure: Applicants must submit a written proposal.
Closing Date: September 27th
No. of awards given last year: 1
No. of applicants last year: 100
Additional Information: The winner is trained by the BBC and records their journey in a radio 4 documentary.

Monica Cole Research Grant

Subjects: Earth and geological sciences.
Purpose: To enable the winner to undertake original fieldwork overseas.
Eligibility: Open to female physical geographers only. Applicants must be registered at a United Kingdom university.
Level of Study: Doctorate, postdoctorate, postgraduate
Type: Grant
Value: UK £1,000
Frequency: Every 3 years
Country of Study: Outside the United Kingdom
No. of awards offered: 1
Application Procedure: Applicants must download guidelines from the website or contact the Grants Co-ordinator. There is no application form.
Closing Date: January 25th
Funding: Private

Neville Shulman Challenge Award

Subjects: The geographical sciences and exploration.
Purpose: To further the understanding and exploration of the planet, while promoting personal development through the intellectual or physical challenges involved.
Eligibility: Open to any United Kingdom national over the age of 25.
Level of Study: Unrestricted
Type: Grant
Value: Normally up to UK £10,000
Length of Study: Unrestricted
Frequency: Annual
Country of Study: Any country
No. of awards offered: Normally 1
Application Procedure: Applicants must submit a proposal, following the guidelines, to the Grants Co-ordinator by the closing date. There is no application form. Details are available from the website.
Closing Date: October 28th (Last Friday in October)
Funding: Private
No. of awards given last year: 1
No. of applicants last year: 24

Peter Fleming Award

Subjects: Geographical research.
Purpose: For the advancement of geographical science.
Eligibility: Individuals of teams. Must be British or registered at a United Kingdom institution.
Level of Study: Postdoctorate
Type: Grant
Value: UK £9,000
Length of Study: Unspecified
Frequency: Annual
No. of awards offered: 1
Application Procedure: Applicants must submit a typed proposal.
Closing Date: March 16th
Funding: Private
No. of awards given last year: 2 (split award)
No. of applicants last year: 2
Additional Information: Equipment costs should not be more than 10 per cent of total. Conference attendance will not be funded.

Ralph Brown Expedition Award

Subjects: Natural sciences.
Purpose: To support and encourage objectives that involve the study of rivers, inland or coastal wetlands or shallow marine environments.
Eligibility: Open to applicants over 25 from any country. The applicant must be a Fellow or Associate Fellow of the Society.
Level of Study: Postgraduate, research
Type: Grant
Value: UK £15,000
Frequency: Annual
Country of Study: Any country
No. of awards offered: 1
Application Procedure: Applicants must contact the Grants Co-ordinator or refer to the website for detailed guidelines.
Closing Date: November 30th
Funding: Private
No. of awards given last year: 1
No. of applicants last year: 15

Ray Y. Gildea Jr. Award

Subjects: Geography education.
Purpose: To support innovation in teaching and learning in higher and secondary education directly beneficial to students of geography.
Type: Grant
Value: UK £2,750
Frequency: Annual
No. of awards offered: 1
Application Procedure: There is no application form. Applicants are asked to submit a word-processed proposal to the Society's Grants Officer.
Closing Date: October 31st
Funding: Private
Contributor: Professor Ray Gildea

Royal Geographical Society Geographica Fieldwork Grants

Subjects: Geographical, Earth, life and human sciences.
Purpose: To support British expeditions carrying out geographical field research and exploration overseas.
Eligibility: Open to multidisciplinary teams, rather than individuals, the majority of which must be British and over 19 years of age.
Level of Study: Unrestricted
Type: Grant
Value: UK £750–3,000
Length of Study: Must be over 5 weeks
No. of awards offered: 60–70
Application Procedure: Applicants must complete an application form. These can be obtained from the Society's website or by writing to the Grants Co-ordinator.
Closing Date: January 25th or August 25th
Funding: Commercial, private
No. of awards given last year: 52
No. of applicants last year: 61

Slawson Awards

Subjects: Social and behavioural sciences and development studies.
Purpose: To assist students intending to carry out geographical field research in developing countries to increase knowledge, awareness and understanding of the world in which we live.
Eligibility: Applicants must normally be United Kingdom citizens, currently be registered for a PhD at a United Kingdom Institute of Higher Education and be Fellows of the Society.
Level of Study: Postgraduate
Type: Grant
Value: Normally up to UK £3,000
Frequency: Annual
Country of Study: Outside the United Kingdom, preferably in developing countries
Application Procedure: Applicants must submit a proposal, following the guidelines, to the Grants Co-ordinator by the closing date. There is no application form and more details are available from the website.
Closing Date: February 18th
Funding: Private
No. of awards given last year: 2
No. of applicants last year: 20

Small Research Grants

Subjects: Geographical, Earth, life and human sciences.
Purpose: To provide grants for desk or field-based postdoctoral research.
Eligibility: Individual researchers within 10 years of the start of their PhD.
Level of Study: Postdoctorate
Type: Grant
Value: Up to UK £3,000
Length of Study: Unspecified
Frequency: Annual
Country of Study: Unrestricted
No. of awards offered: 510
Application Procedure: Application form.
Closing Date: December 31st
No. of awards given last year: Approx. 12
No. of applicants last year: Approx. 20
Additional Information: Only available to RGS-IBG members.

Thesiger-Oman Research Fellowship

Subjects: Research in arid lands: physical environment and human environment.
Purpose: To support research in arid environments.
Level of Study: Doctorate, postdoctorate
Type: Grant
Length of Study: UK £8,000
Frequency: Annual
No. of awards offered: 2
Application Procedure: Not yet finalized.
Closing Date: May 13th

Violet Cressey-Marcks Fisher Travel Scholarship

Subjects: Natural sciences and geography.
Purpose: To finance research in the field.
Eligibility: Applicants must be registered at a United Kingdom university. There is no age limit.
Level of Study: Postgraduate, research
Value: UK £350
Length of Study: More than 6 months
Frequency: Annual
Country of Study: Outside the United Kingdom
No. of awards offered: 1
Application Procedure: Applicants must submit a formal proposal following guidelines to the Grants Co-ordinator. Guidelines can be downloaded from the website. There is no application form.
Closing Date: January 25th
Funding: Private
No. of awards given last year: 1
No. of applicants last year: 16

ROYAL HISTORICAL SOCIETY

University College London, Gower Street, London, WC1E 6BT, England
Tel: (44) 207 387 7532
Email: rhsinfo@rhs.ac.uk
Website: www.rhs.ac.uk
Contact: The Executive Secretary

The Royal Historical Society has limited funds to assist postgraduate students (and some others) with expenses incurred in the pursuit of advanced historical research. These funds are intended principally for postgraduate students registered for a research degree at United Kingdom Institutions of Higher Education, both full-time and part-time.

Royal Historical Society Postgraduate Research Support Grant

Subjects: History.
Purpose: To assist postgraduate students with expenses incurred in the pursuit of advanced historical research.
Eligibility: Applicants must be postgraduate students registered for a research degree at a United Kingdom Institution of Higher Education, either full-time or part-time, or individuals who have completed doctoral dissertations within the last 2 years and who are not in full-time employment.
Level of Study: Postgraduate
Type: Grant
Value: Approx. UK £250
Frequency: Annual
Study Establishment: United Kingdom Institutions of Higher Education
Country of Study: United Kingdom
Application Procedure: Applicants must download application form from website. Applications should include a well-costed budget, a proposal that indicates the scholarly value of the proposed project and letters of reference.
Additional Information: Preference will be given to members of the Royal Historical Society.

ROYAL HOLLOWAY, UNIVERSITY OF LONDON

Egham, Surrey, TW20 0EX, England
Tel: (44) 1784 443399
Fax: (44) 1784 471381
Email: liaison-office@rhul.ac.uk
Website: www.rhul.ac.uk
Contact: Ms Claire Collingwood, Schools & International Liaison Officer

All departments of Royal Holloway, University of London seek to provide taught programmes that reflect the latest developments and are responsive to the needs of students and society, together with research and scholarship, which contribute to the advancement of knowledge and the enhancement of public policy, wealth creation and the quality of life.

Royal Holloway, University of London College Overseas Entrance Scholarships

Subjects: All subjects.
Purpose: To award outstanding academic achievement.
Eligibility: Open to overseas students only for full-time Master's or research.
Level of Study: Research, postgraduate
Type: Scholarship
Value: Up to a maximum of UK £10,000 depending on the number of awards available and the strength of the applicant. This award pays fees and/or some maintenance depending on level of award
Frequency: Annual
Application Procedure: Students who accept the offer of a place will automatically receive an application form.
Closing Date: Students must be in receipt of a conditional or an unconditional offer of admission by May 31st in order to be eligible for nomination
Additional Information: Further details of the awards can be found on the University's website or in the booklet Funding Postgraduate Studies, available from the college.

Royal Holloway, University of London College Research Studentship

Subjects: All subjects.
Level of Study: Doctorate
Type: Studentship
Value: Tuition fees at the home rate
Length of Study: Tenable for 3 years full-time or 6 years part-time
Frequency: Annual
Application Procedure: Applicants must indicate if they wish to be considered, but departments nominate their candidates.
Closing Date: Applicants should contact the relevant academic department
Additional Information: These studentships cannot be held with a research council, AHRB or similar major award. Further details of the awards can be found on the University's website or in the booklet Funding Postgraduate Studies, available from the college.

Royal Holloway, University of London Departmental Assistantships

Subjects: All subjects.
Level of Study: Postgraduate
Type: Other
Value: Up to UK £4,000 per year for a maximum of 6 hours work per week, 48 weeks per year
Length of Study: Tenable for 1 year full-time or 2 years part-time
Frequency: Annual
Application Procedure: Applicants must indicate on their application form that they wish to be considered.
Closing Date: Applicants should contact the relevant academic department
Additional Information: These assistantships cannot be held with a research council, AHRB or similar major award. Departmental assistantships require research students to support teaching and research in the department for up to 6 hours each week. Further details of the awards can be found on the University's website or in the booklet Funding Postgraduate Studies, available from the college.

Royal Holloway, University of London Endowed Postgraduate Scholarships

Subjects: All subjects.
Eligibility: This award cannot be held with a research council, AHRB or similar major award.
Level of Study: Research, postgraduate
Type: Scholarship
Value: Varies
Length of Study: Tenable for 3 years full-time. For part-time maintenance elements are reduced pro rata
Frequency: Annual
No. of awards offered: Varies
Application Procedure: Applicants must indicate if they wish to be considered, but departments nominate their candidates.
Closing Date: Applicants should contact the relevant academic department
Additional Information: Availability varies from year to year and is restricted to certain departments. Interested parties should contact the academic department for availability. More details of the awards can be found on the University's website or in the booklet Funding Postgraduate Studies, available from the college.

Thomas Holloway Research Studentship

Subjects: Arts and humanities, business administration and management, music, drama, cinema and television, mathematics and computer science, natural sciences and social science or behavioural science.
Eligibility: This studentship cannot be held with a research council, AHRB or similar major award.
Level of Study: Doctorate
Type: Studentship
Value: Tuition fees at the home rate plus maintenance of up to UK £9,000 per year. Rates vary between departments
Length of Study: Tenable for 3 years full-time. For part-time maintenance elements are reduced pro rata
Frequency: Annual
Application Procedure: Applicants must indicate if they wish to be considered, but departments nominate their candidates.
Closing Date: Applicants should contact the relevant academic department

ROYAL HORTICULTURAL SOCIETY (RHS)

Wisley, Woking, Surrey, GU23 6QB, England
Tel: (44) 1483 212380
Fax: (44) 1483 212382
Email: bursaries@rhs.org.uk
Contact: Secretary of RHS Bursaries Committee

The Royal Horticultural Society (RHS) is a membership charity holding a Royal Charter for horticulture. The Society promotes the science, art and practice of horticulture in all its branches through a wide range of educational, research and advisory activities. It also maintains some major gardens, shows and the internationally renowned Lindley Library.

Blaxall Valentine Trust Award

Subjects: Horticulture.
Purpose: To help finance worldwide plant collecting in natural habitats and study expeditions that will provide real benefits to horticulture.
Eligibility: Open to applicants worldwide, but preference is given to United Kingdom and Commonwealth citizens. Applicants should preferably be within the age bracket of 20–35 years and satisfy the Society that their health enables them to undertake the project proposed. Financial sponsorship will be available to both professional and amateur horticulturists and consideration for an award is not restricted to RHS members.
Level of Study: Unrestricted
Type: Bursary
Value: Funds are limited. High-cost projects are expected to receive supplementary finance from other sources, including personal contributions
Frequency: Annual
Country of Study: Any country
Application Procedure: Applicants must complete an application form available on request. Candidates may be called for interview.
Closing Date: December 24th, March 31st, June 30th or September 30th
Funding: Private
No. of awards given last year: 15

Coke Trust Award

Subjects: Horticulture.
Purpose: To broaden professional gardeners' and student gardeners' knowledge, skills and experience, and to finance horticultural projects that demonstrate a distinct educational or historic value, as submitted by institutions, charities or gardens.
Eligibility: Submissions are welcomed from applicants worldwide, but preference is given to United Kingdom and Commonwealth citizens. Applicants should preferably be within the age bracket of 20–35 years and satisfy the Society that their health enables them to undertake the project proposed. Financial sponsorship will be available to both professional and amateur horticulturists and consideration for an award is not restricted to RHS members.
Level of Study: Unrestricted
Type: Bursary
Value: Funds are limited. High-cost projects are expected to receive supplementary finance from other sources, including personal contributions
Frequency: Annual
Country of Study: United Kingdom
No. of awards offered: Unlimited
Application Procedure: Applicants must complete an application form, available on request.
Closing Date: December 24th, March 31st, June 30th or September 30th
Funding: Private
No. of awards given last year: 55
Additional Information: Recipients must submit a brief factual report within 3 months of completion, along with an outline of achievements or difficulties, including any unusual problems, eg. medical or political, and an account of expenses.

EA Bowles Memorial Bursary

Subjects: Horticulture.
Purpose: To aid project regarding the work of EA Bowel, his garden at Myddelton House, Essex, or one of his particular horticultural interests eg. bulbs or alpines.
Eligibility: The award is open to students and trainees in horticulture and relevant related topics eg. garden history and design. There are no age restrictions.
Level of Study: Unrestricted
Type: Bursary

Value: UK £500
Frequency: Every 2 years
Country of Study: United Kingdom
No. of awards offered: Unlimited
Application Procedure: Applicants must complete an application form available on request.
Closing Date: December 24th, March 31st, June 30th or September 30th
Funding: Private
No. of awards given last year: None
Additional Information: The award was set up by the EA Bowels of Myddleton House Society in memory of EA Bowles VMH, one of the most eminent plantsmen of the first-half of the 20th century. Recipients must submit a brief factual report within 3 months of completion, along with an outline of achievements or difficulties, including any unusual problems eg. medical or political and an account of expenses.

Jimmy Smart Memorial Bursary

Subjects: Horticulture.
Purpose: To provide financial support to a working (employed) gardener for travel and/or accommodation during visits overseas with the prime intention of seeing or studying plants and/or trees growing in their natural habitats. Other gardening-related travel may also be funded.
Eligibility: The award is open to experienced working gardeners in the British Isles, particularly those whose work includes responsibilities in relation to National Collections. There is no age restriction.
Level of Study: Unrestricted
Type: Bursary
Value: UK £1,000 maximum
Frequency: Annual
Country of Study: Any country
No. of awards offered: Unlimited
Application Procedure: Applicants must complete an application form available on request.
Closing Date: December 24th, March 31st, June 30th or September 30th
Funding: Private
No. of awards given last year: 1
Additional Information: Recipients must submit a brief factual report within 3 months of completion, along with an outline of achievements or difficulties, including any unusual problems eg. medical or political, and an account of expenses. Applications to visit Australia or New Zealand are particularly encouraged. Additional support may be offered to gardeners spending time in either of these countries.

Osaka Travel Award

Subjects: Horticultural-related study or work experience will be considered.
Purpose: To allow young people from the United Kingdom and Japan to study in each other's country and benefit from a cross-cultural exchange of ideas.
Eligibility: Open to British and Japanese citizens with a horticultural background. Applicants should preferably be within the age bracket of 20–35 years. Financial sponsorship will be available to both professional and amateur horticulturists and consideration for an award is not restricted to RHS members. The awards are made to individuals, not to groups or expeditions.
Level of Study: Unrestricted
Type: Bursary
Value: Funds are limited. High-cost projects are expected to receive supplementary finance from other sources, including personal contributions
Frequency: Annual
No. of awards offered: 1–2
Application Procedure: Applicants must complete an application form, available on request. Candidates may be called for interview.
Closing Date: December 24th, March 31st, June 30th or September 30th
Funding: Private
No. of awards given last year: 2
Additional Information: Recipients must submit a brief factual report within 3 months of completion, along with an outline of achievements or difficulties and an account of expenses.

Queen Elizabeth the Queen Mother Bursary

Subjects: Horticulture.
Purpose: To help finance related projects, eg. study tours, horticulturally-related expeditions, minor research projects possibly working with an acknowledged expert on short-term research, taxonomic studies, specialized courses and programmes of study such as specific subject symposia. The award is reserved for proposal of particular excellence.
Eligibility: Submissions are welcomed from applicants worldwide but preference is given to United Kingdom and Commonwealth citizens. Applicants should preferably be within the age bracket of 20–35 years and satisfy the Society that their health enables them to undertake the project proposed. Financial sponsorship will be available to both professional and amateur horticulturists and consideration for an award is not restricted to RHS members. The awards are made to individuals, not to groups or expeditions.
Level of Study: Unrestricted
Type: Bursary
Value: Funds are limited. High-cost projects are expected to receive supplementary finance from other sources, including personal contributions
Frequency: Variable
Country of Study: Any country
No. of awards offered: 13
Application Procedure: Applicants must complete an application form, available on request. Candidates may be called for interview.
Closing Date: December 24th, March 31st, June 30th or September 30th
Funding: Private
No. of awards given last year: None
Additional Information: Recipients must submit a brief factual report within 3 months of completion, along with an outline of achievements or difficulties, including any unusual problems, eg. medical or political, and an account of expenses. Recipients must also be prepared to give a lecture on their project at the Society's headquarters at Vincent Square in London, within 18 months of completing the project.

RHS Financial Awards

Subjects: Horticulture.
Purpose: To help finance horticulture-related projects and to further the interests of horticultural education along with horticultural work experience.
Eligibility: Submissions are welcomed from applicants worldwide, but preference is given to United Kingdom and Commonwealth citizens. Applicants should preferably be within the age bracket of 20–35 years and satisfy the Society that their health enables them to undertake the project proposed. Financial sponsorship will be available to both professional and amateur horticulturists, and consideration for an award is not restricted to RHS members. The awards are made to individuals, not to groups or expeditions.
Level of Study: Unrestricted
Type: Bursary
Value: Funds are limited. High-cost projects are expected to receive supplementary finance from other sources, including personal contributions
Frequency: Annual
Country of Study: Any country
No. of awards offered: Unlimited
Application Procedure: Applicants must complete an application form, available on request. Candidates may be called for interview.
Closing Date: December 24th, March 31st, June 30th or September 30th
Funding: Private
No. of awards given last year: 8
Additional Information: Recipients must submit a brief factual report within 3 months of completion, along with an outline of achievements or difficulties, including any unusual problems, eg. medical or political, and an account of expenses.

ROYAL INCORPORATION OF ARCHITECTS IN SCOTLAND (RIAS)

15 Rutland Square, Edinburgh, EH1 2BE, Scotland
Tel: (44) 13 1229 7545
Fax: (44) 13 1228 2188
Email: info@rias.org.uk
Website: www.rias.org.uk
Contact: Ms Linda Connolly, Awards Administrator

The RIAS was founded in 1916 as the professional body for all chaptered architectures in Scotland. It has charitable status and offers a wide range of services and products for architects, students of architectures, construction industry professionals and all those with an interest in the built environment and the design process.

Martin Jones Memorial Scholarship and Award

Subjects: Architecture.
Purpose: To support an outstanding student in pursuing a personal line of creative investigation and research.
Eligibility: Open to students and graduates of the School of Architecture in Duncan of Jordanstone, College of Art, Dundee University.
Level of Study: Postgraduate
Type: Scholarship
Value: UK £7,500
Frequency: Annual
Country of Study: Any country
No. of awards offered: 1
Application Procedure: Invitations are issued in the Autumn each year.
Closing Date: The end of January
Funding: Private

For further information contact:

The Martin Jones Award, c/o School of Architecture, Duncan of Jordanstone, Perth Road, Dundee, DD1 4HT, Scotland

RIAS Award for Measured Drawing

Subjects: Architecture and measured drawing.
Purpose: To encourage and recognize original hand-measured drawing as essential to an architect's training.
Eligibility: Open to student members and members of the RIAS.
Level of Study: Postgraduate
Value: The premier award for student members is UK £200 and the prize for full members is UK £100
Frequency: Annual
Country of Study: Any country
No. of awards offered: 1
Closing Date: The end of January
Additional Information: The Committee will judge competitors on the following points: the choice of architectural fabric for the measured study, such as buildings under threat, the clarity of understanding and accuracy revealed by the drawing and the elegance with which the analysis is presented. Adjudication will normally take place in March. If confirmed by the RIAS Council the result of the competition will be notified to the competitors. The presentation of the award will be made at the RIAS Annual Convention. The winning drawing will form part of a travelling exhibition of RIAS Awards and Prizes and may, at the Incorporation's discretion, subsequently form part of the RIAS Archive.

Sir John Burnet Memorial Award

Subjects: Architecture.
Purpose: To test a student's skill in architectural design and communicating by drawing, within a predetermined time limit, their proposals in response to a client's brief.
Eligibility: Open to student members of the RIAS who should be first year full-time post Part I.
Level of Study: Postgraduate
Value: UK £150 and a certificate
Frequency: Annual
Country of Study: Any country
No. of awards offered: 1
Additional Information: Submissions will be judged by the RIAS Awards Committee. The Committee may be assisted by distinguished critics, co-opted by the Committee. The judges will consider skills in interpreting a brief within a time deadline, flair in architectural design and skill in methods of communication and presentation. The drawings will remain the property of the RIAS.

Sir Robert Lorimer Memorial Award

Subjects: Architecture.
Purpose: To encourage students to keep sketch books or notebooks, as in Lorimer's time.
Eligibility: Open to student members and members of the RIAS under the age of 29.
Level of Study: Postgraduate
Value: A book voucher to the value of UK £125 and a certificate
Frequency: Annual
Country of Study: Any country
No. of awards offered: 1
Closing Date: The end of January
Additional Information: The assessors prefer working sketch books, which are a record of study and travel, and will look for careful observation and sensitive draughtsmanship. Adjudication will normally take place in March. If confirmed by the RIAS Council, the result of the competition will be notified to the competitors. The presentation of the award will be made at the RIAS Annual Convention.

Sir Rowand Anderson Silver Medal

Subjects: Architecture.
Purpose: To recognize the best student member in Scotland.
Eligibility: Open to student members of the RIAS within a year of passing Part II.
Level of Study: Postgraduate
Value: A silver medal and a certificate
Frequency: Annual
Country of Study: Scotland
No. of awards offered: 1
Closing Date: October 31st
Additional Information: The RIAS Awards Committee may interview candidates before making their selection. The award and presentation will be made at the RIAS Annual Convention, for which the winner may be asked to make available a selection of his or her portfolio for exhibition.

ROYAL IRISH ACADEMY

19 Dawson Street, Dublin, 2, Ireland
Tel: (353) 1 676 2570
Fax: (353) 1 676 2346
Email: admin@ria.ie
Website: www.ria.ie
Contact: Ms Laura Mahoney, Assistant Executive Secretary

The Royal Irish Academy is the senior institution in Ireland for both the sciences and humanities. It publishes a number of journals and monographs. It is Ireland's national representative in a large number of international unions, and through its national committees runs conferences, lectures and workshops. It also manages a number of long-term research projects. The Academy participates in the Royal Society European Science Exchange Programmes in pure and applied science, in the British Academy European Exchange Programmes in the humanities, and in the Austrian, Hungarian, or Polish academy exchange schemes in science and the humanities. Small grants for work in all disciplines are available annually from the Academy's own funds.

Eoin O'Mahony Bursary

Subjects: History.
Purpose: To assist Irish scholars undertaking overseas research on historical subjects of Irish interest.
Level of Study: Unrestricted
Type: Bursary
Value: Varies

Length of Study: Varies
Frequency: Annual
Country of Study: Any country
No. of awards offered: 1
Application Procedure: Applicants must complete an application form, available from the Academy.
Closing Date: End of January
Funding: Private
Contributor: Trust fund
No. of awards given last year: 8
Additional Information: Preference will be given to projects concerning family history, in particular those which are associated with the 'Wild Geese' (genealogy). Special consideration will be given to those who have been active in local learned societies.

Royal Irish Academy Award in Biochemistry

Subjects: Biochemistry.
Eligibility: Open to anyone who is actively engaged in biochemical research in Ireland. The award may be made to scientists at any stage of their scientific career and will primarily recognize scientific work carried out in the past decade.
Level of Study: Professional development, postdoctorate
Value: A silver medal
Frequency: Annual
Country of Study: Ireland
No. of awards offered: 1
Application Procedure: Applicants must be nominated. Nomination must be made by two scientists who also supply the names of two independent referees, one of whom must reside outside Ireland.
Closing Date: Please contact the Academy
Funding: Private
Contributor: Schering Plough (Brinny) Company
No. of awards given last year: 1
Additional Information: The recipient delivers a review lecture at the Royal Irish Academy and also at a meeting of the Irish Area Section of the Biochemical Society.

Royal Irish Academy Award in Microbiology

Subjects: Microbiology.
Purpose: To recognize research contributions in referred international journals.
Eligibility: Open to people who are resident in either Northern Ireland or the Republic of Ireland. Only applicants less than 40 years of age on January 1st of the year of the award are eligible.
Level of Study: Unrestricted
Value: A silver medal
Frequency: Every 2 years
Country of Study: Ireland
No. of awards offered: 1
Application Procedure: Applicant must be nominated independently by two scientists who are familiar with his/her work.
Closing Date: February 23rd
Funding: Private
No. of awards given last year: 1
Additional Information: The recipient will deliver a review lecture at the Royal Irish Academy. A copy of the lecture must be deposited in the Academy's library.

Royal Irish Academy Award in Nutritional Sciences

Subjects: Dietetics and microbiology.
Purpose: To recognize research contributions in nutritional sciences in referred international journals.
Eligibility: Open to people who are resident in either Northern Ireland or the Republic of Ireland. Only applicants who are less than 45 years of age on January 1st of the year of the award are eligible.
Level of Study: Postdoctorate, professional development
Value: A silver medal
Frequency: Every 2-4 years
Country of Study: Ireland
No. of awards offered: 1
Application Procedure: Applicants must be nominated independently by two scientists who are familiar with the work of the nominee.
Closing Date: Applications are accepted at any time
Funding: Private
Additional Information: The recipient will deliver a review lecture at the Royal Irish Academy. A copy of the lecture must be deposited in the Academy's library.

Royal Irish Academy Award in Pharmacology and Toxicology

Subjects: Pharmacology and toxicology.
Purpose: To recognize achievement.
Eligibility: Open to all those who work in or close to the areas of pharmacology and toxicology and who are resident in either Northern Ireland or the Republic of Ireland.
Level of Study: Professional development, postdoctorate
Value: A silver medal
Frequency: Every 2 years
Country of Study: Ireland
Application Procedure: Applicants must be nominated by not less than two persons who will have obtained the prior agreement of the nominee.
Closing Date: Applications are accepted at any time
Funding: Private
Contributor: The Élan Corporation
No. of awards given last year: 1
Additional Information: The medal will be presented at a function to be held at the Royal Irish Academy. The recipient will be required to speak on this occasion and a copy of the address must be deposited in the Academy's library.

Royal Irish Academy European Exchange Fellowship

Subjects: Humanities, social sciences and natural sciences.
Purpose: To promote academic exchange between Ireland and Austria, Great Britain, Hungary, France and Poland.
Level of Study: Postdoctorate, professional development
Type: Fellowship
Value: Varies
Length of Study: Varies
Frequency: Annual
Country of Study: Other
Application Procedure: Applicants must complete an application form, available from the Academy.
Closing Date: October 30th
Funding: Government
No. of awards given last year: 17

Royal Irish Academy Science Writing Competition

Subjects: Biochemistry.
Eligibility: Open to graduate students in third level institutions in either Northern Ireland or the Republic of Ireland.
Level of Study: Predoctorate, research, postgraduate
Value: €1,000 for the winner and €400 for the runner-up
Frequency: Annual
Country of Study: Ireland
No. of awards offered: 2
Application Procedure: Applicants must submit five copies of the article.
Closing Date: March 26th
Funding: Private
Contributor: Yamanouchi Ireland and the Irish Times newspaper
No. of awards given last year: 2
Additional Information: The newspaper article must be suitable for a non-scientific reader explaining the development of any new topic in biochemistry and its significance to medical, agricultural or industrial practices. The winner's article will appear in the Irish Times newspaper.

THE ROYAL LITERARY FUND RLF

3 Johnson's Court, London, EC4A 3EA, United Kingdom
Email: rlitfund@btconnect.com
Website: www.rlf.org.uk

The RLF has been continuously helping authors since it was set up in 1970. It is funded by requests and donations from writers who help other writers. Its committee members came from all walks of literary life and include novelists, biographers, poets, publishers, lawyers and agents.

RLF Fellowships

Subjects: Higher education in literature and authorship.
Purpose: To provide former RLF fellows with an opportunity to continue working in the field of education.
Eligibility: Open to professional, published writers of literary merit with at least two books of any genre already published (or mainstream theatre works performed or scripts broadcast).
Level of Study: Professional development
Type: Fellowship
Value: A UK £13,000 stipend
Length of Study: 1–2 years
Frequency: Annual
Country of Study: United Kingdom
Closing Date: November
Contributor: RLF
No. of awards given last year: 62

For further information contact:

Royal Literary Fund, 3 Johnson's Court, London, EC4A 3EA
Tel: 020 7353 7160
Email: rlitfund@btconnect.com
Contact: Steve Cook, Fellowship Officer

RLF Grant

Subjects: Literature, authorship.
Purpose: To support prolific writers suffering financial hardship.
Eligibility: Open to applicants who have published several works for a general readership and are suffering financial hardship (books stemming from a parallel career as an academic or practitioner are not eligible).
Level of Study: Professional development
Type: Grant
Value: Funds are decided by the committee case by case.
Length of Study: 1 year
Frequency: Annual
Country of Study: United Kingdom
No. of awards offered: Varies
Application Procedure: Contact the RLF General Secretary.
Closing Date: There is no deadline
Contributor: RLF
No. of awards given last year: 12

For further information contact:

The Royal Literary Fund, 3 Johnson's Court, Off Fleet Street, London, EC4A 3EA
Tel: 020 7353 7159
Email: egunnrlf@globalnet.co.uk
Contact: Eileen Gunn, General Secretary

ROYAL PHILHARMONIC SOCIETY (RPS)

10 Stratford Place, London, W1C 1BA, England
Tel: (44) 20 7491 8110
Fax: (44) 20 7493 7463
Email: admin@royalphilharmonicsociety.org.uk
Website: www.royalphilharmonicsociety.org.uk
Contact: General Administrator

The Royal Philharmonic Society (RPS) offers support for young musicians and composers, sponsorship of new music events, debate and discussion about the future of music and has an active commissioning policy. It recognizes achievement through the prestigious annual RPS Music Awards and with the Society's Gold Medal. Full information is available on the RPS website.

RPS Composition Prize

Subjects: Musical composition.
Purpose: To encourage young composers.
Eligibility: Open to past and present registered students of any conservatoire or university within the United Kingdom, of any nationality, under the age of 29. Former winners are not eligible.
Level of Study: Postgraduate
Type: Prize
Value: UK £5,000 commission plus a guaranteed performance of commissioned work
Frequency: Annual
No. of awards offered: 2
Application Procedure: Applicants must complete an application form. There is a UK £20 entry fee but this is free to RPS members.
Closing Date: March 31st annually
Funding: Private
No. of awards given last year: 2
No. of applicants last year: 70

THE ROYAL SCOTTISH ACADEMY (RSA)

The Mound, Edinburgh, EH2 2EL, Scotland
Tel: (44) 44 (0) 131 225 6671
Fax: (44) 44 (0) 131 220 6016
Email: info@royalscottishacademy.org
Website: www.royalscottishacademy.org
Contact: Secretary

Founded in 1826, the RSA, Scotland's foremost body of artists, has promoted the works of leading contemporary painters, sculptors, printmakers and architects. It also gives practical and financial help to young artists through scholarships as well as the annual Student's Exhibition.

The Alastair Salvesen Art Scholarship

Subjects: Painting in any medium.
Purpose: To encourage young painters who have made the transition from college to a working environment.
Eligibility: Open to painters who have been trained at one of four Scottish colleges of art in Aberdeen, Dundee, Edinburgh or Glasgow and are living and working in Scotland.
Level of Study: Postgraduate
Type: Scholarship
Value: Up to UK £10,000 depending on the plan submitted, and an exhibition that lasts approx. three weeks to take place in November or December in a gallery
Length of Study: 3–5 months
Frequency: Annual
Study Establishment: Any of the main art colleges
Country of Study: Scotland
No. of awards offered: 1
Application Procedure: Applicants must contact the RSA.
Closing Date: January 19th
Funding: Private
Contributor: The Alastair Salvesen Trust
No. of awards given last year: 1

The John Kinross Memorial Fund Student Scholarships/ RSA

Subjects: Painting, sculpture, architecture and printmaking.
Purpose: To allow young artists from the established training centres in Scotland to spend time in Italy.
Eligibility: Open to all final year and postgraduate students from the four main colleges of art in Scotland.
Level of Study: Postgraduate
Type: Scholarship
Value: UK £1,400
Length of Study: 3 months
Frequency: Annual
Country of Study: Italy
No. of awards offered: 13
Closing Date: Late April
Funding: Private
Contributor: The Kinross Scholarship Fund, which is administered by the RSA

No. of awards given last year: 15
No. of applicants last year: 80

RSA Annual Student Competition

Subjects: Painting, sculpture, architecture and printmaking.
Eligibility: Candidates should be residents of Scotland. Painting, printmaking and sculpture students should be in their final or postgraduate years of study at one of the Scottish schools of architecture or one of the main Scottish colleges of art in Aberdeen, Dundee, Edinburgh or Glasgow. Applicants should submit one work. Architecture students should be in their final year and present work normally related to the requirements of the RIBA Part II syllabus.
Level of Study: Postgraduate
Type: Competition
Value: More than UK £6,000 worth of prizes and awards
Frequency: Annual
Study Establishment: All main colleges of art and architecture
Country of Study: Scotland
No. of awards offered: Varies
Application Procedure: Applicants must submit applications via their college, which must be countersigned by their tutor.
Closing Date: February
Funding: Commercial
Contributor: The RSA
No. of awards given last year: 15
No. of applicants last year: 400
Additional Information: The Academy also sponsors an annual exhibition of painting, sculpture, printmaking and architecture, with special awards for students. Entry forms are available in January. Various monetary awards are also made from May 2nd to July 5th.

Sir William Gillies Bequest–Hospitalfield Trust

Subjects: Painting, sculpture, architecture and printmaking.
Purpose: To provide young professional artists who are Scottish or have studied in Scotland, with a period for personal development and the exploration of new directions.
Eligibility: Open to all emerging professional artists.
Level of Study: Postgraduate
Type: Residency
Value: UK £1,666
Length of Study: 1 or 3 months
Frequency: Annual
Study Establishment: Hospitalfield House, Arbroath
Country of Study: Scotland
Application Procedure: Applicants must contact the RSA.
Funding: Private
Contributor: The Bequest Fund administered by the RSA

THE ROYAL SOCIETY

6–9 Carlton House Terrace, London, SW1Y 5AG, England
Tel: (44) 20 7451 2500
Fax: (44) 20 7930 2170
Email: info@royalsoc.ac.uk
Website: www.royalsoc.ac.uk
Contact: Research Appointments Officer

The Royal Society is the independent scientific academy of the UK dedicated to promoting excellence in science. It plays an influential role in national and international science policy and supports developments in science engineering and technology in a wide range of ways.

Copus Public Understanding of Science Development Fund

Subjects: All areas of science.
Purpose: To encourage and support major new initiatives that aim to improve the public understanding of science and technology.
Eligibility: Applicants must be resident in the United Kingdom.
Level of Study: Unrestricted
Type: Grant
Value: Up to UK £20,000
Frequency: Annual
Study Establishment: Varies
Country of Study: Other
No. of awards offered: Varies
Application Procedure: Applicants must complete an application form. Further information is available on request. Requests must quote the name of the scheme or programme. If requests are made by email applicants must include their full name and postal address.
Funding: Government
Contributor: OST
No. of awards given last year: 7
No. of applicants last year: 34
Additional Information: Further information is available on the website or by contacting Scott Kier on (44) 20 7451 2513.

Copus Public Understanding of Science Seed Fund

Subjects: All areas of science.
Purpose: To assist pump-priming activities or initiatives directly concerned with the promotion of the public understanding of science at a local level.
Eligibility: Open to residents of the United Kingdom.
Level of Study: Unrestricted
Type: Grant
Value: Up to UK £3,000
Frequency: Annual
Study Establishment: Varies
Country of Study: Any country
No. of awards offered: Varies
Application Procedure: Applicants must complete an application form. Further information is available from the website or by contacting Natasha Martineau on (44) 20 7451 2579. Requests must quote the name of the scheme or programme. If requests are made by email applicants must include their full name and postal address.
Funding: Government
Contributor: OST
No. of awards given last year: 25
No. of applicants last year: 68
Additional Information: Further information is available on the website or by contacting Scott Kier on (44) 20 7451 2513.

For further information contact:

6 Carlton House Terrace, London, SW1Y 5AG, England
Tel: (44) 20 7451 2547
Contact: Mr Keith Wylde, Research Appointments Officer

ROYAL SOCIETY FOR THE ENCOURAGEMENT OF ARTS, MANUFACTURERS AND COMMERCE (RSA)

8 John Adam Street, London, England
Tel: (44) 20 7930 5115
Fax: (44) 20 7839 5805
Email: lizzie.tulip@rsa.org.uk
Website: www.rsa-afa.org.uk
Contact: Project Co-ordinator

The Royal Society for the Encouragement of Arts, Manufactures and Commerce (RSA) is an instrument of change, working to create a civilized society based on a sustainable economy. It is a charity that uses its independence and the resources of its international fellowship to stimulate discussion, develop ideas and encourage action. Its main fields of interest today are business and industry, design and technology, education, the arts and the environment.

RSA Art for Architecture

Subjects: Art and architecture.
Purpose: To encourage collaboration between design professionals, by giving grants to support the artists places in design teams at the early stage of the design process.
Eligibility: Open to visual artists who are to be employed at the earliest stage of a building project as part of the design team. The

award is restricted to projects within the British Isles, but is also open to individuals of any nationality if attached to a project.
Type: Varies
Value: UK £2,000–15,000. Awards are in the form of payment towards the design fees of artists appointed
Country of Study: United Kingdom
No. of awards offered: 2
Application Procedure: Applicants must complete an application form. Other documentation such as slides, plans and letters of support should be submitted with all applications to Lizzie Tulip.
Closing Date: See the website at www.rsa-afa.org.uk
Funding: Government, commercial
Contributor: The Commission for Architecture and the Built Environment (CABE)
No. of awards given last year: 8
No. of applicants last year: 50
Additional Information: There is also a Publication Award, intended to help fund publications that focus on issues and practice relating to collaboration.

RSA Design Directions

Subjects: A range of design projects, many encouraging cross-disciplinary working, which urge students to consider the role of design within a broad societal context.
Purpose: The awards are given as prizes to winning students in the scheme and can be used for research, travel, funding for further study, funding for internships or other purposes agreed with the RSA.
Eligibility: Open to students within the EU and studying at further or higher education level.
Level of Study: Graduate, postgraduate
Type: Competition
Value: These vary from amounts beginning at UK £500 up to UK £10,000
Length of Study: Varies
Frequency: Annual
Study Establishment: An appropriate institution
Country of Study: European Union
No. of awards offered: Varies
Application Procedure: Applicants must visit the website for project briefs and details for application.
Closing Date: Varies according to project – applicants should check website (www.rsa-design.net)
Funding: Private, government, commercial
Contributor: Commercial organizations
No. of awards given last year: 72
No. of applicants last year: 2,200 (Competition Entrants)
Additional Information: RSA design directions does not offer grants; it is an annual competition open to design students.

THE ROYAL SOCIETY OF CHEMISTRY

Burlington House Piccadilly, London, W1J 0BA, England
Tel: (44) 20 7437 8656
Fax: (44) 20 7734 1227
Email: langers@rsc.org
Website: www.rsc.org
Contact: Mr S S Langer

The Royal Society of Chemistry is the learned society for chemistry and the professional body for chemists in the United Kingdom with 46,000 members worldwide. The Society is a major publisher of chemical information, supports the teaching of chemistry at all levels, organizes hundreds of chemical meetings a year and is a leader in communicating science to the public. It is now the United Kingdom National Adhering Organization (NAO) to the International Union of Pure and Applied Chemistry (IUPAC).

Corday-Morgan Memorial Fund

Subjects: Chemistry.
Purpose: To allow members of any established chemical society or institute in the Commonwealth to visit chemical establishments in another Commonwealth country.
Eligibility: Open to citizens of, and those domiciled in, any Commonwealth country.
Level of Study: Professional development
Type: Grant
Value: Up to UK £500. The grants will complement, where appropriate, those for visits to developing countries available from the International Committee's fund, and funding would cover the additional travel costs involved, together with appropriate subsistence. Applicants should also see the Visits to Developing Countries awards
Frequency: Annual
Country of Study: Any country
No. of awards offered: Approx. 4
Application Procedure: Applicants must submit applications on the official form and will normally be considered within 1 month of receipt.
Closing Date: Applications are accepted at any time
No. of awards given last year: 6
No. of applicants last year: 8
Additional Information: Applicants must be travelling to another country (not necessarily in the Commonwealth) and would normally stop en route to visit a third country that must be in the Commonwealth.

Hickinbottom/Briggs Fellowship

Subjects: Organic chemistry.
Purpose: To assist research.
Eligibility: Open to applicants domiciled in the United Kingdom or Republic of Ireland. Candidates must already hold a PhD or equivalent in chemistry and be not more than 36 years of age on October 31st.
Level of Study: Postdoctorate
Type: Fellowship
Value: Approx. UK £17,000/year
Length of Study: 3 years
Frequency: Dependent on funds available
Study Establishment: A British or Irish university or college
Country of Study: Other
No. of awards offered: 1
Application Procedure: Applicants must apply by application forms or be nominated.
Closing Date: June 1st
No. of awards given last year: 1

J W T Jones Travelling Fellowship

Subjects: Chemistry.
Purpose: To promote international co-operation, to enable chemists to carry out short-term studies in well established scientific centres abroad and to learn and use techniques not accessible to them in their own country.
Eligibility: Open to members of the Royal Society of Chemistry who hold at least a Master's or PhD degree in chemistry or a related subject and are already actively engaged in research. Candidates must produce evidence that the theoretical and practical knowledge or training to be acquired in the foreign laboratory will be beneficial to their scientific development and must also return to their country of origin upon termination of the fellowship.
Level of Study: Professional development
Type: Fellowship
Value: A lump sum of up to UK £5,000, designed to cover part or all of an economy class air or rail ticket and a subsistence allowance. It is expected that the institution of origin and/or the host institution will contribute to defray any remaining expenses incurred by the fellowship holder
Length of Study: Normally 1–3 months
Country of Study: Any country
No. of awards offered: Approx. 6
Application Procedure: Applicants must apply for application forms, together with full details, from the International Affairs Officer.
Closing Date: January 1st, April 1st, July 1st or October 1st
No. of awards given last year: 4
No. of applicants last year: 5
Additional Information: Fellowships will not be awarded to attend scientific meetings. Applications will be considered by a Fellowship Committee and the holder will be required to submit a formal report on the work accomplished.

Royal Society of Chemistry Journals Grants for International Authors

Subjects: Chemistry.
Purpose: To allow international authors to visit other countries in order to collaborate in research, exchange research ideas and results, and to give or receive special expertise and training.
Eligibility: Open to anyone with a recent publication in any of the Society's journals. Those from the United Kingdom or Republic of Ireland are excluded.
Level of Study: Professional development
Type: Grant
Value: A lump sum of up to UK £2,000, designed to cover part or all of an economy class air or rail ticket and a subsistence allowance. It is expected that the institution of origin and/or the host institution will contribute to defray any remaining expenses incurred by the grant holder
Length of Study: Normally 1–3 months
Country of Study: Any country
No. of awards offered: 100
Application Procedure: Applicants must apply for application forms, together with full details, from the International Affairs Officer.
Closing Date: January 1st, April 1st, July 1st or October 1st
No. of awards given last year: 83
No. of applicants last year: 107

Royal Society of Chemistry Research Fund

Subjects: Chemistry and chemical education.
Purpose: To provide financial support to those working in less affluent institutions.
Eligibility: Open to members of the Society.
Level of Study: Professional development
Type: Grant
Value: Up to UK £1,200 for the purchase of chemicals, equipment or for running expenses of research
Length of Study: 1 year
Frequency: Annual
Country of Study: Any country
No. of awards offered: 20–30
Closing Date: October 31st
No. of awards given last year: 30
No. of applicants last year: 50
Additional Information: Funds are limited, so preference will be given to those working in less well-endowed institutions. The Selection Committee is especially anxious to see inventive applications of a 'pump priming' nature. Members in developing countries should note particularly that additional funds have been made available by the Society's International Committee to provide grants for successful applicants from such countries. Preference will be given to those able to cite collaborative research projects with United Kingdom institutions.

Royal Society of Chemistry Visits to Developing Countries

Subjects: Chemistry.
Purpose: To promote international co-operation, specifically, to enable chemists to carry out short-term studies in well established scientific centres abroad and to learn and use techniques not accessible to them in their own country.
Eligibility: Open to members of the Society.
Level of Study: Professional development
Type: Grant
Value: Up to UK £500. The grants will complement, where appropriate, those for visits to Commonwealth countries, and funding would cover the additional travel costs involved, together with appropriate subsistence. Applicants should also see the Corday-Morgan Memorial Fund
Frequency: Annual
Country of Study: Any country
No. of awards offered: Approx. 4
Application Procedure: Applicants must submit applications on the official form and will normally be considered within 1 month of receipt.
Closing Date: Applications are accepted at any time
Additional Information: Applicants must be travelling to another country and would normally stop en route to visit a third country. This must be a developing country.

THE ROYAL SOCIETY OF EDINBURGH (RSE)

22-26 George Street, Edinburgh, Scotland
Tel: (44) 131 240 5000
Fax: (44) 131 240 5024
Email: resfells@royalsoced.org.uk
Website: www.ma.hw.ac.uk/RSE
Contact: Research Awards Manager

The Royal Society of Edinburgh (RSE) is Scotland's National Academy. It is an independent body, founded in 1783 by Royal Charter for the Advancement of Learning and Useful Knowledge and governed by an elected council of Fellows.

Auber Bequest

Subjects: All subjects.
Purpose: To provide assistance for the furtherance of academic research.
Eligibility: Open to naturalized British citizens or individuals wishing to acquire British nationality who are over 60 years of age, resident in Scotland or England and are bona fide scholars engaged in academic, but not industrial, research. Applicants should not have been British nationals at birth, nor held dual British nationality, and must have since acquired British nationality.
Level of Study: Unrestricted
Value: Varies, not normally exceeding UK £3,000
Length of Study: Up to 2 years
Frequency: Every 2 years
Country of Study: Other
No. of awards offered: Varies
Application Procedure: Applicants must complete an application form, available from the Research Awards Manager.
Closing Date: October 31st
Funding: Private
Contributor: The Auber Bequest
No. of awards given last year: 2
No. of applicants last year: 4

BP/RSE Research Fellowships

Subjects: Mechanical engineering, chemical engineering, control engineering, solid state sciences, information technology, non-biological chemistry and geological sciences.
Purpose: To support independent research in specific fields.
Eligibility: Open to persons of all nationalities who have a PhD or equivalent qualification. Applicants should be aged under 35 on the date of appointment and must show they have a capacity for innovative research and a substantial volume of published work relevant to their proposed field of study.
Level of Study: Postdoctorate
Type: Fellowship
Value: Salaries within the scales RGIA-2 for research and analogous staff in Institutes of Higher Education with annual increments and superannuation benefits. Financial support towards expenses involved in carrying out the research is available, including a start up grant of UK £1,000 in the first year only and a further allowance of up to UK £1,500 for travel and subsistence each year. Up to UK £2,500 is also available by competitive bid from the support fund pool each year
Length of Study: Up to 3 years
Frequency: Annual
Study Establishment: Any Institute of Higher Education approved for the purpose by the Council of the Society
Country of Study: Scotland
No. of awards offered: 1
Application Procedure: Applicants must complete an application form, available from the Research Fellowships Secretary. Candidates must negotiate directly with the relevant head of department of the proposed host institution.
Closing Date: Mid-March

Funding: Private
Contributor: British Petroleum (BP)
No. of awards given last year: 1
No. of applicants last year: 26
Additional Information: Fellows will be expected to devote their full time to research and will not be allowed to hold other paid appointments without the express permission of the Council of the RSE.

CRF (Caledonian Research Foundation)/RSE European Visiting Research Fellowships

Subjects: Archaeology, art and architecture, economics and economic history, geography, history, jurisprudence, linguistics, literature and philology, philosophy and religious studies.
Purpose: To create a two-way flow of visiting scholars in arts and letters between Scotland and continental Europe.
Eligibility: Open to members of the academic staff of a Scottish Institute of Higher Education or equivalent continental European institution. Applicants must be aged 60 or under on the date of the appointment, which is variable, but must be within 16 months of date of award. Applicants from continental Europe must be nominated by members of staff from a Scottish Institute of Higher Education.
Level of Study: Professional development
Type: Fellowship
Value: Up to UK £6,000 for visits of 6 months, which is reduced pro-rata for shorter visits, to cover actual costs of travel, subsistence and relevant study costs
Length of Study: Up to 6 months
Frequency: Annual
Study Establishment: A Scottish Institute of Higher Education or a recognized Institute of Higher Education in a continental European country
Country of Study: Other
No. of awards offered: 8
Application Procedure: Applicants must complete an application form, available from the Research Fellowships Secretary in August and September each year.
Closing Date: Early November
Funding: Private
Contributor: The CRF
No. of awards given last year: 6
No. of applicants last year: 10
Additional Information: Successful applicants will be required to submit a report within 2 months of the end of the visit.

CRF (Caledonian Research Foundation)/RSE Personal Research Fellowships

Subjects: Biological, biochemical, physical and clinical sciences.
Purpose: To aid independent research.
Eligibility: Open to students of all nationalities who have a PhD and are aged 32 or under on the date of appointment, or who have 2–6 years of postdoctoral experience.
Level of Study: Postdoctorate
Type: Fellowship
Value: A salary according to age, qualifications and experience. Salaries are within the scales RGIA-2 for research staff in Institutes of Higher Education. Financial support towards expenses involved in carrying out the research is available, including a start up grant of UK £1,000 in the first year only. Fellows receive UK £1,000 for travel and subsistence each year
Length of Study: Up to 3 years
Frequency: Annual
Study Establishment: Any Institute of Higher Education
Country of Study: Scotland
No. of awards offered: Varies
Application Procedure: Applicants must complete an application form, available from the CRF. Candidates must negotiate with the relevant Head of Department of the proposed host institution.
Closing Date: Mid-March
Funding: Private
Contributor: The CRF
No. of awards given last year: 2
No. of applicants last year: 20
Additional Information: The fellowships are administered by the Caledonian Research Foundation (CRF). Fellows will be expected to devote their full time to research and will not be allowed to hold other paid appointments without the express permission of the Council of the RSE.

For further information contact:

The CRF (Caledonian Research Foundation), 39 Castle Street, Edinburgh, EH2 3BH, Scotland
Contact: Grants Management Officer

CRF (Caledonian Research Foundation)/RSE Support Research Fellowship

Subjects: Biology, biochemical, physical and clinical sciences related to medicine.
Purpose: To enable fellows to take study leave, either in their own institution or elsewhere, while remaining in continuous employment with their present employer.
Eligibility: Open to existing members of academic staff aged 40 or under on date of appointment and employed on the lecturer scale, who have held a permanent appointment for at least 5 years in any Scottish Institute of Higher Education.
Level of Study: Professional development
Type: Fellowship
Value: The actual cost for non-clinical staff will be reimbursed according to the lecturer A scale (maximum RGI-3) with the placement determined by the employer. If clinically qualified, the salary will be within clinical senior lecturer grade. A provision of UK £1,000 is made for a start up grant. There is also a grant of UK £1,000 for travel and subsistence
Length of Study: 1 year
Frequency: Annual
Study Establishment: Any Institute of Higher Education
Country of Study: Scotland
No. of awards offered: 1
Application Procedure: Applicants must complete an application form, available from the CRF.
Closing Date: Mid-March
Funding: Private
Contributor: The CRF
No. of awards given last year: 1
No. of applicants last year: 4

For further information contact:

The CRF (Caledonian Research Foundation), 39 Castle Street, Edinburgh, EH2 3BH, Scotland
Contact: Grants Management Officer

Henry Dryerre Scholarship

Subjects: Medical and veterinary physiology.
Purpose: To support postgraduate research.
Eligibility: Open to European citizens holding a First Class (Honours) Degree from a Scottish university.
Level of Study: Postgraduate
Type: Scholarship
Value: Fees, research costs and travel expenses up to UK £850 per year and a maintenance grant of UK £5,956 if living away from home
Length of Study: 3 years full-time research
Frequency: Dependent on funds available, Other
Study Establishment: A Scottish institution
Country of Study: Scotland
No. of awards offered: 1
Application Procedure: Applicants must be nominated by a professor, reader or lecturer in a Scottish university.
Closing Date: March
Funding: Private
No. of awards given last year: 1
No. of applicants last year: 1
Additional Information: The scholarships are administered by the Carnegie Trust for the Universities of Scotland.

For further information contact:

Carnegie Trust for the Universities of Scotland,
Cameron House, Abbey Park Place, Dunfermline, Fife,
KY12 7PZ, Scotland
Tel: (44) 1383 622148
Fax: (44) 1383 622149
Email: carnegie.trust@ed.ac.uk
Contact: Miss J Gray

John Moyes Lessells Scholarships

Subjects: All forms of engineering.
Purpose: To enable well-qualified engineering graduates of Scottish Institutes of Higher Education to study some aspect of their profession overseas.
Eligibility: Applicants must be graduates of a Scottish Institute of Higher Education.
Level of Study: Professional development, predoctorate, postgraduate
Type: Scholarship
Value: Normally up to UK £15,000 per year. Additional research or travel expenditure may be sanctioned
Length of Study: Initially for 1 year but shorter periods or extension for a second year may be considered. Acceptance of a scholarship implies a willingness to spend at least 2 years in the United Kingdom following the period of tenure
Frequency: Annual
Country of Study: Other
No. of awards offered: Varies
Application Procedure: Applicants must complete an application form, available from the Research Awards Manager or the RSE website.
Closing Date: February 15th
Funding: Private
No. of awards given last year: 5
No. of applicants last year: 7

Royal Society of Edinburgh Wellcome Research Workshops

Subjects: Biomedical science, veterinary science, history of medicine.
Purpose: To bring together research staff, academic staff and clinicians from a wide spectrum of backgrounds and levels to discuss research topics of common concern. Attendance will be by invitation of the organizer.
Eligibility: Open to academic research or clinical staff in Scottish Higher Education or Research Institutes. Joint applications welcome.
Level of Study: Professional development, postgraduate, research, doctorate, postdoctorate
Type: Other
Value: Up to UK £2,000 per workshop
Frequency: Dependent on funds available
Study Establishment: In the Society's rooms or at a suitable research centre
Country of Study: Scotland
No. of awards offered: 3
Closing Date: End of April
Funding: Private
Contributor: The Wellcome Trust
No. of awards given last year: 3
No. of applicants last year: 5
Additional Information: The workshops, which may be specialist or multidisciplinary, are organized by the applicant and are restricted to a maximum of 40 participants, including five speakers. The workshops are advertised annually. They are sponsored by the Wellcome Trust.

For further information contact:

22-24 George Street, Edinburgh, EH2 2PQ, Scotland
Tel: (44) 131 225 6057
Fax: (44) 131 220 6889
Contact: Research Fellowships Secretary

Scottish Executive Personal Research Fellowships

Subjects: All subjects. The fellowships are awarded in fields likely to enhance the development of industry and encourage better uses of resources in Scotland.
Purpose: To encourage independent research in any discipline.
Eligibility: Open to persons of all nationalities who have a PhD or equivalent qualification. Applicants must be aged 32 or under on the date of appointment (October 1st) or have between 2 to 6 years of postdoctoral experience. They must also show they have a capacity for innovative research and have a substantial volume of published work relevant to their proposed field of study.
Level of Study: Postdoctorate
Type: Fellowship
Value: Annual stipends are within the scales RGIA-2 for research and analogous staff in Institutes of Higher Education with annual increments and superannuation benefits. Expenses of up to UK £7,000 in year one, UK £6,000 in years two and three for travel and attendance at meetings or incidentals may be reimbursed. No support payments are available to the institution but Fellows may seek support for their research from other sources
Length of Study: Up to 3 years full-time research
Frequency: Annual
Study Establishment: Any Institute of Higher Education, research institution or industrial laboratory approved for the purpose by the Council of the Society
Country of Study: Scotland
No. of awards offered: 4
Application Procedure: Applicants must complete an application form, available from the Research Fellowships Secretary. Applicants should negotiate directly with the proposed host institution.
Closing Date: Mid-March
Funding: Government
Contributor: The Scottish Executive
No. of awards given last year: 4
No. of applicants last year: Approx. 50
Additional Information: Fellows may not hold other paid appointments without the express permission of the Council, but teaching or seminar work appropriate to their special knowledge may be acceptable.

Scottish Executive/RSE Support Research Fellowships

Subjects: All subjects. The fellowships are awarded in fields likely to enhance the development of industry and encourage better uses of resources in Scotland.
Purpose: To enable support Fellows to take study leave, either in their own institution or elsewhere, while remaining in continuous employment with their present employer.
Eligibility: Candidates must be existing members of staff who have held a permanent appointment for not less than 5 years in any Institution of Higher Education in Scotland. Applicants should be aged under 40 on the date of appointment (January 1st) and employed on the lecturer grade or equivalent.
Level of Study: Professional development
Type: Fellowship
Value: The actual cost of replacement staff will be reimbursed according to the Lecturer A scale (maximum RGI-3) with the placement determined by the employer. Superannuation costs and employer's National Insurance contributions will also be reimbursed
Length of Study: Up to 1 year of full-time research
Frequency: Annual
Study Establishment: Any Institute of Higher Education, research institution or industrial laboratory approved for the purpose by the Council of the Society
Country of Study: Scotland
No. of awards offered: 4
Application Procedure: Applicants must complete an application form, available from the Research Fellowships Secretary. Applicants must negotiate directly with the proposed host institution.
Closing Date: Mid-March
Funding: Government
Contributor: The Scottish Executive
No. of awards given last year: 3

No. of applicants last year: Approx. 15
Additional Information: Further information is available on request or on the website.

THE ROYAL SOCIETY OF MEDICINE (RSM)

1 Wimpole Street, London, W1G 0AE, England
Tel: (44) 20 7290 2900
Fax: (44) 20 7290 2909
Email: events@rsm.dc.uk
Website: www.rsm.ac.uk
Contact: Section Manager Alademic Department

The Royal Society of Medicine (RSM) provides academic services and club facilities for its members as well as publishing a monthly journal and an annual bulletin, and providing over 400 educational conferences and meetings per year.

Colyer Prize

Subjects: Odontology.
Purpose: To reward the best original work in dental science completed during the previous five years.
Eligibility: Open to dental surgeons educated at a United Kingdom dental school who have not been qualified for more than 10 years. Open to all dental surgeons educated at any recognized dental school in the UK.
Level of Study: Postdoctorate
Type: Prize
Value: Varies, at least UK £100
Frequency: Every 3 years
Country of Study: United Kingdom
No. of awards offered: 1
Application Procedure: Further details are available from the Academic Registrar at the RSM.
Closing Date: March 30th
No. of applicants last year: 1

John of Arderne Medal

Subjects: Coloproctology.
Purpose: To award the presenter of the best paper presented at the short papers meeting of the section of coloproctology. Applicants have to submit an abstract for presentation at the meeting.
Eligibility: Open to applicants of any nationality.
Level of Study: Professional development
Type: Award
Value: Approx. UK £500
Frequency: Annual
Study Establishment: Varies
Country of Study: Any country
No. of awards offered: 1
Application Procedure: Further details are available from the RSM administrator.
Closing Date: September and November
Funding: Private
No. of awards given last year: 16
No. of applicants last year: 80

Karl Storz Travelling Scholarship

Subjects: Laryngology and rhinology.
Purpose: To assist with the cost of travel to overseas centres.
Eligibility: Open to senior registrars or consultants of not more than two years standing, who must be members of the section of laryngology and rhinology of the RSM.
Level of Study: Postdoctorate
Type: Scholarship
Value: UK £1,000
Frequency: Annual
Country of Study: Any country
No. of awards offered: 1
Application Procedure: Applicants must submit a paper to the RSM section of laryngology and rhinology. Further details are available from the RSM administrator.
Closing Date: December 9th
Funding: Commercial
Contributor: Karl Storz Endoscopy Limited
No. of awards given last year: 1
No. of applicants last year: 25
Additional Information: The recipient will be required to submit a brief report on the visit within three months of his or her return.

Nichols Fellowship

Subjects: Obstetrics and gynaecology.
Purpose: To encourage research to advance knowledge in the field.
Eligibility: Open to suitably qualified United Kingdom citizens.
Level of Study: Postdoctorate
Type: Fellowship
Value: UK £500 per year for two years, the second year being at the discretion of the Section Council
Length of Study: 2 years
Frequency: Every 3 years
Country of Study: Any country
No. of awards offered: 1
Application Procedure: Applicants must apply to the academic administrator at the RSM.
Funding: Private

Norman Gamble Fund and Research Prize

Subjects: Otology.
Purpose: To support specific research projects.
Eligibility: Open to British nationals.
Level of Study: Unrestricted
Type: Prize
Value: UK £100 for the research prize and UK £1,500 for the grant-in-aid. Awards alternate every two years
Frequency: Annual
Country of Study: Any country
No. of awards offered: 1
Application Procedure: Further details are available from the RSM administrator.
Closing Date: December 9th
Funding: Private
No. of awards given last year: 1
No. of applicants last year: 4

Norman Tanner Medal and Prize (1st Prize) Glaxo Travelling Fellowship (2nd Prize)

Subjects: Surgery.
Purpose: To enable the recipient to travel to a recognized institution to further his or her knowledge of surgery, or to attend an overseas conference in the speciality. To enable the recipient to attend the annual 'Out-of-Town Meeting' of the section of Surgery. The use of the fund to attend an alternative conference is permitted by agreement of council.
Eligibility: Open to Surgeons in training of any nationality.
Level of Study: Professional development
Type: Travel grant
Value: UK £250 (1st Prize) UK £250 (2nd Prize)
Frequency: Annual
Country of Study: Any country
No. of awards offered: 2
Application Procedure: Abstracts are submitted and selected papers are presented at the December meeting. Papers should be clinically orientated. Further details are available from the Academic Administrator at the RSM.
Closing Date: Early October
No. of awards given last year: 2
Additional Information: The recipient will be required to submit a brief report on the visit within three months of his or her return.

Ophthalmology Travelling Fellowship

Subjects: Ophthalmology.
Purpose: To enable British ophthalmologists to travel abroad with the intention of furthering the study or advancement of ophthalmology, or to enable foreign ophthalmologists to visit the United Kingdom for the same purpose.

Eligibility: Open to ophthalmologists in the British Isles of any nationality who have not attained an official consultant appointment, nor undertaken professional clinical work or equivalent responsibility for any substantial period before or during the execution of original work.
Level of Study: Professional development
Type: Fellowship
Value: UK £500–2,000
Frequency: Every 2 years
Study Establishment: Varies
Country of Study: Any country
No. of awards offered: Varies
Application Procedure: Applicants must apply to the academic administrator at RSM.
Closing Date: Entries are evaluated in December and May
No. of awards given last year: 4
No. of applicants last year: 6

Royal Society of Medicine Travelling Fellowship

Subjects: Urology.
Purpose: To enable the holder to enhance his or her knowledge and experience by visiting an overseas unit.
Eligibility: Open to members of the section of urology of RSM, who should be in urological training or within three years of a consultant appointment. No restriction of age, nationality or residency.
Level of Study: Professional development
Type: Fellowship
Value: UK £1,000
Frequency: Annual
Country of Study: Any country
No. of awards offered: Varies
Application Procedure: Further details are available from the RSM administrator. No application form needs to be completed.
Closing Date: End of October
Contributor: Prize fund setup to cover worthy Academic Activity.
No. of awards given last year: 1
No. of applicants last year: 5

RSM Medical Insurance Agency Prize

Subjects: Surgery.
Purpose: To enable the recipient to travel to a recognized institution to further his or her knowledge of surgery, or to attend an overseas conference in the speciality. To enable the recipient to attend the annual 'Out-of-Town' meeting of the Section of Surgery. The use of the fund to attend an alternative conference is permitted by agreement of council.
Eligibility: Open to surgeons in training, holding the post up to the grade of registrar or senior registrar.
Level of Study: Professional development
Type: Prize
Value: UK £250 (Varies)
Frequency: Annual
Study Establishment: A recognized institution in the United Kingdom or overseas
Country of Study: Any country
No. of awards offered: 1
Application Procedure: Further details are available from the RSM administrator. Abstracts are submitted and selected papers are presented at February meeting. Papers should be laboratory-based research papers.
No. of awards given last year: 1
Additional Information: The recipient will be required to submit a brief report on the visit within three months of his or her return.

RSM Mental Health Foundation Essay Prize

Subjects: Psychiatry.
Purpose: To award an essay.
Eligibility: Open to candidates practising medicine in the United Kingdom or the Republic of Ireland who are in training at any grade from senior house officer to senior registrar or equivalent. Applicants need not be members of RSM.
Type: Prize
Value: Varies, approx. UK £500–250 depending on available finance. It also includes a subscription to RSM if funds are available, 1st prize UK £750, 2nd prize UK £500
Frequency: Annual, SHO or SPR
Country of Study: United Kingdom
No. of awards offered: 2
Application Procedure: Essays should be submitted in triplicate to the RSM section of psychiatry.
Closing Date: Early January
Funding: Private
No. of applicants last year: 1
Additional Information: The subject is chosen by the Council. Essays should be approx. 5,000 words in length.

RSM Presidents Prize

Subjects: Clinical neurosciences.
Purpose: To reward summaries of cases for clinical presentation.
Eligibility: Open to applicants of any nationality.
Level of Study: Professional development
Type: Prize
Value: UK £100
Frequency: Annual
Country of Study: Any country
No. of awards offered: 1
Application Procedure: Further details are available from the RSM administrator.
Closing Date: November
Funding: Private
No. of awards given last year: 1
No. of applicants last year: 12
Additional Information: Presentations take place in February.

Sylvia Lawler Prize

Subjects: Oncology.
Purpose: To provide prizes in the field of oncology.
Eligibility: Open to medically or scientifically qualified trainees.
Level of Study: Postgraduate
Type: Prize
Value: Details on application
Frequency: Annual
Country of Study: United Kingdom
No. of awards offered: 2
Application Procedure: Applicants must submit an abstract of one side of A4 to the annually held Sylvia Lawler prize meeting. Abstract forms are available from the Academic Administrator at the RSM.
Closing Date: Please contact the Foundation
Funding: Trusts
No. of awards given last year: 1
No. of applicants last year: 12

ROYAL TOWN PLANNING INSTITUTE (RTPI)

41 Botolph Lane, London, EC3R 8DL, England
Tel: (44) 20 7929 9473
Fax: (44) 20 7929 8199
Email: judy.woollett@rtpi.org.uk

The Royal Town Planning Institute (RTPI) was founded in 1914 and is a registered charity. Its aim is to advance the science and art of town planning in all its aspects, including local, regional and national planning for the benefit of the public. The Institute is primarily concerned with maintaining high standards of competence and conduct within the profession, promoting the role of planning within the country's social, economic and political structures, and presenting the profession's views on current planning issues.

George Pepler International Award

Subjects: Town and country planning or some particular aspect of planning theory and practice.
Purpose: To enable young people of any nationality to visit another country for a short period to study.
Eligibility: Open to persons under 30 years of age of any nationality.

Level of Study: Research, professional development
Value: Up to UK £1,500
Length of Study: Short-term travel outside the United Kingdom for United Kingdom residents or for visits to the United Kingdom for applicants from abroad
Frequency: Every 2 years
Country of Study: Any country
No. of awards offered: 1
Application Procedure: Applicants must submit a statement showing the nature of the study visit proposed, together with an itinerary. Application forms are available on request from the RTPI.
Closing Date: March 31st
Funding: Private
Contributor: Trust fund
No. of awards given last year: 1
No. of applicants last year: 20
Additional Information: At the conclusion of the visit the recipient must submit a report.

RUSSELL SAGE FOUNDATION

112 East 64th Street, New York, NY, 10021, United States of America
Tel: (1) 212 750 6012
Fax: (1) 212 371 4761
Email: info@rsage.org
Website: www.russellsage.org
Contact: Vice President of Administration

The Russell Sage Foundation is the principal American foundation devoted exclusively to research in the social sciences. Located in New York City, the Foundation is a research centre, a funding source for studies by scholars at other academic and research institutions and an active member of the nation's social science community.

Russell Sage Foundation Visiting Scholar Appointments

Subjects: Social sciences.
Eligibility: Open to scholars in the social sciences. The Foundation particularly welcomes groups of visiting scholars who wish to collaborate on a specific project during their residence at the foundation. In order to develop these projects fully, support is sometimes provided for working groups prior to their arrival at the foundation. Awards are not made for the support of graduate degree work, nor for institutional support.
Level of Study: Doctorate, postdoctorate
Type: Fellowship
Value: Varies
Length of Study: 1 academic year
Frequency: Annual
Study Establishment: The Foundation
Country of Study: Any country
No. of awards offered: Varies
Application Procedure: Applicants should consult the website or contact the organization for details.
Closing Date: October 15th prior to the year of residence
Funding: Foundation
No. of awards given last year: 21
No. of applicants last year: 110
Additional Information: Awardees are expected to offer the Foundation the right to publish any book-length manuscripts resulting from Foundation support.

RUTH ESTRIN GOLDBERG MEMORIAL FOR CANCER RESEARCH

885 Gloucester Road, Union, NJ, 07083, United States of America
Tel: (1) 908 688 1725
Contact: Mrs Myrna Abramson, Past President

Ruth Estrin Goldberg Memorial for Cancer Research

Subjects: Cancer research.
Eligibility: Open to candidates from the eastern United States of America, preferably New York, New Jersey, Pennsylvania, Connecticut, Massachusetts, Delaware or Maryland.
Level of Study: Unrestricted
Value: US$10,000–20,000
Frequency: Annual
Country of Study: United States of America
No. of awards offered: 2
Application Procedure: Applicants must write for an application form and guidelines.
Closing Date: February 28th
Funding: Private
Contributor: Members and friends
No. of awards given last year: 2
No. of applicants last year: 1015
Additional Information: The Ruth Estrin Goldberg Memorial for Cancer Research is a volunteer organization.

For further information contact:

653 Colonial Arms Road, Union, NJ, 07083, United States of America
Contact: Mrs Rhoda Moodman, Past President

RYAN DAVIES MEMORIAL FUND

1 Squire Court, The Marina, Swansea, SA1 3XB, Wales
Tel: (44) 1792 301500
Fax: (44) 1792 301500
Contact: Mr Michael D Evans, Secretary

The Ryan Davies Memorial Fund honours the memory of the great Welsh performer, Ryan Davies, and gives awards in the performing arts to postgraduate students of Welsh extraction.

Ryan Davies Memorial Fund Scholarship Grants

Subjects: Music, drama and all performing arts.
Purpose: To enable Welsh artists to continue studies following their formal training.
Eligibility: Open to Welsh artists or artists of Welsh extraction only.
Level of Study: Professional development
Type: Grant
Value: Up to UK £2,500 each
Length of Study: Up to 1 year
Frequency: Annual
Study Establishment: Unrestricted
Country of Study: Any country
No. of awards offered: Up to 8
Application Procedure: Applicants must apply by forwarding all relevant information including their reason for application, qualifications, referees and any further background information to the Secretary.
Closing Date: May 30th
Funding: Private
Contributor: The general public
No. of awards given last year: 8
No. of applicants last year: 50
Additional Information: The Fund was set up in memory of Ryan Davies, Wales' most versatile entertainer. Artists will be notified of their application by July 31st.

S S HUEBNER FOUNDATION FOR INSURANCE EDUCATION

3000 SH-DH, 3260 Locust Walk, Philadelphia, PA, 19104-6302, United States of America
Tel: (1) 215 898 9631
Fax: (1) 215 573 2218
Email: hcalvert@wharton.upenn.edu
Website: www.huebnergeneva.org
Contact: Associate Director

The S S Huebner Foundation is an educational foundation with the objective of promoting education and research in risk management and insurance. It provides PhD fellowships for the study of risk management and insurance economics at the Wharton School of the University of Pennsylvania, and publishes books and working papers.

S S Huebner Foundation for Insurance Education Predoctoral Fellowships

Subjects: Managerial science and applied economics, with a specialization in risk management and insurance economics.
Purpose: To increase the supply of college professors specializing in risk management and insurance economics.
Eligibility: Open to citizens of the United States of America and Canada who hold a Bachelor's degree from an accredited United States of America or Canadian university or college and intend to pursue a teaching career in insurance.
Level of Study: Doctorate, postdoctorate
Type: Fellowship
Value: Full tuition fees of the Wharton School of the University of Pennsylvania plus an annual living stipend of US$20,000
Length of Study: 4 years
Frequency: Annual
Study Establishment: The Wharton School of the University of Pennsylvania
Country of Study: United States of America
No. of awards offered: Varies
Application Procedure: Applicants must apply to the Wharton School doctoral programme for admission and to the Huebner Foundation for funding.
Closing Date: December 15th (Wharton admission), January 15th (Huebner funding)
Funding: Corporation, foundation, individuals
Contributor: Leading insurance companies in the United States and Canada
No. of awards given last year: 2
No. of applicants last year: 8
Additional Information: Candidates are required to certify that it is their intention to follow a teaching career in insurance and that they will major in insurance and risk management for a graduate degree. Applicants must take the admission test for graduate study in business. For information concerning these examinations, candidates should write directly to the Educational Testing Service (ETS). Applicants should apply separately and directly to the Wharton School Doctoral Programme Office for admission into the Insurance and Risk Management Doctoral Programme.

SAINT ANDREW'S SOCIETY OF THE STATE OF NEW YORK SCHOLARSHIPS, THE CARNEGIE TRUST FOR THE UNIVERSITIES OF SCOTLAND

Cameron House, Abbey Park Place, Dunfermline, Fife, KY16 7PZ, Scotland
Tel: (44) 13 8362 2148
Fax: (44) 13 8362 2149
Email: jgray@carnegie-trust.org
Contact: Chairman, Scottish Selection Commitee

The Carnegie Trust for the universities of Scotland offers scholarships to students of Scottish descent or birth for study at a university in the United States of America, within a radius of 250 miles from New York City or the Washington, DC area.

St Andrew's Society of the State of New York Scholarship Fund

Subjects: All subjects.
Purpose: To support advanced study exchanges between the United States of America and Scotland.
Eligibility: Open to newly qualified graduates of a Scottish university or of Oxford or Cambridge. Candidates are required to have a Scottish background. The possession of an Honours Degree is not essential. Personality and other qualities will influence the selection.
Level of Study: Postgraduate
Type: Scholarship
Value: US$20,000 to cover university tuition fees, room and board and transportation expenses
Length of Study: 1 academic year
Frequency: Annual
Study Establishment: A university within 250 miles of New York City or the Washington, DC area
Country of Study: United States of America
No. of awards offered: 2
Application Procedure: Applicants must write for details. Each Scottish university will screen its own applicants and nominate one candidate to go forward to the final selection committee to be held in Edinburgh in early March. Oxford and Cambridge applicants should apply directly to the Society.
Closing Date: December 15th
Funding: Private
No. of awards given last year: 3
No. of applicants last year: 25
Additional Information: Only in unusual circumstances will the Society consider other locations. Thereafter, the scholar is expected to spend a little time travelling in United States of America before returning to Scotland. Applications should be made via the principal of the university attended (ing) in the case of the Scottish universities.

SAINT PAUL'S COLLEGE

115 College Drive, Virgima, Lawrenceville, 23868, United States of America
Tel: (1) 434 848 3111
Fax: (1) 434 848 0229

The Saint Paul's College is a private, historically black college in Virginia and its mission is to serve each student as a family member and as an individual, pooling its human and financial resources to nurture those who make the wise choice to pursue their education here.

Saint Paul's Academic Presidential Scholarship

Subjects: All subjects.
Purpose: To provide financial support.
Eligibility: Open to students enrolled in Saint Paul's College.
Level of Study: Postgraduate
Type: Scholarship
Value: US$9,700
Frequency: Annual
Study Establishment: Saint Paul's College
Country of Study: United States of America
No. of awards offered: 8
Application Procedure: A completed application form must be submitted.

SAMUEL H KRESS FOUNDATION

174 East 80th Street, New York, NY 10021, United States of America
Tel: (1) 212 861 4993
Fax: (1) 212 628 3146
Website: www.kressfoundation.org

The Samuel H. Kress Foundation, since its creation in 1929, has devoted its resources almost exclusively to programmes related to European art. The Foundation devoted its resources to advancing the history, conservation, and enjoyment of the vast heritage o European art, architecture, and archaeology.

Samuel H Kress Foundation 2-Year Research Fellowships at Foreign Institutions

Subjects: Art history.
Purpose: To facilitate advanced dissertation research in association with a selected institute of art history in either Florence, Jerusalem, Leiden, London, Munich, Nicosia, Paris, Rome or Zurich.
Eligibility: Open to PhD candidates in the history of art for the completion of their dissertation research. Candidates must be citizens of the United States of America or matriculated at an institution in the United States of America.
Level of Study: Predoctorate
Type: Fellowship
Value: US$22,500 per year
Length of Study: 2 years
Frequency: Annual

Study Establishment: One of a number of art historical institutes in Florence, Jerusalem, Leiden, London, Munich, Nicosia, Paris, Rome or Zurich
No. of awards offered: 4
Application Procedure: Applicants must be nominated by their art history department. There is a limit of one applicant per department. The Foundation does not accept grant materials by fax.
Closing Date: November 30th
Funding: Private
No. of awards given last year: 4
No. of applicants last year: Approx. 25

Samuel H Kress Foundation Fellowships for Advanced Training in Fine Arts Conservation

Subjects: Specific areas of fine art conservation.
Purpose: To enable young American conservators to undertake post-MA advanced internships.
Eligibility: Open to those who have completed their academic training in conservation.
Level of Study: Postgraduate
Type: Fellowship
Value: US$30,000
Frequency: Annual
Study Establishment: Appropriate institutions
Country of Study: United States of America
No. of awards offered: 10
Application Procedure: Applicants must write for details. The Foundation does not accept grant materials by fax. Application procedures and contact information available at www.kressfoundation.org
Closing Date: February 28th
Funding: Private
No. of applicants last year: Approx. 25–30
Additional Information: Emphasis is on hands-on training. These grants are not for the completion of degree programmes. Enquiries should be directed to Ms Ackerman or Wyman Meers.

Samuel H Kress Foundation Travel Fellowships

Subjects: Art history.
Purpose: To facilitate travel for PhD candidates in the history of art to view materials essential for the completion of dissertation research.
Eligibility: Open to predoctoral candidates at United States of America universities.
Level of Study: Doctorate
Type: Fellowship
Value: Varies between US$3,500–10,000
Frequency: Annual
Country of Study: Any country
No. of awards offered: 10–15
Application Procedure: Applicants must be nominated by their art history department. There is a limit of one applicant per department. The Foundation does not accept grant materials by fax. Procedures and forms available to download at www.kressfoundation.org
Closing Date: November 30th
Funding: Private
No. of awards given last year: 10
No. of applicants last year: Approx. 50

SASAKAWA FUND

School of Economics, University of São Paulo 908, FEA 1, room D105, São Paulo, Buntantã, SP 055 (080) 10, Brazil
Tel: (55) 11 3091 6075
Email: sylff@usp.br

Generally known as SYLFF, The Ryoichi Sasakawa young leaders fellowship fund established in 1987 aims to nurture future leaders who will transcend the geopolitical, religious, ethnic, and cultural boundaries and actively participate in the world community for peace and the well- being of humankind.

Sasakawa Young Leader Fellowship (SYLFF) Program

Subjects: Social sciences and humanities.
Purpose: To provide grants for graduate students is social sciences areas.
Eligibility: Open to post-graduate students from the university of Sao Paulo with research projects proposals that relate to approved subject areas and aim to assist Brazil in its global insertion.
Level of Study: Postgraduate
Type: Fellowship
Length of Study: 2 years
Frequency: Annual
Study Establishment: São Paulo University
Country of Study: Brazil
Funding: Foundation
Contributor: The Tokyo Foundation
No. of awards given last year: 9

For further information contact:

Tel: +55 11 3091 6075
Email: sylff@usp.br
Contact: Professor Luciano Gualberto

SAVOY FOUNDATION

230 Foch Street, St Jean Sur Richelieu, QC, J3B 2B2, Canada
Tel: (1) 450 358 9779
Fax: (1) 450 346 1045
Email: epilepsy@savoy-foundation.ca
Website: www.savoy-foundation.ca
Contact: Secretary

The Savoy Foundation's main activity is to support and encourage research into epilepsy.

Savoy Foundation Postdoctoral and Clinical Research Fellowships

Subjects: Medical and behavioural science, as they relate to epilepsy.
Purpose: To support a full-time research project in the field of epilepsy.
Eligibility: Candidates must be scientists or medical specialists with a PhD or MD.
Level of Study: Research, postgraduate, postdoctorate
Type: Research grant
Value: Canadian $25,000
Length of Study: 1 year, in the first instance, but will be renewable once and, exceptionally, twice upon request
Frequency: Annual
Country of Study: Canada
No. of awards offered: Varies
Application Procedure: Applicants must contact the Foundation or visit the website for application forms and further information.
Closing Date: January 15th
Funding: Foundation, private
Contributor: The Savoy Foundation endowments
No. of awards given last year: 3
No. of applicants last year: 11
Additional Information: The period of support may begin at any time between May and October.

Savoy Foundation Research Grants

Subjects: Medical and behavioural science, as they relate to epilepsy.
Purpose: To support further research into epilepsy.
Eligibility: Only available to clinicians and established scientists.
Level of Study: Research, postgraduate, postdoctorate
Type: Research grant
Value: Up to Canadian $30,000
Frequency: Annual
Country of Study: Canada
No. of awards offered: Varies
Application Procedure: Applicants must contact the Foundation or visit the website for application forms and further information.
Closing Date: January 15th
Funding: Private, foundation
Contributor: The Savoy Foundation endowments
No. of awards given last year: 5
No. of applicants last year: 10

Additional Information: The grant is only available to Canadian citizens or for projects conducted in Canada.

Savoy Foundation Studentships

Subjects: Biomedicine, neurology and epileptology.
Purpose: To support training and research in a biomedical discipline, the health sciences or social sciences related to epilepsy.
Eligibility: Candidates must have a good university record, eg. a BSc, MD or equivalent diploma and have ensured that a qualified researcher affiliated to a university or hospital will supervise his or her work. Concomitant registration in a graduate programme is encouraged. The awards are available to Canadian citizens or for projects conducted in Canada.
Level of Study: Predoctorate, doctorate, postgraduate
Type: Studentship
Value: The stipend will be Canadian $12,000 for the 1st year, with a Canadian $1,000 increase for each year of renewal. An annual sum of Canadian $1,000 will be allocated to the laboratory or institution as additional support for the research project
Length of Study: 1–4 years
Frequency: Annual
Country of Study: Canada
No. of awards offered: Varies
Application Procedure: Applicants must contact the Foundation or visit the website for application forms and further information.
Closing Date: January 15th
Funding: Foundation, private
Contributor: The Savoy Foundation endowments
No. of awards given last year: 7
No. of applicants last year: 19

SCHOOL OF ORIENTAL AND AFRICAN STUDIES (SOAS)

University of London, Thornhaugh Street, Russell Square, London, WC1H 0XG, England
Tel: (44) 20 7074 5091
Fax: (44) 20 7074 5089
Email: jt26@soas.ac.uk
Website: www.soas.ac.uk
Contact: Mrs Jean Tullett, Scholarships Officer

The School of Oriental and African Studies (SOAS) regards its role as advancing the knowledge and understanding of the cultures and societies of Asia and Africa and of the School's academic disciplines through high-quality teaching and research.

Bernard Buckman Scholarship

Subjects: Chinese studies with an emphasis on modern and contemporary China, although it is possible to study aspects of premodern China.
Purpose: To provide fee remission for a student taking an MA in Chinese studies.
Eligibility: Open to those candidates who qualify to pay for home or European Union tuition fees. Applicants must possess a good Honours Degree from a United Kingdom university or its equivalent.
Level of Study: Postgraduate
Type: Scholarship
Value: Home or European Union postgraduate fee
Length of Study: 1 year
Frequency: Annual
Study Establishment: SOAS
Country of Study: United Kingdom
No. of awards offered: 1
Application Procedure: Applicants must complete an application form, which can be obtained from the registry or downloaded from the website.
Closing Date: March 31st
Funding: Private
No. of awards given last year: 1
No. of applicants last year: 7

SOAS Bursary

Subjects: Oriental and African studies in archaeology area studies, economics, ethnomusicology, history, law, languages, linguistics, phonetics, politics, religious studies, social anthropology and development studies.
Purpose: To provide financial assistance to study for a Master's or postgraduate diploma.
Eligibility: Applicants must possess a good Honours Degree, preferably First Class, from a United Kingdom institution or overseas equivalent.
Level of Study: Postgraduate
Type: Bursary
Value: UK £7,855
Length of Study: 1 year, non-renewable
Frequency: Annual
Study Establishment: SOAS
Country of Study: United Kingdom
No. of awards offered: 8
Application Procedure: Applicants must complete and submit an application form obtainable from the academic registrar, with two references and a 500-word submission. Application forms are also available on the website.
Closing Date: March 31st
Funding: Government
No. of awards given last year: 8
No. of applicants last year: 350

SOAS Research Student Fellowships

Subjects: The languages and cultures of Africa, East Asia, near and Middle East, South Asia and South East Asia, focusing on anthropology and sociology, art and archaeology, development studies, economics, ethnomusicology, financial and management studies, history, law, linguistics, political studies and the study of religions.
Purpose: To support research study at SOAS.
Eligibility: Applications are invited in respect of all subject areas offered by the School. Applicants must possess a good Master's degree from a United Kingdom university or its equivalent.
Level of Study: Doctorate
Type: Fellowship
Value: UK £10,065 plus remission of home or European Union fees
Length of Study: 3 years
Frequency: Annual
Study Establishment: SOAS
Country of Study: United Kingdom
No. of awards offered: 4
Application Procedure: Applicants must complete and submit an application form that is obtainable from the academic registrar, with two references, a 500-word submission and five photocopies. Application forms are also available on the website.
Closing Date: March 31st
Funding: Government
No. of awards given last year: 9
No. of applicants last year: 120

SCHOOL OF VETERINARY MEDICINE, HANNOVER

Buenteweg 2, PO Box 71 11 80, D-30559 Hannover, Germany
Tel: (49) 511 523 111
Fax: (49) 511 523 165
Email: hanslinnemann@tiho-hannover.de
Website: www.tiho-hannover.de
Contact: Executive Member of the Board

The School of Veterinary Medicine, Hannover is a centre for teaching and research in veterinary medicine and zoology with approximately 300 scientists and 2,000 students. Among the 26 institutes and clinics is the Institute for Parasitology, where the Karl-Enigk Foundation was founded.

Karl-Enigk Scholarships

Subjects: Parasitology, mainly veterinary parasitology.
Purpose: To support research in experimental parasitology, mainly veterinary parasitology.
Eligibility: Applicants must not be older than 32 years and must be from European countries where German is spoken.
Level of Study: Postdoctorate, doctorate
Type: Scholarship
Value: Please contact the organization for further information
Length of Study: Varies
Frequency: Annual
Country of Study: Any country
No. of awards offered: Varies
Application Procedure: Applicants must submit a curriculum vitae, publication list, short research proposal and references from the head of the research institute. Applications must be addressed to the Karl Enigk-Stiftung, School of Veterinary Medicine, Hannover.
Closing Date: Applications are accepted at any time
Funding: Private
No. of awards given last year: 3
No. of applicants last year: 5

SCIENCE FOUNDATION IRELAND

Wilton Park House, Wilton Place, Dublin 2, Ireland
Fax: (353) 353 1 607 3201
Email: info@sfi.ie
Website: www.sfi.ie
Contact: William C Harris, Director

SFI Fellow Awards

Subjects: Science and engineering.
Purpose: To support senior distinguished researchers in science and engineering that underpin biotechnology and information and communications technology (ICT).
Eligibility: Applicants must be senior distinguished researchers in science and engineering.
Level of Study: Research
Type: Grant
Value: Up to €1 million per year
Length of Study: 5 years
Frequency: Annual
No. of awards offered: 3
Application Procedure: Application forms and support notes can be downloaded from the website.
Closing Date: No deadline
Funding: Foundation
Contributor: Science Foundation Ireland

SFI Fellows–Research Professorships

Subjects: Information and communications technology (ICT) and biotechnology.
Purpose: To assist research bodies in Ireland in attracting outstanding scientists to their institutions.
Eligibility: Applicants must be research bodies that can attract investigators of distinguished international reputation from outside Ireland. Applicants must be research bodies that can attract investigators or distinguished international reputation from outside Ireland.
Level of Study: Research
Type: Professorship
Value: €50,000 per year
Length of Study: 5 years
Frequency: Annual
Application Procedure: Application forms and supports notes can be downloaded from the website.
Closing Date: No deadline
Funding: Foundation
Contributor: Science Foundation Ireland

SFI Investigator Programme Grants

Subjects: Biotechnology and information and communications technology (ICT).
Purpose: To support fields of science and engineering that underpin biotechnology and ICT.
Eligibility: Applicants must be distinguished researchers in biotechnology and ICT.
Level of Study: Research
Type: Grant
Value: Up to €250,000 per year
Length of Study: Up to 4 years
Frequency: Annual
Application Procedure: Application forms and support notes can be downloaded from the website.
Funding: Foundation
Contributor: Science Foundation Ireland

SCOULOUDI FOUNDATION

The Institute of Historical Research, University of London, Senate House, London, WC1E 7HU, England
Tel: (44) 20 7862 8740
Fax: (44) 20 7862 8740
Website: www.history.ac.uk
Contact: James Lees, Fellowships Officer

The IHR is an important resource and meeting place for scholars from all over the world. It contains an outstanding open access library, runs courses and major conferences, offers research fellowships and other awards and produces many significant research aids and tools.

Economic History Society Research Fellowships

Subjects: Economic and social history.
Purpose: To help candidates at an advanced stage of a PhD to complete their doctorates or to fund 1 year of postdoctoral study in history.
Eligibility: Open to postdoctoral candidates who have recently completed a doctoral degree in economic or social history or to graduates who are engaged in the completion of a doctoral degree in economic or social history and who have completed 2 years, but not more than 4 years of full-time or 8 years part-time research on their chosen topics. Fellowships are open to citizens of the United Kingdom or to candidates with a degree from a university in the United Kingdom.
Level of Study: Doctorate, postdoctorate
Type: Fellowship
Value: In line with ESRC rates (approx. UK £10,000 per year)
Length of Study: 1 year
Frequency: Dependent on funds available
Study Establishment: An institute of historical research
Country of Study: England
No. of awards offered: 3
Application Procedure: Applicants must complete an application form, available from the Fellowship Officer in early January.
Closing Date: End of March
Funding: Foundation
Contributor: The Economic History Society
No. of awards given last year: 3

Scouloudi Foundation Historical Awards

Subjects: History or a related subject.
Purpose: To provide subsidies towards the cost of publishing a book or article in the field of history, incorporating an academic thesis or other scholarly work already accepted by a reputable publisher or learned journal or to pay for special expenses incurred in the completion of advanced historical work such as the cost of fares and subsistence during visits to libraries or record repositories.
Eligibility: Open to graduates of United Kingdom universities who possess a relevant Honours Degree, or United Kingdom citizens with a similar qualification from a university outside the United Kingdom. These awards are not made for study or research towards a postgraduate qualification, eg. work on thesis for higher degrees.
Type: Varies
Value: UK £100–1,000. Applicants should not ask for more than their minimum requirements for the year concerned
Frequency: Dependent on funds available, Publication
Study Establishment: None

Country of Study: Any country
No. of awards offered: Varies
Application Procedure: Applicants must complete an application form.
Closing Date: Early March
Funding: Private
Contributor: The Scouloudi Foundation

SEMICONDUCTOR RESEARCH CORPORATION (SRC)

PO Box 12053, Research Triangle Park, NC, 27709, United States of America
Tel: (1) 919 941 9400
Fax: (1) 919 941 9450
Email: students@src.org
Website: www.src.org
Contact: Fellowships Office

The Semiconductor Research Corporation (SRC) is a consortium of about 60 semiconductor manufacturers and equipment makers. The SRC manages a research portfolio in major research universities throughout the world. At any given time it supports about 700 advanced degree students on contract research, 45 graduate Fellows and 15 Master's scholars. The SRC supports a pragmatic approach to developing student programmes and provides industry interactions and other opportunities for its students.

SRC Graduate Fellowship Program

Subjects: Electrical engineering, computer engineering, chemical engineering, mechanical engineering, materials science, physics and related areas.
Purpose: To attract academically outstanding students to doctoral programmes in areas of interest to the semiconductor industry.
Eligibility: Open to students who have United States of America citizenship or permanent resident status. Students are also required to perform their doctoral research under the guidance of an SRC-funded faculty member.
Level of Study: Doctorate
Type: Fellowship
Value: Please contact the organization
Length of Study: 5 years or until completion of the PhD degree, whichever comes first
Frequency: Annual
Study Establishment: Universities having SRC-funded contracts. A list is available at the website
Country of Study: United States of America
No. of awards offered: Varies
Application Procedure: Applicants must complete an application form. Applications are distributed through SRC-funded faculty in November. Applications are also distributed through other avenues outside the SRC community and applications are encouraged from non-SRC-funded colleges.
Closing Date: February 15th
Funding: Commercial
Contributor: The semiconductor industry
No. of awards given last year: 7
No. of applicants last year: 98
Additional Information: Recipients are required to be associated with an SRC-funded contract. Resources are available to assist qualified students in identifying suitable faculty within SRC-funded universities. SRC contracts support precompetitive research areas of interest to the semiconductor industry.

SRC Master's Scholarship Program

Subjects: Electrical engineering, computer engineering, chemical engineering, mechanical engineering, materials science, physics and related areas.
Purpose: To attract underrepresented minorities and women to disciplines of interest to the semiconductor industry.
Eligibility: Open to students having United States of America citizenship or permanent resident status. Students are also required to be from underrepresented minorities, eg. African American, Native American, Hispanic.
Level of Study: Postgraduate
Type: Scholarship
Value: Please contact the organization
Length of Study: 2 years or until completion of the Master's degree, whichever comes first
Frequency: Annual
Study Establishment: Universities having SRC-funded contracts. A list is available at the website
Country of Study: United States of America
No. of awards offered: Varies
Application Procedure: Applicants must complete an application form. Applications are distributed through SRC-funded faculty in November with a due date early in February. Applications are also distributed through other avenues outside the SRC community and applications are encouraged from non-SRC-funded colleges.
Closing Date: February 15th
Funding: Commercial
Contributor: The semiconductor industry
No. of awards given last year: 14
No. of applicants last year: 30
Additional Information: Recipients are required to be associated with an SRC-funded contract. Resources are available to assist qualified students in identifying suitable faculty within SRC-funded universities. SRC contracts support precompetitive research in areas of interest to the semiconductor industry.

SEOUL NATIONAL UNIVERSITY

San 56-1, Shinrim-dong Kwamk-gu, Seoul, Kawnak-Ku, 151-747, Korea
Tel: (82) 2 880 5488
Fax: (82) 2 871 6907
Website: www.snu.ac.kr
Contact: MBA Admissions Officer

Korea Foundation Fellowship

Subjects: Fields of Korean research in the humanities and social sciences.
Eligibility: Preference is given to Korean nationals residing abroad.
Level of Study: Postdoctorate, postgraduate, research
Type: Fellowship
Value: To be determined by the review committee
Length of Study: 1 academic year
Frequency: Annual
Study Establishment: Seoul National University
Country of Study: Korea
Application Procedure: Contact the Office of international Affairs.
Closing Date: January
Funding: Foundation
Contributor: The Korean Foundation

For further information contact:

Tel: 2 880 8635
Fax: 2 880 8632
Email: yss@snu.ac.kr
Contact: Mr Sung Sub Yoon

Korea-Japan Cultural Association Scholarship

Subjects: Humanities and social-science.
Eligibility: Open to outstanding Japanese scholars receiving an education in Korea.
Level of Study: Postdoctorate, postgraduate, research
Type: Scholarship
Value: KRW 3,500,000
Length of Study: 1 academic year
Frequency: Annual
Study Establishment: Seoul National University
Country of Study: Korea
Application Procedure: Contact the Office of International Affairs.
Closing Date: March

Funding: Foundation
Contributor: Korea-Japan Cultural Association

For further information contact:

Tel: 2 880 8635
Fax: 2 880 8632
Email: yss@snu.ac.kr
Contact: Mr Sung Sub Yoon

Korean Government Scholarship

Subjects: Korean studies.
Purpose: To further international bilateral cultural agreement with Korea.
Eligibility: Applicants must be under 40 years of age as of September 1st.
Level of Study: Postgraduate, research, postdoctorate
Type: Scholarship
Value: All airfares, living expenses, tuition fees, research allowance, settling and repatriation allowance, language training expenses, dissertation publication costs and insurance
Frequency: Annual
Study Establishment: Seoul National University
Country of Study: Korea
Application Procedure: Contact the Korean Embassy in residing country or see website.
Closing Date: No deadline
Funding: Government

For further information contact:

Website: www.studyinkorea.go.kr

Overseas Korean Foundation Scholarship

Subjects: Korean studies.
Purpose: To support students with an outstanding academic record.
Eligibility: Preference is given to Korean students with majors related to Korean studies, in particular: language, literature, medicine, education or IT, which are beneficial to the development of Korea.
Level of Study: Postgraduate, postdoctorate, research
Type: Scholarship
Value: KRW 2,000,000
Length of Study: 1 year
Frequency: Annual
Application Procedure: Contact the Overseas Korean Foundation.
Closing Date: March–April

For further information contact:

Education Department, Overseas Korean Foundation, Seocho 2-dong, Seocho-gu, Seoul, (137-072)
Tel: 2 3463 5322 (ext. 405)
Fax: 2 3463 3999
Email: yhs6543@okf.or.kr
Contact: Coordinator

SERONO FOUNDATION FOR THE ADVANCEMENT OF MEDICAL SCIENCE

12 Chemin des Aulx, 1228 Plan-les-Ouates, Geneva, Switzerland
Tel: (41) 22 706 9368
Fax: (41) 22 706 9398
Email: renee.beaudry@serono.com
Website: www.serono-foundation.org
Contact: The Secretary

The Serono Foundation for the Advancement of Medical Science is an independent non-profit organization dedicated to supporting educational activities in basic and clinical research. The aim of the Foundation is to improve human health and welfare through the advancement of medical sciences. The Foundation promotes and supports scientific research-orientated investigators by fostering an open exchange of information, experience and knowledge within the scientific and medical communities. Specifically, the Foundation facilitates the exchange of information on relevant topics between universities, research institutes, industries, national agencies and international organizations. The Foundation accomplishes its mission by sponsoring independent scientific workshops and conferences, and by supporting peer-reviewed research fellowships, primarily in the fields of reproduction, endocrinology, immunology, neurology and oncology.

Serono Foundation for the Advancement of Medical Science Fellowships in Biomedicine

Subjects: Reproductive endocrinology.
Purpose: To support postdoctoral research.
Eligibility: Applicants must have completed PhD/MD preferably not more than 3 years prior to the start of the fellowship, should be changing institution laboratory, and must communicate fluently in English.
Level of Study: Postdoctorate
Type: Fellowship
Value: US$90,000 over 2 years
Length of Study: 2 years
Frequency: Annual
Study Establishment: Academic institutions
Country of Study: Any country
No. of awards offered: 2–4
Application Procedure: Applicants must visit the website for application forms and guidelines.
Closing Date: February 28th
Funding: Private
Contributor: Serono Foundation for the Advancement of Medical Science
No. of awards given last year: 3
No. of applicants last year: 48

SHASTRI INDO-CANADIAN INSTITUTE (SICI)

1402 Education Tower, 2500 University Drive, NW, Calgary, Alberta, T2N 1Nr, Canada
Tel: (1) (403) 220 7467
Fax: (1) (403) 289 0100
Email: sici@ucalgary.ca
Website: www.sici.org
Contact: Dr Arun Prabha Mukherjee, President

The Shastri Indo-Canadian Institute (SICI) is a unique educational enterprise that promotes understanding between Canada and India, mainly through facilitating academic activities. The Institute funds research, links institutions in the two countries and organizes seminars and conferences.

SICI India Studies Fellowship Competition

Subjects: Subjects relating to India in the social sciences and humanities including education, law, management and the arts, science and technology.
Purpose: To support candidates wishing to undertake research or training in India.
Eligibility: Applicants must be Canadian citizens or landed immigrants.
Level of Study: Postgraduate, postdoctorate, research, doctorate, professional development
Type: Fellowship
Value: Varies
Length of Study: 3 months–1 year
Frequency: Annual
Study Establishment: Varies
Country of Study: India
No. of awards offered: Varies from year to year
Application Procedure: Applicants must contact the Canada head office for the application procedure.
Closing Date: June 30th
Funding: Government
No. of awards given last year: 15
No. of applicants last year: 65

SHEFFIELD HALLAM UNIVERSITY

Graduate Studies Team, City Campus, Howard Street, Sheffield, S1 1WB, England
Tel: (44) 11 4225 5555
Fax: (44) 11 4225 4055
Email: reseng@shu.ac.uk
Website: www.shu.ac.uk
Contact: Senior Administrative Officer

Sheffield Hallam University received one of the highest ratings of all new universities in the 2001 research assessment exercise. The university has a postgraduate population of 8,000 students and is one of the United Kingdom's major providers of postgraduate, post-experience and research opportunities.

Sheffield Hallam University Studentships

Subjects: All subject areas covered by the University, eg. business, computing, cultural studies, education, finance, health studies, materials and metallurgy, sport and exercise, science, mathematics, engineering, social studies, psychology, environmental science courses and town planning.
Purpose: To support study towards a PhD degree.
Eligibility: Open to European Union nationals only.
Level of Study: Doctorate
Type: Studentship
Value: A maintenance award of approx. UK £12,300
Length of Study: Up to 3 years, full-time
Frequency: Annual
Study Establishment: Sheffield Hallam University
Country of Study: United Kingdom
No. of awards offered: Up to 4 year (Dependent on individual faculties)
Application Procedure: Applicants must direct initial enquiries to the Graduate Studies Team. If there are studentships for the chosen area of study then an application form must be completed.
Closing Date: Applications are accepted when the studentships are advertised, usually from May to September
Funding: Government, commercial
Contributor: Sheffield Hallam University, external collaborators

SHELBY CULLOM DAVIS CENTER FOR HISTORICAL STUDIES

Shelby Cullom Davis Center for Historical Studies, Department of History, 129 Dickinson Hall, Princeton University, Princeton, NJ 08544-1017, United States of America
Tel: (1) 609 258 4997
Fax: (1) 609 258 5326
Website: www.princeton.edu
Contact: Ms Jennifer Houle, The Manager

The Davis center for historical studies was founded in 1968 to assure the continuance of excellence in scholarship and the teaching of history at Princeton University.

Shelby Cullom Davis Center Research Projects, Research Fellowships

Subjects: History.
Purpose: To support research.
Eligibility: Applicants must have completed a PhD.
Level of Study: Postdoctorate
Type: Fellowship
Length of Study: 1–2 semesters
Frequency: Annual
Study Establishment: Shelby Cullom Davis Center
Country of Study: United States of America
No. of awards offered: Varies
Application Procedure: Applications are available online.
Closing Date: December 1st
Funding: Private
No. of awards given last year: 7

SIDNEY SUSSEX COLLEGE

Cambridge, Cambridgeshire, CB2 3HU, England
Tel: (44) 12 2333 8810
Fax: (44) 12 2376 5744
Email: gradtutor@sid.cam.ac.uk
Website: www.sid.cam.ac.uk
Contact: Tutor for Graduate Students

Founded in 1596, Sidney Sussex College admits men and women as undergraduates and graduates. The college presently has 180 graduate students, including 100 working for the PhD degree. The college has excellent sporting, dramatic and musical facilities.

Evan Lewis Thomas Law Bursaries and Studentships

Subjects: Law.
Purpose: To support students carrying out research or taking advanced courses.
Eligibility: There are no eligibility restrictions. Candidates must have shown proficiency in Law and Jurisprudence, normally by obtaining a university degree in Law by August 2006, and they must be or become candidates for the PhD Degree, the Diploma in Legal Studies, the Diploma in International Law, the M.Phil Degree (one-year course) in Criminology, or the LL.M Degree. Only candidates for the PhD Degree may apply for Evan Lewis Thomas Studentship offered by the College.
Level of Study: Doctorate, postgraduate
Type: Studentships and bursaries
Length of Study: 1–3 years
Frequency: Annual
Study Establishment: The University of Cambridge
Country of Study: United Kingdom
No. of awards offered: 3–4
Application Procedure: Those wishing to apply for this award may either go to the link http://www.admin.cam.ac.uk/offices/gradstud/admissions/forms/Cambridge graduate.pdf and print pages 7-12 or make a copy of the corresponding on-line application pages. (this is the form you should have already completed for your application to the University) You must send this duplicate form directly to Sidney Sussex, fully completed, including the names of your references and your photograph. You must also send us a copy of your research proposal as submitted to the Faculty to which you have applied. Please do not send transcripts and indicate on the top of the front page of the application form Even Lewis Thomas Studentship/Bursaries.
Closing Date: Febuary 1st
Funding: Private
Contributor: Sidney Sussex College
Additional Information: For further information contact the Tutor for Graduate Students. gradtutor@sid.com.ac.uk

For further information contact:

Email: gradtutor@sid.cam.ac.uk

Sidney Sussex College Research Studentship

Subjects: All subjects.
Purpose: To provide full support for research leading to a PhD degree.
Eligibility: Applicants must apply for a postgraduate place at the University of Cambridge. Preference is given to candidates under 26 years of age.
Level of Study: Doctorate
Type: Studentship
Length of Study: 3 years
Frequency: Annual
Study Establishment: The University of Cambridge
Country of Study: United Kingdom
No. of awards offered: 1
Application Procedure: Those wishing to apply for this award may either go to the link http://www.admin.cam.ac.uk/offices/gradstud/admissions/forms/Cambridge graduate.pdf and print pages 7-12 or make a copy of the corresponding on-line' application pages (this is the form you should have already completed for your application to the University). You must send this duplicate form directly to Sidney Sussex, fully completed, including the names of your references and your photograph. You must also send us a copy of your research proposal

as submitted to the Faculty to which you have applied. Please do not send transcripts and indicate on the top of the front page of the application form The Sidney Sussex Studentship.
Closing Date: March 1st
Funding: Private
Contributor: Sidney Sussex College
Additional Information: For further information contact the Tutor for Graduate Students. gradtutor@sid.car.ac.uk

SIGMA THETA TAU INTERNATIONAL

550 West North Street, Indianapolis, IN, 46202, United States of America
Tel: (1) 317 634 8171
Fax: (1) 317 634 8188
Email: research@stti.iupui.edu
Website: www.nursingsociety.org
Contact: Research Grant Programme

Sigma Theta Tau International exists to promote the development, dissemination and utilization of nursing knowledge. It is committed to improving the health of people worldwide through increasing the scientific base of nursing practice. In support of this mission, the society advances nursing leadership and scholarship, and furthers the utilization of nursing research in healthcare delivery as well as in public policy.

Doris Bloch Research Award

Subjects: Nursing.
Purpose: To encourage qualified nurses to contribute to the advancement of nursing through research. Multidisciplinary and international research is encouraged.
Eligibility: Applicants must be a registered nurse with a current licence, must have received a Master's degree, must have submitted an application package, must be ready to start the research project and must have signed a Sigma Theta Tau International research agreement. Allocation of funds is based on the quality of the proposed research, the future promise of the applicant and the applicant's research budget. Applications from novice researchers who have received no other national research funds are encouraged and will receive preference for funding, other aspects being equal. See website www.nursingsociety.org
Level of Study: Predoctorate, postgraduate, doctorate, postdoctorate, master's prepared
Type: Research grant
Value: Up to US$5,000
Frequency: Annual
Country of Study: Any country
No. of awards offered: 1
Application Procedure: Applicants must write for an information booklet and application form.
Closing Date: March 1st
Funding: Private
Contributor: Sigma Theta Tau International
No. of awards given last year: 1
Additional Information: Preference is given to Sigma Theta Tau International members. Funding date is June 1st.

Rosemary Berkel Crisp Research Award

Subjects: Women's health, oncology and infant or child care.
Purpose: To support nursing research in the critical areas of women's health, oncology and infant or child care.
Eligibility: Open to registered nurses with a current licence who have a Master's or higher degree (those with baccalaureate degrees may be co-investigators), have submitted a complete research application package, are ready to initiate the research project and are Sigma Theta Tau International members. Some preference is given to applicants residing in Illinois, Missouri, Arkansas, Kentucky and Tennessee. See website www.nursingsociety.org. Some preference is given to applicants residing in Illinois, Missouri, Arkansas, Kentucky or Tennessee.
Level of Study: Postdoctorate, postgraduate, doctorate, predoctorate, master's prepared
Type: Research award
Value: US$5,000
Frequency: Annual
Country of Study: Any country
No. of awards offered: 1
Application Procedure: Applicants must submit a completed Sigma Theta Tau International research application and agreement.
Closing Date: December 1st
Funding: Private
Contributor: The Harry L Crisp II and Rosemary Berkel Crisp Foundation to Sigma Theta Tau International's Research Endowment
No. of awards given last year: 1
No. of applicants last year: 52
Additional Information: The allocation of funds is based upon a research project in the area of women's health, oncology or paediatrics that is ready for implementation, the quality of the proposed research, future potential of the application, appropriateness of the research budget and feasibility of the time frame.

Sigma Theta Tau International Small Research Grants

Subjects: Nursing.
Purpose: To encourage qualified nurses to contribute to the advancement of nursing through research.
Eligibility: Open to registered nurses with a current licence who have submitted a complete research application package, have a project ready for implementation, hold a Master's degree, are enrolled in a doctoral programme and have signed a Sigma Theta Tau International research agreement. See website www.nursingsociety.org
Level of Study: Doctorate, postgraduate, postdoctorate, predoctorate, master's prepared
Value: Up to US$5,000
Frequency: Annual
Country of Study: Any country
No. of awards offered: 10–15
Closing Date: December 1st
Funding: Foundation, private
Additional Information: This grant has no specific focus; however, multidisciplinary, historical and international research is encouraged.

Sigma Theta Tau International Workforce Grants sponsored by Cardinal Health Pyxis Products

Eligibility: See website www.nursingsociety.org
Level of Study: Postdoctorate, doctorate, predoctorate, postgraduate, master's prepared
Frequency: Annual
Funding: Corporation

Sigma Theta Tau International/American Association of Critical Care Nurses

Subjects: Critical care nursing practice.
Purpose: To encourage qualified nurses to contribute to the advancement of nursing.
Eligibility: Open to registered nurses with a current licence who have received a Master's degree and submitted a grant proposal relevant to critical care nursing practice. Research must be related to critical care nursing practice. See website www.nursingsociety.org
Level of Study: Doctorate, postdoctorate, predoctorate, postgraduate, master's prepared
Type: Research grant
Value: Up to US$10,000
Frequency: Annual
Country of Study: Any country
No. of awards offered: 1
Application Procedure: Applicants must write for an information booklet and application form.
Closing Date: October 1st
Funding: Foundation, private
Contributor: The American Association of Critical Care Nurses and Sigma Theta Tau International
Additional Information: January 1st is the funding date.

For further information contact:

American Association of Critical Care Nurses, Department of Research, 101 Columbia, Aliso Viejo, CA, 92656-1491, United States of America
Tel: (1) 949 362 2000
Fax: (1) 949 362 2020

Sigma Theta Tau International/American Association of Diabetes Educators Grant

Subjects: Diabetes education and care.
Purpose: To encourage qualified nurses to contribute to the enhancement of quality and increase the availability of diabetes education and care.
Eligibility: The applicant must be a registered nurse but team members may be from other disciplines. The principal investigator must also have received a Master's degree, and have the ability to complete the project in 1 year from the funding date. Preference will be given to Sigma Theta Tau International members, other qualifications being equal. The grant must be dedicated to diabetes education and care research. See website www.nursingsociety.org
Level of Study: Doctorate, postdoctorate, postgraduate, predoctorate, master's prepared
Type: Research grant
Value: Up to US$6,000
Frequency: Annual
Country of Study: Any country
No. of awards offered: 1
Application Procedure: Applicants must write for an information booklet and application form.
Closing Date: October 1st
Funding: Foundation, private
Contributor: The American Association of Diabetes Educators and Sigma Theta Tau International
Additional Information: January 1st is the funding date.

For further information contact:

American Association of Diabetes Educators (AADE) Awards, 100 West Monroe Street, Suite 400, Chicago, IL, 60603, United States of America
Tel: (1) 312 424 2426
Fax: (1) 312 424 2427

Sigma Theta Tau International/American Nurses Foundation Grant

Subjects: Any clinical topic.
Purpose: To encourage the research career development of nurses through the support of research conducted by beginning nurse researchers, or experienced nurse researchers who are entering a new field of study.
Eligibility: Open to registered nurses with a current licence and a Master's degree who have submitted a complete research application package, are ready to start the research project and have signed a Sigma Theta Tau International research agreement. Preference will be given to Sigma Theta Tau International members, other qualifications being equal. See website www.nursingsociety.org
Level of Study: Doctorate, postdoctorate, postgraduate, predoctorate, master's prepared
Type: Research grant
Value: Up to US$7,500
Frequency: Annual
Country of Study: Any country
No. of awards offered: 1
Application Procedure: Applicants must write for an information booklet and application form. Proposals should be sent to the Sigma Theta Tau International headquarters in even-numbered years (for which applicants should use the Sigma Theta Tau International application), and to the American Nurses Foundation in odd-numbered years (for which applicants should use the American Nurses Foundation application).
Closing Date: May 1st
Funding: Foundation, private
Contributor: The American Nurses Foundation (ANF) and Sigma Theta Tau International
Additional Information: Allocation of funds is based on the quality of the proposed research, the future promise of the applicant and the applicant's research budget. October is the funding date.

For further information contact:

American Nurses Foundation, 600 Maryland Avenue South West, Suite 100 West, Washington, DC, 20024-2571, United States of America
Tel: (1) 202 651 7071
Fax: (1) 202 651 7354

Sigma Theta Tau International/Association of Perioperative Registered Nurses Foundation Grant

Subjects: Perioperative nursing practice.
Purpose: To encourage nurses to conduct research related to perioperative nursing practice and contribute to the development of perioperative nursing science.
Eligibility: Applicants must be a registered nurse with a current license in the perioperative setting, or a registered nurse who demonstrates interest in or significant contributions to nursing practice. The principal investigator must have, as a minimum, a Master's degree in nursing. Applicants must submit a completed Association of Perioperative Registered Nurses (AORN) research application. Membership of either organization is acceptable, but not required. See website www.nursingsociety.org
Level of Study: Predoctorate, postgraduate, postdoctorate, doctorate, master's prepared
Type: Research grant
Value: US$5,000. Allocation of funds is based on the quality of the research, the future promise of the applicant and the applicant's research budget
Frequency: Annual
Country of Study: Any country
No. of awards offered: 1
Application Procedure: Applicants must write to the AORN for an application form and general instructions.
Closing Date: April 1st
Funding: Private, foundation
Contributor: The Association of Perioperative Registered Nurses and Sigma Theta Tau International
Additional Information: July is the funding date.

For further information contact:

Association of Perioperative Registered Nurses (AORN), 2170 South Parker Road, Suite 300, Denver, CO, 80231-5711, United States of America
Tel: (1) 800 755 2676 ext. 277
Fax: (1) 303 750 2927
Email: sbeya@aorn.org
Website: www.aorn.org

Sigma Theta Tau International/Emergency Nurses Association Foundation Grant

Subjects: Topics relating to the specialized practice of emergency nursing. All relevant subjects will be considered, although priority will be given to studies that relate to the Association's Research Initiatives, which include, but are not limited to, mechanisms to assure effective, efficient and quality emergency nursing care delivery systems, factors affecting healthcare cost, productivity and market forces to emergency services, ways to enhance health promotion and injury prevention, and mechanisms to assure quality and cost-effective educational programmes for emergency nursing.
Purpose: To support research related to the specialized practice of emergency nursing.
Eligibility: Applicants must be a registered nurse, but team members may be from other disciplines. Applicants must have a Master's degree, submit a complete application with signed research agreement and be ready to or have already started the research project. See website www.nursingsociety.org
Level of Study: Doctorate, predoctorate, postdoctorate, postgraduate, master's prepared
Type: Research grant
Value: Up to US$6,000

Frequency: Annual
Country of Study: Any country
No. of awards offered: 1
Application Procedure: Applicants must write for an information booklet and application form.
Closing Date: February 1st
Funding: Foundation, private
Contributor: The Emergency Nurses Association Foundation and Sigma Theta Tau International
Additional Information: July 1st is the funding date.

For further information contact:

Emergency Nurses Association (ENA) Foundation, 915 Lee Street, Des Plaines, IL, 60016-6569, United States of America
Tel: (1) 847 460 4100
Fax: (1) 847 460 4005

Sigma Theta Tau International/Hospice and Palliative Nurses Foundation End of Life Nursing Care Research Grant

Eligibility: See website www.nursingsociety.org
Level of Study: Doctorate, predoctorate, postgraduate, postdoctorate, master's prepared
Frequency: Annual
Funding: Foundation

Sigma Theta Tau International/Midwest Nursing Research Society Research Grant

Eligibility: See website www.nursingsociety.org
Level of Study: Doctorate, predoctorate, postdoctorate, postgraduate, master's prepared
Frequency: Annual
Funding: Foundation

Sigma Theta Tau International/Oncology Nursing Society Grant

Subjects: Clinical oncology.
Purpose: To encourage the research career development of nurses through the support of clinically orientated oncology research.
Eligibility: Open to registered nurses who are actively involved in some aspect of cancer patient care, education or research and hold a Master's degree. Preference will be given to Sigma Theta Tau members, other qualifications being equal. See website www.nursingsociety.org
Level of Study: Postdoctorate, predoctorate, postgraduate, doctorate, master's prepared
Type: Research grant
Value: Up to US$10,000
Frequency: Annual
Country of Study: Any country
No. of awards offered: 1
Application Procedure: Applicants must send proposals for this grant to the Oncology Nursing Society and must write for an information booklet and application form. See website www.nursingsociety.org
Closing Date: November 1st
Funding: Private, foundation
Contributor: The Oncology Nursing Society and Sigma Theta Tau International
Additional Information: The funding date is in May.

For further information contact:

Oncology Nursing Society, 501 Holiday Drive, Pittsburgh, PA, 15220-2749, United States of America
Tel: (1) 412 921 7373
Fax: (1) 412 921 6565

Sigma Theta Tau International/Rehabilitation Nursing Foundation Grant

Subjects: Rehabilitation nursing.
Purpose: To encourage research related to rehabilitation nursing.
Eligibility: Applicant must be a registered nurse in rehabilitation or a registered nurse who demonstrates interest in and significant contributions to rehabilitation nursing. Proposals that address the clinical practice, educational or administrative dimensions of rehabilitation nursing are requested. Quantitative and qualitative research projects will be accepted for review. The principal investigator must have a Master's degree in nursing and an ability to complete the project within 2 years of initial funding. See website www.nursingsociety.org
Level of Study: Postdoctorate, postgraduate, doctorate, predoctorate, master's prepared
Type: Research grant
Value: Up to US$6,000
Frequency: Annual
Country of Study: Any country
No. of awards offered: 1
Application Procedure: Applicants must write to the Rehabilitation Nursing Foundation for details.
Closing Date: April 1st
Funding: Foundation, private
Contributor: The Rehabilitation Nursing Foundation and Sigma Theta Tau International
Additional Information: The funding date is the following January.

For further information contact:

Rehabilitation Nursing Foundation, 4700 West Lake Avenue, Glenview, IL, 60025, United States of America
Tel: (1) 847 375 4710
Fax: (1) 847 375 4710
Email: info@rehabnurse.org

Sigma Theta Tau International/Virginia Henderson Clinical Research Grant

Subjects: Clinical research.
Purpose: To encourage the research career development of clinically based nurses through support of clinically orientated research.
Eligibility: Open to registered nurses actively involved in some aspect of healthcare delivery, education or research in a clinical setting, who are Theta Tau International members, hold a Master's degree in nursing or are enrolled in a doctoral programme. The allocation of funds is based on a research project ready for implementation, the quality of the proposed research, the future potential of the applicant, appropriateness of the research budget and feasibility of the time frame. See website www.nursingsociety.org
Level of Study: Postgraduate, predoctorate, postdoctorate, doctorate, master's prepared
Type: Research grant
Value: US$5,000
Frequency: Every 2 years
Country of Study: Any country
No. of awards offered: 1
Application Procedure: Applicants must complete a Sigma Theta Tau International research grant application.
Closing Date: December 1st in odd-numbered years
Funding: Private
Contributor: The Virginia Henderson Clinical Research Endowment Fund
Additional Information: June is the funding date.

Sigma Theta Tau International/Western Institute of Nursing Research Grant

Eligibility: See website www.nursingsociety.org
Level of Study: Doctorate, postdoctorate, predoctorate, postgraduate, master's prepared
Frequency: Annual
Funding: Foundation

SIR HALLEY STEWART TRUST

22 Earith Road, Willingham, Cambridge, Cambridgeshire, CB4 5LS, England
Tel: (44) 19 5426 0707
Website: www.sirhalleystewart.org
Contact: Mrs Sue West, Administrator

The Sir Halley Stewart Trust has a Christian basis and is concerned with the development of body, mind and spirit, a just environment and international goodwill. The Trust aims to promote innovative research activities or developments. It emphasizes the prevention rather than alleviation of human suffering.

Sir Halley Stewart Trust Grants

Subjects: Medical, social or religious research within certain priority areas.
Purpose: To assist pioneering research.
Eligibility: Not open to general appeals, building, capital, running costs or personal education including educational and travel costs.
Level of Study: Research, doctorate, postgraduate, predoctorate
Value: Salaries and relevant costs for innovative and imaginative young researchers in the region of UK £15,000–20,000
Length of Study: 2–3 years
Frequency: Dependent on funds available
Study Establishment: A United Kingdom charitable institution, eg. a hospital, laboratory, university department or charitable organization
Country of Study: Mainly United Kingdom but some overseas, Africa (west/south) given priority
Application Procedure: Applicants must contact the Trust for further details. There is no application form and applications will not be accepted if sent by fax or email.
Closing Date: Applications are accepted at any time
Funding: Private
No. of awards given last year: 65
No. of applicants last year: 650
Additional Information: Further information is available from the Trust's office by obtaining a copy of Notes for those Seeking Grants. The website contains the most up-to-date details.

SIR JOHN SOANE'S MUSEUM FOUNDATION

636 Broadway, Suite 720, New York, NY, 10012, United States of America
Tel: (1) 646 654 0085
Fax: (1) 646 654 0089
Email: soane@mindspring.com
Contact: Mrs Cynthia Sanford, Joint Executive Director

The Sir John Soane's Museum Foundation assists the Museum in London to further Soane's commitment to educate and inspire the general and professional public in architecture and the fine and decorative arts. Programmes have attracted students, collectors, architects, decorators and arts enthusiasts since 1991 to its events, lectures, tours and dinners.

Sir John Soane's Museum Foundation Travelling Fellowship

Subjects: Art, architecture and the decorative arts.
Purpose: To enable scholars to pursue research projects related to the work of Sir John Soane's Museum and its collections.
Eligibility: Open to candidates enrolled in a graduate degree programme in a field appropriate to the Foundation's purpose.
Level of Study: Postgraduate
Type: Fellowship
Value: US$4,000
Frequency: Annual
Study Establishment: The choice of the fellowship recipient
Country of Study: Usually the United States of America or the United Kingdom
No. of awards offered: 1
Application Procedure: Applicants must submit a formal proposal of not more than five pages describing the goal, scope and purpose of the research project, in addition to three letters of recommendation. An interview may be required.
Closing Date: February 1st
Funding: Private
Contributor: The Board of Directors and the Advisory Board
No. of awards given last year: 1
No. of applicants last year: 6
Additional Information: At the end of each research project the award recipient must submit a written documentation or a sketch book on the progress of the research as outlined in the original proposal with respect to goal, scope and allocation of funds, and give a lecture on the research, arranged by the Foundation. The scholar usually spends some time at Sir John Soane's Museum at 13 Lincoln's Inn Fields, London, studying architectural drawings, models and paintings.

SIR RICHARD STAPLEY EDUCATIONAL TRUST

North Street Farmhouse, Sheldwich, Near Faversham, Kent, ME13 0LN, England
Email: admin@stapleytrust.org
Website: www.stapleytrust.org
Contact: Mrs Christine Ford, Administrator

The Sir Richard Stapley Educational Trust awards grants to graduates studying for higher degrees without subject restriction. The Trust will support only one postgraduate degree at a university in the United Kingdom.

Sir Richard Stapley Educational Trust Grants

Subjects: Medical, dental and veterinary science and higher degrees in other subjects.
Purpose: To support postgraduate study.
Eligibility: Open to graduates holding a First Class (Honours) Degree or an Upper Second Class (Honours) Degree and who are more than 24 years of age on October 1st of the proposed academic year. Students in receipt of a substantial award from local authorities, the NHS Executive Industry, Research Councils, the British Academy or other similar public bodies will not normally receive a grant from the Trust. Courses not eligible include electives, diplomas, professional training and intercalated degrees. The Trust does not support students for full-time PhD studies beyond a 3rd year. Applicants must already be resident in the United Kingdom at the time of application.
Level of Study: Postgraduate
Type: Grant
Value: UK £300–1,000
Length of Study: Grants are awarded for 1 full academic year in the first instance
Frequency: Annual
Study Establishment: Any appropriate university
Country of Study: United Kingdom
No. of awards offered: Dependent on availability of funds
Application Procedure: Applicants making enquiries must include a large stamped addressed envelope before February 28th. Application forms will be sent out and must be returned complete with one academic reference in sealed envelopes on or before February 28th. Applicants will be notified in June.
Closing Date: March 31st
Funding: Private, commercial
No. of awards given last year: 280
No. of applicants last year: 390
Additional Information: Grants are only paid upon receipt of official confirmation of participation in the course as well as confirmation that a financial shortfall still exists. All matters concerning application are communicated by email and letter only.

SIR ROBERT MENZIES MEMORIAL FOUNDATION

210 Clarendon Street, East Melbourne, VIC, Australia
Tel: (61) 394 195 699
Fax: (61) 394 177 049
Email: menzies@vicnet.net.au
Website: www.menziesfoundation.org.au
Contact: Ms S K Mackenzie, General Manager

The Sir Robert Menzies Memorial Foundation was formed as a memorial to Sir Robert Menzies in 1979. It is a non-profit and non-political organization with two principal activities. One is directed to the health and fitness of the Australian community and the other to the promotion of academic excellence.

Sir Robert Menzies Memorial Research Scholarships in the Allied Health Sciences

Subjects: Occupational therapy, speech pathology, physiotherapy, psychology, nursing, optometry and physical education.
Purpose: To allow an outstanding applicant to carry out doctoral research work that is likely to improve the health of Australians.
Eligibility: Open to Australian citizens of at least 5 years standing. Applicants will generally have completed the first year of their PhD project.
Level of Study: Doctorate, postgraduate
Type: Scholarship
Value: Australian $25,000 free of income tax
Length of Study: 2 years
Frequency: Annual
Study Establishment: A tertiary institute with appropriate facilities
Country of Study: Australia
No. of awards offered: 2
Application Procedure: Applicants must complete and submit an application form, academic transcripts and other documents. Further information is available on request.
Closing Date: June 30th
Funding: Private
Contributor: The Sir Robert Menzies Memorial Foundation
No. of awards given last year: 2
No. of applicants last year: 30

Sir Robert Menzies Memorial Scholarships in Law

Subjects: Law.
Purpose: To enable Australian citizens to pursue postgraduate studies in the United Kingdom, generally leading to a higher degree.
Eligibility: Open to Australian citizens of 5 years of standing with at least an Upper Second Class (Honours) Degree in law at the time of application.
Level of Study: Postgraduate
Type: Scholarship
Value: Tuition fees or a research grant equivalent, return airfare, examination and other compulsory fees, UK £300 for books and equipment in the 1st year and UK £150 in the 2nd year, up to UK £120 towards the typing and binding of a thesis, a quarterly living allowance of UK £2,000 and an additional allowance of UK £150 per month for spouse and UK £30 per month for each dependent child under 16
Length of Study: 1–2 years
Frequency: Annual
Study Establishment: The Universities of St Andrews, Edinburgh, Cambridge or Oxford and occasionally elsewhere
Country of Study: United Kingdom
No. of awards offered: 1–2
Application Procedure: Applicants must complete and submit an application form along with academic transcripts and other documents.
Closing Date: August 31st
Funding: Private
Contributor: The Sir Robert Menzies Memorial Trust in London, the Foreign and Commonwealth Office and the Foundation in Australia
No. of awards given last year: 2
No. of applicants last year: 40

THE SKIDMORE, OWINGS AND MERRILL FOUNDATION

224 South Michigan Avenue, Suite 1000, Chicago, IL, 60604, United States of America
Tel: (1) 312 427 4202
Fax: (1) 312 360 4551
Email: somfoundation@som.com
Website: www.somfoundation.som.com
Contact: Ms Lisa Westerfield, Administrative Director

The mission of the Skidmore, Owings and Merrill Foundation is to help young architects and engineers broaden their professional education, instil a heightened sense of responsibility as future practitioners to improve the quality of the built and natural environments and to encourage them to appreciate the influence of place making, culture and technology on the design of buildings and their settings.

Architecture Master's Degree Travelling Fellowship

Subjects: Architecture.
Purpose: To help young architects to broaden their education and take an enlightened view of society's need to improve the built and natural environments.
Eligibility: Open to candidates of any citizenship who are graduating from a university in the United States of America. Fellowship winners must receive, prior to commencement of the fellowship, a Master's degree in architecture. Students are eligible for nomination in the Spring of the academic year that they are due to graduate.
Level of Study: Graduate
Type: Fellowship
Value: US$15,000
Frequency: Annual
Study Establishment: Accredited schools, colleges or universities
Country of Study: United States of America
No. of awards offered: 1 for Bachelor's level graduating students and 1 for Master's level
Application Procedure: Applicants must submit a portfolio with a proposed travel itinerary and a signed copyright release statement provided by the Foundation. Complete guidelines are available on request and on the website. Students must be nominated by the United States of America school of attendance.
Funding: Private
No. of awards given last year: 2
Additional Information: Information is sent to schools between February and March.

Building Systems Technology Research Grant

Subjects: Topics such as energy-efficient design, the application of new technologies, the appropriate use or re-use of natural resources and the integration of building systems as components of a work of architecture.
Purpose: To expand the vision and imagination of young engineers in the design and engineering of building systems.
Level of Study: Graduate
Type: Grant
Value: US$7,500
Frequency: Annual
Study Establishment: Accredited schools
Country of Study: United States of America
No. of awards offered: 1
Application Procedure: Applicants must submit their application through the American Society of Heating, Refrigerating and Air Conditioning's Grants-in-Aid Program.
Funding: Private
Additional Information: For further information visit the Society's website: www.ashrae.org under the student zone.

Interior Architecture Travelling Fellowship

Subjects: Architecture and design, including awareness and skilful handling of the full range of elements that support a designed interior space, including furniture and finishes, lighting and artwork.
Purpose: To encourage young designers to explore the relationship between architecture and interiors, with particular emphasis on the three-dimensional modelling of space and the integration of interior spaces and elements with building architecture and systems.
Eligibility: Applicants must be graduating with a Bachelor's or Master's degree from either an accredited United States of America architectural school, the Foundation for Interior Design Education Research (FIDER) or the Association of Independent Colleges of Art and Design (AICAD). Applicants must be nominated by the faculty and endorsed by the chair of the department from which they will receive the degree.
Level of Study: Postgraduate, graduate
Type: Fellowship

Value: US$7,500
Frequency: Annual
Study Establishment: Accredited schools
Country of Study: United States of America
No. of awards offered: 1
Application Procedure: Applicants must submit a portfolio with two copies each of a letter of recommendation, proposed travel itinerary and a signed copyright release statement provided by the Foundation. Complete guidelines are available on request or from the website. Students must be nominated by the United States of America school of attendance.
Funding: Private
No. of awards given last year: 1
Additional Information: Information is sent to schools between February and March.

Structural Engineering Travelling Fellowship

Subjects: The role of aesthetics, innovation, efficiency and economy in the structural design of buildings, bridges and other structures.
Purpose: To foster an appreciation of the aesthetic potential inherent in the structural design of buildings, bridges and other major works of architecture and engineering.
Eligibility: Open to candidates of any citizenship who are graduating from a university in the United States of America with a Bachelor's, Master's or PhD degree in civil or architectural engineering and a specialization in structural engineering. Applicants must be nominated by the faculty and endorsed by the chair of the department from which they will receive the degree. Applicants must intend to enter the professional practice of structural engineering in the field of buildings or bridges.
Level of Study: Postgraduate, doctorate, graduate
Type: Fellowship
Value: US$10,000
Frequency: Annual
Study Establishment: Accredited schools
Country of Study: United States of America
No. of awards offered: 1
Application Procedure: Applicants must submit four copies of a letter of recommendation, a curriculum vitae, recent graduate and undergraduate transcripts, a brief essay between two and four pages in length plus figures, a proposed travel itinerary, a computer disk containing the essay and itinerary and a signed copyright release provided by the Foundation. Complete guidelines are available on request.
Funding: Private
No. of awards given last year: 1
Additional Information: The fellowship hopes to encourage an awareness of the visual impact of structural engineering among engineering students and their schools. It also helps to strengthen the connection between aesthetics and efficiency, economy and innovation in structural design.

Urban Design Travelling Fellowship

Subjects: Pertinent urban design issues such as appropriate development character, sense of place, preservation and adaptive reuse, way finding, ease of access and movement and sustainable patterns of densification and growth.
Purpose: To encourage young architects with an interest in urban design to broaden their knowledge of the design of modern, high-density cities.
Eligibility: Open to candidates of any citizenship who are graduating from a university in the United States of America with a Master's Degree concentrating on urban design. Applicants must be nominated by the faculty and endorsed by the chair of the department from which they will receive the degree.
Level of Study: Graduate
Type: Fellowship
Value: US$7,500
Frequency: Annual
Study Establishment: Accredited schools
Country of Study: United States of America
No. of awards offered: 1
Application Procedure: Applicants must submit a portfolio with two copies each of a letter of recommendation, a curriculum vitae, recent transcript, proposed travel itinerary and a signed copyright release statement provided by the Foundation. Complete guidelines are available on request and on the website.
Funding: Private
No. of awards given last year: 1
Additional Information: Information is sent to schools between February and March.

THE SMITH AND NEPHEW FOUNDATION

Heron House, 15 Adam Street, London, WC2N 6LA, England
Tel: (44) 20 7960 2276
Fax: (44) 20 7960 2298
Email: barbara.foster@smith-nephew.com
Website: www.snfoundation.org.uk
Contact: Ms Barbara Foster, Foundation Coordinator

The Smith and Nephew Foundation aims to develop research capacity and capability of nurses in the field of tissue damage, tissue viability and skin integrity by offering awards for doctoral and post-doctoral research.

Smith and Nephew Foundation Doctoral Nursing Research Studentship

Subjects: Nursing care of patients with skin or tissue damage and vulnerability.
Purpose: To aid nursing research as part of a PhD programme.
Eligibility: Applications are invited from outstanding nurse researchers who will contribute to the evidence base for the nursing care of patients with skin or tissue damage and vulnerability.
Level of Study: Doctorate
Type: Studentship
Value: Up to UK £90,000
Length of Study: Up to 3 years
Frequency: Annual
Country of Study: United Kingdom
No. of awards offered: 1
Application Procedure: Application forms must be completed shortlisted candidates are interviewed in London.
Closing Date: Advertised usually at the beginning of March with a closing date approximately 6 weeks later
Funding: Foundation
Contributor: The Smith and Nephew Foundation
No. of awards given last year: 2
No. of applicants last year: 6

Smith and Nephew Foundation Postdoctoral Nursing Research Fellowship

Subjects: Nursing care of patients with skin or tissue damage and vulnerability.
Purpose: To aid nursing postdoctoral research and to support outstanding career nurse researchers.
Eligibility: Applications are invited from potential Fellows and the proposed host research team or unit. The host research team must be a university school, faculty or department of nursing and have a proven track record of research and development in the nursing care of patients with skin damage or tissue damage or vulnerability.
Level of Study: Postdoctorate
Type: Fellowship
Value: Up to UK £120,000
Length of Study: Up to 3 years
Frequency: Annual
Country of Study: United Kingdom
No. of awards offered: 1
Application Procedure: Application forms must be completed; shortlisted candidates are interviewed in London.
Closing Date: Advertised usually at the beginning of March with a closing date approximately 6 weeks later
Funding: Foundation

Contributor: The Smith and Nephew Foundation
No. of awards given last year: 1
No. of applicants last year: 6

SMITHSONIAN ASTROPHYSICS OBSERVATORY (SAO)

60 Garden Street, Mail Stop 47, Cambridge, MA, 02138, United States of America
Email: predoc@cfa.harvard.edu
Website: www.cfa-www.harvard.edu
Contact: Christine A Crawley, Fellowship Program Co-ordinator

SAO Predoctoral Fellowships

Subjects: Astronomy, astrophysics, atomic and molecular physics, planetary science, radio and geoastronomy, solar and stellar physics and theoretical astrophysics.
Purpose: To allow students from other institutions throughout the world to undertake their thesis research at the SAO.
Eligibility: Applicants must have completed their preliminary course work and examinations and be ready to begin dissertation research at the time of the award.
Level of Study: Predoctorate
Type: Fellowship
Value: A stipend of US$25,800. Some funds may also be available for relocation, travel and other expenses
Length of Study: 1 year, with a possibility of renewal for up to a total of 3 years
Frequency: Annual
Study Establishment: The Smithsonian Astrophysics Observatory
Country of Study: United States of America
No. of awards offered: Varies
Application Procedure: Applicants must directly contact Smithsonian scientists in their area of interest to discuss possible research topics. Applicants must complete an application form available from website.
Closing Date: April 15th
No. of awards given last year: 8
No. of applicants last year: 16

SMITHSONIAN INSTITUTION-NATIONAL AIR AND SPACE MUSEUM

Rm. 3313, MRC 312, PO Box 37012, 6th and Independence Ave, SW, Washington, DC, 20013-7012, United States of America
Tel: (1) 202 633 2648
Fax: (1) 202 786 2447
Email: collette.williams@nasm.si.edu
Website: www.si.edu/ofg/
Contact: Ms Collette Williams, Fellowships Program Coordinator

A Verville Fellowship

Subjects: The history of aviation and space flights.
Purpose: To fund the analysis of major trends, developments and accomplishments in the history of aviation or space studies.
Eligibility: Open to all interested candidates who can demonstrate skills in research and writing. An advanced degree is not a requirement.
Level of Study: Postgraduate
Type: Fellowship
Value: A stipend of US$45,000 with limited additional funds available for travel and miscellaneous expenses
Length of Study: 9 months–1 year, normally beginning June 1st and October 1st
Country of Study: United States of America
No. of awards offered: 1
Application Procedure: Applicants must submit a summary description, research proposal, bibliography, estimated schedule, research budget, curriculum vitae and letters from three referees. Six copies of the complete application must be submitted. Further information and an application pack are available on request or downloadable from the website.
Closing Date: January 15th
Additional Information: Residence in the Washington, DC metropolitan area during the fellowship term is a requirement of this fellowship.

The Guggenheim Fellowships

Subjects: Historical research related to aviation and space.
Purpose: To promote research into, and writing about, the history of aviation and space flight.
Eligibility: Postdoctoral fellowships are open to applicants who have received a PhD degree or equivalent within 7 years of the beginning of the fellowship period. Predoctoral fellowships are open to applicants who have completed preliminary coursework and examinations and are engaged in dissertation research. All applicants must be able to speak and write fluently in English.
Level of Study: Postdoctorate, predoctorate
Type: Fellowship
Value: Postdoctoral stipend US$30,000 for 1-year term and predoctoral stipend US$20,000 for 1-year term, with limited additional funds available for travel and miscellaneous expenses
Length of Study: 3 months–1 year
Frequency: Annual
Study Establishment: A major portion of the research must be conducted at the Smithsonian Institution
Country of Study: United States of America
No. of awards offered: Varies
Application Procedure: Applicants must submit a summary description, research proposal, bibliography, estimated schedule, research budget, transcripts from all graduate institutions, English training with test scores and level of proficiency in reading, conversing and writing (if English is not the applicant's native language), a curriculum vitae and letters from three referees. Six copies of the complete application must be submitted.
Closing Date: January 15th
Additional Information: Residence in the Washington, DC metropolitan area during the fellowship term is a requirement of the fellowship. Further information is available on the website.

Ramsay Fellowship in Naval Aviation History

Subjects: The history of aviation at sea and in naval service, particularly the United States of America Navy.
Eligibility: Open to all interested candidates who can demonstrate skills in research and writing. An advanced degree is not a requirement.
Level of Study: Postgraduate
Type: Fellowship
Value: A stipend of US$45,000 with additional limited funds available for travel and miscellaneous expenses
Length of Study: 9 months–1 year
Country of Study: United States of America
No. of awards offered: 1
Application Procedure: Applicants must submit a summary description, research proposal, bibliography, estimated schedule, research budget, curriculum vitae and letters from three referees. Six copies of the complete application must be submitted. Further information and an application pack are available on request or downloadable from the website.
Closing Date: January 15th
Additional Information: Residence in the Washington, DC metropolitan area during the fellowship term is a requirement of this fellowship. Further information is available on the website.

THE SNOWDON AWARD SCHEME

22 City Business Centre, 6 Brighton Road, Horsham, West Sussex, RH13 5BB, England
Tel: (44) 14 0321 1252
Fax: (44) 14 0327 1553
Email: infor@snowdonawardscheme.org.uk
Website: www.snowdonawardscheme.org.uk
Contact: Laura Hanlon, Administrator

The Snowdon Award Scheme provides grants of up to UK £2,000 to physically disabled students for disability-related costs of further or higher education or training in the United Kingdom.

Snowdon Award Scheme Grants

Subjects: All subjects.
Purpose: To support physically impaired students for further or higher education or training in the United Kingdom.
Eligibility: Physically impaired students studying in the United Kingdom.
Level of Study: Postgraduate
Type: Award
Value: UK £250–2,000 (UK £2,500 in exceptional circumstances)
Frequency: Annual
Study Establishment: All recognized further, higher education or training centres
Country of Study: United Kingdom
No. of awards offered: Up to 100 per year, depending on funds
Application Procedure: Applicants must submit an application form and at least four specialized references. The application form is available online from January to September.
Closing Date: May 31st
Funding: Individuals, commercial, private, trusts
Contributor: Trusts and commercial sponsors
No. of awards given last year: 78
No. of applicants last year: None

SOCIAL SCIENCE RESEARCH COUNCIL (SSRC)

810 Seventh Avenue, New York, NY, 10019, United States of America
Tel: (1) 212 377 2700
Fax: (1) 212 377 2727
Email: info@ssrc.org
Website: www.ssrc.org
Contact: Mr John Meyers, Director of Development

Founded in 1923, the Social Science Research Council (SSRC) is an independent, non-governmental, non-profit, international association devoted to the advancement of interdisciplinary research in the social sciences. The aim of the organization is to improve the quality of publicly available knowledge around the world.

ACLS/SSRC/NEH International and Area Studies Fellowships

Subjects: Humanities.
Purpose: To encourage humanistic research in area studies.
Eligibility: Open to United States citizens who have lived in the United States for at least three years and completed their PhD more than two years prior to application.
Level of Study: Postdoctorate
Type: Fellowship
Length of Study: 6–12 months
Frequency: Annual
Country of Study: Other
No. of awards offered: Approx. 10
Application Procedure: Applicants must apply for information, available on request from ACLS.
Closing Date: October
Contributor: The National Endowment for the Humanities

For further information contact:

ACLS 633 Third Avenue, New York, NY, 10017-6795, United States of America
Fax: (1) 212 697 1505
Email: grants@acls.org
Website: www.acls.org

SSRC Abe Fellowship Program

Subjects: The social sciences and humanities relevant to any one or combination of the following themes: global issues, problems common to industrial and industrializing societies and issues that relate to United States of America–Japan relations.
Purpose: To develop a new generation of researchers who study policy-relevant topics of long-range importance and who will become members of bilateral and global research networks.
Eligibility: Open to citizens of Japan and the United States of America and other nationals who can demonstrate serious and long-term affiliations in research communities Japan or the United States of America. Applicants must hold a PhD or have attained an equivalent level of professional experience as evaluated in their country of residence. Applications from researchers in non-academic professions are welcome.
Level of Study: Postdoctorate
Type: Fellowship
Value: Research and travel expenses as necessary for the completion of the research project in addition to limited salary replacement
Length of Study: Up to 1 year
Frequency: Annual
Study Establishment: An appropriate institution
No. of awards offered: Approx. 14
Application Procedure: Applicants must submit a reference and an optional language evaluation form.
Closing Date: September 1st
Funding: Private
Contributor: The Japan Foundation's Center for Global Partnership
No. of awards given last year: 15
No. of applicants last year: 60–100
Additional Information: In addition to receiving fellowship awards, Fellows will attend annual conferences and other events sponsored by the programme, which will promote the development of an international network of scholars concerned with research on contemporary policy issues. Funds are provided by the Japan Foundation's Center for Global Partnership. Further information is available by emailing abe@ssrc.org

SSRC Africa Program Advanced Research Grants

Subjects: African studies.
Purpose: To support field research in Africa and comparative, theoretical research that proposes more than the analysis of previously gathered materials.
Eligibility: Open to citizens and permanent residents of the United States of America for at least 3 consecutive years, who hold a PhD or an equivalent degree. Applicants working in underrepresented areas such as literature, philosophy, religion and art history are especially encouraged to apply.
Level of Study: Postdoctorate
Type: Research grant
Value: Up to US$15,000
Frequency: Annual
Country of Study: Africa
No. of awards offered: Varies
Application Procedure: Applicants must complete an application form.
Closing Date: December 1st
Additional Information: If travel to Africa is planned, applicants must try to arrange for affiliation with an African university or research institute. Grants are for Sub-Saharan regions. North Africa is included in the Near and Middle East program.

SSRC Africa Program Dissertation Fellowships

Subjects: The social sciences and humanities in Africa, south of the Sahara.
Eligibility: Open to full-time students, regardless of citizenship, who are enrolled in doctoral programmes in the United States of America, and to citizens and permanent residents of the United States of America enrolled in full-time doctoral programmes abroad.
Level of Study: Doctorate
Type: Fellowship
Value: Varies
Length of Study: 9–18 months
Frequency: Annual
Country of Study: Africa
No. of awards offered: Varies

Application Procedure: Applicants must complete an application form.
Closing Date: November 1st
Funding: Private
Additional Information: Applicants are expected to have achieved a level of fluency in African and European languages sufficient to enable them to accomplish the goals of their project satisfactorily. Limited support for additional language training and dissertation write-up support may be included in awards. Please contact SSRC in May for further information.

SSRC Africa Program Predissertation Fellowships

Subjects: African studies.
Purpose: To support short-term field trips to Africa to encourage preliminary field activities, the identification of local scholars and contacts and planning for students preparing for dissertation research on Africa.
Eligibility: Open to students who have completed 1 year of graduate study in the social sciences or humanities at a United States of America university, or who are citizens or permanent residents of the United States of America who have completed this study abroad, and have been accepted into a full-time PhD programme.
Level of Study: Postgraduate
Type: Varies
Value: Up to US$2,500
Frequency: Annual
Country of Study: Africa
Application Procedure: Applicants must complete an application form.
Closing Date: November 1st
Funding: Private
Additional Information: Grants are for Sub-Saharan regions. North Africa is included in the Near and Middle East program.

SSRC Eurasia Program Postdoctoral Fellowships

Subjects: The social sciences and humanities, with a specific focus on Eurasia.
Purpose: To improve the academic employment and tenure opportunities of new PhDs and junior faculty.
Eligibility: Applicants for Postdoctoral Fellowships must have the PhD in hand at the time of application (ABDs will not be considered), must have received the degree no more than 5 years prior to the application deadline, and must have accumulated no more than 3 consecutive years in a tenure-track teaching position (although they need not currently be in a tenure-track position). They must be citizens or permanent residents of the United States of America. Detailed information on eligibility criteria and conditions of awards will be in the application materials.
Level of Study: Doctorate, postdoctorate
Type: Fellowship
Value: A stipend of US$24,000 to provide 2 years of Summer support plus one semester free of teaching for postdoctorates
Length of Study: 2 years
Frequency: Annual
Country of Study: United States of America
No. of awards offered: Varies
Application Procedure: Awards are made on the basis of evaluations and recommendations by the Title III Program Committee, an interdisciplinary committee and composed of scholars of the region. The committee rewards proposals with clarity of argument, purpose, theory, and method, written in a style accessible to readers outside the applicant's discipline. Applicants must submit a completed application, a narrative statement, a curriculum vitae and references. Full information is available online.
Closing Date: November
Funding: Government
Contributor: US Department of State under the Program for Research and Training on Eastern Europe and the Independent States of the Former Soviet Union (Title VIII)
No. of awards given last year: Approx. 3
No. of applicants last year: Approx. 20
Additional Information: No funding is available for research on the Baltic States.

For further information contact:

Email: eurasia@ssrc.org
Website: www.ssrc.org/fellowships/eurasia
Contact: SSRC, Eurasia Program

SSRC Eurasia Program Predissertation Training Fellowships

Subjects: The social sciences and humanities, with a specific focus on Eurasia.
Purpose: To provide graduate students with the opportunity to enhance their research skills in the field of Eurasian Studies.
Eligibility: Applicants for Predissertation Training Fellowships must be enrolled in a doctoral programme in the social sciences or humanities or equivalent degree, but not yet advanced to the PhD candidacy. ABD's are not eligible for these fellowships. They must be citizens or permanent residents of the United States of America. Detailed information on eligibility criteria and conditions of awards will be available in the application materials.
Level of Study: Doctorate, graduate
Type: Fellowship
Value: US$3,000–7,000
Length of Study: Up to 9 months
Frequency: Annual
Country of Study: United States of America
No. of awards offered: Varies
Application Procedure: Awards are made on the basis of evaluations and recommendations by the Title VIII Program Committee, an interdisciplinary committee composed of scholars of the region. The committee rewards proposals with clarity of argument, purpose, theory, and method, written a style accessible to readers outside the applicant's discipline. Applicants must submit a completed application, a narrative statement, transcripts, a course list and language evaluation form and references. Full information is available online.
Closing Date: November
Funding: Government
Contributor: US Department of State under the Program for Research and Training on Eastern Europe and the Independent States of the Former Soviet Union (Title VIII)
No. of awards given last year: 6
No. of applicants last year: Approx. 20
Additional Information: No funding is available for research on the Baltic States.

For further information contact:

Email: eurasia@ssrc.org
Website: www.ssrc.org/fellowships/eurasia
Contact: SSRC, Eurasia Program

SSRC Eurasia Program Teaching Fellowships

Subjects: The social sciences and humanities, with a specific focus on Eurasia.
Purpose: To encourage and support faculty members at all career levels in their efforts to impart their own knowledge and expertise to their students.
Eligibility: Applicants for the Teaching Fellowships must have the PhD in hand and currently be teaching full-time in an accredited United States of America university, and the must be citizens or permanent residents of the United States of America. The home institution of the Teaching Fellowship recipient is expected to provide a letter of intent stating that the institution or relevant department intends to support the implementation of the Fellow's new course into the offered curriculum at least once within a period of no more than 2 years. Detailed information on eligibility criteria and conditions of awards will be available in the application materials.
Level of Study: Postdoctorate
Type: Fellowship
Value: US$10,000
Length of Study: Maximum 2 years
Frequency: Annual
Country of Study: United States of America
No. of awards offered: Varies

Application Procedure: Awards are made on the basis of evaluations and recommendations by the Title III Program Committee, an interdisciplinary committee and composed of scholars of the region. The committee rewards proposals with clarity of argument, purpose, theory, and method, written in a style accessible to readers outside the applicant's discipline. Applicants must submit a completed application, a narrative statement, a curriculum vitae and references. Full information is available online.
Closing Date: November 1st (may change annually)
Funding: Government
Contributor: U.S. Department of State (Title VIII)
No. of awards given last year: 3
No. of applicants last year: 15

For further information contact:

Email: eurasia@ssrc.org
Website: www.ssrc.org/fellowships/eurasia
Contact: SSRC, Eurasia Program

SSRC Eurasia Title VIII Dissertation Write-Up Fellowships

Subjects: Social sciences and humanities, with a specific focus on Eurasia.
Purpose: To provide support to students who have completed the research for their doctoral dissertations and expect to complete the writing of their dissertations during the next academic year.
Eligibility: Applicants for Dissertation Write-up Fellowships must have attained ABD status (must have completed all requirements for the PhD degree except for the dissertation) by the fellowship start date. They must be citizens or permanent residents of the United States of America. The Fellow's home institution is expected to make a cost-sharing contribution of no less than 10 per cent of the fellowship award. Detailed information on eligibility criteria and conditions of awards will be available in the application materials.
Level of Study: Doctorate, graduate
Type: Fellowship
Value: Up to US$15,000
Length of Study: Up to 1 year
Frequency: Annual
Country of Study: United States of America
No. of awards offered: Varies
Application Procedure: Awards are made on the basis of evaluations and recommendations by the Title VIII Program Committee, an interdisciplinary committee composed of scholars of the region. The committee rewards proposals with clarity of argument, purpose, theory and method, written in a style accessible to readers outside the applicant's discipline. Applicants must submit a completed application, a narrative statement, transcripts, a course list and language evaluation form, and references. Full information is available online.
Closing Date: November
Funding: Government
Contributor: US Department of State under the Program for Research and Training on Eastern Europe and the Independent States of the Former Soviet Union (Title VIII)
No. of awards given last year: 7
No. of applicants last year: Approx. 30
Additional Information: No funding is available for research on the Baltic States.

For further information contact:

Email: eurasia@ssrc.org
Website: www.ssrc.org/fellowships/eurasia
Contact: SSRC, Eurasia Program

SSRC International Dissertation Field Research Fellowship

Subjects: Humanities and social sciences, with a focus on cultures, societies, aesthetics, economics and/or polities outside the United States of America.
Purpose: To provide support for international dissertation field research for students in the social sciences and humanities.
Eligibility: Open to candidates who will complete all PhD requirements except fieldwork before the commencement of research and are able to provide evidence of language fluency adequate to complete the project.
Level of Study: Doctorate
Type: Fellowship
Value: Support in the field, plus travel expenses. Awards rarely exceed US$17,000
Length of Study: 9 months–1 year
Frequency: Annual
No. of awards offered: Approx. 50
Application Procedure: Applicants must complete an application form, available from the SSRC website.
Closing Date: November
Funding: Private
Contributor: The Andrew W Mellon Foundation
Additional Information: Applicants must contact the programme for further information by emailing idrf@ssrc.org

SSRC Japan Program JSPS Postdoctoral Fellowship

Subjects: Social sciences and humanities.
Purpose: To provide qualified researchers with the opportunity to conduct research at leading universities and other research institutions in Japan.
Eligibility: Open to citizens or permanent residents of the United States of America. Applicants will need proof of an affiliation with an eligible host research institution. For 1–2 years of study, scholars must have received a PhD no more than 6 years prior to April 1st of the year for which they are applying. For 3–11 months of study, scholars must have received a PhD no more than 10 years prior to April 1st of the year for which they are applying. Previous awardees are not eligible.
Level of Study: Postdoctorate
Type: Fellowship
Value: Round-trip airfare, insurance coverage for accidents and illness, a monthly stipend of Yen 392,000 and a settling-in allowance of Yen 200,000. Applicants will also be eligible for up to an additional Yen 1,500,000 annually for research expenses for stays of 1–2 years and a domestic travel allowance of Yen 150,000 for stays of 3–11 months
Length of Study: 1–2 years
Frequency: Annual
Study Establishment: An approved institution
Country of Study: Japan
No. of awards offered: 1
Application Procedure: Applicants must apply for information, available on request by emailing japan@ssrc.org
Closing Date: December. Please contact the SSRC for the exact date
Funding: Private
Contributor: The Japan Society for the Promotion of Science
No. of awards given last year: 13
No. of applicants last year: 34

SSRC Japan Studies Dissertation Workshop

Subjects: Japan studies.
Purpose: To create a network of advanced graduate students and faculty.
Eligibility: Open to full-time advanced graduate students, regardless of citizenship, who are enrolled at United States of America institutions. Applicants must have an approved dissertation prospectus, but cannot have completed writing for final submission.
Level of Study: Doctorate
Value: In most cases, the SSRC will fully cover participants' travel, lodging and meals for the duration of the workshop
Frequency: Annual
Country of Study: Japan
No. of awards offered: 10–12
Application Procedure: A narrative description of the dissertation topic and a letter of reference from the student's advisor are required as part of the application. Applicants must apply for information, available on request by emailing japan@ssrc.org
Closing Date: October 1st
Funding: Private
Contributor: The Japan Foundation
No. of awards given last year: 12
No. of applicants last year: 33

SSRC Program on the Corporation as a Social Institution Fellowships

Subjects: Economic sociology, political economy, business history and corporate law.
Purpose: To develop a stronger, conceptually richer and potentially more interdisciplinary approach to the study of firms and other business institutions.
Eligibility: Open to graduate students from all fields conducting research in economic sociology, political economy, business history, corporate law or related fields who must be advanced to PhD candidacy before taking up the fellowship.
Level of Study: Doctorate
Type: Fellowship
Value: US$10,000
Length of Study: 2 years
Frequency: Annual
Application Procedure: Applicants must submit an approved dissertation proposal, a two-page summary of the project, a budget, and two letters of recommendation to the Program on the Corporation as a Social Institution, SSRC, at the main address.
Closing Date: January
Contributor: The Alfred P Sloan Foundation
Additional Information: Students will participate in four workshops over the course of 2 years with senior scholars working in sociology, economics, law and business. Please contact the programme director by emailing guthrie@ssrc.org for additional information.

SSRC Sexuality Research Fellowship Program

Subjects: Human sexuality research.
Purpose: To fund social and behavioural research.
Eligibility: There are no citizenship, residency or nationality requirements. Dissertation students must have completed all requirements for a PhD, except the dissertation, in a full-time graduate programme leading to a PhD in a social, health or behavioural science department of a nationally accredited United States of America college or university. Postdoctoral candidates must hold a PhD or equivalent in a social or behavioural science from a state or nationally accredited university in the United States of America, or an equivalent PhD degree from an accredited non-United States of America university.
Level of Study: Doctorate, postdoctorate
Type: Fellowship
Value: US$28,000 at doctoral level and US$38,000 at postdoctoral level
Length of Study: 1 year for dissertations, 1–2 years for postdoctorate
Frequency: Annual
Country of Study: United States of America
No. of awards offered: 10 dissertation fellowships and 4–6 postdoctoral fellowships
Application Procedure: Applicants must apply for information. All application materials are available online at www.ssrc.org/programs/sexuality or by emailing srfp@ssrc.org
Closing Date: December
Funding: Private
Contributor: The Ford Foundation
No. of awards given last year: 15
No. of applicants last year: 100
Additional Information: Members of minority groups are especially encouraged to apply. Applicants must contact the programme for further information.

SSRC South Asia Regional Fellowship Program: Fellowships for the Study of Migration

Subjects: Humanities.
Purpose: To enable successful applicants to take leave from teaching and other responsibilities to write up completed research.
Level of Study: Postdoctorate
Funding: Private

SSRC South Asia Regional Fellowship Program: Fellowships for the Study of Sexuality

Subjects: Social sciences or humanities as related to the study of sexuality.
Purpose: The primary intent of the fellowships is to enable successful applicants to take leave from teaching and other responsibilities to write up completed research. Proposed fellowship outputs may include preparation of syllabi. Applications proposing new research seeking support for ongoing field research will not be rejected but given much lower priority.
Eligibility: Eligibility is restricted to college and university-based researchers who teach in any social science, humanities or related discipline. Applicants must hold an earned PhD from an accredited university. Applicants must hold a permanent, full-time position in an accredited college or university in Bangladesh, India, Nepal, Pakistan or Sri Lanka.
Level of Study: Postdoctorate
Type: Short-term fellowship
Value: Junior scholars are eligible for a maximum fellowship amount of US$2,200 and senior scholars are eligible for a maximum fellowship amount of US$3,000
Length of Study: 3–6 months
Frequency: Annual
Study Establishment: Fellows must be affiliated with a local research center of institute during their fellowship tenure
Country of Study: Current place of residence (Bangladesh, India, Nepal, Pakistan or Sri Lanka)
No. of awards offered: A total of 20 fellowships are available each year. Up to 15 fellowships are reserved for junior scholars (below Professor rank), and no more than 5 for senior scholars (Professor rank and above)
Application Procedure: Applicants may download application forms from www.ssrc.org/fellowships/southasia or may contact our partner institutes listed below for an application form. Applications should be sent to the partner institutes listed below for an application form. Applications should be sent to the partner institute located in the country from which you are applying. Please email all your inquiries to sur@ssrc.org
Closing Date: May 15th
Funding: Private
Contributor: Ford Foundation
No. of awards given last year: 13
No. of applicants last year: 80
Additional Information: Applications forms are also available through our partner institutes in the region. For more information, please contact: Center for Alternatives, Bangladesh: ssrc-cfa@proshikanet.com; Center for Studies in Social Sciences, Calcutta, India: ssrccal@csssc.ernet.in; Social Science Baha, Nepal: ssrc@himalassociation.org; Social Scientists' Association, Sri Lanka: ssrc-ssa@eureka.lk; Sustainable Development Policy Institute, Pakistan: ssrcpakistan@sdpi.org

SSRC Summer Institute on International Migration

Subjects: Social science.
Purpose: To enable attendance at a workshop/conference training young scholars in the field of migration studies.
Eligibility: Open to advanced doctoral candidates currently involved in research or writing for their dissertations and recent PhDs revising their dissertations for publication or initiating new research.
Level of Study: Postgraduate, postdoctorate, predoctorate
Type: Award
Value: Flights, meals and lodging necessary for participation in the institute are fully subsidized
Length of Study: 1 Week
Frequency: Dependent on funds available
Study Establishment: The University of California at Irvine
Country of Study: United States of America
No. of awards offered: 20
Application Procedure: Applicants must download the application form from the website www.cri.uci.edu
Closing Date: February 18th
Funding: Private
Contributor: UCT and SSRC
No. of awards given last year: 20
No. of applicants last year: 250
Additional Information: The Institute is a collaboration between the SSRC and the Center for Research on Immigration, Population and Public Policy (CRI) at the University of California, Irvine.

For further information contact:

CRI
Tel: (1) 949 824 1361
Email: cbramle@uci.edu
Contact: Carolynn J Bramlett, Administrative Assistant

SSRC-Mellon Mays Predoctoral Fellowships

Subjects: The processes of migration and settlement of the USA, and the outcomes for both immigrants and native-born Americans.
Purpose: To offer intensive training to students of minority background in developing dissertation and funding proposals.
Eligibility: Applicants must be citizens or permanent residents of the United States of America who are of African, Latino, Asian, Pacific Island, or Native American ancestry. Applicants have to be graduate students who are matriculated in doctoral programmes in the social sciences, including history, have taken coursework related to international migration, have completed their 1st year of graduate study, and have developed a preliminary research focus for their dissertation.
Level of Study: Postgraduate
Type: Fellowship
Value: US$5,000
Frequency: Annual
Study Establishment: A recognized university
Country of Study: United States of America
No. of awards offered: 10–15
Application Procedure: Applicants must write for further information and application materials.
Closing Date: November 15th
Funding: Private
Contributor: The Andrew W Mellon Foundation
Additional Information: The awards will be announced in April.

SOCIAL SCIENCES AND HUMANITIES RESEARCH COUNCIL OF CANADA (SSHRC)

350 Albert Street, PO Box 1610, Ottawa, ON, K1P 6G4, Canada
Tel: (1) 613 992 8092
Fax: (1) 613 992 2803
Email: jta@sshrc.ca
Website: www.sshrc.ca
Contact: Mr Joel Tatelman, English Editor

The Social Sciences and Humanities Research Council of Canada (SSHRC) is the federal agency responsible for promoting and supporting research and research training in the social sciences and humanities in Canada. SSHRC supports research on the economic, political, social and cultural dimensions of the human experience.

Aboriginal Research: Development and Research Grants

Subjects: Social sciences and humanities.
Purpose: To help teams of Aboriginal organizations and university researchers develop partnerships to investigate issues of concern to Aboriginal peoples.
Eligibility: Applicants must be researchers affiliated with Canadian postsecondary institutions. Or members of Canadian Aboriginal community, voluntary or cultural organizations.
Type: Grant
Value: Development Grants: up to Canadian $10,000 annually Research Grants: up to Canadian $100,000 annually with a maximum of $250,000 over 3 years
Length of Study: Development Grants: 2 years Research Grants: 3 years
Frequency: Annual
Application Procedure: Applicants must visit the website for application forms and instructions.
Closing Date: September 15th
Funding: Government

Aid to Research and Transfer Journals

Subjects: Social sciences and humanities.
Purpose: To assist in the effective dissemination of original research findings and in the transfer of knowledge to practitioners.
Eligibility: Open to candidates who are either Canadian citizens or permanent residents of Canada at the time of application and are established researchers in the social sciences or in the humanities. They must also be a member of the sponsoring institution or organization and not be under SSHRC sanction for financial or research misconduct. A research or transfer journal must have as its main objective the publishing of the results of advanced research and scholarly work by specialists for a readership of specialists or practitioners. The journal must also have a subscription level over 200, be in either English or French and be sponsored, edited and published in Canada, by a Canadian institution or a Canadian association.
Level of Study: Research
Type: Grant
Value: The maximum value of a General Grant is Canadian $30,000 per year or Canadian $90,000 over 3 years; the maximum value of a Special Initiative Grant is Canadian $10,000
Frequency: Every 3 years
Country of Study: Canada
Application Procedure: Applicants must make the case for the funding requested. For full details on application visit the website.
Closing Date: June 30th
Funding: Government

Aid to Research Workshops and Conferences in Canada

Subjects: Arts and humanities and social sciences.
Purpose: To support workshops and conferences held in Canada that will facilitate essential knowledge transfer.
Eligibility: Applicants must be either Canadian citizens or permanent residents of Canada at the time of application, researchers in the social sciences or humanities, and members of the conference's or congress's organizing committee. Applicants for Congress Grants must also be members in good standing of the international scholarly association in question, be affiliated with a Canadian university that agrees to administer the grant and not be under SSHRC sanction for financial or research misconduct. For a conference to be eligible, it must take place after the date specified for SSHRC's announcement of competition results, have a defined theme and be devoted to scholarly research issues in the social sciences or humanities, be held in Canada or at a Canadian academic institution abroad, not be receiving support for the same activity under another SSHRC programme, and not be an association's annual general meeting. For a congress to be eligible, it must be sponsored by an international scholarly association that has as its main objective the furthering of advanced scholarly research in a discipline of the social sciences or the humanities, and that shows evidence of a membership with broad international representation.
Level of Study: Research
Type: Grant
Value: A maximum of Canadian $20,000–50,000 depending on number of participants.
Country of Study: Canada
Application Procedure: Applicants must consult the organization or visit the website.
Closing Date: May 1st or November 1st
Funding: Government

Aid to Scholarly Publications

Subjects: Social sciences and humanities.
Purpose: To promote the sharing of research results by assisting the publication of individual works that make an important contribution to the advancement of knowledge.
Eligibility: Applicants must consult the website for eligibility requirements.
Level of Study: Postdoctorate, research
Type: Grant
Frequency: Annual
Application Procedure: Applicants must refer to the website or email the Humanities and Social Sciences Federation of Canada.
Closing Date: Applications are accepted at any time.
Funding: Government
Additional Information: The programme is administered on behalf of SSHRC by the Humanities and Social Sciences Federation of Canada (HSSFC).

For further information contact:

The Humanities and Social Sciences Federation of Canada (HSSFC), 151 Slater Street, Ottawa, ON, K1P 5H3, Canada
Tel: (1) 613 238 6112 ext 350
Email: secaspp@aspp.hssfc.ca
Website: www.hssfc.ca/aspp/homee.htm

Aid to Small Universities

Subjects: Arts, humanities and social sciences.
Purpose: To promote the focused development of social sciences and humanities research capacity in small universities.
Eligibility: Open to institutions that have degree-granting status for social sciences and humanities disciplines at the graduate level or beyond, and are institutional members of the Association of Universities and Colleges of Canada (AUCC), or members of the AUCC and affiliated with an institution itself too large to be eligible for the ASU Program. They must also have fewer than 250 full-time faculty in SSHRC fields and be independent of the federal government for the purpose of faculty employment status.
Level of Study: Research
Type: Grant
Value: Determined using a formula based on the number of full-time social sciences and humanities faculty at the institution. Awards are usually up to Canadian $30,000 over 3 years
Length of Study: 3 years
Frequency: Every 3 years
Country of Study: Canada
Application Procedure: Applicants must contact the organization or visit the website.
Closing Date: December
Funding: Government

Aileen D Ross Fellowship

Subjects: Sociology.
Purpose: To support an outstanding SSHRC doctoral or postdoctoral fellowship holder who is conducting research in sociology, especially in poverty.
Eligibility: Open to Canadian citizens or permanent residents living in Canada at the time of application who are not under SSHRC sanction resulting from financial or research misconduct, or already in receipt of SSHRC, NSERC or MRC (now CIHR) funding to undertake or complete a previous doctoral degree. At the time of taking up the award, applicants must have completed either a Master's degree or at least 1 year of doctoral study, and be pursuing either full-time studies leading to a PhD or equivalent, with a research specialization in sociology and with the intention of pursuing an academic career. Candidates wishing to study at a foreign university may only do so if one of their previous degrees was earned in Canada.
Level of Study: Doctorate, postdoctorate
Type: Fellowship
Value: Canadian $10,000 plus the value of the fellowship
Length of Study: 1 year
Country of Study: Canada
No. of awards offered: 1
Application Procedure: Applicants must indicate their interest on the doctoral or postdoctoral application form. Further details can be found on the website.
Closing Date: Postdoctoral applications are due October 1st. Doctoral application dates are set by the applicant's university
Funding: Government, trusts
Additional Information: Preference will be given to postdoctoral applicants.

Bora Laskin National Fellowship in Human Rights Research

Subjects: Human rights, as relevant to Canada.
Purpose: To support research, preferably of a multidisciplinary or interdisciplinary nature, and to develop Canadian expertise in the field of human rights, with an emphasis on themes and issues relevant to the Canadian human rights scene.
Eligibility: Open to Canadian citizens or permanent residents of Canada. Preference will be given to applicants with at least 5 years of proven research experience in their field, as this fellowship is not intended for scholars just beginning their research careers.
Level of Study: Postdoctorate, research
Type: Fellowship
Value: Canadian $45,000 plus a research and travel allowance of Canadian $10,000
Length of Study: 1 year, non-renewable
Frequency: Annual
No. of awards offered: 1
Application Procedure: Applicants must complete an application form, available from the website. (http://www.sshrc.ca/web/apply/program_descriptions/fellowships/bora_laskin_e.asp or... bora_laskin_f.asp)
Closing Date: October 1st
Funding: Government

Boreas: Histories from the North-Environments, Movements, Narratives

Subjects: Social sciences and humanities.
Purpose: To support multidisciplinary research on the circumpolar North.
Eligibility: Applicants must be researchers affiliated with Canadian postsecondary institutions. See programme description on website for additional details.
Level of Study: Research
Type: Grant
Value: Dependent on nature and scope of proposed research project
Length of Study: Up to 4 years
Frequency: Annual
Application Procedure: Visit SSHRC website to access program description follow hyperlink to European Science Foundation website.
Closing Date: See website
Funding: Government
Contributor: SSHRC, European Science Foundation

For further information contact:

Website: www.esf.org

Canada Graduate Scholarship Program (CGS): Master's Scholarship

Subjects: Social sciences and humanities.
Purpose: To support graduate students working towards a Master's degree at a Canadian University.
Eligibility: Open to citizens or permanent residents of Canada who are applying for, or registered in a Master's programme in the social sciences or humanities at a Canadian University.
Level of Study: Graduate, predoctorate
Type: Scholarship
Value: Canadian $17,500
Length of Study: 1 year
Frequency: Annual
Country of Study: Canada
No. of awards offered: Several hundred
Application Procedure: Applicants must visit the website for further information.
Closing Date: Applicants must consult the programme description on the website to determine their applicant status, which in turn determines the application deadline
Funding: Government
No. of awards given last year: Hundreds
No. of applicants last year: Thousands

Canadian Forest Service Graduate Supplements

Subjects: Forestry and related fields.
Purpose: To promote Canadian doctoral research into forestry, to encourage the use of Canadian Forest Service (CFS) centres and to increase contacts between CFS researchers and Canadian universities.
Eligibility: Open to SSHRC Doctoral Fellows who are conducting research in an area related to forestry in Canada and who are in the 3rd or 4th year of their programme. Candidates must have at least one CFS scientist on their supervisory committee and must carry out all or part of their research at a CFS forestry centre.

Level of Study: Doctorate, predoctorate, research
Type: Supplement or Fellowship
Value: Canadian $5,000 supplement to the Canadian $20,000 doctoral fellowship
Length of Study: Up to 2 years
Frequency: Annual
No. of awards offered: 5
Application Procedure: Applicants must visit the website.
Closing Date: Interested doctoral students should contact their department for the SSHRC Doctoral Fellowship application deadline
Funding: Government, foundation
Contributor: The Canadian Forest Service

For further information contact:

Canadian Forest Service Graduate Supplements, Science Branch, Natural Resources Canada, 580 Booth Street, Ottawa, ON, K1A 0E4, Canada
Tel: (1) 613 947 8992
Fax: (1) 613 947 9090
Email: mlamarch@nrcan.gc.ca
Contact: Programme Co-ordinator

Canadian Initiative on Social Statistics: Data Training Schools

Subjects: Social sciences.
Purpose: To promote research and training in the application of Canadian social statistics.
Eligibility: Eligible applicants include research groups, departments and centres that are operating in a Canadian university eligible participants include students and researchers at a variety of levels.
Level of Study: Doctorate, predoctorate, research, graduate, postdoctorate
Type: Grant
Value: Up to Canadian $50,000 annually
Length of Study: 3 years
Frequency: Annual
Application Procedure: Applicants must visit the website for application forms and instructions.

Community-University Research Alliances (CURA)

Subjects: Social sciences and humanities.
Purpose: To support research projects jointly developed and undertaken by university-based researchers and community organizations.
Eligibility: Open to community or other not-for-profit organizations in Canada that are teaming up with university-based researchers to address issues of mutual interest and concern.
Level of Study: Professional development, postdoctorate, research
Type: Grant
Value: Up to Canadian $200,000 annually over 5 years
Length of Study: Up to 5 years
Frequency: Annual
Country of Study: Canada
Application Procedure: Applicants must visit the website for further information on the two-stage application process.
Closing Date: See programme description on website
Funding: Government

Geomatics for Informed Decisions (GEOIDE) Networks of Centers of Excellence Graduate Supplement Program

Subjects: Geomatics.
Purpose: To support SSHRC doctoral award holders conducting research in geomatics-related fields.
Eligibility: Open to applicants for or holders of an SSHRC doctoral fellowship.
Level of Study: Doctorate
Value: Canadian $5,000 in addition to the value of the doctoral award
Length of Study: Up to 2 years
Frequency: Annual
Country of Study: Canada
Application Procedure: Applicants must indicate their interest on the doctoral fellowship application form. Further details can be found on the website.
Closing Date: November 15th or date set by the applicant's university, whichever is earlier
Funding: Government

Image, Text, Sound and Technology: Networking Summer Institute, Workshop and Conference Grants

Subjects: Social sciences and humanities.
Purpose: To help scholars, especially in the humanities, apply innovative digital technologies to research on image, text and sound.
Eligibility: Applicants must be researchers affiliated with Canadian postsecondary institutions.
Level of Study: Research
Type: Grant
Value: Up to Canadian $50,000
Length of Study: 1 year
Frequency: Annual
Country of Study: Canada
Application Procedure: Applicants must visit the website for application information and forms.
Closing Date: September 15th
Funding: Government

International Opportunities Fund: Development and Project Grants

Subjects: Social sciences and humanities.
Purpose: To support developmental activities and projects.
Eligibility: Applicants must be researchers affiliated with Canadian postsecondary institutions.
Level of Study: Research
Type: Grant
Value: Development Grants: Up to Canadian $25,000. Project Grants: up to Canadian $75,000.
Length of Study: 1 year
Frequency: 4 times per annum
Application Procedure: Applicants must visit the website for application forms and instructions.
Closing Date: Applications may be submitted at any time

Jules and Gabrielle Léger Fellowship

Subjects: The Crown and Governor General in a parliamentary democracy.
Purpose: To encourage research and writing on the historical and contemporary contribution of the Crown and its representatives, federal and provincial, to the political, constitutional, cultural, intellectual and social life of the country, including comparisons between Canadian and Commonwealth systems.
Eligibility: Open to Canadian citizens or permanent residents of Canada who have proven experience in the proposed field of research and are not under SSHRC sanction for financial or research misconduct.
Level of Study: Research, postdoctorate
Type: Fellowship
Value: Canadian $40,000, plus Canadian $10,000 for research and travel costs
Length of Study: 1 year, non-renewable
Frequency: Every 2 years
Study Establishment: A recognized university or research institute
Country of Study: Any country
No. of awards offered: 1
Application Procedure: Applicants must visit the website for full application details.
Closing Date: October 1st
Funding: Government

Knowledge Impact in Society

Subjects: Social sciences and humanities.
Purpose: To support university-based knowledge mobilization initiatives that will enable non-university stockholders to benefit from existing human sciences research.
Eligibility: The programme offers institutional grants, which are available only to universities, eligible for SSHRC Institutional Grants. See website for full details.

Level of Study: Research
Type: Grant
Value: Up to Canadian $100,000 per annum
Length of Study: Up to 3 years
Frequency: Annual
Application Procedure: Applicants must visit the website for application forms and instructions.
Closing Date: Visit website
Funding: Government

Major Collaborative Research Initiatives (MCRI)

Subjects: Arts, humanities and social sciences.
Purpose: To strengthen Canadian research capacity by promoting high-quality, innovative, collaborative research and unique student training opportunities in a collaborative research environment.
Eligibility: Open to leading scholars with a solid track record and past experience in collaborative research, student training and grant management. Please consult the programme description on the website.
Level of Study: Research
Type: Grant
Value: Up to Canadian $500,000 per year with a minimum budget of Canadian $100,000 per year. A Canadian $20,000 development fund will also be offered to assist the research team's planning and preparation for its formal application
Length of Study: 5 years
Frequency: Annual
Application Procedure: Applications must be submitted by the Project Director on behalf of the research team. There is a two-stage application process, the first being a letter of intent, followed by a formal application.
Closing Date: January 31st for the first stage and September 1st for the second
Funding: Government

For further information contact:

Tel: (1) 613 996 2994
Email: pierrette.tremblay@sshrc.ca
Contact: Pierrette Tremblay, Research Grants Co-ordinator

Multiculturalism in Canada: Research Grants

Subjects: Social sciences and humanities.
Purpose: To support research on diverse issues that arise from Canada's increasingly multicultural and multiethnic population.
Eligibility: Applicants must be researchers affiliated with Canadian postsecondary institutions.
Level of Study: Research
Type: Grant
Value: Up to Canadian $50,000 per year
Length of Study: 1 year
Frequency: Annual
Country of Study: Canada
Application Procedure: Applicants must visit the website for application forms and instructions.
Funding: Government

Northern Research Development Program

Subjects: Social sciences and humanities.
Purpose: To support research in and about the Canadian North, with emphasis on involving local stakeholders.
Eligibility: Applications should come from research teams made up of university-based researchers and community or non-profit organizations. See programme description on website for details.
Level of Study: Research
Type: Grant
Value: Up to Canadian $40,000
Length of Study: Up to 2 years
Frequency: Annual
Country of Study: Canada
Application Procedure: Applicants must visit the website for application information, forms and instructions.
Closing Date: See programme description on website
Funding: Government

Queen's Fellowships

Subjects: Canadian studies.
Purpose: To assist an outstanding candidate who intends to enter a doctoral programme in the relevant field.
Eligibility: Open to Canadian citizens and permanent residents who, by the time of taking up the fellowship, will have completed 1 year of graduate study or all the requirements for the Master's degree beyond the Bachelor's (Honours) Degree or its equivalent, and will be registered in a programme of studies leading to a PhD or its equivalent. This award is offered to one or two outstanding and successful doctoral fellowship candidates.
Level of Study: Doctorate
Type: Fellowship
Value: Tuition fees and travel to the main place of tenure and travel for research purposes
Length of Study: 1 year, non-renewable
Frequency: Annual
Study Establishment: A recognized university
Country of Study: Canada
No. of awards offered: 1–2
Application Procedure: Applicants cannot apply for this award, but are automatically eligible if they intend to study Canadian studies at a Canadian university. The Queen's Fellowship is not a programme, but a special award given to a doctoral Fellow.
Funding: Government

Research/Creation Grants in Fine Arts

Subjects: Fine arts and related disciplines.
Purpose: To support programmes of research/creation by artist-researchers affiliated with Canadian postsecondary institutions.
Eligibility: Artist-researchers affiliated with Canadian postsecondary institutions.
Level of Study: Research
Type: Grant
Value: Up to a total of Canadian $250,000 over 3 years
Length of Study: Up to 3 years
Frequency: Annual
Country of Study: Canada
Application Procedure: Applicants must visit the website for application forms and instructions.
Closing Date: November 1st each year
Funding: Government

SSHRC Doctoral Awards

Subjects: Social sciences and humanities.
Purpose: To develop research skills and to assist in the training of highly qualified academic personnel by supporting students who demonstrate a high standard of scholarly achievement.
Eligibility: Open to Canadian citizens or permanent residents living in Canada at the time of application, who are not under SSHRC sanction resulting from financial or research misconduct, or already in receipt of SSHRC, NSERC or MRC (now CIHR) funding to undertake or complete a previous doctoral degree. At the time of taking up the award applicants must have completed either a Master's degree or at least 1 year of doctoral study, and be pursuing either full-time studies leading to a PhD or equivalent. Candidates wishing to study at a foreign university may only do so if one of their previous degrees was earned in Canada.
Level of Study: Doctorate
Type: Fellowship /Scholarship
Value: SSHRC doctoral fellowships: Canadian $17,700 per year, up to and including the 4th year of doctoral study (tenable in Canada and abroad) CGS doctoral scholarship: Canadian $35,000 per year for 3 years (tenable only at Canadian universities)
Length of Study: 6 months–4 years
Frequency: Annual
Study Establishment: Any recognized universities
Country of Study: SSHRC doctoral fellowships: tenable in Canada or abroad; CGS doctoral scholarships: tenable in Canada only
No. of awards offered: Varies

Application Procedure: Applicants must complete an application form along with a detailed description. Forms are available from the website. For complete application information, go to: http://www.sshrc.ca/web/apply/program_descriptions/fellowships/doctoral_e.asp or...doctoral_f.asp
Closing Date: For applicants registered at a Canadian university, the university sets the deadline; for all others, November 15th
Funding: Government
No. of awards given last year: 572
No. of applicants last year: 1,521

SSHRC Institutional Grants

Subjects: Social sciences and humanities.
Purpose: To help universities develop and maintain a solid base of research and research-related activities.
Eligibility: Open to Canadian postsecondary institutions only.
Level of Study: Postgraduate
Type: Research grant
Value: Minimum Canadian $5,000 per annum
Length of Study: 3 years
Frequency: Every 3 years
Country of Study: Canada
No. of awards offered: Varies
Application Procedure: Applicants must complete an application form, available from the website. For complete application information, see the official programme description: http://www.sshrc.ca/web/apply/program_descriptions/institutional_grants_e.asp or...institutional_grants_f.asp
Closing Date: December 1st
Funding: Government

SSHRC Postdoctoral Fellowships

Subjects: Social sciences and humanities.
Purpose: To support the most promising new scholars and to assist them in establishing a research base at an important time in their research career.
Eligibility: Open to candidates who are Canadian citizens or permanent residents living in Canada at the time of application. They must also be able to demonstrate skill in research, not be under SSHRC sanction resulting from financial or research misconduct and have earned their doctorate from a recognized university no more than 3 years prior to the competition deadline or have completed their degree within 6 years prior to the competition deadline, but have had their career interrupted or delayed for the purpose of child rearing. Candidates must also have finalized arrangements for affiliation with a university or a research institution and have applied not more than once before for a SSHRC postdoctoral fellowship. At the time of taking up the award, applicants must have completed all requirements for the doctoral degree, must intend to engage in full-time postdoctoral research and not hold a tenure or tenure-track position.
Level of Study: Postdoctorate
Type: Fellowship
Value: Up to Canadian $35,028 per year, plus a research allowance of up to Canadian $5,000
Length of Study: A minimum of 1 year and a maximum of 2 years
Frequency: Annual
Study Establishment: For applicants who earned their doctorate at a Canadian University, there is no restriction on the location of the tenure
Country of Study: Any country, under certain conditions
No. of awards offered: Approx. 100
Application Procedure: Applicants must complete an application form. To do this, go to the programme description the SSHRC website.
Closing Date: October 1st
Funding: Government
No. of awards given last year: 100
No. of applicants last year: 380
Additional Information: Applicants wishing to hold their award at a foreign university may do so only if their PhD was earned at a Canadian university.

SSHRC Relationships in Transition

Subjects: Public policy issues relating to law reform.
Purpose: To support the writing of research papers relevant to law reform in Canada.
Eligibility: Participants must meet SSHRC's general eligibility criteria. Proposals for interdisciplinary papers are invited from researchers and teams of researchers affiliated with Canadian postsecondary institutions. Please see the website for full details.
Level of Study: Research
Type: Grant
Value: Average Canadian $25,000, but up to Canadian $40,000 per paper
Length of Study: 1 year
Frequency: Annual
No. of awards offered: Varies
Application Procedure: Applications must consist of a research proposal and a budget proposal. Applicants must visit the website for further details.
Closing Date: Please contact the organization
Additional Information: Each year the focus is on one of the following four themes: economic relationships, personal relationships, social relationships and governance relationships. Successful candidates will be invited to present their papers at a conference held in the Spring.

SSHRC Research Development Initiatives

Subjects: Humanities, the social and cognitive sciences and the educational sciences.
Purpose: To support research that defines new conceptual and methodological perspectives and challenges. Research should define new priorities to be taken into account when conducting research, disseminating research results or training new researchers. The programme supports research that both addresses and elicits the changing directions of research and the evolution of the relevant disciplines.
Eligibility: Candidates should visit the website for eligibility requirements.
Level of Study: Research
Value: A maximum of Canadian $50,000 per year
Length of Study: Up to 2 years
Frequency: 3 times a year
Application Procedure: Applicants must visit the website for further details as there are two parts to the application process, a form and a project description. Applications must be addressed to the Strategic Programmes and Joint Initiatives Division at the main address or emailed to collaborative@sshrc.ca
Closing Date: See website
Funding: Government

SSHRC Standard Research Grants

Subjects: Social sciences and humanities.
Purpose: To support and develop excellence in research, with the research projects proposed by the researchers themselves.
Eligibility: Open to scholars who are Canadian citizens or permanent residents of Canada and who are affiliated with a Canadian university or recognized postsecondary institution.
Level of Study: Research
Type: Research grant
Value: Up to a maximum of Canadian $100,000 per year, but not totalling more than Canadian $250,000 over a 3-year period. A minimum of Canadian $5,000 in at least one of the years is required unless the applicant is at an institution not receiving a General Research Grant
Length of Study: Grants in support of research programmes will ordinarily be expected to cover 3-year periods
Frequency: Annual
Study Establishment: An approved institution
Country of Study: Any country
No. of awards offered: Varies
Application Procedure: Applicants must visit the website for full application details.
Closing Date: October 15th

Funding: Government
Additional Information: Approx. 1800.

SSHRC Strategic Research Grants

Subjects: Social sciences and humanities.
Purpose: To support research and research-related activities in areas of national importance. SSHRC offers many separate programmes to support strategic research. See the website for current offerings.
Eligibility: Applicants should visit the website for requirements.
Level of Study: Research
Type: Grant
Frequency: Annual
Country of Study: Canada
Application Procedure: Applicants must visit the website for full application details.
Closing Date: Varies according to programme
Funding: Trusts, foundation, government

Thérèse F Casgrain Fellowship

Subjects: Canadian women and social change.
Purpose: To carry out research in the field of social justice, particularly in the defence of individual rights and the promotion of the economic and social interests of Canadian women.
Eligibility: Open to Canadian citizens or permanent residents. At the time of taking up the fellowship, the successful candidate must have obtained a doctorate or an equivalent advanced professional degree, as well as have proven research experience and not be under SSHRC sanction for financial or research misconduct.
Level of Study: Postdoctorate
Type: Fellowship
Value: Canadian $40,000, paid in three instalments, of which up to Canadian $10,000 may be used for travel and research expenses
Length of Study: 1 year, non-renewable
Frequency: Every 2 years
Country of Study: Canada
No. of awards offered: 1
Application Procedure: Applicants must complete an application form, available from the website. Application forms and instructions are available on the SSHRC website: http://www.sshrc.ca/web/apply/program_descriptions/fellowships/casgrain_e.asp or...casgrain_f.asp
Closing Date: October 1st
Funding: Private
Contributor: The Thérèse F Casgrain Foundation
No. of awards given last year: 1
No. of applicants last year: 21
Additional Information: The fellowship was created by the Thérèse F Casgrain Foundation and is administered by the Social Sciences and Humanities Research Council. Affiliation with a university or an appropriate research institute or similar organization is desirable, but is not a condition of the award. Recipients must submit a final report to the Foundation outlining conclusions of the research, accompanied by a complete financial statement for all expenses.

Virtual Scholar in Residence Program

Subjects: Law reform and related issues.
Purpose: To allow an individual to work with the Law Commission of Canada (LCC) to advance research in a particular area.
Eligibility: Open to researchers affiliated with a Canadian postsecondary educational institution.
Level of Study: Research, postgraduate
Type: Research grant
Value: A maximum of Canadian $50,000 to cover a period of intensive research with the LCC. Financial details regarding this grant will be negotiated between the LCC, SSHRC and the successful applicant's institution following the 2nd stage of the competition. In addition the Commission will also provide up to Canadian $10,000 for research expenses
Length of Study: 8 months
Frequency: Annual
Country of Study: Canada
No. of awards offered: 1
Application Procedure: Applicants must visit the website for application details.
Closing Date: January 10th
Funding: Government, foundation

SOCIAL WORKERS EDUCATIONAL TRUST

British Association of Social Workers,
16 Kent Street, Birmingham, West Midlands,
B5 6RD, England
Tel: (44) 12 1622 3911
Fax: (44) 12 1622 4860
Email: swet@basw.co.uk
Website: www.basw.co.uk/swet
Contact: Ms Gill Aslett, Honorary Secretary

The Social Workers Educational Trust offers grants and scholarships to experienced social workers for postqualifying training or research, with the overall aim of improving social work practice in the United Kingdom.

Anne Cummins Scholarship

Subjects: Health-related social work.
Purpose: To support study or research on health-related social work practice.
Eligibility: Open to qualified social workers who have completed 2 years of work practice postqualification, resident in the United Kingdom.
Level of Study: Postgraduate, professional development
Type: Scholarship
Value: UK £1,000–1,500
Frequency: Annual
Country of Study: United Kingdom
No. of awards offered: 1
Application Procedure: Applicants must complete an application form. Details and forms are available on written request from the Social Workers Educational Trust at 16 Kent Street, Birmingham B5 6RD. Applicants should state whether their application is for a grant or scholarship.
Funding: Private
No. of awards given last year: 1

SOCIETY FOR ENDOCRINOLOGY

22 Apex Court, Woodlands, Bradley Stoke, Bristol,
BS32 4JT, England
Tel: (44) 14 5464 2200
Fax: (44) 14 5464 2222
Email: julie.cragg@endocrinology.org
Website: www.endocrinology.org
Contact: Julie Cragg, Society Services Manager

The Society for Endocrinology aims to promote the advancement of public education in endocrinology.

Society for Endocrinology/Clinical Endocrinology Basic Science Research Fellowship

Subjects: Endocrinology.
Purpose: To enable a suitable candidate to advance their research career in endocrinology.
Eligibility: The sponsor where the research is to be carried out must be a member of the Society for Endocrinology.
Level of Study: Postdoctorate, postgraduate
Type: Fellowship
Length of Study: 3 years
Frequency: Dependent on funds available
Study Establishment: United Kingdom medical research institutions
Country of Study: United Kingdom
No. of awards offered: 1
Application Procedure: Applicants must complete an application form.
Funding: Corporation, private

Contributor: Society for Endocrinology/Clinical Endocrinology Basic Science Research Fellowship
No. of awards given last year: None

Society for Endocrinology/Clinical Endocrinology Trust Clinical Fellowship

Subjects: Endocrinology.
Purpose: To enable a suitable candidate to advance their research career in the field of endocrinology.
Eligibility: The sponsor where the research is to be carried out must be a member of the Society for Endocrinology.
Level of Study: Postgraduate, postdoctorate
Type: Fellowship
Value: Up to an average of UK £40,000 per year
Length of Study: 3 years
Frequency: Dependent on funds available, every 6 years
Study Establishment: United Kingdom medical research institutions
Country of Study: United Kingdom
No. of awards offered: 1
Application Procedure: Applicants must submit an application form.
Funding: Corporation, trusts
Contributor: Society for Endocrinology/Clinical Endocrinology
No. of awards given last year: None

SOCIETY FOR RENAISSANCE STUDIES

12A Manley Street, London, NW1 8LT, England
Tel: (44) 20 7862 8703
Fax: (44) 20 7862 8722
Email: richard.simpson@sas.ac.uk
Website: www.sas.ac.uk/srs

The Society for Renaissance Studies, founded in 1967, provides a forum for those interested in any aspect of the study of the Renaissance. The Society provides support for interdisciplinary teaching and research, organizing and supporting conferences and lectures and publishing the journal *Renaissance Studies*, in conjunction with Blackwell. Topics covered in talks, articles and reviews include the history, art, architecture, philosophy, science, technology, religion, music, the literatures and languages of Europe and of countries in contact with Europe, during the Renaissance. The Society has branches in Ireland, Wales and Scotland that also organize events for members.

Renaissance Society Fellowships

Subjects: Renaissance studies.
Eligibility: Open to any postgraduate student registered in the United Kingdom. There are no age or nationality restrictions.
Level of Study: Predoctorate, postgraduate
Type: Travel grant
Value: Up to UK £1,500
Frequency: Annual
Country of Study: Any country
No. of awards offered: Up to 2
Application Procedure: Applicants must submit a text of not more than 1,000 words describing the research projects to be undertaken, noting the title of the dissertation and the relationship of the proposed travel project to the dissertation and requesting a specific amount of funding. In addition, the applicant must include a short budget detailing the expenditure planned for travel, accommodation and subsistence during the trip. While the maximum amount to be awarded for a single fellowship is UK £1,500, the Society welcomes applications for projects requiring smaller sums. Applications should be sent to Dr Michelle O'Malley.
Closing Date: January 31st
Funding: Private
Contributor: The Society for Renaissance Studies
No. of awards given last year: 2
Additional Information: Fellows will be required to produce a written report to the Society that will be published in the Society's bulletin. They may also be invited to give a 15-minute paper on their project to the Society's annual meeting or at the Society's national conference.

SOCIETY FOR TECHNICAL COMMUNICATION

901 North Street, Suite 904, Arlington, VA 22203, United States of America
Tel: (1) 4522-4114 extn 208
Email: maurice@stc.org
Website: www.stc.org
Contact: Maurice Martin

The Society for Technical Communication is an individual membership organization dedicated to advancing the arts and sciences of technical communication.

Major STC Research Grant Program

Subjects: Technical communication.
Purpose: To promote awareness of the latest trends and technology in the field of technical communication.
Eligibility: Open to all talented individuals.
Level of Study: Postgraduate
Type: Grant
Value: US$10,000
Length of Study: 1 year
Frequency: Annual
No. of awards offered: 1
Application Procedure: See the website for details.
Closing Date: June 30th
Contributor: Society for Technical Communication

STC International Scholarship Program

Subjects: Technical writing.
Purpose: To assist students who are pursuing programmes in some area of technical communication.
Eligibility: Open to full-time students studying communication of information about technical subjects.
Level of Study: Postgraduate
Type: Scholarship
Value: US$1,500
Frequency: Annual
Study Establishment: Society for Technical Communication
Application Procedure: A completed application form must be sent. See the website for complete details.
Closing Date: February 15th

For further information contact:

Scholarships 901 North Stuart Street, Suite 904, Arlington, VA 22203-1822

STC Lone Star Community Scholarship

Subjects: Technical communication.
Purpose: To assist students who wish to pursue a career in the field of technical communications.
Eligibility: Open to students living or attending institution in Arizona Arkansas, Louisiana, New Mexico, Oklahoma, Texas and Utah.
Level of Study: Postgraduate
Type: Scholarship
Value: Varies
Frequency: Annual
Application Procedure: See the website www.stc-dfw.org for details.
Closing Date: October 15th
Contributor: STC Lone Star Community

For further information contact:

Post office Box 515065, Texas, Dallas, 75251-5065
Contact: STC LSC Scholarship Committee Manager

THE SOCIETY FOR THE PROMOTION OF HELLENIC STUDIES

Senate House, Malet Street, London, WC1E 7HU, England
Tel: (44) 20 7862 8730
Fax: (44) 20 7862 8731
Email: officehellenicsociety@org.uk
Website: www-hellenicsociety.org.uk
Contact: Secretary

The Society for the Promotion of Hellenic Studies, generally known as the Hellenic Society, was founded in 1879 to advance the study of Greek language, literature, history, art and archaeology in the ancient, Byzantine and modern periods.

The Dover Fund

Subjects: Greek language and papyri.
Purpose: To further the study of the history of the Greek language in any period from the Bronze Age to the 15th century AD, and to further the edition and exegesis of Greek texts from any period within those same limits.
Eligibility: Open to currently registered research students and lecturers, teaching Fellows, research Fellows, postdoctoral Fellows and research assistants who are within the first 5 years of their appointment.
Level of Study: Postgraduate, postdoctorate, doctorate
Type: Grant
Value: Grants will be made for such purposes as books, photography, including microfilm and photocopying, and towards the costs of visits to libraries, museums and sites. The sums awarded will vary according to the needs of the applicant, but most grants will be in the range of UK £50–250. Larger grants may be made from time to time at the discretion of the awards committee
Frequency: Annual
Study Establishment: The Society for the Promotion of Hellenic Studies
Country of Study: United Kingdom
No. of awards offered: Varies
Application Procedure: Applicants must complete an application form, available from the Society. Applications should be marked for the attention of the Dover Fund and sent to the main address.
Closing Date: February 14th of the year in which the award is sought
Funding: Private
Contributor: Membership subscriptions
No. of awards given last year: 3
No. of applicants last year: 8

SOCIETY FOR THE PROMOTION OF ROMAN STUDIES

Senate House, Malet Street, London, WC1E 7HU, England
Tel: (44) 20 7862 8727
Fax: (44) 20 7862 8728
Email: office@romansociety.org
Website: www.romansociety.org
Contact: Dr Helen M Cockle, Secretary of Society

The Society for the Promotion of Roman Studies aims to promote the study of history, architecture, archaeology, language, literature and the art of Italy and the Roman Empire, including Roman Britain, from the earliest times to about 700 AD.

Hugh Last and Donald Atkinson Funds Committee Grants

Subjects: The history, archaeology, language, literature and art of Italy and the Roman Empire including Roman Britain.
Purpose: To assist in the undertaking, completion or publication of work that relates to any of the general scholarly purposes of the Roman Society.
Eligibility: Open to applicants of graduate, postgraduate or postdoctoral status or the equivalent, usually of United Kingdom nationality.
Level of Study: Postgraduate, graduate, postdoctorate, research
Type: Grant
Value: Varies, but usually UK £200–1,500
Frequency: Annual
No. of awards offered: 20
Application Procedure: Applicants must ensure that two references are sent directly to the Society. Completion of an application form is not essential.
Closing Date: January 15th
Funding: Private
No. of awards given last year: 16
No. of applicants last year: 25
Additional Information: Grants for the organization of conferences or colloquia and symposia will only be considered in exceptional circumstances.

SOCIETY FOR THE PSYCHOLOGICAL STUDY OF SOCIAL ISSUES (SPSSI)

SPSSI Central Office, 208 I Street NE, Washington, DC, 20002, United States of America
Tel: (1) 202 675 6956
Fax: (1) 202 675 6902
Email: spssi@spssi.org
Website: www.spssi.org
Contact: Dr Shari Miles, Executive Director

The Society for the Psychological Study of Social Issues (SPSSI) is an interdisciplinary, international organization of over 3,000 social scientists who share an interest in research on the psychological aspects of important social issues. The Society's goals are to increase the understanding of social issues through research and its dissemination and to support policy efforts consistent with such research.

Clara Mayo Grants

Subjects: Aspects of sexism, racism and prejudice.
Purpose: To support the writing of a Master's thesis or predissertation research.
Eligibility: Open to individuals who have matriculated in graduate programmes in psychology, applied social science and related disciplines.
Level of Study: Graduate, postgraduate
Type: Research grant
Value: Up to US$1,000
Frequency: Annual
Country of Study: United States of America
No. of awards offered: Varies
Application Procedure: Applicants must send five copies of a cover sheet with the title of the thesis and address details, an abstract of no more than 100 words, a budget request and other relevant details. Further details can be found on the website.
Closing Date: May 1st or October 1st
Funding: Private
No. of awards given last year: 5

Gordon Allport Intergroup Relations Prize

Subjects: Intergroup relations.
Purpose: To recognize the best paper or article of the year on intergroup relations.
Eligibility: Open to non-members, as well as members of SPSSI. Graduate students are especially urged to submit papers.
Level of Study: Postgraduate, doctorate, graduate, postdoctorate
Type: Prize
Value: US$1,000
Frequency: Annual
Country of Study: Any country
No. of awards offered: 1
Application Procedure: Applicants must submit four copies of their entry. Entries can be either papers published during the current year or unpublished manuscripts. Applicants must include contact information for all authors. Entries cannot be returned.
Closing Date: November 1st
No. of awards given last year: 1
Additional Information: Originality of the contribution, whether theoretical or empirical, will be given special weight. The research area of

intergroup relations includes such dimensions as age, sex and socio-economic status, as well as race.

Louise Kidder Early Career Award

Subjects: Social and community psychology.
Purpose: To recognize social issues researchers who have made substantial contributions to the field early in their careers.
Eligibility: Nominees should be social issues investigators who have made substantial contributions to social issues research within 5 years of receiving a graduate degree and who have demonstrated the potential to continue such contributions.
Level of Study: Professional development, postdoctorate
Type: Award
Value: US$500 plus plaque
Frequency: Annual
Country of Study: Any country
No. of awards offered: 1
Application Procedure: Applicants must send five copies of a covering letter stating the nominee's accomplishments to date and future contributions, a curriculum vitae and three letters of support. For full details visit the website.
Closing Date: June 1st
Funding: Private
No. of awards given last year: 1

Otto Klineberg Intercultural and International Relations Award

Subjects: Intercultural and international relations.
Purpose: To recognize the best paper or article of the year.
Eligibility: Open to non-members, as well as members of SPSSI. Graduate students are especially urged to submit papers. The originality of the contribution, whether theoretical or empirical, will be given special weight.
Level of Study: Graduate, doctorate, postdoctorate, postgraduate
Type: Prize
Value: US$1,000
Frequency: Annual
Country of Study: Any country
No. of awards offered: 1
Application Procedure: Applicants must submit five copies of their entry. Entries can be either papers published in the current year or unpublished manuscripts. Applicants must include contact details for all authors. Entries cannot be returned. Further details can be found on the website.
Closing Date: February 15th
Funding: Private

SPSSI Applied Social Issues Internship Program

Subjects: The application of social science principles to social issues in co-operation with a community, city or state government organization, public interest group or other non-profit entity.
Purpose: To encourage intervention projects, non-partisan advocacy projects, applied research and writing and implementing policy.
Eligibility: Open to graduate students and 1st year postdoctorates in psychology, applied social science and related disciplines. Applicants must be SPSSI members.
Level of Study: Postgraduate, postdoctorate, graduate
Type: Grant
Value: US$300–2,500 to cover research costs, community organizing, Summer stipends, etc.
Frequency: Annual
Country of Study: Any country
No. of awards offered: Varies
Application Procedure: Applicants must submit an application consisting of three copies of a two- to five-page proposal including a budget, a short curriculum vitae, a letter from a faculty sponsor or supervisor of the project, including a statement concerning protection for participants if relevant and a letter from an organizational sponsor, though this is waived if the applicant is proposing to organize a group. Further details can be found on the website.
Closing Date: March 31st
Funding: Private

SPSSI Grants-in-Aid Program

Subjects: Scientific research in social problem areas related to the basic interests and goals of SPSSI and particularly those that are not likely to receive support from traditional sources.
Eligibility: Open to students at the dissertation stage of a graduate career or beyond.
Level of Study: Graduate, postgraduate, doctorate, postdoctorate
Type: Grant
Value: Up to US$2,000. Up to US$1,000 for graduate students that must be matched by the student's university. Funds are not normally provided for travel to conventions, travel or living expenses while conducting research, stipends of principal investigators or costs associated with manuscript preparation
Country of Study: Any country
No. of awards offered: Varies
Application Procedure: Applicants must submit four copies of a statement that includes a cover sheet stating the title of the proposal, the contact details of the investigator, an abstract of 100 words or less summarizing the proposed research, project purposes, theoretical rationale and specific procedures to be employed, the relevance of research to SPSSI goals and grants-in-aid criteria, a curriculum vitae of the investigator and the specific amount requested including a budget. A faculty sponsor's recommendation must be provided if the investigator is a graduate student as support is seldom awarded to students who have not yet reached the dissertation stage. A recommended length for the entire proposal is five to seven double-spaced, typed pages. Further information can be found on the website.
Closing Date: October 1st and May 1st
Funding: Private
Contributor: The Sophie and Shirley Cohen Memorial Fund and membership contributions

SPSSI Social Issues Dissertation Award

Subjects: Social issues in psychology or in a social science with psychological subject matter.
Eligibility: Open to doctoral dissertations on a relevant topic accepted between March 1st of the year preceding that of application and March 1st of the year of application.
Level of Study: Postgraduate
Type: Prize
Value: First prize of US$750 and a second prize of US$500
Frequency: Annual
Country of Study: Any country
No. of awards offered: 2
Application Procedure: Applicants must visit the website for details.
Closing Date: May 1st
Funding: Private
No. of awards given last year: 2

THE SOCIETY FOR THE SCIENTIFIC STUDY OF SEXUALITY (SSSS)

PO Box 416, Allentown, PA 18105, United States of America
Tel: (1) 319 895 8407
Fax: (1) 319 895 6203
Email: thesociety@sexscience.org
Website: www.sexscience.org
Contact: Mr David L Fleming, Executive Director

The Society for the Scientific Study of Sexuality (SSSS) is an international organization dedicated to the advancement of knowledge about sexuality. The Society brings together an interdisciplinary group of professionals who believe in the importance of both production of quality research and the clinical, educational and social applications of research related to all aspects of sexuality.

FSSS Grants-in-Aid Program

Subjects: Human sexuality.
Type: Grant
Value: US$ 1,000
Length of Study: 1 year
Frequency: Annual

No. of awards offered: Varies
Application Procedure: Contact the society.
Closing Date: No deadline for applications.
Funding: Foundation
Contributor: The foundation for the scientific Study of sexuality
Additional Information: Preference will be given to research areasunlikely to receive support from other sources.

SSSS Student Research Grants

Subjects: Human sexuality.
Eligibility: Applicants must be a member of the SSSS.
Level of Study: Doctorate, postgraduate
Type: Scholarship
Value: US$ 1,000
Length of Study: 1 year
Frequency: Annual
No. of awards offered: 2
Application Procedure: Contact the society.
Closing Date: February 1st
Funding: Foundation
Contributor: The Foundation for the Scientific study of sexuality

SOCIETY FOR THE STUDY OF FRENCH HISTORY

Department of Modern History, University of St. Andrews, St Watharine's Lodge, The Scores, Saint Andrews, FIFE WY16 9AL, Scotland
Tel: (44) 1334 462 886
Fax: (44) 1334 462 927
Email: gr30@st-andrews.ac.uk
Website: www.frenchhistorysociety.ac.uk
Contact: Dr Guy Rowlands, Secretary

The Society for the Study of French History was established to encourage research into French history. It offers a forum where scholars, teachers and students can meet and exchange ideas. It also offers bursaries for research and conferences to postgraduates registered in the United Kingdom undertaking research into French history.

Society for the Study of French History Bursaries

Subjects: Any aspect of French history.
Purpose: To enable postgraduates to undertake research in French history.
Eligibility: Open to postgraduate students registered at a United Kingdom university. Students at any level at postgraduate study may apply, provided that their dissertation is on some aspect of French history.
Level of Study: Postgraduate
Type: Bursary
Value: Up to UK £500
Length of Study: Dependent on the project for which the award is given
Frequency: Annual
Country of Study: France
No. of awards offered: Approx. 8
Application Procedure: Applicants must give details of the research being pursued and the use to which the money would be put, along with the names of two referees. There is no application form and applications by email are acceptable. Applicants are responsible for writing to their referees. Successful applicants will be required to submit, in the first instance, a brief outline of their research proposal and then, after the research trip, a synopsis of their findings, both for publication in the Society's bulletin, *The French Historian.*
Closing Date: February 1st
Funding: Private
Contributor: The Society for the Study of French History
No. of awards given last year: 5
No. of applicants last year: 5

THE SOCIETY FOR THEATRE RESEARCH

The Theatre Museum, 1E Tavistock Street, London, WC2E 7PA, England
Email: e.cottis@btinternet.com
Website: www.str.org.uk
Contact: Chairman, Research Awards Sub-Committee

The Society for Theatre Research was founded in 1948 for all interested in the history and technique of British theatre. It publishes annually one or more books, newsletters and three issues of the journal *Theatre Notebook*, holds lecture meetings and other events, and gives an annual book prize as well as grants for theatre research.

Society for Theatre Research Awards

Subjects: The history and practice of the British theatre, including music hall, opera, dance and other associated performing arts.
Purpose: To aid research into the history and practice of British theatre.
Eligibility: Applicants should normally be 18 years of age or over, but there is no other restriction on their status, nationality or the location of the research.
Level of Study: Unrestricted
Value: From a total of approx. UK £4,000. Major awards are normally UK £1,000–1,500 and other awards are normally UK £200–500
Frequency: Annual
Country of Study: Any country
No. of awards offered: 2 major awards and a number of lesser awards
Application Procedure: Applicants must write to the Chairman of the Research Awards Sub-Committee after October 1st of the preceding year for an application form and guidance notes. All applications and enquiries must be made by post to the Society's accommodation address.
Closing Date: February 1st
Funding: Private
Contributor: Members' subscriptions, donations and bequests
No. of awards given last year: 9
No. of applicants last year: 25
Additional Information: While applications will need to show evidence of the value of the research and a scholarly approach, they are by no means restricted to professional academics. Many awards, including major ones, have previously been made to theatre practitioners and amateur researchers who are encouraged to apply. The Society also welcomes proposals, which in their execution extend methods and techniques of historiography. In coming to its decisions, the Society will consider the progress already made by the applicants and the possible availability of other grants.

SOCIETY OF APOTHECARIES OF LONDON

Black Friars Lane, London, EC4V 6EJ, England
Tel: (44) 20 7236 1189
Fax: (44) 20 7329 3177
Email: clerk@apothecaries.org
Website: www.apothecaries.org
Contact: Wallington Smith, Clerk

Gillson Scholarship in Pathology

Subjects: Pathology.
Purpose: To encourage original research in any branch of pathology.
Eligibility: Open to candidates under 35 years of age who are either licenciates or freemen of the Society, or who obtain the licence or the freedom within 6 months of election to the scholarship.
Level of Study: Postgraduate
Type: Scholarship
Value: UK £1,800 in total. Payments are made twice annually for the duration of the scholarship
Length of Study: 3 years, renewable for a second term of 3 years
Frequency: Every 3 years
Country of Study: Any country

No. of awards offered: 1
Application Procedure: Applicants must submit two testimonials and present evidence of their attainments and capabilities as shown by any papers already published, and a detailed record of any pathological work already done. Candidates should also state where the research will be undertaken.
Closing Date: December 1st
Funding: Private
Additional Information: Preference is given to the candidate who is engaged in the teaching of medical science or in its research. Scholars are required to submit an interim report at the end of the first 6 months of tenure, and a complete report 1 month prior to the end of the 3rd year. Any published results should also be submitted to the Society.

SOCIETY OF ARCHITECTURAL HISTORIANS (SAH)

1365 North Astor Street, Chicago, Illionis 60610-2144, United States of America
Tel: (1) 312 573 1365
Fax: (1) 312 573 1141

The SAH is an international not-for-profit membership organization that promotes the study and presentation of the built environment worldwide.

Annual Meeting Fellowship–Beverly Willis Architectural Foundation Travel Fellowship

Subjects: Gender issues in the history of architecture, landscape architecture and associated fields.
Purpose: To advance the status of women in architecture.
Eligibility: Applicants must be members of the SAH.
Level of Study: Doctorate
Type: Fellowship
Value: US$1,500 travel stipend
Frequency: Annual
Country of Study: United States of America
No. of awards offered: 1
Application Procedure: Apply online.
Closing Date: November 1st

For further information contact:

1365 N. Astor Street, Chicago, Il 60610
Email: ksturm@sah.org
Contact: Kathy Sturm, Manager, Meetings and Tours

Carroll LV Meeks Fellowship

Subjects: Architectural history.
Purpose: To enable an outstanding student to participate in the annual SAH domestic study tour. The location of this is different every year.
Eligibility: Open to SAH members who are students engaged in graduate work in architecture, or architectural history, city planning or urban history, landscape or the history of landscape design.
Level of Study: Postdoctorate, postgraduate
Type: Fellowship
Value: Covers all expenses included in the cost of the four.
Frequency: Annual
Country of Study: Any country
No. of awards offered: 1
Application Procedure: Applicants must complete an application form, available on request by writing to SAH for guidelines or visiting the SAH website.
Closing Date: The date changes each year, please contact the organization
Funding: Commercial, private
No. of awards given last year: 1
No. of applicants last year: 4

Edilia and Francois-Auguste de Montequin Fellowship

Subjects: Spanish, Portugese and Ibero-American architecture.
Eligibility: Applicants must be members of the SAH.
Level of Study: Doctorate, postdoctorate
Type: Fellowship
Value: US$2,000–6,000 stipend
Length of Study: 1 year
Frequency: Annual
No. of awards offered: 2
Application Procedure: Apply online.
Closing Date: October 15th
Funding: Foundation
Contributor: The Auguste de Montequin Foundation

Edilia and François-Auguste de Montequin Fellowship in Iberian and Latin American Architecture

Subjects: Spanish, Portuguese or Ibero American architecture, including colonial architecture produced by the Spaniards in the Philippines and what is today the United States of America.
Purpose: To fund travel for research into Spanish, Portuguese and Ibero American architecture.
Eligibility: Open to SAH members who are junior Scholars, including graduate students.
Level of Study: Postgraduate, postdoctorate, doctorate
Type: Fellowship
Value: US$2,000 for junior scholars awarded each year and US$6,000 for senior scholars offered every two years
Frequency: Annual for junior scholars and every 2 years for senior scholars
Country of Study: Any country
No. of awards offered: 2
Application Procedure: Applicants must complete an application form, available on request by writing to SAH for guidelines or visiting the SAH website.
Closing Date: November 15th
Funding: Private
No. of awards given last year: 1
No. of applicants last year: 5

Keepers Preservation Education Fund Fellowship

Subjects: Historic preservation.
Purpose: To enable a graduate student to attend the annual meeting of the Society, held each April.
Eligibility: Open to members of any nationality who are currently engaged in the study of historic preservation.
Level of Study: Postdoctorate, postgraduate, doctorate
Type: Fellowship
Value: US$1,000 travel stipend and complimentary meeting registration
Frequency: Annual
Country of Study: Any country
No. of awards offered: 1
Application Procedure: Applicants must write to SAH for application guidelines or download an application from the Society's website.
Closing Date: November 15th
Funding: Private
No. of awards given last year: 1
No. of applicants last year: 7

Rosann Berry Fellowship

Subjects: Architectural history or an allied field, eg. city planning, landscape architecture, decorative arts or historic preservation.
Purpose: To enable a student engaged in advanced graduate study to attend the annual meeting of the Society.
Eligibility: Open to persons of any nationality who have been members of SAH for at least one year prior to the meeting, and who are currently engaged in advanced graduate study, normally beyond the Master's level, that involves some aspect of the history of architecture or of one of the fields closely allied to it.
Level of Study: Postgraduate, postdoctorate
Type: Fellowship
Value: US$1,000 travel stipend and complimentary meeting registration
Frequency: Annual
Country of Study: Any country
No. of awards offered: 1

Application Procedure: Applicants must complete an application form, available on request by writing to SAH for guidelines or visiting the SAH website.
Closing Date: November 15th
Funding: Private
No. of awards given last year: 1
No. of applicants last year: 15

SAH Fellowships for Senior Scholars

Subjects: European artistic traditions before 1800.
Eligibility: Applicants must be members of the SAH.
Level of Study: Doctorate, postdoctorate
Type: Fellowship
Value: US$1,000 travel stipend
Frequency: Annual
Country of Study: United States of America
No. of awards offered: 10
Application Procedure: Apply online.

SAH Study Tour Fellowship

Subjects: South Indian architecture of historical significance.
Eligibility: Applicants must be members of the SAH.
Level of Study: Doctorate
Type: Fellowship
Length of Study: 30–40 days
Frequency: Annual
Country of Study: India
No. of awards offered: Varies
Application Procedure: Contact the Society.
Closing Date: December 28th

Sally Kress Tompkins Fellowship

Subjects: Architectural history and historic preservation.
Purpose: To enable an architectural history student to work as an intern on an Historic American Buildings Survey project, during the summer.
Eligibility: Open to architectural history and historic preservation students.
Level of Study: Postdoctorate, doctorate, postgraduate
Type: Fellowship
Value: US$10,000
Length of Study: 12 weeks
Frequency: Annual
Country of Study: United States of America
No. of awards offered: 1
Application Procedure: Applicants must submit an application including a sample of work, a letter of recommendation from a faculty member, and a United States Government Standard Form 171, available from HABS or most United States government personnel offices. Applications should be sent to the Sally Kress Tompkins Fellowship. Applicants not selected for the Tomkins Fellowship will be considered for other HABS Summer employment opportunities. For more information, please contact Catherine C Laudie, HABS/HAER Co-ordinator.
Closing Date: February 1st
Funding: Government
No. of awards given last year: 1
No. of applicants last year: 7

For further information contact:

The Sally Kress Tompkins Fellowship, c/o HABS/HAER, National Park Service, 1849C Street NW, Washington, DC, 2270-20240, United States of America

Samuel H. Kress Foundation Fellowships for Speakers

Subjects: Nationally significant buildings and sites.
Eligibility: Applicants must be members of the SAH.
Level of Study: Doctorate, postdoctorate
Type: Fellowship
Value: US$10,000 stipend
Length of Study: 12 weeks
Frequency: Annual
Study Establishment: HABS Washington Office
Country of Study: United States of America
Application Procedure: Apply online.
Closing Date: February 1st
Funding: Foundation
Contributor: The Historic American Building Survey (HABS)

Scott Opler Fellowships for New Scholars

Subjects: Architectural history.
Eligibility: Applicants must be members of the SAH.
Level of Study: Postdoctorate, postgraduate
Type: Fellowship
Value: A full 1 year membership to the Society of Architectural Historians
Length of Study: 1 year
Frequency: Annual
Country of Study: United States of America
No. of awards offered: 1
Closing Date: November 15th

For further information contact:

Society of Architectural Historians, 1365 N. Astor Street, Chicago, IL 60610
Fax: 312 573 1141
Contact: Kathy Sturm, Manager, Meetings and Tours

Spiro Kostof Annual Meeting Fellowship

Subjects: Architectural history.
Purpose: To enable an advanced graduate student in architectural history to attend the annual meeting of the Society of Architectural Historians.
Eligibility: Open to doctoral candidates only who have been members of the SAH for at least one year.
Level of Study: Predoctorate, doctorate
Type: Fellowship
Value: US$500
Frequency: Annual
No. of awards offered: 1
Application Procedure: Applicants must write for an application form, available after June 1st by mail or by visiting the website.
Closing Date: November 15th
Funding: Commercial, private
Contributor: The Society of Architectural Historians
No. of awards given last year: 1
No. of applicants last year: 15

THE SOCIETY OF AUTHORS

84 Drayton Gardens, London, SW10 9SB, England
Tel: (44) 020 7373 6642
Fax: (44) 020 7373 5768
Email: info@societyofauthors.net
Contact: The Administration Office

The Society of Authors is a non-profit making organization, founded in 1884, to project the rights and further the interests of authors.

Authors' Foundation Grant

Subjects: Authorship.
Purpose: To provide grants to writers to assist them while writing books.
Eligibility: To apply the author must meet either of these conditions: the author has been commissioned to write a work of fiction, poetry or non-fiction and needs funding. The author is without contractual commitment by a publisher but has least one book published already.
Level of Study: Professional development
Type: Grant
Value: UK £1,000–4,000
Length of Study: 1 year
Frequency: Annual
Country of Study: United Kingdom
Application Procedure: Contact Dorothy Sym at the Authors' Foundation.

Closing Date: April 30th
Funding: Foundation
Contributor: The Authors' Foundation
Additional Information: Editors, translators and screenwriters are not eligible.

Elizabeth Longford Grants

Subjects: Historical biography.
Level of Study: Professional development
Type: Grant
Value: UK £2,500
Frequency: Every 6 months
Country of Study: United Kingdom
Application Procedure: Contact Dorothy Sym at the Authors' Foundation.
Closing Date: April 30th
Funding: Private
Contributor: Flora Fraser and Peter Soros

Great Britain Sasakawa Foundation Grants

Subjects: Authorship relating to Japanese culture or society.
Eligibility: Preference will be given to authors whose work helps to interpret modern Japan to the English-speaking world.
Level of Study: Professional development
Type: Grant
Value: UK £2,500
Length of Study: 1 year
Frequency: Annual
Country of Study: United Kingdom
Application Procedure: Contact Dorothy Sym at the Authors' Foundation.
Closing Date: April 30th
Funding: Foundation
Contributor: Sasakawa Foundation

K. Blundell Trust Grant

Subjects: Authorship.
Purpose: To support British cultures who need funding for important research, travel or other expenditure.
Eligibility: Applicants must be British by birth, resident in the UK, under the age of 40 and their work must contribute to the greater understanding of existing social and economic organization.
Level of Study: Professional development
Type: Grant
Value: UK £1,000–4,000
Length of Study: 1 year
Frequency: Annual
Country of Study: United Kingdom
Application Procedure: See the website for guidelines; submissions by fax or email are not acceptable.
Closing Date: April 30th
Funding: Trusts
Contributor: K. Blundell Trust
Additional Information: No author may apply twice to the Trust within one twelve-month period; grants will not be awarded to cover publication costs.

Michael Meyer Award

Subjects: Authorship.
Level of Study: Professional development
Type: Grant
Frequency: Annual
Country of Study: United Kingdom
No. of awards offered: 1
Application Procedure: Contact Dorothy Sym at the Authors' Foundation.
Closing Date: April 30th
Funding: Trusts
Contributor: Michael Meyer

SOCIETY OF CHILDREN'S BOOK WRITERS AND ILLUSTRATORS (SCBWI)

8271 Beverly Boulevard, Los Angeles, CA 90048,
United States of America
Tel: (1) 323 782 1010
Fax: (1) 323 782 1892
Email: scbwi@scbwi.org
Website: www.scbwi.org
Contact: Mr Stephen Mooser, President

The Society of Children's Book Writers and Illustrators (SCBWI) is an organization of 19,000 writers, illustrators, editors, agents and publishers of children's books, television, film and multimedia.

Barbara Karlin Grant

Subjects: Children's picture books.
Purpose: To assist picture book writers in the completion of a specific project.
Eligibility: Open to both full and associate members of the Society who have never had a picture book published. The grant is not available for a project for which there is already a contract.
Level of Study: Unrestricted
Type: Grant
Value: The full grant is US$1,500 and the runner-up grant is US$500
Frequency: Annual
Country of Study: Any country
No. of awards offered: 1
Application Procedure: Applicants must write for details.
Closing Date: May 15th
Funding: Private
No. of awards given last year: 2
No. of applicants last year: 75

Don Freeman Memorial Grant-in-Aid

Subjects: Children's picture books.
Purpose: To enable picture-book artists to further their understanding, training and work in the picture-book genre.
Eligibility: Open to both full and associate members of the Society who, as artists, seriously intend to make picture books their chief contribution to the field of children's literature.
Level of Study: Unrestricted
Type: Grant
Value: The full grant is US$1,500 and the runner-up grant is US$500
Frequency: Annual
Country of Study: Any country
No. of awards offered: 2
Application Procedure: Applicants must submit an application to the Society. Receipt of the application will be acknowledged.
Closing Date: Application requests should be submitted by June 15th and completed applications should be submitted by February 10th
Funding: Private
No. of awards given last year: 2
No. of applicants last year: 48

SCBWI General Work-in-Progress Grant

Subjects: Children's literature.
Purpose: To assist children's book writers in the completion of a specific project.
Eligibility: Open to both full and associate members of the Society. The grant is not available for a project on which there is already a contract. Recipients of previous grants are not eligible to apply for any further SCBWI grants.
Level of Study: Unrestricted
Type: Grant
Value: The full grant is US$1,500 and the runner-up grant is US$500
Frequency: Annual
Country of Study: Any country
No. of awards offered: 1 full grant and 1 runner-up grant
Application Procedure: Applicants must write for details.
Closing Date: May 1st
Funding: Private

No. of awards given last year: 2
No. of applicants last year: 123

SCBWI Grant for a Contemporary Novel for Young People

Subjects: Children's literature.
Purpose: To assist children's book writers in the completion of a specific project.
Eligibility: Open to both full and associate members of the Society. The grant is not available for a project on which there is already a contract. Recipients of previous grants are not eligible to apply for any further SCBWI Grants.
Level of Study: Unrestricted
Type: Grant
Value: The full grant is US$1,500 and the runner-up grant is US$500
Frequency: Annual
Country of Study: Any country
No. of awards offered: 1 full grant and 1 runner-up grant
Application Procedure: Applicants must write for details.
Closing Date: May 1st
Funding: Private
No. of awards given last year: 2
No. of applicants last year: 110

SCBWI Grant for Unpublished Authors

Subjects: Children's literature.
Purpose: To assist children's book writers in the completion of a specific project.
Eligibility: Open to both full and associate members of the Society who have never had a book published. The grant is not available for a project on which there is already a contract. Recipients of previous grants are not eligible to apply for any further SCBWI Grants.
Level of Study: Unrestricted
Type: Grant
Value: The full grant is US$1,500 and the runner-up grant is US$500
Frequency: Annual
Country of Study: Any country
No. of awards offered: 1 full grant and 1 runner-up grant
Closing Date: May 1st
Funding: Private
No. of awards given last year: 2
No. of applicants last year: 45

SCBWI Nonfiction Research Grant

Subjects: Children's literature.
Purpose: To assist children's book writers in the completion of a specific project.
Eligibility: Open to both full and associate members of the Society. The grant is not available for a project on which there is already a contract. Recipients of previous grants are not eligible to apply for any further SCBWI Grants.
Level of Study: Unrestricted
Type: Grant
Value: The full grant is US$1,500 and the runner-up grant is US$500
Frequency: Annual
Country of Study: Any country
No. of awards offered: 1 full grant and 1 runner-up grant
Application Procedure: Applicants must write for details.
Closing Date: May 1st
Funding: Private
No. of awards given last year: 1
No. of applicants last year: 75

SOCIETY OF EXPLORATION GEOPHYSICISTS FOUNDATION (SEG)

SEG Foundation P.O. 702740, Tulsa, OK 74170-2740, United States of America
Tel: (1) 918 497 5500
Fax: (1) 918 497 5560
Email: scholarships@seg.org
Website: www.seg.org
Contact: SEG Scholarship Committee

The Society of Exploration Geophysicists Foundation (SEG) began a programme of encouraging the establishment of scholarship funds by companies and individuals in the field of geophysics in 1956. In 1963, the Foundation's activities were expanded to include grants-in-aid.

SEG Scholarships

Subjects: Applied geophysics and related fields.
Purpose: To encourage careers in applied of geophysics and related fields.
Eligibility: Open to citizens of any country who are entering undergraduate or graduate level and have above average grades and an aptitude for physics, mathematics, and geology.
Level of Study: Unrestricted
Type: Scholarship
Value: US$500–14,000 per academic year. Average awards are approx. US$1,500
Length of Study: 1 academic year, may be eligible for renewal
Frequency: Annual
Country of Study: Any country
No. of awards offered: Varies
Application Procedure: Applicants must submit a completed application form accompanied by three years of transcripts and two letters of recommendation from the mathematics and science faculty.
Closing Date: February 1st of the year in which the award is made
Funding: Corporation, private, trusts, commercial, individuals
No. of awards given last year: 136
No. of applicants last year: 370
Additional Information: Approximately US$200,000 given in scholarship to 100+ students annually.

SOCIETY OF ORTHOPAEDIC MEDICINE

PO Box 223, Patchway, Bristol, BS32 4XD, England
Tel: (44) 14 5461 0255
Email: admin@soc-ortho-med.org
Website: www.soc-ortho-med.org
Contact: Administrative Director

The Society of Orthopaedic Medicine is a non-profit making organization offering grants for work within musculoskeletal medicine.

SOM Research Grant

Subjects: Musculoskeletal medicine.
Purpose: To assist those undertaking programmes of study that will increase knowledge in the field and enhance their professional development.
Eligibility: Applications are considered from those who may be undertaking a research degree leading to an MPhil, a research degree leading to a PhD/DProf, a pilot study or a presentation at a conference. Grants are also available for equipment. Must be member of society of Orthopaedic medicine.
Level of Study: Predoctorate, postdoctorate, professional development, graduate
Value: Up to UK £5,000. UK £2,000 of this allocation will be available in the form of smaller grants of up to UK £500
Frequency: Annual
Country of Study: United Kingdom
No. of awards offered: Varies according to funds
Application Procedure: Applicants must complete an application form available from the organization.
Closing Date: Applications are accepted all year round
No. of awards given last year: 5
No. of applicants last year: 8

SOCIETY OF WOMEN ENGINEERS (SWE)

230 East Ohio Street, Suite 400, Chicago, IL, 60611, United States of America
Tel: (1) 312 596 5223
Fax: (1) 312 596 5252
Email: hq@swe.org
Website: www.swe.org
Contact: Ms Betty Shanahan, Executive Director

The Society of Women Engineers (SWE) was founded in 1950, and is a non-profit educational service organization. SWE is the driving force that establishes engineering as a highly desirable career aspiration for women. SWE empowers women to succeed and advance in those aspirations and be recognized for their life-changing contributions and achievements as engineers and leaders.

B K Krenzer Memorial Re-Entry Scholarship

Subjects: Engineering.
Purpose: To assist women in obtaining the credentials necessary to re-enter the job market as engineers.
Eligibility: Open to women who have been out of the job market as well as out of school for a minimum of 2 years. Recipients may be entering any year of an engineering programme, as full- or part-time students. Preference is given to graduate engineers desiring to return to the workforce following a period of temporary retirement.
Level of Study: Graduate, postgraduate, undergraduate
Type: Scholarship
Value: US$2,000
Frequency: Annual
Study Establishment: An ABET or CSB accredited programme
Country of Study: United States of America
No. of awards offered: 1
Application Procedure: Application forms are available from the website.
Closing Date: February 1st
Funding: Private
No. of awards given last year: 1

Lydia I Pickup Memorial Scholarship

Subjects: Engineering and computer science.
Purpose: To advance the applicant's career in engineering or computer science.
Eligibility: Open only to women majoring in engineering or computer science at a college or university with an ABET accredited programme.
Level of Study: Doctorate, graduate, undergraduate
Type: Scholarship
Value: US$2,000
Frequency: Annual
Country of Study: United States of America
No. of awards offered: 1
Application Procedure: Application forms are available from the website.
Closing Date: February 1st
Funding: Private
No. of awards given last year: 1

Olive Lynn Salembier Scholarship

Subjects: Engineering and computer science.
Purpose: To aid women who have been out of the engineering market and out of school to obtain the credentials necessary to re-enter the job market as an engineer.
Eligibility: Open to women who have not practised engineering or been enrolled in an engineering or other university or college programme in the past 2 years. Applicants must be citizens of the United States of America. Recipients may be entering any graduate year, including doctoral programmes, as full- or part-time students.
Level of Study: Graduate, doctorate, undergraduate
Type: Scholarship
Value: US$2,000
Frequency: Annual
Country of Study: United States of America
No. of awards offered: 1
Application Procedure: Application forms are available from the website.
Closing Date: February 1st
Funding: Private
No. of awards given last year: 1

SWE Caterpillar Scholarship

Subjects: Any engineering subject.
Purpose: To support women in engineering careers.
Eligibility: Applicants must be women engineering students and members of SWE in SWE regions C,D,H or I.
Level of Study: Doctorate, graduate, undergraduate
Type: Scholarship
Value: US$2,400
Frequency: Annual
Country of Study: United States of America
No. of awards offered: 3
Application Procedure: Application forms are available from the website.
Closing Date: February 1st
Funding: Commercial
Contributor: Caterpillar Inc.
No. of awards given last year: 3

SWE Electronics for Imaging Scholarship

Subjects: Engineering.
Purpose: To encourage women engineers to attain graduate engineering degrees.
Eligibility: Open only to women engineering students.
Level of Study: Doctorate, graduate, undergraduate
Type: Scholarship
Value: US$4,000
Frequency: Annual
Country of Study: United States of America
No. of awards offered: 4
Application Procedure: Application forms are available from the website.
Closing Date: February 1st
Funding: Commercial
Contributor: Electronics for Imaging
No. of awards given last year: 4

SWE General Motors Foundation Graduate Scholarship

Subjects: Mechanical engineering, electrical engineering, chemical engineering, industrial engineering, materials science and engineering or manufacturing engineering.
Purpose: To encourage women engineers to attain high levels of education and professional achievement.
Eligibility: Open only to women students entering the 1st year of a Master's degree programme. Applicants must have a career interest in the automotive industry or manufacturing, and have demonstrated leadership potential.
Level of Study: Graduate, postgraduate, doctorate
Type: Scholarship
Value: US$1,000, plus a travel grant of US$500 for each recipient to attend the SWE National Conference
Frequency: Annual
Study Establishment: See the website for list of schools
Country of Study: United States of America
No. of awards offered: 1
Application Procedure: Application forms are available from the website.
Closing Date: February 1st
Funding: Commercial
Contributor: General Motors Foundation
No. of awards given last year: 1

SWE Microsoft Corporation Scholarships

Subjects: Computer science and computer engineering.
Purpose: To encourage women engineers to attain a high level of education and professional achievement.
Eligibility: Open only to women majoring in engineering or computer science in a college or university with an ABET-accredited programme. Applicants must be citizens of the United States of America.
Level of Study: Graduate, undergraduate
Type: Scholarship
Value: US$2,500
Frequency: Annual
Study Establishment: A college or university
Country of Study: United States of America
No. of awards offered: 2

Application Procedure: Application forms are available from the website.
Closing Date: February 1st
Funding: Commercial
Contributor: The Microsoft Corporation
No. of awards given last year: 2
Additional Information: Further information is available on the website.

SWE Past Presidents Scholarships

Subjects: Engineering.
Eligibility: Open only to women majoring in engineering or computer science in a college or university with an ABET-accredited programme. United States of America citizenship is required.
Level of Study: Graduate, postgraduate, doctorate, undergraduate
Type: Scholarship
Value: US$1,500
Frequency: Annual
Country of Study: United States of America
No. of awards offered: 2
Application Procedure: Application forms are available from the website.
Closing Date: February 1st
Funding: Private
No. of awards given last year: 2

SWE-Clare Boothe Luce Program Scholarship

Subjects: Any engineering subject.
Purpose: To encourage and support women in careers as engineering faculty.
Eligibility: Open to women interested in a career in academia.
Level of Study: Doctorate, graduate
Type: Scholarship
Value: 1
Frequency: Annual
Country of Study: United States of America
No. of awards offered: 1
Application Procedure: Application forms are available from the website.
Closing Date: February 1st
Funding: Foundation
Contributor: Henry Luce Foundation
No. of awards given last year: 1

SWE/Bentley Graduate Merit Scholarship

Subjects: MBA.
Purpose: To pursue a full-time MBA at Bentley's McCallum Graduate School of Business.
Eligibility: African American, Latina, Asian or Native American women are especially eligible to apply.
Level of Study: MBA
Type: Scholarship
Value: US$12,600–63,000
Frequency: Annual
Study Establishment: The Bentley McCallum Graduate School of Business
Country of Study: United States of America
No. of awards offered: 1
Application Procedure: Application forms are available from the website.
Closing Date: February 1st
Funding: Private
Contributor: Bentley College
No. of awards given last year: 1

SOIL AND WATER CONSERVATION SOCIETY (SWCS)

945 SW Ankeny Road, Ankeny, Iowa 50023-9723,
United States of America
Tel: (1) 515 289 2331
Fax: (1) 515 289 1227
Email: sueann.lynes@swcs.org
Website: www.swcs.org

The Soil and Water Conservation Society (SWCS) fosters the science and the art of soil, water and related natural resource management to achieve sustainability. The SWCS promotes and practices an ethic recognizing the interdependence of people and the environment.

Donald A. Williams Soil Conservation Scholarship

Subjects: Conservation-related field.
Purpose: To improve technical and administrative competence.
Level of Study: Postgraduate
Type: Scholarship
Value: US$1,500
Length of Study: 1 year
Frequency: Annual
No. of awards offered: 1
Application Procedure: Apply online.

For further information contact:

945 SW Ankeny Road, Ankeny, Iowa, 50023-9723

The Kenneth E. Grant Scholarship

Subjects: Soil science, water science and related natural resource management.
Purpose: To actively promote multi-disciplinary research.
Level of Study: Postgraduate
Type: Scholarship
Value: US$1,300
Length of Study: 1 year
Frequency: Annual
No. of awards offered: 1
Application Procedure: Apply online.
Closing Date: February 13th

Melville H. Cohee Student Leader Conservation Scholarship

Subjects: National resource conservation.
Level of Study: Postgraduate
Type: Scholarship
Length of Study: 1 year
Frequency: Annual
No. of awards offered: 1
Application Procedure: Apply online.
Additional Information: Financial need will not be a factor in selection.

For further information contact:

945 SW Ankeny Road, Ankeny, Iowa, 50023-9723

SONS OF THE REPUBLIC OF TEXAS

1717 8th Street, Bay City, TX, 77414, United States of America
Tel: (1) 979 245 6644
Fax: (1) 979 244 3819
Email: srttexas@srttexas.org
Website: www.srttexas.org
Contact: Administrative Assistant

Sons of the Republic of Texas seeks to perpetuate the memory and spirit of the men and women who settled Texas and won its independence through great personal sacrifice and dedication to the cause of freedom.

Presidio La Bahia Award

Subjects: History.
Purpose: To promote the suitable preservation of relics, appropriate dissemination of data and research into Texas heritage, with particular emphasis on the Spanish colonial period.
Eligibility: Open to all persons interested in the Spanish colonial influence on Texas culture.
Level of Study: Unrestricted
Type: Award

Value: The 1st prize is a minimum of US$1,200, and the 2nd and 3rd prizes are the divided balance from the total amount available of US$2,000 at the discretion of the judges
Frequency: Annual
Study Establishment: Any suitable institution
Country of Study: Any country
No. of awards offered: 3
Application Procedure: Applicants must submit four copies of published writings to the office. Galley proofs are not acceptable.
Closing Date: Entries are accepted from June 1st to September 30th
Funding: Private
No. of awards given last year: 1
Additional Information: Research writings have, in the past, proved to be the most successful type of entry. However, consideration will be given to other literary forms, art, architecture and archaeological discovery. For projects other than writing, contestants should furnish a description of the proposed entry, so that the Chairman may issue specific instructions.

Summerfield G Roberts Award

Subjects: History.
Purpose: To encourage literary effort and research about historical events and personalities during the days of the Republic of Texas 1836–1846, and to stimulate interest in the period.
Eligibility: Open to all writers.
Level of Study: Unrestricted
Type: Award
Value: US$2,500
Frequency: Annual
Study Establishment: Any suitable institution
Country of Study: Any country
No. of awards offered: 1
Application Procedure: Manuscripts must be written or published during the calendar year for which the award is given. There is no word limit. No entry may be submitted more than one time. The manuscripts must be mailed (5 copies, for the use of the judges) to the General Office of the Sons of the Republic of Texas.
Closing Date: January 15th
Funding: Private
No. of awards given last year: 1
Additional Information: The award was made possible through the generosity of Mr and Mrs Summerfield G Roberts.

SOUTH AFRICAN COUNCIL FOR ENGLISH EDUCATION (SACEE)

PO Box 660, Pretoria, 0001, South Africa
Tel: (27) 12 429 8616
Fax: (27) 12 429 8616
Website: www.sacee.org.za
Contact: Ms Patricia Bootland, Administrative Secretary

The South African Council for English Education's (SACEE) mission statement is to support the teaching, learning and appreciation of English. They have branches throughout South Africa, and major national projects are the *English Alive* publication, English Olympiad, language challenge and plays festival.

Norah Taylor Bursary

Subjects: Speech training, oral communication and the teaching of English as a second language.
Purpose: To assist teachers to further their training.
Eligibility: Open to qualified teachers teaching English or other subjects in English, with years of postmatriculation study, and at least 4 years of teaching experience.
Level of Study: Unrestricted, postgraduate, professional development, graduate
Type: Bursary
Value: Varies, depending upon the type of course taken
Length of Study: Varies
Frequency: Annual
Study Establishment: Any educational institution (in South Africa)
Country of Study: South Africa
No. of awards offered: Varies
Application Procedure: Applicants must write for details. An application form, available from the Organization, must be completing.
Closing Date: July 31st of the year preceding that for which the bursary is required
Funding: Private
No. of awards given last year: 1
No. of applicants last year: 7
Additional Information: Applicants not conforming to the requirements cannot be considered and will not be replied to.

SACEE EX-PCE Bursary

Subjects: English and subjects in English, including literature, drama or radio.
Purpose: To assist teachers in service who wish to improve their qualifications and to assist those who wish to take up postgraduate study specializing in the English language.
Eligibility: Applicants who are not normally resident in the Pretoria area will not be considered for an award. Such applications will not be acknowledged.
Level of Study: Postgraduate
Type: Bursary
Value: Varies, depending upon type of course taken
Length of Study: Varies
Frequency: Annual
Study Establishment: Any academic institution
Country of Study: South Africa
No. of awards offered: Varies
Application Procedure: An application form must be completed.
Closing Date: July 31st of the year preceding that for which the bursary is required
Funding: Private
No. of awards given last year: 1
No. of applicants last year: 5

THE SOUTH AFRICAN INSTITUTE OF INTERNATIONAL AFFAIRS (SAIIA)

Jan Smuts House, PO Box 31596, Braamfontein, Johannesburg, 2017, South Africa
Tel: (27) 11 339 2021
Fax: (27) 11 339 2154
Email: saiiagen@global.co.za
Website: www.saiia.org.za
Contact: Mr Tom Wheeler, Chief Operating Officer

The South African Institute of International Affairs (SAIIA) is an independent, non-governmental foreign policy think tank, whose purpose is to encourage wider and more informed interest in international affairs and public education and to focus on policy-relevant research.

SAIIA Bradlow Fellowship

Subjects: Social and behavioural sciences.
Purpose: To provide travel costs and a stipend to enable a senior scholar to reside at the Institute in order to research a subject of importance to South Africa's international relations.
Eligibility: Open to senior scholars.
Level of Study: Research
Type: Fellowship
Value: The stipend covers living expenses and a return economy-class airfare from the candidate's place of residence
Length of Study: 4–6 months
Frequency: Annual
Study Establishment: SAIIA
Country of Study: South Africa
No. of awards offered: 1
Application Procedure: Applicants must send a curriculum vitae including a short research proposal of not more than 1,000 words to the Director of Studies.
Funding: Private
Contributor: The Bradlow Foundation
No. of awards given last year: 1

SAIIA Konrad Adenauer Foundation Research Internship

Subjects: Politics, international relations, journalism and economics.
Purpose: To enable research interns to enroll at the University of Witwatersrand for a Master's degree by coursework while simultaneously working at SAIIA.
Eligibility: Open to South African citizens under 30 years of age.
Level of Study: Postgraduate
Type: Internship
Length of Study: 10 months
Frequency: Annual
Study Establishment: SAIIA and the University of Witwatersrand
Country of Study: South Africa
No. of awards offered: 3
Application Procedure: Applicants must send a curriculum vitae, names and contact details of three referees, letter of motivation, outline of research interests in the field of international relations, three written references, June results and academic transcripts of previous degree's and one example of written work not exceeding 3,000 words on a topic of choice.
Closing Date: October 8th
Funding: Foundation
Contributor: Konrad Adenauer Foundation
No. of awards given last year: 2
No. of applicants last year: 32

For further information contact:

Email: grobbelaarn@saiia.wits.ac.za

SOUTHDOWN TRUST

Holmbush, 64 High Street, Findon, West Sussex, BN14 0SY, England
Contact: Mr John G Wyatt

The Southdown Trust is a small charity that gives limited help to individuals for educational purposes.

Southdown Trust Awards

Subjects: All subjects except law, drama and music, dance, journalism, sociology, women's studies, business studies, arts, sports, IT, counselling, peace studies, Educational costs only supported. Grants not made for equipment such as computers.
Purpose: To encourage personal initiative, education and concern for others.
Eligibility: Open mainly to United Kingdom citizens but other nationalities are considered.
Value: Varies, usually UK £25–500
Frequency: Varies depending on funds available
Country of Study: United Kingdom
No. of awards offered: Varies
Application Procedure: Applicants must write giving full details and include a stamped addressed envelope. All letters must be signed.
Closing Date: May 1st, November 1st
Funding: Private
No. of awards given last year: 106
No. of applicants last year: 2,000

SOUTHEAST EUROPE SOCIETY

Wiedenmayerstrasse 49, D-80538 Munich, Germany
Tel: (49) 89 212 1540
Fax: (49) 89 228 9469
Email: suedosteuropa-gesellschaft@t-online.de
Website: www.suedosteuropa-gesellschaft.com

Southeast Europe Society Short-Term Research Visits

Subjects: Economics.
Purpose: To support research trips that will allow scholarship holders to study in libraries and archives and to contact academic institutions in Germany.
Eligibility: Young doctoral candidates, habilitation candidates, and research institute staff from SouthEast European countries, no older than 40 years of age. The Foundation particularly supports young academics from countries of SouthEast Europe like Albania, Bosnia and Herzegovina, Bulgaria, Croatia, Greece, the Federal Republic of Macedonia, Moldavia, Romania, Slovak Republic, Slovenia, Turkey, Hungary and Cyprus.
Level of Study: Doctorate, research
Type: Research
Value: €50 per day. Travel expenses are not paid additionally
Length of Study: Up to 4 weeks (extension not possible)
Study Establishment: Libraries, archives, academic institutions
Country of Study: Germany
Application Procedure: Applications need not be submitted on a special form.
Closing Date: There are no firm application deadlines

SOUTHERN AFRICAN MUSIC RIGHTS ORGANIZATION (SAMRO) ENDOWMENT FOR THE NATIONAL ARTS

PO Box 31609, Braamfontein, 2017, South Africa
Tel: (27) 11 489 5000
Fax: (27) 11 403 1934
Website: www.samro.org.za
Contact: J C Otto, Liaison & Research Officer

Southern African Music Rights Organization (SAMRO) is Southern Africa's society of composers and lyricists, administering the performing, transmission and broadcasting rights in the musical works of its members and the members of its affiliated societies. Through the SAMRO Endowment for the National Arts (SENA), it currently supports music study at home and abroad for citizens of South Africa, Botswana, Lesotho and Swaziland.

SAMRO Intermediate Bursaries for Composition Study In Southern Africa

Subjects: Music.
Purpose: To support music composition study as a major subject in either the serious classical or jazz popular music genres.
Eligibility: Open to citizens of South Africa, Botswana, Lesotho and Swaziland who have met the requirements for proceeding to the 3rd, 4th or honours year of a senior undergraduate degree or equivalent diploma course. Applicants must have been born after February 15th, 1973. For those entering any year of a Master's or doctoral degree, the age limit is 32. Older students are considered in special circumstances.
Level of Study: Postgraduate
Type: Bursary
Value: Rand 9,000 for 3rd, 4th and honours year students and Rand 6,000 for Master's or doctoral degrees.
Length of Study: 1 year
Frequency: Annual
Study Establishment: A university, institute of technology or other recognized statutory institute of tertiary education approved by the trustees
Country of Study: South Africa, Botswana, Lesotho, or Swaziland
No. of awards offered: 10
Application Procedure: Applicants must complete an application form.
Closing Date: February 15th
Funding: Private
Contributor: SAMRO
No. of awards given last year: 3
No. of applicants last year: 5
Additional Information: Applicants must produce an official letter of acceptance for entering any year of a Master's or doctoral degree.

SAMRO Overseas Scholarship

Subjects: Music.
Purpose: To encourage music study at the postgraduate level in the serious classical or jazz popular music genres.
Eligibility: Open to postgraduate students who are citizens of South Africa, Botswana, Lesotho or Swaziland. The age limit is 34 years.
Level of Study: Postgraduate
Type: Scholarship

Value: Rand 160,000 plus travel expenses of up to Rand 10,000
Length of Study: 2 years
Frequency: Annual
Study Establishment: An institute or educational entity approved by the SAMRO Endowment for the National Arts (SENA)
Country of Study: United Kingdom, Europe or North America
No. of awards offered: 2
Application Procedure: Applicants must complete an application form.
Closing Date: April 30th
Funding: Private
Contributor: SAMRO
No. of awards given last year: 2
No. of applicants last year: 12

SAMRO Postgraduate Bursaries for Indigenous African Music Study

Subjects: Music.
Purpose: To encourage the study of indigenous African music at the postgraduate level in either the traditional, serious classical or jazz popular music genres.
Eligibility: Open to postgraduate students who are citizens of South Africa, Botswana, Lesotho or Swaziland. The age limit is 40 years.
Level of Study: Postgraduate
Type: Bursary
Value: Rand 5,500
Length of Study: 5 years
Frequency: Annual
Study Establishment: A university or other recognized statutory institute of tertiary education approved by the trustees and situated in SAMRO's current territory of operation
Country of Study: South Africa, Botswana, Lesotho, or Swaziland
No. of awards offered: 6
Application Procedure: Applicants must complete an application form.
Closing Date: February 15th
Funding: Private
Contributor: SAMRO
No. of awards given last year: 4
No. of applicants last year: 5
Additional Information: Applicants must produce an official letter of acceptance from a recognized tertiary institute of learning. They must have acceptance into the 1st year or any subsequent year of a postgraduate degree in indigenous African music at such an institute.

SOUTHWEST MINNESOTA ARTS & HUMANITIES COUNCIL (SMAHC)

1210 East College Drive, Suite 600, Marshall, Minnesota, 56258, United States of America
Tel: (1) 800 622 5284
Email: smahcinfo@iw.net
Website: www.smahc.org

The SMAHC, established in 1974, is a non-profit organization committed to encourage the growth and development of the arts and humanities in southwestern Minnesota by serving as a source of funds and technical services.

SMAHC Article Study Opportunity Grant Program

Subjects: Arts and humanities.
Purpose: To aid in career development and arts activities.
Eligibility: Open to applicants who are permanent residents of southwestern Minnesota.
Level of Study: Postgraduate
Type: Scholarship
Value: Up to US$500
Frequency: Annual
Country of Study: United States of America
Application Procedure: See the website for application forms and complete details.
Closing Date: October 1st

SMAHC Career and Development Programs

Subjects: Arts and humanities.
Purpose: To aid in career development of artists.
Eligibility: Open to applicants who are permanent residents of southwestern Minnesota.
Level of Study: Postgraduate
Type: Scholarship
Value: Up to US$2,000
Frequency: Annual
Country of Study: United States of America
Application Procedure: See the website.
Closing Date: March 1st

SMAHC/Mcknight Prairie Star Award

Subjects: Arts and humanities.
Purpose: To recognize an individual whose activities have best exemplified the highest quality of work.
Eligibility: Open to all artists from southwest Minnesota whose work has taken place within the past few years.
Level of Study: Postgraduate
Type: Scholarship
Value: US$1,000
Frequency: Annual
Country of Study: United States of America
No. of awards offered: 1
Application Procedure: See the website.
Closing Date: March 1st

SMAHC/Mcknight Prairie Disciple Award

Subjects: Arts and humanities.
Purpose: To recognize an individual whose activities have best aided in the development of the arts.
Eligibility: Open to applicants from Southwest Minnesota.
Level of Study: Postgraduate
Type: Scholarship
Value: US$500 and a plaque
Frequency: Annual
Country of Study: United States of America
No. of awards offered: 1
Application Procedure: See the website.
Closing Date: March 1st

STANLEY MEDICAL RESEARCH INSTITUTE

5430 Grosvenor Lane, Suite 200, Bethesda, MD, 20814-2142, United States of America
Tel: (1) 301 571 2081
Fax: (1) 301 571 0769
Email: peckk@stanleyresearch.org
Website: www.stanleyresearch.org
Contact: Ms Kelly D. Peck, Executive Administrator

SMRI is a nonprofit organization that supports research designed to find better treatments for schizophrenia and bipolar disorder. Approximately seventy-five percent of its annual expenditures are devoted to the direct clinical testing of new treatments. Twenty-five percent is earmarked for research on the causes of these illness.

Stanley Medical Research Institute Postdoctoral Research Fellowship Program

Subjects: Psychiatry and mental health: causes and treatment of schizophrenia and bipolar disorder.
Purpose: To attract top-quality scientists to specific areas of research in severe mental illness.
Eligibility: Open to researchers worldwide. Applicants must be a doctorate or equivalent professional and must not be more than 2 years past receipt of their doctoral degree.
Level of Study: Research, postdoctorate
Type: Research fellowship

Value: Up to US$150,000 spread over 2 years including indirect costs of up to 15 per cent as part of the total grant budget
Length of Study: 2 years
Frequency: Annual
Country of Study: Any country
No. of awards offered: 1
Application Procedure: Interested applicants must apply online at the website. Detailed instructions for application are available in a printable format (PDF).
Closing Date: January 15th
Funding: Individuals, foundation
Additional Information: Top priority will be given to applications that address the following questions: (a)Synthesis or screening of compounds to be tested against molecular targets identified for servere mental illness (schizophrenia, bipolar disorder, servere depression). (b) Pharmacokinetic and toxicological characterization of potential drugs for servere mental illness. (c) Ethnopharmacology, ie., discovery or characterization of potentially useful psychoactive compounds from non-Western medical traditions.

Stanley Medical Research Institute Research Grants Program

Subjects: Psychiatry and mental health: causes and treatment of schizophrenia and bipolar disorder.
Purpose: To support researchers at all levels of development in fields related to the cause and treatment of schizophrenia and bipolar disorder, as well as from other areas of medicine and biology who wish to initiate new projects in this field.
Eligibility: Open to researchers worldwide. Applicants must be a doctorate or equivalent professional.
Level of Study: Research
Type: Research grant
Value: US$5,000 per year; indirect costs may be paid up to 15 per cent as part of the total grant budget
Length of Study: 2 years
Frequency: Annual
Country of Study: Any country
Application Procedure: Interested applicants must apply online at the SMRI website. Detailed instructions for application are available in a printable formate(PDF).
Closing Date: March 1st
Funding: Individuals, private, foundation

Stanley Medical Research Institute Treatment Trial Grants Program

Subjects: Psychology and mental health: treatments for schizophrenia and bipolar disorder.
Purpose: To support researchers and facilitate the direct testing of new treatments for schizophrenia and bipolar disorder. This programme supports projects involving human subjects and testing a therapeutic intervention (medication; device; putative medication including plant substances and nutritional; psychotherapy).
Eligibility: Open to researchers worldwide. Applicants must be a doctorate or equivalent professional.
Level of Study: Research
Type: Research grant
Value: US$900,000
Length of Study: 3 years
Frequency: Annual
Country of Study: Any country
Application Procedure: Interested applicants must apply online at the SMRI website. Detailed instructions for application are available in printable format (PDF).
Closing Date: March 1st and October 1st
Funding: Individuals, foundation
Additional Information: Please check the master list of Stanley Medical Research Institute awarded trials on the website prior to completing the application. If we are supporting trials with the compound you propose, we are unlikely to support an additional trial until results are available.

STANLEY SMITH (UK) HORTICULTURAL TRUST

Cory Lodge, PO Box 365, Cambridge, Cambridgeshire, CB2 1HR, England
Tel: (44) 12 2333 6299
Fax: (44) 12 2333 6278
Contact: Mr James Cullen, Director

The Stanley Smith (UK) Horticultural Trust supports projects that contribute to the development of the art and science of horticulture, ie. garden conservation and restoration, education and training, publications and travel.

Stanley Smith (UK) Horticultural Trust Awards

Subjects: Horticulture. The Trust supports individual projects in all aspects (including training) of amenity horticulture and some aspects of commercial horticulture.
Eligibility: Open to institutions and individuals. All projects are judged entirely on merit and there are no eligibility requirements, but grants are not awarded for students to take academic or diploma courses of any kind.
Level of Study: Unrestricted
Type: Varies
Value: Varies
Length of Study: Dependent on the nature of the project
Frequency: Twice a year
Country of Study: Any country
No. of awards offered: Varies
Application Procedure: Applicants must apply to the Trust. Trustees allocate awards in Spring and Autumn.
Closing Date: February 15th and August 15th
Funding: Private
Contributor: Donations
No. of awards given last year: 38
No. of applicants last year: 200

STATE LIBRARY OF NEW SOUTH WALES

Macquarie Street, Sydney, NSW 2000, Australia
Tel: (61) 2 9273 1466
Fax: (61) 2 9273 1245
Email: library@sl.nsw.gov.au
Website: www.sl.nsw.gov.au
Contact: Hitchell Librarian

The State Library of New South Wales is the premier reference and research library in New South Wales. The Library consists of the State Reference Library and the Mitchell Library, which contains the famous Australian Research Collections pertaining to the history of Australia and the Southwest Pacific region.

Blake Dawson Waldron Prize for Business Literature

Subjects: Australian corporate and commercial literature, histories, accounts and analyses of corporate affairs as well as biographies of business men and women.
Purpose: To encourage the highest standards of commentary in the fields of business and finance.
Eligibility: The author must be a living Australian citizen or hold permanent resident status. The work must have primary reference to business or financial affairs, business or financial institutions or people directly associated with business and financial affairs, be written in the English language, published in book form and consist of a minimum of 50,000 words.
Level of Study: Professional development
Type: Prize
Length of Study: Australian $30,000
Frequency: Annual
Study Establishment: State Library of New South Wales
Country of Study: Australia
Application Procedure: All nominations must be made on the appropriate form, be submitted with five copies of the nominated work and be accompanied by an entry fee of Australian $66 per title to be

eligible for consideration. A separate form must be completed for each nomination. See State Library of NSW website www.sl.nsw.gov.au/awards/
Closing Date: September 17th
Funding: Private

For further information contact:

Education and Client Liaison Branch, State Library of New South Wales, Australia
Email: smartin@sl.nsw.gov.au
Contact: Stephen Martin, Senior Project Officer

C H Currey Memorial Fellowship
Subjects: Australian history.
Purpose: To promote the writing of Australian history from original sources of information, preferably making use of the collection of the State Library of New South Wales.
Eligibility: Applicants may be residents or non-residents of Australia. Preference will normally be given to applications that support research on a topic or project that is not being pursued as part of a higher degree programme.
Level of Study: Professional development
Type: Fellowship
Value: Australian $20,000
Length of Study: 1 year
Frequency: Annual
Study Establishment: The State Library of New South Wales
Country of Study: Australia
Application Procedure: Applications should be made on forms available from the State Library or the website www.sl.nsw.gov.au/awards/
Closing Date: September

Jean Arnot Memorial Fellowship
Subjects: Librarianship.
Purpose: To reward an outstanding original paper of no more than 5,000 words on any aspect of librarianship by a female librarian or a female student of librarianship.
Eligibility: The author must be a professional librarian or a student at an Australian school of librarianship. The submitted paper must be an outstanding original paper on any aspect of librarianship.
Level of Study: Professional development
Type: Fellowship
Value: Australian $1,000
Length of Study: 1 year
Frequency: Annual
Study Establishment: State Library of New South Wales
Country of Study: Australia
No. of awards offered: 1
Application Procedure: Applicants must complete an application form, available on request. See State Library of NSW website www.sl.nsw.gov.au/awards/
Closing Date: March 30th
Funding: Private
Contributor: National Council of Women of New South Wales Incorporated and the Australian Federation of Business and Professional Women's Association Inc.

For further information contact:

Collection Management Services and Mitchell Librarian, State Library of New South Wales, Australia
Email: eellis@sl.nsw.gov.au
Contact: Elizabeth Ellis, Assistant State Librarian

Kathleen Mitchell Award
Subjects: Writing, literature.
Purpose: To reward a novel by an Australian author.
Eligibility: Applicants must be an Australian author under 30 years of age.
Value: Australian $7,500
Frequency: Every 2 years
Study Establishment: The State Library of New South Wales
Country of Study: Australia
Application Procedure: Applicants must complete an application form, available on request.
Funding: Private

Miles Franklin Literary Award
Subjects: Australian literature.
Purpose: To promote excellence in Australian literature.
Eligibility: Novel must be of the highest literary merit and must present Australian life in any of its phases. Novels submitted must have been published in the year of entry of the award.
Level of Study: Professional development
Type: Award
Value: Australian $42,000
Frequency: Annual
Application Procedure: Application forms can be downloaded from the website www.trustco.com.au/awards/miles_franklin.htm, see also State library of NSW website www.sl.nsw.gov.au/awards/
Closing Date: December 10th
Funding: Individuals

For further information contact:

Cauz Group, Australia
Tel: (61) (02) 9332 1559
Fax: (61) (02) 9332 1298
Email: trustawards@cauzgroup.com.au
Contact: Petrea Salter

Milt Luger Fellowships
Subjects: Australian life, history and culture using the resources of the state library.
Purpose: For projects which investigate and document aspects of Australian life, history and culture.
Eligibility: Persons aged between 18 and 25 years.
Type: Fellowship
Value: US$5,000 and US$3,000
Study Establishment: The state library of NSW
Country of Study: Australia
No. of awards offered: 2 Awards
Application Procedure: Applicants must complete an application form, available on request. See State Library of NSW website www.sl.nsw.gov.au/awards/
Closing Date: August 31st
Funding: Private

For further information contact:

Mitchell Library Office, State Library of New South Wales, Macquarie Street, Sydney, Australia
Tel: (61) (02) 9273 1467
Fax: (61) (02) 9273 1245
Email: awards@sl.nsw.gov.au
Website: www.sl.nsw.gov.au/awards/
Contact: Margaret Bjork

Nancy Keesing Fellowship
Subjects: Australian life and culture.
Purpose: To promote the State Library of New South Wales as a centre of research into Australian life and culture and to provide a readily accessible record of the fellowship project.
Eligibility: Applicants may be either residents or non-residents of Australia. Preference will normally be given to applications that support research on a topic or project that is not being pursued as part of higher degree programme.
Level of Study: Professional development
Type: Fellowship
Value: Australian $10,000
Length of Study: 1 year
Frequency: Annual
Study Establishment: State Library of New South Wales
Country of Study: Australia
Application Procedure: Applications must be made on forms available from the State Library or the website www.sl.nsw.gov.au/awards/
Closing Date: September
Funding: Private

National Biography Award

Subjects: Writing.
Purpose: To encourage the highest standards of writing in the fields of biography and autobiography and to promote public interest in biography and autobiography.
Eligibility: The author must be a living Australian citizen or hold permanent resident status. The work must be classified as either biography or autobiography, be written in the English language, published in book form and consist of a minimum of 50,000 words.
Level of Study: Professional development
Type: Award
Value: Australian $15,000
Frequency: Annual
Study Establishment: The State Library of New South Wales
Country of Study: Australia
Application Procedure: All nominations must be made on the appropriate form and be accompanied by an entry fee of Australian $55 to be eligible for consideration. Five copies of the nominated work must be submitted. A separate form must be completed for each nomination. See state library of NSW website www.sl.nsw.gov.au/awards/
Closing Date: October 22nd
Funding: Private, individuals
Contributor: Geoffrey Cains

Nita B Kibble Literary Awards: Dobbie Literary Award

Subjects: Writing.
Purpose: To reward a first published work by a woman author of fiction or nonfiction classifiable as 'Life Writing'.
Eligibility: Open to a first published work of fiction or nonfiction classifiable as 'Life Writing' by a woman author.
Value: Australian $2,500
Frequency: Annual
Study Establishment: The State Library of New South Wales
Country of Study: Australia
Application Procedure: Applicants must complete an application form, available on request.
Funding: Private

Nita B Kibble Literary Awards: Kibble Literary Awards

Subjects: Writing.
Purpose: To reward women writers of a published book of fiction or nonfiction classifiable as 'Life Writing'.
Eligibility: Open to women writers of a published book of fiction or nonfiction classifiable as 'Life Writing'.
Value: Australian $20,000
Frequency: Annual
Study Establishment: The State Library of New South Wales
Country of Study: Australia
Application Procedure: Applicants must complete an application form, available on request.
Closing Date: December
Funding: Private

State Librarian's Metcalfe Fellowship at UNSW

Subjects: Librarianship.
Purpose: To fund the study of Librarianship.
Type: Fellowship
Frequency: Periodic
Study Establishment: The State Library of New South Wales
Country of Study: Australia
Application Procedure: Applicants must complete an application form, available on request. See State Library of NSW website: www.sl.nsw.gov.au/awards/
Funding: Private

Visiting Scholars-in-Residence (Council of Australian State Libraries Honorary Fellowship; Library Council of New South Wales Honorary Fellowship)

Subjects: All subjects relevant to the Library's collections. (Awarded to two second top shortlisted candidates for the C.H.Currey Memorial Fellowship and the Nancy Keesing Memorial Fellowship).
Purpose: To assist visiting scholars-in-residence to undertake research on specific subjects with a strong emphasis on the library's collections.
Eligibility: Applicants may be residents or non-residents of Australia.
Level of Study: Professional development
Type: Research fellowship
Value: N/A
Length of Study: 1 year
Frequency: Annual
Study Establishment: State Library of New South Wales
Country of Study: Australia
No. of awards offered: 2
Application Procedure: Applicants must complete an application form, available on request. See state library of NSW website www.sl.nsw.gov.au/awards/
Funding: Trusts

STATE THEATRE COMPANY OF SOUTH AUSTRALIA

adelaide Festival Centre, King William Rd, Adelaide, SA 5000, Australia
Tel: (61) 8 82 315151
Fax: (61) 8 82 316310
Email: tabienne@statetheatre.sa.com.au
Website: www.statetheatre.sa.com.au

The company is devoted to the nurturing of new South Australian acting and directing talent.

Adale koh Acting Scholarship

Subjects: Creative arts.
Purpose: To provide funding toward professional career development.
Eligibility: Applicants must be South Australian.
Level of Study: Professional development, postgraduate
Type: Scholarship
Value: Australian $2,000
Length of Study: 1 year
Frequency: Annual
Country of Study: Australia
Funding: Private
Contributor: Mr. Don Dunstan

State theatre Creative Fellowship

Eligibility: Applicants must be South Australian and show a definite commitment to pursuing a career in directing.
Level of Study: Professional development, postgraduate
Type: Fellowship
Value: All costs for professional training
Length of Study: 1 year
Frequency: Annual
Country of Study: Australia
No. of awards offered: 1
Application Procedure: Contact the State Theatre.
Closing Date: November
Funding: Private
Contributor: N.R.G Flinders

STATISTICAL SOCIETY OF CANADA

577 King Edward Avenue, Ottawa, Ontario, K1N 6N5, Canada
Tel: (1) 613 725 2253
Fax: (1) 613 729 6206
Email: ssc@thewillowgroup.com
Website: www.ssc.ca
Contact: Paul Gustafson, Chair, Pierre Robillard Award Committee

The Statistical Society of Canada provides a forum for discussion and interaction among individuals involved in all aspects of the statistical sciences. It publishes a newsletter, Liaison as well as a scientific journal, *The Canadian Journal of Statistics*. The Society also organises annual scientific meetings and short courses on professional development.

Pierre Robillard Award
Subjects: Statistics.
Purpose: To recognize the best PhD thesis defended at a Canadian university and written in a field covered by the Canadian Journal of Statistics.
Eligibility: Open to all postgraduates who have made a potential impact on the statistical sciences.
Level of Study: Doctorate
Type: Award
Value: A certificate, a monetary prize of Canadian $400 and one year's membership of the Society
Frequency: Annual
Country of Study: Canada
No. of awards offered: Varies
Application Procedure: Applicants must submit four copies of the thesis together with a covering letter from the thesis supervisor.
Closing Date: February 15th
No. of awards given last year: 1
No. of applicants last year: 10
Additional Information: The committee may decide that none of the submitted theses merits the award.

For further information contact:

Department of Statistics, University of Toronto, Toronto, ON M5S 3G3
Contact: Professor Mike Evans

STELLENBOSCH UNIVERSITY

Private Bay XI, Matieland, 7602, South Africa
Tel: (27) (0) 808 9111
Fax: (27) (0) 21 808 3822

The raison Dé of the chemistry of Stellenbosch is to create and sustain, in commitment to the academic ideal of excellent scholarly and scientific practice, an environment within which knowledge can be discovered, shared and applied for the benefit of the community.

Harry Crossley Doctoral Fellowship
Subjects: Any subject, with the exception of theology and political science.
Purpose: To reward academically above average students.
Level of Study: Doctorate, postdoctorate
Type: Fellowship
Value: Rand 50,000–85,000
Length of Study: 2 years
Frequency: Annual
Study Establishment: University of Stellenbosch
Country of Study: South Africa
Application Procedure: Request application.
Closing Date: October 21st
Funding: Foundation
Contributor: Harry Crossley Foundation

For further information contact:

The office for Postgraduate Bursaries Division for Research Development Administration Building Block A, Room A2068B
Tel: 021 808 4208/2957
Fax: beurnavre_nagraads@sun.ac.za

Harry Crossley Master's Bursary
Subjects: Any subject, with the exception of technology and political science.
Purpose: To reward academically above average studens.
Level of Study: Postgraduate
Type: Bursary
Value: Rand 30,000–660,000
Length of Study: 2 years
Frequency: Annual
Study Establishment: University of Stellenbosch
Country of Study: South Africa
Application Procedure: Request application form.
Closing Date: October 21st
Funding: Foundation
Contributor: Harry Crossley Foundation

For further information contact:

The Office for Postgraduate Busbaries Division for Research Develepement Administrator Building Block A, Room A206813
Tel: 021 808 4208/2957
Email: beursnavrae_nagraads@sun.ac.za

Stellenbosch Fellowship in Horticultural Science
Subjects: Root studies of fruit trees.
Purpose: To finance research in soil biological, plant physiological and horticultural aspects of root studies.
Eligibility: Open to candidates with a PhD (Agric) Horticultural Science with experience and through knowledge of perennial fruit trees.
Level of Study: Postdoctorate
Length of Study: 1 year
Study Establishment: University of Stellenbosch
Country of Study: South Africa
Application Procedure: Please submit a written application including the completed admissions forms.
Closing Date: August 31st

For further information contact:

Dept of Horticultural Science Private XI, Martieland, 76002, South Africa
Tel: (27) 021 808 2383
Contact: Professor

Stellenbosch Fellowship in Polymer Science
Subjects: New monomer synthesizing and radical polymerization.
Purpose: To fund further study in Polymer Science and synthetic Polymer chemistry.
Eligibility: Open to students with a PhD in Polymer Science or Environmental Engineering and experience in membranes, membrane operations, polymer brushes, grafts and other nano particles.
Level of Study: Postdoctorate
Type: Fellowship
Length of Study: 1 year
Frequency: Annual
Study Establishment: University of Stellenbosch
Country of Study: South Africa
No. of awards offered: 1
Application Procedure: Request application.

For further information contact:

Department of Chemistry, Division of Polymer Science University of Stellenbosch, Stellenbosch, 7600, South Africa
Email: rds@sun.ac.za
Contact: Professor RD Sanderson

Stellenbosch Merit Bursang Fellowship
Subjects: Any subject.
Eligibility: Available to full-time students registered at Stellenbosch University in any postgraduate degree programme.
Level of Study: Doctorate
Type: Fellowship
Value: Rand 30,900 per annum
Length of Study: 3 years
Study Establishment: University of Stellenbosch
Country of Study: South Africa
Application Procedure: Students must submit an application and a certified copy of a complete, official academic record.
Closing Date: October 28th (for foreign students) December 9th (for South Africa students)

For further information contact:

Office for postgraduate bursaries
Tel: (021) 808-4208
Email: beursnarrae_nagraads@sun.ac.za

Stellenbosch Postdoctoral Research Fellowship in Geology

Subjects: Tectono-metamorphic and magmatic evolution of the Archaen Barberton granite-greenstone terrain in South Africa.
Purpose: To finance a student interested in Archaen tectonics and applied structural geology of high-grade metamorphic granite-gneiss terrains.
Eligibility: Open to students with a PhD in geology obtained within the past five years, with a background in regional mapping and structural geology.
Level of Study: Postdoctorate
Type: Fellowship
Value: Rand 60,000 per annum
Length of Study: 2 years
Frequency: Annual
Study Establishment: University of Stellenbosch
Country of Study: South Africa
No. of awards offered: 1
Application Procedure: Submit a covering letter, curriculum vitae and all research outputs.
Closing Date: March 21st

For further information contact:

Department of Geology Private Bag XI, Mtieland, 7602
Fax: +27 (0) 21 808 3129
Email: akister@sun.ac.za
Contact: Professor Allex Kisters

Stellenbosch Rector's Grants for successing against the Odds

Subjects: Any subject.
Purpose: To award students who have achieved exceptional success despite difficult circumstances.
Eligibility: Open to candidate who satisfy the admission requirements of the University and who can provide proof of exceptional achievement despite handicaps and/or specific physical, educational or social challenges.
Type: Grant
Length of Study: Rand 50,000
Frequency: Annual
Study Establishment: University of Stellenbosch
Country of Study: South Africa
No. of awards offered: 3
Application Procedure: Students must submit a complete application form accompanied by a curriculum vitae and 2 references.
Closing Date: September 30th

For further information contact:

Tel: (021) 808-2908
Email: ddreyer@sun.ac.za
Contact: Mr D Dreyer

STOCKHOLM SCHOOL OF ECONOMICS

PO Box 6501, SE-11383, Stockholm, Sweden
Tel: (46) 8 736 9000
Fax: (46) 8 31 81 86
Email: info@hhs.se
Website: www.hhs.se

An international higher educational institution on a comparatively small scale with a dynamic international learning environment to further economic and business study.

Colfuturo Scholarship

Subjects: Business administration.
Purpose: To fund study abroad.
Eligibility: Open to Colombian nationals with atleast one year of work experience only.
Level of Study: Postgraduate
Type: Scholarship
Value: All tuition fees and agreed travel costs
Length of Study: 1 year
Frequency: Annual
Country of Study: Sweden
Application Procedure: Contact the Foundation.
Funding: Foundation
Contributor: Colfuturo Foundation

For further information contact:

Colfuturo, Carera 15 37-15, Santafe de Bogota, Columbia S.A., A.A. 075008
Tel: 340 5394
Website: www.colfuturo.org

Consejo Nacional de Ciencia y Tecnologia (CONACYT) Scholarships

Subjects: Business management.
Eligibility: Open to Mexican students only.
Level of Study: MBA
Type: Scholarship
Value: All agreed fees
Length of Study: 1 year
Frequency: Annual
Country of Study: Sweden
Application Procedure: Contact the Foundation.
Funding: Foundation
Contributor: CONACYT

For further information contact:

Email: ochoa@buzon.main.conacyt.mx

Hans Stahle Scholarship

Subjects: Business management.
Eligibility: Open to candidates of Russian origin only.
Level of Study: MBA
Type: Scholarship
Value: SEK 10,000
Length of Study: 1 year
Frequency: Annual
Study Establishment: SSE
Country of Study: Sweden
No. of awards offered: 1
Application Procedure: Contact the school.
Funding: Foundation
Contributor: Hans Stahle Foundation

The Inlaks Foundation Scholarships

Subjects: Business administration.
Eligibility: The scholarships are not awarded to anyone who has already started a course of study or a project abroad.
Level of Study: MBA
Type: Scholarship
Value: The scholarship covers one way travel tuition fees and adequate living expenses for the period granted
Frequency: Dependent on funds available
Country of Study: Sweden
No. of awards offered: 1
Application Procedure: Candidate can download the application from the website.
Funding: Foundation
Contributor: Inlaks Foundation

For further information contact:

Website: www.inlaksfoundation.org

Petra och Kail Erik Hedborgs Stiftelse Scholarship

Subjects: Business administration.
Level of Study: MBA
Type: Scholarship
Value: All tuition fees and travel costs
Length of Study: 1 year
Frequency: Annual

Country of Study: Sweden
Application Procedure: Contact the institute.
Funding: Private

For further information contact:

Petra och Karl Erik Hedborgs Stiftelse, Vikbyvägen 26, Lidingö, SE-181 43, Sweden
Tel: (46) (0) 8 765 6327
Email: info@pkhedborg.com

Praxis XXI Program

Subjects: Business management.
Eligibility: Open to Portuguese nationals only.
Level of Study: MBA
Type: Scholarship
Value: All tuition fees and travel allowance
Frequency: Annual
Country of Study: Sweden
Application Procedure: See website.
Funding: Government
Contributor: The Portuguese Ministry of Science and Technology

For further information contact:

Website: www.fct.mct.pt

Projeto Start Scholarship

Subjects: Business administration.
Eligibility: Open to Brazilian nationals only.
Level of Study: MBA
Type: Scholarship
Value: All tuition fees
Length of Study: 1 year
Frequency: Annual
Country of Study: Sweden
Application Procedure: Contact the Institute.
Funding: Foundation
Contributor: LING Institute

For further information contact:

Instituto LING, Rua Siqueira Campos, 1163, 5, andar, 90010-001, Porto Alegre RS, Brazil

The Swedish Foundation for International Cooperation in Research and Higher Education (STINT) Scholarship

Subjects: Business administration.
Eligibility: Open to Brazilian nationals only.
Level of Study: MBA
Type: Scholarship
Length of Study: 1 year
Frequency: Dependent on funds available
Country of Study: Sweden
Application Procedure: Contact the institute.
Funding: Government
Contributor: STINT

For further information contact:

STINT, Skeppargatan 8, Stockholm, SE-114 52, Sweden
Tel: (46) 46 8662 7690
Fax: (46) 46 8661 9210
Email: info@stint.se

STOUT RESEARCH CENTRE, VICTORIA UNIVERSITY OF WELLINGTON

PO Box 600, Wellington, New Zealand
Tel: (64) 4 465 5305
Fax: (64) 4 463 5439
Email: lydia.wevers@vuw.ac.nz
Website: www.vuw.ac.nz/stout-centre
Contact: Dr Lydia Wevers, Director

The Stout Research Center was established in 1984 to encourage scholarly inquiry into New Zealand society, history and culture, and to provide a focus for the collegial atmosphere and exchange of ideas that enrich the quality of research.

J D Stout Fellowship

Subjects: New Zealand society, history and culture.
Purpose: To encourage research.
Eligibility: Open to distinguished scholars from New Zealand and abroad.
Level of Study: Postdoctorate
Type: Fellowship
Value: New Zealand $52,348–76,160
Length of Study: 1 year
Frequency: Annual
Study Establishment: The Stout Research Centre
Country of Study: New Zealand
No. of awards offered: 1
Application Procedure: Applicants must write for details.
Closing Date: August 1st of the year preceding the fellowship
Funding: Trusts
Contributor: Stout Trust

STROKE ASSOCIATION

Stroke House 240 City Road, London, EC1V 2PR, England
Tel: (44) 20 7566 0300
Fax: (44) 20 7490 4768
Email: research@stroke.org.uk
Website: www.stroke.org.uk
Contact: Ms M. Bendix, Research Officer

The Stroke Association funds research into rehabilitation, treatment and better methods of rehabilitation, and helps stroke patients and their families directly through community services. It campaigns, educates and informs to increase knowledge of stroke at all levels of society and it acts as a voice for everyone affected by stroke.

Stroke Association Clinical Fellowships

Subjects: The prevention, treatment and rehabilitation of strokes.
Purpose: To equip a trainee for a career in the field.
Eligibility: Awarded to a department in the United Kingdom that can provide an educational programme and the expert supervision required to enable a specialist registrar to gain the appropriate clinical experience required for a career in stroke.
Level of Study: Professional development
Type: Fellowship
Value: UK £40,000
Length of Study: 1 year
Frequency: Annual
Study Establishment: Suitable universities and medical schools
Country of Study: United Kingdom
No. of awards offered: 2
Application Procedure: Applicants must respond to advertisements in the *British Medical Journal* in October of each year. Application forms are available from the website.
Closing Date: Usually March
Funding: Private
No. of awards given last year: 2
Additional Information: Fellowships are assessed by peer review. Awards are made in March.

Stroke Association Research Project Grants

Subjects: Stroke research encompassing epidemiology, prevention, acute treatment, assessment and rehabilitation, psychology of stroke and stroke in ethnic minorities.
Purpose: To advance research into stroke.
Eligibility: Open to medically qualified and other clinically active researchers in the United Kingdom in the relevant fields. Applications are judged by peer review on their merit without limitations of age. Applicants can be from any country but must be based in the United Kingdom.
Level of Study: Research, postdoctorate

Type: Project grant
Value: Salaries for researchers and support staff, some equipment costs, consumables and essential travel. No other overheads, advertising etc. are covered. The maximum award is normally UK £60,000 per year
Length of Study: 1–3 years
Frequency: Twice a year
Study Establishment: A suitable university or hospital in the United Kingdom
Country of Study: United Kingdom
No. of awards offered: Approx. 30 ongoing at any point in time
Application Procedure: Application forms are available from the website.
Closing Date: As advertised, usually February and July
Funding: Private
Contributor: Donations
No. of awards given last year: 11
No. of applicants last year: 80

Stroke Association Therapy Research Bursaries

Subjects: Stroke research.
Purpose: To provide a research training programme and appropriate supervision to equip a trainee for a career in stroke research.
Eligibility: Open to nurses and therapists, but consideration will be given to other health professionals. They will be awarded to departments that can demonstrate a track record and current participation in stroke research.
Level of Study: Postgraduate, professional development
Type: Bursary
Value: UK £30,000 per year
Length of Study: Up to 3 years
Frequency: Annual
Study Establishment: Suitable universities and hospitals
Country of Study: United Kingdom
No. of awards offered: 2
Application Procedure: Applicants must respond to advertisements in *Therapy Weekly* in October of each year. Application forms are available from the website.
Closing Date: Usually January
Funding: Private
No. of awards given last year: 2

THE STUDENT AWARDS AGENCY FOR SCOTLAND

Gyleview House, 3 Redheughs Rigg, Edinburgh,
EH12 9HH, Scotland
Tel: (44) 845 111 1711
Fax: (44) 13 1244 5887
Email: Leia.fitzgerald@scotland.gov.uk
Website: www.saas.gov.uk
Contact: Mr Victor Abela

The brief of the Student Awards Agency for Scotland is to administer the Students' Allowances Scheme, the Postgraduate Students' Allowances Scheme and the Nursing and Midwifery Student Bursary Scheme.

SAAS-Arts and Humanities Postgraduate Scholarships

Subjects: Arts and humanities.
Eligibility: Open to students enrolled in a postgraduate programme in the Arts and Humanities Graduate School.
Level of Study: Postgraduate
Type: Scholarship
Value: UK £9,000
Length of Study: 1 year
Frequency: Annual
Study Establishment: Arts and Humanities Graduate School
Country of Study: United Kingdom
Application Procedure: Application form can be downloaded from the website.
Closing Date: March 31st

SAAS-The Postgraduate Certificate of Education

Subjects: All subjects.
Purpose: To fund Scottish students studying full-time postgraduate courses.
Eligibility: Open to prospective students in need of financial help.
Level of Study: Postgraduate
Type: Scholarship
Value: Fees and maintenance funding
Frequency: Annual
Application Procedure: Contact the website.
Funding: Government

SUDAN CIVIC FOUNDATION (SCF)

SCF House, 37 Monkswell, Cambridge, CB2 2JU, England
Tel: (44) 12 2350 4393
Fax: (44) 12 2350 1125
Email: equiano@sudan21.net
Website: www.sudan21.net/equiano.html
Contact: Dr Salah Al Bander, Director

The Sudan Civic Foundation (SCF) is an independent non-profit group whose purpose is to contribute to public understanding of socio-economic and political issues through research, discussion and publications. It was established in 1996 to provide, among other things, a network for those who share a common concern for better race relations.

Equiano Memorial Award

Subjects: The promotion of race relations.
Purpose: To support a person engaged in the study or promotion of tolerance and peaceful co-existence between communities, and to support research or practical field investigations, leading to a report, essay or dissertation.
Eligibility: There are no eligibility restrictions.
Level of Study: Unrestricted
Type: Research grant
Value: UK £2,000
Length of Study: 1 year. Applicants may reapply for a 2nd year of funding
Frequency: Annual
Study Establishment: An academic or professional establishment
Country of Study: Any country
No. of awards offered: 2
Application Procedure: Applicants must complete an application form and should write for details.
Closing Date: March 31st
Funding: Private
Contributor: Dr Salah Al Bander
No. of awards given last year: 1
No. of applicants last year: 420
Additional Information: Applicants must be registered at a recognized educational institution. The award is based on need as well as academic merit. The area of study must fit in with the research priorities of the Foundation.

SUNY COLLEGE AT BROCKPORT

350 New Campus Drive, Brockport, New York, 14420-2914, United States of America
Tel: (1) 395 2211

Suny College, the state university of New York college at Brockport, is a friendly place to learn, to achieve academic and personal success, to grow and develop, and to shape the future. The focus is up on a learning culture that values strong and effective teaching, yet, is also firmly committed to advancing high-quality scholarship, creative endeavors and service to the college community.

O'Reilly Environmental Science Scholarship

Subjects: Environmental science.
Purpose: To assists students who wish to enroll in the Environmental Science Program.

Eligibility: Open to students committed to environmental issues and the study of science.
Level of Study: Postgraduate
Type: Scholarship
Value: US$900
Frequency: Annual
Study Establishment: Suny College at Brockport
Country of Study: United States of America
Application Procedure: Contact website for application forms and details.
Closing Date: March 11th
Funding: Foundation
Contributor: Brockport College Foundation

SWEDISH INFORMATION SERVICE

One Dag Hammarskjold Plaza, 885 Second Avenue, 45th Floor, New York, NY 10017, United States of America
Fax: (1) 212 755 2732
Email: info@swedennewyork.com
Website: www.swedennewyork.com
Contact: Consulate General of Sweden

The Section for culture and Public Affairs of the Consulate General of Sweden in New York works to promote awareness in the United States of America of Swedish cultural achievement and advancement in scientific research and development, and contributes to the formation of public opinion and policy in an international context.

Bicentennial Swedish-American Exchange Fund

Subjects: Politics, public administration, working life, human environment, mass media, business and industry, education or culture.
Purpose: To provide an opportunity for those in a position to influence public opinion and contribute to the development of their society to make an intensive research trip to Sweden.
Eligibility: Applicants should be citizens or permanent residents of the United States of America. People who have made recurrent visits to or resided in Sweden will only be considered in exceptional circumstances. The grant may not be used to finance participation in conferences or regular ongoing vocational or academic courses. If co-applicants on the same project are selected, the grant will be divided between them. The grant may be used in conjunction with scholarships from other sources.
Level of Study: Research
Type: Travel grant
Value: Krona 25,000 or the equivalent in United States of America dollars to partially cover transportation and living expenses
Length of Study: 2–4 weeks intensive research
Frequency: Annual
Country of Study: Sweden
No. of awards offered: 2
Application Procedure: Application forms are available from the website or can be requested directly from the Swedish Information Service, during the month of November. As a signature is required, application forms should be printed out and signed before sending in the post. Two letters of recommendation are also required. Email applications are not accepted. Application forms to be filled in by hand may be requested by post along with a stamped addressed envelope.
Closing Date: The first Friday in February
Funding: Government
Contributor: The Swedish Institute in Stockholm, Sweden
No. of awards given last year: 5
No. of applicants last year: 40
Additional Information: The project must be completed within 1 year of receipt of the grant. A report must be submitted to the Swedish Information Service 6 months after the research trip is completed. Award recipients are announced during the month of May.

The SASS Swedish Travel Grants

Subjects: Politics, public administration, working life, human environment, mass media, business and industry, education and culture.
Level of Study: Postgraduate
Type: Grant
Value: All agreed travel costs
Frequency: Annual
Country of Study: Sweden
No. of awards offered: Varies
Application Procedure: Contact the Institute.
Closing Date: The first Friday in February
Funding: Government
Contributor: The Swedish Institute in Stockholm

THE SWEDISH INSTITUTE

Skeppsbron 2, Box 7434, Stockholm, 103 91, Sweden
Tel: (46) 46 8453 7800
Fax: (46) 46 820 7248
Email: grant@si.se
Website: www.studyinsweden.se

Sweden has a long and proud history of academic excellence, with outstanding universities dating back to the 15th century. Sweden is also home of the Nobel Prize, the world's most prestigious academic distinction.

Anna Lindh Swedish-Turkish Scholarships

Subjects: Human rights law.
Purpose: To advance the field of European studies.
Eligibility: Open to Turkish students only.
Level of Study: Postgraduate
Type: Scholarship
Value: All tuition fees, plus travel allowance
Frequency: Annual
Country of Study: Sweden
Application Procedure: Apply online.
Closing Date: September
Funding: Government
Contributor: Consulate General of Swedish in Istanbul

Master Programme for Key Personnel in Developing Countries

Subjects: All subjects.
Purpose: To help grow special competencies in targeted countries.
Eligibility: Refer to website.
Level of Study: Postgraduate
Type: Scholarship
Value: A monthly stipend of SEK 8,000, plus travel costs
Length of Study: 1–2 years
Frequency: Annual
Country of Study: Sweden
Application Procedure: There is no application form for this scholarship, please contact the institute.
Closing Date: May
Contributor: Swedish International Development Co-operation Agency (SIDA)

Swedish Institute Bilateral Scholarship

Subjects: All subjects.
Eligibility: Open to nationals of Bulgaria, China, France, Germany, Italy, Japan, Romania, Russia and Ukraine.
Level of Study: Postgraduate, research
Type: Scholarship
Value: All agreed costs
Length of Study: 1 year
Frequency: Annual
Country of Study: Sweden
Application Procedure: Contact the respective Embassy for application guidelines.
Closing Date: September
Funding: Government
Additional Information: Applicants must be fluent in English or proficient in Swedish.

The Swedish Institute Guest Scholarship Programme

Subjects: All subjects.
Purpose: To support advanced level studies at a Swedish institution of higher education.

Eligibility: Open to all nationalities, with the exception of citizens from the Nordic countries-Sweden, Denmark, Finland, Iceland and Norway.
Level of Study: Postgraduate
Type: Scholarship
Value: All tuition fees
Length of Study: 1 year
Frequency: Annual
Country of Study: Sweden
Application Procedure: Apply online.
Funding: Foundation
Contributor: The Swedish Institute

Visby Programme

Subjects: All subjects.
Purpose: To stimulate greater long-term cooperation between institutions of higher education.
Eligibility: Open to all students from the Visby region (see website for definition), priority is given to candidates from Belarus, Ukraine and Russia.
Level of Study: Postgraduate
Type: Grant
Value: All costs for travel, and board and lodging during the study period
Length of Study: 1 month–2 years
Frequency: Annual
Country of Study: Sweden
No. of awards offered: 100
Application Procedure: Apply online.
Closing Date: March 1st
No. of awards given last year: 100

SWISS FEDERAL INSTITUTE OF TECHNOLOGY ZÜRICH

Eidgenössische Technische Hochschule, CH-8092 Zurich, Switzerland
Tel: (41) 1 632 2141
Fax: (41) 1 632 1264
Email: doc.exchange@rektorat.ethz.ch
Website: www.mobilitaet.ethz.ch
Contact: Rita Gilli, Student Exchange Office

The Swiss Federal Institute of Technology Zurich is a science and technology university with an outstanding research record. Excellent research conditions, state-of-the-art infrastructure and an attractive urban environment add up to the ideal setting for creative personalities.

Swiss Federal Institute of Technology Scholarships

Subjects: Architecture, engineering (civil, mechanical, electrical, production, rural and surveying), computer science, materials science, chemistry, physics, mathematics, biology, environmental sciences, Earth sciences, pharmacy, agriculture and forestry.
Eligibility: Open primarily, but not exclusively, to nationals of Canada, Italy, Japan, Poland, Spain, the United Kingdom and the United States of America. Candidates should be 20–30 years of age, have had at least 2 years of university study and have a good working knowledge of German.
Level of Study: Unrestricted
Type: Scholarship
Value: Swiss Francs 1,300–1,500 per month, plus tuition and health insurance allowance
Length of Study: 1 academic year between October and July
Frequency: Annual
Study Establishment: The Institute
Country of Study: Switzerland
No. of awards offered: 8
Application Procedure: Applications must be made to the appropriate address. See the website for further information.
Closing Date: February 15th
Funding: Government

SWISS STATE SECRETARIAT FOR EDUCATION AND RESEARCH (SER)

Hallwylstasse 4, CH-3003, Switzerland, Bern, Switzerland
Tel: (41) 31 323 2676
Fax: (41) 31 323 3020
Email: info@sbf.admin-ch
Website: www.sbf.admin.ch

SER activities are focused on the continuation and development of a high standard of teaching and research in Swiss universities. The SER pursues a policy of efficient use of resources, profile-building allocation of work between individual institutions and the various types of institutions in the field of public education and research as well as of close relations between education, science, society and business.

Swiss Scholarships for University Studies for Central and East European Countries

Subjects: All subjects excluding the arts.
Purpose: To intensity scientific and cultural relations.
Eligibility: Only candidates who excel academically and who have mastered one or more of the languages of instruction (German French, Italian) and are from the countries listed below will be considered: Albania, Belarus, Bosnia and Herzegovina, Bulgaria, Croatia, Macedonia, Moldavia, Romania, Russia, Serbia and Montenegro, Ukraine.
Level of Study: Postgraduate
Type: Scholarship
Value: A monthly stipend of Swiss Francs 1,820
Length of Study: 9 month academic year
Frequency: Annual
Country of Study: Switzerland
No. of awards offered: 30–40
Application Procedure: Application forms are available at the Swiss embassy.
Closing Date: December 15th
Funding: Government
Contributor: The Swiss Federal Commission
Additional Information: Fully completed application documents should be handed over to the Swiss embassy in the corresponding country. For Belarus the embassy in Warsaw is responsible; for Estonia the embassy in Helsinki; for Latvia and Lithuania the embassy in Riga and for Moldavia the embassy in view.

Swiss Scholarships for University Studies, Fine Arts and Music for Foreign Applicants

Subjects: Fine arts and music.
Purpose: To further education and to undertake research work in the fields in which the Swiss universities are particularly active.
Eligibility: Candidates must have a good performance capacity record and clear study goal, and be under 35 years of age when applying. Proficiency in German, French or Italian is required.
Level of Study: Postgraduate
Type: Scholarship
Value: A monthly stipend from Swiss Francs 1,600–4,500
Length of Study: 9 month academic year
Frequency: Annual
Study Establishment: An approved Swiss university or Federal Institute of Technology
Country of Study: Switzerland
Application Procedure: Application forms can be obtained from the ministry of education or institution in change of scholarships in the country of origin of the candidate or from the Swiss diplomatic representation.
Closing Date: October
Funding: Government
Contributor: The Swiss Federal Commission
Additional Information: When accepting the scholarship, candidates may have to give their written agreement to return to their country after completion of studies in Switzerland.

SYMPHONY OF THE MOUNTAINS

1200 E Center Street, Kingsport, TN, 37660, United States of America
Tel: (1) 423 392 8423
Fax: (1) 423 392 8428
Email: info@symphonyofthemountains.org
Website: www.symphonyofthemountains.org
Contact: Ms Ann Myers, Executive Director

Elizabeth Harper Vaughn Concerto Competition

Subjects: Three categories alternate annually in the following sequence: percussion, wind instruments and brass and strings or piano.
Purpose: To encourage and recognize young musicians.
Eligibility: Open to musicians who are 26 years of age or under.
Level of Study: Postgraduate
Type: Competition
Value: US$1,500 plus a concert performance with the orchestra and accommodation
Frequency: Annual
Country of Study: Any country
No. of awards offered: 1
Application Procedure: Applications must be accompanied by a letter of recommendation from a qualified teacher, the entrance fee of US$20 payable to Symphony of the Mountains and a cassette tape. The tape recording must be a concerto, or work of similar importance, written with orchestral accompaniment.
Closing Date: December 1st
Funding: Private
Contributor: Women's Symphony Committee
No. of awards given last year: 1
No. of applicants last year: 30
Additional Information: The competition is held in March.

SYRACUSE UNIVERSITY

Syracuse, NY 13244, United States of America
Tel: (1) 315 443 1870
Fax: (1) 315 443 3423
Email: pdjohso@syr.edu
Website: www.cwis.syr.edu
Contact: Pat Johnson, Associate Director of Scholorship Programs

Syracuse University is a non-profit, private student research university. Its mission is to promote learning through teaching, research, scholarship, creative accomplishment and service.

Syracuse University African American Fellowship

Subjects: African American studies.
Purpose: To support training for graduate students who demonstrate outstanding qualification.
Eligibility: Open to United States citizens who are African American.
Level of Study: Unrestricted
Type: Fellowship
Value: US$11,000
Length of Study: 1–6 years
Frequency: Annual
Study Establishment: Syracuse University
Country of Study: United States of America
No. of awards offered: 6
Application Procedure: Applicants must apply through admission application.
Closing Date: January 15th
Funding: Private
Contributor: The Syracuse University Graduate School
No. of awards given last year: 6
No. of applicants last year: 20

Syracuse University Graduate Fellowship

Subjects: All subjects.
Purpose: To provide a full support package during a student's term of study.
Eligibility: Open to nationals of any country.
Level of Study: Unrestricted
Type: Fellowship
Value: US$11,000
Length of Study: 1–6 years
Frequency: Annual
Study Establishment: Syracuse University
Country of Study: United States of America
No. of awards offered: 101
Application Procedure: Applicants must apply through admission application.
Closing Date: January 10th
Funding: Private
Contributor: The Syracuse University Graduate School
No. of awards given last year: 101
No. of applicants last year: 250

TEAGASC (IRISH AGRICULTURE AND FOOD DEVELOPMENT AUTHORITY)

19 Sandymount Avenue, Dublin, 4, Ireland
Tel: (353) 1 637 6000
Fax: (353) 1 668 8023
Email: corourke@hq.teagasc.ie
Website: www.teagasc.ie
Contact: Dr C O'Rourke, Manager

Teagasc (Irish Agriculture and Food Development Authority) is the parastatal body responsible for agricultural and food research, farm advisory services and farmer education in the Republic of Ireland. Its research programme includes foods, dairy cows, beef cattle, pigs, sheep, crops, horticulture, environment, rural economics and sociology at eight research centres.

Teagasc Walsh Fellowships

Subjects: Any subject relevant to food and agriculture in Ireland, eg. animal sciences, plant sciences, physical or Earth sciences, environment, economics and rural development.
Purpose: To support MSc and PhD projects on topics relevant to the overall Teagasc research programme on agriculture and food.
Eligibility: Applicants must be college faculty members who, in co-operation with Teagasc researchers, submit proposals relevant to the Teagasc programme on agriculture and food in Ireland. If successful, they then select postgraduate students for MSc or PhD programmes as Walsh Fellows. Applications are not accepted from individual students or for taught non-research postgraduate courses.
Level of Study: Doctorate, research, postgraduate
Type: Fellowship
Value: €15,000 per year to cover a postgraduate stipend and all fees. A limited provision for materials and travel is also available
Length of Study: Up to 2 years for an MSc, maximum of 3 years for a PhD
Frequency: Annual
Study Establishment: Any third-level college, in association with a Teagasc Research Centre
No. of awards offered: Approx. 40
Application Procedure: Applicants must apply for an information brochure, which includes an application form, available on request.
Closing Date: Mid-December
Funding: Government
Contributor: Teagasc's own resources, via the Irish government and the European Union agri-food industry
No. of awards given last year: 40
No. of applicants last year: 80

TENOVUS SCOTLAND

Small Research Grants, 234 St Vincent Street, Glasgow, G2 5RJ, Scotland
Tel: (44) 14 1221 6268
Fax: (44) 12 9231 1433
Email: gen.sec@talk21.com
Website: www.tenovus-scotland.org.uk
Contact: E R Read, General Secretary

Tenovus Scotland supports innovative and pilot medical research projects carried out by young researchers who may not have a track record.

Tenovus Scotland Small Research Grants

Subjects: Medicine, dentistry, medical sciences and allied areas.
Purpose: To foster high-quality research within the healthcare professions in Scotland.
Eligibility: Medical professionals of Scotland. 1) No restrictions on age although preference is for young researchers seeking to establish a track record. 2) Grants conditional on the work being carried out in a Scottish University/Teaching an NHS Trust Hospital. 3) No restriction on Nationality provided they meet 1 x 2 above.
Level of Study: Research
Type: Grant
Value: Normally up to UK £10,000 or part thereof
Country of Study: Scotland
Application Procedure: Application forms must be filled, applications from investigators lacking support in the early stages of a new project are encouraged. Applications may be invited for salary support or for research studentships.
Closing Date: February 15th and August 15th of each year
Funding: Trusts
No. of awards given last year: 45
No. of applicants last year: 50

THE MOUNTAINEERING COUNCIL OF SCOTLAND MCOFS

McofS The old Germany West Mill Street, Perth, PH 1 SQP, United Kingdom
Website: www.mountaineering-scotalnd.org.uk
Contact: The National Officer

MCofS administers the Sports Scotland grants for mountaineering.

MCofS Expedition Grant

Subjects: First free ascents of routes I the greater ranges and little or unexplored mountain areas of the world.
Purpose: To award excellence and adventure in sports.
Eligibility: See website.
Level of Study: Research, professional development
Type: Grant
Value: UK £2,000
Frequency: Annual
Country of Study: Any country
No. of awards offered: 1
Application Procedure: Request and expedition grant information pack.
Closing Date: March
Funding: Government
Contributor: Sports Scotland
No. of awards given last year: 1

THIRD WORLD ACADEMY OF SCIENCES (TWAS)

The Abdus Salam International Centre for Theoretical Physics, Strada Costiera 11, I-34014 Trieste, Italy
Tel: (39) 40 224 0327
Fax: (39) 40 224 0559
Email: info@twas.org
Website: www.twas.org
Contact: Professor Mohamed H A Hassan, Executive Director

The Third Word Academy of Sciences (TWAS) is an autonomous international organization that promotes and supports excellence in scientific research and helps build research capacity in the South.

CAS-TWAS Fellowship for Postdoctoral Research in China

Subjects: All areas of the natural sciences.
Purpose: To enable scholars who wish to pursue postdoctoral research to undertake research in laboratories or institutes of the Chinese Academy of Sciences.
Eligibility: Candidates must have a PhD and be nationals of a developing country other than China. They must also be regularly employed at a research or teaching institution in their home country. The maximum age limit is 40 years.
Level of Study: Postdoctorate
Type: Fellowship
Value: Covers food, accommodation and international travel, no provision for family members
Length of Study: Up to 1 year
Frequency: Annual
Study Establishment: CAS
Country of Study: China
No. of awards offered: Up to 15
Application Procedure: Applicants must send one copy of the application form to TWAS and three copies to CAS. Application forms can be obtained from the TWAS website.
Closing Date: October 31st
Funding: Government
Contributor: Chinese Academy of Sciences (CAS) and TWAS
Additional Information: CAS has 5 academic divisions, 11 local branches, 84 research institutes and 3 universities or colleges, distributed throughout the country.

For further information contact:

Division of International Organization Programmes, Chinese Academy of Sciences, 52 Sanlihe Road, Beijing, 100864, China
Contact: Mr Wang Zhenyu, Deputy Director

CAS-TWAS Fellowship for Postgraduate Research in China

Subjects: All areas of the natural sciences.
Purpose: To carry out research towards the final year of a PhD programme in China.
Eligibility: Candidates must have a Master's degree in natural sciences, be nationals of a developing country other than China and be registered for a PhD in their home country. The maximum age limit is 35 years.
Level of Study: Postgraduate
Type: Fellowship
Value: Covers food, accommodation and international travel. There is no provision for family members
Length of Study: 1 year
Frequency: Annual
Study Establishment: CAS
Country of Study: China
No. of awards offered: Up to 20
Application Procedure: Applicants must send one copy of the application form to TWAS and three copies to CAS. Application forms can be obtained from the TWAS website.
Closing Date: October 31st
Funding: Government
Contributor: Chinese Academy of Sciences (CAS) and TWAS
No. of awards given last year: New
Additional Information: CAS has 5 academic divisions, 11 local branches, 84 research institutes and 3 universities or colleges distrubited throughout the country.

For further information contact:

Division of International Organization Programmes, Chinese Academy of Sciences, 52 Sanlihe Road, Beijing, 100864, China
Contact: Mr Wang Zhengu, Deputy Director

CAS-TWAS Fellowship for Visiting Scholars in China

Subjects: All areas of the natural sciences.
Purpose: To pursue advanced research in the natural sciences.

Eligibility: Applicants must have a PhD, a regular research assignment and at least 5 years postdoctoral research experience. Chinese nationals are not eligible. The maximum age limit is 55 years.
Level of Study: Research
Type: Fellowship
Length of Study: 1–3 months
Frequency: Annual
Study Establishment: CAS
Country of Study: China
No. of awards offered: Up to 15
Application Procedure: Applicants must send one copy of the application to TWAS and three copies to CAS. Application forms can be obtained from the TWAS website.
Closing Date: October 31st
Funding: Government
Contributor: Chinese Academy of Sciences (CAS) and TWAS
Additional Information: CAS has 5 academic divisions, 11 local branches, 84 research institutes and 3 universities or colleges distributed throughout the country.

For further information contact:

Division of International Organization Programmes, Chinese Academy of Sciences, 52 Sanlihe Road, Beijing, 100864, China
Contact: Mr Wang Zhenyu, Deputy Director

CNPq-TWAS Doctoral Fellowships in Brazil
Subjects: All areas of the natural sciences.
Purpose: To enable scholars from developing countries (other than Brazil) to undertake research in Brazil.
Eligibility: Applicants must hold a Master's degree or equivalent, and be proficient in either English, French, Portuguese or Spanish. Open to nationals of a developing country other than Brazil. The maximum age limit is 30 years.
Level of Study: Postgraduate
Type: Fellowship
Value: Covers food, accommodation and international travel, no provision for family members
Length of Study: Up to 4 years
Frequency: Annual
Country of Study: Brazil
No. of awards offered: Up to 40
Application Procedure: Applicants must complete an application form, available on request or from the website www.twas.org
Closing Date: October 31st
Funding: Government
Contributor: Brazilian ministry of science and technology, the Conselho Nacional de Desenvolvimento Cientifico e Tecnologico (CNPq) and TWAS
No. of awards given last year: New award

CNPq-TWAS Fellowships for Postdoctoral Research in Brazil
Subjects: All areas of the natural sciences.
Purpose: To enable scholars to pursue postdoctoral research in Brazil.
Eligibility: Applicants must have a PhD in the natural sciences, be proficient in English, French, Portuguese or Spanish and must be regularly employed at a research or teaching institution in their home country. Open to nationals of developing countries other than Brazil. The maximum age limit is 40 years.
Level of Study: Postdoctorate
Type: Fellowship
Value: Covers food, accommodation and international travel, no provision for family members
Length of Study: 6 months–1 year
Frequency: Annual
Country of Study: Brazil
No. of awards offered: Up to 10
Application Procedure: Applicants must complete an application form, available on request or from the website www.twas.org
Closing Date: October 31st
Funding: Government
Contributor: Brazilian Ministry of Science and Technology, the Conselho Nacional de Desenvolvimento Cientifico e Tecnologico (CNPq) and TWAS

CSIR (Council of Scientific and Industrial Research)/ TWAS Fellowship for Postgraduate Research
Subjects: Newly emerging areas of science and technology.
Purpose: To enable scholars from developing countries (other than India) who wish to pursue postgraduate research to undertake research in laboratories or institutes of the CSIR.
Eligibility: Candidates must have a Master's or equivalent degree in science or engineering and should be a regular employee in a developing country (other than India) and be holding a research assignment.
Level of Study: Postgraduate
Type: Fellowship
Value: A monthly stipend of Rs 8,000 per month, extendable to Rs 9,000 in the final year, plus a contingency grant of Rs 20,000
Length of Study: 2–3 years
Frequency: Annual
Study Establishment: CSIR research laboratories or institutes
Country of Study: India
No. of awards offered: Varies
Application Procedure: One copy of the application should be sent to TWAS and three copies to CSIR. Application forms are available on request or from the website www.twas.org or www.ictp.trieste.it/~twas/hg/csir_postgrad_form.html
Closing Date: June 1st
Funding: Government
Contributor: CSIR (India), the Italian Ministry of Foreign Affairs and the Directorate General for Development Co-operation
No. of awards given last year: 8
Additional Information: CSIR is the premier scientific organization of India, and has a network of research laboratories covering wide areas of scientific and industrial research. Further information is available on the CSIR website www.csir.res.in

For further information contact:

International S&T Affairs Directorate, Council for Scientific and Industrial Research (CSIR), Anusandhan Bhavan, 2 Rafi Marg, New Delhi, 110001, India
Fax: (91) 11 2371 0618
Email: rprasad@csir.res.in
Contact: Dr B K Ramprasad, Senior Deputy Advisor

CSIR (The Council of Scientific and Industrial Research)/ TWAS Fellowship for Postdoctoral Research
Subjects: Newly emerging areas of science and technology.
Purpose: To enable scholars from developing countries (other than India) who wish to pursue postdoctoral research to undertake research in laboratories or institutes of the CSIR.
Eligibility: The minimum qualification requirement is a PhD degree in science or technology. Applicants must be regular employees in a developing country (but not India) and should hold a research assignment.
Level of Study: Postdoctorate
Type: Fellowship
Value: A monthly stipend of Rs 11,500 for a maximum of 1 year, plus a contingency grant of Rs 20,000 per year
Length of Study: Up to 1 year
Frequency: Annual
Study Establishment: CSIR research laboratories or institutes
Country of Study: India
No. of awards offered: Varies
Application Procedure: Applicants must complete an application form, available on request or from the website.
Closing Date: June 1st
Funding: Government
Contributor: CSIR (India), the Italian Ministry of Foreign Affairs and the Directorate General for Development Co-operation
No. of awards given last year: 4
Additional Information: CSIR is the premier civil scientific organization of India, which has a network of research laboratories covering

wide areas of industrial research. Further information is available on the CSIR website www.csir.res.in

For further information contact:

Senior Deputy Advisor, CSIR (The Council of Scientific and Industrial Research), Anusandhan Bhavan, 2 Rafi Marg, New Delhi, 110001, India
Tel: (91) 11 331 6751
Fax: (91) 11 371 0618
Email: rprasad@csirhq.ren.nic.in
Contact: Dr B K Ramprasad

DBT-TWAS Biotechnology Fellowship for Postdoctoral Studies in India

Subjects: All areas of biotechnology.
Purpose: To support postdoctoral research in biotechnology in India.
Eligibility: Applicants must have a PhD in the biosciences or biotechnology, be employed at a research or teaching institution and must be a national of a developing country. Indian nationals are not eligible. The maximum age limit is 40 years.
Level of Study: Postgraduate
Type: Fellowship
Value: Rs 11,500, plus a house rent allowance, medical coverage and an Rs 20,000 contingency grant paid to the host institution
Length of Study: 1 year
Frequency: Annual
Study Establishment: More than 80 listed universities and research institutions
Country of Study: India
No. of awards offered: Up to 10
Application Procedure: Applicants must complete an application form, available on request or from the website www.twas.org
Closing Date: October 31st
Funding: Government
Contributor: Indian Department of Biotechnology (DBT) and TWAS

DBT-TWAS Biotechnology Fellowships for Postgraduate Studies in India

Subjects: All areas of biotechnology.
Purpose: To carry out research leading to a PhD in biotechnology.
Eligibility: Applicants must have a Master's degree in science, engineering or equivalent, must be a national of a developing country (except India) and must be registered for a PhD or be willing to register in India. The maximum age limit is 30 years.
Level of Study: Postdoctorate
Type: Fellowship
Value: Rs 8,000 during the first 2 years, rising to Rs 9,000 in the 3rd year. An Rs 20,000 contingency grant is provided to the host institution. Medical coverage and subsidized housing is also provided
Length of Study: Up to 3 years
Frequency: Annual
Study Establishment: More than 80 listed universities and research institutions
Country of Study: India
No. of awards offered: Up to 40
Application Procedure: Applicants must complete an application form, available on request or from the website.
Closing Date: October 31st
Funding: Government
Contributor: Indian Department of Biotechnology (DBT) and TWAS

ICSU-TWAS-UNESCO-UNU/IAS Visiting Scientist Programme

Subjects: All areas of science other than mathematics or physics.
Purpose: To provide institutions and research grants in the South, especially in least developed countries (LDCs), with the opportunity to establish long-term links with world leaders in science and help build scientific capacity in their country.
Eligibility: Candidate must be an internationally renowned expert.
Level of Study: Research, professional development
Type: Consultancy
Value: Travel plus a US$500 honorarium. Local costs will be covered by the host institution
Length of Study: Minimum of 1 month
Frequency: Annual
Study Establishment: Teaching and research institutions
Country of Study: Any developing country, preference will be given to LDCs
Application Procedure: Applicants must complete an application form, available on request or from the website.
Closing Date: October 1st
Funding: International Office, government
Contributor: International Council for Science (ICSU), United Nations Educational, Scientific and Cultural Organization (UNESCO), United Nations University/Institute for Advanced Studies (UNU/IAS) and TWAS
No. of awards given last year: 16 visits
Additional Information: A similar programme for mathematics and physics is run by the Abdus Salam International Centre for Theoretical Physics (ICTP). See the website www.ictp.trieste.it/www-users/oea/vs for more information.

The Trieste Science Prize

Subjects: Biological sciences, chemical sciences, agricultural sciences, Earth, space, ocean and atmospheric sciences, engineering sciences, mathematics, medical sciences, physics and astronomy.
Purpose: To honour outstanding scientists living and working in developing countries.
Eligibility: Candidates must be nationals of developing countries living and working in the South. Individuals who have won the Nobel Prize, Tokyo/Kyoto Prize, Gafoord Prize or Abel Prize are not eligible.
Level of Study: Research
Type: Prize
Value: US$50,000 each
Frequency: Annual
Country of Study: Any developing country
No. of awards offered: 2
Application Procedure: Nomination forms must be downloaded from the website www.twas.org and accompanied by a 5–6 page biographical sketch outlining the nominee's major scientific achievements, pre-prints of up to 20 publications and a complete list of publications.
Closing Date: March 31st
Funding: Commercial, private
Contributor: Illycaffè, Trieste

TWAS Fellowships for Research and Advanced Training

Subjects: All fields of basic sciences.
Purpose: To enhance the research of young promising scientists, specifically those at the beginning of their research career, and to help them to foster links for future collaboration.
Eligibility: Open to nationals of developing countries with permanent positions in universities or research institutes in developing countries holding a PhD or equivalent. Candidates must not be older than 40 years and preference will be given to candidates from less developed countries.
Level of Study: Postdoctorate
Type: Fellowship
Value: Travel support and monthly subsistence of up to US$300. Living expenses are usually obtained from local sources
Length of Study: 3 months–1 year
Frequency: Annual
Country of Study: Developing countries
No. of awards offered: Varies
Application Procedure: Applicants must complete an application form, available on request or from the website.
Closing Date: October 1st
Funding: Government
Contributor: The Italian Ministry of Foreign Affairs and the Directorate General for Development Co-operation
Additional Information: Further information is available on the website.

TWAS Grants for Scientific Meetings in Developing Countries

Subjects: Agricultural, biological, chemical, engineering or geological and medical sciences.
Purpose: To encourage international scientific meetings in Third World countries.
Eligibility: Open to organizers of international scientific meetings in developing countries. Special consideration is given to those meetings that are likely to benefit the scientific community in the Third World and to promote regional and international co-operation in developing science and its applications to the problems of the Third World.
Level of Study: Postgraduate, professional development
Type: Travel grant
Value: Up to US$4,000 for travel expenses of principal speakers from abroad and/or participants from the region
Frequency: Annual
Country of Study: Developing countries
No. of awards offered: Varies
Application Procedure: Applicants must complete an application form, available on request or from the website.
Closing Date: June 1st for meetings held between January and June of the following year, and December 1st for meetings held between July and December of the following year
Funding: Government
Contributor: The Italian Ministry of Foreign Affairs and the Directorate General for Development Co-operation
No. of awards given last year: 30

TWAS Prizes

Subjects: Medical sciences, biology, chemistry, mathematics and physics, agricultural sciences, engineering sciences and Earth sciences.
Purpose: To recognize and support outstanding achievements made by scientists from developing countries. Prizes are awarded to those scientists whose research work has significantly contributed to the advancement of science.
Eligibility: Open to nationals of developing countries who are, as a rule, working and living in these countries. Consideration is given to proven achievements judged particularly by their national and international impact. Members of TWAS are not eligible for such awards.
Level of Study: Postgraduate, professional development, postdoctorate, doctorate
Type: Prize
Value: US$10,000 plus a plaque on which major contributions of the award winner are mentioned
Frequency: Annual
Country of Study: Developing countries
No. of awards offered: 8
Application Procedure: Applicants must be designated on the nomination form. The nomination must be accompanied by a one- to two-page biographical sketch of the nominee including their major scientific accomplishments, a list of twelve of the candidate's most significant publications as well as a complete list of publications and a curriculum vitae. Nominations for the awards are invited from all members of the TWAS as well as from academies, national research councils, universities and scientific institutions in developing countries and advanced countries. A nomination form is available on request or can be downloaded from the website www.twas.org
Closing Date: March 1st. Nominations received after the deadline will be considered in the next year
Funding: Government
Contributor: The Italian Ministry of Foreign Affairs and the Directorate General for Development Co-operation
No. of awards given last year: 8
Additional Information: The awards are usually presented on a special occasion, normally coinciding with the general meeting of the Academy and/or a general conference organized by the Academy. Recipients of awards are expected to give lectures about the work for which the awards have been made. Further information is available on the website.

TWAS Prizes to Young Scientists in Developing Countries

Subjects: Biology, chemistry, mathematics or physics, rotated annually.
Purpose: To enable science academies and research councils in developing countries to award prizes to scientists in their countries.
Eligibility: Open to academies and research councils in developing countries. The age limit for prize winners is 40 years.
Level of Study: Postgraduate
Type: Prize
Value: Usually US$2,000
Frequency: Annual
Country of Study: Developing countries
No. of awards offered: More than 30
Application Procedure: Applicants must write for details to info@twas.org or see the website.
Funding: Government
Contributor: The Italian Ministry of Foreign Affairs and the Directorate General for Development Co-operation
No. of awards given last year: 23

TWAS Research Grants

Subjects: Biology, chemistry, mathematics and physics.
Purpose: To reinforce and promote scientific research in basic sciences in the Third World, to strengthen the endogenous capacity in science and to reduce the exodus of scientific talents from the South.
Eligibility: Applicants must be nationals of developing countries with an advanced academic degree, some research experience and must hold positions at universities or research institutions in developing countries.
Level of Study: Postdoctorate, doctorate, professional development, postgraduate
Value: Up to US$10,000. Grants are to be used to purchase scientific equipment, consumable laboratory supplies and scientific literature (textbooks and proceedings only)
Length of Study: 1 year
Frequency: Annual
Country of Study: Developing countries
No. of awards offered: Varies
Application Procedure: Applicants must complete an application form available on request or from the website. Applications must be submitted in English.
Closing Date: July 1st or December 1st
Funding: Government
Contributor: The Italian Ministry of Foreign Affairs, the Directorate General for Development Co-operation and the Swedish Agency for Research Co-operation with Developing Countries
No. of awards given last year: 90
Additional Information: Further information is available on the request.

TWAS Spare Parts for Scientific Equipment

Subjects: Biology, chemistry and physics.
Purpose: The programme has been established in response to the current difficulty faced by several laboratories in the Third World to obtain badly needed spares and replacement parts for scientific equipment that is required for their experimental research.
Eligibility: Applicants must be research group leaders at universities or research institutes in developing countries.
Level of Study: Professional development
Type: Grant
Value: Up to US$1,000 including insurance and freight charges
Country of Study: Developing countries
No. of awards offered: Varies
Application Procedure: Applicants must first contact the suppliers and obtain a proforma invoice, valid for 3–6 months, including cost, insurance and freight charges for the items they require. Applicants must submit a completed application form with the proforma invoice from the supplier. Application forms are available on request or from the website.
Closing Date: Applications are accepted at any time
Funding: Government
Contributor: The Italian Ministry of Foreign Affairs and the Directorate General for Development Co-operation
No. of awards given last year: 30
Additional Information: Applications by email will not be accepted.

TWAS UNESCO Associateship Scheme

Subjects: Biology, chemistry, physics, mathematics, engineering, agricultural sciences, medical sciences and Earth sciences.
Purpose: To alleviate the problem of isolated talented scientists in developing countries, and strengthen the research programmes of centres of excellence in the South.
Eligibility: Open to associates among the most eminent and promising researchers in developing countries. Special consideration is given to scientists from isolated institutions in developing countries.
Level of Study: Postdoctorate, professional development
Value: Travel costs plus US$300 per month for incidental local expenses. The host centre provides local hospitality and research facilities
Length of Study: 3 years, plus the entitlement to visit the Centre twice for a period of 2–3 months each time. There is a possibility of renewal for a further 3 years depending on funds available
Frequency: Annual
Study Establishment: There are over 116 centres
Country of Study: Developing countries
No. of awards offered: Varies
Application Procedure: Applicants must complete an application form, available on request or from the website.
Closing Date: December 1st
Funding: Government
Contributor: UNESCO, the Italian Ministry for Foreign Affairs and the Directorate General for Development Co-operation

TWAS-S N Bose National Centre for Basic Sciences Postgraduate Fellowships in Physical Sciences

Subjects: Physical sciences.
Purpose: To carry out research leading to a PhD in the physical sciences.
Eligibility: Applicant must have a Master's degree in physics, mathematics or physical chemistry, must be a national of a developing country (other than India) and be employed at a research institution. The maximum age limit is 30 years.
Level of Study: Postgraduate
Type: Fellowship
Value: Rs 8,000 during the first 2 years, rising to Rs 9,000 in the 3rd year. A Rs 20,000 containing grant is provided to the host institution. Travel and subsidized accommodation are covered
Length of Study: Up to 5 years
Frequency: Annual
Study Establishment: S N Bose National Centre for Basic Sciences
Country of Study: India
No. of awards offered: Up to 5
Application Procedure: Applicants must complete an application form, available on request or from the website.
Closing Date: October 31st
Funding: Government
Contributor: S N Bose National Centre for Basic Sciences, Kolkata, India and TWAS
Additional Information: For further information see the website www.bose.res.in

THIRD WORLD NETWORK OF SCIENTIFIC ORGANIZATIONS (TWNSO)

TWAS & The Abdus Salam ICTP, Strada Costiera 11 I-34014 Trieste, Italy
Tel: (39) 040 224 0683
Fax: (39) 040 224 0689
Email: info@twnso.org
Website: www.twnso.org
Contact: Secretariat

The Third World Network of Scientific Organizations (TWNSO) is a non-governmental organization founded in 1988 to promote science-based sustainable economic development in the South. It was founded on the initiative of the Third World Academy of Sciences (TWAS), and by ministers of science, technology and higher education and heads of science academies and research councils in developing countries. In 1990, TWNSO acquired consultative status with UNESCO.

Celso Furtado Award

Subjects: The understanding and promotion of the socio-economic development of countries in the South.
Purpose: To give recognition, encouragement and support to outstanding work in the field of the political economy of developing countries.
Eligibility: Applicants must have worked in the field of political economy resulting in a fundamental contribution to the advancement of socio-economic development and the developing world in the global context.
Type: Prize
Value: US$10,000 and a medallion
Frequency: Every 3 years
Country of Study: Any country
No. of awards offered: 1
Application Procedure: The nomination should be accompanied by a 1–2 page profile of the nominated individual, a list of significant publications relevant to the award, a complete list of publications and a curriculum vitae of the candidate.
Closing Date: January 31st
Funding: Government
Contributor: The Federal Republic of Brazil
Additional Information: Further information is available on the TWNSO website. The award is named after Celso Furtado, one of the leading Latin American economists from Brazil.

TWNSO Grants to Institutions in the South for Joint Research Projects

Subjects: Biotechnology, new materials, microelectronics, information technology, space technology, new and renewable energies, soil erosion and desertification, floods and earthquakes, biodiversity, atmosphere pollution, toxic and chemical waste or fresh water resources.
Purpose: To award grants to joint research projects with well-defined objectives.
Eligibility: Open to institutions in developing countries in the South. Applications must be joint proposals from two to three institutions. At least one co-operating institution must be located in a least developed country (LDC).
Level of Study: Professional development
Type: Grant
Value: Up to US$30,000
Length of Study: Up to 2 years
Frequency: Annual
Country of Study: Developing countries
No. of awards offered: Varies
Application Procedure: Applicants must complete and submit an application form, available on request or from the website. Applications must be submitted from two or three institutions in the South.
Closing Date: December 1st
Funding: Government
Contributor: The OPEC Fund for International Development

THE THOMSON FOUNDATION

37 Park Place, Cardiff, CF10 3BB, Wales
Tel: (44) 29 2035 3060
Fax: (44) 29 2035 3061
Email: enquiries@thomfound.co.uk
Website: www.thomsonfoundation.co.uk
Contact: Mr Gareth Price

The Thomson Foundation provides practical, intensive training both in the United Kingdom and abroad, along with a wide range of consultancies to journalists, managers, technicians and production staff in television, radio and the press.

Thomson Foundation Scholarship

Subjects: Journalism, radio or television broadcasting, internet publishing and photojournalism.

Purpose: To enable recipients to attend Thomson Foundation training courses in Britain.
Eligibility: Open to professional journalists and broadcasters with at least 3 years of full-time experience.
Level of Study: Professional development
Type: Scholarship
Value: Varies
Length of Study: Varies, usually a 12-week Summer course or a shorter 4-week course
Study Establishment: The Thomson Foundation
Country of Study: United Kingdom
No. of awards offered: Varies
Application Procedure: Applicants must complete an application form, available from the Foundation, for the courses they wish to apply for.
Closing Date: April 15th
Funding: Private, government
Contributor: The British Foreign Office Chevening Scholarship Scheme
No. of awards given last year: 6
No. of applicants last year: 20
Additional Information: Annual 3-month courses in television, radio and press journalism run from June to September.

THRASHER RESEARCH FUND

15 East South Temple Street, Salt Lake City, UT, 84150-6910, United States of America
Tel: (1) 801 240 4753
Fax: (1) 801 240 1625
Email: pontslerAV@thrasherresearch.org
Website: www.thrasherresearch.org
Contact: Mr Justin Brown, Research Manager

The Thrasher Research Fund provides grants for paediatric medical research that addresses problems in children's health that are significant in terms of either magnitude or severity. Priority is given to clinical and/or translational research that has a relatively shorter distance to application. The Fund assumes that significant solutions to children's health problems remain undiscovered and invites a broad array of applications designed to remedy these deficiencies.

Thrasher Research and Field Demonstration Project Grants

Subjects: Paediatrics.
Purpose: To promote international and national child health research and child health-related projects. The emphasis is on practical and applied interventions with the potential to improve the health of children worldwide.
Eligibility: Open to research scientists and private voluntary organizations. Pre- and postdoctoral students may be employed on Thrasher funded projects, but the principal investigator is expected to take an active role in the project and assume full responsibility for it. The principal investigator must have a connection with a university, research institution or appropriate private voluntary organization.
Level of Study: Research
Type: Grant
Value: US$100,000–300,000
Length of Study: Up to 3 years
Frequency: 4 times per year
Country of Study: Any country
No. of awards offered: Varies
Application Procedure: Application guidelines are available on the Fund's website. Potential applicants are encouraged to contact Fund staff prior to a formal submission to determine how a potential project will fit with current Fund interests.
Closing Date: Proposals that have completed the external review process will be considered at the subsequent quarterly meeting
Funding: Private
Contributor: The Thrasher Research Fund
Additional Information: Historically, the Fund has supported international research. In an effort to achieve greater balance, the Fund is currently emphasizing research conducted in the United States of America.

THURGOOD MARSHALL SCHOLARSHIP FUND (TMSF)

90 William Street Suite 1203, New York, NY 10038, United States of America
Tel: (1) 573 8888
Fax: (1) 573 8497
Email: rdaniels@tmsf.org
Website: www.thurgoodmarshallfund.org

The TMSF was established in 1987 to support exceptional merit scholars attending American's public historically black colleges and universities (HBCUs), who contribute to science, technology, government, human service, business, education and various communities.

TMSF Scholarships

Subjects: Creative and performing arts.
Purpose: To financially support outstanding students.
Eligibility: Open to candidates who are academically exceptional in the creative and performing arts requiring financial help.
Type: Scholarship
Value: US$2,200 per semester and payment of tuition fees, accommodation and books
Frequency: Annual
Application Procedure: Completed applications must be submitted along with the required attachments. Visit: www.aiplef.org/donors/
Funding: Foundation
Contributor: Thurgood Marshall Foundation

For further information contact:

AIPLEF Scholarship 90 William Street Suite 1203, New York, NY 10038
Email: pallen@tmsf.org

TOKYU FOUNDATION FOR INBOUND STUDENTS

1-21-6 Dogenzaka, Shibuya Ku, Tokyo, 150-0043, Japan
Tel: (81) 3 3461 0844
Fax: (81) 3 5458 1696
Email: info@tokyu-f.jp
Website: www.tokyu-f.jp
Contact: Mr Takashi Izumi, Managing Director & Secretary General

The Tokyu Foundation for Inbound Students grant scholarships to postgraduate students studying in Japan from Asia-pacific areas.

Tokyu Scholarship

Subjects: All subjects.
Purpose: To promote international exchange by fostering the development of international goodwill between Japan and her neighbours in Asia and the Pacific and contributing to international co-operation and cultural exchange in the broadest possible sense.
Eligibility: Open to applicants from Asian countries who will be able to explain about their research plan in Japanese.
Level of Study: Postgraduate
Type: Scholarship
Value: Yen 160,000 per month per student
Length of Study: Up to 2 years
Frequency: Annual
Country of Study: Japan
No. of awards offered: 20–25
Application Procedure: Download application form from the website.
Closing Date: November 10th
Funding: Commercial
Contributor: Tokyu Corporation
No. of awards given last year: 21
No. of applicants last year: 869

Additional Information: Applicants must travel to Japan at their own cost and be admitted to enter university postgraduate school.

TOLEDO COMMUNITY FOUNDATION

608 Madison Avenue, Suite 1540, Toledo, OH 43604-1151, United States of America
Tel: (1) 241 5049
Fax: (1) 242 5549
Email: toledocf@toledocf.org
Website: www.toledocf.org

The Toledo Community Foundation, Inc. is a public, charitable foundation that exists to improve the quality of life in the Toledo region.

Charles Z. Moore Memorial Scholarship Fund

Subjects: Music.
Purpose: To encourage students pursuing a course of study in music with an emphasis on Jazz studies.
Eligibility: Open to residents of northwest Ohio or Southeast Michigan who demonstrate the talent, interest and ability needed to pursue the study of Jazz.
Level of Study: Professional development
Type: Scholarship
Frequency: Annual
Country of Study: United States of America
Application Procedure: A completed scholarship application form and support materials must be sent.
Closing Date: March 31st

Edith Franklin Pottery Scholarship

Subjects: Ceramic arts.
Purpose: To assist promising/accomplished potters in obtaining additional education or training in the ceramic arts.
Eligibility: Open to all applicants who are current residents of northwest Ohio Lenawee or Monroe Countries in Michigan with individual motivation, ability and potential.
Level of Study: Professional development
Type: Scholarship
Length of Study: US$7,000
Frequency: Annual
Study Establishment: Any recognized college, university or nonprofit organization
Country of Study: United States of America
Application Procedure: A completed scholarship application form must be sent.
Closing Date: February 28th

Harold W. Wott-IEEE Toledo Section Scholarship Fund

Subjects: Engineering.
Purpose: To support students studying in the engineering field.
Eligibility: Open to applicants attending institutions or universities in northwestern Ohio and Southeastern Michigan.
Level of Study: Postgraduate
Type: Scholarship
Value: US$1,000
Frequency: Annual
Country of Study: United States of America
No. of awards offered: Varies
Application Procedure: A completed application form and required attachments and transcripts must be sent.
Closing Date: March 3rd

TOURETTE SYNDROME ASSOCIATION, INC. (TSA)

42-40 Bell Boulevard, Suite 205, Bayside, NY, 11361-2874, United States of America
Tel: (1) 718 224 2999
Fax: (1) 718 279 9596
Email: ts@tsa-usa.org
Website: www.tsa-usa.org
Contact: Ms Sue Levi-Pearl, Vice President, Medical & Scientific Programmes

The Tourette Syndrome Association, Inc. (TSA), founded in 1972, is the only national voluntary non-profit membership organization dedicated to identifying the cause, finding the cure and controlling the effects of Tourette Syndrome. Members include individuals with the disorder, their relatives and other interested, concerned people. The Association develops and disseminates educational material to individuals, professionals and agencies in the fields of healthcare, education and government, co-ordinates support services to help people and their families cope with the problems that occur with Tourette Syndrome and funds research that will ultimately find the cause of and cure for it and, at the same time, lead to improved medications and treatments.

TSA Research Grants

Subjects: Basic neuroscience specifically relevant to Tourette Syndrome.
Purpose: To foster basic and clinical research related to the causes or treatment of Tourette Syndrome.
Eligibility: Open to candidates who have an MD, PhD or equivalent qualifications. Previous experience in the field of movement disorders is desirable, but not essential. Fellowships are intended for young postdoctoral investigators in the early stages of their careers.
Level of Study: Doctorate, postdoctorate
Type: Research grant
Value: Varies, depending upon the category and applicants' experience within that category, and is usually US$5,000–75,000. Postdoctoral grants are up to US$40,000
Length of Study: 1–2 years
Frequency: Annual
Study Establishment: Any institution with adequate facilities
Country of Study: Any country
No. of awards offered: Varies
Application Procedure: Applicants must submit a letter of intent briefly describing the scientific basis of the proposed project.
Closing Date: October of each year. Please contact the Association for actual date
Funding: Private
No. of awards given last year: 14
No. of applicants last year: 60
Additional Information: The Association provides up to 10 per cent of overhead or indirect costs within the total amount budgeted.

THE TOYOTA FOUNDATION

37F, Shinjuku-Mitsui Building, 2-1-1, Nishi-Shinjuku, Shinjuku-Ku, Tokyo, Japan
Tel: (81) 3 3344 1701
Fax: (81) 3 3342 6911
Website: www.toyotafound.or.jp

The Toyota Foundation was established in 1974 as a multi-purpose grant-making foundation. It provides financial assistance to carry out projects in Japan and other countries, mainly in the developing world, that address timely issues in a variety of fields.

The Toyota Foundation Research Programme

Subjects: All subjects.
Purpose: To support research.
Eligibility: Open to candidates of all nationalities studying a doctoral programme.
Type: Scholarship
Value: Varies
Length of Study: 1–2 years
Frequency: Annual
Application Procedure: See the website.
Funding: Foundation
Contributor: The Toyota Foundation

TRANSPORTATION ASSOCIATION OF CANADA FOUNDATION

2323 St Laurent Boulevard, Ottawa, ON, K1G 4J8, Canada
Tel: (1) 613 736 1350, ext. 235
Fax: (1) 613 736 1395
Email: skillam@tac-atc.ca
Website: www.tac-atc.ca
Contact: Ms Susan Killam, Secretary-Treasurer

The Transportation Association of Canada Foundation has a mandate to support the educational and research needs of the Canadian transportation industry.

TAC Foundation Scholarships

Subjects: Road- and transportation-related disciplines.
Eligibility: Open to Canadian citizens and landed immigrants who hold university degrees and who are acceptable to the university at which they plan to carry out their postgraduate studies in the transportation field. See website for full details.
Level of Study: Postgraduate, 2 undergraduate scholarships in the 15 offered
Type: Scholarship
Value: Canadian $3,000–5,000, with one Canadian $15,000 scholarship
Length of Study: 1 year
Frequency: Annual
Study Establishment: Universities
Country of Study: Other
No. of awards offered: 15
Application Procedure: Online applications only.
Closing Date: The first working day in March. Applicants should check the website for the exact date, which varies each year
Funding: Private, government, commercial
No. of awards given last year: 15
Additional Information: Scholarships currently offered are from the DELCAN Corporation, Stantec Consulting Limited, provincial and territorial governments of Canada, ND LEA EBA Engineering Consultants Limited, Aimtec, Dillon consulting Limited. IRD and Dr. A.T. Bergan, 3M Company, BA Group, IBI Group, past scholarship winners.

TREE RESEARCH & EDUCATION ENDOWMENT FUND

The Tree Fund, 1402 W Anthony Drive, PO Box 3188, Champaign, IL, 61826-3188, United States of America
Tel: (1) 217 239 7070
Fax: (1) 217 355 9516
Email: treefund@treefund.org
Website: www.treefund.org
Contact: Ms Cindy Stachowski

To identify and fund projects and programmes that advance knowledge in the field of arboriculture and urban forestry that benefit people, trees and the environment.

Hyland R Johns Grant Program

Subjects: Arboricultural, urban and community forestry.
Purpose: To provide funding for research.
Eligibility: Open to qualified researchers of any nationality.
Level of Study: Postgraduate
Type: Research grant
Value: US$7,500–25,000
Length of Study: 2–3 years
Frequency: Annual
Country of Study: Any country
Application Procedure: Applicants must complete an application form.
Closing Date: May 1st
Funding: Private
Contributor: ISA members
No. of awards given last year: 7
No. of applicants last year: 39

John Z Duling Grant Program

Subjects: Arboricultural, urban and community forestry.
Purpose: To provide money to support projects.
Eligibility: Open to qualified researchers of any nationality.
Level of Study: Postgraduate
Type: Research grant
Value: A maximum of US$7,500. Funds cannot be used for expenses associated with attendance at colleges and universities, eg. tuition, books or laboratory fees
Length of Study: 1–3 years
Frequency: Annual
Country of Study: Any country
No. of awards offered: 5–10
Application Procedure: Applicants must complete a two-page application form, available from the ISA Research Trust.
Closing Date: November 1st
Funding: Private
Contributor: International Society of Arboriculture (ISA), National Arborist Association
No. of awards given last year: 10
No. of applicants last year: Approx. 60

TROPICAL AGRICULTURAL RESEARCH AND HIGHER EDUCATION CENTER (CATIE)

Turrialba, 7170, Costa Rica
Tel: (506) 556 1016
Fax: (506) 556 0914
Email: posgrado@catie.ac.cr
Website: www.catie.ac.cr
Contact: Dean of the Graduate School

The Tropical Agricultural Research and Higher Education Center (CATIE) is an international, non-profit, regional, scientific and educational institution. Its main purpose is research and education in agricultural sciences, natural resources and related subjects in the American tropics, with emphasis on Central America and the Caribbean.

CATIE Scholarships

Subjects: Ecological agriculture, biotechnology and genetic resources, management and conservation of tropical forestry and biodiversity, tropical woodlands, tropical agroforestry, tropical crop protection and improvement, integrated watershed management and protected areas and environmental socioeconomics.
Purpose: To develop specialized intellectual capital in clean technology, tropical agriculture, natural resources management and human resources in the American tropics.
Eligibility: Priority is given to citizens of Belize, Guatemala, El Salvador, Honduras, Nicaragua, Panama, Costa Rica, Mexico, Venezuela, Colombia, the Dominican Republic, Bolivia and Paraguay.
Level of Study: Doctorate, postgraduate
Type: Grant-loan system
Value: Tuition and fees
Length of Study: 2 years for a Master's degree and 3–4 years for a PhD
Frequency: Annual
Country of Study: Costa Rica
No. of awards offered: 34
Application Procedure: Applicants must undertake an admission process that constitutes 75 per cent for curricular evaluation and 25 per cent for a domiciliary examination.
Closing Date: Applications are accepted at any time, but the evaluation deadline is October
Funding: Foundation, international office, private, government
Contributor: ASDI, OAS, CATIE, DAAD, Russell Train (WWF), CONACYT (Mexico), Ford Foundation, FUNDAYACUCHO (Venezuela), Gobierno de Noruega, Kellogg Foundation, Fundacióa (Mexico)
No. of awards given last year: 34
No. of applicants last year: 350

TRUSTEES OF THEODORA BOSANQUET BURSARY

28 Great James Street, London, WC1N 3ES, England
Tel: (44) 20 7404 6447
Fax: (44) 20 7404 6505
Email: bfwg.charity@btinternet.com
Website: www.bcfgrants.org.uk
Contact: Mrs Considine, Company Secretary

The Trustees of Theodora Bosanquet Bursary was set up to support female postgraduate students carrying out research in English literature or history requiring the use of libraries and archives in London. It provides accommodation in a hall of residence for up to 4 weeks between mid-June and mid-September.

Theodora Bosanquet Bursary

Subjects: English literature/History.
Purpose: This bursary is offered to women postgraduate students whose research in history or English literature requires a short residence in London in the Summer.
Eligibility: Open to female postgraduate students from the United Kingdom and overseas of any age.
Level of Study: Graduate
Type: Bursary
Value: Will be decided by the BFWG charitable foundation
Length of Study: Up to 4 weeks
Frequency: Annual
Study Establishment: Any approved Institute of Higher Education in the United Kingdom
Country of Study: United Kingdom
Application Procedure: Applicants must request an application form by email or download from the website. Forms should then be returned either by email or post enclosing a large stamped addressed envelope or international reply coupons. The envelope should be marked TBB.
Closing Date: October 31st
Funding: Private, foundation
Contributor: Investment income
No. of applicants last year: 8

TUBEROUS SCLEROSIS ASSOCIATION (TSA)

Tuberous Sclerosis Association, PO Box 12979, Barnt Green, Birmingham, B45 5AN, England
Tel: (44) 0121 445 6970
Fax: (44) 0121 445 6970
Email: research@tuberous-sclerosis.org
Website: www.tuberous-sclerosis.org
Contact: Ms Diane Sanson, Head of Administration

The main aims of the Tuberous Sclerosis Association are to support individuals and families affected by tuberous sclerosis, raise awareness and encourage research. Their services include information, advice, advocacy, training, research conferences and specialist clinics.

Tuberous Sclerosis Association Project Grant

Subjects: Tuberous sclerosis.
Purpose: To support research in Tuberous Sclerosis.
Level of Study: Research
Type: Project grant
Length of Study: Research awards only, not for study
Frequency: Dependent on funds available
Country of Study: United Kingdom
Application Procedure: Application form is available from TSA.
Closing Date: November 30th, March 31st, July 31st
Funding: Trusts
No. of awards given last year: 1
No. of applicants last year: 4

For further information contact:

Church Farm House, Church Road, North Leigh, Oxfordshire, WITNEY, OX29 6TX, United Kingdom
Tel: (44) 19 93 881 238
Contact: Mrs Ann Hunt, Head of Research Tuberous Sclerosis Association

TURKU CENTRE FOR COMPUTER SCIENCE (TUCS)

TUCS Office, Data City, Lemminkäisenkatu 14 A, 4th Floor, FIN-20520 Turku, Finland
Tel: (358) 2 2154 049
Fax: (358) 2 2410 154
Email: tucs@abo.fi
Website: www.tucs.fi
Contact: Ms Pia Le Grand, Administrative Officer, Educational Affairs

TUCS is a joint centre of research and education for the three universities in Turku, Finland: University of Turku, Åbo Akademi University and Turku School of Economics and Business Administration. The TUCS Graduate School offers a framework for studying for the doctoral (PhD) degree in computer science, mathematics, information systems, computer engineering, communication systems, or microelectronics.

TUCS Postgraduate Grant

Subjects: Computer science, information systems and computer engineering.
Purpose: To support students studying for a doctoral degree.
Eligibility: Open to candidates who have a Test of English as a Foreign Language score of at least 550 points or a corresponding level of English proficiency, and an MSc or BSc in computer science or a related field. The Graduate Record Examination test is not required, but can be sent voluntarily.
Level of Study: Postgraduate
Type: Grant
Value: €1,180 per month for postgraduate and €1,430 per month for postdoctoral. Both grants are tax free
Length of Study: 4 years
Frequency: Annual
Study Establishment: An approved graduate school
Country of Study: Finland
No. of awards offered: 2–4 each year
Application Procedure: Applicants must submit an application, a curriculum vitae, financing plan for studies, application for financial support, letters of recommendation with full contact details, official copies of examinations gained with official English translations, a certificate of English proficiency and a statement of research interests.
Closing Date: The deadline for studies starting in September is May 15th and for studies starting in January the deadline is September 30th
Funding: Government
No. of awards given last year: 3
No. of applicants last year: 98

UCLA CENTER FOR 17TH AND 18TH CENTURY STUDIES AND THE WILLIAM ANDREWS CLARK MEMORIAL LIBRARY

310 Royce Hall, UCLA, Los Angeles, CA, 90095-1404, United States of America
Tel: (1) 310 206 8552
Fax: (1) 310 206 8577
Email: c1718cs@humnet.ucla.edu
Website: www.humnet.ucla.edu/humnet/c1718cs
Contact: Fellowship Co-ordinator

The UCLA Center for 17th and 18th-century Studies provides a forum for the discussion of central issues in the field of early modern studies, facilitates research and publication, supports scholarship and encourages the creation of interdisciplinary, cross-cultural programmes that advance the understanding of this important period. The William Andrews Clark Memorial Library, administered by the Center, is known for its collections of rare books and manuscripts concerning 17th and 18th-century Britain and Europe, Oscar Wilde and the 1890s, the history of printing, and certain aspects of the American West.

Ahmanson and Getty Postdoctoral Fellowships

Subjects: Arts and humanities, religious studies and social sciences.
Purpose: To encourage participation by junior scholars in the Center's year-long interdisciplinary core programmes.
Eligibility: Open to postdoctoral scholars who have received their PhD in the last 6 years and whose research pertains to the theme as announced by the Library.
Level of Study: Postdoctorate
Type: Fellowship
Value: US$27,600
Length of Study: 3 consecutive academic quarters
Frequency: Annual
Study Establishment: UCLA and the William Andrews Clark Memorial Library
Country of Study: United States of America
No. of awards offered: Up to 4
Application Procedure: Applicants must submit an application form, a curriculum vitae, a proposal statement, a bibliography and three letters of reference.
Closing Date: February 1st
Funding: Private
Contributor: The Ahmanson Foundation of Los Angeles and the Getty Trust
No. of awards given last year: 4
No. of applicants last year: 30
Additional Information: The award is theme-based and is announced each year. The series intends to be interdisciplinary, with emphasis on both literary and historical perspectives. Participating Fellows will be expected to make a substantive contribution to programme seminars.

ASECS (American Society for 18th-Century Studies)/ Clark Library Fellowships

Subjects: The Restoration and the 18th century.
Eligibility: Open to members of ASECS who are postdoctoral scholars and hold a PhD or equivalent at the time of application. The award is also open to advanced doctoral candidates who are members of ASECS.
Level of Study: Postdoctorate
Type: Fellowship
Value: US$2,000
Length of Study: 1 month
Frequency: Annual
Study Establishment: UCLA and the William Andrews Clark Memorial Library
Country of Study: United States of America
No. of awards offered: Varies
Application Procedure: Applicants must submit an application form, a curriculum vitae, a proposal statement, a bibliography and three letters of reference.
Closing Date: February 1st
Funding: Government
Contributor: ASECS and the Clark Library Endowment
No. of awards given last year: 1
No. of applicants last year: 40

Clark Library Short-Term Resident Fellowships

Subjects: Research relevant to the Library's holdings.
Eligibility: Open to PhD scholars or equivalent who are involved in advanced research.
Level of Study: Postdoctorate
Type: Fellowship
Value: US$2,000 per month
Length of Study: 1–3 months
Frequency: Annual
Study Establishment: UCLA and the William Andrews Clark Memorial Library
Country of Study: United States of America
No. of awards offered: Varies
Application Procedure: Applicants must submit an application form, a curriculum vitae, a proposal statement, a bibliography and three letters of reference.
Closing Date: February 1st
Funding: Private, government
Contributor: The Ahmanson Foundation and the Clark Library Endowment
No. of awards given last year: 16
No. of applicants last year: 60

Clark Predoctoral Fellowships

Subjects: Seventeenth- and eighteenth-century studies or one of the other areas represented in the Clark's collections.
Purpose: To support dissertation research.
Eligibility: Open to advanced doctoral students at the University of California whose dissertation concerns an area appropriate to the collections of the Clark Library.
Level of Study: Predoctorate
Type: Fellowship
Value: US$6,000
Length of Study: 3 months
Frequency: Annual
Study Establishment: UCLA and the William Andrews Clark Memorial Library
Country of Study: United States of America
No. of awards offered: Varies
Application Procedure: Applicants must submit an application form, a curriculum vitae, a proposal statement, a bibliography and three letters of reference.
Closing Date: February 1st
Funding: Private
Contributor: The Ahmanson Foundation
No. of awards given last year: 3
No. of applicants last year: 9

Clark-Huntington Joint Bibliographical Fellowship

Subjects: Early modern literature and history and other areas where the sponsoring libraries have common strengths.
Purpose: To support bibliographical research.
Level of Study: Postdoctorate, professional development
Type: Fellowship
Value: US$4,000
Length of Study: 2 months
Frequency: Annual
Study Establishment: The Clark Library and the Huntington Library
Country of Study: United States of America
No. of awards offered: 1
Application Procedure: Applicants must submit an application form, a curriculum vitae, a proposal statement, a bibliography and three letters of reference.
Closing Date: February 1st
Funding: Private
No. of awards given last year: 1
No. of applicants last year: 15

For further information contact:

William Andrews Clark Memorial Library, 2520 Cimarron Street, Los Angeles, CA, 90018-2098, United States of America
Contact: Fellowship Co-ordinator

Kanner Fellowship In British Studies

Subjects: British history and culture.
Eligibility: Open to both postdoctoral and predoctoral scholars.
Level of Study: Predoctorate, postdoctorate
Type: Fellowship
Value: US$6,000
Length of Study: 3 months
Frequency: Annual

Application Procedure: Applicants must submit an application form, a curriculum vitae, proposal statement, a bibliography and three letters of reference.
Closing Date: February 1st
Funding: Private
Contributor: Penny Kanner
No. of awards given last year: 1
No. of applicants last year: 5

THE UKRAINIAN FRATERNAL ASSOCIATION (UFA)

371 N 9th Avenue, Scranton, PA 18504-2005,
United States of America
Tel: (1) 432 0937
Email: fratrag@apl.com
Website: www.ufa-home.tripod.com

Since 1939 the Association has always been, and continues to be, an ardent supporter of our youth. They represent the future of our society and our communities. From them we will draw our future leaders.

Eugene R. & Elinor R. Kotur Scholarship

Subjects: Any subject.
Eligibility: Applicant must be of Ukranian ancestry a member of the Association and enrolled at an approved university or college.
Level of Study: Postgraduate
Type: Scholarship
Value: US$250,000
Length of Study: 1–3 years
Country of Study: United States of America
Application Procedure: Contact the association.
Closing Date: May 31st
Funding: Trusts
Contributor: Eugene & Elinor Kotur

UNITED DAUGHTERS OF THE CONFEDERACY

Memorial Building 328 North Boulevard, Richmond, VA 23220-4009,
United States of America
Tel: (1) 804 355 1636
Fax: (1) 804 353 1396
Email: hqudc@rcn.com
Website: www.hqudc.org
Contact: Eleanor Kraus, Second Vice President General

The objectives of the United Daughters of the Confederacy are historical, educational, benevolent, memorial and patriotic, to honour the memory of those who served and those who fell in the service of the Confederate States of America.

Mrs Simon Baruch University Award

Subjects: Southern United States history in or near the period of the Confederacy or bearing upon the causes that led to secession and the War Between the States. The life of an individual, a policy or a phase of life may be eligible.
Purpose: To encourage research and to assist scholars in the publication of their thesis, dissertations and other writings.
Eligibility: Open to individuals who have graduated with an advanced degree from a United States university or college within the previous 15 years, or whose thesis or dissertation has been accepted by such institutions as part of graduation requirements.
Level of Study: Postgraduate
Value: US$2,000 to aid in defraying the costs of publication and US$500 to the author
Country of Study: Any country
No. of awards offered: 1
Application Procedure: Applicants must write for details.
Closing Date: May 1st of the award year
Funding: Private

UNITED NATIONS DEVELOPMENT PROGRAMME (UNDP)

304 East 45th street FF-10th Floor, New York, NY 10017,
United States of America

The UNDP launched the Local Initiative Facility for Urban Environment (LIFE) as a global pilot programme at the Earth summit in Rio de Janeiro in 1992. The programme uses environmental deprivation as the entry point for achieving sustainable human development.

UNDP's Local Initiative Facility for Urban Environment (LIFE) Global Programme

Subjects: Urban environmental development.
Purpose: To promote local-local dialogue and partnership between NGOs, CBOs, Local Governments and the private sector for improving conditions of the urban poor.
Eligibility: Application for need-based participatory, community-based projects in Urban poor communities.
Level of Study: Professional development
Type: Grant
Value: Up to US$50,000
Frequency: Annual
Funding: Government
Contributor: Life

UNITED STATES BUSINESS SCHOOL (PRAGUE)

Truhlářská 13-15, 110 00 Prague 1, Czech Republic
Tel: (42) 222 316 960
Fax: (42) 224 814 527
Email: usbsp@usbsp.com
Website: www.usbsp.com
Contact: Ms Ondrej Vobruba, Business Development Director

The United States Business School in Prague offers one of the pre-eminent western MBA programmes under professors from leading business colleges throughout the United States of America. The MBA degree is awarded by the Rochester Institute of Technology and accredited by the Association to Advance Collegiate Schools of Business (AACSB).

United States Business School (Prague) MBA Scholarships

Subjects: MBA.
Purpose: To provide financial support to exceptional students.
Eligibility: Open only to students enrolled in the full-time MBA programme.
Level of Study: Postgraduate, mba
Type: Scholarship
Value: Scholarships are awarded on the basis of results of the Graduate Management Admissions Test scores. For scores of 650–699 US$1,000 is awarded and for scores of 700 or above US$2,000 is awarded. The funds are provided as a discount from the tuition fee
Length of Study: 10 months
Frequency: Annual
Study Establishment: The United States Business School (Prague)
Country of Study: The Czech Republic
Application Procedure: Applicants must contact the organization or visit the website for details.
Closing Date: July 31st
Funding: Private
Contributor: Czech Telecom, the Czech Insurance Company, McKinsey & Company, T-Mobile, Pilsner Urquell
Additional Information: As the United States Business School in Prague was established to help Central and Eastern Europe in the transformation of their economies, financial support is available mainly to the citizens of these countries. For Czech and Slovak citizens up to US$8,000 is available, and for citizens of other Central and Eastern European countries up to US$7,000 is allocated. Please contact the organization for further information.

UNITED STATES CENTER FOR ADVANCED HOLOCAUST STUDIES

United States Holocaust Memorial Museum,
100 Raoul Wallenberg Place South West, Washington,
DC, 20024-2126, United States of America
Tel: (1) 202 314 0378
Fax: (1) 202 479 9726
Website: www.ushmm.org
Contact: Ms Lisa Zaid, Fellowships Office

The United States Holocaust Memorial Museum is the United States of America's national institution for the documentation, study and interpretation of holocaust history, and serves as the country's memorial to the millions of people murdered during the Holocaust. The Center for Advanced Holocaust Studies fosters research in holocaust and genocide studies.

United States Holocaust Memorial Museum Center for Advanced Holocaust Studies Visiting Scholar Programs

Subjects: History, political science, literature, philosophy, sociology, religion and other disciplines, as they relate to the study of the Holocaust.
Purpose: To support research and writing in the fields of holocaust and genocide studies.
Eligibility: Fellowships are awarded to candidates working on their dissertations (ABD), postdoctoral researchers and senior scholars. Applicants must be affiliated with an academic and/or research institution when applying for a fellowship. Immediate postdocs and faculty between appointments will also be considered.
Level of Study: Doctorate, postdoctorate
Type: Fellowship
Value: All awards include a monthly stipend, direct travel to and from Washington, DC and visa assistance, if necessary. The Museum provides office space, postage, and access to a computer, telephone, facsimile machine and photocopier
Length of Study: 3–9 months
Frequency: Annual
Country of Study: United States of America
No. of awards offered: Varies
Application Procedure: Applicants must consult the Museum's website or contact Lisa Zaid, Programme Assistant, for application forms and information.
Closing Date: November. Please consult the website for updated information about deadlines
Funding: Private
No. of awards given last year: 25

For further information contact:

Visiting Scholar Programs, Center for Advanced Holocaust Studies, United States Holocaust Memorial Museum, 100 Raoll Wallenberg Place SW, Washington, DC 20024-2126

UNITED STATES EDUCATIONAL FOUNDATION IN INDIA (USEFI)

Fulbright House, 12 Hailey Road, New Delhi,
110001, India
Tel: (91) 91 11 2332 8944 48
Fax: (91) 2332 9718
Email: info@fulbright-india.org
Website: www.fulbright-india.org
Contact: Programme Officer

The activities of the United States Educational Foundation in India (USEFI) may be broadly categorized as the administration of the Fulbright Exchange Fellowships for Indian and United States scholars and professionals, and the provision of educational advising services to help Indian students wishing to pursue higher education in the United States. USEFI also works for the promotion of dialogue among fulbrighters and their communities as an outgrowth of educational exchange.

Fulbright Doctoral and Professional Research Fellowships

Subjects: These research fellowships are offered in the areas of the United States Special education, conflict resolution, museum studies, arts/culture management and heritage conservation.
Eligibility: Open to Indian citizens resident in India at the time of application who have not been to the United States of America in the previous three years. Applicants must have a high level of academic and professional achievement, proficiency in English and be in good health. Applicants must be registered for a PhD at an Indian institution at least one year prior to application. The fellowship is also open to professionals with postgraduate degrees who are working in areas where study of IPR or special education would be helpful to their institutions.
Level of Study: Predoctorate, professional development
Type: Fellowship
Value: Maintenance in the United States of America, affiliation fees, health insurance and round trip economy class airfare
Length of Study: Up to 9 months
Frequency: Annual
Country of Study: United States of America
No. of awards offered: 6–7
Application Procedure: Application material can be downloaded from the website.
Closing Date: June 30th
Funding: Foundation
Contributor: USEFI
No. of awards given last year: 6
No. of applicants last year: 71

Fulbright Master's Fellowship for Leadership Development (Withdrawn)

Subjects: Designed for outstanding Indians, preferably in the age group of 25–30 years, to pursue master's degree programme at select U.S. colleges and universities in the areas of public administration, economics, communication studies and environment.
Purpose: The program is specially targeted at highly motivated individuals who demonstrate leadership qualities.
Eligibility: Open to Indian citizens resident in India at the time of application who have not been to the United States of America in the preceding three years. Applicants must have completed an equivalent of a U.S. Bachelor's degree from a recognized Indian university with at least 55% marks. Applicants should either possess a four-year Bachelors degree or a completed Master's degree, if the Bachelor's degree is of less than four years duration.
Level of Study: Postgraduate
Type: Fellowship
Value: Maintenance in the United States of America, affiliation fees, health insurance and round trip economy air fare, limited allowance for books
Length of Study: Up to 6 months
Frequency: Annual
Country of Study: United States of America
No. of awards offered: 4–6
Application Procedure: Applicants must complete an application form. Requests for application materials must state the applicant's academic and professional qualifications, date of birth, current position and grant category and be accompanied by a 7 by 10 inch stamped addressed envelope. Requests for application materials must be sent to the USEFI offices in the applicant's region or alternatively can be downloaded from the website.
Closing Date: July 15th
Funding: Government
Contributor: USEFI
No. of applicants last year: 45
Additional Information: Further information is available on request from USEFI.

Fulbright Senior Research Fellowships

Subjects: The United States of America education, society and development, and management.
Purpose: To provide scholars with the opportunity to undertake research on contemporary issues and concerns.

Eligibility: Open to Indian citizens resident in India at the time of application who have not been to the United States of America in the preceding three years. Applicants must have a high level of academic and professional achievement, proficiency in English and be in good health. Applicants must be employed as full-time faculty members in an Indian college, university or research institution, or as a full-time professional at an Indian non-profit organization, hold a PhD degree or have equivalent published work and be under 50 years of age.
Level of Study: Postdoctorate
Type: Grant
Value: Round trip travel, monthly stipend, university affiliation fees, health insurance and a modest settling in allowance, dependent allowance and round trip travel for one dependent
Length of Study: Up to 8 months
Frequency: Annual
Study Establishment: A university or research institution
Country of Study: United States of America
No. of awards offered: 4–5
Application Procedure: Application information can be downloaded from the website.
Closing Date: July 15th
Funding: Foundation
Contributor: USEFI
No. of awards given last year: 4
No. of applicants last year: 162
Additional Information: Applicants must demonstrate the relevance of the proposed research to India and/or the United States, its applicability in India, its benefit to the applicant's institution and the need to carry it out in the United States.

Fulbright Teacher Exchange Program

Subjects: Designed for Indian secondary school teachers (9th to 12th grades) of English, mathematics, and science to participate in direct exchanges of positions with U.S. teachers for semester.
Purpose: To provide Indian teachers the opportunity to work within a U.S. school system and experience U.S. society and culture similarly U.S. teachers will work in an Indian school set up and share their expertise.
Eligibility: Open to Indian citizens resident in India at the time of application who have not been to the United States of America in the preceding three years. Applicants must have a high level of academic and professional achievement, proficiency in English and be in good health. Applicants must have a Master's degree in English, mathematics or science subjects with a teacher training degree and be a full-time teacher (9th to 12th grades) in a recognized secondary school for at least five years.
Level of Study: Postgraduate, professional development, secondary school
Type: Fellowship
Value: Round trip travel, moderate monthly stipend, health insurance
Length of Study: One semester
Frequency: Annual
Country of Study: United States of America
No. of awards offered: 2–4
Application Procedure: Applicants must complete an application form. Requests for application materials must state the applicant's academic and professional qualifications, date of birth, current position and grant category and be accompanied by a 7 by 10 inch stamped addressed envelope. Requests for application materials must be sent to the USEFI offices in the applicant's region. Alternatively, applicants can download information from the USEFI website.
Closing Date: July 15th
Funding: Government
Contributor: USEFI
No. of awards given last year: Under process
No. of applicants last year: 109
Additional Information: Further information is available on request from USEFI.

Fulbright Visiting Lecturer Fellowships

Subjects: Humanities and social sciences.
Purpose: To allow scholars to share their expertise on contemporary issues significant to India and the United States of America.
Eligibility: Open to Indian citizens resident in India at the time of application who have not been to the United States of America in the preceding three years. Applicants must have a high level of academic and professional achievement, proficiency in English and be in good health. Applicants must be permanent full-time faculty members at an Indian college, university or research institute, hold a PhD degree or have equivalent published work, have at least 10 years of college or university level teaching experience and be no more than 50 years of age.
Level of Study: Postdoctorate
Type: Grant
Value: Round trip travel, monthly stipend, university fees, health insurance and a modest settling in allowance
Length of Study: 4 months
Frequency: Annual
Country of Study: United States of America
No. of awards offered: 2–3
Application Procedure: Applicants must complete an application form. Requests for application materials must state the applicant's academic and professional qualifications, date of birth, current position and grant category and be accompanied by a 7 by 10 inch stamped addressed envelope. Requests for application materials must be sent to the USEFI offices in the applicant's region or can be downloaded from the USEFI website.
Closing Date: July 15th
Funding: Foundation
Contributor: USEFI
No. of awards given last year: 8
No. of applicants last year: 44

USEFI Fulbright-CII Fellowships for Leadership in Management

Subjects: Leadership in management.
Purpose: To enable business managers to attend a management programme in the United States of America.
Eligibility: Open to Indian business managers. Age limit, preferably not above 40, Nationality: Indian, Designed for: Mid-level Managers in Indian Industries.
Level of Study: Professional development
Type: Fellowship
Length of Study: 10 weeks
Frequency: Annual
Study Establishment: Carnegie Mellon University
Country of Study: United States of America
No. of awards offered: 5–6
Application Procedure: Applicants must complete an application form, available from the CII.
Closing Date: January 31st
Funding: Foundation, corporation
Contributor: USEFI and employers of selected Managers
No. of awards given last year: 8
No. of applicants last year: 49
Additional Information: For further information contact the Confederation of Indian Industry (CII).

For further information contact:

Confederation of Indian Industry, Mantosh Sondhi Centre, 23, Institutional Area, Lodi Road, New Delhi, 110 003, India
Tel: (91) 24629994-7 Ext. 367
Fax: (91) 24601298, 24626149
Email: ls.rajeshwari@ciionline.org
Contact: Ms S Rajeshwari, Executive Officer

USEFI Fulbright-TATA Travel Fellowships

Subjects: Humanities, social sciences including administration, economics, education, environmental science, language and literature, population studies and women's studies.
Purpose: To assist academics and professionals who have invitations to visit the United States of America for either a research or teaching assignment.
Eligibility: Open to Indian citizens resident in India at the time of application who have not been to the United States of America in the previous three years. Applicants must have a high level of academic

and professional achievement, proficiency in English and be in good health. Applicants must be permanent full-time faculty members at an Indian college, university or research institute, hold a PhD degree or have equivalent published work and be no more than 50 years of age. In addition, applicants must be accepted by a recognized United States university or research institution for postdoctoral research and/or as a visiting lecturer and have assurance of dollar support to cover the expenses in the United States for the duration of the assignment. The letter of acceptance must show the nature and duration of the assignment, and must be accompanied by evidence of dollar support of not less than US$2,000 per month and not more than US$25,000 per academic year. American universities, Indian universities or research institutions could offer the evidence of dollar support in the form of a grant or fellowship. The letters of invitation or sponsorship from United States host institutions must indicate that all expenses towards room and board, local transportation, and related personal expenses will be met. No personal funding or financial support from family or friends is permitted.
Level of Study: Professional development, postdoctorate
Type: Travel grant
Value: Round trip economy class airfare and health insurance
Length of Study: Research or teaching assignments are for 4–12 months and professional visits are for 3–6 months
Frequency: Annual
Country of Study: United States of America
No. of awards offered: 4
Application Procedure: Applicants must complete an application form. Requests for application materials must state the applicant's academic and professional qualifications, date of birth, current position and grant category and be accompanied by a 7 by 10 inch stamped addressed envelope. Requests for application materials must be sent to the USEFI offices in the applicant's region or to the J N Tata Endowment (JNTE) by October 15th or downloaded from the USEFI website.
Closing Date: October 15th
Funding: Foundation, private
Contributor: USEFI and Tata Foundations
No. of awards given last year: 4
No. of applicants last year: 9
Additional Information: Further information is available from the USEFI website.

For further information contact:

J N Tata Endowment (JNTE), Bombay House, 24 Homi Modi Street, Mumbai, 400001, India
Tel: (91) 20 491 31
Contact: Director

USEFI Hubert H Humphrey Fellowships

Subjects: The fellowships are awarded in the fields of Agricultural Development/Agricultural Economics; Communications/Journalism, drug abuse education, treatment and prevention, economic development educational planning and administration, finance and banking HIV/AIDS policy and prevention, human resource management, law and human rights, natural resources and environmental management, nonproliferation studies, public health policy and management, public policy analysis and public administration, technology policy and management, prevention of trafficking in persons and policy development and management for anti-trafficking efforts, teacher training and curriculum development, and urban regional planning.
Purpose: To bring accomplished mid-level professionals from developing countries to the united states for 10 months of non-degree graduate study and related professional experiences.
Eligibility: Open to Indian citizens resident in India at the time of application who have not been to the United States of America in the previous three years. Applicants must have a high level of academic and professional achievement, proficiency in English and be in good health. Preferably applicants will have a First Class Master's or a professional degree of at least four year's duration. Applicants must have at least five years of substantial professional experience in the respective field and not be more than 40 years of age. Applicants applying for the fellowships in drug abuse must hold a PhD or equivalent degree in the health, behavioural or social sciences or an MD.
Level of Study: Professional development
Type: Fellowship
Value: Tuition and fees, a monthly maintenance allowance, modest allowance for books and supplies, round trip international travel to the host institution and domestic travel to Washington, DC and/or Minnesota workshops
Length of Study: 10 months
Frequency: Annual
Country of Study: United States of America
No. of awards offered: Varies
Application Procedure: Applicants must complete an application form. Requests for application materials must state the applicant's academic and professional qualifications, date of birth, current position and grant category and be accompanied by a 7 by 10 inch stamped addressed envelope. Requests for application materials must be sent to the USEFI offices in the applicant's region. Alternatively, applications can be downloaded from the USEFI website.
Closing Date: June 30th
Funding: Government
Contributor: Bureau of Educational and Cultural Affairs, U.S. Department of State, Washington, DC
No. of awards given last year: 9
No. of applicants last year: 57

USEFI Postdoctoral Travel-Only Fellowships

Subjects: Social sciences, humanities, fine arts and the performing arts.
Purpose: To provide travel allowance for academics and professionals who have inventions to visit the U.S. for research, projects other professional visits.
Eligibility: Open to Indian citizens resident in India at the time of application who have not been to the United States of America in the preceding three years. Applicants must have a high level of academic and professional achievement, proficiency in English and be in good health. Applicants must be full-time faculty members of an Indian college, university or research institution, hold a PhD degree or have equivalent published work and be no more than 50 years of age. Applicants must be accepted by a recognized United States university or research institution for postdoctoral research and/or as a visiting lecturer and have assurance of dollar support to cover the expenses in the United States for the duration of the assignment. The letter of acceptance must show the nature and duration of the assignment, and must be accompanied by evidence of dollar support and of not less that US$2,000 per month and not more than US$25,000 per academic year. United States universities, Indian universities or research institutions could offer the evidence of dollar support in the form of a grant or fellowship. The letter(s) of invitation or sponsorship from United States host institutions must indicate that all expenses (towards room and board, local transportation, and related personal expenses) will be met.
Level of Study: Postdoctorate, professional development
Type: Travel grant
Value: Round trip economy class airfare and health insurance
Length of Study: Research or teaching assignments are for 2–12 months. Inter–institutional collaboration is for 2–3 months and social science, humanities, fine arts or performing arts candidates are for 2–3 months
Frequency: Annual
Country of Study: United States of America
No. of awards offered: 2
Application Procedure: Applicants must complete an application form. Requests for application materials must state the applicant's academic and professional qualifications, date of birth, current position and grant category and be accompanied by a 7 by 10 inch stamped addressed envelope. Requests for application materials must be sent to the USEFI offices in the applicant's region or can be downloaded from the USEFI website.
Closing Date: October 15th
Funding: Foundation
Contributor: USEFI
No. of awards given last year: 2
No. of applicants last year: 9

UNITED STATES INSTITUTE OF PEACE (USIP)

1200 17th Street North West, Suite 200, Washington, DC, 20036-3011, United States of America
Tel: (1) 202 429 3842
Fax: (1) 202 429 6063
Email: grant_program@usip.org
Website: www.usip.org
Contact: Ms Cornelia Smith, Grant Programme Administration Assistant

The United States Institute of Peace (USIP) is mandated by the Congress to promote education and training, research and public information programmes on means to promote international peace and resolve international conflicts without violence. The Institute meets this mandate through an array of programmes, including grants, fellowships, conferences and workshops, library services, publications and other educational activities.

Jennings Randolph Program for International Peace Dissertation Fellowship

Subjects: A broad range of disciplines and interdisciplinary fields.
Purpose: To support dissertations that explore the sources and nature of international conflict, and strategies to prevent or end conflict and to sustain peace.
Eligibility: Open to applicants of all nationalities who are enrolled in an accredited college or university in the United States of America. Applicants must have completed all requirements for the degree except the dissertation by the commencement of the award.
Level of Study: Doctorate
Type: Fellowship
Value: US$17,000, which may be used to support writing or field research
Length of Study: 1 year
Frequency: Annual
Study Establishment: The student's home university or site of fieldwork
Country of Study: United States of America
No. of awards offered: 10
Application Procedure: Applicants must complete an application form, available on request from the Institute or from the website.
Closing Date: January 9th
Funding: Government
Additional Information: The programme does not support work involving partisan political and policy advocacy or policy making for any government or private organization.

For further information contact:

Tel: 202 429 3886
Email: jrprogram@usip.org
Contact: Miss Jean Brodeur, Administration Assistant

Jennings Randolph Program for International Peace Senior Fellowships

Subjects: Preventive diplomacy, ethnic and regional conflicts, peacekeeping and peace operations, peace settlements, postconflict reconstruction and reconciliation, democratization and the rule of law, cross-cultural negotiations, United States of America policy in the 21st century and related subjects.
Purpose: To use the recipient's existing knowledge and skills towards a fruitful endeavour in the international peace and conflict management field, and to help bring the perspectives of this field into the Fellow's own career.
Eligibility: Open to outstanding practitioners and scholars from a broad range of backgrounds. The competition is open to citizens of any country who have specific interest and experience in international peace and conflict management. Candidates would typically be senior academics, but applicants who hold at least a Bachelor's degree from a recognized university will also be considered.
Type: Fellowship
Value: A stipend, an office with computer and voicemail and a part-time research assistant
Length of Study: Up to 10 months
Frequency: Annual
Study Establishment: USIP
Country of Study: United States of America
No. of awards offered: 10–12
Application Procedure: Applicants must complete an application form, available on request from the Institute or from the website.
Closing Date: September 15th
Funding: Government

For further information contact:

Tel: 202 429 3886
Email: jrprogram@usip.org
Contact: Miss Jean Bordeur, Adminstration Assistant

USIP Solicited Grants

Subjects: Special priority topics identified in advance by the Institute and current solicited grant topics.
Purpose: To provide financial support for research, education and training, and the dissemination of information on international peace and conflict resolution.
Eligibility: Open to non-profit organizations and individuals from both the United States of America and other countries. These include institutions of postsecondary, community and secondary education, public and private education, training or research institutions and libraries. Although the Institute can provide grant support to individuals, it prefers that an institutional affiliation be established. The Institute will not accept applications that list as participants, consultants or project personnel members of the Institute's Board of Directors or staff. In addition, any application that lists the Institute as a collaborator in the project will not be accepted.
Level of Study: Postdoctorate, research, education, training
Type: Grant
Value: Most awards fall in the range of US$35,000–45,000, although slightly larger grants are also awarded. The amount of any grant is based on the proposed budget and on negotiations with successful applicants
Length of Study: 1–2 years
No. of awards offered: Approx. 35
Application Procedure: Applicants must complete an application form, available on request from the Institute or from the website.
Closing Date: March 1st for the Spring competition and October 1st for the Fall competition
Funding: Government
No. of awards given last year: 48
No. of applicants last year: 294
Additional Information: Subject topics can be found at our website.

USIP Unsolicited Grants

Subjects: Topic areas of interest to the Institute include, but are not restricted to, international conflict resolution, diplomacy, negotiation theory, functionalism and track-two diplomacy, methods of third party dispute settlement, international law, international organizations and collective security, deterrence and balance of power, arms control, psychological theories about international conflict, the role of non-violence and non-violent sanctions, moral and ethical thought about conflict and conflict resolution and theories about relationships among political institutions, human rights and conflict.
Purpose: To provide financial support for research, education and training, and the dissemination of information on international peace and conflict resolution.
Eligibility: The Institute may provide grant support to non-profit organizations and individuals from both the United States of America and other countries. These include institutions of postsecondary, community and secondary education, public and private education,

training and research institutions and libraries. Although the Institute can provide grant support to individuals, it prefers that an institutional affiliation be established. The Institute will not accept applications that list members of the Institute's Board of Directors or staff as participants, consultants or project personnel. In addition, any application that lists the Institute as a collaborator in the project will not be accepted.
Level of Study: Research, postdoctorate, education, training
Type: Grant
Value: Most awards fall in the range of US$25,000–45,000, although somewhat larger grants are also awarded. The amount of any grant is based on the proposed budget and on negotiations with successful applicants
Length of Study: 1–2 years
No. of awards offered: Approx. 65
Application Procedure: Applicants must complete an application form, available on request from the Institute or from the website.
Closing Date: October 1st or March 1st
Funding: Government
No. of awards given last year: 82
No. of applicants last year: 359

UNITED STATES TROTTING ASSOCIATION

750 Michigan Avenue, Columbus, OH, 43215, United States of America
Tel: (1) 614 224 2291
Fax: (1) 614 228 1385
Email: jpawlak@ustrotting.com
Website: www.ustrotting.com
Contact: Mr John Pawlak, Publicity/PR Director

The United States Trotting Association promotes the sport of harness racing and the standardbred breed. It also maintains and disseminates racing information and records and serves as the registry for the breed.

John Hervey, Broadcasters and Smallsreed Awards

Subjects: Journalism, television broadcasting and photography.
Purpose: To honour the best media stories on harness racing in the categories of newspaper, magazines, television and photojournalism.
Eligibility: Stories must have been published or aired in North America.
Level of Study: Unrestricted
Type: Prize
Value: 1st prize US$500, 2nd prize US$250 and 3rd prize US$100 in each division
Frequency: Annual
Country of Study: Any country
No. of awards offered: 12
Application Procedure: Applicants must submit entries to the address shown. There is no application form.
Closing Date: December 1st
Funding: Private
Contributor: The United States Harness Writer's Association
No. of awards given last year: 12
No. of applicants last year: 75
Additional Information: Articles, television programmes and photographs must be published or broadcast in North America.

UNIVERSAL ESPERANTO ASSOCIATION

Nieuwe Binneweg 176, NL-3015 BJ Rotterdam, Netherlands
Tel: (31) 10 436 1044
Fax: (31) 10 436 1751
Email: uea@inter.nl.net
Website: www.uea.org
Contact: Mr O. Buller

The Universal Esperanto Association is dedicated to spreading the use of the international language Esperanto.

Universal Esperanto Association Awards

Subjects: Esperanto.
Purpose: To train young volunteer workers for the advancement of the language and literature of Esperanto.
Eligibility: Open to individuals of all nationalities who are between 18 and 29 years of age. A fluent knowledge of Esperanto, both written and spoken, is essential prior to qualification.
Level of Study: Unrestricted
Type: Award
Value: A monthly stipend of €400 plus accommodation
Length of Study: Up to 1 year, non-renewable
Frequency: Annual
Study Establishment: The Head Office of the Association
Country of Study: The Netherlands
No. of awards offered: 1–2
Closing Date: Applications are accepted at any time
Funding: Individuals
No. of awards given last year: 3
No. of applicants last year: 10

UNIVERSITÉ CATHOLIQUE DE LOUVAIN (UCL)

Department of International Relations, Place de l'Université 1, Louvain-la-Neuve, B-1348, Belgium
Tel: (32) 1047 3095
Fax: (32) 1047 4075
Email: info@adri.ucl.ac.be
Website: www.uclouvain.be/international
Contact: Mr Duque Christian

The Université Catholique de Louvain (UCL) organizes a yearly scholarship contest for postgraduate studies, open to students originating from Developing countries.

UCL Development Co-operation Fellowships

Subjects: Any subject relevant to Third World development.
Purpose: To promote economic, social, cultural and political progress in developing countries by training graduates from these countries.
Eligibility: Open to nationals of developing countries who have an excellent academic background and some professional experience. They should also demonstrate that their study programme is able to promote the development of their home country and that they have a good command of French. Applicants must be less than 40 years of age. Applicants for a DEA must be members of the academic or scientific staff of a university in their own country, be able to demonstrate their interest in an academic career and prove that they will be reintegrated into their home institution upon completion of their DEA.
Level of Study: Postgraduate
Type: Fellowship
Value: Tuition, living expenses, family allowance, medical insurance and transportation costs to the recipient's home country at the end of studies
Length of Study: Up to 4 years
Frequency: Annual
Country of Study: Belgium
No. of awards offered: Up to 25
Application Procedure: All information and documents can be downloaded from the website http://www.uclouvain.be/browser-student.html
Closing Date: December 31st
Funding: International Office
No. of awards given last year: 25
No. of applicants last year: 135

For further information contact:

Administration des relations internationales, Place de l'Université, 1, Louvain-la-Neuve, 1348, Belgium
Tel: (32) 1047 9074

UNIVERSITIES FEDERATION FOR ANIMAL WELFARE (UFAW)

The Old School, Brewhouse Hill, Wheathampstead, Hertfordshire, AL4 8AN, England
Tel: (44) 15 8283 1818
Fax: (44) 15 8283 1414
Email: ufaw@ufaw.org.uk
Website: www.ufaw.org.uk
Contact: The Secretary

The Universities Federation for Animal Welfare (UFAW) seeks to prevent cruelty and promote humane behaviour towards all animals and encourage and promote, through education and scientific research, a proper understanding of the needs of animals.

UFAW Animal Welfare Research Training Scholarships

Subjects: UFAW is particularly keen to receive applicants for studies that may lead to significant developments in the assessment of the welfare of animals or studies aimed at providing new insight into the subjective mental experiences of animals relevant to their welfare. Applications for projects in other aspects of animal welfare science will also be considered.
Purpose: To encourage high-quality science likely to lead to substantial advances in animal welfare and to enable promising graduates to start a career in animal welfare science.
Eligibility: Open to nationals of any country.
Level of Study: Doctorate
Type: Scholarship
Value: Science graduates: UK £15,206–17,952, and veterinary graduates: UK £15,960–20,781. In addition, up to UK £10,000 research costs per year will be met
Length of Study: 3 years
Frequency: Dependent on funds available
Country of Study: Any country
Application Procedure: Applicants must complete a two-stage process. Initially supervisors must submit a brief concept note using an application form available from UFAW. Selected applicants will then be invited to submit more detailed proposals prepared jointly by the supervisor and PhD candidate.
Funding: Private

UFAW Research and Project Awards

Subjects: Full or part funding for self-contained projects or initial funding for studies that may lead to further investigation or welfare benefits. Awards can be used to supplement current work, to extend previous projects that promote animal welfare or to support non-research projects that promote animal welfare, such as preparation and publication of books and teaching materials.
Purpose: To encourage fundamental and high-quality research that is likely to lead to substantial improvements in animal welfare.
Eligibility: Open to nationals of any country.
Level of Study: Unrestricted
Type: Grant
Value: UK £3,500+ (rarely in excess of UK £10,000)
Length of Study: For the duration of the approved works
Frequency: Dependent on funds available
Country of Study: Any country
No. of awards offered: Varies
Application Procedure: Applicants must submit application forms available from the Secretary. Website (www.ufaw.org.uk)
Closing Date: Considered at approx. 3-month intervals
Funding: Private
Additional Information: Annual progress reports are required within 1 month of the anniversary of the start date and a final report must be submitted within 3 months of the completion date.

UFAW Small Project and Travel Awards

Subjects: These awards are to support travel in connection with advancing animal welfare and to support animal welfare research or other projects. Applications are judged on their merits for animal welfare, their scientific quality (in the case of research applications), and also in relation to the other applications received within the same timeframe. Particularly welcomed are applications for pilot studies where there is a likelihood of successful completion leading to further, more substantial work.
Purpose: To support research projects and other activities for the benefit of animal welfare.
Eligibility: Open to nationals of any country.
Level of Study: Unrestricted
Type: Grant
Value: Up to UK £3,500
Length of Study: For the duration of the approved works
Frequency: Dependent on funds available
Country of Study: Any country
Application Procedure: Applicants must complete an application form that must show that the fullest possible account of the welfare of any animals to be used has been taken. Applications must be made on forms available from the Secretary or website: (www.ufaw.org.uk).
Closing Date: Considered at approx. 3-month intervals
Funding: Private
Additional Information: A report is required within 1 month of completion of the project.

UFAW Vacation Scholarships

Subjects: Research that is likely to provide new insight into the subjective mental experiences of animals relevant to their welfare and at understanding their needs and preferences, and also applied research aimed at developing practical solutions to animal welfare problems.
Purpose: To encourage students to develop their interests in animal welfare and their abilities for animal welfare research.
Eligibility: Open to nationals of any country. Candidates must be registered at a university or college in the United Kingdom. Applicants need a nominated supervisor to oversee the project.
Level of Study: Graduate
Type: Scholarship
Value: UK £100 subsistence and UK £20 departmental expenses for each week of study
Length of Study: Maximum of 8 weeks
Frequency: Annual
Country of Study: United Kingdom
No. of awards offered: Varies, approx. 12
Application Procedure: Application form must be completed. Forms are available from the Secretary and must or website (www.ufaw.org.uk) be completed prior to application.
Closing Date: February 28th
Funding: Private
No. of awards given last year: 12
No. of applicants last year: 28
Additional Information: Successful applicants must submit a written report to UFAW by November of the year in which the project was undertaken.

UNIVERSITY COLLEGE LONDON

Gower Street, London, WC1E 6BT, United Kingdom
Tel: (44) 20 7679 2005/4167
Fax: (44) 20 7691 3112
Website: www.ucl.ac.uk

Just 175 years ago, the benefits of a university education in England were restricted to men who were members of the Church of England; University College London (UCL) was founded to challenge that discrimination. UCL was the first university to be established in England after Oxford and Cambridge, providing a progressive alternative to those institutions social exclusivity, religious restrictions and academic constraints. UCL is the largest of over 50 colleges and institutes that make up the federal University of London.

A C Gimson Scholarships in Phonetics and Linguistics

Subjects: Phonetics and linguistics.
Purpose: To financially support MPhil/PhD research.
Eligibility: United Kingdom, European Union and overseas students are eligible to apply.
Level of Study: Doctorate, postgraduate, research

Type: Scholarship
Value: UK £1,000
Frequency: Annual
Study Establishment: University College London
Country of Study: United Kingdom
No. of awards offered: 2
Application Procedure: Applicants should write indicating their intention to compete for the bursaries to the department.

For further information contact:

Department of Phonetics and Linguistics
Contact: Ms Stefanie Anyadi

A J Ayer Scholarship in Philosophy

Subjects: Philosophy.
Purpose: To financially support MPhil/PhD research.
Eligibility: United Kingdom, European Union and overseas students are eligible to apply.
Level of Study: Doctorate, postgraduate, research
Type: Scholarship
Value: Up to UK £2,000
Frequency: Annual
Study Establishment: University College London
Country of Study: United Kingdom
Application Procedure: No separate application is required. All who are admitted to research programmes in philosophy will automatically be considered for the scholarship. Any queries should be directed to the department.
Additional Information: Decisions regarding this award will be made in September.

For further information contact:

Department of Philosophy
Contact: Dr Michael Otsuka

A J Ayer-Sumitomo Corporation Scholarship in Philosophy

Subjects: Philosophy.
Purpose: To financially support MPhil/PhD research.
Eligibility: United Kingdom, European Union and overseas students are eligible to apply.
Level of Study: Research, postgraduate, doctorate
Type: Scholarship
Value: Up to UK £800
Frequency: Annual
Study Establishment: University College London
Country of Study: United Kingdom
Application Procedure: No separate application is required. All who are admitted to research programmes in philosophy will automatically be considered for the scholarship. Any queries should be directed to the department.
Additional Information: Decisions regarding this award will be made in September.

For further information contact:

Department of Philosophy
Contact: Dr Michael Otsuka

AHW Beck Memorial Scholarship

Subjects: Electronic and electrical engineering.
Purpose: To financially support research Master's and MPhil/PhD students.
Eligibility: Applicants should have applied for a place for graduate study at UCL.
Level of Study: Doctorate, postgraduate, research
Type: Scholarship
Value: UK £6,500
Frequency: Annual
Study Establishment: University College London
Application Procedure: Applicants should send an academic curriculum vitae and a letter of more than 500 words describing their areas of interest in the discipline to the address given below. If the applicant has not applied to UCL, they must complete a graduate application form and enclose it with the scholarship application.
Closing Date: August 15th

For further information contact:

Department of Electronic and Electrical Engineering
Tel: (44) 20 7679 7300
Email: n.best@ee.ucl.ac.uk
Contact: The Graduate Tutor

Alfred Bader Prize in Organic Chemistry

Subjects: Organic chemistry.
Purpose: To financially support MPhil/PhD research.
Level of Study: Postgraduate, doctorate, research
Type: Scholarship
Value: UK £1,000
Frequency: Annual
Study Establishment: University College London
Country of Study: United Kingdom
No. of awards offered: 1
Application Procedure: Applicants must contact the department.
Closing Date: Check the website for closing date
Additional Information: The award will be announced in October.

For further information contact:

Department of Chemistry
Tel: (44) 20 7679 4650
Fax: (44) 20 7679 7463
Email: m.l.jabore@ucl.ac.uk
Contact: Ms Mary Lau Jabore

Anvil Scholarship

Subjects: Computer science: data communications networks and distributed systems.
Purpose: To financially support postgraduate study.
Eligibility: United Kingdom, European Union and overseas students are eligible to apply.
Level of Study: Postgraduate
Type: Scholarship
Value: UK £1,000 plus tuition fees at the United Kingdom student rate
Frequency: Annual
Study Establishment: University College London
Country of Study: United Kingdom
Application Procedure: Applicants should indicate on their application for graduate study that they wish to be nominated for this award. Applicants should apply for a place for graduate study at UCL or complete a graduate application form and enclose it with the scholarship application.
Closing Date: Check the website for closing date.

Archibald Richardson Scholarship for Mathematics

Subjects: Pure mathematics.
Purpose: To financially support students to pursue MPhil/PhD research.
Eligibility: United Kingdom, European Union and overseas applicants are eligible to apply.
Level of Study: Doctorate, research, postgraduate
Type: Scholarship
Value: UK £3,000
Frequency: Annual
Study Establishment: University College London
Country of Study: United Kingdom
No. of awards offered: 1
Application Procedure: Applicants must contact the department.
Closing Date: May 15th

For further information contact:

Department of Mathematics
Contact: Ms Helen Higgins

Bentham Scholarships

Subjects: Law.
Purpose: To financially support prospective LLM students.

Eligibility: Applicants must be overseas students from outside the European Union. An applicant must have accepted an offer (either conditional or unconditional) to read for the LLM at UCL to be eligible.
Level of Study: Postgraduate
Type: Scholarship
Value: UK £2,000
Frequency: Annual
Study Establishment: University College London
Country of Study: United Kingdom
No. of awards offered: 10
Application Procedure: Application forms are available from the department at the address given below.
Closing Date: May 31st
Additional Information: The scholarships will be based on academic merit. The faculty will only consider these applicants who have firmly accepted their offer of admission to the LLM by May 31st.

For further information contact:

Faculty of Laws, University College London, Bentham House, Endsleigh Gardens, London, WC1H 0EG, United Kingdom
Tel: (44) 20 7679 1441
Fax: (44) 20 7209 3470
Email: graduatelaw@ucl.ac.uk
Contact: The Graduate Officer

Bioprocessing Graduate Scholarship

Subjects: Biochemical engineering.
Purpose: To financially support study leading to an MPhil/PhD.
Eligibility: Open to students resident outside the United Kingdom. Students domiciled within the United Kingdom are not eligible to apply.
Level of Study: Doctorate, postgraduate
Type: Scholarship
Value: Up to a maximum of UK £11,000 per year. This sum can be set against tuition fees and/or be received as maintenance allowance payable in quarterly installments
Length of Study: Maximum of 4 calendar years
Frequency: Annual
Study Establishment: University College London
Country of Study: United Kingdom
Application Procedure: Applicants must contact the department at the address given below or the British Council Office in Colombo.
Closing Date: May 15th

For further information contact:

Department of Biochemical Engineering, University College London, Torrington Place, London, United Kingdom
Tel: (44) 20 7679 3796
Email: negelth@ucl.ac.uk
Contact: Professor Nigel Titchener-Hooker

Brain Research Trust Prize Studentships

Subjects: Neurology.
Purpose: To financially support MPhil/PhD research.
Eligibility: United Kingdom, European Union and overseas student are eligible to apply.
Level of Study: Postgraduate, research, doctorate
Type: Studentship
Value: Tuition fees at the United Kingdom/European Union student rate, a stipend equivalent to that offered by the Wellcome Trust (UK £15,970 per year), UK £5,000 towards research costs and UK £500 for attendance at scientific meetings
Frequency: Annual
Study Establishment: University College London
Country of Study: United Kingdom
No. of awards offered: 1 or 2
Application Procedure: Applicants should contact the Institute of Neurology.

For further information contact:

Institute of Neurology, Queen Square, London, WC1N 3BG, United Kingdom
Tel: (44) 20 7829 8740
Fax: (44) 20 7278 5069
Email: j.townsend@ion.ucl.ac.uk
Contact: Mrs Janet Townsend

British Chevening/UCL Israel Alumni/Chaim Herzog Award

Subjects: All subjects.
Purpose: To financially support postgraduate study.
Eligibility: Applicants must be Master's students of Israeli nationality residing in Israel.
Level of Study: Postgraduate
Type: Scholarship
Value: Tuition fees, return airfare and living expenses
Frequency: Annual
Study Establishment: University College London
Country of Study: United Kingdom
Application Procedure: Applicants should check the website for details.
Closing Date: December 13th

Chief Justice Scholarships for Students from India

Subjects: Law.
Purpose: To financially support prospective LLM students.
Eligibility: Applicants must be overseas students from India. An applicant must have accepted an offer (either conditional or unconditional) to read for the LLM at UCL to be eligible.
Level of Study: Postgraduate
Type: Scholarship
Value: UK £2,000
Frequency: Annual
Study Establishment: University College London
Country of Study: United Kingdom
No. of awards offered: 10
Application Procedure: Application forms are available from the department.
Closing Date: May 31st
Additional Information: The scholarships will be based on academic merit. The faculty will only consider these applicants who have firmly accepted their offer of admission to the LLM by May 31st.

For further information contact:

Faculty of Laws
Contact: The Graduate Officer

Child Health Research Appeal Trust Studentship

Subjects: Child health.
Purpose: To fund graduate students for MPhil/PhD research.
Eligibility: Applicants must have applied for a place for graduate study at UCL.
Level of Study: Postgraduate, doctorate
Type: Studentship
Value: Tuition fees at the United Kingdom/European Union student rate, a stipend equivalent to MRC levels and UK £3,000 towards research costs
Frequency: Annual
Study Establishment: University College London
Country of Study: United Kingdom
No. of awards offered: 4
Application Procedure: Applicants must contact the department at the address given below. If the applicant has not applied to UCL, he/she must complete a graduate application form and enclose it with the scholarship application.
Closing Date: Mid-January

For further information contact:

Institute of Child Health, University College London, 30 Guilford Street, London, WC1N 1EH, United Kingdom
Tel: (44) 20 7405 6917
Fax: (44) 20 7813 0488
Email: s.fusco@ich.ucl.ac.uk
Contact: Ms Stella Fusco

Civil and Environmental Engineering Graduate Scholarship

Subjects: Civil and environmental engineering.
Purpose: To financially support MPhil/PhD study.
Eligibility: Applicants should hold or except to obtain a First Class (Honours) Degree or equivalent. Applicants should have been offered a place at UCL and should firmly have accepted that offer or be intending to do so. They can be from any country outside the European Union.
Level of Study: Doctorate, postgraduate
Type: Scholarship
Value: UK £5,000 per year
Length of Study: 3 years
Frequency: Annual
Study Establishment: University College London
Country of Study: United Kingdom
No. of awards offered: 1
Application Procedure: Applicants should write indicating their intention to compete for the scholarship to the department.
Closing Date: July 31st
Additional Information: If the applicant has not already applied to UCL, please complete a graduate application form and enclose it with the scholarship application.

For further information contact:

Lecturer in Environmental Engineering, Department of Civil and Environmental Engineering
Tel: (44) 20 7679 7994
Fax: (44) 20 7380 0986
Email: m.khraisheh@ucl.ac.uk
Contact: Dr Majeda Khraisheh

Clinical Psychology Awards

Subjects: Clinical psychology.
Purpose: To financially support doctorate study.
Eligibility: United Kingdom and European Union students are eligible to apply.
Level of Study: Doctorate
Type: Scholarship
Value: Salary, tuition fees and travelling expenses
Frequency: Annual
Study Establishment: University College London
Country of Study: United Kingdom
Application Procedure: Applicants should contact the department.
Closing Date: December 1st
No. of awards given last year: 34

For further information contact:

Head of Department, Department of Psychology
Tel: (44) 20 7679 5332
Fax: (44) 20 7436 4276
Email: psychology-pg-enquiries@ucl.ac.uk

CSC/UCL/FCO Chevening Scholarship

Subjects: Public policy.
Purpose: To financially support students pursuing a 1-year taught MSc degree programme.
Eligibility: Applicants should be citizens and residents of the People's Republic of China. Students pursuing a 1-year taught MSc degree programme in public policy are eligible to apply.
Level of Study: Postgraduate
Type: Scholarship
Value: Tuition fees, a monthly stipend for living expenses and other agreed allowances
Length of Study: 1 year
Frequency: Annual
Study Establishment: University College London
Country of Study: United Kingdom
No. of awards offered: 9
Application Procedure: Applicants should contact the China Scholarship Council at the address given below.
Additional Information: Applicants are expected to return to China at the end of their period of study. The scholarships are awarded on the basis of academic merit.

For further information contact:

China Scholarship Council, 160 Fuxingmennei Street, Beijing, 100031, PR, China
Tel: (86) 10 6641 3119

Dawes Hicks Postgraduate Scholarships in Philosophy

Subjects: Philosophy.
Purpose: To financially support postgraduate research.
Eligibility: United Kingdom, European Union and overseas students are eligible to apply.
Level of Study: Research, postgraduate
Type: Scholarship
Value: Up to UK £5,000
Frequency: Annual
Study Establishment: University College London
Country of Study: United Kingdom
Application Procedure: No separate application is required. All who are admitted to research programmes in philosophy will automatically be considered for the scholarship. Any queries should be directed to the department.
Additional Information: Decisions regarding this award will be made in September.

For further information contact:

Department of Philosophy
Contact: Dr Michael Otsuka

Department of Geography Teaching and Computing Assistantships

Subjects: Geography.
Purpose: To financially support teaching and computer assistants.
Eligibility: Applicants should be United Kingdom or European Union students. Overseas students who can apply the balance of fees to the higher rate, including those receiving an Overseas Research Students award for this purpose.
Level of Study: Postgraduate, doctorate
Type: Assistantship
Value: Stipend based on that paid by the United Kingdom Research Councils and fees at the Home/European Union rate.
Frequency: Annual
Study Establishment: University College London
Country of Study: United Kingdom
No. of awards offered: 4 for teaching and 2 for computer
Application Procedure: Applicants must contact the Department of Geography.

Deputy Prime Minister Bursaries

Subjects: Department and planning: strategic planning and regional development.
Purpose: To financially support part-time study.
Level of Study: Postgraduate
Type: Bursary
Value: UK £1,000
Frequency: Annual
Study Establishment: University College London
Country of Study: United Kingdom
No. of awards offered: 3
Application Procedure: Applicants must contact the department.
Closing Date: Check the website for the closing date

For further information contact:

The Bartlett School of Planning
Contact: Mr Julie Hipperson

DFID Shared Scholarship Scheme (DFIDSSS)

Subjects: Development and planning.
Purpose: To financially help students of high academic ability from developing Commonwealth countries.

Eligibility: Candidates must be from a developing Commonwealth country, must not have undertaken studies lasting a year or more or be currently studying in a developed country. They should hold or expect to attain, a United Kingdom First Degree (Bachelor's degree) with at least Upper Second Class (Honours) Degree or equivalent and should be 35 years of age or under at the time the award begins.
Level of Study: Postgraduate
Type: Scholarship
Value: Tuition fees, maintenance costs, some study expenses and return airfare
Frequency: Annual
Study Establishment: University College London
Country of Study: United Kingdom
Application Procedure: Application forms are available from the Development Planning Unit.
Closing Date: March 31st
Contributor: Department for International Development (DFID) and UCL
Additional Information: Preference is given to candidates unable to afford the cost of studying abroad by themselves. Candidates are expected to return to their home countries to work or study as soon as the award ends.

For further information contact:

Development Planning Unit
Tel: (44) 20 7679 1111
Fax: (44) 20 7387 4541
Contact: The Director

English Heritage Scholarships

Subjects: Archaeology: artefact studies, managing archaeological sites, and the technology and analysis of archeological materials.
Purpose: To financially support postgraduate study.
Eligibility: Applicants need a minimum of 2 years work experience in British archaeology.
Level of Study: Postgraduate
Type: Scholarship
Value: Up to UK £13,210
Frequency: Annual
Study Establishment: University College London
Country of Study: United Kingdom
No. of awards offered: 3 or more
Application Procedure: Applicants must contact the department.
Closing Date: Normally mid-July, check the department website

For further information contact:

Institute of Archaeology
Tel: (44) 20 7679 7495
Fax: (44) 20 7383 2572
Email: k.thomas@ucl.ac.uk
Contact: Professor Ken Thomas

Fielden Research Scholarship

Subjects: German language and literature.
Purpose: To financially support MPhil/PhD study.
Eligibility: Applicants must have applied for a place for graduate study at UCL.
Level of Study: Doctorate, postgraduate
Type: Scholarship
Value: UK £575
Frequency: Annual
Study Establishment: University College London
Country of Study: United Kingdom
Application Procedure: Applicants must contact the department. If the applicants have not applied to UCL they must complete a graduate application form and enclose it with the scholarship application.
Closing Date: May 15th

For further information contact:

FBA, Department of German
Contact: Professor Martin Swales

Follett Scholarship

Subjects: Philosophy.
Purpose: To financially support MPhil/PhD research.
Eligibility: United Kingdom, European Union and overseas students are eligible to apply.
Level of Study: Doctorate, research, postgraduate
Type: Scholarship
Value: Up to UK £13,000
Frequency: Annual
Study Establishment: University College London
Country of Study: United Kingdom
Application Procedure: No separate application is required. Applicants who are admitted to research programmes in philosophy will automatically be considered for the scholarship. Any queries should be directed to the department.
Additional Information: Decisions regarding this award will be made in September.

For further information contact:

Department of Philosophy
Tel: (44) 20 7679 7115
Fax: (44) 20 7209 1554
Email: m.otsuka@ucl.ac.uk
Contact: Dr Michael Otsuka

Franz Sondheimer Bursary Fund

Subjects: Chemistry.
Purpose: To financially support MPhil/PhD research.
Eligibility: Preference is given to overseas applicants.
Level of Study: Doctorate, postgraduate, research
Type: Scholarship
Value: Approx. UK £2,000
Frequency: Annual
Study Establishment: University College London
Country of Study: United Kingdom
No. of awards offered: 1
Application Procedure: Applicants must contact the department.
Closing Date: May 1st

For further information contact:

Department of Chemistry
Tel: (44) 20 7679 4650
Fax: (44) 20 7679 7463
Email: m.l.jabore@ucl.ac.uk
Contact: Ms Mary Lou Jabore

Frederick Bonnart-Braunthal Scholarship

Subjects: Religion.
Purpose: To financially support students who plan to explore the nature of religious, racial and cultural prejudices, and to find ways of combating them.
Eligibility: Open to United Kingdom/European Union nationals. Prospective MPhil/PhD candidates with a First Class (Honours) Degree or equivalent are eligible to apply.
Level of Study: Doctorate, postgraduate
Type: Scholarship
Length of Study: UK £12,000
Frequency: Annual
Study Establishment: University College London
Country of Study: United Kingdom
No. of awards offered: Up to 2
Application Procedure: Applicants must complete the application form available on the website and submit it along with a statement of no more than 1,500 words explaining why and how their research project will fulfil the aims of the scholarship.
Closing Date: April 1st

For further information contact:

Entrance Scholarships Office, Registrar's Division
Tel: (44) 20 7679 2000

Gaitskell MSc Scholarship

Subjects: Economics.
Purpose: To financially support full-time Master's study.
Eligibility: Applicants should have applied for a place for graduate study at UCL.
Level of Study: Postgraduate
Type: Scholarship
Value: UK £5,000
Frequency: Annual
Study Establishment: University College London
Country of Study: United Kingdom
No. of awards offered: Up to 4
Application Procedure: Applicants should send an academic curriculum vitae and a letter of no more than 500 words describing their areas of interest in the discipline to the department. If the applicant has not applied to UCL, they must complete a graduate application form and enclose it with the scholarship application.
Closing Date: May 15th
Additional Information: The scholarship will be awarded to students who are not already receiving full financial support from other sources for fees and living costs.

For further information contact:

Department of Economics
Tel: (44) 20 7679 5861
Fax: (44) 20 7616 2775
Email: d.fauvrelle@ucl.ac.uk
Contact: Ms Daniella Fauvrelle

Gay Clifford Fees Award

Subjects: Arts and humanities, social and historical sciences.
Purpose: To financially support postgraduate study.
Eligibility: Open to prospective female Master's degree students in the faculties of arts and humanities and social and historical sciences with a First Class (Honours) Degree or equivalent.
Level of Study: Postgraduate
Type: Scholarship
Value: UK £2,500
Frequency: Annual
Study Establishment: University College London
Country of Study: United Kingdom
No. of awards offered: Up to 4
Application Procedure: Applicants must complete the application form available on the website and submit it along with a curriculum vitae and a letter of no more than 500 words explaining what difference receiving the scholarship would make to their life.
Closing Date: April 1st
Additional Information: Awarded in memory of Gay Clifford (1943–1998), academic and poet.

For further information contact:

Entrance Scholarships Office, Registrar's Division
Tel: (44) 20 7679 2000

The George Melhuish Postgraduate Scholarship

Subjects: Philosophy.
Purpose: To financially support postgraduate research.
Eligibility: United Kingdom, European Union and overseas applicants are eligible to apply.
Level of Study: Postgraduate, research
Type: Scholarship
Value: Up to UK £3,700
Frequency: Annual
Study Establishment: University College London
Country of Study: United Kingdom
Application Procedure: No separate application is required. Applicants who are admitted to research programmes in philosophy will automatically be considered for the scholarship. Any queries should be directed to the department.
Additional Information: Decision regarding this award will be made in September.

For further information contact:

Department of Philosophy
Contact: Michael Otsuka

Graduate School Master's Awards

Subjects: All subjects.
Purpose: To financially support postgraduate study.
Eligibility: Open to United Kingdom/European Union nationals and prospective Master's candidates with a First Class (Honours) Degree or equivalent.
Level of Study: Postgraduate
Type: Scholarship
Value: Fee deduction up to UK $3,000
Length of Study: 1 year
Frequency: Annual
Study Establishment: University College London
Country of Study: United Kingdom
No. of awards offered: Up to 25
Application Procedure: Applicants must complete the application form available on the website.
Closing Date: April 1st

For further information contact:

Entrance Scholarships Office, Registrar's Division
Tel: (44) 20 7679 2000

Graduate School Research Scholarship

Purpose: To financially support postgraduate study.
Eligibility: Prospective MPhil/PhD candidates with a United Kingdom First Class (Honours) Degree or equivalent are eligible to apply. 1st year MPhil/PhD candidates who have registered on or after the scholarship deadline may also apply.
Level of Study: Postgraduate, doctorate
Type: Scholarship
Value: Fee deduction up to UK £3,000 plus maintenance allowance of UK £14,000 per year
Length of Study: 3 years
Frequency: Annual
Study Establishment: University College London
Country of Study: United Kingdom
No. of awards offered: Up to 22
Application Procedure: Applicants must complete the application form and submit it along with a brief research outline, no more than one side of A4-size paper.
Closing Date: April 1st
Additional Information: Overseas fee-payers are strongly advised to apply for an Overseas Research Student (ORS) award, which can be held together with a Graduate School Research Scholarship.

For further information contact:

Entrance Scholarships Office, Registrar's Division
Tel: (44) 20 7579 2000

Graduate School Research Scholarships for Cross-Disciplinary Training

Subjects: All subjects.
Purpose: To support students in acquiring research skills and knowledge from a different discipline that can be applied in their normal area of research.
Eligibility: Open to United Kingdom/European Union nationals. Prospective and current MPhil/PhD candidates with a First Class (Honours) Degree or equivalent are eligible to apply.
Level of Study: Doctorate, postgraduate
Type: Scholarship
Value: Fee deduction up to UK £3,000 plus maintenance allowance
Length of Study: 1 year
Frequency: Annual
Study Establishment: University College London
Country of Study: United Kingdom
No. of awards offered: Up to 4
Application Procedure: Applications should come from the Head of the Home Department and should include: the student's name and full

curriculum vitae, a proposal indicating the subject of the PhD being studied and the programme for the cross-disciplinary training, and a letter signed by the heads of both the home and host departments certifying that the relevant Research Council has agreed to the proposal. See the website for details.
Closing Date: April 1st

For further information contact:

Entrance Scholarships Office, Registrar's Division
Tel: (44) 20 7679 2000

Health Risk Resources International (HRRI) Scholarship

Subjects: Risk management.
Purpose: To financially support postgraduate study.
Eligibility: Applicants must have applied for a place for graduate study at UCL.
Level of Study: Postgraduate
Type: Scholarship
Value: United Kingdom/European Union tuition fees
Frequency: Annual
Study Establishment: University College London
Country of Study: United Kingdom
Application Procedure: Applicants should contact the department. If the applicants have not applied to UCL they must complete a graduate application form and enclose it with the scholarship application.
Closing Date: Check the website for closing date

For further information contact:

Centre for Health Information and Multiprofessional Education
Tel: (44) 20 7288 3366
Fax: (44) 20 7288 3322
Email: m.jacks@chime.ucl.ac.uk
Contact: Ms Marcia Jacks

Holy Family of Nazareth Polish Scholarship

Subjects: Slavonic and East European studies.
Purpose: To financially support MPhil/PhD research students.
Eligibility: Applicants must be MPhil/PhD research students of Polish descent admitted to the School of Slavonic and East European studies (SSEES) who are not in receipt of a full scholarship (fee plus maintenance) from another source.
Level of Study: Research, doctorate, postgraduate
Type: Scholarship
Value: UK £5,000
Frequency: Annual
Study Establishment: University College London
Country of Study: United Kingdom
Application Procedure: Applicants must contact the Assistant of the Graduate Tutor.
Closing Date: March 1st

For further information contact:

Contact: Andrew Gardner, The Assistant of the Graduate Tutor

Ian Karten Charitable Trust Scholarship (Hebrew and Jewish Studies)

Subjects: Hebrew and Jewish studies.
Purpose: To financially support postgraduate study.
Eligibility: Applicants must have applied for a place for graduate study at UCL.
Type: Scholarship
Value: UK £2,750
Frequency: Annual
Study Establishment: University College London
Country of Study: United Kingdom
No. of awards offered: 3
Application Procedure: Applicants should contact the department. If the applicants have not applied to UCL they must complete a graduate application form and enclose it with the scholarship application.
Closing Date: June 1st

For further information contact:

Department of Hebrew and Jewish Studies
Tel: (44) 20 7679 3028
Fax: (44) 20 7209 1026
Email: n.f.lochery@ucl.ac.uk
Contact: Dr Neil Lochery

J J Sylvester Scholarship

Subjects: Mathematics.
Purpose: To financially support MPhil/PhD research.
Eligibility: United Kingdom, European Union and overseas students are eligible to apply.
Level of Study: Doctorate, postgraduate, research
Type: Scholarship
Value: UK £500 per year
Frequency: Annual
Study Establishment: University College London
Country of Study: United Kingdom
No. of awards offered: 1
Application Procedure: Applicants must contact the department.

For further information contact:

Department of Mathematics
Contact: Ms Helen Higgins

Jacobsen Scholarship in Philosophy

Subjects: Philosophy.
Purpose: To financially support MPhil/PhD research.
Eligibility: United Kingdom, European Union and overseas students are eligible to apply.
Level of Study: Doctorate, postgraduate, research
Type: Scholarship
Value: Up to UK £9,500
Frequency: Annual
Study Establishment: University College London
Country of Study: United Kingdom
Application Procedure: No separate application is required. Applicants who are admitted to research programmes in philosophy will automatically be considered for the scholarship. Any queries should be directed to the department.
Additional Information: Decisions regarding this award will be made in September.

For further information contact:

Department of Philosophy
Contact: Dr Michael Otsuka

The James Lanner Memorial Scholarship

Subjects: Economics, environmental resource economics.
Purpose: To financially support students to pursue MPhil/PhD.
Eligibility: Applicants should have applied for a place for graduate study at UCL.
Level of Study: Doctorate, postgraduate
Type: Scholarship
Value: UK £5,000
Frequency: Annual
Study Establishment: University College London
Country of Study: United Kingdom
Application Procedure: Applicants should send an academic curriculum vitae and a letter of no more than 500 words describing their areas of interest in the discipline the department. If the applicant has not applied to UCL, he/she must complete a graduate application form and enclose it with the scholarship application.
Closing Date: May 15th
Additional Information: Preference is given to candidates who intend to specialize in international economics or an issues of economic policy in Europe.

For further information contact:

Department of Economics
Tel: (44) 20 7679 5861
Fax: (44) 20 7616 2775

Email: d.fauvrelle@ucl.ac.uk
Contact: Ms Daniella Fauvrelle

Jevons Memorial Scholarship in Economic Science

Subjects: Economics.
Purpose: To financially support MPhil/PhD study.
Eligibility: Applicants should have applied for a place for graduate study at UCL.
Level of Study: Postgraduate, doctorate
Type: Scholarship
Value: UK £55
Frequency: Annual
Study Establishment: University College London
Country of Study: United Kingdom
Application Procedure: Applicants should send particulars of the research work they intend to pursue plus an academic curriculum vitae to the department. If the applicant has not applied to UCL, they must complete a graduate application form and enclose it with the scholarship application.
Closing Date: May 15th

For further information contact:

Department of Economics
Tel: (44) 20 7679 5861
Fax: (44) 20 7916 2775
Email: d.fauvrelle@ucl.ac.uk
Contact: Ms Daniella Fauvrelle

John Carr Scholarship for Students from Africa and the Caribbean

Subjects: Law.
Purpose: To financially support prospective LLM students.
Eligibility: Applicants must be overseas students from Africa and the Caribbean. An applicant must have accepted an offer (either conditional or unconditional) to read for the LLM at UCL to be eligible.
Level of Study: Postgraduate
Type: Scholarship
Value: UK £2,000
Frequency: Annual
Study Establishment: University College London
Country of Study: United Kingdom
No. of awards offered: 10
Application Procedure: Application forms are available from the department.
Closing Date: May 31st
Additional Information: The scholarships will be based on academic merit. The faculty will only consider those applicants who have firmly accepted their offer of admission to the LLM by May 31st.

For further information contact:

Faculty of Laws
Contact: The Graduate Officer

John Hawkes Scholarship

Subjects: Pure mathematics.
Purpose: The primary purpose is to support 3rd-year study in pure mathematics but a secondary purpose when there is no suitable candidate or candidates for the whole sum available, is to support a graduate research student.
Eligibility: United Kingdom, European Union and overseas students are eligible to apply.
Level of Study: Research, postgraduate, doctorate
Type: Scholarship
Value: Up to UK £12,000 per year
Length of Study: 3 years
Frequency: Annual
Study Establishment: University College London
Country of Study: United Kingdom
No. of awards offered: Up to 3
Application Procedure: Applicants should write to the Head of the Department, indicating their wish to be considered for the scholarship and providing details of their academic achievements to date. Applicants should also include an up-to-date curriculum vitae.

For further information contact:

Head of Department, Department of Mathematics
Tel: (44) 20 7679 2839
Fax: (44) 20 7383 5519
Contact: Professor David Larman

John S Cohen Foundation Scholarship

Subjects: Holocaust studies.
Purpose: To financially support postgraduate study.
Eligibility: Applicants must have applied for a place for graduate study at UCL.
Level of Study: Postgraduate
Type: Scholarship
Value: UK £2,000
Frequency: Annual
Study Establishment: University College London
Country of Study: United Kingdom
Application Procedure: Applicants should contact the department. If the applicants have not applied to UCL they must complete a graduate application form and enclose it with the scholarship application.
Closing Date: June 1st

For further information contact:

Department of Hebrew and Jewish Studies
Contact: Dr Neill Lochery

John Stuart Mill Scholarship in Philosophy of Mind and Logic

Subjects: Philosophy.
Purpose: To financially support MPhil/PhD research.
Eligibility: United Kingdom, European Union and overseas applicants are eligible to apply.
Level of Study: Postgraduate, doctorate, research
Type: Scholarship
Value: Up to UK £1,400
Frequency: Annual
Study Establishment: University College London
Country of Study: United Kingdom
Application Procedure: No separate application is required. All who are admitted to research programmes in philosophy will automatically be considered for the scholarship. Any queries should be directed to the department.
Additional Information: Decision regarding this award will be made in September.

For further information contact:

Department of Philosophy
Contact: Dr Michael Otsuka

Joseph Hume Scholarship

Subjects: Law.
Purpose: To financially support LLM students or MPhil/PhD research.
Eligibility: LLM students and students with a Master's degree are eligible to apply.
Level of Study: Doctorate, research, postgraduate
Type: Scholarship
Value: UK £1,600
Frequency: Annual
Study Establishment: University College London
Country of Study: United Kingdom
No. of awards offered: 1
Application Procedure: Application forms are available from the department.
Closing Date: August 1st

For further information contact:

Faculty of Laws
Contact: The Graduate Officer

Karim Rida Said Foundation/UCL Joint Scholarship

Subjects: All subjects.
Purpose: To financially support taught Master's study or MPhil/PhD research.
Eligibility: Applicants must be Master's students from Iraq, Jordan, Lebanon, Palestine or Syria.
Level of Study: Doctorate, postgraduate, research
Type: Scholarship
Value: Tuition fees plus a maintenance allowance for taught Master's, maintenance allowance and a contribution towards tuition fees for MPhil/PhD research
Frequency: Annual
Study Establishment: University College London
Country of Study: United Kingdom
Application Procedure: Applicants should check the website for details.
Closing Date: January 31st; May 1st for United Kingdom resident applicants

Keeling Scholarship

Subjects: Philosophy.
Purpose: To financially support MPhil/PhD research.
Eligibility: United Kingdom, European Union and overseas students are eligible to apply.
Level of Study: Doctorate, research, postgraduate
Type: Scholarship
Value: United Kingdom/European Union tuition fees plus a bursary
Frequency: Annual
Study Establishment: University College London
Country of Study: United Kingdom
Application Procedure: No separate application is required. Applicants who are admitted to research programmes in philosophy will automatically be considered for the scholarship. Any queries should be directed to the department.
Additional Information: Decisions regarding this award will be made in September.

For further information contact:

Department of Philosophy
Contact: Dr Michael Otsuka

Liver Group PhD Studentship

Subjects: Hepatology.
Purpose: To financially support students to pursue MPhil/PhD research.
Eligibility: Open to United Kingdom and European Union applicants.
Level of Study: Postgraduate, doctorate, research
Type: Scholarship
Value: United Kingdom/European Union tuition fees plus a maintenance allowance (1st year approx. UK £14,500)
Length of Study: 3 years
Frequency: Annual
Study Establishment: Royal Free and University College Medical School
Country of Study: United Kingdom
No. of awards offered: 1
Application Procedure: Applicants should contact the department.
Closing Date: May 1st

For further information contact:

Centre for Hepatology, Department of Medicine (Royal Free Campus), Royal Free and University College Medicine School, Rowland Hill Street, Hampstead, London, NW3 2PF, United Kingdom
Tel: (44) 20 7433 2854
Fax: (44) 20 7433 2852
Email: c.selden@rfc.ucl.ac.uk
Contact: Dr Clare Selden

The Lloyd's Register Scholarship for Marine Offshore Engineering

Subjects: Marine engineering and naval architecture.
Purpose: To financially support postgraduate study.
Eligibility: United Kingdom, European Union and overseas students are eligible to apply.
Level of Study: Postgraduate
Type: Scholarship
Value: UK £10,000
Frequency: Annual
Study Establishment: University College London
Country of Study: United Kingdom
No. of awards offered: 1
Application Procedure: Applicants should write indicating their interest in being considered for this scholarship to the department.
Closing Date: June 1st

For further information contact:

Department of Mechanical Engineering
Tel: (44) 20 7679 3907
Fax: (44) 20 7388 0180
Email: info@meng.ucl.ac.uk
Contact: The Graduate Tutor

Margaret Richardson Scholarship

Subjects: German.
Purpose: To financially support MPhil/PhD study.
Eligibility: Applicants should have applied for a place for graduate study at UCL.
Level of Study: Postgraduate, doctorate
Type: Scholarship
Value: Tuition fees plus UK £2,800
Study Establishment: University College London
Country of Study: United Kingdom
Application Procedure: Applicants should contact the department. If the applicant has not applied to UCL, they must complete a graduate application form and enclose it with the scholarship application.
Closing Date: May 15th

For further information contact:

Department of German
Tel: (44) 20 7679 3103
Fax: (44) 20 7813 0168
Email: m.swales@ucl.ac.uk
Contact: Professor Martin Swales, FBA

Master of The Rolls Scholarship For Commonwealth Students

Subjects: Law.
Purpose: To financially support prospective LLM students.
Eligibility: Applicants must be overseas students from the Commonwealth countries. An applicant must have accepted an offer (either conditional or unconditional) to read for the LLM at UCL.
Level of Study: Postgraduate
Type: Scholarship
Value: UK £2,000
Frequency: Annual
Study Establishment: University College London
Country of Study: United Kingdom
No. of awards offered: 10
Application Procedure: Application forms are available from the department.
Closing Date: May 31st
Additional Information: The scholarships will be based on academic merit. The faculty will only consider these applicants who have firmly accepted their offer of admission to the LLM by May 31st.

For further information contact:

Faculty of Laws
Contact: The Graduate Officer

Master's Degree Awards in Archaeology

Subjects: Archaeology.
Purpose: To financially support MA and MSc programmes in the Institute of Archaeology.
Level of Study: Postgraduate

Type: Scholarship
Value: Approx. UK £1,000
Frequency: Annual
Study Establishment: University College London
Country of Study: United Kingdom
Application Procedure: Applicants must contact the department.
Closing Date: Mid-July, check the department website for details

For further information contact:

Institute of Archaeology
Tel: (44) 20 7679 7495
Fax: (44) 20 7383 2572
Email: k.thomas@ucl.ac.uk
Contact: Professor Ken Thomas

Momber Scholarship in Statistics
Subjects: Statistics.
Purpose: To financially support full-time graduate study and research.
Eligibility: Applicants should have graduated from UCL or be a candidate for graduation in the term in which the award is made. United Kingdom, European Union and overseas students are eligible to apply.
Level of Study: Postgraduate, research
Type: Scholarship
Value: UK £55
Frequency: Annual
Study Establishment: University College London
Country of Study: United Kingdom
No. of awards offered: 1
Application Procedure: Applicants should write to the department indicating their intention to compete for the scholarship.

For further information contact:

Department of Statistical Science
Tel: (44) 20 7679 1872
Fax: (44) 20 7383 4703
Email: marion@stats.ucl.ac.uk
Contact: Ms Marion Wave

Nederlandse Taalunie Scholarship
Subjects: Modern Dutch studies (literary translation from Dutch into English option).
Purpose: To financially support postgraduate study.
Eligibility: Applicants must have applied for a place for graduate study at UCL.
Level of Study: Postgraduate
Type: Scholarship
Value: UK £2,500
Frequency: Annual
Study Establishment: University College London
Country of Study: United Kingdom
Application Procedure: Applicants should contact the department. If the applicant has not applied to UCL, they must complete a graduate application form and enclose it with the scholarship application.
Closing Date: July 15th

For further information contact:

Head of Department
Tel: (44) 20 7679 3117
Fax: (44) 20 7616 6985
Email: t.hermans@ucl.ac.uk
Contact: Professor Theo Hermans

NHS Bursaries
Subjects: Speech and language sciences.
Purpose: To financially support postgraduate study.
Eligibility: Open to United Kingdom and European Union applicants only. Applicants must have applied for a place for graduate study at UCL. All suitably qualified applicants will be considered for a bursary.
Level of Study: Postgraduate
Type: Bursary
Value: United Kingdom/European Union tuition fees. United Kingdom residents will also normally be eligible for a means tested bursary
Frequency: Annual
Study Establishment: University College London
Country of Study: United Kingdom
Application Procedure: There is no separate bursary application form. If the applicants have not applied to UCL they must complete a graduate application form and enclose it with the scholarship application.
Closing Date: December 1st
Additional Information: When an offer of a place has been made, the NHS Student Grants unit will contact the applicant directly.

OSI/UCL-SSEES/FCO Chevening Scholarship
Subjects: Slavonic and East European Studies.
Purpose: To financially support postgraduate research.
Eligibility: Applicants must be registered in one of the following programmes: MA in political economy of Russia and Eastern Europe, MA in politics, security and integration, and MA in Central and South East European Studies.
Level of Study: Postgraduate
Type: Scholarship
Value: Tuition fees, monthly stipend and other agreed allowances including return economy airfare
Frequency: Annual
Study Establishment: University College London
Country of Study: United Kingdom
No. of awards offered: 5
Application Procedure: Applicants must contact the Assistant of the Graduate Tutor.
Closing Date: March 15th

For further information contact:

Tel: (44) 20 7679 2000
Email: a.gardner@ssees.ac.uk
Contact: Mr Andrew Gardner, The Assistant of the Graduate Tutor

Perren Studentship
Subjects: Astronomy.
Purpose: To financially support graduate study and research.
Eligibility: United Kingdom, European Union and overseas applicants are eligible to apply.
Level of Study: Postgraduate, research
Type: Studentship
Frequency: Annual
Study Establishment: University College London
Country of Study: United Kingdom
No. of awards offered: 1
Application Procedure: Applicants should provide particulars of their academic record and of the work that they intend to pursue to the department.
Closing Date: May 15th

For further information contact:

Department of Physics and Astronomy
Tel: (44) 20 7679 1312
Contact: Dr Alexander Shlyuger

R B Hounsfield Scholarship in Traffic Engineering
Subjects: Traffic engineering.
Purpose: To financially support MPhil/PhD research.
Eligibility: Applicants should hold or expect to obtain a First Class (Honours) Degree or equivalent. Applicants should have been offered a place at UCL and should firmly have accepted that offer or be intending to do so.
Level of Study: Doctorate, postgraduate, research
Type: Scholarship
Value: Not less than UK £120
Frequency: Annual
Study Establishment: University College London
Country of Study: United Kingdom

Application Procedure: Applicants should write indicating their intention to compete for the scholarship to the department.
Additional Information: If the applicant has not already applied to UCL, please complete a graduate application form and enclose it with the scholarship application.

For further information contact:

Centre for Transport Studies
Tel: (44) 20 7679 2710
Fax: (44) 20 7380 0986
Email: civengenquiries@ucl.ac.uk
Contact: Professor R L Mackett

Research Degree Scholarship in Chemical Engineering

Subjects: Chemical engineering.
Purpose: To financially support MPhil/PhD research.
Level of Study: Research, doctorate, postgraduate
Type: Scholarship
Value: UK £2,000
Frequency: Annual
Study Establishment: University College London
Country of Study: United Kingdom
No. of awards offered: 3
Application Procedure: Applicants must contact the department.
Closing Date: Check the website for closing date

For further information contact:

Department of Chemical Engineering
Tel: (44) 20 7679 3835
Fax: (44) 20 7383 2348
Email: h.mahgerefteh@ucl.ac.uk
Contact: Dr Haroun Mahgerefteh

Research Degree Scholarships in Anthropology

Subjects: Anthropology.
Purpose: To financially support research in the field of anthropology.
Level of Study: Postgraduate, doctorate, research
Type: Scholarship
Value: United Kingdom/European Union tuition fees
Frequency: Annual
Study Establishment: University College London
Country of Study: United Kingdom
No. of awards offered: Up to 4
Application Procedure: Applicants must contact the department.
Closing Date: April 30th

For further information contact:

Department of Anthropology
Tel: (44) 20 7679 7085
Fax: (44) 20 7679 7728
Email: Cassue.hill@ucl.ac.uk/anthropology
Website: www.ucl.ac.uk/anthropology
Contact: Ms Cassandra Hill

Ricardo Scholarship

Subjects: Economics.
Purpose: To financially support study and research.
Eligibility: Applicants should have applied for a place for graduate study at UCL.
Level of Study: Postgraduate, research, doctorate
Type: Scholarship
Value: UK £950
Frequency: Annual
Study Establishment: University College London
Country of Study: United Kingdom
Application Procedure: Applicants should send particulars of the research work that they intend to pursue plus an academic curriculum vitae to the department. If the applicant has not applied to UCL, he/she must complete a graduate application form and enclose it with the scholarship application.
Closing Date: May 15th

For further information contact:

Department of Economics, London,
Tel: (44) 20 7679 5861
Fax: (44) 20 7616 2775
Email: d.fauvrelle@ucl.ac.uk
Contact: Ms Fauvrelle Daniella

Richard Chattaway Scholarship

Subjects: History of modern warfare from 1870.
Purpose: To financially support MPhil/PhD study.
Eligibility: Applicants must have applied for a graduate study at UCL.
Level of Study: Postgraduate, doctorate
Type: Scholarship
Value: UK £2,000
Frequency: Annual
Study Establishment: University College London
Country of Study: United Kingdom
Application Procedure: Applicants must contact the department. If the applicants have not already applied to UCL they must complete a graduate application form and enclose it with the scholarship application.
Closing Date: May 15th

For further information contact:

Department of History
Tel: (44) 20 7679 1337
Fax: (44) 20 7413 8394
Email: r.aucott@ucl.ac.uk
Contact: Ms Rachet Aucott

Royal National Orthopaedic Hospital Special Trustees Research Training Scholarship

Subjects: Surgical sciences.
Purpose: To give orthopaedic specialists of the future an early exposure to the first-class research culture at Stanmore.
Eligibility: Open to students enrolled in the MSc in Surgical Sciences programme undertaking a research project at the Royal National Orthopaedic Hospital/Institute of Orthopaedic and Musculoskeletal Science.
Level of Study: Postgraduate
Type: Scholarship
Value: A stipend, tuition and bench fees
Frequency: Annual
Study Establishment: Royal National Orthopaedic Hospital, Stanmore
Country of Study: United Kingdom
Application Procedure: Once students have been accepted by a supervisor, they should contact the R&D office, Royal National Orthopaedic Hospital. Applicants will be asked to send an outline of the research project and their curriculum vitae. Applicant should contact the department at the address given below.
Funding: Private
Contributor: The RNOH Special Trustees and the R&D Subcommittee
Additional Information: Recipients of the scholarships must present their research findings at a symposium to be held at the RNOH. The R&D Director and the Non-Executive Director for research will review applications.

For further information contact:

Royal National Orthopaedic Hospital, Brockley Hill, Stanmore, Middlesex, HA7 4LP, United Kingdom
Tel: (44) 20 8909 5752
Email: lphilpots@rnoh.nhs.uk
Contact: Dr Liz Philpots, R&D Manager

SCALES/SIW Limited Programme Studentship

Subjects: Response of the body to implants or aspects of bioengineering of joint replacement.
Purpose: To financially support postgraduate study.
Eligibility: Applicants should hold a First or Upper Second Class (Honours) Degree in engineering, material science or biology.

Level of Study: Postgraduate
Type: Scholarship
Value: UK £6,500
Frequency: Annual
Study Establishment: University College London
Country of Study: United Kingdom
No. of awards offered: 1
Application Procedure: Applicants should send a curriculum vitae along with a covering letter to the address given below.

For further information contact:

Institute of Orthopaedics and Musculoskeletal Sciences, RNOH Campus, Brockley Hill, Stanmore, Middlesex, HA7 4LP, United Kingdom
Tel: (44) 20 8954 0636
Email: a.bartram@ucl.ac.uk
Contact: Miss J Cheek, Administrator

School of Library Archive and Information Studies Scholarships

Subjects: Library and information studies and information science.
Purpose: To financially support postgraduate study.
Eligibility: Open to part-time applicants who are employees of University of London Libraries that provide placement opportunities for UCL's School of Library Archive and Information Studies.
Level of Study: Postgraduate
Type: Scholarship
Value: United Kingdom/European Union tuition fees
Frequency: Annual
Study Establishment: University College London
Country of Study: United Kingdom
Application Procedure: Applicants must contact the department. No separate scholarship application is necessary. All suitable applicants for the programme will be considered for the award of this scholarship.
Additional Information: Awards will be announced in September.

For further information contact:

School of Library Archive and Information Studies
Tel: (44) 20 7679 2000

Simon LI/UCL China Law Scholarship

Subjects: Law.
Purpose: To financially support graduate students.
Eligibility: Open to citizens of the People's Republic of China other than Hong Kong who are graduates of Tsinghua University. Applicants joining UCL's LLM programme are also eligible.
Type: Scholarship
Value: Tuition fees, return travel and living expenses
Frequency: Annual
Study Establishment: University College London
Country of Study: United Kingdom
No. of awards offered: 1 (full-time)
Application Procedure: Candidates should first contact the Law Faculty of Beijing University. Short-listed candidates must submit no later than May 15th, a UCL graduate application form together with a written notice of their intention to compete for the scholarship. Applicants should also submit an essay of about 1,200–1,500 words on the subject 'How I shall contribute to the development of the legal system in China' and demonstrate in the essay their desire to do so.
Closing Date: May 15th
Contributor: Simon Li and his family, UCL and the China Scholarship Council
Additional Information: The initial short-listing of candidates will be managed by the China Scholarship Council (CSC) working with the Law Faculty of Beijing University. It is a condition that the award holders will return to China upon completion of their study at UCL.

For further information contact:

Entrance Scholarships Office

Sir Frederick Pollock Scholarship for Students from North America

Subjects: LLM.
Purpose: To financially support prospective LLM students.
Eligibility: Applicants must be overseas students from North America. An applicant must have accepted an offer (either conditional or unconditional) to read for the LLM at UCL to be eligible.
Type: Scholarship
Frequency: Annual
Country of Study: United Kingdom
No. of awards offered: 10
Application Procedure: Application forms are available from the department.
Closing Date: May 31st
Additional Information: The scholarships will be based on academic merit. The faculty will only consider those applicants who have firmly accepted their offer of admission to the LLM by May 31st.

For further information contact:

Faculty of Laws
Contact: The Graduate Officer

Sir George Jessel Studentship in Mathematics

Subjects: Mathematics.
Purpose: To financially support MPhil/PhD research.
Eligibility: Applicants must be graduates of University College London.
Level of Study: Research, doctorate, postgraduate
Type: Studentship
Value: UK £1,800
Frequency: Annual
Study Establishment: University College London
Country of Study: United Kingdom
No. of awards offered: 1
Application Procedure: Applicants must contact the department.

For further information contact:

Department of Mathematics
Tel: (44) 20 7679 2839
Fax: (44) 20 7383 5519
Email: h.higgins@ucl.ac.uk
Contact: Ms Helen Higgins

Sir Hilary Jenkinson Scholarship in Archive Studies

Subjects: Archives and records management.
Purpose: To financially support postgraduate study.
Eligibility: United Kingdom, European Union and overseas applicants are eligible to apply.
Level of Study: Postgraduate
Type: Scholarship
Value: UK £1,000
Frequency: Annual
Study Establishment: University College London
Country of Study: United Kingdom
No. of awards offered: 1
Application Procedure: Applicants must contact the department. No separate scholarship application is necessary. All suitable applicants for the programme will be considered for the award of this scholarship.
Additional Information: Awards will be announced in September.

For further information contact:

School of Library Archive and Information Studies
Tel: (44) 20 7679 2000

Sir James Lighthill Scholarship

Subjects: Applied mathematics.
Purpose: To financially support MPhil/PhD research.
Eligibility: United Kingdom, European Union and overseas students are eligible to apply.
Level of Study: Postgraduate, doctorate
Type: Scholarship
Frequency: Annual

Study Establishment: University College London
Country of Study: United Kingdom
Application Procedure: Applicants must contact the department.

For further information contact:

Department of Mathematics
Contact: Ms Helen Higgins

Sir John Salmond Scholarship for Students from Australia and New Zealand

Subjects: Law.
Purpose: To financially support prospective LLM students.
Eligibility: Applicants must be overseas students from Australia and New Zealand. An applicant must have accepted an offer (either conditional or unconditional) to read for the LLM at UCL to be eligible.
Level of Study: Postgraduate
Type: Scholarship
Value: UK £2,000
Frequency: Annual
Study Establishment: University College London
Country of Study: United Kingdom
No. of awards offered: 10
Application Procedure: Application forms are available from the department.
Closing Date: May 31st
Additional Information: The scholarships will be based on academic merit. The faculty will only consider these applicants who have firmly accepted their offer of admission to the LLM by May 31st.

For further information contact:

Faculty of Laws
Contact: The Graduate Officer

SSEES Postgraduate Scholarship

Subjects: Slavonic and East European Studies.
Purpose: To financially support MPhil/PhD research students.
Eligibility: Applicants must be MPhil/PhD research students admitted to SSEES who are not in receipt of a full scholarship (fee plus maintenance) from another source.
Level of Study: Research, doctorate, postgraduate
Type: Scholarship
Value: United Kingdom/European Union tuition fees plus funding for research fieldtrips to the region-up to a combined value of UK £5,000
Frequency: Annual
Study Establishment: University College London
Country of Study: United Kingdom
Application Procedure: Applicants must contact the Assistant of the Graduate Tutor.
Closing Date: March 1st

For further information contact:

Contact: Mr Andrew Gardner, Assistant of the Graduate Tutor

Sully Scholarship

Subjects: Psychology.
Purpose: To financially support MPhil/PhD research.
Eligibility: United Kingdom, European Union and overseas applicants are eligible to apply.
Level of Study: Postgraduate, doctorate, research
Type: Scholarship
Value: UK £2,200
Frequency: Annual
Study Establishment: University College London
Country of Study: United Kingdom
No. of awards offered: 1
Application Procedure: Applicants should contact the department.
Additional Information: Clinical psychology awards are salaried appointments with the Camden and Islington Community Mental Health Trust.

For further information contact:

Department of Psychology
Contact: Head of Department

Teaching Assistantships (Economics)

Subjects: Economics.
Purpose: To financially support MPhil/PhD students.
Eligibility: MPhil/PhD students who have successfully completed their 1st year in the department.
Level of Study: Doctorate, postgraduate
Type: Assistantship
Value: UK £8,500
Frequency: Annual
Study Establishment: University College London
Country of Study: United Kingdom

Ted Hollis Scholarship

Subjects: Wetland hydrology and conservation.
Purpose: To financially support a student pursuing research leading to a PhD.
Eligibility: United Kingdom, European Union and overseas students are eligible to apply. Applicants must have applied for a place for graduate study at UCL.
Level of Study: Doctorate
Type: Scholarship
Frequency: Once in 3 years
Study Establishment: University College London
Country of Study: United Kingdom
No. of awards offered: 1
Application Procedure: Applicants must contact the department at the address given below. If the applicants have not applied to UCL they must complete a graduate application form and enclose it with the scholarship application.

For further information contact:

Graduate Admissions, Department of Geography, University College London, 26 Bedford Way, London, WC1H 0AP, United Kingdom
Tel: (44) 20 7679 5500

Thames and Hudson Scholarship

Subjects: Comparative art and archaeology.
Purpose: To financially support postgraduate study.
Level of Study: Postgraduate
Type: Scholarship
Value: A scholarship up to a maximum value of UK £15,000 or up to 4 scholarships totalling that value
Frequency: Annual
Study Establishment: University College London
Country of Study: United Kingdom
No. of awards offered: 1–4
Application Procedure: Applicants must contact the department for details.
Closing Date: Mid-July, check the department website

For further information contact:

Institute of Archaeology
Tel: (44) 20 7679 7495
Fax: (44) 20 7383 2572
Email: k.thomas@ucl.ac.uk
Contact: Professor Ken Thomas

Thomas Witherden Batt Scholarship

Subjects: Life sciences and mathematical and physical sciences.
Purpose: To financially support students to pursue MPhil/PhD research.
Eligibility: Open to United Kingdom nationals only.
Level of Study: Postgraduate, research, doctorate
Type: Scholarship
Frequency: Annual
Study Establishment: University College London
Country of Study: United Kingdom
Application Procedure: Applicants should contact the department.

For further information contact:

Faculty of Mathematical and Physical Sciences
Tel: (44) 20 7679 3359

UCL Graduate 'Open' Scholarship

Subjects: All subjects.
Purpose: To financially support postgraduate study.
Eligibility: Overseas Master's or MPhil/PhD students are eligible to apply.
Level of Study: Postgraduate
Type: Scholarship
Value: Fee deduction of UK £2,500
Frequency: Annual
Study Establishment: University College London
Country of Study: United Kingdom
Application Procedure: Applicants should check the website for details.
Closing Date: July 31st

University College London Department Awards for Graduate Students

Subjects: Phonetics and linguistics.
Purpose: To financially support Master's and MPhil/PhD programmes.
Eligibility: United Kingdom, European Union and overseas students are eligible to apply.
Level of Study: Doctorate, postgraduate
Type: Scholarship
Value: UK £500
Frequency: Annual
Study Establishment: University College London
Country of Study: United Kingdom
No. of awards offered: 3
Application Procedure: Applicants must contact the department.
Closing Date: May 15th

For further information contact:

Department of Phonetics and Linguistics
Tel: (44) 20 7679 7172
Fax: (44) 20 7383 4108
Email: s.anyadi@ling.ucl.ac.uk
Contact: Ms Stefanie Anyadi

Victor Swoboda Memorial Fund Scholarship

Subjects: Slavonic and East European studies.
Purpose: To financially support postgraduate students.
Eligibility: Applicants must be postgraduate students in Ukrainian studies admitted to SSEES who are not in receipt of a full scholarship (fee plus maintenance) from another source.
Level of Study: Postgraduate
Type: Scholarship
Value: UK £2,000
Study Establishment: University College London
Country of Study: United Kingdom
Application Procedure: Applicants must contact the Assistant of the Graduate Tutor.
Closing Date: March 1st

For further information contact:

Contact: Mr Andrew Gardner, Assistant of the Graduate Tutor

Vinson Chu/UCL China Law

Subjects: Law.
Purpose: To financially support graduate students.
Eligibility: Open to citizens of the People's Republic of China, other than Hong Kong who are graduates of Beijing University. Applicants joining UCL's LLM programme are also eligible.
Level of Study: Postgraduate
Type: Scholarship
Value: Tuition fees, return travel and living expenses
Frequency: Annual
Study Establishment: University College London
Country of Study: United Kingdom
No. of awards offered: 1 (full-time)
Application Procedure: Candidates should first contact the Law Faculty at Beijing University. Short-listed candidates must submit no later than May 15th a UCL graduate application form together with a written notice of their intention to compete for the scholarship. Applicants should also submit an essay of about 1,200–1,500 words on the subject 'How I shall contribute to the development of the legal system in China' and demonstrate in the essay their desire to do so.
Closing Date: May 15th
Contributor: Vinson Chu family, UCL and the China Scholarship Council
Additional Information: The initial short-listing of candidates will be managed by the China Scholarship Council (CSC) working with the Law Faculty of Beijing University. It is a condition that the award holders will return to China upon completion of their study at UCL.

For further information contact:

Entrance Scholarships Office

W M Gorman Graduate Research Scholarship

Subjects: Economics.
Purpose: To financially support students entering the 1st year of the MPhil/PhD degree.
Eligibility: Applicants should have applied for a place for graduate study at UCL.
Level of Study: Doctorate, postgraduate
Type: Scholarship
Value: UK £6,500
Frequency: Annual
Study Establishment: University College London
Country of Study: United Kingdom
No. of awards offered: Up to 6
Application Procedure: Applicants should send an academic curriculum vitae and a letter of no more than 500 words describing the particulars of the research work they intend to pursue to the department. If the applicant has not applied to UCL, they must complete a graduate application form and enclose it with the scholarship application.
Additional Information: The scholarship will be awarded to students who are not already receiving full financial support from other sources for fees and living costs, and will be, awarded on the basis of academic merit.

For further information contact:

Department of Economics
Tel: 20 7679 5861
Fax: 20 7916 2775
Email: d.fauvrelle@ucl.ac.uk
Contact: Ms Daniella Fauvrelle

William Blake Trust Bursary

Subjects: History of British art.
Purpose: To financially support postgraduate or MPhil/PhD study.
Eligibility: Applicants must have applied for a place for graduate study at UCL.
Level of Study: Doctorate, postgraduate
Type: Bursary
Value: UK £2,000
Frequency: Annual
Study Establishment: University College London
Country of Study: United Kingdom
Application Procedure: Applicants must contact the department. If the applicants have not already applied to UCL they must complete a graduate application form and enclose it with the scholarship application.
Closing Date: May 15th

For further information contact:

Department of History of Art
Tel: 20 7679 7546
Fax: 20 7916 5939
Email: d.dethloff@ucl.ac.uk
Contact: Ms D Dethloff

UNIVERSITY INSTITUTE OF EUROPEAN STUDIES

Via Maria Vittoria 26, I-10123 Turin, Italy
Tel: (39) 011 839 4660
Fax: (39) 011 839 4664
Email: info@iuse.it
Website: www.iuse.it
Contact: Ms Maria Grazia Goiettina, Course Secretariat

The University Institute of European Studies promotes international relations and European integration by organizing academic activities. The Institute has a comprehensive library in international law and economics. Since 1952 the Institute has been a European Documentation Centre (EDC), thus receiving all official publications of European institutions.

International Trade Law Postgraduate Scholarships

Subjects: International trade law focusing on the origin and evolution of international trade, instruments and rules of the main economic international organizations, sources of law in international trade, legal aspects of international contracts in international trade, conflict of laws, modes of payment taxation, arbitration and dispute resolution.
Purpose: To allow students to attend the postgraduate course on international trade law, jointly organized by the University Institute of European Studies and the International Trading Centre of the ILO.
Eligibility: Open to Italian and foreign graduates in law, business and economics. Candidates from Turin are not eligible.
Level of Study: Postgraduate
Type: Scholarship
Value: Part of the accommodation expenses or registration fees
Length of Study: 3 months
Frequency: Annual
Study Establishment: The ILO Turin Centre
Country of Study: Italy
No. of awards offered: Varies
Application Procedure: Candidates should fill in the application form, obtainable from the Secretariat or the website. Copies of the applicant's degrees, including a transcript of academic records and a certificate of English knowledge, should be attached.
Closing Date: Mid-January
Funding: Private
No. of awards given last year: 6
No. of applicants last year: 300
Additional Information: The course aims to provide candidates with a common approach to the main legal issues in international trade law and contract drafting. Lecturers are prominent Italian and international experts, university professors or practitioners and senior officials of international institutions. The course, usually held in Spring, is in English. The number of participants is limited and full-time participation is required throughout the programme.

UNIVERSITY OF ALBERTA

114 St- 89 Ave, Edmonton, Alberta, T6G 2E1, Canada
Tel: (1) 780 492 3499
Fax: (1) 780 492 0692
Email: grad.services@ualberta.ca
Website: www.ualberta.ca/gradstudies

Opened in 1908, the University of Alberta has a long tradition of scholarly achievements and commitment to excellence in teaching, research and service to the community. It is one of Canada's five largest research-intensive universities, with an annual research income from external sources of more than Canadian $300 million. It participates in 18 of 21 of the Federal Networks of Centres of Excellence, which link industries, universities and governments in applied research and development.

Alberta Research Council Karl A Clark Memorial Scholarship

Subjects: Computer engineering, computer science, software and information technologies.
Eligibility: Open to students of any nationality who are enrolled in a graduate degree programme and engaged in thesis research at the Master's or doctoral level.
Level of Study: Graduate, doctorate
Type: Scholarship
Value: Canadian $20,000
Length of Study: 1 year, renewable for a further year through open competition
Frequency: Annual
Country of Study: Any country
No. of awards offered: 1
Application Procedure: Applicants must be nominated by the department in which they plan to pursue their studies.
Closing Date: March 1st for submission of nominations from departments. Check with the department for internal deadline
Funding: Government
No. of awards given last year: 1
Additional Information: Awarded annually to a student in an MSc or PhD degree programme engaged in thesis research in the areas of computer engineering or computer science concerned with software and information technologies. Students may apply, in open competition, to hold the award for an additional year at the MSc level, and for an additional 2 years at the PhD level.

Grant Notley Memorial Postdoctoral Fellowship

Subjects: The politics, history, economy or society of Western Canada and related fields.
Purpose: To encourage scholars of superior research ability who graduated within the last 3 years.
Eligibility: Open to persons who have recently completed a PhD programme or who will do so in the immediate future. Applicants should be active and promising young scholars who will perform significantly in fields associated with Grant Notley's interests or related fields. Applicants who have received their PhD degree from the University of Alberta, who will be on sabbatical leave, or who have held or will have held postdoctoral fellowships at other institutions for 2 years are not eligible.
Level of Study: Postdoctorate
Type: Fellowship
Value: Canadian $44,000 per year and a non-renewable research grant of Canadian $4,000
Length of Study: 2 years
Frequency: Annual
Study Establishment: The University of Alberta
Country of Study: Canada
No. of awards offered: 1
Application Procedure: Applicants must visit the website for application information.
Closing Date: December 16th
Funding: Private
No. of awards given last year: 1
No. of applicants last year: 10

Izaak Walton Killam Memorial Postdoctoral Fellowships

Subjects: All subjects.
Purpose: To attract scholars of superior research ability who graduated within the last 3 years.
Eligibility: Open to candidates of any nationality who have recently completed a PhD programme or will do so in the immediate future. Applicants who have received their PhD degree from the University of Alberta, who will be on sabbatical leave, or who have held or will have held postdoctoral fellowships at other institutions for 2 years are not eligible.
Level of Study: Postdoctorate
Type: Fellowship

Value: Canadian $44,000 per year and a non-renewable research grant of Canadian $4,000
Length of Study: 2 years
Frequency: Annual
Study Establishment: The University of Alberta
Country of Study: Canada
No. of awards offered: 8
Application Procedure: Applicants must visit the website for application information.
Closing Date: December 16th
Funding: Private
No. of awards given last year: 8
No. of applicants last year: 48

Izaak Walton Killam Memorial Scholarships

Subjects: All subjects.
Eligibility: Open to candidates of any nationality who are registered in, or are admissible to, a doctoral programme at the University. Scholars must have completed at least 1 year of graduate work prior to beginning the scholarship. Applicants must be nominated by the department in which they plan to pursue their doctoral studies.
Level of Study: Doctorate
Type: Scholarship
Value: Canadian $27,000 per year plus a non-renewable research grant of Canadian $2,000, tuition and fees
Length of Study: 2 years from May 1st or September 1st, subject to review after the 1st year
Frequency: Annual
Study Establishment: The University of Alberta
Country of Study: Canada
No. of awards offered: Approx. 20
Application Procedure: Applicants must visit the website for application information.
Closing Date: February 1st for the submission of nominations from departments. Please check with the department for their internal deadline
Funding: Private
No. of awards given last year: 20
No. of applicants last year: 121

Queen Elizabeth II Scholarships-Doctoral

Subjects: All subjects.
Eligibility: Open to Canadian citizens or permanent residents at the date of application who have completed at least 1 year of graduate study and who are registered in a full-time doctoral programme at the University of Alberta. Applicants must be nominated by the department in which they plan to pursue their studies. Students registered as qualifying graduates or probationary students are not eligible.
Level of Study: Doctorate
Type: Fellowship
Value: Canadian $10,500 for commencement in May and Canadian $7,000 for commencement in September
Length of Study: 1 year from May 1st or 8 months from September 1st
Frequency: Annual
Study Establishment: The University of Alberta
Country of Study: Canada
No. of awards offered: Approx. 63
Application Procedure: Visit the website for application information.
Closing Date: February 1st for the submission of nominations from departments. Please check with the department for their internal deadline
Funding: Government
No. of awards given last year: 40
No. of applicants last year: 245
Additional Information: Recipients must carry out a full-time research programme during the Summer months.

Queen Elizabeth II Scholarships-Master's

Subjects: All subjects.
Eligibility: Open to Canadian citizens or permanent residents who are entering or continuing, at the date of application, in a full-time Master's programme at the University of Alberta. Applicants must be nominated by the department in which they plan to pursue their studies. Students registered as qualifying graduates or probationary students are not eligible.
Level of Study: Graduate
Type: Scholarship
Value: Canadian $9,300 for commencement in May, Canadian $6,200 for commencement in September
Length of Study: 1 year from May 1st or 8 months from September 1st
Frequency: Annual
Study Establishment: The University of Alberta
Country of Study: Canada
No. of awards offered: Approx. 73
Application Procedure: Applicants must visit the website for application information.
Closing Date: February 1st for the submission of nominations from departments. Please check with the department for their internal deadline
Funding: Government
No. of awards given last year: 44
No. of applicants last year: 196
Additional Information: Recipients must carry out a full-time research program during the summer months.

UNIVERSITY OF BERGEN

Post Box 7800 N-5020 Bergen, Norway
Tel: (47) 47 55 580000
Fax: (47) 47 55 509643
Email: post@uib.co
Website: www.uib.no

The university of Bergen is a young, modern university, which is Norway's International university. The academic profile of the university has two major focuses marine research and co-operation with developing countries.

The Holberg International Memorial Prize

Subjects: Arts and humanities, social science, law and theology.
Purpose: To honor scholars who have made outstanding, internationally recognized contributions to research interdisciplinary work.
Eligibility: Open to outstanding researchers from the relevant academic fields.
Level of Study: Postgraduate
Type: Award
Frequency: Annual
Application Procedure: See the website.
Closing Date: February 15th

Nils Klim Prize

Subjects: Arts and humanities, social science, law and theology.
Purpose: To award outstanding research.
Eligibility: Open to Nordic researchers who are below the age of 35 years.
Level of Study: Postgraduate
Type: Award
Value: NOK 250,000
Frequency: Annual
No. of awards offered: 1
Application Procedure: See the website.
Closing Date: February 15th

UNIVERSITY OF BIRMINGHAM

Student Services & Admissions, Edgbaston, Birmingham, West Midlands, B15 2TT, England
Tel: (44) 121 414 3344
Fax: (44) 0121 414 3971
Email: r.groves@bham.ac.uk
Website: www.bham.ac.uk
Contact: Richard Groves, Student Funding Officer

The University of Birmingham is a leading research institution, offering a wide range of programmes, high teaching and research standards, and excellent facilities for academic work.

A E Hills Scholarship

Subjects: Any subjects.
Purpose: To support students who have registered for full-time higher studies.
Eligibility: Open to all students who wish to pursue higher degrees.
Level of Study: Postgraduate
Type: Scholarship
Value: Tuition fees at home rate and maintenance
Length of Study: 1 year
Frequency: Annual
Study Establishment: The University of Birmingham
Country of Study: United Kingdom
Application Procedure: Contact student funding office at the university.

Adrian Brown Scholarship

Subjects: Chemical engineering and biosciences related to brewing sciences and technology.
Eligibility: Open to all students reading a research degree.
Type: Scholarship
Length of Study: Varies
Frequency: Annual
Study Establishment: The University of Birmingham
Country of Study: United Kingdom
Application Procedure: Contact the student funding office at the university for details.

Dudley Docker Research Scholarship

Subjects: Engineering.
Eligibility: Open to students pursuing pure or applied graduate research.
Type: Scholarship
Value: Dependent on funds
Frequency: Annual
Study Establishment: The University of Birmingham
Country of Study: United Kingdom
Application Procedure: Students are nominated from school only.

ESRC Studentships

Subjects: Research and taught programmes is ESRC approved areas of study.
Eligibility: Open to home students only.
Type: Scholarship
Frequency: Annual
Study Establishment: The University of Birmingham
Country of Study: United Kingdom
Application Procedure: Application forms from school should be submitted.
Closing Date: April 30th

Francis Corder Clayton Scholarship

Subjects: Any arts subject.
Eligibility: Open only to existing students of the university.
Type: Scholarship
Length of Study: 1 year
Frequency: Annual
Study Establishment: The University of Birmingham
Country of Study: United Kingdom
Application Procedure: Contact student funding office at the university.

Golden Jubilee Scholarships

Subjects: Any subject.
Purpose: To encourage students of outstanding academic ability who wish to commence one-year full-time taught Master's degrees at the university.
Eligibility: Open to candidates who are home or EU students. Students who already have a Master's degree are not eligible.
Type: Scholarship
Value: UK £1,000
Length of Study: 1 year
Frequency: Annual
Study Establishment: The University of Birmingham
Country of Study: United Kingdom
No. of awards offered: 10
Application Procedure: A completed application form must be reached to the university.
Closing Date: July 29

For further information contact:

Golden Jubliee Scholarship Applications, Student Funding Office, The University of Birmingham, Edgbaston, B 15 2TT, United Kingdom

Guest, Keen and Nettlefolds Scholarship

Subjects: Engineering.
Purpose: To support students reading for a research degree.
Eligibility: Open to candidates reading for a research degree.
Level of Study: Postgraduate
Type: Scholarship
Value: Dependent on funds
Length of Study: 1 year
Frequency: Annual
Study Establishment: The University of Birmingham
Country of Study: United Kingdom
Application Procedure: Details can be obtained from student funding office.

Joseph Chamberlain Scholarship

Subjects: Business, engineering, public policy and social sciences.
Eligibility: Open to students whose parents or guardians have been bona fide residents of the former west midlands country for four years.
Level of Study: Postgraduate
Value: Maintenance at research council rates
Length of Study: 1 year
Frequency: Annual
Study Establishment: The University of Birmingham
Country of Study: United Kingdom
Application Procedure: Contact the student funding office at the university.

Kenward Memorial Fellowship

Subjects: Mechanical engineering.
Purpose: To provide financial assistance to those wishing to undertake research at the University of Birmingham.
Eligibility: Open to graduates in suitable disciplines.
Level of Study: Doctorate
Type: Fellowship
Value: Tuition and maintenance costs
Length of Study: 1 year, possibly renewable for a further 1 or 2 years
Frequency: Dependent on funds available
Study Establishment: The University of Birmingham
Country of Study: United Kingdom
Application Procedure: Applicants must apply through recommendation by school and evidence of academic achievement.
Funding: Private
Contributor: Friends of the late Sir Harold Leslie Kenward
No. of awards given last year: 1
Additional Information: The holder of the fellowship, as well as undertaking research, will undertake a limited amount of teaching in the school, not exceeding two hours each week.

Kirkcaldy Scholarship

Subjects: Business, public policy and social sciences.
Purpose: To support students who wish to pursue higher studies.
Eligibility: Open to all students registered for full-time higher degrees.
Type: Scholarship
Length of Study: 1 year
Frequency: Annual
Study Establishment: The University of Birmingham
Country of Study: United Kingdom

Neville Chamberlain Scholarship

Subjects: Humanities subjects. Preference will be given to studies focusing on modern political, social and economic history, especially concerning Great Britain and its 19th-century sphere of influence.
Purpose: To provide financial assistance to students wishing to study for a higher degree.
Eligibility: Open to non United Kingdom students with a good Honours Degree who have been offered and have accepted admission to study for a higher degree in a humanities subject. Proficiency in English is essential.
Level of Study: Postgraduate
Type: Scholarship
Value: A supplement to student's resources should these be inadequate for taking the degree. An award may be given towards both tuition fees and maintenance but normally should not exceed UK £7,000 per year
Length of Study: 1 year, renewable as funding allows
Frequency: Dependent on funds available
Study Establishment: The University of Birmingham
Country of Study: United Kingdom
No. of awards offered: 1
Application Procedure: Applicants must be nominated by the school at which they wish to attend.
Closing Date: Mid-June
Funding: Private
Contributor: The family of Neville Chamberlain
No. of awards given last year: 2
No. of applicants last year: 8

Richard Fenwick Scholarship

Subjects: Any subject except medicine, dentistry and health sciences.
Purpose: To encourage students who wish to pursue higher studies.
Eligibility: Open to all students who desire to obtain higher degrees.
Level of Study: Postgraduate
Type: Scholarship
Value: Tuition fees at home rate
Length of Study: 1 year
Frequency: Every 3 years
Study Establishment: The University of Birmingham
Country of Study: United Kingdom
Application Procedure: Please contact the student funding office at the university.

University of Birmingham Alumni Scholarship

Subjects: Any subject.
Purpose: To support students reading a research degree.
Eligibility: Candidates must either be an alumnus of the university, or the son or daughter of an alumnus.
Type: Scholarship
Length of Study: Up to 3 years
Frequency: Annual
Study Establishment: The University of Birmingham
Country of Study: United Kingdom
Application Procedure: Contact the university for details.

UNIVERSITY OF BRISTOL

Student Finance Office, Student's Union, Queen's Road, Bristol, BS8 1LN, England
Tel: (44) 11 7954 5785
Fax: (44) 11 7954 5709
Email: std-fin@bris.ac.uk
Website: www.bristol.ac.uk
Contact: Ms Jane Fitzwalier, Student Finance Officer

The University of Bristol is committed to providing high-quality teaching and research in all its designated fields.

University of Bristol Postgraduate Scholarships

Subjects: Any research topic that is covered in the work of the department within the University.
Purpose: To recruit high-quality research students.
Eligibility: Open to new PhD research students with at least an Upper Second Class (Honours) Degree or equivalent. Home/European Union Overseas students must be registered as full-time. Overseas students are only awarded a scholarship if they are successful in obtaining an Overseas Research Student (ORS) award. All scholars must be registered and in attendance for a research degree at the University. Scholarships are awarded for up to 3 years, and are renewed annually, subject to satisfactory academic progress.
Level of Study: Doctorate
Type: Scholarship
Value: UK £5,000 plus home tuition fees of UK £3,160 and UK £500 towards project expenses
Length of Study: 3 years
Frequency: Annual
Study Establishment: University of Bristol
Country of Study: United Kingdom
No. of awards offered: 24 Home/European Union plus a commitment to fund all successful ORS award holders
Application Procedure: Applicants should contact the department where they intend to carry out their research in the first instance, and will then be sent the appropriate form for completion.
Closing Date: May 1st for Home/European Union; February 13th for overseas applicants
Funding: Private
Contributor: University of Bristol
No. of awards given last year: Approx. 50 in total
No. of applicants last year: 180 (overseas only)
Additional Information: For further and up-to-date information, please see the Student Finance Office website www.bris.ac.uk/studentfinance

UNIVERSITY OF BRITISH COLUMBIA (UBC)

2329 West Mall, Vancouver, B.C., V6T 1Z2, Canada
Tel: (1) 604 822 4556
Fax: (1) 604 822 5802
Email: graduate.awards@ubc.ca
Website: www.grad.ubc.ca
Contact: Ms Jiffin Arboleda, Awards Administrator

The University of British Columbia (UBC) is one of North America's major research universities. The Faculty of Graduate Studies has 6,500 students and is a national leader in interdisciplinary study and research, with 98 departments, 18 interdisciplinary research units, 9 interdisciplinary graduate programmes, 2 graduate residential colleges and 1 scholarly journal.

Izaak Walton Killam Postdoctoral Fellowships

Subjects: All subjects.
Purpose: To support all areas of academic research.
Eligibility: Open to candidates who show superior ability in research and have obtained, within 2 academic years of the anticipated commencement date of the fellowship, a doctorate at a university other than UBC. Graduates of UBC are not normally eligible.
Level of Study: Postdoctorate
Type: Fellowship
Value: Canadian $40,000 per year and Canadian $4,000 travel allowance for duration of the award
Length of Study: 2 years, subject to satisfactory progress at the end of the 1st year
Frequency: Annual
Study Establishment: UBC
Country of Study: Canada
No. of awards offered: 8
Application Procedure: Applicants must submit an application form, academic transcripts and three reference letters to the appropriate department. For information and application forms, please visit the website.
Closing Date: November 15th
Funding: Private
No. of awards given last year: 4
No. of applicants last year: 200

Additional Information: Candidates are responsible for contacting the appropriate department at the University to ensure that their proposed research project is acceptable and may be undertaken under the supervision of a member of the department.

THE UNIVERSITY OF CALGARY

Faculty of Graduate Studies, Earth Sciences Building, Room 720, 2500 University Drive North West, Calgary, AB, T2N 1N4, Canada
Tel: (1) 403 220 5690
Fax: (1) 403 289 7635
Email: gsaward@ucalgary.ca
Website: www.grad.ucalgary.ca
Contact: Ms Connie Baines, Graduate Scholarship Officer

The University of Calgary is a place of education and scholarly inquiry. Its mission is to seek truth and disseminate knowledge and it aims to pursue this mission with integrity for the benefit of the people of Alberta, Canada and other parts of the world.

Alberta Art Foundation Graduate Scholarships in the Department of Art

Subjects: Painting, printmaking, sculpture, drawing and photography.
Purpose: To support study.
Eligibility: Open to students entering the second year of the MFA programme.
Level of Study: Postgraduate
Type: Scholarship
Value: Canadian $6,000
Frequency: Annual
Study Establishment: The University of Calgary
Country of Study: Canada
No. of awards offered: 3
Application Procedure: Applicants must be nominated by the Department of Art.
Closing Date: February 1st

Alberta Law Foundation Graduate Scholarship

Subjects: Natural resources, energy and environmental law.
Eligibility: Open to full-time graduates who are registered in or admissible to a programme of studies leading to a Master's degree in the Faculty of Law at the University of Calgary.
Level of Study: Postgraduate
Type: Scholarship
Value: Canadian $13,000 each
Length of Study: 1 year, non-renewable
Frequency: Annual
Study Establishment: The University of Calgary
Country of Study: Canada
No. of awards offered: 2
Application Procedure: Applicants must complete an application form, available from the Director of the graduate programme at the Faculty of Law.
Closing Date: February 1st
Additional Information: In cases where no suitable application is received no awards will be made.

Alberta Research Council Scholarship

Subjects: Agriculture, forestry, fishery, transport, communications, energy engineering, natural sciences and home economics.
Eligibility: Open to graduate students engaged in thesis research at the Master's or PhD level in the relevant fields.
Level of Study: Doctorate, postgraduate
Type: Scholarship
Value: Approx. Canadian $17,300 which is equal to a PGS Master's-level NSERC Scholarship
Length of Study: 1 year. Students may apply in open competition for a subsequent year's award
Frequency: Annual
Study Establishment: The University of Calgary
Country of Study: Canada
No. of awards offered: 1
Application Procedure: Applicants must complete an application form, available from the graduate programme directors of the departments concerned.
Closing Date: February 1st

Canadian Natural Resources Limited Graduate Scholarship

Subjects: Engineering, Earth and geological sciences, home economics and MBA.
Eligibility: Open to full-time graduate students, registered or eligible to register full-time in economics, geology and geophysics, engineering or management.
Level of Study: Postgraduate
Type: Scholarship
Value: Up to Canadian $10,000
Length of Study: 1 year
Frequency: Annual
Study Establishment: The University of Calgary
Country of Study: Canada
No. of awards offered: 1
Application Procedure: Applicants must complete an application form, available from the graduate co-ordinators of the departments concerned of the University of Calgary.
Closing Date: February 1st

Honourable N D McDermid Graduate Scholarship in Law

Subjects: Law.
Eligibility: Open to graduate students enrolled on a full-time basis in the LLM programme in the Faculty of Law at the University of Calgary.
Level of Study: Postgraduate
Type: Scholarship
Value: Canadian $10,000
Frequency: Annual
Study Establishment: The University of Calgary
Country of Study: Canada
No. of awards offered: 2
Application Procedure: Applicants must complete an application form, available from the Dean's office.
Closing Date: February 1st
Additional Information: The scholarship is not renewable. In cases where no suitable applications are received the award will not be made.

Izaak Walton Killam Memorial Scholarships

Subjects: All subjects.
Eligibility: Open to qualified graduates of any university who are admissible to a doctoral programme at the University of Calgary. Applicants must have completed at least 1 year of graduate study prior to taking up the award.
Level of Study: Postgraduate, doctorate
Type: Scholarship
Value: Canadian $25,000. If approved, award holders may also receive up to Canadian $3,000 over the full-term of appointment for special equipment and/or travel in direct connection with the PhD research
Length of Study: 1 year, renewable for a further year upon presentation of evidence of satisfactory progress. Further renewal is available in open competition
Frequency: Annual
Study Establishment: The University of Calgary
Country of Study: Canada
No. of awards offered: 4–5
Application Procedure: Applicants must complete an online application form, available from the University Of Calgary Faculty of Graduate Studies website at: www.grad.ucalgary.ca/funding/htm/scholarship_app_guidelines.htm
Closing Date: February 1st
No. of awards given last year: 4–5

Peter C Craigie Memorial Scholarship

Subjects: Humanities.
Eligibility: Open to full-time registrants from any country who are registered in and have completed one term of study in a programme of

studies leading to an MA degree in a department of the Faculty of Humanities. The recipient must have an outstanding scholastic record and will have been or be involved in activities contributing to the general welfare of the university committee.
Level of Study: Postgraduate
Type: Scholarship
Value: Canadian $5,000
Frequency: Every 2 years
Study Establishment: The University of Calgary
Country of Study: Canada
No. of awards offered: 1
Application Procedure: Applicants must apply to the Faculty of Humanities in the first instance. Recommendations from the Faculty will be submitted for consideration and approval by the University Graduate Scholarship Committee.
Closing Date: April 15th

Queen Elizabeth II Graduate Scholarships
Subjects: All subjects.
Eligibility: Candidates must be registered in, or admissible to, a programme leading to a Master's or doctoral degree. The award is restricted to Canadian citizens and landed immigrants.
Level of Study: Doctorate, postgraduate
Type: Fellowship /Scholarship
Value: The Master's level scholarship consists of Canadian $9,300 per year and the doctoral level scholarship of Canadian $10,500 per year
Length of Study: 1 year, renewable in open competition
Frequency: Annual
Study Establishment: The University of Calgary
Country of Study: Canada
No. of awards offered: 60–70
Application Procedure: Applicants must complete an application form, available from the directors of graduate studies of the departments concerned.
Closing Date: February 1st
Additional Information: Students whose awards begin in May are expected to carry out a full-time research programme during the Summer months.

Robert A Willson Doctoral Management Scholarship
Subjects: MBA.
Eligibility: Open to candidates who are registered in or admissible to a full-time programme leading to a doctoral degree in management at the University of Calgary. While academic excellence is essential, candidates should also present evidence of leadership in their academic or professional background.
Level of Study: Doctorate
Type: Scholarship
Value: Up to Canadian $10,000
Length of Study: 1 year
Frequency: Annual
Study Establishment: The University of Calgary
Country of Study: Canada
No. of awards offered: 1
Application Procedure: Applicants must apply to the Faculty of Management.
Closing Date: May 30th

Sheriff Willoughby King Memorial Scholarship
Subjects: Prevention of family violence and the treatment of the victims of family violence.
Eligibility: Open to candidates registered in the Faculty of Graduate Studies at the University of Calgary who are pursuing a Master of Social Work degree. Candidates must be Canadian citizens.
Level of Study: Postgraduate
Type: Scholarship
Value: Canadian $5,000
Length of Study: 1 year
Frequency: Annual
Study Establishment: The University of Calgary
Country of Study: Canada
No. of awards offered: 1 to a candidate studying in the area of treatment and 1 to a candidate studying in the area of prevention
Application Procedure: Applicants must apply to the Faculty of Social Work. Recommendations from the Faculty will be considered by the University Graduate Scholarship Committee at its annual meeting. Awards are made on the basis of academic excellence.
Closing Date: February 1st
No. of awards given last year: 1 to a candidate studying in the area of treatment and 1 to a candidate studying in the area of prevention

University of Calgary Cogeco, Inc. Graduate Scholarship
Subjects: Mass communication and information sciences.
Eligibility: Open to students admissible to or registered in a Master's programme, either thesis- or course-based, in communication studies programmes at the University of Calgary.
Level of Study: Postgraduate
Type: Scholarship
Value: Canadian $5,000
Length of Study: 1 year
Frequency: Annual
Study Establishment: The University of Calgary
Country of Study: Canada
No. of awards offered: 1
Application Procedure: Applicants must apply to the MA in communications studies programme.
Closing Date: February 1st
Additional Information: The Graduate Scholarship Committee makes the final decision based on departmental recommendations. Awards will be made on the basis of academic excellence.

University of Calgary Dean's Special Master's Scholarship
Subjects: All subjects.
Eligibility: Open to candidates who are or will be registered in a full-time thesis-based Master's programme in a relevant discipline.
Level of Study: Postgraduate
Type: Scholarship
Value: Canadian $5,000
Length of Study: 1 year, renewable in open competition
Frequency: Annual
Study Establishment: The University of Calgary
Country of Study: Canada
No. of awards offered: Up to 5
Application Procedure: Applicants must apply to the appropriate departments at the University of Calgary.
Closing Date: February 1st

University of Calgary Faculty of Law Graduate Scholarship
Subjects: Natural resources, energy and environmental law.
Eligibility: Open to full-time graduate students who are registered in or admissible to a programme of studies leading to a Master's degree in the Faculty of Law.
Level of Study: Postgraduate
Type: Scholarship
Value: Up to Canadian $10,000
Length of Study: 1 year, non-renewable
Frequency: Annual
Study Establishment: The University of Calgary
Country of Study: Canada
No. of awards offered: 1
Application Procedure: Applicants must complete an application form, available from the graduate programme director at the Faculty of Law. Awards will be recommended by a committee of the Faculty of Law based upon academic excellence.
Closing Date: February 1st
Additional Information: In cases where no suitable applications are received no awards will be made.

University of Calgary Silver Anniversary Graduate Fellowships
Subjects: All subjects.
Eligibility: Open to qualified graduates of any recognized university who are registered in or admissible to a doctoral programme

at the University of Calgary. The award is restricted to Canadian residents.
Level of Study: Doctorate
Type: Fellowship
Value: Up to Canadian $20,000, but in no case less than Canadian $16,000
Length of Study: 1 year, renewable for a further year upon presentation of evidence of satisfactory progress
Frequency: Annual
Study Establishment: The University of Calgary
Country of Study: Canada
No. of awards offered: More than 2
Application Procedure: Applicants must apply to the concerned department.
Closing Date: February 1st
Additional Information: Awards are granted on the basis of academic standing and demonstrated potential for advanced study and research.

William H Davies Medical Research Scholarship

Subjects: Medicine.
Eligibility: Open to qualified graduates of any recognized university who will be registered in the Faculty of Graduate Studies at the University of Calgary. Successful candidates must conduct their research programme within the Faculty of Medicine.
Level of Study: Postgraduate
Type: Scholarship
Value: Canadian $3,000–11,000 depending on qualifications, experience and graduate programme
Length of Study: 4 months–1 year, renewable in open competition
Study Establishment: The University of Calgary
Country of Study: Canada
No. of awards offered: More than 1
Application Procedure: Applicants must apply to the Assistant Dean of Medical Science in the first instance. The Graduate Scholarship Committee will make the final decision based on departmental recommendations. Awards are made on the basis of academic excellence.
Closing Date: May 1st

UNIVERSITY OF CALIFORNIA–BERKELEY

Graduate Division, Graduate Fellowships Office,
318 Sproul Hall #5900, Berkeley, CA 94720 5900,
United States of America
Tel: (1) 510 642 0672
Website: www.grad.berkeley.edu

The University of California–Berkeley, founded in 1868, has been hailed as the best balanced distinguished university in the United States of America. It offers the highest quality education in both the arts and sciences, has been the site of pioneering events such as the development of the first cyclotron and the isolation of the human polio virus, and is home to a renowned faculty that includes Nobel laureates in science, literature and economics.

Academic Progress Award

Subjects: All subjects.
Eligibility: Students who will take their qualifying exam and who have not been awarded a university or international fellowship are eligible to apply. Applicants are required to register and may not be employed during the semester of the fellowship.
Level of Study: Graduate
Type: Award
Value: US$7,200 plus fees and non-resident tuition for international students
Length of Study: 1 semester
Frequency: Annual
Study Establishment: University of California–Berkeley
Country of Study: United States of America
Closing Date: October 1st

Albert Newman Fellowship for Visually Impaired Students

Subjects: All subjects.
Purpose: To encourage substantially visually impaired graduate students who demonstrate scholastic achievement.
Eligibility: Applicant must be substantially visually impaired.
Level of Study: Graduate
Type: Fellowship
Frequency: Annual
Application Procedure: Applicants must submit completed application and supporting documents.
Closing Date: April 4th

Chancellor's Dissertation Year Fellowship

Subjects: Humanities and social sciences.
Purpose: To support outstanding students in the humanities and social sciences.
Eligibility: Applicants must be advanced to candidacy at the time of the award and expect to finish their dissertations during the fellowship year.
Level of Study: Doctorate
Type: Fellowship
Value: US$17,000, with an additional US$2,000 if the dissertation is completed before the deadline. For international students, registration fees and non-resident tuition will be covered
Length of Study: 1 year
Frequency: Annual
Study Establishment: University of California–Berkeley
Country of Study: United States of America
No. of awards offered: 13
Application Procedure: The applicant must submit a letter from the department or group chair supporting the nomination, a letter from the dissertation adviser describing the importance of the dissertation project, the Report on Progress in Candidacy in the Doctoral Program' form signed by the dissertation adviser, a copy of the Chancellor's Dissertation Year Fellowship application, a detailed outline of the dissertation, a one-page summary of the dissertation in non-technical language, a copy of the latest chapter completed or other substantive work as evidence of progress on dissertation and an unofficial copy of the University of California-Berkeley graduate transcript showing date of advancement to candidacy.
Closing Date: March 2nd

Conference Travel Grants

Subjects: All subjects.
Purpose: To allow students to attend professional conferences.
Eligibility: Applicant must be registered graduate students in good academic standing. They must be in the final stages of their graduate work and planning to present a paper on their dissertation research at the conference they are attending.
Type: Grant
Value: Maximum US$500
Study Establishment: University of California–Berkeley
Country of Study: United States of America
Application Procedure: Applicants must submit an application form and one letter of support from their graduate advisor attesting to the academic merit of the trip. Applications can be obtained from the website.
Closing Date: 3 weeks before the date of travel

Dr and Mrs James C Y Soong Fellowship

Subjects: All subjects.
Purpose: To financially support graduate students from Taiwan.
Eligibility: Applicants must have graduated from a fully accredited, 4-year college or university in Taiwan, with a grade point average of 3.7 (A-) or higher, must be a citizen of the Republic of China and have lived in Taiwan consecutively for at least 10 years and must have demonstrated financial need in pursuit of advanced degrees.
Level of Study: Graduate
Type: Fellowship
Value: US$14,000 plus fees and non-resident tuition. The fellowship may be renewed one time.
Length of Study: 1 year
Frequency: Annual

Study Establishment: University of California–Berkeley
Country of Study: United States of America
Application Procedure: Applicant must submit a completed application form, available from the website, a one-page typewritten statement of purpose, a copy of the University of California–Berkeley transcript, the international student financial information form and a letter of support from the department chair.
Closing Date: April 16th

Elizabeth Roboz Einstein Fellowship

Subjects: Neurosciences.
Purpose: To fund doctoral candidates in the neurosciences relating to human development.
Eligibility: Applicants must have demonstrated distinguished scholarship as well as the ability to conduct research at an advanced level.
Level of Study: Doctorate
Type: Fellowship
Value: Approx. US$4,000
Length of Study: 1 semester
Frequency: Annual
Study Establishment: University of California–Berkeley
Country of Study: United States of America
No. of awards offered: 2
Application Procedure: Applicants must submit a completed application form, two letters of recommendation in sealed envelopes, a copy of the latest University of California–Berkeley transcript and a one-page description of the research project.
Closing Date: December 1st

Foreign Language and Area Studies (FLAS) Fellowships

Subjects: Foreign languages, humanities, social sciences, area and international studies and professional fields.
Purpose: To enable students to acquire a high level of competence in one or more foreign languages.
Eligibility: Applicant must be graduate students and citizens, nationals or permanent residents of the United States of America.
Level of Study: Graduate
Type: Award
Value: US$14,000 and fees
Frequency: Annual
Study Establishment: University of California–Berkeley
Country of Study: United States of America
Application Procedure: Incoming students should apply using the graduate application for admission and fellowships, which should be submitted directly to their departments by the departmental deadlines.
Closing Date: February 1st

Graduate Division Summer Grant

Subjects: Humanities, social sciences and professional courses.
Purpose: To provide financial assistance to doctoral students during the summer months.
Level of Study: Doctorate
Type: Grant
Length of Study: Summer semester
Frequency: Annual
Study Establishment: University of California–Berkeley
Country of Study: United States of America
Closing Date: October 25th

Graduate Opportunity Program (GOP) Dissertation Year Award

Subjects: All subjects.
Purpose: To support Graduate Opportunity Program (GOP) Fellows who are in or approaching their final dissertation research/writing year and who are also within their department's normative time.
Eligibility: Applicants must be GOP fellows, registered as full-time students, not employed during the tenure of the award and must be advanced to candidacy for the doctoral degree prior to applying for this award.
Level of Study: Doctorate
Type: Award
Value: US$15,000 plus registration fees for 1 year only
Length of Study: 1 year
Frequency: Annual
Study Establishment: University of California–Berkeley
Country of Study: United States of America
Application Procedure: Applicants must submit a completed application form, available from the GOP office or the website.
Closing Date: No fixed deadline. Applications are reviewed throughout the year

Mentored Research Award

Subjects: All subjects.
Purpose: To provide academically promising graduate students the opportunity to conduct research that they would not be able to do otherwise, acquire sophisticated research skills and help strengthen their working relationships with their faculty advisers.
Eligibility: The applicant must be a citizen of the United States of America or permanent resident of high academic potential and promise whose background and life experiences enhance the diversity within in the department on discipline. Priority will be given to 3rd- and 4th-year students.
Level of Study: Doctorate
Type: Award
Value: US$14,000 plus registration fees
Length of Study: 1 year
Frequency: Annual
Study Establishment: University of California–Berkeley
Country of Study: United States of America
No. of awards offered: 15
Application Procedure: Applicants must submit a letter from the department or group chair supporting the nomination and confirming eligibility, a letter from the proposed mentor describing their plans for mentoring the student and past mentoring experience, a letter from the student describing his or her academic progress to date, the nature of the research project in which she or he will be involved, its importance to the student's academic career and how this award would help the student achieve his or her goals, a copy of the Mentored Research Award application and unofficial copies of all graduate transcripts.
Closing Date: March 2nd

Paul J Alexander Memorial Fellowship

Subjects: Ancient history.
Purpose: To encourage the study of Byzantine, ancient and medieval history.
Eligibility: Advanced University of California, Berkeley graduate students studying in the general area of ancient history are invited to apply.
Level of Study: Graduate
Type: Fellowship
Value: Approx. US$3,000
Application Procedure: Applicants must submit an application form, available from the website. The application must also include a letter of endorsement from the applicant's sponsor, a copy of the latest University of California–Berkeley transcript and a one-page description of the dissertation research.
Closing Date: December 1st
Additional Information: A student can receive this award only once during his/her academic career.

University of California Dissertation Year Fellowship

Subjects: All subjects.
Purpose: To support the writing of a doctoral dissertation.
Eligibility: Applicants must be citizens or permanent residents of the United States of America of high academic potential and promise whose background and life experiences enhance the level of diversity within the department or discipline. Applicant must be advanced to candidacy for the PhD at the time of nomination.
Level of Study: Doctorate
Type: Fellowship
Value: US$17,000 and a travel allowance. The Graduate Division will cover the registration fee and an additional US$2,000 if the dissertation is submitted before the deadline
Length of Study: 1 year
Frequency: Annual

Study Establishment: University of California–Berkeley
Country of Study: United States of America
Closing Date: March 2nd

UNIVERSITY OF CAMBRIDGE, JUDGE INSTITUTE OF MANAGEMENT

Trumpington Street, Cambridge, Cambridgeshire, CB2 1AG, England
Tel: (44) 12 2333 9700
Fax: (44) 12 2333 9701
Email: enquiries@jims.cam.ac.uk
Website: www.jims.cam.ac.uk
Contact: Ms Louise Freckleton

The Judge Institute of Management is the University of Cambridge's business school. Founded in 1990, it offers a portfolio of management programmes, including the Cambridge MBA. Accredited by AMBA and EQUIS, the business school now hosts one of the largest concentrations of interdisciplinary business and management research activity in Europe.

Director's Scholarships

Subjects: MBA.
Purpose: To help outstanding candidates with the cost of the Cambridge MBA.
Level of Study: MBA
Type: Scholarship
Value: UK £5,000
Length of Study: 1 year
Frequency: Annual
Study Establishment: Judge Institute of Management, University of Cambridge
Country of Study: United Kingdom
No. of awards offered: Approx. 10
Application Procedure: All applicants who are offered a place on the MBA programme are automatically considered.
Closing Date: May 31st
Funding: Private
Contributor: Judge Institute of Management studies
No. of awards given last year: 10
No. of applicants last year: 104 (all admitted students are considered)
Additional Information: As the number of scholarships is limited, candidates who apply early in the admissions round are more likely to receive this award.

N Boustany MBA Scholarship

Subjects: MBA.
Purpose: To enable a Lebanese national to attend the Cambridge MBA on a full scholarship.
Eligibility: Open to Lebanese nationals who have obtained a good Honours Degree from a recognized university and have at least 2 years of full-time, real-world experience. Candidates will need to demonstrate a high intellectual potential, practical common sense and the ability to put ideas into action. They also need to be highly motivated with a strong desire to learn. Applicants will be asked to take the Test of English as a Foreign Language (TOEFL) where applicable and the Graduate Management Admission Test (GMAT).
Level of Study: MBA
Type: Bursary
Value: US$40,000 including full tuition and travelling expenses
Length of Study: 2 years
Frequency: Every 2 years
Study Establishment: Judge Institute of Management, University of Cambridge
Country of Study: United Kingdom
No. of awards offered: 1
Application Procedure: Applicants must contact or email their curriculum vitae to Mr M Tamar. Applicants must also be applying for the Cambridge MBA programme.
Closing Date: May 31st
Funding: Foundation
Contributor: The Nabil Boustany Foundation
No. of awards given last year: 1
No. of applicants last year: 4
Additional Information: The scholarship recipient is normally required to spend a 1-year internship, carrying no salary, within a Lebanese organization. Applicants must be accepted into the Cambridge MBA programme.

For further information contact:

1 avenue des Citronniers, Monte Carlo, Monaco
Fax: (377) 77 93 15 05 56
Email: metropolegroup@monaco.mc
Website: www.jims.cam.ac.uk
Contact: Mr M Tamar

Sainsbury Bursaries

Subjects: MBA.
Purpose: To support students engaged in charitable, voluntary or public sector work in areas such as housing, health and education, local economic development and social services, as it is difficult for such candidates to secure sponsorship from their employers.
Eligibility: Preference will be given to applicants from the United Kingdom but exceptional candidates working for international aid agencies based outside the United Kingdom will be given consideration. It is expected that applicants will contribute to the sectors in the United Kingdom after completion of the MBA. Candidates must have completed 3 years of work within the charitable, voluntary or public sector prior to submitting their application. The applicants for the 2-year integrated course must have a placement set up within an organization in the charitable, voluntary or public sector. Candidates must also show evidence of a career plan showing how they would use the skills and knowledge gained during the MBA course to develop their career within the charitable, voluntary or public sector.
Level of Study: Postgraduate
Type: Bursary
Value: Ranges from UK £10,000–20,000 at the discretion of The Sainsbury Bursary Scheme Committee. The Committee is also willing to consider higher awards of up to UK £25,000 for candidates who show exceptional ability and potential
Length of Study: 1 year
Frequency: Annual
Study Establishment: Judge Institute of Management, University of Cambridge
Country of Study: United Kingdom
No. of awards offered: 4–7
Application Procedure: Applicants must complete and submit an application form for the MBA along with a covering letter, indicating that they would also like to apply for a Sainsbury Bursary, to the Judge Institute of Management.
Closing Date: The end of March
Funding: Private
Contributor: The Monument Trust
No. of awards given last year: 3
No. of applicants last year: 3
Additional Information: The Monument Trust is one of the Sainsbury Family Charitable Trusts.

St Catharine's College Benavitch Scholarships

Subjects: MBA.
Purpose: To encourage exceptional candidates to pursue the Cambridge MBA.
Eligibility: Applicants must have a First or High Upper Second Class (Honours) Degree, grade point average above 3.5 (out of 4) from a recognized university, minimum Graduate Management Admission Test (GMAT) scores of 680 and 3 years' full-time, postgraduation work experience.
Level of Study: Postgraduate
Type: Scholarship
Value: UK £5,000
Length of Study: 1 year
Frequency: Annual
Study Establishment: Judge Institute of Management, University of Cambridge
Country of Study: United Kingdom

No. of awards offered: 10
Application Procedure: Candidates must apply for admission to the Cambridge MBA in the normal way, and also send a covering letter marked Benavitch Scholarship application' with their MBA form, explaining in not more than 100 words the contribution they expect to make to business and society in the future.
Closing Date: March 15th
Funding: Private
Contributor: The late Maurice Benavitch and his late wife Natalie
Additional Information: Recipients of Benavitch Scholarships will become members of St Catharine's College, Cambridge and be given the option to live in single, college-owned accommodation (some married accommodation may be offered, subject to availability).

UNIVERSITY OF CANTERBURY

College of Arts, University of Canterbury, Private Bag 4800, Christchurch, New Zealand
Tel: (64) 3 364 2426 (ext: 6426)
Fax: (64) 3 364 2683
Email: erin.hird@canterbury.ac.nz
Website: www.canterbury.ac.nz
Contact: Ms Erin Hird, Human Resource Administrator

The University of Canterbury offers a variety of subjects in a few flexible degree structures, namely, first and postgraduate degrees in arts, commerce, education, engineering, fine arts, forestry, law, music and science. At Canterbury, research and teaching are closely related, and while this feature shapes all courses, it is very marked at the postgraduate level.

University of Canterbury and Creative New Zealand Ursula Bethell Residency in Creative Writing

Subjects: Creative writing, fiction, poetry, scriptwriting and literary nonfiction.
Purpose: To foster New Zealand writing by providing a full-time opportunity for a writer to work in an academic environment.
Eligibility: Open to authors of proven merit who are normally resident in New Zealand and to New Zealand nationals temporarily resident overseas.
Level of Study: Unrestricted
Type: Fellowship
Value: Emolument at the rate of New Zealand $46,500
Length of Study: Up to 1 year
Frequency: Dependent on funds available
Study Establishment: University of Canterbury
Country of Study: New Zealand
No. of awards offered: 1
Application Procedure: Applicants must submit details of published writings and work in progress, and include a proposal of work to be undertaken during the appointment only.
Closing Date: October 31st
Funding: Government
No. of awards given last year: 30 since 1979
Additional Information: The appointment will be made on the basis of published or performed writing of high quality. Conditions of appointment should be obtained from the Human Resources Department before applying, available in August from: hr@regy.canterbury.ac.nz

UNIVERSITY OF DELAWARE

Department of History, Newark, DE, 19716, United States of America
Tel: (1) 302 831 8226
Fax: (1) 302 831 1538
Email: pato@udel.edu
Website: www.udel.edu
Contact: Ms Patricia H Orendorf, Administrative Assistant

The Department of History offers M.A. and PhD programmes in American and European history and more limited graduate study Ancient, African, Asian, Latin American, and Middle Eastern history. In conjunction with these, it offers special programmes in the history of industrialization, material culture studies, American Civilization, and museum studies.

E Lyman Stewart Fellowship

Subjects: History.
Purpose: To provide a programme of graduate study leading to an MA or PhD degree for students who plan careers as museum professionals, historical agency administrators or seek careers in college teaching and public history.
Eligibility: Open to nationals of any country.
Level of Study: Doctorate, graduate, predoctorate
Type: Fellowship
Value: US$13,000 plus tuition
Frequency: Annual
Study Establishment: University of Delaware
Country of Study: United States of America
No. of awards offered: 6–8
Application Procedure: Applicants must submit an application form, transcripts, Graduate Record Examination (GRE) scores, Test of English as a Foreign Language (TOEFL) scores where applicable, plus three letters of recommendation and a writing sample.
Closing Date: January 15th
Funding: Private
No. of awards given last year: 8
No. of applicants last year: 20
Additional Information: This is a residential programme.

Fellowships in the University of Delaware Hagley Program

Subjects: The history of industrialization (broadly defined to include business, economics, labour and social history) and the history of science and technology.
Purpose: To provide a programme of graduate study leading to an MA or PhD degree for students who seek careers in college teaching and public history.
Eligibility: Open to graduates of any nationality seeking degrees in American or European history or the history of science and technology.
Level of Study: Graduate, doctorate, predoctorate
Type: Fellowship
Value: US$13,000 for Master's and doctoral candidates. All tuition fees for university courses are paid
Length of Study: 1 year, renewable once for those seeking a terminal MA and up to three times for those seeking the doctorate
Frequency: Annual
Study Establishment: University of Delaware
Country of Study: United States of America
No. of awards offered: Approx. 2–3
Application Procedure: Fellows are selected upon Graduate Record Examination scores, recommendations, undergraduate grade index, work experience and personal interviews.
Closing Date: January 15th
Funding: Government, private
No. of awards given last year: 3
No. of applicants last year: 21
Additional Information: This is a residential programme.

UNIVERSITY OF DUNDEE

Nethergate, Dundee, DD1 4HN, Scotland
Tel: (44) 13 8234 5028
Fax: (44) 13 8234 5343
Email: j.e.nicholson@dundee.ac.uk
Website: www.dundee.ac.uk
Contact: Postgraduate Office

The University of Dundee believes emphatically in the traditional mission of universities, that being the pursuit of excellence in the twin activities of learning and discovery. The University is well placed to fulfil these objectives as it has an established record in teaching and research.

University of Dundee Research Awards

Subjects: Medicine, dentistry, science, engineering, law, the arts, social sciences, environmental studies, town planning, architecture, management and consumer studies, nursing, fine arts, television and imaging.
Purpose: To assist full-time research leading to a PhD.
Eligibility: Open to holders of a First or Upper Second Class (Honours) Degree or equivalent. The Queen's College Scholarship is open to Dundee graduates with a first Class Honours Degree.
Level of Study: Postgraduate, doctorate
Type: Studentship
Value: UK £7,550 plus tuition fees at the National minimum rate
Length of Study: 1 year, renewable annually for up to a maximum of 2 additional years
Frequency: Dependent on funds available
Study Establishment: University of Dundee
Country of Study: United Kingdom
No. of awards offered: 1 Queen's College scholarship
Application Procedure: Applicants can obtain an application form from the website.
Closing Date: March 2nd
No. of awards given last year: 7
No. of applicants last year: 70

UNIVERSITY OF EAST ANGLIA (UEA)

Faculty Of Arts and Humanities, School of Literature and Creative Writing, Norwich, Norfolk, NR4 7TJ, England
Tel: (44) 16 0359 2810
Fax: (44) 16 0350 7728
Email: v.striker@uea.ac.uk
Website: www.uea.ac.uk
Contact: Ms Val Striker

The University of East Anglia (UEA) is organized into 17 schools of study encompassing the sciences, humanities and social sciences, and professional studies. These are supported by central service and administration departments.

Charles Pick Fellowship

Subjects: Fictional and nonfictional literature.
Purpose: To assist and support the work of a new and as yet unpublished writer of fiction or nonfictional prose and to give promising writers time to devote to the development of their talent.
Eligibility: Open to applicants of all ages and nationalities who are writers of fiction or nonfictional prose in English. Applicants must not yet have had a book published but all applicants must provide a reference from either an editor, agent or accredited teacher of creative writing to be sent directly to the Charles Pick Fellowship.
Level of Study: Professional development
Type: Fellowship
Value: UK £10,000 plus free accommodation provided on the university campus
Length of Study: 6 months, starting September 1st
Frequency: Annual
Study Establishment: UEA
Country of Study: United Kingdom
No. of awards offered: 1
Application Procedure: Applicants must submit a completed application form together with a typescript of an original unpublished piece of fiction or nonfiction. This should not be more than 2,500 words, written in English. Emailed and faxed applications and any application form sent without a reference will not be accepted. Late references will also not be accepted. There will be no interviews but candidates will be judged on the quality and promise of their writing, the project they describe and their reference. They will also be expected to provide reasonable proof of writing progress on occasion during their residency.
Closing Date: September 1st
Funding: Private
No. of awards given last year: 1
No. of applicants last year: 93
Additional Information: The Charles Pick Fellowship is dedicated to the memory of the distinguished publisher and literary agent, Charles Pick, whose career began in 1933 and continued until shortly before his death in January 2000. He encouraged young writers at the start of their careers with introductions to other writers as well as practical and financial help. The new fellowship seeks to continue this spirit of encouragement by giving support to the work of a new and as yet, unpublished writer of fictional or nonfictional prose. Please note that for the purposes of this fellowship, nonfictional prose includes, for example, biography, memoir and travel writing but not critical or historical monographs based on academic research.

David T K Wong Fellowship

Subjects: Writing.
Purpose: To support promising writers in producing a work of fiction set in the Far East.
Eligibility: Open to all writers whose projects deal with some aspect of life in the Far East.
Level of Study: Professional development
Type: Fellowship
Value: UK £25,000
Length of Study: 1 year
Frequency: Annual
Study Establishment: UEA
Country of Study: United Kingdom
No. of awards offered: 1
Application Procedure: Applicants must obtain further information and application forms by writing to the School of Literature and Creative Writing at UEA, Norwich.
Closing Date: January 31st
Funding: Private
Contributor: David T K Wong
No. of awards given last year: 1
No. of applicants last year: 57
Additional Information: The Far East is defined as China, Hong Kong, Macau, Taiwan, Japan, Korea, Mongolia, Laos, Cambodia, Vietnam, Thailand, Burma, Philippines, Singapore, Malaysia, Indonesia and Brunei.

THE UNIVERSITY OF EDINBURGH

Old College, South Bridge, Edinburgh, EH8 9YL, Scotland
Tel: (44) 13 1651 4221
Fax: (44) 13 1650 8223
Email: scholarships@ed.ac.uk
Website: www.scholarships.ed.ac.uk
Contact: Robert Lawrie Scholarships and Student Finance Office

The University of Edinburgh is an international centre of excellence in research and teaching, with outstanding resources and facilities for postgraduate students across the whole range of academic disciplines. More than 160 taught postgraduate programmes are available, with around 130 academic units offering subjects for degrees by research.

American Friends of the University of Edinburgh Scholarship

Subjects: All subjects.
Purpose: To foster good relations with students from the United States of America and to enhance graduate study opportunities for deserving students.
Eligibility: Applicants must hold a United States of America passport.
Level of Study: Postgraduate
Type: Scholarship
Value: One scholarship at US$5,000 and two at US$1,000
Frequency: Annual
Study Establishment: The University of Edinburgh
Country of Study: Scotland
No. of awards offered: 2
Application Procedure: Applicants must complete an application form, available from the Scholarship and Financial Aid Office, and enclose a copy of their degree transcript as well as two academic references in sealed envelopes.

Closing Date: April 3rd
Contributor: The University of Edinburgh USA Development Trust, Inc.
No. of awards given last year: 4
Additional Information: For further information visit the website www.scholarships.ed.ac.uk

College of Medicine and Veterinary Medicine PhD Scholarship

Subjects: Applicants are required to select from around 30–40 research projects suggested by Interdisciplinary Research Groups, Interdisciplinary Research Centers and Divisions/Units in the College of Medicine and Veterinary Medicine.
Eligibility: Applicants should hold, or expect to obtain a First or Upper Second Class (Honours) Degree or equivalent qualification in a relevant subject.
Level of Study: Doctorate
Type: Scholarship
Value: An annual stipend of UK £10,000 per academic year, payment of tuition fees at the United Kingdom/European Union rate, payment of bench fees and an annual conference allowance
Study Establishment: The University of Edinburgh
Country of Study: Scotland
No. of awards offered: Up to 6
Application Procedure: Applicants are asked to select from the 30 projects on offer, and to submit a completed application form. Applications not using the application form may not be accepted. Applicants are also required to arrange for two confidential referee reports to be submitted by the closing date.
Closing Date: January 13th

For further information contact:

College of Medicine and Veterinary Medicine, The University of Edinburgh, Teviot Place, Edinburgh, EH8 9AG, Scotland
Contact: Paul McGuire

The Craig Mathieson China Master's Scholarship and The University of Edinburgh China Master's Scholarships

Subjects: All subjects.
Purpose: To support full-time study leading to a Master's degree in any discipline.
Eligibility: Open to Chinese citizens who are normally resident in China and who are entering a full-time Master's programme at the University of Edinburgh.
Level of Study: Postgraduate
Type: Scholarship
Value: UK £3,000
Length of Study: 1 year
Frequency: Annual
Study Establishment: The University of Edinburgh
Country of Study: Scotland
No. of awards offered: 6
Application Procedure: Applicants must complete an application form available from the Scholarships and Financial Aid Office, and enclose a copy of their degree transcript as well as two academic references in sealed envelopes.
Closing Date: April 3rd
No. of awards given last year: 2

For further information contact:

Scholarships and Financial Aid Office, The University of Edinburgh, Old College, South Bridge, Edinburgh, EH8 9YL, Scotland

The Denwyn Dobby Scholarship

Subjects: Philosophy, psychology and language sciences.
Purpose: To support full-time research in the Koestler Parapsychology Unit in the School of Philosophy, Psychology and Language Sciences.
Eligibility: Open to students who are entering a full-time research degree within the Koestler Parapsychology Unit.
Level of Study: Research, postgraduate
Type: Scholarship
Value: United Kingdom tuition fees plus an appropriate living allowance as determined by the Koestler Chair
Length of Study: Tenable for 1 year in the first instance. Renewable for 2 further years pending satisfactory progress
Frequency: Annual
Study Establishment: The University of Edinburgh
Country of Study: Scotland
No. of awards offered: 1
Application Procedure: Candidates should send a written notice of their intention to compete for the scholarships to the Koestler Professor of parapsychology. Along with their application, candidates should submit a statement of not more than 1,500 words explaining their research project and how the award will assist them to carry out their research in parapsychology.
Closing Date: April 15th

For further information contact:

School of Philosophy, Psychology and Language Sciences, 7 George Square, Edinburgh, EH8 9JZ, Scotland

Shell Centenary Scholarships and Shell Centenary Chevening Scholarships at Edinburgh

Subjects: Applied sciences and technology, including environmental sciences.
Eligibility: Students from countries that are not present or applicant members of the Organization for Economic Co-operation and Development (OECD). Candidates should normally be aged 20–35, be resident in one of the non-OECD countries and be intending to return to the country concerned at the end of the period of study. They should normally already hold a degree equivalent to a United Kingdom First Class (Honours) Degree or be expecting to obtain such a degree before the start of their proposed course.
Level of Study: Postgraduate
Type: Scholarship
Value: The scholarships covers tuition fees, accommodation, maintenance costs and a return airfare for the scholarship holder
Length of Study: 1 year
Frequency: Annual
Study Establishment: University of Edinburgh
Country of Study: Scotland
No. of awards offered: 6
Application Procedure: Applicants must apply separately for admission to the University of Edinburgh making a clear statement that they wish to be considered for a Shell Scholarship.
Closing Date: March 1st
No. of awards given last year: 6

Sir Gordon and Lady Ivy Wu Scholarship

Subjects: All subjects.
Purpose: To support full-time study leading to a Master's degree in any discipline.
Eligibility: Open to Chinese citizens who are normally resident in China or the Hong Kong SAR who have studied at the City University of Hong Kong.
Level of Study: Postgraduate
Type: Scholarship
Value: UK £15,000
Length of Study: 1 year
Frequency: Annual
Study Establishment: The University of Edinburgh
Country of Study: Scotland
No. of awards offered: 1
Application Procedure: Applicants must complete an application form available from the Scholarships and Financial Aid Office, and enclose a copy of their degree transcript as well as two academic references in sealed envelopes.
Closing Date: April 3rd
Funding: Individuals
Contributor: Sir Gordon and Lady Ivy Wu

For further information contact:

Scholarships and Financial Aid Office, The University of Edinburgh, Old College, South Bridge, Edinburgh, EH8 9YL, Scotland

The University of Edinburgh Canadian Master's Scholarships

Subjects: All subjects.
Purpose: To support full-time study leading to a Master's degree in any discipline.
Eligibility: Open to Canadian citizens who are normally resident in Canada and who are entering a full-time Master's programme at the University of Edinburgh.
Level of Study: Postgraduate
Type: Scholarship
Value: UK £3,000
Length of Study: 1 year
Frequency: Annual
Study Establishment: The University of Edinburgh
Country of Study: Scotland
No. of awards offered: 2
Application Procedure: Applicants must complete an application form available from the Scholarships and Financial Aid Office, and enclose a copy of their degree transcript as well as two academic references in sealed envelopes.
Closing Date: April 3rd
No. of awards given last year: 2

For further information contact:

Scholarships and Financial Aid Office, The University of Edinburgh, Old College, South Bridge, Edinburgh, EH8 9YL, Scotland

The University of Edinburgh China and Hong Kong Scholarship

Subjects: To support full-time study leading to a Master's degree in any discipline.
Purpose: To support full-time study leading to a Master's degree in any discipline.
Eligibility: Open to Chinese citizens who are normally resident in China or the Hong Kong SAR and who are entering a full-time Master's programme at the University of Edinburgh.
Level of Study: Postgraduate
Type: Scholarship
Value: 1 year - Full tuition fees
Length of Study: 1 year
Frequency: Annual
Study Establishment: The University of Edinburgh
Country of Study: Scotland
No. of awards offered: 1
Application Procedure: Applicants must complete an application form available from the Scholarships and Financial Aid Office, and enclose a copy of their degree transcript as well as two academic references in sealed envelopes.
Closing Date: April 3rd
No. of awards given last year: 1

For further information contact:

Scholarship and Financial Aid Office, The University of Edinburgh, Old College, South Bridge, Edinburgh, EH8 9YL, Scotland

University of Edinburgh College Postgraduate Research Studentship

Subjects: All subjects.
Eligibility: Students should hold, or expect to obtain, a First Class or Upper Second Class (Honours) Degree from the United Kingdom or the overseas equivalent. Candidates who have progressed to obtain a Master's degree with distinction will also be considered.
Level of Study: Doctorate, mphil, 1mlitt
Type: Studentship
Value: United Kingdom tuition fees and a maintenance allowance broadly equivalent to those of the United Kingdom Research Councils and the British Academy. Research costs may also be paid
Frequency: Annual
Study Establishment: The University of Edinburgh
Country of Study: Scotland
Application Procedure: Candidates must be recommended for a studentship by the head of the school in which they wish to study. Candidates who wish to be nominated should contact the relevant school office.

The University of Edinburgh Indian Master's Scholarships

Subjects: All subjects.
Purpose: To support full-time study leading to a Master's degree in any discipline.
Eligibility: Open to Indian citizens who are normally resident in India and who are entering a full-time Master's programme at the University of Edinburgh.
Level of Study: Postgraduate
Type: Scholarship
Value: UK £3,000
Length of Study: 1 year
Frequency: Annual
Study Establishment: The University of Edinburgh
Country of Study: Scotland
No. of awards offered: 2
Application Procedure: Applicants must complete an application form available from the Scholarships and Financial Aid Office, and enclose a copy of their degree transcript as well as two academic references in sealed envelopes.
Closing Date: April 3rd
No. of awards given last year: 2

For further information contact:

Scholarships and Financial Aid Office, The University of Edinburgh, Old College, South Bridge, Edinburgh, EH8 9YL, Scotland

The University of Edinburgh Japanese Master's Scholarship

Subjects: Any discipline.
Purpose: To support full-time study leading to Master's degree in any discipline.
Eligibility: Open to Chinese citizens who are normally resident in China or the Hong Kong SAR and who are entering a full-time Master's programme at the University of Edinburgh.
Level of Study: Postgraduate
Type: Scholarship
Value: UK £3,000
Length of Study: 1 year
Frequency: Annual
Study Establishment: The University of Edinburgh
Country of Study: Scotland
No. of awards offered: 1
Application Procedure: Applicants must complete form available from the Scholarships and Financial Aid Office, and enclose a copy of their degree transcript as well as two academic references in sealed envelopes.
Closing Date: April 3rd

The University of Edinburgh ORS Linked Scholarship

Subjects: All subjects.
Eligibility: Open to overseas postgraduate research students in any discipline who are in receipt of an Overseas Research Student (ORS) Award.
Level of Study: Postgraduate
Value: United Kingdom/European Union tuition fees
Length of Study: A maximum of 3 years
Frequency: Annual
Study Establishment: The University of Edinburgh
No. of awards offered: 15
Application Procedure: As all ORS applicants are automatically considered, no separate application is required for these scholarships.
No. of awards given last year: 15
Additional Information: Further information is available on Scholarships and Financial Aid website: www.scholarships.ed.ac.uk

The University of Edinburgh Thai Master's Scholarship

Subjects: Any discipline.
Purpose: To support full-time study leading to Master's degree in any discipline.
Eligibility: Open to Chinese citizens who are normally resident in China or the Hong Kong SAR and who are entering a full-time Master's programme at the University of Edinburgh.
Level of Study: Postgraduate
Type: Scholarship
Value: UK £3,000
Length of Study: 1 year
Frequency: Annual
Study Establishment: The University of Edinburgh
Country of Study: Scotland
No. of awards offered: 1
Application Procedure: Applicants must complete form available from the Scholarships and Financial Aid Office, and enclose a copy of their degree transcript as well as two academic references in sealed envelopes.
Closing Date: April 3rd

The University of Edinburgh US Master's Scholarships

Subjects: All subjects.
Purpose: To support full-time study leading to a Master's degree in any discipline.
Eligibility: Open to citizens of the United States of America who are normally resident in the United States of America who are entering a full-time Master's programme at the University of Edinburgh.
Level of Study: Postgraduate
Type: Scholarship
Value: UK £3,000
Length of Study: 1 year
Frequency: Annual
Study Establishment: The University of Edinburgh
Country of Study: Scotland
No. of awards offered: 2
Application Procedure: Applicants must complete an application form available from the Scholarships and Financial Aid Office, and enclose a copy of their degree transcript as well as two academic references in sealed envelopes.
Closing Date: April 3rd
No. of awards given last year: 2

For further information contact:

Scholarships and Financial Aid Office, The University of Edinburgh, Old College, South Bridge, Edinburgh, EH8 9YL, Scotland

Wellcome Trust 4-Year PhD Programme Studentships

Subjects: The cellular and molecular basis of disease.
Eligibility: Students should be from a life sciences background and should hold, or expect to obtain, at least an Upper Second Class (Honours) Degree.
Level of Study: Doctorate
Type: Studentship
Value: Tax-free stipend (UK £14,200–16,400), tuition fees and research costs
Frequency: Annual
Study Establishment: The University of Edinburgh
Country of Study: Scotland
No. of awards offered: 5
Application Procedure: Students wishing to apply should supply a covering letter, a curriculum vitae, a one page statement supporting their application and stating the reasons for wishing to follow this programme of research training. Applicants should also have three reference reports sent directly to the graduate school.
Closing Date: January 5th
No. of awards given last year: 5

For further information contact:

The University of Edinburgh, Swann Building, King's Buildings, Mayfield Road, Edinburgh, EH9 3JR
Contact: Programme Secretary, Life Sciences Graduate Programme

UNIVERSITY OF ESSEX

Graduate Admissions Office, University of Essex, Wivenhoe Park, Colchester, C04 3SQ, England
Tel: (44) 12 0687 2719
Fax: (44) 12 0687 2808
Email: pgadmit@essex.ac.uk
Website: www.essex.ac.uk
Contact: Graduate Recruitment and Publications Officer

The University of Essex is one of the United Kingdom's leading academic institutions, ranked 10th nationally for research and 7th for teaching. It offers degrees and research opportunities across 19 academic departments (including government and sociology, which both have 6-star research ratings) and numerous research centres of world renown.

+3 (PhD research) Studentship

Subjects: History from 1500AD to present day.
Purpose: Support full or part-time home/Eu student undertake PhD.
Eligibility: Applicants must be postgraduate students. Need to be undertaking social science based research. Need a 1st or high 2.1.
Level of Study: Postgraduate
Type: Scholarship
Value: British full-time: tuition fees and maintenance of around UK £9,000, British part-time: tuition fees only, Eu: level of support depends on residential status
Frequency: Annual
Study Establishment: University Essex
Application Procedure: Applicants must contact the department concerned.
Contributor: ESRC

British Marshall Scholarships

Subjects: All research degrees.
Purpose: Support American students doing a research degree.
Eligibility: Applicants must be postgraduate students. American students applying for full-time degree.
Level of Study: Research, postgraduate
Type: Scholarship
Value: Tuition fees, living expenses, annual book grant, thesis grant, research and daily travel grant, fares to and from US
Frequency: Annual
Study Establishment: University of Essex
Application Procedure: Applicants must contact the department concerned. See www.marshallscholarship.org
Closing Date: Mid-October of year before tenure
Funding: Foundation

For further information contact:

Email: macc@acu.ac.uk

Don Pike Award

Subjects: Philosophy of social science.
Purpose: Support students over the age of 21 working in one field of philosophy of social sciences at postgraduate or undergraduate level.
Eligibility: Applicants must be students working on philosophy of social science.
Level of Study: Unrestricted
Type: Scholarship
Value: UK £250 towards purchase of books and expenses in preparing a thesis or dissertation
Frequency: Annual
Study Establishment: University of Essex
Country of Study: United Kingdom
Application Procedure: Applicants must contact the department concerned.
Closing Date: Friday of week 31st
Funding: Trusts

Essex Rotary University Travel Grants

Subjects: All subjects.
Purpose: To support students to spend time studying abroad.

Eligibility: Applicants must be a postgraduates at the University of Essex.
Level of Study: Postgraduate
Type: Grant
Frequency: Annual
Study Establishment: University of Essex
Country of Study: United Kingdom
No. of awards offered: 2
Application Procedure: Applicants must send a statement (not exceeding 500 words) indicating what they would do with a rotary travel grant.
Closing Date: Monday of the 2nd week of the Summer term
Funding: Trusts
Contributor: Rotary clubs in Essex
No. of awards given last year: Two
Additional Information: Successful applicants may be invited to give not more than 3 to Rotary Clubs is Essex on their return.

Giulia Mereu Scholarships
Subjects: LLM international human rights law.
Purpose: Support a student on the university of Essex LLM in international human rights law.
Eligibility: Applicants must be postgraduate students on the LLM in international Human Rights Law at Essex.
Length of Study: One year
Frequency: Annual
Study Establishment: University of Essex
Country of Study: United Kingdom
No. of awards offered: One
Application Procedure: Applicants must contact the department concerned.
Funding: Trusts
Contributor: Family and friends of Giulia Mereu
No. of awards given last year: One

ORSAS
Subjects: All subjects.
Purpose: Support high quality international students undertaking research in the UK.
Eligibility: International students wishing to undertaking research.
Level of Study: Research, postgraduate
Type: Scholarship
Value: Covers the difference between home and overseas fees
Frequency: Annual
Study Establishment: University of Essex
Country of Study: United Kingdom
Application Procedure: See www.orsas.ac.uk
Funding: Government
Contributor: Government

Oscar Arias Scholarship
Subjects: All subjects.
Purpose: To enable students of Costa Rican nationality to pursue a full-time Master's or doctoral study at Essex.
Eligibility: Costa Rican nationals.
Level of Study: Postgraduate
Type: Scholarship
Length of Study: 1 year, renewable for not more than 2 further years
Frequency: Annual
Study Establishment: University of Essex
Country of Study: United Kingdom
No. of awards offered: 1
Application Procedure: Applicants must be recommended by the British Ambassador in San Jose, who receives nominations from the University.
Funding: International Office, government
Contributor: Foreign office and British Council

Poulter Studentship
Subjects: Science and archaeology.
Purpose: To enable full-time University of Essex graduates to study archaeology or natural science at graduate level.
Eligibility: Applicants must be University of Essex graduates.
Level of Study: Postgraduate
Type: Studentship
Value: Related to amount given by research councils
Length of Study: 1 year in the first instance, renewable for not more than 2 years
Frequency: Annual
Study Establishment: University of Essex
Country of Study: United Kingdom
Application Procedure: Applicants must visit the website.
Closing Date: Spring
Funding: Trusts
Contributor: Request from the late H W Poulter

Research Preparations Masters Scheme
Subjects: History from 1500AD to present day.
Purpose: Support MA Student (full-time home or Eu).
Eligibility: Applicants must be postgraduate students. Study must be humanities based. Must have first or high 2.1.
Level of Study: Postgraduate
Type: Scholarship
Value: British-fees and around UK £10,000 maintenance Eu-dependent an residency status
Length of Study: One year
Frequency: Annual
Study Establishment: University of Essex
Application Procedure: Applicants must contact the department concerned.
Contributor: AHRB

Sir Eric Berthoud Travel Grant
Subjects: All subjects.
Purpose: To support full-time students wishing to travel as part of their studies/research.
Eligibility: Applicants must be students at the University of Essex.
Level of Study: Unrestricted
Type: Grant
Frequency: Annual
Study Establishment: University of Essex
Country of Study: United Kingdom
Application Procedure: Applicants must visit the website for details.
Funding: Trusts
Contributor: Bequest from Sir Eric Berthoud

University of Essex 1+3 ESRC Competition Award
Subjects: Economics.
Purpose: To support postgraduate study.
Eligibility: Applicants must be postgraduates.
Level of Study: Postgraduate
Type: Studentship
Value: Fees and maintenance for home students. Fees only for European Union students
Frequency: Annual
Study Establishment: University of Essex
Country of Study: United Kingdom
Application Procedure: Applicants must contact the department concerned.
Closing Date: Mid-March
Contributor: ESRC

University of Essex Access to Learning Fund
Subjects: All subjects.
Purpose: To support home students with study.
Eligibility: Applicants must be home students.
Level of Study: Unrestricted
Type: Grant
Value: According to individual needs
Frequency: Annual
Study Establishment: University of Essex
Country of Study: United Kingdom
Application Procedure: Applicants must contact the student support office.
Funding: Government
Contributor: ALF

University of Essex Art History Bursary

Subjects: Art history and theory.
Purpose: To support postgraduate study.
Eligibility: Applicants must be postgraduates.
Level of Study: Postgraduate
Type: Bursary
Value: Approx UK £1,200
Frequency: Dependent on funds available
Study Establishment: University of Essex
Country of Study: United Kingdom
No. of awards offered: 1
Application Procedure: Applicants must contact the department concerned.
Funding: Private

University of Essex BBSRC Studentship

Subjects: Biological sciences.
Purpose: To support postgraduate biological science students.
Eligibility: Applicants must be biological science postgraduates.
Level of Study: Postgraduate
Type: Studentship
Frequency: Annual
Study Establishment: University of Essex
Country of Study: United Kingdom
Application Procedure: Applicants must contact the department concerned.
Contributor: BBSRC

University of Essex Doctoral award for PhD

Subjects: History from 1500AD to present day.
Purpose: Support research students.
Eligibility: Applicants must be postgraduate students. Research must be humanities based.
Level of Study: Postgraduate
Type: Scholarship
Value: British full-time: fees and maintenance of around UK £8,000 part time: fees and around UK £250 per annum EU: dependent on residency status
Frequency: Annual
Study Establishment: University of Essex
Application Procedure: Applicants must contact the department concerned.
Contributor: AHRC

University of Essex Economics Studentship

Subjects: Economics.
Purpose: To support postgraduate study.
Eligibility: Applicants must be postgraduates.
Level of Study: Postgraduate
Type: Studentship
Value: Two scholarships over fees and maintenance. Other smaller amounts are also available.
Frequency: Annual
Study Establishment: University of Essex
Country of Study: United Kingdom
Application Procedure: Applicants must contact the department concerned.
Closing Date: Awards allocated in July so deadline is May/June time
Contributor: University of Essex

University of Essex EPSRC Studentship

Subjects: Computer science.
Purpose: To support postgraduate study.
Eligibility: Postgraduate students with a First or Second Class (Honours) Degree in computer science or a related discipline are eligible to apply.
Level of Study: Postgraduate
Type: Scholarship
Value: Covers fees and UK £12,300 maintenance for home students. Fees only for European Union students
Frequency: Annual
Study Establishment: University of Essex
Country of Study: United Kingdom
Application Procedure: Applicants must contact the department concerned.
Closing Date: July 1st
Contributor: EPSRC

University of Essex MA Scholarship

Subjects: Department of literature, film and theatre studies.
Purpose: To support MA study.
Eligibility: Applicants must be postgraduate students.
Level of Study: Postgraduate
Type: Scholarship
Value: UK £1,000
Length of Study: 1 year
Frequency: Annual
Study Establishment: University of Essex
Country of Study: United Kingdom
Application Procedure: Applicants must contact the department concerned.
Contributor: University of Essex
No. of awards given last year: Three

University of Essex Scholarships

Subjects: Psychology.
Purpose: To support PhD research.
Eligibility: Home or European Union students with a First Class or a High Second Class (Honours) Degree in psychology or related discipline are eligible to apply.
Level of Study: Doctorate
Type: Student bursary
Value: UK £9,000 maintenance per year plus fees
Length of Study: 3 years
Frequency: Dependent on funds available
Study Establishment: University of Essex
Country of Study: United Kingdom
No. of awards offered: 2
Application Procedure: Applicants must first apply for a PhD and then appear for an interview on offer of admission.
Closing Date: May 27th
Contributor: University of Essex and the Department of Psychology
No. of awards given last year: Two

University of Essex Studentships

Subjects: Biological sciences.
Purpose: To support postgraduate biological science students.
Eligibility: Applicants must be biological science postgraduates.
Level of Study: Postgraduate
Type: Studentship
Frequency: Annual
Study Establishment: University of Essex
Country of Study: United Kingdom
Application Procedure: Applicants must contact the department concerned.
Contributor: University of Essex

University of Essex/Department of Computer Science Studentship

Subjects: Computer science.
Purpose: Support postgraduate study.
Eligibility: Applicants must be postgraduate students. Students must be home or Eu or overseas who have secured as ORS award.
Level of Study: Postgraduate
Type: Scholarship
Value: Depends on funds available
Frequency: Annual
Study Establishment: University of Essex
Country of Study: United Kingdom
Application Procedure: Applicants must contact the department concerned.
Closing Date: Mid Jan for overseas students who want to considered for ORS and university scholarship. July 1st for home/Eu applicants
Contributor: University of Essex

University of Essex/Department of Law AHRC Scholarships

Subjects: Law.
Purpose: Support studies that are arts and humanities based.
Eligibility: Applicants must be postgraduate students whose studies have a arts/humanities basis.
Level of Study: Postgraduate, research
Type: Scholarship
Value: Fees and maintenance
Study Establishment: University of Essex
Country of Study: United Kingdom
Application Procedure: Applicants must contact the department concerned.
Contributor: AHRC

University of Essex/Department of Law Scholarships

Subjects: Law.
Purpose: To support research students.
Eligibility: Applicants must be postgraduate research students with an offer for MPhil or PhD in the department of law.
Level of Study: Research
Type: Scholarship
Value: Fees and same maintenance
Length of Study: Up to 3 years
Frequency: Annual
Study Establishment: University of Essex
Country of Study: United Kingdom
Application Procedure: Applicants must contact the department concerned.
Contributor: University of Essex

University of Essex/EPSRC Scholarship

Subjects: Electronic systems engineering.
Purpose: To support postgraduate study.
Eligibility: Applicants must be postgraduates.
Level of Study: Postgraduate
Type: Scholarship
Value: Fees and some maintenance for home students fees only for EU
Frequency: Annual
Study Establishment: University of Essex
Country of Study: United Kingdom
Application Procedure: Applicants must contact the department concerned.
Contributor: EPSRC

University of Essex/EPSRC Studentship

Subjects: Psychology.
Purpose: To support PhD research.
Eligibility: Home or European Union students with a First Class or High Second Class (Honours) Degree in psychology or a related discipline are eligible to apply.
Level of Study: Doctorate
Type: Student bursary
Value: Usually maintenance equivalent to ESCR rate plus fees for home students. Fees only for European Union students
Length of Study: 3 years
Frequency: Dependent on funds available
Study Establishment: University of Essex
Country of Study: United Kingdom
No. of awards offered: Dependent on funds available
Application Procedure: Applicants must first apply for admission to a PhD programme.
Closing Date: July
Contributor: EPSRC

University of Essex/ESRC 1+3 Studentship

Subjects: History from 1500AD to the present day.
Purpose: To support student in pursuing an MA and PhD in history.
Eligibility: British and EU full and part-time proposing to undertake social science based research, with a 1st or high 2.1.
Level of Study: Postgraduate
Type: Studentship
Value: British students-tuition fees and maintenance of up to UK £10,500 for full-time study, fees only for part time EU-level of support depends on residential status
Length of Study: 4 years
Frequency: Annual
Study Establishment: University of Essex
Country of Study: United Kingdom
Application Procedure: Applicants must contact the department concerned.
Contributor: University of Essex ESRC
No. of awards given last year: 1

University of Essex/ESRC 1+3 Studentship

Subjects: Psychology.
Purpose: To support PhD research.
Eligibility: Home or European Union students with a First Class or High Second Class (Honours) Degree in psychology or a related discipline are eligible to apply.
Level of Study: 1-year Master's in research methods followed by a 3 year doctorate
Type: Student bursary
Value: Up to UK £12,000 maintenance plus fees for home students; fees only for European Union students
Length of Study: 4 years
Frequency: Annual
Study Establishment: University of Essex
Country of Study: United Kingdom
Application Procedure: Applicants must first apply for admission to a PhD programme. Their application is then submitted by the department to the ESRC national competition.
Closing Date: April
Contributor: ESRC
No. of awards given last year: Two

University of Essex/ESRC+3 Studentship

Subjects: Psychology.
Purpose: To support PhD research.
Eligibility: Home or European Union students with a First Class or High Second Class (Honours) Degree in psychology or a related discipline are eligible to apply. Applicants must hold an ESRC-approved MSc in psychological research methods.
Level of Study: Doctorate
Type: Student bursary
Value: Up to UK £12,000 maintenance plus fees for home students fees only for European Union students
Length of Study: 3 years
Frequency: Annual
Study Establishment: University of Essex
Country of Study: United Kingdom
No. of awards offered: National competition
Application Procedure: Applicants must first apply for admission to a PhD programme. Their application will then be submitted by the department to the ESRC national competition.
Closing Date: April
Contributor: ESRC
No. of awards given last year: One

University of Essex/MA History Studentships

Subjects: History from 1500AD to the present.
Purpose: To support postgraduates within the Department of History.
Eligibility: Applicants must be postgraduate history students.
Level of Study: Postgraduate
Type: Studentship
Value: UK £1,750–3,500
Length of Study: One year
Frequency: Annual
Study Establishment: University of Essex
Country of Study: United Kingdom
Application Procedure: Applicants must contact the department concerned.
Contributor: University of Essex
No. of awards given last year: 2

Additional Information: Please note that this university award can not be held concurrently with either research council funding or other external awards.

University of Essex/MRC Studentship

Subjects: Biological sciences.
Purpose: To support postgraduate biological science students.
Eligibility: Biological science postgraduates.
Level of Study: Postgraduate
Type: Studentship
Frequency: Annual
Study Establishment: University of Essex
Country of Study: United Kingdom
Application Procedure: Applicants must contact the department concerned.
Contributor: MRC

University of Essex/National Federation of Business and Professional Women's Clubs Travel Grants

Subjects: All subjects.
Purpose: To enable full-time female postgraduates to travel for research/studies.
Eligibility: Female full-time postgraduates.
Level of Study: Postgraduate
Type: Grant
Value: Approx. UK £175
Frequency: Annual
Study Establishment: University of Essex
Country of Study: United Kingdom
No. of awards offered: 1
Application Procedure: See the University website.
Contributor: National Federation of Business and Professional Women's clubs
No. of awards given last year: 1

University of Essex/NERC Studentships

Subjects: Biological sciences.
Purpose: To support postgraduate biological science students.
Eligibility: Applicants must be biological science postgraduates.
Level of Study: Postgraduate
Type: Studentship
Frequency: Annual
Study Establishment: University of Essex
Country of Study: United Kingdom
Application Procedure: Please contact the department concerned.
Contributor: NERC

University of Essex/ORS Awards

Subjects: All subjects.
Purpose: To support postgraduate study.
Eligibility: Overseas Postgraduates.
Level of Study: Postgraduate
Type: Scholarship
Value: Difference between home and overseas tuition fees
Frequency: Annual
Study Establishment: University of Essex
Country of Study: United Kingdom
Application Procedure: Applicants must see the University website and contact the department in which they wish to study.
Closing Date: Application packs are available from departments after November
Contributor: ORS

University of Essex/PhD History Studentship

Subjects: History from 1500AD to the present.
Purpose: To support a PhD student within the Department of History.
Eligibility: Applicants must be PhD students.
Level of Study: Postgraduate
Type: Studentship
Value: UK £5,250–10,500
Frequency: Annual
Study Establishment: University of Essex
Country of Study: United Kingdom
Application Procedure: Applicants must contact the department concerned.
Contributor: University of Essex
No. of awards given last year: 2

University of Essex/PhD Studentship

Subjects: Literature, film and theatre studies.
Purpose: To support PhD study.
Eligibility: Applicants must be PhD students.
Level of Study: Postgraduate
Type: Scholarship
Value: UK £4,000 for up to 3 years study
Frequency: Annual
Study Establishment: University of Essex
Country of Study: United Kingdom
Application Procedure: Applicants must contact the department concerned.
Contributor: University of Essex
No. of awards given last year: 2

University of Essex/Philosophy Graduate Awards

Subjects: Philosophy.
Purpose: To support postgraduate students studying in the Department of Philosophy.
Eligibility: Applicants must be students studying in the Department of Philosophy at postgraduate level.
Level of Study: Postgraduate
Type: Studentship
Value: 2 at UK £3,000, 1 at UK £1,000 (for 1 year)
Length of Study: 2 years for research (renewable for 3 years subject to satisfactory progression); 1 year for 1–year study
Frequency: Annual
Study Establishment: University of Essex
Country of Study: United Kingdom
Application Procedure: Applicants must complete an application form, available from the department's website.
Contributor: University of Essex
No. of awards given last year: Three

University of Essex/Postgraduate Research Studentship

Subjects: Mathematical sciences.
Purpose: To support postgraduate research.
Eligibility: Applicants must be postgraduates.
Level of Study: Postgraduate
Type: Studentship
Value: Up to UK £2,000
Frequency: Annual
Study Establishment: University of Essex
Country of Study: United Kingdom
Application Procedure: Applicants must contact the department concerned.
Closing Date: Spring
Contributor: University of Essex

University of Essex/Sociology PhD Studentships

Subjects: Sociology.
Purpose: To support PhD students studying within the Department of Sociology.
Eligibility: All.
Level of Study: Postgraduate
Type: Scholarship
Value: Up to UK £1,000
Frequency: Annual
Study Establishment: University of Essex
Country of Study: United Kingdom
Application Procedure: Applicants must contact the department for more information.
Closing Date: Applications considered by research committee which meets three times a year: Deadline for applications is week 5, 19 and 33
Contributor: University of Essex

University of Essex/Travel Grants

Subjects: All subjects.
Purpose: To support students who need additional financial assistance.
Eligibility: Graduate students.
Level of Study: Postgraduate
Type: Grant
Frequency: Annual
Study Establishment: University of Essex
Country of Study: United Kingdom
No. of awards offered: 1–2
Application Procedure: Applicants can obtain application forms from the graduate school office.
Closing Date: Monday of the 2nd week of the Summer term
Contributor: University of Essex
No. of awards given last year: 1–2

UNIVERSITY OF EXETER

The Graduate School, Northcote House, The Queen's Drive,
Exeter, Devon, EX4 4QJ, England
Tel: (44) 13 9226 3013
Fax: (44) 13 9226 3108
Email: sradfunding@exeter.ac.uk
Website: www.exeter.ac.uk/gradschool
Contact: Mrs Elaine Cordy, Administrative Officer

The University of Exeter combines a reputation of national and international excellence in research with a record of established excellence in teaching. Providing a superb environment in which to live and work, the University of Exeter is representative of the best in university education in the United Kingdom.

Andrew Stratton Scholarship

Subjects: Engineering and science.
Eligibility: Studying for taught Master's.
Level of Study: Postgraduate
Type: Scholarship
Value: UK £1,000
Length of Study: 1 year
Frequency: Dependent on funds available
Study Establishment: The University of Exeter
Country of Study: United Kingdom
No. of awards offered: 1
Application Procedure: Applicants must consult the University.
Closing Date: Please contact the organization
Additional Information: Further information is available on request.

Anning-Morgan Bursary

Subjects: All subjects.
Purpose: To financially support postgraduate study.
Eligibility: Open to students residing in the Duchy of Cornwall prior to entry or during their postgraduate studies.
Level of Study: Postgraduate
Type: Bursary
Value: Fees only
Length of Study: A maximum of 2 years
Frequency: Dependent on funds available
Study Establishment: The University of Exeter
Country of Study: United Kingdom
No. of awards offered: 1
Application Procedure: Applicants must consult the University.
Closing Date: August 31st
No. of awards given last year: 1
No. of applicants last year: N/A
Additional Information: Further information is available on request.

Anthony Parsons Memorial Scholarship

Subjects: Arabic, Islamic and Middle East studies.
Purpose: To financially support those undertaking postgraduate study.
Eligibility: Open to students conducting research.
Level of Study: Postgraduate
Type: Scholarship
Value: Up to UK £3,000
Frequency: Dependent on funds available
Study Establishment: The University of Exeter
Country of Study: United Kingdom
Application Procedure: Applicants must consult the University.

British Council Awards and Scholarships for International Students

Subjects: All subjects offered by the University.
Purpose: To allow international students to pursue postgraduate study.
Eligibility: Open to candidates for research degrees who have obtained at least an Upper Second Class (Honours) Degree or its equivalent.
Level of Study: Postgraduate
Type: Scholarship
Value: Varies
Length of Study: Varies
Frequency: Annual
Study Establishment: The University of Exeter
Country of Study: United Kingdom
No. of awards offered: Varies
Application Procedure: Applicants must obtain details from the British Council representative in the applicant's own country.
Closing Date: Please contact the organization
Funding: Government
Additional Information: Further information is available on request.

Commonwealth Scholarship Plan

Subjects: All subjects.
Purpose: To allow students to pursue postgraduate study.
Eligibility: Open to students from Commonwealth countries who do not already hold scholarships from their own country.
Level of Study: Postgraduate
Type: Scholarship
Value: Varies, but includes payment of tuition fees
Frequency: Annual
Study Establishment: The University of Exeter
Country of Study: United Kingdom
No. of awards offered: Varies
Application Procedure: Applicants must apply well in advance in their country of permanent residence through the Commonwealth Scholarship Agency.
Closing Date: Please contact the organization
Funding: Government
Additional Information: Further information is available on request.

Cornwall Heritage Trust Scholarship

Subjects: All subjects centering on Cornwall's heritage.
Eligibility: Open to students working towards a Master's degree on a dissertation focussing on an aspect of Cornwall's heritage.
Level of Study: Postgraduate
Type: Scholarship
Value: UK £1,000
Length of Study: 1 year
Frequency: Annual
Study Establishment: The University of Exeter
Country of Study: United Kingdom
No. of awards offered: 1
Application Procedure: Applicants must inform the Graduate School when applying for a place on a programme.
Closing Date: July 31st
Funding: Trusts
No. of awards given last year: Still to be decided
No. of applicants last year: 1
Additional Information: Further information is available on request.

University of Exeter Graduate Research Assistantships

Subjects: All subjects.
Purpose: To assist students by offering them a top-quality scheme that offers excellent career development opportunities.
Eligibility: Open to MPhil and PhD students.

Level of Study: Research, doctorate
Type: Other
Value: Fees and maintenance at research council rates
Length of Study: 4 years
Study Establishment: The University of Exeter
Country of Study: United Kingdom
Application Procedure: Applicants must visit the website of the school in which they wish to study.
Additional Information: Further details of this scheme are available from the website. Graduate research assistants are required to undertake 2 days of research a week for a research team in addition to their own research.

University of Exeter Graduate Teaching Assistantships (GTA)

Subjects: All subjects.
Purpose: To assist students by offering them a top-quality scheme that offers excellent career development opportunities.
Eligibility: Open to MPhil and PhD students.
Level of Study: Research, doctorate
Type: Other
Value: Fees and maintenance at research council rates
Length of Study: Up to 4 years
Frequency: Annual
Study Establishment: The University of Exeter
Country of Study: United Kingdom
No. of awards offered: Varies
Application Procedure: Applicants must visit the website of the school in which they wish to study.
Closing Date: Please contact the organization
Additional Information: Further details of this scheme are available from the Graduate School website. GTAs are given full training with SEDA accreditation and are expected to teach for up to 150 hours per year.

University of Exeter Overseas Research Students Award Scheme

Subjects: All subjects.
Purpose: To assist international students of outstanding merit and research potential undertaking research degrees.
Eligibility: International students holding offers of study for research degrees, or International students already on a research course who do not have an ORS award.
Level of Study: Doctorate, research
Type: Award
Value: The difference between the tuition fees for a home or European Union postgraduate student and that for an international postgraduate student
Length of Study: 3 years
Frequency: Annual
Study Establishment: The University of Exeter
Country of Study: United Kingdom
No. of awards offered: Varies
Application Procedure: Application forms and details are sent to all applicants who are offered a place for MPhil or PhD study before mid-January.
Closing Date: February 3rd
Funding: Government
Contributor: United Kingdom universities
No. of awards given last year: 10
No. of applicants last year: 66

University of Exeter Research Scholarships

Subjects: All subjects.
Purpose: To fund MPhil and PhD study.
Eligibility: Open to international applicants for PhD and MPhil/PhD programmes.
Level of Study: Research, doctorate
Type: Scholarship
Value: Full fees
Length of Study: 3 years
Frequency: Annual
Study Establishment: The University of Exeter
Country of Study: United Kingdom
No. of awards offered: Varies
Application Procedure: Applicants should apply for the ORS scheme. Forms will be sent to eligible offer holders. ORS applications are automatically considered for the ERS scheme.
Closing Date: February 3rd
Contributor: University of Exeter
No. of awards given last year: 10
Additional Information: Further information is available on request.

University of Exeter Sports Scholarships

Subjects: Sports.
Purpose: To assist students of outstanding sporting ability who show evidence of achievement or potential at national level.
Eligibility: Performers from any sport considered, but emphasis is placed on cricket, football, golf, hockey, lacrosse, netball, rowing, rugby, sailing and tennis.
Level of Study: Postgraduate, graduate
Type: Scholarship
Value: Free university residential accommodation and UK £1,000 per year for sporting expenses
Length of Study: 1 year initially, but may be renewed for an additional 2 years
Frequency: Annual
Study Establishment: The University of Exeter
Country of Study: United Kingdom
No. of awards offered: Varies
Application Procedure: Applicants must contact the Secretary of the Sports Scholarship Board at the University.
Closing Date: October 2nd
Additional Information: Students will be provided with a mentor with whom an annual programme of training and competition will be agreed.

UNIVERSITY OF GLAMORGAN

Pontypridd, Wales, CF 37 1 DL, United Kingdom
Tel: (44) (0) 1443 828 812
Fax: (44) (0) 1443 822 055
Email: enquiries@glam.ac.uk
Website: www.glam.ac.uk

The University of Glamorgan is a dynamic institution with an exceptional record for academic excellence, teaching and research.

Crawshays Rugby Scholarship

Subjects: All subjects.
Purpose: To support talented young rugby players through higher education at the University.
Eligibility: Open to applicants who are rugby players studying at the University of Glamorgan.
Level of Study: Postgraduate
Type: Scholarship
Value: UK £1,000
Frequency: Annual
Study Establishment: University of Glamorgan
Country of Study: United Kingdom
Application Procedure: For further details contact the university.
Contributor: Crawshay's Welsh RFC

For further information contact:

Sardis Road, Pontypridd RFC
Contact: Clive Jones, Director of Rugby

The University of Glamorgan Sports Scholarships

Subjects: Sports.
Purpose: To support potential elite athletes and sports people who are competing at national and international level in their chosen field.
Eligibility: Open to students studying on the Treforest or Glyntaff Campus.
Level of Study: Professional development
Type: Scholarship
Value: UK £500

Frequency: Annual
Country of Study: United Kingdom
Application Procedure: Contact the university for further details.

UNIVERSITY OF GLASGOW

Glasgow, G12 8QQ, Scotland
Tel: (44) 141 330 2000
Email: h.ruxton@enterprise.gla.ac.uk
Website: www.gla.ac.uk
Contact: Hazel Ruxton, PG Research Office

The University of Glasgow is a major research led university operating in an international context, which aims to provide education through the development of learning in a research environment, to undertake fundamental, strategic and applied research and to sustain and add value to Scottish culture, to the natural environment and to the national economy.

John & James Houston Crawford Scholarship

Subjects: Veterinary medicine.
Purpose: To assist the advanced study or research into the bovine and equine animals.
Eligibility: Open to university graduates or qualified veterinary surgeons.
Level of Study: Postgraduate
Type: Scholarship
Length of Study: 1–2 years
Frequency: Every 2 years
Study Establishment: Institution approved by the faculty of veterinary medicine
Country of Study: United Kingdom
Application Procedure: Applications to be submitted to the clerk of the Faculty of Veterinary Medicine.
Closing Date: June 1st
Additional Information: Preference is given to graduates in veterinary medicine of the University of Glasgow.

For further information contact:

Faculty of Veterinary Medicine, University of Glasgow Veterinary School, Bearsden, Glasgow, G61 1QH, Scotland

John Crawford Scholarship

Subjects: Veterinary medicine.
Purpose: To assist the advanced study or research into equine animals, with particular reference to blood stock breeding and its improvement.
Eligibility: Open to university graduates of veterinary medicine and qualified veterinary surgeons.
Level of Study: Postgraduate
Type: Scholarship
Value: Please consult the organization
Frequency: Every 2 years
Study Establishment: The University of Glasgow
Country of Study: United Kingdom
Application Procedure: Applicants must write for details.
Additional Information: Preference is given to graduates in veterinary medicine of the University of Glasgow.

For further information contact:

Faculty of Veterinary Medicine, University of Glasgow Veterinary School, Bearsden, Glasgow, G61 1QH, Scotland

University of Glasgow Postgraduate Research Scholarships

Subjects: All subjects.
Purpose: To assist with research towards a PhD degree.
Eligibility: Open to candidates of any nationality who are proficient in English and who have obtained a First or an Upper Second Class (Honours) Degree or equivalent.
Level of Study: Postgraduate
Type: Scholarship
Value: Please consult the organization
Length of Study: 3 year's maximum award
Frequency: Annual
Study Establishment: The University of Glasgow
Country of Study: Scotland
Application Procedure: Applicants must refer to the University's application for graduate studies form that covers application for admission and scholarship. Please refer to the notes for applicants issued with the application form for address details.
Closing Date: Please refer to institution website
Funding: Private
Contributor: Endowments
Additional Information: Scholars from outside the European Union will be expected to make up the difference between the home fee and the overseas fee.

For further information contact:

Postgraduate Research Office, Research & Enterprise, 10 The Square, University of Glasgow, Glasgow, G12 8QQ
Tel: 0141 330 1989
Fax: 0141 330 5856

William Barclay Memorial Scholarship

Subjects: Biblical studies, theology and church history or any subject falling within the faculty of the divinity.
Purpose: To provide an opportunity for a scholar to pursue full-time study or to undertake research.
Eligibility: Open to any suitably qualified graduate of theology from a university outside the United Kingdom.
Level of Study: Postgraduate
Type: Scholarship
Value: £3500
Frequency: Annual
Study Establishment: The Faculty of Divinity at the University of Glasgow
Country of Study: Scotland
Application Procedure: Applicants must request postgraduate study application material. The PG form is used for the Barclay application.
Funding: Private

For further information contact:

Faculty of Divinity, Glasgow, G12 8QQ, Scotland
Tel: (44) 141 330 6525
Fax: (44) 141 330 4943

THE UNIVERSITY OF HONG KONG

Pok Fu Lan Road, Hong Kong, China
Tel: (86) 2859 2111
Fax: (86) 2858 2549
Email: gradsch.@hkucc.hku.hk
Website: www.hku.hk

The University of Hong Kong, as a pre-eminent international university aims to sustain and enhance its excellence as an institution of higher learning through teaching and world-class research, so as to produce well-rounded graduates with the abilities to provide leadership within the societies they serve.

Young Leaders of Tomorrow' Community Leaders Scholarship

Subjects: Any subject.
Purpose: To reward students who have demonstrated excellence and leadership potential, passion and commitment to further study.
Level of Study: Postgraduate
Type: Scholarship
Length of Study: 1 year
Frequency: Annual
Study Establishment: The University of Hong Kong
Country of Study: China
No. of awards offered: 380
Funding: Government
Contributor: A government endowment of $9,000,000

Grace Wei Huang Memorial Fund

Subjects: Business studies.
Purpose: To promote the pursuit of business studies in the University of Hong Kong and recognize outstanding academic performance.
Eligibility: Open to graduates of the University of Hong Kong MBA programme.
Level of Study: Postgraduate
Value: Varies based on the amount of donations raised for the fund
Frequency: Annual
Study Establishment: The University of Hong Kong
Country of Study: China
No. of awards offered: 3
Funding: Trusts
Contributor: Grace Wei Huang Memorial Trust

THE UNIVERSITY OF KENT

Conterbury, Kent, CT2 7NZ, United Kingdom
Tel: (44) (0) 1227 764 000
Fax: (44) 12 2782 7077
Email: web-team@kent.ac.uk
Website: www.kent.ac.uk
Contact: The Registry

The University of Kent is a UK higher education institution funded by the Higher Education Funding Council for England (HEFCE). The university provides education of excellent quality characterized by flexibility and inter disciplinarily and informed by research and scholarship, meeting the lifelong needs of diversity students.

Computing Laboratory Bursary

Subjects: Theoretical computer science, systems, engineering, applied and interdisciplinary informatics lognitive systems, Pervasive computing, information systems security and computing and education.
Purpose: To support postgraduate studies towards a PhD.
Eligibility: Candidates are expected to hold an Upper Second Class (Honours) Degree.
Level of Study: Doctorate
Type: Bursary
Value: Up to 4 awards of fees plus UK £10,500 maintenance for United Kingdom and European Union applicants, and up to 7 awards of fees only for home or overseas applicants, as well as the possibility of a contribution to maintenance for outstanding overseas applicants, particularly those who may be in receipt of funding from other sources
Length of Study: 3 years
Frequency: Annual
Study Establishment: The University of Kent
Country of Study: United Kingdom
No. of awards offered: Up to 4 for maintenance and 7 for fees only
Application Procedure: Applicants must enclose a covering letter and indicate their area of interest. See website www.cs.ukc.ac.uk/research/pg
Closing Date: June 17th
Funding: Government
No. of awards given last year: 3 full (maintenance), 7 for fees only
No. of applicants last year: Approx. 150
Additional Information: Please contact the computing laboratory at computer-science@kent.ac.uk

EPSRC Doctoral Training Awards for Computer Science

Subjects: Applied and interdisciplinary informatics, lognitive systems, computing education, information systems, security pervasive computing, systems, theoretical computer science.
Purpose: To support postgraduate studies towards a PhD.
Eligibility: Primarily open to United Kingdom nationals although European Union citizens may qualify in special circumstances.
Level of Study: Postgraduate
Value: Home fees plus maintenance grant of approx. UK £10,500 per year
Length of Study: 3 years
Frequency: Annual
Study Establishment: The University of Kent
Country of Study: United Kingdom
No. of awards offered: 2
Application Procedure: Applicants must indicate their interest on postgraduate application forms.
Closing Date: June 16th
Funding: Government
Contributor: EPSRC
No. of awards given last year: 2
No. of applicants last year: Approx 150
Additional Information: Please contact the computing laboratory at computer-science@kent.ac.uk

EPSRC Grant for School of Physical Sciences

Subjects: Physical sciences, study in materials science and applied optics.
Purpose: To support research.
Eligibility: Open to candidates who hold or expect to obtain a First Class (Honours) Degree. They should also be citizens of one of the European Union countries.
Level of Study: Postgraduate
Type: Grant
Value: Tuition fees plus the maintenance bursary at the same rate as provided by the EPSRC
Length of Study: 3 years
Frequency: Annual
Study Establishment: The University of Kent
Country of Study: United Kingdom
No. of awards offered: 3
Application Procedure: Applicants must complete an application form.
Closing Date: There is no fixed closing date
Contributor: EPSRC
No. of awards given last year: 3
No. of applicants last year: 15
Additional Information: Holders of the studentships are required to undertake a small amount of teaching assistance.

Ian Gregor Scholarship

Subjects: American literature, postcolonial literature, Anglo-Irish literature, Shakespeare and renaissance studies, Dickens and Victorian studies, modern poetry, theory and cultural ethnography.
Purpose: To support a candidate registered for taught or research MA programmes in English.
Eligibility: Candidates are expected to hold at least an Upper Second Class (Honours) Degree or equivalent. Candidates should also have applied for an external scholarship, such as AHRB.
Level of Study: Research, graduate
Type: Scholarship
Value: Home fees plus UK £500. An equivalent contribution towards fees will be made for overseas students
Length of Study: 1 year
Frequency: Annual
Study Establishment: The University of Kent
Country of Study: United Kingdom
No. of awards offered: 1
Application Procedure: Candidates must complete the postgraduate application form, indicating in the appropriate section that they are interested in being considered for departmental scholarships. A covering letter supporting the scholarship application should be attached.
Closing Date: May 30th
Funding: Trusts
No. of awards given last year: 1

Kent Law School Studentships and Bursaries

Subjects: Banking law, carriage of goods, company law, comparative law, computers and the law, criminal law and penology, critical legal studies, environmental law, emergency powers, European comparative and human rights law, family law, gender, sexuality and law, immigration law, intellectual property law, international law and human rights, international economic and trade law, labor law, law and multiculturalism, legal services, legal theory, modern legal history, multinationals and the law, and private law.

Purpose: To provide funding for 1 year in the first instance, extended to a maximum of 3 years (for registered students only) based on satisfactory progress (including upgrading to a PhD). The retention of the posts will be subject to a review of progress and performance in both research and teaching after the 1st year.
Eligibility: Candidates should hold an Upper Second Class (Honours) Degree or a good postgraduate taught degree in law.
Level of Study: Postgraduate, doctorate, research
Type: Studentship
Value: Home fees plus the Research Council equivalent of a maintenance grant
Length of Study: 1–3 years
Frequency: Annual
Study Establishment: The University of Kent
Country of Study: United Kingdom
No. of awards offered: 2
Application Procedure: Applicants must submit to the University's recruitment and admissions office a research proposal, curriculum vitae and covering letter with an application for their chosen research degree. They should also ensure that the recruitment and admissions office receives two referees' reports by the closing date for applications.
Closing Date: April 7th
Funding: Private
Contributor: Kent Law School
No. of awards given last year: 2
No. of applicants last year: 20–30
Additional Information: Holders of the studentships will be expected to teach for a maximum of 4 hours per week in term time on an undergraduate law module, at the direction of the head of department. For further information contact the Kent Law school at ks-office@kent.ac.uk

Maurice Crosland History of Science Studentship

Subjects: Grant is designed to support postgraduate research in the history of science and technology (excluding history of medicine). The emphasis is on the history of science and technology in cultural contexts (eg. religion).
Purpose: To fund research at the PhD level.
Eligibility: Open to qualified applicants of any nationality.
Level of Study: Postgraduate, doctorate, research
Type: Studentship
Value: Home fees plus a maintenance bursary
Length of Study: 3 years
Frequency: Dependent on funds available
Study Establishment: The University of Kent
Country of Study: United Kingdom
No. of awards offered: 1
Application Procedure: Applicants must apply to Professor Crosbie Smith. Candidates should submit a detailed curriculum vitae together with a 500-word description of their preferred research topic. They may wish to discuss this informally with professor Crosbie Smith first.
Closing Date: June 1st
Funding: Private
No. of awards given last year: 2
No. of applicants last year: 5

For further information contact:

Centre for History & Cultural Studies of Science, Rutherford College, University of Kent at Canterbury, Canterbury, Kent, CT2 7NX, England
Tel: (44) 12 2776 4000
Fax: (44) 12 2782 7258
Contact: Professor Crosbie Smith

University of Kent Anthropology Postgraduate Maintenance Grants

Subjects: Anthropology/ethmobiology (one award), biodiversity management (one award) run by DICE.
Purpose: To offset living expenses.
Eligibility: Candidates are expected to hold an Upper Second Class (Honours) Degree.
Level of Study: Postgraduate, doctorate, research
Type: Bursary
Value: UK £5,500 p.a
Length of Study: 2/3 years
Frequency: Annual
Study Establishment: The University of Kent
Country of Study: United Kingdom
No. of awards offered: 2
Application Procedure: Complete standard university application form and indicate that the applicant wishes to apply for the Departmental Postgraduate Maintenance grant. See website for further details: www.kent.ac.uk/anthropology/prospective_students/funding.html
Closing Date: July 1st for entry in the following academic year
Funding: Government
No. of awards given last year: 0

University of Kent Anthropology Postgraduate Studentships

Subjects: Anthropology and ethmobiology.
Purpose: To offset fees.
Eligibility: Candidates are expected to hold an upper Second Class (Honours) Degree.
Level of Study: Postgraduate, doctorate, research
Type: Studentship
Value: UK £2,000 p.a
Length of Study: 2 years
Frequency: Annual
Study Establishment: The University of Kent
Country of Study: United Kingdom
No. of awards offered: 2
Application Procedure: Complete standard university application form and indicate on the form that the applicant wishes to apply for the Departmental Studentship.
Closing Date: May 1st for entry in the following academic year
Funding: Government
No. of awards given last year: 2
No. of applicants last year: 5

University of Kent Anthropology Taught Master's Studentships

Subjects: Social anthropology, environmental anthropology, vinal anthropology, ethmobotany, ethnicity and nationalism, anthropology and computing.
Purpose: To offset fees.
Eligibility: The awards are open to all applicants. Where an award is offered to an overseas student, or to students registered for high-band programmes, then the recipient will have to cover the difference in fees from other sources. See www.kent.ac.uk/anthropology/prospective_students/funding.html
Level of Study: MA/MSc
Type: Studentship
Value: Home fees (current value UK £3,130) for non-high band programmes
Length of Study: 1 year
Frequency: Annual
Study Establishment: The University of Kent
Country of Study: United Kingdom
No. of awards offered: 2
Application Procedure: All applicants will be considered and the awards will be made to the two students of highest academic caliber.
Closing Date: July 1st for entry in the following academic year
Funding: Government

University of Kent Department of Biosciences

Subjects: Cancer research, cell and developmental biology, infectious diseases and protein science.
Purpose: To support research.
Eligibility: Primarily open to United Kingdom nationals although European Union citizens may qualify in special circumstances. Candidates should hold an Upper Second Class (Honours) Degree.
Level of Study: Research, postgraduate, doctorate
Value: Home tuition fees and a maintenance bursary at the same rate as that provided by the Research Councils

Length of Study: 3 years
Frequency: Annual
Study Establishment: The University of Kent
Country of Study: United Kingdom
No. of awards offered: 7
Application Procedure: Applicants should contact the Department of Biosciences for further information via email on bio-admin@kent.ac.uk
Closing Date: July 31st
Funding: Government
Contributor: BBSRC
No. of awards given last year: 7

University of Kent Department of Economics Bursaries

Subjects: Labour economics, money and development, international finance and trade, migration, defence and energy economics.
Purpose: To support research.
Eligibility: Candidates must have at least a taught Master's degree in economics.
Level of Study: Postgraduate, doctorate, research
Type: Research grant
Value: Up to the equivalent of home fees and/or a maintenance grant of UK £4,250 (current rate)
Length of Study: 3 years
Frequency: Dependent on funds available
Study Establishment: The University of Kent
Country of Study: United Kingdom
No. of awards offered: 2
Application Procedure: Applicants must enclose a separate letter proposing their wish to apply for the bursary along with their university PhD application form. A link to the online application form can be found on the department's website www.ukc.ac.uk/economics/students/postgrad/MPhil/PhD.html
Closing Date: June
Funding: Government
No. of awards given last year: 2
Additional Information: Candidates should note that 4–6 hours of teaching per week and acceptable progress in the programme of study will be expected of the student. The bursary will be subject to review each year.

University of Kent Department of Electronics Studentships

Subjects: Electronics, including image processing and vision, embedded systems, broadband and wireless communications.
Purpose: To enable well-qualified students to undertake research programmes within the department.
Eligibility: Candidates are expected to hold an Upper Second Class (Honours) Degree or equivalent in an appropriate subject, and be nationals of one of the European Union countries.
Level of Study: Postgraduate, research, doctorate
Type: Studentship
Value: Research Council studentships are at a fixed rate determined annually by EPSRC. Departmental bursaries depend on individual circumstances
Length of Study: 3 years
Frequency: Annual
Study Establishment: The University of Kent
Country of Study: United Kingdom
No. of awards offered: Varies
Application Procedure: Applicants should contact the Department of Electronics.
Closing Date: June
Funding: Government
Contributor: EPSRC
No. of awards given last year: 5
No. of applicants last year: 10

For further information contact:

Department of Electronics, University of Kent, Canterbury, Kent, CT2 7NT, England
Email: m.c.fairhurst@ukc.ac.uk
Contact: Professor M C Fairhurst

University of Kent Department of Politics and International Relations Bursary

Subjects: European studies, international relations and international political economy, intergovernmental co-operation in the European Union, political theory and law, politics and conflict analysis.
Purpose: To support research.
Eligibility: Candidates must be citizens of one of the European Union countries. Please write for further details on academic eligibility.
Level of Study: Postgraduate, doctorate
Type: Bursary
Value: Home fees
Length of Study: 3 years
Frequency: Annual
Study Establishment: The University of Kent
Country of Study: United Kingdom
No. of awards offered: 5
Application Procedure: Applicants must apply by letter to the head of the department after being accepted for research study.
Closing Date: Applications may be submitted at any time. Deadline for following academic year is the end of April
No. of awards given last year: 5
No. of applicants last year: 7
Additional Information: A maximum of 6 hours of teaching per week will be required.

University of Kent Department of Psychology Studentships

Subjects: Social psychology, cognitive psychology/neuropsychology, health psychology, developmental psychology, forensic psychology.
Purpose: To support research studies.
Eligibility: Candidates should hold or expect to obtain at least an Upper Second Class (Honours) Degree.
Level of Study: Research, postgraduate
Type: Studentship
Value: Tuition fees at the United Kingdom rate plus a maintenance bursary (at the same rate as provided by the ESRC)
Length of Study: 3 years
Frequency: Annual
Study Establishment: The University of Kent
Country of Study: United Kingdom
No. of awards offered: 2–3
Application Procedure: Applicants must complete an application form.
Closing Date: The deadline changes according to when studentships are advertised. This is usually at the end of July/mid-August
Funding: Private
Contributor: The University of Kent
No. of awards given last year: 3
No. of applicants last year: 20–30
Additional Information: A maximum of 6 hours of teaching per week will be required.

University of Kent English Scholarship

Subjects: American literature, postcolonial literature, Anglo-Irish literature, Shakespeare and renaissance studies, Dickens and Victorian Studies, modern poetry, theory and cultural ethnography.
Purpose: To support research.
Eligibility: Candidates are expected to hold at least an Upper Second Class (Honours) Degree or equivalent. Candidates will normally have also applied for an external scholarship, such as AHRB.
Level of Study: Research, postgraduate, doctorate
Type: Research grant
Value: Home tuition fees for up to 3 years for up to 3 years full-time study. A stipend of £3,500 (subject to change) for the first year of study. Teaching is offered to bursary students in their second and third years
Length of Study: 3 years
Frequency: Annual
Study Establishment: The University of Kent
Country of Study: United Kingdom
No. of awards offered: Several
Application Procedure: Candidates must complete the postgraduate application form, indicating in the appropriate section that they are

interested in being considered for departmental scholarships. A covering letter supporting the scholarship application should be attached.
Closing Date: May 30th
Funding: Private
No. of awards given last year: 2

University of Kent Institute of Mathematics, Statistics and Actuarial Science (IMSAS)

Subjects: Mathematics or statistics.
Purpose: To support studies at the IMSAS.
Eligibility: Candidates for scholarships should hold a First Class (Honours) Degree in mathematics or a related subject.
Level of Study: Doctorate
Type: Studentship
Value: Tuition fees plus the maintenance bursary at the same rate as provided by the EPSRC
Length of Study: 3 years
Frequency: Dependent on funds available
Study Establishment: The University of Kent
Country of Study: United Kingdom
No. of awards offered: 3
Application Procedure: Candidates should complete an application form for postgraduate study and indicate that they wish to be considered for this award.
Closing Date: April 19th
Funding: Private
No. of awards given last year: 2
Additional Information: Holders of the studentships are required to undertake a small amount of teaching assistance. For more information, please email imspg-admiss@ukc.ac.uk or see the website www.kent.ac.uk/IMS

University of Kent Postgraduate Funding Awards

Subjects: Social policy, sociology, criminology, environmental, women's studies or urban studies.
Purpose: To support research.
Eligibility: Candidates should hold a First Class or an Upper Second Class (Honours) Degree.
Level of Study: Postgraduate, doctorate, predoctorate, (not available to ma/msc students)
Type: Studentships and bursaries
Value: Up to 4 awards at UK £9,000 for full-time students, up to 10 awards at UK £4,000 for full-time students or UK £2,000 for a part-time student
Length of Study: 3 years
Frequency: Annual
Study Establishment: The University of Kent, School of Social Policy, Sociology and Social Research
Country of Study: United Kingdom
No. of awards offered: Up to 14
Application Procedure: Applicants must contact The Admissions Secretary, School of Social Policy, Canterbury, Kent, Sociology or Social Research, CT2 7NF, or email: socio-office@kent.ac.uk
Closing Date: June
Funding: Government
No. of awards given last year: 8
Additional Information: A maximum of 2 hours of teaching per week will be required.

University of Kent School of Drama, Film and Visual Arts Scholarships

Subjects: Drama, including performance-making process and theory, theatre history.
Purpose: To support research.
Eligibility: Candidates are expected to hold an Upper Second Class (Honours) Degree and be a citizen of one of the European Union countries.
Level of Study: Postgraduate, research
Type: Bursary - fees only
Value: To cover fees.
Length of Study: The bursary is 1 year
Frequency: One initial bursary for one year only. Opportunity to reapply on a competitive basis.
Study Establishment: The University of Kent
Country of Study: United Kingdom
No. of awards offered: 7
Application Procedure: Applicants must indicate their interest on the postgraduate application form.
Closing Date: July 31st
No. of awards given last year: 6
No. of applicants last year: 9
Additional Information: Some teaching or research assistant work may be required.

University of Kent School of European Culture and Language Scholarships

Subjects: The literature and culture of France, Germany, Italy and Spain. Use opportunities in classical and archaeological studies, comparative literary studies, philosophy and religious studies.
Purpose: To support research.
Eligibility: Candidates are expected to hold an Upper Second Class (Honours) Degree and be a citizen of one of the European Union countries.
Level of Study: Postgraduate, research
Type: Research grant
Value: UK £1,500. Under review for several years we have been able to offer three full fee bursaries.
Length of Study: 3 years
Frequency: Annual
Study Establishment: The University of Kent
Country of Study: United Kingdom
No. of awards offered: Varies (up to 4)
Application Procedure: Application is via the normal U.K form or for further information via email to steel-contacts@kent.ac.uk
Closing Date: June
No. of awards given last year: 5
No. of applicants last year: 14
Additional Information: Some part-time teaching may be required.

University of Kent School of Physical Sciences

Subjects: Physical sciences, study in materials science, applied optics or astronomy and space science.
Purpose: Studentship.
Eligibility: Candidates should hold an Upper Second Class (Honours) Degree or equivalent EU degree and be a citizen of one of the European Union countries or equivalent EU degree.
Level of Study: Postgraduate
Type: Studentship
Value: Home/EU fees plus maintenance at Research Council Rate
Length of Study: 3 years
Frequency: Dependent on funds available
Country of Study: United Kingdom
No. of awards offered: 4
Application Procedure: Applicants must contact Dr Chris Solomon, School of Physical Sciences or by email c.j.solomon@kent.ac.uk
Closing Date: June
Funding: Commercial, government
Contributor: The University of Kent
No. of awards given last year: 5

University of Kent Sociology Studentship

Subjects: Sociological theory and the culture of modernity.
Purpose: To support research.
Eligibility: Candidates should hold a First Class or Upper Second Class (Honours) Degree.
Level of Study: Doctorate, postdoctorate, postgraduate, (not available to ma/msc students)
Type: Studentship
Value: Up to 4 awards at UK £9,000 for full-time students, up to 10 awards at UK £4,000 for full-time students or UK £2,000 for a part-time student
Length of Study: 3 years
Frequency: Annual
Study Establishment: The University of Kent
Country of Study: United Kingdom
No. of awards offered: Up to 14

Application Procedure: Applicants must contact: The Graduate Admissions Secretary, School of Social Research, Kent, CTZ 7NP England or email: socio-office@kent.ac.uk
Closing Date: June
Funding: Government
No. of awards given last year: 8

UNIVERSITY OF KWAZULU-NATAL

Howard College Campus, Durban, 4041, South Africa
Tel: (27) (0) 31 260 3270
Fax: (27) (0) 31 260 2384
Email: harrian@nu.ac.za
Website: www.ukzn.ac.za

The Ernest Oppenheiner Memorial Trust Overseas Study Grant

Subjects: Any subject.
Purpose: To finance the costs of overseas study where the specialization cannot be pursued locally.
Level of Study: Postgraduate
Type: Grant
Value: Varies
Length of Study: 1–3 years
Frequency: Annual
Study Establishment: Any approved overseas university
Country of Study: Any country other than South Africa
No. of awards offered: Varies
Application Procedure: Applicants should submit a detailed motivation for support to the manager of the trust accompanied by: a current curriculum vitae, intended place of study and a full disclosure of personal financial position.
Funding: Trusts
Contributor: The Ernest Oppenheiner Memorial Trust
Additional Information: Third party applications are not accepted.

For further information contact:

The Ernest Openheiner Memorial Trust, PO Box 61593, Marshalltown, 2017
Tel: 011 497 8120
Fax: 011 834 286
Contact: Mr PM Hollesen, The Manager

THE UNIVERSITY OF LEEDS

Research Degrees & Scholarships Office, Leeds, West Yorkshire, LS2 9JT, England
Tel: (44) 11 3233 4007
Fax: (44) 11 3233 3941
Email: ajmorrison@adm.leeds.co.uk
Website: www.leeds.ac.uk
Contact: Ms J Y Findlay, Senior Assistant Registrar

The University of Leeds aims to promote excellence and to achieve and sustain international standing in higher education teaching, learning and research, and to serve a wide range of student constituencies, social and professional communities and industrial, commercial and government agencies, locally, nationally and internationally.

BEIT Trust-FCO Chevening-University of Leeds Scholarships

Subjects: Majority of subjects.
Purpose: To provide awards to students of high academic calibre from Malawi, Zambia and Zimbabwe, who demonstrate both academic excellence and the potential to become who leaders, decision makers and opinion formers in their own countries.
Eligibility: Open to candidates who have obtained, or are about to obtain, the equivalent of a United Kingdom First or good Upper Second Class (Honours) Degree. Candidates must be nationals of Malawi, Zambia or Zimbabwe be under 35 years of age. An adequate standard of English is required.
Level of Study: Postgraduate
Type: Scholarship
Value: Academic fees, living expenses, other allowances, economy return airfares
Length of Study: 1 year
Frequency: Annual
Study Establishment: The University of Leeds
Country of Study: United Kingdom
No. of awards offered: At least 4
Application Procedure: Applications must be made to the BEIT Trust.
Closing Date: August–September in the year preceding the study year
Funding: Government, private
No. of awards given last year: 4
No. of applicants last year: Not known

For further information contact:

The BEIT Trust, BEIT House, Grove Road, Woking, Surrey, GU21 5JB, England

Malawian and Zimbabwean Candidates: The Beit Trust, PO Box CH 7b, Chisipite, Harare, Zimbabwe
Email: beittrust@africaonline.co.zw

BP-FCO Chevening-University of Leeds Scholarships

Subjects: Exploration geophysics, geochemistry, environmental engineering and project management, economics, accounting and finance, business administration and management, international studies, politics of international resources and development, structural geology with geophysics, hydrogeology.
Purpose: To provide postgraduate scholarships to Vietnamese students of high academic calibre, who demonstrate both academic excellence and the potential to become leaders, decision makers and opinion formers in their own countries.
Eligibility: Open to candidates who have obtained, or are about to obtain, a United Kingdom First or Upper Second Class (Honours) Degree or equivalent. Candidates must be nationals of Vietnam and under 35 years of age. An adequate standard of English is required.
Level of Study: Postgraduate
Type: Scholarship
Value: Academic fees, living expenses, other allowances, economy return airfares
Length of Study: 1 year
Frequency: Annual
Study Establishment: The University of Leeds
Country of Study: United Kingdom
No. of awards offered: 4
Application Procedure: Applicants must apply by application form after acceptance into a taught course. Application forms are available from the scholarships office or the British Council.
Closing Date: January 10th
Funding: Commercial, government, private
No. of awards given last year: 2

For further information contact:

Scholarships Office, University of Leeds, Leeds, LS2 9JT, Vietnam

British council Office, 40 Cat Linh Street, Hanoi, Vietnam

Canon Collins Educational Trust-FCO Chevening-University of Leeds Scholarships

Subjects: Majority of subjects.
Purpose: To provide awards to students of high academic calibre, who demonstrate both academic excellence and the potential to become leaders, decision makers and opinion formers in their own countries.
Eligibility: Open to candidates who have obtained or are about to obtain the equivalent of a United Kingdom First or good Second Class (Honours) Degree. Candidates must be nationals of Botswana, Lesotho, Mozambique, Namibia, South Africa or Swaziland and under 35 years of age. An adequate standard of English is required.
Level of Study: Postgraduate

Type: Scholarship
Value: Academic fees, living expenses, other allowances, economy return airfares
Length of Study: 1 year
Frequency: Annual
Study Establishment: The University of Leeds
Country of Study: United Kingdom
No. of awards offered: Up to 20
Application Procedure: Applicants must complete an application form available on request from the CCETSA.
Closing Date: March 1st
Funding: Government, private
No. of awards given last year: 10

For further information contact:

Canon Collins Educational Trust, 2 The Ivories, 6 Northampton Street, London, N1 2HY, England
Email: ccetsa@canoncollins.org.uk

Commonwealth Shared Scholarship Scheme

Subjects: Subjects related to the economic, social and technological development of the student's home country.
Purpose: To provide scholarships to students of high academic calibre.
Eligibility: Applicants must already have obtained a United Kingdom Upper Second Class (Honours) Degree or equivalent. An adequate standard of English is also required and candidates must be nationals of, or permanently resident in, a developing Commonwealth country.
Level of Study: Postgraduate
Type: Scholarship
Value: Academic fees, living expenses, other allowances, economy return airfares
Length of Study: 1 year
Frequency: Annual
Study Establishment: The University of Leeds
Country of Study: United Kingdom
No. of awards offered: Up to 7
Application Procedure: Applicants must complete an application form.
Closing Date: Please contact the organization
Funding: Government, private
No. of awards given last year: 5
No. of applicants last year: 664

Hong Kong Arts Development Council-FCO Chevening-University of Leeds Scholarships

Subjects: Art gallery and museum studies, social history and theory of art, art history, sculpture studies, feminist theory and practice in the visual arts, theatre studies, music, fine art, music and liturgy, arts education, performance studies.
Purpose: To provide awards to students of high academic calibre.
Eligibility: Open to candidates who have obtained or are about to obtain the equivalent of a United Kingdom First or good Second Class (Honours) Degree in a relevant subject. Candidates must be permanent residents of Hong Kong. An adequate standard of English is required.
Level of Study: Postgraduate
Type: Scholarship
Value: Academic fees, living expenses, books, equipment, arrival and departure allowance, economy return airfares and the production of a dissertation
Length of Study: 1 year
Frequency: Annual
Study Establishment: The University of Leeds
Country of Study: United Kingdom
No. of awards offered: 3
Application Procedure: Applicants must complete an application form, available from the Hong Kong Arts Development Council.
Closing Date: May
Funding: Government, private
No. of awards given last year: 3

For further information contact:

HKADC Arts Scholarship, 22/F 181 Queens Road Central, Hong Kong

Kulika Charitable Trust-FCO Chevening-University of Leeds Scholarships

Subjects: Majority of subjects.
Purpose: To provide postgraduate scholarships to students of high academic calibre, who demonstrate both academic excellence and the potential to become leaders, decision makers and opinion formers in their own countries.
Eligibility: Open to candidates who have obtained a United Kingdom First or Upper Second Class (Honours) Degree or equivalent. Candidates must be nationals of Uganda, and under 35 years of age. An adequate standard of English is required.
Level of Study: Postgraduate
Type: Scholarship
Value: Academic fees, living expenses, other allowances, economy return airfares
Length of Study: 1 year
Frequency: Annual
Study Establishment: The University of Leeds
Country of Study: United Kingdom
No. of awards offered: At least 5
Application Procedure: Applicants must apply via an application form after acceptance into a taught course. Application forms for the scholarship are available from the British Council in Uganda.
Closing Date: December 4th
Funding: Government, private
No. of awards given last year: 5

For further information contact:

British Council, Rwenzori Courts, Plot 2 & 4A Nakasero Road, Kampala, PO Box 7070, Uganda

Open Society Institute-FCO Chevening-University of Leeds Scholarships

Subjects: International studies, international political economy, development studies, development studies and gender, gender studies, democratic studies, social and public policy, conflict development and security.
Purpose: To provide awards to students of high academic calibre, who demonstrate both academic excellence and the potential to become leaders, decision makers and opinion formers in their own countries.
Eligibility: Open to candidates who have obtained the equivalent of a United Kingdom First Class or Upper Second Class (Honours) Degree. Candidates must be nationals of Lebanon or Tajikistan and under 35 years of age. An adequate standard of English is required.
Level of Study: Postgraduate
Type: Scholarship
Value: Academic fees, living expenses, other allowances, economy return airfares
Length of Study: 1 year
Frequency: Annual
Study Establishment: The University of Leeds
Country of Study: United Kingdom
No. of awards offered: Up to 6
Application Procedure: Applicants must contact the British Council Office in Lebanon and the OSI Office, Tajikistan, for information and preliminary application forms.
Closing Date: January 31st
Funding: Government, private
No. of awards given last year: 5

For further information contact:

Tajik Branch Open Society Institute, Assistance Foundation, 59 Tolstoy Street, 734003, Dushanbe, Tajikistan,

Overseas Research Students Awards Scheme

Subjects: All subjects.
Purpose: To provide postgraduate scholarships for international research students of high calibre.

Eligibility: Open to applicants who have obtained at least a United Kingdom Upper Second Class (Honours) Degree or equivalent. An adequate knowledge of English is required.
Level of Study: Doctorate, postgraduate
Type: Scholarship
Value: Partial academic fees
Length of Study: Up to 3 years, subject to satisfactory academic performance
Frequency: Annual
Study Establishment: The University of Leeds
Country of Study: United Kingdom
Application Procedure: Applicants must complete an application form.
Closing Date: February 10th
Funding: Government
No. of awards given last year: 26
No. of applicants last year: 347

Shell Centenary/Shell Centenary Chevening Scholarships

Subjects: Engineering geology, exploration geophysics, structural geology with geophysics, geochemistry, hydrogeology, environmental geochemistry, environmental engineering and project management, international construction management and engineering, engineering project management, sustainable waste management, combustion and energy, computational fluid dynamics, automotive engineering, mechanical engineering, integrated design of chemical plant, fire and explosion engineering, modern digital and radio frequency wireless communications, advanced textiles and performance clothing, catchments dynamics and management, and geographical information systems, infrastructure asset engineering and management.
Purpose: To provide postgraduate scholarships to students of high academic caliber, who demonstrate both academic excellence and the potential to become leaders, decision makers and opinion formers in their own countries.
Eligibility: Open to candidates who have obtained, or are about to obtain, a United Kingdom First Class (Honours) Degree or equivalent. An excellent knowledge of English is required. Candidates must be under 35 years of age. Candidates should be nationals of and resident in any country other than Australia, Austria, Belgium, Canada, Denmark, Finland, France, Germany, Greece, Iceland, Ireland, Italy, Japan, Luxembourg, The Netherlands, New Zealand, Norway, Portugal, Spain, Sweden, Switzerland, United Kingdom and United States of America.
Level of Study: Postgraduate
Type: Scholarship
Value: Academic fees, living expenses, other allowances, economy return airfares
Length of Study: 1 year
Frequency: Annual
Study Establishment: The University of Leeds
Country of Study: United Kingdom
No. of awards offered: 6
Application Procedure: Applicants must apply by application form after acceptance onto a taught course.
Closing Date: March 1st
Funding: Government, commercial, private
No. of awards given last year: 6
No. of applicants last year: 305

Tetley and Lupton Scholarships for Overseas Students for Master's Study

Subjects: All subjects.
Purpose: To provide awards to overseas students of high academic calibre.
Eligibility: Open to candidates liable to pay tuition fees for Master's degrees at the full cost for overseas students. Applicants will be required to hold a United Kingdom First Class Honours Degree or equivalent and must meet fully the University's stated English language requirements.
Level of Study: Postgraduate
Type: Scholarship
Value: UK £4,000–£5,200 per year towards academic fees
Length of Study: 1 year
Frequency: Annual
Study Establishment: The University of Leeds
Country of Study: United Kingdom
No. of awards offered: Up to 9
Application Procedure: Applicants must complete an application form.
Closing Date: March 1st
Funding: Private
No. of awards given last year: 9
No. of applicants last year: 605

Tetley and Lupton Scholarships for Overseas Students for Research Study

Subjects: All subjects.
Purpose: To provide awards to international research students of high academic calibre.
Eligibility: Open to candidates liable to pay tuition fees for research degrees at the full rate for overseas students. Applicants must be of high academic calibre and be successful in the ORSAS competition.
Level of Study: Doctorate, postgraduate
Type: Scholarship
Value: The value of the Tetley and Lupton award ensures that all international tuition fees for a successful ORSAS award holder commencing research degree study will be paid in full.
Length of Study: Up to 3 years, subject to satisfactory academic performance
Frequency: Annual
Study Establishment: The University of Leeds
Country of Study: United Kingdom
No. of awards offered: Approx. 40
Application Procedure: Tetley and Lupton Scholarships are available for successful ORSAS award holders who are commencing research degree study. No separate application is required and all ORSAS applicants who are commencing research degree study will be considered.
Closing Date: N/A
Funding: Private
No. of awards given last year: 24

University of Leeds International Fee Bursary–Economics (Vietnam)

Subjects: Economics, economics and finance and accounting and finance and human resource management, development studies, international political economy, international studies, politics of international resources and development, computer science, systems analysis.
Purpose: To provide scholarships to students of high academic calibre in the School of Computing; Politics and International Studies and Leeds University Business School.
Eligibility: Open to nationals of Vietnam who have obtained a degree equivalent to a good Second Class (Honours) Degree. An adequate standard of English is required.
Level of Study: Postgraduate
Type: Scholarship
Value: Academic fees
Length of Study: 1 year
Frequency: Annual
Study Establishment: The University of Leeds
Country of Study: United Kingdom
No. of awards offered: 3
Application Procedure: Applicants must make an application in letter format to the Taught Postgraduate Secretary in the school they intend to study.
Closing Date: June 9th
Funding: Private
No. of awards given last year: 3

For further information contact:

School of Computing/School of Politics and International Studies/ Leeds University Business School, University of Leeds, Leeds, LS2 9JT

University of Leeds International Research Scholarships

Subjects: All subjects.
Purpose: To provide postgraduate scholarships for international research students of high calibre.
Eligibility: Applicants must have applied for an ORSAS award and be commencing PhD research degree study for the 1st time. Applicants must be eligible to pay fees at the international fee rate and hold a degree equivalent to a United Kingdom First Class Honours Degree.
Level of Study: Doctorate, postgraduate
Type: Scholarship
Value: Full maintenance scholarships of UK £12,300 or partial maintenance scholarship of UK £2,500
Length of Study: Up to 3 years
Frequency: Annual
Study Establishment: The University of Leeds
Country of Study: United Kingdom
Application Procedure: Applicants must complete an application form.
Closing Date: February 10th
Funding: Private
No. of awards given last year: 2 Full, 2 Partial
No. of applicants last year: 316

UNIVERSITY OF LONDON INSTITUTE IN PARIS

9-11 rue de Constantine, F-75340 Paris Cedex 07, France
Tel: (33) 1 44 11 73 73
Fax: (33) 145 503 155
Email: c.miller@ulip.lon.ac.uk
Website: www.ulip.lon.ac.uk
Contact: The Director

The University of London Institute in Paris is a United Kingdom Institute of Higher Education specializing in French studies English culture and language (including a comparative perspective), applied linguistics and second language acquisition.

Hamilton Studentship

Subjects: French studies, understood in the widest sense, ie. related to the study of France.
Purpose: To help students pursue an approved programme of research in the field of humanities relating to France.
Eligibility: Candidates must be United Kingdom citizens ordinarily resident in the United Kingdom.
Level of Study: Doctorate, postgraduate, research
Type: Studentship
Value: Tuition fees: UK £3,010, maintenance grant: UK £12,500
Length of Study: The studentship is awarded, in the first instance, for 1 calendar year and is renewable for a further 2 years, subject to a satisfactory annual review of progress
Frequency: Annual
Study Establishment: University of London Institute in Paris
Country of Study: France
No. of awards offered: 1
Application Procedure: Application forms may be requested at any time by writing to: Hamilton Trust, Director's Office, University of London Institute in Paris, 9-11 rue de Constantine, F-75430 Paris Cedex 07, France.
Closing Date: May 15th
Funding: Trusts
Contributor: Hamilton Trust

Quinn, Nathan and Edmond Scholarships

Subjects: French studies.
Purpose: To assist postgraduate research in France.
Eligibility: Open to citizens of the European Union and Commonwealth countries who are graduates and possess sufficient knowledge of French to pursue their proposed studies. Candidates in the early stages of doctoral research or not engaged in research are not eligible.
Level of Study: Postgraduate, doctorate, postdoctorate
Type: Fellowship /Scholarship
Value: UK £450 per month for the scholarship. UK £500 per month for the Junior Research Fellowship
Length of Study: The scholarship is for 1–3 months. The Junior Research Fellowship is for up to 9 months
Frequency: Dependent on funds available
Study Establishment: An approved institute
Country of Study: France
No. of awards offered: Dependent on availability of funds
Application Procedure: Applicants must submit a written recommendation from their professor or tutor along with their application. The name of one academic referee must be given.
Closing Date: March 15th
Funding: Private
Contributor: Trust funds
Additional Information: Scholarships cannot be held concurrently with other major awards. These scholarships are intended for research and not for those following taught courses.

UNIVERSITY OF MARYLAND

National Orchestral Institute School of Music, 2110 Clarice Smith Performing Arts Center, College Park, MD, 20742-1211, United States of America
Tel: (1) 301 405 2317
Fax: (1) 301 314 9504
Website: www.umd.edu
Contact: Mr Richard Scerbo, Orchestra Manager

The University of Maryland, College Park (UMCP) is the flagship institution of the University of Maryland System. As the comprehensive public research university for the state of Maryland and the original 1862 land grant institution in Maryland, UMCP has the responsibility within the University of Maryland for serving as the state's primary centre for graduate study and research, advancing knowledge through research, providing high-quality undergraduate instruction across a broad spectrum of academic disciplines and extending service to all regions of the state.

International Music Competitions

Subjects: Piano (William Kapell), cello (Leonard Rose) and voice (Marian Anderson).
Purpose: To recognize and assist the artistic development of young musicians at the highest levels of achievement in piano, cello and voice.
Eligibility: Open to musicians of all nationalities, fulfilling the following age criteria: piano 18–33 years of age, cello 18–30 years of age and voice 21–39 years of age.
Level of Study: Professional development
Type: Competition
Value: Finalist prizes US$20,000, US$10,000 and US$5,000, semifinalists US$1,000
Study Establishment: The University of Maryland
Country of Study: United States of America
No. of awards offered: 3 finalist prizes and 9 semi-finalist prizes
Application Procedure: Applicants must submit an application form, fee, cassette recording, repertoire list, curriculum vitae, photos and letters of recommendation.
Closing Date: Mid-December of the year preceding the competition
No. of awards given last year: 12
No. of applicants last year: 180
Additional Information: The competition is held in late May–early June. Concurrent festivals offer master classes, recitals and symposia.

For further information contact:

Clarice Smith Performing Arts Center, Suite 3800, University of Maryland, MD, 20742, United States of America
Contact: Mr George Moquin, International Competitions Director

National Orchestral Institute Scholarships

Subjects: Orchestral performance.
Purpose: To provide an intensive 3-week orchestral training programme to enable musicians to rehearse and perform under

internationally acclaimed conductors and study with principal musicians of the United States of America's foremost orchestras in preparation for careers as orchestral musicians.
Eligibility: Open to advanced musicians between 18 and 28 years of age and students and postgraduates of United States of America universities, conservatories and colleges. Others, however, are welcome to apply but must appear at an audition centre. String players, including harpists, who live more than 200 miles away from an audition centre may audition by tape.
Level of Study: Professional development
Type: Scholarship
Value: Full tuition, room and board
Length of Study: 3 weeks
Frequency: Annual
Study Establishment: The University of Maryland
Country of Study: United States of America
No. of awards offered: Approx. 100
Application Procedure: Applicants must submit an application, fee, curriculum vitae and letters of recommendation.
Closing Date: Before regional auditions
No. of awards given last year: 100
No. of applicants last year: 1000
Additional Information: Personal auditions are required at one of the audition centres throughout the country.

UNIVERSITY OF MELBOURNE

Scholarships Office, VIC, 3010, Australia
Tel: (61) 3 8344 8747
Fax: (61) 3 9349 1740
Email: pg-schools@unimelb.edu.au
Website: www.services.unimelb.edu.au/scholarship/

The University of Melbourne has a long and distinguished tradition of excellence in teaching and research. It is the leading research institution in Australia and enjoys a reputation for the high quality of its research programmes, consistently winning the largest share of national competitive research funding.

Melbourne International Fee Remission Scholarships

Subjects: All subjects offered by the University.
Purpose: To enable graduates to undertake a research higher degree in any discipline.
Eligibility: Please see www.services.unimelb.edu/scholarships/pgrad for full details.
Level of Study: Postgraduate, research
Type: Scholarship
Value: Full tuition fees
Length of Study: Up to 2 years at the Master's level and up to 3 years at the PhD and research doctorate level. A 6-month extension is possible at the research doctorate level
Frequency: Annual
Study Establishment: The University of Melbourne
Country of Study: Australia
No. of awards offered: 150. Available only to international students
Application Procedure: International applicants who have not already commenced the course for which they seek scholarship will automatically be considered for scholarship if they receive an unconditional offer of a place in a research higher degree course. Information about applying for courses is available at www.services.unimelb.edu.au/admissions/apply/ A separate application form is not required.
Closing Date: A small number of scholarships may be available throughout the year subject to availability
Funding: Government
Contributor: Scholarship fund
No. of awards given last year: 60
No. of applicants last year: 500

Melbourne Research Scholarships

Subjects: All subjects offered by the University.
Purpose: To enable graduates to undertake a research higher degree in any discipline.
Eligibility: Please see www.services.unimelb.edu.au/scholarships/pgrad for full details.
Level of Study: Doctorate, research, postgraduate
Type: Scholarship
Value: Australian $18,277 per year, payable fortnightly
Length of Study: Up to 2 years at the Master's level and up to 3 years at the PhD and research doctorate level. A 6-month extension is possible at the research doctorate level
Frequency: Annual
Study Establishment: The University of Melbourne
Country of Study: Australia
No. of awards offered: 220, of which approx. 95 may be awarded to international students
Application Procedure: International applicants who have not already commenced the course for which they seek scholarship will automatically be considered for scholarship if they receive an unconditional offer of a place in a research higher degree course. Information about applying for courses is available at www.services.unimelb.edu.au/admissions/apply/ A separate application form is not required.
Closing Date: October 31st for Australian citizens and residents in the main selection round, and September 15th for international students. A small number of scholarships may be available throughout the year subject to availability
Funding: Government
Contributor: Scholarship fund
No. of awards given last year: 210
No. of applicants last year: 1000

UNIVERSITY OF NEBRASKA AT OMAHA (UNO)

College of Business Adminstration, University of Nebraska at Omaha, Omaha, 6001 Dodge Street, NE, 68182-0048, United States of America
Tel: (1) 402 554 2341
Fax: (1) 402 554 4036
Email: cba@unomaha.edu/mba
Website: www.mba.unomaha.edu
Contact: MBA Admissions Officer

The University of Nebraska at Omaha's (UNO) College of Business Administration offers a dynamic, challenging Master's programme designed to help students acquire the knowledge, perspective and skills necessary for success in the marketplace of today and tomorrow. The goal of the programme is to develop leaders who have the ability to incorporate change, use information technology to resolve problems and make sound business decisions. The curriculum focuses on results with an emphasis on how to excel in a rapidly changing world.

UNO Graduate Assistantships

Subjects: MBA, MACC, MA/ECM and MS/ECM.
Eligibility: Open to qualified students who are enrolled in a graduate degree programme.
Level of Study: Graduate, mba
Value: A waiver of tuition costs up to 12 hours of graduate credit per semester
Frequency: Every 2 years
Study Establishment: UNO
Country of Study: United States of America
No. of awards offered: 1–3 each semester
Application Procedure: Applicants must make enquiries in their department about the availability of assistantships, the procedures for applying, and the details of when the application and supporting credentials should be on file in the department or school for consideration. Applicants must complete application for graduate assistantships and submit a curriculum vitae and supporting materials.
Closing Date: June 1st
No. of awards given last year: 3
No. of applicants last year: 40

UNIVERSITY OF NEVADA, LAS VEGAS (UNLV)

Graduate College, 4505 S Maryland Parkway, Box 451017, Las Vegas, NV, 89154-6031, United States of America
Tel: (1) 702 895 3655
Website: www.unlv.edu
Contact: Administrative Officer

UNLV Alumni Association Graduate Scholarships

Subjects: All subjects.
Purpose: To reward outstanding graduate students.
Eligibility: Applicants must have completed at least 12 credits of graduate study at UNLV, have a minimum undergraduate and graduate grade point average of 3.5 and enrol for six or more graduate credits in each semester of the scholarship year.
Level of Study: Graduate, mba
Type: Scholarship
Value: US$1,000
Length of Study: 1 year
Frequency: Annual
Study Establishment: UNLV
Country of Study: United States of America
No. of awards offered: 3
Application Procedure: Applicants must telephone (1) 702 895 3320 or write for application forms or further information.
Closing Date: March 1st

UNLV Graduate Assistantships

Subjects: All subjects.
Purpose: To offer financial assistance and support to students admitted to any graduate degree programme.
Eligibility: Open to students who have already been admitted to any graduate degree programme.
Level of Study: MBA, graduate
Value: A 9 month stipend of US$8,500 for Master's level assistantships plus tuition and fee waivers
Length of Study: 1 year
Frequency: Annual
Study Establishment: UNLV
Country of Study: United States of America
No. of awards offered: Varies
Application Procedure: Applicants must send applications and all supporting materials to the Dean of the Graduate College.
Closing Date: March 1st or November 1st for the Spring assistantship. Applications may be accepted after this date in the event of an unexpected opening for the Autumn semester. On some rare occasions an assistantship is available for the Spring semester
Additional Information: Graduate assistants must carry a minimum of 6 semester hours of credit and are expected to spend 20 hours per week on departmental duties such as instruction or research.

UNLV James F Adams/GSA Scholarship

Subjects: All subjects.
Purpose: To recognize the academic achievements of graduate students.
Eligibility: Applicants must have completed at least 12 credits of graduate study at UNLV, have a minimum undergraduate and graduate grade point average of 3.5 and enrol for six or more graduate credits in each semester of the scholarship year.
Level of Study: Graduate, mba
Type: Scholarship
Value: US$1,000
Length of Study: Varies
Frequency: Annual
Study Establishment: UNLV
Country of Study: United States of America
No. of awards offered: 6
Application Procedure: Applicants must telephone (1) 702 895 3320, or write for application forms or further information.
Closing Date: March 1st

UNIVERSITY OF NEW HAMPSHIRE

The Family Research Laboratory, Department of Sociology, Horton Social Science Center, Durham, NH 03824, United States of America
Tel: (1) 603 862 2594
Fax: (1) 603 862 1122
Email: murray.straus@unh.edu
Website: www.unh.edu
Contact: Mr Murray Straus, Co-Director

The Family Research Laboratory at the University of New Hampshire conducts research studies of interest to state and national policy makers and citizens. Studies include a national survey of families and youth, and the 30-nation international dating violence study. Staff and faculty members associated with the laboratory give lectures and workshops to professionals and provide information to the public about family violence and related family issues. The Family Violence Research Program, which is part of the laboratory, is the first and only research programme concerned with all aspects of family violence and related phenomena. The laboratory maintains a library of about 2,500 books and sponsors national conferences.

University of New Hampshire Postdoctoral Fellowships For Research on Family Violence

Subjects: Family violence including physical, sexual and psychological maltreatment of children, partners in marital, cohabiting and dating relationships and maltreatment of the elderly by members of their family.
Purpose: To provide training and experience in research into all aspects of family violence.
Eligibility: Open to citizens or permanent residents of the United States of America.
Level of Study: Postdoctorate
Type: Fellowship
Length of Study: 1 or 2 years
Frequency: Annual
Study Establishment: The Family Research Laboratory at the University of New Hampshire
Country of Study: United States of America
No. of awards offered: 4
Application Procedure: Applicants must send a brief letter, publications and arrange for three letters of recommendation. Applications are available from the website www.unh.edu/fri
Funding: Government
Contributor: The National Institute of Mental Health
No. of awards given last year: 4
No. of applicants last year: 35

THE UNIVERSITY OF NEWCASTLE

Research Division University of Newcastle, Callaghan, NSW 2308, Australia
Tel: (61) 02 4921 6538
Fax: (61) 02 4921 6908
Email: Kerrie.Carmichael@newcastle.edu.au
Website: www.newcastle.edu.au/research/rhd/
Contact: Kerrie Carmichael, Office of Graduate Studies

The University of Newcastle is one of Australia's top ten research universities. The University has over 1,200 research degree candidates enrolled in five faculties, incorporating a wide range of disciplines including architecture, building, humanities, social sciences, education, economics, management, engineering, computer science, law, medicine, nursing, health sciences, music, drama and creative arts, physcial and natural sciences, mathematics and information technology. Scholarships are available to support research degree students in most disciplines. About 90 new scholarships are awarded each year. In 2005, 347 new and continuing students were supported by research scholarships across the University.

Australian Government Postgraduate Awards

Subjects: All subjects.
Purpose: To support students undertaking full-time higher research degree programmes.

Eligibility: Open to Australian citizens and permanent residents who have lived in Australia for 1 year prior to application. Applicants must have completed 4 years of full-time undergraduate study and gained a First Class (Honours) Degree or equivalent award.
Level of Study: Doctorate, postgraduate, research
Type: Scholarship
Value: A living allowance of approx. Australian $18,000 per year which is tax-exempt and index-linked. Allowances for relocation and thesis production may also be provided
Length of Study: 2 years full-time study for research Master's candidates or 3 years full-time for PhD candidates
Frequency: Annual
Study Establishment: Any university
Country of Study: Australia
No. of awards offered: Approx. 40
Application Procedure: Applicants must complete an application form the Office of Graduate Students or from the website.
Closing Date: October 31st for Australian citizens and permanent residents who have lived in Australia for 1 year prior to application
Funding: Government

UNIVERSITY OF NEWCASTLE UPON TYNE

International Office, 10 Kensington Terrace, Newcastle upon Tyne, NE1 7RU, United Kingdom
Tel: (44) 19 1222 5148
Fax: (44) 19 1222 5219
Contact: Scholarships Officer

The University of Newcastle upon Tyne, established in Newcastle in 1834, is one of the UK's leading universities and known for its quality of teaching, outstanding research, and the works with the regional and local communities, business and industry.

International Alumni Scholarship (IAS)

Subjects: All subjects offered by the University.
Purpose: To provide a partial scholarship for international students.
Eligibility: Candidates for scholarships must have already been offered a place to study at the University of Newcastle upon Tyne.
Level of Study: Research, doctorate, graduate, mba, postgraduate
Type: Partial scholarship
Value: 10 per cent of tuition fees
Length of Study: Duration of programme
Frequency: Annual
Study Establishment: University of Newcastle upon Tyne
Country of Study: United Kingdom
Application Procedure: All eligible applicants who are offered a place to study at the University of Newcastle upon Tyne are invited to apply for one of these scholarships. Applicants must check the website for details or contact the Scholarships Officer at the address given below.
Closing Date: September
Funding: International Office
Contributor: University

International Family Scholarship (IFS)

Subjects: All subjects offered by the University.
Purpose: To provide a partial scholarship for international students.
Eligibility: Candidates for scholarships must have already been offered a place to study at the University of Newcastle upon Tyne.
Level of Study: Doctorate, mba, graduate, postgraduate, research
Type: Partial scholarship
Value: 10 per cent of tuition fees
Length of Study: Duration of programme
Frequency: Annual
Study Establishment: University of Newcastle upon Tyne
Country of Study: United Kingdom
Application Procedure: All eligible applicants who are offered a place to study at the University of Newcastle upon Tyne are invited to apply for one of these scholarships. Applicants must check the website for details or contact the Scholarships Officer at the address given below.
Closing Date: September
Funding: International Office
Contributor: University

International Postgraduate Scholarship (IPS)

Subjects: All subjects offered by the University.
Purpose: To provide a partial scholarship for international students.
Eligibility: Candidates for scholarships must have already been offered a place to study at the University of Newcastle upon Tyne.
Level of Study: Graduate, research, mba, postgraduate, doctorate
Type: Partial scholarship
Value: UK £1,500
Length of Study: Duration of programme
Frequency: Annual
Study Establishment: University of Newcastle upon Tyne
Country of Study: United Kingdom
No. of awards offered: 60
Application Procedure: All eligible applicants who are offered a place to study at the University of Newcastle upon Tyne are invited to apply for one of these scholarships. Applicants must check the website for details or contact the Scholarships Officer at the address given below.
Closing Date: May 23rd
Funding: International Office
Contributor: University
No. of awards given last year: 60

International Research Scholarship (IRS)

Subjects: All subjects offered by the University.
Purpose: To provide a partial scholarship for international students.
Eligibility: Candidates for scholarships must have already been offered a place to study at the University of Newcastle upon Tyne.
Level of Study: Doctorate, research
Type: Partial scholarship
Value: UK £2,000
Length of Study: Duration of programme
Frequency: Annual
Study Establishment: University of Newcastle upon Tyne
Country of Study: United Kingdom
No. of awards offered: 30
Application Procedure: All eligible applicants who are offered a place to study at the University of Newcastle upon Tyne are invited to apply for one of these scholarships. Applicants must check the website for details or contact the Scholarships Officer at the address given below.
Closing Date: May 23rd
Funding: International Office
Contributor: University
No. of awards given last year: 30

International Taught Postgraduate Scholarship (ITPS)

Subjects: All subjects offered by the University.
Purpose: To provide a partial scholarship for international students.
Eligibility: Candidates for scholarships must have already been offered a place to study at the University of Newcastle upon Tyne.
Level of Study: MBA, postgraduate, graduate
Type: Partial scholarship
Value: UK £1,500
Length of Study: Duration of programme
Frequency: Annual
Study Establishment: University of Newcastle upon Tyne
Country of Study: United Kingdom
No. of awards offered: 30
Application Procedure: All eligible applicants who are offered a place to study at the University of Newcastle upon Tyne are invited to apply for one of these scholarships. Applicants must check the website for details or contact the Scholarships Officer at the address given below.
Closing Date: May 23rd
Funding: International Office
Contributor: University
No. of awards given last year: 30

THE UNIVERSITY OF NOTTINGHAM

Graduate School, University Park, Nottingham, Nottinghamshire, NG7 2RD, England
Tel: (44) 11 5951 4664
Fax: (44) 11 584 67799
Email: graduate-school@nottingham.ac.uk
Website: www.nottingham.ac.uk/gradschool
Contact: Ms Claire Jameson, Research Policy Officer

The University of Nottingham is a community of students and staff dedicated to bringing out the best in all of its members. It aims to provide the finest possible environment for teaching, learning and research and has a well-known record of success.

University of Nottingham Doctoral Training Awards

Subjects: All subjects offered by the University.
Purpose: To promote research.
Eligibility: Open to graduates of all nationalities.
Level of Study: Postgraduate, predoctorate
Type: PhD scholarship
Value: Minimum of UK £12,000 maintenance per year where appropriate, plus payment of fees at the home or European Union rate
Length of Study: 3 years leading to PhD submission given adequate academic progress
Frequency: Annual
Study Establishment: The University of Nottingham
Country of Study: United Kingdom
No. of awards offered: More than 75
Application Procedure: Applicants must contact the individual schools for information. Applicants must apply to the school where they intend to study.
Closing Date: Please contact the individual schools for information
Contributor: University of Nottingham
No. of awards given last year: Over 75
Additional Information: The scholarships are awarded internally to the schools and/or institutes. It is then up to those schools receiving awards to advertise the scholarship and set an application deadline.

University of Nottingham Weston Scholarships

Subjects: All subjects from a prescribed list.
Purpose: To provide promising students with full-time home or European Union fees.
Eligibility: There are no eligibility restrictions.
Level of Study: Postgraduate
Type: Studentship
Value: Home or European Union fees only
Length of Study: Usually 1 year full-time or the part-time equivalent
Frequency: Annual
Study Establishment: The University of Nottingham
Country of Study: United Kingdom
No. of awards offered: 4
Application Procedure: Applicants must submit applications to the individual schools and contact them for details. Applicants must apply to the school where they intend to study.
Closing Date: Please contact the individual schools for information
Funding: Trusts
No. of awards given last year: 4
Additional Information: The scholarships are awarded internally to four schools and/or institutes on a competitive basis. It is then up to those schools receiving awards to advertise the scholarship and set an application deadline.

UNIVERSITY OF OTAGO

Scholarships Office, PO Box 56, Dunedin, New Zealand
Tel: (64) 3 479 1100 ext 5291
Fax: (64) 3 479 5650
Email: pgschols@otago.ac.nz
Website: www.otago.ac.nz
Contact: Mr Eddy Vande Pol, Manager, PhD Scholarship

The University of Otago has over 17,000 students, most of whom are based at the Dunedin campus, which is the oldest campus in New Zealand. The University has four divisions: the Division of Commerce (School of Business), the Division of Health Sciences, the Division of Humanities and the Division of Science. The University has a School of Medicine in Christchurch and Wellington, and a campus in Auckland.

University of Otago Dr Sulaiman Daud 125th Jubilee International Postgraduate Scholarship

Subjects: All subjects.
Purpose: To fund research towards a PhD or Master's degree.
Eligibility: Open to citizens of Malaysia with a minimum qualification of a First Class (Honours) Degree.
Level of Study: Doctorate, research, postgraduate
Type: Scholarship
Value: New Zealand $20,000 per year for doctoral study and New Zealand $13,000 per year for Master's study, plus fees
Length of Study: 3 years for doctoral study and 2 years for Master's study
Frequency: Annual
Study Establishment: The University of Otago
Country of Study: New Zealand
No. of awards offered: 1
Application Procedure: Applicants must complete an application form, available from the website.
Closing Date: June 30th

University of Otago International Scholarships

Subjects: All subjects.
Purpose: To assist with funding for study.
Eligibility: Open to all international applicants intending to study at the University of Otago who would normally be charged international fees.
Level of Study: Postgraduate, research
Type: Scholarship
Value: Master's scholarships New Zealand $13,000
Length of Study: 1 year for their Master's study
Frequency: Annual
Study Establishment: The University of Otago
Country of Study: New Zealand
No. of awards offered: 4 Master's scholarships
Application Procedure: Applicants must complete the application for international study at the University of Otago, available from the website.
Closing Date: November 1st
No. of awards given last year: 4 PhD, 4 Master's

University of Otago Master's Awards

Subjects: All subjects.
Purpose: To fund research towards a Master's degree.
Eligibility: Open to permanent residents or citizens of New Zealand or Australia, and to citizens of France and Germany with a minimum qualification of a First Class (Honours) Degree who are entering the thesis year of a Master's degree.
Level of Study: Research, postgraduate
Type: Scholarship
Value: New Zealand $13,000 per year plus fees
Length of Study: 1 year
Frequency: Annual
Study Establishment: The University of Otago
Country of Study: New Zealand
No. of awards offered: 60
Application Procedure: Applicants must complete an application form, available from the website.
Closing Date: November 1st
No. of awards given last year: 60

University of Otago PhD Scholarships

Subjects: All subjects.
Purpose: To fund research towards a PhD degree.
Eligibility: Now any country.
Level of Study: Doctorate
Type: Scholarship
Value: New Zealand $20,000, plus fees

Length of Study: 3 years
Frequency: Annual
Study Establishment: The University of Otago
Country of Study: New Zealand
No. of awards offered: 90
Application Procedure: Applicants must complete an application form, available from the website.
Closing Date: November 1st
No. of awards given last year: 60

University of Otago Prestigious PhD Scholarships

Subjects: All subjects.
Purpose: To fund research towards a PhD degree.
Eligibility: Now any country.
Level of Study: Research, doctorate
Type: Scholarship
Value: New Zealand $25,000, plus fees
Length of Study: 3 years
Frequency: Annual
Study Establishment: The University of Otago
Country of Study: New Zealand
No. of awards offered: 10
Application Procedure: Applicants must complete an application form, available from the website.
Closing Date: November 1st
No. of awards given last year: 10

UNIVERSITY OF OXFORD

University Offices, Wellington Square, Oxford, Oxfordshire, OX1 2JD, England
Tel: (44) 18 6527 0000
Fax: (44) 18 6527 0708
Website: www.ox.ac.uk
Contact: Ms Clare Woodcock, Information Officer

Balliol College Dervorguilla Scholarship

Subjects: Arts and sciences.
Eligibility: Open to overseas students only.
Level of Study: Postgraduate
Type: Scholarship
Value: College and university fees plus a full maintenance grant
Length of Study: 2 years, with the possibility of renewal for a 3rd year
Frequency: Annual
Study Establishment: Balliol College, University of Oxford
Country of Study: United Kingdom
No. of awards offered: 1 award in either arts or sciences
Application Procedure: Applicants must write for details.
Closing Date: In line with the University graduate field deadlines
Contributor: Balliol College, University of Oxford, and the Clarendon Fund Award
Additional Information: This award is held in association with the University Clarendon Fund Award.

For further information contact:

Tutor for Graduate Admissions, Balliol College, University of Oxford, Oxford, OX1 3BJ, England

Balliol College Domus Graduate Scholarships

Subjects: Arts and science.
Eligibility: Open to overseas students only.
Level of Study: Postgraduate
Type: Scholarship
Value: To be decided
Length of Study: 2 years, with a possibility of renewal for a 3rd year
Frequency: Annual
Study Establishment: Balliol College, University of Oxford
Country of Study: United Kingdom
No. of awards offered: Varies
Application Procedure: Applicants must write for details.
Closing Date: In line with the University graduate field deadlines
Contributor: Balliol College and the Clarendon Fund Award
Additional Information: This award is held in association with the Clarendon Fund Award.

For further information contact:

Tutor for Graduate Admissions, Balliol College, University of Oxford, Oxford, OX1 3BJ, England

Balliol College Gregory Kulkes Scholarships in Law

Subjects: Law.
Eligibility: Open to overseas and home/European Union Students.
Level of Study: Postgraduate
Type: Scholarship
Value: To be decided
Length of Study: 2 years, renewable for a 3rd year
Frequency: Annual
Study Establishment: Balliol College, University of Oxford
Country of Study: United Kingdom
No. of awards offered: One award only
Application Procedure: Applicants must contact the tutor for graduate admissions at Balliol College.
Closing Date: In line with the University graduate field deadlines
Funding: Private
Contributor: Balliol College and the Clarendon Fund Award
Additional Information: This award is held in association with the University Clarendon Fund Award.

For further information contact:

Tutor for Graduate Admissions, Balliol College, University of Oxford, Oxford, OX1 3BJ, England

Balliol College Hakeem Belo-Osagie Scholarship held in Association with the Clarendon Fund Award

Subjects: There are no subject restrictions.
Eligibility: Citizen of an African country (no African country excluded).
Level of Study: Postgraduate
Type: Scholarship
Value: To be decided
Length of Study: 2 years, with the possibility of renewal for a 3rd year
Frequency: Dependent on funds available
Study Establishment: Balliol College, University of Oxford
Country of Study: United Kingdom
No. of awards offered: 1
Application Procedure: Applicants must write for details.
Closing Date: In line with the University graduate field deadlines
Contributor: Balliol College, the University of Oxford and the Clarendon Fund Award

For further information contact:

Tutor for Graduate Admissions, Balliol College, University of Oxford, Oxford, OX1 3BJ, England

Balliol College Marvin Bower Scholarship

Subjects: International relations, politics and economics.
Eligibility: Open to overseas, home and European Union students.
Level of Study: Postgraduate
Type: Scholarship
Value: To be decided
Length of Study: 2 years, with a possibility of renewal for a 3rd year
Frequency: Dependent on funds available
Study Establishment: Balliol College, University of Oxford
Country of Study: United Kingdom
No. of awards offered: 1
Application Procedure: Applicants must write for details.
Closing Date: In line with the University graduate field deadlines
Contributor: Balliol College and the Clarendon Fund Award
Additional Information: This award is held in association with the Clarendon Fund Award.

For further information contact:

Tutor for Graduate Admissions, Balliol College, University of Oxford, Oxford, OX1 3BJ, England

Balliol College Snell Exhibition

Subjects: All subjects.
Eligibility: Open to graduates of Glasgow University only.
Level of Study: Graduate, postgraduate
Value: UK £2,000 per year
Length of Study: 3 years
Frequency: Annual
Study Establishment: Balliol College, University of Oxford
Country of Study: United Kingdom
No. of awards offered: 1
Application Procedure: Applicants must contact the Tutor for Graduate Admissions at Balliol College.
Closing Date: In line with the University graduate field deadlines

For further information contact:

Tutor for Graduate Admissions, Balliol College, University of Oxford, Oxford, OX1 3BJ, England

Balliol College Templeton Scholarship in Management

Subjects: Management.
Eligibility: Open only to overseas students.
Level of Study: Postgraduate
Type: Scholarship
Value: To be decided
Length of Study: 2 years, renewable for a 3rd year
Frequency: Dependent on funds available
Study Establishment: Balliol College, University of Oxford
Country of Study: United Kingdom
No. of awards offered: 1
Application Procedure: Applicants must contact the Tutor for Graduate Admissions at Balliol College.
Closing Date: In line with the University graduate field deadlines
Contributor: Balliol College and the Clarendon Fund Award
Additional Information: This award is held in association with the Clarendon Fund Award.

For further information contact:

Tutor for Graduate Admissions, Balliol College, University of Oxford, Oxford, OX1 3BJ, England

Blackfriars Blackwell Scholarship

Subjects: All subjects.
Purpose: Awarded to a graduate student of Blackfriars Hall on merit.
Level of Study: Postgraduate
Type: Scholarship
Value: UK £1,000
Frequency: Annual
Study Establishment: Blackfriars Hall
Country of Study: United Kingdom
No. of awards offered: 1
Application Procedure: Application forms are available from the Hall secretary.
Closing Date: September 1st
Funding: Commercial
Contributor: Blackwell publishing
No. of awards given last year: 1
No. of applicants last year: 2

Brasenose College Senior Germaine Scholarship

Subjects: Economics and management only.
Purpose: Restricted to home/European Union applicants.
Level of Study: Postgraduate
Type: Scholarship
Value: UK £2,000 per year. In the event that the scholars elected are in receipt of full research grant funding the scholarship will be UK £250 per year. Limited dining rights and 1-year guaranteed accommodation will also be provided
Length of Study: 1 year plus a maximum of a further 2 years
Frequency: Dependent on funds available
Study Establishment: Brasenose College, University of Oxford
Country of Study: United Kingdom
No. of awards offered: 2
Application Procedure: Applicants must contact the Brasenose College Admissions Secretary for details.

British Chevening Scholarships (formerly known as Foreign and Commonwealth Office Scholarships and Awards)

Subjects: All subjects.
Purpose: To enable future leaders, decision makers and opinion formers to study in the United Kingdom.
Eligibility: Preference is given to postgraduates or those already established in a career.
Level of Study: Postgraduate, graduate
Type: Scholarship
Value: Varies
Length of Study: 1 year
Study Establishment: University of Oxford
Country of Study: United Kingdom
Application Procedure: Applicants must apply for information available on request from the British Council in the applicant's home country. Candidates are selected by British diplomatic missions overseas. Applicants must apply independently for admission to the University through the Graduate Admissions Office.
Closing Date: Please contact local British Council for details
Funding: Government
Contributor: The Foreign and Commonwealth Office
Additional Information: The scholarships are administered by the British Council on behalf of the Foreign Office. Further information is available on request or from the website www.britishcouncil.org

Chevening Oxford-Australia Scholarships

Subjects: A range of disciplines including economics, environmental studies and law.
Purpose: To assist individuals with overseas study.
Eligibility: Open to Australian nationals.
Level of Study: Graduate, postgraduate
Type: Scholarship
Value: Up to Australian $34,000, to cover fees and living expenses
Length of Study: 1 year
Frequency: Annual
Study Establishment: University of Oxford
Country of Study: United Kingdom
No. of awards offered: 2
Application Procedure: Applicants must write for details or visit the website www.rsc.anu.edu.au/oxford
Closing Date: February 20th

For further information contact:

Oxford-Australia Scholarships Committee, Research School for Chemistry, Australian National University, Canberra, ACT, 0200, Australia
Tel: (61) 2 6125 3578
Fax: (61) 2 6125 4903
Email: jww@rsc.anu.edu.au
Contact: Professor J W White

Christ Church American Friends Scholarship

Subjects: All subjects.
Purpose: The American Friends Scholarship has been established by American alumni of Christ Church to permit qualified Americans to further their education at Christ Church in any academic field or area of interest.
Eligibility: Open to graduate students from the United States of America only.
Level of Study: Postgraduate
Type: Scholarship
Value: US$7,000
Length of Study: 1 year
Frequency: Annual
Study Establishment: Christ Church, University of Oxford
Country of Study: United Kingdom
No. of awards offered: Varies

Application Procedure: Applicants must apply for the scholarship when applying for admission.
Closing Date: May 1st
Funding: Private
No. of awards given last year: 4 full awards, 2 half awards
No. of applicants last year: 20

For further information contact:

The Tutor for Graduates' Secretary, Christ Church, Oxford, Oxfordshire, OX1 1DP, England

Christ Church Hugh Pilkington Scholarship

Subjects: All subjects.
Eligibility: Open to graduate students from outside the United States of America.
Level of Study: Postgraduate
Type: Scholarship
Value: Varies UK £1,000–3,000 per year
Length of Study: 1 year
Frequency: Annual
Study Establishment: Christ Church, University of Oxford
Country of Study: United Kingdom
No. of awards offered: Varies
Application Procedure: Applicants must write to the Tutor for Graduates's Secretary, Christ Church for further information. Applications should be made when applying for admission.
Closing Date: September 1st
No. of awards given last year: 7
No. of applicants last year: 18

For further information contact:

The Tutor for Graduates' Secretary, Christ Church, Oxford, Oxfordshire, OX1 1DP, England

Christ Church Myers Scholarship

Subjects: Law.
Purpose: Established by Christ Church alumnus Allan Myers to enable Australian graduate students to pursue postgraduate studies at Christ Church.
Level of Study: Postgraduate
Type: Scholarship
Length of Study: 1 year
Frequency: Annual
Study Establishment: Christ Church, University of Oxford
Country of Study: United Kingdom
No. of awards offered: 1
Application Procedure: Applications may be made by students on admission to Christ Church, University of Oxford.
Closing Date: May 1st
Funding: Private

For further information contact:

Tutor for Graduates' Secretary, Christ Church, Oxford, Oxfordshire, OX1 1DP, England

Christ Church Senior Scholarship

Subjects: All subjects.
Purpose: To enable graduate scholars to undertake training or a definite course of literary, educational, scientific or professional study.
Eligibility: Open to candidates who will have been reading for a higher degree at the University of Oxford for at least 1 year, but not more than 2 years, by October 1st of the year in which the award is sought.
Level of Study: Postgraduate
Type: Scholarship
Value: Rooms and maintenance at the Research Council level, subject to the deduction of grants from other sources
Length of Study: 2 years, with a possibility of renewal for a further year
Frequency: Annual
Study Establishment: Christ Church, University of Oxford
Country of Study: United Kingdom
No. of awards offered: 2
Application Procedure: Applicants must write for details. Applications should be made in February.
Closing Date: April 1st
No. of awards given last year: 2
No. of applicants last year: 102
Additional Information: Normally, the scholarship is held in conjunction with an award from a government agency that pays the university fees.

For further information contact:

Tutor of Graduates' Secretary, Christ Church, Oxford, Oxfordshire, OX1 1DP, England

Clarendon Fund Bursaries

Subjects: All subjects.
Purpose: To enable outstanding candidates who have been accepted for admission to the University to take up their places.
Eligibility: Open to students who are liable for fees at the overseas rate and who are, therefore, not home or European Union students.
Level of Study: Doctorate, graduate, postgraduate
Type: Bursary
Value: The financial circumstances of applicants will be taken into account in determining the level of awards. It is expected that most awards will be partial although full scholarships will occasionally be provided
Length of Study: Up to 3 years
Frequency: Annual
Study Establishment: University of Oxford
Country of Study: United Kingdom
No. of awards offered: Approx. 100
Application Procedure: Applicants must complete the relevant section of the graduate admission form available at www.admin.ox.ac.uk/gsp
Closing Date: See the website
Funding: Private
Contributor: Oxford University Press
Additional Information: Candidates must apply for an Overseas Research Students (ORS) award if the course they intend to follow makes them eligible.

Corpus Christi College Charles Oldham Graduate Scholarship in Classics

Subjects: Classics.
Eligibility: Open to overseas, home and European Union students.
Level of Study: Postgraduate
Type: Scholarship
Value: Full fees, graduate maintenance grant and some dining rights
Length of Study: Up to 3 years
Frequency: Dependent on funds available
Study Establishment: Corpus Christi College, University of Oxford
Country of Study: United Kingdom
No. of awards offered: 1
Closing Date: Please write for details
Funding: Private

For further information contact:

Corpus Christi College, Merton Street, Oxford, OX1 4JF, England
Contact: The College Secretary

Corpus Christi College E K Chambers Studentship

Subjects: English literature.
Eligibility: Open to candidates who have studied classics at a United Kingdom university.
Level of Study: Postgraduate
Type: Studentship
Value: Full fees and graduate maintenance grant plus some dining rights
Length of Study: 2–3 years
Study Establishment: Corpus Christi College or Somerville College, University of Oxford
Country of Study: United Kingdom

No. of awards offered: 1
Application Procedure: Applicants must write for details.
Closing Date: Please write for details
Funding: Private

For further information contact:

St Cross Building, Manor Road, Oxford, OX1 3UQ, England
Contact: The Faculty of English

Corpus Christi College Garside Scholarship in Mathematics

Subjects: Mathematics.
Eligibility: Open to mathematics DPhil students already registered at the University.
Level of Study: Graduate
Type: Scholarship
Value: UK £1,650 per year, plus limited dining rights
Length of Study: Up to 2 years
Frequency: Every 2 years
Study Establishment: Corpus Christi College, University of Oxford
Country of Study: United Kingdom
No. of awards offered: 1
Application Procedure: Applicants must contact the College Secretary, Corpus Christi College.
Funding: Private

For further information contact:

Corpus Christi College, Merton Street, Oxford, OX1 4JF, England
Contact: The College Secretary

Corpus Christi College Graduate Studentship in Arts

Eligibility: Home, EU and Overseas.
Level of Study: Graduate
Type: Scholarship
Value: Up to UK £15,000
Length of Study: Up to four years
Frequency: Dependent on funds available
Study Establishment: Corpus Christ College, Oxford
Country of Study: United Kingdom
Application Procedure: Send copy of university application to college.
Funding: Private

Corpus Christi College Graduate Studentship in Science

Subjects: Variety of science subjects.
Eligibility: Home, Eu and Overseas.
Level of Study: Graduate
Type: Scholarships
Value: College fee (Approx. £1,800)
Length of Study: Upto four years
Frequency: Dependent on funds available
Study Establishment: Corpus Christi College, Oxford
Country of Study: United Kingdom
No. of awards offered: Up to three
Application Procedure: Send copy of university applications to college
Funding: Private

DFID Shared Scholarship Scheme

Subjects: A subject related to the economic and social development of the student's home country.
Eligibility: Open to students from developing Commonwealth countries. Candidates must not be living or studying in a developed country or be employed by a government department (national or local) or a parastatal organization. Candidates must certify that they would otherwise be unable to afford the cost of study in the United Kingdom and that they will return to work or study in their home country as soon as their award ends. Candidates should normally be under the age of 35 years at the time the award commences.
Level of Study: Postgraduate
Type: Scholarship
Value: University and college fees plus maintenance and return airfare to the United Kingdom
Frequency: Annual
Study Establishment: University of Oxford
Country of Study: United Kingdom
No. of awards offered: 3
Application Procedure: Applicants must complete application forms available on request from the International Office, Wellington Square, or from the website at www.admin.ox.ac.uk/io Applicants must apply separately for admission to the University of Oxford through the Graduate Admissions Office (www.admin.ox.ac.uk/gsp).
Closing Date: See the website www.admin.ox.ac.uk/io
Funding: Government

Dolabani Fund for Syriac Studies

Subjects: Syriac studies.
Purpose: To assist students in meeting the cost of engaging in courses involving Syriac studies at the University and for the provision of grants for the purchase of Syriac manuscripts for the Bodleian Library and the Oriental Institute Library. Also to further Syriac studies within the University and to support students from Syriac churches studying their own tradition in working for formal qualifications of the University.
Eligibility: Open to graduate students of the University who are nationals of the Middle East or the region of the Indian state of Kerala.
Level of Study: Postgraduate
Type: Grant
Value: Varies
Study Establishment: University of Oxford
Country of Study: United Kingdom
No. of awards offered: Varies
Application Procedure: Applicants must submit a statement of purpose for which the grant is requested and, in the case of graduate students, the name of the applicant's supervisor.
Closing Date: March 12th
Funding: Private

For further information contact:

Secretary, Board of the Faculty of Oriental Studies, Oriental Institute, Pusey Lane, Oxford, Oxfordshire, OX1 2LE, England

Dulverton Scholarships

Subjects: All subjects.
Purpose: To provide assistance for students of outstanding academic merit and financial need.
Eligibility: Open to students from Eastern European countries, namely, Albania, Armenia, Azerbaijan, Belarus, Bosnia, Bulgaria, Croatia, Georgia, Macedonia, Moldova, Romania, Serbias Montenegro the Ukraine.
Level of Study: Doctorate, postgraduate, graduate
Type: Scholarship
Value: Full scholarships will cover university and college fees and maintenance for the length of the proposed course of study. Partial scholarships will be awarded on the basis of financial need
Length of Study: Duration of course of study
Frequency: Annual
Study Establishment: University of Oxford
Country of Study: United Kingdom
No. of awards offered: Varies
Application Procedure: Applicants must complete the relevant section of the graduate admission form available at www.admin.ox.ack
Closing Date: See the website
Funding: Private
Contributor: The Dulverton Trust
No. of awards given last year: 4
No. of applicants last year: 362
Additional Information: Also open to undergraduates.

For further information contact:

International Office, University Offices, Wellington Square, Oxford, Oxfordshire, OX1 2JD, England

Felix Scholarships

Subjects: All subjects.
Purpose: To enable graduates accepted for entry to Oxford to read for taught graduate courses or for a Master's or DPhil degree by research, who would be unable, without financial assistance, to take up their place.
Eligibility: Open to Indian nationals under 30 years of age who must have at least a First Class (Honours) Bachelor's Degree from an Indian university or comparable institution. Those who already hold degrees from universities outside India are not eligible to apply.
Level of Study: Postgraduate, doctorate
Value: University and college fees plus maintenance costs
Length of Study: Upto 3 years
Frequency: Annual
Study Establishment: University of Oxford
Country of Study: United Kingdom
No. of awards offered: Up to 6
Application Procedure: Applicants must apply separately for admission to Oxford through the Graduate Admissions Office and should write for further details. Applicants for Felix Scholarships are expected to apply for an Overseas Research Student (ORS) award if the course they intend to take makes them eligible.
Closing Date: See the website

For further information contact:

International Office, University Offices, Wellington Square, Oxford, Oxfordshire, OX1 2JD, England
Website: www.admin.ox.ac.uk/io

Freshfields Studentship in Law

Subjects: Law.
Level of Study: Postgraduate
Type: Studentship
Value: UK £7,500
Length of Study: 1 year
Frequency: Annual
Study Establishment: University of Oxford
Country of Study: United Kingdom
No. of awards offered: 2
Application Procedure: Applicants must contact the International Office for an application form and further details.
Closing Date: See website
Funding: Private

For further information contact:

The International Office, University Offices, Wellington Square, Oxford, Oxfordshire, OX1 2JD, England
Tel: (44) 18 6527 0105
Email: international.office@admin.ox.ac.uk
Website: www.admin.ox.ac.uk/io

Fulbright Oxford University Scholarships

Subjects: All subjects.
Level of Study: Doctorate, graduate, postgraduate
Value: Round-trip travel, a maintenance allowance and approved tuition fees. A candidate gaining three awards, ie. the Fulbright, Overseas Research Award (ORS) and Oxford bursary will have adequate funding for 2 years
Length of Study: 2–3 years
Frequency: Annual
Study Establishment: University of Oxford
Country of Study: United Kingdom
No. of awards offered: 3
Application Procedure: Applicants must complete an application form for Fulbright scholarships and for an ORS award for admission to the University.
Closing Date: October 21st. Those enrolled in United States of America institutions must file applications with their Fulbright Programme Advisor by the deadline set by the campus advisor
Funding: Private
Additional Information: The course must lead to a higher degree and qualify for funding under the Overseas Research Student (ORS) award scheme. Candidates must apply for this award.

For further information contact:

US Student Programs, Institute of International Education (IIE), 809 United Nations Plaza, New York, NY, 10017-3580, United States of America
Website: www.iee.org

Hertford College Senior Scholarships

Subjects: All subjects.
Eligibility: Restricted to students who are about to commence a new research degree course or those about to upgrade their current course.
Level of Study: Postgraduate
Type: Scholarship
Value: UK £1,000 per year, plus priority for housing and some dining rights
Length of Study: 2 years
Frequency: Annual
Study Establishment: Hertford College, University of Oxford
Country of Study: United Kingdom
No. of awards offered: 4–5
Application Procedure: Applicants must write to the College for further details.
Closing Date: January in each year
No. of awards given last year: 5

For further information contact:

Academic Administrator, Hertford College, Oxford, Oxfordshire, OX1 3BW, England

Hill Foundation Scholarships

Subjects: All subjects.
Eligibility: Open to students from the Russian Federation studying for a postgraduate or a 2nd Bachelor of Arts degree. Candidates should not normally be more than 25 years of age and should be intending to return to Russia at the end of their period of study.
Level of Study: Graduate, postgraduate, doctorate
Type: Scholarship
Value: University and college fees, travel to and from the United Kingdom and a grant for maintenance
Length of Study: Up to 3 years
Frequency: Annual
Study Establishment: University of Oxford
Country of Study: United Kingdom
No. of awards offered: Up to 6
Application Procedure: Applicants should complete the funding sections of the graduate admissions form.
Closing Date: See the website
Funding: Private
Contributor: The Hill Foundation
No. of awards given last year: 9
No. of applicants last year: 20
Additional Information: The Foundation particularly wants to encourage applications from candidates for a 2nd BA degree. Further information is available from www.hillfoundation-scholarships.org

Hong Kong Oxford Scholarship Fund Bursaries (China)

Subjects: All subjects.
Eligibility: Open to nationals of the People's Republic of China. Students should be planning to return to and benefit their home country on completion of their studies.
Level of Study: Postgraduate
Value: Up to UK £4,000
Frequency: Annual
Study Establishment: University of Oxford
Country of Study: United Kingdom
No. of awards offered: Varies
Application Procedure: Applicants must apply for admission to the University of Oxford through the Graduate Admissions Office and should write for further details.
Closing Date: June

For further information contact:

International Office, University Offices, Wellington Square, Oxford, Oxfordshire, OX1 2JD, England
Website: www.admin.ox.ac.uk/io

James Fairfax and Oxford-Australia Fund Scholarships
Subjects: Oxford-Australia Fund scholarships are open to any discipline, whereas James Fairfax scholarships are intended for those wishing to study in the arts or social sciences.
Level of Study: Graduate, postgraduate
Value: University fees at the home and European Union rate, college fees and a living allowance of the order of Australian $12,000 per year
Length of Study: Oxford-Australia Fund scholarships are for 2 years, or in the case of DPhil for 3 years, and James Fairfax scholarships are generally of 2 years duration
Frequency: Annual
Study Establishment: University of Oxford
Country of Study: United Kingdom
No. of awards offered: 12
Application Procedure: Applicants must write for details or visit the website at www.rsc.anu.edu.au/oxford
Closing Date: February 21st
Funding: Private
Contributor: Australian scholars who have studied at Oxford and, in particular, Mr James Fairfax
Additional Information: Candidates are also expected to apply for an Overseas Research Student (ORS) award if the course they intend to follow makes them eligible.

For further information contact:

Chairman (Oxford-Australia Scholarships Committee), Research School of Chemistry, Australian National University, Canberra, ACT, 0200, Australia
Tel: (61) 2 6125 3578
Fax: (61) 2 6125 4903
Email: jww@rsc.anu.edu.au
Contact: Professor J W White

Jenkins Memorial Fund Scholarships
Subjects: Humanities and social sciences.
Purpose: To promote academic collaboration between partner members of the Europaeum.
Eligibility: Open to students from partner universities of the Europaeum (see www.europaeum.org)
Level of Study: Postgraduate, doctorate
Type: Scholarship
Value: UK £10,000
Length of Study: 1 year only
Frequency: Annual
Study Establishment: University of Oxford
Country of Study: United Kingdom
No. of awards offered: Up to 4
Application Procedure: Applicants must complete the relevant section of the graduate admissions form available at www.admin.ox.ac.uk/gsp
Closing Date: See the website
Funding: Trusts
No. of awards given last year: 2
No. of applicants last year: 36
Additional Information: Preference will be given to candidates studying for 1-year Master's degrees.

Jesus College Graduate Scholarship
Subjects: All subjects offered by the college.
Purpose: For a high standard of research/study at Jesus College, University of Oxford.
Eligibility: Open to students in the first years of a 2-year course, those in a 1-year course that will lead to a further course at Jesus College, or those in the 1st or 2nd year of a 3-year course at Jesus College.
Level of Study: Postgraduate
Type: Scholarship
Value: UK £750 per year
Length of Study: Up to 3 years
Frequency: Annual
Study Establishment: Jesus College, University of Oxford
Country of Study: United Kingdom
No. of awards offered: Up to 4
Application Procedure: Applications are invited from current eligible postgraduate students at Jesus College.
Closing Date: Write for details
Contributor: Jesus College, University of Oxford
No. of awards given last year: 4
No. of applicants last year: 16

For further information contact:

Senior Tutor, Jesus College, Oxford, OX1 3DW, England

Jesus College Meyricke Graduate Scholarships
Subjects: All subjects.
Purpose: For current graduate members of Jesus College who have taken or are qualified to take a degree at the University of Wales.
Eligibility: Open to graduates of the University of Wales who have been accepted by Jesus College.
Level of Study: Postgraduate
Type: Scholarship
Value: UK £750 per year
Length of Study: Up to 3 years
Frequency: Annual
Study Establishment: Jesus College, University of Oxford
Country of Study: United Kingdom
No. of awards offered: 2
Application Procedure: Applicants must write for details.
Closing Date: End of October
Funding: Trusts
Contributor: The Meyricke endowment at Jesus College
No. of awards given last year: None
No. of applicants last year: None eligible

For further information contact:

Senior Tutor, Jesus College, Oxford, OX1 3DW, England

Jesus College Tarmac Graduate Scholarship
Subjects: Physical and social sciences.
Purpose: Postgraduate study and research on natural research.
Eligibility: Open to candidates from Poland or the Czech Republic only, who have been accepted by the University of Oxford.
Level of Study: Postgraduate
Type: Scholarship
Value: All fees and a maintenance allowance
Length of Study: Up to 3 years
Frequency: Dependent on funds available
Study Establishment: Jesus College, University of Oxford
Country of Study: United Kingdom
No. of awards offered: 1
Application Procedure: Applicants must contact the senior Tutor at Jesus College.
Closing Date: Mid-March, write for details
Funding: Private, commercial
Contributor: Tarmac and Jesus College
No. of awards given last year: 1
No. of applicants last year: 4

For further information contact:

Jesus College, University of Oxford, Oxford, OX1 3DW, England
Contact: Senior Tutor

Jesus College The Alan Hughes' Graduate Scholarship
Subjects: Polynesia and Micronesia.
Purpose: Postgraduate study and research into the language and/or cultures of Polynesia or Micronesia.
Eligibility: Open to applicants who have been accepted by the University of Oxford to undertake research towards a DPhil in the correct subject area.

Level of Study: Doctorate
Type: Scholarship
Value: Home and European Union fees and a maintenance award
Length of Study: Up to 3 years
Frequency: Dependent on funds available, approx. every 3 years
Study Establishment: Jesus College, University of Oxford
Country of Study: United Kingdom
No. of awards offered: Normally only 1 holder at a time
Application Procedure: Applicants must write for details.
Closing Date: Please write for details
Funding: Trusts
Contributor: Alan Hughes Trust at Jesus College
No. of awards given last year: None (insufficient funds)

For further information contact:

Senior Tutor, Jesus College, Oxford, OX1 3DW, England

K C Wong Scholarships

Subjects: All subjects.
Purpose: To assist students studying at doctorate level.
Eligibility: Open to residents of the People's Republic of China only.
Level of Study: Doctorate
Value: University and college fees plus maintenance
Length of Study: 3 years
Frequency: Annual
Study Establishment: University of Oxford
Country of Study: United Kingdom
No. of awards offered: 3
Application Procedure: Applicants must complete an application form for admission to the University at www.admin.ox.ac.uk/gsp
Closing Date: See website
Funding: Private
Contributor: The K C Wong Foundation and the University of Oxford
Additional Information: Applicants for the K C Wong Scholarships are also expected to apply for an Overseas Research Students (ORS) award.

For further information contact:

International Office, University Offices, Wellington Square, Oxford, Oxfordshire, OX1 2JD, England

Karim Rida Said Foundation Scholarships

Subjects: All subjects.
Purpose: To assist students with either a taught Master's degree or a Master's degree by research.
Eligibility: Open to students from Iraq, Jordan, Lebanon, Palestine or Syria.
Level of Study: Postgraduate
Value: University and college fees plus a maintenance grant for the duration of the student's course
Frequency: Annual
Study Establishment: The University of Oxford
Country of Study: United Kingdom
No. of awards offered: Varies
Application Procedure: Applicants must apply separately for admission to the University of Oxford through the Graduate Admissions Office at www.admin.ox.ac.uk/gsp
Closing Date: April 1st
Funding: Private
Contributor: The Karim Rida Said Foundation
Additional Information: Applicants are expected to apply for an Overseas Research Student (ORS) award if the course they intend to follow makes them eligible.

For further information contact:

International Office, University Offices, Wellington Square, Oxford, Oxfordshire, OX1 2JD, England

Linacre College A J Hosier Studentship

Subjects: Husbandry, agricultural economics and statistics and applied agricultural science.
Purpose: To fund graduate study.
Eligibility: Candidates must be honours graduates of a university in the United Kingdom and be citizens of the United Kingdom.
Level of Study: Postgraduate
Type: Studentship
Value: UK £4,000 per year, which may be divided between more than one person
Length of Study: 1 year
Study Establishment: Linacre College, University of Oxford
Country of Study: United Kingdom
No. of awards offered: Varies
Application Procedure: Applicants must contact the Tutor for Admissions for further details.
Closing Date: May 31st
No. of awards given last year: 2
No. of applicants last year: 3

For further information contact:

Tutor for Admissions, Linacre College, Oxford, Oxfordshire, OX1 3JA, England

Linacre College and the Environmental Change Institute Coca-Cola Water Sustainability Scholarships

Subjects: DPhil in water research; Msc in environmental change and management; water science policy and management; nature; society and environmental policy; biodiversity, conservation and management.
Eligibility: Open to suitably qualified graduates admitted to one of the relevant degrees.
Level of Study: Postgraduate
Type: Scholarship
Value: University, college fees and £3,090 towards maintenance
Frequency: Dependent on funds available
Study Establishment: Linacre college, University of Oxford
Country of Study: United Kingdom
No. of awards offered: 3
Application Procedure: Application form available from the college secretary Linacre college Oxford OX1 3JA Website: www.linacre.ox.ac.uk
Closing Date: March 31st
Contributor: The Coca-Cola Foundation
No. of awards given last year: 3
No. of applicants last year: 42

For further information contact:

Linacre college, Oxford, OX1 3JA
Contact: The Principal

Linacre College Applied Materials Scholarships

Subjects: Materials science, environmental studies.
Level of Study: Postgraduate
Type: Scholarship
Value: Up to UK £2,000 per year
Length of Study: Up to 3 years
Frequency: Varies, not available every year
Study Establishment: Linacre College, University of Oxford
Country of Study: United Kingdom
No. of awards offered: Up to 5
Application Procedure: Applicants must contact the Tutor for Admissions at Linacre College.

For further information contact:

Linacre College, Oxford, Oxfordshire, OX1 3JA, England
Website: www.linacre.ox.ac.uk

Linacre College Canadian National Scholarship

Subjects: All subjects.
Eligibility: Open to suitably qualified students of Canadian nationality reading or intending to read for a postgraduate degree.
Level of Study: Postgraduate, graduate
Type: Scholarship
Value: Approx. UK £4,000 per year
Length of Study: 1 year

Frequency: Annual, may not be available every year
Study Establishment: Linacre College, University of Oxford
Country of Study: United Kingdom
Application Procedure: Applicants must write for details or visit the website www.linacre.ox.ac.uk
Closing Date: March 31st
Contributor: Canadian National
No. of awards given last year: 1
No. of applicants last year: 37

For further information contact:

The College Secretary, Linacre College, Oxford, Oxfordshire, OX1 3JA, England

Linacre College Domus Studentships

Subjects: All subjects.
Purpose: To assist postgraduate study.
Eligibility: Open to students with a good First Class Degree who intend to begin reading for a higher degree, or to current members of Linacre College.
Level of Study: Postgraduate
Type: Studentship
Value: UK £250 per year plus priority for accommodation
Length of Study: Up to 3 years
Frequency: Annual
Study Establishment: Linacre College, University of Oxford
Country of Study: United Kingdom
No. of awards offered: Varies
Closing Date: January 31st
Funding: Private
Contributor: College funds
No. of awards given last year: 4
No. of applicants last year: 16

For further information contact:

The Tutor for Admissions, Linacre College, St Cross Road, Oxford, Oxfordshire, OX1 3JA, England

Linacre College EPA Cephalosporin Junior Research Fellowships

Subjects: Biology, biochemistry, medicine, organic chemistry, psychology.
Purpose: To assist postdoctoral research.
Eligibility: Open to persons with a postdoctoral qualification.
Level of Study: Postdoctorate
Type: Fellowship
Value: UK £250 per year
Length of Study: Up to 2 years
Frequency: Annual
Study Establishment: Linacre College, University of Oxford
Country of Study: United Kingdom
No. of awards offered: 3
Closing Date: January 31st
Funding: Private
Contributor: Linacre College
No. of awards given last year: 3
No. of applicants last year: 46

For further information contact:

Linacre College, St Cross Road, Oxford, Oxfordshire, OX1 3JA, England
Tel: (44) 18 6527 1662
Fax: (44) 18 6527 1668
Email: principal.secretary@linacre.ox.ac.uk
Website: www.linacre.ox.ac.uk
Contact: The Principal

Linacre College European Blaschko Visiting Research Scholarship

Subjects: Pharmacology, neuropharmacology.
Purpose: To enable European students to carry out research for 1 year in the department of pharmacology or the MRC anatomical neuropharmacology unit.
Eligibility: Open to students with a doctorate or equivalent degree from Europe.
Level of Study: Postgraduate
Type: Scholarship
Value: College and university fees for visiting student status, stipend and the cost of return travel from the scholar's home country
Length of Study: 1 year
Frequency: Annual
Study Establishment: Linacre College, University of Oxford
Country of Study: United Kingdom
Closing Date: Please write for details
Funding: Private
No. of awards given last year: 1

For further information contact:

The Heart of an Department of Pharmacology, Mansfield Road, Oxford, Oxfordshire, OX1 3QT, England
Contact: Smith

Linacre College Heselton Legal Research Scholarship

Subjects: English or European Union law research degrees.
Purpose: To fund graduate research.
Level of Study: Postgraduate
Type: Scholarship
Value: UK £1,000 per year
Length of Study: 1 year
Frequency: Dependent on funds available
Study Establishment: Linacre College, University of Oxford
Country of Study: United Kingdom
Application Procedure: Applicants must contact the College Secretary at Linacre College in the first instance, or see the website www.linacre.ox.ac.uk
Closing Date: March 31st
Funding: Private
No. of awards given last year: 0
Additional Information: This scholarship may not be available every year.

For further information contact:

Linacre College, St Cross Road, Oxford, Oxfordshire, OX1 3JA, England
Contact: College Secretary

Linacre College Lloyd African Scholarship DFID Shared Scholarships

Subjects: Environmental studies.
Purpose: To enable a qualified graduate student from an African university to pursue a 1-year taught Master's course.
Eligibility: Open to qualified graduate students from developing Commonwealth countries.
Level of Study: Postgraduate
Type: Scholarship
Value: University and college fees, maintenance and return airfare
Length of Study: 1–2 years
Frequency: Annual or biannual
Study Establishment: Linacre College, University of Oxford
Country of Study: United Kingdom
No. of awards offered: 1
Application Procedure: Applicants must write for details.
Funding: Private
No. of awards given last year: 1

For further information contact:

Oxford university centre for the environment, environmental change institute, South parks road, Oxford, OX1 3QY, England
Contact: D. J. Boardman

Linacre College Mary Blaschko Graduate Scholarship

Subjects: Arts and humanities.
Eligibility: Open to suitably qualified students reading or intending to read for a research degree in the arts and humanities.
Level of Study: Research, postgraduate

Type: Scholarship
Value: UK £2,100 per year
Length of Study: 1–2 years
Frequency: Annual, May not be available every year
Study Establishment: Linacre College, University of Oxford
Country of Study: United Kingdom
No. of awards offered: 2
Application Procedure: Applicants must write for details. Forms are also available from www.linacre.ox.ac.uk
Closing Date: January 31st
Funding: Private
No. of awards given last year: 2
No. of applicants last year: 27

For further information contact:

Tutor for Admissions, Linacre College, St Cross Road, Oxford, Oxfordshire, OX1 3JA, England

Linacre College Norman and Ivy Lloyd Scholarship/DFID Shared Scholarship

Subjects: Environmental change and management.
Purpose: To enable a student from developing Commonwealth countries to undertake the MSc.
Eligibility: Open to nationals of developing Commonwealth countries.
Level of Study: Postgraduate
Type: Scholarship
Value: University and college fees plus maintenance and return airfare from the scholar's home country
Length of Study: 1 year
Frequency: Annual
Study Establishment: Linacre College, University of Oxford
Country of Study: United Kingdom
No. of awards offered: Varies
Application Procedure: Applicants must write for details.
Closing Date: Please write for details
Funding: Private
No. of awards given last year: 1

For further information contact:

Environmental Change Institute, 5 Mansfield Road, Oxford, Oxfordshire, OX1 3TB, England
Contact: Dr J Boardman

Linacre College Rausing Scholarships

Subjects: Subjects vary from year to year.
Level of Study: Postgraduate
Type: Scholarship
Value: Up to UK £2,050 per year
Length of Study: Up to 3 years
Frequency: Varies, not available every year
Study Establishment: Linacre College, University of Oxford
Country of Study: United Kingdom
No. of awards offered: 2
Application Procedure: Applicants must be nominated by the faculty. No separate application is required.
No. of awards given last year: 2

Linares Rivas Scholarship

Subjects: All subjects.
Eligibility: Open to students from Spain, studying at or recently graduated from a Spanish university.
Level of Study: Graduate, postgraduate
Value: University and college fees and a grant towards living costs
Length of Study: 1 year only
Frequency: Every 2 years
Study Establishment: University of Oxford
Country of Study: United Kingdom
No. of awards offered: 1
Application Procedure: Applicants must complete the application form for admission to the University at www.admin.ox.ac.uk/gsp
Closing Date: See website
Funding: Private
Contributor: The trustees of the late Lady Consuelo Maria Allen
No. of awards given last year: 1
No. of applicants last year: 10

For further information contact:

International Office, University Offices, Wellington Square, Oxford, Oxfordshire, OX1 2JD, England

Lincoln College Berrow Foundation Scholarships

Subjects: All subjects.
Purpose: To permit graduates of Swiss universities to undertake postgraduate study at Oxford.
Eligibility: Open to graduates of the universities of Berne, Geneva, Lausanne, Fribourg, Neuchâtel or the Ecole Polytechnique Fédérale de Lausanne, of Swiss or Lichtenstein nationality only.
Level of Study: Postgraduate, doctorate
Type: Scholarship
Value: All university and college fees are covered plus maintenance allowance
Length of Study: 2 years, with a possibility of renewal for a further year
Frequency: Annual
Study Establishment: Lincoln College, University of Oxford
Country of Study: United Kingdom
No. of awards offered: Up to 4
Application Procedure: Applicants must write for details.
Closing Date: November
Funding: Private
No. of awards given last year: 4

For further information contact:

The Rector's Office, Lincoln College, Oxford, Oxfordshire, OX1 3DR, England

Lincoln College Berrow Foundation's Lord Florey Scholarships in Medical, Chemical and Biochemical Sciences

Subjects: Medical, chemical and biochemical sciences.
Eligibility: Open to nationals of Switzerland and Lichtenstein.
Level of Study: Doctorate, postgraduate
Type: Scholarship
Value: Tuition fees and maintenance grant
Length of Study: 2 years, with the possibility of extension for a 3rd year
Frequency: Annual
Study Establishment: Lincoln College, University of Oxford
Country of Study: United Kingdom
No. of awards offered: 2
Application Procedure: Applicants must contact the Rector's Office.
Closing Date: November
Funding: Private
No. of awards given last year: 2

For further information contact:

The Rector's Office, Lincoln College, Oxford, Oxfordshire, OX1 3DR, England

Lincoln College Erich and Rochelle Endowed Prize in Music

Subjects: Any discipline other than music.
Eligibility: Open to graduate students who have already been gives a individual place at Lincoln college of exceptional and proven musical ability. The successful candidate will be expected to play a prominent part in the musical life of the college and in particular to act, if requested, as organizing secretary of the college's active Music Society.
Level of Study: Postgraduate
Value: UK £300
Length of Study: 1 year only
Frequency: Annual
Study Establishment: Lincoln College, University of Oxford
Country of Study: United Kingdom
No. of awards offered: 1

Closing Date: Only candidates office of a place at Lincoln college are eligible to apply
Funding: Private
No. of awards given last year: 1

For further information contact:

Admissions Office, Lincoln College, Oxford, Oxfordshire, OX1 3DR, England

Lincoln College Jermyn Brooks Graduate Award

Subjects: Humanities, with a preference for modern languages.
Eligibility: Open to graduate students of the college (other new or continuing) who are studying in the humanities, with a preference for modern languages.
Level of Study: Postgraduate
Type: Scholarship
Value: UK £1,000
Length of Study: One year
Frequency: Annual
Study Establishment: Lincoln college, University of Oxford
Country of Study: United Kingdom
No. of awards offered: One
Application Procedure: Application form available from admissions office at Lincoln College.
Closing Date: Mid-August
Funding: Private
No. of awards given last year: 1

For further information contact:

The admissions office Lincoln College, Oxford, OX1 3DR

Lincoln College Keith Murray Senior Scholarship

Subjects: All subjects.
Purpose: To permit students from outside the European Union to undertake postgraduate study at Oxford University.
Eligibility: Open to holders of a High First Class Degree who are citizens of any country outside the United Kingdom.
Level of Study: Postgraduate, doctorate
Type: Scholarship
Value: All university and college fees are covered, plus maintenance allowance
Length of Study: 2 years, with the possibility of renewal for a 3rd year
Frequency: Every 2 years
Study Establishment: Lincoln College, University of Oxford
Country of Study: United Kingdom
No. of awards offered: 1 or more, depending on funds available
Application Procedure: Applicants must write for details.
Closing Date: January
Funding: Private
No. of awards given last year: 1

For further information contact:

The Rector's Office, Lincoln College, Oxford, Oxfordshire, OX1 3DR, England

Lincoln College Kenneth Seward-Shaw Scholarship

Subjects: Law, history, politics, English.
Eligibility: Open to graduates in Law, history, English or politics who have already been offered a place at Lincoln College.
Level of Study: Postgraduate
Type: Scholarship
Value: UK £1,500
Length of Study: 1 year
Frequency: Annual
Study Establishment: Lincoln College, University of Oxford
Country of Study: United Kingdom
Application Procedure: Applicants must contact the Admissions Office.
Closing Date: Mid-August
Funding: Private
No. of awards given last year: 1

For further information contact:

Admissions Office, Lincoln College, Oxford, Oxfordshire, OX1 3DR, England

Lincoln College Overseas Graduate Entrance Scholarships

Subjects: All subjects.
Eligibility: Restricted to those offered a place at Lincoln College.
Level of Study: Postgraduate
Type: Scholarship
Value: UK £1,500
Length of Study: 1 year
Frequency: Annual
Study Establishment: Lincoln College, University of Oxford
Country of Study: United Kingdom
No. of awards offered: 4
Application Procedure: For further information contact the Admissions Officer, Lincoln College.
Closing Date: Mid-August
Funding: Private
No. of awards given last year: 4

For further information contact:

Admissions Office, Lincoln College, Oxford, Oxfordshire, OX1 3DR, England

Lincoln College Supperstone Law Scholarship

Subjects: Law.
Eligibility: Open to candidates reading for the BCL or the MJuris, with an emphasis or special interest in European or public law. Applicants must have an offer of a college place at Lincoln College.
Level of Study: Postgraduate
Type: Scholarship
Value: UK £650
Length of Study: 1 year
Frequency: Annual
Study Establishment: Lincoln College, University of Oxford
Country of Study: United Kingdom
No. of awards offered: 1
Application Procedure: Applicants must contact the Admissions Office at Lincoln College.
Closing Date: Mid-August
Funding: Trusts
No. of awards given last year: 1

For further information contact:

Admissions Office, Lincoln College, Oxford, Oxfordshire, OX1 3DR, England

Merton College Domus Graduate Scholarships A

Subjects: All subjects accepted by the College. Please refer to the Merton College website www.merton.ox.ac.uk/prospectus/prospectus.html for a comprehensive list of courses not considered by the college.
Eligibility: Open to non-United Kingdom students, of academic excellence who are applying to Oxford for the first time. Joint awards - EU applicants excluded. Scatcherd joint award EU applicants only.
Level of Study: Graduate
Type: Scholarship
Value: Fees and maintenance
Length of Study: Up to 4 years depending on programme of study
Frequency: Annual
Study Establishment: Merton College, University of Oxford
Country of Study: United Kingdom
No. of awards offered: 4, 3 in association with the on fund and 1 in association with the scatchered fund of oxford universtiy
Application Procedure: Application is via the university of oxford application form for graduate study. There is no separate application process. Further information is available at www.merton.ox.uk
Closing Date: Late January
Contributor: From college endowments
No. of awards given last year: 2

No. of applicants last year: 39
Additional Information: It is expected that candidates will apply for ORS awards.

For further information contact:

Merton College, Oxford, Oxfordshire, OX1 4JD, England
Email: julieg@admin.merton.ox.ac.uk
Contact: Secretary for Graduates

Merton College Domus Graduate Scholarships B

Subjects: All subjects accepted by the College. Please refer to the Merton College website www.merton.ox.ac.uk/prospectus/prospectus.html for a comprehensive list of courses not considered by the college.
Eligibility: Open to United Kingdom and EU students who hold a First Class Degree and are still unfunded in September.
Level of Study: Graduate
Type: Scholarship
Value: Fees and maintenance
Length of Study: Up to 4 years depending on programme of study
Frequency: Annual
Study Establishment: Merton College, University of Oxford
Country of Study: United Kingdom
No. of awards offered: 2
Application Procedure: Further particulars and application forms are available from the Merton College website www.merton.ox.ac.uk/vacancies/index.htm or from the Secretary for Graduates.
Closing Date: Late August/early September
No. of awards given last year: 2
No. of applicants last year: 38

For further information contact:

Merton College, Oxford, Oxfordshire, OX1 4JD, England
Email: julieg@admin.merton.ox.ac.uk
Contact: Secretary for Graduates

Merton College Greendale Scholarship

Subjects: All subjects accepted by the College. Please refer to the Merton College website www.merton.ox.ac.uk/prospectus/prospectus.html for a comprehensive list of courses not considered by the college.
Eligibility: Open to nationals and permanent residents of Switzerland who have a degree from a Swiss university.
Level of Study: Postgraduate
Type: Scholarship
Value: Fees and maintenance
Length of Study: Up to 4 years depending on programme of study
Frequency: Annual
Study Establishment: Merton College, University of Oxford
Country of Study: United Kingdom
No. of awards offered: 1
Application Procedure: Further particulars and application forms are available from the Merton College website www.merton.ox.ac.uk/vacancies/index.htm or from the Secretary for Graduates.
Closing Date: Mid-April
Funding: Private
No. of awards given last year: 1
No. of applicants last year: 16

For further information contact:

Merton College, Oxford, Oxfordshire, OX1 4JD, England
Email: julieg@admin.merton.ox.ac.uk
Contact: Secretary for Graduates

Merton College Leventis Scholarship

Subjects: Greek studies from the Bronze Age to 1453 AD.
Eligibility: Open to citizens of Greece or the Republic of Cyprus.
Level of Study: Graduate
Type: Scholarship
Value: Fees and maintenance
Length of Study: Up to 4 years depending on programme of study
Frequency: Every 2 years
Study Establishment: Merton College, University of Oxford
Country of Study: United Kingdom
No. of awards offered: 1
Application Procedure: Further particulars and application forms are available from the Merton College website www.merton.ox.ac.uk/vacancies
Closing Date: End of January
Funding: Private
No. of awards given last year: Not awarded in 2006
No. of applicants last year: C. 10

For further information contact:

Merton College, Oxford, Oxfordshire, OX1 4JD, England
Contact: Secretary for Graduates

Merton College Reed Foundation Scholarship

Subjects: All subjects that the College would normally consider, except medicine, MBA and MSc in management research. Please refer to the Merton college website www.merton.ox.ac.uk/prospectus/prospectus.html for a comprehensive list of courses not offered by the college.
Eligibility: Open to nationals of underdeveloped countries, which are decided on a rotational basis. Please check the website for up-to-date information on countries selected.
Level of Study: Graduate
Type: Scholarship
Value: Fees (maintenance grant)
Length of Study: 2 years
Frequency: Every 2 years
Study Establishment: Merton College, University of Oxford
Country of Study: United Kingdom
No. of awards offered: 1
Application Procedure: The scholarship is likely to be awarded in association with the claredan fund through the international office of the University of Oxford.
Closing Date: Early January. Please check website for further details and updates
Funding: Private
Additional Information: It is expected that candidates will apply for ORS awards.

For further information contact:

Merton College, Oxford, Oxfordshire, OX1 4JD, England
Contact: Secretary for Graduates

Museveni Scholarship

Subjects: African economics.
Purpose: To support DPhil students from Africa.
Eligibility: Open to nationals of Africa, who have been accepted into the DPhil programme in economics at the University of Oxford. Award holders will usually be supervised by a member of the CSAE reserch team.
Level of Study: Doctorate
Type: Scholarship
Value: Up to UK £10,000
Length of Study: 1 year
Frequency: Annual
Study Establishment: The Centre for the Study of African Economies, University of Oxford
Country of Study: United Kingdom
No. of awards offered: 1
Application Procedure: Applications must include a copy of the research proposal, a curriculum vitae and details of other applications for funding and/or funding obtained for DPhil studies.
Closing Date: Mid-October each year
No. of awards given last year: 1
No. of applicants last year: 4

For further information contact:

CSAE, Department of Economics, Manor Road Building, Oxford, Oxfordshire, OX1 3UQ, England
Website: www.csae.ox.ac.uk
Contact: Administrator

Noon/Chevening/OSI Oxford Scholarships
Subjects: All subjects.
Eligibility: Open to nationals of Pakistan, with preference being given to those who have not previously studied outside Pakistan.
Level of Study: Graduate, doctorate, postgraduate
Frequency: Annual
Study Establishment: University of Oxford
Country of Study: United Kingdom
No. of awards offered: Varies. There are a small number of full or partial awards
Application Procedure: Applicants must apply separately for admission to the University of Oxford through the Graduate Admissions Office website www.admin.ox.ac.uk/gsp
Closing Date: See the website
Funding: Private, government
Contributor: The Noon Educational Foundation, the Foreign and Commonwealth Office, the Open Society Institute and the University of Oxford

Nuffield College Funded Studentships
Subjects: Social sciences.
Purpose: To assist students in a postgraduate degree course.
Eligibility: Open to persons with at least an Upper Second Class (Honours) Degree or equivalent.
Level of Study: Postgraduate
Type: Studentship
Value: Maximum UK £14,500 (home and European Union students) UK £19,500 (overseas students), usually partial awards only
Length of Study: For the length of the course, subject to satisfactory progress up to 4 years
Frequency: Annual
Study Establishment: Nuffield College, University of Oxford
Country of Study: United Kingdom
No. of awards offered: Varies
Application Procedure: All students offered a place at Nuffield College will automatically be considered for a studentship without the need for further application, other than the University of Oxford Graduate Admissions application form.
No. of awards given last year: 0 full awards, 7 part awards
No. of applicants last year: 160
Additional Information: Requests for information should be addressed to the College Secretary.

For further information contact:

Nuffield College, Oxford, Oxfordshire, OX1 1NF, England
Email: academic.administrator@nuf.ox.ac.uk
Website: www.nuffield.ox.ac.uk
Contact: Academic Administrator

Nuffield College Prize Research Fellowships
Subjects: Economics, politics, sociology, broadly construed to include, for example, social science approaches to history, social and medical statistics, international relations and social policy.
Purpose: To allow scholars who have recently completed, or who are close to the completion of, a doctoral dissertation, to enable in independent scholarly research in the social sciences.
Eligibility: Open to men and women who have not spent more than 8 years in postgraduate study, teaching or research in social sciences.
Level of Study: Postgraduate, postdoctorate
Type: Fellowship
Value: UK £10,219 per year for predoctoral Fellows, UK £18,601 per year for postdoctoral Fellows, plus accommodation or housing allowance, children's allowance and research expenses
Length of Study: 2 years, extendable for 1 further year provided a doctorate is completed within an appropriate time
Frequency: Annual
Study Establishment: Nuffield College, University of Oxford
Country of Study: United Kingdom
No. of awards offered: 3–6
Closing Date: Beginning of November
No. of awards given last year: 4

For further information contact:

Nuffield College, Oxford, OX1 1NF, United Kingdom
Email: justine.crump@nuf.oxac.uk
Website: www.nuff.ox.ac.uk
Contact: Administrative officer

Oppenheimer Fund
Subjects: All subjects.
Level of Study: Postgraduate
Value: Up to UK £5,000
Length of Study: Duration of the student's course, subject to satisfactory progress
Frequency: Annual
Study Establishment: University of Oxford
Country of Study: United Kingdom
No. of awards offered: Small number of partial awards
Application Procedure: Applicants must apply for admission to the University. Forms are available from the website www.admin.ox.ac.uk/gsp
Closing Date: See the website www.admin.ox.ac.uk/io
Funding: Private

ORISHA (Oxford Research in the Scholarship and Humanities of Africa) Studentships
Subjects: Social and cultural anthropology, archaeology, Egyptology, history, human geography, African literature, politics and international relations and sociology, subject to appropriate supervision being available.
Purpose: To support postgraduate study of Africa in the humanities.
Eligibility: Open to candidates for admission, or those already registered as graduate students. The successful applicant, if not already a member of an Oxford College, may be offered a place at St Antony's College or St Cross College.
Level of Study: Postgraduate
Type: Studentship
Value: University fees plus maintenance allowance. University fees will normally be covered at the home rate, although in exceptional circumstances supplemental grants may be made in order to meet, or to go some way towards meeting, the difference between the home and overseas fee
Length of Study: 2 years with the possibility of extension for 3 and occasionally 4 years
Frequency: Annual
Study Establishment: University of Oxford
Country of Study: United Kingdom
No. of awards offered: 1
Application Procedure: Applicants must write to the Secretary of the Interfaculty Committee for African Studies c/o St Antony's college for further details.
Closing Date: See the website www.admin.ox.ac.uk/gps

OSI (Open Society Institute)/FCO Chevening Scholarships
Subjects: Humanities, social sciences, environmental sciences.
Purpose: To assist candidates studying for a Master's degree in the relevant subjects or conducting research for 9 months as a visiting student.
Eligibility: Open to citizens of Central and Eastern Europe namely Albania, Armenia Belarus, Bosnia, Bulgaria, Croatia, Georgia, Kazakhstan, Hyrgyzstan, Macedonia, Moldova, Romania, Russia, Serbia and Montenegro, the Ukraine, Uzbekistan.
Level of Study: Research, postgraduate
Type: Scholarship
Value: University and college fees, basic maintenance costs, travel to and from Oxford
Length of Study: 1 year
Frequency: Annual
Study Establishment: University of Oxford
Country of Study: United Kingdom
No. of awards offered: Up to 40
Application Procedure: For a research attachment as a visiting student, applicants must submit a single application which will serve

for both the scholarship and for entry to the university. These application forms and further details are available from the OSI/SOROS Foundation office in the applicant's country of residence or from the website www.soros.org For study for a 1-year Master's degree, candidates must also apply for admission to the university at www.admin.ox.ac.uk/gsp
Closing Date: See the website www.admin.ox.ac.uk/io
Funding: Private, government
Contributor: The OSI and the Foreign and Commonwealth Institute
No. of awards given last year: 39
No. of applicants last year: 475
Additional Information: Students will be selected both on the basis of academic excellence and the potential to become leaders, decisionmakers and opinion formers in their own country.

Overseas Research Student (ORS) Awards Scheme

Subjects: All subjects.
Eligibility: Some limitations on type of degree apply; competition is severe.
Level of Study: Graduate, doctorate, postgraduate
Value: Equivalent to the difference between home and overseas fees
Length of Study: Renewable for as long as a student is liable for university fees
Study Establishment: University of Oxford
Country of Study: United Kingdom
No. of awards offered: Varies
Application Procedure: Further details can be found at the website www.admin.ox.ac.uk/io
Closing Date: January
Funding: Government
Contributor: The British Government
Additional Information: For further information please see the website.

For further information contact:

International Office, University Offices, Wellington Square, Oxford, Oxfordshire, OX1 2JD, England

Oxford Kobe Scholarships (Japan)

Subjects: All subjects.
Eligibility: Open to citizens of Japan taking up places to study for a graduate degree.
Level of Study: Postgraduate, graduate
Type: Scholarship
Value: University and college fees plus a maintenance allowance and the cost of travel to and from Japan at the start and end of the course
Length of Study: 1 year, with a possibility of renewal for a further 2 years
Frequency: Annual
Study Establishment: University of Oxford with one scholarship normally tenable at St Catherine's College
Country of Study: United Kingdom
No. of awards offered: 2
Application Procedure: Applicants must complete the application form obtainable from the International Office and should visit www.admin.ox.ac.uk/io for further information.
Closing Date: December 30th
Additional Information: Applicants must apply separately for admission to the University at www.admin.ox.ac.uk/gsp

For further information contact:

International Office, University Offices, Wellington Square, Oxford, Oxfordshire, OX1 2JD, England

Oxford University Theological Scholarships (Eastern and Central Europe)

Subjects: Theology.
Purpose: To enable students to pursue further studies in the University's Faculty of Theology.
Eligibility: Open to candidates aged 22–40, who already have, or expect to obtain, a theological degree from a recognized university or theological college. Applications are invited from citizens of Russia, the Ukraine and any other countries of the former Soviet Union (apart from the Baltic States), Slovakia, Slovenia, Croatia, Bosnia, Macedonia, Bulgaria, Albania and Yugoslavia.
Level of Study: Graduate
Type: Scholarship
Value: Fees, a maintenance allowance and, where necessary, a return airfare
Length of Study: Up to 1 year
Study Establishment: The Faculty of Theology, University of Oxford
Country of Study: United Kingdom
No. of awards offered: Up to 4
Application Procedure: Applicants must contact Mrs Elizabeth Macallister for further information.
Closing Date: December 31st
Funding: Government, private
Contributor: Member churches of the Council of Churches for Britain and Ireland, the Foreign and Commonwealth Office and Oxford University
Additional Information: Scholarships are open to members of any Christian denomination.

For further information contact:

Humanities and Social Division, University of Oxford, 34 St Giles, Oxford, Oxfordshire, OX1 3LH, England
Email: elizaeth.macallister@admin.ox.ac.uk
Contact: Mrs Elizaeth Macallister

Pirie-Reid Scholarships

Subjects: All subjects.
Purpose: To enable persons who would otherwise be prevented by lack of funds to begin a course of study at Oxford.
Eligibility: Preference will be given to candidate's who have lived in or been educated in Scotland, who are applying from other universities (ie not already studying at Oxford.
Level of Study: Doctorate, postgraduate
Type: Scholarship
Value: University and college fees normally at the home rate plus maintenance grant, subject to assessment of income from other sources
Length of Study: Renewable from year to year, subject to satisfactory progress and continuance of approved full-time study
Frequency: Annual
Study Establishment: University of Oxford
Country of Study: United Kingdom
No. of awards offered: Varies
Application Procedure: Candidates must apply for admission to the University through the Graduate Admissions Office (www.admin.ox.ac.uk/gsp). Scholarship application forms are available at www.admin.ox.ac.uk/io
Closing Date: May 1st
Funding: Private
No. of awards given last year: 1
No. of applicants last year: 70
Additional Information: Preference will be given to candidates domiciled or educated in Scotland. Candidates not fulfilling these criteria are unlikely to be successful.

For further information contact:

Student Funding and International Office, University Offices, Wellington Square, Oxford, OX1 2JD, England
Email: international.office@admin.ox.ac.uk

Prendergast Bequest

Subjects: All subjects.
Eligibility: Open to applicants born in the Republic of Ireland whose parents are also citizens of the Republic of Ireland. Applicants must already be at the University of Oxford, or have received a firm offer of both a faculty and college place for a 1-year taught Master's course.
Level of Study: Graduate, postgraduate, doctorate, undergraduate
Type: Grant
Value: Varies, approx. UK £250–2,000 and is means-tested
Length of Study: 1 year
Study Establishment: University of Oxford

Country of Study: United Kingdom
No. of awards offered: Varies
Application Procedure: Applicants must complete an application form. Further information and application forms are available from www.admin.ox.ac.uk/io
Closing Date: August
Funding: Trusts
No. of awards given last year: 13
No. of applicants last year: 18

For further information contact:

Prendergast Bequest, University Offices, Wellington Square, Oxford, Oxfordshire, OX1 2JD, England
Contact: Secretary to the Board of Management

Queen's College Holwell Studentship

Subjects: Religion and theology.
Eligibility: Open to home and overseas students.
Level of Study: Postgraduate
Type: Studentship
Value: UK £2,000 per year
Length of Study: 2 years, renewable for a 3rd year
Frequency: Annual
Study Establishment: The Queen's College, University of Oxford
Country of Study: United Kingdom
No. of awards offered: 1
Funding: Private

For further information contact:

41 St Giles, Oxford, Oxfordshire, OX1 3LW, England
Contact: Faculty of Theology

Queen's College Cyril and Phyllis Long Studentship

Subjects: All subjects.
Eligibility: Overseas students only.
Level of Study: Postgraduate
Type: Studentship
Value: Equivalent of a Research Council maintenance grant
Length of Study: 3 years
Frequency: Annual
Study Establishment: The Queen's College, University of Oxford
Country of Study: United Kingdom
No. of awards offered: 1
Application Procedure: Award associated with a Clarendon Fund Award. Applications will be considered as part of the Clarendon Award process.
Funding: Private

For further information contact:

International Office, University Offices, Wellington Square, Oxford, OX1 2JD, England

Queen's College Florey EPA Scholarship

Subjects: Medical, biological and chemical sciences.
Eligibility: Open to nationals of European Union countries (excluding the United Kingdom and Ireland) Finland, Norway and Sweden.
Level of Study: Postgraduate
Type: Scholarship
Value: UK £2,000 per year. Assistance may also be given with fees to a maximum of half the cost
Length of Study: 1 year, renewable for a 2nd and 3rd year
Frequency: Annual
Study Establishment: The Queen's College, University of Oxford
Country of Study: United Kingdom
No. of awards offered: 1
Application Procedure: Applicants must contact the Tutor for Graduates at the Queen's College in the first instance.
Funding: Private

For further information contact:

The Queen's College, Oxford, Oxfordshire, OX1 4AW, England
Contact: Tutor for Graduates

Queen's College George Oakes Senior Scholarship

Subjects: Aspects of the culture of the United States of America.
Eligibility: Open to citizens of the United Kingdom.
Level of Study: Postgraduate
Type: Scholarship
Value: UK £2,000 per year
Length of Study: 1 year, renewable for a 2nd and 3rd year
Frequency: Dependent on funds available
Study Establishment: The Queen's College, University of Oxford
Country of Study: United Kingdom
No. of awards offered: 1
Application Procedure: Applicants must contact the Tutor for Graduates at the Queen's College in the first instance.
Funding: Trusts

For further information contact:

The Queen's College, Oxford, Oxfordshire, OX1 4AW, England
Contact: Tutor for Graduates

Queen's College Hastings Senior Scholarship

Subjects: All subjects.
Eligibility: Open to graduates with First Class (Honours) Degrees from the Universities of Bradford, Hull, Leeds, Sheffield or York.
Level of Study: Postgraduate
Type: Scholarship
Value: UK £2,000 per year. Assistance may be given with fees if the holder is not eligible for Research Council or British Academy Studentships
Length of Study: 1 year, renewable for a 2nd and 3rd year
Frequency: Annual
Study Establishment: The Queen's College, University of Oxford
Country of Study: United Kingdom
No. of awards offered: 1
Application Procedure: Applicants must contact the Tutor for Graduates at the Queen's College in the first instance.
Funding: Trusts

For further information contact:

The Queen's College, Oxford, Oxfordshire, OX1 4AW, England
Contact: Tutor for Graduates

Queen's College Wendell Herbruck Studentship

Subjects: All subjects.
Eligibility: Open to residents of the United States of America who are not older than 26 when appointed. Preference will be given to residents of Ohio.
Level of Study: Postgraduate
Type: Studentship
Value: UK £2,000 per year
Length of Study: 1 year, renewable for a 2nd and 3rd year
Study Establishment: The Queen's College, University of Oxford
Country of Study: United Kingdom
No. of awards offered: Varies
Application Procedure: Applicants must contact the Tutor for Graduates at the Queen's College in the first instance.
Funding: Private

For further information contact:

The Queen's College, Oxford, Oxfordshire, OX1 4AW, England
Contact: Tutor for Graduates

Sasakawa Fund Scholarships

Subjects: All subjects that require some period of study in Japan.
Eligibility: Candidates must be Japanese nationals or students from countries other than Japan whose course at the University of Oxford requires some period of study in Japan.
Level of Study: Postgraduate, graduate, doctorate
Type: Scholarship
Value: Up to UK £5,000
Length of Study: 1 year in the first instance, with the possibility of renewal for a maximum of 3 years, subject to satisfactory progress
Frequency: Annual

Study Establishment: University of Oxford
Country of Study: United Kingdom
No. of awards offered: Up to 2
Application Procedure: Applicants must complete the relevant section of the graduate admission form available at www.admin.ox.ac.uk/gsp Applicants from the United Kingdom should contact the Secretary of the Sasakawa Fund.
Closing Date: March 1st
Additional Information: Applicants must either have been accepted by the University of Oxford to undertake a research degree as a probationer research or DPhil student, or be currently undertaking such a course.

For further information contact:

The Sasakawa Fund, The Oriental Institute, Pusey Lane, Oxford, Oxfordshire, OX1 2LE, England
Tel: (44) 18 6527 8225
Fax: (44) 18 6527 8190
Contact: Secretary

Scatcherd European Scholarships

Subjects: All subjects.
Eligibility: Open to nationals of any European country, excluding the United Kingdom and Turkey and including the Russian Federation and countries to the West of the Urals. Applicants must be taking up places to read either for a postgraduate degree, a 2nd Bachelor of Arts degree or to spend a period of study as a visiting graduate student at the University of Oxford.
Level of Study: Doctorate, graduate, postgraduate
Type: Scholarship
Value: University and college fees plus maintenance grant
Study Establishment: University of Oxford
Country of Study: United Kingdom
No. of awards offered: Varies
Application Procedure: Applicants must complete the application form for admission to the university available at the website www.admin.ox.ac.uk/gsp
Closing Date: See the website www.admin.ox.ac.uk/io
Funding: Trusts
No. of awards given last year: 4
No. of applicants last year: 778

Shell Centenary Scholarships and Shell Centenary Chevening Scholarships

Subjects: Applied statistics, biodiversity, conservation and management, computer science, mathematics and foundations of computer science, environmental change and management, environmental geomorphology, economics for development, industrial relations and human resources management, public policy in Latin America, forced migration, criminology and criminal justice.
Purpose: To assist with Master's degrees.
Eligibility: Open to students from countries that are not current or applicant members of the Organisation for Economic Co-operation and Development (OECD) or from the Czech Republic, Hungary, Mexico, Poland, Slovakia or Turkey. Candidates should normally be aged between 20 and 35 years of age and be intending to return to the home country at the end of the period of study. They should normally already hold a degree of an equivalent standard to a United Kingdom First Class (Honours) Degree or be expecting to obtain such a degree before the start of their proposed course.
Level of Study: Postgraduate, graduate
Value: University and college fees, maintenance and return air travel to the United Kingdom
Frequency: Annual
Study Establishment: University of Oxford
Country of Study: United Kingdom
No. of awards offered: Up to 9
Application Procedure: Applicants must apply separately for admission to Oxford through the Graduate Admissions Office by mid-January. Forms are available at the website admin.ox.ac.uk.gsp Scholarship applications are available from the International Office. For further details see the website www.admin.ox.ac.uk/io
Closing Date: March 1st
Funding: Commercial, international office, government

For further information contact:

International Office, University Offices, Wellington Square, Oxford, Oxfordshire, OX1 2JD, England

Sir John Rhys Studentship in Celtic Studies

Subjects: Celtic studies.
Purpose: To enable the successful candidate to complete a research programme on which he or she is already engaged.
Eligibility: Open to candidates engaged in graduate research in Celtic studies who need financial support in respect of living expenses or fees. The award is not intended for those who hold full-time university posts.
Level of Study: Postgraduate
Type: Studentship
Value: Normally similar to that of a graduate studentship from a United Kingdom research council. The amount is dependent on the applicant's circumstances
Length of Study: 1 year, renewable only in exceptional circumstances
Frequency: Annual
Study Establishment: University of Oxford, normally Jesus College
Country of Study: United Kingdom
No. of awards offered: 1
Application Procedure: Applicants must send applications to the Secretary of the Taylor Institution and should include a curriculum vitae, a brief outline of the research proposed, an indication of the size of grant required, ie. any necessary expenses in addition to the normal living costs of a graduate student and of other sources of financial support, brief details of any other awards or appointments for which the candidate is applying, the names of two academic referees and the candidate's address for the Easter period if different from the term time address. Applicants who are not already members of the university should apply for admission through the Graduate Admissions Office.
Closing Date: March 1st
Funding: Private
Contributor: The Sir John Rhys Fund
Additional Information: The successful applicant, if not already a member of the University of Oxford, would normally become a member of Jesus College and would be expected to reside in Oxford for the greater part of the academic year.

For further information contact:

41 Wellington Square, Oxford, Oxfordshire, OX1 2JF, England
Email: enquiries@modern-languages.ox.ac.uk
Contact: Secretary of the Taylor Institution

St Antony's College EFG Bank Group Scholarship

Subjects: All subjects in which the College specializes.
Eligibility: Open to graduate students of Greek nationality who are reading for a higher degree.
Level of Study: Graduate
Type: Scholarship
Value: Fees, maintenance and travel costs
Length of Study: 2 years
Frequency: Annual
Study Establishment: St Antony's College, University of Oxford
Country of Study: United Kingdom
Application Procedure: Applicants must contact the College Secretary.
Funding: Private

For further information contact:

St Anthony's College, Oxford, Oxfordshire, OX2 6JF, England
Contact: College Secretary

St Antony's College Ismene Fitch Scholarship

Subjects: Humanities.
Eligibility: Open to graduate students of Greek nationality reading for a doctorate in the humanities.

Level of Study: Doctorate
Type: Scholarship
Value: Fees and maintenance
Length of Study: 3 years
Frequency: Every 6 years
Study Establishment: St Antony's College and Wolfson College, University of Oxford
Country of Study: United Kingdom
Additional Information: comment this scholarship is rotated between St. Antony's, Wolfson the next scholar will be offered a place at Wolfson. Current scholar is put to complete in 2007.

For further information contact:

St Anthony's College, Oxford, Oxfordshire, OX2 6JF, England
Contact: College Secretary

St Antony's College Ronaldo Falconer Scholarship

Subjects: All subjects in which the college specializes 1-3 years depending on the course open to graduate students who have already undertaken higher education in Costa Rica.
Eligibility: Open to graduate students from Costa Rica studying for a higher degree.
Level of Study: Graduate
Type: Scholarship
Value: Fees, maintenance and some travel costs
Length of Study: 1–3 years depending on the course
Frequency: Annual
Study Establishment: St Antony's College, University of Oxford
Country of Study: United Kingdom
Application Procedure: Applicants must write for details.
Closing Date: Please write for details
Funding: Private

For further information contact:

Latin American Centre, St Antony's College, Oxford, OX2 6UF, England
Email: enquiries@lac.ox.ac.uk
Contact: Dr Ronaldo Cerdas, The Director

St Antony's College Sir John Swire Scholarship

Subjects: All subjects in which the college specializes.
Eligibility: Open to graduate students from North East and South East Asia studying for a higher degree.
Level of Study: Graduate, new scholarship offers when current scholars completes
Type: Scholarship
Value: Fees, maintenance and some travel costs
Length of Study: 2 years, with a possibility of renewal for a further year
Study Establishment: St Antony's College, University of Oxford
Country of Study: United Kingdom
No. of awards offered: 1
Application Procedure: Applicants must write for details.
Funding: Commercial

For further information contact:

St Antony's College, Oxford, Oxfordshire, OX2 6JF, England
Contact: College Secretary

St Antony's College Swire Centenary and Cathay Pacific Scholarship (Japan)

Subjects: All subjects in which the college specializes.
Eligibility: Open to students from Japan studying for a higher degree.
Level of Study: Graduate
Type: Scholarship
Value: Fees, maintenance and some travel costs
Length of Study: 2 years, with a possibility of renewal for a further year
Frequency: Annual
Study Establishment: St Antony's College, University of Oxford
Country of Study: United Kingdom
Application Procedure: Applicants must write for details.
Closing Date: Please write for details
Funding: Commercial

For further information contact:

Cathway Pacific Airways Limited, 7/8/F Ginza Namikidori Building, 3-6, Ginza 2-chome, Chuo-ku, Tokyo, 104-0061, Japan

St Antony's College Swire/Cathay Pacific Scholarship (Hong Kong)

Subjects: All subjects in which the college specializes.
Eligibility: Open to permanent residents of Hong Kong who have completed the majority of their education there.
Level of Study: Graduate
Type: Scholarship
Value: Fees, maintenance and some travel costs
Length of Study: 2 years, with a possibility of renewal for a further year
Frequency: Annual
Study Establishment: St Antony's College, University of Oxford
Country of Study: United Kingdom
Application Procedure: Applicants must write for details.
Closing Date: Please write for details
Funding: Commercial

For further information contact:

John Swire & Sons (HK) Limited, 35/F Two Pacific Place, 88 Queensway, Hong Kong
Contact: Assistant Manager, Group Public Affairs

St Antony's College Swire/Cathay Pacific Scholarship (Republic of Korea)

Subjects: All subjects in which the college specializes.
Eligibility: Open to graduate students from the Republic of Korea studying for a higher degree.
Level of Study: Graduate
Type: Scholarship
Value: Fees, maintenance and some travel costs
Length of Study: 2 years, with a possibility of renewal for a further year
Frequency: Annual
Study Establishment: St Antony's College, University of Oxford
Country of Study: United Kingdom
Application Procedure: Applicants must write for details.
Closing Date: Please write for details
Funding: Commercial

For further information contact:

Personnel & Administration Department, Cathay Pacific Airways Limited, J P Morgan Plaza Building, 34-35 Jung-dong, Choong-ku, Seoul, 100-120, Korea

St Antony's College Swire/Chevening Scholarship (Hong Kong)

Subjects: All subjects in which the college specializes.
Eligibility: Open to graduate students who are permanent residents of Hong Kong and who have completed the majority of their education there.
Level of Study: Graduate
Type: Scholarship
Value: Fees, maintenance and some travel costs
Length of Study: 2 years, with a possibility of renewal for a further year
Frequency: Annual
Study Establishment: St Antony's College, University of Oxford
Country of Study: United Kingdom
Application Procedure: Applicants must write for details.
Closing Date: Please write for details
Funding: Commercial

For further information contact:

John Swire & Sons (HK) Limited, 35/F Two Pacific Place, 88 Queensway, Hong Kong
Contact: Assistant Manager, Group Public Affairs

St Antony's College Wai Seng Senior Research Scholarship

Subjects: Subjects concerning the Asia Pacific region.
Level of Study: Doctorate
Type: Scholarship
Value: Fees and maintenance
Length of Study: 2 years
Frequency: Every 2 years
Study Establishment: St Antony's College, University of Oxford
Country of Study: United Kingdom
No. of awards offered: 1

For further information contact:

Asian Studies Centre, St Antony's College, University of Oxford, Oxford, Oxfordshire, OX2 6JF, England
Email: asian@sant.ox.ac.uk
Contact: The Director

St Catherine's College Glaxo Scholarship

Subjects: Medicine.
Purpose: To assist graduates who are, or will be registered for the Oxford University 2nd BM or the accelerated graduate entry medicine course.
Eligibility: Open to graduates who have a confirmed place in the Oxford University 2nd BM or the accelerated graduate entry medicine course.
Level of Study: Graduate
Type: Scholarship
Value: UK £1,500 per year
Length of Study: Up to 2 years
Frequency: Annual
Study Establishment: St Catherine's College, University of Oxford
Country of Study: United Kingdom
No. of awards offered: 1
Application Procedure: Applicants must remember to specify which scholarship(s) they are applying for. In addition, candidates should arrange for two people acquainted with their recent academic work to send a confidential report directly to the Academic Registrar before the closing date. There is no application form for this scholarship. Applicants should send a curriculum vitae with a covering letter including a research outline (where appropriate) and statement of other means of financial support to the Academic Registrar at the address given below.
Closing Date: February 16th
No. of awards given last year: 1
No. of applicants last year: 12

For further information contact:

St Catherine's College, Oxford, Oxfordshire, OX1 3UJ, England
Email: academic.registrar@stxatz.ox.ac.uk
Contact: Academic Registrar

St Catherine's College Graduate Scholarship in the Arts

Subjects: Arts.
Purpose: To assist graduates who are, or will be reading for an Oxford University DPhil, MLitt, or MSc by research degree.
Eligibility: Open to new graduates commencing graduate study at Oxford and to current graduate students who will have completed no more than 2 years of graduate study.
Level of Study: Postgraduate, graduate
Type: Scholarship
Value: UK £2,000 per year
Length of Study: Up to 3 years while the recipient is liable to pay university and college fees
Frequency: Annual
Study Establishment: St Catherine's College, University of Oxford
Country of Study: United Kingdom
No. of awards offered: 1
Application Procedure: Applicants must remember to specify which scholarship(s) they are applying for. In addition, candidates should arrange for 2 people acquainted with their recent academic work to send a confidential report directly to the Academic Register before the closing date. There is no application for this scholarship. Applicants should send a curriculum vitae with a covering letter including a research outline (where appropriate) and statement of other means of financial support to the Academic Registrar.
Closing Date: March 11th
No. of awards given last year: 2
No. of applicants last year: 25

For further information contact:

St Catherine's College, Oxford, Oxfordshire, OX1 3UJ, England
Email: academic.registrar@stcatz.ox.ac.uk
Contact: Academic Registrar

St Catherine's College Graduate Scholarship in the Sciences

Subjects: Mathematical and physical sciences, medical sciences, biochemistry, plant sciences and zoology.
Purpose: To assist students who are, or will be reading for an Oxford University DPhil, MLitt, or MSc by research degree.
Eligibility: Open to new graduate students commencing graduate study at Oxford and to current graduate students who will have completed no more than 2 years of graduate study at Oxford.
Level of Study: Graduate, postgraduate
Type: Scholarship
Value: UK £2,000 per year
Length of Study: Up to 3 years while the recipient is liable to pay university and college fees
Frequency: Annual
Study Establishment: St Catherine's College, University of Oxford
Country of Study: United Kingdom
No. of awards offered: 1
Application Procedure: Applicants must remember to specify which scholarship(s) they are applying for. In addition, candidates should arrange for 2 people acquainted with their recent academic work to send a confidential report directly to the Academic Registrar before the closing date. There is no application form for this scholarship. Applicants should send a curriculum vitae with a covering letter including a research outline (where appropriate) and statement of other means of financial support to the Academic Registrar.
Closing Date: March 11th
No. of awards given last year: 1
No. of applicants last year: 29

For further information contact:

St Catherine's College, Oxford, Oxfordshire, OX1 3UJ, England
Email: academic.registrar@stcatz.ox.ac.uk
Contact: Academic Registrar

St Catherine's College Great Eastern Scholarship

Subjects: All subjects.
Purpose: To assist students who are, or will be reading for an Oxford University DPhill, MLitt, or MSc by research degree.
Eligibility: Open to new graduate students commencing graduate study at Oxford and to current graduate students who will have completed no more than 2 years of graduate study at Oxford, and restricted to Indian nationals.
Level of Study: Graduate
Type: Scholarship
Value: UK £2,000 per year
Length of Study: Up to 3 years whilst the recipient is liable to pay university and college fees
Frequency: Dependent on funds available
Study Establishment: St Catherine's College, University of Oxford
Country of Study: United Kingdom
No. of awards offered: 1
Application Procedure: Applicants must remember to specify which scholarship(s) they are applying for. In addition, candidates should arrange for 2 people acquainted with their recent academic work to

send a confidential report directly to the Academic Registrar before the closing date. There is no application form for this scholarship. Applicants should send a curriculum vitae with a covering letter including a research outline (where appropriate) and statement of other means of financial support to the Academic Registrar.
Closing Date: March 12th
No. of awards given last year: 1
No. of applicants last year: 3

For further information contact:

St Catherine's College, Oxford, Oxfordshire, OX1 3UJ, England
Email: academic.registrar@stcatz.ox.ac.uk
Contact: Academic Registrar

St Catherine's College Leathersellers' Company Graduate Scholarship

Subjects: Biochemistry, chemistry, computing, Earth sciences, engineering science, materials science, mathematics, physics, statistics and zoology.
Purpose: To assist students who are, or will be reading for an Oxford University DPhil, MLitt, or MSc by research degree.
Eligibility: Open to new graduate students commencing graduate study at Oxford and to current graduate students who will have completed no more than 2 years of graduate study at Oxford, and restricted to graduates of European (including United Kingdom) universities.
Level of Study: Graduate
Type: Scholarship
Value: UK £2,500 per year
Length of Study: Up to 3 years while the recipient is liable to pay university and college fees
Frequency: Annual
Study Establishment: St Catherine's College, University of Oxford
Country of Study: United Kingdom
No. of awards offered: 1
Application Procedure: Applicants must remember to specify which scholarship(s) they are applying for. In addition, candidates should arrange for 2 people acquainted with their recent academic work to send a confidential report directly to the Academic Registrar before the closing date. There is no application form for this scholarship. Applicants should send a curriculum vitae with a covering letter including a research outline (where appropriate) and statement of the other means of financial support to the Academic Registrar.
Closing Date: May 5th, March 10th, March 11th
No. of awards given last year: 1
No. of applicants last year: 18

For further information contact:

St Catherine's College, Manor Road, Oxford, Oxfordshire, OX1 3UJ, England
Email: academic.registrar@stcatz.ox.ac.uk
Contact: Academic Registrar

St Catherine's College Overseas Graduate Scholarship

Subjects: All subjects.
Purpose: To assist students who are, or will be reading for an Oxford University DPhil, MLitt, or MSc by research degree.
Eligibility: Open to new graduate students commencing graduate study at Oxford and to current graduate students who will have completed no more than 2 years of graduate study at Oxford, and restricted to students from outside the European Union.
Level of Study: Graduate, postgraduate
Type: Scholarship
Value: UK £1,800 per year
Length of Study: Up to 3 years while the recipient is liable to pay university and college fees
Frequency: Annual
Study Establishment: St Catherine's College, University of Oxford
Country of Study: United Kingdom
No. of awards offered: 1
Application Procedure: Applicants must remember to specify which scholarship(s) they are applying for. In addition, candidates should arrange for 2 people acquainted with their recent academic work to send a confidential report directly to the Academic Registrar before the closing date. There is no application form for this scholarship. Applicants should send a curriculum vitae with a covering letter including a research outline (where appropriate) and statement of other means of financial support to the Academic Registrar.
Closing Date: March 10th, March 11th
No. of awards given last year: 1
No. of applicants last year: 21

For further information contact:

St Catherine's College, Oxford, Oxfordshire, OX1 3UJ, England
Email: academic.registrar@stcatz.ox.ac.uk
Contact: Academic Registrar

St Peter's College Bodossaki Foundation Graduate Scholarship in Science

Subjects: Any field of science including mathematics, engineering and medicine (with preference for immunology, oncology and cardiovascular diseases).
Eligibility: Open to Greek or Cypriot citizens under the age of 30 (35 for candidates in medicine).
Level of Study: Postgraduate, research
Type: Scholarship
Value: Up to UK £12,500 per year
Length of Study: Up to 3 years
Frequency: Annual
Study Establishment: St Peter's College, the University of Oxford
Country of Study: United Kingdom
No. of awards offered: 1 (but may be divided between 2 candidates)
Application Procedure: Applicants must contact the Tutor for Graduates at St Peter's College in the first instance.
Closing Date: Currently February 28th, but subject to change in future years
Funding: Foundation
Contributor: The Bodossaki Foundation
No. of awards given last year: 1

For further information contact:

St Peter's College, Oxford, Oxfordshire, OX1 2DL, England

St Peter's College Leonard J Theberge Memorial Scholarship

Subjects: All subjects.
Eligibility: Open to students admitted to the College only. Candidates must be citizens of the United States of America and preference will be given to mature students over 30 or those who have been employed for 5 years.
Level of Study: Postgraduate
Type: Scholarship
Value: A modest contribution to maintenance and personal expenses
Length of Study: 1–2 years
Frequency: Annual
Study Establishment: St Peter's College, University of Oxford
Country of Study: United Kingdom
No. of awards offered: 1
Application Procedure: Applicants must contact the Tutor for Graduates in the first instance.
Closing Date: Normally August 15th
Funding: Foundation

For further information contact:

St Peter's College, Oxford, Oxfordshire, OX1 2DL, England
Contact: Tutor for Graduates

Trinity College Birkett Scholarship in Environmental Studies

Subjects: Environmental change and management.
Purpose: To promote graduate education in the environment.
Eligibility: Open to any graduate accepted for the MSc in environmental change and management.
Level of Study: Postgraduate
Type: Scholarship

Value: UK £2,400 p.a.
Length of Study: 1 year
Frequency: Annual
Study Establishment: Trinity College, University of Oxford
Country of Study: United Kingdom
No. of awards offered: 2
Application Procedure: Indicate wish to be considered for the scholarship on the university application form.

Trinity College Cecil Lubbock Memorial Scholarship

Subjects: Philosophy.
Purpose: To promote research in philosophy.
Eligibility: Open to any home graduates accepted for a research degree in Philosophy.
Level of Study: Doctorate, postgraduate
Type: Scholarship
Value: UK £10,000 p.a.
Length of Study: 1–4 years, depending on the course
Frequency: Dependent on funds available
Study Establishment: Trinity college, University of Oxford
Country of Study: United Kingdom
No. of awards offered: 1
Application Procedure: Indicate wish to be considered for the scholarship on the university application form.

Trinity College Grabowski Postgraduate Scholarship in Polish Studies

Subjects: Polish studies-language and literature or history.
Purpose: To promote graduate studies in Polish.
Eligibility: Open to any graduate accepted for a degree involving polish studies.
Level of Study: Doctorate, postgraduate
Type: Scholarship
Value: UK £6,000 p.a.
Length of Study: 1–4 years depending on the course
Frequency: Dependent on funds available
Study Establishment: Trinity college, University of Oxford
Country of Study: United Kingdom
No. of awards offered: 1
Application Procedure: Indicate wish to be considered for the scholarship on the university application form.

Trinity College Junior Research Fellowship

Subjects: Biological sciences, history, geography, theology, law, philosophy, economics, politics, physical sciences, English, classics, modern languages, mathematics.
Purpose: To promote and encourage research among those at the start of an academic career.
Eligibility: Open to suitably qualified candidates having some research experience (eg. a completed doctoral thesis).
Level of Study: MBA, postdoctorate, doctorate
Value: Approx. UK £20,000 p.a.
Length of Study: 3 years, non renewable
Frequency: Annual
Study Establishment: Trinity College, University of Oxford
Country of Study: United Kingdom
No. of awards offered: 1
Application Procedure: Please see application form on Trinity College website www.trinity.ox.ac.uk
Closing Date: Autumn of the year preceding the start of the appointment

For further information contact:

Trinity College, Oxford, Oxfordshire, OX 13BH, England
Contact: Academic Administrator

Wadham College Brookman Organ Scholarship

Subjects: All subjects.
Eligibility: Candidates must be graduates or undergraduates or at Wadham College at the period of the post.
Level of Study: Postgraduate
Type: Scholarship
Value: UK £1,850–2,500 plus benefits
Length of Study: 1 year
Study Establishment: Wadham College, University of Oxford
Country of Study: United Kingdom
No. of awards offered: 1
Application Procedure: Applicants must apply to The Registrar, Wadham College.
Closing Date: February
Funding: Trusts
No. of awards given last year: 1
Additional Information: The award entails certain chapel and choir duties. See the website www.wadham.ox.ac.uk for further information.

For further information contact:

Wadham College, Oxford, Oxfordshire, OX1 3PN, England
Website: www.wadham.ox.ac.uk
Contact: The Registrar

Wadham College Donner Canadian Foundation Scholarship

Subjects: Law (BCL or MJur courses only).
Eligibility: Canadian citizens reading for the BCL or MJUR at Wadham College Oxford.
Level of Study: Postgraduate
Type: Scholarship
Value: Canadian $35,000
Length of Study: 1 year
Study Establishment: Wadham College, University of Oxford
Country of Study: United Kingdom
No. of awards offered: 1
Application Procedure: Applicants must apply to the Registrar at Wadham College.
Closing Date: January 31st
Funding: Private
Contributor: Donner Canadian Foundation, Allen E Gotlieb
No. of awards given last year: 1
Additional Information: For further information see the website www.wadham.ox.ac.uk

For further information contact:

Wadham College, University of Oxford, Oxford, Oxfordshire, OX1 3PN, England
Website: www.wadham.ox.ac.uk
Contact: The Registrar

Wadham College Norwegian Scholarship

Subjects: All subjects.
Eligibility: Open to registered students or graduates of Oslo University, who are Norwegian citizens.
Level of Study: Postgraduate
Type: Scholarship
Value: Fees and maintenance
Length of Study: 1 year
Frequency: Annual
Study Establishment: Wadham College, University of Oxford
Country of Study: United Kingdom
Application Procedure: Applicants must submit applications in August of each year to the committee for the Norsk Oxford-Stipendium ved Wadham College at the University of Oslo.
Closing Date: August

For further information contact:

Website: www.wadham.ox.ac.uk

Wadham College Philip Wright Scholarship

Subjects: All subject.
Eligibility: Recipient must be an ex-student of the Manchester Grammar school, Manchester, United Kingdom. And must be accepted by the university of Oxford and by Wadham college for graduate study.
Level of Study: Postgraduate
Type: Scholarship

Value: All fees plus UK £8,000
Length of Study: 1 year, renewable for a further two
Frequency: Annual
Study Establishment: Wadham College, University of Oxford
Country of Study: United Kingdom
No. of awards offered: 1
Application Procedure: Applicants must apply to the Registrar, Wadham College.
Closing Date: May
Funding: Trusts
No. of awards given last year: 1

For further information contact:

Website: www.wadham.ox.ac.uk

Wadham College Senior Scholarship

Subjects: All subjects.
Eligibility: Students must be already reading for a higher degree at Wadham College, Oxford, or have been accepted to do so. Senior scholarships and Keeley senior scholarships are unrestricted in subject area. Eprime eshag graduate scholarships are restricted in area.
Level of Study: Postgraduate
Type: Scholarship
Value: UK £500
Length of Study: 1 year
Study Establishment: Wadham College, University of Oxford
Application Procedure: Contact the Registrar, Wadham College for information.
Closing Date: April
No. of awards given last year: 11

For further information contact:

Wadham College, Oxford, Oxfordshire, OX1 3PN, England
Website: www.wadham.ox.ac.uk

Wadham College Stinton Scholarship

Subjects: All subjects.
Eligibility: The scholarship is restricted to students reading for a higher degree at Wadham College, Oxford (or who have been accepted to do so) who do not have fees paid by any other body. The subject area may be restricted (see college website for further details).
Level of Study: Postgraduate
Type: Scholarship
Value: UK £1,875
Length of Study: 1 year
Frequency: Annual
Study Establishment: Wadham College, University of Oxford
Country of Study: United Kingdom
No. of awards offered: 1
Application Procedure: Applicants must apply to the Registrar, Wadham College. For further information see the website www.wadham.ox.ac.uk
Closing Date: July
Funding: Individuals, trusts
Contributor: Stinton Bequest, in memory of Tom and Sylvia Stinton
No. of awards given last year: 1

For further information contact:

Wadham College, Oxford, Oxfordshire, OX1 3PN, England
Website: www.wadham.ox.ac.uk
Contact: The Registrar

Winter William's Studentship in Law

Subjects: Law.
Level of Study: Doctorate, postgraduate
Type: Studentship
Value: UK £7,500
Length of Study: Up to 3 years
Frequency: Annual
Study Establishment: University of Oxford
Country of Study: United Kingdom
No. of awards offered: 2
Application Procedure: Applicants must contact the International Office for an application form and further details.
Closing Date: See the website www.admin.ox.ac.uk/io
Funding: Private

For further information contact:

The International Office, University Offices, Wellington Square, Oxford, Oxfordshire, OX1 2JD, England
Tel: (44) 18 6527 0105
Email: international.office@admin.ox.ac.uk
Website: www.admin.ox.ac.uk/io

UNIVERSITY OF PUNE

Pune-411 007, Maharashtra, India
Tel: (91) 020-5656061
Fax: (91) 020-5653899
Website: www.unipune.ernet.in

The University stands for humanism and tolerance, for reason for adventure of ideas and for the search of truth. It stands for the forward march of the human race towards even higher objectives. If the universities discharge their duties adequately then it is well with the nation and the people – Jawaharlal Nehru

Department of Biotechnology (DBT) - Junior Research Fellowship

Subjects: Biotechnology and applied biology.
Purpose: To support candidates pursuing research in areas of biotechnology and applied biology.
Eligibility: Open to candidates from the centres supported by the DBT, New Delhi.
Level of Study: Research
Type: Fellowship
Value: Rs 8,000 per month; Rs 9,000 for SRF; and a research contingency of Rs 20,000 per year
Length of Study: 5 years
Frequency: Annual
Study Establishment: University of Pune
Country of Study: India
Application Procedure: A written application along with application fee of Rs 500/- in the form of a DD in favour of Registrar, University of Pune' should be sent.
Contributor: Government of India

For further information contact:

Department of Biotechnology University of Pune, Pune, 411 007, India
Contact: Professor J. K. Pal, Co-ordinator, DBJ-JRF Programme

THE UNIVERSITY OF READING

Whiteknights, PO Box 217, Reading, Berkshire, RG6 6AH, England
Tel: (44) 11 8987 5123
Fax: (44) 11 8931 4404
Email: studentships@reading.ac.uk
Website: www.rdg.ac.uk
Contact: Student Financial Support Office

The University of Reading offers postgraduate taught and research degree courses in all the traditional subject areas except medical sciences. Vocational courses are also offered. Research work in many areas is of international renown.

University of Reading Access to Learning Fund

Subjects: All subjects.
Purpose: To enable postgraduate students to continue a chosen course of study.
Eligibility: Open to all postgraduate students enrolled at the university.
Level of Study: Postgraduate
Type: Grant
Value: UK £3,500
Length of Study: 1–3 years

Frequency: Annual
Study Establishment: The University of Reading
Country of Study: United Kingdom
Application Procedure: Contact the students financial support office.
Closing Date: No deadline

University of Reading Career Development Loan

Subjects: All subjects.
Eligibility: Open to all students registered on a vocational learning course.
Level of Study: Postgraduate, professional development
Type: Grant
Value: UK £200–8,000
Length of Study: 1–2 years
Frequency: Annual
Study Establishment: The University of Reading
Country of Study: United Kingdom
Application Procedure: Contact the student financial support office.
Closing Date: No deadline

University of Reading Dorothy Hodgkin Postgraduate Award

Subjects: Science, engineering, medicine, social science and technology.
Eligibility: Open to nationals of either India, Mainland China, Hong Kong, Russia or a country in the developing world only.
Level of Study: Postgraduate
Type: Scholarship
Value: All tuition fees and a grant for living costs
Length of Study: 1–3 years
Frequency: Annual
Study Establishment: University of Reading
Country of Study: United Kingdom
No. of awards offered: Varies
Application Procedure: Contact the Jonathan Lloyd at the faculties of science and life science.
Closing Date: May 6th

For further information contact:

Tel: (0) 1 18 378 8341
Email: j.d.lloyd@reading.ac.uk

University of Reading Felix Scholarship

Subjects: All subjects.
Eligibility: Open to international postgraduate taught and research students who have Indian citizenship, under 30 years of age holding at least a first class honours degree and who have not studied outside India.
Level of Study: Postgraduate
Type: Scholarship
Value: All tuition fees, UK £10,248 and generous allowances for clothes, books, and a return flight home
Length of Study: 1–3 years
Frequency: Annual
Study Establishment: University of Reading
Country of Study: United Kingdom
No. of awards offered: 1
Application Procedure: Contact Richard Brown at the Student Financial Support Office.
Closing Date: March 1st

For further information contact:

Tel: (0) 118 378 7430

University of Reading General Overseas Scholarships

Subjects: All subjects, subject to the availability of appropriate supervision at the University.
Purpose: To enable students to obtain a postdoctoral degree.
Eligibility: Open to applicants from Mainland China only.
Level of Study: Postgraduate, doctorate
Type: Studentship
Value: Full tuition fees and maintenance at a rate related to that offered by the relevant United Kingdom Funding Council
Length of Study: Up to 3 years
Frequency: Annual
Study Establishment: The University of Reading
Country of Study: United Kingdom
No. of awards offered: 5
Application Procedure: Applicants must fulfil the eligibility criteria and express an interest in the scholarships to be considered.
Closing Date: Please contact the University
Funding: Private
Contributor: University of Reading
No. of awards given last year: 3
No. of applicants last year: 135

University of Reading MSc Intelligent Buildings Scholarship

Subjects: Construction management and engineering.
Eligibility: In order to be considered for this Scholarship you must hold the offer of a place on the MSc Intellegent Buildings course.
Level of Study: Postgraduate
Type: Scholarship
Value: UK £2,000
Length of Study: 1 year
Frequency: Annual
Study Establishment: University of Reading
Country of Study: United Kingdom
No. of awards offered: 1
Application Procedure: Contact Gulay Ozkan, Programme Coordinator at the School of Construction Management and Engineering.
Closing Date: June 16th

For further information contact:

Tel: (0) 118 378 6254
Email: g.ozkan@rdg.ac.uk

University of Reading Music Scholarship

Subjects: Music.
Purpose: To support excellence in music.
Eligibility: In order to be considered for this scholarship you must already hold an offer of a place at the university.
Level of Study: Postgraduate
Type: Scholarship
Value: All tuition fees
Length of Study: 1 year
Frequency: Annual
Study Establishment: University of Reading
Country of Study: United Kingdom
No. of awards offered: 1
Application Procedure: Apply online.
Closing Date: March 1st
Additional Information: Students must be available for audition on March 21st.

For further information contact:

Email: music@rdg.ac.uk

University of Reading Postgraduate Mercia Prize

Subjects: Medical engineering.
Eligibility: In order to be considered for this bursary you must hold a place at the university of reading.
Level of Study: Postgraduate
Type: Grant
Value: UK £500
Length of Study: 1 year
Frequency: Annual
Study Establishment: University of Reading
Country of Study: United Kingdom
No. of awards offered: 1
Application Procedure: Contact the student financial support office.

Closing Date: January 31st
Additional Information: To apply for this bursary you need to be nominated by your department to the worshipful company of Engineers.

University of Reading Postgraduate Studentship

Subjects: All subjects, subject to the availability of appropriate supervision at the University.
Purpose: To enable students to obtain a doctoral degree.
Eligibility: Open to candidates holding a first degree qualification.
Level of Study: Doctorate, postgraduate
Type: Studentship
Value: The composition fee at the home standard rate plus a maintenance award related to the relevant Research Council rate
Length of Study: Up to 3 years
Frequency: Annual
Study Establishment: The University of Reading
Country of Study: United Kingdom
No. of awards offered: 4
Application Procedure: Applicants must be nominated to the Financial Support Office. Full details are available at the website www.reading.ac.uk/studentships
Closing Date: February of the year of entry
Funding: Private
Contributor: The University of Reading
No. of awards given last year: 4
No. of applicants last year: 90
Additional Information: Applications are assessed on the quality of their research proposal and short-listed applicants will be asked to attend an interview.

University of Reading Research Endowment Trust Fund (RETF)

Subjects: Arts and humanities, economics and social sciences.
Eligibility: In order to be considered for this funding you must hold the offer of a place on a PhD or MPhil at the university.
Level of Study: Postdoctorate, doctorate, postgraduate
Type: Fellowship
Value: All tuition fees and living costs of UK £12,000
Length of Study: 1–3 years
Frequency: Annual
Study Establishment: University of Reading
Country of Study: United Kingdom
No. of awards offered: 1
Application Procedure: Contact the admissions officer at the Joint Postgraduate Admissions Office.
Closing Date: February 15th

For further information contact:

Tel: (0) 118 378 8067
Email: faspg@rdg.ac.uk

University of Reading Research Studentships within the Social Sciences

Subjects: Social sciences.
Purpose: To enable students to obtain a doctoral degree.
Level of Study: Doctorate, postgraduate
Type: Scholarship
Value: Composition fee at the home standard rate plus a maintenance award related to the rate paid by the relevant Research Council
Length of Study: Up to 3 years
Frequency: Annual
Study Establishment: The University of Reading
Country of Study: United Kingdom
No. of awards offered: Up to 10
Application Procedure: Applicants must complete an application form available from the Faculty Office via email, faspg@reading.ac.uk
Closing Date: February of the year of entry
Funding: Private
Contributor: The University of Reading
No. of awards given last year: 4
No. of applicants last year: 17

University of Reading Research Studentships: Faculty of Arts and Humanities

Subjects: Research areas within those covered by the Faculty of Arts and Humanities.
Purpose: To enable students to obtain a doctoral degree.
Level of Study: Doctorate, postgraduate
Type: Studentship
Value: Composition fee at the home standard rate plus a maintenance award related to that paid by the relevant United Kingdom Research Council
Length of Study: 3 years
Frequency: Annual
Study Establishment: The University of Reading
Country of Study: United Kingdom
No. of awards offered: Varies
Application Procedure: Applicants must complete an application form, available from the Faculty Office via email, faspg@reading.ac.uk. Eligible applicants are expected to apply for, and accept if offered, a scholarship from the relevant United Kingdom Research Council or an ORS award.
Closing Date: February of the year of entry
Funding: Private

UNIVERSITY OF SOUTH AUSTRALIA

Research Services, Mawson Lakes Boulevard, Mawson Lakes, SA, 5095, Australia
Tel: (61) 8 8302 3615
Fax: (61) 8 8302 3997
Email: research.international@unisa.edu.au
Website: www.unisa.edu.au/resdegrees/default.asp
Contact: Ms Jayne Taylor, Research Degrees Manager

The University of South Australia's mission is to educate professionals, create and apply knowledge and serve the community.

International Postgraduate Research Scholarships (IPRS)

Subjects: All subjects.
Eligibility: Available to international research candidates generally with first-class honours degree or equivalent.
Level of Study: Doctorate, postgraduate
Type: Research scholarship
Value: Approx. Australian $19,231 per year
Frequency: Annual
Study Establishment: The University of South Australia
Country of Study: Any country
Application Procedure: Applicants must submit an application form, which can be obtained from the website.
Closing Date: The end of August
Funding: Government
Contributor: Department of Education, Science and Training (DEST)
No. of awards given last year: 6
No. of applicants last year: 160

UNIVERSITY OF SOUTHAMPTON

Corporate and Marketing Services Highfield, Southampton, Hampshire, SO17 1BJ, England
Tel: (44) 23 8059 4730
Fax: (44) 23 8059 5789
Website: www.soton.ac.uk
Contact: Student Marketing Office

The University of Southampton was granted its Royal Charter in 1952. Today, the University is one of the United Kingdom's top ten research universities, offering a wide range of postgraduate taught and research courses in engineering, science, mathematics, law, arts, social sciences, medicine and health and life sciences.

University of Southampton Postgraduate Studentships

Subjects: All subjects.
Purpose: To provide financial assistance to graduate students with their studies and research.

Eligibility: Open to candidates who hold a good Honours Degree and are eligible for admission to the academic school in which they intend to study.
Level of Study: Doctorate, mba, research, postgraduate
Type: Studentship
Value: Varies; (awards may cover tuition fees and/or maintenance)
Length of Study: The duration of the course of study and research
Frequency: Annual
Study Establishment: The University of Southampton
Country of Study: United Kingdom
No. of awards offered: Varies
Application Procedure: Applicants should make initial enquiries to the academic school in which study is to be undertaken.
Closing Date: Varies
Funding: Government, commercial
Additional Information: Applicants should contact each academic school for further details.

World Universities Network (WUN) Global Exchange Programme

Subjects: A wide range of subject areas reflecting the research interest of the WUN network.
Purpose: To support research visits to WUN partner universities in the United States of America, China and Europe.
Eligibility: Open to candidates currently registered for an MPhil or PhD degree in one of the University of Southampton's departments participating in the WUN scheme.
Level of Study: Postgraduate, research, predoctorate, doctorate
Type: Scholarship (travel and subsistence grant)
Value: Varies, usually up to around UK £5,000
Length of Study: The duration of the research visit, which is normally between 1 and 6 months
Frequency: Annual, annual budget but awards made twice a year in November and March
Study Establishment: Partner Universities
Country of Study: United States of America, China, Norway, Netherlands
No. of awards offered: Varies
Application Procedure: Applicants must make initial enquiries to the head of the academic department in which they are registered for their research degree. Information can also be obtained from the WUN coordinator via Email at eliso@soton.ac.uk
Closing Date: November 30th, March 15th
Contributor: The University of Southampton
No. of awards given last year: 16
No. of applicants last year: 24
Additional Information: For subject details see the website at www.wun.ac.uk

UNIVERSITY OF ST ANDREWS

School of Modern Languages, Buchanan Building, Union Street, St Andrews, Fife, KY16 9PH, Scotland
Tel: (44) 13 3447 6161
Website: www.st-andrews.ac.uk
Contact: Dr William Henry Jackson

Barron Bequest

Subjects: Any field of Arthurian studies.
Purpose: To support postgraduate research in Arthurian studies.
Eligibility: Open to graduates of any university of the United Kingdom or the Republic of Ireland.
Level of Study: Postgraduate Research
Type: Grant
Value: Up to UK £1,250 towards academic fees
Length of Study: 1 year. Candidates may apply for further years on a basis of parity with those applying for the first time
Frequency: Annual
Country of Study: United Kingdom, Republic of Ireland
No. of awards offered: Varies
Application Procedure: For application details applicants must contact Dr W. H. Jackson at the address given below.
Closing Date: April 30th
Funding: Private
Contributor: The Eugène Vinaver Trust
No. of awards given last year: 3

For further information contact:

Administrator of the Research Support Fund, School of Languages, University of St Andrews, Buchanan Building, Union Street, St Andrews, Fife, KY16 9PH
Contact: Dr W.M. Jackson

UNIVERSITY OF STRATHCLYDE

16 Richmond Street, Glasgow, Scotland, G1 1XQ, United Kingdom
Tel: (44) 14 1552 4400
Website: www.strath.ac.uk

British Gas (BG) Group/Strathclyde/Chevening Scholarships

Subjects: Engineering, applied science, business administration.
Purpose: The scholarships are intended for candidates who will benefit from a year's study in the United Kingdom before beginning or resuming key positions in their countries.
Eligibility: Applicants must be a First Class (Honours) Degree and minimum 1-year work experience. Applicants should not have undertaken full-time study in the last 2 years.
Level of Study: Postgraduate
Type: Scholarship
Value: UK £668 per month plus allowances
Length of Study: 1 year
Frequency: Annual
Study Establishment: University of Strathclyde
Country of Study: United Kingdom
Application Procedure: Application forms are available from local BG managers, British embassies in the countries mentioned or can be downloaded from the website www.io.strath.ac.uk
Funding: Corporation, international office
Contributor: BG group, University of Strathclyde, Foreign and Commonwealth Office

Department for International Development (DFID) Shared Scholarships Scheme

Subjects: All subjects.
Purpose: To assist students from developing Commonwealth countries to come to the United Kingdom for a 1-year taught Master's degree.
Eligibility: Candidates must be of outstanding academic calibre. They should not be employed by a government or a parastatal organization and should be below 35 years of age.
Level of Study: Postgraduate
Type: Scholarship
Value: UK £668 per month plus allowances
Length of Study: 1 year
Frequency: Annual
Study Establishment: University of Strathclyde
Country of Study: United Kingdom
Application Procedure: Application forms and more information are available from the website www.io.strath.ac.uk
Funding: International Office

The Hold and Young Distinguished Scholars Award

Subjects: International management.
Purpose: To assist applicants and students who are seeking sources of financial assistance to pursue full-time postgraduate study at the University of Strathclyde.
Eligibility: The applicants should be high-potential candidates with first-rate academic qualifications and relevant business education or experience.
Level of Study: Postgraduate
Type: Scholarship
Value: UK £3,500 plus tuition fees
Length of Study: 1 year
Frequency: Annual

Study Establishment: University of Strathclyde
Country of Study: United Kingdom

For further information contact:

Tel: (44) 14 1548 3455
Email: internationalmanagement@strath.ac.uk
Website: www.internationalmanagement.strath.ac.uk
Contact: Mrs Christine Donald

International Marketing Bursaries

Subjects: MSc in international marketing.
Purpose: To assist applicants who are seeking sources of financial assistance to pursue full-time postgraduate study in international marketing.
Eligibility: First Class (Honours) Degree or equivalent.
Level of Study: Postgraduate
Type: Departmental bursaries
Value: UK £3,500
Length of Study: 1 year
Frequency: Annual
Study Establishment: University of Strathclyde
Country of Study: United Kingdom
Application Procedure: Applicants must contact the Department of Marketing.

For further information contact:

Tel: (44) 14 1548 4590
Fax: (44) 14 1552 2802
Email: pghelpdesk.marketing@strath.ac.uk

International Scholarships

Subjects: All subjects.
Purpose: To assist applicants and students who are seeking sources of financial assistance to pursue full-time postgraduate study at the University of Strathclyde.
Eligibility: Applicants should be students of outstanding academic calibre and new students who are about to begin a 1-year full-time taught Master's course.
Level of Study: Predoctorate
Type: Scholarship
Value: Up to UK £4,000
Length of Study: 1 year
Frequency: Annual
Study Establishment: University of Strathclyde
Country of Study: United Kingdom
Closing Date: May 27th
Additional Information: For more information, applicants must visit the website www.io.strath.ac.uk

For further information contact:

Email: cathy.bonner@mis.strath.ac.uk or s.kirk@mis.strath.ac.uk

John Mather Scholarship

Subjects: Postgraduate instructional courses in business administration and management, economics, hospitality management and tourism.
Purpose: To encourage potential rising stars in the business world, selected on the basis of academic merit.
Eligibility: Open to students from the vicinity of the former Strathclyde Region area enrolled in postgraduate instructional courses.
Level of Study: Postgraduate
Type: Scholarship
Value: UK £5,000
Length of Study: 1 year
Frequency: Annual
Study Establishment: Strathclyde Business School
Country of Study: United Kingdom
No. of awards offered: 5
Application Procedure: Applicants must be nominated by their Head of Department on forms available from the Faculty Officer.
Closing Date: July 22nd
Funding: Trusts
Contributor: John Mather Charitable Trust
No. of awards given last year: 4
No. of applicants last year: 10

Mac Robertson Travelling Scholarship

Subjects: All subjects.
Purpose: To provide funding that will enrich and further the award holder's academic experience and research achievements.
Eligibility: Applicants should be postgraduate research students currently registered at Strathclyde or Glasgow Universities.
Level of Study: Postgraduate, research
Type: Scholarship
Value: UK £2,000–3,000
Length of Study: Varies
Frequency: Annual
Study Establishment: University of Strathclyde
Country of Study: United Kingdom
Application Procedure: Application forms can be downloaded from the website www.io.strath.ac.uk

For further information contact:

Email: cathy.bonner@mis.strath.ac.uk

Overseas Research Students Awards Scheme (ORSAS)

Subjects: All subjects.
Purpose: To assist applicants and students who are seeking sources of financial assistance to pursue full-time postgraduate study at the University of Strathclyde.
Eligibility: Candidates must have a First Class (Honours) Degree or equivalent. Candidates entering the 3rd year of a PhD are not eligible. Candidates from European Union countries are not eligible.
Level of Study: Postgraduate
Type: Award
Value: The balance between the overseas and United Kingdom/European Union rate for tuition fees
Length of Study: Up to 3 years
Frequency: Annual
Study Establishment: University of Strathclyde
Country of Study: United Kingdom
Application Procedure: Application forms can be downloaded from the website www.io.strath.ac.uk
Closing Date: February 4th

Pakistan 50th Anniversary Fund

Subjects: Engineering, computing and business management.
Purpose: To provide an opportunity for well-qualified but needy Pakistan nationals to pursue 1-year MSc study in the United Kingdom.
Eligibility: Applicants should be Pakistan nationals with a First Class (Honours) Degree from a recognized Pakistan university.
Level of Study: Postgraduate
Type: Scholarship
Length of Study: 1 year
Frequency: Annual
Study Establishment: University of Strathclyde
Country of Study: United Kingdom
Application Procedure: Application forms will be available from British Council offices in Pakistan, or can be downloaded from the website www.io.strath.ac.uk, normally in February.
Funding: Foundation

Strathclyde Business School International Management

Subjects: International management.
Purpose: To assist applicants in seeking sources of financial assistance and to provide them with the capabilities and confidence to operate successfully as international executives in a global environment.
Level of Study: Postgraduate
Type: Scholarship
Value: UK £3,500
Length of Study: 1 year
Frequency: Annual
Study Establishment: University of Strathclyde
Country of Study: United Kingdom

For further information contact:

Tel: (44) 14 1548 3455
Email: internationalmanagement@strath.ac.uk

University of Stratchclyde Scholarships

Subjects: All subjects.
Purpose: To assist applicants and students who are seeking sources of financial assistance to pursue full-time postgraduate study at the University of Stratclyde.
Eligibility: Applicants should be students of outstanding academic merit.
Level of Study: Doctorate, research
Type: Scholarship
Value: A minimum of UK £7,000 per year
Length of Study: Up to 3 years
Frequency: Annual
Study Establishment: University of Strathclyde
Country of Study: United Kingdom
Application Procedure: Applicants seeking nomination for the awards should contact the department they wish to join. Existing research students should contact their head of department or supervisor.
Closing Date: There is no central deadline
Additional Information: For more information, visit the website www.io.strath.ac.uk

University of Strathclyde and Glasgow Synergy Scholarships

Subjects: All subjects, but the project must be jointly supervised between Glasgow and Strathclyde universities.
Purpose: To assist applicants and students who are seeking sources of financial assistance to pursue full-time postgraduate study at the University of Strathclyde.
Eligibility: Applicants should be PhD candidates of outstanding academic merit.
Level of Study: Doctorate
Type: Scholarship
Value: UK £10,500 per year
Length of Study: Up to 3 years
Frequency: Annual
Study Establishment: University of Strathclyde
Country of Study: United Kingdom
Application Procedure: Applicants seeking nomination for the awards should contact the department they wish to join. Existing research students should contact their head of department or supervisor.
Closing Date: Check the website
Additional Information: For more information, visit the website www.strath.gla.ac.uk/synergy or email c.gauld@enterprise.gla.ac.uk

UNIVERSITY OF SUSSEX/ASSOCIATION OF COMMONWEALTH UNIVERSITIES

Postgraduate Office, Sussex House, Falmer, Brighton, East Sussex, BN1 9RH, England
Tel: (44) 12 7360 6755
Fax: (44) 12 7367 8335
Email: t.o-donnell@sussex.ac.uk
Website: www.sussex.ac.uk
Contact: Mr Terry O'Donnell

The University of Sussex is one of the United Kingdom's foremost research institutions. The University boasts a distinguished faculty that includes 17 Fellows of the Royal Society and four Fellows of the British Academy. The University has around 15,000 students, 25 per cent of whom are postgraduates.

Chancellor's International Scholarships

Subjects: Scholarships are available in all subjects at all schools (except the Institute of Development Studies and Brighton and Sussex medical school).
Purpose: To provide scholarships to new overseas fee-paying students at the postgraduate taught degree level.
Eligibility: Candidates must have applied for and accepted a place to start a postgraduate degree (eg. MA, MSc, LLM, postgraduate studies and graduate diploma) at the University of Sussex.
Level of Study: Graduate, postgraduate
Type: Scholarship
Value: UK £2,200
Length of Study: Duration of the degree programme
Frequency: Annual
Study Establishment: University of Sussex
Country of Study: United Kingdom
No. of awards offered: 40
Application Procedure: Completed application forms should be returned by email, post or fax.
Closing Date: May 1st
Funding: Private
Additional Information: Scholarships are awarded on the basis of academic merit and potential.

For further information contact:

International and Study Abroad Office, Mantell Building, University of Sussex, Falmer, Brighton, BN1 9RF, United Kingdom
Fax: (44) 12 7367 8640
Email: cisscholarships@sussex.ac.uk

Geoff Lockwood Scholarship

Subjects: All subjects.
Eligibility: Open to United Kingdom students.
Level of Study: Postgraduate
Type: Scholarship
Value: UK £1,000
Frequency: Annual
No. of awards offered: 1
Additional Information: Applicants should see the website.

Sasakawa Scholarship

Subjects: Science, economic and environmental policy, internationalism or gender roles in modern society.
Purpose: To educate graduate students with high potential for future leadership in international life as well as in private endeavour.
Eligibility: Applications are usually accepted from students from the United Kingdom, China, Eastern Europe or former Soviet Republics.
Level of Study: Postgraduate
Type: Scholarship
Value: Fees, maintenance award and return airfare
Length of Study: 1 year
Frequency: Annual
Study Establishment: University of Sussex
Country of Study: United Kingdom
No. of awards offered: 3
Application Procedure: Applicants must complete and submit an application form with transcripts and academic references.

University of Sussex Overseas Development Administration Shared Scholarship Scheme

Subjects: Subjects related to the economic and social development of overseas countries.
Purpose: To help students of high academic calibre in developing Commonwealth countries who would not be eligible for awards to study in the United Kingdom under existing British Government schemes, and would not be able to afford to pay for the cost themselves.
Eligibility: Candidates must be below the age of 35, have sufficient fluency in English, not have studied in the United Kingdom before, be a national of a developing Commonwealth country, not be living in a developed country and not be employed by a government department.
Level of Study: Postgraduate
Type: Scholarship
Value: Fees and maintenance grant
Length of Study: 1 year
Frequency: Annual
Study Establishment: University of Sussex

Country of Study: United Kingdom
No. of awards offered: 2
Application Procedure: Applicants must complete and submit an application form with academic transcripts and references.
Closing Date: Mid-March
Additional Information: Only applicants from targeted countries are eligible to apply and this information is usually known in January preceding the start of the academic year. Targeted countries are decided annually. Successful applicants must agree to return to their home country upon completion of their studies.

University of Sussex Overseas Research Studentships

Subjects: Arts and humanities, education science, English, law, mathematics and computer science, communication and information science, natural sciences and social sciences.
Purpose: To assist overseas students of outstanding merit and research potential.
Eligibility: Open to students applying for research degrees, eg. MPhil or DPhil who are assessed as liable to the overseas rate of fee. Applicants are allowed to submit an award through only one institution.
Level of Study: Postgraduate
Type: Scholarship
Value: Part of tuition fee
Length of Study: Up to 3 years
Frequency: Annual
Study Establishment: University of Sussex
Country of Study: United Kingdom
No. of awards offered: 15
Application Procedure: Applicants must complete and submit an application form with academic transcripts and references.
Closing Date: Early April

University of Sussex/Association of Commonwealth Universities Access Fund Bursaries

Subjects: All subjects.
Purpose: To financially support postgraduate study.
Eligibility: Open to United Kingdom students.
Level of Study: Postgraduate
Type: Bursary
Value: UK £2,000
Frequency: Annual
No. of awards offered: 20
Additional Information: Applicants should visit the website for further details.

University of Sussex/Association of Commonwealth Universities Graduate Teaching Assistantships

Subjects: All subjects.
Eligibility: Applicants must visit the website for full eligibility requirements.
Level of Study: Postgraduate
Type: Other
Value: Includes at least a fee waiver but possibly more, depending on whether the student undertakes teaching
Length of Study: Varies
Frequency: Annual
No. of awards offered: 20
Application Procedure: Applicants must visit the website for details of the application procedure.
Closing Date: Please contact the organization

THE UNIVERSITY OF SYDNEY

Research Office, Main Quadrangle A14, Sydney, NSW, 2006, Australia
Tel: (61) 2 9351 3250
Fax: (61) 2 9351 4812
Email: research.training@usyd.edu.au
Website: www.usyd.edu.au/su/reschols/scholarships
Contact: Mrs Carmen NG, Research Training

The role of the University of Sydney is to create, preserve, transmit, extend and apply knowledge through teaching, research, creative works and other forms of scholarship. In carrying out its role, the University affirms its commitment to the values and goals of institutional autonomy, recognizes the importance of ideas and intellectual freedom to pursue critical and open enquiry, as well as social responsibility, tolerance, honesty and respect, as the hallmarks of relationships throughout the University community. It also understands the needs and expectations of those whom it serves and constantly improves the quality and delivery of its services.

Australian Postgraduate Award (APA)

Subjects: All subjects.
Purpose: To enable candidates with exceptional research potential to undertake a higher degree by research.
Eligibility: Open to Australian citizens and permanent residents, and citizens of New Zealand.
Level of Study: Doctorate, research, postgraduate
Type: Scholarship
Value: Australian $19,231 per year
Length of Study: 2 years for Research Master's by research candidates, and 3 years with a possible 6-month extension for Research Doctorate candidates
Frequency: Annual
Study Establishment: The University of Sydney
Country of Study: Australia
No. of awards offered: 148
Application Procedure: Applicants must complete a form, available from the Research Office between late August and October. Forms can also be downloaded from the website or emailed on request.
Closing Date: October 31st
Funding: Government
No. of awards given last year: 148

International Postgraduate Research Scholarships (IPRS) and University of Sydney International Postgraduate Awards (IPA)

Subjects: All subjects.
Purpose: To support candidates with exceptional research potential.
Eligibility: Open to suitably qualified graduates eligible to commence a higher degree by research. Australia and New Zealand citizens and Australian permanent residents are not eligible to apply.
Level of Study: Postgraduate, research, doctorate
Type: Scholarship
Value: Tuition fees for IPRS, and for IPA Australian $19,231 per year
Length of Study: 2 years for the Master's by research candidates, and 3 years with a possible 6-month extension for PhD candidates
Frequency: Annual
Study Establishment: The University of Sydney
Country of Study: Australia
No. of awards offered: 32
Application Procedure: Applicants must complete an application form, available between May and August from the International Office.
Closing Date: August 31st
Funding: Government
No. of awards given last year: 29

For further information contact:

International Office, Services Building G12, Sydney, NSW, 2006, Australia
Tel: (61) 2 9351 4161
Fax: (61) 2 9351 4013
Email: infoschol@io.usyd.edu.au
Contact: International Scholarships Officer

University of Sydney Postgraduate Award (UPA)

Subjects: All subjects.
Purpose: To enable candidates with exceptional research potential to undertake a higher degree by research.
Eligibility: Open to Australian citizens and permanent residents and New Zealand citizens.
Level of Study: Doctorate, postgraduate, research
Type: Scholarship
Value: Australian $19,231 per year

Length of Study: 2 years for the Research Master's by research candidates, and 3 years with a possible 6-month extension for Research Doctorate candidates
Frequency: Annual
Study Establishment: The University of Sydney
Country of Study: Australia
No. of awards offered: 60
Application Procedure: Applicants must complete a form, available from the Research Office between late August and October. Forms can also be downloaded from the website or emailed on request.
Closing Date: October 31st
Funding: Government
No. of awards given last year: 60

UNIVERSITY OF ULSTER

Research Office, Cromore Road, Coleraine, Co. Londonderry, BT52 1SA, Northern Ireland
Tel: (44) (28) 7032 4729
Fax: (44) (28) 7032 4905
Website: www.ulst.ac.uk
Contact: Mrs H Campbell, Administrative Assistant

The University of Ulster's vision is to be a model of an outstanding regional university with a national and international reputation for quality. The University makes a major contribution to the economic, social and cultural advancement of Northern Ireland as a region within a national and international context and plays a key role in attracting inward investment. Core business activities are teaching and learning, research and technology and knowledge transfer.

Vice Chancellor's Research Scholarships (VCRS)

Subjects: All subjects.
Purpose: To assist candidates of a high academic standard to complete research degrees (PhD).
Eligibility: Open to all eligible applicants for admission to full-time research studies, as advertised on website.
Level of Study: Doctorate, postgraduate
Type: Scholarship
Value: Fees and maintenance grant
Length of Study: Up to 3 years
Frequency: Annual
Study Establishment: University of Ulster
Country of Study: United Kingdom
No. of awards offered: Varies
Application Procedure: Applicants must complete an application form.
Closing Date: Check the website
Funding: Private
No. of awards given last year: 40
No. of applicants last year: 700
Additional Information: Further information is available on the website www.ulster.ac.uk/researchstudy

UNIVERSITY OF VICTORIA

Faculty of Law, PO Box 2400, STN CSC, Victoria, British Columbia, V8W 3H7, Canada
Tel: (1) 721 8150
Email: lawrecep@uvic.ca
Website: www.law.uvic.ca

One of the unique aspects of legal education at the university of Victoria, which came into being on July 1, 1963, is the overwhelming commitment to a supportive learning environment. Today UVic is a major western Canadian university and continues to expand at a rapid place.

The Alexander, Holburn, Beaudin & Lang Scholarship

Subjects: Law.
Purpose: To recognize high academic standing.
Eligibility: Open to students who demonstrate the qualities required for the practice of law.
Level of Study: Postgraduate
Type: Scholarship
Value: Canadian $1,000
Frequency: Annual
Country of Study: Canada
Application Procedure: See the website.

The Baker & McKenzie Prize in Asia-Pacific Comparative Law

Subjects: Law.
Purpose: To recognize academic and scholarly excellence in legal studies.
Eligibility: Open to students in the Southeast Asian Legal Systems course.
Level of Study: Postgraduate
Type: Award
Value: Canadian $500
Frequency: Annual
No. of awards offered: 1
Application Procedure: A completed application form must be sent.
Contributor: International Law Firm of Baker & McKenzie

The Blakes Scholars Scholarship Award

Subjects: Law.
Purpose: To award students who demonstrate academic excellence.
Eligibility: Open to students who demonstrate a financial need.
Level of Study: Postgraduate
Type: Scholarship
Value: Canadian $5,000
Frequency: Annual
Country of Study: Canada
Application Procedure: See the website.
Contributor: Blake, Cassels & Graydon LLP

The David Roberts Prize in Legal Writing

Subjects: Legal writing.
Purpose: To award the presentation of a legal subject in a literate and persuasive manner.
Eligibility: Open to all students of Faculty of Law.
Level of Study: Postgraduate
Type: Award
Value: Canadian $3,000
Frequency: Annual
Country of Study: Canada
Application Procedure: See the website.
Closing Date: June 1st

The Diana M. Priestly Memorial Scholarship Award

Subjects: Law.
Eligibility: Open to Applicants who are members of the Canadian Association of Law Libraries.
Type: Scholarship
Value: Canadian US$2,500
Frequency: Annual
Study Establishment: An approved Canadian Law School.
Country of Study: Canada
No. of awards offered: 1
Application Procedure: Letters of experience and reference along with the of application must be sent.
Closing Date: February 15th

The Guild, Yule & Company Advocacy Award

Subjects: Law.
Purpose: To award excellence in academic studies.
Eligibility: Open to students with outstanding potential as an advocate.
Level of Study: Postgraduate
Type: Award
Value: Canadian US$1,500
Frequency: Annual
Country of Study: Canada
Application Procedure: See the website.
Contributor: Guild, Yule & Company

The Howard Petch Scholarship in Law

Subjects: Law.
Purpose: To recognize highest academic standing.
Level of Study: Postgraduate
Type: Scholarship
Length of Study: Canadian US$5,000
Frequency: Annual
Country of Study: Canada
Application Procedure: See the website.

Victoria Bar Association Founders Committee Award

Subjects: Law.
Purpose: To recognize students who have demonstrated a commitment to public service and relations with the profession.
Eligibility: Open to students of University of Victoria, Faculty of Law.
Level of Study: Postgraduate
Type: Award
Value: Canadian $500
Frequency: Annual
Study Establishment: University of Victoria, Faculty of Law
Country of Study: Canada
Application Procedure: See the website.
Contributor: The Victoria Bar Association

THE UNIVERSITY OF WAIKATO

Gate 1 Knighton Road Private Bag 3105, Hamilton, New Zealand
Tel: (64) 7 856 2889
Fax: (64) 7 838 4300
Email: info@waikato.ac.nz

The University of Waikato was formed in 1964 and is now home to 13,500 students as a breeding ground for independent thought and progressive learning. It prides itself for being the first university in New Zealand to have cyber-graduates.

Bachelor of Engineering Fees Scholarships

Subjects: Engineering.
Purpose: To provide financial assistance to student enrolled full-time for a Bachelor of Engineering degree.
Eligibility: Open to applicants who are New Zealand citizens or permanent residents with high academic caliber.
Level of Study: Postgraduate
Type: Scholarship
Value: NZ $4,000
Study Establishment: University of Waikato
Country of Study: New Zealand
No. of awards offered: 5
Application Procedure: Applicants must submit a completed application form along with a curriculum vitae and one referee's report, which supports their academic achievements.
Closing Date: December 30th
Contributor: School of Science and Engineering

Gallagher Group Master's Scholarship

Subjects: Business management.
Purpose: To assist students undertaking research in a business-relevant topic.
Eligibility: Open to New Zealand citizens or permanent residents.
Type: Scholarship
Value: US$10,000
Study Establishment: Waikato Management School
Country of Study: New Zealand
Application Procedure: Further information and application forms are available from the website.
Closing Date: November 15th
Contributor: The Gallagher Group

ICCS Student Scholarships

Subjects: Canadian studies.
Purpose: To assist candidates in short research trips to Canada.
Eligibility: Open to all Master's and Doctoral candidates who are undertaking research in the field of Canadian studies.
Type: Scholarship
Value: Up to Canadian $3,5000
Length of Study: 4–6 weeks
Frequency: Annual
Study Establishment: Any accredited university or institute
Country of Study: Canada
No. of awards offered: 10
Application Procedure: Application forms and information available at www.powerup.com
Closing Date: November 15th
Contributor: The International Council for Canadian studies (ICCS)

New Zealand Law Society Centennial Scholarship

Subjects: Law.
Purpose: To provide financial assistance to law students.
Eligibility: Open to aw students who require financial assistance.
Level of Study: Postgraduate
Value: NZ $2,000
Frequency: Annual
Study Establishment: University of Waikato
Country of Study: New Zealand
Application Procedure: Further information can be found at www.nzlawsoc.org.nz
Closing Date: November 30th

New Zealand Postgraduate Study Abroad Awards

Subjects: All subjects.
Purpose: To support students from New Zealand institutions who wish to study or research abroad.
Eligibility: Open to New Zealand citizens or permanent residents who are enrolled full-time at a New Zealand institution.
Level of Study: Postgraduate
Type: Scholarship
Value: Up to NZ $10,000
Frequency: Annual
Study Establishment: Any accredited educational institution
Country of Study: Any country
Application Procedure: Further information and application forms are available on www.newzealandeducated.com
Closing Date: December 1st
Funding: Government
Contributor: New Zealand Government

New Zealand Tourism Research Scholarships

Subjects: Tourism.
Purpose: To increase research targeted to the needs of the tourism industry.
Eligibility: Open to New Zealand citizens or permanent residents who are undertaking a tourism-related research thesis.
Type: Scholarship
Value: NZ $15,000
Length of Study: 1 year
Frequency: Annual
No. of awards offered: 7
Application Procedure: For further information and application forms, visit www.tourism.govt.nz
Closing Date: November 21st
Funding: Government
Contributor: The Ministry of Tourism

For further information contact:

PO Box 5640, Wellington,
Tel: 462 42 96
Email: chrisana.archer@tourism.govt.nz
Contact: Chrisana Archer, Ministry of Tourism

Sir Edmund Hillary Scholarship Programme

Subjects: Sports and arts.
Purpose: To support students to achieve a high academic standard and excellence in sports or creative and performing arts.
Eligibility: Open to New Zealand citizens or permanent residents who have not previously been enrolled at the university.
Level of Study: Postgraduate

Type: Scholarship
Value: Tuition fees and associated charges
Length of Study: 1 year, renewable
Frequency: Annual
Study Establishment: University of Waikato
Country of Study: New Zealand
Application Procedure: Further information available on the website.
Closing Date: October 31st

The University of Waikato Alumni Association Master's Scholarships

Subjects: All subjects.
Purpose: To support students who wish to obtain a Master's degree at the university.
Eligibility: Open to New Zealand citizens or permanent residents who are enrolled for a Master's degree at the university.
Level of Study: Postgraduate
Type: Scholarship
Value: NZ $5,500 plus tuition fees up to NZ $4,000
Frequency: Every 2 years
Study Establishment: University of Waikato
Country of Study: New Zealand
Application Procedure: A completed application form must be submitted to the scholarship office at the university.
Closing Date: October 31st
Contributor: The University of Waikato Alumni Association

The University of Waikato Doctoral Scholarships

Subjects: All subjects.
Purpose: To support candidates applying for doctoral studies.
Eligibility: Open to New Zealand citizens or permanent residents.
Type: Scholarship
Value: NZ $22,000
Length of Study: 3 years
Frequency: Twice a year
Study Establishment: University of Waikato
Country of Study: New Zealand
Application Procedure: Contact the scholarships office at the university.
Closing Date: October 30th and April 30th

UNIVERSITY OF WALES, ABERYSTWYTH

Old College, King Street, Aberystwyth, Ceredigion, SY23 2AX, Wales
Tel: (44) 19 7062 2023
Fax: (44) 19 7062 2921
Email: pg-admissions@aber.ac.uk
Website: www.aber.ac.uk
Contact: Dr Rhys Williams, Postgraduate Admissions Officer

Located in beautiful surroundings, the University of Wales provides an ideal learning environment. Its information services are among the best in the United Kingdom, and students also enjoy free access to one of the six copyright libraries in the United Kingdom, the National Library of Wales, which is adjacent to the University.

University of Wales Aberystwyth Postgraduate Research Studentships

Subjects: Studies leading to the award of a PhD in any of the University's 17 academic departments. The university offers a wide range of research opportunities within the faculties of science, social sciences and arts.
Purpose: To enable United Kingdom and European Union students to undertake full-time doctoral study at the University of Wales, Aberystwyth.
Eligibility: Open to United Kingdom and European Union candidates who have obtained at least an Upper Second Class (Honours) Degree or equivalent in their degree examination and who wish to study full-time. To be eligible you must: (i) be a uk/eu fee payer. (ii) have or expect to obtain at least a second upper class honours degree. (iii) apply and be offered a place for doctoral study at UW Aberystwyth.
Level of Study: Postgraduate, doctorate, research
Type: Studentship
Value: United Kingdom fees plus a subsistence allowance based on UK research council rates
Length of Study: 1 year, in the first instance, but usually renewable for up to 3 years subject to satisfactory academic progress
Frequency: Annual
Study Establishment: The University of Wales, Aberystwyth
Country of Study: United Kingdom
No. of awards offered: Usually 12 per year
Application Procedure: Applicants must complete an application form, available from the Postgraduate Admissions Office or from the website. Selection is based on the application for admission including a research proposal and references. There are no additional forms for this competition.
Closing Date: March 1st
Funding: Private
Contributor: The University of Wales, Aberystwyth
No. of awards given last year: 12
No. of applicants last year: 120
Additional Information: For all enquiries, please contact the Postgraduate Admissions Office: pg-admissions@aber.ac.uk

UNIVERSITY OF WALES, BANGOR (UWB)

Academic Registry, College Road, Bangor, Gwynedd, LL57 2DG, Wales
Tel: (44) 12 4838 2025
Fax: (44) 12 4837 0451
Email: aos057@bangor.ac.uk
Website: www.bangor.ac.uk
Contact: Dr John C T Perkins, Assistant Registrar

The University of Wales, Bangor (UWB) is the principal seat of learning, scholarship and research in North Wales. It was established in 1884 and is a constituent institution of the Federal University of Wales. The University attaches considerable importance to research training in all disciplines and offers research studentships of a value similar to those of other United Kingdom public-funding bodies.

Llewellyn and Mary Williams Scholarship

Subjects: All biological sciences, including marine biology.
Purpose: To support doctoral studies and research training in the biological sciences.
Eligibility: Open to First Class (Honours) Degree holders who are classified as home or European Union students for fee purposes.
Level of Study: Doctorate, postgraduate
Type: Scholarship
Value: Equal to that of a British Research Council Studentship
Length of Study: 3 years
Frequency: Annual
Study Establishment: The University of Wales, Bangor
Country of Study: United Kingdom
No. of awards offered: 2
Application Procedure: This scholarship is allocated annually. Applicants must contact the Head of the School for details. Nominations are sought by the school of Biological Science and the school of Decan Science.
Closing Date: May 15th
Funding: Private
No. of awards given last year: 3
No. of applicants last year: 10

Mr and Mrs David Edward Memorial Award

Subjects: All subjects offered by the University.
Purpose: To support doctoral studies in any subject area.
Eligibility: Open to holders of a relevant First Class (Honours) Degree or, exceptionally, Upper Second Class (Honours) Degree, who are classified as United Kingdom or European Union students for fee purposes.
Level of Study: Doctorate, postgraduate
Type: Award

Value: No less than that of a Research Council or British Academy Research Studentship, including fees
Length of Study: 1 year, renewable for a maximum of a further 2 years if satisfactory progress is maintained
Frequency: Dependent on funds available
Study Establishment: The University of Wales, Bangor
Country of Study: United Kingdom
No. of awards offered: 1
Application Procedure: Nominations are made by the University, nominee are invited to submit formal applications.
Funding: Private
No. of awards given last year: 1
No. of applicants last year: 20

Sir William Roberts Scholarship

Subjects: Agriculture and agricultural science.
Purpose: To fund research training at the PhD level.
Eligibility: Open to candidates classified as 'home based' who have attained a First Class (Honours) Degree or Upper Second Class (Honours) Degree. These scholarships are allocated to the School of Agricultural and Forest Sciences and the School of Biological Sciences.
Level of Study: Postgraduate, doctorate
Type: Scholarship
Value: Equal to that of a British Research Council Research Studentship
Length of Study: 1 year, renewable for a maximum of 2 additional years
Frequency: Annual
Study Establishment: The University of Wales, Bangor
Country of Study: United Kingdom
No. of awards offered: 2
Application Procedure: Applicants must contact the Head of the relevant School.
Closing Date: June 1st
Funding: Private
No. of awards given last year: 2
No. of applicants last year: 20

UWB Departmental Research Studentships

Subjects: All subjects offered by the University.
Purpose: To fund research training at the PhD level.
Eligibility: Open to candidates classified as United Kingdom and European Union students for fee purposes who have attained a First Class (Honours) Degree or, exceptionally, an Upper Second Class (Honours) Degree or equivalent.
Level of Study: Doctorate, postgraduate
Type: Studentship
Value: Equal to that of a British Research Council Studentship
Length of Study: 1 year, renewable for a maximum of 2 additional years
Frequency: Annual
Study Establishment: The University of Wales, Bangor
Country of Study: United Kingdom
No. of awards offered: 12–15
Application Procedure: Applicants must contact the relevant department of proposed study. The department will nominate the most worthy eligible students.
Closing Date: April 30th
Funding: Private
No. of awards given last year: 11
No. of applicants last year: 90

UWB Research Studentships

Subjects: All subjects offered by the University.
Purpose: To support students for the duration of a PhD programme.
Eligibility: Open to recent graduates, classified at the lower European Union rate for payment purposes, who hold a First Class (Honours) Degree or Upper Second Class (Honours) Degree or equivalent in a relevant subject.
Level of Study: Postgraduate
Type: Studentship
Value: Equal to that of a British Research Council Studentship
Length of Study: 3 years
Frequency: Annual
Study Establishment: The University of Wales, Bangor
Country of Study: United Kingdom
No. of awards offered: 10–14
Application Procedure: Applicants must contact the Senior Postgraduate Tutor in the department of the proposed research programme.
Closing Date: May 15th. Those interested should make enquiries well before this date
Funding: Private, government
Contributor: The UWB Research Committee and local bequests
No. of awards given last year: 14
No. of applicants last year: Approx. 100
Additional Information: In exceptional circumstances an award may be made to an international student classified for the full cost fee. In such a case the student would be required to pay the difference between the full cost fee and the home or European Union fee.

UNIVERSITY OF WALES, LAMPETER

Lampeter, Ceredigion, Wales, SA48 7ED, England
Tel: (44) 15 7042 2351
Fax: (44) 15 7042 3423
Email: t.rodervick@lamp.ac.uk
Website: www.lamp.ac.uk
Contact: R C Jarman, Registrar and Secretary

At Lampeter research is greatly prized by our academic staff and we can offer a wide range of supervision in the humanities and social sciences. There is simply no other long-established university with our pedigree that operates on such an intimate scale.

Delahaye Memorial Benefaction

Subjects: Theology.
Purpose: To financially support a graduate of UWL who is accepted to read Honours Theology at Cambridge.
Eligibility: Graduates.
Level of Study: Graduate
Value: UK £60
Frequency: Annual
Study Establishment: Magdalene College, University of Cambridge
Country of Study: United Kingdom
No. of awards offered: 1
Application Procedure: Applications for postgraduate awards should be made to the Postgraduate Office, which writes, during the Michaelmas term, to all registered postgraduate students reminding them of the awards and enclosing the official application forms.
Closing Date: March 7th
No. of awards given last year: None
No. of applicants last year: None

Helen McCormack Turner Memorial Scholarship

Subjects: All subjects.
Purpose: The Applicant must be a postgraduate student who graduated recently from the University of Wales, Lampeter.
Eligibility: The recipient must be less than 25 years of age on 1 August 2004 and must be registered to support graduates pursuing research for the degrees of MPhil or PhD.
Type: Scholarship
Value: UK £250
Frequency: Annual
No. of awards offered: 1
Application Procedure: Applications for postgraduate awards should be made to the Postgraduate Office, which writes, during the Michaelmas term, to all registered postgraduate students reminding them of the awards and enclosing the official application forms.
Closing Date: March 7th
No. of awards given last year: 1
No. of applicants last year: 1

Herbert Hughes Scholarship

Subjects: Theology.
Purpose: To support postgraduate or undergraduate students of any discipline who intend to serve in the Ministry of the Church in Wales.
Eligibility: Postgraduate or undergraduate. (Preference may be given to candidates from the parish of Silian, Ceredigion).
Type: Scholarship
Value: UK £170
No. of awards offered: 1
Application Procedure: Applications for postgraduate awards should be made to the Postgraduate Office, which writes, during the Michaelmas term, to all registered postgraduate students reminding them of the awards and enclosing the official application forms.
Closing Date: March 7th
No. of awards given last year: None
No. of applicants last year: None

Mary Radcliffe Scholarship

Subjects: Theology.
Purpose: To support graduates of UWL to study theology.
Eligibility: Applicants must be graduates of UWL.
Level of Study: Graduate
Type: Scholarship
Value: UK £150
Frequency: Annual
No. of awards offered: 1
Application Procedure: Applications for postgraduate awards should be made to the Postgraduate Office, which writes, during the Michaelmas term, to all registered postgraduate students reminding them of the awards and enclosing the official application forms.
Closing Date: March 7th
No. of awards given last year: 1
No. of applicants last year: 2

RHYS Curzon-Jones Scholarship

Subjects: Theology.
Purpose: To support a postgraduate student of any discipline who is a candidate for Holy Orders in the Church in Wales.
Type: Scholarship
Value: UK £50
Frequency: Annual
No. of awards offered: 1
Application Procedure: Applications for postgraduate awards should be made to the Postgraduate Office, which writes, during the Michaelmas term, to all registered postgraduate students reminding them of the awards and enclosing the official application forms.
Closing Date: March 7th
No. of awards given last year: None
No. of applicants last year: None

Ridley Lewis Bursary

Subjects: All subjects.
Purpose: To support a postgraduate student funding his/her studies in whole or in part from his/her own resources.
Eligibility: Applicants must be postgraduate students.
Value: UK £50
Frequency: Annual
No. of awards offered: 1
Application Procedure: Applications for postgraduate awards should be made to the Postgraduate Office, which writes, during the Michaelmas term, to all registered postgraduate students reminding them of the awards and enclosing the official application forms.
Closing Date: March 7th
No. of awards given last year: 1
No. of applicants last year: 29

W D Llewelyn Memorial Benefaction

Subjects: All subjects.
Purpose: To support graduates of UWL for further degrees or research at Lampeter or at other universities.
Eligibility: Applicants must be graduates of UWL.
Value: Six awards of UK £100 each
Length of Study: 1 year
Frequency: Annual
No. of awards offered: 6
Application Procedure: Applications for postgraduate awards should be made to the Postgraduate Office, which writes, during the Michaelmas term, to all registered postgraduate students reminding them of the awards and enclosing the official application forms.
Closing Date: March 7th
No. of awards given last year: 6
No. of applicants last year: 16

UNIVERSITY OF WALES, NEWPORT

Caerleon Campus, PO Box 179, Newport, NP18 3YG, Wales
Tel: (44) 16 3343 0088
Fax: (44) 16 3343 2006
Website: www.wales.ac.uk

The University of Wales, Newport, has been involved in higher education for more than 80 years, and its roots go back even further to the first Mechanics Institute in the town, which opened in 1841.

Pilcher Senior Research Fellowship

Subjects: Welsh and Celtic studies.
Purpose: To support a student in advanced research in the fields of Welsh and Celtic studies.
Level of Study: Postdoctorate
Type: Fellowship
Frequency: As needed
Study Establishment: University of Wales
Country of Study: Wales
Application Procedure: Applicants must check with the website or the University.
Funding: Private
Contributor: The late Sophia Margaretta Pilcher

The Stott Fellowship

Subjects: Welsh and Celtic studies.
Purpose: To support a student in advanced research in the fields of Welsh and Celtic studies.
Level of Study: Postgraduate
Type: Fellowship
Frequency: As needed
Study Establishment: University of Wales
Country of Study: Wales
Application Procedure: Applicants must check with the website or the University.
Funding: Private
Contributor: Miss Muriel Stott of Colwyn Bay

University of Wales Postgraduate Studentship

Subjects: All subjects approved by the University.
Purpose: To support a student with a First Class (Honours) Degree at the university to progress to postgraduate research.
Level of Study: Doctorate
Type: Scholarship
Frequency: Annual
Study Establishment: University of Wales
Country of Study: Wales
Application Procedure: Applicants must check with the website or the University.
Funding: Private
Contributor: Private benefactions

UNIVERSITY OF WARWICK

Coventry, CV4 7AL, England
Tel: (44) 24 7652 3523
Fax: (44) 24 7646 1606
Email: pgoffice@warwick.ac.uk
Website: www.warwick.ac.uk

The University of Warwick offers an exciting range of doctoral, research-based and taught Master's programmes in the humanities, sciences, social sciences and medicine. In the 2001 Research Assessment Exercise, Warwick was ranked 5th in the United Kingdom for research quality. Postgraduate students make up around 35per cent of Warwick's 18,000 students. The University is located in the heart of England, adjacent to the city of Coventry and on the border with Warwickshire.

Argentina Chevening Scholarship

Subjects: All subjects. Not MBA.
Eligibility: Applicants should be nationals of Argentina not currently registered at the University.
Level of Study: Postgraduate
Type: Scholarship
Value: UK cost of Academic fee and maintenance
Length of Study: 1 year
Frequency: One-off award
Study Establishment: Argentina Ministry of Foreign Affairs
Country of Study: United Kingdom
No. of awards offered: 1
Application Procedure: Applicants must complete an application form, available from the British Council.
Contributor: University of Warwick, Foreign and Commonwealth office

For further information contact:

The British Council, Marcelo T de Alvear, 590, 4th Floor, 1058, Buenos Aires, Argentina
Email: info@britishcouncil.org

Brazil Chevening Scholarship (Law)

Subjects: Law.
Eligibility: Applicants must be nationals of Brazil not currently registered at the University of Warwick.
Level of Study: Postgraduate
Type: Scholarship
Value: Cost of academic fees and full maintenance
Frequency: One-off award
Study Establishment: University of Warwick
Country of Study: United Kingdom
No. of awards offered: 1
Application Procedure: Applicants must complete an application form.
Contributor: The University of Warwick, British Council

For further information contact:

The British Council, Eo. Centro Empresarial Varie, SCN Quadra 04, Block B, Torre Oeste Consunto 202, Brasilia, DF, Brazil
Email: brasilia@britishcouncil.org.br
Contact: Irene Taitson

Lord Rootes Memorial Fund

Subjects: Economic, environmental, social and technological problems.
Purpose: To support a student's or society's project.
Eligibility: Applicants must be either full- or part-time postgraduate or undergraduate students belonging to a student society at the University of Warwick.
Level of Study: Unrestricted
Type: Grant
Value: From UK £200 for individuals to UK £3,000 for groups
Length of Study: At least 2 years
Frequency: Annual
Study Establishment: University of Warwick
Country of Study: United Kingdom
No. of awards offered: Variable
Application Procedure: Applicants must submit an application form plus a detailed project proposal of up to six A4 pages including financial plan. Short-listed applicants are interviewed.
Closing Date: The 1st week of the Spring term (approx. January 9th)
Funding: Private
Contributor: Lord Rootes Memorial Fund
No. of awards given last year: 15
No. of applicants last year: 53

Mexico Chevening/Brockmann/Warwick Award

Subjects: All subjects. (Not MBA).
Eligibility: Applicants must be nationals of Mexico, not currently registered at the University of Warwick.
Level of Study: Postgraduate
Study Establishment: University of Warwick
Country of Study: United Kingdom
No. of awards offered: 1
Application Procedure: Applicants must complete an application form.
Closing Date: Contact the British Council for details
Contributor: The British Council, The Brockmann Foundation, University of Warwick

For further information contact:

The British Council, Lope de Vega, 316, Col Chapultepec Morales, Delègacion Miguel Hidalgo, CP 11570, DF, Mexico

Russia Postgraduate Chevening Award

Subjects: All subjects. Not MSc Economics and MBA.
Purpose: To support postgraduate study.
Eligibility: Open to nationals of Russia.
Level of Study: Postgraduate
Type: Scholarship
Value: Academic fees and maintenance
Frequency: One-off award
Study Establishment: University of Warwick
Country of Study: United Kingdom
No. of awards offered: 1
Application Procedure: Applicants must complete an application form.
Closing Date: October 20th
Contributor: University of Warwick
Additional Information: Tuition fees and monthly stipend.

Sports Bursary

Subjects: Sports.
Purpose: To support outstanding sports people.
Eligibility: Candidates should be already competing in their sport at a national standard, or should by their presence in national or regional training squads, show the potential to achieve their standard.
Level of Study: Postgraduate
Type: Bursary
Value: Approx. UK £300 (more may be provided for exceptional cases)
Length of Study: At least 1 year
Frequency: Annual
Study Establishment: University of Warwick
Country of Study: United Kingdom
No. of awards offered: Varies
Application Procedure: Applicants must apply by letter at the start of the academic year to the Department of Physical Education and Sport.
Closing Date: No deadline
Funding: Government
No. of awards given last year: 10
No. of applicants last year: 12

University of Warwick Busary for Postgraduate Study (French Studies)

Subjects: French culture and thought, French studies.
Purpose: To support students registered for an MA in French studies.
Eligibility: Candidates must have accepted a place for the taught MA and must apply to AHRB or any other source of funding for which they may be eligible.
Level of Study: Postgraduate
Type: Scholarship
Value: Dependent on funding, normally up to UK £4,500
Length of Study: 1 year
Frequency: Dependent on funds available
Study Establishment: University of Warwick
Country of Study: United Kingdom
No. of awards offered: A small number

Application Procedure: There is no separate application form. All applications for the MA will automatically be considered.
Closing Date: February 14th
Contributor: University of Warwick
No. of awards given last year: 4
No. of applicants last year: 4

University of Warwick LLM in Development Postgraduate Award (India)
Subjects: Law.
Eligibility: Applicants must be nationals of India, not registered for a postgraduate course.
Level of Study: Postgraduate
Type: Scholarship
Value: 3 æ UK £3,000
Length of Study: 1 year
Frequency: One-off award
Study Establishment: University of Warwick
Country of Study: United Kingdom
No. of awards offered: 3
Application Procedure: Applicants must complete an application form.
Closing Date: May 13th
Contributor: University of Warwick
Additional Information: Award deducted from academic fees and accommodation expenses.

University of Warwick Music Scholarships
Subjects: Music.
Purpose: To support students with outstanding musical ability.
Eligibility: Applicants should be undergraduate or postgraduate students, should have applied for admission to the University for a full-time scheme and have satisfied the entry requirements.
Level of Study: Postgraduate
Type: Scholarship
Value: UK £450 per year (with an additional subsidy on music tuition fees)
Length of Study: At least 1 year
Frequency: Annual
Study Establishment: University of Warwick
Country of Study: United Kingdom
No. of awards offered: 2
Application Procedure: Application forms are available online or from the Music Centre Secretary.
Closing Date: February 10th in proposed calendar year of entry
Funding: Private
No. of awards given last year: 4
No. of applicants last year: 40

University of Warwick Postgraduate Award (Caribbean)
Subjects: All subjects.
Eligibility: Caribbean nationals including nationals of non-commonwealth countries, and not currently registered in a postgraduate course.
Level of Study: Postgraduate
Type: Scholarship
Value: UK £5,000
Length of Study: 1 year
Frequency: One-off award
Study Establishment: University of Warwick
Country of Study: United Kingdom
No. of awards offered: 1
Application Procedure: Applicants must complete an application form.
Closing Date: May 13th
Contributor: University of Warwick
No. of awards given last year: 1
Additional Information: Award deducted from the academic fees.

University of Warwick Postgraduate Award (Ghana)
Subjects: All subjects.
Eligibility: Applicants must be nationals of Ghana, not currently registered for a postgraduate course.
Level of Study: Postgraduate
Type: Scholarship
Value: UK £3,000
Length of Study: 1 year
Frequency: One-off award
Study Establishment: University of Warwick
Country of Study: United Kingdom
No. of awards offered: 1
Application Procedure: Applicants must complete an application form.
Closing Date: May 13th
Contributor: University of Warwick

University of Warwick Postgraduate Award (India)
Subjects: All subjects.
Eligibility: Applicants must be national of India, not currently registered for a postgraduate course.
Level of Study: Postgraduate
Type: Scholarship
Value: UK £3,000–5,000
Length of Study: 1 year
Frequency: One-off award
Study Establishment: University of Warwick
Country of Study: United Kingdom
No. of awards offered: 3
Application Procedure: Applicants must complete an application form.
Closing Date: May 13th
Funding: International Office
Contributor: University of Warwick
Additional Information: Award deducted from academic fees and accommodation expenses.

University of Warwick Postgraduate Award (Japan)
Subjects: All subjects.
Eligibility: Applicants must be nationals from Japan.
Level of Study: Postgraduate
Type: Scholarship
Value: UK £5,000 each
Frequency: One-off award
Study Establishment: University of Warwick
Country of Study: United Kingdom
No. of awards offered: 2
Application Procedure: Applicants must complete an application form.
Closing Date: May 13th
Contributor: University of Warwick

University of Warwick Postgraduate Award (Latin America)
Eligibility: Applicants must be nationals from one of the countries in this region not currently registered for a postgraduate course at the university.
Type: Scholarship
Value: UK £6,000 (Taught Master's only)
Frequency: One-off award
Study Establishment: University of Warwick
Country of Study: United Kingdom
No. of awards offered: 1
Application Procedure: Applicants must complete an application form.
Closing Date: May 13th
Contributor: University of Warwick, International Office

University of Warwick Postgraduate Award (Pakistan)
Subjects: All subjects.
Eligibility: Applicants should be nationals of Pakistan, not currently registered for a postgraduate course at the University.
Level of Study: Postgraduate
Type: Scholarship
Value: UK £8,000
Length of Study: 1 year
Frequency: One-off award

Study Establishment: University of Warwick
Country of Study: United Kingdom
No. of awards offered: 1
Application Procedure: Applicants must complete an application form.
Closing Date: May 13th
Contributor: University of Warwick

University of Warwick Postgraduate Awards (North America)

Subjects: All subjects.
Eligibility: Applicants should be nationals of the United States of America or Canada, not currently registered for a postgraduate course at the University.
Level of Study: Postgraduate
Type: Scholarship
Value: UK £4,000
Length of Study: 1 year
Frequency: One-off award
Study Establishment: University of Warwick
Country of Study: United Kingdom
No. of awards offered: 4
Application Procedure: Applicants must complete an application form.
Closing Date: May 13th
Contributor: University of Warwick

University of Warwick Postgraduate Research Fellowship

Subjects: All subjects.
Purpose: To support PhD students.
Eligibility: Applicants must be registered for a PhD, should have outstanding academic ability, must have applied for external funding and be a current or new PhD student not in their final year.
Level of Study: Doctorate
Type: Fellowship
Value: Home fees and UK £11,500 for maintenance. Between 15 and 20 awards
Length of Study: 3 years
Frequency: Annual
Study Establishment: University of Warwick
Country of Study: United Kingdom
No. of awards offered: 15–20
Application Procedure: Application forms can be downloaded from the website and sent to the department.
Closing Date: First round: January 31st, Second round: July 1st
Funding: Government
No. of awards given last year: 25
No. of applicants last year: 361

University of Warwick Psychology Department Studentship (Master's)

Subjects: Psychology and related subjects.
Purpose: To support students for an MSc in research methods.
Eligibility: Applicants must have a First Class (Honours) Degree in psychology or a related subject.
Level of Study: Postgraduate
Type: Studentship
Value: Home fees
Length of Study: 1 year
Frequency: Annual
Study Establishment: University of Warwick
Country of Study: United Kingdom
No. of awards offered: 5
Closing Date: Varies, see the department website for further details
Funding: Government
No. of awards given last year: 3

University of Warwick Psychology Department Studentship (PhD)

Subjects: Psychology.
Purpose: To support PhD students in psychology.
Eligibility: Applicants must be registered for a PhD, must have outstanding academic ability, must have applied for external funding and must be a current/new PhD student not in their final year.
Level of Study: Doctorate
Type: Studentship
Value: Home fees plus maintenance (for overseas fee payers, the overseas portion of the fee is waived)
Length of Study: 3 years
Frequency: Annual
Study Establishment: University of Warwick
Country of Study: United Kingdom
No. of awards offered: 5
Application Procedure: Applicants must apply directly to the department.
Closing Date: Varies, see the department website for further details
Funding: Government
No. of awards given last year: 1
No. of applicants last year: 10

University of Warwick Research Studentship in Computer Science

Subjects: Computer science.
Purpose: To support PhD students in computer science.
Eligibility: Applicants must demonstrate outstanding academic ability.
Level of Study: Doctorate
Type: Studentship
Value: Fees (full or part) and/or maintenance, based on EPSRC levels
Length of Study: 3 years
Frequency: Dependent on funds available
Study Establishment: University of Warwick
Country of Study: United Kingdom
No. of awards offered: Up to 15 in operation at any one time
Application Procedure: There is no separate application form. The department will automatically consider all PhD candidates.
Closing Date: Early application for the PhD is advised
Funding: Government
No. of awards given last year: 12

University of Warwick Scholarship Scheme (East European)

Subjects: All subjects except MBA.
Purpose: To fund a Master's student at Warwick.
Eligibility: Applicants must be nationals/residents of Bulgaria, Moldova, Belarus, Romania or Georgia, must show potential to make a contribution to home country after graduation and be registered on or applying for a 1-year taught Master's programme. Preference is given to those who have not studied outside their home countries before.
Level of Study: Postgraduate
Type: Scholarship
Value: UK £6,470 fees plus maintenance. Flight allowance given
Length of Study: 1 year
Frequency: Annual
Study Establishment: University of Warwick
Country of Study: United Kingdom
No. of awards offered: 10
Application Procedure: Application forms are distributed by SOROS offices in the relevant countries.
Closing Date: January 14th
Funding: Private, government
Contributor: SOROS, FCO
No. of awards given last year: 10
Additional Information: Address for application: apply to SOROS offices in the relevant country.

THE UNIVERSITY OF WESTERN ONTARIO

1151 Richmond Street, Suite 2, Ontario, London, N6A 5B8, Canada
Tel: (1) 661 2111
Fax: (1) 519 661 3032
Email: ccp@uwo.ca
Website: www.uwo.ca/ccp
Contact: Director

The University of Western Ontario is a modern, well-equipped university offering programmes in all major academic disciplines. With its enrollment of over 25,000 students, the University of Western Ontario is the 5th largest Canadian university and the second largest university in Ontario.

University of Western Ontario Senior Visiting Fellowship

Subjects: Research interests span a wide range of theory and experiment from mathematical physics through chemistry, physics, macro and micro-electronics to many aspects of the biosciences and medicine.
Purpose: To bring established senior scientists to the Centre for Interdisciplinary Studies in Chemical Physics to work on problems that are interdisciplinary in nature and of interest to Centre members.
Eligibility: Open to senior scientific researchers of established standing. There are no nationality restrictions.
Level of Study: Postdoctorate
Type: Fellowship
Value: Varies
Length of Study: 3 months–1 year
Frequency: Annual
Study Establishment: The Centre
Country of Study: Canada
No. of awards offered: Varies
Application Procedure: Applicants must complete an application form, available on the website.
Closing Date: October of the year preceding tenure
Funding: Government

UNIVERSITY OF WOLLONGONG (UOW)

Deborah Porter Academic Registrar's Division Building 36,
Wollongong, NSW 2522, Australia
Tel: (61) 2 4221 3555
Fax: (61) 2 4221 4322
Email: scholarships@uow.edu.au
Website: www.uow.edu.au

The UOW is a university of international standing with an enviable record of achievement in teaching and research, which aims to nurture quality graduates who are experts in their fields and who can work anywhere in the world.

UOW Academic Excellence Regional Scholarship

Purpose: To recognize academic excellence.
Eligibility: Candidates must be from lilwarra, Southern Sydney, South Western Sydney, Southern Highlands and/or the South Coast of New South Wales.
Level of Study: Postgraduate
Type: Scholarship
Value: Australian $3,000
Length of Study: 1 years
Frequency: Annual
Study Establishment: University of Wollongong
Country of Study: Australia
No. of awards offered: 100
Application Procedure: Apply online.
Closing Date: October

For further information contact:

Scholarships Office Northfields Avenue, Wollongong, NSW 2522, Australia

UOW Engineering Scholarships

Subjects: Engineering, materials, mechanical, mechatronics, mining, physics, medical radiation physics, photonics.
Purpose: To award students for academic excellence.
Eligibility: Open to students with strong academic records. Student must not hold any other scholarship or cadetship.
Level of Study: Postgraduate
Type: Scholarship
Value: Australian $3,000
Length of Study: 1 year
Frequency: Annual
Study Establishment: University of Wollongong
Country of Study: Australia
No. of awards offered: 30 (15 of the scholarships will be reserved for women)
Application Procedure: Apply online.
Closing Date: October
Contributor: Bluescope steel Industrial markets and Bluescope steel research laboratories port kembla

For further information contact:

Scholarships Office Northfields Avenue Wollongong, NSW, 2522, Australia

UOW Eurobodalla Shire Council Community Scholarships

Eligibility: Applicants must intend to enroll at Bateman's Bay Education center.
Level of Study: Postgraduate
Type: Scholarship
Value: Australian $500
Length of Study: 1 year
Frequency: Annual
Study Establishment: Bateman's Bay Education Centre
Country of Study: Australia
No. of awards offered: 2
Application Procedure: Students must apply with a complete copy of student enrollment record along with a brief curriculum vitae.
Closing Date: February 26th
Contributor: Eurobodalla Shire Council
No. of awards given last year: 2

For further information contact:

Academic Registrars Division (ARD) Ground Floor, Building 36 Northfields Avenue, Wollongong, NSW 2522

UOW Eurobodalla Shire Council Residential Scholarships

Purpose: To support the students in their first year of studies at UOW.
Eligibility: Applicants must intend to enroll at University of Wollongong, Wollongong Campus.
Level of Study: Postgraduate
Type: Scholarship
Value: Australian $1,500
Length of Study: 1 year
Frequency: Annual
Study Establishment: University of Wollongong, Wollongong campus
No. of awards offered: 3
Application Procedure: Applicants must apply with copies of recent academic records and a brief resume.
Closing Date: February 26th
Contributor: Eurobodalla Shire Council
No. of awards given last year: 3

For further information contact:

Academic Registrars Division Ground Floor, Building 36 North fields Avenue, Wollongong, NSW 2522

UOW Iron & Steal Society Scholarships

Subjects: Materials Engineering.
Purpose: To support students enrolled in a Bachelor of Engineering degree in Materials Engineering.
Eligibility: Candidate must join the Iron & Steel Society before completion of the degree.
Level of Study: Postgraduate
Type: Scholarship
Value: Australian $10,000
Length of Study: 4 years
Frequency: Annual
Study Establishment: University of Wollongong
Country of Study: Australia

No. of awards offered: 2
Application Procedure: Apply online.
Closing Date: October
Funding: Commercial
Contributor: BlueScope Steel Ltd
Additional Information: There is an opportunity for vacation employment at BlueScope Steel Ltd.

For further information contact:

Scholarships Office, Northfields Avenue, Wollongong, NSW 2522, Australia
Contact: Mrs Debby Porter

UOW Loftus Education Centre Teaching Innovation

Subjects: Mathematics, science.
Purpose: To support students with a proven interest in mathematics and/or science.
Eligibility: Applicants must be commencing study as a first-year, full-time undergraduate student in the Bachelor of Science Education or the Bachelor of Mathematics Education at the UOW Loftus Education center.
Level of Study: Postgraduate
Type: Scholarship
Value: Australian $6,000
Length of Study: 4 years
Frequency: Annual
Study Establishment: University of Wollongong
Country of Study: Australia
No. of awards offered: 5
Application Procedure: Apply online.
Closing Date: October
Contributor: Loftus education centre

For further information contact:

Scholarships Office, Northfields Avenue, Wollongong, NSW 2522, Australia

Uow Work-Integrated Learning Scholarship

Purpose: To reward outstanding academic achievements.
Eligibility: Open to students with outstanding academic achievements.
Level of Study: Postgraduate
Type: Scholarship
Value: Australian $3,000–$9,300
Frequency: Annual
Study Establishment: University of Wollongong
Country of Study: Australia
No. of awards offered: Varies
Application Procedure: Apply online.
Closing Date: October
Additional Information: Scholarship holders are required to undertake a period, usually 6–10 weeks of professional work experience each year with an appropriate sponsor organization.

For further information contact:

Uniadvice University of Wollongong, NSW 2522, Australia
Tel: (61) 1300 367 869
Fax: (61) 612 4221 3233
Email: uniadvice@uow.edu.au

UNIVERSITY OF WOLLONGONG IN DUBAI (UOWD)

Blocks 5 & 15, Knowledge village, Dubai, PO Box 20183, United Arab Emirates
Tel: (971) 4 367 2400
Fax: (971) 4 367 2760
Email: info@uowduabi.ac.ae

The UOWD in Dubai, established in 1993, is one UAE's oldest and most prestigious universities. The university strives to provide a fertile environment for bright young minds to flourish, and maintains a long and proud tradition of excellence in education.

UOWD Postgraduate Scholarships

Purpose: To reward the academically outstanding postgraduates.
Eligibility: Open to all outstanding postgraduate students enrolled at the university.
Level of Study: Postgraduate
Type: Scholarship
Value: Payment of tuition fees
Frequency: Annual
Study Establishment: University of Wollongong in Dubai
Country of Study: United Kingdom
No. of awards offered: 9
Application Procedure: Contact the University.
Closing Date: September
No. of awards given last year: 1

For further information contact:

University of Wollongong in Dubai Room G-05, Block 15, knowledge village PO Box 20183, Dubai, United Arab Emirates
Fax: (971) 4367 8047
Email: info@uowdubai.ac.ae

UNIVERSITY SYSTEM OF WEST VIRGINIA

Suite 1100, Charleston, WV 25301, United States of America
Tel: (1) 304 558 0530
Fax: (1) 304 558 0532
Website: www.wvu.edu
Contact: Alicia Tyler, Project Coordinator

The University System of West Virginia works in cooperation with the state college system of west Virginia to deliver quality education to the citizens of the state. The University System and its institutions are governed by the Board of Trustees.

The University System Health Sciences Scholarship

Subjects: Health sciences.
Purpose: To assist students studying in field of health sciences and to practice in rural areas of the state.
Eligibility: Open to all fourth year medical students at a West Virginia school of medicine. Preference is given to West Virginia residents.
Level of Study: Postgraduate
Type: Scholarship
Length of Study: US$10,000
Frequency: Annual
Study Establishment: West Virginia School of Medicine
Country of Study: United States of America
Application Procedure: A completed application form must be submitted.
Closing Date: October 31st

THE US–UK FULBRIGHT COMMISSION

Fulbright House, 62 Doughty Street, London, WC1N 2JZ, England
Tel: (44) 20 7404 6880
Fax: (44) 20 7404 6834
Email: programmes@fulbright.co.uk
Website: www.fulbright.co.uk
Contact: Ms C Norman-Taylor, Awards Director

The US–UK Fulbright Commission has a programme of awards offered annually to citizens of the United Kingdom and United States of America. The United States Educational Advisory Service deals with enquiries from the public on all aspects of United States of America education including sources of funding for study in the United States of America.

Fulbright AstraZeneca Research Scholarship

Subjects: Cell biology, molecular biology, bioinformatics, biochemistry and chemistry.
Purpose: To enable a postdoctoral scientist to carry out research at a top centre in the United States of America.
Eligibility: Open to United Kingdom scientists.
Level of Study: Postdoctorate
Type: Scholarship
Value: UK £15,000 plus round-trip travel
Length of Study: A minimum of 10 months
Frequency: Annual
Study Establishment: An approved establishment
Country of Study: United States of America
No. of awards offered: 1
Application Procedure: Applicants must complete an application form.
Closing Date: Early March
Funding: Private
No. of awards given last year: 1
No. of applicants last year: 12
Additional Information: Short-listed candidates will usually be interviewed in April or May.

Fulbright British Friends of HBS MBA Awards

Subjects: MBA.
Purpose: To enable MBA candidates to participate in United States of America MBA programmes.
Eligibility: Open to European Union citizens normally resident in the United Kingdom. Applicants must hold the minimum of an Upper Second Class (Honours) Degree, have a minimum of 2–3 years of work experience and be able to demonstrate leadership qualities.
Level of Study: Postgraduate, mba
Type: Scholarship
Value: Tuition fees for the 1st academic year
Length of Study: 9 months
Frequency: Annual
Country of Study: United States of America
No. of awards offered: 2
Application Procedure: Applicants must complete an application form and submit this with two references.
Closing Date: Early March
Funding: Commercial, government
No. of awards given last year: 7
No. of applicants last year: 50
Additional Information: Short-listed candidates will be interviewed in February.

Fulbright Distinguished Scholar Awards

Subjects: All subjects.
Purpose: To allow outstanding academics or professionals who are established or potential leaders in their field to undertake a period of professional development in the United States of America.
Eligibility: Open to European Union citizens who are normally resident in the United Kingdom and are planning a minimum stay of 10 months, normally with an affiliation to one academic institution in the United States of America. Proof of this affiliation and details of its nature are necessary. Medical doctors intending to work with patients in any capacity while in the United States of America are not eligible. Awards are not available for peripatetic visits or attendance at conferences only.
Level of Study: Professional development
Type: Fellowship
Value: UK £15,000, visa paperwork fees and visa paid by the Commission and health and accident insurance
Length of Study: A minimum stay of 10 months
Frequency: Annual
Country of Study: United States of America
No. of awards offered: 2
Application Procedure: Applicants must draw up a detailed project outline and provide evidence that a United States of America institution will agree to act as host and supervisor. Lecturers and researchers must have an invitation from the host institution. Completed applications should reach the Commission by the deadline and may not be emailed.
Closing Date: Late March
Funding: Government
No. of awards given last year: 2
No. of applicants last year: 20

Fulbright Graduate Student Awards

Subjects: All subjects.
Purpose: To enable students to pursue postgraduate study or research in the United Kingdom.
Eligibility: Open to citizens of the United States of America, normally resident in the United States of America. Applicants must have a minimum grade point average of 3.5 and be able to demonstrate evidence of leadership qualities. Applicants should be adventurous and be able to demonstrate that they will maximize academic, social and cultural opportunities available in the United Kingdom. A full profile of the ideal candidate is available from the website.
Level of Study: Postgraduate, research
Value: Maintenance allowance and approved tuition fees are covered
Length of Study: 9 months
Frequency: Annual
Study Establishment: Any approved Institute of Higher Education
Country of Study: United Kingdom
No. of awards offered: Approx. 11
Application Procedure: Applicants must submit a formal application with four references.
Closing Date: October
Funding: Commercial, government, private
Contributor: The United States and United Kingdom governments
No. of awards given last year: 20
No. of applicants last year: approx. 600
Additional Information: A telephone interview is required of 48 short-listed candidates.

For further information contact:

Institute of International Education, 809 United Nations Plaza, New York, NY, 10017, United States of America
Tel: (1) 212 984 5466
Fax: (1) 212 984 5465
Contact: Student Program Division

Fulbright Police Studies Fellowship

Subjects: Policing.
Purpose: To enable serving police officers to spend 3–6 months in the United States of America researching an aspect of policing.
Eligibility: Open to United Kingdom police officers (minimum Inspector level).
Level of Study: Professional development
Type: Fellowship
Value: UK £7,500
Length of Study: 3 months
Frequency: Annual
Study Establishment: An approved United States of America Institute of Higher Education
Country of Study: United States of America
No. of awards offered: 2
Application Procedure: Applicants must complete a formal application.
Closing Date: March 30th
Funding: Government
No. of awards given last year: 2
No. of applicants last year: 6
Additional Information: Short-listed candidates will usually be interviewed in June.

Fulbright Postgraduate Student Awards

Subjects: All subjects Except MBA and journalism.
Purpose: To enable students to pursue postgraduate study or research in the United States of America.
Eligibility: Open to European Union citizens who are normally resident in the United Kingdom, hold a minimum of an Upper Second

Class (Honours) Degree and demonstrate outstanding leadership qualities.
Level of Study: Postgraduate
Value: Tuition and maintenance for 9 months and round-trip travel
Length of Study: A minimum of 9 months
Frequency: Annual
Study Establishment: An approved Institute of Higher Education
Country of Study: United States of America
No. of awards offered: 6–10
Application Procedure: Applicants must submit a formal application with two references. Applications can be obtained from the British programme manager or by visiting the website.
Closing Date: End of October
Funding: Government
No. of awards given last year: 6
No. of applicants last year: 300
Additional Information: Short-listed candidates will be interviewed in mid-February.

Fulbright Scholar Grants

Subjects: All subjects.
Purpose: To enable scholars to carry out lecturing and research in the United Kingdom.
Eligibility: Open to United States of America scholars who took their first degree more than 5 years ago. Young academics in their 20s and 30s are actively encouraged to apply.
Level of Study: Postdoctorate, research, professional development, lecture
Value: UK £15,000 inclusive of round-trip travel, pro rata
Length of Study: 3 months–10 months
Frequency: Annual
Study Establishment: An approved Institute of Higher Education
Country of Study: United Kingdom
No. of awards offered: 4
Application Procedure: Applicants must submit a formal application with four references.
Closing Date: August 1st
Funding: Government
No. of awards given last year: 5

For further information contact:

Council for International Exchange of Scholars (CIES), 3007 Tilden Street North West, Suite 5M, Washington DC, 20008-3009, United States of America
Tel: (1) 202 686 6245
Email: we1@ciesnet.cies.org
Contact: Grants Management Officer

Fulbright-Robertson Visiting Professorship in British History

Subjects: British history.
Purpose: To enable a British scholar to spend 10 months lecturing in British history at Westminster College, Fulton, Missouri.
Eligibility: Open to scholars of British history, with 1–2 years of experience of teaching undergraduates.
Level of Study: Professional development
Value: Up to US$40,000 plus round-trip travel for the grantee and up to four accompanying dependants
Length of Study: 10 months
Frequency: Annual
Study Establishment: Westminster College, Fulton, Missouri
Country of Study: United States of America
No. of awards offered: 1
Application Procedure: Applicants must submit a formal application with two references.
Closing Date: Usually at the end of January
Funding: Private
Contributor: Westminster College, Fulton, Missouri
No. of awards given last year: 1
No. of applicants last year: 5
Additional Information: Short-listed candidates will usually be interviewed in March.

US-UK Fulbright Commission Police Research Fellowship.

Subjects: Criminal law.
Purpose: To enable active domestic police officers and police administrators to extend their professional expertise and experience in conducting research into any aspect of policing, in the UK.
Eligibility: Applicants should ideally hold a Bachelor's degree in criminal justice, police studies or a related discipline within the social sciences.
Level of Study: Professional development
Value: UK £7,500
Length of Study: 3 months
Frequency: Annual
Study Establishment: Institutes of Higher Education or a police force
Country of Study: United Kingdom
No. of awards offered: 2
Application Procedure: Applicants must complete an application form available from the organization.
Closing Date: August 1st
Funding: Government
No. of awards given last year: 2
No. of applicants last year: 3

For further information contact:

3007 Tilden Street, Suite 5M, Washington DC, 2008-3009, United States of America

THE US-UK FULBRIGHT COMMISSION

Fulbright Awards Programme Staff, Fulbright House,
62 Doughty Street, London, WC 1N 2JZ,
United Kingdom
Tel: (44) 020 7404 6880
Fax: (44) 020 7404 6834
Email: programmes@fulbright.co.uk
Website: www.fulbright.co.uk

The US-UK Fulbright Commission, supported by both governments, was founded in 1948 and since then over 20,000 scholars have benefited from exchanges between the United States and the United Kingdom. Today, the US-UK Fulbright Commission offers awards for postgraduate study in any discipline as well as a number of professional fellowships.

UK Fulbright Alistair Cooke Award in Journalism

Subjects: Journalism.
Purpose: To finance an aspiring journalist.
Eligibility: US nationals.
Level of Study: Postgraduate
Type: Scholarship
Value: Tuition fees, maintenance and health insurance
Length of Study: 9 months
Frequency: Annual
Country of Study: United Kingdom
No. of awards offered: 1
Application Procedure: See website.
No. of awards given last year: 1

US Fulbright Alistair Cooke Award in Journalism

Subjects: Journalism.
Purpose: To finance an aspiring journalist.
Eligibility: UK nationals and EU nationals residents in the UK.
Level of Study: Postgraduate
Type: Scholarship
Value: Tuition fees, maintenance and health insurance
Length of Study: 9 months
Frequency: Annual
Country of Study: United States of America
No. of awards offered: 1
No. of awards given last year: 1

VANCOUVER PREMIER COLLEGE

200-1338 West Broadway, Broadway, Vancouver, B.C., V6H 1H2, Canada
Tel: (1) 730 1628
Fax: (1) 730 1633
Email: info@vpcollege.com
Website: www.vpcollege.com

Vancouver Premier College of Hotel Management is a learning environment where a multinational student is taught the professional, intellectual, personal and practical leadership skills necessary in providing superior customer care in the hospitality industry worldwide.

Student Ambassador Awards for Hotel Management

Subjects: Food and beverage management, hospitality, hotel and restaurant management, human resource and personnel management, marketing and management, marketing and sales.
Purpose: To offer opportunities to students to learn other cultures and share their own unique experiences.
Eligibility: Open to candidates whose nationalities are not yet or rarely represented at the College.
Level of Study: Postgraduate
Type: Scholarship
Length of Study: Canadian $1,000
Frequency: Annual
Study Establishment: Vancouver Premier College of Hotel Management
Country of Study: Canada
Application Procedure: A completed application form and other related details must be submitted.

For further information contact:

Contact: Ms Silvia Nadeau, Admissions Executive

The Vancouver Premier College Outstanding Student Scholarships

Subjects: Hotel and restaurant management.
Purpose: To award a student for academic excellence.
Eligibility: Open to applicants who are entering or in the first year of hotel and restaurant management.
Level of Study: Postgraduate
Type: Scholarship
Value: Canadian $1,000
Frequency: Annual
Study Establishment: Vancouver Premier College of Hotel Management
Country of Study: Canada
Application Procedure: A completed application form, transcripts and reference letters must be submitted.

For further information contact:

Contact: Ms Silvia Nadeau, Admissions Executive

VATICAN FILM LIBRARY

Mellon Fellowship Program, Pius XII Memorial Library, Saint Louis University, 3650 Lindell Boulevard, St Louis, MO, 63108-3302, United States of America
Tel: (1) 314 977 3090
Fax: (1) 314 977 3108
Email: vfl@slu.edu
Website: www.slu.edu/libraries/vfl

The Vatican Film Library at Saint Louis University in St Louis, Missouri, is a microfilm repository for the Vatican Library manuscripts housed in Rome and a research centre for medieval and Renaissance manuscripts studies in general. The research collections contain a wide range of primary source manuscript materials on microfilm, microfiche and in digital reproduction, in addition to slides and printed facsimile editions ranging in date from the 5th to the 19th centuries, and a large number of incunabula and early-printed books also on microfilm and microfiche. At the core of these collections are the microfilmed copies of approximately three-quarters of the Vatican Library's Greek, Latin and Western European vernacular manuscripts, as well as Hebrew, Ethiopic and Arabic manuscripts.

Vatican Film Library Mellon Fellowship

Subjects: Classical languages and literature, palaeography, scriptural and patristic studies, history, philosophy and sciences in the Middle ages and the Renaissance and early Romance literature. There are also opportunities for supported research in the history of music, manuscript illumination, mathematics and technology, theology, liturgy, Roman and canon law or political theory.
Purpose: To assist scholars wishing to conduct research in the manuscript collections in the Vatican Film Library at Saint Louis University.
Eligibility: Open to candidates who are at the postdoctoral level, or graduate students formally admitted to PhD candidacy and working on their dissertation.
Level of Study: Postdoctorate, postgraduate, research, doctorate, predoctorate, graduate
Type: Fellowship
Value: Travel expenses and per diem expenses (currently US$73)
Length of Study: 2–8 weeks
Study Establishment: The Vatican Film Library
Country of Study: United States of America
Application Procedure: Applicants must write, in the first instance, to describe the topic of the planned research and to indicate the exact dates during which support is desired. A formal application should then be submitted, which should include a cover letter stating the title and proposed dates of research, a detailed statement of the project proposal of not more than two or three pages in length, a list of the manuscripts or other archival materials to be consulted, a selective bibliography of primary and secondary sources relating to the research topic and a curriculum vitae. Applications submitted by PhD candidates should also include a letter of recommendation from their advisor with reference to the applicant's palaeographical and language.
Closing Date: March 1st for research in June to August, June 1st for research in September to December and October 1st for research in January to May

VERNE CATT MCDOWELL CORPORATION

PO Box 1336, Albany, OR, 97321-0440, United States of America
Tel: (1) 541 926 6829
Contact: Ms Emily Killin, Business Manager

The Verne Catt McDowell Scholarship educates pastoral ministers of the Christian Church (Disciples of Christ) by providing supplementary financial grants to graduate theology students.

Verne Catt McDowell Corporation Scholarship

Subjects: Religion, theology and church administration.
Purpose: To provide supplemental financial grants to men and women for graduate theological education for ministry in the Christian Church (Disciples of Christ) denomination.
Eligibility: All scholarship candidates must be ministers ordained or studying to meet the requirements to be ordained as a minister in the Christian Church (Disciples of Christ). Candidates must be members of the Christian Church (Disciples of Christ) denomination. Preference is given to Oregon graduates and citizens of the United States of America.
Level of Study: Postgraduate
Type: Scholarship
Value: US$350 per school month
Length of Study: 1–3 years
Frequency: Annual
Study Establishment: A graduate institution of theological education, accredited by the general assembly of the Christian Church (Disciples of Christ)
Country of Study: United States of America
No. of awards offered: 6

Application Procedure: Applicants must complete an application form and provide details of qualifications, transcripts, three references and state where they obtained information about the scholarship. An interview may be requested.
Closing Date: May 1st
Funding: Private
Contributor: I A McDowell
No. of awards given last year: 6
No. of applicants last year: 12

VERNON WILLEY TRUST

Vernon Willey Trust Guardian Trust, PO Box 9, Christchurch, 8001, New Zealand
Tel: (64) 3 366 6764
Fax: (64) 3 366 7616
Email: gary-anderson@nzgt.co.nz
Website: www.nzgt.co.nz
Contact: Mr G Anderson

Vernon Willey Trust Awards

Subjects: The sheep and wool industry of New Zealand.
Purpose: To assist with research and education into the production, processing and marketing of wool and the general development of the industry for the national benefit of New Zealand.
Eligibility: Open to New Zealand citizens, permanent New Zealand residents or overseas researchers working in New Zealand.
Level of Study: Doctorate, postdoctorate
Type: Fellowship
Value: Varies, usually between New Zealand $30,000–35,000
Length of Study: Up to 3 years
Frequency: Dependent on funds available
Country of Study: New Zealand
No. of awards offered: 1
Application Procedure: Applicants must complete an application form.
Closing Date: The first week in November
Funding: Private
No. of awards given last year: None
No. of applicants last year: 6
Additional Information: Applicants for financial grants must satisfy the Committee that their activities are of general or public benefit. The results of the research or studies are expected to be covered by material suitable for publication in recognized scientific or technical journals.

VICTORIAN COLLEGE OF THE ARTS

The School of Film and Television, 234 St. Kilda Road, South Bank, VIC 3006, Australia
Tel: (61) 3 9685 9300
Fax: (61) 3 9682 1841
Website: www.vca.unimelb.edu.au

Australia's premier visual and performing arts training institution offers training across all artistic disciplines. The teaching philosophy of the college reflects a long held belief that learning comes from doing.

Film Victoria Brian Robinson Script Award

Subjects: Creative film arts.
Value: Australian $250
Frequency: Dependent on funds available
Country of Study: Australia
No. of awards offered: Varies
Application Procedure: Contact the school.
Funding: Trusts
Contributor: Brian Robinson

Film Victoria John Harrison Script Awards

Subjects: Creative film arts.
Level of Study: Postgraduate
Type: Scholarship
Value: Australian $1,500
Frequency: Annual
Country of Study: Australia
Application Procedure: Contact the school.
Funding: Trusts
Contributor: John Harrison

VICTORIAN INSTITUTE OF FORENSIC MEDICINE (VIFM)

57-83 Kavanagh Street, Southbank 3006, Victoria, Australia
Tel: (61) 9684 4444
Fax: (61) 9682 7353
Email: assist@vifm.org
Website: www.vifm.org

The VIFM is a body corporate with perpetual succession that was established by the Coroners Act 1985. VIFM aims to provide timely, high quality and high value forensic medicine and related services, including teaching and research, for Victoria.

VIFM Scholarship in Forensic

Subjects: Forensic medicine.
Purpose: To support students who are likely to make a significant contribution to the field of forensic medicine.
Eligibility: Open to all medical graduates from developing countries.
Level of Study: Postgraduate
Type: Scholarship
Value: Cost of tuition fees and accommodation
Length of Study: 2 years
Frequency: Annual
Country of Study: Any country
Application Procedure: See the website.
Contributor: Indo-pacific Association of Law, Medicine and Science (in PALMS)

VIRGINIA CENTER FOR THE CREATIVE ARTS

154 San Angelo Drive, Amherst, VA 24521, United States of America
Tel: (1) 434 946 7236
Fax: (1) 434 946 7239
Email: vcca@vcca.com
Website: www.vcca.com
Contact: Ms Suny Monk, Director

The Virginia Center for the Creative Arts is an international working retreat that provides a supportive environment for superior national and international visual artists, writers and composers, of all cultural and economic backgrounds, to pursue their creative work without distraction in a pastoral residential setting.

Virginia Center for the Creative Arts Fellowships

Subjects: Writing, musical composition, visual arts, including photography and printmaking.
Purpose: To support literary, musical and visual artists during the most crucial creative phase of their work.
Eligibility: Open to artists with professional competence and promise, regardless of age, sex, citizenship or academic background. Writers, visual artists, composers, choreographers, photographers, film-makers, interdisciplinary and multimedia artists are all eligible. Admission is through a jury selection process.
Level of Study: Unrestricted
Type: Residential fellowships
Value: Subsidized residence at the Center. No cash stipends or travel allowances are provided
Length of Study: 2–8 weeks
Frequency: Annual
Study Establishment: The Center
Country of Study: United States of America
No. of awards offered: Approx. 300 a year
Application Procedure: Applicants must submit an application form, work samples and letters of reference.
Closing Date: January 15th, May 15th or September 15th

Funding: Individuals, commercial, government, corporation, private, foundation
No. of awards given last year: 300
No. of applicants last year: 850
Additional Information: Type of Award: Residential Fellowships. Lasting from 2 to 8 weeks.

THE VITILIGO SOCIETY

125 Kennington Road, London, SE11 6SF, England
Tel: (44) 20 7840 0855
Fax: (44) 20 7840 0866
Email: all@vitiligosociety.org.uk
Website: www.vitiligosociety.org.uk
Contact: Mr Marion Lesage, Administrative Assistant

The Vitiligo Society was established in 1985 as a support group for people who suffer from the skin condition vitiligo, where patches of skin become hypopigmented. This is a chronic, unstable and disfiguring condition that can cause extreme distress and ensuing psychological problems due to loss of self esteem and stigmatization. The Vitiligo Society exists to further the physical, social and emotional well-being of those who are affected by vitiligo. Its mission statement is to promote a positive approach to living with vitiligo and an important aspect of this aim is to support research.

Vitiligo Society Grants

Subjects: Vitiligo-related research in areas such as dermatology, psychology and biochemistry.
Purpose: To facilitate research.
Eligibility: Open to research undertaken in the United Kingdom only.
Level of Study: Postgraduate
Type: A variable number of grants
Value: Dependent on resources available at the time of application
Length of Study: No restrictions
Country of Study: United Kingdom
No. of awards offered: Varies according to funds available
Application Procedure: Application forms are available from the website.
Closing Date: March 31st for the May meeting and September 30th for the November meeting
Contributor: Members of the Vitiligo Society
No. of awards given last year: 1
No. of applicants last year: 3
Additional Information: Although it is keen to fund research, applicants should be aware that the Society is quite a small charity and that its resources are limited. Therefore, it is not usually possible to support long-term salaries or the purchase of expensive technical equipment.

VOLKSWAGEN FOUNDATION

Kastanienalle 35, Hannover, 30519, Germany
Tel: (49) 511 838 1290, ext 212
Fax: (49) 511 838 1344
Email: noellenburg@volkswagenstiftung.de, levermann@volkswagenstiftung.de
Website: www.volkswagenstiftung.de

Volkswagen Foundation Between Europe and the Orient Programme Grants

Subjects: Humanities, social science, natural science (including theoretical medicine) and engineering science.
Purpose: To provide funding aimed at stimulating the research interest of German scholars in the region as well as promoting co-operation projects, and to secure the active participation of scholars and scientists of all disciplines working in the region of Central Asia and the Caucasus.
Eligibility: Open to highly qualified young scientists from those states in Central Asia and the Caucasus that became independent following the collapse of the Soviet Union, especially Armenia, Azerbaijan, Georgia, Kazakhstan, Uzbekistan, Tadzhikistan, Turkmenistan and Kyrgystan. The funding initiative also includes Afghanistan and some parts of the Russian Federation in the lower Volga (Tatarstan, Bashkortostan) and the northern Caucasus regions.
Level of Study: Research
Type: Grant
Value: Varies with the project. The Foundation expects the German partner to administer the allocated funds. For further details on funding, see the Foundation's website
Length of Study: 2–3 years for research projects, 2–3 years for individual scholarships and 6 months–1 year for research visits, co-operation or training visits
Study Establishment: German universities or research institutes
Country of Study: Germany
Application Procedure: Applications need not be submitted on a special form. In the case of joint projects involving scholars and academic institutions in the region (also applications for funding visits to Germany), the German partner needs to submit the application on behalf of all participants. For further details see the Foundation's website.
Closing Date: There are no firm application deadlines
Additional Information: Special consideration will be given to research projects that investigate the political, socio-economic, cultural or natural characteristics of these regions with a view to gain a better understanding of the complex interplay between these factors.

Volkswagen Foundation Symposia and Summer School Grants

Subjects: All subjects.
Purpose: To support the development of new ideas and to promote the discussion of topics and approaches not yet dealt with, in an interdisciplinary and international forum.
Eligibility: Young academics (doctoral candidates, postdoctoral researchers and those working towards qualification as university lecturers) from Germany and abroad are encouraged to apply. The Foundation can grant funding only to scientific institutions and cannot process applications from individuals for travel and accommodation.
Level of Study: Doctorate, postdoctorate
Type: Grant
Value: The Foundation's support is limited to subsidies for travel and accommodation costs for those participants who are unable to finance their study through other means. Summer school participants may also be eligible for funding to prepare and conduct the event, to draw up the working material and to publish or duplicate documents
Length of Study: Varies
Study Establishment: German universities or research institutes
Country of Study: Germany
Application Procedure: Applications need not be submitted on a special form. Applications should be submitted with all required information, allowing sufficient time for the planning and preparation of the event.
Closing Date: At least 4 months before the intended date. Any application beyond this deadline will not be considered
Additional Information: The Foundation will not supplement already existing funding from other institutions. For further details on funding see the Foundation's website.

VON KARMAN INSTITUTE FOR FLUID DYNAMICS (VKI)

Chausse de Waterloo 72, B-1640 Rhode-Saint-Genese, Belgium
Tel: (32) 2 359 9611
Fax: (32) 2 359 9600
Email: secretariat@vki.ac.be
Website: www.vki.ac.be

The Von Karman Institute for Fluid Dynamics (VKI) is an international postgraduate training and research centre specializing in the fluid dynamic aspects of aircraft, spacecraft, turbomachines, wind flows and industrial processes.

VKI Fellowship

Subjects: Fluid dynamics.
Purpose: To support the living costs of recipients who attend the VKI postgraduate diploma course.

Eligibility: Open to citizens of NATO countries, with the exception of Canada, Denmark, Greece, the Netherlands and the United Kingdom, who have the equivalent of a 5-year engineering degree. Applicants must have a working knowledge of English.
Level of Study: Postgraduate
Type: Fellowship
Value: Varies
Length of Study: 9 months
Frequency: Annual
Study Establishment: The VKI
Country of Study: Belgium
No. of awards offered: Varies
Application Procedure: Applicants must submit two application forms, one endorsed by the RTO National Delegate (NATO Research and Technology Organization). Copies of college transcripts and three references are required.
Closing Date: Applications received before March 1st will be given priority
Funding: Government
No. of awards given last year: 21
No. of applicants last year: 52
Additional Information: Please contact the organization or visit the website for further details.

W EUGENE SMITH MEMORIAL FUND, INC.

c/o International Center of Photography, 1133,
Avenue of the Americas, New York, NY 10036,
United States of America
Tel: (1) 212 857 0038
Website: www.smithfund.org
Contact: Ms Helen Marcus, President

The W Eugene Smith Memorial Fund, established in 1979, is a memorial fund to honour W. Eugene Smiths' compassionate dedication exhibited during his 45-year career as a photographic essayist.

W Eugene Smith Grant in Humanistic Photography

Subjects: Photojournalism.
Purpose: To support a photographer working on a project in the humanistic tradition of W Eugene Smith, in order to continue to pursue the work.
Eligibility: Open to outstanding photographers of any nationality.
Level of Study: Professional development
Type: Grant
Value: One grant of US$30,000 with a possible second grant of US$5,000
Frequency: Annual
Country of Study: Any country
No. of awards offered: 2
Application Procedure: Applicants must send a stamped addressed envelope for application information. Application form must be completed, also obtained from website www.smithfund.org
Closing Date: July 15th
Funding: Commercial
Contributor: Nikon, Inc.
No. of awards given last year: 2
No. of applicants last year: 171

For further information contact:

W Eugene Smith Fund, c/o ICP, 1133 Ave of Americas, NYC 10036

THE WALLACE FOUNDATION

General Management, 5 Penn Plaza, 7th Floor, New York, NY 10001, United States of America

The Foundation's mission is to expand learning and enrich opportunities for all people. To achieve our mission we have three objectives strengthening education leadership to enhance student achievement and expanding participation in arts and culture.

Leadership and Excellence in Arts Participation

Subjects: Arts.
Purpose: To build arts participation in communities and as a result provide knowledge and leadership for others.
Level of Study: Professional development
Type: Grant
Value: US$10,000,000
Length of Study: Varies
Frequency: Annual
Country of Study: United States of America
No. of awards offered: Varies
Application Procedure: Contact the Foundation.
Closing Date: No deadline.
Funding: Foundation
Contributor: The Wallace Foundation

Start Arts Partnerships for Cultural Participation

Subjects: Arts.
Purpose: To promote arts participation.
Level of Study: Professional development
Type: Grant
Value: US$700,000
Length of Study: Varies
Frequency: Annual
Country of Study: United States of America
No. of awards offered: Varies
Application Procedure: Contact the Foundation.
Closing Date: No deadline
Funding: Foundation
Contributor: The Wallace Foundation

State Action for Education Leadership Project

Subjects: Arts.
Purpose: To prepare future leader to perform effectively in schools and districts.
Level of Study: Professional development
Type: Grant
Value: US$240,000
Length of Study: 1 year (renewable for up to an additional 2 years)
Frequency: Annual
Country of Study: United States of America
No. of awards offered: 15
Application Procedure: Contact the Foundation.
Closing Date: No deadline
Funding: Foundation
Contributor: The Wallace Foundation

THE WARBURG INSTITUTE

University of London, Woburn Square, London, WC1H 0AB, England
Tel: (44) 20 7862 8949
Fax: (44) 20 7862 8955
Email: warburg@sas.ac.uk
Website: www.sas.ac.uk/warburg
Contact: E A Witchell, Administrative Assistant

The Warburg Institute is concerned with the interdisciplinary study of continuities between the ancient Mediterranean civilizations and the cultural and intellectual history of postclassical Europe before 1800 AD. Its collections are arranged to encourage research into the processes by which different fields of thought and art interact.

Albin Salton Fellowship

Subjects: Cultural and intellectual history that led to the formation of a new worldview, understood in the broadest cultural, political and socioeconomic terms as Europe developed contacts with the world in the late medieval, renaissance and early modern periods and that world came into contact with Europe.
Purpose: To enable a younger scholar to spend 2 months at the Warburg Institute, pursuing research.
Eligibility: Fellowships are generally for younger scholars under 35 years of age as on October 1st; candidates may be pre- or postdoctoral, but should have completed at least 1 year of research on their

doctoral dissertation by the time they apply. Postdoctoral candidates, if over 35 years, must have been awarded their doctorate within the preceding academic year. If it was awarded before, then they should explain the reasons for interruption in their academic career in a covering letter.
Level of Study: Doctorate, postdoctorate
Type: Research fellowship
Value: Applicants domiciled abroad: UK £2,000; Applicants domiciled: UK £1,600
Length of Study: 2 months
Frequency: Annual
Study Establishment: The Warburg Institute, London
Country of Study: United Kingdom
Application Procedure: Applications should made by letter to the Director, enclosing a curriculum vitae, an outline of proposed research, particulars of grants received, if any, for the same subject, and not more than three reference letters written to the Director by the referees, specifying the length of time they wish to spend at the Institute.
Closing Date: December 1st
Funding: Private
No. of awards given last year: 1
Additional Information: Samples of published or written work should be sent, if possible. Applications may be sent by post or fax, but not by email.

Brian Hewson Crawford Fellowship

Subjects: The classical tradition.
Purpose: To support research into any aspect of the classical tradition.
Eligibility: Fellowships are generally open to younger scholars and preference will normally be given to those under 35 years of age on October 1st. Candidates may be pre- or postdoctoral, but must have completed at least 1 year of research on their doctoral dissertation by the time they submit their application. Postdoctoral candidates, if they are over 35 years of age, must normally have been awarded their doctorate within the preceding academic year. If their doctorate was awarded before this they should explain the reasons for the interruption in their academic career in a covering letter.
Level of Study: Doctorate, postdoctorate
Type: Fellowship
Value: United Kingdom-based holders: N/A; overseas holders: UK £2,000
Length of Study: 2 months
Frequency: Annual
Study Establishment: The Warburg Institute, London
Country of Study: United Kingdom
No. of awards offered: 1
Application Procedure: Applications should be made by letter to the Director enclosing a full curriculum vitae comprising name, date of birth, address (including email address) and present occupation, school and university education, degrees, teaching and research experience, publications, an outline of proposed research (of not more than two pages), particulars of grants received, if any, on the same subject and the names and addresses of three persons who have agreed to write, without further invitation, in support of the application.
Closing Date: December 1st of the preceding year
Funding: Private
No. of awards given last year: 1
Additional Information: Those employed as professor, lecturer or equivalent in a university or learned institution may normally hold an award only if they are taking unpaid leave for the whole of the period. The fellowship may not be held concurrently with another fellowship or award. Applications may be sent by post or fax, but not by e-mail.

Frances A Yates Fellowships

Subjects: Any aspect of cultural and intellectual history with emphasis the on medieval and renaissance periods. Preference will be given to those areas of knowledge to which Dame Frances made a contribution.
Purpose: To promote research in any aspect of cultural and intellectual history.
Eligibility: Fellowships are generally for younger scholars under 35 years of age as of October 1st. Candidates may be pre- or postdoctoral, but should have completed at least 1 year's research on their doctoral dissertation before they apply. Postdoctoral candidates, if over 35 years, must have been awarded their doctorate within the preceding academic year. If awarded before, an explanation for the interruption of their academic career should be provided in a covering letter.
Level of Study: Postdoctorate, doctorate
Type: Fellowship
Value: UK holders: UK £2,400–3,200; overseas holders: UK £2,000, £2,900, £3,800
Length of Study: The long-term fellowship is 1–3 years, not normally renewable, and short-term fellowships are 2–4 months, non renewable
Frequency: Annual
Study Establishment: The Warburg Institute, London
Country of Study: United Kingdom
Application Procedure: Applications should be made by letter to the Director, (enclosing) a curriculum vitae, outline of proposed research and particulars of grants received, if any, for the same subject. Samples of published or written work, and the names and addresses of three persons who have agreed to write, without further invitation, in support of the application should also be submitted.
Closing Date: December 1st
Funding: Private
Additional Information: Applications must not be sent by email.

Henri Frankfort Fellowship

Subjects: The intellectual and cultural history of the ancient Near East, with reference to society, art, architecture, religion, philosophy and science; the relations between the cultures of Mesopotamia, Egypt and the Aegean, and their influence on later civilizations.
Purpose: To promote research.
Eligibility: Fellowships are generally for younger scholars under 35 years of age as on October 1st, candidates may be pre- or postdoctoral, but should have completed at least 1 year of research on their doctoral dissertation before they apply. Postdoctoral candidates, if over 35 years of age, must have been awarded their doctorate within the preceding academic year. If awarded before, an explanation for the interruption of their academic career is to be provided.
Level of Study: Postdoctorate, doctorate
Type: Fellowship
Value: UK holders: UK £1,600 and 2,400; overseas holders: UK £2,000 and 2,900
Length of Study: 2–3 months
Frequency: Annual
Study Establishment: The Warburg Institute, London
Country of Study: United Kingdom
Application Procedure: Applications should be made by letter to the Director (enclosing) a curriculum vitae, outline of proposed research and particulars of grants received, if any, for the same subject. Samples of published or written work, and the names and addresses of three persons who have agreed to write, without further invitation, in support of the application should also be submitted.
Closing Date: December 1st
Funding: Private
Additional Information: This fellowship not intended to support archaeological excavation. Application must not be sent by email.

Sophia Fellowship

Subjects: Any aspect of the theory of astrology in historical times, the history of the practice of astrology, astrological iconography, astrology in relation to other arts and sciences and astrology in both Western and non-western societies, particularly in the period before 1800 A.D.
Purpose: To promote research in the history of astrology.
Eligibility: Applicants must normally be 29 years of age or over on 1 October of the academic year prior to which the fellowship is to be taken up.
Type: Fellowship
Value: UK holders: £1,600–£3,200, Overseas holders: £2,200–£3,800
Length of Study: 2, 3 or 4 months, non-renewable

Frequency: Dependent on funds available
Study Establishment: The Warburg Institute, London
Country of Study: United Kingdom
No. of awards offered: 1
Closing Date: December 1st
Funding: Trusts
Additional Information: Applications must not be sent by e-mail.

Warburg Mellon Research Fellowship

Subjects: Humanities in the pre-1800 period.
Purpose: To fund Eastern European scholars in the humanities.
Eligibility: Fellows should have obtained a doctorate or equivalent experience. There is no age limit, but preference may be given to those under 40 years of age and to those who have not previously held an award. Candidates who have held 2 Mellon Fellowships or 1 within the last 3 years are not eligible to apply.
Level of Study: Postdoctorate
Type: Fellowship
Value: Sterling equivalent of US$11,500 each
Length of Study: 3 months; 2 of the 3 months must fall within the Institute's terms
Frequency: Annual
Study Establishment: The Warburg Institute. The applicant may teach elsewhere with the permission of the Director
Country of Study: United Kingdom
No. of awards offered: Three 3-month fellowships
Application Procedure: Applications should be made by letter to the Director. A curriculum vitae giving full details, an outline of proposed research, particulars of grants received earlier, two or three references and to samples of published or written work should be submitted if possible.
Closing Date: April 4th
Funding: Private
Contributor: Andrew W. Mellon Foundation
Additional Information: Applications may be sent by post or fax but not by email.

WARWICK BUSINESS SCHOOL

University of Warwick, Coventry, CV4 7AL, England
Tel: (44) 24 7652 4306
Fax: (44) 24 7652 3719
Email: enquiries@wbs.ac.uk
Website: www.wbs.ac.uk
Contact: Ms Diana Holton, Assistant Communications Manager

Warwick Business School is an international school with 320 staff and 4,100 students from 125 countries worldwide, and is accredited with management associations in North America, Europe and the United Kingdom. Its high-calibre research feeds into top-quality teaching on undergraduate, specialist Master's, doctoral, MBA and MPA degrees.

Warwick Business School Bursaries (for Doctoral Students)

Subjects: Business, management and social science.
Purpose: To aid outstanding applicants to the doctoral programme to complete their studies.
Eligibility: Warwick Business School accepts applications for entry into its doctoral programme from suitably qualified students across a range of business, management and social science backgrounds.
Level of Study: Doctorate
Type: Scholarship
Value: Approx. UK £3,000
Frequency: Annual
Study Establishment: Warwick Business School
Country of Study: United Kingdom
No. of awards offered: Up to 20
Application Procedure: Applicants must contact the Doctoral Programme Office for further application details.
Closing Date: February 9th
No. of awards given last year: 20
No. of applicants last year: 35

Warwick Business School Scholarships (for MBA Study via Distance Learning)

Subjects: MBA.
Purpose: To allow candidates to pursue the distance-learning MBA course.
Eligibility: Au international candidates for distance learning applying for the programme are eligible.
Type: Scholarship
Length of Study: Up to UK £2,500
Frequency: Dependent on funds available
Study Establishment: Warwick Business School
Country of Study: United Kingdom
No. of awards offered: 10
Application Procedure: Applicants must submit a competitive essay to the Business School. This is in addition to the essay that is a requirement of the normal application procedure.
Closing Date: April for the July intake, September for the January intake

Warwick Business School Scholarships (for MBA Study)

Subjects: MBA.
Purpose: To allow candidates to pursue the full-time MBA course.
Eligibility: Students applying for entry into the full-time programme in September are eligible to apply.
Level of Study: Professional development, mba
Type: Scholarship
Value: The scholarships provide up to 50 per cent of the tuition fees, up to a maximum of UK £12,000
Length of Study: 1 year
Frequency: Dependent on funds available
Study Establishment: Warwick Business School
Country of Study: United Kingdom
No. of awards offered: 20
Application Procedure: Applicants must submit a competitive essay to the Business School. This is in addition to the essay that is a requirement of the normal application procedure.
Closing Date: May 31st

WASHINGTON UNIVERSITY

Graduate School of Arts and Sciences, Box 1187,
1 Brookings Drive, St Louis, MO, 63130,
United States of America
Tel: (1) 314 935 6818
Fax: (1) 314 935 4887
Email: graduateschool@artsci.wustl.edu
Website: www.artsci.wustl.edu
Contact: Ms Nancy P Pope, Associate Dean

Mr and Mrs Spencer T Olin Fellowships for Women

Subjects: All subjects.
Purpose: To encourage women of exceptional promise to prepare for professional careers.
Eligibility: Open to female graduates of a baccalaureate institution in the United States of America who plan to prepare for a career in higher education or the professions. Applicants must meet the admission requirements of their graduate or professional school at Washington University. Preference will be given to those who wish to study for the highest earned degree in their chosen field, do not already hold an advanced degree, and are not currently enrolled in a graduate or professional degree programme.
Level of Study: Doctorate, graduate
Type: Fellowship
Value: Full tuition and in some cases a living expense stipend
Length of Study: 1 year, renewable for up to 4 years, or until the completion of the degree programme, whichever comes first
Frequency: Annual
Study Establishment: Washington University
Country of Study: United States of America

No. of awards offered: Approx. 10
Application Procedure: Applicants must complete an application form. Finalists must be interviewed on campus at the expense of the University.
Closing Date: February 1st
Funding: Private
Contributor: The Monticello College Foundation
No. of awards given last year: 8
No. of applicants last year: 450
Additional Information: Candidates must also make concurrent application to the department or school of Washington University in which they plan to study.

Washington University Chancellor's Graduate Fellowship Program

Subjects: Arts and sciences, business, engineering and social work.
Purpose: To encourage students who are interested in becoming college or university professors, and who bring diversity to the campus environment.
Eligibility: Open to doctoral candidates. Applicants must meet the admission requirements of their graduate or professional school at Washington University, and provide evidence that they will contribute to diversity on our campus.
Level of Study: Graduate, doctorate
Type: Fellowship
Value: Doctoral candidates will receive full tuition plus US$21,500 stipend and allowances
Length of Study: 5 years, subject to satisfactory academic progress
Frequency: Annual
Study Establishment: Washington University
Country of Study: United States of America
No. of awards offered: 5–6
Application Procedure: Applicants must complete an application form. Finalists will be interviewed on the campus at the expense of the University. Applications should be addressed to Assistant Dean, Sheri Notaro.
Closing Date: January 25th
No. of awards given last year: 9
No. of applicants last year: 105
Additional Information: The fellowship includes other Washington University programmes providing final disciplinary training for prospective college professors.

WEIMAR CLASSIC FOUNDATION

Marstallstrasse 3, D-99423 Weimar, Germany
Tel: (49) 364 354 5270
Fax: (49) 364 354 5290
Email: lothar.ehrlich@swkk.de
Website: www.weimar-klassik.de
Contact: Professor Dr Lothar Ehrlic

Weimer Classic Foundation Research Scholarships

Subjects: Academic, literary and artistic projects on the cultural history of Europe from the 18th to the 20th century.
Eligibility: Applicants are required to hold a doctorate or show a proof of comparable academic, literary or artistic achievement.
Level of Study: Research
Type: Scholarship
Value: €1,000 per month
Length of Study: 1–6 months (extension possible)
Country of Study: Germany
Application Procedure: Applications need not be submitted on a special form.
Closing Date: There are no firm application deadlines. The selection committee meets in June and December
Additional Information: The Foundation particularly supports: academic, literary and artistic projects funded from budgetary funds; research projects on the Goethe era primarily by foreign academics and funded by the Fritz Thyssen Foundation; and work by young academics on the historical critical edition of Arnim's works, funded by the Globus Holding.

WEIZMANN INSTITUTE OF SCIENCE

Feinberg Graduate School, PO Box 26, IL-76100 Rehovot, Israel
Tel: (972) 8 934 2924
Fax: (972) 8 934 4114
Email: nfinfo@weizmann.ac.il
Website: www.weizmann.ac.il/feinberg
Contact: The Grants Management Officer

The Weizmann Institute of Science is one of the top-ranking multidisciplinary research institutions in the world. Noted for its wide-ranging exploration of the sciences and technology, the Institute houses 2,400 scientists, technicians and research students devoted to a better understanding of nature and our place within it.

Weizmann Institute of Science MSc Fellowships

Subjects: Life sciences, including brain research, cell biology, molecular genetics, biochemistry, biophysics, immunology, biological regulation, plant sciences and bioinformatics; chemistry, including physical, theoretical, organic, biological, environmental sciences and energy research and material sciences; physics, including theoretical, experimental, applied, semiconductor and biological; and mathematics, including pure and applied, computer science and science teaching.
Purpose: To enable study at the Feinberg Graduate School of the Weizmann Institute of Science.
Eligibility: Open to holders of a BSc degree from an accredited Institute of Higher Education in Israel or of an equivalent degree from a recognized overseas university.
Level of Study: Postgraduate
Type: Fellowship
Value: Living expenses
Length of Study: 2 years
Frequency: Annual
Study Establishment: The Institute
Country of Study: Israel
Application Procedure: Applicants must write for details.
Closing Date: May 31st
Funding: Private
No. of awards given last year: 230
No. of applicants last year: 700

Weizmann Institute of Science PhD Fellowships

Subjects: Life sciences, including brain research, cell biology, molecular genetics, biochemistry, biophysics, immunology, biological regulation, plant sciences and bioinformatics, chemistry, including physical, theoretical, organic, biological, environmental sciences and energy research and material sciences; physics, including theoretical, experimental, applied, semiconductor and biological, and mathematics, including pure and applied, computer science or science teaching.
Purpose: To enable study at the Feinberg Graduate School of the Weizmann Institute of Science.
Eligibility: Open to holders of an MSc or MD degree.
Level of Study: Doctorate
Type: Fellowship
Value: Living expenses
Length of Study: 4.5 years
Frequency: Annual
Study Establishment: The Institute
Country of Study: Israel
Application Procedure: Applicants must write for details.
Funding: Private
No. of awards given last year: 656
Additional Information: A special programme is offered to students wishing to take a direct BSc to PhD route.

Weizmann Institute of Science Postdoctoral Fellowships Program

Subjects: Life sciences, including brain research, cell biology, molecular genetics, biochemistry, biophysics, immunology, biological regulation, plant sciences and bioinformatics; chemistry, including physical, theoretical, organic, biological, environmental sciences and energy research and material sciences; physics, including theoretical,

experimental, applied, semiconductor and biological; and mathematics, including pure and applied, computer science or science teaching.
Purpose: To enable study at the Feinberg Graduate School of the Weizmann Institute of Science.
Eligibility: Open to holders of a PhD degree.
Level of Study: Postdoctorate
Type: Fellowship
Value: Living expenses
Length of Study: 1–3 years
Frequency: Annual
Study Establishment: The Institute
Country of Study: Israel
Application Procedure: Applicants must write for details.
Closing Date: January 1st and May 15th
Funding: Private
No. of awards given last year: 204
No. of applicants last year: 350

WELLBEING OF WOMEN

27 Sussex Place, London, NW1 4SP, England
Tel: (44) 20 7772 6326
Fax: (44) 20 7724 7725
Email: jyoung.wellbeingofwomen@rcog.org.uk
Website: www.wellbeingofwomen.org.uk
Contact: Mrs Julia Young, Research Grants Manager

WellBeing of Women is the only UK charity funding vital research into all aspects of reproductive health in three key areas; gynaecological cancers, pregnancy and birth, and quality of life problems.

WellBeing of Women Entry-Lever Scholarship

Subjects: All subjects of relevance to obstertics, gynaecology.
Purpose: To provide Pump-Priming' funds to enable trainees to obtain pilot data for bids for definitive funding.
Eligibility: Work must be undertaken in the UK. Applicants must be from individuals who have not previously been involved in substantial research projects.
Level of Study: Graduate
Type: Scholarship
Value: A maximum of UK £20,000
Length of Study: 1–3 years
Frequency: Annual
Study Establishment: A hospital or university
Country of Study: United Kingdom
No. of awards offered: Varies depending on the amount of disposable income
Application Procedure: Applicants must write for details or access the website.
Closing Date: March
Funding: Commercial, individuals

WellBeing of Women Project Grants

Subjects: All subjects of relevance to obstetrics and gynaecology.
Purpose: To fund research projects.
Eligibility: Open to specialists in any obstetrics/gynaecology interrelated field.
Level of Study: Professional development, research
Type: Grant
Value: A maximum of UK £125,000 over 3 years, with not more than UK £55,000 in the first year
Length of Study: 1–3 years
Frequency: Annual
Study Establishment: A hospital or university
Country of Study: United Kingdom
No. of awards offered: Varies depending on the amount of disposable income
Application Procedure: Applicants must write for details or access the website.
Closing Date: September
Funding: Individuals, trusts, commercial, private
No. of awards given last year: 7
No. of applicants last year: 77

WellBeing of Women/RCOG Research Training Fellowship

Subjects: All subjects of relevance to obstetrics and gynaecology.
Purpose: To fund training in basic science or clinical research techniques and methodology for a medical graduate embarking upon a career in obstetrics and gynaecology.
Eligibility: Research training fellowships are to be undertaken in the UK or the republic of Ireland.
Level of Study: Postdoctorate, research, postgraduate
Type: Fellowship
Value: The upper limit for this award is UK £150,000
Length of Study: 1–3 years
Frequency: Annual
Study Establishment: A hospital or university
Country of Study: United Kingdom
No. of awards offered: Varies depending on the amount of disposable income
Application Procedure: Applicants must write for details or access the website.
Closing Date: March
Funding: Private, trusts, individuals
No. of awards given last year: 2
No. of applicants last year: 16

WELLCHILD INTERNATIONAL

33 Rodney Road, Cheltenham, Gloucester, GL50 1HX, England
Tel: (44) 12 4253 0007
Email: info@wellchild.org.uk
Website: www.wellchild.org.uk
Contact: The Administrator

WellChild is committed to caring for and supporting all sick children, whatever their illness, through research, treatment, prevention and cure, and providing information and advice for all those who care for them.

WellChild Pump-Priming Grants

Subjects: Diseases in children.
Purpose: To enable a student to run a pilot study.
Level of Study: Postgraduate, doctorate, postdoctorate
Type: Grant
Value: Up to UK £10,000
Frequency: Annual
Study Establishment: Accredited institute in the United Kingdom
Country of Study: United Kingdom
Application Procedure: Applicants must download application and guidelines from the website.
Closing Date: September 26th
Funding: Private
Additional Information: Assessment by peer review and the Scientific Medical Advisory Committee.

WellChild Research Fellowships

Subjects: Diseases in children.
Purpose: To support clinicians working towards the development of their own research projects.
Level of Study: Postgraduate, doctorate, postdoctorate
Type: Fellowship
Value: Appropriate salary costs
Length of Study: Up to 3 years
Frequency: Annual
Study Establishment: Accredited institute in the United Kingdom
Country of Study: United Kingdom
Application Procedure: Applicants must download application and guidelines from the website.
Closing Date: September 26th
Funding: Private
Additional Information: Assessment by peer review and the Scientific Medical Advisory Committee.

WELLCOME TRUST

215, Euston Road, London, NW1 2BE, England
Tel: (44) 20 7611 8888
Fax: (44) 20 7611 8545
Email: grantenquiries@wellcome.ac.uk
Website: www.wellcome.ac.uk

The Wellcome Trust's mission is to foster and promote research with the aim of improving human and animal health. The Trust funds most areas of biomedical research and funds research in the history of medicine, biomedical ethics, public engagement of science.

Wellcome Trust Grants

Subjects: Biomedical sciences, from the basic sciences related to medicine to the clinical aspects of medicine and veterinary medicine. The Trust also operates a portfolio of schemes to support research in the history of medicine, biomedical ethics and the public engagement of science.
Purpose: The mission of the Wellcome Trust is to foster and promote research with the aim of improving human and animal health. The Trust aims to: (a) Support research to increase understanding of health and disease, and its societal context; (b) support the development and use of knowledge to create health benefit; (c) engage with society to foster an informed climate within which biomedical research can flourish; (d) foster a research community and individual researchers who can contribute to the advancement and use of knowledge; (e) promote the best conditions for research and the use of knowledge.
Eligibility: Please refer to our website for full information on eligibility, but in brief: Eligible institutions in the UK and Republic of Ireland are normally universities, medical schools, or NHS Trusts. Institutions outside the UK and Republic of Ireland must confirm their status with the welcome Trust. Principal applicants are established researchers who are applying from an eligible institution and are able to sign up to the Trust's grant conditions, and will normally hold an academic or research post (or equivalent) in the UK/Republic of Ireland and have at least five yeas' postdoctoral or equivalent research experience. There are different criteria for the various fellowship schemes.
Level of Study: Professional development, research, postdoctorate
Type: Research grant or fellowship
Value: Varies
Length of Study: Varies
Frequency: Applications are considered throughout the year
No. of awards offered: Varies
Application Procedure: Applicants must submit a preliminary outline for all schemes, except United Kingdom-based projects and programme grants, consisting of a brief curriculum vitae of the applicant, including their source of salary, an outline of the proposed research project and the approximate cost of project. Further information on application procedures is available on the website.
Closing Date: Preliminary applications are accepted at any time. Please visit the website for scheme deadlines
Contributor: Endowment
Additional Information: The Wellcome Trust is one of the most richly endowed of all charitable institutions that fund general medical research in the United Kingdom. The Governors review their policy annually in response to proposals from their advisory committees and professional staff.

WENNER-GREN FOUNDATION FOR ANTHROPOLOGICAL RESEARCH

220 Fifth Avenue, 16th Floor, New York, NY, 10001, United States of America
Tel: (1) 212 683 5000
Fax: (1) 212 683 9151
Email: inquiries@wennergren.org
Website: www.wennergren.org
Contact: The Fellowships Office

The Wenner-Gren Foundation for Anthropological Research supports research, conferences, training, archiving and collaboration in all branches of anthropology, including cultural and social anthropology, ethnology, biological and physical anthropology, archaeology and anthropological linguistics, and in closely related disciplines concerned with human origins, development and variation.

Richard Carley-Hunt Postdoctoral Fellowship

Subjects: Anthropology.
Purpose: To aid the writeup of research results.
Eligibility: Open to scholars within 10 years of the receipt of their PhD.
Level of Study: Postdoctorate
Type: Fellowship
Value: Up to US$40,000
Frequency: Annual
Additional Information: Qualified scholars are eligible without regard to nationality or institutional affiliation.

Wenner-Gren Foundation Dissertation Fieldwork Grants

Subjects: Anthropology.
Purpose: To aid doctoral dissertation or thesis research.
Level of Study: Doctorate
Type: Grant
Value: Up to US$25,000
Frequency: Annual
Application Procedure: Applicants must complete a formal application on an up-to-date form that should be downloaded from the website.
Closing Date: May 1st and November 1st

Wenner-Gren Foundation Post-PhD Grants

Subjects: Anthropology.
Purpose: To support a researcher in postdoctoral fieldwork.
Eligibility: Applicants must have the PhD in hand before they apply.
Level of Study: Postdoctorate
Type: Grant
Value: Up to US$25,000
Frequency: Annual
Application Procedure: Applicants must download an up-to-date form from the website.

WESLEYAN UNIVERSITY

Center for the Humanities, Middletown, CT, 06459-0069, United States of America
Tel: (1) 860 685 3044
Fax: (1) 860 685 2171
Email: bkeating@wesleyan.edu
Website: www.wesleyan.edu
Contact: Ms Brenda Keating, Administrative Assistant

Wesleyan University offers instruction in 41 departments and programmes and 50 major fields of study and awards the Bachelor of Arts and graduate degrees. Master's degrees are awarded in 11 fields of study and doctoral degrees in six. Students may choose from about 960 courses each year and may be asked to devise, with the faculty, some 1,500 individual tutorials and lessons.

Andrew W Mellon Postdoctoral Fellowship

Subjects: Humanities and humanistic social sciences.
Purpose: To provide scholars with free time to further their own work in a cross-disciplinary setting, and to associate them with a distinguished faculty.
Eligibility: Open to persons who have received their PhD within the last 4 years. Scholars who have received their PhD degree after June 2004 in any field of inquiry in the humanities or humanistic social sciences, broadly conceived, are invited to apply.
Level of Study: Postdoctorate
Type: Fellowship
Value: US$45,000
Frequency: Annual
Country of Study: Any country
No. of awards offered: 1 or possibly 2
Application Procedure: Applicants must request a brochure detailing the application process. There is no formal application form.

Applicants should refer to the Center for the Humanities website for instructions on how to apply.
Closing Date: Varies from year to year, but is typically in mid-November
Funding: Private
No. of awards given last year: 2
No. of applicants last year: 285
Additional Information: The Fellow must reside in Middletown during the tenure of the fellowship, give one public lecture and teach one course for 20 students.

THE WHITE HOUSE FELLOWSHIP

The President's Commission on White House Fellowships, c/o O.P.M-Shelia Coates, 1900 E.Street, NW, Room B431, Washington, D.C. 20415, United States of America
Tel: (1) 606-1818
Fax: (1) 395-6179
Website: www.whitehouse.gov/fellows
Contact: White House Fellowships

To maintain the healthy functioning of our system it is essential that we have a generous supply of leaders who have an understanding, gained first hand, of the challenges that our national government faces.

White House Fellowships

Subjects: Domestic and international policy studies.
Purpose: To offer exceptional young men and women first-handed experience working at the highest levels of the federal government.
Eligibility: Civilian employees of the Federal government are not eligible.
Level of Study: Postgraduate
Type: Fellowship
Value: A full-time, paid assistantship to the Vice President, Cabinet Securities, and other top-ranking government officials.
Length of Study: 1 year
Frequency: Annual
Study Establishment: The White House
Country of Study: United States of America
Application Procedure: Application instructions are available on the website.
Closing Date: February 1st

WILFRID LAURIER UNIVERSITY

75 University Avenue West, Waterloo, N2L 3C5, Canada
Tel: (1) 519 884 1970
Fax: (1) 519 884 8826
Email: ahecht@wlu.ca
Website: www.wlu.ca
Contact: Mr Al Hecht, International Relations

Hans Viessmann International Scholarship

Subjects: All subjects.
Purpose: To assist students wanting to study in Germany.
Level of Study: Postgraduate
Type: Scholarship
Value: Canadian $1,050
Length of Study: 1 year
Frequency: Annual
Country of Study: Germany
Application Procedure: Contact University.
Closing Date: June

President Marden Scholarship

Subjects: All subjects.
Purpose: To reward a strong student who best exemplifies the mission of Laurier.
Level of Study: Postgraduate
Type: Scholarship
Value: Canadian $3,900
Length of Study: 1 year
Frequency: Annual
Study Establishment: Laurier University
Country of Study: Canada
No. of awards offered: 1
Application Procedure: Apply online.
Closing Date: September 29th

Ross and Doris Dixon Special Needs Awards

Subjects: All subjects.
Purpose: To create a positive environment for students with special needs.
Eligibility: No restrictions.
Level of Study: Postgraduate
Type: Scholarship
Value: Varies
Length of Study: 1 year
Frequency: Annual
Study Establishment: Laurier University
Country of Study: Canada
No. of awards offered: 20
Application Procedure: Apply online.
Closing Date: September 29th
Funding: Trusts
Contributor: Ross and Doris Dixon

Viessmann/Marburg Travel Scholarship

Subjects: All subjects.
Purpose: To assist students wanting to study in Germany.
Level of Study: Postgraduate
Type: Scholarship
Value: €767
Length of Study: 1 year
Frequency: Annual
Study Establishment: An approved place of study in Marburg
Country of Study: Germany
Application Procedure: Contact University.
Closing Date: June

Wilfrid Laurier University Postdoctoral Fellowship

Subjects: All subjects.
Purpose: To provide full-time research opportunities for recent graduates who wish to pursue independent and collaborative research under the supervision of Laurier faculty.
Eligibility: Applicants must be within 5 years of the completion of all PhD requirements.
Level of Study: Postdoctorate
Type: Fellowship
Length of Study: 1–2 years
Study Establishment: Wilfrid Laurier University
Country of Study: Canada
Application Procedure: Self-funded applicants must submit a copy of their SSHRC or NSERC PDF application, curriculum vitae and a detailed research plan for each year. Applicants who wish to teach will be interviewed by the chair.

William and Marion Marr Graduate Award

Subjects: All subjects.
Purpose: To aid graduate students with special needs.
Level of Study: Postgraduate
Type: Scholarship
Value: Canadian $1,000
Length of Study: 1 year
Frequency: Annual
Study Establishment: Laurier University
Country of Study: Canada
Application Procedure: Apply online.
Closing Date: December 9th
Funding: Private
Contributor: Drand Mrs Marr

WLU Bursaries

Subjects: All subjects.
Level of Study: Postgraduate
Type: Bursary

Value: Up to Canadian $3,525
Length of Study: 1 year
Frequency: Annual
Study Establishment: Laurier University
Country of Study: Canada
No. of awards offered: Varies
Closing Date: November 1st

WLU Graduate Incentive Scholarships

Subjects: All subjects.
Purpose: To reward graduate students who are successful in major external scholarship competitions.
Level of Study: Postgraduate
Type: Scholarship
Value: Varies
Frequency: Annual
Study Establishment: Laurier University
Country of Study: Canada
No. of awards offered: Varies
Application Procedure: Contact University.
Closing Date: No deadline

WLU Graduate Scholarships

Subjects: All subjects.
Level of Study: Postgraduate
Type: Scholarship
Value: Canadian $1,000
Length of Study: 1 year
Frequency: Annual
Study Establishment: Laurier university
Country of Study: Canada
Application Procedure: Apply online.
Closing Date: August 25th
Additional Information: A scholarship is awarded on academic merit, not financial need.

WLU President's Scholarship

Subjects: All subjects.
Purpose: To reward significant contribution to the community as a volunteer or to the discipline as a scholar.
Level of Study: Postgraduate
Type: Scholarship
Value: Canadian $1,985
Length of Study: 1 year
Frequency: Annual
Study Establishment: Laurier University
Country of Study: Canada
Application Procedure: Apply online.
Closing Date: October 24th
Funding: Trusts
Contributor: Dr Neale H Taylor

WLU Student International Travel Scholarship

Subjects: All subjects.
Purpose: To assist Laurier students with travel costs associated with an academic exchange programme.
Level of Study: Postgraduate
Type: Scholarship
Value: Varies
Length of Study: 1 year
Frequency: Annual
Study Establishment: An approved University or Institute
Application Procedure: Contact University.
Closing Date: June

WILLIAM HONYMAN GILLESPIE SCHOLARSHIP TRUST

Tods Murray LLP, Edinburgh Quay, 133 Fountain Bridge, Edinburgh, EH3 9AG, Scotland
Tel: (44) 131 656 2000
Fax: (44) 131 656 2020
Email: maildesk@todsmurray.com
Contact: Trustees

William Honyman Gillespie Scholarships

Subjects: Theology.
Purpose: To allow the recipient to engage in a full-time approved scheme of theological studies or research.
Eligibility: Open to graduates of a theological college of one of the Scottish universities.
Level of Study: Postgraduate
Type: Scholarship
Value: UK £1,000 per year
Length of Study: 2 years
Frequency: Annual
Study Establishment: An approved university or similar institution
Country of Study: Any country
No. of awards offered: Varies, usually 1 to 2
Application Procedure: Applicants must submit applications through the principal of the theological college of which the applicant is a graduate. Application guidelines are available from the Trust or the candidate's university department.
Closing Date: May 15th
Funding: Private
No. of awards given last year: 2
No. of applicants last year: 2

WILLIAM J CUNLIFFE SCIENTIFIC AWARDS

Dessau medical Center, Department of Dermatology and Immunology
Auenweg 38, D-06847 Dessau, Germany
Tel: (49) 340 501 4000
Fax: (49) 340 501 4025
Email: Christos.zouboulis@klinilium-dessau.de

The William J Cunliffe Scientific Awards aim to recognize and encourage innovative and outstanding research in the areas of endocrine dermatology and skin pharmacology, conferring great benefit upon understanding the function of the pilosebaceous unit as well as the pathophysiology and treatment of its disease.

William J Cunliffe Scientific Awards

Subjects: The significance of skin, and especially of the pilosebaceous unit, as hormone target and endocrine organ, the development of new molecules to target skin diseases and the understanding of the molecular action of therapeutic compounds.
Purpose: The William J Cunliffe Scientific Awards aim to recognize and encourage innovative and outstanding research in the areas of endocrine dermatology and skin pharmacology.
Eligibility: Open to persons for any nationality. Living individuals or public or private institutions of any nation, are eligible for nomination.
Level of Study: Professional development
Type: Lectureship/Prize
Value: €12,500 (prize), €15,000 (lectureship)
Length of Study: Nominees will be considered for the year of their nomination
Frequency: Annual
No. of awards offered: 1 per year (major), several per year (small, targeted)
Application Procedure: Applicants must complete an application form. Guidelines can be found on the website www.cunliffe-awards.org Applicants should be nominated.
Closing Date: May 31st
Funding: Corporation
Contributor: Galderma
No. of awards given last year: 6 The William J.Cunliffe Lectureship 2005 (1) The Albert M. Kligman Travel Fellowships 2005 (5)
No. of applicants last year: 8

For further information contact:

Departments of Dermatology and Immunology Dessau Medical Center Auenweg 38, 06847 Dessau, Germany
Contact: Professor Christos C. Zouboulis, Committee Chair Director

WILSON ORNITHOLOGICAL SOCIETY

Fort Collins Science Centre, 2150 Centre Avenue, Building C, Fort Collins, CO, 80526-8118, United States of America
Tel: (1) 970 226 9466
Email: jim_sedgwick@usgs.gov
Website: www.ummz.lsa.umich.edu/birds/wos.html
Contact: The Administrative Assistant

Founded in 1888 and named after Alexander Wilson, the father of American ornithology, the Wilson Ornithological Society publishes a scientific journal, the *Wilson Bulletin*, holds annual meetings, provides research awards and maintains an outstanding research library.

George A Hall/Harold F Mayfield Award

Subjects: Any aspect of ornithology.
Purpose: To encourage and stimulate research projects on birds, by amateurs and students.
Eligibility: Open to independent researchers without access to funds and facilities available at colleges, universities or governmental agencies. The award is restricted to non-professionals.
Level of Study: Unrestricted
Type: Award
Value: US$1,000
Frequency: Annual
Country of Study: Any country
No. of awards offered: 1
Application Procedure: An application form must be completed and submitted with three letters of recommendation and a research proposal. Forms are available from the website.
Closing Date: February 1st
Funding: Private

Louis Agassiz Fuertes Award

Subjects: Any aspect of ornithology.
Eligibility: Open to all ornithologists, although graduate students and young professionals are preferred. Any avian researcher is eligible.
Level of Study: Unrestricted
Type: Award
Value: US$2,500
Frequency: Annual
No. of awards offered: 1
Application Procedure: Application forms are available from the website.
Closing Date: February 1st

Paul A Stewart Awards

Subjects: Ornithology, especially studies of bird movements based on banding, analysis of recoveries and returns of banded birds, with an emphasis on economic ornithology.
Purpose: To support research projects on birds.
Eligibility: Open to students, amateurs and professionals without preference.
Level of Study: Unrestricted
Type: Award
Value: US$500
Frequency: Annual
Country of Study: Any country
No. of awards offered: Up to 4
Application Procedure: An application form must be completed and submitted with three letters of recommendation and a research proposal. Forms are available from the website.
Closing Date: February 1st
Funding: Private

THE WINGATE SCHOLARSHIPS

2nd Floor, 20-22 Stukeley Street, London, WC2B 5LR, England
Email: clark@wingate.org.uk
Website: www.wingate.org.uk
Contact: Ms Faith Clark, Administrator

Wingate Scholarships are awarded to exceptional individuals who need financial support to undertake creative or original work of intellectual, scientific, artistic, social or environmental value of great potential or proven excellence, and to outstanding musicians for advanced training.

Wingate Scholarships

Subjects: All subjects except medical research, fine arts, performing arts (except music), business courses or courses leading to professional qualifications and electives.
Purpose: To fund creative or original work of intellectual, scientific, artistic, social or environmental value and advanced music study.
Eligibility: Open to United Kingdom, Commonwealth, Irish, Israeli or other European Union country citizens provided that they are, and have been for at least 3 years, resident in the United Kingdom. Applicants must be over 24 years of age. No upper age limit. No academic qualifications are necessary.
Level of Study: Postdoctorate, research, doctorate
Type: Scholarship
Value: Costs of a project, which may last for up to 3 years. This is an average of UK £6,500 total to a maximum in any 1 year of UK £10,000
Length of Study: 1–3 years
Frequency: Annual
Study Establishment: Any approved institute
Country of Study: Any country
No. of awards offered: Approx. 40–45
Application Procedure: Applicants must complete application forms, available from the administrator (send an A4 S.A.E) or the website. Applicants must be able to satisfy the Scholarship Committee that they need financial support to undertake the work projected, and show why the proposed work (if it takes the form of academic research) is unlikely to attract the Research Council, British Academy or major agency funding.
Closing Date: February 1st
Funding: Private
Contributor: HHW Foundation
No. of awards given last year: 42
No. of applicants last year: 600
Additional Information: The scholarships are not intended for professional qualifications, taught courses or electives, or the following subject areas: performing arts, fine art, business studies. Musicians are eligible for advanced training, but apart from that all applicants must have projects that are personal to them and involve either creative or original work.

WINSTON CHURCHILL FOUNDATION OF THE USA

PO Box 1240, Gracie Station, New York, NY 10028, United States of America
Tel: (1) 212 879 3480
Fax: (1) 212 879 3480
Email: churchillf@aol.com
Website: www.thechurchillscholarships.com
Contact: Mr Harold Epstein, Executive Director

The Winston Churchill Foundation of the United States was established in 1959 as an expression of American admiration for one of the great leaders of the free world. The foundation was established to encourage and enable outstanding American students to attend graduate school at Churchill College, Cambridge University.

Winston Churchill Foundation Scholarship

Subjects: Engineering, mathematics, computer science and natural and physical sciences.
Purpose: To encourage the development of American scientific and technological talent and foster Anglo-American ties.
Eligibility: Open to citizens of the United States of America only. Applicants must be enrolled in one of 80 institutions participating in the programme, may not have enrolled a PhD and must be no older than 26 at the time of taking up the scholarships.
Level of Study: Postgraduate
Type: Scholarship
Value: Approx. US$40,000
Length of Study: 1 year
Frequency: Annual

Study Establishment: Churchill College, the University of Cambridge
Country of Study: United Kingdom
No. of awards offered: 11
Application Procedure: Applicants must request an application form from the Foundation.
Closing Date: November 15th
Funding: Private
No. of awards given last year: 11
No. of applicants last year: 100

WINSTON CHURCHILL MEMORIAL TRUST (AUS)

Churchill House, 30 Balmain Crescent, Acton, ACT, 2601, Australia
Tel: (61) 26 2478 333
Fax: (61) 26 2498 944
Email: churchilltrust@bigpond.com
Website: www.churchilltrust.com.au
Contact: Ms Louise Stenhouse, Senior Executive Officer, Finance and Administration

The principal objective of the Winston Churchill Memorial Trust (Aus) is to perpetuate and honour the memory of Sir Winston Churchill by awarding memorial Fellowships known as Churchill Fellowships.

Churchill Fellowships

Subjects: All subjects.
Purpose: To enable Australians from all walks of life to undertake an overseas research project of a kind that is not fully available in Australia.
Eligibility: All Australian citizens over the age of 18 years are eligible to apply. Merit of the proposal and benefit to the Australian community at either a local, State or National level are the primary tests. Applications to further tertiary qualifications will not be eligible.
Level of Study: Unrestricted
Type: Fellowship
Value: Approx. Australian $25,000, return economy airfare to the country or countries to be visited and a living allowance plus fees if approved
Length of Study: 4–8 weeks, depending upon the project
Frequency: Annual
Country of Study: Any country
No. of awards offered: 75–100 per year
Application Procedure: Applicants must complete and submit an application form supported by 3 references. For an application form contact the National Office or visit the website.
Closing Date: Last day of February
Funding: Private
No. of awards given last year: 87
No. of applicants last year: 850
Additional Information: Further information is available from the website www.churchilltrust.com.au or the National Office on 1 1800 777 231 (Australia) or 61 2 6247 8333

For further information contact:

Applicants need to apply in their States or Territory of residency.

WINSTON CHURCHILL MEMORIAL TRUST (UK)

15 Queen's Gate Terrace, London, SW7 5PR, England
Tel: (44) 20 7584 9315
Fax: (44) 20 7581 0410
Email: office@wcmt.org.uk
Website: www.wcmt.org.uk
Contact: Ms S Matthews, Trust Office Manager

Winston Churchill Memorial Trust (UK) Travelling Fellowships

Subjects: Approx. ten categories that vary annually and are representative of culture, social and public service, technology, commerce and industry, agriculture and nature, recreation and adventure.
Purpose: To enable British citizens from all walks of life and all ages to travel abroad in pursuit of a worthwhile purpose and so to contribute more to their trade or profession, their community and their country.
Eligibility: Open to British citizens whose purposes must be covered by one of the categories chosen for the year.
Level of Study: Unrestricted
Type: Fellowship
Value: The average award is UK £5,500. This covers all travel and living expenses by individual assessment. The fellowship scheme does not cover attending courses, academic studies, student grants or gap year projects
Length of Study: 4–8 weeks
Frequency: Annual
Country of Study: Any country
No. of awards offered: Approx. 100
Application Procedure: Applicants must complete an application form.
Closing Date: September to October
Funding: Private
Contributor: The public
No. of awards given last year: 100
No. of applicants last year: 100
Additional Information: Awards are announced at the beginning of February, and Fellows may travel after April 1st.

WOLF FOUNDATION

39 Hamaapilim Street, PO Box 398, IL-46103 Herzlia Bet, Israel
Tel: (972) 9 955 7120
Fax: (972) 9 954 1253
Email: wolffund@netvision.net.il
Website: www.wolffund.org.il
Contact: Mr Yaron Gruder, Director General

The Wolf Foundation was established in 1976 by Dr Ricardo Wolf (1887–1981), inventor, diplomat and philanthropist, and his wife Francisca Subirana-Wolf (1900–1981), in order to promote science and art for the benefit of mankind.

Wolf Foundation Prizes

Subjects: In science the fields are agriculture, chemistry, mathematics, medicine and physics, and in the arts the fields are architecture, music, painting and sculpture.
Purpose: To recognize the achievements of outstanding scientists and artists in the interest of mankind and friendly relations among people.
Eligibility: There are no eligibility restrictions.
Level of Study: Postgraduate
Type: Prize
Value: The prize in each field consists of a diploma and US$100,000
Frequency: Annual
Country of Study: Any country
No. of awards offered: 4 prizes in sciences and 1 in the arts
Application Procedure: Applicants must request an application form.
Closing Date: August 31st
Funding: Private
Contributor: The founder, Richard Wolf
No. of awards given last year: 5 fields, to 10 recipients

THE WOLFSON FOUNDATION

8 Queen Anne Street, London, W1G 9LD, England
Tel: (44) 20 7323 5730
Fax: (44) 20 7323 3241
Contact: The Executive Secretary

The aim of the Wolfson Foundation is the advancement of the arts and humanities, science, health and education. Grants are given to back excellence and talent, and provide support for promising projects that may be under funded, particularly for renovation and equipment. The emphasis is on science and technology, research, education, health and the arts.

Wolfson Foundation Grants

Subjects: Medicine and healthcare, including the prevention of disease and the care and treatment of the sick, disadvantaged and disabled, research, science, technology and education, particularly where benefits may accrue to the development of industry or commerce in the United Kingdom and the arts and humanities, including libraries, museums, galleries, theatres, academies or historic buildings.
Eligibility: Open to registered charities and to exempt charities such as universities. Eligible applications from registered charities for contributions to appeals will normally be considered only when at least 50 per cent of that appeal has already been raised. Grants to universities for research and scholarship are normally made under the umbrella of designated competitive programmes in which vice chancellors and principals are invited to participate from time to time. Applications from university researchers are not considered outside these programmes. Grants are not made to private individuals.
Level of Study: Postgraduate
Type: Grant
Value: The Trustees make several types of grants, which are not necessarily independent of each other. Capital Project Grants may contribute towards the cost of erecting a new building or extension, or of renovating and refurbishing existing buildings. Equipment Grants supply equipment for specific purposes and/or furnishing and fittings. Recurrent costs are not normally provided
Frequency: The Trustees meet twice a year
Country of Study: United Kingdom or Israel or The Commonwealth countries
No. of awards offered: Varies
Application Procedure: Applicants must submit in writing a brief outline of the project with one copy of the Organization's most recent audited accounts before embarking on a detailed proposal.
Closing Date: March 1st or September 1st
Funding: Private
No. of awards given last year: 194
No. of applicants last year: 1,200

THE WOLFSONIAN-FLORIDA INTERNATIONAL UNIVERSITY

1001 Washington Avenue, Miami Beach, FL, 33139, United States of America
Tel: (1) 305 535 2613
Fax: (1) 305 531 2133
Email: research@thewolf.fiu.edu
Website: www.wolfsonian.fiu.edu
Contact: Mr Jonathan Mogul, Fellowship Co-ordinator

The Wolfsonian-Florida International University is a museum and research centre that promotes the examination of modern material culture. Through exhibitions, publications, scholarships, educational programmes and public presentations, the Wolfsonian strives to enhance the understanding of objects as agents and reflections of social, cultural, political and technological change. The collection includes works on paper, furniture, paintings, sculpture, glass, textiles, ceramics, books and many other kinds of objects.

Wolfsonian-FIU Fellowship

Subjects: Modern material culture.
Purpose: To conduct research on the Wolfsonian's collection of objects and library materials from the period 1885 to 1945, including decorative arts, works on paper, books and ephemera.
Eligibility: The programme is open to holder of Master's or doctoral degrees, PhD candidates, and to other who have a record of significant professional achievement in relevant fields.
Level of Study: Postdoctorate, doctorate, professional development
Type: Fellowship
Value: Approx. US$425 per week plus travel and accommodation
Length of Study: Approx. 3–5 weeks
Frequency: Annual
Study Establishment: The Wolfsonian-Florida International University
Country of Study: United States of America
No. of awards offered: Varies, approx. 5
Application Procedure: Applicants must complete an application form and submit this with three letters of recommendation. Contact the Fellowship Co-ordinator for details and application materials. Applicants may also download programme information and an application form from the website www.wolfsonian.fiu.edu/education/research/
Closing Date: December 31st
No. of awards given last year: 5
No. of applicants last year: 26

WOMEN BAND DIRECTORS INTERNATIONAL (WBDI)

296 Dailey Hills Circle, Ringgold, GA, 30736, United States of America
Tel: (1) 706 866 9644
Fax: (1) 706 820 1342
Email: robyn509@aol.com
Website: www.womenbanddirectors.org
Contact: Ms Robyn Wilkes, Scholarships Chair

Women Band Directors International (WBDI) is an organization in which every woman band director is represented at the international level, regardless of the length of her experience or the level at which she works. It is the only international organization for women band directors.

WBDI Scholarship Awards

Subjects: Music education.
Purpose: To support young college women presently preparing to be band directors.
Eligibility: Any female student enrolled in college and majoring in music education with the purpose of becoming a band director.
Level of Study: Unrestricted
Type: Scholarship
Value: US$1,500
Frequency: Annual
Country of Study: United States of America
No. of awards offered: 5
Application Procedure: Download the application from our website-essay, 2 letters of recommendations transcript, statement of philosophy, completed application.
Closing Date: December 1st
Funding: Private
No. of awards given last year: 4
No. of applicants last year: 50 per year

WOMEN OF THE EVANGELICAL LUTHERAN CHURCH IN AMERICA (ELCA)

8765 W. Higgins Road, Chicago, IL 60631-4101, United States of America
Tel: (1) 800 638 3522, ext. 2730
Fax: (1) 773 380 2419
Email: women.elca@elca.org

The mission of ELCA is to mobilize women to act boldly on their faiths. As an organization with an anti-racist identity, it offers opportunities for growth by cross-cultural ministry and leadership development.

Amelia Kemp Scholarship

Subjects: All subjects.
Purpose: To provide assistance to women studying for a career other than the ordained ministry.
Eligibility: Open to female citizens of the United States who are members of the ELCA.
Level of Study: Professional development
Type: Scholarship
Value: US$600

Length of Study: 1 year
Frequency: Annual
Country of Study: United States of America
Application Procedure: A completed application form must be submitted.
Closing Date: February 15th
Contributor: Lutheran Church in America

Arne Administrative Leadership Scholarship

Subjects: Church administration.
Purpose: To provide assistance to ELCA women interested in reaching the top of their field as an administrator.
Eligibility: Open to women citizens of the United States who are members of the ELCA.
Level of Study: Professional development
Type: Scholarship
Value: US$500
Frequency: Annual
Application Procedure: See the website.
Closing Date: February 15th

Belmer/Flora Prince Scholarship

Subjects: Theology.
Purpose: To assist ELCA women as they prepare for ELCA service abroad.
Eligibility: Open to women citizens of the United States who are members of the ELCA.
Level of Study: Professional development
Type: Scholarship
Value: US$800–1,000
Frequency: Annual
Country of Study: United States of America
Application Procedure: Application forms are available on the website.
Closing Date: February 15th
Contributor: Lutheran Church in America

Chilstrom Scholarship for Ordained Ministry

Subjects: Theology.
Purpose: To provide assistance to ELCA women during their final year at an ELCA seminary.
Eligibility: Open to women candidates of the United States who are members of the ELCA.
Level of Study: Professional development
Type: Scholarship
Value: US$600–1,000
Frequency: Annual
Application Procedure: Application form available on the website.
Closing Date: February 15th

WOMEN'S INTERNATIONAL LEAGUE FOR PEACE AND FREEDOM (WILPF)

PO Box 28, CH-1211 Geneva 20, Switzerland
Tel: (41) 22 919 7080
Fax: (41) 22 919 7081
Email: inforequest@wilpf.ch
Website: www.wilpf.int.ch
Contact: The Internships Programme

Founded in 1915 to protest against the war then raging in Europe, the Women's International League for Peace and Freedom (WILPF) aims to bring together women of different political and philosophical conviction, united in their determination to study, make known and help abolish the political, social, economic and psychological causes of war and to work for a constructive peace.

WILPF Internship in Disarmament and Economic Justice

Subjects: Disarmament or economic justice, in the context of the United Nations (UN) and international organizations.
Purpose: To focus on the work of the UN and non-governmental organizations (NGOs) in their promoting and strengthening efforts for disarmament and the peaceful settlement of conflict, as well as their involvement in economic justice and North–South relations.
Eligibility: The internships are reserved for women in recognition of the fact that women remain largely excluded from positions concerned with questions of foreign policy and international relations, although their presence in these crucial areas is much needed. Priority is given to women between 20 and 30 years of age and preference is given to WILPF members. Fluency in oral and written English is essential, and Spanish and French speaking skills are an advantage for the work of the interns.
Level of Study: Professional development, postgraduate, graduate
Type: Internship
Value: Round-trip travel from home to Geneva and a small stipend that covers basic living expenses in an expensive city. Accommodation is also provided
Length of Study: From mid-January to mid-December
Frequency: Annual
Study Establishment: WILPF, Geneva
Country of Study: Switzerland
No. of awards offered: 1
Application Procedure: All applications must be submitted a hard copy in English and should state clearly the internship for which the application is submitted. Applications must include a curriculum vitae, a covering letter giving reasons for wanting to follow the programme, a 1,000- to 1,500-word essay about a emails and incomplete applications will not be considered disarmament issue stating why this is of interest and two recommendations from non-family members.
Closing Date: July 30th of the previous year
Funding: Private

WILPF Internship in Human Rights

Subjects: Human rights in the context of the United Nations (UN) and international organizations.
Purpose: To provide leadership training for young women.
To focus on the annual session of the UN Commission on Human Rights, its working groups, the Committee on Economic Social and Cultural Rights and meetings of UN Agencies.
Eligibility: The internships are reserved for women in recognition of the fact that women remain largely excluded from positions concerned with questions of foreign policy and international relations, although their presence in these crucial areas is much needed. Priority is given to women between 20 and 30 years of age, and preference is given to WILPF members. Fluency in oral and written English is essential and Spanish and French speaking skills are an advantage for the work of the interns.
Level of Study: Graduate, postgraduate
Type: Internship
Value: Round-trip travel from home to Geneva and a small stipend that covers basic living expenses in an expensive city. Accommodation is also provided
Length of Study: Early March–Early May
Frequency: Annual
Study Establishment: WILPF, Geneva
Country of Study: Switzerland
No. of awards offered: 1
Application Procedure: All applications must be submitted as a hard copy in English and should state clearly the internship for which the application is submitted. Applications must include a curriculum vitae, a covering letter giving reasons for wanting to follow the programme, a 1,000- to 1,500-word essay about a human rights emails and incomplete applications will not be considered issue stating why this is of interest and two recommendations from non-family members.
Closing Date: July 30th of the previous year
Funding: Private
No. of awards given last year: 1
No. of applicants last year: 75
Additional Information: The intern follows the annual session of the UN Commission on Human Rights, its working group, the Committee on Economic Social and Cultural Rights and meetings of UN Agencies, as well as participating in non-governmental organization meetings and WILPF activities.

WOMEN'S STUDIO WORKSHOP (WSW)

PO Box 489, Rosendale, NY, 12472, United States of America
Tel: (1) 845 658 9133
Fax: (1) 845 658 9031
Email: info@wsworkshop.org
Website: www.wsworkshop.org
Contact: Ms Ann Kalmbach, Executive Director

The Women's Studio Workshop (WSW) is an artist-run workshop with facilities for printmaking, papermaking, photography, book arts and ceramics. WSW supports the creation of new work through an annual book arts grant programme and an ongoing subsidized fellowship programme. WSW offers studio-based educational programming in the above disciplines through, a new annual studio grant programme, its annual Summer Arts Institute.

Geraldine R Dodge Residency Grant

Subjects: Books, printmaking, papermaking, photography and clay.
Purpose: To provide artists with time and resources to create a new body of work or to edition a new bookwork.
Eligibility: Open to applicants resident in New Jersey. Emerging artists are encouraged to apply.
Level of Study: Unrestricted
Type: Grant
Value: A stipend of up to US$2,000 plus materials of up to US$450 and housing
Length of Study: 6 weeks
Frequency: Annual
No. of awards offered: 2
Application Procedure: Applicants must submit an application form, a one-page project description on a separate sheet of paper, a curriculum vitae, ten slides of recent work, a slide script including title, medium, size and date and a stamped addressed envelope for return of materials. Forms are available from the website.
Closing Date: April 1st
Funding: Private
No. of awards given last year: 2
No. of applicants last year: 35

Studio Residency Grant

Subjects: Books, printmaking papermaking, photography and clay.
Purpose: To provide artists with time and resources to create a new body of work or to edition a new bookwork.
Eligibility: Open to applicants national and international applicants. Emerging artists are encouraged to apply.
Level of Study: Unrestricted
Type: Grant
Value: A stipend of up to US$2,000 plus materials of up to US$450 and housing.
Length of Study: 6 weeks
Frequency: Annual
Study Establishment: WSW
Country of Study: United States of America
No. of awards offered: 2
Application Procedure: Applicants must submit an application form, a one-page project description on a separate sheet of paper, a curriculum vitae, ten slides of recent work, a slide script including title, medium, size and date and a stamped addressed envelope, for return of materials. Forms are available from the website.
Closing Date: April 1st
Funding: Government, foundation
No. of awards given last year: 2
No. of applicants last year: 80

WSW Artists Fellowships

Subjects: Intaglio, water-based silkscreen, photography, papermaking or ceramics, letterpress, book arts, ceramics.
Purpose: To provide a time for artists to explore new ideas in a dynamic and co-operative community of women artists in a rural environment.
Eligibility: Open to women artists only.
Level of Study: Unrestricted
Type: Fellowship
Value: The award includes on-site housing and unlimited access to the studios. Cost to artists will be US$200 per week, including their own material
Length of Study: Each fellowship is 2–4 weeks long. Fellowship opportunities are from September to June
Frequency: Annual
Study Establishment: WSW
Country of Study: United States of America
No. of awards offered: 10–20
Application Procedure: Applicants must complete an application form, available on request or online at the website.
Closing Date: March 15th or November 1st
Funding: Government, private
Contributor: Private foundations
No. of awards given last year: 25
No. of applicants last year: 100

WSW Artists' Book Residencies

Subjects: Art books.
Purpose: To enable artists to produce a limited edition book work at the Women's Studio Workshop.
Level of Study: Unrestricted
Type: Residency grant
Value: A stipend of up to US$2,000, plus materials of up to US$450 and housing
Length of Study: 6 weeks
Frequency: Annual
Study Establishment: WSW
Country of Study: United States of America
No. of awards offered: Varies, usually 3–5
Application Procedure: Applicants must submit an application including a one-page description of the proposed project, the medium or media used to print the book, the number of pages, page size, edition number, a structural dummy, materials budget, a curriculum vitae, 10 slides and a stamped addressed envelope for return of materials. Applications are reviewed by past grant recipients and a WSW staff artist. Applicants should write for an application form is on website.
Closing Date: November 15th
Funding: Government, private
Contributor: Private foundations
No. of awards given last year: 2
No. of applicants last year: 150

WSW Book Production Grants

Subjects: Artist's books.
Purpose: To assist artists working in their own studios with the creation and publication of a bookwork.
Eligibility: Open to all artists.
Level of Study: Unrestricted
Type: Grant
Value: Production costs of up to US$1,000
Frequency: Annual
Country of Study: Any country
No. of awards offered: 2 per year
Application Procedure: Applicants must submit an application including a one-paragraph description of the proposed project, the medium or media used to print the book, the number of pages, page size, edition number, a structural dummy, materials budget, a curriculum vitae, 6–10 slides and a stamped addressed envelope for return of materials. Applications are reviewed by past grant recipients and a WSW staff artist. Applicants can download an application form from the website.
Closing Date: November 15th
Funding: Private, government
Contributor: Private foundations
No. of awards given last year: 2
No. of applicants last year: 100

WSW Hands-On-Art Visiting Artist Project

Subjects: Artist's books.
Purpose: To assist an emerging artist in the creation of a new artist's book, while also working with school children in WSW's studio-based Art-In-Education programme.

Eligibility: Open to all artists. Emerging artists are encouraged to apply.
Level of Study: Unrestricted
Type: Grant
Value: A stipend of up to US$2,500, plus materials of up to US$450 and housing
Length of Study: 8 weeks
Frequency: Annual
Study Establishment: WSW
Country of Study: United States of America
No. of awards offered: 2
Application Procedure: Applicants must apply through a two-part application. Artists apply to WSW, WSW juries and then applies to other funding sources. Artists must submit a one-page description of their intended artist book project, including details of the medium to be used for printing the book, number of pages, page size, edition size (100 preferred), a structural dummy, materials budget, a curriculum vitae, a one-page description of relevant work experience with young people, ten slides of recent work and a stamped addressed envelope.
Funding: Government, foundation
No. of awards given last year: 2
No. of applicants last year: 30

WSW Internships

Subjects: Book arts, papermaking, printmaking, ceramics and photography.
Purpose: To provide opportunities for young artists to continue development of their work in a supportive environment, while learning studio skills and responsibilities.
Eligibility: Open to young women artists or students who are aged between 20 and 30.
Level of Study: Unrestricted
Type: Internship
Value: US$150 per month plus housing
Length of Study: 2–6 months
Frequency: Annual
Study Establishment: WSW
Country of Study: United States of America
No. of awards offered: 8
Application Procedure: Applicants must submit a curriculum vitae, 10–20 slides with slide list, three current letters of reference, a letter of interest that addresses the question of why an internship at WSW would be important and a stamped addressed envelope.
Closing Date: October 15th for the Spring-Summer session (January–June) and April 1st for the Autumn-Winter session (July–December. October 15th for Chili Bowl Internship (January–February). April 1st for Summer Intern (June–August)
Funding: Government, private
Contributor: Private foundations
No. of awards given last year: 8
No. of applicants last year: 65

THE WOODROW WILSON NATIONAL FELLOWSHIP FOUNDATION

Po Box 5281, Princeton, NJ, 08543-5281, United States of America
Tel: (1) 609 542 7007
Fax: (1) 609 542 0066
Email: webmaster@woodrow.org
Website: www.woodrow.org
Contact: Ms Judith L Pinch

The Woodrow Wilson National Fellowship Foundation, an independent, non-profit organization, attempts to maximize human potential through education. The Foundation seeks to sponsor excellence in education and thus develop a new generation of leaders.

Andrew W Mellon Fellowships in Humanistic Studies

Subjects: Humanistic studies.
Purpose: To allow exceptionally promising students to prepare for careers of teaching and scholarship in humanistic studies by providing top-level, competitive, portable awards, and to contribute to the continuity of teaching and research of the highest order in America's colleges and universities.
Eligibility: Open to college seniors or recent graduates who are citizens of the United States of America or permanent residents entering into a programme leading to a PhD in the humanities. Applicants must not be enrolled in a graduate or professional study or hold an MA degree.
Level of Study: Doctorate
Type: Fellowship
Value: US$17,500 plus tuition and mandated fees
Length of Study: 1 year
Frequency: Annual
Country of Study: United States of America or Canada
No. of awards offered: 85
Application Procedure: Applicants must provide their full name, current address and telephone number, their address in March, details of their undergraduate institution, major and year of graduation, the intended discipline in graduate school, details of their mailing address and United States of America mail or email. These must be provided by mail, phone, fax or email.
Closing Date: Early December
Funding: Foundation, private
Contributor: The Andrew W Mellon Foundation
No. of awards given last year: 85

Charlotte W Newcombe Doctoral Dissertation Fellowships

Subjects: Topics of religious or ethical values in all fields.
Purpose: To encourage new and significant research.
Eligibility: Open to students enrolled in doctoral programmes in the humanities and social sciences at a university in the United States of America. Students must have completed all predissertation requirements by November 1st.
Level of Study: Doctorate
Type: Fellowship
Value: US$18,000
Length of Study: 1 year, full-time
Frequency: Annual
Study Establishment: Any appropriate graduate school
Country of Study: United States of America
No. of awards offered: 28
Application Procedure: Applicants must write for details.
Closing Date: November 1st
Funding: Private
No. of awards given last year: 35
No. of applicants last year: 450

The Millicent C. McIntosh Fellowship

Subjects: Humanities.
Purpose: These fellowships are specifically intended for recently tenured faculty who would benefit from additional time and resources.
Level of Study: Postgraduate
Type: Fellowship
Value: A US$15,000 stipend
Length of Study: 1 year
Frequency: Annual
No. of awards offered: 6
Application Procedure: Contact the Foundation.
Closing Date: March 31st
Funding: Private
Contributor: Gladys Krieble Delmas Foundation

For further information contact:

Tel: 609 452 7007 ext. 301
Email: mcintoshfellowship@woodrow.org

Woodrow Wilson Grants in Women's Studies

Subjects: Women's studies, the history, education and psychology of women and women's health.
Purpose: To assist those writing dissertations.

Eligibility: Open to doctoral candidates at American universities who have completed all the requirements for the degree course, except the dissertation.
Level of Study: Doctorate
Type: Grant
Value: US$3,000
Length of Study: 1 year
Frequency: Annual
Country of Study: United States of America
No. of awards offered: 20
Application Procedure: Applicants must write for details.
Closing Date: October 11th
Funding: Private
No. of awards given last year: 25
No. of applicants last year: 250

Woodrow Wilson Teaching Fellowship

Subjects: Arts and sciences education.
Level of Study: Professional development
Type: Fellowship
Length of Study: 1 year
Frequency: Annual
No. of awards offered: 1
Closing Date: Please visit website
Funding: Private

For further information contact:

Tel: 609 452 7007 ext. 305
Email: caddeau@woodrow.org

Woodrow Wilson Visiting Fellows

Subjects: All subjects.
Purpose: To encourage the flow of ideas between the academic and non-academic sectors of society.
Level of Study: Postgraduate
Type: Fellowships
Value: US$5,000
Length of Study: 1 year
Frequency: Annual
Application Procedure: Contact the Foundation.
Funding: Private
Contributor: Lilly Endowment

For further information contact:

Visiting Fellows Program
Tel: 609 452 7007 ext. 181
Email: sanford@woodrow.org
Contact: Beverly Sanford, Director

WOODS HOLE OCEANOGRAPHIC INSTITUTION (WHOI)

Woods Hole Oceanographic Institution Bell House, MS #39 221
Oyster Pond Road, Woods Hole, MA, 02543-1531,
United States of America
Tel: (1) 508 289 2219
Fax: (1) 508 457 2188
Email: jfields@whoi.edu
Website: www.whoi.edu/education
Contact: Janet Fields, Coordinator

The Woods Hole Oceanographic Institution is a private, independent, non-profit corporation dedicated to research and higher education at the frontiers of ocean science. Its primary mission is to develop and effectively communicate a fundamental understanding of the processes and characteristics governing how the oceans function and how they interact with the Earth as a whole.

WHOI Geophysical Fluid Dynamics (GFD) Fellowships

Subjects: Classical fluid dynamics, physical oceanography, meteorology, astrophysics, planetary atmospheres, geological fluid dynamics, hydromagnetics, physics and applied mathematics.
Purpose: To bring together graduate students and researchers from a variety of fields who share a common interest in the non linear dynamics of rotating, stratified fields.
Eligibility: There are no eligibility restrictions.
Level of Study: Graduate
Type: Fellowship
Value: A stipend of US$4,150 and travel allowance
Length of Study: 10 weeks
Frequency: Annual
Study Establishment: Woods Hole Oceanographic Institution
Country of Study: United States of America
No. of awards offered: Up to 10
Application Procedure: Application forms may be obtained from the GFD section of the education website or by writing directly to the Fellowship Committee.
Closing Date: February 15th
Funding: Government
Contributor: The United States office of Naval Research and the United States National Science Foundation

WHOI Marine Policy Fellowship Program

Subjects: Marine policy issues.
Purpose: To provide support to research fellows interested in marine policy issues.
Eligibility: Open to candidate with a doctoral level degree or equivalent professional qualifications.
Level of Study: Postgraduate
Type: Fellowship
Value: A stipend of US$51,000 and eligibility for group health insurance
Length of Study: 1 year
Frequency: Annual
Application Procedure: Applications are available online.
Closing Date: January 15th

WHOI Postdoctoral Awards in Marine Policy and Ocean Management

Subjects: Novel proposals in such fields as political science, international affairs, decision theory, economics, diplomacy, management, geography, law, engineering and anthropology will be considered.
Eligibility: Open to Scholars and practitioners from relevant fields in the social sciences, natural sciences, law and management who are interested in applying their disciplinary training and experience to investigations which require a significant component of marine research. Applicants must have completed their doctorate degree or possess equivalent professional qualifications through career experience.
Level of Study: Postdoctorate
Value: Please contact the organization
Length of Study: 1 year
Frequency: Annual
Study Establishment: Woods Hole Oceanographic Institution
Country of Study: United States of America
No. of awards offered: Varies
Closing Date: January 15th for notification in March
Additional Information: Award recipients in the programme have pursued such studies as the implications of oil exploration along the North eastern coast of the United States of America, problems of international law created by new developments in aquaculture and fish farming, economic benefits of some oceanographic research, a perceptual study of New England fishermen, and oceanic waste disposal.

WHOI Postdoctoral Fellowships in Ocean Science and Engineering

Subjects: Oceanography and oceanographic engineering.
Purpose: To further the education and training of recent recipients of doctoral degrees in engineering science or with interests in marine science.
Eligibility: Open to United States citizens and foreign nationals who have earned a PhD degree in biology, physics, microbiology, molecular biology, chemistry, geology, geophysics, oceanography, meteorology, engineering or mathematics. Scientists with more than three years of postdoctoral experience are not eligible.

Level of Study: Postdoctorate
Type: Fellowship
Value: Please contact the organization
Length of Study: 1 year
Frequency: Annual
Study Establishment: Woods Hole Oceanographic Institution
Country of Study: United States of America
No. of awards offered: 7–10
Application Procedure: Applicants must complete and submit an application form with transcripts, reference letters, complete transcripts of undergraduate and graduate records, and a concise statement describing research interests. Further information and application forms may be obtained from the postdoctoral section of the website.
Closing Date: January 15th for notification in March
Funding: Private, government
Additional Information: Award holders work in the laboratory under the general supervision of an appropriate member of the staff, but are expected to work independently on research problems of their own choice.

WHOI Postdoctoral Scholarship Program

Subjects: Chemistry, engineering, geology, geophysics, mathematics, meteorology, physics, biology and oceanography.
Purpose: To further education and training.
Eligibility: Open to applicants who have related their doctoral degree within the past 2–3 years.
Level of Study: Postdoctorate
Type: Scholarship
Value: A stipend of US$52,000 plus a relocation allowance
Length of Study: 18 months
No. of awards offered: 5–6

WHOI Research Fellowships in Marine Policy

Subjects: Oceanography, social and behavioural sciences, political science, international relations, economics and law as related to marine policy.
Purpose: To provide support and experience to scientists interested in marine policy issues, to provide opportunities for interdisciplinary application of social sciences and natural sciences to marine policy problems, and to conduct research and convey information necessary for the development of effective local, national and international ocean policy.
Eligibility: Open to citizens of the United States and foreign nationals with a PhD or equivalent professional experience.
Level of Study: Professional development, postdoctorate
Type: Fellowship
Value: Please contact the organization
Length of Study: 1 year
Frequency: Annual
Study Establishment: Woods Hole Oceanographic Institution
Country of Study: United States of America
No. of awards offered: 1
Application Procedure: Applicants must complete and submit a formal application form with transcripts, three references and a proposal for a research project to undertake whilst at the Institution.
Closing Date: January 15th
Funding: Government, private

WHOI/NOAA Co-operative Institute for Climate and Ocean Research Postdoctoral Fellowship

Subjects: Coastal ocean and near shore processes, the ocean's participation in climate and climate variability and marine ecosystem processes analysis.
Purpose: To build ties between WHOI investigators and colleagues at NOAA laboratories and to develop co-operative NOAA funded research at academic institutions in the Northeastern United States of America. The fellowship also aims to further the education and training of recent recipients of doctoral degrees in the marine sciences.
Eligibility: Open to United States citizens and foreign nationals who have earned a PhD degree in biology, physics, microbiology, molecular biology, chemistry, geology, geophysics, oceanography, meteorology, engineering or mathematics. Scientists with more than three years of postdoctoral experience are not eligible.
Level of Study: Postdoctorate
Type: Fellowship
Value: US$49,000 per year
Length of Study: 18 months
Frequency: Annual
Study Establishment: Woods Hole Oceanographic Institution
Country of Study: United States of America
No. of awards offered: 1
Application Procedure: Applicants must complete and submit an application form with transcripts, reference letters, complete transcripts of undergraduate and graduate records and a concise statement describing research interests. Further information and application forms may be obtained from the education section of the website.
Closing Date: January 15th for notification in March
Funding: Government
Contributor: The NOAA
Additional Information: Award holders work in the laboratory under the general supervision of an appropriate member of the staff, but are expected to work independently on research problems of their own choice.

WORLD BANK INSTITUTE

1818 H Street, Washington, NW, DC 20433, United States of America
Tel: (1) 473 1000
Fax: (1) 477 6391
Website: www.worldbank.org
Contact: Communications Officer

One of the largest sources of funding and knowledge for transition and development councils; The World Bank uses its financial resources, staff and extensive experience to help developing countries reduce poverty, increase economic growth and improve their quality of life.

World Bank Grants Facility for Indigenous Peoples

Subjects: Indigenous culture, intellectual property and human rights.
Purpose: To support sustainable and culturally appropriate development projector planed and implemented by and for Indigenous People.
Eligibility: Applicants must belong to an Indigenous Peoples' community or organization.
Level of Study: Research, professional development
Value: 20% of total project cost ranging between US$10,000 and US$30,000
Frequency: Annual
Application Procedure: A complete application, not more than 10 pages, should be submitted.
Closing Date: November 15th
Contributor: The World Bank

For further information contact:

World Bank Grants Facility for Indigenous Peoples, Social Development Department, Mailstop MC 5-52b, World Bank, 1818 H Street, Washington, NW, DC 20433, United States of America
Fax: (1) 1 202 522 1669
Email: indigenouspeoples@worldbank.org

World Bank Small Grant Program

Subjects: Civil engagement.
Purpose: To strengthen the voice and influence of poor and marginalized groups.
Eligibility: Visit the website, requester and proposals should not be sent to the World Bank Office in Washington, D.C.
Level of Study: Postgraduate
Type: Grant
Value: US$3,000–7,000 with a maximum of US$15,000
Frequency: Annual
Application Procedure: Guidelines and application forms available from the participating World Bank country office.
Closing Date: The small grants program makes decisions only once a year by June; applicant organizations should apply at least four to six months in advance of the date of the grant activity.
Contributor: The World Bank

WORLD LEARNING

School for International Training (SIT), Kipling Road, PO Box 676, Brattleboro, VT, 05301, United States of America
Tel: (1) 802 258 3510
Fax: (1) 802 258 3500
Email: admissions@sit.edu
Website: www.worldlearning.org
Contact: Ms Shannon Simrell, Enrolment Services

The School for International Training (SIT) at World Learning educates leaders capable of bridging differences between people and nations in an effort to build a more peaceful and sustainable world. Accredited by the New England Association of Schools and Colleges, SIT offers Master's degrees in international and intercultural fields, as well as continuing education opportunities, management development courses and peace and conflict transformation training.

School for International Training (SIT) Extension

Subjects: Teacher education, organizational management, web-based research and instruction and conflict transformation.
Purpose: To offer continuing education opportunities for professionals through innovative, high-quality courses.
Eligibility: Open to persons of any nationality.
Length of Study: 1 week–1 month
Study Establishment: SIT
No. of awards offered: Varies
Application Procedure: Applicants must write for details or visit the website.
Additional Information: Online and on-campus intensive formats allow professionals from around the world to engage in reflective learning and practice while working in their chosen fields. For information on deadlines and other aspects of the awards please visit the website www.sit.edu/extension

School for International Training (SIT) Master of Arts in Teaching Program

Subjects: Reflection, observation, self-evaluation, experiential learning and skills development within a strong learning community.
Purpose: To prepare language teachers committed to professional development and service in their field.
Eligibility: Open to persons of any nationality who are preparing for a language teaching career. Awards are available only to students studying at the School for International Training.
Level of Study: Graduate
Type: Scholarship
Value: Varies
Length of Study: A period that includes a time of student teaching and homestay. The programme is offered in a 1-year or 2-Summer format designed for working professionals
Frequency: Annual
Study Establishment: SIT
Country of Study: Any country
No. of awards offered: Varies
Application Procedure: Applicants must complete an institutional financial aid application and should contact the Financial Aid Office for further details, by email at finaid@sit.edu
Closing Date: Rolling admissions
Additional Information: Students master technical teaching methodologies through language classroom practice, on campus coursework and a supervised teaching internship. Further information is available on the website www.sit.edu/mat

School for International Training (SIT) Programmes in Intercultural Service, Leadership and Management

Subjects: International student services, international recruitment, student advising, community education, citizen exchange and educational travel, theory and history of international education, immigration law and practice, advising and management, multicultural organization development, citizen capacity building, multinational human resource development, community development and social action, human resource development and training, diversity leadership, programme planning, proposal writing, policy advocacy and training, cultural, political, economic and environmental context of management, strategic planning, management of human and financial resources, marketing and the theory and practice of sustainable development, conflict and identity or conflict analysis.
Purpose: To provide funding for competency-based, professional level training for intercultural managers through the following courses: SIT's Master of Arts in International Education, SIT's Master of Arts in Conflict Transformation, SIT's Master of Arts in Intercultural Relations, SIT's Master of Arts in Sustainable Development, SIT's Master of Science in Organizational Management and SIT's Master of Arts in Intercultural Service, Leadership and Management.
Eligibility: Open to persons of any nationality.
Level of Study: Graduate
Type: Scholarship
Value: Varies
Frequency: Annual
Study Establishment: SIT
Country of Study: Any country
No. of awards offered: Varies
Application Procedure: Applicants must complete an institutional financial aid application and should contact the Financial Aid Office for further details by email at finaid@sit.edu
Closing Date: Rolling admissions
Additional Information: Further information is available on the website www.sit.edu/degree.html

WORLD METEOROLOGICAL ORGANIZATION (WMO)

Education & Training Department, 7 bis Avenue de la Paix, Case postale No 2300 CH-1211 Geneva, Switzerland
Tel: (41) 22 730 81 11
Fax: (41) 22 730 81 81
Email: ipa@www.wmo.ch
Website: www.wmo.ch
Contact: Director

The World Meteorological Organization (WMO) is an inter-governmental organization with a membership of 185 member states and territories. It originated from the International Meteorological Organization, which was founded in 1873. Set up in 1950, WMO became the specialized agency of the United Nations for meteorology, weather and climate, operational hydrology and related sciences.

WMO Education and Training Fellowships

Subjects: Atmospheric science, meteorology, operational hydrology and related sciences.
Purpose: To educate and train meteorological personnel on individually tailored or group-study training programmes.
Eligibility: Open to nationals from WMO member countries. Potential candidates should meet the requirements for academic qualifications, relevant experience, language proficiency, age limits and other specific requirements, as stipulated by the host training institutions concerned.
Level of Study: Professional development
Type: Fellowship
Value: According to United Nations rates
Length of Study: Varies
Frequency: Dependent on funds available
Study Establishment: Dependent on the required training or education
Country of Study: The applicants home country
No. of awards offered: Approx. 300
Application Procedure: Applicants must be designated officially through the permanent representative with WMO, which will normally be the Director of the National Meteorological Service in the requesting country concerned.
Funding: Government
Contributor: United Nation Development Programme (UNDP), Trust Funds and the Voluntary Co-operation Programme (VCP) and the Regular Budget (RB) of WMO
No. of awards given last year: 310
No. of applicants last year: 590

THE WORSHIPFUL COMPANY OF MUSICIANS

6th Floor, 2 London Wall Buildings, London, EC2M 5PP, England
Tel: (44) 20 7496 8980
Fax: (44) 20 7588 3633
Email: deputyclerk@wcom.org.uk
Website: www.wcom.org.uk
Contact: Ms Margaret Alford, Deputy Clerk

The Worshipful Company of Musicians supports young musicians particularly in the wilderness years between graduating and setting out on their musical careers.

Allcard Grants

Subjects: Music.
Purpose: To support the advanced training of performers at home or abroad for string, voice or piano accompanists, and wind instruments in exceptional circumstances.
Eligibility: Open to individuals wishing to undertake a relevant training or research programme. The grants are not available for courses leading either to a first degree at a university or to a diploma at a college of music, and only in exceptional circumstances will assistance towards the cost of a 4th or 5th year at a college of music be considered. Grants are not available towards the purchase of instruments. Applicants must have studied at a British institution for at least 3 years.
Level of Study: Postgraduate
Type: Grant
Value: Up to UK £3,000
Frequency: Annual
Country of Study: Any country
No. of awards offered: A limited number
Application Procedure: Applicants must be nominated by principals or heads of music departments at the Royal Academy of Music, the Royal College of Music, the Guildhall School of Music, the Royal Northern College of Music, the Royal Scottish Academy of Music, the Welsh College of Music, the Birmingham Conservatoire, the Trinity College of Music, City University, Huddersfield University, Goldsmiths or other university departments.
Closing Date: Applications are to be made after January 1st and before April 30th
No. of awards given last year: 4
No. of applicants last year: 30

Carnwath Scholarship

Subjects: Music.
Purpose: To support young pianists.
Eligibility: Open to any person permanently resident in the United Kingdom and 21–25 years of age. The scholarship is intended only for the advanced student who has successfully completed a solo performance course at a college of music.
Level of Study: Postgraduate
Type: Scholarship
Value: UK £4,150 per year
Length of Study: Up to 2 years
Frequency: Every 2 years
Country of Study: United Kingdom
No. of awards offered: 1
Application Procedure: Applicants must be nominated by principals of the Royal Academy of Music, the Guildhall School of Music, the Royal Northern College of Music, the Royal Scottish Academy of Music, Trinity College of Music, London College of Music, the Welsh College of Music, the Birmingham School of Music or the Royal College of Music. No application should be made directly to the Worshipful Company of Musicians.
Closing Date: June 1st in the year of the award

John Clementi Collard Fellowship

Subjects: Music.
Eligibility: Open to professional musicians of standing and experience who show excellence in one or more of the higher branches of musical activity, such as composition, research and performance including conducting.
Level of Study: Postgraduate
Type: Fellowship
Value: UK £5,000 per year
Length of Study: 1 year
Frequency: Dependent on funds available, approx. every 3 years
Country of Study: United Kingdom
No. of awards offered: 1
Application Procedure: Applicants must be nominated by professors of music at Oxford, Cambridge or London Universities, directors of the Royal College of Music, principals of the Royal Academy of Music, the Guildhall School of Music or the Royal Northern College of Music. No application should be made directly to the Worshipful Company of Musicians.

Maisie Lewis Young Artists Fund

Subjects: Musical performance.
Purpose: To assist young artists of outstanding ability who wish to acquire experience on the professional soloist concert platform.
Eligibility: Open to instrumentalists including organists up to 28 years of age and to singers of up to 32 years of age.
Level of Study: Postgraduate
Value: Reimbursement of recitalists' expenses
Frequency: Annual
Country of Study: United Kingdom
No. of awards offered: 4–6 half recitals per year
Application Procedure: Applicants must complete an application form, available from January 1st.
No. of awards given last year: 4
No. of applicants last year: 80
Additional Information: Auditions are held in March.

YONSEI UNIVERSITY

134 Sinchon-dong, Seodaemun-gu, Seoul, 120-749, Korea
Tel: (82) 2 212 33291-4
Fax: (82) 2 392 3321
Email: gsis@yonsei.ac.kr
Website: www.yonsci.ac.kr/yu/eng/contact.html
Contact: Jisook Han, Admissions Officer

Yonsei University offers Master's and PhD programmes in English.

Hwa Am Scholarship

Subjects: All subjects.
Purpose: To financially assist students.
Eligibility: Students with promise in the field of international co-operation are eligible to apply.
Level of Study: Postgraduate
Type: Scholarship
Value: Approx. US$840, up to US$1,670
Length of Study: 1 semester
Frequency: Each semester
Study Establishment: GSIS
Country of Study: Korea
No. of awards offered: 2–3
Application Procedure: Applicants are selected by the GSIS.
Closing Date: The end of May for Autumn entry and the end of November for Spring entry
Funding: Private
No. of awards given last year: None
No. of applicants last year: None

International Students Award

Subjects: All subjects.
Purpose: To financially assist students.
Eligibility: Open to incoming students from respective continents with good academic records and in need of financial support.
Type: Award
Value: US$770–3,077
Length of Study: 1 semester
Frequency: Each semester

Study Establishment: GSIS
Country of Study: Korea
No. of awards offered: 2–3 from each continent
Application Procedure: Applicants must complete an application form.
Closing Date: The end of May for Autumn entry
Funding: Private

Korea Foundation Fellowship

Subjects: Korean studies.
Purpose: To financially assist foreign students specializing in Korean studies.
Eligibility: Korean nationals are not eligible to apply.
Level of Study: Postgraduate, doctorate
Type: Fellowship
Value: Approx. US$3,340 (PhD) and US$1,670 (MA)
Length of Study: 1 semester
Frequency: Each semester
Study Establishment: GSIS
Country of Study: Korea
No. of awards offered: 3–5
Application Procedure: Applicants must complete an application form.
Closing Date: The end of May for Autumn entry and the end of November for Spring entry
Funding: Private

Korea-Japan Cultural Association Scholarship

Subjects: All subjects.
Purpose: To financially assist students.
Eligibility: Open to Japanese students with good academic records.
Level of Study: Postgraduate, doctorate
Type: Scholarship
Value: US$1,347
Length of Study: 1 semester
Frequency: Each semester
Study Establishment: GSIS
Country of Study: Korea
No. of awards offered: 1–2
Application Procedure: Applicants are selected by KJCAS.
Closing Date: The end of May for Autumn entry and the end of November for Spring entry
Funding: Private

Kwanjeong Scholarship for Chinese Young Leaders

Subjects: All subjects.
Purpose: To financially assist students.
Eligibility: Open to incoming or current Chinese students with academic and professional promise.
Type: Scholarship
Value: US$3,330
Length of Study: 1 semester
Frequency: Each semester
Study Establishment: GSIS
Country of Study: Korea
No. of awards offered: Up to 30
Application Procedure: Applicants must complete an application form.
Closing Date: The end of May for Autumn entry and the end of November for Spring entry
Funding: Private

Scholarship for Academic Excellence

Subjects: All subjects.
Purpose: To financially assist students.
Eligibility: Open to students with a grade point average of over 3.7 and in need of financial aid.
Level of Study: Doctorate, postgraduate
Type: Scholarship
Value: US$840–3,340
Length of Study: 1 semester
Frequency: Each semester
Study Establishment: GSIS
Country of Study: Korea
No. of awards offered: Unlimited
Application Procedure: Applicants must complete a financial Aid application reviewed by GSIS.
Closing Date: The end of May for Autumn entry and the end of November for Spring entry
Funding: Private

Underwood Fellowship

Subjects: All subjects.
Purpose: To financially assist students with a high grade point average and a commitment to good citizenship.
Eligibility: Korean nationals are eligible to apply.
Level of Study: Postgraduate
Type: Fellowship
Value: Approx. US$1,670
Length of Study: 1 semester
Frequency: Each semester
Study Establishment: GSIS
Country of Study: Korea
No. of awards offered: 3–4
Application Procedure: Applicants must complete an application form.
Closing Date: The end of May for Autumn entry and the end of November for Spring entry
Funding: Private

Yonsei University Incoming Students Award

Subjects: All subjects.
Purpose: To financially assist students.
Eligibility: Incoming students who show outstanding academic potential.
Level of Study: Doctorate, postgraduate
Value: Not specified
Length of Study: 1 semester
Frequency: First semester only
Study Establishment: GSIS
Country of Study: Korea
No. of awards offered: Up to 10
Application Procedure: Applicants are selected by the GSIS.
Closing Date: The end of May for Autumn entry
Funding: Private

YORKSHIRE SCULPTURE PARK

Bretton Hall, West Bretton, Wakefield, Yorkshire, WF4 4LG, England
Tel: (44) 19 2483 0579
Fax: (44) 19 2480 0044
Website: www.ysp.co.uk
Contact: Dr Peter Murray, Administrator

Yorkshire Sculpture Park is one of Europe's leading open-air art organizations showing modern and contemporary work by leading United Kingdom and international artists.

Feiweles Trust Dance Bursary

Subjects: Dance, music, art, sculpture.
Purpose: To support an artist at the beginning of their career, after training.
Level of Study: Postgraduate
Type: Bursary
Value: UK £10,000
Length of Study: 3 months
Frequency: Annual
Study Establishment: Workshops within the community
Country of Study: United Kingdom
Application Procedure: Applicants must send a letter, explaining exactly how the bursary would benefit the development of their career and a full curriculum vitae.
Closing Date: February 20th
Funding: Private
Contributor: Feiweles Trust

Additional Information: It is expected that the appointed artists will use this bursary experience to develop their own artistic practice. A different art form is supported each year.

ZONTA INTERNATIONAL FOUNDATION

557 West Randdph Street, Chicago, Illinois 60661-2202,
United States of America
Tel: (1) 930 5848
Fax: (1) 930 0951
Email: aubides@zonta.org
Website: www.zonta.org
Tel: 190200 UT
Contact: Ms Ana L Ubides, Programme Co-ordinator

The Foundation is a worldwide service organization of executives in business and the professions working together to advance the status of women. The Amelia Earhart Fellowship was established in 1938 in honour of Amelia Earhart, famed pilot and member of Zonta International.

Zonta Amelie Earhart Fellowships

Subjects: Aerospace-related sciences and aerospace-related engineering.
Purpose: The Fellowships are granted to women pursuing graduate PhD degrees.
Eligibility: Open to women of any nationality who demonstrate a superior academic record in the field of aerospace-related sciences and engineering.
Level of Study: Doctorate
Type: Fellowship
Value: US$6,000
Frequency: Annual
Study Establishment: Any University
No. of awards offered: Approx. 35
Application Procedure: Complete an official application in English.
Closing Date: November 15th
Funding: Foundation
Additional Information: Recipients are not permitted to defer the Fellowship although Zonta will consider a new application the following year.

SUBJECT AND ELIGIBILITY GUIDE TO AWARDS

AGRICULTURE, FORESTRY AND FISHERY

General
Agronomy
Animal husbandry and animal production
- Sericulture

Horticulture and viticulture
Crop husbandry and crop production
Agriculture and farm management
Agricultural economics
Food science and production
- Meat and poultry
- Dairy
- Fish
- Oenology
- Brewing
- Harvest technology

Soil and water science
- Water management
- Soil conservation

Veterinary medicine
Tropical/Sub-tropical agriculture
Forestry
- Forest soils
- Forest biology
- Forest pathology
- Forest products
- Forest economics
- Forest management

Fishery
- Aquaculture

ARCHITECTURE AND TOWN PLANNING

General
Structural architecture
Architectural restoration
Environmental design
Landscape architecture
Town and community planning
Regional planning

ARTS AND HUMANITIES

General
Interpretation and translation
Writing (authorship)
Native language and literature
Modern languages and literatures
- English
- French
- Spanish
- Germanic languages
- German
- Swedish
- Danish
- Norwegian
- Italian
- Portuguese
- Romance languages
- Modern Greek
- Dutch
- Baltic languages
- Celtic languages
- Finnish
- Russian
- Slavonic languages (others)
- Hungarian
- Fino Ugrian languages
- European languages (others)
- Altaic languages
- Arabic
- Hebrew
- Chinese
- Korean
- Japanese
- Indian languages
- Iranic languages
- African Languages
- Amerindian languages
- Austronesian and oceanic languages

Classical languages and literatures
- Latin
- Classical Greek
- Sanskrit

Linguistics and philology
- Applied linguistics
- Psycholinguistics
- Grammar
- Semantics and terminology
- Phonetics
- Logopedics

Comparative literature
History
- Prehistory
- Ancient civilisations
- Medieval history
- Modern history
- Contemporary history

Archaeology
Philosophy
- Philosophical schools
- Metaphysics
- Logic
- Ethics

BUSINESS ADMINISTRATION AND MANAGEMENT

General
Business studies
International business
Secretarial studies
Business machine operation
Business computing
Management systems and techniques
Accountancy
Real estate
Marketing and sales management
Insurance management
Finance, banking and investment
Personnel management
Labour/industrial relations
Public administration
Institutional administration
MBA

EDUCATION AND TEACHER TRAINING

General
Nonvocational subjects education
- Education in native language
- Foreign languages education
- Mathematics education
- Science education
- Humanities and social science education
- Physical education
- Literacy education

Vocational subjects education
- Agricultural education
- Art education
- Commerce/business education
- Computer education
- Technology education
- Health education
- Home economics education
- Industrial arts education
- Music education

Pre-school education
Primary education
Secondary education
Adult education
Special education
- Education of the gifted
- Education of the handicapped
- Education of specific learning disabilities
- Education of foreigners
- Education of natives
- Education of the socially disadvantaged
- Bilingual/bicultural education

Teacher trainers education
Higher education teacher training
Educational science
- International and comparative education
- Philosophy of education
- Curriculum
- Teaching and learning
- Educational research
- Educational technology
- Educational and student counselling
- Educational administration
- Educational testing and evaluation
- Distance education

ENGINEERING

General
Surveying and mapping science
Engineering drawing/design
Chemical engineering
Civil, construction and transportation engineering
Environmental and Sanitary Engineering
Safety engineering
Electrical/electronic and telecommunications engineering
Computer engineering
Industrial and management engineering
Metallurgical engineering
Production engineering
Materials engineering
Mining and minerals engineering
Petroleum engineering
Energy engineering
Nuclear engineering
Mechanical/electromechanical engineering
Hydraulic/pneumatic engineering
Sound engineering
Automotive engineering
Measurement/precision engineering
Control engineering (robotics)
Aeronautical and aerospace engineering
Marine engineering and naval architecture
Agricultural engineering
Forestry engineering
Bioengineering and biomedical engineering

FINE AND APPLIED ARTS

General
History and Philosophy of Art
- Aesthetics

Art management
Drawing and painting
Sculpture
Handicrafts
Music
- Musicology
- Music theory and composition
- Conducting
- Singing
- Musical instruments (performance)
- Religious music
- Jazz and popular music
- Opera

Drama
Dancing
Photography
Cinema and television
Design
- Interior design
- Furniture design
- Fashion design
- Textile design
- Graphic design
- Industrial design
- Display and stage design

HOME ECONOMICS

General
Household management
Clothing and sewing
Nutrition
Child care/child development
House arts and environment

LAW

General
History of law
Comparative law
International law
Human rights
Labour law
Maritime law
Law of the air
Notary studies
Civil law
Commercial law
Public law
- Constitutional law
- Administrative law
- Fiscal law

Criminal law
Canon law
Islamic law
European community law

MASS COMMUNICATION AND INFORMATION SCIENCE

General
Journalism
Radio/television broadcasting
Public relations and publicity
Mass communication
Media studies
Communications skills
Library science
Museum studies and conservation
Museum management
Restoration of works of art
Documentation techniques and archiving

MATHEMATICS AND COMPUTER SCIENCE

General
Statistics
Actuarial science
Applied mathematics
Computer science
Artificial intelligence
Systems analysis

MEDICAL SCIENCES

General
Public health and hygiene
- Social/preventive medicine
- Dietetics
- Sports medicine

Health administration
Medicine and surgery
- Anaesthesiology
- Cardiology
- Dermatology
- Endocrinology
- Epidemiology
- Gastroenterology
- Geriatrics
- Gynaecology and obstetrics
- Haematology
- Hepathology
- Nephrology
- Neurology
- Oncology
- Ophthalmology
- Otorhinolaryngology
- Parasitology
- Pathology
- Paediatrics
- Plastic surgery
- Pneumology
- Psychiatry and mental health
- Rheumatology
- Urology
- Virology
- Tropical medicine
- Venereology

Rehabilitation medicine and therapy
Nursing
Medical auxiliaries
Midwifery
Radiology
Treatment techniques
Medical technology
Dentistry and stomatology
- Oral pathology
- Orthodontics
- Periodontics
- Community dentistry

Dental technology
- Prosthetic dentistry

Pharmacy
Biomedicine
Optometry
Podiatry
Forensic medicine and dentistry
Acupuncture
Homeopathy
Chiropractic
Osteopathy
Traditional eastern medicine

NATURAL SCIENCES

General
Biological and life sciences
- Anatomy
- Biochemistry
- Biology
- Histology
- Biophysics and molecular biology
- Biotechnology
- Botany
- Plant pathology
- Embryology and reproduction biology
- Genetics
- Immunology
- Marine biology
- Limnology
- Microbiology
- Neurosciences
- Parasitology
- Pharmacology
- Physiology
- Toxicology
- Zoology

Chemistry
- Analytical chemistry
- Inorganic chemistry
- Organic chemistry
- Physical chemistry

Earth and geological sciences
- Geochemistry
- Geography (Scientific)
- Geology
- Mineralogy and crystallography
- Petrology
- Geophysics and seismology
- Palaeontology

Physics
- Atomic and molecular physics
- Nuclear physics
- Optics
- Solid state physics
- Thermal physics

Astronomy and astrophysics
Atmosphere science/ meteorology
- Arctic studies
- Arid land studies

Oceanography

RECREATION, WELFARE, PROTECTIVE SERVICES

General
Police and law enforcement
Criminology
Fire protection/control
Military science
Civil security
Peace and disarmament
Social welfare and social work
- Public and community services

Vocational counselling
Environmental studies
- Ecology
- Natural resources
- Environmental management
- Wildlife and pest management

Physical education and sports
- Sports management
- Sociology of sports

Leisure studies
Parks and recreation

RELIGION AND THEOLOGY

General
Religious studies
- Christian
- Jewish
- Islam
- Asian religious studies
- Agnosticism and Atheism
- Ancient religions

Religious education
Holy writings
Religious practice
Church administration (pastoral work)
Theological studies
Comparative religion
Sociology of religion
History of religion
Esoteric practices

SERVICE TRADES

General
Hotel and restaurant
Hotel management
Cooking and catering
Retailing
Tourism

SOCIAL AND BEHAVIOURAL SCIENCES

General
- Economics
- Economic history
- Economic and finance policy
- Taxation
- Econometrics
- Industrial and production economics

Political science and government
- Comparative politics

International relations
Sociology
- History of societies
- Comparative sociology
- Social policy
- Social institutions
- Social communication problems
- Futurology

Demography
Anthropology
- Ethnology
- Folklore

Women's studies
Urban Studies
Rural studies
Cognitive sciences
Psychology
- Experimental psychology
- Social and community psychology
- Clinical psychology
- Personality psychology
- Industrial/organisational psychology
- Psychometrics
- Educational psychology

Geography (social and economic)
Development studies
Area and cultural studies
- North African
- Subsahara African
- African studies
- African American
- Native American
- Hispanic American
- American
- Canadian
- Asian
- South Asian
- East Asian
- Southeast Asian
- European (EC)
- Eastern European
- Western European
- Nordic
- Caribbean
- Latin American
- Pacific area
- Aboriginal
- Middle Eastern
- Islamic
- Jewish

Preservation of cultural heritage
Ancient civilisations (Egyptology, Assyriology)

TRADE, CRAFT AND INDUSTRIAL TECHNIQUES

General
Food processing techniques
Building trades
Electrical/electronic equipment and maintenance techniques
Metal trades techniques
Mechanical equipment and maintenance techniques
Wood technology
Heating, air conditioning and refrigeration technology
Leather techniques
Textile techniques
Paper and packaging technology
Graphic arts techniques
- Printing
- Publishing and book trade

Laboratory techniques
Optical technology

TRANSPORT AND COMMUNICATIONS

General
Air transport
Marine transport and nautical science
Railway transport
Road transport
Transport management
Transport economics
Postal services
Telecommunications services

ANY SUBJECT

ANY SUBJECT

Any Country

African Nations

Australia

Britain-Australia Bicentennial Scholarships for Postgraduate Study 172
British Chevening Cambridge Australia Trust Scholarships for Postgraduate Study 172
British Chevening Cambridge Scholarships for Postgraduate Study (Australia) 174
Christ Church Hugh Pilkington Scholarship 673
Christ Church Myers Scholarship 673
Churchill Fellowships 721
Clarendon Fund Bursaries 673
Commonwealth Scholarships 112
Department of Education and Science (Ireland) Exchange Scholarships and Postgraduate Scholarships Exchange Scheme 256
French Government Postgraduate Scholarships 269
Fulbright Professional Award 126
Fulbright Senior Scholar Awards 127
International Alumni Scholarship (IAS) 669
International Family Scholarship (IFS) 669
International Postgraduate Scholarship (IPS) 669
International Research Scholarship (IRS) 669
International Taught Postgraduate Scholarship (ITPS) 669
James Fairfax and Oxford-Australia Fund Scholarships 676
Lincoln College Keith Murray Senior Scholarship 680
Lincoln College Overseas Graduate Entrance Scholarships 680
The Lionel Murphy Australian Postgraduate Scholarships 413
The Lionel Murphy Overseas Postgraduate Scholarships 413
Ministry of Foreign Affairs (France) Tertiary Studies in French Universities (Baudin Travel Grants) 269
Overseas Research Students Awards Scheme 664
PEO International Peace Scholarship 372
Queen's College Cyril and Phyllis Long Studentship 684
The Robert Gordon Menzies Scholarship to Harvard 431
Royal Holloway, University of London College Overseas Entrance Scholarships 547
SAAWG International Fellowship 152
St Catherine's College Overseas Graduate Scholarship 688
Tetley and Lupton Scholarships for Overseas Students for Master's Study 665
Tetley and Lupton Scholarships for Overseas Students for Research Study 665
UK Commonwealth (Cambridge) Scholarships for PhD Study 195
UK Commonwealth (Cambridge) Scholarships for Postgraduate Study 195
University of Leeds International Research Scholarships 666
University of Otago Master's Awards 670
University of Sydney Postgraduate Award (UPA) 696
UOW Eurobodalla Shire Council Residential Scholarships 705

Canada

AAUW International Fellowships Program 4
AAUW Rose Sidgwick Memorial Fellowship 147
AAUW/IFUW International Fellowships 147
Action Canada Fellowships 7
AFUW Georgina Sweet Fellowship 148
Association of Rhodes Scholars in Australia Scholarship 113
British Columbia Asia Pacific Students Awards 144
Canada Cambridge Scholarships for PhD Study 178
Christ Church American Friends Scholarship 672
Clarendon Fund Bursaries 673
Commonwealth Scholarships 112
First Canadian Donner Foundation Research Cambridge Scholarships for PhD Study 181
Hans Viessmann International Scholarship 718
IAFC Foundation Scholarship 359
International Alumni Scholarship (IAS) 669
International Family Scholarship (IFS) 669
International Postgraduate Research Scholarships (IPRS) and University of Sydney International Postgraduate Awards (IPA) 696
International Postgraduate Scholarship (IPS) 669
International Research Scholarship (IRS) 669
International Taught Postgraduate Scholarship (ITPS) 669
Killam Prizes 198
Linacre College Canadian National Scholarship 677
Lincoln College Keith Murray Senior Scholarship 680
Lincoln College Overseas Graduate Entrance Scholarships 680
Margaret McWilliams Predoctoral Fellowship 205
Overseas Research Students Awards Scheme 664
President Marden Scholarship 718
Queen Elizabeth II Graduate Scholarships 643
Queen Elizabeth II Scholarships-Doctoral 639
Queen Elizabeth II Scholarships-Master's 639
Queen's College Cyril and Phyllis Long Studentship 684
Royal Holloway, University of London College Overseas Entrance Scholarships 547
SAAWG International Fellowship 152
St Catherine's College Overseas Graduate Scholarship 688
Tetley and Lupton Scholarships for Overseas Students for Master's Study 665
Tetley and Lupton Scholarships for Overseas Students for Research Study 665
Tidmarsh Cambridge Scholarship for PhD Study 195
UK Commonwealth (Cambridge) Scholarships for Postgraduate Study 195
University of Calgary Silver Anniversary Graduate Fellowships 643
The University of Edinburgh Canadian Master's Scholarships 650
University of Leeds International Research Scholarships 666
University of Warwick Postgraduate Awards (North America) 704
Viessmann/Marburg Travel Scholarship 718
William and Marion Marr Graduate Award 718
WLU Bursaries 718
WLU Graduate Incentive Scholarships 719
WLU Graduate Scholarships 719
WLU Student International Travel Scholarship 719

Caribbean Countries

AAUW International Fellowships Program 4
AAUW Rose Sidgwick Memorial Fellowship 147
AAUW/IFUW International Fellowships 147
ADB Research Fellowships 106
ADB-Japan Scholarship Program 106
AFUW Georgina Sweet Fellowship 148
British Chevening Cambridge Scholarships for Postgraduate Study (Cuba) 174
British Prize Cambridge Scholarships 176
Cambridge DFID Scholarships for Postgraduate Study 177
Christ Church Hugh Pilkington Scholarship 673
Clarendon Fund Bursaries 673
Commonwealth Academic Fellowships 111
Commonwealth Academic Staff Scholarships 111
European Development Fund Awards for Citizens of ACP Countries 478
International Alumni Scholarship (IAS) 669
International Family Scholarship (IFS) 669
International Postgraduate Research Scholarships (IPRS) and University of Sydney International Postgraduate Awards (IPA) 696
International Postgraduate Scholarship (IPS) 669
International Research Scholarship (IRS) 669
International Taught Postgraduate Scholarship (ITPS) 669
Lincoln College Keith Murray Senior Scholarship 680
Lincoln College Overseas Graduate Entrance Scholarships 680
One World Scholarship Program 11
Overseas Research Students Awards Scheme 664
PEO International Peace Scholarship 372
Prince of Wales (Cable and Wireless) Cambridge Scholarships for PhD Study 190
Queen's College Cyril and Phyllis Long Studentship 684
Royal Holloway, University of London College Overseas Entrance Scholarships 547
SAAWG International Fellowship 152
St Catherine's College Overseas Graduate Scholarship 688
Tetley and Lupton Scholarships for Overseas Students for Master's Study 665
Tetley and Lupton Scholarships for Overseas Students for Research Study 665
UCL Development Co-operation Fellowships 623

University of Leeds International Research Scholarships 666
University of Warwick Postgraduate Award (Caribbean) 703

East European Countries

AAUW International Fellowships Program 4
AAUW Rose Sidgwick Memorial Fellowship 147
AAUW/IFUW International Fellowships 147
AFUW Georgina Sweet Fellowship 148
BAT Cambridge Scholarships for PhD Study (Russia) 170
BAT Cambridge Scholarships for Postgraduate Study (Russia) 171
BP Cambridge Chevening Scholarships for Postgraduate Study (Russia) 171
British Chevening Cambridge Scholarships for Postgraduate Study (Eastern Europe) 174
Canon Foundation Award 219
Canon Foundation Research Fellowships 219
CEU FCO Cambridge Non-Degree Research Scholarships 179
Christ Church Hugh Pilkington Scholarship 673
Clarendon Fund Bursaries 673
Copernicus Award 257
Cyprus Cambridge Scholarships For PhD Study 180
Department of Education and Science (Ireland) Exchange Scholarships and Postgraduate Scholarships Exchange Scheme 256
Department of Education and Science (Ireland) Summer School Exchange Scholarships 257
Dulverton Scholarships 674
Eugene R. & Elinor R. Kotur Scholarship 618
Fulbright Postgraduate Student Awards 707
Graduate School Master's Awards 629
Graduate School Research Scholarships for Cross-Disciplinary Training 629
Hill Foundation Scholarships 675
International Alumni Scholarship (IAS) 669
International Postgraduate Research Scholarships (IPRS) and University of Sydney International Postgraduate Awards (IPA) 696
Isaac Newton Trust European Research Studentships 183
ISH/London Metropolitan Scholarship Scheme 414
Kapitza Cambridge Scholarships 184
Lincoln College Keith Murray Senior Scholarship 680
Mehmed Fuad Köprülü Scholarships for Turkey 187
NFP Netherlands Fellowships Programme for Development Co-operation 478
PEO International Peace Scholarship 372
President Árpad Göncz Scholarship for Postgraduate Study 190
Queen's College Cyril and Phyllis Long Studentship 684
Research Scholarships: Eastern Europe Programme 223
Royal Holloway, University of London College Overseas Entrance Scholarships 547
Russia Postgraduate Chevening Award 702
SAAWG International Fellowship 152
Scatcherd European Scholarships 685
St Catherine's College Overseas Graduate Scholarship 688
Tetley and Lupton Scholarships for Overseas Students for Master's Study 665
Tetley and Lupton Scholarships for Overseas Students for Research Study 665
TNK/BP Kapitza Cambridge Scholarships for Russia 195
UCL Development Co-operation Fellowships 623
UFA Student Aid Programme 13
University of Warwick Scholarship Scheme (East European) 704
Young Scientist PhD Fellowships (NIS) 358
Young Scientist Postdoctoral Fellowships 358

European Union

AAUW/IFUW International Fellowships 147
Crawshays Rugby Scholarship 657
Czech Republic Scholarships 435
Fulbright Distinguished Scholar Awards 707
International Postgraduate Research Scholarships (IPRS) and University of Sydney International Postgraduate Awards (IPA) 696
Liechtenstein Scholarships and Loans 516
Marie Curie Development Host Fellowships 277
Merton College Domus Graduate Scholarships B 681
PEO International Peace Scholarship 372
SAAWG International Fellowship 152
Scatcherd European Scholarships 685

Middle East

AAUW International Fellowships Program 4
AAUW Rose Sidgwick Memorial Fellowship 147
AAUW/IFUW International Fellowships 147
AFUW Georgina Sweet Fellowship 148
Arab-British Chamber Charitable Foundation Scholarships 169
BP Cambridge Scholarships for PhD Study (Egypt) 171
BP Cambridge Scholarships for Postgraduate Study (Egypt) 171
Christ Church Hugh Pilkington Scholarship 673
Clarendon Fund Bursaries 673
International Alumni Scholarship (IAS) 669
International Family Scholarship (IFS) 669
International Postgraduate Research Scholarships (IPRS) and University of Sydney International Postgraduate Awards (IPA) 696
International Postgraduate Scholarship (IPS) 669
International Research Scholarship (IRS) 669
International Taught Postgraduate Scholarship (ITPS) 669
ISH/London Metropolitan Scholarship Scheme 414
Karim Rida Said Cambridge Scholarship for PhD Study 184
Karim Rida Said Cambridge Scholarship for Postgraduate Study 185
Karim Rida Said Foundation Scholarships 677
Lincoln College Keith Murray Senior Scholarship 680
Lincoln College Overseas Graduate Entrance Scholarships 680
Minerva Fellowships 434
Minerva Seed Grants 435
Minerva Short-Term Research Grants 435
NFP Netherlands Fellowships Programme for Development Co-operation 478
One World Scholarship Program 11
Open Society Institute-FCO Chevening-University of Leeds Scholarships 664
Overseas Research Students Awards Scheme 664
PEO International Peace Scholarship 372
Queen's College Cyril and Phyllis Long Studentship 684
Research Scholarships: Programme I 223
Research Scholarships: Programme II 223
Royal Holloway, University of London College Overseas Entrance Scholarships 547
SAAWG International Fellowship 152
St Catherine's College Overseas Graduate Scholarship 688
Tetley and Lupton Scholarships for Overseas Students for Master's Study 665
Tetley and Lupton Scholarships for Overseas Students for Research Study 665
UCL Development Co-operation Fellowships 623
University of Leeds International Research Scholarships 666

New Zealand

AAUW International Fellowships Program 4
AAUW Rose Sidgwick Memorial Fellowship 147
AAUW/IFUW International Fellowships 147
AFUW Australian Capital Territory Bursary 148
AFUW Georgina Sweet Fellowship 148
Australian Postgraduate Award (APA) 696
Christ Church Hugh Pilkington Scholarship 673
Clarendon Fund Bursaries 673
Commonwealth Scholarships 112
International Alumni Scholarship (IAS) 669
International Family Scholarship (IFS) 669
International Postgraduate Scholarship (IPS) 669
International Research Scholarship (IRS) 669
International Taught Postgraduate Scholarship (ITPS) 669
Lincoln College Keith Murray Senior Scholarship 680
Lincoln College Overseas Graduate Entrance Scholarships 680
Link Foundation/FCO Chevening Cambridge Scholarships for Postgraduate Study 186
Overseas Research Students Awards Scheme 664
PEO International Peace Scholarship 372
Prince of Wales Scholarships for PhD Study 191

Queen's College Cyril and Phyllis Long Studentship 684
Royal Holloway, University of London College Overseas Entrance Scholarships 547
SAAWG International Fellowship 152
St Catherine's College Overseas Graduate Scholarship 688
Tetley and Lupton Scholarships for Overseas Students for Master's Study 665
Tetley and Lupton Scholarships for Overseas Students for Research Study 665
UK Commonwealth (Cambridge) Scholarships for PhD Study 195
UK Commonwealth (Cambridge) Scholarships for Postgraduate Study 195
University of Leeds International Research Scholarships 666
University of Otago Master's Awards 670
University of Sydney Postgraduate Award (UPA) 696
The University of Waikato Alumni Association Master's Scholarships 699
The University of Waikato Doctoral Scholarships 699
William Georgetti Scholarships 481

South Africa

AAUW International Fellowships Program 4
AAUW Rose Sidgwick Memorial Fellowship 147
AAUW/IFUW International Fellowships 147
AFUW Georgina Sweet Fellowship 148
Association of Rhodes Scholars in Australia Scholarship 113
Christ Church Hugh Pilkington Scholarship 673
Clarendon Fund Bursaries 673
Commonwealth Academic Staff Scholarships 111
Commonwealth Scholarships 112
The Ernest Oppenheiner Memorial Trust Overseas Study Grant 663
Guy Clutton-Brock Scholarship for Postgraduate Study 182
International Alumni Scholarship (IAS) 669
International Family Scholarship (IFS) 669
International Postgraduate Research Scholarships (IPRS) and University of Sydney International Postgraduate Awards (IPA) 696
International Postgraduate Scholarship (IPS) 669
International Research Scholarship (IRS) 669
International Taught Postgraduate Scholarship (ITPS) 669
Lincoln College Keith Murray Senior Scholarship 680
Lincoln College Overseas Graduate Entrance Scholarships 680
Mandela Cambridge Scholarships for PhD Study 186
Mandela Cambridge Scholarships for Postgraduate Study 187
Mandela Magdalene College Scholarships for Postgraduate Scholarships 187
NFP Netherlands Fellowships Programme for Development Co-operation 478
One World Scholarship Program 11
Overseas Research Students Awards Scheme 664
Patrick and Margaret Flanagan Scholarship 528
PEO International Peace Scholarship 372
Queen's College Cyril and Phyllis Long Studentship 684
Royal Holloway, University of London College Overseas Entrance Scholarships 547
South African College Bursaries 194
St Catherine's College Overseas Graduate Scholarship 688
Tetley and Lupton Scholarships for Overseas Students for Master's Study 665
Tetley and Lupton Scholarships for Overseas Students for Research Study 665
University of Leeds International Research Scholarships 666
Zimbabwe Cambridge Scholarships for PhD Study 197
Zimbabwe Cambridge Scholarships for Postgraduate Study 197

United Kingdom

AAUW Rose Sidgwick Memorial Fellowship 147
AAUW/IFUW International Fellowships 147
AFUW Georgina Sweet Fellowship 148
Anglo-Danish (London) Scholarships 94
Anning-Morgan Bursary 656
ASBAH Bursary Fund 107
Association of Rhodes Scholars in Australia Scholarship 113
Auber Bequest 555
Bourses Scholarships 274
BUNAC Educational Scholarship Trust (BEST) 164
Canada Memorial Foundation Scholarship 111
Canon Foundation Award 219
Canon Foundation Research Fellowships 219
Christ Church Hugh Pilkington Scholarship 673
Commonwealth Scholarships 112
Crawshays Rugby Scholarship 657
Cross Trust Grants 251
East Lothian Educational Trust General Grant 265
Friends of Israel Educational Foundation Academic Study Bursary 294
Fulbright Distinguished Scholar Awards 707
Fulbright Postgraduate Student Awards 707
Geoff Lockwood Scholarship 695
Graduate School Master's Awards 629
Graduate School Research Scholarships for Cross-Disciplinary Training 629
International Postgraduate Research Scholarships (IPRS) and University of Sydney International Postgraduate Awards (IPA) 696
James Pantyfedwen Foundation Grants 387
Marie Curie Development Host Fellowships 277
Merton College Domus Graduate Scholarships B 681
PEO International Peace Scholarship 372
Pirie-Reid Scholarships 683
Reid Trust For the Higher Education of Women 522
SAAS-The Postgraduate Certificate of Education 604
SAAWG International Fellowship 152
University of Reading Access to Learning Fund 690
University of Sussex/Association of Commonwealth Universities Access Fund Bursaries 696
University of Wales Postgraduate Studentship 701

United States of America

AAUW Career Development Grants 3
AAUW Community Action Grants 3
AAUW Educational Foundation American Fellowships 4
AAUW Selected Professions Fellowships 4
Abe & Esther Hagiwara Student Aid Award 388
Abrahamson Family Endowed Scholarship 440
Adelphi University Dean's Award 9
Adelphi University Presidential Scholarship 9
Adelphi University Provost Scholarship 9
Adelphi University Trustee Scholarship 9
AFUW Georgina Sweet Fellowship 148
Alberta Blue Cross 50th Anniversary Scholarships 234
Alpha Sigma Nu Graduate Scholarship 421
Amelia Kemp Scholarship 722
America-Norway Heritage Fund Grant 486
American Friends of the University of Edinburgh Scholarship 648
American-Scandinavian Foundation (ASF) 486
Arkansas Single Parent Scholarships 97
ASF Grants and Fellowships for Advanced Study or Research in Denmark, Finland, Iceland, Norway and Sweden 93
Briggs Distributing Co., Inc/John & Claudia Decker Endowed Scholarship 441
The Bruce H. Carpenter Non-Traditional Endowed Scholarship 441
Business and Professional Women's (BPN) Foundation Career Advancement Scholarship 98
Christ Church American Friends Scholarship 672
Clarendon Fund Bursaries 673
Ellen Shields Endowed Scholarship 441
EU Parker Scholarship 456
Frances S. Barker Endowed Scholarship 441
Fulbright Commission (Argentina) Awards for US Lecturers and Researchers 296
Fulbright Commission (Argentina) US Students Research Grant 296
Fulbright Graduate Student Awards 707
Fulbright Oxford University Scholarships 675
Fulbright Scholar Awards for Research and Lecturing Abroad for US Citizens 245
Fulbright Scholar Grants 708
The Haynes Foundation Scholarships 441
Henry Cogswell Active Duty Military Scholarship 323

West European Countries

AGRICULTURE, FORESTRY AND FISHERY

GENERAL

Any Country

African Nations

Australia

Canada

Caribbean Countries

East European Countries

Middle East

New Zealand

South Africa

United Kingdom

Fulbright Postdoctoral Research and Lecturing Awards for Non-US Citizens 245
Hilda Martindale Exhibitions 326
John Radford Award for Geographical Photography 545
Linacre College A J Hosier Studentship 677
Mr and Mrs David Edward Memorial Award 699
Neville Shulman Challenge Award 546
Silsoe Awards 249
Sir William Roberts Scholarship 700
Swiss Federal Institute of Technology Scholarships 606
University of Wales Aberystwyth Postgraduate Research Studentships 699
UWB Departmental Research Studentships 700
UWB Research Studentships 700
Wingate Scholarships 720

United States of America

Budweiser Conservation Scholarship 458
Congress Bundestag Youth Exchange for Young Professionals 224
Cranfield University Overseas Bursary 249
Foundation for Science and Disability Student Grant Fund 291
Fulbright Distinguished Chairs Program 245
Fulbright Scholar Program for US Citizens 245
Ian Axford (New Zealand) Fellowships in Public Policy 239
Norwegian Thanksgiving Fund Scholarship 487
Olin Fellowship 118
Swiss Federal Institute of Technology Scholarships 606

West European Countries

Fulbright Postdoctoral Research and Lecturing Awards for Non-US Citizens 245
John Radford Award for Geographical Photography 545
Mr and Mrs David Edward Memorial Award 699
Silsoe Awards 249
Sir William Roberts Scholarship 700
UWB Departmental Research Studentships 700
UWB Research Studentships 700
Wingate Scholarships 720

AGRONOMY

Any Country

Perry Postgraduate Scholarships 503
Perry Research Awards 503
Teagasc Walsh Fellowships 607
University of Otago International Scholarships 670

African Nations

Canadian Window on International Development 364
IDRC Doctoral Research Awards 365

Australia

Wingate Scholarships 720

Canada

Canadian Window on International Development 364
CIC Montreal Medal 213
IDRC Doctoral Research Awards 365
Wingate Scholarships 720

Caribbean Countries

Canadian Window on International Development 364
IDRC Doctoral Research Awards 365

New Zealand

Wingate Scholarships 720

South Africa

Canadian Window on International Development 364
IDRC Doctoral Research Awards 365
Wingate Scholarships 720

United Kingdom

Mr and Mrs David Edward Memorial Award 699
Sir William Roberts Scholarship 700
Swiss Federal Institute of Technology Scholarships 606
UWB Departmental Research Studentships 700
UWB Research Studentships 700
Wingate Scholarships 720

United States of America

Swiss Federal Institute of Technology Scholarships 606

West European Countries

Mr and Mrs David Edward Memorial Award 699
Sir William Roberts Scholarship 700
UWB Departmental Research Studentships 700
UWB Research Studentships 700
Wingate Scholarships 720

ANIMAL HUSBANDRY AND ANIMAL PRODUCTION

Any Country

CATIE Scholarships 615
Perry Postgraduate Scholarships 503
Perry Research Awards 503
Teagasc Walsh Fellowships 607
Thesiger-Oman Research Fellowship 547
TSA Research Grants 614
UFAW Animal Welfare Research Training Scholarships 624
UFAW Research and Project Awards 624
UFAW Small Project and Travel Awards 624
UFAW Vacation Scholarships 624
University of Bristol Postgraduate Scholarships 641

African Nations

Canadian Window on International Development 364
IDRC Doctoral Research Awards 365

Australia

Wingate Scholarships 720

Canada

Canadian Window on International Development 364
IDRC Doctoral Research Awards 365
John Hervey, Broadcasters and Smallsreed Awards 623
Wingate Scholarships 720

Caribbean Countries

Canadian Window on International Development 364
IDRC Doctoral Research Awards 365

New Zealand

Vernon Willey Trust Awards 710
Wingate Scholarships 720

South Africa

Canadian Window on International Development 364
IDRC Doctoral Research Awards 365
Wingate Scholarships 720

United Kingdom

Linacre College A J Hosier Studentship 677
Mr and Mrs David Edward Memorial Award 699

United States of America

West European Countries

SERICULTURE

Any Country

African Nations

Australia

Canada

Caribbean Countries

New Zealand

South Africa

United Kingdom

West European Countries

HORTICULTURE AND VITICULTURE

Any Country

African Nations

Australia

Canada

Caribbean Countries

New Zealand

South Africa

United Kingdom

United States of America

West European Countries

CROP HUSBANDRY AND CROP PRODUCTION

Any Country

African Nations

Australia

Canada

Australia
Wingate Scholarships 720

Canada
Wingate Scholarships 720

New Zealand
Wingate Scholarships 720

South Africa
Wingate Scholarships 720

United Kingdom
Wingate Scholarships 720

West European Countries
Wingate Scholarships 720

FISH

Any Country
WHOI Research Fellowships in Marine Policy 727

Australia
Wingate Scholarships 720

Canada
Olin Fellowship 118
Wingate Scholarships 720

New Zealand
Wingate Scholarships 720

South Africa
Wingate Scholarships 720

United Kingdom
Wingate Scholarships 720

United States of America
Olin Fellowship 118

West European Countries
Wingate Scholarships 720

OENOLOGY

Australia
Wingate Scholarships 720

Canada
Wingate Scholarships 720

New Zealand
Wingate Scholarships 720

South Africa
Wingate Scholarships 720

United Kingdom
Wingate Scholarships 720

West European Countries
Wingate Scholarships 720

BREWING

Australia
Wingate Scholarships 720

Canada
Wingate Scholarships 720

New Zealand
Wingate Scholarships 720

South Africa
Wingate Scholarships 720

United Kingdom
Wingate Scholarships 720

West European Countries
Wingate Scholarships 720

HARVEST TECHNOLOGY

Any Country
Perry Postgraduate Scholarships 503
Perry Research Awards 503

Australia
Wingate Scholarships 720

Canada
Wingate Scholarships 720

New Zealand
Wingate Scholarships 720

South Africa
Wingate Scholarships 720

United Kingdom
Wingate Scholarships 720

West European Countries
Wingate Scholarships 720

SOIL AND WATER SCIENCE

Any Country
Alberta Research Council Scholarship 642
Andrew Mellon Foundation Scholarship 527
CATIE Scholarships 615
CDU Senior Research Fellowship 230
CDU Three Year Postdoctoral Fellowship 230
Donald A. Williams Soil Conservation Scholarship 594
Earthwatch Field Research Grants 265
Edmund Niles Huyck Preserve, Inc. Graduate and Postgraduate Grants 266
Gilbert F White Postdoctoral Fellowship 525
Horton (Hydrology) Research Grant 52
HRF Graduate Fellowships 330
Joseph L Fisher Dissertation Award 525
Melville H. Cohee Student Leader Conservation Scholarship 594
National Geographic Conservation Trust Grant 241
NERC Advanced Research Fellowships 476
NERC Postdoctoral Research Fellowships 476
Perry Postgraduate Scholarships 503
Perry Research Awards 503
Rhodes University Postgraduate Scholarship 528

West European Countries

International Postgraduate Research Scholarships (IPRS) 692
Mr and Mrs David Edward Memorial Award 699
NERC Advanced Course Studentships 476
NERC Research Studentships 476
Sheffield Hallam University Studentships 567
Silsoe Awards 249
Synthesys Visiting Fellowship 477
UWB Departmental Research Studentships 700
UWB Research Studentships 700
Wingate Scholarships 720

VETERINARY MEDICINE

Any Country

The Airey Neave Trust Scholarship 12
Horserace Betting Levy Board Senior Equine Clinical Scholarships 329
Horserace Betting Levy Board Veterinary Research Training Scholarship 329
James M Harris/Sarah W Sweatt Student Travel Grant 255
John & James Houston Crawford Scholarship 658
John Crawford Scholarship 658
Perry Postgraduate Scholarships 503
Perry Research Awards 503
Sir Richard Stapley Educational Trust Grants 571
UFAW Animal Welfare Research Training Scholarships 624
UFAW Research and Project Awards 624
UFAW Small Project and Travel Awards 624
UFAW Vacation Scholarships 624
University of Bristol Postgraduate Scholarships 641
Wellcome Trust Grants 717

Australia

Wingate Scholarships 720

Canada

Dodge Foundation Frontiers for Veterinary Medicine Fellowships 302
Wingate Scholarships 720

East European Countries

FEMS Fellowship 284

New Zealand

Wingate Scholarships 720

South Africa

Wingate Scholarships 720

United Kingdom

FEMS Fellowship 284
Harry Steele-Bodger Memorial Travelling Scholarship 164
Mr and Mrs David Edward Memorial Award 699
Petsavers Award 503
Sir William Roberts Scholarship 700
UWB Departmental Research Studentships 700
Wingate Scholarships 720

United States of America

Dodge Foundation Frontiers for Veterinary Medicine Fellowships 302

West European Countries

FEMS Fellowship 284
Henry Dryerre Scholarship 556
Karl-Enigk Scholarships 564
Mr and Mrs David Edward Memorial Award 699
Sir William Roberts Scholarship 700
UWB Departmental Research Studentships 700
Wingate Scholarships 720

TROPICAL/SUB-TROPICAL AGRICULTURE

Any Country

CATIE Scholarships 615
CDU Senior Research Fellowship 230
CDU Three Year Postdoctoral Fellowship 230
Earthwatch Field Research Grants 265
National Geographic Conservation Trust Grant 241

African Nations

Canadian Window on International Development 364
IDRC Doctoral Research Awards 365
Postgraduate Studies in Physical Land Resources Scholarship 362
TWNSO Grants to Institutions in the South for Joint Research Projects 612
Use of Fertility-Enhancing Food, Forage and Cover Crops in Sustainably Managed Agroecosystems: The Bentley Fellowship 365

Australia

Wingate Scholarships 720

Canada

Canadian Window on International Development 364
IDRC Doctoral Research Awards 365
Use of Fertility-Enhancing Food, Forage and Cover Crops in Sustainably Managed Agroecosystems: The Bentley Fellowship 365
Wingate Scholarships 720

Caribbean Countries

Canadian Window on International Development 364
IDRC Doctoral Research Awards 365
Postgraduate Studies in Physical Land Resources Scholarship 362
TWNSO Grants to Institutions in the South for Joint Research Projects 612
Use of Fertility-Enhancing Food, Forage and Cover Crops in Sustainably Managed Agroecosystems: The Bentley Fellowship 365

Middle East

Postgraduate Studies in Physical Land Resources Scholarship 362
TWNSO Grants to Institutions in the South for Joint Research Projects 612
Use of Fertility-Enhancing Food, Forage and Cover Crops in Sustainably Managed Agroecosystems: The Bentley Fellowship 365

New Zealand

Wingate Scholarships 720

South Africa

Canadian Window on International Development 364
IDRC Doctoral Research Awards 365
Postgraduate Studies in Physical Land Resources Scholarship 362
TWNSO Grants to Institutions in the South for Joint Research Projects 612
Use of Fertility-Enhancing Food, Forage and Cover Crops in Sustainably Managed Agroecosystems: The Bentley Fellowship 365
Wingate Scholarships 720

United Kingdom

Mr and Mrs David Edward Memorial Award 699
Sir William Roberts Scholarship 700
UWB Departmental Research Studentships 700
UWB Research Studentships 700
Wingate Scholarships 720

West European Countries

Mr and Mrs David Edward Memorial Award 699
Sir William Roberts Scholarship 700
UWB Departmental Research Studentships 700
UWB Research Studentships 700
Wingate Scholarships 720

FORESTRY

Any Country

African Nations

Australia

Canada

Caribbean Countries

Middle East

New Zealand

South Africa

United Kingdom

United States of America

West European Countries

FOREST SOILS

Any Country

Australia

Canada

East European Countries

New Zealand

South Africa

United Kingdom

United States of America

West European Countries

FOREST BIOLOGY

Any Country

Australia

FOREST MANAGEMENT

Any Country

CATIE Scholarships 615
Edmund Niles Huyck Preserve, Inc. Graduate and Postgraduate Grants 266
Trinity College Birkett Scholarship in Environmental Studies 688

Australia

Wingate Scholarships 720

Canada

Canadian Forest Service Graduate Supplements 580
Community Forestry: Trees and People - John G Bene Fellowship 364
Wingate Scholarships 720

New Zealand

Wingate Scholarships 720

South Africa

Wingate Scholarships 720

United Kingdom

Mr and Mrs David Edward Memorial Award 699
Sir William Roberts Scholarship 700
UWB Departmental Research Studentships 700
UWB Research Studentships 700
Wingate Scholarships 720

United States of America

Earthwatch Education Awards 265

West European Countries

Mr and Mrs David Edward Memorial Award 699
Sir William Roberts Scholarship 700
UWB Departmental Research Studentships 700
UWB Research Studentships 700
Wingate Scholarships 720

FISHERY

Any Country

Andrew Mellon Foundation Scholarship 527
Earthwatch Field Research Grants 265
NRC Research Associateships 471
Rhodes University Postgraduate Scholarship 528
UFAW Animal Welfare Research Training Scholarships 624
UFAW Research and Project Awards 624
UFAW Small Project and Travel Awards 624
UFAW Vacation Scholarships 624
WHOI Research Fellowships in Marine Policy 727
WHOI/NOAA Co-operative Institute for Climate and Ocean Research Postdoctoral Fellowship 727

African Nations

Austrian Academy of Sciences, MSc Course in Limnology and Wetland Ecosystems 127
Austrian Academy of Sciences, Short Course Tropical Limnology 127
IDRC Doctoral Research Awards 365

Australia

Wingate Scholarships 720

Canada

IDRC Doctoral Research Awards 365
Olin Fellowship 118
Wingate Scholarships 720

Caribbean Countries

IDRC Doctoral Research Awards 365

New Zealand

Wingate Scholarships 720

South Africa

IDRC Doctoral Research Awards 365
Wingate Scholarships 720

United Kingdom

Mr and Mrs David Edward Memorial Award 699
UWB Departmental Research Studentships 700
UWB Research Studentships 700
Wingate Scholarships 720

United States of America

Olin Fellowship 118

West European Countries

Mr and Mrs David Edward Memorial Award 699
UWB Departmental Research Studentships 700
UWB Research Studentships 700
Wingate Scholarships 720

AQUACULTURE

Any Country

CDU Senior Research Fellowship 230
CDU Three Year Postdoctoral Fellowship 230
WHOI Research Fellowships in Marine Policy 727

African Nations

Austrian Academy of Sciences, Short Course Tropical Limnology 127

Australia

Wingate Scholarships 720

Canada

Wingate Scholarships 720

East European Countries

Synthesys Visiting Fellowship 477

New Zealand

Wingate Scholarships 720

South Africa

Henderson Postgraduate Scholarships 527
Wingate Scholarships 720

United Kingdom

Mr and Mrs David Edward Memorial Award 699
UWB Departmental Research Studentships 700
UWB Research Studentships 700
Wingate Scholarships 720

West European Countries

Mr and Mrs David Edward Memorial Award 699
Synthesys Visiting Fellowship 477
UWB Departmental Research Studentships 700
UWB Research Studentships 700
Wingate Scholarships 720

ARCHITECTURE AND TOWN PLANNING

GENERAL

Any Country

African Nations

Australia

Canada

Caribbean Countries

East European Countries

European Union

Middle East

New Zealand

South Africa

United Kingdom

United States of America

West European Countries

STRUCTURAL ARCHITECTURE

Any Country

African Nations

Australia

Canada

Caribbean Countries

East European Countries

Middle East

New Zealand

South Africa

United Kingdom

United States of America

West European Countries

ARCHITECTURAL RESTORATION

Any Country

Australia

Canada

New Zealand

South Africa

United Kingdom

United States of America

West European Countries

ENVIRONMENTAL DESIGN

Any Country

African Nations

Australia

Canada

Caribbean Countries

East European Countries

European Union

Middle East

New Zealand

South Africa

United Kingdom

United States of America

West European Countries

LANDSCAPE ARCHITECTURE

Any Country

African Nations

Australia

Canada

Caribbean Countries

East European Countries

European Union

Middle East

New Zealand

South Africa

United Kingdom

United States of America

West European Countries

TOWN AND COMMUNITY PLANNING

Any Country

African Nations

Australia

Canada

Caribbean Countries

East European Countries

Middle East

Ecosystem Approaches to Human Health Awards 364
George Pepler International Award 559
International Postgraduate Research Scholarships (IPRS) 692

New Zealand

George Pepler International Award 559
Wingate Scholarships 720

South Africa

Ecosystem Approaches to Human Health Awards 364
George Pepler International Award 559
International Postgraduate Research Scholarships (IPRS) 692
Wingate Scholarships 720

United Kingdom

George Pepler International Award 559
International Postgraduate Research Scholarships (IPRS) 692
Sheffield Hallam University Studentships 567
Swiss Federal Institute of Technology Scholarships 606
Wingate Scholarships 720

United States of America

George Pepler International Award 559
International Postgraduate Research Scholarships (IPRS) 692
Swiss Federal Institute of Technology Scholarships 606

West European Countries

George Pepler International Award 559
International Postgraduate Research Scholarships (IPRS) 692
Sheffield Hallam University Studentships 567
Wingate Scholarships 720

REGIONAL PLANNING

Any Country

University of Dundee Research Awards 648
Urban Design Travelling Fellowship 573

African Nations

George Pepler International Award 559
International Postgraduate Research Scholarships (IPRS) 692

Australia

George Pepler International Award 559
Wingate Scholarships 720

Canada

George Pepler International Award 559
International Postgraduate Research Scholarships (IPRS) 692
Public Safety and Emergency Preparedness Canada Research Fellowship in Honour of Stuart Nesbitt White 115
TAC Foundation Scholarships 615
Wingate Scholarships 720

Caribbean Countries

George Pepler International Award 559
International Postgraduate Research Scholarships (IPRS) 692

East European Countries

George Pepler International Award 559
International Postgraduate Research Scholarships (IPRS) 692

Middle East

George Pepler International Award 559
International Postgraduate Research Scholarships (IPRS) 692

New Zealand

George Pepler International Award 559
Wingate Scholarships 720

South Africa

George Pepler International Award 559
International Postgraduate Research Scholarships (IPRS) 692
Wingate Scholarships 720

United Kingdom

George Pepler International Award 559
International Postgraduate Research Scholarships (IPRS) 692
Sheffield Hallam University Studentships 567
Swiss Federal Institute of Technology Scholarships 606
Wingate Scholarships 720

United States of America

George Pepler International Award 559
International Postgraduate Research Scholarships (IPRS) 692
Minorities and Women Educational Scholarship Program 95
Swiss Federal Institute of Technology Scholarships 606

West European Countries

George Pepler International Award 559
International Postgraduate Research Scholarships (IPRS) 692
Sheffield Hallam University Studentships 567
Wingate Scholarships 720

ARTS AND HUMANITIES

GENERAL

Any Country

AAS 'Drawn to Art' Fellowship 25
AAS Reese Fellowship 26
AAS-North East Modern Language Association Fellowship 26
ACLS/Andrew W Mellon Fellowships for Junior Faculty 45
ACLS/SSRC/NEH International and Area Studies Fellowships 45
Adolfo Omodeo Scholarship 384
AFUW Western Australian Bursaries 148
American Historical Print Collectors Society Fellowship 27
American Society for Eighteenth-Century Studies (ASECS) Fellowship 481
Andrew W Mellon Postdoctoral Fellowship 717
ARIT Humanities and Social Sciences Fellowships 77
Arthur Weinberg Fellowship for Independent Scholars 481
ASCSA Advanced Fellowships 78
ASCSA Fellowships 78
ASECS (American Society for 18th-Century Studies)/Clark Library Fellowships 617
AUC Assistantships 89
AUC Graduate Merit Fellowships 90
AUC Ryoichi Sasakawa Young Leaders Graduate Scholarship 90
AUC University Fellowships 91
Audrey Lumsden-Kouvel Fellowship 481
Austro-American Association of Boston Scholarship 129
Balliol College Dervorguilla Scholarship 671
Balliol College Domus Graduate Scholarships 671
Banff Centre Financial Assistance 130
Barry Bloomfield Bursary 134
Bibliographical Society Small Grants 134
British Academy Larger Research Grants 142
British Academy Overseas Conference Grants 142
British Academy Small Research Grants 142
British Academy Worldwide Congress Grant 142
British Conference Grants 142
Camargo Fellowships 169
Canadian Department of Foreign Affairs Faculty Enrichment Program 205

Canadian Department of Foreign Affairs Faculty Research Program 206
Center for Great Lakes Culture/Michigan State University Fellowship 481
Charlotte W Newcombe Doctoral Dissertation Fellowships 725
Clark-Huntington Joint Bibliographical Fellowship 617
Concordia University Graduate Fellowships 240
Council of the Institute Awards 513
David J Azrieli Graduate Fellowship 241
Delahaye Memorial Benefaction 700
Earthwatch Field Research Grants 265
Endeavour International Postgraduate Research Scholarships (EIPRS) 403
Equiano Memorial Award 604
ERASMUS Prize 292
Foundation Praemium Erasmianum Study Prize 292
Frances A Yates Fellowships 713
Frances C Allen Fellowships 482
Franklin Research Grant Program 72
Frederico Chabod Scholarship 384
The Fredson Bowers Award 135
The Getty Trust Curatorial Research Fellowships 306
Harold White Fellowships 468
Helen McCormack Turner Memorial Scholarship 700
Helen Wallis Fellowship 156
Henrietta Hotton Research Grants 545
Henry Moore Institute Research Fellowship 323
Henry Moore Senior Fellowships 323
Herbert Hughes Scholarship 701
Herzog August Bibliothek Wolfenbüttel Fellowship 482
Hong Kong Research Grant 545
HRC Visiting Fellowships 332
IAUW International Scholarship 151
IHS Humane Studies Fellowships 343
IHS Liberty & Society Summer Seminars 343
Institute for Advanced Studies in the Humanities Visiting Research Fellowships 341
Institute of Irish Studies Research Fellowships 348
Institute of Irish Studies Senior Visiting Research Fellowship 348
IRCHSS Postdoctoral Fellowship 525
Irish Research Funds 383
J Franklin Jameson Fellowship 54
Jacob Hirsch Fellowship 79
JSPS Invitation Fellowship Programme for Research in Japan 387
Kanner Fellowship In British Studies 617
Kennan Institute Short-Term Grants 397
Korea Foundation Advanced Research Grant 398
Korea Foundation Fellowship for Field Research 399
Korea Foundation Fellowship for Graduate Studies 399
Korea Foundation Fellowship for Korean Language Training 399
Korea Foundation Postdoctoral Fellowship 399
Library Resident Research Fellowships 72
Linacre College Mary Blaschko Graduate Scholarship 678
Lincoln College Erich and Rochelle Endowed Prize in Music 679
Lincoln College Jermyn Brooks Graduate Award 680
Lincoln College Overseas Graduate Entrance Scholarships 680
Lindbergh Grants 229
Lloyd Lewis Fellowship in American History 482
M Alison Frantz Fellowship in Post-Classical Studies at the Gennadius Library 80
Mary Isabel Sibley Fellowship 510
Mary Radcliffe Scholarship 701
Mellon Postdoctoral Fellowships in the Humanities 502
Mellon Postdoctoral Research Fellowship 483
Monash International Postgraduate Research Scholarship (MIPRS) 440
Monash University Silver Jubilee Postgraduate Scholarship 440
Monticello College Foundation Fellowship for Women 483
NEH Fellowships 80
Newberry Library British Academy Fellowship for Study in Great Britain 483
Newberry Library Ecole des Chartes Exchange Fellowship 483
Newberry Library Short-Term Resident Fellowships for Individual Research 484
Nila Banton Smith Research Dissemination Support Grant 373
ORISHA (Oxford Research in the Scholarship and Humanities of Africa) Studentships 682
Paul D. Fleck Fellowships in the Arts 130
Paul Mellon Centre Rome Fellowship 161
Peter C Craigie Memorial Scholarship 642
Postdoctoral Fellowships (Getty) 306
Queen Mary Research Studentships 518
Renaissance Society Fellowships 585
Residential Grants at the Getty Center 307
Rhodes University Postdoctoral Fellowship and The Andrew Mellon Postdoctoral Fellowship 528
Rhodes University Postgraduate Scholarship 528
RHYS Curzon-Jones Scholarship 701
Ridley Lewis Bursary 701
Royal Irish Academy European Exchange Fellowship 551
Sabbatical Fellowship for the Humanities and Social Sciences 73
SCBWI Grant for Unpublished Authors 592
Sir Allan Sewell Visiting Fellowship 312
Sir Richard Stapley Educational Trust Grants 571
Smuts MCSC Bursaries for Commonwealth Studies 193
Smuts ORS Equivalent Awards 194
Society for the Humanities Postdoctoral Fellowships 242
South Central Modern Language Association Fellowship 484
SSRC Africa Program Advanced Research Grants 575
SSRC Africa Program Dissertation Fellowships 575
SSRC Summer Institute on International Migration 578
St Catherine's College Graduate Scholarship in the Arts 687
Stanley G French Graduate Fellowship 241
United States Holocaust Memorial Museum Center for Advanced Holocaust Studies Visiting Scholar Programs 619
University of Otago International Scholarships 670
University of Otago PhD Scholarships 670
University of Otago Prestigious PhD Scholarships 671
University of Reading Research Studentships: Faculty of Arts and Humanities 692
University of Southampton Postgraduate Studentships 692
University of Sussex Overseas Research Studentships 696
Vera Moore International Postgraduate Research Scholarships 440
W D Llewelyn Memorial Benefaction 701
Weiss/Brown Publication Subvention Award 484
Wolfsonian-FIU Fellowship 722
Woodrow Wilson Grants in Women's Studies 725
World Universities Network (WUN) Global Exchange Programme 693

African Nations

AUC African Graduate Fellowship 89
Endeavour International Postgraduate Research Scholarships (EIPRS) 403
Fulbright Postdoctoral Research and Lecturing Awards for Non-US Citizens 245
International Postgraduate Research Scholarships (IPRS) 692
Lincoln College Overseas Graduate Entrance Scholarships 680
Merton College Reed Foundation Scholarship 681
NUFFIC-NFP Fellowships for Master's Degree Programmes 478

Australia

AAH Humanities Travelling Fellowships 120
Australian Postgraduate Awards 402
Endeavour International Postgraduate Research Scholarships (EIPRS) 403
Fulbright Postdoctoral Fellowships 125
Fulbright Postdoctoral Research and Lecturing Awards for Non-US Citizens 245
James Fairfax and Oxford-Australia Fund Scholarships 676
Japanese Government (Monbukagakusho) Scholarships Research Category 388
Lincoln College Overseas Graduate Entrance Scholarships 680
Marten Bequest Travelling Scholarships 224
University of Essex/ORS Awards 655

Canada

Caribbean Countries

East European Countries

European Union

Middle East

New Zealand

South Africa

United Kingdom

African Nations

Australia

Canada

Caribbean Countries

East European Countries

European Union

Middle East

New Zealand

South Africa

United Kingdom

United States of America

West European Countries

NATIVE LANGUAGE AND LITERATURE

Any Country

African Nations

Australia

Canada

Caribbean Countries

East European Countries

European Union

Middle East

New Zealand

South Africa

United Kingdom

United States of America

West European Countries

MODERN LANGUAGES AND LITERATURES

Any Country

African Nations

Australia

Canada

Caribbean Countries

East European Countries

European Union

Middle East

New Zealand

South Africa

United Kingdom

United States of America

West European Countries

ENGLISH

Any Country

African Nations

Australia

Canada

Caribbean Countries

East European Countries

European Union

Middle East

New Zealand

South Africa

United Kingdom

United States of America

West European Countries

FRENCH

Any Country

African Nations

Australia

Canada

Edouard Morot-Sir Fellowship in Literature 340
Gilbert Chinard Fellowships 341
Harmon Chadbourn Rorison Fellowship 341
International Postgraduate Research Scholarships (IPRS) 692
Quinn, Nathan and Edmond Scholarships 666
Wingate Scholarships 720

Caribbean Countries

International Postgraduate Research Scholarships (IPRS) 692

East European Countries

International Postgraduate Research Scholarships (IPRS) 692

European Union

AHRC Doctoral Awards Scheme 103
Professional Preparation Master's Scheme 103
Research Preparation Master's Scheme 103

Middle East

International Postgraduate Research Scholarships (IPRS) 692

New Zealand

Quinn, Nathan and Edmond Scholarships 666
University of Otago Master's Awards 670
Wingate Scholarships 720

South Africa

International Postgraduate Research Scholarships (IPRS) 692
Quinn, Nathan and Edmond Scholarships 666
Wingate Scholarships 720

United Kingdom

AHRC Doctoral Awards Scheme 103
Hamilton Studentship 666
International Postgraduate Research Scholarships (IPRS) 692
Mr and Mrs David Edward Memorial Award 699
Professional Preparation Master's Scheme 103
Quinn, Nathan and Edmond Scholarships 666
Research Preparation Master's Scheme 103
University of Kent School of European Culture and Language Scholarships 662
University of Wales Aberystwyth Postgraduate Research Studentships 699
UWB Departmental Research Studentships 700
UWB Research Studentships 700
Wingate Scholarships 720

United States of America

Edouard Morot-Sir Fellowship in Literature 340
Fulbright Teacher and Administrator Exchange 297
Gilbert Chinard Fellowships 341
Harmon Chadbourn Rorison Fellowship 341
International Postgraduate Research Scholarships (IPRS) 692
The Walter J Jensen Fellowship for French Language, Literature and Culture 510

West European Countries

International Postgraduate Research Scholarships (IPRS) 692
Language Assistantships in Australia 269
Mr and Mrs David Edward Memorial Award 699
University of Kent School of European Culture and Language Scholarships 662
University of Otago Master's Awards 670
UWB Departmental Research Studentships 700
UWB Research Studentships 700
Wingate Scholarships 720

SPANISH

Any Country

Ahmanson and Getty Postdoctoral Fellowships 617
ASECS (American Society for 18th-Century Studies)/Clark Library Fellowships 617
Barron Bequest 693
CC-CS Scholarship Program 225
Clark Library Short-Term Resident Fellowships 617
Clark Predoctoral Fellowships 617
Clark-Huntington Joint Bibliographical Fellowship 617
Katherine Singer Kovacs Prize 438
Queen Mary Research Studentships 518
Queen Sofia Research Fellowship 282
Thomas Holloway Research Studentship 548
United States Holocaust Memorial Museum Center for Advanced Holocaust Studies Visiting Scholar Programs 619
University of Bristol Postgraduate Scholarships 641
University of Southampton Postgraduate Studentships 692
World Universities Network (WUN) Global Exchange Programme 693

Australia

Wingate Scholarships 720

Canada

Wingate Scholarships 720

European Union

AHRC Doctoral Awards Scheme 103
Professional Preparation Master's Scheme 103
Research Preparation Master's Scheme 103

New Zealand

Wingate Scholarships 720

South Africa

Wingate Scholarships 720

United Kingdom

AHRC Doctoral Awards Scheme 103
Mr and Mrs David Edward Memorial Award 699
Professional Preparation Master's Scheme 103
Research Preparation Master's Scheme 103
University of Kent School of European Culture and Language Scholarships 662
University of Wales Aberystwyth Postgraduate Research Studentships 699
UWB Departmental Research Studentships 700
UWB Research Studentships 700
Wingate Scholarships 720

United States of America

Fulbright Teacher and Administrator Exchange 297

West European Countries

Mr and Mrs David Edward Memorial Award 699
University of Kent School of European Culture and Language Scholarships 662
UWB Departmental Research Studentships 700
UWB Research Studentships 700
Wingate Scholarships 720

GERMANIC LANGUAGES

Any Country

Ahmanson and Getty Postdoctoral Fellowships 617
Aldo and Jeanne Scaglione Prize for Studies in Germanic Languages and Literatures 437

Australia

Canada

European Union

New Zealand

South Africa

United Kingdom

United States of America

West European Countries

GERMAN

Any Country

Australia

Canada

European Union

New Zealand

South Africa

United Kingdom

United States of America

West European Countries

SWEDISH

Any Country

Australia

Canada

European Union

New Zealand

South Africa

United Kingdom

Research Preparation Master's Scheme 103
Wingate Scholarships 720

West European Countries

Wingate Scholarships 720

DANISH

Any Country

Aldo and Jeanne Scaglione Prize for Studies in Germanic Languages and Literatures 437
Barron Bequest 693
United States Holocaust Memorial Museum Center for Advanced Holocaust Studies Visiting Scholar Programs 619

Australia

Wingate Scholarships 720

Canada

Wingate Scholarships 720

European Union

AHRC Doctoral Awards Scheme 103
Professional Preparation Master's Scheme 103
Research Preparation Master's Scheme 103

New Zealand

Wingate Scholarships 720

South Africa

Wingate Scholarships 720

United Kingdom

AHRC Doctoral Awards Scheme 103
Professional Preparation Master's Scheme 103
Research Preparation Master's Scheme 103
Wingate Scholarships 720

West European Countries

Wingate Scholarships 720

NORWEGIAN

Any Country

Aldo and Jeanne Scaglione Prize for Studies in Germanic Languages and Literatures 437
Barron Bequest 693
United States Holocaust Memorial Museum Center for Advanced Holocaust Studies Visiting Scholar Programs 619

Australia

Wingate Scholarships 720

Canada

Wingate Scholarships 720

European Union

AHRC Doctoral Awards Scheme 103
Professional Preparation Master's Scheme 103
Research Preparation Master's Scheme 103

New Zealand

Wingate Scholarships 720

South Africa

Wingate Scholarships 720

United Kingdom

AHRC Doctoral Awards Scheme 103
Professional Preparation Master's Scheme 103
Research Preparation Master's Scheme 103
Wingate Scholarships 720

United States of America

Fulbright Teacher and Administrator Exchange 297
Norwegian Emigration Fund of 1975 487

West European Countries

Wingate Scholarships 720

ITALIAN

Any Country

Ahmanson and Getty Postdoctoral Fellowships 617
Aldo and Jeanne Scaglione Prize for Italian Studies 437
ASECS (American Society for 18th-Century Studies)/Clark Library Fellowships 617
Barron Bequest 693
Clark Library Short-Term Resident Fellowships 617
Clark Predoctoral Fellowships 617
Clark-Huntington Joint Bibliographical Fellowship 617
Howard R Marraro Prize 438
Thomas Holloway Research Studentship 548
United States Holocaust Memorial Museum Center for Advanced Holocaust Studies Visiting Scholar Programs 619
University of Bristol Postgraduate Scholarships 641

Australia

Wingate Scholarships 720

Canada

Wingate Scholarships 720

European Union

AHRC Doctoral Awards Scheme 103
Professional Preparation Master's Scheme 103
Research Preparation Master's Scheme 103

New Zealand

Wingate Scholarships 720

South Africa

Wingate Scholarships 720

United Kingdom

AHRC Doctoral Awards Scheme 103
Balsdon Fellowship 160
Professional Preparation Master's Scheme 103
Research Preparation Master's Scheme 103
Rome Awards 161
Rome Fellowship 161
Rome Scholarships in Ancient, Medieval and Later Italian Studies 162
University of Kent School of European Culture and Language Scholarships 662
University of Wales Aberystwyth Postgraduate Research Studentships 699
Wingate Scholarships 720

United States of America

Gladys Krieble Delmas Foundation Grants 308

West European Countries

University of Kent School of European Culture and Language Scholarships 662
Wingate Scholarships 720

PORTUGUESE

Any Country

Barron Bequest 693
CC-CS Scholarship Program 225
Katherine Singer Kovacs Prize 438
United States Holocaust Memorial Museum Center for Advanced Holocaust Studies Visiting Scholar Programs 619
University of Bristol Postgraduate Scholarships 641
University of Southampton Postgraduate Studentships 692
World Universities Network (WUN) Global Exchange Programme 693

Australia

Wingate Scholarships 720

Canada

Wingate Scholarships 720

European Union

AHRC Doctoral Awards Scheme 103
Professional Preparation Master's Scheme 103
Research Preparation Master's Scheme 103

New Zealand

Wingate Scholarships 720

South Africa

Wingate Scholarships 720

United Kingdom

AHRC Doctoral Awards Scheme 103
Professional Preparation Master's Scheme 103
Research Preparation Master's Scheme 103
Wingate Scholarships 720

West European Countries

Wingate Scholarships 720

ROMANCE LANGUAGES

Any Country

Ahmanson and Getty Postdoctoral Fellowships 617
ASECS (American Society for 18th-Century Studies)/Clark Library Fellowships 617
Camargo Fellowships 169
Clark Library Short-Term Resident Fellowships 617
Clark Predoctoral Fellowships 617
Clark-Huntington Joint Bibliographical Fellowship 617
United States Holocaust Memorial Museum Center for Advanced Holocaust Studies Visiting Scholar Programs 619
University of Bristol Postgraduate Scholarships 641

Australia

Wingate Scholarships 720

Canada

Gilbert Chinard Fellowships 341
Harmon Chadbourn Rorison Fellowship 341
Wingate Scholarships 720

European Union

AHRC Doctoral Awards Scheme 103
Professional Preparation Master's Scheme 103
Research Preparation Master's Scheme 103

New Zealand

Wingate Scholarships 720

South Africa

Wingate Scholarships 720

United Kingdom

AHRC Doctoral Awards Scheme 103
Professional Preparation Master's Scheme 103
Research Preparation Master's Scheme 103
Wingate Scholarships 720

United States of America

Gilbert Chinard Fellowships 341
Harmon Chadbourn Rorison Fellowship 341

West European Countries

Wingate Scholarships 720

MODERN GREEK

Any Country

Aristotle University of Thessaloniki Scholarships 97
M Alison Frantz Fellowship in Post-Classical Studies at the Gennadius Library 80
Mary Isabel Sibley Fellowship 510
NEH Fellowships 80
United States Holocaust Memorial Museum Center for Advanced Holocaust Studies Visiting Scholar Programs 619

Australia

Wingate Scholarships 720

Canada

Homer and Dorothy Thompson Fellowship 199
Wingate Scholarships 720

European Union

AHRC Doctoral Awards Scheme 103
Professional Preparation Master's Scheme 103
Research Preparation Master's Scheme 103

New Zealand

Wingate Scholarships 720

South Africa

Wingate Scholarships 720

United Kingdom

AHRC Doctoral Awards Scheme 103
Hector and Elizabeth Catling Bursary 159
Professional Preparation Master's Scheme 103
Research Preparation Master's Scheme 103
Wingate Scholarships 720

West European Countries

Wingate Scholarships 720

DUTCH

Any Country

Aldo and Jeanne Scaglione Prize for Studies in Germanic Languages and Literatures 437
Barron Bequest 693
United States Holocaust Memorial Museum Center for Advanced Holocaust Studies Visiting Scholar Programs 619

Australia

Wingate Scholarships 720

Canada

Wingate Scholarships 720

European Union

AHRC Doctoral Awards Scheme 103
Professional Preparation Master's Scheme 103
Research Preparation Master's Scheme 103

New Zealand

Wingate Scholarships 720

South Africa

Wingate Scholarships 720

United Kingdom

AHRC Doctoral Awards Scheme 103
Professional Preparation Master's Scheme 103
Research Preparation Master's Scheme 103
Wingate Scholarships 720

West European Countries

Wingate Scholarships 720

BALTIC LANGUAGES

Any Country

M Alison Frantz Fellowship in Post-Classical Studies at the Gennadius Library 80
United States Holocaust Memorial Museum Center for Advanced Holocaust Studies Visiting Scholar Programs 619

Australia

Wingate Scholarships 720

Canada

Wingate Scholarships 720

European Union

AHRC Doctoral Awards Scheme 103
Professional Preparation Master's Scheme 103
Research Preparation Master's Scheme 103

New Zealand

Wingate Scholarships 720

South Africa

Wingate Scholarships 720

United Kingdom

AHRC Doctoral Awards Scheme 103
Professional Preparation Master's Scheme 103
Research Preparation Master's Scheme 103
Wingate Scholarships 720

United States of America

IREX Individual Advanced Research Opportunities 374

West European Countries

Wingate Scholarships 720

CELTIC LANGUAGES

Any Country

Barron Bequest 693
Cornwall Heritage Trust Scholarship 656
Delahaye Memorial Benefaction 700
Dublin Institute for Advanced Studies Scholarship in Celtic Studies 263
Helen McCormack Turner Memorial Scholarship 700
Herbert Hughes Scholarship 701
Mary Radcliffe Scholarship 701
RHYS Curzon-Jones Scholarship 701
Ridley Lewis Bursary 701
Sir John Rhys Studentship in Celtic Studies 685
W D Llewelyn Memorial Benefaction 701

Australia

Wingate Scholarships 720

Canada

Wingate Scholarships 720

European Union

AHRC Doctoral Awards Scheme 103
Professional Preparation Master's Scheme 103
Research Preparation Master's Scheme 103

New Zealand

Wingate Scholarships 720

South Africa

Wingate Scholarships 720

United Kingdom

AHRC Doctoral Awards Scheme 103
Mr and Mrs David Edward Memorial Award 699
Professional Preparation Master's Scheme 103
Research Preparation Master's Scheme 103
University of Wales Aberystwyth Postgraduate Research Studentships 699
UWB Departmental Research Studentships 700
UWB Research Studentships 700
Wingate Scholarships 720

West European Countries

Mr and Mrs David Edward Memorial Award 699
UWB Departmental Research Studentships 700
UWB Research Studentships 700
Wingate Scholarships 720

FINNISH

Any Country

United States Holocaust Memorial Museum Center for Advanced Holocaust Studies Visiting Scholar Programs 619

Australia

Wingate Scholarships 720

Canada

Wingate Scholarships 720

European Union

AHRC Doctoral Awards Scheme 103
Professional Preparation Master's Scheme 103
Research Preparation Master's Scheme 103

New Zealand

Wingate Scholarships 720

South Africa

Wingate Scholarships 720

FINO UGRIAN LANGUAGES

Any Country

United States Holocaust Memorial Museum Center for Advanced Holocaust Studies Visiting Scholar Programs 619

Australia

Wingate Scholarships 720

Canada

Wingate Scholarships 720

European Union

AHRC Doctoral Awards Scheme 103
Professional Preparation Master's Scheme 103
Research Preparation Master's Scheme 103

New Zealand

Wingate Scholarships 720

South Africa

Wingate Scholarships 720

United Kingdom

AHRC Doctoral Awards Scheme 103
Professional Preparation Master's Scheme 103
Research Preparation Master's Scheme 103
Wingate Scholarships 720

West European Countries

Wingate Scholarships 720

EUROPEAN LANGUAGES (OTHERS)

Any Country

United States Holocaust Memorial Museum Center for Advanced Holocaust Studies Visiting Scholar Programs 619

Australia

Wingate Scholarships 720

Canada

Wingate Scholarships 720

European Union

AHRC Doctoral Awards Scheme 103
Professional Preparation Master's Scheme 103
Research Preparation Master's Scheme 103

New Zealand

Wingate Scholarships 720

South Africa

Wingate Scholarships 720

United Kingdom

AHRC Doctoral Awards Scheme 103
Professional Preparation Master's Scheme 103
Research Preparation Master's Scheme 103
University of Wales Aberystwyth Postgraduate Research Studentships 699
Wingate Scholarships 720

West European Countries

Wingate Scholarships 720

ALTAIC LANGUAGES

Australia

Wingate Scholarships 720

Canada

Wingate Scholarships 720

European Union

AHRC Doctoral Awards Scheme 103
Professional Preparation Master's Scheme 103
Research Preparation Master's Scheme 103

New Zealand

Wingate Scholarships 720

South Africa

Wingate Scholarships 720

United Kingdom

AHRC Doctoral Awards Scheme 103
Professional Preparation Master's Scheme 103
Research Preparation Master's Scheme 103
Wingate Scholarships 720

United States of America

ARIT-Bosphorus University Language Fellowships 77

West European Countries

Wingate Scholarships 720

ARABIC

Any Country

Anthony Parsons Memorial Scholarship 656
AUC International Graduate Fellowships in Arabic Studies, Middle East Studies and Sociology/Anthropology 90
AUC Teaching Arabic as a Foreign Language Fellowships 91
British Academy Ancient Persia Fund 141
SOAS Bursary 563
SOAS Research Student Fellowships 563

Australia

Wingate Scholarships 720

Canada

Wingate Scholarships 720

European Union

AHRC Doctoral Awards Scheme 103
CBRL Travel Grant 244
Professional Preparation Master's Scheme 103
Research Preparation Master's Scheme 103

New Zealand

Wingate Scholarships 720

South Africa

Wingate Scholarships 720

United Kingdom

AHRC Doctoral Awards Scheme 103
CBRL Research Award 244
CBRL Travel Grant 244
Professional Preparation Master's Scheme 103
Research Preparation Master's Scheme 103
Wingate Scholarships 720

Center for Hellenic Studies Junior Fellowships 226
Corpus Christi College Graduate Studentship in Arts 674
Delahaye Memorial Benefaction 700
Frederico Chabod Scholarship 384
Helen McCormack Turner Memorial Scholarship 700
Herbert Hughes Scholarship 701
Mary Isabel Sibley Fellowship 510
Mary Radcliffe Scholarship 701
NEH Fellowships 80
Onassis Foreigners' Fellowship Programme Educational Scholarships Category B 16
RHYS Curzon-Jones Scholarship 701
Ridley Lewis Bursary 701
W D Llewelyn Memorial Benefaction 701

Australia

Wingate Scholarships 720

Canada

Homer and Dorothy Thompson Fellowship 199
Wingate Scholarships 720

European Union

AHRC Doctoral Awards Scheme 103
Professional Preparation Master's Scheme 103
Research Preparation Master's Scheme 103

New Zealand

Wingate Scholarships 720

South Africa

Wingate Scholarships 720

United Kingdom

AHRC Doctoral Awards Scheme 103
The Dover Fund 586
Hector and Elizabeth Catling Bursary 159
Professional Preparation Master's Scheme 103
Research Preparation Master's Scheme 103
University of Kent School of European Culture and Language Scholarships 662
Wingate Scholarships 720

United States of America

Fulbright Teacher and Administrator Exchange 297

West European Countries

Merton College Leventis Scholarship 681
University of Kent School of European Culture and Language Scholarships 662
Wingate Scholarships 720

SANSKRIT

Any Country

SOAS Bursary 563
SOAS Research Student Fellowships 563

Australia

Wingate Scholarships 720

Canada

Wingate Scholarships 720

European Union

AHRC Doctoral Awards Scheme 103
Professional Preparation Master's Scheme 103
Research Preparation Master's Scheme 103

New Zealand

Wingate Scholarships 720

South Africa

Wingate Scholarships 720

United Kingdom

AHRC Doctoral Awards Scheme 103
Professional Preparation Master's Scheme 103
Research Preparation Master's Scheme 103
Wingate Scholarships 720

West European Countries

Wingate Scholarships 720

LINGUISTICS AND PHILOLOGY

Any Country

Aldo and Jeanne Scaglione Prize for French and Francophone Literary Studies 437
Aldo and Jeanne Scaglione Prize for Studies in Germanic Languages and Literatures 437
Aldo and Jeanne Scaglione Prize for Studies in Slavic Languages and Literatures 438
ASCSA Advanced Fellowships 78
ASCSA Fellowships 78
British Academy Overseas Conference Grants 142
British Academy Postdoctoral Fellowships 142
British Academy Small Research Grants 142
British Conference Grants 142
Camargo Fellowships 169
CDU Senior Research Fellowship 230
CDU Three Year Postdoctoral Fellowship 230
Fondation Fyssen Postdoctoral Study Grants 286
Gypsy Lore Society Young Scholar's Prize in Romani Studies 314
Jacob Hirsch Fellowship 79
James Russell Lowell Prize 438
Kenneth W Mildenberger Prize 438
M Alison Frantz Fellowship in Post-Classical Studies at the Gennadius Library 80
Marusia and Michael Dorosh Master's Fellowship 207
Mina P Shaughnessy Prize 439
MLA Prize for a Distinguished Bibliography 439
MLA Prize for a First Book 439
MLA Prize for Independent Scholars 439
NEH Fellowships 80
Neporany Doctoral Fellowship 208
Onassis Foreigners' Fellowships Programme Research Grants Category AI 17
Phillips Fund Grants for Native American Research 72
Queen Mary Research Studentships 518
Renaissance Society Fellowships 585
SOAS Bursary 563
SOAS Research Student Fellowships 563
St Catherine's College Graduate Scholarship in the Arts 687
Trinity College Junior Research Fellowship 689
United States Holocaust Memorial Museum Center for Advanced Holocaust Studies Visiting Scholar Programs 619
University of Otago International Scholarships 670
University of Otago PhD Scholarships 670
University of Otago Prestigious PhD Scholarships 671
University of Southampton Postgraduate Studentships 692
World Universities Network (WUN) Global Exchange Programme 693

African Nations

British School of Archaeology in Iraq Grants 163

Australia

AAH Humanities Travelling Fellowships 120
British School of Archaeology in Iraq Grants 163

APPLIED LINGUISTICS

PHONETICS

Any Country

A C Gimson Scholarships in Phonetics and Linguistics 624
Camargo Fellowships 169

Australia

Wingate Scholarships 720

Canada

Wingate Scholarships 720

European Union

AHRC Doctoral Awards Scheme 103
Professional Preparation Master's Scheme 103
Research Preparation Master's Scheme 103

New Zealand

Wingate Scholarships 720

South Africa

Wingate Scholarships 720

United Kingdom

AHRC Doctoral Awards Scheme 103
Mr and Mrs David Edward Memorial Award 699
Professional Preparation Master's Scheme 103
Research Preparation Master's Scheme 103
University of Essex Access to Learning Fund 652
UWB Departmental Research Studentships 700
UWB Research Studentships 700
Wingate Scholarships 720

West European Countries

Mr and Mrs David Edward Memorial Award 699
UWB Departmental Research Studentships 700
UWB Research Studentships 700
Wingate Scholarships 720

LOGOPEDICS

Australia

Wingate Scholarships 720

Canada

Wingate Scholarships 720

European Union

AHRC Doctoral Awards Scheme 103
Professional Preparation Master's Scheme 103
Research Preparation Master's Scheme 103

New Zealand

Wingate Scholarships 720

South Africa

Wingate Scholarships 720

United Kingdom

AHRC Doctoral Awards Scheme 103
Mr and Mrs David Edward Memorial Award 699
Professional Preparation Master's Scheme 103
Research Preparation Master's Scheme 103
University of Essex Access to Learning Fund 652
Wingate Scholarships 720

West European Countries

Mr and Mrs David Edward Memorial Award 699
Wingate Scholarships 720

COMPARATIVE LITERATURE

Any Country

Adolfo Omodeo Scholarship 384
Ahmanson and Getty Postdoctoral Fellowships 617
Aldo and Jeanne Scaglione Prize for Comparative Literary Studies 437
Aldo and Jeanne Scaglione Prize for French and Francophone Literary Studies 437
Aldo and Jeanne Scaglione Prize for Italian Studies 437
Aldo and Jeanne Scaglione Prize for Studies in Germanic Languages and Literatures 437
Aldo and Jeanne Scaglione Prize for Studies in Slavic Languages and Literatures 438
ASCSA Advanced Fellowships 78
ASCSA Fellowships 78
ASECS (American Society for 18th-Century Studies)/Clark Library Fellowships 617
Bilkent Turkish Literature Fellowship 136
British Academy Larger Research Grants 142
British Academy Overseas Conference Grants 142
British Academy Postdoctoral Fellowships 142
British Academy Small Research Grants 142
British Academy Worldwide Congress Grant 142
British Conference Grants 142
Camargo Fellowships 169
CC-CS Scholarship Program 225
Charlotte W Newcombe Doctoral Dissertation Fellowships 725
ChLA Beiter Scholarships for Graduate Students 231
ChLA Research Fellowships and Scholarships 231
Clark Library Short-Term Resident Fellowships 617
Clark Predoctoral Fellowships 617
Clark-Huntington Joint Bibliographical Fellowship 617
Fenia and Yaakov Leviant Memorial Prize 438
Foundation Praemium Erasmianum Study Prize 292
Frederico Chabod Scholarship 384
Howard R Marraro Prize 438
IHS Humane Studies Fellowships 343
Institute of Irish Studies Senior Visiting Research Fellowship 348
Jacob Hirsch Fellowship 79
James Russell Lowell Prize 438
Katherine Singer Kovacs Prize 438
Kennan Institute Short-Term Grants 397
M Alison Frantz Fellowship in Post-Classical Studies at the Gennadius Library 80
Mary Isabel Sibley Fellowship 510
MLA Prize for a Distinguished Bibliography 439
MLA Prize for a First Book 439
MLA Prize for Independent Scholars 439
NEH Fellowships 80
Queen Mary Research Studentships 518
Renaissance Society Fellowships 585
SOAS Bursary 563
SOAS Research Student Fellowships 563
United States Holocaust Memorial Museum Center for Advanced Holocaust Studies Visiting Scholar Programs 619
University of Southampton Postgraduate Studentships 692
William Sanders Scarborough Prize 439
World Universities Network (WUN) Global Exchange Programme 693
Yaddo Residency 243

Australia

AAH Humanities Travelling Fellowships 120
Quinn, Nathan and Edmond Scholarships 666
University of Essex/ORS Awards 655
Wingate Scholarships 720

Canada

Caribbean Countries

East European Countries

European Union

Middle East

New Zealand

South Africa

United Kingdom

United States of America

West European Countries

HISTORY

Any Country

African Nations

Australia

Canada

Caribbean Countries

East European Countries

European Union

Middle East

New Zealand

South Africa

United Kingdom

United States of America

West European Countries

PREHISTORY

Any Country

African Nations

Henry Moore Institute Research Fellowship 323
Herbert Hughes Scholarship 701
Institute of Irish Studies Research Fellowships 348
Institute of Irish Studies Senior Visiting Research Fellowship 348
Isobel Thornley Research Fellowship 347
J Franklin Jameson Fellowship 54
Jacob Hirsch Fellowship 79
JCB William Reese Company Fellowship 391
Littleton-Griswold Research Grant 54
M Alison Frantz Fellowship in Post-Classical Studies at the Gennadius Library 80
Mary Isabel Sibley Fellowship 510
Mary Radcliffe Scholarship 701
Mellon Postdoctoral Research Fellowships 333
NEH Fellowships 80
Neil Ker Memorial Fund 143
Queen Mary Research Studentships 518
Renaissance Society Fellowships 585
RHYS Curzon-Jones Scholarship 701
Ridley Lewis Bursary 701
Royal History Society Fellowship 347
Scouloudi Fellowships 347
Thomas Holloway Research Studentship 548
W D Llewelyn Memorial Benefaction 701

Australia

Wingate Scholarships 720

Canada

Mary McNeill Scholarship in Irish Studies 348
Medieval History Seminar 304
Wingate Scholarships 720

East European Countries

Medieval History Seminar 304
Young Scholars Forum 304

European Union

AHRC Doctoral Awards Scheme 103
CBRL Travel Grant 244
Professional Preparation Master's Scheme 103
Research Preparation Master's Scheme 103

New Zealand

Wingate Scholarships 720

South Africa

Wingate Scholarships 720

United Kingdom

AHRC Doctoral Awards Scheme 103
Balsdon Fellowship 160
British Institute in Eastern Africa Research Grants 155
CBRL Research Award 244
CBRL Travel Grant 244
Economic History Society Research Fellowships 564
Hector and Elizabeth Catling Bursary 159
Medieval History Seminar 304
Mr and Mrs David Edward Memorial Award 699
Professional Preparation Master's Scheme 103
Research Preparation Master's Scheme 103
Rome Awards 161
Rome Fellowship 161
Rome Scholarships in Ancient, Medieval and Later Italian Studies 162
University of Wales Aberystwyth Postgraduate Research Studentships 699
UWB Departmental Research Studentships 700
UWB Research Studentships 700
Wingate Scholarships 720
Young Scholars Forum 304

United States of America

ARCE Fellowships 77
Earthwatch Education Awards 265
Mary McNeill Scholarship in Irish Studies 348
Medieval History Seminar 304
National Endowment for the Humanities Fellowships 333
William B Schallek Memorial Graduate Fellowship Award 529
Young Scholars Forum 304

West European Countries

Medieval History Seminar 304
Mr and Mrs David Edward Memorial Award 699
UWB Departmental Research Studentships 700
UWB Research Studentships 700
Wingate Scholarships 720
Young Scholars Forum 304

MODERN HISTORY

Any Country

AAS Joyce Tracy Fellowship 26
Adelle and Erwin Tomash Fellowship in the History of Information Processing 229
Ahmanson and Getty Postdoctoral Fellowships 617
Albert J Beveridge Grant 54
ASCSA Fellowships 78
ASECS (American Society for 18th-Century Studies)/Clark Library Fellowships 617
Barbara Thom Postdoctoral Fellowship 332
Bernadotte E Schmitt Grants 54
British Academy Elie Kedourie Memorial Fund 141
Bucerius Seminar 302
Camargo Fellowships 169
Charles C Price Fellowship 230
Clark Library Short-Term Resident Fellowships 617
Clark Predoctoral Fellowships 617
Clark-Huntington Joint Bibliographical Fellowship 617
Delahaye Memorial Benefaction 700
Dixon Ryan Fox Manuscript Prize of the New York State Historical Association 480
E Lyman Stewart Fellowship 647
Fellowships in the University of Delaware Hagley Program 647
Fernand Braudel Senior Fellowships 280
Gypsy Lore Society Young Scholar's Prize in Romani Studies 314
Hagley/Winterthur Arts and Industries Fellowship 314
Harry S Truman Library Institute Dissertation Year Fellowships 317
Helen McCormack Turner Memorial Scholarship 700
Henry Moore Institute Research Fellowship 323
Herbert Hoover Presidential Library Association Travel Grants 324
Herbert Hughes Scholarship 701
IEEE Fellowship in Electrical History 335
Institute of European History Fellowships 346
Institute of Irish Studies Research Fellowships 348
Institute of Irish Studies Senior Visiting Research Fellowship 348
Isobel Thornley Research Fellowship 347
J Franklin Jameson Fellowship 54
Jacob Hirsch Fellowship 79
JCB William Reese Company Fellowship 391
Jean Monnet Fellowships 280
Kanner Fellowship In British Studies 617
Lewis Walpole Library Fellowship 410
Library Company of Philadelphia and Historical Society of Pennsylvania Research Fellowships in American History and Culture 411
Library Company of Philadelphia Dissertation Fellowships 411
Littleton-Griswold Research Grant 54
M Alison Frantz Fellowship in Post-Classical Studies at the Gennadius Library 80
Marine Corps Historical Center Research Grants 420
Mary Isabel Sibley Fellowship 510
Mary Radcliffe Scholarship 701
Mellon Postdoctoral Research Fellowships 333

NEH Fellowships 80
Neville Chamberlain Scholarship 641
Paul H. Nitze School of Advanced International Studies (SAIS) Financial Aid and Fellowships 139
Queen Mary Research Studentships 518
Renaissance Society Fellowships 585
RHYS Curzon-Jones Scholarship 701
Ridley Lewis Bursary 701
Roosevelt Institute Research Grant 292
Royal History Society Fellowship 347
Scouloudi Fellowships 347
Thank-Offering to Britain Fellowships 143
Thomas Holloway Research Studentship 548
United States Holocaust Memorial Museum Center for Advanced Holocaust Studies Visiting Scholar Programs 619
University of Dundee Research Awards 648
W D Llewelyn Memorial Benefaction 701
Wolfsonian-FIU Fellowship 722

Australia

University of Essex/ORS Awards 655
Wingate Scholarships 720

Canada

Mary McNeill Scholarship in Irish Studies 348
University of Essex/ORS Awards 655
Wingate Scholarships 720

Caribbean Countries

University of Essex/ORS Awards 655

East European Countries

Elisabeth Barker Fund 142
EUI Postgraduate Scholarships 279
University of Essex/ORS Awards 655
Young Scholars Forum 304

European Union

+3 (PhD research) Studentship 651
AHRC Doctoral Awards Scheme 103
CBRL Travel Grant 244
EUI Postgraduate Scholarships 279
Professional Preparation Master's Scheme 103
Research Preparation Master's Scheme 103
Research Preparations Masters Scheme 652
University of Essex Doctoral award for PhD 653
University of Essex/ESRC 1+3 Studentship 654

Middle East

University of Essex/ORS Awards 655

New Zealand

J M Sherrard Award 220
Wingate Scholarships 720

South Africa

University of Essex/ORS Awards 655
Wingate Scholarships 720

United Kingdom

+3 (PhD research) Studentship 651
AHRC Doctoral Awards Scheme 103
Balsdon Fellowship 160
British Institute in Eastern Africa Research Grants 155
CBRL Research Award 244
CBRL Travel Grant 244
Economic History Society Research Fellowships 564
EUI Postgraduate Scholarships 279
Fulbright-Robertson Visiting Professorship in British History 708
Hector and Elizabeth Catling Bursary 159
Mr and Mrs David Edward Memorial Award 699
Professional Preparation Master's Scheme 103
Research Preparation Master's Scheme 103
Research Preparations Masters Scheme 652
Rome Awards 161
Rome Fellowship 161
Rome Scholarships in Ancient, Medieval and Later Italian Studies 162
University of Essex Access to Learning Fund 652
University of Essex Doctoral award for PhD 653
University of Essex/ESRC 1+3 Studentship 654
University of Wales Aberystwyth Postgraduate Research Studentships 699
UWB Departmental Research Studentships 700
UWB Research Studentships 700
Wingate Scholarships 720
Young Scholars Forum 304

United States of America

Earthwatch Education Awards 265
Fritz Stern Dissertation Prize 302
Fulbright Distinguished Chairs Program 245
Fulbright Senior Specialists Program 245
German Historical Institute Collaborative Research Program for Postdoctoral Scholars 303
German Historical Institute Doctoral and Postdoctoral Fellowships 303
Library Company of Philadelphia Postdoctoral Research Fellowship 412
Mary McNeill Scholarship in Irish Studies 348
National Endowment for the Humanities Fellowships 333
Thyssen–Heideking Fellowship 304
University of Essex/ORS Awards 655
Young Scholars Forum 304

West European Countries

Elisabeth Barker Fund 142
EUI Postgraduate Scholarships 279
German Historical Institute Collaborative Research Program for Postdoctoral Scholars 303
German Historical Institute Doctoral and Postdoctoral Fellowships 303
Kade-Heideking Fellowship 303
Mr and Mrs David Edward Memorial Award 699
UWB Departmental Research Studentships 700
UWB Research Studentships 700
Wingate Scholarships 720
Young Scholars Forum 304

CONTEMPORARY HISTORY

Any Country

Albert J Beveridge Grant 54
Barbara Thom Postdoctoral Fellowship 332
Bernadotte E Schmitt Grants 54
Camargo Fellowships 169
Charles C Price Fellowship 230
Delahaye Memorial Benefaction 700
Dixon Ryan Fox Manuscript Prize of the New York State Historical Association 480
E Lyman Stewart Fellowship 647
Fellowships in the University of Delaware Hagley Program 647
Fernand Braudel Senior Fellowships 280
Gypsy Lore Society Young Scholar's Prize in Romani Studies 314
Helen McCormack Turner Memorial Scholarship 700
Henry Moore Institute Research Fellowship 323
Herbert Hoover Presidential Library Association Travel Grants 324
Herbert Hughes Scholarship 701
IEEE Fellowship in Electrical History 335
Institute of European History Fellowships 346
Institute of Irish Studies Research Fellowships 348
Institute of Irish Studies Senior Visiting Research Fellowship 348
Isobel Thornley Research Fellowship 347
J Franklin Jameson Fellowship 54
Jean Monnet Fellowships 280

Australia

Canada

Caribbean Countries

East European Countries

European Union

Middle East

New Zealand

South Africa

United Kingdom

United States of America

West European Countries

ARCHAEOLOGY

Any Country

African Nations

Australia

Canada

East European Countries

European Union

New Zealand

South Africa

United Kingdom

United States of America

West European Countries

PHILOSOPHY

Any Country

Australia

Canada

Caribbean Countries

East European Countries

European Union

Middle East

New Zealand

South Africa

United Kingdom

United States of America

West European Countries

PHILOSOPHICAL SCHOOLS

Any Country

Australia

Canada

European Union

New Zealand

South Africa

United Kingdom
AHRC Doctoral Awards Scheme 103
Hector and Elizabeth Catling Bursary 159
Professional Preparation Master's Scheme 103
Research Preparation Master's Scheme 103
Wingate Scholarships 720

West European Countries
Wingate Scholarships 720

METAPHYSICS

Any Country
ASCSA Advanced Fellowships 78
Camargo Fellowships 169
Kanner Fellowship In British Studies 617
NEH Fellowships 80
University of Dundee Research Awards 648

Australia
Wingate Scholarships 720

Canada
Wingate Scholarships 720

European Union
AHRC Doctoral Awards Scheme 103
Professional Preparation Master's Scheme 103
Research Preparation Master's Scheme 103

New Zealand
Wingate Scholarships 720

South Africa
Wingate Scholarships 720

United Kingdom
AHRC Doctoral Awards Scheme 103
Professional Preparation Master's Scheme 103
Research Preparation Master's Scheme 103
Wingate Scholarships 720

West European Countries
Wingate Scholarships 720

LOGIC

Any Country
ASCSA Advanced Fellowships 78
Camargo Fellowships 169
John Stuart Mill Scholarship in Philosophy of Mind and Logic 631
Kanner Fellowship In British Studies 617
NEH Fellowships 80
University of Dundee Research Awards 648

Australia
Wingate Scholarships 720

Canada
Wingate Scholarships 720

European Union
AHRC Doctoral Awards Scheme 103
Professional Preparation Master's Scheme 103
Research Preparation Master's Scheme 103

New Zealand
Wingate Scholarships 720

South Africa
Wingate Scholarships 720

United Kingdom
AHRC Doctoral Awards Scheme 103
Professional Preparation Master's Scheme 103
Research Preparation Master's Scheme 103
Wingate Scholarships 720

West European Countries
Wingate Scholarships 720

ETHICS

Any Country
ASCSA Advanced Fellowships 78
Camargo Fellowships 169
Charlotte W Newcombe Doctoral Dissertation Fellowships 725
CIHR Fellowships Program 208
Delahaye Memorial Benefaction 700
Helen McCormack Turner Memorial Scholarship 700
Herbert Hughes Scholarship 701
Kanner Fellowship In British Studies 617
Mary Radcliffe Scholarship 701
NEH Fellowships 80
RHYS Curzon-Jones Scholarship 701
Ridley Lewis Bursary 701
United States Holocaust Memorial Museum Center for Advanced Holocaust Studies Visiting Scholar Programs 619
University of Dundee Research Awards 648
W D Llewelyn Memorial Benefaction 701

Australia
Wingate Scholarships 720

Canada
Wingate Scholarships 720

European Union
AHRC Doctoral Awards Scheme 103
Professional Preparation Master's Scheme 103
Research Preparation Master's Scheme 103

New Zealand
Wingate Scholarships 720

South Africa
Wingate Scholarships 720

United Kingdom
AHRC Doctoral Awards Scheme 103
ESU Chautauqua Institution Scholarships 273
Professional Preparation Master's Scheme 103
Research Preparation Master's Scheme 103
Wingate Scholarships 720

West European Countries
Wingate Scholarships 720

BUSINESS ADMINISTRATION AND MANAGEMENT

GENERAL

Any Country

African Nations

Australia

Canada

Caribbean Countries

East European Countries

European Union

Middle East

New Zealand

South Africa

United Kingdom

United States of America

West European Countries

BUSINESS STUDIES

Any Country

African Nations

Caribbean Countries

East European Countries

European Union

Middle East

South Africa

United Kingdom
ESRC 1+3 Awards and +3 Awards 265
Mr and Mrs David Edward Memorial Award 699
Sheffield Hallam University Studentships 567
University of Wales Aberystwyth Postgraduate Research Studentships 699
UWB Departmental Research Studentships 700
UWB Research Studentships 700

United States of America
Congress Bundestag Youth Exchange for Young Professionals 224
ETS Summer Program in Research for Graduate Students 267
Fulbright Senior Specialists Program 245

West European Countries
ESRC 1+3 Awards and +3 Awards 265
Mr and Mrs David Edward Memorial Award 699
Sheffield Hallam University Studentships 567
UWB Departmental Research Studentships 700
UWB Research Studentships 700

INTERNATIONAL BUSINESS

Any Country
CDU Senior Research Fellowship 230
Frederick Douglass Institute Postdoctoral Fellowship 293
Frederick Douglass Institute Predoctoral Dissertation Fellowship 294
ISM Doctoral Grants 344
ISM Senior Research Fellowship Program 344
Kennan Institute Short-Term Grants 397
LCCIEB Examinations Board Scholarships 414
Rhodes University Postdoctoral Fellowship and The Andrew Mellon Postdoctoral Fellowship 528
School for International Training (SIT) Programmes in Intercultural Service, Leadership and Management 728
Thomas Holloway Research Studentship 548
University of Dundee Research Awards 648

Australia
Wingate Scholarships 720

Canada
Wingate Scholarships 720

European Union
ESRC 1+3 Awards and +3 Awards 265
Transatlantic Fellows Program 305

New Zealand
Wingate Scholarships 720

South Africa
Wingate Scholarships 720

United Kingdom
ESRC 1+3 Awards and +3 Awards 265
John Mather Scholarship 694
John Speak Trust Scholarships 140
Sheffield Hallam University Studentships 567
University of Wales Aberystwyth Postgraduate Research Studentships 699
UWB Research Studentships 700
Wingate Scholarships 720

United States of America
Congress Bundestag Youth Exchange for Young Professionals 224
Fulbright Distinguished Chairs Program 245
Fulbright Senior Specialists Program 245
Kennan Institute Research Scholarship 397
Transatlantic Fellows Program 305

West European Countries
ESRC 1+3 Awards and +3 Awards 265
Sheffield Hallam University Studentships 567
UWB Research Studentships 700
Wingate Scholarships 720

SECRETARIAL STUDIES

Any Country
LCCIEB Examinations Board Scholarships 414

BUSINESS MACHINE OPERATIONBUSINESS COMPUTING

Any Country
Jacob's Pillow Intern Program 385
Rhodes University Postdoctoral Fellowship and The Andrew Mellon Postdoctoral Fellowship 528
University of Southampton Postgraduate Studentships 692
World Universities Network (WUN) Global Exchange Programme 693

United Kingdom
John Mather Scholarship 694
Sheffield Hallam University Studentships 567

United States of America
Congress Bundestag Youth Exchange for Young Professionals 224

West European Countries
Sheffield Hallam University Studentships 567

MANAGEMENT SYSTEMS AND TECHNIQUES

Any Country
CDU Senior Research Fellowship 230
CDU Three Year Postdoctoral Fellowship 230
Hamdard Fellowship in Business Administration 316
ISM Doctoral Grants 344
ISM Senior Research Fellowship Program 344
LCCIEB Examinations Board Scholarships 414
Queen Mary Research Studentships 518
Rhodes University Postdoctoral Fellowship and The Andrew Mellon Postdoctoral Fellowship 528
School for International Training (SIT) Programmes in Intercultural Service, Leadership and Management 728
Thomas Holloway Research Studentship 548

African Nations
MCTC Assistance for Courses 309
MCTC Tuition and Maintenance Scholarships 309

Caribbean Countries
MCTC Assistance for Courses 309
MCTC Tuition and Maintenance Scholarships 309

East European Countries
The Evrika Award for Young Manager 281
Evrika Foundation Awards 281
MCTC Assistance for Courses 309
MCTC Tuition and Maintenance Scholarships 309

Middle East
MCTC Assistance for Courses 309
MCTC Tuition and Maintenance Scholarships 309

South Africa

MCTC Assistance for Courses 309
MCTC Tuition and Maintenance Scholarships 309

United Kingdom

John Mather Scholarship 694
Sheffield Hallam University Studentships 567
University of Wales Aberystwyth Postgraduate Research Studentships 699

United States of America

Congress Bundestag Youth Exchange for Young Professionals 224

West European Countries

Sheffield Hallam University Studentships 567

ACCOUNTANCY

Any Country

Jacob's Pillow Intern Program 385
La Trobe University Postgraduate Scholarship 403
LCCIEB Examinations Board Scholarships 414
Rhodes University Postdoctoral Fellowship and The Andrew Mellon Postdoctoral Fellowship 528
University of Dundee Research Awards 648
UNO Graduate Assistantships 667
World Universities Network (WUN) Global Exchange Programme 693

African Nations

IATF IATA Aviation Training and Development Institute (ATDI) Scholarships 357

Caribbean Countries

IATF IATA Aviation Training and Development Institute (ATDI) Scholarships 357

East European Countries

IATF IATA Aviation Training and Development Institute (ATDI) Scholarships 357

European Union

ESRC 1+3 Awards and +3 Awards 265

Middle East

IATF IATA Aviation Training and Development Institute (ATDI) Scholarships 357

South Africa

Allan Gray Senior Scholarship 527
Henderson Postgraduate Scholarships 527
IATF IATA Aviation Training and Development Institute (ATDI) Scholarships 357

United Kingdom

ESRC 1+3 Awards and +3 Awards 265
John Mather Scholarship 694
Mr and Mrs David Edward Memorial Award 699
Sheffield Hallam University Studentships 567
University of Wales Aberystwyth Postgraduate Research Studentships 699
UWB Departmental Research Studentships 700
UWB Research Studentships 700

United States of America

AICPA Accountemps Student Scholarship 381
Congress Bundestag Youth Exchange for Young Professionals 224
John L Carey Scholarship 382
Kenneth W. Heikes Family Endowed Scholarship 442

West European Countries

ESRC 1+3 Awards and +3 Awards 265
Mr and Mrs David Edward Memorial Award 699
Sheffield Hallam University Studentships 567
UWB Departmental Research Studentships 700
UWB Research Studentships 700

REAL ESTATE

Any Country

RICS Education Trust Award 529

United States of America

Appraisal Institute Education Trust Scholarship 95

MARKETING AND SALES MANAGEMENT

Any Country

Equiano Memorial Award 604
Hamdard Fellowship in Business Administration 316
Jacob's Pillow Intern Program 385
LCCIEB Examinations Board Scholarships 414
Student Ambassador Awards for Hotel Management 709

African Nations

IATF IATA Aviation Training and Development Institute (ATDI) Scholarships 357
MCTC Assistance for Courses 309
MCTC Tuition and Maintenance Scholarships 309

Canada

Horticultural Research Institute Grants 329

Caribbean Countries

IATF IATA Aviation Training and Development Institute (ATDI) Scholarships 357
MCTC Assistance for Courses 309
MCTC Tuition and Maintenance Scholarships 309

East European Countries

IATF IATA Aviation Training and Development Institute (ATDI) Scholarships 357
MCTC Assistance for Courses 309
MCTC Tuition and Maintenance Scholarships 309

European Union

ESRC 1+3 Awards and +3 Awards 265

Middle East

IATF IATA Aviation Training and Development Institute (ATDI) Scholarships 357
MCTC Assistance for Courses 309
MCTC Tuition and Maintenance Scholarships 309

South Africa

IATF IATA Aviation Training and Development Institute (ATDI) Scholarships 357
MCTC Assistance for Courses 309
MCTC Tuition and Maintenance Scholarships 309

United Kingdom

ESRC 1+3 Awards and +3 Awards 265
John Mather Scholarship 694
University of Wales Aberystwyth Postgraduate Research Studentships 699

United States of America

Billings Broadcasters MSU-Billings Media Scholarship 441
Congress Bundestag Youth Exchange for Young Professionals 224
Fulbright Distinguished Chairs Program 245
Fulbright Senior Specialists Program 245
Horticultural Research Institute Grants 329

West European Countries

ESRC 1+3 Awards and +3 Awards 265

INSURANCE MANAGEMENT

Any Country

Ernst Meyer Prize 359
Geneva Association 359
International Association for the Study of Insurance Economics Research Grants 359

Canada

S S Huebner Foundation for Insurance Education Predoctoral Fellowships 561

United Kingdom

Mr and Mrs David Edward Memorial Award 699
UWB Departmental Research Studentships 700
UWB Research Studentships 700

United States of America

S S Huebner Foundation for Insurance Education Predoctoral Fellowships 561

West European Countries

Mr and Mrs David Edward Memorial Award 699
UWB Departmental Research Studentships 700
UWB Research Studentships 700

FINANCE, BANKING AND INVESTMENT

Any Country

Adams Foundation Banking School Scholarship 12
German Chancellor Scholarship Program 19
Hamdard Fellowship in Business Administration 316
ISMA Centre Doctoral Scholarship 384
LCCIEB Examinations Board Scholarships 414
University of Dundee Research Awards 648
University of Southampton Postgraduate Studentships 692
World Universities Network (WUN) Global Exchange Programme 693

Australia

ADB Fully funded Internships 106

Canada

S S Huebner Foundation for Insurance Education Predoctoral Fellowships 561

Caribbean Countries

ADB Fully funded Internships 106
Prince of Wales (Cable and Wireless) Chevening Cambridge Scholarships for Postgraduate Study 191

East European Countries

Citigroup Cambridge Scholarships for Postgraduate Study (Czech Republic, Hungary, Poland and Slovakia) 179
German Chancellor Scholarship Program 19

European Union

ESRC 1+3 Awards and +3 Awards 265

United Kingdom

ESRC 1+3 Awards and +3 Awards 265
John Mather Scholarship 694
Mr and Mrs David Edward Memorial Award 699
University of Wales Aberystwyth Postgraduate Research Studentships 699
UWB Departmental Research Studentships 700
UWB Research Studentships 700

United States of America

AICPA Accountemps Student Scholarship 381
Appraisal Institute Education Trust Scholarship 95
Fulbright Senior Specialists Program 245
German Chancellor Scholarship Program 19
Kenneth R. McCartha Scholarship 12
S S Huebner Foundation for Insurance Education Predoctoral Fellowships 561

West European Countries

ESRC 1+3 Awards and +3 Awards 265
Mr and Mrs David Edward Memorial Award 699
UWB Departmental Research Studentships 700
UWB Research Studentships 700

PERSONNEL MANAGEMENT

Any Country

Equiano Memorial Award 604
Hamdard Fellowship in Business Administration 316
Student Ambassador Awards for Hotel Management 709
University of Southampton Postgraduate Studentships 692
World Universities Network (WUN) Global Exchange Programme 693

African Nations

IATF IATA Aviation Training and Development Institute (ATDI) Scholarships 357

Canada

Horticultural Research Institute Grants 329

Caribbean Countries

IATF IATA Aviation Training and Development Institute (ATDI) Scholarships 357

East European Countries

IATF IATA Aviation Training and Development Institute (ATDI) Scholarships 357

European Union

ESRC 1+3 Awards and +3 Awards 265

Middle East

IATF IATA Aviation Training and Development Institute (ATDI) Scholarships 357

South Africa

IATF IATA Aviation Training and Development Institute (ATDI) Scholarships 357

United Kingdom

ESRC 1+3 Awards and +3 Awards 265
John Mather Scholarship 694
Sheffield Hallam University Studentships 567

United States of America

Fulbright Senior Specialists Program 245
Horticultural Research Institute Grants 329

University of Southampton Postgraduate Studentships 692
UNLV Alumni Association Graduate Scholarships 668
UNLV Graduate Assistantships 668
UNLV James F Adams/GSA Scholarship 668
UNO Graduate Assistantships 667
Warwick Business School Scholarships (for MBA Study) 714
World Universities Network (WUN) Global Exchange Programme 693

African Nations

IATF Aviation MBA Scholarship 357
INSEAD Alumni Fund (IAF) Scholarships 338
INSEAD Eli Lilly and Company Innovation Scholarship 338
INSEAD Jean François Clin MBA Scholarship 339
Shell and IMD MBA Alumni Scholarships 370
Warwick Business School Scholarships (for MBA Study via Distance Learning) 714

Australia

NTU APEC Scholarship 448

Canada

Bank of Montréal Pauline Varnier Fellowship 240
Frank Knox Memorial Fellowships 115
INSEAD Canadian Foundation Scholarship 338
INSEAD Eli Lilly and Company Innovation Scholarship 338
JCCA Graduate Education Scholarship 389
NTU APEC Scholarship 448
Warwick Business School Scholarships (for MBA Study) 714

Caribbean Countries

IATF Aviation MBA Scholarship 357
INSEAD Alumni Fund (IAF) Scholarships 338

East European Countries

Fulbright British Friends of HBS MBA Awards 707
IATF Aviation MBA Scholarship 357
INSEAD Alumni Fund (IAF) Scholarships 338
INSEAD Eli Lilly and Company Innovation Scholarship 338
INSEAD Sisley-Marc d'Ornano Scholarship 340
N Boustany MBA Scholarship 646
Shell and IMD MBA Alumni Scholarships 370
United States Business School (Prague) MBA Scholarships 618
Von Muralt-Lo Scholarship 370
Warwick Business School Scholarships (for MBA Study via Distance Learning) 714
Warwick Business School Scholarships (for MBA Study) 714

Middle East

IATF Aviation MBA Scholarship 357
INSEAD Alumni Fund (IAF) Scholarships 338
INSEAD Antoine Rachid Irani/Bissada Scholarship 338
INSEAD Eli Lilly and Company Innovation Scholarship 338
Warwick Business School Scholarships (for MBA Study via Distance Learning) 714

New Zealand

NTU APEC Scholarship 448

South Africa

IATF Aviation MBA Scholarship 357
INSEAD Alumni Fund (IAF) Scholarships 338
Warwick Business School Scholarships (for MBA Study via Distance Learning) 714

United Kingdom

Frank Knox Fellowships at Harvard University 292
Fulbright British Friends of HBS MBA Awards 707
INSEAD Henry Grunfeld Foundation Scholarship 339
INSEAD Lord Kitchener National Memorial Scholarship 340
INSEAD Louis Franck Scholarship 340
John Mather Scholarship 694
Postgraduate Student Allowance Scheme (PSAS) (Queen Margaret) 517
Sainsbury Bursaries 646
Sainsbury Management Fellowships 535
University of Wales Aberystwyth Postgraduate Research Studentships 699

United States of America

INSEAD Judith Connelly Delouvrier Scholarship 339
JCCA Graduate Education Scholarship 389
NTU APEC Scholarship 448
Warwick Business School Scholarships (for MBA Study) 714

West European Countries

Fulbright British Friends of HBS MBA Awards 707
INSEAD Belgian Alumni and Council Scholarship Fund 338
INSEAD Børsen/Danish Council Scholarship 338
INSEAD Elof Hansson Scholarship Fund 339
INSEAD Giovanni Agnelli Scholarship 339
Warwick Business School Scholarships (for MBA Study via Distance Learning) 714
Warwick Business School Scholarships (for MBA Study) 714

EDUCATION AND TEACHER TRAINING

GENERAL

Any Country

Acadia Graduate Awards 7
Andrew Mellon Foundation Scholarship 527
AUC Teaching Arabic as a Foreign Language Fellowships 91
AUC Teaching English as a Foreign Language Fellowships 91
Barry R Gross Memorial Award 451
Blanche E Woolls Scholarship for School Library Media Service 133
Canadian Department of Foreign Affairs Faculty Enrichment Program 205
Canadian Department of Foreign Affairs Faculty Research Program 206
CDU Three Year Postdoctoral Fellowship 230
Concordia University Graduate Fellowships 240
David J Azrieli Graduate Fellowship 241
Doctoral Dissertation Scholarship 133
Endeavour International Postgraduate Research Scholarships (EIPRS) 403
Equiano Memorial Award 604
Field Psych Trust Grant 284
Foundation Praemium Erasmianum Study Prize 292
Helen Darcovich Memorial Doctoral Fellowship 207
HSA Grant for Educators 324
Humanitarian Trust Awards 332
James M Harris/Sarah W Sweatt Student Travel Grant 255
Kennan Institute Short-Term Grants 397
Korea Foundation Advanced Research Grant 398
Korea Foundation Fellowship for Field Research 399
Korea Foundation Fellowship for Graduate Studies 399
Korea Foundation Postdoctoral Fellowship 399
Lindbergh Grants 229
Monash International Postgraduate Research Scholarship (MIPRS) 440
Monash University Silver Jubilee Postgraduate Scholarship 440
Neporany Doctoral Fellowship 208
NUT Page Scholarship 473
Rhodes University Postdoctoral Fellowship and The Andrew Mellon Postdoctoral Fellowship 528
Rhodes University Postgraduate Scholarship 528
Royal Irish Academy European Exchange Fellowship 551
Sarah Rebecca Reed Award 133
School for International Training (SIT) Extension 728
School for International Training (SIT) Master of Arts in Teaching Program 728

African Nations

Australia

Canada

Caribbean Countries

East European Countries

European Union

Middle East

New Zealand

South Africa

United Kingdom

United States of America

NEA Foundation Learning and Leadership Grants 455
North Dakota Indian Scholarship 485
Nurses' Educational Funds Fellowships and Scholarships 488
Sally S Jacobsen Scholarship 458

West European Countries

Endeavour International Postgraduate Research Scholarships (EIPRS) 403
Fulbright Postdoctoral Research and Lecturing Awards for Non-US Citizens 245
International Postgraduate Research Scholarships (IPRS) 692
Sheffield Hallam University Studentships 567
University of Otago Master's Awards 670
UWB Departmental Research Studentships 700
UWB Research Studentships 700
Wingate Scholarships 720

NONVOCATIONAL SUBJECTS EDUCATION

Any Country

Camargo Fellowships 169
Equiano Memorial Award 604
Snowdon Award Scheme Grants 575

United Kingdom

Innovation and Creative Practice Award 518

United States of America

The Walter J Jensen Fellowship for French Language, Literature and Culture 510

EDUCATION IN NATIVE LANGUAGE

Any Country

AUC Writing Center Graduate Fellowships 91
ETS Summer Program in Research for Graduate Students 267

Canada

Horticultural Research Institute Grants 329

South Africa

Norah Taylor Bursary 595

United Kingdom

Mr and Mrs David Edward Memorial Award 699
University of Wales Aberystwyth Postgraduate Research Studentships 699
UWB Departmental Research Studentships 700
UWB Research Studentships 700

United States of America

ETS Summer Program in Research for Graduate Students 267
Fulbright Teacher and Administrator Exchange 297
Horticultural Research Institute Grants 329

West European Countries

Mr and Mrs David Edward Memorial Award 699
UWB Departmental Research Studentships 700
UWB Research Studentships 700

FOREIGN LANGUAGES EDUCATION

Any Country

AUC Arabic Language Fellowships 89
Camargo Fellowships 169
Equiano Memorial Award 604
ETS Summer Program in Research for Graduate Students 267
KSTU Rector's Grant 397
LCCIEB Examinations Board Scholarships 414
School for International Training (SIT) Master of Arts in Teaching Program 728

Australia

Ministry of Foreign Affairs (France) International Teaching Fellowships 269

South Africa

Norah Taylor Bursary 595
SACEE EX-PCE Bursary 595

United Kingdom

Prix du Québec Award 143
University of Wales Aberystwyth Postgraduate Research Studentships 699

United States of America

ETS Postdoctoral Fellowships 267
ETS Summer Program in Research for Graduate Students 267
ETS Sylvia Taylor Johnson Minority Fellowship Educational Measurement 267
Fulbright Teacher and Administrator Exchange 297
The Walter J Jensen Fellowship for French Language, Literature and Culture 510

MATHEMATICS EDUCATION

Any Country

ETS Summer Program in Research for Graduate Students 267

United Kingdom

Mr and Mrs David Edward Memorial Award 699
Sheffield Hallam University Studentships 567
UWB Departmental Research Studentships 700
UWB Research Studentships 700

United States of America

ETS Postdoctoral Fellowships 267
ETS Summer Program in Research for Graduate Students 267
ETS Sylvia Taylor Johnson Minority Fellowship Educational Measurement 267

West European Countries

Mr and Mrs David Edward Memorial Award 699
Sheffield Hallam University Studentships 567
UWB Departmental Research Studentships 700
UWB Research Studentships 700

SCIENCE EDUCATION

Any Country

Carski Foundation Distinguished Undergraduate Teaching Award 83
Crohn's and Colitis Foundation Career Development Award 250
Crohn's and Colitis Foundation First Award 250
Crohn's and Colitis Foundation Research Fellowship Awards 250
Crohn's and Colitis Foundation Research Grant Program 251
ETS Summer Program in Research for Graduate Students 267
Glenn E and Barbara Hodsdon Ullyot Scholarship 231
Gordon Cain Fellowship 231
Hastings Center International Visiting Scholars Program 318
IAU Travel Grant 360
Joseph H. Hazen Education Prize 327
Lord Dowding Fund for Humane Research 415
Société de Chimie Industrielle (American Section) Fellowship 231
UFAW Animal Welfare Research Training Scholarships 624
UFAW Research and Project Awards 624

HUMANITIES AND SOCIAL SCIENCE EDUCATION

PHYSICAL EDUCATION

Any Country

GNC Nutritional Research Grant 472
NSCA Challenge Scholarship 472
NSCA Graduate Research Grant 472
NSCA Minority Scholarship 472
NSCA Power Systems Professional Scholarship 473
NSCA Women's Scholarship 473

African Nations

International Postgraduate Research Scholarships (IPRS) 692

Canada

International Postgraduate Research Scholarships (IPRS) 692
JCCA Graduate Education Scholarship 389

Caribbean Countries

International Postgraduate Research Scholarships (IPRS) 692

East European Countries

International Postgraduate Research Scholarships (IPRS) 692

European Union

Our World-Underwater Scholarship Society Scholarships 496

Middle East

International Postgraduate Research Scholarships (IPRS) 692

South Africa

International Postgraduate Research Scholarships (IPRS) 692

United Kingdom

International Postgraduate Research Scholarships (IPRS) 692
Mr and Mrs David Edward Memorial Award 699
UWB Departmental Research Studentships 700
UWB Research Studentships 700

United States of America

Adephi University Athletic Grants 9
ETS Postdoctoral Fellowships 267
International Postgraduate Research Scholarships (IPRS) 692
JCCA Graduate Education Scholarship 389
Our World-Underwater Scholarship Society Scholarships 496

West European Countries

International Postgraduate Research Scholarships (IPRS) 692
Mr and Mrs David Edward Memorial Award 699
UWB Departmental Research Studentships 700
UWB Research Studentships 700

LITERACY EDUCATION

Any Country

Albert J Harris Award 372
AUC Writing Center Graduate Fellowships 91
Dina Feitelson Research Award 372
Elva Knight Research Grant 372
ETS Summer Program in Research for Graduate Students 267
Helen M Robinson Award 373
International Reading Association Outstanding Dissertation of the Year Award 373
International Reading Association Teacher as Researcher Grant 373
Jeanne S Chall Research Fellowship 373

African Nations

International Postgraduate Research Scholarships (IPRS) 692
Reading/Literacy Research Fellowship 373

Australia

Reading/Literacy Research Fellowship 373

Canada

International Postgraduate Research Scholarships (IPRS) 692

Caribbean Countries

International Postgraduate Research Scholarships (IPRS) 692
Reading/Literacy Research Fellowship 373

East European Countries

International Postgraduate Research Scholarships (IPRS) 692
Reading/Literacy Research Fellowship 373

Middle East

International Postgraduate Research Scholarships (IPRS) 692
Reading/Literacy Research Fellowship 373

New Zealand

Reading/Literacy Research Fellowship 373

South Africa

International Postgraduate Research Scholarships (IPRS) 692
Norah Taylor Bursary 595
Reading/Literacy Research Fellowship 373
SACEE EX-PCE Bursary 595

United Kingdom

International Postgraduate Research Scholarships (IPRS) 692
Reading/Literacy Research Fellowship 373

United States of America

ETS Postdoctoral Fellowships 267
ETS Summer Program in Research for Graduate Students 267
International Postgraduate Research Scholarships (IPRS) 692

West European Countries

International Postgraduate Research Scholarships (IPRS) 692
Reading/Literacy Research Fellowship 373

VOCATIONAL SUBJECTS EDUCATION

Any Country

LCCIEB Examinations Board Scholarships 414
Lincoln College Erich and Rochelle Endowed Prize in Music 679
Snowdon Award Scheme Grants 575

Australia

Fulbright Professional Award for Vocational Education and Training 126

United Kingdom

Hilda Martindale Exhibitions 326

United States of America

NFID Advanced Vaccinology Course Travel Grant 458

AGRICULTURAL EDUCATION

Any Country

UFAW Animal Welfare Research Training Scholarships 624
UFAW Research and Project Awards 624
UFAW Small Project and Travel Awards 624
UFAW Vacation Scholarships 624

East European Countries

Middle East

New Zealand

South Africa

United Kingdom

United States of America

West European Countries

HOME ECONOMICS EDUCATION

European Union

United Kingdom

INDUSTRIAL ARTS EDUCATION

MUSIC EDUCATION

Any Country

PRE-SCHOOL EDUCATION

Any Country

African Nations

Canada

Caribbean Countries

East European Countries

Middle East

South Africa

United Kingdom

United States of America

West European Countries

PRIMARY EDUCATION

Any Country

African Nations

Canada

Caribbean Countries

East European Countries

European Union

Middle East

South Africa

International Postgraduate Research Scholarships (IPRS) 692
MCTC Tuition and Maintenance Scholarships 309
Norah Taylor Bursary 595
SACEE EX-PCE Bursary 595

United Kingdom

All Saints Educational Trust Personal Awards 21
International Postgraduate Research Scholarships (IPRS) 692
Mr and Mrs David Edward Memorial Award 699
University of Wales Aberystwyth Postgraduate Research Studentships 699
UWB Departmental Research Studentships 700
UWB Research Studentships 700

United States of America

ETS Postdoctoral Fellowships 267
ETS Summer Program in Research for Graduate Students 267
ETS Sylvia Taylor Johnson Minority Fellowship Educational Measurement 267
International Postgraduate Research Scholarships (IPRS) 692

West European Countries

International Postgraduate Research Scholarships (IPRS) 692
Mr and Mrs David Edward Memorial Award 699
UWB Departmental Research Studentships 700
UWB Research Studentships 700

SECONDARY EDUCATION

Any Country

Electrochemical Society Summer Fellowships 268
Equiano Memorial Award 604
ETS Summer Program in Research for Graduate Students 267
Innovative Geography Teaching Grants 545
University of Southampton Postgraduate Studentships 692
World Universities Network (WUN) Global Exchange Programme 693

African Nations

International Postgraduate Research Scholarships (IPRS) 692

Canada

International Postgraduate Research Scholarships (IPRS) 692

Caribbean Countries

International Postgraduate Research Scholarships (IPRS) 692

East European Countries

FEMS Fellowship 284
International Postgraduate Research Scholarships (IPRS) 692

European Union

All Saints Educational Trust Personal Awards 21

Middle East

International Postgraduate Research Scholarships (IPRS) 692

South Africa

International Postgraduate Research Scholarships (IPRS) 692
Norah Taylor Bursary 595
SACEE EX-PCE Bursary 595

United Kingdom

All Saints Educational Trust Personal Awards 21
FEMS Fellowship 284
International Postgraduate Research Scholarships (IPRS) 692
Mr and Mrs David Edward Memorial Award 699
University of Wales Aberystwyth Postgraduate Research Studentships 699
UWB Departmental Research Studentships 700
UWB Research Studentships 700

United States of America

ETS Postdoctoral Fellowships 267
ETS Summer Program in Research for Graduate Students 267
ETS Sylvia Taylor Johnson Minority Fellowship Educational Measurement 267
International Postgraduate Research Scholarships (IPRS) 692
The Walter J Jensen Fellowship for French Language, Literature and Culture 510

West European Countries

FEMS Fellowship 284
International Postgraduate Research Scholarships (IPRS) 692
Mr and Mrs David Edward Memorial Award 699
UWB Departmental Research Studentships 700
UWB Research Studentships 700

ADULT EDUCATION

Any Country

Equiano Memorial Award 604
ETS Summer Program in Research for Graduate Students 267
Snowdon Award Scheme Grants 575
University of Southampton Postgraduate Studentships 692
World Universities Network (WUN) Global Exchange Programme 693

African Nations

International Postgraduate Research Scholarships (IPRS) 692

Canada

International Postgraduate Research Scholarships (IPRS) 692

Caribbean Countries

International Postgraduate Research Scholarships (IPRS) 692

East European Countries

International Postgraduate Research Scholarships (IPRS) 692

Middle East

International Postgraduate Research Scholarships (IPRS) 692

South Africa

International Postgraduate Research Scholarships (IPRS) 692
SACEE EX-PCE Bursary 595

United Kingdom

International Postgraduate Research Scholarships (IPRS) 692

United States of America

ETS Postdoctoral Fellowships 267
ETS Summer Program in Research for Graduate Students 267
ETS Sylvia Taylor Johnson Minority Fellowship Educational Measurement 267
International Postgraduate Research Scholarships (IPRS) 692

West European Countries

International Postgraduate Research Scholarships (IPRS) 692

SPECIAL EDUCATION

Any Country

CDU Senior Research Fellowship 230
CDU Three Year Postdoctoral Fellowship 230

EDUCATIONAL RESEARCH

EDUCATIONAL TECHNOLOGY

EDUCATIONAL AND STUDENT COUNSELLING

EDUCATIONAL ADMINISTRATION

EDUCATIONAL TESTING AND EVALUATION

Caribbean Countries

East European Countries

Middle East

New Zealand

South Africa

United Kingdom

United States of America

West European Countries

DISTANCE EDUCATION

Any Country

ENGINEERING

GENERAL

Any Country

African Nations

Australia

Canada

Caribbean Countries

East European Countries

European Union

Middle East

New Zealand

South Africa

United Kingdom

United States of America

West European Countries

SURVEYING AND MAPPING SCIENCE

Any Country

African Nations

Australia

CIVIL, CONSTRUCTION AND TRANSPORTATION ENGINEERING

QUEST C H Roberts Bequest 350
Sheffield Hallam University Studentships 567
Wingate Scholarships 720

ENVIRONMENTAL AND SANITARY ENGINEERING

Any Country

AWWA Academic Achievement Award 92
AWWA Thomas R Camp Scholarship 93
The Bernard Butler Trust Fund 384
Civil and Environmental Engineering Graduate Scholarship 627
John Moyes Lessells Scholarships 557
QUEST Institution of Civil Engineers Overseas Travel Awards 351
University of Dundee Research Awards 648
World Universities Network (WUN) Global Exchange Programme 693

African Nations

The Bernard Butler Trust Fund 384
Canadian Window on International Development 364
International Postgraduate Research Scholarships (IPRS) 692
School of Industrial and Manufacturing Science Overseas Scholarships 249
Shell Centenary/Shell Centenary Chevening Scholarships 665

Australia

The Bernard Butler Trust Fund 384
Cranfield University Overseas Bursary 249
Fulbright Postgraduate Student Award for Engineering 126
Fulbright Postgraduate Student Award for Science and Engineering 126
School of Industrial and Manufacturing Science Overseas Scholarships 249
Wingate Scholarships 720

Canada

AWWA Abel Wolman Fellowship 92
AWWA Larson Aquatic Research Support 93
The Bernard Butler Trust Fund 384
Canadian Window on International Development 364
Cranfield University Overseas Bursary 249
DEED (Demonstration of Energy-Efficient Developments) Student Research Grant/Internship 77
Horticultural Research Institute Grants 329
International Postgraduate Research Scholarships (IPRS) 692
School of Industrial and Manufacturing Science Overseas Scholarships 249
TAC Foundation Scholarships 615
Wingate Scholarships 720

Caribbean Countries

The Bernard Butler Trust Fund 384
Canadian Window on International Development 364
Cranfield University Overseas Bursary 249
International Postgraduate Research Scholarships (IPRS) 692
School of Industrial and Manufacturing Science Overseas Scholarships 249
Shell Centenary/Shell Centenary Chevening Scholarships 665

East European Countries

The Bernard Butler Trust Fund 384
CERN Technical Student Programme 228
International Postgraduate Research Scholarships (IPRS) 692
School of Industrial and Manufacturing Science Overseas Scholarships 249
VKI Fellowship 711

European Union

The Bernard Butler Trust Fund 384

Middle East

The Bernard Butler Trust Fund 384
Cranfield University Overseas Bursary 249
International Postgraduate Research Scholarships (IPRS) 692
School of Industrial and Manufacturing Science Overseas Scholarships 249
Shell Centenary/Shell Centenary Chevening Scholarships 665

New Zealand

The Bernard Butler Trust Fund 384
Cranfield University Overseas Bursary 249
School of Industrial and Manufacturing Science Overseas Scholarships 249
Wingate Scholarships 720

South Africa

The Bernard Butler Trust Fund 384
Canadian Window on International Development 364
Cranfield University Overseas Bursary 249
International Postgraduate Research Scholarships (IPRS) 692
School of Industrial and Manufacturing Science Overseas Scholarships 249
Shell Centenary/Shell Centenary Chevening Scholarships 665
Wingate Scholarships 720

United Kingdom

The Bernard Butler Trust Fund 384
CERN Technical Student Programme 228
International Postgraduate Research Scholarships (IPRS) 692
Silsoe Awards 249
Wingate Scholarships 720

United States of America

AWWA Abel Wolman Fellowship 92
AWWA Holly A Cornell Scholarship 93
AWWA Larson Aquatic Research Support 93
The Bernard Butler Trust Fund 384
Cranfield University Overseas Bursary 249
DEED (Demonstration of Energy-Efficient Developments) Student Research Grant/Internship 77
Horticultural Research Institute Grants 329
International Postgraduate Research Scholarships (IPRS) 692
School of Industrial and Manufacturing Science Overseas Scholarships 249
VKI Fellowship 711
Winston Churchill Foundation Scholarship 720

West European Countries

The Bernard Butler Trust Fund 384
CERN Technical Student Programme 228
International Postgraduate Research Scholarships (IPRS) 692
Silsoe Awards 249
VKI Fellowship 711
Wingate Scholarships 720

SAFETY ENGINEERING

Any Country

ANS Ray Goertz Award 66
John Moyes Lessells Scholarships 557
University of Southampton Postgraduate Studentships 692

African Nations

International Postgraduate Research Scholarships (IPRS) 692

Australia

Fulbright Postgraduate Student Award for Engineering 126
Fulbright Postgraduate Student Award for Science and Engineering 126
Wingate Scholarships 720

Canada

Caribbean Countries

East European Countries

Middle East

New Zealand

South Africa

United Kingdom

United States of America

West European Countries

ELECTRICAL/ELECTRONIC AND TELECOMMUNICATIONS ENGINEERING

Any Country

African Nations

Australia

Canada

Caribbean Countries

East European Countries

European Union

Middle East

New Zealand

South Africa

United Kingdom

United States of America

Congress Bundestag Youth Exchange for Young Professionals 224
DEED (Demonstration of Energy-Efficient Developments) Student Research Grant/Internship 77
International Postgraduate Research Scholarships (IPRS) 692
SRC Graduate Fellowship Program 565
SRC Master's Scholarship Program 565
SWE General Motors Foundation Graduate Scholarship 593
Swiss Federal Institute of Technology Scholarships 606
University of Essex/ORS Awards 655
Winston Churchill Foundation Scholarship 720

West European Countries

CERN Technical Student Programme 228
International Postgraduate Research Scholarships (IPRS) 692
Mr and Mrs David Edward Memorial Award 699
Sheffield Hallam University Studentships 567
University of Kent Department of Electronics Studentships 661
UWB Departmental Research Studentships 700
UWB Research Studentships 700
Wingate Scholarships 720

COMPUTER ENGINEERING

Any Country

CDI Internship 226
ESRF Postdoctoral Fellowships 279
Ferrari Innovation Team Project Scholarship 284
John Moyes Lessells Scholarships 557
KSTU Rector's Grant 397
Queen Mary Research Studentships 518
SWE Microsoft Corporation Scholarships 593
TUCS Postgraduate Grant 616
University of Bristol Postgraduate Scholarships 641
University of Southampton Postgraduate Studentships 692
University of Western Ontario Senior Visiting Fellowship 705

African Nations

International Postgraduate Research Scholarships (IPRS) 692
School of Industrial and Manufacturing Science Overseas Scholarships 249

Australia

Fulbright Postgraduate Student Award for Engineering 126
Fulbright Postgraduate Student Award for Science and Engineering 126
School of Industrial and Manufacturing Science Overseas Scholarships 249
Wingate Scholarships 720

Canada

DEED (Demonstration of Energy-Efficient Developments) Student Research Grant/Internship 77
International Postgraduate Research Scholarships (IPRS) 692
School of Industrial and Manufacturing Science Overseas Scholarships 249
Wingate Scholarships 720

Caribbean Countries

International Postgraduate Research Scholarships (IPRS) 692
School of Industrial and Manufacturing Science Overseas Scholarships 249

East European Countries

CERN Technical Student Programme 228
International Postgraduate Research Scholarships (IPRS) 692
School of Industrial and Manufacturing Science Overseas Scholarships 249

Middle East

International Postgraduate Research Scholarships (IPRS) 692
School of Industrial and Manufacturing Science Overseas Scholarships 249

New Zealand

School of Industrial and Manufacturing Science Overseas Scholarships 249
Wingate Scholarships 720

South Africa

International Postgraduate Research Scholarships (IPRS) 692
School of Industrial and Manufacturing Science Overseas Scholarships 249
Wingate Scholarships 720

United Kingdom

CERN Technical Student Programme 228
ESRF Thesis Studentships 279
International Postgraduate Research Scholarships (IPRS) 692
Mr and Mrs David Edward Memorial Award 699
Royal Academy of Engineering International Travel Grants 534
Sheffield Hallam University Studentships 567
Swiss Federal Institute of Technology Scholarships 606
University of Kent Department of Electronics Studentships 661
University of Wales Aberystwyth Postgraduate Research Studentships 699
UWB Departmental Research Studentships 700
UWB Research Studentships 700
Wingate Scholarships 720

United States of America

Congress Bundestag Youth Exchange for Young Professionals 224
DEED (Demonstration of Energy-Efficient Developments) Student Research Grant/Internship 77
International Postgraduate Research Scholarships (IPRS) 692
School of Industrial and Manufacturing Science Overseas Scholarships 249
SRC Graduate Fellowship Program 565
SRC Master's Scholarship Program 565
SWE General Motors Foundation Graduate Scholarship 593
Swiss Federal Institute of Technology Scholarships 606
Winston Churchill Foundation Scholarship 720

West European Countries

CERN Technical Student Programme 228
ESRF Thesis Studentships 279
International Postgraduate Research Scholarships (IPRS) 692
Mr and Mrs David Edward Memorial Award 699
Royal Academy of Engineering International Travel Grants 534
Sheffield Hallam University Studentships 567
University of Kent Department of Electronics Studentships 661
UWB Departmental Research Studentships 700
UWB Research Studentships 700
Wingate Scholarships 720

INDUSTRIAL AND MANAGEMENT ENGINEERING

Any Country

John Moyes Lessells Scholarships 557
Johnson's Wax Research Fellowship 421
Kenward Memorial Fellowship 640
KSTU Rector's Grant 397
University of Bristol Postgraduate Scholarships 641

United States of America

American Electroplaters and Surface Finishers Society Scholarship 382
DEED (Demonstration of Energy-Efficient Developments) Student Research Grant/Internship 77
International Postgraduate Research Scholarships (IPRS) 692
School of Industrial and Manufacturing Science Overseas Scholarships 249
Winston Churchill Foundation Scholarship 720

West European Countries

International Postgraduate Research Scholarships (IPRS) 692
Sheffield Hallam University Studentships 567
Wingate Scholarships 720

PRODUCTION ENGINEERING

Any Country

John Moyes Lessells Scholarships 557
Kenward Memorial Fellowship 640

African Nations

International Postgraduate Research Scholarships (IPRS) 692
School of Industrial and Manufacturing Science Overseas Scholarships 249

Australia

Fulbright Postgraduate Student Award for Engineering 126
Fulbright Postgraduate Student Award for Science and Engineering 126
School of Industrial and Manufacturing Science Overseas Scholarships 249
Wingate Scholarships 720

Canada

DEED (Demonstration of Energy-Efficient Developments) Student Research Grant/Internship 77
International Postgraduate Research Scholarships (IPRS) 692
School of Industrial and Manufacturing Science Overseas Scholarships 249
SME Education Foundation Grants Program 266
Wingate Scholarships 720

Caribbean Countries

International Postgraduate Research Scholarships (IPRS) 692
School of Industrial and Manufacturing Science Overseas Scholarships 249

East European Countries

International Postgraduate Research Scholarships (IPRS) 692
School of Industrial and Manufacturing Science Overseas Scholarships 249

Middle East

International Postgraduate Research Scholarships (IPRS) 692
School of Industrial and Manufacturing Science Overseas Scholarships 249

New Zealand

School of Industrial and Manufacturing Science Overseas Scholarships 249
Wingate Scholarships 720

South Africa

International Postgraduate Research Scholarships (IPRS) 692
School of Industrial and Manufacturing Science Overseas Scholarships 249
Wingate Scholarships 720

United Kingdom

International Postgraduate Research Scholarships (IPRS) 692
Sheffield Hallam University Studentships 567
Swiss Federal Institute of Technology Scholarships 606
Wingate Scholarships 720

United States of America

DEED (Demonstration of Energy-Efficient Developments) Student Research Grant/Internship 77
International Postgraduate Research Scholarships (IPRS) 692
School of Industrial and Manufacturing Science Overseas Scholarships 249
SME Education Foundation Grants Program 266
Swiss Federal Institute of Technology Scholarships 606
Winston Churchill Foundation Scholarship 720

West European Countries

International Postgraduate Research Scholarships (IPRS) 692
Sheffield Hallam University Studentships 567
Wingate Scholarships 720

MATERIALS ENGINEERING

Any Country

Electrochemical Society Summer Fellowships 268
ESRF Postdoctoral Fellowships 279
Ferrari Innovation Team Project Scholarship 284
John Moyes Lessells Scholarships 557
Johnson's Wax Research Fellowship 421
Kenward Memorial Fellowship 640
KSTU Rector's Grant 397
Linacre College Applied Materials Scholarships 677
Malcolm Ray Travelling Scholarship 349
Queen Mary Research Studentships 518
University of Southampton Postgraduate Studentships 692
University of Western Ontario Senior Visiting Fellowship 705
Welch Foundation Scholarship 379
World Universities Network (WUN) Global Exchange Programme 693

African Nations

International Postgraduate Research Scholarships (IPRS) 692
School of Industrial and Manufacturing Science Overseas Scholarships 249

Australia

Fulbright Postgraduate Student Award for Engineering 126
Fulbright Postgraduate Student Award for Science and Engineering 126
School of Industrial and Manufacturing Science Overseas Scholarships 249
UOW Iron & Steal Society Scholarships 705
Wingate Scholarships 720

Canada

DEED (Demonstration of Energy-Efficient Developments) Student Research Grant/Internship 77
International Postgraduate Research Scholarships (IPRS) 692
School of Industrial and Manufacturing Science Overseas Scholarships 249
TAC Foundation Scholarships 615
Wingate Scholarships 720

Caribbean Countries

International Postgraduate Research Scholarships (IPRS) 692
School of Industrial and Manufacturing Science Overseas Scholarships 249

East European Countries

CERN Technical Student Programme 228
International Postgraduate Research Scholarships (IPRS) 692
School of Industrial and Manufacturing Science Overseas Scholarships 249

European Union

IPTME (Materials) Scholarships 417

Middle East

International Postgraduate Research Scholarships (IPRS) 692
School of Industrial and Manufacturing Science Overseas Scholarships 249

New Zealand

School of Industrial and Manufacturing Science Overseas Scholarships 249
Wingate Scholarships 720

South Africa

International Postgraduate Research Scholarships (IPRS) 692
School of Industrial and Manufacturing Science Overseas Scholarships 249
Wingate Scholarships 720

United Kingdom

CERN Technical Student Programme 228
International Postgraduate Research Scholarships (IPRS) 692
Royal Academy of Engineering International Travel Grants 534
Sheffield Hallam University Studentships 567
Swiss Federal Institute of Technology Scholarships 606
University of Wales Aberystwyth Postgraduate Research Studentships 699
Wingate Scholarships 720

United States of America

ANS Mishima Award 65
DEED (Demonstration of Energy-Efficient Developments) Student Research Grant/Internship 77
International Postgraduate Research Scholarships (IPRS) 692
School of Industrial and Manufacturing Science Overseas Scholarships 249
SRC Graduate Fellowship Program 565
SRC Master's Scholarship Program 565
SWE General Motors Foundation Graduate Scholarship 593
Swiss Federal Institute of Technology Scholarships 606
Winston Churchill Foundation Scholarship 720

West European Countries

CERN Technical Student Programme 228
International Postgraduate Research Scholarships (IPRS) 692
Royal Academy of Engineering International Travel Grants 534
Sheffield Hallam University Studentships 567
Wingate Scholarships 720

MINING AND MINERALS ENGINEERING

Any Country

Bosworth Smith Trust Fund 348
G Vernon Hobson Bequest 349
John Moyes Lessells Scholarships 557
NERC Advanced Research Fellowships 476
NERC Postdoctoral Research Fellowships 476
The Tom Seaman Travelling Scholarship 349

African Nations

International Postgraduate Research Scholarships (IPRS) 692

Australia

Edgar Pam Fellowship 348
Fulbright Postgraduate Student Award for Engineering 126
Fulbright Postgraduate Student Award for Science and Engineering 126
Wingate Scholarships 720

Canada

DEED (Demonstration of Energy-Efficient Developments) Student Research Grant/Internship 77
Edgar Pam Fellowship 348
International Postgraduate Research Scholarships (IPRS) 692
Wingate Scholarships 720

Caribbean Countries

International Postgraduate Research Scholarships (IPRS) 692

East European Countries

International Postgraduate Research Scholarships (IPRS) 692
NERC Advanced Course Studentships 476
NERC Research Studentships 476
Synthesys Visiting Fellowship 477

Middle East

International Postgraduate Research Scholarships (IPRS) 692

New Zealand

Edgar Pam Fellowship 348
Wingate Scholarships 720

South Africa

Edgar Pam Fellowship 348
International Postgraduate Research Scholarships (IPRS) 692
Wingate Scholarships 720

United Kingdom

Edgar Pam Fellowship 348
International Postgraduate Research Scholarships (IPRS) 692
Mining Club Award 349
NERC Advanced Course Studentships 476
NERC Research Studentships 476
Wingate Scholarships 720

United States of America

DEED (Demonstration of Energy-Efficient Developments) Student Research Grant/Internship 77
International Postgraduate Research Scholarships (IPRS) 692
Winston Churchill Foundation Scholarship 720

West European Countries

International Postgraduate Research Scholarships (IPRS) 692
NERC Advanced Course Studentships 476
NERC Research Studentships 476
Synthesys Visiting Fellowship 477
Wingate Scholarships 720

PETROLEUM ENGINEERING

Any Country

ACS PRF Type AC Grants 34
ACS/PRF Scientific Education Grants 35
ACS/PRF Type B Grants 35
Exxon Mobil Teaching Fellowships 533
John Moyes Lessells Scholarships 557
NERC Advanced Research Fellowships 476
NERC Postdoctoral Research Fellowships 476

West European Countries

CERN Technical Student Programme 228
International Postgraduate Research Scholarships (IPRS) 692
VKI Fellowship 711
Wingate Scholarships 720

HYDRAULIC/PNEUMATIC ENGINEERING

Any Country

Horton (Hydrology) Research Grant 52
John Moyes Lessells Scholarships 557
Kenward Memorial Fellowship 640
KSTU Rector's Grant 397

African Nations

International Postgraduate Research Scholarships (IPRS) 692

Australia

Fulbright Postgraduate Student Award for Engineering 126
Fulbright Postgraduate Student Award for Science and Engineering 126
Wingate Scholarships 720

Canada

DEED (Demonstration of Energy-Efficient Developments) Student Research Grant/Internship 77
Horticultural Research Institute Grants 329
International Postgraduate Research Scholarships (IPRS) 692
Wingate Scholarships 720

Caribbean Countries

International Postgraduate Research Scholarships (IPRS) 692

East European Countries

International Postgraduate Research Scholarships (IPRS) 692

Middle East

International Postgraduate Research Scholarships (IPRS) 692

New Zealand

Wingate Scholarships 720

South Africa

International Postgraduate Research Scholarships (IPRS) 692
Wingate Scholarships 720

United Kingdom

International Postgraduate Research Scholarships (IPRS) 692
Wingate Scholarships 720

United States of America

DEED (Demonstration of Energy-Efficient Developments) Student Research Grant/Internship 77
Horticultural Research Institute Grants 329
International Postgraduate Research Scholarships (IPRS) 692
Winston Churchill Foundation Scholarship 720

West European Countries

International Postgraduate Research Scholarships (IPRS) 692
Wingate Scholarships 720

SOUND ENGINEERING

Any Country

John Moyes Lessells Scholarships 557
Kenward Memorial Fellowship 640
University of Southampton Postgraduate Studentships 692
World Universities Network (WUN) Global Exchange Programme 693

Australia

Fulbright Postgraduate Student Award for Engineering 126
Fulbright Postgraduate Student Award for Science and Engineering 126
Wingate Scholarships 720

Canada

Wingate Scholarships 720

East European Countries

VKI Fellowship 711

New Zealand

Wingate Scholarships 720

South Africa

Wingate Scholarships 720

United Kingdom

Wingate Scholarships 720

United States of America

VKI Fellowship 711
Winston Churchill Foundation Scholarship 720

West European Countries

VKI Fellowship 711
Wingate Scholarships 720

AUTOMOTIVE ENGINEERING

Any Country

Ferrari Innovation Team Project Scholarship 284
John Moyes Lessells Scholarships 557
Kenward Memorial Fellowship 640
KSTU Rector's Grant 397
University of Bristol Postgraduate Scholarships 641
University of Southampton Postgraduate Studentships 692
World Universities Network (WUN) Global Exchange Programme 693

African Nations

International Postgraduate Research Scholarships (IPRS) 692
School of Industrial and Manufacturing Science Overseas Scholarships 249
Shell Centenary/Shell Centenary Chevening Scholarships 665

Australia

Fulbright Postgraduate Student Award for Engineering 126
Fulbright Postgraduate Student Award for Science and Engineering 126
School of Industrial and Manufacturing Science Overseas Scholarships 249
Wingate Scholarships 720

Canada

International Postgraduate Research Scholarships (IPRS) 692
School of Industrial and Manufacturing Science Overseas Scholarships 249
Wingate Scholarships 720

Caribbean Countries

International Postgraduate Research Scholarships (IPRS) 692
School of Industrial and Manufacturing Science Overseas Scholarships 249
Shell Centenary/Shell Centenary Chevening Scholarships 665

East European Countries

Middle East

New Zealand

South Africa

United Kingdom

United States of America

West European Countries

MEASUREMENT/PRECISION ENGINEERING

Any Country

African Nations

Australia

Canada

Caribbean Countries

East European Countries

Middle East

New Zealand

South Africa

United Kingdom

United States of America

West European Countries

CONTROL ENGINEERING (ROBOTICS)

Any Country

African Nations

Australia

Canada

Caribbean Countries

East European Countries

AERONAUTICAL AND AEROSPACE ENGINEERING

MARINE ENGINEERING AND NAVAL ARCHITECTURE

Hastings Center International Visiting Scholars Program 318
HRB Equipment Grants 320
John Moyes Lessells Scholarships 557
Queen Mary Research Studentships 518
Welch Foundation Scholarship 379

African Nations

Hastings Center International Visiting Scholars Program 318
International Postgraduate Research Scholarships (IPRS) 692
School of Industrial and Manufacturing Science Overseas Scholarships 249

Australia

Australian Clinical Research Postdoctoral Fellowship 460
Biomedical (Dora Lush) and Public Health Postgraduate Scholarships 460
C J Martin Fellowships (Overseas Biomedical) 460
Career Development Awards 461
Fulbright Postgraduate Student Award for Engineering 126
Fulbright Postgraduate Student Award for Science and Engineering 126
Hastings Center International Visiting Scholars Program 318
Howard Florey Centenary Fellowship 461
Industry Fellowships 461
NHMRC Medical and Dental and Public Health Postgraduate Research Scholarships 461
NHMRC/INSERM Exchange Fellowships 461
Peter Doherty Fellowships (Australian Biomedical) 462
School of Industrial and Manufacturing Science Overseas Scholarships 249
Training Scholarship for Indigenous Health Research 462
Wingate Scholarships 720

Canada

International Postgraduate Research Scholarships (IPRS) 692
School of Industrial and Manufacturing Science Overseas Scholarships 249
Wingate Scholarships 720

Caribbean Countries

Hastings Center International Visiting Scholars Program 318
International Postgraduate Research Scholarships (IPRS) 692
School of Industrial and Manufacturing Science Overseas Scholarships 249

East European Countries

FEMS Fellowship 284
Hastings Center International Visiting Scholars Program 318
International Postgraduate Research Scholarships (IPRS) 692
School of Industrial and Manufacturing Science Overseas Scholarships 249
VKI Fellowship 711

Middle East

Hastings Center International Visiting Scholars Program 318
International Postgraduate Research Scholarships (IPRS) 692
School of Industrial and Manufacturing Science Overseas Scholarships 249

New Zealand

Hastings Center International Visiting Scholars Program 318
School of Industrial and Manufacturing Science Overseas Scholarships 249
Training Scholarship for Indigenous Health Research 462
Wingate Scholarships 720

South Africa

Hastings Center International Visiting Scholars Program 318
International Postgraduate Research Scholarships (IPRS) 692
School of Industrial and Manufacturing Science Overseas Scholarships 249
Wingate Scholarships 720

United Kingdom

FEMS Fellowship 284
Hastings Center International Visiting Scholars Program 318
International Postgraduate Research Scholarships (IPRS) 692
Swiss Federal Institute of Technology Scholarships 606
Wingate Scholarships 720

United States of America

International Postgraduate Research Scholarships (IPRS) 692
School of Industrial and Manufacturing Science Overseas Scholarships 249
Swiss Federal Institute of Technology Scholarships 606
VKI Fellowship 711
Winston Churchill Foundation Scholarship 720

West European Countries

FEMS Fellowship 284
Hastings Center International Visiting Scholars Program 318
International Postgraduate Research Scholarships (IPRS) 692
VKI Fellowship 711
Wingate Scholarships 720

FINE AND APPLIED ARTS

GENERAL

Any Country

Adolfo Omodeo Scholarship 384
Ahmanson and Getty Postdoctoral Fellowships 617
Alberta Art Foundation Graduate Scholarships in the Department of Art 642
Andrew Mellon Foundation Scholarship 527
ArtsLink VisArt Central Asia 225
ASECS (American Society for 18th-Century Studies)/Clark Library Fellowships 617
Austro-American Association of Boston Scholarship 129
Banff Centre Financial Assistance 130
Barbara Thom Postdoctoral Fellowship 332
British Academy Larger Research Grants 142
Camargo Fellowships 169
Canadian Department of Foreign Affairs Faculty Enrichment Program 205
Canadian Department of Foreign Affairs Faculty Research Program 206
CIUS Research Grants 207
Clark-Huntington Joint Bibliographical Fellowship 617
Concordia University Graduate Fellowships 240
David J Azrieli Graduate Fellowship 241
Earthwatch Field Research Grants 265
Endeavour International Postgraduate Research Scholarships (EIPRS) 403
Equiano Memorial Award 604
ERASMUS Prize 292
Feiweles Trust Dance Bursary 730
Findel Scholarships and Schneider Scholarships 325
Fine Arts Work Center in Provincetown Fellowships 285
Foundation Praemium Erasmianum Study Prize 292
Frederico Chabod Scholarship 384
Hagley/Winterthur Arts and Industries Fellowship 314
Hambidge Residency Program Scholarships 315
Harold White Fellowships 468
Henry Moore Senior Fellowships 323
The Hurston-Wright Writer's Week Scholarships 334
IHS Humane Studies Fellowships 343
IHS Liberty & Society Summer Seminars 343
Institute for Advanced Studies in the Humanities Visiting Research Fellowships 341
Korea Foundation Advanced Research Grant 398
Korea Foundation Fellowship for Field Research 399
Korea Foundation Fellowship for Graduate Studies 399

African Nations

Australia

Canada

Caribbean Countries

East European Countries

European Union

Middle East

New Zealand

South Africa

United Kingdom

International Postgraduate Research Scholarships (IPRS) 692
Oppenheim-John Downes Trust Grants 491
Portia Geach Memorial Award 224
Professional Preparation Master's Scheme 103
Quinn, Nathan and Edmond Scholarships 666
Research Preparation Master's Scheme 103
Rome Scholarships in the Fine Arts 162
Sheffield Hallam University Studentships 567
University of Kent School of Drama, Film and Visual Arts Scholarships 662
University of Wales Aberystwyth Postgraduate Research Studentships 699
Wingate Scholarships 720
Wolfson Foundation Grants 722

United States of America

ACC Fellowship Grants Program 106
Artist Fellowship Program 102
BNS Arts Administrator Renewal Fellowship 138
Congress Bundestag Youth Exchange for Young Professionals 224
Endeavour International Postgraduate Research Scholarships (EIPRS) 403
Eric Robert Anderson Memorial Scholarship 441
Fellowship for American College Students 524
Fulbright Distinguished Chairs Program 245
Fulbright Scholar Program for US Citizens 245
Fulbright Senior Specialists Program 245
GAP (Grants for Artist Projects) Program 102
Geraldine R Dodge Residency Grant 724
Guggenheim Fellowships to Assist Research and Artistic Creation (USA and Canada) 394
Harriet Hale Woolley Scholarships 286
International Postgraduate Research Scholarships (IPRS) 692
Lincoln College Overseas Graduate Entrance Scholarships 680
Louise Wallace Hackney Fellowship 71
The Nadine Blacklock Nature Photography for women 138
National Endowment for the Humanities Fellowships 333
North Dakota Indian Scholarship 485
Rabun Gap-Nacoochee School Teaching Fellowship 316
Twining Humber Award for Lifetime Artistic Achievement 102
Virginia Liebeler Biennial Grants For Mature Women (Art) 467
Virginia Liebeler Biennial Grants For Mature Women (Music) 468
Virginia Liebeler Biennial Grants For Mature Women (Writing) 468

West European Countries

Endeavour International Postgraduate Research Scholarships (EIPRS) 403
Fulbright Postdoctoral Research and Lecturing Awards for Non-US Citizens 245
International Postgraduate Research Scholarships (IPRS) 692
The Metropolitan Museum of Art Annette Kade Art History Fellowship 433
Sheffield Hallam University Studentships 567
University of Kent School of Drama, Film and Visual Arts Scholarships 662
Wingate Scholarships 720

HISTORY AND PHILOSOPHY OF ART

Any Country

AAS 'Drawn to Art' Fellowship 25
Adolfo Omodeo Scholarship 384
Ahmanson and Getty Postdoctoral Fellowships 617
Albert J Beveridge Grant 54
ARIT Humanities and Social Sciences Fellowships 77
ASCSA Advanced Fellowships 78
ASCSA Fellowships 78
ASECS (American Society for 18th-Century Studies)/Clark Library Fellowships 617
Barbara Thom Postdoctoral Fellowship 332
Bernadotte E Schmitt Grants 54
British Academy Larger Research Grants 142
British Academy Overseas Conference Grants 142
British Academy Postdoctoral Fellowships 142
British Academy Small Research Grants 142
British Academy Worldwide Congress Grant 142
British Conference Grants 142
Camargo Fellowships 169
Carroll LV Meeks Fellowship 589
CDU Senior Research Fellowship 230
Clark Library Short-Term Resident Fellowships 617
Clark Predoctoral Fellowships 617
Clark-Huntington Joint Bibliographical Fellowship 617
Council of the Institute Awards 513
Duquesne University Graduate Assistantship 263
Edilia and François-Auguste de Montequin Fellowship in Iberian and Latin American Architecture 589
Essex Rotary University Travel Grants 651
Fondazione Roberto Longhi 530
Foundation Praemium Erasmianum Study Prize 292
Frances Weitzenhoffer Memorial Fellowship in Art History 489
Frederick Douglass Institute Postdoctoral Fellowship 293
Frederick Douglass Institute Predoctoral Dissertation Fellowship 294
Frederico Chabod Scholarship 384
The Getty Trust Collaborative Research Grants 306
The Getty Trust Curatorial Research Fellowships 306
Helen Wallis Fellowship 156
Henry Moore Institute Research Fellowship 323
Henry Moore Senior Fellowships 323
Hugh Last and Donald Atkinson Funds Committee Grants 586
Huntington Short-Term Fellowships 332
Interdisciplinary Internship: Early German and Netherlandish Paintings, Department of European Paintings 433
Jacob Hirsch Fellowship 79
Kanner Fellowship In British Studies 617
Keepers Preservation Education Fund Fellowship 589
Kennan Institute Short-Term Grants 397
Korea Foundation Advanced Research Grant 398
Korea Foundation Fellowship for Field Research 399
Korea Foundation Fellowship for Graduate Studies 399
Korea Foundation Postdoctoral Fellowship 399
Lewis Walpole Library Fellowship 410
Library Company of Philadelphia and Historical Society of Pennsylvania Research Fellowships in American History and Culture 411
Littleton-Griswold Research Grant 54
M Alison Frantz Fellowship in Post-Classical Studies at the Gennadius Library 80
Mellon Postdoctoral Research Fellowships 333
Metropolitan Museum of Art 6-Month Internship 433
Metropolitan Museum of Art Lifchez/Stronach Curatorial Internship 433
Metropolitan Museum of Art Summer Internships for College Students 434
Metropolitan Museum of Art Summer Internships for Graduate Students 434
NEH Fellowships 80
Paul Mellon Centre Rome Fellowship 161
Postdoctoral Fellowships (Getty) 306
Renaissance Society Fellowships 585
Residential Grants at the Getty Center 307
Rhodes University Postdoctoral Fellowship and The Andrew Mellon Postdoctoral Fellowship 528
Rosann Berry Fellowship 589
Samuel H Kress Foundation 2-Year Research Fellowships at Foreign Institutions 561
Samuel H Kress Foundation Fellowships for Advanced Training in Fine Arts Conservation 562
Samuel H Kress Foundation Graduate Fellowships in Archaeology and the History of Art 78
Samuel H Kress Foundation Travel Fellowships 562
Sir Eric Berthoud Travel Grant 652
Spiro Kostof Annual Meeting Fellowship 590
St Catherine's College Graduate Scholarship in the Arts 687
Trinity College Junior Research Fellowship 689

African Nations

Australia

Canada

Caribbean Countries

East European Countries

European Union

Middle East

New Zealand

South Africa

United Kingdom

United States of America

West European Countries

AESTHETICS

Any Country

African Nations

Australia

Canada

Caribbean Countries

East European Countries

European Union

Middle East

New Zealand
Wingate Scholarships 720

South Africa
International Postgraduate Research Scholarships (IPRS) 692
Wingate Scholarships 720

United Kingdom
AHRC Doctoral Awards Scheme 103
International Postgraduate Research Scholarships (IPRS) 692
Professional Preparation Master's Scheme 103
Research Preparation Master's Scheme 103
Wingate Scholarships 720

United States of America
ACC Fellowship Grants Program 106
International Postgraduate Research Scholarships (IPRS) 692

West European Countries
International Postgraduate Research Scholarships (IPRS) 692
Wingate Scholarships 720

ART MANAGEMENT

Any Country
The Getty Trust Curatorial Research Fellowships 306
Metropolitan Museum of Art 6-Month Internship 433
Metropolitan Museum of Art Summer Internships for College Students 434
Metropolitan Museum of Art Summer Internships for Graduate Students 434
WSW Internships 725

African Nations
International Postgraduate Research Scholarships (IPRS) 692

Australia
Wingate Scholarships 720

Canada
International Postgraduate Research Scholarships (IPRS) 692
Wingate Scholarships 720

Caribbean Countries
International Postgraduate Research Scholarships (IPRS) 692

East European Countries
ArtsLink Independent Projects 225
ArtsLink Jubliee Fellowship Program 225
International Postgraduate Research Scholarships (IPRS) 692

European Union
AHRC Doctoral Awards Scheme 103
Professional Preparation Master's Scheme 103
Research Preparation Master's Scheme 103

Middle East
International Postgraduate Research Scholarships (IPRS) 692

New Zealand
Wingate Scholarships 720

South Africa
International Postgraduate Research Scholarships (IPRS) 692
Wingate Scholarships 720

United Kingdom
AHRC Doctoral Awards Scheme 103
International Postgraduate Research Scholarships (IPRS) 692
Professional Preparation Master's Scheme 103
Research Preparation Master's Scheme 103
Wingate Scholarships 720

United States of America
ACC Fellowship Grants Program 106
Congress Bundestag Youth Exchange for Young Professionals 224
International Postgraduate Research Scholarships (IPRS) 692

West European Countries
International Postgraduate Research Scholarships (IPRS) 692
Wingate Scholarships 720

DRAWING AND PAINTING

Any Country
Abbey Harris Mural Fund 5
The Alastair Salvesen Art Scholarship 552
Alberta Art Foundation Graduate Scholarships in the Department of Art 642
ASCSA Advanced Fellowships 78
Banff Centre Financial Assistance 130
BCUC Research Student Bursary (Art and Design) 167
Camargo Fellowships 169
CDU Senior Research Fellowship 230
Don Freeman Memorial Grant-in-Aid 591
Fine Arts Work Center in Provincetown Fellowships 285
Foundation Praemium Erasmianum Study Prize 292
Frederick Douglass Institute Postdoctoral Fellowship 293
Frederick Douglass Institute Predoctoral Dissertation Fellowship 294
Gottlieb Foundation Emergency Assistance Grants 10
Gottlieb Foundation Individual Support Grants 10
Hambidge Residency Program Scholarships 315
Haystack Scholarship 318
Jacob Hirsch Fellowship 79
The John Kinross Memorial Fund Student Scholarships/RSA 552
MacDowell Colony Residencies 418
MICA Fellowship 423
Paul D. Fleck Fellowships in the Arts 130
Pollock-Krasner Foundation Grant 513
Rhodes University Postdoctoral Fellowship and The Andrew Mellon Postdoctoral Fellowship 528
RSA Annual Student Competition 553
Sir William Gillies Bequest–Hospitalfield Trust 553
St Catherine's College Graduate Scholarship in the Arts 687
Studio Residency Grant 724
University of Dundee Research Awards 648
University of Southampton Postgraduate Studentships 692
Virginia Center for the Creative Arts Fellowships 710
Wolf Foundation Prizes 721
World Universities Network (WUN) Global Exchange Programme 693
Yaddo Residency 243

African Nations
International Postgraduate Research Scholarships (IPRS) 692
Royal Over-Seas League Travel Scholarship 532

Australia
AAH Humanities Travelling Fellowships 120
Fulbright Postgraduate Student Award for the Visual and Performing Arts 126
Marten Bequest Travelling Scholarships 224
Portia Geach Memorial Award 224
Royal Over-Seas League Travel Scholarship 532

Canada

International Postgraduate Research Scholarships (IPRS) 692
Royal Over-Seas League Travel Scholarship 532
Vatican Film Library Mellon Fellowship 709

Caribbean Countries

International Postgraduate Research Scholarships (IPRS) 692
Royal Over-Seas League Travel Scholarship 532

East European Countries

ArtsLink Independent Projects 225
International Postgraduate Research Scholarships (IPRS) 692

European Union

AHRC Doctoral Awards Scheme 103
Professional Preparation Master's Scheme 103
Research Preparation Master's Scheme 103
Wingate Rome Scholarship in the Fine Arts 163

Middle East

AICF Sharett Scholarship Program 23
International Postgraduate Research Scholarships (IPRS) 692

New Zealand

Royal Over-Seas League Travel Scholarship 532

South Africa

International Postgraduate Research Scholarships (IPRS) 692
Royal Over-Seas League Travel Scholarship 532

United Kingdom

Abbey Fellowships in Painting 5, 159, 160
AHRC Doctoral Awards Scheme 103
Arts Council of England Helen Chadwick Fellowship 160
Arts Council of Northern Ireland Fellowship 160
Derek Hill Foundation Scholarship 160
ESU Chautauqua Institution Scholarships 273
Friends of Israel Educational Foundation Young Artist Award 295
Hector and Elizabeth Catling Bursary 159
International Postgraduate Research Scholarships (IPRS) 692
Portia Geach Memorial Award 224
Professional Preparation Master's Scheme 103
Research Preparation Master's Scheme 103
Rome Scholarships in the Fine Arts 162
Royal Over-Seas League Travel Scholarship 532
Sainsbury Scholarship in Painting and Sculpture 162
Sargant Fellowship 162
Sheffield Hallam University Studentships 567
University of Wales Aberystwyth Postgraduate Research Studentships 699
Wingate Rome Scholarship in the Fine Arts 163

United States of America

Abbey Fellowships in Painting 5, 159, 160
ACC Fellowship Grants Program 106
Fulbright Senior Specialists Program 245
Geraldine R Dodge Residency Grant 724
International Postgraduate Research Scholarships (IPRS) 692
John F and Anna Lee Stacey Scholarships 394
Selma Naifeh Scholarship Fund 489
Twining Humber Award for Lifetime Artistic Achievement 102
Vatican Film Library Mellon Fellowship 709
Virginia Liebeler Biennial Grants For Mature Women (Art) 467
Virginia Liebeler Biennial Grants For Mature Women (Music) 468
Virginia Liebeler Biennial Grants For Mature Women (Writing) 468

West European Countries

International Postgraduate Research Scholarships (IPRS) 692
Sheffield Hallam University Studentships 567

SCULPTURE

Any Country

The Alastair Salvesen Art Scholarship 552
Alberta Art Foundation Graduate Scholarships in the Department of Art 642
ASCSA Advanced Fellowships 78
ASCSA Fellowships 78
Banff Centre Financial Assistance 130
BCUC Research Student Bursary (Art and Design) 167
Camargo Fellowships 169
CDU Senior Research Fellowship 230
Fine Arts Work Center in Provincetown Fellowships 285
Foundation Praemium Erasmianum Study Prize 292
Frink School Bursary 295
Gilroy Roberts Art of Engraving Fellowship 308
Glenis Horn Scholarship 489
Gottlieb Foundation Emergency Assistance Grants 10
Gottlieb Foundation Individual Support Grants 10
Hambidge Residency Program Scholarships 315
Haystack Scholarship 318
Henry Moore Institute Research Fellowship 323
Henry Moore Senior Fellowships 323
Hugh Last and Donald Atkinson Funds Committee Grants 586
Jacob Hirsch Fellowship 79
The John Kinross Memorial Fund Student Scholarships/RSA 552
MacDowell Colony Residencies 418
MICA Fellowship 423
NEH Fellowships 80
Paul D. Fleck Fellowships in the Arts 130
Pollock-Krasner Foundation Grant 513
Rhodes University Postdoctoral Fellowship and The Andrew Mellon Postdoctoral Fellowship 528
RSA Annual Student Competition 553
Sir William Gillies Bequest–Hospitalfield Trust 553
St Catherine's College Graduate Scholarship in the Arts 687
Studio Residency Grant 724
University of Dundee Research Awards 648
University of Southampton Postgraduate Studentships 692
Virginia Center for the Creative Arts Fellowships 710
Wolf Foundation Prizes 721
World Universities Network (WUN) Global Exchange Programme 693
Yaddo Residency 243

African Nations

International Postgraduate Research Scholarships (IPRS) 692

Australia

AAH Humanities Travelling Fellowships 120
Fulbright Postgraduate Student Award for the Visual and Performing Arts 126
Marten Bequest Travelling Scholarships 224

Canada

International Postgraduate Research Scholarships (IPRS) 692

Caribbean Countries

International Postgraduate Research Scholarships (IPRS) 692

East European Countries

ArtsLink Independent Projects 225
International Postgraduate Research Scholarships (IPRS) 692

La Trobe University Postgraduate Scholarship 403
Leeds International Pianoforte Competition Award 406
Lincoln College Erich and Rochelle Endowed Prize in Music 679
London International String Quartet Competition 415
MacDowell Colony Residencies 418
Manoug Parikian Award 445
Maria Callas Grand Prix 117
Maria Callas Grand Prix for Pianists 117
Maria Callas International Music Competition 117
MBF Awards for Accompanists and Repetiteurs 446
MBF Music Education Awards 446
Miriam Licette Scholarship 446
MSM Scholarships 419
Myra Hess Trust 446
National Orchestral Institute Scholarships 470
Onassis Foreigners' Fellowships Programme Research Grants Category AI 17
Paul A Pisk Prize 65
Paul D. Fleck Fellowships in the Arts 130
Peter Whittingham Award 446
Prize Winner of the ARD International Music Competition Munich 97
Renaissance Society Fellowships 585
Rhodes University Postdoctoral Fellowship and The Andrew Mellon Postdoctoral Fellowship 528
Royal Academy of Music General Bursary Awards 536
Royal College of Music Scholarships 538
Ryan Davies Memorial Fund Scholarship Grants 560
Sir James McNeill Foundation Postgraduate Scholarship 440
SOAS Bursary 563
SOAS Research Student Fellowships 563
St Catherine's College Graduate Scholarship in the Arts 687
Susan and Graeme Mc Donald Music Scholarships 131
Sybil Tutton Awards 446
Thomas Holloway Research Studentship 548
University of Bristol Postgraduate Scholarships 641
University of Otago International Scholarships 670
University of Otago PhD Scholarships 670
University of Otago Prestigious PhD Scholarships 671
University of Southampton Postgraduate Studentships 692
University of Warwick Music Scholarships 703
WBDI Scholarship Awards 722
Wolf Foundation Prizes 721

African Nations

ROSL Annual Music Competition 532

Australia

AAH Humanities Travelling Fellowships 120
Fulbright Postgraduate Student Award for the Visual and Performing Arts 126
International Market Development Program 118
Marten Bequest Travelling Scholarships 224
OZCO Music Project Fellowship 120
ROSL Annual Music Competition 532
University of Otago Master's Awards 670
Wingate Scholarships 720

Canada

Alfred Einstein Award 64
Canada Council Grants for Professional Artists 198
Choirs President's Leadership Award 234
Gilbert Chinard Fellowships 341
Harmon Chadbourn Rorison Fellowship 341
Homer and Dorothy Thompson Fellowship 199
Howard Mayer Brown Fellowship 64
J B C Watkins Award 198
Otto Kinkeldey Award 64
ROSL Annual Music Competition 532
Vatican Film Library Mellon Fellowship 709
Wingate Scholarships 720

Caribbean Countries

ROSL Annual Music Competition 532

European Union

AHRC Doctoral Awards Scheme 103
CBRL Travel Grant 244
Professional Preparation Master's Scheme 103
Research Preparation Master's Scheme 103

Middle East

AICF Sharett Scholarship Program 23

New Zealand

ROSL Annual Music Competition 532
University of Otago Master's Awards 670
Wingate Scholarships 720

South Africa

ROSL Annual Music Competition 532
SAMRO Intermediate Bursaries for Composition Study In Southern Africa 596
SAMRO Overseas Scholarship 596
SAMRO Postgraduate Bursaries for Indigenous African Music Study 597
Wingate Scholarships 720

United Kingdom

AHRC Doctoral Awards Scheme 103
Cardiff University PhD Music Studentship 221
Carnwath Scholarship 729
CBRL Research Award 244
CBRL Travel Grant 244
Countess of Munster Musical Trust Awards 249
ESU Chautauqua Institution Scholarships 273
Francis Chagrin Fund 292
John Clementi Collard Fellowship 729
Mr and Mrs David Edward Memorial Award 699
Professional Preparation Master's Scheme 103
Research Preparation Master's Scheme 103
ROSL Annual Music Competition 532
University of Reading Music Scholarship 691
UWB Departmental Research Studentships 700
UWB Research Studentships 700
Wingate Scholarships 720

United States of America

ACC Fellowship Grants Program 106
Alfred Einstein Award 64
American Music Center Composer Assistance Program 63
ARCE Fellowships 77
ASCAP Foundation Morton Gould Young Composer Awards 105
Charles Z. Moore Memorial Scholarship Fund 614
Fromm Foundation Commission 295
Fulbright Senior Specialists Program 245
Gilbert Chinard Fellowships 341
Harmon Chadbourn Rorison Fellowship 341
Harriet Hale Woolley Scholarships 286
Howard Mayer Brown Fellowship 64
Margaret Fairbank Jory Copying Assistance Program 63
Meet The Composer Fund 429
Music Alive 429
Otto Kinkeldey Award 64
TMSF Scholarships 613
Vatican Film Library Mellon Fellowship 709
Virginia Liebeler Biennial Grants For Mature Women (Art) 467
Virginia Liebeler Biennial Grants For Mature Women (Music) 468
Virginia Liebeler Biennial Grants For Mature Women (Writing) 468

West European Countries

Donatella Flick Conducting Competition 261
Maisie Lewis Young Artists Fund 729

Mr and Mrs David Edward Memorial Award 699
University of Otago Master's Awards 670
UWB Departmental Research Studentships 700
UWB Research Studentships 700
Wingate Scholarships 720

MUSICOLOGY

Any Country

Ahmanson and Getty Postdoctoral Fellowships 617
AMS Subventions for Publications 64
ARIT Humanities and Social Sciences Fellowships 77
ASECS (American Society for 18th-Century Studies)/Clark Library Fellowships 617
British Academy Overseas Conference Grants 142
British Academy Small Research Grants 142
British Academy Worldwide Congress Grant 142
British Conference Grants 142
Camargo Fellowships 169
Clark Library Short-Term Resident Fellowships 617
Clark Predoctoral Fellowships 617
Clark-Huntington Joint Bibliographical Fellowship 617
Earthwatch Field Research Grants 265
Findel Scholarships and Schneider Scholarships 325
Kanner Fellowship In British Studies 617
Kurt Weill Foundation for Music Grants Program 401
Noah Greenberg Award 64
Paul A Pisk Prize 65
Royal College of Music Scholarships 538
Thomas Holloway Research Studentship 548
United States Holocaust Memorial Museum Center for Advanced Holocaust Studies Visiting Scholar Programs 619

Australia

Wingate Scholarships 720

Canada

Wingate Scholarships 720

East European Countries

Mellon Postdoctoral Fellowships In Turkey For East European Scholars 78

European Union

AHRC Doctoral Awards Scheme 103
Professional Preparation Master's Scheme 103
Research Preparation Master's Scheme 103

New Zealand

Wingate Scholarships 720

South Africa

SAMRO Postgraduate Bursaries for Indigenous African Music Study 597
Wingate Scholarships 720

United Kingdom

AHRC Doctoral Awards Scheme 103
Frank Knox Fellowships at Harvard University 292
Kennedy Scholarships 398
Mr and Mrs David Edward Memorial Award 699
Professional Preparation Master's Scheme 103
Research Preparation Master's Scheme 103
UWB Departmental Research Studentships 700
UWB Research Studentships 700
Wingate Scholarships 720

United States of America

ACC Fellowship Grants Program 106
ARCE Fellowships 77
Fulbright Distinguished Chairs Program 245
Fulbright Senior Specialists Program 245
Gladys Krieble Delmas Foundation Grants 308
IREX Individual Advanced Research Opportunities 374

West European Countries

Mr and Mrs David Edward Memorial Award 699
UWB Departmental Research Studentships 700
UWB Research Studentships 700
Wingate Scholarships 720

MUSIC THEORY AND COMPOSITION

Any Country

Camargo Fellowships 169
Cleveland Institute of Music Scholarships and Accompanying Fellowships 237
Hambidge Residency Program Scholarships 315
MacDowell Colony Residencies 418
National Association of Composers Young Composers Competition 450
Queen Elisabeth International Music Competition of Belgium 517
Royal College of Music Junior Fellowship in Performance History 538
Royal College of Music Junior Scholarship 538
Royal College of Music Scholarships 538
RPS Composition Prize 552
Ryan Davies Memorial Fund Scholarship Grants 560
Susan and Graeme Mc Donald Music Scholarships 131
Thomas Holloway Research Studentship 548
United States Holocaust Memorial Museum Center for Advanced Holocaust Studies Visiting Scholar Programs 619
Virginia Center for the Creative Arts Fellowships 710
Wolf Foundation Prizes 721
Yaddo Residency 243

Australia

Wingate Scholarships 720

Canada

Robert Fleming Prize 198
Ruth Watson Henderson Choral Composition Competition 235
Wingate Scholarships 720

European Union

AHRC Doctoral Awards Scheme 103
Professional Preparation Master's Scheme 103
Research Preparation Master's Scheme 103

Middle East

AICF Sharett Scholarship Program 23

New Zealand

Wingate Scholarships 720

South Africa

SAMRO Intermediate Bursaries for Composition Study In Southern Africa 596
SAMRO Overseas Scholarship 596
Wingate Scholarships 720

United Kingdom

AHRC Doctoral Awards Scheme 103
Countess of Munster Musical Trust Awards 249
Francis Chagrin Fund 292
Frank Knox Fellowships at Harvard University 292
Kennedy Scholarships 398
Mr and Mrs David Edward Memorial Award 699
Professional Preparation Master's Scheme 103
Research Preparation Master's Scheme 103
UWB Departmental Research Studentships 700

United Kingdom

AHRC Doctoral Awards Scheme 103
Countess of Munster Musical Trust Awards 249
Philip and Dorothy Green Award for Young Concert Artists in Association with Making Music 419
Professional Preparation Master's Scheme 103
Research Preparation Master's Scheme 103
Richard Tauber Prize for Singers 94
ROSL Annual Music Competition 532
Wingate Scholarships 720

United States of America

ACC Fellowship Grants Program 106

West European Countries

Philip and Dorothy Green Award for Young Concert Artists in Association with Making Music 419
Richard Tauber Prize for Singers 94
Wingate Scholarships 720

MUSICAL INSTRUMENTS (PERFORMANCE)

Any Country

AMSA World Piano Competition 63
ARD International Music Competition Munich 97
Arthur Rubinstein International Piano Master Competition 102
Associated Board of the Royal Schools of Music Scholarships 107
Banff Centre Financial Assistance 130
Brandon University Graduate Assistantships 140
Budapest International Music Competition 168
Chopin Piano Competition 400
Clara Haskil Competition 237
Cleveland Institute of Music Scholarships and Accompanying Fellowships 237
Elizabeth Harper Vaughn Concerto Competition 607
Eric Thompson Charitable Trust for Organists 276
Foundation Busoni International Piano Competition 283
Guilhermina Suggia Gift 445
Hambidge Residency Program Scholarships 315
Hattori Foundation Awards 318
Henry Rudolf Meisels Bursary Awards 406
Ian Fleming Charitable Trust Music Education Awards 445
International Beethoven Piano Competition 360
International Chamber Music Competition 362
International Frederic Chopin Piano Competition 293
International Géza Anda Piano Competition 307
International Harp Contest in Israel 367
International Music Competitions 666
International Paulo Cello Competition 501
International Robert Schumann Competition 380
International Violin Competition 380
International Violin Competition Permio Paganini 380
International Violin Competition of Sion Valais 371
Jean Sibelius International Violin Competition 389
John E Mortimer Foundation Awards 510
June Allison Award 510
Leeds International Pianoforte Competition Award 406
London International String Quartet Competition 415
Manoug Parikian Award 445
Maria Callas Grand Prix 117
Maria Callas Grand Prix for Pianists 117
Maria Callas International Music Competition 117
Martin Musical Scholarships 511
MBF Awards for Accompanists and Repetiteurs 446
MBF Music Education Awards 446
Myra Hess Trust 446
National Orchestral Institute Scholarships 470
National Orchestral Institute Scholarships 470
Noah Greenberg Award 64
Paloma O'Shea Santander International Piano Competition 496
Paul D. Fleck Fellowships in the Arts 130
Peter Whittingham Award 446
Prize Winner of the ARD International Music Competition Munich 97
Queen Elisabeth International Music Competition of Belgium 517
RCO Various Open Award Bequests 543
Reginald Conway Memorial Award for String Performers 511
Royal College of Music Junior Fellowship in Performance History 538
Royal College of Music Junior Scholarship 538
Royal College of Music Scholarships 538
Ryan Davies Memorial Fund Scholarship Grants 560
Sidney Perry Scholarship 511
Susan and Graeme Mc Donald Music Scholarships 131
Thomas Holloway Research Studentship 548
Trevor Snoad Memorial Trust 511
William Robertshaw Exhibition 543
Wolf Foundation Prizes 721

African Nations

ROSL Annual Music Competition 532

Australia

Marten Bequest Travelling Scholarships 224
Philip and Dorothy Green Award for Young Concert Artists in Association with Making Music 419
ROSL Annual Music Competition 532
Wingate Scholarships 720

Canada

Philip and Dorothy Green Award for Young Concert Artists in Association with Making Music 419
ROSL Annual Music Competition 532
Wingate Scholarships 720

Caribbean Countries

ROSL Annual Music Competition 532

East European Countries

ArtsLink Independent Projects 225
ArtsLink Residencies 225

European Union

AHRC Doctoral Awards Scheme 103
Professional Preparation Master's Scheme 103
Research Preparation Master's Scheme 103

Middle East

AICF Sharett Scholarship Program 23

New Zealand

Philip and Dorothy Green Award for Young Concert Artists in Association with Making Music 419
ROSL Annual Music Competition 532
Wingate Scholarships 720

South Africa

Philip and Dorothy Green Award for Young Concert Artists in Association with Making Music 419
ROSL Annual Music Competition 532
SAMRO Overseas Scholarship 596
Wingate Scholarships 720

United Kingdom

AHRC Doctoral Awards Scheme 103
Countess of Munster Musical Trust Awards 249
Emanual Hurwitz Award for Violinists of British Nationality 510
Mr and Mrs David Edward Memorial Award 699
Philip and Dorothy Green Award for Young Concert Artists in Association with Making Music 419
Professional Preparation Master's Scheme 103
Research Preparation Master's Scheme 103
ROSL Annual Music Competition 532

United States of America

West European Countries

RELIGIOUS MUSIC

Any Country

Australia

Canada

European Union

New Zealand

South Africa

United Kingdom

United States of America

West European Countries

JAZZ AND POPULAR MUSIC

Any Country

Australia

Canada

European Union

Middle East

New Zealand

South Africa

United Kingdom

United States of America

West European Countries

OPERA

Any Country

Australia

Canada

Australia
AAH Humanities Travelling Fellowships 120
Fulbright Postgraduate Student Award for the Visual and Performing Arts 126
Lady Mollie Askin Ballet Travelling Scholarship 224
Marten Bequest Travelling Scholarships 224
OZCO Dance Fellowship 119
OZCO Dance Grant Initiative: Take Your Partner 119

Canada
Canada Council Grants for Professional Artists 198

East European Countries
ArtsLink Independent Projects 225
ArtsLink Residencies 225

European Union
AHRC Doctoral Awards Scheme 103
Professional Preparation Master's Scheme 103
Research Preparation Master's Scheme 103

Middle East
AICF Sharett Scholarship Program 23

United Kingdom
AHRC Doctoral Awards Scheme 103
Professional Preparation Master's Scheme 103
Research Preparation Master's Scheme 103
University of Kent School of Drama, Film and Visual Arts Scholarships 662

United States of America
ACC Fellowship Grants Program 106
Fulbright Senior Specialists Program 245
TMSF Scholarships 613

West European Countries
University of Kent School of Drama, Film and Visual Arts Scholarships 662

PHOTOGRAPHY

Any Country
Alberta Art Foundation Graduate Scholarships in the Department of Art 642
Banff Centre Financial Assistance 130
British Academy Larger Research Grants 142
British Academy Overseas Conference Grants 142
British Academy Small Research Grants 142
British Academy Worldwide Congress Grant 142
British Conference Grants 142
Camargo Fellowships 169
Hambidge Residency Program Scholarships 315
Jacob's Pillow Intern Program 385
Library Company of Philadelphia and Historical Society of Pennsylvania Research Fellowships in American History and Culture 411
Light Work Artist-in-Residence Program 413
MacDowell Colony Residencies 418
MICA Fellowship 423
Onassis Foreigners' Fellowships Programme Research Grants Category AI 17
Paul D. Fleck Fellowships in the Arts 130
Rhodes University Postdoctoral Fellowship and The Andrew Mellon Postdoctoral Fellowship 528
Virginia Center for the Creative Arts Fellowships 710
W Eugene Smith Grant in Humanistic Photography 712
WSW Artists Fellowships 724
WSW Artists' Book Residencies 724
WSW Book Production Grants 724
WSW Hands-On-Art Visiting Artist Project 724
WSW Internships 725
Yaddo Residency 243

Australia
Fulbright Postgraduate Student Award for the Visual and Performing Arts 126
Wingate Scholarships 720

Canada
John Hervey, Broadcasters and Smallsreed Awards 623
Wingate Scholarships 720

European Union
AHRC Doctoral Awards Scheme 103
Professional Preparation Master's Scheme 103
Research Preparation Master's Scheme 103
Wingate Rome Scholarship in the Fine Arts 163

Middle East
AICF Sharett Scholarship Program 23

New Zealand
Wingate Scholarships 720

South Africa
Wingate Scholarships 720

United Kingdom
AHRC Doctoral Awards Scheme 103
Arts Council of England Helen Chadwick Fellowship 160
Professional Preparation Master's Scheme 103
Research Preparation Master's Scheme 103
Rome Scholarships in the Fine Arts 162
Sargant Fellowship 162
University of Kent School of Drama, Film and Visual Arts Scholarships 662
Wingate Rome Scholarship in the Fine Arts 163
Wingate Scholarships 720

United States of America
ACC Fellowship Grants Program 106
David McCopy Photography Scholarship 253
Fulbright Senior Specialists Program 245
Geraldine R Dodge Residency Grant 724
Individual Photographer's Fellowship 3
John Hervey, Broadcasters and Smallsreed Awards 623
The Nadine Blacklock Nature Photography for women 138
Twining Humber Award for Lifetime Artistic Achievement 102

West European Countries
Janson Johan Helmich Scholarships and Travel Grants 387
University of Kent School of Drama, Film and Visual Arts Scholarships 662
Wingate Scholarships 720

CINEMA AND TELEVISION

Any Country
ABSW Student Bursaries funded by the Wellcome Trust 109
Austro-American Association of Boston Scholarship 129
Banff Centre Financial Assistance 130
British Academy Larger Research Grants 142
British Academy Overseas Conference Grants 142
British Academy Small Research Grants 142
British Academy Worldwide Congress Grant 142
British Conference Grants 142
CDI Internship 226
Don and Gee Nicholl Fellowships in Screenwriting 6

Australia

Canada

European Union

Middle East

New Zealand

South Africa

United Kingdom

United States of America

West European Countries

DESIGN

Any Country

African Nations

Australia

Canada

Caribbean Countries

East European Countries

European Union

Middle East

New Zealand

South Africa

United Kingdom

United States of America

African Nations
International Postgraduate Research Scholarships (IPRS) 692

Canada
International Postgraduate Research Scholarships (IPRS) 692

Caribbean Countries
International Postgraduate Research Scholarships (IPRS) 692

East European Countries
Audi Design Foundation Award 118
International Postgraduate Research Scholarships (IPRS) 692

European Union
AHRC Doctoral Awards Scheme 103
Audi Design Foundation Award 118
IPTME (Materials) Scholarships 417
Professional Preparation Master's Scheme 103
Research Preparation Master's Scheme 103

Middle East
AICF Sharett Scholarship Program 23
International Postgraduate Research Scholarships (IPRS) 692

South Africa
International Postgraduate Research Scholarships (IPRS) 692

United Kingdom
AHRC Doctoral Awards Scheme 103
Audi Design Foundation Award 118
Breast Cancer Campaign Project Grants 140
Industrial Design Studentship 417
International Postgraduate Research Scholarships (IPRS) 692
Professional Preparation Master's Scheme 103
Research Preparation Master's Scheme 103
Royal Commission Industrial Design Studentship 544
RSA Design Directions 554
Sheffield Hallam University Studentships 567

United States of America
International Postgraduate Research Scholarships (IPRS) 692

West European Countries
Audi Design Foundation Award 118
International Postgraduate Research Scholarships (IPRS) 692
RSA Design Directions 554
Sheffield Hallam University Studentships 567

DISPLAY AND STAGE DESIGN

Any Country
Banff Centre Financial Assistance 130
Paul D. Fleck Fellowships in the Arts 130

African Nations
International Postgraduate Research Scholarships (IPRS) 692

Canada
International Postgraduate Research Scholarships (IPRS) 692

Caribbean Countries
International Postgraduate Research Scholarships (IPRS) 692

East European Countries
International Postgraduate Research Scholarships (IPRS) 692

European Union
AHRC Doctoral Awards Scheme 103
Professional Preparation Master's Scheme 103
Research Preparation Master's Scheme 103

Middle East
AICF Sharett Scholarship Program 23
International Postgraduate Research Scholarships (IPRS) 692

South Africa
International Postgraduate Research Scholarships (IPRS) 692

United Kingdom
AHRC Doctoral Awards Scheme 103
International Postgraduate Research Scholarships (IPRS) 692
The Patterns of Fashion Award 243
Professional Preparation Master's Scheme 103
Research Preparation Master's Scheme 103
The Student Bursary 243

United States of America
International Postgraduate Research Scholarships (IPRS) 692

West European Countries
International Postgraduate Research Scholarships (IPRS) 692

HOME ECONOMICS

GENERAL

Any Country
Alberta Research Council Scholarship 642
Canadian Natural Resources Limited Graduate Scholarship 642
Frederick Douglass Institute Postdoctoral Fellowship 293
Frederick Douglass Institute Predoctoral Dissertation Fellowship 294

African Nations
Fulbright Postdoctoral Research and Lecturing Awards for Non-US Citizens 245
Merton College Reed Foundation Scholarship 681

Australia
Fulbright Awards 125
Fulbright Postdoctoral Research and Lecturing Awards for Non-US Citizens 245
Fulbright Postgraduate Awards 126

Canada
Fulbright Postdoctoral Research and Lecturing Awards for Non-US Citizens 245
Killam Research Fellowships 198
Mary A Clarke Memorial Scholarship, Silver Jubilee Scholarship and Fiftieth Anniversary Scholarship 206
Robin Hood Multifoods Scholarship 206
Ruth Binnie Scholarship 206

Caribbean Countries
Fulbright Postdoctoral Research and Lecturing Awards for Non-US Citizens 245
Merton College Reed Foundation Scholarship 681

East European Countries
Fulbright Postdoctoral Research and Lecturing Awards for Non-US Citizens 245
Merton College Reed Foundation Scholarship 681
Swiss Scholarships for University Studies for Central and East European Countries 606

European Union
All Saints Educational Trust Personal Awards 21

Middle East
Fulbright Postdoctoral Research and Lecturing Awards for Non-US Citizens 245
Merton College Reed Foundation Scholarship 681

New Zealand
Fulbright Postdoctoral Research and Lecturing Awards for Non-US Citizens 245

South Africa
Fulbright Postdoctoral Research and Lecturing Awards for Non-US Citizens 245

United Kingdom
All Saints Educational Trust Corporate Awards 20
All Saints Educational Trust Personal Awards 21
Fulbright Postdoctoral Research and Lecturing Awards for Non-US Citizens 245

United States of America
Fulbright Scholar Program for US Citizens 245
North Dakota Indian Scholarship 485

West European Countries
Fulbright Postdoctoral Research and Lecturing Awards for Non-US Citizens 245

HOUSEHOLD MANAGEMENT

CLOTHING AND SEWING

Any Country
CSA Adele Filene Travel Award 244
CSA Stella Blum Research Grant 244
CSA Travel Research Grant 244

NUTRITION

Any Country
Allen Foundation Grants 21
Earthwatch Field Research Grants 265
University of Otago International Scholarships 670
University of Otago PhD Scholarships 670
University of Otago Prestigious PhD Scholarships 671

African Nations
International Postgraduate Research Scholarships (IPRS) 692

Australia
University of Otago Master's Awards 670

Canada
International Postgraduate Research Scholarships (IPRS) 692
Robin Hood Multifoods Scholarship 206

Caribbean Countries
International Postgraduate Research Scholarships (IPRS) 692

East European Countries
International Postgraduate Research Scholarships (IPRS) 692

Middle East
International Postgraduate Research Scholarships (IPRS) 692

New Zealand
University of Otago Master's Awards 670

South Africa
International Postgraduate Research Scholarships (IPRS) 692

United Kingdom
International Postgraduate Research Scholarships (IPRS) 692

United States of America
International Postgraduate Research Scholarships (IPRS) 692
Nurses' Educational Funds Fellowships and Scholarships 488

West European Countries
International Postgraduate Research Scholarships (IPRS) 692
University of Otago Master's Awards 670

CHILD CARE/CHILD DEVELOPMENT

Any Country
Earthwatch Field Research Grants 265
Equiano Memorial Award 604
Tim Brighouse Scholarship 137

HOUSE ARTS AND ENVIRONMENT

LAW

GENERAL

Any Country
AALL and West–George A Strait Minority Scholarship Endowment 30
AALL James F Connolly LexisNexis Academic and Library Solutions Scholarship 30
AALL Scholarship (Type II) 31
AALL Scholarship (Type V) 31
The Airey Neave Trust Scholarship 12
Alberta Law Foundation Graduate Scholarship 642
Andrew Mellon Foundation Scholarship 527
Balliol College Gregory Kulkes Scholarships in Law 671
British Academy Larger Research Grants 142
British Academy Overseas Conference Grants 142
British Academy Postdoctoral Fellowships 142
British Academy Small Research Grants 142
British Academy Worldwide Congress Grant 142
British Conference Grants 142
Canadian Department of Foreign Affairs Faculty Enrichment Program 205
Canadian Department of Foreign Affairs Faculty Research Program 206
CIUS Research Grants 207
Endeavour International Postgraduate Research Scholarships (EIPRS) 403
Equiano Memorial Award 604
ERASMUS Prize 292
Evan Lewis Thomas Law Bursaries and Studentships 567
Field Psych Trust Grant 284
Freshfields Studentship in Law 675
H Thomas Austern Memorial Writing Competition–Food and Drug Law 287
Helen Darcovich Memorial Doctoral Fellowship 207
Honourable N D McDermid Graduate Scholarship in Law 642
Howard Drake Memorial Fund 344
Humanitarian Trust Awards 332
IALS Visiting Fellowship in Law Librarianship 345
IALS Visiting Fellowship in Legislative Studies 345

African Nations

Australia

Canada

Caribbean Countries

East European Countries

European Union

Middle East

New Zealand

Pegasus Cambridge Scholarships for Postgraduate Study 189
University of Otago Master's Awards 670
Wingate Scholarships 720

South Africa

Allan Gray Senior Scholarship 527
Endeavour International Postgraduate Research Scholarships (EIPRS) 403
Fulbright Postdoctoral Research and Lecturing Awards for Non-US Citizens 245
NUFFIC-NFP Fellowships for Master's Degree Programmes 478
Shell Centenary Scholarships and Shell Centenary Chevening Scholarships 685
Wingate Scholarships 720

United Kingdom

AHRC Doctoral Awards Scheme 103
Balsdon Fellowship 160
CBRL Research Award 244
CBRL Travel Grant 244
Endeavour International Postgraduate Research Scholarships (EIPRS) 403
ESRC 1+3 Awards and +3 Awards 265
Frank Knox Fellowships at Harvard University 292
Fulbright Postdoctoral Research and Lecturing Awards for Non-US Citizens 245
Hilda Martindale Exhibitions 326
Kennedy Scholarships 398
Professional Preparation Master's Scheme 103
Research Preparation Master's Scheme 103
Rome Awards 161
Rome Fellowship 161
Rome Scholarships in Ancient, Medieval and Later Italian Studies 162
Sheffield Hallam University Studentships 567
University of Wales Aberystwyth Postgraduate Research Studentships 699
Wingate Scholarships 720

United States of America

AAUW Selected Professions Fellowships 4
ARCE Fellowships 77
Congress Bundestag Youth Exchange for Young Professionals 224
Endeavour International Postgraduate Research Scholarships (EIPRS) 403
Fellowship for American College Students 524
Fulbright Distinguished Chairs Program 245
Fulbright Scholar Program for US Citizens 245
Fulbright Senior Specialists Program 245
Howard Brown Rickard Scholarship 456
Ian Axford (New Zealand) Fellowships in Public Policy 239
IREX Individual Advanced Research Opportunities 374
IREX Short-Term Travel Grants 374
National Academics Christine Mirzayan Science and Technology Policy Graduate Fellowship Program 68
Robert Bosch Foundation Fellowships 530
Vatican Film Library Mellon Fellowship 709

West European Countries

Endeavour International Postgraduate Research Scholarships (EIPRS) 403
ESRC 1+3 Awards and +3 Awards 265
Fulbright Postdoctoral Research and Lecturing Awards for Non-US Citizens 245
Janson Johan Helmich Scholarships and Travel Grants 387
Sheffield Hallam University Studentships 567
University of Otago Master's Awards 670
Wingate Scholarships 720

HISTORY OF LAW

Any Country

Ahmanson and Getty Postdoctoral Fellowships 617
ASCSA Advanced Fellowships 78
ASCSA Fellowships 78
ASECS (American Society for 18th-Century Studies)/Clark Library Fellowships 617
British Academy Postdoctoral Fellowships 142
Clark Library Short-Term Resident Fellowships 617
Clark Predoctoral Fellowships 617
Clark-Huntington Joint Bibliographical Fellowship 617
Findel Scholarships and Schneider Scholarships 325
Foundation Praemium Erasmianum Study Prize 292
Hugh Last and Donald Atkinson Funds Committee Grants 586
J Franklin Jameson Fellowship 54
Jacob Hirsch Fellowship 79
JCB William Reese Company Fellowship 391
Kanner Fellowship In British Studies 617
Littleton-Griswold Research Grant 54
M Alison Frantz Fellowship in Post-Classical Studies at the Gennadius Library 80
NEH Fellowships 80
Renaissance Society Fellowships 585
United States Holocaust Memorial Museum Center for Advanced Holocaust Studies Visiting Scholar Programs 619

Australia

Wingate Scholarships 720

Canada

The Guild, Yule & Company Advocacy Award 697
Viscount Bennett Fellowship 200
Wingate Scholarships 720

East European Countries

CRF (Caledonian Research Foundation)/RSE European Visiting Research Fellowships 556

European Union

AHRC Doctoral Awards Scheme 103
Professional Preparation Master's Scheme 103
Research Preparation Master's Scheme 103

New Zealand

Wingate Scholarships 720

South Africa

Wingate Scholarships 720

United Kingdom

AHRC Doctoral Awards Scheme 103
CRF (Caledonian Research Foundation)/RSE European Visiting Research Fellowships 556
Hector and Elizabeth Catling Bursary 159
Professional Preparation Master's Scheme 103
Research Preparation Master's Scheme 103
Wingate Scholarships 720

United States of America

Fulbright Senior Specialists Program 245
Kennan Institute Research Scholarship 397

West European Countries

CRF (Caledonian Research Foundation)/RSE European Visiting Research Fellowships 556
Wingate Scholarships 720

COMPARATIVE LAW

Any Country

African Nations

Australia

Canada

Caribbean Countries

East European Countries

European Union

Middle East

New Zealand

South Africa

United Kingdom

United States of America

West European Countries

INTERNATIONAL LAW

Any Country

African Nations

Australia

Canada

Caribbean Countries

East European Countries

European Union

Middle East

New Zealand

African Nations
International Postgraduate Research Scholarships (IPRS) 692

Australia
Wingate Scholarships 720

Canada
International Postgraduate Research Scholarships (IPRS) 692
Viscount Bennett Fellowship 200
Wingate Scholarships 720

Caribbean Countries
International Postgraduate Research Scholarships (IPRS) 692

East European Countries
International Postgraduate Research Scholarships (IPRS) 692

European Union
AHRC Doctoral Awards Scheme 103
Professional Preparation Master's Scheme 103
Research Preparation Master's Scheme 103

Middle East
International Postgraduate Research Scholarships (IPRS) 692

New Zealand
Wingate Scholarships 720

South Africa
International Postgraduate Research Scholarships (IPRS) 692
Wingate Scholarships 720

United Kingdom
AHRC Doctoral Awards Scheme 103
International Postgraduate Research Scholarships (IPRS) 692
Professional Preparation Master's Scheme 103
Research Preparation Master's Scheme 103
Wingate Scholarships 720

United States of America
Edward S. Corwin Award 75
Fulbright Senior Specialists Program 245
International Postgraduate Research Scholarships (IPRS) 692

West European Countries
International Postgraduate Research Scholarships (IPRS) 692
Wingate Scholarships 720

COMMERCIAL LAW

Any Country
H Thomas Austern Memorial Writing Competition–Food and Drug Law 287
International Trade Law Postgraduate Scholarships 638
Queen Mary Research Studentships 518
University of Bristol Postgraduate Scholarships 641
University of Dundee Research Awards 648
University of Southampton Postgraduate Studentships 692
World Universities Network (WUN) Global Exchange Programme 693

African Nations
International Postgraduate Research Scholarships (IPRS) 692
University of Sussex Overseas Development Administration Shared Scholarship Scheme 695

Canada
International Postgraduate Research Scholarships (IPRS) 692
Viscount Bennett Fellowship 200

Caribbean Countries
International Postgraduate Research Scholarships (IPRS) 692

East European Countries
International Postgraduate Research Scholarships (IPRS) 692

European Union
AHRC Doctoral Awards Scheme 103
Professional Preparation Master's Scheme 103
Research Preparation Master's Scheme 103

Middle East
International Postgraduate Research Scholarships (IPRS) 692

South Africa
International Postgraduate Research Scholarships (IPRS) 692

United Kingdom
AHRC Doctoral Awards Scheme 103
International Postgraduate Research Scholarships (IPRS) 692
Professional Preparation Master's Scheme 103
Research Preparation Master's Scheme 103
University of Wales Aberystwyth Postgraduate Research Studentships 699

United States of America
International Postgraduate Research Scholarships (IPRS) 692

West European Countries
International Postgraduate Research Scholarships (IPRS) 692

PUBLIC LAW

Any Country
Fernand Braudel Senior Fellowships 280
Jack Nelson Legal Fellowship 523
Jean Monnet Fellowships 280
Lincoln College Supperstone Law Scholarship 680
Reporters Committee Legal Fellowship 523
Robert R McCormick Tribune Foundation Journalism Fellowship 523
Robert R McCormick Tribune Foundation Legal Fellowship 523
United States Holocaust Memorial Museum Center for Advanced Holocaust Studies Visiting Scholar Programs 619
University of Bristol Postgraduate Scholarships 641
University of Dundee Research Awards 648
University of Southampton Postgraduate Studentships 692
World Universities Network (WUN) Global Exchange Programme 693

African Nations
International Postgraduate Research Scholarships (IPRS) 692

Canada
International Postgraduate Research Scholarships (IPRS) 692
Jules and Gabrielle Léger Fellowship 581
Viscount Bennett Fellowship 200

Caribbean Countries
International Postgraduate Research Scholarships (IPRS) 692

East European Countries
EUI Postgraduate Scholarships 279
International Postgraduate Research Scholarships (IPRS) 692

ISLAMIC LAW

Any Country

CDU Three Year Postdoctoral Fellowship 230
USIP Solicited Grants 622

European Union

AHRC Doctoral Awards Scheme 103
CBRL Travel Grant 244
Professional Preparation Master's Scheme 103
Research Preparation Master's Scheme 103

United Kingdom

AHRC Doctoral Awards Scheme 103
CBRL Research Award 244
CBRL Travel Grant 244
Professional Preparation Master's Scheme 103
Research Preparation Master's Scheme 103

United States of America

ARCE Fellowships 77

EUROPEAN COMMUNITY LAW

Any Country

Fernand Braudel Senior Fellowships 280
Jean Monnet Fellowships 280
Lincoln College Supperstone Law Scholarship 680
Paul H. Nitze School of Advanced International Studies (SAIS) Financial Aid and Fellowships 139
United States Holocaust Memorial Museum Center for Advanced Holocaust Studies Visiting Scholar Programs 619
University of Southampton Postgraduate Studentships 692
World Universities Network (WUN) Global Exchange Programme 693

East European Countries

EUI Postgraduate Scholarships 279

European Union

AHRC Doctoral Awards Scheme 103
EUI Postgraduate Scholarships 279
Research Preparation Master's Scheme 103

United Kingdom

AHRC Doctoral Awards Scheme 103
EUI Postgraduate Scholarships 279
Research Preparation Master's Scheme 103
University of Wales Aberystwyth Postgraduate Research Studentships 699

West European Countries

EUI Postgraduate Scholarships 279

MASS COMMUNICATION AND INFORMATION SCIENCE

GENERAL

Any Country

ABSW Student Bursaries funded by the Wellcome Trust 109
Adelle and Erwin Tomash Fellowship in the History of Information Processing 229
Andrew Mellon Foundation Scholarship 527
AUC Graduate Merit Fellowships 90
AUC University Fellowships 91
Canadian Department of Foreign Affairs Faculty Enrichment Program 205
Canadian Department of Foreign Affairs Faculty Research Program 206
Concordia University Graduate Fellowships 240
David J Azrieli Graduate Fellowship 241
Equiano Memorial Award 604
ETS Summer Program in Research for Graduate Students 267
Field Psych Trust Grant 284
HSS Travel Grant 327
IHS Humane Studies Fellowships 343
IHS Liberty & Society Summer Seminars 343
IHS Young Communicators Fellowship 343
Korea Foundation Advanced Research Grant 398
Korea Foundation Fellowship for Field Research 399
Korea Foundation Fellowship for Graduate Studies 399
Korea Foundation Postdoctoral Fellowship 399
Monash International Postgraduate Research Scholarship (MIPRS) 440
Rhodes University Postdoctoral Fellowship and The Andrew Mellon Postdoctoral Fellowship 528
Rhodes University Postgraduate Scholarship 528
Rolf Nevanlinna Prize 371
Scottish Executive Personal Research Fellowships 557
Scottish Executive/RSE Support Research Fellowships 557
Sir Allan Sewell Visiting Fellowship 312
Stanley G French Graduate Fellowship 241
United States Holocaust Memorial Museum Center for Advanced Holocaust Studies Visiting Scholar Programs 619
University of Calgary Cogeco, Inc. Graduate Scholarship 643
University of Otago International Scholarships 670
University of Otago PhD Scholarships 670
University of Otago Prestigious PhD Scholarships 671
Vera Moore International Postgraduate Research Scholarships 440

African Nations

ABCCF Student Grant 95
AUC African Graduate Fellowship 89
Fulbright Postdoctoral Research and Lecturing Awards for Non-US Citizens 245
International Postgraduate Research Scholarships (IPRS) 692
Merton College Reed Foundation Scholarship 681
NUFFIC-NFP Fellowships for Master's Degree Programmes 478

Australia

Coral Sea Business Administration Scholarship 125
Fulbright Awards 125
Fulbright Postdoctoral Fellowships 125
Fulbright Postdoctoral Research and Lecturing Awards for Non-US Citizens 245
Fulbright Postgraduate Awards 126
University of Otago Master's Awards 670
Wingate Scholarships 720

Canada

Community-University Research Alliances (CURA) 581
Fulbright Postdoctoral Research and Lecturing Awards for Non-US Citizens 245
International Postgraduate Research Scholarships (IPRS) 692
J W McConnell Memorial Fellowships 241
Major Collaborative Research Initiatives (MCRI) 582
SSHRC Doctoral Awards 582
SSHRC Standard Research Grants 583
Wingate Scholarships 720

Caribbean Countries

Fulbright Postdoctoral Research and Lecturing Awards for Non-US Citizens 245
International Postgraduate Research Scholarships (IPRS) 692
Merton College Reed Foundation Scholarship 681

RADIO/TELEVISION BROADCASTING

PUBLIC RELATIONS AND PUBLICITY

African Nations

International Postgraduate Research Scholarships (IPRS) 692
MCTC Assistance for Courses 309
MCTC Tuition and Maintenance Scholarships 309

Australia

AAH Humanities Travelling Fellowships 120

Canada

International Postgraduate Research Scholarships (IPRS) 692

Caribbean Countries

International Postgraduate Research Scholarships (IPRS) 692
MCTC Assistance for Courses 309
MCTC Tuition and Maintenance Scholarships 309

East European Countries

International Postgraduate Research Scholarships (IPRS) 692
MCTC Assistance for Courses 309
MCTC Tuition and Maintenance Scholarships 309

European Union

AHRC Doctoral Awards Scheme 103
EMBO Science Writing Prize 278
ESRC 1+3 Awards and +3 Awards 265
Research Preparation Master's Scheme 103

Middle East

International Postgraduate Research Scholarships (IPRS) 692
MCTC Assistance for Courses 309
MCTC Tuition and Maintenance Scholarships 309

South Africa

International Postgraduate Research Scholarships (IPRS) 692
MCTC Assistance for Courses 309
MCTC Tuition and Maintenance Scholarships 309
SACEE EX-PCE Bursary 595

United Kingdom

AHRC Doctoral Awards Scheme 103
EMBO Science Writing Prize 278
ESRC 1+3 Awards and +3 Awards 265
International Postgraduate Research Scholarships (IPRS) 692
Research Preparation Master's Scheme 103
Sheffield Hallam University Studentships 567
University of Wales Aberystwyth Postgraduate Research Studentships 699

United States of America

Fulbright Distinguished Chairs Program 245
Fulbright Senior Specialists Program 245
Ian Axford (New Zealand) Fellowships in Public Policy 239
International Postgraduate Research Scholarships (IPRS) 692

West European Countries

EMBO Science Writing Prize 278
ESRC 1+3 Awards and +3 Awards 265
International Postgraduate Research Scholarships (IPRS) 692
Sheffield Hallam University Studentships 567

COMMUNICATIONS SKILLS

Any Country

ABSW Student Bursaries funded by the Wellcome Trust 109
Fulbright Institutional Linkages Program 296
IHS Humane Studies Fellowships 343
Major STC Research Grant Program 585
STC International Scholarship Program 585

African Nations

International Postgraduate Research Scholarships (IPRS) 692
MCTC Assistance for Courses 309

Canada

BBM Scholarship 199
International Postgraduate Research Scholarships (IPRS) 692

Caribbean Countries

International Postgraduate Research Scholarships (IPRS) 692
MCTC Assistance for Courses 309

East European Countries

EMBO Award for Communication in the Life Sciences 277
International Postgraduate Research Scholarships (IPRS) 692
MCTC Assistance for Courses 309

European Union

EMBO Award for Communication in the Life Sciences 277
EMBO Science Writing Prize 278
ESRC 1+3 Awards and +3 Awards 265

Middle East

International Postgraduate Research Scholarships (IPRS) 692
MCTC Assistance for Courses 309

South Africa

International Postgraduate Research Scholarships (IPRS) 692
MCTC Assistance for Courses 309
SACEE EX-PCE Bursary 595

United Kingdom

EMBO Award for Communication in the Life Sciences 277
EMBO Science Writing Prize 278
ESRC 1+3 Awards and +3 Awards 265
International Postgraduate Research Scholarships (IPRS) 692
Sheffield Hallam University Studentships 567

United States of America

Fulbright Senior Specialists Program 245
International Postgraduate Research Scholarships (IPRS) 692
STC Lone Star Community Scholarship 585

West European Countries

EMBO Award for Communication in the Life Sciences 277
EMBO Science Writing Prize 278
ESRC 1+3 Awards and +3 Awards 265
International Postgraduate Research Scholarships (IPRS) 692
Sheffield Hallam University Studentships 567

LIBRARY SCIENCE

Any Country

AALL and West–George A Strait Minority Scholarship Endowment 30
AALL James F Connolly LexisNexis Academic and Library Solutions Scholarship 30
AALL LexisNexis/John R Johnson Memorial Scholarship Endowment 30
AALL Scholarship (Type I) 31
AALL Scholarship (Type III) 31
AALL Scholarship (Type V) 31
ALA 3M/NMRT Professional Development Grant 57
ALA AASL Frances Henne Award 57
ALA AASL Highsmith Research Grant 58
ALA AASL Information Technology Pathfinder Award 58
ALA Beta Phi Mu Award 58
ALA Bogle-Pratt International Library Travel Fund 58
ALA Bound to Stay Bound Book Scholarships 58
ALA Carroll Preston Baber Research Grant 58

African Nations

Australia

Canada

Caribbean Countries

East European Countries

European Union

Middle East

New Zealand

South Africa

United Kingdom

United States of America

West European Countries

MUSEUM STUDIES AND CONSERVATION

Any Country

African Nations

Australia

Canada

Caribbean Countries

East European Countries

European Union

Middle East

New Zealand

South Africa

United Kingdom

United States of America

West European Countries

MUSEUM MANAGEMENT

Any Country

African Nations

Canada

Caribbean Countries

East European Countries

European Union

Middle East

South Africa

United Kingdom

RESTORATION OF WORKS OF ART

DOCUMENTATION TECHNIQUES AND ARCHIVING

Professional Preparation Master's Scheme 103
Research Preparation Master's Scheme 103
University of Wales Aberystwyth Postgraduate Research Studentships 699
Wingate Scholarships 720

United States of America

Fulbright Senior Specialists Program 245
International Postgraduate Research Scholarships (IPRS) 692
NHPRC Fellowship in Archival Administration 464
NHPRC Fellowship in Documentary Editing 465

West European Countries

International Postgraduate Research Scholarships (IPRS) 692
Wingate Scholarships 720

MATHEMATICS AND COMPUTER SCIENCE

GENERAL

Any Country

Abdus Salam ICTP Fellowships 5
AFUW Western Australian Bursaries 148
Alberta Research Council Karl A Clark Memorial Scholarship 638
Andrew Mellon Foundation Scholarship 527
Association for Women in Science Educational Foundation Predoctoral Awards 108
AUC Assistantships 89
AUC University Fellowships 91
Computer Laboratory ORS Equivalent Awards 179
Concordia University Graduate Fellowships 240
Corpus Christi College Garside Scholarship in Mathematics 674
CSCMP George A Gecowets Graduate Scholarship Program 246
David J Azrieli Graduate Fellowship 241
Endeavour International Postgraduate Research Scholarships (EIPRS) 403
EPSRC Advanced Research Fellowships 271
EPSRC Senior Research Fellowships 272
HSS Travel Grant 327
Humanitarian Trust Awards 332
IMU Fields Medals 371
Institut Mittag-Leffler Grants 341
La Trobe University Postgraduate Scholarship 403
Matsumae International Foundation Research Fellowship 423
Monash International Postgraduate Research Scholarship (MIPRS) 440
Queen Mary Research Studentships 518
Rhodes University Postdoctoral Fellowship and The Andrew Mellon Postdoctoral Fellowship 528
Rhodes University Postgraduate Scholarship 528
Royal Irish Academy European Exchange Fellowship 551
Scottish Executive Personal Research Fellowships 557
Scottish Executive/RSE Support Research Fellowships 557
Sir Allan Sewell Visiting Fellowship 312
Solomon Lefschetz Instructorships 228
St Catherine's College Leathersellers' Company Graduate Scholarship 688
Stanley G French Graduate Fellowship 241
Thomas Holloway Research Studentship 548
University of Bristol Postgraduate Scholarships 641
University of Dundee Research Awards 648
University of Essex/Postgraduate Research Studentship 655
University of Kent Institute of Mathematics, Statistics and Actuarial Science (IMSAS) 662
University of Otago International Scholarships 670
University of Otago PhD Scholarships 670
University of Otago Prestigious PhD Scholarships 671
University of Sussex Overseas Research Studentships 696
Vera Moore International Postgraduate Research Scholarships 440
Weizmann Institute of Science MSc Fellowships 715
Weizmann Institute of Science PhD Fellowships 715
Weizmann Institute of Science Postdoctoral Fellowships Program 715
WHOI Geophysical Fluid Dynamics (GFD) Fellowships 726
WHOI Postdoctoral Fellowships in Ocean Science and Engineering 726
WHOI/NOAA Co-operative Institute for Climate and Ocean Research Postdoctoral Fellowship 727
Wolf Foundation Prizes 721

African Nations

ABCCF Student Grant 95
ANSTI Postgraduate Fellowships 10
CAS-TWAS Fellowship for Postdoctoral Research in China 608
CAS-TWAS Fellowship for Postgraduate Research in China 608
CAS-TWAS Fellowship for Visiting Scholars in China 608
CNPq-TWAS Doctoral Fellowships in Brazil 609
CNPq-TWAS Fellowships for Postdoctoral Research in Brazil 609
CSIR (Council of Scientific and Industrial Research)/TWAS Fellowship for Postgraduate Research 609
CSIR (The Council of Scientific and Industrial Research)/TWAS Fellowship for Postdoctoral Research 609
Endeavour International Postgraduate Research Scholarships (EIPRS) 403
Fulbright Postdoctoral Research and Lecturing Awards for Non-US Citizens 245
International Postgraduate Research Scholarships (IPRS) 692
Lindemann Trust Fellowships 273
Merton College Reed Foundation Scholarship 681
NUFFIC-NFP Fellowships for Master's Degree Programmes 478
PTDF Cambridge Scholarships 191
The Trieste Science Prize 610
TWAS Fellowships for Research and Advanced Training 610
TWAS Grants for Scientific Meetings in Developing Countries 611
TWAS Prizes 611
TWAS Prizes to Young Scientists in Developing Countries 611
TWAS Research Grants 611
TWAS Spare Parts for Scientific Equipment 611
TWAS UNESCO Associateship Scheme 612
TWNSO Grants to Institutions in the South for Joint Research Projects 612

Australia

C T Taylor Studentship for PhD Study 177
Coral Sea Business Administration Scholarship 125
Endeavour International Postgraduate Research Scholarships (EIPRS) 403
Fulbright Awards 125
Fulbright Postdoctoral Fellowships 125
Fulbright Postdoctoral Research and Lecturing Awards for Non-US Citizens 245
Fulbright Postgraduate Awards 126
Lindemann Trust Fellowships 273
University of Otago Master's Awards 670
Wingate Scholarships 720

Canada

AUCC Cable Telecommunications Research Fellowship 114
C T Taylor Studentship for PhD Study 177
DEED (Demonstration of Energy-Efficient Developments) Student Research Grant/Internship 77
Endeavour International Postgraduate Research Scholarships (EIPRS) 403
Fulbright Postdoctoral Research and Lecturing Awards for Non-US Citizens 245
International Postgraduate Research Scholarships (IPRS) 692
J W McConnell Memorial Fellowships 241
Killam Research Fellowships 198
Lindemann Trust Fellowships 273
NSERC Postdoctoral Fellowships 477
Vatican Film Library Mellon Fellowship 709
Wingate Scholarships 720

Caribbean Countries

East European Countries

European Union

Middle East

New Zealand

South Africa

United Kingdom

United States of America

DEED (Demonstration of Energy-Efficient Developments) Student Research Grant/Internship 77
Endeavour International Postgraduate Research Scholarships (EIPRS) 403
Foundation for Science and Disability Student Grant Fund 291
Fulbright Scholar Program for US Citizens 245
Fulbright Senior Specialists Program 245
Gerald C. Pomraning Memorial Award 67
International Postgraduate Research Scholarships (IPRS) 692
North Dakota Indian Scholarship 485
PhRMAF Postdoctoral Fellowships in Informatics 506
PhRMAF Research Starter Grants in Informatics 508
PhRMAF Sabbatical Fellowships in Informatics 509
Renate W Chasman Scholarship 166
Swiss Federal Institute of Technology Scholarships 606
Vatican Film Library Mellon Fellowship 709
Winston Churchill Foundation Scholarship 720

West European Countries

CERN Technical Student Programme 228
Endeavour International Postgraduate Research Scholarships (EIPRS) 403
EPSRC Doctoral Training Grants (DTGs) 272
EPSRC Postdoctoral Fellowships in Mathematics 272
Fulbright Postdoctoral Research and Lecturing Awards for Non-US Citizens 245
International Postgraduate Research Scholarships (IPRS) 692
Janson Johan Helmich Scholarships and Travel Grants 387
Mr and Mrs David Edward Memorial Award 699
Sheffield Hallam University Studentships 567
St Peter's College Bodossaki Foundation Graduate Scholarship in Science 688
University of Otago Master's Awards 670
UWB Departmental Research Studentships 700
UWB Research Studentships 700
Wingate Scholarships 720

STATISTICS

Any Country

Acadia Graduate Awards 7
CIIT-Centers for Health Research Postdoctoral Fellowships 236
CIIT-Centers for Health Research Predoctoral Traineeships 236
Corpus Christi College Graduate Studentship in Science 674
Hugh Kelly Fellowship 528
Pierre Robillard Award 601
Queen Mary Research Studentships 518
Rhodes University Postdoctoral Fellowship and The Andrew Mellon Postdoctoral Fellowship 528
Sir James McNeill Foundation Postgraduate Scholarship 440
Solomon Lefschetz Instructorships 228
Thomas Holloway Research Studentship 548
University of Bristol Postgraduate Scholarships 641
University of Essex/Postgraduate Research Studentship 655
University of Kent Institute of Mathematics, Statistics and Actuarial Science (IMSAS) 662

African Nations

International Postgraduate Research Scholarships (IPRS) 692
Shell Centenary Scholarships and Shell Centenary Chevening Scholarships 685

Australia

Australian Clinical Research Postdoctoral Fellowship 460
Wingate Scholarships 720

Canada

International Postgraduate Research Scholarships (IPRS) 692
Wingate Scholarships 720

Caribbean Countries

International Postgraduate Research Scholarships (IPRS) 692
Shell Centenary Scholarships and Shell Centenary Chevening Scholarships 685

East European Countries

International Postgraduate Research Scholarships (IPRS) 692
Shell Centenary Scholarships and Shell Centenary Chevening Scholarships 685

European Union

ESRC 1+3 Awards and +3 Awards 265

Middle East

International Postgraduate Research Scholarships (IPRS) 692
Shell Centenary Scholarships and Shell Centenary Chevening Scholarships 685

New Zealand

Wingate Scholarships 720

South Africa

Allan Gray Senior Scholarship 527
International Postgraduate Research Scholarships (IPRS) 692
Shell Centenary Scholarships and Shell Centenary Chevening Scholarships 685
Wingate Scholarships 720

United Kingdom

ESRC 1+3 Awards and +3 Awards 265
International Postgraduate Research Scholarships (IPRS) 692
Mr and Mrs David Edward Memorial Award 699
Sheffield Hallam University Studentships 567
UWB Departmental Research Studentships 700
UWB Research Studentships 700
Wingate Scholarships 720

United States of America

ETS Postdoctoral Fellowships 267
ETS Sylvia Taylor Johnson Minority Fellowship Educational Measurement 267
Fulbright Senior Specialists Program 245
International Postgraduate Research Scholarships (IPRS) 692
Winston Churchill Foundation Scholarship 720

West European Countries

ESRC 1+3 Awards and +3 Awards 265
International Postgraduate Research Scholarships (IPRS) 692
Mr and Mrs David Edward Memorial Award 699
Sheffield Hallam University Studentships 567
UWB Departmental Research Studentships 700
UWB Research Studentships 700
Wingate Scholarships 720

ACTUARIAL SCIENCE

Any Country

The AERF/CKER Individual Grants Competition 8
Sir James McNeill Foundation Postgraduate Scholarship 440
University of Essex/Postgraduate Research Studentship 655

African Nations

International Postgraduate Research Scholarships (IPRS) 692

Canada

International Postgraduate Research Scholarships (IPRS) 692

African Nations

Australia

Canada

Caribbean Countries

East European Countries

European Union

Middle East

New Zealand

South Africa

United Kingdom

United States of America

West European Countries

ARTIFICIAL INTELLIGENCE

Any Country

African Nations

Australia

Canada

Caribbean Countries

East European Countries

European Union

Middle East

New Zealand

South Africa

United Kingdom

African Nations

Australia

Canada

United Kingdom

United States of America

West European Countries

PUBLIC HEALTH AND HYGIENE

Any Country

AACR Scholar-in-Training Awards 28
AFSP Distinguished Investigator Awards 51
AFSP Pilot Grants 51
AFSP Postdoctoral Research Fellowships 51
AFSP Standard Research Grants 51
AFSP Young Investigator Award 51
Alzheimer's Society Research Grants 23
AMFAR Basic Research Grant 50
AMFAR Clinical Research Fellowship 50
Barbers Company Clinical Nursing Scholarship 538
BCUC Research Student Bursary (Medicine) 167
CCFF Special Travel Allowances 203
CIHR Fellowships Program 208
Colt Foundation PhD Fellowship 238
CTCRI Community Based Research Grants 216
Elizabeth Washington Award 145
Health Services Research Fellowships 319
HFG Dissertation Fellowship 317
HFG Research Program 317
Hong Kong Research Grant 545
HRB Project Grants-General 320
Meningitis Research Foundation Project Grant 431
Meningitis Trust Research Award 431
PDS Training Fellowships 498
The Pedro Zamora Public Policy Fellowship 12
Population Council Fellowships in Population and Social Sciences 514
Postgraduate Research Bursaries (Epilepsy Action) 274
Roche Research Foundation 531
Sir Allan Sewell Visiting Fellowship 312
Susan G Komen Breast Cancer Foundation Postdoctoral Fellowship in Breast Cancer Research, Public Health or Epidemiology 129
University of Bristol Postgraduate Scholarships 641
WellBeing of Women Project Grants 716

African Nations

ABCCF Student Grant 95
Canadian Window on International Development 364
Ecosystem Approaches to Human Health Awards 364
IARC Postdoctoral Fellowships for Training in Cancer Research 357
International Postgraduate Research Scholarships (IPRS) 692

Australia

Asthma Foundation of New South Wales Biomedical and Medical Postgraduate Research Scholarships 116
Asthma Foundation of New South Wales Medical Research Project Grant 116
Australian Clinical Research Postdoctoral Fellowship 460
Biomedical (Dora Lush) and Public Health Postgraduate Scholarships 460
The Cancer Council NSW Research Project Grants 218
Career Development Awards 461
Howard Florey Centenary Fellowship 461
Neil Hamilton Fairley Fellowships (Overseas Clinical) 461
NHMRC Medical and Dental and Public Health Postgraduate Research Scholarships 461
Public Health Fellowship (Australian) 462
Sidney Sax Fellowship (Overseas Public Health) 462
Training Scholarship for Indigenous Health Research 462
Wingate Scholarships 720

Canada

Alcohol Beverage Medical Research Foundation Research Project Grant 15
Canadian Window on International Development 364
CBS Postdoctoral Fellowship (PDF) 200
CBS Research and Development Program Individual Grants 200
CBS Research and Development Program Major Equipment Grants 200
CTCRI Idea Grants 217
CTCRI Policy Research Grants 217
CTCRI Research Planning Grants 217
CTCRI Research Planning Grants 217
CTCRI Researcher Travel Grant 217
CTCRI Secondary Analysis Grants 217
CTCRI Workshop and Learning Opportunity Grants 217
Ecosystem Approaches to Human Health Awards 364
Frank Knox Memorial Fellowships 115
International Postgraduate Research Scholarships (IPRS) 692
PAHO Grants 497
Wingate Scholarships 720

Caribbean Countries

Canadian Window on International Development 364
Ecosystem Approaches to Human Health Awards 364
IARC Postdoctoral Fellowships for Training in Cancer Research 357
International Postgraduate Research Scholarships (IPRS) 692
PAHO Grants 497

East European Countries

IARC Postdoctoral Fellowships for Training in Cancer Research 357
International Postgraduate Research Scholarships (IPRS) 692

Middle East

ABCCF Student Grant 95
Ecosystem Approaches to Human Health Awards 364
IARC Postdoctoral Fellowships for Training in Cancer Research 357
International Postgraduate Research Scholarships (IPRS) 692

New Zealand

Training Scholarship for Indigenous Health Research 462
Wingate Scholarships 720

South Africa

Canadian Window on International Development 364
Ecosystem Approaches to Human Health Awards 364
IARC Postdoctoral Fellowships for Training in Cancer Research 357
International Postgraduate Research Scholarships (IPRS) 692
Wingate Scholarships 720

United Kingdom

Hospital Savings Association (HSA) Charitable Trust Scholarships 537
Innovation and Creative Practice Award 518
International Postgraduate Research Scholarships (IPRS) 692
Pace Award 145
PDS Training Fellowships 498
WellBeing of Women Entry-Lever Scholarship 716
WellBeing of Women/RCOG Research Training Fellowship 716
Wingate Scholarships 720

United States of America

Alcohol Beverage Medical Research Foundation Research Project Grant 15
The Chris Ebbers Scholarship 70
The Commonwealth Fund/Harvard University Fellowship in Minority Health Policy 238
Fulbright Senior Specialists Program 245
Ian Axford (New Zealand) Fellowships in Public Policy 239
International Postgraduate Research Scholarships (IPRS) 692
IREX Individual Advanced Research Opportunities 374
National Research Service Award for Mental Health and Adjustment in the Life Course 412
NBRC/AMP Gareth B Gish, MS RRT Memorial Postgraduate Recognition Award 28
NIH Research Grants 466
Nurses' Educational Funds Fellowships and Scholarships 488
Packer Fellowships 239
PAHO Grants 497
Parker B Francis Respiratory Research Grant 28
Pfizer Scholars Grants in Public Health 505

PhRMAF Postdoctoral Fellowships in Health Outcomes Research 506
PhRMAF Predoctoral Fellowships in Health Outcomes Research 507
PhRMAF Research Starter Grants in Health Outcomes Research 508
PhRMAF Sabbatical Fellowships in Health Outcomes Research 509
William F Miller, MD Postgraduate Education Recognition Award 28

West European Countries

International Postgraduate Research Scholarships (IPRS) 692
Wingate Scholarships 720

SOCIAL/PREVENTIVE MEDICINE

Any Country

AACR Career Development Awards in Cancer Research 27
AACR Research Fellowships 27
AFSP Distinguished Investigator Awards 51
AFSP Pilot Grants 51
AFSP Postdoctoral Research Fellowships 51
AFSP Standard Research Grants 51
AFSP Young Investigator Award 51
Alzheimer's Society Research Grants 23
AMFAR Basic Research Grant 50
AMFAR Clinical Research Fellowship 50
ASBAH Research Grant 108
BackCare Research Grants 130
Barbers Company Clinical Nursing Scholarship 538
BCUC Research Student Bursary (Medicine) 167
Breast Cancer Campaign Small Pilot Grants 141
CCFF Fellowships 202
CCFF Special Travel Allowances 203
CCFF Studentships 203
CDU Senior Research Fellowship 230
CDU Three Year Postdoctoral Fellowship 230
CRPF Research Grant 235
Distinguished Research Award 96
Earthwatch Field Research Grants 265
GlaxoSmithKline Collaborative Research Projects 309
GlaxoSmithkline Services to Academia 309
Hastings Center International Visiting Scholars Program 318
HDA Research Project Grants 333
Heart Research UK Basic Science Medical Research Grant 320
Heart Research UK Clinical Medical Research Grant 321
Heart Research UK Emerging Technologies Grant 321
The IASO New Investigator Award 359
Meningitis Research Foundation Project Grant 431
PDS Research Project Grant 498
PDS Training Fellowships 498
Queen Mary Research Studentships 518
Savoy Foundation Postdoctoral and Clinical Research Fellowships 562
Savoy Foundation Research Grants 562
Savoy Foundation Studentships 563
Sir Halley Stewart Trust Grants 571
UICC Translational Cancer Research Fellowships (TCRF) 378
University of Bristol Postgraduate Scholarships 641
WellBeing of Women Project Grants 716

African Nations

Canadian Window on International Development 364
Hastings Center International Visiting Scholars Program 318
IARC Postdoctoral Fellowships for Training in Cancer Research 357
International Postgraduate Research Scholarships (IPRS) 692
UICC Trish Greene International Oncology Nursing Fellowships 378

Australia

Ann J Woolcock Research Fellowship 115
Asthma Foundation of New South Wales Biomedical and Medical Postgraduate Research Scholarships 116
Asthma Foundation of New South Wales Medical Research Project Grant 116
Hastings Center International Visiting Scholars Program 318
National Heart Foundation of Australia Overseas Research Fellowships 462

Canada

Canadian Window on International Development 364
CCFF Senior Scientist Research Training Award 202
International Postgraduate Research Scholarships (IPRS) 692

Caribbean Countries

Canadian Window on International Development 364
Hastings Center International Visiting Scholars Program 318
IARC Postdoctoral Fellowships for Training in Cancer Research 357
International Postgraduate Research Scholarships (IPRS) 692
UICC Trish Greene International Oncology Nursing Fellowships 378

East European Countries

Hastings Center International Visiting Scholars Program 318
IARC Postdoctoral Fellowships for Training in Cancer Research 357
International Postgraduate Research Scholarships (IPRS) 692
UICC Trish Greene International Oncology Nursing Fellowships 378

Middle East

Hastings Center International Visiting Scholars Program 318
IARC Postdoctoral Fellowships for Training in Cancer Research 357
International Postgraduate Research Scholarships (IPRS) 692
UICC Trish Greene International Oncology Nursing Fellowships 378

New Zealand

Hastings Center International Visiting Scholars Program 318
National Heart Foundation of New Zealand Fellowships 463
National Heart Foundation of New Zealand Limited Budget Grants 464
National Heart Foundation of New Zealand Maori Cardiovascular Research Fellowship 464
National Heart Foundation of New Zealand Project Grants 464
National Heart Foundation of New Zealand Travel Grants 464

South Africa

Canadian Window on International Development 364
Hastings Center International Visiting Scholars Program 318
IARC Postdoctoral Fellowships for Training in Cancer Research 357
International Postgraduate Research Scholarships (IPRS) 692
UICC Trish Greene International Oncology Nursing Fellowships 378

United Kingdom

Breast Cancer Campaign Project Grants 140
Fight for Sight, British Eye Research Foundation Grants for Research and Equipment (Ophthalmology) 147
Hastings Center International Visiting Scholars Program 318
Helen Tomkinson Research Grant 157
International Postgraduate Research Scholarships (IPRS) 692
NKRF Special Project Grants 467
PDS Research Project Grant 498
PDS Training Fellowships 498
Postgraduate Student Allowance Scheme (PSAS) (Queen Margaret) 517
Samuel Strutt Research Grant 158
T P Gunton Research Grant 158
WellBeing of Women Entry-Lever Scholarship 716
WellBeing of Women/RCOG Research Training Fellowship 716

United States of America

Damon Runyon Cancer Research Foundation Fellowship Award 253
Fulbright Senior Specialists Program 245
Ian Axford (New Zealand) Fellowships in Public Policy 239
International Postgraduate Research Scholarships (IPRS) 692
McMillan Doctoral Scholarships 290
National Research Service Award for Mental Health and Adjustment in the Life Course 412
New Investigator Fellowships Training Initiative (NIFTI) 290

Nurses' Educational Funds Fellowships and Scholarships 488
Promotion of Doctoral Studies (PODS) 291
Research Grants (FPT) 291

West European Countries

Hastings Center International Visiting Scholars Program 318
International Postgraduate Research Scholarships (IPRS) 692

DIETETICS

Any Country

Barbers Company Clinical Nursing Scholarship 538
BCUC Research Student Bursary (Medicine) 167
Elizabeth Washington Award 145
Heart Research UK Basic Science Medical Research Grant 320
Heart Research UK Clinical Medical Research Grant 321
Heart Research UK Emerging Technologies Grant 321
PDS Training Fellowships 498
Rose Simmonds Award 145
Royal Irish Academy Award in Nutritional Sciences 551

New Zealand

National Heart Foundation of New Zealand Fellowships 463
National Heart Foundation of New Zealand Limited Budget Grants 464
National Heart Foundation of New Zealand Maori Cardiovascular Research Fellowship 464
National Heart Foundation of New Zealand Project Grants 464
National Heart Foundation of New Zealand Travel Grants 464

United Kingdom

Pace Award 145
PDS Training Fellowships 498
PWSA UK Research Grants 514

United States of America

Nurses' Educational Funds Fellowships and Scholarships 488

SPORTS MEDICINE

Any Country

Barbers Company Clinical Nursing Scholarship 538
BCUC Research Student Bursary (Medicine) 167
Colt Foundation PhD Fellowship 238
NSCA Challenge Scholarship 472
NSCA Graduate Research Grant 472
OREF Career Development Award 495
OREF Prospective Clinical Research 495
OREF Research Grants 495
OREF Resident Research Award 495
SOM Research Grant 592
University of Bristol Postgraduate Scholarships 641

African Nations

International Postgraduate Research Scholarships (IPRS) 692

Canada

CTCRI Idea Grants 217
CTCRI Research Planning Grants 217
CTCRI Researcher Travel Grant 217
International Postgraduate Research Scholarships (IPRS) 692
OREF Clinical Research Award 495
OREF Fellowship in Health Services Research 495

Caribbean Countries

International Postgraduate Research Scholarships (IPRS) 692

East European Countries

International Postgraduate Research Scholarships (IPRS) 692

Middle East

International Postgraduate Research Scholarships (IPRS) 692

South Africa

International Postgraduate Research Scholarships (IPRS) 692

United Kingdom

Duke of Edinburgh Prize for Sports Medicine 349
International Postgraduate Research Scholarships (IPRS) 692
Sir Robert Atkins Award 349

United States of America

International Postgraduate Research Scholarships (IPRS) 692
McMillan Doctoral Scholarships 290
New Investigator Fellowships Training Initiative (NIFTI) 290
Nurses' Educational Funds Fellowships and Scholarships 488
OREF Clinical Research Award 495
OREF Fellowship in Health Services Research 495
Promotion of Doctoral Studies (PODS) 291
Research Grants (FPT) 291

West European Countries

International Postgraduate Research Scholarships (IPRS) 692

HEALTH ADMINISTRATION

Any Country

AAOHN Professional Development Scholarship 32
AFSP Distinguished Investigator Awards 51
AFSP Pilot Grants 51
AFSP Postdoctoral Research Fellowships 51
AFSP Standard Research Grants 51
AFSP Young Investigator Award 51
Barbers Company Clinical Nursing Scholarship 538
Breast Cancer Campaign Small Pilot Grants 141
CIHR Fellowships Program 208
Hastings Center International Visiting Scholars Program 318
Health Services Research Fellowships 319
HRB Project Grants-General 320
La Trobe University Postgraduate Scholarship 403
PDS Training Fellowships 498
The Pedro Zamora Public Policy Fellowship 12
Population Council Fellowships in Population and Social Sciences 514
Press Ganey Best Practices Research Program 515
Roche Research Foundation 531
Savoy Foundation Postdoctoral and Clinical Research Fellowships 562
Savoy Foundation Research Grants 562
Savoy Foundation Studentships 563
Sir Allan Sewell Visiting Fellowship 312
University of Bristol Postgraduate Scholarships 641

African Nations

ABCCF Student Grant 95
Hastings Center International Visiting Scholars Program 318
International Postgraduate Research Scholarships (IPRS) 692

Australia

The Cancer Council NSW Research Project Grants 218
Fulbright Awards 125
Harkness Fellowships in Healthcare Policy 238
Hastings Center International Visiting Scholars Program 318

Canada

CTCRI Idea Grants 217
CTCRI Research Planning Grants 217
CTCRI Researcher Travel Grant 217
International Postgraduate Research Scholarships (IPRS) 692

PAHO Grants 497
Public Safety and Emergency Preparedness Canada Research Fellowship in Honour of Stuart Nesbitt White 115

Caribbean Countries

Hastings Center International Visiting Scholars Program 318
International Postgraduate Research Scholarships (IPRS) 692
PAHO Grants 497

East European Countries

Hastings Center International Visiting Scholars Program 318
International Postgraduate Research Scholarships (IPRS) 692

Middle East

ABCCF Student Grant 95
Hastings Center International Visiting Scholars Program 318
International Postgraduate Research Scholarships (IPRS) 692

New Zealand

Harkness Fellowships in Healthcare Policy 238
Hastings Center International Visiting Scholars Program 318

South Africa

Hastings Center International Visiting Scholars Program 318
International Postgraduate Research Scholarships (IPRS) 692

United Kingdom

Breast Cancer Campaign Project Grants 140
Harkness Fellowships in Healthcare Policy 238
Hastings Center International Visiting Scholars Program 318
Hospital Savings Association (HSA) Charitable Trust Scholarships 537
International Postgraduate Research Scholarships (IPRS) 692
PDS Training Fellowships 498

United States of America

Congress Bundestag Youth Exchange for Young Professionals 224
Ian Axford (New Zealand) Fellowships in Public Policy 239
International Postgraduate Research Scholarships (IPRS) 692
Nurses' Educational Funds Fellowships and Scholarships 488
Packer Fellowships 239
PAHO Grants 497
Pfizer Fellowships in Health Literary Clear Health Communication 504
Pfizer Scholars Grants in Public Health 505
Pfizer Visiting Professorships in Clear Health Literacy/Clear Health Communication 505
PhRMAF Postdoctoral Fellowships in Health Outcomes Research 506
PhRMAF Sabbatical Fellowships in Health Outcomes Research 509

West European Countries

Hastings Center International Visiting Scholars Program 318
International Postgraduate Research Scholarships (IPRS) 692

MEDICINE AND SURGERY

Any Country

AACR Scholar-in-Training Awards 28
The Airey Neave Trust Scholarship 12
BackCare Research Grants 130
Barbers Company Clinical Nursing Scholarship 538
BMRP for Inflammatory Bowel Disease Grants 164
British Journal of Surgery Research Bursaries 155
CAMS Scholarship 233
Career Development Program 409
CCFF Scholarships 202
CCFF Visiting Scientist Awards 203
Clinical Scholar Research Award 358
Collaborative Career Development Fellowship in Stem Cell Research 425
Cooley's Anemia Foundation Research Fellowship 242
Daland Fellowships in Clinical Investigation 72
Dr Hadwen Trust for Humane Research Grants 261
Dr Hadwen Trust Research Assistant or Technician 262
Dr Hadwen Trust Research Fellowship 262
ECTS Career Establishment Award 276
ECTS Exchange Scholarship Grants 277
Ellison Medical Foundation/AFAR Senior Postdoctoral Research Program 48
FRAXA Grants and Fellowships 293
Frontiers in Anesthesia Research Award 358
HRB Equipment Grants 320
Humanitarian Trust Awards 332
Hypertension Trust Studentship 334
ISH Postdoctoral Award 290
Islamic Organization for Medical Sciences Prize 402
John of Arderne Medal 558
Leslie Bernstein Grant 24
Linacre College EPA Cephalosporin Junior Research Fellowships 678
Lister Institute Research Prizes 413
Lord Dowding Fund for Humane Research 415
Meningitis Research Foundation Project Grant 431
Meningitis Trust Research Award 431
NORD Clinical Research Grants 470
NORD/Rosoe Brady Lysosomal Storage Diseases Fellowships 470
Norman Tanner Medal and Prize (1st Prize) Glaxo Travelling Fellowship (2nd Prize) 558
OREF Career Development Award 495
OREF Prospective Clinical Research 495
OREF Research Grants 495
OREF Resident Research Award 495
PDS Research Project Grant 498
Postgraduate Research Bursaries (Epilepsy Action) 274
Queen Mary Research Studentships 518
RESTRACOMP Research Fellowship 330
Roche Research Foundation 531
RSM Medical Insurance Agency Prize 559
Savoy Foundation Postdoctoral and Clinical Research Fellowships 562
Savoy Foundation Research Grants 562
Savoy Foundation Studentships 563
Serono Foundation for the Advancement of Medical Science Fellowships in Biomedicine 566
Sigma Theta Tau International/Association of Perioperative Registered Nurses Foundation Grant 569
Sir Richard Stapley Educational Trust Grants 571
Teaching Recognition Award 358
Translational Research Program 409
University of Bristol Postgraduate Scholarships 641
University of Southampton Postgraduate Studentships 692
WellBeing of Women Project Grants 716
Wellcome Trust Grants 717
William J Cunliffe Scientific Awards 719
World Universities Network (WUN) Global Exchange Programme 693

African Nations

TWAS Grants for Scientific Meetings in Developing Countries 611
TWAS Prizes 611
TWAS Research Grants 611
TWAS UNESCO Associateship Scheme 612

Australia

Asthma Foundation of New South Wales Biomedical and Medical Postgraduate Research Scholarships 116
Asthma Foundation of New South Wales Medical Research Project Grant 116
Australian Clinical Research Postdoctoral Fellowship 460
Biomedical (Dora Lush) and Public Health Postgraduate Scholarships 460
C J Martin Fellowships (Overseas Biomedical) 460
Career Development Awards 461
Foundation for High Blood Pressure Research Postdoctoral Fellowship 290
Howard Florey Centenary Fellowship 461

Canada

Caribbean Countries

European Union

Middle East

New Zealand

South Africa

United Kingdom

United States of America

West European Countries

ANAESTHESIOLOGY

Any Country

United Kingdom

United States of America

CARDIOLOGY

Any Country

Australia

Canada

East European Countries

European Union

New Zealand

United Kingdom

United States of America

West European Countries

DERMATOLOGY

Any Country

Australia

United Kingdom

United States of America

ENDOCRINOLOGY

Any Country

Australia

Canada

United Kingdom

United States of America

EPIDEMIOLOGY

Any Country

African Nations

Australia

Canada

Caribbean Countries

East European Countries

Middle East

New Zealand

South Africa

United Kingdom

United States of America

West European Countries

GASTROENTEROLOGY

Any Country

AGA Student Research Fellowship Awards 290
Barbers Company Clinical Nursing Scholarship 538
BMRP for Inflammatory Bowel Disease Grants 164
CGD Research Trust Grants 236
Crohn's and Colitis Foundation Career Development Award 250
Crohn's and Colitis Foundation Research Fellowship Awards 250
Crohn's and Colitis Foundation Senior Research Award 251
Crohn's and Colitis Foundation Student Research Fellowship Awards 251
GlaxoSmithKline Collaborative Research Projects 309
GlaxoSmithkline Services to Academia 309
Lister Institute Research Prizes 413
NORD Clinical Research Grants 470
Queen Mary Research Studentships 518
Sir Halley Stewart Trust Grants 571
University of Bristol Postgraduate Scholarships 641

Australia

The Cancer Council NSW Research Project Grants 218

Canada

Alcohol Beverage Medical Research Foundation Research Project Grant 15

United Kingdom

CORE Fellowships and Grants 242

United States of America

AFAR Research Grants 47
AGA Astra Zeneca Fellowship/Faculty Transition Awards 288
Alcohol Beverage Medical Research Foundation Research Project Grant 15
Nurses' Educational Funds Fellowships and Scholarships 488
Paul Beeson Career Development Award 49

GERIATRICS

Any Country

AFSP Distinguished Investigator Awards 51
AFSP Pilot Grants 51
AFSP Postdoctoral Research Fellowships 51
AFSP Standard Research Grants 51
AFSP Young Investigator Award 51
Alzheimer's Research Trust Clinical Research Training Fellowship 21
Alzheimer's Research Trust Network Co-operation Grant 22
Alzheimer's Research Trust Pilot Project Grant 22
Alzheimer's Research Trust Research Fellowships 22
Alzheimer's Research Trust Research Major Grants 22
Alzheimer's Society Research Grants 23
Alzheimer's Research Trust Emergency Support Grant 23
Barbers Company Clinical Nursing Scholarship 538
Ellison Medical foundation/AFAR senior postdoctoral fellows research program. 48
Institute for the Study of Aging Grants Program 344
The Julie Martin Mid-Career Award in Aging Research 48
Lister Institute Research Prizes 413
NORD Clinical Research Grants 470
PDS Research Project Grant 498
PDS Training Fellowships 498
The Pfizer/AGS Foundation Junior Faculty Scholars Program 505
Sir Halley Stewart Trust Grants 571
Stroke Association Research Project Grants 603
University of Bristol Postgraduate Scholarships 641
Wilson-Fulton and Robertson Awards in Aging Research, Cecille Gould Memorial Fund Award in Cancer Research, Richard Shepherd Fellowship 49

Canada

Alcohol Beverage Medical Research Foundation Research Project Grant 15

United Kingdom

PDS Research Project Grant 498
PDS Training Fellowships 498
REMEDI Research Grants 523

United States of America

ACR/REF/Association of Subspecialty Professors Junior Career Development Award in Geriatric Medicine 42
AFAR Research Grants 47
Alcohol Beverage Medical Research Foundation Research Project Grant 15
Ian Axford (New Zealand) Fellowships in Public Policy 239
NIH Research Grants 466
Nurses' Educational Funds Fellowships and Scholarships 488
Paul Beeson Career Development Award 49
The Pfizer/AGS Foundation Junior Faculty Scholars Program 505

GYNAECOLOGY AND OBSTETRICS

Any Country

BackCare Research Grants 130
Barbers Company Clinical Nursing Scholarship 538
Lalor Foundation Postdoctoral Fellowships 404
Lister Institute Research Prizes 413
Meningitis Research Foundation Project Grant 431
MRC Royal College of Obstetricians and Gynaecologists (RCOG) Training Fellowship 427
NORD Clinical Research Grants 470
Queen Mary Research Studentships 518
RCOG Bernhard Baron Travelling Scholarships 540
RCOG Eden Travelling Fellowship 540
RCOG Edgar Gentilli Prize 540
RCOG Ethicon Travel Awards 541
RCOG Green-Armytage and Spackman Travelling Scholarship 541
RCOG Harold Malkin Prize 541
RCOG Overseas Fund 541
Serono Foundation for the Advancement of Medical Science Fellowships in Biomedicine 566
University of Bristol Postgraduate Scholarships 641
University of Dundee Research Awards 648
WellBeing of Women Project Grants 716

Australia

The Cancer Council NSW Research Project Grants 218

Canada

ACOG/3M Pharmaceuticals Research Awards in Human Papillomavirus 37
ACOG/Berlex Laboratories Research Award in PMS/PMDD 38
ACOG/Berlex, Inc. Research Award in Contraception 38
ACOG/Kenneth Gottesfeld-Charles Hohler Memorial Foundation Research Award in Ultrasound 38
ACOG/Ortho Women's Health Academic Training Fellowships in Obstetrics and Gynaecology 39
ACOG/Solvay Pharmaceuticals Research Award in Menopause 39
Warren H Pearse/Wyeth Pharmaceuticals Women's Health Policy Research Award 39

United Kingdom

American Gynecological Club / Gynaecological Visiting Society Fellowship 540
Endometriosis Millennium Fund Award 540
Nichols Fellowship 558
RCOG Research Prize 541
RCOG William Blair-Bell Memorial Lectureships in Obstetrics and Gynaecology 541
RCOG/Wyeth Historical Lecture 541
REMEDI Research Grants 523
Richard Johanson Obstetric Prize 541

Tim Chard Case History Prize 541
WellBeing of Women/RCOG Research Training Fellowship 716

United States of America

ACOG/3M Pharmaceuticals Research Awards in Human Papillomavirus 37
ACOG/Berlex Laboratories Research Award in PMS/PMDD 38
ACOG/Berlex, Inc. Research Award in Contraception 38
ACOG/Kenneth Gottesfeld-Charles Hohler Memorial Foundation Research Award in Ultrasound 38
ACOG/Ortho Women's Health Academic Training Fellowships in Obstetrics and Gynaecology 39
ACOG/Solvay Pharmaceuticals Research Award in Menopause 39
AFAR Research Grants 47
American Gynecological Club / Gynaecological Visiting Society Fellowship 540
Nurses' Educational Funds Fellowships and Scholarships 488
Paul Beeson Career Development Award 49
Warren H Pearse/Wyeth Pharmaceuticals Women's Health Policy Research Award 39

HAEMATOLOGY

Any Country

Barbers Company Clinical Nursing Scholarship 538
Career Development Program 409
CBS Graduate Fellowship Program 200
Cooley's Anemia Foundation Research Fellowship 242
Friends of José Carreras International Leukemia Foundation E D Thomas Postdoctoral Fellowship 295
Gordon Piller Studentships 408
ICR Studentships 345
Lady Tata Memorial Trust Scholarships 403
Leukaemia Research Fund Clinical Research Training Fellowships 408
Leukaemia Research Fund Grant Programme 408
Lister Institute Research Prizes 413
Meningitis Research Foundation Project Grant 431
NORD Clinical Research Grants 470
Queen Mary Research Studentships 518
Translational Research Program 409
University of Bristol Postgraduate Scholarships 641
University of Dundee Research Awards 648

Australia

The Cancer Council NSW Research Project Grants 218

Canada

Alcohol Beverage Medical Research Foundation Research Project Grant 15
American Society of Hematology Minority Medical Student Award Program 85
CBS Postdoctoral Fellowship (PDF) 200
CBS Research and Development Program Individual Grants 200
CBS Research and Development Program Major Equipment Grants 200
CBS Research Fellowship In Haemostasis (RFH) 201
CBS Small Projects Fund 201
LLSC Awards 409

United Kingdom

REMEDI Research Grants 523

United States of America

AFAR Research Grants 47
Alcohol Beverage Medical Research Foundation Research Project Grant 15
American Society of Hematology Minority Medical Student Award Program 85
Nurses' Educational Funds Fellowships and Scholarships 488
Paul Beeson Career Development Award 49

HEPATHOLOGY

Any Country

AGA Elsevier Research Initiative Award 288
AGA June and Donald O Castell, MD, Esophageal Clinical Research Award 289
AGA Miles and Shirley Fiterman Foundation Basic Research Awards 289
AGA Miles and Shirley Fiterman Foundation Clinical Research in Gastroenterology or Hepatology/Nutrition Awards 289
AGA R Robert and Sally D Funderburg Research Scholar Award in Gastric Biology Related to Cancer 289
AGA Research Scholar Awards 289
AGA Student Research Fellowship Awards 290
Barbers Company Clinical Nursing Scholarship 538
Cooley's Anemia Foundation Research Fellowship 242
Lister Institute Research Prizes 413
NORD Clinical Research Grants 470

Canada

Alcohol Beverage Medical Research Foundation Research Project Grant 15
Canadian Liver Foundation Graduate Studentships 210
Canadian Liver Foundation Operating Grant 210

United Kingdom

CORE Fellowships and Grants 242

United States of America

AFAR Research Grants 47
AGA Astra Zeneca Fellowship/Faculty Transition Awards 288
Alcohol Beverage Medical Research Foundation Research Project Grant 15
Nurses' Educational Funds Fellowships and Scholarships 488
Paul Beeson Career Development Award 49

NEPHROLOGY

Any Country

Barbers Company Clinical Nursing Scholarship 538
ISN Travel Grants 376
Lister Institute Research Prizes 413
LSA Medical Research Grant 417
NORD Clinical Research Grants 470

African Nations

ISN Fellowship Awards 375

Australia

Australian Kidney Foundation Medical Research Grants and Scholarships 122
Australian Kidney Foundation Seeding and Equipment Grants 123
ISN Visiting Scholars Program 376

Canada

ASN-ASP Junior Development Grant in Geriatric Nephrology 87
ISN Visiting Scholars Program 376

Caribbean Countries

ISN Fellowship Awards 375

East European Countries

ISN Fellowship Awards 375
ISN Visiting Scholars Program 376

Middle East

ISN Fellowship Awards 375
ISN Visiting Scholars Program 376

New Zealand

South Africa

United Kingdom

United States of America

West European Countries

NEUROLOGY

Any Country

African Nations

Australia

Canada

Caribbean Countries

East European Countries

Middle East

New Zealand

South Africa

United Kingdom

United States of America

West European Countries

ONCOLOGY

Any Country

African Nations

Australia

Canada

Caribbean Countries

East European Countries

Middle East

South Africa

United Kingdom

United States of America

AFAR Research Grants 47
AHNS Career Development Award 52
AHNS Pilot Research Grant 52
AHNS Surgeon Scientist Career Development Award 52
AHNS The Young Investigator Award 52
Alcohol Beverage Medical Research Foundation Research Project Grant 15
BTS Research Grant 140
Damon Runyon Cancer Research Foundation Fellowship Award 253
Damon Runyon Scholar Award 253
The Damon Runyon-Lilly Clinical Investigator Award 253
Nurses' Educational Funds Fellowships and Scholarships 488
Paul Beeson Career Development Award 49
Pfizer Atorvastatin Research Awards Program 504
Pfizer Visiting Professorships in Oncology 505

OPHTHALMOLOGY

Any Country

AHAF Macular Degeneration Research 53
AHAF National Glaucoma Research 53
Barbers Company Clinical Nursing Scholarship 538
Lister Institute Research Prizes 413
LSA Medical Research Grant 417
MRC Royal College of Surgeons of Edinburgh Training Fellowship 427
NORD Clinical Research Grants 470
Ophthalmology Travelling Fellowship 558
Pilot Project Grants Program 308
The Royal College of Ophthalmologists Clinical Research Fellowships – The Keeler Scholarship 542
The Royal College of Ophthalmologists Travel Awards – Ethicon Foundation Fund 542
Royal College of Ophthalmologists Travel Awards – The Dorey Bequest 542
University of Bristol Postgraduate Scholarships 641

Canada

Alcohol Beverage Medical Research Foundation Research Project Grant 15
E A Baker Fellowship/Grant 211

United Kingdom

Albert McMaster Research Grant 156
Fight for Sight, British Eye Research Foundation Grants for Research and Equipment (Ophthalmology) 147
Guide Dogs Ophthalmic Research Grant 313
John William Clark Research Grant 158
The Royal College of Ophthalmologists Clinical Research Fellowships – The Pfizer Ophthalmic Fellowship 542
The Royal College of Ophthalmologists Travel Awards – Sir William Lister Award 542

United States of America

AFAR Research Grants 47
Alcohol Beverage Medical Research Foundation Research Project Grant 15
Nurses' Educational Funds Fellowships and Scholarships 488
Paul Beeson Career Development Award 49

OTORHINOLARYNGOLOGY

Any Country

American Tinnitus Association Scientific Research Grants 89
Barbers Company Clinical Nursing Scholarship 538
Karl Storz Travelling Scholarship 558
Lister Institute Research Prizes 413
NORD Clinical Research Grants 470

Canada

American Otological Society Research Grants 71
American Otological Society Research Training Fellowships 71

United Kingdom

Norman Gamble Fund and Research Prize 558

United States of America

AFAR Research Grants 47
American Otological Society Research Grants 71
American Otological Society Research Training Fellowships 71
Nurses' Educational Funds Fellowships and Scholarships 488
Paul Beeson Career Development Award 49

PARASITOLOGY

Any Country

Barbers Company Clinical Nursing Scholarship 538
Lister Institute Research Prizes 413
NORD Clinical Research Grants 470
Sir Halley Stewart Trust Grants 571

African Nations

AHRI African Fellowship 98
International Postgraduate Research Scholarships (IPRS) 692

Canada

International Postgraduate Research Scholarships (IPRS) 692

Caribbean Countries

International Postgraduate Research Scholarships (IPRS) 692

East European Countries

FEMS Fellowship 284
International Postgraduate Research Scholarships (IPRS) 692
Synthesys Visiting Fellowship 477

Middle East

International Postgraduate Research Scholarships (IPRS) 692

South Africa

International Postgraduate Research Scholarships (IPRS) 692

United Kingdom

FEMS Fellowship 284
International Postgraduate Research Scholarships (IPRS) 692

United States of America

International Postgraduate Research Scholarships (IPRS) 692
Nurses' Educational Funds Fellowships and Scholarships 488
Paul Beeson Career Development Award 49

West European Countries

FEMS Fellowship 284
International Postgraduate Research Scholarships (IPRS) 692
Karl-Enigk Scholarships 564
Synthesys Visiting Fellowship 477

PATHOLOGY

Any Country

AHAF National Heart Foundation 53
Barbers Company Clinical Nursing Scholarship 538
BMRP for Inflammatory Bowel Disease Grants 164
Career Development Program 409
CCFF Fellowships 202
CCFF Special Travel Allowances 203

African Nations

Australia

Canada

Caribbean Countries

East European Countries

Middle East

South Africa

United Kingdom

United States of America

West European Countries

PAEDIATRICS

Any Country

Australia

Canada

United Kingdom

United States of America

PLASTIC SURGERY

Any Country

Canada

United States of America

Leslie Bernstein Investigator Development Grant 24
Leslie Bernstein Resident Research Grants 25
Nurses' Educational Funds Fellowships and Scholarships 488
Paul Beeson Career Development Award 49

PNEUMOLOGY

Any Country

Barbers Company Clinical Nursing Scholarship 538
Fungal Research Trust Travel Grants 298
NORD Clinical Research Grants 470

Canada

Alcohol Beverage Medical Research Foundation Research Project Grant 15
CTS Fellowships 216
Parker B Francis Fellowship Program 498

United Kingdom

British Lung Foundation Project Grants 156
H C Roscoe Research Grant 157
The James Trust Research Grant 157

United States of America

Alcohol Beverage Medical Research Foundation Research Project Grant 15
Nurses' Educational Funds Fellowships and Scholarships 488
Parker B Francis Fellowship Program 498
Paul Beeson Career Development Award 49

PSYCHIATRY AND MENTAL HEALTH

Any Country

AFSP Distinguished Investigator Awards 51
AFSP Pilot Grants 51
AFSP Postdoctoral Research Fellowships 51
AFSP Standard Research Grants 51
AFSP Young Investigator Award 51
Alzheimer's Research Trust Graduate Student Programme 22
Alzheimer's Society Research Grants 23
BackCare Research Grants 130
Barbers Company Clinical Nursing Scholarship 538
Distinguished Research Award 96
FRAXA Grants and Fellowships 293
GlaxoSmithKline Collaborative Research Projects 309
GlaxoSmithkline Services to Academia 309
HDA Research Project Grants 333
HDA Studentship 333
Institute for the Study of Aging Grants Program 344
LSA Medical Research Grant 417
Meningitis Research Foundation Project Grant 431
NARSAD Distinguished Investigator Awards 449
NARSAD Independent Investigator Awards 449
NARSAD Young Investigator Awards 449
NORD Clinical Research Grants 470
PDS Research Project Grant 498
PDS Training Fellowships 498
Postgraduate Research Bursaries (Epilepsy Action) 274
Queen Mary Research Studentships 518
Savoy Foundation Postdoctoral and Clinical Research Fellowships 562
Savoy Foundation Research Grants 562
Savoy Foundation Studentships 563
Stanley Medical Research Institute Postdoctoral Research Fellowship Program 597
Stanley Medical Research Institute Treatment Trial Grants Program 598
TSA Research Grants 614
University of Bristol Postgraduate Scholarships 641

African Nations

International Postgraduate Research Scholarships (IPRS) 692

Australia

The Cancer Council NSW Research Project Grants 218

Canada

Alcohol Beverage Medical Research Foundation Research Project Grant 15
CTCRI Research Planning Grants 217
Heritage Health Research Career Renewal Awards 15
International Postgraduate Research Scholarships (IPRS) 692

Caribbean Countries

International Postgraduate Research Scholarships (IPRS) 692

East European Countries

International Postgraduate Research Scholarships (IPRS) 692

Middle East

International Postgraduate Research Scholarships (IPRS) 692

South Africa

International Postgraduate Research Scholarships (IPRS) 692

United Kingdom

International Postgraduate Research Scholarships (IPRS) 692
Margaret Temple Research Grant 158
PDS Research Project Grant 498
PDS Training Fellowships 498
PWSA UK Research Grants 514
REMEDI Research Grants 523
RSM Mental Health Foundation Essay Prize 559
Vitiligo Society Grants 711

United States of America

AFAR Research Grants 47
Alcohol Beverage Medical Research Foundation Research Project Grant 15
International Postgraduate Research Scholarships (IPRS) 692
Jeanne Spurlock Minority Medical Student Clinical Fellowship in Child and Adolescent Psychiatry 23
Jeanne Spurlock Research Fellowship in Drug Abuse and Addiction for Minority Medical Students 23
Nurses' Educational Funds Fellowships and Scholarships 488
Paul Beeson Career Development Award 49
Pfizer Travel Grants 24
Presidential Scholar Award 24

West European Countries

International Postgraduate Research Scholarships (IPRS) 692

RHEUMATOLOGY

Any Country

ANRF Research Grants 98
Arthritis Society Research Fellowships 101
BackCare Research Grants 130
Barbers Company Clinical Nursing Scholarship 538
ECTS Career Establishment Award 276
ECTS Exchange Scholarship Grants 277
Lister Institute Research Prizes 413
Metro A Ogryzlo International Fellowship 101
NORD Clinical Research Grants 470
OREF Career Development Award 495
OREF Prospective Clinical Research 495

OREF Research Grants 495
OREF Resident Research Award 495
Queen Mary Research Studentships 518
Serono Foundation for the Advancement of Medical Science Fellowships in Biomedicine 566
University of Bristol Postgraduate Scholarships 641
Wilson-Fulton and Robertson Awards in Aging Research, Cecille Gould Memorial Fund Award in Cancer Research, Richard Shepherd Fellowship 49

African Nations

Metro A Ogryzlo International Fellowship 101

Australia

CDRF Project Grants 235
CDRF Research Fellowship 236
Metro A Ogryzlo International Fellowship 101

Canada

Alcohol Beverage Medical Research Foundation Research Project Grant 15
Arthritis Society Industry Program 101
Arthritis Society Research Fellowships 101
Geoff Carr Lupus Fellowship 101
OREF Clinical Research Award 495
OREF Fellowship in Health Services Research 495

Caribbean Countries

Metro A Ogryzlo International Fellowship 101

East European Countries

ACR/REF Physician Scientist Development Award 41
CDRF Project Grants 235
CDRF Research Fellowship 236
Metro A Ogryzlo International Fellowship 101

Middle East

Metro A Ogryzlo International Fellowship 101

New Zealand

Metro A Ogryzlo International Fellowship 101

South Africa

Metro A Ogryzlo International Fellowship 101

United Kingdom

ARC Allied Health Professional Training Fellowship 98
ARC Allied Health Professionals Educational Travel/Training Bursaries 99
ARC Barbara Ansell Fellowships in Paediatric Rheumatology 99
ARC Clinician Scientist Fellowship 99
ARC Educational Project Grants 99
ARC Educational Research Fellowships 99
ARC Non-Clinical Career Development Fellowships 100
ARC Orthopaedic Clinical Research Fellowship 100
ARC PhD Studentships 100
ARC Programme Grants 100
ARC Project Grants 100
ARC Senior Research Fellowships 100
ARC Travelling Fellowships 101
CDRF Project Grants 235
CDRF Research Fellowship 236
Doris Hillier Research Grant 157
REMEDI Research Grants 523

United States of America

ACF/REF/Paula De Merieu Rheumatology Fellowship Award 40
ACR/REF Clinician Scholars Educator Award 40
ACR/REF Health Professional New Investigator Award 41
ACR/REF Rheumatology Fellowship Training Award 41
ACR/REF/Amgen Pediatric Rheumatology Research Award 41
ACR/REF/Arthritis Investigator Award 41
ACR/REF/Association of Subspecialty Professors Junior Career Development Award in Geriatric Medicine 42
ACR/REF/Clinical Investigator Fellowship Award 42
ACR/REF/Resident Research Preceptorship 42
AFAR Research Grants 47
Alcohol Beverage Medical Research Foundation Research Project Grant 15
CDRF Project Grants 235
CDRF Research Fellowship 236
Lawren H Daltroy Fellowship in Patient-Clinician Communication 43
Nurses' Educational Funds Fellowships and Scholarships 488
OREF Clinical Research Award 495
OREF Fellowship in Health Services Research 495
Paul Beeson Career Development Award 49

West European Countries

CDRF Project Grants 235
CDRF Research Fellowship 236
Metro A Ogryzlo International Fellowship 101

UROLOGY

Any Country

ASBAH Research Grant 108
Barbers Company Clinical Nursing Scholarship 538
CRPF Research Grant 235
ICR Studentships 345
Lalor Foundation Postdoctoral Fellowships 404
Lister Institute Research Prizes 413
NORD Clinical Research Grants 470
Prostate Research Campaign UK Research Grants 516
Queen Mary Research Studentships 518
Royal Society of Medicine Travelling Fellowship 559
WellBeing of Women Project Grants 716

Australia

Australian Kidney Foundation Medical Research Grants and Scholarships 122
Australian Kidney Foundation Seeding and Equipment Grants 123

United Kingdom

Prostate Research Campaign UK Research Grants 516
WellBeing of Women/RCOG Research Training Fellowship 716

United States of America

AFAR Research Grants 47
AUAER/Pfizer Visiting Professorships in Urology 504
Nurses' Educational Funds Fellowships and Scholarships 488
Paul Beeson Career Development Award 49
Pfizer Detrol LA Research Awards Program 504

VIROLOGY

Any Country

Barbers Company Clinical Nursing Scholarship 538
Career Development Program 409
CBS Graduate Fellowship Program 200
GlaxoSmithKline Collaborative Research Projects 309
GlaxoSmithkline Services to Academia 309
Lister Institute Research Prizes 413
NARSAD Distinguished Investigator Awards 449
NARSAD Independent Investigator Awards 449
NARSAD Young Investigator Awards 449
NORD Clinical Research Grants 470
Queen Mary Research Studentships 518
Translational Research Program 409

University of Dundee Research Awards 648
Wilson-Fulton and Robertson Awards in Aging Research, Cecille Gould Memorial Fund Award in Cancer Research, Richard Shepherd Fellowship 49

Canada

CBS Postdoctoral Fellowship (PDF) 200
CBS Research and Development Program Individual Grants 200
CBS Research and Development Program Major Equipment Grants 200
CBS Small Projects Fund 201

East European Countries

FEMS Fellowship 284

United Kingdom

British Lung Foundation Project Grants 156
FEMS Fellowship 284
H C Roscoe Research Grant 157

United States of America

Nurses' Educational Funds Fellowships and Scholarships 488
Paul Beeson Career Development Award 49

West European Countries

FEMS Fellowship 284

TROPICAL MEDICINE

Any Country

Barbers Company Clinical Nursing Scholarship 538
CDU Senior Research Fellowship 230
CDU Three Year Postdoctoral Fellowship 230
Earthwatch Field Research Grants 265
Fungal Research Trust Travel Grants 298
Lister Institute Research Prizes 413
Meningitis Research Foundation Project Grant 431
Meningitis Trust Research Award 431
NORD Clinical Research Grants 470
Sir Halley Stewart Trust Grants 571

African Nations

AHRI African Fellowship 98

United States of America

NFID Colin L Powell Minority Postdoctoral Fellowship in Tropical Disease Research 458
Nurses' Educational Funds Fellowships and Scholarships 488
Paul Beeson Career Development Award 49

VENEREOLOGY

Any Country

Barbers Company Clinical Nursing Scholarship 538
Lister Institute Research Prizes 413
NORD Clinical Research Grants 470

United States of America

Nurses' Educational Funds Fellowships and Scholarships 488
Paul Beeson Career Development Award 49

REHABILITATION MEDICINE AND THERAPY

Any Country

Alberta Heritage Full-Time Studentship 14
Alzheimer's Society Research Grants 23
Ataxia UK Project Grant 116
Ataxia UK Research Studentships 116
Ataxia UK Satellite Meeting at Major Symposium on Related Disorders 116
Ataxia UK Travel Award 117
BackCare Research Grants 130
Barbers Company Clinical Nursing Scholarship 538
CCFF Fellowships 202
CCFF Special Travel Allowances 203
Clinical Research Training Fellowship in Nursing and Midwifery 319
CRPF Research Grant 235
DEBRA UK Research Grant Scheme 255
ECTS Career Establishment Award 276
ECTS Exchange Scholarship Grants 277
HDA Research Project Grants 333
Heart Research UK Basic Science Medical Research Grant 320
Heart Research UK Clinical Medical Research Grant 321
Heart Research UK Emerging Technologies Grant 321
HRB Equipment Grants 320
Meningitis Research Foundation Project Grant 431
MND Research Project Grants 443
PDS Research Project Grant 498
PDS Training Fellowships 498
Postgraduate Research Bursaries (Epilepsy Action) 274
Roche Research Foundation 531
Savoy Foundation Postdoctoral and Clinical Research Fellowships 562
Savoy Foundation Research Grants 562
Savoy Foundation Studentships 563
Sigma Theta Tau International/Rehabilitation Nursing Foundation Grant 570
SOM Research Grant 592
UICC Translational Cancer Research Fellowships (TCRF) 378
University of Southampton Postgraduate Studentships 692
World Universities Network (WUN) Global Exchange Programme 693

African Nations

International Postgraduate Research Scholarships (IPRS) 692

Australia

Australian Clinical Research Postdoctoral Fellowship 460
Biomedical (Dora Lush) and Public Health Postgraduate Scholarships 460
C J Martin Fellowships (Overseas Biomedical) 460
Career Development Awards 461
Howard Florey Centenary Fellowship 461
Industry Fellowships 461
Neil Hamilton Fairley Fellowships (Overseas Clinical) 461
NHMRC Medical and Dental and Public Health Postgraduate Research Scholarships 461
NHMRC/INSERM Exchange Fellowships 461
Peter Doherty Fellowships (Australian Biomedical) 462
Public Health Fellowship (Australian) 462
Sidney Sax Fellowship (Overseas Public Health) 462
Sir Robert Menzies Memorial Research Scholarships in the Allied Health Sciences 572
Training Scholarship for Indigenous Health Research 462

Canada

Alberta Heritage Health Research Studentship 14
CCFF Senior Scientist Research Training Award 202
CTS Fellowships 216
International Postgraduate Research Scholarships (IPRS) 692

Caribbean Countries

International Postgraduate Research Scholarships (IPRS) 692

East European Countries

International Postgraduate Research Scholarships (IPRS) 692

European Union

Clinical Research Training Fellowship in Nursing and Midwifery 319

Middle East

ABCCF Student Grant 95
Hastings Center International Visiting Scholars Program 318
International Postgraduate Research Scholarships (IPRS) 692
University of Essex/ORS Awards 655

New Zealand

Hastings Center International Visiting Scholars Program 318
Training Scholarship for Indigenous Health Research 462

South Africa

DENOSA Bursaries, Scholarships and Grants 255
Hastings Center International Visiting Scholars Program 318
International Postgraduate Research Scholarships (IPRS) 692
University of Essex/ORS Awards 655

United Kingdom

The Allen Iswlyn Giles Memorial Nursing Scholarship 538
British Lung Foundation Project Grants 156
Ethicon Nurses Education Trust Fund 538
Hastings Center International Visiting Scholars Program 318
HSA Charitable Trust Scholarships for Nurses and Midwives 539
Innovation and Creative Practice Award 518
International Postgraduate Research Scholarships (IPRS) 692
MND PhD Studentship Award 443
Mr and Mrs David Edward Memorial Award 699
Nuffield Trust/RCN/IHM Joint Travel Awards 539
PDS Research Project Grant 498
PDS Training Fellowships 498
RCN Margaret Parkinson Scholarships 539
Resuscitation Council Research Fellowships 526
Resuscitation Council Research Grants 526
RNPFN Student Nurse Travel Awards 540
Sheffield Hallam University Studentships 567
Smith and Nephew Foundation Doctoral Nursing Research Studentship 573
Smith and Nephew Foundation Postdoctoral Nursing Research Fellowship 573
University of Essex Access to Learning Fund 652
UWB Departmental Research Studentships 700
UWB Research Studentships 700

United States of America

Ian Axford (New Zealand) Fellowships in Public Policy 239
International Postgraduate Research Scholarships (IPRS) 692
Nurses' Educational Funds Fellowships and Scholarships 488
PhRMAF Postdoctoral Fellowships in Health Outcomes Research 506
PhRMAF Predoctoral Fellowships in Health Outcomes Research 507
PhRMAF Research Starter Grants in Health Outcomes Research 508
PhRMAF Sabbatical Fellowships in Health Outcomes Research 509
Scholarships for Émigrés in the Health Professions 390
Sigma Theta Tau International Small Research Grants 568
University of Essex/ORS Awards 655

West European Countries

Hastings Center International Visiting Scholars Program 318
International Postgraduate Research Scholarships (IPRS) 692
Mr and Mrs David Edward Memorial Award 699
Sheffield Hallam University Studentships 567
UWB Departmental Research Studentships 700
UWB Research Studentships 700

MEDICAL AUXILIARIES

Any Country

Barbers Company Clinical Nursing Scholarship 538
HRB Equipment Grants 320
Roche Research Foundation 531

African Nations

International Postgraduate Research Scholarships (IPRS) 692

Australia

Australian Clinical Research Postdoctoral Fellowship 460
Biomedical (Dora Lush) and Public Health Postgraduate Scholarships 460
C J Martin Fellowships (Overseas Biomedical) 460
Career Development Awards 461
Howard Florey Centenary Fellowship 461
Neil Hamilton Fairley Fellowships (Overseas Clinical) 461
NHMRC Medical and Dental and Public Health Postgraduate Research Scholarships 461
NHMRC/INSERM Exchange Fellowships 461
Public Health Fellowship (Australian) 462
Sidney Sax Fellowship (Overseas Public Health) 462
Training Scholarship for Indigenous Health Research 462

Canada

International Postgraduate Research Scholarships (IPRS) 692

Caribbean Countries

International Postgraduate Research Scholarships (IPRS) 692

East European Countries

International Postgraduate Research Scholarships (IPRS) 692

Middle East

International Postgraduate Research Scholarships (IPRS) 692

New Zealand

Training Scholarship for Indigenous Health Research 462

South Africa

International Postgraduate Research Scholarships (IPRS) 692

United Kingdom

International Postgraduate Research Scholarships (IPRS) 692

United States of America

International Postgraduate Research Scholarships (IPRS) 692
Nurses' Educational Funds Fellowships and Scholarships 488

West European Countries

International Postgraduate Research Scholarships (IPRS) 692

MIDWIFERY

Any Country

Barbers Company Clinical Nursing Scholarship 538
CIHR Fellowships Program 208
Clinical Research Training Fellowship in Nursing and Midwifery 319
HRB Equipment Grants 320
RCN Grants 539
RCN Scholarships Fund 539
Roche Research Foundation 531
University of Dundee Research Awards 648
WellBeing of Women Project Grants 716

African Nations

International Postgraduate Research Scholarships (IPRS) 692

Australia

Australian Clinical Research Postdoctoral Fellowship 460
Biomedical (Dora Lush) and Public Health Postgraduate Scholarships 460
Career Development Awards 461
Howard Florey Centenary Fellowship 461

Canada

Caribbean Countries

East European Countries

European Union

Middle East

New Zealand

South Africa

United Kingdom

United States of America

West European Countries

RADIOLOGY

Any Country

African Nations

Australia

Canada

Caribbean Countries

East European Countries

Middle East

New Zealand

South Africa

United Kingdom

United States of America

RSNA Medical Student Departmental Grant Program 520
RSNA Medical Student/Scholar Assistant Program 520
RSNA Research Fellowship in Basic Radiologic Sciences 520
RSNA Research Resident Program 521

West European Countries

International Postgraduate Research Scholarships (IPRS) 692
Mr and Mrs David Edward Memorial Award 699
UWB Departmental Research Studentships 700
UWB Research Studentships 700

TREATMENT TECHNIQUES

Any Country

AFSP Distinguished Investigator Awards 51
AFSP Pilot Grants 51
AFSP Postdoctoral Research Fellowships 51
AFSP Standard Research Grants 51
AFSP Young Investigator Award 51
Alzheimer's Society Research Grants 23
American Tinnitus Association Scientific Research Grants 89
BackCare Research Grants 130
Barbers Company Clinical Nursing Scholarship 538
BMRP for Inflammatory Bowel Disease Grants 164
Breast Cancer Campaign Small Pilot Grants 141
BRPS Research Grants 159
Career Development Program 409
CCFF Fellowships 202
CCFF Special Travel Allowances 203
CCFF Studentships 203
Cooley's Anemia Foundation Research Fellowship 242
CRPF Research Grant 235
CSMLS Founders' Fund Award 215
DEBRA UK Research Grant Scheme 255
FRAXA Grants and Fellowships 293
GlaxoSmithKline Collaborative Research Projects 309
GlaxoSmithkline Services to Academia 309
HDA Studentship 333
Heart Research UK Basic Science Medical Research Grant 320
Heart Research UK Clinical Medical Research Grant 321
Heart Research UK Emerging Technologies Grant 321
HRB Equipment Grants 320
Institute for the Study of Aging Grants Program 344
Meningitis Research Foundation Project Grant 431
Meningitis Trust Research Award 431
NORD Clinical Research Grants 470
NORD/Rosoe Brady Lysosomal Storage Diseases Fellowships 470
OREF Career Development Award 495
OREF Prospective Clinical Research 495
OREF Research Grants 495
OREF Resident Research Award 495
PDS Research Project Grant 498
PDS Training Fellowships 498
Postgraduate Research Bursaries (Epilepsy Action) 274
Roche Research Foundation 531
RSNA Institutional Fellowship in Radiological Informatics 519
SOM Research Grant 592
Stroke Association Research Project Grants 603
Translational Research Program 409

African Nations

AHRI African Fellowship 98
International Postgraduate Research Scholarships (IPRS) 692

Australia

Australian Clinical Research Postdoctoral Fellowship 460
Biomedical (Dora Lush) and Public Health Postgraduate Scholarships 460
C J Martin Fellowships (Overseas Biomedical) 460
The Cancer Council NSW Research Project Grants 218
Career Development Awards 461
Howard Florey Centenary Fellowship 461
Industry Fellowships 461
Neil Hamilton Fairley Fellowships (Overseas Clinical) 461
NHMRC Medical and Dental and Public Health Postgraduate Research Scholarships 461
NHMRC/INSERM Exchange Fellowships 461
Public Health Fellowship (Australian) 462
Sidney Sax Fellowship (Overseas Public Health) 462
Sir Robert Menzies Memorial Research Scholarships in the Allied Health Sciences 572
Training Scholarship for Indigenous Health Research 462

Canada

International Postgraduate Research Scholarships (IPRS) 692
OREF Clinical Research Award 495
OREF Fellowship in Health Services Research 495

Caribbean Countries

International Postgraduate Research Scholarships (IPRS) 692

East European Countries

International Postgraduate Research Scholarships (IPRS) 692

Middle East

International Postgraduate Research Scholarships (IPRS) 692

New Zealand

Training Scholarship for Indigenous Health Research 462

South Africa

International Postgraduate Research Scholarships (IPRS) 692

United Kingdom

Breast Cancer Campaign Project Grants 140
British Lung Foundation Project Grants 156
International Postgraduate Research Scholarships (IPRS) 692
Owen Shaw Award 164
PDS Research Project Grant 498
PDS Training Fellowships 498
Resuscitation Council Research Fellowships 526
Resuscitation Council Research Grants 526

United States of America

The BSN-Jobst Inc. Research Award 92
Damon Runyon Scholar Award 253
International Postgraduate Research Scholarships (IPRS) 692
National Headache Foundation Research Grant 459
Nurses' Educational Funds Fellowships and Scholarships 488
OREF Clinical Research Award 495
OREF Fellowship in Health Services Research 495
Pfizer Detrol LA Research Awards Program 504

West European Countries

International Postgraduate Research Scholarships (IPRS) 692

MEDICAL TECHNOLOGY

Any Country

Alzheimer's Society Research Grants 23
Barbers Company Clinical Nursing Scholarship 538
Breast Cancer Campaign Small Pilot Grants 141
BRPS Research Grants 159
Career Development Program 409
CCFF Fellowships 202
CCFF Special Travel Allowances 203
CCFF Studentships 203
Cooley's Anemia Foundation Research Fellowship 242
Dr Hadwen Trust for Humane Research Grants 261
Dr Hadwen Trust Research Assistant or Technician 262

Dr Hadwen Trust Research Fellowship 262
GlaxoSmithKline Collaborative Research Projects 309
GlaxoSmithkline Services to Academia 309
Hastings Center International Visiting Scholars Program 318
HDA Studentship 333
Heart Research UK Basic Science Medical Research Grant 320
Heart Research UK Clinical Medical Research Grant 321
Heart Research UK Emerging Technologies Grant 321
HRB Equipment Grants 320
Meningitis Research Foundation Project Grant 431
Meningitis Trust Research Award 431
MND Research Project Grants 443
NORD Clinical Research Grants 470
PDS Research Project Grant 498
Queen Mary Research Studentships 518
Roche Research Foundation 531
RSNA Institutional Fellowship in Radiological Informatics 519
Savoy Foundation Postdoctoral and Clinical Research Fellowships 562
Savoy Foundation Studentships 563
Translational Research Program 409

African Nations

Hastings Center International Visiting Scholars Program 318

Australia

Australian Clinical Research Postdoctoral Fellowship 460
Biomedical (Dora Lush) and Public Health Postgraduate Scholarships 460
C J Martin Fellowships (Overseas Biomedical) 460
Career Development Awards 461
Hastings Center International Visiting Scholars Program 318
Howard Florey Centenary Fellowship 461
Industry Fellowships 461
Neil Hamilton Fairley Fellowships (Overseas Clinical) 461
NHMRC Medical and Dental and Public Health Postgraduate Research Scholarships 461
NHMRC/INSERM Exchange Fellowships 461
Peter Doherty Fellowships (Australian Biomedical) 462
Training Scholarship for Indigenous Health Research 462

Canada

CCFF Senior Scientist Research Training Award 202
Quebec CE Fund Grants 216

Caribbean Countries

Hastings Center International Visiting Scholars Program 318

East European Countries

Hastings Center International Visiting Scholars Program 318

Middle East

Hastings Center International Visiting Scholars Program 318

New Zealand

Hastings Center International Visiting Scholars Program 318
Training Scholarship for Indigenous Health Research 462

South Africa

Hastings Center International Visiting Scholars Program 318

United Kingdom

BDF Newlife- Full and Small Grants Schemes 137
Breast Cancer Campaign Project Grants 140
British Lung Foundation Project Grants 156
Hastings Center International Visiting Scholars Program 318
MND PhD Studentship Award 443
PDS Research Project Grant 498
Resuscitation Council Research Fellowships 526
Resuscitation Council Research Grants 526

United States of America

Ian Axford (New Zealand) Fellowships in Public Policy 239
Nurses' Educational Funds Fellowships and Scholarships 488

West European Countries

Hastings Center International Visiting Scholars Program 318

DENTISTRY AND STOMATOLOGY

Any Country

AFUW-SA Winifred E Preedy Postgraduate Bursary 122
Barbers Company Clinical Nursing Scholarship 538
BDA/Dentsply Student Support Fund 145
CAMS Scholarship 233
Colyer Prize 558
HRB Equipment Grants 320
National Association of Dental Assistants Annual Scholarship Award 450
NORD Clinical Research Grants 470
Queen Mary Research Studentships 518
Roche Research Foundation 531
Sir Richard Stapley Educational Trust Grants 571
University of Bristol Postgraduate Scholarships 641
University of Dundee Research Awards 648
Wellcome Trust Grants 717

Australia

Australian Clinical Research Postdoctoral Fellowship 460
Career Development Awards 461
Howard Florey Centenary Fellowship 461
Industry Fellowships 461
Neil Hamilton Fairley Fellowships (Overseas Clinical) 461
NHMRC Medical and Dental and Public Health Postgraduate Research Scholarships 461
NHMRC/INSERM Exchange Fellowships 461
Peter Doherty Fellowships (Australian Biomedical) 462
Training Scholarship for Indigenous Health Research 462

Canada

DCF Biennial Research Award 256
DCF Fellowships for Teacher/Researcher Training 256
Frank Knox Memorial Fellowships 115
Tylman Research Program 40

New Zealand

Training Scholarship for Indigenous Health Research 462

United States of America

ADA Foundation Dental Student Scholarship 9
Scholarships for Émigrés in the Health Professions 390
Tylman Research Program 40

ORAL PATHOLOGY

Any Country

Barbers Company Clinical Nursing Scholarship 538
BDA/Dentsply Student Support Fund 145
Colyer Prize 558
Queen Mary Research Studentships 518

ORTHODONTICS

Any Country

Barbers Company Clinical Nursing Scholarship 538
BDA/Dentsply Student Support Fund 145
Queen Mary Research Studentships 518

University of Bristol Postgraduate Scholarships 641
University of Dundee Research Awards 648

PERIODONTICS

Any Country

Barbers Company Clinical Nursing Scholarship 538
BDA/Dentsply Student Support Fund 145
Queen Mary Research Studentships 518
University of Bristol Postgraduate Scholarships 641
University of Dundee Research Awards 648

COMMUNITY DENTISTRY

Any Country

Barbers Company Clinical Nursing Scholarship 538
BDA/Dentsply Student Support Fund 145
Queen Mary Research Studentships 518
University of Dundee Research Awards 648

DENTAL TECHNOLOGY

Any Country

Barbers Company Clinical Nursing Scholarship 538
Colyer Prize 558
HRB Equipment Grants 320
Queen Mary Research Studentships 518
Roche Research Foundation 531
University of Dundee Research Awards 648

Australia

Career Development Awards 461
Howard Florey Centenary Fellowship 461
Industry Fellowships 461
Neil Hamilton Fairley Fellowships (Overseas Clinical) 461
NHMRC Medical and Dental and Public Health Postgraduate Research Scholarships 461
NHMRC/INSERM Exchange Fellowships 461
Peter Doherty Fellowships (Australian Biomedical) 462
Training Scholarship for Indigenous Health Research 462

New Zealand

Training Scholarship for Indigenous Health Research 462

United States of America

ADA Foundation Allied Dental Health Scholarship 9

PROSTHETIC DENTISTRY

Any Country

Barbers Company Clinical Nursing Scholarship 538
BDA/Dentsply Student Support Fund 145
Queen Mary Research Studentships 518
Research Fellowship in Geriatric Prosthodontics 40
University of Bristol Postgraduate Scholarships 641
University of Dundee Research Awards 648

PHARMACY

Any Country

AACR Scholar-in-Training Awards 28
AFSP Distinguished Investigator Awards 51
AFSP Pilot Grants 51
AFSP Postdoctoral Research Fellowships 51
AFSP Standard Research Grants 51
AFSP Young Investigator Award 51
Alzheimer's Research Trust Clinical Research Training Fellowship 21
Alzheimer's Research Trust Network Co-operation Grant 22
Alzheimer's Research Trust Pilot Project Grant 22
Alzheimer's Research Trust Research Equipment Grant 22
Alzheimer's Research Trust Research Fellowships 22
Alzheimer's Research Trust Research Major Grants 22
Alzheimer's Society Research Grants 23
Alzheimer's Research Trust Emergency Support Grant 23
Andrew Mellon Foundation Scholarship 527
Barbers Company Clinical Nursing Scholarship 538
Breast Cancer Campaign Small Pilot Grants 141
Career Development Program 409
GlaxoSmithKline Collaborative Research Projects 309
GlaxoSmithkline Services to Academia 309
HRB Equipment Grants 320
Hugh Kelly Fellowship 528
Institute for the Study of Aging Grants Program 344
NORD Clinical Research Grants 470
PDS Research Project Grant 498
PDS Training Fellowships 498
Postgraduate Research Bursaries (Epilepsy Action) 274
Queen Mary Research Studentships 518
Rhodes University Postdoctoral Fellowship and The Andrew Mellon Postdoctoral Fellowship 528
Rhodes University Postgraduate Scholarship 528
Roche Research Foundation 531
Savoy Foundation Postdoctoral and Clinical Research Fellowships 562
Savoy Foundation Studentships 563
Translational Research Program 409

African Nations

International Postgraduate Research Scholarships (IPRS) 692

Australia

Asthma Foundation of New South Wales Biomedical and Medical Postgraduate Research Scholarships 116
Asthma Foundation of New South Wales Medical Research Project Grant 116
Australian Clinical Research Postdoctoral Fellowship 460
Biomedical (Dora Lush) and Public Health Postgraduate Scholarships 460
Career Development Awards 461
Howard Florey Centenary Fellowship 461
Industry Fellowships 461
Peter Doherty Fellowships (Australian Biomedical) 462
Training Scholarship for Indigenous Health Research 462

Canada

CTS Fellowships 216
International Postgraduate Research Scholarships (IPRS) 692

Caribbean Countries

International Postgraduate Research Scholarships (IPRS) 692

East European Countries

International Postgraduate Research Scholarships (IPRS) 692

Middle East

International Postgraduate Research Scholarships (IPRS) 692

New Zealand

Training Scholarship for Indigenous Health Research 462

South Africa

International Postgraduate Research Scholarships (IPRS) 692

United Kingdom

Breast Cancer Campaign Project Grants 140
International Postgraduate Research Scholarships (IPRS) 692

United States of America

West European Countries

BIOMEDICINE

Any Country

African Nations

Australia

Canada

Caribbean Countries

East European Countries

Middle East

Middle East
International Postgraduate Research Scholarships (IPRS) 692
VIFM Scholarship in Forensic 710

South Africa
International Postgraduate Research Scholarships (IPRS) 692
VIFM Scholarship in Forensic 710

United Kingdom
International Postgraduate Research Scholarships (IPRS) 692

United States of America
International Postgraduate Research Scholarships (IPRS) 692

West European Countries
International Postgraduate Research Scholarships (IPRS) 692

ACUPUNCTURE

Any Country
BackCare Research Grants 130
Barbers Company Clinical Nursing Scholarship 538
Breast Cancer Campaign Small Pilot Grants 141
PDS Research Project Grant 498
PDS Training Fellowships 498
Roche Research Foundation 531

Australia
Biomedical (Dora Lush) and Public Health Postgraduate Scholarships 460

United Kingdom
Breast Cancer Campaign Project Grants 140
PDS Research Project Grant 498
PDS Training Fellowships 498

HOMEOPATHY

Any Country
Barbers Company Clinical Nursing Scholarship 538
Breast Cancer Campaign Small Pilot Grants 141
PDS Research Project Grant 498
PDS Training Fellowships 498
Roche Research Foundation 531

Australia
Biomedical (Dora Lush) and Public Health Postgraduate Scholarships 460

United Kingdom
Breast Cancer Campaign Project Grants 140
PDS Research Project Grant 498
PDS Training Fellowships 498

CHIROPRACTIC

Any Country
BackCare Research Grants 130
Barbers Company Clinical Nursing Scholarship 538
CRPF Research Grant 235
Roche Research Foundation 531

African Nations
International Postgraduate Research Scholarships (IPRS) 692

Australia
Australian Clinical Research Postdoctoral Fellowship 460
Biomedical (Dora Lush) and Public Health Postgraduate Scholarships 460

Canada
International Postgraduate Research Scholarships (IPRS) 692

Caribbean Countries
International Postgraduate Research Scholarships (IPRS) 692

East European Countries
International Postgraduate Research Scholarships (IPRS) 692

Middle East
International Postgraduate Research Scholarships (IPRS) 692

South Africa
International Postgraduate Research Scholarships (IPRS) 692

United Kingdom
International Postgraduate Research Scholarships (IPRS) 692

United States of America
International Postgraduate Research Scholarships (IPRS) 692

West European Countries
International Postgraduate Research Scholarships (IPRS) 692

OSTEOPATHY

Any Country
BackCare Research Grants 130
Barbers Company Clinical Nursing Scholarship 538
Roche Research Foundation 531

Australia
Australian Clinical Research Postdoctoral Fellowship 460
Biomedical (Dora Lush) and Public Health Postgraduate Scholarships 460

Canada
Alcohol Beverage Medical Research Foundation Research Project Grant 15

United States of America
Alcohol Beverage Medical Research Foundation Research Project Grant 15

TRADITIONAL EASTERN MEDICINE

Any Country
Alzheimer's Society Research Grants 23
Barbers Company Clinical Nursing Scholarship 538
Hamdard Fellowship in Eastern Medicine 316
Roche Research Foundation 531

NATURAL SCIENCES

GENERAL

Any Country
AACR Scholar-in-Training Awards 28
ACS Ahmed Zewail Award in Ultrafast Science and Technology 33

African Nations

Australia

Canada

Caribbean Countries

East European Countries

European Union

Middle East

New Zealand

South Africa

TWNSO Grants to Institutions in the South for Joint Research Projects 612
Wolfson Foundation Grants 722

United Kingdom

BHF Research Awards 154
Copus Public Understanding of Science Development Fund 553
Copus Public Understanding of Science Seed Fund 553
DEL Postgraduate Studentships and Bursaries for Study in Northern Ireland 256
EMBO Award for Communication in the Life Sciences 277
Endeavour International Postgraduate Research Scholarships (EIPRS) 403
Frank Knox Fellowships at Harvard University 292
Fulbright Postdoctoral Research and Lecturing Awards for Non-US Citizens 245
Gilchrist Fieldwork Award 307
Goldsmiths' Company Science for Society Courses 310
Grundy Educational Trust 313
International Postgraduate Research Scholarships (IPRS) 692
John Radford Award for Geographical Photography 545
Journey of a Lifetime Award 545
JSPS Summer Programme Fellowship 388
Kennedy Scholarships 398
Llewellyn and Mary Williams Scholarship 699
Mr and Mrs David Edward Memorial Award 699
NERC Advanced Course Studentships 476
NERC Research Studentships 476
Neville Shulman Challenge Award 546
Royal Geographical Society Geographica Fieldwork Grants 546
Sheffield Hallam University Studentships 567
Swiss Federal Institute of Technology Scholarships 606
University of Wales Aberystwyth Postgraduate Research Studentships 699
UWB Departmental Research Studentships 700
Wolfson Foundation Grants 722

United States of America

Budweiser Conservation Scholarship 458
Congress Bundestag Youth Exchange for Young Professionals 224
Earthwatch Education Awards 265
Endeavour International Postgraduate Research Scholarships (EIPRS) 403
ETS Postdoctoral Fellowships 267
Fellowship for American College Students 524
Foundation for Science and Disability Student Grant Fund 291
Fulbright Scholar Program for US Citizens 245
Fulbright Senior Specialists Program 245
GSA Research Grants 300
Guggenheim Fellowships to Assist Research and Artistic Creation (USA and Canada) 394
Howard Brown Rickard Scholarship 456
International Postgraduate Research Scholarships (IPRS) 692
JSPS Summer Programme Fellowship 388
Lincoln College Overseas Graduate Entrance Scholarships 680
Mark Mills Award 68
North Dakota Indian Scholarship 485
Norwegian Marshall Fund 487
Parker B Francis Fellowship Program 498
Renate W Chasman Scholarship 166
Swiss Federal Institute of Technology Scholarships 606
Vatican Film Library Mellon Fellowship 709
Washington University Chancellor's Graduate Fellowship Program 715
Winston Churchill Foundation Scholarship 720

West European Countries

BAEF Alumni Award 132
BHF Research Awards 154
DEL Postgraduate Studentships and Bursaries for Study in Northern Ireland 256
EMBO Award for Communication in the Life Sciences 277
Endeavour International Postgraduate Research Scholarships (EIPRS) 403
Fulbright Postdoctoral Research and Lecturing Awards for Non-US Citizens 245
International Postgraduate Research Scholarships (IPRS) 692
John Radford Award for Geographical Photography 545
JSPS Summer Programme Fellowship 388
Llewellyn and Mary Williams Scholarship 699
Mr and Mrs David Edward Memorial Award 699
NERC Advanced Course Studentships 476
NERC Research Studentships 476
Sheffield Hallam University Studentships 567
St Peter's College Bodossaki Foundation Graduate Scholarship in Science 688
Synthesys Visiting Fellowship 477
University of Otago Master's Awards 670
UWB Departmental Research Studentships 700

BIOLOGICAL AND LIFE SCIENCES

Any Country

AAC Research Grants 25
AACR Scholar-in-Training Awards 28
Alberta Heritage Full-Time Fellowships 14
Alberta Heritage Full-Time Studentship 14
Alzheimer's Society Research Grants 23
Apex Foundation Annual Research Grants 94
Association for Women in Science Educational Foundation Predoctoral Awards 108
Bermuda Biological Station for Research Grant In Aid 132
BFWG Johnstone and Florence Stoney Studentship 149
BMRP for Inflammatory Bowel Disease Grants 164
BP Conservation Programme Awards 130
Cancer Research UK LRI Clinical Research Fellowships 219
Cancer Research UK LRI Graduate Studentships 219
Career Development Program 409
CBS Graduate Fellowship Program 200
CDU Senior Research Fellowship 230
CDU Three Year Postdoctoral Fellowship 230
CIIT-Centers for Health Research Postdoctoral Fellowships 236
CIIT-Centers for Health Research Predoctoral Traineeships 236
Collaborative Career Development Fellowship in Stem Cell Research 425
Colt Foundation PhD Fellowship 238
Direct Research on Ataxia-Telangiectasia 3
EMBO Long-Term Fellowships in Molecular Biology 277
EMBO Short-Term Fellowships in Molecular Biology 278
Ernst Mayr Travel Grant 445
ESRF Postdoctoral Fellowships 279
Essex Rotary University Travel Grants 651
Foulkes Foundation Fellowship 287
G M McKinley Research Fund 517
GlaxoSmithKline Collaborative Research Projects 309
GlaxoSmithkline Services to Academia 309
Hastings Center International Visiting Scholars Program 318
HFG Dissertation Fellowship 317
HFG Research Program 317
HFSPO Career Development Award (CDA) 368
HFSPO Cross-Disciplinary Fellowships 368
HFSPO Long-Term Fellowships 368
HFSPO Program Grant 368
HFSPO Short-Term Fellowships 369
HFSPO Young Investigator Grant 369
Horton (Hydrology) Research Grant 52
Hudson River Research Grants 331
Hudson River Travel Grants 331
ICSU-TWAS-UNESCO-UNU/IAS Visiting Scientist Programme 610
ISRT Project Grant 376
J Lawrence Angel Fellowship in Human Skeletal Studies 79
Lister Institute Research Prizes 413
Lord Dowding Fund for Humane Research 415
LSRF 3-Year Postdoctoral Fellowships 412

African Nations

Australia

Canada

Caribbean Countries

East European Countries

European Union

Middle East

New Zealand

South Africa

Hastings Center International Visiting Scholars Program 318
HFSPO IFS Research Grant 367
IARC Postdoctoral Fellowships for Training in Cancer Research 357
The Trieste Science Prize 610
TWAS Fellowships for Research and Advanced Training 610
TWAS Grants for Scientific Meetings in Developing Countries 611
TWAS Prizes 611
TWAS Prizes to Young Scientists in Developing Countries 611
TWAS Research Grants 611
TWNSO Grants to Institutions in the South for Joint Research Projects 612
University of Essex/ORS Awards 655

United Kingdom

British Lung Foundation Project Grants 156
EMBO Award for Communication in the Life Sciences 277
EMBO Science Writing Prize 278
ESRF Thesis Studentships 279
FEMS Fellowship 284
Hastings Center International Visiting Scholars Program 318
Llewellyn and Mary Williams Scholarship 699
Martin McLaren Horticultural Scholarship 347
Mr and Mrs David Edward Memorial Award 699
NERC Advanced Course Studentships 476
NERC Research Studentships 476
North West Cancer Research Fund Research Project Grants 485
Sainsbury Management Fellowships in the Life Sciences 535
Swiss Federal Institute of Technology Scholarships 606
Thomas Witherden Batt Scholarship 636
University of Essex Access to Learning Fund 652
University of Wales Aberystwyth Postgraduate Research Studentships 699
UWB Departmental Research Studentships 700
UWB Research Studentships 700

United States of America

AFAR Research Grants 47
Budweiser Conservation Scholarship 458
Earthwatch Education Awards 265
NIH Research Grants 466
Paul Beeson Career Development Award 49
Pfizer International HDL Research Awards Program 505
Swiss Federal Institute of Technology Scholarships 606
University of Essex/ORS Awards 655
Washington University Chancellor's Graduate Fellowship Program 715
Winston Churchill Foundation Scholarship 720

West European Countries

EMBO Award for Communication in the Life Sciences 277
EMBO Science Writing Prize 278
ESRF Thesis Studentships 279
FEMS Fellowship 284
Hastings Center International Visiting Scholars Program 318
Llewellyn and Mary Williams Scholarship 699
Mr and Mrs David Edward Memorial Award 699
NERC Advanced Course Studentships 476
NERC Research Studentships 476
Queen's College Florey EPA Scholarship 684
University of Otago Master's Awards 670
UWB Departmental Research Studentships 700
UWB Research Studentships 700

ANATOMY

Any Country

Alzheimer's Society Research Grants 23
CBS Graduate Fellowship Program 200
EMBO Short-Term Fellowships in Molecular Biology 278
Health Research Board PhD Training Sites 319
HRB Summer Student Grants 320
JILA Postdoctoral Research Associateship and Visiting Fellowships 390
Mount Desert Island New Investigator Award 443
Queen Mary Research Studentships 518
UFAW Animal Welfare Research Training Scholarships 624
UFAW Research and Project Awards 624
UFAW Small Project and Travel Awards 624
UFAW Vacation Scholarships 624
University of Bristol Postgraduate Scholarships 641
University of Dundee Research Awards 648
University of Otago International Scholarships 670
University of Otago PhD Scholarships 670
University of Otago Prestigious PhD Scholarships 671

Australia

University of Otago Master's Awards 670

Canada

CTCRI Research Planning Grants 217

European Union

EMBO Science Writing Prize 278

New Zealand

University of Otago Master's Awards 670

United Kingdom

EMBO Science Writing Prize 278
Mr and Mrs David Edward Memorial Award 699
University of Wales Aberystwyth Postgraduate Research Studentships 699
UWB Departmental Research Studentships 700
UWB Research Studentships 700

United States of America

Paul Beeson Career Development Award 49
Washington University Chancellor's Graduate Fellowship Program 715

West European Countries

EMBO Science Writing Prize 278
Mr and Mrs David Edward Memorial Award 699
University of Otago Master's Awards 670
UWB Departmental Research Studentships 700
UWB Research Studentships 700

BIOCHEMISTRY

Any Country

AFSP Distinguished Investigator Awards 51
AFSP Pilot Grants 51
AFSP Postdoctoral Research Fellowships 51
AFSP Standard Research Grants 51
AFSP Young Investigator Award 51
Agnes Fay Morgan Research Award 380
AHAF Alzheimer's Disease Research Grant 53
AHAF Macular Degeneration Research 53
AHAF National Heart Foundation 53
Alberta Research Council Scholarship 642
Alzheimer's Research Trust Clinical Research Training Fellowship 21
Alzheimer's Research Trust Graduate Student Programme 22
Alzheimer's Research Trust Network Co-operation Grant 22
Alzheimer's Research Trust Pilot Project Grant 22
Alzheimer's Research Trust Research Equipment Grant 22
Alzheimer's Research Trust Research Fellowships 22
Alzheimer's Research Trust Research Major Grants 22
Alzheimer's Society Research Grants 23
Alzheimer's Research Trust Emergency Support Grant 23
The Biochemical Society General Travel Fund 136

African Nations

Australia

Canada

Caribbean Countries

East European Countries

European Union

Middle East

New Zealand

South Africa

United Kingdom

United States of America

West European Countries

BIOLOGY

Any Country

African Nations

Australia

Canada

Caribbean Countries

East European Countries

European Union

Middle East

New Zealand

University of Otago Master's Awards 670

South Africa

IDRC Doctoral Research Awards 365
University of Essex/ORS Awards 655
Use of Fertility-Enhancing Food, Forage and Cover Crops in Sustainably Managed Agroecosystems: The Bentley Fellowship 365

United Kingdom

EMBO Science Writing Prize 278
ESRF Thesis Studentships 279
Fulbright AstraZeneca Research Scholarship 707
Llewellyn and Mary Williams Scholarship 699
Martin McLaren Horticultural Scholarship 347
Mr and Mrs David Edward Memorial Award 699
NERC Advanced Course Studentships 476
NERC Research Studentships 476
University of Essex Access to Learning Fund 652
University of Wales Aberystwyth Postgraduate Research Studentships 699
UWB Departmental Research Studentships 700
UWB Research Studentships 700

United States of America

AFAR Research Grants 47
APS Conference Student Award 73
APS Minority Travel Fellowship Awards 73
Budweiser Conservation Scholarship 458
Caroline tum Suden/Frances Hellebrandt Professional Opportunity Awards 74
Earthwatch Education Awards 265
Fulbright Senior Specialists Program 245
MARC Faculty Predoctoral Fellowships 465
NIGMS Fellowship Awards for Minority Students 465
NIGMS Fellowship Awards for Students With Disabilities 465
NIGMS Postdoctoral Awards 465
NIGMS Research Project Grants 466
NIGMS Research Supplements for Underrepresented Minorities 466
NIH Research Grants 466
Paul Beeson Career Development Award 49
Pfizer International HDL Research Awards Program 505
Procter and Gamble Professional Opportunity Awards 74
University of Essex/ORS Awards 655
Washington University Chancellor's Graduate Fellowship Program 715
William T Porter Fellowship Award 74

West European Countries

EMBO Science Writing Prize 278
ESRF Thesis Studentships 279
Fulbright AstraZeneca Research Scholarship 707
Llewellyn and Mary Williams Scholarship 699
Mr and Mrs David Edward Memorial Award 699
NERC Advanced Course Studentships 476
NERC Research Studentships 476
Synthesys Visiting Fellowship 477
University of Otago Master's Awards 670
UWB Departmental Research Studentships 700
UWB Research Studentships 700

HISTOLOGY

Any Country

Alzheimer's Society Research Grants 23
EMBO Short-Term Fellowships in Molecular Biology 278
Health Research Board PhD Training Sites 319
HRB Postdoctoral Research Fellowships 320
HRB Project Grants-General 320
HRB Summer Student Grants 320
Lister Institute Research Prizes 413
Meningitis Research Foundation Project Grant 431
Muscular Dystrophy Research Grants 445
Savoy Foundation Postdoctoral and Clinical Research Fellowships 562
Savoy Foundation Studentships 563
University of Otago International Scholarships 670
University of Otago PhD Scholarships 670
University of Otago Prestigious PhD Scholarships 671

Australia

University of Otago Master's Awards 670

European Union

EMBO Science Writing Prize 278

New Zealand

University of Otago Master's Awards 670

United Kingdom

EMBO Science Writing Prize 278
Llewellyn and Mary Williams Scholarship 699
Mr and Mrs David Edward Memorial Award 699
UWB Departmental Research Studentships 700
UWB Research Studentships 700

United States of America

Paul Beeson Career Development Award 49

West European Countries

EMBO Science Writing Prize 278
Llewellyn and Mary Williams Scholarship 699
Mr and Mrs David Edward Memorial Award 699
University of Otago Master's Awards 670
UWB Departmental Research Studentships 700
UWB Research Studentships 700

BIOPHYSICS AND MOLECULAR BIOLOGY

Any Country

Abdus Salam ICTP Fellowships 5
AHAF Alzheimer's Disease Research Grant 53
AHAF Macular Degeneration Research 53
AHAF National Glaucoma Research 53
AHAF National Heart Foundation 53
Alzheimer's Society Research Grants 23
BMRP for Inflammatory Bowel Disease Grants 164
Cancer Research UK LRI Clinical Research Fellowships 219
Cancer Research UK LRI Graduate Studentships 219
Career Development Program 409
CBS Graduate Fellowship Program 200
CDU Senior Research Fellowship 230
CDU Three Year Postdoctoral Fellowship 230
CGD Research Trust Grants 236
Children's Medical Research Institute Graduate Scholarships and Postgraduate Fellowships 232
Children's Medical Research Institute Postdoctoral Fellowship 232
Direct Research on Ataxia-Telangiectasia 3
ECTS Career Establishment Award 276
ECTS Exchange Scholarship Grants 277
Electrochemical Society Summer Fellowships 268
EMBO Long-Term Fellowships in Molecular Biology 277
EMBO Short-Term Fellowships in Molecular Biology 278
EMBO Young Investigator 278
ESRF Postdoctoral Fellowships 279
Fanconi Anemia Research Award 283
Foulkes Foundation Fellowship 287
FRAXA Grants and Fellowships 293
GlaxoSmithKline Collaborative Research Projects 309
GlaxoSmithkline Services to Academia 309

African Nations

Australia

Canada

Caribbean Countries

East European Countries

European Union

Middle East

New Zealand

South Africa

United Kingdom

United States of America

West European Countries

BIOTECHNOLOGY

Any Country

African Nations

Australia

Canada

Caribbean Countries

East European Countries

European Union

Middle East

New Zealand

South Africa

United Kingdom

United States of America

Cranfield University Overseas Bursary 249
Fannie and John Hertz Foundation Fellowships 283
International Postgraduate Research Scholarships (IPRS) 692
MARC Faculty Predoctoral Fellowships 465
NIGMS Fellowship Awards for Minority Students 465
NIGMS Fellowship Awards for Students With Disabilities 465
NIGMS Postdoctoral Awards 465
NIGMS Research Project Grants 466
NIGMS Research Supplements for Underrepresented Minorities 466
University of Essex/ORS Awards 655

West European Countries

EMBO Award for Communication in the Life Sciences 277
EMBO Science Writing Prize 278
FEMS Fellowship 284
Hastings Center International Visiting Scholars Program 318
International Postgraduate Research Scholarships (IPRS) 692
Mr and Mrs David Edward Memorial Award 699
Silsoe Awards 249
University of Kent Department of Biosciences 660
University of Otago Master's Awards 670
UWB Departmental Research Studentships 700
UWB Research Studentships 700

BOTANY

Any Country

ASCSA Research Fellowship in Environmental Studies 79
CDU Senior Research Fellowship 230
CDU Three Year Postdoctoral Fellowship 230
Darbaker Botany Prize 516
Earthwatch Field Research Grants 265
Edmund Niles Huyck Preserve, Inc. Graduate and Postgraduate Grants 266
EMBO Long-Term Fellowships in Molecular Biology 277
EMBO Short-Term Fellowships in Molecular Biology 278
EMBO Young Investigator 278
Grants for Orchid Research 71
Hugh Kelly Fellowship 528
Jessup and McHenry Awards 6
La Trobe University Postgraduate Scholarship 403
National Geographic Conservation Trust Grant 241
NERC Advanced Research Fellowships 476
NERC Postdoctoral Research Fellowships 476
Perry Postgraduate Scholarships 503
Perry Research Awards 503
Queen Mary Research Studentships 518
Rhodes University Postdoctoral Fellowship and The Andrew Mellon Postdoctoral Fellowship 528
St Catherine's College Leathersellers' Company Graduate Scholarship 688
Stanley Smith (UK) Horticultural Trust Awards 598
Teagasc Walsh Fellowships 607
University of Bristol Postgraduate Scholarships 641
University of Dundee Research Awards 648
University of Otago International Scholarships 670
University of Otago PhD Scholarships 670
University of Otago Prestigious PhD Scholarships 671

African Nations

IDRC Doctoral Research Awards 365

Australia

University of Otago Master's Awards 670
Wingate Scholarships 720

Canada

IDRC Doctoral Research Awards 365
Wingate Scholarships 720

Caribbean Countries

IDRC Doctoral Research Awards 365

East European Countries

EMBO Award for Communication in the Life Sciences 277
NERC Advanced Course Studentships 476
NERC Research Studentships 476
Synthesys Visiting Fellowship 477

European Union

EMBO Award for Communication in the Life Sciences 277
EMBO Science Writing Prize 278

New Zealand

University of Otago Master's Awards 670
Wingate Scholarships 720

South Africa

Henderson Postgraduate Scholarships 527
IDRC Doctoral Research Awards 365
Wingate Scholarships 720

United Kingdom

EMBO Award for Communication in the Life Sciences 277
EMBO Science Writing Prize 278
Jerusalem Botanical Gardens Scholarship 295
Llewellyn and Mary Williams Scholarship 699
Martin McLaren Horticultural Scholarship 347
Mr and Mrs David Edward Memorial Award 699
NERC Advanced Course Studentships 476
NERC Research Studentships 476
University of Wales Aberystwyth Postgraduate Research Studentships 699
UWB Departmental Research Studentships 700
UWB Research Studentships 700
Wingate Scholarships 720

United States of America

Budweiser Conservation Scholarship 458
Earthwatch Education Awards 265
Fulbright Senior Specialists Program 245
Washington University Chancellor's Graduate Fellowship Program 715

West European Countries

EMBO Award for Communication in the Life Sciences 277
EMBO Science Writing Prize 278
Llewellyn and Mary Williams Scholarship 699
Mr and Mrs David Edward Memorial Award 699
NERC Advanced Course Studentships 476
NERC Research Studentships 476
Synthesys Visiting Fellowship 477
University of Otago Master's Awards 670
UWB Departmental Research Studentships 700
UWB Research Studentships 700
Wingate Scholarships 720

PLANT PATHOLOGY

Any Country

ASCSA Research Fellowship in Environmental Studies 79
CDU Senior Research Fellowship 230
CDU Three Year Postdoctoral Fellowship 230
Earthwatch Field Research Grants 265
EMBO Long-Term Fellowships in Molecular Biology 277
EMBO Short-Term Fellowships in Molecular Biology 278
EMBO Young Investigator 278
LSRF 3-Year Postdoctoral Fellowships 412

African Nations

Australia

Canada

Caribbean Countries

East European Countries

European Union

Middle East

New Zealand

South Africa

United Kingdom

United States of America

West European Countries

EMBRYOLOGY AND REPRODUCTION BIOLOGY

Any Country

African Nations

Australia

Caribbean Countries

East European Countries

European Union

Middle East

New Zealand

South Africa

United Kingdom

United States of America

West European Countries

GENETICS

Any Country

African Nations

Hastings Center International Visiting Scholars Program 318
IARC Postdoctoral Fellowships for Training in Cancer Research 357
International Postgraduate Research Scholarships (IPRS) 692

Australia

The Cancer Council NSW Research Project Grants 218
Children's Medical Research Institute Postgraduate Scholarship 232
Hastings Center International Visiting Scholars Program 318
Neil Hamilton Fairley Fellowships (Overseas Clinical) 461
University of Otago Master's Awards 670

Canada

Alcohol Beverage Medical Research Foundation Research Project Grant 15
CBS Small Projects Fund 201
CTCRI Research Planning Grants 217
International Postgraduate Research Scholarships (IPRS) 692

Caribbean Countries

Hastings Center International Visiting Scholars Program 318
IARC Postdoctoral Fellowships for Training in Cancer Research 357
International Postgraduate Research Scholarships (IPRS) 692

East European Countries

EMBO Award for Communication in the Life Sciences 277
FEMS Fellowship 284
Hastings Center International Visiting Scholars Program 318
IARC Postdoctoral Fellowships for Training in Cancer Research 357
International Postgraduate Research Scholarships (IPRS) 692
NERC Advanced Course Studentships 476
NERC Research Studentships 476

European Union

EMBO Award for Communication in the Life Sciences 277
EMBO Science Writing Prize 278

Middle East

Hastings Center International Visiting Scholars Program 318
IARC Postdoctoral Fellowships for Training in Cancer Research 357
International Postgraduate Research Scholarships (IPRS) 692

New Zealand

Hastings Center International Visiting Scholars Program 318
University of Otago Master's Awards 670

South Africa

Hastings Center International Visiting Scholars Program 318
IARC Postdoctoral Fellowships for Training in Cancer Research 357
International Postgraduate Research Scholarships (IPRS) 692

United Kingdom

British Lung Foundation Project Grants 156
EMBO Award for Communication in the Life Sciences 277
EMBO Science Writing Prize 278
FEMS Fellowship 284
Goldsmiths' Company Science for Society Courses 310
Hastings Center International Visiting Scholars Program 318
International Postgraduate Research Scholarships (IPRS) 692
Llewellyn and Mary Williams Scholarship 699
MND PhD Studentship Award 443
Mr and Mrs David Edward Memorial Award 699
NERC Advanced Course Studentships 476
NERC Research Studentships 476
PDS Research Project Grant 498
PDS Training Fellowships 498
University of Wales Aberystwyth Postgraduate Research Studentships 699
UWB Departmental Research Studentships 700
UWB Research Studentships 700
WellBeing of Women Entry-Lever Scholarship 716
WellBeing of Women/RCOG Research Training Fellowship 716

United States of America

AFAR Research Grants 47
Alcohol Beverage Medical Research Foundation Research Project Grant 15
Fulbright Senior Specialists Program 245
International Postgraduate Research Scholarships (IPRS) 692
MARC Faculty Predoctoral Fellowships 465
NIGMS Fellowship Awards for Minority Students 465
NIGMS Fellowship Awards for Students With Disabilities 465
NIGMS Postdoctoral Awards 465
NIGMS Research Project Grants 466
NIGMS Research Supplements for Underrepresented Minorities 466
NIH Research Grants 466
Paul Beeson Career Development Award 49
Pfizer International HDL Research Awards Program 505
PhRMAF Postdoctoral Fellowships in Informatics 506
PhRMAF Research Starter Grants in Informatics 508
PhRMAF Sabbatical Fellowships in Informatics 509
Washington University Chancellor's Graduate Fellowship Program 715

West European Countries

EMBO Award for Communication in the Life Sciences 277
EMBO Science Writing Prize 278
FEMS Fellowship 284
Hastings Center International Visiting Scholars Program 318
International Postgraduate Research Scholarships (IPRS) 692
Llewellyn and Mary Williams Scholarship 699
Mr and Mrs David Edward Memorial Award 699
NERC Advanced Course Studentships 476
NERC Research Studentships 476
University of Otago Master's Awards 670
UWB Departmental Research Studentships 700
UWB Research Studentships 700

IMMUNOLOGY

Any Country

AACR Scholar-in-Training Awards 28
Abbott Laboratories Award in Clinical and Diagnostic Immunology 82
AHAF Macular Degeneration Research 53
Alzheimer's Society Research Grants 23
ANRF Research Grants 98
BMRP for Inflammatory Bowel Disease Grants 164
Cancer Research UK LRI Clinical Research Fellowships 219
Cancer Research UK LRI Graduate Studentships 219
Career Development Program 409
CBS Graduate Fellowship Program 200
CGD Research Trust Grants 236
CRPF Research Grant 235
Ellison Medical foundation/AFAR senior postdoctoral fellows research program. 48
EMBO Long-Term Fellowships in Molecular Biology 277
EMBO Short-Term Fellowships in Molecular Biology 278
EMBO Young Investigator 278
Foulkes Foundation Fellowship 287
Fungal Research Trust Travel Grants 298
Gordon Piller Studentships 408
Health Research Board PhD Training Sites 319
HRB Postdoctoral Research Fellowships 320
HRB Project Grants-General 320
HRB Summer Student Grants 320
Leukaemia Research Fund Clinical Research Training Fellowships 408
Leukaemia Research Fund Grant Programme 408
Lister Institute Research Prizes 413
LSRF 3-Year Postdoctoral Fellowships 412

African Nations

Australia

Canada

Caribbean Countries

East European Countries

European Union

Middle East

New Zealand

South Africa

United Kingdom

United States of America

West European Countries

MARINE BIOLOGY

Any Country

LIMNOLOGY

MICROBIOLOGY

Any Country

Abbott-ASM Lifetime Achievement Award 82
ASBAH Research Grant 108
ASM BD Award for Research in Clinical Microbiology 82
ASM Graduate Microbiology Teaching Award 82
bioMérieux Sonnenwirth Award for Leadership in Clinical Microbiology 82
BMRP for Inflammatory Bowel Disease Grants 164
Career Development Program 409
Carski Foundation Distinguished Undergraduate Teaching Award 83
CBS Graduate Fellowship Program 200
CDU Senior Research Fellowship 230
CDU Three Year Postdoctoral Fellowship 230
Corpus Christi College Graduate Studentship in Science 674
Dade Behring MicroScan Young Investigator Award 83
Edmund Niles Huyck Preserve, Inc. Graduate and Postgraduate Grants 266
EMBO Long-Term Fellowships in Molecular Biology 277
EMBO Short-Term Fellowships in Molecular Biology 278
EMBO Young Investigator 278
ESRF Postdoctoral Fellowships 279
Foulkes Foundation Fellowship 287
Fungal Research Trust Travel Grants 298
GlaxoSmithKline Collaborative Research Projects 309
GlaxoSmithkline Services to Academia 309
Health Research Board PhD Training Sites 319
HRB Postdoctoral Research Fellowships 320
HRB Project Grants-General 320
HRB Summer Student Grants 320
Hugh Kelly Fellowship 528
La Trobe University Postgraduate Scholarship 403
Lister Institute Research Prizes 413
LSRF 3-Year Postdoctoral Fellowships 412
Meningitis Research Foundation Project Grant 431
Meningitis Trust Research Award 431
NARSAD Distinguished Investigator Awards 449
NARSAD Independent Investigator Awards 449
NARSAD Young Investigator Awards 449
NERC Advanced Research Fellowships 476
NERC Postdoctoral Research Fellowships 476
NRC Research Associateships 471
Procter & Gamble Award in Applied and Environmental Microbiology 83
Queen Mary Research Studentships 518
Rhodes University Postdoctoral Fellowship and The Andrew Mellon Postdoctoral Fellowship 528
Royal Irish Academy Award in Microbiology 551
Royal Irish Academy Award in Nutritional Sciences 551
Sanofi-Aventis Pharmaceuticals Award 84
Teagasc Walsh Fellowships 607
Translational Research Program 409
University of Bristol Postgraduate Scholarships 641
University of Dundee Research Awards 648
University of Otago International Scholarships 670
University of Otago PhD Scholarships 670
University of Otago Prestigious PhD Scholarships 671
Weizmann Institute of Science MSc Fellowships 715
Weizmann Institute of Science PhD Fellowships 715
Weizmann Institute of Science Postdoctoral Fellowships Program 715
Wellcome Trust Grants 717
William A Hinton Research Training Award 84

African Nations

AHRI African Fellowship 98
International Postgraduate Research Scholarships (IPRS) 692

Australia

The Cancer Council NSW Research Project Grants 218
Neil Hamilton Fairley Fellowships (Overseas Clinical) 461
University of Otago Master's Awards 670

Canada

CBS Postdoctoral Fellowship (PDF) 200
CBS Small Projects Fund 201
CTCRI Research Planning Grants 217
Eli Lilly and Company Research Award 83
ICAAC Young Investigator Award 83
International Postgraduate Research Scholarships (IPRS) 692

Caribbean Countries

International Postgraduate Research Scholarships (IPRS) 692

East European Countries

EMBO Award for Communication in the Life Sciences 277
FEMS Fellowship 284
International Postgraduate Research Scholarships (IPRS) 692
NERC Advanced Course Studentships 476
NERC Research Studentships 476
Synthesys Visiting Fellowship 477

European Union

EMBO Award for Communication in the Life Sciences 277
EMBO Science Writing Prize 278

Middle East

International Postgraduate Research Scholarships (IPRS) 692

New Zealand

University of Otago Master's Awards 670

South Africa

Henderson Postgraduate Scholarships 527
International Postgraduate Research Scholarships (IPRS) 692

United Kingdom

EMBO Award for Communication in the Life Sciences 277
EMBO Science Writing Prize 278
ESRF Thesis Studentships 279
FEMS Fellowship 284
International Postgraduate Research Scholarships (IPRS) 692
Llewellyn and Mary Williams Scholarship 699
Mr and Mrs David Edward Memorial Award 699
NERC Advanced Course Studentships 476
NERC Research Studentships 476
University of Essex Access to Learning Fund 652
University of Kent Department of Biosciences 660
University of Wales Aberystwyth Postgraduate Research Studentships 699
UWB Departmental Research Studentships 700
UWB Research Studentships 700

United States of America

AFAR Research Grants 47
Eli Lilly and Company Research Award 83
ICAAC Young Investigator Award 83
International Postgraduate Research Scholarships (IPRS) 692
MARC Faculty Predoctoral Fellowships 465
NIGMS Fellowship Awards for Minority Students 465
NIGMS Fellowship Awards for Students With Disabilities 465
NIGMS Postdoctoral Awards 465
NIGMS Research Project Grants 466
NIGMS Research Supplements for Underrepresented Minorities 466
Paul Beeson Career Development Award 49
Washington University Chancellor's Graduate Fellowship Program 715

West European Countries

EMBO Award for Communication in the Life Sciences 277
EMBO Science Writing Prize 278
ESRF Thesis Studentships 279
FEMS Fellowship 284

NEUROSCIENCES

Any Country

African Nations

Australia

Canada

Caribbean Countries

East European Countries

European Union

Middle East

New Zealand

South Africa

United Kingdom

United States of America

West European Countries

PARASITOLOGY

Any Country

African Nations

Australia

Canada

Caribbean Countries

East European Countries

European Union

New Zealand

South Africa

United Kingdom

West European Countries

PHARMACOLOGY

Any Country

African Nations

Australia

Canada

Caribbean Countries

East European Countries

European Union

Middle East

New Zealand

South Africa

United Kingdom

United States of America

West European Countries

PHYSIOLOGY

Any Country

Australia

Canada

East European Countries

European Union

New Zealand

South Africa

United Kingdom

United States of America

West European Countries

TOXICOLOGY

Any Country

African Nations

Australia

Caribbean Countries

East European Countries

European Union

Middle East

New Zealand

South Africa

United Kingdom

United States of America

West European Countries

ZOOLOGY

Any Country

African Nations

Australia

Canada

East European Countries

European Union

New Zealand

South Africa

Henderson Postgraduate Scholarships 527
Wingate Scholarships 720

United Kingdom

EMBO Science Writing Prize 278
Llewellyn and Mary Williams Scholarship 699
Mr and Mrs David Edward Memorial Award 699
NERC Advanced Course Studentships 476
NERC Research Studentships 476
University of Wales Aberystwyth Postgraduate Research Studentships 699
UWB Departmental Research Studentships 700
UWB Research Studentships 700
Wingate Scholarships 720

United States of America

Budweiser Conservation Scholarship 458
Earthwatch Education Awards 265
PhRMAF Sabbatical Fellowships in Informatics 509

West European Countries

EMBO Science Writing Prize 278
Llewellyn and Mary Williams Scholarship 699
Mr and Mrs David Edward Memorial Award 699
NERC Advanced Course Studentships 476
NERC Research Studentships 476
Synthesys Visiting Fellowship 477
University of Otago Master's Awards 670
UWB Departmental Research Studentships 700
UWB Research Studentships 700
Wingate Scholarships 720

CHEMISTRY

Any Country

AACR Scholar-in-Training Awards 28
Acadia Graduate Awards 7
ACS Award for Achievement in Research for the Teaching and Learning of Chemistry 33
ACS Award for Creative Research and Applications of Iodine Chemistry 33
ACS Award for Encouraging Disadvantaged Students into careers in the Chemical Sciences 33
ACS Award for Encouraging Women into Careers in Chemical Sciences 34
ACS Award in Chromatography 34
ACS National Awards 34
ACS Petroleum Research Fund 34
ACS PRF Type AC Grants 34
ACS Summer Research Fellowships 35
ACS/PRF Scientific Education Grants 35
ACS/PRF Type B Grants 35
Agnes Fay Morgan Research Award 380
Alfred Burger Award in Medicinal Chemistry 35
Alzheimer's Society Research Grants 23
Anselme Payen Award 35
Association for Women in Science Educational Foundation Predoctoral Awards 108
CDU Senior Research Fellowship 230
CDU Three Year Postdoctoral Fellowship 230
CIC Fellowships 214
CIIT-Centers for Health Research Postdoctoral Fellowships 236
CIIT-Centers for Health Research Predoctoral Traineeships 236
Cognis Corporation Graduate Research Fellowship in Colloid and Surface Chemistry 36
Electrochemical Society Summer Fellowships 268
EPSRC Advanced Research Fellowships 271
EPSRC Senior Research Fellowships 272
ESRF Postdoctoral Fellowships 279
Essex Rotary University Travel Grants 651
Franz Sondheimer Bursary Fund 628
Frederic Stanley Kipping Award in Silicon Chemistry 36
Gladys Anderson Emerson Scholarship 381
GlaxoSmithKline Collaborative Research Projects 309
GlaxoSmithkline Services to Academia 309
Glenn E and Barbara Hodsdon Ullyot Scholarship 231
Glenn T. Seaborg Award for Nuclear Chemistry 36
Gordon Cain Fellowship 231
Herbert C. Brown Award for Creative Research in Synthetic Methods 36
Horton (Hydrology) Research Grant 52
Hugh Kelly Fellowship 528
ICR Studentships 345
ICSU-TWAS-UNESCO-UNU/IAS Visiting Scientist Programme 610
International School of Crystallography Grants 375
Iota Sigma Pi Centennial Award 381
Iota Sigma Pi National Honorary Member Award 381
Ipatieff Prize 36
J W T Jones Travelling Fellowship 554
Johnson's Wax Research Fellowship 421
La Trobe University Postgraduate Scholarship 403
McDonnell Graduate Fellowship in the Space Sciences 424
Members-at-Large (MAL) Reentry Award 381
NCAR Postdoctoral Appointments in the Advanced Study Program 454
NRC Research Associateships 471
Queen Mary Research Studentships 518
R A Bournique Memorial Fellowship 422
Rex Williamson Prize 254
Rhodes University Postdoctoral Fellowship and The Andrew Mellon Postdoctoral Fellowship 528
Roche Research Foundation 531
Ronald Breslow Award for Achievement in Biomimetic Chemistry 37
Royal Society of Chemistry Journals Grants for International Authors 555
Royal Society of Chemistry Research Fund 555
Royal Society of Chemistry Visits to Developing Countries 555
Société de Chimie Industrielle (American Section) Fellowship 231
St Catherine's College Graduate Scholarship in the Sciences 687
St Catherine's College Leathersellers' Company Graduate Scholarship 688
University of Bristol Postgraduate Scholarships 641
University of Dundee Research Awards 648
University of Otago International Scholarships 670
University of Otago PhD Scholarships 670
University of Otago Prestigious PhD Scholarships 671
University of Southampton Postgraduate Studentships 692
University of Western Ontario Senior Visiting Fellowship 705
Violet Diller Professional Excellence Award 381
Weizmann Institute of Science MSc Fellowships 715
Weizmann Institute of Science PhD Fellowships 715
Weizmann Institute of Science Postdoctoral Fellowships Program 715
WHOI Postdoctoral Fellowships in Ocean Science and Engineering 726
WHOI Postdoctoral Scholarship Program 727
WHOI/NOAA Co-operative Institute for Climate and Ocean Research Postdoctoral Fellowship 727
Wolf Foundation Prizes 721
World Universities Network (WUN) Global Exchange Programme 693

African Nations

ABCCF Student Grant 95
Corday-Morgan Memorial Fund 554
International Postgraduate Research Scholarships (IPRS) 692
Lindemann Trust Fellowships 273
PTDF Cambridge Scholarships 191
The Trieste Science Prize 610
TWAS Fellowships for Research and Advanced Training 610
TWAS Grants for Scientific Meetings in Developing Countries 611
TWAS Prizes 611
TWAS Prizes to Young Scientists in Developing Countries 611
TWAS Research Grants 611
TWAS Spare Parts for Scientific Equipment 611

Australia

Canada

Caribbean Countries

East European Countries

European Union

Middle East

New Zealand

South Africa

United Kingdom

United States of America

West European Countries

ANALYTICAL CHEMISTRY

Any Country

African Nations

Australia

Canada

Caribbean Countries

East European Countries

Middle East

South Africa

United Kingdom

United States of America

West European Countries

INORGANIC CHEMISTRY

Any Country

African Nations

Australia

Canada

Caribbean Countries

East European Countries

Middle East

South Africa

United Kingdom

United States of America

West European Countries

ORGANIC CHEMISTRY

Any Country

African Nations

Australia

Canada

Caribbean Countries

East European Countries

Middle East

South Africa

United Kingdom

United States of America

West European Countries

PHYSICAL CHEMISTRY

Any Country

African Nations

Australia

Canada

Caribbean Countries

East European Countries

International Postgraduate Research Scholarships (IPRS) 692

Middle East

International Postgraduate Research Scholarships (IPRS) 692
TWAS-S N Bose National Centre for Basic Sciences Postgraduate Fellowships in Physical Sciences 612

South Africa

International Postgraduate Research Scholarships (IPRS) 692
TWAS-S N Bose National Centre for Basic Sciences Postgraduate Fellowships in Physical Sciences 612

United Kingdom

International Postgraduate Research Scholarships (IPRS) 692
Mr and Mrs David Edward Memorial Award 699
UWB Departmental Research Studentships 700
UWB Research Studentships 700

United States of America

ACS/PRF Type G Starter Grants 35
International Postgraduate Research Scholarships (IPRS) 692
PhRMAF Research Starter Grants in Pharmaceutics 508
Washington University Chancellor's Graduate Fellowship Program 715

West European Countries

International Postgraduate Research Scholarships (IPRS) 692
Mr and Mrs David Edward Memorial Award 699
UWB Departmental Research Studentships 700
UWB Research Studentships 700

EARTH AND GEOLOGICAL SCIENCES

Any Country

AAC Research Grants 25
ACS PRF Type AC Grants 34
ACS/PRF Scientific Education Grants 35
ACS/PRF Type B Grants 35
American Association of Petroleum Geologists Foundation Grants-in-Aid 32
ASCSA Research Fellowship in Environmental Studies 79
ASCSA Research Fellowship in Geoarchaeology 79
Association for Women in Science Educational Foundation Predoctoral Awards 108
BFWG Beryl Mavis Green Scholarship 149
BFWG Eila Campbell Scholarship 149
BFWG Johnstone and Florence Stoney Studentship 149
Canadian Natural Resources Limited Graduate Scholarship 642
CDU Senior Research Fellowship 230
CDU Three Year Postdoctoral Fellowship 230
Earthwatch Field Research Grants 265
ESRF Postdoctoral Fellowships 279
Horton (Hydrology) Research Grant 52
HRF Graduate Fellowships 330
Hudson River Graduate Fellowships 331
ICSU-TWAS-UNESCO-UNU/IAS Visiting Scientist Programme 610
Linacre College Applied Materials Scholarships 677
McDonnell Graduate Fellowship in the Space Sciences 424
National Geographic Conservation Trust Grant 241
NCAR Postdoctoral Appointments in the Advanced Study Program 454
NERC Advanced Research Fellowships 476
NERC Postdoctoral Research Fellowships 476
NSF Division of Earth Sciences 471
Queen Mary Research Studentships 518
Robert K. Fahnestock Memorial Award 301
SEG Scholarships 592
St Catherine's College Graduate Scholarship in the Sciences 687
St Catherine's College Leathersellers' Company Graduate Scholarship 688
Stellenbosch Postdoctoral Research Fellowship in Geology 602
University of Bristol Postgraduate Scholarships 641
University of Dundee Research Awards 648
University of Otago International Scholarships 670
University of Otago PhD Scholarships 670
University of Otago Prestigious PhD Scholarships 671
University of Southampton Postgraduate Studentships 692
University of Western Ontario Senior Visiting Fellowship 705
Weizmann Institute of Science MSc Fellowships 715
Weizmann Institute of Science PhD Fellowships 715
Weizmann Institute of Science Postdoctoral Fellowships Program 715
WHOI Geophysical Fluid Dynamics (GFD) Fellowships 726
WHOI Postdoctoral Fellowships in Ocean Science and Engineering 726
WHOI/NOAA Co-operative Institute for Climate and Ocean Research Postdoctoral Fellowship 727
Wolf Foundation Prizes 721
World Universities Network (WUN) Global Exchange Programme 693

African Nations

ABCCF Student Grant 95
International Postgraduate Research Scholarships (IPRS) 692
Postgraduate Studies in Physical Land Resources Scholarship 362
PTDF Cambridge Scholarships 191
The Trieste Science Prize 610
TWAS Fellowships for Research and Advanced Training 610
TWAS Grants for Scientific Meetings in Developing Countries 611
TWAS Prizes 611
TWAS Prizes to Young Scientists in Developing Countries 611
TWAS Research Grants 611
TWAS Spare Parts for Scientific Equipment 611
TWAS UNESCO Associateship Scheme 612
TWNSO Grants to Institutions in the South for Joint Research Projects 612

Australia

C T Taylor Studentship for PhD Study 177
Cranfield University Overseas Bursary 249
Fulbright Postgraduate Student Award for Science and Engineering 126
Wingate Scholarships 720

Canada

C T Taylor Studentship for PhD Study 177
Cranfield University Overseas Bursary 249
GSA Research Grants 300
International Postgraduate Research Scholarships (IPRS) 692
Public Safety and Emergency Preparedness Canada Research Fellowship in Honour of Stuart Nesbitt White 115
Wingate Scholarships 720

Caribbean Countries

Cranfield University Overseas Bursary 249
International Postgraduate Research Scholarships (IPRS) 692
Postgraduate Studies in Physical Land Resources Scholarship 362
TWAS Fellowships for Research and Advanced Training 610
TWAS Grants for Scientific Meetings in Developing Countries 611
TWAS Prizes 611
TWAS Prizes to Young Scientists in Developing Countries 611
TWAS Research Grants 611
TWAS Spare Parts for Scientific Equipment 611
TWAS UNESCO Associateship Scheme 612
TWNSO Grants to Institutions in the South for Joint Research Projects 612

East European Countries

International Postgraduate Research Scholarships (IPRS) 692
NERC Advanced Course Studentships 476
NERC Research Studentships 476
Synthesys Visiting Fellowship 477

Australia

Canada

East European Countries

United Kingdom

United States of America

West European Countries

GEOPHYSICS AND SEISMOLOGY

Any Country

African Nations

Australia

Canada

Caribbean Countries

East European Countries

Middle East

New Zealand

South Africa

United Kingdom

United States of America

West European Countries

PALAEONTOLOGY

Any Country

United States of America

ANS Outstanding Achievement Award 66
ANS Pioneer Award 66
ANS Training Excellence Award 66
Everitt P Blizard Scholarship 66
Mary Jane Oestmann Professional Women's Achievement Award 68
Octave J. Du Temple Award 68
Samuel Glasstone Award 68
Samuel Untermyer Award 68
Theos J. (Tommy) Thompson Award 69
U.S. Nuclear Regulatory Commission Master's and Doctoral Fellowship in Science and Engineering 69
Walter Meyer Scholarship 69

West European Countries

CERN Technical Student Programme 228

OPTICS

Any Country

Abdus Salam ICTP Fellowships 5
BP/RSE Research Fellowships 555
ESRF Postdoctoral Fellowships 279
JILA Postdoctoral Research Associateship and Visiting Fellowships 390
Weizmann Institute of Science MSc Fellowships 715
Weizmann Institute of Science PhD Fellowships 715
Weizmann Institute of Science Postdoctoral Fellowships Program 715

East European Countries

CERN Technical Student Programme 228

United Kingdom

CERN Technical Student Programme 228
ESRF Thesis Studentships 279

West European Countries

CERN Technical Student Programme 228
ESRF Thesis Studentships 279

SOLID STATE PHYSICS

Any Country

Abdus Salam ICTP Fellowships 5
BP/RSE Research Fellowships 555
ESRF Postdoctoral Fellowships 279
International School of Crystallography Grants 375
JILA Postdoctoral Research Associateship and Visiting Fellowships 390
SISSA Fellowships 375
Thomas Holloway Research Studentship 548
Weizmann Institute of Science MSc Fellowships 715
Weizmann Institute of Science PhD Fellowships 715
Weizmann Institute of Science Postdoctoral Fellowships Program 715
Welch Foundation Scholarship 379

African Nations

TWAS-S N Bose National Centre for Basic Sciences Postgraduate Fellowships in Physical Sciences 612

Caribbean Countries

TWAS-S N Bose National Centre for Basic Sciences Postgraduate Fellowships in Physical Sciences 612

East European Countries

CERN Technical Student Programme 228

Middle East

TWAS-S N Bose National Centre for Basic Sciences Postgraduate Fellowships in Physical Sciences 612

South Africa

TWAS-S N Bose National Centre for Basic Sciences Postgraduate Fellowships in Physical Sciences 612

United Kingdom

CERN Technical Student Programme 228
ESRF Thesis Studentships 279
University of Wales Aberystwyth Postgraduate Research Studentships 699

West European Countries

CERN Technical Student Programme 228
ESRF Thesis Studentships 279

THERMAL PHYSICS

Any Country

JILA Postdoctoral Research Associateship and Visiting Fellowships 390
Weizmann Institute of Science MSc Fellowships 715
Weizmann Institute of Science PhD Fellowships 715
Weizmann Institute of Science Postdoctoral Fellowships Program 715

African Nations

International Postgraduate Research Scholarships (IPRS) 692

Canada

International Postgraduate Research Scholarships (IPRS) 692

Caribbean Countries

International Postgraduate Research Scholarships (IPRS) 692

East European Countries

International Postgraduate Research Scholarships (IPRS) 692

Middle East

International Postgraduate Research Scholarships (IPRS) 692

South Africa

International Postgraduate Research Scholarships (IPRS) 692

United Kingdom

International Postgraduate Research Scholarships (IPRS) 692

United States of America

International Postgraduate Research Scholarships (IPRS) 692

West European Countries

International Postgraduate Research Scholarships (IPRS) 692

ASTRONOMY AND ASTROPHYSICS

Any Country

Abdus Salam ICTP Fellowships 5
Association for Women in Science Educational Foundation Predoctoral Awards 108
Dublin Institute for Advanced Studies Scholarship in Astronomy, Astrophysics and Geophysics 262
IAU Travel Grant 360
Jansky Fellowship 471
JILA Postdoctoral Research Associateship and Visiting Fellowships 390

McDonnell Graduate Fellowship in the Space Sciences 424
NCAR Postdoctoral Appointments in the Advanced Study Program 454
NRC Research Associateships 471
PPARC Research Grants in Astronomy and Particle Physics 500
Queen Mary Research Studentships 518
SAO Predoctoral Fellowships 574
SISSA Fellowships 375
St Catherine's College Graduate Scholarship in the Sciences 687
St Catherine's College Leathersellers' Company Graduate Scholarship 688
University of Bristol Postgraduate Scholarships 641
University of Southampton Postgraduate Studentships 692
Weizmann Institute of Science MSc Fellowships 715
Weizmann Institute of Science PhD Fellowships 715
WHOI Geophysical Fluid Dynamics (GFD) Fellowships 726
Wolf Foundation Prizes 721
World Universities Network (WUN) Global Exchange Programme 693

African Nations

Lindemann Trust Fellowships 273
PTDF Cambridge Scholarships 191
The Trieste Science Prize 610
TWAS Fellowships for Research and Advanced Training 610
TWAS Grants for Scientific Meetings in Developing Countries 611
TWAS Prizes 611
TWAS Research Grants 611
TWAS Spare Parts for Scientific Equipment 611
TWAS UNESCO Associateship Scheme 612
TWNSO Grants to Institutions in the South for Joint Research Projects 612

Australia

Lindemann Trust Fellowships 273
Wingate Scholarships 720

Canada

Cottrell College Science Awards 524
Cottrell Scholars Awards 524
Lindemann Trust Fellowships 273
Research Corporation (USA) Research Opportunity Awards 525
Wingate Scholarships 720

Caribbean Countries

TWAS Fellowships for Research and Advanced Training 610
TWAS Grants for Scientific Meetings in Developing Countries 611
TWAS Prizes 611
TWAS Research Grants 611
TWAS Spare Parts for Scientific Equipment 611
TWAS UNESCO Associateship Scheme 612
TWNSO Grants to Institutions in the South for Joint Research Projects 612

East European Countries

PPARC Postgraduate Studentships 500

European Union

PPARC Spanish (IAC) Studentship 500

Middle East

The Trieste Science Prize 610
TWAS Fellowships for Research and Advanced Training 610
TWAS Grants for Scientific Meetings in Developing Countries 611
TWAS Prizes 611
TWAS Research Grants 611
TWAS Spare Parts for Scientific Equipment 611
TWAS UNESCO Associateship Scheme 612
TWNSO Grants to Institutions in the South for Joint Research Projects 612

New Zealand

Lindemann Trust Fellowships 273
Wingate Scholarships 720

South Africa

Henderson Postgraduate Scholarships 527
Lindemann Trust Fellowships 273
The Trieste Science Prize 610
TWAS Fellowships for Research and Advanced Training 610
TWAS Grants for Scientific Meetings in Developing Countries 611
TWAS Prizes 611
TWAS Research Grants 611
TWAS Spare Parts for Scientific Equipment 611
TWAS UNESCO Associateship Scheme 612
TWNSO Grants to Institutions in the South for Joint Research Projects 612
Wingate Scholarships 720

United Kingdom

Goldsmiths' Company Science for Society Courses 310
Lindemann Trust Fellowships 273
PPARC Advanced Fellowships 499
PPARC Daphne Jackson Fellowships 499
PPARC Postdoctoral Fellowships 500
PPARC Postgraduate Studentships 500
PPARC Senior Research Fellowships 500
University of Wales Aberystwyth Postgraduate Research Studentships 699
Wingate Scholarships 720

United States of America

Cottrell College Science Awards 524
Cottrell Scholars Awards 524
Fannie and John Hertz Foundation Fellowships 283
Fulbright Senior Specialists Program 245
McDonnell Center Astronaut Fellowships in the Space Sciences 423
Norwegian Thanksgiving Fund Scholarship 487
Research Corporation (USA) Research Opportunity Awards 525
Winston Churchill Foundation Scholarship 720

West European Countries

ESO Fellowship 279
PPARC Postgraduate Studentships 500
Wingate Scholarships 720

ATMOSPHERE SCIENCE/METEOROLOGY

Any Country

AAC Research Grants 25
Abdus Salam ICTP Fellowships 5
Association for Women in Science Educational Foundation Predoctoral Awards 108
BFWG Johnstone and Florence Stoney Studentship 149
Earthwatch Field Research Grants 265
ICSU-TWAS-UNESCO-UNU/IAS Visiting Scientist Programme 610
McDonnell Graduate Fellowship in the Space Sciences 424
National Geographic Conservation Trust Grant 241
NCAR Graduate Visitor Programme 454
NCAR IAI/NCAR Postdoctoral Fellowship 454
NCAR Postdoctoral Appointments in the Advanced Study Program 454
NCAR Postdoctoral Fellowships 454
NERC Advanced Research Fellowships 476
NERC Postdoctoral Research Fellowships 476
Queen Mary Research Studentships 518
Weizmann Institute of Science MSc Fellowships 715
Weizmann Institute of Science PhD Fellowships 715
WHOI Geophysical Fluid Dynamics (GFD) Fellowships 726
WHOI Postdoctoral Fellowships in Ocean Science and Engineering 726

African Nations

Australia

Canada

Caribbean Countries

East European Countries

Middle East

New Zealand

South Africa

United Kingdom

United States of America

West European Countries

ARCTIC STUDIES

Any Country

East European Countries

United Kingdom

United States of America

West European Countries

ARID LAND STUDIES

Any Country

East European Countries

United Kingdom

West European Countries

OCEANOGRAPHY

Any Country

African Nations

Australia

Canada

Caribbean Countries

East European Countries

Middle East

New Zealand

South Africa

United Kingdom

United States of America

West European Countries

RECREATION, WELFARE, PROTECTIVE SERVICES

GENERAL

Any Country

African Nations

Australia

Canada

POLICE AND LAW ENFORCEMENT

CRIMINOLOGY

United Kingdom

United States of America

West European Countries

FIRE PROTECTION/CONTROL

United Kingdom

MILITARY SCIENCE

Any Country

United Kingdom

United States of America

CIVIL SECURITY

Any Country

African Nations

Canada

Caribbean Countries

South Africa

United Kingdom

United States of America

PEACE AND DISARMAMENT

Any Country

African Nations

Canada

Caribbean Countries

South Africa

United Kingdom

United States of America

SOCIAL WELFARE AND SOCIAL WORK

Any Country

African Nations

International Postgraduate Research Scholarships (IPRS) 692
MCTC Assistance for Courses 309
MCTC Tuition and Maintenance Scholarships 309

Australia

Wingate Scholarships 720

Canada

Canadian Milleniuni Excellence Awards 234
International Postgraduate Research Scholarships (IPRS) 692
JCCA Graduate Education Scholarship 389
Sheriff Willoughby King Memorial Scholarship 643
SSHRC Doctoral Awards 582
SSHRC Standard Research Grants 583
Terry Fox Humanitarian Award 234
Wingate Scholarships 720

Caribbean Countries

International Postgraduate Research Scholarships (IPRS) 692
MCTC Assistance for Courses 309
MCTC Tuition and Maintenance Scholarships 309

East European Countries

International Postgraduate Research Scholarships (IPRS) 692
MCTC Assistance for Courses 309
MCTC Tuition and Maintenance Scholarships 309

European Union

ESRC 1 + 3 Awards and + 3 Awards 265

Middle East

International Postgraduate Research Scholarships (IPRS) 692
MCTC Assistance for Courses 309
MCTC Tuition and Maintenance Scholarships 309

New Zealand

Wingate Scholarships 720

South Africa

International Postgraduate Research Scholarships (IPRS) 692
MCTC Assistance for Courses 309
MCTC Tuition and Maintenance Scholarships 309
Wingate Scholarships 720

United Kingdom

ESRC 1 + 3 Awards and + 3 Awards 265
General Social Care Council Additional Graduate Bursary 299
International Postgraduate Research Scholarships (IPRS) 692
Mr and Mrs David Edward Memorial Award 699
Sheffield Hallam University Studentships 567
University of Wales Aberystwyth Postgraduate Research Studentships 699
UWB Departmental Research Studentships 700
UWB Research Studentships 700
Wingate Scholarships 720

United States of America

Congress Bundestag Youth Exchange for Young Professionals 224
CSWE Doctoral Fellowships in Social Work for Ethnic Minority Students Preparing for Leadership Roles in Mental Health and/or Substance Abuse 248
CSWE Doctoral Fellowships in Social Work for Ethnic Minority Students Specializing in Mental Health 248
CSWE Mental Health Minority Fellowship Program 248
Fulbright Senior Specialists Program 245
Ian Axford (New Zealand) Fellowships in Public Policy 239
International Postgraduate Research Scholarships (IPRS) 692
IREX Short-Term Travel Grants 374
JCCA Graduate Education Scholarship 389
Robert Bosch Foundation Fellowships 530
Washington University Chancellor's Graduate Fellowship Program 715

West European Countries

ESRC 1 + 3 Awards and + 3 Awards 265
International Postgraduate Research Scholarships (IPRS) 692
Mr and Mrs David Edward Memorial Award 699
Sheffield Hallam University Studentships 567
UWB Departmental Research Studentships 700
UWB Research Studentships 700
Wingate Scholarships 720

PUBLIC AND COMMUNITY SERVICES

Any Country

ASBAH Research Grant 108
Memorial Foundation for Jewish Culture International Scholarship Programme for Community Service 430

African Nations

International Postgraduate Research Scholarships (IPRS) 692
MCTC Assistance for Courses 309
MCTC Tuition and Maintenance Scholarships 309

Canada

International Postgraduate Research Scholarships (IPRS) 692
JCCA Graduate Education Scholarship 389
SSHRC Doctoral Awards 582

Caribbean Countries

International Postgraduate Research Scholarships (IPRS) 692
MCTC Assistance for Courses 309
MCTC Tuition and Maintenance Scholarships 309

East European Countries

International Postgraduate Research Scholarships (IPRS) 692
MCTC Assistance for Courses 309
MCTC Tuition and Maintenance Scholarships 309

Middle East

International Postgraduate Research Scholarships (IPRS) 692
MCTC Assistance for Courses 309
MCTC Tuition and Maintenance Scholarships 309

South Africa

International Postgraduate Research Scholarships (IPRS) 692
MCTC Assistance for Courses 309
MCTC Tuition and Maintenance Scholarships 309

United Kingdom

International Postgraduate Research Scholarships (IPRS) 692

United States of America

Congress Bundestag Youth Exchange for Young Professionals 224
International Postgraduate Research Scholarships (IPRS) 692
JCCA Graduate Education Scholarship 389

West European Countries

International Postgraduate Research Scholarships (IPRS) 692

VOCATIONAL COUNSELLING

Any Country

Equiano Memorial Award 604

United States of America

Ian Axford (New Zealand) Fellowships in Public Policy 239

ENVIRONMENTAL STUDIES

Any Country

ACS Award for Creative Advances in Environmental Science and Technology 33
Alberta Law Foundation Graduate Scholarship 642
American Association of Petroleum Geologists Foundation Grants-in-Aid 32
ASCSA Research Fellowship in Environmental Studies 79
CDU Senior Research Fellowship 230
CDU Three Year Postdoctoral Fellowship 230
Earthwatch Field Research Grants 265
Edmund Niles Huyck Preserve, Inc. Graduate and Postgraduate Grants 266
George A Hall/Harold F Mayfield Award 720
German Chancellor Scholarship Program 19
Gilbert F White Postdoctoral Fellowship 525
Hastings Center International Visiting Scholars Program 318
Honda Prize 328
Hudson River Expedition Grants 330
Hudson River Graduate Fellowships 331
Hudson River Research Grants 331
Hudson River Travel Grants 331
Joseph L Fisher Dissertation Award 525
Lindbergh Grants 229
Louis Agassiz Fuertes Award 720
NCAR Postdoctoral Appointments in the Advanced Study Program 454
NERC Advanced Research Fellowships 476
NERC Postdoctoral Research Fellowships 476
O'Reiuy Environmental Science Scholarship 604
Paul A Stewart Awards 720
RFF Fellowships in Environmental Regulatory Implementation 526
Rhodes University Postdoctoral Fellowship and The Andrew Mellon Postdoctoral Fellowship 528
Robin Roussean Memorial Mountain Achievement Scholarship 234
Sir Eric Berthoud Travel Grant 652
St Catherine's College Graduate Scholarship in the Arts 687
Tibor T Polgar Fellowship 331
Trinity College Birkett Scholarship in Environmental Studies 688
University of Bristol Postgraduate Scholarships 641
University of Dundee Research Awards 648
University of Southampton Postgraduate Studentships 692
University of Sussex Overseas Research Studentships 696
Ursula M. Handel Animal Welfare Prize 259
WHOI Research Fellowships in Marine Policy 727
World Universities Network (WUN) Global Exchange Programme 693

African Nations

Canadian Window on International Development 364
Corpus Christi ACE Scholarship for Postgraduate Study 180
Ecosystem Approaches to Human Health Awards 364
Hastings Center International Visiting Scholars Program 318
HFSPO IFS Research Grant 367
IDRC Doctoral Research Awards 365
International Postgraduate Research Scholarships (IPRS) 692
NUFFIC-NFP Fellowships for Master's Degree Programmes 478
Shell Centenary Scholarships (Developing Countries of the Commonwealth) 192
Shell Centenary Scholarships and Shell Centenary Chevening Scholarships 685

Australia

Cranfield University Overseas Bursary 249
Fulbright Postgraduate Student Award for Science and Engineering 126
Hastings Center International Visiting Scholars Program 318
University of Essex/ORS Awards 655
Wingate Scholarships 720

Canada

Canadian Window on International Development 364
Community Forestry: Trees and People - John G Bene Fellowship 364
Cranfield University Overseas Bursary 249
Ecosystem Approaches to Human Health Awards 364
Horticultural Research Institute Grants 329
IDRC Doctoral Research Awards 365
International Postgraduate Research Scholarships (IPRS) 692
University of Essex/ORS Awards 655
Wingate Scholarships 720

Caribbean Countries

Canadian Window on International Development 364
Cranfield University Overseas Bursary 249
Ecosystem Approaches to Human Health Awards 364
Hastings Center International Visiting Scholars Program 318
HFSPO IFS Research Grant 367
IDRC Doctoral Research Awards 365
International Postgraduate Research Scholarships (IPRS) 692
Shell Centenary Scholarships and Shell Centenary Chevening Scholarships 685
University of Essex/ORS Awards 655

East European Countries

Corpus Christi ACE Scholarship for Postgraduate Study 180
German Chancellor Scholarship Program 19
Hastings Center International Visiting Scholars Program 318
Intel Public Affairs Russia Grant 356
International Postgraduate Research Scholarships (IPRS) 692
NERC Advanced Course Studentships 476
NERC Research Studentships 476
OSI (Open Society Institute)/FCO Chevening Scholarships 682
Shell Centenary Cambridge Scholarships (Countries Outside of the Commonwealth) 192
Shell Centenary Scholarships (Developing Countries of the Commonwealth) 192
Shell Centenary Scholarships and Shell Centenary Chevening Scholarships 685
Synthesys Visiting Fellowship 477
University of Essex/ORS Awards 655

Middle East

Cranfield University Overseas Bursary 249
Ecosystem Approaches to Human Health Awards 364
Hastings Center International Visiting Scholars Program 318
HFSPO IFS Research Grant 367
International Postgraduate Research Scholarships (IPRS) 692
NUFFIC-NFP Fellowships for Master's Degree Programmes 478
Shell Centenary Cambridge Scholarships (Countries Outside of the Commonwealth) 192
Shell Centenary Scholarships and Shell Centenary Chevening Scholarships 685
University of Essex/ORS Awards 655

New Zealand

Cranfield University Overseas Bursary 249
Hastings Center International Visiting Scholars Program 318
Wingate Scholarships 720

South Africa

Canadian Window on International Development 364
Cranfield University Overseas Bursary 249
Ecosystem Approaches to Human Health Awards 364
Hastings Center International Visiting Scholars Program 318
HFSPO IFS Research Grant 367
IDRC Doctoral Research Awards 365
International Postgraduate Research Scholarships (IPRS) 692
NUFFIC-NFP Fellowships for Master's Degree Programmes 478

United Kingdom

United States of America

West European Countries

ECOLOGY

Any Country

African Nations

Australia

Canada

Caribbean Countries

East European Countries

Middle East

New Zealand

South Africa

United Kingdom

United States of America

FFGC Scholarship in Ecology 286
Fulbright Senior Specialists Program 245
International Postgraduate Research Scholarships (IPRS) 692
Welder Wildlife Foundation Fellowship 529

West European Countries

International Postgraduate Research Scholarships (IPRS) 692
Mr and Mrs David Edward Memorial Award 699
NERC Advanced Course Studentships 476
NERC Research Studentships 476
Synthesys Visiting Fellowship 477
UWB Departmental Research Studentships 700
UWB Research Studentships 700
Wingate Scholarships 720

NATURAL RESOURCES

Any Country

Alberta Law Foundation Graduate Scholarship 642
American Association of Petroleum Geologists Foundation Grants-in-Aid 32
AWWA Thomas R Camp Scholarship 93
Canadian Embassy (USA) Faculty Enrichment Program 203
CDU Senior Research Fellowship 230
CDU Three Year Postdoctoral Fellowship 230
Earthwatch Field Research Grants 265
Edmund Niles Huyck Preserve, Inc. Graduate and Postgraduate Grants 266
Hudson River Expedition Grants 330
Hudson River Graduate Fellowships 331
Hudson River Research Grants 331
Hudson River Travel Grants 331
NERC Advanced Research Fellowships 476
NERC Postdoctoral Research Fellowships 476
Rhodes University Postdoctoral Fellowship and The Andrew Mellon Postdoctoral Fellowship 528
Tibor T Polgar Fellowship 331
University of Calgary Faculty of Law Graduate Scholarship 643

African Nations

IDRC Doctoral Research Awards 365
International Postgraduate Research Scholarships (IPRS) 692

Australia

Cranfield University Overseas Bursary 249
Fulbright Postgraduate Student Award for Science and Engineering 126
Wingate Scholarships 720

Canada

AWWA Abel Wolman Fellowship 92
Cranfield University Overseas Bursary 249
IDRC Doctoral Research Awards 365
International Postgraduate Research Scholarships (IPRS) 692
Wingate Scholarships 720

Caribbean Countries

Cranfield University Overseas Bursary 249
IDRC Doctoral Research Awards 365
International Postgraduate Research Scholarships (IPRS) 692

East European Countries

International Postgraduate Research Scholarships (IPRS) 692
NERC Advanced Course Studentships 476
NERC Research Studentships 476
Synthesys Visiting Fellowship 477

Middle East

Cranfield University Overseas Bursary 249
International Postgraduate Research Scholarships (IPRS) 692

New Zealand

Cranfield University Overseas Bursary 249
Wingate Scholarships 720

South Africa

Cranfield University Overseas Bursary 249
IDRC Doctoral Research Awards 365
International Postgraduate Research Scholarships (IPRS) 692
Wingate Scholarships 720

United Kingdom

International Postgraduate Research Scholarships (IPRS) 692
Mr and Mrs David Edward Memorial Award 699
NERC Advanced Course Studentships 476
NERC Research Studentships 476
Silsoe Awards 249
UWB Departmental Research Studentships 700
UWB Research Studentships 700
Wingate Scholarships 720

United States of America

AWWA Abel Wolman Fellowship 92
Congress Bundestag Youth Exchange for Young Professionals 224
Cranfield University Overseas Bursary 249
Earthwatch Education Awards 265
Fulbright Senior Specialists Program 245
International Postgraduate Research Scholarships (IPRS) 692

West European Countries

International Postgraduate Research Scholarships (IPRS) 692
Mr and Mrs David Edward Memorial Award 699
NERC Advanced Course Studentships 476
NERC Research Studentships 476
Silsoe Awards 249
Synthesys Visiting Fellowship 477
UWB Departmental Research Studentships 700
UWB Research Studentships 700
Wingate Scholarships 720

ENVIRONMENTAL MANAGEMENT

Any Country

AWWA Academic Achievement Award 92
CDU Senior Research Fellowship 230
CDU Three Year Postdoctoral Fellowship 230
Earthwatch Field Research Grants 265
Hudson River Expedition Grants 330
Hudson River Graduate Fellowships 331
Hudson River Research Grants 331
Hudson River Travel Grants 331
Linacre College and the Environmental Change Institute Coca-Cola Water Sustainability Scholarships 677
NERC Advanced Research Fellowships 476
NERC Postdoctoral Research Fellowships 476
Rhodes University Postdoctoral Fellowship and The Andrew Mellon Postdoctoral Fellowship 528
Stanley Smith (UK) Horticultural Trust Awards 598
Tibor T Polgar Fellowship 331
UFAW Animal Welfare Research Training Scholarships 624
UFAW Research and Project Awards 624
UFAW Small Project and Travel Awards 624
UFAW Vacation Scholarships 624
University of Calgary Faculty of Law Graduate Scholarship 643
University of Kent Anthropology Postgraduate Maintenance Grants 660

African Nations

Corpus Christi ACE Scholarship for Postgraduate Study 180
IDRC Doctoral Research Awards 365
International Postgraduate Research Scholarships (IPRS) 692

Australia

Cranfield University Overseas Bursary 249
Fulbright Postgraduate Student Award for Science and Engineering 126
Wingate Scholarships 720

Canada

AWWA Abel Wolman Fellowship 92
CIC Environmental Improvement Award 213
Cranfield University Overseas Bursary 249
Horticultural Research Institute Grants 329
IDRC Doctoral Research Awards 365
International Postgraduate Research Scholarships (IPRS) 692
Wingate Scholarships 720

Caribbean Countries

Cranfield University Overseas Bursary 249
IDRC Doctoral Research Awards 365
International Postgraduate Research Scholarships (IPRS) 692

East European Countries

Corpus Christi ACE Scholarship for Postgraduate Study 180
International Postgraduate Research Scholarships (IPRS) 692
NERC Advanced Course Studentships 476
NERC Research Studentships 476
Synthesys Visiting Fellowship 477

Middle East

Cranfield University Overseas Bursary 249
International Postgraduate Research Scholarships (IPRS) 692

New Zealand

Cranfield University Overseas Bursary 249
Wingate Scholarships 720

South Africa

Cranfield University Overseas Bursary 249
IDRC Doctoral Research Awards 365
International Postgraduate Research Scholarships (IPRS) 692
Wingate Scholarships 720

United Kingdom

International Postgraduate Research Scholarships (IPRS) 692
Mr and Mrs David Edward Memorial Award 699
NERC Advanced Course Studentships 476
NERC Research Studentships 476
Sheffield Hallam University Studentships 567
Silsoe Awards 249
University of Wales Aberystwyth Postgraduate Research Studentships 699
UWB Departmental Research Studentships 700
UWB Research Studentships 700
Wingate Scholarships 720

United States of America

AWWA Abel Wolman Fellowship 92
AWWA Holly A Cornell Scholarship 93
Congress Bundestag Youth Exchange for Young Professionals 224
Cranfield University Overseas Bursary 249
Earthwatch Education Awards 265
Fulbright Senior Specialists Program 245
Horticultural Research Institute Grants 329
International Postgraduate Research Scholarships (IPRS) 692

West European Countries

International Postgraduate Research Scholarships (IPRS) 692
Mr and Mrs David Edward Memorial Award 699
NERC Advanced Course Studentships 476
NERC Research Studentships 476
Sheffield Hallam University Studentships 567
Silsoe Awards 249
Synthesys Visiting Fellowship 477
UWB Departmental Research Studentships 700
UWB Research Studentships 700
Wingate Scholarships 720

WILDLIFE AND PEST MANAGEMENT

Any Country

CDU Senior Research Fellowship 230
CDU Three Year Postdoctoral Fellowship 230
Charles Dobbins Memorial Scholarship 473
Earthwatch Field Research Grants 265
Hudson River Expedition Grants 330
Hudson River Graduate Fellowships 331
Hudson River Research Grants 331
Hudson River Travel Grants 331
NERC Advanced Research Fellowships 476
NERC Postdoctoral Research Fellowships 476
Paul A Stewart Awards 720
Tibor T Polgar Fellowship 331
UFAW Animal Welfare Research Training Scholarships 624
UFAW Research and Project Awards 624
UFAW Small Project and Travel Awards 624
UFAW Vacation Scholarships 624
University of Kent Anthropology Postgraduate Maintenance Grants 660

African Nations

IDRC Doctoral Research Awards 365
International Postgraduate Research Scholarships (IPRS) 692

Australia

Wingate Scholarships 720

Canada

IDRC Doctoral Research Awards 365
International Postgraduate Research Scholarships (IPRS) 692
Wingate Scholarships 720

Caribbean Countries

IDRC Doctoral Research Awards 365
International Postgraduate Research Scholarships (IPRS) 692

East European Countries

International Postgraduate Research Scholarships (IPRS) 692
NERC Advanced Course Studentships 476
NERC Research Studentships 476

Middle East

International Postgraduate Research Scholarships (IPRS) 692

New Zealand

Wingate Scholarships 720

South Africa

IDRC Doctoral Research Awards 365
International Postgraduate Research Scholarships (IPRS) 692
Wingate Scholarships 720

United Kingdom

International Postgraduate Research Scholarships (IPRS) 692
Mr and Mrs David Edward Memorial Award 699
NERC Advanced Course Studentships 476
NERC Research Studentships 476
UWB Departmental Research Studentships 700
UWB Research Studentships 700
Wingate Scholarships 720

United States of America

Congress Bundestag Youth Exchange for Young Professionals 224
Earthwatch Education Awards 265
Fulbright Senior Specialists Program 245
International Postgraduate Research Scholarships (IPRS) 692
Welder Wildlife Foundation Fellowship 529

West European Countries

International Postgraduate Research Scholarships (IPRS) 692
Mr and Mrs David Edward Memorial Award 699
NERC Advanced Course Studentships 476
NERC Research Studentships 476
UWB Departmental Research Studentships 700
UWB Research Studentships 700
Wingate Scholarships 720

PHYSICAL EDUCATION AND SPORTS

Any Country

Acadia Graduate Awards 7
BCUC Research Student Bursary 167
Essex Rotary University Travel Grants 651
Explorers Club Exploration Fund 283
The Katrina Mihaere Scholarship 415
Rhodes University Postdoctoral Fellowship and The Andrew Mellon Postdoctoral Fellowship 528
Sir Eric Berthoud Travel Grant 652
University of Bristol Postgraduate Scholarships 641
University of Exeter Sports Scholarships 657
University of Otago International Scholarships 670
University of Otago PhD Scholarships 670
University of Otago Prestigious PhD Scholarships 671

African Nations

International Postgraduate Research Scholarships (IPRS) 692

Australia

University of Essex/ORS Awards 655

Canada

International Postgraduate Research Scholarships (IPRS) 692
JCCA Graduate Education Scholarship 389
John Hervey, Broadcasters and Smallsreed Awards 623
University of Essex/ORS Awards 655

Caribbean Countries

International Postgraduate Research Scholarships (IPRS) 692
University of Essex/ORS Awards 655

East European Countries

International Postgraduate Research Scholarships (IPRS) 692
University of Essex/ORS Awards 655

European Union

Loughborough Sports Scholarships 417
MCofS Expedition Grant 608

Middle East

International Postgraduate Research Scholarships (IPRS) 692
University of Essex/ORS Awards 655

New Zealand

Sir Edmund Hillary Scholarship Programme 698

South Africa

International Postgraduate Research Scholarships (IPRS) 692
University of Essex/ORS Awards 655

United Kingdom

Alpine Ski Club Kenneth Smith Scholarship 158
BMC Grant 159
International Postgraduate Research Scholarships (IPRS) 692
Mr and Mrs David Edward Memorial Award 699
Sheffield Hallam University Studentships 567
University of Essex Access to Learning Fund 652
University of Wales Aberystwyth Postgraduate Research Studentships 699
UWB Departmental Research Studentships 700
UWB Research Studentships 700

United States of America

AAC Mountaineering Fellowship Fund Grants 25
International Postgraduate Research Scholarships (IPRS) 692
JCCA Graduate Education Scholarship 389
John Hervey, Broadcasters and Smallsreed Awards 623
University of Essex/ORS Awards 655

West European Countries

International Postgraduate Research Scholarships (IPRS) 692
Mr and Mrs David Edward Memorial Award 699
Sheffield Hallam University Studentships 567
UWB Departmental Research Studentships 700
UWB Research Studentships 700

SPORTS MANAGEMENT

Any Country

Harness Track of America Scholarship 317
University of Bristol Postgraduate Scholarships 641

African Nations

International Postgraduate Research Scholarships (IPRS) 692

Australia

Cranfield University Overseas Bursary 249

Canada

Cranfield University Overseas Bursary 249
International Postgraduate Research Scholarships (IPRS) 692
JCCA Graduate Education Scholarship 389

Caribbean Countries

Cranfield University Overseas Bursary 249
International Postgraduate Research Scholarships (IPRS) 692

East European Countries

International Postgraduate Research Scholarships (IPRS) 692

European Union

Our World-Underwater Scholarship Society Scholarships 496
The University of Glamorgan Sports Scholarships 657

Middle East

Cranfield University Overseas Bursary 249
International Postgraduate Research Scholarships (IPRS) 692

New Zealand

Cranfield University Overseas Bursary 249

South Africa

Cranfield University Overseas Bursary 249
International Postgraduate Research Scholarships (IPRS) 692

United Kingdom

International Postgraduate Research Scholarships (IPRS) 692
Mr and Mrs David Edward Memorial Award 699

Sheffield Hallam University Studentships 567
Silsoe Awards 249
The University of Glamorgan Sports Scholarships 657
University of Wales Aberystwyth Postgraduate Research Studentships 699
UWB Departmental Research Studentships 700
UWB Research Studentships 700

United States of America

Congress Bundestag Youth Exchange for Young Professionals 224
Cranfield University Overseas Bursary 249
International Postgraduate Research Scholarships (IPRS) 692
JCCA Graduate Education Scholarship 389
Our World-Underwater Scholarship Society Scholarships 496

West European Countries

International Postgraduate Research Scholarships (IPRS) 692
Mr and Mrs David Edward Memorial Award 699
Sheffield Hallam University Studentships 567
Silsoe Awards 249
UWB Departmental Research Studentships 700
UWB Research Studentships 700

SOCIOLOGY OF SPORTS

African Nations

International Postgraduate Research Scholarships (IPRS) 692

Canada

International Postgraduate Research Scholarships (IPRS) 692
JCCA Graduate Education Scholarship 389

Caribbean Countries

International Postgraduate Research Scholarships (IPRS) 692

East European Countries

International Postgraduate Research Scholarships (IPRS) 692

European Union

ESRC 1+3 Awards and +3 Awards 265
Our World-Underwater Scholarship Society Scholarships 496

Middle East

International Postgraduate Research Scholarships (IPRS) 692

South Africa

International Postgraduate Research Scholarships (IPRS) 692

United Kingdom

ESRC 1+3 Awards and +3 Awards 265
International Postgraduate Research Scholarships (IPRS) 692
Mr and Mrs David Edward Memorial Award 699
University of Wales Aberystwyth Postgraduate Research Studentships 699
UWB Departmental Research Studentships 700
UWB Research Studentships 700

United States of America

International Postgraduate Research Scholarships (IPRS) 692
JCCA Graduate Education Scholarship 389
Our World-Underwater Scholarship Society Scholarships 496

West European Countries

ESRC 1+3 Awards and +3 Awards 265
International Postgraduate Research Scholarships (IPRS) 692
Mr and Mrs David Edward Memorial Award 699
UWB Departmental Research Studentships 700
UWB Research Studentships 700

LEISURE STUDIES

Any Country

BCUC Research Student Bursary 167
British Airways Travel Bursary 545

African Nations

International Postgraduate Research Scholarships (IPRS) 692
NUFFIC-NFP Fellowships for Master's Degree Programmes 478

Canada

International Postgraduate Research Scholarships (IPRS) 692
JCCA Graduate Education Scholarship 389

Caribbean Countries

International Postgraduate Research Scholarships (IPRS) 692

East European Countries

International Postgraduate Research Scholarships (IPRS) 692

Middle East

International Postgraduate Research Scholarships (IPRS) 692
NUFFIC-NFP Fellowships for Master's Degree Programmes 478

South Africa

International Postgraduate Research Scholarships (IPRS) 692
NUFFIC-NFP Fellowships for Master's Degree Programmes 478

United Kingdom

International Postgraduate Research Scholarships (IPRS) 692
Mr and Mrs David Edward Memorial Award 699
UWB Departmental Research Studentships 700

United States of America

International Postgraduate Research Scholarships (IPRS) 692
JCCA Graduate Education Scholarship 389

West European Countries

International Postgraduate Research Scholarships (IPRS) 692
Mr and Mrs David Edward Memorial Award 699
UWB Departmental Research Studentships 700

PARKS AND RECREATION

Any Country

Stanley Smith (UK) Horticultural Trust Awards 598

African Nations

International Postgraduate Research Scholarships (IPRS) 692

Canada

International Postgraduate Research Scholarships (IPRS) 692
JCCA Graduate Education Scholarship 389

Caribbean Countries

International Postgraduate Research Scholarships (IPRS) 692

East European Countries

International Postgraduate Research Scholarships (IPRS) 692

Middle East

International Postgraduate Research Scholarships (IPRS) 692

South Africa

International Postgraduate Research Scholarships (IPRS) 692

United Kingdom

International Postgraduate Research Scholarships (IPRS) 692
University of Wales Aberystwyth Postgraduate Research Studentships 699

United States of America

Ian Axford (New Zealand) Fellowships in Public Policy 239
International Postgraduate Research Scholarships (IPRS) 692
JCCA Graduate Education Scholarship 389

West European Countries

International Postgraduate Research Scholarships (IPRS) 692

RELIGION AND THEOLOGY

GENERAL

Any Country

Ahmanson and Getty Postdoctoral Fellowships 617
ARIT Humanities and Social Sciences Fellowships 77
ASECS (American Society for 18th-Century Studies)/Clark Library Fellowships 617
Bertram Maura Memorial Entrance Scholarship 270
Blackfriars Blackwell Scholarship 672
Bloor Lands Entrance Scholarship 271
British Academy Larger Research Grants 142
British Academy Overseas Conference Grants 142
British Academy Postdoctoral Fellowships 142
British Academy Small Research Grants 142
British Conference Grants 142
Camargo Fellowships 169
Charlotte W Newcombe Doctoral Dissertation Fellowships 725
Clark-Huntington Joint Bibliographical Fellowship 617
Concordia University Graduate Fellowships 240
Council of the Institute Awards 513
David J Azrieli Graduate Fellowship 241
Delahaye Memorial Benefaction 700
Earthwatch Field Research Grants 265
Emmanuel College Finishing Scholarships 271
Episcopal Church Foundation Graduate Fellowship Program 276
Equiano Memorial Award 604
ERASMUS Prize 292
Exeter College Senior Scholarship in Theology 282
Field Psych Trust Grant 284
Foundation Praemium Erasmianum Study Prize 292
Frank P Fidler Memorial Award 271
Hastings Center International Visiting Scholars Program 318
Helen McCormack Turner Memorial Scholarship 700
Herbert Hughes Scholarship 701
IHS Humane Studies Fellowships 343
In-Course Scholarships 271
Institute for Advanced Studies in the Humanities Visiting Research Fellowships 341
Institute for Advanced Study Postdoctoral Residential Fellowships 342
Kennan Institute Short-Term Grants 397
Korea Foundation Advanced Research Grant 398
Korea Foundation Fellowship for Field Research 399
Korea Foundation Fellowship for Graduate Studies 399
Korea Foundation Postdoctoral Fellowship 399
Lincoln College Erich and Rochelle Endowed Prize in Music 679
Mary Radcliffe Scholarship 701
Monash International Postgraduate Research Scholarship (MIPRS) 440
Monash University Silver Jubilee Postgraduate Scholarship 440
Oxford University Theological Scholarships (Eastern and Central Europe) 683
Queen's College Holwell Studentship 684
Rhodes University Postdoctoral Fellowship and The Andrew Mellon Postdoctoral Fellowship 528
RHYS Curzon-Jones Scholarship 701
Ridley Lewis Bursary 701
Sir Halley Stewart Trust Grants 571
Stanley G French Graduate Fellowship 241
United States Holocaust Memorial Museum Center for Advanced Holocaust Studies Visiting Scholar Programs 619
University of Bristol Postgraduate Scholarships 641
University of Otago International Scholarships 670
University of Otago PhD Scholarships 670
University of Otago Prestigious PhD Scholarships 671
USIP Solicited Grants 622
USIP Unsolicited Grants 622
Vera Moore International Postgraduate Research Scholarships 440
Vernon Hope Emory Entrance Scholarship 271
Victoria University Graduate Student Assistantships 271
W D Llewelyn Memorial Benefaction 701
William Barclay Memorial Scholarship 658
Woodrow Wilson Grants in Women's Studies 725

African Nations

Fulbright Postdoctoral Research and Lecturing Awards for Non-US Citizens 245
Hastings Center International Visiting Scholars Program 318
Merton College Reed Foundation Scholarship 681

Australia

AAH Humanities Travelling Fellowships 120
Fulbright Postdoctoral Research and Lecturing Awards for Non-US Citizens 245
Fulbright Postgraduate Awards 126
Hastings Center International Visiting Scholars Program 318
Wingate Scholarships 720

Canada

Fulbright Postdoctoral Research and Lecturing Awards for Non-US Citizens 245
J W McConnell Memorial Fellowships 241
Killam Research Fellowships 198
Ministry Fellowship 298
North American Doctoral Fellowship 298
SSHRC Doctoral Awards 582
SSHRC Standard Research Grants 583
Vatican Film Library Mellon Fellowship 709
Wingate Scholarships 720

Caribbean Countries

Fulbright Postdoctoral Research and Lecturing Awards for Non-US Citizens 245
Hastings Center International Visiting Scholars Program 318
Merton College Reed Foundation Scholarship 681

East European Countries

Andrew W Mellon Foundation Fellowships in the Humanities 341
Frederick Bonnart-Braunthal Scholarship 628
Fulbright Postdoctoral Research and Lecturing Awards for Non-US Citizens 245
Hastings Center International Visiting Scholars Program 318
Mellon Postdoctoral Fellowships In Turkey For East European Scholars 78
Merton College Reed Foundation Scholarship 681

European Union

AHRC Doctoral Awards Scheme 103
All Saints Educational Trust Personal Awards 21
CBRL Travel Grant 244
The Holberg International Memorial Prize 639
Nils Klim Prize 639
Professional Preparation Master's Scheme 103
Research Preparation Master's Scheme 103

Middle East

Fulbright Postdoctoral Research and Lecturing Awards for Non-US Citizens 245
Hastings Center International Visiting Scholars Program 318
Merton College Reed Foundation Scholarship 681

New Zealand

Fulbright Postdoctoral Research and Lecturing Awards for Non-US Citizens 245
Hastings Center International Visiting Scholars Program 318
Wingate Scholarships 720

South Africa

Fulbright Postdoctoral Research and Lecturing Awards for Non-US Citizens 245
Hastings Center International Visiting Scholars Program 318
Wingate Scholarships 720

United Kingdom

AHRC Doctoral Awards Scheme 103
All Saints Educational Trust Corporate Awards 20
All Saints Educational Trust Personal Awards 21
Balsdon Fellowship 160
CBRL Research Award 244
CBRL Travel Grant 244
Frank Knox Fellowships at Harvard University 292
Frederick Bonnart-Braunthal Scholarship 628
Fulbright Postdoctoral Research and Lecturing Awards for Non-US Citizens 245
Glasgow Bursary 262
Hastings Center International Visiting Scholars Program 318
Kennedy Scholarships 398
Mr and Mrs David Edward Memorial Award 699
Professional Preparation Master's Scheme 103
Research Preparation Master's Scheme 103
Rome Awards 161
Rome Fellowship 161
Rome Scholarships in Ancient, Medieval and Later Italian Studies 162
UWB Departmental Research Studentships 700
UWB Research Studentships 700
Wingate Scholarships 720

United States of America

ARIT-National Endowment for the Humanities Advanced Fellowships for Research in Turkey 77
Expanding Horizons-Dissertation Fellowship for African Americans 298
Expanding Horizons-Doctoral Fellowship for African Americans 298
Fulbright Scholar Program for US Citizens 245
Fulbright Senior Specialists Program 245
Kennan Institute Research Scholarship 397
Ministry Fellowship 298
North American Doctoral Fellowship 298
Vatican Film Library Mellon Fellowship 709

West European Countries

Frederick Bonnart-Braunthal Scholarship 628
Fulbright Postdoctoral Research and Lecturing Awards for Non-US Citizens 245
Hastings Center International Visiting Scholars Program 318
Mr and Mrs David Edward Memorial Award 699
UWB Departmental Research Studentships 700
UWB Research Studentships 700
Wingate Scholarships 720

RELIGIOUS STUDIES

Any Country

Ahmanson and Getty Postdoctoral Fellowships 617
ASECS (American Society for 18th-Century Studies)/Clark Library Fellowships 617
British Academy Larger Research Grants 142
British Academy Overseas Conference Grants 142
British Academy Postdoctoral Fellowships 142
British Academy Small Research Grants 142
Clark Library Short-Term Resident Fellowships 617
Clark Predoctoral Fellowships 617
Clark-Huntington Joint Bibliographical Fellowship 617
Council of the Institute Awards 513
Delahaye Memorial Benefaction 700
Findel Scholarships and Schneider Scholarships 325
Foundation Praemium Erasmianum Study Prize 292
Frederick Douglass Institute Postdoctoral Fellowship 293
Frederick Douglass Institute Predoctoral Dissertation Fellowship 294
Helen McCormack Turner Memorial Scholarship 700
Herbert Hughes Scholarship 701
Institute of European History Fellowships 346
M Alison Frantz Fellowship in Post-Classical Studies at the Gennadius Library 80
Mary Radcliffe Scholarship 701
NEH Fellowships 80
RHYS Curzon-Jones Scholarship 701
Ridley Lewis Bursary 701
SOAS Research Student Fellowships 563
USIP Solicited Grants 622
USIP Unsolicited Grants 622
W D Llewelyn Memorial Benefaction 701

Australia

AAH Humanities Travelling Fellowships 120
Wingate Scholarships 720

Canada

Bishop Thomas Hoyt Jr Fellowship 342
Ministry Fellowship 298
Wingate Scholarships 720

East European Countries

CRF (Caledonian Research Foundation)/RSE European Visiting Research Fellowships 556

European Union

AHRC Doctoral Awards Scheme 103
All Saints Educational Trust Personal Awards 21
CBRL Travel Grant 244
Professional Preparation Master's Scheme 103
Research Preparation Master's Scheme 103

New Zealand

Wingate Scholarships 720

South Africa

Wingate Scholarships 720

United Kingdom

AHRC Doctoral Awards Scheme 103
All Saints Educational Trust Personal Awards 21
Balsdon Fellowship 160
CBRL Research Award 244
CBRL Travel Grant 244
CRF (Caledonian Research Foundation)/RSE European Visiting Research Fellowships 556
Mr and Mrs David Edward Memorial Award 699
Professional Preparation Master's Scheme 103
Research Preparation Master's Scheme 103
Rome Awards 161

United States of America

West European Countries

CHRISTIAN

Any Country

Australia

Canada

European Union

New Zealand

South Africa

United Kingdom

West European Countries

JEWISH

Any Country

Australia

Canada

European Union

New Zealand

South Africa

United Kingdom

AHRC Doctoral Awards Scheme 103
Mr and Mrs David Edward Memorial Award 699
Professional Preparation Master's Scheme 103
Research Preparation Master's Scheme 103
UWB Departmental Research Studentships 700
UWB Research Studentships 700
Wingate Scholarships 720

United States of America

Fellowship Programme for Émigrés Pursuing Careers in Jewish Education 389
JCCA Graduate Education Scholarship 389

West European Countries

Mr and Mrs David Edward Memorial Award 699
UWB Departmental Research Studentships 700
UWB Research Studentships 700
Wingate Scholarships 720

ISLAM

Any Country

Ahmanson and Getty Postdoctoral Fellowships 617
ASCSA Advanced Fellowships 78
Delahaye Memorial Benefaction 700
Helen McCormack Turner Memorial Scholarship 700
Herbert Hughes Scholarship 701
M Alison Frantz Fellowship in Post-Classical Studies at the Gennadius Library 80
Mary Radcliffe Scholarship 701
NEH Fellowships 80
RHYS Curzon-Jones Scholarship 701
Ridley Lewis Bursary 701
SOAS Bursary 563
W D Llewelyn Memorial Benefaction 701

Australia

Wingate Scholarships 720

Canada

Wingate Scholarships 720

European Union

AHRC Doctoral Awards Scheme 103
Professional Preparation Master's Scheme 103
Research Preparation Master's Scheme 103

New Zealand

Wingate Scholarships 720

South Africa

Wingate Scholarships 720

United Kingdom

AHRC Doctoral Awards Scheme 103
Professional Preparation Master's Scheme 103
Research Preparation Master's Scheme 103
UWB Departmental Research Studentships 700
Wingate Scholarships 720

United States of America

ARCE Fellowships 77

West European Countries

UWB Departmental Research Studentships 700
Wingate Scholarships 720

ASIAN RELIGIOUS STUDIES

Any Country

Ahmanson and Getty Postdoctoral Fellowships 617
SOAS Bursary 563

Australia

Wingate Scholarships 720

Canada

Wingate Scholarships 720

European Union

AHRC Doctoral Awards Scheme 103
Professional Preparation Master's Scheme 103
Research Preparation Master's Scheme 103

New Zealand

Wingate Scholarships 720

South Africa

Wingate Scholarships 720

United Kingdom

AHRC Doctoral Awards Scheme 103
Professional Preparation Master's Scheme 103
Research Preparation Master's Scheme 103
Wingate Scholarships 720

West European Countries

Wingate Scholarships 720

AGNOSTICISM AND ATHEISM

Australia

Wingate Scholarships 720

Canada

Wingate Scholarships 720

European Union

AHRC Doctoral Awards Scheme 103
Professional Preparation Master's Scheme 103
Research Preparation Master's Scheme 103

New Zealand

Wingate Scholarships 720

South Africa

Wingate Scholarships 720

United Kingdom

AHRC Doctoral Awards Scheme 103
Professional Preparation Master's Scheme 103
Research Preparation Master's Scheme 103
Wingate Scholarships 720

West European Countries

Wingate Scholarships 720

ANCIENT RELIGIONS

Any Country

ASCSA Advanced Fellowships 78
ASCSA Fellowships 78
Hugh Last and Donald Atkinson Funds Committee Grants 586

Jacob Hirsch Fellowship 79
M Alison Frantz Fellowship in Post-Classical Studies at the Gennadius Library 80
Mary Isabel Sibley Fellowship 510
NEH Fellowships 80
SOAS Bursary 563

Australia

Wingate Scholarships 720

Canada

Wingate Scholarships 720

European Union

AHRC Doctoral Awards Scheme 103
Professional Preparation Master's Scheme 103
Research Preparation Master's Scheme 103

New Zealand

Wingate Scholarships 720

South Africa

Wingate Scholarships 720

United Kingdom

AHRC Doctoral Awards Scheme 103
Hector and Elizabeth Catling Bursary 159
Professional Preparation Master's Scheme 103
Research Preparation Master's Scheme 103
Wingate Scholarships 720

United States of America

ARCE Fellowships 77

West European Countries

Wingate Scholarships 720

RELIGIOUS EDUCATION

Any Country

Dempster Fellowship 299
Equiano Memorial Award 604

African Nations

International Postgraduate Research Scholarships (IPRS) 692

Canada

International Postgraduate Research Scholarships (IPRS) 692
Ministry Fellowship 298

Caribbean Countries

International Postgraduate Research Scholarships (IPRS) 692

East European Countries

International Postgraduate Research Scholarships (IPRS) 692

European Union

All Saints Educational Trust Personal Awards 21
CBRL Travel Grant 244

Middle East

International Postgraduate Research Scholarships (IPRS) 692

South Africa

International Postgraduate Research Scholarships (IPRS) 692

United Kingdom

All Saints Educational Trust Personal Awards 21
CBRL Research Award 244
CBRL Travel Grant 244
International Postgraduate Research Scholarships (IPRS) 692
Mr and Mrs David Edward Memorial Award 699
UWB Departmental Research Studentships 700
UWB Research Studentships 700

United States of America

Expanding Horizons-Dissertation Fellowship for African Americans 298
Expanding Horizons-Doctoral Fellowship for African Americans 298
Fellowship Programme for Émigrés Pursuing Careers in Jewish Education 389
International Postgraduate Research Scholarships (IPRS) 692
Ministry Fellowship 298

West European Countries

International Postgraduate Research Scholarships (IPRS) 692
Mr and Mrs David Edward Memorial Award 699
UWB Departmental Research Studentships 700
UWB Research Studentships 700

HOLY WRITINGS

Any Country

Council of the Institute Awards 513
IAUW International Scholarship 151
SOAS Bursary 563
SOAS Research Student Fellowships 563

Australia

AAH Humanities Travelling Fellowships 120
Wingate Scholarships 720

Canada

Wingate Scholarships 720

European Union

AHRC Doctoral Awards Scheme 103
CBRL Travel Grant 244
Professional Preparation Master's Scheme 103
Research Preparation Master's Scheme 103

New Zealand

Wingate Scholarships 720

South Africa

Wingate Scholarships 720

United Kingdom

AHRC Doctoral Awards Scheme 103
CBRL Research Award 244
CBRL Travel Grant 244
Professional Preparation Master's Scheme 103
Research Preparation Master's Scheme 103
UWB Research Studentships 700
Wingate Scholarships 720

United States of America

ARCE Fellowships 77

West European Countries

UWB Research Studentships 700
Wingate Scholarships 720

RELIGIOUS PRACTICE

Any Country

SOAS Bursary 563
SOAS Research Student Fellowships 563

Canada

Ministry Fellowship 298

European Union

AHRC Doctoral Awards Scheme 103
CBRL Travel Grant 244
Professional Preparation Master's Scheme 103
Research Preparation Master's Scheme 103

United Kingdom

AHRC Doctoral Awards Scheme 103
CBRL Research Award 244
CBRL Travel Grant 244
Mr and Mrs David Edward Memorial Award 699
Professional Preparation Master's Scheme 103
Research Preparation Master's Scheme 103
UWB Departmental Research Studentships 700
UWB Research Studentships 700

United States of America

Fellowship Programme for Émigrés Pursuing Careers in Jewish Education 389
Ministry Fellowship 298

West European Countries

Mr and Mrs David Edward Memorial Award 699
UWB Departmental Research Studentships 700
UWB Research Studentships 700

CHURCH ADMINISTRATION (PASTORAL WORK)

Canada

Ministry Fellowship 298

European Union

AHRC Doctoral Awards Scheme 103
CBRL Travel Grant 244
Professional Preparation Master's Scheme 103
Research Preparation Master's Scheme 103

United Kingdom

AHRC Doctoral Awards Scheme 103
CBRL Research Award 244
CBRL Travel Grant 244
Hilda Martindale Exhibitions 326
Mr and Mrs David Edward Memorial Award 699
Professional Preparation Master's Scheme 103
Research Preparation Master's Scheme 103
UWB Departmental Research Studentships 700
UWB Research Studentships 700

United States of America

Arne Administrative Leadership Scholarship 723
Ministry Fellowship 298
Verne Catt McDowell Corporation Scholarship 709

West European Countries

Mr and Mrs David Edward Memorial Award 699
UWB Departmental Research Studentships 700
UWB Research Studentships 700

THEOLOGICAL STUDIES

Any Country

British Academy Overseas Conference Grants 142
British Academy Small Research Grants 142
Delahaye Memorial Benefaction 700
Episcopal Church Foundation Graduate Fellowship Program 276
Essex Rotary University Travel Grants 651
Findel Scholarships and Schneider Scholarships 325
Foundation Praemium Erasmianum Study Prize 292
Helen McCormack Turner Memorial Scholarship 700
Herbert Hughes Scholarship 701
Institute of European History Fellowships 346
M Alison Frantz Fellowship in Post-Classical Studies at the Gennadius Library 80
Mary Radcliffe Scholarship 701
RHYS Curzon-Jones Scholarship 701
Ridley Lewis Bursary 701
University of Bristol Postgraduate Scholarships 641
W D Llewelyn Memorial Benefaction 701
William Honyman Gillespie Scholarships 719

Australia

AAH Humanities Travelling Fellowships 120
University of Essex/ORS Awards 655
Wingate Scholarships 720

Canada

Ministry Fellowship 298
University of Essex/ORS Awards 655
Wingate Scholarships 720

Caribbean Countries

University of Essex/ORS Awards 655

East European Countries

University of Essex/ORS Awards 655

European Union

AHRC Doctoral Awards Scheme 103
CBRL Travel Grant 244
Professional Preparation Master's Scheme 103
Research Preparation Master's Scheme 103

Middle East

University of Essex/ORS Awards 655

New Zealand

Wingate Scholarships 720

South Africa

University of Essex/ORS Awards 655
Wingate Scholarships 720

United Kingdom

AHRC Doctoral Awards Scheme 103
CBRL Research Award 244
CBRL Travel Grant 244
Hector and Elizabeth Catling Bursary 159
Hilda Martindale Exhibitions 326
Mr and Mrs David Edward Memorial Award 699
Professional Preparation Master's Scheme 103
Research Preparation Master's Scheme 103
University of Essex Access to Learning Fund 652
UWB Departmental Research Studentships 700
UWB Research Studentships 700
Wingate Scholarships 720

United States of America

Chilstrom Scholarship for Ordained Ministry 723
ELCA Educational Grant Program 280
Expanding Horizons-Dissertation Fellowship for African Americans 298
Expanding Horizons-Doctoral Fellowship for African Americans 298
Ministry Fellowship 298
University of Essex/ORS Awards 655

West European Countries

Mr and Mrs David Edward Memorial Award 699
UWB Departmental Research Studentships 700
UWB Research Studentships 700
Wingate Scholarships 720

COMPARATIVE RELIGION

Any Country

Ahmanson and Getty Postdoctoral Fellowships 617
ASECS (American Society for 18th-Century Studies)/Clark Library Fellowships 617
British Academy Overseas Conference Grants 142
British Academy Small Research Grants 142
Camargo Fellowships 169
Clark Library Short-Term Resident Fellowships 617
Clark Predoctoral Fellowships 617
Clark-Huntington Joint Bibliographical Fellowship 617
Delahaye Memorial Benefaction 700
Findel Scholarships and Schneider Scholarships 325
Foundation Praemium Erasmianum Study Prize 292
Helen McCormack Turner Memorial Scholarship 700
Herbert Hughes Scholarship 701
Institute of European History Fellowships 346
M Alison Frantz Fellowship in Post-Classical Studies at the Gennadius Library 80
Mary Isabel Sibley Fellowship 510
Mary Radcliffe Scholarship 701
RHYS Curzon-Jones Scholarship 701
Ridley Lewis Bursary 701
SOAS Bursary 563
SOAS Research Student Fellowships 563
University of Bristol Postgraduate Scholarships 641
W D Llewelyn Memorial Benefaction 701

Australia

AAH Humanities Travelling Fellowships 120
Wingate Scholarships 720

Canada

Wingate Scholarships 720

European Union

AHRC Doctoral Awards Scheme 103
CBRL Travel Grant 244
Professional Preparation Master's Scheme 103
Research Preparation Master's Scheme 103

New Zealand

Wingate Scholarships 720

South Africa

Wingate Scholarships 720

United Kingdom

AHRC Doctoral Awards Scheme 103
CBRL Research Award 244
CBRL Travel Grant 244
Mr and Mrs David Edward Memorial Award 699
Professional Preparation Master's Scheme 103
Research Preparation Master's Scheme 103
UWB Departmental Research Studentships 700
UWB Research Studentships 700
Wingate Scholarships 720

West European Countries

Mr and Mrs David Edward Memorial Award 699
UWB Departmental Research Studentships 700
UWB Research Studentships 700
Wingate Scholarships 720

SOCIOLOGY OF RELIGION

Any Country

Ahmanson and Getty Postdoctoral Fellowships 617
ASECS (American Society for 18th-Century Studies)/Clark Library Fellowships 617
British Academy Overseas Conference Grants 142
British Academy Small Research Grants 142
Camargo Fellowships 169
Clark Library Short-Term Resident Fellowships 617
Clark Predoctoral Fellowships 617
Clark-Huntington Joint Bibliographical Fellowship 617
Delahaye Memorial Benefaction 700
Findel Scholarships and Schneider Scholarships 325
Foundation Praemium Erasmianum Study Prize 292
Helen McCormack Turner Memorial Scholarship 700
Herbert Hughes Scholarship 701
M Alison Frantz Fellowship in Post-Classical Studies at the Gennadius Library 80
Mary Radcliffe Scholarship 701
NEH Fellowships 80
RHYS Curzon-Jones Scholarship 701
Ridley Lewis Bursary 701
SOAS Bursary 563
SOAS Research Student Fellowships 563
University of Bristol Postgraduate Scholarships 641
W D Llewelyn Memorial Benefaction 701

Australia

AAH Humanities Travelling Fellowships 120
Wingate Scholarships 720

Canada

Wingate Scholarships 720

European Union

AHRC Doctoral Awards Scheme 103
CBRL Travel Grant 244

New Zealand

Wingate Scholarships 720

South Africa

Wingate Scholarships 720

United Kingdom

AHRC Doctoral Awards Scheme 103
CBRL Research Award 244
CBRL Travel Grant 244
Mr and Mrs David Edward Memorial Award 699
UWB Departmental Research Studentships 700
UWB Research Studentships 700
Wingate Scholarships 720

United States of America

Fulbright Senior Specialists Program 245

Merton College Reed Foundation Scholarship 681
Swiss Scholarships for University Studies for Central and East European Countries 606

Middle East

Fulbright Postdoctoral Research and Lecturing Awards for Non-US Citizens 245
International Postgraduate Research Scholarships (IPRS) 692
Merton College Reed Foundation Scholarship 681
NUFFIC-NFP Fellowships for Master's Degree Programmes 478

New Zealand

Fulbright Postdoctoral Research and Lecturing Awards for Non-US Citizens 245

South Africa

Fulbright Postdoctoral Research and Lecturing Awards for Non-US Citizens 245
International Postgraduate Research Scholarships (IPRS) 692
NUFFIC-NFP Fellowships for Master's Degree Programmes 478

United Kingdom

Fulbright Postdoctoral Research and Lecturing Awards for Non-US Citizens 245
Hilda Martindale Exhibitions 326
International Postgraduate Research Scholarships (IPRS) 692
Postgraduate Student Allowance Scheme (PSAS) (Queen Margaret) 517
Sheffield Hallam University Studentships 567

United States of America

Congress Bundestag Youth Exchange for Young Professionals 224
Fulbright Scholar Program for US Citizens 245
International Postgraduate Research Scholarships (IPRS) 692

West European Countries

Fulbright Postdoctoral Research and Lecturing Awards for Non-US Citizens 245
International Postgraduate Research Scholarships (IPRS) 692
Janson Johan Helmich Scholarships and Travel Grants 387
Sheffield Hallam University Studentships 567

HOTEL AND RESTAURANT

Any Country

Student Ambassador Awards for Hotel Management 709
University of Dundee Research Awards 648

African Nations

International Postgraduate Research Scholarships (IPRS) 692

Australia

BMHS Hospitality and Tourism Management Scholarship 138
Food Media Club Australia Scholarship 405
International Association of Culinary Professionals (IACP) and culinary Trust Scholarship 406
Le Cordon Bleu Master of Arts in Gastronomy Scholarship 406
Le Cordon Bleu Master of Business Administration Scholarship. 406

Canada

International Postgraduate Research Scholarships (IPRS) 692

Caribbean Countries

International Postgraduate Research Scholarships (IPRS) 692

East European Countries

International Postgraduate Research Scholarships (IPRS) 692

Middle East

International Postgraduate Research Scholarships (IPRS) 692

South Africa

International Postgraduate Research Scholarships (IPRS) 692

United Kingdom

International Postgraduate Research Scholarships (IPRS) 692

United States of America

Congress Bundestag Youth Exchange for Young Professionals 224
International Postgraduate Research Scholarships (IPRS) 692

West European Countries

International Postgraduate Research Scholarships (IPRS) 692

HOTEL MANAGEMENT

Any Country

Savoy Educational Trust Scholarships 415
University of Dundee Research Awards 648

African Nations

International Postgraduate Research Scholarships (IPRS) 692

Australia

BMHS Hospitality and Tourism Management Scholarship 138
Food Media Club Australia Scholarship 405
International Association of Culinary Professionals (IACP) and culinary Trust Scholarship 406
Le Cordon Bleu Master of Arts in Gastronomy Scholarship 406
Le Cordon Bleu Master of Business Administration Scholarship. 406

Canada

International Postgraduate Research Scholarships (IPRS) 692

Caribbean Countries

International Postgraduate Research Scholarships (IPRS) 692

East European Countries

International Postgraduate Research Scholarships (IPRS) 692

Middle East

International Postgraduate Research Scholarships (IPRS) 692

South Africa

International Postgraduate Research Scholarships (IPRS) 692

United Kingdom

International Postgraduate Research Scholarships (IPRS) 692
John Mather Scholarship 694

United States of America

Congress Bundestag Youth Exchange for Young Professionals 224
International Postgraduate Research Scholarships (IPRS) 692

West European Countries

International Postgraduate Research Scholarships (IPRS) 692

COOKING AND CATERING

Any Country

James Beard Scholarship 386
James Beard Scholarship II 386

African Nations

Australia

Canada

Caribbean Countries

East European Countries

European Union

Middle East

New Zealand

South Africa

United Kingdom

United States of America

ACLS Library of Congress Fellowships in International Studies 45
ACLS/SSRC/NEH International and Area Studies Fellowships 45
ACLS/SSRC/NEH International and Area Studies Fellowships 45
ARCE Fellowships 77
ASA Minority Fellowship Program 88
Canadian Embassy (USA) Graduate Student Fellowship Program 204
Canadian Embassy (USA) Research Grant Program 204
Clara Mayo Grants 586
Endeavour International Postgraduate Research Scholarships (EIPRS) 403
ETS Summer Program in Research for Graduate Students 267
Fellowship for American College Students 524
Foundation for Science and Disability Student Grant Fund 291
Fulbright Scholar Program for US Citizens 245
German Historical Institute Doctoral and Postdoctoral Fellowships 303
GMF Research Fellowships Program 305
Guggenheim Fellowships to Assist Research and Artistic Creation (USA and Canada) 394
Ian Axford (New Zealand) Fellowships in Public Policy 239
International Postgraduate Research Scholarships (IPRS) 692
IREX Individual Advanced Research Opportunities 374
IREX Policy-Connect Collaborative Research Grants Program 374
IREX Short-Term Travel Grants 374
Kennan Institute Research Scholarship 397
Lincoln College Overseas Graduate Entrance Scholarships 680
North Dakota Indian Scholarship 485
Norwegian Thanksgiving Fund Scholarship 487
SSRC Abe Fellowship Program 575
SSRC Eurasia Program Postdoctoral Fellowships 576
SSRC Eurasia Program Teaching Fellowships 576
SSRC Eurasia Title VIII Dissertation Write-Up Fellowships 577
SSRC Japan Program JSPS Postdoctoral Fellowship 577
SSRC Sexuality Research Fellowship Program 578
SSRC-Mellon Mays Predoctoral Fellowships 579
University of Essex/ORS Awards 655

West European Countries

DEL Postgraduate Studentships and Bursaries for Study in Northern Ireland 256
Endeavour International Postgraduate Research Scholarships (EIPRS) 403
Eoin O'Mahony Bursary 550
ESRC 1+3 Awards and +3 Awards 265
Fulbright Postdoctoral Research and Lecturing Awards for Non-US Citizens 245
Gay Clifford Fees Award 629
German Historical Institute Doctoral and Postdoctoral Fellowships 303
International Postgraduate Research Scholarships (IPRS) 692
John Radford Award for Geographical Photography 545
Lady Gregory Fellowship Scheme 473
Mr and Mrs David Edward Memorial Award 699
University of Kent School of Physical Sciences 662
UWB Departmental Research Studentships 700
UWB Research Studentships 700
Wingate Scholarships 720

ECONOMICS

Any Country

AIER Summer Fellowship 54
Alzheimer's Society Research Grants 23
Association for Women in Science Educational Foundation Predoctoral Awards 108
Balliol College Marvin Bower Scholarship 671
Bilkent MIAPP Fellowship 136
Canadian Embassy (USA) Faculty Enrichment Program 203
CDU Senior Research Fellowship 230
Celso Furtado Award 612
Eli Ginzberg Award 328
Ernst Meyer Prize 359
Fernand Braudel Senior Fellowships 280
Geneva Association 359
German Chancellor Scholarship Program 19
Graduate Institute of International Studies (HEI-Geneva) Scholarships 310
Hagley Museum and Library Grants-in-Aid of Research 314
Hagley/Winterthur Arts and Industries Fellowship 314
Harry S Truman Library Institute Dissertation Year Fellowships 317
Houblon-Norman Fellowships/George Fellowships 330
Humanitarian Trust Awards 332
ICCS Doctoral Student Research 363
International Association for the Study of Insurance Economics Research Grants 359
Jean Monnet Fellowships 280
Nuffield College Funded Studentships 682
Nuffield College Prize Research Fellowships 682
Paul H. Nitze School of Advanced International Studies (SAIS) Financial Aid and Fellowships 139
Population Council Fellowships in Population and Social Sciences 514
Queen Mary Research Studentships 518
Rhodes University Postdoctoral Fellowship and The Andrew Mellon Postdoctoral Fellowship 528
Russell Sage Foundation Visiting Scholar Appointments 560
SAIIA Bradlow Fellowship 595
Shell Centenary Scholarships at Cambridge (Non-OECD Countries) 193
SSRC Program on the Corporation as a Social Institution Fellowships 578
Teagasc Walsh Fellowships 607
Thank-Offering to Britain Fellowships 143
Thomas Holloway Research Studentship 548
Trinity College Junior Research Fellowship 689
University of Bristol Postgraduate Scholarships 641
University of Dundee Research Awards 648
University of Kent Department of Economics Bursaries 661
University of Otago International Scholarships 670
University of Otago PhD Scholarships 670
University of Otago Prestigious PhD Scholarships 671
University of Southampton Postgraduate Studentships 692
WHOI Postdoctoral Awards in Marine Policy and Ocean Management 726
World Universities Network (WUN) Global Exchange Programme 693

African Nations

International Postgraduate Research Scholarships (IPRS) 692
Museveni Scholarship 681
Shell Centenary Chevening Scholarships for Postgraduate Study 192
Shell Centenary Scholarships (Developing Countries of the Commonwealth) 192
Shell Centenary Scholarships and Shell Centenary Chevening Scholarships 685
University of Sussex Overseas Development Administration Shared Scholarship Scheme 695

Australia

ADB-Japan Scholarship Program 106
Chevening Oxford-Australia Scholarships 672
University of Essex/ORS Awards 655
Wingate Scholarships 720

Canada

Alcohol Beverage Medical Research Foundation Research Project Grant 15
Gilbert Chinard Fellowships 341
Harmon Chadbourn Rorison Fellowship 341
International Postgraduate Research Scholarships (IPRS) 692
Public Safety and Emergency Preparedness Canada Research Fellowship in Honour of Stuart Nesbitt White 115
University of Essex/ORS Awards 655
Wingate Scholarships 720

Caribbean Countries

ADB-Japan Scholarship Program 106
International Postgraduate Research Scholarships (IPRS) 692

East European Countries

European Union

Middle East

New Zealand

South Africa

United Kingdom

United States of America

West European Countries

ECONOMIC HISTORY

Any Country

African Nations

Australia

Canada

International Postgraduate Research Scholarships (IPRS) 692
University of Essex/ORS Awards 655
Wingate Scholarships 720

Caribbean Countries

International Postgraduate Research Scholarships (IPRS) 692
University of Essex/ORS Awards 655

East European Countries

CRF (Caledonian Research Foundation)/RSE European Visiting Research Fellowships 556
International Postgraduate Research Scholarships (IPRS) 692
University of Essex/ORS Awards 655

European Union

CBRL Travel Grant 244
ESRC 1+3 Awards and +3 Awards 265
University of Essex 1+3 ESRC Competition Award 652

Middle East

International Postgraduate Research Scholarships (IPRS) 692
University of Essex/ORS Awards 655

New Zealand

Wingate Scholarships 720

South Africa

International Postgraduate Research Scholarships (IPRS) 692
University of Essex/ORS Awards 655
Wingate Scholarships 720

United Kingdom

Balsdon Fellowship 160
CBRL Research Award 244
CBRL Travel Grant 244
CRF (Caledonian Research Foundation)/RSE European Visiting Research Fellowships 556
ESRC 1+3 Awards and +3 Awards 265
International Postgraduate Research Scholarships (IPRS) 692
Molson Research Awards 143
Mr and Mrs David Edward Memorial Award 699
Prix du Québec Award 143
Rome Awards 161
Rome Fellowship 161
Rome Scholarships in Ancient, Medieval and Later Italian Studies 162
University of Essex 1+3 ESRC Competition Award 652
University of Essex Access to Learning Fund 652
University of Wales Aberystwyth Postgraduate Research Studentships 699
UWB Departmental Research Studentships 700
UWB Research Studentships 700
Wingate Scholarships 720

United States of America

ARCE Fellowships 77
Fritz Stern Dissertation Prize 302
Fulbright Distinguished Chairs Program 245
Fulbright Senior Specialists Program 245
International Postgraduate Research Scholarships (IPRS) 692
Newcomen Society Dissertation Fellowship in Business and American Culture 485
Thyssen–Heideking Fellowship 304
University of Essex/ORS Awards 655

West European Countries

CRF (Caledonian Research Foundation)/RSE European Visiting Research Fellowships 556
ESRC 1+3 Awards and +3 Awards 265
International Postgraduate Research Scholarships (IPRS) 692
Kade-Heideking Fellowship 303
Mr and Mrs David Edward Memorial Award 699
UWB Departmental Research Studentships 700
UWB Research Studentships 700
Wingate Scholarships 720

ECONOMIC AND FINANCE POLICY

Any Country

Fernand Braudel Senior Fellowships 280
Harry S Truman Library Institute Dissertation Year Fellowships 317
Jean Monnet Fellowships 280
Nuffield College Prize Research Fellowships 682
Paul H. Nitze School of Advanced International Studies (SAIS) Financial Aid and Fellowships 139
Queen Mary Research Studentships 518
Thomas Holloway Research Studentship 548
University of Bristol Postgraduate Scholarships 641
University of Dundee Research Awards 648

African Nations

International Postgraduate Research Scholarships (IPRS) 692

Australia

University of Essex/ORS Awards 655
Wingate Scholarships 720

Canada

International Postgraduate Research Scholarships (IPRS) 692
S S Huebner Foundation for Insurance Education Predoctoral Fellowships 561
University of Essex/ORS Awards 655
Wingate Scholarships 720

Caribbean Countries

International Postgraduate Research Scholarships (IPRS) 692
University of Essex/ORS Awards 655

East European Countries

EUI Postgraduate Scholarships 279
International Postgraduate Research Scholarships (IPRS) 692
University of Essex/ORS Awards 655

European Union

CBRL Travel Grant 244
ESRC 1+3 Awards and +3 Awards 265
EUI Postgraduate Scholarships 279
University of Essex 1+3 ESRC Competition Award 652

Middle East

International Postgraduate Research Scholarships (IPRS) 692
University of Essex/ORS Awards 655

New Zealand

Wingate Scholarships 720

South Africa

International Postgraduate Research Scholarships (IPRS) 692
University of Essex/ORS Awards 655
Wingate Scholarships 720

United Kingdom

CBRL Research Award 244
CBRL Travel Grant 244
ESRC 1+3 Awards and +3 Awards 265
EUI Postgraduate Scholarships 279
International Postgraduate Research Scholarships (IPRS) 692
John Mather Scholarship 694
Molson Research Awards 143

African Nations

Australia

Canada

Caribbean Countries

East European Countries

European Union

Middle East

New Zealand

South Africa

United Kingdom

United States of America

Washington University Chancellor's Graduate Fellowship Program 715
White House Fellowships 718
World Security Institute Internship 226

West European Countries

ESRC 1+3 Awards and +3 Awards 265
International Postgraduate Research Scholarships (IPRS) 692
UWB Research Studentships 700
Wingate Scholarships 720

COMPARATIVE POLITICS

Any Country

Balliol College Marvin Bower Scholarship 671
Bilkent International Relations Fellowship 135
Bilkent Political Science Fellowship 136
Camargo Fellowships 169
Fernand Braudel Senior Fellowships 280
Institute of Irish Studies Research Fellowships 348
Institute of Irish Studies Senior Visiting Research Fellowship 348
Jean Monnet Fellowships 280
Nuffield College Funded Studentships 682
Nuffield College Prize Research Fellowships 682
Paul H. Nitze School of Advanced International Studies (SAIS) Financial Aid and Fellowships 139
Queen Mary Research Studentships 518
United States Holocaust Memorial Museum Center for Advanced Holocaust Studies Visiting Scholar Programs 619
University of Bristol Postgraduate Scholarships 641
University of Dundee Research Awards 648

African Nations

International Postgraduate Research Scholarships (IPRS) 692

Australia

University of Essex/ORS Awards 655
Wingate Scholarships 720

Canada

International Postgraduate Research Scholarships (IPRS) 692
Jules and Gabrielle Léger Fellowship 581
Mary McNeill Scholarship in Irish Studies 348
University of Essex/ORS Awards 655
Wingate Scholarships 720

Caribbean Countries

International Postgraduate Research Scholarships (IPRS) 692
University of Essex/ORS Awards 655

East European Countries

EUI Postgraduate Scholarships 279
International Postgraduate Research Scholarships (IPRS) 692
University of Essex/ORS Awards 655
Young Scholars Forum 304

European Union

CBRL Travel Grant 244
ESRC 1+3 Awards and +3 Awards 265
EUI Postgraduate Scholarships 279

Middle East

International Postgraduate Research Scholarships (IPRS) 692
University of Essex/ORS Awards 655

New Zealand

Wingate Scholarships 720

South Africa

International Postgraduate Research Scholarships (IPRS) 692
University of Essex/ORS Awards 655
Wingate Scholarships 720

United Kingdom

CBRL Research Award 244
CBRL Travel Grant 244
ESRC 1+3 Awards and +3 Awards 265
EUI Postgraduate Scholarships 279
International Postgraduate Research Scholarships (IPRS) 692
University of Essex Access to Learning Fund 652
University of Wales Aberystwyth Postgraduate Research Studentships 699
Wingate Scholarships 720
Young Scholars Forum 304

United States of America

ARCE Fellowships 77
Frank Goodnow Award 75
Fritz Stern Dissertation Prize 302
Fulbright Senior Specialists Program 245
International Postgraduate Research Scholarships (IPRS) 692
IREX Individual Advanced Research Opportunities 374
IREX Short-Term Travel Grants 374
Mary McNeill Scholarship in Irish Studies 348
Thyssen–Heideking Fellowship 304
University of Essex/ORS Awards 655
William Anderson Award 76
Young Scholars Forum 304

West European Countries

ESRC 1+3 Awards and +3 Awards 265
EUI Postgraduate Scholarships 279
International Postgraduate Research Scholarships (IPRS) 692
Kade-Heideking Fellowship 303
Wingate Scholarships 720
Young Scholars Forum 304

INTERNATIONAL RELATIONS

Any Country

The Albert Einstein Fellows Programme 13
Balliol College Marvin Bower Scholarship 671
Bilkent International Relations Fellowship 135
British Academy Overseas Conference Grants 142
British Academy Postdoctoral Fellowships 142
British Academy Small Research Grants 142
British Academy Worldwide Congress Grant 142
British Conference Grants 142
CDI Internship 226
Equiano Memorial Award 604
Essex Rotary University Travel Grants 651
Fernand Braudel Senior Fellowships 280
Foundation Praemium Erasmianum Study Prize 292
Frederick Douglass Institute Postdoctoral Fellowship 293
Frederick Douglass Institute Predoctoral Dissertation Fellowship 294
Gilbert Murray Trust Junior Awards 307
HFG Dissertation Fellowship 317
HFG Research Program 317
ICCS Doctoral Student Research 363
Institute of Current World Affairs Fellowships 345
Jean Monnet Fellowships 280
Joseph L Fisher Dissertation Award 525
Kennan Institute Short-Term Grants 397
M Alison Frantz Fellowship in Post-Classical Studies at the Gennadius Library 80
Mackenzie King Travelling Scholarship 418
Marusia and Michael Dorosh Master's Fellowship 207
Nuffield College Funded Studentships 682
Nuffield College Prize Research Fellowships 682

African Nations

Australia

Canada

Caribbean Countries

East European Countries

European Union

Middle East

New Zealand

South Africa

United Kingdom

United States of America

West European Countries

SOCIOLOGY

Any Country

African Nations

Australia

Canada

Caribbean Countries

East European Countries

European Union

Middle East

New Zealand

South Africa

United Kingdom

CBRL Research Award 244
CBRL Travel Grant 244
ESRC 1+3 Awards and +3 Awards 265
EUI Postgraduate Scholarships 279
Hector and Elizabeth Catling Bursary 159
International Postgraduate Research Scholarships (IPRS) 692
Joshua Feigenbaum Award 328
Mr and Mrs David Edward Memorial Award 699
Rome Awards 161
Rome Fellowship 161
Rome Scholarships in Ancient, Medieval and Later Italian Studies 162
Sheffield Hallam University Studentships 567
University of Essex Access to Learning Fund 652
University of Kent Sociology Studentship 662
UWB Departmental Research Studentships 700
UWB Research Studentships 700
Wingate Scholarships 720

United States of America

AAUW University Scholar-in-Residence 4
ASA Minority Fellowship Program 88
Bishop Thomas Hoyt Jr Fellowship 342
Fulbright Distinguished Chairs Program 245
Fulbright Senior Specialists Program 245
Gilbert Chinard Fellowships 341
GMF Research Fellowships Program 305
Harmon Chadbourn Rorison Fellowship 341
Ian Axford (New Zealand) Fellowships in Public Policy 239
International Postgraduate Research Scholarships (IPRS) 692
IREX Individual Advanced Research Opportunities 374
IREX Short-Term Travel Grants 374
Kennan Institute Research Scholarship 397
National Research Service Award for Mental Health and Adjustment in the Life Course 412
University of Essex/ORS Awards 655
University of New Hampshire Postdoctoral Fellowships For Research on Family Violence 668

West European Countries

ESRC 1+3 Awards and +3 Awards 265
EUI Postgraduate Scholarships 279
International Postgraduate Research Scholarships (IPRS) 692
Mr and Mrs David Edward Memorial Award 699
Sheffield Hallam University Studentships 567
University of Kent Sociology Studentship 662
UWB Departmental Research Studentships 700
UWB Research Studentships 700
Wingate Scholarships 720

HISTORY OF SOCIETIES

Any Country

Ahmanson and Getty Postdoctoral Fellowships 617
Albert J Beveridge Grant 54
ASCSA Advanced Fellowships 78
Bernadotte E Schmitt Grants 54
Bernard and Audre Rapoport Fellowships 55
Camargo Fellowships 169
CIUS Research Grants 207
Clark-Huntington Joint Bibliographical Fellowship 617
CSA Adele Filene Travel Award 244
Earthwatch Field Research Grants 265
Equiano Memorial Award 604
Ethel Marcus Memorial Fellowship 55
Findel Scholarships and Schneider Scholarships 325
Frederick Douglass Institute Postdoctoral Fellowship 293
Frederick Douglass Institute Predoctoral Dissertation Fellowship 294
The Joseph and Eva R Dave Fellowship 56
Liberty Legacy Foundation Award 493
Library Company of Philadelphia and Historical Society of Pennsylvania Research Fellowships in American History and Culture 411
Littleton-Griswold Research Grant 54
Loewenstein-Wiener Fellowship Awards 56
M Alison Frantz Fellowship in Post-Classical Studies at the Gennadius Library 80
Marguerite R Jacobs Memorial Award 56
The Natalie Feld Memorial Fellowship 56
NEH Fellowships 80
Queen Mary Research Studentships 518
Rabbi Frederic A Doppelt Memorial Fellowship 56
The Rabbi Harold D Hahn Memorial Fellowship 56
The Rabbi Joachin Prinz Memorial Fellowship 57
Rabbi Levi A Olan Memorial Fellowship 57
Rabbi Theodore S Levy Tribute Fellowship 57
Starkoff Fellowship 57

Australia

University of Essex/ORS Awards 655
Wingate Scholarships 720

Canada

University of Essex/ORS Awards 655
Wingate Scholarships 720

Caribbean Countries

University of Essex/ORS Awards 655

East European Countries

University of Essex/ORS Awards 655
Young Scholars Forum 304

European Union

ESRC 1+3 Awards and +3 Awards 265

Middle East

University of Essex/ORS Awards 655

New Zealand

Wingate Scholarships 720

South Africa

University of Essex/ORS Awards 655
Wingate Scholarships 720

United Kingdom

British Institute in Eastern Africa Research Grants 155
ESRC 1+3 Awards and +3 Awards 265
Mr and Mrs David Edward Memorial Award 699
University of Essex Access to Learning Fund 652
UWB Departmental Research Studentships 700
UWB Research Studentships 700
Wingate Scholarships 720
Young Scholars Forum 304

United States of America

ACLS Fellowships for Postdoctoral Research 45
ACLS/SSRC/NEH International and Area Studies Fellowships 45
ARCE Fellowships 77
Earthwatch Education Awards 265
Fritz Stern Dissertation Prize 302
Fulbright Senior Specialists Program 245
Japanese Residencies Program 493
Thyssen–Heideking Fellowship 304
University of Essex/ORS Awards 655
Young Scholars Forum 304

West European Countries

ESRC 1+3 Awards and +3 Awards 265
Kade-Heideking Fellowship 303
Mr and Mrs David Edward Memorial Award 699

COMPARATIVE SOCIOLOGY

Any Country

Australia

Canada

Caribbean Countries

East European Countries

European Union

Middle East

New Zealand

South Africa

United Kingdom

United States of America

West European Countries

SOCIAL POLICY

Any Country

African Nations

Australia

Canada

Caribbean Countries

SOCIAL INSTITUTIONS

South Africa

Joshua Feigenbaum Award 328
University of Essex/ORS Awards 655
Wingate Scholarships 720

United Kingdom

ESRC 1+3 Awards and +3 Awards 265
Joshua Feigenbaum Award 328
Molson Research Awards 143
UWB Research Studentships 700
Wingate Scholarships 720

United States of America

ARCE Fellowships 77
University of Essex/ORS Awards 655

West European Countries

ESRC 1+3 Awards and +3 Awards 265
UWB Research Studentships 700
Wingate Scholarships 720

DEMOGRAPHY

Any Country

Alzheimer's Society Research Grants 23
Association for Women in Science Educational Foundation Predoctoral Awards 108
BackCare Research Grants 130
British Academy Overseas Conference Grants 142
British Academy Postdoctoral Fellowships 142
British Academy Small Research Grants 142
British Academy Worldwide Congress Grant 142
British Conference Grants 142
Danish Cancer Society Psychosocial Research Award 254
Kennan Institute Short-Term Grants 397
Marusia and Michael Dorosh Master's Fellowship 207
Paul H. Nitze School of Advanced International Studies (SAIS) Financial Aid and Fellowships 139
Population Council Fellowships in Population and Social Sciences 514
SOAS Bursary 563
SOAS Research Student Fellowships 563
St Catherine's College Graduate Scholarship in the Arts 687
University of Glasgow Postgraduate Research Scholarships 658
University of Southampton Postgraduate Studentships 692
World Universities Network (WUN) Global Exchange Programme 693

Australia

Wingate Scholarships 720

Canada

Alcohol Beverage Medical Research Foundation Research Project Grant 15
Wingate Scholarships 720

European Union

ESRC 1+3 Awards and +3 Awards 265

New Zealand

Wingate Scholarships 720

South Africa

Wingate Scholarships 720

United Kingdom

Balsdon Fellowship 160
ESRC 1+3 Awards and +3 Awards 265
Rome Awards 161
Rome Fellowship 161
Rome Scholarships in Ancient, Medieval and Later Italian Studies 162
UWB Research Studentships 700
Wingate Scholarships 720

United States of America

Alcohol Beverage Medical Research Foundation Research Project Grant 15
ARCE Fellowships 77
ETS Postdoctoral Fellowships 267
Ian Axford (New Zealand) Fellowships in Public Policy 239
IREX Individual Advanced Research Opportunities 374
Kennan Institute Research Scholarship 397
NIH Research Grants 466

West European Countries

ESRC 1+3 Awards and +3 Awards 265
UWB Research Studentships 700
Wingate Scholarships 720

ANTHROPOLOGY

Any Country

Ahmanson and Getty Postdoctoral Fellowships 617
ASCSA Advanced Fellowships 78
ASCSA Fellowships 78
ASCSA Research Fellowship in Environmental Studies 79
ASCSA Research Fellowship in Faunal Studies 79
ASCSA Research Fellowship in Geoarchaeology 79
Association for Women in Science Educational Foundation Predoctoral Awards 108
AUC International Graduate Fellowships in Arabic Studies, Middle East Studies and Sociology/Anthropology 90
British Academy Overseas Conference Grants 142
British Academy Postdoctoral Fellowships 142
British Academy Small Research Grants 142
British Academy Worldwide Congress Grant 142
British Conference Grants 142
Camargo Fellowships 169
CDU Senior Research Fellowship 230
CDU Three Year Postdoctoral Fellowship 230
Charlotte W Newcombe Doctoral Dissertation Fellowships 725
Clark-Huntington Joint Bibliographical Fellowship 617
CSA Adele Filene Travel Award 244
CSA Stella Blum Research Grant 244
CSA Travel Research Grant 244
Danish Cancer Society Psychosocial Research Award 254
Earthwatch Field Research Grants 265
Eli Ginzberg Award 328
Equiano Memorial Award 604
Fondation Fyssen Postdoctoral Study Grants 286
Foundation Praemium Erasmianum Study Prize 292
Frederick Douglass Institute Postdoctoral Fellowship 293
Frederick Douglass Institute Predoctoral Dissertation Fellowship 294
Gypsy Lore Society Young Scholar's Prize in Romani Studies 314
Henry A Murray Dissertation Award Program 322
HFG Dissertation Fellowship 317
HFG Research Program 317
Institute of Irish Studies Research Fellowships 348
Institute of Irish Studies Senior Visiting Research Fellowship 348
J Lawrence Angel Fellowship in Human Skeletal Studies 79
Jeanne Humphrey Block Dissertation Award 322
Kennan Institute Short-Term Grants 397
Library Resident Research Fellowships 72
Linacre College Rausing Scholarships 679
M Alison Frantz Fellowship in Post-Classical Studies at the Gennadius Library 80
Marusia and Michael Dorosh Master's Fellowship 207
NEH Fellowships 80
Onassis Foreigners' Fellowships Programme Research Grants Category AI 17
Population Council Fellowships in Population and Social Sciences 514
Postgraduate Research Bursaries (Epilepsy Action) 274

Primate Conservation Inc. Grants 515
Richard Carley-Hunt Postdoctoral Fellowship 717
Russell Sage Foundation Visiting Scholar Appointments 560
SOAS Bursary 563
SOAS Research Student Fellowships 563
St Catherine's College Graduate Scholarship in the Arts 687
United States Holocaust Memorial Museum Center for Advanced Holocaust Studies Visiting Scholar Programs 619
University of Glasgow Postgraduate Research Scholarships 658
University of Kent Anthropology Postgraduate Maintenance Grants 660
University of Kent Anthropology Postgraduate Studentships 660
University of Otago International Scholarships 670
University of Otago PhD Scholarships 670
University of Otago Prestigious PhD Scholarships 671
University of Southampton Postgraduate Studentships 692
Wenner-Gren Foundation Dissertation Fieldwork Grants 717
Wenner-Gren Foundation Post-PhD Grants 717
WHOI Postdoctoral Awards in Marine Policy and Ocean Management 726
WHOI Research Fellowships in Marine Policy 727
World Universities Network (WUN) Global Exchange Programme 693

African Nations

Canadian Window on International Development 364
IDRC Doctoral Research Awards 365
Primate Conservation Inc. Grants 515
University of Kent Anthropology Taught Master's Studentships 660
University of Sussex Overseas Development Administration Shared Scholarship Scheme 695

Australia

University of Kent Anthropology Taught Master's Studentships 660
Wingate Scholarships 720

Canada

Alcohol Beverage Medical Research Foundation Research Project Grant 15
Canadian Window on International Development 364
Homer and Dorothy Thompson Fellowship 199
IDRC Doctoral Research Awards 365
Mary McNeill Scholarship in Irish Studies 348
University of Kent Anthropology Taught Master's Studentships 660
Wingate Scholarships 720

Caribbean Countries

Canadian Window on International Development 364
IDRC Doctoral Research Awards 365
University of Kent Anthropology Taught Master's Studentships 660

East European Countries

Research Degree Scholarships in Anthropology 634
Sasakawa Scholarship 695
University of Kent Anthropology Taught Master's Studentships 660

European Union

CBRL Travel Grant 244
ESRC 1 + 3 Awards and + 3 Awards 265

Middle East

University of Kent Anthropology Taught Master's Studentships 660

New Zealand

University of Kent Anthropology Taught Master's Studentships 660
Wingate Scholarships 720

South Africa

Canadian Window on International Development 364
IDRC Doctoral Research Awards 365
University of Kent Anthropology Taught Master's Studentships 660
Wingate Scholarships 720

United Kingdom

Balsdon Fellowship 160
British Institute in Eastern Africa Graduate Attachments 155
CBRL Research Award 244
CBRL Travel Grant 244
Emslie Horniman Anthropological Scholarship Fund 536
ESRC 1 + 3 Awards and + 3 Awards 265
Hector and Elizabeth Catling Bursary 159
Prix du Québec Award 143
Research Degree Scholarships in Anthropology 634
Rome Awards 161
Rome Fellowship 161
Rome Scholarships in Ancient, Medieval and Later Italian Studies 162
Sasakawa Scholarship 695
University of Kent Anthropology Taught Master's Studentships 660
Wingate Scholarships 720

United States of America

ACC Fellowship Grants Program 106
Alcohol Beverage Medical Research Foundation Research Project Grant 15
ARCE Fellowships 77
Earthwatch Education Awards 265
Fulbright Senior Specialists Program 245
GMF Research Fellowships Program 305
Ian Axford (New Zealand) Fellowships in Public Policy 239
IREX Individual Advanced Research Opportunities 374
IREX Short-Term Travel Grants 374
Kennan Institute Research Scholarship 397
Mary McNeill Scholarship in Irish Studies 348
NIH Research Grants 466
University of Kent Anthropology Taught Master's Studentships 660
Washington University Chancellor's Graduate Fellowship Program 715

West European Countries

ESRC 1 + 3 Awards and + 3 Awards 265
Research Degree Scholarships in Anthropology 634
University of Kent Anthropology Taught Master's Studentships 660
Wingate Scholarships 720

ETHNOLOGY

Any Country

ASCSA Fellowships 78
Earthwatch Field Research Grants 265
Fondation Fyssen Postdoctoral Study Grants 286
Institute of Irish Studies Research Fellowships 348
Institute of Irish Studies Senior Visiting Research Fellowship 348
M Alison Frantz Fellowship in Post-Classical Studies at the Gennadius Library 80
NEH Fellowships 80

Australia

Wingate Scholarships 720

Canada

Homer and Dorothy Thompson Fellowship 199
Mary McNeill Scholarship in Irish Studies 348
Wingate Scholarships 720

European Union

CBRL Travel Grant 244
ESRC 1 + 3 Awards and + 3 Awards 265

New Zealand

Wingate Scholarships 720

South Africa

Wingate Scholarships 720

United Kingdom

CBRL Research Award 244
CBRL Travel Grant 244
ESRC 1+3 Awards and +3 Awards 265
Wingate Scholarships 720

United States of America

ACC Fellowship Grants Program 106
ARCE Fellowships 77
Earthwatch Education Awards 265
Mary McNeill Scholarship in Irish Studies 348

West European Countries

ESRC 1+3 Awards and +3 Awards 265
Wingate Scholarships 720

FOLKLORE

Any Country

ASCSA Fellowships 78
Earthwatch Field Research Grants 265
Institute of Irish Studies Research Fellowships 348
Institute of Irish Studies Senior Visiting Research Fellowship 348
M Alison Frantz Fellowship in Post-Classical Studies at the Gennadius Library 80
NEH Fellowships 80

Australia

Wingate Scholarships 720

Canada

Mary McNeill Scholarship in Irish Studies 348
Wingate Scholarships 720

European Union

CBRL Travel Grant 244
ESRC 1+3 Awards and +3 Awards 265

New Zealand

Wingate Scholarships 720

South Africa

Wingate Scholarships 720

United Kingdom

CBRL Research Award 244
CBRL Travel Grant 244
ESRC 1+3 Awards and +3 Awards 265
Wingate Scholarships 720

United States of America

ACC Fellowship Grants Program 106
ARCE Fellowships 77
Earthwatch Education Awards 265
Mary McNeill Scholarship in Irish Studies 348

West European Countries

ESRC 1+3 Awards and +3 Awards 265
Wingate Scholarships 720

WOMEN'S STUDIES

Any Country

The Acacia ICT R&D Grants Programme 5
AFFDU Jeanne Chaton Award 147
Ahmanson and Getty Postdoctoral Fellowships 617
ASCSA Advanced Fellowships 78
ASCSA Fellowships 78
ASECS (American Society for 18th-Century Studies)/Clark Library Fellowships 617
BCUC Research Student Bursary 167
British Academy Overseas Conference Grants 142
British Academy Postdoctoral Fellowships 142
British Academy Small Research Grants 142
British Academy Worldwide Congress Grant 142
British Conference Grants 142
Camargo Fellowships 169
Clark Library Short-Term Resident Fellowships 617
Clark Predoctoral Fellowships 617
Clark-Huntington Joint Bibliographical Fellowship 617
Essex Rotary University Travel Grants 651
Foundation Praemium Erasmianum Study Prize 292
Frederick Douglass Institute Postdoctoral Fellowship 293
Frederick Douglass Institute Predoctoral Dissertation Fellowship 294
Hastings Center International Visiting Scholars Program 318
Henry A Murray Dissertation Award Program 322
HFG Dissertation Fellowship 317
HFG Research Program 317
Jeanne Humphrey Block Dissertation Award 322
Kennan Institute Short-Term Grants 397
La Trobe University Postgraduate Scholarship 403
Lee Kuan Yew School of Public Policy Scholarships (LKYSPPS) 474
Library Company of Philadelphia and Historical Society of Pennsylvania Research Fellowships in American History and Culture 411
M Alison Frantz Fellowship in Post-Classical Studies at the Gennadius Library 80
Marusia and Michael Dorosh Master's Fellowship 207
NEH Fellowships 80
Russell Sage Foundation Visiting Scholar Appointments 560
Sir Eric Berthoud Travel Grant 652
St Catherine's College Graduate Scholarship in the Arts 687
United States Holocaust Memorial Museum Center for Advanced Holocaust Studies Visiting Scholar Programs 619
University of Bristol Postgraduate Scholarships 641
University of Dundee Research Awards 648
University of Glasgow Postgraduate Research Scholarships 658
University of Otago International Scholarships 670
University of Otago PhD Scholarships 670
University of Otago Prestigious PhD Scholarships 671
Wolfsonian-FIU Fellowship 722
Woodrow Wilson Grants in Women's Studies 725

African Nations

Hastings Center International Visiting Scholars Program 318
IDRC Doctoral Research Awards 365
International Postgraduate Research Scholarships (IPRS) 692
MCTC Assistance for Courses 309
MCTC Tuition and Maintenance Scholarships 309
University of Sussex Overseas Development Administration Shared Scholarship Scheme 695

Australia

Hastings Center International Visiting Scholars Program 318
University of Essex/ORS Awards 655
Wingate Scholarships 720

Canada

Alcohol Beverage Medical Research Foundation Research Project Grant 15
CTCRI Idea Grants 217
CTCRI Research Planning Grants 217
Gilbert Chinard Fellowships 341
Harmon Chadbourn Rorison Fellowship 341
IDRC Doctoral Research Awards 365
International Postgraduate Research Scholarships (IPRS) 692
Thérèse F Casgrain Fellowship 584
University of Essex/ORS Awards 655
Wingate Scholarships 720

Caribbean Countries

Hastings Center International Visiting Scholars Program 318
IDRC Doctoral Research Awards 365
International Postgraduate Research Scholarships (IPRS) 692
MCTC Assistance for Courses 309
MCTC Tuition and Maintenance Scholarships 309
University of Essex/ORS Awards 655

East European Countries

Hastings Center International Visiting Scholars Program 318
International Postgraduate Research Scholarships (IPRS) 692
MCTC Assistance for Courses 309
MCTC Tuition and Maintenance Scholarships 309
Sasakawa Scholarship 695
University of Essex/ORS Awards 655

European Union

ESRC 1+3 Awards and +3 Awards 265

Middle East

Hastings Center International Visiting Scholars Program 318
International Postgraduate Research Scholarships (IPRS) 692
MCTC Assistance for Courses 309
MCTC Tuition and Maintenance Scholarships 309
University of Essex/ORS Awards 655

New Zealand

Hastings Center International Visiting Scholars Program 318
Wingate Scholarships 720

South Africa

Hastings Center International Visiting Scholars Program 318
IDRC Doctoral Research Awards 365
International Postgraduate Research Scholarships (IPRS) 692
MCTC Assistance for Courses 309
MCTC Tuition and Maintenance Scholarships 309
University of Essex/ORS Awards 655
Wingate Scholarships 720

United Kingdom

Balsdon Fellowship 160
ESRC 1+3 Awards and +3 Awards 265
Hastings Center International Visiting Scholars Program 318
Hector and Elizabeth Catling Bursary 159
International Postgraduate Research Scholarships (IPRS) 692
Mr and Mrs David Edward Memorial Award 699
Rome Awards 161
Rome Fellowship 161
Rome Scholarships in Ancient, Medieval and Later Italian Studies 162
Sasakawa Scholarship 695
University of Essex Access to Learning Fund 652
UWB Departmental Research Studentships 700
UWB Research Studentships 700
Wingate Scholarships 720

United States of America

AAUW Eleanor Roosevelt Teacher Fellowships 4
AAUW University Scholar-in-Residence 4
Alcohol Beverage Medical Research Foundation Research Project Grant 15
Annual Meeting Fellowship–Beverly Willis Architectural Foundation Travel Fellowship 589
ARCE Fellowships 77
ASECS Women's Caucus Editing and Translation Fellowship 80
Emilie Du Chatelet Award for Independent Scholarship 80
Fulbright Distinguished Chairs Program 245
Fulbright Senior Specialists Program 245
Gilbert Chinard Fellowships 341
Harmon Chadbourn Rorison Fellowship 341
Ian Axford (New Zealand) Fellowships in Public Policy 239
International Postgraduate Research Scholarships (IPRS) 692
IREX Individual Advanced Research Opportunities 374
IREX Short-Term Travel Grants 374
Kennan Institute Research Scholarship 397
Samuel H. Kress Foundation Fellowships for Speakers 590
University of Essex/ORS Awards 655
University of New Hampshire Postdoctoral Fellowships For Research on Family Violence 668

West European Countries

ESRC 1+3 Awards and +3 Awards 265
Hastings Center International Visiting Scholars Program 318
International Postgraduate Research Scholarships (IPRS) 692
Mr and Mrs David Edward Memorial Award 699
UWB Departmental Research Studentships 700
UWB Research Studentships 700
Wingate Scholarships 720

URBAN STUDIES

Any Country

The Acacia ICT R&D Grants Programme 5
ASCSA Fellowships 78
British Academy Overseas Conference Grants 142
British Academy Postdoctoral Fellowships 142
British Academy Small Research Grants 142
British Academy Worldwide Congress Grant 142
British Conference Grants 142
Eli Ginzberg Award 328
Equiano Memorial Award 604
Frederick Douglass Institute Postdoctoral Fellowship 293
Frederick Douglass Institute Predoctoral Dissertation Fellowship 294
Gypsy Lore Society Young Scholar's Prize in Romani Studies 314
HFG Dissertation Fellowship 317
HFG Research Program 317
John L Stanley Award 328
Joseph L Fisher Dissertation Award 525
Joshua Feigenbaum Award 328
Kennan Institute Short-Term Grants 397
Lee Kuan Yew School of Public Policy Scholarships (LKYSPPS) 474
M Alison Frantz Fellowship in Post-Classical Studies at the Gennadius Library 80
Queen Mary Research Studentships 518
Robert K Merton Award 329
Russell Sage Foundation Visiting Scholar Appointments 560
University of Bristol Postgraduate Scholarships 641
University of Glasgow Postgraduate Research Scholarships 658
University of Kent Postgraduate Funding Awards 662
Wolfsonian-FIU Fellowship 722

African Nations

Ecosystem Approaches to Human Health Awards 364
IDRC Doctoral Research Awards 365
International Postgraduate Research Scholarships (IPRS) 692
Joshua Feigenbaum Award 328

Australia

Joshua Feigenbaum Award 328
Wingate Scholarships 720

Canada

Alcohol Beverage Medical Research Foundation Research Project Grant 15
Ecosystem Approaches to Human Health Awards 364
IDRC Doctoral Research Awards 365
International Postgraduate Research Scholarships (IPRS) 692
Joshua Feigenbaum Award 328
Wingate Scholarships 720

Caribbean Countries

Ecosystem Approaches to Human Health Awards 364
IDRC Doctoral Research Awards 365

East European Countries

European Union

Middle East

New Zealand

South Africa

United Kingdom

United States of America

West European Countries

RURAL STUDIES

Any Country

African Nations

Australia

Canada

Caribbean Countries

East European Countries

European Union

Middle East

New Zealand

South Africa

United Kingdom

United States of America

West European Countries

COGNITIVE SCIENCES

Any Country

African Nations

Australia

Canada

Caribbean Countries

East European Countries

European Union

Middle East

New Zealand

South Africa

United Kingdom

United States of America

West European Countries

PSYCHOLOGY

Any Country

MRC Royal College of Surgeons of England Training Fellowship 427
MRC Senior Non-Clinical Fellowship 428
MRC Special Training Fellowships in Health Services and Health of the Public Research 428
MRC/Academy of Medical Sciences Tenure Track Clinician Scientist Fellowship 428
NARSAD Distinguished Investigator Awards 449
NARSAD Independent Investigator Awards 449
NARSAD Young Investigator Awards 449
Onassis Foreigners' Fellowships Programme Research Grants Category AI 17
Parapsychology Foundation Grant 497
PDS Research Project Grant 498
PDS Training Fellowships 498
Postgraduate Research Bursaries (Epilepsy Action) 274
Rhodes University Postdoctoral Fellowship and The Andrew Mellon Postdoctoral Fellowship 528
Robert K Merton Award 329
Russell Sage Foundation Visiting Scholar Appointments 560
Sir Eric Berthoud Travel Grant 652
Sir James McNeill Foundation Postgraduate Scholarship 440
Sully Scholarship 636
Thomas Holloway Research Studentship 548
TSA Research Grants 614
UFAW Research and Project Awards 624
UFAW Small Project and Travel Awards 624
UFAW Vacation Scholarships 624
United States Holocaust Memorial Museum Center for Advanced Holocaust Studies Visiting Scholar Programs 619
University of Bristol Postgraduate Scholarships 641
University of Dundee Research Awards 648
University of Glasgow Postgraduate Research Scholarships 658
University of Kent Department of Psychology Studentships 661
University of Otago International Scholarships 670
University of Otago PhD Scholarships 670
University of Otago Prestigious PhD Scholarships 671
University of Southampton Postgraduate Studentships 692
University of Warwick Psychology Department Studentship (PhD) 704
Wellcome Trust Grants 717
World Universities Network (WUN) Global Exchange Programme 693

African Nations

International Postgraduate Research Scholarships (IPRS) 692
Joshua Feigenbaum Award 328

Australia

Joshua Feigenbaum Award 328
University of Essex/ORS Awards 655
Wingate Scholarships 720

Canada

Alberta Heritage Health Research Studentship 14
Alcohol Beverage Medical Research Foundation Research Project Grant 15
CTCRI Idea Grants 217
CTCRI Research Planning Grants 217
Heritage Health Research Career Renewal Awards 15
International Postgraduate Research Scholarships (IPRS) 692
Joshua Feigenbaum Award 328
University of Essex/ORS Awards 655
Wingate Scholarships 720

Caribbean Countries

International Postgraduate Research Scholarships (IPRS) 692
Joshua Feigenbaum Award 328
University of Essex/ORS Awards 655

East European Countries

International Postgraduate Research Scholarships (IPRS) 692
Joshua Feigenbaum Award 328
University of Essex/ORS Awards 655

European Union

ESRC 1+3 Awards and +3 Awards 265

Middle East

International Postgraduate Research Scholarships (IPRS) 692
Joshua Feigenbaum Award 328
University of Essex/ORS Awards 655

New Zealand

Joshua Feigenbaum Award 328
Wingate Scholarships 720

South Africa

International Postgraduate Research Scholarships (IPRS) 692
Joshua Feigenbaum Award 328
University of Essex/ORS Awards 655
Wingate Scholarships 720

United Kingdom

Breast Cancer Campaign Project Grants 140
ESRC 1+3 Awards and +3 Awards 265
International Postgraduate Research Scholarships (IPRS) 692
Joshua Feigenbaum Award 328
Mr and Mrs David Edward Memorial Award 699
PDS Research Project Grant 498
PDS Training Fellowships 498
Sheffield Hallam University Studentships 567
University of Essex Access to Learning Fund 652
UWB Departmental Research Studentships 700
UWB Research Studentships 700
Wingate Scholarships 720

United States of America

Alcohol Beverage Medical Research Foundation Research Project Grant 15
ETS Postdoctoral Fellowships 267
ETS Summer Program in Research for Graduate Students 267
Fulbright Distinguished Chairs Program 245
Fulbright Senior Specialists Program 245
International Postgraduate Research Scholarships (IPRS) 692
IREX Individual Advanced Research Opportunities 374
IREX Short-Term Travel Grants 374
Kennan Institute Research Scholarship 397
National Research Service Award for Mental Health and Adjustment in the Life Course 412
NIH Research Grants 466
University of Essex/ORS Awards 655
University of New Hampshire Postdoctoral Fellowships For Research on Family Violence 668
Washington University Chancellor's Graduate Fellowship Program 715

West European Countries

ESRC 1+3 Awards and +3 Awards 265
International Postgraduate Research Scholarships (IPRS) 692
Mr and Mrs David Edward Memorial Award 699
Sheffield Hallam University Studentships 567
UWB Departmental Research Studentships 700
UWB Research Studentships 700
Wingate Scholarships 720

EXPERIMENTAL PSYCHOLOGY

Any Country

Alzheimer's Society Research Grants 23
D Scott Rogo Award for Parapsychological Literature 497
Eileen J Garrett Scholarship 497
NARSAD Distinguished Investigator Awards 449
NARSAD Independent Investigator Awards 449
NARSAD Young Investigator Awards 449

CLINICAL PSYCHOLOGY

PERSONALITY PSYCHOLOGY

Any Country

Alzheimer's Society Research Grants 23
BackCare Research Grants 130

African Nations

International Postgraduate Research Scholarships (IPRS) 692

Canada

International Postgraduate Research Scholarships (IPRS) 692

Caribbean Countries

International Postgraduate Research Scholarships (IPRS) 692

East European Countries

International Postgraduate Research Scholarships (IPRS) 692

European Union

ESRC 1+3 Awards and +3 Awards 265

Middle East

International Postgraduate Research Scholarships (IPRS) 692

South Africa

International Postgraduate Research Scholarships (IPRS) 692

United Kingdom

ESRC 1+3 Awards and +3 Awards 265
International Postgraduate Research Scholarships (IPRS) 692
Mr and Mrs David Edward Memorial Award 699
PWSA UK Research Grants 514
UWB Departmental Research Studentships 700
UWB Research Studentships 700

United States of America

International Postgraduate Research Scholarships (IPRS) 692
NIH Research Grants 466

West European Countries

ESRC 1+3 Awards and +3 Awards 265
International Postgraduate Research Scholarships (IPRS) 692
Mr and Mrs David Edward Memorial Award 699
UWB Departmental Research Studentships 700
UWB Research Studentships 700

INDUSTRIAL/ORGANISATIONAL PSYCHOLOGY

Any Country

BackCare Research Grants 130

African Nations

International Postgraduate Research Scholarships (IPRS) 692

Australia

University of Essex/ORS Awards 655

Canada

International Postgraduate Research Scholarships (IPRS) 692
University of Essex/ORS Awards 655

Caribbean Countries

International Postgraduate Research Scholarships (IPRS) 692
University of Essex/ORS Awards 655

East European Countries

International Postgraduate Research Scholarships (IPRS) 692
University of Essex/ORS Awards 655

European Union

ESRC 1+3 Awards and +3 Awards 265

Middle East

International Postgraduate Research Scholarships (IPRS) 692
University of Essex/ORS Awards 655

South Africa

International Postgraduate Research Scholarships (IPRS) 692
University of Essex/ORS Awards 655

United Kingdom

ESRC 1+3 Awards and +3 Awards 265
International Postgraduate Research Scholarships (IPRS) 692
Mr and Mrs David Edward Memorial Award 699
UWB Departmental Research Studentships 700
UWB Research Studentships 700

United States of America

International Postgraduate Research Scholarships (IPRS) 692
National Research Service Award for Mental Health and Adjustment in the Life Course 412
University of Essex/ORS Awards 655

West European Countries

ESRC 1+3 Awards and +3 Awards 265
International Postgraduate Research Scholarships (IPRS) 692
Mr and Mrs David Edward Memorial Award 699
UWB Departmental Research Studentships 700
UWB Research Studentships 700

PSYCHOMETRICS

Any Country

Alzheimer's Society Research Grants 23
ETS Summer Program in Research for Graduate Students 267

Australia

University of Essex/ORS Awards 655

Canada

University of Essex/ORS Awards 655

Caribbean Countries

University of Essex/ORS Awards 655

East European Countries

University of Essex/ORS Awards 655

Middle East

University of Essex/ORS Awards 655

South Africa

University of Essex/ORS Awards 655

United Kingdom

Mr and Mrs David Edward Memorial Award 699
UWB Departmental Research Studentships 700
UWB Research Studentships 700

United States of America

ETS Summer Program in Research for Graduate Students 267
NIH Research Grants 466

West European Countries

EDUCATIONAL PSYCHOLOGY

Any Country

African Nations

Australia

Canada

Caribbean Countries

East European Countries

European Union

Middle East

New Zealand

South Africa

United Kingdom

United States of America

West European Countries

GEOGRAPHY (SOCIAL AND ECONOMIC)

Any Country

African Nations

Australia

Canada

Caribbean Countries

East European Countries

CRF (Caledonian Research Foundation)/RSE European Visiting Research Fellowships 556
International Postgraduate Research Scholarships (IPRS) 692
Joshua Feigenbaum Award 328

European Union

CBRL Travel Grant 244
ESRC 1+3 Awards and +3 Awards 265

Middle East

International Postgraduate Research Scholarships (IPRS) 692
Joshua Feigenbaum Award 328

New Zealand

Joshua Feigenbaum Award 328
Wingate Scholarships 720

South Africa

IDRC Doctoral Research Awards 365
International Postgraduate Research Scholarships (IPRS) 692
Joshua Feigenbaum Award 328
Wingate Scholarships 720

United Kingdom

Balsdon Fellowship 160
CBRL Research Award 244
CBRL Travel Grant 244
CRF (Caledonian Research Foundation)/RSE European Visiting Research Fellowships 556
ESRC 1+3 Awards and +3 Awards 265
Grundy Educational Trust 313
International Postgraduate Research Scholarships (IPRS) 692
Joshua Feigenbaum Award 328
Rome Awards 161
Rome Fellowship 161
Rome Scholarships in Ancient, Medieval and Later Italian Studies 162
Royal Geographical Society Geographica Fieldwork Grants 546
Sheffield Hallam University Studentships 567
University of Wales Aberystwyth Postgraduate Research Studentships 699
Wingate Scholarships 720

United States of America

Fulbright Distinguished Chairs Program 245
Fulbright Senior Specialists Program 245
IGU Travel Grant 109
International Postgraduate Research Scholarships (IPRS) 692
IREX Individual Advanced Research Opportunities 374
IREX Short-Term Travel Grants 374
Kennan Institute Research Scholarship 397
Visiting Geographical Scientist Program 109

West European Countries

CRF (Caledonian Research Foundation)/RSE European Visiting Research Fellowships 556
ESRC 1+3 Awards and +3 Awards 265
International Postgraduate Research Scholarships (IPRS) 692
Sheffield Hallam University Studentships 567
Wingate Scholarships 720

DEVELOPMENT STUDIES

Any Country

The Acacia ICT R&D Grants Programme 5
British Academy Postdoctoral Fellowships 142
Earthwatch Field Research Grants 265
Equiano Memorial Award 604
Gilbert F White Postdoctoral Fellowship 525
Gilbert Murray Trust Junior Awards 307
Hastings Center International Visiting Scholars Program 318
Henry A Murray Dissertation Award Program 322
Jeanne Humphrey Block Dissertation Award 322
John L Stanley Award 328
Joseph L Fisher Dissertation Award 525
Joshua Feigenbaum Award 328
Kennan Institute Short-Term Grants 397
M Alison Frantz Fellowship in Post-Classical Studies at the Gennadius Library 80
Paul H. Nitze School of Advanced International Studies (SAIS) Financial Aid and Fellowships 139
Rhodes University Postdoctoral Fellowship and The Andrew Mellon Postdoctoral Fellowship 528
Robert K Merton Award 329
School for International Training (SIT) Extension 728
SOAS Bursary 563
SOAS Research Student Fellowships 563
St Catherine's College Graduate Scholarship in the Arts 687
University of Bristol Postgraduate Scholarships 641
WILPF Internship in Disarmament and Economic Justice 723
World Bank Cambridge Scholarships for Postgraduate Study 197
World Bank Grants Facility for Indigenous Peoples 727

African Nations

Canadian Window on International Development 364
Hastings Center International Visiting Scholars Program 318
IDRC Doctoral Research Awards 365
International Postgraduate Research Scholarships (IPRS) 692
Joshua Feigenbaum Award 328
Shell Centenary Scholarships and Shell Centenary Chevening Scholarships 685
University of Sussex Overseas Development Administration Shared Scholarship Scheme 695
World Bank Grants Facility for Indigenous Peoples 727

Australia

Hastings Center International Visiting Scholars Program 318
Joshua Feigenbaum Award 328
Wingate Scholarships 720

Canada

Alcohol Beverage Medical Research Foundation Research Project Grant 15
Canadian Window on International Development 364
CIDA Research Grant 209
Community Forestry: Trees and People - John G Bene Fellowship 364
IDRC Doctoral Research Awards 365
International Postgraduate Research Scholarships (IPRS) 692
Joshua Feigenbaum Award 328
Organization of American States (OAS) Fellowships Programs 364
SICI India Studies Fellowship Competition 566
Wingate Scholarships 720

Caribbean Countries

Canadian Window on International Development 364
Hastings Center International Visiting Scholars Program 318
IDRC Doctoral Research Awards 365
International Postgraduate Research Scholarships (IPRS) 692
Joshua Feigenbaum Award 328
Prince of Wales (Cable and Wireless) Chevening Cambridge Scholarships for Postgraduate Study 191
Shell Centenary Scholarships and Shell Centenary Chevening Scholarships 685

East European Countries

Hastings Center International Visiting Scholars Program 318
International Postgraduate Research Scholarships (IPRS) 692
Joshua Feigenbaum Award 328
Sasakawa Scholarship 695
Shell Centenary Scholarships and Shell Centenary Chevening Scholarships 685

European Union

ESRC 1+3 Awards and +3 Awards 265

Middle East

Hastings Center International Visiting Scholars Program 318
International Postgraduate Research Scholarships (IPRS) 692
Joshua Feigenbaum Award 328
Open Society Institute-FCO Chevening-University of Leeds Scholarships 664
Shell Centenary Scholarships and Shell Centenary Chevening Scholarships 685

New Zealand

Hastings Center International Visiting Scholars Program 318
Joshua Feigenbaum Award 328
Wingate Scholarships 720

South Africa

Canadian Window on International Development 364
Hastings Center International Visiting Scholars Program 318
IDRC Doctoral Research Awards 365
International Postgraduate Research Scholarships (IPRS) 692
Joshua Feigenbaum Award 328
SAIIA Konrad Adenauer Foundation Research Internship 596
Shell Centenary Scholarships and Shell Centenary Chevening Scholarships 685
Wingate Scholarships 720

United Kingdom

ESRC 1+3 Awards and +3 Awards 265
Goldsmiths' Company Science for Society Courses 310
Hastings Center International Visiting Scholars Program 318
International Postgraduate Research Scholarships (IPRS) 692
Joshua Feigenbaum Award 328
Sasakawa Scholarship 695
Wingate Scholarships 720

United States of America

Alcohol Beverage Medical Research Foundation Research Project Grant 15
International Postgraduate Research Scholarships (IPRS) 692
IREX Individual Advanced Research Opportunities 374
IREX Short-Term Travel Grants 374
Kennan Institute Research Scholarship 397

West European Countries

ESRC 1+3 Awards and +3 Awards 265
Hastings Center International Visiting Scholars Program 318
International Postgraduate Research Scholarships (IPRS) 692
Wingate Scholarships 720

AREA AND CULTURAL STUDIES

Any Country

AAS Joyçe Tracy Fellowship 26
ACLS/SSRC/NEH International and Area Studies Fellowships 45
Albert J Beveridge Grant 54
Albin Salton Fellowship 712
Andrew W Mellon Postdoctoral Fellowship 717
ASCSA Fellowships 78
ASCSA Research Fellowship in Environmental Studies 79
ASCSA Research Fellowship in Faunal Studies 79
ASCSA Research Fellowship in Geoarchaeology 79
Austro-American Association of Boston Scholarship 129
Bernadotte E Schmitt Grants 54
Bernard and Audre Rapoport Fellowships 55
British Academy Overseas Conference Grants 142
British Academy Postdoctoral Fellowships 142
British Academy Sino-British Fellowship Trust 142
British Academy Small Research Grants 142
British Academy Worldwide Congress Grant 142
British Conference Grants 142
C H Currey Memorial Fellowship 599
Camargo Fellowships 169
CDI Internship 226
CDU Senior Research Fellowship 230
CDU Three Year Postdoctoral Fellowship 230
CSA Adele Filene Travel Award 244
CSA Stella Blum Research Grant 244
CSA Travel Research Grant 244
Earthwatch Field Research Grants 265
Equiano Memorial Award 604
Ethel Marcus Memorial Fellowship 55
Foundation Praemium Erasmianum Study Prize 292
Frederick Douglass Institute Postdoctoral Fellowship 293
Frederick Douglass Institute Predoctoral Dissertation Fellowship 294
Gypsy Lore Society Young Scholar's Prize in Romani Studies 314
Henry A Murray Dissertation Award Program 322
HFG Dissertation Fellowship 317
HFG Research Program 317
IFUWA Sarojini Naidu Memorial Scholarship 151
Irish Research Funds 383
The Isi Leibler Prize 254
Jeanne Humphrey Block Dissertation Award 322
John L Stanley Award 328
The Joseph and Eva R Dave Fellowship 56
Joshua Feigenbaum Award 328
Kennan Institute Short-Term Grants 397
La Trobe University Postgraduate Scholarship 403
Lee Kuan Yew School of Public Policy Scholarships (LKYSPPS) 474
Loewenstein-Wiener Fellowship Awards 56
M Alison Frantz Fellowship in Post-Classical Studies at the Gennadius Library 80
Marguerite R Jacobs Memorial Award 56
The Natalie Feld Memorial Fellowship 56
NEH Fellowships 80
Paul H. Nitze School of Advanced International Studies (SAIS) Financial Aid and Fellowships 139
Paul Mellon Centre Rome Fellowship 161
Queen Mary Research Studentships 518
Rabbi Frederic A Doppelt Memorial Fellowship 56
The Rabbi Harold D Hahn Memorial Fellowship 56
The Rabbi Joachin Prinz Memorial Fellowship 57
Rabbi Levi A Olan Memorial Fellowship 57
Rabbi Theodore S Levy Tribute Fellowship 57
Robert K Merton Award 329
SAIIA Bradlow Fellowship 595
St Catherine's College Graduate Scholarship in the Arts 687
Starkoff Fellowship 57
United States Holocaust Memorial Museum Center for Advanced Holocaust Studies Visiting Scholar Programs 619
Wolfsonian-FIU Fellowship 722
World Bank Grants Facility for Indigenous Peoples 727

African Nations

IDRC Doctoral Research Awards 365
International Postgraduate Research Scholarships (IPRS) 692
Joshua Feigenbaum Award 328
World Bank Grants Facility for Indigenous Peoples 727

Australia

AAH Humanities Travelling Fellowships 120
Joshua Feigenbaum Award 328
Wingate Scholarships 720

Canada

Alcohol Beverage Medical Research Foundation Research Project Grant 15
Gilbert Chinard Fellowships 341
Harmon Chadbourn Rorison Fellowship 341
IDRC Doctoral Research Awards 365
International Postgraduate Research Scholarships (IPRS) 692
Joshua Feigenbaum Award 328

Caribbean Countries

East European Countries

European Union

Middle East

New Zealand

South Africa

United Kingdom

United States of America

West European Countries

NORTH AFRICAN

Any Country

African Nations

Canada

Caribbean Countries

European Union

South Africa

United Kingdom

United States of America

SUBSAHARA AFRICAN

Any Country

African Nations

Canada

Caribbean Countries

European Union

South Africa

United Kingdom

AFRICAN STUDIES

Any Country

African Nations

Canada

Caribbean Countries

European Union

South Africa

United Kingdom

United States of America

AFRICAN AMERICAN

Any Country

European Union

United Kingdom

United States of America

NATIVE AMERICAN

Any Country

European Union

United Kingdom

United States of America

HISPANIC AMERICAN

Any Country

European Union

European Union

United Kingdom

United States of America

West European Countries

EASTERN EUROPEAN

Any Country

East European Countries

European Union

United Kingdom

United States of America

West European Countries

WESTERN EUROPEAN

Any Country

Canada

European Union

United Kingdom

United States of America

NORDIC

Any Country

Canada

East European Countries

European Union

United Kingdom

Starkoff Fellowship 57
Touro National Heritage Trust Fellowship 392
United States Holocaust Memorial Museum Center for Advanced Holocaust Studies Visiting Scholar Programs 619

Canada

JCCA Graduate Education Scholarship 389

European Union

AHRC Doctoral Awards Scheme 103
CBRL Travel Grant 244
Professional Preparation Master's Scheme 103
Research Preparation Master's Scheme 103

United Kingdom

AHRC Doctoral Awards Scheme 103
CBRL Research Award 244
CBRL Travel Grant 244
Professional Preparation Master's Scheme 103
Research Preparation Master's Scheme 103

United States of America

Fellowship Programme for Émigrés Pursuing Careers in Jewish Education 389
JCCA Graduate Education Scholarship 389
LBI/DAAD Fellowship for Research at the Leo Baeck Institute, New York 407
LBI/DAAD Fellowships for Research in the Federal Republic of Germany 407

PRESERVATION OF CULTURAL HERITAGE

Any Country

Albert J Beveridge Grant 54
ASCSA Advanced Fellowships 78
ASCSA Fellowships 78
Bernadotte E Schmitt Grants 54
Bernard and Audre Rapoport Fellowships 55
British Academy Postdoctoral Fellowships 142
CDU Senior Research Fellowship 230
CDU Three Year Postdoctoral Fellowship 230
CSA Adele Filene Travel Award 244
CSA Stella Blum Research Grant 244
CSA Travel Research Grant 244
Equiano Memorial Award 604
Ethel Marcus Memorial Fellowship 55
Irish Research Funds 383
Jacob Hirsch Fellowship 79
The Joseph and Eva R Dave Fellowship 56
Loewenstein-Wiener Fellowship Awards 56
M Alison Frantz Fellowship in Post-Classical Studies at the Gennadius Library 80
Marguerite R Jacobs Memorial Award 56
Milt Luger Fellowships 599
The Natalie Feld Memorial Fellowship 56
NEH Fellowships 80
Rabbi Frederic A Doppelt Memorial Fellowship 56
The Rabbi Harold D Hahn Memorial Fellowship 56
The Rabbi Joachin Prinz Memorial Fellowship 57
Rabbi Levi A Olan Memorial Fellowship 57
Rabbi Theodore S Levy Tribute Fellowship 57
Starkoff Fellowship 57
United States Holocaust Memorial Museum Center for Advanced Holocaust Studies Visiting Scholar Programs 619

African Nations

International Postgraduate Research Scholarships (IPRS) 692

Australia

Wingate Scholarships 720

Canada

International Postgraduate Research Scholarships (IPRS) 692
Wingate Scholarships 720

Caribbean Countries

International Postgraduate Research Scholarships (IPRS) 692

East European Countries

International Postgraduate Research Scholarships (IPRS) 692
Synthesys Visiting Fellowship 477

European Union

CBRL Travel Grant 244

Middle East

International Postgraduate Research Scholarships (IPRS) 692

New Zealand

Wingate Scholarships 720

South Africa

International Postgraduate Research Scholarships (IPRS) 692
Wingate Scholarships 720

United Kingdom

CBRL Research Award 244
CBRL Travel Grant 244
International Postgraduate Research Scholarships (IPRS) 692
UWB Research Studentships 700
Wingate Scholarships 720

United States of America

ACC Fellowship Grants Program 106
David Baumgardt Memorial Fellowship 407
Earthwatch Education Awards 265
Fritz Halbers Fellowship 407
Fulbright Senior Specialists Program 245
Ian Axford (New Zealand) Fellowships in Public Policy 239
International Postgraduate Research Scholarships (IPRS) 692
Norwegian Ministry of Foreign Affairs Travel Grants 487

West European Countries

David Baumgardt Memorial Fellowship 407
Fritz Halbers Fellowship 407
International Postgraduate Research Scholarships (IPRS) 692
Synthesys Visiting Fellowship 477
UWB Research Studentships 700
Wingate Scholarships 720

ANCIENT CIVILISATIONS (EGYPTOLOGY, ASSYRIOLOGY)

Any Country

ASCSA Advanced Fellowships 78
ASCSA Fellowships 78
ASCSA Research Fellowship in Environmental Studies 79
ASCSA Research Fellowship in Faunal Studies 79
ASCSA Research Fellowship in Geoarchaeology 79
British Academy Postdoctoral Fellowships 142
Frances M Schwartz Fellowship 69
Grants for ANS Summer Seminar in Numismatics 70
J Lawrence Angel Fellowship in Human Skeletal Studies 79
Jacob Hirsch Fellowship 79
NEH Fellowships 80
SOAS Research Student Fellowships 563

African Nations

British School of Archaeology in Iraq Grants 163

TRADE, CRAFT AND INDUSTRIAL TECHNIQUES

GENERAL

FOOD PROCESSING TECHNIQUES

BUILDING TRADES

ELECTRICAL/ELECTRONIC EQUIPMENT AND MAINTENANCE TECHNIQUES

METAL TRADES TECHNIQUES

MECHANICAL EQUIPMENT AND MAINTENANCE TECHNIQUES

WOOD TECHNOLOGY

HEATING, AIR CONDITIONING AND REFRIGERATION TECHNOLOGY

LEATHER TECHNIQUES

TEXTILE TECHNIQUES

PAPER AND PACKAGING TECHNOLOGY

GRAPHIC ARTS TECHNIQUES

PRINTING

PUBLISHING AND BOOK TRADE

East European Countries

United Kingdom

United States of America

West European Countries

LABORATORY TECHNIQUES

African Nations

United States of America

OPTICAL TECHNOLOGY

Any Country

United States of America

TRANSPORT AND COMMUNICATIONS

GENERAL

Any Country

African Nations

Australia

Canada

Caribbean Countries

East European Countries

European Union

Middle East

New Zealand

South Africa

United Kingdom

United States of America

West European Countries

ESRC 1 + 3 Awards and + 3 Awards 265
Fulbright Postdoctoral Research and Lecturing Awards for Non-US Citizens 245
International Postgraduate Research Scholarships (IPRS) 692
Janson Johan Helmich Scholarships and Travel Grants 387
Wingate Scholarships 720

AIR TRANSPORT

African Nations

International Postgraduate Research Scholarships (IPRS) 692

Canada

International Postgraduate Research Scholarships (IPRS) 692

Caribbean Countries

International Postgraduate Research Scholarships (IPRS) 692

East European Countries

International Postgraduate Research Scholarships (IPRS) 692

Middle East

International Postgraduate Research Scholarships (IPRS) 692

South Africa

International Postgraduate Research Scholarships (IPRS) 692

United Kingdom

Handley Page Award 536
International Postgraduate Research Scholarships (IPRS) 692

United States of America

Congress Bundestag Youth Exchange for Young Professionals 224
International Postgraduate Research Scholarships (IPRS) 692

West European Countries

International Postgraduate Research Scholarships (IPRS) 692

MARINE TRANSPORT AND NAUTICAL SCIENCE

Any Country

De Paepe - Willems Award 371
WHOI Research Fellowships in Marine Policy 727

United States of America

Congress Bundestag Youth Exchange for Young Professionals 224

RAILWAY TRANSPORT

African Nations

International Postgraduate Research Scholarships (IPRS) 692

Canada

International Postgraduate Research Scholarships (IPRS) 692

Caribbean Countries

International Postgraduate Research Scholarships (IPRS) 692

East European Countries

International Postgraduate Research Scholarships (IPRS) 692

Middle East

International Postgraduate Research Scholarships (IPRS) 692

South Africa

International Postgraduate Research Scholarships (IPRS) 692

United Kingdom

International Postgraduate Research Scholarships (IPRS) 692

United States of America

Congress Bundestag Youth Exchange for Young Professionals 224
International Postgraduate Research Scholarships (IPRS) 692

West European Countries

International Postgraduate Research Scholarships (IPRS) 692

ROAD TRANSPORT

Any Country

Rees Jeffreys Road Fund Bursaries 522
Rees Jeffreys Road Fund Research Grants 522

African Nations

International Postgraduate Research Scholarships (IPRS) 692

Canada

International Postgraduate Research Scholarships (IPRS) 692
TAC Foundation Scholarships 615

Caribbean Countries

International Postgraduate Research Scholarships (IPRS) 692

East European Countries

International Postgraduate Research Scholarships (IPRS) 692

Middle East

International Postgraduate Research Scholarships (IPRS) 692

South Africa

International Postgraduate Research Scholarships (IPRS) 692

United Kingdom

International Postgraduate Research Scholarships (IPRS) 692

United States of America

Congress Bundestag Youth Exchange for Young Professionals 224
International Postgraduate Research Scholarships (IPRS) 692

West European Countries

International Postgraduate Research Scholarships (IPRS) 692

TRANSPORT MANAGEMENT

African Nations

International Postgraduate Research Scholarships (IPRS) 692

Australia

Cranfield University Overseas Bursary 249
Wingate Scholarships 720

Canada

Cranfield University Overseas Bursary 249
International Postgraduate Research Scholarships (IPRS) 692
TAC Foundation Scholarships 615
Wingate Scholarships 720

Caribbean Countries
Cranfield University Overseas Bursary 249
International Postgraduate Research Scholarships (IPRS) 692

East European Countries
International Postgraduate Research Scholarships (IPRS) 692

European Union
ESRC 1+3 Awards and +3 Awards 265

Middle East
Cranfield University Overseas Bursary 249
International Postgraduate Research Scholarships (IPRS) 692

New Zealand
Cranfield University Overseas Bursary 249
Wingate Scholarships 720

South Africa
Cranfield University Overseas Bursary 249
International Postgraduate Research Scholarships (IPRS) 692
Wingate Scholarships 720

United Kingdom
ESRC 1+3 Awards and +3 Awards 265
International Postgraduate Research Scholarships (IPRS) 692
Sheffield Hallam University Studentships 567
Silsoe Awards 249
Wingate Scholarships 720

United States of America
Congress Bundestag Youth Exchange for Young Professionals 224
Cranfield University Overseas Bursary 249
International Postgraduate Research Scholarships (IPRS) 692

West European Countries
ESRC 1+3 Awards and +3 Awards 265
International Postgraduate Research Scholarships (IPRS) 692
Sheffield Hallam University Studentships 567
Silsoe Awards 249
Wingate Scholarships 720

TRANSPORT ECONOMICS

Any Country
Rees Jeffreys Road Fund Bursaries 522
Rees Jeffreys Road Fund Research Grants 522

African Nations
International Postgraduate Research Scholarships (IPRS) 692

Canada
International Postgraduate Research Scholarships (IPRS) 692
TAC Foundation Scholarships 615

Caribbean Countries
International Postgraduate Research Scholarships (IPRS) 692

East European Countries
International Postgraduate Research Scholarships (IPRS) 692

European Union
ESRC 1+3 Awards and +3 Awards 265

Middle East
International Postgraduate Research Scholarships (IPRS) 692

South Africa
International Postgraduate Research Scholarships (IPRS) 692

United Kingdom
ESRC 1+3 Awards and +3 Awards 265
International Postgraduate Research Scholarships (IPRS) 692

United States of America
Congress Bundestag Youth Exchange for Young Professionals 224
International Postgraduate Research Scholarships (IPRS) 692

West European Countries
ESRC 1+3 Awards and +3 Awards 265
International Postgraduate Research Scholarships (IPRS) 692

POSTAL SERVICES

United States of America
Congress Bundestag Youth Exchange for Young Professionals 224

TELECOMMUNICATIONS SERVICES

Any Country
Equiano Memorial Award 604
Essex Rotary University Travel Grants 651
Sir Eric Berthoud Travel Grant 652

African Nations
International Postgraduate Research Scholarships (IPRS) 692

Australia
University of Essex/ORS Awards 655

Canada
International Postgraduate Research Scholarships (IPRS) 692
University of Essex/ORS Awards 655

Caribbean Countries
International Postgraduate Research Scholarships (IPRS) 692
University of Essex/ORS Awards 655

East European Countries
International Postgraduate Research Scholarships (IPRS) 692
University of Essex/ORS Awards 655

Middle East
International Postgraduate Research Scholarships (IPRS) 692
University of Essex/ORS Awards 655

South Africa
International Postgraduate Research Scholarships (IPRS) 692
University of Essex/ORS Awards 655

United Kingdom
International Postgraduate Research Scholarships (IPRS) 692
University of Essex Access to Learning Fund 652

United States of America
Congress Bundestag Youth Exchange for Young Professionals 224
International Postgraduate Research Scholarships (IPRS) 692
University of Essex/ORS Awards 655

West European Countries
International Postgraduate Research Scholarships (IPRS) 692

INDEX OF AWARDS

Norah Taylor Bursary 595
NORD Clinical Research Grants 470
NORD/Rosoe Brady Lysosomal Storage Diseases Fellowships 470
Norman Gamble Fund and Research Prize 558
Norman Tanner Medal and Prize (1st Prize) Glaxo Travelling Fellowship (2nd Prize) 558
North American Doctoral Fellowship 298
North Dakota Indian Scholarship 485
North West Cancer Research Fund Research Project Grants 485
Northern Research Development Program 582
Norwegian Emigration Fund of 1975 487
Norwegian Information Service Fulbright Stipend 487
Norwegian Marshall Fund 487
Norwegian Ministry of Foreign Affairs Travel Grants 487
Norwegian Thanksgiving Fund Scholarship 487
Norwich Jubilee Esperanto Foundation Grants-in-Aid 488
NRC Research Associateships 471
NREF Research Fellowship 31
NREF Young Clinician Investigator Award 32
NSCA Challenge Scholarship 472
NSCA Graduate Research Grant 472
NSCA Minority Scholarship 472
NSCA Power Systems Professional Scholarship 473
NSCA Women's Scholarship 473
NSERC Postdoctoral Fellowships 477
NSF Division of Earth Sciences 471
NSPS Forum for Equal Opportunity/Mary Feindt Scholarship 43
The NSPS Scholarships 43
NSW Architects Registration Board Research Grant 488
NTU Alumni Scholarship 448
NTU APEC Scholarship 448
NTU ASEAN Postgraduate Scholarship 448
NTU MBA Scholarship 448
NTU SCCCF Business Scholarship 449
NUFFIC-NFP Fellowships for Master's Degree Programmes 478
NUFFIC-NFP Fellowships for PhD Studies 478
Nuffield College Funded Studentships 682
Nuffield College Prize Research Fellowships 682
Nuffield Trust/RCN/IHM Joint Travel Awards 539
Nurses' Educational Funds Fellowships and Scholarships 488
NUS Asean Scholarship 474
NUS Design Technology Institute Scholarship 475
NUT Page Scholarship 473
The O'Reilly Scholarship Programme 489
O'Reiuy Environmental Science Scholarship 604
OAH Awards and Prizes 494
Octave J. Du Temple Award 68
The ODASS Scheme 415
OFAS Grants 491
Oligo Brain Tumor Fund 451
Olin Fellowship 118
Olive Lynn Salembier Scholarship 593
Onassis Foreigners' Fellowship Programme Educational Scholarships Category B 16
Onassis Foreigners' Fellowship Programme Educational Scholarships Category C 16
Onassis Foreigners' Fellowships Programme Research Grants Category AI 17
Onassis Foreigners' Fellowships Programme Research Grants Category AII 17
One World Scholarship Program 11
ONS Foundation Research Awards 490
Open Russia Foundation Grant 490
Open Society Institute-FCO Chevening-University of Leeds Scholarships 664
Operations and Power Division Award 68
Ophthalmology Travelling Fellowship 558
Oppenheimer Fund 682
Oppenheim-John Downes Trust Grants 491
OREF Career Development Award 495
OREF Clinical Research Award 495
OREF Fellowship in Health Services Research 495
OREF Prospective Clinical Research 495
OREF Research Grants 495
OREF Resident Research Award 495
Organic Films/Fertile Ground Ltd. Grant 104
Organization of American States (OAS) Fellowships Programs 364
ORISHA (Oxford Research in the Scholarship and Humanities of Africa) Studentships 682
ORSAS 652
Osaka Travel Award 549
Oscar Arias Scholarship 652
OSI (Open Society Institute)/FCO Chevening Scholarships 682
OSI Chevening Cambridge Scholarships for Postgraduate Study 189
OSI Noon Chevening Cambridge Scholarships 189
OSI/UCL-SSEES/FCO Chevening Scholarship 633
Osserman/Sosin/McClure Research Fellowship 447
Otto Benecke Foundation Scientific Internships 496
Otto Kinkeldey Award 64
Otto Klineberg Intercultural and International Relations Award 587
Our World-Underwater Scholarship Society Scholarships 496
Overseas Korean Foundation Scholarship 566
Overseas Research Student (ORS) Awards Scheme 683
Overseas Research Students Awards Scheme (ORSAS) 694
Overseas Research Students Awards Scheme 664
Overseas Scholarship for MS (Engineering) in South Korean Universities 326
Owen Shaw Award 164
Oxford and Cambridge Society of Bombay Cambridge DFID Scholarship 189
Oxford Kobe Scholarships (Japan) 683
Oxford University Theological Scholarships (Eastern and Central Europe) 683
OZCO Community Cultural Development Fellowship 119
OZCO Community Culture Development Grant Residency 119
OZCO Dance Fellowship 119
OZCO Dance Grant Initiative: Take Your Partner 119
OZCO Literature Fellowships 119
OZCO Literature Grants Initiative: Write in Your Face 119
OZCO Music Fellowship 119
OZCO Music Project Fellowship 120
OZCO New Media Fellowship 120
OZCO New Media Residency 120
OZCO Theatre Fellowship 120
OZCO Visual Arts Fellowship 120
Pace Award 145
Packer Fellowships 239
PAHO Grants 497
Pakistan 50th Anniversary Fund 694
Paloma O'Shea Santander International Piano Competition 496
Panasonic Trust Awards 534
Parapsychology Foundation Grant 497
Paris International Singing Competition 362
Parke D. Snavely, Jr., Cascadia Research Award Fund 301
Parker B Francis Fellowship Program 498
Parker B Francis Respiratory Research Grant 28
Partial Support for PhD Studies Abroad 326
Paterson 4-Year Studentship 501
Paton/Masser Memorial Fund 144
Patrick and Margaret Flanagan Scholarship 528
The Patterns of Fashion Award 243
The Paul & Daisy Soros Fellowship for New Americans 501
Paul A Pisk Prize 65
Paul A Stewart Awards 720
Paul Beeson Career Development Award 49
Paul D. Fleck Fellowships in the Arts 130
The Paul Foundation Postgraduate Scholarship 501
Paul H. Nitze School of Advanced International Studies (SAIS) Financial Aid and Fellowships 139
Paul J Alexander Memorial Fellowship 645
Paul Mellon Centre Rome Fellowship 161
Paul W McQuillen Memorial Fellowship 392
PDS Research Project Grant 498
PDS Training Fellowships 498
The Pedro Zamora Public Policy Fellowship 12

INDEX OF DISCONTINUED AWARDS

Action Cancer
Pilot Grants

Adelphi University
Adelphi University Graduate Assistantships
Adelphi University Scholarships

Age-in-Action
Zerilda Steyn Memorial Trust

American Bar Foundation (ABF)
ABF Fellowships in Law and Social Science

American College of Prosthodontics (ACP)
George H. Moulton Award for Outstanding Achievement

American Council of Learned Societies (ACLS)
ACLS Charles A Ryskamp Research Fellowships
ACLS Chinese Fellowships for Scholarly Development
ACLS Dissertation Fellowships in East European Studies
ACLS East European Language Training Grants
ACLS Frederick Burkhardt Residential Fellowships for Recently Tenured Scholars
ACLS Humanities Program in Belarus, Russia, and Ukraine
ACLS/New York Public Library (NYPL) Fellowships
Advanced-Mastery Language-Training Grants for Institutions
Chiang Ching-Kuo Foundation for Scholarly Exchange (CCK) New Perspectives on Chinese Culture and Society
Contemplative Practice Fellowship Program
Contemplative Program Development Fellowships
Fellowships for Postdoctoral Research in Southeast European Studies

American Federation for Aging Research (AFAR)
AFAR Research Grants
AFAR/Pfizer Research Grants in Metabolic Control and Late Life Diseases
Merck/AFAR Junior investigator award in geriatric clinical pharmacology
Paul B. Beeson Career Development Awards in Aging Research Program

American Nuclear Society (ANS)
Gerald C. Pomraning Award
Henry Dewolf Smyth Nuclear Statesman Award
Samuel Glasstone Award

American Society for Engineering Education (ASEE)
Army Research Laboratory Postdoctoral Fellowship Program
International Fellowships
Office of Naval Research Summer Faculty Research Program and Sabbatical Leave Program
SRC International Graduate Fellowship Program

The American University in Cairo (AUC)
Faculty Support Grants
Frank G. Wisner Award
Jameel MBA Fellows Program
MAL/MUN Fellowship
Student Support Grants
Tewfick Pasha Doss Award

Arthritis Foundation
Arthritis Clinical Translational Award
Emerging Opportunities Grant
Innovative Research Grant
New Investigator Grant for Arthritis Health Professionals
Training Award

The Arts Council of Wales
ACW Capital Grants
ACW Community Touring Night Out
ACW Lottery Film Funding

Arts International
The Artists Exploration Fund
The Fund for US Artists
INROADS

The ASCAP Foundation
The ASCAP Foundation Johnny Mercer Award
The ASCAP Foundation Lifetime Achievement Award
The ASCAP Foundation Music Teacher Recognition Award

Association of Commonwealth Universities (ACU)
ACU Anastasios Christodoulou International Conference Grants

Association of Universities and Colleges of Canada (AUCC)
Paul Sargent Memorial Linguistic Scholarship Program
Petro-Canada Graduate Research Award Program

The Bush Foundation
Bush Artist Fellows Program

Canadian Embassy (USA)
Canadian Embassy (USA) Senior Fellowship Program

Canadian Society for Chemical Engineering
Enantioselective Synthetic Chemistry Research Grants Program

Canadian Society for Chemical Technology
J.E.Zajic Postgraduate Scholarship in Biochemical Engineering (not offered in 2005)
Nova Chemicals Award
Travel Awards & Grants

Cancer Association of South Africa (CANSA)
CANSA Research Grants
CANSA Travel and Subsistence (Study) Grants

Cancer Research Institute
Grant Research Program on T-cell Rich B-cell Lymphoma

The Cancer Research Society, Inc.
Cancer Research Society, Inc. Studentship

CEC Artslink
FACE Croatia awards

Children's Literature Association
ChLA Beiter Grants For Graduate Students
International Sponsorship Grant

The Crohn's and Colitis Foundation of America
Research Fellowships Awards
Senior Research Award

Delta Society
AAT Instructor Course Scholarship

European Association for the Study of Diabetes
EASD-ADA Transatlantic Fellowships
EASD/Amylin-Paul Langerhans Research Fellowship

European Commission
Marie Curie Experienced Researcher's Fellowships
Marie Curie Incoming International Fellowships (IIF)
Marie Curie Individual Fellowships
Marie Curie Industry Host Fellowships
Marie Curie Intra-European Fellowships
Marie Curie Training Sites Fellowships

Foundation for Digestive Health and Nutrition
AGA Merck Clinical Research Career Development Award

German Historical Institute
German Historical Institute Summer Program
Volkswagen Research Fellowship

Golden Key International Honor Society
2005 U.S. Regional Awards
Advisor Awards
Chapter Awards
Chapter Specific Awards
Community Service Award
Council President's Award
The Golden Key Graduate Scholar Award
Golden Key International Honor Society Art International
Golden Key International Honor Society Business Achievement Awards
Golden Key International Honor Society Earth Ethics Award
Golden Key International Honor Society Education Achievement Awards
Golden Key International Honor Society Engineering Achievement Award
Golden Key International Honor Society Excellence in Speech and Debate Awards
Golden Key International Honor Society GEICO Adult Scholar Awards
Golden Key International Honor Society Information Systems Achievement Awards
Golden Key International Honor Society International Student Leader
Golden Key International Honor Society Literary Achievement Awards
Golden Key International Honor Society Performing Arts Showcase
Golden Key International Honor Society Research Travel Grants
Golden Key International Honor Society Service Award
Golden Key International Honor Society Student Scholastic Showcase
Golden Key Scholar Award
Member Scholarships and Awards
Partner Scholarships

Heed Ophthalmic Foundation
Heed Fellowship Stipend

Institute for Humane Studies (IHS)
Charles G Koch Summer Fellowship
Liberty and Society Week-Long Summer Conferences

Institution of Mechanical Engineers (IMechE)
James Bates Grants
James Bates Prize
Labrow Grants
Solids Handling Award
Spencer Wilks Scholarship/Fellowship
Thomas Andrew Common Grants

International Council for Canadian Studies (ICCS)
Canada - Latin America - Caribbean Awards
ICCS Commonwealth Scholarship and Fellowship Plan
National Capital Research Scholarship

John E Fogarty International Center (FIC) for Advanced Study in the Health Sciences
Brain Disorders in the Developing World Grants
Comprehensive ICGB Awards
ICGB Planning Grants

Meningitis Research Foundation
Meningitis Research Foundation Small Project Grant

National Federation of the Blind (NFB)
Sixteen National Federation of the Blind Scholarships
Two National Federation of the Blind Scholarships

National Research Council (NRC)
NRC Twinning Program

National University of Singapore (NUS)
NUS Graduate Scholarships for ASEAN Nationals
NUS Research Scholarship

Novartis Foundation
Novartis Foundation Symposium Bursaries

Organization of American Historians (OAH)
Horace Samuel and Marion Galbraith Merrill Travel Grants
La Pietra Dissertation Travel Fellowship in Transnational History

Paralyzed Veterans of America
Spinal Cord Injury Research Foundation Grants

Pfizer Inc.
AAFPF/Pfizer Visiting Professorships in Family Medicine
ACCF/Pfizer Postdoctoral Fellowship Awards in Cardiovascular Medicine
The ACCF/Pfizer Postdoctoral Fellowship Awards in Cardiovascular Medicine
Pfizer Scholars Grants in Clinical Psychiatry
Pfizer Scholars Grants in Clinical Rheumatology
Pfizer Visiting Professorships in Allergic Diseases and Asthma
Pfizer/AFAR Innovations in Aging Research Awards

The Population Council
Transmission of Immunodeficiency Viruses: Postdoctoral Research Position

Royal Agricultural College, School of Business
Alltech Biotechnology, Inc. MSc/MBA Studentships

Royal College of Organists (RCO)
Dr D E Braggins Prize
The Eddie Palmer Memorial Award
Mary Layton Organ Exhibition
Sir John Goss Exhibition

Royal College of Paediatrics and Child Health (RCPCH)
Rcpch / Well Child Clinical Research Training Fellowships
Research Training Opportunities in Paediatrics

Savoy Foundation
Savoy Foundation International Grant

Sigma Theta Tau International
Sigma Theta Tau International/Hospice and alliative Nurses Foundation End of Life Nursing Care Research Grant

Society for the Study of French History
Society for the Study of French History Conference Bursaries

The South African Institute of International Affairs (SAIIA)
SAIIA Barratt Rotary Award

University of Birmingham
Neville Chamberlain Scholarship

University of East Anglia (UEA)
UEA Writing Fellowship

University of Essex
University of Essex/ESRC Case Studentship

The University of Leeds
Derek Fatchett Memorial Scholarships (Palestine)

University of Louisiana at Monroe (ULM)
ULM Graduate Assistantships

University of Oxford
Joint Modern History Faculty/St Antony's College Scholarship
St Antony's College Sassoon Scholarship

University of Rhode Island
URI Assistantships
URI Fellowships

Whatcom Museum of History and Art
Jacobs Research Fund

Yale University Press
Yale Younger Poets Prize

ZEIT Foundation
ZEIT Foundation Doctoral Fellowships

INDEX OF AWARDING ORGANISATIONS